twayne

companion to contemporary world literature

from the editors of *world literature today*

twayne

companion to contemporary world literature

from the editors of *world literature today*

pamela a. genova
editor

volume

1

parts I–V

TWAYNE
PUBLISHERS™

New York • Detroit • San Diego • San Francisco • Cleveland • New Haven, Conn. • Waterville, Maine • London • Munich

GALE

Twayne Companion to Contemporary World Literature: From the Editors of *World Literature Today*

Pamela A. Genova

Twayne/Gale
Frank Menchaca, Publisher, Twayne Publishers
Stephen Wasserstein, Senior Editor

Project Editor
Ken Wachsberger

Proofreading, Copyediting
Bill Kaufman
Gina Misiroglu

Indexer
J. Naomi Linzer

Data Capture
Gwen Tucker

Permissions
Shalice Shah-Caldwell

Product Design
Michelle DiMercurio

Imaging and Multimedia
Lezlie Light
Kelly Quin
David G. Oblender
Dan Newell
Leitha Etheridge-Sims

Composition
Evi Seoud

Manufacturing
Rhonda Williams

LIBRARY OF CONGRESS CATALOG-IN-PUBLICATION DATA

Twayne companion to contemporary world literature : from the editors of World Literature Today / edited by Pamela A. Genova.
     p. cm.
Includes bibliographical references and index.
   ISBN 0-8057-1700-5 (hard : set) — ISBN 0-8057-1701-3 (v. 1) — ISBN 0-8057-1702-1 (v. 2)
   1. Literature, Modern—20th century—History and criticism. I. Genova, Pamela Antonia, 1961- II. World Literature Today.

   PN771 .T93 2003
   809'.04—dc21

2002152498

Revised

Printed in the United States of America
10 9 8 7 6 5 4 3 2 1

Contents

III. Africa and the Caribbean

Africa

■ **VOLUME 2**

VI. Eastern Europe, Russia, and the Balkans

VII. Northern Europe

VIII. Western Europe

Introduction

These journals, as they reach a wider public, will contribute most effectively to the universal world literature we hope for; we repeat, however, that there can be no question of the nations thinking alike, the aim is simply that they shall grow aware of one another, understand each other, and even when they may not be able to love, may at least tolerate one another.

■ WOLFGANG VON GOETHE, COMMENT ON *WELTLITERATUR*, INCORPORATED INTO THE *BOOKS ABROAD/WORLD LITERATURE TODAY* MASTHEAD SINCE 1927.

■ *WORLD LITERATURE TODAY*: HISTORY AND LEGEND

The history of the oldest international English-language literary quarterly, *World Literature Today*, housed at the University of Oklahoma in Norman, Oklahoma, presents an engaging tale, full of anecdote and adventure, a story of men and women of letters deeply committed to questions of literature, art, culture, and the global scheme of things.[1] The emergence of an internationally acclaimed journal in a small campus town of the American heartland embodies a phenomenon that may appear unlikely, and yet in a sense it seems also quite normal, conceived as a natural extension of the intellectual encounters of scholars, students, and the reading public, within a large academic research institution. Indeed, as the 1980 Nobel Laureate and 1978 Neustadt Prize winner Czesław Miłosz once declared, "If *WLT* were not in existence, we would have to invent it. It fulfills the unique role of bringing information about works little known or inaccessible in English-speaking countries." For her part, Joyce Carol Oates, the novelist, poet, and playwright, describes the journal by highlighting one of its most original aspects, the inclusion in every issue of an unprecedented number of book reviews: "*World Literature Today* is an extraordinary journal, one very much needed, handsomely produced and edited with skill and discretion. No other journal begins to do what

WLT does routinely—the conscientious reviewing of over 300 books in each issue from approximately 60 languages." It is true that the reviewing of numerous titles of fiction, poetry, drama, autobiography, and many other literary genres, from writers based all over the world, is a prominent and unusual component of *WLT*. Yet, equally importantly, the journal also publishes articles, interviews, and many other features, while its offices function as a vital site for a variety of cultural activities, as the editorial staff organizes conferences and symposia, bestows important literary prizes, and encourages the work of students, scholars, researchers, and readers of world literature everywhere. Devoted to the presentation and discussion of current literature in all the major and many of the lesser-known languages of the world, *WLT* is the only international review focused on comprehensive and informative coverage of developments in contemporary literatures worldwide. In its pages readers can find timely and stimulating discussions of the work of a vast diversity of authors, from many different languages and cultures; *WLT* frequently represents in fact the sole source available anywhere for information on the less-familiar, often unjustly overlooked, literary traditions of the twentieth century.

The journal was founded in 1927 by Roy Temple House at the University of Oklahoma under the name *Books Abroad*. At that time, House was chair of the Department of Modern Languages, Literatures, and Linguistics (MLLL), and his work with the journal launched a long and active relationship between the academic unit of MLLL and the editorial offices of what would later become *WLT* (I myself am a faculty member in the department, as well as a senior contributing editor at *WLT*). House's driving idea for the publication was fueled by his desire to try to offer non-ideological commentary on a variety of foreign literatures as a means of aiding America to move away from what he saw as a dangerous trend toward isolationism. House hoped thus to promote more extensive and more thoughtful international understanding through the communication of a variety of opinions on art, litera-ture, and ideas. As he wrote in the first issue of *Books Abroad*, he was very much aware of the difficulties of his new enterprise, of the myriad looming challenges and obstacles, but also, he could clearly sense the satis-faction and rewards the future would bring:

> [The editors] are undertaking to distribute four times a year a little magazine of really useful in-formation concerning the more important book publications of Germany, France, Italy, Spain, Belgium, Switzerland, the South American re-publics, and perhaps other countries. They are hard-worked modern language teachers in a modest institution, without the leisure, the equipment, or the experience to do this work as well and thoroughly as they wish it might be done. They will be criticized for their omissions and inclusions, for their lack of a hard and fast plan as to just what types of books shall be treat-ed and what types left to other publications, for the amateurish character of some of their matter, for the opportunism which fully expects to change their policy here and there as circum-stances may demand it. They offer their first number with fear and trembling, but with the conviction that they are undertaking a work which very much needed doing.[2]

In the recounting of the legends and lore surround-ing *WLT*, and of the infamous tales associated with the frequent visits of literary celebrities who traveled to the University of Oklahoma campus under the auspices of the journal's affiliated programs,[3] one often encounters the anecdote relating how House and his editors began their work, a genuine labor of love, for no extra com-pensation or release time from their duties as professors at the university; even production costs were paid for a time out of their own pockets. In 1931, however, these costs were becoming more onerous, and the edi-tors were obliged to impose a subscription rate—an amount charming to nostalgic readers and editors of today—of one dollar per year, though the editorial staff still received no extra salary. As a metaphoric emblem, House devised as the journal's Latin motto "Lux a Pere-gre," which can be translated as "Light from Abroad," or "Light of Discovery." The phrase accompanies the logo, also conceived by House, of a full-rigged ship, a rich image which not only calls to mind adventure, as in venturing out toward unknown horizons, but also evokes harbor and beacon, as the academic community and university institution are perceived as a safe haven for the daily operation of the journal. In 1927, the quar-terly (which today is the second-oldest literary periodi-cal in the United States, younger only than *The Sewanee Review*) began as a short publication of thirty-two pages; by the end of its fiftieth year, *Books Abroad* had grown

to more than 250 pages (the average length of an issue of the journal still today).

At its origins, the quarterly was truly democratic in its selection criteria regarding books to review, even ex-cessively so perhaps, and for the first years, every kind of publication—from entomological studies and naval histories to grammar books and reissued classics—was reviewed in its pages. Soon, however, a clearer, more sophisticated focus on literary works per se was formu-lated, as the editors opened the frontiers of their publi-cation to a broader geographical and cultural scope, ex-panding the perimeters of the journal significantly to include reviews and articles addressing the work of non-European writers. House also encouraged the in-clusion of features of more popular style and wider ap-peal, as with the surveys of celebrated writers on ques-tions of general cultural interest and a variety of symposium topics, such as the 1932 discussion, the first of many more to come, on the Nobel Prize. Related top-ics for symposia included "Transplanted Writers," "Women Playwrights," "Foster-Mother Tongue," and "Can't Book Reviewers Be Honest?" By the early 1930s, such celebrated authors as Sinclair Lewis, H. L. Menck-en, Upton Sinclair, and Henry Van Dyke were publish-ing critical texts in *Books Abroad*.

House served as editor from 1927 until his retire-ment in 1949, and was succeeded by the German critic and novelist Ernst Erich Noth, who went on to edit the journal for ten highly productive and formative years. As a European-born writer and editor, Noth was the first of a series of cosmopolitan, foreign-born intellectu-als who would continue to lead the journal's editorial staff for more than forty more years. One of Noth's major contributions to the ongoing process of establish-ing a distinctive identity for the quarterly was the move to streamline the inclusion policy, to focus solely on writers of the twentieth century while reviewing only books that had been published no more than two years earlier. He also introduced a new feature, "Periodicals in Review" (sometimes appearing as "Periodicals at Large"), which surveyed the policies and initiatives of a number of literary journals from Europe, the Ameri-cas, and throughout the world.

In 1959, Noth was succeeded by Wolfgang Bernard Fleishmann, a Viennese-born scholar who directed the quarterly for two years. His major contribution to the development of *Books Abroad* was the publication of a continuing symposium on twentieth-century poetry from the western world. He was followed in 1961 by the Czech émigré Robert Vlach, who had been appoint-ed as a professor in the Department of Modern Lan-guages at the University of Oklahoma. Vlach established a new review section in the journal devoted to Slavic languages, and he also initiated the *Books Abroad* symposia which took place at the annual convention of the Modern Language Association. After Vlach's untimely death in 1966, Assistant Editor Bernice Duncan carried on his duties with noted success until Ivar Ivask became editor in 1967.

With the arrival of Ivask, a long and significant era of development began for *WLT*, and the journal underwent many major transformations, in its style and presentation format as well as in its subject matter and intellectual perspective. Stylistically, the cover was redesigned, the internal page arrangement was transformed into a layout of double columns, and vignettes were added to diversify the visual and thematic organization of the pages. As for the content of the journal, more emphasis was placed on the development of special issues devoted to a single author or topic, while many new symposium proceedings were published, such as those on "The Writer in Exile," "Nationalism in World Literature," and "The Writer as Critic of His Age." Ivask, of Estonian and Latvian heritage, also established a new section of reviews of books in Finno-Ugric and Baltic languages. The staff of associated reviewers had grown to more than 800 by 1970, and fifty percent more books were being reviewed in the quarterly issues. In 1977, a truly significant initiative was reflected in the change of name from *Books Abroad* to *World Literature Today*, an innovative title that suggests both global and contemporary reflections on a diversity of literary forms of art, and transcends the more limited implications of the former title that could be interpreted as excessively Eurocentric. The journal's coverage and reputation had expanded so impressively since its inception that a new name seemed only appropriate to reflect the increasingly rich nature of the overall enterprise.

In 1991, at the end of the sixty-first year of the publication of *WLT*, a new editor replaced Ivask, the Cyprus native Djelal Kadir. In a unique double essay that appeared in the Autumn 1991 issue, the outgoing and incoming editors shared their views on the past, present, and future of the publication, both invoking the seagoing imagery of the masthead. As Ivask points out, a mere six editors in more than six decades is an unusual record for any publication, and each brought an undeniably original style and personal vision to the journal. Kadir, a scholar in English, Spanish, and Portuguese literatures, led the editorial process at *WLT* until 1996, when William Riggan (who joined *WLT* in 1974, and who subsequently served as assistant editor, associate editor, assistant director, and editor of the journal) took over until 1999.

In that year, the current executive director at the journal, R. C. Davis-Undiano, professor of English at the University of Oklahoma, came to work at the offices of *WLT* and was named the Neustadt Professor of Comparative Literature. Today, Davis-Undiano collaborates with the current editor, David Draper Clark (who has been with *WLT* since 1983), and has worked to enact many modifications, among the most significant in the history of the journal. The new format and the expansion of affiliated programs currently enjoying evident success at *WLT* will be discussed in more detail further in this introduction.

▪ NEUSTADT, PUTERBAUGH, NOBEL

One of the most important facets to the *WLT* enterprise is the Neustadt International Prize for Literature, which was launched in 1969 under Ivask's editorial leadership. This biennial award, which brought an original purse of $10,000 and in 2002 bestowed $50,000, is supported by an endowment through the University of Oklahoma, from the Oklahoma-based Neustadt family. The Neustadt Prize was the first international prize for literature of this scope to originate in the United States, and it remains one of the few literary prizes on an international scale for which novelists, playwrights, and poets are equally eligible (the only stipulation dictates that at least a representative portion of the author's work must be available in English, Spanish, and/or French, the three languages used in the jury's deliberations). Each Neustadt Prize winner is selected by a different jury of ten to twelve individuals, chosen by the executive director of the journal (who is the only permanent member), in consultation with the journal's editorial board and the president of the University of Oklahoma. Each juror nominates one author, and all nominations are made public six months before the jury convenes on the campus. The group meets for two to three days behind closed doors and the award ceremonies culminate with a banquet in the following fall semester, an event attended by the laureate, while a special issue of the journal is devoted entirely to that author's work. An overview of the sixteen prizes awarded to date offers a telling perspective into the undeniably esteemed group of winners selected over the past thirty years: Giuseppe Ungaretti (1970, Italy), Gabriel García Márquez (1972, Colombia), Francis Ponge (1974, France), Elizabeth Bishop (1976, United States), Czesław Miłosz (1978, Poland), Josef Škvorecký (1980, Czechoslovakia), Octavio Paz (1982, Mexico), Paavo Haavikko (1984, Finland), Max Frisch (1986, Switzerland), Tomas Tranströmer (1990, Sweden), João Cabral de Melo Neto (1992, Brazil), Kamau Brathwaite (1994, Barbados), Assia Djebar (1996, Algeria), Nuruddin

Farah (1998, Somalia), David Malouf (2000, Australia), and Alvaro Mutis (2002, Colombia).

The second major event associated with *WLT*, a particularly important occasion with regard to outreach and visibility, is the Puterbaugh Conference on World Literature, sponsored by the journal in collaboration with the University of Oklahoma Departments of English and Modern Languages. The Puterbaugh series of conferences began in 1968 and was originally named the Oklahoma Conference on Writers of the Hispanic World; it was endowed in perpetuity in 1978 by the Puterbaugh Foundation of McAlester, Oklahoma. In that year, the scope of the conference was expanded to include writers of the French-speaking world, as well as from Spain and Spanish America. In 1993, all restrictions were removed, and since that date, all living writers have been potentially eligible for the honor. Now an annual event (previously it was biennial), the Puterbaugh Conference brings a prominent author to the Norman campus for approximately one week, during which he or she offers classes and seminars, as well as free public lectures and readings, followed by a symposium featuring scholars and specialists who have concentrated in their research on the author's work. Again, the list of those who have been featured in the Puterbaugh Conference is striking in the highly visible nature and exceptional quality of the writers honored (some of whom have also won the Neustadt Prize): Jorge Guillén (1968, Spain), Jorge Luis Borges (1969, Argentina), Octavio Paz (1971, Mexico), Dámaso Alonso (1973, Spain), Julio Cortázar (1975, Argentina), Mario Vargas Llosa (1977, Peru), Yves Bonnefoy (1979, France), Michel Butor (1981, France), Carlos Fuentes (1983, Mexico), Guillermo Cabrera Infante (1987, Cuba), Edouard Glissant (1989, Martinique), Manuel Puig (1991, Argentina), Maryse Condé (1993, Guadeloupe), Luisa Valenzuela (1995, Argentina), J. M. G. Le Clézio (1997, France), Czesław Miłosz (1999, Poland), and Kenzaburō Ōe (2001, Japan). In April 2002, the nineteenth Puterbaugh Conference on World Literature featured the Cuban poet and essayist Roberto Fernández Retamar.

Another particularly interesting element in the identity of *WLT*, as well as of the Neustadt Prize and the Puterbaugh Conference, is the relationship between these entities and the cultural institution of the Nobel Prize for literature. Since the inception of *Books Abroad*, the editors associated with the journal have encouraged lively debate about the annual announcement of the Nobel Prize, as with the 1939 "Super-Nobel" election sponsored in *Books Abroad*, in which contributors and other specialists were invited to each choose the writer whom they felt had offered the most significant contri-

bution to world literature in the first third of the twentieth century, whether or not that writer had won the Nobel Prize.[4] At the top of the "Super-Nobel" list were several non-Nobel winners, such as Marcel Proust, Franz Kafka, and Theodore Dreiser, but the award went to Thomas Mann, who had in fact won the Nobel in 1929, and who became a frequent contributor to *WLT*. Over the years, *Books Abroad* often featured the topic of the Nobel Prize, as with the series of symposia published periodically in the journal: "Prodding the Nobel Prize Committee" (1932), "Nominations for the Nobel Prize for Literature" (1935), "*Books Abroad*'s Super-Nobel Election" (1940), "What's Wrong with the Nobel Prize?" (1951), and "Nobel Prize Symposium" (1967). In these remarkable symposia, critics, scholars, and authors discussed the policies and procedures of the Swedish academy, as well as the secretive selection process and the sometimes curious choices of winners for an inherently literary prize (such as Winston Churchill, the 1953 laureate, and Bertrand Russell, the 1951 laureate). The Spring 1981 issue of *WLT* was devoted entirely to the presentation of the members of the Swedish academy, many of whom were successful creative writers in their own right. Interestingly, in 1951, the Nobel Foundation chose the University of Oklahoma Press to issue the first English-language edition of its own authoritative volume, entitled *Nobel: The Man and His Prizes*. Also, the often-synchronistic relationship between the Neustadt Prize, once infamously described by *The New York Times* as the "Oklahoma Nobel," and the Nobel Prize itself is in fact quite amazing. Between 1970 and 1980, for example, no fewer than six writers associated in one way or another with the Oklahoma prize (usually as jurors, candidates, or winners of the Neustadt Prize) also received the Nobel.[5]

▪ A NEW ERA OF WORLD LITERATURE

Since 1999, *WLT* has undergone many changes, as the current executive director, R. C. Davis-Undiano, has worked with contributors, readers, and editorial staff to rethink the identity of the journal and the functions it fulfills. At issue are several important goals, especially that of expanding the readership and widening the horizons of the journal, as well as working toward the establishment of an active and diverse humanities center, to be housed at the *WLT* offices. Not surprisingly, throughout the history of the journal, the majority of its reading public has been made up primarily of librarians, research scholars, and literary specialists. These groups remain important subscribers to *WLT*, but a critical recent priority has been to work toward opening the ideological and stylistic parameters of the journal and to present material that is interesting, useful, and accessible to a more general public, one made up of discerning and curious readers who are not specialists in literary criticism, cultural theory, or the history of letters. With this goal in mind, the editors of *WLT* aim to reach the kind of reader who may feel that the realm of purely scholarly and academic writing and research represents a closed, even elitist enterprise, as they seek out a well-rounded reader attracted instead by lively discussions of topics of general cultural and artistic import.[6]

To begin, Davis-Undiano decided to expand the scope of the original periodical extensively, by launching two new related publications. The first, entitled *WLT Magazine*, is, like the journal, quarterly (with the primary difference that the magazine format presents far fewer book reviews). Available at newsstands at half the cost of the original *WLT*, the magazine offers a variety of often-provocative styles of writing and topics for discussion. Of course, in the past *WLT* has offered a few recurring features, such as the "Notes on Contributors," the "Literary Necrology," and the "Last Page" (a kind of bulletin board posting announcements and information regarding international literary events), but the guiding idea now is to develop and augment these supplemental columns substantially. Among the new features, "Currents" presents brief and thoughtful commentaries on new works, literary prizes, and colloquia, as well as subjects of artistic and literary controversy; many of these pieces center on the social and contextual issues affecting literary culture today, such as Ilán Stavan's exploration of the hybrid linguistic forms of "Spanglish," Sudeep Sen's study of recent Indian poetry in English, and Warren Motte's "Ten Fables of the Novel in French of the 1990s." "Travel Writing" is a feature that showcases notes, musings, and essays discussing a diversity of cultural sites around the world (as with Evelyne Accad's reminiscences of the city of Beirut and Marcel Cohen's thoughts on travel after World War II). "Essential Books" presents texts by scholars, specialists, and creative writers who consider the impact of a single book or of a series on the formation of the contemporary canon (see Rainer Schulte on Marcel Proust and Moacyr Scliar on Isaac Babel, for example). Under the rubric of "Children's Literature," readers discover a guide to the leading authors, publishers, and prizes awarded in the field of literature for younger readers. The "*WLT* Interview" furnishes original interviews with internationally recognized writers (such as Mario Vargas Llosa, Aleksandr Kushner, and Amitav Ghosh), and in the "Poetry" columns appears original work in verse composed by a variety of global figures (Ha Jin, Cyril Dabydeen, Claudio Rodríguez, and Czesław Miłosz, for example).

By including features such as these, Davis-Undiano and his colleagues are striving to bring a renewed sense of diversity to the global enterprise of the journal, and new ideas for expansion and experiment are always under review. In late 2000, for example, the editors worked with almost forty scholars to establish a list of the "Most Important Works in World Literature, 1927–2001," a project organized and timed to help celebrate the seventy-five years of uninterrupted publication enjoyed by *WLT*.[7] The top forty list was chosen by specialists, but with the non-specialist in mind, with the intention of inviting response and debate among readers and writers everywhere. A forum for readers' correspondence was also initiated, and since 2000 it has helped spark dialogue among the editors of *WLT* and the reading public, contributors, and reviewers, as they discuss such issues as possible thematic frameworks for new symposia and potential ideological directions for the journal to explore.

In addition, the editorial staff at *WLT* has acted on the resolution to communicate directly with a specific population, at the University of Oklahoma and beyond, the student body. With outreach in mind, a student publication, entitled *WLT 2*, was inaugurated in the fall of 1999. Produced, edited, and designed by undergraduate and graduate students at the University of Oklahoma, the enterprise enables younger scholars to gain valuable insight and practical experience in the editorial world; recent issues have focused on "Latina Literature" and "Literature of the Cuban Diaspora." The new publication is distributed free of charge in creative writing classes and elsewhere, and is also available in an online version. The renewed interest of *WLT* in the student population is also highlighted through the Neustadt Student Fellowship, which allows students to earn three hours of university-level credit free of charge, while the fellows are invited to participate in all events associated with the Neustadt Prize. With the aim of reaching a cross-section of students from various fields of study, *WLT* has also sponsored classes that highlight interdisciplinary topics and methodologies, as with the course on Chicano and Latino Studies offered by Davis-Undiano. Further, a projected endeavor to continue to engage more students into the journal's development will be the *WLT* Virtual Book Club, which will be interactive, while keeping students informed about the various activities planned for visiting authors. A conventionally styled book club, sponsored in conjunction with the University of Oklahoma Hispanic-American Student Association, has already begun. And, *WLT* has now put into place a series of student internships, for both undergraduate and graduate students, to introduce students to the editorial process, marketing practices, and overall dynamics of the world of literary publishing.

Closely related to the goal of reaching a wider reading public, including students and younger readers, is the plan to work toward the establishment of a humanities center, sponsored by the editorial offices of *WLT*. The staff at the journal is currently seeking funding opportunities and examining renovation plans with the aim of constructing a new media center connected to its offices and expanding the space available to accommodate the activities of more classes, visitors, writers, speakers, and guests. The diversification of the content of *WLT*, as well as the exploration of various publication formats directed toward different sectors of the reading public, will be reflected in the wide array of daily projects and special events organized through the humanities center. Welcoming students and faculty, the local community, and visiting writers into an interactive and productive space for cultural, artistic, and literary expression will represent the driving force of the center.

Along with these more pragmatic developments, Davis-Undiano has endeavored to reinvigorate the stylistic form, as well as the subject matter, of the primary critical texts published in each issue. In "Back to the Essay: *World Literature Today* in the Twenty-First Century," a piece by Davis-Undiano that appeared in the Winter 2000 issue, he argues for a move away from the increasingly more stilted academic style of the scholarly article, favoring instead the more creative, experimental, and unrestrained form of the essay. As Davis-Undiano explains:

> The essay tradition is not a prescriptive one of writing in a certain mold, but a capacious one defined mainly by a strategy for maintaining effective ties among writing form, the material being discussed, and the intended audience. Essays in the main tradition tend to have a definable perspective, even on occasion a personal one, and they speak in an idiom that reaches a broad audience. They tend to emphasize the occasion for foregrounding a question or issue as important, and they tend to demonstrate the argument in the form of the essay itself.[8]

In such a way, Davis-Undiano links the contemporary editorial project embodied in *WLT* with a time-honored literary tradition, illustrated by the works of such renowned essayists as Michel de Montaigne and Francis Bacon. Specifically, Davis-Undiano emphasizes the etymology of the word "essay," which evokes experimentation, trial and error, and the exploration of a curious mind faced with the adventures of world culture. Grounded in innovation, interpretation, and hypothesis, essay writing presents a necessarily personal and subjective perspective, as an author explores myriad possibilities surrounding a chosen topic. The key is to encourage lively, provocative writing in essays that address literary issues, while political, economic, and other cultural factors are heartily welcomed into the discussion. Indeed, the influence of social and contextual forces on the formulation of both centuries-old and newly emerging national literatures rises to the forefront in these essays; as Davis-Undiano suggests: "Essays, perhaps unique among literary genres, helpfully mirror the culture back to itself in an immediate or powerful way" (7), and it is this concept of the text, perceived both as a window from which to view the world and as a glass that reflects back to us our own identity, that most succinctly and creatively describes the writing featured in today's *WLT*.

In the end, the contemporary era of *WLT* is characterized especially by heightened visibility; in the editorial offices of the journal, a concerted effort at expansion continues, as new ideas and experimental methods are discussed with editors, contributors, students, faculty, and the increasingly diverse reading public. Many initiatives are underway. Beginning in 2003, *WLT* will award a new juried prize to an author of children's literature; the *NSK*/Neustadt Prize for Children's Literature, which carries a monetary award of $25,000, will be presented every other fall at the University of Oklahoma.[9] Also, there are now among the staff of *WLT* six contributing editors (whose specializations span literatures in French, Japanese, Portuguese, Russian, Spanish, and general traditions of poetry); these individuals work with the core editorial staff to review proposals, establish translations, and recruit new reviewers, essayists, and interviewees; they also represent *WLT* at a variety of national and international conferences and symposia.

The newest initiatives in outreach and development were recently acknowledged in Spring 2002 when *WLT* was awarded the 2002 Arrell Gibson Award for Lifetime Achievement by the Oklahoma Center of the Book (dating from 1986, the Oklahoma center represents the fourth to be established among the forty-four that exist nationwide). This marks the first time that this Lifetime Achievement Award has been bestowed upon an institution rather than an individual writer. (Previous winners include mystery writer Tony Hillerman, an alumnus of the University of Oklahoma, and poet N. Scott Momaday, Pulitzer-Prize winning novelist and Oklahoma native). With an acclaimed and diverse history that reaches back more than three-quarters of a century, today's *WLT* strives to combine the excellence of its past tradition with exciting future plans, as the editors build upon the solid groundwork of many years of literary work and pleasure. Through a renewed perspective and a diversification of methodology, format, and vision, the revitalization of *WLT* is definitely underway.

▪ THE PRESENT ESSAY COLLECTION: METHODS AND MODALITIES OF SELECTION AND ORGANIZATION

The current enterprise—the project to choose, categorize, and present approximately 300 essays and 150 book reviews—has been a challenging, thought-provoking, and ultimately rewarding process. Yet despite the undeniable editorial pleasures that surfaced along the way, when faced with such a task, one cannot help but be reminded of the sentiment shared by Roy Temple House, quoted earlier in this introduction, that any such undertaking is bound to be ambiguous and many-sided, and that those who attempt it "will be criticized for their omissions and inclusions, for their lack of a hard and fast plan. . . ." Indeed, many hours of consideration and discussion, thinking and rethinking have gone into the establishment of the current table of contents, which has seen many versions, and was truly a work in process for some time, flexible and kaleidoscopic.[10] The question of which essays to include, as well as which appendices to provide, involves a series of factors, including fundamental organizational considerations such as chronology, geography, language, political and ethnic identity, gender issues, and regional culture.

On a primary level, we concentrated in our choice on those literatures that have been the most influential during the relative time period in question (the contemporary era as conceived as approximately the past twenty-five years); those writers and languages usually the most underrepresented in other collections of literary essay selections and thus calling for attention here; and those essays that distinguish themselves as the most indicative of the unique nature and function of the journal, *WLT*. Further, working from a foundation of some of the most stylistically sophisticated essays to appear in the pages of the journal over the years, one goal has been to supplement the highly influential pieces composed by celebrated authors (such as Elie Wiesel's 1984 "A Vision of the Apocalypse," Mario Vargas Llosa's 1978 "Social Commitment and the Latin American Writer," and Max Frisch's 1986 "We Hope") with more oblique and specialized essays treating "minority" literatures and languages with which the general reading public may well be much less familiar. By concentrating then on offering a diverse spectrum of literary voices from a perspective firmly grounded in the contemporary era, and originating in a multitude of cultural and linguistic contexts, the aim is to address the interests of a more

diverse readership, one particularly curious about recent developments in worldwide literary history. It is in this spirit that the current two-volume collection of essays has been conceived, as both a narrative of and a guide to the dynamic systems of contemporary literature from across the globe. Further, through the endeavor to choose the best and most representative essays to appear in recent decades in the pages of *WLT* (texts notable both for the quality of the writing and for the significance of the subject matter), we hope to impart to the reader the sense of an era and to communicate the distinctive character of the collaborative editorial project that *WLT* has become.

One of the most important elements in determining which essays should be included in this collection is that of chronology. The reader will note that the time span of critical essays and articles presented begins in 1977, which, were one unfamiliar with the history of *WLT*, might appear as a rather random date. Yet 1977 embodies in fact the pivotal year of transition and revision that accompanies the shift from the former name of *Books Abroad* to the current title of *World Literature Today*, and marks an important moment of self-reflection on the part of the editorial staff at that time. Given that one of the primary aims of the present collection is to offer the reader an overview of the most significant voices in modern literature as seen through the unique perspective of *WLT*, the original idea from which the project sprang was to focus on approximately twenty-five years, a substantial period presenting much radical variation in the history of modern literatures worldwide. Since it is true that within the more concentrated history of the journal itself, 1977 indeed represents such a formative year, the decision was made to limit this collection to works appearing from that date up to 2001, when this introduction was written. If one of the most consequential factors guiding the organizational approach of this collection is the question of time, another is certainly space, as the element of geographical location arises in our project as perhaps even more sophisticated and complex than that of time. For some of the literatures discussed in these essays, the notion of a strong, even oppressive nation state is undeniable, as political and topographical lines of distinction are revealed to be formidable; for others, national boundaries come across as blurred, even transparent, vacillating as they follow the forces of culture and will, as certain artworks aim to transcend the contingencies of daily life; others still consider the context and situation of artistic identity and meaning as well defined but unfettered by the limitations of concrete space, as like-minded writers bond together across borders, mountains, and seas.

Another possible methodology of categorizing the essays is that of language group: presenting together all the texts that address works of literature written in French, for example. However, in this system one quickly confronts a significant problem, most glaring perhaps in the case of English-language writers, given that they span the entire globe, but also discernible of course with other language cases. The Francophone question is a good example of the formidable problem of the categorization of essays, suddenly more complicated from this point of view, for the cultural elements involved are immense; the obviously consequential differences among literatures written in France and those written in North Africa or the Caribbean clearly cannot be ignored if the reader wishes to gain a meaningful sense of the most central issues affecting the formulation of these literatures. Spanish, too, obviously represents a language that has come to be used in cultures, nations, and regions that are distinct from one another to such an extent that to lump together the literatures originating in Colombia, say, with those coming out of Spain could only prove futile in the current enterprise. Language, considered alone, reveals itself to be a decidedly unsatisfactory methodological principle on which to ground this enterprise.

Moreover, to return to the ambition of remaining faithful to the general ideology of the journal itself, when considered from one perspective, little guidance is offered in this sphere, since a substantial number of issues of *WLT* are devoted to a single author or national literature, or, less frequently, an issue presents collections of texts described as "varia," that is, a selection of essays in no way necessarily connected by topic. Thus, the question of organization within a single issue is not normally at play for the editors of *WLT*. In the book review section, however, the editors do categorize the reviews, to facilitate the location of a given literature for the readers, but this choice—the primary categorization is by language family, but geographical factors also affect the decision—is in large part determined by the nature of the selection of books to be reviewed that happen to be received during a specific quarterly period.[11] Thus one issue of *WLT* may arbitrarily contain many more entries in "Asia and the Pacific," for example, than in "Africa and the West Indies," a numerical difference due entirely to coincidental factors. Given the representative design of the current collection of essays, it quickly became clear that this particular system would not prove useful or appropriate as a basis for a coherent and systematic approach.

Therefore, what the reader will discover as a guiding organizational scheme in the present collection is a notion one might describe as that of cultural geography,

a methodology in which the foremost intention is to take into account not only questions of language, but also issues of nation states and geographical borders, regional and personal identities, and ideological identifications. In the combination of elements such as these, our hope is that the reader will find grouped together essays that complement one another, leading toward a thought-provoking and multifaceted overview of a given cultural question and its relationship to literary history, such as the status of women in the Middle East, the impact of poverty in African nations, the obstacles of spiritual isolation in Scandinavia, or the intricacies of post-colonial transition in the Philippines.

Perhaps as important as the question of inclusion is that, inevitably, of exclusion and absence. The decision was made to follow the general model and guidelines of *WLT* itself, in the sense that we have included no section to treat North American authors; throughout the long history of the journal, only twice were authors from the United States showcased specifically (Elizabeth Bishop was featured in the first issue of *WLT* in 1977, and in 1992 a special issue was devoted to Native American literatures). We decided to extend this limitation to Canada, as well, guided by the central logical principle that what we hope to accent in the thinking of *WLT* is its presentation and consideration of literatures originating in countries outside the North American arena. Further, throughout the volumes, the choice of countries or authors featured may seem sometimes arbitrary, even patently non-representative, but again, a basic working principle of this collection is to remain true to *WLT*; the choice of countries and literatures is not so much imposed by an external source, such as the weight of economic influence, political heft, or cultural celebrity in the contemporary global sphere, as it is dictated by that which the journal has truly come to be. Since the literature of Iraq, for instance, has not yet been featured in *WLT*, it does not appear in our collection. Similarly, since no contributor to the journal has written on the work of Iris Murdoch, her name is necessarily absent from the section reserved for Irish literature. Finally, although acceptance speeches of Nobel Prize winners, many of which were reprinted in the journal over the years, certainly present great interest and undeniable creative originality, they have been reprinted so often in other venues and are thus so widely available today that we rejected the option of including them here.

Finally, as the reader peruses the twenty-five years of essays, interviews, and reviews included in this collection, certain inconsistencies and irregularities in format and style will become apparent. Given the vast diversity of languages, regional dialects, and alphabetical systems involved in these discussions, and the frequency with which writers treat literatures of non-Western scripts and systems (such as Cyrillic, Arabic, Hebrew, Chinese, Japanese, and Hindi), it is not surprising that the most obvious of these inconsistencies is to be found in the use of diacritical marks and in transliteration. An example such as the name of the Egyptian Nobel Prize winner—rendered sometimes as "Najib Mahfus," sometimes as "Naguib Mahfouz," and sometimes finally as either one of these forms with the addition of various diacritical marks—illustrates the changing guidelines of standardization in place at *WLT* over the years, while it also underscores the desire of some essay writers to remain as true as possible to the original linguistic form, with the final product often embodying a complex, diacritic-filled transliteration. Other writers prefer to use a version of a name that appears, to the average North American reader, to correspond more closely to how the name sounds when spoken orally. Over the twenty-five years detailed in our collection, reviewers and contributors have clearly been divided in their final decisions on linguistic and stylistic issues such as these, and have often fashioned their own unique solutions to these challenges. Therefore, although the editors at the journal have aimed to standardize usage and style within a given text or issue of the quarterly, when twenty-five years of writing are grouped together, undeniable divergences in orthographic, diacritical, transliterary, and stylistic forms appear. In the end, instead of imposing retrospectively one overarching system of format and style, we decided to keep—as we have kept the unique discursive tones, singular writing styles, and original thematic motifs—the peculiarities of transliteration and linguistic style as they appear originally in our many pieces.

■ THE TABLE OF CONTENTS

The first section of the table of contents, "Perspectives on World Literature," offers a variety of essays in which authors treat questions of literary culture on a global scale, in discussions that bring thoughtful commentary to issues that necessarily cross ideological boundaries and linguistic divisions. Thus well-established critics such as Anna Balakian, Mary Ann Caws, Jonathan Culler, Linda Hutcheon, and Marjorie Perloff discuss in their texts the fluctuating dynamics of the field of Comparative Literature, as they reflect upon its past and contemplate its future as a form of academic inquiry that has undergone much transformation in recent years. Other essays in this section focus on political and ideological factors, especially as they relate to the formulation of new modes of literary art; Alfred Kazin, J. Hillis Miller, Henri Peyre, and Paul Nizon, for example, exam-

ine such questions as the consideration of world topics that resurface throughout various cultures and the problematics of writing literary works in a world in which the technical and scientific advances have become so fast paced that the individual author may find himself or herself isolated, considered as an anachronistic artifact from a quickly receding past. Still other essays in the first section address questions of form, structure, genre, and the fluctuations of the literary canon. Thus Yves Bonnefoy considers the systems of linguistic and semantic activity and the mutations they undergo in the process of translation, Michel Butor discusses the notion of inspiration and the dynamics of writerly production, Michael Hamburger explores poetry as an international and timeless literary form, and Leslie Schenk questions the nature of the world classics as they have been defined in Western culture. In a way, then, the first section was the least difficult category to visualize, given that the articles grouped therein all share a certain universality of perspective, no matter the specific literatures chosen to illustrate the guiding ideas of the essay writers. Much more complicated was formulating a universal, systematic methodology of organization for the rest of the essays included in this collection, the vast majority of texts by far. It is in this arena that the modalities of what we have described as "cultural geography" come into play.

The second section of essays, "The Arab World and the Middle East," presents first a general selection of texts that address issues spanning many countries, such as Roger Allen's examination of Arabic literature and the Nobel Prize or Muhammad Siddiq's study of the contemporary Arabic novel. We then present selections categorized as to geography and nation, listed alphabetically: Algeria, Egypt, Israel, Lebanon, Syria, Turkey, and Yemen. In some of these writings, authors explore the confluence of the cultures of ancient lands with the trends of modern society, such as Yair Mazor's 1984 examination of feminism and the work of the Israeli poet Daliah Rabikovitz; other articles concentrate on the utilization of classical rhetorical figures and universal generic forms as reconstructed from contemporary viewpoints (see Admer Gouryh's 1986 "Recent Trends in Syrian Drama"). Also, as the reader may expect, the conflicts and struggles that have besieged these regions in recent decades play a major role in the analysis of many of these national literatures, as with Eisig Silberschlag's 1980 "Redemptive Vision in Hebrew Literature" and Mohja Kahf's 2001 "The Silences of Contemporary Syrian Literature."

Section III, "Africa and the Caribbean," features first several texts addressing issues prevalent throughout African literatures, such as Charles R. Larson's thoughtful 1986 essay, "The Precarious State of the African Writer," or Isidore Okpewho's study, published in 1981 yet still meaningful for today's Africa, "Comparatism and Separatism in African Literature." This subsection is followed by several others centering on specific countries: Angola, Cameroon, Congo, Ghana, Kenya, Nigeria, Senegal, Somalia, and South Africa. As for the Caribbean authors treated, such as Derek Walcott, Caryl Phillips, Kamau Brathwaite, Edouard Glissant, Simone Schwarz-Bart, and Cristina García, we follow in these subsections a secondary level of categorization—linguistic—with Anglophone and Francophone authors followed by those from Cuba, which happens to be the sole Spanish-speaking Caribbean literature that has been showcased in *WLT*. As might be expected, questions of the hybrid nature of language and cultural identity appear in much of the writing associated with the Caribbean literary scene: exile, territorialism, Negritude, neocolonial social systems, and the changing landscapes of culture animate essays written by well-known literary figures from this part of the world, such as Maryse Condé, Cyril Dabydeen, and Guillermo Cabrera Infante.

Our fourth section, "Asia," has been divided into five subsections, again closely following geographically defined regions: "East Asia" offers writings on China, Japan, Korea, and Taiwan; "Central Asia" presents texts about the literary art of Azerbaijan, Iran, Kazakstan, Kyrgyzstan, Tajikstan, Turkmenistan, and Uzbekistan; "South Asia" includes essays focusing on India, Pakistan, and Sri Lanka; "Southeast Asia" features studies of the literatures of Malaysia, the Philippines, and Singapore. A final section, "Australia and New Zealand," may appear incongruous in this category, when considered from a purely cultural point of view, but again, our central logic within these smaller sections remains primarily geographical. Throughout the essays in which authors consider various aspects of the literatures originating in Asia, it is interesting to note certain basic trends, progressively more discernible, such as the strong impact of political issues in texts treating Chinese literature (as with John Marney's 1991 "PRC Politics and Literature in the Nineties" and K. C. Leung's 1981 "Literature in the Service of Politics: The Chinese Literary Scene since 1949"), while the essayists treating Japanese literature tend to focus on aspects in the work of an individual author, analyzed from a primarily aesthetic point of view (see Bettina L. Knapp's 1980 "Mishima's Cosmic Noh Drama: *The Damask Drum*" and Celeste Loughman's 1999 "The Seamless Universe of Ōe Kenzaburō"). Not surprisingly, issues of cultural turmoil and social unrest permeate much of the discussion of literary art from Central Asia, as with Ahmad Karimi-

Hakkak's 1986 "Poetry against Piety: The Literary Response to the Iranian Revolution" and Bektash Shamshieu's 1996 "Post-Socialist Kyrgyz Literature: Crisis or Renaissance?" As for "Australia and New Zealand," we have endeavored to bring together texts that address general literary traditions in the region (such as Peter Pierce's 1993 "Australian Literature since Patrick White") and those that highlight less familiar modes (see Norman Simms's 1978 "Maori Literature in English: An Introduction").

The fifth major division of essays, "Latin America," opens with a series of discussions of the more ubiquitous issues of the region, such as the 1988 piece by Manuel Durán, "The Nobel Prize and Writers in the Hispanic World: A Continuing Story," while the subsections divided according to national literatures include explorations of the writing of Argentina, Brazil, Colombia, Costa Rica, Mexico, Peru, and Uruguay. In these sections, one is struck by certain commonalities of style and approach, as with the notable number of essays focusing on celebrated literary figures associated with the art of a specific country: Manuel Puig in Argentina, Octavio Paz in Mexico, Mario Vargas Llosa in Peru, or Gabriel García Márquez in Colombia, for example. Here, timely social issues often receive marked attention (see for example Roberto Reis's 1988 "Who's Afraid of [Luso-] Brazilian Literature?"), while a preoccupation with questions of literary form and style is also evident (Wilson Martins's 1979 "Carlos Drummond de Andrade and the Heritage of *Modernismo*" and Gregory Rabassa's 1982 "García Márquez's New Book: Literature or Journalism?" serve as examples).

"Eastern Europe, Russia, and the Balkans," the sixth section, reflects in its organizational logic the radically transformed cultural landscapes of the region. Included in this section are writings on the literatures of Albania, Bulgaria, Croatia, the Czech Republic and Slovakia, Greece, Hungary, Poland, Romania, Russia, Slovenia, Ukraine, and Yugoslavia. The size of this category, one of the largest in the collection, not only illustrates the importance of the geographical proportions of the region in question, but also indicates the impressive number of essays published in *WLT* on literatures from this fast-changing cultural sphere. Over the years, *WLT* has presented a variety of texts focusing on these regions, by such illustrious writers as Milan Kundera, Joseph Brodsky, and Chingiz Aitmatov, as well as a variety of essays that treat the work of these and other celebrated authors from the area (Aleksandr Solzhenitsyn, Andrei Bitov, and Karol Wojtyła—better known as Pope John Paul II—for example). While some of the earlier entries, such as Marketa Goetz-Stankiewicz's 1981 piece on Václav Havel, reflect the intellectual preoccupations of a more traditional eastern Europe, the most recent texts, such as Regina Grol's 2001 article, "Eroticism and Exile: Anna Frajlich's Poetry," demonstrate the extent to which the literary climate of the area has changed dramatically over recent decades.

"Northern Europe," the seventh section, includes a selection of general essays on Scandinavian literatures, followed by subsections on the Baltic States, Denmark, Finland, Iceland, Norway, and Sweden. Many of these pieces treat the artful combination of centuries-old sagas and mythic leitmotiv with truly contemporary issues of society and culture, as with Robert Bly's 1990 study of Tomas Tranströmer or Helena Forsås-Scott's 1984 examination of Sara Lidman. Other essayists focus on the impact of topics that affect a number of different nations in the area, such as George C. Schoolfield's 1988 study of the history of the Nobel Prize in relation to Scandinavian letters.

Section eight, "Western Europe," includes the literatures that may well represent those most familiar to contemporary North American readers, such as works from France, Germany, Ireland, Italy, the Netherlands, Portugal, Spain, Switzerland, and the United Kingdom. Here, readers not only will find essays devoted to some of the most widely recognized names in twentieth-century literature, such as Albert Camus, Günter Grass, Seamus Heaney, Italo Calvino, and Tom Stoppard, but also will discover analyses and appreciations of writers about whom they may know much less, as with Séamus Mac Annaidh, Dario Fo, Albert Verwey, and Jorge de Sena. Provocative cultural issues are also addressed as becomes clear in essays such as H. M. Waidson's 1990 "Silvio Blatter: Realism and Society in Modern Switzerland" and Giose Rimanelli's 1997 "The Poetry of 'Limited' Exile and Its Revealing Trek among Italy's Small Presses."

In the end, we hope that the eight classifications of texts that we include in these volumes will provide the contemporary reader with a manageable and pragmatic reference tool, particularly in light of questions of access and retrievability, while we also hope that the final selection will offer a sense of the logical distinctions, as well as the unexpected correspondences, that can materialize among these many literary perspectives. Regarding the thematic motifs and formal considerations that circulate throughout the collection, a more substantial overview will be presented later in this introduction.

To clarify the motivation of including two substantial appendices, again, a series of factors is involved, most pressingly perhaps, to remain true to the nature of the journal, and to present those elements that are important and interesting but that do not happen to fall within the necessarily limited framework of the present volumes. Appendix A supplies therefore the articles that were reprinted in a special issue of WLT (Spring 1989), entitled "The Best of Books Abroad." Given that the current collection of essays begins only in 1977, when Books Abroad becomes WLT, and since Books Abroad actually began publication in 1927, there are fifty years of engaging and original texts that appeared in the pages of the journal that fall outside the historical scope of the current collection. Appendix A allows readers to explore some of the most significant of these articles (designated as such by the editors of WLT in 1989), some of which are particularly celebrated, such as Czesław Miłosz's 1970 "On Pasternak Soberly," Jorge Guillén's 1971 "Remembering Valéry," Northrop Frye's 1955 "English Canadian Literature 1929–1954," and Mario Vargas Llosa's 1970 "The Latin American Novel Today." Other essays from this retrospective issue address pertinent moments in literary history, especially in relation to fundamental cultural and political paradigm shifts, as with A. A. Roback's 1934 "Yiddish Writing in America," Seán O'Fáolain's 1952 "Ireland after Yeats," and Taha Hussein's 1955 "The Modern Renaissance of Arabic Literature."

In Appendix B, entitled "World Literature in Review" (a title borrowed from the pages of WLT itself to designate the substantial book review section included in each issue), the reader will find an assortment of book reviews published in the period featured in the collection, 1977–2001. Given that the number of book reviews that have consistently appeared in WLT is startlingly high—approximately 300 per quarterly issue, which, for our twenty-five-year collection, amounts to a total nearing 30,000—this selection is hardly meant to be inclusive. Rather, because of the fundamental role bestowed upon book reviews by the editors of WLT throughout its history, Appendix B offers contemporary readers an overview of the diverse variety of reviews that illustrate the far-reaching nature of the material presented in WLT. Perhaps more interestingly, our purpose is also to give an idea of the evolving nature of the genre of the book review itself, as it moves, in the late 1970s, from a more informative, descriptive summary to, in the late 1990s, an original and creative form in itself, explored by review writers as an independent generic space to be sounded and expanded, in which to offer new ideas and to provoke thought and reaction.

For each year included within the time span, the reader will find six reviews, chosen for a variety of logistical and methodological reasons. Many of the reviews concentrate on important and influential books, a majority of which are prize winners. Some are written by authors whose own creative work has become particularly successful. Others stand out as especially provocative, either in form or in content, particularly controversial in viewpoint or suggestive in framework. Although many excellent reviews of extremely influential North American books appeared in the pages of *WLT*, the decision was made to include only reviews on literatures originating in cultures outside North America, to be consistent with the systemic foundation of the main body of the table of contents. Finally, as with the selection of essays, criteria for selection of book reviews involve such factors as language, culture, and the inclusion of both "minority" literatures and the work of internationally recognized authors, as the fundamental purpose remains to offer a diverse and far-reaching selection to contemporary readers, introducing evaluations both of well-known books and of much more specialized creative publications.

▪ TOPICAL MOTIFS AND FORMAL CROSSCURRENTS

One of the most striking impressions likely to occur to the reader of this collection is the increasingly more significant presence, as one advances in time toward the most recent texts, of the elements of history and culture, of the consideration (often reconsideration) of the art of literary expression as a phenomenon always deeply ensconced in a situation. Indeed, the notion of the contextualization of literature becomes a crucial leitmotif in these pieces, as the authors of the articles examine and discuss novels, poems, and plays by writers from vastly different geographical, ideological, and artistic settings. Given the astonishing number of substantial transformations in society, government, technology, and the role of the individual that surface between 1977 and 2001, both on a global level and in specific regional zones, this accent on questions of politics, history, and cultural identification hardly seems surprising. The ambivalent connections among such factors as history and memory, truth and fiction, emerge as well in the rethinking of recent world politics and art. A text such as Leon I. Yudkin's "Memorialization in New Fiction" (1998), for example, explores the genres of the novel, diary, and memoir as potentially powerful modes of expression in the mediation of the past in the work of contemporary writers. Similarly, in Tomas Venclova's 1978 study of Czesław Miłosz, the figure of the writer as conceived as the conscience of the world and the keeper of tradition emphasizes the ethical dimensions of literature and the committed nature of poetry and art. André Brink, in a particularly lucid and eloquent 1996 essay on history and writing in South Africa, suggests that, in the relationship of historiography to the genre of the novel, narrative is revealed to embody a touchstone, both for the community and for the individual. Other essays describe the work of authors who, conversely, do not wish to participate actively in politics and society through their writing, and in texts such as D. C. R. A. Goonetilleke's 1992 piece on Sri Lankan literature in English, we find a rejection of recent trends in some literatures to take advantage of the crises of politics, such as war and ethnic conflict, to meld art into a tool of propaganda.

One particularly significant example of a cultural and historical phenomenon that resurfaces insistently throughout these essays as a primary thematic framework is that of colonialization. Since so many different countries and peoples fought for and won their independence over the past twenty or thirty years, the dramatic new cultural landscapes fashioned through radical social, economic, and artistic renewal give rise to innovative literary artworks in which the notions of oppression, slavery, racism, and domination impact pervasively the tone of the writing. An essay such as Murray S. Martin's 1994 "Who Is the Colonist? Writing in New Zealand and the South Pacific" portrays the inherent ambiguities implied in questions of territory and possession, nation state and tradition, while Rocío G. Davis's 1999 text on the Philippines presents the imagistic notion of the nation as protagonist in a drama of power and propaganda, within a particular social and conceptual space. The move from a colonialist system to one grounded in a postcolonial reality is frequently underscored in works originating in the diverse countries of Africa, in which concerns of the overlapping of cultures merge with issues of linguistic and literary tradition and the encounters among different, often opposing priorities of various cultural hierarchies. See Charles P. Sarvan's piece on French colonialism in Africa, especially Cameroon, and Gerise Herndon's 1993 study of gender construction and neocolonialism in the Francophone Caribbean. Each highlights distinct facets of this complex and multiform cultural issue, as various literatures revisit the notions of history, power, and nation.

Along with the undeniably prevalent existence of heightened cultural consciousness comes quite naturally the reevaluation of the notions of ethnicity and race, of gender and age, of regional and national senses of self. The problem of the other, viewed as either hostile invader or sympathetic compatriot, stimulates frequent discussion regarding the dynamics of encounter, including the exciting possibilities of communication, or the unfortunate lack thereof. As the authors of the creative works under discussion—as well as the writers of the critical articles that address these works—take into account the refashioning of the self, along with the reformulation of the other, we discover authorial perspectives that take nothing for granted, even those elements that may have seemed the most stable and comforting, such as the belief in a coherent, logical, integrated ego. Sylvia Li-Chun Lin examines the problematic relationship of individual and collective values in her 2001 study of Gao Xingjian, for example, while Luiza Lobo, in her 1987 essay, explores the ambivalent condition of Brazilian women writers. Many of these texts illustrate thus the aim to universalize the individual, to impart to the readers a sense of shared community through their very subjectivity.

In part, of course, this revival of debate focusing on the most central issues of the human condition grows out of a more globally progressive trend of intellectual and ideological development throughout the twentieth century, as seemingly every realm of human knowledge and activity—from philosophy and literature to communication and transportation to science and sociology—undergoes a crucial transfiguration from the outmoded nineteenth-century model of rationalist, positivist systems of thought and method. In the West alone, the remarkably rapid development of such twentieth-century aesthetic perspectives as Modernism, Dada, Surrealism, Existentialism, Postmodernism, and Cultural Studies has brought an almost familiar sense of change as natural, of refusal and response directed toward the past as an integral and necessary element in the move toward the future. A selection of essays from throughout Europe, for example—such as A. Leslie Willson, "Entering the Eighties: The Mosaic of German Literatures: Introduction" (1981); Glauco Cambon, "Modern Poetry and Its Prospects in Italy" (1985); and Manuel Durán, "Vicente Aleixandre, Last of the Romantics: The 1977 Nobel Prize for Literature" (1978)—offers a panoramic view of the dynamic variations of aesthetic form and function born from a particularly energetic artistic era. The spirit of experimentation, of the search for innovation and difference, is certainly still present—if not even more powerful and compelling—in the years at issue in this collection.

On one side of what might be conceived as a kind of theoretical and thematic dichotomy between negative and positive impulses that arises in the reading of these essays, we sense an indisputably dark, anxious, even fearful voice of the modern writer that seems, sadly, increasingly universal. Thus the motifs of violence, poverty, oppression, ennui, and exile appear as primary in texts that treat countries as far removed from one another as Sri Lanka and Ireland, and it becomes evident to today's reader that the years in question represent in many ways an era of destabilization and deception, illu-

sion and deceit. As an example, the theme of alienation represents a powerfully evocative motif, widespread throughout these global literatures. The fictional subject of the novels and other creative works seems often irrevocably alone, cut off from family and friends, unable to formulate or to communicate to another his or her deeply felt loneliness and desperation. As examples, Ruth Hottell, in a 1997 piece, examines effects of the entangled relations among sexuality, nationality, and war in the work of Evelyne Accad, while Frederick Hale, in his 1983 "Tor Edvin Dahl and the Poverty of Norwegian Prosperity," underscores the ambivalent fortune of modern economic progress and its effect on the individual. Frequently this sensation of inexplicable, even unutterable, frustration and angst is expressed in these narratives through the figure of exile, sometimes in the most literal sense, as authors and protagonists find themselves, often through the intervention of forces over which they feel completely powerless, cut off from hearth and home, suffering a profound rupture from their own pasts.

Revolutions, invasions, colonization, and turbulent political change frequently precipitate these drastic transformations that can simultaneously affect large percentages of a given population, and are often carried out along ethnic or racial lines. Gila Ramras-Rauch, in a 1998 essay, "Aharon Appelfeld: A Hundred Years of Jewish Solitude," explores the archetypes of catastrophe and atonement in relation to the literature of the Shoah/Holocaust, while David Gillespie, in his 1993 text on the bonds between the Russian writer and the past, comments on the effects of such emblematic phenomena as the gulag and glasnost in the formulation of a new kind of literature, based in large part on the reinterpretation of history. Yet sometimes the implacably pervasive sense of exile emerges in the hearts and minds of authors and characters who remain in their native lands, often surrounded by those with whom they have carried on relations of the most intimate kind, friends and lovers, colleagues and family members. This more abstract and possibly more unsettling sense of difference often forces individuals to the margins of their respective societies, for they are considered (or they perceive they are considered) as pariahs, ostracized at the borders of the ideological and geographical homelands, where they had always found comfort and support. In Fernando Ainsa's 1994 study of Juan Carlos Onetti, for example, the essayist explores the presence in Onetti's work of the dark forces of passivity and fatalism, solitude and futility, in the figuration of the universal metaphysical sadness of the human condition. The sense of belonging—to a family, a nation, the human race—thus is undermined by the gnawing forces of doubt often perceptible in the ambiguities of modern times. Such characters, seeped in estrangement, embody dramatic figures of troubling otherness, from the criminal to the homeless, from the genius to the insane.

Yet it seems both inappropriate and untrue in the end to judge the literatures of the world during these particularly formative years as irrevocably helpless or hopeless, ultimately desperate or victimized. There is a remarkably vibrant presence in these literatures of an emerging sense of self, of a right to entitlement and authority, a drive for self-affirmation and the freedom of choice. As the individual, whether Chinese, French, Iranian, or Greek, comes to assert a sense of independent autonomy, necessarily more subtle and sophisticated than the conventions and clichés shared among larger, more anonymous groups, he or she is presented as having discovered a new path, in the forward-looking process toward the actualization of happiness, authenticity, and freedom. Thus John Scheckter, in his 2000 essay on the recent writings of David Malouf, shows how the Australian author explores the notion of individualism in process, as his fictional characters undergo a fundamental metamorphosis toward self-awareness and a sense of unity and cohesiveness on both temporal and spatial planes. As the disquieting figures of alienation and misgiving move toward the promise of genuine communication and cooperation, the reader is left with the sense of a concerted, energetic effort to perceive and understand the world around us, and to translate those impressions and connect to an increasingly knowing readership.

From these concerns with identity and struggle, purpose and freedom springs the popular central motif of movement. The world, as viewed through these literatures, is in constant flux, with nothing fixed rigidly in time and space, and the animated nature of the cosmos is reflected in the makeup of the individual, whose innate character is one of process and transition. In a piece such as the 1997 essay co-authored by Mohammed Saad Al-Jumly and J. Barton Rollins, "Emigration and the Rise of the Novel in Yemen," the figure of mobility, from one world to another, from one imaginary space to another, is revealed to be closely related to the development of the generic form of novelistic writing in the region. Thus the theme of travel permeates these studies, as do the topics of distance, deterritorialization, and a kind of new nomadism of modern urban peoples. In Rufus Cook's 1994 "Place and Displacement in Salman Rushdie's Work," the critic examines the conflicts that can arise between the impulse toward mobility and innovation and the instinctive desire to remain meaningfully connected to a time-honored cultural heritage, as the effects of immigration and emigration continually

influence the creation of art. The figure of progress, of making one's way from point A to point B, repeatedly embodies the metaphoric pivot in these works, as readers witness the evolution of a central character, on the road to success or artistry or, simply, happiness. Space itself has become somehow fluid in these works of art, as boundaries and borders are often revealed to be imaginary, perceived as metaphoric spaces for transition and progress. Frequently in these texts, what happens on the periphery of the storyline can become as evocative to a reader as that which is presented as taking place on center stage; narratives open outward, embracing limitless possibility and infinite interpretation.

Another important thematic framework that recurs throughout the cultural and geographical categories we have chosen is the portrayal of the career of a single author, often a writer who has won celebrated prizes and gained worldwide recognition, as with the pieces on Seamus Heaney, Czesław Miłosz, Marguerite Yourcenar, Manuel Puig, Nadine Gordimer, Edouard Glissant, and Gao Xingjian. Some essays describe the history of the relationship of a writer to his or her public, as illustrated in Sophie Jollin's 1997 examination of the reception of the work of J. M. G. Le Clézio. Yet also we find studies of the works of single literary figures much less well known, especially from a Western viewpoint, yet grounded in solid literary traditions. Eric Sellin's examination of the work of the Algerian author Moloud Mammeri (1989), Chinyere G. Okafor's study of the Nigerian playwright Ola Rotimi (1990), and John Zubizarreta's essay on the Iranian poet Forugh Farrokhzad (1992) all illustrate the influence and originality of authors who remain largely unfamiliar to today's Western audience. Some studies widen the scope beyond the work of a single author, and introduce an underrepresented group of authors belonging to literary traditions usually quite unfamiliar to the general Anglophone reading public: See for instance the articles by Valérie Orlando on Francophone women writers of Africa and the Caribbean, Nada Elia on Beur fiction, Kathleen Osgood Dana on Sámi literature, Iman O. Khalil on Arab-German writers, and Gerald M. Moser on the writers of Lusophone Africa.

In these essays we also discover examples of celebrated writers who are also the authors of the texts, as they take retrospective looks back at their own work; thus Peter Schneider meditates in a 1995 piece on the presence of the foreigner in his writing, while Maryse Condé considers the role of the family and cultural traditions on the individual literary artist (1993), and Carlos Fuentes ponders, in one of the most beautifully constructed essays in this collection, the development of one of his celebrated works, *Aura*, as an artistic product of the combined forces of context, intertext, and the author's own memory and imagination (1983). Essays such as these are complemented by interviews, such as the one Ronald Christ conducted with Manuel Puig—the last one to be completed before Puig's untimely death in 1990—in which the author discusses the social and artistic issues at play in his work, and suggests that for him writing is primarily a mode of seduction. In such a way, readers become attuned to a variety of often personal perspectives of authors reflecting on the meaning of their art; as Leon S. Roudiez explains in his 1982 text on Michel Butor, for this particular writer, the relationship of literary criticism to primary literary texts is particularly important in that it can reveal parts of a writer's work to that writer that he or she may have never before suspected. In this same vein, other particularly engaging essays are the work of one successful writer who addresses the work of another: See Ngũgĩ wa Thiong'o on Kamau Brathwaite, Jean Starobinski on Yves Bonnefoy, and Evelyne Accad on Assia Djebar.

One interesting expression of the reconsideration of the function and nature of the individual as perceived within a communal context comes through in the large number of essays that describe the work not of a single author presented alone, but of a group of writers considered in close relation to their surroundings, as new aesthetic schools and intellectual coteries are formed. Many of these texts address questions of climate, as they survey specific historical moments and geographical sites that together produce a particularly original cohesiveness in literary expression. The decade of the 1990s presents such an example, worldwide, of an overarching framework for numerous texts included here: Dietger Pforte examines in his 1997 essay the often conflictual dynamics of literary life in Germany after reunification; R. M. Davis explores the situation of Hungarian literature during these same years, describing the predicaments stemming from a literary community in disarray, threatened by ideological factionalism and economic hardship; Rimvydas Šilbajoris reflects on post-Soviet literature in Lithuania; Agnes Lam addresses the changing identity and function of poetry in Hong Kong in the 1990s; and Karl E. Jirgens treats writing in Latvia since independence. The list of essays that could be grouped together from this historical and cultural perspective is extensive and illustrates a growing sense of community, a desire, discernable on an international scale, of writers to form close and meaningful associations among themselves. Often these identities are formulated in terms of generations, as various groups of writers converge after especially momentous social changes, such as revolution and war, as they frequently critique the ideological motivations and modes of art of

those who came before them, often along political lines. Within our collection, it is particularly interesting to note that sometimes two or more essays treating a single national literary issue will display diametrically opposed opinions, as is the case with the controversial topic of the Americanization of the Philippines.

Thus we arrive at a parallel and equally significant sphere of development and experimentation in these works, that of form. The reconsideration of the conventional categories of literature, through the examination of problems of definition (an ongoing process of course since the origins of human art) blossoms during the period treated in these essays. Genre, for example, is aggressively reevaluated as a structural framework for the expression of art. Some authors turn back to ancient or archaic forms, while others move toward figures more specifically focused on the dynamics of individual expression, such as autobiography. History once again asserts its influential presence through primarily historical novels and more experimental forms that combine fact and fiction to such a degree that the reader is obliged to reconsider notions of "true" or "real." Robert E. DiAntonio, in his 1988 piece on the metafiction of Murilo Rubião, explores the dynamic systems of magical realism and the gradual transition into more complex forms in Brazilian literature, combining aspects of anti-realist fiction and Postmodernism.

This blending of forms originating in both poetry and prose produces new collages of textual discourse, and leads readers to rethink that which has conventionally come to be considered as canonical. Mythical and folkloric elements combine with science fiction and metafictional styles, as the notion of the writing itself as always already complete in itself sees the day, revolutionizing the notions of "story," "character," "theme," and "genre." See for example Yoshio Iwamoto's 1993 "A Voice from Postmodern Japan: Haruki Murakami," in which the author explores the marriage of popular discursive elements with phenomenological musings on the nature of the concrete world and on the unsettling relationship of words and things. Also, in Edna Aizenberg's 1992 "Borges, Postcolonial Precursor," the concept of art as a challenge to tradition and convention, particularly through the modes of parody and pastiche, encourages the reconsideration, not only of an aesthetic canon but of a political and social domain as well. Cross-over writing, texts that jump from one generic sphere to another, thus lead the modern reading public into new queries centered on issues of representation and mimesis, as timeworn aesthetic prescripts and strictures fall away, no longer slavishly obeyed. The significant impact of the expressive modes of orality, song, and other artforms manifests itself through the interest in hybrid constructions discernable in numerous essays: See Brendan P. O Hehir on the revival of Irish and its combinations with the English language (1980), Ezenwa-Ohaeto's exploration of Nigerian Pidgin poetry (1995), and E. Anthony Hurley on lyricism in French Caribbean trends in verse (1997). A prevalent related issue visible throughout these essays is that of the political, ideological, and even moral questions raised by the decision of an author on whether to write in English, as opposed to his or her native language; the dilemma of linguistic loyalty is revealed to be of worldwide concern, as with David Lloyd's 1992 article, "Welsh Writing in English," Wong Ming Yook's 2000 text on Malaysian fiction in English, Rajeev S. Patke's 2000 examination of English-language writing in Singapore, and Louise Viljoen's 1996 presentation of women's writing in Afrikaans.

Ultimately, what we have aimed to offer in compiling these volumes for the reading public is a broad perspective into global contemporary literature, characterized both by familiar names and titles and by new writers and literatures rarely discussed or analyzed elsewhere in the West besides in the pages of *WLT*. Another editor surely would have made different selections, would have followed a contrasting organizational plan, and would have offered, through these very differences, what we can only consider as an equally viable project, one clearly as subjective as our own. And that subjectivity, in fact, is precisely the point: Any editor, critic, author, or general reader who peruses the pages of the last twenty-five years of publication of *WLT* will necessarily come away with his or her own impressions—a fortunate thing—forming a sense of modern global literary reality constructed not only from the texts themselves but also from what that reader brings to the essays: experience and learning, original notions and private connections. The hope remains that our readers will use this diverse and rich sampling of texts to make their own distinctions and construct new bridges among these literatures. For when one comes across a surprisingly similar idea or parallel mode of expression in two literatures that appear at first glance to share little in common, connections such as these reveal much about what it has come to mean to be a writer in an international context over the past twenty-five years. Through the voices of these authors and critics—some represent time-honored traditions, while others test the limits and expand current ideological assumptions—we gain fresh awareness of a paradoxical global culture in which we ourselves participate, a culture defined by specific regional variations, yet ultimately surpassing the limitations of them all. The unanticipated affiliations generated throughout the collection also inform us about

ourselves, and about the world that surrounds us, while they suggest possible new directions of thought and art that await, just over future horizons.

Pamela A. Genova

[1] In the gathering of historical details, I have drawn extensively from the texts published by William Riggan, "The Nobel Connection," *Sooner Magazine* 1:1 (Spring 1981): 16–20; "The Puterbaugh Conferences," *Sooner Magazine* 3:4 (Summer 1983): 26–31; and "*World Literature Today* at 60," *Sooner Magazine* 7:2 (Spring 1987): 25–29. Also useful is a piece by David Draper Clark, "*Books Abroad/World Literature Today*: Past, Present and Future," *Publishing Research Quarterly* 18 (Spring 2002): 38–45. I would also like to take this opportunity to thank both of these gentlemen, as well as R. C. Davis-Undiano, for their invaluable editorial help, their efficient technical support, and the gracious access they provided me to the insiders' version of the history of *World Literature Today*.

[2] Roy Temple House, "Foreword to the First Issue—By the Editor," *Books Abroad* 1:1 (January 1927): 1–2.

[3] One case in point involves Michel Butor, the celebrated French author and critic, who was the featured writer at the 1981 Puterbaugh conference; he had already established a productive history with the University of Oklahoma as he had lectured on the campus in 1971 and had served as a juror for the Neustadt Prize in 1974 (in fact, the candidate he championed, Francis Ponge, won the award that year). During the 1981 visit, Butor gave seminars and delivered lectures on such topics as "Literature and Dream" and "The Origin of the Text," but perhaps the most memorable Butor text connected to his visit was the poem he wrote, adapted from the French by Ivar Ivask, entitled "An Evening in Norman," of which the first stanza reads: "My window faces west just as it does in Nice/ where it's deep night now/ the rays of the moon's first quarter/ illuminate the sky both here and there."

[4] It is actually quite surprising to examine the list of some of the most celebrated writers of the twentieth century who never won the Nobel, such as James Joyce, Franz Kafka, Marcel Proust, Jorge Borges, Theodore Dreiser, Henry James, Joseph Conrad, Vladimir Nabokov, Italo Calvino, Paul Valéry, Bertold Brecht, and Federico García Lorca. For more detail, see William Riggan, "The Swedish Academy and the Nobel Prize in Literature: History and Procedure," *WLT* 55:3 (Summer 1981): 399–405.

[5] Over the past thirty-two years, a total of twenty individuals associated in some close fashion with the Neustadt prize have won the Nobel Prize for Literature, including four Neustadt jurors (Henrich Böll, Odysseus Elytis, Joseph Brodsky, and Derek Walcott), three Neustadt laureates (Gabriel García Márquez, Czesław Miłosz, and Octavio Paz), and thirteen Neustadt candidates (Pablo Neruda, Aleksandr Solzhenitsyn, Eugenio Montale, Eyvind Johnson, Claude Simon, Elias Canetti, Wole Soyinka, Nadine Gordimer, Kenzaburō Ōe, Toni Morrison, Seamus Heaney, Günter Grass, and V. S. Naipaul). Elie Wiesel, who served as a juror, was later awarded the Nobel Peace Prize.

[6] *WLT* editor David Draper Clark describes the new direction of the journal as based in large part on widening the reading public: "While honoring *World Literature Today*'s traditions and striving to maintain an expected level of excellence, the current editors believe that they must also find new ways to reach a wider audience for the journal and to seek opportunities for

improvement and continued expansion of its programs. Throughout the journal's history, the majority of its readers have been librarians, research institutions, and individuals from more than seventy countries and six continents. In order to capture a more general audience, however, the staff of *World Literature Today* is committed to a renewed emphasis on clear and lively essays on contemporary literary topics that are accessible to a general, well-informed public—say, a similar readership in the United States to that of the *New Yorker* and *Atlantic Monthly*—as well as to professionals and academics" ("*Books Abroad/World Literature Today*: Past, Present and Future," 42).

7 This list, ranging from the first year of publication of *Books Abroad* to the year the list appeared in *WLT*, is arranged chronologically, and is found in the Summer/Autumn 2001 issue. The forty books chosen are: (1927): *To the Lighthouse* (Virginia Woolf, England); (1928): *The Gypsy Ballads* [*Romancero gitano*] (Federico García Lorca, Spain); (1928): *The Tower* (William Butler Yeats, Ireland); (1929): *The Sound and the Fury* (William Faulkner, United States); (1931): *The Turning Point* [*I strofi*] (George Seferis, Greece); (1933–47): *Residence on Earth* [*Residencia en la tierra*] (Pablo Neruda, Chile); (1934): *Independent People* [*Sjálfstætt fólk*] (Halldór Laxness, Iceland); (1935–40): *Requiem* [*Rekviem*] (Anna Akhmatova, Russia); (1941): *Mother Courage and Her Children* [*Mutter Courage und ihre Kinder*] (Bertold Brecht, Germany); (1942): *The Stranger* [*L'étranger*] (Albert Camus, France); (1943): *The Four Quartets* (T. S. Eliot, England/United States); (1944): *Ficciones* (Jorge Luis Borges, Argentina); (1945): "The Day Before Yesterday" [*Tmol shilshom*] (S. Y. Agnon, Spain/Israel); (1948): *Snow Country* [*Yukiguni*] (Yasunari Kawabata, Japan); (1950): *The Labyrinth of Solitude* [*El laberinto de la soledad*] (Octavio Paz, Mexico); (1952): *Waiting for Godot* [*En attendant Godot*] (Samuel Beckett, Ireland); (1952): *Invisible Man* (Ralph Ellison, United States); (1952): *The Old Man and the Sea* (Ernest Hemingway, United States); (1952): *In Country Sleep* (Dylan Thomas, Wales); (1953): *The Lost Steps* [*Los pasos perdidos*] (Alejo Carpentier, Cuba); (1956): *The Devil to Pay in the Backlands* [*Grande sertão: veredas*] (João Guimarães Rosa, Brazil); (1956–57): *The Cairo Trilogy* [*Al-Thulāthiyya*] (Naguib Mahfouz, Egypt); (1957): *Voss* (Patrick White, England/Australia); (1958): *Things Fall Apart* (Chinua Achebe, Nigeria); (1958): *The Guide* (R. K. Narayan, India); (1959): *The Tin Drum* [*Die Blechtrommel*] (Günter Grass, Germany); (1961): *A House for Mr Biswas* (V. S. Naipaul, Trinidad); (1961): *The Book of Disquiet* [*Livro do desassossego*] (Fernando Pessoa, Portugal); (1962): *The Golden Notebook* (Doris Lessing, Zimbabwe/England); (1962): *Pale Fire* (Vladimir Nabokov, Russia/United States); (1962): *The Time of the Doves* [*La Plaça del Diamant*] (Mercé Rodoreda, Spain);

(1962): *One Day in the Life of Ivan Denisovich* [*Odin den' Ivana Denisovicha*] (Aleksandr Solzhenitsyn, Russia); (1964): *A Personal Matter* [*Kojinteki-na taiken*] (Kenzaburō Ōe, Japan); (1966): *Collected Shorter Poems, 1927–1957* (W. H. Auden, England); (1967): *One Hundred Years of Solitude* [*Cien años de soledad*] (Gabriel García Márquez, Colombia); (1968): *House Made of Dawn* (N. Scott Momaday, United States); (1972): *Invisible Cities* [*Le città invisibili*] (Italo Calvino, Italy); (1974): *The Conservationist* (Nadine Gordimer, South Africa); (1978): *Bells in Winter* (Czesław Miłosz, Poland); and (1987): *Red Sorghum* [*Hung kao liang*] (Mo Yan, China).

8 R. C. Davis-Undiano, "Back to the Essay: *World Literature Today* in the Twenty-First Century," *WLT* 74:1 (Winter 2000): 5.

9 The initials "N," "S," and "K" in the title refer to the first letter of the first names of the Neustadt daughters who have established the prize: Nancy Barcello, Susan Neustadt Schwartz, and Kathy Neustadt Hankin.

10 In the deliberations regarding the establishment of the table of contents and the organization of these volumes, again I would like to thank William Riggan, David Draper Clark, and R. C. Davis-Undiano for their thoughtful input. Also, my deepest gratitude goes to Stephen Wasserstein, senior editor at Schirmer Reference and Twayne Publishers, whose useful suggestions and prescient advice proved to be truly valuable in the compilation and arrangement of the current volumes.

11 See R. C. Davis-Undiano on the reorganization of the substantial book review section in *WLT*: "While the recent introduction of page 'tabs' to provide better navigation through the 'World Literature in Review' section is no large event, in its own modest way this addition highlights the spirit of *WLT*'s more significant changes. We introduced tabs in the Winter 2000 issue, simply to organize a review section of some 300 entries, but soon we were putting the tabs in alphabetical order—in effect, decolonizing the tradition of emphasis on European literature in 'world literature' (our old order ran 'French, Spanish, Italian, Other Romance Languages, German,' et cetera). Now beginning alphabetically with 'Africa & the West Indies,' the 'World Literature in Review' section reflects, in its own way, a new order and a new idea of 'world literature'" ("Introduction: Looking Just Ahead," *WLT* 74:3 [Summer 2000]: 470). As an example, taken from the same issue as Davis-Undiano's essay, the book review section tabs run: "Africa and the West Indies," "Asia and the Pacific," "English," "Finno-Ugric and Baltic Languages," "French," "German," "Germanic Languages," "Italian," "Russian," "Slavic Languages," "Spanish," and "Various Languages."

Perspectives on World Literature

Theorizing Comparison: The Pyramid of Similitude and Difference

The comparatist function has swung in the twentieth century from a search for similitude to an emphasis on difference in a trend parallel to that of politics. After World War I, transnational bonding manifested itself in several forms and levels, among them Marxism, surrealism, and comparative literature. The universal man in the framework of a one-world image was the basis of all three movements, which of course were far apart in terms of the particular content of such images. In contrast, the second part of the century will be noted in history for its drive to split: split the atom, split nations into underlying ethnicities, split the ego in a formidable diaologism with the "other," even split the two sexes into five. I do not intend to pass judgment on the recent targets of the analytical mind and the various resulting forms of deconstruction, but rather to posit two problems that confront comparative literature because of this change of venue: how this tendency to split has affected comparative literature, and what we can do to establish a balance between oneness-vision and the urge for multiplicity of visions that has become popular today.

I present my perception in the form of a pyramid because my image of our domain is broad-based on its most elementary level and the broad bottom level is not separated by a gap from other levels but integral to a structure that grows gradually, becoming higher and narrower, eventually rising to a tip where the subject matter moves from fundamental sameness to diversity and where the diversity is eventually amalgamated and ultimately absorbed into a unity. From the bottom to the peak of the pyramid opportunities for comparison abound.

The bottom of the pyramid encompasses all literature. It constitutes primordial subject matter common to all literatures. Its collective character resembles that of myth; but there is a point where myth stops and literature begins, and who can better give us insight into that junction than Claude Lévi-Strauss with his knowledge of both myth and literature. In his discussion of myth in *Le cru et le cuit* he demonstrates that whereas myth has structure, the expressors of the myth are not conscious of it. Proceeding from that notion, we can say that when the expression of a phenomenon or universal image has a structure which the narrator has created or of which he is aware, then it deserves inclusion in the realm of literature. However, on this level of the pyramid the literary texts as well as the myths have universal linkage. There is nothing new about this observation. Almost all literary materials can be and indeed have been reduced by recent critics to mathematical dimensions at the primary base of similitude. There are two or three basic themes, basic plots, basic images, and many basic human emotions that one can discover in literature, whether simple or sophisticated, wherever they may emerge on the planet Earth;[1] and there are a number of narrative devices that renew themselves continually. Umberto Eco has shown the mathematics of such comparisons; I have heard Oxford scholars argue over the rule of two or three in the plays of T. S. Eliot. On this basis, Tennessee Williams can be compared to Sophocles, and Shakespeare's *The Merchant of Venice* with Molière's *L'Avare*. There is a stark, primordial homogeneity that makes the most unfamiliar literature accessible in comparing it to known ones.

On this level, anthropologists, archeologists, ethnographers, and mythographers supply a convenient frame of reference for the literary critic, because the methodologies they have developed in comparing ancient rites and myths can be applied to certain basic elements that prevail in the literary script. Lévi-Strauss's delineation of the passage from "le cru" to the "cuit" is here at play; the basis of comparison in reference to myths is what Lévi-Strauss calls "reciprocal intelligibility discerned between several myths."[2] Lévi-Strauss established "sets" by looking for patterns in neighboring tribes, and he attributed the syncretism to physical intermovements of such tribes. The same reciprocity occurs between primordial literary texts, but the literary comparison can go much further: it is obvious that at this broad level what unites literatures all over the world is dependent not on circumstantial conditions due to exterior mobility but on essential human elements that bring them together, such as the simple fact that the characters all possess a nose, a mouth, a heart, a mind, and built-in neuro-psychological responses. Equally fundamental and unifying are such human propensities as, to name but a few: lust, greed, jealousy, vengeance, incest, rape, stealing the forbidden, searching for lost or unknown identity, nostalgia for immortality, belief in the transformation of the human and the sacred, and even an inclination to search for fraternity between the species, etcetera. They are the *stuff* that myths are made of, and they are encrusted in both realistic and fantastic literature. In this type of text we look to language not to *shape* thought but to *convey* it. In the comparing of writings based on such primordial drives and images, comparisons can appropriate legends, fairy tales, god substitutions such as Osiris/Orpheus or receivers of gods such as Leda / the Virgin Mary. The task of the comparatist is not simply to show common sources but to study the inception of common structures at points where the myth becomes literature.

The danger lurking in archetypal studies is that the documentary interest may overwhelm other concerns and cause oversights of the various degrees of creativity possible to discover in individual works that lift the primary elements into the realm of the literary. The process of reducing to a common denominator can blind the critic to the complexity of the structure of which the basic similitudes are the foundation.

As we build up the pyramid, ingredients of the multicultural emerge, and the search for distinction uncovers differences of social settings and group mentalities: there occurs an adaptation of the archetypal to a specific locality, time, and race. Comparing literatures becomes a study in contrasts; the barrier language of discriminative criticism sets in: words such as *difference, exile, displacement, outsiderdom,* and *cultural otherness* creep in to describe the conflicting elements that often lead to the study of the heteronomous, emphasizing isolation and disjunction, resulting in a loss of the sense of recognition and of the euphoria of the déjà vu; a newly discovered literature comes to be viewed with blinders, and the notion of influence becomes taboo because it seems to steal something of the uniqueness of the particular. The ethnic perspective starts out innocently perhaps but often ends in a chauvinism that for-

sakes judgmental comparisons with other writings from other nations or ethnicities. To quote a disastrous enthusiast of ethnicity: "The highest purpose of a folkish state is concern for the preservation of those original racial elements which bestow culture and create beauty and dignity of a higher mankind."[3] Politically such concepts have led to the horrors of racial cleansing; unless carefully handled, ethnic studies of literature can lead to arid lands of investigation annulling the very notion of comparative literature. Here again we can learn from the mythographer, who in comparing sets suggests that in their juxtaposition such texts "should display an increasingly intelligible structure as a result of the double reflexive forward movement of two thought processes acting one upon the other either of which can in turn provide the spark or tinder *whose conjunction will shed light on both*" (the emphasis is mine).[4] Here in a nutshell is the essential of all reception theory and the major reason why the comparative optic can provide enriching dimensions to the national or ethnocentric study of literature.

As the layers of cultural strata pile up, their differentials are legitimate pursuits for the comparatist only if they feed each other into a better and broader understanding of each and of each other. This process might be called *the search for complementarity*. The much-abused concept of "influence" should be viewed not as imitation but as a process of transformation.[5] The linguistic differences should become a path to the better grasp of language itself. Why did Cervantes have to write *Don Quixote* in Spanish? Why did Rabelais say it best in French? Why did Shakespeare—the protests of German translators to the contrary—give his best scope in English? Why is it that, even when national literatures try to convey an exotic setting, the exoticism is but a trapping? Why, if in identifying the foreign setting of *Salammbô* Flaubert calls it "the Orient of my imagination," should his statement not be taken as offensive to Arab readers?

The perspective of the multicultural optic is also very fruitful in studies of reception, because variations in culture bring about the outsider's cultural identity to the interpretation and evaluation of the text in question. The sociologist and the political scientist offer supportive resources to the comparatist in this area of study; but the focus is different and the priority of interest for the comparatist has to be—by the very nature of the discipline—on the literary work rather than on the social background. Many archetypal studies in comparative literature can progress into the multicultural as they move from the study of sameness to the ingredients reflecting differences in the cultural base. The comparison of Shakespeare's *Merchant of Venice* and Molière's

L'Avare is a case in point. Both plays are basically studies in the primordial human drive of greed, but the cultures in which these characters are imbedded create enormous differentials. Shylock's usury is not just human greed but a recourse against European treatment of the Jew at a certain time and place in history. His powerful primordial emotions of anger, anguish, and vengeance, consummated in what is taken by the others as a form of intense greed, is really an attempt to preserve his material possessions, which to him is synonymous with self-preservation. His passionate discourse is put in sharp—but not sufficiently noted—contrast with the supercilious dialogues that Shakespeare has written for Shylock's courtly, gambling Venetian (but really English) enemies. Even the presumed heroine, Portia, a product of that mercantile society, is made to utter a stilted, rhetorically contrived tirade about mercy and in the rest of the play engages in trivial discourse.

The cultural difference between *The Merchant of Venice* and *The Miser* is telling. Whereas Orgon's behavior can also be included under the primordial label of *greed,* his motivation is of course quite different. He is defending himself against French seventeenth-century mores dealing with the financial transactions surrounding marriage contracts. As for Shylock, so for Orgon does money become a solace against isolation. Because it brings others into each protagonist's sphere of control, it becomes an important weapon and a major factor in the existence of each. Both will therefore go to extremes to preserve it: Shylock to horrifying cruelty, Orgon to ludicrous behavior. Orgon, however, is threatened not by prejudice but by the standard mores involving on the one hand the threat of depleting his treasure by offering his daughter a dowry, and on the other the temptation to increase his existing fortune by marrying as a widower an attractive woman who would bring *him* a dowry. From the acceptance of greed as a primordial human characteristic to its manifestation as a weapon to combat social mores, we have progressed from an archetypal study to a multicultural one. With a basis in a common elementary emotion, we arrive at the differential of the cause of such a manifestation: in one case racial prejudice, in the other marriage customs. The two cases are cultural manifestations of different nations, different centuries, both brought subtly under attack by the authors. In a study which juxtaposes two such canonical works the comparatist can demonstrate similarity, difference, and something additional that distinguishes comparative literature from other types of criticism dealing with intertextuality: the highlighting of the complementary character of such works, both tested for their universal appeal.[6]

The top of the pyramid is a place of cohesion and unity. Great religious, philosophical, and literary movements create such transcultural manifestations that override or overpower national or ethnic differences: the fifteenth-century passion plays rising out of a community of Christian references; the European literary movements of the nineteenth and twentieth centuries that spread beyond the boundaries of Europe, works reflecting a certain zeitgeist which marks them in fraternal ways, transnational intellectual rebellions such as the one currently being called "postmodernism" for lack of a better word. The interdisciplinary factor here engaged is philosophy.

The local color becomes secondary, parole easily interchangeable from one language to another. Acultural perceptions such as chaos, "le neant," hell, entropy, and changing notions of mortality and happiness, mutations in gender relationships, etcetera, are all shared by a relatively small number of creators in all the arts and received by a number of readers or beholders as small in proportion to the population of the globe. For these creative artists and receivers, language recuperates from the Tower of Babel to *create* rather than to *convey* thought; and the work, becoming self-reflexive, is no longer restricted to national or ethnic boundaries. In fact, it generally becomes more easily translatable. In a 1994 book by Olivier Donnat entitled *Les Français face à la culture* the author recognizes serenely (as only a statistician can) the remoteness, numerically speaking, of the native French population from its high culture, which he calls throughout his book "la culture cultivée." He suggests that only the collective efforts of the cultivated in all cultures can preserve it.[7] We can associate with this notion the fact that if we cannot understand Nathalie Sarraute, it is not because she writes in French. And a bilingual reader may have as much difficulty reading Nabokov in Russian as in English. The philosophic writer, like the scientist, has no country. Such authors are bonded to other philosophers and scientists and to those who can read them. The comparatist who engages in literary studies of this acultural nature demonstrates the interchangeability of such writers. As I was reading a modern Flemish novel called *Celibat* by a certain Gérard Walschap,[8] I thought I was reading Sartre or Ionesco or Cortázar. Here we see concordances, connections, correspondences regardless of ethnic separations.

On the other hand, let us not be misled by the occasional appearance of kinship between the elementary and the sophisticated artist; the mind that has found it necessary to free or distill itself from an overload of associations of established concepts and imagery has a longing to identify with levels of pristine perception and simple expression, whether in writing or in the plastic arts or even in music. But if so many modern artists are drawn to naïve art or writing, the comparison in terms of similitude is a tenuous one. In the one instance the lack of complexity arises from a lack or paucity of cultural associations with other "sets," whereas the second instance involves a process of ultimate triage, and the simplicity of line or verbal concept or image thus achieved is a triumph over miscellany and variation.

André Breton, seeing the cave drawings of the Hopi Indians, exclaimed that these were surrealists. His effervescent desire to expand the domain of surrealism in time and space sometimes resulted in overreach and hasty conclusion. The desire for "l'œil sauvage" by the sophisticated, supremely learned[9] writers and artists from many cultures who formed the surrealist movement resulted in a search for a universal innocence: to recuperate the original freshness of sensations. But they refused to admit the fact that perceptions heavy with cultural connotations could not be cast off so easily. The efforts of the culturally overloaded to embrace the culturally light could only produce an artificial minimalism, an important art form of response, indeed, but one quite different from the primitive model. The simplicity of line in Mondrian or in Miró is symptomatic of a collective reaction that brings them together, as in the case of writers practicing ostensibly simple writing that is in fact highly involuted.

If the bonding of the culturally complex with the culturally simple is misleading, the linking of authors and artists characterized by excessive cross-referentiality brings cultures closer to each other and creates a field day for comparative study in similarities. The danger here is that the critic who juxtaposes such writings to extricate from them generalities often leaves behind the texts that instigated the comparison. Theory has its place at the tip of the pyramid, where all cultures become one. But the danger in the practice of theory is that it can make the comparatist as inaccessible as those writers themselves who have, on their loaded disks, taken the text out of the range of accessibility and produced among themselves a unity so tight that one may assume they are writing principally for one another. Texts that become virtually dialogues between writers are not essentially literature; likewise, in my opinion, theoretical writings belong in the realm of literary criticism only when they retain close contact with the literature that provoked the theory.

Which aspect of these levels is more or less appropriate to comparative literature study? It is a matter of choice. What is significant is to become aware of what one is doing and not be pushed around by passing trends and fashions. What is essential is not to lose sight

of the integrity and independence of the work of art, not to turn a piece of literary writing into a study of archeology or clinical psychology, nor to transform a legendary image such as the labyrinth into a demonstration of an ancient sewer system, as I remember one guide did while leading tourists through the island of Crete, oblivious to the famous legend with its many literary ramifications. Neither is it the less puzzling to observe a manifestation of ethnic pride condemned as an anti-Semitic document as in the case of *The Merchant of Venice,* a drama that focuses on a moral struggle in which the avenging power of money is brought to bear upon the subjugating power of the Establishment. Neither is it fair to attack a narrative of an imaginary dreamland as a dogmatic misunderstanding of Islam under the aegis of critics who have realigned historical time and perspective according to their perceived division of the world into colonial and postcolonial.

We are having disputes and disagreements over what constitutes "great literature" or whether there is in fact such a thing. In terms of the pyramid, when a work of art can be perceived from the primordial base of core substance, proceed to the nuances and variations of a particular culture in which it blossomed and flourished, and have enough resonance to reach the cohesiveness of a vision that synthesizes differences due to time and place, then it possesses the density necessary for literary survival in the face of rising and falling civilizations. I have briefly demonstrated my position in reference to particular works by Shakespeare and Molière that have had the power to sustain universal readership through several centuries, but I believe it can be tested against all literary works that time has preserved as canonical. The examples are not the exception but a fundamental development in literature. Intertextuality was invented not by critics but by artists in all the media. Across differing cultures they have responded to one another in the broader complementarity that binds the world of the arts, and at times by their collective vigor they have produced Golden Ages.

There is a wave of critical attitudes that would dilute what has earned its place as "great literature"; an understandable but hasty spirit of democratization prompts such a judgmental lapse. By introducing into the body of literature on an equal footing with works recognized as "literary" the kind of texts that are indeed sociological documents and fragmentary, minimal, archetypal expressions both oral and written, the proponents of equal time and equal space for all are eliminating the notion of "quality" identifiable with organization, selection, and referentiality. The disdainful branding of "elite" in the literary sorting out is a shirking of the fact that "elite" means "educated"[10] in the literary lexicon, applicable to professional writers as to ordinary people. Purely archetypal writings are interesting and associative on the broad base of the pyramid, but if they do not proceed to other levels, they are unlikely to attain universal and lasting appeal in spite of all the talk and coercion or of any theoretical justification for their inclusion in the mainstream of literature.

My pyramid is not a totem pole or a spiral but a structure of density; it rises on sustained craftsmanship all the way to the top, demonstrating the difference between pure mathematical abstraction and a fleshy, concrete build-up that creative expression distills to form literature.

Anna Balakian, Spring 1995

1   Newly discovered caves in the South of France and burial sites recently uncovered in Honduras have general traits of kinship with those already registered in the annals of archeology.

2   Claude Lévi-Strauss, *The Raw and the Cooked: Overture,* tr. Doven Weightman, Chicago, University of Chicago Press, 1969, p. 13.

3   Adolf Hitler, as quoted from *Mein Kampf* (U.S. ed., Boston, 1943, p. 394) in William Shirer, *The Fall of the Third Reich,* New York, Simon & Schuster, 1963, p. 89.

4   Lévi-Strauss, p. 13.

5   See Anna Balakian, "Influence and Literary Reception," in her book *The Snowflake on the Belfry,* Bloomington, Indiana University Press, 1994.

6   It is interesting to note that whereas the multicultural optic in this instance brings out the diversity in the two situations in terms of the culture in which each of the two characters is framed, the basic psychological motivations bring them together.

7   Olivier Donnat uses the term "la culture cultivée" (the cultivated culture) throughout his book and ascertains statistically that half of the French population has a "nonexistent, feeble, or episodic rapport with the book." *Les Français face à la culture,* Paris, La Découverte, 1994, p. 285.

8   See Gérard Walschap, *Celibat,* Paris, Editions Universitaires, 1968.

9   It is appropriate to note that several of the leading French surrealists had gone through high levels of academic formation, some had studied medicine, and the rest were autodidacts with a very wide range of readings; the Germans, Spanish, and Central Europeans had similar erudition. Even Dali, who clowned to attract public attention, had an extraordinary intellectual background, as the field of reference of his writings demonstrates. In Latin America most of those interested in following the surrealist mode were lawyers by profession as well as the proud possessors of a wide frame of literary reference and a knowledge of several languages, sociology, and psychology. An interesting exception, the Chilean Rosamel del Valle, who portrayed in *Eva y la fuga* a simpleminded dream figure, had had virtually no formal education but was one of the most widely read authors in philosophy and psychology as well as in European and American literature. In fact, what brought the surrealists together was the cohesion in their literary and philosophical framework regardless of the diversities of race and ethnic culture.

10   This "educated" frame of reference is acquired not necessarily in school but through autodidacticism, as in the case of socially disadvantaged writers who aspire to creative expression and build up in their own way a wide frame of reference. It takes a very subtle mind, with a highly charged mental battery, to create what appears to be "simple" literary communication. In this respect surrealists have misled us in popularizing automatic writing. Literature demands organizational control of data, whether randomly culled from the unconscious or selectively collected by the observing mind.

On the Translation of Form in Poetry

Five years ago, on 7 February 1974, Joseph Brodsky published in the *New York Review of Books* an essay about some problems in the translation of poetry. The occasion of this article was the recent rendering into English of poems by Mandelstam done by two American writers, Clarence Brown first, then the noted poet W.S. Merwin; and the problem which had particularly retained Brodsky's attention was the fact, certainly significant, that both the authors had chosen to make their translations in free verse, while the original poems were an illustration of perfectly regular patterns. In his paper Brodsky firmly rejects this decision of the American translators and explains why he cannot accept any translation of a regular or "classical" prosody into free verse. But Brodsky is wrong in this matter, and I shall try tonight to give the reasons why I believe in the virtue of free verse.

What are Brodsky's reasons for refusing a translation in free verse of Mandelstam's poetry? "Mandelstam is a *formal* poet in the highest sense of the word," he writes in the beginning. "For him, a poem began with a *sound,* with a sonorous molded shape of form." And he adds, which seems rather logical indeed, that the translator should find not a *substitute* for this original form, but an *equivalent,* a metrical equivalent which consequently could be nothing—at least he believes so—but the same sort of regular verse handled by the other poet with the same respect and seriousness as Mandelstam did. "Meters," Brodsky writes, "meters in verse are kinds of spiritual magnitudes for which nothing can be substituted. . . . They cannot be replaced by each other and *especially not by free verse.*" In fact, Brodsky goes as far as saying that free verse is another sort of art—presumably inferior, or at least more limited, as drawing is (or would be; this is only Brodsky's opinion) in its relationship to painting: so that, in the field of translation, non-regular patterns should be proscribed and even morally condemned. "Carolyn Kyzer once said in jest," Brodsky remarks, "that international legislation

Yves Bonnefoy (*Gil Jain*)

should be introduced to prohibit the translation of classical verse into free verse." And he adds very seriously, "Something really should be done. Russian poetry does not deserve being treated like a poor relation."

Let us stop here for a while, for we must understand right now that there are in fact two very distinct arguments in this condemnation of free verse, while Brodsky seems to accept as self-evident that they are simply two aspects of the same truth. He emphasizes the value and meaning of poetic form; he shows its relatedness with the most inner quality of the poem, stating: "A poem is the result of a certain necessity: it is inevitable and so is its form. . . . Form is *noble*. . . . It is the vessel in which meaning is cast. They need each other and sanctify each other reciprocally—it is an association of soul and body. Break the vessel and liquid will leak out"—and I cannot but agree with these ideas so beautifully formulated. But there is this other point about the inferior, the "drawing-like" quality, of free verse in general, and even more surprising, this moral judgment which Brodsky makes, in unequivocal terms indeed, by saying assertively, even scornfully: "Russian poetry has set an example of moral purity and firmness which to no small degree has been reflected in the preservation of so-called classical form"; and: "What was

done to Mandelstam by Merwin . . . is a product of profound moral and cultural ignorance." Are these latter propositions really the same unquestionable truth as the former one? We must check them most carefully perhaps, and the more so as Brodsky makes it very clear that he does not limit their condemnation of free verse to its use in the translation of regular ones, but rejects every use of it, every poem written with its help. Actually, he finds in free verse the main distinction between Russian poetry and what he calls "her Western sisters" and makes us suspicious that he believes his own poetic tradition the only one inflexible, if not heroic—a quality which the difficulty of regular verse would underline— while the decadent literatures of the West, with their free verse as a proof of their laziness, would indulge in all the easy delights of their corrupted civilization. Once more, the old idea of holy Russia, whose historical misadventures could even be signs of qualities and aspirations inaccessible to our lower ones!

I will certainly object to this bold discrimination, and in order to answer the questions raised by Brodsky, my first step will be to reformulate in terms of contradiction and perplexity what seems to be for the Russian poet a matter of certitude. Yes, it cannot be doubted that poetry is form as well as meaning, so that I surely do not believe that the Russian poets, for instance, must be deprived, by our ways of translating them, of their rights to be understood as formal artists—the more so as this former quality is the core of their specific and quite meaningful spiritual tradition. More generally, I know that we should lose terribly if we were to read Mallarmé, or Yeats or Leopardi, all of whom used regular verse, without being able to understand and repeat their own experience of form. And yet, when I began to translate Shakespeare and later some poems of John Donne or Yeats, I did not hesitate to adopt free verse, and I still believe I was right. Was it not a renunciation, if not an outright betrayal? I was aware of this risk. But I also knew that the laws of reading, understanding, translating a poem are not simple and that perhaps we must lose in the beginning in order to be able later to recover more fully.

And, first, I will propose to your attention this idea which cannot be doubted and must be applied to our problem, so it seems to me: Nothing can be rightly analyzed in itself, independently of the whole to which it belongs; we must think in terms of structure. In the case of poetry this means that *no part of a poem, not even its form,* has a detached or constant meaning; it is only an element which receives its value from a totality in which certainly are active all the other functional aspects of writing: for instance, the serious or sarcastic intention of the author, or the religious connotations of speech in its society, but also the characteristics of the language, Russian or English or French, and, last but not least, the historical moment, which has perhaps engraved into the very matter of this poetry its special spiritual features, and that far beyond the will and even the understanding of the poet. This proposition may seem to you too general or too nebulous, but I hope that I will make myself clearer in the example of verbal patterns, which is our subject today. In other words, I will try to show how poetic form can contain, in its very regularity, meanings diverse if not contradictory, along with the passage of time and the transformation of social values; to show, therefore, that a regular, conventional type of verse may signify today in America or France something very different from what Mandelstam felt, with the consequence that using it in our 1970s for the translation of his verse would make of our poem quite the opposite of a faithful rendering.

This "regular," this "classical" verse! Strange to say, but nobody seems to have endeavored to discover what regularity meant by itself in these periods when, for the longest part of its history, it was not yet the object of the conscious and explicit attention of the poet: I mean, before the nineteenth century, in which poets began to question its use and find in it expressive possibilities very different from its former ones. According to my feeling, however, the regular form had at the origin in its very conventionality a precise meaning and function which it is important to analyze. Since it was a conventional form, the line—for instance, the English pentameter—was, in a sense, always the same, whoever the poet using it might be. But every particular pentameter remained nevertheless in its content, as the expression of a very definite person, very different from all the others, and consequently the regular verse as such had the same structure and ambiguous duality as the social order, which was a unique pattern, generally and consciously accepted, while being at the same moment also the personal experience and even the personal expression of everybody in that society. In other words, *practice* of conventional prosodic forms resembled then the relation of the human being to the beliefs and values, to the form of his society. If this practice was universally accepted and capable of beautiful and meaningful achievements, the reason was—and that was its innermost significance—that this relationship of man to society was itself, and above all, a positive and full experience as well as a common form and truth: what I could call also an *orthodoxy*. In sum, the conventions in the prosody of this first period, which lasted until romanticism, were in themselves the *metaphor* of the social law, and the beauty of at least many poems in this frame reflected the fact that this law was one and alive: that man participated happily in a common meaningful order.

If I had time, I could now give many examples of this value of regular verse as a mirror and proof of social orthodoxy—a good key indeed to understanding the successive stages of poetry since Homeric verse, in which so many generations found the perfect expression of ideas and beliefs they accepted in their social life, until the dawn of our contemporary world. We could speak of Dante, whose *terza rima* wanted explicitly to reflect the fusion of the finite and infinite which characterized the Christian cosmos in the Middle Ages; or of the classical *alexandrine,* this closed, dignified structure which expresses so well the little world of Versailles, itself so tightly closed and ceremonious. Lacking time, however, I will only underline the reason why these reflections of social order by verse took the particular forms we know: that is, in the predominance of the pentameter in English and the line of ten or twelve syllables in French. Of these verses it can be said that they are the best possible union of a form which remains as such perceptible and imperative—as a representation of social orthodoxy—and of a content, the individual experience, which can find in it room enough for an exploration of itself. A shorter line would have given too much predominance to the formal pattern over its content; the seriousness of the form would not have been supported by a personal experience free enough in its movements to be carried seriously; the verse would have been a game, a playful activity and not a complete image of the social act. On the other hand, had our common verse been longer, the concrete aspects of the individual experience would have been more visible than the common form and we would then be on the verge of prose, which is a rupture with the sacredness of the common law. The average length of the conventional verse in Western tradition signifies, in brief, like a needle upon a dial, that there is, or rather that there was, in these centuries, a good balance and stability in the interplay of social order with these individual experimentations which constantly threaten to break it.

Thereupon, perhaps, will it be easier to understand that, if the use of regular verse signifies thus the actual existence of an orthodoxy, of a common set of beliefs, then free verse, reciprocally, can appear only when no common truth rules any longer the spirits of men—that is, when everybody is fumbling about for his own personal system of values, for his *form*: a variety of possible solutions which the infinite potentialities of the new prosody alone will be able to reflect. As a matter of fact, it is almost exactly at the same moment that Nietzsche himself exclaims, "God is dead," a sentence which means that no spiritual unity remains alive in society, so that men will be entitled from now on to try everything; and the same moment that Mallarmé observes, in his famous lecture at Oxford, that "On a touché au vers," that some young poets have, for the first time in history, broken the great conventional forms which till then had ruled poetic invention. At the end of the nineteenth century Christianity is no longer a universal evidence, the Orient is nearer, the specter of revolution is haunting Europe, terrible wars are at hand, Freud is born—and, simultaneously, some rather obscure symbolist poets decide to break up prosody. No mere coincidence, I believe; perhaps the crystal ball of the clairvoyante. At first in France, but later everywhere in the Western world, will free verse be only the broken mirror or, in the fragments, a new light?

In any case, it will be a *fact,* of changing but precise meaning, and to go back now to Brodsky's problem, we can deduce from these first remarks that it is not as simple as this poet seems to think. In Western Europe at least nobody can use today the regular, the conventional patterns of verse as they were employed before Mallarmé's younger friends, or Nietzsche. In France, for instance, the alexandrine is dead, surviving only in some imitations of the past, void of any substance or sincerity. Sometimes, of course, it can appear accidentally or even sustain itself for a while as a pseudo-regular structure, because of a flash of nostalgia or of hope in a poet's mind; but any true questioning of its sense must nevertheless place it against the background of predominant free verse. In England or America, on the other hand, regular forms are certainly more frequent, and more authentic, since your English prosody has always been more supple than ours, and consequently does not so urgently ask the poet to enter the pure realm of forms and take cognizance of their meaning or requirements. But your prosodic conventions have lost, nevertheless, this remarkable self-assurance and assertiveness which they showed in Shakespeare's or Milton's work. Were your fragile regular schemes of today to be used for ideas or feelings of the old vintage, their vessel would break and the liquid would leak out. None of us can use instinctively, unambiguously, the old regular forms, deprived as we are of the old spirit, which had been for such a long time their principal cause. And even in the case of a translation we cannot but experience this impediment, since the translator of poetry, as Brodsky surely would agree, must react as a poet does.

Against Brodsky I therefore affirm that, even when we have to translate some of these poems of the past, whose regularity was so important an aspect, almost the soul, we can no longer sincerely and seriously use regular, "classical" meters. Indeed, the more regularity was intense or significant in the original poetry, the more our faked or dispirited regularity of now must be, at the very first, dismissed.

But be careful, you will say perhaps; there were cases, in an intermediate period, just after the centuries of social orthodoxy and before the contemporary pluralism or anarchy, in which regular verse and the whole set of its conventions were used very seriously once again, as if a new substance, a new sort of being, had been discovered in the old vessel: no longer, this time, the essence of man's participation in the social myth, but an absolute nevertheless, the distinct and supreme reality which one can find in artistic creation and then oppose to the emptiness of the Universe or to the worn-out laws of a decaying society. In this new sort of poetry, form is no longer a reflection, but an autonomous experience, the possible creation of another world; and regularity can be found often in this use of form, but with a very different meaning: no longer the conventional structure happily accepted as the common ground which is the metaphor of the common truth, but quite the contrary, as a way by which to escape the particular aspects of our social commitment, which are felt to be of a lesser value than the pure intuitions of art and would invade a free verse too easily. Regularity becomes in this perspective the difficulty which helps the poet to go beyond himself, to be born in a higher world.

This formal practice, this poetics of form as a way of being has been very important of course in our modern history; it is what we called "l'art pour l'art," then symbolism, from Gautier and Mallarmé to the young Yeats, and certainly it was of great consequence also for the Russian poets whom Brodsky evokes, saying that they cling with resolution and even courage to meters as "spiritual magnitudes." I recognize readily that, on these occasions, regularity in the original line seems to take an intemporal and autonomous quality which could be reactivated in the translation, and perhaps the more naturally, we may think, as our common social truth continues to fall apart. Will it be sufficient then to make the remark that no Western poet of some importance has used regularity in this special way in recent years? As if we were discovering that regular lines of the past are in any case too narrow a frame to answer the needs of our more complex psychic structures? In other words, are we incapable of accepting the former patterns, alexandrine or pentameter, because they are too simple, too artificially restricted to a small number of solutions, too unfaithful to the multi-dimensionality of the contemporary mind? I believe so, but the whole matter could possibly be discussed. . . .

■ II

. . . Except that this discussion would be of no use, for there is another reason why regular meter must be proscribed from all serious translations. Whatever the resources of regular verse can be today, we must not forget that we cannot think only in terms of what is desirable, without checking what can actually be made. And this examination will rule out, at the level of the translator's word-by-word work, any possibility of satisfying regularity. Why? Because exactly as we discovered awhile ago that a poem is a whole whose formal elements have no meaning as such independently of the others, so now we must understand that writing, the act of writing, is in itself an unbreakable unity whose formal operations are conceived and executed in constant interaction with, for example, the invention of the images and the elaboration of meaning. If the meaning of the future poem were totally given in advance, let us say, there could conceivably be a way for the author to make it known, and this even clearly; but that would be a prosaic expression, and every attempt to adorn this precooked meaning with the feathers of a beautiful prosody would be artificial and lifeless. In other words, when Victor Hugo, for instance, decided at the beginning of a poem to write it in alexandrines or opted for a shorter verse, this sort of decision could preserve his poetic possibility only to the extent that the *content* of the piece was still to be invented: the vessel and the liquid determining each other, as Brodsky would say.

But this necessary freedom is not, unfortunately, within reach of the translator. In his case, meaning, the whole meaning of the poem, is already determined; he cannot invent anything about it without betraying the intent of the author. Consequently, were he to decide to adopt the alexandrine or the pentameter, this regular pattern would be for him nothing but a frame to which the meaning would have to adjust itself, obliging him to pure virtuosity. In brief, he would have to be a *versifier*, not a *poet*. And the only future accessible to his will being this sort of perhaps clever but futile craft, passiveness instead of responsibility and freedom would be his joyless destiny, with discouragement at the end. The translation of a given poem—that is, a given meaning— in the overly demanding structure of regular verse brings about a reversal whereby that which could have been quality becomes poverty, that which could have been plenitude becomes a void. And the only conclusion I can draw from this sad phenomenon is that even in the case of Mallarmé, even for Mandelstam, for whom the classical form was so important, the translation must renounce regularity, must out of necessity be free verse.

But let us now go back to this "free" verse which has been so rapidly and scornfully discarded, as we saw, by Brodsky and which would have been condemned also by Mandelstam, I presume, or by Mallarmé, who watched with such anxiety these young poets "reconsid-

ering the old verse," Mallarmé who nevertheless himself wrote "Un coup de dés jamais n'abolira le hasard," a poem which is among other things the most extraordinary breach ever made of the ancient laws of prosody. There was in all these authors, and there remains sometimes among our contemporaries, what I would call a *suspicion* of free verse. As Brodsky was suggesting, this sort of poetry which seems to be without demanding rules may seem consequently of a lesser quality or scope, exactly as drawing itself can be judged, very unfairly of course, in opposition to painting. Is then free verse only, at its best, the simple beginning of a formal act which only more severe patterns would have helped us to complete? Is it really, like some lazy and irresponsible scribbling, the renunciation of effort, the loosening of the spiritual knots of regular form, a sort of semiprose through which would disappear, as from a broken vessel, the poetic beverage?

I would rather say that there is no reason at all to restrict our idea of verbal form and poetical experience to a set of patterns which, when they no longer benefit from a general endorsement, are nothing but the rules of a sort of game. Beyond these rules, we can easily perceive the presence and activity in our speech of other phonetic structures which are natural phenomena of language and open us more naturally to the understanding of its laws. Far from considering free verse as a minor way of approaching the musicality of language, I will therefore say that it is the full exercise of it, since this fuller verbal substance is not narrowed by the new practice, is deprived only of those conventions, the regular forms, and since the poet is free at last to concentrate on the laws instead of being tempted to seek refuge in the rules! Free verse indeed is, in a world deprived of the protection of myths or traditions or divine figures, the coming of age of man's relationship to himself, the decision to substitute the invention of new structures to the repetition of old ones. If it is often used very poorly, the same regrettable event happened with classical verse in the past, and nothing can impede the best of us from reaching the core of form through its open space.

You will notice, by the way, that in its revolution free verse has done nothing but repeat or foresee the changes which were experienced in the same period by the other arts, principally painting and music. Far from being in comparison to painting the less ambitious or serious activity which Brodsky called "drawing," free verse is analogous to painting itself in its recent metamorphoses, which have made it abandon the conventional procedures of classical mimesis. It is also connected, and even more intimately so, with the revolution which put to an end the long domination of melody in music. In brief, free verse is only one aspect among others of modernity as such, and if it is not recognized in this quality in Russia today, the reason is probably not so much a better understanding of classical forms by Russian poets as it is a consequence of the distance which keeps all the arts in Leningrad or Moscow so isolated from the evolution of their counterparts in the Western world.

Free verse is poetry, in its necessary freedom of expression and research. And one of the consequences of this, which I now must emphasize, is that it is as such the only place where the contemporary poet can define and solve the problems he meets in his existential or cultural condition: for instance, in his relationship with the poets of the past and his task of translating them. It is within the frame of free verse, it is only through this way of questioning the world and the mind that this poetical translation which is our concern tonight must be undertaken. And then regularity, this fundamental aspect of ancient verse, will not be put in opposition to our new vision of the world, but be submitted to it as a lost way of being whereby only that which is alive in us—that is, free verse—can try from now on to understand and possibly make live again.

This means practically that regular verse must not be continued, must not be massively preserved through translation as a foreign word appearing with its own spelling in our French or American poem but *translated* itself, translated like every other element of the original poem into the new idiom of free verse. And the most important point I must make today in answer to Brodsky's remarks will be that this translation is quite possible, while suggesting some of the means which may allow us to begin it. Of course, technical considerations would take us too far. But it will suffice to make apparent the general principles which will permit us to keep the memory of regular verse, of the meaning and richness of its conventions. The first imperative is to keep in mind the problem: that is, to understand that the conventional patterns are not in themselves the necessary condition of a self-revelation of the virtualities of rhythms or sounds that we expect in language, but only the way this revelation has been affected at diverse moments of history by the desire of men to benefit from widely accepted forms, expressing widely accepted beliefs. In particular, we must understand that even this remarkable experience of *expectation* which can make, with classical texts, the next line both expected and unknown, as are the events of life to come, does not imply the absolute regularity of the lines and is not consequently a specific quality of this regularity, which would make it the best metaphor of fate. As translators, then, we must know that there is buried in the soil of

words a treasure of rhythms, of alliterations, of sound patterns which can *imitate,* each in its own way, the old regularity of meters and consequently convey to us its spirit. There is no reason indeed to confine the substance of form in the limits of a count of syllables. Sometimes it will be our treatment of alliterations, for instance, which will allow us to reflect in its mirror the assertiveness, the bold clarity of the pentameter of an old poet.

But the best thing I can do now, I suppose, is to draw more explicitly from personal experiences, and I will say how it seemed to me that I could translate the tragedies of Shakespeare into free verse without having to feel that, at least from this point of view, I was betraying their spirit. Many French translations of Shakespeare exist, written in twelve-syllable lines, sometimes with rhymes at the end, but they always gave to me the intolerable feeling of acrobatics, when Shakespeare is of course so natural. And the very decision to render the English pentameter with the French alexandrine is in my view a mistake, because this French verse, which normally has two equal and symmetric parts, works spontaneously as a closed system, existing in itself and by itself, that is quite apart from the realities of existence, from the throes of time and labor and death through which Shakespeare's pentameters are walking, sometimes even faltering. If Racine was able to write his tragedies in alexandrines, it is precisely because the very spirit of these plays, their metaphysical endeavor, was to deny the existence of the world outside, to reduce life to a rational and intemporal exchange between the archetypes of the mind. Conversely, writing freely does not mean to go very far from the average length of the Shakespearean pentameter, and I soon discovered that, while my sequence of verses was indeed without any formal regularity, something of it was still present there, as if by reflection in a broken mirror. Why? Because among these verses, whose syllables usually number from nine to fifteen, a particular one was reappearing fairly often, as if trying to reinvent, in my own irregularity, the repetitive pattern of the original poetry. The insistence of this line is not sufficient in itself to dissipate the atmosphere of free verse. Nevertheless, it is enough, I presume, to *speak* even faintly what the Shakespearean line has been and to pervade what is said in my modern words with some color of the old relationship between the poet and the world. This is what free verse can do with regular verse.

And, incidentally, I can say that this recurrent line in my translation of Shakespeare is composed of eleven syllables. Beginning like an alexandrine—that is, with these six syllables which lead in the alexandrine to their symmetrical image in the second hemistich—it ends with only five syllables and thus breaks the arrogant symmetry of the great verse of Racine or Mallarmé, with its refusal of time, of everyday life, of death. Why did this new line appear so frequently in my translations? First, because I was discovering the spiritual quality of Shakespeare's verses, which are a form, a reference to the absolute, but also this encounter with life of which I spoke. But also because I was free to move among the multiple combinations of rhythms looking for the one which could make us revive this dual quality of the English verse. This tool, free verse, was able to find an image of the pentameter more faithful to it than any traditional renderings could be. . . . Except that the worst mistake would be to begin to think at this point that since the eleven-syllable line can work so well for the translation of Shakespeare, it would be even more satisfying to have it in our French text from the beginning to the end. A mistake, yes, because all the limitations and failures of the artificial regularity would very rapidly appear. While continuing to write with no prosodic restraint, I can from time to time come across some words which spontaneously organize themselves in a twelve-syllable pattern, adding then to my translation this *indication of plenitude* which the alexandrine alone is able to give in French, despite all its ambiguities or defects.

And I will simply add that after having translated Shakespeare with the occasional help of this particular meter which was very rare indeed in the past—Verlaine and Rimbaud alone had made use of it seriously—I found myself employing it more often in my own verse. This meter was making me more able to apprehend the relationship between the act of writing and existence, between form and time. It was helping me to live.

Yves Bonnefoy, Summer 1979

The Origin of the Text

▪ FIRST AND LAST ANSWERS

Very often people ask you, when you write, where the things which are in your books come from; what is the origin of these things. It is as if, finding some lode inside, they would like to have a guide to lead them into the mine so that they might dig for themselves in that vein of ore. But it is of course a question which is very difficult to answer. I'll try this evening* to offer a few proposals. Most of the time when a writer is asked such a question, he gives unsatisfactory answers, replies which are at the same time almost unavoidable and to which, even if he wants to be as generous as possible, he has to return.

Michel Butor (*Gil Jain*)

His first answer is to say that he doesn't know where the text comes from, and this is quite natural, because if you want to write a text, it is because you have something to say which has not been said before. Or perhaps it is something that in some respects was not possible, or almost not possible, to say. With some work and some luck the writer is able to tell what he was not able to tell before. So when the thing is done, when at last he has said it, it is extremely difficult for him to go back to the preceding stage, to the way it was when it was still obscure. So he can answer: well, the origin of the text is what you can find in the text itself. When the thing is done, somebody else—a university professor, for instance—can take the result, and then he can say, well, this, which is quite clear here, comes from this or that in literature or elsewhere. But for the writer the textual "baby" has still with him the veil of darkness and obscurity from which he comes.

When the text is there, it is something clear, even if it seems for many of us very obscure. So it is possible for the writer to have a more subtle answer and to say that the text comes from itself. And when you see this from the point of view of the student or the reader, it means something quite precise. When you compare, for instance, the first drafts, the intermediate sketches and the final product, it is then very easy to see how a particular sentence will go somewhere. We know where it has to go, and it is very easy to order the sketches and to see the steps in which the text is forming itself. So it is as if the words, the sentences, were attracted by the final product, by that form which now stands clear. It is the experience of many writers that the text exists before the actual writing takes place—much as with a sculptor who sometimes says that the statue is inside the block of marble and he has only to take it out, that everything is already there. We very often have that experience, and many writers have said, "The text was there before it was written." It is somewhere in the ether, in Eden, in paradise, with the gods, and you have only to copy it, or to obey what is called inspiration, or the dictation.

But we have to go further than that. Sometimes the text gives the impression of arriving suddenly. We want to say something, we don't know exactly what; of course, when it is there we know what it is. Sometimes it is quite sudden. In only a moment what was obscure is now clear. Most of the time it takes some work, it takes time. You have these drafts and corrections, so it is evident that the structure which is already there will impose itself on new pieces, and at the end you generally don't write what you wanted to write in the beginning. Very often you try to please somebody—a publisher, for instance, or a teacher or the general public. But when it is good, this doesn't work, because the text itself is so imposing that you have to change your mind; and what is most interesting is that something really new occurs. You need to have, for example, in that whole something of a specific color or tone, and you go to look for it and attempt to insert it inside that extremely demanding structure. In poetry the consciousness of that structural demand is what is called prosody. Prosody, or the rules of versification of any literary genre, is the way some aspect of the structure of the work being done appears to the consciousness of the writer; and that is generally what he is able to speak of. When you ask a writer or a painter, "What did you want to convey?" very often his response is: "I did it in such-and-such a way." In order to make you understand the "what," he will explain to you the "how," because it is *how* the task is done which is the most clear in the process of writing.

So we have the three traditional answers: first, we don't know where it comes from, and anyway, even if we try, we will know only a part of it, and we have always to come back to that; second, the text comes from what it will be; third, the text comes from what is coming, what it comes to be now. But when you are at the same time a writer and a university professor, you can try to see the thing from both sides, from an internal and an external point of view; and any conscious writer is ambiguous in that respect. When I have finished a

text, a university professor can study and compare it with others and be able to say that this thing comes from that; but I can also do it myself, with some difficulties, and do it even before the text is finished. In some sense, the text is never completely finished. When I publish a book, it is not that I consider it to be good; it is because I don't know how to work any more on it. I publish it by a kind of despair. It's not really finished, and it has for me to be continued by other people, by readers. It has to go on.

■ I) WHERE DOES THE MATERIAL COME FROM?

I certainly am able in many cases to answer the question as to where the text comes from. But if I begin to think about it, I see that it may have several different meanings: 1) where the material comes from—the blocks with which you will build your construction; 2) where the difference comes from—you do things strangely, and how does it happen that you are not writing the same things as other people do; 3) what is the origin of the energy you exert in bringing out that difference.

1) It Comes from the Dictionary. For the first question there is an easy first answer. A text is always made with words. One of the great French painters of the impressionist era, Edgar Degas, said one day to Stéphane Mallarmé, "I would very much like to write poems. I have plenty of ideas." Mallarmé answered, "It's not with ideas that you make poems. It is with words." We write texts with words which are all around us. So when somebody asks where the text comes from, you can answer, "It comes from where you are." You are inside that mine. Even if you invent new words, as Joyce did in *Finnegan's Wake,* they are made with old ones, and it is with the attention to these words that the text begins.

It is quite easy to see this with the novel. A great novelist is somebody who is able to make his characters speak, to give them a voice, a recognizable voice. With a dramatist you have the mediation of the actor. When you are all by yourself in your room reading a novel, you are yourself all the troupe, all the actors of the play. In order to convey the feeling that a character has a specific voice, it is absolutely necessary that the choice of the words be made in such a way that the combination of these words will lend itself to a specific pronunciation, a specific tone. For instance, one of the great achievements of Henry James is that in his novels he is able to give to each person a different, distinct voice. It is the same with Proust. This is possible because the writer does not start from a character imagined, asking afterward what will be his words. It goes the other way around. A novelist is somebody who, in reading but especially in conversation, is able to pinpoint certain sentences, certain frequencies of words, which in writing will retain a personality. It is from the personality of speech, if you wish, that the personality of the character will bud.

2) It Comes from the Encyclopedia. But it is not of course only individual words. It is sentences, it is *ensembles* of words; and it is of course texts, the entire world of texts which are already written—which means that the big mine of literature is the library or the encyclopedia. Very often you have to find a word, or you have to find a whole paragraph, a quote, a story, and you go to the stacks, the shelves, the galleries in order to find that.

Before coming to Oklahoma for this conference about some of my books, I wanted, during my stay here, to make a small gift for the participants of this event; so I looked around in Victoria and saw plenty of ravens in the streets, and they were very interesting in many ways. The raven called back to my mind different things, in different tiers of the library. I know that for the Indians of the Northwest Coast the raven was a very important person, and I know that there was in American literature a famous poem about the raven—famous not only in American literature but in French literature as well, because it has been translated into French by two of the greatest French poets, once by Baudelaire and once by Mallarmé. So I went to the library in quest of the translation of Poe's "The Raven" by Mallarmé, and fortunately it was there. So I have used the Mallarmé translation, with some very important alterations. You know that that bird in Poe's poem answers always "Nevermore"; that was not good for me, however, and I have changed it to have the raven tell an Indian tale. I made eighteen versions of that text, which is called "Reminiscences of the Raven," and to find enough Indian tales for that, I went to the library and dug in Franz Boas's ethnography, where I found plenty of marvelous ore in order to make my small metal. Something was dormant in the library, waiting to be awakened by somebody, and the structure of the text, which was already in Poe's poem and in Mallarmés translation, asked me to seek a certain number of texts. I have made eighteen different versions because in Poe's poem there are eighteen stanzas, and so it makes for me a nice symmetrical block.

3) It Comes from Travel. But even all the libraries of the world are insufficient, and that is why we write. We write because the books are at the same time too numerous and unsatisfactory. We have plenty of books but not the books we would like to have. There is a discrepancy between what is inside the library and the general conversation, and a bigger one between all human language and what I may call the language of things. We feel always that something remains not said. We see almost everything through language, but we see through language that language is inadequate. When we look at something which is very interesting, the first thing we say is that it is indescribable. Then the writer comes and tries to describe the indescribable, to augment the whole sphere of language from the want which comes from without and from within at the same time.

■ **II) WHERE DOES THE DIFFERENCE COME FROM?**

You start from words, but you make new combinations of words. In the library you read the unread. You travel in quest of different places. What is the origin of this difference? What is the origin of the originality of the writer? (And of course these two words are quite closely related.)

1) It Comes from Childhood. The first answer to this second question is: the difference comes from the discrepancies which are already inherent in language, literature and landscape. Any word is already a world in itself because it has numerous attachments with other words and with other things, so numerous that they are extremely difficult to handle; and these connections among words are not the same for everybody. There are such complicated associations that it is absolutely necessary in ordinary life to cross out the biggest part of the meaning of a word; otherwise life would not be able to go on. A word means many different things for different people, but these differences in most cases, for practical purposes, must be hidden. So we act as if words were univocal. They tend to be univocal in science but not at all in general language, and literature works upon the ambiguity of words, a dangerous ambiguity.

When you begin to look properly at words, you are in a dangerous situation, because all the differences in our society are reflected inside the complications of vocabulary. We act as if it were easy to understand what somebody says, and in some situations it *is* easy. Within a given level of society it is quite easy to understand what is said, but if you go to another part of the city, the same word will have quite a different meaning. The fact is much more evident when you think about the plurality of languages: one word in French, even if it is the same spelling, or almost the same, does not have the same meaning as it has in English or in German, and so on. If you speak two languages, you are already upon a linguistic frontier where many conflicts arise, and you must keep these conflicts down in order to go on, in order not to have always a war within yourself or with other people. When a word is charged with problems and ambiguities, you need a kind of shield against that. Under the surface of that word you have a turmoil which goes on and on, an accumulation of problems, and the difference between interior and surface becomes stronger and stronger. The shield stiffens, and someday it will crack. It is the upturning of the word which will mark the appearance of the difference in the text, the origin of a new text. I will give you an instance of that.

In traffic lights you need to have very simple symbols, and you know what they are: green is "go," red is "stop"—because in Western mythology red is associated with danger. During the Cultural Revolution in China some young Chinese petitioned Mao Tse-tung asking him to reverse the traffic lights because red had to mean "go," since it was the color of revolution, of progress and so on; but the surface of the symbols was so strong that still in China today red means "stop."

A very important word in our own society is *white;* it is related to almost everything. It has enormous impact in political science. It is related to racial problems, to morality, to cleanliness and so on. And in education and in everyday life we have generally the equation: white is right. White is good, elevated, et cetera. In some cases we know that white is not so good, but most of the time we have to ignore these instances. They are very dangerous ground. In American literature you have a very striking instance of the upturning of the iceberg of the word *white.* It is the famous chapter (seventeen) in Herman Melville's *Moby Dick* which is called "The Whiteness of the Whale." As you know, Moby Dick is a white whale and is in many ways a symbol of evil. Melville, in this chapter, tries to explain this, to make this understandable. He takes from the library and from the encyclopedia greatly diverse instances of the link between white and good in order to make that link as universal as possible, and at the apex of a wonderful sentence he says, "Yet. . . ." This is the hinge.

> Though in many natural objects, whiteness refiningly enhances beauty, as if imparting some special virtue of its own, as in marbles, japonicas, and pearls; and though various nations have in some way recognised a certain royal preeminence in this hue; even the barbaric, grand old kings of Pegu placing the title "Lord of the White Elephants" above all their other magniloquent ascriptions of dominion; and the modern kings of Siam unfurling the same snowy-white quadruped in the royal standard; and the Hanoverian flag bearing the one figure of a snow-white charger; and the great Austrian Empire, Cæsarian, heir to overlording Rome, having for the imperial color the same imperial hue; and though this pre-eminence in it applies to the human race itself, giving the white man ideal mastership over every dusky tribe; and though, besides all this, whiteness has been even made

significant of gladness, for among the Romans a white stone marked a joyful day; and though in other mortal sympathies and symbolizings, this same hue is made the emblem of many touching, noble things—the innocence of brides, the benignity of age; though among the Red Men of America the giving of the white belt of wampum was the deepest pledge of honor; though in many climes, whiteness typifies the majesty of Justice in the ermine of the Judge, and contributes to the daily state of kings and queens drawn by milk-white steeds; though even in the higher mysteries of the most august religions it has been made the symbol of the divine spotlessness and power; by the Persian fire worshippers, the white forked flame being held the holiest on the altar; and in the Greek mythologies, Great Jove himself being made incarnate in a snow-white bull; and though to the noble Iroquois, the midwinter sacrifice of the sacred White Dog was by far the holiest festival of their theology, that spotless, faithful creature being held the purest envoy they could send to the Great Spirit with the annual tidings of their own fidelity; and though directly from the Latin word for white, all Christian priests derive the name of one part of their sacred vesture, the alb or tunic, worn beneath the cassock; and though among the holy pomps of the Romish faith, white is specially employed in the celebration of the Passion of our Lord; though in the Vision of St. John, white robes are given to the redeemed, and the four-and-twenty elders stand clothed in white before the great white throne, and the Holy One that sitteth there white like wool; yet for all these accumulated associations, with whatever is sweet, and honorable, and sublime, there yet lurks an elusive something in the innermost idea of this hue, which strikes more of panic to the soul than that redness which affrights in blood.

Then he makes another visit to the library and takes some striking instances of bad whitenesses, thus being able to make the word *white* and its associations turn upon itself and reveal to us its own other side, and also the other side of many other words and of all history. It is of course the other side of our own society, the other side of not only the word *white* but of whiteness itself and what we mean by that. Such an inversion of meaning in a word or in a story will provoke extensive reorganization of the library and the emergence of new texts.

This is possible when you become free from the urgency of everyday life. You have to take a look from a distance. You have first to dissolve the ordinary associations. You have to unbind the chains and play with the words and the structures. You must agitate them.

If a painter has asked me for a text to go with a catalogue for an exhibition, I am always flattered and generally say yes; and I'm interested, I see a few things. But at the beginning I don't know at all what I'll do. The day of the exhibition comes nearer and nearer, so I have to find something. Then I go out and walk. When the weather is fair, that is very good for me because I can go outside, and there things occur. Walking provokes a sweet agitation of the landscape and with it a movement inside the vocabulary, the ideas; and then at some turning, well, it occurs, it's there, I know how it will be. I had some problems when I began drafting this lecture, for example. I had a few ideas but didn't know exactly how to put them together. So I went into the woods, and the things began to organize themselves into a neat structure.

That link between inspiration and play points to a very strong link between inspiration and childhood. It's quite understandable. You had these difficulties with words. You knew that a word was linked with this or that, but after some time you had to act as if it were not. You knew before that "white" was not always "good," but in order to be an adult, you had to act as if it were. When you look on the other side of the word, you go back to something which you had forgotten. Things forgotten wait in the library, and you have plenty of things waiting in the library of your mind. The moment when inspiration occurs, when things begin to take form, is very generally linked with the coming back of some forgotten experience.

Very often when people speak to me about one of my books, I have forgotten what I have written in that book. They know much better than I do, because I have to forget it in order to make new things. When they speak with some precision, it comes back like a thunderstorm. And with it come many other things. It is a kind of memory cyclone, and it can be very unsettling; but it is fascinating. It is a new "myself" which appears at that time. You know of course the famous opening of *À la recherche du temps perdu*. Proust describes a memory storm coming from the dipping of a small French cake called a *madeleine* in a cup of tea. With the taste of it a whole forgotten portion of his childhood comes flooding back.

2) *It Comes from the Night*. The text comes, then, from a special connection between the writer and his past, through language and through some types of experience. That agitation of the material in order to bring out the differences needs some leisure, and the deepest leisure we can have in our life is the one we find in sleep, deepest sleep, in that profound level of sleep where the great dreams appear. In dream you have a kind of wholesale agitation of material, as if your memory, your experiences, were transformed into dice and these dice were thrown and formed new combinations. In these new combinations your feelings—and especially the repressed feelings—will find a way to express themselves. In dream, things can be turned around much more than in the wakefulness of day, because in that profound recess, that dungeon of sleep, all the other levels of sleep are like guards to protect you. In that deep dungeon of sleep your brain experiences a special kind of freedom. When what occurs can pass through the awakening, you very often have new works of art. The classical instance in English literature is of course Coleridge's "Kubla Khan," which was written entirely in a dream state.

3) *It Comes from Silence*. The origin is in childhood and in dream; and of course you know that in dream many forgotten aspects of our childhood come back, and many repressed aspects of our affective life and of our language can return. It is then very important to be able to preserve or to establish a link between the dream and the writing and to make the writing a kind of awakened dream. Prosody, of which I have already spoken, is extremely useful in that respect. There is a physical element in writing which is almost forgotten today but which was well recognized in other literatures—in classical Greek and Roman literature, for instance. There is a kind of dancing in writing, and much more manual work than is generally believed. In order to establish that link between dream and writing and to maintain that interplay during the day, a sufficient amount of silence is necessary. You have to work, you have to find things here and there, you have to try this and try that, but you also have to wait. You need to wipe your mind clean, make it a blank, establish a certain quality of silence, obliterate some references. You have to go through a kind of ordeal.

You have to be able to go into uncharted waters, and that is one of the reasons why I give lectures which are not readings. I never read a lecture, because I want to take advantage of the stage fright. I always have stage fright, and I know it can be very useful. When I begin, I find myself facing a kind of white fog; I have to plunge into it, and in this trespassing, things occur. The stage fright will engender agitation in the silence before and during the lecture, and so things will happen. Of course I have made hundreds and hundreds of lectures, so I know that it works; but I still get stage fright. When I give several lectures about the same subject, each time I try to do something different; but after ten times the lecture is permanently fixed. At that point I feel like a tape recorder, and I simply wait until the tape is finished. That is boring for me, and it becomes boring for the audience. It is then that I know I must not give that lecture any more, that it is time to write it and publish it; the text is there. If one day I should no longer have stage fright, well, I would stop giving lectures, because it would not be useful—it would not be useful for me, nor would it be useful for anybody.

■ III) WHERE DOES THE ENERGY COME FROM?

The use of stage fright is the use of silence, of shock, and of course it is the use of a kind of anguish. It is a reversal of anguish in the same way that the use of dream is a reversal of nightmares. And here we arrive at the most difficult part of the lecture; but unfortunately time flies, so I will just give you a few very rapid hints about where the energy comes from.

1) It Is Misery Becoming Wealth. It is not enough to have different things appearing to you. You need also to struggle in order to make them appear, be published and so on; and it takes an enormous amount of energy, because when you turn upside down a very important word, a very important element of society, you generally get a very angry reaction. It is a struggle, and you have to keep struggling. We are very surprised, when we look at the works of great writers or musicians or painters, to see the amount of work they were able to do. No one works as much as did Beethoven, or Schubert in his very short life, or Mozart. What made them able to do that? What was the urge? Of course, behind all that is a kind of suffering. It is a want, a misery, and in art you have a transformation of misery into wealth. It is not only an overflow of life. No. It must come from a deep urge, one which is not only an individual urge. It is a want in society. It is the contradiction in society which becomes embodied in some part of this society and sometimes in one individual in particular. What other people can stand, that individual is not able to tolerate. He is crushed by it, or he finds in it the energy to change it—generally with the help of some other people.

Very often at the origin of a work of art you have an expressed order. Someone commissioned Michelangelo to paint the ceiling of the Sistine Chapel. That means there was something lacking in that building, a sense of absence which was becoming worse and worse for someone. And there was a possibility to fill that want, a possibility which could then be expressed in the language of money. Money for us is a very important kind of language with its contradictions, and when you have too many contradictions in the monetary language, you have a revolution somewhere. And you have not only contradictions inside monetary language but plenty of contradictions as well between monetary language and other languages.

In order to make a work of art, the artist has to survive; so there must be, somewhere in the monetary flux, a kind of pool where some leisure can be found. This need is related to all the complications, complexities and contradictions of the monetary system and of all the economic systems. And of course it is related also to the basic urges of human nature, or animal nature. It comes from hunger, thirst, sexuality, the wish to move and the wish to see and know. From these sources the energy will come. But there will be sufficient energy only when the contradictions in society will have matured to such a point that it becomes possible to use the contradictions against themselves, to make the differences work against themselves, to make the hatred of novelty itself work against itself in order to produce something really new. After some time the accumulations and the waste become such that the abscess bursts, and then you have that turmoil, thunderstorm and revolution instigated by writing or painting or anything else.

2) It Is Madness Becoming Reason. But it is not only words which must be turned upside down, or transformed into much more complex figures. It is also the person himself.

In order to have that energy, you have to be the center of a kind of cyclone of energy, of latent energy working inside society. You are yourself an embodiment of contradictions. In the classical literature of the seventeenth century, for instance, any writer was always between two languages. He or she had the classical languages—Latin and Greek—and his or her own language. These were like two poles in an electric arc, and sparks were continually occurring between them. These conflicting languages led, in turn, to conflicting personalities. And you have conflicting parts in society. Even in a single individual you may have conflicting behavior: we all have split personalities because we all think both that white is good and that white is also something else. There is always a hidden face of ourselves which communicates with hidden faces of society, the dark waters of society which are sometimes so dangerous that a boundary has to be placed around them, that they must be removed to a reservation.

The text comes from the reservation. It comes from any kind of jail, and it comes from any kind of hospital. The text comes from the madhouse. And the writer, or the painter, is a madman who has succeeded. We are all madmen, and some of us are so mad that we have to be put inside an enclosure. That enclosure is something extremely active. It is burning. A writer or a painter is somebody who is able to be at the same time mad and reasonable. He is able to manage the reservation inside himself. Your dreams are the madhouse in yourself. But you have plenty of other reservations, and that is why I go to the special collections in libraries. There are reservations in the library, and in French we have the same word *réserve* for special collections of a library and for an Indian reservation. Both are gold mines, mines of something much more precious than gold. In working seriously with art you are always touching madness, and from all the forces that are linked in order to make that madness quiet comes a reserve of energy that you can upturn, that you can use in a completely different way.

3) It Is Sickness Becoming Health. And it is not only the hospital of the mind or the hospital of society, but also the hospital of the body, because all these contradictions are embodied in that very strange personality that we call an artist. I have said it is extraordinary that people like Mozart, Schubert and others have done such an enormous amount of work, and it is especially extraordinary because all of them seem to have had problems with their health, often culminating in early death. The contradictions occur inside the body, and it is in the fever, if you wish, that the energies gathering around are accumulating inside the writer. Here we can really speak of "expression," because you have a pressure inside and then the explosion of that pressure to make an issue. In art illness is transmuted in a new health.

■ **LAST AND FIRST QUESTIONS**

Inspiration comes from misery. It comes from the madhouse, from segregation, frustration, and it comes from sickness. If you take all that together, if you go all the way along that path, you will find that there is a strong relation between literature and death. You can say the text comes from the dead. It is a way the dead may speak. When I write, it is not only I who am writing. I write with you, with your words, and I write for you, I write with your help, I speak with your help. If you were not here, there would not be such a lecture. I read my lecture in your eyes. The lecture I give depends upon the way you are listening; but something else comes through, namely the voices of the dead. Because in the library are many dead writers, and in our society the dead are very efficient. Words are a legacy from the dead, and the biggest contradiction is that between the living and the dead. The dead are not only dead; they are still here. They knew things that we have forgotten and must find again. We do not go back only to our childhood; we go also to our parents and grandparents.

There is something very comforting in the thought that when we write or paint we accomplish in many ways the design of the dead. What these dead people wanted, we begin to make. But it is at the same time a very nagging thought because, if we begin to accom-

plish their desire, they will not have enjoyed it. There will always be a gap in that realization, and that means there will always be new texts, because there will always be these contradictions between the dead and ourselves, who are not yet dead but who will die someday and are dying every day. Plato says that "philosophy is a preparation to death," and Montaigne made that line the title of one of his essays ("Que philosopher, c'est apprendre à mourir"). Writing is also a contemplation of death. It is a changing of death into life; but that transformation will never be finished, and in a way that is nice. We will never finish writing. The great abstract painter Mondrian said that when he had succeeded in doing what he wanted, then there would be no more art. Art would no longer be necessary because society and the world would be entirely beautiful. But there will always be some kind of art, perhaps completely different from what we know today; and there will always be something like writing, because the dead will never be satisfied.

The link between death and literature is a very traditional one, and one of the prosodical urges in writing is the fact that the text has to finish somewhere, even if the matter is infinite. You have very often the comparison between a text and the life of a man: it has a birth and a progress, and it ends. This text which I am delivering is nearing its end. It will not be completely dead, I hope. I hope that it will live in your mind. It is recorded, embalmed, and it will be written, and I'll revise it, and it will be printed. Then it will be truly a text. You will know where the text comes from. It comes from here. Now the time is finished, and there is no more text.

Michel Butor, Spring 1982

*"The Origin of the Text" was delivered in English by Michel Butor on the evening of 12 November 1981 at the University of Oklahoma, concluding two weeks of seminars and lectures on his work by Butor for the Eighth Puterbaugh Conference on Writers of the French-Speaking and Hispanic World. An earlier version of the lecture was presented in September 1981 at the University of Victoria in British Columbia.

Reading, the Cast Shadows: A Reflection

To care for the cast shadows, surely, and to care for nothing else. . . .
■ **YVES BONNEFOY**[1]

1. Shadows Against Light. For Mallarmé, Yves Bonnefoy reminds us, the noblest action is that of sight:

the following comments are meant merely as a sighting on Bonnefoy's own vision, a more-than-modest homage to his light and the necessary shadows which clarify that light. In a general illumination—since light is general, a concept in Bonnefoy's terms—the shadows cast by specific objects are irrevocably associated with a present and with a presence: "What the cast shadow profoundly designates . . . is *a certain place at a certain moment*" (RM, 36).[2] The reality of encounter, shadowed, entails an ontological imperfection and all the opaque resistance of the chanced-upon, within the being of this fleeting moment now marked and held in its exact length and direction. Insofar as the shadows keep the trace of even the most tenuous aspects of being—the odd profile of a top hat or an ox's horn as it prolongs the shadow of an angel's guitar in a Piero della Francesca—they represent the opposite pole to the orangery, that perfect place of light and form, unlivable but present to the thought.

In this way, I think I see the shadows linked both to presence and to the realization of lack, of the essential cleavage in the object and in the instant, of the eternal absence of a key to understanding, especially in that country beyond, that *arrière-pays* just on the other side of our sight. Here the poet is moved to a dark vision, and as elsewhere, the sun is black from it and the land suddenly bare: "if real life is over there, in that elsewhere with no place to it, that is enough for the land here to take on the aspect of a desert" (A, 21). Nerval's blackest sun has its own shadows cast here, in a terrible prolongation, and Hölderlin's Hyperion too, while closer to us De Chirico's hyper-lengthened forms take a terrible and sure hold on our consciousness, attached as they are to "a glove, a mannequin, or a piece of fruit, elementary objects in which the reflection of an arcade's alignment is effaced forever" (SS, 37).

To this suddenly lost fullness, the poetic spirit reacts violently. For the reader, in turn, the importance of this dark spot seen on the sun cannot be overestimated: to the reader the poet has communicated, as his greatest gift, his own "ardent melancholy," and indeed the richness is incalculable. I trust this hypothesis will be taken not as a precious wordplay but as a serious statement of belief: it is not always by a light that one can best read, but sometimes by a shadow, providing that this shadow is clearly seen.

The reader on whose experience these shadows are cast, by sympathy imposed, may well give another sense to the expression "ombres portées," these cast shadows being brought or "portées" in all their terrible dark glory to the attentive vision: not as some casual interruption of the whiteness of a Mallarmean page to be contrasted with the print marking it as text, but rather as a sign, irreversibly natural and specifically sensible to mind

and eye. If in fact the qualification "sensible" appears with such frequency in Bonnefoy's essays, holding in itself all the attributes of the tangible, the concrete and the sensed, it is an indication of the same sort of intelligence, sharply conscious of the intensity of the real, there before us, a consciousness itself intensified by these shadows of the specific, carried far, as they are cast by objects at once immobile and mobile, fixed and yet transformable in their over whelming presence. "Our painting is the place of shadows" (NR, 52), says Bonnefoy in an essay on Balthus, and this statement must be read against its basic background, an evident luminous faith in shadow's opposite: "I believe, for example, in light" (A, 23).

Thus the fascination of the baroque vision which marks, at moments strongly, Bonnefoy's own. The art of the baroque has as a characteristic the serious play of light and dark, and the chiaroscuro rendering casts its own shadow and its own illumination into the reading of painting and text. The hope of the present reading is that some of this complexity and depth can be rendered, with obscurity as the starting point.

2. Ripeness, Grass and Ruin. Bonnefoy's recent essay on Shakespeare,[3] an extraordinary play upon two words in two plays, uses just such contrast for its tones, both visual and sounded, whose parallel depth and modeling are mutually enhanced by the correspondence. So *Lear* is read against and with *Hamlet* as bright zones correspond to the dark which they complement, and positive to negative in photography. To Hamlet's "something is rotten" there responds a mysterious prideful sickness of the soul, not in an exterior state, but an interior one; Hamlet's "readiness is all," in its acceptance of chance in a world destructive and stripped of sense, sounds still (or reads still) in its echoes, for the audience hearing or seeing Edgar's "ripeness is all," that act of faith in the face of Hamlet's despairing doubt. "We learn," says Shakespeare's best and most poetic translator, "that the structures of meaning are only a bridge of thread cast over the horrendous abyss, but that these strands are of steel." As ripeness, a sign of unity and response to meaning, replaces Hamlet's call to a simple readiness empty of sense in a senseless world, light takes its source in a preceding shadow, and "the grass grows once more among the ruins."

As an example of what a cast shadow or tone might represent in an individual reading, in this grass and its regrowth I hear, from *L'arrière-pays*—surely the most impassioned land of poetry—a line coming to the traveler, who is the poet, falling upon the stones at Arezzo: "But the grass is always the same" (A, 82). And then the traveler, refreshed and reilluminated, starts his travels once more. This luminous moment, epiphanic and echoing, identical in essence and yet reborn, serves as a telescoping of the texts, as shadow for the substance of the journey between specific stone and stone as ornament or idea, mediates between stone and ruin, between individual leaf and general nature: shadows connect and join, mediate, echo and prolong, render real at last. The image is here a figure of the text in its own destruction apparent, and in its real rebirth. Each reader's presence and hearing, silent and visible, casts its interpretive shadow through the work, haunting and transmissible in its dark tones, infinitely sensitive.

3. *Place of Reflection.* I would like to maintain that the shadow is not only exterior, is not cast merely as a horizontal but as the deeply sensed anguish of finitude, rending the heart and separating the partial being from its full potentiality: "Something touches me so that being is cloven apart, with its light, and I am in exile" (A, 24).

At the sensed summit of vision, shadow does not cover all the space of earth; rather, it renders present the conscious vertical journey and its real dimension of effort, giving its true worth to "the real place." Not the "vrai lieu" of the Greek formula, where each object was situated in its right and proper place, but the notion as Bonnefoy conceives it, made still of exile and of night, based still on darkness, accepting still the imperfection of its own undoing by time. The cast shadow holds this place as its right and due: "Happy, those men of the rising sun if they can, like Piero della Francesca, find their footing in a wisdom, but truer those men of shadow" (SS, 39).

So the baroque reaffirms the object, sensible and specific, and fated, within absolute and undying Form; reaffirms, against the Greek daylight, another reign illuminated this time from the inside, that of existence and of fate: "The baroque loves and transubstantiates what is limited, what passes by" (A, 150). Baudelaire's sonnet "À une passante" resounds again in the mind, like the sounded shadow of a passerby, all the more desirable in her impossibility: "O toi que j'eusse aimée, ô toi qui le savais." So Bonnefoy's *arrière-pays,* that country beyond but also here, responds to a certain art as to its own true place, its counter in time passing; and for all its vivid imperfection, it alone reveals the place we might live.

> And soon the baroque, the Roman baroque, rose with mystery in its hands, this time in broad daylight, the mystery of the place of existence now assumed. (A, 153–54)

As a bit of earth—Poussin's discovery stated at the conclusion of this volume—can be called Rome, as Moses can be saved, so the nearby place, which is the place of shadow and of earth, is also and forever the place of *reflection.* The reader's own place, then, and his richest imagination, lies where our readings dream us: "Mais si c'étaient nos lectures qui nous rêvent?" (A, 127).

4. *Reading in the Dusk.* In a castle, one empty room where strains of music are no longer heard except in the memory in its mingled peace and pain "is now the altar in its afternoon of shadow toward which converge all the remaining hope of meaning, all thought of a *place,* the only value which can be opposed to the drifting of *signs*" (RT, 51). This afternoon of shadow glimpsed in *Rue Traversière* returns the anxious reader to a line from one of Bonnefoy's works on the baroque, *Rome 1630:* here he defines the baroque gesture and its essential importance for our understanding (once we grasp its attitude), its purpose and, above all, its suggestion, framed here by the dusk of a chapel, like the afternoon altar in the castle. The place is dimly lit, for inner perception: the baroque is not a trompe-l'oeil, but an experience

> . . . of being through illusion, and its eloquence designates this illusion at the very moment when it creates it—thus rejoining the invisible. . . . We see then that what the baroque suggests is not of the nature of the senses, because it has as its object our relation with being, our adherence to destiny: and from that it follows that its most intense moments may be, in the dusk of a chapel, some painted plaster figurine, some "Neapolitan" saint totally unknown, but bearing on its forehead a crown of roses, or of paper, or a tiny light. (R, 39–40)

The exterior sign often is a sign of absence, but one whose mediation in our relations with being is nevertheless entire and efficacious: discussing Poussin's *Appearance of the Virgin to Saint James the Greater,* Bonnefoy points out that there is a physical sensation echoing throughout in its strongly accentuated lines rather than an ecstasy detached from the human and the sensual. But the dream of a poet goes beyond this surface and this sensation to a possible mending someday of absence and presence, to the hope of a true place where shadow is implicated forever in light.

So in Bonnefoy's reflections on literature, this convergence or hope motivates a series of subtle readings of myth and of text. So, for instance, the contrary forces in the *Song of Roland* are seen to vivify: Saracen against French, Roland against Oliver, to be sure, but also French against French, Roland against Roland.

> Against whom do we ever struggle if not our double? Against this *other* in us which would convince us that the world has no meaning, which would have us, wounded and deprived of hope,

turn toward the stream where the blood of the ending day drains away from the lost battle? (NR, 171)

The enemy is not just that meaninglessness, for it at least has color, "as with the red of a victory or a loss," but rather, and far more terrible, "the indifference of everything that is, its resonance like an empty jar."

In the war on indifference, the landscape is sensed in a luster other than that offered by Cartesian rationality: here transparency and clarity are played against their opposite: "From the trees to the Emperor, from abundance to duty, through great transparent words arches the presence of God. And nothing unexplored, nothing future. Except those 'high dark mountains' over there, at the southern border" (171–72). Of this landscape Bonnefoy says that it is space itself, and depth, and luminous hierarchy, but within that limpid world a fierce unease: "I look gladly at these trees of the first day, these 'shining' stars, this 'clear' night—everything is at peace, it seems, in the depth of nature; but why this troubled voice, which speaks to us of an evil always begun anew?" (172).

The question itself as it is posed is the shadow to the splendid structure composed of an army in its moral mobilization: the enemy is able to transmute the sign from one side to the other. Were he to win, would the sun and trees not alter, from horror rather than from hatred? "Would they not from then on be a 'black sun' and absurd forms?" The landscape shifts, then, with the drama it contains, even if finally that drama is played out by two opposing sides within the self.

But as for the enemy, hidden in ourselves, he is further proof of an architecture of the same, not the other. Now is it not fair to say that this reduplication of political and personal and psychological structure, the mirror imagery of one side and the other within the same, that its working yet once more echoes the dark against the light, shadow and certainty? The question persists, with its implied positive for an answer.

What then is the evil that menaces this harmony? And from what exterior space might it come? There is no exterior to a form which appropriates the real, no *other* conceivable in the architecture of the *same*. Matter, certainly, and resistances, dangers, but which acquire a face only once they are in the center of the structure which encounters them. The obstacle to the expansion of the form is not lived, cannot be lived as a concurrent order; it is the formless, and "evil," but in the inert. Then why this moral mobilization in the Song against an "Infidel"? And if evil has its own structure, is it not already hidden, in one way or another, within the lovely dwelling in which we live? (172–73)

Evil, like shadow, places a minus mark against the evidence of an object, rescuing it from its obviousness: this is, then, the passage of shadow or the moment of greatest risk: "A terrible moment: this must be emphasized. For without anything having changed, everything may lose its value. . . . What can one construct, on what can one base one's action, if the good remains beyond its most concrete ciphers, if even the orchard can signify the desert?" (174). And then, too, significance is nothing without substance. Words too are insufficient, and we need the presences of which they are only traces, which they cannot bring back to life; and for life, intelligibility cannot substitute.

A "world" is nothing in itself. The same key for the same door, the same labors as yesterday, around one, the same exchanges whose meaning is known, . . . above and everywhere the same galaxy of values, of tastes, of connivances or conflicts with the distant and the near, and all of that in the rustling of more familiar presences—but "all that" can suddenly, without changing its form, become *empty routine* when just one attachment gives out which supported all the others. . . . And it is not that our reason has failed, having for its task to verify that the key is the right one for the room, and the room the right one for a certain work or a certain game, and these, finally, for life, with its open circles seeing elsewhere still, like infinite aeolian wells, their fresh beginnings of deep waters: no, it is always available, and the internal relationships are more intelligible than ever. (174–75)

Absence masks the other side of Roland's mental landscape, and a sure perishing: "And how to find again what will have disappeared?" The wasteland is perhaps the basic metaphor of all the song and legend underlying the most noble scene, as a shadow deepens a sight. That is my concern here, and there is joined to it the knowledge that the French landscape is pervaded not just by the dark of Saracen might, but by an inner betrayal, undoing the French tongue: "Guenes i vint, ki la traïsun fist. / Dès or (e) cumencet le cunseill que mal prist" (Ganelon then came, who carried out the treason. / From that moment began the advice with evil ending; II. 178–79). This is the division from within, and the menace of pride, the possibility and then the certitude of defeat.

Except for one more thing: Roland, dying, reinvents sacrifice, destroys the limit of those "high dark mountains." The landscape shifts into the poetry of fate: heroic possibility and the certainty of death are met together.

While Roland fights, a transformation takes place, we are aware of it—a change of horizon, a slippage of these real mountains, of these armies, into the space of a consciousness, a transmutation accomplished of the event into symbol, of the memory into a poem. On this theatre of Roncevaux, which will become eternal thereby—a "spiritual battle" as Rimbaud will say—everything is from now on interior, as in the creation (or the contemplation) of an icon. (179)

Roland is conscious always not only of honor, but of death. In the recent film of the *Chanson de Roland* the fourteenth-century pilgrims shown in wandering and in their nightly celebrations of the *Song of Roland* are also dubious as to the Roland role itself. Klaus Kinsky, playing the pilgrim who plays Roland, inveighs against the role, calling it a Song of Death. And of Roland, Bonnefoy says:

> But he knows full well that what saves from death is the acceptance of death. . . . By virtue of Roland, the dark is only virtual in the work. . . . The waters of presence are formed again. (179–80)

The sun is suspended for justice, as Charlemagne demands, and time will stand quite still in the fixed shadows thus associated with an extraordinary event. But these now are not the others of an object or a landscape, rather the return of the same to the same. Roland is made possible by the collective meanings agreed upon—"symbols, myths: the vocabulary and syntax of Presence"—and with them went the time of heroes. Of Roland, perhaps, we keep only the shadow.

Finally for the reading of the shadow, a passage from *Dans le leurre du seuil* (In the Lure of the Threshold) reveals luminous doubt and dark certainty, as does the Song which Roland sings. Here are the obscurity of a wandering and the darkness of grief, together with the resolution to understand; here in my paper, as on the high pass of some mountain, the moment of passage is only suggested by the poem itself, like another song of defeat and triumph, on some threshold between day and death.

Et tant vaut la journée qui va finir,
Si précieuse la qualité de cette lumière,
Si simple le cristal un peu jauni
De ces arbres, de ces chemins parmi des sources,
Et si satisfaisantes l'une pour l'autre
Nos voix, qui eurent soif de se trouver
Et ont erré côte à côte, longtemps
Interrompues, obscures. (P, 280)

(And so rich the day about to end,
So cherished the quality of this light,
So simple the slightly yellowed crystal
Of these trees, the paths among the springs,
And how our voices satisfy
Each the other, eager to be found

And have long wandered side by side
Interrupted and obscure.)

5. Lack and Limit. To accept the act and the art of shadow entails, first, the acknowledgment of incompletion, of a piece with the imperfection we too have learned to call our summit: "Manquait, je me souviens, la première page" (I remember the first page was missing; A, 85). So the beginning lacks, and with it the hope of reader and writer for a text entire—a Book, "Le Livre"—in its impossible and absolute completion. The true place is elsewhere, and more open.

> It is in my becoming, whose openness I can maintain, and not in the closed text, that this vision, this nearby thought, if it has a meaning for me, as I believe it does, must be inscribed and flower and bear its fruit. It must be the crucible where, once dissipated, the country beyond takes new form. And where a few words, finally, will shine perhaps, simple and transparent like the nothing of language, being nevertheless everything, and real. (A, 149)

A few words, radiant as they are real, take the place of the former absolutes, and in full light and knowledge. Simple and sufficient, sure as the shadows of some larger hope, they link, as with threads or lines of steel, the two shores of the abyss Shakespeare sensed. Here, as in the Renaissance paintings in whose own light Bonnefoy's essays can be seen sometimes to stand, time joins with the timeless, perspective with fate.

Specific present is joined by language to specific past. As the words of Mallarmé form the cross-reflections of his "feux croisés," glancing off each other in their multiple facets, so these shadows too reflect upon and measure each other, as they reflect and measure the objects casting them originally in their roles, never without some measureless mystery. Against a profile closed in its sharp definition, the shadow might well be this unknowing, the paradoxical sureness of uncertainty, "le frémissement du possible," the quivering openness of what might be. Against knowing in its certainty, the passing poetry of a shade, whose intensity dapples bright with black.

6. Cloud, Leaf and Sign. As into negative theologies light is cast from beneath and above ("lumière d'endessous, d'au-dessus"; NR, 73), so now the shadows are cast up and down, the necessary precedent and companion of the crimson cloud which replaces that rising Renaissance sun. From Bonnefoy's thoughts on Mondrian to his essays gathered under the sign of *Le nuage rouge,* that single image, more than a single image, balances the art of shadow by its own triumphant color. Is it an exaggeration to see in that play of crimson against dark a contemporary reflection par excellence of the baroque colors? Of some red sonnet by La Ceppède, whose figures are not absent either in the poetry of this movement and this immobility,[4] this yesterday and yesteryear, whose reign marks our own present, and this written stone?

Aux monarques vainqueus la rouge cotte d'armes
Appartient justement. Ce Roi victorieux
Est justement vêtu par ces moqueurs gens d'armes
D'un manteau qui le marque et prince et glorieux.

O pourpre, emplis mon tête de ton jus précieux
Et lui fais distiller mille pourprines larmes,
A tant que, méditant ton sens mystérieux
Du sang trait de mes yeux j'ensanglante ces carmes.

Ta sanglante couleur figure nos péchés
Au dos de cet Agneau par le Père attachés:
Et ce Christ t'endossant se charge de nos crimes.

O Christ, o saint Agneau, daigne-toi de cacher
Tous mes rouges péchés, brindilles des abîmes,
Dans les sanglants replis du manteau de ta chair.

(Jean de La Ceppède, "Théorèmes spirituels")

(To conquering monarchs the tunic of red
Justly belongs. This victorious King
Is justly clad by these mocking men
In a cloak marking him a prince in full glory.

Oh crimson, fill my head with your precious stream
And have it distill a thousand crimson tears,
Until, in meditation on your mysterious meaning,
I stain these songs with blood milked from my eyes.

Your bleeding color figures forth our sins
Bound by the Father to the back of this Lamb:
And this Christ taking you up takes on our crimes.

Oh Christ, oh holy Lamb, deign now to hide
All my red sins, kindling of Hell,
Within the bleeding folds of the cloak of your flesh.)

As for the threshold's lure—that threshold once more stressing the idea of limit like some country beyond, separating here from there and yet joining them in a nearby reading of a moment in its fullest acceptance—it begins as if by an answer to an unspoken question. What of the shadow falling now across the poet's path and setting its limit, and ours, and our measure: is it too to be accepted, unprotestingly? "Oui," the threshold poem begins, and it is one of the great long poems of our century, to be placed alongside *The Waste Land* of Eliot, Stevens's "Rock" and Tzara's *Approximate Man,* these markers of our epoch. But to return to my own question, what of the shadow cast across the threshold, what of the lack and the sign fallen silent? The monumental essay "Baudelaire against Rubens" bears the answer, again prefaced by the positive "Oui,"

a yea-saying devoid of sentimentality, and the clue to the crimson cloud, a positive and prolonged response whose depth is never to be caught by the thin hissing of an English "yes."

> Redness, yes, of the God of yesteryear, that lack, that writing consequently a death—but in the dark fire a transparency, the God to be born who is no one, will be nothing, shining nevertheless on the farm roof over there, transfigured, shining here in some words redeemed. (NR, 73)

And in those words redeemed we hear the others, heard already in the country beyond, the simple and transparent words which will be, however, everything, and real ("qui seront pourtant tout . . . et réels"). There too the triumphant assurance of the "nevertheless" rules and brightens the tone, resurrects and restores the faith. And the radiance of the redemption is illuminated further by the modesty and the limits, those limits which the shadows, glimpsed or not, spoken or unspoken, forever mark. Their falling may well signal a vision on the rise.

Lastly, in the dusty tree, more real and closer in its imperfection, that torn and dirtied leaf of ivy, a truer representation of the human consciousness than some unwithered brilliance, the wounded presence of poetry finds its real place, full of shadow and darkened by passing time.

> I shall say, allegorically: it is this fragment of the somber tree, this broken leaf of ivy. The entire leaf, building its immutable essence from all its veinings, would already be the concept. But this broken leaf, green and black, dirtied, this leaf revealing in its wound all the depth of what is, this infinite leaf is pure presence and consequently my salvation. Who could take away from me its having been mine, and in a contact with me beyond destinies and sites, within the absolute? Who could destroy it, already destroyed? (I, 28–29)

And the shadow cast bears the same witness to a wounded presence as the torn leaf, being the same indication of human vision, and of human art, in its multiplicity of ambivalent signs, and of contradictory signals. What reader of contemporary poetry—what dweller in contemporary time—could not say, with Bonnefoy, "It is clear that we have long wandered, and doubted, among the signs" (NR, 353)? The way has never been less easy, less certain, less absolute, for the voyagers of poetic language.

Words need, says Bonnefoy, a grid to see them by: "our chance, our own place, our existence" (RM, 23). And our chance might well be this quite simple one, made of light, but more surely of shadow; at this point our outward vision might well merge with another, toward the deepest and most private of insights, that nearest place and the most tragic that poetry alone provides.

> What could I use as a grid? The representation of the earth and the sky because the country beyond is first of all a gaze upon the place nearby? (A, 74)

To take the dark as the measure of clarity, and imperfection as the measure of presence, is perhaps to bring, as Bonnefoy says of the *Song of Roland,* a language back to life. After the text as an object seen outwardly, the word as shadow should now be revalued, in quiet and perhaps also in anguish, searchingly. For it is in the depth of these inner shadows that we must at present and at last reread Yves Bonnefoy, in reflection, and in their light: "Art has taken place, and we are saved" (RT, 35).

Mary Ann Caws, Summer 1979

[1] Yves Bonnefoy, "L'humour, les ombres portées," in his *Unréve fait à Mantoue,* Paris, Mercure de France, 1967, p. 37. All translations in this essay are my own.

[2] A = *L'arrière-pays;* I = *L'Improbable;* NR = *Le nuage rouge;* P = *Poèmes;* R = *Rome 1630;* RM = *Un rêve fait à Mantoue;* RT = *Rue Traversière;* SS = *La seconde simplicité.*

[3] Yves Bonnefoy, "Readiness, Ripeness: Hamlet, Lear," preface to *Hamlet / Le Roi Lear,* Yves Bonnefoy, tr., Paris, Gallimard, 1978.

[4] I have pointed out the analogy in my *Inner Theater of Recent French Poetry: Cendrars, Tzara, Péret, Artaud, Bonnefoy,* Princeton, N.J., Princeton University Press, 1972, in the chapter entitled "Not the Peacock but the Stone."

World Literature Tomorrow

I am honored to speak under the aegis of *Books Abroad* on the eve of its golden anniversary. The contribution of this distinguished magazine has been fulsomely acknowledged in the recent Autumn issue by such conspicuous scholars and writers that I feel indeed, like Dante, the last *tra cotanto senno.* The dedication, imagination and sheer energy of Ivar Ivask and his eminent predecessors have made *Books Abroad* unique among literary journals, a tribute I am happy to pay here, having long since paid it in print. I remember that when Norman Cousins was trying to convert *Saturday Review* into a so-called *World Magazine,* I protested that this was an empty title unless his magazine had a world content and outlook. I reminded him that the only American literary magazine with such an outlook was *Books Abroad.* Thus it seems most appropriate to me that Ivask and his editors are renaming their journal *World Literature Today.* This recognition of the imminence of World Literature as a well-defined, carefully-constructed discipline is

welcome. It is a statement of faith that a long-dreamed goal is drawing ever closer and that there is no need to wait for the next jubilee year to celebrate its being commonly discussed and taught. If I have cautiously substituted "tomorrow" in my title for the "today" of Ivask's journal, I am no less optimistic than he that this discipline, consistently defined and ethically presented, will before long become part of school curricula.

For World Literature is the logical third stage of Comparative Literature. The first stage was of course the Western Heritage, which Dean Weisinger too severely branded as "a confining concept" to which "many comparatists enslave themselves." The second step of courses is East-West Literature, in which tentative courses are being tried. I shall return to this step below. Finally, there remains the goal of World Literature, encompassing the two previous categories. This *littérature universelle* is becoming at last an academic reality to which we may legitimately, if cautiously, aspire, but one on whose demands even Goethe probably never reflected while making his titillating remark about *Weltliteratur.* Indeed, as François Jost has made clear, Goethe's call was actually for an East-West (*West-Östliche*) dimension to literature. *Weltliteratur* is something even further, the *Krönung* (to use a favorite word of Goethe) and utmost demonstration of comparatism. René Wellek writes in his *Theory of Literature:* "Goethe himself saw that this [*Weltliteratur*] is a very distant ideal, that no single nation is willing to give up its individuality. Today we are possibly even further removed from such a state of amalgamation, and we would argue that we cannot even wish that the diversities of national literatures should be obliterated." Obviously Comparative Literature often departs from similarities to the examination of meaningful contrast. The real excitement of our discipline, however, and indeed its challenge, remains in the mythic, generic and other homogeneities inexplicably occurring over two millennia on our five continents. It is more exciting to discover that a great number of folk epics include a trip to the afterworld than to observe that a lesser number do not. Little is to be gained by proving that there are exceptions to Otto Rank's comparative observation about the birth and death of the epic hero. It is intriguing to discover that epic heroes even among the Araucanian pagans must have twelve paladins (i.e., disciples), even at the cost of their individuality.

I should like first today to dwell on the remaining problems in achieving world literature, and then proceed to some of the resources which will help us to resolve these problems. The first difficulty to be eliminated is the misuse of the phrase "World Literature" in academia itself. I can find no more striking example of this than in a recent report circulated by the South Central Comparative Literature Association bearing the incredible statistic that 91% of college departments surveyed in that region rather than Senior level, whereas few Comparative Literature courses exist. SUNY-Albany, in our own area, boasted a Department of Comparative and World Literature, with no World Literature courses listed. Indeed the department has folded. We know from *The Teacher's Guide to World Literature,* prepared for the National Council of Teachers of English, that the term is applied at best, as in the SCCLA survey, to Western classics in translation. When I was preparing for a major publisher a Western Heritage undergraduate anthology in English, I was informed that the book was to be advertised as "World Literature" to increase sales. We must not accept easy outs. World Literature as a discipline means the study of literature from the maximum geographical extent where major authors are found (see below), taught as often as possible by teachers who read those authors in the original language. Its method must be that of comparatism rather than of random samplings.

World Literature, our third phase, must establish in its wide area meaningful points of contact and assimilation, most conveniently through the familiar approaches of theme, form and movement. We may have to adjust our definitions and critical vocabulary. Some years ago, while planning with R. K. Das Gupta three East-West courses to be given alternately at NYU and his university in India, I proposed a course on five Western and five Asian tragedies. He reminded me that whereas Aristotle's generic approach might have some value for epic poetry, it was irrelevant to Indian theatre. The course would have to deal instead with "drama." The first World (like the first East-West) Literature courses will have to sift out common denominators which may best bring differing literatures into juxtaposition.

The greatest deterrent to World Literature is of course the language problem, already a challenge to any comparatist, especially if we are to sample the major literary works of the five continents. Africa, which would seem at first to present the major language problem, presents fortuitously little difficulty, for the literary vehicles will remain French and English. Portuguese will surely decline, especially as the chief theme of its poetry, liberation, has been achieved. The same fate awaits Afrikaans. Although the Negro poet Samuel Allen defines the negritude movement as "representative of the Negro African poet's endeavor for his race a normal self-pride," the leaders, with their European schooling and syncretic tendencies, do not espouse black native languages. Their writing and their editing of *Présence Afri-*

caine is in French or English. Some Africans wrote in English as early as the eighteenth century. The common native languages—Bantu, Swahili and Yoruba—have a small literate audience. Yet their themes and concerns are of course based on what Langston Hughes calls the African heritage. Thus, when Patrice Lumumba stirred the Congolese natives with his verses on the white man's savagery and rapine, he wrote in the white man's language. In her anthology *Black Poets in French* Marie Collins explains simply: "More than 400 different tribal languages are spoken in Africa. . . . For the time being at least, French and English are a unifying means of communication." The languages of Alan Paton in the South and the francophone Kateb Yacine in the North are preferred to a continent-wide Babel.

Black African literature is of course the most visibly lacking component in the plans for World Literature. Its major oral tradition of myths, poetry and folktales—with its novels, derivative in form but local in character—could play a modest but useful role in World Literature classes. Any course on myths or oral literature could hardly exclude Africa. In the area of oral poetry Africa contributes odes of praise, oracles, incantations, dialogues and of course political polemic. Prose forms to consider would vary from the sociopolitical novel and autobiography to folktales, bestiaries, picaresque narratives and dilemma tales, where the hearers are invited to supply a conclusion.

Since Africa has contributed fewer literary works which satisfy the first of the dual criteria established by Fritz Strich (international acclaim and enduring values), African authors will play a minor role in the new Universal Literature curricula. Similar massive areas, like Indonesia with a population of 100,000,000, would be minimally represented. Yet even as we accept this reality, we reject the conclusion of Pichois and Rousseau (African literature was also curiously omitted from Étiemble's list quoted below), who write: "Les littératures africaines et polynésiennes occuperont d'autres chercheurs." This same French logic and prudence is expressed in their proverb, "Qui trop embrasse, mal étreint." Excepting this exclusion of Africa, one may agree with their general premise about World Literature: "l'histoire de la littérature n'est pas l'histoire de la littérature universelle." Aficionados of African or Polynesian literatures can of course feature them in theses written for their degrees in World Literature.

No such linguistic capitulation as Africa's is visible in Asia and Indonesia. English, although an official "third" or "international" language in India, is now spoken by only some 5% of the population, although there is strong sentiment in the Indian P.E.N. Club for Indo-Anglian narrative and poetry, voiced typically by Bhabani Bhattacharya as follows: "The Indian writer must be free to use any language he likes, unharassed by criticism, either tacitly implied or plainly stated, and by any kind of compulsion, direct or indirect, which may come out of the strengthening mood of linguistic chauvinism." Yet nationalism is strong throughout Asia. The Indonesians have rejected Dutch for Bahasa Indonesia. Philippine writers reject Spanish and English for Pilipino. China retains its linguistic xenophobia. The greatest problem for World Literature courses in this area is that there are almost no Asian specialists who could participate knowing Asiatic languages other than their own—or even other Asian literatures, which is still more serious for literary internationalism. Fortunately the linguistic imperialism of English and French still clings in Asia, though less than in Africa, of course, and this enables Asians to have indirect access to their continental literatures. Thus, at a recent triennial meeting of the Asian Writers' Conference, the Korean Ko Yo Sup complained that Koreans wishing to translate Asian works must get hold of the English, French or German versions of such works before turning them into Korean. So complicated are Asian languages even to close neighbors that Ryoto Sato of Tokyo claimed that it takes him an entire year to translate one Chinese novel into Japanese.

Thus Americans and Asians face the identical problem in mastering Asian literatures. This problem of linguistic intercommunication within Asia, where more natives know English or French than the *Sprachräume* of their neighbors, has reduced Indian Comparative Literature courses to feature English-Indian literary relations and led the University of Tokyo to emphasize English-Japanese relations, at least at the time I was last in Asia. (Similarly, the dean of Cairo University assured me that his teachers were secular pioneers in Comparative Literature through their Hispano-Arabic researches.)

As suggested above, the inability of Asians to read Asian languages other than their own parallels an ignorance of their neighbors' literatures. Thus the aforementioned joint NYU-Indian program of East-West Literature, although finalized on paper and assured a subsidy from the Fulbright Commission, lurched to a sudden halt. It was only during the FILLM congress in Australia years later that Das Gupta explained what had gone wrong: he could find no Indian colleagues who could or would read in the original (or conceivably even in translation) the various Asian epics and poetry which were to constitute the Asian component of the projected courses. I have of late wondered whether the World Literature courses we are hoping for in America might not be partially staffed by the young comparatists of Asian

birth we are training in our own graduate schools. Their course work makes them familiar with the great texts of the Western Heritage, while their theses often encompass Indian, Chinese, Korean or Japanese authors.

Let me turn now to another dream we have all shared: the institute of World Literature. It has been widely accepted that a dissemination of such institutes would support the spread of the discipline of Universal Literature. Étiemble writes, "The Institute I dream of would naturally include Hellenists, Latinists, Egyptologists, Slavicists, Hindi and Bengali specialists, sinologists, Semiticists, Germanic, Romance, Turko-Mongol, Dravidian and Japanese scholars." Such an institute would have to be in Paris, says Étiemble (who ironically claims to be an internationalist surrounded by chauvinists). "In Paris only can one learn all those languages which I believe indispensable." London and New York are apparently out of the running.

It was this same dream, strengthened by some political motivation, which created Moscow's Gorki Institute of World Literature. It was Gorki's dream that such a clearinghouse could bring the peoples of the world together through literature. It is a research center, a library and an advisory resource to the state publishers on their extensive programs. Many of the books recommended for translation and printing derive from Asia, Africa and the uncommitted nations whose favor the government is currying. The Institute favors the "scientific" approach to literature, which Gorki chose to call social realism. In a *New York Times* report which I wrote after visiting the Institute I concluded that whereas the bibliographies and translations and researches cannot fail to be useful, the Institute's subjugation to political pressures cannot fail to hamper its prestige. It has not even begun to be effective in shaping curricula in World Literature.

Holland has also shown an interest in an institute of World Literature, as have some of us in New York. We had some meetings at New York University about such a project, encouraged by the many surrounding resource bodies: the Asian Literature Committee (chaired so effectively by Bonnie Crown), the Afro-American Research Institute, the American Library Association, P.E.N. Club International, UNESCO and so many others. However, it turned out that to carry on such an institute's five areas of activity (translation, publication, bibliography, symposia and study groups) would require an annual subsidy of $250,000. Such a project was impossible when NYU was selling its uptown campus as a measure for survival. *Nil desperandum.* An institute of World Literature in America, England or France would be useful, yet its absence need not hold back the tide of literary cosmopolitanism.

There are other, more attainable projects to be carried out.

Here let us pause over an inevitable problem which will become intensified by the creation of World Literature curricula. Syllabi of all Comparative Literature courses, whether Western Heritage or East-West or World, must of course acquaint the student with a bibliography of background readings, comment and interpretation of the assigned texts. Time was when such a bibliography should be sure to include criticism by individuals of other nationality than the author evaluated. François Jost reminds us of the venerable attitude that "because foreign criticism is not immediately 'involved,' 'committed' or 'engaged,' it can sometimes reach more valid verdicts than indigenous criticism." It was traditional, he adds, to hold that the Abbé Desfontaines wrote better criticism on Fielding than anyone in London and that Swinburne for this reason was a superior analyst of Hugo. Indeed it was thought that criticism of an author by a conational tended toward shortsighted or one-sided judgments, over-generous or over-hostile.

The politicization of literature after Marx to a point unheard of since feudal-clerical scholasticism makes a luxury of discussions such as the one above. Such politicization may have embarrassed even its chief apostle Gorki, who in September 1923 invited Stefan Zweig to write an article for *Beseda,* a journal which, he assured, "has nothing to do with politics." Controlled criticism, often fickle, spares insiders no more than outsiders. One day the *Hungarian Quarterly* equates József Lengyel with "some of modern literature's greatest writers," whereas the next he is a villain whose *Confrontation* must be suppressed. Literary criticism of outsiders is best illustrated by the two massive cultures of Russia and China, both of which would be inevitably well represented in East-West or World Literature curricula. Let me illustrate how this replacement of criticism by polemics becomes a very real problem for the future development of World Literature.

The monthly journal *Chinese Literature,* which I have received from Peking since 1968, is the most valid document from which to learn the trends of Chinese letters and criticism. It contains original writing in the form of poetry, narrative, drama, filmscripts and opera libretti, such as the famous *Red Lantern,* recalling the war of resistance against Japan. Perhaps its most vigorous element is its literary criticism. Indeed the section reviewing books has borne the significant rubric "Literary Criticism and Repudiation." To illustrate its international tenets of criticism, we shall sample expressions of disapproval of three books well known to the West: Mikhail Sholokhov's *And Quiet Flows the Don,* Ilya Ehrenburg's *People and Life* and Konstantin Simonov's *Days and Nights,* the epochal novel centered on the Battle of Stalingrad.

Russia's third Nobel laureate is branded by critic Shih Hung-yu as a counterrevolutionary and lackey of revisionism who has been betraying the October Revolution since his 1926 *Tales of the Don.* After a lengthy indictment, the review concludes: "Today we expose Sholokhov to the bright light of Mao Tse-tung's thought, and tomorrow Sholokhov will not be able to escape a trial before the revolutionary peoples of the Soviet Union. It is certain that the Soviet people will sweep him into the dust-bin of history, alongside Brezhnev, Kosygin, and company." Critic Chung Yenping turns his attention to Ehrenburg's memoirs written under the brief thaw of Khrushchev, memoirs arraigning that Stalinism which the Maoists still view as a beneficial dictatorship of the proletariat. Chung's repudiation reads: "This big poisonous weed is a long, revolting series of anecdotes dealing with certain historical events and figures from the time of the February Revolution to the eve of the Great Patriotic War. Ehrenburg's intention was to borrow the tongues of the dead to attack the road of the October Revolution, to resuscitate ghosts to take part in the fight for a capitalist restoration." To clinch his point, Chung recalls that the revered pioneer writer Lu Hsün (called by Mao in 1940 "an unprecedented hero on the cultural front") dismissed Ehrenburg thirty years ago as a right-wing bourgeois author.

Finally, critic Hsieh Sheng-wen demythicizes the Siege of Stalingrad as chronicled by Simonov. "Analyzed and examined critically with the sharp weapon of Mao Tse-tung's thought, *Days and Nights* proves to be a black specimen of revisionist war literature, and Simonov a cowardly traitor who traded upon the glory and dignity of the soldiers of the Red Army." In sum, by an insistence on the people's sufferings, Simonov is accused of interpreting Stalingrad as "an unprecedented catastrophe which brought the people nothing but death and destruction" instead of viewing it, in Chairman Mao's words, as "the turning-point in the history of all mankind."

This type of criticism obviously must be prevented from plaguing and impeding the development of World Literature. Such polemicization of criticism, albeit more subtly presented, has found its way into Comparative Literature congresses in both Eastern and Western Europe. A great effort is needed to conciliate views to the point of producing intellectually honest manuals, literary histories and bibliographies for the implementation of future courses in World Literature. The bibliographies on symbolism, Renaissance literature and other topics now being undertaken by the International Comparative Literature Association will hopefully demonstrate that zones of varying political persuasion can produce useful tools for the study of World Literature. If not, then the syllabus and bibliography for a course in contemporary poetry will be different in Western Europe and America from those in Russia or in China.

Mention of bibliographies brings us back to what we were characterizing as "more attainable projects to be carried out." The first and most lengthy step is to undertake a census of the texts available for a pilot graduate program in World Literature, as well as existing translations of these texts. Bilingual texts will be especially desirable. The M.A. in World Literature could in prospect require a knowledge of seventy-five or more texts on the part of a candidate, including twenty to thirty in his own native literature. The Ph.D. would require considerably more but would demand also a far greater number of background and theoretical works, which ideally should exist also in translations. The books selected for these literary courses are those which, as Fritz Strich has qualified them, have already won international recognition and display enduring values. In addition, they will be clearcut examples of the themes, forms and movements which will structure the World Literature courses.

For this essential first step there are many bibliographical tools. UNESCO has been most useful in two ways, not only by the remarkable registry of translations all over the world in its *Index Translationum* but by its remarkable *Connaissance de l'Orient* series. Other bibliographical tools include *Books in Print,* England's *Bookseller* and the European national bibliographies subsidized by governments. New retrieval-of-information techniques in our libraries will be most helpful. Microfilm and microfiche bibliographies will facilitate our enormous task. The Franklin Book Programs, a nonprofit organization with fifteen offices on three continents, has made a useful contribution. The P.E.N. Clubs in many corners of the world publish literary bulletins, some of which I receive and which contain important bibliographical news. University presses and those of learned societies will have to be canvassed. Our own *Books Abroad* as *World Literature Today* will continue its dissemination of information useful to World Literature courses. All the bibliographical sources of the West will require investigation in our search for translations of Asian and African works into a Western language, hopefully into one of the three foreign languages which we shall continue to require of our doctoral candidates. We are at this moment at NYU entering a request for a two-year subsidy to undertake such a census.

Naturally, the same preparations for World Literature courses have to be undertaken as we have all done for Comparative Literature courses: curricular requirements established, course syllabi written, lectures, readings and reports determined. The technical aspects of World Literature we are all familiar with. It might be useful if we in addition requested the ICLA or FILLM— or possibly even our friends in Oklahoma, who have demonstrated that they can achieve what is impossible for others: the compilation of a roster-by-region of comparatists whose knowledge of literature bridges East and West or two totally dissimilar areas.

Once the syllabi are constructed and the bibliographies compiled, we confront one last time the linguistic vehicle of our courses. We have committed ourselves to the principle that the texts of World Literature, like those of the Western Heritage, should be taught by instructors who read them in the original. Let us see how this principle operates in a hypothetical course on the world's great national epic poems, perhaps the most challenging and productive genre of all. Ideally, in a course including six Western and four Asian epics (leaving Africa and other areas in abeyance for our demonstration) a polyglot Western and a polyglot Asian scholar should suffice for the teaching. However, we have already observed that Asian professors usually choose as their second or third foreign language one from the West. Thus the course planner faces one of three solutions.

First, he may resort to group teaching by instructors of differing nationalities and specializations not too alien to epic, a practice occasionally tried in Comparative Literature departments. This is sometimes possible in a large metropolitan university or community. Yet there are inevitable difficulties of scheduling, teaching load and lack of remuneration. Furthermore, a guest lecturer cannot always grasp the direction a course is taking and make the most pertinent contribution. Second, the instructor may lean on foreign-language-speaking graduate students as resource personnel, entrusting to them the reading aloud of a text, adjudicating the assigned translation (when necessary) and making further clarifications. Finally, the instructor may build his course with a maximum of Western epics (nine? ten?) he can read and teach himself and take a chance on finding a willing *suppléant* to teach the others. In case of failure, he must hope to have assigned the best possible translations and rest his case at that point. Certainly, if he feels that *Gilgamesh* must be included as one of the world's greatest national epics (and one which probably influenced the *Odyssey*), he may be forgiven for not reading Babylonian, Hittite or Hurrian. It must be conceded that in Comparative (and especially World) Literature there will be rare cases—when an instructor will have to discuss a book he cannot read in the original, whether an assigned text or a background commentary. As the first Report on Professional Standards of the American Comparative Literature Association put it, "It would be highly puristic to exclude some reading from more remote languages in translation."

Paradoxically, this point is often raised by carping nonlinguists as yet another objection to comparative studies. It is a logical and facile argument, like the insistence that no graduate student in fine arts should work from slide projections but only from studying the original paintings or sculpture, or that historians, philosophers, anthropologists and theologians should not use sources they cannot read in the original. We all stand behind the principle, but it is of course a question of degree. For someone to teach a course, graduate or undergraduate, on Dante without knowing Italian and Latin is unethical and reprehensible. Yet we should not suggest that the planner of the course on world epic described above abandon it. Many English or joint departments which administer the undergraduate literature-in-translation courses impose the *quot opera, tot linguae* principle on graduate literature departments while their instructors abandon it totally at the undergraduate level. When we have developed several World Literature graduate programs in several major universities, we shall have a good idea of what constitutes an ethical compromise on this issue.

Rather than conclude with a bad conscience, I return for a moment to those 91% of college courses entitled "World Literature" listed by the SCCLA. If one is truly devoted to literature, one can only have mixed feelings about them. One may object that they tend to follow without method the random Homer-to-Arthur-Miller zigzag path through Western literature. One may object that they are often taught by instructors who do not read easily two or three European languages, that they usually require not one single command of a foreign language on the part of the student, that they are tokenist in their approach (see below). Still, any literature is good literature in these days of simplified college curricula and abolition of the foreign-language requirement. Furthermore, the schools' misuse of the term "World Literature" is not entirely of their own doing.

Our textbook compilers and editors have indeed decided that "World Literature" is a "sexy" rubric, to quote one publisher. Time was when a Western Heritage anthology would be called by Ginn *The Heritage of European Literature,* by Lippincott *Readings in Western Civilization* or by Ronald Press *Literature of Western Civilization.* When the dike broke, Dryden (*Masterworks of World Literature,*) Norton (*World Masterpieces,*) Odyssey (*Types of World Literature*) and others opportunistically claimed a global viewpoint which was totally lacking.

More ethically entitled were Scott Foresman's *The World in Literature,* American Book's *World Literature,* Holt-Rinehart-Winston's *Heritage of World Literature,* and Macmillan's *Anthology of World Literature,* which led the American undergraduate to a few well-edited samplings of texts from the Orient and the Near East. There seems to be no reason why publishers cannot separate such clearly identifiable areas of literature as Western, East-West and World and describe their anthologies accordingly.

We are sometimes soothed by assurances that such piecemeal phenomena as Pound's interest in Japanese haiku, Yeats's interest in Tagore, Joyce's knowledge of the Koran testify that we are on the way to World Literature. To paraphrase Joseph Bédier's shattering question, one may ask, "Mais où sont les programmes d'études?" Once we organize our courses and syllabi and get on with the task, getting the bugs out of them, as the scientists say, we shall achieve Ivar Ivask's goal of World Literature today. Goethe's challenging words of January 1827 echo within us: "The epoch of world literature is at hand, and everyone must hasten its approach." We are getting closer. As the Russian proverb reminds us, "Patience is the mother of genius."

World Literature courses as we have conceived them in this essay are intended for gifted and motivated graduate students. A candidate in this outermost extension of Comparative Literature, I caution him, "If you keep at it for another ten or fifteen years, you may be a comparatist in your forties." The World Literature professionist will be in command of his discipline by his fifties. And even then there will be uncharted territories beckoning him or her further onward.

Robert J. Clements, Spring 1977

Ed. Note: Robert Clements's essay is an expanded version of his address to the *Books Abroad* Golden Anniversary session at the Modern Language Association convention in New York on 27 December 1976.

Comparability

What makes comparison possible? If we are reflecting theoretically on the nature of comparative literature, then we need to attempt to work out the basis of comparison in literary studies, the nature of comparability itself. Although the question is not often explicitly debated, it underlies important shifts in the discipline. Everyone interested in the field is likely to know one story of comparative literature: once upon a time, comparative literature focused on sources and influence, bringing together works where there seemed a direct link of transmission which subtended and served to justify comparison. But then comparative literature liberated itself from the study of sources and influence and acceded to a broader regime of intertextual studies—broader but less well defined—where in principle anything could be compared with anything else. At this point we began to hear talk of a "crisis of comparative literature," no doubt because of the difficulty of explaining the nature of the new comparability that served to structure and, in principle, to justify comparative literature as a discipline.

The problem of the nature of comparability is rendered more acute by the shift of comparative literature from a Eurocentric to a global discipline, though that may not appear to be the case. We are now in a phase, it seems, where the problem can apparently be set aside, because a good deal of new work in comparative literature is focusing on cross-cultural contacts and hybridity within postcolonial societies and within the literatures of colonizing powers. There is a sense in which the most exciting work in the field is based on a modernized version of the study of sources and influences: insofar as comparative study is based on the diverse literary and cultural influences at work in Derek Walcott's *Omeros,* or Salman Rushdie's *Satanic Verses,* or Ousmane Sembène's *Les bouts de bois de Dieu,* or Rodolpho Gonzalez's *I Am Foaquín / Yo soy Foaquín,* comparison is based on direct cultural contacts and traceable influences. But in principle the problem of comparability remains unsolved—more acute than ever. What, in this newly globalized space, justifies bringing two or more texts together?

In this brief paper I can scarcely do more than pose the problem, but I propose to approach it obliquely, in homage to a brilliant young comparatist, a teacher in the Département de Littérature Comparée at the Université de Montréal, who was killed in the crash of an American Eagle plane outside Chicago in the fall of 1994. His name was Bill Readings. Educated at Oxford, he had taught at the Université de Genève, Syracuse University, and the Université de Montréal. If I approach my topic by asking what Bill might have said about it, I do so with the realization that in losing Bill Readings we have lost someone whose response to a particular topic could not be predicted, except that it would be enormously shrewd and interesting.

At the time of his death Bill was finishing revisions to a book on the university—not the most exciting of topics. Most books about the university are written by retiring university administrators and seem destined for the remainder table even as they come off the press. And perhaps this one will be no different, but it does take as its point of departure the fact that today the tone

of self-satisfaction that has marked so many books on the university, from Jacques Barzun to Jaroslav Pelikan, is no longer available. Today, Readings writes, "No one of us can seriously imagine himself or herself as the hero of the story of the university, as the instantiation of the cultured individual that the entire great machine labors day and night to produce. . . . The grand narrative of the university centered on the production of a liberal, reasoning subject, is no longer available to us."[1] This is in part, of course, because we have come to see that the subject is gendered, racialized.

Kant gave us the model of the modern university organized by a single regulatory ideal, the principle of Reason. Humboldt and the German Idealists replaced the notion of Reason with that of Culture, centering the university on the dual task of research and teaching, the production and inculcation of national self-knowledge. But now the model of the University of Culture, the university whose task was to produce cultured individuals, citizens imbued with a national culture, has in the West been replaced by what Readings calls, in a phrase that resonates for those of us in the American academy, "The University of Excellence."

The crucial thing about excellence, he points out, is that it has no content (there need be no agreement about what is excellent). In that sense, it is like the cash nexus. It has no content and thus serves to introduce—here we come to my topic—comparability. As Readings explains, "Its very lack of reference allows excellence to function as a principle of translatability between radically different idioms."[2] As British and American academics hear endlessly from administrators these days, every unit of the university, from Classics to Transportation and Parking, can and will be judged by its success in achieving excellence. And excellence is determined not by intrinsic characteristics of one's activity, nor by a relation to some external purpose, but, most often, by something like polls: ratings of some sort, where people supposed to be more or less knowledgeable, usually other administrators, are asked to produce rankings based on their perceptions of excellence. And if you are asked to fill out such a survey, you are likely to do so (however much or little knowledge you may possess) by asking yourself, "Well, let's see now. Which are the departments in my field that people generally think are the best?" Excellence is determined by what people think other people might think excellent.

I am reminded of a remark in George W. S. Trow's wonderful book *In the Context of No Context,* which deserves to be better known as a guide to our condition. Trow identifies as a crucial though unrecognized watershed in the history of American modernity "the moment when a man named Richard Dawson, the host of a program called *Family Feud*, asked contestants to guess what a poll of a hundred people had guessed would be the height of the average American woman. Guess what they've guessed. Guess what they've guessed the average is."[3] This about our invention of processes of producing rankings while evading problems of knowledge and referentiality.

In the University of Excellence the question becomes, "Are you in the top ten or twenty or fifty of whatever it is you are?"—judged by criteria that need not be specified, so accustomed are we now to this abstract, nonreferential idea of excellence. (Even surveys that seek to be more serious by refining their questions must, in order to retain comparability, make them essentially empty of reference to any specific standard. Thus a question about the excellence of units and programs might be broken into questions about the excellence of faculty, the excellence of students, the excellence of facilities, and so on.) The idea of excellence enables us to make comparable entities which have little in common as to structure or function, input or output. But that is only half of its bureaucratic usefulness. It also makes possible the avoidance of substantive arguments about what teachers, students, and administrators should actually be doing. Everyone's task is to strive for excellence, however that might be defined.

For example, our Department of Transportation and Parking at Cornell received an award for excellence from its professional organization, apparently for its success in discouraging parking on campus (success in "decreasing demand," they call it) by charging increasingly higher fees and progressively eliminating convenient parking spaces. But it is not utterly impossible to imagine that excellence here might have been assigned precisely the opposite content: excellence might conceivably consist of making it easier for faculty to park on campus, though I agree that this is not very likely.

At the moment I am serving on a task force on graduate education, with representatives from the schools of law, business, veterinary medicine, engineering, and hotel administration on my campus. We have very different ideas, I would guess, about what the goals and means of education should be and about what sort of things our graduate students should be doing, but all this seems to be bracketed as irrelevant as we all agree that "excellence" should be our goal and (alas!) that everybody should be reviewed to see that they are working toward it. As Bill Readings writes, "Excellence shares with Machiavelli's *virtù* the advantage of permitting calculation on a homogenous scale." It is a principle of accounting and bureaucratic control. Bureaucracy works more efficiently if it can avoid becoming involved in arguments about the contents of various activities with

people who know more than the administrators, if it can operate at the level of the quantification of excellence, where the comparability it establishes provides justification for the allocation of resources. As a principle of unrestricted accounting, excellence draws only one boundary, writes Readings, "the boundary that protects the unrestricted power of the bureaucracy."

But it is important to stress, I think, that excellence is not an idea foisted on universities by corporate management and its representatives on boards of trustees. It has, on the contrary, come to be the way in which the university, in the United States, achieves the self-consciousness supposed to guarantee its intellectual autonomy. Unlike business, which is interested only in the bottom line, we in the university are defined by our pursuit of excellence. A thousand reports and brochures tell the same tale. Contentless excellence—our comparability.

I am interested in the relationship between the comparability of comparative literature and the comparability instituted by excellence, which, to sum up, has the following characteristics: 1) it purports to have content but actually does not; 2) it grants groups considerable freedom (it doesn't matter what you do so long as you do it excellently), which is crucial to bureaucratic efficiency; but 3) ultimately it is a mechanism for the reduction or exclusion of activities that do not succeed by this measure. How does the comparability of comparative literature compare with this?

The intertextual nature of meaning—the fact that meaning lies in the differences between one text or one discourse and another—makes literary study essentially, fundamentally comparative, but it also produces a situation in which comparability depends upon a cultural system, a general field that underwrites comparison. The meaning of a text depends on its relations to others within a cultural space, such as that of West European culture, which is in part why comparative literature has been so much inclined to remain Western and European in its focus. The more sophisticated one's understanding of discourse, the harder it is to compare Western and non-Western texts, for each depends for its meaning and identity on its place within a discursive system—disparate systems that seem to make the putative comparability of texts either illusory or, at the very least, misleading.

What sort of comparability, then, could guide the transformation of comparative literature from a Eurocentric discipline to a more global one? There is a difficult problem here, it seems to me. On the one hand, as my colleague Natalie Melas argues, comparison such as justifies a discipline consolidates a standard or norm which then functions to give value to works that match up to it and to exclude those that do not, so that comparison—the principle of comparability—rather than opening new possibilities for cultural value, more often than not restricts and totalizes it.[4] But, on the other hand, as we try to avoid this imposition of particular norms, we may risk falling into the alternative practice, which Readings's account of excellence describes, where the standard is kept nonreferential—vacuous—so that it is not imposing particular requirements but where, in the end, it provides a *bureaucratic* rather than an intellectual mechanism for regulation and control.

The problem of comparison is that it seems inevitably to generate a standard, or ideal type, of which the texts compared come to function as variants. And comparatists today are eager to avoid this implicit result of measuring one culture's texts by some standard extrinsic to that culture. Yet the more we try to deploy a comparability that has no implicit content, the more we risk falling into a situation like that of the University of Excellence, where an apparent lack of concern for content—your department can do what it likes, provided it does it excellently—is in the end only the alibi for a control based on bureaucratic rather than academic and intellectual principles.

The virtue of a comparability based on specific intellectual norms or models—generic, thematic, historical—is that they are subject to investigation and argument in ways that the vacuous bureaucratic norms are not. One solution, then, is to attempt to spell out the assumptions and norms that seem to underwrite one's comparisons, so that they do not become implicit terms. A model here might be Erich Auerbach's conception of the *Ansatzpunkt*: a specific point of departure, conceived not as an external position of mastery but as a "handle" or partial vantage point that enables the critic to bring together a variety of cultural objects. "The characteristic of a good point of departure," writes Auerbach in his essay "Philology and *Weltliteratur*," "is its concreteness and its precision on the one hand, and on the other, its potential for centrifugal radiation."[5] This might be a theme, a metaphor, a detail, a structural problem, or a well-defined cultural function. I can imagine basing cross-cultural comparison on linking principles whose very arbitrariness or contingency will prevent them from giving rise to a standard or ideal type, such as comparing works by authors whose last name begins with *B*, or works whose numerical place in a bibliography is divisible by thirteen. I confess, though, that this is scarcely the sort of thing Auerbach had in mind and not a general or principled solution to the problem of comparability. A further possibility is to attempt to locate the comparative perspective geo-

graphically and historically: instead of imagining the comparative perspective as a global overview, one might stress the value, for instance, of comparing European literatures *from* Africa, for their relations to the cultural productions of a particular African moment. Better such points of departure that impose criteria and norms than the fear that comparisons will be odious. The danger, I repeat, is that comparatists' fear that their comparisons will impose implicit norms and standards may give rise to a vacuousness that is as difficult to combat as is the notion of excellence which administrators are using to organize and reorganize the American university.

The difficulty of the problem makes me regret the more that Bill Readings, who might have had enticing suggestions to offer, is no longer with us. I hope that his book will help us to think about comparative literature as well as about the institutions in which we labor and to which he devoted so much energy and intelligence.

Jonathan Culler, Spring 1995

[1] William Readings, *The University Beyond Culture: The Idea of Excellence,* page 17 of the unpublished manuscript.

[2] Further quotations are all from "The Idea of Excellence," chapter 2 of *The University Beyond Culture.*

[3] George W. S. Trow, *In the Context of No Context,* Boston, Little, Brown, 1981, p. 58.

[4] See Natalie Melas's paper, "Versions of Incommensurability," elsewhere in this issue of *WLT.*

[5] Erich Auerbach, "Philology and *Weltliteratur*," tr. Marie and Edward Said, *Centennial Review,* 13:1 (Winter 1969), p. 15. I owe this reference to David Chioni Moore's stimulating discussion in "Comparative Literature to *Weltkulturwissenschaft:* Remedying a Failed Transition," a paper for the Twentieth Southern Comparative Literature Association meeting, October 1994. See also his unpublished Duke University dissertation, "Geo/graphy Without Borders: Metaphors of Structure in 20th Century World Literature and Culture."

We Hope

"I was frightened," wrote Sigmund Freud to Albert Einstein, who had asked in a letter of 1932 what one could do to defend mankind against the fate of war: "I was frightened first of all at the impression of my—I almost said 'our'—incompetence, for that seemed to me a practical task to be dealt with by statesmen." The postscript could have come from the so-called man on the street: "Then, however, I understood," Freud continued, "that you raised the question not as a natural scientist and physicist, but as a friend of mankind who was following the initiatives of the League of Nations." His analysis of

Max Frisch *(Jerry Bauer)*

why war among men was coming was preceded once more by the modesty of this learned man: "I remembered also that I am not expected to make practical suggestions." Seven years later, world war erupted. . . . Our wishful thinking after Hiroshima—namely, the view that the atomic bomb leaves only the choice between peace or the suicide of mankind and therefore has contributed to eternal peace—did not last long: war in Korea, war in the Middle East. Do we content ourselves with the hope that such conflicts can take place without nuclear weapons? The war in Vietnam, conducted and lost by the power that protects us, exceeded the last world war in numbers of destructive weapons used—without the atomic bomb—and also repeated what since Nuremberg have been defined as war crimes. The latest hope, one knows, is that an exchange of nuclear strikes (*war* becomes a romantic word here) can by no means be excluded but will not destroy the entire human race, only about half of it, or possibly only a third. Whoever speaks today of peace and understands by that word something other than a temporary ceasefire amid the mutual and steadfast cultivation of hostility toward the enemy, so that the strategy of deterrence by fear remains the only conceivable alternative, speaks of a Utopia, and the same applies to freedom, without

which (as has been presented on this very spot) there is no peace. What we need to question, therefore, are our political dealings with Utopia.

Let's begin with freedom. In the rejection of every kind of dictatorship, including the so-called dictatorship of the proletariat as well as the dictatorship of the propertied classes—who of course would never call themselves such—I am certainly a democrat, though not euphorically so. One is a democrat in the hope that dominion will be transformed into rational authority. We need the state, not its deification as a governing body, which is a relic of feudal rule. It is well known that the more mature and self-reliant we become, the less necessary we find the state, and precisely this fact is a constant irritant to the state: its necessity indicates our lack of solidarity, our unreliability, our paucity of imagination as to how an individual's actions affect his neighbors or future generations.

"Property obligates," so the law states, adding: "Its use shall simultaneously serve the general good." Can it be put more politely? Noblesse oblige. However, what happens when power-wielding property holders—for example, in real-estate speculation—place no value whatsoever on such *noblesse,* which the founding fathers of the law imputed to them? We therefore need the state. The call for freedom, more freedom from the state, is worth examining; if it comes from fellow citizens who would also like to see the police strengthened, we know whose freedom is meant; freedom for the few who prefer to call the state, once they have it in their grasp, not "state" but "fatherland," which demands sacrificial victims from the majority. . . . The reason why I am not euphorically a democrat is the following: the parliamentary-democratic apparatus, permanently geared to compromise, inculcates not only tolerance—which would certainly be a humane trait outside the realm of citizenship—but also, to an even greater degree, resignation, the surrender of every Utopia. Among the practitioners of democracy, Utopia is the facile synonym for the purest fancy, the most elusive chimera. What is left one day is a technocracy, efficient as such; the spiritual substance of politics vanishes. There remains only politics as the continuation of business by other means, a certain state of well-being for most as bait to renounce all self-determination, the atrophy of our humanity in luxuriant bondage. . . . The young people who emerged in the late 1960s as an extraparliamentary opposition noticed this insidious resignation and resisted: in France, through out-of-the-ordinary actions recalling the storming of the Bastille, creating scenes that evoked the memory of Delacroix; in West Germany, through rabid theories and with the intransigence of revolutionaries who saw themselves without any common ground. So it was. Schoolchildren and apprentices, even university students, when asked their thoughts about the tasks of democracy, shrug their shoulders today. They know what the cost can be if they make use of the constitutional right to freedom of expression. The fact that even young people have been successfully coerced into resignation is no triumph of democracy. The frantic search for enemies of the Constitution—in which one considers oneself loyal to the Constitution—without fulfilling the great promises of the Constitution (i.e., the search for a scapegoat), accompanied by pharisaical mercy toward dissidents elsewhere, characterizes a society that is afraid of having its confession, its very democratic nature, taken at its word: a profit-and-competition society with a democratic vocabulary, wherein it would be a lie to say that competition itself guarantees that performance is the decisive factor; however liberal one presents oneself in speech, there remains competition between the favored and the disadvantaged. In order to banish from public discussion whatever the favored parties dislike hearing—namely, criticism of the underlying structure of our society and our conceived goals, democratic ones—it is sufficient today almost everywhere to apply the label *leftist,* as it once sufficed, long ago, to say "degenerate." Now, I do not mean that history repeats itself with such precision. I am merely pointing out a climate of animosity: not deadly hostility, but only a sort of allergic sensitivity to political consciousness capable of analysis; not protective custody, but only the refusal of discourse, as in the matter of the so-called *Radikalen-Erlass* or Decree on Radicals, the legitimization of one particular animus via an administrative pact with it.

Ladies and gentlemen, as a foreigner obliged not to become involved in the internal affairs of the Federal Republic—whose intellectual power leads one to marvel, whose economic power gives her the self-consciousness to serve as a model (whether for Italy and France as well is a matter to be decided by Italian and French voters)—as a foreigner, on this occasion where peace is the subject of discussion, I would point out a phenomenon that is pertinent to the question of peace and transcends national boundaries. In my native country we follow approximately the same course: the protection of democracy through the dismantling of democracy but without any formal, legal decree. As a writer, I have paid particular attention to the genesis of hostile perceptions of foes: how a certain animus, a projection of one's own contradictions onto a scape-goat, a community of attitudes takes hold and goes astray; the epidemic of blind insinuation that different-thinking individuals do not really mean what they say; how out of fear of self-recognition (which proves difficult to us all)

there arises a collective hatred that requires a certain perceived target or enemy, whether this one or that; the ostracizing of a minority, with the paradoxical result that the majority thereby relinquishes self-determination and control. Whereas ultimately every individual who, because his conscience forbids him, does not participate in such ostracism ostracizes himself, the majority loses its conscience and becomes craven—i.e., governable as a majority of vassals.

■ NO PEACE WITHOUT FREEDOM

The prevailing situation elsewhere became perhaps especially clear during the Cold War years in a small nation that militarily would have been lost in any event: namely, that the conceptualization of the enemy as developed during the Cold War and still cultivated today has the ultimately internal political purpose of maintaining a dominion that could not endure without deterrence. The sheer inhumanity on the other side (and nothing else can be perceived in the Cold War) serves as dispensation from any and all self-examination; there arises the utterly inane idea that whoever voices criticism of his own country is in his enemy's sway. Not that the citizens who have propagated this idea for two decades desire real war, which China but not Europe is likely to survive; the Cold War's purpose is to render the current form of governance taboo. . . . That would mean that peace (as a situation not without conflict but without the threat of catastrophe) is not first and foremost, as daily depicted, a matter of strategy, both military and diplomatic. Moreover, it cannot be achieved through personal gentleness until the day when marching orders arrive, the oath to the flag is sworn, the order to fire is given. It can be achieved only—in the sense of the thesis "No Peace without Freedom"—through the conversion of society into a community.

■ WHY UTOPIA?

Whether the Utopia of a fraternal society without the dominion of people over people, or the Utopia of a marriage without subjugation, the Utopia of an emancipation of both sexes; whether the Utopia of human love that does not make unto itself a graven image of the beloved, or the Utopia of bliss in the Kierkegaardian sense of succeeding at the most difficult task of all, namely choosing ourselves and thus entering a state of freedom; whether the Utopia of a permanent spontaneity and readiness for shaping and reshaping (according to Goethe, "the eternal mind's eternal entertainment"); in short, the Utopia of a creative and therefore realized existence between birth and death—a Utopia is not debased because we do not stand before it. It is the thing which confers value on us in failure. It is indispensable, the magnet which does not lift us above this earth but gives our lives direction over the course of some twenty-five thousand routine days. Without Utopia we would be creatures without transcendence.

▪ WHENCE THE ANIMUS TOWARD THE LEFTIST UTOPIA?

This doubtless has something to do with the various manifestations of student unrest, although they did not change property relations in the slightest. *L'imagination au pouvoir!* General de Gaulle (which is to say, the state) withstood the tumults, not least thanks to the Communist Party. (I was in Moscow at the time and heard a functionary express the fear that spontaneity could establish a precedent.) In the U.S. there emerged the Free Speech Movement, the first awakening from the American Dream during the pseudocrusade in Vietnam, together with the flower children, revolts set to guitar accompaniment, naïve, "Let us be," without any deafening theory; the power of the state, which did not escape without murders at Kent State, remained secure. In West Germany too—the student Benno Ohnesorg, who did not prevent the Shah of Iran from enjoying the German opera, was inadvertently shot by a guard—the power of the state was never in danger for even a quarter of an hour. Why does a shock nevertheless remain, as if one remembered massacres or at least a total strike? It was not the working class that took to the streets or occupied the universities; sons and daughters of the bourgeoisie wanted to know on what basis authority is founded in our society. A valid question, even though unexpected during a boom period that promised success and prosperity. Instead of the quiet pursuit of business opportunities that stood open to these children of the bourgeoisie, there came the sudden rise of political consciousness; the university, the erstwhile training ground for careers, suddenly became a forum. In the process, it became evident that what the property-owning powers, hitherto certain of their authority, had to offer, except for an abundance of consumer goods, was paltry—in terms of prospects for a more humane world, in ethical values not contradicted in practice, in a hope for all or even for merely that which inspired them—aside from the belief in the free market. Profit as the rapture of the personality? There was, to my mind, a void here.

In the interim, in addition to the polemics in leading papers and magazines, which are part of the property-owning powers, a conservative brand of Utopia criticism has arisen that possesses scientific stature. Is there (I must ask, since I am not a specialist) a code of social ethics which confers authority upon the power of ownership—upon, say, a Nestlé Company or a Hoffmann-La Roche? In connection with the attempt to discredit intellectuals, we hear the loudly voiced concern for constitutional law, which in fact has been violated by several despairing and misguided parties; but constitutionality is thereby elevated to a prerequisite of an ethical society, to the status of a value in and of itself, as if we lived, as always, solely for the constitutional state. Likely, what is meant is that property relationships should be unassailable. It is no help at all to tell people to keep their own houses and gardens in order and not admit the possibility that power through property can be overturned by a popularly elected government when that same power, for example, instigates crises and supplies weapons, as in the case of Chile, where torture has previously been practiced. It is no help at all, for the issue is not about houses and gardens and what should be allowed to everyone, but rather about an axiom: an existence without power over others is an existence unworthy of human beings, and any other kind of self-realization (in which one could perhaps get along without psychiatrists) is unthinkable. Those raised and caught up in this conception of human worth cloak themselves in talk of their responsibility. As a consequence, they cannot offer a hope for human worth to all, for as long as human worth consists in having power over others, these others must of course exist. If one desires a parliamentary majority, fear remains as the common denominator: fear of crisis, of unemployment, of the enemy, whose military armament is indeed threatening. Only we do not disarm him through instituting reforms in our own country.

The property-owning powers: the term makes me think of persons whom one has the opportunity to meet as an honored writer and who, when I listen politely, strive for a lapidary consensus even over aperitifs with comments such as: "A single atomic bomb on Hanoi would have spared the Americans all those difficulties"; or, on the situation in Argentina, "Such people can only destroy. They are not like you and me, Herr Doktor; they have never read a book. One must wipe them out like the Indians in earlier times"; or "It may be true that babies are dying there en masse, but they will die anyway without this powdered milk; these young academics are not concerned about babies and mothers in the Third World, however; it's all purely political, and they are leftist romantics." Comments such as these cannot be invented and are made quite casually, before one repairs to the dinner table and actual conversation.

The animus toward leftists that characterizes the public climate in our nations at present and unhesitatingly equates any leftist project with the Gulag or the Baader-Meinhof gang is plausible in the case of the property-owning powers, but it also appeals to other people, since antipathy is always more comfortable than the exercising of political consciousness. The fact that the New Left has long practiced a sort of self-criticism is not at issue. It is understandable too that the multinational property-owning powers, traumatized by the late sixties and specifically by the evidence that possession in fact conveys power but no authority legitimizing this de facto power, have adopted a particularly patriotic tone and terminology. Their hope is for an irrationally based authority, while they, being multinational in business, teach us at home what *Swiss* or *American* or *German* means. A power without authority is left with nothing but arrogance, as in the proclamation that socialism (which does not yet exist at all) belongs to the Stone Age, so as not to admit that it can offer no alternative of its own to the present state of the world—which is threatening to all, including the property owners—at most, the defensive fiction that the environment (on a worldwide scale) can be ordered via proper management in such a way that mankind can remain as it is and society as it is.

■ **TO SAY SOMETHING ABOUT PEACE**

The prognosis for the human race is well known: thanks to man's irreversible technology, the conflict with the environment is becoming larger than any thinkable conflict between nations or power blocs. While the deterrence strategy makes it difficult for nations to confront together the destruction of all life on this planet, this destruction is already under way despite the absence of war. What diplomacy has achieved to date under the unstable balance of nuclear forces, a case-by-case nonwartime arrangement between two power blocs whereby smaller states must at times make sacrifices, is no small matter: the maintenance of nonwar, a prolongation of the grace period. A prerequisite of peace would be the dismantling of conceptions about the enemy. In terms of domestic politics, who can afford such an action? On the other side, if there were no stereotypical reminders about the inhuman practice of private capitalism, the sheer spiteful pleasure at unemployment, say, or criminality, et cetera, how could the populace diligently and mutely bear state capitalism's economic failures and the total subjugation of the individual citizen?

In part (but only in part), these conceptions of the enemy have a historical justification; peoples have had grievous experiences with other peoples—for example, the Poles and Czechoslovaks with the Germans and the Russians—and there exists a natural mistrust that can be allayed only over a lengthy period of time through new experiences with each other. This is possible; the Federal Republic is not Hitler's Germany. The concern

that a policy of detente (a new experience with each other) will lead not to peace but solely to a weakening of one's own power position follows from the logic of power politics, which seek an expansion of power without war, to be sure, but through the threat of war. To that end, such politics require a different conception of the enemy, one based not on memory but on anticipation. The Soviet Union, for instance, has never attacked the American people; the two nations were even allies. Remarkably, it is anticipatory conceptions of the enemy that are the most difficult of all to overcome; they are set in the future. Where the hegemony of a given *system* is involved, the conception of the enemy is no longer nationalistic: "perfidious Albion," "the Teutonic hordes," et cetera, no longer serve as mobilizing forces. The most obstinate set of bilateral conceptions in Europe (if we disregard the tragic case of Ireland) exists between the two German states, a palpable animosity that can scarcely be dismantled even through familial ties and through reason, since it involves, I suspect, a certain need for identity. As Karl Jaspers stated from this very podium in 1958: "Both regimes have their bases in the will of the Occupation forces." I would add that both have become model pupils of their respective systems' protective powers and that both are on the point of seeing themselves as preceptors to the fellow states within their respective systems.

■ **OUR QUESTION**

When we speak of peace—and let us suppose that we believe in its possibility—how do we imagine peace to be? In 1946, as the guest of bombed-out Germans in Frankfurt, I understood peace as simply no more bombs, no more victories, the release of POW's. In Prague, where there were scarcely any ruins, I visited Theresienstadt and saw gallows and thousands of bags containing human ashes; after this, the answer again seemed simple: peace as the end of fear, no uniforms of foreign rule. In Warsaw, in 1948, following an hourslong walk through the stillness of the rubble, I suddenly heard the drone of riveting hammers at work on the first columns of a new bridge over the Vistula—peace! There as here, conversation (while smoking halved cigarettes) with contemporaries who possessed nothing except the grand hope that out of the ruins would emerge the new man. Some expected him to be a communist, others Christ. Now we know that the new man has not emerged. Our rational rejection of war as a political expedient does not mean that we are capable of peace. Societies built upon a framework of force may desire a state of nonwar; peace would contradict their very nature. Since no government would ever admit that it also needs an army for possible deployment under certain circumstances against its own populace, it is compelled, for the purpose of camouflaging this martial function, to engage in an arms build-up that promises to protect the fatherland from the entire world; through this arms build-up, in turn, it is compelled to cultivate a particular conception of the enemy that justifies such enormous expenditures and hardships, which in no way imply that anyone desires a third world war. The simple fact is that the arms build-up exists, enervating neighbors, verifying the opponent's conception of the enemy and thus the arms race, whereby each respective conception of an enemy always betrays as well one's own nature: how is anyone with the blood of an extortionist in his veins ever to trust that his opposite is not plotting extortion? The scientific study of peace accomplishes several things in this vicious cycle: it calculates the risk of such power politics; it provides instruction in the technological innovations that demand a revision of strategy; it computes the actual changes at present for nonwar between immanently hostile societies, though without being able to guarantee that tomorrow or the day after things might not explode nevertheless because of some unexplored cause or even through some inane incident (for example, a sudden lapse of reason by one's opponents or a stupid error in their calculations). A society capable of peace would be a society which could get along without conceptualization of an enemy. There are phases when we cannot get along without conflict, without anger, but can get along without hatred, without a conceived enemy, as when we (simply put) are happy or at least alive: for instance, due to a kind of labor that not only earns us money but also gives us satisfaction (nonalienating work), or due to a kind of coexistence between people that permits self-realization. What else, in essence, does such a misused word as *freedom* mean? Not the "right of might" for the strong, not freedom through power over others. Self-realization: let's say, when it is possible to live creatively. How many people in today's societies, however, have the possibility of living creatively? Such a state is not granted through prosperity alone. . . . Whether the specie's will for survival will be sufficient for the conversion of our societies into ones capable of peace, I do not know. We hope it will. It is urgent. Prayer does not absolve us from the question of our political dealings with this hope, which is a radical one. The belief in a possibility of peace (and therefore in the survival of mankind) is a revolutionary belief.

Max Frisch, Autumn 1986

Ed. Note: This address was delivered on the occasion of the awarding of the Peace Prize of the German Book Trade, Frankfurt A.M., September 1976. It was first published in the *Börsenblatt für den deutschen Buchhandel*, 32:76 (21 September 1976),

pp. 1412–18, and was reprinted in Max Frisch, *Gesammelte Werke in zeitlicher Folge*, 7 vols., Frankfurt A.M., Suhrkamp, 1976/86, vol. 7, pp. 7–19. It appears here for the first time in English.

Distant Relations: French, Anglo-American, Hispanic

As one begins to consider interrelations between "Hispanic, French, and Anglo-American literatures," it is apparent that two of these terms (Anglo-American and Hispanic) bridge the Atlantic Ocean, while the other traditionally does not. This could mean, hopefully, two things: that the identity of each of these literatures is basically linguistic, thus superseding the concept of national literature; and that, in the process, the contrast or distance or dialectic America/Europe is being transcended as well. Is the latter really the case? And is this a question that can be answered in merely literary terms?

The subject is complex enough in merely literary terms. It is even more so if we take into consideration what used to be called "images"—national or continental—a much-traveled path of research in the past: "mirages franco-américains" (Henri Peyre), "transatlantic refractions" (Harry Levin), and the like. This sort of dominant mental stereotype exists and is doubtless operative. It interferes with cultural interrelations, and we would be unduly exquisite to disregard it.

If we view our environment as plural and perhaps also as amenable to the geological metaphor of strata, we might cut across some of the complexities and discern two levels of contemporary reality: cultural and sociopolitical. I have in mind the levels of life in, for example, New York, Bogotá, Paris, or Barcelona. Since our focus is on relations between these spaces, we face a tangled web involving mutual images and preconceptions on more than one level—and especially certain tensions and differences among the levels themselves. Thus the image of the United States in Bogotá may be quite negative yet compatible with positive perceptions of American novelists and poets. The sociopolitical level of life in Bogotá or Mexico City may not seem enviable to those who read and admire García Márquez and Octavio Paz. The onset of the Cold War at the end of the 1940s and the rising wave of intolerance called McCarthyism affected the image of the U.S. in Italy no end, but not the esteem in which a Vittorini or a Pavese held Hemingway or Faulkner.

Fernand Braudel brought out in a recent interview (*Le Nouvel Observateur*, 10–16 May 1985) that at the time when Venice was the greatest power in Italy and the Mediterranean, the cultural center was Florence: there was no "confusion" between the "material center" and the "cultural center." I agree with Braudel and think that the impact of political and economic behavior on the cultural activity of other nations can be easily overestimated. A culture itself embraces a number of strata, and it often occurs that what economic or military power favors is the most rudimentary and utilitarian stratum, thereby promoting a visible yet superficial influence. Such was not the case of eighteenth-century France and the widespread knowledge of, say, both Montesquieu and the technology outlined in the *Encyclopédie*. The general admiration and translation today into many languages of the great Latin American writers is inversely proportional to the economic prosperity of their countries of origin.

Surely the United States was not a world power during the first decades of its existence as an independent republic, yet Benjamin Franklin and James Fenimore Cooper were presences to be reckoned with even then. The themes of primitivism, youthful vigor, and virile struggle with nature were being sounded already. Cooper came into fashion about 1824, and high praises of his skills as a storyteller are still to be found in Balzac's rave essay of 1840. Cooper was reduced some fifty years later to the status of an author of children's books, but his popularity had given long life to the image of a certain American hero: the pioneer and fighting man, and the Indian himself—loyal, fearless, hard.

The case of Edgar Allan Poe, who was thought to embody opposite values, demonstrates the polyphony of these interrelations and the degree to which the most technical of literary linkages can move away from stereotype and circumstance. Baudelaire found in Poe a confirmation of his needs, and I would be inclined to hold with those who think that this was not a gross misreading. As Heinrich Straumann has shown, Poe did not merely contribute to the development of the short story, through techniques of repetition, musicality, and startling vocabulary, or to that commitment to selfless craftsmanship without which the symbolist tradition in Europe would be inconceivable; he also made possible the passage from late and wearied romanticism to fin-de-siècle decadentism, fascination with evil, crime, compulsive states, and problems of individual identity. Forms, in his case, as later in that of a Dos Passos or a Faulkner, were not innocent of meaning.

The power of literary communication itself, against all odds, as well as its ability to impose its own priorities, is exemplified by the travel book. Often enough the voyage is a confrontation of experience with the previously written word. The voyage is from literature to personal observation. About Chateaubriand's *Voyage en*

Amérique (1827), R. Lebègue says that one cannot notice enough all that it has in common with the same author's fictional *Atala* (1801): "La frontière s'affaçait entre ce qu'il avait lu et ce qu'il avait vu."[1] I have been impressed with the weight of the *déjà lu* in nineteenth-century reports on voyages to Spain such as Edgar Quinet's *Mes vacances en Espagne* (1843) and the first important account by a Russian traveler, B. P. Botkin (1845). This is particularly so in the book by Quinet, a goodly portion of which could have been written without his leaving Paris; or rather, it appears that Quinet sincerely believed to be seeing in Castile what he had read in Paris.

It has seemed to many that the impact of preconception on perception is to be found with singular frequency in European attitudes toward America. Gilbert Chinard, returning to the earlier contacts, stressed the degree of idealization that was thus implied, "le décalage entre l'imaginaire et le réel que nous constatons quand il s'agit de l'Amérique." Sartre would not say anything different in the essays collected in *Situations III* (1949): "Nulle part peut-être on ne trouvera un tel décalage entre les hommes et les mythes, entre la vie et la représentation de la vie." Sartre, however, is talking about the Americans themselves, who generate the idealization. In the words of a British commentator, Marcus Cunliffe, "The United States will continue to be a semi-mythical place for Europeans, but mainly to the extent that Americans see it thus."[2] The interrelationship becomes not so much one involving distinct societies as the nexus between image and experience. From the beginning America was associated with hope and pictures of the future. After Tocqueville, French travelers saw in America an "adumbration of the democratic future" (writes Levin). To what extent does this hold true today? That is, does America continue to export a future-oriented image of itself? Is it the future that others believe visible through the United States? Early in the last century, the answer was yes. Thomas Paine was published in Spanish in Philadelphia in 1811, a brief time before the declaration of independence in Venezuela, where his writings were well known. Vicente Rocafuerte, later a president of Ecuador, had translated Paine in 1821 under the title *Ideas necesarias a todo pueblo americano independiente que quiera ser libre*. During a large part of the nineteenth century the northern and southern halves of the American continent shared a good many themes and aspirations, while ignoring each other's poets and storytellers—the very opposite of the situation today.

The North American public, in Owen Aldridge's words, was "for the most part totally unaware of the intellectual life in Hispanic America." Aldridge thinks that the reason for this was "the Anglo-Saxon distrust of the Spanish character prevailing in the eighteenth and early nineteenth century, which was based on Protestant suspicion of the Catholic religion, particularly the notorious Spanish Inquisition, together with horror of the alleged mistreatment of the Indians during the period of the conquest, the equally notorious Black Legend."[3] I am not denying that such a negative image blocked the road, while allowing the Northerners to look away from their own fleeing Indians and Puritan bonfires. It was most unlikely, however, that the rich Latin American literature of the baroque age could appeal to any other literature of the romantic period.

Later in the nineteenth century a process would begin that has not ceased down to the present day, the economic and political domination of the South by the North on the American continent. Now, since our subject is three-cornered, we must recall too that the balance of power was quite different with respect to relations between North America and Europe. Still, these two sets of relations could be viewed as having in common a widespread instinct implying an "awareness of the Other": in Latin America, as a consequence of subordination; in Europe, for different reasons, or so it seemed until recent years, when subordination also began to apply.

Edward W. Said published in 1978 a powerfully stimulating book titled *Orientalism,* a term denoting for him the special place reserved in European experience for representations of the so-called Orient. Orientalism is a mode of thought based on radical distinctions between the Orient and the Occident. These sharp distinctions were put to the use not merely of Eurocentric but also of dominating intellectual and political behavior, in Said's persuasive judgment. I wonder whether, in comparable terms, it would be fruitful to ask whether an "Americanism" has existed and still exists: a sense of the difference, the otherness of America, whether antithetical or complementary, that would be functional in the European sense of self and pride in identity. It would be interesting to notice, if such were the case, that images of Otherness are bred by both domination and subordination.

Foreign-born "Americanism" appears to have grown since World War II and has much to do with the fact that it is America now that protects the continent across the Atlantic, shapes its policies, and predominates in its military and economic councils. Now it is *our* turn, Melvin Lasky writes in a 1962 issue of *Encounter,* to be constantly aware of the other side of the ocean. It was clear to him that this was a fresh experience for the European: dependency. It was to be hoped that it would accelerate the decline of the old Eurocentric po-

sitions. This is a debatable outcome, though, and it could be argued that an Americanism arises that remains Eurocentric in spirit, particularly in those countries where Orientalism had been strongest—namely, England and France. The subordination that these countries share for the first time with Latin America revives their need to differ from the prevalent superpowers.

This does not mean that the American arts and sciences are not appreciated, imitated, and at times even worshiped in these nations. From the start of this paper I have postulated the frequent coexistence of opposite forces on the sociopolitical and cultural strata. It is precisely the sense of distance and contrast that makes appreciation keener and more self-aware. Shifting attitudes in France have made this quite clear in recent decades. Harry Levin writes that "intercultural exchange is contingent and episodic in nature."[4] I am inclined to agree with him and can only recall here some features of the episode we are in. You are all familiar with the exceptional prestige of French writing all over the Western world during the first half of this century, when Paris was the capital of capitals, the modern novel, from James to Joyce, unimaginable without the French predecessors, and modern poetry, from Eliot and Stevens to Lorca and Paz, inconceivable without the symbolist tradition and the surrealist movement. This central role seemed to perpetuate itself during the years following World War II through the extraordinary vitality of the French reaction to defeat and foreign occupation, which were turned into intellectual triumphs, as in the case particularly of Camus, Sartre, and early existentialism—and of Malraux, whose legend only grew. A generation of G.I.'s visited Saint-Germain des Prés, and, though no longer expatriates, a number of future writers of importance, from Bellow and Paz to Baldwin and Goytisolo, experienced significant Parisian times. The outstanding French writers were widely read in translation; and some playwrights even made it to Broadway (Giraudoux), off-Broadway (Genet), or the campus stages (Anouilh). Obviously the function of French letters is quite different today. French novelists may lecture in American universities, but the *nouveau roman,* an acute but narrow neo-avant-garde, did not hold the interest of a broad readership. Perse and Char reach the buyers of expensive university-press editions. Only Marguerite Duras, known also by way of the cinema, has, it seems, more than technical appeal. *La cage aux folles* enjoys commercial success, but otherwise it is only Beckett who is regularly produced for larger audiences.

This phenomenon—the fragmentation of the theatrical scene in New York—is generally characteristic of the day, and particularly of the presence of French writing, limited generally to equivalents of off-Broadway or the universities. Readers are parceled into neatly separate zones that do not add up to a cultural circumstance accepting or admiring a common group of first-rate writers. Angel Rama describes the situation in Latin America as follows:

> It is at this moment that leadership in cultural matters of official elites ceases in almost all Latin American countries, as marked by the entry of the novel in the market economy of cities and the development of the mass media. [The novel] conquers its freedom, to be sure, at the price of a substantially reduced communication with the social totality. It accepts it. It is going to choose a section of the public by acknowledging first the fragmentation of reality, characteristic of a vast cultural crisis in the midst of which the novelist works. From then on there will be several publics, but the reduction of communication is inseparable in the writer from a nostalgia of the homogeneous society that he seeks everywhere.[5]

Today it is probably the corpus of French classics that is known by a greater number of readers in the United States. These great writers belong to the constellation of models and authorities that specialists call the literary system of the time. Most of the interest otherwise is aroused by the talented critics (Roland Barthes), innovative historians (Michel Foucault), and arcane theorists (Jacques Derrida), mostly in academic circles, where some of these voices are echoed long after they have sounded in Paris. We might still think with Harry Levin, writing twenty years ago, that "the eastward trend across the Atlantic has been largely a traffic in images, whereas the ideas have tended to cross in the other direction."[6]

It is the hour of Latin America where the imagination is concerned. An array of outstanding writers has had the good fortune of having gifted translators in the United States like Gregory Rabassa (García Márquez and Cortázar), Suzanne Jill Levine (Cabrera Infante and Puig), Anthony Kerrigan and Alastair Reid (Borges). Once again it seems to be the imaginative function in literature—Dante, *Amadís,* Ariosto, Cervantes, Byron, Dostoevsky, Kafka—that translates best, peopling the most brilliant pages with the irrational, the extravagant, and the insane. Mario Vargas Llosa has expressed fully his admiration for romances of chivalry such as *Tirant lo Blanch* (just translated into English by David Rosenthal), memories of which are visible in the Peruvian novelist's *La guerra del fin del mundo* (1981). This fantastic factor goes hand in hand with what one might term the syncretic ability of these writers, whose works show an unusual degree of breadth, range, and coherence—a breadth no longer based, as in the nineteenth-century

realists, on the sociological *état civil.* It is common knowledge that in Latin America poetry and the essay or historical prose have been for centuries the principal channels of communication. It is generally observed that contemporary Hispanic fiction embraces the critical restlessness of the essay (Cortázar, Borges, Vargas Llosa) and what Emir Rodríguez Monegal calls the "revolutionary" impulse of the poets of the twenties and after (Huidobro, Neruda, Drummond de Andrade, Paz). The objective world of the middle class assumed by the realistic novel, Rama points out, is first replaced in poetry with the subjectivity presiding over human relations. This opening of the compass makes possible the recovery, as in Rulfo and Carpentier, of mythical, magical, metaphorical, and simple storytelling gifts, rooted in Indian and African as well as Iberian traditions.

This syncretic process has also been operative with respect to artistic developments outside Latin America. Periods and movements that appeared successively in Europe may coincide and overlap in the Hispanic countries. Aldridge showed that neoclassicism and romanticism arrived almost simultaneously there, in the work of a poet like José Joaquín de Olmedo. An even richer convergence can obviously be seen in the achievement of Rubén Darío, who knew of Hugo, Gautier, Leconte de Lisle, Verlaine, Mallarmé, and Moréas, to mention but a few names. In our day, similarly, it is the Central or South American writer who can encompass at once the heritage of Cervantes and Flaubert, Quevedo and Whitman, Balzac and Henry James, Proust and Faulkner. Of the three linguistic areas examined here, the Hispanic is the central, centripetal, absorbing, all-gathering one. In closing, I shall recall some basic North American and French creative personalities and moments, while asking you to keep in mind that it is a Fuentes, a Vargas Llosa, a Borges who is able to know and make use of both cultural sources.

An important moment in the impact of American novelists on modern fiction is the 1930s, shortly before the outbreak of World War II. You will remember the well-known phases of a familiar story: Faulkner's *Sanctuary* prefaced by Malraux in 1931; *As I Lay Dying,* in 1934, by Valery Larbaud; *Sartoris* reviewed by Sartre in 1938; Dos Passos extolled to the skies by Sartre in 1938. Meanwhile, Camus commented in his early notebooks upon Melville, and irresistibly the rapprochement carried through the years of the war and the 1940s in Giono's and Camus's approaches to Melville and, characteristically, in the techniques and themes encapsulated by Claude-Edmonde Magny in her study *L'âge du roman américain* (1948), the cinematic forms, the "traumatisms of time," the anguish and guilt in Faulkner above all. What is not so familiar is that shortly after his publication in French and before his appearance in other languages, Faulkner was translated into Spanish: *Santuario* came out in 1934, translated by the fine Cuban writer Lino Novás Calvo for a Madrid series called "Hechos Sociales," published by Espasa-Calpe with a preface by the talented critic and essayist Antonio Marichalar. Marichalar mentions in passing the names of Hemingway, Dos Passos, and Sherwood Anderson as he struggles to cope with the contrasts and the decay in Faulkner ("aire seco y combustible, pasión en celo, sangre rota") by associating him with the somber *Allegory of Death* by the Sevillian painter Valdés Leal, inscribed with the words: "Ni más, ni menos." Suddenly Faulkner seemed Andalusian. A fleeting fancy, for it must be owned that several of the Latin American writers who matter read Faulkner either in English or in M.-E. Coindreau's superior French translations.

The influence, obviously crucial, was partly that of Coindreau. Rodríguez Monegal says that a "triangular system of communications" developed between the literatures of the U.S., Europe, and Latin America, following the flood of translations and criticism of North American fiction in France and Italy.[7] True, but some of the Hispanic writers are more broadly cultured and mutilingual than the critics: Borges, Paz, Vargas Llosa, Fuentes, and others. Borges translated *The Wild Palms* in 1939, even as he later translated and praised Whitman and Melville, prefaced Henry James, and wrote, inter alia, a poetic monologue called "Emerson," whose titular figure resembles the author of the poem: "Por todo el continente anda mi nombre. / No he vivido. Quisiera ser otro hombre." Monegal shows some of the ways in which James interested José Donoso and Carlos Fuentes and indicates the shifting narrative techniques à la Faulkner in *La muerte de Artemio Cruz* and of course in Vargas Llosa's *La ciudad y los perros,* which, published in Barcelona in 1963, burst onto the Spanish literary scene like a fragmentary bomb. Innumerable typewriter ribbons have been worn through in studies of Faulkner in Latin America. Students of the subject notice that Gabriel García Márquez, after the influence on his early stories of the writer he called "mi maestro William Faulkner," turned in his first masterpiece, *El coronel no tiene quien le escriba (No One Writes to the Colonel;* 1957), toward a novelist less concerned with the depiction of inwardness and intimate perspectives, Ernest Hemingway. The intertextuality in this case is not reduced to the character of the old man who waits and waits ("The Killers") and remains undefeated in his defeat. With the probable aid of Hemingway, Márquez has perfected the art of showing without telling, of describing merely the acts and the gestures, as if misunderstanding and talking at cross-purposes were the basic conditions of communication. You may recall how the first paragraph of *No One Writes to the Colonel*—"The colonel took the top of the coffee can and saw that there was only one little spoonful left. He removed the pot from the fire, poured half the water onto the earthen floor, and scraped the inside of the can with a knife. . . ."—echoes in the reader's mind the intense care of Nick Adams's coffee-brewing in "Big Two-Hearted River": "The coffee boiled as he watched. The lid came up and coffee and grounds ran down the side of the pot. . . . He was a very serious coffee drinker." The point is not to say for a while or even know what it is that makes a serious coffee drinker out of a man.

The interaction of image and experience is still meaningful in many a case, it seems, but no longer massively, and especially not in national literary terms. "Americanism" in Europe and the Hispanic world—the need to differ from the United States—does not coincide with the idea of American letters for the simple and sufficient reason that the notion of local literary tradition has lost its vigor and relevance. The idea of national literature is in crisis in the West at all levels.

If the Latin American novelist or poet occupies a central position today, within the coordinates of this paper, it is perhaps because his approach to other cultures is both syncretic and highly personal. The breakdown of linguistic frontiers is due to more than intellectual interests; it corresponds to the facts of communication in our time. Everything happens as if the writer were not ultimately integrated into a group of colleagues belonging to a particular city, region, or nation, but to a singular cross section of contemporaries across the entire world. The creative reader or writer shapes his own conception of literature. The principal categories and genres are being constantly challenged and reconstituted, shattered and resurrected. Call it the Phoenix, Sisyphus, Penelope's web—there are enough ancient figurations to denote what I am alluding to. Man is, in Oskar Kokoschka's words, "doomed to re-create his own world."

Thus the foundation for the arts is one's own chosen canon of norms and models. When Carlos Fuentes accepted the National Literary Prize of Mexico in December 1984, he spoke of a constellation of contemporary writers who confront comparable tasks as authors of fiction: Italo Calvino, Milan Kundera, Nadine Gordimer, William Styron, Juan Goytisolo, Gabriel García Márquez (I quote from memory and the list may be incomplete). No matter, what should be stressed is the significance of such a supranational constellation as an enveloping environment for the work of the creative writer. We are coming closer every day not to grandiose notions of *Weltliteratur* as objective condition but to widening networks of contacts and connections, to an inventive and ever-renewed exploration and vision of forms and themes cultivated by others in other climates and latitudes, in a manner that is in fact akin to Goethe's original idea of exchange and communication, though only in selective, provisional, shifting, highly individual ways.

The idea of literature rests on each reader's or writer's own critical and creative anthology. But nationalism, prejudice, or the will to ignore and subordinate Others still flourishes on levels usually foreign to the arts. Single cultures where this occurs are not harmonious polyphonies but battlegrounds between competing and interacting strata. To differ from North America—"Americanism"—is today, as I suggested earlier, a continuing necessity in certain minds and moments of Europe and Latin America. These products of image and stereotype, however, are in collision with those circumstances of universal crisis, of problems and injustices and absences shared by all, which tend to suppress all distinctions. The paradox is that nonidealized America no longer appears so remote. America inches closer to other spaces, precisely insofar as it no longer offers an adumbration of the future.

Claudio Guillén, Autumn 1985

1 R. Lebègue, "Structure et but du *Voyage en Amérique* de Chateaubriand," in *Connaissance de l'étranger: Mélanges offerts à la mémoire de Jean-Marie Carré,* Paris, 1964, p. 285. The earlier reference to Heinrich Straumann is to his "Zur Bedeutung der amerikanischen für die europäische Literatur," in *Die amerikanische Literatur in der Weltliteratur,* C. Uhlig and V. Bischoff, eds., Berlin, 1982, pp. 1–13. Henri Peyre's "Mirages franco-américans" is in *Connaissance de l'étranger,* pp. 374–84.

2 M. Cunliffe, "Europe and America: Transatlantic Images," *Encounter,* 17 (December 1961), p. 29. Also, G. Chinard, "La littérature comparée et l'histoire des idées dans l'étude des relations franco-américaines," in *Proceedings of the 2nd Congress of the ICLA,* Werner P. Friederich, ed., Chapel Hill, N.C., 1959, vol. 2, p. 352.

3 A. Owen Aldridge, "The Enlightenment in the Americas," *Proceedings of the 7th Congress of the ICLA,* M. V. Dimić and E. Kushner, eds., Stuttgart, 1979, vol. 1, p. 63.

4 Harry Levin, "France-Amérique: The Transatlantic Refraction," in *Refractions,* New York, 1966, p. 219.

5 Angel Rama, "Formation du roman et modèles narratifs en Amérique latine," in *Proceedings 7,* vol. 1, p. 74 (my translation).

6 Levin, p. 220.

7 Emir Rodríguez Monegal, "A Game of Shifting Mirrors: The New Latin American Narrative and the North American Novel," in *Proceedings 7,* vol. 1, p. 270.

The Survival of Poetry

If in recent decades there have been fewer controversies about the "death of poetry" than about the "death of the novel," one obvious reason is that novels receive more attention in any case, because they can become best sellers as books and can also be processed for the stage, radio, film, television, or video tape. Another is that poetry was recognized to be an anachronism as early as the First Industrial Revolution in Britain. Its obsolescence was predicted in the early decades of the nineteenth century, when Thomas Carlyle, among others, declared that poetry can have no true function in what he called "the Mechanical Age." The prediction, of course, was not dialectical enough to allow for the Romantic movement, with its antimechanical, antirealistic impetus and its return not only to preindustrial but preliterary paradigms—folk song, ballad, and fairy tale. It was in the Victorian period up to World War I that European poetry won an unprecedented readership, thanks to the spread of literacy, a mechanized publishing industry to supply it, a much larger leisured class, and the very need of that class for brief imaginative or sentimental respites from the economic realities of the "Mechanical Age." For centuries it had been illiteracy that restricted the readership for poetry, together with the decline of oral traditions in those countries and regions that had been industrialized, mechanized and/or educationally homogenized by a central bureaucracy.

Now, during the Second—the electronic—Industrial Revolution, it is literacy, not illiteracy, that threatens the survival of poetry, though not the survival of literature as a medium of communication, however diminished that function may turn out to be in relation to the other, electronic, media. The reason is that literature still serves to convey information of many kinds regarded as useful, including information about poetry and the lives of poets! Literature is part of the information industry, as poetry, by its nature, never could and never will be. In the words of the Spanish poet Juan Ramón Jiménez, written in 1941, "Literature is a state of culture, poetry is a state of grace, before and after culture."

Since man does not live by technology alone—though he is doing his best to die by it—once again the very developments that threaten the survival of poetry ensure that it will be needed as long as the species survives. The electronic revolution is also in the process of creating a new leisured class, that of the millions made "redundant" by the automation of industry and the destruction of whole crafts and professions. The more monstrously inhuman our civilization becomes, the more probable it is that at least a small proportion of the permanently unemployed will turn away from other media to a "state of grace before and after culture," to the anachronism of poetry.

So far I have used *anachronism* in the prevalent sense of "at odds with the trends of the age," restricting myself to the civilization which I know, that of the so-called developed nations. Like all the pure—as distinct from applied—arts, however, poetry is also anachronistic in another, more literal sense: that of timelessness. However unfashionable that word, an impulsion toward timelessness remains part of the act of writing poems, regardless of the poet's subject matter, allegiances, manner, vocabulary, or the degree of modernity intended or attained by that poet. Without that impulsion a verse writer can produce literature, but not poetry. Because the poet's medium, words is more easily mistaken for a vehicle of information than the musician's and the visual artist's media—though images and sounds, increasingly, are also being used by the information and advertising industries—a great many readers, teachers, and even writers of verse frequently fall into the error of confusing the functions that a poem can perform with the nature of poetry, which is to carry its temporal and occasional baggage into the dimension of timelessness.

Here I am not advocating any one kind of poetry— the hermetic, for instance—rather than another, and I am very much aware that poetry has had, and continues to have, many different functions within different cultures and civilizations. Verse has served as a mnemonic (Mnemosyme was the mother of the Muses), as a means of telling stories, as a close associate of science and philosophy, ritual, celebration, prophecy, and revelation, but also as play, entertainment, social reportage, social satire, social criticism, and moral exhortation. I am not saying that any of these functions is inadmissible, though they are shared with other media, those of literature. What I am saying is that those functions do not and must not detract from the primacy of language in the art of poetry, and that this language, unlike the language of information, does not lose its power or relevance even when many of the data it has drawn upon have ceased to be the common property of any one historically conditioned audience or readership. This also accounts for the fascination of dictionaries—especially etymological ones—for many practicing poets, as well as for the habit of poets so up to date in other regards as W. H. Auden or Bertolt Brecht of incorporating archaic words and idioms in their poetic vocabularies, words and idioms they would avoid in prose texts that serve to inform or persuade. To a poet it can be more essential to know that the words *real* and *royal* or *matter* and *mother* have sprung from a common root than to be well informed about things that everyone is writing

or talking about. To a poet, language is all it has ever been and is capable of becoming, all it has ever done or is capable of doing. In a sense too, every poet who has ever written anywhere can be his or her contemporary, a contemporary in timelessness.

Just as poetry is anachronistic in the sense of being outside time, it is also utopian, both in the prevalent sense of the word and in the more literal sense of being out of place, in no place—and this, once more, regardless of whether a poet wishes to be so, thinks of himself or herself as being so, considers himself or herself rooted in a particular environment or way of life. If they are to become poetry, such particularities too will be carried into a dimension that is nowhere and everywhere.

Outside their poetry, poets can be anything they are disposed or forced to be. They can be committed to causes, institutions, and powers that no one would call "utopian," or they can be the victims of those same causes, institutions, and powers. They can be employed in any profession or trade that has a use for them, as a brief look at the lives of the outstanding twentieth-century poets will show. What those professions or trades are will depend largely on the public status accorded to poets in different countries, as well as on personal circumstances and qualifications. In a number of European and Latin American countries, for instance, the prestige of poets remains such that some have been considered fit for a diplomatic post. In other countries they are more likely to be found in universities and libraries. Where even universities and libraries are treated as potentially dangerous places, nations have become expert in giving poets economic security while holding a tight rein on their liberties and keeping them out of any occupation in which their utopianism could prove subversive. Interesting though they are, these political and social differences have little to do with the survival of poetry, because poetry has survived in all circumstances, under all conditions, including those as adverse as can be to the survival of its makers.

What is relevant to the survival of poetry is the re-emergence, even in highly technical, commercialized, and pluralistic cultures, of the most ancient, seemingly atavistic functions of poets and poetry. Even the mythical archetype of Orpheus is among the recurrent figures. The vatic or bardic tradition had a great deal to do with the extraordinary appeal of Dylan Thomas to readers and audiences in the forties and early fifties in Britain and the USA, though much of his work must have been obscure to the point of unintelligibility to most of his devotees. The resurgence of oral poetry, sometimes combined with music, that followed in the sixties owed much to that precedent, as the choice of the name Dylan by one of its most famous practitioners attests, however different his practice and person. Other practitioners assumed other functions: that of the prophet, shaman, or guru in North America; that of the clown, tumbler, or folk entertainer in Britain; that of the satirist in Germany. (That Wolf Biermann, the satirist, lived in East Germany, making recordings for a West German public, is one of the many ironies of the decade.) Public readings won large audiences in Eastern Europe also, in response to needs much older than the political systems that permitted and censored them.

It is in economically "backward" cultures that poets are most widely and spontaneously loved and revered as voices of the people; and that traditional relationship is not broken if the work of such poets makes intellectual demands that, elsewhere, would be thought quite incompatible with a mass appeal. In Latin America the work of Pablo Neruda is one of many instances. In Greece the funeral of George Seferis was a public event that honored not only him but the threatened values he stood for; and as recently as 1984 a great crowd followed the body of Nodar Dubarskay, the Georgian poet, as it was carried in an open coffin from the Writers Union in Tiflis to the cemetery. In all these cases, popularity has preserved its true meaning; it is a loyalty and affection not measured in sales or publicity. Under totalitarian regimes it can be manipulated and contained, but neither imposed nor eradicated, by the political system.

Although it has often been suggested that no major and consistent body of work can be produced by a poet without a sense of some such community, which is certainly more sustaining than any honor or recognition available to poets in societies that have ceased to be communities, ever since the late eighteenth century poets have learned to make do with a minimal response. Thanks to the anachronistic and utopian nature of their art, they could address themselves to anyone or no one among the living, or to Rilke's Orpheus, or to the "necessary angel of the earth" posited both by Rilke and Wallace Stevens. Long before them, Hölderlin's poetry had been sustained by a sense of community with the dead and unborn. More and more too, the writing of excellent poetry has been felt to be a privilege so rare as to need no palpable recognition or response.

Deliberate attempts, like Brecht's, to make poetry useful again above all, to make a socially and politically effective art, have come up against a formidable barrier. What Brecht proved was that poetry could be stripped again of all its Romantic and post-Romantic finery and speak in a language as unemotive as that of some of the Latin poets who were among his models. Hence his classical exemplariness, which was widely taken up in both East and West Germany. By revolutionizing him-

self, Brecht succeeded in producing the kind of poetry he thought suitable for his didactic purposes, but its usefulness and effectiveness were beyond his control. That is why his exemplariness too has begun to look utopian.

Like any other poet of the "Mechanical Age," then, Brecht could only cast his bread upon the waters or—in the metaphor chosen by a poet as difficult as Brecht wished to be plain, Paul Celan—launch his message inside a bottle "in the faith, not always supported by hope, that it could be washed up somewhere, at some time, on land, heartland perhaps." The plain messages have fared no better and no worse than the cryptic, enciphered ones.

This uncertainty is inseparable not only from the act of writing and publishing poems but from the special pleasure still to be derived from reading them. Because poets take that risk, cannot be sure that they know what they are about or whether their bottles will be picked up at all, poetry satisfies a need that no other language can satisfy. The opposite of that language is not prose, since there is prose that takes the same risk. Nor is it silence, which remains the source and precondition of poetry, as of music. Rather, it is the noise of literature, with its stock exchange of reputations and personalities, its schools and trends and camps, its ups and downs of acclaim or rejection. As critics and journalists, poets may contribute to that noise. If they are deafened by it, though, anything they write in verse will be literature at best; and their true readers, those who do not read out of vanity or curiosity, will be aware of it, because those readers are also in search of a language that takes risks, an immediate and urgent language that may not reveal where it's coming from or where it's going. As long as there are such readers and writers, poetry will survive.

Michael Hamburger, Spring 1985

Productive Comparative *Angst:* Comparative Literature in the Age of Multiculturalism

The current explosion of interest in the state of the discipline called comparative literature may be a sign of institutional anxiety or intellectual excitement—or perhaps both. The rapid publication of the book *Comparative Literature in the Age of Multiculturalism,* edited by Charles Bernheimer,[1] is more than a tribute to the efficiency and publishing savvy of the Johns Hopkins University Press; it is a sign of the urgency felt by comparativists to rethink and even to reconfigure their affiliations in the light of recent intellectual and academic realignments. Within a year of the December 1993 Modern Language Association convention, at which the newest public debate formally began, this collection of essays has made available for even wider discussion the American Comparative Literature Association's 1993 Bernheimer Report entitled "Comparative Literature at the Turn of the Century." Following on books like *The Comparative Perspective on Literature: Approaches to Theory and Practice,*[2] this volume joins a host of others[3] in examining what it calls the "anxiogenic" state of comparative literature in the United States (and elsewhere) today.

This state of anxiety may well feel familiar to those who recall René Wellek's 1958 worries (in "The Crisis of Comparative Literature")[4] about the lack of both subject matter and methodology in what many refer to by the contraction "CompLit." Indeed, as Bernheimer notes in his introduction, the various shifts in the discipline's focus "since World War II can be viewed as a series of attempts to cure, contain, or exploit the anxiety of comparison" (3). The most recent in this series of attempts was brought about by that new ACLA document: just like the Levin Report of 1965 and the Greene Report of 1975, the 1993 Bernheimer Report is unavoidably the product of a particular generation of comparativists.[5] The reprinting in this volume of these three reports makes possible the kind of comparison that clearly reveals the generational shift from the Americanization of the work of those postwar European émigré philologists and literary historians, through to the domestication of what was called "theory" when it was housed in comparative literature departments, to the current questioning of the centrality of the "Lit" in CompLit. Tellingly, perhaps, the first two were called reports "on standards"; the most recent one has been amended by the ACLA to bear the title of a report on "the state of the discipline."

The second section of *Comparative Literature in the Age of Multiculturalism* contains the three responses to the Bernheimer Report—by K. Anthony Appiah, Mary Louise Pratt, and Michael Riffaterre—that were presented for debate at the 1993 MLA convention. The third and largest section is given over to thirteen "position papers" from respected comparativists of several generations, responding in turn not only to the reports themselves but also to the very different stances taken in the three MLA papers. Chosen for the "diversity in critical perspective and institutional affiliation" (xi) they represented, these scholars offer a wide range of opinion and position. In short, if you come to *Comparative Literature in the Age of Multiculturalism* looking for a single answer

to any of your worries about the discipline, or if you are not comfortable with the postmodern-ly plural and contingent, you will not find your anxieties lessened by your reading. This is not a book for the faint of (meta-narrative) heart.

It is, however, a book for provoking thought, specifically thought on four major areas of concern for comparativists today, as reflected in the Bernheimer Report: 1) the historical Eurocentrism of the CompLit tradition and its relation to the multicultural reality of the present; 2) the continuing concerns about the desirability of reading—and comparing—literatures in their original languages and not in translation; 3) the position of theory in the discipline today; 4) the debate between what might be called the "formalists" and the "contextualists"—or, in institutional terms, literary studies versus cultural studies.

Few would deny that the history of comparative literature in North America is the history of its European émigré founding fathers; for some, that past has lived on as a kind of cosmopolitan, "poetic Euro-chic"[6] that may still be worn as a "'classy' designer label" today.[7] While even the 1965 Levin Report stressed the need to transcend that cultural limitation and the 1975 Greene Report emphasized the "global" nature of literature, the discipline has nonetheless largely remained based in European literary and historical traditions. The essays in this volume thoughtfully combat any knee-jerk rejection of this fact, however. K. Anthony Appiah urges: "Study these interconnected European literatures, I say. They make sense together. They were made for each other."[8] However, he goes on, study as well other interconnected bodies of writing that cohere around other cultural notions in other parts of the world. David Damrosch also reminds us that, in the face of the enormous scope of comparative literature's "mission," working within only the European languages may have been, for European-trained scholars, "less a matter of cultural imperialism than it was a melancholy acceptance of unbridgeable limits."[9]

The early constructions of the field—like those of other fields of literary study—have now been called into question because of their omissions, omissions made more evident through the increasingly diverse demographics not only of North American society but of the North American academy itself. As an internationalist discipline, comparative literature could not remain untouched by the pluralistic demands for canon revision and the ethical considerations vis-à-vis minoritized groups that were part of the contested academic and intellectual climate of the 1980s. In fact, it has faced particular and particularly troublesome problems because of its comparative function. These included problems as different as accusations of implied universalism, on the one hand, and, on the other, charges of essentializing in the face of the mimetic imperative that often accompanies notions of authenticity. There have been problems caused by geopolitical complexities and the historical processes of globalization, democratization, and decolonization that are collectively changing how literature and culture have been understood and studied.[10] And, of course, there have been problems caused by the image of the comparativist as colonizing imperialist taking over individual linguistic and literary domains.

The Bernheimer Report's advocacy of "a pluralized and expanded contextualizing of literary studies" (11) is one response to these diverse problems, one to which I will return shortly. But a number of the contributors to this volume suggest that comparative literature, by its very nature, is already a particularly "hospitable space" for what Mary Louise Pratt calls "the cultivation of multilingualism, polyglossia, the arts of cultural mediation, deep intercultural understanding, and a genuinely global consciousness" (62). This utopian view of CompLit as the "site for powerful intellectual renewal in the study of literature and culture" (62) is part of its history too, in a way: in the nervous postwar years of its North American founding, it was seen as representing "the spirit of peace, sincerity, reasonableness, and hope."[11] Inherently pluralist, CompLit is argued to be "aware of but not defined by Difference in all its powerful forms: language, religion, race, class, and gender."[12] This idea of the discipline as "a theoretical free space and a more cosmopolitan environment for multilingual and multiaccentual community"[13] goes a long way toward making comparative literature into the "humanities counterpart to international relations."[14]

The dissenting view in the volume is that of those like Emily Apter who suggest that CompLit's day may in fact have passed, that now is the time for postcolonial and not comparative studies: "With its interrogation of cultural subjectivity and attention to the tenuous bonds between identity and national language, postcolonialism quite naturally inherits the mantle of comparative literature's historical legacy."[15] While Apter and others reject that implied consensual or utopian model in favor of a dissensual one that would confront First with Third World cultures, Rey Chow offers an important reminder: "Instead of being a blank space ready to be adopted or assimilated by comparative literature, non-Western language and literature programs have been sites of production of knowledge which function alongside United States State Department policies vis-á-vis the particular nations and cultures concerned" (108). From another angle, David Damrosch stresses the need to historicize

and contextualize imperialism. Empire is not a recent phenomenon; it is not only a European one (126).

Postcolonial work is, of course, being done in national literature departments as well, largely because of its frequently unilingual focus: the cultural power of colonialism lives on in language. This brings me to the second source of anxiety for comparativists—the familiar one of linguistic competence and of the pedagogic and ethical issues involved in "engaging" two or more literatures adequately in their original languages. The question of the use of translations has provoked a predictable "elitist versus populist" debate.[16] However, multilingualism, as we are reminded in this volume, is in itself trans-ideological in the sense that it can "as easily serve the agenda of reactionary politics as it can serve progressive ones."[17] Thus, its intrinsic positive value (assumed in the Levin and Greene Reports) is called into question, even as the limits of unilingualism are recognized: not all literary concerns can be satisfactorily investigated through translations. Elizabeth Fox-Genovese takes a strong stand on this issue, urging the seeking of alternatives to the use of translations with its implicit throwing up of hands because "we are too limited (read imperialist) to appreciate it in the original" (135). A sensible and attractive alternative is the one offered by Damrosch: collaborative work for scholars and collaborative training for students (132).

The issue of translation merges with that of Eurocentric critique in the third area of common concern among the contributors to *Comparative Literature in the Age of Multiculturalism*. The ready availability of English versions of the European structuralist and poststructuralist theorists' work has threatened CompLit departments' housing of theory: national literature departments of all kinds can now "do" theory. There is little doubt that the rise and fall of the institutional power and cohesion of the Yale Comparative Literature group has left its mark on the discipline and, many would argue, upon the very process of reading. The comparativists who write for this volume, however, are divided in their views of the continuing importance of theory to CompLit's self-definition. Yale's current chair of Comparative Literature, Peter Brooks, feels theory is still the lingua franca of the discipline (103), and Elizabeth Fox-Genovese feels it would "be difficult to imagine comparative literature without theory, not least since the mere posing of the comparative problem is inherently theoretical" (139). Appiah, on the other hand, while agreeing that theory has been important historically to CompLit, does not see it as either the goal or the defining uniqueness of the discipline (53).

The theories of textuality that the Yale School represented are not, of course, the only components of what we lump together these days as "theory," and that comes through loud and clear in the position papers published in this book. With the increasing importance of feminist theory in North America, a major interest in context—social, cultural, historical, political context—was added to the concern with textuality. The impact of feminist work dovetailed with the theories of Foucault, Bakhtin, and Benjamin, and of Marxist, postcolonial, New Historical, gay and lesbian (and queer) theorists to make ideology an unavoidable issue in literary studies, comparative or otherwise. One of the results of this shift of focus has been the rise of a North American version of what in Britain had been dubbed cultural studies. The Bernheimer Report expresses this shift in quite cautious terms as a broadening of the field of inquiry that "does not mean that comparative study should abandon the close analysis of rhetorical, prosodic, and other formal features but that textually precise readings should take account as well of the ideological, cultural, and institutional contexts in which their meanings are produced" (43).

This may sound like a safe-enough compromise, but the strong reactions of contributors would suggest otherwise. While accepting that formal and contextual studies are necessarily complementary, Michael Riffaterre asserts the need to "decontextualize" and focus on the esthetic features of literature.[18] Peter Brooks protests the "abjectly apologic tone" of the Report which suggests that the teaching of literature is "an outmoded mandarin practice" (99) instead of the study of the "processes by which meaning is made, the grounds for interpretation" (101). Warning of the dangers of interdisciplinary amateurism, Brooks eloquently argues that "real" interdisciplinarity "comes when thought processes reach the point where the disciplinary boundary one comes up against no longer makes sense—when the internal logic of thinking impels a transgression of borderlines. And to the extent that this is teachable at all, it requires considerable apprenticeship in the disciplinary that is to be transcended" (102).

Many contributors attest to their belief in what one calls the "valuable specificity" of literature.[19] For some, this is a reason for remaining, in Brooks's terms, a "viable interlocutor to cultural studies," one that can insist that "contextualizations of literature in ideological and cultural terms remain aware of literature's institutional definitions and of the uses of poetics and rhetoric in understanding the ways in which literature creates meanings that both resemble and differ from those produced in other discourses" (103). But need CompLit's position here merely be one of interlocutor? Has any comparativist, even the most formalist, ever really read literature outside of some context, as *not* inextricably embedded

in a vast set of cultural practices? This is not a rhetorical question; nor is it an utterly naïve one, despite appearances. It points to my genuine puzzlement over what feels like a false dichotomy.

The disciplinary training of a comparativist, like that of any scholar who studies English or French or Korean or Nigerian literature, teaches us all that interpretation does not happen in a vacuum, that it is always relational and dynamic. Our literary disciplines may well traffic, not in political wisdom, but in "metrics, narrative structure, double, triple and quadruple meanings," as Stanley Fish has argued;[20] but the analysis of, say, narrative structure just might have to deal with the fact that stories are written—and read—in certain ways for certain reasons (conscious or unconscious reasons) in certain contexts at certain times. These are the insights that our formal training allows us to carry forward to the interpretation of other cultural artifacts or other discourses. We never stop being comparative *literature* trainees; our "déformation professionnelle" is permanent. At least it is *if* we have had that training.

The ACLA document is not only a report on the state of research in the discipline as it now stands; it is a provocative challenge to broaden the scope of what we teach in CompLit departments. Like many of us, the Report's authors were formed and "deformed" as comparativists; they have that to build upon and to deploy in new areas. The inevitable danger for our students in broadening what is already an impossibly broad discipline is the loss of any useful and distinctive training, even in skills of interpretation. The result, laments Appiah, may not be interdisciplinarity but "an unstructured postmodern hodge-podge" (57). This is a warning we as teachers must heed—for our students' sakes. But I still do not think the institutional or pedagogic answer is to leave cultural studies to the national language and literature departments—where cultural specificity may indeed make such a focus logical. This is Jonathan Culler's solution, one that would leave comparativists to study "literature comparatively" and attempt "to attend to its global manifestations."[21] But the question of cultural specificity will not go away so easily—either as a problem or as a temptation—for those engaging more than one literary or cultural tradition.[22] Culture is no more or less "translatable" than literature. Culture, like literature, is a matter of form as much as of content.[23]

The Bernheimer Report had advised caution for comparative literature vis-à-vis cultural studies, "where most scholarship has tended to be monolingual and focused on issues in specific contemporary popular cultures" (45). But the historical commitment of comparative studies, conjoined with the archival work of historians themselves, might be precisely what the emerging field of cultural studies could most profit from. And the seeming expansion of the scope of the discipline to include not only high art but also popular culture is maybe more apparent than real: minimal historicizing is needed to remind us that Shakespeare's plays were not what we would now call high art for the entire audience of the Globe Theater, and that writers like Rabelais deliberately chose to write in the vernacular, not in Latin.[24] The monolingual and often parochial nature of much cultural-studies work in the recent past need not stand as the final definition of this emerging field. The addition of the work of comparativists could serve to expand it in significant ways.

Comparative literature's major disciplinary strength and major intellectual attraction have always seemed to me to lie in a positive version of what Emily Apter considers its "unhomely" quality (90) and what Bernheimer calls its "quality of dispossession—a kind of haunting by otherness" (12). I remain as worried as ever, both in pragmatic and in political terms, about its vast scope—even vaster in this new definition "charged with the study of discourses and cultural productions of all sorts throughout the entire world."[25] I also share many of the contributors' worries about the possible institutional consequences of a move outward from the literary: in these days of financial constraints, unstable disciplinary boundaries can mean unstable funding.[26] Of course, the inherent versatility of comparativists can also mean the kind of institutional flexibility that could spell survival.[27]

If you have ever taught or been taught in a CompLit program, you will know that comparatists may appear to have little in common with one another: "As a discipline with no common body of knowledge other than literary studies, and without a central purpose except to carry out its astringent or stimulant motions, comparative literature appears to invite misunderstanding even from its own family of scholars."[28] But what *Comparative Literature in the Age of Multiculturalism* reveals is that any such misunderstanding is part of the intellectual vitality of the field and part of the continual self-criticism of a protean discipline that has never been willing (or able) to fix its self-definition. That is what is frustrating about CompLit, but it is also what attracted many of us to it. The ACLA, as an important professional voice for comparativist studies, has provoked productive and continuing debate on the future of the discipline through the Bernheimer Report. This is not the last word, of course. There can, luckily, be no last word on this subject.

Linda Hutcheon, Spring 1995

[1] *Comparative Literature in the Age of Multiculturalism*, ed. Charles Bernheimer, Baltimore, Johns Hopkins University Press, 1995. Most page references to this volume will appear in parentheses in the text. Subsequent references in the notes will use the abbreviation *CL*.

[2] *The Comparative Perspective on Literature: Approaches to Theory and Practice,* eds. Clayton Koelb and Susan Noakes, Ithaca, N.Y., Cornell University Press, 1988.

[3] See *Borderwork: Feminist Engagements with Comparative Literature,* ed. Margaret R. Higonnet, Ithaca, N.Y., Cornell University Press, 1994; *Building a Profession: Autobiographical Perspectives on the Beginnings of Comparative Literature in the United States,* eds. Lionel Gossman and Mihai I. Spariosu, Albany, N.Y., State University of New York Press, 1994; and the recent translation by Cola Franzen of Claudio Guillén's book *The Challenge of Comparative Literature,* Cambridge, Ma., Harvard University Press, 1993.

[4] René Wellek, "The Crisis of Comparative Literature," in *Concepts of Criticism,* ed. Stephen Nichols, New Haven, Ct., Yale University Press, 1963.

[5] For a detailed consideration of these generational changes, see Roland Greene, "Their Generation," in *CL*, pp. 143–54.

[6] Peter Brooks, "Must We Apologize?" in *CL*, p. 97. Further references will be in parentheses in the text.

[7] Rey Chow, "In the Name of Comparative Literature," in *CL*, p. 107. Further page references will appear in parentheses in the text.

[8] K. Anthony Appiah, "*Geist* Stories," in *CL*, p. 54.

[9] David Damrosch, "Literary Study in an Elliptical Age," in *CL*, p. 130. Further page references will appear in parentheses in the text.

[10] Mary Louise Pratt, "Comparative Literature and Global Citizenship," in *CL*, p. 59. Further page references will appear in parentheses in the text.

[11] Tobin Siebers, "Sincerely Yours," in *CL*, p. 195. Siebers questions whether such a worthy social aim, however, is an adequate or even appropriate foundation for a discipline.

[12] Ed Ahearn and Arnold Weinstein, "The Function of Criticism at the Present Time: The Promise of Comparative Literature," in *CL*, p. 78. They go on to note: "There is no period or place of artistic production which is not similarly mixed, cross-cultural, cross-pollinated. Virgin literatures, like the virgin land, are a myth. Comparativists are the people trained to bring us this news" (79).

[13] Mary Russo, "Telling Tales Out of School: Comparative Literature and Disciplinary Recession," in *CL*, p. 189.

[14] Ahearn and Weinstein, p. 81.

[15] Emily Apter, "Comparative Exile: Competing Margins in the History of Comparative Literature," in *CL*, p. 86. Further page references will appear in parentheses in the text.

[16] See Elizabeth Fox-Genovese, "Between Elitism and Populism: Whither Comparative Literature?" in *CL*, p. 134. Further page references will be in parentheses in the text.

[17] Chow, p. 110.

[18] Michael Riffaterre, "On the Complementarity of Comparative Literature and Cultural Studies," in *CL*, pp. 67, 70.

[19] Françoise Lionnet, "Spaces of Comparison," in *CL*, p. 172. Further page references will appear in parentheses in the text.

Alfred Kazin (*Gil Jain*)

[20] Stanley Fish, "Why Literary Criticism Is Like Virtue," *London Review of Books,* 10 June 1993, p. 12.

[21] Jonathan Culler, "Comparative Literature, at Last!" in *CL,* p. 121.

[22] See the important points made by Marjorie Perloff, "'Literature' in the Expanded Field," in *CL,* p. 180; Damrosch, p. 123.

[23] See Siebers, pp. 196–97.

[24] Lionnet, p. 172.

[25] Culler, p. 117.

[26] See Perloff, p. 182.

[27] Russo, p. 193.

[28] Greene, p. 145.

We See from the Periphery, Not the Center: Reflections on Literature in an Age of Crisis

One obvious thing about literature in our day is that the very concept of the *masterpiece,* with all that this old-fashioned word suggests of the exceptional, the all-superior, the unique, and therefore of duration and permanence and lasting influence, is positively disliked by our good contemporary writers. The English critic Cyril Connolly advised me that keeping first editions of the important books he reviewed was a wise investment. Connolly was thoroughly trained in the classics and surely believed in what Matthew Arnold pronounced in *Culture and Anarchy* as the function of culture: "a pursuit of our total perfection by means of getting to know, on all the matters which most concern us, the best that has been thought and said in the world." So what Cyril Connolly—this clever, world-weary, easily disenchanted but still respectful and traditionalist epicure of literature, who divided the great books like different wines that he was always tasting, rejecting or putting away into the deep, deep cellars of his library—finally came out with was this: "*The only reason for writing at all is to create a masterpiece.*"

Cyril Connolly died bankrupt, leaving his family and friends with a staggering debt to pay. He would have been the last person in the world to claim that his charming and sometimes valuable books, which are such clever records of his wide reading—*Enemies Of Promise, The Unquiet Grave, The Condemned Playground,* even his novel-record of the old hedonist life of the 1920s, *The Rock Pool*—were masterpieces or even attempted to be masterpieces. It is not irrelevant to add that Connolly turned his pronounced capacity for melancholy into Spengler-like judgments on the decline of practically everything. One of his famous lines is that it was "closing time in the gardens of the West." He seems to have thought of himself and his friends as Greeks among the new barbarians who had taken over the world. His highest ambition for England was that it become the "Middle Kingdom" between those two horrid superstates, America and Russia.

Collecting first editions of ultimately valuable contemporary books is second nature, of course, to certain bookdealers and to those many university libraries in this country that assiduously seek twentieth-century letters, manuscripts, proofs. I am told by one enterprising bookdealer in New York that even the bound proofs of forthcoming books (usually sent to reviewers ahead of publication date) are worth *money.* But only if the author in question has good prospects on the literary stock exchange and if you collect all the proofs of books by the same author. One set alone is likely to be worthless.

So investing in "masterpieces," commodities likely to last if the *name* does, has not altogether gone out of style. We have the busy bookdealers and university libraries buying everything connected with certain writers, even their old canceled checks. And we have the great graduate school industry, now turning out eleven Ph.D.'s in English for every available job teaching freshman composition. In these factories of learning, where as Spinoza said of the human condition, our task is not to laugh or cry but to understand, the dutiful melancholics who are our students are still churning out papers on "The Unity of *The Faerie Queen*," "Religious Symbolism in Flannery O'Connor," "Myth and Symbol in *The Scarlet Letter*" and "The Character of Satan in *Paradise Lost*." One publisher recently advised me to buy up all first editions of the new American poets in San Francisco—"the crazier they look, especially in cheap pamphlet form, the harder they'll be to find in the 1980s." But English Departments, whose younger members are equally obsessed by every current tribal novelty from Afro-Jewish poetry to Radical Lesbians in Manitoba, are officially mired in that hopeless pursuit of "total perfection"—nothing less!—that is supposed to consist in, to thrive on, the best that has been thought and said.

Actually, that "total perfection," that illusion of *der gebildete Mensch,* the man of perfect cultural development, is one of the sillier secular ideals passed on by great poets like Goethe. All that belongs to the age when man deprived of the church was to become his own church by reading many books. The "intellectual," not yet threatened by science, was a European culture type who confused piety about great writers with his ability to transform society. He transformed it all right—Lenin, Mao, Castro, even Mussolini, have all been intellectuals, sometimes even literary theorists, subjecting helpless millions to their insistence on total perfection—which means the total obedience acquired by studying the wisdom of the Leader himself.

But of course not even the most conservative prelates in the Vatican now believe in total perfection on earth. Sainthood has been a preoccupation of independent radicals and God-seekers on the left like Simone Weil, Ignazio Silone, Albert Camus. Camus said that the task was to become a saint "without God." It has been the victims of, and witnesses to, totalitarianism—Silone, Solzhenitsyn, Osip and Nadezhda Mandelstam, Isaac Babel, Pasternak—who have understood that without some *ideal* of perfection there is no shield from modern despotism. They have been dismayed by the seeming irreversibility of totalitarian dogma and cruelty. So they have put themselves to the agonizing task of a new heaven if not a new earth. But not all the great writers of our time understand that "total perfection" is a cruel and even stupid device for tyranny. Jean-Paul Sartre, the last pure disciple of the Enlightenment and a utopian—for countries *he* does not have to live in—believes in an ideal person who is nothing but pure liberty. "Bad faith" consists in trusting that anyone before you had the morality by which you must now, in total and unflagging independence of spirit, try to live your life.

Departments of literature still invoke the best that has been thought and said and honor masterpieces by dragging students through every jot and title in them. But the most exciting teaching just now honors the "masterpiece" only to the extent that it makes the critic equal to the work by showing the daring of what Richard Poirier calls the "imaginative confrontation of the text." Of course I don't believe that the old-fashioned study of literature on historical principles—whatever *that* was, from "background" studies to examples of how tradition operated by showing that everyone was influenced by his predecessor—did more for the understanding and appreciation of literature than the many critical perspectives that have been in force since The New Criticism began among poet-critics as a way of explicating the novelty of modernist poetry. The New Criticism was institutionalized as the only way of spelling out a text, any text—word for word, line for line, image for image—to students who had never read poetry for themselves. But I do say that the major effect of critical reading in the universities, of so many methods of interpretation sometimes born of nothing but the idiosyncrasy and dogmatism of the instructor, has been to give the critic-teacher delusions of grandeur. Many people far less talented and informed than Harold Bloom now foolishly believe, along with him, that "imaginative confrontation of the text" makes the critic a "creator" of sorts and, according to the new emphasis on reading, so necessary to the text that he may in some sense be said to replace it.

You cannot isolate a text from the creative process that belongs to the creator alone, you cannot isolate it from the historical context which is *in* it, you cannot reduce it to the terms of your own critical method for the examination of text after text inherently different from each other without putting yourself above the text and *attempting* to replace it. As a teacher, I know how easy it is to mislead my students. No matter how genial and encouraging I am with them, every good one thinks that he has everything to learn—which may be true. So any teacher is expected to be able to do a perfect job on him, which is impossible and even undesirable but does turn the class into a captive audience for a strong-minded critic with special views of his own.

However this may be, there is many a critical ideologist in the classroom who no longer believes that *Hamlet, The Rape of the Lock, The Marriage of Heaven and Hell* or *Wuthering Heights* is more important than anything he may have to say about it. Even to understand these classics may require too much knowledge of kingship, the English aristocracy, the theology of Emmanuel Swedenborg, the landscape of Yorkshire. It seems easier for the dutiful follower of critical fashion to show that

Hamlet was an Oedipal case, Wordsworth a precursor of A. R. Ammons and Emily Brontë a feminist.

Personal interest takes over in all departments, and it takes over remorselessly, like the sea eating the land. Nothing lasts. History does not exist, only Historians. Because we are egalitarians, we see no reason to believe that one culture is better than another or that the reasons for believing otherwise are founded, like everything else, on the rationalization of self-interest. There is no qualitative difference even between types of activity. Anyone can be creative, if only in the kitchen. Above all, there is no difference between men and women, and there must not be any. That would lead to the consideration that the truly feminine qualities Emily Dickinson possessed in excelsis may become a caricature of helplessness in Anne Sexton. Adrienne Rich in *Diving into the Wreck* complains that Beethoven's music has too loud a voice. So the masculine qualities are not only disliked by the unisex mind but held untenable. All judgment is so subjective, sexual, tribal, group-think, that the only social context we can admit to exist is that power is as much the issue between the sexes as it is in politics and society. Or as Lenin said, "Who whom?"

There are deeper, more powerful, more unconscious reasons why the contemporary fashion hates and supplants the idea of continuity that was once behind the veneration and the use of masterpieces. We live, as William Blake feared and foretold, in a universe of death. He meant that secularism and materialism run riot, deprive man of the necessary myth of immortality, then give him the excuse—nothing lasts—that is the rationale for manipulation, exploitation, domination, persecution. Dostoevsky said in the nineteenth century that socialism was above all the atheistic question. As we now know, socialism can have no gods but itself. André Malraux said that the purpose of the Nazi terror camps was to reduce the prisoner's regard for himself, to make him contemptible in his own eyes—and so material to torture, murder, incinerate.

Ours is a universe of death, because more and more we regard each other as we do nature—material to be used. Perhaps this contemporary crisis began even before modernization, when nature became *entirely* raw material rather than something "not ourselves" to be contemplated, enjoyed, venerated, propitiated. But ours has turned out to be, in a far deeper sense than Marx could have realized when he castigated the acquisitive bourgeois ego and his fellow Victorian inveighed against the cash nexus, a period peculiarly concerned with exploitation and savagely defensive of it. Conrad said that his aim as an artist was to render the highest possible justice to the created universe. But the "universe" as a term belongs now to astronomy, not to the tragic sense in art. We have seen psychology as the science of character misused as a way of "getting" people, a concentration of specific achievements and satisfactions at the expense of others, a reduction of our once integral conceptions of the human in a friendless universe to the idea of power.

Power, even the most brilliantly technical conversion of anything to our immediate and particular use, sooner or later obliterates the object at whose expense we employ power. We are all painfully conscious of living in a cultural economy of planned obsolescence, of books that are published in order to perish, of diminishing returns on our vaunted traditions. Sisyphus, in the myth retold by Camus, at least tried to roll the stone all the way up the mountain. Now the effort seems futile. People, societies, cultures, all forcibly expressing themselves as commodities for a season, are continually passing away. We cannot hold on to anything for very long—least of all a book. The traditional idea of a masterpiece was that its excellence was recognized in a way that made it good for all seasons and for all types of men. The lifeblood of a master spirit, said Milton, a refuge against trouble, a sealed treasure, said Bellow about the unknown people who find their consolation in secret private reading. Whether the masterpiece was supposed to help tell your future, as the Romans did with a passage from Virgil, or whether it became our favorite form of history, nineteenth-century novels, it was supposed to offer a model, above all to enable you to live better. "What are works of art for?" asked Gerard Manley Hopkins, the good Jesuit teacher. "To educate, to be standards." Certainly no one can deny the use of the book as a sealed treasure. In her remarkable memoir of life in Stalin's camps, *Journey into the Whirlwind*, Evgenya Semyonovna Ginzburg recounts how the women prisoners, locked into boxcars on their long journey to the Arctic, recited poetry from memory, as Russians do, so that even the stony-faced guards were mollified for a brief period.

But that is consolation, inner strengthening, not living better. How in 1977 can any great book help *me* to live better, I who am a creature of anxiety, involved against my will in all twentieth-century injustices and cruelties? How can Kafka relieve me of guilt, he who knew as a Jew even before the Nazis murdered his sisters, since powerlessness is a crime that invites exploitation, that "not the murderer but the victim is considered guilty"? How can Proust, who died to the world in order to live again through his great book retracing the past—how can he relieve me of my dread of death, when I can no longer accept the next world, the world of imagination, promised to me by his last-minute discovery of art in the volume *Time Recaptured?*

But these are rhetorical questions whose emptiness I do not wish to conceal. Because no book has enabled anyone to live better. The influence of any book on my consciousness is necessarily intermittent, a flash, a hope, an illusion, a picture. No more than any other external agent can a book effect a transformation that lasts. What a great literary work does do for me is to clear my mind, to rearrange the order of my thinking, to show me, in the immortal words of *Porgy and Bess,* that "it ain't necessarily so." The real power of a literary work consists in presenting us with alternatives. If the work is emotionally effective enough, it can be an antidote to our usual mental confinement. It is the vision of *another mind,* another way of thinking, not a lasting way out.

Masterpieces are a lost illusion. They presupposed, like all illusions of a lasting state, a continuity of tradition behind us and before us that doesn't exist in a world where literature flourishes as information, entertainment, propaganda, and is constantly denatured of its true substance by furnishing plots to the popular visual arts like film and television. The center does not hold and will not. That is a Western and Christian plaint based on the memory of the Christian church as the world's exclusive moral order. Yeats, who wrote that famous line, was himself no Christian and even offered a rival mythology. There is no center. The classical idea of a center rested on the unchallenged supremacy of the Roman Empire, then of the Catholic Church, then of the Enlightenment's gift—chiefly to America!—of the myth that the individual is a self-sustaining and rational being whose chief aim is freedom in which to think. Dante's idea of poets as a universal band of prophets and teachers was replaced by the Enlightenment's recreation of the thinker as representing perfect liberty of opinion. With the triumph of the so-called free individual in the French and American Revolutions, this resulted in a vortex of competing *opinions* (with the individual known to himself only by *having* certain opinions): "liberal" society.

Modernism began in the twentieth century as a revolt against this confusion of opinions, this modern Babel of tongues. Modernism opposed modernization, improvement, the education of the masses and everything else that the good liberal held dear. Modernism indeed insisted that the only available strategy left to literature and art was the unconscious, the primitive and primeval that united us in common myths. Not the bourgeois individual for civil society, competing in the struggle for existence with other individuals, which naturalists from Zola to Dreiser thought would be the Darwinian literature of the future, but the individual located in universal myths, the individual as a repository of the past. Symbolism, not naturalism; personal consciousness, not society as pictured for us by the historians and journalists, would unexpectedly dominate the literature of a century racked by world war, world revolution, the fiercest nationalism and tribalism.

Cocteau said that literature is a force of memory that is not understood. Rilke wrote that poetry is the past that breaks out in our hearts. William James discovered the stream of consciousness in his classic textbook of scientific psychology. Freud and Jung in their different ways showed that the individual unconscious recapitulates the history of the race. It was this idea of the secular individual—the nineteenth century's representative man—involuntarily returning to the sacred wood which led Eliot to that idea so crucial for literature between the two wars. He saw in Stravinsky's *Rites of Spring* "that vanished mind of which our mind is a continuation." The "primitive mind" still survives in the "obscurities of the soul." His most famous and influential essay, "Tradition and the Individual Talent" (1917), told a whole generation that

> the historical sense is nearly indispensable to anyone who would continue to be a poet beyond his twentyfifth year; and the historical sense involves a perception not only of the pastness of the past, but of its presence; the historical sense compels a man to write not only with his own generation in his bones, but with a feeling that the whole of the literature of Europe from Homer and within it the whole of the literature of his own country has a simultaneous existence and composes a simultaneous order. . . . He must be aware that the mind of Europe . . . is a development which abandons nothing *en route,* which does not superannuate either Shakespeare, or Homer, or the rock drawing of the Magdalenian draughtsman.

Eliot felt that his case was proved, his own example justified, by myth in Joyce's *Ulysses:* "It is simply a way of controlling, of ordering, of giving shape and significance to the immense panorama of futility and anarchy which is contemporary history."

The period between the two world wars was indeed one of the summits of human creativity in poetry, fiction, physics, architecture. In literature it brought to a dizzy culmination all the modernist strivings that had begun as a revolution of the superior individual against mass society. In Russia it produced Pasternak, Mandelstam, Akhmatova, Babel, Kandinsky, Chagall, Gabo; in France, Proust, Cocteau, Malraux, Céline, Picasso; in German, Rilke, Kafka, Jünger, Heidegger, Buber; in English, Eliot, Lawrence, Joyce, Waugh, Frost, Cummings, Stevens, Fitzgerald, Hemingway, Wilson, O'Neill, Orwell, Virginia Woolf.

This constellation of names is now our tradition, along with Stravinsky, Klee, Munch. It dominates the academy. Literature since the late 1930s takes its historical meaning as a continuation of modernism or as a reaction against it. These great artists and originals flourished in a false peace (1918–39) that was wracked with mass unemployment ended only by the most destructive war in history. Intellectuals and writers turned everywhere to totalitarian Communism or Fascism and gladly consigned millions to death or sustained persecution. But the original basis of modernism, which was to reverse the modern age, to restore us to the ancient bond that Eliot called the sacred wood, was exactly and especially the aim that *art* could *not* accomplish. Which was why the idea of the masterpiece as a teacher and inspirer of humanity, a force for change, died out.

The basic reason why *we* in the last twenty years of this century cannot believe in masterpieces is the failure of conservative and reactionary thinkers—modernists all: Eliot, Lawrence, Pound, Yeats, Mann, Pasternak, Mandelstam, Woolf, Proust, et cetera—to affect the modern age that they hated so bitterly. Poetry makes nothing happen. Mandelstam and Babel could do nothing about Stalinism except to die at its hands. Evelyn Waugh could lament the modern and everything about it, thought it sinful for his country to aid Russia in its mortal struggle with Nazi Germany, was a Catholic convert more absolutist than any Pope and lived like a country gentleman in total disdain of the masses, popular education and socialism. He was viewed as an amusing maniac. Americans like Hemingway, Fitzgerald and Faulkner lamented the passing of their old America, of the great race. And so they became culture heroes to the young precisely because *they* became the world they replaced and lamented. This was certainly a misunderstanding on the part of the young. Yet it remains one that is perpetuated by every teacher who ignores the real opinions of the modernists they teach. These great writers were, as a group, antidemocratic to an extreme. Although it is fashionable now among critics like Hugh Kenner to treat Ezra Pound's Fascism as a temporary aberration, the fact is that Pound's "eccentric" broadcasts from Fascist Italy represented a long-standing grievance not only against Jews, Roosevelt and Churchill, but a violent and uncontrolled contempt for the masses, general liberty of opinion, et cetera.

Madness can be an intellectual thing, an obsession with one's favorite ideas, a delusion of grandeur about oneself as a thinker and world-saver. Ezra Pound was a beautiful lyric poet, an indispensable friend to T. S. Eliot in the editing of *The Waste Land,* to Robert Frost in England when *A Boy's Will* came out. And of course he was the tireless spokesman for the modern movement in poetry. But Pound did consider the imagination required to write great poetry as not merely the highest good but as the greatest possible *intelligence,* and therefore so necessary in instructing the human race that those who did not agree with him were criminals, subhuman, deserving extermination.

Here is the key to our present impatience with masterpieces. Poets are not the unacknowledged legislators of the world, as Shelley said; they are not necessarily legislators at all. The brilliance of twentieth-century poets and novelists made no political changes except for the worse. Pound said on the Fascist radio that he was speaking for the "American heritage." On 3 February 1942 this took the following form: "Politically and economically the US has had economic and political syphilis for the past eighty years"; "it becomes increasingly difficult to discuss American affairs except on a racial basis"; "an old-style killing of small Jews is no good whatsoever. Of course, if some man had a stroke of genius, and could start a pogrom up at the top, there might be something to say for it."

Thomas Mann said that in our time every consideration of human fate takes on a political character. But the political *opinions* of great modernist writers are no help to our human interests as a group. It was said of D. H. Lawrence, a very great writer, that he literally kept himself alive "by sheer rage." Bertrand Russell, who was frightened by the influence Lawrence could exert on gifted individuals, said that Lawrence saw himself as the supreme ruler when a dictatorship had been established. He charged that Lawrence had developed the whole philosophy of Fascism before the politicians had thought of it. When Lawrence, who could be the most lyrical and realistic of novelists in the same book, laid down the law about women, society, peasants, he was as repulsive as he was ridiculous. This miner's son said that the lower classes should be relieved of all responsibility. They should not even learn how to read or write. "The secret is to commit into the hands of the sacred few the responsibility which now lies like torture on the mass. . . . Leaders—this is what mankind is craving for." Auden noticed a strain of personal cruelty in Lawrence, a fantasy of unlimited domination over others. It allowed him to praise the most bestial "executions" among the Aztecs and to speak of "blood knowledge."

T. S. Eliot, who, like all our great modernists between the wars, felt that civilization was in the balance, was narrow in his sympathies, advocated inequality of education and was a sympathizer with Fascism. William Butler Yeats, the greatest poet in English of our century, saw the present as a mere transition back to archaic grandeur. He significantly thought that Mussolini's Fascism was "individualist," supported the Irish Fascist Blue Shirts. Perhaps he encouraged the unending violence in Ireland when he wrote: "Politics are growing heroic. . . . A Fascist opposition is forming behand the scenes to be ready should some tragic situation develop. . . . It is amusing to live in a country where men will always act. Where nobody is satisfied with thought."

As Kurt Vonnegut likes to say, so it goes. And so it went. The modernists against modern life, as I call them, the apostles of modern art who disliked everything else in our century, did not change anything: they became the Establishment. They became favorites of the academy because they alone seemed to promise all the old virtues identified with masterpieces: genuineness of inspiration, solidity of purpose, originality of form. As Emerson said to Whitman "rubbing his eyes" over *Leaves of Grass,* such works had a long background somewhere. As indeed they did, and so many of our present books do not.

But the basic reason why the modernists became our heroes, in the academy sometimes our only heroes, is that they promised to last. Western civilization between the wars was threatening to collapse, and it did. Capitalist society could give full employment only in war. The values of American democracy became shoddy to the most obstinate patriots when mass destitution was tolerated in the 1930s and war in Vietnam, corruption at Watergate, seemed the way powerful government operated when it has too much power. The center was not holding. The church was not holding. God was dead, especially in theology courses given by former Jesuits.

By contrast there was a long, long background indeed to the philosophic credo that Proust said had enabled him to write his masterpiece: memory makes an immortal self, presently hidden within us, that becomes the form of forms, the form that fashions order out of our personal chaos. Art, said Thomas Mann, is the fusion of suffering and the desire for form. Form was the magic key to art and the secret talisman of what would last. Our civilization was, is, obsessed by its vulnerability. Art promised immortality through form. In Eliot, Hemingway, Stevens, Valéry, all who valued perfection of the line, the perfect balance and subtlety of images, the belief in form—and to the academy the study of form as a thing in itself—art seemed a counterculture to the pervasive hedonism, pornography, war, terrorism, mass entertainment, the visual media, the tyranny of the daily murder spread over the daily tabloid.

But the example of Céline, the greatest figure in French literature after Proust, the determined antihu-

manist who became the most repellent yet most prophetic writer of the period that ended with him as a fugitive in the ashes of Nazi Germany, shows that even in the late 1920s the real problem of literature was to surmount disintegration by expressing it *fully.* Céline found a language exactly equal in diction and spastic rhythm, even in punctuation, to the realization that dominates writing in our day. Man is completely under the control of events. All expectations are inherently absurd, because they express a mental freedom essentially unrelated to the life of action. Literature thrives on a sense of the ridiculous so unappeasable that the greatest writers of this school, like Samuel Beckett, have finally found a verbal equivalent of silence.

But absurdity as a genre is an expression of relativity and the uncertainty principle in twentieth-century physics. Heisenberg said that to the outer limits of space man carries only his reflection of himself. Céline saw his books as "self-consuming artifacts" and disclaimed any lasting value to books whose deepest aim was to catch the innermost voice of his anguish. He was not modest and despised postwar writers like Camus. But of his own books he said firmly, "Great art is not personal like that."

Céline haunts me, because his aggressiveness and hatred for the contemporary world led him into a violent comedy of style. Beckett, just the opposite type in his passivity, anonymity, nevertheless ends up in the same spirit of limitless comedy. The prose is naked to the point of silence, as I say, but the point is the same: we are no longer even the masters of our own language. The muse uses us instead of the other way around. As Beckett showed in the pauses that are the most dramatic interventions in his plays, and as Céline had shown in the sputtering separation of phrase from phrase, language in our time is an effort, not a rhetorical triumph; it is a confrontation, is not and cannot hope to be an example of that self-confidence once known as "style." There is even an inescapable sense of travesty about writing; for the world of action, the remorseless productivity of "History," is so far in excess of anything we may hope to say about it that there is something inevitably self-mocking and a form of parody about key books that touch on the horrors of World War II—Céline's *D'un chateau l'autre, Nord, Rigodon,* Waugh's *Men at Arms* and *Officers and Gentlemen* are far better examples than Vonnegut's *Slaughterhouse-Five* and Heller's *Catch-22.*

Man created the death camps, the torture and murder of millions on the grounds of class and race. Man was the inventor, the artist, the veritable genius of this demonic "creation." The mind that conceived and sustained the world of the Gulag Archipelago could not be matched in energy and steadfastness by any mere account of it. That led to Solzhenitsyn's whiplash style in *Gulag,* just as a touch of the fundamental anomie in decaying Ireland led Beckett to a style whose fundamental aim is to imitate inertia, to give life the form of death. The extraordinary capacity for destruction and systematic cruelty challenges the writer whose highest dramatic creation was once "Evil, be Thou My Good." Blake in more innocent times said that Milton was of the Devil's Party without knowing it. But as the dying and proscribed Freud began to see, devilishness was not the repressed sexuality of Victorian ladies and of the nineteenth-century capitalists whose passion for gold was really shit. Devilishness, the itch to destroy, was indeed a fundamental passion of man. But even the most pro-Fascist writer maddened by contemporary life, like Céline, could not admire evil as Hitler did. To write is still to respect the economy of life.

Existentialism thus came in, significantly on the eve of the most terrible war in history, as the need to save man from himself. Sartre's great insight in that perilous and haunting novel, *La nausée,* was that there are no connections between man and his surroundings except those he makes for himself by sheer force of a desperately summoned sense of liberty which says: *I will Be.* Freedom—absolute, naked, frightening, desolating, all-lonely freedom is man's only *duty.* It can be his captivity as well; but since it is his destiny, his only nature, freedom is the only possible grace.

We live, Sartre insisted, in a world made impossibly moral and dangerous by the iron necessity of absolute free self-determination. The task is to be human—it is not *conferred* upon us. To *be* in a world essentially of nothingness means a perpetual vigilance in behalf of what Sartre called "good faith"—perfect independence of all institutions, established morality, Nobel Prizes, even settled domiciles.

Man, it seems, is only what he creates. He must continually reinvent himself. Yet even Sartre, who permits himself the fantasy of human renaissance through agrarian revolution and party dictatorship on the Chinese model, is like the exile Nabokov and the ex-prisoner Solzhenitsyn in giving moral supremacy to words rather than to traditions and systems. As language, often wrested out of any context, becomes the only symbol of the human, language becomes the obsession of all of us in a period when "realistic" literature is journalism and the old idea of it as a universal power over the hearts of men seems unreal. For we are trying to retrace, back to its inherent beginning in our minds, what as a finished product literature no longer offers: a clue to the human condition.

What is central to these language studies is the need to discover what is specifically and genetically

human in our instinctive connection with language. Is it possible that *we* are language systems more than we are anything else? Have we all been language makers, language repositories, even language victims without our knowing it? Is it from language itself that we may get the kind of information we no longer get from social novels?

However this may be, the obvious subject matter in poetry and advanced fiction just now is the sense of disruption, the falling back on alienated but haunting forms of a consciousness entirely private. There is nothing for John Ashbery, Thomas Pynchon, Vladimir Nabokov, A. R. Ammons, William Gass to learn from transmitted forms. Saul Bellow at Stockholm piously urged writers to return from the periphery to the center. What center? John Cheever said in a recent interview: "I don't think that a writer has any responsibility to view literature as a continuous process. I believe that very little of literature is immortal. I've known books in my lifetime to serve beautifully, and then to lose their usefulness, perhaps briefly."

What does it mean just now to "serve beautifully"? It means to sustain us by surprising us. Thomas Pynchon in *Gravity's Rainbow* has written an epic in anti-epic form and style, a sustained mockery of the connection between the Bomb and sexuality, those two forms of illusory power that obsess the age. What surprises us is that such a book is everything which a young man who was not there in London 1945 can tell us about a war that has never really ended, a war that continues to ridicule our potency in love and death. In poetry it means something like John Ashbery's uncanny ability to reveal discontinuous human states through stray forms in nature. As the creation may have been an accident, an ultimate secret we are not likely to discover, so consciousness is a series of slides that take the form of the sweetest, most natural disconnection between line and line, memory and memory, image and image. We see from the periphery, not the center. The center is for gods. There is a separation—a silence really—between the items in an Ashbery poem that sustains me. It presents not the supposed logic of the external world in which science no longer believes, not the supposed continuity of history which only textbook writers uphold, but moment after moment of our actual existence, as *quiet,* inevitable, as it is uncertain. As Ashbery puts it in "Definition of Blue," in long lines smilingly reminiscent of prose or of Whitman's old romanticism:

In our own time, mass practices have sought to
   submerge the personality
By ignoring it, which has caused it instead to branch
   out in all directions

Far from the permanent tug that used to be its
   notion of "home."

. . . .

But today there is no point in looking to imaginative
   new methods
Since all of them are in constant use. The most that
   can be said for them further
Is that erosion produces a kind of dust or
   exaggerated pumice
Which fills space and transforms it, becoming a
   medium
In which it is possible to recognize oneself.

. . . .

. . . the blue surroundings drift slowly up and past
   you
To realize themselves some day, while you, in this
   nether world that could not be better
Waken each morning to the exact value of what you
   did and said, which remains.

Alfred Kazin, Spring 1977

Ed. Note: Alfred Kazin's essay was delivered at the University
of Oklahoma on 28 January 1977 as the keynote address of the
Books Abroad Golden Anniversary Symposium.

"World Literature" in the Age of Telecommunications

All those books on my shelves are powerful instruments
for conjuring ghosts. They are there by powerful tools
for reinforcing the ideologies embodied in the medium
of the printed book: the shades of Hegel's "Geist" or
Heidegger's "Sein" when I read either of those two philosophers, the ghosts of Freud's patients Irma, Anna, or
Dora when I read psychoanalysis, the swarming specters of such characters as Fielding's Tom Jones, Stendhal's Fabrizio, Flaubert's Emma Bovary, George Eliot's
Dorothea, Henry James's Isabel, Joyce's Leopold Bloom
when I read works of fiction. All books, as Friedrich Kit-
tler says, "are books of the dead, like those from Egypt
that stand at the beginning of [Western!] literature."
Books are so many powerful conjuring devices for raising all those phantoms.

   The ghosts on the television or cinema screen,
however, seem much more objective, public, and
shared, much less dependent on my own effort of con-
juration than are those specters raised by the private act
of reading a book. Moreover, these new telecommunications technologies, so many new devices for raising
ghosts in a new way, also generate new ideological ma-

trices. They break down, for example, the barrier between consciousness and the objects of consciousness
presupposed in Hegel's *Phenomenology* and leave us
wondering about the fate of "literature" and "world literature" that, as huge constellations of conventions, the
prior culture produced.

   In spite of the fading of the culture that produced
print and literature, I believe the openness of the new
telecommunications can still be appropriated for the
creation of new alliances. How can this happen? One
answer is to recognize that critique or diagnosis always
has a performative as well as a constative dimension.
Though the new telecommunications technologies have
a powerful effect on the meaning of what is encoded in
the new forms, they can nevertheless be appropriated
for new forms of cooperative human praxis. We are not
simply at their mercy. The appropriation of new communications technology can take place in the name of
new cyberspace communities of diversity. I call these,
following Bill Readings, communities of dissensus.
Giorgio Agamben calls this association of diversities
"the coming community."

   The new communications technologies can also be
used to facilitate performative acts of political responsibility. Those acts respond to a demand coming from the
future anterior of that "democracy to come" as a sort of
possible impossibility. If this perfect democracy were
programmed as an inevitable future, if it were "possible"
in the sense of being certainly foreseeable, it would not
require our praxis. It is only as unforeseeable and as impossible without a break in the programmed continuity
that it invites or demands or obliges our performative
praxis. A model for this might be that sentence in the
United States Declaration of Independence: "We hold
these truths to be self-evident, that all men are created
equal, that they are endowed by their Creator with certain inalienable rights, that among these are life, liberty,
and the pursuit of happiness." On the one hand, this
sentence asserts that these truths are self-evident. They
do not require political action to be made true. On the
other hand, the sentence says "*we hold* these truths to
be self-evident." "We hold" is a performative speech act.
It creates the truths it claims are self-evident and invites
whoever reads these words to endorse them, to counter-
sign them, to work for their fulfillment. The words invite us to work toward their fulfillment in further performative acts. The promise embodied in those words
has by no means yet been entirely fulfilled in the United
States. Though the words belong to the past, the past
of the moment of the founding of our country, they invite from the future, as a future anterior, their more perfect fulfillment. The words call to us from the horizon
of that democracy to come.

Well, what about "literature," "world literature," and literary study? Will they survive? Literary study's time is surely up. There is never time any more to study literature "for itself," detached from theoretical or political reflection. It would be anachronistic to do so. I doubt very much that there will ever again be time. This gives yet another meaning, or perhaps the same one, to Hegel's famous dictum that art is a thing of the past: "In allen diesen Beziehungen ist und bleibt die Kunst nach der Seite ihrer höchsten Bestimmung für uns ein Vergängenes" (In all these respects art, as far as its highest determination [or calling] is concerned, is and remains for us a thing of the past [ein Vergängenes—a something past, a past thing]; tr. Warminski). This means too, though Hegel perhaps did not quite know it, that art, including literature as a form of art, is also always a thing of the future. It never quite successfully gets spirit (Geist) into sensuous form so we can get on to the end of getting spirit into spiritual form. It is never time yet for art and literature. We dwell, as far as literature and literary study are concerned, in that perpetual in between, always too late and always too early, untimely.

To shift, on Hegel's back, so to speak, to a slightly different register, I assert that there never has been time for literary study. It was never the right time for it. Literary study always was, is now, and always will be untimely. Literature is a name for that component in whatever medium or mode that is incapable of being rationalized in any form of collective institutionalized pragmatically valuable study in the university, whether in the old Cold War university or in the new global university with new departmental configurations now coming into being. This means that "literary study" is an oxymoron. What this oxymoron names will continue to take place, whenever it does, if it does, in odd moments stolen from more practical concerns, such as making California competitive in the global economy. That is the goal stated for the nine-campus University of California system by its president, Richard Atkinson. Literary study's time is always up. It will survive as it has always survived, as a ghostly revenant, as a somewhat embarrassing or alarming spectral visitant at the feast of reason. Literature is a series of potholes on the Information Superhighway, of black holes in the Internet Galaxy. Nevertheless, though there's never time, though it's never the time, these holes, potholes or black holes, "literature" as survivor, as a feature of absolute singularity within any cultural forms in whatever medium, will continue to demand urgently to be "studied," here and now, within whatever new institutional and departmental configurations we devise and within whatever new regime of telecommunications we inhabit.

Comparative Literature as a discipline is caught at this moment between Scylla and Charybdis, two alternatives almost equally problematic. One choice is to move, as is widely happening now, back to "world literature" (or "World Literature Today") as a paradigm. I think this move is inevitable and in itself all to the good. Partly as a response to the new telecommunications and globalization, many new courses are springing up called "World Literature," usually at the undergraduate level. What starts as a trend in undergraduate courses, however, will soon begin to deflect graduate preparation. Someone with authority and training has to teach those courses in world lit.

The problems with this trend are easy to see. It is unlikely that anyone will ever be competent in "world literature"—that is, know enough languages, literatures, and cultures to be competent in all the literatures of the world, even just the so-called "major" ones. The most likely form such courses will take, even if they are taught by people who have the best will in the world, is a selection of old or new chestnuts, taught in English translation by people who do not know all the original languages. To represent Chinese "literature," for example, by selections from The Dream of the Red Chamber (The Story of the Stone) and a handful of lyrics from Classics of poetry would be like representing English literature by several scenes from Hamlet plus a few short poems by Wordsworth. The synecdochic ratio is too large. So much is represented by so little that it is hardly representative at all. Stephen Owen's admirable Anthology of Chinese Literature: Beginnings to 1911 (Norton, 1996) is twelve hundred pages long and is still controversial both in the choices made and in the translations themselves.

Moreover, with the best will in the world, courses in "world literature," in the West at least, are almost certain to be Eurocentric or United States-centric, partly because they are taught in English, thereby perpetuating, however inadvertently, the ideological assumption that anything can be translated, more or less without loss, into English, partly because the concepts about literature and reading that underlie courses in world literature are almost certain to be Eurocentric. The notion of "literature," as we know it in the West, is an overdetermined, historically conditioned concept, hardly more than two or three hundred years old. It is not even appropriate for so-called Renaissance literature, much less for Greek tragedy. The Chinese, it might be argued, have never had "literature" in just our sense, nor are the protocols for reading Wordsworth and Classics of Poetry the same. These differences are not trivial or superficial. The journal in which this essay is appearing is devoted to confronting all these problems and to dealing with them in the most productive way possible.

The Charybdis for the new global Comparative Literature raises equal problems. This would consist of adding specialists, say, in Chinese or Japanese or Arabic or subcontinental Indian literature to those specialists in European and American languages and literatures who make up most departments of Comparative literature. The problems with this are easy to see. The old Eurocentric Comparative Literature made sense as a discipline because graduate dissertation committees, for example, could be made up of professors all presumed to be competent in all the languages and literatures covered in the dissertation. The situation is different when, as is often the case nowadays, the committee is made up, for example, of several professors who know European languages but not Chinese, plus one specialist in Chinese. The latter is more likely to know European languages and methodologies than the former are likely to know anything about Chinese culture or literature or language, but the old rule that all the committee members have at least minimum competence in all of the work covered in the dissertation is broken in such cases. The methodologies employed in such cases, moreover, the "literary theory" presupposed, are likely to remain determinedly European or North American. In the long run, the new global Comparative Literature is in danger of becoming, despite the goodwill of its practitioners, just one more example of U.S. intellectual imperialism, its domination of the new processes of globalization through making English a universal language.

What is to be done to avoid these bad alternatives? I shall, in conclusion, make ten suggestions for a new global Comparative Literature in the form of aphorisms, not presented in any particular causal or dialectical order, but pell-mell, though they are interconnected. Each demands some commentary.

1. It is better to read and teach *The Dream of the Red Chamber* in translation than not to read it at all.

2. All texts should be read and taught in their original languages.

3. The question of translation is the central problematic in global Comparative Literature.

4. These first three assertions mean that if there are to be courses in world literature, they should be team taught, even if entirely in translation, by those who, in each case, are expert in the language, literature, and culture of the original text. By calling attention to problems of translation, such teachers can entice students, some students at least, to study the original languages. Comparative Literature will therefore be more and more

the guardian and justifier of foreign-language study within departments organized by nation states is conspicuously weakening, for example by being amalgamated, absurdly, into one single "Department of Foreign Languages."

5. Comparative Literature, though it is not a social science and will destroy itself if it becomes one, should nevertheless learn from the social sciences, especially anthropology. One thing it can learn is the responsibility to acquire, by hook or by crook, the languages of the cultures studied, however exotic or out of the way they may be. The institutionalized protocols of anthropology show this can be done.

6. Cultural studies in the humanities are a temporary, though necessary and inevitable, stage on the way to new forms of global Comparative Literature.

7. A major error of Comparative Literature as traditionally institutionalized has been to accept more or less at face value the traditional organization of literary study according to the presumed separateness and monolithic unity of nation-states and their literatures. Comparative Literature has, for example, compared Bulgarian with Outer Mongolian literature as if each of those were a homogeneous monolingual entity. One advance made by cultural studies has been to recognize that each nation-state tends to be endlessly subdivided within itself, to be multilingual, multicultural, multiethnic, hybridized. Comparative Literature must become a form of "glocalization," intranational and local as well as transnational. It must compare different literatures in different languages within a given nation-state as well as bring non-European countries within the space of comparison. The new American Studies is actually a branch of Comparative Literature.

8. All texts should be read on their own terms—that is, with language derived from the text itself and according to methodologies of reading and assumptions about literature derived from the culture in which the text was originally embedded. Chinese "literature" should be read in the light of Chinese "poetics," not have Western theory imposed on it, as I am doing at this moment by using the words *literature* and *poetics*.

9. Eclecticism in methodology and critical theory is a hideous vice in Comparative Literature. No good work was ever done by someone pretending to be a Bakhtinian or a Marxist or a deconstructionist. The imposture will be instantly un-

masked. You must do Comparative Literature with your whole heart. A critical methodology or particular habit of reading is a vocation. No sane man or woman can have more than one vocation at a time, any more than he or she can have more than one beloved at a time.

10. Though a given critical theory or methodology is universalizable, able to be appropriated by others, institutionalized, and translated, what is most valuable in a given critic or scholar is a distinctive tone or note that is unique to him or her and cannot be successfully imitated. This means that other critics should be read as literature, with the same care, the same attention to detail. Any critic not worth such careful reading is not worth reading. It is better to spend one's time reading primary works in their original languages. In fact, that is better *tout court*.

J. Hillis Miller, Summer 2000

Exile: Multiculturalism as Stimulant

For a writer who chose exile, multiculturalism is manifest not only in his desires but also in his everyday life. For almost twenty years I have lived in Paris, another sphere of language and culture. My everyday language is French. My newspaper is French. For that matter, a large part of my reading is in French. Even my marriage is French. French translations of my books circulate, such that I receive letters from my French readers, and French authors, some of whom are young and unknown, send me their books. French students write about me. The desk clerk at the police station recognizes me as a well-known Parisian writer simply from my name. Nevertheless, I remain a German-language author. I could characterize myself as a Parisian writer of Swiss descent who writes in German.

Accordingly, my two- to threefold literary affiliation could certainly be called multicultural. I suppose that multiculturalism has surreptitiously found its way into my language, as a stylistic agent.

The French cultural component expresses itself, purely from a superficial perspective, in books and texts that could only grow in French or, better yet, Parisian soil. I am referring to the novel *Das Fahr der Liebe* (1981), the capriccio *Im Bauch des Wals* (1989), the Parisian journal *Die Innenseite des Mantels,* and larger essays such as "Exkurs über die französische Frau" (1982) or "Im dunklen Erdteil von Paris: Der Rassismus in dir selber" (1984), both of which were published in the collection *Über den Tag und durch die Fahre: Essays, Nachrichten, Depeschen* (1991).

I am indebted to Paris for the aforementioned texts, or even to my bicultural situation, just as I am indebted to Rome for my first longer work, *Canto* (1963), and to Barcelona for the novella *Untertauchen* (1972). I am indebted to cities for everything, even my book *Im Hause enden die Geschichten* (1971), which is lodged within my childhood in Bern. The exception is *Stolz* (1975), a book which I venture to label German: it takes place in the cryptic, fairy-tale landscape of the Spessart Forest.

When I use the word *indebted,* I am not simply implying local color, scenery, or ambience. I mean something archeological in the sense that I have come upon gold mines or graves in these places, which allow me to excavate elements of my own continent and make them existentially and literarily fruitful. These named cities and places have released creative forces and made possible confrontations that pertain to nothing less than a rebirth. I consider Rome to be my literary birthplace. I reflected on this in my 1985 lecture on poetics, "Am Schreiben gehen."

I place myself elsewhere in order to discover a deeper meaning within myself.

If I allude to archeology or, better still, "self-archeology" in the context of foreign places, I am then obligated to entertain the idea of autobiography. Instead of "autobiography" I prefer to speak of "autofiction." I once defined myself as "a fiction writer who passes through the autobiographical station." I am writing *to* myself of a lost life. I.

As I see it, the self is hardly a neglected zone, but rather a through station with thousands of trains that pass through me, the station. The self is an intersection. A greatly riddled self. Dovecote, battlefield, sealing wax: not to preserve a clearcut possession or to place it on a pedestal, but rather to lure a wealth of unfamiliar things into the net of language. Where hope or inclination persists, a genuinely plundered self is able to intone something like the sound of a saga.

But where can the self be riddled, saturated, and charged, if not in the city? I am and have always been a denizen of the city. The city is like a foreign place. Foreign places are nowhere so extravagant, so unyielding, and ultimately so incomprehensibly present as in the big city. For someone who could call himself at best a specialist in the art of experiencing but never a settler in the state of reality, there is no more suitable a place than the city. As in a power failure, darkness threatens if this experiencing is absent. He must therefore stir up his experience and transform his sympathy into high spirits. He can manage this in the city. To rub oneself along its flanks is to come alive.

City. It is the most profound clarification of life, the turmoil of life. It is the most complex condensation of reality and memory, a hermetic poem. And the most luminescent sum of a conceivable, no, unimaginable present, an anarchic sound. It is a synonym of foreignness, foreignness as an enticement. It is the foreign lover who cannot be conquered, who can never be possessed—close but never within reach. It is a bewitchment. It is the blackmailer who loosens your tongue. An object of incessant desires. Predominance. Eternity. Its walls ransom your memories.

The condition of being a foreigner within the city coincides with a life-style that I call nomadic or urban and vagrant. To be constantly on the move by means of public transportation or by foot keeps the foreigner's gaze fresh and assures a certain amazement or even fright at life, the creative challenge.

The underlying scheme is being on the move. The most important factor: the friction that produces the linguistic sparks, shreds of language, images. It is a patchwork of details, small islands of language as scraps of reality.

The corporeality of the event: every day is an experience at the front, placing oneself on the line, commitment. The creative process has its physical syncopation, above all its existential quality.

The narrating "I" in my metropolitan books is, among other things, a city tramp, a marcher—not to be confused with a dawdler who loiters pleasurably and who is out to feast his eyes. No, my city ramblers are not seeking culture or education. They are looking for the torrential downpour, if not the deluge, a kind of great inundation; they are looking for the crisis that leaves them speechless until a survival instinct drives them in the space of a minute to the surface, where the flame of consciousness or cognizance leaps upward and illuminates their vantage point—something that has just as much to do with the world as with one's own self. Cognizance can be compared, for instance, to a flying fish. The fish would be the freed, liberated word. The city ramblers pursue the words and sentences. Every sentence must be a so-called homecomer who could survive the war.

Running around is a form of participation. My marchers could ultimately have neither real access nor a picture of the city; but still they are able to have a part of the city, if they constantly insinuate themselves within it.

According to my marchers there is no insight, only the transition of foreignness into another galaxy that permits them to be in tune with a premonition of insight. Insight, in the definitive sense of the word, be-comes suspected of being unsettled knowledge, like a possession that turns out to be merely a possession of power. Instead of knowledge and insight, the physical provocation of authentically experienced existence. Instead of having, participating. Should I say: coexistence?

My marchers have no clear history and identifiable past. They see themselves as a throng among many. Sometimes they collectively look for themselves in the city like street people, in that they set themselves apart and receive shares or interest thrown back by the city. In their thoughts they could assemble from these scraps an actual figure or at least the beginnings of one. If they should chase after themselves, they would chase after a longing for authenticity. The hope would be to come to one's senses at last. They are in their awkward way creators of the self—autobiographical fiction writers. Above all, they would like to be born into this world. "I want to come into the world" goes the battle cry of my protagonists in the early work *Canto.*

Every truly large city that earns the title "metropolis" contains the world in its hotchpotch. Paris is the French capital, but in its anarchic everyday life it still reflects, alongside the European spectrum, northern and southern Africa and many parts of the Middle East. Every metropolis is a multicultural entity. In my own urbomanic inclination too, the longing for a multicultural polyphony remains. I am sure of it. My childhood served as godfather to this desire. All this is prefigured in childhood.

I was born and grew up in Bern. My father, however, was an immigrant from Russia who married a woman from Bern. It is true that my childhood acquaintances were residents of Bern, but equally important were two Parisian aunts. The one, a great-aunt, lived with us in her old age, and the other, whom I visited at a young age, lived in Paris. Extremely important were the children of Italian and Spanish guest workers, with whom I attended school and played dodgeball in the streets. During school vacations spent with my uncle in the country I saw the interned Polish troops and the mounted North African soldiers march and ride out. As an adolescent I was an internment assistant; I helped house and delouse refugees, including Italian partisans. In our family guesthouse there were foreign students, even Americans. My education was not much different than that of German schoolchildren—I mean, as it had been before the Nazis. I was molded by a humanistic secondary school, but was influenced equally as much by the early Parisian images I absorbed and by an Italian mentality.

After graduation there were the first trips to Italy—in hindsight it is an experienced neorealistic film. There was an extended academic stay in Munich, and my first marriage to a German minister's daughter, which lasted many years and led me to German landscapes and relationships. There was an interim year in Rome. There was a life-threatening Spanish chapter. There was a series of sojourns in London that together would have added up to a two-year stay. There were periods in Berlin and several in the United States. And there is the almost twenty-year-old address in Paris that I would consider as my definitive territory. There is a French wife and a young son born in Paris, who, unlike his father, holds French citizenship.

As a writer I do not play on any national team. I am neither a provincial writer nor a business representative affixed to any national backdrop. My artistic pastureland is divided among many places and nations, and it sneers at the border- or customs-station barrier. And the flag, had I one to hoist, could be emblazoned with a thirst for life and global love.

As mentioned, prior to Paris I lived in Germany, Italy, Spain, London, and elsewhere, but naturally the longest in Switzerland. And I have evoked corresponding experiences in my books. Yet these books have nothing to do with travel literature. I am not a traveler. I am one who passes through stations. I would like to plunk myself down elsewhere and then sponge off that foreign place, but also be invigorated by it. What prods me is the foreign locale as stimulant, everything that is triggered by the shock of being foreign. The self-mobilization connected with this can turn out to be a kind of reincarnation.

After the first shock in a foreign place, I often have the perplexing impression that I have already been there. Where does this impression come from? And the ability not only to communicate with a foreigner despite the linguistic, national, and cultural differences, but also to sense a certain kinship? Obviously, we are not made solely from the stuff of our homeland, but from everything else as well.

Why should we, for example, be able to deal spontaneously with African sculpture and Incan art no less than with a Michelangelo or a Goya without collecting any further knowledge, unless the appropriate sounding-board were already inside us? Strangers bring us together with all sorts of cultures and other capillary systems; we are closely united with everyone and can learn this at first hand, if we put ourselves in a foreign place. Only then can the shock from a confrontation rouse the foreignness that is stored or buried within us all. We consist of nothing more than Trojan horses that are stacked inside one another, smuggled goods, and we can readily communicate with one another on the human level.

Long ago, when I was in Sumatra, I met an old man who was believed to have been a cannibal in his younger days. He did not come across as either repulsive or even especially exotic. Rather, he somehow seemed familiar to me, possibly because he reminded me of an old and rather boring acquaintance from Bern.

While the search for the foreign conforms to my artistic stipulation, my passion all the while is the present. The practice of writing would be the fore-grounding of the present. Instead of homeland, the present. If I am entirely of the present, I am alive or in this world. What does the homeland matter to me? Everything can be considered to be homeland. It becomes a linguistic homeland. In the context of cultural affiliation, does this sound like the making of the global village? I hope not. I would say that I hopefully belong to my time; I am a contemporary. One who declares oneself as a contemporary could thereby assume that this title is befitting, because one would have acquired a suitable contemporary consciousness and thereby would have become an authority. That is not the case with me. I would maintain that, according to my condition and my hopes and wishes, I am, to use the words of Elias Canetti, "a dog of my time."

Paul Nizon, Summer 1995, translated by Richard Langston

The Liberal Tradition

If I were to allow only my feelings to speak, these words would be a long and interminable expression of gratitude. But my emotion is not blind. I am well aware that the symbolic act of this event is more real than the fleeting reality of my person. I am hardly an episode in the history of our literature, the transitory and fortuitous incarnation of a moment of the Spanish tongue. The Cervantes Prize, when it is awarded to this or that writer of our language, without distinction of nationality, affirms each year the reality of our literature. And what is a literature? It is not a collection of authors and books, but rather a society of works. The novels, the poems, the stories, the plays and the essays are converted into works through the creative collaboration of the readers. A work becomes a work thanks to the reader. It becomes an instantaneous monument perpetually erected and perpetually demolished, for it is subject to the criticism of time: the successive generations of readers. A work is created by the conjunction of author and reader; hence literature is a society within society, a community of works that simultaneously creates a public of readers and is re-created by those readers.

It is said that ideologies, classes, economic structures, technology and the sciences, by nature international, are the basic and determining realities of history. The theme is as old as historical reflection itself, and I cannot dwell on it. I find nevertheless that the beliefs, the myths, the customs and the traditions of each social group are equally as determinant, if not more so. The Cervantes Prize with justification reminds us that the language we speak is a reality no less decisive than the ideas we profess or the profession we practice. To say the word *language* is to say *civilization:* a community of values, symbols, customs, beliefs, visions, questions about the past, the present and the future. When we speak we not only speak with those who are present with us; we speak with the dead and with the trees, the cities, the rivers, the animals and things. We speak with the animate world and with the inanimate, with the visible and with the invisible. We speak with ourselves. To speak is to live with others, to live in a world that is this world and worlds to come, this time and other times: a civilization.

Since I was very young I have had an intense feeling of belonging to civilization. I owe this to my grandfather Ireneo Paz, a lover of books who managed to accumulate a small library which contained many of the fine writers of our language. I must have been about sixteen years of age when I read the first two series of the *Episodios Nacionales,* which contain perhaps some of the best writings of Pérez Galdós. It was an edition in octavo with gilded covers and illustrated by various artists of the time; the ten volumes were printed between 1881 and 1885 in Madrid by La Guirnalda. That novelized and novelistic history of modern Spain struck me as being my own history as well as that of my country. When I had reached the second series, the figure of Salvador Monsalud captivated me immediately. He became my hero, my prototype. My identification with the young liberal led me to confront his half-brother and his adversary, the terrible Carlos Garrote, a Carlist guerrilla: a dualism that was both real and symbolic, the legitimate son and the illegitimate son, the watchdog of order and the vagabond, the man of the land and the cosmopolitan, the conservative and the revolutionary. But Carlos Garrote, as the reader little by little realizes, is not only the adversary who is the incarnation of the other Spain, the Spain of religion and of arrogance; he is also Salvador Monsalud's double. In the final episode, "One More Rebel and Fewer Monks," a gloomy picture of the two Spains and their opposite and symmetrical fanaticisms, we are present at the death and transfiguration of Carlos Garrote. He began as the enemy and the persecutor of Salvador Monsalud: he ends as Monsalud's brother and protégé: they are condemned to live as one. Each of them is the other and is the same. I discovered then that in all of us there dwells an adversary

Octavio Paz (*Gil Jain*)

and that to struggle with him is to struggle with oneself. That struggle, no longer personal but rather social, has been the substance of the history of our countries during the past two centuries. Thus I learned that a civilization is not an immutable essence always identical to itself; it is a society inhabited by discord and possessed by the desire to restore unity, a mirror in which, in contemplating ourselves, we lose ourselves, and in losing ourselves, find ourselves.

Many times I have thought about the Hispanic-American parallels to Salvador Monsalud. Even though some of these figures belong to history and others to fiction, all of them, real or imaginary, fought and are still fighting against obstacles that Galdós's hero never dreamed of. For example, apart from confronting Carlos Garrote, an ungovernable and wild guerrilla, the incarnation of a past sometimes obtuse and at other times sublime, the Mexican Salvador Monsaluds have had to struggle against other realities and to exorcise other phantoms: Spain and Mexico have different pasts. In our history there appears an element unknown in that of Spain: the world of the Indian. It is a dimension of my country at once both intimate and inscrutable, familiar and unknown. Without it we would not be what we are. The existence of Islam and Judaism in medieval Spain could give us an idea of what the Indian presence signifies in the conscience of Mexicans, a presence that is not outside us, facing us, but rather within us. Yet there is a fundamental difference: Islam and Judaism are, like Christianity, variants of monotheism; Meso-American civilization, however, came into being and developed without any contact with the Old World. The same can be said of Incan Peru. The Indian world was, from the beginning, the "other" world in the strongest sense of the word: "otherness," which for us Mexicans resolves itself in identity; distance, which is proximity.

The appearance of America with its great exotic civilizations radically modified the dialogue of Hispanic civilization with itself. It introduced an element of uncertainty, so to speak, which since that time has challenged our imagination and questioned our identity. The Indian presence tells us that man is an unpredictable creature, that he is a double being. In other Hispanic-American nations the agents of displacement and transformation of the dialogue were the nomads, the blacks, the geography. Instead of "another" history, as in Peru and in Mexico, it was the absence of any history. From its origin Spain was the land of shifting frontiers, and its last great frontier was America. Because of this and through this, Spain borders on the unknown: America or the vastness, lands without people, distances without names, coasts that look toward Asia and Oceania, civilizations that know nothing of Christianity but have discovered the Zero—diverse forms of the unlimited.

The diversity of their pasts and of their interlocutors always provokes two contradictory temptations: dispersion and centralization. At one extreme our countries have suffered fragmentation, as in Central America and the Antilles, and at the other extreme have encountered rigid centralism, as in Castile and Mexico. Dispersion culminates in dissipation; centralization, in petrification. A double threat: become air or turn into stone. For two centuries we sought the difficult balance between freedom and authority, centralism and disintegration. The temper of our tradition has not been very favorable to these efforts for reform. The eighteenth century, the century of criticism and the first since pagan antiquity to prize once more the intellectual virtues of tolerance, did not have in the Hispanic world the brilliance possessed by the sixteenth and seventeenth centuries. An example of the persistence of authoritarian attitudes and tendencies concealed by liberal opinions is found precisely in the aforementioned concluding pages of Galdós. A character known for the fervor

of his liberal sentiments maintains without blinking an eye that "all Spaniards ought to embrace the banner of liberty and accept the progress of the century. . .; if not everyone wishes to follow this path, the rebels ought to be driven to do so by force, and in order to carry this out it would be a good idea for the free to arm themselves and organize a militia." This curious liberal was a devotee of Rousseau, he of the omnipotence of "the general will," a democratic mask of Jacobean tyranny. Armed with a general theory of freedom, Carlos Garrote enters the twentieth century. He has changed his mode of dress but not his soul: he no longer intimidates his adversary with worn-out scholastic syllogisms; but rather with wave upon wave of dialectics. New chimeras absorb his thoughts, but the smell of blood continues to fascinate him. He has leaped from the Inquisition to the Committee for Public Safety without changing his location.

The moment freedom becomes an absolute, it ceases to be freedom: its true name is despotism. Freedom is not a general system of explaining the universe and mankind. Neither is it a philosophy: it is an act both irrevocable and instantaneous, which consists of selecting one possibility among many. There is no general theory of freedom, nor can there be, since freedom is an affirmation of what in each one of us is unique and personal, something that cannot be reduced to any generalization. Better said, each of us is a singular and unique creature, with the result that freedom becomes tyranny as soon as we try to impose it upon others. When the Bolsheviks dissolved the Russian Constituent Assembly in the name of liberty, Rosa Luxemburg told them: "Freedom of opinion is always the freedom of that person who does not think as we do." Freedom which begins by the affirmation of my uniqueness becomes the recognition of the other person and of other people: their freedom is the condition of my freedom. Robinson Crusoe is not really free on his island, even though there is no other will opposing him and no one constrains him: his freedom unfolds in a vacuum. The freedom of the solitary is similar to the solitude of the despot, teeming with specters. For freedom to be realized, it must incarnate and confront another consciousness and another will: the other person is simultaneously the limit and the source of my freedom. At one extreme freedom is singularity and exception; at the other it is plurality and coexistence. Because of all this, even though freedom and democracy are not equivalent terms, they are complementary: without freedom, democracy is despotism; without democracy, freedom is a chimera.

The union of freedom and democracy has been the great achievement of modern societies. A precarious, fragile achievement disfigured by many injustices and horrors, it is likewise an extraordinary achievement and has something of the accidental and miraculous about it. Other civilizations had no acquaintance with democracy, and in our civilization only a few nations, during limited periods, have enjoyed free institutional systems. At this very time, in the vast expanses of the American continents, many of the nations using our tongue suffer under iniquitous powers. Freedom is as precious as water; and like water, if we do not protect it, it is spilled, it escapes from us and dissipates. I have alluded to the relative poverty of our eighteenth century, which gave rise to the political philosophy of the modern age. Nevertheless in our past—both of the Spaniard and of the Hispanic-American—there exist uses, customs and institutions which are the well-springs of freedom, sometimes buried but still alive. For freedom to take root in our lands, we would have to reconcile these ancient traditions with modern political thought. But for a few timid and isolated attempts, we have done nothing. I deplore this: the task is one not of historical piety but of political imagination.

The word *liberal* appears early in our literature, not as an idea or as a philosophy, but as a humor or disposition of the soul; rather than an ideology, it was a virtue. When I say this, I turn to Cervantes, the writer of ours who incarnates most completely the different meanings of the word *liberal*. With him begins the modern novel, the literary genre of a society which since its inception has identified itself and its history with criticism. Dante's *Commedia* is the reflection of a world governed by analogy: that is to say, by the correspondence between this world and the world hereafter. The *Quijote* is a work animated by the contrary principle, irony, which is the rupture of correspondence and which emphasizes with a smile the fissure between the real and the ideal. Criticism of the absolute begins with Cervantes: freedom begins. And it begins with a smile, not of pleasure, but of wisdom. Man is a precarious being, complex, double or triple, inhabited by phantoms, spurred on by appetites, consumed by desires: a marvelous and lamentable spectacle. Each individual is a unique being, and each individual is resembles every other individual. Each individual is unique, and each individual is many individuals whom he does not know: the "I" is plural. Cervantes smiles: to learn to be free is to learn to smile.

Octavio Paz, Autumn 1982, translated by Lowell Dunham

Ed. Note: "The Liberal Tradition" was delivered by Paz at Alcalá de Henares, Spain (the birthplace of Cervantes), in April 1982 before King Juan Carlos upon acceptance of the 1982 Cervantes Prize, the Spanish-speaking world's highest literary acco-

lade. The Spanish text was published in several periodicals, including the 28 April edition of the weekly *ABC Internacional* of Madrid, on which our translation is based. This is the first authorized English-language publication of the text.

Barthes and the Zero Degree of Genre

J'aime le romanesque, mais je sais que le roman est mort.

▨ ROLAND BARTHES[1]

It is a commonplace that the central influence of contemporary French writing on our own is in the domain of theory. For every American student who has heard of, let alone read, say, Yves Bonnefoy or Michel Deguy, there are a hundred, perhaps a thousand, who have some familiarity with Derrida, Foucault, and Lacan. Again, although we still have no authoritative English translation of Blaise Cendrars, the translations of Michel Serres, Pierre Macherey, Julia Kristeva, and the Deleuze-Guittari *Anti-Oedipe* are to be found in every university bookshop. Roland Barthes, whose presence in our literature is the subject of my paper, is one of the bestselling authors published by the commercial house of Farrar, Straus & Giroux.

On the face of it, this homage to French theory at the expense of new French novels or poems may seem faintly absurd. All of us have occasionally sighed—or have friends who have sighed—at the notion of the student or colleague who has read *S/Z* but not Balzac, *Sur Racine* but not *Phèdre*, *Glas* but not Genet. Yet the rapt attention devoted to these seemingly secondary works by a large literary audience suggests that something else may be happening. *S/Z* may well have less value as a commentary on Balzac, let alone as a methodological model (and I find appalling the slavish taking over of the Barthes codes—hermeneutic, symbolic, proairetic—in solemn articles in *PMLA* or *ELH*), than as an obsessive, highly stylized and personal meditation on the nature of the reading process and its attendant desires, a meditation somewhat in the vein of Richard Burton's *Anatomy of Melancholy*. In order to understand why a writer like Barthes has been so influential, we must begin by dispensing with our conventional notions of genre, stop dividing our literary Gaul into three parts called poetry, fiction, and drama, with "criticism" as a secondary discourse mediating between "imaginative" writing and its public.

"J'aime le romanesque, mais je sais que le roman est mort." Asked in a 1975 interview what he meant by this distinction, Barthes replied:

The novelistic is a mode of discourse unstructured by a story [*une histoire*]; a mode of notation, investment, interest in daily reality, in people, in everything that happens in life. The transformation of this novelistic material into a novel seems very difficult to me because I can't imagine myself elaborating a narrative object where there would be a story, which to me means essentially verbs in the imperfect and past historic, characters who are psychologically believable—that's the sort of thing I could never do, that's why the novel seems impossible to me. (INT, 222–23; *GV,* 210)

And again, he tells Stephen Heath of his longing for "the novelistic without the novel, the novelistic without its characters: a writing of life, which could perhaps rejoin a certain moment of my own life" (INT, 130; *GV,* 124).

Why is Barthes, himself such a brilliant commentator on Balzacian "character" or Racinean "plot," so opposed to the very notion of *fictionality?* We can interpret his predilection for "work[ing] *in* the signifier" as the next step beyond the *nouveau roman,* which had already posited an inability to "invent" coherent psychological characters and plot structures. However, whereas Robbe-Grillet and Sarraute still maintain the "fiction" that there is a story to be told and that this story involves invented persons, explicitly distinguished from the author himself or herself, Barthes wants to create a "novelistic" texture that is no longer "dominated by the superego of continuity, a superego of evolution, history, [and] filiation" (INT, 132; *GV,* 126).

By the same token, but somewhat more puzzlingly in view of his absorption in the nuances of language, Barthes has little taste for the modernist lyric poem. Indeed, one of the anomalies of Barthes's oeuvre is that, given his interest in such diverse texts as those of Sade and Fourier, Flaubert and the Goethe of *Werther,* and in such diverse media as photography and film, landscape design and architecture, he has paid almost no attention to poetry. Evidently, as the brief discussion of modern poetry in *Le degré zéro de la littérature* (1953) suggests, Barthes is suspicious of the symbolist claim for poetry as autonomous language, above and beyond nature.

> Under each Word in modern poetry there lies a sort of existential geology, in which is gathered the total content of the Name. . . . The Word is no longer guided *in advance* by the socialized discourse; the consumer of poetry, deprived of the guide of selective connections, encounters the Word frontally, and receives it as an absolute quantity, accompanied by all its possible associations. The Word . . . therefore achieves a state which is possible only in the dictionary or in poetry—places where the noun can live without its article—and is reduced to a sort of zero degree. . . . This Hunger of the Word, common

to the whole of modern poetry, makes poetic speech terrible and in-human.[2]

Terrible and inhuman in its overdetermination of the sign. "Contemporary poetry," writes Barthes in *Mythologies* (1957), "is *a regressive semiological system . . .* [in that] it attempts to regain an infra-signification, a pre-semiological state of language; in short, it tries to transform the sign back into meaning; its ideal, ultimately, would be to to reach not the meaning of words, but the meaning of things themselves."[3]

The Barthean paradox is thus that, even as nonfictional narrative may be more "novelistic" than the novel, so prose has the capacity to be more "poetic" than poetry. Whereas modern poetry has the "essentialist ambition" of trying to "actualize the potential of the signified in the hope of at last reaching something like the transcendent quality of the thing," it is *prose* that is the language of arbitrary rather than motivated signs, the language of what Barthes calls "open-work meaning" (*M,* 132). To put it another way: whereas poetry, in its modernist form, "wants to be an anti-language" (*M,* 133), "ordinary" prose—say, a fashion article in *Elle* or an advertisement for the new Citroën model—can provide the imaginative reader with any number of "poetic" possibilities.

The aim is not, of course, to replace Balzac and Mallarmé with Citroën ads. To find the "poetic" outside the lyric poem, the novelistic outside the novel, Barthes turns to such models as Japan—a Japan, one should note, that is less a real country with such and such attributes than, in Barthes's own words, "my Japan, a system of signs I call Japan" (INT, 82; *GV,* 82), a locus that, as Barthes puts it in *L'empire des signes* (1970), is characterized by "the ethic of the *empty sign.*"

> Japan offers the example of a civilization where the articulation of the sign is extremely delicate, sophisticated, where nothing is left to the non-sign; but this semantic level, expressed in the extraordinary finesse with which the signifier is treated, in a way means nothing, says nothing: it doesn't refer to any signified, especially not to any ultimate signified, and thus for me it expresses the utopia of a world both strictly semantic and strictly atheistic. (INT, 83; *GV,* 82)

The emblem of this utopia is the Japanese house, a dwelling that is "delightful" in that "it can be emptied-out, un-furnished, de-centered, dis-oriented, dis-originated" (INT, 87; *GV,* 85).

Such dis-orienting is central to Barthes's own verbal structures. Questioned about his fondness for the haiku, Barthes replies: "I have long had a taste for discontinuous writing, a tendency reactivated in *Roland*

Barthes. . . . My mode of writing [is] never lengthy, always proceeding by fragments, miniatures, paragraphs with titles, or articles. . . . The implication from the point of view of an ideology or a counter-ideology of form is that the fragment breaks up what I would call the smooth finish, the composition, discourse constructed to give a final meaning to what one says" (INT, 209; *GV,* 198). In the preface to the appropriately titled *Fragments d'un discours amoureux* (1977), Barthes explains that "no logic links the figures (i.e. the incidents or schema in the book), determines their contiguity: the figures are non-syntagmatic, non-narrative, they are Erinyes; they stir, collide, subside, return, vanish with no more order than the flight of mosquitoes."[4] The lover's discourse can only be horizontal: "no transcendence, no deliverance, no novel (though a great deal of the fictive)" (*LD,* 7; *FDA,* 11). How does the nonfictional "fictive" manifest itself? In "L'empire des signes" everything depends upon the processes of dis-ordering and dis-continuing—what Barthes calls *arthrologie.*

> At every moment of my life, wherever I go, even walking in the street, when I think, react, I constantly find myself on the side of thought that grapples with what is discontinuous and combinatory. Today, for example, I was reading a text by Brecht, admirable, as always, a text on Chinese painting, in which he says that Chinese painting puts things next to each other, side by side with each other. That's a very simple way of putting it, but very beautiful, and quite true, and what I want, after all, is precisely to feel the juxtaposition of things, the "next to" [*l'à côté de*]. (INT, 132; *GV,* 125–26)

Let us consider how this "next to," this "à côté de," works in a text like *Roland Barthes par Roland Barthes.*[5] In the frontispiece we read, "It must all be considered as if spoken by a character in a novel." This "novel," however, begins with a scrapbook of captioned family photographs, a series of childhood images that, as the author tells us, are at once disturbingly familiar and yet seem to portray an unfamiliar other, "whose units are teeth, hair, a nose, skinniness, long legs in knee-length socks which don't belong to me, though to no one else." What Barthes calls "the fissure in the subject" is thus immediately introduced, for who is Roland Barthes? Is he the little boy held by his mother in the first unnumbered photograph, which is labeled "La demande d'amour"? Was his consciousness shaped by "Bayonne, ville parfaite," by the two Proustian grandmothers, by the father, "mort tres tôt (à la guerre)"?

The possibility of finding narrative or psychological continuity in these photographs is precluded by the introduction of a series of *dictées* (dictations), commentaries on given photographs that take the form of

schoolboy exercises, written, says Barthes, "the way we were taught to write" (INT, 210). So the *dictée* called "Les trois jardins," facing the photograph of the family house, begins as follows:

> That house was something of an ecological wonder: anything but large, set on one side of a considerable garden, it looked like a toy model (the faded gray of its shutters merely reinforced this impression). With the modesty of a chalet, yet there was one door after another, and French windows, and outside staircases, like a castle in a story.

The effect of such *dictées,* interspersed in the text, is a kind of Brechtian *Verfremdung* (and Brecht was, we know, one of Barthes's idols). How can the reader identify with an autobiographer who writes (if indeed it is "he" who writes) such set dictations? Or with an autobiographer who provides us with a photograph of himself and a smiling young woman, seated in the grass and captions it with the words, "Where does this expression come from? Nature? Code?"

The "image-repertoire," in any case, gives way to writing with the coming of Barthes's adulthood. Now the possibility of "understanding" Roland Barthes, as the child of such and such parents, growing up in such and such a place and attending a particular lycée, is called into question by the series of fragments that constitute the rest of the book. These fragments are introduced by short titles arranged in alphabetical order, from the *A* of "Actif/réactif" to the *T* of "Le monstre de la totalité," a fragment that ends with the passage:

> Different discourse: this August 6, the countryside, the morning of a splendid day: sun, warmth, flowers, silence, calm, radiance. Nothing stirs, neither desire nor aggression; only the task is there, the work before me, like a kind of universal being: everything is full. Then that would be Nature? An absence . . . of the rest? Totality? (BBB, 180)

Of course the question is left open, the final page containing a pictograph called "La graphie pour rien" ("Doodling") and an illegible line of writing labeled ". . . ou le signifiant sans signifié."

Between *A* and *T* (notice that Barthes does not give us the expected *A* to *Z* sequence with its inevitable move toward closure), the fragments are arranged so as to "be kept from 'taking,' from solidifying" (*INT,* 210; *GV,* 198). Not that anarchy, Barthes is quick to point out, is the signified of the system. "The position," he explains, "is a bit paradoxical in relation to avant-garde style, but perhaps the best way to prevent this solidification is to pretend to remain within an apparently classical code, to keep the appearance of a writing subject to certain stylistic imperatives, and thus to attain the dissociation of an ultimate meaning through a form that is not spectacularly disorganized" (INT, 210, GV, 198).

By "apparently classical code," Barthes refers, of course, to the alphabetical order of titles, each followed by a paragraph or two of what seems to be commentary, as in a Commonplace Book. But consider the choice of the thirteen A titles: "Actif/réactif," "L'adjectif," "L'aise," "Le démon de l'analogie," "Au tableau noir," "L'argent," "Le vaisseau Argo," "L'arrogance," "Le geste de l'aruspice," "L'assentiment, non le choix," "Vérité et assertion," "L'atopie," "L'autonymie." No two are quite parallel: *actif* is an adjective, *l'adjectif* a noun. In the heading "Actif" the A is the first letter; in "L'adjectif" it follows the article. In "L'aise" it isn't sounded at all, and in the fourth title the A only appears in the fourth word. Again, some of the titles are abstractions ("Verité et assertion"), whereas others designate a specific place ("Au tableau noir") or a proper name ("Le vaisseau Argo"). The seemingly orderly sequence of parallel items is thus no more than a form of etiquette, as if to say that once these codes are established, the author can then do precisely as he pleases.

Consider what happens in a relatively long text under *F* called "Le cercle de fragments." It begins with an infinitive.

> Ecrire par fragments; les fragments sont alors des pierres sur le pourtour du cercle; je m'étale en rond: tout mon petit univers en miettes; au centre, quoi? (*BPB*, 96–97)

> To write by fragments; the fragments are then so many stones on the perimeter of a circle: I spread myself around: my whole little universe in crumbs; at the center, what? (*BBB*, 92–93)

But then the "I" whose universe is dispersed in little crumbs (*miettes*) becomes a "he": "His first, or nearly first text (1942) consists of fragments." A little narrative of Barthes's career follows—its Gidean beginnings, the lexias of *S/Z*, the fact that "he already regarded the wrestling match as a series of fragments"—and here the author pauses to cite himself in *Mythologies*. Here is the "novelistic" without the continuity of the "novel," the narrative that presents its subject from different pronominal perspectives and then, once removed, in his own earlier writings. In the fourth paragraph, however, narrative gives way to a rumination on the word.

> Not only is the fragment cut off from its neighbors, but even within each fragment parataxis reigns. This is clear if you make an index of these little pieces; for each of them, the assemblage of referents is heteroclite; it is like a parlor game: "Take the words: *fragment, circle, Gide, wrestling match, asyndeton, painting, discourse, Zen, inter-*

mezzo; make up a discourse which can link them together." And that would quite simply be this very fragment. The index of a text, then, is not only an instrument of reference; it is itself a text, a second text which is the *relief* (remainder and asperity) of the first: what is wandering (interrupted) in the rationality of the sentences.

Here Barthes's "parlor game" ("Jeu de bouts rimés") links together nine nouns that stand synecdochically for the whole: the "circle" of "fragments," first learned from Gide and observed in the "wrestling match"; the "figure of short-circuiting" which is "asyndeton" and which operates in the picture Barthes tries to paint (paragraph 5), wherein the "naïve" attempt to "connect detail to detail" leads to the most "unexpected 'conclusions'"; the "abrupt, separated, broken openings" of Zen (paragraph 7). (In Zen Buddhism, says Barthes, "the fragment [like the haiku] is *torin;* it implies an immediate delight: it is a fantasy of discourse.") This fantasy of "discourse" (the eighth word in Barthes's lyric string) can, says Barthes, come to you anywhere: "in the café, on the train, talking to a friend (it arises laterally to what he says or what I say); then you take out your notebook, to jot down not a 'thought' but something like a strike, what would once have been called a 'turn' (*un vers*)."

And indeed, the whole "circle of fragments" has now taken a lyric verse "turn." The last of Barthes's key words is *intermezzo,* and in paragraph 8 we read:

> The fragment is like the musical idea of a song cycle . . . each piece is self-sufficient and yet it is never anything but the interstice of its neighbors. . . . The man who has best understood and practiced the aesthetic of the fragment (before Webern) is perhaps Schumann; he called the fragment an "intermezzo"; he increased the intermezzi within his works as he went on composing: everything he produced was ultimately *intercalated:* but between what and what? What is the meaning of a pure series of interruptions?

The musical analogy leads into the coda of what is surely a poetic discourse, even if Barthes never allows it to "solidify" into the prose poem which is its intertext.

> The fragment has its ideal: a high condensation, not of thought, or of wisdom, or of truth (as in the Maxim), but of music: "development" would be countered by "tone," something articulated and sung, a diction: here it is *timbre* which should reign. Webern's *small pieces:* no cadence: with what sovereignty he *turns short!* (*BBB*, 94–95)

Note that the "small pieces" bring us back to the "universe in crumbs" of the opening paragraph, to the stones on the perimeter of the writer's circle. The "development" of the whole has been, as Barthes says of the Webern fragment, not one of thought or wisdom or truth, but of music; it is a "development" characterized by "a high condensation"—it "turns short."

To reach the conclusion of this particular section of *Barthes par lui-même* is to realize that the "circle of fragments" of the title has been not so much described or talked about as enacted. Barthes invents no characters or plot, yet the fragment is surely fictive, if not fictional, in its development. The speaking subject is dispersed in the circle of fragments; pronouns and tenses shift, abstraction alternates with image, and bits of narrative are *intercalated* into the meditative structure. The form of the whole is what Barthes calls "discontinuous and combinatory": the "juxtaposition of things," the "next to," creates a postmodern analogue to the definition poem or riddle. The prose, highly condensed, alliterative, and assonantal (e.g., "les pierres sur le pourtour du cercle"), mimes "le cercle des fragments," moving, as it does, from writing to reading to wrestling, from parlor game to painting to Zen koan, to the musical phrase. There are nine key words and nine paragraphs: in the ninth we read that the musical fragment has a "'tone,' something articulated and sung, a diction." And of course "diction" is Barthes's own domain.

One of the later fragments in *Barthes par Barthes* provides an interesting transition to some of the American texts I now want to talk about briefly. It is called "On le sait," which Richard Howard, in the Farrar, Straus edition, translates as "As we know."

> An apparently expletive expression ("as we know," "it is well known that . . .") is put at the start of certain developments: he ascribes to current opinion, to common knowledge, the proposition from which he will start out: his endeavor to react against a banality. And often what he must oppose is not the banality of common opinion but his own; the discourse which comes to him initially is banal, and it is only by struggling against the original banality that, gradually, he writes. Suppose he is to describe his situation in a Tangier bar—what he first manages to say is that the place is the site of an "interior language": a fine discovery! He then attempts to get rid of this importuning banality and to fish out of it some fragment of an idea with which he might have some relation of desire: the Sentence! Once this object is named, everything is saved; whatever he writes (this is not a question of performance), it will always be a vested discourse, in which the body will make its appearance (banality is discourse without body).
>
> In other words, what he writes proceeds from a *corrected* banality. (*BBB,* 137)

Within four years of Barthes's rumination on "On le sait," John Ashbery published a volume of poems called *As We Know,* whose title poem reads as follows:

All that we see is penetrated by it—
The distant treetops with their steeple (so
Innocent), the stair, the windows' fixed flashing—
Pierced full of holes by the evil that is not evil,
The romance that is not mysterious, the life that is
     not life,
A present that is elsewhere.
And further in the small capitulations
Of the dance, you rub elbows with it,
Finger it. That day you did it
Was the day you had to stop, because the doing
Involved the whole fabric, there was no other way to
     appear.
You slid down on your knees
For those precious jewels of spring water
Planted on the moss, before they got soaked up
And you teetered on the edge of this
Calm street with its sidewalks, its traffic,

As though they are coming to get you.
But there was no one in the noon glare,
Only birds like secrets to find out about
And a home to get to, one of these days.

The light that was shadowed then
Was seen to be our lives,
Everything about us that love might wish to examine,
Then put away for a certain length of time, until
The whole is to be reviewed, and we turned
Toward each other, to each other.
The way we had come was all we could see
And it crept up on us, embarrassed
That there is so much to tell now, really now.[6]

One's first impulse is to read this as a kind of riddle poem. Its rhetoric of paradox prompts us to try to name the mysterious "it" that penetrates the "distant treetops" and "the windows' fixed flashing," the "it" with which "you rub elbows" in the second stanza and which finally "crept up on us" in the fourth. Ashbery's, however, is not a romantic longing for what Harold Bloom has called the "slight transcendence," nor do I take the speaking subject of the poem to be, in the Bloomian sense, a "spent seer."[7] On the contrary, Ashbery's "As We Know" is the Barthean "On le sait," the "apparently expletive expression" from which the poet "start[s] out" in his urge "to react against a banality." And the banality, as in Barthes's case, is not that of common opinion but Ashbery's own. "The distant treetops with their steeple (so / Innocent)," "the windows' fixed flashing," "the precious jewels of spring water / Planted on the moss"—these are the "banal" items of discourse against which the poet must struggle if he is to write.

"Suppose," writes Barthes, "he [the author] is to describe his situation in a Tangier bar—what he first manages to say is that the place is the site of an 'interior language': a fine discovery! He then attempts to get rid of this importuning banality and to fish out of it some fragment of an idea with which he might have some relation of desire." Just so, the "I" of "As We Know" begins by referring to childhood settings as if they were stills in some old Hollywood movie: the "distant treetops with their steeple (so / Innocent)" of small-town America, a "staircase" down which a "you" presumably "slid down on your knees" and who "teetered on the edge of this / Calm street with its sidewalks, its traffic, / As though they are coming to get you." And of course, just when you think "they are coming to get you," there is, mysteriously, "no one in the noon glare"—no one, that is, except "birds like secrets to find out about."

Here is what Barthes calls "a *corrected* banality," for in the lexicon of childhood cliché, birds are not really "like secrets to find out about." Indeed, we cannot penetrate their "secrets" any more than we can determine whether the "home" of the following line is a place where the poet has already been or simply the projection of his desire. Indeed, the poem introduces clichés only to subvert them in its refusal to make the necessary connections. The "windows' fixed flashing" admits no possibility of seeing through the glass. We know neither what "That day you did it" refers to nor why this was also "the day you had to stop." The explanatory phrase "because the doing / Involved the whole fabric" is a proposition as emptied of signification as is the title "As We Know." Throughout Ashbery's poem, the speaker's "present" continues to be, as he says, "elsewhere."

"At the center, what?" asks Barthes in "Le cercle des fragments." Ashbery's poem poses the same question. The final stanza opens with the proposition "The light that was shadowed then / Was seen to be our lives." So reasonable, so relaxed is this statement, that we are all but persuaded by its "argument," until we stop to consider that the syntactic equation between "light" and "lives" is never justified semantically. The passive construction ("Was seen to be"), moreover, gives us no clue as to who it is that "sees" things this way. Indeed, the passage is dominated by what Barthes calls "the aesthetic of the empty sign." "Everything," "a certain length of time," "until," "The way we had come"—none of these pseudoconnectives constructs a coherent story about "us." There is only the recognition that "there is so much to tell now, really now," and it is this urgent need to keep "telling" that is the poet's final "corrected banality." "There is so much to tell!" is a standard cliché of conversation when two people who have been separated for some time meet. "Really now" is a standard explea-

tive of reinforcement, yet, given the context, what can "really now" intensify but the poem's pervading stress on absence, on the intangibility of identity? Even such separate particles as the words "no one" in stanza 3 coalesce into the glare of "noon."

"As We Know" is, as we know, a poem and hence, so the common wisdom would have it, quite different from a slice of Barthean prose. Or is it? "As a rule," writes Lawrence Kramer in *Music and Poetry: The Nineteenth Century and After,* "an Ashbery poem does not articulate a process, but simply lets a textured consciousness persist shimmeringly for a given duration, which is presented as something like an *objet trouvé.* Within that duration, the voices of the poem participate in the continuous flow of the present, without imposing any shape on it. . . . The nature of this flow is to be quirky, inconsistently coherent, and, contrary to conventional expectations, non-linear."[8]

To put it another way, lineation, stanzaic structure, indeed the whole visual arrangement of the poem, constitute one aspect of the "original banality" against which the contemporary poem must struggle. The lineation is, for that matter, purposely unobtrusive, the lines ranging from six to sixteen syllables and seeming to succeed one another as best they can. No sooner is an iambic flow established, as in "the way we had come was all we could see," than Ashbery, so to speak, "makes it ugly": "And ît crépt úp ôn us, | embárrassed / That thére îs só múch to téll nôw, réally nów." Ashbery's sound structure is almost willfully antilyric even as his images refuse to be anchored in any coherent system. "The continuity of the ego," as Kramer says, "dissolves experience instead of integrating it. The mind becomes the only constant presence, and it presides over a continuous recession of objects into absence, some of which it is reluctant to let go" (LK, 219).

The same thing could be said of the Barthes fragment. Lineation aside, we are dealing with two very similar modes of writing. In both cases, the fragmentary, discontinuous form breaks up what Barthes calls "the smooth finish, the composition, discourse constructed to give a final meaning to what one says, which is the general rule of all past rhetoric" (INT, 209; *GV,* 198). Again, in both cases, the personal pronoun is unstable, the author representing himself sometimes as "I," sometimes as "he" or "you." "'I'" says Barthes, "is the pronoun of the image-repertoire; 'he' . . . is the pronoun of distance. . . . 'You' can be taken as the pronoun of accusation . . . but also as the 'you' of the writing operator, who puts himself . . . in position to disengage the scriptor from the subject" (INT, 216). Similarly, Ashbery says:

The personal pronouns in my work very often seem to be like variables in an equation. "You" can be myself or it can be another person, someone whom I'm addressing, and so can "he" and "she" for that matter and "we." . . . . my point is that it doesn't really matter very much, that we are somehow all aspects of a consciousness giving rise to the poem. . . . I find it very easy to move from one person in the sense of a pronoun to another and this again helps to produce a kind of polyphony in my poetry.[9]

Polyphony, in such writing, replaces the pattern of crisis and resolution to which we are accustomed in nineteenth-century writing. The conflict between self and other that animates such poems as Keats's "Ode to a Nightingale" gives way to a fluidity of consciousness, a loosening of syntactic connections that allows experience to *happen* rather than make sense.

Literature, Barthes argues, can no longer coincide with the function of *mathesis,* which is his word for "a complete field of knowledge." We live "in a profuse world, and what we learn about it is made known immediately, but we are bombarded by fragmentary, controlled bits of information. . . . For centuries, literature was both a *mathesis* and a *mimesis,* with its correlative metalanguage: reflection. Today the text is a *semiosis*"—that is to say, "a *mise en scène* of *signifiance*" (INT, 237–38; GV, 225).

Such mise-en-scène characterizes contemporary texts as otherwise diverse as Guy Davenport's collage stories, Laurie Anderson's performance pieces, John Cage's conversations with Daniel Charles collected in *For the Birds,* David Antin's talk poems, and Jay Cantor's series of linked essays on the literature and politics of the late sixties and seventies, appropriately called *The Space Between.*[10] One of the most interesting American versions of the Barthean longing for a "fictive" narrative that is not fictional, a poetic text that is not a poem, may be found in *The Writings of Robert Smithson,* assembled by the artist's widow Nancy Holt in 1979. Peppered with citations from Barthes and Burroughs, Flaubert and Williams, these are "writings" that usually take the form of collage, juxtaposing photographic image, illustration, blueprint, graph, chart, commentary, and narrative. "The Spiral Jetty," for instance, opens with a citation from the popular Catholic writer G. K. Chesterton: "Red is the most joyful and dreadful thing in the physical universe; it is the fiercest note, it is the highest light, it is the place where the walls of this world of ours wear the thinnest and something beyond burns through."[11] Smithson, as his narrative makes clear, hardly shares Chesterton's simple faith in the "something beyond" that "burns through," yet his feeling about *red* is equally

intense and is reinforced by his readings, in a book by William Rudolph romantically titled *Vanishing Trails of Atacama,* about the salt lakes of Bolivia "in all stages of desiccation and filled with micro bacteria that give the water surface a red color." According to Rudolph, "The pink flamingos that live around the salars [salt lakes] match the color of the water" (RS, 109).

Given this citational prelude, the creation of the *Spiral Jetty* in the Great Salt Lake of Utah can be read as the artist's struggle against the "banality" of the Chestertonian "highest light" and the equally banal exoticism of the unknown red lakes of Bolivia. As in Barthes's "On le sait," however, it is such banalities that point one in the right direction. "From New York City," writes Smithson, "I called the Utah Park Development and spoke to Ted Tuttle, who told me that water in the Great Salt Lake north of the Lucin Cutoff, which cuts the lake in two, was the color of tomato soup. That was enough of a reason to go out there and have a look." From red as "the most joyful and dreadful thing," to the red lakes and pink flamingos of exotic Bolivia, to "tomato soup"—this deflation of red on the verbal level is juxtaposed to the black-and-white photographs of the actual *Spiral Jetty,* as if to say "No ideas but in things."

These mysterious angle and detail shots of the jetty are now set side by side with the narrative of how Smithson discovered the site he was to transform into his earthwork. Just as the photographs in *Barthes par Barthes* cannot quite "match" the verbal texts that follow, so these photographs are not really "explained" by the detailed account of Smithson's journey, culminating in "my first view of the wine-red water." The photographs present us, not with the actual Utah locale ("Driving West on Highway 83, late in the afternoon, we passed through Corinne, then went on to Promontory," and so on), but with the landscape of dream, of a timeless present, which Smithson now describes in the text: "The road on the map became a net of dashes, while in the far distance the Salt Lake existed as an interrupted silver band. Hills took on the appearance of melting solids, and glowed under amber light. . . . Sandy slopes turned into viscous masses of perception" (RS, 111). To lineate this passage is to recognize its inherent poeticity.

The road on the map became
　　a net of dashes, while
　　　　in the far distance
the Salt Lake existed as
　　　　　　an interrupted silver band

and so on. But Smithson won't leave it there either. The dream landscape now gives way to the perspective of Geology: "The mere sight of the trapped fragments of junk and waste transported one into a world of modern prehistory. The products of a Devonian industry, the remains of a Silurian technology, all the machines of the Upper Carboniferous Period were lost in those expansive deposits of sand and mud" (RS, 111).

Between such alternate systems of signs, the contemporary text oscillates, itself a kind of "jig-saw puzzle . . . compos[ing] the salt flats."

> This site was a rotary that enclosed itself in an immense roundness. From that gyrating space emerged the possibility of the Spiral Jetty. No ideas, no concepts, no systems, no structures, no abstractions could hold themselves together in the actuality of that evidence. My dialectics of site and nonsite whirled into an indeterminate state, where solid and liquid lost themselves in each other. . . . No sense wondering about classifications and categories, there were none. (RS, 111)

No sense wondering about classifications and categories. Here is the Barthean skepticism regarding genre. Given such a state of affairs, what does one do? We Americans are, as the cliché has it, more pragmatic than the French. "After securing a twenty year lease on the meandering zone," says Smithson drily, "and finding a contractor in Ogden, I began building the jetty in April, 1970. Bob Phillips, the foreman, sent two dump trucks, a tractor, and a large front loader out to the site."

Perhaps, after all, so much depends upon a red wheelbarrow. Smithson is never a pragmatist for long, however. Contemplating the scale of his Spiral Jetty, and recalling Brancusi's sketch of James Joyce as a "spiral ear," Smithson observes: "One ceases to consider art in terms of an 'object.' The fluctuating resonances reject 'objective criticism,' because that would stifle the generative power of both visual and auditory scale. Not to say that one resorts to 'subjective concepts,' but rather that one apprehends what is around one's eyes and ears, no matter how unstable or fugitive. One seizes the spiral, and the spiral becomes a seizure" (RS, 112).

From the center of the Spiral Jetty, as the chart on page 113 tells us, every compass point (Smithson lists twenty) yields the same information: "Mud, salt crystals, rocks, water." Still, the chart is no more "accurate" than the detail photograph on the left-hand page, in which the tumbleweed coated with salt crystals looks like a giant rock orchid, placed on the moon. When Smithson decides to "disentangle" the "scale of centers" of the jetty, his list—(a) to (h)—is no more coherent than the alphabetized fragments in Barthes par Barthes.

(a) ion source in cyclotron

(b) a nucleus

(c) dislocation point

(d) a wooden stake in the mud

(e) axis of helicopter propeller

(f) James Joyce's ear channel

(g) the Sun

(h) a hole in the film reel. (RS, 114)

Neither a mathesis nor a mimesis, Smithson's list could easily enter the world of Williams's Paterson or of Pound's Cantos. Its fictiveness is appropriate to a discourse that culminates in the account of the making of the film about the Spiral Jetty, which is described as a kind of science-fiction fantasy. Consider the "shot" filmed in the Hall of Late Dinosaurs at the Museum of Natural History.

> The ghostly cameraman slides over the glassed-in compounds. These fragments of a timeless geology laugh without mirth at the time-filled hopes of ecology. From the soundtrack the echoing metronome vanishes into the wilderness of bones and glass. Tracking around a glass containing a "dinosaur mummy," the words of The Unnamable are heard. The camera shifts to a specimen squeezed flat by the weight of sediments, then the film cuts to the road in Utah. (RS, 115)

Eliot's "fragments," "shored against" the poet's "ruin," here give way to a delight in the very discontinuity and recombination of the fragments. As in the Chinese scroll that Barthes takes as his paradigm, it is the "next to" (l'à côté de) that provides the pleasure of the text.

Marjorie Perloff, Autumn 1985

1 "Twenty Key Words for Roland Barthes," interview conducted by Jean-Jacques Brochier in Le Magazine Littéraire, February 1975; reprinted in The Grain of the Voice: Interviews 1962–1980, Linda Coverdale, tr., New York, Hill & Wang, 1985, p. 222; subsequently cited as INT. For the French original, see Roland Barthes. Le grain de la voix: Entretiens 1962–1980, Paris, Seuil, 1981, p. 210; subsequently cited as GV.

2 Roland Barthes, Writing Degree Zero, Annette Lavers and Colin Smith, trs., New York, Hill & Wang, 1967; p. 48; subsequently cited as WDZ. Barthes, Le degré zéro de l'écriture, Paris, Seuil, 1953, pp. 37–38; subsequently cited as DZE.

3 Roland Barthes, Mythologies, Annette Lavers, tr., New York, Hill & Wang, 1972, pp. 133–34; subsequently cited as M. Barthes, Mythologies, Paris, Seuil, 1957; subsequently cited as MY.

4 Roland Barthes, A Lover's Discourse: Fragments, Richard Howard, tr., New York, Hill & Wang, 1978, pp. 6–7; subsequently cited as LD. Barthes, Fragments d'un discours amoureux, Paris, Seuil, 1977, p. 10; subsequently cited as FDA.

5 Roland Barthes by Roland Barthes, Richard Howard, tr., New York, Hill & Wang, 1977; subsequently cited as BBB. Roland Barthes par Roland Barthes, Paris, Seuil, 1975; subsequently cited as BPB. In the Hill & Wang edition the forty-two pages of photographs and captions are unnumbered; the first page of text is thus page 43.

6 John Ashbery, As We Know, New York, Viking, 1979, p. 74.

7 See Harold Bloom, Figures of Capable Imagination, New York, Seabury, 1976, esp. pp. 123–46, 169–208.

8   Lawrence Kramer, *Music and Poetry: The Nineteenth Century and After,* Berkeley, University of California Press, 1984, p. 218; subsequently cited as LK.

9   See Janet Bloom and Robert Losada, "Craft Interview with John Ashbery," *New York Quarterly,* 9 (Winter 1972), pp. 24–25.

10   *For the Birds: John Cage in Conversation with Daniel Charles,* Boston, Boyars, 1981; Jay Cantor, *The Space Between: Literature and Politics,* Baltimore, Johns Hopkins University Press, 1981. The most recent works of the other authors mentioned are Laurie Anderson, *United States,* New York, Harper & Row, 1984; David Antin, *Tuning,* New York, New Directions, 1984; Guy Davenport, *Apples and Pears and Other Stories,* San Francisco, North Point, 1984. This is, of course, a highly selective list of possible examples.

11   "The Spiral Jetty" (1972), in *The Writings of Robert Smithson: Essays with Illustrations,* Nancy Holt, ed., New York, New York University Press, 1979, p. 109; subsequently cited as *RS.*

"Living in the Same Place": The Old Mononationalism and the New Comparative Literature

A nation? says Bloom. A nation is the same people living in the same place.

By God, then, says Ned, laughing, if that's so I'm a nation for I'm living in the same place for the past five years.
So of course everyone had a laugh at Bloom and says he, trying to muck out of it:

Or also living in different places.

■ **JAMES JOYCE,** *ULYSSES*

Leopold Bloom's definition of nationhood is not as foolish as his fellow Dubliners in Kiernan's Pub took it to be. As citizens of the United States we are, after all, "the same people living in the same place." And when we travel or go abroad, thus "living in different places," we retain a good measure of our "Americanness." Whenever I watch the bleary-eyed plane travelers divide into those two passport lines—U.S. and "Foreign"—at Kennedy Airport or LAX, I am aware that national identity still plays a marked role in one's sense of self.

In his much-cited essay "DissemiNation" Homi K. Bhabha speaks eloquently of the inherent "porosity" of modern nation states, what he calls the "intermittent time, and intersticial space, that emerges as a structure of undecidablity at the frontiers of cultural hybridity."[1] But when Bhabha adds that we are entering an era in which "the liminal figure of the nation space [will] ensure that no political ideologies could claim transcendent or metaphysical authority for themselves" (HKB, 299), he is, I think, engaging in wishful thinking. The "nation space"—*pace* Chechnya and Serbia, *pace* the

People's Republic of China—shows no signs of opening itself up to the sort of dissolution Bhabha and like-minded critics desire. What is the case, however, is that the nation as we know it today can no longer be understood according to the nineteenth-century paradigm which continues to be regarded as normative, at least in the academy.[2] We still, for example, divide literary study into such areas as "Modern British Fiction," "Victorian Poetry," "French Renaissance Literature," "the German Enlightenment," and so on. And the most powerful literary subgroup in the academy, American Literature, together with its more sociohistorical sibling American Studies, acts on the premise that our first (and often our last) obligation is to know those works that, however diverse the race, ethnicity, and gender of their author, have been made in the USA. Hence the emphasis on Chicano rather than Latin American literature, on James Baldwin and Toni Morrison rather than on Aimé Césaire, and the exclusion of Canadian (both anglo- and francophone) or Australian literature from the canon.

This, I shall argue here, is where comparative literature can—indeed must—play a central role. For, given the migrations and emigrations, the exiles (sometimes voluntary, more often forced) that have created U.S. citizenry in the late twentieth century, how can we continue to take "American literature," as it continues to be called in survey courses and textbooks, as a mononational entity? And what about an earlier period like the Renaissance? Given the movement from nation to nation in that period, coupled with the exploration of the New World, is it meaningful to study, say, English Renaissance lyric in isolation?

I am thinking not so much about comparisons between national literatures—the old comparative literature, which was, in many ways, a natural response to nineteenth-century national paradigms—as about the simple reality that today the national literatures are themselves assemblages of many "other-national" strands, sedimentations where different national and hence linguistic elements won't separate out, compost heaps, so to speak, in which nations of origin become curiously conflated. To understand this new situation, we must begin by looking at the nineteenth-century model of a "nation space."

Take a book all of us have come across, at one time or another, no matter what our speciality: the standard-bearing *Norton Anthology of American Literature,* used in freshman and sophomore courses from Fort Lauderdale, Florida, to Anchorage, Alaska, as well as in nations around the globe. The third edition of the Norton (1989) includes forty-five writers in the nineteenth-century (1822–1914) sections, writers whose names alone are revealing: Washington Irving, James Fenimore

Cooper, Augustus Baldwin Longstreet, William Cullen Bryant, Ralph Waldo Emerson, Nathaniel Hawthorne, Henry Wadsworth Longfellow, John Greenleaf Whittier, Edgar Allan Poe, Abraham Lincoln, Oliver Wendell Holmes, Margaret Fuller, Harriet Beecher Stowe, George Washington Harris, T. B. Thorpe, Johnson Jones Hopper, Henry David Thoreau, Frederick Douglass, James Russell Lowell, Walt Whitman, Herman Melville, Emily Dickinson, Rebecca Harding Davis, Mark Twain (Samuel Clemens), Bret Harte, William Dean Howells, Ambrose Bierce, Henry James, Joel Chandler Harris, Sarah Orne Jewett, Kate Chopin, Mary Wilkins Freeman, Booker T. Washington, Charles W. Chesnutt, Hamlin Garland, Charlotte Perkins Gilman, Jane Adams, Edith Wharton, W. E. B. Du Bois, Frank Norris, Stephen Crane, Theodore Dreiser, Jack London, Gertrude Simmons Bonnin (Zitkala-Sa), and Henry Adams.

The Norton editors were, of course, making every effort to include women and minority groups: this edition has eleven women, one of whom is a Native American, and five African American men. No doubt newer editions will feel called upon to include an even larger percentage of women and minority writers,[3] but this is not the issue that concerns me here. For what is fascinating, from the perspective of the comparatist, is the national, cultural, and religious uniformity of the writers who really *were* the leading writers of the U.S. nineteenth century. Of the forty-five (so many of them Boston-bred and Harvard-educated), all but three were born and died in the U.S. Henry James and Edith Wharton lived their later lives abroad (London and Paris respectively), but their careers were very much formed in their native country, as was that of Ambrose Bierce, who died in Mexico. And further: whether these writers were male or female, white or black, all but two—Kate Chopin, who was Catholic, and the Sioux Indian Gertrude Simmons Bonnin—were Protestant (Bonnin, for that matter, was brought up in a Quaker missionary school). Again, almost all the white writers here included were of English descent—an ancestry, by the way, that, judging from their middle names, includes both sides of the family. Theodore Dreiser, whose parents were impoverished German immigrants, is a grand exception.

A similar mononationalism characterizes English, French, and German writers of the nineteenth century. From William Blake, William Wordsworth, Samuel Taylor Coleridge, George Gordon Lord Byron, Percy Bysshe Shelley, John Keats, Jane Austen, William Hazlitt, Charles Lamb, and Felicia Hemans down to Alfred Lord Tennyson and Robert Browning, George Eliot and Elizabeth Gaskell, Charles Dickens and William Makepeace Thackeray, John Ruskin, John Stuart Mill, Matthew Arnold and Walter Pater, English writers were,

well, English writers. There are, of course, certain class and regional differences: Byron was aristocratic, Keats lower-middle-class, Dickens a child of urban poverty. But ethnically and religiously, English writers of the nineteenth century are an astonishingly uniform English Protestant lot: when Gerard Manley Hopkins, following John Henry Newman, converted to Catholicism in the late 1860s, it was considered a major event.

There are three basic ways for literary critics and historians to respond to this situation. The first, and perhaps the most common in the age of multiculturalism, is to deny special status to, say, the six great Romantic poets in England or the American Renaissance writers in the U.S. and elevate to equal (or superior) status the work of "forgotten" women and African American writers, to insist that these writers are "just as important" or "valuable" as are Blake and Byron, Emerson and Hawthorne and Melville. There are two difficulties here. First, the typical "forgotten" writer—say, Susan Warner—is often just as "authentically" Anglo-American as her canonical counterpart—say, Harriet Beecher Stowe. And second, sooner or later readers discover for themselves that Melville's *Moby Dick* is, after all, a more interesting novel than *Wide, Wide World.*

A second response to the mononationalism of the nineteenth century is to retain the existing canon, as, say, Edward Said does in his 1993 *Culture and Imperialism,* but to reread Austen and Dickens and Thackeray for the light they shed on imperialism, colonialism, and capitalism. This approach has generated a whole growth industry of nineteenth-century studies: I note that the prospective sessions listed in the most recent MLA Newsletter have a high preponderance of titles like "Race, Travel and Imperialism in Late Nineteenth-Century American Literature," "Imperial Fantasies in German Nineteenth-Century Literature," and so on.

But the imperialist-colonialist paradigm is already showing signs of strain as everything written has to be ground through its mill. And the irony for comparatists, as the above titles suggest, is that these studies continue to be conducted along strictly national lines: those expert in British imperialism seem to know little about the German situation and viceversa. A third—and, to my mind, more satisfactory—approach would be to recognize that our current drive to discover national porosity, hybridity, difference, dissolution, intersticial space, and all those other positives Homi K. Bhabha and like-minded critics speak of, stems not from some kind of new and definitive theoretical paradigm, a new canon law, but from the simple and practical reality that the writers, artists, and composers of our own time who are "living in the same place" no longer represent the mononationalism which really was the norm in the nineteenth century and which hence inevitably influenced historians and theoreticians of the period. "Philosophy," as Wittgenstein reminds us, "does not attempt to deal with questions which do not really arise."[4]

"The discipline of comparative literature," writes Emily Apter in her essay responding to the Bernheimer Report, "is unthinkable without the historical circumstances of exile . . . the psychic legacy of dislocation."[5] Apter is referring, of course, to the first wave of comparative literature in this country, the European refugee culture of what she calls the "founding fathers"—Leo Spitzer, Erich Auerbach, René Wellek, Wolfgang Kaiser—and she argues that the American "converts to the field" in the fifties and sixties—Fredric Jameson, J. Hillis Miller, Neil Hertz—suffered from "Euro-envy," an "ethic of linguistic estrangement, a secessionism from mainstream American culture" (EA, 89). By contrast, Apter suggests, the current generation of exilic critics— the generation of postcolonialists whom she regards as normative for the "new" comparative literature—are "often . . . deeply antithetical to their Eurocentric counterparts: non-German speaking, nonmetropolitan, non-white, antipatriarchal, and, in varying degrees, hostile to elite literariness" (EA, 90). And she cites Homi Bhabha and Gayatri Spivak, Anthony Appiah and Sara Suleri, V. I. Mudimbe, Edward Said, and Rey Chow as examples (EA, 94). The contemporary situation thus becomes, in Apter's words, "a border war, an academic version of the legal battles and political disputes over the status of 'undocumented workers,' 'illegal aliens,' and 'permanent residents'" (EA, 94).

This now-fashionable formulation is not without its ironies. For one thing, all the theorists mentioned above were themselves educated in elitist Western institutions and, in the case of Spivak and Bhaba, are the direct heirs of those European—which is to say French and German—fathers (especially Derrida) Apter now takes to be so retro. But more important, the teleology proposed here (the "old" comparative literature must be succeeded by the "new" postcolonialism) replicates precisely the blind spot of the earlier model: it demands an exotic other (Pakistan or Nigeria replaces France and Italy) in place of the literature close to home, the literature, that is to say, actually written in the United States today.

It is a commonplace that English literature on the eve of World War I was largely the creation of a few Irishmen (Wilde, Yeats, Joyce, Shaw), two Americans (Ezra Pound and T. S. Eliot), a Pole who knew no English before he was twenty (Joseph Conrad), and a second-generation German who changed his last name from Hueffer to (Ford Madox) Ford. And it is a second commonplace that after the war, dozens of American writers lived in Paris as expatriates, even as, in the World War II years, the flow was reversed, New York becoming the home for André Breton and Max Ernst, Kandinsky and Mondrain, Willem de Kooning and Hans Hofmann, not to mention an entire colony of German exile writers and British expatriates like Auden and Isherwood living in New York and Los Angeles. But what is less well understood is that, by midcentury, the language of American poetry, to take just one example, had become something quite different, not only from its English model but also from the Emerson-Whitman-Dickinson poetics which was its more immediate source. And here, I want to argue, a comparatist approach is needed in order to locate the peculiar momentum of the work.

By 1910, according to the census, it is estimated that roughly one person in four in the continental U.S. learned English as a second language. Five years earlier, Henry James warned the graduating class at Bryn Mawr that the new immigrants were destroying the "ancestral circle" of the American language, turning it into "a mere helpless slobber of disconnected vowel noises," an "easy and ignoble minimum," barely distinguishable from "the grunting, the squealing, the barking, or the roaring of animals."[6] "The forces of looseness," James warned, "are in possession of the field," and they "dump their mountain of promiscuous material into the foundations" of the language itself (QS, 43).

One such immigrant, herself to come under the influence of Henry James, as of his philosopher brother, was Gertrude Stein. Born in Allegheny, Pennsylvania, to an affluent Jewish-German but wholly secularized immigrant family, she was eight months old when her German-speaking family moved to Vienna and stayed there until she was four-and-a-half, when they moved to Paris (which they left when Stein was five). She grew up in Oakland, California (of "no there there" fame), attended Radcliffe, where she studied with a great Anglo-Saxon Protestant American, William James, and then enrolled as one of the first women in the Johns Hopkins Medical School. But she did not matriculate and soon moved to Paris, where she lived the now legendary life recounted in *The Autobiography of Alice B. Toklas*, returning to the U.S. only once, in 1934, on a very successful lecture tour.

How did Gertrude Stein respond to the "force of looseness" of immigrant and then emigrant language? Criticism has been largely silent on this question. For all the discussions of her friendship with Picasso, her debt to cubism, her place in the Paris art world and in the lesbian salon of Natalie Barney, and for all the talk of gender definition in her work, the actual determination of Stein's language field remains largely misunderstood. The headnote in the recent *Norton Anthology,* which includes only Stein's early and accessible "The Good Anna" along with the introduction to *The Making of Americans,* informs us that, because of her cubist connection, "[Stein] came to think of words as they were thinking of brush strokes on canvas, as tangible entities in themselves rather than vehicles conveying meaning or representing reality." And again, "She treated words as things, carefully ignoring or defying the connection between words and meanings."[7] In other words, her texts don't really "mean" anything; they engage in what various scholars have called "non-referential play."

Interestingly, French poets and critics from Jacques Roubaud to Emmanuel Hocquard have taken Stein's meanings more seriously. In an essay called "L'écriture sans rature," Françoise Collin remarks:

> She has accomplished her *depaysement* once and for all by the age of twenty, taking up residence in a country where her language isn't spoken. This is her only exoticism but it is a radical one. . . . Living in a foreign environment, Gertrude Stein distances herself from the language that she hears all around her—French—which is not her own, and which is for her an object of fascination to the point where she appropriates any number of its elements and formulae. But she is also distancing herself from her own language, American, which is not spoken around her, which has become the language of the other, even if it is the language of intimacy. The writing of Gertrude Stein is ex-centric with respect to two languages, according to different formulae: it is a third language.[8]

Once we become aware of the element of appropriation, many of Stein's so-called impenetrabilities open up. Take "Ladies Voices: Curtain Raiser," written in 1916 in Mallorca, where Gertrude and Alice had retreated from the war and were living the hotel life of the international set. Here is "Act IV":

What are ladies voices.

Do you mean to believe me.

Have you caught the sun.

Dear me have you caught the sun.

In French (the lingua franca for the international set populating Mallorca hotels during the war), to take the sun or sunbathe is "prendre le soleil." Now, one of the most common meanings of *prendre* is "to catch" as in "prendre un voleur" (to catch a thief). So "Have you caught the sun. Dear me have you caught the sun" is simply Stein's way of showing, as realistically as possible, what "ladies voices," overheard at a beach resort, sound like and what they say. "Dear me, have you

caught the sun" also contains a double entendre: when retranslated into English, it sounds as if the "you" has "caught" a disease: "Dear me, 'have you caught the flu? Have you caught sunstroke?" and so on.

There is, in any case, nothing meaningless about Stein's locution. At the same time, we find, in Stein's "French-English," traces of childhood German as well: for example, in her predilection for "this one" (*dieser/diese*) and "one" (*Einer*).

But the larger question would be to explore why Stein felt so compelled to write in a "third language," why the very fabric of language—its syntax, vocabulary, punctuation, and semantic possibilities—became such an obsession for her. The case of William Carlos Williams is similar. The son of an English father and a Catholic, Puerto Rican mother who had both French Basque and Dutch Jewish blood, Williams was born in Rutherford, New Jersey. Spanish was the predominant language in the house when Williams was a small child; his mother, who shifted easily from Spanish to French, learned English only reluctantly. In Rutherford, the Williamses, who wanted very much to "belong," joined the Unitarian Church, and, although they were not affluent, they sent their son to an expensive private school (Horace Mann) in New York, despite the fact that the commute, which the poet has described lovingly in his *Autobiography,* took hours. One year, he attended a French boarding school at Annecy, and later he did postdoctoral work in Leipzig. But in contrast to Stein, as to Eliot and Pound, Williams is always cited as the poet who "stayed home," who practiced medicine in his New Jersey hometown for the rest of his life.

Like Stein, Williams was aggressively American: *In the American Grain* reconstructs American history as a kind of contest between redskin and paleface, and his long poem *Paterson* purports to tell the story of the quintessential American polis. But, again like Stein, Williams invents a language (though not as deconstructionist as hers), highly self-conscious in its representations of "authentic" speech idiom, as in the "retarded" language of the "Billy" section of *Paterson* 1, the stilted flowery language of "Cress" in 1 and 2, and the medical case histories throughout. Thus, whereas Americanists have emphasized Williams's debt to Emerson and Whitman, his relationship with Ezra Pound and H.D., his close bonds with the art world of the Arensberg circle, comparatist critics have paid more attention to the "Carlos" strain and have read the love poetry against its Petrarchan and Dantean models. Not that Williams "translated" French or Spanish into English equivalents as did Stein, or that he relied heavily on foreign phrases and locutions as did Ezra Pound. But when Williams explains that his poetic practice is informed by prosodic adjustments, for example, the transformation of the five-line stanza "My shoes as I lean / unlacing them / stand out upon / flat worsted flowers / under my feet" to a four-line stanza by eliminating the last line ("See how much better it conforms to the page, how much better it looks?"),[9] one has the sense, as in Stein, of a peculiar linguistic self-consciousness, a struggle that would not take this particular form in the native speaker.

A third and especially striking example of the multinationalism of the interwar period is that of Mina Loy. Born Mina Gertrude Lowy in London in 1882 to Sigmund Lowy, a Hungarian Jew, and Julia Brian, she left England when she was seventeen to study art in Munich. At nineteen, she married a fellow artist, and they moved to Paris, where she changed her name to Loy and exhibited in the Salon d'Automne. In 1906 they moved on to Italy, where her children were born, her marriage dissolved, and she came under the spell of Futurism, having an affair first with Marinetti and then with the writer Papini. In 1916, when war was declared, she moved to New York, where she immediately became the center of New York Dada and had her fabled meeting with Arthur Cravan. By now she was writing poetry as well as producing art work; Eliot praised her in *The Egoist,* and Pound chose her poetry as an example of the term *logopoeia,* the "dance of the intellect among words." After the war, when Cravan disappeared mysteriously in Mexico, she returned to Paris and again became a "figure" in the literary and art world. But the last twenty-seven years of her life (1926–53) were spent back in the U.S.; in these "silent years" she more or less vanished from public view.

What nationality was Mina Loy and under what rubric should her work be studied? She wrote under so many anagrammatically and numerologically derived pseudonyms and misdated so many of her paintings that in the twenties a rumor circulated around Paris that Mina Loy was not a real person at all, but some sort of hoax. Upon hearing this, her editor Roger Conover tells us, Mina Loy turned up at Natalie Barney's salon and declared: "I assure you I am indeed a live being. But it is necessary to stay very unknown. . . . To maintain my incognito the hazard I chose was—poet."[10] This is, I think, an exemplary tale, for the title *poet* is always something of an incognito, in Loy's case especially so since she was fluent in English, French, Italian, and German. But what is most curious, the English of her poems, as the "Love Songs" and her long poem "Anglo-Mongrels and the Rose" attest, is neither quite British nor yet American but a curious hybrid, a kind of café-society overlay on an English "school-girl" base. And that hybrid—phrases like "conundrums of finance / to

which unlettered immigrants are instantly / initiate" (*LLB,* 115)—is now receiving the recognition it has long deserved, even though much U.S. scholarship has been stymied by its inability to read Loy's work in its French and Italian contexts.

What we might call the "thick" nationalism of Loy, Stein, and Williams has become almost the norm today. In London, at this very moment, one might be able to see a play by Samuel Beckett (whose French/English bilingualism is now understood as a form—but a very individual form—of Irish speech), by Harold Pinter, born and raised in the East End in a Jewish household, or by Tom Stoppard, whose adopted Anglo name belies his Jewish Czech ancestry. Last season the West End had a production of *Death and the Maiden* by the Chilean Jewish writer Ariel Dorfman, who, incidentally, has for several years been on the faculty at Duke University. And there is the further irony that Beckett's later plays and his works for radio like *Eh Foe* and *Quad* have been more frequently produced in Germany and in Japan than in London or Dublin. Some forms of exile exact a price: at the Yeats Summer School in Sligo some years ago, I heard a well-known Irish professor declare that Beckett wasn't nearly as good as the American poet John Berryman. What linguistic and thematic qualities, one wonders, create this kind of transatlantic flow?

Before one can make generalizations about British literary culture based on the theater, one must come to terms with the fact that the poetry situation is, for various reasons, antithetical. After Pound, after Eliot, the English Establishment turned back to its own roots, Donald Davie memorably declaring in the seventies that the tradition of English poetry was not that of the Americans (Pound and Eliot, and certainly not "Carlos Williams," as Davie dismissively called him) but of Thomas Hardy. Hardyesque poetry from Philip Larkin and Donald Davie himself to Andrew Motion and Blake Morrison seems all but incomprehensible to, say, U.S. as to French readers—incomprehensible not because it is difficult but because we have difficulty in seeing what its importance is. And surely this again has to do with the Englishness (old style) of these poets, an Englishness self-consciously assumed in imitation of the nineteenth-century model, vis-à-vis our own polyglot, multinational, multidialect poetry. And it explains why "Contemporary British Poetry" is not a popular subject in U.S. universities.

The opposite situation—and it is the one with which I want to close—is that of the French movement of the 1970s and 1980s called "Oulipo" ("Ouvroir de littérature potentielle"), whose leading figure is the late novelist Georges Perec. I say French movement, but how French is it? In his *W, ou le souvenir d'enfance*

(1975; English translation by David Bellos, 1988) Perec gives us two alternating narratives—the two V's of the *double-V* (W). The first narrative is an allegorical adventure story about a sports Utopia, "a land in thrall to the Olympic ideal"; the second an autobiography, "a fragmentary tale of a wartime childhood."[11] The latter takes its point of departure from Perec's own history: his Polish Jewish father, who had emigrated from Warsaw to Paris in 1926 and worked as a hairdresser, was killed in the war when Perec was four; his mother, née Cyrla (then Cecile) Shulevitz, died at Auschwitz when her son was six. The double text traces the complexities of postmodern identity, using, as is typical of this novelist, the seemingly most scrupulous factual documentation, only to make us more aware of the wide gap between fact and meaning. In chapter 8, footnote 8, for example, we find this etymology of the name *Perec*.

> My family name is Peretz. It is in the Bible. In Hebrew it means "hole," in Russian it means "pepper," in Hungarian (in Budapest, to be more precise) it is the word used for what in French we call "pretzel" ("pretzel" or "bretzel" is in fact merely a diminutive form [Beretzele] of Beretz and Beretz, like Baruch or Barek, is formed from the same roots as Peretz—in Arabic, if not in Hebrew, B and P are one and the same letter). The Peretzes like to think they are descended from Spanish Jews exiled by the Inquisition (the Perezes are thought to be Marranos, or converted Jews who stayed in Spain), whose migrations can be traced to Provence (Peiresc), then to the Papal States, and finally to central Europe, principally Poland and secondarily Romania and Bulgaria. One of the central figures of the family is the Polish Yiddish writer Isaac Leib Peretz, to whom every self-respecting Peretz is related even if it occasionally requires a feat of genealogical juggling. As for me, I am supposed to be Isaac Leib Peretz's great-great-nephew. Apparently he was my grandfather's uncle.

> My grandfather was called David Peretz and lived in Lubartow. He had three children: the eldest was called Esther Chaja Perec; the second, Eliezer Peretz; and the last-born, Icek Judko Perec. In the period between the first and third births, that is to say, between 1896 and 1909, Lubartow was, in succession, Russian, then Polish, then Russian again. An official hearing in Russian and writing in Polish, it has been explained to me, will hear Peretz and write Perec. But it is not impossible that the opposite is also true: according to my aunt, the Russians are supposed to be the ones who wrote "tz," and it was the Poles who wrote "c." This explanation signals but by no means exhausts the complex fantasies, connected to the concealment of my Jewish background through

my patronym, which I elaborated around the name I bear, a name which is distinguished, moreover, by a minute discrepancy between the way it is spelled and the way it is pronounced in French: it should be written Pérec or Perrec (and that's how it always is written spontaneously, either with an acute accent or with a double "r"; but it is Perec, despite the fact that it is not pronounced Peurec. (*W, 36*).

On the following page (footnote 12) the narrator recalls that in 1955 or 1956 he made the pilgrimage to his father's grave: "Seeing the words PEREC ICEK JUDKO followed by a regimental number, stencilled on the wooden cross and still perfectly legible, gave me a feeling that is hard to describe. The most enduring impression was that I was playing a role, acting in a private play: fifteen years after, the son comes to meditate on his father's grave. But beneath the role-playing there were other things" (*W, 37–38*), and the narrator goes on to extricate the complex feelings engaged in finally "put[ting] a boundary around that death which I had never learnt of, never experienced or known or acknowledged, but which for years and years I had had to deduce hypocritically from the commiserating whispers and sighing kisses of the ladies" (*W, 38*).

Here, I want to suggest, is a comparatist paradigm of our times. For if Georges Perec is a "French" author, his Frenchness must be read as the sedimentation of complex strata of Eastern European and Near Eastern cultural, national, and linguistic layers. When, for example, in the other narrative the nameless narrator has been mysteriously summoned to a meeting with the unknown Otto Apfelstahl at the Berghof Hotel in Hamburg, the following exchange takes place:

> "*Do you want some pretzels?*"
> "*Excuse me?*" *I said not grasping.*
> "*Pretzels. pretzels to eat with your beer.*"
> "*No thank you. I never eat pretzels. Give me a newspaper instead.*" (*W, 16*)

This takes place in chapter 5, before we have learned that the name Perec/Peretz is the same word as "pretzel." Only when we reread *W* does the connection between "never eating pretzels" and the question of Perec's origins become apparent. And indeed, the whole text is a language game where clues are distributed in this fashion.

So far as I know, neither Derrida nor Lyotard nor Deleuze has ever written a word on Georges Perec, their "French" deconstructionist contemporary, and neither have the postcolonial theorists whom Emily Apter takes to be *the* comparatists today. Nor is Perec's work taught in courses in the contemporary American novel. Theory, the wisdom here goes, may—indeed must—be read in translation, but when it comes to *literature,* the line continues to be drawn in the sand. American means American, even as it did in the nineteenth century, right? And this despite the simple fact that nationally, culturally, and ethnically, Perec may well be closer to many contemporary Americans than he is to "the French tradition" and to the language in which he writes.

But the irony is that for U.S. fiction writers and to their students, Perec is now a kind of cult figure, that those "pretzels" constitute something of a hidden signifier, rather like the missing *e* in Perec's novel *La Disparition,* just translated into English (as *The Void*). And the ACLA thus has its work cut out for it. For if we are to place and understand literature as it is being composed at the end of the twentieth century, we must rediscover the simple truth that the USA is not an island and that its writing is not only ethnically and racially diverse but always already bears the imprint of the nations, not only of the exotic Third World, but also, closer to home, of the nations in the neighborhood. To put it another way, in the age of the information highway, it is American literature that must begin to "comparatize" itself.

Marjorie Perloff, Spring 1995

[1] Homi K. Bhabha, "DissemiNation: time, narrative, and the margins of the modern nation," in *Nation and Narration,* ed. Homi K. Bhabha, London, Routledge, 1990, p. 312. Subsequently cited in the text as HKB.

[2] That the sense of collective identity which we call nationhood became dominant in the nineteenth century is the central theme of Benedict Anderson's *Imagined Communities: Reflections on the Origin and Spread of Nationalism,* London, Verso, 1983. But if this sense of nationhood was primarily an "imagined community," as Anderson argues, the fact remains that the citizens of a given nation *were* much more identifiable as nationals than they were in earlier periods or than they are today.

[3] As I was writing this essay, I received the new [1994] edition of the *Norton Anthology of American Literature,* and predictably, two new names have been added to the 1820–65 section: the Cherokee Memorials and the Native American writer William Apess.

[4] From the "Notes" of John King and Desmond Lee in Ludwig Wittgenstein, *Lectures Cambridge, 1930–32,* ed. Desmond Lee, Chicago, University of Chicago Press, 1980, p. 74.

[5] Emily Apter, "Comparative Exile: Competing Margins in the History of Comparative Literature," in *Comparative Literature in the Age of Multiculturalism,* ed. Charles Bernheimer, Baltimore, Johns Hopkins University Press, 1995, p. 86. Apter's essay is subsequently cited as EA and the collection as CB.

[6] Henry James, *The Question of Our Speech; The Lesson of Balzac: Two Lectures,* Boston, Houghton Mifflin, 1905, pp. 3, 16. Subsequently cited as QS. I was put onto this amazing essay by Peter Quartermain, who discusses it in his seminal *Disjunctive Poetics: From Gertrude Stein and Louis Zukofsky to Susan Howe,* Cambridge (Eng.), Cambridge University Press, 1992, pp. 9–12. The census statistics are found in Quartermain, p. 10.

[7] *The Norton Anthology of American Literature,* 3d ed., ed. Nina Baym et al., vol. 2, New York, Norton, 1989, p. 1032.

[8] Françoise Collin, "L'écriture sans rature," in *Gertrude Stein encore,* Amiens (Fr.), Trois Cailloux, 1983, pp. 107–8. My translation. This whole collection is very important.

[9] William Carlos Williams, *I Wanted To Write a Poem: The Autobiography of the Works of a Poet,* ed. Edith Heal, New York, New Directions, 1958, p. 66.

[10] Roger Conover, "Introduction," in Mina Loy, *The Last Lunar Baedeker,* Highlands (N.C.), Jargon Society, 1982, p. xviii. Subsequently cited as *LLB.* Conover's edition, by no means complete, is the best text we have today, and I have derived my biographical information from his chronology.

[11] Georges Perec, *W, or the Memory of Childhood,* tr. David Bellos, Boston, Godine, 1988, headnote. Subsequently cited in the text as *W.*

Beyond Cultural Nationalism

The honor is great for me to have been invited to address this distinguished company of poets, scholars, students, and devoted friends of the American periodical which lives up with éclat to its ambitious title; it embraces the whole world as its province, and it is fully worthy of the ideal motto once proposed by Coleridge: "To keep the past alive, in the present, for the future." For many years it bore the name of *Books Abroad,* and it won a faithful audience literally in five continents, out of all proportion to the number of its printed copies. The diversity and quality of its collaborators as well as the large and eclectic choice of books in many languages that it reviewed testified to the generous cosmopolitan spirit of American scholarship in an age when the temptation of isolationism had lured the generations which preceded ours. Several of us had been trained abroad and deplored that the momentous achievement of American culture was not adequately known in other parts of the world; we even suggested to the Department of State that it might well place this review, along with a few other distinterested cultural journals, more generously within the reach of foreign readers. A country in which advertising, often with its loud voice and with its most insistent mechanical devices, had been developed into a huge industry failed to realize that the word *propaganda,* originally a Latin gerund used by the Church ("de propaganda fide"), might well be honored anew; it implied the presentation and the diffusion abroad of what we consider the worthiest in us. The Neustadt International Prize for Literature, often more discriminating in its impartial choice of laureates than the glamorous awards bestowed in Stockholm, and the Puterbaugh Conferences on Writers of the Hispanic and French-Speaking World, with their attendant series of learned talks, have brought renown to America and more particularly to the state of Oklahoma. Norman has gained the fame of an intellectual Mecca for those who, from Finland to Australia and from Buenos Aires to Canada, care for the life of the mind.

Much of that achievement is due to the guiding spirits of the quarterly, of the prize-giving committees, and of the Puterbaugh Conferences: Ivar and Astrid Ivask. They live, feel, and think as poets. They come from countries by the northern seas of Europe which have often haunted the dreams and the longings of some of us, nurtured closer to what Swinburne called "the tideless dolorous midland sea." Because their native languages were known to relatively few and since their lands were trampled upon by foreign soldiers and invaders, they had, early, to respect the broadening values of cosmopolitanism. They became experts in several tongues while continuing to sing their nostalgic memories of the lands of their ancestors. Eventually they migrated to the "paradise of exiles" which, in Shelley's time, was Italy and which, in our century, is America. Ivar Ivask represents to all of us who have collaborated on his review and attended his conferences that rare and paradoxical combination: a poet who is also the most infallible of organizers, all-seeing and all-planning; a uniquely patient, gentle host to his guests, who knows how to elicit from those "Latin" temperaments—Horace's "genus irritabile vatum"—the sweetness and the grace which lie deep in their poetical egos. He bears with the idiosyncrasies of our often prickly selves and, with a touch of humor, remembers those honored visitors who vent their wrath at their luggage misplaced at airports, at snowstorms in a climate they had expected to be Edenic, or at an excess of light in their rooms. He had even, for the gathering of an April weekend, announced (and probably invoked in poetical language) one or two tornadoes driven by some "wild west wind," which would have afforded his sedate academic guests the thrill of "living dangerously" à la Nietzsche. But no such internal or external fury interfered with our debates. With a smile and only an occasional frown of dissent, we listened to each other. The eminent critic Harry Levin once hinted that, if scholars and poets ever utter prayers to "the unknown gods," they probably ask that the whole of their profession be afflicted with chronic insomnia; they could then devote their sleepless hours to the reading of our multitudinous books and articles. We have in fact devised the next-best means: conferences at which we provide the captive audience for the papers of our colleagues, euphemistically calling them "symposia" since we drown our faint velleities to dissent in comforting imbibition.

The present speaker, who has long read and admired *Books Abroad / World Literature Today* and en-joyed the poetry of Ivar Ivask, had never before traveled to Norman. He wonders at the mysterious motives which may have prompted the organizers of the tenth biennial Puterbaugh Conference to invite him here. He happens to have shared with the Ivasks a warm admiration for the great Spanish poet Jorge Guillén, whose *Cántico* he had discovered early, just before the Spanish Civil War: he enjoyed Jorge's friendship after the poet came to the United States during the war years. To the example of the invincible poet who liked to declare with a smile that he had started composing his most ardent love poetry after reaching the biblical age of threescore years and ten, I perhaps owe my own prosaic survival beyond the age of eighty—merely as an obscure critic and interpreter of inspired bards. I am proud to have known his son Claudio Guillén as a boy and to have touched on the questions of influences and of literary originality which have preoccupied him and another Harvard professor, Guillén's son-in-law Stephen Gilman. Both of them are the inheritors of that exquisite Spanish humor which alternated with the fervor and the "clamor" of one of the greatest poets of our century.

It is thus as an aged man that I am addressing this group. I lay no claim to having acquired wisdom through the accumulation of years. Long ago, I was impressed by T. S. Eliot's lines in "East Coker," where he spurns the would-be wisdom of old men and denounces their folly and their fear of fear and frenzy. I have taught so long in several lands that I may well have turned into a dull lay preacher. Like all Frenchmen, I was early imbued with the maxims of La Rochefoucauld, one of which warns us that "old men like to dispense good precepts, because they are no longer in a position to provide bad examples." I shall probably indulge some—valid or tedious—precepts here and utter some prophecies, at scant risk, since I cannot count on seeing them fulfilled or contradicted. The nearness of the last decade of the century turns many of us into millenarian announcers of impending doom. Let us also seek ways of escape from the perils confronting this age.

At the core of any prophecies I might venture to put forward there lies an invincible act of faith in the value of literature and the conviction, unfashionable as it may sound, that there is, or can be, a content to literature, more significant to me than any theory of criticism and any speculation on language. I refuse to smile at the rash prophecy of Matthew Arnold, envisaging an era in which, "the sea of faith" on which he meditated at Dover Beach having receded, literature might replace religion as the provider of ethical values. In the face of some who today hail in Mallarmé the pioneer of a strange form of linguistics and who prize his ludicrously amateurish volume *Les mots anglais,* I choose to remember the severe and lofty statement in which the mission of poetry is defined by him as being nothing less than "the Orphic explanation of the earth." Elsewhere, in replying in 1891 to the question of a journalist, he declared that mission to be "the only possible human creation." We may, at some of our professional gatherings, cultivate esoteric subtleties, coin pedantic formulas, deny all content and significance to literary texts, and declare the recipient of books to be the equal of the creator. All the while, we are losing the audience of the generations whose training is entrusted to us as educators.

There subsists in many of the young a yearning for the expression of emotions, for the understanding of their fellow beings and of their own selves through fiction and drama, an earnest desire to rise up to the momentous demands made upon the youth of a country whose fate, for the next fifty or hundred years, is to lead the rest of the world. Science, technology, exploration of space and remote planets, vertiginous speed of communication are, and will remain, essential. Economics, sociology (which some of its ablest practitioners have defined as, at its best, "an art form"), microbiology, and a score of other sciences have put forward their claims to a greater mastery of the expanding universe and to American preeminence among nations. Still, our progress since the conclusion of World War II has met with disconcerting setbacks. Spanish American intellectuals, whom *World Literature Today* has done much to help us respect and read, have repeatedly warned us that we are dismally failing in our attempts to win their countries over to North American aims. Emigré writers from Europe, who had come to these shores with an eager determination to help deepen and spread "the American dream," have, in the voice of one of the most discerning among them, Hannah Arendt, expressed their dismay at the feeble echoes aroused in 1976 by the celebration of the bicentennial of the American Revolution. That revolution, if indeed it was one, seemed to leave the rest of the world, and many in this country also, altogether unconcerned. It failed, among other things, to excite the imagination of novelists and poets.

Those of us whose life goal has been to help mature and broaden the thousands of students entrusted to us have not failed to remark upon the anxiety underlying their lip service to the pursuit of happiness. They have watched with dismay the accumulation of blunders committed in Vietnam, in Lebanon, in Central America, and the imperious threats thrown at European nations by successive secretaries of state. Theirs will be someday the task of devising a new orientation. Like the Prince of Denmark complaining that the time was out of joint, many of our best-educated young people mourn "that

ever they were born to set it right." Neither sophisticated technology nor learned speculation couched in a language far removed from that of common men is of much avail. Critical spirit and an informed and tactful understanding of other nations are more urgently needed. Literature has a role to play there, as it has if the message of the United States is to be conveyed abroad in noble words and in slogans such as Woodrow Wilson, F. D. Roosevelt, and J. F. Kennedy knew how to devise. I once, in my raw and youthful years, proposed to our colleagues gathered at a convention the motto, "Never underestimate the power of a professor." I would, at the evening of my life, alter the phrase to read: "Do not underestimate the power of literature." Literature has wrought evil more than once, spread hatred or contempt of other races or nations, even rallied to Mussolini, Goebbels, Vichy France, Franco's Spain, and indulged anti-Semitic and other racist denunciations. It has also advocated broad-mindedness and wise tolerance, with Montaigne, Voltaire, and Goethe. Can it help, before the time proves too late, in transcending or at least transforming nationalism?

There is a multiplicity of threats hovering around us in this age. The proverbial curse flung by Chinese sages at their opponents, "May you live in an interesting age!" has not been spared our closing years of the second millennium: overpopulation, chronic drought in Africa, an eventual dearth of energy, the spread of nuclear weapons, others still. Nationalism, however, is the most conspicuous threat, and potentially the most baneful, since it could lead to wars of annihilation, and it is this threat which it is clearly the duty to fight for those of us who deal with ideas and train the future generations. We cannot avert our eyes and, as devotees of esthetic pursuits, hint that this is none of our business. German professors did that, before and in the early years of the Hitler regime, choosing unconcern in political matters and concentration on their sole specialized areas of research. Their successors remember what ensued; they have come to accept the disorders of democratic polemics and of ideological debates. Risks have to be incurred, naturally. It is relatively easy for science to be international. There may be an entity such as "national character," even if we fail to agree on what constitutes it. There is in all likelihood typically French music, Italian sculpture, Jewish painting, Japanese architecture, and American poetry—different in tone and perhaps even in nature from that of Great Britain. It is relatively easy to leave nationalism out of sculpture and even of music, except for passing phases of collective hysteria in wartime at which we subsequently blush. It is far more difficult in fiction, criticism, philosophical speculation, history, and all the disciplines which depend upon language and pursue, or combat, inherited national traditions.

The Age of Enlightenment cherished cosmopolitanism. To a large extent, the internationalism in literary and artistic matters, in manners, in taste was tantamount to the acceptance of French intellectual fashions as they had been predominant under Louis XIV. Still it was the French who first went in for Anglomania, and writers in the French language, Mme de Staël most notably, first encouraged other nations to shake off the yoke of French taste. That internationalism, however, was mostly spread among the aristocrats and intellectuals. It never reached the masses, which were hardly cognizant of literary debates and even of political speculation. With the collapse of the French monarchy and the wars waged by the European princes, egged on by the émigrés from the French nobility, nationalism raised its head. The symbolic cleavage may be dated from the battle of Valmy, on 20 September 1792. The Duke of Brunschweig (or Brunswick, in French) had, with his army, proceeded as far as that village in the Ardennes, near Verdun. He was facing an untrained army of French volunteers alongside troops surviving from the monarchy. The mud and the brush of the Argonne Forest impeded the invaders. When the French revolutionary troops with-stood their cannonade and sang "Vive la Nation!" the invading army retreated, to everyone's astonishment. Young Goethe (he was then forty-three years old) was with the German troops. He later related the event in his *Campagne in Frankreich*. On that evening he sat with a group of officers, who asked the renowned author of *Werther* and *Egmont* what he thought of the puzzling incident. As he reports, in his sententious style of an analyst of history, he solemnly declared: "From this place and from this day begins a new era in world history, and you may declare: I was there."

With the revolutionary and Napoleonic wars, the Spaniards, the Prussians, the Russians, the compatriots of Pitt and Wellington, and even the ethnic groups which the defeat of Napoleon had not yet freed (Poles, South Slavs, Balkan populations fretting under Turkish domination), all became carried away by a wave of nationalist passion. They eventually asserted their identity. The whole of the nineteenth century in Europe, as in South America, thought in terms of nationalism. Literature, history, philosophy, folklore provided the substratum and the impulse for that momentous liberation from medievalism and submission. The role of Herder, of Fichte and Hegel—cured from their youthful enthusiasm for the French conquest of liberty—of the several successors to Hegel (Marx included), later of Nietzsche and Treitschke, is well known. Nietzsche professed to scorn the Germans and warned them sternly after their victory of 1870–71 not to become intoxicated with power and to honor and even imitate the defeated French. He has been cleared of the suspicion of anti-Semitism, and among his often contradictory aphorisms, he aimed his most scornful ones at Christian humility and the ethics of slaves. Almost every one of his exegetes offers his own interpretation of Nietzschean (successive or simultaneous) philosophical attitudes. French interpreters, from Henri Lichtenberger and Charles Andler down to Gilles Deleuze, have done more than the Germans or the British to naturalize the thought of Nietzsche. After the outburst of Nazism, a number of Germans such as Karl Jaspers have proved more reticent.

In a posthumously published essay, Thomas Mann, once carried away by the Schopenhauerian and Nietzschean assertion of the primacy of the will, reconsidered his earlier enthusiasm for Nietzsche. "His destiny was his genius, and another name for his genius is disease," the author of *Doktor Faustus* blandly declared in "Nietzsche's Philosophy in the Light of Recent History."[1] To the Nietzschean praise of life, myths, illusions cherished by the masses, heroic estheticism, Mann, sobered by Hitlerism and exile, wished that respect for reason and truth be opposed, that yearning for mere justice might have been preached to the people—as indeed his brother Heinrich had much earlier advocated. Thomas Mann excerpted blatantly brutal aphorisms from the Nietzschean canon and scathingly condemned them to oblivion: "A good war sanctifies any cause"; "To renounce war is to renounce the grandeur of life itself"; "Be robbers and conquerors." The admirer of the classical understatement of the French moralists who heaped up opprobrium on Bismarck's Reich forbore his restraint when he exclaimed, "A sword wants to drink blood and glistens with desire." In his late years, looking at his former compatriots with a lucid, or jaundiced, eye, Thomas Mann asked in that essay, "Who, in the end, was more German than he?" He admonished, "Eternally necessary is the correction of life by mind, or by morality." The great novelist, who died in Switzerland in 1955 at eighty years of age, was forgetting that he had himself, up to his fortieth year, scornfully denounced all humanitarian and democratic philosophies, in a raving pan-Germanist volume, *Friedrich und die große Koalition* (1915), and three years later in *Betrachtungen eines Unpolitischen* (*Considerations of Nonpolitical Man;* 1918, reprinted in 1933). To the contemptible French, optimistic, Catholic (hence pagan), and addicted to inflated words, he had opposed the Germans, pessimistic, Protestant, preferring music to eloquence and "life" to liberty. Let the Cathedral of Reims, "a flower of fanaticism and superstition," be bombed! "Peace is an element of civil corruption. . . . The greatest and most important contribution to the moral apology of war was done by German minds." In 1915 the novelist, then forty and no longer a naïve youth, had not hesitated to announce: "Only the victory of Germany will guarantee the peace of Europe."[2]

Hundreds of such quotes might be culled from some of the most respected European thinkers and men of letters. Max Weber, just before his death in 1920, dispensed peremptory bellicose advice to General Ludendorff, who, after the 1918 armistice, had turned to pro- and pre-Hitlerian propaganda: "In a democracy, the people choose a leader in whom they trust; then the chosen leader says: shut up and obey." Heidegger is reported to have regretted and perhaps repented, before his death in 1976, his rabid anti-Semitism and his 1933 praise of Hitler: he was forty-four when Hitler acceded to power legally. Solemnly, he had asserted, "History has always sacrificed truth and justice to power and race." In May 1933 he hailed the advent of Nazism as the fulfillment of all his dreams. He closed the gates of the University of Freiburg to his former teacher, the great Husserl, because Husserl had been born a Jew. Addressing his faculty as rector, he urged them to devote themselves to "the mysterious, higher demands of race and heroic leadership," and in a speech which was printed in thousands of copies, he declared, "The Führer himself, and he alone, is Germany's reality and law today and in the future." No wonder Heidegger's picture adorned the official *Führer-Lexikon!*[3]

Nor was such jingoism the monopoly of the Germans. Nicolas Chauvin, whose name gave us the word *chauvinism,* was a French soldier under Napoleon I famous and derided for his repetitious bragging about his native land. Michelet, Hugo, and scores of other widely read French writers advocated peace, better understanding among European nations, and even a United States of Europe, but always under the aegis of Paris, the City of Light. The nationalist Barrès, who turned from an early "enemy of the law" to revanchist Boulangism and to the cult of "the earth and the dead" (a variation on "Blut und Boden"), fascinated thousands of writers, even those who, like Gide, opposed him and coveted his role as "the Prince of the youth." His impact was great—and not only of short duration—on the prose and the sensibilities of Jewish writers such as Proust and Emmanuel Berl, of liberal Catholics such as the editor of *Esprit* Jean Marie Domenach and the Academician Henri Gouhier, even on Montherlant, Malraux, and Camus. He praised the message of "magnanimousness" which he claimed he read in the ruins of militaristic Sparta and spurned the traditional praise of decadent, turbulently democratic Athens. Charles Maurras, who

had been nurtured on the classics, had paid lip service to Catholicism (although a total agnostic himself),[4] had advocated a return to the monarchy and held democracy in contempt, promptly turned pro-German and fierce anti-Semite once France was defeated and occupied by German troops. His newspaper, *L'Action Française,* clamored loudly for "integral nationalism," then ended by bowing to Hitler's design to crush France for a thousand years and to reduce her to a pleasure ground for the benefit of the master race.

Britain too was not immune to the taint of nationalism in her literature. By the end of the long reign of Queen Victoria, William Ernest Henley, whose *Song of the Sword,* a book of verse, had won fame in 1892, published in his magazine Rudyard Kipling's *Barrack Room Ballads* and wrote glowingly in praise of the Empire. Kipling's prestige was immense. Swinburne, who had once been branded as a scandalous practitioner of "fleshly poetry" and as an advocate of liberal revolution (in Italy, at any rate), turned reactionary in his last phase. Early in the new century he penned multiple odes to England, poems celebrating "Trafalgar Day" and "Cromwell's England," praising him "who made England out of weakness strong" (and incidentally made a holocaust of thousands of Irishmen and was greeted by a "Te Deum" in St. Paul's Cathedral on his return from the ravaged green island). One year before Henley's death, in 1903, Cecil Rhodes, a devotee of Marcus Aurelius, whose *Meditations* he pondered over daily, but also a man of action and wealth, adopted as his professed life purpose "the government of the world by the British race." G. B. Shaw had subscribed to some form of socialism and was later to propose it to "intelligent women"; still he unabashedly declared that the Boers deserved to be crushed by the superior British, superior "because more aggressive." Later he was effusive in praise of Mussolini. The memories of the Spanish-American War, encouraged if not engineered by the Hearst press, of Theodore Roosevelt's Rough Riders, and of his bellicose declarations during his two presidencies have remained vivid in the United States, as has the blunt exclamation "My country, right or wrong," uttered a century earlier by a hardy admiral, Stephen Decatur, repeatedly victorious against Tripoli, today's Libya. Decatur died in 1820, in a duel fought with another naval officer; four American cities are proud to bear his name.

Already in those years, at the end of the age of democratic revolutions in Europe and in the early nineteenth century, observers of nationalist movements had prophesied that two great and young countries, Russia and the United States, would one day share the dominion of the world and face each other as two antagonistic empires, one of "evil" and the other presumably of good, since it is "God's own country."[5] Long before Dostoevsky, who spared neither the Catholics nor the Jews in his vituperations and who loved Mother Russia all the more even as she treated him harshly, Russian writers had managed to be both cosmopolitan in their literary interests and rabid patriots, often professing pan-Slavism. Pushkin was steeped in eighteenth-century French and English letters and appeared to the West as a more inspired André Chénier or as a second Byron, yet he was suspect to the Czar's entourage. In 1831, however, he composed an inflamed poem, "To the Slanderers of Russia," justifying the harsh crushing of a Polish uprising by the Russian army. Tiutchev, a delicate and sensitive poet, whose two wives spoke only French and who resorted to French himself in daily life and in his letters, died happy in 1873 because he had just heard that the Russian troops had captured the Khanate of Khiva, somewhere in Asiatic Russia.

There was, however, bestriding the two centuries, one great exception, that of Goethe. Almost to his dying day in 1831, he took a keen interest in the young writers of France, who were asserting their noisy romantic claims against the effete partisans of the classicists. He lauded Vigny, Stendhal, and even Béranger, and balked only at *Notre Dame de Paris,* which he judged to be immoral. At seventy-eight, on 31 January 1827, unresigned to placidly reliving his own past, he declared to Eckermann: "The words 'national literature' have little meaning today. We are advancing toward an era of universal literature, and everyone of us should strive to hasten the advent of that era." The following year, in a letter to Thomas Carlyle, who wanted to know his opinion of an English version of his *Tasso,* Goethe stressed the importance of translations as a means of encouraging the dawning of a world "transcending national boundaries." He devoted his own periodical, *Kunst und Altertum* (founded in 1816), to what we would today call "comparative literature" and informed his readers about Walter Scott, Byron, Carlyle, Manzoni. Diversity would not disappear, he stressed; like that which is to be observed in plants, it is but the visible manifestation of a higher unity, "the Eternal oneness, displayed under many forms." Repeatedly he contended that "the sure way of achieving universal toleration is to leave untouched what is peculiar to each man or each group, keeping in mind that all that is best in the world is the property of all mankind." With rash confidence, he asserted, "It is the destiny of Germany to become the representative of all the citizens of the world." After the defeat of Germany in 1945, a great scholar, Fritz Strich, found some solace in turning to Goethe, whom he presented as an inspirer of an eventual spiritual renaissance

for Germany. His volume *Goethe und die Weltliteratur* appeared in 1945 in Switzerland, where Strich had gone in 1929; it was translated into English in 1949 in London (Routledge & Kegan Paul).

Those lofty hopes have been frustrated, for the present at least. The collapse of Austro-Hungary in 1918 has aroused many a regret and disrupted a frail order which had, somehow, survived since the 1815 Congress of Vienna. That collapse was inevitable from the day when an ultimatum tried to punish the Sarajevo murder of June 1914 and ushered in a European war. The South Slavs, the Poles, the Czechs, the Italians from the "irredentist" provinces were all bound to clamor for their national independence. They could not be expected to learn the need for interdependence overnight and in the flush of their long-delayed autonomy. History had intoxicated the leaders of the European nations: Mussolini invoked the Roman empire and brandished the slogan of "Mare nostrum," defying all sense of the ridiculous; later Israel put forward her claim to the lands mentioned in the Old Testament. French children were gravely taught that the *patrie* was a nearly perfect hexagon; French nuns piously offered to Moslem girls in Morocco and Algeria the holy model of Joan of Arc, expelling the "goddams" (as she called the English) out of the kingdom of France. The pupils then put the lesson to use against their colonial masters. Lay teachers had their black pupils in Senegal and Guinea recite French history textbooks which praised the hardiness of "our ancestors the Gauls, blond and fearless." Eventually, the Africans, having served in the French army in defense of "civilization," were to expel the French. The Egyptians expelled the British. Soon the Basques, the Catalans, the Corsicans, the Lebanese, and the French-speaking Canadians would assert their national and cultural originality. John Stuart Mill had pronounced, "It is in general a necessary condition of free institutions that the boundaries of governments should coincide in the main with those of nationalities." Napoleon III, a former revolutionary idealist and a denouncer of "pauperism," used the new and explosive Principle of Nationalities to further his country's ambitions. Others did likewise in the Balkan peninsula and the Middle East. A former history professor, Woodrow Wilson, generalized the application of the principle at the 1919 Versailles conference. Twenty years later, Hitler invoked it to disrupt and annex Polish and Czech provinces, to spread dissent and revolt in other nations of Central Europe, and to absorb them into his Reich. The catastrophic trend proved irreversible; warnings from some intellectual leaders were few and went unheeded.

Nationalism has proved, in the second half of this century, a formidable force, and within limits it has been a force for the good. It fulfills an eagerness in people to belong to a group, to join a community and thereby feel reassured and comforted. It liberates an energy which is in part spiritual. It inspired the Italian Risorgimento, the independence of Greece, the rebirth of Poland, the assertion of Norwegian originality among the Scandinavian nations, that of Finland as well, and home rule for Ireland. It nurtures the dreams and at times the terrorist fury of Kurds and Armenians. It pits Chile against Argentina, Bolivia against Paraguay, Hispanics against Amerindian peoples having similar names, similar traditions, and parallel interests in Nicaragua, Honduras, El Salvador. The explosive force unleashed by the French revolutionaries has swept away all other creeds, all faiths, and all counsels of mutual tolerance. Socialist and international faiths have faded before that onslaught. The call "Proletarians of the world, unite!" of the 1848 Communist Manifesto has been a fruitless exhortation. Industrial workmen threatened by unemployment or by an influx of cheaper labor from other lands cannot overnight learn how to think and behave internationally. The launching of the first International in 1864, and of the second in 1889, has had but a paltry impact on the working class. The eloquent and warm lines of "L'Internationale" written in 1871 by the touching idealist Paul Pottier (for a time after the Commune a refugee in America) were sung ritually by strikers on May Day, by the Petrograd workmen overthrowing the Czar and defying the Duma in 1917–18. Socialist leaders acceded to power in several lands, apparently eager to help the masses get work, better wages, greater dignity, and cease to serve as mere cannon fodder. Pilsudski, Mussolini, German Social Democrats before 1914 and again before 1933 began as internationally-minded socialists; in France so did Millerand, Briand, Laval, later Doriot and Déat, and in Belgium Henri de Man. Soon they discovered that their socialism had to incorporate into itself a great deal of nationalism or else it would lose the following of the masses. Trotsky organized the Red Army, and Lenin, likewise a man of the "left," ruthlessly crushed dissenters.

Lenin's favorite question, "What is to be done?" (the title of an 1864 novel by Chernyshevsky, who spent nineteen years at hard labor in Siberia), is the inevitable one. None of us advocates uniformity of minds, because—or while—the so-called first and second worlds, soon to be joined by the third, watch similar films on their television sets, rush for the same blue jeans, acclaim the same rock singers, read the same bestsellers. There may run parallel currents through the philosophies, the novels, the critical works of diverse countries on the two sides of the Atlantic, even the shores of the eastern Mediterranean and of the Pacific

Ocean. Still, existentialism, constructivism, *modernismo,* atonalism in music, Lacanism, and a score of other movements or currents, periodically brought up to date by the addition of a Latin or Greek prefix (*post-* or *meta-*), quickly take on an original hue in different countries. The Catholic republics of South America or the Moslem countries of Asia and Africa have not been reduced to dull uniformity. It is said in the Koran, "We have made peoples and tribes different, so that you would know one another." Still, interdependence within different frameworks and solidarity in continents exposed to the same economic threats and between lenders and debtors are values which should be stressed in educational institutions and in the press. For a decade or so after the 1945 victory, a spirit of determination to avoid the recurrence of another catastrophe moved thinkers and statesmen to a common spirit of building a resurgent united Europe: Karl Jaspers, the German psychoanalyst and philosopher, wrote courageously about *die Schuldfrage,* the question of his country's guilt. In 1958 he uttered another warning in his volume on the atom bomb and the future of man. Jean Monnet succeeded in persuading French, German, and other statesmen to make it impossible in the future to return to their former rivalry; there ensued the first unreserved reconciliation between the two countries bordering the Rhine since the peace of Westphalia. However, Britain, weakened by the war, laden with the task of renouncing her empire, hesitated and balked at assuming the leadership of a renascent Western Europe. The United States did not count enough courageous intellectual and political leaders to add to the Marshall Plan a bold scheme insuring solidarity among the ravaged yet hopeful nations. They distrusted their own spiritual and moral prestige, which might then, between 1947 and 1960, have opened the way to closer cooperation. Their fascination with pursuing their rivalry with obdurate Russia turned into an obsession. A subconscious sense of guilt haunted them in the midst of their victory. They should have been ready to develop their armed forces and armaments and to enter the inevitable war before the proclamation of the four freedoms by Roosevelt in August 1941. They might have heeded their president's appeal in his "quarantine speech" of 1938, if only their intellectual leaders had been a little more prescient. It is easy and perhaps vain to rewrite history and to dwell longingly on what might have happened. Still, if the elite of this nation had shaken off, three years before the Japanese attack, the complacent illusion of isolationism, America could very well have been in a position to effect a landing on the Normandy beaches in 1942 and 1943 instead of June 1944, Berlin would have been captured by the Western allies, Poland freed before the arrival of the Russians.

Political scientists, lawyers, and historians had, during the years of the Depression, failed to shake off the isolationist rancor caused by the ingratitude of the European allies who failed to repay their war debts and the incredible shortsightedness of the Republican businessmen who raised the tariffs in 1930. The passionate force which impels the nationalisms of young countries probably cannot be fought frontally. It has been compared by one of the shrewdest analysts of history in our age, Isaiah Berlin, to the bent twig which lashes back if forced to bow.[6] Momentous changes in sensibilities and intellects, even in collective ones, have, however, taken place in the past, through the power of faith and of education. John Stuart Mill had wisely offered a warning: "When society requires to be rebuilt, there is no sense in attempting to rebuild it on the old plan. No great improvements in the lot of mankind are possible, unless a great change takes place in the fundamental constitutions of their mode of thought." Historians of revolutions in the second half of the present century (Crane Brinton, Robert Palmer, Hannah Arendt) have agreed, against the claims of materialistic determinism, that revolutions begin in the minds of men. They did not in the past proceed primarily from food riots, war weariness, peasant uprisings, envy, destructive irrational folly. The events of 1789, analyzed in detail by Robert Palmer in the two volumes of his *Age of the Democratic Revolutions* (Princeton, 1964), should have occurred in a half-dozen European countries, all poorer and more oppressed and humiliated than was the France of Louis XVI, but only in France had there taken place the movement of dissatisfaction of many intellectuals from the prevailing order of things. Though impossible to be measured in quantitative terms, the thought and the literature of the Enlightenment played a considerable part in fomenting, then in guiding, for better or for worse, the positive and the negative achievement of the three revolutionary assemblies which succeeded each other in Paris between 1789 and 1795.

We in America are reluctant to speak of intellectuals—that is, of educated persons specializing in the affairs of the mind who, as the phrase goes, perhaps never had to meet a payroll and who propose to do our thinking for us. Of course, they *are* fallible. They were in Germany around Goebbels, in France, in Oxford. The best and the brightest in this country hailed the Gulf of Tonkin resolution, the domino theory, the fallacy that Vietnam was the ally, or the pawn, of Communist China. Still they can, and do, learn from their mistakes. The world at large entertains lofty and almost impossible expectations from American leaders. They dimly realize that the burden of leading the world into a livable twenty-first century has, at present, fallen upon the shoul-

ders of Americans. This country stands more than ever before in need of a large number of educated citizens with a sense of the past, with imagination, and with the courage needed to rid themselves of what a great historian, Henry Steele Commager, has called "outmoded assumptions."[7] They, we, must, in Shelley's noble words at the end of his *Defense of Poetry,* "imagine that which we know." The ineptitude displayed in disturbing recent catastrophes in Vietnam, in the Guyana mass self-slaughter, in Lebanon, in the rhetorical condemnations of the "empire of evil" and of Nicaraguans impudent enough to appeal to the World Court in The Hague is an insult to the millions in this country who continue to reflect and to work for a livable future. Stephen Graubard, the editor of one of our most thoughtful reviews, *Daedalus,* submitted, in a 1982 survey titled "U.S. Defense Policy in the 1980s," that "our most urgent need may be for a vastly increased store of intellectual and conceptual material." There are more than ten million students in the colleges, junior colleges, and graduate schools of America; probably fifty million or more alumni or former students, and easily over a million teachers. They do not all feel, think, vote alike, but enough of them might provide leaders (in industry, finance, engineering, medicine, law, diplomacy, politics), both women and men, eager to envisage and prepare an era less prone to bow to the easy allurements of nationalism. The challenge is pressing; it can be met. "The irresistible is often that which is *not* resisted," observed Judge Brandeis.

We have fought, transcended, exploded other would-be "irresistible" myths: the supposedly fatal subordination of females to males; slavery; the racial superiority of self-styled higher classes; the superstition that class society was a providential and unshakable order; the idea that an established church and a state religion should forever prevail against dissidents and nonconformists. Literature and education have within their reach ever-growing captive audiences, most of them in their years of greatest receptivity. Those of us who teach, write, reflect, and eagerly attend conferences such as the one here convened by *World Literature Today* need not be bashful about our faith in a better and wiser future which, in this decade, it is the responsibility of the United States to prepare and bring about. The most visionary of American poets, Walt Whitman, in "the greatest book of criticism written in this country," as Lewis Mumford called *Democratic Vistas* (1871), defined a goal at which we should take aim: "Viewed today, from a point of view sufficiently overarching, the problem of humanity all over the civilized world is social and religious, and is to be finally met and treated by literature."

Henri Peyre, Autumn 1985

[1] Thomas Mann, "Nietzsche's Philosophy in the Light of Recent History," in his *Last Essays,* New York, Knopf, 1959.

[2] Taking issue with the great novelist then urging Americans to champion democracy and uphold the liberal tradition, I reminded readers of the *Atlantic Monthly* of July 1944 that Mann had not always been so discerning. He would have given a better example if he had openly confessed and regretted his pan-Germanist ravings lavished over the six hundred pages of his *Betrachtungen.* The epigraph of the book was culled from Molière's *Fourberies de Scapin* (2.7): "Qu'allait-il faire dans cette galère?" What, indeed?

[3] The quotes in the text, and other high-sounding statements of fidelity to Nazism (by the dramatist Gerhart Hauptmann and the poet and physician Gottfried Benn), are to be found in Robert G. Waite's book *The Psychopathic God: Adolf Hitler* (the phrase is from Auden's poem "September 1, 1939"), New York, Basic Books, 1977.

[4] The ancestor and model for that strange Catholic but hardly Christian position was the 19th-century writer Barbey d'Aurevilly, who declared without hesitation, "I established myself in Catholicism, as on a convenient balcony from which to spit on democracy."

[5] I take the liberty here to refer to my essay "History as Prophecy: French Predictions of Russian-American Antagonism," in *Laurels* (the magazine of the American Society of the French Legion of Honor), 53:1 (Spring 1982).

[6] Isaiah Berlin, "The Bent Twig," *Foreign Affairs,* October 1972, pp. 11–30.

[7] Henry Steele Commager, "Outmoded Assumptions," *Atlantic Monthly,* March 1982, pp. 13–18.

Nobel medal with figure of Alfred Nobel (*The Nobel Foundation*)

The Swedish Academy and the Nobel Prize in Literature: History and Procedure

In presenting separate essays on the ten literary members among "The Eighteen" of the Swedish Academy, the Spring 1981 issue of *WLT* (55:2, pp. 197–256) was an attempt to introduce "The Swedish Writers Behind the Nobel Prize" as the ten prominent, engaging and highly individualistic authors that they are, in contrast to the occasional public image of them abroad as a monolithic group of aged men given to "musing the obscure"[1] in their annual Nobel selections. The criticism which these yearly choices call forth—whether of a literary, a journalistic or an ideological nature—often betrays a comparable misapprehension of the way in which the Academy approaches the task and reaches its decisions. Critics outraged at the failure to honor Tolstoy with the first Nobel Prize in 1901, for example, neglected to note that the great Russian novelist had not been formally nominated by any outside individual or group and thus could not even be considered by the Academy under the statutes it had formulated for selecting the prizewinner (*NMP,* 91);[2] and charges of political

opportunism in the 1980 choice of Polish poet and novelist Czesław Miłosz during a well-publicized labor crisis in Gdańsk evidently were prompted by a confusion of the *announcement* of the prize with the lengthy *deliberations* which had begun months if not years earlier and had, for all practical purposes, been concluded before the strikes became a daily page-one item. As a complement to the Spring issue's essays on ten of the Academicians, then, the following descriptive history may serve to clarify, at least in some measure, the Swedish Academy's work in choosing the recipients of the world's most well-known and remunerative literary award.

▪ ▪ ▪

In an 1893 will Alfred Nobel included no specific bequest in regard to literature, making only general reference to rewards "for the most important and original discoveries or the most striking advances in the wide sphere of knowledge or on the path of human progress" and therefore evidently wishing to aid the exact sciences first and foremost (*NMP,* 85). The final will of November 1895, however, stipulated that one of five annual awards for "those who, during the preceding year, shall have conferred the greatest benefit on mankind" was to be given to "the person who shall have produced in the field of literature the most outstanding work of an ideal tendency"[3] and that this prize be distributed by "the Academy in Stockholm." Nobel's wish to promote the cause of letters, writes Academy member Anders Österling,

. . . was inspired, first and last, by his own interest in literature, which had been developed in his earliest youth and was later stimulated by his continued language studies. He not only read but mastered five languages, including Russian; his poems in English, written in his late teens and still preserved, show an astonishing mastery of poetic diction and an unmistakably poetic instinct.

Throughout his life, Alfred Nobel gave serious attention to literature and, as far as his absorbing and hectic existence permitted it, kept in touch with the literary developments of his time. In regard to his tastes, it is also known that he preferred works of an ideal tendency and consequently strongly disapproved of the contemporary naturalism represented, for example, by Zola. . . . As a reader of literature, he looked for the living core; the ideas expressed interested him more than the forms.

Consequently, it was not by chance that he expressly stipulated that "an ideal tendency" was an essential qualification of literary works to be judged for the prize, even though the expression was vague and has caused endless arguments. What he really meant by this term was probably works of humanitarian and constructive character, which, like scientific discoveries, could be regarded as of benefit to mankind. (*NMP*, 85–86)

The Svenska Akademien itself was founded in 1786, under the reign of King Gustavus III. Although based on the model of the Académie Française, the Swedish Academy is composed of only eighteen members instead of the former's forty—reputedly because Gustavus preferred the resonant sound of *En av De Aderton* (One of The Eighteen) to that of all other possible numbers, particularly the pinched nasal tones of *En av De Fyrtio* (One of The Forty). The Academy's principal duties were originally the promotion and preservation of Swedish language, literature, history and culture; since 1893 it has also published and periodically updated the *Svenska Akademien ordbok* (Dictionary of the Swedish Academy). The organization awards numerous grants and scholarships to individuals, to journals and to groups, with the total annual amount allocated for such awards, philological work, magazine publication and research roughly corresponding to that of three Nobel Prizes. Funds for these programs "are derived chiefly from an old newspaper monopoly and from donations which the Academy administers," writes current Permanent Secretary of the Academy Lars Gyllensten (*NPL*, 5).[4] The Swedish Academy also participates with the Music Academy and the Art Academy in the publication of *Artes,* a bimonthly journal devoted to literature and the arts. The journal is not an official organ of the three organizations, but the articles and features published there do represent their various areas of interest. Swedish Academy member Östen Sjöstrand is the Editor, and the Editorial Board includes his fellow authors Lars Gyllensten and Artur Lundkvist as well as essayist and art critic Ulf Linde.

Members of the Academy, who are elected by the group itself for life and occupy specific "chairs" within the organization, are drawn "from Swedish cultural life and the humanities"; approximately half are themselves writers, the others being elected on the basis of their "literary leanings and expert knowledge of the Academy's various spheres of responsibility," Gyllensten continues. The organization "is not subordinate to any state or other authority. The governing body consists of a Director (chairman) and a Chancellor (vice chairman), who are elected for six months at a time, and of a Secretary, who usually remains until the age of 70—all of them members of the Academy. The Academy meets weekly and conducts its business in its own premises on the upper floor of the Stock Exchange (from the 18th century) in the old part of Stockholm" (*NPL*, 5).

Within a month of Nobel's death on 10 December 1896 the Swedish Academy was informed of the task entrusted to it by the magnate's will. There was evidently considerable hesitation and even reluctance among the members to assume this new responsibility, which some felt would so increase the Academy's workload as to force that body to neglect its traditional duties. That a majority of the Academicians did in fact ultimately vote in favor of acceptance was doubtless due to the persuasive force of the group's Permanent Secretary, Carl David af Wirsén, who argued:

> If the Swedish Academy refuses to assume this responsibility, the whole donation will be forfeited as far as literary awards are concerned, and by that very act the leading men of letters throughout Europe will be deprived of the opportunity to enjoy the financial rewards and the exceptional recognition for their long and brilliant literary careers which Nobel had in mind. A storm will blow up, a storm of indignation. The Academy's responsibility is great; if it definitely rejects the task, it will suffer sharp reproaches; in these reproaches may join future generations of our eighteen members who are to succeed us and who may find it strange that for reasons of personal convenience the members of today deliberately declined an influential role in the world of letters. The task is said to be foreign to the true purposes of the Academy. The work will, no doubt, be both new and arduous, but it can hardly be called foreign since it is of a literary character. A body that is to judge the literature of its own country

cannot afford to be ignorant of the very best produced abroad; the projected prizes are to be
given to the best living writers anywhere, and,
consequently, as a rule, to the very men whose
work ought to be familiar to the Academy members anyway. (*NMP,* 91)

To administer the huge fortune made available
from the Nobel estate for the five prizes and to coordinate the work involved in the judging and presentation
of the awards—though exercising no influence whatsoever on the prize deliberations and decisions themselves—the *Nobel Foundation* was established in early
1897. The Foundation is headed by an Executive Director and is managed by a Board of Directors whose members are elected by the several prize-awarding institutions,[5] to which they are responsible; the Executive
Director is chosen by the Board, but the Chairman and
Deputy Chairman of the Board are appointed directly
by the Swedish government (*NPL,* 2). As of this writing
(March 1981) the Chairman is Sune Bergström, a physician and professor at the Caroline Medico-Surgical Institute in Stockholm, and the Executive Director is Stig
Ramel, a Doctor of Law; the other Board members are
bank director Tore Browaldh (Deputy Chairman), pro-
fessor Carl Gustaf Bernhard (Permanent Secretary of the
Royal Academy of Sciences), bank director Lars-Erik
Thunholm, and medical professor and novelist Lars
Gyllensten (as noted above, Permanent Secretary of the
Swedish Academy).[6] "In the course of the years," Gyllensten writes,

> . . . the Foundation has received a number of do-
> nations and grants from other quarters and has
> engaged in various scientific and cultural projects
> in line with the principal aims of the Nobel Prizes
> but in addition to the actual prize work. The in-
> ternational conferences known as the Nobel
> Symposia are one example. The Nobel Founda-
> tion acts as arranger and host at the ceremonies
> and festivities in connection with the presenta-
> tion of the prizes, which takes place on 10 De-
> cember, the anniversary of Alfred Nobel's death.
> The Foundation has nothing to do with the actual
> prize decisions, the choice of candidates, the
> practical work of assessment etc. All this is en-
> tirely in the hands of the prize-awarding
> bodies. . . . The ambition in administering the do-
> nation has been, and is, to maintain as far as pos-
> sible the real value of the fortune and of the reve-
> nue (and thereby also of the prizes), and to place
> sufficient financial means at the disposal of the
> prize-awarding institutions for their increasingly
> widespread and expensive work of investigation.
> In 1901 . . . a prize was worth 150, 800 kronor.
> In 1978 each prize amounted to 725,000 kronor
> [over $180,000]. (*NPL,* 2–3)

Upon the establishment of the Nobel Foundation,
the prize-awarding institutions began drawing up formal statutes and regulations detailing the procedures by
which they would carry out the work of assessment and
selection in their respective areas. The Swedish Academy's final proposals (submitted in the spring of 1900)
placed particular stress on the need for strict and specific rules regarding the right to nominate candidates for
the prize. Österling explains:

> In the case of the Swedish Academy the problem
> was all the more complicated as there were no
> other institutions of the same type anywhere in
> the world, except the French and Spanish acade-
> mies. It would obviously have been unfair to
> limit the nominating rights to these two bodies,
> and it would have been equally inappropriate to
> grant such rights to any institution as a body,
> since the Academy's freedom of action might
> thereby be hampered by overwhelming external
> pressure. It was therefore proposed that the right
> to nominate candidates should be granted to the
> individual members of such institutions and not
> to the institutions themselves. The Academy felt,
> it was further stated, that by distributing the
> nomination rights so widely, it had tried to make
> sure that proposals could be made by duly quali-
> fied persons in all parts of the world and that no
> domestic or foreign literary organization of any
> importance should have cause to complain that
> the rights and privileges of its members had been
> slighted. The proposed text for the special statute
> was formulated as follows: "The right to nomi-
> nate candidates for the Prize in Literature is
> granted to members of the Swedish Academy;
> and of the French and Spanish Academies which
> are similar to it in character and objectives; to
> members of the humanistic sections of other
> academies, as well as to members of the humanis-
> tic institutions and societies as enjoy the same
> rank as academies, and to university professors
> of aesthetics, literature, and history." (*NMP,* 91–
> 92)

The statute was altered in 1949 to broaden the range
of groups regarded as competent to make nominations.
The field now includes, according to Gyllensten, "members of the Swedish Academy and of other academies,
institutions and societies similar to it in membership
and aims; professors of languages or in the history of
literature at universities and university colleges;[7] Nobel
laureates in literature; and presidents of authors' organizations which are representative of the literary activities
of their respective countries" (*NPL,* 7). Detailing the actual nomination procedure, Gyllensten continues:

> In order for anyone to be considered for a Nobel
> Prize, he or she must be proposed as a candidate

for the prize by someone qualified to make such a proposal. . . . Nominations must be sent in writing to the Swedish Academy or its Nobel Committee before the end of January of the year in which the award is made. The reason for a nomination should be stated, but detailed analysis is not necessary. A person who has once been proposed for a Nobel Prize is not automatically regarded as a candidate in following years but can be proposed again. Also, the Nobel Committee or the Academy can, if it sees fit, reconsider a previously proposed name, if this is not among the nominations from outside. Applications to receive a prize are disregarded.

In order to stimulate nomination, the Nobel Committee during the autumn sends out reminders or invitations to nearly 600 persons within the groups having the right to nominate candidates. The Committee endeavours to distribute such invitations all over the literary world and to vary the recipients each year. This procedure does not mean that others who are entitled to submit proposals do not have the right to do so—this right holds good even if no special invitation has been received.

The Academy receives between three and four hundred nominations each year before 1 February. Many of the proposers nominate the same candidates, so that the number of suggested prizewinners is much smaller than the number of proposers—of recent years, the number of nominees has usually amounted to 100–150. Of these, only a few are new names which have not been proposed before—about a dozen. It does not occur that a candidate of any literary importance is proposed who is unknown to the Academy or the Nobel Committee. The names of the more important ones are sent in year after year. It is very unusual for anyone who has been proposed for the first time to receive the prize. As regards appraisal of the most qualified candidates, there is a clear consensus of opinion between many of the proposers from different parts of the world. (*NPL,* 7–8)

In setting up a mechanism whereby it might handle the nominations most efficiently, the Swedish Academy established, prior to the very first prize, a *Nobel Committee,* which consists of five regular members plus one or more co-opted members appointed by the Academy. (The Committee presently includes Johannes Edfelt, Karl Ragnar Gierow, Lars Gyllensten, Artur Lundkvist and Anders Österling, with Östen Sjöstrand as a co-opted member.) Committee members are elected for three-year terms, receiving a yearly honorarium of approximately $1,200 (otherwise the Academicians receive no salary or stipend for their Academy work), and

may be reelected without restriction; in fact, Österling has served on the panel continuously since 1921! The Nobel Committee, Gyllensten writes,

> . . . is responsible for the adjudication work necessary in dealing with the questions concerning the Nobel Prize in Literature. . . . This work goes on all the time, the whole year round. It is the Committee which gathers in the nominations from outside, supplementing the list if necessary, and which sees to it that the merits of the nominees are scrutinized sufficiently to give the [Academy] a solid basis for its opinion. . . . The Committee is aided in its work by a secretary (the head librarian of the Nobel Library) and a literary scholar engaged as professor at the Academy. [Presently these posts are held by Anders Ryberg and Knut Ahnlund respectively.] . . . The Nobel Committee's adjudication work is of course decisive for the Academy's choice, but this work is done in continual contact with the Academy as a whole and during discussions which can be carried on all the year round in connection with the Academy's regular meetings each week. (*NPL,* 6, 4)

Assisting the Academy and the Nobel Committee in their work is the Academy's *Nobel Institute,* which consists of the *Nobel Library,* housed in the Academy's premises in the Royal Stock Exchange. The Library maintains a large collection of Swedish fiction, poetry, drama, essays and criticism for use in the Academy's regular activities, and also procures some 1,500–2,000 books annually in modern literature from throughout the world, in accordance with each year's list of Nobel Prize candidates. The total collection numbers approximately 150,000 volumes, making the Nobel Institute "the largest library in the Nordic countries as regards modern literature," adds Gyllensten. Moreover, "it is available to the public and is part of an interurban library service together with other public libraries. It is financed, however, entirely by private means from the Nobel Foundation and the Academy, without state or municipal grants. In addition to the head librarian and his assistants, the previously mentioned literary scholar works at the Academy's Nobel Institute" (*NPL,* 6–7).

All candidates proposed prior to 1 February by eligible individuals or organizations are placed on the year's list of nominations by the Nobel Committee, which may not exclude anyone so proposed. "This list," explains Gyllensten, "is put before the Academy as a whole during the first days of February. The Academy can then add new names, if necessary supplementing with those which for some reason, perhaps mere chance, have not been included. Nowadays the Academy, as well as the Nobel Committee, is more active in making such nominations than it was in the early days of the prize, when the members thought they should be very restrictive with their own proposals" (*NPL*, 8). All nominees on the supplemented list are appraised by the Academy, but "for one reason or another, many are unthinkable as Nobel laureates—perhaps because their production must be regarded as scholarship without the stipulated literary qualities, perhaps because their work, even if it does belong to literature, is far from having the necessary weight or quality, perhaps because they have obviously been proposed on grounds other than factual or literary ones (in some cases political, provincial, ideological and other motives appear as the decisive ones for the nomination in question)" (*NPL*, 9). The remaining names are then turned over to the Committee for thorough scrutiny. Gyllensten outlines the procedure at this stage of evaluation as follows:

> [The candidates'] works are procured in the original or in translation, if they are not already in the library. In cases where there is a paucity of translations and where candidates write in a language unfamiliar to the Academy's members or the experts, sample translations can be commissioned. With the aid of reference books, magazines, critical or scholarly reviews of literature etc. the Nobel Committee and its assistants familiarize themselves further with the nominees and their position in the literary world. Experts within or outside the Academy, at home and abroad, are commissioned to submit reports. Sometimes such assignments are given to individual writers, sometimes they are extended to include specific language areas or countries and certain literary schools or genres etc. Several investigations are made concerning most of the candidates of any importance and extensive information is collected about them. At the same time, the members of the Committee themselves read as much as they can of the candidates' works in the original or in translation and recommend books for the other members of the Academy to read. (*NPL*, 9)

Several factors pertaining to Alfred Nobel's will must be considered by the Committee and subsequently by the Academy as a whole in weighing each year's candidates: the nature of "literature," the "work" to be recognized, the "recentness" of that work, its benefit to "mankind" and the "ideal tendency" which it reflects. In 1900 the original Committee decided that "under the term 'literature' shall be comprised, not only belles lettres, but also other writings which, by virtue of their form and method of presentation, possess literary value" (*NMP*, 93); hence the subsequent selection of such laureates as Henri Bergson (1927), Bertrand Russell (1950) and Sir Winston Churchill (1953), although the Academy has adhered to a more purely belletristic

line since Churchill's award. The will's stipulation that the prizewinners must have rendered their noteworthy service "during the preceding year," Österling writes, "is interpreted to mean that 'the awards shall be made for the most recent achievements in the fields of culture referred to in the will, and for older works only if their significance has not become apparent until recently.' The purpose of the new phrasing was, obviously, to clarify in a legally proper way the testamentary requirement which, in most instances, it would have been impossible to interpret in any other way" (*NMP*, 93). Gyllensten reasons:

> Literary works in particular often do not acquire their full importance until they are seen as a life's work or parts of a whole, as distinct from more ephemeral lucky shots in the literary market. This is also the background to the fact that many literary laureates receive their prize when they are well up in years and the greatness and creative context of their work is clearly apparent or when their significance to the age in which they live begins to be discerned. The insistence on topicality and on the benefit to mankind implies, however, the condition that what is to be rewarded shall still be a vigorous and fruitful literary creativeness on which the prize and its prestige can be expected to have a stimulating effect. This point of view has explicit support in what is known of Alfred Nobel's intentions with his donation. (*NPL*, 12–13)

The statutory regulation that the prizes be given for *a work* or *a writing* posed no dilemma for the prize-awarding institutions in the sciences and medicine, "but for the Swedish Academy it has been much more difficult to observe," Österling says. "Usually the literary awards have been given for an author's entire production, without specifying any particular work. At times it has been done, however, 'with special reference' to a particular book, as in the case of . . . Hamsun's *Growth of the Soil*, . . . Mann's *Buddenbrooks,* Galsworthy's *Forsyte Saga,* and Martin du Gard's *Les Thibault*" (*NMP*, 93). The condition that the prizes benefit "mankind" has been taken at least since World War II as an enjoinder to look beyond the somewhat limited geographic and cultural views of Nobel's day, to adopt a more "universalist" outlook, to take into account what is being offered by civilizations other than those of Scandinavia or Europe or North America, and to honor their outstanding achievements too (*NPL*, 13). Lastly, the will's directive that the prize in literature honor the person who has produced the most outstanding work "of an ideal tendency" has caused much perplexity over the years. Gyllensten explains:

> Just what Alfred Nobel intended is not clear. With the knowledge we have of his person and

life, and of what he has expressed about his general outlook and aims, the words "of an ideal tendency" have been taken to mean a striving for the good of mankind, for humaneness, common sense, progress and happiness. The fundamental idea has been interpreted as applying to literary achievements with constructive aims. All the same, there have sometimes been violent differences of opinion as to what was intended by "ideal tendency" in the strict sense. When considering the candidates nowadays, this expression is not taken too literally. It is realized that on the whole the serious literature that is worthy of a prize furthers knowledge of man and his condition and endeavors to enrich and improve his life. (NPL, 15)

In December 1900 Esaias Tegnér, in his capacity as Director of the Academy, delivered an address which became something of a program declaration regarding the organization's approach to its new duty. He emphasized that the task was one which the Academy did not assume lightly, one which it in fact could not shirk, since the donor's millions had been given not to the Academy itself but to all mankind as represented by its foremost writers. His fervent hope was that a prize of such magnitude would in any event "have the effect of making a good piece of work known in much wider circles than would otherwise have been the case—and that it would be an excellent piece of work, if not in every instance the best available for a prize, he felt could be taken for granted" (NMP, 94). He foresaw the difficulties involved, but pointed up as well the Academy's uniquely favorable position for accepting such a task as that assigned by Alfred Nobel's will.

> "The Swedish Academy," [Tegnér] proceeded, "certainly does not cherish the illusion that even once it may be able to award a prize in such a way as to escape criticism. Nay, it anticipates with certainty that such criticism will often be merited. But it consoles itself with the assurance that in the whole world there is no other institution which would not meet the same fate. . . . If there are drawbacks to being a small nation situated on the outskirts of the civilized world, there are also certain advantages. And when it is a question of a responsibility like this, a few of them become clearly evident. A person living on the border of a province is better able to decide which peaks inside it are the highest than an observer standing amidst the mountains themselves. In a different sense, this is also true of us. And in the fact that we are a small nation we have, in a way, a safeguard against partiality which the big nations lack: we shall less often be able to appear as contenders for the prize ourselves." (NMP, 94–95)

Once its studies and preliminary discussions are completed—usually by early summer—the Nobel Committee submits to the full Academy a ranked listing of the candidates it deems most deserving of full consideration in the current year, together with information on the nominees' principal works, suitable secondary-source materials and available reports by Committee members and/or outside specialists. The Academy is in no way bound by the Committee's recommendations and may alter or add to the list as it wishes. Upon receiving the Committee's list, the Academy begins its deliberations, which occupy the major portion of the time at the group's weekly meetings until a decision is reached, usually by mid-October (NPL, 9–10). All nominations, investigations, deliberations and pollings are secret, and only the final choice is officially made public, at a time fixed by the awarding institution (NPL, 4). "In order for the voting within the Academy to be valid," Gyllensten notes, "it is required that at least twelve members shall take part and that a candidate shall receive more than half of the votes. The choice is made by secret ballot in writing. As a rule, all members of the Academy take part in the voting; if one or two cannot be present they send in their ballot papers. Usually the result is apparent after lengthy discussions and scrutiny, so that a large majority, or all, can agree on the prizewinner. No reservations concerning the majority's decision may be expressed, still less made public" (NPL, 10).[8] The awards, moreover, cannot be appealed against. In addition, the following regulations apply:

> All prizes may be shared jointly by more than one person (a maximum of three). . . . The literary prize, however, is shared very seldom, as literary achievements rarely show the kind of affinity which often justifies a division of the scientific prizes. . . . A prize can be withheld and awarded the following year. Prizes may only be given to persons, except the peace prize which may also be given to an institution or a society. A deceased person cannot be put on the list of candidates for a prize, but if someone dies after having been chosen a prizewinner and before the prize has been presented, the prize can nevertheless be given. This is the exception, however. Any criteria other than actual merit may not be observed when the decisions are made—in other words, no regard shall be paid to race, sex, nationality etc. (NPL, 4)

Once the final vote has been taken, the Academy notifies the new laureate (usually by telegram or phone), announces the decision publicly and issues a brief citation which is later printed on the Nobel diploma presented to the prizewinner by the Swedish King at the official award ceremonies on 10 December. Responsibility is then passed to the Nobel Foundation for issuing invitations to the recipient and his or her family and for arranging the round of festivities held in conjunction with the presentation ceremonies. The Academy does host a luncheon in honor of the laureate, however, and also sponsors the *Nobel Lecture* that most recipients consent to give, generally on 8 December or at another time shortly before or after the award presentations: "It is a rule for [the Nobel Lecture] to be given by the prizewinners in the other spheres, but not always in the case of the literature prize. If the lecture is not held, the prizewinner writes an essay or an article which the Nobel Foundation issues in its publication *Les Prix Nobel*" (*NPL*, 10).

▪ ▪ ▪

Kipling, Yeats, Shaw, Thomas Mann, Pirandello, O'Neill, Eliot, Faulkner, Pasternak, Seferis, Beckett—like them or not, as you will, they are writers whose fame has endured and who are still read and admired the world over. Many of these were at the time by no means obvious choices for the Nobel Prize in Literature: Faulkner was lionized in France and Sweden and was prominent in the States in 1949 (though success at home had been long and slow in coming, and many of his books were in fact out of print) but enjoyed only a modest reputation in most other countries; and Seferis was only slightly more well known outside Greece in 1963 than was his compatriot Odysseus Elytis in 1979. The Prize focused the reading world's attention on their work, however, and that work has proved itself worthy of the scrutiny. The same is true to varying degrees in the cases of Lagerlöf, Tagore, Hamsun, Undset, Hesse, Lagerkvist, Asturias and Kawabata, and probably will prove so with 1978 laureate I. B. Singer. Meanwhile the fame of, say, Heyse, Sillanpää and Frédéric Mistral has shrunk from international to merely national or regional dimensions in literary history. "At the same time," concludes Österling,

> . . . it could be objected that a number of equally significant names are conspicuous by their absence; . . . and it is not to be denied that the history of the Nobel Prize in Literature is also a history of inexpiable sins of omission. But even so, it may perhaps be said that the mistakes have been comparatively few, that no truly unworthy candidate has been crowned, and that, if allowances are made for legitimate criticism, the results have reasonably matched the requirements and difficulties of an almost paradoxical assignment.

> Just as there are older prizewinners in whom a younger generation can take only a slight interest, so there are recent winners who, to the older people, would have seemed unthinkable. The

coming of new generations, with inevitable changes in literary tastes, must obviously be reflected in the history of the Nobel Prize, and all the more clearly as time goes on. But under any circumstances it would be presumptuous to expect the Nobel Prizes to exercise any kind of guiding influence on the direction of literary progress. This has so far followed its own course, independently of the prizes, and will continue to do so in the future. (*NMP*, 133)

To point up the unique difficulties in choosing each year's recipient of the Nobel Prize in Literature is not to offer any apology for past choices but rather to state what should be readily apparent upon serious reflection. The criteria for assessment here "are necessarily more varied and often, too, more contradictory than in the case of medicine and other natural sciences," writes Gyllensten, himself both a teaching physician and a novelist; and those criteria are also more readily discernible—and, therefore disputable—by the layman than are those for the exact sciences.

> A literary work has its roots in the traditions and the cultural setting of the age and country in which its author lives. The work reflects this background and acquires its full richness only through this interplay and only in those readers who are, or can put themselves, in sympathy with it. Literary works are more or less bound to the literary environment in which they are created, and the farther away from it one is, the harder it is to do them justice.

> The task of awarding the Nobel Prize in Literature involves the obligation of trying to find methods for keeping oneself *au fait* with what is happening in literature all over the world and for appraising it, either on one's own or with the aid of specialists. Finally, the prize awarders must try to familiarize themselves with the works of most value, directly or via translations, and to make a careful assessment of their quality with all the viewpoints conceivably necessary for a reasonable evaluation. It is obvious that no hard and fast criteria for such an appraisal can ever be laid down. One must accept a kind of pragmatical procedure and look to the fundamental idea in Alfred Nobel's will as a whole: it was a matter of encouraging science and literature and of disseminating them in an international perspective for the benefit of mankind, but not of handing out empty status rewards. (*NPL*, 11)

A given year's laureate may well turn out to be, in time, another Sully-Prudhomme, who received the very first award in 1901 yet today is all but forgotten even by his French countrymen. But he or she may also be another Pasternak, a Hamsun, a Seferis. Whatever posterity may reveal about a particular prizewinner, the Academicians take their year-round labors seriously, as I hope this outline of their history and procedures will indicate. The annual shots fired by much of the fourth estate at the Academy's choices thus are often as ill-considered as they are unoriginal, a perhaps natural ("the general public naturally does not like to be surprised by names it has never heard of before," *NMP*, 134) though regrettable reaction totally alien to the spirit of the Prize selections. Current fame is not a major criterion. Quality is. The Nobel Prize in Literature is not intended merely to echo and confirm popularity. It may also attempt to point out talent not yet recognized by most of the world's readers and critics. It may educate the many as it celebrates the one.

William Riggan, Summer 1981

Ed. Note: We would like to thank the Swedish Academy's Permanent Secretary Lars Gyllensten for taking the time to read over this essay and check its accuracy prior to publication. His comments and corrections were most helpful in clarifying several points left unclear in the available published materials on the Prize procedures.

[1] In its issue of 3 November 1975 *Time* wrote (p. 95): "In one of his great poems, Wallace Stevens speaks of 'musing the obscure.' That phrase seems to be the unspoken motto of the Swedish Academy. Last week it again passed over such notables as Vladimir Nabokov, Graham Greene and Saul Bellow to award the Nobel Prize in Literature to Eugenio Montale, 79, an Italian poet virtually unknown to the public outside his native land." The view is surprising, to say the least; in light of the same magazine's comments nine years earlier (3 June 1966), when "transatlantic ignorance [was] relieved" by the appearance of Montale's *Selected Poems* in English: "a European writer of enduring importance, indisputably the most profound Italian poet of the 20th century. . . . Like Eliot, he has written very little . . . but that little he has written with iridescent precision." Evidently "times" change.

[2] Anders Österling, "The Literary Prize," in *Nobel: The Man and His Prizes,* Norman, Ok., University of Oklahoma Press, 1951; second and third revised and enlarged editions were published in New York by Elsevier in 1962 and 1972 respectively. Parenthetically abbreviated as *NMP.*

[3] The word used in Nobel's will is *idealisk* (ideal) and not *idealistisk* (idealistic), although the latter form is often used in translations of the will such as that which appears in *Nobel: The Man and His Prizes.* As Österling indicates, the term is best understood as expressing a preference for works possessing some positive, constructive purpose, although widely varying interpretations have been offered. Astronomer and mathematician M. G. Mittag-Leffler, for example, a good friend of Nobel, wrote that "he was an anarchist; by *idealisk* he meant anything that comprehends a polemic or critical attitude toward religion, royalty, marriage, or social organization in general" (see Richard Vowles, "Twelve Northern Authors," *BA* 41:1 [1967], p. 22). In any event, writes Lars Gyllensten, "*idealisk* is about as bewildering in Swedish as *ideal* is in English" (letter of 1 April 1981). For consistency, I have changed all references here to read *ideal* and not *idealistic.*

[4] Lars Gyllensten, *The Nobel Prize in Literature,* Alan Blair, tr., Stockholm, Swedish Academy, 1978. Parenthetically abbreviated as *NPL.*

[5] In addition to the Swedish Academy, the prize-awarding institutions are the Royal Academy of Sciences (physics and chemistry awards), the Nobel Assembly of the Caroline Medico-Surgical Institute (physiology and medicine) and the Norwegian Nobel Committee (peace). The prize in economics was added in 1969 and is actually sponsored by the Bank of Sweden "in memory of Alfred Nobel;" it is awarded by a special Prize Committee of economists from the Royal Academy of Sciences.

[6] *Nobel Foundation Directory: 1979–1980,* Stockholm, Nobel Foundation, 1979.

[7] The *Nobel Foundation Directory* (p. 11) qualifies this category as "professors of languages or in history of literature at universities and university colleges *selected by the Swedish Academy*" (my stress).

[8] However, in the three editions of *NMP* Österling does give brief summaries of the Academy members' thinking and a hint of the course which the deliberations followed in many of the Nobel selections through 1970.

Memory and Reconstruction of Self in Contemporary Yiddish Literature

To establish a terminus a quo for any major movement in literature is a matter of arbitrary selection. As for Yiddish literature, the beginning of the twentieth century seems an adequate point of departure: it was both the last breath of the major center in Eastern Europe which lasted till 1945, the end of World War II, and the beginning of what seemed to be the end for Yiddish as a spoken and written language. Most Yiddish writers are dead; few older critics and writers are still contributing to sundry Yiddish newspapers. Thus, I. B. Singer (see *WLT* 53:2, pp. 197–201) still contributes to *Forwerds* (Forward) in New York, and cognoscenti of Yiddish in Russia contribute to *Sovietishe Heimland* (Soviet Homeland).

In the first half of the twentieth century, the classical Yiddish establishment was still alive; Sholom Aleichem died in 1916 in Brooklyn, Mendele Mokher Sefarim in 1917 in Odessa, and Yehuda Leib Peretz in 1915 in Zamość. Yiddish, a mélange of many languages, chiefly Hebrew and German with admixtures of East European and Slavic languages, was by the end of the 1930s spoken by some ten million Jews.

As a folk literature, Yiddish had its inception in medieval Germany less than a thousand years ago, whereafter it flourished especially in Eastern Europe: Poland, Russia, Bohemia, Galicia, Romania. For a hundred years it had a brief efflorescence on the American continent in the U.S., Canada, and Latin America, and finally in the former Palestine and the Israel of today. Still, Yiddish has never lost its dependence on Hebrew literature.

Most Hebrew writers, interestingly, were bilingual, creating their literary works also in Yiddish. A good example is Samuel Joseph Agnon (1888–1970), the corecipient of the 1966 Nobel Prize in literature (with the German-Jewish poet Nelly Sachs). In a foreword to a collection of his Yiddish works, Agnon tells with a good deal of humor how he wrote his first Yiddish stories in Palestine.[1] It was Mendele Mokher Sefarim, however, who may be regarded as the major architect of Yiddish literature. In his autobiographical notes he states, "[Hebraists] looked on Yiddish with conceit and contempt and tried to reduce its value and influence."[2] Nevertheless, he decided in his early years to write in Yiddish such works as *Fishke der Krumer* (Fishke the Lame), a tale of poverty-stricken people published in 1869; *Di Klatshe* (My Mare), better known in its Hebrew version as *Susati,* published in Warsaw in 1886; as well as *The Travels of Benjamin the Third,* also known by its Hebrew title of *Masot Benjamin ha-Shlishi.* All these works created an unforgettable monument to East European Jewry in the nineteenth century.

Sholom Aleichem, the second of the great trio of Yiddish literature, derided the quixotism of his people, while Sefarim's work is actually a sociological document surpassing the scholarly tracts of Simon Dubnow in assessing the period. Aleichem was also the first to concentrate on the shtetl, the townlet, a nucleus of Jewish life in Eastern Europe, and thus introduced a major theme into Hebrew and Yiddish literatures; Shalom Asch, Yehuda Leib Peretz, and Isac Dov Berkowitz owe Aleichem this ancestral drive toward the shtetl theme. While Aleichem and Sefarim were preoccupied with the humanistic side, Yehuda Leib Peretz, the third in the trio, was the prose poet among them. He created a romantic attitude toward a major movement of Eastern Jews—Hasidism—and infused a new mystical dimension into Yiddish literature. Despite rejection by eminent contemporary historians (Heinrich Graetz, for example), who claimed Hasidism was a movement unfit for Jews, Peretz lent it dignity and began a complete volte-face in appreciation of the folk culture in Hasidism.

For a hundred years or so, up to World War I, Eastern Europe was the home of Yiddish literature. Between the wars, this literature still had its focus in Poland and Russia, but under drastically changed conditions. In Poland it was nurtured by vicious anti-Jewish regimes, and in Russia it was transformed into a communist tool by the so-called *Yevsektsiia* (the bureaucratic branch under the Russian Bolshevik government charged with Jewish affairs).

For a brief period of time between the two world wars, Yiddish literature wandered to the American continent. The U.S., Canada, and South America became the adopted homes for this newly evolving immigrants' literature. Arriving in America in 1906, I. J. Schwartz, winner of Israel's 1970 Manger Prize for poetry, belonged to a group of young poets known as *Di Yunge* (the Young Ones) and helped in the establishment of the first literary school in Yiddish literature. Schwartz's *Kentucky,* the first American Yiddish epic, is unique in its depiction of Jewish immigrants, their new rural reality in America, and its effect on Jewish life. Despite material prosperity, the spiritual component disappears and only memory remains of bygone times.[3]

Other poets of the Young Ones group were Mani Leib (1883–1983), Zishe Landan (1889–1937), Peretz Markish (1895–1952), Itzik Manger (1901–69), and Aaron Zeitlin. These American poets became an active group with political differences and various regional roots. Mani Leib arrived in New York in 1905 after a period of political activity in the Russian revolutionary movement, joined the Young Ones, and published poetry of strong emotive power.

There they were many, O God, so many
Such vital ones and unafraid,
Such noble ones, with beard and braid—
And talking in a marvelous strange way.
But above their heads only the sun in its stare
Saw the raw fury, the killer's cold blade,
How with wild force it descended,
And what massacres were there.
Now there are but a trace of that fury:
An axed forest, a couple of trees.
("They")

Other poets like Jacob Glatstein (1896–1971) and Abraham Glanz-Leyeles were of a more experimental bent. Glatstein also founded the *Inch-Zich* (Introspective) group of Yiddish writers.

. . . I dreamed that
The gentiles crucified Mozart
And buried him in a pauper's grave.
But the Jews made him a man of God
And blessed his memory.
("Mozart")

Steadily, Yiddish literature began to function as a substitute for a "would-be territory." For the Jewish immigrant writers, national pride and a sense of the collective self were met by this new evolving literature. Yiddish became the linguistic tool endowed with this capacity for nurturance and charged with the task of re-constructing the missing collective self. Soon Yiddish emerged as a healing and redemptive literature, especially in the poetry of the Young Ones and their contemporaries in the various Yiddish centers. So, it was the wind of history and psycholinguistic dynamics, coupled with political and social upheavals, which sowed the seeds of Yiddish and were the contributing elements for its redemptive qualities, a fact which makes Yiddish a curious phenomenon in modern linguistics.

Relationships between peoples and their languages generally follow a dialectical dynamism with universal implications. Ancient languages such as Chinese, Japanese, the Indian tongues, and Arabic underwent such dialectical changes and became vast repositories of moral, religious, political, and ethical knowledge of its people millennia ago. A relatively modern language, Yiddish is nevertheless suffused with these qualities. Whereas Hebrew was seen as a wholly religious and formal language, Yiddish inherited the folkloristic layers, but also embodied a moral and ethical vision of *Mentshlekhkayt*. Naturally, it soon became the preferred I-and-thou language of communication and healing among Jews.

Reconstruction is not a new concept in Jewish history. The social reconstruction of a historical reality was always tied somehow with the history of the Jews. After the Chemielnitsky massacres in 1648 and the doomed messianic aspiration led by Shabbatai Zvi, East European Jewry found itself isolated and demoralized. Whole communities were left once again with the task of re-constructing their psychical and social void. Settling in villages owned by feudal gentile aristocrats, enduring a harshly hostile environment, Jews turned to Talmudic debates (among the intellectual elite) and Yiddish (for the *populos*) to fill that vacuum. The shtetl incorporated this new, reconstructed reality. Hasidism, Jewish ethics, family life, and folklore thrived and served to revitalize the otherwise depressing economic and social milieu.

The *Khaliastre* (Gang) was a group of Yiddish poets active in postwar Warsaw. Theirs was a different tone; they depicted the horrors of the age, the chaos, the pogroms of the Ukraine and of Bolshevik power with unusual poetic strength. Peretz Markish (1895–1952) and Melech Ravitch (1893–1976) drew also on Russian life anchored in the rural landscape.

Now lambs of snow seek white wool for your shelter,
And somewhere now a royal frost sucks up
The Dnieper's dream, the Volga's helter-skelter,
And sips a white salve all your rivers yield. . . .

And everywhere you halt, there bows a hope,
A wayside hamlet on your twilit field.

The more socially oriented poets in the group, Yisroel Shtern and Kadia Molodovsky, raised Yiddish consciousness in Poland to new heights.

My heart is so small
that it won't hide all
of my tears. . . .

My life is so hard
that no boats at sea
or trains on the land
can even take me
where I want to go,
my dears.
And yet—
with death stalking me
hiding my tears,
desperate—
I am an arrow set in the bow
and my will is the hand
that aims me
where I will go
and will arrive,
my dears.

Romania, another center in Eastern Europe where Yiddish theatre and poetry thrived, produced two major Yiddish poets, Eliezer Steinberg and Itzik Manger. Manger (1901–69), recognized for his folkloristic poetry, was familiar with German verse and was highly influenced by Rilke. Most of his poems and ballads are suffused with biblical themes and religious motifs of an unusual, modernistic bent.

Avremele, when will we have our own child?

We've already reached our old age,
A woman who has lived as long as I have,
Has by now mothered many a babe.

Father Abraham smiles and thinks,
And smoke from his pipe fills the air,
Faith my wife, if the Holy One wants,
Even a deaf mute can hear.

Avremele, you hear how every night
My body and soul are torn with strife,
And Hagar is only your servant girl,
And I am your loving wife.
("Abraham and Sarah")

This trend of ballad and epic writing continued in New York with the work of I. J. Schwartz and the folk-verse plays of Halper Leivick, especially *The Colem* (1921).

Yung Vilne (the Young of Vilna) was the last of the literary groups formed between the wars and claimed poets such as Chaim Grade and Abraham Sutzkever. Grade, born in Vilna in 1910, began publishing poetry in *Vilna Tog* (Vilnius Day) and helped bring Yiddish closer to European literary trends. He became a voice for a new collective self.

Sometimes I cross a street and ask:
Did I just walk over a covered grave?
Sometimes I stand before my house, forgetting
because everything I build is built on a miracle,
And may become topsy-turvy in a flick of an eyelash.
("The Miracle")

Sutzkever, born in 1913 near Vilnius, (escaped the Nazi Occupation by fleeing to Russia. Influenced by the poet Moishe Leib Halpern and the Introspective poets, he is now the editor of the Yiddish literary magazine *Golden Keit* (Golden Chain) and resides in Israel. His poetry harkens to distant memory with a need to come to terms with a new self and leans toward a prophetic stance.

How and with what will you fill
Your cup on the day of freedom?
In your joy are you willing to feel
Yesterday's dark screaming
Where skulls of days congeal
in a pit with no bottom, no floor?

They will compare your memory
to an ancient buried town.
And your alien eyes will tunnel down
like a mole, like a mole.
("How?")

The third major cultural and geographical center of Yiddish literature, in addition to Eastern Europe and the U.S., was the Soviet Union. Around 1913 the young Yiddish writers of Kiev, including the novelists David Bergelson and Der Nister and the poet David Hofstein, began to coalesce as a group. After the 1917 revolution, a revival of Yiddish sprang up in Petrograd (today's Leningrad), Minsk, Kharkov, and Kiev. Between 1917 and 1921, about 850 Yiddish books were published in Russia. Yiddish theatre, under the direction of Shlomo Mikhoels, also flourished. Kiev, the Yiddish cultural hub, claimed two Yiddish daily newspapers and a few Yiddish publishing houses, as well as literary journals like *Der Shtern* (The Star) and *Shtrom* (Stream), which first appeared in Moscow in 1922. The new Russian poets Itzik Feffer, Leib Kvitko, David Hofstein, Jacob Sternberg, and Izzy Kharik adopted a new thrust of revolt and called for a renewed self and a new future in their poetry, as in this excerpt from Feffer's "So What If I've Been Circumcised?":

So what if I've been circumcised?
With rituals, as among the Jews?

. . . .

I'm a quiet guy and hardly a villain,

My honesty has no great appeal,
I'm never known to put on tefillin,
I'm never known to wheel and deal.

So what if I've been circumcised?

In 1932, a volume of verse entitled *The Building of Birobidzhan* went on sale in Moscow, Kharkov, Minsk, and other cities in the Soviet Union. It was the first publication from Birobidzhan, not yet a regional center. (The Jewish Autonomous Region, located in the Far East of the USSR, was formed in 1934.) Emanuel Kazakevick, editor of the volume, was one of the first settler-writers of Birobidzhan. Birobidzhan Yiddish literature saw its inception in 1928, when a train pulled into the Far East station of Tikhonkaya with settlers from all over the USSR. From Kharkov came the Yiddish writer Meyer Alberton, who left a year later with a volume entitled *Birobidzhan*. David Bergelson, the foremost Soviet-Yiddish novelist, was connected with Birobidzhan since the early 1930s. Moshe Goldstein, the poet, wrote there, died in combat in 1943, and lies somewhere near Smolensk.

Other colleagues—Buze Olevsky, Henry Korfman, Aaron Hofstein, Vladimir Shulman, and Samuel Eisenwarg—also died during the war of 1941–45.[4] From Moscow came Grigori Rabinkov, who wrote short stories, plays, and historical novellas. Boris Miller and Lyubov Vasserman also settled and wrote of the joys and sorrows of life at Birobidzhan. From Brazil came Salvadore Borges, who wrote his novel *Rio de Janeiro* when not attending to his physical labor. In the village of Amurzet on the Amur, Isac Bronfman wrote poetry and Aaron Vergelis took his first steps as a poet. Birobidzhan literature is one of reconstruction and transformation: the harnessing of the taiga by man and the emerging new self constitute a recurrent theme in most Birobidzhan literature. Samuel Gadiner, in his short story "The Sun Rises in the East," writes:

> In time they learned that Birobidzhan lay beyond the Urals, beyond Siberia, beyond the Baikal, that the land was rich, that people had only to come and take all they needed for a good happy life. . . . Their heart was full of sweet beginnings and heavy with the unknown ahead—what would it be like, this misty future happiness, when would it come?

Bergelson's story "To the Hills" depicts different pioneers. The characters are young people prepared for a hard, cruel life but also hopeful about the future, ready for their initiation.

During the 1960s and 1970s, Yiddish writers were still active, but some have left Birobidzhan. Aaron Vergelis's novel *Time and the Chermisters* and his verse volume "By the Stream" are permeated with the motif of transforming the land via transforming the individual in Birobidzhan. Other writers still active are Roman Shoikhet, a short-story writer who published in *Birobidzhan Zvezda* and also contributes to *Dalny Vostok* and *Sovietishe Heimland.*

The majority of Jews emigrating from Yiddish-speaking countries in Eastern Europe relocated in Argentina, which became a central community in 1889, when Baron de Hirsh started to settle Jews in agricultural communities there. Buenos Aires slowly became the center for Yiddish schools and for the Yiddish press, which included *Die Yiedishe Zeitung* (founded in 1914) and *Die Presse* (founded in 1918). After the Holocaust, Argentina was surpassed in the 1950s and 1960s only by the U.S. and Israel in the number of Yiddish books published.

One hundred and fifty volumes of the series *Dos polishe Yiedenturm* (Polish Jewry) was published, as well as a large number of volumes of Yiddish literary masters, edited by Shmuel Rozhansky. By 1970 the Jewish population of Argentina was close to half a million, but was later depleted by emigration to Israel. Among the early Argentine Yiddish writers was Mordecai Alperson (1860–1947), the chronicler of three decades of pioneering Jewish life in the three-volume *Memoiren fun a yiedishen Kolonist* (Memoirs of a Jewish Colonist; 1922, 1926, 1928). Other Yiddish prose writers included Michel Hachen Sinai (1877–1958), who in 1898 founded the first Yiddish periodical, *Der Viederkol* (The Echo), and Y. S. Liachovitzky (1874–1937), the first editor of *Die Yiedishe Zeitung* (The Yiddish Newspaper). Pinie Katz (1882–1959) arrived in Buenos Aires in 1906, later became the editor of *Die Presse,* and also translated *Don Quixote.*

Poets in Argentina included Aba Kliger, who wrote of the Andes Mountains before emigrating to the U.S., and Moshe Pinchevsky, who came from Bessarabia to Argentina in 1913 but got caught up in the Russian Revolution and lived there until his arrest in 1948 during Stalin's liquidation of Yiddish writers. He spent his final years in Siberian labor camps, where he died. Kehos Kliger (b. 1908) came to Argentina in 1937 and wrote ballads about the pampas and the unfortunates in his *Gezang oif der Erd* (Song of the Earth; 1941); his other poetry and prose was compiled in a volume entitled *Die Velt farbet mikh shtarben* (The World Invites Me to Die; 1950), a bitter cry for the lost collective Jewish identity destroyed by the Nazis. Other Yiddish poets active after World War II are Abraham Zak (b. 1891), Mordecai Bernstein (1905–66), Barnch Hager (b. 1898), and Israel Ashendorf (1906–56).

Chile's Yiddish culture was closely linked with Argentina's Jewish population. The most talented of its Yiddish poets was Moshe David Giser (1893–1952), who lived nine years in Argentina before moving in 1933 to Santiago, where he edited the biweekly *Zied-Amerika* (South America) and the *Chilener Yiedishes Vochenblat* (Chilean Yiddish Weekly). His coeditor, the novelist Noah Vital (1886–1961), spent twenty years in Argentina before coming to Chile in 1926. Yitzkhok Blumstein (b. 1897) was a balladeer of the Andes even before relocating to Chile in 1936 to become editor of Yiddish periodicals there. *Idishe Presse* (The Yiddish Press) was founded in Santiago in 1930, and seven years later the weekly *Dos Vort* (The Word) began to appear as the Yiddish community's voice.

Israel is one of the thriving centers of Yiddish today. Under the auspices of the labor organization *Histadrut,* the literary quarterly *Di Goldene Keyt* (The Golden Chain) was founded in 1949, and a chair in Yiddish was established at Jerusalem's Hebrew University in 1951. The poets Pinski, Opatoshu, Leivick, Reiser, and Kadie Molodovsky have enjoyed a popularity much greater in Israel than what they had known previously in Yiddish-speaking centers. It is a matter of irony that Yiddishism, which opposed Hebraism bitterly, found a new home in Israel, where Yiddish newspapers, periodicals, and books are published and read with assiduity.

The older generation of Jewish immigrants to the land of Israel forms one of the best consumer groups for Yiddish literature. Scholars like Dov Sadan, the first incumbent of the Yiddish chair at Hebrew University, and H. Shmerok, one of the foremost specialists in Yiddish literature, have also contributed to the efflorescence of Yiddish in Israel. It is curious too that Dan Miron, one of the most respected critics of Hebrew literature, also plays an important role in Yiddish creativity. Israel is probably the safest haven anywhere for a future flowering of Yiddish literature.

Dalia Ross-Daniel, Winter 1985

---

[1] S. Y. Agnon, *Shriftin* (Selected Works), Jerusalem, Hamenora, 1969, pp. 7–12.

[2] Mendele Mokher Sefarim, *Kol Kitve Mendele Mokher Sefarim,* Tel Aviv, Devir, 1963.

[3] Schwartz left New York and actually went to live in Kentucky for twelve years, where he resided with his sister and helped run a women's-wear store. *Kentucky* was later translated by Schwartz into Hebrew and published.

[4] Interestingly, these poets also called themselves *Di Yunge.*

The Western Canon

Like most readers, I am deeply grateful to Harold Bloom for his having written *The Western Canon* at all. Like most readers too, I may have my own minor complaints, but, upon reflection, even those disappear. For example, I think it is regrettable that the Greeks and Romans are not given Bloom's full treatment in at least one separate chapter, but I have to admit Bloom is right, in the context of his task. In the nineteenth century, Greek and Latin ceased constituting the obligatory bases of studies indoctrinating the Educated Westerner, so it is only right, however lamentable, that Homer, Plato, Thucydides, Herodotus, Aristophanes, Aeschylus, Sophocles, Euripides & Co. are for the most part relegated to the back of the book, in lists of writers who have counted in the West, although I note the sublime Sappho is merely tagged on to a kind of afterthought miscellany, alas. I myself, no doubt in abysmal ignorance, have never developed the love for Roman writers that I have for the Greeks, and can only theoretically lament their exclusion from the main body of the book. Also, at the other end of time, I could wish that Bloom had reserved individual chapters to Stendhal and Byron and, most particularly, W. H. Auden, surely the greatest poet of our century, rather than merely inserting passing remarks on them. And Cavafy could at least have been *mentioned* in the body of Bloom's text. But still, all in all, I can have no argument with any aspect of Bloom's realization of what it was, after all, he set out to do. His book really is an invaluable record of what constitutes the Western Canon.

What I do find argument with is how ramshackle and makeshift, when all is said and done, our Western Canon turns out to be. It is first and foremost *too* . . . Western, i.e. provincial. Also, too many accidents entered into its creation. Finally, too many worthies are omitted not for lack of merit but on the basis of time and chance or geography, or on the choice and deficiencies of translators. Whether their names are listed at the back of the book or not (and many such are not), shouldn't certain other writers *become* part of our Western Canon, even if it is quite accurate to state that they are not yet? Bloom is quite right not to include one single Japanese or Chinese anywhere in our Canon, but, I wish to ask, does that make our Canon right? I think it makes our Canon appallingly wrong. In short, what Bloom's book leaves me panting for, craving for, is a *Worldwide* Canon. This is not so farfetched as it may sound upon first hearing. The Japanese, for example, are well along in establishing just that. But I had better plunge into details.

The first disaster to befall Western letters was doubtless the burning of the library in Alexandria, by Christianized Romans, in the earliest centuries of our era. History does not tell us whether their battle cry was "Why should we read the writings of Dead White Pagan Males?," but it might as well have been. If we still possess any Greek manuscripts whatever, it is almost entirely due to assiduous Arab scholars in their universities in Muslim Spain. Despite this extraordinary stroke of luck, we idiotically banned the Greeks from our basic studies around a century ago, I repeat, which, as the French say, was worse than a mistake (*erreur*); it was a downright sin (*faute*). Well, many such accidents prevailed in the establishment of our Western Canon, for or against. Would Shakespeare have been rediscovered centuries later if someone somewhere had not put up the money to print his First Folios? My bones tell me *he* would never have been forgotten, no matter what; but had Chaucer's manuscripts and rare printed versions disappeared for a few centuries, to be discovered only later, would many of us spend a year learning Middle English (as I have) to be able to read him in the original, infinitely preferable to reading him in modern translation? Those nonanglophone writers Bloom includes are all writers in European languages that at one time or another stood some chance of being translated (and, it must be emphasized, would stand less chance of being translated today) from French, German, Italian, Spanish, Portuguese, or Russian. But what if the utterly misguided and inept English-language mangler of the German Spengler's *Decline of the West* had been as good a translator as Scott-Montcrieff (as revised by Kilmartin) of the French Proust? Wouldn't that German work now be one of the major pillars of our Canon? What if Gibbon, arguably the best writer of English prose ever to have set pen to paper, had not criticized Christian religions and had thereby been more Politically Correct? Surely, surely, his *Decline and Fall of the Roman Empire* would have at least equal stature with, say, Montaigne, who *is* included? That Stendhal has never caught on as one of the very greatest novelists of all time (Dickens is a comic book in comparison) is a great mystery, and so for that matter, in a completely different fashion, is the later Anthony Trollope; but just suppose T. S. Eliot or someone of that ilk had become the champion of one or the other or both somewhere along the line. If our convention would be to take Sigmund Freud as a writer—which to my mind is the only way to take him—rather than as a scientist, surely he should figure high in our Pantheon? Is it because they were women that Molly Keane, Edna St. Vincent Millay, and Jean Rhys are not awarded so much as a nod? Given these few bewilderments, I hope it is clear that the time and chance that happeneth to everyone hath also played a huge role in determining membership in this particular club, and that with more time and chance perhaps there might one day be a rejuggling of which writers get chapters and which get merely listed in the back. Also, it is at least possible that, for these same reasons, great masterpieces lie buried somewhere, crying out for disinterment, recognition, and admission.

But these are minor quibblings, inevitable and obvious. More to the point, and indeed the sole reason I attempt this essay at all, is that our Canon has indeed remained so Western, so adamantly impervious not only to the masterpieces but also to the merely damned good writing that has been produced outside the West. We pride ourselves on our wisdom, and yet permit our obtuseness to flourish without the least hint of shame. From here on in we no longer can even so much as comment on Bloom, for he did his job only too well. But the fact remains we in the West are inexcusably ignorant of the literatures that have been produced elsewhere. Oh, excusable in previous centuries perhaps, but *today*, with Internets, World Wide Webs, and other instantaneous resources of information, certainly not.

Of course, this attitude is symptomatic of the West in more ways than one. We generally think that only what has been assimilated into Western culture can matter. If other things mattered, it is a basic assumption of ours, they would long since have been assimilated into our culture. Well, we are wrong, dead wrong.

Compare our *Iliad* and *Odyssey* epics, the neglected bases of our literature and civilization, untaught in our schools because willfully banished from our curricula, and then consider the entirely comparable *Ramayana* epic, still alive and breathing in countries with a population of roughly *one billion people* no less, its stories by chapter and verse known by heart to uncountable millions throughout Southeast Asia, from India through Sri Lanka and Thailand to Bali and Lombok, where episodes are not only read and/or recited but also dramatized and/or danced to this day (I speak of temple dancing, not performances for tourists); and we Westerners know nothing whatever about it, nothing, which is scandalous, disgraceful, given our intellectual pretensions. And please note: the well-educated Southeast Asian knows about Homer.

In present-day mainland China, political disasters have marred what would otherwise be a similar awareness of that megacountry's great classics, but those classics are immortal nonetheless and will inevitably reenter the national consciousness. But if communist fiends have outlawed great *littérateurs* of genius such as Mencius, is that any excuse for our doing likewise? If political censorship is wrong in China, and it certainly is, is our equivalent of censorship through ignorance right? I'm here to tell you that Mencius (371?-288? B.C.) in particular is one of the greatest thinkers and writers of all time, on a par with Plato, and I consider it one of the privileges of my life that, through my knowledge of Japanese *kanbun,* I have been able to read him in the original. I will spare you the pages of dithyrambs I could expend on T'ang poetry and other superb excrescences of the Chinese creative imagination. In political theories several millennia old, such as Confucianism, there may be much to discard, certainly the idea of a *hereditary* chief of state/government with a mandate from heaven, but how can we be sure there are no germs of ideas applicable to the political conundrums of our own day if we do not even familiarize ourselves with these writings? (Personally, I hold that a certain dosage of Confucianism is precisely what our abusive capitalistic democracies, especially in our inner cities, are in dire need of.) And Lu Xun! What abysmal provincialism can hold that Hemingway is to be read but that Lu Xun is not? In my humble opinion, the former is a midget compared to the latter. And again please note: the well-educated Chinese reader in Hong Kong, Singapore, Taipei, et cetera, knows as much about the Western Canon as he knows about the Chinese Canon.

But in my meanderings through some forty countries of the globe, partly on behalf of the United Nations but mostly by my taking more side jaunts on my own than I could really afford, the country that widened my outlook the most, without question, was Japan. No, I am not an apologist for either the military past or economic present of the powers-that-be in that archipelago, nor is my judgment swayed by the sociological niceties that make of the Japanese the most courteous and therefore most civilized people on earth. After my seven-year sojourn in Japan, I held that the Japanese sine qua non of interpersonal deference and respect was indeed the very definition of "civilization," until I realized my rule would relegate the booby prize to the independent and egotistical French as the *least* civilized people on earth, and, whatever else can be said, the French are not that. They are only the rudest, but even in that connection, to be absolutely accurate, I should speak of Parisians as contrasted to other French.

This widening of my literary weltanschauung is only partly due to the many well-worth-reading classical and modern Japanese authors I have had occasion to discover, by which I hasten to add I do not refer to the second-rate Mishima or to the somewhat underwhelming Ōe Kenzaburō, Nobel Prize notwithstanding. Similarly, it is only partly due to my sincere admiration for the genuinely *original* forms of expression the Japanese have invented, such as haiku, tanka, and renga.

By the way, one of our many misconceptions about things Japanese is that we think a three-line poem in five, seven, and five English syllables constitutes a haiku, and this cries out for setting to rights. Consider one of my early attempts at the genre: "Blossoming branches / in swirling snow vaunt both still / and moving white flakes." My purpose in quoting such a feeble, nay, miserable effort is to demonstrate that these fourteen English syllables would be counted as *fifty* syllables by Japanese reckoning. You don't believe me? Here it is in Japanese syllabification, bearing in mind that long English vowels as well as doubled consonants like the s's in *blossom* or the l's in *still* are counted as two syllables in Japanese, and an *n* not followed by a vowel is counted as one: "Bu-ro-s/so-mi-n-gu bu-ra-n-che-zu / i-n su-wa-a-ri-n-gu su-no-o ba-a-n-to bo-su su-ti-r/ru / a-n-do mu-u-bi-n-gu u-a-i-to fu-re-i-ku-su." In other words, Japanese haiku are even more miraculously brief than we can barely conceive. End of digression.

Now, it is perfectly accurate to report that the great *Genji Monogatari* (Eng. *The Tale of Genji*) does not yet form part of our Canon, but it is absolutely unarguable that it should. Alas, translation problems arise. Arthur Waley's version captures the poetic fragrance with scarcely any attempt at accuracy, so that whole sections of his attempt are imagined synoptic equivalents of certain passages; and Edward Seidensticker's more contemporary version, while accurate as can be, has tenth-century Japanese nobility speaking as flat an idiom as American hillbillies of the 1930s, *deliberately,* to bring them down to the level we mere mortal and egalitarian Americans are supposedly capable of understanding. The very recent French version is even worse, at the other extreme, for René Sieffert modeled his stilted prose on Saint-Simon's, from the court of Louis XIV, rendering the original author absurd as well as unreadable. Remember my use of *accident* above?

Since one of the reasons Bloom wrote his *Western Canon* was to retort to feminists who rave and rant about their "needing" to read other female writers, I should point out that *Genji Monogatari* was written by a lady, Murasaki Shikibu, and that two other earthshaking landmarks in classical Japanese literature were also written by ladies: *The Pillow Book* by Sei Shōnagon, and Sarashina's diary *As I Crossed a Bridge of Dreams,* both beautifully translated by Ivan Morris and therefore highly readable. I wouldn't be at all surprised if these three ladies should one day be recognized in the West as the greatest women writers of all time (except that I hold the term "women writers" as repugnant as "men writers"), and our American feminists apparently do not even know these ladies ever existed and wrote. Of course not, since they are not part of our Canon. But

then even best-selling (i.e., big-bucks-making) present-day Japanese authors are not often translated into English any more. I think particularly of Minakami Tsutomu as only one example, a marvelous novelist on several levels. In actual fact, one of his novels *has* been translated into English, by me, and it got me a Master's degree in Japanese from the Langues Orientales in Paris (I took early retirement from the UN in order to study Japanese language and literature). Can you imagine *The Catcher in the Rye* being known in Japan only through one translation by one student? In fact, more copies of J. D. Salinger's novel have probably been sold in Japan than in the USA. Now ponder that likelihood for a moment, and please note: the well-educated Japanese knows the Western Canon as well as he knows the Japanese *and* the Chinese Canons. And literally hundreds of guidebooks already exist to help him through, so that he reads Tanizaki *and* Dostoevsky *and* Lu Xun!

It is this latter fact that broadened my literary weltanschauung, brought me face to face, for the first time, with a widening awareness of the provinciality of our West, and now, thanks to Harold Bloom, of our Western Canon. For please note: Harold Bloom is about as well-educated a Westerner as can be, but he seems not to know beans about non-Western literature. What on earth is wrong with us that we be so blinkered, and what can be done about it?

We are blinkered because for two hundred years or so the British Empire and now the United States have played the role of Number One in World Society, the role previously played for two hundred years or so by France, and earlier still for two hundred years or so by Italy. In actual fact, and English-language bias constitutes another blinkering in Bloom's book: it is written from a strictly monolingual anglophone reader's point of view, so that many of Bloom's first choices (Chaucer, Milton, Samuel Johnson) would not even be recognized by francophone or hispanophone readers, theoretically as much a part of the West as we are. Not only that, but there has been a basic shift all over the world in the latter half of the twentieth century. Three elements govern the literary situation that never governed it before: 1) a general mindlessness, engendered by the elevation of the lowest common denominators of our societies to be the models and judges of all things, to a certain extent due to movies and television, and in consequence 2) general economics rules supreme, so that basketball champions can earn tens of millions of dollars during their careers while poets are lucky to receive two copies of the minuscule reviews deigning to publish their poetry, and literary translators can barely survive in business. At the same time, however, 3) it has to be granted that modern technology enables works *already admitted to the Canon* to become more readily available and in greater numbers than ever before, notably in the form of paperbacks. The trouble is that if there ever was a time to resort to that tired cliché, "a vicious circle," here it is: these three factors join to limit the development and growth of our Western Canon. Publishers can no longer afford even to read, let alone publish, promising *new* writers of value; they can consider only "agented" blockbusters.

As for what to do about all this, ah, that is the question. After the burning of the Alexandrian library, I would say that here indeed is the second disaster to befall Western letters: we do not know how to go about incorporating the rest of the world's Canon into our own. And it is time we learn, now or never.

It is not necessarily idle daydreaming therefore to speculate on what might be done. Ideally, we need some kind of Académie, not Française but Universelle, to establish which works of all languages deserve our attention. Where might the money come from? Certainly not from Washington, not now. But, if one percent of France's national budget can be allocated to the furtherance of artistic and cultural activities, is it beyond the realm of possibility that a few other enlightened governments of the world might agree to allocate one percent, not of their budgets, but of the extravagant amounts dispensed on armaments and other killing apparatus, i.e. risking the death of our civilizations, to the furtherance of culture, i.e. furthering the life of our civilizations? Specifically, who might do the work? Japan, because it has already begun it. At almost precisely the same moment the West ruthlessly cut itself off from its roots in Greek and Latin writings, Japan equally ruthlessly elected the opposite course. Japan determined to *maintain* cognizance of its Japanese and Chinese literatures and concurrently to *assimilate* the literature of the West, including our Greeks and Romans. Moreover, it so happens there is an embryo of an international organization in Tokyo that has never yet found a satisfactory reason for being, the UN University, without a student body, teaching staff, or football team, but autonomous, i.e. nonpolitical. With its already well-established infrastructure. . . .

Ah, but perhaps this *is* idle daydreaming. Reality raises its ugly head. This is here and this is now. FM stations play rock "n" roll, and Bach is out. College graduates as well as their textbooks write "different *than*" and get away with it. Bloom thinks multiculturalists and "all six branches of the School of Resentment: Feminists, Marxists, Lacanians, New Historicists, Deconstructionists, Semioticians" will succeed in their "irreversible . . . Balkanization of literary studies," and perhaps he is right. The second edition of *The Western Canon* may

consist solely of anglophone writers, the third of Yanks only.

When and if space ships carrying inhabitants from some other planet eventually come to visit our earth, it's nice they will have Harold Bloom's record of our Western Canon to help them get acquainted. But wouldn't it be nicer still if we could provide them with a Worldwide Canon? If we the living could establish it in a hurry, it might even do *us* some good, no? What else is literature for, if not to get to know as much about ourselves, *all* of us, together and individually, as we possibly can?

Leslie Schenk, Spring 1996

A Vision of the Apocalypse

In evoking apocalyptic messianism, a famous Hasidic Master said, "At that time, summer will be without heat, winter without frost, the wise will have forgotten their wisdom, and the elect their fervor." Another Master expressed the same idea, but in a different way: "At that time, one will no longer distinguish light from what negates light, twilight from dawn, silence from speech and speech from its content; there will no longer be any relation between man and his face, desire and its object, metaphor and its meaning."

Orwellian premonitions and predictions before their time. The enemy resides not in the triumph of evil but in chaos. The confusion of values is worse than their disappearance. Satan will be punished not for having tempted man to sin, but rather for having pretended it was in the name of Good. As long as day and night are separate, everything is possible; should their realms intermingle, both will be cursed.

Such is the stirring lesson of the Jewish tradition. It is in discernment that truth becomes manifest. For creation to be revealed, God must recede within His secret. "Blessed be the Lord for having given the rooster the ability to distinguish between darkness and light," says the Jewish man every morning. And after the seventh day, as twilight falls, what does he say? "Blessed be the Lord for having set apart the Sabbath from the rest of the week, the sacred from the profane." Let the separations be abolished, and it will be Apocalypse.

As a child I dreaded the messianic times, and yet I prayed they would come. I was not the only one to have such conflicting feelings. Already in the Talmud we find a Sage exclaiming, "I wish for the coming of the Messiah, but I do not want to be around to welcome Him." Too many torments will usher Him in. Too many wars. Too many massacres. Kafka was right in saying that the Messiah will not arrive on the last day, but on the day after—too late for too many people.

However, unlike the Talmudic Sage, I was ready to accept the event in its totality. I lived in expectation of it. It told myself and I was told: to be Jewish is to wait. What sets my people apart from others? We have not gone beyond waiting; we are going beyond ourselves while waiting.

You see, for us the Apocalypse was not in the distant future, but in the immediate present. Some days we needed only to go into the street to perceive it. Danger was everywhere. For us, there was no solid ground anywhere. Always in exile, always in flight. The world of men, human happiness, eluded us. Often we had the feeling that we were living out the curses of the Scriptures: at night we waited for day to dawn; in the morning we waited for night to fall.

Driven out of every place, pursued everywhere, accused of every misdeed, blamed for every evil, we did not understand what was happening around us. We seemed to live in a separate universe, to speak a separate language. When they looked at us, people seemed to glimpse an ancient vision of terror. We, on the other hand, had nowhere to look: expelled from geography, we sought refuge in books.

Therein we discovered the glory and suffering of another time, and we used it for guidance and support. We recounted the suffering of our ancestors in Egypt, and suddenly our own seemed more tolerable. We spoke of the destruction of the Temple of Jerusalem, the murderous persecutions at the time of the Crusades from Mayence to Blois to Jerusalem, the victims of the Inquisition, the burning of the synagogues during the pogroms. We felt strangely reassured, even encouraged. Times were tough? Well, hadn't they always been? Yet we were still around, unchanged. The Apocalypse? We knew how to survive it. Through endless dying we had learned the art of survival.

We considered the future—I mean the immediate future—with apprehension. Any change is for the worse: that was our conviction. Even our friends treated us differently when they came to power. "Whoever persecutes Jews establishes himself as a leader," according to the Talmud. And conversely, "Whoever attains a position of power takes to persecuting Jews." So it was better to endure the known, familiar punishments of those already in power. In our prayers we spoke of the days that passed, not of those to come. Rooted in the past, we responded to the present. To look beyond was to sense the imminence of the final age, that of the Apocalypse.

Now, that is something one must not do. The Apocalypse does not have good press in Jewish tradi-tion. We admire Ezekiel and we like Isaiah because, like Jeremiah, they do not let their vision and their discourse sink into melancholy. They offer consolation and hope. Certain works of merit, both from an ethical and literary standpoint, have not been included in the sacred canon because they are imbued with too much despair.

Ben Sira and Baruch Dalet, for example, inspire too much pessimism, which is why they are found in the Apocrypha. Even Job nearly had the same fate. Numerous scholars discussed his case for generations before deciding in his favor. Undoubtedly, that was because of the optimistic conclusion of the drama. After the catastrophe, Job becomes happy again, at peace with heaven and obedient to His will.

For us, today, it is not so easy to close the parentheses. More than ever, the future, a source of terror, reflects our past, a cemetery of illusions. To the extent that my contemporaries believe in the Apocalypse, they refer to the one they lived through. They speak of memory more than of vision. They are afraid. They are afraid because they remember. The tragic imagination does not attain the limit of pain; the tragic memory goes further. When the two meet, there is no way out of the nightmare.

Now, that is the case of the survivor: his memories, linked to an Event of an absolute character, weigh on the future as much as on the past. What was in the realm of fantasy or premonition for Orwell is for the survivor of Auschwitz a life experience. For Orwell, it was before the event; for us, it is after—and before. In other words, for us, time stopped between Auschwitz and Hiroshima.

But please, no comparisons. In the realm of the concentration camps, analogies can only be false—and blasphemous. Despite, or because of, its universal implications and applications, the Holocaust remains unique: its universality lies in its very singularity. And yet, negating History, Auschwitz represents a kind of aberration and culmination of History. Everything brings us back to it. Illuminated by its flames, the present appears more understandable, if only at the existential level. Today's commitments can be explained by the indifference of the past, which they strive to challenge and condemn. Dehumanized and dehumanizing, the Nazi system showed the way for many other systems. If our language is corrupt, it is because at that time language itself was perverted. Fine and innocent words were used to designate the most abject crimes. Night and fog, selection or evacuation or special treatment— we know now that these terms meant torture and torment by starvation, isolation and terror. The first crime committed by the Nazis was against language. It excluded from the experience all those who were not directly involved. Only the executioners and their victims understood each other. The others listened and read without understanding.

Do people understand now? I am not sure. I would be more certain of the contrary. The concentration-camp experience will forever defy any possibility of understanding. In that respect, it differs from the Orwellian vision of society, where, in spite of everything, things are held together by a rigorous and implacable logic. For Orwell, the antinomian principle asserts itself as an immutable law. When the roles are reversed, the relations between the actors remain constant. Changing signs would be inconceivable in the Realm of Night: there, it is not a question of pure metamorphosis per se, or just of metamorphosis. Auschwitz and Treblinka are something else entirely—and they will forever remain something else—*other*. To say that Good was replaced by Evil, truth by lie, life by death, would not suffice to grasp the profound significance of it. As a permanent questioning of the human condition, the concentration-camp phenomenon wounds and challenges us, but it never offers an answer, That is what we learned from Auschwitz: it is possible to live and die exclusively in a climate of questioning—that is, deprived of solutions. Just as there is no reasoning to explain Majdanek, to us, so there is none to tell us how we managed to live after Majdanek.

Perhaps we should evoke Noah here rather than Job. After the Flood, Noah makes a new home. How does he manage to forget? He has forgotten nothing. It is because he forgets nothing that he decides to begin everything anew, to confer meaning on his survival and to justify the work of God by refuting death. Is he happy? If he were, he would not seek refuge in drunkenness. How could he be happy? All those dead haunting him, calling out to him, accusing and repudiating him. Worse still, he knows what will happen next. Already the horizon is clouding over: a new storm approaches. Driven by immense, unreasoned pride, men are rushing to erect a Tower that would touch the heavens. But don't they know that human salvation is defined in relation to one's fellow human beings? Haven't they learned anything? Drawn by space, they betray the earth and its inhabitants. Therein lies the tragedy of Noah. He, the survivor, realizes that history continues as if nothing happened, that it repeats itself. For Noah, the Apocalypse is at the same time a reminder and a warning. It is his task to make of it a revelation—and a lesson.

But such is the nature of men. They refuse to listen. Eager for diversion, they shun the testimony of witnesses. How have the survivors not gone mad? They spoke, yet nothing changed. Their works, dealing with the common destiny of men, are not received. Hence their despair. If Auschwitz has not forced society to come to its senses, what hope is there? The tragedy of the Apocalypse is this: instead of confronting it, men turn away from it. They act as if they had not discovered the ways to the abyss.

Hence the anguish that permeates my generation, or at least its thinkers, writers and artists. Will they succeed in saving from oblivion everything that could save humanity? In order to manage this, they would have to believe in their mission. But they no longer do.

All the heritage gained from philosophers and creative individuals over centuries and centuries, from various cultures and collective quests, could not prevent the civilization of self-repudiation. The triumphs of the mind, inscribed in the history of diverse peoples with a variety of titles, could not keep away defeat. Socrates and Spinoza, Dante and Dostoevsky, Bach and Michelangelo bear their share of responsibility for what has been done in Christian countries, proud of their progress, to serve Death. The murderers of Treblinka had all read Goethe and admired Schiller. There were scientists and doctors, psychiatrists and opera singers among the officers of the *Sonderkommandos*. Imagine them at work, and you have a glimpse of true Apocalypse. Mad, savage killers cutting the throats of children and old people while screaming their hatred are less terrifying than cultivated individuals massacring their victims with absolute calm, their actions not in the least evident in their faces. The Apocalypse is well-dressed barons slaughtering ten thousand Jews a day at Babi Yar; it is doctors welcoming the crowds at Birkenau and sending the weak and the children straight to the gas chambers while their sleep goes undisturbed; it is doctors of letters and doctors of law drawing up, in Wannsee, the Final Solution. The Apocalypse is a spacious and well-lighted office, well-bred technocrats, efficient secretaries. It is government employees working together with or without passion, with or without conviction, first to imagine, then to bring about, Auschwitz.

The Apocalypse, then, is no longer great beasts spewing forth flames, or horsemen ushering in destruction, or homes ransacked and collapsing in an earthquake imparting to History a hallucinatory, fiery end. The Apocalypse is individuals who appear gentle, generous and intelligent, for whom the disappearance of a person, a family or a community seems to have no real significance. It is individuals for whom abstraction alone counts.

Originally a virtue, abstraction, or the power of abstraction, now reveals itself as a source of calamity. It is abstraction, which, pushed to its ultimate, insane consequence, has ended by condemning our century, one in which all the ideals have failed because they turned against the very men whom they had intended to save.

Marx and Lenin led to the Gulag, and National Socialism to scientific massacres. In both cases, the human being was stripped of his identity, his right to individuality.

I think about what I myself saw, felt and experienced. The Enemy forbade us to live first in our family home, then on our street, then in our neighborhood, eventually in our town and in our country. He took away from us first our house, then our belongings, next our clothes, our hair and finally our identity: we had become numbers, objects, functions. An abstraction. An invisible sign in the vast scheme of the mute, mysterious Apocalypse.

Can we transpose this into the future? Yes and no. I do not believe the Jewish people are threatened as they were in my time. I do not believe a system, a legal government, could conceive of appropriating for its own use the methods tested by Hitler's Germany. Ghettos and gas chambers? Impossible. We will be shielded by memory.

But I do fear something else. I fear a different kind of transfer. I fear that what happened to us will now happen to all peoples. Born of indifference, the Holocaust has proved the malevolent power of indifference. Humanity need only be sufficiently apathetic for a few individuals to usurp the right to trigger, from their air-conditioned offices, the nuclear Apocalypse. And

then—no, I can't go on. I am incapable of imagining what would follow.

To imagine it would be, somehow, to accept it, hence to suppose it possible—that is, somehow, to make it possible. Although unreal in its initial phase, the vision of the Apocalypse carries the risk of becoming reality. Would it be better not to speak of it? Not at all. A contradiction? So be it. I am ready to assume it. Since the war, since the liberation of the camps, I have learned not to evade paradoxes, but to accept them. Otherwise, where would I have found the strength to sanctify life and to trust in man?

To speak of the Apocalypse that was is as difficult as—and no less dangerous than—to articulate the one to come. The solution? It is imperative for creative individuals to keep the vision in mind, but without putting it into words. They must be able to speak of children who are happy—or still happy—even as they imagine the planet in flames. They must be able to describe the poor daily ambitions of their poor selves, even as they see in their mind's eye the heavens being covered by that mortal cloud which the prophets of science have portrayed so well for us.

Yet, by looking, we risk losing our taste for, if not our knowledge of, discourse. How can we use words while knowing, while recognizing their futility?

Perhaps it would be useful to speak no longer of the vision of Apocalypse, but rather of the voice: the voice of the witness rendered mute by his inability to say what he might to help men live. And hope.

Elie Wiesel, Spring 1984, translated by Joan Grimbert and the Author

The Arab World and the Middle East

■ ■ ■

GENERAL

Tension in the House: The Contemporary Poetry of Arabia

One of the interesting but highly telling semantic junctures in Arabic poetics is that the word designating the basic unit of a poem, *bayt* (a line divided into two parts or hemistichs), also means "house" or "home," which is why it cannot be translated simply as "line." For the ancient Arabs of the desert, the nomadic Bedouins who are still with us, the house is essentially a tent, a fact that explains why the eighth-century Arab linguist Al-Khalīl ibn Ahmad, who laid the foundations for the study of Arabic prosody as poetry passed down from its ancient oral origins, chose the Arab tent as model. Later scholars came to compound this domestic model by talking about the thematic progress of the classical poem as if it formed *'amud,* "pillar" or "pole" (that which props up the tent). Until now the term *shi'r 'amudi* (literally, verse that follows the pillar model) has referred, though not accurately, to all poems based on the *bayt* as nucleus.

Today, however, the semantic and poetic dimensions of the *bayt* are not so easily recognizable, not only because the old tent is almost extinct, but also because the modern poem has largely replaced the *bayt* with the culturally different Western line. The gradual transformation of Arabic culture since the eighteenth century left a deep impression on Arabic poetics. The change acquired a stronger momentum toward the middle of the twentieth century. Around that time, the traditional structure of the classical poem was drastically and finally revised, creating two major forms, one preserving essential features of the classical structure and the other breaking that form to constitute what came to be called, again not quite accurately, "the free-verse poem." This latter change took place under the impact of a Western culture that filtered through the minds of poets and critics who either traveled to the West or studied Western literature at home, and who in turn communicated their knowledge to others.

These momentous changes took place first in Egypt, Lebanon, and Iraq, but it wasn't long before other parts of the Arab World followed suit. Of course, those changes did not go unchallenged; a stiff resistance accompanied them, forcing some changes and modifications on the outcome. The ensuing battle of books centered on something that certainly went beyond the technicalities of prosody; it was a battle of basic cultural concepts and values. Tampering with the poem meant to many a tampering with the essence of culture, an encroachment upon the sacrosanct, not so much upon the "house" of poetry as upon the "house" of culture as a whole. Despite the fact that early modernist poets of the forties and fifties did not go beyond the traditional meters, that they simply wanted to break free from the unity of the *bayt* as an enclosed unit inside the poem and replace it with lines that flowed into one another, thus giving the poet more space to move, the innovation was still seen by many as a serious breach of an essential component of Arab cultural identity. The well-known story goes that when the Egyptian critic Abbas El Akkad was chairing the poetry committee at a national contest in the fifties, he rejected a poem written in the new verse form because he insisted that it belonged within the purview of the prose committee instead.

The irony in El Akkad's position was that he himself was part of an earlier wave of modernization that brought, among other innovations, a Western-oriented romantic flair into the arena of Arabic letters. As a consequence of the efforts of people like him, Egypt became a leading country in the process of modernization that swept the Arab world, a process that basically meant embracing Western models in various areas of cultural and social life. The resistance to a drastic change in verse forms while accepting other forms of Western culture was one of many ironic yet telling anomalies that still persist in several areas of life in Arab countries. But if the irony is clear in countries such as Egypt, which were closer to Western models in several areas of cultural life, it is all the more glaring in places such as the Arabian Peninsula, that remained for a long time far from Western influence.

The Peninsula, or "Arabia" as it is sometimes known in the West, is historically regarded as the cradle of Arab culture. Over the centuries, it has remained the place that supplies the description "Arab" with its etymological and semantic base. When modernity began to shake dormant life in the Peninsula around the second half of the nineteenth century, the Arab identity there retained a strength scarcely to be found elsewhere. To this day, numerous social and cultural phenomena in the life of Arabia are less prone to change, or at least to drastic change. Whether one looks on the surface at the continuing traditional (un-Westernized) dress, or the lingering and largely characteristic modes of architecture, or, more deeply, at the persistently dominant forms of oral culture, the scenery is highly suggestive of an anxious guardianship over the remnants of Arab identity. First-time visitors to contemporary Saudi Arabia (where the second part of the country's name retains the historical designation of the Peninsula), or to any of the five Gulf states, are likely to be struck by this seemingly anachronistic situation, which becomes all the more obvious and paradoxical as one contemplates the other side of the coin: the relatively high degree of modernization that those countries have achieved in many other sectors of life.

One of the familiar sights in the modern cities of Gulf countries in recent years is the architectural curiosity of combining a modern, Western-style villa with a traditional tent in the middle. The latter customarily serves mainly as a reception hall, exactly as it used to be in nomadic life. The combination is emptied of any sense of clash, as is the case with the sporadic presence of folkloric literature, particularly oral, Bedouin poetry on state-run television and radio stations. The architectural and technological innovations are not seen as serious threats to cultural identity—a tolerant, almost magnanimous attitude largely denied to changes that touch upon something like language. It is as if the *bayt* that needs to be kept intact is not the one where people live, but rather the one where they articulate their views of life.

This public opposition has not, however, prevented poetry in the Arabian Peninsula from adopting a variety of modern forms, or from finding a receptive audience. The opposition that faced the earlier "free verse" (or *taf'ila*) has reached unprecedented hostility in the case of the prose poem, yet even this highly controver-

sial form succeeded in securing a prominent position in the poetic output of several countries in the area. The interesting thing, however, is that the success achieved by modernity has not resulted in unchecked progress, but has too often been accompanied by a revisionist stand. Instead of basking in their success, the leading figures of the movement have themselves often found it necessary to modify their positions by adapting their innovations to local culture. More often, this did not occur for practical or pragmatic reasons, but rather because of genuine attachment to that local culture. It is this interesting situation that I have found worth discussing in the following remarks, which are bound to be introductory, given the expected lack of familiarity with the literature of the area among the majority of non-Arab readers. My objective is to paint a picture of the tensions occasioned by modernization in the contemporary poetry of Arabia, a picture as comprehensible as it is comprehensive. The ironies and paradoxes of modernization, however, have, as usual, dictated their own choices, and the final picture is certainly more selective than I would have liked. It goes without saying that the examples chosen are not to be seen as the best there are. They are mainly representative of the argument.

The need to modernize while maintaining a distinct cultural identity is of course a global dilemma. In non-Western regions of the world, this dilemma is increasingly aggravated in proportion to the accelerated process of globalization exercised by Western systems—political, economic, cultural, and otherwise. What is of concern in the following remarks is the particular form this dilemma has taken in the literature of a specific area, the Arabian Peninsula. I am concerned, in other words, with the particular manner in which the poets of modern Arabia have tried to overcome the impasse of adopting Western poetic forms and techniques while maintaining an indigenous identity that is both personally meaningful and locally acceptable.

The poets I am referring to are those who generally came to the fore during the 1970s. Those who belonged to earlier generations found little problem in continuing to use traditional forms in order to articulate themes either totally classical or colored by shades of romantic interest. A notable exception within that earlier generation is the Yemeni poet Abdullah al-Baradduni (1922–99), who came up with the rare combination of traditional form and a strikingly modernized set of themes and verbal structures. Yet there is no indication that al-Baradduni went through any identity crisis similar to that suffered by the younger members of the modernist generation before they produced their best work.

A somewhat different case is that of the younger 'Abd al-'Aziz al-Maqalih, another notable Yemeni poet and critic. Al-Maqalih belongs to a transitional generation that still exerts influence throughout the Peninsula. He achieved eminence by early espousing, both critically and poetically, the modern literary trend in the Arab world, especially in Yemen. His poetic modernity stops, however, at "free verse," having already composed in the traditional *bayt* or *'amūdī* verse. Nevertheless, his critical or theoretical modernity includes discussion of poetic prose, defending its legitimacy as part of the poet's freedom and right to experiment. In an article published in the first volume of the Yemeni literary periodical *Aswat* (Voices) in 1993, al-Maqalih identifies the current stage of Arabic verse as "the stage of the newer poetry, that type of writing which tries to go beyond the poetic forms, both traditional and liberal, that Arabic language is accustomed to" (*Aswat*, 13).

At the end of the same article, the writer refers to himself as someone who "has always written rhythmic poetry, which is not devoid sometimes of rhyme." In this, al-Maqalih could be taken to exemplify the response of an entire generation to the advent of modernization in Arabic. The writer is split between what he rationally espouses and is willing to defend but cannot be entirely part of, on the one hand, and, on the other, what he, as a consequence of education or training and therefore of taste and creative skills, can actually engage in. Al-Maqalih will defend prose poetry, accepting the famous pioneering study of this genre by the French critic Suzanne Bernard, but he cannot or will not write prose poetry himself. At the beginning of his creative efforts he straddles the two forms: the traditional *bayt* poem and the *taf'ilah*, as in some of the verse he produced in the early seventies (e.g., in *Hawamish Yamaniyah* [Yemeni Margins]). But in some of his later work, as in two poems published in 1989 in the London-based journal *Mawaqif*, we find him adopting the *taf'ilah* form.

In almost all these poems, the early ones and the more recent alike, the Yemeni poet is driven by essentially the same concern: the Yemeni struggle to overcome the variety of political, social, and economic problems facing the country's effort to join the modern world. Whether he falls back on the rich past of Yemen itself, the part of Arabia once known as "Arabia Felix," or meditates on the distinguished heritage shared by all Arabs, including those as far away as Andalusia, the poet is painfully reminded of a tragically inferior present, not only in Yemen, his main concern, but throughout the Arab world.

A flood flows out of the body of a banner-covered homeland:

A banner with a sword in the middle
A banner with a barrel in the middle
A banner with a grave in the middle
A banner with nothing in the middle.
(*Mawaqif*, 129)

This multiplicity of banners strongly evokes an agonizing multiplicity of identities, a maze of dizzying political identifications that serve only to thwart the historical Arab longing for unity. It is a state of dismemberment and weakness that came about in modern times as a consequence of a long history of Western colonialization. The experience of modernity has been gruesome from this perspective. The resulting distress is summed up more suggestively, though from a slightly different standpoint, by another, somewhat younger Yemeni poet, 'Abd al-Wadud Saif, who addresses his readers as follows:

Ask us about the distress deified on the throne of our
    dismembered bodies:
Are we to leave it in the lips of silence
Until the ice wall falls
— on the ground — ?
Or are we to throw it in the lightning of the first
    elegy

Alighting on our ears?
(*Aswat*, 26)

The dilemma is one of a nation that has lost its features, a nation that looks like nobody, like nothing: "We belong — perhaps — / To that which doesn't look like us!. . . / We look neither like this . . . nor like that" (*Aswat*, 27). These questions about identity are not entirely philosophical; the immediate political, social, and cultural anxieties are too pressing to allow the luxury of philosophical speculation.

One of those pressing anxieties is silence, "the silence that has bred silence in us / That will ignite all the snow mountains" (*Aswat*, 25). The politico-social implications of silence here are perhaps too obvious, but they do not preclude another implication: the difficulty of poetic articulation within a cultural environment that sets limits on innovation. Saif is one of several Yemeni poets who accepted the risks of experimentation, writing the *taf'ila* as well as the prose poem in a milieu wherein orality and conservative forms predominate. In this he had to face strong attacks from those who, according to al-Maqalih, considered "the new poet a heretic on the level both of religion and of language" (Fadhil, 349).

Attacks upon modernization efforts are rampant on the Peninsula. The responses to them have varied, but a common denominator has been compromise: no one could afford simply to ignore the consequences, which could sometimes be serious, threatening both the persons themselves and their livelihood. But political pressure has not been the sole motive behind such compromise. There is much to indicate that the cultural legacy each poet carries was a conditioning force behind the modernization project, in addition to the pragmatic but vital need to reach out to the poetry-reading audience. Thus the issues of political dispersal and its impact on identity that we have seen in the two Yemeni poets are found almost everywhere in the countries of Arabia, but the responses to those issues are not at all the same.

In Saudi Arabia, which covers the largest part of Arabia, the tensions of modernism over the last three decades have been at least the most visible, if not always the strongest. The long process of political unification that the country has been through since 1902, the year the capital Riyadh was conquered, was the result of geographic distance and diversity, something that resulted in diverse responses to cultural modernization in general. Thus, the province of Hijaz, where the holy city of Makkah (or Mecca) is located, was the earliest to respond to changes taking place in Egypt and other parts of the Arab World. Movements like Romanticism, for example, found early echoes in the work of Hijazi intellectuals well before the country became part of the political entity that joined Najd (the middle province) and other parts of Arabia, mostly constituting what the Greeks and Romans knew as Arabia Deserta. This is perhaps why, when modernism touched the traditional *bayt* or "house" of poetry in the seventies, violent reactions did not come from Hijaz or from any other similar region, for that matter, but rather from Najd, the vast central province and the conservative citadel of the country—this is in spite of the fact that poets and critics of the movement came from all different parts of the country.

One of the more prominent poets of the movement is Ali al-Dumayni, who came from the southwest, an area whose geographic nature is similar to that of Yemen. In the sixties, al-Dumayni moved to the eastern region, where oil is produced, only to find himself beset by agonies not so very different from those of Yemen's 'Abd al-Wadud Saif:

Sir,
You who are hiding at the end of the garment
Will you feel ashamed that you are smaller than all
    these wounds?
Will you laugh secretly,
When your candor hugs you switched between the
    damp ceiling
And the eternal loneliness at night? . . .
When people exhaust you

Or when they are exhausted by me
I search my chest, searching
For a green seagull
A small country.
Have the birds left there their virginity yet?
Or have the Bedouins erected their tents?
(*Riyah al-Mawaqi'* [Winds of Sites], 51)

Behind this reticence and pain lies the poet's daring choice to bring tension into the house of poetry. He is "accused of swallows / and bleeding language" (*Riyah*, 50), of being too poetic, as he would like to put it.

At the same time, however, the poet's venture into modernity is not an exercise in masochism, but an acceptance of responsibility. He is aware that "a street is seeking refuge in you from the heat of the sun / and the wind is sheltering in your arms" (*Riyah*, 50). This is why it becomes vitally important for him to find a language that reaches out to that human, natural reality outside without sacrificing his modernist quest. One of the options here is to create a poem that accommodates the local element, the homegrown, by resorting to folklore and to common heritage. Al-Dumayni's poem quoted above, for example, is titled "They Ask You About the Hour," a phrase taken directly from the Holy Qur'an, where the sacred verse refers to the Day of Judgment. For the poet, it is an hour open to several implications, but "change" and "truth" seem to be prominent. The poet is invested with a leading role, which is why he is asked about the time. That the time is not exactly a religious one becomes clear at the end of the poem, where the speaker refers to himself as "still not lost, but having not yet found the right path." A true modern dilemma.

Another strategy for dealing with such a situation is to use folklore, and this is done by deploying expressions from colloquial Arabic as well as by injecting the text with specimens of relevant oral poetry, or simply by recalling an idyllic nomadic life in desert homes. We find these strategies in the verse of al-Dumayni and several other poets of the seventies and eighties in Saudi Arabia and the Gulf countries (although it seems to have disappeared from the more urban prose poem of the nineties). Among the poets who use this strategy are the Bahraini author 'Ali al-Sharqawi, the Kuwaiti woman poet Sa'diyya Mufarrih, and the Omani writer Sayf al-Rahabi. Al-Sharqawi is well known as an accomplished poet both in classical Arabic and in the Bahraini dialect. In both forms of expression, but perhaps more so in the colloquial, he makes heavy use of oral tradition familiar to everyone, especially the illiterate. His modernity extends at times to delicate, single-image poems, as in "Desert":

She enacts laws for the sea
Pulls its blueness

Pollutes it with common pebbles
Sands
Preparing nets
To catch the fish's water.
(*Ma'idat al-Qurmuz* [The Kermes Table], 107)

Yet the presence of such flights into modernity is always qualified by strict attention to traditional rhythm and the accessibility of colloquial verses, many of which have become popular songs in the Gulf area.

Qualifying modernity is also an outstanding feature in the work of the Kuwaiti Mufarrih, especially in her early publications. One of the poems in her first collection is titled "Confessions of a Bedouin Woman," a text entirely focused on a heritage shared by both the poet and a large part of her community. The confession concerns the poet's sense of a split between an urban modernity into which she was born and a nomadic culture she cannot deny in her background. It is when "the winds of change blow in [her] chest," she says, that she recalls the Bedouin tent, "the house made of hair" (*Akhir al-halimin Kan* [He Was the Last of the Dreamers], 33) The details of such a house are all related to the body: "Its black color is in my eyes / Its wooden nails deep and sarcastic in the heart" (33). It is at such moments of identification that she longs for "a smell that / Despite all the perfumes of civilization / is still stuck to my clothes" (34).

One decade later, Mufarrih's most recent work appears to veer away from these torturous memories, both formally and thematically. The prose-poem form that she adopts to articulate modern (or postmodern) urban concerns is accomplished by a series of complex metaphors that bear little resemblance to what the author has written previously. Still, it is not difficult to sense the old concern in a short poem like "Forlornness," in the collection *Mujarrad Mir'at Mustalqiya* (Just a Mirror Lying, 1999). Here a paradoxical situation unfolds: the emptiness and abandonment of urban houses and streets, which ought to be full, force the poet to seek refuge in a vast, vacant, yet more intimate desert: "How much I miss it in the space of cities / Where streets are endlessly wide and long / In the midst of low-flying planes" (34).

Highlighting a similar, though more direct view of the desert, the Omani poet Sayf al-Rahabi addresses the adjacent Empty Quarter, the most expansive and awe-inspiring of Arabia's deserts: "We look into your dense darkness / Begging your mysterious gifts, / Your scattered members in the distances / Have been refuge to an outcast / Wisdom for a deception crowded with mountain goats" (*Yadun fi akhir al-A'lam,* 9). Al-Rahabi's vigorous experimentation in poetic form, which put

him from the outset on the road toward the prose poem, did not prevent him from launching a critique of modernity, whether in his poetry or in the essays he wrote as editor of the avant-garde Omani journal he edits, *Nazwa*. In a poem from a recent collection, he looks homeward, only to find his people, having abandoned the desert camel, blindly straddling "the camel of technology / Now so popular in markets." This disappointment with technology is the impetus behind the search for refuge in the desert. Yet the poet is not consistent in his search. In one of his essays he looks at the Empty Quarter and sees it "changed from a limited geographic area into a symbolic universe spreading cruelty, emptiness, and loss, from which the young generation find no refuge except in . . . language" (*Hiwar al-Amkina wa al-wujuh* [A Dialogue of Places and Faces], 34). The poet's dissatisfaction with Western culture, and his citing of the failure of enlightened reason as proof of that culture's inefficacy (26), mean that he is not far from his Saudi counterpart al-Dumayni's proclaimed oscillation between not having been lost and not having found the right path as yet.

These intellectual dilemmas take another turn in the case of a female poet who sees herself caught up in her femininity within a society that imposes strict codes of behavior and expression on the female. Examples of such a situation are plentiful in modern Arabia: Ashjan al-Hindi from Saudi Arabia, Maysun Saqr from the United Arab Emirates, Hamda Khamis from Bahrain, and Sa'diyya Mufarrih from Kuwait, to whom I have already referred, are but four among the numerous examples that could be cited in this context. The Emirati writer Maysun Saqr is a particularly interesting case, not only because she is a noted poet and painter, but also due to her personal history as a member of the ruling family of Sharja, one of the constituent Gulf emirates forming the UAE.

In a poem titled "Flowing in the Body Matter" ("Jarayan fi Maddat al-Jasad," 1992), in a collection bearing that same title, Saqr stages a bold but generally delicate protest against a social ambience that can scarcely tolerate female freedom: "Each tribe is a draft copy of my suppression / They are all a door leaf repressing my stature." The climax of the poem comes in a passage found toward the end. A series of paradoxes contribute to the esthetic pleasure of reading this passage:

Half of my body is paralyzed in movement
The other half is still
Dreaming only of that half where suicidal thoughts
Are extinguished.
I set fire in my room
Hoping to save a flooding motherhood

Hoping to burn down a country of cardboard
To burn myself in it.
Fire is intimate with me
Eager to sting my ego.

The paradoxical reference to the intimate fire is reminiscent of the equally intimate desert in the verse of the Kuwaiti poet Sa'diyya Mufarrih. Both fire and desert form a bulwark, a refuge, as the Omani writer Sayf al-Rahabi put it, against the atrocities of excessive social control. The image of the cardboard country, and the fragility this implies, recalls the political protest suggested in the image of a many-bannered Arab world in the poem by al-Maqalih from Yemen. From another standpoint, however, the image bears a significance that translation cannot convey. The Arabic for "cardboard," waraq muqawwa, literally means "hardened paper," an expression that opens up implications of writing in a way that "cardboard" does not. The most immediate implication is that the country is fragile, but the presence of "paper," in the Arabic original, opens a space for writing as a way out of the local confinement, in a fashion similar to that found in al-Rahabi's poem.

The paper country in Saqr's poem, the small country in al-Dumayni's, the desert tent in the work of Mufarrih are all variations in a continuum of hope and disillusionment. The fact that they are all related to the "house" of poetry, the bayt, seems completely self-evident. Poetry, or writing, or art in general, has functioned in this way in various cultures. It forms the "raw towns that we believe and die in," as W. H. Auden put it in his famous elegy on W. B. Yeats. The difference lies in the particular forms it takes in each culture or individual work, the diversity of expressions, images, metaphors, et cetera into which it formulates itself.

One of the noted poets of modernism in Saudi Arabia, Muhammad al-Thubayti, paints a fantastic portrait of the artistic refuge in a poem called "Taghribat al-Qawafil wa al-Matar" (The Westward Movement of Caravans and Rain). The country appears here as a drink to be served to a group of nomadic travelers who have stopped to rest. A necessary complement to the relaxation is the sound of the rababa (rebec), the stringed instrument predominantly used by the Bedouin Arabs in their desert tents. The tribal soothsayer (the kahin) is asked to deliver his prophecy about the future of this group as they try to find their way in an endless desert. That this soothsayer represents the poet himself is obvious to the reader.

Pour down the mourning heartblood
Pour down a country in cups
To turn heads around,
Give us more of "shadhiliyya" until the cloud covers
    us

Pour down the mourning heartblood
Shed on people's heads your sour but delicious coffee
(Attadharis [Land Undulations], 50–51)

The image of pouring a country in a cup recalls Keats's famous beaker which is "full of the warm south"—with, however, one big difference: the Arab poet wants the drink to be a sobering instead of a numbing tool. The drink, after all, is coffee (although an argument to the contrary could be made on the basis that the word for coffee in Arabic, qahwa, which is said to be the basis of the European word, formerly meant wine).

Al-Thubayti's poem narrates a symbolic trip that epitomizes the quandary of modern Arabs. By selecting his symbols, images, and characters from the desert culture, the poet simultaneously raises the vital question of identity and selects the poetic vehicle that facilitates his crossing of the modernity bridge to a potentially alienated audience. The taghribah recalls a famous, part-historic, part-legendary exodus by a tribe known as Banu Hilal from Najd in the middle of the Arabian Peninsula to North Africa. The poem is full of direct allusions to the life of such a tribe and the hard circumstances that forced them to leave, thus addressing a collective memory among the poet's audience. But this is all done in a highly sophisticated language and with imagery that is full of complex metaphors and expressions of the sort indicated above.

From this perspective, one could argue that al-Thubayti's poem may also be seen as epitomizing the modernist enterprise as a whole. For at the nucleus of the enterprise there lies the movement westward—in the direction, that is, of Western culture, from which came the very idea of breaking the forms of traditional Arabic poetry. At the same time, however, the westward movement is inherently eastward, a journey into the heart of Arabic culture, as exemplified by a well-known saga. The conflict between these two directions has created the tension of modernity in the work of Arabian poets, a tension that constitutes at once the impediment and the impetus of that movement.

Saad Al-Bazei, Spring 2001

Arabic Literature and the Nobel Prize

For many centuries the Arabs have constituted for the Western world an alien and often confrontational entity, a quintessential "other." The posture can be traced back at least to the Crusades, and as we know to our cost from current conflicts in Ireland, Lebanon, and the Gulf, wars based on religious belief are particularly capable of engendering misinformation and misunderstandings of prolonged duration. In spite of recent developments in what is known both about the Arab world and also about the processes by which that knowledge is interpreted, many Western attitudes of considerable antiquity still persist. The "Middle East" was so designated by the Western imperialist interests of previous generations (to which the Middle East was "middle"), and the inhabitants of the region seem to have been condemned by their very proximity to Europe, and therefrom by the frequency of military confrontations with the European political powers throughout the ages, to be the subject of a wide variety of religious and cultural polemics. By contrast, the nations of what was simultaneously designated as the "Far East" were a more remote and "exotic" entity, something which, within a less directly confrontational context, seems to have promoted among Western scholars (perhaps automatically) a closer attention to the literary production of the region. More recently, events such as the series of conflicts following the foundation of the State of Israel and the emergence of a newly invigorated fundamentalist Islam have given the Western nations their share of anxiety and often annoyance. However, rather than being seen as offering opportunities for a renewed interest in the history and nature of Arabo-Islamic culture, these contemporary confrontations and conflicts have tended to cement still further attitudes which lead to a widespread unfamiliarity with this elaborate complex of nations and peoples and a concomitant reluctance to change the situation.

The reception of Arabic literature in the West has thus always been set within a complicated array of cultural attitudes. The intricate questions of "influence" and cultural exchange between the two remain the subject of much controversy. While research on the implications of the presence of Arabic lyric poetry and picaresque narrative in ninth-century al-Andalus (as Spain was termed) continues to tantalize some scholars and antagonize others, the influence of Sir William Jones's translations of Eastern poetry and of Galland's translation of *The Thousand and One Nights* on the history of European literature is scarcely open to debate. More recently, and particularly following the colonization of many countries in the Arab world by Europe in the nineteenth century, the process has been predominantly unidirectional. The genres of the novel and drama were to a large degree transplanted into modern Arabic literature direct from the Western tradition, rapidly superseding any attempts at reviving older genres. It was in the realm of poetry, the most vigorous of the classical genres, that the neoclassical tendency persisted longest, but it too came under the influence of Western

"schools" of poetry. As one of the participants in the process, Jabra Ibrahim Jabra, a Palestinian poet, points out: "Influences reaching the Arabs had a way of being thirty or forty years late. Up to 1950 most of these influences belonged to pre-World War I, if not to the end of the 19th century."[1] Jabra continues by noting that European influences were not only late, but also compressed and occasionally out of sequence vis-à-vis their European chronology.

It is within the context of this confusing set of influences and attitudes that modern Arabic literature and the West confront each other. That there should be misunderstanding and "anxiety" on both sides is hardly surprising. It would also seem unreasonable to expect that any exercise in transcultural evaluation such as that essayed by the Nobel Prize Committee should not be a reflection of the general situation. With that in mind, I will address some of the issues raised within the framework of the prize and its selection committee under three headings: access to Arabic literature in the West; the Nobel Prize criteria; and finally, a short segment concerning those Arab authors whose candidacy seems plausible within the current terms of reference.

Many Western readers are exposed to a monument of Arabic literature at a relatively early age in the form of *The Thousand and One Nights,* a work which has for a long time provided a rich source of entertainment for children. I myself can vividly remember being taken to see pantomime versions of both "Aladdin" and "Ali Baba" as a child. Ironically, this huge collection of tales was never regarded as literature by the Arabs themselves, and current scholarly interest is largely the result of Western attention, initially to the sources and, more recently, to narrative structure and techniques. The popularity and exoticism of these tales within Western culture seems to have produced two major results. In the first place, it fostered a fantastic view of Middle Eastern culture, something which has been documented by a large number of sources[2] and which finds what is perhaps its extreme representation in such media as the cinema (from the Sindbad films of Douglas Fairbanks Sr. to more recent examples such as *The Jewel of the Nile*). Second, the almost automatic selection of tales from this collection for anthologies of "world literature" succeeded to a large degree in blocking any further interest in searching for other examples of literature written in Arabic. The wealth of classical Arabic poetry remained essentially a closed book except to a few scholars, and even they were not of any great assistance: the German scholar-poet Nöldeke gave his opinion (in the introduction to a collection of Arabic poetry) that the esthetic pleasure gained from a reading of the poems hardly justified the pain involved.[3] Thus, the general

Western readership, endeavoring to evaluate examples of literature produced in today's Arab world, may perhaps be considered to be at a double disadvantage: not only are they presented with works which seem to show a strong reliance on Western models with which they are already familiar; but also the history of the Arabic literary tradition, available to them through their own general education and the more direct avenue of translation of the "classics," is incomplete and distorted. There is thus an unsettling lack of context.

If we turn now to a consideration of the criteria under which the Swedish Academy's Nobel Committee operates, some of the issues which need to be raised in connection with the above survey become clear.[4] One of the members of the jury itself, the Swedish physician-novelist Lars Gyllensten, readily acknowledges a point which has already been made: "Literary works are more or less bound to the literary environment in which they are created, and the farther away from it one is, the harder it is to do them justice." I might observe that, on the basis of my comments above, the epithet *far* in this instance needs to be interpreted within the context of cultural attitudes rather than pure geographic distance. The same writer then goes on to make what is, for the purposes of Arabic literature, a statement of major importance.

> The task of awarding the Nobel Prize in Literature involves the obligation of trying to find methods for keeping oneself *au fait* with what is happening in literature all over the world and for appraising it, either on one's own or with the aid of specialists. Finally, the prize awarders must try to familiarize themselves with the works of most value, directly or via translations, and to make a careful assessment of their quality with all the viewpoints conceivably necessary for a reasonable evaluation.[5]

Two issues emerge here: first, the question of evaluation; and second, that of translation. On the matter of translation, one has to state fairly bluntly that, as far as English is concerned, modern Arab *littérateurs* have not been particularly well served by translation (although the situation seems at least marginally better in French). A number of things are implied within this statement: that there are relatively few qualified people in the West interested in translating works of modern Arabic literature (and most of them are academic scholars with other responsibilities); that the works selected for translation show some peculiar preferences and omissions (the emphasis on the Egyptian novel at the expense of other national traditions, for instance); that the translations are sometimes not of a high standard; and above all, that the publishing outlets for such efforts are exiguous in

the extreme. Although small and adventurous presses such as Sindbad (France) and Three Continents (USA) produce as many translated editions as their limited budgets will permit, the record of larger publishing companies with regard to the publication of works of Arabic literature can only be described as deplorable. We can once again refer to the above comments about attitudes, although the formulation "lack of market" apparently becomes a more satisfactory substitute phrase within the demands of modern economics and thus becomes a self-fulfilling prophecy, as in the recent decision to discontinue the Arab Authors series at Heinemann (England) following the firm's takeover by a large industrial concern. Thus is a major world literature apparently declared "unmarketable."[6]

The second issue raised by Gyllensten's statement involves evaluation, and most particularly the phrase "with the aid of specialists." If we assume the phrase "Arabic literature" to incorporate literary works written in the Arabic language throughout the Arabic-speaking world, then we have to acknowledge that the Nobel Committee is presented with an enormous and probably impossible task; for few indeed are the critics and scholars, whether Arab or non-Arab, whose knowledge of the field is sufficiently broad to encompass the entire region and the variety of genres involved and to present the committee with a list of nominees which will transcend political, religious, and cultural boundaries. Here we must refer to the documentation regarding the nomination procedure itself.

> The right to nominate candidates for the Prize in Literature is granted to members of the Swedish Academy; and of the French Academies which are similar to it in character and objectives; to members of the humanistic sections of other academies, as well as to members of the humanistic institutions and societies as enjoy the same rank as academies and to university professors of aesthetics, literature and history.[7]

In view of the extremely small number of "specialists" in Arabic literature to whom the members of the Nobel Committee might have access and indeed of the relatively few contacts between Western scholars in the field and Arab *littérateurs* and literary critics, it is hardly surprising that this nominating procedure has not worked in favor of nominations from the field of Arabic literature.

Another feature of the criteria for nominations which has been much debated concerns the stipulation in Alfred Nobel's will that the prize honor someone whose writings have been "of an ideal tendency," a phrase which is interpreted by Gyllensten to mean "a striving for the good of mankind, for humaneness, common sense, progress and happiness . . . literary achievements with constructive aims."[8] While this rubric has been liberally interpreted, several critics have suggested dropping it altogether.[9] Those who have any familiarity with the history of the Arab world during the course of this century, and most particularly in the decades since World War II, will perhaps realize that "common sense, progress and happiness" have not been attributes which have provided the driving force for the majority of Arab authors. Alienation, rebellion, confrontation, rejection, revolution, self-sacrifice, struggle—these have been far more characteristic of the literature of the last several decades.

All this said, it will perhaps not be a surprise if I eschew the opportunity to compare recent prizewinners with potential nominees from the Arab world. No Arab has as yet won the prize; whether one will (or can) under the current criteria seems open to doubt. That is not to say, of course, that there are not Arab *littérateurs* who are worthy of nomination. I would like to devote just a few lines to a consideration of my own short list: Najīb Mahfūz (sometimes written as Naguib Mahfouz) of Egypt and Adunis (or Adonis) of Lebanon. Both manage to combine two considerations: in the first place, they are preeminently great writers; second, translations of many of their works are available in at least English and French. However, this availability in English translation itself presents us with a problem. In the case of Mahfūz, the novels which are now available in translation are, in the main, part of a series being published by the American University in Cairo Press. Because of the order in which the translations were completed, the novels have appeared in essentially random sequence; most especially, Mahfūz's major monument and contribution to modern literature as a whole, *Al-Thulathiyya* (The Trilogy; 1956–57), has yet to appear. The slightly earlier *Al-Bidaya wa-al-Nihaya* (1951; Eng. *The Beginning and the End*) is now available, along with *Zuqaq al-Midaqq* (1947; Eng. *Midaq Alley*), but the bulk of the published translations are from novels which were written in the 1960s; though all are of extreme interest within the perspective of the recent history of Egyptian society, they are of varying literary quality in both the original and in translation.[10]

Adunis has been particularly poorly served in translation, although some critics would suggest that the very nature of his own poetic language and vision encourages translators to indulge in some extreme pieces of creativity of their own. Whatever the role of cause and effect here, the fact remains that there are very few translations of Adunis's poetry into any Western language which manage to convey to the reader the complex and multilayered significances of the original

poetry. That said, it must be affirmed that, more than any other modern Arab poet, Adunis has succeeded in radically reforming attitudes toward the great tradition of Arabic poetry, and using that and his own immense creativity as a base, he has established new terms of reference for poetry and the poetic and has applied his vision in poems of striking originality and beauty.[11]

It is, however, with Mahfūz that I choose to conclude. Although Herbert Howarth may have complained about the emphasis on novelists in awarding the Nobel Prize,[12] it was in the new and largely imported field of fiction that enormous efforts had to be made by Arab *littérateurs* during the early decades of this century. Najīb Mahfūz is acknowledged throughout the entire Arab world as the great pioneer in the mature Arabic novel, and he has achieved that distinction by dint of sheer hard work, tenacity, patience in adversity (both political and medical), and a disarming humility. He is recognized as the Arab world's leading writer of fiction because he has not only produced a whole stream of excellent novels over a period of four decades, but also turned the novel, as a means of societal comment and criticism, into an accessible and accomplished medium. His is a nomination which, the normalities of Arab politics aside, would be welcomed throughout the Arab world.

Roger Allen, Spring 1988

[1] Jabra Ibrahim Jabra, "Modern Arabic Literature and the West," *Journal of Arabic Literature*, 2 (1971), p. 81.

[2] Such as Muhsin Jassim Ali's *Scheherezade in England*, Washington, D.C., Three Continents, 1981.

[3] For an interesting experiment in the reading of translations of classical Arabic poetry, see "'And heard great argument': An Essay in the Practical Criticism of Arabic Poetry," *Journal of Arabic Literature*, 1 (1970), pp. 49–69.

[4] I shall be referring to the article by William Riggan, "The Swedish Academy and the Nobel Prize in Literature: History and Procedure," *WLT* 55:3 (Summer 1981), pp. 399–405.

[5] Cited in Riggan, p. 404.

[6] The recent foundation of the Project for the Translation of Arabic (PROTA), directed by the famous Palestinian poet and critic Salma Khadra' al-Jayyusi, has shown through its publications (three novels and two major anthologies as of 1987) that excellent and accessible translations of works of modern Arabic literature can be produced and published with the necessary cooperation between translators and editors. The volume *Modern Arabic Poetry: An Anthology* (New York, Columbia University Press, 1987) is exemplary in this regard.

[7] See Riggan, p. 401.

[8] See Riggan, p. 403.

[9] Herbert Howarth, "Nobel Prize Symposium: A Petition to the Swedish Academy," *BA* 41:1 (Winter 1967), p. 6.

[10] On Mahfūz, see both Roger Allen, "Aspects of Technique in the Modern Arabic Short Story," and Muhammad Siddiq, "The

Contemporary Arabic Novel in Perspective," in *WLT's* special issue on the literatures of the Middle East, 60:2 (Spring 1986), pp. 199–206 and 206–11 respectively.

[11] On Adunis, see Samuel Hazo and Mirene Ghossein, "Adonis: A Poet in Lebanon," *BA* 46:2 (Spring 1972), pp. 238–42.

[12] See Howarth, p. 6.

Literary History and the Arabic Novel

■ INTRODUCTION

One of the more necessary, and perhaps unfortunate, duties of literary historians is continually to remind themselves of a corollary to the rules of the process of change: namely, that literary histories also have their own history. When the topic and region upon which a scholar focuses is as vast and varied as the tradition of novel-writing in the Arab world, and indeed when one realizes the pace of change that forces, both internal and external, have brought to bear on this complex region during the course of the twentieth century, it should come as no surprise to learn that versions of literary history penned as recently as a few decades ago are in need of at least revision and, more often than not, rewriting. Thus, a history of the Arabic novel, viewed from the perspective of today (2001) looks very different from that of, say, the pre-1967 period, in terms of the nature and direction of the novel itself, and of the volume and variety of examples of it written in Arabic. In this short essay I would like to consider some of the ramifications of this situation as reflected in the projection of the Arabic novel genre through its modes of study and, in particular, from a Western perspective.[1]

■ RETROSPECT I

Within such an investigative framework the year 1988 may be seen as a significant watershed, in that the Egyptian novelist Najīb Mahfūz (b. 1911) was announced as that year's winner of the Nobel Prize in Literature (an event, incidentally, in which this journal and the present writer were closely involved; see "The Nobel Prizes in Literature 1967–1987: A Symposium," *WLT* 62:2 [Spring 1988], pp. 201–3). At the time Mahfūz (often transliterated as "Mahfouz" in the West) was hailed by the Nobel Committee and by literary commentators as "the Dickens of Cairo" or "the Balzac of Cairo." Along with the usual supply of political sour grapes and pretentious nonsense that accompanies the annual Nobel announcement in October, a number of questions were raised by Arab critics as to precisely what the longer-term implications of this award to an Arab novelist

might be. I shall refer to some of those issues below, but at this juncture the major point I wish to emphasize is that, from a historical perspective, the 1988 date is already chronologically misleading. Even though Mahfūz had continued writing novels and short stories right up to the time of the announcement of the award and indeed thereafter, the Nobel citation made no mention of his recent works and concentrated instead on those published before the June War of 1967 (the so-called "setback" or *al-naksah*), lavishing particular praise on one work, *Al-Thulāthiyyah* (The Trilogy), a three-novel family saga set in inter-world-war Cairo that was originally published in the Egyptian capital in 1956 and 1957 (the three volumes were published in English by Doubleday between 1990 and 1992 under the titles *Palace Walk, Palace of Desire,* and *Sugar Street*). These novels have long since come to be regarded as a kind of capstone to a particular phase in the Arabic novel's development, and indeed as the most visible sign of a rigorous and carefully planned process whereby Mahfūz brought the development of the Arabic novel to a stage of complete maturity. In the words of more than one critic, the European novel had thereby become a fully domesticated literary genre within the Arab world.

Mahfūz's own career as a published writer extended back into the 1930s. He himself had started with the short-story genre, the mode of fiction which, for a number of reasons, had reached a level of maturity earlier than its longer fictional cousin; in Egypt this was largely due to the efforts and artistry of a group of writers known as *jamā'at al-madrasah al-hadīthah* or the "New School Group," many of whom Mahfūz admired greatly. During this particular decade, a whole host of Egyptian litterateurs decided to "try their hand" at novel writing, most notably Ibrāhīm 'Abd al-Qādir al-Māzinī (d. 1949) with *Ibrāhīm al-Katīb* (1931; Eng. *Ibrahim the Writer,* 1976), and Tawfīq al-Hakīm (d. 1987), with several novels, of which *'Awdat al-rūh* (1933; Eng. *Return of the Spirit,* 1990) and *Yawmiyyāt nā'ib fī al-aryāf* (Diaries of a Public Prosecutor in the Provinces, 1937; Eng. *The Maze of Justice,* 1947, repr. 1989) are the most accomplished. Mahfūz appears to have been drawn into this arena of experiment, but, in an absolutely typical gesture, he went about it in a methodical manner, setting himself to read John Drinkwater's introductory work, *The Outline of Literature,* and then doggedly making his way through examples (mostly in English or English translation) of many of the novels listed there. The notion of *The Trilogy* as a final stage in a process of experiment toward the completion of a transplanted European novel of family life composed in Arabic, as noted above, thus seems entirely reasonable.

These "novelists of the '30s" were the inheritors of a process of novelistic development that traces its beginnings to what is regarded as the cultural renaissance of the nineteenth century (known in Arabic as *al-nahdah*), a movement that involved in varying degrees a combination of, first, an encounter with the West and its different and more "advanced" culture, and second (and subsequently), a retrospect into the Arab-Islamic past. One of the great problems connected with this approach to "the modern" in the Arab world context is that this retrospective process did not involve an engagement with the immediate past (which was, and often still is, regarded as a literary and cultural wasteland, tarred with that kiss-of-death epithet, "decadent") but rather a huge chronological leapfrog to an idealized "classical" era some seven centuries earlier. The ongoing effects of this process of retrospect on the emergence of "neoclassical" movements and on critical (and historical) attitudes to generic development have been profound and retain their ability to obfuscate and obliterate the investigation of possible continuities right up to the present.

Convenience and economy being basic principles of human endeavor, not least in the writing of literary history, it has been customary to use the cultural history of Egypt as a general model for the development of genres, and especially fictional genres, in the Arab world. Certainly, there are a number of reasons to justify such a choice: the centrality of the country within the larger region, the dominant political and cultural role that the country played from an early stage in the modern history of the Middle East, the large number of citizens living within its borders, and the warm welcome it has provided to exiles from other regions, most particularly the Christian communities of Syro-Lebanon during the second half of the nineteenth century. Certainly also, the basic matrix of generic importation that the case of Egypt presents is applicable, albeit within very different time frames—some earlier, some later—to the other regions of the Arab world. The first stage involves translation, and Egypt, with its Translation School (under the directorship of the renowned Rifā'ah al-Tahtāwī [d. 1873]), is certainly a pioneer in that regard. The initial priority in the translation endeavor was toward more practical matters (technical manuals), but it was not long before versions appeared in Arabic (and other Middle Eastern languages) of swashbuckling adventure romances. Bearing in mind the strong influence of *The Arabian Nights* on Alexandre Dumas, it comes as no surprise that one of the very first works to be published was *The Count of Monte Cristo*. A second stage in the matrix involved imitation, and the 1880s and 1890s witnessed a flood of weekly and monthly magazines

publishing works by such writers as Sa'īd al-Bustānī, Ya'qūb Sarrūf, and, above all, Jūrjī Zaydān, whose historical novels, still popular today, presented a wide variety of historical episodes from Arab and Islamic history in attractive novelistic frameworks. It needs to be noted in this context that women were, as in the European model, primary readers of these works and that there were also publications produced by and aimed specifically at a women's readership.

Within this historical model, certain other works of a more neoclassical mode are always mentioned and frequently honored. For example, Ahmad Fāris al-Shi-dyāq's (d. 1887) *Al-Sāq 'alā al-Sāq fī-mā huwa al-Fār-Yāq* (approximately, One Leg Over Another / The Pigeon the Tree-Branch / Concerning the Doings of Fār-Yāq, 1855) announces in the very complexity of its title (including double entendres and rhymes) that its author relishes the opportunity to play with the Arabic language in ways that are utterly characteristic of earlier tastes in prose composition and its reception. Even within this pioneering work in fictional autobiography, Al-Shidyāq feels somehow compelled to insert some examples of the most popular genre of "elite" prose narrative from the premodern period, the *maqāmah,* and indeed to provide glossaries of their lexical complexities. Such essays in prose writing were written to appeal to the tastes of an educated elite and clearly, in terms of reader popularity, presented no challenge to the increasingly popular novel-romance genre. Even Muhammad al-Muwaylihī's (d. 1930) highly critical and witty *Hadīth 'Īsā ibn Hishām* (1907; Eng. *A Period of Time,* 1974, 1992), also written in a style that would appeal to an elite readership, did not manage to serve as a counterweight to the growing popularity of the "imported" genre of the novel in spite of its highly realistic portrayal of life in Egypt under British occupation. While other writers in Egypt and elsewhere in the Arab world used the *maqāmah* genre—whether its form, language, ironic tone, or picaresque themes—to serve as a kind of "bridge" between classical and modern prose writing, the genre was reckoned to have seen its "swan song," at least within this historical approach to the Arabic novel, with al-Muwaylihī (the phrase is that of the great French scholar Régis Blachère).

While Al-Shidyāq and Al-Muwaylihī receive polite tips of the hat in this procession toward the 1930s, *The Trilogy,* and the Nobel Prize of 1988, it is a single novel, *Zaynab,* that has consistently been awarded a prize of its own as "the first Arabic novel," "the first real Arabic novel," "the first artistic Arabic novel" (and so on). Muhammad Husayn Haykal's (d. 1956) novel was written in France in 1911 and published in Egypt in 1913 under a pseudonym (a sign of the new fictional genre's continuingly suspect moral probity). It is indeed a major monument in modern Arabic fiction, but, as I have argued elsewhere (see, for example, *Modern Arabic Literature,* ed. M. M. Badawi, Cambridge University Press, 1992), its significant advances in the treatment of social themes (especially the status of women within the family structure) and in the use of language need to be relieved of the burden of "firstness" and placed within a broader historical and developmental framework. This notion that the Arabic novel "begins" in 1913 is merely one of the problems associated with the retrospective matrix that I have just tried to outline.

▪ QUESTIONS

This type of historical analysis applied to a novelistic tradition within a particular world culture leads, almost automatically, to a number of questions concerning the processes of "translation," used here in the literal sense to describe the process whereby an artifact or genre is "carried across" the divide between two literary traditions, and therefrom to a (re)examination of the origins and development of the novel genre itself—issues of definition and development, of "the novel before the novel," and so on. Much ink has been expended on these topics, and I do not propose to enter the lists here. However, the Western world's plaudits in 1988 for Najīb Mahfūz as the author of an Egyptian family saga written in Arabic and published in 1956–57 do point to some interesting questions regarding cultural hegemony and future directions for the Arabic novel. It is those I wish to address in what follows.

Is it the fate of the Arabic novel, for example (and by extension those of other non-Western / Third World cultures) to play a continuous and eventually unsuccessful game of "catch-up" with the various subdivisions of the Western novel? According to the matrix that we have explored above, does *The Trilogy* of Mahfūz represent the (now "certified") culmination of a "Western" phase in the development of the Arabic novel, after which he, along with his contemporary and successor novelist colleagues, could and can explore more intrinsically "Arab" narrative elements in their compositions? What might the "particularities" of such novels be? And, most fascinating from the Western point of view in the post-1988 era of the Arabic novel, what is the likely reception of translations of narratives that add other elements of cultural difference to those already furnished by language and social/cultural setting (and perhaps an interest in the "exotic" as a residue from the reception history of *The Arabian Nights*)? In Walter Benjamin's terms (in his famous essay in *Illuminations*), what is the potential "translatability" of such works? In this instance, we already have an interesting test case in the reception of translations of Mahfūz's novels into English during the post-1988 period. For, while the majority of his novelistic oeuvre has now been rendered into English and published by Doubleday in attractive editions, it is very noticeable to someone such as myself who keeps track of such trends that the only work(s) that consistently remain on the shelves of bookstores at this point are the volumes of *The Trilogy* (in their often less than satisfactory English titles). By contrast, none of those works written by the Nobel laureate in which he follows the more "particularizing" trend noted above, by attempting to utilize the styles and structures of more indigenous narrative genres (albeit for the purpose of thoroughly contemporary commentary)—for example, *Rihlat Ibn Fattūmah* (1983; Eng. *The Journey of Ibn Fattouma,* 1992) and *Layālī Alf Laylah* (Nights of a Thousand Nights, 1982; Eng. *Arabian Nights and Days,* 1995)—none of these translated works has earned a broad readership in European or Anglo-American markets. These observations regarding the English translations of Mahfūz's works provide further evidence, if required, of the urgent need, within the realm of reception theory, for critical analysis of the factors involved in the process of reading translated works from noncontiguous literary traditions.

▪ PARAMETERS OF CHANGE

The novel being a most effective mirror of society and the circumstances within which it functions, any attempt to reformulate a history of Arabic versions of the genre from a different, more recent perspective must of necessity take into consideration a whole host of contributors to political and social change (although here I will try to summarize them as briefly as possible).

The June War of 1967 came as a devastating blow to all those political institutions and social structures that the Arabic novel, fulfilling its most direct generic purpose, had striven to foster and reflect. From that point of view at least, the selection of works mentioned in Mahfūz's Nobel citation (all written before 1967) was an accurate reflection of a genuine watershed in the modern history of the Arab world. After a prolonged and often bitter era of struggle against occupation by European powers (beginning in the nineteenth century) and of aspiration toward an Arab nationalism (culminating in the establishment in Cairo of the League of Arab States in 1945), the 1950s had ushered in a new age of independence for a number of nations within the Middle Eastern region. This process is seen at its most bitter in Algeria, where the depth of French political and cultural penetration (beginning as early as 1830) led to a vicious war that resulted in independence but did not resolve many internal issues which continue to beset that society to this very day.

The dominant figure in this postindependence period had undoubtedly been the President of Egypt, Jamāl ʿAbd al-Nāsir (Nasser), but the heady days represented by the Bandung Conference, the creation of the United Arab Republic (1958–61), the building of the Aswan High Dam with Soviet help—all these faded into the background in the wake of a total defeat of forces and institutions in 1967. During those six days the propaganda machines that Arab regimes had put together to foster a new spirit of élan and optimism systematically lied to the Arab people. As several writers ruefully observed, the word itself had become totally discredited. Such was the scale of this "setback" (naksah) that a period of the most profound self-reflection was called for; as part of it, many intellectuals undertook a wholesale reexamination of the very bases of Arab values. Which elements in Arab culture were asīl (an epithet implying an authenticity to one's cultural roots)? What was there in the Arab-Islamic heritage (turāth) that might provide lessons for the present? Thus, while certain Arab novelists such as Salim Barakat almost immediately addressed themselves with a new and devastating candor to the events of the war itself, including the media's deliberately misleading information (in ʿAwdat al-tāʾir ilā al-bahr [Return of the Flying Dutchman to the Sea, 1969; Eng. Days of Dust, 1974]), others chose to pause for thought and then to invoke texts from the past, often with a heavily ironic overlay, all in order to suggest bitter lessons for the present. Emīl Habībī's Al-Waqāʾi ʿal-gharībah fī-ikhtifāʾ Saʿīd Abī al-Nahs al-Mutashāʾil (The Strange Events Surrounding the Disappearance of Saʿīd, Father of Misfortune, the Pessoptimist, 1972, 1974; Eng. The Secret Life of Saeed the Pessoptimist, 1982, 1985) and Jamāl al-Ghīṭānī's Al-Zaynī Barakāt (1971; Eng. Al-Zayni Barakat, 1988) are two early and brilliant contributions to this new trend in the Arabic novel.

The carefully fostered image of Arab nationalism and unity was to be further buffeted in the years that followed the June War. Nasser's successor, Anwar al-Sādāt, turned to the West for support, opened the Egyptian economy to the outside world, and in 1979 signed the Camp David Accords with Israel. Egypt, with its class structure increasingly polarized by the processes of economic change he had initiated, was now ostracized by the Arab League (which moved its headquarters to Tunis). While a concept of Arab unity remained a reality, particularly in times of crisis, regionalism and localism were now to an increasing extent the preferred models (and perhaps, one might suggest, the more natural ones in view of the size of the region and the diversities involved).

The 1970s were to see at least two other major events in the Middle East region that were to have an enormous impact on every conceivable aspect of society. During the 1973 conflict between Israel and its Arab neighbors, the Organization of Petroleum Exporting Countries (OPEC) severely restricted the flow of oil to the West, causing a major economic crisis. Oil, already an economic weapon, now became a strategic one as well. Furthermore, the Arab states with the smallest populations and the most traditional lifestyles now found themselves in control of the flow and pricing of the world's largest reserves of a vital commodity and accruing staggering amounts of money. The devastating impact of this new wealth on the inherited values of those traditional economies is graphically captured in the renowned quintet of novels by the Saudi-born novelist ʿAbd al-Rahmān Munīf (b. 1933), Mudun al-milh (Cities of Salt, 1984; Eng. Cities of Salt, 1987; The Trench, 1991; Variations on Night and Day, 1993). Less well known but equally significant for Arab societies was the effect of workers' migration from the most populous (and poorer) countries—in particular, Egypt—to the Gulf states, and the concomitant effect on family life and its authority structures. This issue of gender roles and women's status has been a major topic of the Arabic novel since Haykal's Zaynab and before, and remains so. In that, it finds itself in frequent opposition to the second event of the 1970s, the revolution in Iran (1979) that created the first Islamic Republic and thereafter fostered (and sometimes financed) popular religious movements elsewhere in the region (most notably in Lebanon, which suffered through its own gruesome civil-war experience between 1975 and 1988). While it is obviously not the case that Shiʾite Iran has single-handedly been responsible for the appearance of all the popular religious movements that have sprung up across the Arab world in recent decades, it is certainly true that the model of an Islamic state, with its consistent reliance on Islamic tradition for precedents, has found a ready reception among those disillusioned inhabitants of Arab nations who see in the adoption of Western economic and political systems a future of never-ending dependence.

"A disturbance of spirits" is the apposite phrase used by Albert Hourani (A History of the Arab Peoples, 1991) to describe the set of events and transformations in the Middle Eastern region that I have just surveyed. The ongoing conflicts, the economic disparities between and within nations, the clash of generations within the family, the struggle for women's rights, the parlous state of individual liberties—not least of those individuals who choose to express their views and aspirations in literary form—all these political and social phenomena have indeed been "disturbed" by the rapidity of the changes that have affected the Middle East in recent times. It almost goes without saying that all of them have also provided fruitful topics for the Arabic novel. Indeed, as Gaber Asfour suggests in his *Zaman al-riwāyah* (Time of the Novel, 1999), the very rapidity and intensity with which these factors have impinged upon the societies of the region is a major contributor to the prolific way in which Arab litterateurs are now producing distinguished examples of the novel genre.

▪ PARTICULARITIES

Of all these "disturbances," it is the marked shift to regionalism and localism that has had a profound effect on recent developments in the Arabic novel. Needless to say, local trends have always been in evidence since the earliest stages as each subregion—Palestine, Egypt, and Algeria, for example—has seen its own struggles reflected in fictional form. This feature has also characterized studies of the Arabic novel. For, while the adjective *Arabic* may have been used in a very large number of studies, the number of works that have sought to survey the genre throughout the entire Arabic-speaking region has been very small. Those, such as my own (*The Arabic Novel*, 2d ed., 1995), that have endeavored to do so have found the process of summarizing such novelistic depth and variety as has recently emerged increasingly difficult. It needs to be emphasized that the application of modern narratological approaches by contemporary critics has served to improve the situation considerably as the focus has shifted more to subgenres of the novel and to various critical evaluations of them, but the situation with regard to the distribution and availability of books between the Arab world nations is a constant source of frustration for writers and critics alike throughout the region.

One of the first casualties of these fresh configurations should clearly be the adoption of the Egyptian model of cultural development as a model for the entire region (a trend particularly common in English writing on the subject, my own included). As novel writing in many regions of the Arabic-speaking world has developed to a stage of maturity, critics have written literary histories of the genre and of linkages to its precedents, a process that has often revealed striking dissimilarities between regions and, in certain cases, required the rewriting of earlier versions composed during the initial fervor of postindependence and nationalist rhetoric. As an example, I will cite the countries of the Maghrib (Northwest African) region. Quite apart from issues connected with the multilingual situation (to be discussed below), the region differs from the "Mashriq" (countries of the Middle East) in at least two major ways: first, the region of the far west was not subsumed under the aegis of the Ottoman Empire, and so cultural perceptions regarding premodern history are considerably different from those of countries further to the east; second, the somewhat later time frame for the development of fictional genres in the Maghrib implies that many incipient litterateurs had direct access to early examples from the countries of the Mashriq that were already available *in Arabic,* so that the relative role of translated European works differed from that encountered at an earlier stage in eastern regions.

What exactly are some of the particularities that can be identified within this more localist framework? One of the most marked is, ironically, that single element that binds the Arab world together: namely, the Arabic language. Thus, there are a large number of novelists who, acknowledging the region-wide applicability of written Arabic, choose to write their novels—including dialogue—in that level of the language. Chief among them is, of course, Najīb Mahfúz himself, who—unfortunately, in my opinion—has termed the different colloquial dialects of Arabic a "disease" and yet is not averse to including individual items from the local vocabulary of Egypt in his novels. He is joined in this approach by a large number of other novelists, among whom Jabrā Ibrāhīm Jabrā and 'Abd al-Rahmān Munīf are two of the most renowned. However, alongside the "pan-Arabic" approach implicit in this choice of language level, there has from the outset been an expressed unease with the couching of dialogue—the "dramatic" element in fiction—in a language which is not that of daily conversation. For some pioneers in the development of the Arabic novel—for example, Muhammad Husayn Haykal and Ibrāhīm al-Māzinī in Egypt, or al-Bashīr Khurayyif in Tunisia—the need to use the colloquial to give authentic coloring to novelistic dialogue has ruled out any other alternative. A listing of contemporary novelists who resort to the colloquial in novelistic dialogue would be extremely long, but in such a context the principal point to observe is that, while there may be a certain "universality" to the dialect of Cairo thanks to the general distribution of Egyptian films and television, the same cannot be said of the "outlying" dialects: those, say, of Iraq and Morocco. Thus, those novelists, such as the Iraqi Fu'ād al-Tikirlī or the Tunisian 'Aliyā' al-Tābi'ī, who utilize their own colloquials in novels are, almost automatically, restricting the marketability of their fiction. (In her novel *Zahrat al-Subbār* [Thorn-Flower, 1991], al-Tābi'ī follows her illustrious predecessor, al-Bashīr Khurayyif, in providing footnotes that "translate" the Tunisian colloquial phrases into standard Arabic.)

Adding to the complexities of the Arabic language situation itself is the fact that the Arabic novel is now a vigorous literary presence in those areas of the Arab world that are intrinsically multilingual. One of the most prolifically talented of novelists writing today is the Libyan Ibrāhīm al-Kūnī, who makes abundant use of his Tuareg origins deep in the southern Sahara to produce unforgettably rich fantasies of desert existence far from the city, full of references to myth, folktales, and animistic beliefs. His frequent invocation of phrases in the indigenous Amazigh language (often termed Berber) enriches his novelistic world while at the same time interjecting yet another linguistic level into the reading process. However, most famous and well researched of all the multilingual situations is that which has been the natural consequence of French colonial policy in the Maghrib. The extensive gallicization of the educational systems in Tunisia, Morocco, and (especially) Algeria has led to a situation in which, in spite of determined efforts at *ta'rīb* (arabization) on the official level, a substantial number of writers and intellectuals in those countries have continued to write in French, thus enriching the repertoire of French fiction to a considerable extent, as the popularity of the works of Ṭāhir ibn Jallūn (Tahar Ben Jelloun), Muhammad Dib, 'Abd al-Kabīr al-Khatībī, Kātib Yāsīn, Assia Djebar, Rashīd Abū Jadrah, and others clearly shows. (One might note here *en passant* that the willingness of the French government to subsidize the publication of books written in French is a not unpersuasive factor in this complicated situation.) Those Maghribi novelists who have taken on the task of developing the novel genre in Arabic within this creative environment have faced a prolonged struggle, but a major feature of recent decades has been the emergence of a younger generation of writers who have made major contributions to the Arabic novel, although it needs to be added with regret that, book distribution within the Arab world being as atrocious as it is, their efforts have not been widely noticed. And, in the midst of these linguistic complexities, there is a wide arena within which creative writers and critics have explored the postcolonial phenomenon that Lyotard has termed "métissage," that central space, that "mingling," within which writers such as al-Khatībī and Abū Jadrah find themselves exploring new approaches to culture and language. In fact, the career of Abū Jadrah, who began writing in French and earned a high reputation in France (particularly with his novel *La répudiation* [1969]), may be considered emblematic of the complexities involved here. Having announced in 1981 that he was now going to compose his works in Arabic, he has since been the focus of considerable debate, as critics have wondered out loud whether the publication of the Arabic version of his works (which regularly appear in both Arabic and French) before the French one actually reflects original composition in Arabic.

Thus, linguistic realities and the practicalities of cultural politics impinge in direct ways on the Arabic novel and its course of development, for good and for ill. Nor are they the only factors involved. The variable and mostly lamentable state of civil liberties in the majority of Arab states (one that can be seen as deteriorating in more than one region, most notably Egypt) means that the Arab novelist needs courage as well as artistry. A listing of those who have been imprisoned or exiled would be regrettably long. In spite of that, many writers continue to address themselves to the crucial societal and political issues of their time and region. Nor is the phenomenon confined to male writers. Laylā Ba'albakkī (Lebanon), Nawāl al-Sa'dāwī (Egypt), and Laylā al-'Uthmān (Kuwait) are all women novelists who have been subjected to trial and/or imprisonment, yet they and their fellow writers have not flinched in addressing the needs of women, both within the family structure and in the public domain, in a forthright manner. In so doing, they have made crucial contributions to the ability of the Arabic novel to confront genuine social concerns, and in particular gender roles, in a much more convincing fashion than heretofore. Writers of both genders have joined forces in order to express their anger and frustration at the violence and oppression that has afflicted their societies from within and without, most notably in Lebanon but also in Palestine and Algeria. And, no doubt as a consequence of these circumstances and the generally inimical atmosphere within which the vast majority of Arab novelists attempt to eke out a living, alienation and exile, real and fictional, are frequent resorts as an escape from the intolerable.

In order to give fictional expression to these often unpleasant realities, Arab novelists have adopted a number of creative strategies, prime among which has been a resort to texts from other sources, both contemporary and historical, within the narrative. These range from Sun'allāh Ibrāhīm's use of newspaper clippings in his novel *Dhāt* (Self, 1992) to the insertion into novels by Jamāl al-Ghītānī, 'Abd al-Rahmān Munīf, and BenSālim Himmīsh of actual documents from classical narrative sources, but all for thoroughly contemporary purposes. In this way the invocation of materials from the cultural heritage of Arabic becomes not merely a revival of an earlier style or form but also a powerful commentary on the political circumstances of the present. Other novelists who confront this same set of circumstances choose to remain resolutely with the present, but refuse to provide their readers with any sort of ordering or reordering of the totally fractured world within which they find themselves living. In a series of disturbing novels, the Lebanese writer Ilyās Khūrī (Elias Khoury) has perfected a craft of complete narrative uncertainty in which a "speaker" is unable to explain much of the causality of what he endeavors to report (*Al-Jabal al-saghīr,* 1977 [Eng. *Little Mountain,* 1989]; *Abwāb al-madīnah,* 1981 [Eng. *Gates of the City,* 1992]; *Rihlat Ghandī al-saghīr,* 1989 [Eng. *The Journey of Little Gandhi,* 1994]). Khūrī's Lebanese colleagues Rashīd al-Da'īf and Hasan Dā'ūd reflect the same sense of disillusion by depicting the mundane elements of daily existence in truly obsessive detail.

In moving from a previous more overtly public role to one that sees the world through the eyes and angst of the individual, the Arabic novel now adopts oppression of all kinds—political, social, gender-based—as a major theme and reflects its disillusion with prevailing norms and structures through a search for alternative models. In such a context the reexamination of national myth(s) and the revival of earlier modes of expression are currently playing a key role.

▪ RETROSPECT II

In returning now to the historical framework I invoked above, I trust it is clear that this somewhat lengthy yet still recklessly brief survey of recent trends in Arabic novel writing illustrates a need to reexamine the Arabic novel's literary history and heritage. To provide one concrete example, I will use the novelistic output of Tawfīq al-Hakīm. Within a model of novelistic history that seeks a process of development toward an acme that is Mahfūz's *Trilogy,* the novels of al-Hakīm that have taken pride of place in the historical record are *'Awdat al-rūh* (1933; Eng. *Return of the Spirit,* 1990) and *'Usfūr min al-Sharq* (1938; Eng. *A Bird from the East,* 1966), and it is certainly true that their themes and experiments with novelistic technique do represent significant advances within the context of a quest for an imported novel genre. If, on the other hand, we now look back from a perspective that seeks inspiration from a rereading and rewriting of traditional narrative forms and styles, then clearly the annalistic structure and picaresque qualities of al-Hakīm's *Yawmiyyāt nā'ib fī al-aryāf* (Diaries of a Public Prosecutor in the Provinces, 1937) come to assume a more central role (quite apart from the fact that, in my view, it is a much better novel). Using this same perspective to move back in time, it emerges that the structures of al-Shidyāq's *Al-Sāq 'alā al-sāq* (One Leg Over Another, 1855) and al-Muwaylihī's *Hadīth 'Isā ibn Hishām* (1907; Eng. *A Period of Time,* 1979, 1992), both formerly regarded as neoclassical precursors to a tradition of modern fiction, now become important attempts at combining autobiography and fiction (in the former case) and in utilizing

a traditional picaresque genre (and its accompanying style) for some highly accurate social criticism (in the latter case)—a level of critical realism that was, in fact, not equaled until the novels of the 1930s. Of more recent works that fit this same mold, Emīl Habībī's carnivalesque intertextual romp through the daily life of an Israeli Palestinian, *Al-Waqā'i 'al-gharībah fī-ikhtifā' Sa'īd Abī al-Nahs al-mutashā'il* (Eng. *The Secret Life of Saeed the Pessoptimist*) is the outstanding example.

From the perspective of the post-1967 (and perhaps even the post-1988) era, there is clearly a need to revisit the literary history of the Arabic novel; and indeed, the critics of several Arab world nations have begun to do precisely that. If we acknowledge first that the nineteenth-century cultural renaissance known as *al-nahdah* involved, to varying degrees, two primary forces—the exposure to and importation of Western literary genres on the one hand, and on the other the rediscovery of the cultural heritage of the past—and, second, that early developments in the Arabic novel were placed into a literary-critical and literary-historical framework that emphasized the role of the former over the latter, then we have now to suggest that more recent trends in novel writing demand a change of balance between the two. It has immediately to be acknowledged that, as soon as this need is identified, a number of interfering factors become evident. I have already alluded to the first, a literary-historical issue of major importance within the Arabic tradition: namely, that our knowledge of the period (say, the sixteenth to the eighteenth centuries) immediately anterior to the beginnings of a "modern" period—whenever that is seen to take place—is very poor indeed, whether we talk about indigenous or Western research. A second factor, which is in effect a subset of the same literary-historical dilemma, is that the values attached to the different levels of the Arabic language (to which I alluded briefly above) have prevented the vast repertoire of premodern narratives composed in an Arabic that is not the "classical" standard—thus including, for example, *The Arabian Nights*—from incorporation within the canon of what is "literary." This situation is changing rapidly as the social-scientific approaches to folklore and cultural traditions make their way into the educational systems of the Arab world countries and impinge upon the national conscience. Lastly, the sheer variety of the literary production within the Arab world (to which I have also drawn attention) now almost demands an approach to the literary history of the Arabic novel that is more concerned with the particular features of each regional tradition rather than an attempt to identify those common features that unite the Arabic tradition as a whole.

▪ CONCLUSION

From the post-1988 perspective, by which I imply the "translation" or "exportation" of the Arabic novel to a larger readership, the Arabic novel clearly enjoys a higher profile than was the case before the award of the Nobel Prize. This is, of course, largely thanks to Najīb Mahfūz, the laureate himself, but other novelists—Jamāl al-Ghītānī, Hanān al-Shaykh, 'Abd al-Rahmān Munīf, and Ilyās Khūrī, for example—have been able to share some of the limelight of Western (and Eastern) interest. That said, however, the current situation poses an interesting dilemma for Arab novelists. If the novel has now been recognized in the Arab world as being a literary genre, or, as some critics would have it, *the* literary genre of this era (the "time of the novel," as Gaber Asfour's book title has it), and if a Western readership has now become somewhat familiar with a few examples of that productivity, then how does the Arabic novel proceed to fulfill its role as an agent of change within the context of the Arab world, its cultural values, and its sense of heritage? And, if it chooses to do so, then what will be the reception of such works both within the different regions of the Arab world itself and, via translation, in the broader context of world literature? Those are, of course, open questions, but I hope to have pointed in this study to some of the complex issues that are involved in the process of answering them.

Roger Allen, Spring 2001

---

[1] I would like to acknowledge here that these thoughts on the Arabic novel tradition are much influenced by readings of the work of two colleagues in the Arab world itself. One is the Moroccan critic and novelist Muhammad Barrādah, in his *As'ilat al-riwāyah, as'ilat al-naqd* [Questions on the Novel, Questions on Criticism], Rabāt, Sharikat al-Rābitah, 1996. The second is Jābir 'Usfur [Gaber Asfour], Egyptian critic and Secretary-General of the Supreme Council for Culture in Egypt, in his collection of essays, *Zaman al-Riwāyah* [The Time of the Novel], Beirut, Dār al-Madā, 1999.

[2] I should note here that, with the readership in mind, I will endeavor in what follows to cite works that are available in translation.

Telling Their Lives: A Hundred Years of Arab Women's Writings

The year is 1899. In America Kate Chopin's controversial novel *The Awakening* and in Egypt Qasim Amin's *Tahrīr al-mar'a* (Liberation of Women) have just been published. In Europe and America women have been mobilizing for half a century. In the Arab world urban women of the upper classes are cloistered in the heart of the home. With the publication of these two texts, two worlds, divided by what has appeared to be an insuperable cultural gulf, are beginning to come together. The furor over Amin's plea for the recognition of women's rights obscured activity in some Arab countries that now, in the light of current feminist literary criticism, is being discovered and disseminated. In her *Mudhakkirāt 1917–1977* (Memoirs 1917–1977) Wadad al-Maqdisi Qurtas writes:

> When we look at feminist literature today we find it limited in comparison with what it had been. . . . Leaders of the feminist movement wrote about social problems and they gained many victories in social legislation. . . . In a time of great stress women helped alleviate the suffering of the deprived classes. Their pioneering works attest to their sacrifice and selflessness.[1]

Contrary to popular assertion, Qasim Amin was not the first to write of women's plight in a repressive traditional society, though he was the first to receive widespread recognition and notoriety. Preceding him were women in Egypt, Lebanon, and Syria such as Aisha al-Taimuriya (1840–1902), Warda al-Yazigi (1838–1924), and Zainab Fawwaz (1850–1914),[2] who had begun contributing poems, articles, and essays to newly founded papers and magazines. Although their publications were classical in form (*ghazal, ritha, madih*) and theme, the discerning reader can distinguish a muted protest. The feminist critic Elaine Showalter writes of her own sense of discovery when rereading women's literature that she had been taught to read as descriptive. She realized that far from being docile, much of the literature "was often covertly subversive, even volcanic, and almost always profoundly revisionary."[3] In fact, Aisha al-Taimuriya's poems challenge a patriarchal society that nips women's talents in the bud. She cites as models of feminine creativety the pre-Islamic and Umayyad women poets, whose elegies in particular had been acclaimed by their society.[4]

By the turn of the twentieth century, women, like their male counterparts, were coming under the influence of Western ideas and styles which Arab translators of contemporary French, English, American, and Italian literature began introducing into the Arab world. A change in literary genres and themes mirrored social and political change. Female and male writers adopted prose (mainly articles and essays in papers and magazines) as the most appropriate medium. After an initial flirtation with romanticism at the end of the nineteenth century, their works began to reflect current social concerns, foremost among which was the plight of women in the Arab world.[5]

During this early period of modern Arabic literature, May Ziadeh (1886–1941) was a leading literary exponent of feminist ideas. May, a convent-educated Lebanese Christian born in Palestine, went to Egypt in 1908. She stayed there for over thirty years, writing French and Arabic articles, essays, short stories, plays, poetry, and biographies of contemporary feminist leaders. In 1912 she established a literary salon, which each week for twenty years brought together the leading thinkers and writers of a Cairo that was at the forefront of change and modernization. The blind Egyptian scholar Taha Hussein called May's salon

> . . . democratic; in the sense that it was open to various classes of intellectuals and to literary men and women of different nationalities: Egyptian, Lebanese, Syrians, Europeans and others. They discussed all sorts of topics, local and international. . . . Unique in character, this salon had a decided influence on its habitués, who spoke highly of it in their memoirs and their reminiscences.[6]

May was well regarded by her male colleagues. Although she never met the Lebanese-American poet and writer Gibran Khalil Gibran, they did correspond, and their correspondence, recently brought to light, is evidence of mutual respect and admiration.

When May Ziadeh died in the Asfuriya mental hospital in Lebanon at the age of fifty-five, her loss was deeply felt. Abbas Mahmud al-Aqqad (who has been accused of misogyny) wrote an elegy to her which is now regarded as one of the best of his works, and the Bengali poet Rabindranath Tagore dedicated his poem "The Morning Bird" to her memory. The Lebanese writer, artist, and poet Etel Adnan (b. 1925) explains the incongruity between the status of the Arab women as writer and as civilian:

> In Arab countries society does not like women in politics, but does respect women writers. There is such reverence for literature in the Arab world and such love for poetry, that even women share in that respect. . . . They are not censured because they are women.[7]

One of the writers who attended May Ziadeh's salon was Malak Hafni Nasif (1886–1918), better known by her pen name of Bahithat al-Badiya. She wrote and lectured extensively on contemporary feminist and social issues, and scholars are now beginning to accord her Nisā'iyāt (Feminist Texts) the importance they deserve. Without mincing words, the Nisā'iyāt texts call for compulsory female education at the primary level and access to secondary and tertiary levels. Malak was particularly concerned that women have the chance to study medicine and economics. This latter demand may appear strange until it is realized that many middle- and upper-class women in the nineteenth-century Arab world were property owners who needed to learn management skills so as to better administer their holdings. The call for education fell on fertile ground, and in 1929, only fifty-six years after the opening of the first primary school for girls in Egypt, five women enrolled in Fuad University in Cairo. The Nisā'iyāt also called for the abolition of polygamy, forced marriage, and the invidious institution of the house of obedience.[8] These demands were echoed in statements published in the contemporary women's press—e.g., L'Egyptienne (1925), Al-Misriya (1937), and Bint al-Nil (1949?)—as well as in public forums by the leaders of the Egyptian Feminist Union.[9]

The founder of the Egyptian Feminist Union, Huda Sharawi (1879–1947), who was betrothed at twelve and married to her cousin a year later, recognized her life to be a model in which others might find their own reflected. Affluence notwithstanding, Huda had always been discontent. She became deeply disturbed by her own inability, as well as that of all women in Egypt, to participate directly in society. Her memoirs, published in the 1940s, eloquently describe the life of upper-class women at the end of the nineteenth century. She gathered around her women who discussed issues of burning concern to a society entering a new era. Although their social, economic, and political positions removed them from the mass of Arab women on whose behalf they presumed to speak, they did use their public position to advance crucial social issues.

By the 1930s a few upper-class women like the Kurdish Egyptian Qout al-Qouloub and the Cairene Suhair Qalamawi were writing short stories and novels about women's predicament. Although some of these writers were disappointed that the public largely ignored their literary productions, their works did constitute a voice that some later noted. Qout al-Qouloub's Ramza (1931) and Le harem (1934) are sad but searing indictments of a society in which women are theoretically accorded rights that in practice they are denied. Ramza tells the surprising story of a girl who, when faced with the shock of betrothal, does not submit as most did but rejects her father's choice in favor of a man she herself has chosen. They elope and she discovers that he is not the man she had thought him to be. The novel is bitter (so much had been risked for so little) but also triumphant (risk had been taken, convention defied). It was also during this period that the first Francophone North African writings appeared, and one of the first writers was the Algerian Djamila Debèche, whose works evince a concern for women who are prime victims in a society torn between two cultures: Arab and French.

In the first half of this century feminists throughout the Arab world joined with nationalists to combat an anachronistic colonialism and to forge a future that would respond to everyone's needs. As Ceza Nabarawi (b. 1893), a close associate of Huda Sharawi, has said: "How could women hope to gain their freedom when Egypt herself was not free?"[10] World War II was being waged not only on the military battlefields of Europe, but also on the cultural and intellectual battlefields of the Middle East and North Africa. This new future had to be expressed in a new way, and the 1940s, particularly after the establishment of the state of Israel in 1948, witnessed a wave of experimentation in all genres. Men as well as women earnestly sought new methods to convey new realities. The most profoundly revolutionary change, however, came in poetry. The Palestinian poet Salma Khadra Jayyusi describes the beginning of the free-verse movement as "an artistic phenomenon which succeeded because it was both artistically mature and timely in that it suited the historic and psychological moment in the Arab world."[11]

Free verse was introduced into the poetic canon by a woman. In 1949 the Iraqi poet Nazik al-Malaika published a collection of verse called *Shadhāyā wa ramad* (*Splinters and Ashes*). Only eleven of these poems were in free verse, but the iron hold of classical and neoclassical poetry had been broken. True, men had experimented with free verse, but their attempts had encountered stiff opposition. Experimentation had been tolerated in the new, Western genres such as the novel and the short story, but poetry, the literary art of the Arabs par excellence, could not submit to such treatment. Critics condemned all experimentation in poetry as evidence of weakness on the part of the poet, who clearly could not master the arduous techniques of the classical ode, elegy, eulogy, et cetera. However, when Nazik al-Malaika risked the critics' scorn and published *Splinters and Ashes,* the reaction was astounding. The collection was hailed as a breakthrough, and two of al-Malaika's countrymen, Badr Shakir al-Sayyab and Abd al-Wahhab al-Bayyati, started composing poetry in this new liberated form.[12] Only a woman who was barred by gender from entry into the magic circle of the literary canon could risk such a challenge. She was outside criticism, good or bad; she had nothing much to lose but a great deal to gain. In the same year, 1949, the Jordanian poet Thurayya Malhas published a collection of free verse entitled *The Wandering Song,* wherein she attacked tradition in literature as in thought. Free verse had come to stay.

Throughout this period, stretching from the late nineteenth century into the middle of the twentieth, women writers had found an outlet for their writing in women's newspapers and magazines. Between 1892 and 1950 over forty such papers were founded and edited by women.[13] Most women writers started their careers as journalists, and only when they had attained a measure of success did they consider turning to fiction or poetry writing as a full-time occupation. The Lebanese writer Emily Nasrallāh (b. 1938) is a case in point. She left her village in the south as a young girl and eventually attended the American University in Beirut. Due to her financial circumstances she had to work her way through school, and she started contributing articles to magazines like *Al-Sayyad*. It was also at this time that she published the novel *Tuyūrailūl* (September Birds; 1962), which first appeared serially in *Al-Sayyad* and has since been reprinted six times. By 1970 she was sufficiently well known to be able to devote herself full-time to writing novels, short stories, and children's books.

In Saudi Arabia of the 1980s women journalists are becoming active in current literary production. Khairiya al-Saqqaf (b. 1950), for example, the director of the women journalists at the national paper *Al-Riyad,* has published three collections of short stories.

According to Ceza Nabarawi, the Egyptian revolution of 1952 brought women many human and political rights. However, the gains in the political field did not ease the psychological pressure suffered by women caught between the modern and the traditional worlds. As Evelyne Accad has stated, many women writers' works at that time evinced a "Saganian existentialism": melancholic boredom, which leads to revolt against tradition and, particularly, seclusion. They are "selfish, highly strung and always egocentric."[14] The writings of the Lebanese Laila Baalbaki (b. 1934) and the Syrian Colette Khuri (b. 1931) echo this mood.

In 1958 Baalbaki published her novel *Anā ahya* (Eng. *I Live*), which signaled a bold rebellion against the hypocrisy and injustice of a society that considers women to be sex objects. Lina Fayad rebels against her family and goes to work and to university. At the university she meets a young communist, with whom she falls in love. Illusion soon gives way to reality, as it becomes clear that ideology is only skin-deep. In despair at her discovery of this stereotypical chauvinist, Lina decides to kill herself, but her society will not allow her such control. As she is about to throw herself under the wheels of a passing truck, she is saved by a friendly passerby. In her next novel, *Āliha mamsūkha* (Deformed Gods; 1960), Baalbaki, like al-Malaika in Iraq and Venus Khuri in Lebanon and Paris, protests against a society that demands unimpeachable modesty and chasti-ty of women and mandates that men fulfill their man-hood by displays of sexual prowess. The heroine may protest, but she is at the mercy of her society's expecta-tions. Colette Khuri is often paired with Baalbaki, but her work is less pessimistic. In *Ayyāmī ma'ah* (Days with Him; late 1950s?) the heroine overcomes her disap-pointment at the hollowness of her lover's ideals, rejects him, and leaves for Europe.

At this stage the preoccupations of the women writ-ers in Egypt, Syria, Lebanon, and Tunisia were emotion-al and male-oriented. Their options were rebellion, es-cape, madness, or suicide. However, in Algeria the situation was quite different. From 1954 until 1962 the Algerians fought for their independence. As had hap-pened in other movements of Arab resistance toward European colonial powers, women were drawn into the public realm to help their country realize its indepen-dence, and some of them began to write.

During the early years of the Algerian War most of these women wrote of the evils of biculturism forced on them by 150 years of French colonial rule. There was little hint of what was to come. It was only Assia Djebar, now living in Paris, who intimated that women should beware lest their combined revolution not become the men's victory. Her novel *La soif* (The Thirst; 1957) was condemned by critics as a subversive work designed to divide Algerian women from their men and to allow the French to conquer. Djebar's next work, *Les impatients* (1958), claimed to be about the past, yet the message was the same: women must beware of their men's need to rule at home. Her warning went unheeded, and in 1964 Zoubeida Bittari wrote *O mes sœurs musulmanes, pleurez!,* which, as the title suggests, laments the lost revolution. Bittari, like many other North African Fran-cophone writers, eventually chose to leave home for Paris in order to write freely what she felt about the con-dition of women in her native land.

In the wake of the 1967 defeat there was a wave of despair and self-criticism throughout the Arab world. Women writers also expressed the general anguish, yet one can already detect the distinctive character of women's writings: the urge to survive and resist despite the seemingly overwhelming odds. In Morocco, Khan-natha Bannuna wrote *Al-nār wa'l-ikhtiyār* (Fire and Choice; 1969). In Lebanon, the Syrian Ghada al-Samman (b. 1942) condemned the Zionist enemy, yet her concern was feminist also: women are responsible for their liberation; escape (whatever form it takes) is no longer a viable option. Women must change a society that is as oppressed as they are. Al-Samman's numerous novels and short stories are extremely popular through-out the Arab world, and in some countries, like Saudi

Arabia, they are considered to be manifestos for an Arab women's movement.

Of all the literatures in the Arab world, the most politicized is that of the Palestinians. The foremost ex-ponent of Palestinian feminine writing is Fedwa Tuqan. Since 1948 she has been living in Nablus (on the West Bank) and has been writing freedom poetry that has gal-vanized the masses. Her poetry calls for love, justice, co-operation, and resistance. Although she is regarded as a spokesperson for the Palestinian—rather than the Pal-estinian *women's*—cause, she has also recognized the importance of women's separate contribution to the struggle. In a recent interview she said: "If there is any good to be found in the long drawn-out nature of the Palestinian struggle, it is that mass and women's partici-pation may have irreversibly changed sex and class rela-tions."[15] Her poetry, which emphasizes a shared Arab heritage and responsibility, has often been banned, and it is only during funerals that she is allowed to hold po-etry-reading sessions.

Another Palestinian women who has written of contemporary political problems is Raymonda Tawil. In contrast with Tuqan, Tawil's primary concern is femi-nist: *My Home My Prison* (1980) faces the dilemma of a women who wants to fight for her country but who refuses to risk her rights as a woman. The novel focuses on the tensions a women and an Arab must daily con-front on the West Bank. Tawil's work reflects the atti-tude of the camp women who have organized into women's unions, which will join with the men's move-ments but not sacrifice their autonomy. Algeria's lessons have been learned: nationalism must not be allowed to reinforce women's oppression.

The literature that reflects most vividly how far women writers have come in this century is that pro-duced in Lebanon during and immediately after the civil war of 1975–76. As in all wars, a cultural efflores-cence occurred. Women who had never written a word for publication produced poems, novels, and short sto-ries. Those who had already written found that the war had sharpened their literary skills. What began for many in catharsis finally became honed into works of art. Hanan al-Shaikh (b. 1945), who had written a few novels of average merit before the war, wrote *Hikāyat Zahra* (1980; Eng. *Zahra,* 1985), a powerful account of the war from the viewpoint of a madwoman. The war is experienced in all its horror and pain. The fine line between reality and dream is rarely drawn, and survival in such a situation is shown to be what it is: a prolonged nightmare of intensity and boredom, terror and normal-ity. Emily Nasrallāh's work reflects a profound change in women's identity that emerged as the war continued. Her two novels on the war, *Tilka al-dhikrayāt* (Those

Memories; 1980) and *Iqla' 'aks al-zaman* (Flight against Time; 1981), criticize those (usually men) who left Lebanon; she even goes so far as to question their right to call themselves Lebanese. Since it was the women who had stayed, it is they who are the real Lebanese. The civil war allowed women to find a discursive identity that challenged the foundations of their patriarchal society.

This angry rejection can be read in an increasing number of women's writings in the seventies and eighties. Egypt is again at the center of the feminist debate, but the matter has now acquired an Islamic coloration. How can a woman realize herself in contemporary Islamic society? Some women have joined in the Islamic revivalist movements: they are returning to the veil that their mothers fought so hard to abolish, and they are protesting against the values of a society which, they claim, has abdicated its right to be Egyptian and opted to become pseudo-American. Intellectuals are faced with a dilemma: in such a movement, can women retain their separate identity with the rights so dearly bought? Is this not a return to the nationalist struggles of the first half of this century, struggles that subsumed women's rights to those of the emerging political entity? Or is this in fact, as some claim, a feminist-inspired revolution that neutralizes sexuality under heavy clothing and thus allows women to penetrate the public sphere?[16]

Zaynab al-Ghazali al-Jabili, founder of the Muslim Women's Association in 1937, has recently published her memoirs, *Ayyām hayātī* (Days of My Life). They tell of her association with and later rejection of the secular liberal Feminist Union of Huda Sharawi. In the memoirs Zaynab al-Ghazali traces the checkered fortunes of the religiously zealous Muslim Brethren from their foundation in the late twenties until today. Their hardships, she affirms, have only made them stronger and more worthy of women's support. By contrast, Nawal al-Saadawi (b. 1931), the Egyptian feminist doctor and writer, is outspoken in her criticism of the Brethern and others because they represent, in her view, a regressive movement. A prolific writer who has produced seventeen volumes of short stories and novels, including the controversial *Al-mar'a wa'l-jins* (Women and Sex), she has devoted herself to condemning a society that will not tolerate women who dare, or need, to leave the sanctum of the home.

A possible middle line between Zaynab al-Ghazali and Nawal al-Saadawi is struck by Alifa Rifaat (b. 1926). In her collection of short stories *Man hādha al-rajul?* (Who Is This Man?; 1978) she describes women's lives as a painful drudgery that only fantasy can render tolerable. None of the women protagonists protests, openly, for they all believe; and it is their belief that beings comfort.

It remains to be seen what direction contemporary women's writings will take, what effect, if any, the wave of Islamization now washing over much of the Muslim world will have. Can the raised feminist consciousness gained during the Lebanese civil war persist beyond and in spite of a reactionary religiopolitical trend? This is a time of political and cultural turmoil, when all voices have at least a chance to be heard. Let us hope that women's voices will outlast the chaos, preparing for a new society at once reconciled to its past and inclusive of all its members.

Miriam Cooke, Spring 1986

[1] Wadad al-Maqdisi Qurtas, *Mudhakkirāt 1917–1977* (Memories 1917–1977), Beirut, Al-Dhikrayat, 1982, pp. 82–83.

[2] Unlike most of the writers of her generation, Zainab Fawwaz was not upper-class. A poor orphan from southern Lebanon, she had started work as a child in a rich house. Her mistress soon discovered her young servant's intelligence and determined to teach her to read and write. Zainab later moved into the employ of another family, with whom she eventually went to Egypt. Here she earned her independence of domestic service by contributing articles to Cairene papers and magazines. She also wrote two novels. The first was a historical novel, the second was a lightly fictionalized chronicle of the tribal customs and heroic deeds of her kinfolk in the Jabal Amel in southern Lebanon. She also wrote a four-act play, a collection of poems, and a volume chronicling the lives of 456 famous women. For further information, see *Al-Raida*, June 1978, pp. 2–3.

[3] *The New Feminist Criticism: Women, Literature and Theory*, Elaine Showalter, ed., New York, Pantheon, 1985, p. 35.

[4] Al-Khansa and Laila al-Ukhailiya are two well-known examples.

[5] Fawzia al Ashmawi-Abouzeid asserts that feminist consciousness in the Arab world coincides with the rise of modern Arabic literature. See *La femme et l'Egypte moderne dans l'œuvre de Naguib Mahfuz*, Geneva, Labor & Fides, 1985, pp. 13, 17.

[6] Rose Ghorayeb, "May Ziadeh (1886–1941)," *Signs: Journal of Women in Culture and Society*, 1979, 5:2, p. 376.

[7] Hilary Kilpatrick, "Interview with Etel Adnan (Lebanon)," in *Unheard Words: Women and Literature in Africa, the Arab World, Asia, the Caribbean and Latin America*, Mineke Schipper, ed., London, Allison & Busby, 1985, p. 117. See this issue, p. 369.

[8] The house of obedience was an institution that allowed a man whose wife had left him to demand that she return into his possession. He was then free to do with her as he pleased.

[9] At an AUB conference in May 1928 Ibsan al Koussi declaimed: "Sirs, the house of obedience is more dangerous than houses of detention. Criminals who have been detained are put under the surveillance of guards whose authority is defined by the law. They are not driven by hatred or vengeance to overstep legal bounds. The husband, on the other hand, is clearly partial. No one has any authority over him: what recourse does the unfortunate woman entrusted into his care have?"

[10] *Al-Raida*, 4:16 (May 1981), p. 2.

[11] Salma Khadra Jayyusi, *Trends and Movements in Modern Arabic Poetry,* Leiden, Brill, 1977, p. 557.

[12] There was much debate about who it was that had actually written the very first Arabic poem in free verse. See Jayyusi, pp. 557–560.

[13] The number of women's journals and magazines has dwindled from forty in the 1950s and 1960s to about ten in the whole Arab world today. Women journalists are now being employed in mainstream journalism. In February 1981 a seminar of Arab women journalists was held in Beirut. Forty participants from Lebanon, Tunisia, Morocco, Iraq, Egypt, and Syria attended. They talked of journalists' contributions to the nationalist struggles in Palestine and Iraq, but they also pointed out that coverage of women in the Arabophone press has been less than 4 percent.

[14] Evelyne Accad, "La longue marche des héroïnes des romans modernes du Machrek et du Maghreb," *Présence Francophone,* 12 (Spring 1976), p. 10.

[15] *Women and the Family in the Middle East: New Voices of Change,* Elizabeth W. Fernea, ed., Austin, University of Texas Press, 1985, p. 197.

[16] Fadwa El Guindi, "Veiling *lufitah* with Muslim Ethic: Egypt's Contemporary Islamic Movement," *Social Problems,* 28:4 (April 1981), pp. 481–83.

Major Currents in North African Novels in French since 1966

Alongside a literature in Arabic, there also exists in the Maghreb (Tunisia, Algeria, Morocco) a literature in French, a fact explained by a long-lasting French presence in those countries. The first Algerian novel written in French was published in 1920, but it was mainly the "Generation of 1952," including writers from one end of the Maghreb to the other, that revealed to the world the names of Tunisia's Albert Memmi, Algeria's Mouloud Feraoun, Mohammed Dib and Mouloud Mammeri and Morocco's Ahmed Sefrioui and Driss Chraïbi. These three countries gained their independence in 1956 (Tunisia and Morocco) and 1962 (Algeria), and their literary production in French does not show any signs of slowing down.

On the contrary, one can even say that the year 1966 marks a starting point, the beginning of a sometimes bold renewal of themes and styles. The 1970s and early 1980s have emphasized the new features even more, and new authors have made themselves heard. In 1966 the Moroccan writer Abdellatif Laâbi started the review *Souffles* with several poets of the younger generation: among them, Mohammed Khaïr-Eddine, Mohammed Loakira, Tahar Ben Jelloun, Mostefa Nissaboury, Abdelkébir Khatibi, Mohammed Bouharate and Abdallah Bounfour. In Algeria, while established authors such

as Mohammed Dib (see *BA* 50:1, pp. 98–99), Mouloud Mammeri and Assia Djebar remain active, other writers are rapidly beginning to command attention: Rachid Boudjedra, Nabile Farès, Yamina Mechakra, Tahar Djaout, Hamid Tibouchi, Rachid Mimouni. As far as Tunisia is concerned, Albert Memmi, while residing in France, continues his high-quality work in novels as well as in essays, but new names are appearing there too: Mustapha Tlili, Abdelwahab Meddeb and Souad Guellouz, to list only the principal figures.* The poets are numerous, but the quality of their works is very uneven. Some critics had predicted the rapid death of this literature as the consequence of the recent re-Arabization campaign. However, up to now, twenty and twenty-five years after the recovery of national independence, there is still an appreciable production every year, even if strict criticism would retain as quality work only a little part of what is published.

It is difficult and risky to generalize about the whole of the Maghreb, for each of the three countries has its own particular character and its own problems. However, if one keeps to the great names and the great works of the period since 1966–70, a few major currents become evident in the North African novel: subjects to which the writers have returned or are now returning, preoccupations and recurrent themes which are common to authors from each of the Maghrebine countries. The same could be said about the poets, if they had been included here. It should be observed, moreover, that several of today's more important North African novelists have also published noteworthy books of poetry.

The first trend I would mention (and one which declines as the years go by) is self-assertion through wars of independence, a trend found most prominently in Algerian and Moroccan novels. Many short stories and narratives from Algeria have featured the good, positive hero who is fearless, blameless and without conflicts or qualms, and they have done so with all the stereotypes and clichés common to this kind of literature. Fortunately, there exist other approaches to the theme of the liberation war. Mohammed Dib in *La danse du roi* (1968), Reda Falaki in *Le milieu et la marge* (1964) and Mouloud Mammeri in *L'opium et le bâton* (1965) are very critical or even skeptical, on the verge of disillusionment. In *Ciel de porphyre* (1978) Aïcha Lemsine refuses to adopt the oversimplified language of conventional, semiofficial literature: the good characters on one side, the bad ones on the other. Ali Boumahdi's story *Le village des asphodèles* (1970) ends by acknowledging that the future is not so bright. In Nabile Farès's novels, especially *Yahia pas de chance* (1970), any epic vein is definitely out of the question; one does not cele-

126

brate war. In *L'insolation* (1972) Rachid Boudjedra says that he does not want to dwell on the war by looking back on it; he does come back to the topic in *Le vainqueur de coupe* (1981), but the event which he relates (the murder of a collaborator with the French) is only a pretext to a text, since the author is more interested in compositional techniques than in the facts themselves. In *La mémoire tatouée* (1971) by the Moroccan writer Abdelkébir Khatibi, only a few lines about the independence and the struggles that led to it are to be found. The point of view here is more and more "demythifying." True enough, some Algerians go on publishing stories about the war in either a flat, anecdotal style or in highly bombastic fashion, but the poet and essayist Mostefa Lacheraf (now the Algerian ambassador to UNESCO) said what was necessary on the subject during a December 1968 conference in Hammamet (Tunisia).

The last noteworthy novel specifically about the liberation war was written by a young Algerian woman psychiatrist, Yamina Mechakra. *La grotte éclatée* (1979) is a highly lyrical and very introspective work. Its title, "The Exploded Cave," is significant, referring not only to the explosion of bombs or even of writing techniques, but also to the explosion of the very subject itself. The war has shattered old structures, old patterns of behavior and the enclosed space of the protective ancestral cavern. The heroes are dead; one cannot sound the trumpet of glory, for the aftermath is tragic. Ahmed Azeggah, an Algerian poet and novelist, begins one of his poems with the lines, "Arrêtez de célébrer les massacres / Arrêtez de célébrer des noms" (Stop celebrating massacres / Stop celebrating names).

A second trend, and one which seems to be growing stronger, consists of more or less veiled sociopolitical opposition. The official images, views and truths in the political discourse—or some of them at least—are rejected, for one cannot identify with them. These images are meant to be reassuring; they celebrate the great leap forward and the road to a glorious future. But introspection unveils other realities. People are, as the novelist Mourad Bourboune exclaims in *Le muezzin* (1968), "fed up with all the countries that look for positive heroes."

In Morocco it is Mohammed Khaïr-Eddine who, from one novel to the next since *Agadir* in 1967, most strongly opposes a world which he views as rotten and gangrenous, rejecting his ancestors, his father and all blood ties. The catastrophic 1961 earthquake in Agadir has shaken the very core of the individual and mutilated the unconscious. Khaïr-Eddine's first two books of poems were called *Nausée noire* and *Faune détériorée*. These are significant titles, as are those of his novels:

Corps négatif suivi de Histoire d'un bon Dieu (1968), *Moi l'aigre* (1970) and *Une vie, un rêve, un peuple arrant* (1978), where the author continues unveiling the frustrations, the crushed hopes, the other side of an "enchanting Morocco" which others have seen only under a spell. Tahar Ben Jelloun cries out against the misery of the poor and the humble, the sexual loneliness of the immigrants in the Paris streets, the degradation of the ridiculed man in works such as *Harrouda* (1973), *La réclusion solitaire* (1976) and *Moha le fou, Moha le sage* (1978). Driss Chraïbi, who created a scandal in 1954 with *Le passé simple* and has lived for a long time outside his country, returns to it in his 1981 novel *Une enquête au pays,* where he uses a healthy irony to demystify and vituperate an administration and a bureaucracy which are unable to function in the interest of people. What all these writers have in common is the critical way in which they observe daily reality, thereby rejoining their compatriots who write novels in Arabic. They make "madmen" speak, "madmen" who play the fool but who, on the margin of folly, can allow themselves to tell bitter truths. The official accounts of victory, they say, are not to be taken for granted.

One may observe the same tendency in Algeria. A well-established author like Mohammed Dib, in *Dieu en barbarie* (1970) as in *Le maître de chasse* (1973), carries to the point of bloody confrontation the opposition between the long-forgotten peasants and a technocrat who is the prefect's assistant, an urban man and a representative of soulless development plans. In *Habel* (1977) the eponymous hero, who has been forced to emigrate under the pressure of an older brother more terrible than his father, pays off old scores at the end of his adventures. This difficult but lofty novel deals with much more than the mere geographical facets of emigration: it is in fact a "spiritual" quest in the larger sense of the word. Habel is reborn to a new life thanks to his meeting with Lili, his "chimera" (but who is Lili?); at the same time he tells a few bitter truths to his brother, who represents the state apparatus or the castrating superego. This brother believes himself to be a man but is actually a mere caricature of one; he takes himself seriously and feels secure about what is apparent, not about what really *is.* The novelist therefore turns indirectly and symbolically upon the authorities, who force the writer to play the "revolutionary" game, to conform to the expected official image of him, or who practically force him to go into exile if he has any hope of regaining the freedom to criticize and to rouse consciences.

Rachid Boudjedra, who became known in 1969 with his then audacious book *La répudiation,* wherein he attacks both a bigoted bourgeoisie and castrating fathers who encourage incest, has carried on with the same denunciatory rage in *L'insolation* (1972) and *L'escargot entêté* (1977). In the latter novel he tells the ironic tale of a small and somewhat neurotic civil servant, whose main quality is "blind submission" and whose dream is to destroy all the rats which proliferate in the town. He likes to say that he is "too faithful to the state to be able to believe in God," although the Constitution declares Islam to be the religion of the state! In fact, this sociopolitical fable also conceals—as in Boudjedra's other works—the narcissistic obsessions and sexual fantasies of the author.

One of the subjects which is being treated more and more often in this type of oppositional fiction is that of the compromised and betrayed revolution. In Boudjedra's *La répudiation* revolt already figured as an aborted fetus. In *Le démantèlement* (1982) by the same author, the history student Selma uncovers certain contradictions and also the arrivistes, who have taken a place in the sun thanks to the blood of the martyrs and now use religion to justify themselves. The tortured heroes died for nothing. Revolution has failed here too, and Selma is sick of it all. The theme of *Le muezzin* by Bourboune leads to the same conclusion: the people are frustrated in their aspirations and have not been liberated; they are born by Caesarean section, not by natural means. The stammering, atheistic hero, who "lives in a scar," proclaims his own truth: one must start from square one, get out of the mess. "The battle has stopped on the verge of victory," we read; "you're hopping along." The muezzin lives in a "vaginal land" which cries (*vagit*) like a newborn child or which is not yet completely born, not come into the light, much as revolution here is a fetus in the hands of abortioners.

Along the same lines, Mouloud Mammeri's novel *La traversée* (1982) clearly ends up in disenchantment. A journalist writes one last article before handling his resignation to his chief editor. The apologue which he narrates could not be more symbolic: the caravan of "revolution" moves through the desert on its way to an oasis (the supposedly bright future) with the leaders and positive heroes at its head, followed by a crowd of simple soldiers, those who have believed and who have marched in spite of and against everything, hoping for glory and rest when they arrive. But then the trap is sprung. They have been channeled, controlled, guided; the leaders have blocked all the exits, and the magicians have done their work. Already at the end of *L'opium et le bâton* Mammeri had shown a disappointed hero, facing the ruins and calling for the healer, whom he is able to distinguish from the sorcerer. In *La traversée*, however, the healer has not come, and the masses have been abandoned to all sorts of magicians—principally to the magicians of political discourse who corrupt and exploit

the people. As for the hero, he really does cross the Sahara and goes south to purify himself, but his "road to Damascus" unveils hard facts to him. When he returns, his only choice is between committing suicide and letting himself die. Mysticism in fact has relapsed into politics. At the end of the story, a foreign woman who also has made the journey imparts her last thoughts, which are against dogma and programmed slavery. Mourad, the hero, is dead, the other principal characters are opportunistic or dogmatic and sectarian, or they manage to survive by being pragmatic. In this case too, the revolution has been compromised.

Another example of the same trend is Rachid Mimouni's novel *Le fleuve détourné* (1982). The starting point is an idea used earlier by the Algerian novelist Tahar Ouettar (who writes in Arabic) in his short story "Les martyrs reviennent cette semaine" (which is also the title of the book in which it was published). A freedom fighter, believed to have been killed, returns to his native village. There is no longer any place for him there, except on the memorial to the dead. Nobody recognizes him, and he must face one affront after another. He observes the established bureaucracy, the niggling administration, the suspicious "brothers" who dictate the law "in the name of the people and for the people." It is all like a bad dream. In fact, those who had come down from their mountains in 1954 were dreaming when they picked up the gun. But they were naïve. The course of the "revolution" has been diverted for the benefit of others who are less naïve.

The narrative is cutting, and the picture may be too dark. However, we do recognize once more a great disillusionment. In an interview given to the Algerian press, the author has emphatically declared that the story is neither a pamphlet nor an essay and that there are no autobiographical features in it. Since he lives in Algeria, where the press is nationalized, he was bound to be somewhat reserved in his statements. His novel, however, is virulent: the naïve have been caught in a trap, and "one fine morning we woke up with a bitter taste in our mouths."

Once the Algerians spoke out against the foreigners, who were to be driven out of the country. Now they have begun to examine themselves and to deal with the monsters which haunt the depths of the cavern. Mustapha Tlili, the Tunisian author of two novels wherein troubled heroes flee to some distant "elsewhere," declared in an interview that the people of the Maghreb "have never had the courage to look at themselves in a mirror," for "looking at oneself is destructive." This new generation of North African novelists does not hesitate any longer to deal with the troubles at home and to look themselves straight in the face. A certain courage is necessary when it comes to speaking out against the official public policy, which often attempts to be reassuring and unifying.

■ ■ ■

The third trend in Maghrebine fiction involves the problems of identification, the search for identity, for one's roots and ancient heritage. The search for a father and for an identity, both individual and collective, was one of the main themes in the books of the Generation of 1952; but now that independence has been won, one finds analogous questions and approaches. At the end of *L'œil et la nuit* (1969) Abdellatif Laâbi asked, "Now we are dead tired of the past . . . but who are we?" And one page earlier came the question, "How can we get out of the cavern?" The choice is between a geographical wandering "elsewhere" and internal exile, a state of paralysis in the depths of the cavern. In his latest novel the Moroccan author recalls his itinerary of 1969, "this confused feeling for my roots, this furious search for an identity. I retrace the curve of cursed times to unearth my deep-rooted memory." This disarray can be felt in several books where the characters are dispossessed of their lives and thrown into history. The Algerian Tahar Djaout, for example, has titled his book *L'exproprié*. Its protagonist is doubly expropriated: of both his native country's legends and its words (Berber words, that is, for he writes in French and has been taught Arabic).

In *La rage aux tripes* (1975) the Tunisian Tlili introduces an Algerian at grips with his "bastardy." The author himself in fact explains that the problem of this Algerian concerns "self-questioning: how to set oneself free after liberating oneself from France. . . . The question is: what are we now? What's the future of our societies?" The Algerian novelist and poet Nabile Farès opts for a pluralistic world, refusing the monolithic system of his native country and telling his father that he wants to go beyond the Book (the Koran), to be free, to live. In *L'exil et le désarroi* (1976) he declares clearly: "What is the meaning of your independence if you reject what is multiple."

In Boudjedra's *La répudiation* this identity quest takes the form of a repudiated son's search for his lost father, with much overcompensation in eroticism and incest. The quest also manifests itself in another book by Boudjedra, *Les 1001 années de la nostalgie* (1979), through a return to the ancient collective memory. This resorting to memory can also be found in the works of contemporary Moroccan poets and in the latest novel by Driss Chraïbi, *La mère du printemps* (1982), which is set in the seventh century, the period when the Arabs arrived in the country of the Berbers. Abdelkébir Khatibi gives his "autobiography of a decolonized individual"

the explicit title *La mémoire tatouée* (1971). Memory is etched, "tatooed" by the successive invasions of the Maghreb, but, at the same time, the decolonized individual remains amnesiac. In Kateb's *Nedjma* (1956) the pages of the book of ancient history were scattered, torn out; one could gather only bits and pieces of them. Memory, which does not show any "chronological order" (Kateb in *Le polygone étoilé,* 1966), rises to the surface only in bits and pieces, more or less glorious moments from the "days of the Arabs." For Khatibi this search for identity is a complex one; there are "no means to dissociate identity and difference," since the Other (i.e., the colonizer) has invested the place. "We admit," writes Khatibi, "that the West has fascinated us to death, that we are divided to death." In *La mémoire tatouée* he also admits: "When I dance in front of you, West, without relinquishing my people, know that this dance is one of mortal desire."

Sometimes, in order that the protagonist might find his identity, the novelist sends him southward, to the desert, synonymous with depth and roots. In *Le désert* (1977) Albert Memmi is in search of his ancestor in the deepest Sahara in the fifteenth century, and in *Une enquête au pays* (1981) Chraïbi goes far into the mountains to get nearer to the people, who are simple and close to the earth, the wellspring of life. This journey into the depths sometimes looks like an initiation quest. In *La prière de l'absent* by Tahar Ben Jelloun, for example, we find a road—again leading back to buried memories and ancestral tombs—which resembles the route of a mystic pilgrimage with its allusions to Muslim mysticism (*tasawwuf*). Memory has gone to shreds, but little by little a certain coherence is restored. However, for the hero of Mustapha Tlili's *Le bruit dort* (1978) there remains only nostalgia on the pavement of Manhattan, "place of solitude, disarray and exile above all others." One does not glue together what has crumbled to dust," says Jalal Ben Cherif, the protagonist of Tlili's earlier book, *La rage aux tripes*. With Tlili one is reduced to wandering "elsewhere," without any pilgrimage to the sources. In a recent interview Abdelwahab Meddeb, author of *Talismano* (1979), insisted on the theme of travel, "which illustrates," he says, "the theme of wandering." He himself likes to place his works in the tradition of the quest as it is frequently expressed in the spiritual heritage of both the West and the East. In so doing, this Tunisian author resembles the Moroccan Khatibi.

Some authors admittedly feel a sensual pleasure in writing French (Khaïr-Eddine, Boudjedra) and want to share that pleasure with the reader. They multiply metaphors and neologisms, playing on words as if in fun, frolicking aimlessly in the sheer joy of getting intoxicated on words, of making them bounce and clash. It gives the writers pleasure, but for whom do they write? This is one of the problems of the North African Francophone novel today. Some critics in Algeria, for example, want to impose strict guidelines on "intellectual workers" and go as far as to insist on their writing "good novels" for the "people," novels that will be "useful" to them. Others, writers who are neither demagogic nor submissive, want to test their wings to the limits, delirious with creative freedom, disturbing the orthodox, the censors and the decorous conventions of official discourse. The contemporary Maghrebine novel is therefore facing formidable problems: between writing for oneself in the context of current social changes (which means telling striking and salutary truths), on the one hand, and writing for the "others," for semioticians who will know how to play with the texts. Which is the better choice? Must one either write in a flat, trite style which affords no pleasure to readers who understand less and less French, or produce excessively subtle texts, using dictionaries to find rare words and consequently being read by only a few small circles?

"You speak to those who hear man's call," Laâbi writes in *Le chemin des ordalies* (1982). This call is heard, but the words are not necessarily understood. Still, Laâbi tells himself, "You are a kind of fanatic of the written word." This could just as well apply to many other North African Francophone writers of today, or at least to the most talented among them; and that is, in sum, all to their credit.

Jean Déjeux, Summer 1983

*In addition to the biographical sketch of Mohammed Dib in *BA* 50:1, pp. 98–99 (when Dib served on the 1976 Neustadt International Prize jury), we refer the reader to the following reviews of recent works by authors discussed in this essay: Tahar Ben Jelloun, *A l'insu du souvenir* (*WLT* 55:2, p. 365) and *Les amandiers sont morts de leurs blessures* (51:3, p. 490); Rachid Boudjedra, *L'escargot entêté* (52:2, p. 328); Driss Chraïbi, *Une enquête au pays* (56:4, p. 738); Dib, *Habel* (53:1, p. 170), *Omneros* (53:3, p. 546) and *Mille hourras pour une gueuse* (55:4, p. 719); Abdelkébir Khatibi, *Le livre de sang* (55:1, p. 165); Abdellatif Laâbi, *Histoire des sept crucifiés de l'espoir* (55:3, p. 518); Mouloud Mammeri, *Poèmes kabyles anciens* (55:3, p. 516), Albert Memmi, *La terre intérieure* (51:2, p. 323), *Le désert* (52:2, p. 331) and *La dépendance* (54:2, p. 400). — The Editors.

In the Making: Beur Fiction and Identity Construction

"Beur" is the label used to refer to the children of North African (Maghrebi) immigrants to France, previously known as "second-generation immigrants." They are not immigrants in the traditional sense of the word, for the Beur generation consists of children born into involuntary minority status, with none of the dreams and illusions that prompted their parents to leave North Africa in hopes of a better life. Yet Beur literature reflects the tensions resulting from another type of migration, the daily commuting between a Muslim, Arabic-speaking home where tradition-upholding parents reminisce about North Africa as they prepare couscous and meschwi, and the streets of the only city they know, the French metropolis with its corner bistros, its secular culture, and the growing racism of Jean-Marie Le Pen supporters and neo-Nazi skin-heads. Today, the Beurs number approximately one and a half million. They share to a large extent the culture of the majority of young people in French, yet are denied equal opportunity because of perceived differences, based on ethnic origin. Indeed, anti-Beur racism is such that, while they make up 40 percent of the foreign population in France, they are the victims of 90 percent of the hate crimes.[1]

In 1983 Mehdi Charef published his first novel, *Le thé au harem d'Archi Ahmed* (Eng. *Tea in the Harem*, 1989), depicting the underside of Paris with its public-housing projects and transient shelters that foster a life of violence, alcoholism, drug addiction, prostitution, and pimping. The blunt, occasionally vulgar novel won unanimous acclaim and became a best seller almost overnight. Charef was the guest of numerous radio and television shows, including France's most popular literary television program, Bernard Pivot's "Apostrophes." Following the success of his novel, Charef was asked to direct a film based on the book. The latter (with a slight variation in the title: *Le thé au harem d'Archimède*) won the Prix Jean Vigo for best first feature at the Cannes Film Festival.

Today *Le thé au harem* is considered the first work of Beur fiction, a literature still at an embryonic stage and featuring little more than a handful of titles. Only one Beur novel had been published before Charef's, Hocine Touabti's 1981 book *L'amour quand même*, which met with little critical acclaim. Hence it is Charef, and his *Thé au harem*, who is credited with bringing unprecedented attention to the plight of the Beurs. As I write this, Beur literature is a mere twelve years old, and there is only one full-length study in English devoted to it, Alec Hargreaves's *Voices from the North African Immigrant Community in France: Immigration and Identity in Beur Fiction* (1991). Only one work of Beur fiction has been translated into English, Charef's *Tea in the Harem*. What Beur novels have in common is the desire to affirm one's presence through self-expression, a feeling of ever-elusive identity, of missing roots, of disintegration, and of unresolved angst, as evidenced by their open-ended final chapters.

Charef's second novel, *Le harki de Meriem* (1989), further elaborates on the cultural homelessness of the Beurs. In it, Sélim is murdered by three ultranationalists as he comes out of a public phone booth. Had he been Algerian, the thugs would have let him go. It is upon finding out that he is a French citizen that they decide to kill him: a "basané" (darkie) has no business claiming the same nationality as they: "Si par malheur tu as une carte d'identité française on te fait la peau, on ne veut pas de basanés dans les memes registres que nous, Bicot tu es, Bicot tu resteras. Tes papiers?" (If by misfortune you have a French I.D. card, we'll get your skin. We want no darkies in the same registers as us. You're Arab and you will stay Arab; 28).[2] The neo-Nazi thugs search Sélim and find his papers indicating he is indeed a French citizen: "Lui plaquant sa photo sur les yeux, le châtain dit a Sélim: —T'as vu la tête que t'as? Réfléchis bien! . . . Tu ne peux pas être français avec la gueule que t'as" (Rubbing the photo over Sélim's eyes, the light-haired one tells him: — Do you see your mug? Think about it! You can't be French with a mug like this; 31).

Like its predecessor *Tea in the Harem, Le harki de Meriem* is a groundbreaking novel in that it touches on an extremely sensitive subject, the Algerians who fought alongside the French occupier during Algeria's War of Independence. Those *harkis* were then "repatriated" to France for their own safety, having earned the hatred of their fellow Algerians. They were also "rewarded" with French citizenship, unlike their compatriots, who retained Algerian nationality. The children of harkis and "immigrants" alike, however, experience similar discrimination in France, and have overcome the old political demarcation that separated their parents under French occupation. In Algeria, on the other hand, hatred of the harkis did not subside with independence, for they had engaged in some of the ugliest acts of violence during the war. Hence they are not embraced as Arabs by the North Africans. Charef, by choosing the son of a harki as the central character in his novel, is symbolically illustrating the practical impossibility for Beurs to "return" to their parents' homeland.

Sélim's bereaved father wants his son buried in Algeria. But an airport officer in Algiers will not allow the dead body in, because of the father's treason. Yet it is this treason that earned Sélim his French identity, and his death, for racists do not distinguish between the children of harkis and freedom-fighters, looking no further than skin color. To the ultranationalists, all are "Bicot" (a pejorative term for Arab), or, as one of Sélim's assassins says with disgust, "Beurk! . . . Beeuurk! . . . Beeeuuurk!" (29). Racism against the harkis adds a further dimension to their alienation. Having allied them-

selves politically with the French, they did not anticipate the discrimination that the rest of the Algerians took for granted from their enemies. Sélim, however, "feels" French, even as he is reminded of his fateful origins.

> Malgré lui sa différence lui revint. . . . Il savait qu'avec un visage plus clair il rentrerait tranquillement chez lui. Il n'était pas d'ailleurs et ne se sentait pas d'ailleurs. Sélim n'imaginait pas d'issue de secours, ville ou pays de retour. Il était de Reims, de France, depuis la clinique Saint-Charles où il était né. Il avait même de la peine à l'idée qu'il pourrait un jour quitter cette ville qu'il aimait tant, à laquelle il avait donné une première place de français au concours général et un podium au championnat de France cadets de fleuret à Coubertin. (24)

> (Despite himself, his difference came back to him. He knew that with a lighter skin shade he would safely go home. He was not from elsewhere, nor did he feel from elsewhere. Sélim could not imagine an emergency exit, a town or country to return to. He was from Reims, from France, ever since the Saint-Charles clinic where he was born. He was even pained at the thought he might someday leave this city he loved so much, for which he had won a first place in French at the national contest, and a runner-up position at the junior fencing championship in Coubertin.)

An incident of racial violence is also at the center of two other Beur novels. Ahmed Kalouaz's *Point Kilométrique 190* (1986) recounts the death, ten years earlier, of Habib Grimzi, thrown out of a moving train by French soldiers. Kalouaz had seen a brief mention about this real-life event in the French newspapers and decided it merited a full-length narrative. Jean-Luc Yacine's 1986 book *L'escargot* is also about the senseless murder of a young Beur. It is closer to *Harki* in that it is a fictional account of a young man's death on the eve of a major event in his life. Here the fictional Amar is killed by a night watchman as he is about to receive an unexpected inheritance. The unsettling murder takes place in Paris, a city unfamiliar to Amar, and one to which he had to travel from his hometown of Aras in a northward movement which, for the French-born Beurs, replicates the North Africans' emigration to France.

France, then, is fated to be the home, if not refuge, of the Beurs, a disenfranchised minority ever on the defensive, welcome nowhere. Clearly representative of this subculture, Majid, the central character in *Le thé*, lives in constant fear.

> La crainte domine la cité et ses habitants. Avec tous ces jeunes qui se droguent et qui détrous-

sent, qui violent les vieilles, à ce qu'on dit, c'est l'angoisse! C'est du délire: ils veulent tous s'armer. . . . Il paraîtrait meme qu'il y a des viols dans les caves (*Thé*, 23–24)

Fear dominates this estate and its inhabitants. There's an atmosphere of dread, or so it seems, with all these people taking drugs, thieving, raping old women and so on. It's madness. People are talking about getting arms to defend themselves. . . . They even say that women get raped in the basements of the flats. (*Tea*, 18–19)

Unlike the United States, another multicultural society with much racial tension, it is noteworthy that, in France, most crimes are committed by members of the dominant culture, the Euro-French. Similarly, the Euro-French have a significantly greater tendency to bear, and use, weapons. This issue is brought up in both of Charef's novels, where the xenophobic French neighbors arm themselves while the Arabs live in terror. Here is one of the final thoughts to cross Sélim's mind as he agonizes outside the phone booth:

"Pour se protéger chez soi et sortir sans peur, il faut s'armer . . ."

Ces mots de Pierre vinrent à l'esprit de Sélim. Pierre qui, gagné par la psychose de l'insécurité, s'était aussi payé un fusil au cas où on l'attaquerait chez lui. Mais pour Pierre c'était aussi la crainte de l'étranger, de l'adolescent basané, même si dans son quartier, à part Sélim, il n'y avait guère de cette racaille, comme il disait. (29)

("To protect yourself at home and to go out without fear, you need to arm yourself . . ." Pierre's words came to Sélim's mind. Pierre who, overcome by the psychosis of insecurity, had bought himself a gun in case he was attacked at home. But for Pierre it was also the fear of the foreigner, of the dark adolescent, even if, in his neighborhood, besides Sélim, there was no "riffraff," as he called it.)

Uncomfortable in their physical environment, the Beurs also find themselves in a linguistic limbo. Thus Majid can barely communicate with his mother, who speaks to him in Arabic, while he knows only French. Under French colonialism, his parents' lived reality, access to the dominant discourse had its benefits; hence their move to the metropolis. But in Majid's postcolonial world, joining the center of a collapsed structure brings no benefits.

Tout jeunes mariés, les parents ont émigré. Ils voulaient faire des gosses qui aillent à l'école pour devenir des médecins, ou des avocats, ou des maîtres d'école, comme on dit à la campagne.

Et déjà le chomâge pour Madjid et le père . . . (*Thé*, 21)

The parents had married young and then they emigrated. They wanted to send their kids to school so that they could grow up to be doctors, lawyers, schoolteachers, the Third World dream. But already Majid and his father are unemployed. (*Tea*, 16–17).

The shattered illusions of the North African immigrants are rendered more powerfully in *Harki*. Sélim is killed on his twenty-second birthday, shortly after having celebrated it with his family, who proudly boast:

— Avocat! Mon fils sera avocat!

Un project qui revenait souvent dans le F4 depuis que le fiston étudiait le droit.

— Juge, c'est mieux! avait retorqué Saliha.

— Moins brillant, avait repris le père, plus attiré par latchatche et les projecteurs.

Il rêvait tout haut l'avenir de son fils. . . .

On comptait sur la réussite du fils pour effacer tout regret d'exil. Son adolescente de sœur bûchait, quant à elle, pour un diplôme d'infirmiere.

— Ça me suffit, disait-elle. (25)

(— A lawyer! My son will be a lawyer!

This topic was frequently brought up since the kid started studying law.

— Judge, that's even better, his sister jumped in.

— Not as flashy, replied the father, more attracted to glitz and show.

He fantasized aloud about his son's future.

They were counting on the son's success to erase all bitterness of exile. His young sister was a nursing student.

— That's good enough for me, she would say.)

Like most first Beur novels, *Le thé au harem* contains autobiographical elements, which Charef has tried to attenuate in an attempt to achieve greater objectivity and credibility—reality is too ugly to be readily believed, he says. Thus, whereas Charef was born in Algeria in 1952 and was taken to Paris by his family in 1964, his fictional namesake was born in Paris, thanks to an authorial intervention possibly revealing of Charef's own allegiance to the European metropolis. Yet Majid, the novel's central character, falls into the same age group as the author and is a "transplant," brought over by his parents. Similarly, the central character's mother is depicted as constantly struggling with French, while Charef's mother, the author indicates in the dedication of his novel, is illiterate. In an interview, Charef explains that his writing is a palliative for the pain of spiritual homelessness: "Si j'étais resté en Algérie, j'aurais été peut-être bien, je n'aurais peut-être paseu besoin de m'exprimer" (If I had stayed in Algeria, I might have been fine, I may not have felt the need to express myself).[3] Majid, in the novel, experiences the same fragmentation and mental orphanhood, the result of unwanted displacement. Speaking to him in Arabic, his mother is a painful reminder that, because of his status as North African in France, he belongs nowhere.

> — Je vais aller au consulat d'Algérie, elle dit maintenant à son fils, la Malika, en arabe, qu'ils viennent te chercher pour t'emmener au service militaire là-bas. . . . Parfois Madjid comprend un mot, une phrase et il répond, abbatu, sachant qu'il va faire du mal à sa mère:

> — Mais moi j'ai rien demandé! Tu serais pas venue en France je serais pas ici, je seràis pas perdu . . .

> Elle quitte la chambre et Madjid se rallonge sur son lit, convaincu qu'il n'est ni arabe ni français depuis bien longtemps. Il est fils d'immigrés, paumé entre deux cultures, deux histoires, deux langues, deux couleurs de peau, ni blanc ni noir, à s'inventer ses propres racines, ses attaches, se les fabriquer. (Thé, 17)

> Then Malika informs her son, in Arabic, that she's going to see the Algerian consul. . . .

> Majid understands the occasional phrase here and there, and his reply is subdued, because whatever he says is bound to hurt her.

> "I never asked to come here. If you hadn't decided to come to France, I wouldn't be finished, would I, eh?" . . . She leaves the room and Majid flops down on the bed, reflecting that for a long time he's been neither French nor Arab. He's the son of immigrants—caught between two cultures, two histories, two languages, and two colours of skin. He's neither black nor white. He has to invent his own roots, create his own reference points. (Tea, 12–13)

With its articulation of the dilemma of identity construction in the diaspora, highlighting not the both/and of biculturalism, but the neither/nor of homelessness, Beur literature constitutes one of the most recent developments in postcolonial writing. The titles of the works themselves reflect the ruptured experiences that characterize the Beurs' everyday existence. Thus Charef got the title of his first novel from a real-life incident in which a schoolchild wrote, in his notebook, "Le thé au harem d'archi Ahmed" instead of "Le théorème d'Archimède," a confusion that resulted from his lack of adjustment to his two cultures. This confusion occurs again in Farida Belghoul's Georgette! (1986), where the young school-girl writes her homework at the place indicated by her father: the blank page closest to the right-hand cover. At school, the teacher looks to the left-hand flap, and does not see the exercise, in an incident illustrating the incompatibility of the two cultures. The schoolgirl decides that, if she is to get any credit for her work, she must write from left to right. The title of the novel is taken from a passage where her father berates her, telling her she might as well be called "Georgette," considering her behavior. Georgette!, with the exclamation mark, focuses the reader's attention on the oddity of such a French persona created by an Arab author—the literary representation of the hybridity of the Beurs. At no point are we told the schoolgirl's real name, an omission clearly symbolic of the Beurs' lack of identity.

In Akli Tadjer's book Les ANI du 'Tassili' (1984) ANI is an acronym for "Arabes Non-Identifiés," highlighting the problematic identity of the Beurs. In Touabti's L'amour quand même we are again not told the immigrant protagonist's name, only that of the French woman he loves, Sylvie. And Sakinna Boukhedenna's Journal. 'Nationalité: Immigré(e)' encapsulates the decentering that has become the defining characteristic of the Beurs. This decentering is further illustrated in the novel, where the protagonist describes herself as "Bougnoule en France . . . immigrée en Algérie" (nigger in France, immigrant in Algeria; 91). The title of Tassadit Imache's 1989 novel Une fille sans histoire alludes to the silence surrounding the Beurs' circumstances. This silence itself was an imposed political reality in France until 1981, when the Socialist Party and President François Mitterand came to power. As Alec Hargreaves explains, among the first actions undertaken by the Socialists was the abolition of a law forbidding foreigners from organizing without the prior approval of the Ministry of the Interior, as well as making public funds available to the immigrant community on an unprecedented scale, the result being "a veritable explosion of new organizations set up and run by members of the immigrant community, particularly the younger generation" (28).

The collapse of the society that has produced such repression and misery is reflected in the structure and circumstances of Majid's friends' families. There is no mention of a single "traditional" household living on the estate, fake to its very name: "Flower City."

> La cité des Fleurs, que ça s'appelle!!!

> Du béton, des bagnoles en long, en large, en travers, de l'urine et des crottes de chiens. Des bâtiments hauts, longs, sans cœur ni âme. Sans joie ni rire, que des plaintes, que du malheur. . . .

> Les fleurs! les fleurs! . . .

Et sur les murs de béton, des graffiti, des slogans, des appels de détresse, des S.O.S. en forme de poing levé.

Des grosses couilles avec des grosses bites, bien poilues, peintes. (*Thé,* 24–25)

Flower City—that's what they call it!

Acres of concrete. The smell of piss. Cars, cars and more cars. And dog turds. Row after row of tall, soulless apartment blocks. No joy, no laughter, just heartache and pain.

. . . Flower City!

Concrete walls, covered with slogans. . . . Cries from the heart . . . anti-racist graffiti in the form of raised fists . . . great long cocks and hairy testicles spray-painted down the walls. (*Tea,* 19–20)

Majid never mentions the possibility of returning to Algeria, which he does not think of as his "homeland." On the other hand, Charef the author voices ambiguity, if not bitterness, toward the country of his origins, which he has visited as an adult.

Mais qu'est-ce que l'Algérie a fait pour nous, les jeunes? . . . Peu tentés par le retour en Algérie, poussés, au contraire, je dirais même condamnés à vivre en France, écorchés vifs, les jeunes de la migration pensent que maintenant le meilleur moyen de s'affirmer, c'est de vivre tels qu'ils sont, de se poser en fils de migrants vivant en France, en mettant en valeur ce qui a pu etre sauvé de la culture d'origine, mais en affirmant aussi qu'ils appartiennent déjà de plus en plus à la société française.

(What has Algeria done for us, the young ones? Condemned to live in France, skinned alive, the young of the migration think that the best way to affirm themselves is to live as they are, to present themselves as children of migrant people living in France, while valuing what has been salvaged of the original culture, but also affirming thus that they belong more and more to the French society.)[4]

The incongruity of a "return" to North Africa is a thread that runs through many Beur novels and is expressed most strongly in *Le harki de Meriem,* in which the dead young man is legally denied entry into Algeria. The problematic return is also at the heart of Boukhedenna's novel, where the protagonist (also named Sakinna), angered by racism in France, travels to Algeria, only to be even more exasperated by the sexism of "her" culture.

Si la culture arabe, c'est de réduire la femme à l'état oùelle est, je ne veux pas de cette arabité. . . . La France est raciste, mais en France je peux vivre seule sans mari, sans père, mèpie,

et la police ne m'épie pas tous les jours. Je peux crier, 'non' au racisme, 'non à l'exploitation de la femme, je me sens up peu plus libre que surma terre. (100–1)

(If Arab culture reduces woman to the state she is in, I want nothing to do with Arabism. France is a racist country, but at least in France I can live alone, without husband, father, or mother, and the police do not spy on my every movement. I can shout "no" to racism, to the exploitation of women, I feel a little more free than in my homeland.)[5]

The duality of her decentering is rendered most explicitly by Sakinna's reference to Algeria, the country she cannot relate to, as her homeland, "materre." Boukhedenna, like Charef, feels more at home in France, but needed her trip to Algeria to realize where her allegiance lies.

Most Beur writers refer, in their work, to their feelings upon visiting, or considering a visit to, their parents' country. These vary from mere disappointment (Algeria is no vacation paradise!) to bitter disillusion, the confirmation of the fact that they have been uprooted. Thus Bouzid, in *La marche,* recalls his pain upon being called "fils de Française" (son of a Frenchwoman-which he is not) while vacationing with his family in Algeria.

J'eus l'impression que tous les pays me claquaient la porte au nez. Ils étaient privés. Il fallait la carte pour entrer. J'étais condamné à vivre dans les *no man's lands* que j'imaginais comme des couloirs froids où le vent soufflait à tout rompre. (35)

(I felt as if all countries were slamming their doors in my face. They were exclusive clubs, I needed a membership card. I was condemned to live in the no-man's lands which I imagined as cold hallways where the wind blew with destructive gusts.)[6]

Significantly, Beur writers seem undaunted by their use of the French language, an issue the earlier generation of postcolonial subjects dealt with at great length. Yet many, just like Charef, acknowledge that it constitutes a problem in communicating with their parents. The "French" that Charef speaks, however, is by no means the imperial language, and is best compared to one of the multitude of "englishes" spoken by members of the former British colonies.[7] It has even earned itself a distinct name, Beur, after its speakers ("parler beur," "écriture beure," et cetera).

"Beur," a form of backslang, operates as counterdiscourse by reversing the order of the syllables of a word. As such, it has a rich vocabulary consisting not of newly coined terms but of French inverted, spitting its guts out. Beur is French, then, but read against the grain, from left to right, as an Arab eye would read— even if French schoolteachers disapprove of the practice, as we see in *Georgette!* The very word *Beur* is a distortion and contraction of "arabe," read backward. Being neither Arabic nor French, Beur is the natural vehicle of expression for second-generation immigrants and constitutes a shift from polyglossia, which Bakhtin saw as "the interanimation of major national languages . . . each of which was in itself already *fully formed* and *unitary*" (66), to heteroglossia, the coexistence of a number of voices "*within* a language, that is, . . . internal differentiation, the stratification characteristic of any national language" (67). Thus backslang is punctuated with words such as *renoi* for "noir" (black), *kefri* for "fric" (slang for money), but also *clebard* for "chien" (dog), derived obviously not from "chien" but from "kelb," Arabic for dog.

As it provides no closure in the traditional sense, *Le thé au harem* suggests that there is no clear way out for the victims, that the protagonists are born into a vicious cycle of violence, pain, crime, and misery. When, in the last chapter, the cops finally arrest Majid and expect, through him, to arrest his friends, they are right. Again, there is a slight twist: the forces of law and order are successful, but not through traditional interrogation techniques. It would seem instead that the physical and psychological torture that usually accompanies arrests and investigations has plagued the young gang members throughout their lives. Constantly under surveillance, always the prime suspects in the event of wrongdoing, presumed guilty until proven innocent, they have been on trial since birth, and their arrest is not the beginning of a legal process but the pronouncement of the final verdict: the Beurs are guilty. Majid does not even attempt to resist.

> Madjid ne bougeait pas. Il regardait droit devant lui, les yeux mi-clos, las, dégoûté, fatigué.
>
> Alors, Pat partit en courant derrière les autres. Un gendarme prit les fuyards en chasse, mais n'insista pas trop longtemps. Il revint essoufflé. Le brigadier se pencha à l'intérieur de la B.M.W. Il observa longuement Madjid et lui dit de sortir. Madjid obéit sans un mot. La tête baissée, il prit place dans l'Estafette. (*Thé*, 183–84)
>
> Majid looked like he didn't want to leave his seat. He just stared in front of him, his eyes half-closed, fed up and tired. Pat ran off behind the others. One of the cops gave chase, but then gave up and came back all out of breath. The sergeant leaned into the BMW. He took a long look at Majid and told him to come out. Majid obeyed without a word. His head bowed, he went and sat in the patrol car. (*Tea*, 156)

With the young men's sincere friendship and solidarity working against them, the novel ends on a truly pessimistic note. Yet it is less than realistic, for Charef has actually kept out some of the more disturbing elements, such as his imprisonment and the fact that Josette's suicide, a failed attempt in the novel, was successful in real life. Hargreaves observes that Beur writers frequently indulge in omissions and attenuations when basing their novels on personal experience. He cites, for example, an interview with Charef conducted when *Le thé au harem* was made into a film:

> Asked to explain why he had toned things down in this way, Charef replied: 'On aurait dit que j'en faisais trop. . . . J'ai préféré une chronique allègre plutôt qu'un film accusateur conçu pour choquer systématiquement le spectateur.'
>
> (They would have accused me of exaggerating. I preferred a light chronicle to an accusing film conceived to deliberately shock the viewer.)[8]

Clearly, Charef seeks to express, not impress. Indeed, such is his eagerness to break the silence about the misery of the Beur community that he is willing to compromise, to tone down his narrative, if that ensures that it will reach a greater public. This approach may well be the factor behind the overwhelming success of his first novel, which then paved the way for more visceral accounts of Beur experiences.

Yet the educated reader cannot help but wonder just how violent the reality of the immigrant community is, that it should be minimized in fiction. It is also, at times, too painful to be articulated, recorded, put into words. We know, for instance, that Charef, whose own adventures are the model for Majid's, spent time in prison; but that episode is totally excluded from *Le thé au harem*. Charef also kept silent regarding some of the details of his escapades, in order to protect friends who might be implicated. Indeed, objectionable as some may find it, *Le thé au harem* is a sanitized, socially acceptable version of ghetto life. In this new fiction we are very far from the realism of such authors as Dostoevsky, who delighted in an exquisitely accurate description of a toothache, because art must render the ugliness of life as well as its beauty. In *Le thé au harem* we have a highly lyrical description of the painful, traumatic, and permanently destructive effects of life in the concrete world of housing projects, yet one which falls short of specifics.

> Faut surtout pas chialer, parce que la faiblesse est alors reconnue, citée, criée, répandue. Faut pas pleurer. Faut pas, petit!
>
> Emmagasiner encore et toujours en attendant, avec l'espoir peut-être de se réconcilier avec soi-même et avec la vie. Sinon c'est l'explosion, ça se

réveille comme unvolcan qui a longtemps ruminé sa vengeance contre tout ce qui lui a été bourré dans la gueule. Il évacue l'énergie somnolente en ses tripes. De bonne elle est devenue mauvaise, dévastatrice, et c'est la violence. Le refus. Le refus de se laisser étouffer. Contre la récupération de soi. (*Thé*, 62–63)

No tears. Don't cry—never! Just store it all up, and wait, wait forever, with perhaps a small hope of being able to reconcile yourself with your life. Because if you don't, the explosion will come, and it will come like the awakening of a volcano that has long planned its revenge for everything that it's had to endure. . . . It turns destructive, and that means violence . . . a refusal . . . a refusal to let yourself be silenced . . . a refusal to allow yourself to be swallowed. When you try to break the silence and the self-destructiveness, violence takes the upper hand, and you turn savage. You never recover from the concrete. (*Tea*, 51–52)

But Charef does not suggest that a successful life is unattainable for the Beurs, only that it is a long, arduous process as they overcome the trauma of displacement and fragmentation, question and confront their alienation from their direct environment, and forge themselves a living space. In *Tea in the Harem* Majid and his friends do none of this; they engage strictly in escapist activities: alcohol and drug use, occasional minimum-wage dead-end jobs, sexual promiscuity. To quote Glenn Fetzer: "Like Beckettian heroes these characters spend their energies waiting for something undefined and undefinable, something which will intervene and which will somehow restore meaning to their existence" (335). No such "thing," however, will materialize for society's outcasts, unless they take it upon themselves to reify it. Sélim, on the other hand, seems to have accepted his status as outsider and thrives on his isolation.

Coincé toute sa vie entre le rejet d'une communauté française et les insultes de l'autre, l'algérienne, Sélim se frayait un chemin à coups de poing. Jamais il ne se plaignait et toujous il cherchait à distancer ceux qui le narguaient. Premier en tout, et regrettant de ne pas en savoir davantage, inquiet d'être rattrapé par la meute. Seul contre tous, c'était sa force. (*Le harki*, 45)

(Stuck all his life between the rejection of the French community and the insults of the Algerian, Sélim cleared his path open with his fists. He never complained, always trying to distance those who mocked him. First in everything, eager to learn even more, afraid of the mob catching up with him. Alone against all, there lay his strength.)

His loneliness, however, proves detrimental when he is approached by the ultranationalist bigots. Significantly,

Sélim had not told his family he would be celebrating his birthday alone—by going to a prostitute, an appropriate social symbol for solitude. Instead, he lied to them, claiming he was going out with his best friend Marc.

In Charef's two characters, then, we have two extreme reactions to diasporic fragmentation. Majid is an average adolescent trying to establish collective turf while completely neglecting his personal identity: he even shares his lovers with with best friend and alter ego Pat. Deterritorialized as a Beur, he seeks membership in gang life that further ghettoizes him and fixes his status as outcast. His utter passivity, leading to his arrest and incarceration, illustrates the fruitlessness of escapism in a hostile society. Sélim, on the other hand, claims membership in no community whatsoever, and even uses Marc as an alibi, making of friendship an excuse for being alone. His murder is a visceral reminder of the vital importance of belonging. Charef has also created a third character, however, who illustrates the successful combination of the ethnic and cultural components of the Beur identity, Sélim's sister Saliha. Her conscious search for her identity began when she was nine, when she first learned that her father was a harki.

— Mais c'est quoi un harki?

— C'est un Arabe qui, pendant la guerre entre les Français et les Arabes, s'est battu contre les Arabes.

— Contre nous! Pourquoi?

Elle avait eu un choc. Elle revoyait le graffiti sur le mur de l'école: "Le Arabes dehors."

("But what is a harki?" "It's an Arab who, during the Franco-Algerian war, fought against the Arabs."

"Against us! Why?" She was shocked. She remembered the graffiti on the school wall: "Arabs keep out.")

As is obvious from her spontaneous response, "Against us?," young Saliha identifies as Arab. Yet she was born in Reims, France, and, like the rest of her immediate family, has given little consideration to Algeria. As she accompanies her brother's casket to her parents' homeland, she realizes she does not know much about that country.

Saliha n'avait jamais poussé son imagination très loin derrière la Mediterranée. Elle se sentait, comme sa famille, abandonnée par ceux de "labas," qui ne répondaient pas au courrier. Alors elle evitait d'imaginer quoi que ce soit." (48)

(Saliha had never pushed her imagination very far beyond the Mediterranean. Like her family, she felt abandoned by those from "over there," who did not respond to the mail. So she avoided imagining anything.)

Yet it is this voyage, occasioning at once the painful denial of burial privileges for her brother and her own ultimate reconciliation with her family roots and ancestral ties, that allows for the full expression of the two parts of her identity. Indeed, even the Arabic language, which she had not used since her childhood in Koranic school, returns to her as she embraces her grandmother at the airport. A long conversation ensues, during which Saliha learns all about her family's past and informs her grandmother about more recent developments, creating a continuity across generations and continents.

Shortly after her return to France, Saliha obtains her diploma, moves away from Reims and the painful memories of her brother's murder, and sets up a successful practice among the immigrant community just outside Paris. The novel ends with a rosy picture of her happy marriage to a fellow Beur she met during a political protest, a man who has now given her twin sons, Abdennebi and Malik. Healed both as an individual and as a member of a broader social community, she is forging her own space, refusing to be deterritorialized, pushed to the margins of society. No longer stuck between two antagonistic cultures, she is now comfortable in her chosen environment, the Beur community to whose well-being she tends.

Majid is yearning for self-expression; he seeks "to break the silence and the self-destructiveness," yet is incapable of doing anything positive or constructive. Sélim is initially better off, a law student with a first prize in French who carries French papers and "feels" French. Yet this is viewed by ultranationalists as intolerably arrogant, a "crime" punishable by death, the ultimate gag. The refusal to be silenced, however, is one that Charef, the author, stresses as essential, for it alone can allow for self-inscription. Commenting on his work, he says:

> Le meilleur moyen de s'affirmer, c'est de s'exprimer, de parler. Les médias nous en ont longtemps dénié le droit, en laissant entendre qu'un bougnoule était incapable de s'exprimer et qu'il n'avait que le droit de setaire. Cette réflexion, à propos de mon bouquin, je l'ai souvent entendue.

> Maintenant, la condamnation au silence, c'est fini. Les jeunes veulent parler, dire ce qu'ils ont sur le cœur, dialoguer.

> (The best way to affirm one's presence is to express oneself, to speak. The media have long denied us this right, by suggesting that niggers cannot express themselves and only had the right to remain silent. I have frequently heard this comment made about my book. But the condemnation to silence is finally over. The young want to speak, to say what's on their heart, to engage in dialogue.)[9]

A dialogue may finally become possible, as more Beur novels are published, teasing the readers out of their complacence. Within a decade of the publication of *Le thé au harem,* which has been called "the first and best" of this new and dynamic literary practice, well over a dozen Beur writers have produced highly successful novels. Through their depictions of the difficulty, alienation, and humiliation of a new French subculture, they represent a strongly worded plea for, and create the grounds for, respect and recognition. It is now up to postcolonial scholars to familiarize themselves with this body of work, in order better to engage with the multitude of "minorities" that make up the Majority World.

Nada Elia, Winter 1997

▪ WORKS CITED

Ashcroft, Bill, Gareth Griffiths, Helen Tiffin. *The Empire Writes Back: Theory and Practice in Post-Colonial Literatures.* London. Routledge. 1989.

Bakhtin, M. M. *The Dialogic Imagination: Four Essays.* Caryl Emerson, Michael Holquist, trs. Michael Holquist, ed. Austin. University of Texas Press. 1981.

Belghoul, Farida. *Georgette!* Paris. Barrault. 1986.

Boukhedenna, Sakinna. *Journal. 'Nationalité: Immigré(e).'* Paris. L'Harmattan. 1987.

Bouzid [Bouzid Kara]. *La marche.* Paris. Sindbad. 1984.

Charef, Mehdi. *Le thé au harem d'Archi Ahmed.* Paris. Mercure de France. 1983.

———. *Le harki de Meriem.* Paris. Mercure de France. 1989.

———. *Tea in the Harem.* Ed Emery, tr. London. Serpent's Tail. 1989.

Djaout, Tahar. "Black 'Beur' Writing." *Research in African Literature,* 23:2 (Summer 1992), pp. 217–21.

Fetzer, Glenn W. "Memory, Absence, and the Consciousness of Self in the Novels of Mehdi Charef." *College Language Association Journal,* 38:3 (March 1995), pp. 331–41.

Hargreaves, Alec G. *Voices from the North African Immigrant Community in France: Immigration and Identity in Beur Fiction.* New York. St. Martin's. 1991.

———. "Violent Symbols: The *Beurs* and the *Banlieues.*" Presentation at the Modern Language Association 111th Annual Convention, Chicago, 29 December 1995.

Imache, Tassadit. *Une fille sans historie.* Paris. Calmann-Lévy. 1989.

Kalouaz, Ahmed. *Point Kilométrique 190.* Paris. L'Harmattan. 1986.

Tadjer, Akli. *Les ANI du 'Tassili.'* Paris. Seuil. 1984.

Touabti, Hocine. *L'amour quand même.* Paris. Belfond. 1981.

Yacine, Jean-Luc. *L'escargot.* Paris. L'Harmattan. 1986.

[1] Hargreaves, MLA presentation.

[2] All translations from *Le harki de Meriem* are mine.

[3] Cited in Hargreaves, 1991, p. 26; my translation.

[4] Cited in Hargreaves, 1991, p. 27; my translation.

[5] All translations from Boukhedenna's *Journal* are mine.

[6] All translations from *La marche* are mine.

[7] I have in mind the use of "english" adopted by the authors of *The Empire Writes Back: Theory and Practice in Post-Colonial Literatures.*

[8] Cited in Hargreaves, 1991, pp. 93 and 86–87; my translation.

[9] Cited in Hargreaves, 1991, p. 27; my translation.

Middle Eastern Literature and the Conditions of Modernity: An Introduction

> My voice echoes
> Like a worn record
>
> Ah, Iram of great pillars
> Ah, Iram
> Give him back the reins of his horse
> And the books of dawn
> And some bread
> For his heart split in two
> Lies within the lotus flower, in exile.

▓ **AMAL DUNQUL**

Like their Egyptian counterpart, the late Amal Dunqul, poets, writers, and thinkers in the Middle East, that meeting ground of three continents, speaking many languages and in many tongues, fear that their voices, like worn-out records, can only echo in exile. The past two decades have intermittently observed this part of the world caught in turmoil and strife and repeatedly catapulted onto center stage. From Morocco to Caucasia, writers and thinkers have equally felt the seismic waves that have been sweeping through their domains. They witnessed the most massive transfer of wealth in history inundating the oil-rich Muslim nations with Western technology. They watched their peoples, in the majority conservative in religion and politics, resist and resent the Western values and attitudes that arrived with the bank drafts. They stood bewildered before attempts to impose artificially the trappings of a secular, powerful, technologically advanced West on their societies, which were not prepared for it. They looked on helplessly as their human rights were wrenched away from them; many experienced prison torture and sometimes even death. They were bitterly disillusioned in revolution, which had held so much promise for them, and came to realize that only other forms of tyranny were awaiting them. Once more they were faced with gnawing

choices: either to compromise or to send themselves into dreaded exile. The violent conflicts of civil wars, border wars, and armed resistance to occupation, conflicts of the most savage kind, were the muses inspiring them to challenge the status quo with a vision of a future that, however distant and elusive, nonetheless contained some glimmer of hope. Those writers, men and women, a "transnational" caste indeed, have many essential interests in common.

The invited articles in this special issue are perceptive "reflections" (to borrow a cliché, albeit a useful one) on the state of the art in the respective regions and literatures of the Middle East. Each and every study draws nourishment from the best traditions of critical discourse. Almost a decade and a half ago, *World Literature Today* (then called *Books Abroad*) pioneered a special first issue on the subject "The Literatures of the Near East." That first and this second number are in accordance with the editors' commitment to serve as a guide to the best work of unfamiliar authors of the Second and Third Worlds, bringing their masterworks to the consciousness of Western scholarship. The present issue continues in this tradition, and more. A collection of impressively vibrant critiques of Arabic, Armenian, Hebrew, Judeo-Spanish, Soviet Caucasian, Persian, and Turkish literatures and specifically of writers who have made their mark during the past two decades or so is surveyed and analyzed. With this issue, we come perhaps to a new definition of the term *regionalism,* which can no longer be exclusively based upon self-limiting geographical or material considerations. We discover here that what binds those writers from farflung areas is not some vague sense of geography or history, but rather an underlying tender scrutiny of their subject, finely attuned broodings, and finally, their intents and attempts to respond to "the conditions of modernity." Each and every one echoes and refracts the intractable predicaments of their Middle East.

George Steiner, commenting in a recent article on the PEN International Congress held in New York this past January, writes: "One point is evident, in the current part of our century, almost all of the best fiction is more or less explicitly political. This is as true of Günter Grass and of Solzhenitsyn as it is of García Márquez and Nadine Gordimer." One would have wished that he had mentioned a few of the equally essential writers from the Middle East: Yashar Kemal, Fazil Iskander, Vehanoush Tekian, Füruzan, Shamlu, Golshiri, Raymonda Tawil, Mahfūz, Idrīs, Yehoshua, Oz, among many, many others, for the cumulative recitation of their names reads like an incantation to one of the most tortured regions of the world in the latter part of the twentieth century. Steiner further adds, "The haunting parodox is this: historical evidence goes a long way to suggest that great literature flourishes under political social repression." The men and women authors of the contemporary Middle East are indeed writing great literature.

Each of the authors discussed in this collection of essays has had a growing and lasting impact on the cultivated audience of his or her respective country. The fast-changing social and political realities of the region have led to a general retreat to more conservative stances in almost all domains, especially in the realm of esthetics. This has inevitably engendered bitter polemics between states and writers, between writer and writer, and between religious establishment and minority liberals. The traditional function of *littérateurs* to question honestly and seriously the moral values of a civilization at a particular historical moment is being daily and fiercely challenged. In response, our writers fall back on their creative impulses to unveil rampant spiritual bankruptcy and corruption, the demeaning condition of women, the hopelessness of the rural environment, the squalid character of city life.

The mood and intellectual climate for the majority of these writers is one of indecisiveness and confusion. They grope their way through a "blind alley," as the Persian poet Shamlu so aptly notes: "In this crooked blind alley at / the turn of the hill // they feed the fire / with logs of song and poetry." Poets and writers in Iran today, those who think for themselves and are capable of elaborating a criticism of prevalent mystifications, have bravely confronted the political and religious censorship which has not spared their works, and once more many are forced to flee to a West that is paradoxically the only place where they can freely express their anguish. Elsewhere, artistic ferment and sociopolitical conditions still continue to be the dominant factors in Israeli literature. A. B. Yehoshua, Uri Zvi Greenberg, Amos Oz, and Yehuda Amichai, to name but four, have forged a formal esthetic for Hebrew literature, whose thematic and rhythmical origins, combined with their modern-day Israeli experience, may provide authentic models to future generations.

A special feature of this collection is the attention given to women writers of the Middle East. In the last two decades these writers have found an audience prepared and eager to read what they have to say, and so they have produced a literature that is written both by and about, but not exclusively for, an audience of women, stating their point of view and their ideologies. Contemporary women writers in Turkey such as Nazh Eray, Füruzan, and Latife Tekin, while experimenting with new modes of writing, have succeeded in firmly establishing their positions within the male hierarchy.

Their stories resonate with the vast social and political changes of their worlds. They deal more concretely with the loneliness and anguish women are forced to endure. Beings shackled by social conventions and prejudices, they nevertheless struggle in creative ways to gain their unassailable rights. Arab women writers, we are told, for the last hundred years have been striving to have their voices heard. Unsung heroines have valiantly tried to fulfill themselves as individuals and not merely submit to their traditional role as mother and wife. Today they write with passion and compassion, not only of their beleaguered sisters, but of their societies as a whole. Improved education for the middle and working classes has changed the equation in favor of women, making them a formidable resource to contend with. Regressive forces opposed to their enfranchisement are valiantly assailed in their writings.

The growing influence of television and cinema vis-à-vis the fate of fiction has become a factor directly instrumental in giving birth to a more commercial type of literature throughout the area, much to the chagrin of many. These instruments of change do not necessarily bring about improvement in literary taste. However, many distinguished writers throughout the region have contributed their talents to these fields, fully cognizant of the formidable role and influence they can exert through reaching millions of eager viewers instantly.

A shining star in the firmament of Arab letters is the literary journal *Fusul,* which serves as a forum for free discussion and exchange of ideas ranging from the purely ideological to the highly technical in the realm of semiotics and literary studies in general. Its contributors come from throughout the Arab world and occasionally from Europe and the United States. One can detect temptations, rarely resisted by poets and writers, of intellectualizing their oeuvres. In their works one sees structural techniques and stylistic modes of some of the most celebrated Western poets, dramatists, and novelists of this century, from Valéry to Sartre, Beckett, Ionesco, Sarraute, Robbe-Grillet, and myriad others. They grapple with the realization that if science could unquestionably help us understand and define human problems, it would nevertheless be incapable of providing solutions. They are consumed by the fragility of existence and the insoluble enigmas of life. The heroes and heroines of Middle Eastern literatures, like those in certain writings of the existentialists, reach for a wholeness and identity through action, but they almost always fail. The representative hero (if we can at all risk such a generalization), like modern man in Camus's definition, feels himself a stranger in "a universe suddenly emptied of illusion and light."

Another dominant aspect of these literatures is a stubborn determination to confront the irrationality of life. Interestingly, this sometimes takes the guise of flights from reality and, in extreme cases, total withdrawal into the self and narcissistic obsessions. In the wake of 1967, Arab writers such as Kharrat, Idrīs, Al-Ghitani, Hanan al-Shaikh, Sun'allah Ibrāhīm, Muhammad Barrada, Emile Habibi, Majid Toubya, and Alifa Rifaat, to mention only a few, embarked on flights of fantasy in desperate attempts at coping with the paradoxes of life and the incongruities of their political realities. It was their creative way of explaining away, primarily to themselves, the external chaos that engulfed them. They have also succeeded in bringing Arabic prose to new heights, for in the process a dry, nervous, electric style denuded of embellishments was developed. The documentary and investigative style that some of them adopted contrasts with the phantasmagoric worlds they conjure up. Critics have equally noted the significant linguistic changes that took root in Turkish prose, most notably the elimination of words of foreign origin and the coining of new ones exploiting the vast resources of the inflectional feature of the language.

Be it Judeo-Spanish, Armenian literature of the diaspora, literature written in Soviet Caucasia, or Palestinian literature, these beleaguered voices still speak of deep pride in ancestral beginnings. Dispersed and fragmented by history, they stand as the custodians of their national identities and seek cohesion and continuity through their literary legacies. In the vanguard of their literatures, Middle Eastern writers alternate both tragic and comic touches, sustaining an enticing tale of the irony and humor of life and the inescapable absurdity of its events.

Mona N. Mikhail, Spring 1986

Ed. Note: This special issue was conceived and organized by *WLT* Associate Editor William Riggan. The articles are grouped alphabetically by language—Arabic, Armenian, Hebrew, Judeo-Spanish, Persian, Russian, Turkish—and within sections proceed from general surveys to specific analyses (as in Arabic) or in chronological sequence (as in Persian). Commissioned essays on Soviet Armenian literature and on recent Turkish poetry unfortunately did not materialize to complete the symposium's planned coverage.

The Contemporary Arabic Novel in Perspective

The contemporary Arabic novel is the product of a complex interaction among constraints that originate in three major realms. These realms can be variably defined in terms of the novelistic traditions to which the

Arabic novel relates, the artistic standards it sets out to meet, or the geographic distribution of the reading public it seeks to address. Each one of these realms has a local, a pan-Arab, and an international dimension. In general, the Arabic novel seems to have effected a division of labor to deal with the different and not infrequently conflicting demands and pressures emanating from these different realms. This division invests the novel's thematic concerns with local interests, its language with pan-Arab significance and appeal, and its narrative technique and artistic form with universal or international affinities.

With rare exceptions the themes, issues, and characters the novel dramatizes readily give away the Arab writer's country of origin. Two probable causes may account for this phenomenon: on one hand there is the inescapable influence of the novelist's personal experience on his or her imaginative works;[1] on the other—and this seems to be a congenital characteristic of the Arabic novel—the act of writing fiction in Arabic is never undertaken for its own sake, nor is it ever entirely divorced from politics. In fact, the matter can, and perhaps should, be stated more categorically: the intimate and direct relation Arabic fiction has always maintained with Arab politics invariably results in the subordination of the literary and esthetic concerns of the novel to political and discursive ones.[2] The reasons for this historical development are many and varied and need not detain us here; the fact itself, however, deserves recognition, because as a rule, the novel's universal significance relates inversely to its involvement in current events.

Two intrinsic safeguards have proven effective so far in preventing local concerns from confining the Arabic novel to irrelevant parochialism. First, as aspects of Arab culture, both Arabic fiction and modern Arabic literature in general have contributed to and benefited from this culture's assertion of its vital oneness and viable unity in the face of the insidious political divisions plaguing the Arab world. Certainly to date no major Arab poet, short-story writer, or novelist has risen to prominence on the basis of local acclaim alone. Second, the universal adoption of a functionally updated version of classical Arabic as the primary medium of expression in the Arabic novel puts within the novelist's linguistic reach the entire range of the Arab and Islamic cultural heritage and, by so doing, enhances the novel's appeal to the wider reading public of the Arab world at large. (I might note parenthetically here that in Arabic drama, for precisely the opposite thematic and linguistic reasons, the local traditions have developed more autonomously of each other than has the novel in the various Arab countries.)

Beyond the local and regional Arab horizons the contemporary Arabic novel displays acute awareness of developments in the novel worldwide. This awareness takes many forms and manifests itself in many ways. One such manifestation is the novel's increasingly more frequent engaging of other literary and historical works through direct formal reference or implicit allusion. The utilization of narrative techniques and styles that tend to problematicize the very act of fiction writing is yet another such manifestation.

One more general point deserves bearing in mind when considering the contemporary Arabic novel: namely, the relatively short history of the genre in Arabic. In its recognizable Western form, the debut of the Arabic novel dates no farther back than the second decade of this century. Furthermore, artistically sound and esthetically defensible species in the genre begin to appear only in the forties. At the risk of slightly oversimplifying a rather complex historical process, it may be possible to switch to a more appropriate literary yardstick and date this phase of maturity from the appearance of Arabic novels written in the mode of social realism. The tremendous progress the Arabic novel has made since then seems utterly incommensurate with the short time within which it has occurred. To dramatize the relevance of this fact of history, it may suffice to note that practically all the phases in the development of the mature Arabic novel fall within the creative career of a single Arab novelist: Najīb Mahfūz of Egypt.

With this brief and necessarily general overview in mind, let me turn to consider a sample of contemporary Arabic novels to show how the various constraints mentioned above figure in specific works. The four novels I have chosen for this purpose come from four different Arab countries and thus reflect fairly accurately, I believe, some major concerns of the contemporary Arabic novel, though they by no means exhaust its immense diversity. These novels are *Allāz, al-'Ishq wa-al-Mawt fī al-Zaman al-Harāshī* (Allaz: Love and Death in Terrible Times; 1982) by the Algerian writer Al-Tāhir Wattār, *Mudun al-Milh: Al-Tīh* (Cities of Salt: The Wilderness; 1984) by the Saudi-born writer 'Abd al-Rahmān Munīf, *Al-Rabī' wa-al-Kharīf* (Spring and Autumn; 1984) by the Syrian writer Hannā Mīna, and *Beirut Beirut* (1984) by the Egyptian writer Sun'allah Ibrāhīm.

Both the title and the front cover of Al-Tāhir Wattār's most recent novel announce it as a sequel to his earlier novel *Allāz* (1974). Whereas the events of the earlier novel occur in the fifties during the war of independence, however, the action of the present novel takes place in the seventies in independent Algeria. The major thematic concern of both volumes remains the same: namely, the ideological direction of the Algerian Revolution.

In the preface to book 1 Wattār sketches the chronology of the genesis of his novel, and his views on the matter warrant summarizing here because they bear on other Arab novelists as well. Wattār states that he began thinking about the novel in 1958, at the time of the formation of the first temporary government of the Algerian Republic, but actually started writing it in 1965, after the internal conflicts within the ranks of the FLN (Front de Libération Algérienne) had come into the open. He goes on to note that during the seven years it took to finish the novel (1965–72) he was gripped by feelings of guilt for spending his time looking backward and exposing the problems of the past instead of participating in the gigantic effort being spent to transform Algerian society in the present. At the end of this short but impassioned preface, Wattār promises the reader that he will spend an equal number of years in the future writing a novel that will celebrate the glorious achievements of the Algerian Revolution in agriculture, industry, education, and, above all, self-reliance, social justice, and solidarity with the peoples of the world struggling for freedom, peace, and justice. Book 2 of *Allāz* is presumably that promised novel, but as we shall see, the news it brings is hardly good news.

How typical this intimate involvement of Arab writers in current politics is can be gathered from the ebbs and flows in the creative career of the paragon of the Arabic novel, Najīb Mahfūz. From the onset of the Egyptian Revolution in 1952 until 1957 Mahfūz abstained entirely from writing fiction. The reason for this, he later explained, was his feeling that the revolution, whose declared objective was to cure the economic, social, political, and moral ills of Egyptian society, had rendered superfluous the need to draw attention to these ills in his fiction.[3] It was not until 1957, when he had become disenchanted with the revolution, that he resumed writing fiction. The haunted symbolic fiction he wrote then and throughout the sixties, however, was drastically different not only in content but also in form and style from his earlier fiction of social realism. The catastrophic Arab defeat in the 1967 war with Israel caused a similar interruption in Mahfūz's novelistic output. His response to the incredible magnitude of the defeat was a spate of surrealistic and hallucinatory short stories. When he finally returned to the novel proper in 1974, the result was perhaps the most directly political novel he ever wrote: *Al-Karnak*.[4] (Under the impact of the same momentous event and for the identical purpose of bringing fiction closer to reality, the literary technique and style of the Palestinian writer Ghassān

Kanafānī underwent a similar change during the same period.)[5]

To return to the two volumes of *Allāz,* I would first note that the events of book 1 revolve around two central characters: Zaydān and his son Allāz, who was born out of wedlock. The plot, however, is not about the traditional theme of fathers and sons. In fact, the two meet here only briefly at the beginning and the end of the novel. For most of the span of the action they remain separated, and the narrative constantly shifts back and forth between the two loci they occupy: the hideout of the guerrilla fighters in the mountains, and the French garrison in the adjacent town, where Allāz operates clandestinely. Zaydān, nicknamed The Red, is an outstanding member of the Algerian Communist Party who has spent most of his adult life either underground fighting the foreign occupation of his country or traveling extensively in communist countries to study Marxist strategies of national and social liberation. As the novel opens, we find him commanding a guerrilla cell in the mountains and tirelessly striving to educate his subordinates in Marxism through the good example of his brave, democratic leadership.

Meanwhile in town Allāz emerges at the age of twenty-three as a wild, indomitable, and, most important, enigmatic character. Not only the identity of his father is shrouded in mystery, but also his intimate relation with the homosexual French commander of the garrison, and especially his true identity as an FLN plant.

The two lines of action finally converge when Allāz's cover is blown and he flees in the nick of time to join his father's cell in the mountains. The happy reunion between father and son does not last long, however. Soon after Allāz's arrival he is ordered to witness the execution of his father at the hands of a higher-ranking Muslim sheikh in the ranks of the FLN. Four other French and Spanish communist volunteers also die with Zaydān when, like him, they refuse to disavow communism and, in addition, convert to Islam. Book 1 thus ends with the onset of the purge of communists from the ranks of the Algerian Revolution.

As can be guessed from the foregoing brief summary of the plot, *Allāz* is essentially an action novel written in the realistic mode and informed by an undisguised political commitment. The progression of the narrative remains remarkably clear in spite of the frequent shuttling back and forth between the two major loci, the different layers of consciousness, and the various temporal frames. The present comes into view as it unfolds in action and dialogue, the past is recalled through limited and well-demarcated flashbacks, and the working of the

"unconscious" manifests itself in the form of fully articulated but unvoiced speech—all, it may be added, in modern literary Arabic.

From an artistic point of view, Waṭṭār's novel suffers from a certain degree of schematization in the choice of its characters as well as in its account of their psychological motivation. To note just two examples of this weakness, I would mention the French commander of the garrison and Ba'ṭūsh, the Algerian lackey turned hero. Though central to both the plausibility of the plot and the political and cultural symmetry which informs the novel, the character of the French commander remains hopelessly one-dimensional. Neither the faint attempt to provide an existentialist underpinning to his sadomasochistic perversity nor the positive example of the French communist volunteers in the service of the revolution really succeeds in breaking the stereotypical mold in which the French occupier is cast. The diametrically inverse treatment of Ba'ṭūsh clearly shows that the novel's abiding interest is not with the departing French but with the Algerians staying behind. Originally a degenerate and selfish brute who would refrain from no act, however abominable, to advance his career in the service of the French, Ba'ṭūsh at one point becomes so outraged by the personal perversity of the commander that he sets the entire garrison on fire and flees to the mountain, where he is welcomed as hero. From his survival and rise to high office in book 2, one gathers that his sudden and largely unmeditated change of heart has a lasting effect. Nowhere, however, do we find a plausible explanation of this drastic and highly improbable metamorphosis.

In contrast, the characters of Zaydān and Allāz are drawn with exquisite care and subtlety. Zaydān in particular emerges as one of the most fully and satisfactorily developed communist characters in all Arabic fiction. His credibility as a fictional entity rests on his realized individuality and psychological depth; his considerable value as a spokesman for an ideology, on the other hand, derives from his lucid analysis of the class structure of Algerian society and the revolution, the predicament of the left in the Arab and Islamic world, and the daunting difficulties associated with the attempt to transform the struggle for national independence into a social revolution. This last quest has been the rock on which most national liberation movements in the Third World founder. The physical liquidation of Zaydān and his comrades at the end of book 1 indicates with oppressive clarity the general drift of the Algerian Revolution toward that rock. Against the inexorable force of this actuality the novel poses Zaydān's integrity, his sound analysis, and the abstract notion that truth and justice will ultimately prevail. This notion is captured in the linguistic formula which serves as Allāz's pass-word while underground and which recurs in the novel like a musical refrain: "Nothing remains in the valley but its stones."

The events composing the plot of book 2 of *Allāz* are even more particularly Algerian than those of book 1. The novel's meager plot dramatizes a tense encounter between a group of progressive university students, mostly women, who volunteer their time to work in agricultural projects and cooperatives in support of the Algerian agrarian reform of the early seventies, and a group of reactionary students, political functionaries, and opportunists opposed to it. Since the time of the novel's writing is contemporaneous with the internal time of the novel's action, and since the issue with which the work deals was an urgently pressing one during that period, the reader cannot fail to detect the primary intention behind the act of writing: namely, to influence the actual course of events.

Equally transparent are the strategies deployed to balance this localizing thematic thrust of the plot. Thus, for example, the amorous correspondence one of the characters maintains with a pen-friend in India adds a geographic dimension to the local setting, and from this addition a host of linguistic, religious, cultural, and literary consequences flow. On the linguistic level, the inclusion of Hindi words in the Arabic text imparts a cosmopolitan ring to the novel's language. More substantially, the presence of the girl in a religiously and culturally pluralistic society inevitably invites a comparison between Islam and the other Eastern religions with which the girl is familiar. This comparison acquires added poignancy from the fact that whereas these tolerant religions prove irresistible to the Muslim girl of India, Islam fares even worse at home at the hands of reactionary Algerians who cynically abuse it for opportunistic political ends. It falls to the positive characters of the novel to salvage what remains of the spirit of Islam from the fictional Hizb Allah (Party of God) in the novel, years before actual political parties bearing this same name came into being in the Arab world. (The phrase itself, of course, originates in the Koran—e.g., 5:56 and 58:22, where it has a general meaning rather than a specific referent.)

Frequent allusion to other works of literature serves a similarly universalizing function here. These allusions range from the mention of writers and poets such as Kātib Yāsīn, Pablo Neruda, and Shakespeare, to a more substantive engagement of texts such as the memoirs of the Algerian patriot Al-Aurasī, André Malraux's novel *Man's Fate,* and especially the first volume of *Allāz.* Aspects of these works which shed light on the novel's events are brought up either in the form of inte-rior monologues going through the mind of the heroine Jamīla, or as simulated dialogues between her and a fictionalized Al-Tāhir Wattār. Utilizing the Indian connection, the author is cast in the role of Brahma and is thoroughly quizzed about all sorts of matters ranging from the meaning of *Allāz* and the significance of its characters to the nature of truth in fiction and the role of the intellectual in modern history.

This type of self-conscious novel has of course been familiar in Western literature at least since *Don Quixote.* As this volume of *Allāz* and other recent novels, especially those of the Egyptian writer Muhammad Yūsuf al-Qaʾīd, show, the type seems finally to be gaining a foothold in Arabic fiction as well.

Perhaps the most effective antidote to the localizing drift in the novel, however, is the mythopoeic transformation of Allāz. Here Allāz's past, including his very birth, is shrouded in complete mystery and he is invested with mystical powers and revered by all as a saint. Though poor and homeless, he nevertheless is generously provided for and appears immune to change and the forces of nature as he roams the streets totally oblivious to the reality around him. His talismanic phrase "Nothing remains in the valley except its own stones" acquires an incantatory force here and readily evokes the events and atmosphere of the earlier novel. Each time it recurs it implicitly condemns the aberrant present, for, we are reminded, its original encoded meaning is that nothing in the end prevails except truth and justice. Since neither is much in evidence during these terrible times, the present may not be the legitimate offspring of the revolutionary past. In fact, this interpretation seems implicit in the desire expressed by women and tacitly approved by men that Allāz should father as many children through as many women as he can. Allāz thus represents a living and lasting testimony to the revolutionary past and the vital force that lies dormant in the Algerian people. Allāz's momentary awakenings signify the return of the revolutionary spirit to the novel; his permanent reawakening, we are meant to understand, will also usher in the alternative to the present terrible time.

■ ■ ■

Although there is a region in northern Saudi Arabia called Qaryat al-Milh (Villages of Salt) which has primarily archeological significance, the title of Munīf's intended fictional trilogy, "Mundun al-Milh," more appropriately invokes the proverbially wicked cities of Sodom and Gomorrah. More specifically, the title suggests the injustice associated with the emergence of the modern cities of salt in the desert. The rest of the novel is devoted to describing in the minute detail of epic plenitude the suffering of generations of indigenous Bedouins and villagers as they are forcibly removed from their historical habitat to make room for "diabolic" Americans and "fiendish" machines that ravage the landscape in search of oil. As the carnivorous machines devour one sacrificial victim after another, resistance to the American-Saudi encroachment on the local landscape assumes a mythic character. Much like his Algerian counterpart Allāz, the Bedouin patriarch Mut'ib al-Hadhdhāl undergoes a mythopoeic transformation in *Al-Tīh,* and when, long after his death, both the indigenous population and the Saudi rulers still see his hand in every natural disaster that befalls the Americans and disrupts work in the oil fields, we realize that the myth of a political saint has taken firm hold in the land. However, since the present volume stops at the threshold of the cataclysmic expansion in the oil industry that sets in motion the irreversible transformation of the desert in the late thirties, it remains to be seen how this carefully nourished mythic past is brought to bear on the political and social struggles in the Gulf oil kingdoms when the cities of salt are no longer isolated exploration spots in the desert but bustling metropolitan centers like Riyadh, Dammam, and Kuwait. This, no doubt, will be the formidable political and literary challenge for the subsequent volumes of Munīf's promising trilogy.

In both *Allāz* and *Al-Tīh,* as indeed in many other Arabic novels, the presence of foreigners in the Arab landscape often imparts a broadening intercultural dimension to the local setting and plot. Hannā Mīna's "Spring and Autumn" follows an older and immeasurably richer tradition of Arabic novels that send their protagonists to foreign lands and enact the cultural encounter there, but instead of Paris or London, the two traditional loci for such encounters in Arabic fiction, Mīna sends the hero of his novel to two communist capitals: Peking and Budapest. This change of destination reflects an ideological and cultural preference for socialism over the capitalistic (Western) context in relation to which Arabic fiction has traditionally sought to define Arab national identity in modern times. In fact, Mīna's novel critically engages that tradition by reworking some familiar stock themes, motifs, and narrative situations. Thus, for example, the reference to seasons in the title of the novel readily and teasingly echoes the title of *Season of Migration to the North* by the Sudanese writer al-Tayyib Sālih. By far the greatest single work in that tradition, Sālih's novel treats in strikingly melodramatic fashion the fatal impact of the cultural conflict between East and West (and North and South) on the troubled psyche of Mustafā Sa'īd, a Sudanese intellectual impostor whose sexual machinations claim the lives of a number of English women in London before he

himself falls victim to his own twisted life and perishes mysteriously in the Nile.

Though no less virile or extroverted than Mustafā Sa'īd, Karam, the Syrian protagonist of Mīna's novel, is considerably less flamboyant and complex than his Sudanese counterpart. A professor of Arabic by profession, Karam is also a novelist and a political exile from his native Syria. After spending five culturally rich but socially impoverished years in China in the early sixties, he arrives in Budapest shortly before the outbreak of the 1967 Arab-Israeli war. Here he experiences firsthand the liberating effects of socialism on all aspects of the individual's life, especially interpersonal relations, where sex is demystified and is predicated solely on the existence of a community of feeling between the partners. Karam quickly and joyfully learns to give and take in this and all other areas of human relations in his hospitable land of exile. The contrast between Karam's positive experience in socialist Hungary and Mustafā's tragic entrapment in capitalistic England are quite transparent throughout Mīna's unabashedly ideological novel. Nowhere is this contrast sharper, however, than in the ultimate fate of the two protagonists after their return to their respective countries. Haunted by his traumatic experience in the West, Mustafā leads a fugitive life for a short time in a secluded Sudanese village and then dies mysteriously in the Nile. Karam's fortifying experience enables him to terminate his exile and take a personal risk by returning to his homeland to help chart its course into a brighter future. His resolve remains intact when he is picked up and driven away for interrogation by the Syrian police upon arrival at Damascus airport.

The implied thematic contrast with *Season of Migration to the North* is only one of several effective measures Mīna takes to enhance his novel's literary and esthetic appeal and check the obtrusiveness of its ideological charge. The twists of the intricate triangular relations involving the middle-aged Karam, the young and infatuated Berushka, and the older and more mature cabaret artist Erijka enliven the plot and further dilute the ideological import. A similar effect accrues from the frequent allusions to other literary and cultural works such as the poetry of Badr Shākir al-Sayyāb of Iraq and Nazim Hikmet of Turkey (who is said to have lived, during his exile in Hungary, in the same house Karam now occupies), the music of the Greek composer Mikis Theodorakis, the *Arabian Nights,* and Chinese culture. Perhaps the most intriguing technical feature of the novel, however, is the casting of Karam in the role of a leftist Syrian novelist in exile writing a novel about the experience of exile, which is, of course, the novel we are reading. The discussion of the novel within a novel as well as the airing of germane questions involved in the transmuting of lived experience and historical facts into artistic creation imparts a significant literary quality to the novel.

The same technical ploy of embedding one text within another is what holds together Sun'allah Ibrāhīm's latest novel, *Beirut Beirut*. Whether the technique is pliable enough to mold into an artistic unity materials presumably from different media such as film and fiction or from different genres like the documentary and the novel is more difficult to ascertain, but as the following brief summary of the novel's plot will show, this is precisely what *Beirut Beirut* attempts to do.

An Egyptian writer travels to Beirut to inquire about the fate of the manuscript of a novel he had submitted for publication there because Egyptian censorship under Sādāt made its publication in Egypt impossible. Upon arriving in Beirut late in 1980, he learns that the publishing house to which he had sent the manuscript has recently been destroyed by a bomb. He stays on in Beirut to look for a new publisher while living with an Egyptian boyhood friend who has become a bureau chief for a major Egyptian newspaper in the city. In the meantime he accepts a temporary job as editor of a documentary film made by a leftist group on the 1975–76 civil war in Lebanon. His specific task is to transcribe in narrative the visual content of the film. While doing this, he becomes involved in casual affairs with two Lebanese women. The novel before us is the composite account of events that occur on both planes.

I use the word *composite* advisedly to describe the two narrative thrusts, which frequently intersect but never completely merge in the novel. No thematic, structural, or symbolic correspondence, let alone causal relation, is perceptible between these two sets of events. Far greater in both volume and significance, the documentary part stands in no obvious need of the feeble fictional plot contrived presumably to support it. Still more paradoxically, perhaps, it is the imaginative ordering of the documentary material that reveals both Ibrāhīm's remarkable craftsmanship and the inherent capacity of history to turn into a moving story at the touch of the artist. To date, no account of the Lebanese civil war in any discipline has captured with such accuracy and pathos the various factors, dimensions, and ramifications of this conflict as has the unpretentious and seemingly artless documentary collage contained in *Beirut Beirut*. Methodically and fearlessly, Ibrāhīm exposes the responsibility of the various states and groups in the region and the world whose interests and schemes nourish the ongoing civil strife in Lebanon.

This political frankness, plus the explicit sexual scenes in which the fictitious writer within the novel is involved, occasions an interesting twist in the relationship of the actual novel we are reading to the one the fictitious writer is supposed to have written, for these same two features are attributed to the fictitious novel and are also said to have obstructed its publication and distribution in the Arab countries. Whereas the novel before us was actually published in Egypt, the fate of the fictitious one remains undecided. An enterprising Lebanese publisher suggests to the fictitious writer a politically insane but commercially sound idea: to publish the novel in Switzerland but market it in Israel, where it can be read by the 1.2 million Arabs under Israeli control! The writer walks away from this suggestion in shocked disbelief.

It may be worthwhile to ponder briefly the cause of the failure to connect more meaningfully the two narrative threads, which, incidentally, are set apart in the text by the use of different-size print. This failure is all the more striking because the ingenious use of the illusion of mixed media synchronizes the time schemes of the two sets of events and is thus singularly conducive to integrating them. One plausible explanation may be found in the simple fact that Ibrāhīm, an Egyptian, is not sufficiently intimate with the Lebanese social scene to fashion a convincingly realistic representation of it in fiction. Hence also, it seems, the author's instructive recourse to the documentary as a politically and ideologically acceptable expression of identification with the cause of the Lebanese left in lieu of the empathy which experience alone imparts to the writer and he, in turn, imparts to his imaginative creation.

One readily detects here a negative demonstration of the working of the constraints that shape the contemporary Arabic novel postulated at the beginning of this discussion. The felt need to venture beyond indigenous concerns into pan-Arab and, ultimately, universal ones appears severely circumscribed by the Arab writer's lived experience and his commitment to local political and social causes. A twofold challenge thus confronts the contemporary Arabic novel: a political imperative dictating involvement in current indigenous affairs, and an artistic imperative advising esthetic detachment and greater attention to literary form and technique.

Muhammad Siddiq, Spring 1986

[1] In answer to the question of why the Arab-Israeli conflict has figured so marginally in his fiction, Najīb Mahfūz singled out the lack of direct experience of the Palestine tragedy as the cause. Direct treatment of this conflict, he went on to say, "is possible only to a writer such as Ghassān Kanafānī, who has been burned by the tragedy or has experienced it from close quarters." See Ahmad Muhammad 'Atiyya, *Ma' Najīb Mahfūz* (With Najīb Mahfūz), Beirut, Dār al-Jīl, 1977, p. 14.

2   Contributors to previous issues of *Books Abroad / World Literature Today* have in one way or another noted this pervasive influence of politics on modern Arabic literature. See, for example, E. G. Von Grunebaum, "Contemporary Literature in the Middle East: An Overview," *BA* 46:2 (Spring 1972), pp. 244–47; Salih J. Altoma, "Postwar Iraqi Literature: Agonies of Rebirth," ibid., pp. 211–17; Mona Mikhail, "*Iltizam*: Commitment and Arabic Poetry," *WLT* 53:4 (Autumn 1979), pp. 595–600.

3   Fu'ād Duwwāra, *'Asharat 'Udabā' Yatahaddathūn* (Ten Writers Speak), Cairo, Dār al-Hilāl, 1965, pp. 283–84.

4   Mahfūz readily recognizes the conflict between the political and artistic imperatives but goes on to defend the political nature of *Al-Karnak* as his direct contribution to the debate about the future of his country during a severe national crisis. During such a crisis, Mahfūz says, "What the homeland needs is fast-shooting agitprop art, to accompany the battle, not fine art." See Najīb Mahfūz, *Atahaddath Ilaykum*, Beirut, Dār al-'Awada, 1977, p. 22. The reference to *Al-Karnak* is on page 111.

5   See Muhammad Siddiq, *Man Is a Cause: Political Consciousness and the Fiction of Ghassān Kanafānī*, Seattle, University of Washington Press, 1984.

Modernism and Metaphor in Contemporary Arabic Poetry

But metaphorical language is the most important. The right use of metaphors is a sign of inborn talent and cannot be learned from anyone else.

▓ ARISTOTLE, *POETICS*

In his Short Essay for the "metaphor" (*isti'ara*, literally "borrowing") entry in the *Encyclopedia of Arabic Literature*, W. P. Heinrichs aptly laments the remarkable dearth of studies on the nature and function of metaphor in Arabic poetry: "A history of metaphor and its function in Arabic poetry (or literature in general) has not been yet written, and studies of metaphor in circumscribed corpora of texts, such as the *oeuvre* of a particular poet, are few and far between." Even in S. Moreh's *Modern Arabic Poetry 1800–1970: The Development of Its Forms and Themes under the Influence of Western Literature* (1976), a work that has been considered crucial in delineating the main characteristics of modern Arabic poetry, there is a jarring absence of discussion of the modernistic uses of metaphor. Yet Aristotle, whose *Poetics* and *Rhetoric* were translated into Arabic around the ninth century and became profoundly catalytic in the formative period of Arabic literary criticism, postulates the centrality of metaphor in the very act of the literary creation. Reverently labeled as "the First Teacher," Aristotle put forth a concept of metaphor that not only made many Arab critics and poets conscious of metaphor as the essence of great literature but also inspired them to experiment with it. Hence the nature

of literary *tajdid* (innovation) throughout Arabic literary tradition cannot be fully appreciated without a careful examination of the historical evolution of metaphor. In this paper, I will first highlight the transforming power of metaphor in Arabic poetic tradition, then examine its nature and function in belletristic modernism, focusing on the poetry of three contemporary Arab poets, each of whom represents distinct aspects of modernism. These are the Iraqi Badr Shakīr al-Sayyab (1926–64), the Egyptian Muhammad 'Afifi Matar (b. 1935), and the Palestinian Mahmūd Darwīsh (b. 1941).

As a literary term, *metaphor,* though it is epistemologically saturated with cultural significations, does mean and function in Arabic as it does in English and other Western literatures. A survey of literary studies of metaphor indicates that the concept is generally defined, even in its mushiness and unruliness, in similar terms in Arabic and in English literary criticism. Twentieth-century studies of languages have aided literary critics in further studies of metaphor. One of the revolutionary landmarks in the study of metaphor is I. A. Richard's classic, *The Philosophy of Rhetoric* (1939), in which he convincingly expands the traditional function of metaphor from merely creating verbal pictures to creating new meanings. His crucial idea is that metaphor "is the omni-present principle" of all language, for "the metaphors we are avoiding steer our thought as much as those we accept" (92). In other words, metaphor, Richards argues, makes language possible. Building on Richards's theory, Owen Barfield, Philip Wheelwright, and Winfred Nowottny, among others, recognize the omnipresence of metaphor not only in poetry but even in everyday language. Recent investigations of metaphor, such as Paul de Man's *Aesthetic Ideology* (1996) and Paul Ricoeur's *Rule of Metaphor* (1973), have identified the function of metaphor as not merely a figure of speech that helps expand the language by fusing a word with another one in order to produce a Hegelian synthesis, but as the essence of all figurativeness that makes even our expanding thought possible.

▪ METAPHOR AND INNOVATION IN CLASSICAL ARABIC POETRY

Before I discuss the modernistic manifestations of metaphor in selected poems, I think it is imperative to outline the evolution of metaphor in classical and *muhdath* ("new poetry," after the early Islamic period from around the ninth century) Arabic poetry. Arab scholars were exposed to Aristotelian definitions of literary terms much earlier than were European scholars. Hence, metaphor has a longer and more complicated history in Arabic literature. Yet the abovementioned recent Western studies of language and metaphor have had a profound impact on modern Arabic literary criticism. Literary historians usually attribute the emergence of Arabic literary criticism and literary theory to two historical factors: 1) the challenges of the Qur'an and the subsequent active Qur'anic exegesis that primarily focused on the hermeneutic significance of the literal and the figurative or tropical (*majaz*), on the one hand, and on the location of meaning and truth in the interaction between the literal and the figurative, on the other; and 2) the translation of the Greek works, especially the philosophical works of Aristotle and Plato around the second century of Hijra (approximately the ninth century A.D.). Around this time major critical theories and schools began to become established, with Umayyad philologist al-Asma'ī (d. 213/828) founding his poetic standards for good poetry. Later, Ibn Sallam al-Jumahī (139–232/ 756–846) reflected his critical evaluation of poetry in his *Tabaqāt Fūhūl al-Shu'ara'* (Classes of Great Poets). Al-Jahiz (b. 160/776) postulated his theory of style and was the first to define metaphor. According to him, metaphor is the borrowing of one aspect of a word and attributing it to another (Azzam, 36). He did not distinguish between metaphor and other figures of speech as we know them now, assuming, probably following Aristotle, that metaphor is the quintessential trope or figure of speech, in that all figures of speech are essentially metaphorical.

Frequently the particular use of metaphor seems to have defined the nature of *tajdid* (innovation) and of the individual talent of a poet; that is, the more imaginative the poet, the more sophisticated his or her metaphor. Significantly, the literary battles between the traditionalists and the innovators in Arabic poetry as they are reflected in the history of literary criticism from early medieval times to the present were in most cases fought over the nature of metaphor and figures of speech (*majaz*). The major innovators throughout Arabic literary history were usually initially attacked because of the nature and function of their metaphor. In other words, change in metaphor has been considered change in the very nature of poetics and of meaning in general. In *Jahiliyyah* (pre-Islamic) poetry, simile rules supreme in the poetic landscape, though we find occasional uses of metaphor that do not go beyond conceptual comparison, as in the famous elegy by the *mukhadram* ("a poet who lived in Jahiliyyah and Islam") Abu Dhu'ayb al-Hudhalī on the death of his sons: "I have stayed behind after they [have gone], with a life that is full of misfortune. I see myself trying to follow them and overtake them. / [How] eager I was to protect them; but when Fate advances it cannot be warded off. / When Fate fixes its claws [into its prey], you find every charm [against it] to be of no avail" (ll. 7–9; Jones, vol. 2, p. 259). A

Mahmūd Darwīsh (*Banipal Magazine*)

clear use of implied metaphor occurs in line 9, in which Fate, an abstraction, is given the claws of a wild animal. Yet in its sixty-two lines, the poem seems to reach its peak of power when it uses metaphor as in line 9.

In the *Mu'allaqa* (Ode) of Imru' al-Qays (sixth century), which is traditionally considered the jewel of *Jahiliyyah* poetry, one finds in its eighty-two lines twenty-four uses of simile and only six metaphors. These six are primarily one-line metaphors, and in most cases are genitive:

When they stood up, the scent of *musk* wafted from them like breath of the east wind bearing the fragrance of cloves (l. 8)

I said to her, "Ride on, but slacken the reins of [your camel].

Do not put me at a distance from *the fruit* that can be *plucked* time and time again from you (l. 15)

And if there is some trait of mine that has vexed you, draw my *garments* from yours [and] they will slip away (l. 20)

Your eyes have shed their tears only that you may smite with *the two arrows* of you[r eyes that strike] into the fragments of a slaughtered heart (l. 22)

When either of us gets something, it slips away from him.

Whoever tills your *tilth* or mine will find lean pickings (l. 52)

From time to time I used to journey in the morning, whilst the birds were still in their nests, on a well-built short-haired [horse], *able to rein in* wild game (l.53)

(Jones, vol. 2, pp. 239–43; italics added)

Obviously, to contemporary readers these are very simple and vapid metaphors, and the translation has reduced their poetic power by failing to reflect either their cultural connotations or their linguistic delight. Language, especially in poetry, not only becomes more cultural; it even becomes more tactile, providing special pleasures for the mouth and the ear. The italicized words in the above lines are metaphors in the Arabic original, though in line 8 the translation reduces the metaphor to a simile by using "like." And in line 53, a classical example of metaphor is totally lost in the translation. In the Arabic text, the line describes the lean, fast horse as a chain or lock of wild animals. It is interesting to note that most of the metaphors in this *mu'allaqa* are simple and are constructed in one single line or phrase. Yet, by the standard of pre-Islamic and early Islamic poetry, they were probably as striking as Homer's similes.

The historical evolution of figures of speech in Arabic poetry reveals that metaphor is a creation of a sophisticated imagination and bold semantic and syntactic adventures. When the Qur'an was introduced, it caused a linguistic and figurative revolution so stunning to the Arab poets and orators that they believed it was a divine or Satanic work (Azzam, 67–68), considering it impossible for humans to compose anything even remotely similar. Thus, the Qur'an, perceived as a challenge and/or a miracle, triggered literary activism that inaugurated the idea of exegesis, which in turn gave birth to literary criticism. A prominent aspect of the powerful eloquence of the Qur'an is no doubt its figurative language. Major Qur'anic exegetes painstakingly tried to account for the miraculous power in its divinity, claiming, for example, that it is the very word of God or that God naturally would not endow a human with the ability to produce a text similar in its spiritual power to the Qur'an, thus making His Book inimitable.

Even by the poetic standard of medieval Arabic poetry, pre-Islamic metaphor was considered dead metaphor, and poets sought fresh ways to respond to a relatively more complex life. Al-Mutanabbi (c. 303–54/c. 915–65), considered the most prominent Arab poet of all times, became the epicenter of one of the longest and fiercest literary debates in history, primarily because of his radical innovations in metaphor. To a lesser extent, other major poets such as Abu Nuwas (c. 140-c. 198/c. 755-c. 813), Abu Tammam (c. 189-c. 232/c. 805–45), and Bashshar Ibn Burd (c. 95-c. 167/c. 714–84), who are called *muhdathun* or "modernist poets" in the early Abbasid period, faced harsh criticism from both traditional critics and poets. In all of these cases the change in metaphor was the evidence of their poetic sin, so to speak (Heinrichs, 1984, 185–89; Stetkevych 8–19; 'Abbas, 167–68).

During the early Abbasid period, the new urban life, the active translation movement, and the stimulating encounter with more advanced civilizations of Persia, Greece, and Rome inspired Arab poets to modernize their poetic styles and themes. The emergence of new poetry called *muhdath* ("novel" or "modern") and its practitioners, *muhdathun* ("creators of novel poetry"), necessitated the invention of new critical discourse and critical terminology. The battle between the innovators and the traditionalists gave birth to what is now called Arabic literary criticism when Ibn al-Mu'tazz (d. 296/908) published his *Kitab al-Badi'* (The Book of the Original Style). Ibn al-Mu'tazz defines *al-Badi'* by five major characteristics and considers the new use of metaphor as the first criterion in the production of the new poetry (Heinrichs, "Badi'," 122). Thus, metaphor and its particular uses seem to have always been at the center of any innovation in literature. Let us examine some of the convoluted metaphors in al-Mutanabbi's poetry that outraged many critics during medieval times. In one famous poem, he describes his encounter with several social problems: "The age has hurled rough times at me my heart is numb from its missiles / And neatly where the arrows struck me the point of one struck the other" (al-Mutanabbi, 3, ll. 101–2). In another example, he describes his hero Sayf al-Dawlah, the ruler of Syria, during one of his battles:

With other shepherds, not you, have the wolves trifled; other blades, not you, have the blows blunted.
You in your possession the souls of men and jinn. How would Kilab [the enemy tribe] hold on to theirs?
They did not flee you [literally, forsake you] out of rebellion, but one shrinks from going to water when death is the drink.
You pursued them all the way to their watering places, [till the clouds were frightened that you would search it for them].

(Hamori, ll. 1–4)

These metaphors are typical of al-Mutanabbi, whose poetry represented the highest artistic creation in the renaissance of Arabic verse. Compared with traditional metaphors, his manifest both a complex, agile imagination and a linguistic playfulness that usually bend the sacred syntactic rules in order to produce recherché metaphors.

More than any other critic, 'Abd al-Qahir al-Jurjani (d. 471/1087 or 474/1081), the most prominent literary theorist of medieval times, devoted significant attention to the study of metaphor in the Qur'an, in the Hadith (the Prophet's sayings), and in Arabic poetry. Although he does not mention Aristotle, many modern critics, such as Taha Husayn and others (Matlub, 291–304), believe that al-Jurjani was influenced by Aristotle's *Poetics* and *Rhetoric,* which were available in Arabic early in the ninth century. In his treatment of metaphor, al-Jurjani cites examples to illustrate what he considers effective metaphor. The most effective metaphor, he believes, is one that is based on imagination or one that requires imagination to be appreciated, such as "Follow the light that has been revealed for you," with "light" as metaphor for the Qur'an; or "Beware of the greenness of dung," an example of the paired metaphor in which greenness stands for a beautiful young woman and "dung" for her corrupted family or tribe (al-Jurjani, 41–89). Clearly, al-Jurjani seems to have appreciated the new poetic style introduced by "modern" poets in the Abbasid period, rejecting the simple, worn-out clichés or dead metaphors of the traditional poets. Yet, by modern poetic standards, al-Jurjani's concept of metaphor, which continued in use until the middle of the twentieth century, is dated and would no longer explain the new complex metaphor.

■ MODERNISM AND METAPHOR

In the twentieth century, poetic modernism, mostly influenced by the West, has been so radical that it involves not only changes in perception of metaphor but also a rejection of some of the revered fundamentals of Arabic poetics, usually called 'Amud al-Shi'r (literally "the pillar of poetry"), such as the unity of the poem (wahdat al-qasidah) manifested in the required use of monometer and monorhyme in a poem composed of two hemistiched lines. Needless to say, it is impossible to separate modernism in Arabic literature from Western colonialism and imperialism, but the focus of my discussion of modernism and its impact on metaphor will be limited to the impact of the Western influence, whether in the form of translation of Western literatures or the westernization of Arabic education or the impact of war and occupation. Literary historians of Arabic literature seem to agree that the modern period in Arabic letters began around 1800 and continued through the typical phases of neoclassicism and romanticism to the

present. The metaphorical forms in poetry have gone through radical changes. Now one can talk not only about paired metaphor, complex metaphor, subtle metaphor, organic metaphor, and telescoped metaphor, but also about psychological metaphor and surrealistic metaphor.

Let us begin by examining the status of metaphor in the poetry of al-Ruwwad (the pioneers), who rebelled around 1940, especially in Iraq, against traditional poetic forms, including the romantic ones, and started what is called now al-Shi'r al-Hurr or "free verse," which has become the dominant poetic form in most of the Arab world. The deconstruction of the traditional poetic form seems to have opened up the Arabic poem for new themes and freer play of metaphor. An example of the new metaphor can be seen in the following stanza from "Rain Song" by al-Sayyab, one of the leading practitioners of free verse:

Your eyes are two palm tree forests in early light,
Or two balconies from which the moonlight recedes
When they smile, your eyes, the vines put forth their
    leaves,
And lights dance . . . like moons in a river
Rippled by the blade of an oar at break of day;
As if stars were throbbing in the depths of them.
(al-Sayyab, 1987, 427)

The traditional concept of metaphor as a primarily visual or conceptual similarity between two dissimilar things obviously does not seem to work in the example above. Linguistically and grammatically, the metaphor seems to expand beyond the limit of one line. When this poem was first published (1960), many critics objected to the apparent absence of visual similarity between the eyes and the two forests of palm trees in the first line and the balconies under the moon in the second line. But this innovative use of metaphor in a poem that does not adhere to the traditional monorhymed hemistich clearly allows the poet to be more precise in depicting the complexity of his emotional and spiritual reality. By describing her eyes in more than one definite metaphor, the poet expresses both the complex reality of her eyes as he experiences them and the limitation of language, even poetic language, in fully capturing his imagination. The result is an esthetic ambiguity central to the modernistic sensibility as William Empson has elaborated it in his *Seven Types of Ambiguity* (1930).

In the Arabic original, the metaphor, which takes the entire stanza, conveys a mysterious beauty of the eyes whose tantalizing depth is emphasized by endless layers of lights intensified by mirrors of sky, moon, and water. A traditional metaphor would have drastically reduced the complexity to one dimension, creating only a surface picture of the eye. Another crucial aspect of the metaphor that is definitely lost in translation (and no translation can really capture it) is the full cultural connotation of palm-tree forests. In Arabic culture, the word for palm trees (*nakhil*) has extensive connotations essential to the very sense of Arab identity. Furthermore, metaphor, meter, and rhythm represent the defining limits of any serious translation primarily because they express the very ethos of any culture. In the above-translated stanza, the meter and rhythm are clear casualties, and the metaphor has lost not only its musical context but also its cultural connotations.

Another example of modernistic metaphor is found in al-Sayyab's poem "A Stranger at the Gulf," which is recognized by readers and critics alike as one of his most powerful lyrics. It was written while the poet was in exile in Kuwait in 1953 and was published as the first poem in his most acclaimed collection, *Unshudat al-Matar* (The Rain Song), in 1960. The poem is so visceral and intensely emotional that it is usually hard to read even a single line or stanza without being carried by its sweeping rhythm, which uncannily echoes two realities at the same time: the roar of the sea and the rage of the speaker/poet's emotion. The poem hits the reader like successive relentless waves. Here is one of them in which the poet yearns to go back to Iraq but is so poor that he cannot afford a ticket to cross the sea:

Like a homeless stranger I walked among strange
   cities and fearful villages
Yet I sang your beloved soil (my homeland)
And carried it with me, for I have been Christ
   dragging his cross in exile
And I heard the footsteps of hungry masses, their
   bare feet bleeding while stumbling
Throwing into my eyes dust from you (homeland)
   and from their feet.
Disheveled, I still wander on the roads, with my
   soiled feet,
Under foreign suns
In my fluttering rags, stretching my moist hand for
   alms
Yellow hand because of shame and fever: disgrace of
   a strange beggar
Among foreign eyes
Among contempt, rejection, evasion, and charity
And death is much easier than pity
That *charity* foreign eyes shed
Drops of *water,* of *metal* [coins]
Out, out you damned *drops, blood,* you *coins*
You *wind,* you *needles* that would sew the sail for me
   — when do I return?
To Iraq? When do I return?

You the *shimmer* of the waves tossed by an oar in the
   Gulf
You *big stars* of the Gulf sky . . . you damned *money.*

Oh, I wish that ships did not charge passengers
Or the earth were just flat land without seas!
I am still counting you, *money,* and dream of *increase*
I still *decrease* by you, money, the days of my exile
I still *light* with your *glow* my window and my door
On the other shore there [in Iraq], so speak to me,
   money, tell me
When will I *return?* When will I return?
(*Dīwān al-Sayyab,* my translation, italics added)

The italicized words constitute this single, extended, multilayered metaphor. To use I. A. Richards's very useful terms *tenor* and *vehicle* in talking about the work of metaphor, the tenor, the drift of the meaning in the lines, is the yearning for home and the vehicle is money. The yearning is embodied in money, and money has to be earned through begging, humiliation, and contempt. In a string of metaphors, money becomes tears of pity, becomes the blood desire of the speaker, becomes the wind that pushes the sail, and becomes the very sewing needles that make the sail. Yet the speaker is painfully aware that money is so distant that it becomes the elusive shimmers of the waves, and finally he poignantly realizes that money is as far away from him as the stars in the Gulf sky. The wave of the stanza is utterly shattered on the rock of reality. Unlike the first metaphor in "The Rain Song," in which ambiguity functions as an esthetic dimension, metaphor in this poem clusters so many meanings around it that its vehicle, money, is fused with the tenor and is rendered symbolic of the yearning itself. This kind of metaphor is called "organic" (Cuddon, 660), primarily because the metaphor blends with reality and the reality becomes metaphorical.

Influenced by T. S. Eliot and other modernist poets in English, al-Sayyab introduced a very fruitful property of modernism by deftly grafting myth onto the traditional structure of the Arabic poem, steering the poem into new adventuresome spaces. The experiment gave the poem more narrative elements, such as characterization, dialogue, and the use of masks. It also opened up the metaphor by offering it new dimensions: namely, the mythical and the intertextual. In a ten-part poem titled "The Book of Job," published in his collection *Manzil al-Aqnan* (The House of the Slaves), al-Sayyab lyrically fuses personal suffering (he wrote the poem when he was dying of Lou Gehrig's disease) with the existential and the biblical and the Qur'anic. In this context, metaphor branches out to interact with more levels of imagination and thought. I am here translating part 1 only, due to limited space:

Praise be to You, no matter how long the plight will
  last,
And no matter how relentless the pain becomes,
Praise be to You, for *disasters are gifts*
And *calamities are some of your bounties.*
Haven't You given me this darkness?
And haven't You given me this dawn?
Would the earth thank You for the drops of rain
And feel insulted if rain has not come?
For long months these wounds
Like knives tear my sides
And the disease does not relent in the morning
Nor does the night cease its pains by killing [me].
Yet, if Job ever cried, he would cry:
"Praise be to You, for *disasters are magnanimity,*
And these wounds are the Beloved's gifts,
I press them to my bosom,
Your gifts are never absent from my heart!"
I hold my wounds and tell my visitors:
"Behold and envy me, for *these are my Beloved's gifts.*"
And when fever's fire touches my forehead
I pretend it was Your fiery kiss.
My sleeplessness is beautiful, for I shepherd Your sky
Until the stars disappear
And Your grandeur touches my window.
Splendid is the night: Owl's hooting
And a car's honking in the distance
And moaning of the sick, and a mother retelling
Her ancestors' stories to her child.
The forests of the sleepless night, the clouds
Keep covering and uncovering the face of the sky
And brighten it under the moon.
But when the pain forces Job to scream, his cry is:
"Praise be to You, *who shoots with Fate*
And who decrees, later, the remedy."
(*Dīwān al-Sayyab,* 249–50; italics added)

The use of myth is an essential characteristic in al-Sayyab's poetry, in which metaphor acquires a new role in addition to its above-discussed functions. In "The Book of Job," if we examine the italicized phrases, the metaphors effectively function to characterize the speaker, and the speaker's relationship to God and to the biblical Job. One may call this kind of metaphor intertextual metaphor, as it engages in profound intertextuality that, together with the myth, the hymnal rhythm (which is lost in translation), makes the speaker / poet's cosmic vision linguistically possible.

In general, though not always, the poet's particular vision seems to forge the nature and function of metaphor. Badr Shakir al-Sayyab, until his untimely death in 1964, was a towering figure who mastered both romanticism and modernism. Arabic modernism reached its highest point after the 1960s, when visions were

more complex, translations from Western literatures began to play the privileged Muse, and the race for new poetic styles and techniques produced both fine and vapid verse. One of the interesting figures of modernistic poetry is the Egyptian Muhammad 'Afifi Matar. His poetry is a balanced blend of Western poetic styles and the best tradition of Sufi and mystic poetry in Arabic. It aptly reminds Edward W. Said of Blake, Smart, and T. S. Eliot. And Andrei Codrescu believes Matar's rich poetic world has the "ecstatic expansiveness of Saint-John Perse's oceanic vision. . . . Yet Matar's work springs fully from an ancient Islamic tradition."

Matar's poetry "has grown in complexity, and he is now one of the most difficult poets in contemporary Arabic, using many allusions and images from his Arab, Egyptian, and contemporary local heritage" (Jayyusi, 347). The following selections of metaphor are from Matar's collection *Ruba'iyyat al-Farah* (written 1970–88 and published in Arabic in 1990 in London), translated into English as *Quartet of Joy* by Ferial Ghazoul and John Verlenden (1997). The four sections of this long poem (hence "quarter") are consecutively titled "Earth Joy," "Fire Joy," "Water Joy," and "Air Joy," reflecting the poet's cosmic vision that celebrates the four basic constituent elements of the universe. Interestingly, Matar employs the traditional Arabic convention of *ghazal* and *nasib* (love poetry), usually devoted to a female beloved, in his mystical love of the elements, which, in his particular vision, are each in love.

The fired shot of glassy water
with translucent bullet:
the sea aimed it — between resting
    and rising up —
and it felled me with rapturous blow;
I blanked out from glare
    of high-distancing noon . . .

My limbs: a mare.
The sea: a spring season
        of flesh well toned,
spreading for me its tables of hunger,
    dish after dish.
And my dreams: wild birds,
    night surprised them with bafflement
            and the call of space
(Matar, 1)

There is metaphor within metaphor to the point that semantics, syntax, and meter, all traditional elements of poetry, become subordinate to the pursuit of metaphor and rhythm. The result is crystal ambiguity, which is delightful to the eye, mouth, and ear but very hard to understand fully. The modernist's cultivation of esthetic ambiguity is not really entirely new. It has been an essential aspect of Sufi and mystical poetry, not to mention the many enchanting esoteric passages in the Qur'an. Interestingly, the style of the Qur'an, though received in the seventh century, has always been viewed as new, even by most iconoclastic modernists. Matar's poetry is laden with Qur'anic phrases and echoes, as in the following lines: "So Speak up, O my Certitude, / and blow my blood in the Trumpet. / Let my right hand attest that cities / of the living and the dead / under the pure touch quiver, / stirring the eruption of the daily scene / with apocalyptic vision" (Matar, 8). The visionary context, which is the tenor of the metaphor, that introduces the metaphorical vehicles "Trumpet" and "apocalyptic" makes the lines quiver with Qur'anic imagery and cadence.

Unlike al-Sayyab's metaphor, which is profoundly informed by his use of myth and mythmaking, Matar's is totally informed by his vision. It relies heavily on imagism in which metaphor becomes an integral part of the vision, which is definitely Sufistic. In other words, metaphor in Matar becomes a mirror that at once expands his vision and embodies it. By subordinating the metaphor to the larger picture of his mystical vision, Matar sacrifices some clarity and lyricism for the sake of mysticism. In the following lines from the section "Air Joy," one can sense Matar's systematic fragmentation of his metaphor, which is ingeniously appropriate in describing the act of making love.

Now is that singular time for the onset
of beginning or the last of ending —
everything ends:
    they are two bodies on a spot of blood,
    a magic killing; she is killed
        and he is killed,
Who between the two aimed the blade?
Who between the two initiated the act and the
    passion?

It is the one stab.

Who between the two was ablaze
    in the burning ember,
    by a kiss sneaking up
    until the mixing
    of the vigorous blood;
    or by the cry of ecstasy
    meshing its *ah* with death?
(Matar, 53)

Within this consciously fragmented metaphor for the sexual act are smaller metaphors or implied metaphors such as "a kiss sneaking up," fittingly suggesting the archetypal snake of sexuality in the biblical and Qur'anic story of Adam and Eve. Though it is interesting, even delightful, to reconstruct this scattered metaphor,

which may be called a puzzle metaphor, it is predictable, after all. Most of the metaphors in Matar's *Quartet of Joy* are purposely fragmented in an effort to subordinate language, even figurative language, to the mystical or philosophical vision.

Poetic visions inform the very nature of modernism in Arabic poetry, which in its elegant and effective form is a synthesis of Sufi and Qur'anic tradition on the one hand and the impact of Western modernism on the other. Modernism is brilliantly manifest in the poetry of Adonis, Muzaffar al-Nawwab, Sa'di Yusuf, Fadil al-'Azzawi, and Mahmūd Darwīsh. The idea of having a vision or being possessed by a vision seems to be very attractive to all poets, probably because it legitimates their assumed personae as prophets whose visions or missions are inspired by some sort of divine or supernatural powers. This vision or mission (not message) is very evident in the poetry of Darwīsh, who introduced into Arabic letters a new perfection of the poetic genre: the poetics of place and space. Many Arab poets wrote about places and spaces from the ancient theme of *al-Buka'a 'ala al-Atlal* ("weeping over the ruins") to the modernistic interest in place and nature. Intensely lyrical and desperately meticulous in depicting Palestinian places, trees, soil, animals, food, and smells, Darwīsh's poetry powerfully employs the Arabic convention of Sufi love in his Palestinian poetic epic. His metaphors are so extended and detailed that they verge on becoming elaborate conceits and symbols. In the opening of his "Qasidat al-Ard" (Poem of the Land), written in celebration of the Palestinian Day of the Land on 30 March, the speaker describes the day when the Israeli army fired at student demonstrators, killing five young girls. The metaphor elegantly moves from land to plant to girls to blood, weaving mournful lyricism and love poetry.

In the month of March
    in the year of the uprising
        earth told us her blood secrets
In the month of March
    five girls at the door
        of the primary school
Came past the violet
Came past the rifle
        burst into flame

With roses
    and thyme
        they opened
*the song of the soil
    and entered the earth
        the ultimate embrace*
March comes to the land
    out of earth's depth
        out of the girls' dance

The violets leaned over a little
　　so that the girls' voices
　　　　could cross over

the birds
　　pointed their beaks
　　　　at that song and at my heart
(Darwīsh, 1992, 145–46; italics added)

The dominant metaphor is violent death, described in terms of wedding and rebirth, in which all things inanimate and animate participate. The poet utilizes the symbolic connotations of March as the month of rebirth in many ancient Middle Eastern mythologies and religions. Here, however, March comes not only from the earth but also from the girls' dance of death, which promises new life. Violets and birds and the speaker's heart and even the soil join the girls' singing while bursting into flame, roses, and thyme. The metaphor, gathering all these images and colors and smells, acquires inexhaustible mythical and ritualistic dimensions. An essential part of this dramatic, colorful metaphor is "the rifle," a metonym which appears in the drama as an inhuman, antilife entity but is defeated by the persistent continuity of life.

The speaker goes on mourning (in a stanza not translated by Jayyusi and Middleton), becoming the earth itself while talking apparently with one of the murdered girls: "I am the land / and the land is you / O Khadija, do not close the door / do not enter into absence. / We will drive them [the enemies] out of the flowerpot and the laundry line / we will drive them out of the rocks of this long road / and out of the air of Galilee" (my translation). By identifying with the occupied land, the speaker is able to express the desire of the rocks, the air, the flowerpot, and the laundry line. Every intimate detail is enlisted in his struggle without weapons.

I name the soil I call it
　　an extension of my soul
I name my hands I call them
　　the pavement of wounds
I name the pebbles
　　wings
I name the birds
　　almonds and figs
I name my ribs
　　trees
Gently I pull a branch
　　from the fig tree of my breast
I throw it like a stone
　　to blow up the conqueror's tank
(Darwīsh, 146)

Here is a highly detailed metaphor that seems very close to a conceit in which the comparison is elaborately and fancifully constructed. Although Darwīsh's is poetry of resistance, his elegant, labyrinthine use of metaphor saves his verse from deteriorating into propaganda.

For Darwīsh, most tragically conscious of the loss of his homeland and his roots, metaphor has become a synthesizing power that magically reconstructs his atomized world. This power of re-creating what has been destroyed is brilliantly manifested in the metaphors in a poem titled "I See What I Want," from which I quote stanzas 4 and 7:

I see what I want in the soul: the face of a stone
scratched by lightning — green, oh land, green is the
　　land of my soul —
haven't I been a child playing at the edge of a well?
I am still playing . . . this space is my playground
　　and the stone is my wind

I see what I want in prison: days of a flowering
that led from here to two strangers in me
seated in a garden — I close my eyes:
How spacious is the earth! How beautiful the earth
　　from the eye of a needle
(Darwīsh, 1998–99, 81)

The fifteen quatrains in this poem all utilize various metaphors as windows for new seeing and for freedom. Hence, metaphor becomes an empowering outlet for the powerless and a home for the homeless. Much has been written about the power of the arts to reconstruct new worlds out of ruined or deteriorating ones. Darwīsh's poetry, and especially his unsparing metaphors, which seem so omnipresent that they lyrically embrace every corner in his homeland, is an artistic re-creation of lost Palestine. Crucial aspects of modernism in Arabic culture are largely found in the literary response to Western challenges, exile, war, and uprooting.

Modernism has radically transformed the traditional structures and styles in Arabic poetry. While there have been vigorous studies of metaphor in Western modernism, there is almost no serious study of the transformation and the transforming power of metaphor in Arabic modernism. Recent Western studies of metaphor, in light of modern literary, critical, and linguistic theories and methodologies, are very informative and can be fruitful in studying the interactions between metaphor and modernism in any national literature; nevertheless, historicity and cultural studies rightly warn against the pitfalls of universality. One does not need to be a translator or bilingual to realize the complex interlacing of language and culture. Despite many basic similarities between metaphor in Western poetry and Arabic poetry, metaphor in Arabic modernism requires careful examination that takes into account historical, cultural, and linguistic factors. The three examples of modernistic metaphor discussed in this paper are by no means exclusive, nor do they represent all the metaphorical innovations in contemporary Arabic poetry. In my treatment of metaphor in three modernist Arab poets, I hope that I have examined to the reader's satisfaction how such major characteristics of modernism as the free-verse movement, the use of myth, the rediscovery of Arabic heritage, and the impact of the West have radically changed the traditional ways in which metaphor was constructed, received, and evaluated in Arabic verse.

Saadi A. Simawe, Spring 2001

■ **WORKS CITED**

'Abbas, Ihsan. *Tarīkh al-Naqd al-Adabi 'inda al-'Arab.* 4th edition. Beirut. Dar al-Thakafa. 1971.

Aristotle. *Poetics.* In *Aristotle on Poetry and Style.* G. M. A. Grube, tr. Indianapolis. Hackett. 1989.

Azzam, Muhammad. *Mustalahat Naqdiyya min al-Turath al-Adabi al-'Arabi.* Damascus. Manshurat Wizarat al-Thaqafa. 1995.

Barfield, Owen. *Poetic Diction.* London. Faber & Faber. 1952.

Codrescu, Andrei. Back-cover text. In Muhammad 'Afifi Matar. *Quartet of Joy.* Ferial Ghazoul and John Verlenden, trs. Fayetteville. University of Arkansas Press. 1997.

Cuddon, J. A. *A Dictionary of Literary Terms and Literary Theory.* 3d edition. Oxford, England. Blackwell. 1991.

Darwīsh, Mahmūd. "From: Poem of the Land." Lena Jayyusi and Christopher Middleton, trs. In *Anthology of Modern Palestinian Literature.* Salma Khadra Jayyusi, ed. New York. Columbia University Press. 1992. Pp. 145–51.

———. "I See What I Want." Saadi A. Simawe and Ellen Dore Watson, trs. *Modern Poetry in Translation: Palestinian and Israeli Poets,* 14 (Winter 1998–99), pp. 81–82.

de Man, Paul. *Aesthetic Ideology.* Andrzej Warminski, ed. Minneapolis. University of Minnesota Press. 1996.

Empson, William. *Seven Types of Ambiguity.* 2d edition. London. Chatto & Windus. 1947.

Hamori, Andras. *The Compositions of Mutanabbi's Panegyrics to Sayf al-Dawla.* Leiden, Netherlands. Brill. 1992.

Heinrichs, Wolfhart. "Isti'ara and Badi' and Their Terminological Relationship in Early Arabic Literary Criticism." *Zeitschrift für Geschichte der Arabisch-Islamischen Wissenschaften,* 1 (1984), pp. 180–211.

———. "Badi'." In *Encyclopedia of Arabic Literature.* 2 vols. Julie Scott Meisami and Paul Stakey, eds. London. Routledge. 1998.

———. "Metaphor." In *Encyclopedia of Arabic Literature.*

Jones, Alan. *Early Arabic Poetry.* 2 vols. Reading, England. Ithaca Press, for the Faculty of Oriental Studies, Oxford University. 1996.

Matar, Muhammad 'Afifi. *Quartet of Joy.* Ferial Ghazoul and John Verlenden, trs. Fayetteville. University of Arkansas Press. 1997.

Matlub, Ahmad. *'Abd al-Qahir al-Jurjani: Balaghatuhu wa Naqduh.* Beirut. Wakalat al-Matbu'at. 1973.

Meisami, Julie Scott, and Paul Stakey, eds. *Encyclopedia of Arabic Literature.* 2 vols. London. Routledge. 1998.

Moreh, S. *Modern Arabic Poetry 1800–1970: The Development of Its Forms and Themes under the Influence of Western Literature.* Leiden, Netherlands. Brill. 1976.

al-Mutanabbi, Ahmad ibn Husayn. *Poems from the Dīwān of Abu Tayyīb Ahmad ibn Husayn al-Mutanabbi.* Oxford, England. Oxford University Press. 1968.

Nowottny, Winfred. *The Language Poets Use.* 2d edition. London. Athlone. 1965.

Richards, I. A. *The Philosophy of Rhetoric.* New York. Oxford University Press. 1936.

Ricoeur, Paul. *The Rule of Metaphor.* Robert Czerny with Kathleen McLaughlin and John Costello S.J., trs. Toronto. University of Toronto Press. 1977.

Said, Edward W. Back-cover text. In Muhammad 'Afifi Matar. *Quartet of Joy.*

al-Sayyab, Badr Shakir. *Dīwān Badr Shakir al-Sayyab.* Beirut. Dar al-Awda. 1971.

———. "Rain Song." Lena Jayyusi and Christopher Middleton, trs. In *Modern Arabic Poetry.* Salma Khadra Jayyusi, ed. New York. Columbia University Press. 1987.

Stetkevych, Suzanne Pinckney. *Abu Tammam and the Poetics of the 'Abbasid Age.* Leiden, Netherlands. Brill. 1991.

Wheelwright, Philip. *Metaphor and Reality.* Bloomington. Indiana University Press. 1962.

ALGERIA

Assia Djebar's Contribution to Arab Women's Literature: Rebellion, Maturity, Vision

Young Arab women have unsuspected reserves of romanticism; too brutally thrown against men, they seldom regain their injured innocence. And their husbands will never know the exalted face of their adolescence. Only the dry look, barely touching, of submissive beasts, of the weak.

■ ASSIA DJEBAR, *LA SOIF*

For Arabic women I see only one single way to unblock everything: talk, talk without stopping, about yesterday and today, talk among ourselves . . . and look. Look outside, look outside the walls and the prisons!

■ ASSIA DJEBAR, *WOMEN OF ALGIERS IN THEIR APARTMENT*

Women come and go, between Algeria and France, haunted by yesterday's war. . . . They come and go in their own way, . . . women who write, till the final adieu! Adieu I receive a little later, or much later, in the depth of today's death narrative, procession I organize, hoping thereby to unravel, in them, an irresistible flight.

▦ **ASSIA DJEBAR**, *LE BLANC DE L'ALGÉRIE*[1]

Fiction by women writers in North Africa and the Middle East goes back for sixty years.[2] In this relatively short time we can trace a remarkable pace—and breadth—of development in theme, form, and technique. Beginning with a preoccupation with bicultural anxiety and loss of identity (especially among the North African writers), the genre progresses to a self-empowering, inward look at problems and the search for the self. Although the works often seem to reflect the most self-centered aspects of romanticism, such preoccupation is understandable: in the face of legalized oppression and social degradation, it is not too surprising that the first concern of women novelists has been their female characters' private struggles for a personal identity, seen alternately as a search for personhood or an escape from "thinghood."

What is particularly interesting, however, is that the fiction of women writers in North Africa and the Middle East does not stop at this stage of development, even though it might be expected to do so, given the general powerlessness of the group from which the characters of the genre are drawn. Instead, the romantic egotism of the 1950s and 1960s gives way, in the works of many of these writers, to clear rebellion in the face of newly recognized oppression. Personal rebellion, however, is of little use when the entire structure of the surrounding society militates against the exercise of individual freedom. Much of the fiction of these writers ultimately escapes this impasse by universalizing the questions of individual freedom that confront the female characters in this genre. In addition, the social milieu begins to be explored with a new clarity and frankness that moves it from the background to the front of the fictional stage. It becomes clear that not only individuals but also the society in which they live must be reborn.

Because of this overwhelming concern with finding a personal identity, Djebar's early works, along with other women novelists, were not always warmly received by the critics. In the late 1950s and early 1960s there was a strong tendency to compare her works—either outright unfavorably or in an act of condemnation by association—with Françoise Sagan's *Bonjour tristesse*. In fact, it may well be that adolescent rebellion

Assia Djebar (*Robert H. Taylor*)

and the search for identity are not the stuff of the great novels of tomorrow; whether or not this is the case is irrelevant. What matters is that these works were in many ways authentic and necessary; you must know some basic things about yourself before you can begin to write about your place in the millennium.

The next stage in the evolution of the genre is rebellion in the face of the realization of the oppression that women must undergo in North Africa and the Middle East; this is a thing apart from the fairly universal human experience of rebellion on the way to maturity. The pattern is brutally simple in most parts of North Africa and the Middle East: women are born to fill the roles of daughter, wife, and mother, to be successively subservient to their fathers, husbands, and sons. Education for women is in most cases regarded as superfluous, few occupations outside the home are open to women, and in most cases the legal status of women is determined by the *shari'a* or Muslim religious code. In court, a woman's testimony is accorded only half the weight of a man's, a husband may divorce his wife without recourse to legal action, often merely by stating aloud that he repudiates her, and the law permits a husband or father to force his wife or daughter to remain at home, often literally under lock and key. Revolt against such customs and conditions leads to political awakening in the hope of finding solutions to women's problems through political commitment. Engagement is often mixed with a sense of nationalism and national identity, because the countries from which the women write are either struggling against foreign domination or are striving toward national identity and development.

Then comes disillusionment with the realization that political movements use women instead of serving or working together for their liberation. Those novelists who find a productive solution to this impasse usually do so by universalizing the feminist cause and expressing women's problems in the context of Middle Eastern and North African societies.

Assia Djebar exhibits all the stages mentioned above. She even goes one step further with her latest work, *Le blanc de l'Algérie,* in which she expresses a strong vision starting with the personal and the national to reach the political and the universal. It is because of this progression that I suggest that her fiction has achieved a true maturity, a realization that the self—and its freedom—cannot be separated from the entire social context. Obviously, this evolving vision has important political implications.

Djebar, a writer of middle-class Muslim and Algerian origins, was able to synthesize her traditional Muslim background and her European education. By the age of twenty-six she had published three novels (*La soif, Les impatients, Les enfants du nouveau monde*) and had obtained a *licence* (B.A.) in history from the Sorbonne. During the revolution she taught in Tunis and Rabat, where she completed a fourth novel (*Les alouettes naïves*). She went back to Algeria after its independence, in 1962, and taught at the University of Algiers. In 1969 she co-produced a play, *Rouge l'aube,* for the Third Pan-African Cultural Festival in Algiers, and her *Poèmes pour l'Algérie heureuse* was published by SNED (the National Algerian Publishing House)—all signs that she had been accepted by and was willing to make peace with the authorities of her country. In 1969 she stopped publishing and producing and fell silent for about ten years, which led many critics to speculate over the reasons for her withdrawal. Clarisse Zimra probably gives the best analysis for this silence, which she sees as "a cycle that opens on an enlarged version of the female self. The resulting figure is one of disclosure rather than closure" (Zimra, "Writing Woman").

It was with a film, *La nouba des femmes du Mont Chenoua* (1979), that Djebar broke her silence. The film received the first prize at the Venice Film Festival. It was followed by a collection of short stories, *Femmes d'Alger dans leur appartement* (1980), named after the 1832 Delacroix painting. She has since published three volumes of a quartet—*L'amour, la fantasia* (1985), *Ombre sultane* (1987), and *Vaste est la prison* (1995)—in a style increasingly worked out, refined, and perfected and in which she blends historical events with autobiographical elements in a complex sense of time and space. *Loin de Médine* (Far from Medina), which appeared in 1991, was an interruption, an interlude to her quartet and a reflection on the life of the Prophet Mohammed which we will analyze later. Another interruption, stirred by Djebar's desperate concern for the events in her country, was the publication in 1996 of *Le blanc de l'Algérie,* written after she was shaken by the death of a loved one.

> The worst moment for me, the strongest, was in March of last year [1994], when a friend and relative, Abdel Kader Alloula, died. He was an extraordinary man . . . the only one in my opinion who, for the last thirty years, had forged an Arabic language between the popular language of the street and the literary one. . . . He died at the age of fifty-three. He was forging this language for us. It was a song at the crossroads of several traditions. The fact that this man was killed, a man who was also francophone, was for me—how shall I say—as if danger were being instilled, establishing itself in the heart of Algerian culture. My reaction was to close myself into my apartment for three months and to do my own anamnesia, going back into my mother's, my grandmother's memories, and into my own, of thirty years in which I lived pushed back and forth between Europe and Algeria. ("Territoires des langues," 73–74)

This recall of one's relatives and of one's own memory is at the core of *Vaste est la prison,* but grief also inspired *Le blanc de l'Algérie,* which is an amazingly courageous and honest narrative that raises vital questions about Algeria's present, past, and future political and cultural situation.

Djebar now spends most of her time in France as a practicing writer, film producer, and literary critic. This year she received the Neustadt International Prize for Literature awarded by *World Literature Today,* a very prestigious award which, in the last twenty-five years, has seen eighteen of its laureates, candidates, and jurors subsequently receive the Nobel Prize in Literature. (Djebar was a Neustadt juror in 1990.) In the future we may increasingly see Djebar in the States, for she has been invited by various universities here as a lecturer and/or writer in residence.

I would like to trace the evolution of Assia Djebar's works from rebellion to maturity as expressed by the various plots and characters of her novels. Since a lot has been written on her recent works, I will dwell more on the early ones. I will trace the unifying themes of those early works which can be found again in her latest ones. I hope to show the evolution and progression into maturity of an author who can be considered one of the most important women writers in North Africa.

The central figure of Djebar's first novel, *La soif* (1957; Eng. *The Mischief,* 1958), resembles other bicultural characters in novels of that period. Nadia is the issue of a marriage between an Algerian man and a French woman. Because her mother died in childbirth, Nadia lives with her father and her half-sister's family. She has been educated in French schools, and her lifestyle does not appear to be circumscribed by traditional Muslim customs. She goes where she pleases, drives her own sports car, and associates with men. While the plot is often melodramatic and reminiscent of Sagan's *Bonjour tristesse,* at the same time the central figure espouses some of the qualities of Meursault in Camus's classic, *L'étranger:* her life was "placid, superficial, empty." Nor is this all, for Nadia is also capable of displaying a striking combination of fatalism and existentialism: "I wanted to think of nothing except the wind blowing against my temples and the restless course of my life. Hussein hated me, and Jedla considered me of no importance whatever. As for Ali, he was gone and I had forgotten about him. . . . Rage, violence, insults—life was made up of these. I would do what Jedla expected of me. (*M,* 77–78)

Briefly, the plot goes as follows: Nadia has a friend, Jedla, who is married to a lawyer, Ali. Nadia also has a boyfriend, Hussein, but she thinks that she is in love with Ali and flirts with both of them. When Jedla manifests psychotic behavior and attempts suicide, Nadia feels she must delve into her friend's psychological background. What she discovers is that Jedla once lost a baby through miscarriage and now fears that she will be childless. Childlessness is considered the supreme curse that can be visited upon a woman in the North African Muslim culture; not only is it a cause of social mortification, but it also constitutes grounds for the husband to terminate the marriage. The problem here has become exacerbated by Jedla's discovery that Ali once had a French mistress who bore him a son, since such proof of Ali's fertility places the stigma of barrenness squarely on Jedla.

The discovery of the French mistress has another effect, however, in that it makes Jedla insanely jealous and leads her to plot a complicated revenge on Ali. Nadia is to tempt Ali into a sexual relationship, whereupon Jedla will have an excuse to free herself from him on grounds of infidelity. It is a daring scheme for an Al-

gerian woman to attempt and is probably indicative of the gradual breakdown of the old male-dominated culture in the face of European influences. Before this plot can be put into action, however, there is yet another turn of events: Ali goes off on a trip to France, and Jedla discovers that she is pregnant. Acting in accordance with cultural expectations, she is at first overjoyed with her pregnancy, an attitude for which the more liberated Nadia despises her: "Yes, she was just like the common run of women, so easily contented, so quick to submit to convention; she was morbidly anxious to proclaim her happiness from the rooftops and see it unfold, like a poisonous plant, in front of other people" (*M,* 93). She introduces doubt into Jedla's heart by telling her that even her pregnancy will not keep Ali from being unfaithful to her if he wants to be. Given Ali's background, there is probably a certain amount of truth to this, however despicable Nadia's intentions may be for pointing out the fact to Jedla. In any case, Jedla is easily convinced and asks Nadia to take her to the abortionist. Nadia is frightened at the consequences of her meddling and regrets her words. She tries to reason Jedla out of her decision by telling her:

> "What I think is that you'd better take Ali as he is. There's no use loving him as an exception. You must show some understanding. . . . Almost any man, even Ali, can have his moments of . . . instability. . . .

> "Don't be too proud! You ought to be content with your lot as a woman. I've come around, myself, to the point of view of our mothers and grandmothers. As long as women have a home of their own where they can serve and obey their husbands, they need ask nothing more. What if their husbands do have affairs on the outside? As long as their wifely position is respected, what does it matter? Of course they know that as they grow old, other and younger wives may take their place. But they're not jealous; they remain calm and submissive, and who's to say they haven't the right idea?" (*M,* 99–100)

Unfortunately, this litany of the old ways does not convince Jedla; on the contrary, it drives her to furious rebellion. She goes through with the abortion and dies as a result of the operation. When Ali returns from France to find that the wife he adored is dead, he turns to drink. Nadia, on the other hand, marries Hussein and tries to forget "the tumult of that summer when I was twenty years old" (*M,* 111). She is no longer thirsty for rebellion and notices that, "in the lethargy of my heart there is not even a trace of shame" (111). Her marriage is calm and banal, and in its anticlimactic mood there is an unconvincing attempt to create a moralized ending with the message: "What I possess is a certain physical

well-being, the companionship of Hussein, and the sensation that life is running out, drop by drop, inexorably"
(110–11).

In essence, however, the novel is not as superficial
as it may seem from this summary of the main plot. In
addition to the valid overtones of cultural conflict, at the
center of the novel there seems to be the possibility of
a beautiful friendship between Jedla and Nadia, a relationship which would transcend their day-to-day banalities and desires. Passages which describe this relationship manage to evoke a peaceful security and calmness,
but without slipping into the spiritual flaccidity which
characterizes Nadia's marriage to Hussein: "After establishing a great calm on the veranda, where we sat together, we went off to sleep, like sisters, in the same
room. We pulled the beds close to each other, and often
we whispered for long hours in the dark" (M, 63).

What precludes this gentle and sisterly relationship
is the "thirst" (la soif) or "craving" which pervades the
novel. Jedla is "thirsty" for a child, Nadia is "thirsty" for
men. "Thirst," then, revolves around children and men,
both of which are required by society before a woman
can consider herself successful. Conversely, there is no
social utility to prompt a deep friendship between two
women. Jedla has been so well trained in her role as an
Arab female that she thinks that a childless marriage is
sure to drive away her husband; neither can the liberated Nadia escape the pressure to find the focus of her life
through a man. But la soif also involves "rebellion"
against this same slavery imposed by society. Speaking
of Jedla, Nadia says: "What I had cared most for in her
so far was her refusal to compromise and be like everyone else, her vaguely dissatisfied craving, which was
even deeper than my own" (M, 92). But Nadia too has
a "vaguely dissatisfied craving," and therefore she understands Jedla better than she thinks she does. It is this
spirit of rebellion against society's norms which attracted her to Jedla in the first place. The tragedy of the
novel arises out of the fact that the two women are enemies in their struggle or thirst for independence; it is
essentially Nadia's thirst for Ali that leads her to incite
Jedla to rebel against her thirst for a child. Unable to see
the need to unite, they only exacerbate each other's
problems. Nadia, had she been more mature, would
have understood the necessity of uniting with Jedla instead of either admiring her blindly or trying alternately
to persuade her to rebel or submit, depending on her
own capricious moods. The weakness of Djebar's novel
lies in her failure to stress the possibility of unity among
women, and not in the book's sexual overtones, which
the Algerian revolutionaries found indecent. The revolutionaries considered La soif's subject particularly inappropriate because the book ignored the revolution pre-

cisely at a time when the country was engaged in a fierce
war. This reaction was more or less to be expected inasmuch as the political activists of Algeria have never been
greatly concerned with the liberation of women. In fact,
the political programs of Arab nationalists frequently
call for a return to ancient Muslim social customs, including the cloistering of women.

In Djebar's second novel, Les impatients (The Impatient Ones; 1958), one can see a certain oblique response to the revolutionaries' criticism of La soif. This
work depicts the awakening consciousness of a young
Algerian girl rebelling against tradition. Djebar still
seems unconcerned with the revolution taking place in
her country, and the emphasis of Les impatients is as
firmly centered on the problems of women as was that
of La soif. This time, however, Djebar seems to have
taken care to disarm her critics by setting the novel a
few years in the past, thereby sidestepping any need to
mention the revolution. As the title indicates, the emphasis of the novel is slightly less personal, slightly
more social. Instead of dealing with a thirst, a feeling
centered entirely in the individual, Les impatients deals
with an individual's "impatience" with the existing social order.

Dalila, the heroine, is similar to Nadia in that she
is French-educated. Both of her parents are dead, and
she lives in Algiers with her stepmother, her brother's
family, and a house full of other relatives. Like Nadia,
Dalila is bored, but unlike Nadia, she is not free to go
where she pleases. She is cloistered like the other
women in the house, but occasionally she visits girl-
friends, attends weddings, and goes to the Turkish bath.
This humdrum existence gives her an insight into the
desperation which drives cloistered women to seek adventure even at the risk of social disgrace.

> Then I understood the agitation that drives
> women to say "yes." In the face of the confusion
> of their hearts, filled at the same time with sloth,
> compassion, and an inexplicable tenderness, in
> the face of the multiple void of their hearts, they
> give themselves to men, even if only by way of
> being raped, in order that, when the act is over
> they may rediscover themselves definitively, face
> to face with an image of themselves. (I, 121)

Even the meetings with her schoolmates during which
they discuss important questions such as "the problem
of the evolution of the Muslim woman, the problem of
mixed marriages, the problem of the social responsibilities of women" (17) are empty because they are approached without sincerity: "They discussed these
questions because it was fashionable to do so." Indeed,
given the cloistered lives the girls are forced to live, such
discussions could hardly be expected to have any greater effect than relieving boredom.

Dalila, however, finds a more effective means of combatting the flatness of life. Secretly, she starts dating the brother of one of her friends. Selim is an *évolué,* a "liberated man" who seems to share Dalila's convictions concerning the right of every girl to choose her friends and to exercise the freedom to come and go as she pleases. In order to see Selim more often, Dalila blackmails her stepmother Lella. Dalila has pieced together bits of conversations that she has overheard and has deduced that Lella was once an "easy" woman—in fact, she was Selim's mistress before she married Dalila's father. By threatening to reveal what she knows, Dalila forces Lella to lie to Dalila's brother whenever she wants to go out. It is of course heavily ironic, and indicative of the incomplete state of her "evolution," that Dalila is in effect using the sanctions of the old order to gain her own freedom.

Dalila's blackmail is very effective, because Lella, having gained respectability through marriage, now goes to great lengths to lead an exemplary life: "In our household the image of the exemplary woman has as much charm as that of the femme fatale has in the outside world. Perhaps it is more reassuring. Unfortunately it's just another image" (I, 224). Dalila, forgetting that it is this very image that makes it possible for her to deceive her brother and leave the house, takes Lella to task for hypocrisy and adherence to a double standard: "It's prostitution. And of the worst sort. . . . As I understand it, you don't even want to give it up. It has its advantages: security, honor, and all the attentions of men, not only those under this roof but others whom you imagine to be forever raising their eyes to your famous virtue, as to a flag" (152). Lella, on the other hand, is quite sensible of the advantages of the orderly though limited life which she leads. She begs Dalila to think twice before destroying this order, pointing out that this order is necessary to the happiness of others, even though it may not suit Dalila's purposes at the moment: "Before spreading trouble in this way, stop and *think,* be prudent. Don't upset anything in this house, in this order. . . . You are insensible to the unhappiness and disappointment of other people. You're nothing but an egoist" (153).

In fact, Dalila is selfish. Nevertheless, the reader admires her desire to break away from restrictive conventions at the same time that he is repelled by her underhanded methods. Dalila never does actually expose her stepmother's past, and when Dalila's father dies, Lella ultimately remarries and thus can no longer serve the interests of Dalila's petty blackmail. However, it is evident in the blackmail of her stepmother that the young girl who seeks her own freedom from custom and convention is not averse to using these same conventional

forms for her own ends. Like Nadia in *La soif,* Dalila lacks compassion for and solidarity with the other women surrounding her.

Dalila also undergoes a process of disillusionment. When she joins Selim in Paris, where he has gone on business, she discovers to her great surprise that he has become extremely jealous and possessive. He even resents her friendship with a French girl. He slaps her when she goes out without telling him and locks the door of her room to prevent her from going out during his absence. The action of the novel takes a melodramatic turn when Dalila receives a letter from home informing her of Lella's remarriage. Selim leaves to meet secretly with his former mistress, and both are killed by her new husband. Dalila then realizes that she is at last alone but free.

> Escape, freedom, what can that mean? Nothing. Suddenly there had been a scene which only a few days ago I would have found degrading. Now I accepted it the way one accepts something that happened several years ago. Even if that tempest should return, what did it matter to me, seeing that, immediately afterward, I could be perfectly happy in spite of it? Seeing that I could seize that pure, immobile exaltation by the throat and thus feel alone, sure of myself. (I, 230)

An inherent weakness of the novel arising from the melodramatic resolution of the plot is that Dalila gains her freedom through the fortuitous exercise of the very conventions against which she is rebelling. Not only was it possible for her to see Selim in the first place through the agency of blackmail arising from the sexual cloistering of women, but her final "freedom" from Selim is achieved when *he leaves her* to visit his former mistress and is murdered by Lella's new husband as an affair of honor. Like Nadia, Dalila achieves her ends primarily by negative means, by profiting from the misfortune of others. Even though the ends in *Les impatients* are more worthy and less selfish than those in *La soif,* the means the two women use are similar, and they both end up alienated from the other women around them. They are both stubborn, independent, and selfish, and both finally resolve their conflicts with society by submitting to life on a plane of reduced expectations.

Selim's death, while it is convenient for Dalila, constitutes a weakness in the novel because it overextends the reach of coincidence and thereby significantly reduces the meaning of Dalila's resulting "freedom." Djebar herself may have been conscious of this shortcoming, because she does not end the novel with Dalila's attainment of freedom but instead adds another event which substantially modifies and extends the meaning of the novel. In the closing scenes Dalila appears to move out of her egotistical isolation and toward a new consciousness of the world around her. She has returned home, and one day as she walks the streets of Algiers she sees a boy being arrested by the French police and hears him screaming out his innocence in Arabic, joyfully rebellious: "I asked myself whether it was only youth which lent to this joy overtones of hate, of despair. If it was not rather a kind of grace reserved for certain beings, certain people. . . . Had I lost that grace?" (238). She compares herself to the boy perhaps guilty, perhaps innocent, but nevertheless screaming in revolt, "the chant of a child victorious under the strokes of the cane" (239). "Impatience," then, which was at first merely an expression of selfish desire, takes the form of courage and willingness to speak in the midst of injustice.

Assia Djebar's third novel, *Les enfants du nouveau monde* (The Children of the New World; 1962), moves further in the direction of the developing consciousness indicated at the end of *Les impatients*. Here she shows the awakening of a new nation and its people by describing the growing awareness of several women. Stylistically, in *Les enfants du nouveau monde* Djebar makes use of a circular technique reminiscent of the male Algerian writer Kateb Yacine.

Unlike Djebar's previous novels, this work deals directly with the Algerian Revolution. Not only does the action take place during that conflict, but the focus is upon the various reactions to the revolution in a small town adjacent to a guerrilla-held mountain range. In particular, Djebar focuses on the role of women under these circumstances. There are, for instance, certain necessary social adjustments to the fact that many of the men are off fighting: "In every house where, ordinarily, four or five families were living, one family to a room, there is always one woman, young, old, it doesn't matter, who takes charge" (*E,* 14). Some insight is also given into the attitude of the Algerian male, who, oppressed by the French, exhibits his helpless frustration by oppressing his wife at home. At the same time, returning to his cloistered wife provides the Algerian with a source of cultural identity.

> Yes, to forget the French oppressor, that's almost easy, he thinks as he comes back home in the evening and looks at his wife which the other, the all-powerful master of the outside, will never know; "cloistered" they say of her, but the husband thinks "liberated." . . . That body which he embraces, a body which gives itself without flinching because it is unfamiliar with the language of glances. (17)

Although a number of women are described, Djebar focuses on Chérifa, the uneducated wife of Youssef,

a merchant and also a member of the underground. Because she cannot have children, Chérifa is bored with her life and passes the time playing with the children of her neighbor Amna. Amna, also uneducated, is married to a police inspector, Hakim, a traitor to the Arabs who is also distrusted by the French police for whom he works. Chérifa's consciousness was awakened through the experiences of her first marriage. She had lived for three years with a man who had been forced upon her, "a man whom everything in her had rejected" (23). Every night for three years she had given herself to him like a cold statue, a possession worse than rape. Her decision to break away from him was not only her first act of rebellion but also the first manifestation of the consciousness of her own existence: "'I should leave,' and she thought with vehemence that it would be a lie to continue living there. This impetus which had pushed her, she felt it also as an awakening; yes, all her life before today had been only a long slumber" (27).

A second significant step in Chérifa's awakening takes place during the revolution. When she discovers that Youssef, her second husband, is in danger because of his clandestine activities with the underground, she leaves her home alone for the first time in her life and crosses town on foot to warn him of the imminent danger of his capture. This one act gives a significance to her life which it had never had before.

> She herself had forgotten the danger; perhaps it was not the danger, in fact, which had driven her, but rather a cunning desire to know at once whether she could not perhaps consecrate herself to something besides waiting in her room, to patience and love. Besides, she had crossed town forthrightly, despite feeling so many hostile eyes upon her, and at the end of her walk she had discovered that she was not merely a target for the curiosity of males, a form which passes, a veiled mystery which the first glance solicits, a fascinating weakness which one ends up hating, spitting upon. . . . No, she did exist; a driving obsession had possessed her and thereby made her unstoppable. "Get to Youssef! He is in danger." (162)

Once Chérifa sees herself as an active agent, capable of taking initiative outside the home, she is a changed woman.

Djebar depicts another type of awakening through the character of Lila, a highly educated young woman whose husband Ali has left her to join the guerrillas in the mountains. Lila is sympathetic to the Arab cause, but she is too tied to her French education to be totally committed. In both personality and situation the twenty-four-year-old Lila resembles Nadia and Dalila in Djebar's previous novels. Like them she is an orphan, and

like them she is bored, selfish, and lazy. Her friend Suzanne, a Frenchwoman married to an Arab lawyer who
has left for France, thinks of Lila, "She conceived of
friendship the same way she did of love: egotistically"
(83). But unlike the central figures of Djebar's previous
novels, Lila's selfishness and boredom are turned into
positive action and courage. She is arrested because she
hides Bachir, a relative who has just performed an act
of sabotage. Significantly, instead of feeling sorry for
herself because of her arrest, she rises above such selfish
concerns and accepts her lot as the price she must pay
for the honor of participating in the struggle for her
country's independence. She forgets about herself and
feels fulfilled: "What wonderful luck to finally be just
anybody on an earth, in an age that will never be repeated" (217).

Another woman who exhibits a similar involvement in the national cause is Salima, a thirty-one-year-
old teacher who is imprisoned for her participation in
the underground. She too feels lucky to have been able
to participate actively in the revolution. In prison, her
past unfolds before her eyes: "Was it really just yesterday, that epoch? Here it is fifteen or sixteen years
ago. . . . Then she was the only Muslim girl in town who
pursued her studies. A father who just happened to die
when she was at the age where she should have been
cloistered, like the other girls; in other words, a stroke
of luck" (128). During the night she cannot go to sleep
because the guards are torturing a man in the next cell
and she can hear him screaming. She shivers with horror, but she listens with all her might: "'This is the song
of my country, this is the song of the future,' she mur-
mured" (128).

To round out the picture of women in the revolution, Djebar also depicts Hassiba, a girl in her early
teens who joins the guerrillas, and Touma, a "loose"
girl, semi-educated in the French schools. The portrayal
of Touma is particularly significant because her fate reveals the degree to which the "new order" of the revolutionaries is merely a continuation of the old order of
Muslim Algeria: Touma's younger brother Tewfiq is required to kill her in order to clear the honor of his family before the guerrillas will permit him to join their organization.

Overall, in *Les enfants du nouveau monde* Djebar's
orientation toward the condition of women is markedly
different from her attitude in the previous novels. Here
the female characters are made to feel that they should
seek solutions to their problems *within themselves*. Their
rebellion should be directed toward political goals, and
such qualities as commitment, independent thinking,
and decision-making are desirable for the sake of political change. While directing criticism at women's per-

sonal goals in life, Djebar makes it clear that society is
no longer to be considered the culprit with respect to
the condition of women, as was the case in her previous
novels.

Critics generally praised Djebar for *Les enfants du
nouveau monde,* which they found sensitive in its inner
prise de conscience or grasp of the awareness of a people,
of women as well as men. Further, this is the first North
African novel in which a woman writer focuses on the
inner conflicts of some of her male characters. Khatibi
found that, whereas in other women's novels the heroines are occupied with private self-realization, the
women in *Les enfants du nouveau monde* are seen to unite
among themselves and with their menfolk for group
solidarity, to create not a Third World society but a new
society entirely, where women work beside men,
though within their own roles (64).

Assia Djebar's early novels reflect a progression in
her ideas from an insistence upon the necessity of self-
preoccupation in a world hostile to women, to a recognition of the importance of awareness of others, to the
resolution of personal problems through immersion in
a national cause. Her first novel reveals a selfishly unhappy woman preoccupied with herself; her second
shows one more aware of society but still bored and
selfish; and finally, her third depicts women who lose
themselves to gain their country's independence. This
reflects the approximate path of women's liberation in
Algeria, which lost almost all its impetus after national
independence was gained. According to Fadéla
M'Rabet, women were simply used during the revolution, only to be pushed down to a lower level after independence. Reflecting occurrences in Algeria, Djebar's
early novels indicate a simultaneous—and perhaps related—progression in the cause of nationalism and regression in the cause of women's rights. The nationalism which was so necessary for the revolutionaries to
oust the French colonialists turned counterrevolutionary after the oppressor had been evicted. As part of this
counterrevolution, traditional laws were reinstituted
which deprived women of the rights they had enjoyed
under colonial rule. Although Djebar's first novels give
us the impression that she is revolutionary in her ideas
of women's role and their liberation, her theoretical
ideas presented to us at that time, in an introduction to
a book of photographs called *Women of Islam,* showed
her to be a moderate.

Djebar believed then that it was dangerous to speak
of *the* Muslim woman, because she could be seen in so
many contexts throughout the Islamic world. Even
within the confines of Algeria, attitudes toward the liberation of Algerian women varied widely, often reflecting what the individual stood to gain or lose by such

liberation. For example, there was the French-educated Muslim man who deplored the seclusion of women but married a European, or the Muslim father who was in favor of having his daughter receive a bicultural education but then became alarmed when she gained a wide knowledge of the world and began to behave like a European. Finally there was the feminist who decided that the dominating male to whom she happened to be married really possessed only illusory power! Neither did Djebar find true liberation to be an unmixed blessing. She pointed out, for instance, that the Eastern mindset tended to emphasize and value private rather than public life, in contradistinction to the Western approach, which tended to value the public display and outward control of others. Essentially, this was the difference between *being* and *doing*. Thus, according to Djebar, liberating a woman in an Eastern culture often resulted in thrusting her into a cruel and competitive world for which she was unprepared and in which she might have no wish to participate.

Djebar denied that in Islam women were inferior to men. Instead she insisted that they were complementary. Furthermore, she emphasized that women were in fact becoming emancipated as the traditional family disintegrated, a process which had reached the point where women were beginning to hold jobs outside the home. Djebar also noted, however, that this emancipation as a result of the disintegration of the family structure was creating problems rather than solving them.

In his study *Women of Algeria* David Gordon saw a similarity between Djamila Debèche's and Djebar's directions: if women were to be emancipated, the process had to be accompanied by harmony with society as a whole, for the liberating of women demanded the liberation of men as well from the framework of traditional Muslim thought (Gordon, 49). In short, while Djebar was acutely aware of and poignantly depicted the plight of the Algerian woman, she was far from convinced that total liberation of women—say by legislative fiat—would be a wise course of action for her country. Indeed, since she saw liberation primarily as a process of individual mindset adjustment, she would probably have viewed "legal" liberation as irrelevant.

In contrast to the few novels written by women in the Mashrek and the Maghreb which lashed out against brutalizing social conditions, the majority presented, in the first decades of women's literary production, a more moderated view. Often pampered and bored, the women writers of North Africa and the Middle East frequently began their careers by imitating the West. Djebar and Ba'labakki, for example, imitated Françoise Sagan in drawing melancholic characters and featuring plots filled with sudden outbreaks of violence and fre-

quent violations of normal fictional causality. Later they tried to grasp more of themselves through increased sensitivity to their Eastern heritage, producing self-searching, introspective literature which revealed the inward turn of their rebellion. The critic Abdelkebir Khatibi tried to explain the reasons for this inwardness which characterized so many of the women writers of that period: "Considered, and perceiving herself, as an object, the woman is more sensitive, more centered on her own psychological problems. Bullied, obliged to be always on the defensive, she interiorizes her complexes and neuroses. This is why one finds in feminine literature this constant taste for introspection, this obstinate search for the other, this feverish puritanism" (Khatibi, 61–62). This preoccupation with the self may account for the writers' inability to engage themselves in political and social problems outside their own immediate environment. Thus it was that the writers of that period, while dwelling on their own oppression in some detail, generally lacked sympathy for and awareness of the sufferings of women from the lower strata of their own societies. A number of cultural problems which directly affected women found no expression in the fiction of women writers of that period. Little attention was paid to crimes of honor, for example. Djebar mentioned them in *Les enfants du nouveau monde* but passed no judgment on the act itself. It was merely mentioned in passing as evidence of traditional thinking among political revolutionaries.

The inability to express women's problems and to be heard by the public she wanted to reach, combined with personal problems and the dilemma over which language to use, rendered more acute through a search for cultural and national identity, can probably account for Djebar's long hiatus from writing and publishing after the release of *Enfants*. In a recent interview with Lise Gauvin she stated:

> It seemed to me I could have been a poet in the Arabic language. *Vaste est la prison* starts with an introduction called "The Silence of Writing." I talk about why I went almost ten years without publishing. I show what I had not yet perceived in *L'amour, la fantasia*. In that book I was in a relationship between French and Arabic. French had liberated me from my body at the age of eleven. But it was also a Nessus tunic—meaning that I had been able to escape from the veil thanks to the French language, thanks to having a father in the French language. It was evident that at the age of sixteen, seventeen, I conceived of myself, externally, as as much a boy as a girl. ("Territories des langues")

Language is a dilemma Djebar reflects upon in many instances. Like many North African novelists who have been outspoken on the topic,[3] Djebar also experiences bilingualism as a problem which "enriches only the one who truly possesses two cultures. And this is rarely the case in Algeria."[4] But unlike many of her male counterparts who express this dilemma in violent terms, Djebar has a more tender relationship with language.

> I started by writing one day, on the first page of a notebook, a rule of behavior to myself: "To recover the Arab tradition of love in the language of Giraudoux." Then, after a few trials, I chose, as a defiance to myself a kind of: "Even though I write in French, can I be as Arab as possible?". . . Each time I find different justifications, the least of evils being to re-create in French a life lived or felt in Arabic. This movement from one language to another has probably helped some North African writers of French expression achieve a certain lyricism, others a tone of aggressiveness or, on the contrary, of nostalgia. As for me, my desire is to find, in spite of this movement, a profound fluidity and intimacy—which seems difficult. ("Le romancier dans la cité arabe")

Ten years of silence were broken with the film *La nouba des femmes du Mont Chenoua* (1979). Like the Senegalese writer and director Sembène Ousmane, Djebar felt she could reach her people at last, and especially the women, in a language understandable through spoken Arabic and through sounds and images. The film is a very beautiful one, with reflections on memory and portraying the gaze. A young woman plunges into her past and allows women to speak out, giving them a voice and telling their stories mixed with the stories of their ancestors and flashbacks of war. In it one already finds many elements of her future novels.

With the short stories of *Femmes d'Alger dans leur appartement* (Eng. *Women of Algiers in Their Apartment*), an offshoot from Djebar's film turned into narratives, women's voices come out even more strongly. It is as if millennial oppression had been finally unleashed, veils dropped, and bodies restored to their beauty and full integrity: "New women of Algiers, who have been allowed to move about in the streets just these last few years, have been momentarily blinded by the sun as they cross the threshold, do they free themselves—do we free ourselves—altogether from the relationship with their own bodies, a relationship lived in the shadows until now, as they have done throughout the centuries?" (*WA*, 2).

L'amour, la fantasia (Eng. *Fantasia: An Algerian Cavalcade*) is a carefully worked-out narrative that functions on two levels, reflecting two journeys: one into the author's inner self, partly autobiographical, the other historical, tracing the history of Algeria from the con-

quest of 1830 to the liberation of 1962. It is also a reflection on language. These two themes, the autobiographical elements mixed with history and the reflection on language, are crafted beautifully within the narratives. They can be found again in the next two volumes of Djebar's quartet. In addition to these two levels, Djebar gives us interwoven narratives through various voices set into different time frameworks. For example, her reflections on language are in one voice, lyric passages in praise of Algerian women are in another. She successfully constructs a polyphonic narrative resembling a symphony; hence the allusion to Beethoven's *Fantasia* and her division of the novel into five parts, like a symphony. The condition of women is also very much present and continues in the line of her preceding works with more strength and determination to give them a greater voice and visibility. Djebar studied the archives and looked for women's achievements and participation in political and historical events. She demonstrates that women were active participants in the resistance against the French. As Mildred Mortimer has well analyzed:

> By alternating historical accounts of the French conquest, oral history of the Algerian revolution, and autobiographical fragments, Djebar sets her individual journey against two distinct and yet complementary backdrops: the conquest of 1830 and the Algerian Revolution of 1954. The former introduced the colonial era; the latter brought it to a close. In this way, the narrator establishes links with Algeria's past, more specifically with women of the past whose heroism has been forgotten. Giving written form to Algerian women's heroic deeds, Djebar as translator and scribe succeeds in forging new links with traditional women of the world she left behind. ("Fleeing the Harem," 156–57)

In *Ombre sultane* (Eng. *A Sister to Scheherazade*) Djebar continues on the musical theme she started with *L'amour, la fantasia*, alternating the voices of two women—one traditional, the other liberated, married to the same man. The inner and outer journeys are still present but are reflected by the two women. Hajila, the traditional woman, decides to leave the confinement of her home and explore the city, whereas Isma, the emancipated one, embarks on a reflection of her past, her childhood as well as her married life. She resembles the heroines of Djebar's earlier works. It is almost as if *La soif* were being repeated in this novel, with Isma, like Nadia, choosing Hajila, who is submissive, as a second wife to her husband and then pushing her into a revolt that is bound to end in tragedy. But here the complexity of the narrative gives way to various interpretations, one of which is that Hajila could be the double of Isma or her subconscious. The intermingling of Scheherazade's story adds to this complexity and gives yet another reading of the tale. Specifically, it recalls the *Arabian Nights,* in which Scheherazade, a princess, tries to escape the fate a cruel sultan inflicts on all the virgins of the town. He has sex with them and at the end of the night kills them. Scheherazade succeeds in saving her life by inventing tales that never end, thereby keeping the sultan interested in hearing the next one every night. In order to do so, Scheherazade calls upon her sister Dinarzade for help. Dinarzade sleeps under the nuptial bed and helps her sister remember stories: "To throw light on the role of Dinarzade, as the night progresses! Her voice under the bed coaxes the story-teller up above, to find unfailing inspiration for her tales, and so keep at bay the nightmares that daybreak would bring" (*SS,* 95).

As for *Vaste est la prison* (Vast Is the Prison), it is probably the most obviously autobiographical work by Djebar, who recalls the memories of her mother, her grandmother, and herself, who talks about her father, who recalls her childhood and her adolescence. It is also a novel on Algeria's present situation with its frightening war. Djebar tells us:

> The true interrogation of my last novel, and in which I have found myself for at least two years, is how does one explain, or give an account of blood. The conclusion of *Vaste est la prison* is called "The Blood of Writing." How does one explain violence? Autobiographical writing is necessarily a retrospective writing where "I" is not always "I." It is an "I/us" or a multiplied "I." But in *Vaste est la prison* there is a regression into autobiographical and historical time; the impetus of this book was the death of someone close, inscribed in the present, a violent death, an assassination. The last few pages of the novel bear on this interrogation: to know if, writing in Berber or in Arabic, I would be able to explain better, give an account of this violence, if I could *inscribe* it. . . . I would convert within six months to any language if it could account for blood. . . . Throughout the book, I have lived an interrogation I would call ethical. In writing, there is a sort of impossibility; writing runs away, it is replaced by screaming, it is silence. ("Territoires des langues," 87)

In a foreword to her narrative *Loin de Médine* (Far from Medina; 1991) Djebar tells us why she applies the label "novel" to this collection of tales, narratives, visions, scenes, and recollections inspired by her readings of some of the Muslim historians who lived during the first centuries of Islam. Fiction allows freedom in reestablishing and unveiling a hidden space. Through it, Djebar gives a voice and a presence to the many women

forgotten by the recorders and transmitters of Islamic tradition. This is quite an ambitious undertaking, and Djebar does it well in her usual careful, sensual, well-worked-out language. In a beautiful style, she re-creates the lives of women who surrounded the Prophet Mohammed, the influence they had on his thinking and in the debates of the times. The unofficial, occulted history of the beginning of Islam becomes very real and present with its women through Djebar's powerful pen. There is Aisha, the Prophet's favorite wife, and Fatima, his proud daughter. They both died soon after him. There is Sadjah the woman prophet, Selma the healer, and so many others. They all seem to act freely and are not afraid to stand up for what they believe, especially when it pertains to their belief in the Prophet. The Prophet himself is described as soft-spoken and very kind to his women, whom he treats with respect and care and whose advice he takes seriously.

This is certainly a revolutionary outlook and program for women's role in contemporary Arab society, if it would take its tradition seriously as an example to follow. And I have no doubt Djebar intended it this way. Nevertheless, such a tactic raises many problems, not the least of which are to be found in the text itself. The final message is that one ought to leave Medina (as implied in the title of the novel): "If Aisha one day decided to leave Medina? Ah, far away from Medina, to rediscover the wind, the breathtaking, incorruptible youth of revolt!" (300). But actually, the whole novel is a paean to Medina, a glorification of the Prophet and of his women! This is the most problematic contradiction one finds throughout the book: if, in order to free oneself, one ought to leave tradition and its enslavement, then how can one look upon it as a beautiful past filled with role models?

Other questions raised by this narrative as it inscribes itself in today's contemporary Arabic and North African literature are: what message can today's writers give, and ought they give one? If, like Rushdie or El-Saadawi, they bring out the contemporary issues with clarity, frankness, and irony, are they doomed to ostracism, house arrest, threats of death, imprisonment, and persecution? Is there no middle way between glorification and reinterpretation of tradition to show how today's Islam has been twisted or radically transformed?

Djebar must have been aware of or unconsciously gripped by all these questions, because her latest work, *Le blanc de l'Algérie* (The White of Algeria; 1996), inscribes itself into the most daring, courageous, outspoken reflections of today's world problems and pressing conflicts, most specifically as enacted in the Algerian War. It dares look at the roots of the conflict and raises vital questions on the works and deaths of well-known writers, intellectuals, thinkers (Frantz Fanon, Albert Camus, Mouloud Feraoun, Jean Amrouche, Jean Sénac, Malek Haddad, Mouloud Mammeri, Kateb Yacine, Anna Gréki, Taos Amrouche, Josie Fanon, Bachir Hadj Ali, Tahar Djaout, Youssef Sebti, Said Mekbel, Mahfoud Boucebci, M'Hamed Boukhobza, Abdelkader Alloula), and others. Djebar associates the destiny of Algiers in 1957 with the present, noting that violence and carnage are taking the same form: "On both sides, death launchers, one in the name of legality, but with mercenaries, the other in the name of historical justice—or ahistorical, transcendental, therefore illuminated and with 'demons.' Between these two sides . . . a field is open where a multitude of innocents are falling, too many humble people and a number of intellectuals" (134). Djebar is not afraid to attack the powers that be: "Those who continue to officiate in the confusion of the hollow political theater . . . the well-kept, more firmly established every year, with their bellies, their self-right-eousness, their ever larger spaces, their swelling bank accounts. . . . This is how the caricature of a past is amplified, with indistinctly sublimated heroes and fraternal killings all mixed together" (150). She wonders who is going to talk about all this now and in which language, noticing that the two who could have done so with irony, humor, and strength, Kateb Yacine and Abdelkader Alloula, are now dead and much missed. Indirectly, Djebar is setting herself in their place by giving us this strong, beautiful text.

Le blanc d'Algérie is also a reflection on death, and on the yearning, the possibility/probability of her own demise. The grief and sadness she feels over the death of loved ones and the destruction of her country leads her to express a death wish: "Desire takes hold of me, in the middle of this funeral gallery, to drop my pen or my brush and to join them, to dip my face in their blood (the blood of the assassinated)" (162). She barely resists the temptation, finally noticing that the earth calls her, that other countries invite her. She will heal, forget. I agree with Clarisse Zimra, who says:

> "The White of Algeria" marks a turning point in Djebar's career, because it is the first time she has come publicly, in voice as well as in print, to an openly political position regarding current events in her country. . . . She indicts the official governmental policy that would render the complex and multilayered ethnicity of past and present-day Algeria into a single entity. But she also indicts a whole generation of writers and thinkers, herself among them, who have not spoken soon enough and loudly enough. Not any more. ("Introduction to Assia Djebar's 'The White of Algeria'")

The blunter and more open treatment of the oppressive aspects of North African societies that we find in the more recent literary inscriptions by Assia Djebar are not simply a more daring exercise of literary freedom—although we must never lose sight of the courage she has shown. Rather, the increasing clarity and frankness with which the social context is presented suggests that it is no longer merely a backdrop for the action of the story. In these works, North African society itself emerges as a character in the play, a character complete with principles of choice and action, and with both trivial and tragic flaws.

It is not necessarily the role of fiction to provide blueprints for concrete social action—and much bad fiction has resulted from attempts to do so—but the recent fiction of Assia Djebar, with its greater openness and its integration of individual struggle into the larger social context, may well become a force for positive and creative change in the Arab world and in her native Algeria, which so much needs it at this time and at this point in history.

Evelyne Accad, Autumn 1996

▪ WORKS CITED

Accad, Evelyne. *Contemporary Arab Women Writers and Poets* [with Rose Ghurayyib]. Beirut. Institute for Women's Studies in the Arab World. 1965.

———. *Veil of Shame: The Role of Women in the Contemporary Fiction of North Africa and the Arab World.* Sherbrooke, Québec. Naaman. 1978.

———. *Sexuality and War: Literary Masks of the Middle East.* New York. New York University Press. 1990.

Adnan, Etel. *Sitt Marie Rose.* California. Post-Apollo. 1982.

Ahmed, Leila. *Women and Gender in Islam: Historical Roots of a Modern Debate.* New Haven, Ct. Yale University Press. 1992.

Altomah, Salih. "Westernization and Islam in Modern Arabic Fiction." *Yearbook of Comparative and General Literature,* 20 (1971).

———. "The Contemporary Arabic Novel." *The Cry of Home.* Knoxville. University of Tennessee Press 1972.

Ba'labakki, Layla. "Nous, sans masques." *Orient* (Paris), 11 (1959).

———. *Ana Ahya.* Beirut. Al-Tijari. 1958. Published in French as *Je vis,* Paris, Seuil, 1961.

Barbot, Michel, "Destinée de femmes arabes." *Orient,* 17:1 (1965).

Beauvoir, Simone de. *The Second Sex.* London. Cape. 1968. (Original French published in 1949.)

Beck, Lois, and Nikki Keddie. *Women in the Muslim World.* Cambridge, Ma. Harvard University Press. 1978.

Bittari, Zoubeida. *O, mes sœurs musulmanes, pleurez!* Paris. Gallimard. 1972.

Boullata, Kamal. *Women of the Fertile Crescent.* Washington, D.C. Three Continents. 1978.

Chedid, Andrée. *Le sommeil délivré.* Paris. Stock. 1952. (Reissued by Flammarion in 1976; translated as *From Sleep Unbound.*)

———. *Cérémonial de la violence.* Paris. Flammarion. 1976.

———. *La maison sans racines.* Paris. Flammarion. 1985.

Cooke, Miriam. *War's Other Voices: Women Writers on the Lebanese Civil War.* Cambridge, Eng. Cambridge University Press. 1988.

Debèche, Djamila. *Aziza.* Algiers. Imbert. 1955.

Déjeux, Jean. *Assia Djebar: Romancière algérienne, cinéaste arabe.* Sherbrooke, Québec. Naaman. 1984.

———. *La littérature féminine de la langue française au Maghreb.* Paris. Karthala. 1994.

Djebar, Assia. *La soif.* Paris. Julliard. 1957.

———. *Les impatients.* Paris. Julliard. 1958. [I]

———. *The Mischief.* Frances Frenaye, tr. New York. Simon & Schuster. 1958. [M]

———. "Introduction." *Women of Islam.* London. Deutsch. 1961. Pp. 1–25.

———. *Les enfants du nouveau monde.* Paris. Julliard. 1962. [E]

———. *Les alouettes naïves.* Paris. Julliard. 1967.

———. "Le romancier dans la cité arabe." *Europe,* 474 (October 1968).

———. *Femmes d'Alger dans leur appartement.* Paris. Des Femmes. 1980.

———. *L'amour, la fantasia.* Paris. Lattès. 1985.

———. *Ombre sultane.* Paris. Lattès. 1987.

———. *Loin de Médine.* Paris. Albin Michel. 1991.

———. *Women of Algiers in Their Apartment.* Marjolijn de Jager, tr. Charlottesville. University Press of Virginia. 1992 [WA]

———. "Fugitive, et ne le sachant pas," *L'Esprit Créateur,* 33:2 (Summer 1993), pp. 129–33.

———. "Ecrire, sans nul héritage." *Trans-européennes,* 5 (Winter 1994–95), pp. 25–29.

———. *Vaste est la prison.* Paris. Albin Michel. 1995.

———. *Le blanc de l'Algérie.* Paris. Albin Michel. 1996.

———. with Lise Gauvin. "Territoires des langues: Entretien." *Langue et Littérature en Suisse Romande,* 101 (February 1996), pp. 73–87.

Donadey, Anne. "Assia Djebar's Poetics of Subversion." *L'Esprit Créateur,* 33:2 (1993), pp. 107–17.

El-Saadawi, Nawal. *The Hidden Face of Eve.* Boston. Beacon. 1981.

———. *Woman at Point Zero.* London. Zed. 1983.

———. *Memoirs from the Women's Prison.* London. Women's Press. 1986.

———. *Searching.* Shirley Eber, tr. London. Zed. 1991.

Fanon, Frantz. *Peau noire, masques blancs.* Paris. Seuil, 1952.

Farraj, 'Afif. *Al-Huriyyat Fi Adab Al-Mar'a.* Beirut. Dar Al-Farabi. 1975.

Gadant, Monique. "La permission de dire je: Réflexions sur les femmes et l'écriture à propos d'un roman de Assia Djebar, *L'amour, la fantasia." Peuples Méditerranéens,* 48–49 (July-December 1989), pp. 93–105.

Ghaussy, Soheila. "A Stepmother Tongue: 'Feminine Writing' in Assia Djebar's *Fantasia: An Algerian Cavalcade." World Literature Today,* 68:3 (Summer 1994), pp. 458–62.

Gracki, Katherine. "Assia Djebar et l'écriture autobiographique au pluriel." *Women in French Studies,* 2 (Fall 1994), pp. 55–65.

Johnson-Davis, D. *Modern Arabic Short Stories.* London. Oxford University Press. 1967.

Khatibi, Abdelkebir. *Le roman maghrébin.* Paris. Maspero. 1968.

Khoury-Ghata, Vénus. *Au sud du silence.* Paris. Saint-Germaindes-Près. 1975.

———. *Vacarme pour une lune morte.* Paris. Flammarion. 1983.

———. *La maûresse du notable.* Paris. Seghers. 1992.

Malti-Douglas, Fedwa. *Woman's Body, Woman's Word: Gender and Discourse in Arabo-Islamic Writing.* Princeton, N.J. Princeton University Press. 1991.

Marx-Scouras, Danielle. "The Poetics of Maghrebine Illegitimacy." *L'Esprit Créateur,* 26:1 (Spring 1986).

———. "Muffled Screams / Stifled Voices." *Yale French Studies,* 82 (1993), pp. 172–82.

Mernissi, Fatima. *Beyond the Veil.* Cambridge, Eng. Shenkman. 1975.

Mikhail, Mona. *Images of Arab Women.* Washington, D.C. Three Continents. 1979.

Mortimer, Mildred. "The Evolution of Djebar's Feminist Conscience." *Contemporary African Literature,* 1983, pp. 7–14.

———. "Entretien avec Assia Djebar, écrivain algérien," *Research in African Literatures,* 19:2 (Summer 1988), pp. 197–205.

———. "Fleeing the Harem: Assia Djebar." In her *Journeys Through the French African Novel.* Portsmouth, N.H. Heinemann. 1990.

M'Rabet, Fadéla, *La femme algérienne, suivi de Les Algériennes.* Paris. Maspero. 1969. Pp. 97–142.

Murdoch, H. Adlai. "Rewriting Writing: Identity, Exile and Renewal in Assia Djebar's *L'amour. la fantasia." Yale French Studies,* 83 (1993), pp. 71–92.

Page, Andrea. "Rape or Obscene Copulation? Ambivalence and Complicity in Djebar's *L'Amour." Women in French Studies,* 2 (Fall 1994), pp. 42–53.

Rezzoug, Simone. Cited by Winifred Woodhull in *Transfigurations of the Maghreb.* Minneapolis. University of Minnesota Press. 1993. Pp. 78–79.

Roche, Anne. "Women's Literature in Algeria." *Research in African Literatures,* 23:2 (Summer 1992), pp. 209–15.

Tahon, Marie-Blanche. "Women Novelists and Women in the Struggle for Algeria's National Liberation (1957–1980)." *Research in African Literatures,* 23:2 (Summer 1992), pp. 39–50.

Taos, Marguerite Amrouche. *La Rue des tambourins.* Paris. Table Ronde. 1960.

Tuéni, Nadia. *Liban, vingt poèmes pour un amour.* Beirut. Zakka. 1979.

———. *Archives sentimentales d'une guerre au Liban.* Paris. Pauvert. 1982.

———. *La terre arrêtée.* Paris. Belfond. 1984.

Turk, Nadia. "Assia Djebar: Voix au féminin." *Constructions,* 1988–89, pp. 89–98.

Yetiv, Isaac. *Le thème de l'aliénation dans le roman maghrébin d'expression française.* Sherbrooke, Québec. CELEF. 1972.

Zimra, Clarisse. "Afterword" [including a 1991 interview with Djebar]. In Assia Djebar's *Women of Algiers in Their Apartment.* Marjolijn de Jager, tr. Charlottesville. University Press of Virginia. 1992. Pp. 159–211.

———. "Writing Woman: The Novels of Assia Djebar." *Sub-Stance,* 69 (1992), pp. 68–84.

———. "Introduction to Assia Djebar's 'The White of Algeria'." *Yale French Studies,* 87 (1995), pp. 140–41.

———. "Disorienting the Subject in Djebar's *L'amour, la fantasia.*" Yale French Studies, 87 (1995), pp. 149–70.

[1] Citations from *La soif, Femmes d'Alger,* and *Ombre sultane* are taken from their respective published translations: *The Mischief, Women of Algiers in Their Apartment,* and *A Sister to Schehera-zade.* All other translations from French sources are my own.

[2] Fiction, the novel, is a relatively recent genre in the Arab world for both men and women. Its origins are usually tracted back to the Egyptian Muhammad Husayn Haykal's *Zaynab* (Cairo, 1914). For more information on Arab literary history, see my book *Veil of Shame.*

[3] See my articles on the topic: "Writing to Explore (W)Human Experience," *Research in African Literatures,* 23:1 (Spring 1992), pp. 179–85; "L'écriture (comme) éclatement des frontières." postcolonial Women' Writing in French: *L'Esprit Créateur,* ed. Elisabeth Mudimbe-Boyi, 33:2 (Summer 1993), pp. 119–28.

[4] Interview, *L'Afrique littéraire et artistique,* no. 3 (February 1969).

Algerian Fiction and the Civil Crisis: Bodies under Siege

Nul n'a aujourd'hui en Algérie le monopole de la souffrance.

▨ SÉVERINE LABAT, *LE DRAME ALGÉRIEN*

During Algeria's anticolonial struggle, French-language (as well as Arabic-language) novelists took up their pens in order to oppose the violence and injustice of French colonial rule. Since the 1950s, French-language fiction in Algeria has been committed to bringing about social, political, and cultural change. Regardless of the somewhat ambiguous status that French-language writing in Algeria has previously occupied,[1] Algeria's current civil crisis, which began at the end of 1991, has witnessed an outpouring of fictional writing devoted to exposing both the political and historical complexities of the civil crisis and the numbing horror of daily life in Algeria since the start of this decade.[2] Not only have writers with long-established international reputations such as Mohammed Dib and Assia Djebar published works that deal with the civil crisis, but many young writers are publishing their first novels during this distressing state of siege.[3]

In his essay "Une société en mal d'expression," Benamar Mediene points out that "comme il y a quarante ans, l'Algérie d'aujourd'hui s'exprime par et dans le tragique" (105). During the Algerian War, as in recent years, Algerian fiction expresses "the tragic" by providing semifictional accounts of the Algerian people's sufferings and their political struggles, but today Algerian novelists also attempt to transcend through their fictional writings the very real threats of violence and death which seek to silence and censor their voices and their art. For novelists like Tahar Djaout and Rachid Mimouni, the struggle against the forces of obscurantism through the pen of committed literature has tragically ended too soon. Other writers, fearing for their lives, continue from exile the struggle for freedom of expression.

In her introduction to a special issue of *La Nouvelle Revue Française* entitled "L'Algérie des Ecrivains," Denise Brahimi rightly points out that although Algerian writers are today threatened by extremists, another significant threat they face is that of being "held hostage" by their positions as representatives of Algeria on the world stage. They also run the risk of being cast as proponents of one side or another in the conflict.[4] As Brahimi observes, "Cependant, menacés dans leur vie, les écrivains algériens affrontent un autre risque: celui de voir chacun de leurs actes exclusivement dicté par l'urgence de l'instant, l'effet simplificateur du crime" (34–35). The novelists grouped together for the purpose of this essay demonstrate that they are indeed aware of the risk of reductive representation to which Brahimi alludes. In order not simply to *react* to the crisis through literature, Algerian writers consciously attempt to transcend basic political references as well as the immediate need simply to bear witness to current events, in order to engage the reader in a compelling exchange. Recent Algerian novels do not so much *directly* and *concretely* speak to current political and social issues in Algeria as evoke an atmosphere of urgency, terror, and confusing contradictions in which the very sacredness and dignity of human life are callously discarded. My argument in this essay is that by focusing on creating a portrait of a society in which a "reign of terror" is suggested by the climate of bureaucratic confusion, nearly anonymous violence, and physical constriction, many Algerian novelists transcend a "reactive" impulse by creating works of fiction that are hauntingly effective in making the reader feel the consequences of living under siege. In this way, it may be suggested that by underscoring the body's relationship to the civil crisis, Algerian writers speak to the very real horror of violence.

Out of the nearly one dozen Algerian novels in French that have been published since early 1991, four novels in particular share a common thread: the centrality of the human body. The body is omnipresent in much recent fiction from Algeria. The very real threat of horrible violence done to the body is clearly a source for the corporeal theme in Algerian writing; bodies at risk of decapitation, emasculation, shooting, bombing, stabbing, rape, or incarceration are recurring images. For virtually all the novels published since the civil crisis began, the metaphor of Algeria the nation as a body suffering from illness, cancer, or gangrene also manifests the authors' anxiety about the "health" of the nation and its citizens. The novels chosen for this analysis include *Les vigiles* by Tahar Djaout (1991), *La malédiction* by Rachid Mimouni (1993), *Une femme à Alger* by Fériel Assima (1995), and *Un été de cendres* by Abdelkader Djemaï (1995).

In the field of literary criticism, there is presently a great deal of interest in the close relationship between the creation of narrative meaning and the depiction of the human body in literature. In *Body Works: Objects of Desire in Modern Narrative* (1993) Peter Brooks raises the question "Are we to conclude that ultimately the text itself represents the body, and the body the text?" (6). Brooks posits this query in order to arrive at what he views as the heart of the notion of representing the human body in literature: narrative constantly returns to the body, as it is the ultimate source of symbolism and, by extension, of most referential meaning. According to Brooks: "Narratives in which a body becomes a central preoccupation can be especially revelatory of the effort to bring the body into the linguistic realm because they repeatedly tell the story of the body's entrance into meaning . . . they dramatize ways in which the body becomes a key signifying factor in a text: how . . . it embodies meaning" (8).

For Algerian fiction originating in the civil crisis, the human body "embodies" meanings that are political and sectarian. The violence with which "the Other" is mutilated or violated is symptomatic of a desire to inscribe political meaning unto the Other and ultimately to defile the humanity of the victim. Recent Algerian fiction clearly illustrates Elaine Scarry's notion on the inherent inexpressibility of human physical pain. As difficult as it may prove to be, writers strive to overcome language's resistance to translating pain in order to share it and find a cathartic release. Furthermore, in *The Body in Pain* (1985) Scarry points out that there are very definite political ramifications linked to one's inability to express pain. In matters of war or torture, Scarry reminds us of just "how intricately the problem of pain is bound up with the problem of power" (12). For Algerian novelists portraying a society racked by seemingly random sectarian violence and political repression, the inexpressibility of physical pain manifests itself through a parallel representation of mental anguish and emotional pain brought on by unsettling social and political circumstances.

■ LES VIGILES: EARLY WARNING SIGNS OF AN ILLNESS

Assassinated in May 1993, Tahar Djaout published four novels and two poetry collections before his murder by a man who admitted acting on behalf of Islamic militants. Djaout's fiction was marked throughout by his uncompromising stance toward FLN corruption and what he considered to be their betrayal of history and of the Algerian Revolution's ideals. In addition to being a poet and novelist, Djaout was a highly regarded journalist living and working in Algiers, writing mainly for *Algérie-Actualité*. His dedication to exposing the truth about Algeria's real difficulties and political and social realities led him to collaborate on the creation of an independent weekly newspaper in January of 1993 entitled *Ruptures*. One of more than a hundred Algerian "intellectuals" to have been killed since 1992,[5] Djaout produced fiction that is characterized by an insistence upon the existence of universal values and truths. His fiction at first appears deceptively simple; the plots involve journeys or itineraries, and his narrators avoid bitter tirades about politics and religion. Djaout's work stands out within the scope of recent Algerian fiction because of its originality, sincerity, and humanist values.

In the novel *Les vigiles* Djaout presents a Kafkaesque tale about a young inventor (he has developed an improved loom) who runs the gauntlet of bureaucratic procedures in order first to obtain a patent application, then to secure a passport to attend an inventors' product fair in Germany, and finally to retrieve his loom model from customs officials several days after his return. Perhaps parodying the fate of Rachid Mimouni, whose novels were praised and allowed to circulate in Algeria only after they were acclaimed by the French media,[6] the inventor Mahfoudh Lemdjad is feted by the local mayor and city council after news of his award is made public. In order to expiate their crime of having harassed so noteworthy a citizen, the city administrators seek a scapegoat to take the blame. Menouar Ziada, a former maquisard in the Algerian war for independence and now an insomniac who once reported the strange all-night lights in the inventor's studio, is instructed to kill himself in order to assuage the collective guilt.

Peter Brooks, referring to Kafka's fiction, notes that "the body can be made to bear messages of all kinds" (22). For Djaout's novel, those messages inscribed unto the body include a very strong one that society as a body is in the early stages of a disease. Besides the simple narrative plot outlined above, in *Les vigiles* the third-person narrator relates each man's thoughts about the society he observes. The diagnosis is simple: the society around them is like a human body suffering from an illness; more precisely, Algerian society is likened to a body suffering from malnutrition or perhaps some kind of eating disorder.

When Mahfoudh Lemdjad goes to city hall to request the necessary documents to initiate the patent process, he encounters a singular reaction: his invention meets with skepticism, as it is not deemed vital to a society organized solely around the task of rampant consumption. The bureaucrat attempts to enlighten Mafoudh:

> Mais l'inventeur—auquel se rattachent des notions aussi dépaysantes que l'effort, la patience, le génie, le désenteressement—relève d'une race encore inconnue chez nous. Vous venez perturber notre paysage familier d'hommes qui quêtent des pensions de guerre, des fonds de commerce, des licences de taxis, des lots de terrain, des matériaux de construction; qui usent toute leur énergie à traquer des produits introuvables comme le beurre, les ananas, les légumes secs ou les pneus. Comment voulez-vous, je vous le demande, que je classe votre invention dans cet univers œsophagique? (42)

Mafoudh is a problem because he works with "his head" instead of "his stomach" (42). Djaout's underlying reference is no doubt to all Algerian writers, journalists, and intellectuals who in the past have been scorned (or even harassed) by the authorities for valuing "intellect" over consumption. Like a foreign object or a contaminant, the inventor's project cannot be introduced into a system whose sole function is to provide sustenance to an undernourished "body"—that is, Algerian society as a whole.

Furthermore, society is presented under the guise of a body that is ailing, as Mafoudh confronts his brother who has joined an Islamic party and is teaching his children that strict adherence to the sacred texts is the only salvation for a society slipping into social and political chaos. As the two men argue, the heart of their opposing ideas is made clear: which ideology can create a more "human" or "humane" society? In Mafoudh's view, his brother and like-minded citizens believe that the denigration and denial of the human body will be the path to salvation. Society's illness is expressed in the oftenheard curse "Maudite soit cette vie" (73), an insult to the very existence of human life.

In *Les vigiles,* as in many other recent novels from Algeria, another symptom of the disease is the overwhelming number of citizens who surround foreign embassies each day in the hope of being able physically to leave their country in the near future. Aware of his society's intractable illness with its numerous symptoms, a café philospher expounds his own macabre theory of how to cure the disease: "Je crois bien que l'humanisme ne vaut pas mieux. . . . Ce qu'il faudrait promouvoir, c'est une éthique du suicide. Apprendre aux gens à franchir le pas, à transcender cette lâcheté qui les empêche de s'accomplir dans le néant définitif" (72). In Djaout's Kafkaesque style, all the disturbing symptoms of a society at war with its own corporeal nature are exposed. Human beings have less and less of a role to play in creating a healthy environment. Bodies are expendable, as suicide, ultimately to be the fate of Menouar Ziada, is proposed as the "final solution" in an increasingly anarchistic society.

The absurd social order symbolized by a bloated bureaucracy that exists only to perpetuate itself is also shown in *Les vigiles* to be another root cause of the illness. Not satisfied with keeping citizens in the dark about their motives and the existence of secret dossiers on each citizen, through a mirror-effect tactic the government hopes to make each citizen feel personally responsible for the evil that affects their society: each citizen must come to see him- or herself as "contaminated." Samia, Mafoudh's lover, urges him to resist giving up when confronted with the faceless bureaucracy that at first refuses him a passport: "Ils cherchent à culpabiliser les gens, à semer en eux le doute. Ils veulent les forcer à fouiller au fond d'eux-mêmes jusqu'à découvrir le mal ou à le créer au besoin" (97–98). By implicitly creating an atmosphere of self-blame, the powers that be in *Les vigiles* hope to make citizens believe that the cancer comes solely from within. If all citizens are implicated as "contaminants" or "cancer cells," then their possible eradication, it is hoped, will be met with little resistance.

Perhaps the most telling example Mafoudh uncovers about the illness affecting his society is that some of the small bookseller stalls have disappeared, to be turned into snack bars and fast-food eating establishments. The head has again lost out in the struggle with the stomach; nourishment for the soul and mind has been deemed less vital than filling society's ravenous appetite: "Aujourd'hui, deux de ces kiosques ont été transformés en snacks; le rêve de culture et d'élévation du pays s'est englué dans une immense bouffe, s'est noyé dans une kermesse stomacale. Un pays en forme de bouche vorace et boyau interminable, sans horizon et sans rêves" (100). If society has been transformed into a gigantic stomach that only hopes to process foodstuffs, it is because of the rampant corruption on all levels of government. *Les vigiles* demonstrates Djaout's belief those who should be acting as society's guardians (vigiles) are in fact more like quack doctors, ministering to a hungry body (a being whose hyperhunger is symptomatic of a deeper malaise) as if it were gangrenous and diseased.

To avoid looking foolish after having initially refused a passport to Mafoudh Lemdjad, the city council meets to decide upon a course of action. Their words are a feeble attempt to position themselves as dedicated guardians of society's "health." Using body metaphors, they justify their project of finding a suitable scapegoat: "Comme dit je ne sais quel proverbe ou tout simplement ma logique, lorsque la main est gangrenée il ne faut pas hésiter à la couper afin de préserver la santé du reste du corps. . . . Il ne faut pas s'apitoyer sur les membres malades qui peuvent contaminer tout le corps" (162). Their self-justifying logic is meant to be read as ironic; what obviously needs pruning from the society depicted in Les vigiles are the shadowy and corrupt public officials. Menouar Ziada is chosen to be sacrificed, allegedly for the public good—the health of society. His death is not only tragically ironic, since he had already survived a near-death experience at the hands of his own comrades among the maquis during the Algerian War, but also because it was he who first brought the inventor's presence to the attention of authorities when he mistook the mysterious lights and odd evening hours kept by the apartment's tenant as a sign that political agitators were operating in his neighborhood. A true and politically disinterested vigile for the well-being of his neighborhood, Ziada cannot hope to survive in a climate of increasing corruption and political oppression.

■ LA MALÉDICTION: LES FIS CONTRE LES PÈRES

Rachid Mimouni became known as one of Algeria's leading French-language novelists with the publication of four important novels in the 1980s. His work is characterized by its links to its literary predecessors, "la tradition d'une littérature algérienne de combat, de contestation, et de remise en question qui va des nos aînés à nos plus jeunes écrivains" (Gafaïti, 33). La malédiction (1993) is Mimouni's last fictional work to be published before his death in 1995 from hepatitis. It is also very clearly a work that portrays the Algerian civil crisis in an overt and pointed fashion. Mimouni, more than the three other novelists discussed in this essay, creates characters who evidently represent the spectrum of competing ideological positions in the civil crisis. Yet again, the body in its need for dignity and the violation of that supposedly inviolable right by the forces of obscurantism serve as the unifying principles.

The events depicted in La malédiction take place during the summer of 1991, in the city of Algiers. The young obstetrician Kader and his group of friends become embroiled in a struggle to protect the privacy of the patients in the maternity ward after local electoral victories and government concessions to striking militants have allowed members of a conservative Islamic group to gain access to the hospital's administration. Kader's father died in the Algerian Revolution, and since that time Kader has benefitted from the tutelage of Si Morice, now a drunkard eccentric but in his youth a rebel against his own property-owning class and a maquisard in the revolution. In a development that evokes Kateb Yacine's masterpiece Nedjma, Si Morice (like Si Mokhtar for Rachid) is actually responsible for the death of Kader's father during the war for independence. The events of the present in La malédiction are clearly linked to unresolved tensions and ambiguities from the Algerian War. The generation of the fathers—that is, the generation of FLN party founders—has "sired" the generation of Islamic militants who are currently attempting to reformulate Algerian society along new ideological lines.

In Mimouni's novel the question of paternity and legitimacy functions as a direct body metaphor that attempts to explain the origins of the actual civil crisis.

> [Kader] se demandait si le pays n'était pas en train de payer le prix des monstruosités autrefois commises au nom d'une cause juste. N'était-ce pas le passé qui resurgissait à la faveur des derniers événements? Le médecin se souvint de la phrase de Si Morice qui annonçait l'heure du réglement de tous les vieux comptes. Il craignait que le sang ne coulât encore, tout en estimant qu'il était temps que le pays se débarrassât des boulets qu'il traînait depuis si long temps. (266)

Kader sees the source for the present-day political and social violence in Algeria as stemming from repressed violence and crimes from the war of independence. Kader, by the novel's close, has made his peace with Si Morice and the latter's role in his father's death. However, Kader's brother Hocine exemplifies "the son" who rejects the birthright passed down to him from "the father." Hocine is a member of a society that Benamar Mediene describes as "une société des fils" who no longer recognize themselves in "la société des pères" (109). La malédiction opens with Kader visiting a Paris morgue looking for his missing brother. Hocine reappears when Kader is kidnapped and brought before a self-appointed Islamic Revolutionary Court. Hocine, a former soldier for Islam in Afghanistan, acts as the judge. He has secretly returned to Algiers (allowing his mother and wife to continue believing him dead) in order to pursue his project of instituting an Islamic regime in Algeria. Hocine will ultimately appoint himself judge and executioner over his brother and sentence Kader to die for his role in hiding the patient files at the maternity ward.

To become a successful Islamic fighter, Hocine not only adopts a new identity that symbolically cuts off all birth ties to his family and to the ideals of the Algerian Revolution for which his father died, but he also physically cuts himself off from his family by carrying out the execution of his own brother Kader, condemned as an enemy of Islam. Hocine's rejection of the blood ties that bind him to his family are symptomatic of a larger "filiation" crisis, identified by Benamar Mediene as one of the root causes of Algeria's civil crisis. In his essay "Une société en mal d'expression" Mediene notes that the charter members of the FLN had set themselves up as "founding fathers" to succeeding generations of young men in Algerian society without realizing that their own betrayal of the revolution's ideals would lead to the current state of affairs, in which the "fathers" have lost all legitimacy with the "sons": "Pères biologiques transportant l'image de l'échec total, patent, insupportable: la culture et l'idéologie patriarcales se fragilisent et ne peuvent plus permettre le maintien des cohésions familiales et des repères sociaux. Progressivement l'autorité du fils se substitue à celle du père" (110). As patriarchy is challenged and an attempt is made to substitute the authority of sons acting on behalf of God, the biological and symbolic authority of the fathers of the new nation-state is compromised. As Hocine sits in judgment of his brother, one of Hocine's followers makes a scornful reference to their father, who died a martyr in the Algerian Revolution. This lack of respect brings tears to Kader's eyes, but Hocine remains impassive, indicating he no longer recognizes the link between himself and his biological (and symbolic) father.

In *La malédiction* society and its governing body are suffering from corruption and decay, symbolized by body metaphors of rot and gangrene. One character, speaking of the FLN Party, observes: "Du centre de pouvoir n'émane qu'une odeur de cadavre en putréfaction" (81). On an even more symbolic level, not only is the single-party system suffering from the cancer of corruption and illegitimacy, but so many men's minds and their attitudes toward sexuality have been infected as well. As Louisa—a young woman forced out of medical school by her peers and professors because of her sensual charms—tells Kader: "Il faudra bien un jour se décider à extirper ce chiendent sexuel qui gangrène vos esprits" (186).

The Islamic militants who assume control of the hospital administration believe they are acting as legitimate replacements for corrupt secular authorities. They believe they have a divinely appointed right to take charge of the women who are patients in the maternity ward. At stake in the power play between Kader and his friends on the one side and the Islamic militants on the other is the right of the individual (in this case, women) to safeguard their privacy and to maintain doctor-patient confidentiality. Like Hocine, who feels he must deny the bonds of biological fraternity (and paternity) for the sake of his "brothers" in the ideological struggle, the men who now control the hospital feel they must prove their political and civil authority by targeting notions of paternity and legitimacy. Msili, a former ambulance driver dismissed for having too many accidents, now revels in his usurped authority to order physicians to comply with the new statutes erected by the local Islamic authorities. His reasons for wanting to obtain the women's files is chilling and strikes at the very heart of the women's right to privacy regarding their own bodies. Msili tells Kader that the files must be investigated, because "Nous savons que vous recevez des dévergondées qui viennent ici se soulager du produit de leurs fornications" (140).[7] Kader is tempted to tell Msili that these procedures are legal under the current national law, but he realizes that hatred and a determination to act without compassion are the overriding factors pushing the Islamic militants to these actions.

In *La malédiction* the body is central to the concerns expressed in the narrative. Kader's act of conviction, for which he pays with his life, is a symbolic attempt to guard the dignity of the human body in the face of efforts to defile the women at the maternity ward and to make their bodies—women as the sum of all sins in the eyes of the Islamic party members—targets which may be blamed for all the social ills that afflict that society.[8]

At the end of *La malédiction* Kader feels defeated by the knowledge that his own brother is determined to kill him, and he expresses his bewilderment at the state of affairs in which a doctor— taught to prize human life above all else—loses his authority to practice medicine for the benefit of the human body. Hatred has become the common currency, and the body has become the target of this hatred.

> Sa pratique de médecin lui avait pourtant enseigné la nécessité de lutter pied à pied pour contenir les ravages d'une affection. Mais il ne savait pas se défendre contre la haine. On lui a appris les gestes qui sauvent, non pas ceux qui tuent, et il ne comprenait pas cette obscure perversion qui poussait tant de frères et de voisins à vouloir assassiner leurs frères et voisins. Il prit soudain conscience qu'un terrible monstre venait d'émerger des abysses et qu'il allait tout dévaster. (279).

The normal order in which a doctor can practice his or her skill no longer exists in the society depicted by Mimouni. The body is a target: its sufferings and the violence it endures are symbolically referred as the "monster" that has emerged from the darker, sinister side of humanity. The infection plaguing Algerian society is evoked by a memory Kader has of a previous statement made by a friend who is also a militant for the Islamic cause. His friend scolds him for his desire to "soigner des individus quand la société est malade. Si vous voulez continuer à faire votre métier, il vous faudra prendre le pouvoir." Kader's answer reveals that, as a physician, he is dedicated to helping mankind one body at a time; the physical ailments can be addressed, but the psychological illness affecting Algerians which pits brother against brother is beyond his skill: "Nous n'avons pas cette prétention. Nous nous contentons, selon nos modestes connaissances, de limiter les dégâts. Vos poumons sont mal en point, mais votre tête est plus gravement atteinte. Le mal qui la ronge dépasse mon savoir" (280).

■ UNE FEMME À ALGER: WOMEN'S BODIES UNDER SIEGE

Une femme à Alger: Chronique du désastre (1995) is Fériel Assima's first novel. She has subsequently published another remarkable work, *Rhoulem ou le sexe des anges* (1996), which paints the contemporary Algerian scene even more vividly as kind of nightmarish landscape. Her stream-of-consciousnes style of narration allows her to evoke the horrors of daily life in Algeria, in which citizens are beleaguered from all sides, without sliding into melodrama or political diatribe. The unnamed female narrator of *Une femme à Alger* is practically impersonal as she describes the effects of living under siege in a large apartment in Algiers with the extended family that surrounds her. This novel (or is it the author's own journal?) is distinguished by a terse and restrained narrating voice. The narrator's observations of the chaos and the physical and psychic disintegration affecting the city and its inhabitants are hauntingly evocative for their detached simplicity and relative objectivity.

At the heart of *Une femme à Alger* is the narrator's growing awareness that she too is implicated in the civil crisis by the very fact of her gender and her class: "Les agressions contre les femmes se multiplient. La police n'y peut rien. Elle même a du mal à se protéger. Il me faut être prudente" (59). Her insight into the heart of the state of siege and the reigning disorder is striking for its lucidity: "Chaque individu devient victime potentielle, ou criminel en puissance. C'est cette situation qui creuse un fossé entre nous tous. Cette aberration nous isole et nous rend plus fragiles" (59). Every citizen is implicated; it is no longer possible to stand in a neutral corner. The narrator's flash of insight regarding the

true state of affairs underscores the banality of violence; its frequency and anonymity push each protagonist into an isolated position. Even the narrator's stance of simply observing and documenting "the disaster" in her "chronicle" means that she too is now no longer a completely innocent party.

The climate of terror evoked in Assima's narrative is underscored by the constant threat of violence, especially violence against women. In this haunting narrative, their bodies become a lightning rod for the ideological battle being played out in the streets of Algiers. Women like the narrator who are not wearing modest dress are the primary objects of insults, threats, and violent demonstrations that reveal the extent to which a woman's body in public, dressed in "Western" clothes, is transgressive and thereby a fitting target. While visiting an acquaintance with a friend who is wearing a sundress, the narrator's friend is given a violent warning that her body is deemed an affront to members of the extremist movement. Bearded men driving past the house lash her with a steel wire, drawing blood from a gash in her neck. This aggression is matched by the threat yelled from the truck: "Sales putes, c'est pas la culotte qu'on va arracher, c'est la tête!" (14). A neighbor assures the young women that the men just mean to frighten and intimidate them. The threat of decapitation and the suggestion of rape circulate, as men's voices—angry and insistent—are described as rising from all sides in the city.

Women's bodies are clearly marked as targets in the growing struggle. What will the domestic incarceration of women accomplish? How will the siege against women bring about the new social order demanded by the throngs of agitators who fill up the city squares? Assima's work suggests that the rhetoric against women is merely an excuse to vent many forms of hatred that have lain dormant in the society portrayed in *Une femme à Alger*.

The narrator describes the present state of affairs as a world whose "normal" order has been reversed. Clothing for women, which has previously marked the "tradition" versus "modernity" binary, has been reversed: "C'est le monde à l'envers. Les femmes en hidjab sont dans les rues, les autres, habillées à l'européenne, restent enfermées chez elle" (66–67). Whether those women wearing modest dress have adopted it out of conviction or for safety's sake, the narrator wants to suggest that ideological walls between segments of the population are being constructed.

Class conflict in which women and their bodies are portrayed as the culprits is also presented in *Une femme à Alger*. Chahine, a woman doctor, gives birth to her second child in a maternity clinic during the night of a particularly tense period of unrest in the city. The nurse on duty strikes another woman in labor for crying out. In the nurse's opinion, the woman, who is giving birth to her eleventh child, is a kind of social "criminal"; even worse, the nurse likens the woman to a piece of garbage and calls her "une pondeuse de malheur" (88). When Chahine reprimands the nurse for her cruelty toward the woman in labor, the nurse rejects her counsel by pointing out that Chahine, as an educated woman in a nice apartment with only two children, is in no position to pass judgment on those who have to deal with the lower classes. For the nurse in question, the lower classes are scapegoated as the cause of the nation's misfortunes: women who give birth to too many children, "traditional" mothers who insist their sons marry in spite of housing shortages, women who stand on their balconies and take pleasure in the scenes of violence in the streets below (88). In *Une femme à Alger* the acrimonious discourses about politics, religion, and the need for social change which circulate in the public and private spaces of Algiers point to women as the source of so much evil.

Not all the women portrayed in the novel accept their treatment in this climate of terror. Outside city hall an elderly widow asks passers-by for assistance in claiming her widow's pension. A bearded young man responds by insulting her for being out in public making "a spectacle of herself," adding that if she were his own mother, he would feel no remorse at "beating her" (129). Enraged, the woman unleashes her fury and frustration on the man who dared speak to her in that fashion; she draws attention to her gender and, by extension, to a social order that has become so corrupt and tainted that mothers no longer have the respect and protection of their sons. Lifting her skirts, she shrieks:

> Tu le vois, ce trou, dit-elle dans un râle animal, c'est de là que ta mére t'a chié. C'est d'ici qu'on vous a tous chiés, bâtards que vous êtes, pédés, femmelettes qu'on a élevés comme des dieux et qui nous le rendent par des menaces, qui osent menacer celles qui leur ont donné la vie. Parce qu'elles n'ont plus personne pour les protéger, on les traite de traînées. Parce qu'elles refusent de mourir comme des misérables, on se permet de les insulter. (129)

"Génétrices" and "matrices," women are shown to be under siege for their biological essence, for their role in creating the millions of young men who now throng the streets of Algiers and who are "agonisés de l'estomac et du sexe" (145).

As in *Les vigiles,* one of the causes here for the climate of terror is that the Algerian populace has become one great hungering body. The lack of basic foodstuffs such as oil, butter, and flour drives people into the streets with the demand that their hunger be satisfied: "Le peuple n'est qu'un ventre dilaté qui aspire la terre. Ces pénuries volontaires ne profitent à personne. Une foule, un flot de boue, un éboulement déferlent sur nous, déracinent nos jours de ce trop long sommeil" (36). The trope of the entire populace being transformed into one single belly symbolizes that the nation has become one giant "need" or "appetite." All the political, economic, and social frustrations felt by the people are transformed into a basic human need for food.

The society chronicled in Assima's narrative is one at war with itself and with its biological nature. Those who can, seek escape in other countries; they seek escape from a nation that makes its citizens "dingues" (54). Those like the narrator who remain in Algiers must face the truth of their situation. Living in a state of siege destroys all points on the moral compass. As children turn against parents (one character bemoans the fact that there are many more children than adults, and this state of affairs is to blame as well) and siblings turn against each other, people must acknowledge the fact that their humanity has been compromised: "Nous avons semé la haine, nous récoltons l'absurde haine qui fait de nous des monstres" (157). Human beings transformed into monsters: how can an explanation be found to account for the violence? The novel has no closure; as the violence continues, the narrator's chronicle will continue as well. The narrator's tale ends with a reference to the waking nightmare that has engulfed the nation. Life under a state of siege has given people a single-minded desire to escape and leave their country. The narrator imagines a possible future date when this episode will be evoked by a near-mythic statement: "Quand il était une fois un peuple, un pays, une terre que tout le monde rêvait de quitter" (187).

▪ UN ÉTÉ DE CENDRES: LIVING ON THE EDGE

Abdelkader Djemaï, now living in France and contributing articles to *Le Monde,* has published two novels in Algeria (*Saison de pierres* in 1986 and *Mémoires de nègres* in 1991) before releasing *Un été de cendres* (1995). The narrator-protagonist of this very brief third novel is Sid Ahmed Benbrik, a government statistician who has been demoted due to his inopportune claims that, in fact, the population of Algiers is actually several million higher than the official statistics indicate (30). Benbrik's superiors also ostracize him for suggesting that someone in the government statistical bureau should be keeping count of the "personnes assassinées dans la rue ou chez elles, devant leurs enfants, leurs épouses" (17).

Is Benbrik mad, as his former supervisors and colleagues wish to imply? His first-person narrating voice is one of detached lucidity; Benbrik describes the events that torment the city (and himself) during a single month, and indeed they are events that could make even the strongest person slip into insanity.

Disgraced in his profession, the narrator now lives in a minuscule room in his former office building. Recently widowed, he passes the time by looking out his window, methodically preparing his meals, and polishing his shoes. *Un été de cendres* is a Kafkaesque tale of one man's efforts to keep his sanity as chaos, violence, suicide, and corruption surround him. The narrative takes place during one summer month in Algiers. An intense heat wave is roasting the countryside and its inhabitants. For lack of spare parts, the city morgue's refrigeration system has broken down, and the narrator cannot help but dwell on the bodies that are piling up and rotting in a morgue with no refrigeration (85). To make matters worse, the trash collectors are on strike and garbage is piling up in the streets, stinking and raising the specter of pestilence in an already-martyred city.

The tone of *Un été de cendres* is one of quiet desperation. In spite of his own sufferings, the narrator has a gentle word for those despairing even more than himself, especially the elderly guardian of the building, whose eldest son is in an insane asylum, where he eventually commits suicide. Madness and confinement in *Un été de cendres* are recurring body metaphors that translate the atmosphere of deep despair swallowing up the city and its inhabitants. Speaking of the deplorable conditions at the asylum housing his son, the guardian notes, "Le pays entier avait besoin d'être interné" (27).

In order not to go insane living in the tiny office, the narrator concentrates all his energies on his physical body. He stores food and plans out his meals in detail at the start of the day. He suffers from tremors brought on by too much coffee and too many cigarettes. Once a month, he visits a prostitute in a small brothel in a nearby neighborhood in order to reassure himself that "je n'ai pas encore perdu le goût de l'amour" (75). The body must resist decay and madness through regimented living: Benbrik shaves carefully, exercises in the empty building after nightfall, and methodically washes his socks and underwear once a week.

Benbrik can no longer sleep; at night he listens to the noises that drift up to his window from the city below. Part of the city is burning under the assault from security forces; the ashes also drift through his window: "Je referme alors la fenêtre sur la rumeur belliqueuse et sanglante de la ville. Têtue, animale, elle s'infiltre, à travers les huit cent dix murs et les mille deux cents

vitres dont soixante-cinq ont été soufflés par l'explosion d'une voiture piégée. Victorieuse, vorace, la guerre finit par me rejoindre jusque dans mon lit de camp" (85). Living on the edge of sanity, perched precariously on the edge of the violence that threatens to overwhelm the methodical nature of his mind, the narrator finds solace in the detached accounting of bodies, fires, bombs, and eventually the flies that begin to swarm in the city—the ultimate symbol of the state of decay taking over all life in the metropolis below.

Besides being surrounded by death everywhere in the city, Benbrik makes it a habit to go to the cemetery to visit the grave of his late wife, barren yet dead from uterine cancer. There the narrator sees another side of the state of affairs. Each time the city extends the cemetery walls, the need for more and more graves outstrips the city's expansions. Benbrik notices: "Le cimetière a quadruplé de surface depuis trois ans" (109). As in the city morgue, the bodies are multiplying so quickly that their disposal presents a serious problem. The horrific nature of this dilemma translates the urgency of the situation in nightmarish fashion.

Un été de cendres is the tale of one man's withdrawal into a numbing state of lucid evaluation. The narrative is not fiction in the traditional sense; of what use is fiction in a world where "la réalité dépasse souvent la fiction" (46)? Death is omnipresent here; the narrator reads reports of atrocious killings, and he redoubles his efforts to live in as organized a fashion as is possible while camped out in a small public office. He increases his consumption of coffee and cigarettes. He is perhaps slowly killing himself with nicotine and caffeine, but, as he reasons, "au moins, j'aurai choisi ma mort" (46).

By the end of the novel, Benbrik's sanity is even more questionable. He describes for a second time the "gros lézards qui remuent dans ma tête pleine de murs fissurés" and the "bruits de ferraille qui déchirent mon cerveau" (112). For how much longer can he hold out against his supervisors and colleagues, who wish to have him taken away to an insane asylum with the thousands of other citizens who have succumbed (as has virtually the entire nation) to "cette violence venue du plus profond de ses entrailles, de sa peur" (51). His only course of action to stave off the threat of madness is to plan his next statistical project: counting the flies which now infest the city. In an ironic homage to the narrator's lifelong career as a statistician for the city of Algiers, contrasting his former usefulness with his present-day hermitlike state of existence, he thinks, "Cette importante mission, sur laquelle je fonde beaucoup d'espoir, constituera, sans nul doute, le couronnement de ma longue et fructueuse carrière à la Direction générale des statistiques" (112).

Recent Algerian fiction describing the current civil crisis reveals how the multiple layers of violence affect all citizens. At the heart of the civil crisis as depicted in these four novels is the human body as a specific target and as a metaphor for the causes and manifestations of chaotic political and sectarian violence in Algeria since 1992. These four authors refuse to abdicate their responsibility as committed writers even in an atmosphere of horror and mindnumbing confusion, and the reader must acknowledge the courage of all such writers who resist every effort to muzzle their pens and their voices. Perhaps more so than the most precise journalistic account of the terrors facing Algeria today, fiction from this period will contribute to our understanding of how the dignity of the human spirit resists the forces of obscurantism (from all ideological positions) in order to create art. It is important to recall Tahar Djaout's words from his first editorial in *Ruptures:* "L'Algérie vit la période des combats décisifs où chaque abdication, chaque pouce de terrain cédé peuvent s'avérer fatals." Novelists who assume their role even in the face of life-threatening circumstances are to be appreciated for heeding Djaout's "call to arms." Only silence (refraining from writing or speaking in *any* language) may be a potential victory for the forces of oppression seeking control over Algeria today.

Patricia Geesey, Summer 1997

■ WORKS CITED

Addi, Lahouari. "Les intellectuels qu'on assassine." *Esprit,* special issue "Avec l'Algérie," January 1995, pp. 130–38.

———. "Algeria's Tragic Contradictions." *Journal of Democracy,* 7:3 (July 1996), pp. 94–107.

Assima, Fériel. *Une femme à Alger: Chronique du désastre.* Paris. Arléa. 1995.

———. *Rhoulem ou le sexe des anges.* Paris. Arléa. 1996.

Bekkar, Rabia. "Femmes, filles et villes." *Demain l'Algérie.* Gérard Ignasse, Emmanuel Wallon, eds. Paris. Syros. 1995. Pp. 89–103.

Bonn, Charles. *Le roman algérien de langue française.* Paris. L'Harmattan. 1985.

———. "Deux ans de littérature maghrébine de langue française." *Hommes et Migrations,* no. 1197 (April 1996), pp. 46–52.

Boudjedra, Rachid. *FIS de la haine.* Paris. Denoël. 1992.

Brahimi, Denise. "L'Algérie des écrivains." Introduction to a special issue of *La Nouvelle Revue Française,* no. 521 (June 1996), pp. 34–35.

Brooks, Peter. *Body Work: Objects of Desire in Modern Narrative.* Cambridge, Ma. Harvard University Press. 1993.

Burgat, François. *L'Islamisme en face.* Paris. La Découverte. 1995.

CISIA *Cahier,* no. 1: "Tahar Djaout: Ruptures et Fidelités." Paris. CISA. 1993.

Déjeux, Jean. *Littérature maghrébine d'expression française.* Paris. PUF. 1992.

Dib, Mohammed. *La nuit sauvage.* Paris. Albin Michel. 1995.

Djaout, Tahar. *Les vigiles.* Paris. Seuil. 1991.

Djebar, Assia. *Le blanc d'Algérie.* Paris. Albin Michel. 1995.

Djemaï, Abdelkader. *Saison de pierres.* Algiers. ENAL-Alger. 1986.

———. *Mémoires de nègre.* Algiers. ENAL-Alger. 1991.

———. *Un eété de cendres.* Paris. Michalon. 1995.

Entelis, John P. "Political Islam in Algeria: The Nonviolent Dimension." *Current History,* 94:588 (January 1995), pp. 13–17.

Gafaïti, Hafid. "Mimouni entre la critique algérienne et française." *Itinéraires et contacts de cultures,* no. 14 (1991), "Poétiques croisées." Charles Bonn, ed. Paris. L'Harmattan. 1991. Pp. 26–34.

Grandguillaume, Gilbert. *Arabisation et politique linguistique au Maghreb.* Paris. Maisonneuve & Larose. 1983.

Imache, Djedjiga, and Inés Nour. *Algériennes entre Islam et Islamisme.* Aix-en-Provence, Fr. Edisud. 1994.

Khan, Amin. "Algerian Intellectuals: Between Identity and Modernity." *Algeria: The Challenge of Modernity.* Ali El-Kenz, ed. London. CODESRIA. 1991. Pp. 281–306.

Malley, Robert. *The Call from Algeria: Third Worldism, Revolution, and the Turn to Islam.* Berkeley. University of California Press. 1996.

Mediene, Benamar. "Une société en mal d'expression." In *Demain l'Algérie.* Ignasse and Wallon, eds. Paris. Syros. 1995. Pp. 105–20.

Mimouni, Rachid. *De la Barbarie en général et de l'intégrisme en particulier.* Paris. Le Pré aux Clercs. 1992.

———. *La malédiction.* Paris. Stock. 1993. Republished in Casablanca by EDDIF in 1995.

Mortimer, Robert. "Islam and Multiparty Politics in Algeria." *Middle East Journal,* 45:4 (Autumn 1991), pp. 575–93.

Reporters Sans Frontières. *Le drama algérien: Un peuple en otage.* Paris. La Découverte. 1994.

Scarry, Elaine. *The Body in Pain: The Making and Unmaking of the World.* New York/Oxford. Oxford University Press. 1985.

Zoubir, Yahia. "The Painful Transition from Authoritarianism in Algeria." *Arab Studies Quarterly,* 15:3 (Summer 1993), pp. 83–110.

———. "Review of *FIS de la haine* and *De la barbarie.*" *Arab Studies Quarterly,* 16:2 (Spring 1994), pp. 100–4.

[1] The limited scope of this essay does not allow for a thorough examination of the relationship between French-language and Arabic-language writing. As in most former French colonies, indigenous languages suffered under French colonial rule. To this day, under the auspices of Francophone Development Programs, the French government actively promotes continued use of French. This state of affairs quite naturally causes professional jealously and resentment between French-language authors, who benefit from these attentions, and those who choose to express themselves in other languages. For more information on language choice and Algerian intellectuals, see Lahouari Addi, Gilbert Grandguillaume, François Burgat, and Amin Khan. For a history of French-language Algerian literature, see Charles Bonn and Jean Déjeux.

[2] The current crisis, which nowadays is more often referred to as a civil war, began in January 1992, following the December

1991 cancellation of national election results that indicated the FIS (Front Islamique du Salut) had won a majority. Algeria's military-backed government, led by the FLN (Front de Libération Nationale) since the nation's independence in 1962, feared the consequences of the FIS victory and subsequently revoked many of the multiparty election reforms. Since the start of 1992, the government's security forces and various groups (Islamic militants) opposed to the continued rule of the FLN have engaged in both open and clandestine terrorist violence. To date, more than 60,000 Algerians from all backgrounds have been killed in the fighting. For more detailed information on the civil war, see François Burgat, Yahia Zoubir, Lahouari Addi, Robert Mortimer, John P. Entelis, and Robert Malley.

3 This essay deals with works of fiction. Assia Djebar's recent work *Le blanc d'Algérie* (1995) is not so much a novel as it is a meditation on the fate of many well-known intellectuals and writers—Algerian or strongly associated with Algeria—who became martyrs to the cause of democracy and freedom of expression, from the 1950s to the present day. In 1992 Rachid Boudjedra published a polemical nonfiction essay condemning the FIS for their extreme positions. In 1992 the novelist Rachid Mimouni also published a treatise against the two main groups locked in a heartless battle for the political soul of Algeria, namely the FLN and the FIS. For a more detailed look at these teo nonfiction works written by two of Algeria's leading writers, see Yahia Zoubir's review published in *Arab Studies Quartely*.

4 At the Cornell conference "Algeria: In and Out of French," Hafid Gafaïti pointed out that, tragically, the events in Algeria are viewed in some circles as a "godsend" (*du pain bénit*) for neocolonialist discourses related to "la Francophonie."

5 For further information on Algerian intellectuals and their role in society, see Lahouari Addi and Amin Khan.

6 For a detailed description of how the reception of Mimouni's work in France affected his treatment in Algeria, see Hafid Grafaïti's essay "Rachid Mimouni entre la critique algérienne et la critque française."

7 The women characters who are patients at the clinic in *La malédiction* have ended up in their present situation because of the deceitfulness and cruelty of men. Seduced and abandoned, or raped by their employers or stepfathers, the patients on the maternity ward are in no way guilty of what Msili suspects.

8 For a summary of how Islamic Party rhetoric in Algeria has focused on women, see Djedjiga Imache and Inès Nour, *Algériennes entre Islam et Islamisme,* and Rabia Bekkar's essay "Femmes, filles et villes."

Moloud Mammeri Returns to the Mountains

During the night of 25–26 February 1989 the Algerian novelist Mouloud Mammeri died in an automobile accident near Ain-Defla, two hundred kilometers west of Algiers. He had attended a threeday colloquium on "Literary Creation and the Greater Maghreb: From the Specific to the Universal," held at Mohammed I University in Oujda, Morocco, during which he had delivered a talk entitled "Is Specificity in Literature a Problem?," and was returning to Algiers when his car struck a tree.

Mammeri's contribution to Maghrebian culture developed on several fronts and covered the entire span of modern Maghrebian Francophone literature. A member of the so-called "Generation of 1952" (Mouloud Feraoun, Mammeri, Mohammed Dib, Kateb Yacine) which launched the explosion of Maghrebian literature in French, Mammeri was the author of two "ethnographic" novels about Kabyle life and customs and about culture conflict with the colonial overlay (*La colline oubliée,* 1952, and *Le sommeil du juste* [Eng. *The Sleep of the Just*], 1955), a more epic novel about contemporary Algerian history (*L'opium et le bâton,* 1965), and an oneiric fable which ostensibly describes a trans-Saharan crossing but which may be interpreted symbolically on several levels (*La traversée,* 1982). When asked, a few days before his death, about his work in progress, Mammeri replied that he had almost finished a novel, that it was in rough form and only needed a good bit of rewriting.

Besides being a novelist, Mammeri was one of the world's leading authorities on Berber language and literature. He had published a Berber grammar (1976), a collection of traditional poems or *isefra* by the great nineteenth-century wandering Kabyle bard Si Mohandou-Mhand (1969), and an anthology titled *Poèmes kabyles anciens* (1980).[1] Mammeri had also written plays, essays, and short stories and had translated traditional tales. In 1984 Mammeri was a member of the jury for the Neustadt International Prize for Literature; his nominee for the prize, Jorge Amado of Brazil.[2]

Mammeri was a quiet, tactful man, but events in his life were often surrounded by controversy. A prize awarded by the French to his first novel was maligned by some compatriots as a deliberate wedge between Kabyle and Arab. In 1980 Mammeri was scheduled to deliver a lecture on traditional Kabyle poetry at the largely Berber university at Tizi-Ouzou. The lecture was canceled by authorities at the last minute. Mammeri had only been prevented from giving the lecture; but rumors spread that he had been arrested, and riots ensued.

On 23 February 1989, just two days before Mammeri's death, Algerians had voted in a new constitution, and Mammeri was brimming over with optimism concerning the future of his country. He felt that the open discussion in the press since the October 1988 riots, regardless of the direction future events would take, had been a healthy, wonderful happening. One had a feeling that Mammeri's longawaited time had come. Algeria was entering a decisive period in its history, and Mammeri was at the peak of his creative and intellectual powers. His place in literature is assured; the real tragedy is Algeria's loss of this man at this particular moment in the country's history.

■ ■ ■

Mammeri was a gentle man with a warm laugh and charming manners. I am glad to have had the opportunity to know him. I shall always remember his unstinting kindness, intellectual curiosity, modesty, and trenchant wit. Two anecdotes from the final days may demonstrate the charm and the wit.

One morning I came to breakfast in the Hotel Terminus in Oujda, where the colloquium participants were staying. It was early and Mammeri was alone in the dining room, seated at a table set for two. I said: "May I join you, or were you waiting for someone?" "Yes I was; *you,*" he replied gently, smiling and gesturing to the empty chair opposite him.

One evening, when we returned from dinner, we went to the front desk to get our keys. I was in room 424, Mammeri in Room 3. Wishing to use what little Arabic I had learned in my recent studies, I laboriously asked for the key to room number "arba'a mi'a wa arba'a wa 'ashrin," by the middle of which phrase the clerk, knowing my room number, was holding out my key. He then turned to Mammeri who smiled and quickly said, in English, "Room Three, please." We all laughed at this teasing yet benevolent bit of humor.

Kabylia, where Mammeri was born in 1917, has an essentially oral tradition. Mammeri was thus influenced at an early age by the foreign classic writers, notably Racine, by the Russian novelists, and by such Americans as Hemingway and Caldwell. He was always concerned with the multivalent nature of the literary product, ever mindful of the form, the content, and the reader for whom the work was intended. In an interview published posthumously in Algiers[3] he conveys this three-pronged concern.

> In the culture in which I was born, books did not count (or hardly). . . . I love book places but not to the point of fetishizing them, not to the point of preferring the particular manner books have of saying something to that which they say. A beautiful bottle (or perhaps no bottle at all)! But if there weren't inside the bottle a fine beverage, and, perhaps more important still, the use one can put it to. . . .

On 28 February, in the Beni-Yenni region of Kabylia, Mouloud Mammeri was buried in the earth whose spirit he somehow defined in his works and anthologies. His funeral was attended by an enormous crowd. At the end of Mammeri's latest novel, *La traversée,* the hero comes home to die alone in the village *djemaa* or

Najib Mahfuz *(AP/Wide World Photos)*

square. So too was Mammeri's crossing done; he too had come home, but he was not alone.

Eric Sellin, Summer 1989

[1] For reviews of *La traversée* and *Poèmes kabyles anciens,* see respectively *WLT* 58:1 (Winter 1984), p. 151, and 55:3 (Summer 1981), p. 516.

[2] For a biobibliographical profile on Mammeri as a member of the 1984 Neustadt Prize jury, see *WLT* 58:1 (Winter 1984), p. 49.

[3] "La dernière interview," *Horizons* (Algiers), 28 February 1989, p. 2.

EGYPT

Najib Mahfuz: Nobel Laureate in Literature, 1988

It was, I seem to recollect, quite early in my British school career that I was made aware of the value of using the anonymous voice in scholarly discourse. My use of it last year in writing the article "Arabic Literature and the Nobel Prize" (see *WLT* 62:2, pp. 201–3) was to the following effect: "No Arab has as yet won the prize; whether one will (or can) under the current criteria seems open to doubt." Never has the process of having doubt removed so quickly and convincingly provided such pleasure! This is the more the case, in that the same article finishes by identifying Najib Mahfuz (sometimes written as Naguib Mahfouz) as the clear candidate for the award from the contemporary tradition of Arabic literature.

This year's Nobel laureate is an Egyptian writer of fiction. Born in Cairo on 11 December 1911, he has rarely left his homeland. He is a quintessential Egyptian, educated in the schools of Cairo, steeped in the culture and history of his homeland, full of wit and personal charm. Married with two daughters, he lives in a modest apartment in 'Aguza, a suburb of Cairo on the western bank of the Nile. From this apartment he travels on Thursdays to the building of the famous Cairene newspaper *Al-Ahram,* for which he has been writing a weekly column for a number of years. In an echo of earlier practice in the Western world, the press has provided the medium for the initial publication of almost his entire fictional output. Thursday evening in the week will often find him at his preferred café in the city, participating in discussions about culture and politics—two areas discussed, more often than not, in tandem within Third World societies. During the summer he travels to Alexandria, a city which he describes with obvious affection in several of his works.

Mahfuz makes it clear that he likes to live a thoroughly organized life. This must have served him in good stead as a civil servant within the Ministry of Culture, a post that he held until his retirement. It accounts, no doubt, for the disarming accuracy with which he is able to portray characters from the petty bureaucracy in his fiction. Though the need to ration his time carefully between the demands of the ministry post and his own writing obviously provided instigation enough to organize his days with care, an additional incentive has been the fact than an eye condition makes it impossible for him to work in bright light, a considerable impediment in a country with a climate such as that of Egypt. For that reason, he has always tended to write at specific times of day and to work in closely shuttered spaces (as was the case when I first visited him in his office in the Ministry of Culture building in 1970).

In spite of his distaste for travel abroad, one should not conclude that his vision is in any way a purely local one. After his school studies he attended the University of Cairo and completed an undergraduate degree in philosophy. He was in fact embarking on a graduate degree in the same subject when his interest in the writing of fiction diverted him from further formal academic studies. Almost from the outset, his fictional oeuvre shows the influence of his earlier academic pursuits on his writing: for example, his very early short story "The Mummy Awakes" makes several references to famous European philosophers.[1] To these interests garnered while a student he was to add other influences from an avid reading of fictional literature from a variety of world traditions. On several occasions, for example, he has acknowledged a particular affinity for the works of Kafka and Camus, but they are merely two of a number of authors of fiction whom he has read.

Mahfuz's early reputation results from a series of social-realist novels that he wrote during the 1940s, culminating in what is clearly his most famous work, *Al-Thulathiyya* (The Trilogy; 1956–57), for which he was awarded the State Prize for Literature in 1957. Whereas the earlier novels in this series had been reviewed at the time of their appearance, it was the timing of the publication of "The Trilogy"—in the early years of the Egyptian revolution (1952) and in the wake of the repulsion of the Tripartite (Suez) Invasion of 1956—which led to an amplified interest in Mahfuz's works not only in Egypt but throughout the Arab world. In fact, Mahfuz had begun his career as a writer of fiction with the publication of a collection of short stories, *Hams al-junun* (The Whisper of Madness; 1939), and with three historical novels set in ancient Egypt, but the social and political turmoil engendered by World War II and its aftermath turned his attention away from the ancient period to the present plight of his fellow countrymen. If we may suggest that the historical novel in Arabic had previously played a valuable role in developing a sense of national consciousness among the larger Arab nation, then Mahfuz's advocacy of social-realist fiction in the 1940s points to a seizing of the prerevolutionary moment which was indeed felicitous. His developing mastery of novelistic technique, so evident in these novels, laid the groundwork on which a whole generation of postrevolutionary novelists have been able to build.

"The Trilogy" itself tells the story of a single family as it moves from one quarter of Cairo to another: from Bayn al-Qasrayn, to Qasr al-Shawq, and finally to Al-Sukkariyya (the names provide the titles for the three volumes), all this between the years 1917 and 1944. A whole generation of political and social turmoil and change is enfolded within a lovingly accurate depiction of both place and time. Since this masterpiece of modern Arabic fiction is not yet available in translation,[2] we can refer to the work's immediate predecessor as an example of an another elaborate portrait of a family in translation: *Al-Bidaya wa-Nihaya* (1949; Eng. *The Beginning and the End*).[3] Here too the setting in both time and place serves as a backdrop for the story of a Cairene family whose members respond to the pressures and demands of life in their own unique way.

The novel opens with the news of the death of the family's wage-earner, the father. Each member of the bereaved family—the mother, her three sons, and a daughter—has to learn to cope with the consequences of this dire news. The emotional makeup of each child—the selfishness and depravity of the drug dealer Hasan, the humility and loyalty of Husayn, the driving social ambition of Hasanayn (who becomes an army officer), and the irrepressible sexual appetite of Nafisa—are all drawn together into a series of events which lead to a tragic conclusion. Hasan is terribly wounded in a fight with his adversaries from another thug gang. It is almost part of the "canon" of social realism that Hasanayn, "the respected officer" and social climber of the family, is the one who has to go the police station to collect his sister after her arrest on charges of prostitution. Hasanayn tells his sister to commit suicide by jumping off a bridge into the Nile. After watching her do so and considering the implications of what has happened for his family, he follows her example. By implication, it is Husayn, the humble school administrator whose sense of duty goes so far as to make him propose to the jilted fiancée of his brother Hasanayn out of a sense of shame, who is left with his mother and shattered elder brother to face the future.

Of this series of novels, *Zuqaq al-Midaqq* (1947; Eng. *Midaq Alley*) has always been among the most popular.[4] It clearly represents one of Mahfuz's most brilliant efforts in portrayal of place; the very title of the work perhaps conveys best of all to the reader the primary role of the Alley as a unifying factor in the work. If this attention to spatial detail is a particular characteristic of the set of novels written before the 1952 revolution, then the novels written in the wake of 'Abd al-Nasir's rise to power represent a significant change of emphasis. The minute details which were previously compounded into a large picture now become more symbolic and suggestive of atmosphere; with a shift away from the family structure to the inner world of the individual, the depiction of place becomes more economical and often poetic.

When *Awlad Haratina* (literally "Children of Our Quarter," translated as *Children of Gebelawi*) was serialized in *Al-Ahram* in 1959, readers familiar with Mahfuz's earlier "quarter" novels may have assumed that he was resuming where he had left off in 1952.[5] Instead Mahfuz chose to tell a highly allegorical tale in which five successive "leaders" endeavor to keep the quarter in order while maintaining varying relations with the mysterious Gabalawi, who lives in a house set apart and controls the *waqf* or religious endowment. The fifth and last of these leaders kills Gabalawi. The import of this work as a survey of mankind's religious history and the modern confrontation between religion and science (the latter already addressed in *Qasr al-Shawq*, the second volume of "The Trilogy") was not lost on the conservative establishment in Egypt, and the work was immediately banned. It was subsequently published in Beirut in 1967.

Between 1961 and 1967 Mahfuz published no fewer than six novels and two collections of short stories, a truly astonishing outpouring of creativity. That it accompanied some of the darkest years in recent Egyptian history, characterized by an oppressive level of governmental control over every aspect of society and a great deal of disillusion among the intellectual community after the heady days of the late 1950s, is no accident. *Al-Liss wa-al-Kilab* (1961; Eng. *The Thief and the Dogs*) recounts the story of a released prisoner who, in seeking vengeance on those who framed him, kills innocent bystanders by accident and is hounded down.[6] *Al-Summan wa-al-Kharif* (1962; Eng. *Autumn Quail*) traces the downfall of a civil servant who is "purged" following the 1952 revolution (the events of which are described in some detail).[7] Although couched in a fictional mode heavily overlaid with symbolism, the intensity of Mahfuz's distress at the direction his country was taking becomes increasingly clear; by *Miramar* (1967) it reaches its acme.[8] A group of Egyptian men, of all classes, political persuasions, and ages, come together at a pensione in Alexandria; a peasant girl, Zahra, serves as the catalyst whereby they reveal their attitudes toward life in Egypt in the 1960s. Above all, Sirhan al-Buhayri, the personification of success under the revolution, commits suicide when his plan to steal from the company he supervises goes awry. A few months after the publication of this novel the June War of 1967 and its aftermath demanded a new agenda for the entire region.

Many writers responded in intense anger to the revelations that followed *al-naksa* (the setback), as this total defeat was termed. Others resorted to silence. For his part, Mahfuz responded in quick succession with a series of short stories which painted a dark and deeply symbolic vision of external and internal oppression and civic responsibility. Once again political events had radically altered the agenda; the death of 'Abd al-Nasir brought Anwar al-Sadat to the Egyptian presidency. The focus was now on a reexamination of the past and a new "openness" in economic terms. Mahfuz's first contribution to this process is a unique work in his fictional output, *Al-Maraya* (translated as *Mirrors*), a series of vignettes through which a narrator paints a character portrait of an entire generation (significantly coterminous with that of its author).[9] In what is probably his most notorious novel, *Al-Karnak* (Eng. *Al-Karnak* and *Karnak Café*)—made into a somewhat sensationalist film during the Sadat era—Mahfuz records in frank and gruesome detail the practices of the secret police against dissenters in Egypt during the 1960s.[10]

I must confess to a feeling of difficulty in assessing Mahfuz's more recent works of fiction but can find some slight comfort in that I do not seem to be alone in facing this quandary. One may perhaps begin by noting that, in attempting to evaluate such works, we do not have the benefit of that historical perspective which now allows us to place his earlier novels within a clear developmental framework incorporating the Arabic novel tradition as a whole. Beyond that, however, lies the clear fact that his recent works have not been subjected to the same almost-universal critical attention which greeted his earlier ones. As I survey my own recent interests, it becomes clear that a reason for my own failure to keep up with Mahfuz's continuing creativity with the same degree of assiduity is due in no small part to the attractions provided by the large number of other novelists who have emerged in all parts of the Arab world: Al-Tayyib Salih from the Sudan, Jabra Ibrahim Jabra from Palestine, Al-Tahir Wattar from Algeria, 'Abd al-Rahman Munif from Saudi Arabia, Hanna Mina from Syria, to compile just a short list. There is a real sense here in which all these Arab novelists represent branches emerging from that trunk which is Mahfuz himself, the one who established the roots of the genre in the Arab world; indeed, more than one of the novelists listed above has acknowledged as much.

As writers throughout the Arab world have expanded the scope of the Arabic novel in terms of themes (and therefrom venues) and techniques, Mahfuz has continued to concentrate on issues confronting his own Egyptian society and indeed to return to themes and techniques essayed in previous works; to a degree, that has tended to restrict his readership to those who are familiar with the particular local circumstances being discussed: namely, those closely acquainted with Egypt itself. Furthermore, whereas in previous decades the course of political and social development in Egypt brought about by the socialist revolution managed to serve as a general paradigm for intellectuals throughout the region, the emergence of new and diverse centers of influence which have inevitably followed the multifarious political and economic developments throughout the Arab world in recent decades has produced a different kind of cultural situation. As contacts among Arab creative writers, critics, and scholars have increased and publication outlets have expanded in both number and output, there has developed an awareness of the novel as a literary phenomenon which expresses the aspirations and concerns of different countries of the region in a wide diversity of styles and forms. Instead of one country providing a model or one author a particular lead, the directions and focuses are now as broad as the region itself.[11] In such a context Mahfuz now occupies a revered position, but his more recent works clearly have a more local and traditional appeal than novels written by those who may be termed his successors.

Wherein does Mahfuz's "pioneer" status within the tradition of modern Arabic fiction reside? The novel is, needless to say, a highly complex phenomenon, and arguments concerning both its history and definition have ranged far and wide. What is clear is that Balzac and Flaubert, Tolstoy and Dostoevsky, Mann and Hesse, Dickens and Trollope, Faulkner and Hemingway, all these great figures have, within their own literary tradition and that of Western culture in general, built upon a narrative tradition which emerged gradually in response to particular social and cultural forces and which also showed clear links to previous narrative traditions and types, not least of which is the picaresque. In the case of modern Arabic fiction the process has been somewhat different, and for two main reasons. In the first place, the imported genre of the novel, with its focus on an urban middle class and its emphasis on the processes of change, presented a challenge to would-be Arab novelists in terms not only of subject matter but also of language itself. The process of depicting "real" Arab characters in a variety of situations, talking to each other in a language which could reflect the natural exchange of facts, ideas, and emotions, was not achieved quickly or easily. The second reason concerns the historical moment. The emergence of the novel in the Arab world coincided with a large-scale movement of modernization and rediscovery of the past during the nineteenth century, a movement generally termed in Arabic *al-nahda*. This process was accompanied, and indeed stimulated, by the incursions of Western colonization throughout the region and the resulting emergence of an Arab nationalist movement. These trends (which, albeit within different time frames, were substantially of the same kind throughout the Arab world) led to an initial focus on historical and romantic novels which aimed at reviving the past glories of the Arab nation and painting both them and present realities in an idealized way. In the wake of World War I, calls for independence and self-determination became more insistent, and a whole series of separate and local nationalist movements began to emerge. This provided the context for the emergence of a tradition of fiction which would concentrate on the realities of the present, and in Egypt in particular the 1930s were a decade rich in experiment, as famous authors such as al-Mazini (d. 1949), al-Hakim (d. 1986), al-'Aqqad (d. 1964), and Taha Husayn (d. 1973) applied themselves to novel writing.

Following a prolonged and extensive process of reading in Western fiction and refining his own novel-writing technique, Najib Mahfuz was to provide the capstone for all these earlier attempts. It is here that his "pioneer" status resides, in that Mahfuz was the first Arab novelist to transcend the various difficulties, cultural and technical, which I have outlined briefly above, to set himself to reflect and criticize the social and political realities of his own contemporary environment, and to make the fullest possible use of the many facets of the novel genre. As we follow the course of his career, it is possible to trace elements of stability and change in his writing. Among the former is his choice of themes and venues. It is useful to recall that in his educational background Mahfuz differs from many other earlier writers of fiction, in that he studied philosophy. "What is madness?" is the question with which the title story of his first collection, Hams al-junun, begins.[12] Alongside a concern with the mundane but crucial issues of survival in the inimical environment of the modern city, Mahfuz shows a continuing and particular concern for such questions as the nature of madness, the alienation of modern man and his search for consolation, and the role of religion in contemporary societies dominated by humanistic values. His choice of venue for the various fictional worlds he has created has been the city, with a particular concentration on Cairo but also involving a number of "excursions" to his beloved Alexandria. Unlike other Egyptian novelists such as 'Abd al-Rahman al-Sharqawi and Yusuf Idris, he has not used the countryside and its peasant population as a focus for criticism of the course of socialist policies in his country, but has concentrated instead on the sector with which he is extremely familiar: the bureaucrat class in the city. Within such a framework the quarters of the old city are initially the object of lovingly detailed description and are often named; but as his style became more symbolic, the "quarters" became less particular in their location and more generalized as paradigms for larger areas and focuses of attention. The very word hara (meaning "quarter") appears in the title of a number of his works.[13]

The move to a more symbolic style just mentioned provides a clear, if gradual, illustration of the way in which Mahfuz has changed and developed his writing techniques. This can be illustrated with relative ease by contrasting the descriptive method of an early work such as Midaq Alley with that of a later work like Miramar. In the early pages of the former we read:

Two shops, however, Uncle Kamil's, the sweets seller to the right of the alley entrance and the barber's shop on the left, remain open until shortly after sunset. It is Uncle Kamil's habit, even his right, to place a chair on the threshold of his shop and drop off to sleep with a flywhisk resting on his lap. He will remain there until customers either call out to him or Abbas the barber teasingly wakes him. (MA, 2)

The close attention to detail here stands in sharp contrast with the opening of Miramar, which in its evocative power is akin to a prose poem: "Alexandria. At last, Alexandria, Lady of the Dew. Bloom of white nimbus. Bosom of radiance, wet with sky-water. Core of nostalgia steeped in honey and tears" (MM, 1). In the following passage from Autumn Quail the description of place only provides those details which will serve the author's particular symbolic purpose:

Everything around seemed to promise a death-like repose. Grief-stricken people are apt to welcome any kind of sedative, even if it is poison. This small, furnished flat showed that civilization was not entirely devoid of a little mercy at times. There was the sea stretching away into the distance till it sank over the horizon; from the mildness of October it derived a certain wisdom and tenderness. (AQ, 66)

As Mahfuz has honed his style into an instrument of powerful, evocative force, so too he has managed to turn that wonderful self-deprecating wit for which Egyptians are justly famous into a hallmark of his recent works. A few examples follow:

Many people ask me why the theater is flourishing these days. Do you know why? It's because we've all become actors! (MR, 88)

So with him philosophy begins with Ibn Rushd [Averroes] and now it's finishing with Ibn Kalb. (MR, 164)[14]

Just look how filthy these streets are, right in the middle of the city; pretty soon, flies will start demanding their citizen's rights! (MR, 172)

We're living in times when sex has become a national pursuit.[15]

I'm liberated. I belong to the good old days, before religion and moral behavior became all the rage. (WS, 37)

Najib Mahfuz has contributed to modern Arabic fiction in a vast outpouring of writing unmatched by any other writer. Uniquely placed to seize the particular historical moment and to reflect the aspirations and concerns of newly emerging classes and societies as the Arab world began its postrevolutionary phase, he has been able to provide a succession of models in Arabic to place alongside the great traditions of the Western novel as both reflection and catalyst of change and as a mirror of mankind's highest hopes and bitterest moments of despair and alienation. In commenting on and criticizing aspects of modern life in Egypt he has occasionally incurred official opprobrium in his own homeland and elsewhere, but such limited readings of certain works have failed to divert him from his chosen course. The Nobel Prize in Literature for 1988 is a well-earned reward for such a combination of artistry, honesty, and diligence.

Roger Allen, Winter 1989

1 Translated with commentary by Roger Allen in *The Worlds of Muslim Imagination,* Alamgir Hashmi, ed., Islamabad, Gulmohar, 1986, pp. 15–33 and 212–15.

2 I have been told that at least the third volume, *Al-Sukkariyya,* is in press at the American University in Cairo Press. One can only hope that the other two volumes will follow in rapid succession following the award of the Nobel Prize.

3 Najib Mahfuz, *The Beginning and the End,* Ramses Awad, tr., Cairo, American University in Cairo Press, 1985. For a review, see *WLT* 62:3 (Summer 1988), p. 504.

4 Najib Mahfuz, *Midaq Alley,* Trevor Le Gassick, tr., Washington, D.C., Three Continents, 1974. All citations use the abbreviation *MA.*

5 Najib Mahfuz, *Children of Gebelawi,* Philip Stewart, tr., Washington, D.C., Three Continents, 1981. For a review, see *WLT* 56:2 (Spring 1982), p. 398.

6 Najib Mahfuz, *The Thief and the Dogs,* Trevor Le Gassick and Mustafa Badawi, trs., Cairo, American University in Cairo Press, 1984. For a review, see *WLT* 60:1 (Winter 1986), p. 684.

7 Najib Mahfuz, *Autumn Quail,* Roger Allen, tr., Cairo, American University in Cairo Press, All citations use the abbreviation *AQ.* For a review, see *WLT* 61:1 (Winter 1987), p. 148.

8 Najib Mahfuz, *Miramar,* Fatma Moussa-Mahmoud, tr., Cairo, American University in Cairo Press, 1978. Citations use the abbreviation *MM.* For a review, see *WLT* 53:4 (Autumn 1979), p. 739.

9 Najib Mahfuz, *Mirrors,* Roger Allen, tr., Minneapolis, Bibliotheca Islamica, 1977. All citations use the abbreviation *MR.* For a review, see *WLT* 52:4 (Autumn 1978), p. 686.

10 Najib Mahfuz, *Al-Karnak,* Saad el-Gabalawi, tr., Fredericton, N.B., York Press, 1979; also translated as *Karnak Café,* Roger Allen, tr., forthcoming.

11 A sign of these changes is that a number of works in both Arabic and Western languages have begun to focus on the Arabic novel as a regional rather than a local literary phenomenon. Among these I would cite: Roger Allen, *The Arabic Novel: An Historical and Critical Introduction,* Syracuse, N.Y., Syracuse University Press, 1982; idem, "The Arabic Novel outside Egypt," *Cambridge History of Arabic Literature,* vol. 4, ch. 6 (forthcoming); Shukri 'Ayyad, "Al Riwayah al-'Arabiyyah al-mu'asirah wa-azmat al-damir al-'Arabi," *'Alam al-fikr,* 3:3 (Oct.-Dec. 1972), pp. 619–48; Halim Barakat, *Visions of Social Reality in the Contemporary Arab Novel,* Georgetown (Washington, D.C.,), Center for Contemporary Arab Studies, 1977; Muhammad Barradah, *Al-Riwaya al-'Arabiyya,* Beirut, Dar Ibn Rushd, 1981; Ilyas Khuri, *Tajribat bahth 'an ufq,* Beirut, Markaz al-Abhath, Munazzamat al-Tahrir al-Filastiniyyah, 1974; Shukri 'Aziz Madi, *In'ikas hazimat Huzayran 'ala 'l-riwayah al-'Arabiyyah,* Beirut, Al-Mu'assassah al-'Arabiyyah li-'l-Dirasat wa-'l-Nashr, 1978; 'Isam Mahfuz, *Al-Riwayah al-'Arabiyyah al-tali'iyyah,* Beirut, Dar Ibn Khaldun, 1982; Muhsin Jasim al-Musawi, *Al-Mawqif al-thawri fi 'l-riwaya al-'Arabiyya al-mu'asira,* Baghdad, Manshurat Wizarat al-I'lam, 1975; Sayyid Hamid al-Nassaj, *Panorama al-riwaya al-'Arabiyya al-haditha,* Beirut, al-Markaz al-'Arabi li-'l-Thaqafah wa-'l-'Ulum, 1982; 'Abd al-rahman Majid al-Rubay'i, *Al-Shati' al-jadid: Qir'a fi kuttab al-qissa al-'Arabiyya,* Tunis, Al-Dar al-'Arabiyya li-'l-Kitab, 1983; Jurj Salim, *Al-Mughamara al-riwa'iyya,* Damascus, Manshurat Ittihad al-Kuttab al-'Arab, 1973; Muhammad Siddiq, "The Contemporary Arabic Novel in Perspective," *WLT* 60:2 (Spring 1986), pp. 206–11.

12 The story is included in *God's World,* Akef Abadir and Roger Allen, trs., Minneapolis, Bibliotheca Islamica, 1973, pp. 47–54.

13 In addition to the famous *Awlad haratina* (translated as *Children of Gebelawi*), there is "Harat al-'ushshaq," a lengthy story published in the collection *Hikaya bi-la bidaya wa-la nihaya* (Story with No Beginning or Ending; 1971), and *Hikayat haratina* (literally "Tales of Our Quarter," translated as *Fountain and Tomb* in 1988). In addition to these, *Malhamat al-harafish* (The Epic of the Riffraff; 1977), which Mahfuz counts among his personal favorites, is also set in the context of "the quarter" and squabbles among successive generations of its inhabitants.

14 Ibn Rushd is a famous medieval Arab philosopher. "Ibn Kalb" means "son of a bitch."

15 From *Afrah al-Qubba,* translated by Olive Kenny as *Wedding Song,* Cairo, American University in Cairo Press, 1984, p. 15. Subsequent citations are abbreviated as *WS.* For a review, see *WLT* 61:1 (Winter 1987), p. 149.

Modern Egyptian Theatre: Three Major Dramatists

This essay is basically addressed to the reader who knows hardly anything about the theatrical movement in Egypt. Books on the history of world drama quite often begin with the earliest drama humanity has known, namely the Passion plays of ancient Egypt. Ironically, a modern European or American reader with some modest interest in the theatre knows more about the Passion play of Isis and Osiris than he does about the modern theatre of Egypt. More often than not, he knows next to nothing about a dramatic movement the roots of which go even deeper than those of the young American theatre. We find this difficult to accept in an age that knows no communications barriers, where instantaneous coverage of events has been made possible in the second half of the twentieth century through the highly organized mass media of radio, television and satellite. In the midst of all these technological achievements one is puzzled by the paucity of information about a dramatic movement that has been active and prolific for the last seventy years. With the exception of a few articles here and there, either in English or French, the only serious study of Egyptian theatre is the invaluable *Studies in the Arab Theatre and Cinema* by Jacob Landau (1958).

Significantly enough, the study appeared at a time when the Egyptian theatre was on the threshold of its golden age, from 1958 to 1968. One need not point out that this fact postdates the study; so much has happened in the Egyptian theatre since. Modern Egyptian theatre proper actually begins after the publication of Landau's book. The only dramatist who dominated the scene before that date is Tawfiq Al-Hakim (see *BA* 50:1, p. 99 and 46:2, p. 187). But this by no means undercuts the value of the study up to 1958.

The crucial year, then, is 1958, or just a couple of years before, when our first dramatist of stature other than Al-Hakim, Nu'man 'Ashour, appeared on the scene with his play of social criticism, "The People Downstairs." In the following decade Egyptian theatre witnessed the apex of its fulfillment. That milieu boasted many playwrights, but only three major figures will be discussed here in an attempt to give the foreign reader a fair idea of what Egyptian drama is about in terms of theme and technique: Al-Hakim, 'Ashour and Rashad Rushdy.

■ ■ ■

Tawfiq Al-Hakim is the father of modern Egyptian drama, in the opinion of many Egyptian critics and orientalists who have studied our dramatic movement. Although Al-Hakim started writing for the theatre in the early 1920s, he continued well into the sixties. In addition to this, his influence today is too strong to be ignored. Nu'man 'Ashour made dramatic history when he first introduced Egyptian audiences to Egyptian comedy in the full sense of the word. Rashad Rushdy, on the other hand, can be considered the real founder of modern Egyptian drama and the bedrock of the tragic form in this country. It is worth mentioning here that these three major dramatists had a European education, a fact we will return to later on for a fuller discussion of its implications in their art.

The case of Al-Hakim is something of a paradox. His tremendous achievement in Egypt as thinker, novelist and playwright is uncontested. When he turned his back on family tradition and wrote pieces like "The New Woman" and "The Unwelcome Guest," which were adumbrations in the popular vein of the time of farce, folklore, satire and music, he was actually opening new vistas for an Egyptian theatre that had been living on

adaptations and translations of European texts for years. Al-Hakim's appearance on the scene was the grand entrance of the first Egyptian dramatist. The young man's break with his family proved to be the beginning of a long, prolific and profitable career in the theatre.

As a dramatist, he has demonstrated varied interests. He has written plays of social bias and plays of intellect. He has even tried his hand at the Theatre of the Absurd in "The Tree Climber" and "The Fate of a Cockroach." There is no denying that he was greatly influenced by the years he spent in France studying for a law degree. The contact with French culture and theatre in the twenties left in indelible mark on his art. And significantly, one of his major idols was George Bernard Shaw.

Al-Hakim now seems to be ashamed of his early period. The texts of "Ali Baba" and "The Unwelcome Guest" have never been available for publication or even private scrutiny. It is difficult to accept Al-Hakim's contention that they are lost. As for the published text of "The New Woman," it seems to have undergone some major changes that the playwright himself saw as necessary. After his return from France he assumed the pioneering role of introducing the theatre proper to the Egyptian scene. But "proper" simply signifies a theatre in the French tradition of Corneille and Racine rather than Molière, for instance. Hence the works of this period, such as "The Cave Men," "Scheherazade," "Solomon the Wise," "Pygmalion," "Oedipus" and "Journey into the Future," are all "plays of intellect." Ironically, the first one to use this label in describing his work was the author himself. He first used the phrase to justify his coyness in presenting his plays to the professional theatre, saying that he preferred to have them read. But the description was an unfortunate one, because the label stuck, and critics and scholars engaged in enthusiastic defense of his work find it difficult to convince audiences of their stageworthiness. Critics begin either by outright refusal to accept the classification or by a simple attempt to establish the value of his works as dramas of intellect. Even after an active career of fifty years he has never really shaken off his preoccupation with intellectual struggle as the core of his dramatic conflict.

The key word in regard to almost all his plays, regardless of period, is *abstraction*. Al-Hakim formulated his concept of dramatic conflict in his preface to "Pygmalion": "Today I set up my theatre inside man's intellect. I make of my characters ideas moving in absolute values and dressed up in symbols." Nothing could be more succinct. His plays certainly substantiate this concept. Whether their plots are taken from mythology, religion or life, the plays usually revolve around intellectual conflict of one sort or another. The playwright ordinarily begins with an intellectual hypothesis in the abstract and moves on to show the consequences of this hypothesis if carried out. In the process his vision of life classifies and passes value judgments on the consequences. In "Scheherazade," for instance, the playwright presupposes that Shahriyar, the tyrannical king, has developed into pure intellect, to the utter renunciation of emotional needs. The dramatist then proceeds to examine the king's indecision and frustration as the immediate result of the hypothesis. The process is repeated in other works, including "The Cave Men," "Solomon the Wise" and "The Return of Youth."

A closer examination of one of the works will underscore Al-Hakim's habit of placing a central idea before character or action. In "A Journey into the Future" two people with death sentences hanging over them are given the choice between execution and a journey into outer space, where they will be facing the unknown. They choose the latter and are launched into space. After a crash landing they discover they are on a strange planet where most of man's biological needs are simply satisfied by radiation. Bored with ease and monotony, they manage to repair the damaged parts of the rocket and head for earth. To their consternation, they find that the short span of time the round trip took comes to three hundred years, a period that has brought about complete change—machines have taken over, making life easy and comfortable beyond man's wildest dreams. Politically, people are divided into two main parties, the Radicals and the Conservatives. The two protagonists make their commitments, with each joining a party. When the Radicals (who, it seems, always have a better chance) come to power, the Conservative partner is arrested and put in prison again.

The play fails to develop into a conflict between two human wills but continues, as do Al-Hakim's other works, to be a simple duel between two ideas. From the traditional or Aristotelian point of view, then, the play fails to persuade the audience to become involved, to side with one party or the other. Neither catharsis nor pity and fear seem to be present in Al-Hakim's concept of tragedy. When the two conflicting or warring parties are mere ideas, one tends to accept one side to the rejection of the other, a fact which brings us closer to the didactic theatre of someone like Brecht. Can Al-Hakim's plays therefore be called didactic or epic? Hardly. His plays come very near to epic theatre without renouncing their claim to traditional form; thus they claim the merits of neither theatre.

The result, more often than not, is a theatre where characters become walking ideas and mouthpieces for the author's direct and immediate vision of life. The dialogue suffers at the hands of a dramatist who admits

writing plays to be read. It is replete with lengthy passages and monologues or *longueurs* that are no longer accepted vehicles for the development of dramatic action. In fact, one comes across passages that seem to interrupt the action or actually to stop it. Characters speak out of character, saying things they hardly know anything about, tending to go on and on without adding anything new to the dramatic action.

A passage from "The Game of Death" will suffice to show the qualities of a typical dramatic situation. In this play a scholar discovers that he has been exposed to radiation and, consequently, has only a few months to live. He decides to put an end to his life, but instead of dying alone in peace, he is determined to blow up the world around him. He deliberately chooses a secondrate belly dancer, Cleopatra, for his experiment. The heroine of his choice has little formal education and was launched into night life at the age of twelve. The girl's partner in her nightly program is an acrobat by the name of Antonio. The historian lays a trap for the girl and starts pulling the strings by first convincing her of his love, a proof of which is the big fortune he is leaving her in his will. He expects the nightclub girl to act in accordance with his own preconceived idea of her: to conspire with her partner and boyfriend Antonio to kill him for the fortune. To his surprise, the scholar discovers in the confrontation scene that the girl neither desires his money nor his death. She simply loves him for himself. The following dialogue ensues:

Historian: You make me ashamed of myself.

Cleopatra: You should be. Everything you said on that tape is downright shameful! How could one like you think of these ugly things?

Historian: I can't deny they are ugly. Yet, think of what happened to me, wasn't it ugly?

Cleopatra: The atomic radiation?

Historian: Yes.

Cleopatra: The worst thing that happened to you was your inner distortion.

Historian: Inner distortion . . . an amazing diagnosis.

Cleopatra: Yes. It destroyed in you the man who believes in goodness and love . . . and left a black empty shell . . . except for suspicion, hatred and revenge, and hurting others.

Historian: You think so?

Cleopatra: This alone filled me with terror. . . . This is the real disaster. Man with a distorted soul.

The belly dancer who has hardly any schooling and who has probably never heard of psychoanalysis is teaching the scholar a lesson. Her diagnosis is that of someone other than the character, someone who well knows that external distortion or ugliness is nothing compared to inner distortion. Naïvely enough, the scholar is the first to admire the diagnosis. It is the playwright who is talking. The given situation does not—cannot—justify what the character utters onstage.

This is only a sample of what Al-Hakim does quite often. Even in his best plays, like "The Sultan Who Couldn't Make up His Mind" and "The Tree Climber," he evinces symptoms of the same repetition. The paradox lies in the fact that access to European dramatic literature, which Al-Hakim provided, resulted in a burden bequeathed to the next generation which they had to shake off before they could write plays to be performed and not just to be read.

The first dramatist to offer such works was Nu'man 'Ashour. He was able to shake off much of Al-Hakim's influence. This was due perhaps to the fact that he had access to another school—English theatre. Like Rashad Rushdy, he is a graduate of an English department; his eyes were opened to beauties other than those of French theatre. Yet in being introduced to English literature and drama 'Ashour was attracted by someone who never wrote a word in English and who exercised a great influence on modern world drama, Anton Chekhov. The young Egyptian playwright modeled himself not on Shakespeare or Ben Jonson, but on a Russian dramatist whom he studied in English translation. His choice of Chekhov, however, was far from accidental or haphazard. 'Ashour's active career in the Egyptian theatre began about five years after the Revolution of 1952, with its drastic changes for Egyptian society. The fresh hopes and glamour of the promised reforms, together with the young dramatist's dreams of change, made the Russian writer especially attractive. No wonder Chekhov has been the most popular dramatist in Egypt for the last twenty years.

An examination of Nu'man 'Ashour's active decade of playwriting becomes also an examination of revolutionary ideas and dreams in Egypt. 'Ashour is the faithful mirror for a young revolutionary's development—from hope and enthusiasm, unlimited and innocent, to frustration and loss of innocence. In his first and best play, "The People Downstairs," the closing scene shows the basement people (a symbol too obvious to elaborate) moving out of their rat-infested holes to a New Egypt, above ground. The only character who cannot break away from his roots in the basement is the hero Raja'i, who speaks enthusiastically of the need for change but cannot move out of the basement—a typical Chekhovian perspective. Yet there is hope. Almost ten years later the young revolutionary, in the guise of another name, comes to a full realization of what is going on in his New Egypt: the older generation have quickly adapted to the new circumstances and at least on the surface are considered members of the revolutionaries. The younger generation, the real upholders of revolution, have not been taking their mission seriously. Consequently, according to 'Ashour, they have allowed themselves to be cheated and robbed of their gains by the same older class, who turned profiteers and bloodsuckers. When this realization dawns on them, at the end of *Bellad barrah* (Abroad), they suddenly realize the need for new people, new land, a new Nile, for a complete uprooting of the past in order to have a really new Egypt. When the hero's wife Sou'ad shows him a scarab she has inherited from her mother, telling him of her intention to use it as a charm for their unborn son, he snatches it violently from her hand and smashes it.

El-Nems: Your baby has to be different from these [*pointing to the characters on stage*], away from them, different. He has to come out from the sands of the desert, the water of the Nile, the soil. [*Continues crushing the scarab*]

Sou'ad: [*In her usual innocence*] Isn't he mine?

El-Nems: Ours . . . from other sands, other water, other soil. [*Throwing the atoms of the scarab away*]

Sou'ad: Isn't he ours!!!

El-Nems: The future's different from all these. [*Full turn, pointing to both backstage and auditorium*]

Considering the social, political and economic conditions that surrounded the young playwright's early days in the theatre, it was natural for him to be primarily occupied with the class struggle in Egypt. The decade during which he was an active participant in the dramatic movement represents to Egypt what the "fervent years" of the thirties represent to American theatre and history of thought. Ideological conflict, to be blunt, is the core of the dramatic conflict in Nu'man 'Ashour's plays.

But his plays are not concerned with ideas moving in the realm of abstract values, the way Al-Hakim's are. On the contrary, 'Ashour's real contribution to Egyptian theatre lies in his introduction of realistic characters of blood and flesh that do stand on their own, regardless of whether one believes in his ideology or not. Whether in "The People Downstairs," "The People Upstairs," "The Doughry Family" or "Abroad," his major plays, Nu'man 'Ashour has been able to create memorable characters. His serious comedy is something different from many of the cheap farces one is bound to see on the commercial boards nowadays. His concern with a "message," however, does not blemish the worth of his plays as works of art. Far from being naïve agitprops, they manifest the author's mastery of dramatic technique. The message is so skillfully woven into the texture and overall structure of his work that one does not find it difficult willingly to suspend disbelief. 'Ashour's second major contribution to Egyptian theatre lies in his use of language. He is the first dramatist of weight to have the audacity to use Egyptian spoken Arabic onstage. Up to "The People Downstairs" classical Arabic was the language of dramatic dialogue, a phenomenon which often led to interesting discrepancies in dramatic performance. This was obvious in Al-Hakim's plays in particular—indeed, it was behind that dramatist's failure to create the illusion of reality even in plays with realistic themes. The discrepancy becomes more obvious when a dramatist makes a maid with no schooling whatsoever speak the beautiful classical Arabic of centuries ago. The difference between classical and spoken Arabic may not be readily apprehended by, say, an American audience, to whom the gap between spoken and written English is not so frightening. In Arabic it is. When Al-Hakim, in his attempt to remedy the situation, introduced what he called "the third language," the result was even more objectionable. Only against such a background can Nu'man 'Ashour's achievement be measured. He was the first dramatist to give spoken Arabic its due respect, against very strong odds. The result was a full-fledged realistic theatre.

The trend was fortunately continued, developed and perfected by our third playwright, Rashad Rushdy. Before he was launched into his long career in the theatre, Rushdy was for years the leading Egyptian critic. He introduced the modern school of analytical criticism to Egypt and championed it until it struck roots in the Arab world. As Chairman of the Department of English at Cairo University with a Ph.D. in English Literature, he was qualified to reject both the abstraction of Al-Hakim and the ideology of 'Ashour, to initiate interest in the theatre as theatre. Naturally the opposition was strong and even fanatical to Rushdy's endeavor, writing as he did during the socialist tide in Egypt. But fortunately for the theatrical movement, drama was never really strictly censored. It is true that Rushdy's first two plays, "The Butterfly" (1959) and "The Game of Love" (1961), were performed at the Théâtre Libre in Cairo, a joint project sponsored not by the government but by a group of enthusiasts who included actors, actresses and directors. But even when the government began to be interested in the theatre on a large scale in the early sixties (as a means of diverting interest away from politics and economics), the subsidized theatres, of which ten were opened in one year, were a blessing in disguise. Unlike other socialist or Eastern countries, the fully subsidized state theatre had almost complete freedom in presenting texts and authors. No wonder it was

the Egyptian dramatists, more than the novelists and poets, who were able to predict the military defeat of 1967 years before it occurred. They could see through the false façade and detect the prevailing attitude of frustration and defeat.

Rushdy was one of the dramatists who could see what was coming and express it in his later plays like "Journey Beyond the Fence," "Behold and Wonder" and "Egypt, My Love." His starting point was neither the abstract idea of Al-Hakim strutting on an empty stage nor the sometimes stark ideology of 'Ashour, but people—the individual in his relation to other individuals in his early plays and in his relation to political power in the later ones. As for the early period of "The Butterfly," "The Game of Love" and "Shadows" (1964), Rushdy could be called a poetic realist who is concerned with unmasking the falsity of social values relating to love, marriage, sex and family relations. In this respect, he could easily be called a social critic. The message, however, is never in the foreground but something indirectly felt. As a master technician Rushdy could never have been as direct as the other two dramatists. Again, the same technical skill becomes more obvious when the dramatist moves to express political consciousness. Political criticism is not naïvely presented in the foreground, in the manner of some political plays of the period. Political theatre was indeed rampant in the sixties; unfortunately most of the figures who tried their hand at this genre had neither the training nor the talent necessary to write for the theatre. The result was, more often than not, a decade of superficial agitprop works that are not even remembered. But when Rashad Rushdy turns to political awareness, he never forgets that he is a dramatist.

In his early stage Rushdy is mainly concerned with man's search for love and the discovery of his self-image. The two themes run almost parallel throughout his plays. In "The Game of Love," for instance, the playwright takes upon himself the responsibility of unmasking man's values about himself and others in an attempt to open his eyes to his self-image. The vehicle for this is a love story, or rather love stories. The Egyptian male is shown in this play as husband, lover and brother. In his relationship with his wife his falsity is exposed the moment we know about his love affair. The play comes to an end, later, when the wife comes to know too. As a typical traditional Egyptian he gives himself the liberty to love while denying it to his sister. The play ends when both wife and mistress discover the extent of his selfishness. The wife decides to leave, à la Ibsen. But more devastating is the mistress's blow. She too rejects his offer of marriage once the wife leaves. Her eyes are opened to the fact that when she becomes his wife he will have to find himself another mistress. She sees through his oriental weakness for the harem.

In "Journey Beyond the Fence" the playwright becomes more aware of the intricate relationship between individual corruption and the corruption that gnaws at the very marrow of the social system. The hero's fight against one single engineer who laid the "false" foundation for a bridge across the river soon becomes a hopeless fight against a majority of shockingly corrupt engineers and administrators. His tragic sense of life is intensified through a series of shocks by which he gradually loses his innocence as he discovers the extent of defilement around him. The conflict, then, is no longer between the individual and the rotten traditions from which he has to free himself, but against a corrupt, unjust social force created by the new status introduced by the Revolution. Things are not the milk and honey the revolutionaries promised. But the dramatist's tampering with politics is cleverly masked as social criticism.

When political consciousness became too strong to ignore, Rushdy produced dramas with political bias which are considered among the best plays of the decade. His two masterpieces in this respect are "Behold and Wonder" and "Egypt, My Love." Here he combines clarity of vision with mastery of dramatic technique. But the political force against which the dramatist is fighting is tyrannical; hence he resorts to distancing for the first time in his plays. He sets the scene of his politically-oriented plays in the past, leaving it to the audience to grasp the connotations. And they have loved it. In "Egypt, My Love," which was conceived and written just before the humiliating military defeat of 1967, the playwright takes us back to a period 800 years ago. His hero is something of a Muslim saint, Ahmad El-Badawi, who came to Egypt at a time when it was pressed hard by corruption within and the last European Crusaders without. He is determined to clean up everything and unite the Egyptians against their external enemy. But he is soon besieged by a train of corrupt profiteers who gradually and systematically change the reformer's image in the people's eyes until he becomes a god.

When man relegates his troubles to a miraculous god, what need does he have for work or struggle? The reformer's image of himself is different. He is by no means aware of his real image in the people's eyes. When the French are finally knocking at the gates of Egypt, the leader descends to the people to ask them to take up arms in defense of their country. He is shocked to discover that they do not even recognize him. He has simply become a legend, a miracle worker, a god. The result is defeat, for which he is partly to blame because he allowed himself to be isolated and deified.

Such daring articulation of the social and political situation under Nasser was admirable enough in itself. Yet it seems that the authorities welcomed this on the part of Rushdy and other dramatists because it helped deflate people's anger and dissatisfaction. Plays like "Behold and Wonder" and "Egypt, My Love" absorbed people's indignation and worked as a buffer.

Rushdy's contribution to the theatrical movement remains uncontested. As a scholar the man is able to write masterpieces of technique by any standard. Undoubtedly he formed his plays on the model of Aristotle's theory of drama. In his works we hardly find one loose end. The Aristotelian concept of organic structure, for instance, is faithfully followed. But most important of all is Rushdy's mastery of the complex action that depends on several different threads. From the very beginning of his career he showed his interest in complex action in variations that played upon, through repetition, parallels or contrast. This technique appears at its best in "Journey Beyond the Fence," "Behold and Wonder" and "The Light of Darkness." His plays therefore represent an advantageous breaking away from the thinness of Al-Hakim's plots. Nu'man 'Ashour, it is true, was interested in the complex or multilevel structure; but it is Rashad Rushdy who has developed this technique and carried it to its logical conclusions.

Abdel-Aziz Hammouda, Autumn 1979

ISRAEL

Writing in Hebrew

A century ago few visionaries conceived of the Jewish people reconstituting itself as a nation after a hiatus of two millennia. Even fewer imagined that the ancient language of the Jews could similarly be resurrected. And if Paul Johnson, historian and author of the monumental *History of the Jews,* gets it just about right when he calls the State of Israel a "miracle," the rebirth of Hebrew is similarly wondrous.

The Hebrew language is most widely associated with its magisterial literary document, the Hebrew Bible. In Christendom as well as in Jewry it was the "Holy Tongue" by which the world had been created and through which the Divine Will had been revealed.[1] Extrapolating from the Bible itself, what other language could have been used by God in Creation, or by humanity before the babble of languages ensuing from the Babel rebellion?

By the very beginning of the Christian era, however, it had become necessary to translate the Hebrew Bible into Greek and into Aramaic, due both to demographic dispersion and to linguistic erosion of Hebrew as a spoken language. The ambivalence of the Pharisaic-Rabbinic translators reflects their recognition that, in fact, *traduttori traditori,* whether the translator be literal or *ad sensum:* "He who translates a verse verbatim is a liar! And he who alters it is a villain and heretic."[2] This attitude toward the translation of hallowed Hebrew texts manifests insights articulated by modern semanticists: "The medium is the message." For the medium of human thought—language—not only *conveys* the "message" but significantly shapes, guides, and determines it.

Like all languages, Hebrew *itself* is a message independent of whatever specific message someone thinks he is conveying. Thus, the terms *medium* and *message* are multiordinal; their use in any specific case is dependent not on any permanent meaning but on the context. They do not have unchanging referents but indicate relationships between two things, like figure and ground in psychology: they actually define each other through their reciprocal relationship. Hence, despite the myriad difficulties involved, although Jews were not native speakers of the language, formal Jewish worship and study was conducted in Hebrew.

This retention of Hebrew had profound influences upon the individual Jew as well as upon the people as a whole, for experientially the *inner* world was involved. And once the individual is considered as an integral part of the process, it would be irrational to ignore this inner world, where much of what goes on is, in fact, language. Briefly put, a person spends much of his time "thinking"—i.e., "talking to himself"—and responding with corresponding feelings and actions. Thus, "inner talking" in Hebrew was a fundamental Jewish concern, for it was a communication process which created both awareness and self-awareness. Hebrew had its own unique input apparatus, its choice of symbols and abstracting system, and each user of the language had some awareness of these factors. Thus did religious tradition maintain a Jewish language, a specifically Jewish way of discriminating shades of meaning and feeling, a sensory system, intuitive evaluation, subliminal perception, perceived attitudes, goals, and beliefs. And on the collective level it is historically verifiable that to the degree that the Jews preserved Hebrew, Hebrew preserved the Jews.

The notable paradox of secularized Israeli life and literature is the fact that despite whatever cynicism, alienation, and humanism a person wants to convey, the Hebrew language itself is both textually and texturally religious, laden with religious terms and idioms. For example, whereas "welcome" in English is a secular term, the Hebrew equivalent *Baruch Ha Ba',* "Blessed be he who comes," is a quotation from Psalms. And whereas "science" is a secular term par excellence in English, its Hebrew equivalent *madda'* involves a theological dimension as well; witness Maimonides' *Sefer ha-Madda',* not "The Book of Science" but "The Book of Knowledge (of God)."[3] The paradox derives from the fact that in contemporary Hebrew literature, conscious historicism is almost invariably secular,[4] yet the rampant secularization has not significantly affected the character of the Hebrew language; the vocabulary is significantly larger than it was 3,500 years ago, to be sure, but strong bonds of idiom and grammar extend from biblical antiquity to modern Hebrew diction, particularly in literature.[5]

One of the most amazing successes of the Jewish national liberation movement was the revival of Hebrew as a spoken, living language. The likelihood of success seemed so remote that even Theodore Herzl, the visionary architect of political Zionism, deemed German to be the most appropriate lingua franca for the eventual *Judenstaat.* Many of the original settlers were of similar opinions, preferring Russian, Yiddish, Turkish, German, or English, rather than attempt to breathe life into an archaic language that had long been relegated to the study hall and the synagogue. Yet Hebrew won out, as it had to, and not solely because only Hebrew could provide some linguistic commonality to the settlers coming from widely divergent language communities. Rather, only Hebrew could provide the Zionist enterprise with its spiritual roots, its cultural continuity, and its historical associations.[6] A nation reborn requires its authentic language to be reborn. Weaving the textual threads of a language that had not been natively spoken for almost two thousand years into a medium of modern communication and cerebration remains a challenge for every Israeli author to this day. Whether for better or for worse, the writer is affecting the emerging tapestry.

Throughout the centuries, Hebrew linguistics was historically prescriptive: determining the norms of classical Hebrew. Grammarians, largely biblical scholars, defined what constituted correct Hebrew. Modern grammarians followed suit, proclaiming criteria for words, phrases, and sentences. In brief, they wrote prescriptions for correctness in modern Hebrew. Yet adherence to prescriptive Hebrew was an unrealistic expectation: pedant grammarians are unlikely linguistic leaders. The inevitable inadequacy of prescriptive Hebrew may be illustrated by the anecdote about the newly arrived European intellectual who managed to fall into the deep end of Tel Aviv's municipal pool. Unable to extricate himself by his own efforts, he frantically pleaded in flawless biblical Hebrew, "Hosi'uni na'," rather than the modern call for help, "Hasilu!" According to reports, passersby were heard to remark, "I don't know what the guy wants, but he sure speaks a beautiful Hebrew!"

According to expert testimony, "Spoken Hebrew can now perhaps best be described as a substandard immigrant speech that developed in the absence of any native population to serve as a corrective guide . . . or, rather, in which the role of 'native population' has been played entirely by the written word, which alone has continued to provide an organic linguistic link with the past."[7] Present-day Hebrew grammarians must cope with five basic realities: a) an inadequate supply of words for the diverse needs of modern life; b) confusion as to whether grammatical norms should correspond to biblical, mishnaic, medieval, or modern forms;[8] c) the accommodation of pronunciation and accent to Ashkenazi or Sephardi traditions; d) the likelihood of sociocultural corruption; and e) the assimilation of foreign terms and expressions. It is small wonder that a comprehensive, consistent grammar of Israeli Hebrew has yet to be composed; serious attempts at resolving the questions of "good Hebrew" continue, but, like the search for answers to Talmudic enigmas, these too apparently require superhuman assistance.[9]

By virtue of sheer necessity, therefore, there has evolved a shift in emphasis from prescriptive linguistics to descriptive linguistics. For even as simple a question as asking for the time could not be solved by reference to precedent. Should it be "Which hour is it?" (*ezohi hassa ah*), "How many hours is it?" (*kamma hassa ah*), or "What is the hour?" (*ma hassa ah*)? In fact, the last is the accepted form today, yet numerous alternatives would be equally correct in principle.

Studies of contemporary Israeli Hebrew involve the well-known structural transformation of the language in recent decades: grammatical issues involving morphology (e.g., conjugation of verbs, declension of nouns), syntactical issues (the use of the genitive, the continuous relative clause), et cetera. Common usage and consensus are employed as the criteria for "rightness" or "wrongness"; and although some observers accept and encourage innovations to facilitate ease of declension and conjugation, others lament this process, which is increasingly converting the typology of the language itself, for foreign constructions are causing modern Hebrew to lose its historical Semitic structure. Prescriptive linguists therefore advocate conservatism: faithfulness to the "sources" (i.e., the Bible, postbiblical and medieval texts), purism (opposition to foreign terminology and constructs), and loyalty to what is sensed as constituting the "spirit of the language" (*ruah ha lason*).

The Academy of Hebrew Language has attempted to stem the inundation of foreign terms by the creation of appropriate Hebrew equivalents. Sometimes these innovations take root, sometimes they coexist with a foreign equivalent, and sometimes they wither into obscurity, preserved only in Hebrew dictionaries.[10] In assimilating Israeli Hebrew, an immigrant must learn to mispronounce English words, adopt Yiddishisms, add Slavic and German diminutives, and intersperse Arabic—and all this in the name of learning "Hebrew." For although Hebrew is a Semitic language, the original settlers hailed almost exclusively from European countries. Speakers of Arabic and cognate Semitic languages arrived only later, adding atomistic elements but not affecting the structure of the language. And then, due largely to Western mass media, came the inundation by English, radically affecting grammar, idiom, and morphology. It is on this profound level of articulation and thought that Hebrew is being most drastically altered. It is true that in late antiquity Greek, Aramaic, Latin, and other morphemes were assimilated into the Hebrew language, but these borrowings came gradually into a living language equipped with a functioning selection system for adaptation or rejection of foreign terminology. Today, however, indiscriminate borrowing of morphemes destroys syntax[11] as well as frequently displacing perfectly adequate Hebrew terms. Thus it weakens and impoverishes the language rather than strengthening and enriching it.

The fundamental importance of Hebrew as a sociocultural medium is self-evident. First, it is the bond of the individual with Jewish history, cerebration, and values that cannot be duplicated by any other medium. Second, it is the bond uniting the potpourri of Israelis, regardless of religion, country of origin, political posture, educational level, et cetera. The vexing question, however, is the degree to which Hebrew can be altered, transformed, and inundated with foreignisms and yet retain its ability to bond a Hebrew-speaker or Hebrew-reader to a Jewish past, a Jewish present, and a Jewish future, however these be defined. And on the pragmatic level, the question is whether the present trend can be ameliorated and possibly even reversed. For Hebrew, like any other language, is not merely a means of communication; it is a virtual organ of perception, despite the necessity of distinguishing between the world and our means of symbolizing it. Hebrew is not a neutral mechanism through which our evolving culture transacts its affairs. It is, by its very form and content, a shaper of values, an advocate of ideologies, a stimulus of senses, and an instructor of the mind.

Today, as in the past, the single most positive architect of the Hebrew language is the serious writer of poetry and of prose. A host of erudite and creative authors have coined neologisms, revived long-dormant terms and phrases, adapted Hebrew to modern use, and re-created it as a language with a rich treasury and variety of expression. This endeavor has involved both linguistic conservatism and creativity. The most successful of the conservatives was Israel's Nobel laureate S. Y. Agnon (1888–1970), who, more than other writer, utilized to good advantage the Hebrew language from its biblical origins, through its rabbinic continuation, onward through medieval diction, to its modern renaissance. His style is not simply eclectic. Rather, "It is an artistic blend of various strands of language at an unusual pitch of intensity. Any paragraph in any story or any novel of Agnon's teems with half-phrases and quarter-phrases from the Bible, the Talmud, the medieval tract, the hassidic tale, the philosophic homily. And these language pebbles form a mosaic of unusual splendor and unusual brilliance. How they do this is Agnon's secret. In an age which has enriched but also vulgarized the Hebrew language, Agnon stands out as the self-appointed guardian of its purity, its wealth and its Semitic character."[12]

The most creative revitalizer of the Hebrew language was the poet Abraham Shlonsky (1900–73), whose poems constitute a trove for researchers into Semitic philology. His virtuoso creativity earned him the affectionate nickname "Lashonsky" or "Mr. Language."[13] The language is female in Hebrew, and the endearments lavished on her beauty, felicity, and creativity (by writers who until recently were all males!) is typified by Shlonsky's encomium: "I like to struggle with the language, with the sentence, with the word. And when I am victorious and when I feel that I have found the correct expression, I smile and say to myself: Shlonsky, it is not you. It is she: It is the Hebrew language that is victorious."[14]

Traditionally, Hebrew had been invariably described as being aristocratic and holy, like the beautiful maiden described by the early-thirteenth-century poet Judah Al-Harizi in the introduction to *Tahkemoni*. There he relates how this exquisite creature, like the biblical Rebecca, comes to the well and offers him the "liquid of her thoughts" and the "milk and honey that are under her tongue." When he asks who she is, she replies: "I am your mistress, the Holy Tongue. And if I find favour in your eyes, I shall be your companion, provided that . . . you sanctify my great name." Consequently, although Jews utilized Arabic, Latin, and European languages for mundane writing, Hebrew was the medium of their poetic and inspirational expression.

The modern metamorphosis of Hebrew from a literary trove into a living language has required that the regal lady change radically. As the contemporary Israeli novelist Aharon Megged observed, "The revival of the Hebrew language is not like Lazarus arising miraculously from the dead. It is more like Sleeping Beauty awakened by the Prince. She was not dead, she had only lain dormant for a long time; and she was not rotten bones but a genuine beauty. But when you betroth her and bring her into your house, your problem is how to make this noble, aristocratic princess, adorned with jewels and clad in purple, do all the domestic work, soil her hands, break her back cooking, washing and tending the backyard garden. Contrary to Liza Doolittle of *Pygmalion,* she is quite all right at fancy parties, but she misbehaves in the market place."[15]

Since few contemporary Israeli writers today are at home in the text-world of classical Hebrew, many perforce join forces with the recurrent waves of untutored immigrants in carrying the secularization and vulgarization of the language to extremes. Still other authors adopt the spoken language, "street Hebrew," as a matter of principle, as though barbarization of language were equivalent to relevance. The best Israeli authors today avoid the extremes and balance linguistically on a *media via* between classical Hebrew and colloquial language. The linguistic dilemma facing the contemporary creator of Hebrew literature is well described by the novelist Amos Oz:

> You compose a Hebrew sentence, combine a few Hebrew words: a palace full of echoes and reverberations answers you. . . . I and people like me stand before a difficult challenge without precedent in the entire history of Hebrew literature. We have to write in a language which, on the one hand, belongs to us more than to former generations, and on the other hand, belongs to us less than to former generations because its treasures were opened before them daily, in a live reality.[16]

Over the past century, the creative revival of Hebrew in the Land of Israel has produced a corpus of literature that is generally adequate and occasionally even sublime. The eternal themes of life and death, war and peace, love and hate, the human and the divine, humanity and nature, along with the themes unique to Jewish experience and the Zionist revolution, have been articulated with insight and sensitivity. In large measure the question of whether "Torah" will emerge from Zion will be determined by how Israeli Hebrew evolves. And despite whatever offensive and unnecessary neologisms, unidiomatic foreignisms, and shoddy syntax may have been inflicted on the language, many of the *disjecta membra* of "dry bones" have come to life, albeit not without scarring. Also, one recalls a somewhat analogous historical precedent: although Nehemiah, the leader of the emerging second Jewish commonwealth after the destruction of Jewish independence in 586

B.C.E., was properly concerned about the inadequate and corrupt Hebrew of the populace, in time Hebrew flourished as an elegant, precise, dexterous medium of Jewish literature for 2,500 years.

As to the future of Israeli Hebrew, nobody has stated it better than the acknowledged dean of Hebrew translators, Hillel Halkin:

> If the visionaries of the Hebrew revival miscalculated at all, their miscalculation lay rather in the failure to consider that even miracles have their price and that a conquered language and a cultivated one are two different things. But if it was shortsighted of them to believe otherwise, it would be equally so today to assume that just because spoken Hebrew has taken a certain tack up until now, it must necessarily continue to do so. Linguistic change is a constant whose precise nature and rate remain variable, and this is especially so in an age of mass media and mass education, in which for the first time in history the forces working to conserve and standardize language are as great as if not greater than those tending to corrode and fragment it. Indeed, it is not out of the question that with the intelligent harnessing of these forces, it may yet prove possible to salvage for a living Hebrew much of its classical heritage that already appears irretrievably lost. The prospect may seem unlikely, yet it is hardly as farfetched as the notion one hundred years ago that Hebrew would someday be spoken at all.[17]

In sum, the present, like the past, is but prologue: it has a vote, but not a veto. And *that* is the "Good News"![18]

Étan Levine, Summer 1998

[1] See Étan Levine, *The Aramaic Version of the Bible*, 1988, p. 14. Thus, Germany's greatest humanist, Johannes Reuchlin, in his *De Verbo Mirofico* (1494 C.E.), attests that Hebrew is "the language in which God, angels, and men spoke together, not through the ambiguous murmur of a Castalian spring, Typhonian cave or Dodonian wood, but as friends talk face to face." Consequently it is hardly surprising to read of medieval Christian monks who, upon approaching old age, would hurriedly study Hebrew, "knowing" that when their earthly days were over, they would have to know biblical Hebrew in order to converse with the heavenly angels! (See M. Lowenthal, *The Jews of Germany*, 1936, p. 145.) The esthetic appreciation of Hebrew is best described by the renowned nineteenth-century French scholar Joseph Ernest Renan: "It is a quiver full of steel arrows, a cable with strong coils, a trumpet of brass crashing through the air with two or three sharp notes—such is the Hebrew language. The letters of its books are not to be many, but they are letters of fire. A language of this sort is not destined to say much, but what it does is beaten out upon an anvil. It is to pour floods of anger and utter cries of rage against the abuses of the world, calling the four winds of heaven to the assault of the citadels of evil. Like the jubilee horn of the sanctuary, it will be put to no profane use, but it will sound the notes for the holy war against injustice, and the call of the great as-

sembles; it will have accents of rejoicing, and accents of terror. It will become the trumpet of judgment." (See H. Orlinsky, *Bible Culture and Bible Translation,* 1974, pp. 425 ff.)

[2] Babylonian Talmud, *Qiddushin* 49a. For rabbinic attitudes toward translation, see Levine, pp. 3–17.

[3] These observations are made by Eisig Silberschlag in *From Renaissance to Renaissance,* vol. 2: *Hebrew Literature in the Land of Israel: 1870–1970,* 1977, p. 315. Let it be admitted, however, that today's Israelis more frequently greet each other by the English slang "Hi," the Arabic slang "Ahalan," or the standard Hebrew "Shalom," with "Baruk Ha-Ba" regarded as a self-conscious archaism.

[4] As the noted novelist and playwright Moshe Shamir explains: "The bridge which the younger generation seeks to build between ourselves and our great past does not resemble bridges of yore. We lost the religious, physical ties with the heritage of our People. All those wonderful things which our predecessors regarded as slices of life, essential experiences, eternal verities—the prayer book, the traditional holy days, the traditional modes of thought, the world of the Law, the customs—all these are history as far as we are concerned, and their value is only the value of a historical heritage" ("Renaissance," *Al-Hamishmar,* 26 April 1958).

[5] Consequently, even without my etymological, semantic, or syntactical comments, my more literate students of Biblical literature at the University of Haifa read the ancient texts with a significant degree of comprehension and exactitude. I am unaware of any other language community able to decipher texts 3,000 years old with equal facility.

[6] As succinctly put, linguistic zeal "was not uncommon among settlers in Palestine, nor could language's rebirth—perhaps the most extraordinary aspect of the entire Zionist venture—possibly be imagined without it." To these romantic nationalists, "Zionism itself was unimaginable without Hebrew, that sleeping beauty which once awakened would again become a princess among tongues." From the very beginning *kibbush ha-lashon,* "the conquest of the language," ranked in Palestinian Zionist ideology alongside *kibbush ha-avodah,* "the conquest of labor," and *kibbush ha-adamah,* "the conquest of the soil." Every new word forged from an ancient root, every foreignism banished and replaced, was the equivalent of another house built by Jewish hands, another *dunam* of land reclaimed by Jewish toil (Hillel Halkin, "Hebrew as She Is Spoke," *Commentary,* December 1969, p. 56).

[7] Although it is the coterie of Israel's best poets and prose writers who most retain classical Hebrew diction, even the mass media utilize a Hebrew that is more conservative than the spoken language today. One cannot help but wonder whether the frequent high volume, repetitions, and gesticulations characteristic of Israeli conversation largely derive from linguistic impoverishment.

[8] In fact, even in the Bible itself there are different verb forms. Thus, using *qtl* as a model of verb conjugations, we find: *qotelalqotalet, qittallqittel,* and *yiqtolnaltiqtolna.* Today no consistent principle is at work; contradictory reasons are presented as justifications for particular decisions. For example, the most archaic third-person plural feminine future form of the word meaning "to kill" (*qtl*) is *yiqtolna.* This ancient form corresponds to Aramaic, Arabic, and other Semitic languages. At some point in history, people began changing *yiqtolna* to *tiqtolna* (as an analogy to the second-person plural feminine). No doubt, the innovators of this alteration were at first "corrected"

by both teachers and peers. However, in time this new form became acceptable. It was widely utilized until it too suffered a similar fate and was subsequently replaced by *yiqtelu* (with no difference between masculine and feminine in the plural future). Thus *yiqtolna*, which later was replaced by *yiqtelu*. In modern Hebrew, although the three are theoretically "valid," the latest form—i.e., *yiqtelu*—is considered "correct." Similarly, the Hebrew verb "to find" (*ms'*) has in its past tense *masa'n, masinu,* et cetera. Yet in Mishnaic Hebrew (and in late biblical Hebrew), the *Lamed Heh* or *ultima "h"* verbs prevailed and penetrated into *Lamed Aleph* or *ultima "a"* verbs. Thus, *masa'nu* became *masinu.* This "mistake" became accepted as the correct form during the Mishnaic period. However, in our day, the revivers of the Hebrew language have generally emphasized biblical grammar, so that once again *masanu* is the "correct" form. Interestingly, in the past participle it is correct to say "*masuy*" (i.e., as though from *ultima "h"*), and no contemporary grammarian has objected. No rational explanation of this internal contradiction has been given, nor is any available.

9   See Mordecai Ben-Asher, *The Crystallization of Normative Grammar in Modern Hebrew* (in Hebrew), 1969, and my brief review in *Reconstructionist,* February 1970, pp. 74 ff.

10   Some of these authentic Hebrew innovations prove acceptable (e.g., "establishment" is *mimsad,* "telegram" is *mibraq,* and "delegation" is *mislahat*). Frequently these created terms prove unacceptable: Israelis prefer "babysitter" to *smartaf,* "radio" to *allhut,* "decentralized" to *irkuz,* "autobus" to *asmona,* and "telephone" to *sah-rahoq.* Foreignisms almost invariably remove the existing Hebrew term from currency. Thus, a sweater is no longer a *simri'ah* (from the Hebrew *semer* or "wool'") but simply a *sveter,* nor is a small shop a *hanuti'ah* (the diminutive of the Hebrew *hanut* or "store") but a "kiosk." One may still ride in a *rekeb* as well as an *auto* or take a *monit* as well as a *taxi.* But if one should hitchhike, one must "take a tramp" like any "trampist," and should there be a flat, it is not a *teqer* but a *puncher* (from "puncture"), and one must bring it to a *puncher-macher.* Then again, a mobile mechanic (*mosaknik*) might pass by in his *tender* and put his *jeck* under the *bekexel,* as the rear axle is called. Should it be the front axle, that would be the *bekexel kidmi,* the "front back axle"! Needless to say, perfectly adequate Hebrew terms exist, though their currency in ordinary speech is limited.

11   The distinction between the organic assimilations of antiquity and the inorganic invasions of modernity is best illustrated by Hillel Halkin, who writes (op. cit., p. 57): "The curious case history of a word that has been twice 'lent' to Hebrew illustrates the difference. When the Greek *spongos,* 'sponge,' was adopted by Mishnaic Hebrew (the Jews of biblical times, not a sea-dwelling people, apparently never possessed such a term), it was first metamorphosed into the phonetically Hebraic *s'fog,* which in time productively yielded the verb *safag,* 'to absorb,' the adjective *s'fogi,* 'sponge-like, absorbent,' and the noun *maspeg,* 'a blotter,' all in accordance with the regular laws of Hebrew grammar and morphology. When the same root, on the other hand, redundantly reentered Hebrew via English in the present century to signify the common household sponge—the sea animal continues to be called *s'fog*—it did so rudely untransmuted as *sponja,* a phonetic barbarism (the soft *j*-sound is not even represented in the traditional Hebrew alphabet), so unmanipulable that one has to do violence to the idiomatic integrity of the language simply to use it in a sentence. That is, because *sponja* yields no verb or any other derivable form, one cannot 'sponge the floor' as one would ordinarily; one must 'make a *sponja.*'"

12   See Silberschlag, p. 185. If Agnon is not as widely read as his magnificent writing deserves, it is not solely because he is basically a *lauditor temporis acti,* but because his myriad allusions escape modern readers.

13   This sobriquet was coined by his colleague Shneour by consonantal metathesis of the name Shlonsky into "Lashonsky," itself a clever pun.

14   *Ma'ariv,* 26 August 1966, p. 14, translated by Silberschlag. The twin giants of modern Hebrew poetry, H. N. Bialik and Saul Tschernichowsky, were similarly innovative, the latter especially in the fields of medicine, biology, and zoology. The list of other contributors is both lengthy and distinguished, yet they were all too hesitant for Shlonsky, who once described the great Bialik as a huge bus blocking a one-way street!

15   In "How Did the Bible Put It?," *Encounter,* January 1971, pp. 39 ff.

16   See *Moznayyim,* July 1966, p. 134.

17   Halkin, p. 60. For a survey of Hebrew language and poetry, the reader is advised to continue with *The Penguin Book of Hebrew Verse,* ed. T. Carmi, New York, 1981. Its introductions (pp. 13–72) are concise and judicious, and its bibliography (581–85) is genuinely selective.

18   A highly readable account of Hebrew's modern revivification is Robert St. John, *Tongue of the Prophets,* 1952. In his historical survey "Shalom Means Peace" the author unwittingly demonstrates the inadequacy of all translation, for *shalom* does not mean "peace." Whereas "peace" (e.g., *pax*) constitutes the agreement which the victor imposes and the vanquished, however reluctantly, must accept, *shalom* derives from the root *slm,* signifying wholeness, completeness, well-being, and the like. (See the semantic field in S. Mandelkern, *Veteris Testamenti Concordantiae Hebraicae atque Chaldaicae,* 1978, p. 1182.)

Besieged Feminism: Contradictory Rhetorical Themes in the Poetry of Daliah Rabikovitz

All was ended now, the hope, and the fear, and the sorrow,
All the aching of heart, the restless, unsatisfied longing,
All the full, deep pain, and constant anguish of patience.

▨ **LONGFELLOW,** *EVANGELINE*

Even a quick reading of the poetry of Daliah Rabikovitz will reveal its strong emotion, evoked by a hurt, deprived and rejected narrator who complains about her alienating and hostile environment. The narrator's penetrating complaint is set against a general human background shared by any individual who yearns for personal redemption, yet it is also a feminist complaint; it reflects a woman's desire to extricate herself from her subordinate position in a male-dominated environment. Though the male characteristics of the hostile environment, in many of the poems, are indirectly conveyed, being metaphorically shaped, the nature of the environment can easily be traced. In the poem "An-aqim" (Giants) from the collection *Hasefer Hashelishee* (The Third Book), for example, we read:

Ants found in the grass a half cadaver of a fly
And it was hard for them to get it out of the grass.
Their small hips were crumbling because of the hard
  labor.
And as if in spite, the grass suddenly
Swelled, turning into crop spikes, as if it were a
  barley field.
It is such madness for grass to think that it is a
  barley field.
I knew that the end of the ants would be bitter
Much hard labor with no longevity.
Some thick insects were walking as well in the grass
Whistling in the ears of the silly ants.[1]

The mistreatment by the grass (a masculine noun in Hebrew) of the agonizing ants (a feminine noun) is demonstrated in two ways: 1) the swelling of the grass makes the ants' mission of pulling out the fly from the grass more difficult; and 2) the swelling of the grass implies a male attempt to annex a feminine function, reproduction. The grass's pretense that it is a barley field—which is criticized by the narrator—emphasizes its arrogant attempt to adopt a feminine reproductive function; and the erotic male characteristics of the grass—its swelling also implies an erection—underline the feminist nature of the ants' distress. Hence the grass, a metonymic representation of a male-dominated environment, is not only an intruder, but also an impostor. It not only sabotages the ants' productive labor, but also tries to hide its own barren nature by putting on a false disguise of pregnancy.

The "thick insects" which whistle in the ears of the "silly ants" share the repulsive role of the grass: their thickness likens them to the swelling grass, and their whistle demonstrates a malicious rejoicing at the ants' calamity. The adjective *silly* can be seen either as a mocking judgment by the insects or as a rebuke by the narrator, who is castigating the ants for accepting the unbearable situation. However, the end of the poem exposes the "tenor" beyond the "vehicle": "Afterward I wept. Everybody beside me became a giant." The metaphorical cover drops; the narrator identifies herself with the ants and adopts their tormented standpoint. The male-dominated environment appears threatening indeed through that lattice. The very same view is repeated in the poem "Hakarpodim" (The Male Toads; *HH,* 19): "In a small pond, in an assembly of male toads / There is hidden a yellow rose. / Only because of its wonderful bravery / It does not look for another pond." The description of the toads as male (in Hebrew this is

quite rare) and the female characteristics of the rose (the word for rose is a feminine noun, heavy with feminine connotations) direct the reader to notice the feminist foundations of the situation: one single rose set in a crowded male environment. Also, the end of the poem again drops the "figurative epidermis," and the poem extricates itself from the stratum of metaphorical gesticulations to reveal its naked message. The oppressiveness of the male-dominant environment is exposed in its full repugnance: "Like the wonderful yellow rose / Many will never reach another pond / The male toads, they are blind to / The dreadful fear of our heart." The blindness of the male toad is a passive indifference with a destructive result. The distress demonstrated in the poem is undoubtedly a general human distress, but it has unmistakably feminist overtones.

The metaphorical expression of the narrator's distress is widespread in Rabikovitz's poetry. "Hayonah" (The Dove) from the collection *Ahavat Tapouach Hazahav* (The Love of the Orange; 42) provides one such example. The poem depicts the agonizing odyssey of a dove as it confronts a crow, a flock of wolves, a hostile band of fowl and seventy-seven other foes, until it is finally devoured. There is one clause which is repeated incessantly throughout the poem: "Ehevou na et zot hayonah" (Do love that dove). The obstinate repetition gives this clause the feel of a desperate oath uttered only by those who know that they are doomed from the very beginning. The moving supplication to love the dove, on the one hand, and the awareness of its unavoidable demise on the other produce a tense irony that emphasizes the shadowy fate of the dove. Toward the end of the poem the metaphorical riddle is cracked: "And the dove is a parable, by its eye, by its wing." The narrator's complaint echoes again beyond the figurative sheath, and its feminist tone is not to be missed.

In other poems the poet drops the metaphorical mask, and her complaint is naked and biting, as in "Qaf Yad Resh'ah" (A Wicked Hand's Palm; *ATH,* 15): "Strings of smoke have been bent diagonally / And my father hit me. / All those who stood beside were laughing as / They saw it." The childish point of view adopted by the narrator emphasizes this brutal and humiliating experience. One could argue that the complaint is not just a feminist one, but the fact that the oppressive environment is again male cannot be denied.

In still other poems the narrator's complaint is a crossbreeding of metaphorical and literal rhetoric. We see this, for example, in "Zichronot Chamim" (Warm Memories) from the collection *Choref Kashe'* (Hard Winter; 33).

Imagine: it was only the dust which accompanied me
. . . .

Imagine: who was the one who accompanied me
And how much I wished to have another companion

. . . .

Imagine how much I was deprived
For having it as my only companion.

The combination of a complaining human narrator and
a symbolic companion creates a surprising rhetorical
equation, giving the imploring complaint a unique feel.
Moreover, the fact that the object of the narrator's complaint is again male (dust is masculine in Hebrew) colors the complaint with a feminist hue.[2]

Undoubtedly, one of Rabikovitz's effective "complaint poems" is "Buba Memouqenent" (Mechanical
Doll; *ATH*, 35), which narrates the story of a mechanical
doll that is mistreated by an exploitative environment.
In the poem the doll finds her way to a ball. Once there,
she is repelled by the dancing and is outrageously neglected "in a company of dogs and cats." The poem ends
with a moving description of the tender, pretty doll.
The main literary device in the poem is the selective use
of allusion, especially to the fairy-tale figure of Cinderella: both Cinderella and the doll are mistreated in a hostile environment, both are trapped in that environment,
and both find their way to "the ball." But here we come
to a crucial difference: for Cinderella, the ball becomes
a turning point which extricates her from misery to happiness; but for the mechanical doll, the ball becomes
one more step toward brutal humiliation. The doll is exiled from the ball to the revolting company of dogs and
cats. Hence, wishing to establish a bleak atmosphere in
the poem, the "implied author" (to use Wayne Booth's
term) employs the allusion to Cinderella in a most selective and calculating way. As long as the allusion fits the
poem's mood of gloom, it is followed most obediently,
but as the allusion starts to move from its path of gloom,
it is dropped. The effect of this deviation heightens the
somber atmosphere of the poem as a result of a rhetorical refutation of expectations. The allusion to Cinderella
induces in the reader the hope of future happiness for
the mechanical doll. The disappointment of this expectation emphasizes the sadness of the ending and adds
a touch of bitterness.

Another literary device enlisted by the implied author to intensify the bleak atmosphere of the poem is
compositional. The suspension of the moving description of the lovely doll until the very end of the poem
seems at first a questionable choice. One would expect
the poem to start with this expositional description of
the doll, before the narration of her story. But the delay
is significant, for it links the moving description of the
doll with its unhappy fate. This compositional linkage
heightens the melancholy of that fate.[3]

A third technique enlisted by the poet for heightening the atmosphere in the poem is ironic allusion. The
poem opens with the clause "On that night I was a mechanical doll." The phrase "on that night" is an allusive
fragment from the Haggada—the tale of the Exodus
read on Passover night. Since the expression is originally set in a context which emphasizes a move from slavery to freedom, its use in a poem that speaks about
hopeless servitude creates a bitter irony that sharpens
the gloomy fate of the enslaved doll. Hence the poem
mobilizes the thematic stratum (the selective adoption
of the allusion), the rhetorical stratum (the process of
frustrated expectation) and the compositional stratum
(the suspension of the expository description of the
doll) with one principal goal in view: to stress the outrageous, malicious attitude of society toward the doll and,
consequently, its agonizing condition.

The wicked oppression which restlessly haunts the
narrator in Rabikovitz's poetry urges her to look for a
refuge, to seek redemption. That wish is strongly demonstrated in many poems, such as "Tirtzah Vehaolam
Hagadol" (Tirtzah and the Large World; *CK*, 42).

Take me to the northern edges
Take me to the Atlantic Ocean
Put me among other people . . .

. . . .

Take me to the Pacific Ocean
Take me to the brown fish

. . . .

Take me to the weeping rivers

. . . .

Take me to the shores of Norway
Take me to the desert of Australia

. . . .

Tell them that I will be
Next year in the heart of the ocean.

The insistent devotion of many of Rabikovitz's poems
to exotic and remote places demonstrates the narrator's
yearning to remove herself from her unhappy reality.
Her longing for salvation is translated into a tireless
naming of places such as Hong Kong, Manchuria, Chad,
Zanzibar, Cameroon, China, Madagascar, Africa and
Scandinavia, among others, each of which represents
shelter. Thus Rabikovitz's poetry frequently deals with
extremities, with polarities; the sense of "edge" is widespread. The depth of the mines, the bottom of the seas,
the very top of the mountains, the heart of darkness, the
end of the West—all populate her poems; all comprise
an utterance of her desperate attempts to flee her oppressive reality.

The many references to voyages in Rabikovitz's
verse serve the very same aim. It is not accidental that

she titled a large cluster of poems "The Viking," convey-ing via obvious metonymy a sense of wandering, of per-manent exile. In that light, verses like "Here, another painful thing: / A seashore without ships" in "Hama'rav Haqachol" (The Blue West; *CK*, 20) or "Today I am a hill / Tomorrow I am a sea / Each day I wander" in "Qishoufim" (Magics; *CK*, 44) are very typical. The poet's eternal search for absent horizons makes her sor-rowfully proclaim, in "Qoulam Tsomchim" (Everybody Is Growing Up; *HH*, 12), "So many are growing up, but nobody flies." Her restless cry "I want to arrive at the other side of the hill / I want to arrive / I want to go" ("The Blue West") might be considered the "slogan" of a principal theme in her poetry.

In light of the above, the motif of the bird in Ra-bikovitz's poetry appears to be of great importance in-deed. Even a superficial reading of her verse cannot fail to reveal the frequent presence of this motif, and statisti-cal examination shows it to be present in approximately 25 percent of the poems.[4] Among the many references to the bird which are included in Rabikovitz's work are: a wild turkey, a crane, a peacock, "a bird that madly twitters" (*CK*, 38), another "that is not hunted" (*CK* 42), a parrot, a kingfisher, a raven, a lark and a starling. In other cases the motif is present through metonymy: for example, a wasp, or a wing which is "whitely flashing" (*CK*, 46). There are cases in which the metonymic mark of the bird motif is even more remote, but a close read-ing shows that its connection to the base motif is there: for instance, the references to airplanes, as in the poem "Sof Hanefilah" (The End of the Falling; *HH*, 25), which starts, "If a man falls from an airplane in the middle of the night . . . ."; or the poem "In Memory of Antoine de Saint-Exupéry" (*HH*, 44), which adoringly speaks of the airplane of the famous French nobleman and author that "fell to the Mediterranean Sea / Swinging in the strong spring winds." The fact that the narrator identi-fies with the airplane of the author of *The Little Prince*, a book that became a symbol of innocent wandering, is not accidental; it reflects her constant wish to escape, to extricate herself from her despotic environment. And it is significant that the most intense presence of the bird motif is found in the book "Hard Winter": more than 33 percent of the book's poems include references to various birds. Since this collection's title hints at an extreme and difficult reality, it is not surprising that the bird motif—which stands for the narrator's yearning for escape—fills the volume.

Not all the occurrences of the bird motif are set in a context which is directly related to the narrator's wish to extricate herself from her environment, but its fre-quent presence in her poetry has a cumulative meta-phorical resonance of flight. Thus the motif of the bird

plucks the same rhetorical string as do the references to remote, exotic places, daring voyages and extreme situ-ations: a desperate yearning for salvation. In light of this, the expression of a contradictory impulse in the very same clusters of poems, an impulse which appears to move against the desired extrication, is most aston-ishing indeed. Moreover, the holding back from the wishful redemption, the lack of preparedness to realize the extrication and the willing compliance with the op-pressive reality are not accidental or sporadic; they con-stitute a major rhetorical strain whose presence in the poems is as strong as the one evoked by the yearning for extrication. The reader, familiar with the imploring complaint of the narrator who wishes to flee her humili-ating distress, could not be more surprised. It is as if he were confronting a hidden alter ego of a divided narra-tor, as if he were suddenly facing an unexpected antago-nist bursting forth from behind the familiar protagonist.

This splitting of the narrator's personality in Ra-bikovitz's poetry, though it seems arbitrary in a most disturbing way, is actually anchored in a well-wrought and monitored rhetorical system, with an explainable poetic-psychological rationale. Before any discussion of that comprehensive rhetorical-psychological system, however, it is necessary to observe the major character-istics of this surprising impulse. One may identify three forms of this opposing theme. In the first stage the pre-vious rejection of the depriving, humiliating and mali-cious environment becomes a submissive attraction to and even a docile adoration of that environment. A con-spicuous illustration of this impulse is found in the poem "Matnot Melachim" (Kings' Presents; *ATH*, 26). Here the king's beloved is expressing her unrestrained attraction to the king's headstone (in Hebrew, "Haeven Harosha"). The headstone is not only the king's most precious gift waiting for his beloved; metonymically, it *is* the king, his very essence, his realization. As his be-loved states, "Hamelech hou haeven haroshah" (The king is the headstone). Hence the beloved's attraction to and desire for the king, which is partly sexual, makes her set aside her self and leads her toward total self-abasement: "I want the headstone / To touch the head-stone / To lick the headstone / To gore my head on the headstone."

The chorus, which as in Greek drama serves here as "la voix de raison," expresses a warning: "The head-stone, the headstone. Alas for the one who takes and in-herits it." This danger is not hidden from the king's be-loved ("I knew that my desire would bring a disaster upon me"), yet her submission to her lust, her servility toward the man, is much stronger than her clear-eyed judgment. Her docile addiction to the male influence blunts her monitoring capability and leads her to participate in the perpetuation of male dominance. The same self-destructive addiction to male authority is suggested metaphorically in the poem "Ahavat Tapouach Hazahav" (The Love of the Orange; *ATH*, 5), which opens with a biting expression of that submissive impulse: "An orange / Loved its eater." Like the chorus in "Kings' Presents" that sounded an alarm against destructive servility, the citron (*etrog* in Hebrew) and the tree warn: "Sarah hee vachet hee" (It is a revolt as well as a sin). But "la voix de raison" is denied again: "An orange / Loved its eater / Loved its beater / In all its organs."

In other poems the narrator demonstrates an ardent and passionate admiration of masculine tyranny. In "Oshek" (Extortion; *CK*, 47) we read: "In that place / In one of those places / the flowers have been devoured violently / the flowers have been devoured like prey . . . Lord / such a beauty there was!" The wish for extrication from the exploitative, male-dominated environment is fleeting and is replaced with blind devotion. The same adoration of "manly might" is expressed in "Qarney Chitin" (The Mighty Summits of Chitin; *HH*, 23),[5] as the narrator describes in a sympathetic light the brutal rapes committed by the Crusaders: "How their blue eyes were shining / As they saw the palm tree waving in the wind. / How they tainted their beards with their spittle / As they pulled the women to the bushes' thicket." Here the most violent antifemale aggression is not only tolerated but also welcomed wholeheartedly: malicious suppression is painted with a romantic tint. The alter ego of the narrator is fully exposed; the pining for escape from the male-dominated environment is radically converted into an obsequious addiction to male exploitation.

The second form of this surprising rhetorical tendency is more moderate and restrained, but still the previous yearning for redemption is clearly contradicted. In this form the narrator demonstrates a certain passivity; though she does not enjoy her subservient position, she avoids any opportunity to extricate herself from it. In "Milmoolim" (Stammerings; *CK*, 15) this passivity is strongly emphasized through contrast to the strenuous activity of industrious birds.

They twitter in flutes' sounds . . .
They twitter in rivers' sound . . .
They twitter in a sound which shakes
The sun from its place in the depth of the night . . .
They extricate the forest from the dark
They count the sparkles
They count the weeks . . .
They tell about the day's tenderness.

The poem ends with its only reference to the narrator: "Though I am still sleeping." The placement of the clause highlights the contradiction between the active birds and the passive speaker; consequently, the narrator's lack of readiness to escape her oppressive situation is underscored. The same rhetorical technique, involving even the very same thematic components, is echoed in "Sheon Hamayim" (The Uproar of the Water; *CK*, 37).

A bird twittered madly
'Til her strength gave out
And then she wept;
And I sank in a cloud of gracefulness
I sank
And I was evaporating.

The passive "evaporation" of the narrator marks the end of her formerly proclaimed wish to escape. She lacks the necessary strength of will.

In this context it should be noted that some of the "voyage poems" are narrated as reports of nocturnal dreams. "Hazman Hanitzod Bareshet" (The Time Trapped in the Net; *CK*, 13), for instance, begins: "Again I was like one of those small girls / who travel in one night around the whole world"; and "Eretz rechoqah" (Remote Land; *CK* 14) opens: "Tonight I returned in a sailboat / From the sun islands and the coral bushes." The fictional shaping of the voyage in dream form may be considered another indication of passivity, another step that was never taken, that will never be taken.

The passive response of the narrator to her exploitation is revealed even in those poems which also express a deep longing for salvation. In a poem like "Tirtzah and the Large World" we face the often-heard request, "Take me to the sterns of the north / Take me to the Atlantic Ocean / Put me among other people. / . . . Take me to the Pacific ocean / Bring me to the brown fish / Bring me to the weeping rivers / . . . Bring me . . . Put me . . . Take me . . . Prepare for me . . . Wait for me . . . ." and so on. All these demonstrate the narrator's passivity. She is waiting for the man to take her, to lead her, to direct her (all the verbs are conjugated in the masculine), without even considering an active step of her own. The very same impulse is reflected in other poems such as "Qiseot Lemishpat" (Chairs for the Judgment; *ATH*, 30): Please, take me by your hand / Please, approve of me / . . . / Please, take me by your very hands / To chant a praise among your worshipers." And again, in the poem "Portrait" (*HH*, 33), we find:

She is sitting in her home for many a day.

. . . .

She does not do what she would wish to do
She has inhibitions
She wants vanilla, a lot of vanilla

Give her vanilla.

The implied sexual meaning of vanilla in Rabikovitz's poetry emphasizes a dependence upon the man, maintaining the passive and barren expectation of being saved by others.[6] Hence even the most urgent desire for salvation cannot release the narrator from her caged circumstance. She disdains her chains, yet she keeps choosing and rechoosing them. The narrator continues to cultivate the defeatist belief that any attempt at extrication is hopelessly doomed. In the poem "Lashanah Haba-ah" (Next Year; *HH*, 56) she rebukes a female figure who seems to be badly deprived.

Why are you sitting here,
Don't you have another place?
Why does she sit here like a spider?
. . . .
Why are you sitting here always confused,
Always frightened of what will happen?
Try for once, recall what is written in the books
Leave the Vale of Tears.

But the narrator knows that all is in vain. The woman she addresses will never release herself from the Vale of Tears. The narrator herself never did, and never will. And the way that she ends the poem demonstrates a clear-eyed irony: "Next year / In Jerusalem." Since this saying is not only a symbol of hope but also a symbol of "lip service," of a promise to leave that will never be realized, the ending of the poem implies in bitterly ironic fashion that the exploitation will be perpetuated.

This confusing gap between the desire to escape oppression and the inability to realize it leads the narrator to look for a convenient refuge in various justifications. In "Eich Hong Kong Neherssah" (How Hong Kong Was Destroyed; *HH*, 14) the narrator proclaims, "And I was the only one who knew / That there is nothing in the West / That there is nothing in the East." Another statement echoes in the poem "Dimyon hou Davar She-ein Lo Shiour" (An Imagination Is a Measureless Thing; *HH*, 28): "The view of the yellow river does not deceive me / As there is nothing in the river except water." The message is clear: since there is nothing either in the West or in the East, there is no point in leaving. And even though the yellow river does exist, there is no point in going there either, since its enchanting reputation is deceiving—there is nothing there except water. In this same spirit the narrator claims in the poem "Afilou Elef Shanim" (Even a Thousand Years; *HH*, 53), "I cannot rebuild the world from the beginning / And there is also no point." It is a repetition of a docile, defeatist spirit. All is doomed and nothing can be changed, and even if it could, it is not worth the effort. Hence it is no wonder that the speaker comes to

the following conclusion: "The really beautiful things do not happen outside / Sometimes they happen in the room when the doors are locked and the shutters are also closed / Sincerely, the really beautiful things are not rivers or mountains or seashores."

The narrator, who realizes that she is too weak to "rebuild the world from the beginning," that she is too indolent to leave for remote, exotic places, that she is too passive to extricate herself from her reality, attempts to lessen her frustration by adopting a new view: there is no salvation. And since there is no salvation, there is no point in feeling sorry or guilty for not achieving it. The unbridged gap between constant yearning for salvation and its perpetuated frustration is too great a burden for the clear-eyed narrator. And though she is aware that her refuge is fragile, she must stay there. As long as she is weak and passive, that is all she can have.

The third form in which the narrator's passivity is reflected is not as caustic as the two previous ones, yet it expresses faithfully the very same impulse. As noted, the speaker demonstrates a strong desire for remote, exotic places, and indeed, many of the poems are brimful of references to enchanting places, voyages and various kinds of birds, which function metonymically to indicate extrication, hovering, escape from agonizing burdens. But the strain of passivity is found even in these very images of hovering, soaring flight. They all concentrate on the act of leaving and avoid the act of arriving, settling down. Hence the passivity is still there. Decision-making, stand-taking, the burden of responsibility—they are all rejected and prevented. The narrator who wishes "to fly with a right wind" does not wish to land, because landing means obligation and commitment; and for those, she is not ready—at least not yet.

It appears appropriate to end this discussion by quoting from "The Marionette" (*HH*, 63). The yearning of the poem's narrator for the marionette's delicate chains, her willing identification with its enslaved position, extends the theme of the narrator's passivity to the full.

To be a marionette . . .
Passing under the new day
By diving
In the low currents
To be a marionette
A porcelain puppet, lean and pale
Bound with cords
. . . .
In the twentieth century, in a gray darling dawn
How good it is to be a marionette.

Reading these lines, one cannot but recall the bitter complaint of another marionette wrought by the very same poet, the agonizing puppet in "Mechanical Doll." The great gap between these two poems is undoubtedly the best example of the contradictory, ambivalent feminism in Rabikovitz's poetry.

The contradictory feminist rhetorical trends in Rabikovitz's verse are not reflected in each of her poems; they are revealed only by a panoramic view of her work as a whole. Hence that dialectic ambiguity is not just a marginal, sporadic component in her poetry; it is rooted in the very heart of her ars poetica and has a pervasive effect. On the psychological level, the split personality of the narrator, whose action—or rather, lack of action—invalidates her proclaimed longings, might appear rather embarrassing. The speaker's inability to satisfy her yearning can be considered the bitter offspring of an uncontrolled weakness. Any change, any act of realization, demands the burden of responsibility, of venture. On the other hand, an oppressive situation is not only a burden; it is also a convenient shelter from the difficult task of conducting one's own life. Any failure can find, in this way, its justification. Hence the splitting of the narrator's personality perpetuates her oppressed position; the feminist impulse lays siege to itself.

But the psychological flaw of the split narrator is fully compensated for on the esthetic level. The unbridged gap between the preaching and the breaching, the tense dialogue between the two polar tendencies, gives Rabikovitz's poetry a continuous vitality, a vigorous dialectic. Here "To be or not to be" is never the question. In Rabikovitz's verse "To be *and* not to be" is an enduring answer. The psychological fallacy is translated into an esthetic virtue.

Yair Mazor, Summer 1984

1 See Daliah Rabikovitz, *Hasefer Hashelishee* [The Third Book], 2nd ed., Tel Aviv, Levin-Epstein, 1970. Subsequent references to this collection use the abbreviation *HH*. All translations from the Hebrew are my own. Other books by Rabikovitz mentioned and discussed in this paper are: *Ahavat Tapouach Hazahav* [The Love of the Orange], Tel Aviv, Sifriyat Happoalim/Hakibbutz Ha-artzee, 1967; and *Choref Kashe'* [Hard Winter], Tel Aviv, Devir, n.d. Subsequent references to these two titles use the abbreviations *ATH* and *CK* respectively.

2 A thorough discussion of the various characteristics of the narrator's complaint in Rabikovitz's poetry is included in Miri Baruch, *Iyounim Beshirat Daliah Rabikovitz* [Studies in the Poetry of Daliah Rabikovitz], Tel Aviv, Eked, 1973, pp. 9–33.

3 For a detailed discussion (in Hebrew) of the literary devices of the poem "Mechanical Doll" and their rhetorical-ideational functions, see Yair Mazor, "On the Selective Use of Allusions in Poetry: A Study of Two Poems by Daliah Rabikovitz and Yehuda Amichai," *Rosh* (Quarterly for Poetics and Modern Poetry), 2 (April 1978), pp. 23–27.

4 The precise statistical analysis is as follows: in "The Third Book," 15.4 percent of the poems include the bird motif; in

"The Love of the Orange," 17.9 percent; in "Hard Winter," 33.3 percent. The general mean is 22.2 percent.

5 Karney Chitin is a moutainous area in the lower Galilee, not far from Tiberias.

6 The etymology of the word *vanilla* gives the word its erotic connotation: In Latin vanilla means "vagina," a case, a pod, a sheath, probably because of the affinity between the fruit of the vanilla plant and a capsule. That meaning of the word is recaptured in Rabikovitz's poetry by being set in erotic contexts; see "Shivron Lev Bagan" (A Broken Heart in the Park; *CK*, 39): "On the opposite side, in the delicate café, a vanilla smell was dispersed / Pleasant men picked up their wives' coats." In the poem "Shunrah" (Cat; *CK*, 61) the sexual meaning of vanilla is metaphorically conveyed: "Shunrah put a napkin on her knees and was licking a vanilla cake." The act of eating (which is filled with sexual connotations) and the immediate context ("somebody was waiting for her . . . then . . . he kissed her as if she were a cake") both intensify and emphasize the implied sexual meaning.

Aharon Appelfeld: A Hundred Years of Jewish Solitude

The Holocaust has already engendered more historical research than any single event in Jewish history, but I have no doubt whatever that its image is being shaped, not at the historian's anvil, but in the novelist's crucible.

▓ Y. H. YERUSHALMI, IN *ZAKHOR*

■ INTRODUCTION

The literature of the Shoah is complex, varied, and multifaceted. It is a literature of commemoration, testimony, and document. It is a literature of both fact and fiction, and occasionally the barriers between the two blend and become unclear. It is ultimately an attempt against all odds to give verbal expression to an experience that challenges and defies the boundaries of language yet emerges through it. Indeed, some scholars challenge the clear division between "fact" and fiction: "The role of the critic here is not to sort 'fact' from fiction in Holocaust literary testimony, but to sustain an awareness of both the need for unmedicated facts in this literature and the simultaneous incapacity in narrative to document these facts."[1] By comparison, the words of George Steiner carry an emotive tone: "The world of Auschwitz lies outside speech as it lies outside reason. To speak of the unspeakable is to risk the survivance of language as creator and bearer of humane, rational truth."[2] And yet, the restoration of memory through language allows for a modicum of re-creation, conceptualization, and representation. Geoffrey Hartman claims that even in the case of the Shoah "there are no limits of representation, only limits of conceptualization."[3]

The issue of representation is a major issue when the fiction of the Shoah is discussed. Fictional representation may and does have historical underpinnings. However, a personal point of view, a personal tone or attempt to grapple with the event is simultaneously a major consideration. As such, pitting history against fiction in the master narrative of the Shoah may be erroneous. All attempts to come to terms with the enormity of the Shoah are of crucial importance. They all wrestle with these issues of conceptualization and representation.

To a certain extent, as a historical event of such gigantic proportions, the Shoah almost inherently dooms all attempts to grapple with it. The Shoah is a metatext bequeathed to us and to the generations to come. The last fifty years have seen a major attempt on the part of theologians, philosophers, and historians to come to terms with it more fully. Under the heading "the Narrative of the Shoah," a new discipline has emerged that grapples with the phenomenon from all aspects of human epistemology: a human quest to place a map of understanding on the phenomenon.

The liminal line between "story" and history continues to challenge all thinking on and interpretation of the phenomenology of the Shoah. The creative artistic mode, especially in literature, continues to search for a verbal and personal narrative as a proxy for comprehending the catastrophe. The Shoah is the most extensive communal catastrophe in Jewish history. Until the nineteenth century, the Jewish response to catastrophe mostly occurred within the traditional liturgical literature and the Jewish canon—deep piety justifying God's judgment.

Shoah literature can be viewed as part of Destruction Literature in Hebrew and Jewish literature. It is possible to trace its early appearances in Deuteronomy, Jeremiah, Daniel, and other prophetic books of the Hebrew Bible. To an extent, the destruction of the First Temple is a model for Destruction (*Hurban*) Literature. Sacred texts—from the Bible through the Talmud, Midrash, and liturgy—form a continuous literature that has canonized the verbal memory of the people. It is a code, a history rife with persecution and destruction, reinforced by repetitive patterns which have shaped this literature. The collective memory is intertwined with the personal. Events moored in history enter a metahistorical heritage of a continuous presence of past events. Jewish history is studded with words and names serving as markers and signs that continue to carry meaning despite elapsed time. The last to have been added to the list is Auschwitz.

Aharon Appelfeld (*Frederick Brenner*)

Thus, collective memory and personal response coalesce into a totality, making the past not a cold historical fact but vital, ever-present experience. This synoptic view creates what Harold Fisch calls "historical archetypes." All this assumes a collective cultural consciousness that can be evoked by means of a text.

The question how to approach Shoah literature is still an issue of discussion and disagreement. Critics who endorse an open-ended reading of texts insist on a particular approach and understanding of our relationship to the event and its depiction. Notably, David Roskies takes a clear, unequivocal position.

> It now seems to me that to approach the abyss as closely as possible and to reach back over it in search of meaning, language, and song is a much more promising endeavor than to profess blind faith or apocalyptic despair. The alternative, to focus solely on the Event itself, succeeds only in robbing the dead of the fullness of their lives and in inviting the abstraction of survivor into Everyman, the Holocaust into Everything.[4]

Modern Hebrew secular writers relate to traditional Jewish archetypes by incorporating them into modern texts. Sometimes the dialogue between these modern texts and canonic texts is negative, yet it is evoked. Thus, at the heart of many modern literary works there are classical allusions and modernistic ironic perceptions.

■ AHARON APPELFELD

Aharon Appelfeld has chosen a different path.[5] He introduces irony by facing the unresolvable tension between what seemed and what was, as he probes the psyche of those who died and those who survived. His highly stylized fiction summons the Shoah not through direct depiction, but through metaphorical connotations. In his 1990s fiction—after more than three decades of writing—he has finally touched directly on the death-camp experience. Yet it would be incorrect to perceive him as a realistic writer. He is still the master of the fable despite his attempts to moor his characters in a defined time and space.

Appelfeld (b. 1932) is a unique modernistic writer who creates a unique fictional universe for his characters. The Shoah is *the* experience that shaped their lives. Appelfeld expands his historical scope and depicts the life of the Jews in Central Europe prior to, during, and after World War II. In the 1980s he said that he aimed to write about "a hundred years of Jewish solitude," and indeed he has continued in this vein. Appelfeld's stories and novels create a singular world during the age of the Shoah, and very often in his fiction the Shoah takes on a mythic, timeless quality. In his earlier narratives the traumatized individual is devoid of memory or desire.

Appelfeld's earlier narratives can be read as postmodernist in nature. The atomistic, decentralized, nonresolvable nature of the narrative exposes a protagonist detached from any definite social framework, cultural matrix, or historical continuity. The experience of the protagonist in this framework is nonaccumulative and often devoid of self-perception. This allows for a certain open-endedness, unhindered by demands of probability and resolvability.

Appelfeld is fascinated with the assimilated, cultivated European Jew of the late 1930s. The existence of the assimilated Jew is tinged with a deep sense of impending catastrophe. Appelfeld's fiction has evolved in its treatment of characters. His early stories all contain three or four characters but have no main protagonist at the center of the unfolding tale. Since the 1970s he always centers his fiction on one individual. If Appelfeld can be said to depict the "Jewish archetype" before and after the war, he is also concerned with the fragmentation of that archetype. If words cannot encompass the impenetrable experience of the Shoah, can they at the very least heal?

Amid the ruination of reason and meaning, Shoah literature has been one of the most profound attempts to find meaning in the realm of the inexplicable. Appelfeld's fiction is a deep and moving testimony to experience and to its expression and limitations. In his earlier postmodernistic fables Appelfeld creates a limited and restricted universe for his characters to inhabit. Regardless whether we find them in an elegant resort town,

wandering across unidentifiable vistas as persecuted refugees, or on a train, they move in a world that gains its inner meaning from their presence, their movement, and their experience. Although his characters are often fragmented and dislocated, his fiction is not. Terms such as *abyss* and *void,* often used by postmodernist writers, aptly characterize the daily, suppressed experience of his characters. The unarticulated self carries an unexpressed sense of horror. The human being as a "torn fabric" is depicted in highly metaphorical language, and this gives Appelfeld's fiction its power. Moreover, the frequent omission of causal relationships between events, the technique of juxtaposition rather than comprehensible continuity, and the depiction of an almost "flat" character tie his early narratives to postmodernist fiction.

▪ "ANI KOTEV U'MOHEK"

When asked how he is doing, Appelfeld frequently answers, "Ani Kotev U'mohek"—that is, "I write and erase." This refers to the actual writing process, of course, but it can be applied as well to other aspects of his work, mainly to the relationship between autobiographical experience and fictional depiction. Appelfeld erases raw memory and writes metaphorical tales. The relationship between the expressed and the suppressed is essential in his work. However, even his more detailed and "realistic" novels of the 1990s are still highly stylized, probably touching upon personal experiences but not elaborating on them. In his novel *Ha'kutonet Vehapassim* (1983; Eng. *Tzili: The Story of a Life*) he tells the story of a young girl who survives the Shoah. Tzili, not unlike Appelfeld himself, spends four years separated from her family, escaping the Nazis by living in the forests, marshes, and bunkers nearby. Eventually, again like Appelfeld, she joins the hordes of refugees in their journey south toward Italy: "Perhaps it would be better to leave the story of Tzili Kraus's life untold. Her Fate was a cruel and inglorious one, and but for the fact that it actually happened we would never have been able to tell her story."

Appelfeld's early characters consciously or subconsciously sever their ties with their past and their memories. For these traumatized individuals there occurs a basic dislocation of the "self" and the "I." Accordingly, the reader cannot—freely—paint the character with data unattached to the Shoah. It is a stark drama of the suppression of memory and the prior self that allows a mode of survival and a limited mode of functioning in the post-Shoah world. Thus, the reader's process of filling in the gaps is extremely difficult. This ties in with the suspension of all ethical considerations, as observed in the behavior of various characters who, in the post-Shoah experience, dwell in a wholly different world.

Appelfeld weaves highly sensitive tales about individuals in both the pre- and post-Shoah world. All his characters from the early 1960s to the 1990s are constantly on the move. Movement is their raison d'être. They roam through these tangential and fantastic narratives in a state of suppressed quest. As noted, in his early works Appelfeld consciously suspends the framework of both the historical and the endured time of the Shoah experience to raise it to the plane of mythic narrative. With the partial suspension of any temporal frame of reference, there emerges the theme of the Fall of Man. It is a fall wherein humanity has been stripped not only of its usual categories of understanding, but, even more profoundly, of its accustomed self-image *qua* humanity, thrusting the individual into an elemental, precognitive state of existence. The suffering that is experienced—repeated and intensified daily—occurs within a definite span of time. Often, Appelfeld's characters retreat into an insular existence, into oblivion, into inaccessibility and silence—all within an opaque and tenacious existence.

How is the modern reader to come to terms with Appelfeld's unique form of narrative? Can the literature of the Shoah retreat into the fantastic? In regard to the literature of the fantastic, the suspension of disbelief is a matter of volition. In regard to the Shoah there is nothing volitional: just as we cannot suspend believing that it happened, so no fictive suspension is applicable. Nothing here happened "once upon a time." Everything happened at a definite place or places. Neither is there a fictive refuge for the characters; the reality allows no escape. Yet the authors of Shoah literature can make use of the fantastic—by transcending the flow of the narrative and inserting a different reality within it, thereby suspending realistic time, and placing within it a character of an insular type.

The inconceivability of these events serves to dispel our hesitation between the real and the imaginary. In Appelfeld's fiction, the fantastic is a quality of the individual, the consequence of a torn psyche. During the Shoah, the impossible and the inconceivable became reality. For Appelfeld's characters, as for Shoah victims and survivors, it was all too real, yet cannot be explained by the laws pertaining to the familiar world. The effect of this is shattering, and is internalized by Appelfeld's characters.

With the suspension of the consecutive unfolding of time, space gains a central importance in Appelfeld's fiction. The effort to encapsulate the solipsistic individual within an airless bubble enhances the depiction of outwardly and inwardly passive individuals. In his later novels, his characters are more active, leaving behind or emerging from their total insularity. However, since

the 1980s Appelfeld has ceased to depict the life of Jewish survivors in Israel and has begun to delve deeper into past Jewish intellectual life in Europe, giving it a historical or chronological as well as spatial existence. He has expanded the archetype of the Wandering Jew in the post-Shoah world, and as such, this period, this mode of existence, allows for movement to function as the lifeline of Jewish existence. However, movement is not only a mode of existence; it is also a state of mind.

Europe after the Shoah is a Jewish wasteland in Appelfeld's world: there are few Jewish survivors, and those who have survived are constantly on the move. These dynamics, however, do not bring an essential change in the lives of the characters. It seems as if the Jew moves yet continues to stand in the same spot on the map—that is, he continues to be the stranger, "the other," the hovering shadow of an extinct reality. For Appelfeld's characters, Europe of the post-Shoah period is an archeological site, the largest Jewish cemetery in history. Appelfeld's characters remain in Europe. An almost sick fascination draws them to return to their hometowns in Europe. Notably, this applies to the protagonists in *For Every Sin* and *Mesilat Barzel* (1991; Eng. *The Iron Tracks*). The life of the protagonist in *The Iron Tracks* is a loose compilation of the post-Shoah experience of Appelfeld's characters throughout his stories: Italy, smuggling, black-marketeering, love of the German language. The extent to which *The Iron Tracks* represents a cross-section of Appelfeld's work is readily apparent in the fact that even the names of several previous characters are repeated, now taking different roles.

On the whole, then, Appelfeld's fiction depicts two movements: first, the narrative of assimilated Jewish society before the war, including the excessive cultivation and intellectualism which brought him to the point of atrophy; and second, the narrative of the survivor with suppressed memories and the fundamental need to be on the move.

■ THE THREE PERIODS

In a sense, then, one can divide Appelfeld's work into three distinct periods. In the 1960s he published surreal short fiction with strong fantastic elements. This fiction consists of five books of short stories, some of which have been translated into English. His early novels relate to Israeli experience. Of these, the most personal, *Michvat Ha'or* (The Searing Light; 1980), about the adjustment of young refugees to life in Israel, was not translated. Appelfeld made his mark in his "second period," with the novels of the 1970s, *Badenheim, Ir Nofesh* (1980; Eng. *Badenheim 1939*), *Tor Ha'pelaot* (1978; Eng. *The Age of Wonders*), and others, among them the beautiful short novel *Ke'Ishon Ha'ayin* (The Pupil of the Eye; 1973), as yet not published in English. In his third period, the novels of the 1990s, the actual events of the Shoah are incorporated directly into his fiction. An examination of three works by Appelfeld from his various periods will serve to elucidate the richness of his prose and its unique nature.

"Kitty." One of his early stories, "Kitty,"[6] combines Appelfeld's plastic, almost sensory depiction of the rapport between the psyche and the surrounding world. Like much of his fiction, this story is dominated by the image of a monastery. The intricate pictoriality, the detailed depiction of mood and atmosphere by means of impressionistic technique, and the diminution of dialogue all contribute to the highly stylized quality of the text.

The story centers on an eleven-year-old girl who finds herself in a French convent toward the end of the war, devoid of both language and memory. She emerges from her insulated, autistic state through a series of revelations, discovering life through her senses. This synesthetic "conversion" lifts her from an elemental, preverbal creature into a person who relates to the world through her body. As she grows, she becomes open to touch, sound, and sight, and while opening up she continues to weave her own unique, enclosed, solipsistic self. With the onset of puberty she acquires language and begins to ask questions in the context of a possible loss of innocence. The silence of the convent has protected her like a womb. It bursts open with encroaching reality as the Germans approach. In the meantime, she discovers her Jewishness and, with it, anti-Semitism as well as greed. Through it all she maintains her world of fantasy and epiphany. As the war draws to a close, the Germans shoot her.

Appelfeld is especially attuned to the fate of young girls whose stories carry autobiographical elements. In Kitty we encounter a solipsistic young woman whose trauma, undetailed in the story, is connected with Christian symbolism. Kitty feels that in her rebirth she is the daughter of God, whose tormented body on the cross she observes. Like other characters of Appelfeld, she senses a mysterious flow of movement which points to another reality embedded in the visual signs of the world. And yet, outside the world of the imagistic, the protracted silence of the convent functions as her salvation.

Her transition from innocence to experience comes with the posing of questions, whether about puberty or war, all portending penetration. German soldiers, their half-naked bodies suggesting the sensuality and sexuality that have penetrated Kitty's existence, surround the convent. Peppi, a vulgar local cleaning woman, exposes Kitty to a world unexpressed by her tutor, the nun Maria, not hiding her sexual encounters with the Germans. She suggests that Kitty steal the convent's golden candelabra. Kitty's refusal to go along with this scheme unleashes a barrage of anti-Semitic slurs. Peppi calls her "a dirty Jewess" and threatens to expose her. As a result, Kitty is confined to the cellar, yet in her descent there is an element of ascent: through spiritual resignation and calm she weaves a new relationship with the things that surround her.

Two voices are at war within Kitty. One, a sense of divine grace, leads her to think that she is one of God's chosen children and as such must suffer until His light shines upon her. The other voice repeats the question, "Am I a hairy Jewess?" Despite everything, in an act of spiritual resignation, she awaits her fate. As the war draws to an end, the convent is attacked and invaded.

> Kitty had grown taller in the cellar and when she was brought out into the light, dressed in her white nightgown, she looked even taller. The gown trailed behind her. She was led along narrow paths behind the fence. How marvelous it all seemed — like floating in space. Now all the people were gone. Angels embraced her arms and when the shot was heard, she stood for a *moment,* marveling at the miracle revealed. (K, 246)

A spiritual, almost hagiographic element combined with the irreversible reality of the Shoah concludes the story. The fear of womanhood, of growing up, is typical of many of the young women in Appelfeld's narratives. Both fear and guilt accompany Kitty's emerging womanhood and the beginning of her menstruation. Only in a state of childhood, protected by a father figure or the convent, can the traumatized girl's wounded psyche survive. If indeed she is a dirty Jewess, she is responsible for the crucifixion. Sexuality, suppressed and expressed, is depicted by the women in the story; and yet, the nuns and Peppi send starkly differing messages to Kitty. There is a fundamental conflict here between sublimation and repression, which ultimately serve to engulf the girl, who has to withdraw into her encased self and to the cellar to await her inevitable fate.[7]

Appelfeld's fiction employs several basic motifs and archetypes. One of the most prominent, which applies to the assimilated Jew in his fiction, is self-denial and self-deceit as a mode of existence. Appelfeld admits that he admires assimilated Jews. Despite their uprootedness, despite the fact that they function as cosmopolitan outsiders, they reach a height of sensibility.

> The assimilated Jew had a feeling that he should deny his being, his culture, his heritage, his being a Jew. This was a part of it. To become a univer-

salist you should deny yourself. This is of course a tragedy, you can't deny yourself. The moment that you deny yourself, you are punishing yourself. Another danger is that you become a superficial person, because you are an uprooted person without a past. This is a kind of ambiguity. . . . Being a part of the great world on one side and then you are punished by the world they do not accept you. They accept you as Jewish.[8]

The Coming Storm: **Badenheim 1939.** Appelfeld's fiction portrays the attitude of the Germans and the Austrians toward Jews: an alien element, demons from another world that penetrated their culture and contaminated it. In *Badenheim 1939*[9] two movements inform the slowly unfolding plot: the forthcoming spring cultural festival and the presence of Sanitation Department inspectors. The town faces a slow and irreversible invasion. The festival, like mythical spring rites, revives the visitors, whose need for the yearly pilgrimage is acute. This reality is a form of madness, of sickness and intoxication, which has beset the town and its inhabitants. The visitors are Jews who have married gentiles, Jews who have married into the aristocracy and nobility of Europe as well as Jewish intellectuals.

The novel has no central protagonist, with the exception of Dr. Pappenheim, the impresario of the cultural festival. Pappenheim emerges from the forest, like a Hassidic miracle worker, to preside over the festivities. A variety of characters are introduced, and each character contributes to the novel's architecture. Bitter irony pervades the work, bordering on the grotesque and the tragic and resembling at times the sketches of George Gross. As noted, the novel chronicles the development of two movements: the preparations for the festival and the slow, almost imperceptible turning of the town into a concentration camp. Appelfeld's orchestration is deft: "The inspectors of the Sanitation Department were now spread all over the town. They took measurements, put up fences, and planted flags. Porters unloaded rolls of barbed wire, cement pillars, and all kinds of appliances suggestive of preparations for a public celebration" (*B,* 15).

In a highly stylized manner, *Badenheim 1939* presents Badenheim as a microcosm of the assimilated existence of Central European Jews on the eve of World War II. As the novel unfolds, a feeling of impending doom settles in on all the characters and a sense that no exit is possible takes hold more and more. The preparations for the festival correspond to the preparations for the deportation. The posters put up by the Sanitation Department are chilling: "The Sanitation Department now resembled a travel agency festooned with posters; Labor is our Life . . . The air in Poland is fresher . . .

Sail on the Vistula . . . The development areas need you . . . Get to know the Slavic culture" (*B,* 29–30). Remote, alien Poland begins to seem a pastoral place to many of the assimilated visitors on holiday. The vacationers at Badenheim seem to be captivated by powers beyond their control. Like marionettes, they go through the motions of assimilation, featuring in a most civilized manner the stylized horror story of the twentieth century.

Appelfeld does not try to come to terms openly with the cause of assimilation. However, through careful signs and symbols he depicts the detrimental effects of assimilation and the psychological dislocation it has produced in his characters. What was the source of the breach in the Jewish psyche in the twentieth century? What was the cause of the tragic excess? Was it man's attempt to erase stereotypical Jewish traits? A deep guilt at leaving the fold? Self-hate and/or self-denial? A quest for the unattainable? Appelfeld is posing questions for the last one hundred years of modern Jewish history in Europe. Madness serves as a form of self-negation, and self-denial as a way out.

Superimposing a transparency of common sense and causality on the Appelfeldian universe does not enlighten the reader. In a parallel to the world of Kafka, Appelfeld's fiction in many cases creates an enclosed verbal universe that answers only to its own inner laws. In *Badenheim 1939* the message of doom is transmitted through the actions of the Sanitation Department and through Rilke's "Sonnets to Orpheus" and "Duino Elegies," recited by twin poetry readers from Vienna. These two readers, whose voices touch the infected cells of their listeners, represent the motif of the double or doppelgänger, portraying the double nature of existence in Badenheim and the fractured psyche of the vacationers, who are intoxicated by the sickness in their voice.

As the novel unfolds, the return of the Jews parallels the expanding activity of the Sanitation Department. A barrier is placed at the entrance to the town, and the movement of the vacationers is limited more and more. Appelfeld does not expose us to the inner thoughts and feelings of his characters. We observe only their movements and their conversations. Outer agents represent the mood: the anaerobic atmosphere is depicted through locutions such as "cold light," "leaden sun," and "cold horizons," all indices of the abnormality of the situation. A state of expectation characterizes the inhabitants of Badenheim. Expectation grows, for example, for the arrival of the famous Mandelbaum Trio. Upon his arrival, Mandelbaum tells of the Jews of Reizenbach, who were placed in quarantine even as he himself managed to escape. At the same time, Dr. Pappenheim is elated: for years he has tried to bring Mandelbaum to the festival. Pappenheim promises him a most memorable experience, to which promise Mandel-baum replies, "Me? I'm just a Jew, a number, a file. . . . What do you need me for? Am I a rabbi, a cantor?" (B, 67).

Appelfeld portrays music as a possessive force that overpowers the artist. Mandelbaum buries himself in his room, tormenting his musicians in a quest for utmost perfection. Simultaneously, restriction and confinement continue: telephone service is terminated, and the town becomes totally cut off from the outside world. It begins to live "a life inside itself" (B, 70). A quiet conversion to Jewish consciousness is enhanced by the return of Badenheim's former rabbi. Dr. Pappenheim and the rabbi become the leaders of the community. When asked how the transfer to Poland will take place, Dr. Pappenheim answers, "By train. Train journeys are nice, aren't they?" (B, 74).

The cold horror of the narrative lies in its slow pace and in the quiet process of the telling of the tale. The strength of Badenheim 1939 rests in its power to portray the macabre though not garish colors and harsh sounds. Muffled utterances, everyday small talk, and bizarre behavior seemingly within the boundaries of order paint the picture. And yet the novel challenges the claims of order, culture, and civilization. Appelfeld shuns the melodramatic. He remains a student of such Central European Jewish writers as Wassermann, Schnitzler, and Kafka (as well as, obviously, the Thomas Mann of The Magic Mountain). The tone of the narrative is stoic despite the underlying madness in man.

The infrastructure of Appelfeld's novel feeds on irony, the tension between seeming and being. The characters remain within the domain of the seeming, whereas the reader combines the two realities, knowing full well that the train is carrying the vacationers to their doom. The novel's final paragraph reads:

> An engine, an engine coupled to four filthy freight cars, emerged from the hills and stopped at the station. Its appearance was as sudden as if it had risen from a pit in the ground. "Get in!" yelled invisible voices. And the people were sucked in. Even those who were standing with a bottle of lemonade in their hands, a bar of chocolate, the headwaiter with his dog — they were all sucked in as easily as grains of wheat poured into a funnel. Nevertheless Dr. Pappenheim found time to make the following remark: "If the coaches are so dirty it must mean that we have not far to go." (B, 147–48)

The 1990s: The Iron Tracks. Until the 1990s, Appelfeld's stories, characters, and plots were situated geographically far from the war and the concentration camps. We do not encounter a camp directly until his

1991 novel The Iron Tracks. Appelfeld's stories, both shorter and longer, are frequently fictional recastings of his personal autobiography. The importance of the text as a chronicle of time, memory, and history is of major importance in Appelfeld's latest narratives. Self-consciousness and a sense of continuity, which were mostly absent from his earlier narratives, now appear in Katerina (1989), Ad Sh'yaleh Amud Ha'schar (Until the Dawn's Light; 1995), and other novels. The personal chronicle is inseparable from that of the community.

Healing and atonement are permanent features in Appelfeld's world: the search for roots as the search for meaning moves many characters in his later novels. Forever fascinated with the terminally intellectual Jew of Europe, Appelfeld begins to expand on the archetype of the Wandering Jew in the post-Shoah period. This mode of depiction releases him from historical constraints and allows for movement as the lifeline for Jewish existence. Movement, as observed by Appelfeld, is not only a mode of existence; it is also a state of mind.

The refusal or inability to venture toward basic change is enhanced by the unique nature of those who belong to the tribe of the survivors. The characters in The Iron Tracks adapt to a paradoxically open yet underground existence. Ideas of conspiracy and secret cells still prevail. The Jewish subterranean existence, in bunkers and other hiding places, becomes a conceptual underground.

In The Iron Tracks, a modern picaresque tale, the first-person narrator is one Irwin Ziegelbaum (Irwin is Appelfeld's given name), who recounts in the 1980s his forty years of wandering in Europe. A Shoah survivor, he continues to move about in trains, like a modern land-surveyor in the European countryside, from South to North and back. Trains make him a free man, unattached. Haunted by his memories, he nevertheless visits all the stations in his life and his parents' lives. He maintains a yearly cycle—like the reading of the Torah in weekly portions—consisting of twenty-two stations, paralleling the number of letters in the Hebrew alphabet. He returns compulsively to a forlorn train station where, during the war, after three days in a sealed car, the Jews inside were deserted by the Germans. Along his way, he redeems Jewish holy artifacts at fairs, collecting them and selling them to those who will maintain them, eventually shipping them to Jerusalem.

A personal quest appears as a subtext beneath the novel's surface text when Ziegelbaum learns that Nachtigel, the German officer who killed the former's parents, is about to return to his hometown. This allows the protagonist to fulfill his task: he kills Nachtigel. The novel concludes as follows: "It was clear that my life in this place had burned up and come to an end. If I had a different life, it wouldn't be happy. As in all my clear and drawn-out nightmares, I saw the sea of darkness, and I knew that my deeds had neither dedication nor beauty. I had done everything out of compulsion, clumsily, and always too late" (195).

The combination of a mission on the one hand and the sense of delay on the other is reminiscent of Agnon's *Book of Deeds* and Kafka's *Castle*. The elements of suppression and concealment, so prevalent in Appelfeld's previous texts, are partially lifted here, and a direct depiction of the Shoah and the experience within the camps enters his fiction for the first time. The belated act of revenge does not bring the expected sense of relief, but perhaps it does provide a degree of closure.

The act of killing underscores finality as a major thread in the book. *The Iron Tracks* is a novel rich in its numerous characters, minor as well as major, traveling in the insular compartments of their lives and never getting off. Appelfeld's earlier narratives often had no distinct turning point, no resolution, no clearly individuated characters. The later narratives, in their longer form, are still highly stylized, and Appelfeld continues to write the saga—often predicated on solitude—of European Jewry in the twentieth century.

Gila Ramras-Rauch, Summer 1998

[1] James Young, *Writing and Rewriting the Holocaust,* Bloomington, Indiana University Press, 1990, p. 11.

[2] George Steiner, *Language and Silence,* New York, Athenaeum, 1966, p. 123.

[3] Geoffrey Hartman, in *Probing the Limits of Representation: Nazism and the "Final Solution",* ed. Saul Friedländer, Cambridge (Ma.), Harvard University Press, 1992, p. 320.

[4] David G. Roskies, *Against the Apocalypse,* Cambridge (Ma.), Harvard University Press, 1984, p. 9.

[5] For a general discussion of Appelfeld, see Gila Ramras-Rauch, *Aharon Appelfeld: The Holocaust and Beyond,* Bloomington, Indiana University Press, 1994.

[6] Aharon Appelfeld, "Kitty," in *Modern Hebrew Stories,* ed. E. Spicehandler, New York, Bantam, 1971, p. 22. Subsequent references use the abbreviation K.

[7] For another view, see N. Aschkenasy, *Eve's Journey,* Philadelphia, University of Pennsylvania Press, 1986, pp. 236–39.

[8] Aharon Appelfeld, *The Iron Tracks,* tr. Jeffrey M. Green, New York, Schocken, 1997.

[9] Aharon Appelfeld, *Badenheim 1939,* tr. Dalya Bilu, Boston, Godine, 1980. Subsequent references use the abbreviation B.

Israel's Theatre of Confrontation

Israel, as an open, democratic society existing in a state of siege, is a country in which all the measures of artistic and individual expression are daily put to the test of whether they do—or should—serve the nation's interests. In those circumstances Israeli theatre, especially in the past few years, has moved into the vanguard of the arts in taking a didactic tack that has often brought it into outright confrontation with the public. That approach is hardly an Israeli invention, but it does represent a departure from the mainstream of Western theatre, recently dominated by a focus on self-discovery and the relationship of individuals rather than ethical or cultural values. In this article the Israeli stage is examined as a forum for expression of the artist's vision of a higher law, the roots of that attitude are traced, and its implications explored.

Theatre attendance is very high in Israel, with some three million tickets reliably estimated to have been sold in 1980, a number equal to the total population of the country.[1] That gives Israel the highest per capita theatre attendance in the world, about eight times that of the United States. Nor is attendance class-related. It cuts across all social and economic lines, making the stage a truly demotic forum for ideas: "In Israel . . . bringing the blue-collar worker and lower classes to the theatre was never a problem" (Levy, 40). Then too, the country is small enough that almost everyone knows almost everyone else in the professional world, and because of its strong egalitarian outlook there is more offstage fraternization between actors and their audiences than one finds in most Western countries. Being so deeply entwined in the society, actors, playwrights, and directors have always been unusually sensitive to national moods. It would come as no surprise, then, to see the present depression and frustration reflected on the stage. What does strike an observer as unusual is to find professional theatre acting as a brutal goad rather than a sympathetic nurse. Where one might expect to find solace, Israeli theatre doses its public with wormwood and gall. Sartre's *Trojan Women,* for example, was set in a refugee camp with the guards wearing Israeli uniforms and carrying Israeli weapons. This was not a random choice for dramatic updating, but was staged during the turmoil that followed charges of Israeli negligence in permitting Phalangist massacres in Lebanon's Sabra and Shatila refugee camps. "It was very hard to take, but it had some truth in it," said actor Misha Asherov.[2] To make a play of the past come to grips with the present is hardly a new idea; but methodically to create a setting with the intent of affronting the audience is not simply "relevant," to use a word with hackneyed overtones; it is provocative. It is a theatre of confrontation.

Such a stance produces practical, not just theoretical, problems in the politics of art. When poet Yitzchak Laor, seething with anger, wrote a poem for the literary journal *Siman Kri'ah* that included the phrase, "and in our *matzot* the blood of Palestinian youths," he enlisted two thousand years of blood libel against the Jews as a powerful yet extremely offensive ally in opposition to the government's internal policies. The potency of burning Israel's sacred Torah onstage, as was done in the play *Tashmad,* cannot be denied; but must any society stand by and watch its most cherished symbols desecrated, its history flogged, and its recent wounds torn open publicly in the name of "Art"?

The answer, of course, is clear if one lives in Switzerland, Denmark, or the United States. There society is strong enough and the freedom great enough to withstand such attacks. The long-range value to the culture far outweighs the shock to community delicacy, and the principle of untrammeled artistic expression is of greater import than any temporary discomfort. In more stringently regulated countries such as the Soviet Union or Chile, the question is moot. Whether by consensus or fiat, those societies have subscribed to the Platonic vision of art regulated in support of a prescribed political vision. Violation of that aim, however courageous, is viewed as a thoughtless or selfish aberration, like someone who insists on driving through red lights or absconding with his neighbor's goods, and is treated accordingly.

Israel presents a more problematic situation. Maintaining the ideal of an open society, it is beset by external enemies and internal tensions that threaten imminent destruction in very real terms. Those who widen existing fissures or diverge from the common purpose can easily be viewed as insurgents or dangers to the integrity of the body politic. One need only think of the treatment accorded to American Vietnam protesters of the sixties and seventies under much less stringent circumstances to imagine the situation. This is further complicated by the fact that the performing arts are publicly subsidized in Israel, with all that implies, from government intervention in their content and presentation to the right of the artist to bite the hand that feeds him.

During a brief return of several weeks to Israel I spoke about this to a number of people in the theatre and uncovered not a festering sore, as I had expected, but a pot boiling with philosophical currents and crosscurrents, arguments and convictions on every side of the issue. In a country where 26 percent of the population are theatregoers,[3] the events of the 1983–84 season outline the main themes of that debate, as the arts, with theatre in the vanguard, attempt to delineate the ethical and moral center of the country's national life. Israeli theatre sees itself as a voice of opposition, probing at national ideals from the stage in an abrasive way that is

uniquely and aggressively Israeli. Art in the public market has once again become a vehicle for reform, as it had been in an earlier Jewish commonwealth for Jeremiah, Ezekiel, and Hosea.

Some fundamental assumptions about theatre's place in modern society were made and questioned in such presentations as Moshe Shamir's *Judith of the Lepers,* a 1968 play based on the biblical story of Judith and Holofernes. Shamir's *Judith* was not simply a Bible story. It carried a bitter message that there is no morality in war or international relations. "For Jews, even fanatical ones," laments Uri Rapp in his review, "the play is a rejection of whatever they believed in."[4] The content may have been about characters from the Bible, but the subject was today's world, and an unpleasant view of it at that.

This is not to say that the entire season is an unrelieved succession of head-on collisions between the theatrical establishment and its public. *Much Ado about Nothing* was on the boards at the Haifa Municipal Theatre, and the national theatre, the Habimah, presented the Neapolitan farce *Caviar and Lentils* in Tel Aviv along with a setting of *Hamlet* as "readapted" by David Avidom and directed by Dino Cernescu. *Mephisto* was imported, based on Klaus Mann's novel by Ariane Minouchkine, founder of the Théâtre de Soleil in Paris, and for local color, *Behind the Fence,* an adaptation of a Bialik love story by Avi Koren, was presented. Those only served, though, to make the Israeli plays of confrontation and the controversies surrounding them stand out in bolder relief.

Nola Chilton, 1972 winner of the Tel Aviv Prize for directing and developing Israeli drama and twice winner of the "David's Harp" Award (1974, 1982), staged a play by Yehoshua Sobol, *The Seamen's Mutiny,* dealing with a scandal from the early days of the state in which many felt that the ideals of Zionism were sacrificed to the exigencies of politics. Motti Barhav's *Sanjer* dealt with drug addiction and Haim Marin's *Bunker* with the unpleasant but ever-present topic of war. A new play called *Ali the Galilean* by François Abu Salem, a Palestinian theatre director living in Jerusalem, was produced. In spite of many trials, at the end Ali is still an Arab and not "a hollow man calling himself Eli and trying to pass for a Jew."[5]

> The messsage of the play for an Arab audience is . . . keep your chins up and hang on to your culture. . . . The message for a Jewish audience is: Here's what you look like to the people who clean your streets and bake your bread. (Grossman, 17)

Hanoch Levin's cynical and scatological play *The Patriot* was excoriated by the government censorship board, which sued to have it banned. *The Patriot* rubbed Israeli sensibilities the wrong way. The protagonist is a cynic who, unwilling to participate in the spiritual or physical defense of the country, falls back on Johnson's "last refuge of a scoundrel" to profiteer from his fellow citizens' plight. Another committee of the same government, though, awarded the author the Leah Porat Prize for Literature only a few months later, confusing the issue still further.

In December 1983 Haim Druckman, a conservative member of the Knesset, had had enough and initiated a parliamentary debate on the "offence to the basic values of Judaism, the nation and the state in theatre productions."[6] That, in turn, sparked a March 1984 meeting of two hundred Israeli writers, artists, and academics in Tel Aviv's Tzavta Theatre, where a resolution was unanimously adopted establishing a watch-dog committee to "defend freedom of expression in the arts." In fact, the Israeli arts in general have come under increasing fire from the country's conservative elements. Deputy Minister of Education and Culture Miriam Ta'asa-Glaser referred to poet Yona Wallach as a "beast in heat" in an interview for the now-defunct newspaper *Rehov Rashi*. The remark was made in reference to a poem published in the monthly literary magazine *Iton 77* entitled "T'fillin," in which "the phylacteries of the title are used to embellish sexual intercourse" (Pomerantz, 12). Tel Aviv University suspended support of the literary review *Siman K'riah* when it printed an offensive political poem by Yitzchak Laor. "Liturgica," an international festival of religious music held annually in Jerusalem, had a performance of Bach's *Passion According to St. John* disrupted by an organized demonstration of students from one of the yeshivas.[7]

The case of *The Patriot,* which engendered angry censorship on the one hand and inspired a national award on the other, was just one of a series of contradictions. Another play, *The Soul of a Jew,* by Yehoshua Sobel (directed by Gedalia Besser), had a run at the Riverside in London and was a hit at the 1983 Edinburgh Festival, where "the audience gave it a rapturous reception."[8] Theatre critic John Clifford, writing in *The Scotsman,* praised it as "intellectually enthralling and very deeply moving . . . it is easy to understand its impact in Israel, given its intense relevance to the country's current crisis of ideals and identity." In Israel, though, the play met with a mixed reception, to say the least. Performances were disrupted by zealous demonstrators, and even erstwhile supporters occasionally walked out of the theatre in distaste. Professionals and audiences alike were divided in their opinion of the play, which may be as it should be, for the work deals, in explosive language, with a Jewish protagonist living in Europe at the

end of the nineteenth century who represents an assault on every value held dear to the Israeli: a sexist, self-hating, homosexual nihilist who finally commits suicide.

A speech in Martin Sherman's *Messiah,* given at the Haifa Municipal Theatre, resulted in threatening letters and two bomb scares at the theatre. The play is about Shabetai Zvi, the sixteenth-century poseur and false messiah, and the particular lines cited as so offensive are those of a young woman who, in an intense dialogue with God, cries out, "Cursed be You, God Almighty," then "You do not exist" and "I hate you." The embattled government and the religious establishment did not take this lightly. Moshe Blimenthal, head of the three-member United Religious Front of the Haifa City Council, filed a complaint with the city police, who finally decided that there were insufficient grounds on which to act.

The artistic director and playwright, of course, stood firm on leaving the lines in. At that point, in this already overheated atmosphere, Shlomo Lorincz, an Orthodox rabbi, member of Agudat Yisrael (a right-wing religious-political party), and chairman of the Knesset Finance Committee, threatened to withhold some two billion shekels in government funds owed to the city unless mayor Arieh Gurel forced the theatre to remove the lines. The issue was finally resolved with the lines' being stricken, but the intervention of Israel's president, Chaim Herzog, was required. Without having seen the play, Herzog asked that those lines be deleted "in the spirit of tolerance and mutual respect."[9] The president's polite request, however, did not neglect to bring up the matter of a little-used 1973 law that could be used to impose a one-year jail sentence for any person who "offends in speech or writing the religious faith and feelings of others." Israeli political scientist Allan Shapiro explains:

> Offending religious sensibilities was a punishable offense under the Ottoman code, and was perpetuated in British-ruled Palestine even before the formal inception of Mandatory rule. In independent Israel it has been evoked to protect Christian sensibilities, as in the banning of Amos Kenan's play, *Friends Tell about Jesus* in 1972, which resulted in a high court decision referred to . . . by president Chaim Herzog in the matter of the Haifa production of *The Messiah.*[10]

In reaction to Herzog's plea, the author Aharon Megged, president of the Israeli branch of PEN, released a statement attacking the president for his interference with free speech.

Somewhere in this mixed bag of provocations and responses one can sense a confused search for a principle that would harmonize the heritage of openmindedness with the fears of a religious-political establishment that feels beset from within the country as well as from without. What is taking place is something more complex than a descent down the dreary path of repression already trod by so many nations. Having inherited censorship laws from both Turkish and British administrations together with a centuries-old tradition of individualism and the free exchange of ideas, Israel is wrestling anew with the question of the mutual responsibilities of the artist and society. Time-honored arguments over the purpose of art have become pressing, practical issues in Israel today, perhaps more so than anywhere else, and the answers are making headlines and lawsuits on the eastern edge of the Mediterranean.

For every attempt to quash the confrontational nature of Israeli theatre there has been a counterploy to support it. The parliamentary debate on theatre as an "offense to the basic values of Judaism" was met by another motion opposing any intervention whatsoever in the country's artistic, creative, and intellectual life. Given the complex structure and party discipline of Israeli politics, it is heartening to note that even though it was defeated, the countermotion proposed by M.K. Yossi Sarid received forty-seven votes, whereas the floor had been opened to the original debate on a vote of only fifty.[11]

The theatre critic Uri Rapp wrote, quite reasonably, in *The Jerusalem Post:*

> The girl [in Martin Sherman's *Messiah*] who curses God and denies his existence in one breath . . . is an ardent believer. Only a deeply religious person could give vent to such disillusionment. . . . The offending sentences are part of a very intimate relationship with God.
>
> There are few other forums [besides theatre, in Israel] where issues can be thrashed out publicly. Thus constant vigilance is imperative against any attempt to silence the debate. Art is not a matter of consensus but of controversy, at least in a pluralistic society. A play like Martin Sherman's *Messiah* could have been a case in point . . . but no genuine debate materialized for two reasons. First *Messiah* is simply a bad play . . . [but] this is not the first time that artists and intellectuals have had to fight over a piece of little artistic value all for the sake of freedom of expression. The second problem was the attempt to get the play taken off the stage, or at least to get the theatre to delete a passage which "offended" the kind of people who don't go to the theatre anyway.[12]

What is taking place in this pragmatic pressure cooker appears to be a gradual redefinition of theatre's sociopo-

litical role in the country. Aharon Megged, who had castigated President Herzog for his attack on free speech, also said, following the protest meeting at the Tzavta Theatre in Tel Aviv: "Someone coming to the Tzavta meeting from the outside might have thought this was Chile. We don't have to act as if we're in a fascist regime."[13] The Haifa police found no cause to close the municipal theatre over Martin Sherman's *Messiah,* and the fuss, as might be imagined, contributed greatly to the financial success of the play, as it had for Levin's *Patriot.*

Is it possible for a government that holds the purse strings of the arts and carries a public censorship law on its books to maintain even a façade of freedom of expression? Most in the West would answer no. It can only lead, one would think, to state control of the arts, a horror that seems to follow logically from state support of the arts, at least in American eyes. It is also clear, though, that official attempts at repression have put no appreciable brake on the assault emanating from the state-subsidized stage, and that until the issue is finally resolved, it will bear close observation.

That all this should be coming to the fore now is no accident. A national culture grows out of the weaving of threads into a fabric that becomes a cloth of assumptions against which value judgments can be projected by members of the society. The Israeli stage has a history of political awareness dating back to the birth of the Habimah in Moscow during the second decade of the century as a Hebrew theatre-in-exile. From the earliest days of its existence, "Most of the idea-elements in the *Habimah* ideology, artistic and non-artistic, were based primarily on moral and ethical, rather than aesthetic, considerations."[14]

The establishment of a national theatre was an early priority to the founding fathers of the state. That meant more than simply creating a paid troupe of actors with a performance venue; it meant developing the language and creating new plays relevant to the culture expressed in modern Hebrew as well as transmitting the heritage of the past. At the same time that new literature came into being in a revived Hebrew, Haim Nahman Bialik translated *Don Quixote* and Saul Tchernikovsky brought out the *Iliad,* the *Odyssey,* and the *Kalevala* in Hebrew as part of the earliest stages of revitalizing the national language and culture.

The Habimah was performing in Hebrew in Moscow by 1918 and established itself in Tel Aviv by 1926. Its first production, opening on 18 October 1918, was the Hebrew-language composite *Neshef Bereshit* (An Evening of Beginning), composed of *The Eldest Sister* by S. Asch, *The Hot Sun* by I. Katznelson, *The Fire* by I. L.

Peretz, and *The Bone* by I. D. Berkowitz. The balance between theatre as national expression and theatre as world art has seesawed back and forth since then, but "The topic of the play, i.e., Jewish or non-Jewish, did not in itself guarantee a successful or popular production. . . . What accounted for the popularity of these plays was not their topic or ideas, but their artistic level" (*H,* 48–49).

By 1948, when the nation gained official recognition, state support of theatre was well established. The theatre had played a significant role in setting the standard of a reconstituted Hebrew language as well as disseminating Zionist ideals of the collective future of the land, the value of physical labor, and aspirations to intellectual achievement. In the next twenty years Israeli theatre grew in a climate of financial and intellectual expansion, developing new performance venues throughout the country and strengthening an already solid popular base.

Emanuel Levy, in his 1980 study of the Habimah, concluded that Israeli theatre has been, from its outset, internationally oriented, with artistic quality being the most important factor in establishing a play's success (*H,* 48–49). He also noted a high proportion of new native plays produced by the country's four major theatres, remarking as an aside to the main thrust of his interest, "Indeed, most of the Hebrew-Israeli plays were topical and realistic . . . for their subject matter they drew upon current events and issues" (*H,* 43). His point was that an affinity for "imported" culture exists in Israel as a manifestation of opposition to ethnocentrism and that Israeli theatre strives for universality in repertoire and outlook, downplaying parochial interests and local playwrights.

There has been a change in the mood of the country, though, in reaction to the situation in Lebanon, and in response, confrontational theatre has come to play a more important role in Israel within the last few years than in the period covered by Levy's study. Productions that "draw upon current events and issues" have promoted the sense of social commitment, always an important secondary role in Hebrew drama, into a frothing, cudgel-swinging main character prowling the forestage. There are two principal reasons for this. The first is based on the particular social and financial circumstances in which the theatre establishment finds itself today; the second, and more far-reaching, grows naturally out of the traditional mission of theatre within the Zionist enterprise.

To understand the first of those reasons, it is necessary to recall as background that until 1969 all the theatres in Israel were cooperatives, with actors and profes-

sional staff enjoying a beneficent system that virtually assured tenure. A few years of work guaranteed, if not assignments, then at least a low-pressure sinecure followed by a comfortable pension. It took a fortunately-timed financial and administrative crisis in the government to impose belt-tightening, which resulted in the present structure of public corporations. Those corporate theatres were provided with substantial subsidies jointly from the central government and their local municipalities in order to maintain what was perceived as a central role for theatre in Israeli cultural life. While standards have risen in the permanent repertory troupes, the division of responsibilities and loyalties has produced an administrative ambiguity that has, in effect, given artistic directors greater independence than they might have enjoyed under the earlier system.

The second reason is far more compelling, for it grows out of the reactions of artists themselves to frustration with their society and its loss of innocence. Zionism, whatever else it may have been, was based on a unique mélange of political and spiritual ideology envisioning the reentry of a people into the realities of history after a two-thousand-year hiatus. That reentry, though, was to have been on a basis that would establish new societal standards for humanitarian and egalitarian behavior among nations as well as among its own citizens. The facts of the matter have resisted that idealization. The triumph of the 1967 "Six-Day War" may have done more damage to the values of Zionism than any other single event. Culturally, it was a pyrrhic victory. "It killed us," said sixty-year-old Misha Asherov.

> You can't even imagine what happened. . . . I was in Chicago the day it happened [6 June 1967] and I couldn't come [home]. And when I arrived it was four days after the war was finished. When I arrived I took a Jeep with a friend to the Golan Heights, and when I came there and saw the things, the defeated [Syrian] army . . . all of a sudden I felt myself like—no use! I felt, maybe, like Alexander the Great when he is in his prime. And if you are not sane, at that moment you start to become the megalomaniac. . . . With the inflation we had and the boom we had, everyone [thought] we could buy America!

A great euphoria, almost akin to megalomania, swept the country. At that moment many of the younger generation of Israeli artists began to see their homeland not as the conquering lion of Judah portrayed in the world press, but as a defector from the social ideal toward which all their history had aspired. The stage was set for a generation of socially-oriented artists to charge their elders with living up to their teachings. Nola Chilton put together her emotionally charged "docudrama," *Soldiers Talk,* a powerful series of dialogues assembled from interviews with young Israelis still hot from the battlefield. A generation of artists looked at what had been foisted on them by friends as much as by enemies and were dissatisfied. What they saw was a country aspiring to wealth, power, and material values, not to freedom and justice. Israel was to have become a "light unto the nations," but it appeared to be only one more country on the map, no different than the others.

Actors and directors took every opportunity to express their opinion of the wrong turn they saw the country taking. Asherov recounts a typical story describing the forms that expression took.

> You know that I played in *Who's Afraid of Virginia Woolf?* . . . We planned this play as a political play, a social/political play. We planned the subject of false belief, that they believed that they had a child. We planned it for Israel to [relate to] the actual life that we have here now. What's the actual life that we are living and dreaming? That we are big, that we are rich, that we can afford everything. Then all of a sudden, all the banks are down and all the economy is down: the child is dead. That's the thing we turned into the play. You see, it depends what drives you to give the interpretation.

Prodded as to whether such an interpretation was legitimate for a group of actors to take upon themselves, he responded, "Yes, especially now." It wasn't, he explained, that they favored this or that political party as much as it was that artists needed to be on guard against government itself.

> Look, from one side it doesn't matter if it is Russia or the way it was in the Nazi time; they wanted that the artist will serve the regime. Artists here say that we have to serve the ideas that we believe are right. As I told you about *The Trojan Women*, if you play it in Athens or Troy in that time, what do you care about it? But if things [are represented], actual things that happen to you now, and you have to give the answers now, it turns the theatre . . . the theatre becomes a live theatre. You see, we have to say what we have to say because . . . I don't know how it is in America . . . maybe what happened now with the Marines. . . . My dear friend, two hundred and some people killed in Lebanon. Isn't it your relative, isn't it your neighbor, isn't it an American? Why did people not ask [in 1982], "What are Americans doing in Lebanon?"

Viewed in this way, every play becomes more than a theatre event. It becomes, as well, a tool for the artist to shape society. In Haifa, at the Municipal Theatre, manager Noam Semel and artistic director Omri Nitzan have developed a policy in which they see each new Israeli play as "another point in a sort of connect-the-dots game: it's our self-portrait. With local material, by necessity, we make more mistakes. But point by point we begin to see ourselves."[15] That approach carries through even in the choice and staging of foreign plays. *The Island,* for instance, was not set in South Africa with prisoners of Soweto, but in Israel, and was performed by two Arab actors—in Arabic.

It is clear that the recent theatre seasons were not simply an aberration of dirty words, offensive phrases, and antigovernment sentiments, as may appear at first glance. They were the fruits of a scenario that had its roots in the earliest principles of public theatre in Israel, then grew to maturity in the atmosphere of disgust with a '67 victory that smacked of too much triumph and despair at the '73 victory that tasted too much of defeat. The disastrous Lebanon adventure, a divisive and perhaps pointless exercise, ground an additional sense of bitter disillusionment into Israeli idealists.

Conventional wisdom has it that, to the extent that art remains pure, it better serves the muse. "The arts as a political weapon proved impotent,"[16] wrote Robert Corrigan, who found that politics proved "deaestheticizing" to American theatre of the sixties. It has certainly been true that for every *Guernica* there have been hundreds of polemical works that have not survived their immediate political point. There is no reason, though, to believe that a work's subject matter must necessarily weaken its artistic thrust. Corrigan's concern, and thus his conclusion, was less with the uses of theatre than with its form; but theatre has been a didactic art since its beginnings. In all its rituals and expressions it has served the purposes of education, propaganda, and public morality from time immemorial. Whether demonstrating the fate of Oedipus, the prayer of the *Pattukaran,* or the postadolescent problems of Laverne and Shirley, a principal impetus for theatre through most of its history has been the transmission and explication of culture.

The theatrical establishment in Israel is imbued with a fierce sense of mission. Only in a brief period toward the end of the Vietnam War did American theatre attempt to serve as the country's political conscience, and as important as that effort may have been as a political gesture, its impact on either history or theatre in the United States was infinitesimal. Israeli writers, though, have taken the tough stance of biblical prophets with their audience and have touched off a predictably heated reaction. Hardly a single new play has appeared in the last few years that did not have some such component, and many productions of traditional and foreign works gained a dimension in their direction and staging that put them into just such a posture. Seen from that perspective, the recent swirl of conflict takes on a pattern that reflects a view of theatre as a sociocritical voice actively creating and maintaining the values of a cultural system.

Emanuel Rubin, Spring 1986

[1] Emanuel Levy, "National and Imported Culture in Israel," *Sociological Focus,* 13 (January 1980), p. 40.

[2] Misha Asherov was a student of Stanislavsky and has been a member of the Habimah's staff in Tel Aviv since 1946. The direct quotes from him in this paper are taken from a personal interview which I conducted with him at his home in Tel Aviv on 3 January 1984.

[3] Augustine Zycher, "Israeli Theatre Is Now Developing Its Own Character," *New York Times,* 3 December 1978, pp. 6 ff.

[4] Uri Rapp, "Kill or Be Killed," *Jerusalem Post* (International Edition), 22–28 January 1984, p. 18.

[5] Ed Grossman, "A Palestinian's Message," *Jerusalem Post* (International Edition), 3–9 October 1984, p. 17.

[6] Marsha Pomerantz, "Muzzling the Muses," *Jerusalem Post* (International Edition), 15–21 April 1984, p. 12.

[7] Exception was taken to specific anti-Jewish sentiments expressed in St. John's account of the Passion, not to the work as a whole or its other theological content. Berlioz's setting of the Te Deum, for example, met no objections when it was performed in that same series, because the text conveyed no such offense.

[8] "Israeli Play Is Edinburgh Hit," *Jerusalem Post* (International Edition), 28 August–3 September 1983, p. 16.

[9] "Herzog in Flap over Haifa Play's 'Blasphemous Line,'" *Jerusalem Post* (International Edition), 5–11 February 1984, p. 9.

[10] Allen E. Shapiro, "A Question of Blasphemy," *Jerusalem Post* (International Edition), 12–18 February 1984, p. 14.

[11] There are a total of 120 members in the Israeli Knesset or Parliament. Members are designated, in English, by the letters M.K. ("Member of the Knesset") preceding their name, or sometimes by H.K. ("Haver Knesset," Hebrew for the same).

[12] Uri Rapp, "A Challenge Missed," *Jerusalem Post* (International Edition), 12–18 February 1984, p. 17.

[13] Pomerantz, p. 12.

[14] Emanuel Levy, *The Habimah. Israel's National Theatre, 1917–77,* 1980, p. 27. Subsequent citations use the abbreviation *H.* For a review, see *WLT* 54:3 (Spring 1980), p. 482.

[15] Marsha Pomerantz, "Shakespeare and the Jewish Question," *Jerusalem Post* (International Edition). 6–12 November 1983, p. 19.

[16] Robert Corrigan, "The Search for New Endings: The Theatre in Search of a Fix, Part III," *Theatre Journal,* 36:2 (May 1984), p. 153.

Redemptive Vision in Hebrew Literature

Within the framework devoted to declining and reviving literatures, Yiddish is assumed to be a declining, He-brew a reviving literature. The assumption is partially correct as far as Yiddish literature is concerned; it is totally incorrect as far as Hebrew literature is concerned.

Yiddish literature, a folk literature to a great extent, had its birth in medieval Germany a thousand years ago;[1] it achieved its greatest efflorescence in the Slavic countries of Eastern Europe—notably in Russia, Poland, Bohemia, Galicia and Romania—and, in the last hundred years, in the United States. It even had a brief period of growth in a few Latin American countries in the closing decade of the previous century and in the twentieth century and, finally, in Israel in the later decades of this century. Originally intended for women and also for men of slight education, it became in the early decades of the twentieth century a vehicle of sophistication even for the very sophisticated. But its origins in biblical translation kept a firm link with the biblical origin of Hebrew literature. And *Zene Urene*—the phrase is from the Song of Songs 3:11—was not only the most popular Yiddish paraphrase of the Pentateuch; it became the source of moral knowledge and practice for the culturally underprivileged. Interspersed as it was with rabbinic laws and legends, cabalistic snippets and free renditions of Aramaic translations of the Bible, it achieved the status of a major classic of Yiddish literature for four centuries, though its author, Jacob ben Isaac Ashkenazi (1550–1628) of the Polish town of Yanov, was hardly known by name.[2]

The language of Yiddish literature is a variant of German with a strong admixture of Hebrew and Aramaic, as well as components of Slavic and even West European languages. Yiddish is one of several languages and literatures created by Jews in the diaspora. Ladino, Judeo-Arabic, Judeo-Berber, Judeo-Persian and Judeo-Greek are a few other prominent examples. If Yiddish achieved the greatest notoriety, it was because, on the eve of World War II, it was spoken by almost ten million Jews where the concentration of Jews was at its densest, notably in Eastern Europe and in the United States.[3] In quality its literature was superior to all the other Jewish literatures, with the sole exception of Hebrew literature. That this literature is moribund is by no means a certainty. Though fewer and fewer Jews seem to know it, millions admire its folklike thrust. That is its dominant characteristic. It permeates the oeuvre of Mendela Mokher Sefarim as well as of Isaac Leibush Peretz, Isaac Bashevis Singer, the Nobel Prize winner for literature in 1978 (see *WLT* 53:2, pp. 197–201), and another American, Harry Sackler, who had his origins in Galicia. In the stories of Sholem Aleichem, who spent the last years of his life in America, it is veined with incomparable humor. A literature capable of creating first-rate works of folkloristic and comic impact cannot be written off as moribund. Before consigning the patient to a hasty grave, it is perhaps safer to watch or even encourage his recovery.

The assumption that Hebrew literature is a reviving literature is totally incorrect. Revival is resuscitation. But Hebrew literature has never been dead; it is a continuum of 3,500 years of uninterrupted activity. As such it is the oldest living literature in the Western world. But the West is aware of the earliest segment of that literature, the Bible. There is either total ignorance or dim perception of the existence of a post-biblical literature which extends from about 200 years before Christianity till the present day. Hence the facetious assumption: Hebrew literature is one book, the Bible, plus 100,000 commentaries. That book—through its language, its style, its divine sanction—is still a paramount presence in world literature, as it had been in the Middle Ages and as it was a few centuries before the birth of Christianity. Indeed, it is still a formidable presence in world literature. Its continuous contribution to the humanization and refinement of the West through its ethical fervor is an assumption with the force of an axiom. That its redemptive vision has been embraced by Christianity and, to a certain extent, by Islam, is also an undeniable fact.

But post-biblical literature has not enjoyed persistent study and popularity in the Western world. The historical reason for the neglect of post-biblical literature is the Christian notion that Judaism found its fullest efflorescence in Christianity. The Old Testament was absorbed in the New Testament, the old faith was superseded by the new faith, the old Israel was succeeded by the new Israel. The Old Testament was not rejected, though Marcion of Pontus, the Christian Gnostic of the second century, advocated rejection. And so did Montanists and Novatians. The former were followers of Montanus, whom Tertullian (160–240) admired to such an extent that he became, for a number of years, a convert to Montanism, which emerged in Phrygia in the last decades of the second century; the latter were followers of anti-pope Novatian in the third century. Slowly but inevitably the Old Testament came to be regarded as a prediction of the new faith, as a prolegomenon to the New Testament. In time it was integrated with the New Testament as a divinely inspired document.

But Hebrew literature did not accept absorption by Christian literature and continued its development on biblical foundations with stubborn independence. Since Hebrew ceased to be the spoken idiom of daily communication among Jews in the third century of the Christian era, it was assumed that Hebrew literature also had died. But that was not the case. Myriad books—some of them seminal works of philosophy, ethics and, above all, messianic visions of redemption—have been produced throughout the ages. And even spoken Hebrew was not as dead as has been thought. In daily prayer and in daily study it was a living reality. By dint of its antiquity and sacredness it has won its battle with minor contenders as the language of Jewry in former Palestine and become the official language of present-day Israel. Critics argue—and Hebrew critics like Baruch Kurzweil are among them—that modern Hebrew literature is not a continuity: it is a revolutionary discontinuity. Modern Hebrew was supposed to have broken with the past which was sacral and to have become a profane vehicle of daily communication and literary expression. This is a superficial view on two counts: it assumes that modern Hebrew literature began in the era of enlightenment in the eighteenth century, and it postulates a nonexistent dichotomy of the sacred and profane.

Though all periodizations suffer from arbitrary compulsions of historians of literature to impose order on a disorderly mass of literary artifacts, some periodizations are more justifiable than others. For Hebrew literature, dispersed like its people in many lands, only an escalating periodizations is possible. Before the apocalyptic events of Jewish history in this century—the Holocaust and the establishment of the State of Israel—the exile of Jews from Spain in 1492 marked a new era in Hebrew literature. It was the root of a mystical and, subsequently, a rationalist trend; it colored the cultural regeneration of Jewry in Turkey, in the Land of Israel and in Italy in the sixteenth century, in Holland in the seventeenth, in Germany in the eighteenth, in Eastern Europe in the nineteenth, in Israel and in the United States in the twentieth century. It cannot be denied, therefore, that modern Hebrew literature begins at different times in different countries. Acceptance of secularism as a criterion of modernity and of enlightenment in the eighteenth century as the beginning of modern Hebrew literature—that is the imposition of an artificial chronology and of nonexistent sequiturs. All Western literatures were theocentric before the Renaissance. It was the Renaissance which, through the work of humanists, ushered in an era of anthropocentrism. That era gained ground in the seventeenth and eighteenth centuries and hastened erosion of a religious view of life.

■ ■ ■

In what sense is modern Hebrew literature an extension of biblical literature? One of its main themes is the uneasy coexistence of Arab and Jew in Israel. Yet that theme in its literary deposits is orchestrated, with all its overtones and undertones, as the redemptive drive which has its origins in the Isaianic fantasies of world peace. Another theme of primary importance is the development of Jerusalem as the spiritual capital of the world and the national capital of Israel. A third theme is the creation of an ideal society in rural areas under various forms of cooperative endeavor. Within these three themes, rooted in the Bible, Hebrew literature made its significant strides.

Jewish statehood has not changed the development of Hebrew literature perceptibly. Political and literary events do not run on principles of coincidence. Jewish independence—after two millennia of dependence and exile, alienism and martyrdom—was an event of geopolitical impact, as has been amply demonstrated by more than three decades of Jewish statehood. But it was not an event of immense significance in Hebrew literature. Poets—even such celebrated poets as S. Shalom and Nathan Alterman—rushed into print with poems of ephemeral patriotism. But no major work represented the major event of independence. In theme and style, Hebrew literature between 1948 and 1980 was a continuation of the literature of pre-independence. In the realm of poetry, one of the stronger segments of Hebrew literature since its inception in the Bible, there was a definite decline. None of the major representatives of that art who began their careers in the thirties or forties—Alterman, Amichai, Leah Goldberg—reached the authoritative stature of the two major poets Hayyim Nahman Bialik (1873–1934) and Saul Tschernichowsky (1875–1943) who dominated the literary scene in the early decades of the century. Both had faithfully represented the particularist and universalist facets of Judaism. Bialik was the nationalist: the singer of a past-centered preoccupation with study of traditional lore in the small town—the shtetl—in the Slavic countries and of the future-oriented revival of his people in the Land of Israel. Tschernichowsky was the universalist: the linker of Hebraic and Hellenic cultures, the importer of new prosodies and themes, the translator of classics of world literature. Both had immortalized themselves with poems which provided new slogans for their contemporaries: Bialik in "The Dead of the Desert" had proclaimed that his contemporary generation—like the desert generation which escaped from Egyptian bondage to the threshold of freedom in the Promised Land—was "the last generation in slavery, the first in freedom." Tschernichowsky in "Before the Statue of Apollo" linked the Greek God of the Sun and leader of the nine muses with the God of the Hebrew conquerors of Canaan who was bound by later generations with straps of phylacteries. A synthesis of the elemental forces of nature and culture in Hellenic and Hebrew forms was the new directive he wished to impose on his contemporaries.

Both Bialik and Tschernichowsky had the poetic means at their disposal to popularize their innermost inspirations and aspirations: Bialik imparted the enormous knowledge of the totality of the Hebrew language to his lyric lightness of touch and to his depth of perception, which few masters in the entire range of Hebrew literature equaled or surpassed. Tschernichowsky utilized his wide knowledge of world poetry and his epic powers of portrayal with unequaled expertise. Poets like Alterman, Amichai and Goldberg, who made their debut in the forties, were authentic practitioners of their art; but they lacked the strength and the resonance of the two former masters: Bialik and Tschernichowsky. There were others of lesser stature who began publishing in the fifties and sixties, but the progress of their maturation is still a matter of chronological uncertainty.

It is as a balladist that Alterman made an indelible impact on Hebrew literature. While traditional balladists borrowed their themes from a real or legendary past, Alterman concentrated on the present and transmuted ephemeral events into poems of eternal significance. In time he became the poetic journalist of Israel: his poems in the seventh column of the Labor daily *Davar*—hence the title *Ha-tur ha-shevi'i* (The Seventh Column) of two volumes of his verse which appeared in 1948 and 1954 respectively—were read by young and old with an expectant eagerness. They were studied and recited, they were set to music and sung in the streets and at public festivities.

Irony and wrath were Alterman's favorite poetic devices, irony more than wrath. And a tragic sense of life permeated most of the ballads. At their best they expressed that sense in folklike verses and used the sad-faced fool or harlequin as spokesman. Even when a single ballad like *Shir 'asarah ahim* (The Song of Ten Brothers), based on the Yiddish ballad *Tsen brider zenen mir geven* (Ten Brothers Were We), reached the size of a book, it retained the simplicity of the Yiddish original. But the author, who provided an inn as a locale for the ballad and convivial din as a mood, managed to infuse a sense of the tragicomedy of life into its verses.

In *Sefer ha-tevah ha-mezammeret* (The Hurdy-Gurdy Book) Alterman attempted to reach an audience of children and adults with catchy lines which lend themselves to singing and dancing. Historical personages like the famed medieval traveler Benjamin of Tudela and the medieval poet Samuel the Prince, legendary figures like the sailors of King Solomon, contemporary figures like early pioneers—these are the cast of "The Hurdy-Gurdy Book." Over and above them are the circus, the animals and the inevitable jongleur. The hurdy-gurdy itself is the subject of a poem.

What's a hurdy-gurdy? Where's the wit
That will enclose its notes, its gear?
You open it a weeny bit:
The voice of song assails your ear.
A tiny mechanism within
Wakes at once in sweetest din
And makes it sing and makes it play.
Such is the hurdy-gurdy's way.[4]

Love of a mechanical instrument transforms, for the poet and his audience, simple notes into magical music, simple existence into existential mystery. Illusionism succeeds where reality fails.

Such is the magnetic pull of the ballad on the poet that even some of his plays are ballads in dramatic form. This is especially true of *Pundak Ha-Ruhot* and *Esther Ha-Malkah* (The Inn of the Winds; Queen Esther). In the former he presents to his audience the owner of a hurdy-gurdy with parrot and ape. The parrot draws the folded pieces of paper with predictions of future fates for the inquisitive customers. The ape turns the handle of the instrument; the owner of the instrument sings his song, a popular discourse on man's fate.

It's a matter of luck,
A slip of paper—You ask.
You draw. And that's it.
No return to the basket.
No law and no rule.
Only luck. It's a play.
All matters of luck
Are matters of luck.[5]

In "Queen Esther" there is a wandering jester over and above the biblical characters—a whole array of invented characters and animated objects. The play opens with the song of the rug in a rug emporium.

Everything is rug.
A great illumined rug,
Common, yet uncommon,
Always there yet rare and strange.
He talks and tells a story
And sings from time to time.
A rug and not a rug,
Woven between yesterday and tomorrow.[6]

To sum up, Alterman is a troubadour reincarnated as a modern bard, a verbal acrobat who uses acrobatics for nationalist purposes. He has found the appropriate medium of his art and practiced it as an inventor and translator. His versions of Scottish and English ballads are the best in modern Hebrew literature.

There is another Alterman: a young poet of great lyrical promise, a delicate observer of landscape, a romantic admirer of womanhood, a dedicated lover, a compassionate student of the deprived and dispossessed. That phase is particularly noticeable in *Kokabim ba-huz* and *Simhat'aniyyim* (Stars Without; Joy of the Poor). But even in these early works he showed an addiction to the ballad, and as balladist of Israel he made an immeasurable impact on his generation.

In the period that elevated Alterman to fame and popular recognition, Yehuda Amichai made his debut with poetry which—like modernist poetry in England and America, Germany and France—was but a step removed from prose. The themes were untraditional and unconventional. In the poem "They Call Me" the poet could paint a triptych of taxis and angels and himself.

Taxis below,
Angels above.
Impatiently,
Simultaneously
Both call me with awesome voice.

I come, I
Come.
I descend,
I ascend.[7]

The terrestrial symbol in the form of taxis is commonplace; angels are the expected symbols of the celestial realm. The poet is the guest in both worlds, and he achieves his guesthood by sparsest use of simplest vocabulary. Anything and anybody serves as pretext for an Amichai poem: a historical personage, a legend, a city, a relative. But the thing or the person is seen in new perspectives or in new combinations. Nothing, nobody appears in expected stance. The unexpected creates the tension; the tension creates the poetry. Association is replaced by dissociation; dissociation operates in solitary splendor. But dissociation is more in keeping with the poet's talents than association. And so is discontinuity, which also affects English and American poetry.

Amichai replaces the traditional categories of poetry, the associative stance, the magisterial continuum, with simultaneity and the insistent present. Though he lives in Jerusalem, he clings to the diaspora. With the slight change of one word in Psalm 137:5 he achieves simultaneity of Israel and the diaspora: "If I forget you, diaspora," substituting for the biblical half-verse, "If I forget you, Jerusalem," effects the simultaneity. Small wonder that the poet's favorite stance is *now*. A volume of his poetry is entitled *Now in Noise*. His surrealistic novel is called *Not from Now, Not from Here*. Even Jerusalem, encrusted in hoary tradition, is "now" rather than "then."

On a roof in the Old City,
Wash illumined with day's last light.
A white sheet of a female enemy,

A towel of a male hater
To wipe his sweat with.

In the skies of the Old City
A kite.
At the end of the thread
A child
I have not seen
Because of the wall.

We raised many flags.
They raised many flags.
So we may think they are happy.
So they may think we are happy.[8]

The Old City as the scene of new strifes: Arabs and Jews hang their inimical laundries; a child hides behind a wall. Between the visible hatreds and the fear of a child—as victim of these hatreds—is the deception played by both sides. With a few inanimate objects like sheet and towel and flags the poet succeeds in presenting the living reality of hate and deception. Nobody is happy with the hatred, but everybody pretends happiness with his stance. This is Jerusalem today. Amichai's facility, though not his stature, has an Audenesque quality. Plays, novels, stories flow from his pen. But his essentiality must be recovered from his poetry, an obedient mistress rather than a dominant and demanding persona.

Alterman and Amichai made serious assaults on tradition. So did Leah Goldberg with her penchant for verses suitable to adult and childish mentalities. To win the human being in early growth with fun and exaggeration and an attachment to small animals was an ambition she cultivated in many memorable volumes. For the mind of the adult she developed a technique which has many points of resemblance to that of Edna St. Vincent Millay: a conversational tone and an epigrammatic verve coupled with elements of satire and surprise in brief lyrics or in elegant sonnets. Her vast knowledge of literature, especially Russian literature, infused her poetry with Slavic melancholy and moodiness. Too wise to trust wisdom, she knew that somewhere, somehow, wisdom and folly meet, the wise and the fool are one.[9] She had an intimate need and knowledge of love which dominates her poetry.

One bird only. How can it bear
All the heavens
On weak
Wings
Above the desert land?
They are big and blue,
They lie on its wings,
They stand by the strength of its song.

It was thus that my heart bore my love,

The big and the blue,
The love that was higher than high
Above the desert land,
Above the ruins
And the depths of rue.

Till the song of my heart was stilled,
Till its strength faded,
Till it was stone
And fell.

My love, wounded and mute.
One bird only. How can it bear
All the heavens?[10]

Bird, heaven, love, desert: the seemingly common ingredients of a lyric on an immortal theme. In her delicate juxtaposition of a bird's burden and her heart's burden, Leah Goldberg achieves an uncommon intensity. The frail bird carries the sky on its frail wings in an unfriendly land; the tender heart carries in the deserted land a love too strong to bear. Yet both survive, wounded but not vanquished. How? The poet has not answered the question. The mystery remains. The poetic mind may not achieve peace of mind, but it acquires wealth through its transforming sorrows.

Leah Goldberg had a special gift: she knew how to shield sentiment against debilitating sentimentality. In her posthumous *Remnant of Life* she contrasted the youthful and the mature poet.

A young poet grows silent suddenly:
He is afraid to tell the truth.

An old poet grows silent, he is afraid
That the best in poetry
Is poetry's lie.

By the end of her life Leah Goldberg achieved that delicate balance between truth and untruth. In the fear of truth, in the assumption that the poetic lie is superior to so-called truth, she sought and found her peace of mind.

■ ■ ■

The three most representative poets in the State of Israel—Alterman, Amichai and Goldberg—have not dominated the literary scene in Israel as Bialik and Tschernichowsky had before the birth of the State. In spite of that preeminent trio and a host of poets who had achieved fame and recognition—S. Shalom and Bat-Miriam as well as younger poets like Carmi and Mar, Zach and Rübner, Pagis and G. Hillel, Wieselthier and Reuben ben Yosef—it is undoubtedly evident that Hebrew poetry under independence is infinitely inferior to Hebrew prose. It may be said almost axiomatically: the reign of poetry was superseded by the reign of prose under independence. This is a surprising event, for poetry has dominated Hebrew literature from its biblical inception. It differed from the poetry of the West: it was not structured in symmetries of feet but in symmetries of syntactic units, in parallelism, *parallelismus membrorum.* The term was coined more than 200 years ago by Robert Lowth (1710–87), Professor of Poetry at Oxford, in his *Praelectiones Academicae de Sacra Poesi Hebraeorum,* which was translated into English by G. Gregory as *Lectures on the Sacred Poetry of the Hebrew.* No other ancient device has managed to convey intensity so well as the parallelism in the Prophets and in the Psalms and Job.

The great masterpieces of Hebrew prose were published in the centuries following Christ's birth. The *Mishnah,* idiomatically translated into English by Herbert Danby of Oxford, was edited at the end of the second century and became the great source of Jewish Law. And in the succeeding centuries prose was dominant in legal and ethical, theological and philosophical works.

The transition from poetry to prose during the last few decades was no less dramatic than the similar transition at the dawn of Christianity. Though poetry was produced in the State of Israel in substantial quantity and in remarkable quality, it did not reach the stature of the prose in the works of Agnon and Hazaz, who were the acknowledged literary leaders until their deaths in 1970 and 1973 respectively. Both made their initial reputation in the 1920s, and both continued producing first-rate work until the seventies. The voluminous commentaries on Agnon and the less voluminous critiques of Hazaz have this in common: they often obfuscate the authors' intent and shed little light where interpretation is expected to illuminate the hidden meaning of the text.

In spite of the hyperbolic praise of his work, Agnon is not a figure of universal magnitude. As the master portraitist of the Hasidic past he has no equals. The centerpiece of his work, *Haknasat kallah (The Bridal Canopy* in the English translation by J. M. Lask), is an inexhaustible source of Jewish folklore, Jewish mores and Jewish religiosity in the early decades of the nineteenth century. The protagonist of the novel, Reb Yudel, symbolizes by his very name the totality of Jewry. He is the knight-errant who visits villages and towns and entertains his co-religionists with jousts of learning. Though his peregrinations represent realistic searches for husbands for his three daughers Gittele, Blume and Pessele, they suggest worship and scholarship which lead to ethical accomplishment. Almost every chapter represents a story, each story enriches the preceding and succeeding story, and every appearing and disappearing personage enhances his spiritual adventurism. In spite of

the loose thread of narrative which holds the chapters together, there is a firm texture underlying the novel: the Bible and the Talmud, the medieval and modern works of sacred content. These sources have shaped the characters, who are represented as people dedicated to Jewish law and lore and permeated by messianic dreams of justice and peace for mankind in addition to redemption from exile and from humiliation and suffering. The chief protagonist, the Jewish Don Quixote, is accompanied by his Sancho Panza and his Rosinante: note the coachman and the two horses Drawme and Willrun, whose names have been lifted from the first chapter of the Song of Songs. The two horses are Jewish horses. They talk like Jews, they sigh like Jews, they even reminisce like Jews.

> Said Drawme to Willrun: Remember, brother, days gone by when roads were no roads, when traveling was not done by night because it was dangerous, when travelers stopped at an inn when it was still day and the horses would stay in the stable and rest their weary limbs? Now that the roads are roads, traveling is done by day and by night, and there is no time to gather strength and to rest one's limbs. . . . The horse forgets he is a horse, and he runs like a crazy beast.

> Said Willrun to Drawme: Shut up, don't remind me of days gone by.

> Willrun had been pampered when he grew up in his early years. He ate and drank, he enjoyed himself and he was happy. But his fortune changed; he was like a beast ready for the yoke and like a horse prepared to bear this burden. That's why he didn't like to reminisce. . . . Then both Drawme and Willrun turned their heads and sighed for the days of their youth that fled and could not be recovered.[11]

Neither the horses nor the personages of Agnon live merely in the past. Some of the novels and stories, written in the realistic vein of the fin de siècle, have appeared during his lifetime and posthumously. They confronted the two worlds he knew intimately: his native Galicia and his adopted and beloved Land of Israel in the first decades of the century. This contemporaneity linked his name to Kafka in the view of several critics, though he denied repeatedly (to me and to others) any knowledge of Kafka's works. The linkage was effected by Edmund Wilson, who made his reputation as an American critic and who had scant knowledge of the Hebrew language and literature. The rooted characters of Agnon have little in common with the uprooted Europeans of Kafka. Both express the misery of modernity, the torn warp and woof of life's tapestry, the individual in shredded isolation. Kafka knows no way out; Agnon points to renewal in the solidity of tradition, to transhuman authority in human affairs. And he does it in a style which is elegant and erudite. Out of the fullness of his linguistic resources he blends his masterpieces which, in spite of their fine polish, stand out as paradigms of splendor in an age of lingual debasement and vulgarization. This total concentration of Agnon on style, this immense lingual sophistication, may have been responsible for the simplistic and static stance of his characters.

The restitution of Hasidism as a positive force to Hebrew literature was not Agnon's rediscovery. Other contemporaries, Perez and Berdyczewski, have contributed a major share to the reappreciation of Hasidism. But Agnon's oeuvre confronts the modern reader with no less an impact than Eliot's rediscovery of Donne. It was a major volte face in Hebrew literature, and it has fed this literature's subterranean springs to this day.

The literary reputation of Hayyim Hazaz has not attained the unassailable solidity of his older contemporary. But his literary stature surpasses Agnon's. Both enjoy access to all resources of the Hebrew language; both are predominantly Jewish and both regard concern with Jewry as identical with absorption in the problems of humanity. For Marx the status of woman was the barometer of civilization in a given epoch; for Agnon and Hazaz the status of Jewry was the barometric indication of civilization. But they achieve their goals by totally different means. In his first novel, an unfinished masterpiece by the name of *Be-yishuv shel ya'ar* (Home in the Woods), Hazaz achieves a bucolic reconstruction of the lonely life of a Jewish family in a rural Russian milieu. For some unknown reason he treated the work as a stepchild. Ostensibly he was dissatisfied with the printer's errors and the publisher's attitude. But other factors have undoubtedly contributed to the author's disregard for his firstling. Ita Kalish maintained in her reminiscences that Hazaz regarded his novel as a "very beautiful book," that he planned six volumes for the novel and that some people thought it was the best piece of work he had ever done.[12] But that statement contradicts a later opinion by Hazaz, a total rejection in fact: "This book does not exist. . . . Since its publication I have not read it."[13] This unexplainable attitude, maintained by Hazaz with real adamance, is an unfair critique of a work which is rather unique as a monument to an island of Jewishness in a sea of hostility.

The shattering experience of youth in the life of Hazaz was the the Russian Revolution. In 1924 and 1925 he published his three stories of Jewry in the throes of the Bolshevik upheaval and won instant recognition. Eventually, after more than three decades, they were redone as a novel, and half a century after their first appearance they were published as a novel which, in the English translation of 1975, bore the title *Gates of Bronze.* The rich orchestration of impotence and helplessness amidst revolutionary ardor and ruthlessness, the banalization and the perversion of the redemptive drives of ageless Jewry by Jews and Russians—these were given powerful expression in the novel of Hazaz. That redemptive drive was also the central theme of his solitary play *Be-kez ha-yamim* (At the End of Days), which reflected the turbulence caused by the pseudo-messianic fantasies of Sabbatai Zevi.

Among the Jews of Yemen messianism was a dominant force. After Hazaz settled in the Land of Israel, he became absorbed in their ways of life. And he was the first Hebrew writer who authored two novels on Yemenite Jewry—one on Yemenite Jewry in Israel, another on Yemenite Jewry in Yemen. In both works the dwelled on their rich traditions and the unsophisticated craving for redemption which dominated their simple lives as artisans and petty merchants in the oppressive and repressive society of rigid Islam. But he was not unaware of the corrosive forces of modernity which affected Yemenites in Israel and bridged the gaps between Western and Eastern Jewry. It is a supreme irony of modern Jewish history that repudiation rather than retention of tradition built the bridge of common concern between Jewries of the West and Jewries of the East. Yet it is precisely Jewish history as seen through the prism of contemporaneous Jewry that shaped one of the great themes, if not the greatest, of concern in the stories and novels of Hazaz. In his story "Ha-derashah" (The Sermon) Hazaz attempted to reinterpret Jewish history through Yudkah, the protagonist of the story. A simple, almost inarticulate pioneer like the unsophisticated but learned Reb Yudel in Agnon's novel *The Bridal Canopy,* he represents in his very name the whole of Jewry. The chief complaint of Yudkah about Jewish history is the fact that Jews have no history.

> Exile is our pyramid. The base—martyrdom, the apex—messiah. . . . Jews are commanded to stay in exile until redemption. . . . They sit and wait. . . . They believe . . . and yet, in their heart of hearts . . . they don't believe. . . . Redemption is their chief desire . . . but at the same time . . . they pledged themselves . . . not to be redeemed forever and ever. . . . Because they don't want to be redeemed. . . . They don't ever want to return to the Land of their fathers. . . . Zionism and Judaism are not the same. . . . Zionism is not continuation . . . it is the opposite of what has been . . . it is the seed of a different people.[14]

In a threefold, unintentional analysis of Jewish fate a simple worker has enunciated a new theory of Jewish history: exile is Jewish root and rootlessness; redemption from exile is a belief which is deeply connected with hope for nonredemption; Zionism and Judaism are antithetic entities. Hazaz was not only concerned with Yudkah's ideas, which may be seen as the essence of Jewish historiosophy in Eastern Europe. He leveled incisive criticism against German and American Jewry in his fictive work. For German Jewry rushed into assimilationism immediately after the proclamation of the so-called Edict of Toleration by Joseph II in 1782. And then, under Hitler, it was forced into Judaism again. American Jews, like their German confrères, believe that the prophetic message of redemption is intended—through exile—for all peoples. The State of Israel is a diminution of Jewish stature: it is as if Jesus, after the tragic drama of crucifixion, had gone back to carpentry in Nazareth. Slowly, but with firm determination, partly conscious, partly unconscious, Hazaz arrived at the idea that Jewish history is the myth of mankind and that the Jewish people is the hero of the mythological universe in perpetual war with the forces of Satanism. And he viewed Salvation as annihilation of these Satanic forces by Jews.

No Hebrew writer has submitted diaspora and Israel to an analysis of such imaginative depth as has Hazaz. And no one else has aspired to and achieved the impossible task: to enshrine the totality of modern Jewry in fictive work. These two accomplishments, created in a playful, swiftly moving and richly erudite style, have raised Hazaz above all contemporary Hebrew writers. His oeuvre is the crowning glory of Hebrew literature under independence.

Eisig Silberschlag, Spring 1980

Ed. Note: The essays by Eisig Silberschlag, Peter Cocozzella and Brendan P. O. Hehir were originally delivered at *WLT*'s special session on "Declining and Reviving Literatures," held on 28 December 1979 at the annual meeting of the Modern Language Association in San Francisco.

[1] Translations of biblical words and phrases precede the oldest Yiddish document: two rhymed verses in a *Mahzor*, a prayer-book for Jewish holidays, are dated 1272/73 in Worms. They contain a blessing for the person who carries the *Mahzor* to the synagogue: "Gut Tak Im Betage / Se' Waer Dis Mahzor in Beshakkenesses trage" (A good day may be the lot / of the one who carries this Mahzor to the synagogue). For a thorough discussion of the verses, see Walter Roll, "Das älteste datierte jüdisch-deutsche Sprachdenkmal: Ein Verspaar in Wormser Machsor von 1272/73," *Zeitschrift für Mund-artforschung*, 33 (June 1966), pp. 127–38.

[2] Jews preferred quoting names of books rather than names of authors: *Moreh nevukim* (The Guide of the Perplexed) rather than its author Moses Maimonides, or *Shulhan 'aruk* (Set Table) rather than its author Joseph Karo. And these are only two of the most prominent examples.

[3] For this estimate, probably exaggerated, see Helmut Dinse and Sol Liptzin, *Einführung in die jiddische Literatur*, Stuttgart, Met-

zler, 1978, p. vii. Today the number must be reduced to about half that estimate. See Otto F. Best, *Mameloschen*, Frankfurt a. M., 1973, p. 51. The three chief factors for the decline of Yiddish-speaking Jews are 1) the genocide perpetrated by Hitler and his Nazi cohorts in World War II, 2) the inimical attitude of the Russian government for the past half-century and the discouragement of Yiddish by the State of Israel, and 3) the swift pace of assimilation in the twentieth century.

[4] Nathan Alterman, *Sefer ha-tevah ha-mezammeret*, in *Kol kitve Nathan Alterman*, Tel Aviv, 1973, p. 5.

[5] Nathan Alterman, *Mahazot*, in *Kol kitve Nathan Alterman*, p. 152.

[6] Ibid., pp. 267–68.

[7] Yehuda Amichai, *Shirim*, Tel Aviv, 1967, p. 186.

[8] Ibid., pp. 163–64.

[9] Leah Goldberg, *Shirim*, in *Ketavim III*, Tel Aviv, 1973, p. 205.

[10] Leah Goldberg, *Shirim*, in *Ketavim II*, Tel Aviv, 1973, p. 108. For a different translation, see Dov Vardi's version in *New Hebrew Poetry*, Tel Aviv, 1947, p 74.

[11] *Haknasat kallah I*, in *Kol sippurav shel Shemuel Yosef Agnon*, Berlin, 1931, pp. 129–30. For a different translation, see I. M. Lask's version of *The Bridal Canopy*, New York, 1937, pp. 110–11.

[12] Ita Kalish, *Sihot 'im Hazaz*, Tel Aviv, 1976, p. 51.

[13] *Ma 'ariv*, 29 December 1967.

[14] Ben Halpern's rendition of "The Sermon" in *Partisan Review*, Spring 1956, pp. 171–87.

Memorialization in New Fiction

The Past in the Present. Distinctions between fiction and biography blur. In the literature of the past, the reader was normally aware of the generic nature of the material that was being read. There was little presumed doubt as to whether the thrust was documentary, whether it was a historical and factual account, or whether it was fictional, invented. And, if there was such doubt, this was incorporated into the overall opus and became integral to the genre. We see this, for example, in Daniel Defoe's account of the plague year, where the author adopted the pose of a diarist recording the events from an earlier age but as though writing at the time, experiencing the dreadful spectacle and himself, naturally, under threat.[1] On the other hand, when the assumption of biography or autobiography was made, it was clear that such an assumption served as an agreed convention, either for the purposes of the fiction or for the establishment of the unadorned fact.

Or so it seemed. But this distinction between historiography representing undiluted facticity, on the one hand, and literariness, the fact including its interpretation and the response of the writer, is itself a fairly modern one. This seems to derive from the ambition to see historiography as an empirical science, stripped of the subjectivity of the historian, on the assumption that a story of the unfolding of events might be told as it "actually" happened. But if we examine the ancient testimonies, the act of interpretation constantly accompanied the fixing of facts. Otherwise, it might have been asked, why tell the story? In the Bible, for example, the events discussed are promulgated together with a confirmation of significance.[2] The point of the narrative text is to confirm and promulgate the kingship of God and His dominion over the events of history. Thus it is that an apparently convenient dichotomy created between fact and interpretation breaks down in our examination of the actual practice of literature. To put it in another way, matters of fact are also mediated.

A hallmark of the contemporary writer is perhaps the recognition of this unavoidable mediation, followed by narrative qualification. Certainly, one of the characteristics of contemporary writing is the uncertainty created in regard to the borders between the two, between fact and interpretation, either because such divisions are regarded as irrelevant, or in order, deliberately, to allow uncertainty to surface in the mind of the reader. "Crossover" (the term is taken from the current music scene) writing invokes variety and mixture. We may be uncertain in such narrative as to whether we are dealing with an accurate and literal representation of lives and situations, or with an imagined variation on a theme.

We find an example of this in the novel by the young Israeli writer Ronit Matalon, *Im hapanim elenu* (Facing Us),[3] where the family background is offered up with a variety of historical commentary, dialogue, and pictorial support. Here the past is described with such loving detail and passion that these become part of the essence of the novel. An overall picture is created through the dual medium of photographs, or their absence, and verbal commentary, explicating the visual material with background elucidation and further amplification.[4] As in a collage, materials from sources other than the pen of the author are imposed on a primary narrative, presumably gaining credence from the duplication of complementary sources.

The story is told by the seventeen-year-old Esther, who opens with a photo of her uncle, standing with his back to the camera, arms folded, facing his African workers in the Cameroons. This is followed by a detailed analysis of their relative positioning and individual shapes. This sets the tone for the opening of the story, which takes place at the African home of this uncle, Sicurel, where Esther is visiting at his request. The next chapter, headed by the "missing photo," tells of the uncle's need to reestablish contact with "someone from the family" (*I*, 21). There is, however, a "mystery," without which the narrative would no doubt lack tension and substantial interest. This mystery consists of how a member of this Cairene Jewish family, most of whom, including the narrator relocated in Israel, came to settle in this part of Africa. So, the scene is set for a background roundup of how this all happened, with some introduction to the family members, particularly the uncle's siblings, and the dominant role of his brother, Moïse, the single-minded Marxist Zionist. We are taken further into a reconstruction of the family history and how the uncle moved originally to Brazzaville, as a "first stop on the black continent" (66).[5]

But there is of course one more character here of vital significance in the story, and that is the narrator herself. How did she come to compose the novel, and what was its genesis? The uncle comes into her room to discover her writing a "diary," and he asks her what she is writing about. Her reply is that it is "about everything happening, what I think, imagine . . . but chiefly about the present" (68). This then is our novel—the record, observation, and also the product of the imagination of the narrator. And there is a darker side to this act of record too, as it is, she adds in the explanation offered to her uncle, "'like an inscription on a tombstone." The necessary implication that follows then is that we are closing the cover on a book of the past. This is a life that is gone, and the novel here presented is a record of recall. Esther is always writing in her notebook, and it is fair to assume that the material which she notes down constitutes the kernel of the novel before us. The materials for the novel then are the writer's own notes, her recollections, her scrap-books, and her photographs.

In order to reinforce the solid basis of the narrative, there are also added some substantial extracts, interposed from an autobiographical account of the Israeli writer Jacqueline Kahanoff, who grew up in Cairo. This internationally known author also appears in a photograph together with the narrator's family, taken in Cairo in 1946, and this confirms not only a thematic connection but a family link too. Kahanoff is concerned with the issue of the minorities there, among whom were Jews like herself. It was particularly these minorities who cultivated European education, as well as taking over the position of the ideological opposition. Why does our novel introduce such apparently extraneous material? Well, it seems to broaden the potential base of the fiction, and to suggest alternative and refreshing ways of looking at a situation which is not necessarily "fiction," in the sense of unfettered invention. There is a social foundation to Esther's story which cuts in odd directions. The supplementary aids are also part of the story, and these are offered thematically rather than chronologically. Presumably, a piece of autobiographical analysis, with its sociological tendency, contributes to the overall understanding of the situation, including the Levantine attitudes of this social sector. A constant contrast is implied between the past and the present. But the starting point is the concrete representation in the photograph, and the novel only arrives at the apparent nub—the manner in which the father got involved with Africa—well over halfway through the text (193). At this point, she relates of her relative's restlessness, his curiosity, his ambition, which might have collided awkwardly with his pan-Arab sympathies, and his admiration of the Egyptian leader, Nasser. Thus, he landed up in black Africa, still trying to make money. Our narrator attempts a reconstruction of the past, as it involved him, and of his character, through inspection of the image, supported by recollection.

But it is not only the presentation of photographs that comprises a necessary element in the reconstruction of the overall picture. It is also the technique of perusal that must be taken into account. There is an almost infinite multiplicity of materials. But how does one absorb them all? Another relative, the niece Zuza, now living as a journalist in New York and currently writing a book about the family's "roots," comes to interview her aunt for information and background to their Cairene life and general awareness: "'In order to see a photograph properly, one must take one's eyes away from it, or just close them,' declares Zuza, closing her own eyes, and thrusting her chin forward" (285). This distancing should presumably put the artifact in context and enable one to see it more objectively, as the visitor attempts to recapture the family atmosphere in Egypt through the medium of the novel.

For a very different sort of example we may consider the book *The Emigrants* by the Austro-German writer W. G. Sebald, now a British academic.[6] Here we have a description of four separate people, and their stories, including photographs illustrating their stories. These elements are formed of separate units, but they combine into one rather mournful narrative. In the first account, headed "Dr. Selwyn," Selwyn and his friend Edwin show slides of Switzerland to the narrator: "I sensed that, for both of them, this return of their past selves was an occasion for some emotion" (*E,* 16–17). But the primary object of Selwyn's longing is the village near Grodno, in Lithuania, which he had left at the age of seven. His account relates of his emigration to London (where the family had disembarked, thinking it was New York) and his disguised identity (his surname was changed from Seweryn to Selwyn, for example). The

narrator virtually loses contact with Selwyn, but later hears of his suicide: "And so they are ever returning to us, the dead" (23), this story ends. The cumulative effect of the four accounts gathers strength from the notion of mutual enforcement around a single theme. The emotional charge and implications of the totality assume a knowledge of the historical events that have led to the later and present circumstances. The understatement of the restrained narrative contains all the more power for being implicit.

The second account in Sebald's book tells of the narrator's primary-school teacher, Paul Bereyter, who put an end to his life at the age of seventy-four, in January 1984. The narrator goes to investigate the case in the small town of S in the new Germany, and, in so doing, meets up with Lucy Landau, who had been a friend of Bereyter and had also arranged his burial. The narrator then discovers that Lucy had kept a "large album which contained photographs documenting . . . almost the whole of Paul Bereyter's life, with notes penned in his own hand" (45). The overt source of Paul's dislocation emerges in the discovery that he was one-quarter Jewish on his father's side, a factor that disqualified him from teaching under the Nuremberg laws. Still, despite or perhaps even because of this, he returned to his home country, to Berlin no less, into the lion's den, at the outbreak of the war, in which he could serve even with his racial disability, and after the war he resumed his teaching. He was always consumed by "a loneliness within" (44), however, a sense that was presumably to deprive him of the will to continue to live.

The third section deals with a great-uncle of the narrator, Ambros Adelwarth. The narrator had only met him once, but again his curiosity was aroused by photographs (71). The narrator's Aunt Fini recalls this fascinating character's accounts of the past, when the narrator visits her in the USA. Ambros had fallen into a deep depression and, of his own free will, had entered a psychiatric institution. This section concludes with a reading of his journal (with which the narrator had been presented by the aunt) from a much earlier period, the year 1913. What the narrator chooses to highlight from that record is the note about memory, that it is "a kind of dumbness" and that "it makes one's head heavy and giddy" (145). But the book is all about memory, and it does indeed have that effect.

The fourth and final subject of this series of reconstructions and inquiries is the single-minded artist Max Ferber, for the purposes of which the narrator takes us back to the time he spent in Manchester, for him a place of fascination and strangeness. Not much is known originally of this Max Ferber, who had erased all memories of a past before he arrived in England at the age of fifteen in 1939. But the narrator catches up with the painter some twenty-five years later, after having by chance seen a work of his at the Tate Gallery. Ferber is now an artist much in demand. The narrator's return to Manchester in pursuit of his old friend is as bleak as was the original contact, but now he receives from Max a memoir penned by his mother many generations ago. The next stage is for the narrator to visit Kissingen, site of the family memoir, and to seek out the Jewish cemetery, where that Jewish community came to an end. The principal feature that the narrator notes in the Germany around him is "the mental impoverishment and lack of memory that marked the Germans" (225). Unable to bear this any longer, he returns to England, and thus to his own attempt at a memorial.

The adoption of an ultimate adherence to authenticity can serve very different purposes, however. Binjamin Wilkomirski's recent work, *Fragments*,[7] is a long-delayed response to the events described in the text, coming fifty years or so after the subject matter contained therein. The title, and its uncertain genre, indicate the apparently impenetrable nature of the material, the difficulty of its absorption and the near impossibility of its communication. The author attempts to convey his own experiences, those of a child sent to Majdanek to be exterminated, who miraculously and painfully survived—just about—in body. This was against all the odds, and also against the intentions of the Nazi regime, making such survival not only improbable but also illogical. As the material had not been properly assimilated and absorbed into the author's conscious mind, it could only be brought to the surface very partially, very gradually, and in small pieces, "shards" (as he has it), or "fragments" (hence the title). But the effort was supremely important for him, and so all means available are conjured up to bring obscured memories into focus. This is a story, but it is the author's own, a memoir.

Even language constitutes a difficulty. Yiddish is the author's mother tongue, but that was cut off early by the intervention of his camp experience, when he was sent to Majdanek. That language was replaced by what he calls the "Babel-babble" of the camps, a confused concatenation of tongues, with an admixture of the primary Yiddish. The author's later languages, the adult tongues which superseded his first experience of speech, are not regarded as integrally his own but rather as acquired imitations of foreign voices. More primary then than language indicators for the recovery of this dreadful but transcendent and dominant phase is the instrument of vision. It is the recording eye that can be imprinted on the memory, his own inner "camera," a metaphorical camera, acting in similar ways to the actu-

al cameras of Matalon and Sebald. This is how he builds up this heavily overladen past: "My early childhood memories are planted, first and foremost, in exact snapshots of my photographic memory and in the feelings imprinted in them, and the physical sensations" (*F,* 4). Memory, the recall of the eye, and the impression created by these, become the organizing principle, rather than any other sort of externally imposed logic or chronological sequence. He enters the child's world, because that is the world that has to be recalled. So, in order to achieve the recovery of that world, he must become a child once more, thus abandoning adult postures, which were a later accretion: "If I'm going to write about it, I have to give up on the ordering logic of grown-ups; it woud only distort what happened" (4). The object of all this effort is "to try to use words to draw as exactly as possible what happened, what I saw, exactly the way my child's memory has held on to it; with no benefit of perspective or vantage point" (4, 5). He wants to reproduce the clear pictures that surface: "Just pictures, no thoughts attached."

We must add a rider to this ambition. The pictures are not, to be frank, unaccompanied. There is no doubt that the stark picture itself, without context or clarification for the reader, would hardly make sense. The author does offer at least a minimum of commentary, or, sometimes, some necessary words that allow the reader in on the basis of his own historical orientation. There is then some intervention of an adult observer, looking over the shoulder of the child. But the narrator holds this to a minimum, attempting to recover the horror, and specifically the sense of betrayal, on the part of the child at the hand of the sadistic adult. He was taken to what he thought was an orphanage, and found himself in a concentration camp. The names for these types of institutions were lacking to the child, but the experience can now be conveyed. The child portrayed here gradually loses all childlike mental features. He even loses the capacity to feel: "There are no feelings left . . . / I'm just an eye, taking in what it sees, giving nothing back" (87). The words used are clearly adult words, as are the formulated sentiments. But the feeling behind them can be recaptured. And the feeling that he wants to communicate is of the end of feeling, for that matter, of the end of the world as we have known it: "I just feel that this is a place where everything ends, not just the embankment and the rails. This is where the world stops being the world" (94). It is at such points that the flashbacks are crisscrossed with flashforwards. Later, in Switzerland, where the author was first taken and where he still lives, he looks back on himself with horror at his own apparent lack of feeling, treading over the heads of nursing babies to save himself. His self-disgust had reached such proportions that not only had he virtually forgotten his own name, but he even came to forget that he actually possessed a name. In Switzerland too, he still retained the marks of his background, long after the circumstances of that terror had disappeared. But the child, now presumably becoming a young adult, does not easily grasp the nature of such boundaries, and still sees things in their original terms. That after all was his formative period. Adults, these others, are still the enemy. "Liberation," an adult term, never occurred. The subtitle of the book gives the cutoff point for the subject as 1948 rather than 1945. The narrator has no clear recollection of 1945 as a turning point, but only as a phase when peculiar things started to happen, and when he continued to expect the inevitable calamities. He can never trust anyone. For him, the SS man has invaded the person of the Swiss hero, William Tell, and the child with the apple on his head will be murdered, an act to precede the consumption of the apple by the adult. He is constantly told to forget. But he can never forget, and he rather needs to verify his own experience continually in order to check it against the accounts of others. For this reason, he can only find genuine communication with those whose experiences match his own. The act of writing here, the setting down of his story to the best of his ability and as truthfully as he can, is a necessary act of purgation, a sort of belated self-discovery.

■ **THE NEW ISRAELI NOVEL**

One of the typical new novels in Israel is constituted of an exercise in memorialization. In Judith Katzir's *Lematis yesh et hashemesh babeten* (Matisse Has the Sun in His Belly)[8] a love story is not only recorded long after the event, but is searched out, fixed in the memory, memorialized. Rather than integrated into the life of the principal character, the lovely Rivi, twenty-one years old at the time of the affair, the story is elevated as the high point and guiding light of her life. Rivi falls in love with a much older man, Yigal, her mentor, a lecturer in mathematics at the Haifa Technion. It is Yigal who is specifically marked out by a search for place, he whose original home was not Israel but somewhere in Central Europe. Rivi acquires her habit of yearning from him, even as she learns so many other things as well. And this makes "yearning" the central theme of the novel, the looking back to a time or place that was. Rivi then travels with Yigal to Europe and becomes his lover. They go to Italy and to Paris, and the photos that they take there become the sign and monument of the formative phase of her life: "And she was already longing for this house that she was leaving behind her, not that she might be coming back here in a week or two, but as though she had lost it forever, as she would long for it

following the passage of many years" (L, 34). Here, the expected mark in memory becomes a fact of life and establishes her very being.

In the "Italian" chapter, there is a flashforward, and we read: "Often she would pore over their photographs—what else do I have left apart from them?" (43), she asks herself. The problem is that experience in its actuality is so short-lived. Even while the affair is taking place, the person undergoing it is aware of its transience and feels the need to perpetuate its sense and texture. This has become the function of the photograph, but it is reflected in the title of the novel as well, where the title phrase—i.e., that Matisse has "the sun in his belly" (as reportedly uttered by Picasso)—becomes a motto for the book and the model for her supreme experience. It is not only Rivi, however, who draws out the past here. She manages to extract memories from her partner as well, memories that he has hitherto buried deep inside himself. Time, then, is not equally spread in its significance, and this short span, the snatched holiday in Europe, becomes the hinge of the central figure, and so of the book as a whole. The uneven quality of time is a recurrent theme in modernist writing. Of course, moments of significance have always been afforded a greater degree of focus; events are not treated equally, but instead receive an amount of space proportional to their importance. Now, however, there is heightened awareness of the erratic impression made separately by various time spans, as captured by memory and recall. These "fragments" are an extreme exemplification of such recognition.

Rivi looks both backward and forward; her memorialization is both recollection of the past and protection against the vicissitudes of the future. She can proceed to a new life henceforth, following the passing away of her mother and the end of her affair with Yigal. The flashforwards shadow the future (43), with the significance of the pictures as evidence to imprint memory for a later period (48). Her passion is unique, not to be repeated, and so must be recoverable as a thing that was (77). In terms of narrative perspective, the voices alternate between the first person, when the emotion is not contained, and a detached third person. All the trips that they have made together (these are the high points of their passionate union, as they were then together, separate from others, intensively and extensively together as an isolated couple). Egypt, which she also recalls as a country associated with her grandfather, is appropriately mummified, embalmed, in her recollection. This all becomes a monument for the future.

Rivi's attempts at memorialization of her lover constitute a considerable part of the novel, pictures and all (162). She is informed by the haunting figure of the fortune teller in Tel Aviv that something of this necessarily doomed affair will always remain. The past then, however it is sealed up, confined, and cast away, will always be with her. Yigal too appreciates this, and what he values in her is precisely her capacity to preserve this kernel, and to make something of it in written form: "It is in this that your power lies, in inscribing the meteorological map of your stormy soul" (187). This is said in the wake of their separation. What is preserved as a residue is precisely the book. So the novel here, in front of the reader, is the replay of what is recorded in that original document.

Another new Israeli novel, Eleanora Lev's *Haboqer harishon began eden* (First Morning in Paradise),[9] takes the form of a sort of long memoir, built around the female narrator and her married lover. There is a detailed dissection of the narrator's feelings, and a meditation on her loss of youth and attractiveness. She leaves home for an apartment, so as to acquire the necessary freedom of movement. She mourns the loss of her lover Saul, as well as the loss that he represents to Hebrew drama, to which he had contributed so much as one of Israel's leading playwrights. And there is also the wife's loss, contrasted with the narrator's very different sort of loss (*H,* 284). The chaos of Tel Aviv, as described here (131–34), acts as an objective correlative to her own feelings, as does her description of the impoverishment of immigrant life. The inevitable happens, and she waits, as she says, "like a piece of meat" for an abortion. She is an *eshet tselalim* (shadow wife) or a *gevavah urbanit shelahar yeush* (urban heap in the wake of despair; 303) in regard to Tel Aviv. Here we have the relationship between the pictorial representation and the verbal, where the sometimes more accurate and penetrating equivalent of words is a photograph, although this latter is supplemented by words. The photograph is an attempt to grasp the moment, and imprint it on the memory (260). Ira Bernowitz, her friend and advisor, presses in one direction, arguing strongly that an abortion is an absolute necessity, whilst her own instincts move her in the opposite direction. She has become convinced that she needs the life of the child to supplement her own uncertain vitality. The text is addressed to this new life, to the potential and then the actual child, from conception through birth. At the end, Rivi is visited by the memory of a picture of Eve, newly set down in Eden (hence the title). The narrator gradually comes to terms with the basic human fact of male domination, because, if she were not able to do so, "Then, in that event, she would never bear a child: it was this hunger that was decisive." (These are the closing words of the novel: "Haraav hazeh hu shehikhria et hakaf.")

Shifra Horn, in her novel *Arba imahot* (Four Mothers),[10] adopts a very complex and subtle narrative approach. The first-person narrator is born in the summer of 1948, in Jerusalem. The mother of the narrator is Geulah, the father "unknown." Amal, the narrator, grows up in an atmosphere of maternal hostility toward boys. She herself marries Yaakov, who leaves her when their son is born. This Yaakov believes in his multiple genetic role, as dominant male, and so when this particular function is fulfilled, he feels free to leave and search for another female.

The four successive mothers raise their children by themselves. Amal's own son breaks the pattern of the exclusively female line. The first recorded member of this line, Mazal, flourished a hundred years earlier, bore Sara (the beauty and central figure of the novel), and was then divorced, at age sixteen, for not providing satisfaction to her husband. Sara had an ongoing affair with the well-known British photographer Edward, whose brilliant daughter was Pnina-Mazal. Pnina-Mazal married David, who was killed. Her daughter, Geulah, grew up wild, and remained so in later life too, exclusively attached to the Arab child with whom she was reared. In the Israeli context, it was understandable that she turned into a revolutionary. But she was then raped, and her baby, called Amal (a common name in both Hebrew and Arabic), is our narrator here. Amal wants to discover her origins, and, by means of a tape recorder, produces an oral transmission from a member of a communist cell that she joins (*H,* 262). Sara, the great-grandmother, feels that she can die when new baby boy is born. This is the end of the saga of the mothers. The son, still unnamed at the conclusion of the novel, brings this exclusively matrilineal tradition to an end. Amal's son marks both the novel's termination and the end of this deviant line.

The view here of the woman's place is unexpected. We are accustomed to seeing feminism as a modern phenomenon, with the stress that it places on either the equality of the sexes or, beyond that, the primacy of the female. But here, the further that we go back in time, the greater is the degree of female domination, and it is only as we approach our own day that the male seems to come into his own. Now, arriving at the contemporary scene—i.e., the period of the composition of the novel—the balance of the genders is restored.

Irit Linur is one of the new brand of demotic female Israeli novelists, a writer conveying her material in the common language of current Israeli speech. Her first novel, *Shirat hasirenah* (The Siren's Song),[11] is cast in a local argot and is related in the first person as though it were a diary, written straight from the sleeve. The narrator has a feeling that she is aging (she is thirty-two years old), a common enough obsession in life as in literature. She works as a senior administrator in an advertising agency, responsible for budgets. The novel presents an unfiltered ego, through the medium of idiomatic language, and articulates uninhibited thought. The narrator offers a deflated view of herself: witty, self-effacing, fully admitting to the need for love, and thus to her own limitations.

The diary genre offers a medium of memorialization. It records directly and confidentially. It does not have to pass through the sieve of public acceptability or stand before the court of public opinion. It is, by definition, addressed to oneself. It is unconcerned with embarrassment and unencumbered by structural or conventional considerations. The introduction of the diary (or quasi-diary) form into the novel can offer a glimpse of narrative intimacy not normally granted to the reader, and thus extend the imaginative and expressive borders of the genre.

The question is often raised as to whether there is a distinctly feminine fictional voice in Israeli literature. But the sheer quantity of this production, amounting to predominance, testifies to the growing strength and confidence of the Israeli woman writer. Still, we may legitimately pose the question of whether there is a qualitative difference from the male voice. From what we have seen here, the expression of this tendency is characteristically Israeli in language, character, and tone. But it is nonideological, except to assert the strength of the needs of the woman, the narrator or the prime mover in the story. There has been a shift of focus. The shift is from the consideration of such weighty themes as, for example, the Jew as Israeli, the position of Israel in the world, or the place of the fighting soldier. This does not mean that the woman does not play a central role in fiction written by male authors. The feminine figure is certainly important in, for example, the work of the well-known male novelist Amos Oz. But there she is an object of interest, the representation of the unpredictable and the mysterious, very much the "other." In the works discussed here, the point of view adopted is that of the woman, taken on as natural, central, the assumed given. Desire, love, emotional fulfillment, the needs of a woman as lover and mother are primary and all-encompassing. Interpersonal relationships, rather than serving symbolic functions or as a kind of national allegory, come up for critical inspection. Domestic themes stand out here: sex, love, growing up, growing old, the nature of changing affections, death and memory. These are what invest the narrator and the fiction with such zest as they possess and evince.

■ AND IN FRANCE

Patrick Modiano (b. 1945 in Paris to a Flemish mother and a Sephardic Jewish father) is a contemporary French writer. An early work of his is titled *La Place de l'Etoile*,[12] which can stand for various things. The "place" of the title name can imply a public square, a badge, or a heart. The name of the "hero," Schlemilovitch, indicates his status as a schlemiel or ne'er-do-well, but also ensures that this particular Jew can don a variety of guises: martyr, king, clown, and also avenger. He always remains a foreigner, because he bears that dislocated experience within. The novel is written in the first person. The main character, our Schlemilovitch, abandons his Venezuelan background, lives as a foreigner in France, and is known widely as a Jew: "Aux journalistes qui me questionnaient devant le *Carlton,* le *Normandy* ou le *Miramar,* je proclamais inlassablement ma juiverie," he says (To the journalists who question me in front of the Carlton, the Normandy, or the Miramar, I proclaim my Jewishness indefatigably; *P,* 14). He wants to be a great French Jewish writer. But now "Le juif était une marachandise prisée, on nous respectait trop. Je pouvais entrer à Saint-Cyr et devenir le maréchal Schlemilovitch: l'affaire Dreyfus ne recommencera pas" (The Jew is acceptable merchandise; everyone respects us too much. I can go into Saint-Cyr and become Marshall Schlemilovitch: the Dreyfus Afffair won't come back again; 38). In the later prizewinning novel *Rue des Boutiques Obscures*[13] the main character, deprived of his identity, sets out as a detective (his profession, appropriately enough) in search of his past, his existence, and therefore his identity: Guy Roland, "sur la piste de mon passé" (on the track of my past; *R,* 14). Once more, the narrative is presented in the first person, although we have a heavily disguised narrator. The novel opens with the words "Je ne sais rien. Rien qu'une silhouette claire, ce soir là, à la terrasse d'un café" (I know nothing. There was nothing but a distinct silhouette that evening, on the café terrace; 11). The sense of a dislocated Jew seeking some sense of location is reminiscent of Romain Gary, the great French novelist of an earlier generation, born in Vilnius, in his novel *La danse de Genghis Cohn,*[14] where the executed Jew Moishe, also known as Genghis Cohn (although "murdered" by the Nazis), cannot die and so, after the war, invades the body of the Nazi officer Schatz. Here the torment and the unresolved tensions are exemplified in a metaphor become grotesque reality. Present-day Germany, in this view, has not absorbed (that is to say, has not totally consumed or swallowed) the events of previous years. Rather than state this in banal and transparent language, the author vividly encapsulates this notion through the penetration of the clownish Moishe into the physical body of the Nazi. But the form of presentation seems to tease the reader and to leave him in some doubt as to whether what is offered is a memoir, a diary, or a fiction. These are the narrative options, and the lines of demarcation merge into one another.

We normally associate a diary with the uncensored recording of feeling, where there is no need for disguise and so where the truth is more likely to emerge. The author, after all, does not have to feel that there is a reader looking over his shoulder, and so he is presumably at liberty to offer an unvarnished version of the narrative that he presents. A novel, on the other hand, as the term *fiction* suggests, can be the product of the imagination, in the traditional sense of invented material. We certainly would not rebuke the author of fiction for lying about the factual material conveyed. A memoir, though, does make a claim to veracity, and the reader may reasonably expect literal truth in its pages. However, unlike a diary, it is not a private work; rather, it is presented to the public. What seems to be happening in recent work is that the traditional boundaries are collapsing amid the search for new forms of presentation.

It might be thought that the discussion thus far has revolved around empty questions of technique rather than content, that we have been dealing with the "how" rather than with the "what." However, the variety of technical resources brought to bear on the material itself predicates new needs, as well as a dissatisfaction with what is already in place. The writer must invoke new and multiple ways of achieving the desired effects. But there is naturally a wide range of disparate concerns represented in literature. Some of it aspires to reveal the turmoil of the individual, and the need to impress the significance of external events on personal development. In the case of other types of writing, personal concerns may play no smaller part, but the implications may have public and political reverberations. Both are significant in equal measure, and the writer makes the effort to seek out the means adequate for their expression.

▪ TURNS OF THE NOVEL

The evidence of current writing does not square with the notion of the death of the novel. The novel is taking on new forms, and presents the narrative in many guises. What is distinctive about the novel as a genre is its cultivation of a cognate relationship of the novel form to the contemporary setting. That is to say, the novel stands alongside the recognizable life of ordinary humanity. It comments on life, while preserving the necessary distance in order to sharpen the objective preception (the view from the outside) of character and its development. The flexibility of language, the shifts of

scene, the deployment of paradoxical devices, the options of time and space, and the involvement of the reader can all shift the perspective, deepen understanding, and open the mind to differences of approach. This takes us back to the original discussion and to the question of generic distinctions within literature. Facts are accompanied by commentary, whether explicit or implicit. There can be no statement without a narrator, the one who frames the statement. An event has its meaning; otherwise we would not record it in human terms for human consumption and understanding.

This is made manifest in our modern fiction, where additional materials are brought to bear on the text. These do not veil the voice of the narrator, but they do provide supplementary sources of bombardment that are designed to concretize the narrative. Whether this deepens the experience of the reader or not may be an open question. On that issue the reader will no doubt arrive at an independent judgment. But as is the case with all such innovation, possibilities like these can certainly broaden the range of available narrative technique. It is this range which is being explored and exploited in current fiction, both Israeli and European.

Leon I. Yudkin, Summer 1998

[1] Daniel Defoe, *A Journal of the Plague Year,* London, 1722. This work was initially published in 1722, but was presented by the author as though it were a diary written during the events described—i.e., in the year 1665. Anthony Burgess, in his introduction to the Penguin English Library edition of 1966, writes that the work reads as though it were "[a] genuine book of memoirs. This is what it reads like and is meant to read like—a rapid, colloquial, sometimes clumsy setting down of reminiscences of a great historical event that was lived through by a plain London merchant with a passion for facts, a certain journalistic talent, but . . . no literary pretensions whatever" (6). The book is signed by "H.F.," presumed to be a man living contemporaneously with the events, perhaps a relative of the author, Henry Foe, who was thirty-seven at the time that the plague broke out. Despite the unambiguous "fictionality" of the account, a pseudopigrophon, Burgess calls it "the most reliable and comprehensive account of the Great Plague that we possess."

[2] For a discussion of this issue, see James Young, *Writing and Rewriting the Holocaust: Narrative and the Consequences of Interpretation,* Bloomington, Indiana University Press, 1988, pp. 20–25.

[3] Ronit Matalon, *Im hapanim elenu* (Facing Us), Tel Aviv, Am Oved, 1996. Abbreviated as *I* where needed for clarity.

[4] It is interesting to understand why this use of the extra medium is seen to be useful. Young comments: "One of the reasons that narrative and photographs are so convincing together is that they seem to represent a combination of pure object and commentary on the object, each seeming to complete the other by reinforcing a sense of contrasting functions." See Young, op. cit., pp. 57–58.

[5] See also Marcel Proust, *Le temps retrouvé,* in *A la recherche du temps perdu* (vol. 6, Paris, La Pléiade, p. 451), for a presentation

of this image of the fictional word as an inscription on a tombstone.

6 W. G. Sebald, *The Emigrants,* London, Harvill, 1996. Orig. *Die Ausgewanderten,* 1993. Subsequent references abbreviated as *E* where needed for clarity.

7 Binjamin Wilkomirski, *Fragments: Memories of a Childhood, 1939–1948,* London, Picador, 1996. Original German, 1995. Abbreviated as *F* where needed for clarity.

8 Judith Katzir, *Lematis yesh et hashemesh babeten* (Matisse Has the Sun in His Belly), Tel Aviv, Hakkibutz Hameuchad, 1996. Abbreviated as *L* where needed for clarity.

9 Eleanora Lev, *Haboqer harishon began eden* (First Morning in Paradise), Tel Aviv, 1996. Abbreviated as *H* where needed for clarity.

10 Shifra Horn, *Arba imahot* (Four Mothers), Tel Aviv, Maariv, 1996. Abbreviated as *A* where needed for clarity.

11 Irit Linur, *Shirat hasirenah* (The Siren Song), Tel Aviv, Zmora-Bitan, 1991. Abbreviated as *S* where needed for clarity.

12 Patrick Modiano, *La Place de l'Etoile,* Paris, Gallimard, 1968. Abbreviated as *P* where needed for clarity.

13 Patrick Modiano, *Rue des Boutiques Obscures,* Paris, Gallimard, 1978. Abbreviated as *R* where needed for clarity.

14 Romain Gary, *La danse de Genghis Cohn,* Paris, Gallimard, 1968.

LEBANON

Literature and War, Beirut 1993–1995: Three Case Studies

Unstable
I stand
looking in front of me
looking behind me
I call you
I stretch out to you
come to me
don't let me fall
don't let me lose you
don't let me lose myself.

▓ **MONA TAKIEDDINE AMYUNI**[1]

The eminent literary critic Edward W. Said rightly believes that texts are worldly, are events, "a part of the social world, human life, and of course, the historical moments in which they are located and interpreted." A little further down in that same essay, titled "Secular Criticism," Said adds that what he wants to explore in this type of *criticism* is the individual consciousness which is "placed at a sensitive nodal point . . . this consciousness at that critical point."[2] Similarly, my commitment to a study of the literature of what I have called "Wounded Beirut"[3] springs from the tragic feeling of loss and disintegration which hit us, the Lebanese people, when the war exploded in our country (1975–90)

and threatened us with total annihilation. We lost our bearings during our long war, and my preoccupation with the artistic rendering of this experience saved my soul and allowed me to carry on with reading and writing. The process was certainly cathartic, and an immediacy was constantly established between the text, its author, its reader, and myself. In this sense, the text was a living thing with its own secrets, ambiguities, resistance, and the many "games" it plays with the reader.

Moreover, a generalized condition of despair and alienation prevails in times of crisis, a condition which defines the three texts I have chosen to analyze. Their authors were certainly part of the social order, but they witnessed and recorded its tragic disintegration. In their late thirties, Hoda Barakat, Abdo Wazen, and Sabah al-Kharrat Zuweyn all came of age during the war. They wrote their respective war novels during the conflict's final, extremely violent phase, and they published them a little later, between 1993 and 1995. Journalists as well, the three authors were deeply involved in the daily events of their country. They recorded such events in the best Arab newspapers to earn a living,[4] but they also transmuted those same historical moments into literary works which effectively ushered in a new mode of writing in Lebanon, a new sensibility placed at a "nodal point," a consciousness at a "critical point."

Thus, in the three texts I have chosen as case studies of writing in "Wounded Beirut," geographic boundaries have broken down. The categories of "ours" and "theirs" have lost all meaning, at every level. There are deep ruptures within the self, between the self and others, the self and society, the self and reality at large. Dialogue is broken off, and so is communication. The world is become deaf and mute. Silence prevails. The three texts, moreover, are all built on the interior monologue of a totally isolated narrator. These narrators' links with the community are nonexistent, and they are all caught up, graphically, in fragile postures which dominate their tales: a large man sitting on a high rock ecstatically merging with the moonlit night after having killed his beloved, in Hoda Barakat's novel *Ahl lil-hawa* (Of Dust and Love); a man half-bent over his table in the darkness of a night which reflects his innermost somber core, in a text by Abdo Wazen titled *Hadiqat al-hawass* (Garden of the Senses); and finally, a woman standing hesitantly at the doorstep of an oblique house, unable to decide whether to go in or out, in Sabah al-Kharrat Zueyn's dramatic poem *Al-Bayt al-ma'il, wal-waqt, wal-jidran* (The Oblique House, and Time, and the Walls).[5]

As for the other, the sexual partner, whether man or woman, he/she is completely occluded. We hear only the interior monologue of the narrator. In a postmodern stance, the self, like the other, is anonymous, with hardly any physical description, any history, any personal name. The authors deal with what Raymond Williams calls "structures of feeling"[6] rather than events, against the backdrop of a city, breaking down as it is being dismembered and burned to the ground by its own inhabitants. All points of reference thus disappear, all sense of orientation is lost, movement disintegrates, and feelings are pushed to the absolute limit.[7] Such "structures of feeling" convey fear, loss, despair, dispossession, and emptiness, in an often fragmented, syncopated style. Maurice Blanchot's fragmented modern man, fragmented writing—*l'écriture fragmentée*—readily come to mind.[8]

Hoda Barakat's protagonist in *Ahl lil-hawa* has just killed his beloved. Perched now on a high rock, he feels suddenly peaceful, having mended his fragmented body when he murdered his lover. The novel opens in arresting fashion:

> I stood on a high rock after killing her. I closed my eyes for a long time until I recollected myself. My muscles relaxed, my limbs rested and reconnected, like water calming down and reintegrating, following much turmoil. My skin gently grew cooler with the soft breeze, now that I had regained it, now that I had recovered the strong envelope which keeps me intact without any holes — a new man.

The scene is lyrical, the moon lovely, the night harmonious. Anyone who has never experienced the ecstasy of killing his beloved, of fully absorbing her soul, knows nothing of life, says the narrator. Dawn is about to break. The man sings loudly to welcome the sun that will warm him up.

Thus begins Barakat's novel, which later doubles back on itself at its conclusion, erasing what it had stated at the outset by letting the narrator say: "But all this may not have happened. She may very well have gone back to her husband. I may well have invented the murder scene. I am mad, after all, am I not? and he sings comically: 'Ya leyl!'" Framed in this fashion, Barakat's tale is a parody of the Lebanese war. Her protagonist was kidnapped and tortured. He went mad and was placed in the (psychiatric) Hospital of the Cross, above Nahr el-Kalb on the east side of Beirut. The hospital (which is still in operation) becomes the emblem of a sick nation murdering itself. Through its clever play with spatiotemporal shifts, Barakat's novel unfolds as a tale recounted by her deranged narrator. He first met the woman during a heavy bombardment, the narrator says. She took refuge in his village and in his home. They made love under heavy shelling. He did not want to pull out of her. He wanted to breathe in her very soul.

She, however, never spoke, never reacted, yielding compliantly to his insatiable desire. The two bodies became one, boundaries fell, and in a maddening "nodal point" he absorbed her completely by killing her.

In her narrator's inner monologue, Barakat creates an incredible amalgam of jarring elements, juxtaposing lyric, erotic, humorous, and highly realistic scenes all set among the mentally ill in the hospital. A kind of shock treatment seems to be at work here, as human behavior is conditioned by the savage bombardment going on outside, and shock creates parody, a forceful parody of the Lebanese war, as the male protagonist loses his mind in the midst of collective hysteria. Barakat had prepared us for this parody in her first novel, *The Stone of Laughter* (orig. 1990, Eng. 1994), where the protagonist was also marginalized in the midst of a mad society. In "Of Dust and Love" he literally loses his mind—or so the doctors say. The ambiguity is maintained against the Freudian reality of prolonged sexual intercourse, leading to the ecstasy of murder with which the novel opens. Now her protagonist sits on a high rock singing "Ya leyl!," as we have seen. Witness the disturbed condition of the narrator, one night in the hospital:

> At first, I used to be quiet in the shelter. But when I heard screams, my whole body shook. My hair stood up on my head, my limbs were electrified, and an incredible force would swell me up. I would yell and hit my head against the wall until blood gushed out. And a deep, fragmented sound would overcome me, would erase, would absorb the sound of the shelling. The total delight of that new sound. (20)

But witness as well the lyricism of the love scenes:

> For the first time I make love without looking at her. I don't see her body, some flowing liquid for drink. . . . I lie down next to her, I look at her face with ecstasy. I pull out of her but I know I shall never leave her. . . . I breathe over her mouth to catch her breath. . . . One day she will leave, I say to myself. (64)

Thus, personal and collective dramas are looked at through a "de-centered perspective," as defined by Linda Hutcheon. The boundaries between Barakat's protagonist, his beloved, and the world at large are not only unbalanced but ever moving, for the self has lost all sense of reality. Hutcheon adds, in her study *A Poetics of Postmodernism,* that postmodern parody often conveys "ironic discontinuity." She thinks that "parody is a perfect postmodern form, . . . for it paradoxically both incorporates and challenges that which it parodies."[9] In fact, Barakat does incorporate and challenge, with intense dramatic irony, the cruel practices in which people indulged during the Lebanese war. Her parody is even more ferocious in that it is based on the "de-centered perspective" of her crazy narrator.

In contrast to Barakat, Wazen and Zueyn neither incorporate nor challenge those wartime practices. Dramatic irony, however, runs through their two texts, and the war is continually present/absent. Individual dramas are recollected almost mutely, with hardly any sound. As a result, a kind of restrained violence lurks everywhere, but it is never rendered with the factual realism found in Barakat. Thus, Wazen's protagonist in "Garden of the Senses" is immersed in total darkness. Dead to his own body, dead to the world, he adds that he himself has no history, for he has lost his memory. Caught up in the small confined space of his bedroom, he knows he will never be able to overcome his feelings of desolation, despair, and emptiness. His inner monologue is a kind of murmur, his utter alienation caught up in the space of the text like a deep wound.[10]

His story is quite simple, and contains hardly any "event" at all. It unfolds through his inner monologue by means of images, metaphors, and symbols. Highly poetic, the narration makes abrupt halts, shifts fluidly backward and forward, repeating musically in a kind of "theme and variations" fashion the same few obsessions which haunt the narrator. "Structures of feeling" take shape, and the narrator says, in one typical passage, "I bend over myself at night to confront the fear which invades me, to kill the slowly ramping coldness which sneaks into my body, to overcome the choking inner feeling of isolation, of incapacitation and paralysis" (10).

Images of numbness and paralysis recur; others speak of broken glass similar to his broken soul, of his body crumbling down like a heap of ashes, et cetera. He feels fragmented and scattered, and seems to be standing at the edge of an abyss, which once again sheds light on the theme of human instability and vacillation in the midst of the shambles of a city called Beirut. A sense of unreality dominates the narration, and the lovers are often described as shadows about to disappear. Elsewhere they are dislocated, dispersed, absent/present at the surface of the narrator's psyche. Their story is stripped down to a stark double movement, which will be the case as well for Sabah al-Kharrat Zueyn's dramatic poem. In Wazen's "Garden of the Senses" the woman arrives one day from nowhere and departs another day to nowhere. Silently, at dawn, she goes out, leaving the door half-open. The narrator watches her without any sound. He then struggles with the white paper lying on his table, struggles to write down their story. His solitude is primordial. His only link with reality is a small patch of sky he can see through his window, plus the sound of waves breaking on the shore. The shimmering moon sheds some faint light on an otherwise dark scene. Isolation and strangeness prevail everywhere.

> We were strangers [he says], complete strangers, absent. Time was not ours, nor was the window overlooking the sea. . . . Anguish burned us up. We became the shadows of bodies which had been alive, of creatures that ceased to exist, present/absent to the world. . . . We looked at ourselves as we were quickly scattered in the darkness of our prison. Our faces were many and we had no faces. . . . Silence united us. . . . When we met we were absent, fading away like the destruction around us, like the debris we became at the end of our love. (30–31)

The woman slowly metamorphoses into a symbol, and a pseudoreligious level is contrapuntally introduced, with political overtones. The narrator discovers scars all over her body, old wounds which continue to bleed. She never explains them, and he is both intrigued and moved. Thus she reflects obliquely, in her own body, the wounds of Beirut. Wazen here joins scores of poets and novelists who have addressed Beirut as their (female) beloved.[11]

She leaves. Bent over his desk, he is obsessed with the single haunting *idée fixe* of the white paper before him. Whiteness connotes death in Wazen's text, from beginning to end.[12] Will he be able to write, or will he die? Struggling for meaning, Wazen builds up a multilayered construct he calls *nass* (a text), refusing to pin it down more precisely. In this fashion, he entertains much ambiguity and develops, in counterpoint, one more level for his composition. The theme of writing echoes intimately that of the sexual relationship. Unstable boundaries between the self and itself, between the self and the other, between the self and the world threaten to annihilate the couple. Unstable boundaries threaten writing as well with its own impossibility. "To be or not to be" rests on "to write or not to write." Each word Wazen uses, each assemblage of words, images, and metaphors, creates new harmonies among several levels of reality. Or, rather, new disharmonies invest the fragmented poetic prose. Reality has been irremediably shattered outside. Will writing mend it within the author?

In fact, the conclusion of the text releases language, endowing the function of writing with great ambiguity.

> Silent I am. Far away, muffled voices are heard. Voices out of my own night, out of the universe's night. Black papers in front of me. . . . I expect nobody . . . . Her face fades away. I don't remember her face any more. . . . The white papers fill my eyes. My eyes close. The dense white papers in front of me.

Alone. I realize I am alone. I don't remember exactly what has happened. I only remember I am writing. I write so that I won't die. I write to die the death we did not die together.

Alone. I face my papers. They are wet with her water, her blueness, her smell, which spreads over my face, over my hands. I write to acknowledge her absence, writing will not imprison her. Writing is born out of the instant of her vanishing away. That instant which burnt her up. Like desire which remains alive in an ever absent longing. (134)

Desire is fixed on the white paper, as Wazen salvages life through the completion of his text.

Sabah al-Kharrat Zueyn's dramatic poem "The Oblique House, and Time, and the Walls" bears fascinating parallels with Wazen's text. Silence and isolation prevail as in "Garden of the Senses." A first-person narrator is described with neither name nor features, except for her very white skin and her slim fragile body. She stands at the doorstep of an "oblique house," undecided. Will she go in or will she return to where she came from, one day, by train? Unstable boundaries threaten her, as she walks in circles in a misty city. She stands at the doorstep of that house as if at a razor's edge, with abysmal depths ever present in her psyche. In counterpoint here, as was the case with Wazen's text, she weaves her tale between what had happened a year ago and the need to capture those events in writing at the present moment. The theme of writing as an act of consciousness, giving life to the self, acquires existential importance due to the total absence of any other points of reference.

Zueyn's story is stripped down to a few essential occurrences, as was the case with Wazen's text. The woman narrator comes to the city by train. She hesitantly steps into the "oblique house," where four white walls stare at her, walls she often feels coalescing into a single huge cement edifice about to enfold and crush her. She meets the man immediately upon her arrival inside the house. With great hostility, she refers to him in practically every scene as *he or the other*. They play out an extremely violent sexual relationship. She feels broken down, dead, scattered. She leaves, comes back, then departs for good. A year later, she reenacts their devious relationship in writing. Here is her recollection of their last day together, as she was about to leave:

I woke out of a sleep that was not sleep, the sun warmed up the windows and the corners of the cold house, so painfully quiet, I smiled to the other, the other who came toward me without a smile, who was so deeply still when I writhed with pain, when I writhed under my destruction,

I could not sleep, I had been subjected to such perversion, such perversion he exercised on me, and my time went out of hand, I lost my face in the dim light . . . , and when I tried to come closer to his body, for it was time [to leave] and time and space were annihilated, when I tried to come closer, he stepped back, empty space stretched out in front of me, the impossible mad space, my body stood still, such pain, such pain on my white body, my body crumbling down during that last morning, I couldn't stand up, darkness all around me, and he fell down and went away without turning to look at me, and the maddening silent space as if language too had gone mad, totally paralyzed. . . . (32–33)

Highly charged language captures the recollected past experience, while body language rather than speech conveys the lived moment. Interestingly, Zueyn's dramatic poem is constructed in seventy-five vignettes called "scenes." The text could be performed beautifully by two mute actors, playing out a recitation by a backstage narrator. Highly visual, the scenes are evoked in syncopated style, with full-stops only at the end of each part. Thus, an accumulation of short, gasping sentences with commas—brief pauses needed to catch one's breath—evoke this extreme relationship on the verge of a madness unto death. Pattern and rhythm are created through desperate leitmotivs (encountered in Barakat and Wazen as well). Words such as *fear, despair, annihilation, anguish, emptiness, madness,* and *guilt* fill the space of each scene, charged with an almost unbearable intensity.

Such extreme "structures of feeling" are dramatized by bodies bent over, crouched, bleeding, dislocated, fragmented, at the edge of an abyss, or otherwise terrified, hiding in bed beneath several blankets. To convey such outer limits of living and perceiving, the language Zueyn uses so brilliantly is composed of a succession of sentences which accumulate vertically, endlessly. As a result, those syncopated sentences thrown onto the page as if by blasts of wind create waves of highly compressed emotions at the point of explosion—and indeed they do often explode. In the chaos of each instant, not only do sentences accumulate like blasts announcing the approach of a destructive tornado, but thoughts, feelings, and action follow in the same brutal way, contradictory, stubborn, submitting to the tyranny of the instant and the arbitrary reign of desire. Fear, hatred, love, attraction, and repulsion—all merge to convey an atmosphere of tremendous violence and passion. Language and silence, living and nonliving, the scarred faces, the shattered selves are imitated stylistically by a broken-down language and the failure of words to express a primitive, sinful human condition.

Moreover, Zueyn's spatiotemporal units seem to crush or smother the female narrator, who strains for air. The walls which are featured in the title stand for this claustrophobic feeling of being crushed as if by cement, by entire buildings, by the city itself, crumbling down on the horizon. In perfect mimesis, words are lost. They struggle and break down under tremendous pressures. Like the wounded and bleeding bodies, words as well are injured and incapacitated. Rescuing words, language, and meaning, as was the case with Abdo Wazen, becomes the only reality for Zueyn, an impossible reality.

The final scene before the fall of the "curtain" presents the debris of time and dismembered bodies yearning for death. The narrator recalls, ultimately, their pain, their distorted selves, their memories and madness, even as she tries to escape and to glean some meaning from it all. But words fail her, and she can find no such meaning whatsoever. Utter chaos usurps the space while the white walls observe her constantly. The closing sentence is about writing itself, which is as sinful as the protagonist's own soul: "I did not find the meaning . . . our things in our death ended up taking us unawares, no memory of a city, our souls escaped our bodies, our bodies washed away our sins, but I came back every day committing the sin of writing, and every day I wished I were dead, I wished to abolish the abyss from which I came" (96).

To recapitulate: an absolutely desperate stance at the end of Sabah al-Kharrat Zueyn's dramatic poem; the highly ambiguous function of writing in Abdo Wazen's text; and self-parody in Hoda Barakat's novel ("I am mad! Ya leyl!"). Could one perhaps understand such a new type of writing in Beirut as the result of a harrowing situation in a fragmented epoch and a destroyed city? We should pause for a moment and recall that when the fighting finally ceased in Lebanon, the Lebanese failed to understand both the war and the ceasefire. What were the reasons for the destruction of a city and a nation by its own people? What had been achieved? How would we reconstruct and reinvent our boundaries and our identities? We found no answers to those haunting questions.

But our artists did. They did not so much give us answers as dramatize in their works a completely mad situation, a "no exit" condition. Witness this one last passage from "The Oblique House":

> Our bodies went through tunnels, walked in narrow streets, I was separated from him, I stopped seeing him, I was in deep pain hoping for a time outside this space, I was at the zenith of violence, bending my shattered body, and he in his silence tried not to lose me . . . , and the city was dreamlike, its houses reflecting a lost language with their closed doors and windows, its houses in the paralysis of my voice, . . . its dead houses, . . . our ghostlike bodies trying to patch up reality and madness. (95–96)

Are we about to see the end of such tunnels? we wonder along with our young authors. Barakat, Wazen, and Zueyn have certainly ushered in a new epoch in the literature of Lebanon, an epoch marked by radical demands and new languages. Texts are worldly, after all. The absence of such new literary pressures would be unimaginable amid the debris of a city both hated and loved by her own people.

Mona Takieddine Amyuni, Winter 1999

[1] I dedicate this short poem to the companion who held me tight, during the war, when we watched Beirut aflame and the collapse of what we thought of as our stable boundaries.

[2] Edward W. Said, *The World, the Text and the Critic,* Cambridge (Ma.), Harvard University Press, 1983, pp. 4 and 15. My essay is a revised version of a paper delivered at an international conference ("For a Critical Culture") honoring Edward Said, held 29 June to 1 July 1997 in Beirut.

[3] I used the expression "Wounded Beirut" for the first time in an essay titled "The Image of the City: Wounded Beirut," published in *Alif: Journal of Comparative Poetics* (the American University in Cairo), 7 (Spring 1987), pp. 27–52. The essay was reprinted in *The View from Within: Writers and Critics on Contemporary Arabic Literature,* eds. F. J. Ghazoul and B. Harlow, Cairo, American University in Cairo Press, 1994, pp. 53–76. Also, a book on the literature of Wounded Beirut is in preparation.

[4] Barakat lives in Paris today, writes for *al-Hayat,* and broadcasts news on Radio al-Sharq. Wazen also writes for *al-Hayat* and Zueyn for *An-Nahar.* Both live in Beirut.

[5] Hoda Barakat, *Ahl-lil-hawa,* Beirut, Dar an-Nahar, 1993, p. 7. The author uses *hawa* ambiguously, for it means "wind" but also "love." It was my friend the novelist Dominique Eddé who suggested to me the beautiful translation of the title as "Of Dust and Love," but the novel has not yet come out in English. Barakat's first novel, *Hajar al-dihk* (London, Riad el-Rayyes Books, 1990), has appeared in English as *The Stone of Laughter* (tr. Sophie Bennett, New York, Interlink Books, 1994) and in French as *La pierre du rire* (tr. Nadine Acoury, Paris, Actes Sud, 1996). Abdo Wazen, *Hadiqat al-hawass* (Garden of the Senses), Beirut, Dar al-Jadid, 1993. See my review in *The Beirut Review* (Beirut, 7 [Spring 1996], pp. 145–52), which has inspired parts of the present discussion. Sabah al-Kharrat Zueyn, *Al-Bayt al-ma'il wal-waqt wal-jidran* (The Oblique House, and Time, and the Walls), Beirut, Dar Amwaj, 1995). Excerpts from all three texts are in my own translation; parenthetic page references are to the original Arabic texts.

[6] This expression recurs in Raymond Williams, *The Country and the City,* New York, Oxford University Press, 1973.

[7] See Nathalie Sarraute, *L'ère du soupçon: Essais sur le roman,* Paris, Gallimard, 1956, where her discussion of Kafka in the wake of Dostoevsky applies to the ethos of the three Lebanese authors I am analyzing here. Sarraute writes what I have partly

translated: "Ici, où des distances infinies comme les espaces planétaires séparent les êtres les uns des autres, où vous avez, à tout moment, 'l'impression qu'on a coupé avec vous toute liaison', tous les points de repère disparaissent, le sens de l'orientation s'émousse, les mouvements peu à peu se dérèglent, les sentiments se désagrègent (ce qui subsiste encore de l'amour n'est qu'une mêlée brutale dans laquelle les amants sous les yeux indifférents des spectateurs, 's'acharnent l'un sur l'autre, déçus impuissants à s'aider' . . ." (51–52).

8 Maurice Blanchot, *Le livre à venir*, Paris, Gallimard, 1959, pp. 153–72. Blanchot writes of a fateful disintegration ("disintegration inévitable"), of the dislocated, discordant, fragmented individual, or all that the individual has missed out on ("le caractère disloqué, discordant et fragmenté de l'être ou . . . les manques de l'homme"); such elements abound in my three case studies.

9 Linda Hutcheon, *A Poetics of Postmodernism: History, Theory, Fiction,* New York, Routledge, 1988, p. 11.

10 Maurice Blanchot expresses this feeling beautifully when he writes, "La solitude au niveau du monde est une blessure"; see *L'espace littéraire*, Paris, Gallimard, 1955, p. 9.

11 Suffice it here to mention Nizar Qabbani, Mahmoud Darwish, Adonis, and Nadia Tuéni among others. See my book, *La ville, source d'inspiration: le Caire, Khartoum, Londres, Beyrouth, Paola Scala,* Stuttgart, Steiner, 1998.

12 Maurice Blanchot's *L'espace littéraire* comes to mind here, as the following subtitles suggest: "La solitude essentielle" (Essential Solitude), "L'œuvre et l'espace de la mort" (The Book and the Space of Death), and "Recherche d'une juste mort" (Search for the Proper Death). Interestingly, Abdo Wazen told me recently that he was obsessed with death as he wrote his text inside the city at war. He wanted to go to the extreme limit of the sexual relationship and beyond, into that symbolic dimension I have indicated here. He also confirmed that he greatly admires Maurice Blanchot and the latter's concepts of "fragmented modern man" and "fragmented writing."

A Poetics of Pain: Evelyne Accad's Critical and Fictional World

Poetic and *personal* are two adjectives that fit Evelyne Accad's political and critical philosophy, for references to the personal domain and its political relevance permeate her work, from her earliest writings to her most recent ones. Her first published treatise, *Veil of Shame: The Role of Women in the Contemporary Fiction of North Africa and the Arab World* (1978), represents a theoretical and political preoccupation with lived and witnessed reality—the position afforded women in North Africa and the Arab world and the manifestation of those roles in fiction. She returns often to this topic and, in a later novel, admits that she left her own native Lebanon to escape oppression and limitations placed on women.

Accad's academic career began in Lebanon, with an Associate of Arts degree from the Beirut College for Women. She continued her education in the U.S. at the age of twenty-two. Having completed a Bachelor of Arts in English and a Master of Arts in French, she returned to her native Lebanon in 1968 to teach and contribute to society there. It would seem that the constraints in Lebanese society were still too rigid for her, for she returned to the States in 1971 to complete a doctorate in comparative literature at Indiana University. During the twenty-four years since the completion of her degree, she has divided her time between a vibrant academic career in the United States, Lebanon, North Africa, and various regions of the Arab world and writing, research, and political activism in Paris.

Accad's personal roots evince multiplicity, since she is the child of an intercultural union between a Swiss mother and a Lebanese father. The result is a hybrid of poetic expression: Accad is a novelist, a poet, a scholar, a singer, and a songwriter. Interestingly, we find that her fictional narratives tend to be expressed in French, while her critical works are composed in English. Her poetry and songs marry all three of her "native" languages: Arabic, English, and French. This multilingual multiculturalism continues to play itself out in her life as well. I have never had the opportunity to observe Accad in her native Lebanon, but I have been fortunate enough to work with her in the U.S., Paris, and Tunisia. Of these three environments, she seems most at home in Tunisia, itself a mixture of Arabic, Mediterranean, and French cultures.

Tunisia has recognized the honor and sought to return the gift, for Tunisian women have paid tribute to Accad in a most compelling manner: they have transformed her novel *Blessures des mots: Journal de Tunisie* (Wounded by Words: A Tunisian Journal; 1993) into a play that includes her songs and even incorporates her own renditions of these songs. The result is a moving testimony to women's theater and women's relationships as well as a powerful commemoration of Accad's work and her contributions to their lives and activities.

This creative celebration of the connection between the personal and the political and of writing as political activity reflects the quest that has always functioned at the heart of Evelyne Accad's writing, whether it be fiction or literary criticism. Her first work, *Veil of Shame,* is a critical analysis of women's place in the literature and culture of North Africa and of the Arab world in general. In this book she begins by discussing the connections between scholarly work, literature, and the personal and the political. She explains: "The most direct reason [for this study] is that when I first became interested in the subject, I was already a student of literature. I had run away from my country precisely to avoid some of the practices described in this study; this experience gave me the background knowledge to enable me to read between the lines of the literature, to sense the personal human suffering reflected, however dimly, in the fiction" (11).

Twelve years later she addresses even more precisely the links between literature and culture/society in *Sexuality and War: Literary Masks of the Middle East* (1990), her study of reactions to war as they differ along gender lines. Here she eloquently answers critics of "politicized" criticism: "The questions I am often asked when treating and illustrating my topic are: Is literature an adequate field to understand political and social realities? Can novels be used as social, anthropological, and political documents? What about the imagination, the fantasy of the author? What about his or her 'distortions'? My immediate response is to say that creative works are more appropriate than other works. They give us the 'total' picture because they not only include all the various fields—social, political, anthropological, religious, and cultural—but they also allow us to enter into the imaginary and unconscious world of the author. In expressing his or her own individual vision, an author also suggests links to the collective imaginary" (4).

Accad's most recent novel, *Blessures des mots,* is a deft mixture of autobiography, documentary, and fictional material based on a year she spent in Tunisia as a Fulbright Scholar. She further recognizes the links between the personal and the political, exposing also the importance of looking inward before turning to societal ills: "Ne vaut-il pas mieux être profondément honnête vis-à-vis des autres et de soi-même? Comment résoudre les problèmes politiques si nous ne commençons pas par nous-mêmes? Le privé n'est-il pas politique?" (Isn't it better to be deeply honest concerning others and yourself? How can we solve political problems if we don't start with ourselves? Isn't the private political? [59]).[1] These reflections also echo Julia Kristeva's theory of alterity as expressed in *Strangers to Ourselves,* where she describes the other in Lacanian terms, applying those distinctions to sociocultural conditions: "Etrangement, l'étranger nous habite: il est la face cachée de notre identité. . . . De le reconnaître en nous, nous nous épargnons de le détester en lui-même" (9; "Strangely, the foreigner lives within us: he is the hidden face of our identity. . . . By recognizing him within ourselves, we are spared detesting him in himself" [1]).[2]

Accad herself is pushed to write as a means of political activity and, through writing, to discover a path away from hatred of the other. She seeks to delineate the destructive forces of exclusionary nationalism, a nationalism that would eradicate difference, and to work toward a "reformed nationalism stripped of its male chauvinism, war, and violence" (*SW,* 25). In *Veil of Shame* she tells us that "my sleepless nights over a subject which agonizes me because I am personally as well as intellectually involved have compelled me to put this situation on paper" (11). Similarly, in *Sexuality and War* it is "the anguish, sadness, and despair over the senseless war and destruction of my beautiful country of birth, Lebanon . . . [that is] at the core of what led me to write this book" (xi). Indeed, throughout her writing, no matter what the form of expression, Accad exposes the roots of oppression and seeks solutions to painful situations, both personal and political/societal.

Kristeva calls for a subversion of modern individualism, where "le citoyen-individu cesse de se considérer comme uni et glorieux, mais découvre ses incohérences et ses abîmes" (*Etrangers,* 11; "the citizen-individual ceases to consider himself as unitary and glorious but discovers his incoherences and abysses" [2]). She envisions a system where relevant questions deal no longer with "l'accueil de l'étranger à l'intérieur d'un système qui l'annule, mais de la cohabitation de ces étrangers que nous reconnaissons tous être" (ibid.; "welcoming the foreigner within a system that obliterates him but promoting the togetherness of those foreigners that we all recognize ourselves to be" [2–3]). Rather than searching to repress the other within ourselves, she recommends celebrating otherness and difference, thereby alleviating the psychic pain and fear caused by the "misrecognized" plenitude of the real.[3] She explains: "Ne pas chercher à fixer, à chosifier l'étrangeté de l'étranger. . . . L'alléger aussi, cette étrangeté, en y revenant sans cesse—mais de plus en plus rapidement. S'évader de sa haine et de son fardeau, les fuir non par le nivellement et l'oubli, mais par la reprise harmonieuse des différences qu'elle suppose et propage" (ibid.; "Let us not seek to solidify, to turn the otherness of the foreigner into a thing. . . . Let us also lighten that otherness by constantly coming back to it—but more and more swiftly. Let us escape its hatred, its burden, fleeing them not through leveling and forgetting, but through the harmonious repetition of the differences it implies and spreads" [3]).

Accad also calls for a harmonious integration and embrace of difference, reminding us that "recognition of the other also applies to sexual differences, to the relationship between men and women" (*SW,* 4). She practices and finds communities that demonstrate what she calls *femihumanism,* a concept discussed in *Sexuality and War.* As she explains: "I am using this expression rather than *feminism* because I believe that both women and men must work together to bring about the changes. In these terms, a new movement, with a redefined *femihumanism,* working with a reformed nationalism stripped of its male chauvinism, war, and violence, is being conceptualized" (25). Accad's redefined femihumanism resembles Kristeva's call for a subversion of modern individualism, the latter tied directly to totalitarian, intolerant nationalisms. As Kristeva explains: "Issu de la révolution bourgeoise, le nationalisme est devenu le symptôme d'abord romantique, ensuite totalitaire, des XIXᵉ et XXᵉ siècles. Or, s'il s'oppose aux tendances universalistes (qu'elles soient religieuses ou rationalistes) et tend à cerner, voir pourchasser l'étranger, le nationalisme n'en aboutit pas moins, par ailleurs, à l'individualisme particulariste et intransigeant de l'homme moderne" (Etrangers, 11; "Stemming from the bourgeois revolution, nationalism has become a symptom—romantic at first, then totalitarian—of the nineteenth and twentieth centuries. Now, while it does go against universalist tendencies [be they religious or rationalist] and tends to isolate or even hunt down the foreigner, nationalism nevertheless ends up, on the other hand, with the particularistic, demanding individualism of contemporary man" [2]).

In point of fact, Accad's entire body of work can be viewed as the representation of what femihumanism means to her and how it can be used to overcome chauvinist forms of aggression and totalitarian nationalism.[4] Integral to her concept of femihumanism is the role of exile in contributing to the building of new communities and to rejuvenating political discussions and activities. In discussing Andrée Chedid's treatment of multiculturality (a term coined by Accad), Accad reveals indirectly yet clearly her own thoughts on the mixture of cultures: "Chedid insists on the positive aspects of such hybridization, affirming cosmopolitanism and the enrichment, tolerance, and openness it brings" (SW, 86). In Accad's world, exile creates a mixture of cultures, a hybridization, that is embodied in the exiled individual; furthermore, l'exilé becomes a source of inspiration and new ideas. In Blessures des mots Hayate, the main character, is introduced to a group of women as "Hayate, libanaise, en exil parmi nous cette année, pour nous inspirer, nous apporter des idées nouvelles, pour que nous nous soutenions dans l'engagement au côté des opprimés!" (Hayate, a Lebanese woman, in exile among us this year, to inspire us, to bring us new ideas, so that we can support one another in struggle alongside the oppressed; 20). Exiled from power in the intransigent and divisive individualism of modern man, the stranger is always excluded, foreign to the system. Both Kristeva's and Accad's theories lead to the conclusion that the presence of the stranger in communities working to subvert rigid hierarchies of group identification and power serves to bring to the surface otherwise hidden (i.e., repressed from the collective unconscious) practices of exclusion and intolerant individualism.

Accad's remarks regarding the role of exile were made in the context of studying preoccupations of female and male writers of the Middle East in literary texts. In contemplating the differences, she remarks: "The search for roots can be an expression of nostalgia for one's childhood or a need for security and love. Male authors tend to depict multiplicity as confrontation. They search for purity, multiplicity meaning dishonor. Multiculturality increases their schizophrenia and makes them uneasy and depressed. Roots are a search for identity, and exile is a terrible fate" (SW, 168–69). Accad's conclusions are that male authors tend to find exile traumatic, whereas female authors see multiplicity as something positive—exile often means freedom (SW, 168). Foremost in her criticism is the search for the non-dit of narratives in an effort to understand the cultural underpinnings at work in texts. At times these studies lead her to interpretations regarding connections between sexuality, nationalism, and war; at other times, her analyses lead to an understanding of the cohesive elements holding together women's political groups.

In her fiction Accad often demonstrates her philosophy of political action and progressive communities through interpersonal dynamics, and we find that concepts repressed in traditionalist literature occupy a central role. Specifically, expressing and transcending pain functions as the driving force behind many of Accad's narratives and much of her philosophical theorizing. She is not alone in affording a central role to psychic pain, for its configuration and manifestation have been explored by several other leading feminist theorists and artists working in French. For example, Marguerite Duras published an entire novel entitled La douleur, and Kristeva has produced a long study titled Soleil noir: Dépression et mélancolie (Black Sun: Depression and Melancholia). In her final chapter Kristeva studies "la maladie de la douleur" (the malady of grief) in the Durasian world. In L'amant the retelling of the pain endured by Duras and her siblings seems crucial to the narrator, and the reader is induced to seek the guilty parties along with the narrator. For Marie Cardinal in Au pays de mes racines, the retrieval of a repressed memory and the reliving of the resultant primal pain indicate the path toward acceptance of the maternal terre/mer/mère and toward eventual liberation.

Pain and its expression in Accad's work plays various roles. At times she recognizes a transformative power in pain itself. For example, the novel Coquelicot du massacre (Poppy from the Massacre; 1988) is a metaphor of the pain inflicted by the destruction of her beautiful homeland as well as of her own guilt for having left. The main character, Nour, wanders through the surreal cityscape of war-torn Beirut in a desperate attempt to cross the line of demarcation to the peaceful side, where she and her child will be sheltered from physical harm. Along her path, Nour seeks and finds her former voice teacher. As the two women discuss their lives since they last met, the voice teacher echoes parts of Accad's philosophy of pain and suffering: "J'ai parcouru de longs trajets de souffrance à l'intérieur de moi-même. J'ai compris que la douleur conduit à de grandes plénitudes. Je suis parvenue à un autre état de grâce et de foi qui m'aide à vivre aujourd'hui, quand tout s'effondre autour de nous" (I have crossed long periods of suffering in my innermost being. I have understood that pain leads to great fulfillment. I have attained a higher state of grace and faith that helps me live today when everything is crumbling all around us; 70).

At the opposite end of the spectrum of pain, Accad feels the need to express the pain but fears its paralyzing effects. Although earlier in *Coquelicot* she exalted the transcendent powers of pain, she later feels overwhelmed by the horror of the wounds: "Elle ne trouve pas les mots pour lui exprimer la blessure, qui, tout au fond d'elle, vient de se rouvrir. C'est une douleur sourde et profonde qui la prend aux tripes, la paralyse et l'empêche de parler. . . . La vie est une répétition des mêmes blessures" (She cannot find the words to express the wound that has just reopened in the very depths of her being. The pain is mute and deep and seizes her entrails, paralyzes her and prevents her from speaking; 112). Elsewhere in *Coquelicot,* horror and suffering have forced her into an impasse: "Je ne sais pas si j'arriverai à décrire l'horreur qui les rongent, et la souffrance que je ressens. J'ai l'impression de pousser des cris aïgus que personne ne veut écouter. Je suis dans une impasse dans ce que j'écris, et dans ma vie" (I don't know if I can manage to describe the horror that gnaws at them and the suffering I feel. It's as if I were screaming sharp cries that no one would listen to. I've reached an impasse in my writing, in my life; 132).

But Accad, not unlike Cardinal, must conquer the paralysis and bring the pain into the open to be analyzed—in a phase I call reworking/retrieval. Confronting and analyzing pain now allows her characters to cope with the hypocrisy of so-called self-exile and personal betrayals. She explores the parameters of her own exile, a self-imposed one because she was neither literally forced to leave her native Lebanon nor kidnapped into slavery (as was the case with the characters in Euzhan Palcy's 1983 book *La Rue Cases-Nègres,* for instance); instead, she was compelled to choose between remaining in a repressive/oppressive environment or relocating to a milieu which allowed freedom of movement and expression. She describes her "condition as an Arab woman, which made me leave my country of birth, Lebanon, at the age of twenty-two, in order to free and assert myself as an autonomous human being" (*SW,* 165).

As we have seen, the concept of exile also plays an important role in Accad's narratives from a philosophical standpoint and in her studies of community dynamics. I would propose examining as well its place in the configuration of psychic pain, for the exiled condition is a significant feature both of her texts and of groups portrayed in those texts. Accad does not see either exile or the multiplicity resulting from changing situations and mixing with other cultures as damaging to the psyche; she seems to agree with the female authors she studies when she explains: "Another major preoccupation of female and male writers is their outlook on multiculturality and the question of roots, exile, and pluralism mixed with violence and war, and how these are reflected in interpersonal relationships. Female authors tend to see multiplicity as something positive. Exile often means freedom" (*SW,* 168). Accad indicates that she might never have felt drawn back to Lebanon if the war had not torn the country apart, hence implying that exile has meant freedom for her rather than the dishonor, confrontation, depression, and schizophrenia manifested by male authors she has studied. She tells us: "I would not have felt the same concern for Lebanon had it not been for the war and for what I perceived as real suffering in my friends and many of the people I came in contact with. I shared their pain and desire to remedy" (*SW,* 165, 166).

If Accad does not suffer alienation through exile, she does undergo scrutiny and a kind of double-edged xenophobia in *Blessures des mots.* Although this book is presented as fiction, it is largely based on facts, for she declares that Hayate "voulait écrire un roman mais comme un documentaire de la vie des femmes en Tunisie" (Hayate wanted to write a novel that would be like a documentary of women's lives in Tunisia). In the novel Hayate represents Accad herself, and the action takes place during the year that Hayate/Accad spends in Tunisia on a Fulbright research grant. She meets with fear and rejection from some of the women, who accuse her of CIA connections; for example, she is told: "Hay, je dois te dire: un Libanais, une Libanaise vivant aux Etats-Unis ne peut qu'être suspect" (Hay, I have to tell you: a Lebanese man or woman living in the United States is, by definition, suspect; 84). Not only is she a Lebanese living in the U.S., but her Fulbright fellowship gives her contacts at the American Embassy—a status some take as proof positive of government connections. Hayate's surprise turns to mute agony: "Pourtant, comme toujours dans ces situations de violence verbale, elle demeure muette, incapable de prendre part ou de rompre la virulence des propos" (Conversely, as always happens in such situations of verbal violence, she remains mute, incapable of participating in or rupturing the virulence of the remarks; 87). Although the solidarity Hayate had hoped to find is tinged with resentment and jealousy from some, the reader is reminded that this *blessure* is offset by true, deep relationships: "Il y a des êtres avec lesquels on sait tout de suite que ça va être très fort et très beau. . . . Elle avait comme ça, à travers le monde, quelques amitiés sûres, sur lesquelles elle pouvait compter. Ces êtres merveilleux et enrichissants la portaient au-dessus des déceptions et amertumes de la vie" (There are some people with whom you know right away that your relationship will be strong and beautiful. . . . She had some solid friendships like that around the world, people whom she knew she could count on and who carried her above all the disappointment and bitterness of life; 48).

In *Coquelicot* pain and suffering lead to a state of grace that allows the heroine (also based on Accad) to live even as everything around her is crumbling. In *Blessures des mots* the pain functions as a sad reminder that jealousy and envy arise in all situations and conspire to prevent progress toward resolution of conflicts. Here, true friendships counteract the superficial *mesquineries* and function as a balm on the wounds inflicted by mean-spirited gossips and the aggression inherent in their words. Additionally, the expression of pain becomes a catharsis, a means of rising above the noxious effects of the wounds: "C'est merveilleusement cathartique de pouvoir exprimer sa douleur et ses souffrances passées avec d'autres femmes blessées elles aussi dans leur être" (It's wonderfully cathartic to be able to express your pain and past suffering with other women who have also been wounded at their very core; 56).

Accad's first novel, *L'excisée* (1982), is the story of a young woman who is metaphorically excised because she leaves home to follow a dream and a love that turn out to represent even greater repression than that which she suffered during her childhood. She escapes physical excision by leaving the community, taking with her a young girl. In guaranteeing the girl a life without direct oppression, she creates an aura of hope for other young women. This first novel is partially autobiographical in that it depicts some lived experiences and characters from the author's own life. In *Blessures des mots,* speaking through Hayate, Accad gives a succinct rationale for autobiography within fiction: "Mon premier roman est aussi en partie autobiographique. Tout ce que j'écris l'est un peu, car pour exprimer des choses profondes, il faut sans doute en avoir fait réellement l'expérience, non?" (My first novel is also autobiographical in part. Everything I write is to some extent, because, in order

to present deep things, you undoubtedly have to have lived them, don't you think?; 58).

As we have seen, much of *Blessures des mots* deals with how to rise above and even use pain inflicted both by others and by the system itself. *L'excisée,* on the other hand, deals with a young girl who has not yet experienced suffering but who instead chooses to leave her country with her lover in order to find fulfillment. She chooses to run risks and indulge her desire rather than stay with her family, where she is "safe" both from danger and from *jouissance:* "Elle ne veut pas mourir, mourir déjà dans son être, avant d'avoir vécu, avant d'avoir compris le pourquoi de ces bouillonnements qui la soulèvent, qui la tourmentent. Même l'angoisse est préférable à cette abnégation. Même la souffrance vaut mieux que le renoncement" (23; "She doesn't want to die, to die in her very soul now before having lived, before having understood the whys of these agitations that arouse her, that torment her. Anguish itself is preferable to the abnegation of oneself. Even suffering is better than renunciation" [10]).[5] She does indulge her desire, but falls victim to broken promises and disillusionment at best; at worst, she suffers mental abuse from her husband and witnesses the physical abuse of young girls— in the form of genital mutilation. The descriptions of the "cleansing ceremony" convey vividly the author's rage at this atrocity enacted on the bodies of the girls.[6]

Ahlame, one of the characters in *Blessures des mots,* characterizes eloquently the strength of the narrative style in *L'excisée:* "Ce n'est pas une expression ici et là. C'est rempli de passages extraordinaires. Par exemple, là où tu décris ton premier contact physique avec un homme, et la description de la femme derrière le voile, et celle sur le bateau, et les petites filles qu'on excise dans la cour. C'est aussi ta manière très sensuelle de t'exprimer, une violence dans ta douceur. Je suis éblouie!" (It's not just an expression here and there. It's full of incredible passages. For example, when you describe your first physical contact with a man, and the description of the woman behind the veil, and the one on the boat, and the little girls circumcised in the courtyard. It's also the very sensual manner in which you express yourself, a violence in your gentleness. I'm overwhelmed!; 68).

Unlike Hayate in *Blessures des mots,* E., the main character in *L'excisée,* does not find a community of women with which to share her pain; instead, she witnesses violence carried out against young girls by women. Where Hayate is bolstered by true friendships, E. despairs at the physical violence perpetuated by women against women and seeks solace by joining with the sea (the *mer/mère*). The one note of hope in the novel is the Egyptian woman who has escaped the constraints of her world and who takes E.'s surrogate child away from the danger of excision.

In *L'excisée* and in her short stories Accad attempts to exorcise those ghosts that would call her a traitor for having "abandoned" family, homeland, students, and traditions in general. In parts of *Coquelicot du massacre* she seems to be seeking release from the psychic pain brought about by the machinations and manipulations of people she had trusted in the "liberated" world. These personal concerns are interwoven with a narrative which treats large-scale oppression and mutilation of women in a way that powerfully paints and conveys the pain to the reader. In these instances she uses the expression of pain as a way to escape the long-term paralysis caused by personal deceptions and large-scale injustices.

Throughout most of *Coquelicot* and *Sexuality and War,* pain takes on a transcendent role. At times in *Coquelicot,* however, it becomes a paralyzing force which grips her entrails and stops her from speaking. Overcoming the silencing effects of pain, she moves from the specific protagonist-centered narrative to multiple narratives woven around Lebanon and the war. Although a protagonist still exists, it is that character's interaction with others and their political action(s) which plays the central role. In *Blessures des mots* experiencing and working through pain become central themes, even part of the title of the book. Unlike the cases of Cardinal and Duras, Accad's pain bypasses bitterness, retaining instead a profound sadness and melancholy. Contrary to the vague *mal* found in much of French film and literature, her angst has tangible causes, and she does not recoil from the task of exposing those causes. The songs and novels of this phase go beyond her personal pain and use her position as outsider to her own culture to lament the suffering and physical violence inflicted by brothers on brothers. In the acknowledgments to *Sexuality and War* she informs us, "My commitment to women and peace issues has given [the book] its main form and content, and my deep concern about oppression and injustice has marked its tone" (xi). *Coquelicot* and the songs whose texts are reprinted therein represent a poignant cry for compassion and sanity in an insane situation; her critical work accomplishes something very similar by offering suggestions for escape from the unbroken cycle of fratricide.

As we have seen in Accad's novels, pain is a recurring theme that even becomes a motivational element of the narrative. It remains clear and palpable throughout, making itself constantly felt by the reader. As a critical reader, I have always admired Accad's courage in confronting pain and suffering and her gift for communicating those feelings to the reader. The "violence dans

la douceur" that Ahlame discusses in *Blessures des mots* can be described as an unforgiving, relentless sensitivity to which Accad holds tenaciously in spite of opposition. To critics who have found her philosophy and style naïve and unrealistically utopian, she responds with a refusal to be censored and/or to remove the personal from the political, acknowledging those who understand the direct relationship between the two (e.g., "Pat Cramer corrected my manuscript and encouraged me to develop even further the personal and emotional statements that other readers had found unnecessary and distracting" [*SW,* xi]).

In point of fact, the "violence dans la douceur," the relentless sensitivity that characterizes Accad's work, reflects theories of nonviolent resistance versus passivity as they are presented in *Sexuality and War.* Accad quotes Laure Moghaïzel on nonviolence: "I am not a pacifist. I am revolted, revolted by injustices and violence. That is why I use the term *nonviolence.* There is a nuance. Pacifism is a form of passivity, which nonviolence is not. . . . Nonviolence is a struggle, and those who say struggle also say activity, dynamism. . . . It is a political action, sustained and energetic, that refuses to exercise violence" (*SW,* 37). Accad believes that "nonviolent active struggle is the only viable and hopeful strategy" (*SW,* 94). Like nonviolence, the *douceur* apparent in Accad's work is not passive but active resistance to hate, injustice, and oppression. Her sensual style and her resolute affirmation of hope become a form of nonviolent political activity; pain may sometimes temporarily disable her pen, but the silencing techniques of the order will not still it. The conclusion of *Sexuality and War* outlines succinctly the ties linking political action and writing; it clarifies once again the philosophy behind Accad's work and discloses the strength behind her gentleness: "Only a different vision, new actions, and altered relationships based on trust, recognition, and acceptance of the other can help heal the wounds and bring about the cure necessary to project a new future for Lebanon and for the world. Such a change has already started taking place with personal and political actions aimed at solving the problems rooted in oppression, domination, and the victimization of women. Writing this book has been one of these actions" (174).[7]

Ruth A. Hottell, Summer 1997

■ **WORKS CITED**

Accad, Evelyne. *Veil of Shame: The Role of Women in the Contemporary Fiction of North Africa and the Arab World.* Sherbrooke, Québec. Naaman. 1978.

———. *L'excisée.* Paris. L'Harmattan. 1982.

———. *Coquelicot du massacre.* Paris. L'Harmattan. 1988.

———. *L'Excisée.* David K. Bruner, tr. Washington, D.C. Three Continents. 1989. Reissued in 1994 as *The Excised.*

———. *Sexuality and War: Literary Masks of the Middle East.* New York. New York University Press. 1990. (*SW*)

———. *Blessures des mots: Journal de Tunisie.* Paris. Indigo & Côté-Femmes. 1993.

Cardinal, Marie. *Au pays de mes racines.* Paris. Grasset. 1980.

Duras, Marguerite. *L'amant.* Paris. Minuit. 1984.

———. *La douleur.* Paris. P.O.L. 1985.

Hottell, Ruth A. "Blinding the Other: *La Morte Amoureuse* by Théophile Gautier." *Misogyny in Literature: An Essay Collection.* Katherine Ackley, ed. New York. Garland. 1992. Pp. 183–201.

———. "The Delusory Dénouement and other Narrative Strategies in Maupassant's Fantastic Tales." *Romanic Review,* 85:4 (1994), pp. 573–85.

———. "The Diabolic Dialogic: *Les Diaboliques* by H. G. Clouzot." *Literature/Film Quarterly,* 24:3 (1996), pp. 255–60.

Kristeva, Julia. *Soleil noir: Dépression et mélancolie.* Paris. Gallimard. 1987.

———. *Etrangers à nous-mêmes.* Paris. Fayard. 1988.

———. *Strangers to Ourselves.* Leon S. Roudiez, tr. New York. Columbia University Press. 1991.

Lionnet, Françoise. *Postcolonial Representation: Women, Literature, Identity.* Ithaca, N.Y. Cornell University Press. 1995.

Palcy, Euzhan. *La Rue Cases-Nègres.* 1983.

Saadawi, Nawal El. *Woman at Point Zero.* Sherif Hetata, tr. London. Zed. 1983.

Said, Edward. *Orientalism.* New York. Pantheon. 1978.

———. *Culture and Imperialism.* New York. Random House. 1993.

[1] All translations from *Blessures des mots* are my own.

[2] All translations from Kristeva are by Leon S. Roudiez, taken from *Strangers to Ourselves.*

[3] This fear of the return of the repressed has figured as the motivating force behind much of mainstream literature and, most specifically, has provided for the entrance of the uncanny element in traditionalist fantastic literature. (See Edward Said for attempts in Occidental literature to trivialize the Oriental Other, particularly during imperialist moments of history, and Hottell for discussions of the fantastic as expressions of sexual difference and desire.)

[4] See Lionnet's succinct discussion of Accad's femihumanism and its "ethical imperative that governs their [Accad's and other authors'] search for new cultural forms and hybrid languages that better represent the particularisms of the communities about which they write, without locking them into idiosyncratic dead ends and narrow views of history" (19).

[5] Translation by David Bruner.

[6] Lionnet also attests to the power of the narrative in *L'excisée* and in Nawal El Saadawi's *Woman at Point Zero.* She heralds the two novels as "among the few fictional accounts written with moving sincerity and autobiographical details" (131). She further describes them as "a more effective and convincing denunciation than many pragmatic or political treatises because [they] allow the reader to enter into the subjective processes of the individual, to adopt her stance" (131).

[7] Research for this project was funded in part by the University of Toledo Office of Research and the Humanities Institute.

The Fiction of Hanan Al-Shaykh, Reluctant Feminist

In the fiction of the Lebanese writer Hanan Al-Shaykh, only a portion of whose work has been translated into English, women play the major roles, but only in the sense of plot and conflict. In some cases her female protagonists are more acted upon than active: the victims of an Islamic patriarchy that treats them as second-class citizens, powerless both politically and economically. Bewildered and passive, they permit themselves to drift along from event to event (and often from man to man) with little sense of fulfillment or awareness that their situations might be altered. In other instances, when they attempt to assert some kind of independent stance from male authority, it is only with a sense of reluctance— not that this is their right, but simply a matter of happenstance. It is impossible to think of her characters as committed feminists, though the mere fact that Hanan Al-Shaykh herself painstakingly describes the situations that entrench women within the contemporary Islamic world implies that she herself identifies her role as that of a reluctant spokesperson for change in women's lives.

Hanan Al-Shaykh's career as an Arabic writer has been shaped both by her own rather peripatetic life (including the obstacles she has encountered in publishing individual works), coupled with the rigidity of her traditional upbringing in Lebanon. She was raised in a strict Shiite Moslem household, in which she covered her hair and wore full-length dresses with long sleeves. Beginning in 1963, she studied in Cairo at the American College for Girls. She worked as a journalist after her return to Beirut four years later. With her husband, she moved to Saudi Arabia for a year, followed by a return to Lebanon (at the beginning of the war) and then a subsequent move to London. Her four novels and a collection of short stories—all published in Beirut—have encountered frequent censorship in other Islamic countries. *The Story of Zahra* (her first novel translated into English) was sufficiently troubling to Lebanese publishers that she published it herself.

Perhaps the metaphor that best typifies the conflict between the male and female worlds in Al-Shaykh's writing is the unknowable. Too many of her male characters act as predators, stalking women because they know little about them: sexually, emotionally, mentally. Others merely endure the situation in which they find themselves, demonstrating little or no curiosity about the opposite sex. In a two-page story called "The Unseeing Eye" an old man searches for his wife in a hospital the day after she has had a heart attack. First he is told that he cannot enter her ward, "because there are other women there,"[1] a remark that reveals the context of the problem. When he tells the nurse his wife's name, he is informed, "There are two women called Zeinab Mohamed. One of them, though, has only one eye. Which one is your wife so that I can call her?" (148). The question throws the old man into a state of confusion.

> One eye? How am I to know? He tried to recall what his wife [of thirty or forty years] looked like, with her long gown and black headdress, the veil, and sometimes the black covering enveloping her face and sometimes removed and lying on her neck. He could picture her as she walked and sat, chewing a morsel and then taking it out of her mouth so as to place it in that of her first-born. Her children. One eye. How am I to know? (148).

Somehow one feels that the old man's wife (one-eyed or two-eyed) perceives far more about her husband than he has ever known of her.

In *The Story of Zahra*—certainly a major work of Middle Eastern fiction—the situation is even more unsettling. In this novel, set both in Lebanon and in Africa, women are depicted as extraneous, as not fitting in, as mere pawns of the men around them. Their lives are precarious, always in such flux and in such control by men that they are little more than victims. The men themselves, however, are ineffectual, sexually repressed, spineless spouses, perhaps because of their pampered and favored status. Needless to say, there are no positive male-female relationships, nor is there a hint that there can be until women are no longer oppressed.

Zahra herself is directionless. While still young, she enters into a lengthy affair with a married man, which provides her with no genuine satisfaction. After two abortions, she decides to join her uncle Hashem, a political refugee who has fled to Africa. The move appears to be precipitated only by her desire to try a change of venue, since she herself is basically apolitical. Unfortunately, Hashem in his frustration turns toward Zahra, whom he regards as the personification of his lost motherland. Though she repeatedly thwarts his sexual advances, she is propelled into a loveless marriage and immediately denounced by her husband because she is not a virgin. Zahra's sexual encounters take one final permutation after she returns to Lebanon, now in a state of war. For reasons that initially make little sense to her, she gives herself freely to a sniper, once again becoming pregnant and trapped by the possibility of motherhood.

Almost at the end of the narrative the story takes an unusual turn both thematically and structurally. Zahra informs the sniper that she is pregnant, only to encounter the typical masculine response: get an abor-

tion. However, her lover shortly changes his stance and implies that he will marry her. The thought of legitimacy makes her momentarily believe that the war has ended, but then as she leaves him (and the rooftop where they have held their clandestine meetings), she feels such excruciating pain that she believes she is suffering a miscarriage or—worse—that her sniper/lover has shot her. Whichever it is, she lies in the street, blood draining from her body.

> The pain is terrible, but I grow accustomed to it, and to the darkness. As I close my eyes for an instant, I see the stars of pain. Then there are rainbows arching across white skies. He kills me. He kills me with the bullets that lay at his elbow as he made love to me. He kills me, and the white sheets that covered me a little while ago are still crumpled from my presence. Does he kill me because I'm pregnant? Or is it because I asked him whether he was a sniper? It's as if someone tugs at my limbs. Should I call out one more time, 'Please help!'[2]

Miscarriage or bullet, it hardly matters, since the result is the same: her continued plight as a woman at the pursuit of many men.

In the last sentence of the novel Zahra's thoughts juxtapose the horror of her situation with the beauty of transcendence: "I see rainbows processing [sic?] towards me across the white skies with their promises only of menace" (184). The war metaphor has been fused with male aggression. Wars kill, but so do men. The difference is inconsequential. Women are still victims, and it makes little difference what one wants to call it. Moreover, the fallacy of having a first-person narrator relate her own death (the "I am dying, I am dead" violation) is totally convincing within the context of the novel's ending.

Interestingly, there is a possible source for Zahra's sexual indecisiveness regarding the men in her life. The opening scenes of the story describe her mother's multiple liaisons with men who are not her husband, encounters perceived by Zahra as a child, since her mother drags her along in order to help conceal these activities. The purpose of these scenes is not to suggest that Zahra is like her mother (they are worlds apart) as much as to establish a cycle of repetition within the family (and perhaps the culture) itself. As one reviewer wrote of the novel, "Rarely can the family life of Islam have been portrayed in such an unattractive light."[3]

This depiction of a Moslem family with no sense of cohesiveness (and the mother's adultery) is apparently the primary reason for the novel's being banned in several Islamic countries. Zahra's father is portrayed as a tyrant with little control over his wife's promiscuity.

Zahra is ever fearful of him. Her brother Ahmad is little more than a spoiled lout. The attention lavished on him as a child manifests itself in his adulthood in his addiction to hashish, masturbation, and stolen goods (often stripped from the bodies of the dead). The war, in short, serves him well. He lives on other people's miseries, though he is certainly one of the sources of misery (or menace) in Zahra's immediate world.

The wonder of Hanan Al-Shaykh's novel ultimately resides in Zahra herself, ever controlled by the people around her (initially her mother, father, and brother; followed by her various lovers; and finally the war itself, represented by her sniper/lover). So convincing is the narrative that the reader feels the immediacy of autobiography, yet with all the frustration that can only be conveyed by a failed life. One hazards to guess how many other Zahras populate Al-Shaykh's homeland, how much of their story has been told in this raw account of one woman's inability to step outside the circle of contempt.

That continuing circle also begs the question of for whom *The Story of Zahra* was written—Al-Shaykh's own Lebanese people, a wider Muslim audience, or one outside the Islamic world? Posing such a question often places the critic (especially the Western critic of non-Western literature) on dangerous ground. The answer, however, belies Al-Shaykh's dilemma as a woman novelist within an Arabic context, faithfully attempting to write of the world as she knows it. Her subject matter quite naturally becomes that of women in a patriarchy, and that alone can often guarantee a limited readership in many areas of the Third World. This is not to imply that Arabic fiction is devoid of male writers who expound women's rights. One thinks immediately of Zohra in Naguib Mahfouz's *Miramar* (and wonders at the similarity of their names) or Hamida in his *Midaq Alley*. Recalling the years that Hanan Al-Shaykh spent as a student in Cairo, it is impossible not to assume some kind of kinship between the two writers' works.

Women of Sand and Myrrh, Al-Shaykh's fifth published book and her second translated into English, would not seem so disturbing were it not for the fact that four female characters dominate the narrative, quadrupling the bleakness of *The Story of Zahra*. The setting is an Arab country somewhere in the Gulf, most probably Saudi Arabia, where Al-Shaykh lived for a time with her husband. The four women referred to in the title of the English version represent differing perspectives and degrees of entrapment within the patriarchal order, though often the confinement is more figurative than literal.

The first of these is Suha, who, along with her husband, is in flight from the war in Lebanon. Well educat-ed, she is what would be regarded as a career woman if the setting were not so conservative. Tamr, the second, is largely self-educated, twice divorced, and diligently struggling for survival as a seamstress. The third, Suzanne, is a middle-aged American housewife, no longer attractive to her husband but sought after by Arab men. Nur, the last, is rich and spoiled, an international playgirl when she is away from the Arabic world. The lives of these four characters are only loosely intertwined. The story itself is plotless, connected thematically by images and incidents of repression that control both the men and the women within an ultraconservative society.

If Al-Shaykh's picture of life in an Islamic gulf state is accurate, it then becomes a question of who is fooling whom. The activities of both the men and the women in this novel are dominated by sex, liquor, and videos—not the sand and the myrrh of the English title but rather what can be imported, especially in the form of consumer goods. Air-conditioners, telephones, and swimming pools (whatever money can buy)—all these material objects are vehicles for escaping the traditional world. One is left with the impression of a medieval society that has been transported into the modern world. When all else fails, the government can resort to censorship and repression.

Suha responds to the loss of the freedom she knew in Lebanon by frequently hiding herself in a packing box in the department store where she works. (Zahra, it might be noted, was forever hiding in bathrooms, the one place apparently off limits to her male pursuers.) Suha pleads with her husband to leave the country, to take her away. "I'll go mad. I could accept life in the fighting, but not this," she tells him.[4] She cannot stand the stultifying atmosphere; she constantly states that she is miserable. At the end of the novel, as she is about to return to Lebanon without her husband, Suha notes the literal barriers that have restricted her activities during her symbolic imprisonment in the gulf.

> As if I had just arrived I noticed the walls; every house had a different wall, made of marble, cement, natural stone like the stone you see in the mountains: tiles, factory-made stones, patterned and plain; there was a wall that took the form of a series of arches, so high that only the water storage tank was visible. New young branches were tied to one wall to give them support; electricity cables and telephone cables dangled down from another: no building, nothing in this place, was ever completely finished. The walls were high; the newer they were, the higher they seemed to be . . . walls constricting everybody. (278)

If Suha's education helps her only marginally, Tamr's lack of schooling restricts her in numerous other ways. The closest character to mere chattel, Tamr is married when she is twelve. That "marriage" ends in divorce, as does a second one lasting but a month. Though she eventually learns to read and write—in preparation for starting her business as a seamstress—she still finds herself hampered in every direction. Men have the authority to close down her shop; she has no true home of her own (as a divorcee, she is largely restricted to her brother's household); the inheritance from her father has not been left to her but instead passed on to her son. When she attempts to take economic matters into her own hands and enters a bank, she is told, "You're not allowed to come in" (104). As she remarks on one occasion apropos of the difficulty of starting even a modest business, "I didn't remember signing my name on a single official document in my life" (105). She is, in short, a woman with no rights at all, a nonperson.

Suha hides in a packing box and ultimately escapes the claustrophobic atmosphere by leaving the country, Tamr is under symbolic house arrest within her brother's family, but Suzanne (as a Western woman) has little denied to her—at least as long as Arabic men find her attractive. She represents for them all that has been denied sexually. Since she wears no veil or restrictive clothing and enjoys freedom of movement and availability, it is no surprise that men follow her like a bitch in heat. These perks (if one wants to consider them that) initially make her feel as if she is the only woman in the world—not exactly a feminist goal. As she wryly comments:

> It wasn't difficult to find men. The men in their white robes searched for women among the freezers and food-stuffs in the supermarkets. They tailed foreigners and car passengers who weren't wearing veils. As they walked along the street they stole glances at the gates of houses just in case a woman going in behind the high walls gave them a smile: telephone and electricity workers and private gardeners were the worst offenders. (213)

Suzanne is in sexual heaven—or so she believes for a time. She even considers becoming the second wife of her lover, an alcoholic businessman, who can indulge his own sexual fantasies by trips overseas, where even more attractive women are readily available. In the end, however, sex becomes Suzanne's downfall. She fears that she will be apprehended for her indiscretions and deported. The last time she visits Maaz, her lover, she nearly retches at the sight of the poor man's newborn syphilitic child. If that is what sexual liberation leads to, then it is time for her to leave the gulf also.

Of Al-Shaykh's fourth character, Nur, little need be said. Great wealth has brought her no more happiness

than the others. Overseas, like her masculine counterparts, she is able to indulge herself freely, at least until her husband hears of her activities and takes away her passport. At home there are brief affairs with both men and women. In one of the final images the author presents of her, Nur is dressed as a man, coming to visit Suha, with whom she has had an earlier liaison. Is this the ultimate freedom of an Arabic woman: assuming the identity (sexual or otherwise) of a man?

The men in *Women of Sand and Myrrh* are a faceless lot, except for Suzanne's lover Maaz. Otherwise, they are best typified as controlling forces (or menaces, as in the author's earlier novel). Tamr refers to them as "traps set ready for [women]" (152). On one occasion when Suha goes swimming, she watches a man nearly drown, so concerned is he with the impropriety of viewing the seminaked bathing women. Suha's husband seems oblivious to her complaints about life in the gulf and much more concerned with watching videos. Nur's first husband is bisexual. Maaz, however, has the final word on male-female relationships. As he tells Suzanne after she has had the audacity to enjoy herself in bed with him, "God created you to bear children, and to give pleasure to a man, and that's all" (210). When she says she does not understand what he means, he replies, "God created women to make children, like a factory. That's the exact word, Suzanne. She's a factory, she produces enjoyment for the man, not for herself" (210).

It is not only sexuality that restricts the women in Al-Shaykh's novel, though many of the restraints apply to one gender only. Suha complains to Tamr, "There's no freedom here. You can't play tennis, go to the cinema, go for walks. There's no entertainment" (96). Newspapers and magazines are censored: advertisements with scantily clad women are excised from them. Western music is referred to as "the work of the devil" (35). Playing cards are illegal. The stuffed toys and dolls that were shipped to the store where Suha worked for a time "had [to be] destroyed, every one that was meant to be a human being or animal or bird, since it was not permissible to produce distortions of God's creatures" (13).

Are all these incidents in *Women of Sand and Myrrh* a challenge to traditional Islam? When I asked Hanan Al-Shaykh that question, she responded:

> Of course not. I have never thought only of religion when I was writing [*Women of Sand and Myrrh*]. I knew that I wanted to open a curtain on a way of living which is part of the Middle East and yet different. This closed atmosphere attracted me and became juicy material for my imagination . . . for the unusual daily life there which carries many social problems, tempted me to write about my feelings. That women are still op-

pressed, etc . . . Even when I write [about] what appears to be Islamic behaviour, it is really more under the domain of social habits—which don't relate to the true teaching of Islamic societies.[5]

Nevertheless, Al-Shaykh adds that her second novel ("The Praying Mantis," yet to be translated into English) shows "how a young girl who belongs to a pious religious family can suffer!!"

It seems proper to conclude that what Al-Shaykh means by her answer to my question—and what her fiction clearly demonstrates—is the condition of exploitation that women in certain areas of the Moslem world experience. I would call this exposé spontaneous feminism without the more familiar dogma of some of her Western counterparts. Without that rhetoric, her writing soars above the commonplace. Certainly it is only a matter of time before her dialogue with the Islamic patriarchy is no longer one-sided.

Charles R. Larson, Winter 1991

[1] Hanan Al-Shaykh, "The Unseeing Eye," Denys Johnson-Davies, tr., in *Storia 2,* 1989, p. 148.

[2] Hanan Al-Shaykh, *The Story of Zahra,* Peter Ford, tr., London, Quartet, 1986, p. 183.

[3] Robert Irwin, "On the Treadwheel," *Times Literary Supplement,* 16 May 1986, p. 535.

[4] Hanan Al-Shaykh, *Women of Sand and Myrrh,* Catherine Cobham, tr., London, Quartet, 1989, p. 34.

[5] Hanan Al-Shaykh to the author, in a letter posted (but not dated) 10 March 1990.

SYRIA

Recent Trends in Syrian Drama

As a distinct genre designed to be performed by actors onstage and according to certain theatrical conventions, drama has no historical roots in the Arab world. Despite the popularity of the shadow play and the storyteller for over seven centuries, they did not contribute to the rise of Syrian drama; the modern founders—Marun al-Naqash (1817–55), Salim Marun al-Naqash (d. 1884), Khalil Qabani (1833–1902), and others—wrote plays in the Western vein. Though Arab drama originated in Syria around 1850, it did not live long enough to mature and take root. In this article I intend to survey the rejuvenation of Syrian theatre in the last two decades and its contribution to the rise of interest in playwriting. Plays by five contemporary Syrian dramatists will be analyzed to point out their genres, modes, and techniques, and their social, political, and ideological import.

Drama and theatre in Syria remained in a dormant state until the 1950s, gaining strength in the early 1960s, when the Ministry of Culture established official theatres. Such troupes as the National Theatre, the Itinerant Theatre, and the Military Theatre are subsidized and supervised by the government.

During the early years of the establishment of official theatres, Syrian directors—Western- or Arab-trained—were preoccupied with the production of Western masterpieces. Among the sixty-one plays that the National Theatre staged from 1961 to 1972, forty were Western and the rest were written by Egyptian or other Arab dramatists. Obviously, the production of plays such as *King Lear, Life Is a Dream, School for Scandal, Ghosts, The Glass Menagerie, Tartuffe, Death of a Salesman,* and *The Visit* appealed to Syrian intellectuals, college students, and the elites, not to the average Syrian. However, the rapid social and political changes that swept Syria and the Arab world in the early 1950s gave rise to plays inspired mostly by those changes and their underlying national and political ideologies. The growing number of Syrian plays portraying the lives and experiences of Syrians and Arabs has attracted middle-class people and workers to the theatre. As a result, at the beginning of the 1970s the production of Western plays gave way to the staging of more Syrian and Arab works.

Among the most prolific playwrights whose dramas have been produced and have caught the imagination of Syrian spectators since the early sixties, one can mention Mustafa al-Halaj, Hassib Kaiali, Ali Uqla Ursan, Sadala Wanus, and Walid Ikhlasi. Due to space limitations, playwrights such as Farhan Bulbil, Riad Usmat, Mamduh Adwan, Mohamad Al-Maqhout, and others are excluded here.

Mustafa al-Halaj was first known as a short story writer. In the 1960s he took to playwriting and has since published six full-length plays and several short ones, all focused on the question of freedom and justice in the social and political arenas. The influence of existentialism is evident in most of his plays. "Killing and Regret" (1957) shows the Tunisian revolt against the French mandate. The hero kills several French soldiers, reaches a moment of regret, loses faith in the revolution, then reviews his past attitudes and makes new choices. Thus he develops along an existential line: through awareness of his past, he makes the choice to transcend it and proves he is a free individual.

Al-Halaj's reputation has often been associated with "A Special Night Festival for Dresden" (1970) and "Dervishes in Search of Truth" (1970). These two plays, unlike most Syrian stage works, have a broad human interest. In "A Special Night Festival" Al-Halaj focuses on the destruction of the beautiful city of Dresden by the Allies and the loss of human lives during the Nazi era. He sets his play in a basement where people of different classes are trapped and have no other choice but to face an inevitable death. The basement symbolizes the city, which turned into a grave for thousands of people.

"A Special Night Festival for Dresden" is a drama without action. The war is presented as an insurmountable devastation about which the characters can do nothing but react helplessly. The conflict has already determined their fate. This state of helplessness makes the characters think of the past, reminisce about the war, and reflect upon its motivations and consequences. Thus the play rewrites the history of Dresden to disclose the underlying motivations and to reveal the actual forces that were responsible for the war. The question of human responsibility is the backbone of this drama. Though it considers the war the work of capitalists and the military, it holds the working class no less responsible for not taking any action before hostilities broke out. The play, in general, points out that we are all responsible for whatever happens to our world.

In "Dervishes in Search of Truth" Al-Halaj posits the question of freedom and responsibility as the essence of human existence. Darwish, the protagonist, is an innocent man thrown in jail and later charged with plotting against the ruling order. For a while he rejects the charges, but he gradually finds out that there is no room for innocence in the real world. As he learns more about himself in relation to others, he identifies with the image that others have assigned him. He turns what was forced on him into a consciously chosen identity.

Al-Halaj presents Darwish as an intellectual whose nature is not totally determined by class or heredity. Regardless of his social affiliation, Darwish is able to free himself of his past and project himself into a future of his choice. This choice, however, occurs in a historical context, so the individual can only select from among the possibilities available in a given situation.

The name Darwish has two meanings: the first recalls an Islamic sect that searched for truth inwardly and remained aloof from any social and political involvement; the second, which is relatively new, symbolizes the poor and the deprived. The play makes clear that there is no room for neutrality. Man is doomed to make choices that serve to change both himself and the world of which he is part. "Dervishes" calls for the integration of the individual into the whole. The "other" is not hell, and Darwish realizes the truth about himself through others. He finds out that what has happened to him could happen to millions like him; no one can change the world alone, without others.

The prominent playwright and director Ali Uqla Ursan has headed the National Theatre for a number of years and has directed and produced several works. In "The Night Visitors" (1965), the first of his seven published plays, Ursan discloses the destructive nature of traditional marriage, how it dehumanizes both men and women. Ahmad, the protagonist, is in love with Hind, but he cannot marry her for a number of social reasons. When Hind's brother discovers that his sister is pregnant, he murders her. Ahmad, who later marries Sauad, develops guilt feelings and lives a restless life, haunted by the specter of Hind. He finally breaks with Sauad and follows the ghost of his beloved.

In "The Night Visitors" Ursan explores the contradiction between the genuine inner world of his hero and the masks that the social world assigns to him. The discrepancy between the realm of conscience and that of tradition lies at the core of the dramatic action. As in French symbolist drama, Ursan stresses the authenticity of inner spiritual feelings as opposed to the inauthenticity of socially derived values. Following the symbolist approach, he objectifies whatever is subjective—that is, he reveals Ahmad's concealed and turbulent emotions in the guise of a ghost chasing him at night and urging him to be honest with his feelings for his murdered beloved. Thus the play's action fluctuates between the world of dreams and that of reality in order to disclose the true nature of Ahmad's character.

In "The Old Man and the Road" (1971) Uqla sets out to discover the roots of sociopolitical disorder. His world is split into conflicting classes and bickering ideological groups representing the division and disunity among Arab countries. The four main characters, who espouse different ideologies, are always on a road that symbolizes the course of history and are in constant search for ways to solve the problems that plague their world. The Old Man, who has never stopped working, is still poor. He believes that his poverty is determined by luck and that no one can do anything about it. Jaser opposes the Old Man's philosophy, asserting that whatever happens to people is the outcome of actual social conditions that can be identified, studied, and changed. Abdou is a romantic rebel caught in the web of abstraction. The Prince, who clashes with these characters, is rich and has the support of the establishment. At the end, Jaser confronts the Prince and the establishment and wins several peasants to his side.

"The Old Man and the Road" thus attacks deterministic and abstract beliefs that often keep people from understanding their oppressive conditions and block them from working toward change. The process of social change is contingent upon the concerted efforts of the oppressed, the deprived, and the intellectuals. The play shows the political movements of the Arab world as embroiled in ideological controversies instead of standing united against the oppressive forces of society.

Uqla has always been interested in situations that encompass the collective. Even when he focuses on the individual's predicament, as in "The Masks" (1979), his primary concern is to explore the whole through the part. "The Masks" portrays a world gradually turning into a jail guarded by state police. Anis, the protagonist, is an intellectual who was involved in the war of liberation and is still trying to carry out his revolutionary mission in a world whose people are alienated, oppressed, and indifferent to everything but survival. After the war is over, he comes home to learn that his wife has been carrying on affairs with different men and now refuses to recognize him as her husband. As he talks politics with some men, he is harassed by the secret police, who put him in a jail surrounded by houses inhabited by masked people.

Anis's cell occupies the center of the play and is constantly tightening, keeping him out of touch with the people, who are themselves reduced to masks. Most of the characters wear masks, which they change according to the changing conditions. Ursan uses the masks to designate the loss of self and the erosion of human communication. They have turned these men into mere observers, incapable of taking any action against whatever happens to their world.

The sixties also witnessed the plays of Hassib Kaiali. He started out as a short-story writer, but during his stay in Paris he made the acquaintance of Jean Vilar, attended Vilar's theatrical workshops and rehearsals, and subsequently wrote more than fifteen full-length and short comedies and social dramas. The focus of Kaiali's plays, except those that deal with political issues, is the relationship between men and women. Even the works that explore intellectual questions have subplots revolving around love and marriage.

"The Carpenter's Daughter" (1968) takes its story line, characters, and framework from an Arabian tale. Its socially relevant philosophical thesis explores the dichotomy between creativity and life or the relation of life to creativity. The major plot alternates with two related subplots, and the characters all suffer from boredom and sterility. The principal plot line involves a barren woman who asks her husband, the carpenter, to make her a wooden doll. Both dream of the doll's producing embroidery that will make them famous and wealthy. The carpenter's scenes fuse with others centering on Arjwan, a jinn prince, and his sister Zumurda. The prince has fallen ill at the loss of his girlfriend but gradually recovers as he takes to writing poetry; his sis-

ter becomes involved in making embroidery, which she delivers to the carpenter's house. Parallel scenes portray the king, Al-Aldin, who falls in love with the maker of the embroidery. When Zumurda realizes that Al-Aldin is in love with the wooden doll, which he hasn't seen, she takes on the form of the doll and marries him.

Kaiali holds that life has no meaning or significance unless it is fused with the world of imagination. The carpenter and his wife find in the doll a means to rise above their familiar world. It is the contrived doll that makes their life livable. Zumurda, though a supernatural being, makes embroidery in order to get closer to the world of human beings. By nature, she belongs to the realm of imagination and lacks the domain of human life. To achieve her dream, she merges her supernatural origin with the natural world. Kaiali's ideal realm is always torn between the real and the unreal. It seeks their constant fusion.

The play draws heavily on the fictional techniques of the storyteller, for at the end of every scene a character relates a fragment of what will occur in the next in order to establish a kind of continuity. Furthermore, many of the events are narrated rather than acted out, in keeping with the oral tradition from which the work derives.

In 1978 Kaiali wrote "The Sultan and the Shepherdess," a play modeled after "The Carpenter's Daughter" and again a dramatization of an Arabian folktale. As in the earlier work, the characters are drawn from opposite ends of the social spectrum, royalty and the poor, which are ultimately united by the bond of love. Again, in order for love to be consummated, productivity is essential.

"The Sultan and the Shepherdess" is traditional in form: that is, the first few scenes serve as exposition, establishing atmosphere and identifying the setting, the characters, and their objectives. In the middle portion a crisis arises as the shepherdess refuses to marry the sultan for not having a craft. The sultan learns rug weaving and marries the shepherdess, but then a surprise crops up, throwing the disguised sultan and his minister into the hands of an evil butcher, who decides to kill them and sell their meat. The sultan proposes to weave a rug that the butcher can sell to the royal family for forty thousand dollars. As the butcher takes the rug to the castle, the queen recognizes the sultan's seal on the rug. She orders her guards to arrest the butcher and save the sultan and his minister.

"The Sultan and the Shepherdess" possesses the characteristics of both melodrama and thesis play. The essential ingredients of the former are evident in the innocent, clever hero and heroine, whose happiness the villainous butcher tries to destroy. The unexpected denouement demonstrates that good always triumphs over evil, and the hero and heroine are reunited. Similarly, one can spot the basic structure of a thesis play: from the outset, the notion of "survival through a craft" is established and emphasized, and plot complication and the development of events are geared to illustrate the thesis, prove its validity, and make the hero (who was not aware of its significance) recognize it as a fact of life.

In both "The Sultan and the Shepherdess" and "The Carpenter's Daughter" Kaiali portrays love as a force that can break down the barriers between social classes. Love alone, however, is not able to create a successful relationship. Kaiali sees the survival of love and marriage as contingent upon the involvement of both men and women in productive activity. His ideal woman is always one who pursues a career and embodies a self-made personality.

In the late 1960s the effort to minimize Western influence and maximize national roots and national identity prompted many playwrights to search for dramatic elements in Syria's ancient heritage. Thus the shadow play and the storyteller found their way into modern Syrian drama. Sadala Wanus and Walid Ikhlasi were the first to unearth and employ local motifs in their plays. Wanus, now regarded throughout the Arab world as Syria's most innovative playwright, is credited with the invention of what is called "political theatre." Like Richard Schechner in the United States, Wanus believes that "the origin of theatre lies in the unison of actor and spectator in a kind of ritualistic or social gathering." He argues that the barrier between the auditorium and the stage should be removed and that the theatrical event must occur either before or within the spectators' space of movement.

Only in his later plays, especially "A Joyous Party for June 5th" (1968), does Wanus use some of the theatrical devices he developed and illustrated in his theory of political theatre. Ignoring linear chronology and traditional plot, he presents events, experiences, and ideas relating to the 1967 war. Despite the disconnected and improvisational nature of the individual scenes, their social and political relevance generate a cohesive impression in the mind of the beholder familiar with the implications of the 1967 conflict. The action occurs both on the stage and in the audience, where Wanus seats some of his actors. Whenever a discussion grows heated onstage, it draws reaction from the actors in the auditorium; as the stage-actor/audience-actor dialogue intensifies, members of the "real" audience loosen up and get in on the discussion. Through this process and the free movement of actors between stage and auditori-

um, Wanus is able to make people relax and encourage their participation in the performance.

Wanus has also made use of the storyteller's technique. The storyteller is a very popular figure in Syria, usually a pleasant, witty old man who frequents cafés to spin tales as a means of earning a living. In an attempt to create a familiar social and physical atmosphere, Wanus sets the events of "The Adventures of Jaber's Head" (1970) in a café, a place frequented by Syrian men. The storyteller narrates part of his tale, then enacts the rest along with other actors. This performance before the café's customers creates a play within a play, and members of the theatre audience become extensions of the café's customers, not via participation in the events, but rather through objective observation.

"The Adventures of Jaber's Head" is a history play depicting an ancient Arab era fraught with political unrest, disorder, and power struggles, a critical exploration of a past whose consequences are still felt in the Arab world today. Wanus points out that whatever happens to people is essentially the outcome of political conditions, and the prospects of change are contingent upon their attitude toward the existing situation. In such a world, innocence, purity, and neutrality always lead to more human frustration, alienation, and destruction. The process of change requires a collective effort armed with political consciousness.

Wanus's interest in interpreting history, this time through a Marxist perspective, is most evident in his last play, "The King Is the King" (1978), which takes its plot from "The Sleeper and the Waker," a tale in *A Thousand and One Nights*. The caliph Al-Rashid and his guard Mansrur roam Baghdad disguised as merchants. As Al-Rashid is walking around, he remembers Abu Al-hassan, who frequently stated that if he ruled the country for one day only, he would right whatever was wrong. Abu Al-hassan is taken to the castle and crowned as the new caliph. However, he fails to accomplish his dream.

Wanus has modified the tale by adding new characters and events in order to make it more universally relevant. The rule of Al-Rashid is stripped of its particularity and presented as a phenomenon whose nature derives from the growing self-interest of an entire class. Thus, whether Al-Rashid is replaced by Abu Al-hassan or by someone else, nothing changes; it is the social class that determines the course of events, not the individual ruler.

The play also stresses the fact that since the emergence of private ownership, people have experienced alienation. People are no longer themselves; they play roles and wear masks. Hence the play is full of masquerading and role playing. All the characters are players hiding their real selves behind a series of masks. In casting his play in the form of a game, Wanus lessens the likelihood that his audience will identify with the depicted events rather than observing them and understanding their nature and development. To keep his audience from empathizing with the characters, he destroys the illusion of reality and stresses the sense of being in a theatre. He narrates events, uses placards to describe scenes, has actors address the audience directly, and makes characters dismantle scenes without blackouts. All these techniques are of course drawn from the epic theatre, with which Wanus is undoubtedly familiar.

Walid Ikhlasi's name is associated with literary experimentation.* The volume of his dramatic output is staggering, and his plays are characterized by unprecedented thematic and dramatic diversity. Ikhlasi, like Wanus, experiments with various Syrian and Arab dramatic modes, including the storyteller, the shadow play, and Islamic rituals. His work also reflects a wide range of human concerns and a variety of artistic expressions, conjoining such genres as tragedy, tragicomedy, mystery, epic drama, and the theatre of the absurd.

Ikhlasi has written several episodic plays that are inspired by the storyteller and the shadow play. "The Straight Path" (1976), for example, owes much to the shadow play, which has held its own as a popular form of entertainment in Syria and in the Islamic world since the thirteenth century. The play echoes a revolt against Western dramatic forms, departing from the linearity of most Western drama and abandoning the law of cansality for an episodic structure with incidents that move in irregular curves and with little logical sequence.

"The Straight Path" explores the relationship between the artist and the state—the contradiction between the artist's free commitment to his art and the cause of justice, on the one hand, and his feeling of being forced to serve the state, on the other. The artist-protagonist, an actor, attempts honestly to live up to his principles, but the pressures exerted on him by social and governmental institutions force him to play roles not of his own choosing. Realizing that his career serves the ruling class rather than a just cause, the actor develops guilt feelings and finds himself stuck on the Syrian border, where he can neither practice his art nor escape into exile. Here Ikhlasi calls for an art independent of the state and more indicative of the artist's free perception of reality. The artist's commitment to a cause, in Ikhlasi's eyes, remains essentially a matter of individual choice and not something imposed on him from outside.

Most Syrian playwrights have been dealing with issues of social, political, and national relevance. Ikhlasi, in plays such as "Oedipus" (1978) and "Garden Song" (1979), has tackled problems of a strictly humanistic and philosophical nature. In "Oedipus" he argues that certain primeval forces are still functioning in disguise in the midst of a world remote from super-stitions and dominated by scientific thinking and achievements. As in Greek tragedy, Ikhlasi's protagonist Suffian asserts that he is the master of his life and future. He subjects everything to the laws of reason and logic. At the end his proclaimed free will, his infatuation with reason, and his determination lead him to find himself a plaything of fate. Like the Greek heroes, he experiences the darkest sides of human existence; he faces defeat but also gains knowledge of himself. The play is not an attack against science or reason; it only criticizes the reductionist view that subjects complex human phenomena to purely scientific or rationalistic analyses.

A similar issue crops up in "Garden Song," which deals with original sin and the fall of man and also poses the age-old dilemma of free will versus predestination. The play focuses on a family in which the father is challenged by the son. This unexpected mutiny drives the father to expel his son from the fold. The latter suffers as a result of the eviction from his father's garden, but he also succeeds in achieving both material and spiritual success. His dream, however, remains that of returning to the garden.

Ikhlasi's vision of man's fall is neither strictly idealistic nor purely materialistic. He sees three forces as inherent in the very being of man. Though at variance, these opposed forces (body or matter, spirit, and reason) are merged in man. The hero's initial violation of the father's will demonstrates that he has the potential for making free choices. Ikhlasi shows man as the source of his own salvation and damnation. He also argues that no matter how man is conditioned by matter, he always strives to rise above its limitations. Man is seen as an unfinished project whose completion is the ultimate aim of his attempt to transcend his own existence and rise toward a higher being.

In these past two decades, during which Syrian playwrights and directors have been engaged in exploration and experimentation with both Western and Arab dramatic forms, dramatic literature and theatre have become essential parts of modern Syrian culture. More plays are being written and produced, and more people are being attracted to the theatre. Some playwrights still write plays along Western lines, whereas others have moved toward indigenous forms. This attempt to integrate Western and Arab approaches, one would like to think, may well lead to the development of forms more expressive of Syrian and Arab culture.

Admer Gouryh, Spring 1986

*See Admer Gouryh. "The Fictional World of Walid Ikhlasi," WLT 58:1 (Winter 1984), pp. 23–27.

The Silences of Contemporary Syrian Literature

■ IS THERE A SYRIAN LITERATURE?

There is, of course, no such thing as Syrian literature. Certainly, citizens of the modern nation-state of Syria write literature, but to claim that "Syrian literature" exists in the same way that, say, Russian literature or German literature exists is misleading. First, it implies that there is a language called Syrian. Syrian literature is, for the most part, written in Arabic and is part of a literary family that includes all literature written in Arabic. Second, anyone familiar with the Middle East will be quick to point out that "Syria" itself is a complicated label. From ancient times until the early twentieth century, the term has been used loosely to describe a region that, in addition to the land defined by the borders of Syria today, included historical Palestine and the area of modern Lebanon (which two places also had their own names), Jordan, and the northwestern parts of the Fertile Crescent (now belonging to Turkey). Syria's present borders were carved out of the former Ottoman Empire by Britain and France in the Sykes-Picot agreement of 1916 in a manner corresponding, not with local goals or sensibilities, but with the imperialist interests of European powers. This turns out to be not that unusual for Syria, a strategic crossroads frequently fought over by powerful neighbors. Its periods of independence, whether in its modern borders or larger ones such as those of the Damascus-based Arabo-Muslim Umayyad Empire, have alternated with periods when Syria was a province or cluster of provinces included in a larger empire ruled by people based elsewhere: Assyrians of Mesopotamia (who probably gave Syria its name), Pharaonic Egyptians, Persians, Greeks, Romans, Byzantines, and, in the Islamic era, the Abbasids of Baghdad and the Ottomans of Anatolia—to name but a few.

Syria has not, historically speaking, had a great deal of ethnic homogeneity; a vast number of ethnic groups have comprised this region's population. Syria has also been a place where many religions and religious sects have been born and have flourished, skirmished, and lived as neighbors. The majority of the people of Syria today are Arab; a Syrian may also be Kurdish, Armenian, Circassian, Chechen, Daghestani, Turkish, Jewish, Assyrian. Sunni Islam is the majority religion, and Syrians are also Christian (Greek Orthodox, Catholic, Maronite, Church of the East, and others), Druze, Ismaili, Alawi, and Jewish. One constant from ancient to modern times is that the cities situated along a north-south axis in its interior—Aleppo, Hama, Homs, Damascus—have always formed the inner core of whatever was designated as Syria (Meisami, 746). Eastward-turned, desert-facing ports of overland trade, they form a strip parallel to the westward-facing ports of the sea—Latakia, Banias, Tartus—on Syria's slender coastal plain. This central strip extends on the southwestern end to the Hauran plateau and the cities of Suweida and Bosra (nearing Irbid, Amman, and Nablus), and at the other, northeastern corner, it includes the Euphrates-watered Jazira region in the northeast and joins with Iraq to form, altogether, the Fertile Crescent. The Syrian Desert, with its oasis cities such as Palmyra, rounds out the area traditionally known as Syria.

What purpose does it serve, aside from that of an unbecoming and narrow Syrian chauvinism, to speak of Syrian literature? It is helpful, here, to point briefly to Egyptian, Palestinian, and Lebanese literatures by comparison. As in the Syrian case, each of these literatures is intrinsically part of the Arabic cultural world. Yet no one disputes the fact that "modern Egyptian literature" makes sense as a category that enriches our appreciation of the works therein considered. The soundness of gathering the literature of Egypt into one sheaf is as self-evident as the Nile. (Is there an Egyptian novel without the Nile running through it?) Geography gives Egypt cohesiveness. Modern Palestinian literature coheres around the catastrophic wrenching of the Palestinian people from their historical homeland in 1948. Having a literature is crucial to the survival of this uprooted and embattled community. Or, take Lebanese literature today: the prolonged civil war of 1975–90 wounded Lebanon, and the wound became a well of words.[1] Syria lacks the geographic cohesiveness of Egypt and has been spared the Palestinian and the Lebanese traumas. Nevertheless, it does enrich our understanding to bundle together the literature of Syria; such a harvesting allows us to become aware of patterns and to experience esthetic pleasures otherwise undetectable. That may be the only good reason—and it is a sufficient one—to endeavor theorizing Syrian literature.

What are we talking about when we speak of contemporary Syrian literature? A survey of the Syrian literary landscape in the last quarter-century or so is in order here. In the 1970s, Arabic literary modernism reigned triumphant, with Syrian-born poet and literary scholar Adonis (b. 1930), who adopted Lebanese citizenship, as one of its influential theorists. Yusuf al-Khal (1917–87), another pioneer of poetic experimentation, is, like Adonis, of Syrian origin but often assumed to be Lebanese. Certainly their chosen country of affiliation is important, and so, for our study of patterns in Syrian literature, is the fact that they began in Syria and left it. (Adonis was imprisoned for political activities in 1955 and left thereafter.) From this, it will be clear that what is meant here by "Syrian literature" is not necessarily the same as "literature from the Syrian Arab Republic." The prolific Nizar Kabbani (1923–98), who was a language innovator in his own right without fitting neatly into any school,[2] was in the 1970s at the peak of his powers as a poet of eros and political protest, having riveted the attention of the poetry-listening and poetry-reading public since the 1940s. Muhammad al-Maghut (b. 1934), who began in Adonis's circle and helped establish the prose poem as an Arabic form, is another major figure.

Perhaps Syria's greatest poet of the neoclassical school, which held sway earlier in the century, is Badawi al-Jabal (1907–81); his collected poems were published in 1978. Prominent in earlier literary movements but still present in the last quarter of the twentieth century were Nadim Muhammad (1910–94) and Umar Abu Risha (b. 1908). Huda Na'mani (b. 1930) is a poet of mystical bent who has lived outside Syria much of her life. Saniyya Saleh (1935–85) was a modernist prose poet. Mamduh Udwan (b. 1941) is a poet and dramatist living in Syria. The poet (and novelist) Salim Barakat is associated with the Palestinian literary journal *al-Karmel,* having been forced to leave Syria in 1982 after the Israeli invasion of Lebanon. Etel Adnan may be counted as being from Syria and Lebanon simultaneously, writes in French and English, and figures in Middle Eastern as well as Arab-American anthologies. Muhyiddin al-Ladhiqani emigrated after persecution for one of his writings in 1971 (Human Rights Watch, 126). Syrian poet Nouri Jarah (b. 1956) launched a literary journal, *al-Qassida,* from London in the 1990s, publishing Arabic poetry and arabophonic translations from Asia and Africa, contesting what he sees as the westward-oriented poetry scene of al-Khal and Adonis (*Aljadid,* 1999, 34). Lina Tibi, in London, is one of many emerging Syrian poets.

The short story is an important genre in the Arab world, perhaps because it is compact enough to be published in daily newspapers or weekly magazines and thus can be read without much expense. Some Arabic literary critics find that it is becoming as important as poetry—quite a coup in the Arab world, where poetry

has always been the privileged genre. Syrians are acknowledged as having made major contributions to the modern short story. The cynical and uncanny stories of Zakaria Tamer (b. 1931), jewels of precision and craft, have gained global acclaim. Abdal-Salam al-Ujayli (b. 1918) is an acknowledged Syrian master of this genre (and has worked his entire life as a full-time physician in his hometown, Raqqa). Widad al-Sakakini (1913–86) was born in Lebanon but spent most of her life in Syria, writing of life in Syria in the realistic, straightforward manner of Ujayli. She and Fuad al-Shayib (1910–70) authored what are reckoned the first modern Arabic short-story collections in 1945 and 1944 respectively. Muzaffar Sultan (b. 1913), Sa'id Horaniyeh (1929–?), Faris Zarzur (b. 1929), George Salem (1933–76), and other Syrians contributed to the development of this genre.

Ghada Samman (b. 1942) has had a powerful voice as the author of short stories, poetry, creative nonfiction, and, most notably, novels, her tone brisk, urbane, sardonic. She is both a high-profile novelist and one of the best-known feminists in the Arabic-speaking world. Samman arrived on a Syrian novel scene already strong with Hanna Mina (b. 1924), prolific since the 1950s. Mina frequently treats themes of class conflict and political change, his early works being considered novels of social realism. Novelist Shawqi Baghdadi (b. 1928) is also associated with the socialist-realism school. Ulfat al-Idilbi (b. 1910 or 1912) has been an active short-story writer since the 1940s, and in the 1990s published novels that are some of her best works. Walid Ikhlasi (b. 1935) is probably Syria's most prolific fiction writer, with over forty books; some of his novels have been adapted for the screen, as have Idilbi's. Hani al-Rahib (b. 1939) and Haidar Haidar (b. 1936) are well-known novelists. The former has suffered beatings from the Syrian state police as well as exile and other state harassment, whereas the latter has lived and worked in Syria since the mid-eighties; one of his novels recently provoked an uproar from the religious right in Egypt. The novelist Colette Khoury (b. 1937) lives and works in Syria. Samar Attar (b. 1945), who began as a poet in Arabic and now writes prose in both Arabic and English, published two novels in the 1990s, translating them into English herself. She lives in Australia. Salim Barakat (b. 1936) is another Syrian novelist living in the West.

The late Sa'dallah Wannous was Syria's leading dramatist. Drama is frequently adapted into television and film, and we may glance there: Nabil Malih, Usama Muhammad, and Muhammad Malas are some of the notable Syrian filmmakers. It would be interesting to make a case for including Hollywood-based filmmaker

Mustafa Aqqad, who is certainly Syrian although he is now American too. His horror-slasher films are very "Hollywood," while the topics of his epic sagas such as *The Message,* about the Prophet Muhammad and the dawn of Islam, reflect his interest in topics related to his Islamic and Arab roots.

■ THE POLITICS OF SYRIAN SILENCE

"Smash our pens!" the Syrian poet Khalil Mutran wrote early in the century from the relative freedom of Egypt, having fled Syria to escape punitive Ottoman measures against proponents of Arab nationalism. "Will smashing them / prevent our hands / from carving on the stones?" (Jayyusi, 82), he asks, which shows that bad government has been good grist for poetry for many decades in modern Syria. Censorship policies pursued by the French Mandate authorities continued the Ottoman tradition of harassing and exiling offending writers; they banned Khalil Mardam and condemned Khairuddin al-Zirakly to death (in absentia) in 1920. Independence in 1945 saw an improvement and growth in civil society, but only briefly. The coup that brought military rule by Husni al-Za'im in 1949 and the military coups that followed him in rapid succession tightened state control of cultural institutions. Another few years of lively and meaningful political contestation followed the series of military governments, but in 1958, Syria's three-year union with Egypt again increased state censorship powers.

The periods of relatively free and diverse public contestation, however brief, are important because they establish that Syrians do indeed understand and have a collective memory of the political freedoms they lack today. President Quwwatli's remarks upon giving up power to the union with Egypt in 1958 attest to the political sophistication and participatory expectations in the country: "You have liberated me from the ingratiating honor of being the head of five million inhabitants all of whom consider themselves politicians emeritus," he said to Egyptian president Nasser. "Half claim for themselves the vocation of leader. One-fourth believe themselves to be prophets; ten percent at the least take themselves to be gods" (quoted in Wedeen, 143). Heirs to unbroken urban and mercantile traditions that go back thousands of years and have outlasted brilliant empires, denizens of several of the world's oldest continually inhabited cities that have seen the rise and fall of the world's most powerful dynasties, and keenly cognizant of the dizzying layers of civilization beneath their feet, Syrians have a measure of urbanity about politics.

In 1963, the Ba'th Party took rule of Syria. With it came the rise of a police state with great repressive powers, achieved in part through the 1963 declaration of

martial law that has not been lifted once to this day. After successive purges of various wings of the party, including its founders, Hafez Asad consolidated his hold on the state in 1970. Political participation by Syrians was severely curtailed; it was limited to rubber-stamp activities in Parliament, Ba'th Party organizations, and a few government-sanctioned other parties, closely monitored. "Asad did not wholly stifle political activity," his biographer Patrick Seale says, "but confined it to in-groups such as the higher echelons of the party, the army commanders, and the security chiefs, all ultimately dependent on himself. Those outside these privileged circles soon learned they could go about their business without undue fear or constraint so long as they accepted that politics was not their domain" (179). The Ba'th increased the censorship powers of the state. Article 4b of the state of emergency straightforwardly permits the state "to control newspapers, books, broadcasting, advertising, and visual arts—in other words, all forms of expression and announcements before publication. It may also stop, confiscate, and destroy any work deemed to threaten state security, or close down offices and places of printing" (Human Rights Watch, 109).

Internal political developments in Syria during the last thirty years with bearing on censorship include purges by the ruling Ba'th Party of other parts of the party itself in 1967–71, and the rise of an Islamist opposition movement among Sunni Muslims from the mid-1970s to the mid-1980s, which encouraged the emergence of other opposition. Oppositional Syrians of various stripes took control of many professional organizations in the late 1970s for the first time since the Ba'th had taken power. The Islamist opposition armed itself enough to pose a military as well as political threat taken seriously by the regime. Dissent underlined the open secret of the sectarian nature of the Ba'thist regime, which was largely dominated by people who shared the Alawite ethnic-religious background of Asad; to dilute this criticism, the regime moved several Sunnis into visible positions.

To be sure, other political developments during Syria's recent history besides the internal ones have bearing on the issue of censorship, human rights, and writing. Hostile external and regional political conditions have created a siege mentality in Syria that has helped justify deprioritizing human-rights issues. This is not unique to Syria; across the Arab world for years, governments have been able to shift attention from their own lack of democracy by pointing to the outside threat, which is indeed a real one, posed by the belligerence and expansionism of Israel. Any dissent could be attributed to conspiracies of external enemies; the writer's duty was the service of the nation. However, whereas this argument began to be more questioned in the post-cold-war 1980s by intellectuals in the Arab world who started demanding increased accountability from Arab leaders for their human-rights transgressions, in Syria it has held fast.

The Asad regime's struggle to put down widespread insurgence culminated in the crushing of rebel forces in Hama in 1982, followed by the punitive massacre of thousands in the city that had given the insurgents refuge. The damage to the city was such that, as late as 1991, Human Rights Watch reported that "virtually every façade is pockmarked with shell holes and people live in the remains of their houses" (21). With "a third or more of the city's housing completely destroyed, between sixty and seventy thousand were left homeless. . . . One credible report states that eighty-eight mosques and five churches were destroyed, along with twenty-one markets, seven graveyards, seven public bath houses, and thirteen residential neighborhoods" (20). To come to the loss of human lives, the opposition's figure for the number massacred is 22,000, while "the most credible analysts put the number at between five and ten thousand people" (Human Rights Watch, 20). Hama's population at the 1981 census was 177,208, which means that, taking the lower estimate of casualties, between three and six percent of the city dwellers died in this event; many times that number were wounded. If the victims of violence in Hama during the entire month of February 1982 are included, "no fewer than 25,000 civilians lost their lives" according to Akram Hurani, a leading figure in the secular, socialist opposition and a Hama native (Batatu, 274). The ensuing government crackdown on dissent of all ideological stripes imprisoned many more and changed the tenor of life for all Syrians. Moreover, the 1982 Hama massacre was only part of a long chain of events beginning about a decade earlier, including massacres at Jisr al-Shughur, Ma'arra, Idlib, the Palmyra political prison, Sarmada, Aleppo, and in Hama itself prior to the big Hama massacre. These events reverberated through the 1980s and 1990s; their effects linger with Syrians in the third millennium.

Regime officials maintain that there is no such thing as a "Hama massacre." There were a few armed criminals, terrorists, agents of foreign governments in Syria's midst, the line goes, and the state eliminated them. Now, while the main force of the rebellion against the Ba'th came from the Muslim Brotherhood, a conservative religious party based mainly in the Sunni middle classes, and while many Syrians did not agree with its ideological orientation, the scale of the insurgency reflected a more widespread dissatisfaction with Ba'th

rule. The extent of the government violence at Hama, and the mass punitive executions of residents of the city, even those without ties to the rebels, was enough, at any rate, to horrify even those unsympathetic to the rebellion.

Mass violence committed on Syrians by their fellow Syrians has not occurred since the Christians of Damascus suffered massacre at the hands of mobs of the city's Muslims in 1860 (despite the efforts of Sheikh Abdal Qadir al-Jaza'iri to protect the Christians from his coreligionists). The numbers killed at Hama are far higher, although this does not decrease the atrociousness of the 1860 carnage. The Hama massacre is one of the top traumas of the twentieth century for Syrians. The first was the Turkish repression, for which the public hanging of twenty-one Arab nationalists in Damascus and Beirut in 1915 serves as an effective symbol. After the brief euphoria of Arab nationalist King Feisal's triumphant 1918 entry into Damascus, Syrian independence forces were crushed in 1920 by the entering French colonizers, who also wiped out a revolt led by Syria's Druze in 1925–27. Midcentury saw the defeat of Syria's troops by the Israeli army taking over Palestine in 1948; the penultimate blow of the century was the 1967 snatching of the Golan Heights from Syria by Israel, which also seized the West Bank, East Jerusalem, and the Sinai in that war. The devastation of 1948 and 1967 touches every life in the region. Hama was Syria's nightmare alone.

Contemporary Syrian literature contains no account of the Hama massacre, as far as I can ascertain. Syrian literature has treated Turkish tyranny, British perfidy, the French onslaught, and the Israeli aggression. Syrian writers have written courageously on the Turkish massacre of the Armenians (Hanna Mina) and the plight of the Kurds (Salim Barakat). The silence on Hama is notable, given the sophisticated levels of political consciousness present among Syrian writers. An episode of this magnitude in a country's third largest city does not just pass unnoticed by the country's major poets and novelists, no matter what their ideological leanings. A book or two on the Palmyra prison massacre and the Hama massacre, of the pulp-fiction sort, were spotted briefly in Iraqi and Jordanian bookstores during the 1980s. But in the literary journals, in the publishing houses, in the novels, short stories, screenplays, and poems of Syria's many writers, the Hama massacre is markedly absent.

Syrian silence on Hama, and on political repression under the Ba'th in general, is not hard to explain, given the plight of Syrians under authoritarian rule. The livelihoods of many excellent writers depend on state agencies. Hanna Mina has worked at the Ministry of Culture;

Walid Ikhlasi is a member of the People's Assembly; Mamduh Udwan works for the Ministry of Information (Jayyusi, 463); Colette Khoury is a consultant for the Ministry of Defense. There are many other examples. Mina tried to support himself as a barber early in his life before becoming a professional writer, and some writers hold nongovernmental jobs or have enough family wealth to be independent; but the fact is that "most of the jobs which will permit writers to pursue their craft are to be found in the area of the state cultural bureaucracy—as editors of newspapers, journals, and the like—positions in which they can often be easily controlled and from which they can be dismissed with equal ease" (Allen, 220). This may apply to most Arab countries, but is truer in countries with leftist governments, such as Syria, because the private sector is smaller in such countries. Even if financially independent, a writer needs to be published to have a meaningful vocation. (It is possible that Syrians have written a great deal of literature on Hama and the events surrounding it; who knows what reams of manuscripts on it have been penned that will never see the light of day. By *writing* here, I am, perhaps unjustifiably, assuming publication.) The Ministries of Culture and Information are Syria's largest publishers. A major "private" press is that of the party-controlled Writers Union. One of the largest private publishing houses is Dar Tlas. The founder and owner is book-loving Mustafa Tlas, Defense Minister since 1971. All colleges and universities in Syria are state schools.

The punitive arm of the state is long. In 1985, novelist Hani al-Rahib was arrested, not for anything he wrote, but just for saying at a Writers Union lecture in Damascus that individual freedoms were greater in Egypt than in Syria. He was fired from his job at the University of Damascus, not allowed to travel out of the country for two years, and beaten by the state police (Human Rights Watch, 134; Frangieh, 82). Syria's wrath has extended to Syrian-controlled areas of Lebanon. Lebanese journalist Salim al-Lawzi, an outspoken critic of Syria, moved his paper to London to avoid Syrian control after publishing articles criticizing Asad's policies, but was killed when he went back to Beirut for his mother's funeral in 1980. Al-Lawzi's body was found with his writing hand cut off. Syrian journalist Ali al-Jundi and Lebanese journalist Riad Taha were killed the same year in what are believed to be assassinations by Syrian government forces. Generally, "Imprisonment and torture are reserved mainly for intellectuals from underground political parties—even though they may simply advocate free speech and a peaceful transition to democracy," while other intellectuals and artists are kept in line "through bullying, praise, threats, bribes,

fines, promotion (or demotion), and social pressures" (Human Rights Watch, 109). Another means by which the Ba'th regime has kept a lid on dissent is by allowing a certain amount of criticism of the government to be aired periodically. Hanna Batatu describes one such event of 1979, when the Writers Union condemned "the stifling of freedoms and the government's scandalous lies"; by allowing this, "Asad let off steam, played for time, drew critics of the regime out into the open" (271). The much-loved films of Doraid Lahham, several of which were co-written by Muhammad al-Maghut with his trademark satiric wit, are typically cited as exemplifying this sort of condoned criticism.

■ THE POETICS OF SYRIAN SILENCE

Contemporary Syrian literature is created under the conditions of repression and censorship that have borne down on Syria from the beginning of the twentieth century to its end, from Ottoman heavy-handedness to Hafez Asad's long dictatorship, with short spates here and there of relatively freer conditions. One would think that such a repressive situation would suffocate creativity, but actually Syria has produced a good many major writers for a small country. Many of the best Syrian writers (Kabbani, Samman, Tamer, Adonis—who merit top ranking not only in Arabic literature but among the world's best contemporary writing) have been driven to leave Syria, and there is a significant lesson in this. However, a refreshing amount of very good literature is written and published inside Syria. Paradoxically, the heaviness of censorship in Syria spurs some writers to new levels of creative development, as they seek more sophisticated ways to express their art and their truths. There are "two responses to the censorship rules" in Syria, according to Syrian filmmaker Usama Muhammad: "One, to make bad art and talk about nothing, or two, to say what you want to say and make art. . . . The trick is to find one's own . . . language that is indirect, so one can make films about political power, religion, sex, and violence in a metaphorical — and often more powerful — way" (Nice, 31). Leo Strauss says of persecution that it "gives rise to a peculiar technique of writing, and therewith to a peculiar type of literature, in which the truth about all crucial things is presented exclusively between the lines." He adds that such literature is addressed "not to all readers, but to trustworthy and intelligent readers only" (26).

The silences created in the spaces between the lines of contemporary Syrian writing are as ripe with meaning as the lines themselves, and the shapes of these silences are as varied and nuanced as the writers and their styles. The nostalgic, moist-eyed silences of Ulfat Idilbi's narratives could not be more different from the chilling, cynical silences in Zakaria Tamer's stories. The impassioned lacunae in Nizar Kabbani's poetry proclaim exactly what it is they are not saying explicitly, while the poet Muhammad al-Maghut's silence is sardonic, sneering both at the authorities and at himself, at the futility and absurdity of the human situation under authoritarian rule.

Ulfat al-Idilbi is a third-generation Damascene with aristocratic Daghestani origins. Her great-grandfather, a Daghestani notable, was forced to settle in Damascus in the nineteenth century due to the annexation of their homeland by Russia's czar and the deceit of the Ottoman sultan. In prose collections such as *Qisas Shamiyeh* (Damascene Stories) and *Wada'an Dimashq* (Farewell, Damascus—the number of her titles with "Damascus" in them is noteworthy), as well as in her novels, Idilbi's work evinces nostalgia for the grand old era of an aristocratic Turco-Arab Syria. We see in sepia tones its well-run public baths and its abundance of luxury goods laid out in the large, well-ordered homes of prominent families. Several of her book covers show the façades, latticed windows, or gardens typical of beautiful old Damascene houses.

Idilbi's words are what they speak about: stately, regular, thick with the stuff of Damascus, the damask itself; her words are brocaded fabric. If a recent (Spring 2000) *World Literature Today* review called her narrative technique conventional, brocade does not need to surprise; the pleasure lies in its supple regularity. *Hikayatu Jaddi* (Eng. *Grandfather's Tale,* translated by Peter Clark) is highly conservationist in spirit. It is hung on the frame-within-a-frame of the narrator's mother telling the story of how her grandfather related the story of his childhood and origins to her, the mother, when she was a child. Idilbi's form alludes obviously to the *Thousand and One Nights* narrative tradition. This is nostalgia multiplied by three or four generations and by the narrative structure itself.

Even when an Idilbi novel delivers a critique of social customs on the level of plot, her words belie a love for the tastes and textures of that world and a belief in this world's inherent potential to return itself to harmony, balance, and beauty, rather than a call for constant struggle and change. *Dimashq ya basmatal huzn* (also translated by Clark, as *Sabriya: Damascus Bitter Sweet*), may be, on one level, about the suicide of the main character, an insightful but self-abnegating woman of 1940s Damascus, whose act is an indictment of her crass, domineering brothers and a triumph over them. But what these brothers represent is their own crassness and snobbery. The only change required is the removal of the outside evils that harry Sabriya, her arms full of lilacs, and that rain down on Damascus itself. Damascus

is the real heroine of the novel, and the strength of Damascus is its ability to turn inward, to fold its wings over itself: "After this calamity [the French bombing of the city during World War II], Damascus became like a humble dove that folds its wings over a fracture and remains silent in steadfast defiance" (96).

The dove image, which derives naturally from the fauna of Damascus and is not a farfetched poetic fancy, keys us to the essence of Idilbi's writing. This dove in its act of feathery retreat and withdrawal strongly implies the primal image of the nest; Idilbi's narrative impulse is a nesting impulse. "The nest, quite as much as the oneiric house," Gaston Bachelard says in *The Poetics of Space,* "knows nothing of the hostility of the world. Human life starts with refreshing sleep, and all the eggs in a nest are kept nicely warm. The experience of the hostility of the world . . . comes much later" (103). Idilbi's narrative powers enter at the moment in the story when the warm nest has already been disturbed. French bombing has pockmarked the city Sabriyya traverses in the last pages, as she sets out to put flowers on a grave. Idilbi's lens is focused on the withdrawal of the dove into itself and into the new period of quiet turning and turning that must follow to allow repair of the nest: "The secret of your eternal survival, dear Damascus, is that silence in the face of disaster. You have suffered so much. Through raids and plunder you remain forever" (96). The silence that fortifies Damascus belongs to Sabriyya too: "I will carry on harboring my grief in silence. I will conceal it in the depths of my soul and disclose it to nobody. I will hoard it as a miser hoards his money" (145). Thus does the main character cultivate within her breast the disciplines of Damascene silence, just as a bird uses its breast—for it has no tools except its own small body, as Bachelard exquisitely tells us (101), with which to fashion its nest. Idilbi's work waters the small, tidy flowers of the inner atrium, what is local and interior about Syria, and mainly Damascus, so much that she may perhaps be considered a regional writer, one who puts her home gently and lovingly into the world's imagination. Idilbi's novels are published with Tlas House in Damascus.

The gesture of the dove folding its wing over itself is a sheltering of self and home from attackers. Muhammad al-Maghut's work is strikingly different from Idilbi's, yet we find there a similar gesture: "Whenever a knock resounds / whenever a curtain moves / I cover my papers with my hand / like a prostitute covers herself during a raid" ("The Tattoo," 21). This time it is no foreign colonizer but the state's own police who threaten. Idilbi's gesture is one that cultivates inner qualities of fortitude and perseverence; the gesture of Maghut's speaker is a political act. This posture of anxiety, the looking over the shoulder by someone who knows he is being watched by the panoptical apparatus of political repression pervading an entire culture, summarizes the condition of the Syrian in the last thirty years of the twentieth century.

A whole subgenre consisting of the literature of the sudden violent knock at the door can be constructed within Syrian literature. Palestinian writers have eloquently given us homelessness and oppression by foreign occupiers but do not excel at the "knock at the door" genre, in which it is one's own countryman who is terrorizing one. We have camped with Palestinian poet Mahmoud Darwish in the airports of the world, and been harried and shot at with Liyana Badr's characters from one sorry shelled building to another, dragging our family behind us. Maghut's exile is neither refugee camp nor occupation; it is the seedy motel of Syrian life, where the security cameras are on all night and you get the feeling the guards can watch you in your room. Paranoia takes hold: "I enter restrooms with identity papers in my hands, / I leave the coffee-bar looking right and left — / even the little bud looks right and left / before it blooms" ("Fear," 14). Nizar Kabbani strikes a similar note in his poem "Taqrir sirri jiddan min bilad Qam'istan" (Top-Secret Report from the Country of Smotherland) when he says:

Do you know who I am?
I am a simple citizen
who lives in Smotherland
A citizen whose greatest dream
is to rise to the level
of an animal if he can

A citizen who can't go out
for a drink on the town,
so nervous that the State Police
— who knows? — might jump up
from the darkest places
at the bottom of his cup
(Translation mine)

One may object that this description of the citizen facing a repressive political culture applies in exactly the same measure to any Arab state; this is not true. A state of emergency decree that has not been lifted since 1963 does not exist in every Arab country, for example. Specific different conditions of repression pertain in each country, and the differences are important. Among all Arab cultures, Syrian culture has become the one most associated with the posture of paranoia stemming from a realistic fear of a police state with a vast surveillance apparatus and great demands of public shows of allegiance. Only in brutally governed Iraq does such paranoia ring as true as it does in Syria (and after the post-

Gulf War falling apart of Iraq, the paranoid cultures of these two Ba'thist states have parted ways, the Iraqi one acquiring new dimensions of intense physical deprivation). Thus, it is all very well that Kabbani calls this place by a fictional name and even specifically says that the repression he describes is everywhere in the Arab world: "Would you like a brief report / on the realm of Smotherland? / It extends from North Africa / to the sands of Petro-stan." And it is true, no activist for human rights need pack up her dossier on any Arab country today. Still, there is no mistaking, in a poem written in 1984, during the peak of the Syrian regime's sweeping post-Hama arrests and massive clampdown on freedoms, that Kabbani's diatribe applies especially pointedly to Syria. In another part of the poem he says he is

a citizen afraid to pray —
What if the State Police
stake out the prayer line?
They might say I tried to contact
the Merciful on High
Worse, they might accuse me
of perpetrating faith
— God, what a place

Kabbani alludes indirectly to surveillance of mosque-goers that, while it of course takes place in many other countries with politicized Islamist movements, was particularly pointed and noticeable in post-Hama Syria because the Hama rebellion had had an Islamist orientation. No Syrian poet, regardless of his or her political stripe, can be writing these lines in 1984 without being very well aware of what would be the first thing they would bring to mind for a Syrian readership. Kabbani is published in Beirut, where he relocated and founded his own publishing house in the 1960s; this poem, like many others, came out first in an Arabic daily based in London. Pirated editions of his books number in the millions.

In Maghut's poetry, when we are not in Syria, we are in a place where we stand looking back at Syria, as when he, like so many of his fellow poets and writers, experienced a period in which the government was displeased with him (in the 1980s, when he left Syria for the Gulf with his wife, poet Saniyya Saleh). Syria clings to him, even in the way he describes the advance of white in his hair in "Domestic Duties": "Now my forehead is singed with white / like Damascene jasmines on each bend / of the road" (16). If Idilbi is a writer of the interior spaces and the silences they induce, Maghut is a poet of the Syrian streetscape and particularly of the threshold and the scream that curdles inside the throat upon the threshold. The threshold is the border line between house and world, paranoia inside and danger outside. Maghut's knuckles are scraped raw on the sidewalk, and the threshold is a place viewed with the mixed longing of the outsider looking in, as in "Ila 'ata-bat bait majhul" (To the Threshold of an Unknown House), where the scene is the front entrance of a house near the pathetically dried-up Barada River of Damascus. The threshold is addressed, "You're a stranger lying calmly at our feet / But also a lowdown thief, full of treachery" (24). It is a poem that is nearly incomprehensible without a cultural sense of the external architecture of Syrian houses, because the threshold, like the stoops of brownstones in Manhattan and the wrap-around porches of Southern U.S. farmhouses in mosquito-bitten summer, is thick with local cultural connotation. Maghut's threshold is also the door whence the state could enter at any moment.

From whom did I inherit this terror?
this jittery blood like a mountain panther?
Whenever I glimpse an official paper on the
  threshold
or a helmet from a crack in the door,
    my bones rattle,
    tears race, and my terrified blood
    jolts in all directions
    as if an eternal legion of police
    chased it from vein to vein
(21)

Maghut cannot decide if he is in or out; he stands restlessly at the threshold casting his wit, caustic and tender, out to the street and back into the little house, his stubborn, insular country, which sits atop the world's civilization reserves but is determined to be parochial today. Maghut's tone is as sardonic as his landscape is urbane: "Tell my little country, vicious as a tiger, / that I raise my hand like a student, / asking permission to depart or die." Maghut's poems were published in Beirut.

Horrified silence is the void around which Zakaria Tamer's stories are built. In story after unsettling story, terrible things happen, crimes are committed, but the bizarre, hallucinatory quality of the narrative numbs us, forces us to watch people go on acting normally in the midst of horror, as if nothing were wrong. "The Orchard" (first published in 1973 in the collection *Dimashq al-Hara'iq* [Damascus of Flames]), begins on a note of whimsy, magic, and love.

Sameeha used to be a fish in bygone days and lived in the sea. Then she became a drop of water in a cloud. The day Sulaiman met her, Sameeha had become a beautiful woman and he craved her mouth with its two delicate lips. Fire her lips cre-

ated and music, and offered them up to the world of air and light and water. (11; translation mine)

Whimsy evaporates when a group of vicious men overtake Sameeha and Sulaiman in the orchard. They knock Sulaiman down physically, but they also beat the couple, with the brunt of misogyny at its most brutish. If Sameeha were not a whore, goes the logic with which they assault Sulaiman, she would not be traipsing alone in an orchard with him. That's when they grab her by the wrist, knock Sulaiman out, and "Sameeha screams but is not able to become a drop of water in a cloud"; and we know what happens next, though it is not narrated. However, the story's power to horrify is carefully placed, not in the gang rape itself, but in the submission to the fact of this rape that takes possession of Sulaiman.

When Sulaiman came to, he opened his eyes stiffly, to spy Sameeha spread under a heaving man, her clothing in shreds. He hurried to close his eyes, submitting to a cold shuddering fright, his body bonding to the matted straw beneath it. He concentrated on a wail emitting from a hollow in the earth, bitter and blended with a panting, as of animals on the prowl for water. (16; my translation)

The numbness that possesses Sulaiman is it, is the evil that lurks in the horrible little heart of a Tamer story. Tamer, without mentioning specific political events, points unnervingly, sometimes with very black humor, to that in human nature which can be trained to numb acquiescence before the assault against one's deepest truth. In the story "Tigers on the Tenth Day" a trainer uses hunger to makes a wild caged tiger submit to the whip, and even, eventually, to *like* submitting to the whip, against the very nature of its being as a tiger. The tiger is fully "trained" by the end of the short, terse story: "On the tenth day the trainer, the pupils, the tiger, and the cage disappeared; the tiger became a citizen and the cage a city" (1985, 17).

Many of Tamer's protagonists are so far gone in this process that they have become willing participants. In one story, a woman is about to be raped by five men in a park. Wait, she says—and begs them, not to reconsider raping her, but to allow her eleven-year-old daughter to help her service the five of them. The pimping or prostitution of whatever is supposed to be inviolable—and, more important, the acquiescence to this—is a primal scene in Tamer's world. The citizen of an authoritarian state recognizes the metaphor in this instantly. In her recent book on the political culture of Syria and the meaning of Asad's cult, Wedeen describes "the regime's demand that citizens provide external evidence of their allegiance to a cult whose rituals of adulation are manifestly unbelievable" (68). The amount of precious energy ordinary citizens are required to expend on this pretense, even keeping tabs on one another for signs of adherence to the cult, is an affirmation of the government's power, even though everyone, including the government, knows that everyone else is dissimulating. Wedeen relates a story that reached her about the beating and discharge of a young army officer she calls "M," an incident that purportedly happened a few days before the story was narrated to her. The anecdote—or "meaningful fiction," as she calls it—goes thus:

> A high-ranking official visited the young officer's regiment and ordered the soldiers to recount their dreams of the night before. A soldier stepped forward and announced: "I saw the image of the leader in the sky, and we mounted ladders of fire to kiss it." A second soldier followed suit: "I saw the leader holding the sun in his hands, and he squeezed it, crushing it until it crumbled. Darkness blanketed the face of the earth. And then his face illuminated the sky, spreading light and warmth in all directions." Soldier followed soldier, each extolling the leader's greatness. When M's turn came, he stepped forward, saluted the visiting officer, and said, "I saw that my mother is a prostitute in your bedroom." The beating and discharge followed. Commenting retrospectively on his act, M explained that he had "meant that his country is a whore." Like state ideologues, M plays off an allusion to the etymological relation between *umma* (nation) and *umm* (mother). . . . His country, he implies, has sold itself to a corrupt military; Syria has become defiled. (67, 70)

The telling part in the narrative is M's standing and watching: "His self-announced voyeurism suggests his awareness of his own complicity" (70).

Like this short story in the raw from Wedeen's source, Tamer's stories are written in a way that leads us over and over to that dark place at the center of the citadel where this primal scene is taking place before the silent acquiescence and fascination, even, of the witness. Far from us now is Idilbi's little nest that only needed a wing folded over it. With Tamer, the innermost nest is exposed and defiled; there is no wing or will to cover the shame, and all the birds are in cages of their own complicity. Tamer constructs the stories so that the ugly shape of our complicit silence becomes evident. We flinch. We can no longer pretend the silence is normal, rationalize it away. His works, now printed in London by Riad al-Rayyes Books, have long been officially banned in Syria. This, of course, only makes Tamer's words better read, in that it gives them the benefit of a more select and alert circle of readers who get them under the table.

■ **MURMURS AT THE THRESHOLD**

Contemporary Syrian literature is created in the crucible of a tenacious authoritarianism. Manifold silence, evasion, indirect figurative speech, gaps and lacunae are striking features of Syrian writing, habits of thought and wary writerly techniques that have developed during an era dominated, in Syria more overwhelmingly than in other Arab countries excepting Iraq and perhaps Libya, by authoritarian governments with heavy-handed censorship policies and stringent punitive measures. Idilbi's silences are sweet and sad; Maghut's are bitter, sarcastic, choked; and silence that is at once terrified, mesmerized, and complicit is Tamer's specialty. Syrian literature today is jittery with what it cannot say, and that is its genius. The ultimate silence of contemporary Syrian literature is its collective silence about the Hama massacre of 1982, "a bloodbath without parallel in the history of modern Syria" according to the late Hanna Batatu, a sober and distinguished Syria scholar (269).[3] That a trauma of the magnitude of the Hama massacre is nowhere to be found in contemporary Syrian literature is stunning and, of course, impossible; Hama, being nowhere in Syrian literature, can be read in it everywhere.

What will happen under Asad the son? The manner in which power passed to the son in what is supposed to be a republic, not a monarchy—the Constitution was amended at breakneck speed to make his assumption "legitimate"—is cause for skepticism. Bashar Asad has released hundreds of political prisoners, some from decades of imprisonment without trial. He has ordered newspapers to tone down the panegyrics to the president. He seems to want to make Syrian society more open. Asad *père* also began his rule with similar pardons and release of prisoners. At the time of this writing, neither the state of emergency nor the constitutional powers allowing arbitrary imprisonment have been repealed, although promises are being floated about lifting the state of emergency. Bashar's current support for opening Syria to new communications technology—satellite television, the Internet—will create a level of cognitive dissonance that is already putting a strain on the culture of carefully cultivated silences and of mental acrobatics around the doublethink authorized by the state. Some Syrians, accustomed to protecting themselves against the dangers of free speech, have already recoiled with vertiginous fear. (This is evident, for example, in the mixed reactions of Syrian viewers to Al-Jazira, the acclaimed Qatar-based Arabic news channel which beams into Syrian homes via satellite news analyses and policy debates far more daring than what Syrians are accustomed to hearing aired publicly.) Other makers of Syrian culture have leapt into the new apertures boldly to widen them. Ninety-nine Syrian writers, including many mentioned in the survey above, courageously signed a petition on 27 September 2000, demanding the broadening of human rights in Syria. They published it, not in Syria of course, but in Lebanese newspapers. In January 2001, a thousand writers signed a petition reiterating these demands, and what is being called the "Movement for Civil Society" is taking the form of informal discussion groups, *muntadayat,* springing up in the homes of intellectuals, writers, and artists. The government has so far played a game of loosening the leash a bit, then jerking it back, such as when a government decree in March 2001 cracked down on the *muntadayat,* demanding that names of people intending to come to such meetings and the topics to be discussed be submitted in advance so that the required license to assemble could be properly obtained before every meeting.

What is encouraging is that, despite the suspicious eye of the government on them, these sorts of initiatives from below are increasing. Perhaps a new spirit is moving in the land. Will Syrians begin to converse in these new cultural spaces, and will they be unafraid to let their voices rise? Or, like Rappacini's daughter in Hawthorne's tale, has the Syrian body become so accustomed to the poison—silence—that the antidote would kill?

Mohja Kahf, Spring 2001

■ **WORKS CITED**

Allen, Roger. "The Mature Arabic Novel Outside Egypt." *Modern Arabic Literature.* M. M. Badawi, ed. Cambridge, England. Cambridge University Press. 1992.

Amnesty International. *Syria: Torture by the Security Forces.* New York. Amnesty International Publications. 1987.

———. *Syria: Indefinite Political Imprisonment.* New York. Amnesty International Publications. 1992.

Bachelard, Gaston. *The Poetics of Space.* Maria Jolas, tr. New York. Orion. 1964.

Batatu, Hanna. *Syria's Peasantry, the Descendants of Its Lesser Rural Notables, and Their Politics.* Princeton, N.J. Princeton University Press. 1999.

Bazei, Saad A. al-. Review of Ulfat Idilbi, *Grandfather's Tale. World Literature Today,* 74:2 (Spring 2000), p. 452.

Chalala, Elie. "Al-Qassida: A New Journal of Arab Poetry." *Aljadid: A Review & Record of Arab Culture & Arts,* Summer 1999, pp. 33–34.

Frangieh, Bassam. "Hani al-Rahib: A Tragic Life in a Tragic Age." *Banipal: Magazine of Modern Arab Literature,* Spring 2000, p. 82.

Human Rights Watch. *Syria Unmasked: The Suppression of Human Rights by the Asad Regime.* New Haven, Connecticut. Yale University Press. 1991.

Idilbi, Ulfat. *Sabriyya: Damascus Bitter Sweet.* Peter Clark, tr. New York. Interlink. 1997.

Jayyusi, Salma Khadra. *Modern Arabic Poetry: An Anthology.* New York. Columbia University Press. 1987.

Kabbani, Nizar. *Al-a'mal al-siyasia al-kamila* [Complete Political Works]. Beirut. Nizar Kabbani Publications. 1993. Volume 6.

Maghut, Muhammad. *Al-athar al-kamila* [Complete Works]. Beirut. Dar al-'Awda. N.d.

———. *The Fan of Swords.* May Jayyusi and Naomi Shihab Nye, trs. Salma Khadra Jayyusi, ed. Washington, D.C. Three Continents. 1991.

Meisami, Julia Scott, ed. *Encyclopedia of Arabic Literature.* 2 volumes. New York. Routledge. 1998.

Nice, Pamela. "Finding the Right Language: A Conversation with Syrian Filmmaker Usama Muhammad." *Aljadid: A Review & Record of Arab Culture & Arts,* Spring 2000, pp. 10, 25.

Seale, Patrick. *Asad: The Struggle for the Middle East.* Berkeley. University of California Press. 1988.

Strauss, Leo. *Persecution and the Art of Writing.* Chicago. University of Chicago Press. 1988.

Tamer, Zakaria. *Dimashq al-Hara'iq.* 3d ed. London. Riad al-Rayyes Books. 1994.

Wedeen, Lisa. *Ambiguities of Domination: Politics, Rhetoric, and Symbols in Contemporary Syria.* Chicago. University of Chicago Press. 1999.

[1] Elise Salem's book *Constructing Lebanon,* due in 2002 from the University of Florida Press, studies the idea of Lebanon in the past hundred years of Lebanese literature.

[2] On Kabbani, see my essay "Politics and Erotics in Nizar Kabbani's Poetry: From the Sultan's Wife to the Lady Friend," *WLT* 74:1 (Winter 2000), pp. 44–52.

[3] Hanna Batatu's book, which has an elaborately boring academic title that disguises its extremely lucid political content, is dedicated "To the people of Syria."

TURKEY

The Turkish Peasant Novel, or the Anatolian Theme

Is there a peasant-novel genre, or are there simply novels with a dominant peasant theme? To the numerous possible classifications which have appeared in the history of the novel—the picaresque novel, the historical novel, the popular novel, the social novel, the *roman à thèse,* the proletarian novel, et cetera—it is possible in the case of Turkish literature to speak of a "peasant novel," with its particular characteristics, flaws, and great merits. If Hegel's celebrated and oft-cited definition of the Western novel as "a modern bourgeois epic, designed to express the conflict between the poetry of the heart and the prose of social relations" (*Ästhetik*) is to a certain extent still valid, it could not easily be applied to the emergence of the art of the peasant novel in Turkey, which is the subject of this study and which takes as its setting the Anatolian region and its inhabitants. But whereas Hegel's definition does not seem quite applicable in this instance, Stendhal's, on the other hand, is illuminating: "A mirror carried along a path." In this case, the novelistic mirror is carried along the great paths of the Anatolian steppes, revealing the problematic condition of the peasants, people whose destiny bears almost no resemblance to that of the men and women who make up the living fabric of the Western novel.

The genre which might be called the peasant novel in Turkey appeared around 1949–50 with the publication of a number of works by young novelists of peasant stock, most of whom had been trained in the so-called village institutes, which I will discuss later in this essay. The first and most famous of them, Mahmut Makal (b. 1930), was to write *Bizim Köy* (Our Village; 1950), the story of Makal's misadventures as a teen-age schoolteacher in his own village but also a merciless portrayal of peasant conditions in Turkey.[1] The little book's almost anthropological account of a village on the Anatolian plateau not only had an explosive impact on both political and literary circles but also possessed the added merit of establishing a literary style that was at once dramatic and unadorned. With Makal, it was not so much the novel itself that was important as it was that his concise, expressive style offered an excellent model of fiction for young peasants with literary talent.

The most important and clearly the most popular novel to come out of the village culture was Yashar Kemal's *Ince Memed* (1955; Eng. *Memed, My Hawk*), which has had, and continues to have, numerous printings in Turkey and in many other countries, giving the Turkish novel a worldwide audience.[2] Following its publication, dozens of young novelists with a similar background began to write novels and short stories inspired by what they knew better than anyone: the village and its daily life, its dramas, and its passions. Fakir Baykurt, Talip Apaydin, Lütfi Ay, and Dursun Akşam, to name just a few, were to form the nucleus of the "peasant novel," opening new perspectives for the novelistic genre in Turkey.

Whatever literary qualities these works displayed or lacked, this novelistic discovery of the village by Turkish readers, city dwellers for the most part, had the undeniable merit of revealing the emotional world, the social conflicts, the language, and the images of the rural majority. The extraordinarily rich vocabulary, the expressive verbal structure, the vivid and evocative language, and the lively dialogues made a major contribution to the development of Turkish literature, guiding or supporting attempts to purify and transform the language of contemporary Turkey, which was undergoing a process of great change. By helping to bring about the divorce between the modern idiom and the old Ottoman language (which was filled with Arabic and Persian words), this new genre contributed to the democratization of the Turkish language and of Turkish literature.

■ ■ ■

Despite the immense talent of the peasant authors, this novelistic current was not the result of spontaneous generation, a genre devoid of history or roots. The literary focus on the peasantry and the desire to purify the language go further back than the 1950s.

One of the very first literary works to concern itself with the Turkish peasantry was *Kara Bibik* (1890), an unfinished narrative which drew its inspiration from the French naturalistic movement. Written by Nabizade Nazim, it describes the life of a peasant from the Antalya region and is less a novel than an attempt at one. Another work of some significance by the same writer, *Küşük Paşa* (The Little Pasha), which dates from 1910, tells the story of a mother and son living in an Anatolian village. The author, who was a governor, a minister, and later a deputy, weighs down his narrative with numerous speeches in order to present his ideas on country schools, village health, and other matters. It is less a novel than a pretext to lecture, but it is not without merit.

The Turkish village did not really become the focus of novelists' interest until the War of Independence (1919–23), led by Mustafa Kemal Atatürk, who managed to rally all the life forces of the nation: numerous civilian and military intellectuals, and especially peasant soldiers, who continued to have faith in their commander, the man who had led the nation to victory in the Battle of the Dardanelles Straits in 1915.

The city of Ankara had become the center of the armed struggle. Writers, novelists, poets, and journalists joined the movement and traveled about the country from village to village, where they got to know the peasants who had taken up arms. They soon realized that these people were imbued not just with the desire to free their country from the foreign invader, but also with the hope of freeing themselves from ancestral poverty. For the Turkish intellectual, this was an agonizing discovery which raised many questions. Who then was this peasant in rags, this "other" who fought courageously at his side but was so different from him? Anatolia was becoming, in the midst of its struggle for survival, the focus of intense curiosity and interest, but this was not to bear fruit until after the founding of the Turkish Republic.

Writers such as Refik Halit had up until then displayed only an attitude of ironic superiority with respect to the world of the peasantry and the Anatolian villages. They would soon be replaced by writers who were determined to probe more deeply into the relationship between city and village, which they perceived as crucial to the cohesion of the new nation. Writing, prose, the short story, the novel, were becoming an essential part of this quest for national and social identity.

This attitude was to encounter considerable friction, misunderstanding, surprise, and fear, however. It was during this period that there emerged at last, in the person of Memduh Şevket Esendal (1883–1952), a great and talented writer capable of conveying his emotional response to the mysteries of the Anatolian plateau. By depicting in several of his stories characters drawn from real life, he managed to communicate to the reader the malaise and confusion with which he himself was grappling. "The Desert" (1946), for example, recounts the author's crossing of the Anatolian steppes in a rented carriage drawn by scrawny horses and guided by a laconic driver who inspires little confidence. After a long drive in the scorching sun, they arrive at last at a remote inn of sorts, run by a man who does not seem any more trustworthy than the driver.

> Leaning once more against the wall, I closed my eyes. The driver and the innkeeper know each other; who knows how often they've met. They're talking about this and that, but I can't make out most of what they're saying. One is probably from Kayseri and the other from Konya. They are speaking very rapidly. However much I pay attention, I miss at least one out of every three or four words. They're talking about a debt, something about a broken contract; they're exchanging all sorts of news. They're talking about Bor, Kayseri, Nigde, Eregli, Aksaray. Once they had finished this conversation, they began to talk about me, but they didn't think it necessary to lower their voices. The driver recounted all he knew about me, where I was coming from, where I was going, and it's strange, he gave quite a bit of information, although I hadn't told him anything and I thought he was not the least bit interested in me. I was curious: how had he found out who I was, I wondered. Since it's hard to say what one is and to hide one's habitual character, I was surprised and at the same time annoyed to discover that the driver knew so much about me. They didn't care the least bit about me, nor were they afraid of me. Especially this innkeeper, this individual who looked like a bandit. If he had come here two or three hundred years ago, he would certainly have laid down the law. An individual who does not bow to destiny, who cares nothing about the whole world. In his own uni-

verse, he has seen and endured many things, overcome numerous worries and misfortunes. But then again, my driver's no better. He's a young boy, but he has bloodshot eyes; he looks at you like a bird of prey perched on a rock.[3]

Esendal was also to write, in his fine, nuanced, unadorned style, stories in which he denounced the inner workings of the patriarchal system in the villages, for there was injustice not only in the relations between city and village but also within each village.

Whereas Esendal expresses his observations by purposely distancing himself, Yakup Kadri Karaosmanoğlu (1889–1974) brings to the description of the realities of village life the subjectivity of a city dweller grappling with his anguished failure to communicate with those living around him. Although he understands why he is cut off from the others, he cannot help feeling tremendous bitterness. His celebrated novel *Yaban* (The Outsider), published in 1932, is the story of an officer whose arm has been amputated and who decides to live out the rest of his life in a settlement located on a remote steppe. His personal misfortune is aggravated by the foreign occupation of the country in 1919. The work is thus a novel about despair, for the disabled officer, living in voluntary exile, is considered a *yaban,* an outsider, by the peasants. Despite all his efforts, communication is never established between the ex-officer, an intellectual from another world, and the peasants living out their own drama. The mistrust which the author senses stems from centuries of virtual slavery. Through his identification with the protagonist of his novel, and through his personal commentary, Karaosmanoğlu indulges in what amounts to self-criticism in the form of direct discourse, establishing the historical guilt of the intelligentsia, which had hitherto ignored its own country and the immense majority of its inhabitants.

If "The Outsider" contains many novelistic elements which were new to Turkish literature, it nonetheless retains the didactic quality characteristic of the novelists who were responsible for the birth of the genre in the second half of the nineteenth century. Still, it has many fine qualities, due largely to the author's sincerity and his desire to create a coherent novelistic style. Karaosmanoğlu's talent is revealed in his description of places, people, and situations, the very differences which form the barrier between the village world and that of the city.

> And the road is long. If you ask the villagers, they will say, "It's very close by," but I know what "very close by" means to a villager. The nearest point indicated by "very close by" is five or six hours down the road. Why is it they have no no-

tion of time or space? As the days go by, I find my own answer. The reason is this: even in myself I feel that since I arrived here, the notion of time has diminished considerably. The first few days I forgot what day of the week it was. Now I no longer keep track of the months; all I notice is the change of seasons. The day I forget my age and the past on which I've turned my back, I will feel indescribable relief. But even when I reach that state, I will not escape the frightening feeling these immense, dry plains awaken in me: this feeling oppresses me continually; it makes me dizzy and destroys my will. But a village in the middle of the desert does not even offer the assurance of a stage. A stage marks a point of departure in the middle of Space. If you are here today, you will reach an oasis tomorrow; the day after tomorrow the waters of a large river will flow forward to meet you. Maybe a village, a village in Anatolia represents a stage fixed in time. Space here seems to swallow you up. In the middle of this space you feel a numbing terror. Truly, in this village which resembles Hittite ruins, what difference is there between the men and the statues that have just been exhumed?[4]

The anguish described by Karaosmanoğlu is similar to Esendal's. These two talented writers, the cream of the Turkish intelligentsia of their time, experience the same fear and anguish, one that is not only physical, but moral and intellectual as well.

These feelings of surprise, fear, and anguish seem no longer to be an issue in the writings of Sabahattin Ali (1906–48). Ali goes beyond the mea culpa of someone like Karaosmanoğlu to denounce in virulent terms the social structure that the reader discovers and understands better in his stories. His work marks a turning point in the development of the Turkish novel; the reality he depicts is a more global vision: the crisis of a whole society. In his story "The Oxcart,"[5] a watershed piece in Turkish literature, he tells of an Anatolian peasant woman whose son was killed by the son of the agha (rich peasant) of the village. The mother is urged not to file a complaint: "'What would you gain by it?' asked the imam. 'Who do you think would testify against the agha's son and say he was a murderer? . . . It was God's will. You aren't going to use a court to go against God's will, now, are you?'" When the police arrive, "Mehmet the Blond's mother did not say anything. She simply repeated, 'I am not filing a complaint against anyone.' . . . Mevout agha had bought her silence with two milk goats, a sack of flour, and a bag of sugar." The idea of having to deal with government officials seems to her worse still than the death of her son, but the police force her to bring her son's exhumed corpse to the city in her oxcart.

The oxcart, which moved along slowly on wheels that screeched more loudly than jackals howling in the shimmering summer moonlight, did not look as though it were carrying a corpse. In this light, which outlined the backbone of the oxen, the animals seemed powerful and full of life; the patched quilt and the worm-eaten cart seemed as beautiful and new as if they had been made of an extraordinarily precious metal. . . . And the woman staggered along. She wanted to cry out to the oxen to halt, but no sound came out. Her hands let go of the cart and she stumbled to the ground. She picked herself up from the dust and began to run. . . . Her bandana floated behind her like a black flag. Before she caught up with the cart, she fell again, face-down in the path, in dust as white and fine as ash.

Then, bumping along, tossing the tied-down corpse here and there, wheels screeching in a wail that was now drawn out, now muffled in the moonlight, trailing a light halo of dust behind it in the silence of the night, the cart continued slowly on its way.

This grandiose image symbolizes centuries of powerless resignation and submission, that of a world cut adrift, allowed to go its own way.

The perspective of critical realism which Sabahattin Ali introduces into his vision of Turkish peasant life is revealed as well in his novel *Kuyucakh Yusuf* (Yusuf the Taciturn; 1937),[6] in which an Anatolian village is dissected in terms of its social life, its prejudices, and its obscurantism, revealing the abuses and corruption of the administration. The story revolves around the son of a peasant who, following the murder of his parents in the village, is taken in and later adopted by the subprefect and eventually marries the latter's daughter. The orphaned Yusuf has trouble adapting to the corruption around him. The network of special interests in the village, the pettiness of the officials, the transformation of the women into objects of derision—all these make his revolt appear socially motivated, even if he himself seems unaware of it.

Sabahattin Ali, like Balzac, Stendhal, and so many other great realists, understood that an essential part of the reality of a given society becomes crystallized in provincial life, which in turn mirrors the realities of big-city life. Reşat Nuri Güntekin (1886–1956), in his famous novel *Cahkuşu* (The Petty King) of 1922 and in *Yeşil Gece* (The Green Night) of 1928,[7] had already taken up the subject of provincial life, but he was content to describe the antiquated customs, the obstinate ignorance, the bigoted fanaticism of life in a small town, and schoolteachers' desperate battles against the kind of reactionary thinking which opposed all attempts at change—in sum, a Kemalist struggle, an attempt to re-form an archaic system and mentality that had existed for centuries.

By denouncing and criticizing the very structures of a society in which the power of the privileged classes seems to go unquestioned, Sabahattin Ali imparted to his work a social dimension that is without precedent in the art of the Turkish novel. Here is the closing passage of "Yusuf the Taciturn," where melodrama is woven into the fabric of daily life:

> After contemplating the town, Yusuf gazed at the hill rising before him. He clenched his fists and bit his lip, but could not hold back the big tears that began to roll down his cheeks, blinding him. He wiped his eyes with his sleeves and leaped into the saddle. He turned around once more, and, shaking his fist at the small town where he had spent the most terrifying years of his existence, he galloped off toward the mountain.
>
> In spite of the distress and pain which filled his soul, he would not surrender. He would share his grief with no one, he would shoulder this burden alone and would give his life a new direction.

It is clear that the stage is set for *Memed, My Hawk* by Yashar Kemal, that other famous rebel.

Before the emergence of the peasant novelists in the 1950s, however, there were, following Sabahattin Ali, other writers who would help prepare the way for a new vision of the Anatolian people and their lives, developing situations and characters using techniques inspired by realism to explore human relations. In successive cross sections, entire segments of Turkish society were revealed to the eye of the spectator-reader in works which sometimes went beyond the scope of literature to provide sociological insights not to be found elsewhere. Although some works were vitiated by this orientation, the trend was inevitable; the rapid pace of social change gave rise to a certain didacticism, creating a new form of bildungsroman. This quest for identity was to pose numerous problems, some of which were ideological.

For one thing, the Republican government declared itself populist while refusing to give up its elitist attitude of state control. Popular expression was accepted and encouraged in the form of folklore, but it was denied and repressed whenever it took up anything involving social change. Therefore, artists who sought to give a true image of society had to tread a narrow path. The ideologists of the sole party (the Republican People's Party) had decreed that Turkey would be a "classless society"; so it was at great personal risk that writers sought to explore the more conflictual aspects of reality,

particularly if they wanted to depict the patriarchal structure of the village, which was morally and materially in the hands of the most influential men, and the exorbitant power that the large landowners and the agha held over the poor, landless peasant. It was a contrast that was almost Manichean in nature; but it was real, and it was played out in the theatre of village life day after day, in total contradiction to the idyllic picture painted by the administration.

Although it would be impossible to list all the urban writers who sought to understand the condition of the Turkish peasantry, I would like to mention a few of the most interesting ones.

- Sadri Erdem (1900–43). After participating as a youth in the War of Independence, he became a journalist, then began working for the Republican government and was eventually elected as a deputy to the National Assembly. His collections of stories reveal a caustic and independent spirit, which is already apparent in the title of his first collection, "The Peasant in Top Hat" (1933).

- Kemal Tahir (1910–73). After training as a navy officer, he was sentenced in 1939 to a long prison term, which was to be a determining factor in his becoming a writer, for he was befriended by the great poet Nazim Hikmet while in the Cankiri prison. He published a collection of stories in 1941, then a novel, *Köyün Kamburu* (The Village Hunchback; 1959),[8] and numerous other novels analyzing the customs and traditions of peasant life. These works, which he wrote before turning to the historical novel and other genres, represented an important contribution to Anatolian literature.

- Abidine Dino (b. 1913). A painter by trade, Dino wrote and published the play *Kel* (The Bald Man) in 1942, while living under surveillance in Adana. Although the work was immediately censored, it did enjoy a certain clandestine distribution. It features a great variety of characters whose vocabulary bears the stamp of the peasant idiom as well as many poetic elements of popular expression. Rich in contrastive social elements, it was read by later peasant writers.

- Reşat Enis (1909–82). This writer, who was on the editorial staff of a newspaper in Adana during the years 1942–44, published the novel *Toprak Kokusu* (The Smell of the Earth) in 1944, revealing an extensive knowledge of the large landowners of the Shukur-Ova region as well as of the problems of the impoverished peasantry.

- Orhan Kemal (1914–70). Orhan Kemal's career as a writer was determined by his incarceration in the prison at Bursa, where, like Kemal Tahir, he was encouraged by the poet Nazim Hikmet to write prose. He decided to remain in Adana when he was released from prison in 1942. Already in his first work, the story collection *Ekmek Kavgast* (The Battle for Bread; 1949), he portrayed the drama of young peasants who try to flee the village and adapt to city life. He sought to document this difficult transition from village life to that of the industrial centers.

This list of writers who prepared the ground for the emergence of the peasant novelists is far from exhaustive, but I would be particularly remiss if I did not add further mention of the major contribution made by the imprisoned poet Nazim Hikmet, for he was to write between 1941 and 1945 a poem comprising several thousand verses (actually a prose poem or poetic prose) and published in five volumes, *Memleketimden İnsan Manzaralari* (Human Landscapes; 1966–67), for which he claims to have drawn inspiration from the works of William Langland, Gogol, and Tolstoy.[9] With this poem, Hikmet sought to break down the barriers between poetry and prose in order to create a new genre capable of depicting his century and those living through it both in Turkey and elsewhere. Peasant themes play a major role in the poem, which brims over with the most diverse situations taken from the War of Independence as well as from the conflicts of daily life in and out of prison; landscapes are depicted along with the people who inhabit them—people driven by love, crime, and passion.

> They who are numberless,
>   like ants in the earth,
>   fish in the water,
>   birds in the air,
> they who are cowardly,
>   courageous,
>   ignorant
>   and wise,
>   they who are children
> they who begin anew,
>   and who create,
> our book will recount only their adventures.

This great poem, which in the course of its composition was passed from hand to hand, circulated outside the prison, and read by a considerable number of people, was important both for its stylistic perfection and the poet's determination to avoid the pitfalls of a superficial kind of realism. "The danger is to schematize," he wrote in a letter to Kemal Tahir.

Whatever the merits, qualities, and flaws of these precursors of the peasant novel, their works alone do not suffice to explain the force and vitality which was to characterize the development of the genre. Despite the limited scope of the populist movement and of the reforms carried out during the first years of Kemalism, these phenomena did nevertheless set in motion a process of change that was extremely important, thanks to certain educational measures for which it would be hard to find anything comparable in other countries. One of the most important of these innovations was the establishment of the "village institutes."

The village institutes were founded in 1940 by a great pedagogue, I. H. Tonguç, in order to accelerate the cultural and material transformation of the Turkish villages. These institutes were innovative in that they were set up and run by peasant boys and girls who were supervised by a new type of monitor, teaching skills in the field that were adapted to regional needs. It was thus in the context of rural production that the elements of a general culture were passed down to students, who would continue the process in their own villages when they returned after completing their studies. The long-awaited agrarian reform announced by Atatürk was thus finally carried out by people who were specially trained to transform the traditional mental and material structures of the rural areas. This bold reform, which was conceived toward the end of Atatürk's life (1938), was implemented two years after his death, during the presidency of Inönü, with the help of a courageous minister of education, Hasan Ali Yücel.

A wave of constructive enthusiasm greeted the reform. The twenty-one institutes had an average of fifteen thousand students. The Institute of Higher Education, designed to prepare highly qualified and specialized teachers, was created in 1942–43. The best students from the village institutes were eligible. There were theoretical and practical courses, but research was also undertaken and published. A group of young authors began collaborating in 1945 on a journal whose title translates simply as "Journal of the Village Institutes." The teaching of foreign languages was also an important activity at the Institute of Higher Education. The courses offered took on an innovative and creative character. This institute, located near Ankara, rapidly became a center which attracted people from the villages as well as from the capital; it sponsored numerous shows, concerts, and lectures and made use of every opportunity to introduce to the public modern trends and modes of thinking.

One of the leading figures at the Institute of Higher Education was Sabahettin Eyuboğlu, whose creative and infectious spirit, which opposed fanaticism in all its forms, made him one of the most influential personalities of his time. He also played a major role in the field of translation: being of Anatolian stock and having studied in France (Dijon), he was tapped by the Ministry of Education to set up a translation bureau, with the help of Nurullah Ataç, the great literary critic of the post-Republican years. This bureau organized a systematic program to translate in a very short time hundreds of classical works from all languages, using the best Turkish translators and writers. This collective activity had a considerable impact on Turkish letters, for the numerous works translated opened new perspectives in the area of thought and literature. These publications, distributed nationwide, provided an opportunity not just to urban intellectuals, but also to rural teachers and institute students as well, to read both classical and modern works of world literature and to be exposed to the values and ideas expressed in these works. The cultural renaissance which resulted from this widening of intellectual horizons combined with that which had originated with the works of the intellectuals mentioned above.

Thus, paradoxically, the exploration of peasant life begun by the leftist intellectuals, who were to pay dearly for their quest for truth, was amplified by the pedagogical efforts initiated under Yücel's ministry. This situation could only lead to violent conflicts, for social developments in Turkey after World War II brought to power the very social classes that were most averse to granting concessions to the underprivileged peasantry. The projects for agrarian reform proposed by the government were rejected in 1946 by the National Assembly, which was dominated by a majority of large landowners supported by their conservative allies. These groups sought a rapid accumulation of wealth, a desire that was in direct conflict with the projects for emancipating and modernizing the villages. Inönü was forced to retreat. Repressive measures led to the deterioration of the village institutes and of the spirit which they represented, putting an end to the pedagogical experiments initiated by Tonguç and Yücel, who were dismissed from public service and punished for their audacity.

Despite this radical break, the impetus resulting from the innovations of the 1940s continued for a long time to bear fruit in the field of literature; young graduates from the village institutes, ignoring the various kinds of persecution which must have been rained on them, began to speak out and took on the task of relating through literary fiction their own lives and their own conception of the world. The great variety of stories and novels which they wrote reflected the diversity of Anatolia itself, its spiritual richness and complexity. The most striking difference between these peasant writers and their predecessors was the radical change in perspective that they adopted toward their universe. Up

to that point, they had been no more than passive objects of observation for urban writers; now they were becoming active subjects of this same literary movement. The peasant writer speaks not of the "other" but of himself, of an individual who was ignored, passed over, for centuries.

This mixing of cultures, this upheaval set off by the first writers to explore Anatolia in their fiction, by the vast movement of the village institutes, by exposure to world literature, and by the effort of modernization initiated by Atatürk, was bearing fruit. The peasant writers provided a vision of their reality that was brutal, forceful, and passionate. They assumed a stance that was denunciatory, accusatory even; but how could they have done otherwise, when they were giving voice to a suffering that had existed and gone unnoticed for centuries?

In what literary category could we classify this movement? Although it shares certain characteristics with the *roman à thèse*, the popular novel, and the historical novel, it does not really fit into any of these categories. It would be unfair, however, to assume that these novels, stories, and writings have no validity other than to reveal the Anatolian Atlantis, a lost continent rediscovered in the literary world! Even in a work that is not particularly literary, such as that of Mahmut Makal, the life experience which the narrative documents, the various seasons and the suffering they bring, the endearing humanity of the village people, their courage but also their passivity, their naïveté, their archaic ways, and what some call ignorance—all these things which make it seem as though contemporary history has had no impact are expressed in a prose that is beautifully simple, in perfect harmony with the nature of the narrative. Here in the prose of Makal and his friends is the spontaneous expression of Roland Barthes's "zero degree of writing." The following passage from Mahmut Makal's work "Our Village" (discussed earlier) reveals the unadorned nature of his style and the vehemence of his message:

> In his head, there was nothing except what he had assimilated in the course of his military service. His contact with the world had lasted only as long as he was a soldier. . . .
>
> "How many years ago was it, uncle, that all that happened?"
>
> "I was born in 1305 [the year of the Hegira]: my late father set my date of birth somewhat later in order to put off my military service: I was called up at the same time as Keunuk Veli. We went to sign up at the same time. . . . We were enrolled on the twenty-second day of the sixth month at Konya. . . ."
>
> But as to the year, however much he searched his mind, he could not remember. . . . So began the

process of figuring out how old he must have been. . . .

"I was born around the time of Uncle's wedding, Halil the Great, who is the oldest man in the village, but the date of his wedding is not known. . . . Nothing Uncle ever did was officially registered."

"So let's forget about Uncle's wedding. At the time of the great famine, I wasn't even in pants. . . . But no one knows when the great famine occurred." . . .

"My mother changes my age constantly."

"While I was over there, across the way, my labor began."

"Well, then, how old *am* I?"

"When the Negro killed Şinaşi the khoja, you were in my belly, and I had two souls."

"Well, then?"

"I gave birth when Corporal Ishak died."

I turn to my father.

"When did Corporal Ishak die?"

"We had been flooded over by the water from the Black Slope and Ali the Cutter's children were drowned. . . . Now then, it wasn't that year, but the following year."

The Anatolian village has changed somewhat since then. This is what Makal wrote fifteen years later, in the second French edition of *Un village anatolien* (1978):

At the town hall they speak only of progress, and money, for which the peasants have become as greedy as they are for land, is eating away at relationships. Reis Timisi, Abdullah, Demir, Adem . . . busy themselves on the telephone [which did not exist fifteen years before]. They call the cooperative, the schools, the café in Turkesh. They talk and talk and talk . . . and to make themselves seem important, they pretend to call Ankara, with the complicity of the telephone operator. . . . One must not lose face in front of people who have worked abroad. So, Reis uses the intercom to talk to his colleagues in the next room.

The need to communicate, to speak, to hear each other, to hear another using modern technology, which made its appearances in the village at the same time as currency, introduces into a world still dominated by myth and archaic modes an explosive dimension which bears no relation to the concerns of Western literature. Other customs, another literature; the novelistic form has entered a world where capitalism is still in its infancy!

The main plot of the peasant novel is usually rather simplistic (though rooted in reality), drawing on social contrasts, conflicts between the rich peasant (the agha) and the poor peasants, all set against a backdrop of religious fanaticism or conservative prejudices. Women are particularly vulnerable and are victimized from all quarters; the process of awareness which these dramas set in motion is somewhat tortuous. A complex and peculiar network of relations is created between the characters and their inner selves. The narrative takes form around these particular structures and remains on the frontiers of the so-called bourgeois novel, from which it borrows many compositional techniques, combining them with resources from its own tradition. Indeed, the oral tradition of the professional folk storytellers from both the country and the city, as well as the half-oral, half-written tradition of the "Hikaye" (a seventeenth-century genre), represented an important legacy for later novelists. This is how writers like Fakir Baykurt, Talip Apaydin, Basaran, and many others came to create a particularly original literary current in Turkish literature, rooted in the origins of that literature.

Fakir Baykurt (b. 1929) wrote a trilogy around the figure of Irazca, an extravagant old Anatolian woman, capricious and quick-tempered, and incorporating the daily life of a village, the very fabric of its existence, its destiny. This impressive figure embodies the frustrations endured by men and women in the face of the indifference and injustice displayed by those successively vested with power throughout the ages.

The first book in the trilogy, *Yilanlarin Öcü* (The Vengeance of the Serpents; 1958), caused a great stir; deputies in the Democratic Party condemned both author and work, even though the case was thrown out of court. As Baykurt himself has pointed out, the novel "is written in a bitter language which troubles us all. In many chapters it is the people's subconscious that speaks." And it is indeed the collective memory that speaks.

"Don't go to Yemen, to Yemen," we have said over and over. Since the beginning of time, no one has paid heed to us women. Women are all just like slaves, aren't we? "Don't go to Yemen!" There was the case of Kamilie, who went crazy repeating "Don't go to Yemen." There were those who left and came back alive, there were those who left and came back sick, who came back with white hair, and what of us? Our horses turned white as well. What terrible times, what ignorant sultans, so ruthless, those men! So many years of neglect toward the country, toward new brides, toward women. How can you expect a new bride to wait—a woman twenty years old, not even thirty—to wait for so many years. We have complained about our lot. And then suddenly it happened and it's past. A riddled past.

The villages have decayed. We have come, through these days of grief and mourning, widows. *My* hunter is dead, left early, we stayed behind, widow. Chali the Black was a hunter, idle. Holding a *saz* [reed] in his hand, he sat alone in a corner, swish, swish, swish. I will never forget, never; his friends would come over in a group, widow. He died and left too. . . . Grasshopper. . . . Taxes for me to bear alone, widow. In the morning I went to gather wood, in the afternoon to plough, widow. What endless nights without faith, without him. They pounded on my door. Bayram was little, widow. I couldn't open for anyone, widow."

An obsessive theme runs through "The Vengeance of the Serpents" from beginning to end, that of the reptiles' hatred for Irazca's family, the Karabayrams, who were responsible for the death of Shahmeram, king of the serpents. Irazca is also engaged in a tragicomic struggle with a powerful neighbor and his ally, the village mayor, for a reason which, though seemingly futile, is of prime importance to the old woman: she hates injustice. The "people's subconscious" mentioned by Baykurt is the communal sensibility of the Anatolian village, the product of a slow historical evolution within a closed world. The individual emerges only with great difficulty from a world that is both real (inequality, climate, injustice) and imaginary (myths, superstitions).

Peasant literature was to take on a new dimension with the first writings of Yashar Kemal. Originally from the village of Adana, he began his career by publishing the remarkable story *Sari Sicak* (Yellow Heat) in 1952. The publication of *Memed, My Hawk* in 1955 brought fame, and he has since turned out many more novels at a rapid pace, all written in an epic style combining real and fantastic elements.

Kemal's novels are generally set in the Chukur-Ova plain or the foothills of the Taurus Mountains and treat a rather broad set of problems: the changes resulting when an archaic rural society is confronted with modern capitalist brutality, new landowners, the destruction of nature, the clash of East and West, of old and new myths, and of ideologies, the transformation of an entire world. Memed the Thin, a rebel and provocateur turned honorable bandit, revolts in the same way as Sabahattin Ali's hero Yusuf the Taciturn, but Kemal manages to transcend the anecdotal character of the adventure novel through his poetic style, the exemplary humanity of his characters, and his vivid epic imagery.

With *Ortadirek* (1960; Eng. *The Wind from the Plain*) Kemal succeeded, like Baykurt before him, in creating a memorable character in the person of an old Anatolian woman named Meryemce. In order to survive another winter in their mountainside settlement, Meryemce and her family must, at all costs, go down to the plain, where day laborers earn meager wages during the cotton-picking season. This transhumance, led by an ailing, tenacious, half-delirious old woman, takes on an allegorical dimension. For the journey, Meryemce saddles up an aged horse, which dies soon after they set out. She is then carried the rest of the long way down on her son's shoulders. The extraordinary dramatic tension of the mother-son relationship, the burden of misfortune, the process of decomposition which grief works on a human being, the will to survive at any cost—all give Meryemce the symbolic stature of a woman from the Third World struggling against adversity.

By using a language enriched with the inexhaustible store of images inspired by southern Anatolia, and by his technique of thematic counterpoint, Kemal manages to draw the reader into a spellbinding world, an unknown universe gradually revealed. His style has the charm of the great Anatolian storytellers, but it also shares the flaws inherent in the oral tradition: incantatory repetition and overlong dialogues and monologues, which make sense when designed for evening recitation to peasant audiences but which weigh down a written text and throw it off balance. Nevertheless, the reader is swept along by the lyrical qualities of the language and the magical descriptions of the landscapes and characters, so that the poetic majesty of the work as a whole causes one to overlook defects that might otherwise seem unforgivable. Kemal had originally wanted to be a poet, and he remained one in his fiction.

Then with all its branches and its trunk, the walnut tree reached toward the sky and stretched out toward the mountains. The whole earth lit up as if it were day. The darkness of the mountains had vanished, and the darkness of the night. Have you ever seen a tree of light as big as the whole earth unfold against the blackness of night? Ah! my God, God whose wisdom I adore! An enormous tree of light reaching to the sun the stars! And the night was so terribly black. I swear to you there wasn't a single star. And the tree grew and grew! A tree streaming toward the sky with its branches and its foliage, a tree of light! . . . The tree remained luminous until dawn. I stayed to contemplate it until the break of day. My eyes were dazzled by it and I was exhausted. The horse I was riding, that blessed beast pricked up its ears and watched too. When dawn broke behind the mountain, the walnut tree became small again, very small; it was divested of its light and returned to earth. When day broke, I again saw the green walnut tree with its foliage standing in front of me, as if nothing had happened.

The agglomerated villages and provincial towns spawned still other works focusing on Anatolia written by urban novelists who had a thorough understanding of the region: Samim Kocagöz, Necati Cumali, Kemal Bilbaşar, Sayar, and Bekir Yildiz. These writers enriched the Turkish novel considerably, adding a great variety of situations and characters. But what is truly remarkable is the progress made by writers *from* the villages, who in the space of a single generation reached the point where they were producing novels. No matter that the route had been sketched out by their predecessors or by their urban contemporaries.

Turkish society, which was predominantly rural up to the 1950s, was to undergo an abrupt change thereafter. The fifty thousand tractors and farm machines allocated to Turkey under the Marshall Plan could only benefit farmers of means—i.e., those who owned a large amount of arable land, possessed bank credit, and enjoyed the support of the Democratic Party, which came to power in 1950. Sharecroppers and poor peasants were forced to leave the villages, and approximately half of them went to lie in slums on the outskirts of cities like Istanbul, Ankara, and Izmit. This caused a wide-scale social upheaval, for the breakdown of the archaic system of production served both to reinforce social inequalities and to put an end to the closed economy of the forty thousand Anatolian villages.

As the once predominantly rural population decreased dramatically, the urban centers grew proportionally, but the cities were incapable of assimilating such a great influx. Industrial growth had not kept pace with the increasing numbers of potential workers. Statistics showed that the agricultural sector was indeed becoming a minority, but it was being replaced by metropolitan centers that were half villages, resulting in a new type of agglomeration: slum cities. Uprooted peasants were transplanted to the inner city, where they formed a social class halfway between the proletariat and the peasantry, in search of a thousand and one little trades and odd jobs that would allow them to survive. Another factor that contributed to the crisis was the growth of Turkey's population from seventeen million to nearly fifty million in the space of sixty years. The exodus toward industrialized Western nations whose economies were expanding during the 1960s led to the integration of a sizable peasant population into the industrial sector of countries like West Germany, France, Switzerland, Belgium, and Holland. This complex social change had repercussions in many areas, including literature. The oft-portrayed and somewhat Manichean (though real) struggle between the agha and the poor peasant was gradually replaced by more complex novelistic structures, which took into account subtler aspects of human relations and raised many questions about the individual and society.

In the development of the Anatolian novel, two specific and very different cases deserve mention. First, the novel by Ferid Edgü, *O* (Him), subtitled "A Season at Hakkari," which deals with a theme that had been treated by Karaosmanoğlu a half-century earlier and by Makal thirty years earlier. Edgü's portrayal of inner motives and his style of writing shed a different light on the problem, however. Although the work concerns the isolation of a snowbound village decimated by an epidemic and abandoned by an indifferent administration, the focus is no longer on the historical guilt of the intellectual (as in "The Outsider") or on the despair over the uneven fight against an archaic system (as in "Our Village"), but rather on the almost metaphysical absurdity of the absence of interaction between two fundamentally different worlds. Although Edgü sets forth the concrete reasons which explain why such a dialogue is impossible, it is an existential sort of anguish that he feels in the face of life, death, and the impossibility of resolving the absurdity of the present. Cut off from the others, he feels dispossessed of himself, of his own self-image.

> I had conserved the memory of no human face. My fright continued, for I had no memory of my own face.
>
> My face (at least mine, o stunned reader). Nowhere to be found. I went out.
>
> I asked the innkeeper for a mirror.
>
> A mirror? he said, staring at me in disbelief. What do you want with a mirror?
>
> Nothing.
>
> I went back to my room. I felt my face with my hands. Like a blind man who sees with his fingers.

Both Karaosmanoğlu and Makal, each in his own way, are disturbed by the notion of time or space; Edgü even feels dispossessed of his physical presence. He is original in that he breaks with the system of imagery and writing that characterizes the peasant authors: using a series of short poetic annotations, he seeks to explore the experience of living via a painful interior monologue aimed at discovering another way of seeing the world.

Among the numerous novelistic subgenres that exist in Turkish literature—the realistic, intimist, and historical novels—it was again in the context of the Anatolian theme that a young woman, Latife Tekin, also of peasant stock, was to contribute something quite new, writing two novels, one after the other, with striking titles, *Sevgili Arsiz Ölüm* (Dear Shameless Death; 1983) and *Berci Kristin Çöp Masallari* (Berci Christine's

Tales of Filth; 1984),[10] which created a sensation among readers and critics and went through four printings in six months. Regarding her strange childhood, she wrote: "I learned to read frolicking under wooden beds with little demons and fairies." Tekin was to become acquainted with the underworld as well as the real world when her family moved to the city: "In order to get my footing in the city, I had to fight constantly. I had bruises and cuts everywhere."

Transplanted to the city (but what a city!), the villages are recreated amid piles of garbage, the refuse of the big city, sprawling shantytowns thrown together out of odds and ends overnight by a desperate population. The new city dwellers bring with them their imaginary world, their poetry, their vocabulary. The author, like her characters, transfigures reality to make it bearable. In the villages as in the shantytowns, the frenzy born of the mingling of imaginary and real worlds creates a style, a narrative in the form of an obsessive interior monologue which transgresses the rules of "good composition." The result is startling. The critic and writer Murat Belge states, "Twenty years of social transformation have finally given us an original cultural harvest." The critic Fethi Naci wrote, "Dream and reality overlap. A fine sense of humor. A story that proceeds at a breathless pace." And the novelist and essayist Atilla Ilhan was also enraptured: "You have given us a breath of fresh air by describing peasants grappling from day to day with genies and fairies, with their illusions and problems."

Tekin ranks with other writers of great talent like Leyle Erbil, Sevim Burak, and Nazh Eray, who have sought to depict the frenzy of the imaginary, the obsessions of the subconscious. In her second book particularly, she creates a kind of collective character, that of men and woman struggling to get their footing in the huge swamp of filth that surrounds the big city. It is a task comparable to that of Sisyphus, a struggle against bulldozers, trucks, and their masters, who seek to demolish shacks built overnight. The high and low points of this incredible struggle, this adventure, this saga, are related in a work that hovers on the frontier between novel and poetry; it is a picaresque lyric, a new kind of epic.

With each demolition and rebuilding, the shantytowns diminished a bit in size. Eventually they lost all semblance of a dwelling, and the people had lost all semblance of humanity. They had blended with the dust, mud, and garbage. Their clothing was full of holes; they were in rags from head to foot. Three babies, overwrought by the demolition and by the cold, fled. They turned into birds and flew off into the sky before the eyes of the wreckers. A woman who had injured a wrecker with an ax was escorted down the hill by two gendarmes. Those who remained behind could barely breathe after salvaging the sheet metal and sorting through the garbage. The last days of the demolition, not a single tree remained on the hill. Anything that people could get their hands on—rusty tin cans, light fixtures, disposable plates, boxes pulled out of the garbage, nylons, bottles—all were used to build the shantytowns: "The hill plunged into deep darkness. The wind attacked the roofs of the shantytowns after midnight. It tore off the roofs and bore them aloft like wings. With the babies attached to the roofs, it flew away."

If we are to reach a conclusion regarding the peasant novel or the novel focusing on Anatolia, we might say that it has a bright future. Moreover, this quest for identity is being pursued in other fields besides literature. A number of prizewinning films, for example, have been directly inspired by the literature of the peasant novel, as the following list attests: *The Arid Summer* by Metin Erksan, winner of the Grand Prize at the Berlin Festival in 1963; *Hope* by Yilmaz Güney, special jury prize in 1970 at Grenoble; *Yol* by the same author and S. Ogoren, winner of the Cannes Festival in 1982; *A Season in Hakkari* by E. Kral, with a script written by Ferid Edgü, winner of the Berlin Festival in 1983; *The Herd,* winner of the Locarno Festival in 1979, *Hazal* (1980) by Özgentürk, and *The Horse* by the same author, winner of the Tokyo Festival in 1985. This vast movement has influenced many other forms of art in Turkey as well, including painting, sculpture, music, and theatre, but a discussion of the impact of the peasant novel in these areas is unfortunately beyond the scope of this article.

Guzine Dino, Spring 1986, translated by Joan Grimbert

[1] *Bizim Köy* is available in French translation as *Un village anatolien,* Paris, Plon, 1963.

[2] For a review of a recent French translation of *Ince Memed,* see *WLT* 51:2 (Spring 1977), p. 329.

[3] Memduh Şevket Esendal, "Cöl," in his *Temiz Sevgiler* (Pure Loves), 1965.

[4] Yakup Kadri Karaosmanoğlu, *Yaban,* as excerpted in *Orient* (Paris), 47/48 (1968), pp. 141–42.

[5] Karaosmanoğlu, "The Oxcart," *Orient,* 47/48, pp. 154 ff.

[6] Available in French as *Youssoufle Taciturne.* Paris, Publications Orientalistes de France, 1977.

[7] Available in French as *Le roitelet* and *La nuit verte* respectively.

[8] Available in French as *Le tors du village,* Paris, Les Editeurs Françaises Réunis, 1958.

[9] Nazim Hikmet, letter to Kemal Tahir, 30 May 1941, as published in *De l'espoir à vous faire pleurer de rage,* Paris, Maspéro, 1973. The five-volume epic is available in French as *Les paysages humains,* Paris, Maspéro, 1973.

[10] Available in French as *Mort Chérie Fantasque* (1983) and *Les contes d'ordure Berdji Christine* (1984).

The Turks Are Coming: Deciphering Orhan Pamuk's *Black Book*

Orhan Pamuk takes his own portrait of the artist very seriously indeed—as he well should. After all, he's being touted as Turkey's new literary prodigy, putting in a timely appearance on the world literature scene. Turkish literature buffs ask one another: how come? After all, there are other Turkish writers who are as good or better but to whom the world pays scant attention. So, why Orhan Pamuk?

Well, for starters, not only does Pamuk's work sell quite briskly at home; it also translates into English like a dream. Educated at the prestigious Robert College (an extension of the American Ivy League in Istanbul), Pamuk can hear his work fall into place abroad. Besides, he has his finger on the pulse of world literature. While his compatriots are still tinkering with the secrets of the well-made modern novel, Pamuk has already graduated into postmodernism. He is part of what might be termed the New International Voice—like Isabel Allende, for example, who too must not be the only good writer in Chile, although she's the one we buy and read, in translation.

Pamuk's achievement is indeed considerable. At thirty-nine, he has four major novels under his belt. The first, *Cevdet Bey ve Oğlulari* (Cevdet Bey and His Sons; unavailable in translation), is a bildungsroman which tells the three-generation saga of an upper-class Istanbul family. The second, *Sezsiz Ev* (The Quiet House; also not translated), a modernist novel told from five different perspectives, deals with a week spent by four siblings, who represent four distinct generations, at their dying grandmother's country house during a dark period in Turkish political history (1981), when the different generations of Turks were actually at one another's throats. The third, which is enjoying a good run in the West, is the recently translated *Beyaz Kale* (Eng. *The White Castle*), an intriguing postmodernist novel ostensibly about a seventeenth-century Venetian slave and his Ottoman master, who resemble each other so much that they end up swapping identities.

In his fourth and most complex postmodernist novel, *Kara Kitap* (Black Book), Pamuk capitalizes on the contemporary psychological insight that all we can know of others are the projections of ourselves. With this insight carried into the novel, it stands to reason that all the characters are figments of the basic enigma which is the mind of the author, as enigmatic to the author himself as it is to the reader who is trying to decipher the text. In an effort to clue in (or to psych out) the reader, the novelist/narrator quotes Sheikh Galip, the eighteenth-century Ottoman mystic poet (who, as well as sharing his name with the protagonist, Galip, provides the book with its literary underpinnings), admonishing his readers: "Enigma is sovereign, so treat it carefully." We will try.

The novel takes the rudimentary form of the detective novel. Being sophisticated readers, however, we know that a detective story is only a setup to lead us through a maze where the entrance and the exit are preordained, strewn with clues and red herrings along the way, its arbitrary coincidences faked by the clever author to beguile, frustrate, and misguide us through a reality that turns out to have been illusion posing as reality—in other words, the fictive world. Of all the novel forms, the detective novel must be the most contrived. The novelist knows at the outset whodunit. With "Black Book" the convention is nevertheless turned on its ear: whodunit is an enigma. He is a voice on the telephone, perhaps.

Pamuk is not going to provide us with something so cheap as a solution. His protagonist remembers telling his lost wife once that the only kind of detective fiction he might find interesting is a story wherein the author does not know the identity of the murderer.

The plot of "Black Book" is deliberately simple: a guy is looking for his missing girl. He suspects that she is off with another fellow. He finds her by causing her demise as well as the other fellow's. What is complex about the work is the structure: a chimerical narrative (polyphonic, polyvalent, allusive, obscurantist, unreliable) in which chapters of the story are interspersed with chapters that are in the form of newspaper columns. No less complex is the content: a labyrinthine quest through Istanbul which encompasses an encyclopedia of Turkish life, past and present, with its cultural delights as well as its public shames.

Galip, an Istanbul lawyer, is abandoned by his wife, who also happens to be his first cousin. He guesses that, although she has vanished, she cannot have gone too far. She must be hiding out with her half-brother (and therefore another first cousin) Celâl, a newspaper columnist. And where could they be hiding? Well, at the family compound, of course, the old apartment building where the family intellectual, the newspaper columnist, lives (where else?) on the top floor. Not finding the missing pair there, Galip moves into the flat, sort of, and begins to lead a double life as himself and also as Cousin Celâl, the columnist.

The protagonist suffers from a case of deep hero-worship for his columnist boy-cousin as well as from unrequited love for his girl-cousin wife, who is his Beauty Incarnate. This is the stuff of a heavy-duty family romance, with incestuous implications strewn about like herrings that are strictly of the red variety. The wife's name, Rüya, inasmuch as it means "dream," clues us that we have here a persona who is not only a Platonic Ideal but an identity closely related to the protagonist's as an Idealized Self: a narcissistic and incestuous anima (or the female double).

Wife-cousin-sister Rüya is a consumer of cheap fiction, especially detective novels, which she devours as she swings her long legs. Galip keeps her craving well supplied with sleazy reading material, but apparently she has other appetites that have gone unsatisfied. Why else would she have absconded? Well, irony of ironies, the heroine as an addict of detective fiction provides this "detective novel" with its mystery.

As the author has named Galip after the Ottoman poet who wrote the long mystical poem in which Love searches for Beauty (*Hüsn-ü Ashk*), Cousin Celâl's appellation obviously alludes to the great Sufi mystic teacher Mevlana, whose name was *Celâl*-ed-din Rümi. If the English-speaking reader gets the names of the two characters mixed up, not to worry; so does your Turkish-speaking literary sleuth. The state of confused identities seems to be a deliberate ploy on the part of the author.

The protagonist, the lawyer called Galip, having sneaked into and taken possession of his cousin's flat, clothes, files, and phone calls, takes on the columnist's function as well as his form. He goes through his cousin's mental and physical furniture, producing columns which he passes off as the work of the missing journalist. However, our lawyer-sleuth, unlike Perry Mason, bungles his quest and manages to get both his idols killed (unintentionally?) by an enigmatic assassin whose identity he never discovers.

The key to finding his wife-sister-cousin Rüya (Dream) seems to be not only to be *like* Cousin Celâl but to *be* Celâl. Remember, this kind of impersonation is exactly what every novelist, working in the interests of "realism," wishes to accomplish successfully so that the reader will be fooled into thinking the person he has come to know so intimately is Emma Bovary when in fact he knows only an aspect of Gustave Flaubert ("Mme Bovary, c'est moi"). Remember also, collaterally, in the language of mystical enlightenment, that to become oneself is to *be* another—a notion that will be explained presently.

There are a couple of threads in "Black Book" (of the many that are dangled, abandoned, or used as false

Orhan Pamuk (*Robert H. Taylor*)

leads) which wind together into a kind of yarn to take us through the labyrinth, the enigma, or the black hole which will not reflect. Though tongue-in-cheek for the most part, Pamuk drags into his novel Gnostic and mystical texts which, to use his own words, are "all the more convincing because [he himself is] a nonbeliever." The first involves Mevlana and his passion for a flimflam man called Shams. When Mevlana fell for his dubious love object, he was already the greatest Sufi master ever; but his passion served only to embarrass family, friends, and students, thereby putting Mevlana (one assumes) into a bad light vis-à-vis the expectations of proper behavior from him as the dean of a famous theological seminary. Mevlana had already achieved "enlightenment," yet, having turned into the Big Cheese, there was nothing else for him to do but dry up. So, he surpassed himself by doing something really cheesy. His most famous catchphrase with which he regaled his students was, "If you wish to increase your perception, then increase your necessity."

Falling in love inappropriately was one way of increasing his own necessity. He unabashedly told the world that he, the Great Mevlana, wanted "not to be *like* Shams, but to *be* Shams." He could surpass himself only by totally submitting his identity to his lover's. (This is the heart of the mysterious paradox, by the way, that Pamuk lifts from Sheikh Galip: "Mystery is to be Oneself and to be Another"—the same mystery that we are admonished to treat carefully.) Well, Mevlana's submission of his exalted identity, under the identity of the town creep's, must have confused and frustrated his friends, relatives, and adherents. Being Oneself and also

Another, indeed! It must have stuck in everybody's craw, and so it was not surprising that, eventually, Shams was thrown down a black well by assassins and killed.

Who had the motive and the opportunity to murder Shams? ponders the postmodern police detective Orhan Pamuk. Who stood most to gain from Shams's death? Mevlana's adherents and sons? Or Mevlana himself? Did Mevlana contrive to get Shams killed? After all, it was Mevlana whose necessity was in fact increased by the death of his lover, thereby increasing his perception. We shall, of course, never know.

Coincidentally, did our lawyer also arrange to get his cousins-idols bumped off (inadvertently on purpose) so that their deaths would illuminate his perceptions? This is the question that Pamuk never seems to tire of begging, obliquely behind his "Black Book," but which he never answers. He misses no opportunity to posit another concentric equation: he himself (as the author) fulfills his *dream* (Rüya) to become the *writer* (Celâl) by submitting his alter selves to the mystery of *art* (death). In terms of the mystery in "Black Book," who stood the most to gain, after all, by his love objects' (alter egos) deaths? The Author, of course! Did not Dante gain as a poet by Beatrice's death? Petrarch of Laura's? Orpheus of Eurydice's? One is reminded of a line by Margaret Atwood involving power politics between lovers in which the poet wants the upper hand: "Please die I said / so I can write about it."

Another fascinating bit of mystic lore Pamuk digs up concerns a sect called Hurufi. At first glance one might even think the author invented the Hurufi Book of Onomancy in the interests of postmodernist high jinks. But no, Hurufism is for real and subject to serious scholarship, even today, involving divination by the letters "written" in faces. Fazlallah of Astarabad (b. 1339) was the founder of the sect, which drew meaning and conclusions from a combination of the letters of the Arabic alphabet. In "Black Book" we learn that, according to Fazlallah, sound was the demarcation line between Being and Nothingness, since everything that crossed over from nothingness into the world of materiality produced a sound. The acme of sound was, of course, the "word," the exalted thing called "speech," the magic known as "words," which were made up of Letters. The origin of Being, its Meaning, and the material Aspect of God were distinguishable in Letters that were clearly written in the faces of men. We all had native-born characteristics of two brow lines, four eyelash lines, and one hairline—seven strokes in all. At puberty this figure increased to fourteen, with the late-blooming nose dividing our faces, and with its poetic doubling (reflection) we reached the number twenty-eight, the number of letters in the Arabic alphabet, which brought the Koran into existence. Fazlallah, in an effort to bring the count up to thirty-two, the number of letters in the Persian alphabet (he was, after all, Persian himself), perused the line under the chin and found two, which he then doubled, reaching thirty-two.

Crackpot stuff? Well, you will find references to what is "written" in the rose, for example—or in the spots of the tiger—in the fiction of the Great Borges himself, as well as in that of many other great Gnostic poets, past and present. Fazlallah, who started it all, proclaimed himself Messiah (the twelfth Imam returned to purify Islam) with seven apostles to help him proselytize in Isphahan on the hidden aspect of the Koran. Accused of heresy, he was tried and executed. The belief passed from Iran to Turkey, thanks to Nesimi, a poet and one of Fazlallah's successors, who put all his writings in a green trunk and went around Anatolia, finding followers for his sect. Nesimi himself was later captured in Aleppo, tried endlessly, and flayed; his body was subsequently exhibited in the city, then cut into seven pieces and buried in seven cities where he had adherents. Hurufism spread quickly among Anatolian Bektashis, who talked about *kanz-i mahfi,* the secret treasury of the universe, which is God's's True Quality. The problem was to decipher the clues in the world in order to achieve the treasury. They set themselves up to decipher this mystery in every thing, every place, every person.

It is all just too much fun for one postmodernist novelist to have by himself, but Pamuk does. He has Galip rifle through his columnist-cousin's treasury of arcane publications to find a weird little book by one F. M. Üçüncü (I still do not know if this Üçüncü is a legitimate commentator), who presumably says in his book *Esrar-i Huruf ve Esrarin Kaybi* (The Mystery of Huruf and the Loss of Mystery) that Fazlallah was a true Easterner. To think of him as part of any platonistic, pantheistic, cabalistic thought was wrong. According to Pamuk's protagonist, Üçüncü postulates that East and West occupied separate halves of the world and that never the twain shall meet. At times one of the two halves was victorious over the other, making it the master and the other the slave. The historic junctures in the seesaw of ascendancy were not coincidental but logical. Whichever half was at any given time successful in viewing the world as a mysterious, double, and magical place was the half that was the ascendant. Those who saw the world as a simple, single-meaninged, unmysterious place were doomed to fail and to end up as slaves.

The second part of Üçüncü's book (as the lawyer-protagonist registers it) is devoted to a detailed discussion of how Mystery was lost. The loss of Mystery was a loss of "center," therefore a loss of order. In the Age of Happiness all of us had "meaning" in our faces, but with the loss of Mystery, our faces lost that "meaning." The fact that faces looked so much like one another was because of the "emptiness" they all showed.

Galip, like the author himself, is also engaged in looking for clues to put together a meaning. None is forthcoming, however. All the clues are red herrings, coincidences that he contrives himself. The object of the search (Platonic Ideal, Beauty, Reality, Identity) is Dead on Arrival—in other words, a setup, the dead duck the author props up in order to shoot several hundred pages later. Art is all illusion, sleight-of-hand, trickery, impersonation, ventriloquism, the creating of mannequins or wax dummies by a master craftsman (which abound in "Black Book" in the subterranean passages of Istanbul). Art is a dark mirror, a black mirror: art does not reflect Life. So what's new?

Well, "Black Book" is very engaging. When it first fell into my hands, I read it with a quivering excitement, filled with both envy and recognition, much like Anton Salieri taking down Mozart's dictation of the *Requiem* at the end of the movie *Amadeus*: "Yes! Of course, yes! Ahh, yes!" I stopped friends on the street to narrate for them whole sections of the novel. No other book had spoken to me so completely, hitting my concerns on the head, grabbing the themes I myself pursued, beating me to the punch line. Granted, Pamuk and I share backgrounds, yet why all the excitement?

I had a hunch, as a watcher of the world literary scene, that here was a Turkish writer who was going to Make It. The Nobel, for example: for years the names of Yashar Kemal and Nazim Hikmet have been submitted, only to be turned down, as the Nobel Committee, one suspects, scratched its illustrious collective head and wondered what Turks see in those two writers; but here was Orhan Pamuk, a kid who was doing the right thing at the right time. I could already hear "Black Book" in English. All it needed was the right translator.

To speak more generally, "Black Book" is made of the stuff that grabs us all. Aside from being pertinent to our times, there is something appealing in Pamuk's unrequited quest for meaning, an innocence in his sophistication, and truth in his trickery. Here is a wide-eyed devourer of books, Pamuk himself, who is heartbroken at the fact that, seductive as literature is, it cannot deliver on its promises, let alone guarantee a good time in bed.

Pamuk, in his fourth and most ambitious novel, seems determined to reposit in this book a revolving index of a culture, high and low, that produces a Turkish intellectual: everything that delights and instructs

the Turkish heart, including an obsession with history, beauty, mystical philosophy. The book derives from the world of the Haves (as opposed to the Have-Nots). Not only is Pamuk the bookish son of a well-heeled family who has inherited the pursuit of happiness as a natural right; he is also an obsessive researcher into odd historical quirks, which come out of the past in recognizable embroidered satin tatters that he works into the crazy quilt called the postmodernist novel.

The modern trend in Turkish "realism" had been the so-called Village Novel, in which the author, more often than not a member of the middle-class intelligentsia, depicts the trials and tribulations of godforsaken peasants in an effort to "educate" the reading public (also composed of the middle class) and to produce a national conscience as well as consciousness: the Writer posing as Teacher, as Pamuk never tires of pointing out. It is perhaps this educator's mask worn by the Turkish novelist that has turned off New York Publishing, which has no taste for teachers. And we all know that what doesn't play in New York doesn't get to play on the rest of the world's playgrounds.

Pamuk, who has deliberately set out to become a world-class writer, has borrowed the attitudes and strategies of Third World authors writing for the consumption of the First World. Not only does he know all the tricks; he never misses one. His work translates like a charm precisely for the same reason Isabel Allende's work travels easily into English: English is, in fact, the common language *behind* the various languages out of which the new world-voice is being created—like world rock music—the destination of which is also the United States.

As John Updike somewhat biliously points out in his *New Yorker* essay on Pamuk and the Czech Ivan Klíma (2 September 1991), it might be the Iowa International Writing Program that fosters a global voice. True, Pamuk has put in an almost obligatory stint at Iowa; but the global voice is more likely to be tied to world economics, I suspect, than to Midwestern schools playing host to world writers. Updike, as a master of the modern novel, justifiably feels left out of the fun and games perpetrated by the slew of international writers and foisted on him to review. "Fantasy and cleverness," he says; "exotic visions," he says; "effortless gymnastics," he says. He is not entirely sure if the new kids on the block are For Real. How does one know if they are any good if one does not have the proper critical tools with which to measure them against the likes of himself, John Updike, or (heaven forbid) Master Hemingway?

True, fantasy and cleverness have taken the place of the restraint and symmetry of the modern novel, apparently because that is the form in which the material from the Third World sells over here. And why not? Vis-à-vis Turkish literature, the English-speaking world has been looking high and low for a Turkish writer with whom to identify. If fantasy or cleverness is the only vehicle on which Turkish literature can arrive upon the world scene, well then, all the more power to Orhan Pamuk.

Güneli Gün, Winter 1992

Turkish Family Romance

Kurban olam kalem tutan ellere . . . .
■ PIR SULTAN ABDAL

Don't say, "It has been said," when I really hear you saying, "Ağa listen to me."
■ GÜNELI GÜN, BOOK OF TRANCES

Shahrazad's presence might yet make things come out all right.
■ GÜNELI GÜN, ON THE ROAD TO BAGHDAD

John Barth has called Güneli Gün "a shrewd and magical Turkish-American storyteller, sired by García Márquez upon Scheherazade." The wily American writer and teacher of writers, who himself has amply suckled from Shahrazad's breast (see his recent novel *The Last Voyage of Somebody the Sailor,* 1991), might have also admitted that he served as midwife in Güneli's delivery upon our writing scene. He does make his appearance, in fact, in Güneli's novel *On the Road to Baghdad* (London, Virago, 1991), where, under the code name of Jann Baath, he engages Güneli's Shahrazad in conversation on the topic of her tale-telling, enjoining her to write *"as if* you already have a gentle heart" (243) that would redeem Shahriyar, her husband and would-be executioner. No doubt, the pedagogical injunction that I have heard Barth reiterate in conversation must have been delivered also to his students, of whom Güneli was one, at the Johns Hopkins Writing Seminars: "Write as who you are." Barth is crafty enough to know that since a version of that injunction, "Know thyself," was delivered by Socrates, the primal teacher of crafty teaching, *his* students have been trying to comply for some two and a half millennia with mixed success. If knowing oneself is a sinuous path and and a circuitous enterprise, writing *as* oneself or, as Jann Baath would have it, *as if,* is treacherous indeed. "The intricate evasions of as" may well be the best characterization of the writer's vocation in this regard, as summed by Wallace Stevens in this pithy verse from one of his better-known poems

("An Ordinary Evening in New Haven"). Evasion and pursuit are, of course, sides of the same coin, a coin whose faces a writer cannot countenance without some trepidation. A common recourse in the face of such peril is the assumption of evasion as tactic when one means to pursue and a course of pursuit when one intends evasion. In the mirrored reversals which inevitably haunt writers and writing's realm, one hopes to stay on course.

The Turkish literary tradition has wrought this strategy to elaborate extremes. Orhan Pamuk and Güneli Gün make their respective ways through the stations of this venerable itinerary. Pamuk's *Kara Kitap,* discussed in the accompanying essay by Güneli, who is in the throes of delivering the novel into English for Farrar, Straus & Giroux, is an exemplary specimen of hide-and-seek, whereas Güneli's own *Book of Trances* (1979) and her more recent *On the Road to Baghdad* bend this strategy to exquisite ends. Her foregoing commentary on Pamuk's novel, then, becomes most revealing, not only with regard to Pamuk's latest opus, but, just as significantly, with regard to her own novel and its intricate way stations along the path of writing's picaresques. This last word is meant, obviously, to rhyme with arabesques, since the spirit of Shahrazad and of the thousand-and-one-night tales hovers playfully in the intricate plots of this writing's family romance, as Güneli points out with regard to Pamuk's novel and as she engagingly dramatizes in her own latest work.

The epigraphs I have placed at the head of these lines may be instructive in how this latter-day Shahrazad demurs in the tradition of pursuit by evasion and evasion through pursuit. The first is from a sixteenth-century Turkish bard who met his untimely demise at the end of a rope knotted by those who could not distinguish between poetry's pursuit and its persecution, not unlike the prosecutorial Galip who forecloses on his fugitive kin's evasion in Pamuk's novel. Pir Sultan Abdal, magnificently brothered to Süleyman the Magnificent in the telling wiles of our Shahrazad, found his demise at the hands of his royal pursuers. He serves Güneli as Virgilian beacon at the framing end of her picaresque *On the Road to Baghdad,* where she persuasively devises a fratricidal fate for the poet, now a classic in Turkey's literary canon. The latter two suggestive epigraphs are from Güneli's own two books. What is suggestive in them is a strategy of attribution whose ploy is unmasked by the admonitory sentence from Güneli's *Book of Trances* I have placed at the head of this commentary. In the case of Pir Sultan Abdal, we know that he did indeed pay the ultimate price in ending up as a sacrifice to the hand that holds the pen, as his verse cited above roughly translates. He, of course, dictated the terms of the challenge, even as he wielded the pen and embodied the poet of his apostrophe. Far from acting as shield, this made him a triple target no tyrant threatened by poetry's clairvoyance could pass up. No extreme of self-effacement could assuage the wrath of worldly interests, even, or especially, since the felt threat originated in the otherworldly condition of one turned away from earthly interests to disinterested investments. *Abdal,* Pir Sultan's surname, refers to one transformed, the Sufi who divests himself of the worldly in order to assume the "simplicity" that in the Socratic legacy we refer to as *docta ignorantia,* or wise ignorance, and in the Christian tradition goes by the designation of *intellegentia spiritualis* and is practiced by those who would adhere to apostolic simplicity. This sort of self-effacement, of course, is an ironic form of self-empowerment, and those in power are usually intelligent enough to recognize the odds such form of enablement could place in their way. Certainly the authorities of Socratic Athens were wakeful to such odds, as were the Pharisees and roman legates of Jerusalem. Süleyman the Magnificent, in whose reign his mirrored obverse and versifying specter Pir Sultan Abdal sang, and whose time serves as the setting for Güneli Gün's novel, appreciated the power of the "transformed" no less than the Greeks, the Jews, or the Romans; hence the inexorable end "the fates" meted the poet. Attribution has never proved sufficient as immunity, whether the authorizing agency be imputed to the *sophia* of philosophy, the holy spirit that moves the *eiron* and the irenic, or the love that moves the poet and the hand that inscribes his breath. As the Ağa of Güneli's *Book of Trances* cuts to it: "Don't say 'It has been said,' when I really hear you saying, 'Ağa listen to me.'" *On the Road to Baghdad* puts the burden of the "messenger" on the most vulnerable—"the weaker gender." That Shahrazad should serve as her mistress *and* rival in one of the picaresque heroine's time-spaces need not surprise us. The primal tale teller's own stories originate in her vulnerability. She is, after all, holding death at bay with her tale-telling wiles. And that the author herself should find ancestral precedent in this mother of novelists is predictable enough. The interest lies, of course, in *how* both heroine (Hürü) and author (Güneli Gün) muster the necessary craft and craftiness to traverse various centuries and the divers vicissitudes that attend not just the traditional wanderer-messenger, worldly pilgrim, or other-worldly *viator,* but one who would also embody the vulnerabilities history has willed to the "weaker sex." In this respect, Güneli also works very much in the gender-bending feminist tradition of Virginia Woolf, whose *Orlando* (1928) is the modern prototype of the female historical picaresque in a decidedly man's world. Güneli's devices are literary, of course, and they pertain to what the Western critical

idiom has lately pegged as postmodernism, though in the Eastern context of Güneli's novel these narrative procedures antedate the West's own modernism and novelistic history. In this guise, the procedures of *On the Road to Baghdad* are doubly literary, since the recourses available to its literary figures (heroine and author) are already part of the inventory of literature's legacy: impersonation and music. That is, fictional representation and its masks animated by the breath of the muses, holy or otherwise, if any distinction really be viable. In this sense, Shahrazad is legion, and Güneli Gün, not unlike her heroine, figures as one of her avatars. And that is why, as the novel itself has it, "Shahrazad's presence might yet make things come out all right." As indeed they do, for *On the Road to Baghdad* is a novel that Shahrazad would be proud to have one of her daughters author. Which brings us back to Güneli's comments on Pamuk's *Kara Kitap,* now in her hands, undergoing a rebirth into another language. Cousin Celâl's reaction is predictably, one could say impishly, reflexive. After all, he is the one who ran off with the writer's dream. And here is the mirror he holds up to his cousin's enigmatic countenance: "Don't say 'It has been said,' when I really hear you saying, 'Ağa listen to me.'" By which this Cousin Djelal, editor and literary columnist, like his *Black Book* counterpart, means to say to his Daydream cousin that what she says has been said by Orhan Pamuk through his prosecutorial and pursuing Galip is what she would have us listen to, or read from her own pen, as we accompany the picaresque heroine of her novel through the centuries of baneful history, enforced metamorphoses, inspired transformations, and breathtaking song. When *On the Road to Baghdad* is born into its Turkish-language life, as it will be shortly, the readers of Orhan Pamuk's *Kara Kitap* will discover that Güneli Gün is not just the commentator of the novel in the pages of *World Literature Today* and its translator and deliverer into English, but could well have been the absconded djinni whose circuitous itinerary has taken her from the "iron-belted people" (as she refers to the folk of Anatolia who engendered her stories) to the "rust belt" of the American Midwest, not far from Cousin Djelal (as his name is now spelled), who goes on, in the spectral spirit of Pir Sultan Abdal's epigrammatic verse, limning out literary calumnies in editorial columns.

Djelal Kadir, Winter 1992

YEMEN

Emigration and the Rise of the Novel in Yemen

Well before the rise of the novel in post–World War II Yemen, emigration and its attendant alienation and dispossession had become a dominant theme in Yemeni poetry in response to harsh social and economic conditions resulting from hundreds of years of war and oppression. Known in classical times as *Arabia Felix,* Yemen had gradually lost its position as a happy land of beauty and wealth, becoming by the dawn of the twentieth century one of the poorest, most backward places on earth. Before the birth of Christ, its location in the heart of the Old World had made Yemen a rendezvous point on many of the most frequented commercial routes between Europe and Asia, a happy geological circumstance that allowed it to control much of the trade between East and West. This domination boosted Yemen's agricultural economy, and the country became famous for its dams and irrigation system. On the other hand, its strategic location made Yemen a target of increasingly formidable invasions from Greece, Rome, Ethiopia, Persia, Egypt, and eventually Turkey and Britain.

The Turkish (Ottoman) occupation, which lasted for over four hundred years (1517–1918), was dominated by conflict and corruption that finally left Yemen an economic wasteland. The Porte's administrators manipulated tax revenues for their private interests, which led to frequent local uprisings against the Turks. In 1839 The British took advantage of this turmoil and seized Aden in order to protect their route to India. Over the next few decades, they gradually established a protectorate in southern Yemen, pushing out the Ottomans as they advanced. In the north, however, the Turks continued to hold sway until forced to evacuate at the end of World War I, a turn of events resulting largely from the campaign waged against them by Imam Yahya, who had acceded to the throne in 1904. The exhausted country became independent in 1918 in a state of famine, destruction, and anarchy (Wenner, 46). At this point in its history Yemen was divided into a British protectorate in the south—including Aden and a group of sultanates, emirates, and sheikdoms—and the imamate in the north.

The British achieved relative stability in the south by allowing the sultans, emirs, and sheiks outside Aden a relatively free hand with their own people. In the north, to forge a semblance of political stability from ruin, Imam Yahya adopted such oppressive policies as the holding of hostages to ensure loyalty. He staffed powerful political and military posts with his own brothers or sons. Although these tactics may have protected the imam from overt opposition, they also encouraged hatred of his regime (Wenner, 18–19). In foreign relations, Yahya adopted isolationist policies to protect his sovereignty as he fought the British over Aden in the south and the Saudis over Asir in the north.

When he was killed in 1948 and his son Ahmad came to power, the enmity Yahya's despotism had engendered grew into ever-widening opposition to the rule of the imams. Several reformist groups attempted to overthrow the government in hopes of changing the direction of Yemen's political system and floundering economy (Wenner, 20). Finally, in 1962, the Free Yemeni Party, which had carried out revolts in 1948 and 1955, succeeded in ending the imamate regime and establishing the Yemen Arab Republic. During this same period, the National Liberation Front was fighting the sultans and other rulers in the British protectorate. The NLF won independence for the south, including Aden, in 1967 and founded the People's Democratic Republic of Yemen.

Unfortunately for both Yemens, political and economic stability did not come with declarations of victory and independence. In the south, numerous coups within the NLF kept the country from true peace until unification of the two Yemens in 1990. In the north, only one month after the 26 September 1962 victory celebration, the country was plunged into a bitter civil war which lasted until 1970. The imam's sympathizers, supported by Saudi Arabia, led a Royalist counterrevolution against the Republican government supported by Egypt. The last Royalist attempt to regain power was the unsuccessful siege of Sana'a in 1970. Instability continued to plague the country, however, until Ali Abdullah Saleh rose to power in 1978. It was he who was elected president of the unified Yemen, the Yemeni Republic, in 1990.

Perhaps the most important social effect of the seemingly innumerable nineteenth- and twentieth-century Yemeni wars was the emigration of legions of Yemenis to other parts of the world. Thousands were forced from their homeland by the poverty and political fragmentation which resulted from conflict with the Turks and the British. Thousands more left in consequence of the high taxation and other repressive policies of the imams and sultans. Recurrent drought brought yet more emigration when farmers were unable to harvest enough to provide for their families after paying taxes to the rulers and rent to the land owners. An especially powerful push factor for Yemeni capital and labor was the economic attraction of Aden during British colonization. Aden also became the main exit port to the outside world for Yemenis who went to sea, eventually reaching India, Southeast Asia, France, Britain, and America. Other Yemeni emigrants found their way to East Africa, especially Ethiopia and the Sudan (Al-Sabah, 47–48). Most hoped simply to improve their own lives and those of their families, but a growing number—chanting "poverty, ignorance, famine,

Imam"—escaped in order to support liberation movements.

Abdulla Al-Baradoni, an eminent Yemeni poet and critic, has declared that being forced to leave one's homeland, the most agonizing of events, produces the saddest, most creative folk songs (272). One of the most widely known songs, which also serves as an excellent example of Yemeni folk poetry, narrates the sufferings of an emigrant who escapes the tyranny of the imam's soldiers only to live a miserable life of loneliness and sorrow.

Al-Balah[1]

And tonight, Al-Bal, why comes tonight the gentle
  breeze
Winding from the East, smelling of kadhia,
Smelling of coffee, with its soothing whisper,
Recalling boyhood memories in our precious land.

Tonight the feast and I far from home,
The despairing flood of my heart overwhelming,
My heart infatuated with the valleys of Bana, Abyan,
  and Zabid,
And my body a captive of cruel emigration.

I set out from my homeland, the land of death.
"The days of the plague season," they said, "are
  near,"
My companions died, and in my misfortune I have
  lived.
I have lived by planting the land and sowing my
  exhausted soul.

I remember my brother, a trader. Wherever he went
  he spread goods.
The demon's soldiers came and took all he had, all
  his bugash.[2]
He set out early. Where are you going? "Ethiopia," he
  said.
And he went. . . . Today they say, "He is doing well."

Like him, I emigrated early; success comes in being
  early.
My provisions were bread and two stony rials.[3]
And I sailed on a ship carrying cow hides and coffee
For the fortunate merchant and the tyrant.

I searched for work at the port of Asab and in the
  city,
In road and building construction, but I did not find
  what I needed.
I complained to my brothers of my trouble and
  prolonged toil.
They said, "The sea." I replied, "The sea. Oh, ship!"

And I lived as a worker on the sea for fifteen years,
On the ship of a one-eyed, severe Greek captain,
And the coal blackened my skin like a chimney.
And I traveled around many a far land.

Like traveling birds, I saw all islands.
I traveled aimlessly until I hated it.
And I chose Adanakil's Plain and selling mats.
From one place to another. Oh, ship without a
  canvas!

A stranger's body put down upon the Western shore,
His soul in the East, his heart gone.
If only the Red Sea were narrowed or bridged
Across to the other shore.

Stranger away from home like me with no resting
  place,
What if you weep and weep the stones and trees.
You weep and weep, and tears pour down like rain,
And you let your tears flow from the heart's blood.

In my emigration I sing, "Oh, God, don't degrade
  us."
And longing consumes my soul in exhaustive flames.
I will return, oh my homeland, oh happy home,
Oh, my paradise! Oh, my refuge! Oh, my precious
  mother!
— Motahar Al-Iryani[4]

Another famous Yemeni emigration poem depicts the torturous loss of identity resulting from life away from the homeland.

Al-Ghareeb[5]

There he lived many years,
His old name but a memory,
His new one engraved on papers written in a non-
  Arabic script.
And he wandered the seas and desolate regions of the
  earth,
Changing names and changing papers.
In his pocket many papers,
And the name! Any name,
Any name—no matter.
— Mohammed An'am Ghalib

That the novel, struggling to gain a foothold within Yemeni literature after World War II, should also focus on what many Yemenis consider the greatest of national tragedies is no surprise. The coming together of such an overarching theme with that of the fight for freedom from despotic government gave Yemeni fiction the cultural authority it needed to find a public. In addition, the surging growth of a cultivated middle class after the end of the civil war in 1970 provided Yemeni novelists with an audience acutely aware of the political and economic difficulties their people had faced for generations. These readers were avid advocates of a new national literature that could attract worldwide attention. They wanted Yemen to break out of its cultural isolation, to take an honored place among the world's nations. Fiction dramatizing the suffering and heroism of the revolutionary generation was the perfect medium through which to present this ancient yet new nation on the world stage.

The first published Yemeni novel appeared in 1959. Written by Ali Mohammed Abdo, it was entitled *The Cart-Horse*.[6] *Wag Al-Wag Tragedy* was published the following year by Mohammed Mahmoud Al-Zubari. In 1966 came Ali Mohammed Abdo's *Labor Memoirs*. Then began what Yemeni scholars sometimes refer to as "the golden age of the Yemeni novel" with the rise of "the Seventies Generation." 1971 brought Mohammed Abdul-Wali's *They Die Strangers*, 1976 Ahmad Mohammed Al-Mu'alime's *Strangers in Their Homelands*, 1977 Hussein Salim Basideeg's *The Fogway*, and 1979 Mohammed Honaybir's *Al-Batool Village*. All of these 1970s novels focused on the expatriation of Yemeni men in search of a better life for themselves and their families at home either through the accumulation of money to be sent back to Yemen or through the overthrow of their people's rulers. In the early 1980s came *The Old Port* by Mahmoud Sa'gheeri and *The Hostage* by Zaid Motie Damag, dealing with the imam's policy of ensuring loyalty among powerful Yemenis by holding their children in prison.

The compelling subject matter of these works notwithstanding, the Yemeni critic Abdul-Aziz Al-Magaleh, writing in the late 1980s, saw the Yemeni novel as "a newborn attempt and stumbling effort." Our writers, he explained, "are unable to express [themselves well] through the novel . . . which requires long contemplation and observation" (11). Following a line of development common to the rise of the novel in other countries, the Yemeni novel began as a weak genre dominated by reporting and moralizing, its art and creativity often overwhelmed by political and social commentary. By the mid–1980s, Al-Magaleh felt, Yemeni novelists had not yet arrived at an advanced state of creativity and mastery of the genre. Al-Magaleh found Honaybir's theme in *Al-Batool Village* effective but his narration too direct and spontaneous: "It does not penetrate into the boiling, uproaring depths" (12). He felt that Basideeg's novel *The Fogway* fails to achieve a "balance between the action and artistic structure" (12).

Despite such reservations, the Yemeni novel deserves attention for its unflinching focus on the displacement and dispossession of a people so tyrannized that emigration becomes their only avenue of hope. The best of these novels develop the idea that, although expatriation may solve an individual's temporary social, economic, and political problems, one pays dearly for leaving the homeland. The emigration of Yemenis, particularly from the late 1940s through the end of the rev-

olution in 1970, almost inevitably turned into a torturous experience for the individual and his family both at home and abroad rather than an easy way out of life's difficulties. Like other Yemeni intellectuals, as well as outside observers, Al-Magaleh feels that emigration is "the problem of problems for the Yemeni people. There are emigrants from almost every home. The villages' strongest youths have been taken away by emigration" (9).

Perhaps the best example of a Yemeni fictionist who devoted himself to the emigration theme is the late Mohammed Abdul-Wali. Among the writers of the "seventies generation," Abdul-Wali is generally accepted by the Yemeni literary establishment as the most accomplished. It is often said in Yemen that Abdul-Wali is one of the most masterful fiction writers not only of Yemen but of the Arab world, particularly among those whose works focus on the flight from their motherland of the persecuted and economically disadvantaged.

Born of Yemeni immigrants in Ethiopia in 1940, Abdul-Wali was raised and educated away from his family's homeland. Not merely a close observer of Yemeni expatriate life, Abdul-Wali was a full participant in it. His novel *They Die Strangers*, often considered by Yemenis to be the greatest work of fiction yet produced by one of their countrymen, brings this experience to literature by developing three main themes connected to emigration and the alienation and dispossession it produces: first, the pain of life in Yemen before the revolution and how most Yemenis accepted misery as their lot in life and refused to fight for liberation from their oppressive rulers; second, emigration as a way to escape misfortune and attain personal goals; and third, the intolerable situation of half-breed children.

Most of the characters in *They Die Strangers* are impotent and defeated. Wahb Romeyah, another Yemeni critic, sees them as "prisoners of historical circumstances. In attempting to challenge these circumstances, they follow a way which leads to nothing but complication of the problem. . . . They all choose emigration" (84). These characters leave their homeland in order to pursue their personal dreams rather than the welfare of their nation. Al-Haj Abdul-Lateef, one of the richest Yemenis in Addis Ababa, is a member of the Yemeni Liberation Party. He is its mouthpiece, collects donations, and delivers enthusiastic speeches in support of the liberation of Yemen; yet he mocks Abdo Sa'id when the latter vows to go home, accusing him of being mad. Naively, Abdul-Lateef insists that the tyrannical imamate regime remains in power because young Yemenis are abandoning religion. On the other hand, although he often speaks of his own virtuous deeds and sees religion as the only way out, he comforts himself with such irreligious activities as drinking alcohol and visiting prostitutes. In defeat, Al-Haj Abdul-Lateef ends up dreaming of nothing but having a grave like Abdo Sa'id's. Salih Safe, who, as the novel progresses, gradually loses enthusiasm for the revolutionary movement, dreams primarily of making money. As a young man, he supports the Liberation Party and plans to return to Yemen to live under the new government. After the failure of the 1948 uprising, however, he loses faith and stops collecting donations for the movement. At that point, his life begins to spiral downward into despair.

Abdul-Wali's most powerful political/moral point in the novel is that the lives of such expatriates are dominated by an egotism and separatism which will never help change the desperate situation in Yemen. This lesson is brought home forcefully by Abdul-Lateef's secretary. Given no other name in the novel, the secretary criticizes the emigrants, represented by his employer, who talk about Yemeni liberation but never do anything to bring it about. He tells his boss disdainfully, "You talk twenty-four hours a day about your country's liberation, but you will never liberate it. You have escaped. You know, from here you can only . . . shout . . . 'We will avenge.' But you open your mouth and no one can hear you except us [in Ethiopia]" (81). The secretary believes that confrontation is essential: "The liberation of your country requires first . . . to liberate yourself . . . not to be afraid and to fight, not from overseas but there, face to face with the enemy. . . . You have escaped from the ghost of the Imam. . . . Frankly speaking, you will never liberate your country, and if anybody does it will be those who remain there" (82).

Romeyah characterizes Abdul-Wali's novel as a depiction of "a collapsing human world. . . . Its people are sick—they carry the seeds of destruction within themselves, and they move toward their demise with determination. Their lives, relationships, and dreams are strong, but emigration kills their souls as they get used to it and submit to it. . . . And from the heart of this split world which is about to break apart and fall come the half-breeds torn apart by the duality of their allegiance to home or the absence of any allegiance at all (51). Himself half-Yemeni, half-Ethiopian, Abdul-Wali dramatizes his view of the mixed-blood issue through the secretary, a character obviously drawn after himself. That such a central character remains nameless is symbolic of his position, or lack of one, in Yemeni or Ethiopian society. In essence, he is a man without a country, a race, or an identity. The son of a Yemeni immigrant and an Ethiopian mother, he has never been to Yemen. When Abdo Sa'id rejects his own half-breed son born of an illicit relationship with an Ethiopian woman, the secretary takes the child in. His own tragic life has rendered him kindhearted and humanitarian. He knows what it is to feel illegitimate and reviled. He explains to Abdul-Lateef, "Yes, I decided to take him. He will be like a brother, . . . my younger brother. . . . I don't want him to be alienated. Do you know that a person without roots—that would be difficult for you to understand easily, but I do. . . . We are a new nation. . . . [We] don't know you" (81). In his obsessive pondering of the half-breeds' hopeless social situation, he reflects on how Abdo Sa'id's son is

> . . . torn up like him [self], does not know a
> homeland to belong to. . . . His father dreams of
> his land, of the future there in Yemen when they
> 'liberate' it. . . . As for [the child], he is cut off a
> rootless tree. He is 'no one.' Yes, no one. And his
> mother . . . has a land and home, [but] . . . he
> is strange. He cannot say that he is Yemeni, he
> does not know Yemen and has never seen it in
> his life. . . . What if he went there? How would
> it receive him? It might spit him out just as this
> land [Ethiopia] does. (78–79)

Abdo Sa'id himself serves to unify Abdul-Wali's themes of overwhelming oppression in the homeland, the futility of escape, and the agony of mixed blood. Rather than joining with other victims to face his oppressors at home, he abandons his country and people to pursue the individualistic, selfish goal of becoming the richest person in his village. He leaves his family because he envies others'. He becomes a victim of what Al-Baradoni calls "money fever" brought on by the success of some who have left the country and then returned with their earnings. When Salih, a returned emigrant from Abdo Sa'id's village, builds a glimmering semi-palace, Abdo Sa'id determines to seek his own fortune abroad. His decision is confirmed when he hears the talk of women in the field, including his wife: "all who go to sea return wealthy" (27). In an especially powerful scene, Abdo Sa'id's half-naked son reproaches his father for not giving him dates like those Salih hands out to the village children upon his return. Thus Abdo Sa'id embarks for Ethiopia with the desire to build a better house than Salih's, to buy land for his son and silk clothes for his wife.

Once in Ethiopia, Abdo Sa'id never thinks about the liberation of Yemen, never contributes to the revolutionary cause nor attends a community council. When Abdul-Lateef tries to persuade him to abandon his plan to return to Yemen, he answers, "I don't care about the [political] situation. I will return to my village, plow my land, and remain with my wife and son" (72). Naïve and shortsighted, Abdo Sa'id imagines that money will solve all his problems, whatever they are. He thinks he can return home and live peacefully without anything disturbing his fantasy. In pursuing his dream, however,

Abdo Sa'id allows himself to backslide into miserliness, immoral relationships with women—one of which produces his half-breed son—and religious hypocrisy. Although he achieves a measure of prosperity, these actions make him an object of suspicion and fear in the Yemeni and Ethiopian communities. His alienation from both is dramatically expressed in his rejection of his mixed-blood son. In the end, he dies alone on a filthy pile of empty sacks in the back room of his canteen far short of his dream.

Such a life astonishes the Italian physician who examines Abdo Sa'id in the hospital. In a conversation between the physician and a male nurse, the irate doctor powerfully drives home Abdul-Wali's most persistent point as he condemns the inhumane circumstances of Abdo Sa'id's life in particular and those of Yemeni emigrants in general.

> — Uncivilized people. How can they live in this filth?
>
> — But they live.
>
> — To die like animals. . . .
>
> — I can't imagine how this man lives in that hole. How is it possible? My goodness, that life is like hell. . . .
>
> — But what could they do except that? They left their land and their families to make a living.
>
> — . . . A nation that leaves its land betrays it.
>
> — Injustice makes betrayal a simple thing.
>
> — But it doesn't justify escape. (94–95)

In a contemplative moment after Abdo Sa'id's burial, the secretary expresses the pathetic futility of Yemeni emigration.

> "Are graves the end of wandering about, of this struggle and searching? . . . Graves are the right place for individualistic emigration. . . . [Abdo Sa'id] died without leaving anything in his life except pain. A wife deserted for years . . . and a son who doesn't know him. And a land to which he gives no drop of his blood. He died a stranger like hundreds of Yemenis all around the earth. They live and die strangers without knowing solid ground to stand on. As for this grave, it is not his. . . . It is the grave of another people. The graves we [Yemenis] occupy are Ethiopian. Isn't it enough that we take our living from their mouths, much less take their graves? My god, what strangers we are, what strangers we are!!" (95–96)

Although *They Die Strangers* may be one of the works Al-Magaleh had in mind when he wrote that the Yemeni novel is a "stumbling effort," it attains true dra-

matic power in this scene. Abdul-Wali's social/political/moral message may sometimes intrude upon the narration, but the human devastation suffered by the emigrants comes squarely before the reader's eyes and heart in the secretary's words. For a few moments at least, the characters, and particularly the secretary, come to life.

Hussein Salim Basideeg's novel *The Fogway*, published in 1977, is more directly didactic than *They Die Strangers*. In effect, *The Fogway* is a sociopolitical tract written as a proletarian novel. It sees Yemeni society as polarized between a tyrannical ruling class and a downtrodden working class and reads like a revolutionary's manual when it discusses how one should go about organizing the people and then confronting the regime in power. Still, Basideeg achieves notable artistic effect in his emphasis, reminiscent of Abdul-Wali's, on the need to remain in Yemen in order to defeat the forces of oppression which perpetuate the conditions that have forced so many to flee.

Early in the novel, Basideeg points out that leaving the homeland has been the fate of almost every young man in his country. It has been the only way one could make a living for oneself and one's family. As part of his sociopolitical message, Basideeg summarizes the push factors of Yemeni emigration in a chat between Salih, his main character, and the young men with whom Salih discusses Yemen's problems: "The homeland has dried up, the Sultan and the Imam exploit it from all sides. . . . And people have escaped to search for their living abroad. Only women, children, and old men remain at home" (11). A member of the southern lower class victimized by the sultans, Salih is someone we would expect to leave Yemen as such young men had been doing for years, but he is not a quitter like most characters in these novels. He is decisive and stubborn. Rather than accepting emigration as inevitable, Salih insists on remaining in Yemen in order to work with other youth to prepare for the revolution. His group rejects emigration when they realize that, to improve their own lives and those of their loved ones, they must achieve freedom for all the people of their country: "No, no, no, the young men should stay [at home] to work. . . . We will squeeze the stone to get our living" (13). Accordingly, they "decide to work in secret and to continue their march to put an end to injustice and corruption in their land" (8).

To prepare for revolt, the young men determine to build a school "to be followed by other schools, then factories and stores . . . [and] the power which was not in their hands." The school would provide "the strongest base for obtaining other powers" (80). The people's struggle would include two phases, the first concentrating on education. Basideeg emphasizes the importance of education for Yemen by introducing Salih to the reader with a book in his hand. Salih and his companions know the secret behind the authorities' refusal to build a school in their village, so they build one themselves. It is during the construction of the school in Al-Garn village that the novel's first confrontation between irate laborers and ruthless soldiers and officials takes place, and it is upon prevailing in this struggle that the workers first fully comprehend their power.

When Salih becomes the leader of the young men who promise to remain in Yemen rather than emigrate, he realizes that he himself will not be able to remain at home but must "follow a new way" (11). He must find help for his fellows. He must provoke the people into putting an end to the Sultan's rule. This choice to become a political leader in opposition to the despotic government eventually forces him to become a fugitive. To organize the people and to teach the gospel of mass revolution, he must move about the country and work in disguise. Thus he begins a series of clandestine displacements, a sort of internal emigration, which forces upon him "the drudgery and sufferings of travel and migration . . . [for] the accomplishment of the wide-range incitement to revolution in three big cities and some villages . . . for the continuation of their march . . . to his desired aim" (47). The displacement and loss of outward identity he undergoes, however, are essentially positive, not debilitating and defeating like those experienced by the desperate, hopeless characters in other Yemeni emigration novels.

Salih's movements through the narrative and South Yemen form a three-stage journey: 1) determination to remain at home and fight, 2) incitement of the people to revolt, and 3) confrontation with the sultanate regime. The first, which culminates with Salih and his companions' decision not to emigrate, develops along with the growing, unavoidable realization of the Yemeni people that they are mistreated by their government. The second begins with Salih's decision to leave home "in order to press the issue and support his companions successfully" (87). He tells his wife, "Don't be afraid, Nora. Allah is with us. . . . I will disappear . . . to think the matter over with my companions and to end this corrupt situation. We will change the atmosphere for our children" (90). Leaving his home village of Si'on, Saleh introduces people throughout South Yemen to ideas of freedom and independence. Through his efforts, the workers and common people begin to see the necessity of unity in order to confront those rulers who are determined to keep them divided, ignorant, and backward. Salih attracts people, especially oppressed workers, wherever he goes. His sincere desire to help his people endears him to them.

Basideeg finds his surest voice in the second stage of Salih's journey. The series of scenes in which Salih convinces the tobacco planters to stand together against the forces of the Sultan are the most successful in the novel dramatically, although the action is often handicapped by the social and political commentary which characterizes the novel as a whole. These scenes begin with Salih's drawing the attention of the hard-working planters to their trade monopoly, then advising them to establish an association that will allow them to go to market and buy sardine fertilizer without having to deal with greedy middlemen. He also encourages them to employ their own agent for tobacco exports and to form a cooperative with the sardine fishermen. When the planters take his advice, their actions lead to a climax of revolutionary fervor and a conflict with wealthy merchants. Finally, they promise Salih, "We will work together. There is no power on earth that will separate us" (220).

The third stage of Salih's journey, confrontation, is less developed and less convincing than the first two, but it does clarify the novel's most important symbols. The confrontation takes place on two levels—individual and national. Individually, Salih faces the Sultan's most dangerous henchmen—the Chief of Guards, who murders Salih's wife, and Om Al-Sa'ad, the Chief of Guards's sweetheart as well as mistress and confidante of the Sultan. Salih feels that assassinating "these two horrible symbols of betrayal . . . will help bring about the revolution or at least limit the people's pain . . . or perhaps stir up fear in [the Sultan's] followers" (14). On the national level, Salih determines to revolt "whatever the situation is" (230). The people will gather together "and eventually totally destroy the statues" (237) symbolic of the Sultan and his forces. The novel ends with Salih's dream that Si'on has been blessed with heavy rains symbolic of renewal and revolution. The fog, symbolic of tyranny and oppression, is dispersed by the rain, and the sultanate is swept aside by the people.

Like Abdul-Wali, Mohammed Honaybir actually lived emigrant life in North Africa, in his case the Sudan, and used his experience to create a tableau of the losing battle waged by Yemenis who had left their homeland. His novel *Al-Batool Village* (1979) is more overtly political than *They Die Strangers,* more like *The Fogway* in this respect. A strong advocate of unity between North and South Yemen, Honaybir uses his two main characters, Salih Hussein and Fadhl Al-Yafi—a northerner and a southerner respectively—as mouthpieces for his political message.

In the north, Salih decides to leave his pregnant wife and emigrate south to Aden after his father is killed by the imam's soldiers: "I will emigrate like tens of thousands of Yemenis who have spread to the East and West of the earth, escaping injustice and searching for their living. . . . I will do like them . . . [and] others will do like me since the prevailing logic in my homeland is that of injustice" (32). In the south, Fadhl and his mother decide to leave for the north after the deaths of Fadhl's father and sister. The Sultan of lower Yafi, in order to take over the family's land, imprisons the father, who dies in confinement, and causes the rape of Fadhl's eldest sister, Fatima, who then commits suicide. Desperate, Fadhl's mother knows that she and her son must abandon their ancestral home.

> "We will leave Al-Garah," the mother says.
>
> "To where, Ma?" says Fadhl.
>
> "Allah's land is wide."
>
> "I know . . . but to which place . . .?"
>
> "To any place where there are no sultans. . . ."
>
> "But all places around us are sultanates."
>
> "To the land of the Imam, in the north, . . . We will go to Al-Bayda." (108–9)

After a short time in the north, however, Fadhl and his mother realize that tyranny bedevils both parts of Yemen "as if the imams and sultans have sucked oppression from one mother's breasts" (113). After the death of his mother and experiences with the oppression of the imam's governors, sheiks, and soldiers, Fadhl sets out to leave Yemen altogether: "to any land in which there are no sultans, imams, or sheiks" (115). He returns south, to Aden, where he takes a job on board the *Satirani,* an English vessel. Salih already works on that ship, and thus the two men meet and agree that they are victims of the same cruel monster which is ravaging North and South Yemen. To escape this monster, both, like the speaker in Al-Iryani's "Al-Balah," accept the prospect of an endless journey of emigration in which no land, only the sea, will be their home.

Salih and Fadhl dream of nothing in their forced exile but the collapse of the regimes in the north and south. They pity the Yemenis they see toiling desperately in ports all around the world. The only hope for them is in revolt. Listening to Salih tell about the French Revolution, Fadhl declares:

> "If there were men of this kind inciting our people to revolt, there would be neither imams nor sultans in it. . . . How I hope that all the sons of the Yemeni nation will read this story. To know how the French people revolted, crushed the tyrants, and destroyed that prison which they called 'Al-Bastel.' The imams and sultans do not intend to build schools because if we know how

to read and write, and we read such stories as this one about other peoples' lives, no doubt we will revolt against their tyranny and destroy their palaces just as the French people did." (147–48)

Although he has lost all of his family, Fadhl is optimistic about Yemen's future: "The day will come when our nation will take up its position among the civilized nations of the world" (74).

Honaybir's message is clear: only through unity and education can the Yemeni people defeat the oppression that has beset their nation for hundreds of years. Fadhl and Salih agree that the only way to put an end to the imamate and sultanate regimes is through confrontation in all of Yemen, both north and south. Salih's experiences with corruption and disorder have rendered him keenly observant, so he pays careful attention to the foreigner-imposed discipline on board the *Satirani.* In a letter to Haj Manie he declares, "All workers on the ship form one family. . . . Cooperation and hard work are obvious when the sea hinders the peaceful passage of the ship. Then you will see all workers on board become one power to resist its roughness. Despite its strength and tyranny, the crew's unity in resisting always wins victory" (123). But Salih knows that an ignorant people cannot confront tyranny. He tells Fadhl, "We who have understood and know how world nations live should educate our sons so that they can fulfill our dreams. That is why I say to you that my hope is to educate my son" (148).

Haj Manie, who has been away from his village in Yemen for ten years, is pessimistic about his own chances for happiness—his wife is dead and he has lost contact with his only son, who works on a ship he knows not where—but the wisdom which comes from years of dislocation and dispossession allows him to understand what it will take to change the homeland. His advice to Salih upon hearing of the birth of the latter's son back home articulates his hope for the Yemeni people: "He [Salih's son] might be, with his age group, their nation's hope. . . . Accordingly, my son, take care of him and educate [him]. Don't let him face what you and your father did . . . and what all Yemenis are still facing" (46). Following Haj Manie's advice, Salih determines to send home all his earnings. This will be his way of contributing to the welfare of the Yemeni nation. Years later, never having seen his child, he reflects, "My son has reached fourteen by now and I want him to continue his education. I will not leave him without education even if I do not save a pound, and if I have to remain an emigrant all my life" (241).

Honaybir's concern for the children of Yemeni emigrants recalls Abdul-Wali's poignant dramatization of the half-breed problem in Ethiopia. Al-Haythami, a Ye-meni native, hesitates to marry a Yemeni woman who has just arrived in Port Sudan. He fears that although marriage may solve some of his personal problems, it may also result in children who will suffer for being conceived outside Yemen: "If I, who was born in the heart of Yemeni country, feel lost and alienated, how about those who will be conceived in another country? Here, the Sudanese . . . will treat them as Yemeni emi-grants like their father. And if they are destined one day to return to their homeland in Yemen, they might be treated there as Sudanese emigrants or at most half-Yemeni" (233). But Salih responds convincingly: "Don't you know that Yemeni emigrants, all around the world, form the main support for the Yemeni liberation move-ment which struggles to put an end to the Imam's re-gime in our land? . . . Isn't the agony of displacement and the bitterness of emigration enough to give them a fulfilling . . . decent life in their homeland?" (234).

Most characters in *Al-Batool Village* are impotent, intimidated victims who do nothing but pray to "Allah" to demolish the imamate and sultanate systems in Yemen. Salih's mother, Fadhl's mother, and Moham-med Al'Shatibi are powerless when attacked by their rulers' soldiers. As a result, they give up and abandon their homes. They no longer believe life in Yemen will improve. Mahdi Al-Gayfi, who sees no point in talking about Yemen's problems, compares the injustice there to "an incurable disease in a place where there is no doctor" (251). Salih also tries to take vengeance on his rulers by imploring "Allah" to support him and his downtrodden people, but like Abdul-Wali's secretary and Basideeg's Salih, he is against emigration as an es-cape from oppression. Leaving one's homeland, he de-clares, "is the fate of the weak. Allah likes the strong be-liever and hates the weak believer. And since we respond to injustice by escaping through emigration, the injustice will continue" (32).

All Yemenis in *Al-Batool Village* except Salih are de-feated and dispossessed by the end of the novel. Forced to flee, all lose their hopes in the country to which they emigrate, and some die tragically. Haj Manie's long, dif-ficult life ends with his death in the auction-market cof-feehouse in Aden with only poorly paid porters and market mediators to donate money for his burial. Fadhl represents the complete defeat of his family when, the sole survivor, he drowns with the sinking of the *Sati-rani*. Only Salih lends the novel a glimmer of hope. He survives the sinking and, despite the loss of his savings of the last ten years, is more determined than ever to help his son. He vows to save enough money for his son's education whatever the consequences. Taking a

job on the *Shantele,* therefore, he begins another jour-ney.

Nearly every novel written by a Yemeni deals with some aspect of emigration, and nearly all do so with rel-atively heavy-handed didacticism. The three we have examined here, however, achieve at least occasional ar-tistic success, Abdul-Wali's *They Die Strangers* being clearly the most accomplished in this respect. Although Abdul-Wali's writing can be faulted for moments of sty-listic stiffness or narrative inconsistency and may be said to be superficial in its characterizations, his work contributes much of artistic and social value to the body of world literature devoted to the depiction of suffering caused by tyranny and oppression. *The Fogway* and *Al-Batool Village,* despite their more intrusive political/social commentary, should also be taken seriously as fictional records of a people's struggles against unjust government. Most important, Abdul-Wali, Basideeg, and Honaybir have laid a foundation upon which pres-ent and future Yemeni novelists can build more solid lit-erary treasures for their homeland as Yemen, now fully unified between north and south, continues its journey back toward a central place in the world like that it knew in ancient times.

Mohammed Saad Al-Jumly and J. Barton Rollins,
Winter 1997

■ **WORKS CITED**

Abdul-Wali, Mohammed. *Yamutoon Ghuraba* [They Die Strang-ers]. Beirut. Dar Al-Awadah. 1971.

Al-Baradoni, Abdulla. "Aghani Al-Ghurbah" [Migration Songs]. In *Fonoon Al-Adab Al-Sha'bi Fi Al-Yaman* [The Art of Folk Litera-ture in Yemen]. N.p. 1981.

Al-Magaleh, Abdul-Aziz. "Fi *Tareeg Al-Ghiyoom* Wa Al-Bahth Ain Tareeg Lil-Riwaya fi Al-Yaman" [*The Fogway* and the Search for the Novel Route in Yemen]. *Al-Yaman Al-Gadeed,* 11 (1987), pp. 8–16.

Al-Sabah, Aml Yousif. "Al-Heigra Wal-Heigrah Al-Mu'akisah" [Emigration and Counter-Emigration]. *Alam Al-Fikr,* 17 (1986), pp. 47–48.

Basideeg, Hussein Salim. *Tareeg Al-Ghiyoom* [The Fogway]. Bei-rut. Dar Al-Farabi. 1977.

Honaybir, Mohammed. *Garyat Al-Batool* [Al-Batool Village]. Cairo. Alm Al-Kutob. 1979.

Romeyah, Wahb. "Mushkilat Al-Heigrah fi A'mal Mohammed Abdul-Wali" [Emigration Problems in Mohammed Abdul-Wali's Works]. *Al-Yaman Al-Gadeed,* 6 (1987), pp. 27–91.

Wenner, Manfred W. *Modern Yemen, 1918–1966.* Baltimore. Johns Hopkins University Press. 1967.

---

[1] "Sinbad's Song." Thanks to Dr. Patricia Ta'ani for helping make the translation of this poem more poetic in English.

[2] Old Yemeni coin, equal to two and one-half fils (100 fils per rial).

[3] Maria Theresa coins.

4 Motahar Al-Iryani is the most widely known contemporary Yemeni poet of emigration and emigrants.

5 "The Stranger."

6 All English titles referred to in the text of this article, and all quotations from both primary and secondary sources, are translations of the original Arabic by Mohammed Saad Al-Jumly. The original Arabic titles are given in the "Works Cited" listing above, with the English titles in brackets.

Africa and the Caribbean

Africa

GENERAL

Toward a Convention of Modern African Drama

Modern African creative writing has been the subject of intense critical analyses. Critics have taken freely to almost every existing methodology in their attempts to evaluate it. Dan Izevbaye has recently assessed these diverse approaches.[1] It would be superfluous, so soon after his brilliant appraisal, to engage in a similar exercise which, in any case, would lead us away from our immediate concern. However, a significant feature of the criticism of African literature which is relevant to the topic under discussion here is the controversy among critics as to who is qualified or not to participate in the critical evaluation of African literature. So far the protagonists of this debate fall into two broad categories: the *nationalists* and the *universalists*. Since I am concerned here with the criticism of modern African drama, I shall closely examine their respective approaches as applied to this topic.

The nationalist approach grew out of some African critics' reaction to the cultural criteria alien critics adopted in evaluating African literature. The African critics observed that the persistent interest shown by most foreign critics of African literature in exotic cultural trappings often blurred their perception of the true artistic merits of modern African creative writing and made them applaud works of minimal or dubious literary merits. They became apprehensive of the detrimental consequences on the literary quality of the young African literature if ethnographic contents became the major consideration in its evaluation. Consequently, they began to advocate the nationalist approach to modern African literature.[2] They claimed that only Africans, using critical canons derived from African culture and esthetics, were capable of judiciously assessing African creative writings.

Présence Africaine pioneered the call for the nationalist approach, whose aim would also be to retrieve the critical appreciation of African works from aliens: "The soul of our people will not be heard in the concert of nations until they have regained their artists, their authority to judge and their privileges as consumers and interpreters of their works of art."[3] An echo of this view is to be found in Joseph Okpaku's forthright assertion: "The primary criticism of African art must come from Africans using African standards."[4] This claim, we are further told, is based on "a belief that a creative writer cannot completely escape from the established literary traditions of his society, and [on] a recognition that only those who are born to a particular culture are the best qualified to interpret it."[5]

Both the critics who should adopt the nationalist approach and their reasons for doing so are clear enough; what remains obscure is the method. The possibility of Africans' using purely African critical standards to give an African interpretation of a piece of modern African writing presupposes the existence of these "African critical standards" or at least of an established literary tradition from which they can be derived. It is here that the nationalists run into difficulties; there are no clearly defined African literary critical standards at the moment. Even Joseph Okpaku, an eloquent advocate of the nationalist approach, concedes this when he pleads for its establishment "by examining, from the point of view of the African culture and aesthetics, aspects of life and death which writers often dramatise."[6]

The nonexistence of a clearly defined set of literary standards in Africa is not synonymous with the absence of an African literary tradition. Africa has a long literary tradition from which critical canons could be derived—the tradition of its oral literature. This literature, which dates back several centuries, still flourishes today. Over the years it has developed its own genres, and drama is preeminently one of them. But traditional African drama differs in several respects from modern African drama written in European languages. In traditional African drama the arts of dance, music and mime are the salient elements; they play a more important role in dramatic expression than does dialogue. Of course, the language of traditional African drama is indigenous and unwritten, unlike that of modern African drama which is written in European languages. Also, traditional African drama, usually meant for presentation in the public or village square, has no rigidly fixed time limit. On the other hand, modern African drama, influenced by European dramatic tradition, is designed for the proscenium-type theatre, and its duration is conventionally determined.[7] Thus both types of drama have distinctive characteristics. It follows then that modern African drama will need a basically different set of critical canons from those which may be valid for traditional African drama. This evidently invalidates the argument that the evaluation of modern African drama should be based on the existing African literary tradition.

The universalist approach, when critically examined, does not fare better than the nationalist approach. The main advocates of this approach are Western critics of African literature. They also include some Africans who, like their former European and American teachers, equate Western civilization with the universal. They argue that modern African literature, being an integral part of world literature, should be set against universal critical standards. This seemingly convincing argument is essentially specious. What, one may ask, constitutes "universal critical standards"? The universalists do not provide any satisfactory answer to this crucial question. In the absence of a clear-cut definition of "universal critical standards" one is invariably tempted to look for them in the essays of the universalists themselves. The search is vain, for instead of "universal critical standards," one notices in their analyses a conspicuous absence of yardsticks borrowed from non-Western literature. Trained in the Western literary tradition, they do not often extend their frame of reference beyond Western literature. It means therefore that what they present as a universalist approach is nothing other than a Western approach.

Before proceeding further, it is perhaps appropriate to examine quickly the comparative approach, which is derived from Western criticism but which its few African proponents prefer to present as a different or even new critical methodology. After categorically stating that the goal of the comparative approach is to trace and account for influences, one of its most ardent advocates goes on to say:

This [tracing of influences] does not mean examination and compilation of influences on a particular writer. It involves the attempt to distinguish between the treatment of particular themes by African and foreign writers in order to bring out and emphasise those peculiar African themes and attitudes which the African writer deals with. [Critical criteria] for judging modern African literature cannot be arrived at in isolation; *they can be determined through a comparison of the techniques used by African writers with those of western writers.*[8] (My stress.)

I will not delve here into the abuses which have arisen from the quest for influences, such as the refusal to recognize the originality of successful African writers by assigning to them what Earnest Emenyonu has termed Western "literary godfathers."[9] But I should like to emphasize that this declaration unmistakably aligns the comparative approach with the Western approach. To make the acceptability of African writers' techniques depend on how favorably they compare with those of European writers means, in effect, the application of Western critical canons to African literature. This unwillingness to judge African literature on its own terms becomes glaring when it is recalled that, in the absence of any commonly acceptable African critical canons, the only available tools for the proposed comparative approach are invariably Western.

Since, as we have shown, both universalist and comparative approaches derive from, and are consequently much the same as, the Western approach, the question one may ask is whether or not Western criteria are valid for appreciating modern African drama. Theoretically they are, provided the African play conforms to Western dramatic conventions. But in reality this proviso takes on a crucial significance, for a play cannot be decidedly African and conform at the same time to Western dramatic traditions.

It must be remembered here that a play is deeply rooted in the culture from which it is produced. That is why, for instance, an African playwright cannot, unless he wishes to produce some special effects, attribute European mannerisms to his African characters, just as a European author cannot introduce into his play a *griot* as a chorus, commentator and character. In other words, being essentially a collective art, drama relies heavily on the social context. Consequently, unlike fiction and poetry, which may be easily transposed into a new culture, a play remains intimately linked with its original cultural background.

This is not to say that a play necessarily has a limited or local appeal. Of course, a play can and does often have a wide and sometimes even universal appeal if its theme is commonplace enough. But then, for such a play to take on a new cultural identity, it must lose its former one. A classic example of a modern African play which has been successfully transposed from another culture is Ola Rotimi's *The Gods Are Not to Blame*. In reworking the universal incest theme borrowed from Sophocles's *Oedipus Rex*, Rotimi has infused into it so many Yoruba elements—speech patterns, dances, songs, mannerisms—that the play ceases to be Greek and becomes convincingly African.

Similarly, the National Theatre of Zaïre has invested with indigenous cultural identity its adaptation of Molière's *Le bourgeois gentilhomme*, which treats the theme of the social upstart—another theme common to most, if not to all, human societies. The resulting play, entitled *Mundele Ndombe*, like *The Gods Are Not to Blame*, would certainly appear to the uninitiated to be an original African play. This is because in both cases the cultural background is now authentically African and no longer European. As Demas Nwoko has pertinently remarked:

> When a writer is inspired by the work of another author and produces a new play, it is a valid work of art. It should contain artistic values that are true expressions of his own personality and exhibit new theatrical values that can make it a worthy extension of the work that inspired it. Thus it can bear and support proudly its own title.[10]

The Gods Are Not to Blame and *Mundele Ndombe* clearly satisfy these prerequisites. That is why they can be said to have been successfully acclimatized to a new cultural environment. But in the process they have lost their original cultural identity, thus demonstrating the extent to which a play reflects its cultural background. This peculiarity of drama was aptly summarized by Jean Duvignaud when he observed:

> Le théâtre, surtout, est un art qui s'implante profondément dans l'existence collective, tant par ses origines, l'utilisation qu'il fait des rôles et des situations vivantes, que par ses résultats et les publics qu'il touche ou éveille. Plus que tous les autres arts, le théâtre ne saurait être détaché de la région où il prend naissance.
>
> (Drama, especially, is an art which is deeply rooted in collective existence in regard to its origins, the use it makes of living roles and situations, its results and also the audiences it affects or arouses. More than all the other arts, drama cannot be detached from the region from which it springs.)[11]

And more succinctly, Harris Memel-Fote adds: "À chaque société, à chaque époque d'une société, son théâtre" (Every society, every epoch of a society has its own

drama).[12] Thus, for a play to be African, it must possess some identifiably African elements which will distinguish it from a European or Chinese play. These elements confer on the play its "Africanness." The Africanness of modern African plays has not been lost on perceptive Western critics, in spite of their strenuous efforts to underscore the indebtedness of African playwrights to Western dramatists. This is why, for instance, Bernth Lindfors can write: "Clark, like Soyinka, remains a thoroughly African writer even while borrowing from Europe."[13]

This remark is equally applicable to other African playwrights, at least those worthy of note. Martin Banham makes the same point and adds:

> Plays like *The Strong Breed* (Soyinka), *Foriwa* (Sutherland) and *Ozidi* (Clark) amongst many others have their inspiration from and their relevance to the living festivals of Africa. The playwrights' role may be to sophisticate or to develop the themes, but their references are often directly to things familiar and accepted by millions of ordinary people.[14]

In fact, as Bakary Traore points out more specifically:

> [Le théâtre africain] est en tant que transformation du mythe, une formule de vie. Il reflète la vie de la communauté et son éthique.
>
> (Inasmuch as it is a transformation of myth, African drama is a formula for living. It reflects the life of the community and its ethics.)[15]

It follows then that whatever affinities may be detected between them, African drama is different from European drama and, accordingly, requires a different approach. On this point Martin Banham again rightly observes:

> The critic of African playwriting and theatre from outside the Continent of Africa, used to the form and nature of, say, British or American drama, may have to accept a different set of critical criteria if he or she is to come to terms with much African drama, and understand it more readily.[16]

Consequently, Western critical approaches cannot be relied on to elucidate fully the meaning of an African play and to evaluate its artistic value.

Having successfully demonstrated that the nationalist approach and the Western method (with its variants in the so-called universalist and comparative approaches) cannot lead to a valid interpretation of modern African drama, it is time to focus on the main point of this essay: to propose a more viable approach to modern African drama. The inadequacies of the existing methodologies are essentially due to a misconception of the real nature of modern African drama. They stem, in fact, from the failure of critics to recognize in practical terms that modern African drama has its own characteristics despite its links with both traditional African and European drama. And as such, it is necessary to devise for its evaluation a distinct methodology. In order to be viable, the methodology envisaged must necessarily avoid the pitfall of current procedures by coming to grips with the composite nature of modern African drama. This implies that the new methodology must be suitable for the assessment of the traditional as well as the foreign elements in modern African drama.

The traditional elements invariably predominate, since drama relies heavily on the culture from which it emanates. Some of these are self-evident; others are not. The obvious traditional elements are mostly the themes borrowed from the African past and present, real or imaginary, such as history, mythology, legends and contemporary social situations. Music, dances and songs which feature prominently in most modern African plays are easily recognizable. To a large extent, this is equally true of masks, proverbs, idioms or symbols, whose meanings may sometimes elude the uninitiated. The critic of modern African drama must have some deep knowledge of African culture, For instance, Martin Esslin did not find *The Song of a Goat* quite convincing as a tragedy.[17] But if he had been aware that in most African societies, particularly Ijaw, childlessness is regarded as a curse and adultery as an abomination, the tragedy of Clark's play would have appeared credible to him. Similarly, Alain Ricard saw in the all-male cast of *The Road* evidence of Beckett's influence on Soyinka.[18] But if he had known that the Agemo festival on which Soyinka based his play is an all-male affair, he would not have made such an obviously erroneous comment. Thus the mere ability to read and comprehend the text is inadequate when it comes to appreciating the traditional elements which African playwrights may have incorporated in their works; it has to be complemented by a familiarity with African culture.

However, the mere presence of these elements does not necessarily determine the intrinsic artistic value of the play. Art is selection; it involves the discriminatory and harmonious blending of materials to produce a coherent and esthetically valuable work. That is why critics often frown at the inclusion in African plays of some elements which do not contribute directly to the unfolding of the plot. But the choice of the theme and its treatment are not always exclusively determined by esthetic considerations. They are often greatly influenced by the goals the author has assigned himself. Theatre can make a dynamic impact on the audience, and many an African playwright exploits this potential of drama. In such cases the dramatist must attempt to strike a bal-

ance between his social commitment and the demands of drama as an art form and not sacrifice these to the former. Martial Malinda falls into this trap in his *L'enfer, c'est Orfeo*, in which he displays a striking lack of subtlety in expressing his ideological convictions, unlike Dadié, whose discreet condemnation of economic exploitation and political oppression in all his three political plays—*Monsieur Thogognini, Beatrice du Congo* and *Les voix dans le vent*—is not lost on the reader or spectator.

Whatever the social objective of the play may be, its language is central to the author's ability to communicate with his audience or to forge a viable synthesis from the elements at his disposal. The language of modern African drama, which is European—English, French and Portuguese for the most part—is the most evident and the most important foreign borrowing. When an African playwright adopts a foreign language as his medium, he has to conform to its syntactic norms. Nevertheless, the African playwright frequently expresses African modes of thought in the foreign language. Thus the language of modern African drama, like that of the African novel or poetry written in European languages, contains African images, idioms or proverbs. A few examples from Pliya's *Kondo le requin* illustrate this point. After announcing the king's death, the public crier expresses the irreversibility of death thus:

> Qui peut soulever des champs labourés? Nul ne peut griffer le porphyre. Le prestigieux Roi qui a lancé ces défis est parti a Allada.
>
> (Who can lift cultivated fields? No one can graft the Porphyrian tree. The prestigious king who threw out challenges has gone to Allada.)[19]

Later on, with this circuitous sentence, Gbehanzin, the new king, pronounces a death sentence on Kinvo for disrespecting him.

> Dans un cachot, en compagnie de la vermine et des larves suceuses de sang, Kinvo réfléchira au respect dû a Gbéhanzin.
>
> (In the dungeon, in the company of bloodsucking vermin and larvae, Kinvo will think of the respect due to Gbehanzin.)[20]

Other equally interesting examples can be quoted from Soyinka's *Kongi's Harvest*. The traditional Yoruba saying at the beginning of the play expresses the difficult nature of the task Kongi has set himself: "The pot that will eat fat its bottom must be scorched. The squirrel that will long crack nuts. Its footpad must be sore."[21] Then, later on, Oba Sarumi stresses the respect which age and maturity confer on the elder.

Let the dandy's wardrobe
Be as lavish as the shop

Of the dealer in brocades
It cannot match an elder's rags.[22]

The implications of these examples for the criticism of modern African drama are fairly obvious; in addition to his ability to judge the grammatical correctness of the European language used by the African playwright, the critic must be familiar with African expressions and modes of thought in order to grasp their meanings and assess their effectiveness.

A combined sociological and esthetic approach will no doubt be appropriate for explaining and assessing the components (traditional as well as foreign) of the play and its artistic worth. But the efficacy of this approach is limited by the absence of a tradition in modern African drama. The procedure may, however, be used in the first instance in the analysis of whole series of African plays so as to determine the trends of modern African drama. This is necessary, for the critic cannot give appropriate emphases to the various aspects of individual plays in ignorance of the conventions of modern African drama, which can only be determined by its dominant characteristics. The sociological and esthetic approach can then be applied to the study of plays which treat the same or identical themes. It will be interesting in this connection to compare, for example, plays which explore the legend of the Zulu warrior Chaka, such as Abdou Anta Ka's *Les Amazoulous*, Seydou Badian's *La mort de Chaka* and Eugène Dervain's *Chaka*, or those which deal with anti-colonial resistance, such as Amadou Cisse Dia's *Les derniers jours de Lat Dior* and Mamadou Seyni M'Bengue's *Le procès de Lat Dior*. The latter group of plays may even be compared with Jean Pliya's *Kondo le requin*.

It hardly needs to be stressed that a tradition of modern African drama based exclusively on either Anglophone or Francophone African plays cannot be regarded as truly African. That is why the comparison may be extended to the other linguistic zone. The anticolonial plays may eventually be set against Ola Rotimi's *Ovonramwen Nogbaisi* and Evbinma Ogieriaikhi's *Oba Ovonramwen* and similar African plays which may have been written in Portuguese.

Will the critic be justified in rejecting as naïvely exhibitionist a traditional element like dance if the study reveals a general tendency on the part of African playwrights to include it in their plays simply as local color, or more importantly, to bridge the gap between the actors and the audience and consequently to get the audience more involved in the play? Such a study may help to answer this question and also to show that African playwrights have a penchant to write longer plays and by implication not to make the pace of the action in their plays conform to BBC standards or to Radio-France-inspired plays, which are often tailored to suit the taste of the largely European and Europeanized African juries. Obviously such facts will affect the assessment of individual plays, if they are shown to be more or less common in modern African drama. No doubt such a study will make tremendous intellectual demands on the critic. But this is an indispensable pioneering effort, and the critic, African and non-African alike, who wishes to comprehend modern African drama in depth will find his reward if he makes this effort.

Unionmwan Edebiri, Autumn 1978

[1] Dan Izevbaye, "The State of Criticism in African Literature," *African Literature Today*, 7 (1975), pp. 1–19.

[2] Eldred Jones was one of the earliest African critics to warn of the dangers of leaving the criticism of African literature to aliens. Cf. "Academic Problems and Critical Techniques," *African Literature and the Universities*, G. Moore, ed., Ibadan University Press, 1965, 89.

[3] "Language of the Heart," in *Présence Africaine*, 58 (1966), p. 8.

[4] Joseph Okpaku, "Tradition, Culture and Criticism," in *Présence Africaine*, 70 (1969), p. 141.

[5] J. K. Agovi, "Towards a Formulation of Critical Standards for Modern African Literature," *Bulletin of the Association of African Universities*, 1:2 (1976), p. 80.

[6] Okpaku, p. 141.

[7] Cf. "Aspects of Nigerian Drama," in *The Example of Shakespeare*, London, Longman, 1970, pp. 76–96; and Ola Rotimi, "Traditional Nigerian Drama" in *Introduction to Nigerian Literature*, Bruce King, ed., London, Longman, 1970, pp. 36–49.

[8] S. A. Dzeagu, "The Criticism of Modern African Literature," *Bulletin of the Association of African Universities*, 1 (1976), p. 96.

[9] Earnest Emenyonu, "African Literature: What does it take to be its Critic?," *African Literature Today*, no. 5, p. 3.

[10] Demas Nwoko, "Search for a New African Theatre," *Présence Africaine*, 75 (1970), p. 62.

[11] Jean Duvignaud, *Sociologie du théâtre: Essai sur les ombres collectives*, Paris, Presses Universitaires, 1965, p. 35.

[12] Harris Memel-Fote, in "Le théâtre négro-africain: Actes du Colloque d'Abidjan," *Présence Africaine*, 1973, p. 29.

[13] Bernth Lindfors, "Shakespeare and Nigerian Drama," in *Proceedings of the 6th Congress of the International Comparative Literature Association*, Bordeaux, 1970, p. 641.

[14] M. Banham, *African Theatre Today*, London, Pitman, 1976, 2.

[15] Bakary Traore, in "Le théâtre négro-africain," p. 36.

[16] Banham, p. 3.

[17] Martin Esslin, "Two Nigerian Playwrights," in *Introduction to African Literature*, U. Beier, ed., London, Longman, 1967, p. 259.

[18] Alain Ricard, "Les limites de l'étude d'influence: Théâtre nigérian et théâtre anglais," in *Proceedings of the 6th Congress of the International Comparative Literature Association*, pp. 635–38.

[19] *Three Nigerian Plays*, U. Beier, ed., London, Longman, 1967, 19.

Chinua Achebe (*Robert H. Taylor*)

[20] Ibid., p. 61.

[21] Ibid., p. 1.

[22] Ibid., p. 9.

The Precarious State of the African Writer

These are not good times for African writers—or Third World writers almost anywhere, for that matter. Political and economic factors (determinants even in the best of times) have become so unstable in recent years that the African literary scene has begun to resemble a barren wasteland, unprecedented at any time since the early 1960s, the era of independence. What can be more ironic than to glance back to the final days of colonialism and regard them nostalgically as the golden days of African literature—stifled by the increasing political instability across the continent once Africans shook off their colonial shackles? African writers, it appears, have paid for their independence with their creativity.

Before I begin my tale of woe, however, let me illustrate with one lengthy example the economic obstacles operating against African writers even in the best of times (those infrequent periods when publishers are receptive to creativity and the books they publish are widely read, if not sold). For this hypothetical example,

I shall use Chinua Achebe's *Things Fall Apart,* since this work has probably been the most popular African novel of all time. (My students are convinced that Achebe is getting rich.)

To follow the course of Achebe's riches, we have to begin with the original edition of the work, since that is where much of the problem begins for any writer, William Heinemann published the English hardback edition in 1958. Assuming a standard contract between publisher and author, Achebe would have received a 10 percent royalty on all copies of his novel sold within England. Copies sold overseas—and that would include Nigeria, Achebe's homeland—would have earned him half-royalties or 5 percent. African writers have often been shocked to discover that copies of their books sold within their own country earn them reduced royalties, yet this is only one of the prices Third World writers pay for publishing "overseas."

When paperback rights are sold to another publisher, the royalty is traditionally split fifty-fifty between the author and the hardback publisher of the work. No doubt such an arrangement existed between Achebe and the African Writers Series, in 1962, when *Things Fall Apart* first appeared in a paperback edition. It is possible that those terms were subsequently renegotiated when Achebe became the editor of the series, but if they were not, all those copies of his first novel (said to be in the hundreds of thousands) have earned him half-royalties. (This, one hopes, was not a case of a double jeopardy: half-royalties for "overseas" sales and then half-royalties again for the paperback edition.)

Reprint rights in other countries are more complicated. The royalties paid on the American hardback edition of *Things Fall Apart* were probably split in the traditional manner: half to the author and half to William Heinemann. The American publisher was McDowell, Obolensky (1959), which had its own trade paperback in print for a number of years; but then in 1969 the mass-market paperback rights were sold to Fawcett Books, and the novel suddenly became much more widely available.

The explosion in black studies in the United States in the early 1970s undoubtedly helped increase the sales of Achebe's book. It is possible that *Things Fall Apart* sold twenty-five or thirty thousand copies yearly for a while, until black-studies courses experienced declining enrollments. The original Fawcett edition of the novel sold for seventy-five cents, though several years later the price had escalated to $1.95—the figure we can use to demonstrate why Chinua Achebe (or any African writer) will never get rich from American readers.

By rounding off the price to two dollars, increasing the yearly sales to fifty thousand copies, and assuming a 10 percent royalty base (unlikely for a paperback contract negotiated in 1969), the figures look like this: 50,000 copies at $2 = $100,000 gross × 10% royalties = $10,000. That $10,000 in royalties looks quite respectable until one remembers that half of it has to go to Obolensky (the American hardback publisher). That immediately cuts Achebe's potential share to $5,000, a figure that has its own set of restrictions.

Once we earmark $5,000 for Achebe at this stage, we have to figure out the portion that will go to the Internal Revenue Service. I mention this fact because it is inescapable. Just as the United States designates certain countries as most-favored nations and exempts businesses from paying dual income taxes, the United States—and many European countries—offers similar reciprocity to writers within those countries. Thus, when Graham Greene publishes a novel in the United States, he pays income taxes on his American royalties only in England and not in both countries. Norman Mailer pays income taxes to the American government on his English royalties and not both. That reciprocity does not exist with African nations, however, so the IRS takes a 30 percent cut (or $1,500) out of Achebe's American royalties. That reduces the figure to $3,500, which must be split equally between Heinemann and the author, further decreasing Achebe's royalties to $1,750. Since Nigeria and England do have a tax agreement, Achebe gets to keep the full $1,750—except, of

course, for that portion he has to pay in tax to his own government.

African writers who publish outside the continent have the economic cards stacked against them. They'll never get wealthy under these conditions, which give no indication of changing. Pity the poor writer who experiences only modest sales in the United States or any other Western country. For the most part, however, the options for publishing in Africa are still greatly limited. Worse, several African writers have said that when they have chosen to publish on the continent, the publishers have paid them no royalties at all.

Economically, the African writer is hardly better off today than he was during colonial times. Though literacy has improved greatly across the continent in the last twenty-five years, the situation for most writers has barely altered. African governments are so economically strapped that very little money can be spent on the arts. Even funds for education (the most logical area for a trickle-down effect to reach the writer) have been cut because of the servicing of national debts, the financing of defense, and so on. Can one imagine, for example, Samuel Doe or Idi Amin showing much interest in the state of their respective countries' literatures?

There are probably only two writers in all of tropical Africa who can live by their royalties: Chinua Achebe and Wole Soyinka.[1] That in itself belies the pathetic situation for most African writers. They are forced to support themselves by other means—an affinity they share with many writers throughout the world. Few writers anywhere take up the pen expecting to become rich by their efforts. But let's consider what many writers in the West do to supplement their serious writing. They free-lance; they write articles and reviews for newspapers and magazines to help earn their bread and butter. Those outlets do not really exist for the writer in tropical Africa. Economically, almost everything is against him.

Let's be optimistic about this and assume that good writing will always survive and that the writer who struggles hard enough will find a publisher for his work. Thus, the African writer—like his counterpart anywhere else—will find his readers. He may not become wealthy or famous, but he will see his work in print and derive comfort from that. Naïvely, I used to believe that the African writer could overcome all these factors and find his niche in world literature. Lately, however, I've begun to feel differently, as I've looked at what can only be called a decline in African literature—both in quality and quantity. (The former is more upsetting than the latter.)

What's happened to Chinua Achebe, who must be Africa's most famous novelist yet hasn't published a novel since *A Man of the People* (1966)—twenty years ago? What about Ayi Kwei Armah, who looked for a while as if he might become Africa's most prolific novelist? His last novel, *The Healers,* was published in 1978. What about Kofi Awoonor? Bessie Head? Cyprian Ekwensi? Amos Tutuola? Mongo Beti? Cheikh Hamidou Kane? J. P. Clark? Richard Rive? Gabriel Okara? Yambo Ouologuem? Ferdinand Oyono? Lenrie Peters? Taban lo Liyong? Charles Mangua?

The list could go on, but I've tried to name only those writers who demonstrated major talent and then—for the most part—fell silent. Out of fairness, this roster should be balanced with the names of those writers who have continued to be visible; yet that list is much, much shorter: Wole Soyinka, Ngũgĩ wa Thiong'o, Nuruddin Farah. There are also a number of popular writers (such as Buchi Emecheta) whose visibility has increased, but it is difficult to treat their work seriously. More significant, it seems, is the situation in which so many of these writers have found themselves caught during the last few years.

Chinua Achebe is again the best example. After *A Man of the People,* he published other works: a volume of short stories and a collection of poems. Achebe's poems are minor works, however, and even his collection of short stories contains substantial material written prior to his last published novel. Turning instead to his last published book, *The Trouble with Nigeria* (1983),[2] the dilemma becomes immediately apparent. If the continent's major novelist has been reduced to publishing a treatise such as this, the intellectual climate for the African writer has become appalling. One quotation from this work will suffice.

> Nigeria is *not* a great country. It is one of the most disorderly nations in the world. It is one of the most corrupt, insensitive, inefficient places under the sun. It is one of the most expensive countries and one of those that give least value for money. It is dirty, callous, noisy, ostentatious, dishonest and vulgar. In short, it is among the most unpleasant places on earth!

Great writers have always been social critics. *The Trouble with Nigeria* belongs to a distinguished list of polemics written by major writers through the years. Still, shouldn't the Nigerian government be embarrassed by this latest publication by its major writer? And shouldn't those of us who admire Achebe for his creative brilliance be enraged that he's felt compelled to publish a work such as this instead of his long-promised fifth novel? To what extremes will African governments drive their artists?

That is the rub, of course: the African governments, the powers that be, the politicians in charge. Achebe

had fun with this years ago in *A Man of the People.* In that novel he satirically described Chief Nanga (the Minister of Culture of an unnamed African country, though clearly Nigeria) as a man who "announced in public that he had never heard of his country's most famous novel," presumably *Things Fall Apart,* though "he prophesied that before long our great country would produce great writers like Shakespeare, Dickens, Jane Austen, Bernard Shaw, and—raising his eyes off the script—Michael West and Dudley Stamp."

Has Achebe lost his sense of humor? Probably not. Rather, it looks as though he has concluded that satire is meaningless if the objects of that satire no longer realize that they are being attacked. Only a frontal approach will be noticed; hence *The Trouble with Nigeria.* Yet the trouble with Nigeria is the trouble with African governments in general. They will apparently do anything to silence their writers. African governments have a) imprisoned their writers (Soyinka, Ngũgĩ, Awoonor, René Philombe, and too many South African writers to list here); b) censored their writers' works (Ngũgĩ, Philombe, Legson Kayira, Camara Laye, Nuruddin Farah, plus dozens of South African writers); c) forced their writers into exile (Laye, Kayira, Farah, S. Henry Cordor, Solomon Deressa, Achebe [after the civil war], Oswald Mtshali, Dennis Brutus, Bessie Head, Ezekiel Mphahlele, Peter Abrahams, and numerous other South African writers); and d) pushed their writers to the brink of insanity (Head, Laye, Yambo Ouologuem). When all these tactics have failed, African governments have silenced their writers with one of the most effective muzzles: assimilating them into the government bureaucracy or, worse, the diplomatic corps (Laye, Awoonor, Cyprian Ekwensi, Amos Tutuola, Wilton Sankawulo, Abioseh Nicol, Syl Cheyney-Coker).

What impresses one most about African writers' responses to these intrusions on their corporeal and intellectual existence is that so few of them have compromised their positions. Rather, they have met the enemy (the state) with silence, which of course is the reason why so many of the writers mentioned here have apparently stopped publishing. They have seen what has happened to a writer like Ngũgĩ, who has continued publishing. They have fully understood why a novel that satirized the colonial government is acceptable (even de rigueur), whereas one criticizing the postindependent political situation can only get them into trouble.

It is fear of reprisals, then, that has led to the steady decline of African writing during the last twenty-five years. The older generation of writers (those who began publishing in the 1950s and the early 1960s) have been silenced, and the younger ones have quickly followed suit, though some of the latter have chosen another route and written fluff, devoid of any artistic merit or meaningful social context. Still, these are difficult times, no matter what road taken.

Several years ago I was asked to write an article about younger African writers—those who had begun publishing during the 1970s. The intent of the essay (which was to be published in a United States government publication widely distributed in Africa) was to describe as many writers as possible and thereby increase their exposure among African readers. It was only after I agreed to write the piece that I began to reflect upon the sorry state of African writing and realize that there were only a few writers who had demonstrated great promise (comparable to those who had begun writing earlier).

I picked three writers: Nuruddin Farah of Somalia, S. Henry Cordor of Liberia, and T. Obinkaram Eschewa of Nigeria. The article I subsequently wrote was never published but was censored instead, because authorities in the State Department—I was told—decided that the praise I had lavished on Farah would offend officials in Somalia, where he had been declared persona non grata. I was appalled that the censorship of African writers had reached American soil, though I have never had any illusions about Ronald Reagan's political myopia. Examining the careers of these three writers, we can observe a kind of pattern typical of the situation in general.

Of the three, Nuruddin Farah has been the most visible, though he has had to remain in exile for most of his career. His first novel, *From a Crooked Rib,* published in 1970, was written while he was a student in India. It identified Farah immediately as one of his continent's most sensitive and understanding writers about African women. Elba, the young woman in the story, runs away from her village in order to avoid an arranged marriage with an older man. She tells a friend, "That is what we women are—just like cattle, properties of someone or other, either your parents or your husband." What she ponders is why a man can have four wives but a woman only one husband.

Farah's championing of women's rights has been unacceptable to some of his African readers, though it has not been the reason for his exile. That problem has been political, the subject all of his recent novels: *A Naked Needle* (1976), *Sweet and Sour Milk* (1979), *Sardines* (1981), and *Close Sesame* (1983). The last three (powerful and disturbing works) constitute a trilogy with the overall theme of African dictatorship. The pathway of his fiction, then, has been overtly political, with only one possible escape route: exile. His books are not available in Somalia, where they have been banned, and Farah himself—determined to continue writing—

has become a kind of cosmopolite, picking up teaching and journalistic assignments wherever possible to supplement the meager income from his novels.

S. Henry Cordor's situation parallels Farah's. He too has been trapped by politics, though ironically by the regime he initially chose to embrace. The body of his creative work is still quite small because so much of it has never been published. As Liberians often say, they never enjoyed the benefits of being a colony. That has posed special problems for the country's writers, who find it almost impossible to publish overseas. Self-publication tends to be the norm.

Cordor's stories demonstrate a rare sensibility. In a few brief paragraphs he is able to size up character and situation, often with a subtle wit and a polished manner far beyond that of his most daring contemporaries. "In the Hospital," for instance, is an almost perfect example of what can be done with the short-story form. Sadly, however, Cordor has found himself in recent years becoming a spokesman for Liberian intellectuals and compelled to abandon fiction for political commentary. When Doe became president of Liberia, Cordor was enthusiastic, but he quickly soured when he witnessed the president's intolerance of free speech (especially among students). Today Cordor lives in exile in the United States, waiting for the day when politics back home will change.

In contrast to the works by Farah and Cordor, T. Obinkaram Echewa's novel *The Land's Lord* is much more traditional and free of contemporary commentary. The three principal characters (Father Higler, a Catholic priest; his African acolyte, Philip; and a juju priest called Ahamba) are engaged in a kind of philosophic dialogue about good and evil and, by extension, about Christianity and animism, Africa and the West. When *The Land's Lord* was published by Heinemann in 1976, comparisons were made between Echewa and Achebe and Ngūgī, largely because of the novel's traditional setting, though Echewa has also said of his writing: "I expect to go over the social and historical terrain that has been traversed by Achebe and others and till it more deeply. I am interested right now in the problem of 'evil' in African societies without reference to colonialism or the white man."

Although Echewa's novel has been widely praised, it has been followed by a ten-year silence. A second novel, called *The Crippled Dancer* and announced for publication in 1982, has never appeared. It is probable that Echewa's writing career has been stifled by Heinemann's decision to curtail drastically the scope of its African Writers Series, the major publishing outlet for the continent's writers during the last twenty years. At the moment many publishers in the West are interested in publishing only those African writers whose work is already widely known and deemed profitable.

The fact is that Africa cannot afford its writers today—and neither can the West, though their reasons are somewhat different. As long as African governments regard their writers as threats to their longevity, most of the continent's serious writers will be forced to remain silent and the decline of African writing will continue. One has only to think of the career of Ngũgĩ wa Thiong'o and the continual harassment he has experienced both in and out of prison at the hands of the Kenyan government. A lesser man would have caved in long ago.

The West, of course, could help the situation, particularly in the area of publishing, but the indications are that that will not happen. Why is it, for example, that South Africa's white writers are embraced by American publishers (and readers) while the country's black writers still remain virtually unknown? Years ago there was a rumor going around that an African writer who tried to get published in the United States was told that his book wasn't African enough. A similar myopia about Africa on the part of Western publishers still exists, in spite of the commercial success of books about Africa by writers who are not African (Isak Dinesen and Alice Walker, to mention two current favorites).

For years the literary image of Africa in the West was largely controlled by writers who were not African. In the late 1950s and early 1960s it looked as if that were about to change. A dozen or so writers achieved international recognition, though only one of them (Wole Soyinka, the continent's major writer) has enhanced his visibility in the West. Politics and economics have pushed most of the others to the side. If the situation does improve, it will not be the result of worldwide political and economic fluctuations but rather because of the resilience of the writers themselves.

Charles R. Larson, Summer 1986

---

[1] On the various authors discussed or referred to in this essay, see the following articles in *BA/WLT*: Chinua Achebe, 48:1 (Winter 1974), p. 74; Wole Soyinka, 60:1 (Winter 1986), pp. 31–32; Ngũgĩ wa Thiong'o, 59:1 (Winter 1985), pp. 26–30; Nuruddin Farah, 58:2, (Spring 1984), pp. 215–21; Ayi Kwei Armah, 59:3 (Summer 1985), pp. 337–42; Ferdinand Oyono, 59:3 (Summer 1985), pp. 333–37; Buchi Emecheta, 59:1 (Winter 1985), pp. 9–13; J. P. Clark, 52:2 (Spring 1978), pp. 216–23; Dennis Brutus, 55:1 (Winter 1981), pp. 32–40; Bessie Head, 57:3 (Summer 1983), pp. 414–16; Camara Laye, 54:3 (Summer 1980), pp. 392–95.

[2] For a review of Achebe's book *The Trouble with Nigeria*, see *WLT* 59:3 (Summer 1985), p. 478.

Neglected or Forgotten Authors of Lusophone Africa

Não sabias, Amigo,
Nem eu, por bem!
Aonde viveríamos
Ilhados e esquecidos?
(You did not know, my Friend,
Nor, luckily, did I!
Where we would chance to live
Lone and forgotten?)
—Mário António, "Ninguém se ri como nós"

A few novelists painters
sculptors singers
achieve glory and fame
while others of
comparable talent
have neither memory nor name.
—Don Burness, "The Pietà at Valence," 1996

This vast continent of North America possesses many colleges and universities. If you listen in them for echoes of the African literatures that are written in Portuguese nowadays, you will hear a silence that is crying to the high heavens—to borrow an expression coined by Eugénio Lisboa, the sharp-tongued Mozambican critic. I mean the silence that at present is the fate of not just one or two but many good writers who have lived in the five lusophone countries of Africa. It is not my intention to blame anyone, but rather to encourage younger scholars, particularly graduate students, as well as their advisers, to venture beyond the by now all too familiar territory of the internationally acclaimed stars: the Angolans Luandino Vieira and Carlos Pepetela or the Mozambicans José Craveirinha and Bernardo Mia Couto. There are others worthy of attention waiting in the wings, authors of works to be read, studied, appreciated.

To convince you, I have selected just nine among the many neglected authors from the literatures of lusophone Africa. Furthermore, I shall point out aspects of their works which I feel reward investigation, for example, from a comparative angle. I admit that the selection is personal, influenced by interest and preference.

Beginning with contemporary Angola, the first writer I should mention called himself Mário António—by his full name, Mário António Fernandes de Oliveira. This gifted mestizo from Luanda has been neglected by young American scholars and critics. At an early age he converted his acute vision of the *musseques,* the poor districts of Luanda, to intense free verse. While remaining very conscious of his African heritage, he subsequently extended his vision to Europe, where he spent most of his life. As a result, he was also neglected at home for keeping aloof from nationalistic politics. When he was only twenty-four, he wrote these melancholy lines:

Contudo, sou o marginal,
Aberrante, o alheio. . . .
Hoje vejo só passar. Não falo, calo. . . .
Passa. Passa. Passa. Eu não adiro.

(Yet, I remain on the margin,
an aberration, alien.
Today I watch things merely pass, speak not, keep silent.
It passes, passes, passes. I don't take sides.)
("Conta," 1958)

It was not until years after the post-Independence tumult had died down that Mário António's greatness as a poet and story writer was fully recognized in his native land.

Another Angolan example is an author who defies classification. He belongs also to his native Mozambique, to which he remained attached to the end, but Angola was the country to which he gave his best years, as a physician and a creative writer. The manuals omit all references to him. His name? Orlando de Albuquerque, born in 1925 in the capital, which at that time was named Lourenco Marques. He settled in Angola in 1958 and established a medical practice. Reluctantly, he left the country in 1975. He started all over again in Braga, Portugal, and there he died in 1997, ignored by the literary establishment of Angola.

Albuquerque was a prolific writer, proud of having conceived more works than any other Luso-African author. Their extraordinary variety amazes me, ranging from poems, prose sketches, stories, novels, dramas, fictionalized biography, and autobiography, to history, African religions, Portuguese ethnography, travel literature, fables, and books for children. He became known in Portugal while still a university student when his *Batuque negro* (Black Batuque Dance; 1947), a pioneering booklet of poems in the *négritude* mode, was suppressed by the censor. This happened while he and his future first wife, the poet and physician Alda Lara, were active members of the *Casa dos Estudantes do Império*. The future leaders of their countries were among its members.

Both Albuquerque and his wife lived their humanistic convictions, never losing empathy with black and mestizo Africans even after the disasters of the colonial and civil wars. He created such works about black An-

golans as the plays *Ovimbanda* (1967) and *O Filho de Zambi* (Zambi's Son; 1974) or the novel *A Porta Fechada* (The Closed Door; 1968), about an exemplary Catholic missionary fully understanding the Africans' beliefs; that novel remains his most thoughtful and best written work of fiction.

Religious themes attracted him frequently. Another novel, *A última Estrada* (The Ultimate Road to the Cross; completed 1971, published 1995), offers a striking example. Called by the author an *estória africana,* it features as its protagonist an African prophet who is presented as living and suffering much like a black Christ in Angola. The tragedy is rendered vividly poignant via the use of opposing scenes involving Africans and colonials at the time of the first uprisings of 1961.

Now and then Albuquerque displays a satiric kind of humor, as in a farce about the biblical Noah in which the Lord appears as a powerful bureaucrat and Noah's wife as a nagging woman. The farce was written in 1965 but not published until 1996. There can be no doubt in my mind that Orlando de Albuquerque and his excursions into many fields of literature should no longer be ignored.

For good reasons, notably the early existence of good schools and close relations with Portugal, the United States, and Brazil, the small islands of Cape Verde have given rise to more writers proportionate to their population than, I believe, any other country in Africa. I shall mention only two good ones. The first is António Aurélio Gonçalves of São Vicente Island (1901–84), who belonged to the original group that founded the review *Claridade* in 1936 with the aim of exploring the island society, until then a virgin subject. Gonçalves had a marvelous gift for telling stories and keeping his listeners spellbound. I can still recall the as yet unpublished story he told a small group of us sitting comfortably in a bar in a town on Mindelo, in a soft, clear voice, uttering each word with great precision. It was a wonderful yarn about a crew of Cape Verdeans becalmed on their small frigate in the South Atlantic. Their captain passes the time by telling them one of *his* tall tales, this one about another becalmed vessel, and just as food and water are running dangerously low, they are all rescued and taken home to *Son'cente* in time to enjoy Easter dinner with their families. The tale about sailors surprised us; for all of Gonçalves's published stories involved women of São Vicente.

Because he was so exigent as a stylist, Gonçalves published no more than a dozen of his tales during his lifetime. After his death, these were collected under the title *Noite de Vento* (Windy Night). His friend Arnaldo França is about to publish more of his stories, found tucked away *na gaveta* (in a drawer), as they say in Portuguese, so that we shall soon have plenty more material with which to examine his insights into the feminine psyche.

Another writer among the neglected Cape Verdeans who, like Orlando de Albuquerque, practices medicine, is Henrique Teixeira de Sousa, born in 1919 on Fogo Island, which boasts a large and still-active volcano. In 1975 he moved to the outskirts of Lisbon, but he continues to write exclusively on and for Cape Verde. When he was young, Fogo Island still preserved an upper class of landed gentry, proud of their pure whiteness and residing in *sobrados,* fine two-story mansions. Teixeira de Sousa undertook to tell the story of their decline and the concomitant rise of ambitious commoners. This he did more dramatically than could any sociologist in *Ilhéu de Contenda* (Isle of Contention; 1978), the first of six novels bearing the name of a *sobrado.* That work was followed by two other novels about social changes on Fogo. Three subsequent novels which have as their setting the intellectually prominent island of São Vicente are likewise well constructed. One of them, *Djunga* (1989), will interest readers who like to engage in literary theory. In it a young writer discusses, in a series of dialogues with a witty friend nicknamed Djunga, how to write this very novel and receives good advice from the older man, modeled after a real person. It becomes quite obvious that the younger man's ideas coincide more or less with Teixeira de Sousa's own desire for innovation.

The first Mozambican I wish to present was actually born in Lisbon in 1924: Glória de Sant'Anna. Although she hails from Portugal, spending the best part of her life in Africa and devoting all of her published writing to African subjects have made of her a Mozambican. Upon her marriage to a painter in 1951, Sant'Anna went to live in Porto Amélia, now renamed Pemba. There she taught school to African children. In 1975 she returned to Portugal. Reading her poems collected in the volume *Amaranto, 1951–1983,* one discovers a large number of verses on African motifs, inspired by the people and the countryside on the coast facing Madagascar. No other Mozambican poet has attained such purity of form or force and depth of feeling as are found in her verse or in the lyrical prose sketches of *Do Tempo inútil* (1978). Her writing is pervaded by a constant *angústia.* As she put it in "Motivo": "Um poema é sempre / uma qualquer angústia que transborda" (A poem is always / some overflowing anguish).

This anguish grew during the war years from 1961 on, but Sant'Anna's writings prove that she kept her faith in humankind, black and white. To find out how and why would be a rewarding enterprise, as would an examination of her frequent use of nouns and adjectives conveying either serenity or sorrow (*mágoa*). In "Poema sem hora certa," one of her latest poems written in Mozambique, she suggested a fusion with Africa beyond her death:

É a quarenta quilómetros no meio do mato.
e aqui estou
e aqui paro . . .
rodeia-me de borboletas brancas
que me tocam a face . . .
e eu reparo
que a última borboleta me ha deixado.
É a quarenta quilómetros no meio do mato
que hoje estou sepultado.

(Miles away, deep in the woods.
Here I am
and here I stop . . .
and a common, unsuspected fluid
encircles me, of milk-white butterflies
touching my face . . .
and then I notice
that the last butterfly has left me.
There, miles away, deep in the woods
I am interred today.)

Rui (Correia) Knopfli (b. 1932 in Inhambane, d. 1987 in London) stands apart as another unusual Mozambican poet, and not just because he bears a funny Swiss German name. Like some others, he belongs to two countries: the Mozambique of his birth, on the one hand, and Portugal, or more exactly the Europe of his precise diction and humanistic culture on the other, solidified by long years in London, although he considers them years of exile. He was a careful, meditative craftsman, always strictly reducing his poetry to the essentials.

"Expatriate," Knopfli once called himself in an interview, adding that "we expatriates, not due to any fault of our own, or to that of others, suffer the fate of being paid little attention, or of pure and simple oblivion." Perhaps someone will feel inspired to study how expatriation affected the poetry of Knopfli and others like him. Someone else, tempted by theorizing, will discover Knopfli's theory of poetry, particularly as conveyed in his slender 1984 collection *Corpo de Atena* (Athena's Body). Another attractive and intriguing quality is Knopfli's premonition of future defeats, wrecks, catastrophes. This visionary vein manifested itself most strikingly in the closing poem of his final book, "Cair do Pano" (The Curtain Falls): "As acácias já se incendiaram de vermelho / e o zumbido das cigarras enxameia obsidiante / a manhã de Dezembro" (Already the acacias turned a fiery red / and the buzz of locusts swarms obsessively / on the December morning). This apparently normal Mozambican summer introduces the poem's conclusion:

O encenador faz
a vénia de praxe e . . .
esqueira-se pelo
anonimato da esquerda alta.
É Dezembro
a encurtar o tempo, o pouco que nos sobra

(The stage director takes
the customary bow and . . .
steals away
unseen at upstage left.
It is December,
shortening the time, the little we have left)

I shall conclude by mentioning three writers belonging to a couple of small tropical nations with written literatures of small local circulation, as literacy is still minimal there, while oral lore abounds, largely in Creole dialects which are being increasingly used in written form by literate poets. Early in the twentieth century, Guinea-Bissau had the good fortune to produce a talented author in Fausto Duarte (b. 1903 in Praia, d. 1953 in Lisbon), one of the numerous Cape Verdeans active as officials in the Portuguese colonial service. He spent thirty years in Guinea-Bissau, from 1932 on, and his observations of Guinean life led him to write three novels, one long tale, and a volume of seven stories published under the grim title *Foram êstes os Vencidos* (These Were the Vanquished; 1945).

The first work that Duarte published was *Auá* (1934), a *novela* he referred to as an "ethnographic documentary" and "a new chapter of indigenous psychology"—that is, of the Islamic Fulas. The combination of ethnography with psychology and a dramatically resolved plot is well handled, although the form suffers from the adjective-studded style of the fledgling author. His later tragic stories and the novels show great progress in depth and style. Someone ought to study Duarte's writings and restore his reputation, which has been misjudged by Guineans as well as by such a qualified critic as Russell Hamilton.

The revolutionary fervor and hope seem unjustified now in the poems which Helder Proença (b. 1956 in Bolama, Guinea-Bissau) gathered in *Não posso adiar a Palavra* (I Cannot Delay Speaking Out; 1982), his first book. The language, musicality, and imagery are still magnificent when he is not assuming the role of the militant poet who fought in the war and became Secretary of Culture in the first government following independence. His poetry glows with a passionate love for his country and its people, especially girls and children. He

is free of blind partisanship and hatred. Instead, one finds love poems like "Pérola cintilante" (Scintillating Pearl) and "Quando desflorei" (When I Deflowered): "Quando desflorei / o silêncio / e a voz embutida / em flor no peito / teus lábios / se abriram criança e doce" (When I deflowered / the silence / a flower embedded / in the breast / your lips / opened childlike and sweet). Neither does he conceal his many moments of discouragement in "Suspiro poético" (Poetic Sigh):

Foram tantos
os dias de espera,
macabras
       e solitárias
       as horas
       prometedoras!

(They were so many,
those days of waiting,
macabre
       and lonely,
       those hours
       promising much!)

One has to familiarize oneself with Guinean history, places, personalities, and terms to comprehend Proença fully, most of all when he is writing in Creole. I wish I knew his second volume of verse, *O Canto por Vezes tem a Cor das Cordilheiras em Chamas* (Song at Times Takes the Cordilleras' Color; 1985), for its poems were inspired by a stay in Brazil in 1979–80. Had he met the Brazilian poet Ferreira Gullar? Perhaps a connection exists between Brazilian poetry and his own.

Finally, from São Tomé Island hails a forceful woman poet who began her professional career as an elementary-school teacher, Aldo (do) Espírito Santo. The daughter of a mixed couple, she was born in 1928 on one of the island's dozen vast plantations. She lived for a while in Lisbon as a student, returned home in 1951, was jailed as a subversive in 1965–66, became a radical militant in the struggle for liberation, and, after the nationalists' victory, was named Secretary of Culture, like Hélder Proença in Guinea-Bissau. Her earliest writing was apparently a feminist article published in a 1949 issue of *Mensagem,* the organ of the Casa dos Estudantes do Império. She was to reiterate her feminism in poems.

The bulk of her verse appeared in one volume, *É nosso o Solo sagrado da Terra: Poesia de Protesto e Luta* (To Us Belongs the Sacred Soil of our Land: Poetry of Protest and Combat; 1978). Her best poems were written early, using striking symbols and a colorful, idiomatic, yet easily understandable language. They sketch scenes from the daily lives of common folk: washerwomen, fishermen, fishwives, plantation laborers. Other poems lovingly depict children: for example, in

"Em Torno da minha Baía" (Around My Bay), where she tells of teaching her class of children on a beach near a crumbling wharf, of her island's decay and the rise of new young hope. Only in the later poetry do protest and militancy become strident. The successive editions of her book offer numerous variants, so that a critical edition would be a most worthwhile task if undertaken.

With Alda Espírito Santo my parade of neglected or forgotten authors of lusophone Africa ends. I hope that one or the other writer has caught the attention of the younger generation and that my brief remarks will serve as a reminder to older lovers of the African literatures to sample the works of those authors and others like them.

Gerald M. Moser, Winter 1999

Slavery and the African Imagination: A Critical Perspective

This paper is not another attempt to define or even suggest what should be the proper orientation of the African critic. My immediate concern is to point out that whatever ideological stance he may take, the African writer cannot ignore the historical fact that the roots of modern African literature lie outside the African continent. I do not intend to raise any controversy by this statement, because I believe it is self-evident. I would like to add the necessary corollary that as long as this situation remains, African literature will continue to function as an awkward appendage of the major national literatures of Western Europe.

The curious fact that the African imagination has been dominated since the Era of the Slave Trade by the traumatic experience of that racial tragedy has been ignored almost to a point of scandal. Yet for black men all over the world the only genuine, shared racial memory is slavery and what it entailed. It is this experience that has defined and appears to continue to shape our relationship with the rest of the world. It is the one single experience that binds all black people together. For let us remember: slavery was both the misfortune of a few *and* the destiny of the many. It was in practical terms the fate of an entire race. What this means is that with the introduction of slavery, the very basis of African society was considerably altered. It is true that slavery developed because European traders were quick to exploit some defects within the structure of traditional African society; but without the advanced technology of Europe, the continuance of the trade would have been impossible. What sustained the trade was the provision

of European manufactures usually summed up as "gin, gun and powder." We know that Europe was quick to exploit Africa as the dumping ground for poorly and cheaply manufactured goods which Daniel Defoe proudly referred to as "useless gewgaws."[1] The legend of the guinea coast and the grain coast had behind it the colonial reality of the slave coast, and from about the middle of sixteenth century to the end of the eighteenth century, slaves constituted the very basis of British trade—in other words, the basis of the British colonies.[2]

The upshot of the commercial contact between Europe and Africa was the gradual destruction of the basis of traditional African society. The very constructs of traditional African society were dismantled, and although a replacement by European systems has not been totally successful, the ultimate aims of modern African society have been dictated, to a large extent, by European ideals. For the African at home and the African of the diaspora the advent of the European on the African continent has thus tremendously altered his pattern of thought and feeling. The set of ideas which governed the form and content of traditional society has become hopelessly inadequate in terms of the demands of modern life. The mutual antagonism between the continental African and the African of the diaspora springs from the agonizing recognition of the fact that for both of them the future is white, *not* black. This antagonism, I would suggest, arises out of a sobering recognition of a hopeless situation.

The above general observations should enable us to make some valid assessment of the set of ideas that informs the written literature of African peoples. Criticism of African literature has too often assumed that the tradition of written literature in Africa is an ancient one. It is true that individual Africans have written within the European tradition since and after the Roman Empire.[3] But these blacks had written within the prevailing tradition of their respective European societies, and neither the plays of Terence (ca. 195–159 B.C.) nor the *Austriad* of Don Juan de Sessa (alias Don Latino), nor yet the various productions of Dumas and Pushkin can be said to be African even under that nebulous concept. What we now refer to as African literature in modern European languages is a much later affair.

African writing in its modern sense began in the eighteenth century, and it developed inevitably as a protest literature. It is needless to recite the circumstances under which this literature was produced. What is important from the point of view of this essay is to recognize that its primary impetus was derived from the dehumanizing institution of slavery. The most telling indictment of the brutality of slavery is the fact that it took well over two centuries before the black slave could put his thoughts on paper—in other words, before he became tolerably literate in the culture of his masters. And when he did, he was compelled by his new social and religious orientation to play down his African origins and to think in terms of a universal man. As we may expect, the first literary experiment took the shape of poetry, but poetry so public in its nature and so impersonal in its content that it would probably have remained unnoticed had it not been written by slaves. Francis Williams's "Ode" to Governor Haldane and the poems of Phillis Wheatley hardly betray any evidence of intimate acquaintance with the hard lot of the black man in the New World. It was this lack of personal concern for the social and racial problems of their times that made Jefferson smugly dismiss the poetry of Phillis Wheatley.

> Among the blacks is misery enough, God knows, and no poetry. Love is the peculiar cestrum of the poet. Their love is ardent, but it kindles the senses only, not the imagination. Religion indeed has produced a Phyllis Whately [sic]; but it could not produce a poet. The compositions published under her name are below the dignity of criticism.[4]

Jefferson was partially right: the poetry of Phillis Wheatley was only too painfully deficient in feeling. In her social poems she could let flow liberal floods of tears. But in reality these were dry tears, because they came out of the dry rationalization of the Christian faith. And her tears were grotesquely irrelevant, because they flowed outside the mainstream of her experience. When she wrote of Africa and of the African, she totally, completely ignored her feelings and went to the Bible and the Puritan imagination of New England for her models. The promising title of one of her earliest poems, "On Being Brought from Africa to America," turns out to be hugely misleading, because the poem itself lacks depth both in feeling and in thought.

'T WAS mercy brought me from my pagan land,
Taught my benighted soul to understand
That there's a God, that there's a *saviour* too:
Once I redemption neither sought nor knew.
Some view our sable race with scornful eye,
"Their colour is a diabolic die."
Remember, *Christians, Negroes,* black as *cain*
May be refin'd and join th'angelic train.[5]

Today the central thought of the poem may appear repugnant, but in the eighteenth century Phillis Wheatley's plea for the conditional acceptance of the African would have appeared progressive, indeed radical. What is disturbing in this poem is the ideological assumption of Phillis Wheatley. It is an assumption which is central to her imagination and which recurs in every poem. And Jefferson was obviously wrong when he implied that Phillis was merely the product of religion. For she was, in every sense of the word, the product of slavery, and her poetry thus becomes the manifestation of the slave's imagination. All the slave writers—Francis Williams, Phillis Wheatley, Ignatius Sancho and Olaudah Equiano—were unable to transcend the ideological chains clamped on their imagination by the European societies in which they lived. Thus Equiano became the "black Christian" and wrote "Miscellaneous Verses, or Reflections on the State of My Mind during my first conviction; of the Necessity of believing the truth, and experiencing the inestimable benefits of Christianity."[6]

To continue the argument of Jefferson, Equiano was as much the product of religion as Phillis Wheatley ever was. But more than that, Equiano was the product of the white liberal imagination that substituted colonialism for slavery on the basis of an argument first developed by Defoe and later utilitzed by Adam Smith: that the exploitation of the labor of a free people is more productive than the exploitation of the labor of the slave.[7] Thus Equiano himself, after his mighty and roaring indignation against slavery, suggested an alternative, howbeit a more human one, a new system of exploitation.

> As the inhuman traffic of slavery is to be taken into the consideration of the British legislature I doubt not, if a system of commerce was established in Africa, the demand for manufactures would not rapidly augment as the native inhabitants will insensibly adopt British fashions, manners, customs etc. In proportion to the civilization, so will be the consumption of British manufactures.[8]

The argument in the above passage presupposes the necessity for a relationship between Europe and Africa. With the exception of Ignatius Sancho, all black writers in the eighteenth century appear to have shared Equiano's view, and they all wrote in response to the demands of the relationship between black and white; in the eighteenth century the very core of that relationship was slavery.[9] They all wrote outside the African continent, and by the mere fact that they wrote at all, they expressed themselves through an idiom and a medium alien to their own culture. In other words, they wrote as exiles.

▦ ▦ ▦

If we now take a leap of over 100 years, it is not because there was no literature by black Africans between the eighteenth century and the twentieth century. There was plenty, but plenty that was not particularly different. The fact is that there is a sense in which every black writer is an exile and shares with his fellow Africans through the centuries the frustrations inherent in that state. There are apparent differences between the political and social status of the modern black writer and his eighteenth-century counterpart, but there is little change in his imagination and the set of ideas that define his intellectual goals. We must take Wole Soyinka very seriously when he complains:

> To recommend on the one hand that the embattled general or the liberation fighter seek the most sophisticated weaponry from Europe, America and China, while, on the other hand, that the poet totally expunge from his consciousness all the knowledge of foreign tradition in his own craft, is absurdity.[10]

We must take Soyinka seriously not because of the strength of his complaint—it has little worth noting—but because he thought the defense necessary at all. Soyinka, it must be assumed, will be first to admit that shopping for bazookas in European ministries of defense and armament conglomerates is not exactly the same function as acquiring the skills for the metrical form of the English madrigal or the pastoral. Indeed, the disturbing aspect of Soyinka's complaint is its implication, an implication that looks *backward* to Equiano; for Soyinka and Equiano both affirm that our taste must be acquired, and indeed must be acquired from Europe.

As we have seen, Equiano's solution to slavery is colonization. He read his history accurately, and it was only a matter of time before blacks began to acquire the taste for European manufactures. But they went beyond that: they acquired European languages and European cultures. As all colonized peoples know, the first real problem of a colonizing people is one of ideology—how to impose the ideology of the colonizing power on the colonized people. And the first solution is to deemphasize the cultural values of the subject people and proclaim the superiority of the culture of the colonizing power. The Christian religion was particularly instrumental in the colonization of Africa because of its apparent liberating influence, and we should not be surprised that the first Africans to be literate in European languages were deeply religious. So complete is the colonization of the African imagination that the distinguished Wole Soyinka could champion the ideology of the colonizer without knowing it.[11]

It may appear to be an exaggeration to assert that African literature primarily illustrates the success of European colonization, but the facts sufficiently justify the assertion. We cannot deal with the "colonial content" of African literature in any meaningful way here. In a sense, every black writing is a confession of the European influence on the black imagination. Soyinka, for instance, reverts to the slave idiom in *A Dance of the For-*

ests, and in his adaptation of Euripides's *Bacchae* he introduces black slaves and makes the conflict instinctively racial. His class structure is created out of a finely spun racial texture;[12] in *Death and the King's Horseman,* for example, he registers the following dialogue:

Pilkings: Your son honours you. If he didn't he would not ask your blessing.

Elesin: No. Even a thoroughbred is not without pity for the turf he strikes with his hoof. When is he coming?

Pilkings: As soon as the town is a little quieter. I advised it.

Elesin: Yes white man, I am sure you advised it. You advise all our lives although on the authority of what Gods, I do not know.[13]

The case of Soyinka is not peculiar. We realize that the most casual examination of the works of any major African writer will reveal a solid base of European ideological assumptions, and for most Africans ideology in its intellectual sense is European. The case of Chinua Achebe is most intriguing, since this aspect of his writing has generally been ignored. But in spite of the richness of the very structure and texture of Ibo society presented in his three famous novels (*Things Fall Apart, No Longer at Ease* and *Arrow of God*), the ideology which Achebe presents as a viable alternative to traditional Ibo values has a strong foreign tinge. Using the framework of the English novel, Achebe presents his postmortem on the collapse of traditional African societies and the implied triumph of the European world view. Okonkwo, Obi, Ezeulu—these are men for whom the times are definitely out of joint but who, unlike Hamlet, never learn to understand the dynamics of social change. They are totally ignorant of the rhythm of the ebb and flow of social movement, and thus they end wretchedly, a telling testimony to the dynamic force of the social winds of change. They remain what we call men whom Time has passed by.

But the punishment for being out of step with the march of Western ideology is far more severe than mere neglect. Unable to appreciate the centripetal forces that control the movement of history, these eminent characters of Chinua Achebe are helplessly crushed under the pressure of the very society whose values they have sought to protect. It is interesting to note how at the fall of each of the heroes of these three novels, we are reminded—very forcefully reminded—of the new and triumphant ideology: the European administrative machinery which embraces the rule of law and the greater rule of the Christian religion. Achebe's novels thus become the history of the fall of African social systems. And the drama of the fall is played against the background of a new set of ideas and social relations closely associated with the triumphant European colonizers. In the end the white man has the last word; at least in each of Achebe's three novels we witness not only the fragmentation of traditional society but the emergence of new concepts of society. Achebe made the point rather subtly in *Arrow of God*:

> For a deity who chose a time such as this to destroy his priest or abandon him to his enemies was inciting people to take liberties; and Umuaro was just ripe to do so. The christian harvest which took place a few days after Obika's death saw more people than even Goodcountry could have dreamed. In his extremity many an Umuaro man had sent his son with a yam or two to offer to the new religion and to bring back the promised immunity.[14]

One may choose to see the central theme of these novels as the distintegration of traditional African society. But one must add, I think, that the conflict within these novels is generated by the white presence which ultimately dominates the entire world of Achebe's heroes.

The same conclusion emerges from any real study of all major African writers. In other words, to appreciate fully the nature of the African creative imagination as manifested in contemporary African literature, we must be profoundly familiar with the history of the African people. T. S. Eliot has pertinently observed that "Every nation, every race, has not only its own creative, but its own critical turn of mind."[15] Our present business is to seek to establish what constitutes the "African turn of mind," to determine how to identify its critical idiosyncrasies. We must assume that by "turn of mind" both creative and critical, Eliot meant a historically conditioned impetus and response rather than a genetically derived response.

It is obvious from the foregoing discussion that any attempt made at defining African literature, however tentative, must take note of the history of the African people. One of the most sobering experiences that a black man can have is suddenly to realize that suffering and humiliation have been curiously linked with his fate since 1441 or thereabouts. That experience unifies all black sensibilities and has become the pivot of African literary tradition. In other words, the tradition of suffering and humiliation is the *living* tradition of black people all over the world and has become an integral part of the African heritage. It is so total in its embrace and remorseless in its continuity that modern African literature explodes with unremitting intensity of passion. This tradition of suffering and humiliation is the product of the collective experience of the African people. And the African writer with a proper historical per-

spective cannot write outside the limits already defined by the exploratory works of the eighteenth-century African writers. It is this total surrender to the imperatives of history that accounts for the triumph of neocolonialism in Africa; and it is no cynicism to observe that the penetration of Kenya, for example, by Western ideology became complete only *after* the Mau Mau victory.

The criticism of African literature must therefore take note of the necessity to view the African creative turn of mind within the context of the historical relationship between Africa and Western Europe. This relationship appears to have defined the sensibilities of the African psyche and thus dominates the creative expression of the African artist. When T. S. Eliot, in the essay already cited, develops his idea of tradition, he suggests that it must imperceptibly be intertwined with a historical sense which involves an esthetic "perception, not only of the pastness of the past, but of its presence." It is this deep awareness of historical sense, according to Eliot, that compels an Englishman, for instance,

> to write not merely with his generation in his bones, but with a feeling that the whole of the literature of Europe from Homer, and within it the whole of the literature of his own country has a simultaneous existence and composes a simultaneous order. This historical sense which is a sense of the timeless as well as of the temporal and of the timeless and temporal together, is what makes a writer traditional.[16]

"No man is an island unto himself," wrote John Donne, and Donne was a poet. The dictum is particularly expressive of the artist's need to communicate and, like the Ancient Mariner, to search for an audience for his tale—all this within a central tradition. What has happened in the case of African literature is not just a matter of influences. The extraordinary conditioning of the African imagination by centuries of humiliation has resulted in a literature which seeks to establish its authenticity on the acceptance or, at best, acknowledgment of the European side of the African experience. The English poet, the English dramatist, the English novelist can create within the framework of the English literary tradition and within the general European heritage. He need not be aware of an African tradition, indeed of the African continent. And indeed to be relevant, the English writer must ignore such distractions. The African writer, on the other hand, appears most relevant when he acknowledges the European roots of his imagination. He appears to have no alternative; or, to put it another way, his alternative is to escape into a romantic world of a past that is inaccessible to him and, in any case, a past that is totally irrelevant to the social realities of the present.

There is another area in which the tyranny of the West manifests itself. I refer to the linguistic base of modern African writing. Here we have the definite disadvantage of using a second language for creative work. Derek Elders once complained that "density of verbal texture is notably absent in many African novels" and then went on to speak of "the desperate modishness of Soyinka's The Interpreters.[17]

In the end the set of ideas that inspires African literature also affirms the fundamental dependence of the African imagination on the historical experience of the African people. As Julian Mayfield, writing about the black esthetic, put it, "It is our racial memory, and the unshakable knowledge of who we are." Mayfield adds:

> For me the Black aesthetic is in a photograph in the book Harlem on my Mind of two old black women, clinging to one another as they walk along the cold streets of New York City. Their faces, especially their eyes, are tired and worn, and their backs are bent, for they and their mothers before them have been working for centuries for nothing. It is in the remembered face of one of my grandmothers as she lay in her coffin. . . . She washed clothes for one white family for fifty years![18]

The African writer may not put it in exactly the same words. But however he puts it, he almost always says the same thing and thus affirms his common heritage with his American brothers.

As I have suggested, the historical imperatives that define the nature and the structure of the African's imagination also define his ideological position. And for us to understand this position, the dominant control exerted on the African imagination by slavery colonialism and neocolonialism should be recognized. How deeply ingrained in the African psyche the underlying ideologies of these historical imperatives have proved to be may be seen in their continuing position of dominance in the African literary tradition since the eighteenth century. Critical discussions of African literature may therefore be meaningful only when African literature is properly recognized for what it is: the collective expression of the racial memory of black people all over the world. But let us add that wherever and whenever this is properly and genuinely expressed, it is violent, unromantic and untragic because built essentially on a historical structure of deprivation, exploitation and humiliation.

S. E. Ogude, Winter 1981

[1] Daniel Defoe, A General History of Trade, London, 1713, p. 11.

[2] Daniel Defoe, The Review, 8 (1711), p. 591.

[3] For example, Terence, Juan de Sessa alias "Don Latino" (ca. 1516–1606), Pushkin, Alexander Dumas, et cetera.

[4] Thomas Jefferson, Notes on the State of Virginia, 2nd American ed., 1794, p. 208.

[5] Phillis Wheatley, The Poems of Phillis Wheatley, Julian D. Mason Jr., ed., Chapel Hill, University of North Carolina Press, 1966.

[6] Paul Edwards, ed., Equiano's Travels, London, Heinemann, 1967, p. 170.

[7] Daniel Defoe, The Life of Colonel Jacque, 2nd ed., London, 1723, p. 191. See also Defoe, Review, p. 263; Adam Smith, Wealth of the Nations, 1776, 1.471; David Hume, Philosophical Works, T. H. Gree & T. H. Grose, eds., 1875, 111.390, note 2.

[8] Edwards, p. 158.

[9] George Moses Horton, a slave in North Carolina (he was actually employed for some time at the University of North Carolina in Chapel Hill), published three volumes of poetry between 1829 and 1865: The Hope of Liberty (1829), The Poetical Works (1845) and Naked Genius (1865).

[10] Wole Soyinka, ed., Poems of Black Africa, London, Heinemann, 1975, p. 15.

[11] See Soyinka's essay "The Fourth Stage," appended to Myth, Literature and the African World View, Cambridge, Cambridge University Press, 1976, pp. 140–60.

[12] But see Jane Lyman, Perspective on Plays, London, 1976, p. xii.

[13] Wole Soyinka, Death and the King's Horseman, London, Eyre Methuen, 1975, p. 64.

[14] Chinua Achebe, Arrow of God, London, Heinemann, 1965, p. 287.

[15] T. S. Eliot, "Tradition and the Individual Talent," in The Sacred Wood, London, Methuen, 1960, p. 47.

[16] Ibid., p. 49.

[17] African Literature Today, 1 (1965), pp. 51–52.

[18] Julian Mayfield, "You Touch My Black Aesthetic," in Black Aesthetic, Addison Gayle Jr., ed., New York, Anchor, 1972, p. 26.

Comparatism and Separatism in African Literature

In this essay I take *comparatism* in the broadest sense to mean the tendency in humanistic scholarship to resist confinement within a limited body of data, whether in time (e.g., in terms of generations of artists or thinkers) or in space (e.g., in terms of a limited culture or society): the comparatist is thus one who feels sufficiently free to range across cultural and disciplinary boundaries to explore logical and other relationships between ideas and phenomena. By *separatism* is meant the urge to limit the scope of inquiry to a recognizable (though quite often dubiously delimited) zone of cultural life or activity, mostly in the belief that such a zone has a character all its own no matter what the historical relationship or incidental affinity between it and any other zone might be. In its ugliest form this parochial urge breeds an obsessive hunger for empirical data amassed for one cultural area in sheer innocence or disregard of their replication in another area and the light that the latter could therefore have shed on the former. Comparatism sometimes goes under the name of universalism, while separatism is in many respects identical with such tags as historicism or functionalism.

A brief survey of the tidal relationships between these two tendencies in some areas of cultural scholarship will help to put the succeeding discussion in the right perspective. Starting with the history of ethnological research, we can draw a recognizable line between the paths of inquiry pursued by evolutionists on the one hand and functional anthropologists on the other—between, for instance, the scholarship of James George Frazer, guided by a belief in elementary cultural universals, and that of Bronislaw Malinowski, based on the persuasion that every society is unique unto itself, being defined by a body of needs and "functions" unreplicated anywhere else. In cognitionist research we can also draw a line between Freudians and Jungians, that is, between those who hold that the psychological picture presented by a subject under study can best be traced back to his unique experiential history and those who, convinced that an individual's behavior has a larger human (universal) background transcending his limited apperception of reality, conduct their analysis on the basis of archetypal symbols.

The meeting ground between the ethnological and cognitionist traditions may be seen in the ingenious structuralist researches of Claude Lévi-Strauss. Though as an anthropologist he stresses the need for a detailed ethnographic probe of each culture or society, he is Kantian enough to hold that all cultural behavior is subject to the universal constraint on the human mind toward binary classification. The cognitionist implication of this belief is that no *qualitative* distinction can be sustained between the so-called civilized and primitive mentalities, and we can only speak of cultural progress in terms of material sophistication, not of mental development, since the mind of man remains qualitatively the same everywhere. It is this belief in one universal mentality that encourages Lévi-Strauss to engage in the analysis of myths from societies as far apart in time and space as Ancient Greece and contemporary Amerindia. For him the essential quality of these myths lies not so much in their linguistic forms as in their semiotic composition; thus he tells us in his epoch-making essay "The Structural Study of Myth": "Whatever our ignorance of the language and the culture of the people where it originated, a myth is still felt as a myth by any reader anywhere in the world."[1]

Perhaps nowhere has this issue of language generated so much disagreement as in comparative literary studies. Some of the more respectable comparatists seem to feel that no literary analysis can justly be called *comparative* unless it deals with works by writers of linguistic dissimilarity, which would no doubt involve a dependable knowledge of the different languages concerned; other comparatists do not, however, consider language such an indispensable barrier to comparative analysis. A further division, which is in many ways a corollary to the linguistic atomism, can be seen between the claims of "national literature" and "world literature," or at least literature that transcends national or racial boundaries. On the whole, the debate seems to center on the fundamental issue of whether human culture is better understood from the perspective of independent units or by seeing the world as one large cultural geography, albeit a variegated one.

▪ ▪ ▪

The above survey will have helped, I hope, to put into proper perspective the sort of questions which any consideration of comparative literature in Africa may raise. I have never ceased to recall with a certain degree of puzzlement the words of a Nigerian academic on an occasion when I had cause to remark the virtues of the comparative approach. "We *don't* need comparative literature here," I remember his stressing. "When they were doing their own stuff there they never thought about us, so why should we think about them now?" I say "puzzlement" because on one level this statement resounds with the resentment every honest African must feel against the prejudices on which most of the earlier researches by Western scholars into African culture were based; and yet at a deeper level I am worried that statements and sentiments of this kind may reduce the intellectual efforts of native African scholars to the level of myopia which has impaired foreign judgment. If it is true that in their day those foreigners failed to consider us of much cultural account, can we at the present state of knowledge pretend that they do not exist, or exert any influence on our lives, and hope to make any epistemological sense in our researches? It would be naïve, of course, to overlook the point that most cultural studies invariably have a basis in prejudice or ideology, and that indeed most of the great cultures the world has acknowledged took themselves as the standard of measurement of human progress.[2] But there has always been at least the need or tendency for each culture to see itself in the comparative light of others, and the more significant strides in humanistic studies have been achieved largely because the scholars concerned have endeavored to cross cultural as well as political barriers.

The political undercurrents of comparatism do indeed deserve some emphasis, especially in the light of the painful political history of Africa. The colonial and other foreign presences among us did so much savagery to our cultural values that it is no surprise to find some of our scholars looking inward for a rediscovery of our violated essences. But we can also take what seems to me a deeper view of domination and argue that it is essentially an effort toward dehumanization. Here I think we can see the foundations of the two paramount lines of inquiry in African cultural studies, which may help us to determine the relative merits of comparatism and parochialism. If we contend that we have some uniquely African values and essences to which the foreign element or outlook is a dispensable exoderm, then we may either try to exorcise that foreign element or else ignore it completely so that the native element can shine forth in its "unsullied" integrity. But if we believe that there are fundamental human values and outlooks amenable to local adjustment, then the simple ethnographic differences between peoples will have that much less prominence in our researches and the vagaries of global politics will be taken largely for granted. This is not to underestimate the sheer physical or other menace of this politics, but to argue that it is as distractive to basic human goals as foreign domination is to local cultural aspirations.

Let us now look a little more closely at those two paramount tendencies in African cultural scholarship, with particular reference to literature. There is, we may as well admit, a certain naïve piety in the universalist faith, and it may even be argued that similarities between peoples are not so hard to demonstrate. But of course all knowledge, as Emerson reminds us, may be no more than an articulation of obvious natural truths; the novelty consists in the sophistication by which the familiar is transformed into a discovery. There are various ways in which African scholars with a comparatist turn of mind have been inclined to spread a large cultural canvas across societal boundaries, but we will here identify two which correspond to perhaps the two most-consulted methods of comparative scholarship— at least the part of it that explores the points of convergence between one society and another. These are the pursuits of *analogy* and *influence* (or indebtedness).

Analogy studies set out to explore, among other things, the physical, political, psychological and other contexts or backgrounds to cultural behavior across societies. Why, for instance, would two artists who live in societies widely separated from one another in space and sometimes time and who have had no appreciable contact with each other produce similar works? In a recent and very stimulating paper Chikwenye Ogunyemi

discovers a happy correspondence between the lives of Wole Soyinka and LeRoi Jones (Imamu Amiri Baraka) as reflected in their two respective plays *The Strong Breed* and *Dutchman*.[3] She is intrigued by the fact that these two black writers, with seemingly dissimilar social backgrounds and upbringing, were able, at the time they were concurrently thirty years of age (in 1964), to produce two similar works. In her discussion of the two plays Ogunyemi presses the biographical similarities of Soyinka and Jones toward an interpretation of their respective messages: at a time when these playwrights deemed it necessary to abandon the smug indifferences of their earlier youth and become fully involved in the surrounding political ferment of the 1960s, they sought an outlet in protagonists who, as (archetypal) scapegoats, must needs pass through a painful experience to achieve full political awareness; having each been married first to a white woman and then to a black, these chastened playwrights have put their protagonists through equally chastening experiences with women so as to convey "the necessity for complementarity between black men and women"; and as angry young black men, Soyinka and Jones have each adopted a stridently iconoclastic tone designed to unsettle the play audience as thoroughly as it does the insensitive political establishment, for the common good of society.

The element of analogy is, however, somewhat qualified in Oguyemi's comparative analysis. For her these two black playwrights, though lacking in any social contact between them, are primarily of African origin; she even goes so far as to conjure a "black collective unconscious" in her discussion of their techniques. Referring to the scapegoat and other archetypes used by the playwright, she says: "The African heritage speaks for itself; it permits them to take a foreign myth or a foreign idea and combine it with what is essentially African to create a new type of art." But at least Ogunyemi continually stresses the point that these two artists have grown up in two distinct societies, and she also points up certain biographical issues which are not necessarily germane to Africanness.

Some African comparatists of the analogical tradition have spread the canvas somewhat wider, and here perhaps I may be permitted to cite my own recent work on the oral epic.[4] I have, I must admit, never been enamored of archetypal criticism with its ragbag of tired clichés, and in this I find support in K. K. Ruthven's witty remark that "archetypal images are not intrinsically valuable, and may pop up in a toothpaste advertisement as readily as in an epic poem."[5] But in my study of what happens to the content and form of the heroic narrative text as the singer faces a live audience during performance I have allowed myself the kind of ecumenical vision that Jung assumed and so observed some enlightening similarities between evidently distinct cultures. In my introductory chapter I allow that my comparative approach "is based on the simple faith that different peoples, placed under roughly the same circumstances, would behave in roughly the same ways or have similar goals and expectations" (p. 30). Having thus absolved myself of the urgency to document ethnographic differences, I then begin to tackle what seems to me essentially a problem of poetics. At the end of my comparative inquiry I am able to reach conclusions which I am convinced are good for the performance of the oral epic before an audience anywhere. "There seems no doubt," I have proposed,

> that the duty to affect an audience (in an act involving singing, musical accompaniment, and some dramatic movement), and a challenge of avoiding a collapse of the fervid act, impose upon the epic certain distinctive features. In content, not only may the story occasionally distort the accepted facts of a body of belief or of true history but the details of one performance may not be in total agreement with those of another performance of the same story, since each performance reflects the specific context that gave rise to it. In form the oral epic demonstrates, under the pressure of steady delivery, a peculiar combination of economy and extravagance, or what Nagler has called an "intriguing mixture of sameness and variety." In style, the bard employs certain techniques aimed both at manipulating the passions of his audience so that they accept the peculiar terms of his myth and at ensuring that there is enough of the familiar touch and voice in the tale to make it acceptable in contemporary, human terms. (240)

My comparative study of the epic was primarily motivated by the fashionable tendency, recently reenacted by Ruth Finnegan in her *Oral Literature in Africa* (Oxford, Clarendon, 1970), to set Homer up as the yardstick of definition of the epic and to dismiss as inadequate all "primitive" heroic narratives which do not ape the classic devices of Homer (or at least such of them as the scribal culture has passed on to us). I have indeed made the Homeric corpus the major counterpoint of my examination of various African texts and have consequently reached conclusions which raise questions about the validity of the fashionable premises concerning the art of Homer: "Structurally, for instance, a bard under the pressure of the audience out there endeavours to encompass more than rigid metric form can allow, and so some of the fashionable conclusions which have been framed largely on prosodic considerations need a little re-examining. And stylistically, since it is clear that the bard endeavours to impress that audi-

ence with the peculiar appeal of his style, however long-established the tradition which he reenacts, we must go back and look a little deeper into the affective purposes of certain tendencies in the acknowledged classics like Homer whom we have for so long seen in terms not of the pre-literate artistic background from which they derive, but of sophisticated literary culture" (243).

I am of course willing to admit that, in arguing a cross-cultural poetics on the basis of the African evidence, I have proposed an Afrocentric view of human cultural behavior and am therefore no less guilty of cultural chauvinism than most earlier European scholars were. But I can at least claim that I have not dissipated my energies in arguing the superiority of one group of people over the other; my inquiry has stayed safely at the level of esthetics where others may have been drawn into a sterile racial or sociological fray.

■ ■ ■

The study of literary influence or indebtedness is another way in which African scholars have subsumed a transcultural universe. This has been done mostly in the analysis of literary works written by Africans in foreign languages; the elements of the humanistic education which these writers have absorbed from the foreign cultures clearly makes this brand of comparatism inevitable. In a quite readable article published in 1975 Charles Nnolim pursues an archetypalist analysis of characters and events in Ferdinand Oyono's *Houseboy*.[6] In this essay Nnolim probes the well-worn motifs of the "scapegoat" and the "quest" as well as Jungian ideas about "individuation" and the tripartite composition of the human psyche (shadow, anima and persona). But the truly comparatist quality of the essay comes in the concluding part, where Nnolim sees the protagonist Joseph Toundi in the scapegoat plight of the biblical Joseph among his treacherous brothers. Considering Oyono's educational background, which may have influenced the choice of the name Joseph for the protagonist, one cannot help wishing that Nnolim had addressed himself more usefully to an exploration of such an arguable likelihood than to the platitudes of archetypalist scholarship.

There are quite a few contemporary African artists, especially poets, who have unabashedly displayed their indebtedness to some European literary conventions. Even at his Negritude best, Senghor, in his style and versification, is fundamentally attached to the traditions of French symbolist poetry, as Abiola Irele has recently pointed out.[7] In his posthumous volume of poems *Labyrinths* (London, Heinemann, 1971) Christopher Okigbo makes free use of a variety of images and figures from the Indo-European classics and even undertakes, in true

Eliotic fashion, to explicate some of these references for his readers. Here clearly is a writer who seems to invite primarily an influence type of study, a task to which Sunday Anozie has risen with true comparatist ardor, meticulously documenting Okigbo's borrowings from Virgil, Baudelaire, Pound, Eliot, Neruda, Sumerian mythology and various other sources.[8] Some African critics have objected to the undue abstruseness of Anozie's analysis and to the modishness of its structuralist design. It is true, of course, that much of Okigbo's imagery and rhythm are rooted in a demonstrably native African environment—that, for instance, the river goddess Idoto at whose feet the poet begins his "rites of passage" in *Heavensgate* and the Nigerian political crisis which is the subject of *Paths of Thunder* are primarily local references; and indeed Anozie gives due emphasis to the provenance of such references in the poet's local experience. But when the poet surrounds all these with images from a random transcultural sampling, employed both as symbolic backdrop and counterpoint in his exploration of a poet's painful search for a selfhood consecrated to a larger communal vision, surely there is little left for the scholar to do but employ an analytic design that, as we saw in Lévi-Strauss above, views the world as one large cognitive landscape.[9]

The view of the world as an undifferentiated cognitive or cultural landscape is one that not a few African scholars would reject, some with greater sophistication or critical competence than others. In a continent where the wounds of colonial brutality are all too fresh or the scars quite recent, the threat to the comparatist faith is real: the effort to trace any cultural or cognitive affinities with the oppressors of the black race would seem nothing short of racial treason. In recent years a series of articles has appeared from a rather uncompromising troika of Nigerian critics—Chinweizu, Onwuchekwa Jemie and Ihechukwu Madubuike—under the title "Towards the Decolonization of African Literature."[10] In these pieces, as they have put it in a later controversy, the authors have "demonstrated the obscurantism prevalent in Nigeria's euromodernist poetry, the curious severance of this poetry from the African tradition, and its phoney and alienating version of syncretism whereby African elements are inducted into the service of a euromodernist sensibility, instead of euromodernist elements being absorbed into the African tradition to serve it."[11] What these critics are saying is simply that Africa is defined by a unique set of values expressed in a language and an oral tradition which is earthy, simple, unpretentious, and that African writers and scholars have no business sporting with a foreign sensibility when there is more than enough in the native traditions to use.

Such literary chauvinism is of course not new. It has antecedents in medieval European discourse if not in the *Dialogus*. In the early decades of this century it received considerable support from folklore scholarship. One of the highlights of diffusionist research was Carl Wilhelm von Sydow's identification of the so-called *oikotype*—i.e., a tale type that is at home in one society or culture group but may not be favored in another since it reflects the cultural propensities peculiar to that group.[12] More recently Alan Dundes has tried to validate this concept in the contemporary folk traditions of Africa and Amerindia: in discussing their tales involving the violation of friendship he finds that whereas among the American Indians the tales are told outright, among the Africans the tales frequently end with a question inviting communal debate, giving proof of the peculiarly African tendency toward communalism as against the introverted life-style of the American Indian.[13] Chinweizu and his friends would no doubt applaud such arguments. Indeed, their series of polemical essays took its start from Chinweizu's earlier essay in which he recommends the adoption of "an African poetic landscape with its flora and fauna—a landscape of elephants, beggars, calabashes, serpents, pumpkins, baskets, towncriers, iron bells, slit drums, iron masks, hares, snakes, squirrels, etc." in place of images and effects imposed by the British poetic tradition.[14] All African poets who have not embraced this truly native sensibility are "prodigals," and of this number Wole Soyinka has been singled out for a particularly virulent condemnation.

Soyinka's response to this nationalism presents a rather interesting study, for it shows how in a politicocultural climate such as Africa's the parochial imperative can run afoul of the ecumenical conscience. He of course dismisses the attack by the troika as sheer ignorant rubbish, and with some justification. In their articles these critics have formed the habit of counterposing what they consider models of traditional African poetry against the borrowed contortions of the so-called "Ibadan-Nsukka school" of poetry (see the Peter Thomas essay elsewhere in this issue) which they think subserves "alien religious rites" and an alien poetics. Not many Africans would reject their plea that "it is from the oral tradition that we must extract the foundation elements of a modern African poetics." But some of the models they have chosen are simply insipid translations which hardly convey the characteristic nuances (tonal music, et cetera) of oral poetry. In a damaging response to them, Soyinka dubs them "neo-Tarzans" who would perpetuate the jungle image of Africa by upholding serpents, elephants and whatnot as the sustaining imagery most fitting to the continent, when the elements of contemporary life and technology (many of which are non-African anyway) are here with us and just as usable; and he reveals their eclecticism as inadequate by quoting pieces of traditional Yoruba poetry which defy the grasp of the uninitiated and demand nothing short of the terse rendition that Soyinka offers.[15]

Here then is a poet who is prepared to open up his sensibilities to a wider universe. In his poetic portrait of the Yoruba mythic figure Atunda, who is fabled to have splintered the creator-god Obatala with a boulder and thus given rise to countless other deities, Soyinka applauds the regenerative act and puts Atunda in the cosmic company of "the rest in logic / Zeus, Osiris, Jahweh, Christ in trifoliate / Pact with creation."[16] In drama he has done an adaptation of Euripides's *Bacchae* which he sees as "a celebration of life, bloody and tumultuous" and in many ways similar to Yoruba mythic drama, "a prodigious, barbaric banquet, an insightful manifestation of the universal need of man to match himself against Nature."[17] And in fiction he has adapted the Orphic quest motif to the experiences of two Nigerian protagonists Ofeyi (Orpheus) and Iriyise (Eurydice) in the face of the surrounding sociopolitical morass.[18] This is not to say that in his creative work Soyinka has never been moved to urge a parochial African message: nothing, for instance, can be more combative of European pretenses than his recent poetic statement on the situation in southern Africa in which he applauds the belligerent position of Samora Machel against Pretoria.

For Dialogue
Dried up in the home of Protestations [i.e., the
  United Nations]
Sanctions
Fell to seductive ploys of Interests
Twin to dry-eyed arts of Expediency.
Diplomacy
Ran aground on Southern Reefs. . . .[19]

But it would be fair to say that on the whole the creative career of Soyinka has been sustained by a certain universalist, humanist temper.

However, in Soyinka's expository statements—in his essays and articles mostly—we see a certain ambivalence. In a paper presented at a Scandinavian conference in 1967, in which he explores the problems and tasks facing the modern African writer, he declares there is no basis for the long-advertised humanism of the African: "that, given equal opportunity, the black tin god a few thousand miles north of him would degrade and dehumanize his victim as capably as Vorster or Governor Wallace. . . . And the intermittent European exercises in genocide have been duplicated on the African continent admittedly on a lower scale, but only be-cause of a temporary lack of scientific organization."[20] Africans are, that is, like the rest of mankind. In a contribution published in a festschrift to his old professor at Leeds, G. Wilson Knight, Soyinka attempts a comparative equation of the Yoruba god Ogun with the Phrygian Dionysos, which leads him later to adapt the *Bacchae;* leaning heavily on Nietzsche's essay *The Birth of Tragedy,* he conceives each god as an epitome of the tragic sensibility of the race which sees life and death as complementary units of a "cosmic equation."[21] The Yoruba and the Greeks have, then, similar world views.

But the position taken by Soyinka in his most extensive expository statement so far—his book *Myth, Literature and the African World* (Cambridge University Press, 1976)—is considerably different. The essay "The Fourth Stage" is reprinted in this book as an appendix, and perhaps rightly; for though the revolutionary essence of the god Ogun unites that essay with the rest of the book, in the latter the comparatist energy is devoted to urging a parochial black (African) message, whereas the former is essentially a cross-cultural humanist exegesis. The mission of Soyinka's book is simply this: the African world view is fundamentally distinct from that of the Indo-European world, so every intellectual effort must be made to free the native cultural element from all contamination by the foreign toward a "vindication of a separate earth and civilization." In myth, for instance, he sees the Yoruba (African) pantheon in an essentially euhemeristic light. It is thus within the logic of the anthropomorphism of these gods that in their rites of passage they should be tainted with error just like men; hence Yoruba ritual drama calls the gods to account by reminding them of this error and demanding that they bless the race in just recompense. But for the European world, divinity is distant from humanity, is a spiritual essence; thus we can discern in European (or Euro-inspired) drama having to do with divinity or the supernatural a certain esthetic of estrangement and nihilistic severance of the social purpose from the spiritual essence. For myth Soyinka gives us a comparison of the traditional Yoruba story of the imprisonment of Obatala with a Brazilian version of it in Zora Zeljan's play *Oxala;* for ritual drama he defends J. P. Clark's *Song of a Goat* against its poor reception by a London audience and applauds the virtues of Duro Ladipo's *Oba Koso,* both of which plays are seen to reveal the African syncretic fusion of the natural and the supernatural, an outlook alien to the European world.

For the rest of the book Soyinka makes the point that, since in the African religious conscience divinity is basically anthropogenic, it follows that man, not god or God, is the measure of reality and of morality; the reverse is the case in the white man's world. Thus Soyinka on the one hand condemns those African works inspired by the canons of foreign religious sanction, like Lewis Nkosi's *Rhythms of Violence* and William Conton's *The African,* which simply justify the Christian injunction to love thy neighbor and turn the other cheek, or Hampate Ba's *Tierno Bokar* and Cheikh Hamidou Kane's *Ambiguous Adventure,* wherein the word of Allah is not just the medium but the message in the exploration of an essentially social predicament, and he applauds Chinua Achebe's *Arrow of God* where divinity is made to subserve the human will. On the other hand Soyinka systematically urges the expulsion of those "alien gods" that have infiltrated the essentially secular African syncretism: here he makes a sustained attack on the ideology of Negritude, which (under Senghor at least) has chosen to sacrifice the black race to the Marxist goal of leveling all humanity in a raceless, faceless identity, and stoutly upholds those works which reject alien religions like Islam and Christianity (e.g., Ouologuem's *Bound to Violence* and Armah's *Two Thousand Seasons*) or else exemplify the syncretic union of the natural and the supernatural (as Camara Laye's *The African Child*).

The task of separating the African world view from the Indo-European is surely a heroic one, but has Soyinka pulled it off? The plea is moving, yet the logic creaks in a few places. For instance, if it is true that we can separate the "eternal verities" (Soyinka's phrase) of one culture from those of another, how was it possible for the French director Mnouchkine to evoke the archetypal "ritual of revolution" to good effect in her play 1789? Or how is it that "towards the close of the sixties, the company which created the New York version of Euripides' *Bacchae* should draw, among other sources, upon an Asmat New Guinea ritual in its search for the tragic soul of twentieth-century, white bourgeois-hippie American culture" (*Myth, Literature,* pp. 6–7)? Also, in explaining how it comes about that elements of modern technology are subsumed into the tutelage of traditional deities (by Soyinka's deduction, Sango is the god of electricity as well as of lightning), he tells us: "An attitude of philosophical accommodation is constantly demonstrated in the attributes accorded most African deities, attributes which deny the existence of impurities or 'foreign' matter, in the god's digestive system. Experiences which, until the event, lie outside the tribe's cognition are absorbed through the god's agency, are converted into yet another piece of the social armoury in its struggle for existence, and enter the lore of the tribe" (p. 28). One therefore wonders: why would Soyinka spend so much time trying to fight off all "foreign matter" when he knew his culture gave it such ample welcome?

It should perhaps be said that, whether one urges a universalist or a parochial message depends largely on the setting or circumstances in which the effort is made. Chinweizu and his friends wrote up their polemical pieces mostly from the United States. There is obviously something in the American sociopolitical climate that inspires a resentment against domination and a desire to shed it in all its forms: we will recall that the pioneers of the struggle for African liberation—the Nnamdi Azikiwes and the Kwame Nkrumahs—had their education in the United States. The parochial Africanist fervor of the troika's statements is therefore understandable. Soyinka again offers an interesting study. The Scandinavian essay was presented between his two incarcerations by two successive Nigerian governments, one civilian and the other military. The essay "The Fourth Stage" was written as an homage to an old white teacher to whom Soyinka must have felt a considerable attachment. The polemical, anti-white-world book *Myth* was first given as a series of lectures at Cambridge University. Now Cambridge does not recognize (as Soyinka tells us in the preface) "any such mythical beast as 'African Literature,'" thus forcing such a luminary of not just the African but the world literary scene to take refuge in a department of anthropology; the intransigence of the book's message was therefore inevitable. But the preface itself was written in Accra, Ghana under the shadow of a military dictatorship and thus amid a general sociopolitical mess which, it would seem, makes the celebration of a uniquely African world view hardly worth the trouble. These lines from the last paragraph of the preface clearly do not sort well with the spirit of what follows:

> Nothing in these essays suggests a detailed uniqueness of the African world. Man exists, however, in a comprehensive world of myth, history, and mores; in such a total context, the African world, like any other 'world,' is unique. It possesses, however, in common with other cultures, the virtues of complementarity. To ignore this simple route to a common humanity and pursue the alternative route of negation is, for whatever motives, an attempt to perpetuate the external subjugation of the black continent. (xii)

Wole Soyinka, described on the title page as Professor of Comparative Literature in a University of Ife that has seldom offered that course of study, may have written a book which is in one sense a commendable effort toward Africa's "self-apprehension" (as he indeed claims), in another sense a learned waste of time.

⬛ ⬛ ⬛

To conclude, the fortunes of comparative scholarship may be seen in a purely epistemological light as being ultimately bound up with the contending claims of *historicism* (the tendency to see cultural reality from the limited perspective of one individual or group) and *universalism* (the tendency to see the world as one large cultural or cognitive family). In Africa, however, the problem is further complicated by the painful history of relations between Africa and the white world which has so severely threatened the validity of a cross-cultural vision. Africans have an undeniable right to be careful about engaging in a cross-cultural parley with peoples who continue to deny them fundamental human rights. But there are some African scholars who continue to consult the "eternal verities" of humanity, not because they are any less resentful of the assaults on their race or would be any less inclined to fight against these assaults (physically or otherwise), but because they consider these assaults surmountable distractions from an honest quest for those verities. Such scholars should, however, understand that the ecumenical faith all too often turns out to be naïve and feeble unless sustained by painstaking analytical rigor.

The burden of demonstration is nonetheless heavier on the parochialists. Those who shut their eyes on the world beyond their immediate purviews, whether from sheer innocence or from intransigence, have frequently ended by arguing a laughable uniqueness. Even those who have employed comparatist techniques to argue separatism have not, as Soyinka's case clearly shows, always justified the effort. And it may be well to remember that the political circumstances which give rise to these parochial claims may ultimately recede and render the claims somewhat passé. For instance, Willa Muir's declamation against the imperial urge as revealed in the German of Kafka's writing has failed to impress an ex-German Jew like S. S. Prawer, for whom the Teutonic menace is somewhat of a distant history.[22]

Whatever its uses, the search for a separatist poetics should be indulged with caution. When the battle against the oppressors of the black race has been fought and won, whither, we may well ponder, will our bellicose energies be turned? One suspects that in the not-too-distant future it will no longer be enough for us to be told that "we are all Africans" simply because we are black or inhabit an integral land mass or even trace from a demonstrable genetic source. In a continent where linguistic differences are frequently a barrier to true national unity, separatist comparatism may be about to have a field day. But God forbid. I believe that those who see the world as one large cultural or cognitive family should of course not deliberately shirk the responsibility—should indeed welcome every effort—to point up the independent vitalities of the members of that family. "Comparative literature," as Wellek has

rightly observed, "surely wants to overcome national prejudices and provincialisms but does not therefore ignore or minimize the existence and vitality of the different national traditions."[23] Still, the search for affinities is just as fruitful if not more fulfilling. And those pious exegetes who hope to pontificate for the African writer an esthetic that excludes influences he has gainfully embraced may as well save themselves the trouble.

Isidore Okpewho, Winter 1981

[1] Claude Lévi-Strauss, *Structural Anthropology,* London, Allen Lane, 1968, pp. 206–31.

[2] This point has recently been driven home by the polemical recommendation of an "Afrocentric" view of reality: see Molefi K. Asante, *Afrocentricity: The Theory of Social Change,* Buffalo, N. Y., Amulefi, 1980.

[3] Chikwenye O. Ogunyemi, "Iconoclasts Both: Wole Soyinka and LeRoi Jones," *African Literature Today,* 9 (1978), pp. 25–38.

[4] Isidore Okpewho, *The Epic in Africa: Toward a Poetics of the Oral Performance,* New York, Columbia University Press, 1979. All page references are to this edition. [See *WLT* 54:1, p. 160 for a review of Okpewho's book.—Ed.]

[5] K. K. Ruthven, *Myth,* London, Methuen, 1976, p. 77.

[6] Charles E. Nnolim, "Jungian Archetypes and the Main Characters in Oyono's *Une vie de Boy*," *African Literature Today,* 7 (1975), pp. 117–22.

[7] Léopold Sédar Senghor, *Selected Poems of Léopold Sédar Senghor,* Abiola Irele, ed., Cambridge, Cambridge University Press, 1977, pp. 29–36.

[8] Sunday Anozie, *Christopher Okigbo: Creative Rhetoric,* London, Evans, 1972.

[9] Anozie did postgraduate research at the Sorbonne. His book provides enough autobiographical information to suggest he was practically commissioned by Okigbo to write it. But that hardly reduces the enormity of the task or the courage of its execution.

[10] Chinweizu, "Towards the Decolonization of African Literature," *Okike,* 6 (1974), pp. 11–27 and 7 (1975), pp. 65–81. Chinweizu is the author of the stridently polemical *The West and the Rest of Us,* New York, Random House, 1974; and Onwuchekwa Jemie of the no less committed *Langston Hughes: An Introduction to the Poetry,* New York, Columbia University Press, 1976.

[11] Chinweizu, O. Jemie, I. Madubuike, "The Leeds-Ibadan Connection: The Scandal of Modern African Literature," *Okike,* 13 (1978), p. 37.

[12] See C. W. von Sydow, *Collected Papers in Folklore,* Lauritz Bodker, ed., Copenhagen, Rosenkilde & Bagger, 1948, pp. 50–51.

[13] Alan Dundes, "The Making and Breaking of Friendship as a Structural Frame in African Folk Tales," in *Structural Analysis of Oral Tradition,* Pierre Maranda & Elli K. Maranda, eds., Philadelphia, University of Pennsylvania Press, 1971, pp. 171–85.

[14] Chinweizu, "Prodigals Come Home!," *Okike,* 4 (1973), p. 4.

[15] See Wole Soyinka, "Neo-Tarzanism: The Poetics of Pseudo-Tradition," *Transition,* 48 (1975), pp. 38–44. Chinweizu and his friends have come back with a counterargument in *Okike,* 14 (1978), pp. 43–51.

[16] Wole Soyinka, *Idanre,* London, Methuen, 1967, p. 83.

[17] Wole Soyinka, *The Bacchae of Euripides,* London, Methuen, 1973, pp. xi–xii.

[18] Wole Soyinka, *Season of Anomy,* London, Collings, 1973.

[19] Wole Soyinka, *Ogun Abibiman,* London, Collings, 1976, p. 6.

[20] Wole Soyinka, "The Writer in a Modern African State," in *The Writer in Modern Africa,* Per Wästberg, ed., Uppsala, Scandinavian Institute of African Studies, 1968, p. 20.

[21] Wole Soyinka, "The Fourth Stage," in *The Morality of Art,* D. W. Jefferson, ed., London, Routledge & Kegan Paul, 1969. We may recall that Cheikh Anta Diop, in his *L'unité culturelle d'Afrique noir* (Paris, Présence Africaine, 1959), used the same essay by Nietzsche to draw a line between the tragic sensibility of the Aryan (Indo-European) world and the cheery optimism of the Negro race, a reverse position to that of Soyinka.

[22] See S. S. Prawer, *Comparative Literary Studies: An Introduction,* New York, Barnes & Noble, 1973, p. 17.

[23] René Wellek, "The Name and Nature of Comparative Literature," in *Comparatists at Work,* S. Nichols, Jr. and R. Vowles, eds., Waltham, Ma., Blaisdell, 1968, p. 22.

Writing New H(er)stories for Francophone Women of Africa and the Caribbean

Self-sacrifice—as the major ethic of the female culture—has been one of the most effective psychological blocks to women's open rebellion and demand for self-determination. It has also been a major tool of male manipulation of females.

▓ PHYLLIS CHESLER, *WOMEN AND MADNESS*

At the dawn of a new millennium, the work of contemporary francophone women authors must be considered as situated at the crossroads of history and philosophy. On the historical level, women's writing in Africa and the Caribbean was rarely referenced for the first half of the past century. Women have usually had their histories written for them by men, interjecting rarely to alter masculine depictions. Both colonial and even, to some extent, postcolonial historical perspectives have left women in the lurch, with little voice and presence on the page.[1] Philosophically, literary movements such as *Négritude,*[2] while promoting the revitalization (and, as some would say, the reinvention) of African thought, have left women out of the literary loop, circumscribing their selfhood within the larger, what V. Y. Mudimbé calls, African *gnosis.*[3] How do African and Caribbean women writing in French, thus, situate themselves at the crossroads of these historical-philosophical junctures? I would answer: by creating their own unique feminine space wherein they explore new trajectories toward original feminine *becomings.*

Female subjecthood as defined by current African and Caribbean francophone women authors is formed not only from new ideals of the mind but also from the conceptualization of a unique body politics, a corporeal reality that promotes a sexually differentiated structure of the speaking subject. Such a new speaking subject is no longer understood as an ahistorical object, but rather as a body linked to, and interwoven with, a plurality of systems: political, cultural, economic, and historical. The new feminine subject is a site of contestation where sociocultural and political struggles play themselves out, are heard by all, refashioned and retransmitted on a woman's own terms. As the Moroccan sociologist Fatima Mernissi states: "It is [with] access to public space, employment, and education that women's lives have undergone the most fundamental changes. Space, employment, and education seem to be the areas where the struggles which agitate society (especially the class struggle) show up in the life of women with the greatest clarity."[4] The postcolonial theorist Gayatri Spivak also explains that the public sphere is characterized by all that represents culture and politics, as well as the social, professional, economic, and intellectual. Women who step into the public sphere as agents of their destiny are essentially stepping into an environment of marginality and of exile where their numbers are few.[5]

Women authors of francophone Africa and the Caribbean define a separate space in which history and philosophy become something *other* for women. This space may be thought of as the *vel,* a place where the overlap of male history and philosophy takes place, deferring to *a woman's way.*[6] The *vel* is Lacan's *Möbius strip,* where philosophy and history twist around to form a third, uncharted territory. The philosopher and feminist Elizabeth Grosz explains the image of the Möbius strip as "the torsion or pivot around which the subject is generated. The double sensation creates a kind of interface of the inside and the outside, the pivotal point at which inside will become separated from outside and active will be converted into passive."[7] Within this pivotal point, women find their voice—are made active—as they discover new processes of selfhood in both physical and literary form. Writing within the interface is both liberating and terrifying because it is uncharted and unknown. It is a place where women define their feminine ethic, where the self is in process and in metamorphosis. This self can be violent, hysterical, and even self-destructive, as evidenced in novels such as Myriam Warner-Vieyra's *Juletane.*[8] Or, as Aminata Sow Fall's recent work *Douceurs du bercail*[9] demonstrates, the feminine self may be a seeker of tranquillity, peace, paradise, and fulfillment through human contact and the discovery of women's ancient heritage.

As francophone women writers write *in* this new space, their works encompass a variety of issues, the most important being feminine emancipation in both legal and social spheres. At the dawn of this millennium, women francophone authors of the Maghreb, sub-Saharan Africa, and the Caribbean are undertaking feminine research that touches upon religious values, law, society, and culture. Women's emancipation requires first and foremost the breaking away from (and of) traditional phallocratic/centric roles that have hemmed them in the confines of traditional sociocultural spaces. In contemporary francophone literature, women take flight and step out of sociocultural boundaries to explore identity. These women authors are *deterritorializing* to build new social projects where the historical, the cultural, and the economic all come into play. Deterritorialization is, as Gilles Deleuze and Felix Guattari state, a "signifying rupture" that always assures the subject a break with the past: past life histories, past destinies, and past traditions.[10] Such a rupture promotes the re-creation of the subject, forcing her to adapt to new frontiers and fields of reference. Within the *vel*—this tantalizing new public space of agency—a feminine speech is fashioned.

Irène Assiba d'Almeida aptly states in her book *Francophone African Women Writers: Destroying the Emptiness of Silence* that "the dynamics of speech and silence are far from being simple and clear-cut [in francophone Africa]."[11] Speech, or the lack thereof, has been a central theme used by Western literary critics to define African and Caribbean feminine writing within a postcolonial context. For authors such as the Algerian Assia Djebar and the Senegalese Aminata Sow Fall, the importance of women's voices used to rectify history and establish a place in it has been a central topic in their work. As one traverses the literary production of women authors from the regions discussed here, one realizes that speech takes on many forms. In sub-Saharan francophone Africa, not only colonialism but also traditional mores shaped women's roles within their tribes. Cultural constraints determined how women literarily contributed to their respective societies. In Senegal and Cameroon women were, and continue to be, the keepers and transmitters of oral traditions. As *griottes,* women storytellers passed down countless generations of oral lore.

Although modern literature (written in French by Africans) took root in Africa in the 1930s, African francophone women did not begin to write until the 1960s (in the Maghreb, women were writing in the 1950s).[12] However, as African women scholars point out, women in a sense have been speaking for centuries. The difference is that their speech has been contained within tribal and/or family boundaries. Public oral milieus destined for women were usually viewed as marginalized segments of society. Here *griottes* reigned, but often were thought to be possessed by demons.[13] As women authors attest, outside the confinement of village and home, the act of speaking for women becomes a political act. In the case of the Caribbean, although Suzanne Césaire, Suzanne Lacascade, and Paulette and Jane Nardal contributed to the Négritude revue *Tropiques* in the 1920s and 1930s, their impact politically was overshadowed by the notoriety of male authors such as Aimé Césaire, Léopold Senghor, and Léon Damas. It was not until the 1950s and 1960s that major literary works written by women, depicting strong feminine characters, made their mark. Women authors such as Marie Chauvet (Haiti) and Michèle Lacrosil (Guadeloupe), laid the groundwork for later seminal authors such as Maryse Condé and Simone Schwarz-Bart, who continue to draw attention to feminine writing in French from the Caribbean.[14]

Women as active agents, challenging the prerogatives of male public space, place themselves on equal footing with men. In the postcolonial years, women authors of the Maghreb such as Fatima Mernissi and Assia Djebar have sought not only to challenge men's privileged power in their respective societies but also to use the written word as a political act of defiance.[15] In Algeria, the development of women's associations within the emergence of numerous political parties after independence in 1962 supported women who sought to write and to challenge the fundamentalist Islamic traditionalism that slowly took its hold, effacing women's rights. Communication between women was the only way to "understand the relationship between gender and nationalism" and the about-face the Front de la Libération Nationale party (FLN) perfected with regard to women's rights once its pundits were in power.[16]

From feminine authors, researchers, and academics of immense notoriety such as the Algerian Assia Djebar and the Moroccan Fatima Mernissi, to those recently entering the arena of contemporary francophone literature, field, women of Algeria, Cameroon, Guadeloupe, Haiti, Martinique, Morocco, Senegal, and Tunisia are striving to gain an active presence in society and culture in order to shape new roles for women in politics, literature, and history. Francophone authors such as Malika Mokeddem (*L'Interdite*), Myriam Warner-Vieyra (*Juletane*), and Aminata Sow Fall (*Douceurs du bercail*)[17] cultivate a deterritorialized space that does two things: first, it allows women to break the traditional feminized interior area of ultratraditional space; and second, it fosters the building of a new platform of agency in public "exterior" areas (such as those of politics, law, and cultural activism), thus recontextualizing previous representations of women.

■ L'INTERDITE: EXILE AND THE LANGUAGE OF WOMEN

In Malika Mokeddem's novel *L'Interdite* the heroine realizes that it is only after confronting and subsequently persevering over violent political conflicts, exile, and feelings of solitude and marginalization that she is able to reach a place of true self-knowledge. Yet neither author nor heroine is able to right any of the political, social, cultural, or economic wrongs of her country single-handed. The freedom granted to Sultana, the protagonist of *L'Interdite,* does not come without a price to pay. Deterritorialization—a life of nomadism—condemns her to a destiny of wandering and of *étrangeté* (foreignness). This foreignness often throws feminine characters into a new reality that is marginalized, exiled, and full of despair. Julia Kristeva underscores the fact that "liberty" as well as "solitude" fashions a double-edged sword that comes from writing in the margins of established norms.[18] *Étrangeté* is a means of resistance, a price that has been paid for crossing over boundaries to foster communication in a public space of active agency. "In crossing a border," Kristeva remarks, "the *étranger* has changed [her] discomforts into a base of resistance, a citadel of life. . . . Without a home, [she] disseminates . . . , multiplying masks and false selfs."[19]

The world of *étrangeté* generates feelings of duality—of "being split apart," as Malika Mokeddem's heroine, Sultana, remarks (191). It is often in the world of the "shattered" that the African francophone author is able to find the secrets to her selfhood. In order to confront these feelings of "multiplicity" and "duality" so often expressed by feminine authors, Mokeddem places her female characters in spaces of negotiation. These spaces exist outside the normal boundaries within which women are expected (by family, fathers, culture, and society) to operate.[20] In *L'Interdite* Sultana steps out into a space of agency that leads her not only to freedom but also to solitude and self-doubt.

Mokeddem positions Sultana between two worlds; one French, a symbol for an adopted refuge, a place where she has developed her professional career as a doctor and lived freely as a woman; and one Algerian, representing a past full of tormented memories, lost love, religious fundamentalism, and death. "No it's not a tragedy to be foreign, it's a tormented richness" (253), Sultana exclaims as she tries to come to terms with her French present and her Algerian past, from which she has been barred as "l'Interdite"—the Forbidden Woman—by the villagers of her childhood home, Aïn Nekhla. She discovers that returning to Algeria after a long absence allows her slowly to efface the feelings of attachment she once had toward her native country.

Sultana is forced to return and confront her childhood memories because of the death of her former lover, Yacine. A doctor in the village, Yacine dies of unknown causes immediately after posting a letter to Sultana, who resides in Montpellier, France. Yacine's death offers a window to her past and provides a means of closing the gap between the memories of her native village and her new life in France, which she defines as "a privileged corner of exile" (12). Yet what does she find upon returning? Not only the childhood hostility she endured because of her foreignness (her father was considered an "outsider" because of his foreign tribe), but also the new popularity in the village of the ultrareligious fundamentalist party, the Front Islamique du Salut (FIS), which poses a constant threat to her from the first hours of her arrival. In order to combat the fundamentalists and to come to terms with her painful childhood memories and subsequent exile in France, she decides to stay on after Yacine's funeral, taking up his position as town doctor. Her work becomes a lifeline to her own sanity as well as to that of other women. It is only later that we learn the circumstances of her tortured memories. It was here, in her village, that her mother was murdered by her father in front of Sultana. As a village elder explains to the young woman, it was because of her father's *foreignness* and her mother's murder that Sultana was condemned as "l'Interdite." As the old woman points out, "You came from somewhere else, with mannerisms from somewhere else. Bad luck made you even more foreign. So you left also" (254).

Overlaying Mokeddem's story is her political commentary on the current upheaval caused by the FIS, which she does not deny has infested the social fabric of Algeria. The author's disdain over the treatment of women and the deterioration of women's social and political status because of the rise of religious fundamentalism renders her novel more than a story of fiction. It is a critical commentary on the demise of civil liberties for those who have no voice in Algeria. The author draws the reading public's attention to the ongoing sociocultural and political strife of a country laid waste by inner conflict, factionalism, fundamentalism, and abuse of human rights. As Sultana realizes in the closing pages of *L'Interdite,* it is only through the solidarity of women that political, social, and cultural gains favoring change will be made. Standing up in unison to the patriarchal status quo, as one old woman tells Sultana, will be the only solution for women in Algeria: "When one is cornered, one is obligated to counterattack. That's perhaps where our strength comes from. Individually they can enslave and break us. [But] they will think twice if we are unified" (251).

Sultana's predestined life of nomadism leads to the realization that her multiple identity is really made up of her Algerian history, French schooling, and the present bonds she shares with the village women. Although she is eventually forced to leave by members of the FIS ruling the village, Sultana takes with her the knowledge that now she is not alone. The heroine has formed links of feminine connections that will all contribute to the continuation of feminine solidarity and to the struggle against oppression in favor of human rights: "Tell the women, even from far away, I'll be with them," Sultana cries out (264). Mokeddem's novel attests to the new political agendas to which francophone women authors are devoting themselves as they confront a new era of feminine writing that is liberating on a personal level, yet potentially dangerous when met with opposition at home.

▪ JULETANE: IN THE SPACE OF MADNESS

Out on the borders of tradition, within the hostile *vel*, women authors writing from the francophone diaspora discover the intricacies not only of public agency but also of their psyche. "It is debilitating to be any woman in a society where women are warned that if they do not behave like angels they must be monsters," write Sandra M. Gilbert and Susan Gubar in their noteworthy study, *The Madwoman in the Attic*.[21] So often the socialization of women in patriarchal societies has led to hysteria and sickness, creating women-mutants out of pain and stifling access to subjectivity. "The despair of the monster-woman" becomes something "real, undeniable, and infectious" as she tries to grasp mental normalcy.[22]

For centuries, Western women authors have shifted between the "fundamental extremes of angel and monster" to criticize the oppression of the "male text's 'imposition' upon women."[23] The francophone feminine author, like her Western counterpart, not only condemns patriarchal discourse as hindering feminine agency within the African and Caribbean diasporas; she also blames the patriarchal sociocultural systems that continue to bear down upon her, maintaining an oppressive status quo even in our postcolonial era. Shoshana Felman writes that "madness is the impasse confronting those whom cultural conditioning has deprived of the very means of protest or self-affirmation." This madness has characterized the "very status of womanhood," Felman states, and therefore must be contested on all levels.[24] Often writing is the only means to thwart the loss of subjectivity for women who, on a daily basis, confront imminent madness caused by sociocultural barriers often constructed by

men (one need only consider the present condition of women in Afghanistan to understand the extreme results of masculine oppression and misinterpretation of cultural traditions at women's expense). Certainly, since the dawn of the postcolonial era, writing has afforded women authors of the formerly colonized diaspora the means to strike back and reclaim their agency. "Woman must write woman," Hélène Cixous exclaims; by writing, "women will confirm women in a place other than that which is reserved in and by [men]."[25]

In the francophone novels of women authors of the African continent and the Caribbean islands, madness is the result of many factors. It is often caused by exile, isolation, and marginalization—either forced by the masculine-centric power or self-imposed—as women seek to challenge age-old traditions in their respective indigenous societies. In some instances, hysteria is a positive catalyst toward a truer knowledge of the self, a force that empowers and allows her to overcome debilitating obstacles. Perhaps the voice of the hysteric is, as the Cameroonian author Werewere Liking suggests, the result of our modern age, where "a lunatic language must be born to allow lunatics to express themselves in the face of an age of lunacy."[26]

Madness in feminine writing is not a new subject, as Gilbert and Gubar tell us. Since the dawn of civilization, women have *literally* fought men to gain a voice in society and culture through acquisition of the pen. The pen represents one of the few viable tools women have had to *right/write themselves in[to]* history. "Precisely because a woman is denied the autonomy—the subjectivity—that the pen represents, she is not only excluded from culture (whose emblem might well be the pen) but she also becomes herself an embodiment of just those extremes of mysterious and intransigent Otherness which culture confronts with worship or fear, love or loathing."[27] The pen is the maleness, the physical power of subjecthood. Without the pen, women have little agency and access to sociopolitical and cultural domains. Access to the pen puts women on equal footing with men. The female novelist becomes *génétrice* of her own progeny, mistress of her own destiny—a matriarch who has a chance to challenge patriarchy. Yet women francophone novelists of Africa and the Caribbean have discovered, like their Western counterparts, that confronting patriarchy and dominant male sociopolitical systems inevitably generates the possibility of causing harm to their own well-being. However, these women authors also attest that potential personal risk outweighs the alternative, which is silence, folding up on oneself, closing one's mind, and succumbing to the oppressive system. Women win some battles and others they lose.

Often there is a price to pay for speaking out and voicing opinions on certain feminine issues that allude to sociocultural constraints on women. In most cases, speaking out destroys the author's heroine, sending her into an abyss of insanity from which she cannot extract herself. Novels such as the Guadeloupean Michèle Lacrosil's *Cajou,* the Senegalese Mariama Bâ's *Un chant écarlate,* and the Algerian Nina Bouraoui's *La voyeuse interdite* depict madness as a result of the heroine's direct confrontation with masculine sociocultural paradigms that hinder the development of her independence as well as her identity.[28] Curiously, as Elisabeth Mudimbé-Boyi states, writing in/of/about madness also often "functions rather as a metaphor of the female social condition and alienation."[29] Insanity within the realm of the fictional text becomes a means to say what cannot be said. The "unsaid, the unsayable" then "attempts to find an outlet by disguising itself in illness or in madness."[30] Speaking from exile, the Algerian author and feminist Assia Djebar attests that her very existence depends on her writing and that she must always write as if tomorrow were her last day for saying the "unsayable": "When I write, I write always as if I am going to die tomorrow. Each time I finish I ask myself if this is really what one expected of me, because the murders continue [in Algeria]. I wonder what [writing] is good for. If not to clench [my] teeth so as not to cry."[31]

As we have established, the theme of women on the brink of madness or succumbing to it is a trope often found in women's writing; African and Caribbean francophone novels are no exception. However, what is interesting to study are the different manners in which Mokeddem's Sultana and Warner-Vieyra's Juletane struggle against being cut off from tribe, family, and social group and how they confront psychological torment. Where haunting memories, exile, and isolation from family and home country, although painful, were in the end reconciled, liberating Sultana of *L'Interdite,* for the Guadeloupean author Myriam Warner-Vieyra's heroine Juletane they are overwhelming forces that, in the end, lead to death. A variance in the effects of exile and marginalization on these two heroines is also found in the way each author tells her heroine's story. Sultana is master of her own history; her narrative is told in the first person, "je." She is able to survive as an immigrant in France, return to her native village in Algeria, confront her past and its psychological turmoil, and then extract herself from tortured memories to live her life on her own terms in exile. Juletane, on the other hand, has her story *read* for her. Warner-Vieyra's narrator Hélène Parpin finds Juletane's diary among "long-forgotten objects" (11) she has packed up to move to a new apartment. The diary came to her by way of her job as a social

worker in a hospital. Juletane's story, in a sense, is "possessed" by others. Her words are not those of direct speech, but come to the reader via the pages on which she has written her story.

Hélène is everything Juletane is not. "Contrary to the author of the diary, she did not know solitude when she was young. Her childhood had been happy, her parents were still living" (39). Hélène is educated at home in the Antilles and pursues professional studies in Paris. Where Juletane feels alone living in France as an immigrant from "a small island in the Caribbean Sea" (12), Hélène is liberated by her nomadic life crossing between the islands, France, and Africa. Her family roots are strong, yet she does not feel the need to rely on anyone to make her way in life. After the death of her mother, Juletane, as Hélène reads, is raised by an elderly godmother in Paris who watches over the young girl and eventually sends her to university. When her godmother dies, Juletane feels "all of a sudden alone in a hostile world" (29). She finds a small room and continues to work, trying all the while to combat the isolation she feels. Comfort is found in her new Senegalese boyfriend, Mamadou, who becomes "her whole universe" (31). Upon completing his law degree, he asks her to marry him and go back to Senegal to begin life in the newly independent country. Only on the boat crossing does Juletane learn of Mamadou's first wife, Awa, and of his children.

Once the shock subsides, the young woman decides that as soon as she arrives in "his country" she'll return to France (35). But home is elusive. Juletane is without money or means: "My desire to leave, although strong, made me nevertheless realize that it wasn't going to be that simple" (47). Mamadou persuades her to come "home" to his family. Language becomes a torment for her, since few members of the family speak French. Curiously, we note that she now feels more ill at ease in Senegal than in France. "Mamadou becomes another person" (49), slowly forcing her to accept his first wife and her children as well as a third wife, Ndèye. Juletane seeks refuge in her room, refusing to eat or drink. As she slowly wastes away, her mind drifts into "true madness [and] bouts of delirium" (51). Her love for Mamadou withers and dies as she realizes, in her increasingly rarer moments of lucidity, that he is hypocrisy personified, living for his parents the life of "a good Muslim" yet all the while, in reality, being a "broke, egotistical, alcoholic, liar" who does not care about his wives and children (53). Hospitalization for her madness and depression leads Mamadou and his family to ignore her. Juletane's identity, even within the presence of others, is slowly erased: She sinks further into madness and is finally committed to a psychiatric ward after throwing hot oil in the third wife Ndèye's face. Just before, the first wife Awa's three children were found dead. Although no one can prove it, Juletane is suspected of their murder. She herself is not sure if she is innocent: "Did I pour the contents of the flask of barbiturates in the children's ladle of water, or did I leave the flask within their reach? I don't remember" (133).

As Hélène continues to read Juletane's story, she becomes more convinced that "all men, no matter their class or their social origin, [are] perfect egoists who [don't] merit [a] single tear of a woman" (82). She decides her life will be devoted to avenging all that was lost with Juletane's death (85). It is only by traversing Juletane's turbulent life that Hélène finally feels the reality of loneliness and isolation that plagues so many women caught up in lives of marginalization and exile. As she reads the closing pages of the diary writer's tormented life, she learns that Juletane's husband was killed in an auto accident and that the patient's own death followed shortly thereafter. Hélène cannot help admitting that "Juletane's diary broke the ice that encased her heart" (142) and exposed the world of women's mental suffering to her.

Juletane is forced to attempt murder and then suicide in order to rid herself of insurmountable pain. She is a person who is doubly hindered, as Warner-Vieyra points out, because she "has no relatives, no attachments in France" or to her country of origin. Her whole "raison d'être is her husband."[32] Women's sociocultural isolation is brought to the fore as the author explores a very real and widespread problem for women of the developing world, who find themselves manipulated because of their economic dependency on men.[33] Madness and economic power are inextricably linked in Warner-Vieyra's novel. Isolation, exile, the domination of her husband, and financial impoverishment drive Juletane insane. Juletane is a testament of how "women become prisoners of other people's distorted perceptions," traditions, and oppressive cultural mores, and of how one woman seeks to write herself into a place of subjecthood while confronting daunting odds.[34] For Juletane, finding a place of physical agency proves to be impossible. Yet her journal—the story of her life and her madness—remains a legacy to the power of words in the process of inscribing feminine subjectivity. By writing down her story—her speech—Juletane has formed connections with the women who later read her diary.

Myriam Warner-Vieyra's novel reminds us of the importance of the link between power and speech. Those who have access to the pen rule the writing of their history. It is, therefore, important for women to understand this power, to find a way to divert its original male sources to wield it in women's own fashion. "Power and knowledge are mutually conditioning"[35] and lead to development of the ego, the very heart of logos: subjectivity. For women, development of the ego, and therefore identity, is extremely important when considering madness, loss of subjectivity, and women's domination due to phallocentric oppression. Development of the ego relies on the inscription of events and experiences on the surface of Being. Inscribing one's surface places primacy on the outside, the active areas of culture and society (the street, the workplace, politics). Isolation, on the other hand, only leads women down an empty road, as Juletane attests.

In contrast to the negative aspects of madness, however, many contemporary feminists (Western, African, and Caribbean) argue that the realm of insanity can serve the woman author well by enabling her to fight the "male logos that excludes the truly feminine voice from the information system that determines what counts as culture and rationality."[36] Elisabeth Mudimbé-Boyi maintains that if women are forced to adhere to a masculine logos that has ruled their very language and destroyed any hope of creating an original identity for themselves, then perhaps madness—location outside the norm, on the liminal edges of rationality—could offer a means to discover the "affirmative of a self beyond sanity determined by masculine rationality."[37] Writing from a realm of madness is perhaps a way to establish a new set of communicative signifiers that escape male codes; a means to find other systems that will bring women into their own logos. Underlining this possibility, Mudimbé-Boyi notes that "madness or illness is the space that makes possible the constitution of [a woman's] text," and often in women's writing, "illness is the place from which [feminine] discourse emerges."[38]

Affirmation of the outside self is what women strive for, yet embracing madness as a catalyst for truer knowledge of the self is like walking on thin ice. It is certainly a subject that has generated heated debate for Western feminists since the 1970s. Claims to alterity have been championed by French feminists such as Luce Irigaray and Hélène Cixous for years. Yet can we really condemn women to what is considered a pejorative state of being? I argue that we should take that risk. If madness is used by women to embrace a truer sense of self, then perhaps, in some instances, it will empower them. Although Myriam Warner-Vieyra is not herself mad, in Juletane the author does explore a deeper meaning of feminine self and selfhood through the actions and dementia of her heroine and the latter's efforts to seize the "magic of words" (93). It is this extradiegetic madness—a state of being created by the author to study the female condition within the realm of fiction—

that will offer her the power to re-create a woman's way outside the masculine *logos*. This power defines a new set of ethics for and about women. Fictive madness produces a communicating, socially embodied woman who experiences through her liminal, marginalized existence, power on her own terms. In a lucid moment, Juletane attests to this power, stating that, although she fights for her mind, writing in her journal gives her "a more sure sense of herself" (93). Though the heroine loses her mind in the end, her written story becomes both a legacy and a lesson for women who will continue to read it for years to come.

■ DOUCEURS DU BERCAIL: PARADISE AND PEACE

In 1976 Aminata Sow Fall helped break the gender barrier in Senegal by publishing the first major novel in French written by a Senegalese woman.[39] Her novel, *Le revenant,* put forth for the first time a study of the condition of women in Senegal.[40] Sow Fall has continued to write for over two decades. Her recent novel *Douceurs du bercail,* published in 1998, continues to explore the situation of African women with respect to a variety of sociocultural issues, the most important of which are the economic difficulties of the Senegalese people (particularly women) and racism.

Asta Diop, Sow Fall's heroine, is an accomplished divorcee and single mother, traveling to Paris to attend "la Conférence sur l'Ordre Economique Mondial." Knowing the stringent bureaucratic hurdles foreigners must face when trying to enter France, Asta has made sure every possible paper pertaining to her visit is *en règle.*

> She fished in her handbag for a parcel of papers which she placed in the hands of one of the passport officers. Not only the passport and the airplane ticket, but also her professional identity card, certificate of residence (public housing project "Baobab" no. 1022–Dakar, Senegal), a copy of her police record, a national identity card, and assignment papers in triplicate. She added the official letter of the organization inviting her to the Conference on the Economic World Order. Mentioned also was the fact that all transportation and lodging costs were to be paid by the organizers. (15–16)

Despite the plethora of papers, the passport control officer still has the audacity to ask her, "What did you come here for?" (16). In his eyes, Asta is nothing more than another *immigrée* seeking asylum in France. It neither occurs to him, nor is it even a consideration, that she might be happy in her own country and want to go back, even when she is questioned about her return

ticket: "How long are you staying? One week. And your return trip? It's made . . . it's all okayed on the ticket" (18). Reading of Asta's confrontation, we are reminded of Frantz Fanon's words: "I move slowly in the world, accustomed now to seek no longer for upheaval. I progress by crawling. And already I am being dissected under white eyes, the only real eyes. I am fixed . . . I am laid bare."[41] Because she protests the passport official's aggressive attitude toward her, Asta is subjected to a strip search by "a woman in uniform," whose "gloved hands swept all over her body, passing even under her bra, descending down to her knees, going up her skirt. Asta shivers with disgust. She feels as if she is broken" (27). Yet the most humiliating aspect of the strip search occurs when Asta "realizes that a despicable hand goes astray and seeks to penetrate a closed passage. Asta squeezes her legs shut. The hand insists" (27). It is at this point that she defends herself. "Never!" she screams (27). A rage takes over her as she seizes the neck of the female officer. She remembers nothing after that until she wakes up, handcuffed, in the deportation detention center, which "the pensioners have named 'layover'." It is here that "blacks, mulattoes, and Arabs, for the most part, [all wait] for expulsion to their country of origin" (39).

What sets Sow Fall's novel apart as a major contribution to contemporary feminine francophone writing is that it depicts an individual woman's humiliation and how this is turned into a catalyst for positive social change. Asta's story becomes a national sensation in France and Senegal. Her "incident" ends up benefiting not only those with whom she passes a week in the Parisian airport detention center, but also people back home. Sow Fall's characters Yakham, Dianor, Babou, and Séga, fellow deportees, form human links that help Asta reinstall her dignity. She discovers through their stories that the lives of others from her country have been as painful as her own. Yakham, who came to France to "tempt his luck" (98), figures he has nothing to lose, since he lost his chance to attend a highly selective foreign university due to an acceptance letter that was never delivered simply because he lived in a slum area where postmen feared to go. Missing his opportunity to further his education, he left for France, accepting out of necessity the lowest-paid jobs he could find in the bowels of Les Halles, the central market of Paris. There he "transported meat on his back so heavy that it would break your spine" (101). And then there is Dianor, an artist, obliged to live with six other men in a one-room apartment in the Foyer du Quartier de la Gare "with a population five times greater than its capacity [and] sanitary conditions that defy all regulations on hygiene" (125).

The airport's deportation center becomes a forum for discussing the sociocultural and political situations of both France and Senegal. Sow Fall plays devil's advocate on a variety of fronts. On the one hand she condemns France's political policies toward people of color, where "racism is winning ground" (101), while on the other she takes to task modern-day Senegal, which has become unbalanced by materialism and the huge, ever-present socioeconomic gap that has been created between those who have and those who do not. The author's goal in the novel to dispel the misconceptions of her fellow Senegalese that Africa is a wasteland when compared to France (perceived as the summit of perfection) operates as a constant theme. "When we come here [to France], we always believe it will be paradise," Yakham remarks at one point. Yet he follows up this observation by affirming the cold reality that he ended up "heeding the advice of [his] cousin: don't . . . look anywhere except for jobs that are hard and which the people here don't want" (100). France is not paradise, and Africa is not a heart of darkness where intellectual thought processes are held at bay by famine, drought, and poverty. For Sow Fall, Africa and its people share in the hopes and fears of the world. Evidence of considering humanity with all its trials and tribulations is summed up by Anne, Asta's close friend, when she asks two rhetorical questions: "How does one exist in this era of paradoxes where physical or moral misery opens wounds in the stomach even of temples of abundance?"; and "How can modern society promote 'Tolerance' and uphold ideals such as 'All men-Are equal-No to racism-Yes to love-Between people-Beyond race-And religious beliefs'?" (148–49).

It is the need to explore this *beyond,* this *au-delà* (which the author describes as a place where racial and gender differences are nullified and the pain of human suffering is lifted), that brings out the utopian message of Sow Fall's novel. The *au-delà,* a paradise on earth in Africa, is possible and is created by Asta and her companions. Asta's farm, Naatangue (Wolof for "happiness, abundance, and peace"), becomes a sanctuary for her fellow deportees from France. The heroine finds money through financial organizations to fund her project, a lifelong dream which brings "ineffable happiness to smell the earth, to communicate with her when from her breast gushes forth life; food that gives life and consistency" (200). Naatangue is a place which will convince others that "paradise is not necessarily somewhere else" (201).

In the closing pages, Naatangue is "in effervescence." Men, women and children from all over the region come together to help celebrate the first true harvest of Asta's farm worked by *Waa Reewu Takh,* "those who come from concrete cities" (203). Almost ten years have elapsed since Asta's incident at the airport. Despite endless hurdles and obstacles not only because of lack of money but also from the neighboring villagers, who view the newcomers with "a skeptical eye" (204), the heroine succeeds in bringing together her friends whose unique force of "knowing nothing of the earth, but loving it" (205) enables their success. The villagers discover that, like themselves, these urban-misfits-turned-farmers seek to "regenerate all that grows," while also implanting "other cultures, other species in order to enrich the site" (205–6). Working the earth convinces Asta and her compatriots of their "determination never to give in to discouragement and doubt" (210). Their farm products, labeled as "douceurs du bercail" (sweetness of the fold), are sold "everywhere in other countries," promoting "the idea of a generous and hospitable earth capable of giving more than what is offered it" (217).

Sow Fall's novel is a testament to one woman's capacity to construct a world through *a woman's way.* Her heroine finds peace on the margins of society, in a space she constructs for herself. Asta's space (unlike Juletane's, filled with isolation and despondency, and Sultana's, haunted by childhood memories and unsettled by the heroine's dual Algerian/French world) is characterized by tranquillity and spirituality. Naatangue is not only synonymous for a place of celebration for the life it gives forth to the heroine and the band of misfits from the airport detention center; it is also a statement about the power of humanity to conquer the ills of racism, abjection, poverty, and despair.

Women of Africa and the Caribbean, writing in French, those who are exiled and those who live clandestinely fighting for human rights, are conceptualizing new ways to study their past as well as to formulate new plans for their future through literature. They are *becoming* a new identity, fashioned in the *vel,* a beyond where all preconceived notions, whether historically, phallocratically, or traditionally ordained, are taken to task, questioned, and then reconstructed. Their discourse posits a multiple feminine subject that reflects a panoply of connections crisscrossed by many cultures, languages, nationalities, and ways of looking at the world. Instead of essentializing the feminine ideal (either physically or mythically), contemporary African and Caribbean women authors are transgressing boundaries and using their pens to gain access to areas once forbidden to them as they write *their* stories.

Valérie Orlando, Winter 2001

---

[1] According to Christopher Miller, the first book written by an African francophone author was a 1920 school textbook titled

Les Trois Volontés de Malic by Ahmadou Mapaté Diagne, a Senegalese man educated in the French colonial school system (see Christopher Miller, *Theories of Africans,* Chicago, University of Chicago Press, 1990, p. 249). Jean Déjeux estimates the date of the first novel written in French in Algeria by a non-native Frenchman to be 1891. He credits *La vengeance du cheikh* to Algerian author M'Hamed Ben Rahal. The novella was published in *Revue algérienne et tunisienne, littéraire et artistique* (see Jean Déjeux, *Maghreb: Littératures de langue française,* Paris, Aracantère, 1993, p. 31). Writing in the Caribbean by women was sporadic. In Martinique during the 1920s and 1930s, Paulette and Jane Nardal and Suzanne Lacascade contributed to the Négritude movement, writing for the literary journal *Tropiques.* It was not until much later, in the 1960s, 1970s, and 1980s, that women from the Antilles became prolific, with literary contributions by authors such as Michèle Lacrosil, Maryse Condé, and Simone Schwarz-Bart, among others.

2   Négritude, a literary movement begun in the early 1930s by Aimé Césaire, Etienne Léro, Jules Monnerot, and Jacques Romain (among others), sought to "determine a strategy for promoting the individuality of African culture." Négritude soon blossomed into the radical "affirmation of African political thought" and solidified the anticolonial rhetoric of African independence movements in the 1960s (V. Y. Mudimbé, *The Invention of Africa: Gnosis, Philosophy, and the Order of Knowledge,* Bloomington, Indiana University Press, 1988, pp. 86–87). The literary-political movement, however, has been widely criticized by African feminists for its exclusion of women's issues. With the exception of Paulette and Jane Nardal, few women contributed to the Négritude venue during the early 1930s.

3   V. Y. Mudimbé distinguishes *gnosis* as a term to "extend the notion of philosophy to African traditional systems of thought, considering them as dynamic processes in which concrete experiences are integrated into an order of concepts and discourses. . . . Etymologically, *gnosis* is related to *gnosko,* which in the ancient Greek means "to know." Specifically, *gnosis* means seeking to know, inquiry, methods of knowing, investigation, and even acquaintance with someone" (ix).

4   Fatima Mernissi, *Doing Daily Battle: Interviews with Moroccan Women,* New Brunswick (N.J.), Rutgers University Press, 1989, p. 3.

5   Gayatri Spivak, *In Other Worlds,* New York, Routledge, 1988, p. 207. See also my book, *Nomadic Voices of Exile: Feminine Identity in Francophone Literature of the Maghreb* (Athens, Ohio University Press, 1999), for further reading on the link between women, agency, and public space.

6   See Juliet Flower Maccannell, *The Hysteric's Guide to the Future Female Subject,* Minneapolis, University of Minnesota Press, 2000, p. xv.

7   Elizabeth Grosz, *Volatile Bodies: Toward a Corporeal Feminism,* Bloomington, Indiana University Press, 1994, p. 36.

8   Dakar, Présence Africaine, 1982.

9   Abidjan, NEI, 1998.

10   See Gilles Deleuze and Felix Guattari, *Mille Plateaux,* Paris, Minuit, 1980.

11   Irène Assiba d'Almeida, *Francophone African Women Writers: Destroying the Emptiness of Silence,* Gainesville, University Press of Florida, 1994, p. 2.

12   D'Almeida, p. 3.

13   Miller, p. 164.

14   See Christiane P. Makward's article "Cherchez La Franco-Femme," in *Postcolonial Subjects: Francophone Women Writers,*

eds. Mary Jean Green et al., Minneapolis, University of Minnesota Press, 1996, pp. 115–23, 118.

15   Fatima Mernissi's powerful sociocultural studies such as *Beyond the Veil: Male Female Dynamics in Modern Muslim Society* (Bloomington, Indiana University Press, 1987) and *Doing Daily Battle: Interviews with Moroccan Women* (New Brunswick [N.J.], Rutgers University Press, 1989) draw direct links between the political agendas of Morocco's ruling male elite and the deplorable living conditions in which women find themselves locked on a daily basis. Assia Djebar's book *Le blanc de l'Algérie* (Paris, Albin Michel, 1995) also demonstrates how phallocralic laws set into place by the Front de la Libération Nationale government's adoption of strict Shari'a doctrine have set women back centuries since 1962.

16   Marnia Lazreg, p. 195, Lazreg and other historical chroniclers of the Algerian War (including Frantz Fanon) have pointed out that without the aid of women, the Front de la Libération Nationale would have most assuredly lost the struggle against the French during the 1954–62 war. The FLN rebels promised women equal access to society once the revolution was achieved; however, after the war this was not the case. Women found themselves still caught between modernity and traditionalism.

17   Malika Mokeddem, *L'Interdite,* Paris, Grasset, 1993. Myriam Warner-Vieyra, *Juletane,* Dakar, Présence Africaine, 1982. Aminata Sow Fall, *Douceurs du bercail,* Abidjan, NEI, 1998. All translations from these authors' works are my own.

18   Julia Kristeva, *Etrangers à nous-mêmes,* Paris, Gallimard, 1988, p. 23.

19   Kristeva, p. 8.

20   Placing Algerian women in roles they are not normally permitted to play in Algerian traditional society is a theme in all of Mokeddem's works. See her novels *Le siecle des sauterelles* (Paris, Ramsay, 1992), *Les hommes qui marchent* (Paris, Grasset, 1997), *Des rêves et des assassins* (Paris, Grasset, 1995), and *La nuit de lu lézarde* (Paris, Grasset, 1998).

21   Sandra M. Gilbert and Susan Gubar, *The Madwoman in the Attic,* New Haven (Ct.), Yale University Press, 1979, p. 55.

22   Gilbert and Gubar, p. 55.

23   Gilbert and Gubar, p. 20.

24   Shoshana Felman, "Women and Madness," in *Feminisms,* eds. R. Warhol et al., New Brunswick (N.J.), Rutgers University Press, 1991, pp. 6–19, 7.

25   Hélène Cixous, "The Laugh of the Medusa," in *Feminisms,* pp. 334–49, 338.

26   Cited by Anne Adams in her article "To W/rite in a New Language: Werewere Liking's Adaptation of Ritual to the Novel," *Callaloo,* 16:1 (1993), pp. 153–68, 153.

27   Gilbert and Gubar, p. 19.

28   Michèle Lacrosil, *Cajou,* Paris, Gallimard, 1961. Mariama Bâ, *Un chant écarlate,* Dakar, Les Nouvelles Editions Africaines, 1981. Nina Bouraoui, *La voycuse interdite,* Paris, Gallimard, 1991.

29   Elisabeth Mudimbé-Boyi, "Narrative 'Je(ux)' in *kamouraska* and *Juletane,*" in *Postcolonial Subjects: Francophone Women Writers,* eds. M.). Green et al., Minneapolis, University of Minnesota Press, 1996, pp. 124–39, 137.

30   Mudimbé-Boyi, p. 137.

31   Interview with Assia Djebar in *Le Monde,* no. 12, 1993, n.p. (The translation is mine.)

[32] Mildred Mortimer, *Callaloo,* 16:1 (1993), pp. 108–15, 111.

[33] I by no means want to suggest that women's economic dependency on men is solely a phenomenon in the developing world. It is also a First World condition that must be addressed. Phyllis Chesler, in her ground-breaking study *Women and Madness,* frequently notes that economic dependency of women on men has often left them with no hope, outlet, or means of escaping seriously harmful situations which affect their health, both mental and physical. See *Women and Madness,* New York, Four Walls Eight Windows, 1972; reprinted 1997.

[34] Mortimer, p. 112.

[35] Grosz, p. 148.

[36] Allen Thiher, *Revels in Madness: Insanity in Medicine and Literature,* Ann Arbor, University of Michigan Press, 1999, p. 302.

[37] Thiher, p. 302.

[38] Mudimbé-Boyi, p. 138.

[39] Two other women of notable importance writing in the 1970s were Aoua Kéita (*Femme d'Afrique: La Vie d'Aoua Kéita racontée par elle-même,* Paris, Présence Africaines, 1975) and Nafissatou Diallo (*De Tilène au plateau: Une enfance dakaroise,* Dakar, Nouvelles Editions Africaines, 1975). Their works were more autobiographical in scope. (See Miller, p. 250.)

[40] Miller, p. 250.

[41] Frantz Fanon, *Black Skin, White Masks,* New York, Grove, 1967, p. 116.

ANGOLA

The Poetry of Agostinho Neto

Political nationalism was preceded in Angola, as in other African areas, by cultural nationalism. The first meaningful signs of the latter trace back to the postwar period. It is in 1948 that the Movement of the New Intellectuals of Angola lets its cry be heard: "Let's Discover Angola!" This proclamation meant, among other things, that Angolan intellectuals, members of an assimilated African minority, felt the need to go back to the sources of their culture. The negation of the colonizer's culture and the refusal of the apparent benefits of the assimilated status were obviously implicit in their proclamation. Their purpose was to achieve what Mário de Andrade calls a "re-Africanization" of the spirit.[1]

The publication in 1951 of the literary journal *Mensagem* (Message) by the Cultural Department of the Association of the Natives of Angola made clear the intentions of the new generation in establishing the foundations of a truly Angolan literature, the kind of literature that would have nothing to do with the exoticism favored by colonial writing or with the imitation of models far from African reality. The journal did not go beyond its second issue (numbers 2–4), however.

Cultura (II), begun in 1957 and published by the Cultural Society of Angola, continued the nationalistic spirit of *Mensagem* for thirteen issues, to 1961, the year when the armed struggle began in Angola. Among the contributors to both journals was Agostinho Neto, who had come to Portugal in 1947 to begin his medical studies.[2]

The early fifties also saw the creation of the Center for African Studies (1951) in Lisbon. The founders of the Center were Amílcar Cabral, the creator of the PAIGC (African Independence Party of Guinea and the Cape Verde Islands) in 1956; Mário de Andrade, who was to play a most decisive role in the diffusion of Lusophone African writing with the publication of essays and carefully organized anthologies; Francisco José Tenreiro, the first voice of Negritude in the Lusophone areas with his book of poems *Ilha de nome santo* (Island of Holy Name; 1942); and Agostinho Neto.

In the late forties, the fifties and the early sixties the CEI or Casa dos Estudantes do Império (Overseas Students House) in Lisbon did its best to promote cultural and political awareness among students from the colonies. Many of those who were to be the leaders of the emergent nationalist movements used to meet there, exchanging ideas and projects. In 1958 a new impulse was given to the bulletin of the House, *Mensagem (CEI),* which had experienced a vicissitudinous fate since its establishment in 1949, and an intensive editorial program was carried out under the prestigious Colecção de Autores Ultramarinos (Overseas Authors Collection) imprint in the period between 1960 and 1962. As was to be expected—the guerrilla war having started in Angola in 1961, in Guinea in 1963 and in Mozambique in 1964—the House was closed in 1965 by the fascist regime.

Agostinho Neto, an active member of the CEI, was jailed for different periods before obtaining his medical degree in 1958. Born in Kaxikane, Icolo e Bengo, in 1922, the son of a Methodist pastor, Neto completed his high-school education in Angola and worked from 1944 to 1947 in the Luanda Health Services before coming to attend the Medical School at the University of Coimbra. In Portugal he oriented his political activities mainly in two directions, concerning himself with the promotion of African nationalism and joining the Portuguese anti-fascist opposition groups. The second time Neto was imprisoned, from 1955 to 1957, it was only through the intervention of such well-known intellectuals as Sartre, Mauriac, Aragon, Beauvoir, Nicolás Guillén and Rivera that he was ultimately released by Salazar's political police.[3] (The subsequent proceeds from the sale of *Quatro poemas de Agostinho Neto,* published in 1957, were used, by the way, to assist the families of Portuguese political prisoners.)[4]

In 1956 the MPLA (Popular Movement for the Liberation of Angola) had been founded, and in 1959 Neto returned to Angola.[5] In March and in July of 1959, before Neto's arrival, many nationalists had been jailed, among them Ilídio Machado, the first President of the MPLA, "one of the defendants in the famous Trial of the Fifty."[6] The poem "O icar da bandeira"[7] (The Hoisting of the Flag), dedicated to the "heroes of the Angolan people," was written at that time, and the tone pervading it is one of certainty and confidence in the future of Angola. For Neto, his friends Liceu (the founder of the group Ngola Ritmos), Benge, Joaquim, Gaspar, Ilídio and Manuel, in their devotion to the cause of independence, were of a stature equal to that of such past heroes as Ngola Kiluanji and Queen Ginga.

In July 1960 Agostinho Neto was arrested, and as a consequence a movement of protest spread in the vicinity of his birthplace. The repression by the colonial authorities was brutal: thirty people were killed and 200 wounded in what came to be termed the Massacre of Icolo e Bengo.[8] Neto was sent to a prison in Lisbon and later deported to Cape Verde, where he was allowed to practice medicine; but in the autumn of 1961 he was to be imprisoned in Lisbon again. On 4 February of that year the attack on the prisons of Luanda marked the beginning of the armed struggle in Angola.

Again international opinion helped Neto, effecting his release from prison in 1962: *Présence Africaine* in Paris and a group of British intellectuals speaking through *The Times* had voiced their concern over the poet's fate. Despite his fixed residence in Portugal and the continuous surveillance of the political police (the PIDE), he managed to leave the country and join his comrades of the MPLA in Kinshasa in July of that year. Angola became an independent country in November 1975, and Neto is today the President of the People's Republic of Angola and of the MPLA Workers' Party.

Sagrada esperança (Sacred Hope), published in Lisbon in 1974, the year of the April Revolution, includes almost all the known poems of Agostinho Neto. Many of the texts in the volume are not dated, but according to Basil Davidson's preface, the oldest ones "date back from 1945. . . . Most of them were written in the fifties and many in prison in 1960."[9] Neto's essential bibliography comprises the already-mentioned *Quatro poemas de Agostinho Neto* (1957), *Poemas* (1961) and *Con occhi asciutti* (With Dry Eyes), a bilingual edition (Portuguese/Italian) including the same poems as *Sagrada esperança* and taking its title from two of his best-known texts, "The Tears of Africa" ("And love / and the dry

eyes") and "Create" ("Create / create love with dry eyes"). Besides editions in Serbo-Croatian, Russian and Chinese, there is also an English edition of his poems, *Sacred Hope* (Tanzania, 1974), which I was unable to find.

The title of the Italian edition emphasizes the affirmative tone of Neto's poetry, the courage and firmness transmitted by the poet to his fellowmen. It means a resolute refusal of self-pity and fatalism, the embracing of a continually positive and creative attitude toward life. The Portuguese title stresses the prevalence of hope, the certainty that, in spite of all the suffering, oppression and humiliation, the future will be on his people's side. The adjective chosen, on the other hand, points to the deeply religious character of that confidence in the future—religious in the sense that it presupposes a total immersion in reality, the establishment of a sacred relationship with all beings, the radiant feeling of being a part of the whole, harmonious with and at the same time subject to the incessant flux of History. (The theme of hope is, incidentally, recurrent in Lusophone African poetry.[10] Hope kept alive the spirit of resistance against colonialism.)

Neto's poetry is seen by Donald Burness as one of combat.[11] Militancy in Neto's poems, as in those of many other African writers of Portuguese expression (and it is no accident that most of them—for example, Neto himself, Marcelino dos Santos, António Jacinto, Luandino Vieira, Alda do Espírito Santo, Mário de Andrade, Corsino Fortes—combined their literary career with an intense political activity), is a determining factor. Most Lusophone African intellectuals, committed in the liberation struggle, would easily subscribe to Amílcar Cabral's view that the struggle itself was an act of culture. Their militancy, however, did not imply, as Neto's case so well illustrates, that they put aside the specific demands of the means employed. It is difficult to accuse Agostinho Neto of carelessness in his approach to poetry. Images and metaphors are judiciously set in the organic unity of the poem, so that the implicit message may be conveyed more effectively. All stylistic devices—anaphora, alliteration, enumeration, parallelism—contribute to intensify the rhythmic quality of poetry (seen as a counterpart of some black musical forms) and not to overcharge or smother the contents of the text.[12]

To analyze the main topics in Neto's poetry we could follow the useful thematic scheme proposed by Mário de Andrade in his anthology *Na noite grávida de punhais*[13] (In the Night Heavy with Daggers). A good starting point is "Adeus à hora da largada" (Farewell at the Time of Parting; pp. 35–36), the opening poem of the 1974 edition, included in the subsection "Mãe"

(Mother) of the section "Evocação" (Evocation) of the anthology. In an article already mentioned[14] I have extensively compared the two known versions of the poem, one published in *Quatro poemas* and the other opening the collection *Sagrada esperança*. The Mother evoked in the text, as Alexandre Pinheiro Torres has penetratingly observed, "rather than [being] the progenitor, is the Earth-Mother herself, or the Mother-Earth, the Universal Nourisher, the Tellus Mater of the symbolically universal belief of Man born from the Earth (= Mother)."[15] The second version makes the poem obviously more didactic, introducing words like *hoje* (today) and *amanha* (tomorrow) that divide in a clearer way the two dialectical planes which define, in the poet's eyes, Africa's position between the alienated present and the redeemed future.

Today
we are the naked children of the forest villages
the children who don't go to school and play with
  the rag ball
. . . the ignorant black men
who must respect the white man . . .
Tomorrow
we will chant hymns to freedom
when we commemorate
the date of the abolition of this slavery.

The two protest poems selected by Andrade for another subsection, "Terra" (Land), of the same section could easily be considered under the rubric "Identification." In both "Quitandeira" (Street Market Woman; pp. 49–51) and "Meia-noite na quitanda" (Midnight at the Street Market; p. 53) the poet identifies himself with the tragic fate of his people. He gives voice to the drama of those whose voice the colonialist system ignores. The first street vendor comes to the front of the stage and speaks her mind. Her calling the passing lady's attention to the oranges she has for sale is at the same time an accusation, an accusation to an indifferent colonial middle class that knows nothing of the hard life of the poor, of those who have to sell themselves in order to survive. The preoccupation of Sá Domingas, the second street vendor, is to get enough money for her son "to pay the taxes." Non-payment of the latter means for the young man the threat of becoming a contract laborer.

In this poem, as well as in "Partida para o contrato" (Departure for Contract Labor; p. 37), the drama of the contract laborer is not given directly but through the suffering of his closest relatives, in one case his mother and in the other his wife. In this way Agostinho Neto shows that forced labor resulted in a disruption of family ties. The woman in "Partida para o contrato," given no name (which is an indication of the possibility of any wife's being subject to the same kind of separation), says goodbye to her husband Manuel (again ascribing so common a name to a character is a way of stressing how frequent among *indigenas*—non-assimilated Africans—such a destiny was). Manuel leaves for São Tomé, the worst contract that could await him, for distance—São Tomé was "beyond the sea"—made things still worse for the laborer. Night falls and Manuel's wife is still there, looking sadly at the horizon. It is not, however, external night that matters, but the one which darkens the woman's soul, her complete solitude ("There is no light / there is no north in the woman's soul // Darkness / Only darkness").

The *contratado* or contract laborer is for the Angolan intellectual a symbol of his oppressed countrymen, the most evident example of colonialist exploitation. "Contratados" (pp. 65–66) is an example of the open, ambiguous poem whose interpretation is extremely difficult. The singing of the contract laborers amidst the hard conditions of their life may have different readings. How can they sing in such circumstances? Or do they sing because there is some kind of instinctive certainty in their hearts that in the end they will overcome the curse that weighs upon them?

Andrade's anthology includes, in the subsection "Africanidade" (Africanness) of "Evocação," a poem by Neto that was not published in *Sagrada esperança*— "Voz do sangue"[16] (The Voice of the Blood). The poet asserts here his African condition proudly and feels at one with all the oppressed blacks of the world. He just wants to join his "poor voice / his humble rhythms to theirs." He addresses not only the "black of Africa," but also "the blacks of all the world." And the references to "the melancholy rhythms of the blues" and to the "ragged black of Harlem / the dancer from Chicago / the black servant from the South" constitute no surprise for the reader familiar with Lusophone African writing, for the American black's situation is a great concern to the intellectuals of the former Portuguese colonies in the late forties and fifties. If in "Voz do sangue" the poet shares the black man's suffering, in "Bamako" (pp. 92–93), an enthusiastic hymn dedicated to the Pan-African Conference in Bamako (in the then French Sudan) in 1954, he is especially interested in expressing his rejoicing, his hope in the future. The word *hope* appears three times in the poem, and so does *future*. The tone is wholly affirmative. There is no room for anguish or despair. The entire vocabulary points in the same positive direction: truth, brightness, freshness, love, generosity, strength, friendship.

The theme of *identification* is present in one of Neto's most famous poems, "Mussunda amigo" (Mussunda My Friend; pp. 79–81). The text is at the same time a melancholy recollection of a childhood and adolescence in common (the narrator remembers the time when he and his friend Mussunda used to buy mangos, or lamented "the destiny / of the women from Funda" with "clouds" in their eyes) and the expression of a deep confidence in the permanence of a sense of communion that nothing can destroy. The final statement, "We are," avoiding as it does the rhetoric of any exclamatory emphasis, echoes nonetheless a determined militancy, the idea that in spite of everything, of the ditch that colonialism put between the intellectual and the masses ("Here I am / Mussunda my friend / writing poems you can't understand"), they persist, they *are,* they affirm their existence simultaneously as an ontological and a historical barrier against which colonialist violence can do nothing. The African intellectual is fully aware of the contradiction implicit in his literary endeavors inaccessible to his illiterate countrymen; he knows, however, that there is always a point of convergence that makes them, after all, "inseparable."

The presence of a refrain in Kimbundu is a typical stylistic device used by many Angolan poets to stress their respect for the national languages, the languages the masses continue to speak in spite of centuries of Lusitanian "civilization." The poet's friend Mussunda appears again in "O choro de Africa" (The Tears of Africa; pp. 117–18). Africa is about to enter a new age, an age of struggle for freedom from violence and serfdom—the liberation fighters must have their "eyes dry."

The sense of being engaged in the same struggle against colonialism was very strong in the Lusophone African movements right from the beginning. Even before the launching of the liberation struggle, the MAC (Movimento Anti-Colonialista) was founded in 1957 by representatives of all the Portuguese colonies. In 1961, a few weeks after 4 February and the beginning of the armed struggle in Angola, the CONCP (Conferencia das Organizações Nacionalistas das Colónias Portuguesas) was established in Casablanca. Thus it is easy to understand why the massacre of Batepá (in São Tomé) in February 1953 could not leave Neto indifferent.[17] Significantly enough, the poem Neto wrote on the occasion was dedicated to Alda do Espírito Santo, a woman poet from São Tomé who also denounced the massacre in two famous, moving poems.[18]

It should be stressed that both in Neto's poem ("Massacre de S. Tomé," pp. 90–91) and in Alda's texts hope is not defeated. The idea that repression is unable to liquidate the people's resistance unites the three poems. Colonialism may use violence against the nationalists and put them in jail, yet even there theirs is a song of hope, in the comforting feeling that nothing or "nobody / will prevent rain" from coming ("Aqui no carcere" [Here in Jail], July 1960, p. 116). The poet, a few months later, still imprisoned but this time in Lisbon after having been transferred from Luanda, proclaims: "We will come back / to a liberated Angola / an independent Angola." The last text of *Sagrada esperança,* "A voz igual" (The Equal Voice; pp. 130–35), dated December 1960 and written in Cape Verde, is a long, beautifully structured poem which epitomizes the thematic and stylistic obsessions of the poet: the voice of a bard, that is to say the voice of a people preparing to take History in their hands and approach the "vital dawn" of the future, a people finally leaving "chaos" and entering "the harmonious concert of the universal."

Fernando Martinho, Winter 1979

[1] Mário de Andrade, "Amílcar Cabral e a reafricanização dos espíritos," *Nô Pintcha* (Bissau), 12 September 1976.

[2] See Marga Holness, "Introdução" to Agostinho Neto, *Sagrada esperança,* Lisbon, Sá da Costa, 1974, p. 15.

[3] Ibid., p. 16.

[4] See *Africa* (Lisbon), 1 (July 1978), p. 113.

[5] See *O Jornal* (Lisbon), 110 (3 June 1977), p. 10.

[6] Holness, p. 19.

[7] Agostinho Neto, *Sagrada esperança,* pp. 119–21. Subsequent references to the poems in this volume will be by parenthetical page number in the text of this paper.

[8] See *História de Angola,* Oporto, Afrontamento, n.d., pp. 175, 176.

[9] Neto, p. 3. Translations from the Portuguese are my own unless otherwise indicated.

[10] See my article "O tema da *esperança* na poesia africana de língua portuguesa," in *Colóquio-Letras* (Lisbon), 39 (September 1977), pp. 5–16.

[11] See Donald Burness, *Fire: Six Writers from Angola, Mozambique and Cape Verde,* Washington, D.C., Three Continents, 1977, pp. 19–34.

[12] Cf. Russell Hamilton, *Voices from an Empire,* Minneapolis, University of Minnesota Press, 1975, pp. 96–101.

[13] Mário de Andrade, *Na noite grávida de punhais,* Lisbon, Sá da Costa, 1975.

[14] See note 10.

[15] Alexandre Pinheiro Torres, "A poesia de Agostinho Neto: Entre o espaço e o ser," *Diário Popular,* 6 November 1975.

[16] Andrade, *Na noite grávida de punhais,* p. 147.

[17] See Mário Soares, *Portugal amordaçado,* Lisbon, Arcádia, 1974, pp. 437, 438. The author says that "thirty people from the forty-five who were in prison died from asphyxiation" and that "the dead and missing amounted to about a thousand."

[18] Andrade, *Na noite grávida de punhais,* pp. 241–45, 246–48.

CAMEROON

French Colonialism in Africa: The Early Novels of Ferdinand Oyono

In 1956 Ferdinand Oyono published *Le vieux nègre et la médaille* and *Une vie de Boy,* two short novels which together number about three hundred pages.[1] Despite the limited output, the inevitable loss in translation, and the passage of thirty years, Oyono's work is very much alive in Anglophone black African secondary and tertiary institutions. If on publication Amos Tutuola's novel *The Palm-Wine Drinkard* drew much attention in Europe and little in Africa, the opposite seems to be the case where Oyono is concerned. Oyono was born in 1929 in Cameroon. His mother was a devout Catholic and therefore left her polygamous husband.[2] For a while Oyono worked at a local mission as a "boy" (servant) to European missionaries.[3] However, he was encouraged and helped in his studies by his natural father and eventually obtained his doctorate in law from Paris and joined his country's diplomatic service.

To understand Oyono's works, one needs to know something of the history of the Cameroons. The beginning of this century saw the Cameroons as a German "protectorate." The term illustrates how words can conceal the truth—who was protecting whom, and from what? In reality the colonized peoples needed protection from their European "protectors." After World War I the country was divided between France and Britain, with the former gaining the greater share. In *Houseboy* Chief Mengueme's brother is killed during World War I fighting for the Germans and against the French; during World War II, Mengueme's two sons are killed fighting for the French against the Germans, and thereby hangs a tale.

French policy in Africa was known as "assimilation," and the alleged aim was to make Frenchmen of the "natives." French culture, institutions, and language were to be transplanted to Africa, and in due course the African was to become a Frenchman, except for his race and color. Whereas Britain pursued a policy of "indirect rule" through local chiefs, ostensibly preparing the people for that independence of which they had been deprived by Britain in the first place, the French saw their African colonies as an extension of France. French policy implied the total dismissal of African culture as having any value of its own. Furthermore, "In practice remarkably little was done to bring into effect the official policy,"[4] and "The essential aim of education was to supply the subordinate personnel necessary to the effective functioning of the colonial administration."[5] The curricula designed and the texts chosen were intended, on the one hand, to convince Africans of their inherent inferiority, their lack of achievement, and the barbarity of their ancestors, and, on the other, to emphasize the greatness and goodness of Europeans, who brought peace, education, and health assistance. Toundi in *Houseboy* writes on the first page of his diary, "My ancestors were cannibals." The colonized peoples were led to feel ashamed of themselves and of their color. It was a Manichean dichotomy, as Frantz Fanon has brilliantly explained.[6]

Political domination was reinforced by alienating the people from their roots. This led, among other things, to what is even today referred to as a colonial-service mentality in some Third World functionaries: "base servility and obsequiousness" toward Europeans and "arrogance, scorn and cupidity" toward their fellow countrymen (*EA,* 49). The chosen few—and they were very few indeed—were the *évolués,* who were granted civic rights, but the majority under French colonialism were subject to the *indigénat* and *prestation*—that is, to arbitrary punishment and forced labor. (This explains how it was possible for the prison governor to torture Toundi and others with impunity.)

Another element in this colonial scenario was the European missionary. It is now a well-established, almost hackneyed fact that the missionaries, consciously or not, were agents of imperialism. The missionary could not operate freely unless the imperial army subdued the native population and the civil administration imposed "discipline." In return for their protection by the state, the missionaries encouraged a passivity in the people, directing their thoughts to wealth, dignity, and freedom in the next world.[7] A saying heard in many a colonized country was, "When the missionaries came, we had the land and they had the Bible; now we have the Bible and they [the Europeans] have the land." What Christine Bolt states in *Victorian Attitudes to Race* (1971) applies to the early part of this century as well, and the missionaries continued to believe that inasmuch as Christianity was divinely ordained to vanquish "false" religions, so too Europeans were meant to rule nonwhite peoples: the missionary's sense of his spiritual superiority easily shaded into racial and cultural arrogance. White was the color of moral and spiritual purity—and of racial superiority. Moreover, the missionaries confused Christian doctrine with Western culture: Christianity had, in effect, become a European religion. "Why do we insist on imposing our customs?" And again, "Why not present a Christianity . . . in which polygamy is permitted . . . and where sexual chastity is not regarded as the chief of all virtues?" (*PC,* 151, 157).

The Old Man and the Medal is divided into three parts. Within the first thirteen pages, we have old Meka being summoned by the French Commandant, his journey to the Residence, a shift of scene as Meka's wife Kelara anxiously awaits his return, and Meka's triumphant reappearance with the news that the French governor is going to award him a medal during the 14th of July celebrations. (Of course the full significance of Bastille Day and of its relevance to their situation is not explained to the Africans.) The remaining sixty-five pages of part 1 describe the reactions of Meka's relatives and friends and his preparations for the great day. Part 2, the actual presentation ceremony and the events immediately following, take up but twenty-eight pages. The fifty pages of part 3 are divided between Meka's humiliation, imprisonment, and release and his final return "home." This allocation of space affects the reader's focus: we see European colonialism through the treatment and perspective of Africans, and most of our "time" is spent in the village. However, it is a matter not only of emphasis but of treatment. The very first paragraph reads in part: "Meka was already awake when the first ray of sunlight . . . found its way through one of the holes in the rotten raffia thatch . . . and fell . . . into his left nostril." We note the poverty and yet are led to smile at the occupant of the hut. This satiric mixture of serious subject matter and comic treatment persists throughout the work. (There is even the danger of Oyono's perpetuating the colonial stereotype of the black African: childish, fun-loving, incapable of sustained seriousness of thought and purpose.)

The first page also establishes Meka's Christian belief: "Woman, you are as weak as the disciples were on the Mount of Olives." Veritable beasts of (colonial) burden, husband and wife pray, "kneeling on their bamboo bed like camels waiting to be loaded." The European quarter on the hill physically dominates the African township, the forest, and the villages beyond. The white man is held in fear and admiration. Kelara can think of no better comparison and compliment than to say to her husband, "You look very nice . . . like an American missionary" (4). Still, Meka and the others believe that the whites, with their ignorance of African languages and culture, are "easy enough to take in." The novel ironically shows that, in more important ways, it is the African who has been "taken in." Altogether it is a world of knaves and fools. Meka's ancestral land "had proved pleasing to the eye of the Lord," and though his father had fought heroically against the incursions of the white man, Meka obediently offers this land to "the Good Lord." "'To the Catholic mission you mean,' someone corrected" (7). Land in black Africa is almost sacred, the place where ancestors are buried; it is communally owned, and although one may give the use of land, the land itself is not ceded in perpetuity. In addition to this great gift, Meka's two sons had been "sacrificed" during the war while fighting for France. In recompense, Meka is to be awarded a medal, with the result that he incurs further expenses: clothes, shoes, socks, et cetera. Meka and his people are convinced that henceforth he will be a person of status and influence.

On the actual day of the presentation, Meka is kept waiting in the sun, "baking like a lizard," while the Europeans enjoy the shade of a veranda. He is made to stand within a white circle, literally and otherwise isolated: "He was not with his own people, and he was not with the others" (85). There are beads of sweat on his nose; his feet boil in the unaccustomed, ill-fitting shoes, and he feels the pressing "urge to satisfy a need." After the brief ceremony (lower order of medal and no congratulatory embrace from the governor), Meka finds himself *outside* another circle: the one formed round the governor by the Europeans. Found drunk on the road in the night, having lost his medal, drenched in the tropical downpour, Meka is unrecognized and unbelieved by the police, beaten, dragged in the mud, whipped and spat on by the white superintendent of police, and locked up for the night: "He asks me who I am. Tell him I am a very great fool, who yesterday still believed in the white man's friendship" (134–35). *Houseboy* echoes similar sentiments with the rhetorical question, "Is the white man's neighbour only other white men?" (87). The day of his baptism now becomes to Meka "the day he became a slave" (137). Meka's sympathy is not only for himself but for all those deceived by and suffering under colonialism, including the African policemen who had treated him so roughly despite his pleas and his age: "Poor us."

Meka's return to his people, community, and culture is seen by the author as retrogressive: "All these superstitions had sprung up again in his mind like a great tide sweeping away the years of Christian teaching and practice" (142). Faced with this conundrum, the author reestablishes the hilarity which had lately been lessened, and the work ends with a spontaneous "beer-drink." Meka is an old man, respected and loved, and he settles happily back into the old ways. Besides, he is a bit of a rogue. For instance, he drinks the local brew (banned by the civil authorities and by the missionaries so that French products have a market) and, at confession, impresses the priest by saying, "I quenched my thirst when I had no need to" (10–11). He is also given to a frank, Chaucerian sensuality: "My mouth was all salty / When I looked up your armpits, / It was even more salty / When I looked up somewhere else" (12). Though *The Old Man and the Medal* is not intended to be a tragedy, there *are* elements of the tragic hero in Toundi, the protagonist of *Houseboy*.

■ ■ ■

In *Houseboy* we again meet characters like the Commandant, Gullet, and Father Vandermayer. A "troublemaker" in *The Old Man and the Medal,* later identified as "the Commandant's houseboy," turns Kelara's pride and happiness to shame and grief: "I think they ought to have covered [Meka] in medals. . . . To think he has lost his land and his sons just for that." Toundi is the Commandant's houseboy, and *Houseboy* is perhaps the most passionate denunciation in African literature of French colonial rule.[8] Nonetheless, the work is also hilarious; I know of no other African novel which more successfully combines comedy and cruelty.

The novel is in the form of a diary, two exercise books, found by a fellow Cameroonian. The work being a diary and therefore a first-person narrative, 'Toundi is situated within the story he himself narrates.' The perspective is his, and the focus is outward, though the author enables the reader himself to evaluate the narrator. Since we know more (and differently) than Toundi, there is an irony at the narrator's expense. Like Doris Lessing's book *The Grass Is Singing,* the work commences with the death of the central character. An unnamed Cameroonian, taking temporary refuge in Spanish Guinea—"used by us [black] 'Frenchman' . . . as a place to slip away . . . whenever things became a little strained between ourselves and *our white compatriots*" (3; italics are my own)—comes to Toundi's side as he lies dying, fatally tortured by the colonial authorities. This "translator" presents Toundi's diaries to us, and as we read them, the story proper begins. Knowing in advance the manner of his death, we take with caution and irony Toundi's early rhapsodies over colonial Europeans: Toundi was happy; he was going to learn about white men and live like them (16).

On the day before his initiation, Toundi runs away from his father to Father Gilbert. It is more a running away than a running to—Toundi's father is crude, cruel, and dishonest. Literally hiding behind the white priest's cassock. Toundi can now stick out an impudent tongue at his once-dreaded father. At this stage Toundi is but a boy, and we make deductions which he does not make. He is a naïve narrator, and we grasp meanings which elude him: Father Gilbert treats him affectionately, "like a pet animal." The priest is amused at Toundi's "constant amazement," an amazement which is pleasing since it confirms the Father's European superiority. Toundi works hard, starting at five in the morning, but receives no salary: "Now and then he gives me an old shirt or an old pair of trousers." "The Europeans receive Communion separately"; they go into church and sit, separately. Toundi prefers the leftovers from the priest's plate, because sometimes "we find scraps of meat there." (Evidently Toundi is not given meat.)

Father Gilbert, given to riding his motorcycle recklessly and spreading "panic through the village" (a demonstration of power), dies in an accident, but by now Toundi is much less "innocent." (We are not told how many years Toundi worked at the mission.) The death of Father Gilbert coincides with Toundi's rejection of colonial Christianity: "I have died my first death." (Oyono uses the thought ironically, in a sense opposite to the Christian one of being born again spiritually. What is more, there are other deaths awaiting Toundi.) The impact of Christianity on black Africa was great not because its truth was felt to be patent and powerful but because it was identified with a conquering people and with a superior technology. Toundi moves away, nonetheless, as he does later from Madame's attempt to breed a fatalistic acceptance: "You are a houseboy, my husband is Commandant . . . nothing can be done about it. You are a Christian, aren't you?" (66).[9]

The new life for Toundi is at one of the centers of French colonialism: "little Joseph" enters the service of the colonial pharaoh:[10] "I am the thing that obeys." Toundi is initially proud of being chosen to work at the residence: "The dog of the King is the King of dogs: (24). The "dogs" in this case are Toundi's fellow Africans, and we see again his early wish and attempt to distance himself from his own people and to become as "white" as possible. It is a rejection of his people and a seeking of power over them, allied to the white man in the role of collaborator. Toundi thinks and talks as if he weren't black, but together with others, he is chased up a tree by a huge dog, set on them for sport.[11] Perched precariously up a tree, Toundi is not recognized by the amused Commandant: "All Africans look the same to them."

The Commandant is cruel with the sadism of the weak. Again, as Fanon has shown, the colonial situation provided the colonizers with helpless victims on whom to vent their guilt, frustrations, moods, inadequacies. Behind the power and the bluster, the intimidating glare and the kicks, the Commandant is weak. This fact is brought home to Toundi when he sees the man naked: "A great chief like the Commandant uncircumcised. . . . It killed something inside me. . . . I knew I should never be frightened of the Commandant again" (33). The laugh may be on Toundi for his assumption that only circumcised males are real men, but in this particular instance the conclusion is right. The Commandant is a boy masquerading not only as a man but as a chief. If, indeed, the great white chief himself is but a boy, what of the other Europeans and of their rule? (Toundi ran away before his initiation ceremony, the test of his manhood, and so is a boy, like the Commandant.)

At this juncture the news breaks that the Commandant's wife is coming to Yaoundé "tomorrow," and Toundi, stubbornly idealistic, begins to build fresh illusions. Expectations appear to be more than confirmed. Madame is "like a precious jewel," and Toundi waxes lyrical.

> My happiness has neither day nor night. . . . I will sing to my flute, I will sing on the banks of rivers, but no words can express my happiness. . . . Her smile is refreshing as a spring of water. Her look is as warm as a ray from the setting sun. It bathes you in a light that warms the depths of the heart. I am afraid. (55–56)

The above is in deliberate contrast to the earthy reaction of the others: "I'm glad I've met her before I go to confession"; "If she had been the one to pour ointment on our Lord's feet, the Bible story would have been rather different"; "What couldn't I do with what's inside those slacks"; "What a shame it's all reserved for the uncircumcized" (63).

"Madame" is soon bored and resorts to infidelity, just as she has in the past, we later learn. Toundi's adulation turns to contempt, and Madame, guilty and uneasy, cannot forgive that he, a black "boy" (in fact, a young man now), should presume to have superior standards and to judge her. Toundi's broom discovers the illicit contraceptive under Madame's bed ("These whites with their craze for putting clothes on everything"): he is someone who has seen through the pretense and the façade; he is one with "big ideas," a threat to the myths which help sustain colonialism—and he is accordingly destroyed. Madame is sexually persuasive, and Toundi becomes the sacrifice through which the Commandant and his wife are reconciled. Since the Commandant and his wife are representatives and symbols, French rule and civilization, as far as Toundi is concerned, stand or fall with them. It may be unfair to judge the group by a few individuals, but, as Orwell and others have shown, most Europeans in the colonies willingly assumed that particular "burden" of the white man and acted out the role. In being sexually unfaithful to the Commandant, Madame is also unfaithful to Toundi, betraying that elevated conception which he had of her. Neither the Commandant nor Madame keeps faith, and that is more painful to Toundi than their overt, verbal, and physical cruelty.

One puzzle in *Houseboy* is Toundi's failure to make good his escape when he well had the opportunity.

Why didn't he run away? Why did he disregard ominous signs and not heed explicit warnings? Why did he wait to be arrested and tortured? Critics have not confronted this apparent flaw. To say that Toundi remained fatally mesmerized by white civilization is not satisfactory, since long before his death he had shed all illusions about European colonial culture.

Toundi had three possible worlds before him: Christianity, the world of French power and culture, and his own traditional life. Under imperialism, the Europeans scrupulously distanced themselves from the "natives" in order to maintain the belief not only that they were stronger, but that they were superior in morals and values. The domestic servant was, in the colonial past as in the bourgeois present, the spy within the camp, the person able to see into bedrooms and behind public pretensions. The servant is one of the outsiders—in terms of color, race, or class—inside. Rejecting Christianity as preached and practiced by French colonialism, rejecting French imperial power, disillusioned with the French civilizing mission which, he had thought, possessed some beauty and goodness, Toundi has only his own, African world. Had he returned to it like Meka, the quest or epic pattern would have been fulfilled: departure, adventures and experiences in foreign realms, the final return home of one who is wiser and more mature, if sadder. (The medal Toundi wears is that of Saint Christopher, patron saint of travelers.) What, however, does African society under colonialism have to offer? To vary Toundi's image, having known electricity, can one return to the oil lamp?

There are two traditional chiefs in *Houseboy* and neither is admirable: one is comic and the other an escapist. The village elders are a mockery of what one would expect of traditional village leaders.

> The question you ask is . . . the question of a wise man who is seeking to understand. Our ancestors said, "Truth lies beyond the mountains. You must travel to find it." I have travelled. I have made the great journey. . . . I have made war. I have lost my leg and I can answer your question. (67)

The linguistic structure is traditional in its patterning, in its reference to ancestors and ancestral sayings, but the subject of the serious and engrossing meeting is one of the elders' wartime experiences of sleeping with European prostitutes. (Oyono's weapon is satire, and from that sharp and impartial blade not even the colonized escape.) The contrast between style and content is deliberately ludicrous. The elders have no worthwhile subjects to discuss because history has overtaken them, and they are bereft of real power. Colonialism has reduced them to voyeuristic boys deriving vicarious excitement. Similarly, Toundi's fellow workers discuss contraceptives all afternoon. Their defense and "revenge" is to laugh at the white man, though they are excessively respectful when he is physically present. They are dismissed as being men only in the sense that they happen to have the biological appendages of the male: "What would our ancestors say?" (93). There is no one in the book whom Toundi can look to as a model of either private morality or public conduct. If his world is one of "respect and mystery and magic" (93), Toundi fails to perceive it. In this respect, *Houseboy* stands in extreme contrast to Camara Laye's *African Child*.

Toundi is alienated from traditional society and beliefs, from Christianity, and from the colonial order. Western imperialism, as has been observed, turned some into exiles in their own countries, the way Prospero made Caliban an exile on the latter's island.[12] They did not have to journey abroad to experience alienation. (It must be admitted that the fault was also Caliban's for mistaking mere mortals for gods.) The diary form, though improbable, is appropriate. It is improbable because Toundi would not have been permitted to keep a diary in prison, nor would he have been physically able to in the hospital, tortured and dying. Still, it is appropriate in that the form emphasizes Toundi's utter loneliness. A diary is written to oneself; it is circular, beginning and ending with oneself. Toundi listens to conversations, asks questions, is advised and laughed at, but does not engage in discussion. He is reserved by nature and does not have a friend or companion.

Toundi has been seen as "a Christ figure—Christ, the scapegoat *par excellence*."[13] If so, he is a Christ dying between the world he rejected and the one which rejected him. All worlds—traditional, Christian, colonial—have betrayed Toundi, and he waits in the garden to be arrested. Toundi makes himself the pot rubbing itself against the hammer (73). The realization, "How wretched we are," is corrosive, and Toundi can "never stop living through [that] over and over again." Destroyed in his soul, he commits what almost amounts to suicide: there is "a song we sing . . . when someone is dying" (92), and Toundi sings "it out loud." He sings of *himself*. Oyono writes of life under a repressive political system, but he is not a political writer in the sense that Ngũgĩ wa Thiong'o is one: not only describing exploitation but presenting a viable alternative, imparting confidence, urging action.

Toundi's last question, "Brother, what are we?" is not rhetorical, implying the answer, "Nothing." The question is intense and *literal*. At that last moment between life and death, Toundi still hoped to find an answer to the existential question, "What am I?" Finding no answer, he dies "utterly untransfigured." *Houseboy*

is usually described as a work which exposes the extreme cruelty of French colonialism, and by this cruelty is meant the indignities, verbal abuse, and physical assault to which Toundi and others were subjected. As Idi Amin, Bokassa, and others have shown in recent times, however, cruelty is not confined to foreigners and colonialism, not to one people, place, or time. The cruelty and exploitation Toundi experienced were undoubtedly physical and material, but they were also of another kind: destroying one world and denying full and equal admission to another.

In understanding why Toundi could not and did not run away, we also gain a fuller measure of Oyono's achievement in *Houseboy*. However, at the end, Toundi, who had once preferred to be a dog in the white man's world rather than a man in his own, drags himself away in order to deny the colonialist the satisfaction of finishing him off. Though still without orientation, he is clear about what he rejects and dies very much a man. If Toundi were only an impudent, naïve, foolish boy, the work would not arouse that degree of pity, in the classic sense, which it does. The "greed" Toundi's mother warned him against is an inquiring mind and a questing spirit. These qualities, plus courage and a sense of humor even while he is dying, change the "boy" into an admirable man. It is when he is seen in this light that Toundi is transformed into a tragic, rather than a merely pathetic, figure.

C. P. Sarvan, Summer 1985

[1] Ferdinand Oyono, *Le vieux nègre et la médaille* and *Une vie de Boy*, Paris, Julliard, 1956. The two works were translated respectively as *The Old Man and the Medal* (1969) and *Houseboy* (1966), London, Heinemann. Oyono's third novel, *Chemin d'Europe* (1960), also published by Julliard, has not been translated into English.

[2] See Mongo Beti's novel *Le pauvre Christ de Bomba*, Paris, Laffont, 1956; translated as *The Poor Christ of Bomba*, London, Heinemann, 1971. Subsequent references use the abbreviation *PC*.

[3] The use of the term *boy* is in itself interesting. Even mature men in domestic service were, and are in South Africa, called boys, denying them both manhood and adulthood and exposing them to the scolding and "correction" meted out to children.

[4] Michael Crowder, *Senegal: A Study in French Assimilation Policy*, Oxford, Oxford University Press, 1962, pp. 2, 3.

[5] Abdou Moumouni, *Education in Africa*, London, Deutsch, 1968, p. 37. Subsequent references use the abbreviation *EA*.

[6] See Frantz Fanon, *The Wretched of the Earth*, New York, Grove, 1968; and, more pertinently, his *Black Skin, White Masks*, Grove, 1967.

[7] See C. P. Sarvan, "Aspects of the Victorian Age," in *English Literature: Introductory Essays*, C. P. Sarvan, ed., Lusaka, National Educational Company, 1981, p. 132.

[8] Eustace Palmer, *The Growth of the African Novel*, London, Heinemann, 1979, p. 172.

[9] In Doris Lessing's short story "No Witchcraft for Sale" the black servant exclaims reflectively, "Ah missus, these are both children, and one will grow up to be a Baas, and one will be a servant. . . . It is God's will." Doris Lessing, *This Was the Old Chief's Country: Collected African Stories*. vol. 1, London. Michael Joseph, 1973, p. 31.

[10] *Houseboy* refers to "the lean kine in Pharaoh's dream," p. 36.

[11] See Mark Twain, *More Tramps Abroad*, London, 1897, pp. 137–38.

[12] Jan Carew, "The Caribbean Writer and Exile," *Lotus*, 46:4 (1980), pp. 9–25.

[13] Charles Nnolim, "Jungian Archetypes and the Main Characters in Oyono's *Une vie de Boy*," *African Literature Today*, 7 (1975), p. 122.

CONGO

Tchicaya U Tam'Si: Some Thoughts on the Poet's Symbolic Mode of Expression

The death of Tchicaya U Tam'Si on 22 April 1988 at the age of fifty-seven sent shock waves through the world of African literature. Tchicaya, the oldest of a generation of important Congolese writers, is one of the few whose reputation has reached beyond the confines of Francophone Africa and France.[1] During his lifetime, however, he never reached the wide audience that he deserved, not only as a poet but also as novelist and playwright. Despite the fact that *Epitomé* (1958) won him the first prize for poetry at the Festival des Arts Nègres at Dakar in 1966, his reading public has remained limited. While recognizing him as one of the leading contemporary African poets, critics and readers remain strangely reserved. In a recent publication Théophile Obenga puts his finger on one of the main reasons for this reticence: "U Tam'Si n'est l'héritière de personne et de rien: à souhait, et non sans belle ironie" (U Tam'Si inherits from nobody and nothing: by choice and not without beautiful irony).[2] Tchicaya's writing defies classification. His intensely personal world view and poetic expression create his own individual mythology, which sets him apart from all neat literary categories. His poetry is often described as hermetic, which is, in reality, the literary critic's terminology for admitting that it is not easily understood. At the same time the poet's obvious mastery of his medium precludes his being dismissed as obscure or unintelligible. Who then is this poet? What is his significance as a writer?

Perhaps U Tam'Si owes the initial recognition of his work by Western critics to fortuitous historical circumstances. In France the surrealist revolt against traditional poetic norms had opened the way for experimental form and expression, and poets such as André Breton and Robert Desnos had enthusiastically supported the Negritude poets. In his preface to the 1947 edition of Aimé Césaire's *Cahier d'un retour au pays natal* Breton recognized in Césaire's poetry "cette exubérance dans le jet et dans la gerbe, cette faculté d'alerter sans cesse de fond en comble le monde émotionnel jusqu'à le mettre sens dessus dessous qui caractérisent la poésie authentique."[3] At times U Tam'Si's own words would seem to confirm this link with the surrealists, although he himself has said that he had not read their poetry at the time of writing his own first poems: "I lack the intoxication to understand what is plausible. And yet the world is as it appears to the lark: a distorting mirror."[4] However, as this study of U Tam'Si's imagery and symbolism will attempt to make clear, fundamental differences distinguish his verse from that of the French surrealists, who, in advocating automatic writing, deliberately refused all restraint imposed by logic. The surrealist poet's highly individualistic message was "dictated" by his subconscious being, which he believed to be the echo of the universal consciousness. It was expressed by an arbitrary association of words which, at first reading, the poet often understood no better than the reader. This is very different from U Tam'Si's dense and at times esoteric imagery, by which he expresses his profound and passionate identification with the suffering of Africa and, more particularly, of the Congo. U Tam'Si's imagery is distinguishable from that of the surrealists because of its coherent scheme of reference and world view. His poetic universe is that of an individual who expresses both consciously and unconsciously his sense of a collective identity. This will become apparent when a closer look is taken at his image-symbols.

In general, U Tam'Si's merit as a poet was judged in terms of criteria that had evolved out of the European experience, which meant that the full extent of his creative inspiration and originality was not appreciated. This is perhaps still true today. By virtue of his early schooling under the French colonial administration and his having lived almost exclusively in France since the age of fifteen, U Tam'Si inherited from a dual cultural tradition. Nevertheless, his early writing in particular was strongly marked by his non-Western experience, thought modes, speech patterns, and thematic concerns. Although he was in no way traditionalist or limited by a uniquely African perspective, it is no doubt this unfamiliar world of reference which, on first reading, makes his poetry appear impenetrable to the Western reader or even to the Congolese reader who, through the process of "acculturation," has lost touch with "the cultural heart of the land." U Tam'Si is uncompromising in the demands he makes upon his reader: "When I write, I do not recount, I don't chew your food for you. I say to you 'There you are,' and according to the habits that you have acquired, you may take more or less."[5] He has also noted, on the other hand: "If one makes a literal reading of what I write, one understands what I am saying."[6] Similarly, he has indicated that the key to his poems can be found in the titles, just as the proverbs that run as a leitmotiv through his novels point to the meaning.

However, the "literal reading" advocated by U Tam'Si is based on an important assumption: that his work will be read as a whole. This is a crucial factor in "decoding" U Tam'Si's creative writing. Unfortunately, it is very difficult to make the necessary global reading of his work so as to appreciate the extended imagery and thought patterns; not only does little of his work exist in translation, but much of it is out of print as well—the fate suffered by a high proportion of valuable African writing. Perhaps, following upon U Tam'Si's untimely death, there will be a resurgence of interest in his writing, leading to the reprinting of those works that are presently unobtainable.

It is important to read U Tam'Si's oeuvre not only as a whole but also chronologically, in the order of composition. His novels illustrate this very well; the first three, each over 250 pages long, form a trilogy that paints a vast human and sociopolitical fresco of the Congo, although spanning only fifty-some years in the life of the main protagonists, Sophie and Prosper. In fact, it was conceived of as a single narrative and was divided into three in order to satisfy the editors. Thus, although each novel may be read and enjoyed in isolation, characters and events in one of the three may be alluded to in another or may reappear without explanation, with the result that the full significance is lost on the reader. Similarly, certain recurrent images become key symbols, an understanding of which is essential in order to release the full meaning of the text. One such image-symbol is that of the *cancrelat* or cockroach, which lends its name to the first novel, *Les cancrelats*. The word first appears in the enigmatic proverb which introduces the novel: "Le cancrelats. alla plaider une cause au tribunal des poules!" (The cockroach went to plead its cause before the hens' court). Both the proverb and the cockroach image reappear at significant points in the first and last of the three novels, illuminating the meaning of the text and themselves acquiring new connotative dimensions. The semiological role of *le cancrelat* is lost on the reader who reads *Les phalènes* without having first read *Les cancrelats*.

When viewed globally, the overall shape and development of U Tam'Si's poetry and prose can be com-

pared to that of an orchestra. In fact, the importance of music as a structural element is consciously emphasized by the poet in his first collection of poems, entitled *Le mauvais sang,* which has musical terms as subtitles to the two main sections. In a piece of orchestral music the part for a single instrument may be extracted from the score and enjoyed in isolation, but it only acquires its full meaning when integrated into the orchestrated whole. Similarly, the full force of a single poem's expression and vision is released only when it is read in the context of the whole body of U Tam'Si's poetry. His poetic discourse works extendedly: an idea or image, initially introduced almost unobtrusively, will be picked up in successive poems, where a different context or emphasis will add new layers of meaning, until, as with the *cancrelat* image, it attains the value of a symbol. U Tam'Si's discourse at times reads like a form of poetic shorthand, where a single word-sign signifies a complexity of meaning, intelligible only if the reader has followed its development.

The importance of the overall shape or structure as a signifier in U Tam'Si's poetry can be illustrated by the collection entitled *Le ventre.*[7] The final poem, "le ventre reste," takes up successively and almost line by line the titles of the thirteen poems that make up the collection, so that each phrase releases the complexity of emotion and meaning that was developed in the poem of that little. The whole is woven together in a perfectly controlled and unified statement which, in the final stanza, ends with a vision of hope: "God be thanked the prophets fall / most often on their backs / most often with their arms opened wide / most often / their bellies to the sky!" (*SP, 133*).

A study of the way in which the image of *le ventre* is developed into a key symbol reveals the dialectical nature of U Tam'Si's symbolism. Typically, the final statement of "le ventre reste" (quoted above), which is also the final statement of the collection, is not definitive, for U Tam'Si refuses to be categorical. "To identify a thing is to limit its possibilities," he says in *Les cancrelats*. It is by taking cognizance of the dialectical complexity of an idea or an image that one comes to some sort of understanding. U Tam'Si's refusal to simplify is illustrated in the image-symbols that constitute the framework not only of his poetry but also of his prose. It is thus worth making a brief semiological study of the complex *ventre* symbol.

In divinatory practices the opened belly of an animal or fowl reveals the future to the seer. This is particularly significant, for in his poetry and prose U Tam'Si makes frequent allusions to the prophetic vocation of the poet. Furthermore, in traditional African society the storyteller was often believed to have prophetic vision, and, conversely, the seer would express himself in poetic or esoteric language. Lying on his back, open to the sky or the heavens, arms wide and receiving, the seer-poet offers himself to divine inspiration. Yet the opened belly means death, both for the sacrificial animal and for man caught up in violent conflict. Yet again, the belly is associated with fertility and regeneration (*bas-ventre* means "womb"). The navel symbolizes the biological and the cultural link with the mother, Mother Earth/Africa, and therefore the Ancestors. Indeed, the collection entitled *Le ventre* has been interpreted as the poet's attempt to understand his own identity in terms of his origins and his relation with his mother and Africa.[8] The belly is associated too with warmth, with passion, and, particularly in Africa, with dance: "Dance is the best language / in which to make of two bodies / the two parts of a single phrase / which writes the perfect verb to love!" (*SP*, 180).

The concept of the brotherhood of man and, more particularly, of a united Congo, informs all Tchicaya's creative writing; it is something he believed in passionately, and his disillusion and bitterness were all the greater as he witnessed the internecine fighting that crippled the Congo Republic. He was deeply shocked by the assassination of Patrice Lumumba, with whom he had worked and whose ideals he shared. The martyred political leader, epitomized by Lumumba, is the major thematic concern of *Epitomé* (1962) and *Le ventre*. It is a theme which links up with that of the Christ, betrayed and betrayer, and the suffering poet-prophet, thus forming another complex image-symbol, which finds its origin in his first collection of poems: "Christ trahi voici ma croix humaine de bois" (Christ betrayed here is my human cross of wood).[9]

Still, whereas the belly is often associated with warmth and life, refrains such as "The belly / always with that sickening warmth / as of the charnel-house" (*SP*, 127) serve as a reminder not only of death but also, significantly for the Central African countries such as the Congo, of cannibalism: "We shall live no more on flesh or blood / I am eating a dish of meat this evening / why not the flesh of my brothers / burnt in the holocaust?" (*SP*, 56). The belly is associated with greed, the voracious appetites of the exploiters of Africa, both the colonialists and the neocolonialist dictators of the newly independent states.

It is not possible here to do more than touch on some of the main dialectical themes and connotations contained in the symbol of the belly; as one progresses through the poems of *Le ventre,* one is struck by the rich density of allusion, the play and replay of word and image, and one becomes aware that it is probably impossible to give a complete exegesis of the symbol. To

define is to limit, to simplify is to falsify—that is what U Tam'Si would seem to be saying.

Another important factor that contributes to the dynamic force of U Tam'Si's creative writing but is unfortunately lost in a piecemeal or incomplete reading of his work is the role played by rhythm, in terms of both structure and language. The importance of rhythm in African poetry has been more than adequately explained by Léopold Senghor, himself one of the greatest lyric poets of Africa.[10] Like the poets of the *Anthologie,*[11] U Tam'Si is, in the words of Senghor, an "auditory" poet; his poems are to be spoken aloud, not read silently. In a 1986 interview in Paris, U Tam'Si stated, "Everything that I have written is oral." Thus assonance, alliteration, and echoing reverberations reinforce the repeated images, refrains, and ideas. This makes his poetry extremely difficult to translate satisfactorily.

Again it is important to make a chronological reading of U Tam'Si's poetry in order to appreciate the semiological significance of rhythm. As he frees himself of conventional metric form, it is rhythm that determines the shape and progression of the poem. In *Feu de brousse* the insistent and syncopated rhythm of the drum predominates. A selective reading destroys the cumulative effect of the repeated words and phrases, which mark time and then advance the poem, which echo an image from a previous line or poem and then surge forward with a new thematic element. At times the effect is incantatory, creating a profound emotion that in turn releases the poem's significance. In his later poetry rhythm plays a more subtle role; less semiologically significant in itself, it serves to underscore and develop the meaning of the image-symbols. Flexible yet controlled, the dynamics of repetition and variation, suspense and advance, create a complex pattern of sound and movement, which is an integral part of the poem's meaning.

In U Tam'Si's writing, repetition and rhythm are not only semiologically but also structurally significant. The collection *Le ventre* represents one of the most striking illustrations of this. The dialectical nature of the word-symbol *le ventre* has already been discussed, but it is important to consider the *ventre* symbol in the context of the collection as a whole in order to appreciate how the contradictions and contrasts make up a synthetic unity. Space does not allow for the required detailed study of this high-frequency word. However, a chronological reading of the poems in the collection would reveal how the development of the referential value of the *ventre* symbol mirrors the organically integrated structure of the whole. This rhythmic pattern is a constant in U Tam'Si's writing, a structural technique which can be found in his first collections of poems and which is developed to a striking degree in his later works. For example, repeated semiological and linguistic elements link the poems in *Le mauvais sang,* and key recurrent images such as blood, water, the woman/mother/Africa, and the Christ are introduced. In later volumes the title of a poem is often anticipated in the preceding poem, thus reinforcing the sense of pattern in ideas and sounds.[12] This repetition is not static; each reappearance of an image brings to it a new dimension, and its development can be traced through U Tam'Si's work as a whole. It is significant that many of the key images in his verse are important signifiers in his prose.[13]

To understand how repetition determines progression, it is important to consider African music. There the repetition, which is often monotonous to the Western ear, is in fact made up of constant slight variations that mark the forward movement of the song or dance. The development takes place over an extended time span.

One of the most important effects of the rhythmic repetition of image and sound is to give U Tam'Si's work both consistency and homogeneity. As has already been shown, certain core ideas or images inform his entire work, not only as leitmotivs but as part of the structural and referential framework. These images, anchored in the real, material world, are developed by association and correspondence, and they signify at several levels. Thus in *Le mauvais sang,* a chain of ever-widening reference is created, beginning with "blood" and the "wound," through "water" to "thoughts" and "memories," "diving" (back into the stream of time, the past), to "skiff" (canoe), "river" (the Congo River), and "shipwreck." Each of these links in the image chain acquires greater resonance as it is picked up and developed in a later poem or collection. Thus "wound" is inseparable from the Christ figure, which, introduced in *Le mauvais sang,* becomes a dominant image in *Epitomé* and *Le ventre.*

Water and rain link with the immense Congo River, which reflects the past and potential grandeur of the country, the dream of a nation reunited, just as the tributaries of the Congo River link across the land. The Congo River is also the source of identity: "There remains a river and the key of dreams in its flanks."[14] Furthermore, it represents the total giving of self, the poetic vocation, commitment to an ideal (the throwing of oneself into the water). Elsewhere U Tam'Si has compared his poetry to the Congo River, "qui charrie autant de cadavres que de jacinthes d'eau" (that carries along as many cadavers as water lilies).[15] Water, like blood, is a sacrificial and cleansing element, and as the river leads to the ocean, so it links up with another very important and complex image-symbol in U Tam'Si's discourse, the

ocean/salt/ waves/sea gull. Again, space does not allow an adequate treatment of these images, each of which requires close analysis in the context of U Tam'Si's creative writing as a whole.

It is not possible to appreciate the full depth and breadth of U Tam'Si's symbolic universe without taking cognizance of his dual cultural heritage. His early, formative years in the Congo would have had an indelible effect on his thinking and imaginative mind, but at an early age he accompanied his father to France and, from that time, spent most of his life away from Africa, primarily in Paris. An important facet to the study of his poetic imagery would be to trace the gradually increasing incidence of semiological elements originating in the European context. Right from the start of his literate life, however, elements of a French subculture would have influenced his thinking, for all his schooling was in French. In fact, his mother tongue, Vili, was not and still is not taught anywhere, not even at junior school. It is important, then, not only to take into account the way in which language patterns influence thought, but also to remember that the French colonial policy of "assimilation" consistently aimed at imposing a French subculture at the expense of the African cultures.[16]

For a non-Congolese reader, U Tam'Si's writing cannot be understood out of its sociopolitical context. This is not always easy, since few detailed historical, geographic, or sociocultural studies of the Congo are available, and of those that do exist, the majority are written by European historians and ethnologists. U Tam'Si does not make it easy for the non-Congolese reader. He has said that he does not write for a Western public: "That would denaturalize my thinking. I speak of my country to those of my country . . . and then to those who might be led to live there."[17] Thus he assumes a knowledge of the political events leading up to independence in 1960 and the turbulent years that followed. His language is elliptic; images follow each other in quick succession, often specifically Congolese or regional in origin. Even universal images such as the sun or rain or trees must be read in the context of the Congolese heat and tropical rain forests. For example, no European experience of rain can release the full resonance of "The belly trembles, the deluge approaches"[18] or of the lines "the rain is clinging, sticky, / gummy, insistent, petrifying, excreting, / shitty and distressing."[19] It is impossible to convey adequately the musical reverberations of the original French, which reinforce U Tam'Si's earthy, ironic humor as he speaks of the chaos that engulfed the Congo after independence.

In his preface to the 1962 edition of *Epitomé* Senghor speaks of the "kaleidoscope" of images, which erupt with the force of a "geyser." He refers to the "syntax of juxtaposition," which "explodes the hinges of logic." U Tam'Si's poetry translates the "movements of a passion, in offbeat rhythms and syncopation," like African music.[20] At times the asymmetric parallelisms, the enjambments, the breaks and returns make it difficult to follow the movements of the poet's mind and passion. What appear to be linguistic "gymnastics" in fact find their origin in the oral tradition.[21] Learning to understand and use proverbs and *devinettes* (riddles) was as important a part of the young African child's "schooling" as was the learning of mythological and historical stories and fables. Riddles depend upon the clever use of sound and words to create a symbolic language, behind which lies the "hidden" meaning that must be guessed at. Through these games a certain mental and linguistic dexterity is learned. Many of U Tam'Si's poems open with a gnomic utterance which, while not explained, is never gratuitous; it plays an important semiological role, just as the titles of the poems or the lines set in proem serve as an epitome for the poem. This use of proverbs and enigmas is equally significant in U Tam'Si's prose works. For the non-Congolese or even non-Vili reader, the meaning of some of the aphorisms and esoteric utterances will remain hidden. For example, only someone familiar with African and more particularly Congolese or Vili custom would realize the full dialectical force of the phrase "They have spat on me,"[22] since spitting or unction by saliva is a form of benediction.

Two interesting attempts have been made to categorize the major images that inform U Tam'Si's poetry,[23] but the danger of this method is that the essential and dynamic homogeneity of his symbolism is lost. To classify separately such complex symbols as water, blood, and the woman/mother figure is to splinter the "substance"[24] of the writer's creative universe. Théophile Obenga gives a better understanding of the intrinsic unity of U Tam'Si's poetry through a detailed study of the blood image (*le sang*), which he sees as U Tam'Si's "literary fancy," the key to both the logical and the imaginary universe of his poetry.[25] The work of Gaston Bachelard and, more recently, that of Gilbert Durand suggest a similar approach. Their investigations into the psychology of the imagination and their analysis of archetypal and mythical imagery represent a synthetic treatment of image and symbol, whereby contradictions and contrasts form a harmonious whole. Durand demonstrates the inadequacy of the structuralist approach for the analysis of imagery, in that it does not take sufficient cognizance of the dynamic and unifying creative mind behind the poetic discourse, an understanding of which requires an organic rather than a mechanistic approach. Although one would not claim that a piece of creative writing can be fully understood only in the light of the author's personal life and psyche, there is nevertheless a general motivating force behind the symbolism that emanates from a particular emotional and mental universe.

There exists a symbiotic relationship between, on the one hand, the mythical universe created by the poet and augmented with each new piece of writing, and on the other the writer's own mental universe; symbols, rhythm, and structure acquire a dynamism of their own and inform the writer's own philosophical and emotional development. Speaking about his writing, U Tam'Si said: "A creative work should take root in you. The more it takes root in you, the more chance it has of affecting others."[26] This is not a new idea, but its significance is not always taken into account by contemporary literary critics.

U Tam'Si's work is of particular interest in this respect, for his highly integrated poetic universe reflects a holistic world view that stands in sharp contrast to the Manichean Western world view. U Tam'Si's thought processes are firmly rooted in a sense of rhythmic pattern, the cycles of life and man's collective identity. His poetic discourse is strongly individualistic in terms of image and language, yet his concern is for understanding the meaning of "existential anguish" not for the individual alone but for the individual as part of a corporate body, past, present, and future. His poetry is the concrete expression of his conception of the poet-prophet, whose role in the life of society is as important as that of the mason or the carpenter: "The poet is above all a man, a man in the full meaning of the word, a conscious man. A conscious man is he who dreams, and the dream is only a projection into the future of what can be realized."[27] The poet, like Christ and the political martyr, lays himself open to the conflicting forces of life. U Tam'Si's creative writing constitutes the commitment of a life to this task. In his poetry the poetic "I" represents a constant dialectic, an intensely personal expression that crystallizes the experience of a people. He expresses this in an observation from *Notes de veille;* the final ironic comment is typical of his blend of mocking self-deprecation and dedicated belief in the poet's vocation: "En fait l'homme s'élabore dans un temps trop court dans lequel il lui est impossible d'assimiler tous les éléments extérieurs qui pourraient faire de lui une unité solvable. Peu y sont arrivés: Christ, Rimbaud . . . moi ma gloriole défunte" (In fact man develops in too short a time, during which it is impossible for him to assimilate all the external elements which could make of him a creditable unity. Few have managed it: Christ, Rimbaud . . . I, my defunct vainglory).

Betty O'Grady, Winter 1991

¹ Tchicaya's second collection of poetry, *Feu de brousse* (Bruno Durocher, 1957), was translated by Sangadore Akanji (Mbari, 1964) as *Brush Fire,* but the limited circulation made it somewhat inaccessible. Subsequently, selections of his poetry have been translated by Gerald Moore (*Selected Poems,* Heinemann, 1970) and John Reed and Clive Wake (*French African Verse,* Heinemann, 1980). His play *Le destin glorieux du maréchal Nnikon Nniku, Prince qu'on sort* has been translated by Timothy Johns (Ubu Repertory Theater Publications, 1986). Quotations from *Selected Poems* are indicated parenthetically and use the abbreviation *SP.*

² Théophile Obenga, *Sur le chemin des hommes,* Paris, Présence Africaine, 1984, p. 45. Translations are my own unless otherwise indicated.

³ ". . . that exuberant outpouring and bursting forth, that power of alerting the emotional world ceaselessly, from top to bottom, so as to turn it upside down, which characterizes authentic poetry." Aimé Césaire, *Cahier d'un retour au pays natal,* new ed., Paris, Présence Africaine, 1983, p. 81.

⁴ "Je manque d'ivresse pour comprendre ce qui est plausible. Et pourtant le monde est tel qu'il apparaît à l'alouette; un miroir déformant." Tchicaya U Tam'Si, *Notes de veille,* Nubia, 1977, p. 91.

⁵ Tchicaya U Tam'Si, quoted from an interview in *Fraternité Matin,* 6 January 1981.

⁶ Tchicaya U Tam'Si, quoted in *Calao,* 81 (May-June, 1988), p. 11.

⁷ Tchicaya U Tam'Si, *Le ventre,* Paris, Présence Africaine, 1978.

⁸ R. Chemain and A. Chemain-Degrange, *Panorama critique de la littérature congolaise contemporaine,* Paris, Présence Africaine, 1979.

⁹ Tchicaya U Tam'Si, *Le mauvais sang,* Bruno Durocher, 1955, p. 33.

¹⁰ See in particular Senghor's postface to *Ethiopiques,* entitled "Comme les lamantins vont boire à la source," in *Poèmes,* 4th ed., Paris, Seuil, 1984, p. 155–68.

¹¹ Léopold S. Senghor, *Anthologie de la nouvelle poésie nègre et malgache de langue française,* Paris, PUF, 1948.

¹² For example, in *A triche cœur* (A Game of Cheat-Heart) the title "Low Watermark" is introduced in the preceding poem, "Agony." See *Selected Poems,* pp. 6, 4.

¹³ For example, the *cancrelat* appears in both *Le mauvais sang* and *Feu de brousse.* Similarly, the sea is a very important semiological element in *Les méduses* (Sea-Urchins), the second novel in the trilogy. Again it is important to take into account the chronological sequence of U Tam'Si's writing; although his novels were not published until the 1980s, he has said that they were written during the 1950s—that is, at the same time as his early poems.

¹⁴ U Tam'Si, *Feu de brousse,* p. 52.

¹⁵ U Tam'Si, in *Calao,* p. 11.

¹⁶ Bernard Mouralis, in *Littérature et développement,* (Silex/ACCT, 1984), makes an in-depth study of this policy and its effects on the cultural heritage of several generations of young African children.

¹⁷ Tchicaya U Tam'Si, interview, Paris, 1986.

¹⁸ *Le ventre,* p. 113. In the French, "le ventre" echoes "le vent," the wind, which often blows very strongly before a tropical downpour.

¹⁹ ". . . la pluie est collante poisseuse / gluante lancinante pétrifiante filente / chiente et navrante." Tchicaya U Tam'Si, *Le pain ou la cendre,* Paris, Présence Africaine, 1978, p. 165.

²⁰ Senghor was one of the first to recognize the poetic genius of U Tam'Si: in this preface he hails Tchicaya's poetry as being one of the most authentically "négro-africaine," free from Arab-Berber influence and therefore "closer to the source" of pure African inspiration and expression. See "Tchicaya ou de la poésie bantoue à la poésie négro-africaine," in his *Liberté 1: Négritude et humanisme,* Paris, Seuil, 1964, pp. 364–68.

²¹ U Tam'Si himself makes reference to this traditional style of expression: "Go into the villages and listen to the people talking; you will see that they speak by means of parables, proverbs, images. With us, it is images that speak, where the verb is not a grammatical structure but rather a structure by echoes. When I say 'mango', you see a child eating a mango, you see a mango tree, or a countryside where there is a mango tree, etc. All these signifiers are reconstituted by the reader." Quoted from the interview in *Fraternité Matin* of 6 January 1981.

²² U Tam'Si, *Le mauvais sang,* p. 31.

²³ R. Godard, *Trois poètes congolais,* Paris, Harmattan, 1985; R. Chemain and A. Chemain-Degrange, *Panorama critique.*

²⁴ The term *substance* is understood here according to the meaning given to it by the formalists: i.e., "the inert mass, either of the extralinguistic reality (substance of the content) or of the phonetic or other means used by language (substance of expression)." G. Genette, *Figures* 2, Paris, Seuil, 1969, p. 19.

²⁵ Obenga, pp. 40–53.

²⁶ U Tam'Si, interview, Paris, 1986.

²⁷ Tchicaya U Tam'Si, quoted from an interview in *Jeune Afrique,* 278 (24 April 1966).

²⁸ U Tam'Si, *Notes de veille,* p. 98.

The Dancing Masks of Sylvain Bemba

Sylvain Bemba of the Congo is one of the most recent African writers to have achieved an international reputation, first in the theater, then through four novels that seem to puzzle readers. Critics also seem somewhat put off by his works, since they have received little sustained analysis, although Bemba's name is often seen in general discussions of the new African writing. Bemba mixes modern literary technique and complicated psychological and sociological concepts with elements drawn from African folklore, legend, tribal history, and religion in a quite original way. The supernatural aspects of African tradition are crossed with modern fantasy and science fiction in the manner of Third World "marvelous realism" to dig deeper into the double identity of the colonized person.

The theme of dancing masks provides a key to Bemba's main characters and to his literary methodology and style. The image of dancing masks is very close to the central concept behind all of Bemba's work. The masks worn by the characters, the roles they play, are less a disguise or protection than a symbol, a projection of the self, a label, an "identity," serving to relate the individual, especially the inner self (emotions, the subconscious, et cetera), to the ideal self, the collective self, the historical self, the timeless self. Obviously masks are ambiguous, overdetermined, and kaleidoscopic, constantly shifting in valence, like the moods of the mythological gods with whom they are allied; but like all mythic elements they have a positive significance, weaving a web of references while educating those who witness their dance.

Bemba is original in attempting to relate the traditional masks to modern masks based on the identities of the figures of recent African history, the national heroes of Bemba's region. These new masks are useful for the understanding of self and the creation of national institutions in the period of rapid decolonization. The role of literature is to use the stories of these "model" selves to inform the reader of his or her role in society. Bemba studies both the self and the context, throwing both into relief through the ever-shifting dance of the masks. Two historical figures seem particularly to obsess the author; he returns often to Patrice Lumumba and Albert Schweitzer, each time casting them in a different light.

The word *mask* implies a tangle of artistic and psychological realities. The word evidently comes into Europe with the Arabs; their word *maskharah,* meaning "buffoon," enters Italian, then goes into French and English, meaning "mask." In this early period the concept was surrounded with the complex of values associated with the uses of masks in African rituals: festivity, celebration of the gods and forces of nature, ritual, revelry, singing and dancing, momentary change of identity, as when a mortal is possessed by an immortal spirit. Later, Europeans saw African masks as grotesque and devalorized them. Their misunderstanding symbolizes the cultural tensions of colonialism when Europeans destroyed thousands of masks as "fetishes." Twentieth-century anthropologists, however, becoming aware of psychological and artistic values, collected them. The mask is then seen as a mediating force relating the identity of the outer face to the hidden inner face. It is a link between the natural and the supernatural, between the everyday world and various privileged states of being: the ideal, the timeless, the sacred.

An African mask is almost always made of wood. The spirit inherent in the tree is incarnated in the mask. There is an identification with nature and its forces, signifying harmony and cooperation. Bemba uses all these values in the central image of *Le soleil est parti à M'Pemba* (Paris, Présence Africaine, 1982). The traditional solar masks, first seen as the integral image or symbol of tribal African society in the sacred ritual, are later perceived at the colonial exposition in Marseilles, in a profane and commercial setting (60–61). The defiling of the masks parallels the loss of the sun and the vitality of African life. Of Bemba's four novels, this one is the one that deals most directly with the dancing masks.

Bemba is fascinated with the problem of identity and with central African history. There is always a doubling. In *Soleil* he presents two sets of twins, the second set sons of one of the brothers in the first. We can thereby contrast two generations and the difference between urban and rural settings. All Bemba's characters undergo striking transformations as we see them in different settings, playing different roles, assuming various identities, especially when they go to France. The Lumumba- and Schweitzer-like characters come to assume the mask of "hero" or ideal self; like the numerous political-leader characters, they come to represent the group and a kind of "collective self." In *Soleil* we are also given the classic case: the buffoon masker, playful, a clown, who uses a magic phonograph to do a rapid-rerun of recent African history to unmask the evils and distortions of colonialism and their vestiges in the postcolonial world. This madman, like the fool in *Ambiguous Adventure,* has been destabilized by the tensions of living in two cultures but has become wise in revealing alienations.[1]

Comparing Bemba's Lumumba with Aimé Césaire's in *Une saison au Congo* reveals significant differences. Both use a Brechtian technique, but Césaire sticks close to the known facts, seemingly wanting to explain history; the sociopolitical interpretation is left implicit in this example of Negritude. Bemba is more willing to add imaginative details, to play with history by combining and recombining elements of various stories, to graft on dramatic happenings drawn from legends or his own imagination.

Toward the end of *Soleil* one of the sage elders puts forward a sketchy *art poétique* or literary theory, one related to social change.

> En partant des idées de certains grands hommes sur le changement social, je peux parler du Congo comme d'une société hydraulique. . . . Si je transforme cela en parabole, l'avenir du Congo, c'est l'eau plus la justice sociale, pour que revienne ce soleil que les Kongo disent immergé à M'PEMBA. . . Mais le soleil reviendra un jour. Sache qu'un pays qui se construit a besoin absolument de faire un pagne unique avec tous les morceaux du tissu des légendes les plus intéressantes de ses populations. Penser ensemble au

récit embelli d'un passé idéalisé est la meilleure manière d'édifier l'avenir. Tous les peuples, sans exception, embellissent leur histoire. (152–53)

In *Léopolis* Bemba writes, "Chaque pays a besoin d'un héros" (125). These citations make clear Bemba's belief in the role of literature to educate and unify a people.

Although didacticism is out of style as a literary criterion in the West in these days of deconstruction, Third World writers are not bound by European fads and proclaim other conceptions. The Russians too have a different view. A Soviet critic, writing in a recent issue of *Research in African Literature,* sees Bemba, indeed "French-language comedy in tropical Africa," as essentially didactic and "a form of mass literature." Nina D. Lyakhovskaya of the Gorky Institute for World Literature in Moscow states: "One cannot fail to notice features of mass literature in such plays, notably excessive, 'protruding' didacticism, the longing for extreme situations and the working up of tensions."[2] She relates didacticism to melodrama and labels Bemba's plays as being "serious" comedy or "tragicomedy" characterized by the "spirit of uncompromising struggle against everything that prevents Africans from parting with their past" (461).[3] Bemba has a simpler way of stating this: "Ce qui m'intéresse, moi, c'est de raconter une histoire qui a quelquechose dans le ventre" (*Soleil,* 56).

Bemba wrote his first novel, *Rêves portatifs,* at the age of forty, in 1979. The central concern is the relation of film to freedom. Bemba hangs all the diverse happenings on the story of a projectionist who has inadvertently gotten tangled up in drug dealing, just as the country of Palms is coming to independence. The rather rambling narration depicts not only the microcosm of the movies, but also nightclubs, jails, courts, journalism, politics, clinics, and bush hospitals. The author attacks all the cultural changes that accompany the birth of a new nation, which in itself might be seen as a manifestation of the mask theme; in running up the new flag the nation puts on a new mask.

Ignace Kambeya, the projectionist, is presented with fanfare. As a twin he is viewed as an oracle, but the death of his twin brother darkens his life. Ignace dreams of his lost alter ego and ceases to communicate, until he finds his role in life: to project the shadow images on the screen. He considers himself happy in his hidden booth, which transforms him into the equal of the white man. His head crammed full of alien images, he comes to identify with Fernandel, playing the comic role of Ignace Boitaclou. Ignace is a sort of faceless Everyman, the average African bewildered by culture shock and future shock.

Three major characters wear masks derived from the three most famous citizens of Zaïre.[5] The fictional

Kingaboua Yaya resembles Kasavubu, whereas Léonidas resembles Lumumba.[6] There are three passages in the novel which indicate Bemba's understanding of the mask, as both psychological and literary medium.

La magie des gosses. . . . C'est d'un œil attendri que leurs parents les voient se barbouiller de pâte dentifrice ou de rouge à lèvres pour se composer le visage terrifiant de Sitting Bull, Geronimo, Cochise et autres chefs indians célèbres.

Les grandes personnes jouent, elles aussi, mais elles montreraient des faces de vierge outragée si on leur disait qu'elles portent un masque. Depuis l'avènement de monsieur Eddie Constantine sur les écrans de l'Eldorado—l'unique salle de cinéma dans la ville européenne—les femmes se font coiffer et s'habillent comme Dominique Wilms, font onduler leur postérieur comme Brigitte Bardot. (67)

The main white character in *Rêves,* Délurin Brillat, a sort of Don Juan with homosexual tendencies, models himself after Gérard Philippe. The wife of Léonidas, Annabelle, is a nurse and wears a surgical mask in the operating room: "Dans une salle d'opération, le cynisme se porte comme un masque obligatoire servant de rempart contre toute forme d'émotion" (93). This passage adds a new dimension to the analysis of the mask. Beyond the "rampart against emotion," the mask is seen as the projection of an emotionless expression, a blank emotion, just as traditional African masks may project either a serene visage or one of agitation. Emotion is related to mood and expression, which is constantly variable on the human face, whereas in a mask one expression has been set, as a sign of character. The infinitely variable has been objectivized as a sign of social, metaphysical, religious, or political relationships. The face has been transformed into a signifier in order to communicate a social value, in order to instruct.

The mask game is a game of identities and identification in which the wearer of the mask chooses to imitate another person, or an already standardized role. At one point Bemba names Frantz Fanon in an implicit reference to *Black Skin, White Masks:* "Je suis l'homme de deux cultures . . . ces deux cultures coulent également en moi . . . à leur confluent, se forme ma personnalité" (175). In other words, his personality is based on two standardized types or masks, the "Black" and the "White."

There are two references to Lumumba, who apparently has become a type in the Congo, a mask many identify with and want to wear. One character has worked long and hard to "se donner une tête à la Patrice Lumumba" (158). Then there is a picturesque detail that has received much analysis. The last photograph of

Lumumba became an instant classic of journalism; it showed him in an awkward pose in the back of a Jeep, tied, beaten, clothes undone, glasses gone, his head lifted by the hair by a jeering soldier, almost as if the head had been severed. The glasses had become part of Lumumba's mask. In *Rêves* Bemba crosses this image with one from Alfred Hitchcock.

> On le pilonne à coups de crosse. Recroquevillé sur le sol, crachant plusieurs dents, l'ancien universitaire devenu aphone n'a pas la force de recoupérer ses lunettes brisées. Avant de sombrer dans le néant, il revoit avec une netteté saisissante cette séquence du film "L'inconnu du Nord-Express" dans laquelle Hitchcock exposait en gros plan les lunettes de myopie appartenant a une personne assassinée. (169)

Here the loss of the mask signifies the undoing of self-perception as well as perception and dramatizes the necessity of the mask.

The main masks in *Rêves,* however, are those shadowy ones on the movie screen. Already in his plays Bemba had pointed out the nefarious nature of mass culture imported into the Third World, a major factor in the breakdown of African culture. In one of the high points of the novel, Ignace dreams while in prison that he is a Darryl Zanuck-type producer of the African epic.

C'est l'heure du sabbat . . .
. . . d'une messe basse
Le temps d'un relevé débit/crédit
pour faire passer la mort
au compte des pertes et des profits.
Silence, on va tourner
Bloody Mama.
Mère Europe
qui étrangle et jette Negro Baby
avec l'eau du bain (59)

The subject of his film is a page of African history read from the textbook in class. The pupil is horrified by the savagery of his ancestors and identifies only with the benefactors from overseas bringing civilization: "Cinéma s'écrit aujourd'hui avec la lettre Y à la place de I, ce qui rapproche cynéma de cynisme. Allons . . . Que demande notre époque? De la fesse et du sang, du pognon et de l'aventure, voilà l'unique recette du succès" (63). Ignace's dream-film is the best example of an African brain scrambled by exposure to a perverted Eurocentric Africa.

In *Le soleil est parti à M'Pemba* (1982) the protagonist, jester and seer, uses a fantastic "phonovideograph" for a replay of recent history, in which we follow the development of two sets of twins, one which represents the last generation of colonialism, one which represents the first generation of independence. This version of the time machine might be seen as a device which permits the author to put the masking theme into relief by the unmasking made possible by the rapid juxtaposition of different faces presented by characters at different moments of their development. Thus we see N'Gambou Félix's transformation into Félix Gamboux (with a final *x*). Their generation was probably the one forced to make the most abrupt changes in identity and culture. The personal transformations parallel major social changes sketched in the novel.

Curiously, masks are associated both with timeless societies (traditional precolonial Africa) and with societies undergoing rapid transformation, like today's. Bemba counterposes the two kinds. The sacred masks serve as a foil for the kaleidoscopic personal transmutations. (Still, Bemba remains flexible on the theme of identity. The novel shows both the advantages and disadvantages of the various masks. Koumbandza, the jester, reveals himself as a defrocked priest: "Chacun de nous devrait avoir . . . le courage de dépouiller le vieil homme et d'enfiler une nouvelle peau" [125].)[7] Bemba pays tribute to Aladdin and his magic lamp twice in *Soleil;* besides the phono-videograph, there is a simple (but magic) phonograph that plays black music from Africa and the Americas and also has a genie who explains the connection, perhaps another of Bemba's ideas on the role of art, the art of the mask: "Ce phonographe renferme dans son ventre le récit épique du Grand Cavaleur. Unique et pluriel est ce héros. Chez vous, il porte le nom de André Grenard. Aux Etats-Unis, il s'est appelé Gabriel, Nat Turner, John Brown. . . . Tous le peuples enchaînés ont eu leur Grand Cavaleur" (104).

Le dernier des cargonautes (1984), the least substantial of Bemba's novels, relates to the mask theme in emphasizing changing identities in development of character. It combines the apparent simplicity of a Gidean récit with elements of medieval hagiography. It somewhat resembles Camus's *Etranger* in focusing on the vicissitudes of the life of an exceptional Everyman who is also something of a Christ figure; he resembles both Lumumba and Schweitzer to some degree and is named "Emmanuel." The book opens with a quotation from Pierre Klossowski.

> On croit choisir librement d'être ce que l'on est, mais on est en fait contraint de jouer un rôle, n'étant pas ce que l'on est; donc de jouer le rôle de ce qu'on est hors de soi. On n'est pas là où l'on veut, mais toujours là où l'on n'est que l'acteur de cet autre que l'on est. (9)

Our actor wears many masks; like many saints, he bathes in sin, sexuality, and crime before discovering his true role of serving his people, then leading them and saving their lives at his bush hospital. That his is a saintly presence is made clear by the last words of the novel: "Un souverain. C'était un roi, car il voulait conquérir cet ailleurs qui reste, pour le plupart des humains, un royaume inviolé" (168).

Bemba's most recent novel, *Léopolis,* represents something of a new departure and demonstrates a new mastery. The fact that it was published in an inexpensive paperback edition indicates that the publisher believed it might attract a larger audience. This seems paradoxical, since the aspects that characterize the new "popular" literature in Africa have always been present in Bemba's work; but in this novel Bemba combines them with irony and some of the Brechtian distancing elements to create a work to be read on many levels. One may read it as a combination adventure tale, detective story, love story, and historical romance, or see it as a gentle mocking of the quest for the epic. There are really two stories. Parts 1 and 3 present the story of a young Afro-American woman's search for the "historical Lumumba" (here named Fabrice M'Pfum). She ends up lost in the jungle with her young African guide, with whom she has fallen in love. This happily married father feels all too vulnerable "sans masque," having launched the expedition with only picnic supplies, wondering why he couldn't be Tarzan and vanquish the natural elements (341).[8] Framed by the story of the quest in the jungle (parody of the legend of Africa) is part 2, the "Roman de Fabrice M'Pfum," a scrambled version of the life of Patrice Lumumba, in which Bemba seems to enjoy playing with rearranging the story for his own literary purposes. The book, full of surprises yet realistic, puzzling yet satisfying, is hard to put down. It combines aspects of popular literature and serious art; structurally it is streamlined, more coherent, yet still rich in suggestions.

Patrice Lumumba, like Nelson Mandela, became an African mask during his lifetime. His inscrutable face was flashed around the world as an electronic image, a victory of minimalist art, since its essence was a certain pair of spectacles and a certain goatee. Bemba seems to have chosen Lumumba partly because of this "mask" attribute. He can lead us into a psychological hall of mirrors, let us glimpse the fragments of a personality, and attempt to reconstruct an identity, reconstruct a hero to our own liking, one that will be meaningful to us, as he is to Miss Nora Norton from Baltimore.[9]

Léopolis is Bemba's most playful novel, the most comic. Like Robbe-Grillet, he juggles clues, traces, objective correlatives, the projections left by a personality.[10] Bemba presents Fabrice as a Christ figure, a shooting star, a sort of Faust figure who sold his soul to become a national power, a solitary orphan, a black

sphinx, the nameless Everyman (97), the eloquent voice of his people with perfect memory who improvises perfectly structured speeches, but most centrally as "le joueur de dames génial," the crowned champion of a continent.

So far research has failed to turn up evidence that Lumumba played checkers, though it seems plausible. (His biographer Robin McKown mentions checkers being played on the Congo riverboats, an interesting intertextuality.) One wonders. Is this a *jeu de mots?* Fabrice is indeed as intoxicated with women as he is with intellectual problems. Unlike Robbe-Grillet's protagonists, who are good either at formal analysis or at playing the games of life and love, Fabrice is equally gifted in both areas. Like Achilles, he chooses the short yet glorious life, chooses to become a timeless mask, a martyr.

According to McKown, Lumumba was fascinated by the legendary America he discovered in his youth. Bemba emphasizes this connection, especially Fabrice's quick trip to the U.S., where he inspired black Americans. One of the most curious passages recounts a nightmare Fabrice has while flying over America to Mount Rushmore to visit the giant masks of stone. Fabrice foresees the assassination of JFK but is unable to move or cry out, is taken in the grip of the dead president, but finally succeeds in tearing off Kennedy's mask to reveal Xoxo (Kasavubu), his rival, who winks at him.[11]

Bemba puts most of the bizarre details of Lumumba's short life to good use in his imaginative novel but neglects perhaps the strangest of all, the well-documented CIA attempt to dispose of the Congolese prime minister in one of its first efforts at assassination. Most of the facts emerged in the "Interim Report of the Select Committee to Study Government Operations with Respect to Intelligence Activities" of the U.S. Senate in 1975 (pages 13–70), but Madeleine Kalb dug out further details by studying the secret dispatches. Sidney Gottlieb, top CIA scientist, brought a new secret poison to Leopoldville in September 1960 but was unable to get access to Lumumba.[12] Meanwhile, of course, the CIA was subverting Mobutu and conspiring with Tshombe and may have managed Lumumba's death trip to Katanga. It seems to be a significant literary decision on Bemba's part not to use this material, perhaps merely because he wants to emphasize the purely African sources and causes behind Fabrice/Lumumba's life and death.

At the end of the novel Nora Norton is asked, "Belle histoire . . . mais nous . . . qu'allons-nous dire à nos amis? que nous avons vu le Léopolis souterrain, habité par le fantôme de M'Pfum?" To which she responds:

"Pourquoi pas? . . . les héros sont faits pour qu'on les réinvente, chaque fois d'une manière différente" (121). This seems to reflect Bemba's own conception of hero, history, and story. With his characteristic tinge of marvelous realism[13] and his quixotic way of questioning history and established concepts with a quiet joke, Bemba retreats behind his authorial mask. Study the miniportrait on the back cover of *Rêves* and the fine portrait done of Patrice Lumumba by the United Nations. Same glasses, same tie, same suit, same expression. Two very similar masks.[14]

Hal Wylie, Winter 1990

[1] There is one evil genius, Moudandou in *Rêves* (who may be partly based on Mobutu), whose mask is the totally negative one of the impassive tyrant, the Tonton Macoute with impenetrable dark glasses: "A force de se composer un masque, il devient impénétrable jusqu'au mystère . . . sombre, ombrageux" (189).

[2] Nina D. Lyakhovskaya, "French-Language Comedy in Tropical Africa as a Form of Mass-Literature," *Research in African Literature,* Winter 1987, p. 461.

[3] Later in the same article Lyakhovskaya studies Bemba's dramatic methods, concluding: "Bemba used the usual means of the folk narrative tradition, specifically the traditional narration of fairy tales, fables, and legends. The folklore background . . . becomes . . . a stylistic device used for the benefit of mass consciousness—with the aim of explaining the ideological content of the comedy to the mass audience" (465). She adds: "The direct treatment of social ideas and conflicts, the ideologization of the plot, the use of newspaper propaganda language, maxims, declarations and indirect quotations . . . enhances didacticism" (466).

[4] Bemba puts this statement in the mouth of one of his characters, Georges Simon, a Belgian writer.

[5] It is interesting to note that Bemba has written both about his own country, the People's Republic of the Congo, the former French Congo or Congo-Brazzaville (many masks for one little country), and also about Zaïre, the former Belgian Congo, once known as Congo-Kinshasa. The country of Palms resembles Zaïre.

[6] I have already noted that the deadly minister of the interior resembles Mobutu.

[7] The black-skin-white-masks syndrome is critical in Ronald N'Gampika, a magistrate, who confronts his own alienation, especially from his mother and twin brother in the dramatic denouement: "Cet autre . . . se détachait de moi et me laissait seul en face de moi-même" (180). The mother with whom he must converse through an interpreter gives us the last characterization of him: "Pour mener aujourd'hui la vie d'un homme blanc, dois-tu arracher ta peau de Noir?" (181).

[8] This mention of Tarzan is another sign of Bemba's evolution. One of Bemba's first works was titled "Il faut tuer Tarzan" (1971). Now he seems to realize that a better tactic is to co-opt the white legend who had an impact upon black imaginations as well as white and is, for better or for worse, a manifestation of Africa.

[9] Of course, the question of the significance of the past is immediately posed. Nora leaves Africa having discovered that the liv-

ing African, nonhero, non-Tarzan, is more important to her than the legendary father of his country.

[10] Léopolis, the city of lions, was the city Fabrice came to dominate; it was destroyed by the usurper who overthrew him and left to mold back into the jungle, a taboo world off-limits. Lions have also been abolished, both as reality and as image. However, the more one seeks to banish an identity, the stronger it becomes, the more its attributes proliferate.

[11] Robin McKown, *Lumumba,* New York, Doubleday, 1969, p. 80.

[12] Madeline Kalb, *The Congo Cables,* New York, Macmillan, 1982, p. 102. The former U.S. secretary of defense, Frank Carlucci, was also in Leopoldville at the time; there is a body of evidence linking him to the CIA.

[13] See the interview "Le théâtre militant: Entretien avec Sylvain Bemba," *Notre Librairie,* September 1977, p. 91.

[14] This essay was first presented at the 1988 meeting of the African Literature Association in Dakar.

GHANA

Angled Shots and Reflections: On the Literary Essays of Ayi Kwei Armah

In contrast to other major African writers such as Wole Soyinka, Chinua Achebe, and Ngũgĩ wa Thiongo, who quite early in their careers realized the need to discuss their writing constantly in interviews, essays, and symposia, Ayi Kwei Armah has until recently remained a recluse. Believing that communication between the artist and his readers should be through the medium of the work, he once boasted:

> Many African writers discuss their work and themselves quite willingly, sometimes even eagerly, with Western critics, newspapermen, magazine pundits, radio commentators, television hosts and just plain dilettantes. That is their choice. I don't. I have no personal contact whatsoever with any Western critic of African literature. I have never granted any interview about my person or my work, no matter how prestigious the publication asking for it. That is my choice. I have never gone on lecture tours. I have never accepted invitations to go to Writers' Conferences. *And I have never, till now, found it necessary to write any article about my writing.*[1] (Emphasis added)

We should be grateful for Charles Larson's invidious comments,[2] which eventually rattled Armah out of his shell to take up the practice of the artist who is also a critic—a practice that has always been at the foundation of socially committed literature.

The tradition of practical criticism by which literary artists clarify their writings outside the creative works is by no means peculiar to Africa; in Western literature it has its roots in Johnson, Coleridge, and Dryden and was only later extended by such moderns as Woolf, Yeats, Eliot, and Pound. For African writers like Ngũgĩ, Achebe, and Soyinka, who conceive of literature as part and parcel of the liberation struggle of the oppressed African people, the practice naturally became a necessity from the very beginning of their writing, since these writers, who were seen as leading members of the revolution, did not wish to be viewed as aloof or ambiguous. Interview comments, lectures, addresses, articles, and symposia have over time become not only valid but indispensable supplements to the creative work of other African writers.

Armah may have learned in a roundabout way that African writers who discuss "their work and themselves quite willingly, sometimes even eagerly" seek for something far less trivial than fame and its privileges: they cry out for their message of hope, often the African point of view, to be heard in no uncertain terms. Armah, however, has properly taken his place among writers who, in Izevbaye's words, "create taste for [their] own type of literary compositions by prescribing literary criteria and standards which are often more valuable in the appreciation of [their] own works than for the criticism of other works."[3] A possible grouping of Armah's work of this category could be: a) the review essays "The Definitive Chaka" (1975/76), "The Caliban Complex" (1985), and "Battle for the Mind of Africa" (1987); b) incidental responses to criticism of his work, including "Larsony or Fiction as Criticism of Fiction" (1976) and "The Lazy School of Literary Criticism" (1985); c) sociopolitical theories, as elaborated in "African Socialism: Utopian or Scientific?" (1967) and "The Festival Syndrome" (1985); and d) such items as "One Writer's Education" (1985) and "Interview with Dimgba" (1986), which basically provide biographical insights on the writer.

Such a classification, though, is neat and simplistic; it is only valid as a convenient tool of analysis, because all the writings are linked by an obsessive preoccupation with the question of Africa's future. Armah isolates the colonization of the mind of the African—with all the attendant inferiority complexes—as the most devastating legacy of colonialism, an approach that is cultural, as opposed to the materialist view, which lays emphasis on economic exploitation. These are the issues with which the writer is concerned in his novels and short stories as well.

The most frequently recurring element in these works is the issue of an African perspective. It dominates Armah's very first published essay, "African Socialism: Utopian or Scientific?,"[4] which appeared in 1967, a year before the publication of his first novel, *The Beautyful Ones Are Not Yet Born* (1968),[5] with which the essay evinces a convergence of ideas. Deploring the absence of an ideology that could facilitate Africa's decolonization, Armah attacks Africa's leaders for their unimaginativeness. The leaders have been cut off from their roots by Western education. They have become greedy and opportunistic, subscribing to "an ethic that has everything to do with consumption and notoriously little to do with production of any sort" (AS, 15). In their desperation to safeguard their power, the leaders corrupt the urban workers, among whom they base their influence; they aspire to the elitist privileges associated with whites but are frustrated by their color. They are torn between two cultures and belong neither to the black world into which they are born nor to the white world for which their education has prepared them.

Armah presses home his point using the example of Senghor, whose Negritude he describes as an artistic statement that reflects the political leader's inferiority complexes, his slave mentality. Armah is quite harsh on Senghor, whose Negritude he calls a wooden attempt to perpetuate Western assumptions in reverse. His criticism of Senghor for "swooningly" extolling "the beauty of black womanhood" in poetry while being married to a white woman is superficial. Neither is Armah convincing in his declaration that Senghor is "a colonial political boss, necessarily janusfaced, guiltily hating and despising his black roots but being pushed back to them" (AS, 21).

It is all too easy now to overlook the historical significance of Negritude, which has played no mean role in establishing the humanity of black people before a world that denied them such a claim. Armah is a victim of this fallacy. Not even proximity—when Armah moved to Senegal, Senghor's country, in 1985—could temper his attitude; hence ten years later, in 1987, Armah still persisted in his outright condemnation of Negritude, calling the movement "a blind artistic summary of actual relations between Europeans and Africans from about the start of the slave trade to the latest adjustment programme designed in Washington, Paris, London or Rome for adoption and implementation by an African elite that still refuses, out of sheer inertial habit, to do its own thinking."[6]

Armah's commendation of Cheikh Anta Diop, the late Senegalese scholar, in the same breath points up the inconsistency in his thinking, since there is not much difference between Senghor's "false names of famous kings and glorious empires," to which Armah objected, and "the origins . . . indispensable beginnings of the long, continuing process of human civilization" Diop claims for Africa.[7] However, Armah is full of praises for Diop for being able to set out in "his lively, friendly and persistent fashion," to look at "the Western intellectual monument," without being overwhelmed. The significance of Diop, says Armah, is that he was able to probe beyond the fog of white racism to unearth the authentic African personality.

Armah's criticism of Nkrumah and Nyerere is similarly uncharitable. Although in its mood his own writing resembles Nkrumah's beliefs, he tells us that Nkrumah's "African personality and consciencism" are falsifications of African reality, doctrines designed to rehabilitate Nkrumah's battered psyche. Armah wrote that Nkrumah should have backed up his "exhibition of self" by relying on indigenous technology instead of imported Eastern and Western technology. This criticism oversimplifies the issue of self-reliance. Not even Nyerere's imagination appeared to Armah at this point adequate for the task of combating neocolonialism; hence Armah's description of Ujamaa's ideas as "the sort of simplistic formulae dispensed by the less astute religious orders" (AS, 25). Whereas Armah castigated Nkrumah for borrowing from the East, he lashed out at Nyerere for failing to borrow ideas from socialism as practiced in the East.

Armah is erratic on this issue, but there is no doubt the question of greatest concern to him is the nature of the flag independence gained by African nations and the fact that the African elite are slaves of their colonial masters. Armah laments that Africa is cursed with such slaves.

> It is not every age or every continent which can boast of fiery revolutionaries who have never ventured within the smelling distance of a revolution, of freedom fighters whose suits are made in Paris and whose hair-raising campaigns are fought and won in the scented beds of posh hotels, and of militant workers who ride to work in chauffeur-driven German Limousines. This is Africa's heroic age. (AS, 28)

This is the image in which Armah casts Christian Mohamed Tumbo, Africa's representative to the Anti-Drought Organization in "Halfway to Nirvana,"[8] a story in which he aptly employs drought as the symbol of neocolonial domination of Africa. In that story Tumbo, who works against ending Africa's problem instead of eradicating it as he should, symbolizes Africa's political leaders of all religious and ideological persuasion; but his name can also be seen more specifically as an indirect reference to Oliver Tambo, leader of the African National Congress of South Africa, and thus to the leadership of the liberation movements in Africa.

Although in substance Armah's observations reflect the corruption inherent in Africa, he exaggerates and makes sweeping generalizations that fail to take into account exceptions. Such is his criticism of the sumptuous life-style of African leaders in the midst of mass squalor and poverty and the way the ruling elite use ideology as a cover for their materialistic ways. This criticism cannot apply to Nyerere, for example; neither has Armah's prediction that the existing class distinction in Africa will lead to a revolution come about on the scale he has stressed.

Perhaps the most redeeming feature of Armah's criticism is his sincerity of purpose. Writers not infrequently drag out Africa's name to plead selfish causes, but Armah's commitment overrides all personal considerations. His eagerness to be seen as African is not gratuitous self-dramatization. The desire for the revival of Africa's heroic past, expressed in "The Definitive Chaka,"[9] for instance, is deeprooted. In praise of Mofolo's achievement with regard to his authentic picture of the legendary exploits of one of Africa's greatest nationalists, Armah makes the following revealing comment:

> Mofolo's *Chaka* is a masterpiece. It is also a work of art essentially African. By all accounts the book in its original Sesotho language is breath-takingly beautiful. Despite this excellence, or, to put it more accurately, precisely because of this excellence, the book never saw print. That is because its author wrote under the most unfavourable publishing circumstances any black artist has ever faced. He was writing for his fellow Africans, but no African individual or group owned a printing press, much less a publishing house. Mofolo was therefore entirely dependent upon whites—and missionary whites at that—for publication facilities. (DC, 13)

The two problems—of a black writing in an indigenous language and of an authentic African work confronting Western prejudice—are relevant to Armah's own career. Armah's first novel was almost suppressed for being too African.[10] The similarities with Mofolo are legion; and Armah allows us to see that the genius of Mofolo lay in his painstaking "labour of love," which enabled the writer to travel "all over Natal, South Africa, the site of Chaka's Zulu empire, gathering and checking background material for his book" from sources as authentic as "traditional historians, storytellers and poets among the Zulu people" (DC, 13).

This emphasis on fiction as mimesis of life, and on fidelity to actual experience, is equally reflected in Armah's novels and short stories, which are fictional recreations of his experiences around the world. Thus his first novel, *The Beautyful Ones Are Not Yet Born* (1968), and the story "An African Fable" (1968) mirror the spate of corruption that engulfed his native Ghana in the years immediately after independence; "Contact" (1965) and *Why Are We So Blest?* (1972), on the other hand, attempt to convey the feel of Armah's American experience; in the same vein, *Two Thousand Seasons* (1973) and *The Healers* (1978),[11] written when Armah lived in Tanzania from August 1970 to May 1976, demonstrate the influence of Nyerere's Ujamaa. Furthermore, these last two novels are, in a sense, imitative of Mofolo's *Chaka,* whose imaginative indulgence of traditional heroism Armah's work somewhat advances.

Given Armah's obsession with the African image, his belligerence toward George Lamming is justified. The quarrel is ideological and nonpersonal. In "The Caliban Complex"[12] the failure of Lamming, a West Indian, to understand his African roots is attributed to Western education (of which Armah says Lamming is a victim), an education which imparted on the colonial the false notion that "the non-westerner has no culture or literature comparable in historical depth with western culture or literature." Armah's criticism is based on the fact that Lamming succumbs to the equally false notion that to become "really cultured, literate and historically conscious, it will inevitably be through his assimilation into the mainstream of western civilization" (CC, 570).

Lamming's dependence on Shakespeare for "insights" on Africa in *The Pleasures of Exile,* "even when the Shakespearean mind gift is poisoned," is evidence of Lamming's mental unpreparedness to return to his roots. As Armah rightly states, "exile may be an unavoidable human predicament but the only lost soul is the soul that does not seek the way back home." Were exile simply a question of physical distance from home and not essentially spiritual separation, Lamming's brief visit to Africa would have restored his culturally dislocated personality. Armah argues that a more authentic return, of the sort Lamming could not achieve, one that could have had enduring results, "would have involved an intellectual return also." Armah asks the Lammings of the world, "victim(s) of the Western *Weltanschauung* . . . in Port Elizabeth and Durban and Mombasa . . . in London . . . Windhoek and Port Harcourt and Abidjan," to find evidence of Africa's contribution to world civilization left behind by our ancestors on "papyrus sheets, on wooden tablets on shards and Ostraca, and, most reassuringly of all, on lasting stone" (CC, 570).

A more pointed advancement of this conception of the relevance of the past to the present can be found in "The Lazy School of Literary Criticism," where Armah exhorts the critic to cultivate "a particularly solid grounding" in African history with which he can give

direction to contemporary society.[13] His other dictum expressed in this same essay, to the effect that "it is impossible to be a genuine critic of an art one hasn't, in practice, mastered," should not, however, be interpreted literally as an arrogant claim that encourages mystification and obscurity: seen correctly, it is a plea for collaboration between artists and critics in the creative endeavor; for only when readers feel with the same passion as the writer can they get the message.

> Literature is not about literature, any more than physics is about physics. In the same way that physics is about the environment, literature is a life discipline. Its substance consists of life reflections. Reflections of life. Reflections on life. An understanding of literature requires a corresponding understanding of that which it reflects, that on which it is a reflection. (LS, 355–56)

"The human value of literature," Armah adds, must lie in its ability to improve man's life on earth. Literature should stimulate us with questions such as, "What is the quality of our life now? How did it get this way? What are our future options?" Thus Armah lays emphasis on the social value of literature, like such fellow African writers as Sembène Ousmane, Ngũgĩ, Achebe, Okot p'Bitek, and a host of others.

The weight of "Larsony or Fiction as Criticism of Fiction" also lies primarily in the manner in which Armah, overreaching personal indignation, places the discussion in the overall context of African literature (L, 11–14). In addressing some critical responses to his work mainly by Western critics like Charles Larson, Armah naturally devotes a good deal of the paper to the issue of the audience to which he directs his writing, the question being invariably tied to the larger subject of a writer's commitment or lack thereof. The essay is generally expressed with elegance and vigor, in the tradition of Swift's "Modest Proposal." There are snatches of dispassionate and informative writing, however, a candor that is most evident in the passage where Armah cites his publishing history in support of the argument that he is so African that such Western publishing ventures as the Heinemann African Writers Series tried to sabotage the publication of his novels.[14]

The substance of this part of the paper is to adduce facts which refute allegations such as Larson's that Armah is so Western that Africans rejected him, that he had exiled himself in the West, and that he had said he no longer remembered his mother tongue, Akan. The allegation that Armah models his novels on the work of the Irish writer James Joyce is also challenged. Armah asks:

> By what occult means does Larson say I have absorbed the influence of Joyce when I've never

even once placed myself in contact with his work? Does Larson offer any textual evidence to back up his assertion?. . . . Ordinarily, a scholar indicates the source of this type of information [about Armah's having said he no longer remembered his mother tongue] as precisely as he can. But Larson does the opposite. He takes great care not to indicate in any way the source of his expert information about me. (L, 12)

The aphoristic *occult* in the above-quoted excerpt recalls Achebe's image of the harmattan in reference to the hostility of "colonialist criticism,"[15] which is unsympathetic and destructive. Even though Achebe fails to apply his own creed to Armah's work,[16] his disquiet about the framework of superstition within which colonialist criticism operates corresponds with Armah's in many respects. The major difference lies in the fact that whereas Achebe allows—a position of which Irele[17] is another well-known defender—that the Western critic of African literature who does his homework well and overcomes traditional prejudices can contribute meaningfully in the criticism of African literature, Armah makes a blanket condemnation of all Western critics.

What Armah regards as Larson's unaccommodating nature and intransigence leads him, in fact, to the conclusion that all Western critics are enemies of African writers. Larson's determination to damage Armah's image is underscored by the false information he persistently peddles about Armah's art and personality, with claims in *The Emergence of African Fiction* (1971) of Armah's having forgotten his mother tongue, of his exile, and of his debt to Joyce, graduating into the allegation in *Africa Report* (Spring 1974) of Armah's rejection by Africans. The key used by Western critics like Larson in their approach to African writing, Armah states, "and the way to all other pet assumptions of western racism is the claim that Africa is inferior and the West is superior." Larson's rumors attempt to prove the myth of the superiority of the West by denying that creativity, "the highest instance of human intelligence," can take place in Africa.[18]

Armah does not know Larson personally, and he has not revealed to Larson or anyone else information that could possibly be construed to support Larson's assertions: "It is within the framework of white western racist prejudices about Africa that Larson's assertions make sense" (L, 13). "For the benefit of anyone curious to know where I did get the organizing idea for *Fragments*," Armah reveals about the book in question, "it grew out of a conversation with my elder brother concerning the quality of life at home" (L, 12). Armah sends a disclaimer on the issue of exile, over which not only Larson but other critics such as Achebe, Obumselu Ben,

and Arthur Gakwandi[19] have taken him to task, and answers back that he travels outside Africa "by choice, and following a long-standing plan," like any other person: "As for travelling to countries in Africa, I do not even think I am in a foreign country as long as I'm here in Africa" (L, 12). In fact, Armah was "at home in Africa" when Larson placed him "physically in the west" to defend his racist claim that Africa naturally rejects talent.

In conclusion, Armah suggests that, to enable Larson to achieve his ambition of becoming the most popular "Western critic of African literature, his name a house-hold word," Larson's style be christened "Larsony, the judicious distortion of African truths to fit western prejudices" (L, 14). In all fairness, we should add that the cultural frontiers Armah erects are nonexistent, as there are obviously many Westerners who approach African writing with objectivity. Insularity of the sort Armah advocates is surely to be discouraged, although the point should also be conceded to him that honesty and assiduous openmindedness are essential to criticism, whether of African or any other literature. As Armah puts it in "The Lazy School of Literary Criticism": "Genuine scholars and critics address themselves to the author's work; their conclusions and insights, negative or positive, are backed up with serious textual spadework and analysis" (LS, 355). These are qualities that cut across races and are surely not the preserve of any one people.

There is nothing peculiarly African about the values that Armah's writing champions which confers special privilege on African critics. The notion of African culture which his works defend, poignantly articulated in his article "The Festival Syndrome,"[20] consists rather of universal life-giving forces placed in an African context. In that article Armah points out that for the authentic African culture we must go beyond festivals such as FESTAC, for instance, which he describes as "wasteful demonstrations of intellectual bankruptcy." "The most sensible demonstration of cultural awareness," he adds, "would be to use available resources" to ensure that Africans are able to contain the scourge of drought, famine, and poverty ravaging their continent. "Culture is a process, not an event," and its promotion should be regular and continuous, "not a haphazard scattering of spastic shows." Armah states that "the development of culture depends on a steady, sustained series of supportive activities whose primary quality is not a spectacular extravagance but a calm continuity."[21] He cites the examples of the Chinese, the Japanese, Americans, and Europeans as people who rely on their culture to improve their daily lives.

Armah warns that the failure to reactivate African culture will forever force Africans to remain dependent consumers of the products of others who create culture daily from their "publishing houses, television stations and movie industries working full time to promote their culture on the domestic level, but also to export it." This is the view of self-reliance reflected in the objectives of Baako, the central figure in *Fragments,* whose efforts to encourage productivity at Ghanavision (where he works) are, however, frustrated by the established dependency syndrome. Armah asks Africans to look inward into themselves, to improve their inventiveness and management strategies, to shun corruption, and to regain their self-reliance. From the foregoing, it can be seen that it would be simplistic to say that these qualities Armah would like to see restored are unique to Africa, just as are the claims of a critic[22] who argues that Armah leaves the impression in his writing that the same values are alien to Africa.

"Armah's Celebration of Silence,"[23] his first and only interview to date, is a summary restatement of some of the longstanding controversies surrounding his work and personality, but it is not sufficiently comprehensive. For instance, an opportunity is missed to confirm Armah's claim in an earlier paper ("One Writer's Education") as to how he dropped out of his undergraduate studies at Harvard on account of his response to white racism. Another gap that is not filled relates to information on the writer's formative years, childhood, and primary and secondary education, which could throw much-needed light on his writing.

Of the issues touched upon, the most salient are the burning allegations of debt to Western authors; Armah does not reopen the issue with Larson, but he is surprised that Achebe, a fellow African writer with whom Armah has much in common, should have capitulated and become a purveyor of what he regards to be Western racist assumptions: Armah, "who says he defers to Achebe as an elder in the literary world," writes Dimgba Igwe, asked Achebe when they met at Ibadan to substantiate the allegation of Western influences on Armah's work. Armah's wide travels in Africa, which he claims are research trips and further evidence of his pan-African perspective, receive adequate coverage, as do his views on the relationship between history and literature and the relevance of the past to the present. A sense of the past is an essential guide to the present and the future, and is best enhanced by knowledge of African languages; hence Armah has taken to learning Kiswahili and the ancient Egyptian hieroglyphic language in which the wealth of Africa's past civilization is encoded.

His interest is not really literature, however, Armah says, but rather practical action to bring about change for the better in society.

To me writing is still a very weak response to the enormous problems in Africa. If we can survive the multifarious onslaught of these problems, one had to acquire a weapon to match or neutralize the enemies. . . . I don't think writings have done much, created much impact in that regard. (ACS, 12)

Armah tells us he would want to "go into the people's life" to "actually affect them and get involved." This objective is analogous to the goal of the Ghanaian scholar Modin Dofu, in Armah's third novel *Why Are We So Blest?,* who, like Armah, gives up his studies in his final year at Radcliffe and returns to Africa to enlist in a liberation movement. The faith in action also explains Armah's respect for Wole Soyinka. Armah describes Soyinka's novel *Season of Anomy* as "one of the greatest works in the world today if only people will read it carefully and check out his allusions, his imageries and so on" (ACS, 12).

Armah's defense of Soyinka's obscurantism lacks merit, however, for his own works are not as labored, even if his conception of the value of revolutionary violence in *Two Thousand Seasons* corresponds fairly closely to Soyinka's in *Season of Anomy* (we cannot talk of direct borrowing, because the two novels appeared in the same year). Similarly, Armah expresses a lack of faith in the power of the written work but proceeds apace to plead the cause of writers: "The publishers do not promote books in a realistic fashion. Why are there no serious book clubs in Africa? No good marketing strategies and so on? I think the publishers should support writers with appropriate remuneration to sustain them." These issues are part of the paradox of the African writer, who is conscious of the limitations imposed by the form within which he functions in his own kind of setting yet faces a situation in which no viable alternatives suggest themselves.

Often the result is a profound uncertainty, which threatens to bring about a complete paralysis of the creative intellect; it may also explain why, more than a decade since the appearance of *The Healers* in 1978, Armah has not returned to the novel. Writing is surely in some way a poor means of trying to reach the grassroots populace in a largely analphabetic society such as Africa. It is the awareness of this fact that has led writers like Ousmane and Ngūgī to explore other, more direct modes such as the cinema and the theater. Still, there can be no guarantee that a writer who branches out to these other areas will achieve better results. So it will be interesting to see how Armah faces this problem in the future, and his next work will be eagerly awaited.

Because of the crosscurrents of ideas and concerns running through them, all Armah's essays to date should be considered as one unified piece of writing, which helps us more fully to understand his creative work. Vituperation animates the early papers, especially "Larsony, or Fiction as Criticism of Fiction," but there is now a movement toward increasing calm in the more recent articles. Without diminishing his commitment, Armah has continued to speak with greater clarity of vision and openness. Contradictions such as those that bedeviled the earlier work have happily disappeared from the more recent writings, and there is a promise that Armah is yet to produce his best work.

Ode S. Ogede, Summer 1992

[1] Ayi Kwei Armah, "Larsony, or Fiction as Criticism of Fiction," *Asemka,* 4 (1976), pp. 1–4. All quotations are from the reprint in *Positive Review,* 1978, pp. 11–14. Subsequent references use the abbreviation L.

[2] Charles Larson, *The Emergence of African Fiction,* Bloomington, Indiana University Press, 1971; rev. ed., London, Macmillan, 1978; and *Africa Report,* Spring 1974.

[3] D. S. Izevbaye, "Criticism and Literature in Africa," in *Perspectives on African Literature,* Christopher Heywood, ed., London, Heinemann, 1971, p. 27.

[4] Ayi Kwei Armah, "African Socialism: Utopian or Scientific?," *Présence Africaine,* 68 (1967), pp. 7–30. Subsequent references use the abbreviation AS.

[5] Ayi Kwei Armah, *The Beautyful Ones Are Not Yet Born,* Boston, Houghton Mifflin, 1968; reissued in London by Heinemann in 1969.

[6] Ayi Kwei Armah, "Battle for the Mind of Africa," *South,* August 1987, p. 62.

[7] Ibid.

[8] Ayi Kwei Armah, "Halfway to Nirvana," *West Africa,* 24 September 1984, pp. 1947–48.

[9] Ayi Kwei Armah, "The Definitive Chaka," *Transition,* 50 (October 1975—March 1976), pp. 10–13. Subsequent references use the abbreviation DC.

[10] See Armah, "Larsony," pp. 11–12 for detailed information on this sensitive issue.

[11] Ayi Kwei Armah, "Contact," *The New African,* December 1965, pp. 244–46; *Why Are We So Blest?,* New York, Doubleday, 1972; *Two Thousand Seasons,* Nairobi, East African Publishing House, 1973; *The Healers,* Nairobi, East African Publishing House, 1978.

[12] Ayi Kwei Armah, "The Caliban Complex," *West Africa,* 18 March 1985, pp. 521–22, and 25 March 1985, pp. 570–71. Subsequent references use the abbreviation CC.

[13] Ayi Kwei Armah, "The Lazy School of Literary Criticism," *West Africa,* 25 February 1985, pp. 355–56. Subsequent references use the abbreviation LS.

[14] It seems to me that Sandra Barkan's cogent argument in her article "Beyond Larsony: On the Possibility of Understanding Texts Across Cultures" (*WLT* 57:1 [Winter 1983], pp. 35–38) suffers from her omission to tackle this important aspect of Armah's essay.

[15] Chinua Achebe, "Colonialist Criticism," in his *Morning Yet on Creation Day,* London, Heinemann, 1975, pp. 3–18.

[16] For details on Achebe's unsympathetic and subjective criticism of Armah's novels, see "Africa and Her Writers," in *Morning Yet on Creation Day,* pp. 19–29; and *Issue: A Quarterly Journal of Opinion,* 6:1 (Spring 1976), p. 37.

[17] Abiola Irele, "The Criticism of Modern African Literature," in *Perspectives on African Literature,* pp. 9–24.

[18] Sandra Barkan has, of course, exposed the shallowness of this assumption. See her article "Beyond Larsony."

[19] Obumselu Ben, "Marx, Politics and the African Novel, *Twentieth Century Studies,* 10 (1973), pp. 114–17; Arthur Gakwandi, *The Novel and Contemporary Experience in Africa,* London, Heinemann, 1977, pp. 87–99.

[20] Ayi Kwei Armah, "The Festival Syndrome," *West Africa,* 15 April 1985, pp. 726–27.

[21] Ibid., p. 726.

[22] See Ama Ata Aidoo's preface to the American edition of *The Beautyful Ones Are Not Yet Born,* New York, Collier/Macmillan, 1969.

[23] Dimgba Igwe, "Armah's Celebration of Silence," *Concord* (Lagos), 12 April 1987, pp. 11–12. Subsequent references use the abbreviation ACS.

The Metaphysical and Material Worlds: Ayi Kwei Armah's Ritual Cycle

At the beginning of Ayi Kwei Armah's second novel, *Fragments* (1974), the grandmother Naana, who is the novel's repository of traditional wisdom, speaks of "the way everything goes and turns around. . . . All that goes returns."[1] This might serve as a coda for Armah's fiction, in which almost everything moves in circles. In his first novel the cycles through which Africa's political regimes rise and fall shrink satirically to the dimensions of the human physiological circuit's daily cycle of ingestion and evacuation. This is then countered by an outward expansion, through further spirals of weekly and monthly cycles, toward the climactic calendrical evacuation of the nation's corruption at the novel's end.[2] In *Fragments* wheels move within wheels through a web of simultaneous cycles. The traditional religious concept of a continuous circuit of passage through a world of ancestor spirits, into which this world's dying are reborn and from which outgoing spirits become the material world's new births, is given a warped parody in the ritual "death," spiritualization, and ghostly return of modern Ghana's cargo-bringers. "The main export to the other world is people," runs Baako's cargo-theory. "The true dead going back to the ancestors, the ritual dead" (223). In Armah's third novel, *Why Are We So Blest?* (1974),[3] a figurative theology of neocolonialism borrowed from Fanon transforms the familiar circular passage into the carefully monitored voyage of intellectual "factors" between America and Africa, variously represented as the lands of the blessed and the damned, Olympus and Tartarus, the Center and the Periphery, the sacred and the profane worlds.

In each novel the cyclical journey is placed in the context of calendrical ritual. In *The Beautyful Ones Are Not Yet Born* (1969) the decline of the Nkrumah regime is played off against an end-of-the-year purification rite. In *Fragments* the birth and death of Araba's short-lived child, sacrificed to make money at a premature out-dooring ceremony, hinge on the autumnal equinox which marks the changing of the Akan agricultural year.[4] One "traditional" reading of the death invited by the ritual symbolism is that angry earth spirits have re-claimed the child to punish those who abuse its fertility at a time when this is ritually renewed. The murder of Modin at the end of *Why Are We So Blest?*, which pun-ishes his attempt at a Promethean "reverse crossing" from America to Africa, follows his twelfth diary entry and coincides with the start of the twelve-day changeover from the old to the new year on the Western Christian calendar. (Armah's love of numerological symmetries is also evident in the recurrence of the num-bers 5 and 7 throughout his work and the structuring of the chapters of *Fragments* around the thirteen lunar months of the Akan year.)

The novels' ritual metaphors hold out the respec-tive prospects of purification, sacrificial regeneration, and Promethean deliverance, but always against a fore-ground of negative or destructive action. The anony-mous man returns from his purifying sea journey to an unredeemed world where "nothing changes" and cor-rupt regimes come and go, the next no better than the last. Naana's despair of this world's impenitent material-ism and resigned retreat into the next is held in balance, at the end of the second novel, with Baako's despair and disintegration in the world and his escape into madness. The worthwhile Prometheian endeavor with which the myth structure dignifies Modin's death is checked by Solo's verdict of "useless, unregenerative destruction" (*W*, 263). It will be the aim of this short article to take some account of the twofold nature of Armah's ritual cycle and the implications of its ability to operate in two mutually exclusive orders.

▪ ▪ ▪

In traditional African belief the function of ritual is to hold in place the walls of a sacred cycle of being: it en-sures the contiguity of the cycle's interdependent phases of birth and death, arrival and departure, childhood and spirithood, in the light of the belief that a going in one world is always a coming in another. The Akan mean-ings of Naana's name—grandparent, grandchild, ances-

tor—reveal a verbal continuum which reflects the inter-connectedness of their referents in the cycle. Prayers to or through ancestors for fertilility indicate the power of the dead over birth[5] and, proportionately, of outgoing over incoming lives. The not-yet-born turn in a wheel of dependency with the elders who are not yet dead, and the undisturbed continuity of this cycle is para-mount: the neglect of one end of the continuum inter-feres with developments at the other. Thus the inability of Araba's children to be born in *Fragments*—she has five miscarriages, one for each year of Baako's exile—has something to do with the deterioration of Naana's position in the family from that of an elder who can still assert superior rights at libation ceremonies (at Baako's departure) to that of one who, five years later at Baako's return, has no rights at all.

This sacred cycle, however, functions only in one of Armah's two orders of experience, the "metaphysi-cal," as opposed to the "material." Whenever rituality and cyclicality converge in a religious or metaphysical context in the novels, the evaluation is positive; when they meet in a material context, the evaluation is nega-tive. In the first novel the "metaphysical" meeting stands, to a limited extent, in redemptive opposition to the "material" one, playing off ritual hope against nega-tive material events. At the end of the novel the man carries to sea the corruption of the fallen regime in the form of Koomson. In the wake of this definitive purifi-cation ritual and in the presence of the sea's creative-destructive cycle, the man comes to a confirmation of an almost mystical perception of nature, which has been growing steadily, or is at least intermittently present, throughout the novel. In nature's ongoing regenerative process, corruption is seen not as an absolute evil but as a necessary part in a dynamic continuity, out of which grow new flowerings from dung, new seeds from rotten fruit, new life from death and decomposition. The disconnective purification in a rite of separation and expulsion is itself a stage in an unbroken cycle, a part of the interconnectedness of all things. Meanwhile, at the psychological level, this metaphysical mysticism is merely another stage in the man's inner debate, an-other round of moral musings which need have no final value.

In *Fragments,* where Naana's beliefs are of a more specifically religious nature and their value more defi-nite if not more absolute than the man's, the unbroken-ness of the cycle is maintained by the performance of ritual acts such as libation, prayer, sacrifice, and the of-fering of thanks. To honor the dead is to safeguard the living. Only by the flawless observance of these rites, which means balking Foli when he tries to cheat the an-cestors of their due, can the cycle of death and rebirth, departure and safe return, be kept whole and in motion: "Nothing at all was left out. The uncle called upon the nephew the protection of the old ones gone before. The circle was not broken. The departed one will return" (*F,* 5). Thus, although Efua, of the modern generation, fears that Baako may never return from the United States, Naana adheres to a traditional faith in ritual efficacy.

In Armah's early novels the circle has already been irreparably broken by the incursions of the West, its metaphysic undermined by materialism. Ritual is emptied of value by a separation of meaning from form which steers attention away from the inherent power resident within ritual properties and occasions to their outward show. Hence the strangely disembodied descriptive style of *Fragments,* the obsessive lingering on hard shiny surfaces, the awe of language in the presence of material objects. The furniture of festivals is turned into spiritless objects—the kente cloth Brempong tramples on, the libations poured down human throats—which are greedily exploited to procure more of the same. Ritual performance loses its place in a wider religious cycle of events and is connected instead to a cargo circuit of commodities. Its modern degradation leads not to a departure from the psychology of cyclical process but to an impatient acceleration of that process in its diversion to profit-making purposes. The first cycle of the child's life in *Fragments* is shortened from seven to five days, following an already accelerated gestation period: its poetic corollary is the rapid circular motion of the icy electric fan that scatters the collection money at the five-day outdooring and dispatches the child to the other world from which it has barely arrived. The misplaced emphasis on Baako's beneficial return even before his departure has the same effect of blasphemously accelerating the circular process of outward and return passage. At this speed, fragile things—and oversensitive been-to's—fragment. Taken too quickly, things fly apart in giddy atomization, like the whirling banknotes and shattered television screens of the novel.

The higher cyclicalism of the spirit occupies minority space in the novels: the man's nature-metaphysics, Naana's religious beliefs, the mystical concept of return to an African "Way" in Armah's historical fantasy.[6] Its peripheral passage is toward release, restoration, or regeneration, and death is not final but a translation to a different level. Naana's traditional beliefs imply progress or at least a salvaging, holding action. They urge the conservation of value: "Each thing that goes away returns and nothing in the end is lost" (*F,* 1). In its metaphysical form the circle is, traditionally (in Africa and the West), a symbol of perfection, completion, fulfillment. The ritual observances which sustain it have positive associations: for Naana "the traveler's drink of cere-

mony" is a hallowed property and the "perfect words" of the libation ceremonial retain their intrinsic beauty even in the mouth of "the drunken Foli. . . . Even Foli felt their presence" (*F,* 4, 5, 9).

In its material counterpart, however, the cycle signifies only futile repetition and recurrence. Even "renewal" is a misleading word for this process, because what is renewed is the old order which was there before, so that, as the first novel oppressively insists, "nothing changes." The metaphysical spiral of expansive release is here countered by an inward motion of narrowing entrapment. The former's conservation of recycled energy is matched by the modern materialistic ritual's conspicuous waste, as in the squandering of expensive foreign drinks at Brempong's reception ceremony or the gratuitous exhibition of wealth at the outdooring. In the material context the circle has only a negative form: the circle of impending doom closing in upon Baako and the mad dog; the circle of the abandoned, oppressed by the privileged square in Baako's screenplay; the circle of frustrated, self-enclosed art suggested by Ocran's ring of statues; the "senseless cycles" of the poor and the "horrible cycles of the powerless" in the first novel; the endless, immeasurable circumference of the "periphery" magnetized to the oppressive "centre" in Modin's paradigm of neocolonialism.

The deflection back upon itself of the passage from captivity toward liberation is a recurring motif in the novels. In *Two Thousand Seasons* (1979) the return of the escapees from the slave boat to a society which has been entirely enslaved during their absence repeats fictionally, and anticipates historically, the fate of the been-to who returns from America to an Africa which is more Western than the West. It is the manipulative foreign control of these circular operations, notably the system of educational "factorship" that takes intellectual slaves abroad and programs them for an eventual return as Westernized oppressors, which earns for the words *ritual, ceremony,* and *cycle* their darkest and most derogatory connotations in Armah's work. An indigenous equivalent is ceremonialized in Baako's screenplay "The Brand." In this work the periodic isolation and absorption of potential deliverers of the enslaved circle by the privileged of the square is calculated to frustrate any energies directed toward change. The predictable success of this project is crowned with "a repeated ritual of congratulation and sustained praise" (*F,* 213).

Armah often gives to the word *ritual* its ordinarily negative implications: a mechanical, meaningless ceremonial, thoughtlessly gone through; an unprofitably repeated observance, granting an excessive, undue importance to a fossilized form; something merely procedural or gestural, tokenlike or symbolic, unreal rather than vital with magical potency. The manufactured rite of Brempong's reception is wholly illusion, "an invitation into a pretended world, happily given, happily taken, so completely accepted that there had hardly been any of the pretenders to whom it could have seemed unreal" (*F,* 88). In reality little has happened: "A man had gone away, spent time else-where, grown months and years, and then returned. Those he had left behind had spent time too, grown along their different waves, waiting to welcome their traveler" (*F,* 88). The ritual is designed to conceal from feted and feters alike their real power-lessness and emptiness. Korankye, the hunchback who performs a mockery of a sacrifice on the morning of the outdooring ceremony, brings the ram from the Onipa's ancestral village, suggestively named "Kotse-ye-Aboa"—in Akan, "for the ceremony."[7] Shorn of its true significance, the outdooring is mere ceremonial, done for itself. "The ceremony you ought to understand," Naana tells Baako, "or where do you get the meaning of it, even if it is done right?" (*F,* 139).

In *Why Are We So Blest?,* however, rituals are not merely empty but menacing and malign things, in both their real and figurative forms. In Modin's notebook meditations the word *ritual* hammers obsessively at the attention. Here, for example, is his account of the Western education system, which leaves the African student inferiorized, exploited, and dependent.

> I should have stopped going to lectures long ago. They all form a part of a ritual celebrating a tradition called great because it is European, Western, white. The triumphant assumption of a superior community underlies them all, an assumption designed to reduce us to invisibility while magnifying whiteness. My participation in this kind of ritual made me not just lonely, not just one person unsupported by a larger whole, but less than one person: a person split, fractured because of my participation in alien communal rituals designed to break me and my kind. (*W,* 31–32)

The "invisibility" taken on by the liminal in this ritual is not something in process; it is meant to be permanent and to fracture his links with the "larger whole." Since such rituals are intended to isolate and exclude the African, their communality is alien. In this novel "rituals" are actively evil, grotesquely artificial arrangements purposefully "designed" to do harm, and Modin's ritual murder by whites in the desert is the culminating point in a conspiratorial cult-practice. Armah draws upon the word's more sinister associations of occult secrecy and superstition, cabalistic obscurantism and mystification.

> In the imperial situation the educational process is turned into an elitist ritual for selecting slave traders. . . . In the system the factor is a link that must be hidden . . . his functioning is secret. Thick walls, the elaborate rituals of our education. This is all a system for hiding our factorship from the victims we make, our own people. There is no justification in this kind of system. Instead of justification, the rites of secrecy, mystification. (*W,* 222–23)

The occult ritualization of the educational cycle by Western powers releases associations of such horror in Baako that, after his return from America, he is unable to conceive the idea of return, even in memory, without experiencing panic and nausea. The sight of the outgoing students at Oeran's school fills him not with nostalgia but with "a semblance of panic, as if time could absorb him into itself and drive him along the edge of some endless, vertiginous cycle over and over again" (*F,* 112). Even Araba's child is able to evoke a terror of the educational passage: "Babyhood, infancy, going to school . . . the thought of a person having to go through the whole cycle again brought back his nausea, and suddenly the room to him felt too humid, too full with the mother, the child and him" (*F,* 122). In the first half of *Why Are We So Blest?* the sickening oscillation of Modin's monologues between his departure for and departure from the United States, moving alternately backward and forward in time, arouses the same debilitating sensation of entrapment within a closed circle.

The cycle in its metaphysical conception is something which the man and Naana, in their different ways, can find comfort in, become resigned to, and retreat into. Its materialization, however, into a pernicious neo-colonial form in the educational politics practiced by the West is a phenomenon which can only be challenged and resisted. In the case of the former, the most important thing is for ritual to keep unbroken the cycle it inaugurates; in its latter manifestation the cycle must be broken at all costs if Africa is to be released from its eternal roundabout of dependency and exploitation. The ritual forms which Naana alone still prizes are survivals from a traditional Africa, but those which haunt contemporary Ghana's new hearths and altars—the airports and hotel lounges—appear rather as alien forms imposed upon Africa from outside. Baako explains to his horrified grandmother that the outdooring, a wholly Europeanized affair conducted by men in tuxedos and waistcoats, is "a new festival," only distantly related to the traditional rite which marked the child's entry into the material world and offered thanks to the ancestors. The same is essentially true of Brempong's reception ceremony, with its very faint echoes of tribal panegyric and the outdooring of chiefs.

> In the end they had come waiting for him with a ceremony in their hearts, and amazingly it had

happened that whatever strange ceremony he had been rehearsing inside his own being had been a perfect answer to theirs. Amazing, since these had been no mere laid-down ceremonies, but things growing with an obvious, wild freedom right here and now. (*F*, 88)

The ceremony is really a new form, invented with a mystical collective spontaneity and catering, in its own ridiculous way, to the dislocated worshiping impulses left behind by a forsaken religion.

One should be wary of translating the idiosyncratic rituality of Armah's cyclical structures into the terms of conventional rites of passage, except in an ironic way. Armah has written in one of the polemical essays of the been-to's pseudorite of passage, which "includes the heroic initiation drama of the crossing of that geographical gulf separating metropolitan centers from the provincial outlands."[8] This rite, though, may take the "initiate" out of the ritual cycle altogether, leaving him liminally stranded between his phase of passage and the society to which he is unable to make a reverse crossing (Baako and Modin, but also Teacher, an indigenous been-to whose marginality has become a permanent condition). Alternatively, as in the more customary case of Brempong, the completed "rite" returns him to the community, not to reenergize it from within but to deepen its oppression from without. The largely ironic presence of a fatalistic ritual pattern draws attention to the failure of a revolutionary recharging of the system, Modin speaks of his entrapment in a cycle of fragmented isolation and frustrating contact, a cycle not of liberation but destruction (*W*, 157–58). The horrifying parody rite of pubertal circumcision at the end of the novel marks the passage into a senseless death, not a new phase of life. Victor Turner has written of the dialectic between social structures and the recharging energy of "liminal communitas" which is generated in the course of a rite of passage.

> There is a dialectic here, for the immediacy of communitas gives way to the mediacy of structure, while, in *rites de passage*, men are released from structure into communitas only to return to structure revitalised by their experience of communitas. What is certain is that no society can function adequately without this dialectic.[9]

Clearly, this revitalizing cyclical interflow of one form into another does not take place in the moribund structure of Armah's Ghana, a society which seems content to function inadequately. Historically, the been-to has a limited and diminishing value as a ritual passenger, the main reason being that he is not, in any radical sense, changed and shows less and less inclination to change the society he returns to. He is not a force for regeneration, to which his society is not, in any case, susceptible. The liminal death awarded to the outgoing been-to is an empty ceremonial which corresponds to nothing in reality, since the ritualized passage entails no suffering and little personal transformation except for a few sensitive souls: Baako undergoes the mental death of breakdown and madness, Modin the trauma of isolation and then actual death. Only the untypical ones, who bring an intangible and unrecognized cargo, return altered and remain in the grip of a kind of death process. For the average half-westernized African youth of the post-Independence period, who is already, perhaps, in aspiration the "swinging nigger" of the taxi driver's Americanized jargon, residence abroad is no longer the vicious cycle of inferiorization described in *Black Skin, White Masks;* it has long ceased to be the purgatorial process which Armah's Anglophone been-to's have mysteriously inherited from Fanon.[10] For the mundane majority, the been-*to* experience is not an ordeal they have been *through*. The nearest Armah gets to the collective turmoil of a revolutionary return is the traumatized soldiers of the first novel: these are sent back altered from the white war to spread new fashions, needs, and violences, which send shock waves through the colonial society. The Brempongs and Asante-Smiths of the 1960s, however, return full of the materialistic pomp and power that Africa sent them forth to acquire, and they conform to expectations by feeding back into their societies more of what keeps the latter stagnant, unproductive, and dependent. Apart from the Baakos and Modins, who are totally isolated by their exceptional status, Armah's been-to cycle is a complacently monolithic continuum, not a process of transitional upheaval and regenerative chaos like the one undergone by the liminal neophyte in Turner's structural model. In these novels ritual backdrops are used guardedly by an author who is constantly suspicious of their relevance. Predominantly ironic patternings establish what is effectively a series of oppositions between ritual and reality.

Finally, what value have those rituals which do survive, in one debased and corrupted form or another, into contemporary practice? Danièle Stewart has written: "Armah insists particularly on the *degradation* of old customs: not their disappearance, which he probably would not mind, but their absurd adaptation to the demands of a consumer society."[11] Doubtless, there is a pragmatist somewhere in Armah who would prefer that these ancient customs, along with traditional myths, disappear altogether instead of lingering on to lend a spurious legitimacy to evil modern practices. In *The Beautyful Ones Are Not Yet Born* gifts of kola are perverted from honorable tokens of respect and hospitality into shameless bribes, and traditional proverbs are twisted out of their customary meanings to defend the practice. The lengthy funeral rites of ancient village custom become the pretext by which a corrupt urban clerk endlessly extends his holidays. In *Fragments* libation is an excuse for Foli's bibulous indulgence, Korankye's sacrifice of the ram to mark the reception of the child is desecrated by an irreverence more appropriate to a drunken feast, and the Mammy Water myth survives the assault of the modern media only in the form of Akosua Russell's execrable piece of propaganda on the electrification of Amosema village.

There is also a subdued idealistic, perhaps even sentimental element in Armah's vision which prevents these modern desecrations from diminishing entirely the traditional value and importance of custom. In *Fragments,* a work saturated in Akan ritual and mythology, a weight of almost "objective" worth protects hallowed forms, preserves vestiges of their preperverted conditions, and survives their violation by an impatient modern materialism. The elegant, dirgelike solemnity of the words of the libation, surrounded by Naana's poetic reverie, recaptures some of the dignity and wisdom of ancient beliefs about the importance of ancestors in the eternal cycle of being. Naana manages to convey enough of the spiritual meaning and practical wisdom of the original outdooring ritual to convince her grandson, who understands too little to share her anger, that he should listen to her more often. Finally, and most important, ritual has a special relationship with time. It marks off especially significant moments and periods on the event calendar and usually involves, by its temporary suspension of normal activity, a more intense apprehension of time's passage. Mbiti writes of African birth rites.

> His birth is a slow process which is finalised long after the person has been physically born. In many societies, a person is not considered a full human being until he has gone through the whole process of physical birth, naming ceremonies, puberty and initiation rites, and finally marriage (or even procreation). Then he is fully "born", he is a complete person.[12]

In such matters as birth, the moral implications which inform the metaphysic of ritual carry over and have direct consequences in the material world. The failure of Armah's stagnant consumer society to progress beyond an infantile materialism toward full maturity is expressed in the greedy acceleration of the outdooring ceremony which speeds Araba's child in and out of the world before it has completed the first phase of its "birth." This profanity against natural time-process is multiplied by Foli's cargoist eagerness that

Baako should no sooner go than return laden with gifts, and by his mother's impetuous commencement on a dream house for him even before he has returned. Naana compares the sacrifice of the child with the eating of unripe fruit by people "who have forgotten that fruit is not a gathered gift of the instant but seed hidden in the earth and tended and waited for and allowed to grow" (*F,* 282–83). Nothing in Armah's early novels is given sufficient time and care to get properly "born," a gradual process valorized by ritual. Araba's child is premature, Oyo's in the first novel is "dragged out of its mother's womb" (*B,* 98). The newly born Independent Ghana, in *The Beautyful Ones Are Not Yet Born,* is given the symbolic form of a progeric child: like the real child in *Fragments,* this creature is exposed too soon to a deadening, stultifying Western materialism unchecked by any moral vision, with the result that its deathly birth is followed by a rapid decline into age (*B,* 63). The landscapes in the third novel are blasted with a sterility and impotence which match the humanly incomplete characters. If there are no "beautyful ones" among Armah's people, it is because, in the ritual sense, they "are not yet born."

Derek Wright, Summer 1985

[1] Ayi Kwei Armah, *Fragments,* London, Heinemann, 1974, p. 1. Further page references are given parenthetically in the text, using the abbreviation *F.*

[2] Ayi Kwei Armah, *The Beautyful Ones Are Not Yet Born,* London, Heinemann, 1969. Page references are given parenthetically in the text, using the abbreviation *B,* and are taken from the 1975 reset Heinemann edition.

[3] Ayi Kwei Armah, *Why Are We So Blest?.* London, Heinemann, 1974. Page references are given parenthetically in the text, using the abbreviation *W.*

[4] Eva Meyerovitz, *The Sacred State of the Akan,* London, Faber, 1951, p. 142.

[5] Geoffrey Parrinder, *West African Religion,* 3rd ed., London, Epworth, 1969, p. 115.

[6] Ayi Kwei Armah, *Two Thousand Seasons,* London, Heinemann, 1979.

[7] Kofi Yankson, "Fragments: The Eagle That Refused to Soar," *Asemka,* 1:1 (1974), p. 57.

[8] Ayi Kwei Armah, "A Mystification: African Independence Revalued," *Pan-African Journal,* 2:2 (1969), p. 146.

[9] Victor Turner, *The Ritual Process,* Harmondsworth, Eng., Pelican, 1974, p. 116.

[10] Frantz Fanon, *Black Skin, White Masks,* Charles Lam Markmann, tr., New York, Grove, 1967, p. 116.

[11] Danièle Stewart, "Disillusionment among Anglophone and Francophone African Writers," *Studies in Black Literature,* 7:1 (1976), p. 8.

[12] John S. Mbiti, *African Religions and Philosophy,* London, Heinemann, 1969, p. 25.

Ngũgĩ wa Thiong'o (*Robert H. Taylor*)

KENYA

Literary Criticism as Social Philippic and Personal Exorcism: Ngũgĩ wa Thiong'o's Critical Writings

Over the last two decades, Ngũgĩ wa Thiong'o's critical writings have increasingly insisted on the integral relationship between literature and society. His own experiences have confirmed this link. After his detention by the Kenyan government, from 31 December 1977 to 12 December 1978, Ngũgĩ was denied reinstatement to his chair in the department of literature at the University of Nairobi. In April 1982 police and soldiers disrupted, then later pulled down, the theatre which housed his latest collaborative Gikuyu-language play in his hometown of Limuru. Today Ngũgĩ lives in London, far from that region where he had for years been living, working, and learning "at the feet of the Kenyan peasant and worker."

An examination of his essays, articles, and speeches, collected in *Homecoming* (1972) and *Writers in Politics* (1981),[1] reveals the growing rift between Ngũgĩ and his government's cultural and economic policies. They suggest that many of the contradictions that plague contemporary Africa are to be found within Ngũgĩ himself. His introduction to *Homecoming* touches on the contrasts between creative writing and the essay.

> In a novel the writer is totally immersed in a world of imagination which is other than his conscious self. At his most intense and creative the writer is transfigured, he is possessed, he becomes a medium. In essay the writer can be more direct, didactic, polemical . . . his conscious self is here more at work. Nevertheless, the boundaries of his imagination are limited by the writer's beliefs, interests, and experiences in life, by where in fact he stands in the world of social relations. (xv)

These thoughts are echoed yet restructured, to emphasize the latter qualification, in his prefatory remarks for

Writers in Politics. Ngũgĩ stresses the conscious, or committed, persona of the writer when he states:

> Literature cannot escape from the class power structures that shape our everyday life. Here a writer has no choice. Whether or not he is aware of it, his words reflect one or more aspects of the intense economic, political, cultural and ideological struggles in a society. What he can choose is one or the other side of the battle field: the side of the people or the side of those social forces and classes that try to keep people down. (xii)

In this more recent pronouncement the writer can no longer afford to be simply "transformed," "possessed," or the "medium" of creative muses, but must respond to specific social conditions that cry out for attention. Ngũgĩ chooses to make his points, especially in his more recent writings, in a very blunt manner. For scholars who are used to the niceties of criticism couched in dense exposition or tempered phrases, Ngũgĩ's is a particularly disturbing voice, a direct and relentless conscience, repetitive to the point of tedium, and challenging in a most confrontational way. To find a path through the foliage of rhetoric, the key to "reading" Ngũgĩ's ideas is to consider his artistic and scholarly growth, and the audience for his remarks.

Ngũgĩ's position on literature and its intersection with society can be considered in three main groupings. First, he critically appraises the destructive forces, literary-cultural and economic, which stem from the imperial presence of Europe in Africa. These colonial and, later, neocolonial factors are materially and spiritually damaging to the continent's cultural and social institutions. His second focus of attention is the role played by African writer-intellectuals in the artistic reevaluation and reversal of these negative effects. This concern is expressed in three phases of activity. The first is the realistic depiction of the insensitive and destructive nature of colonialism through literary works. In the second phase, African writers create, or rather re-create, images of the positive communal and progressive elements of indigenous cultural and social life. The third phase is envisioned as the merging of the writer with the aspirations and activities of the majority of Africans—the workers and peasants. This phase leads into Ngũgĩ's third major area of concern, the direct role of the African writer in both commenting on contemporary injustice *and* instigating positive, often radical, changes in economic, cultural, and political systems grounded in neocolonial relationships.

Prior to such reforms, however, is the isolation and identification of the root problems which, Ngũgĩ suggests, grow from colonial imperial rule. Throughout *Homecoming* the paternalistic, racist views of some

Western writers are cited as examples of attitudes which not only justified exploitation but also devalued the self-image of Africans raised in colonial contexts.[2] Ngũgĩ decries the fact that the works of Western writers were used in colonial educational systems and continued to predominate in the syllabi of independent nations, creating

> . . . an elite who took on the tongue and adopted the style of the conquerors. They hearkened to the voice of the missionary's God, cried Hallelujah, and raised their eyes to Heaven. They derided the old gods and they too recoiled with a studied (or genuine) horror from the primitive rites of their people. (10)

In order to reverse this process, Ngũgĩ calls for the breaking of the debilitating cycle created by colonial rulers and perpetuated by syllabi emphasizing Western literature. These scenarios and values are often inappropriate to an African context, entrenching standards which reward the internalization of European ideals at the expense of positive African self-images. He writes convincingly on the need for a "national" culture, and his most detailed remedy is contained in a 1969 letter coauthored with Henry Owuor-Anyumbe and Taban lo Liyong, "On the Abolition of the English Department." They prescribe the creation of a *literature* department that focuses on African literature as the core curriculum. Students would, from the beginning, see and hear about the continent's history and culture through the words and experiences of African writers. Western works would be read in a historical context as a specifically foreign literature. The long-term effect of this new curriculum would be that students would never need to unlearn the negative images of Africa purveyed by the West and would be able to interpret all literature from a position secure in its identity and historical place.

Ngũgĩ's second major area of concern focuses on the *creation* of the literature that will form the core of this curriculum. Contemporary African, Caribbean, and Afro-American writers must lead the way for students of literature. In a 1975 lecture, later published in *Writers in Politics,* he describes the dilemma of the African writer who tries to avoid the question of commitment to some form of political action: "He makes a cult of Africanness, of Blackism, of the dignity of the African past, of the African approach to problems; or he simply becomes cynical and laughs at everything equally" (79). To counter this tendency, the writer "must repudiate, and negate his roots in the native bourgeoisie . . . and find his true creative links with the pan-African masses" (80). In his 1966 review of *A Man of the People* Ngũgĩ suggests that one way to do this is to depict the African context prior to, during, and after imperial rule. He finds Chinua Achebe to be both a fine stylist and an excellent teacher, pointing out that his novels span the historical periods mentioned above. Measuring other writers according to the manner in which they portray the colonial and neocolonial experience, their treatment of African culture, and their affinity for the masses and progressive action, he is articulate and uncompromising in his evaluations. In *Homecoming* Ngũgĩ chides Aluko for his cynical portrayal of peasants as "merely ignorant, incapable and half-savage" (59); and, while lauding Soyinka's satirical criticism of corruption and elitism, Ngũgĩ complains that he "does not know where to turn. . . . The cynicism is hidden in the language . . . and in occasional flights of metaphysics" (65).[3] Ngũgĩ praises Okot p'Bitek's *Song of Lawino,* which was first written in Acoli, then translated by its author into English, as belonging to "a new mood of self-questioning and self-examination" (76).

Ngũgĩ's study of Caribbean literature, in the last section of *Homecoming,* translates the racial and political concerns of Anglophone West Indian writers into terms familiar to Africa, noting that "the surprising thing in fact is that, despite the years of lies and distortions about Africa, the African consciousness should still form an important element in West Indian awareness" (83). He notes the ways various writers employ Africa or a black identity in their novels, with some of them downplaying the efficacy of evoking a lost past and others using the idea of a common ancestry as "a necessary psychological prop in the struggle of the socially betrayed to remain human" (85). He also discerns a pattern of biblical allusions in West Indian literature, especially a strong identification with the Jews of the Old Testament, with the "promised land" often considered to be Africa itself. It is not surprising that the overall evaluation of the novels from that region comes down to the same thematic relationship found in Ngũgĩ's appraisal of African writing: racism and class structures growing out of capitalist colonial systems.

In the final, and most controversial, essay of *Writers in Politics* Ngũgĩ studies a number of literary efforts by Afro-American writers. "The Robber and the Robbed: Two Antagonistic Images in Afro-American Literature and Thought" covers a broad spectrum of black American thinking. Ngũgĩ begins by criticizing the conciliatory sentiments contained in a 1773 poem by Phyllis Wheatley, wherein she expressed "gratitude for having been rescued in safety from 'those dark abodes,'" or Africa, then contrasts her belief in Western humanism and superiority with the positive views of Africa drawn from the writings of Olaudah Equiano. Ngũgĩ traces examples of black American writing and themes up to the present era, concluding that certain writers have swal-

lowed the philosophy of the "robbers," the ruling class, while others have identified with and championed the causes of the "robbed," the poor majority, especially its black members. Ultimately, Martin Luther King, James Baldwin, Ralph Ellison, Whitney Young, and Eldridge Cleaver are seen as "sellouts" and are named as descendants of Wheatley and Booker T. Washington, whose *Up from Slavery* is referred to in *Writers in Politics* as "a song in praise of . . . subjugation . . . and self-humiliation" (133). The progressive side includes W. E. B. DuBois, Paul Robeson, Richard Wright, Malcolm X, and George Jackson. This essay, like most of the pieces so far described, equates good literature with commitment; but in contrast to those other articles, it extends the boundaries of what constitutes "literature." Literature is not simply what a person writes, but also what that person says, does, or stands for.

This hardening of critical evaluative criteria parallels Ngũgĩ's own activities in the third phase, which he considers the goal of African writers. As has become an obvious pattern in his life and work, he attempts to follow his own prescription assiduously. In the last decade he has experimented with new, more obviously political themes in his novel *Petals of Blood* and in the play he co-wrote with Micere Githae-Mugo, *The Trial of Dedan Kimathi.* The novel he completed while in prison also examines sociopolitical problems and is written in Kikuyu. The most exciting project Ngũgĩ has participated in, however, is the staging of the Kikuyu-language play he coauthored with Ngũgĩ wa Mirii, *Ngaahika Ndeenda* (1982; Eng. *I Will Marry When I Want*), by the Kamiriithu Community Education and Cultural Centre in Limuru. The play was directed, set, critiqued, reworked, and performed by an essentially peasant-worker crew. The theme revolves around the betrayal of poor peasants by a growing and powerful local landowning class. In *Writers in Politics* Ngũgĩ says of this experience:

> For the first time, the rural people could see themselves and their lives and their history portrayed in a positive manner. For the first time in their post-independence history a section of the peasantry had broken out of the cruel choice that was hitherto their lot: the bar or the church. (47)

In his prison diary he details the work of the community in creating this production, as well as the thousands of people, mostly peasants and workers, who come from miles away to view this landmark event. He derives some comfort, during his imprisonment, in hearing that the Heinemann Kikuyu-language edition of the play has gone into several printings, thereby corroborating his ideas about reaching the preferred audience of peasants and workers and allying himself with their aspirations.

It is this conviction that fosters Ngũgĩ's third major concern: the writer's role as social activist. *Writers in Politics* contains numerous pieces that inexorably focus directly on Kenya and its policies. In two essays, "Kenyan Culture: The Struggle for Survival" and "Handcuffs for a Play," he describes the shameful situation wherein two Kenyan dramas could not get adequate play dates because the national theatre had booked the Jeune Ballet de France and *A Funny Thing Happened on the Way to the Forum.* Two 1975 essays decry the recent assassination of J. M. Kariuki, Kenyan M. P. and author of the groundbreaking autobiography *Mau Mau Detainee,* the story of an intellectual's participation in that essentially peasant revolt. Ngũgĩ's increasingly militant defense of national cultures and the right to dissent takes on its most vociferous form in a talk delivered to a group protesting the imprisonment of South Korean activist poet Kim Chi Ha.[4] The text of his talk, when not evocatively quoting the poet's work, is peppered with such rhetorical epithets as "the South African Hitlerite Vorster," "Zionist collaborators," and "the mad dog, rampaging, imperialist countries." This pedantic and polemical style tends to, and is perhaps intended to, grate on the sensibilities of his academic audience.[5]

The paradox of a writer who condemns Western imperialism, promotes literature in African languages, yet publishes his pronouncements in English for an essentially scholarly readership is not lost on Ngũgĩ himself. He answers the question of why he criticizes foreign cultural imperialism while publishing with Heinemann by remarking, "I have never said that I am above the contradictions which bedevil our society. I have never even said that I have found solutions to these contradictions."[6] Ngũgĩ seems to be searching for a path through these contradictions, as he admits—or perhaps "confesses" is a more appropriate term—to the bourgeois influences in his earlier writings and pronouncements (*Writers in Politics,* 57, 78, 83, 85). Indeed, Peter Nazareth suggests that Ngũgĩ's fervent activism may best be understood, despite his renunciation of Christianity, as a "born again" phenomenon.[7] In a thought-provoking socio-Marxist essay, Ian Glenn notes this continued recourse to Christian imagery in Ngũgĩ's literary efforts, even as late as *Petals of Blood* (1977), and points out that the influence itself reveals much about the intellectual's dilemma in the African context:[8] the novel written in detention (*Caitaani Mutharaba-ĩnĩ*) has the ironic yet nonetheless Christian-influenced English title *Devil on the Cross;* and even in prison, the writer debates the chaplain by engaging in a battle of biblical quotes and allusions, each backing his point of view with certain selections.[9]

Christianity, however, is only one of several ambiguities in Ngũgĩ's critical writing. Though he denies Western literature an important place in Kenyan curricula, his own ideas are in great part shaped and continue to be influenced by this literature, as much of his prison diary shows;[10] and while he adopts a strong Marxist interpretation of economics and class relationships, his applications of these ideas to literature are at times inconsistent with notions of dialectics and history. His blanket condemnations often leave little room for understanding complex cultural and historical issues, as is evidenced by his post-Fanon interpretations of eighteenth- and nineteenth-century Afro-American writers. Ngũgĩ owes much of his basic methods and ideas to Frantz Fanon, especially those on national culture, class, and race. Because the mix of Marxism, pan-Africanism, Christian sensibility, and literary romanticism that swirls through his critical and artistic writing has not been resolved within himself, Ngũgĩ has yet to develop the clarity of vision and style that characterized the more self-assured Fanon. However, this is not necessarily a bad thing, since, as he himself keeps saying, the artist is not removed from the influences of his environment. More and more he has sought the environment that he most wants to learn from, to be influenced by: his peasant-worker neighbors at Limuru. His activist art shows through more clearly in his prison diary than in his critical essays, making effective reading *because* his personal and political life is dramatically merged in detention and allows the reader to see the theorist forced to "practice what he preaches" (if he will forgive the religious analogy).

This raises the question of audience. Most of the pieces collected in *Homecoming* and *Writers in Politics* are not formal essays for a scholarly readership. They are speeches, letters to newspapers, editorials, and lectures. Since his remarks are made before numerous groups and framed in polemical terms, repetition is inevitable (though it could have been more effectively handled by his editors at Heinemann). The fact is that Ngũgĩ is not really trying to reach an "academic" audience. His writings are meant to touch various levels of readers and to stimulate their thinking regarding class and economic relationships in culture and society. On at least one level he has succeeded, since, as a well-known novelist and educator, his critical comments are published for, and perused by, a large readership. Therefore, virtually all scholarly discussions of his essays must confront the question of literature and society. The essays, however, are stylistically limited, and clearly, those who go along with Ngũgĩ's line of thought hardly need to be convinced, while those who do not will simply tune him out. Unfortunately, those in the middle, the undecided, are left to forage in the forest of slogans for the crux of these valuable thoughts and ideas, a search made needlessly difficult. If Ngũgĩ is not an entirely successful proselytizer, it may be that his example will win more converts than his essays.[11] Like Ousmane Sembène, who tired of "enriching the French language" with his prizewinning novels, Ngũgĩ is seeking the audience that is important to him. Whereas Sembène turned to film, then to film in Senegal's languages, Ngũgĩ turns to drama and literature in Kenyan languages—up to this point, Kikuyu. Also like Sembène, who when criticized for accepting sponsorship from the U.S. National Council of Churches replied he would take money from the devil himself if it meant being able to finance a film and get his message across, Ngũgĩ will no doubt continue writing in whatever language suits his communicative purposes and publishing with whatever publisher carries his words to the desired readership.

If in the process Ngũgĩ's standing as a "literary critic" is diminishing, his movement to a form of artistic and pedagogic activism may end up fulfilling his most fervent hope: the creation of a positive union between the writer-artist-intellectual and the most fundamental aspirations of the majority of his people. Here, traditional literary criticism, what he no doubt considers to be "bourgeois" literary criticism, will play only a minor role, if any, or it will have to accommodate the stretching of literary categories and criteria advocated by Ngũgĩ and his contemporaries.

Robert Cancel, Winter 1985

[1] Both *Homecoming* and *Writers in Politics* were published in London by Heinemann.

[2] At one point Ngũgĩ was commissioned by Heinemann to write a book on the early white settlers of Kenya. Though he never wrote the history, his detailed research provided him with the information that has shaped his views on what he terms the "culture of silence and fear" in *Detained: A Writer's Prison Diary,* London, Heinemann, 1982.

[3] Ironically, it was Soyinka who was first detained for "political" activities during the Nigerian Civil War. Nearly a decade later, Ngũgĩ quotes from Soyinka's detention memoirs, *The Man Died,* in his own prison diary.

[4] On Kim Chi Ha, see *WLT* 53:4, pp. 634–35.

[5] See, for example, Reed Way Dasenbrock's review of *Devil on the Cross* in *WLT* 58:1, p. 153; John Povey's review of *Writers in Politics* in *WLT* 55:4, p. 717; and my review of *Writers in Politics* in *African Studies Review,* 26:1, pp. 162–64.

[6] *The Standard,* Nairobi, 28 August 1981, p. 11.

[7] See Peter Nazareth's review of *Writers in Politics* in *World Literature Written in English,* 20:2, pp. 225–30.

[8] Ian Glenn, "Ngũgĩ wa Thiong'o and the Dilemmas of the Intellectual Elite in Africa: A Sociological Perspective," *English in Africa,* 8:2 (1981), pp. 53–66.

[9] Ngũgĩ, *Detained,* p. 25.

[10] See pp. 132–33 of *Detained* for a comprehensive list of the books Ngũgĩ read while in detention. Interestingly enough, one of the writers he most often quotes in that diary is William Blake (e.g., p. 133).

[11] For an example of a more comprehensive radical critique of African literature, see Chinweizu, Jemie, and Madubuike, *Toward the Decolonization of African Literature,* 1: *African Fiction and Poetry and Their Critics,* Washington, D.C., Howard University Press, 1983 (reviewed in *WLT* 58:2 [Spring 1984], p. 313).

NIGERIA

Bridges of Orality: Nigerian Pidgin Poetry[1]

The exploitation of oral traditions through a synthesized creative crucible enables the modern Nigerian writer to produce fresh, exciting, and artistic poetry. The Pidgin language provides an appropriate medium for this exploitation of oral traditions in poetry, for it acts as a bridge between the orality of verbal communication and the formality of the written word. Thus Nigerian Pidgin poetry is constructed as part of this utilization of oral resources, which has revitalized the literary scene and the poetic tradition. However, the development and utilization of Pidgin as a language medium in Nigerian poetry owes its manifestation to the reality of its profuse use along the coast and also in the hinterland, where the indigenous Nigerian languages predominate.

All the same, the origin of Nigerian Pidgin has been stated in a pioneering study as "essentially a product of the process of urbanisation, while its origins lie historically in the early contacts between Africans and Europeans. The rapidly growing towns of Nigeria have increasingly become the melting pots of the many tribes and races which constitute Nigeria, and Pidgin seems to be today a very widely spoken lingua franca, many town and city dwellers being at least bilingual, in Pidgin and an indigenous language" (Mafeni, 98). Similarly, a later study which examines the origins of Nigerian Pidgin confirms that it "arose from the urgent communication needs of the contact between the visiting Europeans (in the end the English) and their multi-lingual Nigerian hosts. Stabilisation of this contact led to the stabilisation and expansion of Nigerian Pidgin (NP)" (Elugbe and Omamor, 21). These assertions emphasize the prevalent view discernible in the definition of Pidgin as a "communication system that develops among people who do not share a common language. In early stages of contact, such as the first encounters between British sailors and coastal West Africans or between American soldiers and the Vietnamese, a make-shift system emerges involving a few simple structures—mostly commands—and a limited number of words, drawn almost entirely from the language of the dominant group" (Todd, 3). Although the issues of domination and its appendage, exploitation, provided a political focus in the areas in which Pidgin was a medium of communication, the development of the language was affected by several other sociocultural factors.

The most prominent sociocultural factor was the fact that Pidgin was associated with a lower social status, which aided in the social stratification of the people who use it. In Jamaica, for instance, as Beryl Loftman Bailey reveals, "Good breeding and a sound education invariably result in the renunciation of creolised speech," because the "retention of Creole speech or admission of one's ability to speak it (except, of course, for stage effect) is condemned and may well spell disaster for the adherent" (Bailey, 2). John Holm notes that "this contempt often stemmed in part from the feeling that Pidgins and creoles were corruptions of *higher,* usually European languages, [by people] who were often perceived as semisavages whose partial acquisition of civilised habits was somehow an affront" (Holm, 1). This feeling of contempt was originally informed by a false sense of racial superiority, which has now been replaced by a misdirected sense of elitist superiority. In his study of Pidgin literature in Cameroon, a literature that possesses a great deal of similarity with Nigerian Pidgin literature, Abioseh Porter says, "Pidgin has made a noticeable linguistic advance in spite of the stigma that has often been attached to its use, especially in elitist circles. Although some educationists and other literates still snobbishly and hypocritically condemn the use of Pidgin, claiming that it leads children to make a poor use of the 'Queen's English,' it is true that among the people in the anglophone region and for quite a sizeable number in the francophone zone, Pidgin is the main linguistic medium of communication" (Porter, 63). Nevertheless, the existence and development of Pidgin are the result of its own internal dynamics, and this internal dynamism of Nigerian Pidgin particularly has been aided in recent times by the production of works of literature in Pidgin and also by the arguments of critics who have found either merit in such works or possibilities in the language.

One of these recent critics is Emeka Okeke-Ezigbo, who, in an interesting but somewhat acerbic article, opines that Pidgin is a "practical, viable, flexible language distilled in the alembic of our native sensibility

and human experience. This lusty language, which transcends our geographical and political boundaries grows daily before our eyes. It is our natural, unifying weapon against the divisive forces of English. In West Africa, English splits; Pidgin unites" (Okeke-Ezigbo, 34). The critic adds that "the adoption of Pidgin will automatically make the writer national by domesticating his outlook and sensibility," and he concludes, "On adopting Pidgin and becoming a real nationalist the Nigerian writer can now speak with the knowledge of an insider" (35). Certainly there are areas in that essay in which Okeke-Ezigbo overstates his case, especially in his illustrations, but the thesis of his argument is sound if one overlooks the connotative exclusivity of his call for the adoption of Pidgin. It is this exclusivity that must have prompted Femi Osofisan's rejoinder, published in the same issue of *Okeke.* Osofisan takes exception to the generalization of Okeke-Ezigbo's postulations when he argues that "the use of Pidgin cannot automatically make any writer patriotic or progressive; that will depend finally on other factors, such as the consciousness and purpose of the particular artist" (Osofisan, 43). However, he agrees that Pidgin is a viable language and capable of sustaining works of literature.

It is clearly this capability of Pidgin to sustain works of literature—since it is a language that bridges orality, a language that absorbs several cultural elements as it communicates—which has made it yield creative possibilities for the Nigerian poet. However, a stress on Pidgin poetry in this study does not mean that it is only in poetry that the Pidgin language has been utilized. Although in the works of the popular Onitsha market literature there is no indication of a sustained use of Pidgin as a language of creative communication, Emmanuel Obiechina points out that "some authors make their illiterate or semi-literate characters speak in West African Pidgin English. Sometimes they take pains to explain such idiosyncratic usages in their prefaces" (Obiechina, 86). But the later works that emerged after the literary outburst of the Onitsha market literature indicated artistic dimensions to the use of Pidgin in Nigerian literature. Tony Obilade, in a study of Chinua Achebe and Wole Soyinka, argues that Pidgin English is "used for humour as well as for character portrayal" and can also be "employed to explore deeper meanings, to explain the reasons behind a character's actions, and to project and foreground certain themes" (Obilade, 22). There is no doubt that Pidgin has been deployed interestingly in the novels of Achebe, Cyprian Ekwensi, and Adaora Lily Ulasi and in the plays of Soyinka and Ola Rotimi. There are also other works that are written entirely or to a great extent in Pidgin, like Ken Saro-Wiwa's *Sozaboy,* Segun Oyekunle's *Kata-kata for Suffer-*

head, and Tunde Fatunde's *No More Oil Boom, No Food No Country, Water No Get Enemy, Blood and Sweat,* and *Oga na Tief-Man*. These works portray the varied dimensions in the use of Pidgin to enhance modern Nigerian literature. However, it is in poetry that this language has been most effectively employed to create a bridge of orality, especially in the attempt to domesticate, develop, and exploit its artistic resources, as we find in the works of Frank Aig-Imoukhuede, Mamman Vatsa, Ezenwa-Ohaeto,[2] Ken Saro-Wiwa, Tunde Fatunde, and Tanure Ojaide.

Historically, among the pioneer poets of West Africa there were writers who made use of Pidgin even as they created other poems in English. In 1948 Gladys Casely-Hayford of Ghana published a small volume of poetry entitled *Take Um So* (Take It Like That). This collection has three poems in what is known as Krio, a language that essentially differs from Pidgin only in name. She writes with insight on the attitude of man to his fate and the role of destiny in life as the persona insists that one should accept one's fate in spite of the fact that other people are in better circumstances: "If God full some ouse wid pickin, en 'E no gree full youn / Or 'E gie you: don 'E take de pickin back; / Or 'E show you road way tranga, en 'E put you for climb hill / En guide some oder person pan broadtrack—take Um So." O. R. Dathorne ably translates this poem as follows: "If God has filled some house with children, but not yours. / Or if He gave you and then recalled the children; / Or if he showed you a dangerous road and made you climb a steep hill / And guided somebody else on a broad track— / Don't quarrel—accept it as it is" (Dathorne, 162). The poem is essentially moralistic, for at this stage in the development of Pidgin poetry the poets have not commenced experimentation with the elasticity of the language. But Casely-Hayford introduces a lyric structure that ends in the interesting phrase "take Um So"— accept life as it is. Dathorne's observation that the poet "has accomplished here a difficult task since it is commonly accepted that dialect English is appropriate only for comical situations" (Dathorne, 162) is relevant, for the poem is pointed, lyrical, and deals with the significant issues of tolerance and harmony in human relationships.

In his collection *Africa Sings* (1952) Dennis Osadebay, another pioneer poet, makes use of Pidgin in one poem entitled "Black Man Trouble." Here he is much more adventurous than even many contemporary Nigerian poets, as he dramatizes the themes through the use of a character who is lamenting not only the injustice of his race but also his oppression as a colonial subject. This four-stanza poem commences with a general examination of the fate of the black man. The syntax of the Pidgin poem is not taxing, for Osadebay is clearly influenced by the ideas associated with the placement of words in English. However, the artistic element in the poem that is portrayed through the deliberate dissociation of the persona from the issue of the lament in the first stanza contributes to the arousal of empathy in the reader. The poet indicates that the black person encounters enormous problems ("face big strife") in order to acquire even "some little food" for "him belly" (his stomach). Thus unconsciously the reader agrees with the poet in the subsequent stanzas that his "heart be clean, my word be true," but "why must my feet be in your chain?" and "you must chase me with your cane?" Even the issue of religion is utilized in this poem to demonstrate the unfair treatment of the black persona, who "no get gun," "no get bomb," and "no fit fight no more." The aspect of this hopeless situation which the poet most detests is the hypocritical use of the "cross" to "make me dumb," with the result that he is asked to close his eyes in prayer as the priest's "brudder thief my land away." The poet therefore laments the use of religion to camouflage materialistic aims. The emphatic note on which the poem ends reiterates the poet's thematic objective.

I no fit listen to more lies
 I done see everything;
Dis tam I open wide my eyes
 And see de tricks you bring;
  You play me fair, I make you glad;
   Play me selfish, I make you sad (17)

There is no doubt that this poem illustrates quite early the blend of serious issues and language experimentation which contradicts some of the recent prevalent views that Pidgin is suited for only comic situations. That erroneous impression must have developed through the popular use of Pidgin in Nigerian newspapers like *Lagos Weekend* and *Lagos Life* and on such television programs as "New Masquerade" and "Samanja." Osadebay's poem may appear humorous in some sections, but it captures with telling accuracy the problems of colonialism during that period of Nigerian history.

The achievement of that pioneer poet is extended in the early sixties by Frank Aig-Imoukhuede, whose poem "One Wife for One Man" was given in manuscript form to Gerald Moore and Ulli Beier and was subsequently published in the 1963 edition of *Modern Poetry from Africa*. In this poem Aig-Imoukhuede adopts a jocular tone to satirize the religious injunction that polygamy is abnormal. The poet does not advocate polygamy, however, and in fact he presents several reasons for questioning the practice. The use of polygamy here as a theme serves the twin function of providing the poet with an issue that is not only traditional but also capable of forming a substantial subject for the interrogation of the cultural-conflict reality. The persona has been inundated by the injunction "One wife for one man" in the churches and law courts, with the result that he is almost deaf or, as he puts it, "my ear nearly cut." In the second stanza he argues that his ancestors "get him wife borku [plenty]," although he agrees that "dat time done pass before white man come" (the time is past). After these seemingly trivial assertions, the persona proceeds to tabulate the reasons of infertility, excessive pride, the lack of home training or formal education, and the issue of producing male children to continue one's lineage as justification for not allowing "one wife for one man." The final stanza ends with the words "Suppose, self, say na so-so woman your wife dey born / Suppose your wife sabe book, no'sabe make chop; / Den, how you go tell man make 'e no' go out / Sake of dis divorce? Bo, dis culture na waya O! / Wen one wife be for one man" (Moore and Beier, 128–29). The ironic implications in this poem materialize through the persona's catalogue of reasons, for those reasons can still be discerned even when a man is polygamous. An infertile man, for instance, cannot produce offspring even if he marries a hundred wives. In effect, the irony here is used to reassert the poet's satiric purposes, which ultimately assure the reader that polygamy is not as advantageous as it was originally conceived to be.

The effect of Aig-Imoukhuede's "One Wife for One Man" is still felt, for almost twenty years later a woman published a rejoinder in *Okike*. Abigail Ukpabi's poem "One Man, One Wife (a Wife's Rejoinder)" commences with a direct statement that establishes the purpose for which she writes: "Na wetin dis, A beg na wetin dis? / Na wetin dis, Aig-Imoukhuede de talk so?" (Ukpabi, 13). Ukpabi does not argue against the reasons projected in the poem that inspired her work; rather, she bases her reaction on the foundation of human feelings. Her argument that if a man is entitled to many wives then a woman should possess the same right to acquire several husbands is clearly advanced in this poem to show that a woman feels hurt when her emotions become a plaything. Just like Aig-Imoukhuede, Ukpabi is not advocating the right to several husbands for women, because she ends her poem this way: "Wetin be white man culture / White man, white woman / Black man, black woman / Yellow man, yellow woman / Red man, red woman / All get same heart for dis world!" (13). She stresses that human beings are the same in spite of their racial differences. Her poem illustrates and subverts satirically the same subject matter that Aig-Imoukhuede ironically treats in his own poem.

The collections of verse published by Mamman Vatsa and Aig-Imoukhuede in the eighties emphasized the progress which Pidgin poetry had made in two decades. But those collections were not the only works of Pidgin verse that the reading public encountered, for such well-known writers as Ken Saro-Wiwa, Tanure Ojaide, and Tunde Fatunde and such lesser-known poets as Pita Okute, A. Ajakaiye, Ogunlowo, Erapi, Udenwa, Ojeifo, Bello, and Osita Ike published Pidgin poems in various anthologies which I have selected for closer attention. Both these well-known and lesser-known poets illustrate the basic orality manipulated through the choice and placement of Pidgin words. For instance, Ojaide, whose reputation[3] has been established by the publication of several collections of verse in English— *Labyrinths of the Delta, The Endless Song, The Eagle's Vision, The Fate of Vultures, The Blood of Peace*—includes one Pidgin poem in *The Eagle's Vision*. In this poem, entitled "I Be Somebody" (Ojaide, 69), he employs contrast as a rhetorical and artistic device as he manipulates the orality of the Pidgin language while choosing and placing his words in a manner to enhance the effect of his ideas. The persona in the poem is proud of his abilities to "shine" shoes "like new one from supermarket" and "carry load for head from Lagos go Abuja." In addition, this persona is fertile, for his "children reach Nigerian Army" in their numbers. It is possible to argue that the fertility which this "poor man" asserts as a quality may not be positive considering his limited financial resources. However, what the poet is indicating ironically is that it is unjust and unwise to regard one's compatriots with contempt, especially when the persona is noble and selfless in helping "push your car from gutter for rain." Although the persona's reward is the splashing of "poto-poto" (watery mud) on his body, the poet still implies that his selfless services are essential.

It is in this use of contrasts, both in terms of creating the characters of the rich man and the poor man in the poem and in terms of the kindness of one character contrasted by the wickedness of the other, that Ojaide stresses the importance of even the least member of the society, for the persona in the poem is described as the "salt for the soup you de chop everyday." That image of salt, a substance best appreciated when it is used to add taste and improve the quality of food, becomes a metaphor for the value of the persona, a "common man." All the same, it is this use of an ordinary member of the society as a persona in Pidgin poems which one reviewer criticizes when he opines that "an apparent danger in Pidgin poetry is to slide into the world-view of the man in the street or the girl next door" (Omoifo, 29). But the "world-view of the man in the street" does not necessarily mean a lack of profundity or relevance, for it is possible to use even the "world-view" of a child or a lunatic in literature to make profound philosophical, psychological, and cultural statements.

In effect, the use of a persona whose ordinariness is obvious is, in most cases, not intended by the Pidgin poet to create the impression of naïveté or simplemindedness. In the articulation of themes, the Pidgin poet, like other Nigerian poets who employ either English or one of the various Nigerian languages, makes use of the parabolic mode associated with the poetic persona in addition to the adoption of proverbial structures, metaphors, symbols, ironies, images, contrasts, refrain, rhythm, alliteration, and onomatopoeia. The language of the poem is mediated, but in this mediation there are varied levels of competence, which is really what determines the success of the works. The writers who have published Pidgin poems in the various widely available journals, in the anthologies *Voices from the Fringe* and *Poets in Their Youth,* or in their own individual verse collections provide enough material for the determination of poetic competence and the manner in which the orality of Pidgin has been bridged.

Tunde Fatunde, for instance, has published three poems in *Okike, The Anthill Annual,* and *Voices from the Fringe* in which he exploits the resources of descriptive poetry. For example, in "Woman Dey Suffer," published in *Okike,* he describes the unpleasant aspects of the experience of women in society. He depicts the woman as receiving little pay despite her hard work at the office, having to return home in the evening to labor for her husband and children, and, in addition to all this responsibility, encountering several religious restrictions on her womanhood. The poet's basic contention is that "as we get beta woman / Na so we get Yeye Koni-Koni man / Yeye woman dey / Beta Man dey / If dis world good / Na man and woman / Make am good / If dis Obodo Nigeria bad / Na woman and man / Make am bad" (98). The poet is advocating equal treatment for all sexes, which is why his conclusion stresses social harmony.

In another poem, "Bad Belle Too Much," published in *The Anthill Annual,* Fatunde again advocates amity and harmony in social interactions. His concern is clearly to highlight the forms of injustice in society, which is probably why he subjects his themes so seldom to complex philosophical ruminations. In addition, his poems are topical, as in the case of "Denis Obi Don Die," published in *Voices from the Fringe.* The poem is based on a real-life incident in which Denis Obi, a ten-year-old schoolboy, drowns while trying to catch fish in a small river near Sabongida-Ora in Bendel State. The poet attributes the boy's death to social injustice, which denies him parental guidance and financial protec-

tion—"Bekos in Papa and Mama / No fit pay in School fees / Na only fifteen naira" (Garuba, 145)—and leads the headmaster to drive him away from school. All the same, it is still possible to read this poem as a metaphor in spite of its topicality, which to some extent militates against Fatunde's utilization of relevant poetic devices. His Pidgin poems are nevertheless faithful to the social and cultural tensions in contemporary Nigerian society.

Other poems in *Voices from the Fringe* present new thematic perspectives for both the creation and the appreciation of Pidgin poetry, as their variety of subjects touch on most aspects of modern reality. The poem "Common Wealth" by A. Ajakaiye takes up the concept of the commonwealth of nations, in which a "former colomaster" and several "former colo servants" are expected to assume a unitary view of reality. The poet argues, however, that their problems are varied, which negates the idea of commonwealth. In the final stanza he reaffirms: "So na common wealth be dis / or common wetin? / Because / if dem be common friends / why their enemy / no be common one?" (Garuba, 136). The argument that "common friends" must possess "common enemies" or even "common problems" is not a trivialization of the issue of intercontinental associations but rather a way of highlighting that even in such international relationships there are selfish and dishonest motives.

These Pidgin poets consider such deviant motives fundamental, and there is confirmation in Anthony Ogunlowo's "Dem Dey Kill Dem Sef," in which the poet condemns the violence of soldiers who periodically exterminate their comrades, especially "for dis time / when war no dey" (137). His comparison of those soldiers with birds, fish, and animals that exist harmoniously brands the degeneration of the soldiers as inhuman. Complementary to this poem is Godwin Erapi's "Chopping Freedom," which demonstrates the dishonesty of one of those soldier-leaders who denies his people freedom of expression, freedom to live, and freedom to acquire education in spite of promises to the contrary. The poet clearly perceives the situation as abnormal, which is why at the end of the poem he twists the phrase "human rights" into "human lefts," eliciting humor as well as magnifying the persona's outrage. This issue of military politics is also prominent in Onuora Udenwa's "Who Send You," a poem in which he challenges the idea of "civilianized Soldiers" as he questions "wetin concern soja / for inside town? / Not to talk of to / Come kick me—Gbaga, gbaga, gbaga?" (141). Udenwa certainly abhors the oppression of soldiers, a phenomenon that has become magnified in Nigerian social activities.

These poems so far discussed clearly contradict Nwachukwu-Agbada's remark, in an otherwise informative study concerning content and form in the Nigerian Pidgin poetry of Aig-Imoukhuede and Mamman Vatsa, that "it seems that at the moment the language of Pidgin is suited to the treatment of a certain category of social ills, especially those which are easily appreciated by the lowly members of society who incidentally have only a smattering knowledge of the English language." Nevertheless, this critic hastens to add, "Pidgin can be a language 'for serious profundity'" (99). The remark that Pidgin can be used in the discussion of profound issues is adapted from the Pidgin poetry of Aig-Imoukhuede. Moreover, the Pidgin poem "Haba! Father" by Haj Bello, which appeared in the anthology *Poets in Their Youth* edited by Uche Nduka and Osita Ike, confirms that profound issues can indeed be discussed in Pidgin, as the poet laments the social disorganization which generates economic devastations. The poet's use of a persona who is beckoning "Father" to intervene is parabolic, for this father is clearly the political leader who created the economic problems in the first place. But it is not only political issues that engage the attention of the Pidgin poets represented in *Poets in Their Youth,* for Osita Ike's poem "Sisi Shakara" in the same anthology criticizes the pretense and hypocrisy in human relationships. The poet uses the word *laff* (laugh) to signify the change of mood and parallelize the action, as the persona obliterates the garbs of pretense adorning his companion "Sisi Shakara" (pretentious sister) until the "bed begin laff" (56) in the end.

The pervasive nature of social criticism in Pidgin poetry reaches a high point in Ken Saro-Wiwa's "Dis Nigeria Sef." The tone of this poem emerges quite early, as the poet compares Nigeria to "water wey dey boil." The personification of Nigeria here is a means for examining the country's prevalent social ills, disorganized social services, and dilapidated infrastructures. One poetic device used by the poet is the creation of a dialogue involving the persona and Nigeria. The poet indicates that the country's soldiers, policemen, and nurses do not provide the necessary services associated with their professions, while the citizens lack originality in their religion, language, and acquisition of names. The exasperation of the persona, which emerges at intervals as the poem progresses, becomes part of the poet's technique in the addition of a folkloric dimension, as Nigeria is scolded: "Oh yes, you be foolish yeye man / Look as you dey laugh as I dey talk / You tink say I dey joke?" (39). This abusive tone becomes clearer as a deliberate shock device when Saro-Wiwa adopts a different tone later in the poem: "But I beg you oh, Nigeria / No talk say I dey cuss you / True to God no be say, I no like you" (41).

It is this patriotic love which the persona has for his country that is behind the poetic attitude, for the poet perceives the ostentatious nature of the people as responsible for the social anomalies despite the fact that the "rivers and de ocean / full of fish and oder good tings."

The final segment of the poem extols the positive qualities of the country in terms of food, and Saro-Wiwa insists that some of the people "na better man / Dey work from morning till night / weder soza nurse or police / or farmer wey dey cut bush plant / or trader wey dey sell petty petty for market / or *akowe* dey siddon for him office" (44). The perception of contraries in terms of the country's positive and negative characteristics takes the poem beyond the level of cataloguing impressions, for this poetic attitude is stressed in the last stanza as "dis I-love-no-love Nigeria" mannerism. This attitude also parallels that of the majority of the people, who are troubled by doubts of patriotism. Thus the poem is both a statement and an injunction, as Saro-Wiwa reflects the syntax and spelling of Pidgin words like *soza* (soldier), which is influenced by his mother tongue. But this development is not outrageous, considering the contention by Chantal Zabus that the "new generation of Nigerian writers like Osofisan, Iyayi, Oyekunle, Ezenwa-Ohaeto and Fatunde, as well as other well-meaning rhetors writing politics from the grassroots, have been said to further contribute to the dismantlement of Pidgin" by subjecting it to some sort of "plastic surgery" that makes "new contradictions" emerge "from coining a pseudo-Pidgin" (Zabus, 125). But these coinages are not abnormal, since all languages grow through the absorption of foreign elements, which are enriching and necessary for language development.

This issue of language development through the absorption of elements from other languages is noticeable in the verse of Mamman Vatsa,[4] whose *Tori For Geti Bow Leg* adds yet another dimension to Pidgin poetry, since his work is the product of cultural experience from the northern region of Nigeria. In the forty-one poems of Vatsa's collection he explores diverse themes in such a way that he "seems to have combined the attentive perception of social ethos with his own natural flair for light-heartedness" (Nwachukwu-Agbada, 1987, 96). The first poem in this collection, "Our Country Law," sets the scene, as it illustrates the devious ways in which laws are fashioned to restrict womanhood. It must be stated that many of these Pidgin poets consider fundamental and worthy of castigation all issues related to the treatment of women in society. Vatsa's poem, for instance, charges that in most segments of society women are forbidden to smoke or to engage in polygamy. But the basic idea which he makes persuasive is that some of these laws are often circumvented, and he turns those instances of circumvention into metaphors in the poem.

Vatsa also criticizes prevalent attitudes that he deems detrimental to the development of society. In the poem "Woman, You Be Manure" (31) it is the punishingly high rate of fertility without commensurate financial weight that merits his displeasure, while in "Wayo Man" (29) he castigates unreliability and dishonesty. As a Pidgin poet, Vatsa is certainly interested in the elimination of social vices and pretentious behavior, like the other Pidgin poets considered here. In a poem entitled "Yanga" (which means "Useless Pride") he feels that many of those people who behave as if they possess physical power are often deluded and weak, like "chicken / im feda / wey wind / dey blow" (15). The admonition is made more forceful by the image of the chicken with its feathers flattened by the wind. It is in this use of apt imagery that Vatsa makes a striking mark as a Pidgin poet. In the poem "Apartai," which is informed by the obnoxious apartheid policy that existed for so long in South Africa, he extends the issue to incorporate all forms of discrimination. For instance, "Bigi man latrine / wey smaller man no fit / use / dat na apartai." Elsewhere we read: "Ten people / wey de rule / ten tousand people / bicos dem / get plenty moni / an' diffren-diffren colour / dat na apartai" (12). Vatsa artistically elaborates upon the subject of discrimination in most human interactions in order to persuade the reader that even the trivial incidents one is likely to ignore are all appendages to the great discrimination that is transformed into the law of "apartheid." It is through this use of familiar symbols to treat social issues via new perspectives that Vatsa's poetry widens in scope.

In his verse Vatsa the military man does not spare the deficiencies of the members of his profession, for the poems "Drink-Drink Soja-Soja" and "Ol' Soja Jolly Time" criticize the habit of soldiers who drink intoxicating wine excessively. At the same time he shows an awareness for some of the unpleasant effects of the profession on low-ranking military personnel, for in the poem "Priva Soja Cry-Cry" he sympathizes with the ordinary soldier who bears the brunt of the labor in the barracks. It is this awareness of social injustice which makes the poet argue in "Judgmenti Day" that, in the final analysis, each person, irrespective of his material possessions, is bound to pay for his unjust actions, since on the day of judgment "argument / no go de" (11). The stress on this "day of judgment" is clearly Vatsa's way of drawing attention to the futile nature of such abnormal habits as the acquisition of expensive cars, as he shows in the poem "Obokun Odabo," where a "man no geti room / for sleep / e dey drive / Obokun" (39). In

using the name "Obokun," said to be a Yoruba name for an expensive fish but also a term applied to Mercedes-Benz cars, the poet is satirizing an excessive acquisitive mentality, as he does again in the poem "Country Make Me Good." This poem admonishes covetousness, which makes "ya troat long," and at the same time asserts the values associated with farm work—an injunction that is needed in a society which craves finished products without appreciating the labor associated with them.

It is certainly this issue of misplaced values that makes the poet criticize the fact that emotions often overcome the senses in human affairs, as in the title poem "Tori For Geti Bow Leg," in which a man confesses to his wife that if he had listened to his friend, she would not have been his wife. This confession leads to altercations, and Vatsa, in presenting this poem, is stressing the importance of applying a dose of wisdom to emotional issues. Thus, in his criticism he tackles all those characteristics that are foolish, like the modern woman in the poem "Modan Moda" who is unwilling to breastfeed her babies so that she can maintain erect breasts, the unpolished woman in the poem "Ye-Ye Woman" (32), the disrespectful woman in the poem "Gara-Gara" (48), and the women who gossip excessively in "Madam Tok-About" (54). Vatsa does not single out only women for censure, for he also criticizes men, as in the poem "Make-Make-Man," and especially when they engage in profitless activities in order to create false impressions. Such men are among the politicians he castigates in the poem "Promise Wey Boku" for not taking beneficial actions but instead only spouting frivolous speeches, with the result that, before the general public can benefit, "dem / Billi for Killam!" This ironic perception indicates that those who are expected to benefit from parliamentary bills put forward by politicians usually become victims of the ill-conceived ideas of those same politicians. It is clearly this perceptive power in Vatsa's poems that persuaded one critic to state that, as in "Tori For Geti Bow Leg," "Vatsa ever wrote genuinely popular poetry, poetry rooted in the accents, rhythms and feelings of common people, not versified banalities masquerading as simple, accessible 'popular' poetry" (Jeyifo, 291). In Vatsa's Pidgin poetry these feelings of common people range from the political to the social, from the personal to the public, from the mundane to the spiritual, from the psychological to the philosophical.

It is this same range that is apparent in the poetry of Frank Aig-Imoukhuede, whose collection *Pidgin Stew and Sufferhead* contains twenty-three poems in Pidgin. This poet explores most of the profound themes to be found in works of modern African literature, and it has been remarked elsewhere that "the predominant style in this poetry is the gradual development of an idea or theme until the denouement when it is unravelled through an ironic twist of the words or phrases" (Ezenwa-Ohaeto, 1991, 159). The first poem in the collection, "Flood Done Come," exemplifies this technique, as it discusses the issues of dictatorship, tyranny, and injustice. The poetic voice laments all instances of tyranny and chaos through the use of "flood" as a metaphor. The flood is described as terrible: "Flood done come / and tear dey borku for eye" (1). In the subsequent stanzas the reader realizes that the poet is not talking of an ordinary flood, because "the flood wey reach us / lef' we man with two head." In addition, we read that "di man wey flood bring / Done seize store key / Butu di money bambam." It is thus clear that "the flood" here is a metaphor either for a derailed revolution or for the arrival of a destructive military regime. The poem ends with a telling observation of the type that characterizes expressions in Pidgin: "Rape na rape / wether na gun or strong prick." This poem illustrates Aig-Imoukhuede's awareness concerning the power of the Pidgin language, which he states in "Pidgin Stew" as portraying "like-joke like joke / Na him serious matter / Dey commot for mout" (2).

Thus the themes of Aig-Imoukhuede's poems are comprehensive, and they are explored with that peculiar humor associated with the language. The poet utilizes earthy imagery, the type that recalls to the mind familiar objects but in a manner that is both fresh and original. Similarly, in the poem "Blackman's Consolation" Aig-Imoukhuede criticizes racism, which makes it possible for the white man to oppress the black man. But in the poem "Independence Done Come" he satirizes the notion of independence as he tabulates those activities and events that contradict it, thereby confirming that oppression emanates from all racial groups. The issue which the poet highlights in the poem is that although independence was touted as the avenue for freedom and equal rights, we now discover that "One year two year done pass / Now we get 'unanimity'; / And Cletus wit' talk of 'human right' / Dey chop bean for prison now. / Shout hurra, shout hurra / Independence done come" (32). The joyful shout of "hurra" which the persona asks the reader to raise after each stanza of the poem becomes a mockery, for independence has not fulfilled the hopes of the people but has led instead to the imprisonment of Cletus because he was sensitive to human rights in his society.

In the poem entitled "Politics" Aig-Imoukhuede ridicules the politician, concluding that "lie too plenty for your throat / and cunnin'cunnin' / Be your proper name" (41). The humor in this poem lies in its assemblage of impossible promises, like the one which says,

"Poor man go turn millionaire." In addition, military politics is satirized in the poem "Coup D'etat" through the use of the meaningless orders that are usually issued by hasty coup plotters. Some of these orders include "Advance to de recognise," "Curfew from dawn to dusk," and "Open bottom, madam make I see." In the end the poet notes that "Bo world head no correct again!" because "General throway salute for corp'l" (45). The fact that a general salutes a corporal in the state of confusion illustrates the poet's perception of the coup as a "ritual in ridicule."

These political poems are successful through the poet's use of disarming humor and exaggerations that appear ridiculous in order to prod the reader into a realization of the enormity of the political abnormalities. It is clear that these Pidgin poems exploring the theme of politics fulfill the requirements of good poetry, because they survive the political circumstances that originate them. However, Ken Goodwin, in his critique of African poetry, states: "For a poet committed to poetry as a political instrument, literary quality may seem of little importance: an irrelevance or even a subversive hindrance. It is not surprising, then, that the politicisation of African poetry in English has been accompanied by a decline in literary quality" (Goodwin, xiii). All the same, he adds that he does not mean to imply that no fine political poems have been written; rather, he is suggesting that the need to make a political statement has often directed a poet's attention away from poetic quality. Aig-Imoukhuede in his Pidgin verse does not write political poems in order to win applause, for the pervasive nature of African politics makes such creative efforts inevitable. What he has achieved is the establishment of an entirely new set of symbols and the expression in Pidgin of a theme that is of the gravest importance to his society.

Sexual metaphors such as "rape na rape / whether na gun or strong prick" are part of this fresh symbolism and are combined with the poet's wit to explore reality from even trivial dimensions in order to reach profound conclusions. In the lyrical and successful poem "Take Me Go for Corner-Place" the persona laments his public embarrassment. This persona had imagined that his "power pass all," because "no man pickin fit face" him; but he realizes with a shock the limitation of his belief and pride, as he laments, "No' be di conk dem conk me for head; / No' be my eye dem turn like coal-tar; / Bot (make una weep for me!) for my wife before, / Braimoh wife knack me down put sand for my mout'" (30). Thus he pleads with his audience, "Take me go for corner-place / make I go hide my face." The idea conveyed by the use of this incident of a man who believes he is strong but who is physically subdued by a woman is that humanity should not let pride be a destructive trait. The poet shows that there is a need for restraint, decorum, and civility in human actions.

Aig-Imoukhuede also uses irony to good effect in his Pidgin poems. In "The Day Samson Die" he begins as if he is praising Samson by itemizing all the incidents that took place on Samson's death-day. These incidents include the numerous people "wey borku like sand," the "traffic stop and man-pickin trek," "Dem gi am big gun salute / Dem bring television camera / And priest to say 'our father' / And he get free medical service too" (38). However, toward the end of the poem it becomes clear that Samson, who received a gun salute (satirically), great publicity, and the attention of a priest, was in fact an armed robber executed by a firing squad, as the poet tells us that he was tied up like a ram because "Sallah ram better pass am / Dem tie am for stick" and "the mess he mess for air / Not small for talk" (39). The irony here, which is enhanced by the arresting imagery, enables the poet make this poem a criticism of violent robberies that is relevant to the social realities of his country.

One critic has commended Aig-Imoukhuede's use of "metaphoric transfer," which is defined as occurring "when a word is placed in a context where it is forced to function as a metaphor, whereas in normal usage the same word cannot be used as a metaphor in such a combination" (Maduakor, 114). Two examples from the poem "Flood Done Come" are cited: "Cat be wrong watch night for fried meat" and "Hawk no be Baby nurse for fowl." This metaphoric transfer is part of the artistic essence of Aig-Imoukhuede's verse, and he has used it to enrich the corpus of Pidgin poetry.

There is no doubt that the thematic range and artistic qualities of the Pidgin poets discussed in the foregoing portray both a development and successful poetic experiments. The lyric quality of the poems and the use of irony, metaphor, and imagistic characterization combine to produce innovations which have helped blend the resources of Pidgin to the needs of serious poetry. The essence of these poems makes it clear that the language is not an end in itself but a means to an end, thus confirming the view that language is used for "the external manipulation of human thoughts [and] for man's understanding of the world in which he lives" (Goody, 259). The use of Pidgin by these poets is intended to make that manipulation and that understanding artistically better, for as has been argued in the essay "The Eighties and the Return to Oral Cadences in Nigerian Poetry," Pidgin serves as a "convenient meeting ground for the mother-tongues and the English Language," thereby producing a "medium quite close to orality"

(Nwachukwu-Agbada, 100), although the language has not been standardized.

These Pidgin poets have established a viable poetic tradition, and in their achievement they have bridged the gap between oral communication and the written medium. In addition, in their use of language they exploit its resources through the use of a folk poetics and a sensitive deployment of a range of rhetorical styles while synthesizing formal features of poetry and verbal resources to generate a new vigor in the Nigerian poetic tradition. Although this study indicates that the strengths of the poets vary and that sometimes their creative works possess flaws, the conclusion is that Pidgin poetry is part of the poetic traditions that coalesce to make modern Nigerian verse worthy of critical attention.

Ezenwa-Ohaeto, Winter 1995

■ **WORKS CITED**

Aig-Imoukhuede, Frank. *Pidgin Stew and Sufferhead.* Ibadan, Nigeria. Heinemann. 1982.

Bailey, Beryl Loftman. *Jamaican Creole Syntax: A Transformational Approach.* Cambridge, Eng. Cambridge University Press. 1966.

Casely-Hayford, Gladys. *Take Um So.* Freetown, S.L. New Era. 1948.

Dathorne, O. R. *African Literature in the Twentieth Century.* London. Heinemann. 1976.

Elugbe, B. O., and A. P. Omamor. *Nigerian Pidgin: Background and Prospects.* Ibadan, Nigeria. Heinemann. 1991.

Ezenwa-Ohaeto. *Songs of a Traveller.* Awka, Nigeria. Town Crier. 1986.

———. *I Wan Bi President.* Enugu, Nigeria. Delta. 1988.

———. "Song of a Labourer: If to Say I Be a Soja." *The Anthill Annual,* 1 (March 1988), pp. 64–65.

———. "The Dimensions of Language in New Nigerian Poetry." *The Question of Language in African Literature Today,* 17 (1991), pp. 155–64.

Fatunde, Tunde. "Woman Dey Suffer." *Okike,* 27/28 (March 1988), pp. 95–98.

———. "Bad Belle Too Much." *The Anthill Annual,* 1 (March 1988), p. 25.

Garuba, Harry, ed. *Voices from the Fringe: New Nigerian Poetry.* Lagos. Malthouse. 1988.

Goodwin, Ken. *Understanding African Poetry.* London. Heinemann. 1982.

Goody, Jack. *The Interface Between the Written and the Oral.* Cambridge, Eng. Cambridge University Press. 1988.

Holm, John. *Pidgins and Creoles. 1: Theory and Structure.* Cambridge, Eng. Cambridge University Press. 1987.

Jeyifo, Biodun. "Mamman J. Vatsa." In *Perspectives on Nigerian Literatures: 1700 to the Present.* Vol. 2. Yemi Ogunbiyi, ed. Lagos. Guardian. 1988. Pp. 287–92.

Maduakor, Obi. "Review of Aig-Imoukhuede's *Pidgin Stew and Sufferhead.*" *Okike,* 22 (June 1983), pp. 112–16.

Mafeni, Bernard. "Nigerian Pidgin." In *The English Language in West Africa*. John Spencer, ed. London. Longman. 1971.

Moore, Gerald, and Ulli Beier, eds. *Modern Poetry from Africa*. Baltimore. Penguin. 1968.

Nduka, Uche, and Osita Ike, eds. *Poets in Their Youth: An Anthology*. Lagos. Osiris. 1988.

Nwachukwu-Agbada, J. O. J. "Content and Form in Nigerian Poetry: The Pidgin Poetry of Aig-Imoukhuede and Mamman Vatsa." *Chelsea*, 46 (1987), pp. 91–105.

———. "The Eighties and the Return to Oral Cadences in Nigerian Poetry." *Matatu*, 10 (1993), pp. 85–105.

Obiechina, Emmanuel. *An African Popular Literature*. Cambridge, Eng. Cambridge University Press. 1973.

Obilade, Tony. "The Stylistic Function of Pidgin English in African Literature: Achebe and Soyinka." In *Research on Wole Soyinka*. James Gibbs and Bernth Lindfors, eds. Trenton, N.J. Africa World. 1993. Pp. 13–23.

Ojaide, Tanure. *The Eagle's Vision*. Detroit. Lotus. 1987.

Okeke-Ezigbo, Emeka. "The Role of the Nigerian Writer in a Carthaginian Society." *Okike*, 21 (July 1982), pp. 28–37.

Omoifo, Isi. "Little Comfort from the Poet-President: Ezenwa-Ohaeto's Use of Pidgin Confirms a Growing Trend—Review of *I Wan Bi President*." *The African Guardian*, 14 November 1988, p. 29.

Osadebay, Dennis Chukude. *African Sings*. Ilfracombe, Eng. Arthur Stockwell. 1952.

Osofisan, Femi. "Enter the Carthaginian Critic?" *Okike*, 21 (July 1982), pp. 38–44.

Porter, Abioseh Michael. "Smohl No Bi Sik: A Preliminary Survey of Pidgin Literature in Cameroon." *African Writing Today: A Special Issue of Pacific Moana Quarterly*, 6:3–4 (July/October 1981), pp. 63–69.

Saro-Wiwa, Ken. "Dis Nigeria Sef." *Songs in a Time of War*. Port Harcourt, Nigeria. Saros. 1985. Pp. 36–44.

Todd, Loreto. *Modern Englishes: Pidgin and Creoles*. Oxford, Eng. / London. Stockwell / Andre Deutsch. 1984.

Ukpabi, Abigail. "One Man, One Wife (A Wife's Rejoinder)." *Okike*, 21 (July 1982), p. 13.

Vatsa, Mamman Jiya. *Tori For Geti Bow Leg and Other Pidgin Poems*. Lagos. Cross Continents. 1985.

Zabus, Chantal. "Mending the Schizo-Text: Pidgin in the Nigerian Novel." *Kunapipi*, 14:1 (1992), pp. 119–27.

---

[1] This paper was presented at the conference of the Société des Anglistes de l'Enseignement Supérieur (SAES), Université de Valenciennes (France), 13–15 May 1994. The author is grateful to the von Humboldt Foundation of Bonn, Germany, for the research funds and facilities.

[2] My Pidgin works entitled *I Wan Bi President, Songs of a Traveller,* and *If to Say I Be Soja* are not part of this study, although they have received significant attention from other critics.

[3] On Tanure Ojaide, see his autobiographical essay "I Want to Be an Oracle: My Poetry and My Generation," *WLT* 68:1 (Winter 1994), pp. 15–21.

[4] Mamman Vatsa was a Nigerian major general who in 1986 was controversially accused of plotting a coup and executed in spite of opposition by the Babangida regime.

Ola Rotimi: The Man, the Playwright, and the Producer on the Nigerian Theatre Scene

The contribution of Ola Rotimi to the development of drama in Nigeria has been significant. His achievement can be understood through his involvement and input not only as a playwright and critic but also as a director and producer. It is perhaps necessary first to take a cursory glance at the personality and background of the man in order to appreciate how these influence his experience in the theatre.

Emmanuel Gladstone Olawale Rotimi, popularly known as Ola Rotimi, was born in 1938 in Sapele, a town in the delta area of Bendel State. As a semiurban community at the time, Sapele still retained aspects of traditional African life through its culture and traditions. Street parties, dancing, and masquerade theatres were very much part of the town, and these early traditional African theatrical influences still show in Rotimi's creativity. His father is Yoruba, his mother Ijo (Bendel State), and this double parentage is also of interesting artistic value in his career. His constant use of Pidgin English (a common language of communication in Bendel State) and of Yoruba myths and rituals in his plays is a clear sign of his dual ethnic origin. Another aspect of his parentage that helped excite Rotimi's creative impulse is the fact that his father, an educated middle-class engineer, was a rhetorician. The young Rotimi was thus exposed to the rudiments of public speaking, which he started practicing at the age of four, when he first participated in a play production.[1]

Rotimi had his postprimary education in Methodist Boys' High School, Lagos, from 1952 to 1957. He proceeded to the USA two years later for undergraduate studies in drama at Boston University. After graduation in 1963, he obtained a Rockefeller Foundation award, which enabled him to undergo further training at Yale University, where he obtained a Master's degree. Rotimi's formal education, both in Nigeria and in the USA, equipped him with a knowledge of the arts of the theatre as well as critical ability and exposed him to the world of literature and the arts in general. All this training and exposure later yielded artistic fruit in his numerous plays and productions. Added to his achievement in the USA is his marriage to a Canadian artist, Hazel, who brings her influence as a musician to bear on her husband's productions.

Rotimi returned to Nigeria in 1966 as a senior research fellow at the Institute of African Studies of the University of Ife. It was during his sojourn in Ife that he had the opportunity to develop his art as a play-wright. The serenity of his position as a fellow at the university also gave him ample time for research and publication. He wrote his two most popular critical essays during this period: "The Drama in African Ritual Display" was published in 1968;[2] "Traditional Nigerian Drama" followed in 1971.[3] These two articles, dealing with the origins, nature, and techniques of drama of the traditional society of Nigeria, reveal Rotimi's keen interest in the precepts of indigenous Nigerian theatre, which was part of his background. It is hardly surprising that this interest is reflected in his theatre experience through his utilization of traditional African performance techniques, an issue to which I shall return later in this essay. Rotimi left Ife for Port Harcourt in 1975. At present he is not a full-time writer. Like most African writers, he is forced by the "exigencies of subsistence"[4] to employ his creative talent part-time. He is full-time professor at the University of Port Harcourt.

Rotimi is responsible and serious yet has the ability to laugh and find fun even when hope appears to be lost. This partly explains why he can infuse humor into his tragic plays even when tension is very high. He believes in justice and fairness as well as in equal opportunity for all, irrespective of sex, religion, and ethnic origin. This philosophy influences his plays, which betray his concern for such oppressed groups as the masses in *If . . . A Tragedy of the Ruled* and *Hopes of the Living Dead,* women in *Our Husband Has Gone Mad Again,* and colonized peoples in *Ovonramwen Nogbaisi.*

Rotimi's knowledge of many Nigerian languages is an indication of his interest in people irrespective of ethnic origin. He speaks English, Yoruba, Ijaw, Igbo, Hausa, and Pidgin and has a little knowledge of a few other Nigerian tongues. His ability to inject these languages into his lectures to create interest and lure his listeners has endeared him to audiences, just as his multilingual approach to playwriting has also yielded success. Rotimi has a vibrant stage voice, which he uses to great advantage as an actor and in his public addresses. His experience with his rhetorician father has combined with his talent and training to make him a good orator. He can use his voice to hold an audience, build up their interest and emotion gradually, swing this emotion, and then withdraw his hold in order to allow a cathartic release. He utilizes this ability tremendously as a University of Port Harcourt orator.[5]

Rotimi's talent in the arts is not limited to the theatre. He is also an art connoisseur. Perhaps his experience at Yale University, where he studied fine arts, has contributed to his taste in the arts. He is also interested in history, and this is of singular importance in his career as a playwright, as I shall note later. His keen appreciation of music is evident in his plays. According to him, "Without music, I can't even get the inspiration to write a play, let alone stage one. I'm inspired by music and I articulate my dramatic formulations through music."[6] As a playwright, Rotimi weaves music into the structure of the play. As a producer, he directs the music and choreographs the dance with the help of his musician wife.

A brief discussion of Rotimi's plays will enhance our appreciation of his creative talent. He has published six major plays: *The Gods Are Not to Blame, Kurunmi, Ovonramwen Nogbaisi, Our Husband Has Gone Mad Again, Holding Talks,* and *If . . . A Tragedy of the Ruled. Hopes of the Living Dead* is not yet published but has been produced. A study of these plays readily shows that Rotimi possesses a tragic vision and a sense of history, a sense that has led to such historical plays as *Kurunmi, Ovonramwen,* and *Hopes.* In addition to these three, which are based on the political struggle of specific groups in the past, the other plays also have concerns which touch on contemporary history. *The Gods* is a reworking of the classical Greek tale of Oedipus in Yoruba cultural terms, yet it is relevant to contemporary history because the Greek mentor fits into the contemporary history of Nigeria. Moreover, the play's questions about the issue of tribalism at a time when Nigeria was going through a war garnished with ethnic sentiments also indicate its historical relevance.

Like the classical Greek antecedents, *The Gods* explores the Oedipal theme in the tragic mode. Rotimi consciously deviates from the tragic style of the classics in order to express his own personality as a Nigerian rooted in his culture. From his background he is able to re-create such traditional African elements as Yoruba myths, songs, Ifa practice, and the narrator technique in the play. He sustains the tragic mood of the dramatic action while swinging the audience's emotions and reactions through his use of song, dance, and comic characters such as Alaka as well as witty and serious dialogue rich in traditional usages. One of the successes of the play has been the character of Alaka,[7] who supposedly tries to dispel the hero's fears and unwittingly commits patricide and incest. Rotimi's ingenuity as a creative adaptor of a foreign work is also seen in his attempt, in the prologue, to familiarize the Nigerian audience with the unfamiliar tale.[8]

Rotimi's popularity in the Nigerian theatre was largely established by his production of *The Gods* in 1968. Consequently, audiences were enthusiastic to receive his next play, *Kurunmi. Kurunmi* is based on Yoruba history, specifically the Ijaiye war of the nineteenth century. It treats the theme of tradition and change against the background of power politics and warfare.

The major character, Kurunmi, is the Are-Ona-Kakanfo (Generalissimo), who leads the Ijaiye people to war in defense of tradition. The play has a tragic denouement for the hero, and his people suffer humiliation, defeat, and destruction.

Rotimi's personality again shows itself here. He uses theatrical structures which are common in the traditional theatres of his background. Clusters of singers, dancers, musicians, warriors, and other groups are part of the stage action. These can become unwieldy if not well handled, but they are so artistically woven into the dramatic action that one can hardly complain about the play's theatricality. For example, the Ijaiye warriors who rush onto the stage are in pursuit of their enemy, the Ibadan soldiers. The dialogue and action of the warriors influence the events of the play. It is the decision of the third warrior that leads the group into the enemy trap and thus influences the tragic turn of the conflict. Although the play is set in the past, it is relevant to contemporary life, because "its comments often seem as pertinent to the tragedies of our age as they are to those of days long ago."[9] For example, the issue of tradition and change and its relevance in determining the course of contemporary Nigerian history still rears its head in the power politics of the country.Ovonramwen is another play which is based on nineteenth-century events in Nigeria. It portrays the tragic consequences of the clash between the powerful Oba of Benin, Ovonramwen Nogbaisi, and the British colonialists who were scheming to control the source of trade. In theatrical terms Rotimi is doing what modern Nigerian historians such as Onwuka Dike and Obaro Ikime are doing: reconstructing African history, correcting false views of the clash between African nations and the colonists.[10] In Ovonramwen Rotimi shows the fall of Benin as an effect of the British scheme to control African nations for economic reasons, not just of the Benin monarch's tyrannical rule. Phillips, the representative of the Queen of England, affirms that they must disregard Benin tradition and enter Benin during the Ague festival, because "the conduct of trade in the Colonies demands direct contact with the interior that produces the goods" (ON, 31). Although the British intrusion into Benin plays an important role in directing the dramatic action toward its catastrophic end, the contradictions within the Benin kingdom aid the foreign element.

The tragic action of the play, from exposition through climax to the fall of the hero, takes place in the first two acts. The third and final act, which deals with the aftermath of the tragic denouement, creates pathos and thus does not enhance the structure of the tragedy. It merely shows Rotimi's attempt at the reconstruction and accurate portrayal of historical reality. His account of Benin history through theatre strikes a concordant note with Ngūgī wa Thiong'o and Micere Mugo's reconstruction of the distorted Kenyan history through their play The Trial of Dedan Kimanthi.[11] As in Dedan Kimanthi, Rotimi uses mime, music, and song as devices for commenting on, underscoring, and anticipating action, a characteristic that permeates most of his plays and betrays his presence as a man who loves music and is rooted in the precepts of traditional African theatre. If . . . A Tragedy of the Ruled also reveals Rotimi's personality and interest in contemporary history. His concern for the oppressed receives theatrical attention here, as the play exposes the exploitation of the people by the rich and powerful men of society. His concern for the masses and his insight into a possible means of solving that problem show in his recognition of group cohesion and franchise as viable tools that can be used for the liberation of the oppressed. However, the people fail to use this power to effect good leadership, and this leads to the tragic conclusion of the play. Thus, If is sociopolitical and ends on a pessimistic note, but through a powerful instrument of mass communication (theatre) Rotimi succeeds in sensitizing the consciousness of the people. The fact that the dramatic personages fail to utilize their power properly served as a warning to the original audience, which was preparing for general elections at the time the play was first produced (1979). The play therefore seemed to foreshadow the political reality of contemporary elections and politics in Nigeria and sounded a warning to the electorate.

In If Rotimi once again shows his love for music, since songs and chants are dynamically integral to the action. For example, the contemporary music of Sunny Okosun, "Fire in Soweto," is not just a melodious element used for entertainment. The message of the music underlines Rotimi's intention of using the South African example to sensitize the audience to their own plight in Nigeria. In addition, the music is used as a basis for awakening the consciousness of the audience through the poignant dialogue between the then-ignorant Betty and the politically conscious Hamidu (55–56). Similarly, the children's song, which follows the rhythm of a religious catechism chanted by rote, contains a message which is directly relevant to them as future leaders of the nation: "Self-reliance, self help / This is the only way . . . / To build a great nation" (58). In this way music becomes a dramatic technique that not only entertains but also serves a political purpose, for it rouses the political consciousness of the people at various levels.

It is in Rotimi's unpublished play, Hopes of the Living Dead, that the oppressed get what they failed to achieve in If, and it shows a new angle to Rotimi's historical plays. The issue of political struggle resurfaces here in the plight of the lepers and their struggle for redemption from their oppressors. As with *Kurunmi* and *Ovonramwen*, the source of *Hopes* is historical, in this case the experience of lepers in Port Harcourt in the late twenties and early thirties. Rotimi's treatment of the subject is serious; even though the play uses a good deal of music and humor, these do not diffuse the pathos of the action. The work does deviate, however, from the usual tragic denouement of Rotimi's plays, as the oppressed lepers triumph and the play concludes on a merely pessimistic note.

The discussion thus far has shown that Rotimi possesses a sense of history and a tragic vision, as well as an ability to laugh even in the face of serious problems. However, it must be noted that Rotimi is also capable of making the audience laugh extensively at itself. The issue of oppression and leadership, for example, is treated comically in *Our Husband Has Gone Mad Again*. The play is based on the experience of Lejoka Brown, a politician who exploits women but is ultimately outwitted by women in politics. He is rejected by the electorate because he lacks the ability to pilot his own domestic affairs, where he is revealed as a cheat and an authoritarian. Through the play Rotimi sends a message to the Nigerian electorate and once more shows his interest in sensitizing the consciousness of the people, who should not waste their votes on those who prove unworthy in smaller tasks. One major achievement of the play lies in its sarcastic and humorous exposition of the bigotry, crudity, selfishness, and exploitation that is part of Nigerian politics. These are qualities hated by the social critic Rotimi, who uses his art "to indurate the people towards grappling with forces inimical to their well-being in the real world.[12]

Language is one very important device for creating laughter in *Our Husband*. Mirth is evoked, for instance, through the characters' use of Pidgin English, a language that has been noted for its creation of humor in drama.[13] Rotimi's background in Bendel State, where Pidgin is freely used, is of artistic advantage here, and he utilizes his knowledge of different levels of Pidgin. Madam Ajanaku's language, for instance, demonstrates the eloquence and showiness of the market woman, whereas Lejoka Brown's speech is a good example of the rhetoric of the loud and crude politician. Rotimi uses Pidgin to characterize as well as to amuse.

One can also see the man behind the play through the music employed to create a sense of fun and to emphasize conflict. Popular tunes are twisted and juxtaposed with new contexts in awkward situations, creating surprise and delight. The contemporary music of the taxi driver, "I Don't Care," takes on new shape and significance in Sikira's rendering of her reply to Liza's

claim as the wife of Lejoka Brown (*OH*, 25). Similarly, Lejoka Brown uses the well-known tune of the national anthem to render "Pig Like Lejoka Brown" (*OH*, 41), a sarcastic song which creates humor through its ridicule of Lejoka Brown's unsuitability for leadership.

Another work that uses the comic mode is *Holding Talks*, an absurdist play which employs humorous and absurd situations to explore the weariness and dissatisfaction resulting from inaction. Rotimi shows his impatience with the contemporary attitude toward events demanding instant action. He admits that the play is a "reaction to a growing preference of our Age for talking even in the face of situations demanding action and obvious solutions."[14] A barber is hungry. Nothing is done. He collapses and still nothing is done. Instead, his appalling situation becomes the subject of discussions and press photographs, at the end of which nothing has changed for him, as he continues to lie there naked. The plot consists of many strange incidents which appear unreal, illogical, and funny, yet on close appraisal we realize that they parody our very existence. For example, the policewoman engages in an argument with Man over the procedure for investigative interrogation instead of taking the dying or dead man to the hospital. Man and Apprentice also waste a lot of time arguing about whether the barber just collapsed or is actually dead. The illogicality of the situation and the triviality of the arguments evoke bitter laughter. It is in this seeming illogicality that the play's historical perspective can be gleaned, for the actions parody contemporary social life's penchant for discourse and the application of bureaucratic red tape even when situations demand instant action.

> France flagrantly exploding bombs in the Pacific, the United Nations "discussing" the situation! The Republic of Guinea under invasion by Portuguese mercenaries, the O.A.U. arranging "Talks" on the incident to take place some two weeks after the deed. Africans in Mozambique being massacred, the world press "sending in observers" and "debating the issue" etc, etc.[15]

Holding Talks shows the playwright's ability to use humor and dialogue to illustrate humankind's frequent inanity even when faced with catastrophe, what Soyinka might call the "recurrent cycle of human stupidity.[16] The play embodies Rotimi's influence as a rhetorician. One appreciates his ability to use words, stretch them in dialogue, and make them yield sense or no sense in accordance with the dictates of the absurdist play.

The foregoing discussion of Rotimi as a playwright shows that he is sensitive to the human predicament and committed to the articulation of various aspects of this predicament in his plays. He weeps, talks, laughs, and sings about human problems in a bid to sensitize the audience into finding possible ways of solving the problems. Thus the theatrical vision of most of Rotimi's plays encompasses the same thematic world, a world that is bitter and tragic yet humorous and musical. The cathartic exploration of man's response to the dynamics of power, change, and fate is structurally designed to evoke the tragic mood of *The Gods, Kurunmi, Ovonramwen, If,* and *Hopes.* With great humor, Rotimi shows a similar concern in *Our Husband* through the main character's quest for leadership. In this way Rotimi dances in the same thematic ambience, albeit in different dramatic modes.

Similarly, his dramatic spectacle, which is largely influenced by his experience in traditional Nigerian theatrical practice, always draws from a pool of stage icons. He uses the icons successfully to make up for the inadequacy of a proscenium stage that is basically unsophisticated when compared to its Western counterparts. Dapo Adelugba calls Rotimi an expert in the creation of stage icons,[17] and Banham and Wake refer to this when they argue that Rotimi's plays are "conceived in generous terms."[18] Rotimi can create a large cast that includes crowds, armies, and musicians to support dramatic action, and these help establish the communal atmosphere that has come to be associated with his work for the stage. This communality is another characteristic which links Rotimi to his background in traditional theatre. In spite of the large casts, the action, movement, dance, and mime are usually well orchestrated by the playwright, who normally directs his own plays.

Nigerian audiences appreciate Rotimi's use of stage icons and have come to expect it. They are sometimes surprised and even disappointed when they do not find theatrical elements in his plays. Although the Port Harcourt audience enjoyed the production of *Holding Talks* in 1979, a few admitted that it was not what they expected from Rotimi because of the absence of the type of music, dance, and crowds that are the usual features of his plays. Rotimi shares his use of music and dance with another notable modern Nigerian dramatist, Meki Nzewi, whose performances also draw "full and spilling" houses, like Rotimi's. Whereas Nzewi uses music and dance to beef up the story line in performances that have been called opera-dramas,[19] Rotimi uses music and dance not just for support but as a dynamic part of the dramatic conflict of extended plots.

The use of music and dance by Rotimi even in his tragedies has puzzled some critics, who feel that this reduces the tragic impact of the action. It must be noted that for Rotimi and for many traditional African performers, music and dance are not distractions but instead are essentially elements that can heighten the trag-

ic mood, as do the dirges in *The Gods* and *Ovonramwen,* for example. Rotimi understands the theatrical sensibility of the Nigerian audience and strives to please them in his productions. Femi Euba says that Rotimi takes apparent joy in his audience.[20] His expertise as a dramatist enables him to manipulate stagecraft in such a way that he can keep his audience even when he reduces the stage icons, as in *If,* or withdraws them, as in *Holding Talks.* His recent experimentation in language is a sign of his interest in the audience and the problem of language in a multiethnic nation such as Nigeria. He is aware of the barriers created by language in his country and tries to lure his audiences by using many Nigerian tongues. In *If* he employs up to six languages to supplement English; in the production of *Hopes,* he used more than ten. These added elements broaden the linguistic framework of his plays and maintain the interest and attention of his audience. They also encourage Nigerians to strive to break the language barrier and seek better understanding with fellow citizens irrespective of ethnic origin. In *Hopes* people of different ethnic backgrounds cooperate to fight the common enemy oppressing them.

Rotimi's popularity with audiences stems from his ability as a playwright and ingenuity as a director and theatre organizer. As a playwright he employs the conventional technique of creating tension through suspense and action that leans on music and dance. As a director he utilizes his experience in theatre and rhetoric. He controls the action and subjects his actors to rigorous rehearsals, paying close attention to details of language, inflection, the slightest movements and gestures, dance patterns, and choreography.[21] In short, he demands the "flesh and blood and even the soul" of his actors.[22] This is largely responsible for the high standard of his productions.

Details of the iconography evident in Rotimi's productions are not usually fully explained in his works. According to Adelugba, the "sense of theatrical iconography is often unrecorded in the published play."[23] This criticism is a tribute to Rotimi's expertise as a director and producer. His competence as a director is used to judge his ability as a playwright. As a playwright, Rotimi does not believe in lengthy stage directions like those of Bernard Shaw.[24] He gives the director a guideline which serves as basis for expressing the latter's own creative resourcefulness as an artist. It is from such guidelines that Rotimi, as director, creates his popular spectacles.

Rotimi's theatre flouts the conventions of the proscenium style of performance. He sees the proscenium as a structure which inhibits the freedom of the actors and audience, unlike the traditional open-air theatre, which promotes the physical and psychological closeness of performers and spectators.[25] He adopts a style which gives the actors the freedom to feel the audience and mingle with them, as can be gleaned from his work as a playwright and producer. As a playwright he does this through stage directions. For example, in a manner reminiscent of Efua Sutherland's seating of members of the audience in a courtyard in *Edufa*,[26] Rotimi places members of Oba Ovonramwen's council among the audience. According to the stage direction, "It is suggested that some chiefs and communality move into the auditorium and share seats with members of the audience" (*ON*, 51).

As in his playscripts, his productions show his attempt at breaking down the constraints of the proscenium stage. There are no strict boundaries marking out the stage. The action defines the acting space, which can include any part of the physical theatre. The actors may walk through the audience area, thus extending their acting space outside the conventional stage of the proscenium theatre, as in *Hopes*. They may also fill the stage and the orchestra pit, as in the crowd scenes of *The Gods*.

Rotimi's interest in the creation of a theatre that is uninhibited and free like the traditional African theatre is given expression not only in his scripts and productions but also in the theatres he has helped found. In 1968, at the University of Ife, he established the Ori Olokun theatre group, which became a center of dramatic experience between townfolk and university people.[27] The meeting place, the group's physical theatre, was an open-air courtyard structure, a kind of theatre in a rectangle. The structure, similar to the courtyard of many traditional palaces and homes, fostered a creative atmosphere that was not totally alien to the theatrical sensibility of the townfolk, who were drawn to the theatre as performers. The Ori Olokun experiment was "a remarkable attempt to design a modern stage loyal to an authentically traditional Nigerian situation."[28]

Rotimi also founded another playhouse, the Crab, which was also adapted from the traditional open-air theatre. The Crab, at the University of Port Harcourt, owes its design to Rotimi's insistence on employing the expertise of Demas Nwoko, a notable Nigerian artist whose reputation as an architect is largely based on his ingenuity in adapting traditional modes to suit modern design. The Crab Theater is an amphitheatre and has the advantage of promoting a physical and psychological rapport between audience and performers much like that which obtains in traditional theatre.

In sum, Ola Rotimi is a giant in the Nigerian stage world. His traditionalism and his sensitivity to the problems of society significantly influence his works, and he takes up these problems in his plays, which adapt traditional African theatre techniques within a modern context. His sense of history also influences his plays, which seem to affirm the fact that the past influences the present and therefore must always be reviewed in order to build the present and the future. The popularity of his productions, resulting from his talent as a playwright, his ingenuity as a director, and his meticulousness as an organizer, has given him a special place in the Nigerian theatre. He is respected both by the cast and crew who work with him and by the audience he strives to impress. Although he has achieved greatness in the field of drama, this is not the end. His career is still flourishing. He is not yet old. Thus, more good things are still expected of this renowned man of the theatre.

Chinyere G. Okafor, Winter 1990

■ PLAYS BY OLA ROTIMI

The Gods Are Not to Blame. London. Oxford University Press. 1971. (G)

Kurunmi. Ibadan, Nigeria. Ibadan University Press. 1971. (K)

Ovonramwen Nogbaisi. Benin City, Nigeria. Ethiope. 1974. (ON)

Our Husband Has Gone Mad Again. London. Oxford University Press. 1977. (OH)

Holding Talks. Ibadan. Ibadan University Press. 1979. (HT)

If . . . A Tragedy of the Ruled. Ibadan. Heinemann. 1983.

Hopes of the Living Dead. Unpublished. First performed in 1985 at the University of Nigeria, Nsukka.

---

[1] Ola Rotimi, production program of *Our Husband Has Gone Mad Again,* University of Ife Institute of African Studies Files; cited by Dapo Adelugba, "Three Dramatists in Search of a Language," in *Theatre in Africa,* Oyin Ogunba and Abiola Irele, eds., Ibadan, Ibadan University Press, 1978, p. 213.

[2] Ola Rotimi, "The Drama in African Ritual Display," *Nigeria Magazine,* 99 (1968).

[3] Ola Rotimi, "Traditional Nigerian Drama," in *Introduction to Nigerian Literature,* Bruce King, ed., London, Evans, 1971.

[4] Ola Rotimi, "The Trials of African Literature," public lecture delivered at the opening of the English and Literature Students' Association Week, University of Benin, 4 May 1987, p. 5.

[5] Rotimi's spectacular introduction of the guest of honor at the installation of the first chancellor of the University of Port Harcourt in 1979 was one of the highlights of the ceremony.

[6] Effiok Bassey Uwatt, "Interview with Professor Ola Rotimi," in "Towards the Evolution of a New Nigerian Theatre: A Study of Form in the Plays of Ola Rotimi," Ph.D. diss., University of Benin, 1988, p. 265.

[7] Martin Banham with Clive Wake, *African Theatre Today,* London, Pitman, 1976, p. 44.

[8] E. J. Asgill, "African Adaptation of Greek Tragedies," *African Literature Today,* 2 (1980), p. 180.

[9] Banham/Wake, p. 45.

[10] See K. O. Dike, *Trade and Politics in the Niger Delta,* Oxford, Clarendon, 1956; and Obaro Ikime, *The Fall of Nigeria,* London, Heinemann, 1971.

[11] Ngũgĩ wa Thiong'o and Micere Mugo, *The Trial of Dedan Kimathi,* London, Heinemann, 1975.

[12] Rotimi, "The Trials of African Literature," p. 14.

[13] Martin Banham, "Note on Nigerian Theatre: 1966," *Bulletin of the Association for African Literature in English,* 4 (1966), p. 32.

[14] Ola Rotimi, production notes of *Holding Talks,* University of Port Harcourt, 1979.

[15] Ibid.

[16] Wole Soyinka, "The Writer in Modern Africa," *Scandinavian Institute of African Studies* (Uppsala), 1968, p. 20.

[17] Adelugba, p. 215

[18] Banham/Wake, p. 45.

[19] Meki Nzewi, "Music, Dance, Drama and the Stage in Nigeria," in *Drama and Theatre in Nigeria,* Yemi Ogunbiyi, ed., Lagos, Nigeria Magazine, 1981, p. 449.

[20] Femi Euba, "The Nigerian Theatre and the Playwright," in *Drama and Theatre in Nigeria,* p. 393.

[21] I cite these facts from firsthand experience in Rotimi's productions as an actress and assistant director.

[22] Production note to *Hopes of the Living Dead,* University of Nigeria at Nsukka, 1985.

[23] Adelugba, p. 215.

[24] Uwatt, p. 264.

[25] *Dem Say: Interviews with Eight Nigerian Writers,* Bernth Lindfors, ed., Austin, University of Texas Press, 1974, pp. 60–61.

[26] Efua Sutherland, *Edufa,* London, 1967, p. 1.

[27] Nzewi, p. 456.

[28] Nzewi, p. 437.

Soyinka's Smoking Shotgun: The Later Satires

Wole Soyinka did not coin the term *shotgun writing*— "you discharge and disappear"—until the 1970s.[1] He had, however, produced occasional subversive satiric sketches throughout the previous decade, and his unpublished one-act Royal Court entertainment *The Invention* (1959), a caustic tour de force on universal racism set in a futuristic South Africa, had been written in the broad satiric tradition of the revue. During the deepening crisis of Nigeria's First Republic, as political murders became more frequent and blatant intimidation by power-addicted local chiefs escalated daily, Soyinka opted increasingly for the direct thrust and immediate corrective impact of the revue sketch performed hot on the heels of the event. In *The New Republican* (1964) and *Before the Blackout* (1965, published in selection in 1971) the targets were various acts of public cowardice

and sycophancy performed before both the new time-serving, opportunistic politicians and Nigeria's traditional rulers, portrayed in the sketches either as lecherous rogues or as corrupt feudal chieftains who had betrayed their people throughout history.

Soyinka, however, acknowledged in his preface to *Before the Blackout* the familiar paradox of the satirist: the acute topicality of the material made it libelous in print and dangerously open to political reprisal, but once its targets were dead or dethroned and it ceased to be a threat, it also ceased to be topical. Thus those sketches have worn least well in which Soyinka, working on the assumption that wrongs are only correctable if identifiable, attacked the individual villain rather than the villainy and took little trouble to camouflage his identity. Possible afterthoughts on the short life of close-range satire prompted him, in his prefatory comments, to leave loopholes for updating and contemporary adaptation, and it is significant that the most enduring and most frequently revived of these sketches make no specific contemporary references (notably, the perennially popular *Childe Internationale,* in which a traditional Yoruba father takes in hand his affected been-to wife and his obnoxious daughter, outrageously Americanized by one of the new international schools).[2] The issues raised by this form of satire served as an example, and also as a warning, for Soyinka's later work in the "shotgun" mold, to which he returned in the midseventies.

The year 1975, which brought *Death and the King's Horseman* and Soyinka's return to Nigeria after five years in exile, was something of a water-shed in his dramatic career. About this time, whether in response to the exigencies of the worsening political situation or to the pressures of criticism leveled at his work by the Nigerian Left, the dramatist chose to strip from his drama its complex ritual and mythological idiom and informing Yoruba world view in favor of the subversive, agit-prop satiric revue, written for performance rather than for publication. This more popular form was adopted for the purpose of urgent political communication with a mass audience, and the works written in it, usually published some years after production and in some case not at all, are theatrical amphibians with one foot in the textual world of Western drama and the other in the improvisational comic folk theater, or *alawada,* of the Yoruba world. Whereas the 1960s revue sketches left occasional loopholes for topical adaptation, this later work was much looser in structure and more openly experimental in approach. "The text of the play was never completely written as it was ever being rewritten and reshaped during rehearsals," Yemi Ogunbiyi has said of Soyinka's production of *Opera Wonyosi* (1977). "Nothing was finally arrived at until the play closed. . . . For him [Soyinka] the text, even his own text, was merely a map with many possible routes."[3] This largely unscripted, hit-and-run kind of street theater, targeting specific political enormities, mounted with minimal publicity, and vanishing before the players could be rounded up by the police of the latest repressive regime, maintained a topical commentary which was best suited to the raw atmosphere of marketplace and lorry park. "The cosy, escapist air of formal theatres tends to breed amnesia much too quickly," Soyinka had remarked of his earlier sketches of the 1960s.[4]

Over the next decade the links between Soyinka's theatrical and political involvements were to be particularly close, and the "shotgun" satires, running a constant caustic calypso on public affairs, were a frontline force in the responses to Nigeria's succession of political and economic crises and subsequent scandals and outrages: shrinking oil revenues, plunging foreign exchange, the chronic shortage of books and information, and multiplying ministerial embezzlements and political murders. Sometimes pointedly Nigerian in reference, as in Before the Blowout (1978) and Priority Projects (1983), and sometimes concerned with evils on the African continent at large, as in Opera Wonyosi, the revue satires have in their favor the urgent relevance of their political comment and the spontaneity of the theatrical "happening," with its capacity for surprise, shock, and audience involvement. In their published form, however, they inevitably suffer from a limiting topicality and ephemerality. Performance here has priority, and when the works' virtuoso satiric techniques are allowed to interfere with the dramatic integrity of fully-crafted stage plays, the results are apt to be disappointing: a satiric meanness of characterization, instanced in the mechanical lining up and wheeling on of slight and unsubstantial targets (Requiem for a Futurologist, 1985); and a linguistic flatness and general thinness of texture (A Play of Giants, 1984), the more noticeable after the verable richness and somber grandeur of Death and the King's Horseman. The invasion of Soyinka's stage drama by the styles and techniques of the opportunistic satiric revue has, I suspect, had much to do with the marked dilution of the substance and quality of his later dramatic writing. Opera Wonyosi, a ballad opera first performed in 1977 but not published until 1981, is the most substantial and sustained of these satires. With the aid of an eclectic medley of English ballads, Kurt Weill songs, jazz and blues, and the tunes of the 1950s Ibo folk singer Israel Ijemanze, Soyinka transposes the eighteenth-century London of Gay's Beggars' Opera and the Victorian Soho of Brecht's Threepenny Opera to a bidonville of Bangui, capital of the former Central African Republic,

on the eve of the imperial coronation of Jean-Bedel Bokassa, who was to be overthrown two years later when his involvement in the murder of schoolchildren became widely known. The obscenely decadent extravaganza of Bokassa's coronation in one of Africa's poorest countries, which took place in the same week as Soyinka's Ife production, substitutes for the royal jubilee that forms the background to the action in the Gay and Brecht originals and provides Macheath with his royal reprieve at the climax. (Significantly, in Soyinka's African version, the royal pardon which liberates vicious criminals is not extended to political detainees.) The emperor "Boky," or "Folksy Boksy," a crazy caricature of feudal barbarism mixed with servile, sentimental Francophilia, makes one unforgettable appearance in the play, during which he drills and clubs senseless his goon squad before stomping off to "pulp the brains" of the children who have refused to wear his uniforms. The motley collection of rogues and thugs who make up the cast of Opera Wonyosi, however, are Nigerian expatriates. These are the "beggarly" racketeers of Chief Anikura (the Peachum of the original); the venal police chief and security expert "Tiger" Brown, on loan to the emperor; the psychopathic Colonel Moses, military adviser to the same; and the thieves, arsonists, drug peddlers, and murderers gathered around the highway robber Macheath. Lest the audience jump to the conclusion that the Nigerian military regime has exported all of its undesirable elements, however, it is made clear at the outset that the expatriate cliques of the Nigerian quarter are meant to serve as a satiric microcosm of the home country during the oil boom of the seventies. In a program note Soyinka insisted that "the genius of race portrayed in this opera is entirely, indisputably and vibrantly Nigerian."

Preferring Gay's ebullient indictment of specific historical vices and corruptions to Brecht's portrayal of universal human depravity, Soyinka uses the wisecracking cynicism of the expatriate scoundrels to draw up a ghastly inventory of Nigerian outrages in the years of the oil dollar or "petro-naira": government-sponsored extortion and assassination; arson and atrocities by a powerdrunk soldiery (notoriously, the burning down of Fela Kuti's "Kalakuta Republic"); the public flogging of traffic offenders and execution of felons; murderously punitive industrial conditions in government cement works and levels of state responsibility so low that month-old corpses were left to decompose on public highways; and a general craze for wealth which was epitomized by the wearing of the gaudy wonyosi, the absurdly ragged-looking but fantastically expensive lace that was the rage of the tasteless Nigerian nouveaux riches in the 1970s. (Ogunbiyi points out that, accented in a certain way, *opera* in Yoruba can mean "the fool buys.")[5]

Anikura's beggars are, of course, more than what they seem, and their feigned physical deformities are more than distant symbolic allusions to the moral deformation of their country. Among the ragged band are lawyers, professors, doctors, and clergymen whose begging is used by Soyinka as a precise metaphor for the shameless sycophancy to "khaki and brass," the groveling in military gutters by which the professional classes won preferment and promotion during the years of "nairomania" ("Khaki is a man's best friend," runs the refrain of one song). Sycophancy, backed up by coercion, is the way to a slice of the national cake. In the words of the garrulous Dee-Jay, who replaces Gay's beggarly poet and Brecht's Moritatensänger, "That's what the whole nation is doing—begging for a slice of the action. . . . Here the beggars say, 'Give me a slice of action, or—give me a slice off your throat.'"[6] But Soyinka literalizes his metaphors, and labors them somewhat, by having his mendicant professionals turn professional mendicants. Professor Bamgbapo, who has "bagged" the chairmanships of a number of industrial corporations as well as his university chair by "sucking up to the army boys" ("To beg is to bag," runs the beggars' anthem), has even come to Anikura for "a refresher course" in the form of fieldwork with full-time beggars! (65). Thus the street beggars become synonymous with fawning bureaucrats, and the small crooks actually turn into big ones before our eyes. Anikura, the brain behind the beggars' protection racket (a "beneficent society for the relief of burdened consciences"), is "chairman of highly successful groups of companies," while Polly plays the stock market and, if we can believe it, amalgamates Macheath enterprises with a multinational corporation: "Let's go legitimate like the bigger crooks" (46, 62, 66). However, though the links between legal business practice and crime, and between capitalism and gangsterdom, are certainly present, Soyinka's play is not the assault on capitalism which Brecht meant his to be; instead it is essentially a satire on power. The culprit is the oil-produced wealth that promoted power and the target the criminal lengths to which people were prepared to go to get the money that would buy them power. *Opera Wonyosi* is devastating, merciless satire, and the government's prompt intervention to prevent a Lagos production was proof that the play had struck powerfully home. There are odd moments of pure hilarity (Anikura's reference to the American habit of "pleading the Fifth Commandment"), and the dialogue crackles with verbal play ("While Mackie and Brown were ripping the insides of foes" in the civil war, the notorious corpse-stripping "attack traders" were "ripping off

both sides"), but the sugar coating on the bitter satiric pill is usually very thin (71, 43). Sometimes the tone is brash, swaggering cynicism in the Brechtian mode, as in Macheath's remark that the stupidity in a Nigerian can be only temporary or feigned because "the smell of money endows the dumbest Nigerian with instant intelligence," or Anikura's comment that fraud by one's fellow countrymen is an infallible alibi for destitution, since everyone knows "that any Nigerian will rob his starving grandmother and push her in the swamp" (54, 4). The latter threatens to have an army of real beggars march on coronation day, not to embarrass tyranny with poverty but to blackmail it into arresting his personal enemy Macheath. At other times the satire is pure vitriolic rage, as in the Bangui equivalent of the Bar Beach Show at Mackie's execution, where schoolchildren are given a holiday to watch the spectacle on television and a deathbed patient from the hospital falls over his wheelchair in righteous bloodlust for a ringside seat and promptly bursts into a gruesome parody of Donald Swann's "Hippopotamus Song": "Blood, blood, glorious blood / Nothing quite like it for offering to God / Banish the gallows / So I can wallow / In the crimson juice of the criminal sod!" (78). Reality here seems always one step ahead of satiric invention, and the unspeakable needs little enhancement from the writer to provoke a sense of outrage.

The terrorizing of civilian populations by megalomaniacal military buffoons and the squalid compliance of the professional classes, cowed by a mendicant mentality, were the painful Nigerian and African realities of the 1970s, and satire targeted at them walks the fine edge between the real and the surreal. Soyinka stated in the playbill to the 1977 Ife production that "the characters in this opera are either strangers or fictitious, for Nigeria is stranger than fiction, and any resemblance to any Nigerian, living or dead, is purely accidental, unintentional and instructive."[7] The repellant historical originals of characters like Boky, more grotesque than any invention, have a way of parodying themselves, but even in the case of the more generalized Nigerian material the preposterous reality keeps breaking through at unexpected moments to dissolve the conventional safe divisions between the stage world and the "real" world. The very closeness of these two worlds made possible a number of surprise effects in performance: Soyinka had the "attack trade" women descend into the audience at the interval to sell their grisly wares, and a coffin, ostensibly containing the real corpse scooped from the roadside the previous day by Tai Solarin, was carried by pallbearers into the auditorium, thus implicating everyone in willful blindness to the daily public obscenity. In one performance the shock tactics of the

Theater of the Real were even turned against his own actors: on Soyinka's secret instructions, his orchestra halted the opening number so that Professor Bamgbapo (played by a real-life academic) could be dragged from the chorus and, in front of a university audience, thrashed by a figure looking very much like a real-life Nigerian army officer.

Time has, inevitably, taken the sting from the satire in these topical allusions, which call for constant updating, but Soyinka has been equal to the task. One year on he reassembled his beggarly crew on Nigerian soil to satirize political opportunism at the lifting of the ban on political activities and a contemporaneous national wave of car thefts: in the two sketches of *Before the Blowout,* "Home to Roost" and "Big Game Safari," Chief Anikura (now Onikura) returns home to pursue the career of a popular philanthropic politician and smuggles in new and stolen cars to sell at inflated prices or use in his electoral campaign (the cars are the "big game," hidden in the jungle and hunted down with metal detectors). In a 1983 revival of the opera itself Soyinka dispensed with Colonel Moses altogether, replacing him with a subtle and slippery academic advisor more suited to the civilian government of the Second Republic. This ability to improvise modifications around basic structures of dialogue, song, and mime to suit changing venues and historical contexts is, along with the amount of audience participation, in the best traditions of the traveling mask theater, the *alarinjo,* which name originated, appropriately, as a term of abuse referring to "rogues, vagabonds and sturdy beggars."[8]

The published text of such works can give only slight indication of their effectiveness in performance, but few critics would single out *Opera Wonyosi* as Soyinka's best work. The musical score has not been widely commended, and even within the loose and highly stylized form of the Brechtian play-with-songs, which attempts no naturalistic blend of lyric and action, the plot creaks with some rather obvious devices. Chief among these is Macheath's invalidation of Anikura's charge against him by having the begging fraternity declared a secret society of the kind banned by the Nigerian military regime: the point is simply to set up the satiric tour de force of the beggar-lawyer Alatako, who succeeds in proving that the government is itself a conspiratorial secret society, a cartel created for mass exploitation and terrorization, implemented always by "unknown soldiers." The extreme length of *Wonyosi* draws attention to its episodic, patchwork structure—neither a full-length play nor a series of revue sketches—and the mechanical tying of the action back to the Gay and Brecht originals proves irksome at times. Mackie's sexual intrigues and betrayals are poorly integrated into the anti-Nigerian satire, and, though Macheath's largely allegorical connection with big business hints cynically at the "moral" of the big fish going free, this is but a faint gesture toward exploding the light opera's conventional happy ending. In accordance with the latter, he turns out to be a lovable rogue whom we feel, in some way, deserves to cheat his fate—an impression quite at odds with that conveyed by the local satire that he is a vicious and evil force rotting society from top to bottom. Macheath, in this version as in the Gay and Brecht models, is a rather artificial villain, something of a satiric dead end, and Soyinka's use of the character has a free rein only when he departs from his originals or takes such liberties with them as to make them say something entirely new.

In his foreword to the play Soyinka envisages his task as "the turning up of the maggot-infested underside of the compost heap" as "a prerequisite of the land's transformation" (iv), and he has said elsewhere that if satire is to have any reformist or revolutionary purpose, the satirist must first arouse "a certain nausea towards a particular situation, to arouse them [people] at all to accept a positive alternative when it is offered to them."[9] For Soyinka, the satirist appears to be a kind of purifying *carrier* who, through ridicule and disgust, clears away the junk of the existing order to make possible the construction of an alternative one; it is the role of another—the reformer—to discover that alternative. He does not take the negative view of satire as a social safety valve, having merely therapeutic or cathartic value, but neither does he see it as offering solutions. *Opera Wonyosi* was criticized, somewhat unfairly, by the Nigerian Left for its failure "to lay bare unambiguously the causal historical and socio-economic network of society" and for its lack of "a solid class perspective."[10] Soyinka has replied to these critics that the satirist's business is not exposition but exposure—in this case of the "decadent, rotted underbelly of a society that has lost its direction" (iii)—and that programs of reform and revolutionary alternatives are the province of the social analyst and ideologist, to whose roles the writer's own distinctive vocation is merely complementary (ii-iii).

Still, there are varying depths and densities of exposure, and if there is in *Wonyosi* suprisingly little penetration, for such a long play, of the forces underlying the crimes and corruptions passingly referred to, then the fault is not that exposure is unaccompanied by analysis but that too much is being exposed for anything to be focused very clearly. In the last third of the play the topical references to guilty parties crowd too thick and fast into the text—some speeches are mere lists of suppressed riots, arson, and lootings—and the result is satiric overkill. The opera takes on too many issues, is too thinly all-embracing, and the overall effect is a diffusion of intensity, a kind of satiric tear-gassing instead of a few carefully aimed bullets, more smoke than shot. Soyinka has always been more of a crusader than a revolutionary, campaigning for selected causes rather than for the total transformation of society, and in the late seventies he advanced some of these causes by directing the Oyo State Road Safety Corps, bombarding the press with letters on police harassment, censorship, and political corruption, and, in 1980, affiliating himself with the short-lived People's Redemption Party. At the launching of his autobiography *Aké* in 1981 he protested that his "faith in an inevitable revolution" had nothing to do with his own actions but was based squarely in the depredations of the Shagari government.[11] Nevertheless, Soyinka's use of his Guerilla Theater Unit to mobilize opinion against the Shagari government and his attempts during the years of the Second Republic (1979–83) to reach a wider audience by experimenting with the more popular mediums of street theater, Gramophone records, and film have all the makings of revolutionary art. *Rice Unlimited* (1981), in which the actors piled sacks marked "rice" in front of a police-guarded House of Assembly, attacked the running down of food production during the years of oil mania and the subsequent government racketeering in the sale and resale of imported rice, which made staple foodstuffs unavailable or unaffordable for most of the population. Another unpublished collection of sketches, *Priority Projects* (1983), provocatively performed under the nose of Shagari's personal security guards during a presidential visit to the University of Ife, targeted abortive agricultural and building schemes designed to enrich a ruling party in open connivance with business tycoons, police commissioners, and traditional chiefs. In these sketches the nation which the civil war was fought to keep united is seen as really being two countries: "Mr Country Hide and his brother Seek." The big political brother hides millions of naira, pouring them down bottomless pits of extravagance and corruption (the futile digging and filling in of holes is a prevailing image) while his brother on the street searches in vain for some visible return from the reckless spending. Some of the songs from *Priority Projects* appear on Soyinka's hit record "Unlimited Liability Company" (1983). The scandals of the anarchic Shagari administration—illegal currency exportation, private jets and helicopters, criminals appointed to company directorships, arson and massacre, deportation of political opponents, municipal breakdowns resulting in part-time electricity and mountains of uncollected refuse—are mercilessly exposed in their sharp, instantly graspable Pidgin lyrics: "You tief one kobo, dey put you in prison / You tief ten million, na patriotism."[12]

This was candidly experimental theater, rehearsing and performing in the public view on street corners, in markets, and in open spaces on university campuses and casually inviting audience participation. It was also dangerously confrontational in its use of guerrilla tactics to deliver bold and brave satire, and Soyinka himself came under some pressure over his record, which quickly made him a household name across the country (government action was taken against radio and television stations which played it). The writer's last word on the Shagari government was the film *Blues for a Prodigal* (Ewuro Productions, 1984), about the political recruitment of scientists as demolition experts to blow up the opposition. Filming commenced in the dying days of the now thoroughly rotten republic but still had to be shot secretly, with minimal scripting and several switches of location to evade the authorities, and to be processed abroad. "We utilized the guerilla tactics of the travelling theatre," Soyinka said in a recent interview.[13] Ironically, the Lagos print of the film was immediately impounded by the security forces of the new military regime, which thus identified itself with the repressions of its civilian predecessor.

Perhaps as a result of overactivity in revue work and in other mediums, Soyinka published only two full-length dramatic works in the eighties, both, predictably, in the "shotgun" mold. Returning, in *Requiem for a Futurologist,*[14] to the theme of religious charlatanism explored in the two earlier *Jero* plays, he pokes fun at the astrologists and parapsychologists who came to exercise considerable influence over public and political life during the Shagari years (the main target was one of Shagari's toadies, the powerful Dr. Godspower Oyewole). The specific model for the play, fully acknowledged by Soyinka in the introductory material, is Swift's satiric prediction and later announcement, in *The Bickerstaff Letters,* of the death of the astrologer John Partridge, who then had great difficulty convincing people that he was still alive. In Soyinka's vision the rogue-futurologist, the Reverend Dr. Godspeak Igbehodan, is caught in the trap of his more cunning protégé Eleazor Hosannah, who, with a view to superseding his master, predicts his death during a television program. As Eleazor has the Godspeak pedigree, everyone instantly believes the prophecy, and when he publishes Godspeak's obituary, an impatient mob of the faithful lays siege to the master's house, determined to pay their last respects and refusing to be swayed in their resolve by any amount of live appearances.

Eleazor, the archmanipulator and master of disguise, tricks his way back into Godspeak's employment under the semblance of the metaphysician Dr. Semuwe, in which guise he causes the hapless Godspeak to doubt the reality of his own existence and to entertain the possibility that he may, after all, be dead. In this cause Eleazor even bribes the local *egungun* to feign recognition of a fellow spirit in Godspeak's figure at the window (no religion is sacred in this play). As the furious mob prepares to storm the house, the bewildered master reluctantly agrees to play dead and lie in state, and the play ends with Semuwe revealing that "everything is under control," becoming Eleazor again and proclaiming himself the reincarnated Nostradamus, a figure who is the source of much comic disquisition in the course of the play.

There is a limited amount of political satire in *Requiem* in the form of parallels between religious and political opportunism. Regimes, like the prophets they refer to and rely upon, promise what they fail to deliver, and cling to power long after their authority has outrun its legitimacy. It was no accident that in the 1985 published version Godspeak's demise is predicted for New Year's Eve 1983, the date of Shagari's downfall. Though the play was written for the celebration of the twentieth anniversary of the University of Ife, Soyinka withdrew it because even its limited political content had drawn the threat of government interference and censorship, and when the play went on a tour of the university campuses, he made a point of opening each performance with a procession of political parties and different religious faiths. There are also a few sideswipes at favorite local abominations, such as "the highly original driving habits" that provide a roaring trade for the play's undertaker, and some satire at the expense of the death industry itself, notably the Ghanaian "Master Carpenter" who allows his clients' vulgar fantasies of wealth and status to carry over into the grave in the form of designer coffins shaped like their Cadillacs and television sets. The bulk of the satire, however, is reserved for the human gullibility that invests superstitious faith in the pseudo-science of charlatans. Because of their automatic and absolute belief in astrological predictions, the prophet's followers, who know a walking corpse when they see one, are unable to accept the idea that Eleazor has merely pretended that Godspeak is dead: they therefore believe that the master is really dead and pretending to be alive. Thus is Godspeak boxed, farcically, into a corner from which every protest that he is alive is taken to be one more proof that he is dead. Underlying the verbal and visual humor of this situation, and the fantastically credulous newspaper cuttings cited in the introductory paraphernalia, there is the disturbing picture of a society caught in a spiritual malaise, thirsting after illusion and virtually begging to be deceived. (The play, with its multiple disguises and costume changes, is itself a kind of conjuring trick, depicting a world where all is trickery.) Still, whatever its darker implications, *Requiem* is essentially lighthearted and acutely local satiric comedy, disappointingly slight as a stage play (it evolved out of a much shorter radio play) and with the elaborate joke on the life-death inversion carried on perhaps a little too long. If *Requiem* is really, as Soyinka has bemusingly claimed, part of a "trilogy of transition," following *The Road* and *Death and the King's Horseman,* then it relates to these two towering achievements as the satyr play related to the tragedy in the Greek festival: as satiric postscript and light counterweight. *A Play of Giants,* written for a fully equipped theater and with at least one eye on international audiences, is more substantial fare and represents the author's political satire at its most ferocious. Soyinka gathers under the roof of the Bugaran (meaning Ugandan) embassy in New York, and under the transparent anagrams "Kamini," "Kasco," "Gunema," and "Tuboum," a gruesome quartet of real-life African dictators: Amin, Bokassa, Nguema of Equatorial Guinea, and Mobutu of the Congo. In the first part of the play, while ostensibly sitting for a sculpture for a Madame Tussaud's exhibition, these strutting, gibbering psychopaths explain with sadistic relish how their appetites for power are satisfied, their people terrorized, and their barbaric despotisms maintained: by voodoo (Gunema), cannibalism (Tuboum), and an imperium of "pure power" (Kasco). Kamini, who has no talent for analysis, does not have to speak of power: he *is* power, in its most fearsome and ridiculous embodiment, and never ceases to exercise it.

The play is a succession of Kamini's psychopathic explosions, which, like those of the real Amin, arise from willful misconceptions, the paranoid twisting of trivial offenses, and pure, groundless delusions, such as his bizarre notion that the Tussaud statuettes are really life-size statues intended for the United Nations Building across the road from the embassy. When the Chairman of the Bugara Bank informs him of the World Bank's refusal of further loans and explains that he cannot print any more banknotes because the national currency is worth no more than toilet paper, Kamini has his head flushed repeatedly in the toilet bowl; and when the British sculptor, revealing the true destination of his work, utters the unguarded aside that its subject properly belongs in the Chamber of Horrors, Kamini has him beaten up and maimed. The sculptor represents symbolically the obsolete, lame Western view of Amin—that he was not a dangerous threat but a circus freak whose savagery could be contained like a waxworks horror in a museum—and it is ironically apt that when the sculptor next appears, *he* is a museum piece, gagged and "mummified" in bandages from head to foot.

Kamini's anxiety complexes are not entirely gratuitous, however, for defections of Bugaran diplomats are constantly reported and the mounting crises culminate in the news of a coup in his absence. Instantly assuming that the coup has been engineered by the superpowers, Kamini reacts by taking hostage a group of visiting Russian and American delegates and threatening to unleash rockets and grenades from his embassy arsenal upon the United Nations Building unless an international force is sent to Bugara to crush the uprising. In the fantastic apocalyptic finale the rockets go off and the last light fades on the sculptor, quietly working away at what is now a living chamber of horrors. Kamini, who in Soyinka's prefatory words "would rather preside over a necropolis than not preside at all,"[15] turns his embassy into a fortress and then into a tomb, a pyramidal monument to his own barbaric excesses and the sycophantic self-interest of the West. The final sculpted work is, in fact, Soyinka's play, which catches in their frozen manic gestures the most monstrous manifestations of power ever spawned by the African continent.

Soyinka was one of the first to see through Amin's buffoonery, and from 1975 onward he waged a determined campaign in the African press against the dictator's reign of terror, lambasting Western and African governments and intellectuals who either supported Amin or cultivated a convenient deafness to the horror stories that were emerging from Uganda. In the play the latter forces are represented by the Scandinavian journalist Gudrun, mindlessly devoted to the dictator out of some romantically twisted concept of racial purity, and by the black American academic Professor Batey, who, out of misplaced loyalty to notions of black brotherhood and pan-Africanism, holds up to the black peoples of the world a mass murderer as a model for emulation. Both play and preface make clear that Kamini and his cronies, like their historical counterparts, are originally the postcolonial products of the Western superpowers. Kasco is a Gaullist, Gunema a Franco-worshiper, and Tuboum a Belgian puppet given to fake Africanization schemes. Kamini is placed in power by the British, financed by the Americans, armed by the Russians (until they refuse him an atom bomb to drop on his socialist neighbor), eulogized by the Western press which had unseated his predecessor, and finally deserted by all of them when support for insane African dictators is no longer in their interest. *A Play of Giants* is a surreal fantasia of international poetic justice in which Western support systems catastrophically backfire and the monster runs out of his maker's control: the Russian-supplied weapons are now trained on their own delegations, and the horror comes home to roost in the American sponsor's own back yard. "I'd rather kill them, but I acknowledge my impotence," Soyinka said of his power-grotesques in an interview at the time of the play's New York production. "All I can do is make fun of them."[16] It is, inevitably, a horrific kind of fun, and they are the more terrifying precisely because their historical originals were once thought to be merely ridiculous comic figures. Soyinka commented in the same 1984 interview that the work was not intended to be "a realistic play," that his "giants" are artificial, composite constructs, endowed with more intelligence, introspection, and eloquence than their originals could muster. Nevertheless, many of their mouthings are reportage material based on original speeches and press statements, and the fantastic virtuoso satirizing of Amin, enough to burst the bounds of any "well-made play," infuses the historical figure's own devilish, manic hysteria into the mood of the play. Soyinka claimed in the interview that the entire rogues' gallery of *A Play of Giants* are "excellent theatrical personalities."[17]

History plus Burlesque does not quite equal Drama, however, and if, as Soyinka remarked, Amin was "the supreme actor," he was a rather obvious, unsubtle one, best suited to broad farce and the 1970s television sketches which made him the constant butt of their satire. The theaters of politics and art are very different. If dramatic effigies of Hitler and Mussolini were put on stage and their mouths stuffed with their speeches and press releases, they would not be much more interesting or authentic as dramatic creations than Soyinka's gruesome foursome. There are odd quirky moments when one of them may spring to life, as in Gunema's chilling, shocking anecdote about his attempt to "taste" the distilled elixir of power by sleeping with the wife of a condemned man and then having them both garrotted. For the rest, they are the vaudeville freaks anticipated by Soyinka's opening circus flourish: "Ladies and Gentlemen, we present . . . a parade of miracle men . . . Giants, Dwarfs, Zombies, the Incredible Anthropophogai, the Original Genus Survivanticus (alive and well in defiance of all scientific explanations)" (*PG*, x). Cartoon puppets that they are, they burble nonsense and twitch at the behest of every passing sadistic whim and crack of the satiric whip, and the fact that their real-life models were much the same does not make them theatrically viable. Though having just enough distance from contemporary history to work as convincing satiric creations, they are too close to it to succeed as autonomous dramatic ones. The result is that *A Play of Giants,* like so much politically engaged art, is dramatically unengaging.

It is also curiously unpenetrating. In the interview Soyinka expressed the hope that the play would "raise certain intellectual and philosophical questions about power,"[18] and the text tosses a few ideas about. It is suggested that power calls to power, that "vicarious power responds obsequiously to the real thing," and that the "conspiratorial craving for the phenomenon of 'success' . . . cuts across all human occupations," which would explain the professor's admiration of the idiot-tyrant (vi–vii). There is also a hint that the African dictator's power mania is the pathological product of colonialism's long suppression of traditional male authority and the continued taunting of African manhood in the postcolonial world (the Russian diplomat describes Kamini as an "overgrown child"). These suggestions, however, are more in the preface than in the play, which is concerned to deride and debunk, not to analyze. *A Play of Giants* is unflaggingly savage burlesque, but it does not add a great deal to the knowledge of the nature of dictatorship already gleaned from Soyinka's earlier *Kongi's Harvest* (1965) or from *Opera Wonyosi,* and it retains all the usual limitations of its medium. Its claustrophobic set and nervous constricted laughter are, of all these later satires, at the furthest cry from the expansive metaphysical universe of the dramatist's middle period, and for the first time in a Soyinka play there is no music, dance, or mime, indeed not a hint of the visual and aural spectacle of festival theater.

In the late seventies and eighties satire came to constitute Soyinka's characteristic response to Nigeria's and Africa's worsening political crises, and as the bitter-satiric element of his dramatic writing deepened, there was a thinning out of its once rich texture which has not, to date, been repaired. It is perhaps unreasonable at the present time to hope that, after more than a decade's work in this vein, he will return to subjects which, though not necessarily more worthwhile, at least have a greater dramatic viability.

Derek Wright, Winter 1992

[1] James Gibbs, "Soyinka in Zimbabwe: A Question and Answer Session," *Literary Half-Yearly,* 28:2 (1987), p. 63.

[2] This sketch was originally published in Soyinka's *Before the Blackout,* Ibadan, Orisun Acting Editions, 1971. It is now available separately as *Childe Internationale,* Ibadan, Fountain Publications, 1987.

[3] Yemi Ogunbiyi, "A Study of Soyinka's *Opera Wonyosi,*" *Nigeria Magazine,* 128–29 (1979), p. 13.

[4] Soyinka, preface to *Before the Blackout,* p. 4.

[5] Ogunbiyi, p. 3.

[6] Wole Soyinka, *Opera Wonyosi,* London, Rex Collings, 1981, p. 1. Further page references are given parenthetically in the text, using the abbreviation *OW* where needed for clarity. For a review, see *WLT* 55:4 (Autumn 1981), p. 718.

[7] Quoted in Bernth Lindfors, "Begging Questions in Wole Soyinka's *Opera Wonyosi,*" *Ariel,* 12:3 (1981), p. 31.

[8] Joel Adedeji, "'Alarinjo': The Traditional Yoruba Travelling Theatre," in *Theatre in Africa,* Oyin Ogunba and Abiole Irele, eds., Ibadan, Ibadan University Press, 1978, p. 34.

[9] Wole Soyinka, "Drama and the Revolutionary Ideal," in *In Person: Achebe, Awoonor and Soyinka at the University of Washington,* Karen L. Morell, ed., Seattle, Institute of Comparative & Foreign Area Studies / University of Washington, 1975, p. 127.

[10] Ogunbiyi, p. 12; Bidun Jeyifo, "Drama and the Social Order: Two Reviews," *Positive Review* (Ile-Ife), 1 (1977), p. 22.

[11] Quoted in James Gibbs, "Tear the Painted Masks, Join the Poison Stains: A Preliminary Study of Wole Soyinka's Writings for the Nigerian Press," *Research in African Literatures,* 14:1 (1983), p. 40.

[12] *Unlimited Liability Company,* featuring Tunji Oyelana and His Benders with music and lyrics by Wole Soyinka, Ewuro Productions, EWP 001, side 2.

[13] Wole Soyinka, interview with Jeremy Harding, *New Statesman,* 27 February 1987, p. 22.

[14] Wole Soyinka, *Requiem for a Futurologist,* London, Rex Collings, 1985.

[15] Wole Soyinka, *A Play of Giants,* London, Methuen, 1984, p. vii. Further page references are given parenthetically in the text, using the abbreviation *PG* where needed for clarity.

[16] Art Borreca, "'Idi Amin Was the Supreme Actor': An Interview with Wole Soyinka," *Theater,* 16:2 (1985), p. 32.

[17] Ibid., p. 34.

[18] Ibid., p. 36.

SENEGAL

Social Vision in Aminata Sow Fall's Literary Work

For the last twelve years the Senegalese novelist Aminata Sow Fall has been relatively prolific. Between 1976 and 1987 she has produced four novels: *Le revenant* (1976), *La grève des bàttu,* (1979; Eng. *The Beggars' Strike,* 1981), *L'appel des arènes* (1982), and *L'ex-père de la nation* (1987).[1] Following the publication of *La grève des bàttu,* she was shortlisted for the Prix Goncourt in 1979 and awarded the Grand Prix de l'Afrique Noire in 1980.

No doubt Fall's work has given a voice to millions of voiceless women in her society. Put together, her four novels also create a literary universe that goes beyond the already-classic theme of women's emancipation to explore the human predicament in a contemporary Senegalese society undergoing tremendous mutations. In each of her four novels the issue of social change is portrayed through the collective and individual dramas of her characters. More specifically, Fall narrates social, cultural, and political behavior to illustrate the negative impact of unbalanced social change.

Published in 1976, *Le revenant* (The Ghost) sets the stage for what could be called a vast *comédie humaine.*

Here Fall defines the milieu in which her characters evolve: the urban area of Dakar, capital of Senegal. It is a society at a crossroad, caught in a process of rapid social change: "Tradition has been pierced to the heart, and what Bakar resented the most in that situation was the corruption of morals."[2] Indeed, the old value system based on *ngor* (nobility), *jom* (dignity), and communal values has been replaced by only one criterion: money or material wealth. Under the impulse of that new divinity, all relationships have become a game, and society itself a stage ruled by money. The negative effect of money over collective and individual life is embodied in the corruption of social life and the drama of Bakar, the main character.

The radical alteration of the meaning of such family rituals as marriage, child-naming, and funerals illustrates that corruption. Under the impact of money, the sacred act of marriage has become a business, even a "lottery game," in which two families invest for better returns. Thus the marriage of Bakar's sister Yama Diop to the rich merchant and *ndaanan* Amar N'diaye serves material purposes. The entire Diop family perceives this alliance with Amar as a way out from poverty and an opening to *le grand monde*. Indeed, after the celebration of the couple's union, the Diops move from their one-bedroom *baraque* in the shantytown of Colobane into a brick house provided by Yama's generous husband in the middleclass neighborhood of Medina. In the same way, when Bakar himself seeks to marry Man Aïssa Gueye, his in-laws investigate only his material status, illustrating the marketing of marital relations. Morality and nobility are no longer the criteria of trust and respect. The wealth of a family determines eligibility for marriage.

Here it is interesting to mention that Fall points to a twofold reality: the transformation of marital relations into a money-making business and, even worse, the new status of women as a product for sale. In the same way, the term *bride price* appears with a striking strength: "Bakar offered 100,000 francs for a bride price, a wardrobe of a higher value, and, one morning, a huge lorry unloaded at the Wéllé's a bed-room set a living-room set and a dining-room set. . . . El hadj Wéllé thought maybe he did well giving his daughter to Bakar in marriage" (37). Marriage and wedlock have thus come to mean an investment for greater accumulation of material wealth.

The corruption of social relations may also be seen in the new aspect taken by child-naming. Initially a symbolic act of conferring an identity on a newborn and a celebration of a new family member, child-naming has grown into an indecent trade in which calculations and mercantilism generate rivalry between two families. For Yama, the naming of her brother's first child is an occasion to humiliate the Wéllé family, his brother's in-laws. According to the new rules, a family unable to display as much material wealth as its daugher-in-law's family experiences shame and public scorn. Therefore for the poor, child-naming ceremonies have come to mean stress, pain, and possible humiliation.

Money also dominates funeral observances. Here Fall deeply and openly deplores the shamelessness which has been introduced into social relations. Death should be an occasion of grief, sorrow, and pain; but as Bakar, disguised, attends his own funeral ceremony, he realizes how death has been transformed into a profit-making opportunity. Under the new social reality lies the advertising of death on the air, using the modern medium of radio. For Yama, death and its attendant publicity increase her fame and make known her extensive connections. Thus the announcement of Bakar's death generates a long list of famous and well-to-do people whom Yama needs to maintain her status in *le grand monde*.

This change from the old value system into a society dominated by money and material wealth has a devasting effect on individual and collective behavior. We may notice how often Fall uses here the word *stage* and other expressions within the same semantic field such as *mask* or *xessal*, a chemical treatment aimed at lightening the skin color, thus conferring a new identity on the individual. Hypocrisy and cupidity dominate social life. Even more interesting is to see how a society corrupted by money becomes a source of tragedy for Bakar. At the beginning of the novel Bakar is described as a young man full of dignity and honesty despite his poverty. His dream is only to get a job and earn enough money in order to create decent living conditions for his loved ones. Very soon his prayers for employment are answered. Hired at the post office, he demonstrates an impressive sense of responsibility, hard work, and honesty. Very soon, however, the dream turns into a nightmare. Caught in the game of a society corrupted by money, Bakar starts spending more than he earns in order to obtain fame and become the pride of his wife, his sister, and his relatives. To satisfy the needs of a greedy society, he commits the self-destructive act of embezzling money from the post office.

Thrown in jail, Bakar undergoes an eye-opening experience: "Then he understood his misfortune and his powerlessness, and he realized he had been a toy absurdly rolled by a capricious society" (49). Praised only yesterday for his generosity and fame, he finds himself isolated, rejected by his sister Yama, and a source of shame for his in-laws. Bakar's new awareness leads him to self-destruction in the world of the pariah and alcoholism. In the closing pages of the novel he uses his new knowledge of society to take revenge. Against a milieu dominated by money and transformed into a theater, he uses the mask of *xessal* to reach his goal: "Now I am going to play their game, enter this counterfeit world. I will play them the worst trick ever played" (106).

Clearly *Le revenant* documents a world torn apart by the belief in money and material wealth. Under the impact of that new god, Aminata Sow Fall introduces her reader to a social stage ruled by cupidity, hypocrisy, lies, and fake emotions. Still, this work, reminiscent of *Tartuffe,* goes beyond the game to explore the human tragedy that results from what the author perceives as unbalanced social change.

As mentioned earlier, *Le revenant* sets the stage for a wider *comédie humaine* that expands as Fall's literary production develops. With the publication of her second novel, *The Beggars' Strike,* Fall gives a new dimension to her vision of Senegalese society. The word *battu* in Wolof designates a gourd bowl used by beggars to collect alms from believers. Literally, the novel recounts a beggars' strike. Symbolically, however, this second work owes its success to a combination of two elements: the acuteness of Fall's observation of the social arena, and the fertility of her imaginative vision.

On the surface, *The Beggars' Strike* appears as mere reportage on a Senegalese society faced with the dilemmas and traumas of economic development or "modernization." Confronting a severe cycle of drought that endangered their agriculturally based economics, public officials sought economic survival through the development of tourist industries. At the same time, hard-hit rural areas saw their population flee and invade the cities in a search for subsistence. With no formal education or skills, that displaced rural populace became beggars in the streets and public places, including those visited by the tourists. In order to maintain the flow of tourists from all over the world, public officials had to rid the city of its beggars. Therefore a campaign was launched to drive "the dregs of society" to a relocation area on the outskirts of the city.

Fall's social vision goes beyond the issue of modernization to explore its implications for humans and their conduct. To reach such a depth of insight, she draws from an imagination fed by a strong knowledge of her countrymen and -women. What would happen if, as a protest, the beggars decided to go on strike, thus depriving the entire population of the possibility of giving alms? In her fictional world Fall brings to life a well-organized group of beggars—Salla Niang, Gorgui Diop, and Nugirane Sarr—who decide to go on strike against the brutalities perpetrated by public officials, represent-

ed by the Director of Health and Hygiene Mour Ndiaye and his assistant Keba Dabo. Exploring the consequences of this strike, Fall highlights the collective and individual dramas generated by the contradictory demands of a changing society.

Following the beggars' withdrawal from the city, the entire population finds itself in semihysteria. Suddenly a daily routine long taken for granted, giving alms, becomes impossible to accomplish because the *battu* holders have vanished from the streets. With this calamity there reappears the strong collective belief attached to almsgiving. In a society deeply influenced by the teachings of the Koran and by traditional values, charity maintains the equilibrium between individual and collective psyche. As a sacred act of exchange, almsgiving also provides the giver a sense of security and, in traditional thinking, opens the door to wealth, prosperity, and peace of mind. The paths to the beggars' retreat are soon crowded by distressed carriers of gifts.

> To listen to the conversations exchanged, the complaints at having to travel so far to make their donations, [Mour's maid] realized that the shortage of beggars is causing a considerable inconvenience to a part of the population; she sees sick people, pale and haggard, who have dragged their suffering this distance in order to make the sacrifice which may perhaps help them to be restored to physical and mental wellbeing. She sees luxurious cars, with their windows tightly closed, speeding down the sandy track that leads to the beggars' house.[3]

The psychological damage of the beggars' disappearance from the city has an even deeper impact at the individual level, judging from Mour Ndiaye's experience. For the main character, the situation approaches tragedy. Mour appears here as a living example of the human drama that often results from social change that fails to find a balance between the demands of "modernization" and of loyalty to a people's cultural genius. He is torn between his position as a public official, liable for the implementation of his government's development plans, and the beliefs with which he had grown up. On the one hand he must be pragmatic, take action, design a strategy to get rid of the beggars; the fulfillment of his ambition depends on this. On the other side, despite his Western education and his display of rationality, he is the product of a culture where marabouts and beggars have a very influential role. He has been raised to believe that almsgiving and blessings from the marabout and the poor bring access to health, social success, and heaven. Thus, to reach his goal of becoming the next vice-president of the republic, Mour is ordered by his marabout Kofi Bokoul to slaughter an ox, divide the meat into seventy-seven packs, and distribute it to beggars around town. Then he realizes the irony of his situation, because no more beggars are to be found. He cannot give the alms as prescribed because he has rid the city of its *battu* holders.

Suddenly Mour sinks into panic and desperation. Like a lunatic, he wanders around the four corners of the city, in a van loaded with meat, in search of absent beggars: "Not a soul at the main market; no talibes, no beggars, no battu. Mour's heart began to beat faster. . . . Then he feels a weight on his chest, he has difficulty in breathing, there is ringing in his ears" (88). This ambiguity is also reflected in his behavior. As a public official, he delivers speeches in which he castigates marabouts and witchcraft, advocating a fight against beggars for economic development; but in private he and all other intellectuals "drank beer when they were thirsty and whiskey when they needed perking up, . . . only spoke French . . . [and] never left home in the morning without daubing themselves with a mixture of powders and fermented roots" (24).

Through a theme of mendicancy, then, Fall explores the dilemma and the duplicity of a society caught in a crossfire between the demands of an imposed model of development and the constraints of its own cultural heritage. More important, using the resources of her rich and creative imagination, she manages to display the devastating effects of such an imbalance on both the individual and the collective psyche.

At this point it is important to remember that before becoming a novelist, Aminata Sow Fall was first a teacher and a specialist in education who participated in a committee for the reform of French programs in public schools. Education and the issues it raises in a changing society lie at the very heart of her third novel, *L'appel des arènes*. Through the simple story of a schoolboy and his family in a small Senegalese town, Fall stresses the disarray of a humanity confused by the content of an imposed educational system that does not correspond to its realities. Ndiogou and his wife Diattou are both professionally successful, Western-educated individuals of a type often referred to as "been-tos," people who have sojourned in Europe for their education. He has returned home with a degree in veterinary medicine, she with a degree in nursing.

Despite their professional success, however, both Ndiogou and Diattou have been victimized by their education abroad. Fascinated by the Western values of progress and civilization, and alienated from Africa, they reject the cultural realities of their country. Desiring to distance herself from everything that reminds her of her past, Diattou seeks a complete personal transformation: "Diattou concentrated on changing herself. She

worked hard to domesticate her vocal cords and polish them. She learned to regulate her walk and gestures on the pace of the West. She became Toutou" (88). What she draws from her Western experience is the intense desire to create an African aristocracy marked by progress and materialism. For her, progress comes to mean a total rejection of all that has belonged to her country's social values as well as to her own past values and cultural identity. Back home she withdraws from her family and neighbors.

Like his wife, but to a lesser extent, Ndiogou also shows signs of cultural alienation. He too distances himself from his relatives and his aristocratic past. Once in Louga, where they work, they retreat into a fictitious universe, cut off from the surrounding reality.

The drama of this couple starts when they seek to educate their only child, Nalla, in their own image, imposing on him concepts and methods drawn from the West and which only fit Western needs and cultural realities. From the West they bring him books that speak to him of snow and relate alien folktales, but for Nalla all these efforts only result in frustration and a sense of castration. While his parents were away, he had stayed in the village with his grandmother Mam Fari. Through tales, songs, and proverbs that dignify and glorify the African past, Nalla had already developed "a certain inclination for an esthetic of form, color, and sounds, magnified by courage and strength in motion" (66). He dreams of becoming a wrestler. At this critical stage of his development, Nalla's parents return from the West with a new ideal of education, which Fall describes as one "which rejects as barbarian any manifestations expressing the vitality of the people not yet spoiled by the unbearable turmoil of Western civilization" (67).

At home, Diattou makes sure that Nalla does not interact with the kids of their neighborhood and tries to discipline him to the Western way of thinking and behaving. In addition to his parents' blindness, however, Nalla's drama also derives from a deeper dilemma. The ideals with which his grandmother raised him exist only in memory, because "tradition is vanishing." Longing for disappearing values and shaped by his parents on the basis of abstract, obscure, vague principles, Nalla rebels against parental authority in order to direct his search toward the wrestling grounds. He is fascinated by Andre and Mallaw, "lelion des arènes." Though at the end of the novel Nalla and his father reconcile with each other and their respective cultural values, for Diattou, the result is a devastating one. In a final act of desperation, with a feeling of betrayal, she flees her house.

Through their family drama, Nalla and his parents send the reader a clear signal. For a community and a country, an educational system that negates cultural reality and the inner need of the people is a destructive one. Here the happy ending, at least for Nalla and his father, is an indication by Fall that a well-balanced educational system ought to be deeply rooted in and fed by a people's cultural vitality.

From a portrayal of social and cultural behavior in her first three works, Fall's most recent novel, *L'expère de la nation,* deals with the hot topic of political life in an imaginary African country easily identifiable as Senegal. This reflection on political behavior is presented as the memoirs of Madiama Niang, former head of state, jailed after his dismissal from office. Through this flashback on his own past reign and personal tragedy, Madiama introduces the reader into the daily intrigues and vices of political life.

The novel develops in three stages depicting Madiama's era: his rise to power, the peak of his reign, and his downfall. Fall portrays Madiama as a man of principles and moral purity changed into an oppressor by the intricacies of political power. His coming to power also clearly reveals the hard realities of African independence. The erstwhile nurse and trade unionist Madiama's political ascendancy illustrates how the former colonizers attempted to perpetuate their control through puppets of their own fabrication. Men rise to power not from popular support but more often against the will of the people.

> I don't know what happened, but three weeks later an open crisis occurred between [former majority leader] Mass and the legislative majority. Mass was dismissed . . . and the Assembly, where I did not count only friends, elected me almost unanimously. (24)

Soon Madiama discovers his imposition on his country by the former colonial master to be a poisonous present. His ideal of humanity, justice, and truth comes into conflict with harsh reality. After the euphoria of the first days, Madiama begins to see political life in a new light. He has been chosen to preside over a huge governmental machine dominated by corruption, bribery, self-interest, and self-serving praises.

Within the circle of political power itself, conflicting interest groups generate a climate of gossip and suspicion, where people spy on one another. That dark side of Madiama's reign is embodied in the dealings of his second wife Yande, who transforms the presidential palace into private property, where the distribution of favors depends only on her goodwill. As the state itself sinks into chaos, the president is blinded by the hypocrisy and self-serving lies of those supposedly helping him manage the public interest: "I no longer believed

I could exercise power in a context where some menused it to plot, to tear each other, . . . where the most talented in indecent maneuvers crushed the others and where hypocrisy has become a way of life" (109). Far from the center of political power and its allies, the majority of the population shares only in drought, poverty, and mystification. That voiceless majority, excluded from any and all progress, wealth, and well-being, has become a tool in the hands of manipulative politicians, who use "the people" only for their own interest.

Progressively, Madiama discovers himself to be a man trapped in a tragic situation, isolated from his relatives and stifled by power. The irony here is that he cannot even resign from the presidency that is killing his ideals of democracy and justice. He finds himself a hostage. Here Fall goes beyond the sphere of domestic politics. The president, those around him, and the entire country are taken hostage by foreign powers through capital investment. As Madiama discovers later, dependence on foreign capital denies his nation its very foundation: the freedom to make choices and preside over its own destiny. This realization of his failure coincides with the last stage in Madiama's rule.

The same hidden threads that brought him to power work to overthrow him. His very decision to find an honorable exit through resignation proves to be self-destructive. After an arranged public disturbance, a shadowy coup d'état topples him and he is thrown into jail, to be replaced by a more willing player. *L'ex-père de la nation* goes beyond the personal drama of an imaginary head of state to explore the tragedy of African political life. The nation Madiama presided over is like a confiscated ship in which, like worms, public officials greedily thrive on the sweat of the people. In this atmosphere of tension and competitiveness, freedom, humanity, and justice are replaced by hypocrisy as a way of life.

As noted in my introductory remarks, Aminata Sow Fall's social vision goes well beyond the issue of feminine emancipation to embrace the general survival of a collectivity and a nation faced with the delicate task of finding a balance between the demands of what is improperly termed "modernization" and the preservation of its very foundation, its cultural genius. As a novelist, however, Fall draws from both social reality and her imagination to bring to life the destructive effects of this unresolved situation on human resources. Indeed, from *Le revenant* through *L'ex-père de la nation,* what she tackles is the human predicament in a changing society. Through Bakar's personal disillusionment, Mour Ndiaye's ambiguity, Nalla's search for threatened values, and Madiama's bitter prison memoirs, the reader discovers a vast *comédie humaine* of people searching for social, cultural, and political solutions to their unhappiness.

Nevertheless, Fall's approach to the issue of social change raises some serious ethical and ideological questions. Her social vision, described through a criticism of social, cultural, and political behavior, is very reminiscent of Molière and Balzac. In suggesting the need to reform individual and collective conduct as a solution to social change, Fall, like these two French predecessors, stands behind the fence, so to speak. Her social realism betrays a failure to question the institutions that generated such conduct. In pointing at the consequences, not at the institutions that support and implement social change, Aminata Sow Fall's ideological stand goes beyond a choice of the status quo to advocate social reformism, but she does not prescribe thoroughgoing or revolutionary solutions.

Samba Gadjigo, Summer 1989

¹ *Le revenant, La grève des bàttu,* and *L'appel des arènes* were all published in Paris by Nouvelles Editions Africaines. *L'ex-père de la nation* was published in Paris by L'Harmattan. For reviews of the second and third titles, see respectively *WLT* 54:2 (Spring 1980), p. 327, and 58:1 (Winter 1984), p. 153.

² All translations are my own unless otherwise noted.

³ Aminata Sow Fall, *The Beggars' Strike,* Dorothy S. Blair, tr., London, Longman, 1981, p. 53. All subsequent citations are from this translation.

Nuruddin Farah *(Gil Jain)*

SOMALIA

Brothers and Sisters in Nuruddin Farah's Two Trilogies

Nuruddin Farah's two trilogies are organized on the basis of political and historical themes. The title of the first set of novels, *Variations on the Theme of an African Dictatorship,* follows the gradual disillusionment with the regime of General Siyad Barre on the part of those who had set their hopes on the new Somalia. More generally, it reflects the hopelessness a nation feels in fighting against a tyranny it has helped create, and the questions raised are broad enough to apply to other times and places. After all, at the time he was composing the opening installment of the first trilogy, *Sweet and Sour Milk* (1979), the author also had in mind the Greece of the Colonels. The titles of the three novels that constitute the second trilogy—*Maps, Gifts,* and *Secrets*—refer to abstract topics, which are explored on various levels, in poetic images, and in intimate human relationships, as well as in contemporary history. Here again, the is-

sues examined—identity through blood or language or territory (*Maps*), the receiving of aid (*Gifts*), and ties of kinship and clan (*Secrets*)—have direct relevance to the more recent events in Somalia, yet they are also echoed in many conflicts both within and outside Africa. The lack of any precise dating and of any readily identifiable incidents helps universalize the reflection. As in many other postcolonial works of fiction, one can see here the difficult birth of the modern nation-state, the rapid changes in a pastoral and rural society, and the growing gap between an educated elite and the new generations who have no contact with either traditional wisdom or modern schooling.

As is true in the works of other novelists concerned with history and society, here the family is the stage whereupon these issues are dramatized. Most of the time, the reader knows about events in the country through conversations that take place in the homes of a few characters, where rumors, reports, and arguments are exchanged. These characters are not mere passive victims or observers. Farah never resorts to simple binary oppositions between, say, colonizer and colonized, or dictator and oppressed citizens. Each member of the community has a share of responsibility in the way his country is faring. In *Sweet and Sour Milk* the text refers explicitly to the theories of Wilhelm Reich, according to which the structure of the family is reproduced in the national structure: "In the figure of the father the authoritarian state has its representative in every family, so that the family becomes its most important instrument of power" (*SSM*, 97). Farah is a moralist who asks his reader not to blame an individual for his tyrannical excesses or a foreign power for its domination without first asking himself whether the dealings at the highest state level are not just a replica on a larger scale of his or her own individual behavior. In this demonstration, the power relationships between generations offer a good model. Like other African writers who explore the handing down of tradition and the weight of authority—the Nigerian Chinua Achebe or the Moroccan Driss Chraibi, for instance—Farah presents vertical plots spanning three or four generations. Harsh fathers and rebellious sons figure frequently in his works, as patriarchy is examined in both the home and the state, as has already been well analyzed (Wright, 1994).

Another aspect of Farah's family histories which deserves attention is the fact that his stories rarely focus on a simple nuclear family, the Oedipal triangle of much Western literature. Brothers and sisters, horizontal relationships within a single generation, play the most important part, as they do in such traditional tales as *King Lear* or in the novels of Virginia Woolf. As in *Antigone,* the opposition to patriarchal power is complicated and made richer by the presence of this group of siblings, with all their differences in gender, in age, and eventually, within a specifically African situation, their different mothers. In what follows, I shall examine the part played by such characters in each trilogy in order to determine what they show regarding the evolution of the novelist's vision and political thinking, and also how they provide patterns, images, and emotions that enrich the range of these original novels, at once poetic and political, susceptible to allegorical readings as well as anchored in warm, recognizable humanness.

The first trilogy, comprising *Sweet and Sour Milk, Sardines* (1981), and *Close Sesame* (1983), is concerned with dictatorial power. The first two novels revolve around conflictual situations: they question the authority of fathers over sons in *Sweet and Sour Milk,* of matriarchs over daughters or daughters-in-law or granddaughters—and especially over excision—in *Sardines.* The third novel reexamines the vertical line within a family—grandfather, sons and daughters, grandchildren—as all try to find ethical and practical guidelines for resisting a tyrant. Each book privileges one type of consciousness in its narrative: sons in *Sweet and Sour*

Milk, daughters in *Sardines,* and the grandfather's perspective in *Close Sesame.* (The same sequence of young hero-woman-grandfather is to be found in the main characters of the second trilogy.) Keynaan, the father in *Sweet and Sour Milk,* is the archetype of the patriarch, as he slices the ball with which his two sons are playing and refuses the impious notion that the earth is round rather than flat, as established in the Koran (*SSM*, 21). And the matriarch Idil in *Sardines* is also seen wielding a knife, here in the nightmares of the granddaughter whom she wants to subject to clitoral excision. Absolute power gone mad is both male and female: it is the ogress of legend, the whale that devours men. As individuals suffer more and more from the harsh effects of the arbitrary power of the "socialist Islamic" regime, we witness the efforts of the various members of the family to cope with the situation, either by trying to adapt to the ruling group or by joining the underground opposition. Most of the chapters relate conversations in the home, a refuge where rumors and propaganda are assessed and where ethical and practical modes of survival are contemplated.

Within this closed space, brothers and sisters enjoy a privileged mode of communication, exchanging secrets in complete trust, much more freely than with their spouses or parents. We see them sharing meals and sharing dreams, in an everyday relationship which is a comfort against a dangerous outside world. For instance, here is a moment of pure fusional joy, as brothers and sister are reunited: "*What do I see?* It was Loyaan. Loyaan in person. For a good five minutes, no one would recall who did what, who said what, who hugged or kissed whom" (*SSM*, 18). The siblings are set in patterns which, as in folktales, help underline a general meaning. In *Sweet and Sour Milk* the similarly named twins Loyaan and Soyaan represent two options for opposing patriarchal power. Soyaan chooses rebellion when he writes a text that will prick the ear of the president, who, like the tyrant Dionysius, listens through a network of informers for signs of subversion. Soyaan soon dies, perhaps poisoned with a glass of milk, and Loyaan, inquiring into the possible murder, discovers a group of underground opponents to the regime: will he join them, or will he be exiled or even killed like his brother? The parallel between the twins illustrates the plot's hesitation on the whole issue of commitment or detachment. In *Sardines* the symmetrical pattern is provided by Nasser and his sister Medina, who also hesitate between acceding to the demands of authority—whether parental or presidential—and acting against them. The book focuses principally on the predicament of women, seen as hemmed in by a tradition with which they feel extremely uneasy. The opposition between brother and sister in this instance underlines how educated women—Medina is a journalist—are beginning to find a freedom of judgment and behavior which unsettles the men, here shown as more ready to compromise.

In *Close Sesame* the atmosphere is more oppressive still. There is no ambiguity this time as to the lethal power of the head of state. Zeinab, a widow, and her brother Mursal care for their aged father, the tolerant and pious Deeriye. The two siblings here are more divided in their opinions than was the case in the two preceding novels. Their heated arguments represent two options: either to play safe or to join an underground movement (*CS*, 118). Their complicity ends when Mursal refuses to share his secrets, acts in conspiracy with several friends, and disappears, probably executed. The father, at the end, tries to accomplish what the young cannot do, but he fails in his attempt to shoot the tyrant and instead is himself gunned down ignominiously. In this pessimistic conclusion to the trilogy, brotherly bonds are no solace. In Deeriye's nightly visions his children are powerless: "In these visions, these dreams, Mursal and Zeinab remained small, innocent as their infant days, toothless" (*CS*, 160).

In contrast with most of their parents' generation, the groups of brothers and sisters are shown as united in their refusal to compromise, but still they are no match for the tyrant. The pathos of the families' doomed fight in the three books is relieved by the human warmth found within the confines of the home. With Farah, however, human emotions are ambivalent blessings. "Do not throttle me with your love," Loyaan implores his sister (*SSM*, 191). Those who would like to take more decisive steps against an unjust order feel hampered by the concern of their kin. The bonds are strong, and conversely, any and every initiative might well involve the safety of siblings: one is reminded of the danger when Mulki is tortured by the security police who are trying to charge her brother Ibrahim. Yet emotional comfort may have a price, the novels imply; it may paralyze action and ultimately greatly curtail individual freedom. The novelist goes even further in exploring the deep attachment of brother and sister. In *Sweet and Sour Milk* intimacy comes close to breaking taboos, as when Ladan awakens her brother Loyaan: "As his concentrated look zoomed in on her, he noticed that she averted her eyes. What was wrong? His sheet had fallen off. He was naked. / 'Sorry.' He covered his indecency" (*SSM*, 63). In *Sardines*, during a relaxed moment, Nasser massages his half-sister Medina, reading her back like a well-known text, and wonders if the scene could be seen by an external observer as incestuous.

He oiled his hands and, with tremendous care and tenderness, massaged, thumbed and squeezed the hard joints. His expert fingers, at times, descended like a hawk hunting on the wing and, at others, crawled like a many-legged insect on a plateau of uneven smoothness. He touched, he pressed, he tickled. He helped orchestrate the rise and fall of her body's temperature. With equal facility, he conducted his hands through a series of annotations: a scar here, a cut too low or too deep there, a burn which his memory couldn't date, another which marked where the blade met the shoulder, then a medicinal burn near the spine. Nasser knew his notes well enough, he hardly needed to improvise a move. (*S*, 82)

As in *Maps*, with its account of Askar's love for his foster mother Misra, the evocation of incest is made more acceptable by being set within an indirect relationship. In *Sardines* the author is not out to shock, but instead to hint at the density of family ties, at once a source of strength and a limitation. Once more the home is the core image and accurate reflection of what takes place in society at large. The ruling elite are described as "an incestuous circle" (*S*, 87) incapable of opening up. Medina and Nasser, Loyaan and Ladan are not allegorical figures of a ruling class which is too inward-looking, but rather individualized instances of the way intimate modes of feeling can be reproduced from family to community to the nation at large. Patriarchal authority eventually destroys the fabric of society, but fraternity, or brotherhood, does not offer an alternative utopia. It makes life more bearable in times of crisis, but paradoxically underlines how vulnerable the younger generations are.

The second trilogy moves away from the theme of dictatorship. Farah implies that a continuation of such a focus would do too much honor to tyrants, who are after all mediocre: Siyad Barre, for example, is contemptuously described in *Secrets* as "the mayor of Mogadiscio." He is one of the symptoms of a dysfunctional community, not just an evil accident in the life of a people who do not deserve such a bad leader. The three books *Maps* (1986), *Gifts* (1992), and *Secrets* (1998) deal primarily with identity, and each weaves a complex network of images, myths, philosophical reflections, and historical examples that induce the reader to think again about accepted wisdom: for instance, what is national identity if it does not lie in territorial borders, in language, in the blood (*Maps*)? The first trilogy's explicit debates and arguments between brothers and sisters in the shelter of their homes now give way to a more complex system of cross-references among fables, press cuttings, and dreams. From one book to the next, the juxtapositioning of such diverse clues and paradoxical questions adopts more and more the mode of the riddle, which is one of the established African ways of engaging the listener's or reader's moral thinking. The first installment, *Maps,* like *Sweet and Sour Milk,* has a young man as protagonist. Askar, however, is no epic hero in spite of his name—it means "the soldier" in Somali—and despite the omens he believes were present at his birth. The fantasies of self-creation and of power in his early days in the Ogaden give way to the realities of a difficult world in his move to Mogadiscio. The novel leaves him on the threshold of adulthood, irresolute and no match for the complexities of a fast-changing world. He embraces a doubtful nationalist creed, yet his isolation seems complete; in contrast with the previous texts, there are no warm family scenes, and Askar has no siblings in whom he can confide. His father, the real soldier-hero, died before Askar was born. The absence of such a direct, accessible parental figure represents a marked change from the first trilogy.

Brothers do exist here, however, though now in the characters of uncles. These are important figures of authority in African society but are not often given space in African novels. In *Maps* the pattern is simple. First, we have the "bad" uncle, Qorrax, the paternal uncle who extends his protection to the young orphan but has also possibly exerted his masculine power by "having his way" with Misra, Askar's foster mother. Once, the young man even wonders whether Qorrax similarly used this power to enforce levirate tradition on his real mother: "'Did Uncle Qorrax abuse my mother's trust?'. . . 'Did he rape my mother?' you asked. 'Did he want to marry her when news about my father's death came?'" (*M,* 140). The ambivalent, paternalistic character of the father's brother is contrasted in a neat symmetry with Hilaal, the urbane, intellectual maternal uncle who lives up to his theories of gender in an egalitarian marriage with Salaado. Where one uncle is an image of the patriarchal power of the father's line,

> It was no secret that you didn't like Uncle Qorrax or his numerous wives: numerous because he divorced and married such a number of them that you lost count of how many there were at any given time, and at times you weren't sure to whom he was married. (*M,* 12)

the other uncle connects the young boy with emotion and intelligence, the mother's side, which in Somali culture, however, does not bestow identity.

> On the other hand, you loved Uncle Hilaal and his wife, Salaado, directly you met them. The flow of their warmth was comforting—sweet as spring water. And everything either of them did or said, once you gave it a thought, appeared as necessary as the blood of life. (*M,* 17)

It is as if each brother were an extension of the absent parent. The two uncles are secondary elements in a plot that revolves around the relationship between Askar and Misra, his Oromo foster mother. Yet the contrasting descriptions of the brothers-in-law create a subplot that echoes the topic of the first trilogy in its indictment of the misuse of the patriarchal order, although now the theme has receded into a fictional world where the real figures of parents are absent.

Gifts, the middle novel in the second trilogy, is, like *Sardines,* centered on a woman who is at the core of a family. After the intricate narrative design of *Maps,* it seems to propose a mere linear romance, as Duniya, in her thirties and twice married, falls in love for the first time. The simplicity of the plot is deceptive, for, once more, family bonds are examined as clues illuminating wider political and ethical concerns. The balance between giving and receiving, the moral issues in helping others and thus curtailing their freedom, are part of an ongoing argument which is woven into the narrative along with instances ranging from folktales about lending pots to articles about U.S. aid to developing countries. Like Medina in *Sardines* and in contrast to Askar in *Maps,* Duniya has a rich network of friends and relatives. Brothers and sisters figure prominently in the novel, contributing to the lively domestic atmosphere yet also providing food for thought—for example, about the way the traditional and modern codes of behavior interact. The cast is numerous, and the reader must memorize the connections among a host of secondary characters who all seem related in one way or another. We feel we are getting acquainted with an extended family in Africa, disentangling the network of assigned roles, jealousies, and affectionate ties.

Duniya has three children, among whom the teenage twins, another fictional boy-girl pair, provide symmetry and gender comparison. Seven-year-old Yarey is the third and youngest of the heroine's offspring. Within Duniya's own generation we have Abshir and Shiriye, two of her brothers. The novelist seems hesitant in attributing totally negative aspects to direct kin. Thus Abshir is the good brother in the story—"my full brother . . . my mother's son" (*G,* 79)—the one who cares for Duniya and her family by sending gifts from Italy while making sure his generosity contributes to her freedom. His love for her has a motherly quality, as he reminds her: "As you refused to breast-feed and our mother was too unwell to take care of you, it was I who fed you the first drop of milk, a gift you wouldn't take from anyone else, including our father, the midwife or other women of the neighbourhood" (*G,* 236). She even muses on the fantasy that her daughter Nasiiba looks so much like her beloved Abshir that she may have been sired by him:

"(Once, albeit in a light-hearted manner, Duniya asked Dr. Mire if it were possible for a woman to carry in her womb two-egg twins emanating from two different sources, when one of the men had never made love to the woman in question.)" (*G,* 37). With his help, she chooses to have a flat of her own, her first independent home.

The bad brother, Shiriye, is not so welcome: "Now what in your elder half-brother's wisdom had you in mind to do for me when you decided to pay me a visit?" (*G,* 79). His authority is an important feature in traditional society. When Qasim asks Farida for the hand of her younger sister Miski, we are reminded that power is not only exerted by fathers. Shiriye exercised his prerogative when Duniya was a child in giving her away to an old man in a transaction that included a thoroughbred horse as well as money. As with the character of Uncle Qorrax in *Maps,* Farah insists on the reverse side of the often idealized African solidarities: sometimes family solidarity just means domination and exploitation. Duniya has nothing but hatred and fear for a brother who even "appeared in her nightmares to whip her for disobedience" (*G,* 78). He is the obtuse leader of the clan: "Shiriye does not give reasons. He spouts opinions, crude prejudices and unlearned pontifications" (*G,* 121).

Another negative image is projected by the character of Waberi, not a direct sister but rather the sister-in-law of Duniya's lover Bosaaso through his late wife. She is a predator of another kind, the female counterpart to Shiriye's pompous military authority. Her style is to wheedle money and gifts out of the man she deems to be richer than she is and thus duty-bound to provide for her. Her insistent visits are little else than euphemistically disguised begging: "'You used to give us a hand in settling some of the bills.' / 'Did I give you a hand or did I settle them all, every cent of your bills?'" (*G,* 219). This contrasts with the attitude of Duniya, who is always at pains not to be in anyone's debt and who inculcates the same attitude in her children. Her daughter Nasiiba makes sure that her younger sister Yarey is not overly attracted by the material goods in her uncle's home. The example of Muraayo, sister-in-law to Duniya's ex-husband Taariq, is a variation on the theme of sisterly excess: being very well off, the childless woman thinks she can buy the affections of the young girl with videos and modern gadgetry, possessiveness being the reverse side of protection.

As we can see, the novelist keeps the pattern clear, as is done in folktales the world over, by ascribing negative values to sibling relationships in the case of in-laws and half-brothers only. The satire in the physical descriptions of Shiriye and Muraayo, fat and pretentious,

or in the whining demands of Waberi balances the harmonious warmth in Duniya's young family, a family also open to strangers. The contrast underlines the risk run by those who rely only on blood ties and refuse to see beyond their clan, as when Shiriye comes across Bosaaso: "Entering, he shouted Duniya's name angrily, not a greeting. Fat-bellied, he met their hostile stare with indifference. He stared back longest at Bosaaso, whose face he couldn't place, a man who, as far as Shiriye was concerned, was not-family" (*G,* 76).

The end of the novel is a move away from the ties of blood. Mire's friendship with Bosaaso is compared with the love between Duniya and Bosaaso and with Duniya's affection for her brother; the three types of love are shown as complementary but also as similar. *Gifts* establishes how brothers, lovers, and friends are careful to construct "symmetrical relationships" without possessiveness and authority. The happy end of the romance is fused with the joy of the brother's return as he gives "an elder brother's love and blessing to a younger sister getting married" (*G,* 242). The book is Farah's first with such a warm atmosphere and so many generous characters. It is as if tenderness between brother and sister, even in the ironic exchanges between the teenage twins, radiates around and throughout Duniya's house. Her bond with Abshir is the real source of the confidence that will allow her to risk a new commitment without losing herself, as in her previous marriages.

The mood could not be more different in the third novel of the later trilogy, *Secrets,* just as the old man Nonno with his paradoxes, his lust for life, and his wicked humor could not be more different from the pious Deeriye of *Close Sesame.* The protagonist, Kalaman, like Askar in *Maps,* is a solitary figure who tries to decipher his destiny by closely examining the moment of origin. Askar's fascination is with the moment of self-creation at birth; Kalaman's search, in a novel abounding with primal scenes, is connected with the moment of his conception. It is fitting that such a character should be an only son; part of the mystery of his family and origin is included in his repeated childhood request to his parents: "Please, give me a sibling." He cannot have one, however, since his mother is now infertile as the result of the gang rape from which he himself issued (a possible reading of the nation figure, once more an abused woman?). In contrast to Kalaman's status as an only child stand his two awful childhood companions Sholoongo and her half-brother Timir, the negative counterparts of the fusional brothers and sisters we have seen in other novels. Their incestuous relationship is repeatedly consummated during their childhood. They grow up promiscuous, and Timir eventually turns out to be gay yet comes back to Somalia in order to acquire a wife as a helpmate at home and bearer of offspring. They are both made even more cynical and manipulative by their settling in the USA.

The characters of Sholoongo and Timir closely resemble some of the grotesques in *Gifts,* but with a more deliberate and sinister capacity to do harm. Their presence in the story here leads to a reading that goes further than the previous novel. *Secrets* states most forcefully that blood ties are not necessarily the best way to organize human relationships. Kalaman's father and grandfather are revealed to be biologically not his kin, yet they are *his* by choice, in a love that binds him just as strongly as does his mother's love. The violence and the satiric gusto of the narrative in the depiction of the brother-sister couple express the rejection of a system that puts family and blood lineage on the father's side— that is, clan—before all other allegiances. The anger and sadness permeating the novel is that of a writer who sees the damage done to his country and many others by such inward-turned loyalties (Farah, 1996). One must remember that in *Maps,* Misra, the Oromo foster mother of Askar, is raped and then condemned as a traitor because she is not a direct relative: "Those who were looking for a traitor and found one in me, rationalize that because I wasn't born one of them, I must be the one who betrayed. Besides, it is easier to suspect the foreigner amongst a community than one's cousin or brother" (*M,* 184).

The family bonds which in the first novels are shown to provide comfort, complicity, and loyalty in a secure nest, as opposed to destructive tyranny, are now represented as a destructive force for society, even if they provide a haven, at a cost, to the individual. The dominance of the father's line is a destructive source of clannish self-centeredness. *Secrets,* finished ten years after the writing of *Gifts,* is the work of a man who has seen his country devastated by lineage feuds: "A land where reason does not reign, a conditional rage." All taboos have been broken when "brothers are getting deadly weapons to kill brothers" (*Secrets,* 293). The power of brother over sister-in-law—that is, of the father's lineage over the despised stranger—is now expressed in the harsh image of "a man raping his sister-in-law and emptying her of her fetus just because the woman belonged to a different bloodline from his" (192). At one point, Kalaman, unable to sort out his complicated emotions, exclaims, "Curse the blood that binds!" (200). Nonno, close to death, embodies a vanishing kind of wisdom and generosity, in that he refuses the abstraction of blood ties into "civil strife": "I can't bear the thought of generalizing. I am a person, a clan is a mob. Talk to me, sell things to me, I am reasonable. Clans are not" (296).

The novelist is at once concerned with individuals and with generalities, and also with the representation of individuals with their ambivalent feelings. He has always been fascinated by the relationships between siblings. Two of his books are dedicated to brothers, and his play *Yussuf and His Brothers* is about a Joseph character in exile, looking after his sometimes jealous kin. The theme lends itself to sociological and political reflection, as we have seen, and it also enriches the human dimension of Farah's stories. In *Gifts* Taariq acknowledges there is "sustenance in myth," but his bonds with his elder brother are also part of an individual, idiosyncratic reality: "For this was closer to home, this was not a Judaic, Christian, Islamic or Mendik myth, this was more real, touching on fraternal realities and truths, on the relationship between elder and younger brother. And Taariq knew it, and he knew that Duniya knew it too" (*G,* 122). And this reality is the flesh and blood of the novels. The relationship allows for a wide range of emotions, from tenderness to jealousy to hatred.

Farah is unique among African novelists in giving so much fictional space to the intimacies of domestic life, a refuge and a forum where outside events reverberate. The presence of brothers and sisters enriches the scene with the calm sensuality of daily life, a warmth which in most cases is at one remove from the passions of desire and power. The characters share meals, they sleep not far from one another, they narrate their dreams in a relaxed mood absent from other types of family encounters. They argue, they show their concern with small gestures and companionable moments of silence. They also touch and hug in a bodily proximity close to the fusion of childhood. Here is Loyaan comforting Ladan after the death of Soyaan:

> Hush. A sob. Quiet again, like a bundle in a corner: that was Ladan. He went to her. He helped her stand. He held her in his embrace as she shook, as she trembled, as she choked on her phlegm of tears. He took out a handkerchief. He wiped her face clean and dry. "Come on." (*SSM,* 32)

The sensuality of such moments connects the characters with the natural elements always present in the descriptions, tales, and narrative images. The emotions thus embodied establish a link with the poetry of microcosm and macrocosm, which itself cannot be separated from the philosophical reflection.

Together with the remembered stories of oral tradition, the warm relation which has its source in childhood is a source of confidence for the adult as he faces the harsh world outside. It is also a part of his or her identity, as important as being a friend, spouse, parent, or child. African novelists have often been criticized for limiting their women characters to roles as mothers or prostitutes and, even worse, for dehumanizing them into allegories of the nation-state or of long-suffering Africa. Farah's women, from his first novel onward, are complex individuals and full subjects in their lives: Ladan, Medina, Duniya remain distinctive and real in the reader's memory. Part of this is due to the way they are portrayed in relationships with their brothers, a bond which is an experience of freedom and exchange, and this may in turn be helped by the level of education attained within the comparatively privileged families represented. Medina has supported Nasser from childhood, in a special bond: "Medina who had known him longer and who loved him more than anybody else" (*S*, 106). In his turn, Nasser helps her find the unity she seeks, just as Abshir contributes to Duniya's shaping of her own life.

The six books making up the two trilogies show a distinct evolution, as the novelist changes generations and as the history of Somalia and Africa offers new developments. In their variety, the novels reveal a remarkable coherence in the way the brother-and-sister pattern explores the links between protection and freedom, between duties and emotions, and the exchanges between genders within a rapidly changing society. The topic has been neglected in many Western novels of post-Freudian times, works frequently preoccupied with desire and individual destinies. African fiction often centers on genealogy, its structure given by a vertical pattern establishing continuities and ruptures in the line that connects ancestors to children yet to come. Farah has enriched both the philosophical questioning and the human and poetic texture of his novels by giving fictional life to a wide range of brothers and sisters.

Jacqueline Bardolph, Autumn 1998

■ **WORKS CITED**

Farah, Nuruddin. *Sweet and Sour Milk*. London. Heinemann. 1980. Originally published by Alllison & Busby in 1979. (*SSM*)

———. *Sardines*. London. Heinemann. 1982. Originally published by Allison & Busby in 1981. (*S*)

———. *Close Sesame*. London. Allison & Busby. 1983. (*CS*)

———. *Maps*. London. Picador. 1986. (*M*)

———. *Gifts*. London. Serif. 1992. (*G*)

———. "The Women of Kismayo." *Times Literary Supplement*, 15 November 1996.

———. *Secrets*. New York. Arcade. 1998.

Wright, Derek. *The Novels of Nuruddin Farah*. Bayreuth, Ger. Bayreuth University. 1994.

André Brink (*Jerry Bauer*)

SOUTH AFRICA

Reinventing a Continent (Revisiting History in the Literature of the New South Africa: A Personal Testimony)

1. "Our continent has just invented another," wrote Montaigne about the discovery of the New World. At the time, of course, *to invent* was a synonym for *to discover*; yet both readings of the word are relevant to a procedure which may well become, increasingly, a preoccupation of the literature produced in postapartheid South Africa. The need to revisit history has both accompanied and characterised the literature of most of the great "thresholds of change," as Kenneth Harrow has called them—those periods in which, as Santayana had it, "mankind starts dreaming in a different key." This need speaks as much from the inventive historiography of Herodotus as from the Icelandic sagas, the heroic epics of the Renaissance, the flowering of the historical novel in the wake of the French Revolution, the

writings of early modernism (from *Kristin Lavransdatter* to *Finnegans Wake*), or the postmodernisms of our fin de siècle, which cover the spectrum from *One Hundred Years of Solitude* to *The Satanic Verses,* from *Terra Nostra* to *The Name of the Rose,* from John Barth to Italo Calvino, from Milan Kundera to Peter Carey.

In South Africa the change of direction signaled by the dismantling of apartheid (against the backdrop of the larger watershed marked by the breakup of the former Second World) coincided with the revisions wrought in historical consciousness by postmodernism, which may well have an impact on a novelist's view of history. It is likely to form part of an intensive endeavour in postapartheid literature to address the silences of the past, and the forms this may assume cannot but be informed by the peculiar concept of history the authors concerned bring to it. In general terms it would involve a choice between two *kinds* of concepts, two ends on a sliding scale: namely, "history as fact" and "history as fiction." I know that in my own work I have moved from one notion to the other, not necessarily in a clear linear development, but as part of a continuing dialectic; and it seems to me that this may hold true of the larger territory of the South African historical novel as a whole. This is what I propose to address in the present essay in order to present, at least tentatively, some personal and subjective comments within a larger perspective.

It is important to remember that within historiography itself there has been a move away from the approach of the past as a set of "data," a "reality behind the text," toward the open-ended perception of history itself as text and as narrative. This move has accompanied the shift in the novel, from the realism of the nineteenth century (which, by and large, persisted in South African literature until well after World War II) to the constructions and inventions of modernism and postmodernism. Throughout this movement its dynamic has been provided by the underlying tussle between Europe and Africa, and informed by the need to bring under words the invention of a new continent.

2. In older South African literature, whether written by black or white authors, in English or in Afrikaans,[1] the historical novel occupied a very minor place; and as might be expected, the approach was largely traditional—in the form of attempts merely to personalise and dramatise accepted renderings of history. In English, Thomas MacIntosh McCombie wrote *Adriaan van der Stel; or, Two Hundred Years After* in 1885, retelling the struggle of Dutch and Huguenot colonists against an autocratic Cape governor during the early years of Dutch settlement; and the black writer Sol Plaatje presented in *Mudhi* (1930, but written much ear-

lier) the first attempt to retell an epoch from the country's history from the point of view of black experience. For much historical writing in the twentieth century, the tone was set by the popular but ideologically suspect novels of Sarah Gertrude Millin (1889–1968), which took the supremacy of the white race as their point of departure. Several other writers, including Stuart Cloete (1897–1976), veered toward an even more sensationalist approach. In Afrikaans, where for the better part of this century the genre has enjoyed considerably more popularity, novels by authors as disparate as J. H. H. de Waal (1871–1937), Elizabeth Vermeulen (1897–1978), and the much more modern F. A. Venter (b. 1916) invariably revisited the great moments of the Afrikaner past—notably the Great Trek and the Anglo-Boer War—to rediscover a divine interest in the trials and tribulations of God's chosen people in darkest Africa. One of the few Afrikaans writers openly to challenge the Eurocentric approach has been Jan Rabie (b. 1920), who dramatically rewrote Afrikaner history from the point of view of "coloured" experience. But not one of these writers revealed any doubt about history as a collection of facts, objectively verifiable; not one of them challenged the underlying ideological assumptions of history as a representation of the real. Even if writers like Plaatje and Rabie do offer an alternative—black or "coloured"—view of the past, their acceptance of the *status* of history is identical to that of the other writers concerned; that is, the assumption that interpretations may differ but that behind the idiosyncrasies of personal perception, history exists as an acceptable record of an accessible reality. It is a map drawn of a real, existing land: the lines and contours and place-names may be refined and revised as we move toward ever greater precision, but given the right tools and the right experience, the map at the very least has the potential of becoming a wholly dependable representation of the thing itself.

The problem of this approach, as Hayden White (89) has so convincingly argued, is that it is erroneous for a theorist/critic/reader to presume that the "context" or "historical milieu" of a literary text "has a concreteness and an accessibility" which the text itself lacks, "as if it were easier to perceive the reality of a past world put together from a thousand historical documents than it is to probe the depths of a single literary work that is present to the critic studying it. But the presumed concreteness and accessibility of historical milieux, these contexts of the texts literary scholars study, *are themselves products of the fictive capability of the historians who have studied those contexts*" (my italics).

3. What is interesting, as a background to postmodernist forages into the historical novel in more re-

cent South African literature, is a small clutch of early fictional writing in which a view of history-as-narrative, history-as-text, is already communicated. It may be significant for future development, as the evolving new South Africa tries to come to grips with its past, that the very first historical novel in the Afrikaans language, S. J. du Toit's *Die Koningin van Skeba* (The Queen of Sheba), first serialised in 1896–98, offered, in the guise of a factual account of a journey to Great Zimbabwe, a wildly imaginative invention about a distant African past, in the form of ancient documents "discovered" in the famous Zimbabwe ruins and allegedly translated by an expert in the group of travelers. So persuasive was the account that contemporary readers were horrified to learn subsequently that the respected clergyman du Toit had in fact "lied" to them. Inserting himself— unwittingly, quite probably—in a tradition of the textualisation of history at least as old as the *Don Quixote*, the Reverend du Toit may have unwittingly provided a model for much later postmodernist writing in South Africa.

Another significant forerunner of this trend may be A. C. Jordan's *Imgqumbo Yeminyana* (The Wrath of the Ancestors; 1940): although it cannot be regarded as a historical novel in any accepted sense of the term (it deals with a young man from the Mpondomise people who has to abandon his university studies in order to assume the kingship), the way in which the protagonist must reconcile his progressive ideas with the whole weight of his historical and traditional milieu does problematise the very notion of history. Of particular importance is the way in which any excessive or fanciful usage of history as an ideological tool in the community is persistently branded in the text as "Nongqawuse tales"—a reference to that key moment in Xhosa history when, in 1857, the young girl Nongqawuse played a Jeanne d'Arc role in persuading her people that mysterious voices had ordered the slaughtering of all the cattle and the burning of all the possessions of the Xhosa people in anticipation of an apocalypse in which the ancestors would rise from the dead to drive the white race into the sea. Jordan's skillful involution of myth and history, fiction and fact, paves the way for future revisitings of the past in order to evoke it, not as fact but as metaphor. In this way his text may be read as a dialectic between written history and oral tradition, producing a new form teeming with possibilities for future exploration.

4. South African fiction began to interrogate history—not just different versions of history, but the very notion of its ontology, status, and structure—well before the rigorous certainties of apartheid began to crumble. In Afrikaans literature the decisive marker of this change was Etienne Leroux's *Magersfontein, o Magersfontein* (1976; Eng. 1983), in which textualisation runs riot. The narrative concerns the attempts of a present-day film company from Britain to make a film based on the crucial battle of Magersfontein, fought during the Anglo-Boer War; in the process there is growing confusion between the historical personalities, their fictionalised counterparts in the script, the actors involved in playing these roles, and the "real-life" characters of the actors. One of the consequences for the narrative (which ends in a literal "send-up" in a hot-air balloon) is that all sense of identity is dissipated in the endless postponements and distancings of Derridean *différance,* and the very notion of "historical origins," of an ur-text, of a reality behind the textualising processes of a self-inventing narrative is left open-ended.

Once again, as Hayden White (91) formulates it, history itself becomes no more than an extended metaphor: "It tells us in what direction to think about the events and charges our thought about events with different emotional valences. The historical narrative does not image the things it indicates; it calls to mind images of the things it indicates, in the same way that a metaphor does."[2]

In English South African fiction this process has been demonstrated in quite a variety of novels, including *The Arrowing of the Cane* (1986) and *The Desecration of the Graves* (1990) by John Conyngham, in both of which "real" or "imagined" texts from the past are reinvented in the present. In the narrative world of the first novel (by far the more convincing of the two) the narrator renounces the possibility of physical and emotional fulfillment in a love relationship with his fiancée to withdraw into a private world where sex is simulated by inserting a manuscript scroll (which represents his own biography and the written record of his white tribe) in a vaginal fissure in the cellar, from which it can be retrieved only in a postapocalyptic world. By reducing, in this way, his private and collective history to a written text, the narrator reminds the reader that, as a character in a novel, he *is* no more than text.

Likewise, the driving force behind Mike Nicols's three novels to date is the fictionalisation of history: in *The Powers That Be* (1989) the entire apartheid experience is reduced emblematically to the fantastic story of a small village in the iron grip of Captain Nunes (who, as a construct, is reminiscent of Brecht's Arturo Ui); in *This Day and Age* (1992) crucial battles from the history of the South African racial conflict are reinvented in a curious synchronic relationship (occasionally with a certain strained urge to allegorise) in which disparate incidents are retextualised to foreground the pervasiveness of evil; in the most allegorical and least successful of the three, *Horseman* (1994), an apocalyptic rider charges through a frightening world that ranges, in time and space, from medieval Europe to present-day Southern Africa to sow terror and confusion. The point is that by turning everything into *story* and thereby "dehistoricising"—and defamiliarising—known events and patterns from European and African tradition, Nicol restores an original violence to the reader's awareness of history. Precisely by shattering the perception of history as "something out there," a record of distant times, people, and events, and drawing into the textual here-and-now of a story that exists within the physicality of a book held in the reader's hands, it assumes a new immediacy and in fact a new urgent "reality."

The most impressive demonstration of the textualisation of history in recent South African fiction has been the novels of J. M. Coetzee, in which it assumes a dazzling variety of forms. It involves the literal rewriting—and reimagining—of a specific historical sequence of events in *The Narrative of Jacobus Coetzee* (in the diptych novel *Dusklands,* 1974); it also embraces the delineation of the patterns of power in *Waiting for the Barbarians* (1980), in which the experience of empire acquires a heightened urgency precisely because the Empire of the text is not identified exclusively with any historical epoch (ranging from the Roman to the apartheid state) but spans and crystallises them all; elsewhere the process ranges from the recovery of a history already fictionalised by Defoe (*Foe,* 1986), to a history of a possible future already perceptible within the present (*Life and Times of Michael K,* 1983), to the diarising of a personal history in the process of unfolding (*Age of Iron,* 1990), to a reimagined and intensely fictionalised life of Dostoevsky (*The Master of Petersburg,* 1994).

Apropos of *Foe,* Malvern van Wyk Smith (128) comments on the text and the writing of *Robinson Crusoe* as "the archetypal text of the colonizing myth . . . capable of generating endless texts and readings . . . all re-inscriptions of the history of conquest which have powerful 'meanings' *but no substance in a reality identifiable outside the discourse itself*" (my italics). This, it seems to me, is precisely the point of the endless array of revisitations of history now opening up to the writer of the new South Africa. For a very long time (for eminently understandable reasons, and perhaps not without effect) South African fiction has been intimately tied up with the need to record, to witness, to represent, and to interpret the unfolding of a historical process and its effects on the lives of women, men, and children caught up in it. At a time when the media were prevented from fulfilling their basic function of reportage, fiction writers had to assume this burden. But as the Russian writer Victor Erofeyev once said, this activity could be com-

pared to the uses to which furniture might be put in time of war, whether as barricades against the enemy, or as firewood in a winter of deprivation, or as blunt weapons of defence and attack; yet when peace returns, furniture is set free to become once again no more—and no less—than "mere" furniture. Similarly, if in a state of emergency writing assumes functions of representation and persuasion, its "true" function ultimately, always, and already lies in *being what it is:* a text and a process of textualisation, a narrative and a process of narrativisation. And when it turns to history, as it may feel inspired to do in a time when the processes of history are themselves highlighted, it can explore the kinship of story and history precisely by recognising the story nature of history itself—that is, its textual status, and its recourse to the forms and processes of storytelling, emplotment, characterisation, et cetera. Hayden White once again: "In general there has been a reluctance to consider historical narratives as what they most manifestly are: verbal fictions, the contents of which are as much *invented* as *found* and the forms of which have more in common with their counterparts in literature than they have with those in the sciences" (82).

5. In looking, with the advantage of hindsight, at a few moments in my own writing as a new kind of historical consciousness surfaced, I do not presume to attempt anything more than to clarify for myself, *après coup,* certain issues of which I may not even have been conscious at the time (which is why I am intrigued enough to look at them now) and which may or may not illustrate, in one concrete example, the development of this consciousness at a time when a "threshold of change"—in contemporary South African history, and in the possibility of a new kind of literature emerging within it—is being crossed.

Returning reluctantly to South Africa in 1961 after two years of study in Paris and still enthralled by the world I'd discovered abroad, I found that the last subject that interested me as a writer was this country; my centre of gravity was elsewhere. But after another year in France, the watershed year of 1968, my second return was different in every respect from the first: this time I *wanted* to come home to "know the place for the first time." What fired my writing was no longer what I had in common with writers in Europe, but what tied me to Africa. For the first time I was possessed by the passionate need to define my roots and invent my subcontinent. And the first form this took was *Looking on Darkness* (1974; first published in Afrikaans in 1973), in which the "coloured" narrator attempts to reconstruct his own history (an exercise which, in one way or another, appears to obsess all my other narrators). His sources are twofold: the oral tradition passed on to him by his mother, in which at least some of the original "voices" attempt to find an articulation within Joseph Malan's reconstructions; and external materials, written documentation in books and archives. He inevitably finds that sources are suspect, and so his preoccupation is not primarily with an "accurate" or "objective" report (although at times his conditioning by traditional mind-sets is still evident) but with the appropriation of a personal history through the imagination. (In later novels like *An Act of Terror* [1991] the writing of a personal or tribal history would be extended to involve the gradual transition from mythology to historiography.) The suspect nature of the verbal construct is signaled to the "objective" spectator/reader—personified by Joseph's jailers, who survey his every move and scrutinise his every word—by the thirteen Shakespeare sonnets he leaves behind as his disguised written testimony. (Whatever else he writes he flushes down the toilet, which means that the text that meets the reader's eye is quite literally an *impossible* text which cannot exist except in the narrator's mind—and he, of course, is dead by the time any outsider can enter the narrative world.) These sonnets are Joseph's "purest" testimony, into which his whole life history has been distilled; and they are literally the words of "someone else" (Shakespeare). Furthermore, even as quotations they are not dependable, as there are errors of transcription in each of them. As an actor, Joseph has a trained memory; it is his only certainty in a world of endless shifts and changes. But the actor's profession is notorious, not only for its "secondhand" quality, but also for the futility and unreliability of its sound and fury. And if the sole dimension of existence in which Joseph presents himself as reliable—his ability to memorise the texts of others—is revealed to be dubious, then everything else in his confession, including most notably his narration of his history, is open to question. But this ambiguity remains vested in the role of the *narrator,* rather than the perception of history as such—except if the interposition of the narrator between reader and story is to be read as a demonstration of the opacity of language, which presents language not as an access toward history but as a displacement of it—i.e., language not as a transparent sheet of glass but as a stained-glass window (which still requires the light from the "real" world to bring it to life, but which focuses the attention on its intrinsic colours and patterns).

Unreliable narrators of one kind or another recur in *Rumours of Rain* (1978) and *A Dry White Season* (1979). In the first, Martin Mynhardt demonstrates the apartheid mind at work, as he desperately tries to impose a rigorous separation on the different clusters of data that constitute his life, one set surrounding his son,

another his best friend, or his father, or his mistress; and this severe ordering of his various worlds—until they are all swept away by a more fluid and chaotic course of events—must inevitably raise questions about his presentation of history as well. In *A Dry White Season* the narrator, a hack writer, is let loose upon an assortment of notes, diaries, press cuttings, et cetera, and the tension between the attempt to "do justice" to the documents and his professional inclination to sensationalise his material coincides with the tussle between different perceptions of history, even though the novel as a whole, geared toward representation-as-protest, does not radically question the status of history.

An altogether different situation obtains in *An Instant in the Wind* (1976; Afrikaans edition 1975), in which the illusion is created of a "true story" based on authentic archival documents. These documents do not exist, however, at least not in the Cape Archives; inasmuch as the story has an original source, it is Sidney Nolan's account of the famous Australian history of Mrs. Frazer, which also formed the ur-text of Patrick White's novel *A Fringe of Leaves,* published—by a curious coincidence—simultaneously with the English edition of *An Instant in the Wind.* The novel is presented explicitly as a modern reconstruction and a reimagination of an "original"; but the point is, of course, that this "original" is transposed to a different century and a different continent, which effectively deauthenticates it as a history (even though most of the historical information about the Cape of Good Hope in the eighteenth century is based on travel documents from that time and place).

This differs from *A Chain of Voices* (1982), in which the narrative of a slave revolt in the Cold Bokkeveld in 1825 is indeed inspired by existing documents (the 2,000-odd pages of documents surrounding the trial of the slave rebels). What struck me at the time was the way in which the depositions of all the witnesses and accused in the trial had been *transcribed* by court officials (and, in fact, the scribe[s] had occasionally left more than one version of his/their transcriptions behind, in various stages of legibility and stylistic competence). Only occasionally, in unguarded moments as it were, one could hear, in an unexpected or ungrammatical turn of phrase, the "original" voice of the speaker sounding through the palimpsest of transcriptions. (And even in these cases it was a mere hunch, a personal opinion, a "feeling"; there was no external proof in the documents themselves.) So here I was exposed to history itself; it was the most direct access to "what really happened" I could ever have hoped for. Yet even in these circumstances my most painful discovery was the *unreliability* of historical documentation. (Even on "basic facts" like the ages or names or family relationships of some deponents the documents turned out to be fairly unreliable.) Moreover, on one absolutely crucial issue the documents were conspicuously silent: toward the end of the proceedings the judge referred to "certain rumours" surrounding the relationship between the slave Galant and the white woman Hester and ordered an *in camera* hearing of evidence in this respect. Nothing further was recorded about the enquiry—which was enough stimulation for the dirty mind of the novelist to take over.

But what is really at issue is that the archival material demonstrated at this point quite dramatically that history, even in the most traditional sense of the word, is not only composed of texts (written and otherwise), but is also strung together from silences. And this, it seems to me, is what primarily attracts the novelist (as it originally attracted the historiographer?). Throughout the apartheid years whole territories of silence were created by the nature of the power structures that ordered the country and defined the limits of its articulated experience. Some of these silences were deliberately *imposed,* whether by decree or by the operations of censorship and the security police; but in many cases the silences arose because the urgencies of the situation presented priorities among which certain experiences simply did not figure very highly. (In crude terms, if at a given moment I had to choose between writing a love story and the story of a life disrupted by the machinations of apartheid, I would opt for the latter—not because it was "expected" of me or "imposed" on me, but because in those circumstances I would *choose* to.) In yet other cases the silences had to be discovered *below* the clamour that filled certain gaps: the clamour of "official versions" and "dominant discourses," which caused such a din that one often did not even realise the noise existed, not for its own sake but purely as a cover-up for the silences below. It is the inverse of what George Eliot intimated in that wonderful line from *Middlemarch,* "There is a great roar at the other side of silence."

A completely different relationship with history informs *The First Life of Adamastor* (1993), originally intended as the first of thirteen chapters in a novel to be entitled *The Lives of Adamastor* (and which was eventually reshaped into Thomas Landman's invention of a family history in *An Act of Terror,* 1991). This was, explicitly, an attempt to counter, from the "inside," two key myths of the dominant historical and ethnographic discourse about Africa: Camões's version of Europe's early encounter with Africa, personified as a monstrous black giant who resists all attempts to be conquered from abroad and who is finally punished by Zeus, the god of European patriarchy, for having dared to love the (white) nymph coveted by the Father himself; and sec-

ond, the persistent European myth about black African sexual potency. In both cases a "send-up" technique of gross exaggeration is used, deliberately couched in the shape of early European narratives but incorporating stories and story forms from various African oral traditions. This, I hoped, would result in something more complex than a simple refutation of the prevalent discourse, or the positing of a simple alternative: because part of the narrative wealth of Africa lies in moving beyond the simple dichotomies of either/or, to arrive at more syncretic and holistic patterns of narrative thinking. (And "narrative thinking" is, of course, what writing is about: discovering for the novel, and rediscovering in each new novel, that which, as Kundera said, can be articulated *only* by the novel and not by any other form of discourse.)

In yet another way my involvement with history expressed itself in *On the Contrary* (1983), where the mendacious and imaginative nature of the historical character Estienne Barbier prompted a continuation, in the novel, of the self-inventions in which Barbier indulged through the writing of his letters (still available in the Archives) to successive governors at the Cape of Good Hope. Accompanied by the fictional character of Don Quixote and by a Jeanne d'Arc as much imagined by Barbier as drawn from the popular mythologies surrounding her historical role, the new hidalgo sets out on several journeys (all three of them imagined, by the writer or by the narrator or by both) into the African interior, an interior whose geography is as suspect as its history; it is, in fact, an interior composed not so much of landscapes and climatological conditions as by the *texts* of numerous eighteenth-century travelers through the Cape hinterland. The key figure among them, whose voice is often allowed to speak for itself in the text, is a German of whose very name we are not quite sure: he might be Peter Kolb, or Kolbe, or Kolben, and he apparently spent some time at the Cape at the beginning of that century—but considerable doubt exists about his veracity. Some commentators have even suggested that he wrote his extensive travelogues without ever setting foot beyond the immediate environs of Cape Town. (And yet, in his imaginative reconstruction of an African Other without which the self could not come to know itself, Kolb[e][n] might have ventured closer to grasping an elusive truth about the continent than many others who observed, named, and recorded, in meticulous detail, every little plant, insect, animal, or human being encountered on their journeys of exploration.)

One step further, and one would not even require the pretext (in the most literal sense of a pre-text) of historical "sources" to reinvent the past in order to valorise—and validate—it for the narrative in which the writer is personally implicated. In *Imaginings of Sand* (1996) the compulsively narrating grandmother, mouthpiece of a long line of silent and/or silenced women in South African history, no longer relies on "evidence" or "references" of any kind: her narratives are their own raîson d'être and derive from the individual's need to insert her/himself, through storytelling, within the larger contexts of space and (historical) continuity. Where sources are used in recognisable form, they function on at least three levels: sometimes they are "informal" by nature, like the Great Trek diaries of Susanna Smit; on other occasions they are subjected to transference, as happens in the case of the well-known seventeenth-century figure of Krotoa (known as Eva to the Dutch), who acted as interpreter between the Dutch and the indigenous Khoikhoin until she became the victim of both groups. This chapter from history is transposed in the novel to the fictitious character of the woman Kamma,[3] whose involvement in the story is based on a particularly illuminating feminist reading of the Adamastor myth (cf. Driver, 455–57). In other words, the concern of the narrative here is not the "facts" but the *patterns* of already-narrativised history. A third level on which "historical sources" function in the narrative involves the complete abandonment of that "reality identifiable outside the discourse itself" to which van Wyk Smith referred: for instance, one of the instigators of a crucial episode in the grandmother's family history is borrowed, not from historiography, but from another novel, *An Act of Terror*.

In all these instances the importance lies in the recognition of the *need to storify,* not in the specifics of the remedies each individual may bring to the situation. Passing beyond the intertextualities of separate documents, and relying more on images and metaphors than on the grammars of language, the grandmother reverts to pure invention—as an acknowledgment of that primal urge described by Russell Hoban in his famous dictum, *"We make fiction because we are fiction."*

6. And this is, ultimately, the only answer one can give to the inevitable question, "Why?" *Why* resort to fiction? *Why* reduce history to storytelling? *Why* confront a demanding and turbulent "real" world with the inventions and fabrications of narrative? *Why,* at a time when South Africans are expected to be preparing to face present and future, should one waste time by an *invention,* rather than a strict discovery, of the past? We are moving toward the persistent objection against all postmodernist writing, but most pertinently against its practices within the dimensions of history and of morality. For surely, if *anything* may be invented, why should any one particular invention carry more weight than an-

other? If all is text and there is nothing outside the text, how can anything be morally or historically valorised?

The answer, I have already suggested, lies in that leap of the imagination (and, it should be added, of reason) that prompted Hoban to say, "We make fiction because we *are* fiction." Whether one composes a c.v. for a job application, or reviews a day or week or year or a life traversed, or relates a crucial experience to someone else, or writes a letter, or describes an event—however one sets about it, it is inevitably turned into narrative, within what Brian Wicker called a "story-shaped world." This, as Hayden White (87) argues, provides a key to psychological analysis as well: "The therapist's problem . . . is not to hold up before the patient the 'real facts' of the matter, the 'truth' as against the 'fantasy' that obsesses him. . . . The problem is to get the patient to 'reemplot' his whole life history in such a way as to change the *meaning* of those events for him and the *significance* for the economy of the whole set of events that make up his life." The same process, he indicates, occurs in historiography: "Historians seek to refamiliarize us with events which have been forgotten through either accident, neglect, or repression."

Whether this occurs in therapy, in historiography, or in literature, the powerful act of appropriating the past through imaginative understanding—that is, through the devices of metaphor rather than through a "scientific objectivity" which tries to mask its own uncertainties—is necessary for the sanity of the whole community. And this is not a random act at all. It is not a matter, as critics of postmodernist discourse often pretend, of "any invention will do." What this kind of invention effects is to open a door to *comparative* reading. The new text *has* to be evaluated against the whole spectrum or palimpsest of available texts, and so a polylogue is opened through which versions of the past are drawn into the present, confronting the reader with the need—and above all with the responsibility—to *choose*.

Since we experience our own lives as a compilation of narrative texts, this approach to historiography within the novel introduces (a) history into the whole collection of narratives that constitute us, both as individuals and as a community. And *because* the text is not offered as definitive, final, absolute, but as the exploration of a possibility among others, it invites the reader to keep her/his critical faculties alive by pursuing the processes of imagination in order to arrive at whatever proves more relevant, more meaningful, or simply more useful in any given context. It intensifies the relationship between the individual and her/his spatial and temporal environment. And learning to inhabit the continent of our invention may well be one of the most rewarding challenges facing South Africans—readers and writers alike—in this time of change, knowing that neither its history nor its moral boundaries are fixed and final, but remain constantly to be reinvented and, in the process, revalorised.

André Brink, Winter 1996

■ **WORKS CITED**

Driver, Dorothy. "Women and Nature, Women as Objects of Exchange: Towards a Feminist Analysis of South African Literature." In Michael Chapman et al. *Perspectives on South African English Literature*. Parklands (Johannesburg). Donker. 1992.

Harrow, Kenneth W. *Thresholds of Change in African Literature: The Emergence of a Tradition*. Portsmouth, N.H. Heinemann. 1994.

Smith, Malvern van Wyk. *Grounds of Conquest: A Survey of South African English Literature*. Kenwyn (Cape Town). Jutalit. 1990.

White, Hayden. *Tropics of Discourse*. Baltimore. Johns Hopkins University Press. 1978.

[1] For equivalents of "historical novels" in Zulu, Xhosa, Sotho, and other indigenous literatures, one would have to explore oral tradition. The influence of this tradition on a novel like A. C. Jordan's *Ingqumbo Yeminyanya* (The Wrath of the Ancestors) is discussed elsewhere in this essay.

[2] This functioning of metaphor White explains by referring to the familiar metaphorical equation of "my love" and "rose": it does not suggest, he points out, that the beloved is *actually* a rose; nor does it suggest that the loved one has the specific attributes of a rose—i.e., that s/he is red, or yellow, is a plant, has thorns, needs sunlight, "should be sprayed regularly with insecticide," et cetera: "It is meant to be understood as indicating that the beloved shares the *qualities* which the rose has come to *symbolize* in the customary linguistic usages of Western culture. . . . The metaphor does not image the thing it seeks to characterize, *it gives directions* for finding the set of images that are intended to be associated with that thing" (91).

[3] The Khoikhoin word *kamma* means "water," which refers to a creation myth in which the first woman (in Africa) emerged from water; in Afrikaans it refers to the realm of the imagination, of illusion, and of fiction.

The Sabotage of Love: Athol Fugard's Recent Plays

In a review of *A Lesson from Aloes* in the *Times Literary Supplement* (23 April 1982), Dennis Walder writes that with this play Athol Fugard "seems to be turning inward, towards a personal past . . . , a movement somewhat alarming in a playwright whose work has generally shown with great power and conviction the inextricability of private and public life." With his next and most recent play, *"Master Harold" . . . and the Boys,* Fugard turned even more deeply inward. The characters and incidents are drawn more or less directly from

his own life: "It is," he has said, "the most totally and immediately autobiographical" of all his work.[1] Yet for all the movement inward, one need not, I think, share Dennis Walder's alarm, for the two most recent plays are the best Athol Fugard has written. While they no doubt lack the immediate political relevance of some of his earlier ones, they manage, without ever ignoring or mitigating the horrors of life in South Africa, to move beyond the particulars of place and affirm, in a world of cruelty and suffering, the value and dignity of human life everywhere.

After its premiere in Johannesburg in 1979, *A Lesson from Aloes* opened in the United States for a limited engagement at the Yale Repertory Theatre on 27 March 1980. The following November it reopened in New York, where it had ninety-six performances on Broadway and was chosen the best play of the season by the New York Drama Critics Circle. Both productions were directed by Athol Fugard, with Harris Yulin, Maria Tucci and James Earl Jones in the cast.

Set in Port Elizabeth, in the backyard of Piet Bezuidenhout, an Afrikaner, and Gladys, his English wife, the play begins slowly and casually as Piet and Gladys (recalling the lonely tramps in *Godot*) await the arrival of Steve Daniels, a Coloured man recently released from prison, who is coming for supper with his wife and children. The stage is covered with Piet's collection of aloes, thorny plants that "are distinguished," as Fugard puts it in his introduction, "above all else for their inordinate capacity for survival in the harshest possible environments."[2]

Piet and Gladys are alone on the stage throughout the long first act. Gladys seems tense and painfully fragile. Piet is determinedly, at times even desperately gentle, patient, solicitous, high-spirited: his manner suggests that Gladys is on the edge of a breakdown. Slowly time passes. Slowly their story unfolds. Gladys has only recently come home from the Fort England Clinic, where she was hospitalized after the Special Branch (the South African secret police) had read and confiscated her diaries. Piet and Steve were once political activists; but now the optimism of the old days is gone, and Steve is about to emigrate with his family to England. Toward the end of the act, Piet, with sudden joy and enthusiasm, recalls his conversion to political action and then reluctantly reveals that he is suspected by his friends of having betrayed Steve to the Special Branch.

Both husband and wife survive the first act, however. Gladys manages, despite a brief period of hysteria, to recover her composure. Piet prepares, with a willed optimism, for the arrival of his friend and seems neither bitter nor disillusioned, even after Gladys suggests that

Steve too may suspect Piet and never come. Piet is determined: the supper for Steve and his family, which is to be both a reunion and a farewell, will be celebrated. Working with deliberate skill against our expectations of this realistic and essentially well-made play, Fugard so extends the uneasy waiting and apparently random talk of the first act that we begin to wonder if anything will ever happen and in the process come to feel the solitude and emptiness of the lives before us. Then, as Piet lights the candles for his friends' imminent arrival, the curtain comes down on Gladys's "Call me . . . if they come."

As the curtain goes up for the second act, it is two hours later and Steve has still not come. In a moment, however, as Piet begins to clear the table, Steve makes his boisterous arrival. He is alone, though, for his wife, as he admits later, believes that Piet is the informer and has refused to join him. The two men at first are in high spirits: they drink, recite poetry, recall the old days together. Then as Steve, who has come upon an old picture in his packing, talks about his father, the tone slowly changes: he begins with a joyous story of their fishing together when he was a boy and ends with the old man's despairing response to his displacement by the Group Areas Act: "*Ons geslag is verkeerd.* . . . Our generation . . . our race is a mistake." Finally, in an attempt to shake her husband's stoic determination to remain in South Africa, Gladys forces the two men to face the issues they both want to avoid: Steve's emigration to England and his suspicion about Piet.

The second act is beautifully written, exquisitely paced and inordinately moving. As the play works toward its end, the three characters are drawn together by their suffering and disappointment. Steve, arguing more for himself than his friends, defends his decision to leave South Africa. Gladys, after listening to Steve explain the psychic tortures of prison, describes her shock treatments at Fort England: "They've burned my brain as brown as yours, Steven." No one escapes. Piet, taking a lesson from aloes, refuses to answer either his wife's deliberately false accusations or his friend's reluctantly articulated doubts. At the end of this devastating second act, Steve has left without ceremony, Gladys is preparing to return to Fort England, and Piet sits, utterly alone, in the backyard with one of his aloes.

For all the cruelty and suffering it portrays, the play does not end in despair. Small things, ordinary things, affirm the dignity, the beauty, the decency of human life: Steve's memories of fishing with his father; his reluctant decision to leave South Africa so that "I can feed and clothe my family"; Gladys's heroic determination to return to Fort England rather than destroy her husband; Piet's celebration of the bus boycott, his generous com-

Athol Fugard (*AP/Wide World Photos*)

passion for his wife, his constant love for his friend. At the end of the play, as it was directed in New York by Fugard, Harris Yulin, sitting as Piet in the darkened backyard, raised his head from the unnamed aloe in his hand and looked out over the audience. With that small movement, he confirmed the play's vision of the world, its belief—to use the words of William Faulkner, whose work Fugard knows and admires—"that man will not merely endure: he will prevail . . . because he has . . . a spirit capable of compassion and sacrifice and endurance."[3]

"*Master Harold*" . . . *and the Boys* had its world premiere at the Yale Repertory Theatre on 12 March 1982. Fugard chose for the first time to open a play outside South Africa, because "the origin of the work was so private and so South African that he was hesitant about exposing it to an audience of his countrymen, at least before he could validate its universality."[4] Fugard directed the production, which cast Zeljko Ivanek as Hally, Zakes Mokae as Sam and Danny Glover as Willie. It reopened in New York on 4 May 1982 (with Lonny Price as Hally) and went on to be Fugard's longest-running play on Broadway, closing finally on 26 February 1983.

"*Master Harold*" is set in the St. George's Park Tea Room (named for the one Fugard's mother ran) in Port Elizabeth on a rainy afternoon in 1950.[5] Although it is performed without an intermission, the play has essentially three movements. It begins in joy and laughter and seems at the start as casual as ordinary life on a rainy day. Two black waiters, Willie and Sam, are preparing the shabby tea room for its afternoon patrons, talking of a ballroom-dancing contest they have entered. In a few moments, Hally (the Master Harold of the title), a prep-school boy whose mother owns the tea room, arrives for lunch. The men, it seems, have been Hally's only friends: their easy intimacy and genuine affection for one another are at once apparent. Sam, moreover, has been a father to Hally, and one of the loveliest parts of the opening movement is their recollection of the day they made and flew a kite together.

The telephone ends the joy and high spirits of the first movement. Hally's mother calls to tell him she is bringing his father, a crippled alcoholic, home from the hospital. Hally, angry and frightened, protests and then sits at his homework, impatient at the jocular conversation of the two men. But Sam finally cheers Hally by convincing him to write his 500-word composition on the upcoming dance contest. At first Hally dismisses the event as mere entertainment, but Sam makes clear to him its beauty: it's "like being in a dream about a world in which accidents don't happen. . . . And it's beautiful because that is what we want life to be like."[6] It is, he tells Hally, a momentary vision of "a world without collisions."

Once again in good spirits, Hally begins his composition; but the telephone rings again, and the third movement of the play begins. His father is home, and the boy turns all his anger and shame against Sam, the father who has loved him and treated him decently all his life. He demands to be called "Master Harold" and then insults the two men with a crude joke about "a nigger's arse" not being fair. Sam, who has been struggling to control his anger, with great sorrow and dignity, drops his trousers in response to Hally's joke, but his painful affirmation of their common humanity does no good. Hally calls him quietly, and as Sam bends over and "looks expectantly at the boy," Hally suddenly spits in his face.

Having come to know Sam's generosity, wisdom and great love for the boy, an audience is shocked and devastated by Hally's act. Willie is shattered and sits behind the table, his head in his hands. Sam, restraining both his anger and his sadness, wipes away the spittle with his handkerchief and recalls how he made the kite for Hally to help him "look up" after they had had to carry his drunken, crippled father home from a bar one night. But he has failed, Sam says, to give the boy what he realized his natural father could not—a sense of his own dignity and worth. And yet, for all his sorrow and

disgust, as Hally is about to go, Sam, in an effort to live out the goodness and love he believes must govern human affairs, asks the boy if they should try again. But Hally, helpless and ashamed, has no answer, and he leaves the two men alone in the tea room.

Again, however, the play does not end in despair. Willie, in an effort to cheer Sam, suddenly decides to spend his carfare, the only money he has, on the jukebox: "To hell with it. I walk home." The machine turns on and colors the darkened stage with soft red light, a record drops, Sarah Vaughan sings "Little Man, You've Had a Busy Day," and just before the curtain falls, the two black men dance a slow foxtrot together across the stage—their beautiful, poignant refusal to abandon the dream of a world that moves "without collisions." After the harrowing events that close the play, their dance is a quiet, moving affirmation, in the face of shocking and painful indignity, of human goodness and love.

In production these two plays have had an extraordinary impact on their audiences. Part of the reason, of course, is the careful, finely paced, exquisitely modulated direction they have received in New Haven and New York from their author. (When James Earl Jones replaced Zake Mokae in "Master Harold" in November 1982, Fugard traveled from South Africa to New York to direct him in the role.) Neither structurally nor technically innovative, both A Lesson from Aloes and "Master Harold" are essentially realistic, more or less conventional well-made plays. They seek not alienation, but engagement, and their real strength, it seems to me, is their ability to involve an audience sympathetically in the world they create. "You can't answer violence with counter-violence," Fugard once said. "Love is the answer. The best sabotage is love."[7]

Opening in what seems to be the familiar, uneventful world of our daily lives, the plays gradually illuminate the goodness and significance of ordinary people and events and then move slowly, imperceptibly to a point at which the characters, in what remains a recognizable representation of the ordinary world, must speak and act with an intense and profound purity—as does Gladys, for example, when she describes her shock treatments at Fort England, or Sam when he explains why he made the kite for Hally. Fugard's great gift as a playwright is his power, through metaphors taken from ordinary life and deft, deceptively simple writing, to draw characters whose lives initially seem utterly unremarkable but whose manifest goodness and worth can finally engage and hold to the end the sympathy and concern of an audience.

Piet's account of his conversion to political activism, Steve's memories of fishing with his father, Hally and Sam's description of the day they flew the kite become, as Fugard writes them, celebrations of human goodness and love. At the same time, with the sure sense of proportion he displays, an audience never loses its sympathy for his characters: not for Gladys, who tries to destroy her husband's last friendship; not even for Hally, who spits in the face of the good man who loves him. These two plays are extraordinarily moving in the theatre, for they draw their audiences deeply into the world they portray and leave them, paradoxically, shattered by human suffering and cruelty yet exultant in the enduring goodness and dignity of human life.

With celebrated productions of *A Lesson from Aloes* throughout the world over the last three years and the resounding success of *"Master Harold"* in New Haven and New York, Athol Fugard has come to be recognized as one of the major dramatists in the world today. While neither of the plays is perfect (the first act of *A Lesson from Aloes,* for example, may in fact be too long, and *"Master Harold"* probably spends too much time spelling out some of its metaphors), the faults seem small ones finally, and the plays are both inordinately effective on the stage. If Fugard has ceased to deal directly with the immediate political situation in South Africa, it is still at the heart of his work, but now in a richer and more resonant way. What I once wrote about *A Lesson from Aloes* (see WLT 56:2, pp. 393–94) should, I think, be extended to include as well *"Master Harold"* . . . *and the Boys.* These plays are set squarely in South Africa, but they transcend the particulars of their setting not only to cry out against human suffering everywhere, but to proclaim, in the face of that suffering, the nobility and significance of human life. *A Lesson from Aloes* and *"Master Harold"* are, in my judgment, great and beautiful plays, and they will continue to be performed long after the social and political horrors of South Africa have been cast from the earth.

Michael J. Collins, Summer 1983

1 Mel Gussow, "Witness: Athol Fugard," *The New Yorker,* 20 December 1982, p. 47. The essay discusses in great detail the autobiographical elements of *"Master Harold".*

2 Athol Fugard, *A Lesson from Aloes,* New York, Random House, 1981, p. xi. Subsequent citations of the play are from this edition.

3 William Faulkner, "Speech of Acceptance upon the Award of the Nobel Prize for Literature," in *The Faulkner Reader,* New York, Random House, 1954, p. 4.

4 Gussow, p. 47.

5 As Gussow points out in his profile of Fugard, the name of the tea room is just one of the autobiographical elements in the play: "It tells the story of the relationship between Fugard as a youngster and Sam Semela, a black waiter who for many years worked for Fugard's mother in a cafe she ran in Port

Elizabeth. . . . Even the names are the same: the playwright was born Harold Athol Lannigan Fugard, and his nickname, as in the play, was Hally; Sam Semela; the other waiter, Willie Malopo. . . . In the play's climactic scene Hally spits at Sam, as Fugard did in real life—an act that has haunted the playwright through all the subsequent years" (p. 47).

6 *"Master Harold"* . . . *and the Boys,* New York, Knopf, 1982, p. 45. Subsequent citations of the play are from this edition. (I would like to thank Esther Sherman of the William Morris Agency for her kindness in permitting me to read a copy of *"Master Harold"* prior to its publication.)

7 Quoted in "Dance Marathon," *Time,* 17 May 1982, p. 86.

Nadine Gordimer: Nobel Laureate in Literature, 1991

The world literary community has noted each year the prevailing tastes and proclivities of the Nobel jury.[1] So rare was the choice of the Nigerian Wole Soyinka in 1986, for example, that it evoked comment from many quarters.[2] John Kwan-Terry has speculated on the reasons for the exclusion of Chinese names from the list of winners.[3] The paucity of women recipients is no less cause for speculation. In addition, commentary on the Nobel Prize traditionally includes the observation voiced here by John Banville: "The committee has always appeared distinctly chary of anything that smacks of art for art's sake, preferring its literature well salted with political or social concerns."[4] Alfred Nobel's stipulation that his money reward literature of benefit to mankind [sic] and many of the jury's choices through the years do contribute to this perennial observation that artists' artists (e.g., Borges and Nabokov) do not win the Nobel Prize. Writers' and critics' common assumption that esthetic experiment and political commitment are incompatible is, however, equally responsible for this Nobel lore. The jury's awarding of the Nobel Prize to Nadine Gordimer in 1991 provides an opportunity not only to congratulate her for a reward earned through a lifetime's work but also to challenge the assumption separating esthetic complexity and political engagement.

Gordimer's receipt of the award in 1991, rather than earlier, speaks to the recent negotiations of the South African apartheid regime and leaders of the black majority population. The overt white supremacy practiced by the South African government has long been, at the very least, an embarrassment to Europeans and other people of primarily European descent, regardless of our own sins. Until that embarrassment had reason to abate, or seemed to,[5] no white South African living in material comfort in South Africa, whatever the individual's stated resistance to apartheid, could receive a

Nadine Gordimer *(AP/Wide World Photos)*

Nobel Prize, the major European prize. As a black African, the moderate but nonetheless worthy Bishop Desmond Tutu could receive the Peace Prize in 1984 for his resistance to the recalcitrant apartheid government. Still, separation of black rights and white rights being what they are in South Africa, the awarding of a Nobel Prize to a white South African would, until this year, have been untenable for the jury—or so I am guessing. This is, of course, not to say that Gordimer's prize also belongs to the South African government or that it deserves it. It is to speculate that, from the jury's point of view, the time is right to reward Nadine Gordimer and the political commitment her work has expressed for over four decades.

In her career, to date, Gordimer has published eight collections of short stories, ten novels, and two nonfiction works, has contributed excerpts from her fiction to two fine collections of photographs by David Goldblatt, and has given numerous interviews, now collected in one volume. This large body of work has prompted some reviewers and critics to assert that Gordimer is at her best in the short story and others to insist that the novel is her milieu. Having succumbed to this comparative thinking in the past, I now suspect my judgment—all these judgments—were based on the

wrong question. Evidence of success in both genres disproves any assertion that Gordimer's talent is better suited to one fictional form than to another. She has also published less-polished pieces in both genres. Her work is not more accomplished in the one than in the other. Reflecting on her body of work, I realize instead that she repeats certain social situations in a number of works and that this repetition sometimes results in powerful work and sometimes not. The question to ask, then, is how repetition of these certain social situations has served Gordimer's fiction.

In a recent essay Irene Gorak points to a situation repeated in much of Gordimer's work. "Interpenetrating white and black bodies . . . forms the hidden center of all her books," Gorak asserts.[6] Gorak criticizes what she calls the political quiescence of this repeated situation, dubbing it "libertine pastoral." I agree that much, though not all, of Gordimer's work describes bodies, explores the role of sex in life, and imagines the possibilities and difficulties of interracial sex. But Gorak is wrong to see this crucial repetition as a separation of private appetite from social choice. Examining the role of repetition in linking Gordimer's esthetics to her politics and ethics, I find that private life and public life, desire and choice, are also inextricably linked.

I use the term *repetition* thinking of Edward Said's essay "On Repetition" and Henry Louis Gates's use of the concept of repetition and reversal to explain signifying as it is practiced primarily by African Americans. Both critics focus on what Said describes as "Marx's method [which] is to repeat in order to produce difference." Said concludes:

> Probably repetition is bound to move from *immediate* regrouping of experience to a more and more *mediated* reshaping and redisposition of it, in which the disparity between one version and its repetition increases, since repetition cannot long escape the ironies it bears within it. For even as it takes place repetition raises the question, does repetition enhance or degrade a fact?[7]

Does Gordimer's repetition of black-white sexual relations "enhance or degrade" the fact? Is the hegemonic fear of rape by the black man that dictates the behavior of the white woman in "Is There Nowhere Else Where We Can Meet?" enhanced by the cruel law and white self-interest imposed upon the young black women with white sexual partners in "Town and Country Lovers"? Is the Utopian interracial union that represents a new nonracial political state in *A Sport of Nature* enhanced by the interracial extramarital affair that finds itself at the margin rather than the center of *My Son's Story*? To both questions I answer yes, in short, and see clear value in the mediated repetition. In other stories of interracial sexual union the repetition is less success-fully reshaped. Even in these stories, however, one can understand the need for and the use in repeating the problem and the question in response to the apartheid government's reiteration of unchanging racialist an-swers and solutions.

But why this particular repetition, this "interpene-trating of black and white bodies"? An answer lies in these repetitions' struggle to elucidate what are the po-litical powers of intimate relations. By this I mean not only how state political powers define the limits of per-sonal desire by such acts as a law against miscegenation; but I mean also how all private spheres, all families of whatever ethnicity, perpetrate sets of gender and racial ideologies. This Gordimer shows masterfully in a num-ber of pieces, among them the early story "Something for the Time Being" and the recent novel *My Son's Story.* Thus when sexual partners of different races meet, Gordimer postulates, a possible interpenetration of these different privately held ideologies occurs. In its best fictional forms this interracial intimacy asserts itself as more than an allegory for a nonracial state.

Racial supremacists' fear of miscegenation—promoted as fear of black man's rape and enforced by laws, lynchings, and torture—occupies considerable space in South African and United States history (to name two). That fear, obscured by violence, derives in part from the possibility that the interpenetration of ethnically different private spheres and their ideologies would result in ideological accommodations threaten-ing to absolute separation and one group's assumption of supremacy. Individuals' attempts to wrest personal appetite or desire from ideological determination are so-cial choices. Interracial sexual relations are one means Gordimer used to explore the possibility of a social choice free from ideological determination. Her fiction repeatedly demonstrates, however, that such choice is rarely, if ever, achievable in any situation. Nevertheless, in repetition is "mediated reshaping," the possibility of change.

South African writers of every ethnic origin face the question, "Am I politically radical enough?" Whether or not they ask it of themselves, it is asked of them by re-viewers and critics both inside the country and out. Be-hind the question is the model of the martyrs, those South Africans, like Steve Biko, who believe that only overcoming fear of death will free them to oppose the apartheid regime as one must. Theirs is a standard of sacrifice difficult to match or to doubt. Reviews and es-says about Gordimer's work frequently raise the ques-tion of political commitment through a comparison of her to another South African writer (often John Coetzee), and often these essayists formulate the com-parison by means of the dichotomy between so-called modernist esthetic experiment and so-called historically determined revolutionary commitment. The usual strat-egy assumes that the modernist esthetic is ahistorical and therefore incompatible with political commitment. In 1983 Rowland Smith compared the work of Gordimer and Coetzee, arguing that her writing is his-torically grounded and, thus, preferable. Richard Martin begins his 1986 comparison with the promising idea that both Gordimer's and Coetzee's uses of history are borderline cases in their treatment of realist and non-realist form and content, but Martin returns in the end to the favored assumption. Paraphrasing Gordimer's re-view of Coetzee's 1983 novel *The Life and Times of Mi-chael K,* Martin asserts that the novel demonstrates a re-vulsion of history. On the other hand, Martin concludes that Gordimer's 1979 novel *Burger's Daughter* is "at home in history and in language, [and so] the text can take its place in the struggle for . . . a solution." Irene Gorak turns the tables of the dichotomy in her 1991 essay, declaring Gordimer the modernist whose "radical aesthetic tradition [is] yoked to a quiescent political one" and quoting Coetzee's review of *The Conservation-ist* (1974), in which he asserts that Gordimer's novel has not laid the Afrikaner pastoral to rest.[8] Although my cursory treatment does not do justice to these argu-ments, it is, I believe an accurate characterization of the tendency to polarize narrative experiment and political engagement, the same tendency which influences Nobel lore. This polarization, together with the tendency also to compare Gordimer to other writers in order to mea-sure relative political merit, elicits in me not the ques-tion "What should the relation of 'modernist' literature and political change be?" but "What *can* the relation be-tween any literature and political change be?"

It is possible that no direct relation exists between literature and political change, regardless of how pre-scriptive or how paradoxical the literary form; but I re-ject the certainty of this idea, just as I do the certainty that literature does produce political change. Instead it is probable that no easily determinable relation exists between literature and political change. Gordimer clari-fies in part why this is true in numerous stories about the difficulty of beginning and maintaining direct politi-cal action and the dubious relationship between that ac-tion and greater justice. *A Sport of Nature* aside, the skepticism with which Gordimer depicts political change in most of her fictions prevails; it is obvious, for example, in *A Guest of Honor,* "A Soldier's Embrace," and "A City of the Dead, a City of the Living."

As a teacher of Gordimer's fiction, I have witnessed what the relation between her fiction and political change might be. All her best work undoes easy outrage and assumption about blame. It demonstrates the complicity with racist injustice of those who seem innocent, uninvolved, or even possessed of the correct sympathies. It teaches the careful student how to read politics as systems of power reaching into private life, lying with lovers. Those who learn what her fiction shows from affiliative bonds, links to consciously learned ideas challenging the intimate ideologies of unexplored assumptions. Whether or not these affiliative ideas provoke action and action produces change are another matter.

The strength of Gordimer's fiction lies less in what her characters say than in her careful descriptions of how they move through different private, public, physical, and political landscapes. Her characters' essential gestures speak. They tell of the characters' cruelty and grace, vulnerability and will, desires and choices.

> The old man from Rhodesia had let go of the coffin entirely, and the three others, unable to support it on their own, had laid it on the ground, in the pathway. Already there was a film of dust lightly wavering up its shiny sides. I did not understand what the old man was saying; I hesitated to interfere. But now the whole seething group turned on my silence.[9]

Characters within a story often repeat a gesture, turning habits of living into statements of belief, and sometimes Gordimer repeats a gesture of a character from one piece in another character of another work, but repeats it with a critical difference. These modest changes are both credible and moving. One such example occurs in two works separated by decades: "Is There Nowhere Else Where We Can Meet?" and *My Son's Story*. The first, the story Gordimer chose to begin her *Selected Stories,* describes a meeting in an isolated field between two strangers, a young white woman and a poor black man.

> . . . any move seemed towards her and she tried to scream and the awfulness of dreams came true and nothing would come out. She wanted to throw the handbag and the parcel at him, and as she fumbled crazily for them she heard him draw a deep, hoarse breath and he grabbed out at her and—ah! It came. His hand clutched her shoulder.[10]

The ambiguity of this isolated encounter in which the woman interprets the man's gestures through the fear she has learned becomes in this second scene a passing encounter in a crowd. Hannah, a white woman, attends memorial services for slain young men in a black township.

> . . . moving over forgotten graves with the party from the combis she stumbled on a broken plastic dome of paper flowers and was quickly caught and put on her feet by a black man in torn and

dirty clothes: *sorry sorry.* They were all around, those who had followed the convoy, and those who were streaming down from all parts of the township to the graveyards.[11]

With the absence of isolation, separation, and unmediated fear in this second scene, the hand that seemed to clutch now quickly put her on her feet. This is repetition with a difference—not necessarily in the black man's hand but in the white woman's head.

While congratulating Gordimer on her achievement, it is important to concede what she herself would concede: her opportunities as an artist in South Africa between the 1940s and 1990s have, because of her "color," surpassed any available to artists of other "colors" whom political conditions have often forced into exile.[12] Ezekiel Mphahlele, one of those exiles, gracefully illustrates this point at the end of his 1959 autobiography *Down Second Avenue.* Having escaped the confines of South Africa and gone to Lagos, he sits in a garden listening to Vivaldi and remembers an afternoon in Gordimer's garden where they also listened to Vivaldi. The memory serves as a reminder that Gordimer's garden could only be a temporary oasis; in Lagos Mphahlele felt the full refreshment of Vivaldi in his own garden.[13] Perhaps the Swedish Academy has contributed to the dismantling of the apartheid government's separate systems of opportunity by honoring Nadine Gordimer's art and its resistance to injustice.

Barbara J. Eckstein, Winter 1992

[1] See especially *WLT* 62:2 (Spring 1988), a special issue on the Nobel Prizes in Literature 1967–1987; *WLT* 55:2 (Spring 1981), a special issue on the Swedish Academy; and William Riggan, "The Swedish Academy and the Nobel Prize in Literature: History and Procedure," *WLT* 55:3 (Summer 1981), pp. 399–405.

[2] See, for example, *Black American Literature Forum,* 22 (Fall 1988), which contains several pieces concerning Soyinka's award, including Soyinka's acceptance speech (pp. 447–48) and an essay by Bernth Lindfors (pp. 475–88); *The Economist,* 309 (29 October 1988), pp. 95–96; Bruce King's comments in *Sewanee Review,* 96 (Spring 1988), pp. 339–45; and Reed Way Dasenbrock's in *WLT* 61:1 (Winter 1987), pp. 5–9.

[3] John Kwan-Terry, "Chinese Literature and the Nobel Prize," *WLT* 63:3 (Summer 1989), pp. 385–90.

[4] John Banville, "Winners" (a review of Nadine Gordimer's *Jump and Other Stories,* Ian Buruma's *Playing the Game,* and Michael Ignatieff's *Asya*), *New York Review of Books,* 21 November 1991, pp. 27–29.

[5] Black South African leaders warn those of us outside the country, through our press, that conditions in South Africa today are still tenuous.

[6] Irene Gorak, "Libertine Pastoral: Nadine Gordimer's *The Conservationist,*" *Novel,* 24 (Spring 1991), pp. 241–56.

[7] Edward W. Said, *The World, the Text, and the Critic,* Cambridge, Ma., Harvard University Press, 1983, pp. 124–25; and Henry

Louis Gates Jr., *The Signifying Monkey,* New York, Oxford University Press, 1988, and *Figures in Black,* New York, Oxford University Press, 1989.

8 See Rowland Smith, "The Seventies and After: The Inner View in White English-Language Fiction," in *Olive Schreiner and After,* Malvern Van Wyk Smith and Dan Maclennan, eds., Cape Town, David Philip, 1983, pp. 196–204; Richard Martin, "Narrative and Ideology in Coetzee and Gordimer," *Ariel,* 17 (July 1986), pp. 3–21; and Irene Gorak's essay (note 6). Brian Macaskill's "Interrupting the Hegemonic: Textual Critique and Mythological Recuperation from the White Margins of South African Writing" (*Novel,* 23 [Winter 1990], pp. 156–81) provides a persuasive defense of *The Conservationist* predicated on a link between narrative sophistication and political acumen. Macaskill, however, also engages in comparison, in this case of *The Conservationist* and André Brink's *Rumours of Rain.*

9 Nadine Gordimer, "Six Feet of the Country," in her *Selected Stories,* New York, Penguin, 1978, p. 78.

10 Nadine Gordimer, "Is There Nowhere Else Where We Can Meet?," in her *Selected Stories,* p. 19.

11 Nadine Gordimer, *My Son's Story,* New York, Penguin, 1991, p. 109.

12 See, for example, "Relevance and Commitment," in *The Essential Gesture,* Stephen Clingman, ed., New York, Knopf, 1988, pp. 133–43.

13 Ezekiel Mphahlele, *Down Second Avenue,* London, Faber & Faber, 1959, p. 220.

Mazisi Kunene (*Robert H. Taylor*)

Some Aspects of South African Literature

It is difficult after a period of thirty-four years of exile to make a fair or even an educated judgment of South African literature. Besides, there are fundamental questions of definition to be asked about this literature, even if one is unable in the end to answer the questions adequately. One may indeed be required to ask as a primary question: when did South African literature become South African? Does a political entity called South Africa presuppose a literature that is South African? A partial answer may well be that South African literature is part of a definable intellectual past that has either culminated in the phenomenon of "a South African literature" or is in the process of doing so. Then one must look carefully at the cultural and intellectual threads that are on their way to becoming an integrated body of literature.

The first problem affecting the development of a South African literature in the past was simply prejudice. Prejudice has been so rampant in the South African political and cultural ethos that few things developed outside its colouring factor. By *prejudice* here I do not mean only the idea of rejecting another person because of his or her race, but rather the extreme quality of subjectivity which makes everything that is threatening or undesirable so powerful that it poisons the mind's judgment. Many causes led to this state of mind, including fear, questionable intellectual capacity, et cetera; but one of the consequences was a delay in the development of anything calling itself South African literature.

Consequently, one can argue that various cultural streams, antagonistic to one another, were unable in the past to construct an integrated body of national literature. First of all, South Africa as the South Africa of our discussion was created as a convenience to meet the economic needs of an expanding or colonising Europe. Europe was concerned with the available resources it so desperately needed in terms both of its expanding population and also of its industrialisation project. It follows that Europe was not interested in expanding the intellectual horizons of peoples in regions "far and wide." The nature of its interest was in the development of some partially qualified artisans.

The colonisers themselves demonstrated little scientific or creative talent. They pursued physical goals of bravery in their search for resources, and a certain degree of curiosity combined initially with a sense of wonderment: hence the diaries and records of adventures by those who were literate. Even those who were part of missionary teams were primarily concerned with extending the interests of their colonial states and brought with them political identities that were primarily national interests couched in terms of religious dogmas. In a situation like this, how does an individual far away from home retain his/her culture, or what literature is likely to emerge in such a situation? We might suppose that, afflicted by homesickness, such individuals inevitably become subject to a fierce desire to re-create the world that has been lost. Imitation becomes a necessity. A sense of inferiority is compensated for by the recreation of the new Londons, new Bremens, new Englands, new Yorks.

What this means in terms of literature is a long-delayed process of cutting the cultural umbilical cord. In short, immigrants from England are English long after the actual reality of being English has been eaten up by the reality of time and distance from the cultural centre of the real English world. Further, a fixation develops that the English cultural reality which once constituted life is an ideal for all time. The England once idealised persists long after the dynamics of English cultural influence have been transformed at the original base. As a consequence, the colonising community is culturally unable to share and/or integrate with the local cultural community, which it inevitably views with disdain and contempt. In addition, this colonising populace can no longer truly claim convincing access to the best of English culture. The tragic result is a gradual barbarisation of the colonisers, who eventually are looked upon as more savage than the people they went out to "civilise." To the horror of the colonisers, the home or metropolitan culture secretly or even publicly may consider the natives more civilised than the barbarised colonisers. At the same time it modifies its controls over the colonised, leading to the horror that the mother country does not understand the mind of the natives.

At this point the hypothetical question is: how do the literary or artistic traditions of the colonisers respond to this challenging situation? The choice for them is either to participate in the spirit of revolt by the colonised or to identify with the liberalism of the mother country. And since it becomes clear that they can only hold on to the colonies with the help of the colonising country or potentially with alliances that are anathema to the mother country and to themselves, their reaction to any revolt is physical, brutal. And the intellectuals of the colonial society, still so deeply culturally indebted to the mother country, respond at best moralistically.

Early Afrikaner "documentary" literature is a record of personal and individual episodes. But the most vigorous literature is found in the powerful oral literature of the African populace, a literature celebratory of its values and traditions and history. It is a literature that is vigorous and satirical, lampooning the colonial lifestyle. As there is not much systematic study of the literature of this era of Euro-African confrontation, we can only point out that much of the oral literature which is available is concerned with a heroic reaffirmation of a society confronting a foreign invasion. This is powerfully represented in the oral literature of the Moshoeshoe era on the one hand and the Hitsa era on the other. The flourishing of this heroic oral literature is no better represented than in the era of the Cetshwayo among the Zulus. One stanza fully summarises the relentless heroic resistance of the Cetshwayo era: "The proud calf Ndaba / That stabs even as it is bending on one knee." The stanza refers to the heroic wars against the English in which the English army was humiliated and defeated by the Zulus (only to recoup its reputation by a second onslaught, which caught the Zulus by surprise).

Our intention here is not to elaborate on the oral literature of this period but to summarise some of the aspects characterising the heroic resistance against the invaders, in an era which is characterised by divisions and in which a segment of the African people is seduced by "Christian" affiliations which purport to bring a new humanistic era but in actuality are fundamentally concerned with reinforcing the colonial armies with political, cultural, and military alliances. The African world is depicted as deeply influenced either by those who advocate resistance or by those who advocate the "civilised" life-style that the colonisers were claiming to bring. Needless to say, this division served, as it was intended to, the interest and strategies of invasion. The converts, led by their chiefs, aspired to illegitimately constructed positions within their own society. Thus the African heroic poetry celebrates on the one hand the "Christian" hero (generally a prince from the Junior Royal House) and the heroic leader from the nationally endorsed segment of the society. The best heroic poetry is represented by the latter. The most cacophonic literature is that allied with the invaders claiming to fight the wars of Christ. The physical confrontation between the African world and the Western world is no better represented than in this division within the African world, projecting as it did the idea of the Christian in battle against the barbarian.

Needless to say, with the evolution of a literate culture the later records reflecting South African literature become more accessible, and this literature can therefore be better analysed. It should not be assumed that the later South African literature was neatly divided along racial lines between those who espoused literary traditions and those who espoused nonliterary traditions. This literature comprised both oral and written literature. While the literary factor dominated the world of the official records, the nonofficial world flourished, particularly through the social and political song. The categories of song were and are both the "musical" song and the chanted poem.

As the South African state formally emerges in 1910, it boasts a heritage of literature dealing with a variety of themes, most dominantly about nature, personal matters, and political issues. Here again, a much deeper study is yet to be be made of the relation between the African stream and the non-African stream. The latter is characterised by what was later to characterise the bulk of South African literature. This non-African South African literature is characterised stylistically and thematically by an imitative quality derived from its European influence. This influence is even deeper than that which affected Australian, American, and Canadian literatures. The European influence persists in countries where European languages are spoken, particularly French and English. Only Latin American literature is vigorously trying to shed this influence and, in the process, create a powerful and original postcolonial literature. South African literature, particularly in English, remains on the whole obsequious to the European models. Thanks to writers like Douglas Livingstone, the model has become less and less dominant and is in the process is being replaced by a more vigorous literature, native-born or natively anchored. Afrikaans literature, both in Afrikaans and in works written by Afrikaners in English, is more vigorously concerned with local themes and local episodes, and handles them more convincingly. In my opinion, Afrikaans literature has shed the curse of Europeanism in literature except insofar as it is a factor of relation in the world context. Its literature seems to have a future from within its native context, even in cases where it deals with European-based themes. Some of the greatest and most innovative South African writers of European origin are possibly going to emerge among the Afrikaners. This is not to say that they will be the greatest on the African continent but rather the greatest within the framework of the postcolonial writers. On the other hand, the seduction of Europe will remain a factor for some time or for many years. The Afrikaners may better resolve the problem of being Europeans in Africa and consequently fashion a literature which in spirit will be closer to Latin American literature. English literature in South Africa may run out of themes and be poisoned by Europeanism or Americanism.

This logically leads us to the question of what African literature will evolve into. Two powerful streams will continue to dominate: namely, the oral and the literary. South African oral literature, like many African oral literatures, is one of the most vigorous and most elaborate extant in the world today. As its credibility is gradually restored by more common usage and exposure via television, radio, the stage, and the desacralisation of literality in modern life, oral literature and its traditions will earn a new respectability.

In recent years oral literature has flourished effectively in public stadiums and in more private venues. Unfortunately, there are numerous quacks rushing to the podiums, becoming famous for their second-rate oral performances. Usually these performers are latter-day converts who do not understand that the greatest oral literature requires a careful balance of theme and performance. In short, shouting a series of statements (usually of a sensational political nature) and prancing about the stage does not constitute a quality performance of this poetry. For the poetry to be great, the theme must be great and the style of presentation must correspond to that theme. The performance of oral literature is an art requiring vigorous training both in the selecting of a public event and in its correct projection in performance. Also, the performance itself requires a participating and highly critical audience. Applauding on such occasions is appropriate only if the work is genuine, intellectual, and possesses potentially universal relevance. There is a mistaken view that the performance is the primary constituent, but in fact the art is in the intelligent interweaving of profound oral statements and their carefully organised projection in various controlled dancelike movements corresponding to the theme.

The best and the greatest artist of the oral tradition in modern times was without doubt Cijimpi Msomi of Zululand, who unfortunately was killed at an early age. Other oral performers do not by any stretch of the imagination equal this great genius of the oral tradition. Although I have listened to many such artists, I can say without qualification that Cijimpi Msomi will remain the greatest, equaling in stature such oral artists as Magolwane, Mshongweni, and their like. The greatest problem of the latter-day oral performer is the choice of a theme, which traditionally must be of universal significance and lasting meaning. It is not, as some latter-day performers think, about the king or sensational themes, but rather about lasting values; the king or theme is merely a peg.

Written literature by Africans in the earlier period, when literacy was low, had a surprisingly great significance and relevance. The reason was that Africans did not look at writing with a sense of awe. On the contrary, to Africans, written literature violated one of the most important literary tenets by privatizing literature. Literature was understood to possess value by being disseminated in communally organised contexts. Thus, people were curious about the new written literature, yet not impressed by the status of the exotic act of writing. What interested the old people of African tradition was the story and not the idea of affiliation into a supposedly intellectual circle. It was in that sense that many old people who were not versed in writing asked those who could write to read the story to them. Literacy in the sense of accessibility of knowledge was more rampant in the early periods than in the present era. Africans who could write wrote books of significance as a service to the community and the nation as a whole. In short, a sense of community and nationhood inspired those who wrote great and significant books more than did financial remuneration. In fact, many Africans used their land and stocks as collateral for their publications. This was particularly true of remnant aristocratic families that still had land. Strangely, then, there were greater and more significant literary works in the earlier period than in later years, when there was comparatively a wider degree of literacy.

The intervention of apartheid as a doctrinaire and controlling system of thought brought about a distorted phenomenon in African literature. Severe censorship and the emergence of government-controlled and -sponsored publications meant an increase in the output of written African literature but with themes carefully steered away from matters political. Those who were able to be published had to be careful to avoid themes that might be deemed suspect by the government monitoring systems. The government's policies thus encouraged a literature that was large in volume and thin in content. Only a few good writers survived the censor's pen. And the books still in use in schools today are in many cases the same ones that were used some forty years ago.

Thus was born the idea of a direct correlation between writing and the market. The market itself was government-controlled through its policy of Bantu Education, a lower quality education but large in volume and geared to producing poorly qualified black people. Further, the government indirectly and directly created a system of monitoring African-language departments through the appointment of whites only partially capable of speaking the African languages. The whole system of education was organised in such a way that an African child could only be exposed to his or her mother tongue at the lowest levels. Thereafter the languages of competence were designed to be Afrikaans and English.

The African child was encouraged, sometimes in the name of language progress, to speak a *fanakalo* language—that is, a crossbreed language blending English and Afrikaans and one or more African tongues. Thus began the process of alienation from the mother tongue, combined with the idea of the nonfunctionality of these languages in places of employment. The new fanakalo African language (slang/creole) challenged what came to be designated as Old Zulu, Xhosa, Sotho, Venda, et cetera—actually a reference to the classical variety of the language.

Needless to say, there emerged a generation which was only partially competent in the mother tongue. The weeding out of African students at the early level guaranteed cheap unqualified labour, people only semiliterate in the mother tongue. The result was that the African literature produced often was and is of low quality and centred on insignificant and innocuous themes. The outstanding works of this period are those written by such figures as as C. Msimang, D. B. Z. Ntuli, Kubheka, and Nyembezi, the once great J. C. Dlamini. It should not be assumed that the censor's lance killed only African writers. There were a sizable number of Afrikaans writers who were censored and/or driven into exile. Some died, desperate and demoralised.

Finally, one must comment on fighting literature, mainly written and performed by ANC cadres. And there were others who wrote literature which we all looked forward to reading. Among the significant writers in this category are Alex la Guma, Ronald Segal, Nadine Gordimer, Wally Serote, Ingrid Jonker, Ingrid de Kok, Alfred Qabula, Alfred Hutchison, James Matthews, and Dennis Brutus. Most of these wrote in English, a factor that tended to limit the circulation of their works to a certain percentage of the population—an accusation that might stick in the future. However, it must be borne in mind that the focus of these writers was on creating a significant critique of apartheid in order to mobilise the intellectuals.

We are now about to enter a new era, a golden age. The often-invoked New South Africa will be new only if its spirit and external reality is refurbished to give birth to a child whose spirit will be firmly anchored in the world in which it is born.

Mazisi Kunene, Winter 1996

Postcolonialism and Recent Women's Writing in Afrikaans

▪ POSTCOLONIALISM AND AFRIKAANS LITERATURE

Although cynical words have been spoken about the current popularity and academic marketability of postcolonial theory, it cannot be denied that it has provided valuable new perspectives on the world's so-called marginal literatures. One's understanding of postcolonialism is largely determined by the way in which the prefix *post-* in postcolonialism is read. If it is read as a reference to temporal succession and even supersession, the term *postcolonialism* applies to that which follows after colonialism. If, however, colonialism is defined as the way in which unequal international relations of economic, political, military, and cultural power are maintained, it cannot be argued that the colonial era is really over. Moreover, viewing colonialism as "a homogeneous thing of the past" (Thomas, 13) in the hope of achieving a break with a blameless present poses the risk of obscuring the historical, geographic, and political specificity of totally different forms of colonization. Anne McClintock has also argued that the reading of postcolonialism as that which follows after colonialism divides history into a series of teleologically directed phases that progresses from the pre-colonial via the colonial to the postcolonial. This description of history as a linear march of time falls into the same trap as the meta-narrative of Western historicism by arranging world history around the single binary opposition of colonial/postcolonial (292–93).

The writers of the well-known book on postcolonialism *The Empire Writes Back* (1989) seem to avoid these pitfalls by defining postcolonialism as that which undermines colonialism rather than that which follows after colonialism. They extend the use of the term *post-colonial* to cover "all the culture affected by the imperial process from the moment of colonization until the present day" and assert that literatures are made distinctively postcolonial by the fact that they "emerged in their present form out of the experience of colonization and asserted themselves by foregrounding the tension with the imperial power, and by emphasizing their difference from the assumptions of the imperial centre" (Ashcroft, 2). Emphasising attributes like syncretism, hybridism, disruption, and polyglossia in postcolonial texts, they see postcolonialism as a potentially subversive presence within the colonial itself. They also declare that "South African writing clearly demonstrates that the political

Antjie Krog *(Robert H. Taylor)*

impetus of the post-colonial begins well before the moment of independence" (83).

The objections most frequently raised against the theory of postcolonial literature proposed by the writers of *The Empire Writes Back* are also those which affect its applicability to Afrikaans literature. Their totalising view of postcolonial literature as a homogeneous category disregards the differences between highly diverse geographic, historical, and cultural contexts like those of the African countries, the Caribbean islands, and former settler colonies like Australia, New Zealand, and Canada (Williams/Chrisman, 13). Even though it is conceded at the outset of *The Empire Writes Back* that the focus will be on the literature produced in English or "english" in the former British colonies, criticism has been leveled at the exclusivist embeddedness of its postcolonial theory in English. It soon becomes clear that this English-based definition of postcolonialism cannot adequately describe the full variety of literatures produced in languages and literary traditions other than the English. Because of its rootedness in English, *The Empire Writes Back*'s account of South African literature is limited to that written in English, which is then described in terms of a simplistic binary division that obscures the heterogeneity of the languages and literatures in South Africa. It is argued that the white English literature of South Africa can be compared to the literature produced in settler colonies while the black English literature in South Africa can be more fruitfully compared to the literature of other African countries (27), thus revealing a nostalgia for the "apartheid" of binary divisions between black and white (Jolly, 21). By disregarding the literature produced in the black languages and Afrikaans, the writers of *The Empire Writes Back* paint an incomplete picture of the literary scene in South Africa (a country in which eleven languages have been given official status since the advent of democracy in 1994). Their description also ignores the interaction between the different literary systems in South Africa. This is an important oversight in the South African situation, in which the Afrikaans and English literatures were institutionally privileged because these languages had official status in predemocratic South Africa while black languages were not afforded the same status and means of literary production. Presenting writers who use English as the sole representatives of South African literature (albeit implicitly) also leaves the non-English reader of *The Empire Writes Back* with the impression of a theoretical imperialism which Aijaz Ahmad argued against in another context.

From this it becomes clear that a variety of "historically nuanced theories and strategies" (McClintock, 303) will have to be developed to describe the specific position of Afrikaans literature in the context of postcolonialism. Recent attempts to describe the history of white supremacy and racism in South Africa draw attention to the fact that its complex origins can be found in the long-drawn-out process of colonization first by the Dutch and then the British, the subjection of different peoples in territorial victories, and the subsequent enslavement of black people (Worden, 1994). In South Africa this developed into a systematic and legalized racial discrimination in the course of the nineteenth century that finally affected the economic, social, and political structures of the whole country. Although white supremacy was also prevalent in other colonial territories such as the British colonies in Africa, Asia, and America, it started declining after 1945 with the rise of the independence movements. In contrast, white supremacy became stronger in South Africa from the late forties onward under the apartheid government established with the coming into power of the Nationalist Party in 1948 (Worden, 65–120). Because of apartheid's entrenchment of the white supremacy associated with colonialism, some writers on colonial discourse and postcolonial theory refer to South Africa under the apartheid regime as a colonial regime (Ashcroft, 83), whereas others describe it as a neo-imperialist system (Carusi, 96). It must also be taken into consideration, however, that many Afrikaners (Afrikaans-speaking whites) regarded themselves as a people colonized by Britain because of the mythologisation of events like the Great Trek in the 1830s and the wars waged by the Boer Republics against Britain in the nineteenth century. For these people the declaration of a Republic by the Nationalist government in 1961 signaled the beginning of postcolonialism in the historical sense of the word (Worden, 87–88; Carusi, 96). Using the terminology of colonial discourse, one would be able to say that Afrikaans-speaking whites or Afrikaners had a "double" status in the course of South African history, that of being the colonizers as well as the colonized. Another complicating factor with regard to Afrikaans literature is that precisely this moment in Afrikaner history (the advent of the "postcolonial" Republic of South Africa in 1961) also marked the beginning of a tradition of dissent against Afrikaner nationalist power by Afrikaans writers (John, 11).

The situation is made even more complex by the peculiar situation of the Afrikaans language. Afrikaans is a separate language that developed out of the Dutch spoken by the first colonizers of South Africa (the Dutch East India Trading Company established a refreshment station at the Cape in 1652), with demonstrable influences of Malay, Portuguese, Khoi, High and Low German, French, Arabic, black languages, and English (Ponelis, 99–120). On the one hand, it can be viewed as a foreign language connected to the colonization of South Africa by the Dutch; on the other hand, it can be seen as an indigenous language that developed in Africa and carries a name which literally means "of Africa." Since the turn of the century Afrikaans has been closely linked with the rise of Afrikaners from what they regarded as colonization and oppression by the British. The language was often used as an argument to culturally legitimate the right to existence and separateness of the Afrikaner nation in its rise to political power, finally achieved with the electoral victory of the National Party in 1948. Afrikaans also came to be identified with the oppressive ideology of apartheid because of events like the Soweto riots in 1976, which centered on the enforced use of Afrikaans in black schools. On the other hand, Afrikaans is not the exclusive property of whites in South Africa. More than half of all the speakers who use Afrikaans as a first language are coloured people (also referred to as black in the context of the political struggle; see Willemse, 237), who were excluded by the racist basis of Afrikaner nationalism. It is therefore also the language of those who could be seen as the colonized because of racial oppression. Voicing the "double identity" of Afrikaans, the black Afrikaans writer Hein Willemse stated in 1987 that one had to accept "that Afrikaans is at once the language of the conqueror and the language of the oppressed" and argued for its continued use as an instrument in the struggle against apartheid (239).

In its earliest stages in the late nineteenth century and the beginning of the twentieth century Afrikaans literature functioned as a tool in the political struggle of the Afrikaner against British rule. This process of decolonization partly effected through Afrikaans literature was at the same time a process of colonization, because it excluded and oppressed Afrikaans-speaking people of colour as well as others. It is also known that the institutionalisation of Afrikaans literature was supported by the Afrikaner nationalist project and that it lent status and legitimacy to that project in its turn. Although Afrikaans literature has been called "a faithful bedfellow of Afrikaner nationalism and Afrikaner identity" (Willemse, 241), it would be a mistake not to recognise the counterhegemonic strain present in Afrikaans literature since the beginning of the sixties. Rosemary Jolly argues convincingly for the need to recognise the heterogeneity of the South African literary landscape, but her own analysis tends toward a view of Afrikaans literature as the monolithic representative of Afrikaner nationalism, thus constituting Afrikaans literature as the "other" of struggle literature in South Africa (22–23). Even though she implies the heterogeneity of Afrikaans literature by referring to the predicament of black Afrikaans writers, she mistakenly states of the well-known dissident writer Breyten Breytenbach that "writing against apartheid in his first language seems impossible" for him (22). Following his debut in 1964, Breytenbach often voiced his criticism of the apartheid government in literary texts written in Afrikaans. As such, he formed part of a strong tradition of dissidence in Afrikaans literary texts from the early sixties onward that counteracted the Afrikaner nationalist nature of earlier Afrikaans texts. During the eighties this tradition grew so strong that it became the dominant strain in Afrikaans literature rather than a marginal one.

To undercut the confusing variety of different postcolonialisms, Vijay Mishra and Bob Hodge distinguish between two kinds of postcolonialism, viewed as ideological orientations rather than historical stages. Although they make the mistake of racializing the distinction between settler and non-settler literatures, as Jolly has pointed out (22), their differentiation between an *oppositional* and a *complicit* postcolonialism can be useful in a description of Afrikaans literature's postcoloniality. Oppositional postcolonialism manifests most

clearly in literatures striving for autonomy and political independence; concern with race, a second language, and political struggle are the fundamental principles of this form of postcolonialism. Complicit postcolonialism is implicitly present in colonialism itself, although not overtly political in nature; it refers to the always-present tendency toward subversion in any literature subordinated by imperial power structures and cultural domination, tending to manifest in "postmodern" features like fracture, interlanguage, and polyglossia (Mishra/Hodge, 284–90). Experience has shown that Afrikaans literature has functioned both oppositionally (in open support of the political struggle) and complicitly (in the tendency toward the rupture and decentering of all totalising discourses), thus leaning toward the "fused postcolonial" in its construction of postcoloniality. The heterogeneity of Afrikaans literature thus necessitates the telling of several smaller narratives which take into account local historical contexts in order to avoid obscuring generalisations and ever-new forms of imperialism (whether it be on the grounds of language, race, gender, sexuality, or theory).

■ **POSTCOLONIALISM AND WOMEN WRITING IN AFRIKAANS**

The parallel between the relationship man-woman and the relationship empire-colony or colonizer-colonized has often been cited in postcolonial theory as well as the "double colonization" of women in colonial situations (see Petersen/Rutherford). Some writers even feel that imperial, colonial, and postcolonial discourses can largely be seen as "allegories of gender contests" (Williams/Chrisman, 18). Although this reduction of the one to the other obliterates historical specificity and difference, it can be said that the history and preoccupations of feminism show certain similiarities with that of postcolonialism. Early feminism, like the oppositional form of postcolonialism, tried to subvert structures of domination, whereas both feminism and postcolonialism have tried to write back the marginalised into the dominant discourse (Ashcroft, 175–76). These superficial similarities between postcolonialism and feminism should not blind one, however, to the fact that the feminist struggle is not neccesarily coterminous with the struggles for political freedom characteristic of oppositional postcolonialism. It has been shown that some postcolonial nationalisms have entrenched rather than dismantled the power of patriarchy, so that women's struggle against domination often continues in these contexts. Much has been said and written about the continuous dialogue between race and gender which considerably complicates the discourse of postcolonialism as far as the situation of women is concerned. In the process, considerable attention has been given to the need to avoid totalising strategies which eradicate difference and presume the unity of concepts like the "third world woman," the "black woman," and the "white woman." Even more than elsewhere, scholars in postcolonial feminism have been forced to elaborate their own subject positions in an attempt to establish the historical specificity of their discussions and to avoid the impression of a theoretical colonization. In contexts of oppositional postcolonialism (like the South African in the past decades) the dialogue between race and gender often centered on questions like: Which comes first, gender or race? Or should one's first loyalty be to gender issues or the political struggle of the racially oppressed? It was not uncommon for women writers to feel pressured to give their political (racial) loyalties priority over their gender loyalties. The debate around this issue in South African literature has been lively, with academic feminists sometimes arguing the case for feminism and the gendering of race against prominent writers (see Lenta).

Without discounting the fact that other categories of writers have contributed significantly to the establishment of a postcolonial discourse in Afrikaans, it is striking that previously marginalised discourses (women's writing, gay writing, and popular literature) have become increasingly important in interrogating the discourses of power in South Africa. It has been suggested by more than one critic that Afrikaans women writers can play an important role in transforming South African culture in the postcolonial context. André Brink maintains that Afrikaans women writers have already shown the ability to utilise feminism's strategies for the subversion of phallocratic systems (Brink, 4), while Kenneth Parker argues that their freedom from any obligations toward the masculinist discourse of the Great South African Nation has already led to experimentation with ways in which to write the new South Africa (Parker, 4–5). It must also be noted, however, that the category of mainstream Afrikaans woman writer does not as yet include coloured or black women, despite the fact that more than half of the speakers who use Afrikaans as a first language are coloured people. Although one can point to a few Afrikaans texts by coloured or black women published in anthologies like I Qabane Labantu: Poetry in the Emergency (1989), no novels, collections of short stories, or volumes of poetry by such women exist in mainstream Afrikaans literature. This silence can undoubtedly be read as an indication of the double colonization effected by Afrikaner cultural domination on the grounds of race as well as gender. Some of the other reasons for this silence have been pointed out by Beverly Jansen: the double oppression of col-

oured and black women in the apartheid society as well as in the family, an inferior education system, debilitating socioeconomic conditions that sapped women's creative energy, the preference for English because of political resentment against Afrikaans as the language of the oppressor, and the neglected status of the oral tradition used by many of these women (Jansen, 79–81).

Although the category of Afrikaans woman writer displays racial homogeneity (in contrast with that of the men writing in Afrikaans), this does not simplify the position of women writing in Afrikaans with regards to race. Afrikaans writing by women until the sixties was influenced by the ambivalent position of Afrikaans women who were part of a group who felt themselves colonized by white British imperialism but who also colonized black South Africans. Therefore it is not strange to find that Afrikaans women's writing up until the sixties displayed patterns of affiliation to Afrikaner nationalism and racial supremacy. It is also interesting to note that women writers achieved considerable prominence in the Afrikaans literary system despite gender oppression, although this does not necessarily imply a well-developed feminist discourse (Van Niekerk, 5). Since the sixties, but especially during the seventies and the political emergency of the eighties, Afrikaans women writers have occupied a strong place in the tradition of dissidence against the apartheid regime in Afrikaans literature. Although they are the racial "others" of women of colour, most of those writing since the sixties have chosen to "betray" (a term used by Trinh Minh-ha in referring to the "triple jeopardy" of writing women; 104) their own race in identifying with the liberation struggle of black people in their texts. Their position is therefore not unlike that of white settler women in previous centuries, whose narrative stance was considerably complicated by their alignment with colonized blacks but simultaneous entrapment in the discourses of imperialism and patriarchy implicit in the mere act of writing in a colonial context (Driver, 12).

My discussion of the following examples of Afrikaans women's writing since the beginning of the eighties will try to demonstrate that an engagement with the problems of race, class, gender, and writing constitutes a common element in the postcoloniality of Afrikaans women's writing. The complex social, historical, and cultural positionality that emerges from these texts again indicates that it would be a mistake to regard even the small Afrikaans literature as a monolithic entity. The power of recent Afrikaans women's writing lies in the multiple voices that enunciate a complex subjectivity and that enable their texts to speak to diverse audiences (see Henderson on black women's writing in America).

■ TEXTS BY AFRIKAANS WOMEN WRITERS

The texts by Lettie Viljoen, Antjie Krog, Emma Huismans, Riana Scheepers, and Marlene van Niekerk I have chosen for discussion represent only a small sample of Afrikaans women's writing since the eighties. Texts by writers like Elsa Joubert, Wilma Stockenström, Jeannette Ferreira, Reza de Wet, Welma Odendaal, Jeanne Goosen, Dalene Matthee, Marita van der Vyver, Rachelle Greeff, and Johnita le Roux could just as well have been used to demonstrate the various forms of oppositional and complicit postcolonialism present in the Afrikaans women's writing of the past decade.

Klaaglied Vir Koos *by Lettie Viljoen.* Lettie Viljoen's first novel, *Klaaglied vir Koos* (Lament for Koos), was published in 1984 during a time of increased militarisation and political repression by the South African government. The narrator in this short novel is a white woman whose husband unexpectedly leaves her and their four-year-old child to join in the armed struggle against apartheid. She angrily confronts the reader with these facts on the first page of the novel as she registers her fury at being left behind by her husband, declaring it to be the starting point of her narrative. (It is interesting to note that anger has been inspirational for more than one Afrikaans woman writer. A few years earlier the poet Antjie Krog declared in one of her poems, "Ek skryf omdat ek woedend is" (I write because I am livid; 1980, 23). After spending time in hospital to recover from the shock caused by her husband's departure, the narrator slowly puts her life together again. Having experienced a nadir of emotional estrangement and inertia, she slowly comes to terms with her feelings of rejection and inadequacy, regaining her independence and the confidence to live her own life.

The psychic trauma that provides the stimulus for the writing of Viljoen's novel foregrounds the narrator's feelings of inferiority, guilt, and inadequacy. The work demonstrates that her trauma is related to the way in which her subjectivity is constructed in terms of gender, race, and class relationships. Her gender identity is mainly constructed in terms of the differences between her and her husband. He is described as intellectual, capable of thinking in macro-political terms, intolerant of contradictions or ambivalence, prepared to go to war and sacrifice the safety of his bourgeois home and nuclear family to achieve his political ideal of freedom for the oppressed. According to her own analysis, she is a vessel filled with ideological content by her husband who dreams of a whole that will accommodate ambivalence and contradiction, wants to entrench the confines of their nuclear family rather than break it open, thinks of opposing the regime but not of leaving their home and joining the war as he did. In comparison to his she

finds hers a small life of no consequence (41), although she is subconsciously warned by an image of herself and her husband as Siamese twins in a bottle that she should free herself from constituting herself as her husband's "other" (53). The narrator's racial identity is constructed in terms of her relationships with black people and also manifests in feelings of inferiority and triviality. She feels that her own life as a white woman is less meaningful and consequential than the lives of black men and women involved in the struggle against oppression. She sees their culture as more sustaining, their people's history as richer in texture and less perverse than the sparse facts of her own history as a white person (12, 38).

Relationships determined by class also feature in the construction of the narrator's subjectivity. As the white owner of a solid bourgeois home, she stands in a relationship of economic as well as racial power toward the homeless couple Frans and Bettie, the destitute woman Sylvia whose house burned down, and the gardener Nevil, who all knock at her door to ask for food or shelter and who depend on her goodwill for their survival. At first she hides from them in her house, frightened and silent (15), but eventually she is prepared to leave the safety of her bourgeois home to negotiate with them and even to join them: "Gaan ek voortaan nie meer van binne die huis onderhandel nie maar saam met die befoktes, die haweloses, die besittingloses, saans so my huis omsirkel, in waaragtige meelewing" (Henceforth I am not going to negotiate from inside my house, I am going to circle my house in the evenings together with the fucked, the homeless, the possessionless, in genuine empathy; 66). She finally achieves the solidarity with the dispossessed that her husband so desperately desired: "Eén met die laagstes . . . die sosiaal uitgeworpenes" (One with the lowest . . . the socially rejected; 66). Thus she succeeds in breaking out of the constricting patterns preordained by gender, race, and class in predemocratic South Africa.

The narrator registers her rebellion against the various forms of domination which gives rise to her feelings of inadequacy and inferiority on a narrative level. The novel disengages itself from traditional narrative patterns (interpreted by feminists as patriarchally determined) by subverting linear causality, closure, and authorial control. The narrative outwardly follows the linear progress of the seasons but gives priority to the chaotic and unresolved inner life of the narrative as a structuring device. The novel also takes as its terrain the personal, the intuitive, the subconscious, and the microphysical domain rather than the public. Whereas the narrator's husband fights the political struggle on a public level, she conducts her struggle within a private domain (symbolised by the bourgeois house and garden). Whereas her husband analyses the political situation in South Africa on an intellectual level (18), she experiences it intuitively in terms of an image. While recovering in hospital, she sees the image of an ants' nest which she relates to the large number of oppressed workers in South Africa (11, 20, 27), with whom she feels a subconscious solidarity when performing her domestic tasks (27). Thus image and fantasy often take the place of intellectual analysis and event in her narrative. At certain points the concentration on the private and personal becomes a preoccupation with the microphysical, as is evident from the scientifically detailed descriptions of sexual organs during intercourse, especially the male organ during erection and ejaculation (2, 7). The discourse of sexual submissiveness one finds elsewhere in the novel (she lies "down for" her husband; 6) is subverted by these moments of masculine, scientific discourse in which the colonizing "male gaze" is momentarily returned. Thus the construction of the narrating subject at the intersection of race, gender, class, and writing is interrogated on a thematic as well as a structural level.

Lady Anne *by Antjie Krog.* Krog's seventh volume of poems, *Lady Anne,* was published in 1989, at the end of a decade marked by such furious political resistance against the apartheid government that it resulted in the unbanning of the ANC in February 1990. In this collection of verse, conceived as a postmodern epic, Krog interrogates her own situation as a white Afrikaans-speaking woman in the politically turbulent South Africa of the late eighties by using the historical figure Lady Anne Barnard as a "guide" (16) for her own life. Lady Anne Barnard (1750–1825) was a Scottish noblewoman who married her husband Andrew, a former soldier twelve years her junior, in 1793. Because she was a friend of Sir Henry Dundas, then Secretary of State for War, she procured for her husband the post of Colonial Secretary at the Cape during the first British occupation from 1795 to 1803. Unusually for a woman of her time and class, she accompanied her husband to the Cape in 1797, and they lived there until 1802. The letters, journals, diaries, and drawings she produced during her stay at the Cape and on travels into the interior have become an important source of information about the people, events, and social life of the time, because she recorded particular male writers considered beneath their notice. She is also retained in popular memory as a socialite, known for entertaining at the Castle at the Cape of Good Hope as the official hostess of Governor Macartney (Lenta, in Robinson, x-xix).

Krog's *Lady Anne* is a collage of poems supplemented by quotations, drawings, an ovulation chart, a property advertisment, an electoral poster, and extracts from a diary. Several poems are written from the perspective of Lady Anne, whereas others are composed from the perspective of an "I" that can be autobiographically linked to the poet. Still another set of poems places the two women together in situations that imaginatively overstep the boundaries of time and space. Similarities as well as dissimilarities in the way the subjectivity of these two women is determined by race, class, and gender in different historical contexts emerge from the poems. Lady Anne's position at the Cape of the late eighteenth century is determined by the fact that she is a member of a privileged race (a European in Africa), a privileged class (of noble descent), and a power that colonized the indigenous peoples as well as the Afrikaners in South Africa (a British subject). She looks at South Africa from the perspective of a temporary inhabitant and voyeuristic traveler, as demonstrated by the poem describing her consciousness of being an outsider who looks at the country as if through a windowpane (56–57). The volume also refers to the fact that Lady Anne lived in a time of political upheaval. Some of the poems show her in Paris during the French Revolution, feeling guilty about the fact that personal sorrow stands in the way of political concern (65–66), while others depict her agitation about the inhumanity of slavery (81–82). The poet Antjie Krog's position in South Africa in the 1980s is determined by her being a member of a privileged race (white in apartheid South Africa), a privileged class (the bourgeois middle class), and a group who colonized black people in South Africa but were also colonized by the British (an Afrikaner). She looks at South Africa from the perspective of a permanent inhabitant who feels morally compelled to take part in the establishment of a just society in that country. Her writing is decisively influenced by the context of political emergency in which she finds herself. In the poem "parool" (parole; 35–38) she questions the validity of poetry about private emotions written from a privileged perspective in an unjust society and remains conscious of the fact that even her most innocent words cannot be detached from the context of political violence in which they were produced (32). She also acknowledges that her poetical project entails a measure of violence toward her subject, Lady Anne, when she admits in the final line of the volume, "onder my duim lê die fyn sintaksis van jou strot" (under my thumb lies the delicate syntax of your throat; 108).

Because the epic usually traces the history of great men and nations, the mere fact that Krog chose a woman as subject of her postmodern epic makes a statement about the importance of gender issues amid the struggle for racial equality in South Africa. Her artistic portrait of Lady Anne ventures further than the conclusion of literary historians that she was both caught up in traditional gender stereotypes and anxious to escape them (Driver, in Robinson, 7). Krog represents her as a strong-willed person, fully conscious of the power play between men and women, as in the poem "ballade van die magspel" (ballad of the power game; 76). One of the poems even depicts her as expressing a militant erotic desire to grow a penis and to possess her husband sexually in the manner of a man (24). The poems referring to the poet Krog herself show the way in which she struggles to reconcile different facets of her gendered position (sexual partner, wife, mother, daughter, domestic manager) and how they interact with her writing as well as political and religious consciousness. Despite the fact that both the "bard" and her "epic hero" (108) are women and that they share many similarities, Krog experiences ambivalent feelings about her subject. These feelings emerge in several poems self-reflexively charting the course of her project of writing about Lady Anne. Her elation at finding a woman she can use as "guide" (16) soon makes way for frustration when she discovers that this British Lady cannot easily be accomodated into her own scheme and has to conclude, "as metafoor is jy fôkol werd" (as metaphor you are worth fuckall; 40).

Because Krog is aware that her perspective on the South African situation is a limited one, she inserts quotations into her text that confirm, supplement, or contradict her own poems. One of these quotations describing a black working-class woman (97) is juxtaposed with a poem in which the poet expresses her affection for Lady Anne but also refers to her "totale stralende nutteloosheid" (total radiant uselessness; 96). By inserting this reference to the black working-class woman, the poet questions her own position as a privileged white woman writing about another privileged white woman. The quotation also deliberately exposes the class and racial divides present in the gender consciousness evident in the volume's focus on women. Krog's brutally honest interrogation of her own subject-position as a white Afrikaans woman writer in the late eighties is another example of the fused postcoloniality of Afrikaans literature, in which elements of oppositionality (the political struggle) and complicity (the postmodernist subversion of dominance and centrism) are combined.

Berigte van Weerstand *by Emma Huismans*.

Berigte van weerstand (Reports of Resistance) by Emma Huismans was published in 1990, shortly after the unbanning of the ANC, but looks back on the author's experiences during the political struggle in Cape Town in 1985 and 1986, when she worked as journalist for the publication *Crisis News* (Odendaal, 45). These stories with their strongly factual content focus on the issues of political struggle, race, and language that are usually associated with the oppositional phase of postcolonialism. The narrator in this collection of interconnected stories takes an active part in the political struggle, writing newspaper reports about the political crisis, carrying guns, nursing the wounded, and doing paperwork like taking down statements from victims of political violence.

Huismans's stories bring to light several complications in the dialogue between race and gender in the South African context. Although she is a privileged white, the narrator identifies herself actively with the struggle of the racially oppressed in South Africa. This does not mean, however, that her position as a white woman in the struggle is unproblematic, as can be deduced from remarks like: "Nog 'n jaar van swart en bruin agterdog oor wie is wie in die struggle en freaked out whiteys wat iets probeer doen" (Another year of black and coloured suspicion about who is who in the struggle and freaked out whiteys trying to do something; 11) and "My usefulness as 'n whitey in die local townships het uitgedien raak. Wit is 'n opvallende kleur" (My usefulness as a whitey in the local townships was wearing thin. White is a conspicuous colour; 12). Some of her assignments are also the direct result of her marginality in the struggle as a white person. In the story "Die verhouding" (The Affair) she is ordered by her young black comrades in the struggle to eliminate a coloured man suspected of defecting from the cause. She realises, "Dis 'n swart-bruin ding hierdie en 'n whitey om die can te carry" (This is a black-coloured thing with a whitey carrying the can; 14). Her conclusion illustrates the dilemma of the person who completes the crossover between races in times of political upheaval: "Maar commitment is commitment, 'n Opdrag 'n opdrag. En waar sal ek, ex-Afrikaner, môre wees as ek dit nie uitvoer nie?" (But commitment is commitment. An order is an order. And where will I, ex-Afrikaner, be tomorrow if I do not carry out the order?; 14).

The narrator's position in the struggle is further compromised by the fact that she is Afrikaans-speaking. Several stories demonstrate that the perception of Afrikaans as the language of the oppressor has been transferred onto the Afrikaans-speaking narrator despite her commitment to the liberation struggle. She comments that her Boer descent was "'n byna onuitputlike bron van wantroue" (an inexhaustible source of distrust) and her use of Afrikaans perceived as "'n persoonlike belediging" (a personal insult; 80) by one of her black comrades in the struggle. Her identity as an Afrikaans-speaking white is complicated by the revelation in another story that her familiy emigrated from Holland to South Africa when she was five years old. She comments ironically: "Verwoerd was vyf toe hy die eerste keer sy Hollandse voet op Afrikaanse grond gesit het, spot ek. Ek ook. Moet minstens nie ons Afrikanerskap in twyfel trek nie" (Verwoerd was five years old when he first set his Dutch foot on Afrikaans soil, I say jokingly. Me too. At least do not doubt our Afrikaner identity; 72). The stories also note with devastating candour the use of Afrikaans by the violent oppressors (18) and demonstrate to what extent English came to dominate the jargon of the liberation struggle. In contrast, the mere writing and publication of these "reports of resistance" in Afrikaans testify to the fact that Afrikaans was also the language of the struggle.

The collection touches as well on the nature of the relationship between the political (commitment to the struggle) and the personal (commitment to a love affair). The story "Die verhouding" (The Affair) describes an affair between the narrator and a woman who is not fully committed to the struggle (as is evident from bourgeois attributes like a state housing subsidy and two carefully groomed poodles). When the narrator is ordered to shoot the young coloured man they are taking leave of at the Johannesburg airport, she shoots her lover's two poodles instead. On the one hand, this action is a manifestation of sexual jealousy because her lover is flirting with the young man who is leaving; on the other hand, it is an expression of political frustration with the intricacy of struggle politics and her lover's superficial attitude toward these issues. Without reducing the importance of either one, the story demonstrates the problematic interaction of the political struggle with personal relationships.

The stories also raise questions about the prioritisation of race and gender issues in the political struggle. It is significant that gender is underemphasised in these stories. The collection contains only three references to the gender of the narrator (56, 68, 94) and only two references to the position of women in the struggle, from which it is clear that race takes priority before gender in the struggle, even if it is against the better judgment of the narrator (56, 63). The relative lack of attention for gender issues in these stories can be interpreted in different ways. It can be read either as an indication that race should be given preference over gender in the political struggle, or as a powerful commentary on the undervalued position of women in the struggle. To my mind, the problematic position of women is accentuated by the narrator's choice to suppress references to gender, something that also has implications for the lesbian relationships portrayed in some of the stories. Thus the dialogue between race and gender is extended to include the issue of sexuality or gay rights. The struggle for the political rights of the racially oppressed was often given priority over the struggle for gay rights in predemocratic South Africa, in the same way that the struggle against gender oppression was subordinated by the struggle against racial oppression (Gevisser). The raising of these issues in Huismans's text shows that marginalized discourses like that of women's and gay writing can contribute significantly to a complex, heterogeneous postcolonialism in Afrikaans.

Die Ding in Die Vuur *by Riana Scheepers.* Like the collection by Huismans, Riana Scheepers's volume of short stories *Die ding in die vuur* (The Thing in the Fire) was published in 1990. Whereas Huismans's text is representative of the oppositional impulse, Scheepers's stories show that these impulses coexist with affirmative tendencies exploring new possibilities for postcolonial writing in Afrikaans. The collection combines a European narrative tradition (as manifested in the use of several postmodernist strategies) with an African narrative tradition (references to Zulu oral narration as carried forth by women) to forge a new narrative strategy for the South African situation. Apart from this, the difficult process of transculturation is achieved through an intricate interplay of focalisations that leads to the dismantling of privileged and patronising vantage points.

Most of the stories included in the collection are situated in rural KwaZulu-Natal, where Scheepers grew up and later taught as a university lecturer at the University of Zululand. The title of the collection refers to the "thing" that will give one horns on the head if one listens to stories before the day's work has been done, according to the Zulu narrative tradition (76). It is also part of this tradition for the *ugogo* or storyteller to spit in the fire after the story has been told in order to destroy all the fictional images called forth so that they cannot give her listeners nightmares (81). To emphasise further the influence of the Zulu narrative tradition on this collection, it is preceded and concluded by traditional storytelling formulas in Zulu. In "Abantu oNgoye" (The People of oNgoye) several stories are combined to create a composite ideological picture of the oNgoye massacre, which took place on the campus of the University of Zululand in the mideighties. The first story is told by an external narrator, who describes the founding of the University of Zululand as an ethnic university by Verwoerd; the second is narrated by an *ugogo* or traditional storyteller, who recounts the massacre from the perspective of the rural inhabitants of Zululand; the third is reported by the external narrator, who tells the story from the viewpoint of the students attacked in the massacre; the fourth is told by an "I" (reminiscent of the author Scheepers) who is trying to find out what really happened. The agile alternation between different narrative modes and ideological viewpoints and the author's relinquishing of a controlling perspective are narrative strategies adapted to the multiculturality of the South African situation.

Other stories in the collection chart the diverse forms of colonization still experienced by women in the remote rural regions of South Africa. In "Ruil" (Exchange) a white shopkeeper who emigrated from Scotland to rural KwaZulu-Natal abuses the financial and sexual power he has over the black women left impoverished and alone in their villages by the migrant labour system, exchanging a small jar of Vaseline for the sexual favours of a black woman. Although this is a potentially degrading situation for the latter, the narrator recovers the dignity of the woman by stressing her nobility at the expense of the shopkeeper's depravity. The story concludes with this image of the woman: "Haar nek en haar skouers het die trots en rysigheid van 'n vrou wat weet dat haar inkope goed afgehandel is" (Her neck and shoulders are proud and tall like that of a woman who knows that her shopping has been well done; 17). In "Tweede kind" (Second Child) the wife of a white missionary and a thirteen-year-old black girl abandoned by her people on instruction of the *Isangoma* (witch doctor) give birth at the same time in a remote missionary hospital. Because the girl dies and her baby cannot keep down cow's milk, the missionary's wife is asked to breastfeed the black baby. She grudgingly gives her "borste vir die barbare" (breasts to the savages; 21), as she terms it, bargaining with God to make her own son even stronger than he would have been, had she fed him herself. Although the black girl (condemned by the power of the male *Isangoma*) and the white woman (negotiating with a patriarchal God) are both subject to male domination, this story shows that gender does not necessarily unify them in a glorious sisterhood but that it is definitively intersected by race and class. "Dom Koei" (Stupid Cow) describes the practice of female circumcision from the uncomprehending perspective of a white student who sees the victim of such a circumcision brought to the rural medical clinic where she is doing postgraduate research. The story forces the reader out of a position of cultural ignorance by placing him/ her in the same position as the white student through a confrontation with a graphic word picture of the circumcision wound. While the black nursing sister is treating the mutilated girl, the student is sent to free a cow that got itself caught in a wire fence outside the clinic. She vents her feelings of incomprehension, shock, disgust, and anger on the defenceless cow, which becomes symbolic of the girl: "Jou simpel fokken

dom koei" (You dumb fucking stupid cow), she screams at the animal. The narrative places the student, the narrator, and the reader in a position of voyeuristic power in relation to the silent and defenceless victim, almost implicating them in this colonizing abuse of women.

"Oor die pornografie van geweld in die Afrikaanse prosa: 'n outbiografiese steekproef" (On the Pornography of Violence in Afrikaans Prose Writing: An Autobiographical Sample) raises the question of literary violence as opposed to literal violence in predemocratic South Africa. In this postmodernist collage of intertwining discourses a discussion about violence is conducted with two men, both Afrikaans authors who have written on violence. One of the stories included in the collage contrasts the situation of a white woman's inexperience of violence with her black housekeeper's daily exposure to it. Another story describes an attack on the black woman's kraal in which her little brother as well as the *ugogo* or storyteller dies. Not only does this tale reflect on its own implication as example of the European narrative tradition in the literary exploitation of violence; it also comments symbolically on the endangered position of the African oral tradition (the killing of the *ugogo*). As such, Scheepers's collection of short stories is aware not only of the variety of narrative possibilities available for the creation of a South African postcolonial discourse but also of that which threatens to impoverish or destroy it.

Triomf *by Marlene van Niekerk.* Marlene van Niekerk's novel *Triomf* was one of the first literary texts in Afrikaans to be published in what can literally be called "postcolonial South Africa." Incorporating references to the first democratic election in South Africa in April 1994, it appeared only a month or two after the election. The novel recounts the monotonous daily lives of a family of poor white Afrikaners, showing how apartheid failed even those it was ideologically designed to benefit. The family lives in the Johannesburg suburb ironically called Triomf (triumph), built on the ruins of the black township Sophiatown, which was demolished in the fifties by the social engineers of apartheid to create a suburb for the white working class.

It is gradually revealed that the Benade family of Triomf is a gross caricature of the nuclear family and all the values it embodies: the old man Pop, his "wife" Mol, and their "relative" Treppie are actually siblings; the epileptic Lambert is their son, though it is not clear whether Pop or Treppie fathered him. Treppie's scheme to establish a refrigerator-repair business having failed and Lambert not being able to finish school or hold down a job because of his epilepsy, they depend on welfare pensions for their livelihood. The suspense in the novel comes from the buildup toward Lambert's fortieth birthday and the national election while the reader also waits for the unsuspecting Lambert to find out the truth about his father and mother. The family prepare themselves to escape to the North in their beat-up Volkswagen Beetle if "the shit hits the fan" after the election, but the end of the novel shows the remaining members of the family (Pop has died in the interim) still caught in the same circumstances as before. Nothing has changed, and the final moments of the novel depict them looking at the constellation of Orion over the roofs of Triomf, without a north they can escape to.

Underneath its naturalistic surface the novel is richly symbolic. On a political level the incestuous and inbred Benade family becomes symbolic of the extremes to which the apartheid philosophy of racial exclusivity led. The novel also discloses the historical circumstances that led to their condition (their ancestors were landowners forced off their land during a depression to become impoverished workers with the railways and in the garment industry in the city). Their history and family setup leads to a situation in which anyone outside the family is regarded with the utmost suspicion, prejudice, and contempt (as manifested in their crude racism toward blacks and their disgust with the "dykes" who live across the road). On a religious level the family, consisting of two brothers and sister together with their ironically innocent son, can be read as a symbolic perversion of the myths of origin found in several world religions, of Christianity's trinity and sacrificial lamb, of the different images of the devil, as well as of the idea of an apocalypse. The novel also drives the idea of the Freudian family romance to grotesque extremes, going so far as to have Lambert accidentally kill his "father" Pop.

Although this novel is not exclusively occupied with gender issues, it demonstrates more eloquently than could any feminist treatise the position of women in such conditions. The objectification of Mol, the sister of Pop and Treppie and the mother of their child Lambert, reaches atrocious depths. She is emotionally, verbally, physically, and sexually abused, especially by her brother Treppie and her son Lambert. She is the sexual tool of all three men, and her status as a (sex) object is underlined by the fact that their beat-up car is also called Mol. Racially she is part of a group who consider themselves superior to blacks (her position is symbolic of the failure of white supremacy); she is of a class looked down upon by other whites and Afrikaners (evident from the reaction of the young Afrikaans couple who try to recruit their votes for the Nationalist Party), and she is of the gender oppressed by the patriarchal system prevalent in the race and class configuration in which she finds herself.

Triomf, as well as a spate of other novels probing the hidden corners of the Afrikaner psyche in a process referred to as "Afrikaans literature's own truth commission" (Swanepoel, 102), signifies an important element in Afrikaans literature's postcoloniality. In her paradoxical ability to evoke feelings of revulsion as well as compassion for the degenerate Benade family, Van Niekerk illustrates the intricate relationship between the colonial and the postcolonial that must be negotiated when writing the new South Africa. Her novel demonstrates an awareness of the fact that the colonial cannot be eliminated from the postcolonial in a simple act of political amnesia and that the past must be confronted rather than evaded when constructing a postcolonial discourse in South Africa.

■ **CONCLUSION**

The texts by Afrikaans women writers discussed in this article have shown different ways of engagement with the postcolonial problematic in South Africa. The works by Lettie Viljoen, Antjie Krog, and Emma Huismans demonstrate their commitment to the project of an oppositional postcolonialism as well as the complexities involved in such a commitment for an Afrikaans woman writer. Riana Scheepers's novel shows an attempt to forge new narrative strategies appropriate for a multicultural situation and an awareness of the narrative subject's implication in discourses of power, while that by Marlene van Niekerk represents a preparedness to confront the colonial in the postcolonial. Afrikaans literature—including these texts written by women—has shown that it is willing and able to make a meaningful contribution to a postcolonial South Africa as well as to the continual process of denning a heterogeneous postcolonialism.

Louise Viljoen, Winter 1996

■**WORKS CITED**

Adam, Ian, and Helen Tiffin, eds. *Past the Last Post: Theorizing Post-Colonialism and Post-Modernism.* Calgary. University of Calgary Press. 1990.

Ahmad, Aijaz. *In Theory: Classess Nationss Literatures.* London. Verso. 1992.

Ashcroft, Bill, Gareth Griffiths, and Helen Tiffin. *The Empire Writes Back: Theory and Practice in Post-Colonial Literatures.* London. Routledge. 1989.

Brink, André P. "Op pad na 2000: Afrikaans in 'n (post)koloniale situasie." *Tydskrif vir Letterkunde,* 29:4 (1991), pp. 1–12.

Carusi, Annamaria. "Post, Post and Post: Or, Where Is South African Literature in All This?" In Adam, pp. 95–108.

Coetzee, Ampie, and Hein Willemse, eds. *I Qabane Labantu: Poetry in the Emergency / Poësie in die Noodtoestand.* Bramley, S.A. Taurus. 1989.

Driver, Dorothy. "Woman as Sign in the South African Colonial Enterprise." *Journal of Literary Studies,* 4:1 (1988), pp. 1–20.

Gevisser, Mark. "A Different Fight for Freedom: A History of South African Lesbian and Gay Organisations from the 1950's to the 1990's." In Gevisser and Cameron, pp. 14–86.

Gevisser, Mark, and Edwin Cameron, eds. *Defiant Desire: Gay and Lesbian Lives in South Africa.* Johannesburg. Ravan. 1994.

Henderson, Gwendolyn Mae. "Speaking in Tongues: Dialogics, Dialectics and the Black Woman Writer's Literary Tradition." In Williams.

Huismans, Emma. *Berigte van weerstand.* Bramley, S.A. Taurus. 1990.

Jansen, Beverly. "Swart Afrikaanse digters en hulle ambag." In Smith, pp. 79–81.

John, Philip. "Resisting Totalisation: Afrikaans Literature and the Postcolonial Project." Paper read at CSSALL conference, University of Durban-Westville, September 1995.

Jolly, Rosemary. "Rehearsal of Liberation: Contemporary Postcolonial Discourse and the New South Africa." *PMLA,* 1995, pp. 17–29.

Krog, Antjie. *Otters in bronslaai.* Cape Town. Human & Rousseau. 1980.

———. *Lady Anne.* Bramley, S.A. Taurus. 1989.

Lenta, Margaret. "The Need for a Feminism: Black Township Writing." *Journal of Literary Studies,* 4:1 (March 1988), pp. 49–63.

McClintock, Anne. "The Angel of Progress: Pitfalls of the Term 'Post-colonialism'." In Williams, pp. 291–304.

Mishra, Vijay, and Bob Hodge. "What Is Post(-)colonialism?" In Williams, pp. 276–90.

Odendaal, Welma. "Betrokke, besmet, gehawend . . . Huismans leef om die storie te vertel." *Die Suid-Afrikaan,* 28 (August-September 1990), p. 45.

Parker, Kenneth. "In the 'New South Africa': W(h)ither Literature?" *Wasafiri,* 19 (Summer 1994), pp. 3–7.

Petersen, Kirsten Holst, and Anna Rutherford, eds. *A Double Colonization: Colonial and Postcolonial Women's Writing.* Mundelstrup/Oxford. Dangaroo. 1986.

Ponelis, Fritz. *The Development of Afrikaans.* Frankfurt a.M. Peter Lang. 1993.

Robinson, A. M. Lewin, ed. *The Cape Journals of Lady Anne Barnard 1797–1798.* Cape Town. Van Riebeeck Society. 1994.

Smith, Julian, Alwyn van Gensen, and Hein Willemse, eds. *Swart Afrikaanse Skrywers.* Bellville, S.A. UWK. 1985.

Swanepoel, Eduan. "Helende terapie." *De Kat,* April 1995, p. 102.

Thomas, Nicholas. *Colonialism's Cultures: Anthropologys Travel and Government.* Cambridge. Polity. 1994.

Trinh Minh-ha. *Womans Natives Other: Writing Postcoloniality and Feminism.* Bloomington. Indiana University Press. 1989.

Van Niekerk, Annemarie. *Vrouevertellers 1943–1993.* Cape Town. Tafelberg. 1994.

Viljoen, Lettie. *Klaaglied vir Koos.* Emmarentia, Transvaal. Taurus. 1984.

Willemse, Hein. "The Black Afrikaans Writer: A Continuing Dichotomy." *TriQuarterly,* 69 (Spring/Summer 1987), pp. 237–47.

Williams, Patrick, and Laura Chrisman. *Colonial Discourse and Post-Colonial Theory: A Reader.* New York/London. Harvester Wheatsheaf. 1993.

Derek Walcott (*Gil Jain*)

Worden, Nigel. *The Making of Modern South Africa: Conquests Segregation and Apartheid.* Oxford, Eng. Blackwell. 1994.

Caribbean

CARIBBEAN IN ENGLISH

Derek Walcott: 1992 Nobel Laureate in Literature

I have been suggesting to colleagues and friends since the mid-1980s that someday soon Derek Walcott would be receiving the Nobel Prize in Literature. My prediction has now come true, perhaps much sooner than many people would have thought. My motive here, however, is not to masquerade as a literary prophet. A much more important reflection may emerge from this consideration: what elements in Walcott's work led me, and later the members of the Swedish Academy, to an acknowledgment of Walcott's work as worthy of the Nobel Prize?

If there is any dominant principle for literary prize-giving that influences the Swedish Academy, it is: a strong regional voice that transcends its topical locality, through the depth and breadth of its poetic resonance and through its global human implications. The publication of Walcott's *Omeros* in 1990 absolutely certified this same long-standing quality of his work. *Omeros,* a rare modern verse epic, places Walcott's birthplace of St. Lucia at the center of his epic cosmos, builds its local islanders into epic heroes, magnifies their conflicts into epic battles, visits the exotic shores of Africa, North America, and Europe on Odyssean journeys, and gives voice (in a lyric mode that departs from traditional epic form) to the epic writer himself, Walcott as the lonely, exiled "Homer." In the manner of Joyce and Yeats, Walcott has merged a profound, rhapsodic reverie upon his remote birthplace—its people, its landscape, and its history—with the central, classical tradition of Western civilization. We can trace back this grand method through his entire oeuvre and locate it as early as his first published works: ". . .where / Canoes brace the sun's strength, as John, in that bleak air / So am I welcomed richer by these blue scapes, Greek there, / So I shall voyage no more from home; may I speak here" ("As John to Patmos," from *In a Green Night,* 1962).

From this, one of Walcott's earliest poems, the poet quickly discovered his lifelong course: the retracing of the Caribbean experience over the essential Judeo-Christian and ancient Greek and Roman mythologies. Such a project may not seem particularly revelational, except that Walcott's intercultural "meld" appears absolutely natural and flawless, with hardly a trace of artificiality or pretension. His sense of the "right image" is so finely tuned that his classical allusions chime as truly as if it were Aeschylus himself writing. The geological affinities between the two archipelagoes—the Antilles and the Greek islands—further add to an intrinsic consonance between Walcott's real and imagined worlds.

However, profound ironies quickly mount up within Walcott's intertextual matrix. Most critically, how does he juxtapose the Caribbean history of transmigration, slavery, and degradation with the Olympian majesty of Greek culture? The poet must eschew a pure-blooded, largely noble, mythic past (such as in Yeats's Celtic world) for a more complex, ironic mode reminiscent of Joyce, Eliot, and Auden. His multiple mythologies begin to cross one another like antipodal harmonies in a majestic fugue, not with a single strain but with multiple cadences, voices, and nuances, the full articulation of which is radically new and ultimately has become Walcott's central contribution to world literature. As early as his poem "Origins" (from *Selected Poems,* 1964) Walcott manifested an intense multicultural consciousness and displayed his central paradox of being a man of letters schooled in the major European tradi-

tions while living on islands populated largely by former slaves and where the indigenous population has been almost completely eliminated.

> I learnt your annals of ocean,
> Of Hector, bridler of horses,
> Achilles, Aeneas, Ulysses,
> But "Of that fine race of people which came off the
>   mainland
> To greet Christobal as he rounded Icacos,"
> Blank pages turn in the wind.

This treacherous irony of Walcott's classical Western education and poetic predilection, in view of his place of origin, has been a thematic and formal knot for him to unravel on a continuing basis, while it has also formed perhaps the richest fabric of meaning that stretches throughout his work. Critics have attacked him on this very subject,[1] and perhaps some of them would continue to protest even his receipt of the Nobel Prize. If Walcott were not so committed to the exploration of so many purely regional Caribbean themes, of racism and discrimination, of the lowest as well as the highest strata of society, and of the bounteous physical beauties of the islands, then his critics might secure more merit for their arguments. It has been said that he has done nothing for "building [the] image" of a new Caribbean literature and culture,[2] or that he has in some sense abandoned his duty to rage as an angry black man from an impoverished, formerly enslaved (and still perhaps economically controlled) colony, and instead that he has embraced the dominant culture of the European imperialists.[3] Nevertheless, his historical themes of the African diaspora, his colorful St. Lucian characters, and the epic largesse of *Omeros* appear to render most of these arguments moot.

Throughout his career Walcott's critics have often missed his passionate and unswerving dedication to his homeland. The vast majority of his lyric verse forms a long and detailed meditation on sea, sand, the mangroves and the fish of the islands. From "The sound of water gnawing at bright stone" ("Brise Marine," from *In a Green Night,* 1962), to "the coconut lances of the inlet" (*Another Life,* 1973), to "the splayed hands of grape-leaves" (*Omeros,* 1990), his imagination has been perennially saturated with figures of the islands' natural beauty. His increasingly crisp, precise natural imagery forms a major part of the essential core of his poetic diction. The language of the coral, of the dreamlike undersea life, of the multiple faces of the sea in seemingly infinite moods, of the brilliant tropical foliage of the rain forests and mountain valleys, is thoroughly interwoven with his cultural and historical concepts, his purely formal lyric and narrative aims, and his unceasing desire to secure portrait-perfect accuracy in his rendering of the visual world.[4] Walcott has for many years practiced as a painter, mostly creating watercolor landscapes of island life and habitats.[5] His preoccupation with the subtle nuances of the physical world has given his poetic diction perhaps its most enduring and vivid ingredient. So precise, intense, and prevailing has been his visual instinct that Walcott can claim without affectation in *Omeros* that it suffuses his other senses: "I smelt with my eyes, I could see with my nostrils" (6.44).

Unlike the Antillean natural paradise, the urban "places" in Walcott's Caribbean setting are not inspirational locations for the poet. Port of Spain, Trinidad, and Castries, St. Lucia, form Walcott's central "cityscapes." The latter is his birthplace (1930), and the former was his residence and workplace for many years when he formed and directed the Trinidad Theater Workshop (1959–77). Although Port of Spain is the most important city in the southern Caribbean island region, it holds little charm or mystery for visitors. Its urban sprawl and the "ghettoization" of its poorer inhabitants find sharp expression in Walcott's poem "Laventille" (from *The Castaway and Other Poems,* 1965), named for one of Port of Spain's slums, "where lank electric / lines and tension cables linked its raw brick / hovels like a complex feud." In "The Spoiler's Return" (*The Fortunate Traveller,* 1981) Walcott makes his disgust for the physical and political putrefaction of the city even more explicit: "all Frederick Street stinking like a closed drain / Hell is a city much like Port of Spain."

The poet reserves a softer, more nostalgic attitude for his hometown, Castries. Smaller than Port of Spain, and not as congested or polluted, Castries is certainly no shining metropolis; rather it is a quiet, overgrown village—discreetly poor yet nevertheless picturesque. Like most people contemplating the "overdevelopment" of their childhood abodes, however, Walcott regrets the "lowland poplars / now, levelled, bulldozed and met-alled for an airstrip" (*Another Life,* 1973).

Throughout his career Walcott has been equally as poignant in his observation of people as in his observation of the natural world. His sense of character, human psychology, and the idiosyncratic inflections of personal speech patterns is displayed most explicitly in his dramas, although closely drawn characters also appear in his two epic-length poems, *Another Life* and *Omeros,* and here and there in his longer lyric verse as well. The epic mode allows him space to develop more generalized human typologies which can blend easily into larger and universal themes. Monsieur Auguste Manoir, for example (in *Another Life*), becomes the emblem for the greedy, mean-spirited, decadent merchant: "His hands

still smelled of fish, of his beginnings, / hands that he'd ringed with gold, to hide their smell, / sometimes he'd hold them out, / puckered with lotions, powdered, to his wife, / a peasant's hands, a butcher's / their acrid odour of saltfish and lard." The other main characters in the autobiographical *Another Life,* Gregorias and Anna, are based on Walcott's real-life relationships with a young painter friend and with his first important lover; their thoughts and actions are drawn with detailed, lyric complexity epitomizing youthful friendship and romantic love.

"Ma Kilman," the proprietor of the village rum shop in *Omeros,* was developed as a character from a St. Lucian *conte* or narrative Creole song recorded in the earlier poem "Sainte Lucie" (from *Sea Grapes,* 1976). She is a superstitious, uneducated, but kind-hearted matron who, through her witchlike manipulations of mysterious, potent herbs and weeds, carries on a dialogue with the spirit world. She indulges her animistic beliefs through pilgrimages into the rain forest to seek out natural remedies, and she becomes the sad repository of the unfulfilled, truncated native religions of the Afro-Caribbean sundered from ancient African traditions—from Erzulie, Shango, and Ogun, who were "subdued in the rivers of her blood."

The wild, wire-haired, and generously featured
apotheosis of the caverned prophetess
began. Ma Kilman unpinned the black, red-berried

straw-hat with its false beads, lifted the press
of the henna wig, made of horsehair, from the mark
on her forehead. Carefully, she set both aside

on the coiled green follicles of moss in the dark
wood. Her hair sprung free as the moss. Ants
  scurried
through the wiry curls, barring, then passing each
  other

the same message with scribbling fingers and
  forehead
touching forehead. Ma Kilman bent hers forward,
and as her lips moved with the ants, her mossed
  skull heard

the ants talking the language of her great-
  grandmother,
the gossip of a distant market, and she understood,
the way we follow our thoughts without any
  language,

why the ants sent her this message to come to the
  wood
where the wound of the flower, its gangrene, its rage
festering for centuries, reeked with corrupted
  blood. . . .

(*Omeros,* 6.48)

Ma Kilman, in her passionate enactment of white magic, the practice of Obeah, attempts to erase not only the flesh wound of her fellow villager Philoctetes but also the terrible wound of a whole people's centuries-long forced separation from their ancestral, spiritual roots.

The grand, larger-than-life persona of Ma Kilman is matched in mythic proportion by many of the characters from Walcott's early dramas. Particularly Makak, the wild, divinely inspired charcoal-burner in *Dream on Monkey Mountain* (1967), and his antagonist, Corporal Lestrade, resonate with hemispheral magnitude as twin representatives of black consciousness in the New World: the inchoate longing for freedom, self-empowerment, and economic independence on the one hand, and obsequious, even righteous acceptance of and subjugation to the codes and manners of imperial Eurocentric society on the other. *Dream on Monkey Mountain,* a paean to emerging black and postcolonial identity that burst forth during the 1960s, forms the culmination of Walcott's early mythic/musical dramas, including *Henri Christophe* (1950), *The Sea at Dauphine* (1954), *Ione* (1957), *Drums and Colours* (1958), *Ti-Fean and His Brothers* (1958), and *Malcochon* (1959). All these early dramas are mythopoeic efforts to express the essence of select cultural representatives, individuals and communities, from the Caribbean, and primarily from St. Lucia. Walcott wrote most of these in verse or song-lyric form; if their parts are in prose dialogue form, as is most of *Dream on Monkey Mountain,* Walcott tells us their "source is metaphor, and it is best treated as a physical poem with all the subconcious and deliberate borrowings of poetry."[6]

In *O Babylon!* (1976) Walcott's exploration of Rastafarian culture in Jamaica, many of the dialogue lines appear as reggae lyrics, but this function of the musical drama remains largely a realistic attempt to capture the essence of the song/speech manner of Rastafarian dialogue and of the lilting, songlike quality of Jamaican speech in general. Rufus Johnson, or "Brother Aaron," the Rastafarian "hero" of *O Babylon!,* symbolizes the strong, proud defiance of the Rastafarian cult, and the partially romanticized stereotyping common to the musical form does not diminish the memorable peculiarities of his "outcast philosopher" personality. *O Babylon!* forms the transition point between Walcott's early poetic and musical drama and his more recent realistic plays. Where Walcott's epic/mythic characters radiate with necessarily blurred edges, projecting wide, powerful circles of symbolic meaning, his more recent dramatis personae etch highly concrete portraits of a variety of island characters and subcultures.

Nearly all the characters in Walcott's plays since *Remembrance* (1977) have been vivid portraits drawn from his experience and knowledge of Trinidad and the drastic cultural changes that have taken place there since the end of World War II. He illustrates the recurrent themes of the painful, awkward emergence from colonialism with a brilliant mastery of multiple texts, or "heteroglottic speech genres," if one applies the conceptualizations of the Russian literary theorist Mikhail Bahktin.[7] Drawing also upon the technique of the *picong,* the satiric "song-duels" common to the Calypso fests, Walcott has created a series of intertextual dialogues and scenes that both capture the peculiar habits and personalities of his characters and establish many of the essential dramatic conflicts between them. Especially prevalent among these texts are a series of "imperial culture" exempla: the poet Shelley, intoned by the black former schoolteacher Albert Perez Jordan in *Remembrance;* Coleridge and Robert Louis Stevenson, parodied by the white/black duo Harry and Jackson in *Pantomime* (1978); Baudelaire, Watteau, and French classical culture, espoused by the French creole painter Victor de la Fontaine, in *The Last Carnival* (1982); Shakespeare's *Antony and Cleopatra,* enacted by the Trinidadian theater troupe in *A Branch of the Blue Nile* (1985). All these writers and texts function both as symbols of the colonial, imperial culture in general and as individual obsessions or states of mind from which many of Walcott's characters are unable to extract themselves. As classical figures and texts, they play the same role in the dramas as the Judeo-Christian and Greco-Roman myths play in Walcott's poetry: in toto they represent European cultural transplantation upon the Caribbean—an immense and complex backdrop, alongside the mute, pristine natural beauty of the islands and the dismal history of racial oppression, genocide, and slavery—against which Walcott attempts to sketch a necessarily troubled, ironic identity.

Respectively counter to each of these imperial texts are the variously parodic island "texts" which document the peculiar hybridizations, degradations, and adaptations that have flourished among the islands—often in a comic mode bolstered by the omnipresent, satiric, and mimicking styles of the Trinidadian carnival and its Calypso lyrics. Jordan attempts a number of derivative, self-admittedly poor poems and stories of his own in *Remembrance;* Harry and Jackson, in *Pantomime,* reverse their traditional roles to become a black Crusoe and white Friday, only to show the pathetically difficult task of role-changing for all races and cultures in a postcolonial world; in silly yet tragic fashion, Victor's family and friends prove unable to reenact faithfully his schizophrenic obsession with Watteau in *The Last Carnival* and slide helplessly, decadently into base slapstick and debauchery; the actors' hilarious Trinidadian dialectal versions of Shakespeare in *A Branch of the Blue Nile,* and their own parodic "playback" of their lives together on and off the stage, form a multiplicity of interwoven texts, both faithfully rehearsed ones and satirically improvised and distorted ones. Walcott's nearly flawless ear for personal, idiosyncratic speech patterns, his mastery of the many different "speech genres," the dialects, the established and transplanted texts of the Caribbean, give his plays their dense, formal structure and their brilliant, scintillating surfaces, always witty and frequently hilarious. His profound understanding of the deeper implications of these multiple, conflicting, and interacting voices provides a rich portrait of the cultural and historical identity and transformation of the English-speaking Caribbean.

From the outset of his poetic career, through his recent completion of *Omeros,* Walcott has sketched and resketched discrete fragments, long passages, and cosmic eons of history unfolded in the Caribbean. Beginning at the zero point, the "blank pages turn[ing] in the wind," and the infinite void of blue azure and Caribbean sea imaged in many of his poems, Walcott has set out to reconfigure and to reprioritize Caribbean history. From his postcolonial vantage point, the poet has been freed to "reverse the sights" on European history, on the prior heralded exploits of imperialist expansion, the "conquest" of indigenous peoples, slave-trading, and colonial cultivation. In most of the "official" European and American histories of colonial grandeur, the slaves have been mere footnotes to essentially white texts. The true history of Caribbean blacks, as of the Caribbean Indians before them, remains largely unwritten. This vast and sad ignorance permeates even the present generation, as Walcott's persona, Shabine, reflects in "The Schooner *Flight*" (from *The Star-Apple Kingdom,* 1979): "Who knows / who his grandfather is, much less his name?" His history is only one that his "masters please." "Official" histories are most frequently promulgated on some notion of "progress," and "progress" is quite hard to discern within the backwash of present-day colonial vacuums, as Shabine goes on to lament in "The Schooner *Flight*": "Progress leaving all we small islands behind. /. . . Progress is history's dirty joke."

Walcott has not failed to note the shortcomings of recent political history within the Caribbean community, for example its aborted attempt to form a Caribbean federation during its new, independent era; he has given a vivid account of his view in "The Star-Apple Kingdom."

One morning the Caribbean was cut up
by seven prime ministers who bought the sea in
  bolts—

one thousand miles of aquamarine with lace
  trimmings,
one million yards of lime-coloured silk,
one mile of violet, leagues of cerulean satin—
who sold it at a markup to the conglomerates,
the same conglomerates who had rented the water
  spouts
for ninety-nine years in exchange for fifty ships,
who retailed it in turn to the ministers
with only one bank account, who then resold it
in ads for the Caribbean Economic Community,
till everyone owned a little piece of the sea,
from which some made saris, some made bandannas;
the rest was offered on trays to white cruise ships
taller than the post office; then the dogfights
began in the cabinets as to who had first sold
the archipelago for this chain store of islands.

Walcott's epic perspective on history provides him with the necessary neutrality to perceive that glory does not necessarily follow from revolution, that all change is a mixed blessing. In his more recent poetry, in many poems from *The Fortunate Traveller* (1981), *The Arkansas Testament* (1987), and *Omeros* (1990), Walcott has turned his attention often to the corruption and demise of the empire itself, and he links the waning of power of England and the United States to the final histories of Rome, Tyre, and Alexandria. From a cosmic or epic perspective, all civilizations follow many of the same patterns of rise, decline, and fall; the struggles of different peoples frequently resemble one another within the vast and ancient currents of human life around the world: "Albion too was once / A colony like ours" ("Ruins of a Great House," from *In a Green Night,* 1962).

Nevertheless, the "mainstream" history of the Caribbean is bankrupt and passé for its contemporary inhabitants, and as its revision takes its course, many great, white idols must in turn be humbled: "I thought next / Of men like Hawkins, Walter Raleigh, Drake, / Ancestral murderers and poets, more perplexed / In memory now by every ulcerous crime" (ibid.).

Still, after such momentous revisions have been made, what remains? Certainly not the stuff of patriotic slogans, national anthems, and glorious "official" histories. The Caribbean, as Walcott is so painfully and acutely aware, will forever remain quixotic among the world's annals. As a region, it may form the paradigm for postcolonial "antihistory," for the overturning of long-cherished myths and the brutal new chronicling of oppression, racism, and genocide. Its cultural history, which Walcott traces so accurately in the complex designs of his heteroglottic "multitexts," provides one of the world's richest models for true multiculturalism—a dense crossroads of human differences, sometimes tragic and sometimes hilarious in their juxtapositions and interrelationships.

If we are entering an era in which multiculturalism is our central ideology, Derek Walcott must be acclaimed as one of our greatest cultural leaders. He repeatedly demonstrates, in dozens of his plays and volumes of verse, the true meaning of "many cultures coexisting in dialogue" within the work of a single writer. His multiple voices with Joycean brilliance range not only among the numerous dialects and speech genres of the English- and French-patois-speaking Caribbean, but also move to the widest limits of our entire treasure house of Judeo-Christian, Greco-Roman, and European cultures. We may detect in Walcott's microcosmic Caribbean a paradigm for the most tolerant, mutually enriching coexistence of all the world's voices. Most wonderful of all, Walcott thoroughly exemplifies a "both/and" global political and cultural philosophy rather than an "either/or" divisive one. The Swedish Academy has certainly perceived this, and my congratulations go to its members for their choice, as well as to this profoundly accomplished, inspirational author whom they have lauded.

Stephen Breslow, Spring 1993

¹ Lloyd King, "Derek Walcott: The Literary Humanist in the Caribbean," *Caribbean Quarterly,* 16:4 (December 1970).

² Ralph Campbell, "The Birth of Professional Theatre in Trinidad," *Sunday Guardian,* 22 July 1973, p. 4.

³ Anonymous, "How Far Are Derek Walcott and Edward Brathwaite Similar?," *Busara,* 6:1 (1974).

⁴ See Robert Benson, "The Painter as Poet: Derek Walcott's *Midsummer,*" *Literary Review,* 29:3 (Spring 1986), pp. 259–68.

⁵ See David Montenegro, "An Interview with Derek Walcott," *Partisan Review,* 57:2 (1990), pp. 202–14; and Clara Rosa de Lima, "Walcott: Painting and the Shadow of Van Gogh," in *The Art of Derek Walcott,* Stewart Brown, ed., Chester Springs, Pa., Dufour, 1991, pp. 171–90.

⁶ Derek Walcott, "A Note on Production," in *A Dream on Monkey Mountain and Other Plays,* New York, Farrar Straus Giroux, 1970. This sentiment and practice in Walcott's early drama conforms well to the concept of "word-song" in black world theater, as articulated by Paul Carter Harrison in his introduction to *Totem Voices: Plays from the Black World Repertory,* New York, Grove, 1989, pp. xi–lxiii.

⁷ See Stephen Breslow, "Trinidadian Heteroglossia: A Bakhtinian View of Derek Walcott's Play *A Branch of the Blue Nile,*" WLT 63:1 (Winter 1989), pp. 36–39.

The Myth of the Fall and the Dawning of Consciousness in George Lamming's *In the Castle of My Skin*

In 1958 George Lamming wrote that the modern black writer's endeavor is like that of "every other writer whose work is a form of self enquiry, a clarification of his relations with other men, and a report on his own highly subjective conception of the possible meaning of man's life." A writer's self-inquiry constitutes his first world—"the world of the private and hidden self, the world hidden within the castle of each man's skin." And if he is honest, he will bear witness to the impact that a second world, the social, has made on his consciousness. Finally, because a man cannot escape "the essential need to find meaning for his destiny," the writer must confront his third world, his "definition of himself as man in the world of men." When he looks fully into these three worlds of his self, he finds a "very concrete example of . . . the human condition . . . a condition which is essentially . . . originally tragic." The contemporary human condition, writes Lamming, involves a "universal sense of separation and abandonment, frustration and loss, and above all, of man's direct inner experience of something missing."¹

All over the world and in different periods, that sense of absence has given rise to a myth of a past time of perfection from which man has fallen, a myth of a golden age or an Eden. In coming to terms with that archetypal sense of absence through the medium of the autobiographical fiction *In the Castle of My Skin* (1953), George Lamming revivifies the archetype of the Fall, now in Barbadian garb, as it touches each of his worlds. Not only is much of his personal life projected into the fictional character G, but the novel articulates the history of an entire village, as the protagonist individually and the villagers collectively come into historical consciousness and in so doing lose their innocence. "Archetypes come to life only when one patiently tries to discover why and in what fashion they are meaningful to a living individual," wrote Carl Jung.² A fascinating example is the particular manner in which the myth of the Fall as a metaphor for maturation infuses Lamming's narrative, dignifying with eternal human significance the life of a poor, black child struggling to adulthood in Barbados.

1. Calling the biblical Fall "one of the most essential symbolic teachings of the Christian religion," Jung argued that the myth expresses the psychic fact that man experiences "the dawn of consciousness as a curse." Adam—the primitive man, responding to instinct, in-

nocent without self-consciousness of his impulses and actions—rested secure in his trust of nature. That things were the way they were was not problematic. But in turning away from instinct and opposing himself to it, modern man, recognizing his nakedness, creates consciousness and with it the inevitability of choice, doubt, fear. Eating the apple from the tree of knowledge marks the sacrifice of the natural man, of the unconscious, of the capacity to live in the world through simple response without judgments of good and evil. And modern man, fallen, in an "orphaned and isolated state where [he is] abandoned by nature and driven to consciousness," aware of the insecurity implied by freedom to choose, said Jung, wishes he could avoid the problems thus engendered and may wonder whether the childlike, preconscious state were not preferable. He experiences loss and absence. Jung further argued that each individual reenacts the psychic history of the race in his emergence from preconsciousness and movement into the dualistic stage, characteristic of "youth" from puberty to mid-life, in which he experiences himself both as "I," the innermost psychic self, and as "also I," the self adjusting to making its way in the physical and social world.[3]

In the early chapters of *In the Castle of My Skin* Lamming frankly acknowledges his use of Old Testament metaphor, but only to mock its simplistic nature. Humorously he compares the flood which opens the novel to the biblical Flood. Only once does he overtly contemplate the Garden of Eden story, which he merges with Lucifer's rebellion against God. In chapter three the schoolboys, having been denied knowledge of Barbadian history by the colonialist school system, speculate as to how Queen Victoria could have freed them from slavery. They arrive at a composite explanation which, though naïve, articulates the assumptions underlying British rationalizations for colonialist rule. Though in origin different, the Garden of Eden or heaven and the empire are identified with one another. Because both are products of God's will and under His dominion, to rebel against either is to become a moral outlaw, a Lucifer, a rebel against God. Rebellion, while offering the exhilaration of new possibility, produces loneliness so terrible that the rebels repent, preferring bondage to freedom. And bondage to the empire will facilitate their return to the true garden in heaven. Thus in his only overt consideration of the myth of the Fall, Lamming blasts the colonialists' exploitation of Christian theology in the interests of perpetuating economic and psychological enslavement. Lamming's analogy affirms that colonial Barbados was no paradise, except perhaps for the British.

Yet on a subtler level the myth does pervade the novel, and metaphorically Barbados is indeed a garden. A matured G, looking back, describes the house of the landlord Creighton as "a castle around which the land like a shabby back garden stretched."[4] While the shabbiness under the colonial regime is never in doubt, neither—it turns out—is its gardenlike quality. In considering how the regime impinges on his second world, Lamming never retreats from resistance; still, when that rule is replaced by the native bourgeoisie, bringing about the sale of the land and destruction of a way of life, then the loss of that simple, harmonious community—poignantly symbolized by Pa's removal to the almshouse—is felt severely enough that village life seems in retrospect like an innocent paradise. The verdure of the land is known only after the trees are downed, and the land's value becomes evident only when it is sold. G's mother voices this truth in an aphorism: "You never miss the water till the well run dry; / You never miss a mother till she close her eye" (294). Just as the child's lack of consciousness of being a person separate from the mother gives way before the evidence that he is himself not her, so man—the villagers—no longer in a monistic relationship with the source of sustenance, the natural world, becomes forcefully conscious of his separateness with profound regret.

2. While the villagers experience the social and political changes as disastrous, the novel's judgment of these changes is more complex. For although throughout most of the novel G's experience of the world is like that of the villagers, their fall is single. His is double. The sociopolitical narrative of social change in a Barbadian village deals with the single fall, which is, it appears, a fall only in part.[5] Even desirable change involves loss: "Whether you were glad or sorry to be rid of [things,] you couldn't bear the thought of seeing them for the last time" (238). The narrator's fall, on the other hand, has a second part and a different quality, for he also becomes alienated from the village community. In gaining access to the narrator's double fall, we enter the writer's first world, the world of the innermost self, and perhaps not surprisingly find ourselves involved with issues of autobiography as a genre.

Of course Lamming, like G, was once a boy growing up in Barbados. But *In the Castle of My Skin* resembles autobiography more than superficially. First, its mode is self-reflective and so has a natural tendency toward irony. In autobiography the narrator is both the observer and the observed, and as such the genre can only be written after the writer has separated himself enough from living experience to objectify it. If the writer, now matured, tries to re-create experiences as he lived them (this Lamming does), his double vision characteristically produces irony. In Lamming's novel the double vision accounts for the humor in the early part of the novel, for he recounts events as the child and the villagers experienced them, but with the hindsight of the matured observer. Naturally by the end, as the ages and perspectives of the observer and the observed converge, the humor disappears, and the ironic distance diminishes.

The novel shares with autobiography a second feature: the use of Edenic imagery to depict childhood. In "The Myth of the Fall: A Description of Autobiography" Martha Lifson explores the curious fact that many autobiographies—those of Augustine, Rousseau, Wordsworth and Thoreau, among others—invoke garden-of-paradise imagery in describing childhood: "The light, the peace, the friendly insect, the stillness, and particularly the timelessness, are all images that recur frequently in autobiographical scenes of childhood." Later she adds to this list a "sense of order" and "abundance of nature."[6]

Atlhough "light" is not a prominent metaphor in his novel, Lamming sometimes uses light-dark imagery in crucial ways, as will be seen. "Peace" and "stillness," while indeed appropriate to the chapters at the beach, would not seem to describe the raucous, often quarreling interchanges of village life unless we understand them as commotion which occurs within the context of the steady rhythms of that life, commotion which signals no disruption. The theme of Edenic harmony emerges strikingly in depictions of the land, the sky, the sea, the sand of the beach with its wondrous crabs appearing and disappearing. The crabs, vibrating with luminous significance, are the Barbadian equivalent of Lifson's "friendly insects," emblematic of the eternal wonder of the universe, with which the child feels at one. It emerges in the fisherman, masterful and at ease in his element, who personifies man's harmony with the natural world and capacity for securing abundance from its unspoiled state. Though the village is poor and ragged, no one appears to be in real want. The rootedness of the village order and the unconscious assumption that the village will remain unspoiled are Edenic qualities too. G's friend Trumper alone voices what others only vaguely intuit.

> When you up here [at the landlord's house] . . . you see how it is nothin' could change in the village. Everything's sort of in order. Big life one side an' small life a next side, an' you get a kin' o' feelin' of you in your small corner an' I in mine. Everything's kind of correct. (193)

Still, as Lifson noted, it is the child's sense of timelessness which most emphatically evokes paradise.

In this novel chronological time belongs to the adult observer reflecting on how the village and he have changed. For the villager and the child, time does not exist. G is aware of time as sequence but not as progression. The villagers similarly cannot imagine the radical changes set in motion by Mr. Slime's formation of the Penny Bank and the Friendly Society. Thus the consequences, unexpected, shock them not just because of specific effects, but because they had not conceived that real change was possible. "This land ain't the sort of land that can be for buy or sell. . . . 'Twas always an' 'twill always be land for we people to live on," protests a bewildered woman (264).

Thus a maturer Lamming joins in choosing Edenic imagery to transcribe his childhood. For G and the villagers, conflicts occur within the unexpected, natural rhythms of life and create neither alienation nor self-division. The paradise Lamming evokes is one of naïve inner harmony, based on the assumption that the world is what it is and everyone has a secure place in it, not on the judgment of it as good in itself. So also affirms the book of Genesis: knowledge of good and evil arises only after the apple is eaten.

3. Although Lamming's evocation of Eden is powerful, equally if not more forceful are the images of disappearance and destruction, of the Fall, which resonate throughout the novel. Sudden, mysterious, unexpected disappearances of objects, emblems of the more catastrophic loss of psychic grounding, punctuate the text. The humorous story of the drunk man's penny and cent—one rolled into the gutter in full view under a full moon, the other was carefully secured under a stone, and both vanished—echoes through the narrator's later, nearly frantic search for the special pebble which, having seized the narrator's attention, vanishes contrary to all logical causality through some strange, indecipherable intervention. In the midst of security, in the Garden of Eden, without source or explanation, without preparation, cataclysmically enters the serpent.

The novel tells of two falls: the simple sale of Eden itself (the village land) through the agency of the serpent Mr. Slime, and the more complex disinheritance of G, who loses his identity. Repeatedly, Lamming projects the predicament precipitating the fall as closed. Only two alternatives (they appear either as opposites or as identical—it makes no difference) are postulated, and the protagonist must choose between them. Although in the predifferentiated state G embraced both alternatives without conflict, yet with the coming of an unforeseen, intervening force he is compelled to choose between illusory alternatives. The refusal to choose places him in limbo; choosing leads him into exile or destroys him. Always he loses the harmony of his pre-lapsarian state.

The tales told by the boys at the beach rehearse G's later experience of this psychological predicament. Boy Blue tells the story of Bots, Bambi and Bambina, of a village man living contentedly with two common-law wives. Under external pressure he arbitrarily marries one of them. All continues the same until, without warning, the formerly warm and sociable man becomes silently morose, takes to drink and dies. The boys explain his enigmatic behavior thus: "Something go off pop in yuh head an' you ain't the same man you think you was" (131). The story is preceded by Trumper's tale of Jon, who, similarly coerced into choosing between two women, Sue and Jen, attempts to watch his wedding from a tree, waiting to discover what will happen as, simultaneously in facing churches, his two brides-to-be vainly await his arrival at the altar. Images of a duality which is no duality repeat elsewhere—two moods of the ocean on either side of the lighthouse, the oppositions of life and death, Creighton and Slime, god and dog in Pa's dream. Always frustration and loss follow choice.[7]

Such predicaments are emblematic of the narrator's situation near the end of the novel, when he finds himself separated from the village by his education and from his intellectual peers by his ties to village life.

> I remained in the village living, it seemed, on the circumference of two worlds. It was as though my roots had been snapped from the centre of what I knew best, while I remained impotent to wrest what my fortunes had forced me into. (244)

Repeatedly as situations necessitate choice between false, arbitrary or meaningless alternatives, the individual remembers that it had formerly been possible to have wholeness, to appropriate all alternatives and so avoid loss. Trumper explains Jon's perspective: able imaginatively to marry both women as well as observe from the tree, he accepts the psychic reality as primary and fails even to consider as problematic the failure of the three events to proceed simultaneously in actuality. Instead he waits patiently for the groom, himself or another, to arrive for the weddings. Trumper comments, "P'raps it ain't [logical] . . . but that don't make it not so." When Boy Blue objects that living a contradiction makes wholeness impossible, Trumper responds, "I don't know. . . . P'raps you can if you feel you can" (142). In dream, in memory, in imagination, the mind contemplates and realizes multiple, incompatible alternatives. Since all perceptions ultimately must be subjective, the subjective projection can become more actual than the objective manipulation of physical matter.

Eden is not just a folk village, a childhood mentality, but also, as in Jung, a psychic position.

Lamming contrasts archetypally the atemporal, paradisiacal Barbadian life and Slime's modern, analytical approach to it. In introducing the novel, Richard Wright, speaking of the clash of the folk and the modern worlds, focuses on its sociopolitical dimensions, highlighting the Third World cultures versus modern industrialism. Wright further argues that the clash occurs in the mind of every man who grows up in the one culture to find himself an adult in the other.[8] For the atemporal, dream-fantasy mode which accounts for the label "poetic" so frequently bestowed on the novel arises from the child's preconscious mode of mental activity, and the temporal perspective of the matured observer is generated from the analytic, linear mode of mental life.

Lamming has embodied the opposed modes, the "atemporal folk" and the "linear modern," within the novel's narrative strategy. The adult observer perceives the causality of events, analytically and linearly, revealing the dynamics of social change. But the villagers' and child's perspective is atemporal.[9] Several narrative strategies create the impression of timelessness. First, the time lapses between chapters vary radically and indefinitely. Rarely does the reader know how old G has become.[10] Second, the narrative voice ranges from primarily first person, to primarily third person, to—in the chapters which are dialogues between Ma and Pa—primarily dramatic. The voices narrate a whole unified by harmony rather than by logic. Third, images felt to be similar to one another in essence, though different in form, emerge at unforeseen points to create a narrative of mood subliminally felt to dominate the linear narrative of events.[11] As in a dream where the insights of the psyche are disguised in symbols and meaning emerges from decoding the emotional reverberations (not from simply remembering the narrative of the dream), so the emotional content of the novel is structured by a process of freely associating images and symbols which resonate against one another, allowing the correspondences to surface.

When he juxtaposes atemporal and analytical narrative modes, Lamming gives concrete form to Jung's concept of the self in youth experiencing its own duality, itself as "I" and "also I." Pa's enigmatic dream in chapter ten exemplifies this. The dream, voice of the unconscious function of the psyche and a balancing corrective to conscious thought, is here presented as the voice of the slave ancestors. It would seem to be a dream emerging from a kind of racial collective unconscious within the individual psyche. That voice describes the origins of Barbados through slavery as a terrible mistake, as the formation of an illusory duality between oppressed and oppressors which never should have been, one begun symbolically here by the sailor Christopher Columbus.

> The only certainty these islands inherit was that sailor's mistake, and it's gone on and on from father to son 'mongst the rich and the poor: in Slime and Creighton, landlord and politician, those who play at ruling and those at being ruled, and those who are neither one nor the other. . . . The fate of these islands I do not know, but man must live like a god or a dog, or be a stone that is neither dead nor alive, a pool no wind will ever wrinkle. For there's always two worlds to one man if you're a man, two darknesses to one light, one light, one light. . . . (234)

The very concept of duality, of alternatives at once opposite and the same, is illusory. The necessity of choosing between Jen and Sue, folk and modern, unconscious and conscious, is an illusion. Here especially images of light, typical of Eden, become relevant. In Pa's dream, darkness represents the fallen state of the present; and light at the end of the dream—Pa's vision for the future—seems to signify a yearning for a final reintegration and return to what long ago, before the fall, had been whole. The hope of reintegration is what prevents Lamming's novel from representing life as in essence tragic, his later comments notwithstanding.

4. Even though Eden collapses and G experiences consciousness as a kind of catastrophe, the novel's ending transcends the tragic view of human experience. The Old Testament is completed by the New Testament; the fall from grace ends with Christ's resurrection and the promise of grace and eternal life for the sinner. A higher, integrating consciousness follows Jung's dualistic state of "youth." The quest myth of world literature describes the same progression. The questing hero, born under unusual circumstances, grows up in a protected environment; as a young adult he leaves home to seek a boon (an object; knowledge). After encountering perils, he finds it and returns home. The variations are legion, but the essential tale remains the same.[12] G, hero of "virgin" birth—"My father who had only fathered the idea of me had left me the sole liability of my mother who really fathered me" (3)—and product of Eden, leaves the island with archetypal optimism. *In the Castle of My Skin* ends with a beginning—not an ending—as the hero, bound first for Trinidad, prepares to cross the magic threshold of the sea.

Lamming published the novel when he was twenty-six years old and very likely experiencing the "I"/ "also I" dualism typical of that age. His comments on the tragic nature of life, appearing five years later

(1958), perhaps represent the feelings of the quester who, in the midst of seemingly endless trials, begins to doubt the existence of the boon. Lamming's subsequent novels, each an adventure in the quest, consider the struggle to integrate the warring dualism and so create a broader, more encompassing Eden. The sociopolitical struggle to shape a Caribbean culture which will transcend the class conflict and racial animosity bequeathed by the colonial experience is a metaphor for the quester's search for the boon. In his major work of nonfiction, *The Pleasures of Exile* (1960), which elucidates the central issues of his novels, Lamming uses Shakespeare's metaphor to argue that the problems for Caliban the natural man arose when Prospero the colonialist gave him language, and so consciousness. Each of Lamming's novels questions how, without accepting Prospero's exploitation, Caliban can use the "gift" of consciousness to achieve a new Eden.

In *The Emigrants* (1954) a band of West Indians seeking a "return" to the nurturing motherland, England, find instead the disillusionment of reality. In the other novels successive protagonists attempt to transform San Cristobal, Lamming's fictional, quintessentially Caribbean island, into Eden. *Of Age and Innocence* (1958) explores the failure of the conquering savior, Shepherd, to join the races—black, Indian, Chinese and, to an extent, white—in establishing political freedom and justice. Fola of *Season of Adventure* (1963), who combines in her person black and white (she claims a "double fatherhood"), native and middle class, seeks integrity by rejecting her "also I" heritage and retreating into the native past. In *Water with Berries* (1971) Teeton must shed his attachment to the patronizing mother Dowager before he can hope to return. *Natives of My Person* (1972) addresses the obstacles to realizing Eden in an early period in San Cristobal's history.

Thus at the end of *In the Castle of My Skin* the truly autobiographical hero G seeks now in an immense universe, one which encompasses all human possibility and not just that in his tiny Eden, a new perfection of light, peace, order, eternity; he seeks harmony within himself and with the universe. Until he achieves that apotheosis, he travels with the memory of Eden and the current reality of strife—with his dualism—and with no certain knowledge of whether his alienation will be final, a tragedy, or just one stage in the journey back to wholeness. Although this quest journey represents psychological passage, for the Third World writer of that single generation caught in the interstices of two cultures, raised in the folk culture but adult in the modern world, expulsion from paradise has an additional, painful dimension.

In confronting his three worlds honestly, Lamming achieves a multiple triumph. For his second world, his sociopolitical life and time, he voices the dilemma and loss felt by that generation and expresses their double perception, as observers and participants, of the anguish and the possibility inherent in their predicament. For his first world, that of the innermost self, he articulates the Edenic joys and modes of perception of the child and villager living out of the unconscious impulses of the psyche. And finally, when he confronts those first two worlds in the fullness of his sensitivity, he discovers himself wrestling with his third world, his "destiny as a man among men"; he embodies and revivifies through Barbadian experience the knowledge of every questing hero who ever trod the Earth. And one hopes that, as with the hero at the end of the journey and with Pa at the point of death, the vision of grace, the reconciliation of the mistake of duality, in the end will also be Lamming's.

Carolyn T. Brown, Winter 1983

[1] George Lamming, "The Negro Writer and His World," *Caribbean Quarterly,* 5:5 (Feburary 1958), pp. 109–15.

[2] Carl G. Jung, "Approaching the Unconscious," in *Man and His Symbols,* Garden City, N.Y., Doubleday, 1964, p. 96.

[3] Carl G. Jung, "The Stages of Life," in *The Portable Jung,* Joseph Campbell, ed., New York, Penguin-Viking, 1971, pp. 5–10.

[4] George Lamming, *In the Castle of My Skin,* New York, Collier-MacMillan, 1970, p. 23. Future citations will provide the page number following the quotation.

[5] Ngũgĩ wa Thiong'o fully discusses this aspect of the novel in "George Lamming's *In the Castle of My Skin,*" in *Critics on Caribbean Literature,* Edward Baugh, ed., New York, St. Martin's, 1978. Several other critics include political issues in their broader discussions. See especially Ian Munro, "The Theme of Exile in George Lamming's *In the Castle of My Skin,*" *World Literature Written in English,* 20 (November 1971), pp. 51–60; and Kenneth Ramchand, *An Introduction to the Study of West Indian Literature,* Kingston (Jamaica), Nelson Caribbean, 1976.

[6] Martha Ronk Lifson, "The Myth of the Fall: A Description of Autobiography," *Genre,* 12 (Spring 1979), pp. 48–49.

[7] Michael Gilkes discusses this problem of choice in terms of the individual's alienation from the group in his book *The West Indian Novel,* Boston, Twayne, 1981, pp. 123–31.

[8] Richard Wright, "Introduction" to *In the Castle of My Skin,* pp. v-vi.

[9] Critics have noted the schism in narrative mode with varying degrees of annoyance and comprehension. Ambroise Kom objects to Lamming's "difficulty in choosing between social analysis and character development" and to G's functioning as both hero and narrator; see "*In the Castle of My Skin:* George Lamming and the Colonial Caribbean," *World Literature Written in English,* 18:2 (November 1979), p. 417. Ian Munro is more sympathetic to the division but treats the two levels as if they were unrelated.

[10] Gerald Moore makes this point in *The Chosen Tongue: English Writing in the Tropical World,* New York, Harper & Row, 1970, p. 70.

[11] Moore also addresses the issues of voices and of imagery as a structuring device but without examining how these strategies relate to the narrative's polarities (pp. 12–14).

[12] The universality of the quest theme is documented in Joseph Campbell, *The Hero with a Thousand Faces,* Princeton, N.J., Princeton University Press, 1968.

V. S. Naipaul: A Wager on the Triumph of Darkness

V. S. Naipaul has traveled far since his Trinidad beginnings. He was born there in 1932, a third-generation West Indian of Hindu ancestry. His father, a reporter with literary ambitions, encouraged his son to study and write. Even as a very young man Naipaul was determined to get away from the narrow, neocolonial world of his birth. At eighteen he left for England, took an Oxford degree, worked for the BBC, began to write. With his early stories of West Indian life he received immediate recognition from British critics as the most talented of contemporary Caribbean writers. He was covered with prestigious English literary prizes, four of them in a little more than ten years. Lately he has begun to pick them up in the United States as well, winning in 1980 the Bennett Award, given to a "writer of literary achievement" who is considered to "have received insufficient attention"—which, to tell the truth, is not really Naipaul's case. In the opinion of some of his disgruntled West Indian colleagues he became a prize exhibit of the London intellectual establishment, living proof of the generous recognition of colonial talents in the capital. He has often been accused, in judgments motivated, it would seem, more by envy than by justice, of "looking down his long Oxonian nose" at the trivialities, the pretensions and the provincialism of the West Indies. One Trinidadian official indeed informed me that "Naipaul is certainly not our favorite native son"—something of an understatement. Naipaul seemed to have adapted swiftly to English life. He married a young English woman, acquired a prose style hailed as masterly. His eye was unerring in observing English scenes, as he demonstrated in *The Mimic Men* and in *Mr. Stone and the Knights Companion.*

But it was clear that Britain wasn't "home" any more than Trinidad had been. Like every other place, it was a place to get out of. Naipaul early recognized in himself that sense of placelessness and of universal insecurity which afflicts the characters of his later novels. He began to travel, more perhaps to prove to himself that he didn't belong anywhere than to find a permanent haven. In 1960 he returned to the Caribbean, a sobering and bitter experience recounted in *The Middle*

V. S. Naipaul *(Lütfi Özkök)*

Passage (1962), which mingles history and sharp, personal observations. He visits Trinidad, British Guiana, Surinam, Martinique and Jamaica, all of them "borrowed cultures." He has few illusions about the future of the entire region, now largely freed from that colonialism which had been so often blamed for its misfortunes. Many of the issues discussed in this volume reappear in *The Mimic Men*. A close relation exists between Naipaul's travel books and his fiction, the travel books often serving as raw material for the novels.

He returns to the West Indies once again in *The Loss of El Dorado* (1969), a historical work in which he explores the origins of modern Trinidad. He highlights two key events: the founding of Port of Spain in 1592 by Antonio de Berrio, a belated conquistador obsessed by the legend of El Dorado and the capture of the island by the British in 1797. Berrio, quite out of his mind, spent the last years of his life in a mad search for the golden city. And the first British governor, a deranged sadist, reveled in hangings and floggings and was finally brought to trial for torturing a young mulatto girl. But by that time the West Indies were already rapidly becoming the backwaters of the empire. Naipaul handles these events with a novelist's skill and sense of drama,

but he also exhibits that vital feeling for history which is apparent throughout his later work. Using unpublished archival material, he vividly evokes what Walter Allen has called "the contradictions and the tragic absurdities, the whole inheritance of cruelty and chaos" which marks the history of the Caribbean.

In 1962 Naipaul went to India for a year, traveling widely: south to Madras, east to Calcutta, north to Kashmir, where he spent several months. He accompanied a crowd of pilgrims to a holy cave high in the Himalayas and visited his grandfather's desolate native village in Uttar Pradesh. He records his impressions in *An Area of Darkness* (1964), which, on its appearance, provoked cries of protest from Indian intellectuals. H. B. Singh branded Naipaul as "a despicable lackey of neocolonialism" who deserves "utter contempt." Another critic claimed that "the area of darkness" is within Naipaul himself. In 1977 came *India: A Wounded Civilization.* For Naipaul, India is "a difficult country." It isn't his home, but he cannot reject it because of his family background. On this second visit he wished to investigate the "Emergency" of 1976, when Indira Gandhi had in effect seized absolute power. He reaches the conclusion that with this suppression of democratic institutions and "with no foreign conqueror to impose a new order," India is now forced to face alone "the blankness of its decayed civilization."

The Return of Eva Perón (1980) contains four essays written between 1972 and 1975: "Michael X and the Black Power Killings in Trinidad," "The Return of Eva Perón," "A New King for the Congo: Mobutu and the Nihilism of Africa" and "Conrad's Darkness." These essays have close links with the novels. The "Author's Note" states: "These pieces . . . bridged a creative gap; from the end of 1970 to the end of 1973, no novel offered itself to me. . . . Out of these journeys and these writings, novels did in the end come to me." Many of Naipaul's articles and some of the more important of his numerous book reviews are included in *The Overcrowded Barracoon* (1972). They include *"Cannery Row* Revisited," a particularly interesting piece, since Steinbeck's book has sometimes been mentioned as a forerunner of *Miguel Street.*

Among the Believers: An Islamic Journey, the most recent (1981) and the least well-received of Naipaul's nonfiction books, contains observations on his seven-month trip to four countries—Iran, Pakistan, Malaysia and Indonesia—which are all undergoing Islamic revolutions. It has been pointed out that, curiously, the volume has nothing to say about any Arab state. Specialists have noted that Naipaul seems inadequately prepared to deal accurately with a complex phenomenon which varies from country to country. And his fondness for anecdote and personal narrative often leads him to pay relatively little attention to crucial events taking place in the Islamic world during his trip: the storming of the American Embassy in Teheran; the violent incidents in the Great Mosque in Mecca; the Russian invasion of Afghanistan; the reign of martial law in Pakistan. In the section on Pakistan there is a chapter titled "Killing History," deploring the violence with which Islam "tramples on the past." Islam's kind of "selective history" fuels the rage that Naipaul encountered wherever he went, the rage to kill and to destroy, a love of violence masquerading as faith ("Islam sanctified rage"). But sometimes he has the fleeting impression that Islam can give people a kind of serenity, a feeling of completeness—if only the world outside, the world of Western technology which the "Believers" hate but without which they cannot get along, could only be cast away.

But remarkable as Naipaul's travel books may be, he is essentially a novelist, and it is as a novelist that his achievement must be evaluated. In the field of fiction he is certainly no innovator. He has mastered the craft of traditional narrative and shows little interest in technical experiment. He is closer to Dickens or Balzac than he is to Joyce or *le nouveau roman;* his concern is to tell a story and also to discuss ideas. He would never subscribe to Flaubert's ideal to "write a book about nothing." *Miguel Street*—the first of his Trinidad stories to be written, although it was published in 1959, after *The Mystic Masseur* and *The Suffrage of Elvira*—consists of a series of sketches about a lower-class neighborhood in Port of Spain. There is the vivacious Laura, mother of eight children by as many fathers, "whose shouts and curses were the richest things I ever heard. She like Shakespeare when it comes to using words." There we also encounter B. Wordsworth, the poet who had never written poetry but who lived it; Man-man, who thought he was the Messiah and who sent out invitations for his crucifixion; Eddoes, "one of the aristocrats of the street" because he drove the garbage truck and only had to work mornings.

Miguel Street differs from most West Indian writing about the poor in that it expresses no overt social protest, but rather a humorous delight in these colorful characters, apparently happy in spite of their poverty. These vignettes, with their mix of sentimentality and irony (and perhaps with a dash of condescension as well), are always charming and occasionally even somewhat coy. The leading character of *The Mystic Masseur* (1957), Ganesh, already appears in *Miguel Street* no longer as a pundit in a dhoti but as a rising politician in "an expensive looking lounge suit." Pundit Ganesh Ramsummari, after having failed in a series of undertakings, finally gains a reputation as a learned man and

a mystic. He then embarks on a political career, is elected to the Trinidad Legislative Council, becomes more and more British and finally assumes the name of G. Ramsay Muir, M.B.E.

The Suffrage of Elvira (1958) also treats of Trinidad politics. A rich Hindu, Harbans, is seeking election to the Legislative Council from the Elvira district. Democracy "had taken everybody by surprise" when it had come to Elvira after the war, and no one is very sure how it should work. So here, as elsewhere, Elvira apes the world outside. Harbans hires a truck with a loudspeaker and a brash young campaign manager to drive it and blat out the campaign slogans. He passes out free "rum vouchers" so that prospective supporters can get drunk free and democratically in the local rumshop. However, success finally depends on buying up the votes. Harbans wins the election, but it has cost him a lot of money. As he leaves Elvira, he shakes his fist at the countryside he is now representing and shouts: "Elvira, you is a bitch." As usual in these Trinidad stories, Naipaul shows an enviable command of local language: "you talking arseness"; "you suckastic and insultive in my pussonal." These electoral antics in Elvira are marvelously entertaining. But Naipaul is also expressing concern about the degradation of democracy in many emerging countries. Only in the emerging countries? Harbans's comment, as he is forced to bribe more and more, has an uncomfortably familiar ring: "'They should pass some sort of law to prevent candidates from spending so much money. . .' But then he pulled out his wallet."

The last of the Trinidad novels, *A House for Mr. Biswas* (1961), goes beyond local color to embrace a universal theme: the desire of a man to have a home of his own, to "be somebody" in his own right. Looking back on his early years, Naipaul has created a "remembrance of things past," a large-scale chronicle teeming with life and rich in feeling. It retraces the history of a tentacular Hindu family, the Tulsis, into which the poor orphan Mr. Biswas marries nearly by accident, admitted only because he is a Brahmin and the Tulsis are of an inferior caste with many daughters to provide for. But they are prosperous. They own a store, a sugar plantation and a big house, where all the tribe live in stifling proximity. The sons-in-law are expected to work on the family properties. As a man who knows how to read, Biswas refuses to work in the fields; so he is assigned to manage a small grocery shop the family owns. But he has no business sense and is given another job as an assistant overseer on the sugar plantation, where he and his family are forced to live in one room in the barracks. Unable to stand it, he manages to build a cheap house on a nearby site. A house of his own! But a tropical storm wrecks it, and he is forced to return to tribal life with the Tulsis. He takes refuge in reading: "He discovered the solace of Dickens." He finds pleasure in transferring Dickens's characters and settings "to people and places that he knew," as perhaps Naipaul himself did in writing *Mr. Biswas*. By a stroke of luck, Biswas gets a newspaper job, and although he is still under the roof (and the thumb!) of the Tulsis, his prestige as a journalist makes life more tolerable. He also derives comfort from his children, especially his only son, a bright boy who eventually wins a scholarship to study abroad.

Conventional, romantic love has little place in Naipaul's world. Biswas's relations with his wife seem without affection. Her deepest loyalties are to the tribe rather than to her husband. Only with his son does Biswas exhibit any real tenderness. Finally, he manages to borrow money to buy a run-down dwelling. After a heart attack he loses his job but is able to take refuge in "a home of his own," and soon afterward he dies there, under his own roof, content in spite of all the disappointments and frustrations of his life. Naipaul, so often lacking in emotional warmth, clearly has a special affection for Biswas. He succeeds admirably in communicating this affection to the reader. Of all his novels, this is perhaps the most appealingly human.

After *Biswas* the novelist's vision of the world grows darker. He will never be able to find his way back to the innocence of *Miguel Street*. The years in England had confirmed his feelings about the secondhand quality of his place of birth. Determined to avoid being categorized as a "West Indian writer," he set out in his next book, *Mr. Stone and the Knights Companion* (1963), to write of British life and proved himself an expert craftsman who could do it extremely well. The protagonist, Mr. Stone, has spent his obscure career as a clerk in a large London firm. On the eve of his retirement he dreams up a program by which the pensioned employees will get together to assist the less fortunate retirees. Management backs the scheme, and Stone hopes that it means he will acquire a prestige he never enjoyed before. But a brash public-relations man takes over, and Stone is once again relegated to obscurity.

The Mimic Men (1967) is set largely in Trinidad (here called "Isabella"), although the opening and closing sections take place in London, where the narrator Ralph Singh studied as a young man and to which he has now returned as an ex-minister in disgrace. He is only forty, but he knows that he is washed up: "The career of a colonial politician is short and ends brutally." Back home from England, he has embarked on a profitable real-estate operation and has become involved in politics. But the exercise of power cannot conceal from him the void of his "bastard world." He and others like

him "in Isabella and in 20 other countries" are all "mimic men." Some readers branded the novel as reactionary, and many of Singh's opinions would seem to justify the accusation. He describes Isabella in the colonial period as "a benevolently administered dependency." He has a nostalgia for "the good old days" on the great cocoa plantations. But the old regime was not as benevolent as that and was marked, as *The Loss of El Dorado* makes clear, by horrifying brutality. Still, it would be an error to label Singh (or his creator) simplistically as neocolonialist. Both "write from both sides." Singh "hates oppression and fears the oppressed." He is aware, like many disillusioned liberals, that the oppressed, once delivered from oppression, are swift to become oppressors in their turn. Singh shares Naipaul's interest in history, deplores that "there is no such thing as history nowadays . . . only the pamphleteering of churls." In both of them there lurks more than a hint of snobbishness, of Brahmin superiority. (Naipaul has written an essay, "What's Wrong with Being a Snob?") And as the exiled Singh meditates on the history of Isabella, with "its hunters and hunted, rulers and ruled," he realizes that its message is cruelly clear: nothing is secure. So, alone in London, he settles down to accept "the final emptiness" which, it is implied, awaits us all.

The short stories in *A Flag on the Island* (1967) restate familiar themes: placelessness, alienation, meaninglessness, the illusion of "progress." The title novella deals with the return to a Caribbean island by an American soldier who had been there during the war and who is saddened at the devastation wrought by tourism and by the vulgarity of a gadget civilization.

In a Free State (1971) consists of the two journal entries "The Tramp at Piraeus" and "The Circus at Luxor," and two short stories—"One Out of Many," about an East Indian trying to adjust to life in Washington, D.C., and "Tell Me Who to Kill," an account of a West Indian and his brother adrift in London—as well as the novella "In a Free State," one of Naipaul's outstanding achievements. All the characters in this last-named work have in one fashion or another escaped the constraints of their own culture to live in a "free state," only to discover that they don't belong anywhere. Geographically, the "free state" is a recently independent African country, torn by civil war between the new president and the old tribal king, who is in flight before the government forces and who is finally murdered by them. The protagonist Bobby, a neurotic, homosexual Englishman, works for the government as a foreign expert. He longs to be a part of African society. He wears native-style shirts, attempts to speak the patois of the region, seeks friendship (and love) among the natives. During his stay in the capital for professional meetings he attempts to pick up a young Zulu, who disdainfully rejects him and spits in his face. The next morning he sets out to drive back to his work in "the Southern Collectorate," accompanied by Linda, the wife of one of his colleagues. During the long trip the two keep talking randomly away, but they have little to say to each other, since Linda does not share Bobby's enthusiasm for Africa.

Naipaul masterfully conveys the feel of the country they are driving through, in all its vastness, emptiness and menace. They stop for the night in a run-down inn, once a tourist attraction, now unfrequented because of civil disorder. The proprietor, a crusty old colonial, reveals in a confrontation with one of the black servants all the hatred that exists between the few whites remaining in the area and the natives bent on taking over. The next day Bobby and Linda press on through the empty land, occasionally surprised by bizarre sights: "Two men ran out into the road . . . they were naked and chalked white from head to toe, white as the rocks." When Bobby stops to inquire about a rumored curfew, he is seized and beaten (for no clear-cut reason) by a group of soldiers and is then permitted to go on his way. On their arrival in the compound, Luke, the houseboy, begins to laugh at the battered Bobby, and Bobby knows that he must "sack" him in order to preserve his own dignity. This unsettling narrative, for all its strangeness, gives an impression of a frightening authenticity, and as we read contemporary African history, we sense that Naipaul's view of things may be uncomfortably close to the unreal reality.

Before the appearance of *Guerrillas* (1975) Naipaul was relatively little known in the U.S. Of course his earlier fiction, even that dealing with revolutionary situations in newly independent countries, had avoided sensationalism, had appealed mostly to a literate minority. *Guerrillas,* on the other hand, struck a new note with its emphasis on brutality and on the explicit treatment of morbid sexuality. A deliberately bleak and nihilistic work, it made nevertheless a greater impact here than anything he had previously written, was extravagantly praised, even overpraised as "the masterpiece of the best novelist now writing." All the characters—from Jimmy Ahmed, the confused, self-dramatizing Black Power leader; to Jane, the Anglo-Canadian victim of his sadistic hate; to Roche, the South African dissident; to Bryant, Jimmy's slum-boy lover—are at once pitiful and repulsive, mini-monsters smelling of "rotten meat" (one of Jimmy's frequently used expressions). The novel itself, however, is no more macabre than the events on which it is based, recounted in the essay "Michael X and the Black Power Killings."

Peter Roche, banned from South Africa after having suffered torture and imprisonment, arrives on a West Indian island as a public-relations man for a foreign company bent on improving its image and also on counteracting any incipient revolutionary disturbances. He is accompanied by his mistress Jane, who (like her real-life counterpart in "Michael X") is looking for thrills and for the excitement she identifies with Black Power. Roche becomes associated with Jimmy Ahmed, half black, half Chinese, who, after having been deported from England where he had achieved a certain notoriety in "radical chic" circles as "the black Pekinese" of salon revolutionaries, has founded an agricultural commune "for the land and for the Revolution." The enterprise is financed in part by Roche's company, who see in it a possible means of defusing certain potentially dangerous elements in the island's urban youth gangs. Jane, bored with Roche, no longer the heroic figure she imagined him to be, takes Jimmy to bed, although it is difficult to see what either one finds attractive in the other. Meanwhile, the slaying by the police of Stephens, a young black gang leader who had briefly belonged to Jimmy's commune, provokes an abortive popular uprising. Houses are burned, stores looted. But soon the government, with the support of "Americans" in helicopters, restores order of a sort. These events persuade Jane that it is time to get out, but, drawn by the odor of "rotten meat," she goes to pay a last visit to Jimmy. Their final sexual encounter, at once savage and absurd (in these matters Naipaul is at his least convincing), ends with Jimmy's offering Jane as a victim to his young lover ("Bryant, the rat, kill the rat"); the hysterical, hate-crazed boy hacks her gruesomely to death with his cutlass. Roche, probably aware that Jane has been done away with, destroys her papers so that there will be no evidence that she ever existed, and, fearful for his own life, prepares ingloriously to flee.

Africa evidently made a deep impression on Naipaul, as *A Bend in the River* (1979) testifies. One of his major achievements, much larger in scale than *In a Free State* and rich in Conradian resonances, it merits the comparison sometimes made to *Heart of Darkness*. Naipaul's characters, however, lack the tragic dimensions of Conrad's Kurtz, who had, at least in the beginning, nourished the hope that humane concern might bring light into the darkness. In Naipaul's work, on the contrary, the characters have long since renounced such an illusion—if indeed they ever had it at all. For its subject matter, *A Bend in the River* draws largely on the essay "A New King for the Congo: Mobutu and the Nihilism of Africa" but demonstrates once again how a novelist of Naipaul's gifts can convey a new density, a deeper significance to "facts," can absorb and transform the document.

Naipaul's preoccupation with history and with historical change is everywhere apparent. Early in the story the narrator Salim, the son of an Indian Moslem family installed for generations on the African coast, realizes that with the rise of revolutionary movements "another tide of history was coming to wash us away." He decides to strike out on his own and acquires a store in a small city in Zaïre, on "a bend in the river." He finds the town in shambles after the disorders which followed the departure of the Belgians: "You were in a place where the future had come and gone." But soon the new president, backed up with tough white mercenaries, succeeds in imposing order of a sort, and the town comes to life again. The little foreign colony draws a breath of relief and settles down to make money. Naipaul hates the greed of the Europeans, but he is swift to point out that the Africans are just as greedy. The native officials, gathered in the newly opened Bigburger, "wore as much gold as possible—gold-rimmed glasses, gold rings, gold pen and pencil sets, gold watches."

On the outskirts of the town, the president ("the Big Man") creates a showy institute for the training of young officials and for international meetings to which Western experts on African affairs, picturesquely clad in native costumes, are invited. The director of the center, a middle-aged Belgian professor, had been "the Big Man's white man," but he is aware that he is on the skids, that his boss has no further need of him. Salim engages in a rather absentminded liaison with the director's young wife. Their couplings are marked by sadistic violence; on one occasion she falls to the floor under Salim's blows: "Then I used my feet on her." Soon conditions again grow worse for the foreign colony. The Big Man nationalizes all foreign property and distributes it to the "people." Salim becomes the manager of his own store, now the property of an illiterate native called Citoyen Théotime. Anxious to make money in order to get out, he engages in illegal traffic in ivory, is flung into jail and later gains release only through the intervention of Ferdinand, a young native whom he had befriended in the past and who had risen to be "a commissioner." But in spite of his official position, Ferdinand too is deathly afraid. He foresees mass killings when the Big Man arrives to conduct a purge: "They're going to kill and kill and kill." Salim manages to get on the steamer—perhaps the last one for some time—that is leaving the next morning. But we know as well as he does that there is nowhere for him to go.

These works of his maturity reveal that Naipaul is far more than "the most gifted West Indian novelist of his generation," more indeed than the most compelling and troubling of the writers who have confronted the tragic contradictions of the Third World. He implies that their problems—placelessness, disorder, violence, racial hatred, irrational frenzy, self-destroying greed—may be ours as well. We can certainly accept the validity of his grim premonitions. It is more difficult, however, to accept the bleak and intransigent hopelessness with which he views the human situation. Throughout his work he has always insisted that he refuses to take a position "for" or "against." But, on a deeper level, he *is* a partisan, indeed a fierce partisan of an apocalyptic conception of history whose dogmatic blackness betrays a romantic immaturity. His knowledge of the past should have shown him that every ending is also a beginning, that neither men or events are inexorably predestined, that the human adventure is an eternally disconcerting mixture of good and evil, of darkness and light—even though the light may often seem very faint and flickering indeed. But so far he has wagered consistently on the triumph of darkness, insufficiently aware that prophets announcing the end of the world have appeared in every generation in the past and that, in spite of their prophecies, new worlds have arisen to take the place of those which have passed away. But of course these past cultures were unprovided with nuclear playthings.

John L. Brown, Spring 1983

Places We Come From: Voices of Caribbean Canadian Writers (in English) and Multicultural Contexts

1. The recent special "Canadian Caribbean Issue" of *Descant* (Summer 1998) suggests a journey and a maturing of Canadian literature in terms of the latter's flexibility and capacity to be all-embracing, without undermining Canada's identity; moreover, this attitude strengthens the nation's spirit and sense of continuing possibilities in a land which, since its inception, has been formed by immigration and continuing to grow on its "triangular foundation" (John Ralston Saul) of First Nations Peoples and English Canadian and French Canadian heritages. Caribbean links and correspondences with Canada, of course, have been manifold, varied, down through the ages and associated early with the Maroons and with the Atlantic trade and mercantilism. Salted cod from Newfoundland exported to the Caribbean is still special to the palate, for instance. And whenever I contribute material to the three main literary magazines in Canada's Maritime—*The Fiddlehead, The Dalhousie Review,* and *The Antigonish Review*—these con-

texts and influences often come into play in my psyche, all part of the polarities and simultaneous evolution of culture and cultural norms that occur in the numinous sense of the spirit of place. Naturally, paradox and irony are integrated in the ongoing flux, and ingrained in one's developing sense of poetics, living in a land becoming less strange or foreign in the widening context of the self, and as the dynamics associated with adaptation dictate.

The early interactions and connections, of course, inevitably resulted in art and literature, some of it oral, undocumented; at other times, as we have seen, much of it written and fully expressed, or in the process of being so, but now especially manifest in the esthetic energy of a range of writers, some relatively new like Andre Alexis and Shani Mootoo with recent first-novel publications, and others—like Austin Clarke—writing for two or three decades and more in Canada, sustaining their reputations as their sensibilities continue to define the Canadian identity. Interestingly, the seminal or inchoate point of reference in my own assessment and appreciation of Canadian Caribbean literature stems from an awareness of a process that goes back to the 1960 issue of *Tamarack* magazine embracing West Indian writers, edited by Robert Weaver—the first Canadian magazine's special issue on this subject, which I nostalgically reflected on while reading the recent *Descant* issue. At that time I was living in Guyana, and *Tamarack,* in a sense, contributed to my view of Canada as an intrinsic place to fashion dreams, all conceived despite the overwhelming, even forbidding, sense of the Great White North, far different from the tropical milieu I grew up in; and, increasingly, Canada became the place of possibilities, unlike the U.K. or the U.S. in my formative years toward acquiring experience akin to what W. H. New calls "a shaping of connections . . . setting dreams into motion" (154), albeit far from a mundane organizational context. Later, I would reflect on less numinous experience as I considered the impact of Liberal prime ministers Lester B. Pearson and, later, Pierre Elliot Trudeau in sustaining one's faith and vision while simultaneously contemplating Canada in the context of geography and climate as influencing destiny. Now, almost four decades later, with the aforementioned special *Descant* issue, Edward T. Chamberlin would write in the introduction about reconciling "attachments to place with allegiances to language, and how to accommodate different allegiances and attachments, different lands and languages, within a single community" (8). Could all this perhaps lead to formation of a world community of literature(s) without imposing artificial boundaries on the creative spirit?

Cyril Dabydeen (*Courtesy of the author*)

The rubric "Canadian Literature" naturally becomes elastic and simultaneously dynamic as much as arguments in favor of multiculturalism when Caribbean Canadian writing is juxtaposed with, say, Jewish Canadian, Italian Canadian, Hispanic Canadian, South Asian Canadian, and other forms of nascent and/or maturing "ethnic" literatures—including regionally formed literatures—in a changing world of the arts and the humanities. As the scholar Joseph Pivato says in the *Toronto Review of Contemporary Writing Abroad*, in advocating recognition of multiculturalism as intrinsic to Canadian writing: "The work of Italian Canadian writers and other ethnic minority authors demonstrates that 'there is setting into shape a nation' of great diversity" (42). And does all this take away from Canadian identity or nativism (so-called), as some have argued? No less a commentator of the liberal imagination than Michael Ignatieff remarks: "Living with racial, religious, ethnic difference is a challenge, but conservative critics are simply wrong when they argue that immigration and the proliferation of multicultural identity threatens us with cultural and social fragmentation" (*Ottawa Citizen,* B7). It is interesting to posit this view against that of the novelist and short-story writer Neil Bissoondath (Trinidadian-born), in some quarters better known for his egregious "cult of multiculturalism" reflected in his *Selling Illusions* (1994) than for his belletristic work. Ironically, Bissoondath has sometimes referred to the philosophically astute Ignatieff to shore up his assertions in decrying identity politics and ethnicity—all part, no doubt, of the Yeatsian "quarrel with ourselves" and bordering on mundane discourse about nationhood in a Canada irrevocably evolving as an adaptive immigrant and multicultural society as the Caribbean-born writers' presence is manifested and formed by the spirit of the place.

Seminal voices such as that of the novelist Austin Clarke, sometimes viewed as "the dean of Caribbean writing in Canada," have challenged, implicitly and explicitly, the sense of the Great White North as the overwhelming paradigm with all its attendant symbolism in asserting his indubitable Canadian literary presence. And in the flux of shaping connection, it is relevant to juxtapose other early Caribbean influences on Canada, such as that of the novelist George Lamming, who would reveal that in contributing to the 1960 *Tamarack Review* special issue, his writing of *The Pleasures of Exile* (an acknowledged postcolonial text) came about at this time, giving voice and nuance to migration and consciousness of the Caribbean while wrestling with the angst of colonialism through his imaginative prism. Significantly, when Lamming first came to Canada and interacted with Canadian writers, not least the novelist Margaret Laurence, it is reasonable to assume that his impact upon them (and vice versa) was immediate; Laurence, for one, would describe Lamming as "not only a talented writer, but the kind of personality that hits you like the spirit of God between the eyes" (King, 168). Of course, other Caribbean writers' voices have also been heard in Canada over the years, some as specially invited guests at conferences and to give readings, all adding to the ongoing influence and cross-fertilization of taste, style, and meaning in setting the stage for the more home-grown Canadian writers of Caribbean background to influence an evolving literature accommodating themes and argot often appearing unaccustomed to their Canadian readership only a few years ago but now gaining acceptance.

Interestingly, Austin Clarke, with his latest book, *Origin of Waves* (1997), has consolidated his particular vision, following on the uncompromising themes of his earlier works, including the classic trilogy (*The Meeting Point, Storm of Fortune,* and *The Bigger Light*) chronicling West Indian immigrants' lives in the 1960s, followed by other works such as *Growing Up Stupid under the Union* (1980). As the Barbadian-born Clarke recently stated in a "Black Writers" pamphlet: "The social and cultural landscape of Canada has changed fundamentally from the 1960's when I wrote the Toronto Trilogy. And even at that time, there was notice being given to the literary establishment, that we had in our midst, the traditional one—albeit an English sensibility—and that this nontraditional perspective could no longer be viewed as a 'minority' point of view."

Clarke's influence on my own early work, for instance, I have acknowledged (cf. Stella Algoo-Baksh, *Austin Clarke: A Biography,* 1994), much as I have heard other writers such as Cecil Foster (Barbadian-born) and the anthologist Ayanna Black (Jamaican background) make similar acknowledgments, while simultaneously recognizing influences of other writers: those referred to as the "first generation" such as Lamming himself, V. S. Naipaul, Roger Mais, John Hearne, Jan Carew, Wilson Harris, Sylvia Winters, Sam Selvon, Kamau Brathwaite, and Derek Walcott—many of whom have lived in the U.K. or in the U.S. for decades at a time when "exile" was the norm, and who have contributed to the steadily shifting grounds and polarities of place with inherent paradoxes stemming from the sense of the hurts of history (slavery and indentured labor), colonialism, and immigrant marginality, while grappling with the politics of race, ethnicity, and class. Language formations as dialectal expression of authentic inner rhythms of voice and place expressed in individual ways, such as Sam Selvon's, continue to form part of the assertion of identity, even with the intent to subvert because of the underpinning or immanent sense of the "outsider" and the sense of alienation, albeit contiguous with the desire for adaptation. In Canada, the irony of the "other" responds to the challenge of citizenship in a country now being described by some as "the Caribbean of the North."

The themes, motifs, and images already referred to are reflected in varying ways and styles by older and many newer Caribbean Canadian writers, each with his or her own unique and personal perspective, such as Dionne Brand, Foster, Bissoondath, Nigel Thomas, Marlene Nourbese Philip, Claire Harris, the dub poets Lillian Allen and Clifton Joseph, Dany Laferrière (writing in French but translated in English), by the late novelists Sam Selvon and Harold Sonny Ladoo, and others. Many of these writers live in Canada's major urban center of Toronto, the "meeting place," once known as Hogtown and still associated with Governor Simcoe, yet with little of the writing, it has been said, reflecting the heartland by focusing on experience in the Prairies or the East and West Coast regions, though one suspects this is beginning to change. Albeit, the writers continue to make their presences felt, including relatively recent ones like Rabindranath Maharaj and Sasenarine Persaud (Trinidadian- and Guyanese-born respectively); and there are others, perhaps seen as singular but lonely voices, like Madeline Coopsammy's in Winnipeg, striving to achieve immediacy by reconciling the breadth of the Prairie and its Red and Assiniboine Rivers with the angst of small-state experiences (often Trinidad) by extension and criss-crossing metaphorical boundaries. Because inevitably all these writers are gifted with their particular visions informing their work, they necessarily call attention to the fluid stream of creativity in Canadian literature, invariably in their verbal reaction to the fluctuating sense of place, even with the dislocated self seen in the voice of someone like the writer Arnold Itwaru (Guyanese-born), or the dissembled presence of Horace Goddard (Barbadian-born) in Québec in view of the unique political and social dynamics in the latter province.

By focusing attention on an orientation of Canada in terms of binaries such as "outsider" and "insider" while mediating experience in a country that is "huge, frightening, beautiful" (as the late Irish-Canadian novelist Brian Moore, himself an immigrant, described it), this forms an integral part of the paradoxical nature of the creative act in bringing polarities, real and imagined, closer to a common yet universal meeting ground in Canada.

In my edition of *A Shapely Fire: Changing the Literary Landscape,* I brought together twenty relatively active Caribbean-born writers (of fiction, poetry, and drama) living in Canada, while considering the evolving literary canon toward a redefinition of the norm of what is considered "Canadian" and "Canadian literature"; in so doing, I was hoping for newer contexts while also attempting to go beyond the merely promising literature in English, including that of writers of French-speaking background (such as Gérard Etienne and Anthony Phelps, both Haitian in origin and both translated in this book), the aim being to help prepare the way for what was yet to come: the nascent or new human possibilities and movement to the literary foreground with the sense or belief in a country with rootedness embedded. Thus I wrote in the introduction: "For these latter-day newcomers, the frontier took a different meaning: like their European counterparts of an earlier period, they too were drawers of water and hewers of wood, roughing it as domestic servants, factory and farmworkers, security guards, railway conductors, and more recently as teachers and doctors—all the while expressing a vitality of spirit stemming from the active imagination that is the birthright of all" (9). I further suggested an interpretation beyond a conventional definition of nationhood, with the construct of the "landscape of the imagination," arguing that Canada could be conceived as the imagined place—not viewed solely in phenomeno-logical terms of physical space or geographic boundary associated singularly with the "idea of the north" (à la Margaret Atwood) in apprehending Canadian reality. Indeed, as I asserted, identity would be

> . . . based on a concept associated with the landscape of the mind, wherein place and psyche become intertwined in nation-building terms through the creative outpouring and meshing of

the spirit. In this context, a real shaping is constantly taking place: the collective Canadian spirit is enhanced and enriched by the varied cultural streams in the fusion of old and new traditions towards a vital celebration of the oneness of the evolving Canadian consciousness. (*Shapely Fire,* 10)

Now in Canada's major urban center we are hearing voices continuing to express the palpability of the "the Caribbean of the North," inspired no doubt by the critical mass of a Caribbean-born immigrant population seeking to validate their diverse heritage and black experiences—for instance, in festival extravaganzas like Caribana, which a writer like Cecil Foster strongly locates in his writings as the new sensibility gains momentum (reflected, for instance, in his 1996 book *A Place Called Heaven*). Moreover, rap music and dub poetry in Toronto have energized the local scene, which scholar Brenda Carr describes as "dub-aesthetics-in-the-diaspora and which necessitates a reconsideration of Western notions of the aesthetic, the literary, and the poetic" (12). Thus the impulses of urbanization invariably add to the unfolding destiny and esthetics circumscribing the immigrant and indigenous energies as the writers continue to cross numinous boundaries, sometimes seen in my own work as I would write about experiences of living close to Lake Superior in the Lakehead with a Great Spirit ambience, while evoking memory with present experience, all in a place Margaret Atwood, because of her own early years living close to the world's largest lake, viewed as "an excellent place to spend your formative years" (14).

Many other writers also re-create the Caribbean past, sometimes combined with the present, such as the Jamaican-born Rachel Manley, Olive Senior, and Louise Bennet, and the Trinidadian-born poet Ramabai Espinet in *Nuclear Seasons* (1991). This is sometimes inevitably contexted by a forceful African Canadian consciousness and presence, as seen in such writers as Marlene Nourbese Philip, Claire Harris, Makeda Silvera, and Althea Prince. In Mairuth Sarsfield, Montréal-born but with a Guyanese father, we see a first-novel appearance in *No Crystal Stair* (1997), which intersects the American Langston Hughes's poem of the same name and other U.S. reference points with other ethno-specific cultures and singular Afrocentric images associated with Montréal in the "Black pioneering days": the forties, fifties, and onward. Worthy of note is George Elliot Clarke's warning that "African Canadians appear blithely acquiescent to the forces of a homogenizing African Americanism," while admitting that this consciousness "is not simply dualistic" (*Essays,* 15, 16). Unique strains of womanhood, in pursuing individual truths, it should be added, are seen in many of the aforementioned writers, mainly Harris, Philip, and Brand, in asserting female identity with African presence in Canada—in the case of Philip, sometimes with blood and/or menstrual experience in fundamental association with Mother Earth as a driving force.

2. The recognition and appreciation of many relatively newer Canadian writers—many Caribbean-born but many more from other parts of the developing world, like Rohinton Mistry (Indian-born) and M. G. Vassanji (Tanzanian-born), Denise Chong (Chinese background), and Joy Kogawa and Keri Sakamoto with their Japanese roots—are persuading scholars like David Staines to refer to it as the current "international phase" in Canadian writing; however, perhaps one could argue that Canadian literature has always been international, albeit influenced mainly by British and American sources from the time of the early pioneering period, with writers like Frances Brooke, Susanna Moodie, and others in the Confederation and post-Confederation periods. In the modern or contemporary period, one finds Earle Birney's poems "Bear on the Delhi Road" and "To George Lamming," with their sense of visions afar. And indeed, Margaret Laurence wrote authentically about Africa when she lived there, and Atwood's novel *Bodily Harm* (1981) has a Caribbean setting. Further examples abound, all as part of the flux of ongoing shaping of connection in a seemingly globalized world. In fundamentally responding to the prevailing sense of the Great White North—the "twin bars" implying the sense of solitude and beauty of the vast landscape and inspiring awe while simultaneously evoking beauty, manifested in such classic twentieth-century Canadian poets as A. M. Klein and E. J. Pratt—all contemporary writers, like Irving Layton, have described it ad nauseam. Northrop Frye would add a new dimension, "satire and exuberance," making for a more interesting if not complex critical context in the enrichment of Canadian literature and culture with other people coming to Canada's shores, all with minds, memories, and emotions from nontraditional immigrant sources eager to establish a niche in the seemingly overwhelming landscape. It is a context particularly significant for the Caribbean-born writers' contribution, leading to what Austin Clarke called giving voice "to the actual putting down of the 'other' side—though not always a vindictive sensibility—to the former 'national' prism. National in the sense, that before the landscape of these writers, the point of view was not intended to express, and did not in fact include a way of seeing that was different from the status quo" ("Black Writers").

Essentially, the way of seeing is enhanced by the use of variations of mother-tongue language and the storyteller's sometimes unconventional technique of combining social consciousness and realism, as in Cecil Foster's latest novel, *Slammin' Tar* (1997), dramatizing Brer Anancy as trickster-cum-story-teller of Caribbean farm workers' experiences in Canada, a form of "putting down" that is very close to magic realism. As one critic observes of *Slammin' Tar:*

> North American readers might feel justifiably guilty while reading this novel, but that's hardly Foster's project. The inequities of the farm labor programs don't need Foster's analysis; they're obvious enough. Instead, his narrator spider simply reports on lives, telling it like it is, or at least how he sees it. . . . A good portion of the book goes to the narrator's own ruminations about himself and his task, how the role of storyteller is changing in these modern times, how quality and experience are being shunted aside by youth and attitude, how one teller's hero is another's clown. (*Paragraph,* 55)

It is significant to point out cross-references and juxtapositions of the trickster that permeate Native writing and the Native weltanschauung—one perhaps truly Canadian—as parallel with innate West Indian narrative and verbal structure. The Native writer Tomson Highway, in his novel *Kiss of the Fur Queen* (1998), contends that the trickster is Weesageeclak (Cree) and Nanabush (Ojibway), or Raven of other tribes, and that it is familiarly the coyote in North American Indian mythology and is sometimes consciousness of man, God, the Great Spirit, or the existence of the Earth itself. Narrative technique and use of language associated with origins and social history form part of the discourse of evolving identity within prevailing Great White North norms. And haven't I been told that I must write about the Franklin Expedition (finding a Northwest Passage) to be considered Canadian when I discussed Canadian Caribbean literature at the University of Miami not so long ago? The metaphysic of "the north" as a defining consideration continues as an underpinning despite changing times, within a metropolitan consciousness shaping sensibilities, compelling as concept for "outsiders" to sustain irony within multicultural landscapes. Thus, Brand, in her prizewinning poetry collection *Land to Light On,* begins: "Out here I am like someone without a street / without a branch but not even safe as the sea, / without the relief of the sky or good graces of a door" (3). Sections such as "Islands Vanish," "I Have Been Losing Roads," and "All That Has Happened Since" reflect the attitude of irony with language rhythms of protest that are Caribbean-based, while the voice is paradoxically concerned with *here.* Here-and-there juxtapositions and polarities are relevant as a kind of continuum in view of historical, social, and esthetic factors.

In a previous collection, *Chronicles of the Hostile Sun,* largely about reactions to the American invasion of Grenada, Brand (who has attested to the influences of African poets, the Chilean Pablo Neruda, and the American Adrienne Rich), both asserting and longing for "place," writes in the poem "For Stuart":

I am a refugee,
I have my papers,
I was born in the Caribbean,
practical in the sea,
fifteen degrees above the equator,
I have a Canadian passport,
I have lived here all my adult life,
I am stateless anyway.

(70)

An intersecting of the longing for place with memory is seen, for example, in Neil Bissoondath's recent novel, *The Worlds Within Her* (1998), where the female character, Yasmin, travels from Canada to return her mother's ashes to the Caribbean, in the process meeting formerly unknown or unheard-of relatives who help her become aware of larger truths about herself while reclaiming her Indian background and thereby fulfilling her self and identity. In Bissoondath's very first book, *Digging Up the Mountains* (1985), especially in the often-anthologized story "Insecurity," we see the symbolic escape from a less-than-proverbial Trinidad because of social and political events as leading to spiritual confinement and constraint; however, in this latest novel a reversal occurs, as Yasmin returns to the island and completes her self through a renewed awareness of kin and ethnicity. Austin Clarke, as critic, however, says of this novel: "All the characters seem to me to be irreconcilably and irredeemably negative. They all want to be somewhere else, something else, somebody else. . . . It is this dependency upon whiteness that expresses Bissoondath's bleating request for cultural acceptance, that drives his characters' unrelenting nihilism" (*Ottawa Citizen,* E3). Is this too political a reading of Bissoondath, without recognizing memory or the force of irony as a way of formalizing affirmation through authentic imaginative experience? Memory, as "mother of the Muse," is seen at work also in Andre Alexis's *Childhood* (1997), the story of forty-year-old Thomas MacMillan's efforts to piece together the elements of his conflicted past and questionable parentage by sifting through layers of memory in a narrative that is self-reflexive almost to the point of being surrealistic; it is a book that "examines lives in ways so subtle that they defy analysis," as Bissoondath himself acknowledges (*Globe and Mail,* A12). Interestingly, both of these two writers came to Canada at a relatively young age—in Alexis's case before he was ten, Bissoondath before he was twenty—which no doubt influenced

their fictional mode and its tendency to veer away from conventional realism to explore different forms of self-reflexiveness, influenced no doubt by other trends in Canada and contemporary literature as a whole.

Shani Mootoo (Irish and Trinidadian background) in *Cereus Blooms at Night* (1996), a work viewed as her "multigenerational novel" depicting life in a small town in Lantanacamara (in the Caribbean), portrays the complex but tragic figure of Mala Ramchandin in the Paradise Alms House as narrator Tyler (her attendant) assists in exploring. Awareness of Indianness as palpably integral to Caribbean experience is seen in other writers, including myself, and notably in such as Sasenarine Persaud, Itwaru, Maharaj, Ladoo, and Selvon, adding multicultural vigor to Caribbean writers' contribution, one juxtaposed and fully expressed with Afrocentric experiences and angst, while voicing a range of feelings, expressions, and attitudes, as well as ways of viewing the world, including through Hinduist, Zen Buddhist, and Muslim prisms, sometimes in purely creolized situations—or, as Mootoo calls it, her "bastardized Indian" self.

The new esthetic energies being released are counterpointed with the singularly or homogenous larger community attitudes, generating the sense of possibilities, yet with an accompanying "identity crisis," as described by Canadian nationalists (not least driven by threats of French Canadian separatism). But as Marshall McLuhan once lamented, "Canada is the only country in the world that knows how to live without an identity"; and, for stronger emotion, Robertson Davies would reputedly say to Mavis Gallant, "You never ask if you love Canada; you only question Canada" (Dabydeen, A17). This attitude also seems to grow from the "strong undercurrents of passion and emotion hidden beneath a thick crust of reticent puritanism," which Henry Kreissel observed more than two decades ago in defining his own "double experience" as a European-immigrant Jewish writer. "To the man who comes from abroad, Canada is not an easy country to come to know and to write about," he adds (Neuman, 139), with the "outsider" capitalizing on self-dramatizing moments in creating the new literature, often with the force of his or her unique language, I suggest.

The Caribbean-Canadian writer's use of language is generally conceived as a two-toned English striving to extract from subjective reality imaginative truths in order to maintain integrity, famously encapsulated in the phrase "No language is neutral" (Derek Walcott, later perhaps a not infrequent visitor to Canada). Undoubtedly, most Caribbean Canadian writers have in one form or another engaged in varying use of demotic or dialectal English as legitimate forms of self-expression stemming from an ongoing, even as yet un-leavened oral tradition (in Brer Anancy and the trickster vision at work), or veering off in new directions in Dionne Brand's novel *In Another Place, Not Here* (1997), a book about Verlia and Elizete's lesbian relationship upon shifting grounds within Oliviere's sugar-plantation and island-upheaval ambience, with revolution and survival memories foregrounded in Canada.

Assumptions of the nature and function of immigrant and culture-based writers are often in respect to questions such as: Whom does the writer write for, the community or himself? Or should one label oneself simply as a "Canadian writer" or "Caribbean writer," or as a hyphenated or hybridized one (perhaps as said of myself)? The newer writers (apologies to those not mentioned) are inclined to view radical issues relating to themes and social issues in evoking images and concepts tied to colonialism and the hurts of history (not least, slavery's legacy), plantation society experience to challenge European-based forms of knowledge and dispensation of this knowledge and esthetics in universalist contexts, to one now perhaps not exclusively African, Asian, or European, but perhaps genuinely Canadian, bearing in mind Native experiences of oppression. These resonances go beyond mere Derrida-like deconstruction, to "reconstruction" (as the poet Kamau Brathwaite and others describe it), perhaps in reaction to place of origin—a Caribbean region seen merely in exotic terms with a vision of ochered beaches, ubiquitous palm trees, and bright sunshine.

The new energies of the changing Canadian literature—gender, racial, sexual, and other social and personal factors—come into play, including the time of settlement in Canada, and associations with the baggage of the postcolonial in purely academic parameters. Binaries related to margin-hinterland, majority-minority, hybridity, multiplicity, creolization, cross-nationalism, diaspora, reflection of the Other, and notions of imagined societies are all integral to the discourse associated with the purportedly "international" in Canadian literature. This has also lent itself to reevaluation by some scholars and thinkers; as the critic Diana Brydon said at a Commonwealth Literature and Language Studies conference: "Deconstruction imperialism keeps us within imperialism's orbit. . . . As a white Canadian, I speak as heir to an invading culture and beleaguered citizens of a colonized one, to an audience whose own participation in these processes is far from simple" (8).

There have been a shaping of connections and an apprehending of correspondences since the *Tamarack Review* West Indian writers issue, and a recognizing of cross-national influences, not least beginning and ending with the image of pan-Caribbean merging with es-sentially a unique Canadian or Canadian-influenced writing. As Austin Clarke suggests, "This writing, emerging into a kind of literary renaissance, stands on its own legs, so to speak, and will be judged harshly when it is flawed: but processionally when it compares with the high standard of Canadian literature" ("Black Writers").

If indeed, in the words of Michael Ondaatje, "we own the country we grow up in, or else we become aliens," then as West Indian-born writers inhabiting Canada we will continue to fashion our own dreams in unique ways as we react to a complex Canadian social and cultural landscape in invoking memory and forming dreams, even as we wrestle with commitment in pursuing individual visions, sometimes in strident or uncompromising ways over issues such as discrimination while simultaneously striving to maintain integrity as artists above all else. I confess that when the writer Earl Lovelace suggested to me (at a University of Miami Caribbean writers' retreat) that Canada is "a mediocre place," I bristled, because of the instinct informing me of the ongoing effort to shape drama, all in possessing and simultaneously learning "to love the land" as more than mere counterpoint—concerned as I am with exploring my own psyche and human fragility while trying to understand or apprehend truths in the particular and the "primordial"; for I believe strongly that art, above all else, as Carl Jung has said, is "nothing but a tremendous intuition striving for expression" (198).

This expression is also longing for perfection, concerned as I have been with finding a voice for my own sometimes amorphous, changing, and perhaps changeable ideas and feelings; all this while engaged in self-exploration and identification in the now ubiquitous or self-same Great White North with Guyanese-formed inner experiences. These experiences, while encompassing elements of metaphysics or mysticism tied to hinterland resonances of the "pool of origins" (Wilson Harris), I now see reflected in my first-ever written story, "Tide at Beach-head," formed while living in Guyana and significantly included in the special Canadian Caribbean issue of *Descant*, as engaging in memory as the deepest possible creative experience toward defining literature, with Eldridge Cleaver, as the combining of the alphabet "with volatile elements of the soul" (97).

Cyril Dabydeen, Spring 1999

■ **WORKS CITED**

Atwood, Margaret. "Margaret Atwood Speaks to the Class of '98." *Nor'Wester*, Fall 1998, pp. 14–15.

Brand, Dionne. *Chronicles of the Hostile Sun*. Toronto. Williams-Wallace. 1984.

———. *Land to Light On*. Toronto. McClelland & Stewart. 1997.

Brydon, Diana. "New Approaches to the New Literatures in English: Are We in Danger of Incorporating Disparity?" *A Shaping of Connections: Commonwealth Literature Studies—Then and Now.* Hena-Maes Jelinek et al., eds. Denmark. Dangaroo. 1989.

Carr, Brenda. "'Come Mek Wi Work Together': Community Witness and Social Agency in Lillian Allen's Dub Poetry." *Ariel: A Review of International English Literature,* 29:3 (1998), pp. 7–40.

Chamberlin, Edward J. "The Canadian Caribbean *Descant:* An Introduction." *Descant,* 29:2 (1998), pp. 7–10.

Clarke, Austin. "Black Writers" (pamphlet). Toronto. Chapters. 1998.

Clarke, George Elliot. "Structures of African Canadiante." *Essays in Canadian Writing,* No. 63 (Spring 1998), pp. 1–55.

Cleaver, Eldridge. *Soul on Ice.* New York. Dell. 1968.

Dabydeen, Cyril, ed. *A Shapely Fire: Changing the Literary Landscape.* Ontario. Mosaic. 1987.

———. "Multiculturalism Has Become One of Our Core Values." *Toronto Star,* 28 March 1995, p. A17.

Degen, John. Review of *Slammin' Tar* by Cecil Foster. *Paragraph,* No. 25 (1998/99), pp. 55–56.

Ignatieff, Michael. "A Defence of the Liberal Imagination." *Ottawa Citizen,* 17 January 1998, p. B7.

Jung, C. G. *Psychological Reflections: A New Anthology of His Writings, 1905–1961.* New ed. Princeton, N.J. Princeton University Press. 1973.

King, James. *The Life of Margaret Laurence.* Toronto. Knopf Canada. 1997.

Neuman, Shirley, ed. *Another Country: Writings By and About Henry Kreissel.* Edmonton. NeWest. 1985.

New, W. H. "A Shaping of Connections." In *A Shaping of Connections: Commonwealth Literature Studies—Then and Now.*

Pivato, Joseph. "The Singing Never Stops: Languages of Italian Canadian Writers." *Toronto Review of Contemporary Writing Abroad,* 16:3 (1998), pp. 35–43.

The Fictional Works of Caryl Phillips: An Introduction

Caryl Phillips was born in St. Kitts in 1958 and was brought by his parents to England in that year. He grew up in Leeds, studied at the University of Oxford, but returned recently to St. Kitts and the Caribbean. (Of course, there are no real returns but always and only onward journeys.) He has traveled extensively in the United States and Europe and has visited Africa.

The Final Passage[1] (winner of the Malcolm X Prize) is the story of Leila, who comes to England, bringing her husband Michael (more burden than baggage) and infant son Calvin. Left alone by her unfaithful husband, living without hope or happiness in slum conditions, she decides to return to her little Caribbean island. However, by this time Leila has suffered a breakdown, is unemployed, and one wonders if she will be able to

give the decision practical, financial expression. It is not that Britain has opened her eyes to previously overlooked positive aspects of her island home; return is merely the lesser of two unattractive alternatives. The author, who himself was taken to England as a baby and who as an adult has made the journey back, writes about "the West Indian wave of immigration" into Britain, the so-called mother country, in the 1960s. Through Leila we gain an inkling of understanding as to why people left the Caribbean and what life was like for those immigrants in Britain, where at that time it was legal and normal to display signs that read, "No coloureds [or 'blacks']. No dogs." (Wole Soyinka records his experiences in the satiric poem "Telephone Conversation.") The novel thus has wider dimensions—of a historical, economic, and cultural nature.

In 1962 V. S. Naipaul published a collection of essays titled *The Middle Passage.*[2] The phrase "the middle passage" comes down from the days of slavery. The "first passage" was when a ship left England for Africa, carrying baubles, cheap industrial products that were bartered for slaves. Then began the dreadful "middle passage," to the American and Caribbean plantations, during which voyage many died and were thrown overboard. (It is estimated that as many as twenty million Africans were abducted from the continent.) The survivors were sold at auction; with the money realized, raw materials were purchased to feed the voracious industrial machines back home, and the ship began "the final passage," so much the richer for the "enterprise." Leila wishes to make her final passage back to the Caribbean, although, as already indicated, she may end up marooned and captive for the rest of her life: a different form of life imprisonment from that experienced by Rudy in *Higher Ground* (more on this later). On the other hand, the first section of the novel bears the subtitle "The End," describing Leila's departure from the Caribbean: the end may also be the beginning of a return after all. Her mother, dying in a London hospital, says, "London is not my home. . . . And I don't want you to forget that either" (124). Naipaul, in *The Middle Passage,* observes with detachment the subdued, bewildered immigrants herding onto the ship for England. Phillips presents us with the case of one out of those anonymous thousands, one from the historical statistics.

In the same collection of essays Naipaul describes St. Kitts as "an overpopulated island of sixty-eight square miles, producing a little sea-island cotton, having trouble to sell its sugar, and no longer growing the tobacco, the first crop of the settlers. . . . We were. . .watching the lights of the toy capital where people took themselves seriously enough to drive cars from one point to another" (24). He records his nightmare, "that I was back in tropical Trinidad" (43), a land indifferent to virtue as well as to vice (58). History, he argues (29), is built around achievement and creation, and nothing was created in the West Indies. (The epigraph of *The Final Passage* is from Eliot: "A people without history / Is not redeemed from time.") Slavery has bred self-contempt (71), and the "West Indian, more than most, needs writers to tell him who he is and where he stands" (73). Phillips undertakes a telling, and absence becomes the essence of the novel: absence of history and achievement, of scope in the present and hope for the future.

The second and longer section of the work is "Home." Michael's grandfather uses a metaphor to convey the island's cultural hybrid: yams from Africa, mangoes from India, and coconuts from the Pacific. The men almost miraculously find money to go drinking day and night, but it is not a glorious riot, a Bacchanalian celebration of life, but rather a drinking through boredom and hopelessness to a state of stupor. The island is a place where the sound of a motorcycle starting up is a sufficient event to attract adult spectators: "There's nothing here for me to do, nothing! . . . Nothing, man!" (53). Michael falls back on physical vanity: great care is taken over the length of his shirt sleeves and trousers; the motorcycle gives him the illusion of power, and he possesses the "freedom" that is a total denial of responsibility. In sleep, with pose and posturing set aside, his tired face crumbles like a bridge collapsing into rubble (62). He gets drunk on his wedding day and spends the night with Beverley, by whom he already has a son. As Leila's pregnancy advances, he moves into Beverley's shack and sees the baby for the first time when it is six weeks old.

In order to escape from the life in which she was trapped (95), Leila decides to emigrate to England. Michael's preparation for the challenges of this new life is to wonder whether or not to grow a moustache. Leila does all the packing; Michael drinks—and almost misses the ship. Leila's beauty, discipline, and determination attract Michael, but he feels inferior and, as a consequence, resentful. He has no understanding of himself, of the forces that have shaped him and account for his circumstances and behavior. He is an unthinking victim: his situation is all vague and confused but, nevertheless, real and damaging. His grandfather had advised, "You must hate enough, and you must be angry enough to get just what you want" (41), but disgruntled, destructive Michael is not clear about what he wants, much less how to set about getting it.

Unqualified, unskilled, and unprepared, Michael and Leila move into a depressed part of London, initially to a boardinghouse, where men sleep "head to toe" for want of space. The house they later rent is squalid.

> Two of the upstairs window panes were broken in, and the door looked like it had been put together from the remains of a dozen forgotten doors. . . .
>
> The light switch did not work. The house was dark and smelled of neglect. . . .
>
> Upstairs there was a solitary bedroom. A soiled double mattress lay prostrate in the middle of an otherwise naked floor. . . . The small bathroom consisted of a toilet bowl and a wash basin. . . . There was no bath, and the door to this room hung from its hinges. (161)

Michael's reaction is to walk out (escape), saying he expected to find the house in better shape on his return. Whether describing scene, house, character, or conduct, the narrator impassively, "factually" gives us the details.

> Michael forced his hand down between her legs and prised them open. Then he hauled himself on top of her, unable to take any of the weight himself. . . . But it was no good. He leaned over and vomited beside her head, catching the edge of the pillow and running back some of the vomit into her hair. Then, having emptied his stomach for the third time, he lay unconscious and draped across her. . . . She looked at the side of his head and waited until morning came. . . . (165)

Leila had booked passage on a ship, but a passage is also a path, an initiation, as in Forster's *Passage to India.* Having learned, she would rather retrace her steps and come to terms with life back home: there she has a friend who loves and understands her. Her experience is one that was shared by many: "home" is a plantation economy in dilapidation, with an imported population (the descendants of slaves and indentured laborers) without history or hope. Attempting to fashion a more meaningful life, they leave their stagnant societies and come to Britain, only to find that she can be as cruel as the heartless stepmother in fairy tales. Lacking education, training, and (especially the men) inner resources, encountering racial prejudice, reduced to mean employment, and restricted to certain areas for accommodation, they neither find nor are able to create opportunities. Since individuals like Michael are unaware of the impersonal forces that have damaged their lives, they continue the pattern: irresponsible, violent, fantasizing, trying to find temporary escape from a reality they do not comprehend and cannot combat. It is the reader who reaches an understanding.

The title of Phillips's second novel, *A State of Independence,*[3] recalls Naipaul's *In a Free State.* Bertram

Francis returns to his Caribbean home (having lived the last twenty years in Britain) three days before the country gains its independence. The island has turquoise coral and green forests, but outside the capital the houses are small fragile boxes with roofs of corrugated-iron sheets: "People seem just as poor as they always been" (*sic*, 19). In the naïve rhymes there are shades of Naipaul's perception of Caribbean politics: "Forward ever—backward never"; "Proud, Dignified and Black / None Can Take My Freedom Back!" There is a touch of satire in the doctor and the funeral director's joint ownership of a rum distillery, in the fire-brigade station's catching fire and burning down. And, as in most of what is hopefully called the "developing" world, there is exploitation: "Our finest minds . . . who all been overseas [*sic*] . . . are so bored with how easy it is to make money off the back of the people that they are getting drunk for kicks and betting on who can lap up the most sewage water from the gutter" (63).

Much of this is embodied in Jackson Clayton, once a close friend of and almost a brother to Bertram and now deputy prime minister as well as minister of agriculture, lands, housing, labor, *and* tourism. Among the things Clayton proudly claims to have done for his country is the bringing in of the luxury liner *Queen Elizabeth II* (with her affluent tourists), Pan American Airlines, and Hollywood films. In short, this man who once referred to himself as Jackson X, following the example of the radical Malcolm X, is a representative of Western capitalism rather than of the island's people. Made calloused and smug by wealth and power, Jackson now advocates closer ties with the United States, not because of a rejection of Britain and her imperial past but because the United States is commercially more promising to him. (Jackson imports Japanese cars via the U.S.) Independence means that, in addition to economic "clout," complete political power will now pass into such hands. To the people, celebrating independence is a patriotic excuse to drink more and longer than usual. It is an inefficient, poor, and polluted island, "And what is the response from the people with the money? The Rotary Club decide to donate a dustbin to every village. . . . As a people we come like prostitutes" (132). The people are not angry, not even cynical, but only apathetic. (Cynicism implies understanding.) Enter Bertram Francis.

Francis went on a scholarship to England but, after two years, was asked to leave college. Thereafter he drifted: "My time just slide away from me . . . there's plenty more just like me. . . . People who went there for five years, then one morning they wake up with grey hair and wonder what happened" (151).[4] Bertram returns with guilt and apprehension, after an absence of two decades. The airport runway is his welcome carpet, but otherwise, to adapt the words of Christopher Okigbo, he was the sole witness of his homecoming. It is not that Bertram has been away so long; it is not that he slacked in his studies and returns with nothing to show for all those years, but that during his absence he did not write to anyone—not to his mother, his brother Dominic, his girlfriend Patsy, or his friend Clayton—much less send the odd bit of money to his long and silently struggling mother. Bertram returns unaware that his brother, who had become an alcoholic, was killed by a hit-and-run driver. This failure in human relationships, and the obligations which go with them, is paralleled by our misgivings about his political stance.

Bertram returns because the country is about to become free. He did not help in the hunt and, in fact, showed no interest in it, but has come to see if he can get a share of the meat. He seems to think that the mere fact of his having lived in Europe is qualification enough, something that makes him superior. An obnoxious Clayton demands, "What do you have to offer us? What is it about yourself that you think might be of some benefit to our young country?" (110). All he has is a vague notion of setting up a commercial venture that will not depend on the white man. It is significant that he wants to "seize the opportunity" (50) by going into business: he does not think of a cooperative project, or rural development, or of education, but only of making money for himself. Neither in personal relationships nor in public matters is he any different from Clayton, and his sense of moral superiority is baseless. Most of the time between arrival and independence (three days later) he spends drinking bottle after bottle of beer. The positive characters are the minor ones (and all female): Bertram's mother; Mrs. Sutton, who, though old herself and having no obligation to do so, cares for Bertram's mother; and Patsy, who loves, forgives, is quietly cheerful, and takes back the failed and directionless man.

Bertram has lived "in a free state," one without commitment and duties, but now accepts his "mediocrity" (157), resumes his relationship with Patsy, and begins to wonder what he can do for his bedridden mother. (Perhaps nineteen-year-old Livingstone is his son.) As Bertram moves away from his selfish, sterile "freedom," the country is moving into *its* state of independence under the likes of the Honourable Jackson Clayton. Are the rains which disrupt the celebrations inauspicious or a sign of fertility and promise? A similar enigma is also faced at the end of Ngũgĩ wa Thiong'o's novel *A Grain of Wheat*.

Higher Ground,[5] subtitled "A Novel in Three Parts," consists of three stories. The first, "Heartland," is told by a "collaborationist" (an anachronistic term), an African who assists in the slave trade: "It is moments such as these . . . marooned between [the European traders and the enslaved Africans] . . . that the magnitude of my fall strikes me" (22). Circumstances have distorted the narrator—"If survival is a crime then I am guilty"—and there is a diminution of human feelings to the point of extinction. Because "Heartland" is a first-person narrative, the reader is situated within the consciousness of this man, and contradictory impulses result: between identification and sympathy, on the one hand, and recoil on the other. The reader must constantly remind her- or himself of the appalling wretchedness the slave trade inflicted, of the terror and misery. The brutality is heightened by the neutral tone of the narrator: "In the corner trading equipment is temporarily stored: whips, flails, yokes, branding-irons, metal masks" (15). Women are kept separate because they often attempt, mercifully, to take the lives of their children (16). The European slavers, who equate literacy, technological (military) superiority, and fine clothes with "civilization," are barbarous in conduct, often perverted and sadistic; but the African chiefs are also guilty of selling their own for baubles and beer (51).

This holocaust is little remembered because it was visited upon "natives" long ago, at a time when that graphic recorder of human cruelty, the camera, had not yet been invented. In the end the narrator resists and is himself transported to the United States as a slave. Beyond degradation, there is regeneration and moral recovery. He decides to feign ignorance of English, for competence in the language is a liability and has led to his being a tool in the exploitation of his own people. Caliban ostensibly forgoes Prospero's language yet is subversive in that he writes his memoir in it, using the language of the slave masters to indict them, to return, if not to his home across the ocean, then to himself: "We are promising ourselves that we will return to our people. . . . And the promise comes from deep inside of our souls" (60).

"Heartland" is told throughout in the present tense, which accords with the narrator's determination to keep the past alive and thus to "return" to it, yet it is more a memoir than a diary. As with that earlier African novel, *Houseboy*,[6] apart from literary conventions and a willing suspension of disbelief, the impact is such that we do not query how the narrator, given his circumstances, contrived to write, and preserve, his testimony.

Prisons have sometimes proved to be places of education, reflection, writing. At random, one thinks of Pandit Nehru of India and, from more recent times, of Kenya's Ngũgĩ and Nigeria's Soyinka. The letters that constitute "The Cargo Rap" (the longest and the most central of the three stories) are the direct descendants of the prison letters of George Jackson, published in 1970 as *Soledad Brother*. In 1960, at the age of eighteen, Jackson was misadvised to plead guilty to a charge of robbery and was sentenced to an indeterminate prison term of one year to life. In Soledad Prison he was accused of the murder of a white prison guard and transferred to San Quentin, pending trial. He was killed there on 21 August 1971 in circumstances that have never been satisfactorily explained. "Rudy," who writes the letters of "The Cargo Rap," is very similar to Jackson. He did not enter prison because of a politically motivated act, and his consciousness developed while he was in prison. As Jackson wrote, "I have almost arrived but look at the cost."

Both Jackson and the fictional Rudy arrive at an understanding of society and what it has done to them, but too late. Indeed, because of their awareness, consequent stance, and political influence, the system does not release them. Jackson's letters were to his parents, whom he loved (but about whose limitations—their mental shackles and timidity—he remained bitter and upbraiding); to his younger brother (shot dead while attempting to free him); to his lawyer Fay and to Angela Davis, the black activist. Rudy, also serving a "one year to life" sentence for robbery, writes to his parents, his sister, and two female lawyers. However, unlike in Jackson's case, finally it is not Rudy's life but his sanity that is killed. In style too, the letters—in one instance real, in the other fictional—are similar, for Jackson's correspondence ranges from sardonic, terse, and witty to impassioned protests of tremendous rhetorical power. Jackson belongs to history, however, and what is interesting in "The Cargo Rap" is the fictional Rudy: the processes by which character is created, the character himself, and his perceptions. Unlike *Soledad Brother: The Prison Letters of George Jackson,* "The Cargo Rap" must provide its own context, its own external data, necessary for an understanding of the fictional present.

The narrator of "Heartland" lived inside a fort, a stockade; Rudolph Leroy Williams is in prison, and prison becomes the metaphor for an unfree society and for captive lives: "It is only logical that two hundred years of exposure to the idea of a 'natural' (inferior) position should have nappied your mind" (63), Rudy writes to his mother. His teacher had told him that he had talent and could, one day, become a clerk: "He did not mention doctor, lawyer, judge, professor, or nuclear physicist. . . . He wanted me to make peace with my mediocrity" (76). Black Americans are released from the womb "only into the greater captivity of American society" (112), and prison brutality is but a reflection of that brutality which is present in society (147). Rudy describes himself as follows: "Name: Homo Africanus; Occupation: Survivor; Age: 200–300 years; Parents: Africans captured and made slaves; Education: American school of life" (91). The reader wonders whether this survivor will survive. Will he succeed in being moved from solitary confinement to the main block? Will he win parole? "In the bosom of this country there is a man who is being stretched and tortured for forty dollars" (163).

Rudy's passing references to a broken arm, a concussion, and to spitting blood indicate that the letters do not tell everything; this is an epistolary story, and the letters are all we have to go by: "I am once again down here on Max Row. I apologize to you for the disappointment that this will no doubt cause you" (162). What happened? Why is he back in the "maximum" (solitary) wing of the prison? His struggles are protracted, and there are increasing signs of irrationality. Don't let mother work so hard and physically, he writes, without confronting the reality that the family needs the money, that his mother cannot find other work. Has his sister lost her virginity? Can he pay his lawyers with fruit from Africa, once he is released and "returns" to that continent? And, writing to his father, he asks whether the latter still derives sexual pleasure from sleeping with Mother or whether he masturbates. Rudy's last letter, poignantly, is addressed to his mother, whose death a month earlier represented the proverbial final nail.

Since there is no narrator other than himself and the replies he receives are not included, Rudy is characterized solely through his letters. These can be direct, with a conversational casualness: "Come a Saturday night Mr Charlie likes nothing better than to go out and crack a coon [black man] or two" (64). Rudy educated himself politically, relying on books, and the language of these works enters his vocabulary with incongruous effects, so that in writing to his family we have "I'll amplify upon this in my next communication. . . . She is being malprogrammed in a hostile and alien culture" (64). He uses words and phrases such as "peruse" or "your senescent body" and pellucid disquisitions, but he can be succinct: "For half an hour each day, I breathe fresh, if not free, air" (68). Life in prison is like being inside not a boxing ring but the boxing glove itself: one passively and helplessly encounters pain. Rudy uses irony ("I tried to liberate some money"), puns ("We are trying to make the white Americans change their attitudes but are we getting any change [results]?"), and paradox ("I sit here in the darkness of constant light")— the last phrase also possessing biblical overtones of a people who sat in darkness and then saw a great light. He can be warm and persuasive, as when writing to his mother—"You describe yourself as an invalid. . . .

In-valid. . . . You are a very valid part of our world" (127)—or sardonic and bitter: "In the mornings, grandfather would get up, take down his cap and jacket, hang up his dignity and his mind, and slope out to slave and giggle for the white man" (73–74). He can rise to tremendous verbal power, reminiscent of protest and revivalist rhetoric: "Do you want mustard for your hot dog, flowers for your hair or bullets for your gun?" (169); "Hang in or hang up" (80). Black women in prison are there "for whoring, not warring." The black man needs "your support, not your scorn. . . . I am a literal and metaphorical prisoner, Moma. I need you to stand by me, not sit on me" (80). His perceptions and his power point to potential, and thus to the waste.

Rejecting the society in which he is a prisoner, Rudy turns (in order to fill the void) to the original home of his people, to Africa and to a "Negro Zionism" (124): "Is this America, the civilized country of satellites and color television? . . . We must flee and burn bridges behind us as we leave. . . . The dice are loaded, the terms are unacceptable, the American odds too long" (106–7). It is here that the setting (in terms of time) throws a cruel irony on Rudy: his (fictional) letters were written between January 1967 and August 1968; *Higher Ground* was published in 1989, and, seen from the perspective of the latter date, Rudy's vision of Africa is undercut and mocked. His heroes are Lumumba, Nyerere, and Kenyatta; he wishes to visit Egypt and Ethiopia, and then settle in Ghana. Patrice Lumumba of the Congo was killed before he could implement his policies, but Nyerere's long experiment with village socialism led Tanzania to economic ruin; indirectly admitting his mistakes and failure, he resigned from office. Jomo Kenyatta "hijacked" the Kenyan revolution and created an exploitative society, with his family and supporters being the beneficiaries—the structures Ngũgĩ condemns and opposes. Egypt has grave economic difficulties; so does Ghana, which has the added bane of military coups and violence. As for Ethiopia, it is now associated with extreme poverty, mass starvation, and the attempt to raise money through international music concerts. These are Rudy's ideal leaders and countries: the irony is gained by placing the story two decades back in time. Events and developments of the seventies and eighties subvert and mock Rudy, even as we are moved by his predicament and words, and leave the reader to make her or his own way out: a disturbed character, and a work that is disturbing in more ways than one.

The third story, "Higher Ground," begins with the narrator telling us that Irene did this, Irene did that, Irene, Irene, Irene. It is winter and the trees are naked; when they put on their clothes, so will Irene. We move from an outer observation of Irene to what she thinks and feels, and we realize that she has passed beyond what is termed normality. A headache is an iron handcuff around her head—again, the prison image. "Stop talking to yourself, you crazy Polish bitch" (177), shouts the incontinent old man next door, throwing a shoe at the dividing wall as an added expletive.

We gradually make sense of it all. Rachel and Irina were daughters of a Jewish shopkeeper in Poland: decent, caring parents; a frugal flat but well stocked with books; a close relationship between the sisters; prospects of university studies. Then Nazism reaches out, Rachel is beaten up and takes to her bed, and the sisters no longer attend school. There is talk of mother and daughters escaping while father remains to tidy up and sell the shop. (How can one abruptly abandon a shop slowly built up over the years? And he could not have known the virulence of the evil coming closer.) The ominous minutes of history tick by, and suddenly it is too late. Time only to hustle Irina, clutching the family photographs, to Vienna and so to England. Working in a factory, she meets and goes out with Reg, gets pregnant, and miscarries; relieved of responsibility in this way, he abandons her. She meets Louis from the Caribbean; he has been in London ten days and has already decided to return home, on the reasoning that "it was better to return as the defeated traveller than be praised as the absent hero and live a life of spiritual poverty" (197). There is a strong affinity between them; but Louis is determined to return, and Irene is left to her loneliness. In the face of her alienation and total loss (parents, sister, home, language, and even name, with *Irina* Anglicized into *Irene*), destruction seems inevitable. In his book-length essay *The European Tribe* Phillips writes that the exploitation and sufferings of black people were not in his school curriculum, nor did they find articulation on television and in the media: "As a result I vicariously channelled a part of my hurt and frustration through the Jewish experience."[7]

Joseph Conrad in his "Author's Note" to *Youth* wrote that the three stories "lay no claim to unity of artistic purpose"; *Higher Ground* is described as a novel in three parts. However, one expects a degree of integration within a novel, and if, for example, the work produces new characters, we assume they will be related, however tenuously, to the preceding characters. The three parts of *Higher Ground* take us from Africa and the slave trade, to the United States of the 1960s, and finally to Britain during and shortly after World War II. The characters are an African, a black American, and a Polish-Jewish woman. Therefore, to claim that *Higher Ground* is a novel—not short stories on the same theme—is to urge readers to see the stories as a unity.

The work is a triptych, and it is not only that when we place the three parts together they form a unity—of damaged and hurt lives—but that there emerges a significance which no one part by itself can communicate with such clarity and force: "If one takes a piece of banal journalistic prose and sets it down on a page as a lyric poem, surrounded by intimidating margins of silence, the words remain the same but their effects for readers are substantially altered."[8] So too, by the simple device of asserting that *Higher Ground* is a novel, Phillips makes us approach it as a single, unified work, and to respond and draw significance accordingly.

Can Phillips be described as a British (or a black British) writer? In the bulk of Conrad's work, Poland—in terms of setting—is not significant, yet his Polish life shaped a part of his basic awareness. So too with Phillips, and even if little of his work thus far is set in England, his British years, from infancy to manhood, have given him great advantages. The term *advantages* may surprise, given the degree of racism—covert or overt, suave or crude—that pervades contemporary Britain. Still, I would argue that having grown up in Britain has heightened Phillips's awareness and fine (in the two meanings of *sharp* and *excellent*) sensitivity. This is not to suggest that Phillips is some bruised plant trembling delicately in unkind winds. His difference and exile have positively defined him; they make up his essential being, and, if often a source of hurt or anger, of alienation and loneliness, they also constitute his awareness and strength. It is the turning of what a hostile society and a denigrating culture would impose as misfortune and limitation into advantage and a wonderful broadening out of understanding and sympathy, a turning of prisons into castles (with acknowledgment to George Lamming and his novel *In the Castle of My Skin*), a moving from pain to knowledge and beyond to joy, pride, and thence to celebration.

To return to the question, can Phillips be labeled "British" despite his "return" to the Caribbean? Not to do so would leave our taxonomic lust unsatisfied. If anything, his latest work, *Higher Ground,* shifting from the days of slavery somewhere on the coast of black Africa to a contemporary maximum-security prison cell in the United States and then to a Polish-Jewish woman suffering incomprehension, loneliness, and a breakdown in Britain during World War II, shows a liberated Phillips, a writer who can penetrate the inner being of people vastly different from himself in time, place, and gender, yet people very much like us all in the common and eternal human inheritance of pain and suffering. In a recent essay Phillips writes that his "branches have developed, and to some extent continue to develop and grow, in Britain" but that his "roots are in Caribbean soil."[9] Eluding labels that will seize and fix him, he finally remains Caryl Phillips.

If one were to ask what unifies the fictional works of Phillips, I would turn to the words of the Spaniard Camilo José Cela (winner of the 1989 Nobel Prize in Literature), who said that he is on the side not of those who make History but of those who *suffer* History. In Phillips's work there is a strong sense of historical violence and its consequences, of resulting journeys and alienation, but also the effort to find (or make for oneself) a little peace. As Rudy urged from prison, don't let anyone take away your dreams.

Charles P. Sarvan and Hasan Marhama, Winter 1991

1 Caryl Phillips, *The Final Passage,* London, Faber & Faber, 1985 (reprinted 1989).

2 Reference to V. S. Naipaul, *The Middle Passage,* is to the Penguin Books edition, London, 1969 (reprinted 1988).

3 Caryl Phillips, *A State of Independence,* London, Faber & Faber, 1986 (reprinted 1989).

4 This so-called urban drift is common not only with Third World migrants to the West but also *within* these countries. Characterized by the attempt to make good in the city, time imperceptibly slips by and one feels a reluctance to return home empty-handed and a failure. See, for example, Meja Mwangi's *Kill Me Quick.*

5 Caryl Phillips, *Higher Ground,* New York, Viking Penguin, 1989. For a review, see *WLT* 64:3 (Summer 1990), p. 518.

6 See C. P. Sarvan, "French Colonialism: The Early Novels of Ferdinand Oyono," *WLT* 59:3 (Summer 1985), pp. 333–37.

7 Caryl Phillips, *The European Tribe,* London, Faber & Faber, 1987. See paperback edition (Faber), 1988, p. 54.

8 Jonathan Culler, *Structuralist Poetics,* London, Routledge & Kegan Paul, 1975, p. 161.

9 Caryl Phillips, "Living and Writing in the Caribbean: An Experiment," *Kunapipi* (Denmark), 11:2, (1989).

Kamau Brathwaite: The Voice of African Presence

In May this year my wife and I called a few friends to our house in Orange, New Jersey, to celebrate the arrival of our daughter, born at the end of April. Among them was Kamau Brathwaite, who later rose to read a poem to honor the new arrival. The poem had lines that repeated the name of our daughter, Mūmbi, Mūmbi, Mūmbi, Mūmbi, almost like a religious chant. Now *Mūmbi* means "creator," and we gave our daughter the name because she is in fact my mother, Wanjikū, who died in 1989 but is now reborn in Mūmbi. Her full name, then, is Mūmbi Wanjikū, creator of my mother. Mūmbi is also the name of the original mother of all

Kamau Brathwaite *(Gil Jain)*

Gīkūyū people. In thinking about the evening afterwards, I was struck anew by Kamau Brathwaite's invocation of the name.

My thoughts took me back to 1972, when Kamau, then Edward Brathwaite, came to the Department of Literature at Nairobi University, Kenya, on a City of Nairobi Fellowship. The department was undergoing tremendous changes. We were trying to break away from the old colonial tradition that emphasized our colonial connections to Europe as primary but not our natural connections to Africa and the rest of the world. We are all familiar with the often-told stories of African children having to learn all about daffodils and snow long before they are able to name the flowers of their own lands. Rebellion against this was the basis of the 1969 Nairobi declaration calling for the abolition of the English Department as then constituted and for its restructuring along entirely new lines. By 1972 we had started breaking away from the centrality of English literature in our syllabus to a new dispensation that emphasized the centrality of the African experience at home on the continent and abroad in the Caribbean, Afro-America, and other parts of the world. We wanted a dialogue among all the literatures of the entire pan-African universe and between them and those of South America, Asia, and

Europe in that order. Central to the enterprise was ora-ture, the long tradition of verbal arts passed from mouth to ear in both their classical and contemporary expressions. Other needs arose from the new centrality. For instance, instead of inviting Shakespearean scholars from England, we now wanted scholars from the rest of Africa, from the Caribbean, and from Afro-America. That kind of academic exchange and communication would be more useful to us in cementing the new foundation of our literary and cultural studies. We were also rebelling against a tradition that taught literature as if it was divorced from its social and historical milieu. We wanted to see, explore connections between phenomena. So we hoped that we would get scholars with a sensitive awareness of the connections between literature and life. Who was going to be our first visitor? This was a crucial question, particularly in our new beginnings: suppose we brought a scholar who would come to reinforce the very traditions we were now fighting against?

I had met Edward Brathwaite in London in 1966 when I was doing research on Caribbean literature at Leeds University. It was a gathering which in fact was the formal beginning of the Caribbean Arts Movement. I did not know then that Brathwaite was its founding spirit. Even less did I know that at different but crucial moments in our literary lives we had both been influenced in a fundamental way by one of the classics of Barabajan and Caribbean literature, George Lamming's *In the Castle of My Skin.* For me, Kamau's brilliant poems in *Rights of Passage,* out in 1967 and followed by *Masks* in 1968 and *Islands* in 1969, had added to that sense of self-discovery. In this I was not alone. Those collections became part of the new syllabus. There was in fact something about their content and form that made everybody feel that they fit the historical moment, this our search for a connection. And so there was really little doubt as to whom we wanted as our first scholar of what we saw as the beginnings of a new era. Brathwaite was then teaching history at the University of the West Indies' Mona Campus in Jamaica. We were very excited when he accepted our invitation, although the fellowship did not really amount to much in terms of money. As a lecturer, he proved a great teacher. He saw no barriers between geography, history, and literature. What formed the African and Caribbean sensibility could not be divorced from the landscape and the historical experience.

This to me is still one of the most remarkable elements in the life and work of Kamau Brathwaite. He is a connecting spirit. Europe, Africa, the Caribbean, and now America, all important landmarks in his life and thought, find expression in his work in their impact on one another. He explores the African presence in Africa,

the Caribbean, and the world, not in its staticness but in its movement, in its changingness, in its interactions. In these interactions the African presence is not a passive element. Whether across the Sahara deserts, through the savannas and tropical forests, across the Atlantic, say, in all its continental and diasporic dimensions, it is a resisting spirit, refusing to succumb, ready to rebuild anew from the ashes of natural disasters and human degradation. In his work, taken as a whole, the physical cannot be divorced from the metaphysical or the material from the religious. In his capacity to move freely from geography to history to literature to cultural criticism, Brathwaite exemplifies a great tradition of the Caribbean intellectual, the tradition of C. L. R. James, Frantz Fanon, Walter Rodney, Aimé Césaire, George Lamming, to mention just a few who readily come to mind. What connects these names, apart from their intellectual versatility, is also their unapologetic claim to Africa as their roots. These islands have given so much to twentieth-century Africa and the world, and our students in Nairobi could now see that for themselves in the presence of the lecturer before them. It was remarkable, and Brathwaite was the talk among the students and faculty.

But it was when Edward Brathwaite performed sections from his poems that we truly appreciated what we had been sensing. The voice. We were being mesmerized by the voice of orature. We were captives of a heritage we knew so well but from which our education had been alienating us. His voice was returning us to our formative roots in *orature.* This was what had been created by our mothers and fathers, and it was there in his performance for us all to see. This orality runs through Brathwaite's entire work and is what gives it its very distinctive quality. This comes out powerfully through performance and makes us realize that, in his literary output, Brathwaite gropes for the word in its oral purity. In doing so, he is groping for the voice of the peasant, the submerged voice of the many who toil and endure.

But alas, our enthusiasm was not necessarily shared by the establishment, who thought they had already given in too much by agreeing to have a scholar who came from places other than England itself, the real home of real literature. Tension was in fact developing between, on the one hand, the students and the faculty, who understood, and on the other the administrative establishment, who could not realize whom we had in our midst and treat him accordingly.

Then something happened that I will never forget. I invited Brathwaite to my rented home in Tigoni, Limuru. The land around Tigoni and Limuru is truly beautiful. Not surprisingly, Tigoni was fairly central to Kenya's history, because it was one of the earliest bones of contention between the British colonial settlers and Kenyans. The demand for the return of the stolen lands of Tigoni to their original owners was one of the key elements in the anticolonial militancy which in the fifties erupted into the Mau Mau armed struggle. The fact that now in the seventies Tigoni was occupied by African landlords, though not the actual original owners, symbolized that Kenya was no longer exclusively a white man's country. Brathwaite was coming into an area hallowed with memories of intense struggles.

I should add that the invitations to meet Brathwaite were sent solely through word of mouth. It turned out to be a big welcome party, with the faculty and some students driving thirty kilometers from Nairobi to attend the gathering. Women led by my mother came from all the villages around. So the peasants from the villages and the men and women of letters from Nairobi, the big city, now gathered in this rural outpost to celebrate Brathwaite's presence. Ceremonial goats were slaughtered in his honor. The women performed. The voice of orality from rural Kenya. It was during the ceremony, with the women singing Gĩtiiro, a kind of dialogue in song and dance, that Edward Brathwaite was given the name of Kamau, the name of a generation that long ago had struggled with the elements to tame the land and make us into what we now were. Edward, the name of the British king under whose brief reign in the 1920s some of the Tigoni lands had been appropriated by blue-blooded aristocrats who wanted to turn Kenya into a white man's country, had now been replaced by Kamau. Naming Brathwaite became the heart of the ceremony, which was also symbolically appropriate.

The right to name ourselves, our landscape; the struggle for the means with which to name ourselves; the search, in other words, for the true voice of our collective being—is this not at the heart of Kamau Brathwaite's work from *Rights of Passage* in 1967 to the *Barabajan Poems* in 1994 and elaborated in his critical works, now collected under the suggestive title *Roots?* The right, the process, and the means to name our world are behind his notion of the Nation Language, that submerged language of the enslaved which, through evolutionary and at times revolutionary subversion of the dominating, asserts itself, often changing the character of what was supposed to be the mainstream.

It was this ceremony way back in 1972 that I was remembering when going over Kamau's invocations on Mũmbi's name in May this year. Little did Kamau know that he was actually invoking the name of my mother and that of all the peasants who welcomed him in 1972 and gave him his name, asserting through song and dance that he was being welcomed in the lands where his ancestral umbilical cord had been buried. Didn't

know? That is not even true, because all his work is really an invocation of the power of the African peasantry in all its struggles in Africa, the Caribbean, and the world. He is saying that if we are to claim the twentieth and twenty-first century properly and creatively, we have to connect ourselves to that power. Acknowledgment of the past becomes the basis of strengthening the present and opening out to the future.

Kamau and I are now in the same Department of Comparative Literature at New York University, for reasons that well go back to what we were trying to do at Nairobi in the seventies and therefore what had made possible that invitation; but that is another story. Tonight, my wife and I are very touched at being asked to be part of this truly great occasion in honor of one of the most remarkable voices of the twentieth century. For we are celebrating thirty years of a continuous creative output in theater, poetry, criticism, and history, from his plays published in 1964 to his most recent production, *Barabajan Poems,* in 1994. We are celebrating a producer who through journals like *Savacou* has created forums for others. We are celebrating a teacher who has drawn from, and given back to, Africa, the Caribbean, Europe, and the USA. We are celebrating a gifted individual who believes in the collective spirit as seen in his work as the founding spirit of efforts like the Caribbean Arts Movement. We are celebrating the voice of connections, because what is so remarkable about him is not that he is a great poet, historian, critic, and teacher, but that these are not separate entities in himself. They are rather expressions of a searching spirit, searching for the connective link in human life and struggles. We are also celebrating a most courageous man who has gone through personal adversities without succumbing to the death of the spirit. In congratulating Kamau for the 1994 Neustadt Prize, we wish him all the best as we eagerly wait for his many future productions. We hope he will continue to inspire us to join hands so that individually and collectively, we, to paraphrase him, can make here, on these broken grounds . . . something torn and new . . . , a communal future of wholeness.

Ngũgĩ wa Thiong'o, Autumn 1994

CARIBBEAN IN FRENCH

The Role of the Writer

Writers are often asked, "When did you start writing?" or "How did you become a writer?" Nobody knows what the answer is, so the writer makes up his or her own clever little story. I have no story to fabricate. I am simply going to tell an episode which is my best possible answer on the matter.

When I was a child of seven or eight, I was very fond of my mother, as little girls are. At the same time I was very much afraid of her, because she was a schoolteacher, and this position in those days carried a lot of prestige. For instance, every morning when she went to school, two of her pupils preceded her. One of them would carry the pile of exercise books that she had corrected the night before. The other would carry her books. She herself followed behind under her parasol. So every morning there was a procession like the one of an African queen. For her birthday I decided to write a one-act play illustrating the many facets of her character such as mother and teacher. When the day came, I read my play to her, and to my surprise she became very upset. She nearly cried. "I'm not at all the person you describe," she said. "I am not at all like this."

Thus at a very young age I discovered that writing is a very perilous exercise. If you write what you believe to be true, you displease. You are in danger of being beaten or jailed or even killed. At the same time, by making my mother cry, I felt a very intoxicating kind of power. I decided to renew the experience. Writing is largely enjoying the pleasure of displeasing.

Tonight I have been asked to talk to you about my book *Tree of Life* (in French *La vie scélérate*). Don't ask me to start with why *La vie scélérate* became *Tree of Life*. That is the secret of my American publisher, like the design of the book jacket. Although the jacket is undoubtedly beautiful, its bright orange color suggests exoticism. It means that the author of the novel comes from a part of the world where life is supposed to be more colorful than in the USA.

However, *Tree of Life* is not, it seems, colorful and exotic. It stems from a bitter experience. When I started it in 1985, it was at the end of a twelve-year stay in Africa. I was in a state of complete confusion, as all the values I used to believe in were shattered. In my younger days I was a convinced Marxist. People of my generation all believed in Marxism. We were convinced that this ideology would bring about the end of colonialism and usher in a new era of happiness and freedom for the Third World. After my years in Africa, however, I could not decide whether Marxism itself was an evil or whether it was turned into evil because leaders were manipulating it. In fact, I had doubts long before the East European countries started rebelling against their political regimes. If Marxism was the wrong path, what other path should I have followed?

Revolution was another concern of mine. I was a very avid reader of Frantz Fanon, who said that revolution was not only the changing of a country's political status but also the changing of the people's inner selves.

After a successful revolution a new man and a new woman would emerge, strong enough to build a new world. Was it possible to have that sort of revolution? I never witnessed any in all my years in Africa.

Race was my third concern. My parents had brought me up in the idea that to be black implied a solidarity, a unique brotherhood with people of the same color. During my student years in Paris I became enthused with the ideals of pan-Africanism. Unfortunately, later on, I was to see black leaders oppressing black people in Guinea; I was to see black people forced into exile because of their political opinions. So I came to the conclusion that race might be an empty word.

Marxism, revolution, race—all these notions had been shattered. I was in this state of confusion when I received a letter from a young lady called Nadia. She told me that she had read and enjoyed my novel *Ségou*. After seeing me on television, she had inquired about me and discovered that her family name was identical to my maiden name. After further inquiries she had discovered that she was a cousin of mine, the granddaughter of my great-uncle, Albert. What did I know about him? Did I know that he had a son named after him, Albert Junior? Albert Junior? When I was a child in our family house in Pointe-à-Pitre there were all sorts of photographs on the walls. Middle-class people in the Caribbean like to have photos everywhere of grandfathers, great-grandfathers, and so on, to show where they come from and their social ascendancy. One of them depicted a mulatto boy of about six or seven, dressed in a blue-and-white sailor suit. It was bizarre to have a mulatto child in my family, where everybody was black and proud to be so. Whenever I asked about that unusual-looking boy, the answers were very vague. Apart from his name, Albert, nobody seemed to know exactly who he was. Nadia and I went to see her grandmother, Marie, who lived in the town of Saumur on the banks of the River Loire, famous for its white wine. She told me the complete story.

Albert Senior was my grandfather's son by a previous wife and was sent to study engineering in Saumur. Can you imagine the life of a black boy in a French provincial town circa 1920? He was lonely, he was desperate, when he met her. She was working in a wine-cork factory. They had an affair, and of course she got pregnant. At that time I must say that my family was very religious. My mother used to get up at five o'clock in the morning to go to first mass. As Albert Senior had been brought up in this tradition, he could not abandon her and proposed marriage. My grandfather was so incensed at his son marrying a white woman that he stopped sending him his allowance to pay for his studies. Poor Albert Senior had to take a job with the

French electric company. Life was hell! Finally one day he committed suicide. He left her with a baby boy who bore his name.

Marie told me how over the years she had sent letters and pictures of the baby to my family in the hope of interesting them in her plight. She never got any answer. When he was twenty, Albert Junior decided to go to Paris and become a musician. Apparently things did not work out, as he too committed suicide, leaving her with his very young daughter, Nadia. Such a story only added to my "angst."

I decided to write about my family, not only the official version but also the untold facts. I decided to present lovable and dignified people who at the same time could be mean and cruel. This story would have larger implications and express my doubts about culture and politics as well. *Tree of Life* garnered an award from the Académie Française, but in Guadeloupe it was not well received. People objected to what they called its cynicism and dark sides. Even now this book is my forgotten novel. At colloquia scholars like to give papers on *Hérémakhonon* or *I, Tituba, Black Witch of Salem* or *Traversée de la mangrove*. It is easy to speak about *Hérémakhonon*, since it is the story of an alienated girl going to Africa. Critics are eager to condemn her lack of political consciousness and her dependency on men. Tituba seems a fascinating character, the embodiment of the entanglement of the visible and invisible in the Caribbean. *Traversée de la mangrove* is more lyrical, with its description of nature and rural life in Guadeloupe. But *Tree of Life* raises too many embarrassing questions.

At what cost do you become middle-class? What sort of compromise should you make? How far must you alienate yourself from your people? There is a scene in the novel which is based on my childhood memories and which for me sums up this painful divorce between the middle class and the poorer classes. My father had a lot of tenement houses all over Pointe-à-Pitre, but he would not go himself to collect the rent. So he used to send my elder brother and myself. Can you imagine two kids coming to collect the rent? The poor tenants, who could not pay, shouted insults at us. One day a man threw a stone at my brother, who, in his eyes, represented my father.

Why does anyone want to become middle-class? What do you gain from it? If one decides that after all it is not worth the trouble, can one go back to the people? In the novel two characters try desperately to return to their roots: first, Thecla, who believes that she must start a revolution to abolish the class structure but never succeeds; second, Jean, who renounces his studies and settles in a village among the peasants. He devotes his energies to writing a book and does not succeed any better than Thecla, since he dies at the end of the novel.

Another reason why *Tree of Life* displeased Guadeloupean readers is the fact that it takes place in Panama, the USA, Jamaica, and Haiti. Even the most superficial study of literature from the West Indies demonstrates that every writer keeps to his or her island. Personally, I do not share this viewpoint, believing instead in a West Indian identity, regardless of colonial language and political status. I feel as much at home in Jamaica as in Martinique or Guadeloupe. People from the Caribbean share a common history and are united by a common experience. Such a belief does not contradict my doubts about pan-Africanism. In fact, it is based on it. The people of the diaspora suffered a common estrangement from their motherland, but they remain as close to one another as orphans. For them it is essential to come to terms with the image of Africa. Too often they see Africa as a myth of beauty and lost grandeur but refuse to be concerned with the actual problems of the continent. I remember my conversation in Berkeley with a Nigerian girl who was working with the African-American-studies program. She complained that she could never speak with her colleagues about present-day Nigeria because they did not want to listen to her. They did not want to hear about coups d'état, military oppression, and boundless suffering. They just wanted to know about the Yoruba bronzes and the Benin masks.

Tree of Life also raised a very important question: what is it like to be a West Indian woman? Male novelists portray women only as mothers or grandmothers. They are interested only in the maternal function. In the French Caribbean classic *La Rue Cases-Nègres* (1950; Eng. *Black Shack Alley*) by the Martinican novelist Joseph Zobel, Man Tine sacrifices her entire life to her grandson José and symbolically dies when he reaches adulthood. As a female I cannot accept being restricted to motherhood, however important it is. Looking at the women in my family, I have the impression that the more educated they became the less liberated they were, so to speak. The educated women of my family tried to conform to "the angel in the house" image, which is so harmful, as demonstrated by Virginia Woolf. A quick parallel between my grandmother and my mother will illustrate my point. My grandmother was born on the small island of Marie-Galante, off the coast of Guadeloupe. She was almost totally illiterate. At the age of sixteen she left her home to go and work in Pointe-à-Pitre, where she soon gave birth to my mother. Who was the father? He seems to have abandoned my grandmother very early on and never took any responsibility for the education of his daughter. This did not seem to matter much to my grandmother. She raised my mother all by herself and managed to make one of the first schoolteachers of her generation out of her. Her story is one of independence and self-assertion. Although highly educated by the standards of that time, my mother voluntarily abandoned all authority to the man she married at an early age, who was twenty years older than she. She "had read books," but she had no say in our education, in the use of the family properties, or in the management of finances. She was extremely conscious of her appearance and was very proud to be termed one of the most beautiful women of her generation. Therefore I come to the striking conclusion that the more you lose your illiteracy, the more you lose confidence in yourself. Because of those contradictory images, I had a hard time choosing a role for myself. Should I fight for a career and get an impressive array of degrees? Should I have children and devote myself to them? Thecla is faced with that impossible choice. Her ambition is to write a highly intellectual book. Therefore she neglects her daughter and does not know how to show her affection.

However, the main concern in *Tree of Life* is with literature. What should a West Indian author write about? Depicting Caribbean society, must he or she respect the canon set by previous writers and conform to committed literature? Coco, the narrator of the novel and the youngest of the family, decides what she is going to write about: a novel in which there will be no heroes, no important personalities, just ordinary human beings; a novel in which capitalism and economic exploitation will not be the only issues dealt with, but also love, dreams, and fantasies.

In conclusion, I wish to touch briefly on a widely discussed topic: *créolité*. This new literary movement is emerging in the wake of Aimé Césaire's *négritude* and Edouard Glissant's *antillanité*. We must return to history. What does it mean to be a Creole? To be a Creole simply means "to be born in the islands." From the sixteenth century, missionaries and travelers alike called "Creole" not only the white people but also the blacks born on the plantation. The Creole people possessed a distinctive way of life and a distinctive way of expressing themselves. If we accept this historical definition, a Creole person enjoys the right and the freedom to express his or her *créolité* as he or she pleases. The expression of this identity is not restricted to the use of the Creole language, which is part of a linguistic continuum. To quote Wilson Harris, the writer can go beyond it, since "language is the ground of an interior and active expedition through and beyond what is already known." Moreover, the end of the twentieth century is

witnessing a massive migration of the peoples of the Caribbean, driven away by political hardship and economic instability. A million Haitians are living outside their native island. Great Britain is inhabited by colonies of Jamaicans and Trinidadians whom she strives to integrate under the false name of "Black British." Guadeloupeans and Martinicans are living in France. Does the word *Creole* not need to be reevaluated? It used to designate the population of the islands at a time when migration and exile were unknown. Nowadays it is a fact that the majority of the West Indians are not Creole. Does it mean that their writing should be excluded from Caribbean literature? Or treated as second-class literature?

I am sorry that I have raised so many questions and have given so few answers. However, this is how I see the role of the writer.

Maryse Condé, Autumn 1993

Gender Construction and Neocolonialism

Between Europe and America I see only specks of dust.

■ *ATTRIBUTED TO CHARLES DE GAULLE ON VISIT TO MARTINIQUE*[1]

The Antilles, Maryse Condé has said, are an artificial construct of the capitalist system: "The paradox is that, taking everything into account, born of a truly artificial creation, the Antillean people nevertheless exist. But if one looks at their origins, one understands that their problems are complex."[2] Given that the origins of the West Indies include elements transplanted from Europe, Africa, and Asia as well as the indigenous population of Arawak and Carib Indians now virtually extinct, Guadeloupeans encounter particular dilemmas because of their diverse cultural heritage. Condé explains the specific context of the colonization of the Caribbean and the resulting predicament.

> The colonial problem was not that of the importation of a foreign culture and of its imposition onto a national reality which it slowly attempted to destroy—as is the case in most colonized countries. Rather, the problem lay in the difficulty inherent in the attempt to construct, from the incongruous and dissimilar elements that coexist in such a general climate of aggression, harmonious cultural forms.[3]

This attempt to construct West Indian culture has been termed *métissage* by Edouard Glissant in *Le discours antillais* (1981; Eng. *Caribbean Discourse*), similar to Claude Lévi-Strauss's notion of *bricolage*. Maryse Condé's first novel, *Hérémakhonon* (1976), addresses this problem encountered by the postcolonial subject who attempts to gain some understanding of her cultural identity by searching for her "roots." Her work raises the important question of representation: how do Caribbean-based authors "represent" their gender, ethnicity, culture, et cetera? How do they use language to construct and reconstruct their ethnic identity? What figures of rhetoric operate in these texts? The discussion which follows will answer these questions by addressing a first-person narrative from the Caribbean, Condé's *Hérémakhonon,* in relation to prevailing theories about gender and identity construction in the Caribbean.

▪ WOMEN'S STRATEGIES IN THE POSTCOLONIAL NARRATIVE

"Francophone" writers use *métissage* or creolization to construct their cultural identity. *Creolization* is the term J. Michael Dash uses in translating Glissant's *Discours antillais,* yet in the present context I prefer to use *métissage* because of its connotations in French of forced racial mixing as opposed to the free choice implied by the English word *creolization. Métissage* is used by Glissant and quoted by Françoise Lionnet in *Autobiographical Voices: Race, Gender and Self-Portraiture;* it implies cross-cultural, nonhierarchical relations across different components in Caribbean history. As Lionnet makes clear, such a mixture of cultural forms involves relational rather than hierarchical systems: for example, West Indian oral traditions are privileged, as can be the influence and tools of the colonizer. When writing as postcolonial or neocolonial subjects, then, Caribbean authors must necessarily demonstrate heterogenous ethnic identities and layered, diverse language systems. In their writing they draw on numerous indigenous components existing in a hostile climate, including remnants of African cultural practices: *quimbois,* Obeah, oral traditions (as exemplified in the use of Creole languages, proverbs, storytelling), an emphasis on dream imagery and "magic" that becomes in "Western" eyes a sort of "marvelous realism." At the same time, the writers borrow from the "colonizer": intertextual references to "high" French literature, reference to colonial education and culture, and the use of both "metropolitan" French or English and slang. The writers use these diverse components to construct that which has become and is becoming Caribbean literature and culture to affirm their colonial and postcolonial identities simultaneously. The signifying practices represented here are common to peoples who had to learn such practices as survival tactics. This mixing or "transculturation" is especially evident in the fiction produced by Caribbean women, whose textual production often mirrors the writers' own production by historical circumstance.

That is, women writers serve a particular function in a *métissage* culture that men may not.

In her *Autobiographical Voices* Lionnet discusses the importance of women writers in the postcolonial situation. They must rediscover their pasts and rewrite their history in their own words, transforming that which has been suppressed by those who have held cultural power. For example, Lionnet calls Condé's writing "an unrelenting search for a different past, to be exhumed from the rubble of patriarchal and racist obfuscations."[4] Lionnet, too, finds Glissant's analysis of *métissage* useful in interpreting texts by so-called Third World women. Calling *métissage* a "braiding of cultural forms" (*AV,* 11), she uses the metaphor of weaving to elucidate the concept for the specific cases of women: "The use women writers make of both Western literary (or religious) traditions and vernacular cultures (or dialects) contributes to a form of intertextual weaving or mé-tissage of styles" (*AV,* 29).

As a "Northern" Euro-American critic, my challenge is not to see how the Caribbean writer does or does not fit into my definitions of feminisms, but to see how she wrestles with the various aspects of being a woman that are particular to her cultural, geographic, and political situation. Overlapping (and even conflicting) issues of gender and race particular to ethnic groups in the Caribbean may well affect the writer's representation of her gender in ways not immediately evident to "Western" readers. Another key distinction is that Caribbean women, unlike most male Caribbean writers, examine specifically gendered issues from the perspective of those who are doubly or triply marginalized in terms of gender, ethnicity, and geography. If the writing to be discussed is feminine, it is in the sense elucidated by Lionnet in *Autobiographical Voices.* She claims that women rewrite the "feminine" by valorizing it, by showing the arbitrary nature of the values and images feminized by patriarchal culture which constructs, distorts, and encodes them as inferior and thus "feminine." Of course, the writers' identity comes not solely from cultural or ethnic groups, but also from their mothers or other women; thus, the matrifocal emphasis is particular to women writers.

"Western" or "Northern" feminist critics may all too easily appropriate works of marginalized women for their own purposes, locating their versions of "feminism" in these works without regard for cultural specificity. A work may emphasize gender without necessarily being "feminist" (that is, stressing gender construction in relation to a specific political agenda). To highlight differences between themselves and "Northern" critics interested in gender, Caribbean feminists use *womanist* as one way to refer to their feminism.

Womanism, a term first used by Alice Walker, need not merely imply essential racial differences between women (Caribbean women versus "Northern" women, women of color versus white women), but signals a redefinition of feminism that does not attribute feminism to what has been constructed as "the West" or white, bourgeois women (certainly not a monolithic category, but the direction in which feminist inquiry tends to veer). The term *womanism* is thus foregrounded by Carole Boyce Davies and Elaine Savory Fido, who note, in *Out of the Kumbla: Caribbean Women and Literature,* "a consistent move to find new language to encompass our experience."[5]

In other words, a term other than *feminism,* a term free of assumptions and cultural baggage, has been needed by Caribbeans to describe the experience of African-Caribbean women, marginalized both geographically and ethnically. Fido interprets feminism as typically having a political agenda, whereas she sees womanism as more of a cultural manifestation: like *métissage,* it encompasses women's discourse, stories, cultural practices such as Obeah, speaking Creole, using proverbs. In the same text Davies also sees womanism as a "redefinition of the term feminism as applied to experiences other than those of Western and white women."[6] Obviously, critics cannot negate their subject positions, but in exploring the theoretical constructions surrounding Caribbean women, they can ground their knowledge in something other than essentialized experience, or a "universalist" position.

Maryse Condé exemplifies this corrective womanist practice of *métissage,* for she illustrates the specificity of how Caribbean women represent gender differently from U.S. or European white women: she is from a postcolonial (or neocolonial) culture, and her writing expresses outrage at injustice. Véronica, the narrator of *Hérémakhonon,* is geographically displaced (in Paris and Africa); she is searching for roots (which changes her course by the end of the novel), and she ends up far from her origins (in an unnamed West African country recognizable as French Guinea). The narrative perspective shifts without warning from memory to present life, from country of origin to country of exile.

By looking at Condé's work, then, readers can trace relevant issues in terms of her treatment of gender construction, geographic and cultural displacement, intertextuality, and representation of history within fiction. *Hérémakhonon* thus explores the political and psychological contradictions of a multiple identity constructed from various warring elements. Through intertextuality, a literary rendering of *métissage,* Condé demonstrates the complexities of Caribbean culture and identity.

▪ SEXUAL POLITICS

Maintaining a cynical distance from her sexual activity, Condé's narrator explores heterosexual relations in a rebellious and experimental fashion by playing with the stereotypes of the whore and black woman as sexual animal. But she discovers that sexuality cannot be expressed in isolation from other elements of her identity: however much she would like to remain neutral, the inevitable conclusion is that her choice of sex partners resonates with the history of colonialism in Africa and the Caribbean. Véronica claims to be dissatisfied with her conversations with Ibrahima Sory (the corrupt defense minister who becomes her sex partner), but rather than continue attempting dialogue with him, she decides on another course: "Transform any questions I might let slip into moans or sighs. All this noise of lovemaking is to get rid of my conscience. I ought to say consciences, both of them. The one you always get rid of when making love."[7] In this way, Véronica silences herself as a woman by ignoring her need to communicate with her sex partner. She transforms not only her questions into sighs but herself into "Marilisse," the slave/whore, a woman whose only useful function is to serve a man sexually. She thus adopts the white stereotype of black female sexuality: "A woman in love, isn't she always a Marilisse? Let the Feminists stone me if they want to!" (18).

Véronica's notions about female sexuality are in no sense "feminist." At the beginning of the novel Véronica does not realize the importance and the consequences of her actions when she first agrees to have sex with Ibrahima Sory. It is her students who make her aware of the implications of her choice when she discovers written in red chalk on the board: "We shall Destroy the Ministers, their Mercedes and their Whores" (68). At first Véronica is slow to recognize that she is the "whore" in the students' message. Whereas she initially has difficulty making this connection, her leftist friend Saliou quickly links Véronica's sexual activity to the country's political plight. When Saliou confronts her about her actions, Véronica satirizes the confessional mode: "I had imagined an interview in the shadows, conducive to self-reproach, whispering and hesitant" (67). Nevertheless, Saliou brings Véronica's private life out of the confessional and into the public arena. The personal is unquestionably political for Saliou, and he even takes partial responsibility for Véronica's choice of sex partners. When he contends that he should have "guided" her, Véronica thinks: "And then guide me where? Into the bed of a militant companion? So that I'm screwed along the same lines? Why not into *his* bed? To make sure the message gets through" (81). Although resistant, she finally realizes, half cynically, half in self-reproach: "If I understand correctly making love in this country comes down to making a political choice" (69). By the end of the narrative, Véronica has realized the futility of her searching for identity by way of her African past and through sexual encounters with an African dictator (her "black prince" or her "Oroonoko") who had come to represent that past. She realizes that both are mythical: "Do I love this man or a certain idea I have to have of Africa? When you think about it, it's the same thing. Loving a man is the myth you create around him" (77).

Véronica finds no secure sense of self—her postcolonial condition of being adrift without a clear construction of subjectivity appears to be a post-modern condition as well. She lacks direction, socially and politically: having sex with Ibrahima Sory has cut her off from both the leftists (some of whom have even been assassinated) and their cause. She succeeds in communicating only with her homosexual friend Pierre-Gilles, though a gulf emerges even here as they realize that each harbors stereotypes concerning the other's identity, she about gays and he about black women. Véronica first recognizes their shared marginality by saying that the two are in the same boat; but then she likens "sodomy" (as she refers to homosexual activity) to prostitution and perversion. In turn, he claims that only a black woman can interest a homosexual and insists that black is a virile color. In searching for community, then, Véronica finds only postcolonial ethnic chaos.

As she becomes increasingly aware of her own stereoyped status (as an exotic sexual object), however, Véronica realizes how societies have repressed her expression of sexuality, especially in its *métissage* or "race mixing" overtones (choosing someone of a slightly different shade to have sex with). When she moves to her first country of exile, France, Véronica is continually assaulted by the ancient stereotypes of black woman as relegated to the instinctual or the libidinal. She becomes aware of the image of herself as exoticized object when she notes, "Because basically for the silent majority the line is very thin between a negress and sex" (72). Awareness of her sexual exoticization, then, becomes an integral first step in her liberation.

Through such representations of sexuality as *Hérémakhonon's*, Antillean women are not only liberating their sexuality but also writing their bodies as part of a larger process of liberation. As the passages above indicate, characters such as Véronica are emblematic of the region from which they come, and their attempts at sexual independence mirror attempts of their islands to become politically independent, with varying degrees of success. Condé the author is active in the Guadeloupean independence movement; but like her charac-

ter Véronica, the island has not yet attained its desired sense of cultural identity through national independence from the metropole.

▪ INTERTEXTUALITY AND LITERACY

As she problematizes gender constructions and cultural identity in her novels, then, Condé foregrounds historical realities within the frames of her fictions. The extensive use of multicultural historical and intertextual reference by Condé also shows the writer's concern for educating her readers about Africa, different areas of the diaspora, and Europe. Such intertextual reference also assumes a broad-based readership: her works are aimed at more than a Caribbean audience.

Condé's frequent use of multicultural reference has been noted by Vèvè A. Clark in her article "Developing Diaspora Literacy: Allusion in Maryse Condé's *Hérémakhonon*." Clark demonstrates how Condé's work, while drawing on cultural elements from Africa and the diaspora in both the U.S. and the Caribbean, also contains massive intertextual reference to both "high" and "popular" European literature and culture. In *Hérémakhonon* Condé makes reference to literature, painting, sculpture, music, architecture, philosophy, and history both as a metaphor for her own multiple identity and as a lesson in multicultural literacy for her readers. *Hérémakhonon* is a thick textual machine that signifies in many ways: it is a literary example of the cultural process of *métissage,* a process by which West Indians represent their identity. As Condé asserts, Caribbean identity necessitates laborious reconstruction: "The terms of one's identity are dictated to him or her. We must glue back together the pieces of a very crumbled history, which we cannot do without pain."[8]

In an attempt to reconstruct her history as an African-Caribbean woman, Condé weaves together discourses from various disciplines. For example, she makes reference to sculpture held in the Louvre. The *Venus de Milo* and the *Victory of Samothrace* represent the accomplishments of whites so admired by Véronica's "assimilated" parents, who take her to France to gaze at the cultural monuments. Véronica's ironic voice satirizes her parents' assumptions.

> "What wonderful things the whites have accomplished!"
>
> "What about us?"
>
> "What about us? They let us stand back and admire. Isn't that enough?" (9)

Given her parents' obsession with assimilating, it is no surprise that Véronica turns away from Europe toward ancient Africa in order to reclaim a different history.

Her parents reveal their shame when forced to confess that their history originated in Africa. They are unable to tell Véronica about what life in Africa was like for their ancestors or why it was forgotten. She thus justifies her trip to Africa by claiming that she wants to "try and find out what was before" (12), before her parents' stories of coming "up from slavery" in the tradition of Booker T. Washington. Thus, the many intertextual references to European and U.S. architecture (Eiffel Tower, Notre Dame, Westminster Abbey, Golden Gate Bridge) demonstrate that until Véronica's trip to Africa, she has had no sense of her own history; her history was borrowed from those cultures that constructed the post—Carib Indian Antilles, with the significant exception of Africa, the continent which gave her the dark skin that sets her apart from most Europeans.

Although unaware of African history, Véronica at least demonstrates an awareness of Caribbean literature when she insists that she has read Césaire, like everybody else from the Caribbean, and when she claims: "I'm no Mayotte Capécia. No! I'm not interested in whitening the race! I swear. . ." (30). Despite her tendency to choose white French men and light-skinned Caribbeans, Véronica claims that "lactifying" the race is not her motive. She may not have read Frantz Fanon's critique of the Capécia, but she is aware of the esthetic of feminine beauty proposed in her novels and prevalent in the Caribbean: the lighter the skin, the more beautiful the woman. Véronica's protests, however, indicate that she tries to deny the beauty esthetic propagated by European media. She cannot acknowledge her preferences consciously, but her sexual history indicates that she has absorbed a French value system. The literary reference to Capécia alludes to the ethnic politics operating in Guadeloupe and Martinique: namely, that gradations of skin color determine social position, that light skin equals sex appeal and power.

In addition to the literary references, Véronica also makes reference to Tegbessu and Agadja, two African kings who sold slaves, and thus emphasizes that corrupt African power existed before neocolonialism. Agadja traded human beings for a portable organ, whereas Tegbessu received a carriage for his human capital, in addition to glass beads and red cotton. Véronica sees the onset of the slave trade as the beginning of another empire, albeit a less-celebrated decline than the Roman one described in one of her father's tomes. Although Véronica contrasts Mwalimwana, the leader currently in power, with Tegbessu (because he expelled the whites, something Tegbessu was unable to do), both have participated in a similar corruption of power. Knowing that leaders have been corrupt in Africa's past, Véronica should not be surprised by the corruption of Mwalimwana's regime and Ibrahima Sory's participation in censorship, detention, and murder. The historical reference

to Tegbessu shows that Véronica, at least initially, values the past to the detriment of the present.

Although preoccupied with the African past, Véronica refers to the African American present, specifically African American music, since she herself is mistaken for an African American. Because African American singers such as Mahalia Jackson, Aretha Franklin, and James Brown have captured the limelight in Africa, the West Indies, with its meager offering of Gilles Sala, cannot compete for cultural representation. With these references, the narrative reflects the frustration of the Caribbean attempting to carve out an identity that belongs to her and her alone, not to France or the U.S. In fact, the Caribbean may even compete with other areas of the diaspora in an attempt to valorize her own specificity: Véronica insists that her problems are more important than those of Salamata, the African-American visitor to Africa who had her hair braided and changed her name.

Although Véronica demonstrates a broad-based knowledge, she has difficulty applying that knowledge to her identity quest. Unlike her young friend Birame III, who reads Marx, as a girl Véronica read *Les liaisons dangereuses*, Marivaux (author of *Le jeu de l'amour et du hasard*), and Ben Jonson. These works, she claims, not *The Principles of Marxism-Leninism*, constitute "healthy" reading. Unfortunately, as with her knowledge of Tegbessu and Agadja, she can neither apply what she has read nor read her own situation in order to make it healthier: she is unable to read her relationship with Ibrahima Sory as a "dangerous liaison" or a "game of chance." The intertextual references here juxtapose Véronica's education with her self-knowledge (and, by implication, her cultural knowledge). Again, although she knows the canon of French and English literature, she cannot interpret herself or her culture.

Like Véronica's knowledge of literary history, her father's bookshelf is replete with "Western" classics such as *Decline and Fall of the Roman Empire*, *A la recherche du temps perdu*, *L'Assommoir*, *Germinal*, *Le ventre de Paris* and *La bête humaine*. While the decline of empire would be applicable to African history, or the search of things past significant in light of Véronica's quest, there is little evidence that Véronica's education by the "great books" has given her any information about her identity crisis. Had she experienced a "multicultural" education, she might have been better prepared for what awaited her in Africa.

Condé's concern with readers' literacy is evident when she is asked by Ina Césaire about the geographic placement of *Hérémakhonon*'s setting. Her answer: "Caribbeans may ask this question, but all Africans recognize the setting."[9] Condé has also been criticized for choosing such an obscure title for the novel. Her response demonstrates her desire that her readers be multiculturally literate.

> C'est une expression malinké qui signifie "Attends le bonheur." Here, le bonheur. Makhonon, attends. On m'a reproché ce titre hermétique. Hermétique pour qui? Le malinké est parlé dans presque tout l'Afrique de l'Ouest: Guinée, Mali, Côte-d'Ivoire, Sierra Leone, un peu au Sénégal.

> (It's a Mande expression meaning "Wait for happiness." *Here,* happiness. *Makhonon,* wait. I've been reproached for this hermetic title. Hermetic for whom? Mande is spoken in nearly all of West Africa: Guinea, Mali, the Ivory Coast, Sierra Leone, a little in Senegal).[10]

As suggested by her article's title, Clark shows how Condé educates readers by placing allusions to diaspora culture alongside allusions to European literature and culture: "Mayotte Capécia and Mahalia Jackson are treated as recognized references sharing a wealth of connotations comparable to *Swann's Way* and the Douanier Rousseau."[11] Thus, Condé's frequent and varied use of intertextual reference reflects cultural and (by implication) political concerns: the placing of reference is not hierarchical (us "over" them) but relational (what we each draw from the other), and it reflects Condé's own relational and multifaceted cultural identity. European culture is thus not valued over African culture, and "high" literature is not privileged at the expense of "popular" culture; again, they are merely related. Historical allusion also serves to increase readers' multicultural literacy, as evident in Condé's explanation that her novel originated in "the tragic events of Sékou Touré's Guinea in 1962 (teachers' and students' uprising, savage police repression, brutalities of all kinds)."[12] This position has been seen as problematic to some definite political agendas. Condé's denunciation of neocolonialist independent African countries was criticized by those who saw it as a "total rejection of Africa."[13] Her rewriting of history was not a complete dismissal of African leaders, however, but grew out of specific circumstances.

During Condé's stay in Guinea there was a teachers' conference at which some participants read papers about Sékou Touré's government. After two days they were arrested, and subsequently students went on strike. Some of Condé's friends were detained and some deported: "It was because of that incident that I began to understand what was happening in the country, to comprehend the real face of African Socialism."[14] As Condé then makes clear, the events in Guinea neatly encapsulate the movement from colonialism to neocolonialism. Although the African-Caribbean middle class

(represented by Véronica's parents) is criticized for its hypocrisy in *Hérémakhonon,* the neocolonial power of leaders like Sékou Touré deserves much stronger condemnation. Her novel, Condé explained, was the earliest denunciation of Sékou Touré in writing, and "some readers were shocked because they wanted to believe *Présence Africaine* and the myth that we people of the black world are one."[15]

■ CONCLUSIONS: THE POLITICS OF IDENTITY

How do the politics of neocolonialism complicate the politics of writing and gender? How does Condé actually construct or define her politics? While harboring a suspicion of unity of any kind (political parties, ideological labels, feminisms, and family bond[age]s), Condé's work is grounded in specific historical circumstances: she wants to illuminate historical and resulting political problems and thus inform her readers. In this way, she demonstrates the difficulty of the Guadeloupean who finds herself between cultures in search of an identity.

Women writers such as Condé are simply making the reading public aware of the conditions of their lives, their gender, and their sexuality, including the contradictions inherent in their identity constructions. Politics under these conditions is defined by recovering personal space. Obviously, Condé's use of *métissage* can be read in sociopolitical terms. Nevertheless, the author herself may appear ostensibly less "political" than we might expect in light of her comments in interviews. She confided to one interviewer that, although "Césaire's generation convinced us literature could change things, . . . perhaps changing things is not the function of literature."[16] This lack of a clear political agenda, however, should not be construed as an avoidance of politics, but rather as a reflection of the relational politics of the postcolonial Caribbean. Although Condé's comments may appear to emphasize an apolitical view of literary activity, her writing increases awareness of "small places" on the "periphery," those "specks of dust" between Europe and America evoked in this article's epigraph. Her affirmation of African-Caribbean women's subjectivity begins to effect a decisive relational and power challenge to the ex-colonial powers. Her first move is to displace racial mythologies of the black woman as exotic object and sexual plaything. The valorization of specific components of Caribbean culture will then replace stereotypes of primitivism. Finally, the awareness and foregrounding of regional Caribbean social formations, the intertextual references to European, African, African-American, and Afro-Caribbean culture, the anticolonial discourses and the history of the African diaspora embodied in the characters, and, not least, the autobiographical womanist emphasis linking woman to language and narrative (a decisive refutation of the male hegemony of the colonial era)—all these narrative moves make Condé's (re)writing a political act that reinscribes African-Caribbean women, ignored by the dominant culture, misnamed by stereotype, and distorted by the tourist's gaze. She takes a "modest approach" to the politics of the region (where postcolonialism is merging with neocolonialism) by turning to the region's more fundamental issue of self-representation.

Gerise Herndon, Autumn 1993

[1] Edouard Glissant, *Caribbean Discourse,* J. Michael Dash, tr., Charlottesville, University Press of Virginia, 1989, p. v. (Originally published as *Le discours antillais,* Paris, Seuil, 1981.)

[2] Marie-Clotilde Jacquey and Monique Hugon, "L'Afrique, un continent difficile: Entretien avec Maryse Condé," *Notre Librairie,* 74 (April-June 1984), p. 24. Translations are my own unless otherwise indicated.

[3] Maryse Condé, "Propos sur l'identité culturelle," in *Négritude: Traditions et dévelopement,* Guy Michaud, ed., Paris, Complexe/PUF, 1978, pp. 82–84.

[4] Françoise Lionnet, *Autobiographical Voices: Race, Gender, and Self-Portraiture,* Ithaca, N.Y., Cornell University Press, 1989, p. 21. Subsequent citations use the abbreviation *AV.*

[5] Carole Boyce Davies and Elaine Savory Fido, *Out of the Kumbla: Caribbean Women and Literature,* Trenton, N.J., Africa World Press, 1990, p. xii.

[6] Ibid.

[7] Maryse Condé, *Heremakhonon,* Richard Philcox, tr., Washington, D.C., Three Continents, 1982, p. 157. Subsequent citations use the abbreviation *H* where needed for clarity. (Originally published as *Hérémakhonon* in Paris by Union Générale in 1976; reissued by Seghers in 1988.)

[8] Jacquey/Hugon interview, p. 24.

[9] Ina Césaire, "Interview de Maryse Condé," in *La parole des femmes: Essai sur les romancières des Antilles de langue française,* Paris, L'Harmattan, 1979, p. 128.

[10] Ibid., p. 129.

[11] Vèvè A. Clark, "Developing Diaspora Literacy: Allusion in Maryse Condé's *Heremakhonon,*" in Davies and Fido, p. 307.

[12] Maryse Condé, "Avant-propos," in *Hérémakhonon,* pp. 11–12.

[13] Ibid., p. 14.

[14] "'Je me suis réconciliée avec mon île': Une interview de Maryse Condé," *Callaloo,* 12:1 (Winter 1989), pp. 102–3. The interview includes a parallel translation by Richard Philcox.

[15] Ibid., pp. 120–21.

[16] Jacquey/Hugon interview, p. 25.

Loving Words: New Lyricism in French Caribbean Poetry

New or rarely heard poetic voices from the French Caribbean, such as Marcelle Archelon-Pépin, Ernest Pépin,

and Gilette Bazile from Guadeloupe, or Michèle Bilavarn and Annick Collineau de Montaguère from Martinique, each of whom has published a collection of poems within the last ten years, have been exploring the link between words of love and love of words. The works of these poets provoke the question: what is the function of poetry in the "new" French Caribbean? This essay examines the different role played by these five poets (four women and one man) as they celebrate love, sensuality, and verbal beauty in their search for a new life. It will provide both brief examples of the productions of these writers that illustrate what I am calling the new lyricism of the French Caribbean and an interpretive synthesis of these new features.

The Guadeloupean Marcelle Archelon-Pépin's poems, published under the title *Ciselures sur nuits d'écume,*[1] are for the most part very short (usually four or five lines long), self-referential, highly imaged, but with little direct political content. The brevity of her poems demands, like the haiku, a condensing of imagery and a maximizing of the associative and evocative force of individual words. There is no attempt to inscribe or proclaim a Caribbean cultural heritage in her poetry. Her very real connection to her native land is expressed allusively at the level of emotion rather than of social commitment. At the same time some aspects of her poetic practice provide a clear link with metropolitan French literary conventions.

One such feature of Archelon-Pépin's poetry is her use of classical allusions, references to figures of Greco-Roman and Greco-Egyptian mythology (Serapis, Persephone, Morpheus). A typical example of this practice is to be found in the poem "Mirages" (6): "Les cases d'ébène / dans un ciel de jade / ont défié Artémis, / Une colombe / de ses ailes blanches / les a parées" (The ebony shacks / in a jade sky / have defied Artemis / A dove / with its white wings / have decked them out). The privileging of Western "classical" traditions that were formerly associated with exposure to the "best" in education is curious in the light of the decline in the value of such an education even in the modern metropole, where "scientific" expertise particularly in relation to electronic technology has created a new elite. Thus Archelon-Pépin's poetic practice in this respect represents a desire for reconciliation with an outmoded but still relevant European cultural tradition. This is a departure from the direction implicitly proposed for French Caribbean poetic creation by Léon-Gontran Damas and Aimé Césaire since the late 1930s. The Negritude-oriented poetry of these two writers was generally "committed" to the reclamation of an African or Caribbean cultural identity and to the liberation of the Caribbean peoples of color. It focused therefore primarily on political and sociocultural "realities" and often took the form of voicing individual and community convictions and aspirations in relation to race and culture and specifically to the African heritage, particularly in response and opposition to the negating and alienating force of metropolitan French culture. This aspect of Archelon-Pépin's poetry thus represents a rejection of cultural separatism.

Archelon-Pépin furthermore links herself to nineteenth-century metropolitan literary conventions through her self-conscious focusing on the exploration and expression of her internal experience as a poet. In "Le désespoir du poète" (The Poet's Despair; 8) she describes herself in these terms: "Je suis le poète / aux mains vides / qui hante le monde / dans sa ronde rituelle" (I am the poet / with empty hands / haunting the world / in its ritual round). This self-consciousness manifests itself, as with other French lyric poets before her (including Ronsard, Hugo, Lamartine, Baudelaire), in meditating on the source of her poetry. Thus, in "Inspiration" (11) she reveals that poetic inspiration for her is inseparable from pain. Water and fire are presented as elemental forces of painful purification and are used as metaphors for her writing: "Comme une cascade, / comme une flamme qui pousse / comme une pluie infinie / cette douleur en un tonnerre / dévale le flanc des écritures" (Like a waterfall / like a growing flame / like an unending rain / this pain in a thunderclap / hurtles down the writings' side).

The pain of creation is related to the experience of love, which is a major theme in Archelon-Pépin's poetry. Two poems in this collection bear the title "Amour" (Love). In the first (30), love is associated metaphorically with sensuous caresses that have the explosive passion of a volcano: "Une main / court / la peau grise du volcan" (A hand / roams over / the gray skin of the volcano). In the second "Love" poem (33), love is associated both with suffering and with the harmful power of words: "Il est des jours / mon cœur sanguinolent / de tes mots en torture / s'ouvre en corolle / pour t'aimer un peu plus" (There are days / my heart bleeding / from your words in torment / opens like a corolla / to love you a little more). In an untitled poem (25) it is the repetition of variations of the words "t'aimer" (love you) throughout the poem that gives it its harmony: "Hier / je t'ai aimé / pour les reflets de ton ombre. / Aujourd'hui, je t'aime / pour la transparence de tes yeux. / Etranger / Vais-je t'aimer demain?" (Yesterday / I loved you / for the reflections of your shadow. / Today, I love you / for the transparency of your eyes. / Stranger / Will I love you tomorrow?). Love is represented as a process that leaves only doubt, in which the loved one remains a stranger and the future only a question without an answer. The conflicting qualities associated with the loved one of reflection and transparency, indicating opposites of impenetrability and penetrability, produce only uncertainty and pain. It is this pain, however, that functions as the spur to creative production. In "Regard" (Look; 26), for example, the pain of love is an exciting source of the words that constitute the poem: "Vos yeux, / ces Océans / m'ont fouettée / avec leur houle de mots" (Your eyes, / those Oceans / have whipped me / with their swell of words). In "Message" (27) the lover's eyes have a different function and a different effect. They represent threats to her existence as a woman: "Dans vos yeux / mon essence de femme / s'est évaporée. / Vous avez voulu de vos mains la tenir en berceau. / Entre vos doigts, elle est passée / Comme vous passez" (In your eyes / my woman's essence / has evaporated. / You wanted to keep it cradled in your hands. / Between your fingers, it has passed / As you are passing). In neither poem is the gender of the love partner specified. What is important is the connection established between the partner's eyes and the woman poet in her twin roles as poet and woman: the partner's eyes have the paradoxical potential both to initiate the creative process and to dissolve gender identity.

The poetic persona projected by Archelon-Pépin is self-consciously and assertively female, sensitive to the possibility of her own existential annihilation as a woman in any love relationship. Pain serves as a stimulus and as the connecting link between poetic creation and love, both of which have special meaning for this woman poet. Not only does the love experience operate as the very substance of poetic activity, but poetry acquires dynamic significance as the affirmative act by means of which the poet retains her freedom and integrity as a woman.

The Guadeloupean Gilette Bazile is similarly self-conscious as a poet. The preface to her 1989 collection *Clins d'Œil*[2] (Winks) characterizes Bazile's verse as "oneiric poetry" and suggests that the poet is beyond theme, instant, subject, and object, since artistic creation is the only thing on earth that allows her to snatch herself away from the constraints of temporality and to fix in the Elsewhere the drafts of ideals to come. Bazile's poetic practice, the preface further asserts, makes her above all a witness, a researcher, and often a guide. These assertions are undoubtedly valid, and Bazile does assume poetic responsibility by placing great emphasis on the "je," on the I-subject of the poetic discourse. What is also striking is the way in which her poems, which are often self-referential, deliberate, and conscious, move constantly toward lyricism.

This fusion of features that may be characterized as traditional and modernist is reflected also in Bazile's tendency to adopt directly or indirectly the rhythm of the classical alexandrine. In "Je chante" (I Sing; 10) poetic ancestry is conveyed somewhat contradictorily in hidden (broken) alexandrines that are firmly linked to a metropolitan French literary tradition: "Je chante quand il pleut. / Je chante comme un cri, / cette ancestrale veine / qui me tient par le goût / par les doigts par le crâne" (I sing when it rains, / I sing like a shout, / this ancestral vein / that holds me by the taste / by the fingers by the skull). While the ancestry alluded to by Bazile is not identified in the poem, the use of the alexandrine as the basic form of the poetic song suggests that the poetic ancestry which prevails here is not the African, reclaimed by so many Caribbean poets since the 1930s, but implicitly the European.

It comes as no surprise, therefore, to find that Bazile reverts in "Dis, poète" (Tell Me, Poet; 21) to the convention of poetic reportage, of self-inquiry following an experiential journey of the type made famous by Baudelaire and Rimbaud. The poem presents itself as an internal dialogue, in which the poet responds to the questions she has posed herself: what have you seen, what did you take, what did you understand? The poet's reply—"Ai appris le fier silence / de toute grandeur innée, l'ordre classant les êtres et les choses" (I have learned the proud silence / of all innate greatness, the order classifying beings and things)—situates her within the universalizing European lineage of cosmic *magi*-philosopher-poets.

In "Attente" (Expectation; 62) Bazile reveals the mysterious word that her poetic search has discovered—Love, the emblem for the poet of all poetic activity: "Moi qui rêvais d'argile et de voix intérieures / Pour façonner au siècle un mot rare, vibrant, /. . . / Je ne trouvai qu'un mot dans l'ardeur éveillée" (I who dreamed of clay and of inner voices / to craft in the century a rare word, resonant, /. . . / I found only one word in fervor awakened). The fixed verse form in which this dependence on love as a poetic panacea is expressed creates a strong impression of anachronism. Even when the form changes, however, and becomes more flexible, more modern, the same impression persists. "Mon cœur chante" (My Heart Sings; 75), for example, is another celebration of love, as the poet seeks to convey the depth of her emotion intensified by separation and anticipation. The capitalized personifications of Hope and Peace impart a flavor of archaism to a text which without them would not have drawn attention to its temporality: "Mon cœur qui vit de toi / A paré son autel / De ses fleurs d'Espérance / Engrangées aux moissons / De mes étés de Paix / Pour t'accueillir bientôt / Au quai des retrouvailles" (My heart that lives on you / Has decked out its altar / With its flowers of Hope / Gathered in the harvests / Of my summers of Peace / to welcome you soon / At the reunion quay). By this device the poet takes a leap backward onto a tradition of writing and feeling with which she evidently feels quite comfortable.

Significantly, it is in the one poem which attempts to explore the identity dilemma that a conspicuously fresh note is struck. The poem "Identité" (92) stands out among all the others, despite its use of a conventional rhyme and versification: "Je suis née d'un arc-en-ciel. / Mes veines, fleuves d'horizons divers, / Sont d'un enfant d'univers. / Charroi d'épices, de tamtam, de miel, / De mistral doux ou de pomme" (I was born from a rainbow. / My veins, rivers of diverse horizons, / Are those of a child of the universe. / A cart full of spices, tom-tom, honey, / Of sweet mistral or apple). This poem echoes the consciousness of racial polyvalency expressed by Damas in *Black-Label:* "trois fleuves coulent dans mes veines" (three rivers flow in my veins).[3] The narrow shoe of Damas's Negritude, however, with its privileging of the African cultural heritage, clearly does not fit Bazile. The focus and themes Bazile adopts are rooted in metropolitan conventions that are already outdated in continental France, and her avoidance of contemporality diminishes the vigor and conviction of her poetry. What her poetry exemplifies is a desire to avoid poetic production grounded in a new sociocultural reality. It is evident from the inconclusive note on which this poem ends that the identity dilemma has not been resolved for this poet. But it is the awareness and the acknowledgment of this dilemma that helps Bazile find her voice.

The Martinican Michèle Bilavarn expresses a different sensibility and different preoccupations. Her highly sensual poetry attempts to capture in impressionistic strokes the outer and inner, the visual and emotional, aspects of her woman's experience. Her primary poetic identity is that of a woman, and the thematic focus of *Les ombres du soleil* (Shadows of the Sun),[4] as the titles of so many of her poems indicate, is women: "Une femme d'ombre" (A Woman of Shadow; 11), "Femmes" (Women; 13), "Mouvement de femme" (Woman's Movement; 15), "Nina" (17), "Femme" (Woman; 19), "Nazila" (23), "Petite fille de l'amour" (Love Child; 86). She explores an inner world ignored or neglected by the poetic patriarchs of the French Caribbean. For her, considerations of gender supersede those of racial or cultural affiliation.

Bilavarn's poetic activity is grounded in and stimulated by her identity as a woman, and it is within this world closed to men that she chooses to let her creative imagination take flight. In "Première rencontre" (First Encounter; 22), for example, the poet evokes an experience of physical and emotional intimacy between two lovers identified clearly by the feminine personal pronouns as women: "Elles s'assirent dos à dos / Sur la crête luisante / De l'écume des jours. / Leurs mains s'élevèrent / Cherchant l'espace immense / Où leurs cœurs et leurs corps / Se comprendraient enfin" (They sat down back to back / On the gleaming crest / Of the foam of the days. / Their hands rose up / Seeking the immense space / Where their hearts and bodies / Would finally understand each other). In "La panthère en folie" (The Crazy Panther; 30) Bilavarn transforms a characterization that in a typical male perception would have reduced the woman to objectified animal sexuality into an image of self-conscious power and beauty. The wild feline is the alter ego and emblem of the woman, in whom violence is transmuted into the essential rhythm by which she is defined. The sensuality conveyed by these female characteristics (violence and rhythm), moreover, is presented not as subject matter that is external to the text but becomes part of its substance and is reinforced by the spatial arrangement of the poem, which moves from left to right in a descending sinuous pattern across the page: "Un matin de printemps / la panthère devint / rythme du corps / immense . . . / La violence meurtrie mourut / pour laisser place / enfin / aux rythmes essentiels / d'une danse / Sensuelle. . ." (One morning in spring / the panther became / the body's rhythm / immense . . . / Bruised violence died / to give way / finally / to the essential rhythms / of a Sensual dance). The use of uppercase characters for "Sensuelle" and of the suspension points immediately following dramatically isolates the word and underscores the importance the poet attributes to sensuality.

Bilavarn conceives of the poem as a form of dance that opens the door of the imagination. She therefore tries to capture the dance rhythms by which for her the essence of the universe is revealed and to reproduce these in her poetry. In "Danse" (34) the cadence of the short lines is underscored by alliteration and the images convey the fusion between human and plant life. Here it is the submission to natural rhythms that permits the transcendence of a purely corporeal existence and guarantees an entry into a reality of true life: "Dans le rythme universel / De la Danse, / Il y a comme un murmure / Comme une blessure. / . . . / Dans le rythme universel / D'une danse innée / Ton corps devient tige / Et le feuillage ardent / De tes mains / De tes yeux / S'envole à tout jamais / Vers l'horizon doré / D'un monde bien réel / Où tu vivras / Enfin" (In the universal rhythm / Of the Dance / There is like a whisper / Like a wound. / . . . / In the universal rhythm / Of an innate dance / Your body becomes a stem / And the ardent foliage / Of your hands / Of your eyes / Flies away for ever / Toward the

golden horizon / Of a very real world / Where you will live / At last).

Rhythm is invested with the same life-giving potential in "Paysage" (Scenery; 79), a poem that is marked by its self-conscious transcription of emotion. The poet's sensitivity to rhythm enables her to move from observation of an external scene of beauty to participation in its essence: "Je vivais au rhythm du paysage / Et j'inscrivais en moi / La paix d'un lieu si beau. / Je me sentais / En mutation intense / Face à un passé / Qui mourait doucement. . ." (I lived by the rhythm of the scene / And I inscribed in me / The peace of so beautiful a place. / I felt myself / In intense mutation / In the face of a past / That was quietly dying). As the poem intimates, the poet's response to the scene is linked to the creative process: the poem is born from and conveys the transforming vibration of her inner rhythm.

There is no suggestion in Bilavarn's poetry of a creative impulse related to a desire for social transformation, nor is there any explicit or implicit political message. For Bilavarn, poetry primarily derives from and transcribes her experience as a woman, which includes her accessibility to universal and cosmic rhythm and dance. It is a profoundly personal and individual activity through which the poet gives expression to a voice that sings its own songs. Her poetic vision is directed internally rather than externally, toward self-transformation rather than toward social change. But it is precisely this concentration on a realm of experience that Bilavarn explores with passionate skill which enables her to produce very strong, highly original poetry.

The poems of the Martinican Annick Collineau de Montaguère in *Nostalgie* (1989)[5] do not consistently convey the intensity of creative imagination exhibited by the other poets under study here. Her poems are for the most part "occasional," in the sense that they are personal reminiscences of family members and friends, or memories of the pains and joys of love. The poems are generally marked by a transparent simplicity with little evidence of figurative or formal boldness. A discussion of recent variations on the poetic representation of love in the French Caribbean would, however, not be complete without reference to one of her poems, "Toi, l'amour" (You, Love), which stands out among Caribbean "love" poems if only because of its candid sexuality: "Comment ne pas frémir / Et mourir de plaisir, / Quand de tes mains gourmandes, / Mes formes tu parcours, / Lorsque mes seins se tendent / A la bouche d'amour? // Demain est encore loin! / Caresse-moi encore, / De tes baisers j'ai faim, / Promène-les sur mon corps! // Quand tes suaves lèvres / Viennent dévorer la fièvre / Et ma gorge se noue! / . . . / Amour incontrôlable, / Qui me rend malléable, / Demeure toujours en moi, / Je suis faite pour toi!" (How can I not tremble / And die with pleasure, / When your greedy hands / You run all over my body, / When my breasts stretch out / To your mouth of love? // Tomorrow is still far away! / Caress me some more, / I am hungry for your kisses, / Run them over my body! // When your smooth lips / Come and devour my neck, / I feel the fever rising / And my throat gets knotted! / . . . / Uncontrollable love, / That makes me malleable, / Stay always in me, / I am made for you!). In this poem the poetic persona speaks for herself, takes responsibility as "je" (I) for the speech act as well as for her own physical pleasure. The frequent rhymes—regular and internal—and assonances intensify the ambience of sensuality by titillating the ear. The poet owns and names her body as well as her reactions and issues instructions to direct the sexual activity.

Such an explicit expression of frank sensuality by a woman poet is rare even in the metropolitan French literary tradition and particularly in the French Caribbean, where male-centered social values have had, to a greater extent than in continental France, a restrictive effect on women's self-expression on the subject of sexual desire. Collineau de Montaguère does have, however, at least one distinguished antecedent within the French Caribbean tradition. Her compatriot, the Martinican Marie-Magdeleine Carbet, the most prolific of French Caribbean women writers from the late 1930s to the 1970s, published similarly sensual poetry, including poems celebrating sexuality between women.[6] Whatever her limitations as a poet, Collineau de Montaguère has asserted her right to her own voice as a woman despite the expectations and restrictions of a cultural milieu that has been unwilling to recognize this strain of poetic activity.

It has been more comfortable for the French Caribbean to recognize, accommodate, and even applaud the use of women, objectified or essentialized, by the male luminaries of the francophone literary tradition (particularly Aimé Césaire, Léopold Sédar Senghor, and to a lesser extent Edouard Glissant) to represent their connection to their native land, in Africa or the Caribbean, as mother or lover. This practice, undoubtedly intended to pay tribute to the importance of women in these societies, carries its own baggage of patriarchy all the more deleterious in that it has generally been unconscious. It could be for this reason that Negritude attracted the wholehearted support of so few women writers of the 1940s and 1950s. One of the most original male voices to adapt and renovate this practice is the Guadeloupean Ernest Pépin, whose poetry provides interesting convergences with the works of the women poets we have examined so far, particularly in the increased attention attached to love and to women, reflected in his 1984

collection *Au verso du silence* (On the Reverse Side of Silence).[7] His poetry is, however, more explicitly rooted in the sociocultural realities of the Caribbean than is that of the women.

The first poem, "Notre amour sans archives" (Our Love with No Archives), sets the trajectory of the whole collection, in its focus on the role of women and the role of love. While the tendency to reification of the woman manifests itself in the opening apposition of the first two lines, the poet's project is to bring to light the forgotten and unrecognized contributions and beauty of African women. Thus he pays tribute to the "Reine du royaume de Guinée / Amphore laquée de noir / laissant ébloui le potier/ Reine du royaume de Guinée / oubliée" (Queen of the kingdom of Guinea / Amphora lacquered in black / leaving the potter dazzled / Queen of the kingdom of Guinea / forgotten) as well as to "Celles qui suivirent Béhanzin / celles que le navire força / celles / effrayées par l'aurore blême arrondi dans leur ventre / Leur chair germée loin d'elles / dans les champs négriers" (Those women who followed Behanzin / those whom the ship forced / those / frightened by the pale rounded dawn in their bellies / Their flesh germinated far from them / in the slavers' fields; 13–14). The motivation, as the title indicates, is love. This is an African-Caribbean love poem, directed not to a single woman as the French lyric convention requires, but to the many black women with whom the poet recognizes a historical and spiritual connection.

Pépin's evocation of African women and their beauty, despite his use of metaphors that are reminiscent of nineteenth-century Parnassian objectification, is, however, never impersonal. His descriptions are colored by and infused with empathy, admiration, and love. Love is presented as the missing component in the history of Caribbean people of color: "nous voilà / tressant les nattes de l'amour / mais notre amour n'a pas d'histoire" (there we are plaiting braids of love / but our love has no history; 14). Other poets, including Césaire and Glissant, have attempted their own historical rewritings out of their awareness of the omissions, inaccuracies, and distortions of the prevailing European narratives of the Caribbean. Pépin introduces another perspective. He alludes to the fact that accounts of the past of the Caribbean peoples have not presented the people of the Caribbean as human beings with human emotions and have not been authored by people with a primary responsibility and emotional attachment to the Caribbean people. Thus it is this form of love that impels Pépin to acknowledge his debt as a man to the women of his race and to recognize poetically the vital role of their heroism throughout the history of slavery and colonization: "Femme / capitale où s'édifie mon courage / . . . / tu as posé sur moi l'étole / et me voilà fait homme" (Woman / capital where my courage is erected / . . . / you placed the stole upon me / and here am I become a man).

Love in Pépin's poetry does not manifest itself solely as admiration and respect. It also takes the form of sexuality. It is evident that his imagination is sometimes stimulated by his own woman-directed sexual desire as a male. Woman is presented in "Alors" (Then; 22) as "femme-pirogue" (canoe-woman), "femme-marronne" (maroon-woman), but this celebration of the woman as heroine and as courageous is fused with sensuality: "l'eau neuve du désir / lavera notre histoire" (the new water of desire / will bathe our history). The poet seeks a new relationship in which adoration and sexual desire may become reconciled. This is not the expression of a spiritually and emotionally sick sensibility such as that reflected in the prurient mixture of religiosity and sexuality prevalent in the decadent strain of French nineteenth-century romanticism, of which Baudelaire was a preeminent exponent. The poet's interest here is precisely to repair the damage done in the past to relations between black men and women and to forge a healthy new alliance based on honesty.

In this collection, therefore, love for women serves as the emotive force on which many of Pépin's poems depend. The relationship between love and poetic practice is illustrated admirably in a brief untitled poem (27) which demonstrates the poetic search for beauty through the concentrated fusion of imagery: "Coupé en deux / l'amour n'a plus sa perfection / de frère siamois" (Cut in two / love no longer has its perfection / of a Siamese brother). The awareness of separation has long been a preoccupation of French Caribbean writers. This separation has usually been conceived of as the result of the slave trade that forcibly isolated Africans in the Americas and the Caribbean from their continental African base communities. While Pépin is conscious of this loss, he focuses on a related form of separation (emotional and spiritual) that has resulted from the same set of historical circumstances and implicitly suggests the practice of love as a solution to the problem of cultural fragmentation.

The voices of these five writers, who have as a common denominator an interest in love, particularly in passionate, sensual love, indicate a new direction in French Caribbean poetry. Since the appearance of *Légitime Défense,* the journal launched in June 1932 by a group of young Martinicans in Paris,[8] there has been a consistent attack on a variety of writing emanating from the French Caribbean perceived as inauthentic. Writings that could be considered as lyrical or "romantic," exploring natural beauty or love, were dismissed as bourgeois, imitative, assimilationist, exotic, *doudouiste,*

and beneath consideration as serious Caribbean literature. The situation of people of color in the French Caribbean was perceived as being so desperate that commitment to the solution of their problems was expected to take precedence over everything else. Poetry, it was felt, should be a weapon of the sociocultural revolution that needed to take place if the French Caribbean were to be free. Césaire himself asserted that literature should be regarded as "sacred": "Artistic creation must, by its force, mobilize virgin emotional forces, so that unsuspected psychic resources would rise to its call and contribute to the restoration of the social body that has been shattered by the shock of colonialism."[9]

These five writers demonstrate that there is now a movement, conscious or not, toward avoiding what might be considered "committed" or directly political poetry. Poets are moving toward a new lyricism and a new estheticism, even when informed by a retrograde movement toward the conventional lyricism of metropolitan poets. The poetic subject is becoming less communal, less the voice of a people, and more an individual voice, conscious of her/himself as a poet, seeking beauty in language, associating beauty with emotional experiences, concerned with passion and desire, and interested in translating these emotional experiences in their poetry. Poetry is reclaiming its territory: that of the word, divorced from political intent and transcending considerations of cultural specificity. This means, in fact, that these French Caribbean poets are making peace with the French language and with the notion of cultural domination with which the language has been associated. They have found a new path between exoticism and commitment, between cultural self-alienation and political activism. The experience of the greatest of the Caribbean poets (Césaire, Damas, and Glissant) indicates that poetic power necessitates self-awareness and vision—the capacity to apprehend present realities with honesty and courage and to envision alternative realities with faith and lucidity. The beauty of their poetry is directly proportional to its "truth" and to its power to transcend the limitations of temporality. The focus of these younger poets on love may well be a new stage in the continuing movement in the French Caribbean toward the reclamation of artistic integrity and freedom.

E. Anthony Hurley, Winter 1997

▪ WORKS CITED

Archelon-Pépin, Marcelle. *Ciselures sur nuits d'écume.* Paris. Silex. 1987.

Bazile, Gilette. *Clins d'Œil.* Nimes. Bené. 1987.

Bilavarn, Michéle. *Les ombres du soleil.* Saint-Estève. IMF. 1984.

Carbet, Marie-Magdeleine. *Point d'orgue.* Paris. La Productrice. 1958.

Césaire, Aimé. "L'homme de culture et ses responsabilités" (Deuxième Congrès des écrivains et Artistes Noirs, Rome, 26 mars-ler avril, 1959). *Présence Africaine,* 24–25 (February-May 1959), pp. 116–22.

de Montaguère, Annick Collineau. *Nostalgie.* Paris. Nouvelles Editions Debresse. 1989.

Hodge, Merle. "Beyond Négritude: The Love Poems." In *Critical Perspectives on Léon-Gontran Damas.* Keith Q. Warner, ed. Washington D.C. Three Continents. 1988. Pp. 119–45.

Léro, Etienne. "Misère d'une poésie." *Légitime Défense,* June 1932. Reprinted in Lilyan Kesteloot, *Les écrivains noirs de langue française: Naissance d'une littérature.* Brussels. Editions de l'Université de Bruxelles. 1975. P. 25.

Pépin, Ernest. *Au verso du silence.* Paris. L'Harmattan. 1984.

1   Marcelle Archelon-Pépin, *Ciselures sur nuits d'ecume,* Paris, Silex, 1987.

2   Gilette Bazile, *Clins d'Œil,* Nimes, Bené, 1987.

3   L.-G. Damas, *Black-Label,* Paris, Gallimard, 1956, p. 9.

4   Michèle Bilavarn, *Les ombres du soleil,* Saint-Estève, IMF, 1984.

5   Annick Collineau de Montaguère, *Nostalgie,* Paris, Nouvelles Editions Debresse, 1989.

6   See particularly "Tourment" and "Rancune" in Marie-Magdeleine Carbet's *Point d'orgue,* Paris, La Productrice, 1958, pp. 16 and 25–27 respectively.

7   Ernest Pépin, *Au verso du silence,* Paris, L'Harmattan, 1984.

8   In an essay entitled "Misère d'une poésie," intensely critical of the kind of literature produced by the French Caribbean bourgeoisie, Etienne Léro stated: "L'étranger chercherait vainement dans cette littérature un accent original ou profond, l'imagination sensuelle et colorée du noir, l'écho des haines et des aspirations d'un peuple opprimé" (It would be impossible for a foreigner to find in this literature a profound or original note, the sensuous and colored imagination of blacks, or the echo of the hatred and aspirations of an oppressed people).

9   See Aimé Césaire, "L'homme de culture et ses responsabilités" (Deuxième Congrès des Ecrivains et Artistes Noirs, Rome, 26 mars-1er avril, 1959), *Présence Africaine,* 24–25 (February-May 1959), p. 122. Translation mine.

The Poetics of Ex-île: Simone Schwarz-Bart's *Ton beau capitaine*

Toi là-bas et moi ici, toi ici et moi là-bas, c'est pareil.

Simone Schwarz-Bart's play *Ton beau capitaine*[1] was inspired by the real-life circumstance of Haitian men who leave their native land in search of work. Set in 1985, it presents agricultural worker Wilnor Baptiste, who lives in Guadeloupe while his wife Marie-Ange remains behind in Haiti. During their years of separation they communicate by way of audio cassette. Wilnor's simultaneous absence from Haiti and presence in Guade-

loupe are the subjects of this 1987 play. Consequently, patterns of isolation, separation, displacement, and exile are found throughout the text.

Even before the play opens, Schwarz-Bart underlines the poverty and isolation of Wilnor. All the action takes place in Wilnor's one-room shack, creating a claustrophobic atmosphere. Furnished with only a stool, an old crate, a stove, and a floor mattress, it resembles a prison cell. Far away from his family, he is indeed condemned to a life of loneliness. His clothes—one suit, one shirt, one tie, one pair of shoes—a few dishes, a plastic mirror, and a borrowed radio/cassette player complete the setting.

There are only two characters listed. Wilnor, described as a tall and thin thirty-year-old, and the tape player. Marie-Ange never appears onstage; her voice is heard only on the tape. That Wilnor is onstage alone throughout the play accentuates his isolation. He even dances two communal dances—the quadrille and the *lérose*—alone. Traditionally the quadrille is performed with a partner and three other couples.[2] Here it functions paradoxically to reinforce his solitude and provide some consolation during his nostalgic moments.

The play is divided into four tableaux of approximately equal length. In the first two Marie-Ange's taped voice is privileged while Wilnor listens and reacts. In the last two tableaux Wilnor's voice predominates as he records a reply to his wife. Although Wilnor's voice is represented in the title *Ton beau capitaine,* Marie-Ange actually has more lines. It is Wilnor, however, who opens and closes the play.

The play opens at night as the protagonist returns home from work. He bumps into a piece of furniture in the darkened room. This entrance is revealing, as it signifies Wilnor's return to an unfamiliar place. After reminding himself to be careful because the furniture does not belong to him, he takes from his sack a cassette that was recorded by his wife and brought to him by a friend who has just arrived by plane from Port-au-Prince. The cassette is his sole possession: "Wilnor, mon cher, je t'apprends que rien ne t'appartient ici, pas même l'herbe des chemins, pas même le vent. Et si tu veux savoir, la seule chose qui soye vraiment à toi: c'est ça vieux camarade, c'est ça" (12). He then places the cassette in the player and listens to its contents.

Marie-Ange's first words, "Allô, allô Wilnor, Wilnor Baptiste," resemble a telephone conversation. She brings greetings from Wilnor's parents, sisters, and "de tous nos exilés de par le monde: Grenade, Saint-Domingue, Portorique" (14). Thus the drama of the displaced Haitian is evoked, all those who have left to "gagner le pain des errants" (18). One such friend picks oranges in Miami. Another, Petrus, drowned along with a group of thirty boat people trying to reach the Americas.

The reader/spectator of *Ton beau capitaine* learns few details about Wilnor's life in Guadeloupe. The play focuses rather on the effects of the separation on both husband and wife. Although Wilnor sends money home regularly, the material comforts that it affords Marie-Ange cannot compensate for his absence. She misses him terribly and urges him to come home, even if it means they will be unable to better their economic situation. Tearfully she confesses that, out of loneliness, she had an affair with another man because he reminded her of Wilnor. She became pregnant as a result. That is why he has not heard from her in three months. For his part, Wilnor does resist the temptation of other women in Guadeloupe, but he lies to Marie-Ange about his life. First, he describes his house as being large and comfortable, when in reality it is a one-room shack. Hardship is his companion as he sacrifices to send money to Haiti. Second, Wilnor has been concealing some of his savings. Realizing that the separation is responsible for the damage to their personal relationship, Wilnor accepts Marie-Ange's transgression, forgives her, and urges her to take care of herself so that the baby will be born healthy.

As a closing to his taped response, Wilnor repeats five times, "Ton beau capitaine," each time with a different intonation. The first time, while looking in the mirror, he says, "Ton beau capitaine. Wilnor." Dissatisfied with that sign-off, he removes his shirt and tie and repeats a second time, "Ton beau capitaine," but "sur un ton moins assuré." The "points de suspension" reflect his hesitancy. Still uncertain, he covers his mouth with his hand and hunches his shoulders in resignation as the third "Ton beau capitaine" audio signature is posed as a question. Then the music begins as Wilnor does a desperation dance. He stops and says, "Ton beau capitaine?" Then he dances to a drumbeat. Hands over his head, he reaches for the sky as if to fly away. This final gesture reflects Wilnor's desire to escape his prisonlike existence and rejoin his wife in Haiti. Then, in the darkness, one last ironic "Ton beau capitaine?" is heard. There is no happy ending here. The couple remain separated.

It is not surprising that words like *errants, exilé, partir, s'en aller, séparé, séparation, s'éloigner, loin, l'absent,* and *s'envoler* recur throughout the text, forming a matrix. The sea is at the center of this displacement. Guadeloupe is an island; Haiti makes up part of an island. Water separates them not only from each other but from other lands as well. Fittingly, Marie-Ange wishes that she were a boat, "un bateau qui s'en va vers la Guadeloupe" (19).[3] Wilnor is her "beau capitaine." The sea thus becomes a metaphor for separation. Wilnor explains, "La séparation est un grand océan et plus d'un s'y noie" (41). On a literal level their friend Petrus did drown. On a figurative level their relationship could have had a similar fate. The image of separation as ocean also appears in the text in this way: "La séparation est un grand océan, elle emmêle toutes choses, elle les secoue comme un cornet à dés" (35). Here Wilnor compares separation to a large, almost limitless open space that swallows some who try to cross it and whose currents mix up, tangle, and thus confuse people's lives in the way that a cup shakes up dice. The allusion to gambling is appropriate. On the one hand, luck plays an important role in the success of a marriage in which the principals are separated. On the other hand, the dice cup scatters its contents in the same way that the economic and political situation in Haiti has led to the Haitian diaspora.

In addition, images of weightlessness are found in the characters' dreams, or rather nightmares. For example, Marie-Ange confesses that while washing Wilnor's shirt in the river she imagined that suddenly his body appeared in the shirt, only to melt and disappear. Wilnor has similar "rêves bizarres." He dreams of being carried away to faraway places, unable to find the road back (50). On another occasion he explains: "Et soudain je me sens léger, léger, m'envole comme si j'étais emporté par deux ballons" (55). These haunting dreams of weightlessness reflect the characters' real uprooting or *déracinement*. In an effort to resist, Marie-Ange tries to hold on to Wilnor's body: "Tu essayais de fuir et moi je voulais te retenir" (16). Wilnor, on the other hand, buries a jar with his savings "pour me donner du poids, de l'assise" (50). Also, when he dances; he deliberately brings his feet to the ground to be sure to make contact with it. The ideas of separation and displacement are thus sustained throughout the text.

Schwarz-Bart has also used the theme of displacement in her novels. In *Un plat de porc aux bananes vertes* (1967), written with her husband André, we read the memoirs of Mariotte, an old Martinican woman living in exile in Paris. In *Pluie et vent sur Télumée Miracle* (1972) Télumée refers to the inhabitants of La Folie as "nègres errants," whereas they call themselves "la confrérie des Déplacés."[4] It is the *errants* who founded the village of l'Abandonnée: "Les gens se sentaient là comme des voyageurs perdus en terre inconnue" (12–13). Amboise, Télumée's lover, feels alienated and isolated during his seven-year stay in Paris. In *Ti-Jean l'Horizon* (1979) the title character journeys from Guadeloupe to Africa and returns to Guadeloupe by way of war-torn France.

One is tempted to compare Wilnor to Manuel in Jacques Roumain's *Gouverneurs de la rosée* and Hilarion Hilarius in Jacques Stephen Alexis's *Compère Général Soleil* on one level. All three are Haitian agricultural workers who left home in search of work: Manuel to Cuba and Hilarion Hilarius to the Dominican Republic. Whereas Manuel and Hilarion's stories focus on their return to Haiti and their attempt to reintegrate themselves into society, Wilnor's story is one of separation and exile, reflecting the worsening conditions in Haiti that have contributed to the most recent exodus. Because the center of the story is the protagonist's absence, *Ton beau capitaine* can be seen as a subversion of the title of Aimé Césaire's *Cahier d'un retour au pays natal*; the *cahier* has become a cassette, the *retour au pays natal* has become an *absence d'un exilé*.

More recent Haitian writers have not ignored the issue of displacement: the novelist Jean-Claude Charles's *Saint-Dérive des cochons* (1977), *De si jolies plages* (1982), and *Manhattan Blues* (1985), the playwright Franketienne's *Pelin tèt*, and the short-story writer Marie-Thérèse Colimon's *Chant des sirènes* (1979) are all good examples. Along those same lines the displaced Caribbean woman in particular is the subject of several recent novels by Caribbean writers. The Guadeloupean Véronica Mercier leaves for France and West Africa and Marie-Hélène for Africa in Maryse Condé's *Hérémakhonon* (1976) and *Une saison à Rihata* (1981) respectively; Juletane in the novel of the same name by Myriam Warner-Vieyra (1982) experiences a similar uprooting, traveling to France and Senegal. Although these female characters are middle-class, their separation from their *pays natal* is still disastrous.

The patterns of displacement, separation, isolation, and exile that characterize the fictional *Ton beau capitaine* are mirrored in the real-life struggles of contemporary migrant workers everywhere.[5] The longing that Wilnor and Marie-Ange feel for each other is a desire for the *pays natal*. Wilnor and Marie-Ange's story can also be seen as a metaphor for the millions of people who were forcibly removed from Africa and brought to the Americas as slaves, victims all of circumstance.

Renée Larrier, Winter 1990

1 Simone Schwarz-Bart, *Ton beau capitaine*, Paris, Seuil, 1987. The play has been performed in Pointe-à-Pitre and Basse-Terre, Guadeloupe; Fort-de-France, Martinique; Casablanca and Marrakesh, Morocco; Paris, Foix, Limoges, Saint-Junien, and Aubusson, France; London, England; Port-au-Prince, Haiti; and in English translation in New York City and Providence, Rhode Island. For a review, see *WLT* 62:4 (Autumn 1988), p. 715.

2 For a more complete discussion of Caribbean dances, see Marie-Céline Lafontaine, "Musique et société aux Antilles," *Présence Africaine*, 121/122 (1982), pp. 72–108.

3 Conversely, in *Pluie et vent sur Télumée Miracle* Elie is compared to a boat and Toussine is compared to a "barque enlisée" (27). For a complete discussion of the image in Schwarz-Bart's novels, see Beverly Ormerod, "The Boat and the Tree," in her *Introduction to the French Caribbean Novel*, London, Heinemann, 1985, pp. 108–31.

4 Simone Schwarz-Bart, *Pluie et vent sur Télumée Miracle*, Paris, Seuil, 1972, pp. 186–87.

5 Schwarz-Bart has indicated in the stage directions that Wilnor could be played by a white man.

Desirada—A New Conception of Identity: An Interview with Maryse Condé

The following interview with Maryse Condé (MC) took place on 12 June 1999 at the author's home in Montebello, Guadeloupe. The interview was recorded, transcribed, edited, annotated, and translated from French into English by Robert H. McCormick Jr. (RM).

RM: I would like to focus, at the beginning, on your most recent novel, *Desirada* [1999]. My first set of questions relates to the origin of the novel. When did you start thinking about writing what eventually became *Desirada*?

MC: A long time ago, but I can't say exactly when. Generally, one works on two novels at the same time. Thus, while I was working on *Windward Heights* [1999; orig. *La migration des cœurs*, 1995], I was thinking about *Desirada*. All together it took me about four years, but I can't say exactly when I started thinking about it.

RM: Is *Desirada* a novel, an idea, that you have nurtured for a long time?

MC: It is the conclusion of a lot of thought, of continual reflection on identity, origin, nationality, language. . . . Yes, it is the result of long periods of reflection. The actual writing of the book, however, took three or four years.

RM: What was the original impulse behind the novel? Was there a particular incident or idea that pushed you to write the novel?

MC: The specific problem is that one always asks me, a West Indian, the question "Where are you from?" as if to say "Define yourself!" Since I am black, people want me to emphasize Africa. I was in Africa, though, and I realized that race is less important than culture. I cannot say that I am African. I must say I am West Indian. Then someone says, "You are West Indian, but you don't live in the West Indies. You don't speak

Creole, or very little. By what criteria do you define your West Indian-ness?" You see, I constantly have to justify my identity. Finally, one day, I came to the conclusion that I was going to stop justifying myself. Too bad for everyone else! Perhaps we can say that I chose my identity and that I was going to stick by it. Marie-Noëlle [in *Desirada*] doesn't know who her father is, and she doesn't know her own family history very well because there are a lot of gaps in it. Her mother gives her one version. Her grandmother another. Everyone around her lies. Thus, she finally says to herself, "It doesn't matter. I am going to live as I am." I think that one has to define one's identity personally without worrying too much about other people.

RM: I am pleased to hear your answer because that is more or less how I interpreted the novel. You dedicated this novel to your daughters, didn't you?

MC: My daughters? Perhaps. I can't remember exactly.

RM: I was going to ask you why.

MC: Perhaps . . . it's because there are many mother-daughter relationships in the book and because my daughters also have daughters. . . . Everyone knows that mother-daughter relationships are very complicated.

RM: I would like to ask you a few questions about the structure of *Desirada*. It's a ternary structure that represents three generations, isn't it?

MC: Yes. There are three generations of women: the grandmother who almost never left Desirada and who returns to die there, the mother who left for France and who represents the first form of emigration, and her daughter who ultimately arrives in Boston. I didn't want those three narratives to be in chronological order whereby one begins with the grandmother, then the mother, and then . . . No. I wanted to deconstruct. The novel begins with the birth of the granddaughter. Thus, we start at the end and, gradually, discover the grandmother, the third generation. One must deconstruct linear structure. There should be some fantasy in the construction. The women, the three panels of the triptych, correspond to three ways of being West Indian, Guadeloupean.

RM: Thus, there are three generations, but they don't really correspond exactly to the three parts of the novel.

MC: Right.

Maryse Condé (*Michael Britto*)

RM: There are three "media" too—i.e., three women in touch with the imaginary world. There is Madame Esmondas in Boston . . .

MC: Yes.

RM: That's not a reiteration of the ternary structure? In each venue where Marie-Noëlle lives, there is a woman allegedly in contact with the "other" world. Each one mysteriously disappears without a trace, without saying anything to Marie-Noëlle.

MC: Not really. They represent memories of people I knew. When one writes an intimate novel, memories resurface, people and even events that one wants to include somewhere, but there is no particular significance.

RM: There were three of them. I thought that perhaps you were subtly trying to echo your tripartite structure. . . . Generally, what is the function of a "récit" in your novels? In *Desirada* there are two récits: one by Nina and the other by Ludovic.

MC: I wanted to show that there is no Truth. Everyone recounts his/her life, life history, differently. It is not possible to find an objective reality basing one's judgments solely on the words of others. Nina relates events her way. Ludovic in his way. Reynalda too.

RM: Fiorella!

MC: Yes, everyone! And poor Marie-Noëlle, who only wants to know the answer to some simple questions—Who is my father? Who am I? What happened?—won't ever find out. Because everyone lies. Not in a conscious and malicious way. Because, ultimately, to tell a story is to embellish it, to fabricate it according to one's tastes and desires, to create fiction.

RM: But Reynalda, for example, Marie-Noëlle's mother, doesn't have a récit. Only Nina and Ludovic. When, in your writing, do you say to yourself, "Aha! Now, I need a récit"?

MC: When I want to interrupt, deconstruct, my narrative by introducing another voice. To create a sort of polyphony, I introduce a voice which is not the narrator's voice, a voice that subverts the narrative that the author, Maryse Condé, is presenting. The récits and the voices are there to create a sort of contradictory polyphony so that the reader can form his own opinion. I don't think the author, the narrator, should always provide the definitive version.

RM: Thus, it would be an error to interpret those récits as being closer to reality, to Truth, than the other voices.

MC: Yes, because they, too, are very subjective. A récit is the presentation of a version of a life history. Not every one is a manifestation of Truth. It's just another version.

RM: A récit, then, is simply another voice, another point of view, in a different—i.e., first-person—narrative form.

MC: A variation.

RM: I also wanted to ask you a couple of autobiographical questions if I could. Where was your mother born?

MC: She was born on the island of Marie-Galante.

RM: Could you please be a bit more precise?

MC: A La Treille.

RM: Yes, Mrs. Thérèse Tyrolien was kind enough to pass that information along to me. I have read that you have great admiration for Guy Tyrolien.

MC: Yes.

RM: He wrote some very pertinent remarks about your early works. . . . And your grandmother? Where was she born?

MC: I believe she was born in Marie-Galante also.

RM: When did your mother die?

MC: That must have been in the 1950s.[1]

RM: Out of curiosity, did you frequently go to Desirada[2] when you were young?

MC: No, never. I only went when I had finished the book.

RM: Really? That's interesting.

MC: I wrote the novel based on travel books. The book by Lasserre[3] gives a good description of Guadeloupe and its surrounding islands. Afterwards, I went there.

RM: Shifting away from the relation of fact to fiction, I wanted to ask a few questions about the role of music in *Desirada*. What is Stanley's role in the novel? Is he a musical genius, but a failure in his private life?

MC: I personally consider him a genius. He is someone who has, with his M.N.A., "Music of the New Age," a broad, panoramic vision of West Indian culture. He wanted to create a harmony, or synthesis, that would encompass all the musical forms of the Caribbean. He was striving for a way to break with *particularismes,* such as zouk.

RM: A sort of musical pan-Caribbeanism?

MC: Exactly. He's a genius, but a genius who isn't able to live.

RM: At times I was confused, but you do use the word *genius* in the text. I assume to make your position clear.

MC: Yes.

RM: After the failure of his group in the Dominican Republic, essentially because they are unknown, he has many problems. And, toward the end, he becomes rhetorical, repetitive.

MC: Bitter. Frustrated. He starts to drink, I believe.

RM: He has a life trajectory that . . .

MC: That declines.

RM: I was puzzled by the title of his symphony, "The Symphony of the New World." Could you explain that title? There is, of course, the passage where he indicates he wants to distance himself from Bob Marley. But when he speaks about Dvořak, no one understands him.

MC: I wanted to say that here, in the West Indies, there is a tendency to have heroes once and for all. West Indian music, especially Jamaican music, is essentially the reggae of Bob Marley. If you talk to West Indians about other forms of European or Western music, they will refuse to accept them. They are not familiar with them, but reject them nonetheless. We need to open ourselves up to new forms of music no matter where they come from. Bob Marley is not the only one capable of creating music we can call

"Caribbean." We must accept the fact that people can produce music that differs radically from the music of the gods venerated by tradition. For example, now in Guadeloupe, there is only "Kassav." O.K, but other musicians can produce other types of music equally significant. We have to stop being narrow-mindedly nationalistic, exaggeratedly patriotic.

RM: I didn't understand whether there was a hint of irony in use of the title "The Symphony of the New World," but . . .

MC: No, the title is not ironic. In fact, it's a tribute to Dvořak, a musician I like very much.

RM: Stanley becomes then the source of certain ideas about migration and creativity, for example, that are dear to you, ideas you developed in your presentation, "O Brave New World" (32), at the 1998 African Literature Association conference held in Austin, Texas.

MC: Yes, it is not at all ironic. On the contrary, Stanley is a sort of spokesperson.

RM: Who has the problem of adapting poorly to everyday life?

MC: He doesn't know how to live. He's too interior. He's very introverted. Thus, he doesn't know how to communicate. He doesn't know how to get people to accept, to appreciate, his ideas.

RM: His experience at the jazz festival in the Dominican Republic is rather brutal. People went to his concert in Santo Domingo because they were expecting to see another group. The one advertised! When Stanley's ensemble arrives, the audience leaves en masse. It's the fear of every artist, I think.

MC: Exactly. And it happens very often. You are there when people are waiting for someone else.

RM: I would like, because it seems to me relevant to your comments about Stanley's music, to refer to another novel of yours that greatly intrigues me: namely, *Tree of Life* [1992; orig. *La vie scélérate,* 1987]. Should we consider Stanley as representing values antithetical to those of Gesner?

MC: Gesner is much more local.

RM: Exactly.

MC: Gesner is Guadeloupe, and that's it!

RM: Because he doesn't leave.

MC: He doesn't leave. He doesn't travel. He represents popular, traditional music. Roots. Stanley, on the other hand, is a visionary. He leaves Guadeloupe. He listens to everything.

RM: I saw the opposition, but I wasn't sure how to evaluate it. According to your explanation, Stanley is more important, even though Gesner is rooted in his people.

MC: Perhaps the shift corresponds to my own evolution. When I was writing *Tree of Life,* I thought the best thing was returning to one's native country and settling in there. Gesner knows the people of his country; he speaks for them. Gradually, though, I realized that this is not enough, that one has to go beyond this.

RM: An orientation like Gesner's could be considered a bit . . .

MC: Parochial!

RM: Yes. Perhaps we could shift our attention to Reynalda, a key protagonist in *Desirada* and a rather ambiguous one. I could almost say a "nega-positive" female protagonist.

MC: Yes.

RM: On the one hand, she is a bad mother. She says so herself. On the other hand, one forgets that she herself was the result of a rape and that she suffered so much from her pregnancy that she tried to drown herself. She is the illegitimate child of a domestic servant who doesn't love her.

MC: Right. She doesn't know who her father is. The man who is in love, one would suppose, with her, allegedly raped her although the reader doesn't know for sure. In short, she had a very difficult and painful past. Thus, she is a character who should be pitied rather than condemned.

RM: Of course, at the beginning one sees Reynalda from the point of view of Marie-Noëlle, who suffers and doesn't know exactly why. Then gradually . . .

MC: One understands why Reynalda, too, is so miserable. There is one thing, however, that she can be blamed for. When she obtains a sort of literary success, she abandons Ludovic. In that case, she is a woman who is only thinking about herself.

RM: Yes. After having listed all the positive things she did—i.e., write two books, avoid, unlike her mother, the submissive role of a domestic servant, et cetera—she becomes rather worldly. Like the bourgeois writer, Elinor, in your short story "Three Women in Manhattan."

MC: Yes. She does all the radio and television shows. She reads everywhere. In doing so, though, she is rejecting her interiority. She becomes . . . exterior.

RM: She doesn't do anything to clarify things for her daughter. Once, Reynalda started to explain everything to Marie-Noëlle, but she stopped abruptly in the middle of her explanation.

MC: True. I don't think she is very interested in the life of her daughter. . . . It's difficult to defend her. She's not a very positive character.

RM: Perhaps we could say, though, that she led the way for Marie-Noëlle. In her writing, for example.

MC: Yes, she opened the door for her daughter. Then, as Marie-Noëlle says, she closed it too. Marie-Noëlle says, "I wanted love, but I didn't get any. I wanted literature, but my mother had already done it." Thus, ultimately, Reynalda opens, and then closes, the door.

RM: I asked myself, though, if Reynalda didn't actually succeed in constructing a new vision of herself, of her personality. Thus, once again, she does, in a certain sense, what Marie-Noëlle will have to do at the end of the novel.

MC: Well, she did start from nothing. She has a lot of energy! And she did in fact reconstruct herself.

RM: Socially and psychologically.

MC: Yes, she moves from wanting to commit suicide to wanting to write, to the act of wanting to express what is inside of her. A nice progression.

RM: But Ludovic says that everything she writes will be a lie.

MC: But everyone lies. Everyone!

RM: Ludovic is an interesting character too. If one can talk about a new Caribbean woman, perhaps, it is not unjustified to talk about a new Caribbean man. Clearly, Ludovic is the opposite of the traditional Caribbean male as you have described him in other texts. For one, he is not the biological father of Marie-Noëlle. Nor does he leave after the birth of his children.

MC: No, he stays.

RM: And even though he isn't the biological father, he's the one who wants Reynalda to bring her daughter back to Paris.

MC: Right. He's the one who wants Marie-Noëlle brought back to Europe.

RM: Perhaps we can consider Ludovic as a sort of counter-father.

MC: Yes, the opposite of the traditional father.

RM: Exactly. Thus, the work you do on male and female roles in this text is prodigious! From the beginning, one is so focused on the role of women that perhaps one overlooks the fact that Ludovic is the narrative depiction of a new role for Caribbean men.

MC: Yes, his role in very important.

RM: If we compare him to masculine protagonists in some of your other novels, again we see how different he is. But perhaps what is most interesting for me is his *métissage*. He is a bit like Stanley in that he has a very broad cultural vision.

MC: He is Haitian, and he is Cuban. He has traveled throughout the world. He speaks many languages. He is the image of what the West Indies will become. He is a sort of future projection of Stanley, of people who don't have a nationality, who don't have a precise homeland or culture, who have a sort of general, global culture, but who often don't have social roles commensurate with their vision.

RM: Yes, he's multilingual. He's an excellent example of the knowledge and wisdom that come from travel, from emigration. . . . Perhaps we could discuss for a minute the novelistic trajectory of Marie-Noëlle. I would say she wants to find a way of life, a way of living, that isn't determined by others. Would you agree?

MC: She wants to be liberated from the opinions of others. She doesn't want to have to answer to others for her identity or for her nationality. She must be the only judge. The only opinion that can be important is her own. She wants to be liberated from all the constructions others make of her. She doesn't want to have to act in accordance with their expectations. She wants to be free. That's very difficult, and it takes a lot of time. Finally, just at the end of the novel, she begins to articulate, hesitantly, a few words.

RM: Yes, and she calls that her "cure" [*guérison*].

MC: It is the beginning of her cure.

RM: One senses she is on the right track.

MC: We hope. For her sake.

RM: I want to try to understand if she really isn't very different from your other female protagonists. She's not determined by geography, for example.

MC: True, but she's the same as the others. She's the same as Veronica, the heroine in my first novel, *Hérémakhonon*. Marie-Noëlle continues along the same path as Veronica, but Veronica stops after her failure in Africa. Veronica leaves— perhaps for France, but it really doesn't matter—

whereas Marie-Noëlle continues along the same trajectory. After all her deceptions and all the negative things that happen to her, Marie-Noëlle finally reaches a point where she says, "O.K. That's enough! From now on, I am going to live without worrying about the opinion others have of me. I am going to try to live for myself and in relation to myself." Ultimately, she is not that different from the other heroines. She simply pushes herself farther down the road of introspection.

RM: Yes, but Veronica is determined, somewhat, by her country of origin, by her language, by her genes too, if I can put it that way.

MC: Perhaps, but Veronica doesn't really know who she is. She knows her father, she knows her country of origin, and she knows her language, but, nonetheless, the entire book demonstrates that she too is in search of her identity. Everyone is searching for his or her identity, but Marie-Noëlle is the only one who finishes her search and says to herself, "I am going to live in harmony with myself without knowing the exact answers to all the questions that have been put to me."

RM: By saying to herself, "No, I am not determined by my country of origin. No, I am not determined by the language I speak. No, I am not determined by . . ."

MC: "My social class."

RM: "By the genetic structure of my father." Thus, in a certain sense, we can say that she overcomes all those so-called determinisms, that she rejects them.

MC: Yes, she succeeds in overcoming them and in finding a definition of her own unique personality.

RM: Thus the importance of her trip to the United States.

MC: Exactly, because it is in the United States that she realizes that having a country is not that important, having a language is not that important, having a specific place of origin is not that important.

RM: I saw a television program the other day on adoption, or rather about women, as children, who had been abandoned by their mothers. Years after the separation, many women still desperately wanted to know who their mothers were. The adoption agencies, on the other hand, defended their policy of never revealing the identity of a child's donor. Especially since those were the original conditions. I started asking myself if that desire wasn't the sociological equivalent of the problematic you are raising. The desire to find out the identity of their parents was so strong that some of the women interviewed were working together on the formulation of a law that would force the agencies to reveal the identity of the donor. I found the discussion of that urge related directly to the problematic of your novel.

MC: Yes, I agree. But I think now that many agencies make information about the biological parents available.

RM: According to the program I saw, that wasn't the case.

MC: It depends on the country.

RM: This particular program was about French women. In the United States . . .

MC: I think they have the right to know. In England too.

RM: Before we finish our discussion of *Desirada,* could we talk a bit about the role of Garvey? He seems to represent the anti-quest. Thus, his mode of being is diametrically opposite to that of Marie-Noëlle.

MC: The small child, the son.

RM: Yes. He's not at all interested in his past. In fact, he seems to consider himself European.

MC: He is born far from the West Indies, and neither his mother nor his father maintains any connection with the place of their origin. He is not familiar with it, nor does he ever return. Many young people of the West Indies consider themselves Europeans. I know a lot of them. I have discussed this with a fellow writer, Caryl Phillips. He's from St. Kitts. He left the island when he was three months old, and he grew up in England. He considers himself a European. Thus, it's another problematic all together. It's not the problem of insular identity.

RM: Being here now, at the time of the elections for the European parliament, I realize how difficult it might be for people living in Guadeloupe to consider themselves European. It seems to give the question of identity, and the question of pan-Caribbeanism, an entirely new dimension. For me, it was strange seeing Sarkosy, and other candidates in the election, walking among voters trying to convince them that they were Europeans when in fact, as we know, they were colonized by Europeans. And their independence was denied by Europeans. I remember asking myself if a Caribbean Common Market wasn't more logical.

MC: We tried that. We just didn't succeed.

RM: A few last questions about *Desirada*. The word *rêve* occurs quite frequently in your novel. Marie-Noëlle, to give just one example, dreams of her birth. Is dreaming more important in *Desirada* than in your other novels?

MC: It seems to me it's important in all my texts, isn't it? Dreams are an extremely important dimension of West Indian culture. Dreams always make us think. What do they mean? What are they telling us? I think that they are important in the other texts too.

RM: I want, perhaps erroneously, to link the word primarily to Marie-Noëlle, to what she must do at the end: i.e., re-imagine herself, re-create her life. I found it fascinating how she tries to imagine the life of her mother in Paris. It is also interesting stylistically because, as she narrates, one starts to think that it's the narrator speaking . . .

MC: And not her!

RM: Yes, there is that intriguing slippage in point of view. In any case, I was thinking that it is precisely this capacity to dream, to reconstruct imaginatively, that allows her to go beyond what she is.

MC: It's a sort of constant in my novels. The capacity and the need to dream have an important function in life, and it seems to me that they are not unique to Marie-Noëlle.

RM: To me, it seems significant that Marie-Noëlle is the one who dreams in your novel. I don't believe, for example, that Ludovic dreams. He even says, on a slightly different level, that the "American dream" is dead. In fact, the novel demonstrates that it is very much alive. Garvey . . .

MC: No, he doesn't dream either. Reynalda dreams because she writes.

RM: Yes, that is what I was trying to get at. *The Last of the African Kings* [1997; orig. *Les derniers rois mages,* 1992] begins with Spero's dream, but the capacity to dream, in *Desirada* in any case, seems limited to the female characters. . . . I was always intrigued by the title of a play by Calderón de la Barca . . .

MC: *Life Is a Dream.*

RM: Yes. The title, polyvalent to be sure, seems to indicate that dreams create life. By dreaming,

conceiving of oneself differently, one can construct a reality greater than . . .

MC: Prosaic reality.

RM: By the way, is the English translation of *Desirada* coming out soon?

MC: It should be out in November 2000.

RM: A final observation about the role of sexuality in *Desirada*. In this novel you portray, it seems to me, sexuality without sensuality. That is not really new in your novels. I am thinking of Thécla in *Tree of Life,* to cite only one example. It is frequently the case in *Segu* too. I am going to translate one sentence from the French as an example: "After Terri's departure, Stanley took over again his place in Marie-Noëlle's bed" (148). We have here a simple changing of the guard; it is banal and without affection.

MC: Yes.

RM: In this regard, I would say it is rather unlike certain of your other novels. I am thinking of *I, Tituba, Black Witch of Salem.* In that novel, Tituba's sexuality is related to her evolution. And, of course, to some of her problems! Nonetheless, it is an important component of her self-expression. In *Desirada,* on the other hand, sexuality is . . .

MC: It's anguish and confusion!

RM: I would like to move now to your most recent text, *Le cœur à rire et à pleurer: Contes vrais de mon enfance,* one that just came out this year [1999]. What was the original impulse behind this text?

MC: Essentially, it represents my response to the loss of a son who died recently. To be honest, we were not very close. In fact, the relationship between us was always somewhat strained. Perhaps partly because of me. Nonetheless, or perhaps because of that, his death was traumatic for me.

RM: Approximately how old was your son when he died?

MC: Around forty.

RM: And so the text was a sort of response . . .

MC: Of therapy.

RM: How would you say this loss affected your writing?

MC: I stopped writing fiction for a long time. For almost a year.

RM: And now?

MC: I am writing again.

RM: The title of your text is taken from a song, isn't it?

MC: Yes, an old, very well known, popular French song called "A la claire fontaine."

RM: I found the subtitle intriguing. There is an intentional ambiguity in the words "contes vrais," isn't there?

MC: When you try to tell the truth about your life, you realize immediately that your truth is fiction and that you are fabricating a reality, a somewhat imaginary life. Nonetheless, the desire to be autobiographical was real.

RM: Is this the first text where you speak autobiographically of your youth?

MC: Yes.

RM: But couldn't we say that the description of Marie-Noëlle's birth is based on your own?

MC: Marie-Noëlle's? No.

RM: Reynalda gives birth to Marie-Noëlle on Mardi Gras. In *Le cœur à rire*. . . this is also the day your mother feels her first contractions.

MC: Yes. And Veronica too. Both are born during the period of Carnival.

RM: Like you, if we can believe *Le cœur à rire*. . .! At one time, I thought that perhaps *Desirada* and *Le cœur à rire* . . . were written at the same time, but that is clearly not the case. The progression is linear if the second text corresponds . . .

MC: To a very specific time period.

RM: And now, are you back to writing novels?

MC: Yes, I am back in the mold of fiction . . . It was difficult, though. I was groping around for a while. I didn't exactly know what I was going to write or what I wanted to say.

RM: You mention, in *Le cœur à rire* . . . , a certain Tertullien family. If I understood correctly, it is in fact the Tyrolien family.

MC: There is a resemblance.

RM: We have already spoken about Guy Tyrolien. I have only recently had the chance to look over his books of poetry. I like the titles: *Balles d'or* and *Feuilles* about your first play.

MC: He wrote a preface.

RM: In *Le cœur à rire* . . . , I believe it's the first time in your work that you mention Alexandre, who called himself "Sandrino" to appear more American.

MC: My brother.[4]

RM: Who wrote too. I found it interesting that you were surrounded by . . .

MC: He was the only one in the family who wrote. He couldn't get his books published, though. He tried. He sent off manuscripts. They came back. I was always there to read them, to correct them for him. . . . There were times when he couldn't write, when his hand trembled.

RM: Did he have a muscular dysfunction?

MC: No! It was his brain. I saw the difficulties of becoming a writer.

RM: In trying to point out possible influences, it is interesting to note that there were people in your proximity who took writing seriously.

MC: He was the only one.

RM: Perhaps there was a small influence exerted by Guy Tyrolien too?

MC: That came much later.

RM: In *Le cœur à rire* . . . there are gaps. For example, you don't relate, in depth, any sentimental experiences, with the possible exception of "The Bluest Eye," the humorous anecdote linked by title, if not really by subject matter, to Toni Morrison's first novel.

MC: No. That wasn't the focus. The focus was my relation to my mother.

RM: To whom you dedicated the book. And to your family.

MC: Yes, O.K.

RM: I read somewhere that *Hérémakhonon* was your favorite novel. Is that true?

MC: Perhaps it was true. Now, however, I prefer *Desirada*.

RM: Both are extremely important texts, but there is a unique tone in your first novel.

MC: Yes, there's a bit of mockery. It's cynical. But it's not my favorite now. Then it was because the novel wasn't understood, nor was it well received.

RM: That tone, however, is especially interesting because it has, for the most part, disappeared from your later work. It indicates . . .

MC: The provocative arrival of a new author on the literary scene.

RM: Was your use of that tone intentionally provocative?

MC: Yes.

RM: Could you say a word or two about the style of *Hérémakhonon*? It has been said that it is a text difficult to follow. I want to discuss a short passage of the Richard Philcox translation. It is interesting because you have written what is essentially a dialogue between Veronica and

Oumou Hawa in paragraph form without quotation marks. It is as if the dialogue takes place in Veronica's head.

MC: The whole book is like that. A dialogue in her head. There are no words spoken, no responses. That's intentional.

RM: But in the very next sequence, Oumou Hawa does respond. She says, "Saliou says you've got to fight even so" (93). Thus, sometimes the interlocutor speaks, and sometimes he/she doesn't. Sometimes there is a real dialogue. Sometimes the dialogue is embedded in an interior monologue.

MC: There are no rules. It was a bit spontaneous.

RM: Upon rereading Hérémakhonon, I found some interesting names embedded in it. Reynalda, for example.

MC: It's a very West Indian name. Those names were very popular in the West Indies at one time. Reynalda. Even Maryse. No one is called Maryse now! Thécla. They were very confining West Indian names.

RM: It is interesting to find, in your first novel, the name of one of the principal protagonists of your last novel, written some twenty-plus years later. You mention Segu too. It is a sort of synonym for home, for Guadeloupe. But again, the word is used some eight years before the publication of *Segu* [1984; Eng. 1987]. There is perhaps another link between the first and last novel. Neither of the female protagonists has children. In fact, the word *sterile*[5] is used in the description of both of the young heroines.

MC: Marie-Noëlle isn't sterile, is she? No. She doesn't have any children. Not yet, but she . . . Veronica says, "Je n'aurai jamais d'enfants." But she doesn't know either. She imagines she's sterile, but there is no proof. It's a sort of cultural sterility. Since they don't know who they are, since they aren't educated about their own identity, how can they give life to another being? It's an emblematic sterility. It doesn't really involve the body. I believe it's a question of spiritual anguish; thus, they cannot communicate or give life to another being.

RM: Then this childlessness, common to the two young women, should be considered more symbolic than physical.

MC: Yes.[6]

RM: I want to ask you a couple of questions about your novel, *The Last of the African Kings,* and more specifically about the chapter called "The

Origins." At first, I thought you invented this passage. Later, after reading a series of interviews you did with Françoise Pfaff, I realized it was the myth of the origins of the royal family of Abomey (97).

MC: Yes, that's true.

RM: Has this myth been recorded?

MC: Yes, it has been recorded in several different places. It's the foundation of the ethnic group. The original myth is a very well known one. Agasu, the panther.

RM: Did you rework it considerably for your novel?

MC: Yes, I completely changed it. I rewrote it in my own way.

RM: Stylistically, or did you rework the content too?

MC: Stylistically! Not the content. The panther and the young girl have a child. Essentially, the content of my version is faithful to the original.

RM: I have compared this myth to the account of the Creation in the book of Genesis. Some of the ideas that came out of that comparison are interesting. For one, the concept of guilt completely disappears. Furthermore, instead of an idyllic garden, we have a jungle forest replete with ferocious animals.

MC: Right. It's the opposition between Africa and the Garden of Eden, the garden imagined in Judeo-Christian thinking.

RM: But isn't there a possible contradiction? Your novel criticizes an exaggerated dependence on the past, the veneration by Spero of a picture of his African ancestor. But with this beautiful text, don't you too, in a certain way, invite us . . .

MC: No, because the myth is rewritten, transformed. It means that you do what you want with the past. One uses the text, or one does what one wants with it. It is not considered as a myth that only has one meaning. It is considered as a story that can be interpreted however you want. It is, in fact, the proof that the past has to be reinterpreted according to one's needs.

RM: O.K. Now I would like to try to trace a relation between this reworking of a myth of origin and the situation of Marie-Noëlle. Couldn't we say there is a link between the two—i.e., that both represent subversions of myths of origin? On one hand, we have the myth of the origin of the Dahomeyan royal family. On the other hand, we have Marie-Noëlle's reflection on the identity of her father, an obsession that is the primary cause of her unsettled state of existence. Thus, both novels undermine myths of origin.

MC: I personally didn't think of that.

RM: No doubt! Perhaps I am totally off base, but isn't it the case that the life of Marie-Noëlle is perverted, stunted, deflected by her obsessive reflection on her origin?

MC: Perhaps. When I was writing the two texts, though, I had no intention, conscious in any case, of going back to myths of origin and perverting them. Perhaps, though, by analyzing them, one could arrive at such a conclusion. At the beginning, however, that wasn't what I intended.

RM: To conclude, I wanted to ask you if have ever, among your extensive writings, made any theoretical formulations about Art?

MC: No, not really.

RM: You are more involved in producing Art than in analyzing it. A couple of final questions. One about teaching French West Indian literature. What are the bases, the most important texts?

MC: Everyone: Césaire, Glissant, Chamoiseau, Confiant, Simone Schwarz-Bart, Gisèle Pineau, et cetera.

RM: Gisèle Pineau too?

MC: Yes, everyone.

RM: Finally, I am thinking of young writers. What bit of advice might you have for them?

MC: You must be very patient. And very courageous. You need to have faith in what you are doing.

RM: Because that faith won't come from the outside world.

MC: No. What you are doing must satisfy you. Don't trust others too much, interviews, articles in newspapers. No, what counts is your own personal judgment.

RM: This is perhaps a good place to stop. I thank you very much for your patience, for the generous gift of your time, and for having received me so cordially here at your home in Montebello.

Robert H. McCormick Jr., Summer 2000

▪ WORKS CITED

Clark, VéVé A. "Je me suis réconciliée avec mon île: Une interview de Maryse Condé." *Callaloo,* 12:1 (1989), pp. 86–133.

Condé, Maryse. *Hérémakhonon.* Paris. Union Générale d'Editions. 1976.

———. *Heremakhonon.* Richard Philcox, tr. Washington, D.C. Three Continents. 1982.

———. *Desirada.* Paris. Laffont. 1997.

———. *Le cœur à rire: Contes vrais de mon enfance.* Paris. Laffont. 1999.

———. "O Brave New World." In *Multiculturalism and Hybridity in African Literatures.* Hal Wylie and Bernth Lindfors, eds. Trenton, N.J. Africa World Press. 2000. Pp. 29–36.

Pfaff, Françoise. *Conversations with Maryse Condé.* Lincoln. University of Nebraska Press. 1996.

[1] Condé's mother died in 1956 or 1957.

[2] A small island to the east of Guadeloupe, called La Désirade in French.

[3] Most probably Guy Lasserre.

[4] Condé indicates elsewhere that her brother's actual name was Guy (Clark, 90).

[5] Cf. *Hérémakhonon,* p. 103 in the original French edition of 1976, and *Desirada,* p. 143.

[6] This common description, or fear, can perhaps be related to an illness Condé suffered as a young woman in Paris. In *Le cœur à rire* . . . Condé relates that her doctors told her, after an operation for an ovarian tumor, that her chances of being a mother would be greatly reduced (132). Nonetheless, she subsequently gave birth to four children.

Whose House Is This? Space and Place in Calixthe Beyala's *C'est le soleil qui m'a brûlée* and *La Petite Fille du réverbère*

The success of Mariama Bâ's novel *Une si longue lettre* (1980) contributed greatly to the female voice's entering the mainstream of francophone African fiction. Clearly announcing women's literature of revolt, the text revealed to Senegalese and foreign readers that one woman's struggle against polygamy could become the catalyst for personal growth and self-definition, and it subsequently opened the way for the second generation of francophone African women novelists. Ken Bugul, Werewere Liking, Calixthe Beyala, and others would take Bâ's attack on African patriarchy a step further with texts that would prove to be more aggressive, more rebellious, and more audacious in content and form.

Beginning with her first novel, *C'est le soleil qui m'a brûlée* (1987), the Cameroonian novelist Calixthe Beyala has engaged in systematic provocation of francophone African literature, presenting protagonists who are politically, socially, and economically marginalized and exploring a range of cultural taboos. She depicts prostitutes, pimps, sadistic parents. Her characters engage in rape, incest, self-mutilation, and murder. As

Calixthe Beyala (*Robert H. Taylor*)

Odile Cazenave and Béatrice Rangira Gallimore have shown, Beyala uses marginality to articulate a feminist response to an African patriarchal tradition that refuses woman's right to self-expression and control of her body.

Although Beyala joins Bâ in charting her protagonist's evolution toward self-realization, her first novel deconstructs the myths of the nurturing mother and the protective hearth that Bâ carefully constructs. In Bâ's text, *Une si longue lettre* (Eng. *So Long a Letter*), it is clear that as her protagonist Ramatoulaye faces the psychological pain caused by her husband's decision to take a second wife, she remains the stable anchor, assuring financial and emotional support for her children after her husband has left. Ramatoulaye never abandons her role as the caring parent affirming the importance of her home as a protective hearth. In *C'est le soleil qui m'a brûlée* Beyala's protagonist, Ateba, is the daughter of an alcoholic prostitute who abandoned her as a child. Consequently, Ateba suffers from a lack of nurturing space in the house she cannot call her home following her mother's departure. Treated as a stranger, a servant, a commodity, in her aunt's cold and forbidding house, she encounters the "unhomely" which Homi Bhabha defines as "the estranging sense of the relocation of the home and the world in an unhallowed place" (1992, 141). The young woman's physical poverty and psychological dislocation mirror the alienation of inhabitants of *bidonvilles,* postcolonial African slums.

Linking the concept of home to the concept of self, I will chart the search for place in two of Beyala's novels,

C'est le soleil qui m'a brûlée and *La Petite Fille du réverbère,* as I explore the hypothesis that the attempt to recover the protective hearth is integral to the protagonist's search for self-realization. Beyala initiates the quest in her first novel, and her latest work, a largely autobiographical novel published a decade later, develops the theme further in surprising and significant ways. In both texts, the protagonist negotiates between physical and imaginative space, the realms of the real and the imaginary. Ateba attempts to recuperate a childhood home situated in memory, and to construct a future home beyond the confines of carceral space. In *La Petite Fille du réverbère* Beyala, nicknamed Tapoussière, inhabits a childhood home that her grandmother's mastery of oral tradition opens to mythic space, and seeks to find her place in her community and the world at large.

In this study, I adopt Yi-Fu Tuan's definition of *place* as space enriched with human experience and understanding, and Gaston Bachelard's analysis of the house as intimate space. In *La poétique de l'espace,* his topoanalysis or study of the sites of intimate life, Bachelard posits home as the crucial site of one's intimate life, the refuge where the human imagination serves to integrate life's experience. In his analysis, he uses the term *espace heureux,* felicitous space, to designate home as interior space, the anchor without which men and women remain fragmented individuals.[1]

Bachelard's topoanalysis, however, does not distinguish between men's and women's experience. The appropriation of space, both physical and imaginative, is an important factor in the process of women's self-realization, and a key element in women's struggle for empowerment in Africa, where patriarchal domination weighs heavily upon women's domestic space. Masculine supremacy is a reality, the important public sphere reserved for man, the less valued domestic sphere given to women. Although the domestic sphere is considered in the broadest sense of the term—in other words, as a household constituting the center of production and consumption of goods—African women are greatly valued as instruments of reproduction but largely unappreciated for their significant contribution to their society's economic production.[2]

Situating both texts in the slums of Douala (Ateba lives with her aunt in the *quartier général* or QG,[3] Tapoussière with her grandmother in Kassalafam), Beyala portrays the lives of rural immigrants who left impoverished villages in the hope of economic gain in the city. Presenting the sociological reality of the uprooted rural poor, she shows rural dislocation often resulting in a "matriarchy by default" with women heads of household replacing absent men, the unemployed who have become transient. Examining the status of Cameroonian women who are single heads of household, Julienne Ayissi Ngono finds that whereas traditional law does not recognize the single mother as the legal head of the family, written law, in contrast, does. Yet despite legal protection, the female head of household most often remains economically and socially disadvantaged, usually earning a living for her family in the informal sector: agriculture, small commerce, or prostitution.

In *C'est le soleil qui m'a brûlée* Beyala depicts Ateba's fight for survival in the QG as a struggle against confinement in two spaces, the real and the imaginary. Throughout the text, Ateba negotiates between the outer visible and tangible world of physical poverty and human misery, and the inner world of dream, memory, and desire. To convey this dynamic, the novelist adopts a double-voiced narrative: the voice of Ateba's soul, "Moi," expressing the protagonist's inner thoughts; and the voice of the narrator, adopting the code of social realism to depict external reality. In both realms, the real and the imaginary, the QG is a carceral space, invisible gates keeping inhabitants locked in and outsiders locked out. Nineteen years old and a high-school graduate, Ateba remains in Aunt Ada's house doing daily chores in exchange for room and board. Monitoring Ateba's daily routine, Ada intends to control her niece's future by negotiating her marriage with a man of means. In the interim, she treats Ateba as a child and a prisoner, her "patriarchal" mentality imprisoning the young woman's body and controlling her movements in accordance with an exacting principle of virginity.

As Ateba is locked in, Jean, the potential tenant of the room for rent in the house, is nearly locked out. Because taxis refuse to venture into the QG, he walks a long distance, crosses a bridge in torrid heat, and faces the hostile interrogation of the proprietor, Aunt Ada, before acquiring the room. Having finally entered this carceral universe, the stranger becomes another threat to Ateba's world. He is a force of disorder disturbing the equilibrium of the house defined as female domestic space. Jean not only keeps a messy room and leaves muddy footprints on clean floors, but also assumes the role of male predator. The room he has rented becomes a dangerous trap for Ateba. After she comes to Jean's room with a neighbor's message, and inadvertently discovers him in bed with a woman, he punishes her for her "transgression."

> Il l'oblige à se baisser, à s'accroupir. La tête dans les odeurs de l'homme, la bouche contre son sexe, elle se dit qu'il est devenu complètement fou, qu'elle est devenue complètement folle, puisqu'elle est responsable de ce qui lui arrive. . . . A genoux le visage levé vers le ciel . . . la position de la femme fautive depuis la nuit des temps . . . assise. Accroupie. (45)

He forces her down low, forces her to crouch. With her head pushed into his manly smells, her mouth against his penis, she says to herself he's gone completely mad, that she's gone completely mad since she is responsible for what happens to her. . . . On her knees, her face raised to the sky . . . the position of the offending woman since time immemorial . . . on the floor. Crouched.(24)[4]

Humiliated, Ateba never allows herself to be trapped again in his room. They meet later in public space—a bar, a street, Ada's living room. However, this man has disturbed her world, by forcing her to recognize not only her own impotence in the face of his aggression but also her own conflicted desire—for love or sex? Her motives are unclear to her. Finally, the encounter in Jean's room foreshadows the violent reversal that will occur later in another man's room, when Ateba, in revenge for violence and humiliation, murders the man who rapes her.

Until Jean's arrival, Ateba's emotional defenses work for her. In public space, she wears a mask, cooperating outwardly although inwardly seething with resentment against her aunt's control and indifference. From the private space of her room, she writes letters to imaginary women, folding her sheets of paper into paper boats and launching them on the waters of the QG sewers. And within the privacy of the room, she maintains her freedom from men, releasing her own sexual tensions by masturbating before falling asleep at night. As Jean attacks the emotional walls Ateba has constructed, he threatens Ada's marriage plans for her as well. Alternating the threat of violence with the danger of seduction, his attempted manipulation of Ateba challenges Ada's control over her niece's movements and the young woman's body. Ironically, Ada remains unaware that her renter menaces Ateba—by rape or seduction. To assure herself and the community of Ateba's virginity, she forces her to endure the humiliating "rite de l'œuf," the egg test, which proves that Ateba is still submissive, obedient, intact. Through the psychological portrait of Ada, Beyala reveals women's complicity in rituals that perpetuate patriarchy and abuse women's bodies.

Threatened by female complicity with patriarchy as well as by male intrusion, Ateba experiences increasing anxiety in the house that is no home. At times the "unhomely" space takes on the characteristics of a haunted house filled with avenging ghosts:

> Les mânes des ancêtres surgissent. Leurs plaintes illuminent la maison et la transforment en un gigantesque brasier. Ateba hurle, sa voix s'enfuit,

les cris refluent pêle-mêle dans son corps, elle ne
peut plus les ordonner, elle ne veut plus les ordonner. (38)

The spirits of the ancestors spring up. Their
groans illuminate the house and transform it into
an enormous inferno. Ateba shrieks, her voice
leaves her, the screams flow back into her body,
one on top of the other. She can no longer command them, she no longer wants to be in command. (19)

As visions of the house haunted by destructive ghosts
terrify Ateba, they risk not only dislodging her public
mask of obedience and passivity, but loosening her grip
on reality as well. As Eloise Brière notes, the stifled voice
is becoming a source of madness (230). Thus, imaginative space that promises refuge may finally imprison
Ateba in insanity.

In traditional and modern societies alike, the house
has generally been conceived of as female domestic
space. In *La poétique de l'espace* Bachelard links the concept of the house to the body of the nurturing mother:
"La vie commence bien, elle commence enfermée, pro-
tégée, tout tiède dans le giron de la maison" (26; "Life
begins well, it begins enclosed, protected, all warm in
the bosom of the house" [7]). However, Mieke Bal reveals the inherent contradiction in the gendering of the
house as female space; it is, she argues, the site of patriarchy: "In the house fatherhood establishes itself; the
house becomes fatherhood's synecdochic metaphor"
(171).

Turning to the history of architecture, we find that
architecture's role has been to control woman's sexuality: the young girl's chastity, the wife's fidelity. Examining the gendering of domestic space, one discovers
woman's complicity in patriarchal domination. The patriarch gives his wife authority to replace him as the
guardian of their daughter's chastity, a role which, once
she accepts, perpetuates patriarchal domination within
apparent female domestic space.[5] Given the history of
patriarchal domination of domestic space, it is not surprising that as Bal challenges the female gendering of
the house, Sandra Gilbert and Susan Gubar find that
domestic space entraps women, producing women's fiction in which spatial imagery of enclosure and escape
is often elaborated with "obsessive intensity" (83). From
Virginia Woolf's "room of one's own" to Charlotte Brontë's "madwoman in the attic," women in literature have
occupied confined inner spaces.

Beyala's text presents spatial imagery of enclosure
and escape as Ateba retreats from painful reality to find
refuge in imaginative space. "Etre ailleurs," to be elsewhere, becomes her strategy for survival in the world
that denies her the comfort of a nurturing mother and

the shelter of a protective hearth. Hence, she withdraws
physically and psychologically into the confined space
of her bedroom. Although the physical space of her
bedroom is disagreeable, a reflection of the physical
misery of the ghetto—"L'odeur de renfermé, d'urine et
de moisissure la prend au nez" (96; "The smell of stale-
ness, urine and moisture fills the nose" [62])—the room
becomes a creative space for writing and reflection.
Here, Ateba, like Ramatoulaye, composes letters to
women, but Bâ's protagonist writes to her closest friend,
whereas Ateba's narratees are imaginary.

The space in which Ateba writes letters to women
opens upon imaginative space, her refuge for meditation, recollection, fantasy. As Ateba retreats into the
inner spaces of dream and memory, the room she
shared with her mother in the past emerges as an impenetrable fortress against outside intrusion. Betty's
bedroom remains anchored in Ateba's memory as a protective hearth, "espace heureux," the place where her
mother expressed maternal love. Ateba recalls its
warmth and comfort: "allongée dans le lit de sa mère,
la tête sur ses genoux" (128; "stretched out on her
mother's bed, her head in her mother's lap" [86]). Although she remembers her mother's care, more often
than not it was the child who nurtured the psychologically fragile parent. Ateba denies the painful truth that
Betty abandoned her to follow a lover; she patiently
awaits Betty's return, dreaming of "their place," the
home where mother and daughter, away from men,
might live in peace. On the one hand, Ateba, in her
search for shelter for her wounded soul, articulates a desire to return to maternal space, a return to the womb.
On the other hand, she expresses the desire for alternative space, a space apart from man where woman may
free her creative potential.

"Their place," however, is an illusion. As if she were
waiting for Godot, Ateba anticipates a return that will
not occur. Refuge in imaginative space, Ateba's strategy
for survival, leads only to an impasse. Closed space,
protecting and reassuring for the person seeking refuge,
eventually becomes a prison when the individual must
get out. As Bachelard reminds us, withdrawal implies
reemergence: "L'être qui rentre dans sa coquille prépare
une sortie" (110; "A creature that hides and 'withdraws
into its shell,' is preparing 'a way out'" [111]).

Ironically, Ateba is blocked by the memory of the
very person whose presence she desires. She fears repeating her mother's trajectory: "Pute aussi: à elle-
même, à son passé, à son impuissance à briser le fil du
désepoir. Doucement, elle se retire en elle-même" (73;
"Whore as well: to herself, to her past, to her helplessness in breaking the thread of despair. Gently she retreats into herself" [45]). Although she never learns why

Betty took to the streets, she knows that once her mother was there she was unable to retrace her steps back to domesticity: "Ici, dans cette rue, Betty a vécu, c'est dans sa boue qu'elle s'est façonnée" (92; "Betty lived here in this street; it's this sludge that shaped her" [59–60]). Contemplating the QG streets, Ateba acknowledges the dual nature of the signifier that haunts her life. For families, the streets are centripetal, leading home to the hearth; for streetwalkers, they are centrifugal, leading out to prostitution:

> C'est l'heure du crépuscule. Celle qui ramène dans les cabanes hommes, femmes et enfants, les genoux fatigués de la journée de travail. Celle qui paradoxalement déverse dans les rues la femme aux baisers et aux caresses infâmes. (63–64)

> It is dusk. The time of day that brings men, women and children back to their shacks, tired of the day's work. The time of day that, paradoxically, pours into the street the women of easy virtue and loathsome caresses. (39)

For the prostitute's daughter attempting to find her way out of the QG, the streets are snares. They are dirty and ugly: "Le boulevard se rétrécit, devient sale, puis crasseux" (73; "The boulevard grows narrow, becomes dirty, then downright filthy" [46]). They are dangerous: "Des soldats, mitraillette au poing, débouchent de partout, cernent la rue" (106; "Soldiers, submachine guns in hand, come out from everywhere, check the street" [70]). Leading nowhere, they define the QG as carceral space: "Le QG ne mène nulle part" (73; "The QG leads nowhere at all" [45]).

Struggling to situate herself elsewhere, however, Ateba is forced to come to terms with the symbolic referents of Betty's life: the streets where she picked up her clients; the rooms where they exchanged money for sex. Her search for place takes on aspects of an epic journey, ritual purification preceding the hero's confrontation with the enemy. First, Ateba descends into the street on a rainy night, cleansing and purifying her body in the falling rain: "Elle a l'impression que chaque goutte d'eau l'immacule et la sort du QG et de ses noirceurs d'égout" (135; "She is under the impression that each drop of water is making her immaculately clean and taking her out of the QG and the black filth of its sewers" [91]). Following the death of a QG prostitute, her closest friend Irène, she takes on the role of prostitute, confronting the male predator in closed space, her client's room. There, in a paroxysm of fury, she murders the man who abuses her.

Through this act of violence, Ateba takes revenge for the physical and psychological harm men have inflicted upon her, her mother, other women. Confusing the man she has killed with her dead friend Irène, and whispering passionately, "Viens dans mes bras. . . . Viens tout contre moi. . . . Je t'aime" (173; "Come into my arms. . . . Come close, close to me. . . . I love you" [119]), Ateba transforms heterosexual violence—man's violence against woman met with woman's violence against man—into homosexual love. The murder, in self-defense, is Ateba's ultimate act of resistance, the passionate and erotic embrace of Irène, her ultimate act of female bonding. In this final scene, Beyala links violence with eroticism to boldly challenge the norms of patriarchal discourse.

The text ends with Ateba leaving the room: "Ses pas résonnent sur le bitume, elle avance lentement, pas à pas, vers la clarté diffuse à l'horizon" (174; "Her footsteps reverberate on the asphalt. Slowly she moves on, step by step, towards the radiating brightness on the horizon" [119–20]). Liberation, however, occurs only in mythic space; it remains symbolic, and incomplete. The young woman leaving the room has lost her grip on reality; she is caught in both the inner spaces of her mind and the outer world of reality. Facing imprisonment in an institution, Ateba becomes yet another "madwoman in the attic," literally and figuratively trapped in carceral space.

In *La Petite Fille du réverbère* Beyala takes key elements from *C'est le soleil qui m'a brûlée* to transform a closed narrative—Ateba's failure to connect past to present, memory to expectation—into an open one, Tapoussière's trajectory toward the future. Borrowing Katherine Platt's distinction between home as centripetal energy enclosing and turning inward and home as centrifugal energy extending its meaning outward into the world, I view Beyala's first novel as enclosed, centripetal, and her latest as open, centrifugal.

In *La Petite Fille du réverbère* the protagonist is a child of the slums whose mother is absent, her father unknown. Although Tapoussière lives in physical poverty, she does not experience psychological deprivation. Unlike Ateba, whose memories of maternal love are stored in memory, Tapoussière's are present in reality. A cherished grandchild, Tapoussière is the center of her grandmother's universe. As they share physical space—a house, a bedroom, a bed—Grandmother's shack becomes the space of Tapoussière's progressive initiation into her grandmother's world. Here, fluid boundaries separate the realms of the real and the imaginary. A healer, Grandmother grows plants in her garden, explaining their medicinal properties to Tapoussière. A storyteller, she teaches the child proverbs, myths, legends, using oral tradition to transmit moral values and complex truths. Like Télumée's grandmother in Simone Schwarz-Bart's *Pluie et vent sur Télumée-Miracle,* Grandmother transforms her tiny cabin into mythic space: "Grand-mère me racontait des histoires, des légendes, certes, mais si vivantes qu'elles vibraient dans mes veines et s'emmêlaient dans mes pensées. Je voyais les esprits courir et les morts danser sur les toits" (41; Grandmother told me stories, legends surely, but so vivid that they stirred the blood in my veins and entered my thoughts. I saw spirits run and the dead dancing on the rooftops). Initiating the child to the power of the word, Grandmother emphasizes the importance of memory and imagination. In their home, Tapoussière, like Ateba, learns to value imaginative space as refuge: "L'expérience m'avait appris à posséder par les images ce que la vie me refusait. Je fermais les yeux et je voyais merveille" (71; Experience had taught me to seize through image what life refused. I closed my eyes and saw marvelous things).

In addition, the home they share is a space for communication. The child comes to value her grandmother's attentive and sympathetic ear: "Je narrais les scènes de la journée. . . . Grand-mère m'écoutait, attentive" (142; I recounted my day. . . . Grandmother listened attentively). Significantly, when Tapoussière's mother returns, treating her daughter as a servant and showing her no love, the child confides her sorrow to her grandmother, who explains that it is more important to love than be loved: "La plus grande joie de l'existence, c'est de vivre auprès de ceux qu'on aime. Tu aimes ta mère, c'est l'essentiel" (226; The greatest joy in life is to live close to the one we love. You love your mother, that's what's important). Thus, by talking to her grandmother, Tapoussière finds comfort and security; their home is her refuge. Clearly, Grandmother's humble shack meets Tuan's definition of *place,* space enriched with human experience and understanding; it is a protective hearth embodying the symbolic value Bachelard attributes to intimate space, the sense of refuge and maternal protection.

Transporting her "magic" from the village, Grandmother represents the force of traditional values within the *bidonville,* which, as intermediate space between village and city, is liminal space between continuity and change. Bringing words (legends, myths, proverbs), herbs, and potions to protect the community of Kassalafam, the old woman passes this lore on to the others, preparing Tapoussière to take her place eventually. Choosing Tapoussière as her link in the transmission of tradition, she puts her through a traditional initiation into her spiritual world. This ritual includes washing the child's eyes so that she, like her grandmother, will perceive the supernatural. Thus, in contrast to Ada's requirement that Ateba remain passive and silent, Grandmother's goal for Tapoussière is agency: "Grand-mère m'aimait parce que j'étais son espoir, celui de recon-

struire un jour le royaume des Issogos" (43; Grandmother loved me because I was her hope for someday rebuilding the Issogo kingdom).

Accepting agency willingly, Tapoussière does not share her grandmother's goal, the return to a traditional world. In the process of individuation, the child moves psychologically beyond her grandmother's "magical kingdom" despite the nurture and protection it provides. For her, agency implies the claim to physical as well as imaginative space. Secure in the inner world, she desires the challenge of the outer world. Structured by reason and logic, interpreted by social discourse, the public arena is dominated by men. Hence, Tapoussière embarks upon the search for her father. We may view her quest as the longing for the male figure representing the power of the phallus, the origin of patriarchy. I believe, however, that we should interpret it as the child's attempt to bond with both parents, assuring access to public and private space which, in post-colonial Africa, is still largely divided into masculine and feminine spheres.

Hence, as Ateba passively awaits her mother's return and their eventual refuge in "no man's land," Tapoussière actively seeks her father—or surrogate—in order to assume her place in public space. In practical terms, a father will give Tapoussière standing in a community that denigrates the child who is poor, dirty, and illegitimate. Tapoussière never meets her father, but she gains her community's praise through intelligence and hard work. By passing her school exams, she earns recognition independently, albeit with the help of her male schoolmaster.

Sustained—but not limited—by her grandmother's strength and wisdom, Tapoussière achieves agency. She finds her place in both private and public spheres, the inner world of imagination, the outer physical world structured by reason and logic. This duality is symbolized through Tapoussière's acquisition of language, African orality and *écriture,* the written word in French. As informal schooling enriches the inner world, formal schooling becomes a blueprint for the larger world.

In contrast to Ateba, who experiences the QG as "lost" space where rituals of community life—circumcision, funerals—have lost their meaning and new structures have not replaced them, and to Grandmother, who criticizes Kassalafam's materialism, Tapoussière views the *bidonville* positively. She finds promise and opportunity in "ce quartier des extrêmes, où la laideur et la beauté avançaient au coude à coude, tant mieux pour l'univers" (57; this neighborhood of extremes, where ugliness and beauty go together, so much the better for the universe). For her, contradictions allow for possibilities; the Douala slum is a dynamic stage, and she believes she will be able to participate in shaping her community's future: "J'étais convaincue qu'un jour viendrait où, d'un seul regard, je transformerais Kassalafam en une ville fantastique, ruisselante de lumière" (55–56; I was convinced that a day would come when, with one glance, I would transform Kassalafam into an amazing city, streaming with light).

Establishing the concept of Kassalafam as a dynamic stage, Tapoussière adds a new dimension to the symbolic representation of the streets. Adapting public space—and city electricity—to her needs, she does her homework in the street, under the light of a streetlamp. Praised in Kassalafam as the first child to obtain a primary-school certificate, Tapoussière is renamed "la petite fille du réverbère," the little girl of the streetlamp. The child who lights her way out of darkness also "reflects" the creativity of those who survive—and thrive—through ingenuity. Hence, an important shift takes place in Beyala's work as she reconceptualizes the African *bidonville;* no longer carceral space, it is a space of possibilities whose inhabitants create, invent, construct. She explains:

> Il suffit de voir combien la créativité est de rigueur dans les bidonvilles. On construit n'importe quoi et n'importe comment. Le fait de vivre au pan de la misère en permanence permet une émulation de l'imaginaire de manière extraordinaire. . . . Je crois fort que ceux qui feront l'Afrique de demain sortiront des bidonvilles. (Matateyou, 606)

> (You just have to see the extent to which creativity is required in the slums. People build all sorts of things in every which way. The fact of always living with misery encourages extraordinary imagination. . . . I strongly believe that those who build the Africa of the future will come from the slums.)

The search for place in these two texts reflects a significant evolution in Beyala's writing. The child of the African slums establishes a new relationship to self and community as the female protagonist with strong ties to her mother—or surrogate—finds her place. With her trajectory to self-expression encouraged and protected by her grandmother, Tapoussière's voice resonates within and beyond the confines of the protective hearth. Articulate, uninhibited, spontaneous, the child becomes the willing and capable narrator of her own story as well as a storyteller of African myth and legend.

As Beyala, through Tapoussière, arrives at autofiction, her readers are left to wonder how the protagonist will deal later with the problems that confronted Ateba: her relationship to men; her life with her cold and indifferent mother following her grandmother's death. This text leaves questions that hopefully another will answer. *La Petite Fille du réverbère* marks an important stage in Beyala's fiction as "le réverbère de la petite fille," Tapoussière's streetlamp, penetrates the darkness. It simultaneously opens the child's world, projecting her into the future, and lights Calixthe Beyala's way back to her grandmother's hearth.

Despite the bold challenge to patriarchal discourse through the depiction of eroticism and violence, Beyala's fiction reveals a quest for domesticity that may seem conventional rather than iconoclastic, conservative rather than revolutionary. Having first marked a radical departure from Bâ's representation of domestic space, Beyala now appears to join her through the process of restructuring the concept of the protective hearth. Readers will recall that in Bâ's text, Ramatoulaye transforms domestic space into refuge, her space for meditation, literary expression, and healing, as she writes to her best friend during the period of mourning required by Islam. Similarly, in *C'est le soleil qui m'a brûlée* Ateba transforms her bedroom into her refuge, the creative space for writing, reflection, memory, and in *La Petite Fille du réverbère* Tapoussière's grandmother, as storyteller, opens their domestic space to myth and legend.

In conclusion, Beyala, like Bâ, depicts home in Bachelardian terms, as the refuge where the human imagination integrates life's experiences. In her texts, the concept of home is crucial to the process of self-realization. In both fiction and reality, however, individuals in search of home often encounter displacement instead. For Beyala, who has found her creative space in Paris, not in Douala, the search for place represents an important and challenging problematic, and one that may continue to engage her in the years to come.[6]

Mildred Mortimer, Summer 1999

▪ WORKS CITED

Mariama Bâ. *Une si longue lettre.* Dakar. NEA. 1980.

Gaston Bachelard. *La poétique de l'espace.* Paris. Quadrige/PUF. 1957. Reprinted 1994.

———. *The Poetics of Space.* Maria Jolas, tr. Boston. Beacon. 1994.

Mieke Bal. *Death and Dissymmetry: The Politics of Coherence in the Book of Judges.* Chicago. University of Chicago Press. 1988.

Calixthe Beyala. *C'est le soleil qui m'a brûlée.* Paris. Stock. 1987.

———. *The Sun Hath Looked Upon Me.* Marjolijn de Jager, tr. Portsmouth, N.H. / London. Heinemann. 1996.

———. *La Petite Fille du réverbère.* Paris. Albin Michel. 1998.

Homi Bhabha. "The World and the Home." *Social Text,* 31/32, 10:2–3 (1992), pp. 141–53.

———. *The Location of Culture.* London/New York. Routledge. 1994.

Eloise Brière. *Le roman camerounais et ses discours.* Paris. Nouvelles du Sud. 1993.

Odile Cazenave. *Femmes rebelles: Naissance d'un nouveau roman africain au féminin.* Paris. L'Harmattan. 1996.

Catherine Coquery-Vidrovitch. *Les Africaines: Histoire des femmes d'Afrique noire du XIXᵉ au XXᵉ siècle.* Paris. Desjonquères. 1994.

Irène Assiba D'Almeida. *Francophone African Women Writers: Destroying the Emptiness of Silence.* Gainesville. University Press of Florida. 1994.

Béatrice Rangira Gallimore. "Ecriture féminine dans la littérature noire: Bâ et Beyala." *Missives*, October 1992, pp. 64–69.

———. *Le renouveau de l'écriture féminine dans l'œuvre romanesque de Calixthe Beyala: Afrique Francophone Sub-Saharienne.* Paris. L'Harmattan. 1997.

Sandra Gilbert, Susan Gubar. *The Madwoman in the Attic: The Woman Writer and the Nineteenth Century Literary Imagination.* New Haven, Ct. Yale University Press. 1979.

Emmanuel Matateyou. "Calixthe Beyala: Entre le terroir et l'exil." *French Review*, 69:4 (March 1996), pp. 605–15.

Julienne Ayissi Ngono. "Statut juridique et rôle économique de la femme chef de famille au Cameroun." In *Femmes du Sud, chefs de famille.* Jeanne Bisilliat, ed. Paris. Karthala. 1996. Pp. 315–22.

Katherine Platt. "Places of Experience and the Experience of Place." In *The Longing for Home.* Leroy S. Rouner, ed. Notre Dame, In. University of Notre Dame Press. 1996. Pp. 112–26.

Simone Schwarz-Bart. *Pluie et vent sur Télumée-Miracle.* Paris. Seuil. 1972.

Yi-Fu Tuan. *Space and Place: The Perspective of Experience.* Minneapolis. University of Minnesota Press. 1977.

Mark Wigley. "The Housing of Gender." In *Sexuality and Space.* Beatriz Colomina, ed. Princeton, N.J. Princeton University School of Architecture. 1992. Pp. 329–89.

[1] Explaining the importance of home, Bachelard writes: "Elle maintient l'homme à travers les orages du ciel et les orages de la vie. Elle est corps et âme. Elle est le premier monde de l'être humain. . . . Et toujours, en nos rêveries, la maison est un grand berceau" (26); "It maintains him through the storms of the heavens and through those of life. It is body and soul. It is the human being's first world. . . . And always, in our daydreams, the house is a large cradle" (*The Poetics of Space*, 7).

[2] For a detailed historical study of African women's role in economic production, see Coquery-Vidrovitch.

[3] QG stands for "quartier général" or military headquarters, an ironic misnomer since this area is one of squalor and poverty.

[4] All translations of *C'est le soleil qui m'a brûlée* are taken from *The Sun Hath Looked Upon Me,* translated from the French by Marjolijn de Jager. The translations of passages from *La Petite Fille du réverbère* are my own.

[5] For a probing analysis of architecture as patriarchal space, see Wigley.

[6] For Beyala's reflections on living abroad, see Gallimore, 202, and Matateyou, 613.

Beyond the Word of Man: Glissant and the New Discourse of the Antilles

The imprisoned source of the Lézarde, guarded by thick walls, surrounded by marble tiles, like an idol bedecked with ornaments.

▓ EDOUARD GLISSANT, *THE RIPENING*

■ INTRODUCTION TO THE ARGUMENT

During his childhood years 1940–44, Edouard Glissant, like all residents of the French colonial island of Martinique, found himself in a lived situation of double blockade. Outside, the United States fleet blockaded the ships of Vichy France. Internally, not only did the presence of the navy and the naval authority of Vichy France as the cause of the U.S. blockade lead to a lack of food on the export-import outpost that was the island, but incidents of direct racism inflicted by the French sailors, as colonial occupiers, led also to an intensified sense of dispossession on the part of the islanders. This second effect was one that was common to all the still colonialized population groups of the Caribbean islands, whether Francophone, Anglophone, or Dutch-speaking, since it was based on the common exclusion from all powers of decision-making with respect to our fate in the context of the global conflagration of World War II, and therefore to the recognition that to be a *colonial* was precisely to be excluded from all autonomous processes of decision-making with respect to one's fate as a collectivity.

There was a *specificity,* however—to touch here on one of the major motifs of Glissant's discourse—to the situation of Martinique, as distinct, for example, from my own parallel childhood experience in the then British colonial island of Jamaica. The population of Martinique found itself, willy-nilly, on the side of a France which, having had to accept German domination, was now both an ally to and a neocolony of a Germany determined to found the empire of its Thousand-Year Reich on European "natives" in place of the series of primary non-European "natives" on whose subordination France, like several other European nation-states, had built hers.

Although on the one hand for British colonies such as Jamaica, however helpless to control events, there was a strong sense among the population as a whole that under all the British propaganda there was indeed a core truth which impelled their allegiances, this was not to be so in Martinique. The core truth in our case was that the delirium of the Nazi system of thought, which was based on the taking to a logical extreme of the social Darwinist discourse of "race" that had been put in place in the nineteenth century as the legitimating "magical thought" of that century's industrial mode of colonialism, would now have to be fought by colonized and colonizers alike. We therefore had the assurance, during the years 1940–44, that we were, as British subjects, on the side of the "good guys," on the side of an opening rather than a regressive dynamics of historical and cultural change.

The situation of Martinique differed not only in the accidental sense of finding itself subordinated to collaborationist rather than to Resistance France, but also in a structural-existential sense; for the dual processes of intellectual and social assimilation specific to the Catholic French model of colonization were already firmly in place in Martinique as distinct from the antithetical processes of intellectual assimilation but of *social exclusion* and economic marginalization which defined the Protestant British model of dominance and subordination specific to the situation of a British colony such as Jamaica.

As a result of these differing models, if a series of widespread social and economic revolts rocked the Anglophone colonies from 1935 onward in the wake of the 1929 economic crash, and if this struggle would lead in Jamaica, for example, to the introduction of limited self-government on the basis of adult suffrage in 1944 and then to formal political independence in 1962, the script of the schema would be different in Martinique, as Glissant reveals in his 1981 essay, *Le discours antillais* (Eng. *Caribbean Discourse*).[1] There the social unrest and psychological awakening of the war and the postwar years led to the French model solution, that of departmentalization, whereby Martinique, Guadeloupe, and French Guiana were made into departments of France and into extensions of the French nation overseas.[2] In the 1970s, as Glissant points out in his chronology of Martinican history from an Antillean perspective, this assimilation would be extended to all areas of economic life. Whatever the increase in "metropolitan privileges" Martinique would enjoy, there would be a decrease in the central privilege of all, that of autonomous input into the processes of decision-making by the collectivity in its own name.

■ THE ARGUMENT

I have given this brief overview in order to introduce the existential ground from which the root metaphor that is central to Glissant's oeuvre, whatever the genre—poetry, fiction, drama, or prose works such as *L'intention poétique* or *Le discours antillais,* which defies generic classification.[3] This metaphor is that of *blocking.* Its re-

ferent is the series of empirical obstacles impeding the Antilles' realization of the full potential of what Glissant defines as "Antilleanity." Glissant sees this blocking at a fundamental level, in the case of both Martinique and the Francophone Caribbean in general, as the effect of the French model of assimilation. Since such a model, although it saves Martinicans from the economic fate of the boat people of independent Haiti, who are turned back almost every day now by the U.S. Coast Guard as they seek to escape in their unseaworthy boats from the inferno of economic misery to which contemporary Haiti is "condemned,"[4] nevertheless imprisons Martinicans in a specific mode of subordination for which there can be no words within the analogic of our present governing order of discourse and its related episteme or global order of knowledge.

Beverley Ormerod entitled her essay on Glissant's 1958 novel *La Lézarde* (Eng. *The Ripening*) "The Freeing of the Waters: Edouard Glissant's *The Ripening.*" Pointing out that Glissant had dedicated one of his latest volumes of poetry, *Boises,* to "every country which is diverted from its course and suffers the failing of the waters" and that one of the final poems in that collection had concluded with a call to "retrace the dried water course, and descend into many absences, to wind along the place of our rebirth, black in the rock," Ormerod shows us how this imperative call and the existential reality of psychocultural "blockade" against which it protests refer us to "the major themes in Glissant's work."

These major themes—namely, the "need to recapture but also to transcend a vanished unrecorded history," and "the struggle to preserve a sense of cultural identity in the face of metropolitan French policies that discourage and inhibit the flow of a specifically Caribbean tradition" in Martinique—are themselves instituted on the basis of the root metaphor and tropic matrix of blocking/blockage. This root metaphor, although already part of what Michael Dash calls "the symbolic patterns" laid down in Glissant's early volumes of poetry from 1953–55,[5] was to be fully developed in his 1958 novel *La Lézarde.* One could argue that this metaphor *is* the novel, explaining why, as Ormerod points out, it is as "bare of everyday domestic detail as a classical French tragedy," since its main concern is "the intellectual and emotional development of the characters and the growth of their sense of commitment to the land"[6] against all the obstacles placed in the way of such commitment.

The metaphor of blocking as the rhetorical strategy of *La Lézarde*'s psychocultural imperative is expressed at the level of the novel's character system in the blocking figure or "villain" Garin. The latter's mimetic ideal of power, based on private ownership and therefore on the autarchy of decision-making which it enables, leads him to build his house, the House of the Spring, over the source of the Lézarde River. Although Thaël, as the Maroon hero and a descendant of those African slaves who had fled to the mountains in repudiation of the plantation system of the lowlands, brings about Garin's death, the process of blocking will be revealed to be, in the trajectory of Glissant's later works, the industrial process itself—in other words, the industrial model of human auto-domestication.

In this context I should note that the term *Maroon,* which was and is used throughout the Caribbean and the Americas to designate the runaway African slaves who took to the mountains in order to escape enslavement and to reestablish the ancestral cultures of Africa in syncretic variants there, is derived originally from the Spanish word *cimarrón:* that is, the nontamed, non-domesticated animal. The figure of the Maroon as the nonassimilated Antillean will therefore be central to Glissant's oeuvre,[7] to its inscription of the "antithetical values" between the rebellious, "non-domesticated" mountains, based on the ancestral African cultural model, and those of the "tamed landscape of the lowlands,"[8] based first on the model of the plantation, then on that of contemporary France—a model which, I hope to show, is itself instituted for both the French and the Martinicans by the Word of "Man" and its related order of discourse.

A shift will therefore take place in Glissant's work in which the blocked symbol of the river's source in the 1958 novel, and the imperative to which its plot line urges us, that of the freeing of the river from its imprisonment in Garin's House of the Spring, is necessarily transformed. If, in the 1958 novel, the Lézarde River provides the central millennial metaphor of hope and liberation (since it is the image of this river which links the mountain, as "the repository of Maroon memories," with "the unfettered sea" and therefore links the tradition of the Maroon repudiation of the plantation to a new future whose synthesis transcends both that gesture of refusal of, and the plantation slaves' submission to, the course of modern history), in Glissant's later work this mode of millennial hope is shown to be as "dried up" as the actual Lézarde River that had provided its founding analogy. If, however, that earlier river of Glissant's childhood, which with "the mud swirling up from its bed and the logs across it singing a chaotically savage song . . . calling out for a life" and "exultantly free" had been the analogue, in the natural order, of the uprising of a "people in revolt" setting out to claim autonomy over the circumstances which controlled its life, had now been reduced to a gutter in the relentless pro-

cess of the shantytown urbanization defining the systemic "Third World" peripheries, this drying up of both river and revolt had led to the paradoxical emergence of a new mode of revolt, one which will be specific to the historico-existential situation of the Antilles.

This new mode of revolt is one against the very roots of our present mode of "conventional reason" and therefore of the order of discourse and of its Word of Man, which now serves as, in Pocock's terms, the non-questionable "paradigm of value and authority"[9] from which our present order of knowledge (episteme) and its disciplining discourses are, in rule-governed fashion, generated. Glissant's discourse is, I shall propose, an instituting act of this new mode of revolt. As such, it takes part in a new uprising, together with the line of intellectual filiation specific to Martinique, from Aimé Césaire's founding Negritude poem *Cahier d'un retour au pays natal* (1939; Eng. *Return to My Native Land*) to Frantz Fanon's epistemological break effected in *Peau noire, masques blancs* (1952; Eng. *Black Skin, White Masks*), as well as with the new postcolonial discourse of other writers from the ex-slave Caribbean islands such as George Lamming (whose classic novel *In the Castle of My Skin* was published in 1953), and also with the post-1960s work of Maryse Condé.[10]

I want to propose here that this uprising is directed not only at our present order of discourse and at its founding Word of Man, as the Word of the human conceptualized as a selected being and natural organism, but also at the tradition of discourse to which its specific discourse of man belongs: that is, at the tradition on whose basis, from 1512 onward, Western Europe was to effect the first stage in the secularization of human existence in the context of its own global expansion and to lay the basis of the plantation structure out of which the contemporary societies of Glissant's Antilles, as well as the specificity of their Antilleanity, as he insists and reinsists, was to emerge. I want to propose further that we look at all the major themes of Glissant's works as themes which cross-link and cross-resonate with each other from one work, one genre to another and as themes which constitute *acts.* I shall therefore define the following major themes of Glissant's works as performative acts of countermeaning directed against the semantic charter[11] or behavior-regulating program, instituted by our present order of discourse and therefore by its related order of rationality or mode of "conventional" or cultural "reason." In this context the major themes of his work are instituted as a magma of themes generated from the tropic matrix of the metaphor of blocking, whose referent is that of the blocked/blockaded existential situation, at the level of the psyche of the Antillean human subject as well as of his or her empirical situation.

Central to this magma, as Beverley Ormerod points out, is history, the theme of an Antillean history which, at present "relegated" to an "obscure" representation, must now be recovered in its fullness in order to reorient our behaviors in the present.[12] Another theme is that of the psychic disorder and cultural malaise, both caused by the nihilated (néantisé) sense of identity of the population groups of the Antilles who, finding themselves subordinated to the universal Word of Man and to the specific view of the past which its Word demands, are also necessarily subordinated to the empirics of the global relation which the behavior-regulating signals of this Word and its story (history) necessarily bring into being.[13] This theme of psychic disorder and cultural malaise will in turn be linked to that of the Relation, of its poetics and its politics, as well as the macrotheme which is centrally linked to that of the Relation: that of the ongoing "economic warfare" waged by the haves against the have-nots within the legitimating semantic charter of the Word of Man. This in turn will be linked to the theme of the consumerism, material and intellectual, imposed on the islands as places assigned for consumption rather than production in the global system, and to the theme of the devastation of entire peoples imprisoned in the roles assigned them by the "transcendental signified" of Man and by what Foucault calls its "true" discourse.[14]

Against the universel généralisant of the Word of Man (and its variants: Proletarian, Woman), the central countertheme that will be enacted again and again in Glissant's work is that of the anti-Universal, the theme of the claim to specificity, of the claim to "rester au lieu" (the remaining-in-place) in the specific oikumene of the Antilles, in the specificity of its "mode of the imaginary." This countertheme of specificity extends from the Antilles as an Other America to that of the Creole languages themselves, of their syntax, sound, and poetics of rhythm, and confronts their orality to the written nature of the "official languages," to the specificity of the Antillean landscape, of its nonorderly seasons as explosive as the flame tree and the poinciana.

The major theme of a "transphysics" in which being is defined as l'étant because it itself is defined by the fact that it relates (DA, 251) and is related—which is then linked to the theme of historical models of structuration as distinct from structure, with the latter an effect of the former—leads to the call for another kind of specificity, for a restructuring based on an endogenous Antillean "work upon itself," able to lead to the putting in play of an autonomous social formation (DA, 93–95). Meanwhile, the call for a "transphysics" is linked in Glissant's

poetry and fiction to a poetics whose primary referent/ topic is, rather than the subjective and intimate life of an individual, that of the blocked individuality and fulfillment of a people, the Antilleans, of their realization as a new collectivity. Against the reality of a colonization of the cultural Imaginary so successful at the level of the assimilation of the psyche, of its mimesis of being, stands Glissant's insistent proposal for the "taking charge of the Word" in order to develop the counterconcept of métissage so as to contest the representation of monofiliation, of Genesis (DA, 250),[15] of, in our terms, "Man." It is this dual call for, and praxis of, "taking charge of the Word" that I have defined in my title as the New Discourse of the Antilles.

▪ THESE THEMES-THAT-CONSTITUTE ACTS: ANTILLEANITY AND THE QUESTION OF BEING

As Glissant said of Fanon, that the latter with his adherence to the Algerian anticolonial revolution had passed over to the act, so I want to propose that with the performative acts of countermeaning put into play by these cross-linking themes, all generated from the phenomenological field of the root metaphor of blocking, Glissant has also "passed over to the act." This act, however, as one impelled by the specific existential circumstances of the Antilles, is defined by a specific mode of uprising, one which calls into question, rising up against, our present mode of being, of subjectivity, the Self.

As long as the human subject, Heidegger pointed out, continued to conceptualize and experience itself as a created being, it would see no necessity to ask questions about being, about in effect our modes of human beingness. After Darwin's Origin of Species and Descent of Man, however, the universal model of being that had been projected by Western Europe from 1512 onward was displaced from that of the human as a created rational being (that is, of the human species as divinely created to be separate from all other organic species by its rational nature) to that of the human as a selected being. In this new representation, in which the human as an evolutionarily selected natural organism now differed from other forms of organic life only by the fact that it created "culture," the same phenomenon would occur, since the pseudoscientific concept of the human as an evolutionarily selected being would also function to block off any questions about being—about, that is, how as humans we attain to human beingness and do so now in a profane or secular rather than sacred modality.

If Foucault was to raise the question of the historical and therefore relative nature of our modes of subjectivity in the wake of the 1968 cultural revolts in

France,[16] this question had been first raised poetically rather than conceptually by Aimé Césaire in his *Cahier*. In the wake of World War II the question was again raised by Fanon and Glissant as well as by writers like George Lamming of the English-speaking Caribbean. However, the question of subjectivity had been impelled, in their earlier case, unlike that of Foucalt, by a recognition specific to the Antilles. This was that of the Abject Otherness of the majority of Antilleans, as the descendants of pure or "mixed-race" Africans (and therefore as Negroes), to the Self of Man and its instituted mode of subjectivity/subject, conceptualized as a selected being and purely natural organism.

The recognition here was therefore psychoexistential, that of the need to reject one's own physiognomic Being in order to attain to the Ideal Self or optimal model of the subject, in order to attain to the universal of "Man." It was this awareness that was to be the basis of the challenge later mounted by Antillean writers both to our own mimeticism of being, at the level of the individual subject, as defined by Fanon in *Black Skin, White Masks,* as well as to our cultural and intellectual mimeticism, as explored and called in question by the discourse of Glissant as well as by the overall post-1945 discourse of the ex-slave and ex-colonial Caribbean. As a result, the new synthesis which this discourse seeks was to be based on a "changed quality of consciousness" impelled by the imperative of a "perspective of struggle" sited on the new terrain of being, of modes of subjectivity. This new terrain and perspective was to define the Antillean educated elite, opening them/us onto the possibility of a new intellectual front, outside the orthodox "fronts" of Marxism, liberal nationalism, and feminism.[17]

Glissant points out that although the popular groups of the Antilles have waged their struggles persistently throughout Caribbean history, the same has not been true generally of the educated elite. If we make use of Foucault's distinction between an intelligentsia that defines itself as the bearer of a "just-and-true-for-all" truth and the "specific intellectual" as one who works not in the name of a universal—i.e., liberal nationalism, Marxism, and/or feminism—but rather as on the terrain and in the mode of struggle provided by the existential conditions of her or his life to which she or he bears witness, with these conditions defining the specific nature of what that intellectual struggle must be,[18] it is clear that it is only where the terrain of struggle has been that of *being* that the Antillean intellectuals have reenacted the empirical struggles of the popular forces at the level of ideas and of imaginative discourse.

In this context the terrain specific to Glissant's "educated elite" can be seen as that of the struggle over which "order of discourse" (the *ordo verborum*) is to provide the system of meanings through whose mechanism our collective behaviors are to be regulated, over which magma of meanings, therefore, and their transformatively generated signaling systems is to be instituted so as to trigger those identifiable patterns of electrochemical activity in the hedonic reward/punishment centers of the brain, by means of which, I want to further propose, our human behaviors are culturally induced and regulated[19] and our models of being (or modes of *l'étant*) thereby instituted; the struggle, therefore, over which behavior-regulating order of discourse and related mode of the subject it is to be, whether one which continues to impose a situationally blocked destiny upon the peoples of the Antilles, or a new one to be consciously put in place as capable of enabling the liberation of the majority of peoples of the Antilles from their enforced role of Other to the Self, their role of abjectly embodying the hypher-sign by means of whose antonymic trigger alone our collective desire for being on the mimetic model of our present mode of optimal being, Man, can continue to be dynamically and stably induced.

The history of the Antilles from its post-Columbus origins, which Glissant urges us to retrace, to reinterpret, has been nothing less than the struggle against this imposed role, that of the lack of being to the first secular models of being in human history. "You suddenly understood," Glissant wrote in *The Ripening,* "that this entire history had been nothing but a fierce collective effort to escape the mean destiny that had been imposed on this world, the petty provincialism that overwhelmed this country, as well as feelings of shame and self-disgust. A supreme effort to identify with the flame tree, the terrible silk-cotton tree, the shimmering sand bar. . . . And you realized . . . that they would no longer tolerate (neither you nor the people) being twisted in a vice, the marks of humiliation. But that also, in this sudden wave of freedom that is suddenly realized, a dark, flaming eruption, reality was already perceived in a new way" (*R,* 168–69).

■ TO PERCEIVE REALITY IN A NEW WAY: FROM A LOSS OF TRUST IN PHYSICAL NATURE TO A LOSS OF TRUST IN OUR MODES OF SUBJECTIVITY, OF BEING

Césaire's *Cahier,* with its calling in question of this Ontological Lack role, had emerged in the same historical landscape as that of the Harlem Renaissance and Langston Hughes as well as that of the Cuban author Nicolás Guillén's *son* poems. As Hughes had brought the form of the blues, of jazz (of Glissant's oral), into the written poetry, Guillén had not only brought the Afro-Cuban musical form of the *son* and its drum poetics into written Spanish poetry but had also, with his *negro bembón* (thick-lipped Negro) thematics—"Why do you get so angry?" one *son* runs, "when they call you *negro bembón?* When you have a most beautiful face, and Caridad [your woman] loves you and gives you everything?"[20]—ironically brought out into the open the imposed role of Physiognomic Other that the black was made to play in the Greek Ideal esthetics of the post-Enlightenment bourgeoisie.[21] Whereas Césaire's *Cahier,* with its symbolic inversion of the "sacral" metaphysics of *blanchitude,* was the founding counterdiscourse of the Antilles, the later discourses of Fanon and Glissant were the continuation of the act of poetic uprising against the role imposed on the black population groups of the New World as the embodied bearers of Ontological Lack to the secular model of being, Man, as the negative conceptual Other term to its instituting Word.

I use the term *Word* here in a special sense. Julia Kristeva has pointed out that the epochal mutation of Christianity lay in the fact that it summed up and conceptualized all the earlier ritual representations of the Abject, or modes of Otherness from which one had to separate oneself aversively if one were to realize being as it was optimally represented, and had done so in the symbolic concept of Original Sin.[22] As a result, the Ontological Lack or absence from "true" being, as one made applicable to all mankind, was now represented as having been brought into the world by the event of Adam's act of disobedience or Fall, within the narrative schema of the Genesis origin text. With this shift, all humans were now made the recipient of this Adamic negative inheritance and were therefore bearers of this universal mode of the Abject. Redemption from this legacy, for the layman, could only be obtained through the ritual processes of baptism into orthodox feudal-Christian identity. Because the original ritual construct of the Abject or of Pariah Otherness had been translated into the *concept* of Ontological Lack, the order of knowledge of scholastic theology had been elaborated, as the Word of the Christian, upon the a priori premise of an Ontological Lack of being as that of human enslavement to Original Sin. Since the concept of enslavement to Original Sin was embodied in the social category of the prebaptismal Laity or lay intelligentsia, whereas that of the "redeemed Christian" was embodied in the category of the celibate Clergy (whose procreation was that of Spirit rather than in that of the "fallen flesh" of Adam's heirs), the empirical binary Clergy/Laity categories of the feudal-Christian order had "verified" the conceptual categories of scholastic theology before the challenge of humanism and the rise of our present "lay" orders of knowledge or *studia humanitatis.*

However, with the political and cultural revolution of humanism, and the establishment of the monarchical state on the basis of the new Machiavellian discourse of civic humanism, the concept of the Abject as that of Adamic enslavement to Original Sin was transferred to that of potential human enslavement to its own lower sensory nature. In place of the Laity, the new hybridly secular and religious mode of Ontological Lack was now embodied, outside Europe, in the binary opposition between the European settlers and the New World peoples (*indios*) and enslaved peoples of Africa (Negroes). Inside Europe itself it would come to be embodied in the oppositional categories of the Sane (rational nature) and the now asylum-interned, the Mad (as Foucault has traced), together with the categories of the jobless and the poor, now coclassified with the Mad as the embodiment of irrational sensory nature. A shift had therefore been effected from the Word of the Christian to that of rational-nature Man.

Humans, as Peter Winch points out, never live merely animate lives.[23] Rather, we live our lives according to the regulatory representations of that which constitutes symbolic *life* and of that which constitutes its Lack, its mode of symbolic *death.* Group categories, whether that of the Laity or that of the indio/Negro/Mad, who embody the Ontological Lack are therefore the signifier of symbolic "death" within the conceptualization of optimal being specific to each order, whereas, as in the case of Original Sin, the construct which embodies the Lack of Being everywhere serves as a nonquestionable paradigm of value and authority on which each culture's order of rationality or mode of conventional reason is then rigorously and objectively elaborated.

At the end of the eighteenth and during the nineteenth century the construct of an atavistic, genetically dysselected Lack of normal human nature took the now purely secular place both of Original Sin and of the earlier hybridly religio-secular construct of Sensory Nature. The new Lack was now conceptualized as that of a lack of racial "normalcy" and was embodied in the recently freed Black/Africoid population, who now took the place of the prebaptismal Laity as conceptual Other, as the embodiment, that is, of the "dysgenic human subject" in place of the "fallen natural man" of the feudal-Christian schema. The negative inheritance was no longer from Adam in Genesis, but rather from, ostensibly, the processes of natural dysselection, within the new secular-origin text of evolution.

In place of the pre-baptized Laity or "fallen natural man" it was the *Nigger* as atavistic human that now had to be aversely withdrawn from as the condition of realizing being according to the criteria of the purely secular and therefore first nonsupernaturally guaranteed model of being in human history. The new order of "true" discourse and of knowledge would be as elaborated on the premise of Ontological Lack as that of dysgenic atavistic human nature as earlier that of the feudal order had been elaborated on the premise of Original Sin and that of the monarchical and landed gentry's on the premise of sensory nature.

Foucault has traced the discursive processes by means of which our present model of being, Man, was instituted on the represented analogy of a natural organism at the same time as the disciplinary discourses of our present order of knowledge that were to institute it as such, was enabled to displace those of the earlier classical episteme and its partly secular, partly religious model of being. The latter model had been grounded on the premise that the hierarchies of its social order had been as divinely ordered as the chain of being of the natural order, which was itself believed to be based on an ascending ladder of the organic species, each of which had been instituted, as a species, by divine fiat, so that once the ground of this analogy and the system of "true" discourse based upon it had crumbled in the wake of Darwin's *Origin of Species* and the rise of the new discourse of evolutionary biology, the supernational "space of Otherness" inhabited by God could no longer serve to stabilize the representation of optimal being as that of the rational human defined by its divinely created rational nature. Instead, in the shift which now occurred from the representation of rational-being Man to that of Man on the model of a pure natural organism, a new "space of Otherness" term now took the place of that of God. This new term was that of "Race."

Wlad Godzich recently defined the role that all "spaces of Otherness" play with respect to the instituting of human societies. He argued that "for a society to know itself" it "must know where its legitimacy lies," that "furthermore it must have a sense that its order is neither anarchic nor nonsensical but must be . . . the realization of true order." Even though "its intelligibility" may be a challenge to our limited cognitive means, it must possess it in principle. "If all these conditions obtain," he continues,

> . . . order and change are both possible and the society is assured of continuity. But for that to occur, the foundational principles cannot be found in the society at large but must be located in a space of otherness that ensures that they remain beyond the reach of human desire and temptation. This space of otherness is either absolute or mediated through the institutions of the state. In other words the society carries a heavy burden of debt to this space of otherness; it owes its meaning, its organization, its capacity to act

upon itself, and thus its ability to manage order and change. This is the foundational debt of meaning that pervades all institutions, including the academic disciplines.[24]

The proposal I want to make here, in the context of Glissant's differentiation of the concept of structuration from structure, is that as the feudal God was the supernatural "space of otherness" of the Christian and was, however remotely, still partly the guarantee of the human, defined as the owner of a "rational nature" which distinguished it as a category from organic species, the construct of *Nigger* as well as that of the non-European *native* now came to serve as the inversion of the divinely instituted realm of the supernatural and therefore as the extrasocietal source, "beyond the reach of human desire and temptation," since both *Nigger* and *native* were now projected as being genetically, if no longer divinely, predetermined to be a mode of Lack defining an ostensibly evolutionarily determined mode of "normal" human being, Man. Both *Nigger* and its transformatively generated semanteme *native* now functioned at the level of empirical reality as the embodiment of the dysgenic Other, as "proof" therefore of the functioning of an infranatural process of genetic selection as the new that-which-is-in-itself that guarantees the now purely secular model of the absolute subject in its bourgeois conceptualization.

Glissant's reconstitution of the hitherto repressed historical beginnings of the Antilles—that is, of the deportation of the ancestors of the majority peoples of the ex-slave polities from their originally autocentric model of being, their reduction to the status of *pieza* (i.e., of being so many units of extractable labor capacity),[25] of their passage in chains across Columbus's newly navigable ocean sea, with the slave trade (*le Traité*) coming to constitute the founding origin of today's Antilles— places a new focus on the question of being, that of the Antilles as well as that of the human in general, for it was the slave trade, as a culture-specific origin, which posed the central dilemma charted by Glissant in his fiction. This dilemma was that of the choice between the alternative thrust of *marronaje,* of Maroon identity, and of its defense of a still-autocentric tribal-lineage model of being secured by a retreat to the mountains and to the ancestral past, or that of the entrance into the mainstream flow of historical events only at the price—paid by the majority—of one's submission to a new imposed and nihilated (*néantisé*) identity.

Nevertheless, it was this second alternative that would lead to the psychic trauma from whose basis, paradoxically, the new discourse of the Antilles would be compelled to initiate its new acts of revolt, since whereas he had been the Other as slave before the abolition of slavery, now, after slavery, the Antillean found himself as colonial "native" and "Nigger," instituted as another mode of Otherness, as the Lack of the autonomous and absolute subject, Man. As a result, in order to realize optimal being according to the specifications of the new model of being, the majority Antillean subject had, and has, to split itself so as not to coincide with itself. Like the layman of medieval-Christian Europe who could realize optimal being as a baptized, redeemed feudal-Christian subject only through his or her autophobic aversion to prebaptismal being as the embodiment of "fallen natural humanity" enslaved to Original Sin, the Antillean subject had also to become reflexively autophobic to its own specific physiognomic being as the condition of its attaining to the middle-class model of desire, of being.

The specificity of the problem particular and unique to the Antilles was and is therefore an existential one, in that in order to attain to optimal being on the model of secular Man, to attain to being human, the Antillean subject had to be against not only the specificity of its own physiognomic being (Césaire, Fanon) and the specificity of its own Antillean kinship based on the "peculiarity of its own history" as the only people who had been denied human status (Césaire), but, as Glissant will further develop and extend, to the specificity of its own Creole language, of its own landscape and lived existential history, the specificity of that to which Glissant gives name, of its Antilleanity. It is the psychic costs of this contradiction which were protested against, in the acts of discursive revolt from Césaire to Glissant, that begins to insert a "new and changed quality of consciousness," that of a new loss of trust which reenacts the earlier loss of trust that had led to the earlier revolt of the Laity and therefore to the rise of humanism, of the natural sciences, and the modern world system.

In *The Legitimacy of the Modern Age* Hans Blumenberg argues that both the post-fifteenth-century epistemological "leap" of Western Europe, which ushered in the Modern Age, and the rise of the natural sciences cannot be understood outside the "changed quality of consciousness" which had been initiated, inter alia, by the counterreaction to the nominalist currents of thought of high scholasticism. The latter's Aristotelianized Unmover of God creating only for the sake of His own glory had implied both that the physical world "is no longer reliably arranged in advance for man's benefit" and that therefore "the truth about it was no longer at man's disposal."[26] Both Columbus and Copernicus, as representatives of the first Christian-humanist counter-reaction to this, had counterprojected the original Christian image of the caring-father-God in whose image man had been made: Columbus asserting that be-

cause God had made land for the salvation of souls, there had to be more land than water, there had to be imaginary islands like Antilia between Spain and India, if one sailed west;[27] and Copernicus asserting that because the "world was intended" by God for man, the heavens could be dependably known precisely because it had been "constructed on our behalf by the best and most trustworthy Master Builder of everything."[28]

However, the second phase put into play by Descartes displaced the first phase of self-assertion with a more total one. Here the Cartesian's discourse's acceptance of the nominalists' destruction of trust in the providentiality of physical nature for man's sake, as well as of their removal of "inherent purpose" from the cosmos, led both to its own consequent prohibition of any "propositions in the natural sciences from a purpose that God or nature could have had in their production" and therefore inevitably to the development of a "new theoretical attitude." In this new attitude, physical reality freed from an a priori anthropocentrism could now be conceptualized as "having to be altered and produced in accordance with human purposes, to the extent [such a] reality proves to be inconsiderable for men" (*DA*, 209).

In our contemporary Antillean case the loss of trust has been that of any necessary providentiality for our sake of the always rhetorico-discursively instituted modes of being/subjectivity, and the modes of cultural reason, and imaginative discourse which sustains them, for our Antillean—for our human—sake. Meanwhile, the new theoretical attitude here is that of the conceptualization of these modes of being/knowing/feeling, and the systems of meaning which induce and institute them, as modes that will now have "to be altered and produced in accordance" with our now-conscious purposes "to the extent that each such mode proves to be inconsiderate" for the full realization of the specific Antillean subject, of the concrete human subject.

One of Glissant's most telling distinctions is that with respect to the uniqueness of both the Antillean and the New World black situation, so that, whereas for the Indochinese or African subject the end of the colonial experience was the *end of an interruption,* this was not to be so in their case. Rather, because Antillean societies "did not pre-exist the colonial act, but were literally the creation of that act," one cannot "speak of structures disturbed by colonialism, of traditions that have been uprooted." For the Indochinese and the African there could be a return, after independence, to the old ancestral bases of identity, on which to meet the challenge of coping with a contemporary reality, but this could not be so for the ex-slave polities of the Caribbean. Only the Maroon in his or her mountain retreats, as exemplified by the Longoué family in Glissant's fiction, re-mained to remind of what that ancestral mode of being, of subjectivity, had originally been. For the majority who had submitted to the "domestication" processes of the plantation order, however, and who had come to live their imposed identity, a unique psychoexistential situation had developed. Once freed from slavery, in order to realize being according to the specifications of the new mode of subjectivity, I had to experience my own Antillean-*nègre* physiognomic features as an object of abjection, of aversive phenomenological loathing—as Other, therefore, to the mode of the ego in which I had been conditioned, as Other to the I in which I thought, acted, had been "domesticated" to desire, dream. I had to become reflexively aversive to the specificity of my concrete being now made into the embodiment of the non-autonomous Nigger-Other, whose signifying nega-tion alone made my mode of the conditioned ideal self experienceable at the level of affect.

In the new governing code of "life" and "death" the slave and Caliban symbol of sensory-nature Otherness had been displaced by the empirical figures and hy-pher-signs of "natives" and "Negroes," both men and women, in the context of the nineteenth-century Euro-pean order of discourse, so that the Hottentot woman with her steatopygous buttocks and Hottentot "apron" became the signifying category of an ostensibly atavistic mode of human female sexuality. The European prosti-tute, like all lower-class women to varying degrees, was therefore assimilated to the abject category of the Hot-tentot woman in medical and criminological dis-courses;[29] similarly, as Fanon shows in his critique of the North African syndrome of the mainstream colonial psychiatry of the time, the mental illness of native Alge-rian men was diagnosed as "proof" of the fact that they were decorticalized, born as atavistic throwbacks with-out a frontal cortex, as proof therefore of a genetically determined mode of human differential value.[30]

If, as Glissant argues, the colonial structures of the Antilles were put in place with Western Europe's first colonial act, Shakespeare's projection of Caliban as a symbol of the first "native" or nihilated (*néantisé*) peo-ples was isomorphic with this originary putting in place and with the instituting of the model of structuration based on the ontological axioms of the rational-nature/sensory-nature dichotomy that was to be as fundamen-tal to the colonial (or Other) social formation of the An-tilles as it was, at the same time, to the secularizing mo-narchical state of Western Europe, in which politics was to be emancipated from morality by the new reasons-of-state discourse of civic humanism. Thus, as Glissant points out in the *Discours,* the Caliban theme had been a constant with Caribbean intellectuals: Fanon, Lam-

ming, Césaire, Fernández Retamar (*DA,* 231). This is due, I propose, to the fact of these writers' recognition of the analogical similarity between Caliban as the first hybrid form of the secular Other and its mode of the self, and the "Nigger" and "native" as the second form of the Other to the *propre* of the now purely secular mode of the self, Man; to their intuitive recognition, therefore, of the Caliban symbol and the native/Nigger symbol as embodied constructs of the code of symbolic "death" for the two variants of the Self by means of which the West would desupernaturalize the represen-tations of "life" and "death" that are instituting of human "forms of life." . . .

■ CONCLUSION

"1492. Les Grands Découvreurs s'élancent sur l'Atlantique, à la recherche des Indes. Avec eux le poème commence."[31] In 1992 it will be five hundred years since Columbus sailed across an ocean sea that was logically nonnavigable within the a priori conceptu-al schema and mainstream mode of "conventional rea-son" of the feudal-Christian episteme. To contradict that a priori schema, Columbus would base on a series of empirical mistakes his insistence that the East and the source of the spice trade could be reached by sailing west across the ocean sea. One of these mistakes was his projection, after Toscanelli, of the existence of imagi-nary islands between "Spain and India." One of these islands was named Antilia. A second mistake was that the islands he *did* reach were indeed the westernmost part of the East Indies.

In his early epic poem *Les Indes* (The Indies; 1955) Glissant had centered on Columbus's misconception within the context of the opposition, as Dash points out, between the reality and "the illusion that they sustain in people's minds." "And if the Indies are not where you are," Glissant has Columbus say in his poem, "I do not care. Indies you will be. West Indies, so that my dream will be" (128). The point was exact. It was the "illusion" of the imaginary geography of Antilia and of the Indies that enabled Columbus to call into question the "sa-cred" and conventional geography of his time. This ge-ography, as Lynn Thorndike points out, was still based on an Aristotelian physics and on its a priori notion of "natural place." In this conceptual a priori view, given that the element of water normally submerged the ele-ment of earth except in cases of "unnatural motion," the ratio of the former element to the latter would have made the voyage impossible, given the vast distance that would have to exist between land-mass and land-mass. Columbus had therefore based his counterargu-ments on the postulate of the Christian humanist an-thropic principle (and on the empirical error) that there had to be more land than water, seeing that God had made the Earth for the "salvation of souls." With his voyage he had therefore sailed out of the conceptual inferential schema in which human knowledge of the geography of the earth had still to be subordinated to the "public languages" of scholastic theology and its "transcendental" behavior-regulating Word of the feudal-Christian, out of the latter's paradigm of value and authority, and "true" discourse. His voyage, in spite of his own factual errors, would therefore, together with Copernicus's challenge to the then still "sacred" Ptolemaic astronomy a half-century later, lay the basis for the emancipation of human knowledge of physical nature (and, after Darwin, of organic nature) from its millennial traditional role of verifying the "paradigm of value and authority" or, in Glissant's phrase, the "transcendentally intolerant" Word of each order's sociogenic principle or code of "life and death." This emancipation of human knowledge and therefore of human autonomy with respect to its knowledge of physical and organic nature is of course expressed in the natural sciences.

This cognitive autonomy with respect to natural science was, however, only won on the basis of an epochal secularization of human modes of being, which, however, in order to effect its own mutation from the sacred to the profane by means of the then-revolutionary counterdiscourse of humanism, also had to reestablish its own absolutizing "space of Otherness" on the basis of a Las Casasian "error of natural reason." This error, which is as founding to our contemporary world system as Columbus's, was based on the self-representation of the two secular models of the human: that of Rational Man (whose symbolic Other was the *indio,* the Negro, the Mad) and, at the end of the eighteenth century, that of Man as a selected being and natural organism (whose dysselected symbolic Other was the Nigger, the native, the poor, the nonfit) as the universal human, "man as man." In consequence, the "conventional reason" or episteme specific to the sociogenic principle of each necessarily represented themselves as firstly reason-in-general, then as the "objective truth" of liberal positivism, and in its proletarian variant as the "scientific truth" of historical materialism.

In both cases, in order to secure the cognitive closure and "hermeneutic circle" necessary to sustain their founding respective a prioris, the orders of rational knowledge that were elaborated had necessarily to continue to institute themselves as processes of symbolic thought and therefore as modes of Lyotard's millennial tradition of "narrative knowledge" rather than as thought on the model of that of the natural sciences. Since both modes of "cultural reason" were enabled to effect the mutation of human social knowledge from the

sacred to the profane only on the condition that they elaborate themselves with rigorous reference to the objective "internal standard" of their codes of antithetical life and death (Prospero/Caliban or Man/Nigger), in order so to provide the rigorous behavior-regulating system of meanings inducing of the collective behaviors that were and are integrative of the first secular modes of kind and of human beingness in history—according therefore to a sociogenic internal standard which specifies, as the genome specifies for organic species, what we are selectively to know of the World.

We cannot, however, given the ongoing destruction of our planetary environment—Glissant's "dried-up" riverbed of La Lézarde—as well as the reality of large-scale global poverty and of the population explosion in the shantytown archipelagoes to which this poverty leads, continue to regulate our behaviors half by process of scientific thought and half by the millennial processes of symbolic thought generated from "the paradigm of value and authority" of our present absolute model of human nature, Man, of its transcendental Word. If at the level of physics Einstein's theory of relativity has put an end to the Newtonian concept of absolute space and time, the theory of the Big Bang revealed that even ostensible constants like the "laws of nature" had their origin in time, whereas the revelation of a subatomic quantum world has deabsolutized our earlier notion of physical reality, this process of relativization has not occurred at the level of our social knowledge, that is of our "human sciences." There our "error of reason" with respect to the premise of an absolute "human nature," as one based on our belief in a relation of *pure* continuity between the genetically regulated modes of organic life and the always rhetorico-discursively regulated modes of human life, still represents our present model of the human, Man, as being as absolute as Newtonian space and time before Einstein.

The "war" waged by the new discourse of the Antilles is a war waged against that error. Since the fixity of "Man" and its model necessarily depends on the fixity and nonvalue of the *nègre,* Césaire's revalorization of the *nègre,* Fanon's genial replacement of ontogeny with sociogeny, and Glissant's projection of *l'étant* in place of *l'Être,* together with his reclaiming of the specificity of the history, landscape, and historical-existential being of Antilleanity, all call into question and refute the premise of an acultural and absolute model of the human. The new discourse of the Antilles therefore goes "beyond the Word of Man" in that it is impelled to replace the latter's postulate of "man as Man," of an ontogenic subject, with that of an everywhere culturally relative—because rhetorico-discursively cum neurophysiologically instituted—mode of the human subject and therefore of the relativity also of its necessarily negatively invested mode of the Abject, of Ontological Lack, of the "Negro" as a "different kind of creature," as the only group (as Césaire pointed out) excluded from human status within the symbolic logic of the Word of Man and of its absolute model of the human.

The postulate of human life as a phenomenon which does not preexist each culture's "order of discourse" but comes into being simultaneously with it, as a third level of existence defined by the fact of its being regulated in its behaviors by the discursive-neuronal patterns of its culture-specific modes of "mind" or systemic consciousness, by, in effect, the hybrid correlation between the *ordo naturae* of our neurochemical brain states and the *ordo verborum* of our systems of meanings, necessarily impels both the Antillean and the human subject beyond our present "order of discourse" and episteme into "realms" beyond "conventional reason." This new realm, I shall propose here, will necessarily be that of a reinvented *studia humanitatis* or science of the human, which takes as its object of inquiry the correlation between our rhetorico-discursively instituted systems of meanings and the neurochemical signaling field that they orchestrate and which can therefore isolate and identify the rules of functioning of the meaning-neural dynamics which govern our behaviors, instituting us as specific modes of that hybrid logos/bios mode of existence: the human. It is clear in this context that Glissant's Antillean human subject, coming to realize *its* cognitive autonomy not merely with respect to its knowledge of physical and organic nature but with respect to its knowledge of itself as a mode of life which exists *outside* the symbolic circuit of organic life, must therefore now accept the full responsibility of its position as a "free outcast" who confronts "the rest of nature as a trial, task, issue and enigma, as an alien abode" and therefore as the causal source of our own Good, our own Evil.

Both the Antillean and the human subject are therefore now called upon to realize the fullest measure of their possible autonomy, on the model of Glissant's hero Thaël; for although all the other young urban people of *La Lézarde* must go through the rite of passage, as Beverley Ormerod points out, it is Thaël for whom the rite will entail the greatest and most final rupture. As the descendant of the Maroons of the mountains, Thaël has been compelled in the wake of World War II and the emerging political struggles of the island to leave the certainty of his ancestral retreat in the mountains in order to join in the struggle for the future that was being fought out in the lowland plantation plains. To do so, however, he must leave behind the "invisible roads" of a nonconscious past in order to attain to a "true age of reason," one that can enable him to take the "measure" of the universe, not only of that which lies around him, but of that inside him as he leaves behind the certainty of the transcendental for the provisional.[32]

It is this imperative of a shift from ontogeny to sociogeny, from *l'Être* to *l'étant,* and the new frontiers of being and knowing that such a shift opens, that is to be, I believe, the gift of the New World to the Old, the gift specifically of that Other America, the Antilia of both Toscanelli's and Columbus's imaginary geography of some five centuries ago; today the Antilia of Glissant's dream for a fully realized archipelago, for the *avenir* of its small countries, for its collective free, as his oeuvre incites them to be, in their acts, in their desire. "Mais les Indes sont vérité" (*I,* 95).

Sylvia Wynter, Autumn 1989

1 Edouard Glissant, *Le discours antillais,* Paris, Seuil, 1981. See his analysis of the difference between the two colonizer models, pp. 206–7. An English edition, *Caribbean Discourse,* J. Michael Dash, tr., is to appear from the University Press of Virginia in late 1989. Citations use the abbreviation *DA* where needed for clarity.

2 Martinicans were educated in the representational system of the French nation-state. The latter's "origin," which all blacks, whites, and in-betweens recited, began with the litany "Our ancestors, the Gaels." Within the context of "the intolerance" of the nation schema there could only be a single Origin. More than one Origin, as in the case of more than one language, would be, as Glissant notes, logically "seditious" (*DA,* 319).

3 In one sense an essay, in another "cultural sociology" or "auto-ethnography," *Le discours antillais* is properly transgeneric. In the line of Fanon's *Black Skin, White Masks,* the book best exemplifies what I have defined as a "new discourse" specific to the Antilles. Both texts defy our present generic classification.

4 The term is taken from the title of Fanon's book *Les damnés de la terre,* Paris, Maspéro, 1961. The term *damnés* is translated literally as "condemned" to mean those systemic areas that are as condemned to "poverty" by the logic of our present order of knowledge as heretics were condemned to burning within the logic of the order of knowledge of scholastic theology. The powerful phrase was coined by Jacques Roumain, the Haitian writer.

5 Michael Dash, introduction to his translation of *La Lézarde* as *The Ripening,* London, Heinemann, 1985, p. 3. Subsequent citations use the abbreviation *R* where needed for clarity.

6 Beverley Ormerod, *An Introduction to the French Caribbean Novel,* London, Heinemann, 1985, p. 39.

7 See *DA,* pp. 104–5, where Glissant discusses the definition of the phenomenon of *marronnage* (running away) as a "fundamental cultural opposition to the new order imposed on the slave."

8 Dash, p. 1.

9 J. G. A. Pocock, *Politics, Language and Time: Essays on Political Thought and History,* New York, Atheneum, 1971, p. 6.

10 Whereas from inside the Francophone literary tradition the comparative *differences* between Glissant and Césaire loom

large, from the perspective of the Caribbean as a whole it is the similarities, the line of filiation, between Césaire, Fanon, and Glissant that stand out. So, although there are differences among their individual perspectives—for example, Glissant's emphasis on cultural *métissage* rather than on Césaire's *négritude,* as well as his stress on the linkages between the Antillean islands rather than on Césaire's return to the African connections—these differences are *not* contradictions. Without Césaire's *négritude* and the revaluation of the African connection, Glissant's later concept of *métissage* would have been meaningless. One should note a "Bloom-type anxiety of influence" at work here that leads Glissant to emphasize his differences with the earlier writer. However, if we see Césaire's *négritude* as an act of uprising against the *blanchitude* by means of which the representation of the generic human (Man) was totemized in the Indo-European population group, in the same way as post-sixties feminism has been an uprising against the representation of the male sex as the generic self, then Glissant's work can be seen as an evolutionary variant, defined by the different moment in history that it is called to address, of Césaire's founding poetic paradigm and can be seen as part of its completion.

11 Pierre Maranda, "The Dialectic of Metaphor: An Anthropological Essay on Hermeneutics," in S. R. Saleiman and Inge Grossman, *The Reader in the Text: Essays on Audience and Interpretation,* Princeton, N.J., Princeton University Press, 1980.

12 Ormerod, p. 36, where she cites Glissant's preface to his play *Monsieur Toussaint,* Paris, Seuil, 1964, p. 219.

13 I have coined the word *empirics* to refer to what Foucault defines as nondiscursive practices in his lecture *The Order of Discourse.* See *The Archaeology of Knowledge,* A. M. Sheridan Smith, tr., New York, Pantheon, 1972.

14 "True discourse," Foucault suggests, can function as a "regime of Truth" only on the basis of processes of exclusion and selectivity and therefore on areas of repressed and forbidden knowledge.

15 My one area of strong disagreement with Glissant is cited here. He proposes that it is *métissage* and its affirmation as a value that contests the West's postulate of "filiation" as the guardian of a unique and single origin of race. I argue, on the other hand, that since the nineteenth century representation of the Indo-European as the generic human as well as the idea of a generic of "normal" mode of human being "totemized" in a one race, with all other population groups being its Lack, was and is a function of the instituting of generic "Man," defined by the Word of Man, Césure's *négritude,* which refused the black's imposed role as conceptual Other to the representation of generic Man, not only calls in question our present order of being and knowing but dispenses with the need for the word *mestizaje* itself, since the syncretism of culture can now be seen as a *recombination* of cultures (Native American, Judeo-Christian, African) into a new Caribbean and American synthesis, whereas the term *mestizo* (mixed) becomes simply the recombination of two variants of the human genome—rather, that is, than a *mestizaje.* The "notion of *race*" therefore ceases to function as it does in the Word of *Man* as the *ground* of human being.

16 Michel Foucault, "The Confessions of the Flesh," in *Power/ Knowledge: Selected Interviews and Other Writings,* C. Gordon, ed., New York, Panther, 1980, p. 207.

17 These "fronts" are essentially part of what Glissant calls the "universal généralisé." As such they have been central to what he defines as the intellectual mimeticism of the thought of many of the Antillean and so-called Third World educated elite. One can speak here of a universal proletarianism and genderism on the model of Glissant's analysis of universal humanism, in *DA,* p. 385.

18 Michel Foucault, "Truth and Power" in *Power/Knowledge,* pp. 127–28.

19 This postulate is based on a seminal article by the biologist Danielli, "Altruism and the Internal Reward System or the Opium of the People," in the *Journal of Social and Biological Structures,* 1980, no. 3, pp. 89–90.

20 Nicolás Guillén, *Motivos de son,* Havana, Imprenta Rambla, Bouza, 1930.

21 See George L. Mosse, *Towards the Final Solution: A History of European Racism,* New York, Fertig, 1978, p. 20.

22 Julia Kristeva, *Powers of Horror: An Essay on Abjection,* Leon S. Roudiez, tr., New York, Columbia University Press, 1982, p. 17.

23 Peter Winch, "Understanding a Primitive Society," *American Philosophical Quarterly,* 1964, pp. 307–24.

24 Wlad Godzich, afterword to Samuel Weber, *Institution and Interpretation,* Minneapolis, University of Minnesota Press, 1987, p. 161.

25 The *pieza* or "piece" was a male slave around twenty-five years old, in top physical condition. Two young boys, for example, would then make up one *pieza* for purposes of the trade. The term reduced the slave to his or her pure physical-labor capacity.

26 Hans Blumenberg, *The Legitimacy of the Modern Age,* R. M. Wallace, tr., Cambridge, Ma., MIT Press, 1983, p. 205.

27 See Bjorn Landstrom, *Columbus: The Story of Don Cristóbal Colón, Admiral of the Ocean Sea, and His Four Voyages to the Indies,* New York, Macmillan, p. 166.

28 Blumenberg, p. 205.

29 Sanders Gilman, "Black Bodies, White Bodies: Towards an Iconography of Female Sexuality in Late Nineteenth Century Art, Medicine, and Literature," in Race, Writing, and Difference," H. L. Gates, ed., *Critical Inquiry,* 12:1 (Autumn 1985), pp. 204–42.

30 Frantz Fanon, *Toward the African Revolution,* Haakon Chevalier, tr., New York, Grove, 1968.

31 Edouard Glissant, *Les Indes,* Paris, Seuil, 1955; reprinted in *Poèmes,* Paris, Seuil, 1965. The citation here is from page 77; subsequent citations refer to the 1965 edition and use the abbreviation *I* where needed for clarity.

32 As Ormerod points out, the members of the young group in *La Lézarde* are shown as following the "paths of questing adolescence"; as such they find themselves on those "fragile invisible roads, which a man leaves behind when he attains the true age of reason, when he . . . takes the measure of the universe around him" (51). See also the original French edition of the novel, p. 106: "Chemins invisibles que quitte l'homme quand il entre dans l'âge de ses vraies raisons . . . et qu'il mesure l'univers autour de lui."

CUBA

Displacements and Autobiography in Cuban-American Fiction

The narratives of Pablo Medina, Omar Torres, and Cristina García are representative of a pivotal moment in contemporary Cuban-American writing. Medina, Torres, and García belong to a generation of younger writers of Cuban heritage who, in the words of Eliana Rivero, "are in the midst of effecting the transition from émigré/exile categories to that of ethnic minority members" (191).[1] These are writers whose literary identity is determined by history, in this case the diaspora which arose after the 1959 Cuban Revolution. Their texts, written in English and published between 1990 and 1992, embody the dislocation of exile as they attempt to recapture a past that is marginal to their present.

In *At Face Value: Autobiographical Writing in Spanish America* Sylvia Molloy tells us that the idea of crisis is tied to the autobiographical moment in Latin American letters.[2] For Cuban-American writers, this crisis originates in two basic issues which they share with other cultures in exile: how do they reconcile their past experiences in their country of birth with present experiences in their adopted country, and how do they negotiate between bicultural and monocultural readers? My study seeks to trace the dramatization of the Cuban voice within the fictional world of these authors and to explore the solutions and substitutions these authors have devised in order to create a voice in a culture other than that of their country of birth. Issues of representation will be concerned with the autobiographical strategies used by these writers and the manner in which each text inscribes the reader in its process of self-revelation.

I have chosen the autobiographical accounts of these authors because their narratives illustrate simultaneous yet different stages in the evolution of contemporary Cuban-American narrative. Medina's childhood memories recall the prerevolutionary Cuba in which he spent his first twelve years. Torres's novel is a fictional autobiography of a young Cuban-American poet very much engaged with his Cuban past and the politics of the exile communities of Miami and New York. Cristina García's autobiographical persona is a Cuban-American ethnic who grows up in New York desperately searching for her Cuban roots. Unlike García, who was only two years old at the time of her departure, Medina and Torres were young boys of twelve and thirteen and as such experienced a Cuban childhood. All three write in English about a past that took place in Spanish.

Any consideration of the creation of fictional selves for these authors must address issues pertinent to autobiography. Autobiography as a narrative form prompts the reader of the novel to consider the act of telling, the protagonist's particular purpose for telling his or her own story, and the links between the teller's own life and the manner in which it is communicated. Clearly, the choice of an autobiographical self, fictional or otherwise, is an appropriate one for these authors, since the narrative act is linked to the achievement of identity and thus is frequently used by writers who belong to ethnic and minority groups. Examining how each author tells the Cuban story will reveal how autobiographical strategies of representation serve to articulate their perceptions of self.

In her essay "Women's Autobiographical Selves: Theory and Practice" Susan Stanford Friedman[3] establishes a workable theory that is useful not only for the explication of autobiography in Anglo-American and European women's texts but also in regard to minority writers such as the ones we are investigating here. Friedman examines the reigning attitudes toward autobiography in contemporary theory and questions "the individualistic concept of the autobiographical self" such as it has been proposed by well-known scholars of autobiography such as Olney and Gusdorf.[4] Friedman argues that for the "marginalized cultures" a definition of autobiography that stresses interdependent identification within a community is a much more useful tool of analysis. The autobiographical consciousness of marginal groups, according to Friedman, results in autobiographical forms that are not only individualistic but also collective (35). Friedman's theories of autobiography are useful to my investigation, since the autobiographical model employed by Cuban-American writers exhibits a desire to connect with a larger community of Cubans as well as Cuban-Americans in the process of telling their life stories.

In *Exiled Memories*[5] Pablo Medina's life in Cuba is chronicled via incidents which occurred in the places where he grew up: his grandparents' farm, the house in coastal Havana, his wanderings and explorations of the city's streets. The book begins with a vignette that illustrates the Narrator's arrival in the U.S. in 1960 and works back in time to return to this same moment in the text's final pages. Specific events of the Narrator's own childhood—his traumas, triumphs, and discoveries—are interspersed with vignettes about the life stories of his ancestors and how they came to settle on the island of Cuba. The incidents Medina narrates are chosen by virtue of the intensity with which they stand in his memory: the frightening experience of a night spent crabbing in the Zapata swamp (14), the finding of human bones belonging to a victim of repression under the Batista dictatorship (100). Medina recalls these events vividly, and his prose at times possesses an eerie intensity.

Even though the author tells us his primary wish is to record his past, the main interest of his text is generated from what the reader learns about Medina's present. According to Louis Renza, the predominant reason for writing an autobiography is the writer's present: "Autobiography is the writer's de facto attempt to elucidate his present rather than his past" (271). In the same vein, Roy Pascal observes that autobiography involves an interplay between the past and the present, that "its significance is indeed more the revelation of the present situation of the autobiographer than the uncovering of the past" (11).[6] For Medina, the genealogical self-exploration which at first seems to be the central issue of his memoirs leads to the Narrator's conclusion that his self will forever and irremediably be split: "My childhood lies inside the bowl of distance and politics, unapproachable and thus disconnected from my adulthood. The two revolve around each other like twin stars, pulling and tugging, without hope of reconciliation" (113).

Although the text is primarily a revisiting of experiences of a Cuban childhood, Medina's story exhibits an emotional and ideological interaction between the writing self and the self recalled. The fact that many Cuban children were violently uprooted in the early sixties challenges the reader's perspective of the Cuban situation. Medina's past is marginal to his present but essential to it.

When the Narrator describes the slaughtering of a pig in the Cuban countryside, the event witnessed by Medina as a child is brought to the present by Medina's ruminations about his own imagined slaughtering.

> He discarded the tools carelessly on the ground, grabbed each side of the crevice . . . and pulled until the ribs let go of the spine and the chest cavity opened like a pulpy fruit exposing a chaos of purple organs and blue and yellow intestines. And then I wondered if I were split so unceremoniously like that whether my organs too would shine amorphously in the sun like multicolored gelatin. (25)

The pig's dismemberment brings to the writer associations of the fragmentation and dislocation of his own exiled condition. Such comments betray the anxiety of the Narrator as he views his uncertain present in the U.S.

Throughout the narrative Medina injects the fears of his present self into the story of his past self: "I am terrified of growing old alone . . . because my children will be too busy to care for me or because my presence makes them feel uncomfortable, put-upon, and limited from pursuing that vacuous activity called self-realization" (36). Cuban and American cultural mores are juxtaposed as the writer tries to make sense of their differences. The author at times is critical of life in both societies, and his criticism becomes an invitation to re-think the way in which life evolves in both cultures.

> As I grow older and sink ever deeper into the loneliness of American society, this sense of family, of openness to others that she [his grandmother] and others of the family have deeded to me, becomes increasingly dear. Because I dread isolation, because I have been taught to define myself through others, I fight that tendency of our society to shut the door on anyone who is not a card-carrying member of the nuclear family. (36)

Medina's commentaries from his present vantage point as a writer in the U.S. reveal a desire to engage the reader in some value questioning: "Life in the United States for me has not been a search for roots (that presumes their loss), but rather a quixotic attempt to become a creature I never was nor can ever be: an American" (preface, x). By asserting his own marginal condition, Medina separates himself from the English-speaking majority. The stories and the events Medina relates took place in Spanish, whereas his narration takes place in English, and this linguistic severance produces anxiety in the Narrator. Spanish, the language of his childhood, is now silenced and replaced by English.

Medina feels that the kind of childhood he lived in Cuba will never be lived again either by the Cuban-American children in the U.S. or by the children in Cuba today. Dislocation for writers such as Medina is, in a sense, more tragic than the experience of adult exiles who were secure in their identities as Cubans at the time they had to leave their country. In his preface Medina explains the reasons for recording the memories of his childhood:

> On visiting my great-aunt and my grandmother . . . I was awakened to the fact that they and the other old folks of the family would not live forever. . . . When they went, they would take with them the myths and folklore I had grown up with. That, I thought, should never be allowed to happen. And who better than I . . . to chronicle our past for those generations who had never lived it? (x)

Historical changes on the island would not allow the children there to live as he had, and Cuban children living in the U.S. would be destined to grow up as Americans. Thus Medina's text assumes the task of preserving a way of life and a tradition which the author feels could be a source of strength and knowledge for other Cuban-Americans. His memories become a means to ensure the survival of a collective identity.

Medina's task of collecting the stories of his family is central in the development of his present self. It is precisely this rich and secure past that will lend stability to the uncertain present of the writer in his adopted country: "the house [of memories] stands and leans freely into the future. Whatever winds may come, welcome" (114). The stories provided to him by his community and his family members render context and become a necessary exercise to confront the present in the U.S.

As in Medina's case, the diaspora resulting from the 1959 revolution becomes the structural and thematic core of Omar Torres's narrative *Fallen Angels Sing*.[7] As opposed to Medina's memoir, which relies on the security of a happy past, Torres's version of his present situation in the U.S. requires the distance of fiction as it conveys the existential anxiety of the divided self. The narrative imitates the structure of autobiography via a protagonist who seeks the capacity to tell his own story.[8]

The narrative takes place in the U.S. and concentrates on the present of a thirty-three-year-old exiled poet as he copes with the shattering experience of dislocation. Although this is a fictional autobiography, there are coincidences between the life of Miguel Saavedra, the protagonist, and that of Omar Torres, the author. Like Torres, Saavedra was born in Victoria de las Tunas in 1945; and like Torres, he is a poet who came to Miami from Cuba at the age of thirteen and eventually settled in the New York City area. Both Torres and Saavedra were thirty-three years old at the time of the publication of the text's original Spanish version in 1981.[9]

The reader meets Miguel Saavedra on his way from Miami to New York City as the protagonist agonizes about his frivolous life and the need to become more involved in the political future of his country: "I had been a Philistine, living on the periphery of my convictions about Cuba. I had dogged the issue, but it was in vain. Cuba was embedded in me; I had to harvest my involvement anew" (78). In New York, Miguel finds himself caught between pro- and anti-Castro groups who wish to use him as a symbol that will further their political causes. However, the protagonist's own inability to decide between these factions contributes to his deep anxiety: "The exiles admired my work, but distrusted me. Now it happened that those in Cuba also admired me, but I distrusted them. They were clearly wanting to use me, but I didn't know for what" (97). In his search for meaning and commitment, the protagonist travels from university poetry readings to Santería

churches to gay bars and finally to Cuba, where he dies in a failed attempt to assassinate Castro.

The hybrid structure of Torres's novel as well as his use of metafictional devices provides a potential avenue for the understanding of the protagonist's evolving self. The mixing of the genres of theater, poetry, and narrative in the telling of Saavedra's tale parallels the protagonist's anxious and undecided condition as he flounders between the Cuban communities of New York and Miami. A section entitled "Memories of My Father's Family" is narrated as a play within the narrative; another segment, entitled "We Interrupt This Program . . . ," takes on the shape of a long poem. The protagonist's dilemma is well articulated when, in a play-within-the-text acted out by Miguel and his friends, his own generation confronts the values of his parents.

> The question is not to forget, Dad. Take me or my friends; you have a life to remember, but in that life we are nothing, we don't belong, because we have nothing to share with you in that life. We don't belong there, and we don't belong here; we just don't belong. We're not Cubans and we're not Americans. (111)

Miguel Saavedra does not achieve a coherent sense of self; he is too involved in the reality of his elders and thus is paralyzed in his attempt to reconstruct his own story. As already noted, the novel's Spanish version (under the title *Apenas un bolero*) had appeared back in 1981. Torres's decision to publish a version of the same novel in English in 1991 points toward the ambiguity and unresolved pull felt by the Cuban-American writer regarding his likely audience. Early in the novel Saavedra addresses his potential reader: "You are what you read, but you are also what you write. I was part of this story, even though it's not autobiographical. I wrote it on my Smith-Corona. How would non-Latin Americans react to this story?" (27).

Saavedra engages the "non-Latin American" reader as an outsider, as someone to be instructed about the details of a country in crisis. Narratorial digressions about specific events in Cuban history abound in the narrative and become a way to inform and instruct the English-speaking reader about U.S.-Cuba relations (33, 83, 123).

The protagonist's frequent dialogues with his readers as well as with his author are examples of the many self-conscious narrative devices used by Torres in the telling of Saavedra's story. Moreover, the central issue in the novel is literature, since Saavedra's writings become the source of his own exploitation by factions from the Right and the Left. As an artist, Saavedra is pictured as a vulnerable element and as a likely victim of the politics that divide Cubans and Cuban-Americans: "You are the Cuban exile; you're all of us with your longing and your endless nostalgia" (131), writes a friend to Miguel as the protagonist sets out for Cuba to meet his death.

In the closing pages of the book the figure of the author appears in the text and states his intention to travel to Havana, ostensibly to meet the same deadly fate as his protagonist Miguel. If the metatext is in fact a dramatization of the construction of the self as the pieces of writing come together within the fiction, in the case of Torres the metatext seems dooming rather than redemptive.[10]

Metafictional narrative strategies are also central to the search undertaken by Pilar, the protagonist of Cristina García's *Dreaming in Cuban*.[11] Unlike Miguel Saavedra's failed attempts to make some sense of his life through his writings, the diary that García's protagonist writes becomes a repository of stories which will help her piece together her life. The stories Pilar compiles describe a family split between two countries due to the harsh realities of the Castro regime. Pilar records their various stories in a diary she keeps in the lining of her winter coat. Her diary eventually becomes the reader's text.

Pilar dramatizes the anxieties felt by an ethnic writer about the issues of voice and identity. At the beginning of the novel she formulates the question she will pursue throughout: "Even though I've been living in Brooklyn all my life, it doesn't feel like home to me. I'm not sure Cuba is, but I want to find out. If I could only see Abuela Celia again, I'd know where I belonged" (58). *Dreaming in Cuban* is significant because it treats the experience of exile from the perspective of an ethnic writer.

Like Cristina García herself, Pilar was born in Cuba but grows up in New York City. Pilar is the daughter of exiles, a kind of skeptical punk who dabbles in art and Santería. The text's story allows García to examine three important dimensions of Cuban exile: the story of the Cubans who remained in Cuba (exemplified in the book by Abuela Celia and Tía Felicia); the story of the Cuban exiles who came to the U.S. in the sixties (the story of Lourdes, Pilar's mother); and, finally, the story of the children of exile—that is, Pilar's story.

The novel is sometimes told in Pilar's first-person voice (when she narrates events related to her own life in the U.S.) and sometimes in her omniscient voice, as in the stories of Celia, Lourdes, and Felicia. The various interpolated sections constitute two moments in time: a Cuban past which goes back to the beginning of the century and incorporates the poverty and corruption under which Celia, the matriarch, grew up; and the present, which takes us all the way to Pilar's visit to Cuba during the early eighties. Although there are contradictions in how each character views events, virtually all the stories from the past of these characters help explain present circumstances and demonstrate the links between past and present.

The tales contained in Pilar's diary seem to fall into two categories: those in which language loss is directly related to the exile experience, and those in which loss of voice transcends exile and becomes a metaphor for existential alienation. For Pilar herself, language loss is a given. After all, she has grown up speaking English, and English is the language in which she writes and records the tales of the Del Pino family. Thematically, Pilar's anxiety about losing the language of her culture is manifested through her obsession with painting and in her ruminations about visual texts. To the dilemma of language loss, Pilar finds that visual images communicate meaning much more effectively than does language: "Painting is its own language. . . . Translations just confuse it, dilute it, like words going from Spanish to English. . . . Who needs words when colors and lines conjure up their own language?" (59, 139).

In terms of the text's narrative process, Pilar uses nontraditional avenues such as telepathy to communicate with her grandmother. Celia, the Cuban matriarch, becomes Pilar's inner voice, and their frequent exchanges help Pilar cope with her daily existence: "I feel much more connected to Abuela Celia than to Mom, even though I haven't seen my grandmother in seventeen years. . . . Even in silence, she gives me the confidence to do what I believe is right, to trust my own perceptions" (63, 176).

In telling the stories of others, Pilar's omniscient voice inverts the relationship to figures of authority who have dominated her in the past. Lourdes, her mother, does not fare well in Pilar's narrative. As a representative of the exile generation that came from Cuba in the sixties, she is ridiculed in the text. Her politics are wrong, she is overweight and unbecoming, and, most of all, she is totally unable to understand her daughter. Not surprisingly, when Lourdes visits Cuba, the language she speaks cannot be understood by the Cubans in Cuba (221).

García does not shy away from the diversity and differences that separate Cubans from Cuban-Americans, yet she understands the challenges common to both groups. Like all the characters in the text, Lourdes is tormented by feelings she does not confront. Her anxiety about her own displacement is evident when she passes the Arab shops in Brooklyn which make her reflect on her condition as an exile: "What happens to their languages?" she asks herself, "the warm burial grounds they leave behind?" (73).

For the women living in the U.S., the loss incurred by exile is clearly expressed though the metaphor of language loss. Pilar knows Spanish but doesn't use it. Her telepathic conversations with Celia and her obsession with painting become the bridges that connect her two cultures. Lourdes, on the other hand, speaks in Spanish but no one knows what she is saying.

As a narrator of and participant in her own story, Pilar believes that if she can get to Cuba she will be able to reconstruct the puzzle of her fragmented family and thus recapture a part of her life she knows has been missing. The stories of Abuela Celia and Tía Felicia will provide her with a context within which her life can be assumed.

The characters left in Cuba experience a loss of voice which can be understood in terms of gender as well as political history. As Rosario Ferré observes in her review of the novel,[12] Celia and Felicia are products of male-dominated Cuban society. Celia's husband tries to punish her for having had a lover before she met him; Felicia's husband abandons her as soon as they are married. As women, Celia and Felicia have been victimized by their men; as Cubans, they have not been served well by their history. Their poverty, their unhappy childhood, and their lonely existence are indirectly tied to events which have rendered them powerless. Both Felicia and Celia suffer from profound unhappiness born out of their inability to share their joy with others (119). Theirs is the silent world of inner exile.

Celia's story is a case in point: When her lover Gustavo leaves for Spain, she becomes inconsolable—in the words of Pilar, "a housebound exile" (117). If there is meaning in Celia's life, it is her magical link with her granddaughter Pilar. Celia will pass on to Pilar the family history which is contained in the unmailed letters she writes to her lover Gustavo during the twenty years she stays married to Jorge Del Pino. When Pilar visits Cuba, Celia will give them to her granddaughter, and these "texts within the text" will become part of Pilar's diary. In one of the letters Celia summarizes how she views her own situation:

> If I was born to live on an island, then I'm grateful for one thing: that the tides rearrange the borders. At least I have the illusion of change, of possibility. To be locked within boundaries plotted by priests and politicians would be the only thing more intolerable. Don't you see how they're carving up the world, Gustavo? How they're stealing our geography? Our fates? The arbitrary is no longer in our hands. To survive is an act of hope. (99)

The novel ends fittingly with one of Celia's letters to Gustavo in which she designates Pilar as a keeper of the family's knowledge: "The revolution is eleven days old. My granddaughter, Pilar Puente del Pino, was born today. It is also my birthday. I am fifty years old. I will no longer write to you. . . . She [Pilar] will remember everything" (245).

This last vignette is chronologically out of sequence, for we have been reading Pilar's diary all along. However, the vignette is significant from the perspective of its author, for here Cristina García identifies her protagonist as the narrator of the book we have just read. Pilar leaves the reader with the conviction that the double consciousness of being both narrator of and participant in her own story has enabled her to find that part of her own identity she knew was missing. Listening to the stories of others binds García into a relationship with a community of tellers. Fictional autobiography functions in this text as a "community binding ritual" (Friedman, 50) in García's search for the ethnic voice.

The novels analyzed in this study focus on the implications of a specified cultural and political condition of displacement. If these narratives look to the community for answers in the reconstruction and healing of their life stories, in the case of Torres and Medina this reconstruction seems next to impossible. Torres fights to be different from the Miami Cubans but somehow does not achieve this goal. His protagonist never acquires verbal control over his experiences because he cannot achieve the needed balance to overcome his fear of not really belonging in the U.S. or in Cuba. Medina, on the other hand, wants to preserve Cuban culture and its traditions through the legacy of his memoirs. Nevertheless, he betrays a great deal of anxiety as he shares with the reader the uncertainties of his divided self. In the case of Cristina García, it is precisely Pilar's gathering of information about the history of her ancestors in Cuba that brings her life back into focus.

Eliana Rivero tells us that a writer's transition from exilic to ethnic concerns entails coming into a personal awareness of biculturalism and takes for granted the reality of permanence in a society other than the one existing in the country of birth ("Immigrants," 193). Bicultural awareness, in the case of these writers, has mainly to do with the way in which they conceive the language and culture of their adopted countries. Although these writers are roughly contemporaries in age and write about the same concerns, their autobiographical perspectives vary significantly according to the degree of interaction they had with the language and culture of their country of birth during their formative years.

The findings of James Ruppert and Reed Way Dasenbrock[13] on the subject of monocultural versus bicultural audiences are pertinent in the assessment of the translatability of these Cuban-American autobiographies. Ruppert coins the term *mediation* to designate the act of negotiation by the writer between two cultural codes. According to Ruppert, the bicultural writer must be free to use the epistemology from both cultures as a way to strike what he calls a "dynamic confluence of values and expectations" (223). The ideal writer of any bicultural text would be able to speak to two audiences at once. Dasenbrock tells us that "multicultural works of literature are multicultural not only in their subject matter, but also as far as how they allow readers into the text" (18).

In the case of Medina and Torres, their stance toward their monocultural readers seems at times critical, and there is a reluctance to allow the English reader into the world of the text. Medina assures us that he "will never become an American," while Torres's protagonist agonizes as to the possible reaction of the "non-Latin American reader" to his narrative. As an ethnic writer, García engages the U.S. experience directly and cannot separate herself from it. Pilar's story tries to reconcile two cultures and two languages and two visions of the world into a particular whole. It is precisely this pull between two places that the ethnic character experiences and that motivates her actions within the text. García's poetic descriptions allow her to display an ability to speak to two audiences at once.

According to Paul John Eakin, the autobiographical act recapitulates the fundamental rhythms of identity formation: "The writing of autobiography emerges as a second acquisition of language, a second coming into being of self, a self-conscious self-consciousness."[14] In the case of the three authors discussed here this double translating act has had different degrees of success. English was not the experiential language for Torres or Medina; thus their task of translating became one in which the English reader could only be engaged from the outside. García's childhood, on the other hand, occurred in English, a fact which allows her to integrate issues of past and present more easily. As one of the first ethnic Cuban-American writers, García envisions questions of identity and heritage with less anxiety and thus greater distance from her material. If autobiography is a "theater of self-expression, self-knowledge, and self-recovery" (Eakin, 3), Cristina García leads a third generation of Cuban-American writers as they walk the path from exile to ethnicity.

Isabel Alvarez-Borland, Winter 1994

[1] In recent years there have been various attempts to classify the writings of Cuban-Americans according to their different waves of migration. Rivero, in particular, makes useful distinctions between the concerns of exiles and ethnic writers. See Eliana Rivero, "From Immigrants to Ethnics: Cuban Writers in the U.S.," in *Breaking Boundaries,* Asunción Horno-Delgado, ed., Amherst, University of Massachusetts Press, 1989, pp. 189–200; and "Cubanos y Cubano-Americanos: Perfil y presencia en los Estados Unidos," *Discurso Literario,* 7 (1989), pp. 81–101. See also Silvia Burunat, "A Comparative Study of Contemporary Cuban-American and Cuban Literature," *International Journal of the Sociology of Language,* 84 (1990), pp. 101–23; and Carolina Hospital, "Los hijos del exilio cubano y su literatura," *Explicación de Textos Literarios,* 16:2 (1987), pp. 103–14.

[2] Although Molloy's study concentrates on nineteenth- and twentieth-century Latin American literary figures, her observations regarding these writers' perceptions of self are relevant to contemporary Cuban-American autobiographical narratives as well. See Sylvia Molloy, "Introduction," *At Face Value: Autobiographical Writing in Spanish America,* Cambridge, Eng., Cambridge University Press, 1991, pp. 1–13.

[3] See Susan Stanford Friedman, "Women's Autobiographical Selves: Theory and Practice," in *The Private Self,* Shari Benstock, ed., Chapel Hill, University of North Carolina Press, 1988, pp. 34–63; In addition to Stanford Friedman, Valery Smith's *Self-Discovery and Authority in Afro-American Narrative* (Cambridge, Ma., Harvard University Press, 1987) provides useful insights regarding autobiography as it applies to the literature of marginal groups. For Smith, autobiography "underscores the importance of naming oneself and shaping one's own story" (153). Smith also studies the role of the community in the autobiographical accounts of Afro-American writers. See her chapter "Tony Morrison's Narrative of Community," pp. 122–55.

[4] James Olney, "Autobiography and the Cultural Moment," and George Gusdorf, "Conditions and Limits of Autobiography," in *Autobiography: Essays Theoretical and Critical,* James Olney, ed., Princeton, N.J., Princeton University Press, 1980, pp. 3–49.

[5] Pablo Medina, *Exiled Memories,* Austin, University of Texas Press, 1990. All page numbers in the text pertain to this edition.

[6] Both Roy Pascal, in *Design and Truth in Autobiography* (Cambridge, Ma., Harvard University Press, 1960), and Louis Renza, in "The Veto of the Imagination: A Theory of Autobiography" (in Olney, pp. 268–95), study the idea of the split self as it applies to autobiography. On the essential division of the narrating subject, see Shlomith Rimmon-Kenan, *Narrative Fiction,* London, Methuen, 1983, pp. 71–106. In addition, Rachel Feldhay Brenner's discussion on the interaction between the "formative and the present self of the autobiographer" is relevant to my work on Cuban-American writers; see Rachel Feldhay Brenner, "In Search of Identity: The Israeli Arab Artist in Anton Shammas's *Arabesques,*" *PMLA,* 108 (1993), pp. 431–45.

[7] Omar Torres, *Fallen Angels Sing,* Houston, Arte Público, 1991. All page numbers refer to this edition.

[8] Paul John Eakin's *Fictions in Autobiography* (Princeton, N.J., Princeton University Press, 1985) offers a stimulating discussion on the role of fiction in autobiography as well as on the different theoretical stances regarding this subject. See his chapter 4, "Self-Invention in Autobiography: The Moment of Language," pp. 181–279.

[9] Torres's Spanish original, *Apenas un bolero* (Miami, Universal, 1981), and its English re-creation, *Fallen Angels Sing,* are sepa-

rated by ten years, although their content is essentially the same. Notable differences in the English version are the absence of a table of contents as well as slightly longer discussions by the Narrator regarding Cuban history.

[10] In using the term *metatext,* I allude to the general subject of reflexivity as it appears in contemporary narrative. Specific studies on embedded texts, readers, and writers within fictional narratives have influenced my investigation. See Gerald Prince, "Introduction a l'étude du narrataire," *Poétique,* 14 (1973), pp. 178–96; and Naomi Schor, "Fiction as Interpretation / Interpretation as Fiction," in *The Reader in the Text,* Susan Suleiman and Inge Crossman, eds., Princeton, N.J., Princeton University Press, 1980, pp. 165–83.

[11] Cristina García, *Dreaming in Cuban,* New York, Knopf, 1992. All textual references pertain to this edition.

[12] Rosario Ferré, "Review of *Dreaming in Cuban* by C. García," *Boston Sunday Globe,* 23 February 1992. Of the three writers studied here, Cristina García has received the greater critical attention. Reviews of *Dreaming in Cuban* have appeared in various mainstream publications. See Thulani Davis, *New York Times Book Review,* 17 May 1992, p. 14; and Michiko Kakutani, *New York Times,* 25 February 1992. In addition, García was a 1992 National Book Award finalist.

[13] See Reed Way Dasenbrock, "Intelligibility and Meaningfulness in Multicultural Literature in English," *PMLA,* 102 (1987), pp. 10–19; and James Ruppert, "Mediation and Multiple Narrative in Contemporary Native American Fiction," *Texas Studies in Literature and Language,* 28 (1986), pp. 209–25.

[14] Eakin, p. 18.

Back to the Future: Mothers, Languages, and Homes in Cristina García's *Dreaming in Cuban*

The complex discourse of the mother-daughter relationship, as well as the imaginative inscription of the lost homeland, occupies a prominent place in the thematics of immigrant literature in the United States. Ethnic writing in general often reflects gender conflicts transmitted through culturally constructed but frequently misinterpreted roles, specifically those of mothers. Emblematic novels such as Maxine Hong Kingston's *Woman Warrior* and Toni Morrison's *Beloved* revolve around ambivalent relationships with the mother or mother figure, as well as other female members of the family. These texts are frequently narrated by protagonists who must necessarily deal with the implications of specific maternal discourse (or the lack thereof) in the process of self-identification and affirmation. The place of the mother—personally, socially, culturally—directs, modifies, and influences the daughters' responses to both individual and cultural demands. Ethnic texts such as these highlight questions of identification with and differentiation from the mother, emphasizing a need for understanding and bonding between mothers and daughters as a fundamental step toward self-awareness and mastery of the culture. Often the texts imply the need for the daughter to take on and continue maternal stories, transforming them literally and metaphorically with their own lives and experiences.

Cultural inscriptions by ethnic women offer an interesting analysis of the hermeneutics of female representation and access to the world, yet cannot be divorced from forms of orientation toward the mother or fore-mother. The pattern of the maternal figure as origin and daughter as perpetuation, extension, or completion repeatedly appears as a necessary starting point to the drama of the tenuous negotiation of identity and difference within the ambivalent universe of filiality. As Nancy Chodorow has pointed out, "In any given society, feminine personality comes to define itself in relation and connection to other people more than masculine personality does" (44). Emphasis on relationships leads to a reevaluation of personal and communal tragedies that oblige the daughters to look back to the mothers, whose image and personality are often inseparable from community history and values. These texts often involve a return to the maternal, which leads to the appreciation of community history and forging of communal bonds with, first, the immediate family and then the larger gender and cultural group.

The novel here analyzed, Cristina García's *Dreaming in Cuban,* centers on the complicated negotiations of mother-daughter bonds. García tells the stories of three generations of Cuban women and their experiences with revolution and immigration through a blending of first-and third-person narrations, with epistolary sections that convey the rich texture of intersecting positionalities and overlapping worlds. At the center of the novel is Pilar Puente, born in Cuba and raised in Brooklyn, who must deal with her antipathetic relationship with her mother, Lourdes, and her longing for her grandmother, Celia. Similarly, Lourdes and Felicia, Celia's two daughters, struggle to unravel their complex ties with their mother as well as those with their own daughters. The novel thus presents a composite portrait of diverse mother-daughter relationships, offering a multiperspective vision of the possibilities for division and unity, adaptation and adjustment, separation and bonding. The mother-daughter dance of approach and withdrawal is mirrored in the separate and interrelated sections on each of the characters, the shifts in temporality, geography, and narrative voice illustrating the tangled web of affinity between and among the characters and their homelands.

In the tradition of breaking silence that has become one of the shaping myths in ethnic writing by women, maternal storytelling becomes a medium of self-inscription and subjectivity, as well as an instrument of inter-subjectivity and dialogue. The separate accounts of all the characters, mothers and daughters, are converted into chronicles of individual empowerment and self-affirmation. García opts for a narrative stance that includes multiple voices, offering individual versions of events and engaging in complex dialogues. There is, further, a sense of collectivity in the text, according to which the diverse voices that speak discern self-referential hints at definition through the juxtaposition of the other voices in the narrative. The concept of the isolated self is continually questioned, as the individual accounts are repeatedly mirrored, contrasting or complementing preceding or succeeding stories. Thus, the individual voices that meditate on the mothers' and daughters' multilayered selves are inseparable from the other voices in the text, coalescing to represent the family to which these women belong. The process of unearthing maternal and communal stories becomes an essential part of the process of self-identification, linked to the discovery of the mother and the mother's history, cultural possibilities, and choices. Cultural identification, and the recovery of a bond with the heritage culture, arises from the irrevocable connection between self and community, as issues of origins and beginnings occupy center stage in the drama of self-affirmation. According to Lorna Irvine, the process of discovery—the "psychological journey"—of the daughter's own identity demands a revision of the relationship with the mother, and this often involves three stages: negation, recognition, and reconciliation (248). The need to go "back to the future" implies the urgency of appropriating the intricate truths about one's self and history as part of the process of self-affirmation. The immigrant characters in García's novel—Lourdes and Pilar—need to return to Cuba in order to come to terms with the tangled meanings of mothering, language, and home, and renew their lives in the United States.

Ethnic and cultural factors, such as the serious difficulty of mutual decoding of social signs, are central to the linguistic misunderstanding between mothers and daughters. Language plays a central role in this process, as the exercise of female self-definition develops within the nuances of meaning, of understandings and misunderstandings, of significance misconstrued or unaccepted. In the isolation enforced by these misunderstandings, the characters explore a widening sphere of forms of communication: from telepathy to painting. The process of self-identification, therefore, involves issues of pain and resistance: remembering, understanding, and

articulating significance within the female matrix. The most important lesson the daughters in the novel learn, as articulated by Chodorow, is that "differentiation is not distinctness and separateness, but a particular way of being connected to others" (II). They learn the distinction between division and differentiation, understanding that while division prevails, there can never be completion. As Chodorow explains, "In the process of differentiation, leading to a genuine autonomy, people maintain contact with those with whom they had their earliest relationships: indeed this contact is part of who we are" (10–11). Separation and death may be overcome by reconstructing both the cultural past and the image of the mother, achieving a reconciliation with the maternal through and within language and by re-creating the idea of home. The final section suggests the protagonist's appropriation of the foremothers' voices and stories, to bring the cycle of generation and regeneration to completion.

Dreaming in Cuban explores the various dimensions of the drama of a family divided by Castro's takeover of Cuba in 1959. As William Luis points out, García's novel weaves intricate layers of Cuban history, politics, literature, and culture, both on the island and in the United States, echoing the work of such Cuban literary masters as Cirilo Villaverde and Reinaldo Arenas, who also abandoned the island and lived in exile (203). Political events and loyalties lead Rufino, Lourdes, and Pilar Puente to immigrate to the United States in 1961, leaving behind Lourdes's parents, Celia and Jorge del Pino, as well as her sister Felicia and the latter's family. Jorge will eventually leave Cuba for medical treatment in the United States, and will die there. Events in recent Cuban history become the central subtext for the novel: Pilar was born ten days after the victory that forced Batista to flee the island and three days after Castro's triumphant march into Havana; the novel ends with Felicia's son Ivanito's escape to freedom.

The present time of the narrative develops between 1972 and 1980 and refers to specific events in the Revolution. Luis has analyzed extensively the specific events of recent Cuban history that García incorporates into the subtext of her narrative: the failed ten-million-ton sugar harvest of 1970, the detention of the poet Heberto Padilla, and the seizing of the Peruvian embassy in April 1980, which was followed by the Mariel boatlift that enabled more than 125,000 Cubans to escape to Miami (206–8).

The blending of historical detail is central to Pilar's search for self, as she comes to terms with her position regarding the Cuban Revolution, the central point of contention with her mother. At the beginning of the novel, she rejects her mother's patriotic American values—"She bought a second bakery and plans to sell tricolor cupcakes and Uncle Sam marzipan. Apple pies, too. She's convinced she can fight Communism from behind her bakery counter" (136)—sympathizing with the Cuban cause embodied in the figure of her grandmother. At the end, after witnessing life in Cuba for herself, and incorporating her grandmother's, aunt's, cousins', and mother's stories, she appears to become independent of her previous ideas. She lies to her grandmother about Ivanito's departure, implicitly assenting to his defection.

Pilar's process is highlighted by García's complex ordering of the narrative. The author frequently juxtaposes present and past tense, blurring and confounding the two time frames: rather than presenting a chronological account, she invites the reader to reconstruct the sequence of events—from the first story, set in 1972, to the last piece, a letter written in 1959. Furthermore, as Jorge Duany explains, the geographic transition from Cuba to the United States is often imperceptible, because that is the way the characters experience the transition: "There is no radical discontinuity in time and space between the two sides of the del Pino family, one in Cuba, the other in the United States. The family is spiritually united by common memories and fantasies, by their image of Cuba" (177).

Section and story titles like "Imagining Winter" and "Going South" are paradigmatic of the journeys many of the characters have to take, away from and back to their original home, emphasizing the search for connection which will be completed in the final section, "The Languages Lost." The last line of the novel, from Celia's final letter to her Spanish lover, presents the charge given to Pilar, which she metafictionally completes through the novel. On 11 January 1959 she writes: "Dear Gustavo, The revolution is eleven days old. My granddaughter, Pilar Puente del Pino, was born today. It is also my birthday. I am fifty years old. I will no longer write to you, *mi amor*. She will remember everything" (245). Pilar's trip to Cuba, when she inherits the letters her grandmother never sent to Gustavo, makes her understand that she belongs to a family as well as to Cuban history and culture. This discovery enables her to decipher the master codes of her increasingly complex subjectivity, allowing her to signify on her own, yet within the network of women of which she forms an inextricable part. Even Pilar's surname, "Puente," highlights her role as a bridge between the place and the people of the past and the future.

Thus, the recounting in Pilar's voice acquires a forceful emotional tone that rings clearly through the entire novel, transforming the story into a female bildungsroman. Furthermore, when questioned in an interview about the nature of the novel, García admits that "emotionally, it's very autobiographical. The details are not. . . . Pilar is a kind of alter ego for me" (López, 610). Cristina García and Pilar Puente share biographical similarities, and the text may be read as both a valedictory and a catharsis for a young woman dealing with the events and characters in her past.

Crucial to the evolving relationship with the past is the figure of the mother, an image expanded in the novel to include both mother language and motherland. In the same movement, Lourdes abandons her mother and motherland, physically and emotionally, rejecting the communism that both espouse. Celia's relationship with her elder daughter is sour from the start, as she suffers from the loss of her Spanish lover and the abuse by Jorge's mother and sister. The awareness of her mother's rejection of her clouds Lourdes's infancy.

> She imagined herself alone and shriveled in her mother's womb, envisioned the first days in her mother's unyielding arms. Her mother's fingers were stiff and splayed as spoons, her milk a tasteless gray. Her mother stared at her with eyes collapsed of expectation. If it's true that babies learn love from their mothers' voices, then this is what Lourdes heard: "I will not remember her name." (74)

Celia's other daughter, Felicia, also abandons her through her consistent indifference to the revolutionary cause, and her eventual sinking into madness: "After all, as her mother points out, the only thing Felicia ever did for the revolution was pull a few dandelions during the weed-eradication campaign in 1962, and then only reluctantly. Her lack of commitment is a source of great rancour between them" (107).

The generational divisions extend to Lourdes and her daughter Pilar, who nonetheless has a powerful sense of connection with Abuela Celia, and also to Felicia and her revolutionary twin daughters, Luz and Milagro. Interestingly, familial and generational patterns develop to which all the characters adhere. The generational opposition between Celia and her two daughters, Lourdes and Felicia, is repeated in the next generation between Lourdes and Felicia and their own daughters, Pilar, Luz, and Milagro (Luis, 211). Still, similarities and connections are perceived between mothers and daughters, even those separated by an ocean. For instance, both Celia and Lourdes serve law and order, the mother as a civilian judge of her neighborhood defense committee and the daughter as an "auxiliary policewoman, the first in her precinct" (127). Pilar also acknowledges seeing her mother in herself: "If I don't like someone, I show it. It's the one thing I have in common with my mother" (135).

The difficulties between Lourdes and Pilar are a metaphor for all the other mother-daughter dyads. Both perceive clearly the gap between them. Pilar notes that "Mom's views are strictly black-and-white. That's how she survives" (26), and Lourdes admits that she "has no patience for dreamers, for people who live between black and white" (129), such as her own mother and daughter. Celia muses: "If I was born to live on an island, then I'm grateful for one thing: that the tides rearrange the borders. At least I have the illusion of change, of possibility" (99), an attitude she shares with her granddaughter. On the one hand, Lourdes is consistently maddened by Pilar's immunity to threats, her "indifference" (128), while the daughter suffers from her mother's unpredictability. When Lourdes asks Pilar to paint a mural for her new bakery, and agrees not to see it before the official unveiling, the daughter cannot fathom her mother's intentions. Lourdes looks at Pilar with an expression "as if to say, 'See, you always underestimate me.' But that's not true. If anything, I overestimate her. It comes from experience. Mom is arbitrary and inconsistent and always believes she's right. It's a pretty irritating combination" (140).

Interestingly, both turn to the past—the dead father and the far-off grandmother—for advice. Jorge del Pino reassures Lourdes: "Pilar doesn't hate you, *hija*. She just hasn't learned to love you yet" (74). Similarly, Pilar takes reassurance from Celia: "I might be afraid of her if it weren't for those talks I have with Abuela Celia late at night. She tells me that my mother is sad inside and that her anger is more frustration at what she can't change. I guess I'm one of those things she can't change" (63). Yet when Pilar's blasphemous punk version of the Statue of Liberty is finally unveiled, the patriotic Lourdes rushes to her daughter's defense and protects the mural from a man who threatens to rip it with a knife: "Then, as if in slow motion, she tumbles forward, a thrashing avalanche of patriotism and motherhood, crushing three spectators and a table of apple tartlets. And I, I love my mother very much at that moment" (144).

As opposed to other mother-daughter narratives, this text highlights the daughters' connections with their fathers, and that of the mothers with their sons. Lourdes and Jorge del Pino, Pilar and Rufino Puente, even Luz, Milagro, and Hugo Villaverde share a relationship that all the mothers envy. Celia perceives the affection between her husband and daughter, a world closed to her: "That girl is a stranger to me. When I approach her, she turns numb, as if she wanted to be dead in my presence. I see how different Lourdes is with her father, so alive and gay, and it hurts me, but I don't know what to do. She still punishes me for the early

years" (163). Moreover, "Lourdes is herself only with her father. Even after his death, they understand each other perfectly, as they always have" (131). The disconnection between mothers and daughters finds a foil in the bond between mothers and sons. Javier del Pino returns to Cuba and his mother when his wife abandons him, taking their daughter. Felicia and Ivanito live happily for a while in a dreamworld of poetry and coconut ice cream. Lourdes fantasizes about the son she miscarried: "He wouldn't have talked back to her or taken drugs or drunk beer from paper bags like other teenagers. *Her* son would have helped her in the bakery without complaint. He would have come to her for guidance, pressed her hand to his cheek, told her he loved her. Lourdes would have talked to her son the way Rufino talks to Pilar, for companionship" (129). She thus, at the end of the novel, adopts the motherless Ivanito and helps him escape from Cuba.

The positive emphasis on the father-daughter and mother-son relationship, as opposed to the problematic mother-daughter one, may also have its roots in Spanish/Cuban culture. Sons tend to be revered over daughters in these families, and García blends this customary dynamic into her text, to complicate the central issue further. Sons traditionally enjoy preferential treatment in these families, though fathers are also inclined to pamper their daughters. The latter are, nevertheless, viewed by the mothers as extensions of themselves and are therefore treated more harshly, for they had to learn to be prepared for life. On the contrary, mothers openly indulge their sons, the future of the family and the country. This reality offers another layer of meaning to the text as a sociocultural construct: García appears to suggest that the dynamic of conventional family relationships becomes another obstacle to the desired mother-daughter attachment.

Knowledge of a shared communication between Pilar and her grandmother serves to help reconstruct the matrilineal bond, forging the link with the mother country and its language as well. Between these two exists the attachment that both lack with Lourdes: "I wonder how Mom could be Abuela Celia's daughter. And what I'm doing as my mother's daughter. Something got horribly scrambled along the way" (178). Celia provides Pilar with the connection to the maternal line, mother tongue, and homeland her mother had severed, as well as a sense of security and self-worth.

> I feel much more connected to Abuela Celia than to Mom, even though I haven't seen my grandmother in seventeen years. We don't speak at night anymore, but she's left me her legacy nonetheless—a love for the sea and the smoothness of pearls, an appreciation of music and words, sym-

pathy for the underdog, and a disregard for boundaries. Even in silence, she gives me the confidence to do what I believe is right, to trust my own perceptions. (176)

This link has loaded implications for the nature of nar rating memory and the constructing of a multivoiced text. Because of their affiliation, Pilar can construct the text, the metafictional implication being the continuation of the cycle of women's stories within a culture-specific ambience: "Women who outlive their daughters are orphans, Abuela tells me. Only their granddaughters can save them, guard their knowledge like the first fire" (222). The diary Pilar keeps becomes a repository of stories which will help her piece together her life, becoming the text the reader receives, as Isabel Alvarez-Borland suggests (46). She will thus appropriate the voices of the women who are part of the del Pino family saga—her grandmother, mother, aunt, cousins, and even her aunt's friend, Herminia Delgado—arriving at a deeper understanding of each one's motivations and actions. The metafictional detail suggests the continuance of the female line, and the narrative becomes the vehicle through which the wounds are healed and the pain of exile overcome.

Language functions in *Dreaming in Cuban* as a measuring device for gauging both connection and separation, loyalty and abandonment, between families and land. The languages each learns, speaks, and passes on illustrate diverse attachments, just as the lack of a common language signals the severance of a bond. As Mary Vásquez points out, Celia's poetic idiom passes to her daughter, Felicia, for example, but not to Lourdes, for whom even her mother speaks a foreign tongue; it is her father's deprecating rhetoric that becomes Lourdes's legacy (23). By extension, foreignness in the novel becomes "a metaphor for separation and estrangement: it can exist as fully within a family home as in exile in an alien land. Indeed, individual language in the novel's world becomes an emblem, and expression of foreignness becomes impenetrability, the ultimate isolation to which each of García's characters is condemned" (Vásquez, 23). In the novel, language loss is directly related to the exile experience, often serving as a metaphor for existential alienation (Alvarez-Borland, 46). Because Pilar left Cuba at the age of two, language loss for her is a given. Celia reflects that "Pilar, her first grandchild, writes to her from Brooklyn in a Spanish that is no longer hers. She speaks the hard-edged lexicon of bygone tourists itchy to throw dice on green felt or asphalt" (7). Although, as an adult, Pilar reflects that "English seems an impossible language for intimacy" (180), it is the language she grows up speaking, and,

more important, the language in which she records her family's story.

Attitudes toward language separate mothers and daughters: Lourdes believes that "immigration has redefined her, and she is grateful. . . . She welcomes her adopted language, its possibilities for reinvention. . . . She wants no part of Cuba, no part of its wretched carnival floats creaking with lies, no part of Cuba at all, which [she] claims never possessed her" (73). Felicia, who learned the language of poetry from her mother, builds her own dreamworld, borrowing "freely from the poems she'd heard, stringing words together like laundry on a line, connecting ideas and descriptions she couldn't have planned. The words sounded precisely right when she said them, though often people told her she didn't make sense at all" (110). Felicia's practical daughters do not share her flights of fancy, though her son Ivanito does. He plays word and color games with her: "'Let's speak in green' his mother says, and they talk about everything that makes them feel green" (84). Her daughter, Luz, judges that "this was just like her. Pretty words. Meaningless words that didn't nourish us, that didn't comfort us, that kept us prisoners in her alphabet world" (121).

The twins find a more authentic language in their burned father's disfigured face: "In his sagging eyes we found the language we'd been searching for, a language more eloquent than the cheap bead necklaces of words my mother offered" (124). Language also separates the twins from Ivanito, who decides "he will never speak his sisters' language, account for his movements like a cow with a dull bell" (86). Diverse idioms antagonize mothers and daughters, just as Cuba, "a country living on slogans and agitation" (107) alienates its exiles. Felicia's death leads Ivanito toward another language and land: "My mother never speaks to me, but sometimes . . . I pick up radio stations in Key West. I'm learning more English this way, but it's a lot different from Abuelo Jorge's grammar books. If I'm lucky, I can tune in the Wolfman Jack show on Sunday nights. Sometimes I want to be like the Wolfman and talk to a million people at once" (191).

Because of the loss of language, characters consistently turn to other, nontraditional forms of expression. Celia and her granddaughter communicate telepathically, in evening conversations that prove vital for both: "I hear her speaking to me at night just before I fall asleep. She tells me stories about her life and what the sea was like that day. She seems to know everything that's happened to me and tells me not to mind my mother too much. Abuela Celia says she wants to see me again. She tells me she loves me" (29). In Cuba, Celia "knows that Pilar keeps a diary in the lining of her winter coat, hidden from her mother's scouring eyes. In it, Pilar records everything. This pleases Celia. She closes her eyes and speaks to her granddaughter, imagines her words as slivers of light piercing the murky night" (7). Felicia turns to *santería* for insight into the real meaning of things, the ceremonies becoming "a kind of poetry that connected her to larger worlds, worlds alive and infinite" (186). Lourdes eats her way to obesity, converting food into the language of her grief as her father undergoes medical treatment. Thematically, Pilar's anxiety about losing the language of her culture is manifested through her obsession with painting and in her ruminations about visual texts (Alvarez-Borland, 46). Pilar finds that visual images communicate meaning much more effectively than words do: "Painting is its own language. . . . Translations just confuse it, dilute it, like words going from Spanish to English. I envy my mother her Spanish curses sometimes. They make my English collapse in a heap. . . . Who needs words when colors and lines conjure up their own language? That's what I want to do with my paintings, find a unique language, obliterate the clichés" (59, 139).

Pilar's obsession with language goes further than mere communication. She worries about the stories recorded, the versions of histories and truths hidden within the metaphors and constructedness of language. "If it were up to me," she says, "I'd record other things. Like the time there was a freak hailstorm in the Congo and the women took it as a sign that they should rule. Or the life stories of prostitutes in Bombay. Why don't I know anything about them? Who chooses what we should know or what's important? I know I have to decide these things for myself. Most of what I've learned that's important I've learned on my own, or from my grandmother" (28). She reflects on the consequences of increasing separation from her roots: "I resent the hell out of the politicians and the generals who force events on us that structure our lives, that dictate the memories we'll have when we're old. Every day Cuba fades a little more inside me, my grandmother fades a little more inside me. And there's only my imagination where our history should be" (38). Pilar's need to see behind the mask of language is part of her strategy of separation from her mother, who she feels never really told her anything important.

> This is a constant struggle around my mother, who systematically rewrites history to suit her views of the world. This reshaping of events happens in a dozen ways every day, contesting reality. It's not a matter of premeditated deception. Mom truly believes that her version of events is correct, down to details that I know, for a fact, are wrong. . . .

Mom's embellishments and half-truths usually equip her to tell a good story, though. And her English, her immigrant English, has a touch of otherness that makes it unintentionally precise. Maybe in the end the facts are not as important as the underlying truth she wants to convey. Telling her own truth is *the* truth to her, even if it's at the expense of chipping away our past. (176–77)

When García entitles the last section of her book "The Languages Lost," she therefore refers to much more than just Spanish, widening the reference to include the breaking of familial bonds between Cubans living on the island and those residing abroad. When they return, Pilar realizes, "The language [my mother] speaks is lost to them. It's another idiom entirely" (221). The novel's title, *Dreaming in Cuban,* suggests a rhetoric of belonging, a collective yet ever-imperfect antidote to isolation and estrangement (Vásquez, 23). Pilar, who begins to dream in Spanish, ultimately becomes embedded within a process of translation that involves a heightened appreciation of the shifting boundaries between language and meaning and the possibilities for the connection and the multiple self. Only then can she inscribe the book of women's stories, as she hovers between languages and belonging, challenging the fixed borders of relationships and loyalties.

The representation of Cuba as motherland becomes another important subtext in García's novel. The country is portrayed through both an insider and an outsider perspective, evocations tinged with the suffering of those who remain and the nostalgia of those who left and wish to return. All the central female characters are somehow exiled from Cuban reality: Celia lives defending an obsolete revolution, Felicia ignores it, Lourdes staunchly fights and deprecates communism, and Pilar idealizes the land her grandmother describes to her. Mary Vásquez argues that, for these four characters, Cuba is present fundamentally as a memory, disconnected from time. For Lourdes, Cuba is present only as an absence chosen and, hence, quite satisfactory: "Time with respect to Cuba has frozen in her perception of 1959: Cuba itself is immutable, lost, and deviant until Castro's fall, which must surely come, and when it does not, can only be delayed by the regime's lies and the people's blindness" (Vásquez, 22). Moreover, when she leaves Cuba, she insists on heading toward the cold, seeking a complete rupture from the heat of Cuba. New York is "cold enough," she proclaims (70), and she "relishes winter most of all—the cold scraping sounds on sidewalks and windshields, the ritual of scarves and gloves, hats and zip-in coat linings. Its layers protect her [from Cuba] . . . which Lourdes claims never possessed her" (73).

Pilar's search is ultimately for roots and connectedness, which she cannot achieve through her mother. Celia and Cuba become, therefore, the idealized objects of personal fulfillment and stability. As Pilar incorporates her grandmother's narrative, we become aware that both have lived for a time in the past, apprehending Cuba only through memory. As Vásquez explains, Celia "seeks to arrest the past and insert herself into it, with both she and the content of that past pristine and simultaneously changed and unchanged. . . . Pilar, on the other hand, practices the paradox of an anticipated, future and need. Of course, both are exercises of invention" (24).

In this vein, García uses the color blue as the primary motif for the representation of Cuba and its powerful link with the characters. "What I had in mind with the color blue is the mental image one has of an island," she explains in an interview. "Cuba is surrounded by water, and that's why there's so much blue in the book. Celia has a house on the beach, and so her entire horizon is blue. It colors her whole life and perspective" (Vorda, 70). Blue is the light that shines from Jorge del Pino's hospital room when he dies (19). He appears on the horizon as Celia stands guard, blue eyes "lasers in the night" and the beams "five hard blue shields" that bounce off his fingernails—a spectacular announcement of death (5). Celia, who "had lived all these years by the sea until she knew its every definition of blue" (7), understands that this is her husband's farewell. When Pilar begins to paint her grandmother, she foregrounds this color, blending the woman and the land: "Mostly, though, I paint her in blue. Until I returned to Cuba, I never realized how many blues exist. The aquamarines near the shoreline, the azures of deeper waters, the eggshell blues beneath my grandmother's eyes, the fragile indigos tracking her hands. There's a blue, too, in the curves of the palms, and the edges of the words we speak, a blue tinge to the sand and the seashells and the plump gulls on the beach. The mole by Abuela's mouth is also blue, a vanishing blue" (233). Her painting will become another metafictional device that will freeze the experience of her Cuban visit and capture her grandmother's last moments.

The denouement of the novel centers on Lourdes and Pilar's journey back to Cuba. Lourdes returns to see her mother and sister again, to share her grief over Jorge's death. Pilar completes a long-deferred spiritual journey to recover her grandmother's dreams, as if to close a circle that began in the 1930s (Duany, 178–79). The latter must deal with an existential question of belonging, whose only response lies in the land of her past: "Even though I've been living in Brooklyn all my life, it doesn't feel like home to me. I'm not sure Cuba is, but I want to find out. If I could only see Abuela Celia again, I'd know where I belonged" (58). Mother and daughter will discern a central truth: that the old Cuba no longer exists, except in the imagination of both the exile and characters such as Celia, who remain loyal to the cause. Pilar realizes that "Cuba is a particular exile. . . . We can reach it by a thirty-minute charter flight from Miami, yet never reach it at all" (219). Still, the affinity with the land remains, making all the characters part of the network which has Cuba as the center that defines them and their relation to the other characters (Vásquez, 26). The realization that all of them are somehow exiles from Cuba permeates the end of the novel. Pilar's catharsis will be her awareness that, though she is captivated by Havana and treasures her grandmother, "sooner or later I'd have to return to New York. I know now it's where I belong—not *instead* of here, but *more* than here. How can I tell my grandmother this?" (36). Even Ivanito perceives the imperative: "I felt that I was meant to live in this colder world, a world that preserved history. In Cuba, everything seemed temporal, distorted by the sun" (146). Abandoning Cuba is imminent and necessary, through a return to the United States, defection, or death. Yet leaving the island, and Celia's walking into the ocean at the end of the narrative, frees Pilar, allowing her to appropriate the voices of the past and narrate personal and cultural histories.

One of Cristina García's central achievements in her inscription of the mother-daughter relationship lies in the manner in which she widens the sphere of this theme within the field of ethnic literature. In *Dreaming in Cuban* the author offers a new perspective on this struggle by further complicating the presentation of the maternal relationships in three ways. First, by analyzing three generations of women and the inclusion of sisters as vital constituents of the female group. Second, by contrasting mother-daughter relationships to those between mothers and sons and fathers and daughters. Finally, she chooses not to offer a more traditionally well-rounded ending to the central conflicts. At the end of the novel, Celia dies without her daughter coming to terms with her choices, and the relationship between Pilar and her mother remains problematic, though each has achieved insight into the other. Though other mother-daughter ethnic texts tend to favor the pattern of separation and later bonding, García chooses to undermine this, preferring instead to maintain her characters' ultimate disconnection. The process of reconciliation typical of mother-daughter ethnic novels is here presented, in the case of most of the characters, as incomplete. In this manner, García hints at the continuing process that moves beyond the text, and perhaps a progressive cyclical dialectic of entanglement.

The complicated mesh of relationships García untangles in *Dreaming in Cuban* has at its center the negotiation with the image of the maternal, in diverse ways. Each of the characters must delve into the implications of mothering, as well as belonging to a family and to a culture. The question of language and exile metaphorically dramatizes the mother-daughter relationships, deepening their implications and broadening possibilities for maternal discourse. Returning to the motherland, going back, gives Pilar the license to speak for the others and build her own future within the universe of maternal difference and connectedness, understood as the key to continuity. The concept of agency is at the heart of the narrative, the appropriation of the voice of mothers as exiles allowing the chronicle simultaneously to articulate and to signify. Cristina García turns to family, language, and motherland to develop and analyze sources of personal identity and creative expression, negotiating the between-world position and illustrating the process of self-identification.

Rocio G. Davis, Winter 2000

Brief Encounters in Havana

Written in an alien tongue, an alien tongue will read it.

Fifty years ago last summer Federico García Lorca was taken from his hiding place in Granada to jail. Later he was led to a secluded spot and shot. It has been said that he was killed because of an imaginary vengeance no more real than a story by Edgar Allan Poe: his killers thought that Jacinto Benavente, the right-wing playwright, had already been executed by the Reds in Madrid. Others say that it was out of envy that Lorca was assassinated: at the time he was Spain's most popular writer. Still others claimed that Lorca was shot out of machismo: the poet was a well-known fragile feminine figure in Granada. The truth is that he was exterminated by the hatred totalitarians feel for the writer in general and the poet in particular. Franco killed Lorca, Stalin killed Mandelstam, Hitler killed Bruno Schulz—and we'll never know how many writers perished, like angels on a hot pin, in Russian and German concentration camps.

In this my encounter with Lorca, the poet is in Havana and living well in a nice revenge. Both the city and the writer are gone forever. I chose to bring them back alive. It is only in this context that my text can be taken for fiction.

The spring of 1930 was summer as usual in Cuba, what Octavio Paz, a poet, calls "the violent season." It was then that Federico García Lorca traveled from New York to Havana by sea, the only way to reach Cuba at that time. Not long ago the American poet Hart Crane, a homosexual and a hopeless drunk, had traveled from Havana to New York—and never arrived. In midtrip he jumped overboard and disappeared for good—or perhaps for bad. Behind him was *The Bridge,* the long poem that led him to suicide, plus a few mild metaphors. That's all he left of his short stay on earth: no grave, not even an epitaph. Lorca's body was never found either, though it was buried in Granada not far from his home.

That year, 1930, Lorca was in the prime of his life. He had asked for the moon and the stars, and all were given him. He in turn was like a gift. He had just finished *Poet in New York* with its splendid "Ode to Walt Whitman" and had escaped from New York. I won't go into a commentary of that Lorquian poem, which is a long, lucid lament. But I will play for you in a moment its musical coda, that happy "Son de negros en Cuba," which not only transformed popular poetry in Cuba but altered Lorca's vision of black literature by listening to music, not to poetry. Contrary to Crane, Lorca traveled from the dark into the sun, from New York to Havana.

At the time, besides a Crane more lamentable than lamented, many American writers and artists, who later on would be as famous as Lorca, visited Havana and left their footprints in the sand like white versions of Friday. Now a cruising Crusoe, I'll tell you who they were and what they did for an anchor. Some lived in Havana for a few free days. But never by fate or dire design did they meet Lorca. Not in Old Havana or in El Vedado or in the barrio of La Víbora or in Jesús del Monte.

Ernest Hemingway, that he-man who also committed suicide like weak Crane, lived in Old Havana then, in a hotel whose name Lorca would have loved: Hotel de Ambos Mundos, the "hotel of two worlds." Come to think of it, Voltaire would have liked that too, with Candide staying in the best of *two* possible worlds.

In this small hotel Hemingway wrote a novel of love and hate, with much violent death, but which offers, at the very beginning, the view of a dream city that could be, at the flicker of a pencil, the writer's wand, a nightmare world: "You know how it is there in the morning in Havana with the bums still asleep against the walls of the buildings, before even the ice wagons come by with ice for the bars?" The novel is titled *To Have and Have Not,* and it portrays a kind of violence Lorca never knew. Not before five in the afternoon in the bullring, or before his end in Granada years later.

> Well, we came across the square from the dock
> to the Pearl of San Francisco Café to get coffee
> and there was one beggar awake in the square
> and he was getting a drink out of the fountain.

Guillermo Cabrera Infante (left) with wife, Miriam Gomez (*Gil Jain*)

But when we got inside the café and sat down, there were three of them waiting for us.

It's fairly possible that Lorca would have known any of those unholy three in Havana in 1930. But now:

> The three of them started for the door and I watched them go. They were good looking young fellows, wore good clothes; none of them wore hats, and they looked like they had plenty of money. They talked plenty of money, anyway, and they spoke the kind of English Cubans with money speak.

(As you can hear, I never had much money in Cuba—or in England, for that matter!).[1]

Lorca never wore a hat either. At the time and in that city he must have dressed like the young Turks who didn't like to be called Turks. Like the thugs' hair, the poet's was as shiny as his shoes. Dark as Lorca was, Hemingway, whose Spanish was never very good—I heard him talk; I heard him call his novel *El viecho y la mar*—and whose eyesight was never very good, would have taken Lorca for a rich Cuban boy or for a singer in the Lecuona Cuban Boys Band. But Hemingway

knew then, as we know now, what usually happens to a rich Cuban boy when he plays a deadly game.

> As they turned out of the the door to the right, I saw a closed car come across the square toward them. The first thing a pane of glass went and the bullet smashed into a row of bottles on the showcase wall. . . . I heard the gun going and bop, bop, bop, there were bottles smashing all along the wall. . . . One of the boys was spread out on the sidewalk, face down. . . . The car was stopped and there were two fellows crouched down by it. One had a Thompson gun and the other a sawed-off automatic shotgun. The one with the Thompson gun was a nigger. . . . One of the boys shot from the rear corner of the wagon and it ricocheted off the sidewalk. The nigger with the Tommy gun got his face almost into the street and gave the back of the wagon a burst and sure enough one came down . . . and at ten feet the nigger shot him in the belly with the Tommy gun. . . . The nigger took the shotgun that was lying against the wheel of the car . . . and blew the side of his head off! *Some nigger.*

Lorca never knew in Havana that terrible, horrible Cuban brand of violence, as native and as sudden as an exploding cigar. He didn't know those Havana blacks either, *sbirri eccenenti*. Lorca's blacks were all rumba dancers, *son* singers, men on the town. He used to sneak out of his hotel to roam the streets at night, bound for the black barrios like Jesús María, Paula, and San Isidro, next to the docks of La Machina. Here is where *To Have and Have Not* begins. Lorca never witnessed the obscene scene with the forgotten beggars asleep against the walls like Mexican *peones* in the afternoon. But Lorca, and Hemingway too, later, knew what a violent death early in the morning was like. Lorca killed himself when he decided to go back to Granada that fateful summer of 1936.

Another American who visited Havana in the early thirties was the photographer Walker Evans. Evans wrote later: "I did land in Havana in the midst of a revolution." These Americans! They always come to Cuba in the "midst of a revolution." (Midst is the mist of spirits.) Evans was in Havana in 1932, and Dictator Machado did not fall until mid-1933, to be replaced after a coup d'état by Batista some time later. Evans couldn't have fallen in the midst of any revolution, except of course, the revolt of a bad hangover after a night out with Señor Rum and Miss Coca Cola. The pair were known in Cuba at the time as Cuba Libre. "Batista was taking over," claims Evans, but it was only ten days that shook Bacardi. Evans did the shaking with ice, lime juice, and sugar. That's what you call a daiquiri.

Evans called it a day and went to see Hemingway at the Ambos Mundos, and they became *ambos* drunk. "I had a few letters to newspapermen" Evans says, "which turned out to be lucky, because it brought me to Ernest." Why so chummy so soon? "So I met him. I had a wonderful time with Hemingway." And why is that? "Drinking every night," writes Evans with a shaky hand. It was then that he had the revolution rum—straight, no chassis. Hemingway, according to Evans, "was at loose ends." How can this be remedied? "He needed a drinking companion"—and that was Evans, the only photographer who saw double through a single lens. He was a constant companion, as a matter of fact. Friends who drink together stink together.

Those were the days of writing *To Have and Have Not,* and Hemingway was having problems with his first Cuban novel, as Evans knew. But Evans also knew where he was headed. His pictures of Havana, like Lorca's "Son of Blacks in Cuba," are shot in the black-and-white shadows near the Gulf Stream. It all was like a romance for Evans, in which the black men of Havana are featured not as killers with a shotgun but as dandies in white. That's a revelation which belongs now in the

museums. I wish I could, like Humbert Humbert, pass around a few picture postcards and other memorabilia. I cannot, of course, but I can describe it in a few clumsy words that will never equal one single image: that of a particular black gentleman dressed in white—white straw boater, white three-piece suit, white of the eye surrounding piercing pupils—with his shining black shoes, recently polished by the shoeshine boy one can still see in the background. He also wears a pocket handkerchief matching his tense, intense tie. He looks like a million dollars, though he perhaps has only a few cents in his pocket: a dandy in drill. He is dressed to kill, no doubt, for he looks like a very dangerous man, his keen eye boring a hole in the photo beyond its frame. It all makes the photograph into a portrait, forever fixed on that corner of Old Havana. Evans's masterpiece is a work of art. *To Have and Have Not* never was. But the "Son" by Lorca I've been telling you about was a work of art too. Hemingway, the charging bully, never saw Havana, though he said he did. He went through it like a bullet.

Havana was not the violent city he wanted it to be. Not at the time anyway. Listen to what a contemporary of Lorca, an American named Joseph Hergesheimer, now unjustly forgotten, has to say about Havana considered as a Mediterranean city. He wrote this a few years before Lorca came to see and to conquer.

> There are certain cities, strange to the first view, nearer to the heart than home. . . . Approaching Havana in the early morning . . . yet, watching the silver greenness of Cuba rising from the blue sea, I had a premonition that what I saw was of peculiar importance to me. . . . It was exactly as though the smooth lustrous hills before me had been created out of an old mysterious desire to realize them in words.[2]

How true! How strange indeed that it was Hergesheimer who first discovered it and not Lorca. But Hergesheimer goes on:

> Undoubtedly their effect belonged to the sea, the sky, and the hour in which they were set. . . . The island seemed unusually solid and isolated, as complete within itself as a flower in air, and saturated with romance. . . . Drawing rapidly nearer to what was evidently the entrance to the harbor of Havana. . . . (10–11)

Naïve alliteration, that one, "the harbor of Havana."

> The Cuban shore was now so close, Havana so imminent, that I lost my story in a new interest. I could see low against the water a line of white buildings, at that distance purely classic in implication. Then it was that I had my first premonition about the city toward which I was smoothly

progressing—I was to find in it the classic spirit not of Greece but of a late period; it was the replica of those imagined cities painted and engraved in a wealth of marble cornices and set directly against the tranquil sea. There was already perceptible about it the air of unreality that marked the strand which saw the Embarkation for Cytherea. (13)

Cytherea is a Greek island off the coast of the Peloponnese. In ancient times it was a center of worship for Aphrodite, so intense that Aphrodite came to be known as Cytherea. The Romans called it simply Venus. That was me. Now let's come back to Hergesheimer:

> Nothing could have made me happier than this realization; an extension of the impression of a haunting dream turned into solid fact. . . . But the narrowness of the harbor entrance, a deep thrust of blue extending crookedly into the land, the sense of crowded shipping and massed city, the steamers of the world and broad shaded avenues at my elbow, impressed me at once with Havana's unique personality. (13–14)

Please observe that this was the Havana Lorca saw when he came from New York. Hergesheimer concludes:

> I heard, then, the voice of Havana, a remarkably active staccato voice, never, I was to learn, sinking to quiet, but changing at night into different yet not less disturbing clamor. . . . Havana was artificial, exotic . . . the special characteristic of a city which had already possessed me. (14–15)

These quotations by Hemingway, Hergesheimer, and Evans, though they sound like a firm of lawyers, are poetic visions of Havana. But—just wait—there is a second opinion of this Havana ancien régime, the city that never wept. I found this dry description in the *Encyclopaedia Britannica,* which sometimes is our contemporary:

> *Havana,* capital, commercial metropolis and major port of the republic of Cuba, . . . one of the leading tropical cities in the new world, lies on the northern coast of the island toward the western end. Its location on one of the fine harbours of the hemisphere made it commercially and militarily important from colonial times and is a major factor in accounting for its steady growth in population. . . . Other factors in its growth have been its salubrious climate, picturesque location and, before the advent of Fidel Castro in 1959, gay entertainment which made it a mecca for tourists. . . . Rain falls throughout the year. . . . The aspect of Havana from the sea is picturesque. Although the country clubs and many of the fashionable residential suburbs along the coast were expropriated by the Castro govern-

ment, from a physical standpoint the view remains no less impressive.

Though I can appreciate *Britannica's* brand of humor, I'd rather not laugh now.

That was also the Havana that Lorca knew. Here he wrote one of his most carefree poems. Here he was an enormous fish in a small pond. From here he writes a letter to his parents telling them about his successes as a poem reader (he should have been a palm reader instead), which were many and true. He also writes of his faked fear during a crocodile hunt not far from Havana. He claimed that he took part with a mixture of sangfroid and excitement. Luckily for the gators (and for us), Lorca was not a hunter, and we are spared the croc count and the stuffed lizards being taken back to Spain to decorate the walls of the family villa at Fuentevaqueros. Could you picture Lorca being photographed wearing a pith helmet, rifle firmly held in one hand, and his foot on a dead crocodile as big as "Jaws"?

It could perhaps amuse Lorca (if anything can amuse him now), to know that in that region of Cuba, the Zapata Swamps, where he saw so many dangerous alligators, there was circa 1960, thirty years after his swamp safari, a cage that was merely a low wooden circular fence. Here a single saurian was kept in captivity. It now slept in the tropical sun and it looked very dead, dead still, as if it were already stuffed and therefore unable to be moved by its own fate. A sign next to the crocodile pleaded with the visitors: "Please don't throw stones at the cayman." End of the species.

Lorca did see in Havana (how could he have missed them?) what he calls "the most beautiful women in the world." Then he turns the parade into a nation: "This island," he writes, "has the most beautiful type of woman." He amplifies: "This is due to the fact that all Cubans have at least one drop of black blood." Lorca must insist: "The blacker the better," which was, you must remember, Walker Evans's opinion too. Evans in fact photographed white Cubans, but they were charcoal burners, coal stevedores, and mine workers with soot faces. Lorca now speaks of black women only. He goes on with his rhapsody: "This island is a paradise"—lost, I must add. He finally mock-warns his parents: "If I get lost . . . look for me in Cuba." The letter ends between hype and hyperbole: "Don't forget that in America to be a poet means more than being a prince." Unfortunately, this wasn't true—then or now. At least not in Cuba. Lorca went to the island for her poets, but like Humphrey Bogart in *Casablanca* with the waters, he was misinformed. I could have told him that I've known all kinds of poets in Cuba. Poor poets and sick poets, poets pursued and poets in prison, dying poets and dead poets finally: all dead as the dodo in the end. Poets I've known who were treated not like princes but like scum—called scum, in fact. Called worms also. Poets as pariahs on the island. Poets considered untouchable, poets suffering from political leprosy. But Havana was for Lorca a moving feast, and I don't want to rain on his parade of beauties. I don't want to contaminate his poetry with my experience.

On his visit to Buenos Aires sometime later, Borges blamed Lorca for a crime of lesser levity. Young Lorca told young Borges that he had just discovered an exemplary character, crucial to mankind, humanity's second savior, in fact. His name? Why, Mickey Mouse, of course. It seems very out of character that Borges, who had a keen sense of humor, couldn't see that Lorca's coy confession was a piece of whimsy: sometimes the poet was a joke gone wild. Unamuno wrote of a tragic sense of life. Lorca had a comic sense of everything. Borges missed the point altogether: all Lorca wanted was to *épater le Borges.*

In Havana, quite the contrary, Lorca delighted his Cuban friends with some little night poetry. It was called "Buster Keaton's Promenade," written by moonlight. Buster Keaton is not a redeemer on his second coming to the screen, but neither is he the whimpering Mickey, the meek mouse. Mickey is, in fact, a pain in the eyes of every filmgoer; Keaton is the true fan's delight. The playlet's subtitle is "There Are Nightingales in America," which is Lorca's way of saying again that poets can be princes. It's easier, alas, for princes to be poets. For in Havana once, Lorca, with the intention of astonishing no one, astonished all.

An anonymous Cuban writer (most Cuban writers are anonymous) describes Lorca's stay in Havana as "the agitated rhythm of the poet's life . . . so crowded with soi-disantes soirees, shattering chats, and homages to Havana." Lorca, however, stayed not only in Havana. He himself had said so many times that he was headed for Santiago de Cuba that he almost didn't make it. Even today many readers think that Lorca never went to Santiago. Poetry might be a metaphor looking for some sense in reality, but after many a tremor of intent, Lorca went to Santiago de Cuba after all: "Iré a Santiago de Cuba / en un coche de aguas negras." He went not in a coach or car made entirely of black water, as he wrote, nor with Fonseca's blond head of hair, but by train with some anonymous friends. In Santiago, Lorca stayed at the Venus Hotel, for Lorca was a poet of love, faithful to Aphrodite only. Those who doubt it must read "The Unfaithful Married Woman." There are not many erotic poems about the naked body—"Sus muslos se me escapaban / como peces sorprendidos"—in Spanish litera-

ture of yesterday. Even today they are few and far between. Love in Spain stays mainly in plain clothes.

Lorca the poet was a major influence on Cuban poetry. After much *modernista* abandon and languor, poetry in Cuba, an island, was for castaways climbing back on Nigger Jim's raft for white boys only. This was *negrismo,* but the only black poet to rhyme to the sound of bongos, guiros, and maracas was Nicolás Guillén. Curiously enough, not only was he steeped in Spanish literature, but he was the sole Cuban poet to be vastly influenced by Lorca. Could you picture Alejo Carpentier, the other eminent writer in the group, reciting "O cintura caliente y gota de madera!"?

Negrismo was a way of talking (or sounding) like black men did in Cuba, orally and musically. But the dialect had an alien echo from afar. It was all very exotic, mind you, in Cuba, where exotic is a Scandinavian sailor, not a shoeshine boy, or a musician singing a *son,* or a stevedore. The best poets of the generation were not *précieux,* but they certainly were *ridicules.* They all looked, poetically, well, like versions of Al Jolson in black face, or even better, like the chorus boys from a black-and-white minstrel show, those who rhyme "Mammy" and "Alabammy." Poetry for them was some sort of sticky bootblack. Any old Walker Evans photo was infinitely truer and therefore closer to art than this poetry that went from verse to worse.

Lorca's brief visit to Havana was like a sudden squall, coming not from Grenada but from Granada. His bardic breath swept the land. There was even a rhyme not without reason: "Federico García Lorca / Pa los poetas cubanos / Pide la horca." Or even better: "García Lorca vino a Cuba / en un barco americano / a enseñar a los cubanos / a ser un poco gitanos."

His kind of poetry was meant to be read aloud, recited, sung, and even played as a tiresome tirade. Poetry can be close to pottery sometimes, but it also is another kind of music. As Verlaine demanded, "De la musique avant toute chose." Lorca in his "Son de negros en Cuba" has music for his muse, an exotic muse that instantly becomes familiar. "Iré a Santiago" is a very effective refrain from a *son.* As you probably know, a *son* is a popular type of song of the 1920s and 1930s which can still be heard in salsa. But salsa is a music with a nostalgia for a past that never was. It is to Cuban music what Dixieland is to jazz. As in the "Cuban Overture" by Gershwin, the harmony is forgettable but the melody lingers on.

Lorca landed in Havana on the Machina docks. The time he lived in New York, though he wrote there "The Shoemaker's Wondrous Wife," a play full of Andalusian sunshine, he composed his dark book in darkness, *Poet in New York.* The poem begins with a phrase of premonition, "Murdered by the Sky," and ends with "Escape from New York." Almost immediately, as an afterthought, the poet writes his "Son de negros en Cuba." Here he invokes the moon as some sort of sorcery: "When the moon is full / I'll go to Santiago de Cuba." The poem has the form of a *son,* it's true, but it's rather like a tropical tune. The poet flies away from rough civilization to the soft soil and to exotic nature. One can almost hear Caliban in *The Tempest.*

> The isle is full of noises,
> Sounds and sweet airs, that give delight and hurt not.
> Sometimes a thousand twangling instruments
> Will him about mine ears; and sometimes voices.

But Lorca wants to travel around the island with sail and soul.

> Cantarán los techos de palmera
> Iré a Santiago
> Iré a Santiago
> Con la rubia cabeza de Fonseca
> Iré a Santiago
> Y con el rosal de Romeo y Julieta . . .
> ¡O Cuba! ¡O ritmo de semillas secas!
> ¡O cintura caliente y gota de madera!
> ¡Arpa de troncos vivos, caimán, flor de Tabaco!

Did Lorca know the romance by Lope de Vega with its constant refrain, "Me voy a Panamá"? It's perhaps the first time that Cuban rhythms and Spanish verse became the true lyrics of a *son,* even if it is an ur-*son.* There is a traditional *son* sung by Miguel Matamoros, a surname Lorca found funny in Cuba. Here's the *son:* "Mamá yo quiero saber / de donde son los cantantes." Lorca knew; those singers, like the *son,* came from Santiago de Cuba: "They are from the hills / And sing in the plains." But Lorca saw it first, heard it first, and went to Santiago, though the poem was written in Havana with sunbeams: this searching light, the poet said, can only be seen in Havana. Like that Wildean character from the South, I could say, "Ah yes, the light of Havana. But you should have seen it before the Revolution!" I have witnesses, you know. It was witnessed here tonight by the fragment of Hergesheimer, which is a frozen frieze of a tropical edifice, and by the photographs of Walker Evans, where the façade of a movie house is an invitation to the voyage every night. In that era of smiles of a summer evening, gone with the wind of history, Lorca too was blinded by Havana. He in turn blinded the Habaneros with his dazzling display of words, verse, and charm, even though the citizens of Havana were, since the dawn of geography, used to the lights of a city that was a capital of sin.

There are those who still remember Lorca in the flesh, the man alive. One of them is Lydia Cabrera, now living in Miami as the doyenne of Cuban writers in exile. She remembers Lorca at the beginning: "He was charm incarnate," she says. "What a vital creature!" Lydia at eighty-six remembers that it took only five minutes of conversation to be charmed forever. Now she speaks of his tragic ending: "When I knew the awful circumstances of his death, I thought of Federico's terrors. He was a very timid person, cowardly even, and his death must have come to him in sheer horror. It was unforgivable!" Lezama Lima had a curious opinion of Lorca's death; it is not a political but a poetical version of his assassination. "It wasn't a political murder," says Lezama, adding cryptically, "What killed Lorca was vulgarity."

That was of course the end. In the beginning Lorca arrived in Havana to astonish everybody with his own introduction: "Call me Federico García." To call himself García and not Lorca gave birth to many comments. Somebody even asked, "Who's this guy? Are you sure this man is the *real* Lorca? Why then does he say he's García?" With so many people called García in Cuba, from the guerrilla general who before independence got a personal letter from the president of the United States, in what is called in history as "A Message to García," to the most vulgar politicians, you could find more Garcías in Cuba than Pérezes in the Madrid phone book. Instantly many Cubans claimed a kinship to Lorca. The poet smiled and said, "Yes, of course, why not?" And everybody was happy to have Lorca in the family. "Isn't it amazing? He looks exactly like my cousin Fico!" The more the merrier, except for a particular poet who saw Lorca as a double rival in poetry and in love.

At the time there lived in Havana a Colombian poet named Porfirio Barba Jacob. What a formidable name! But the man had as many aliases as he had unfinished poems. He lived and wrote under a spreading pseudonym. First it had been his own name, the obscure Osorio. Then there was in quick succession Ricardo Arenales and Main Ximénez, and finally he stumbled on Porfirio Barba Jacob, his last refuge, as it were. See the name, feel the beard, and buy a poem. The whole moniker could easily mean a bearded Jacob ailing from porphyria. Be that as it may (it was March then), all those names formed the shape of a grand *poeta* who thought he was great but who was only gray. He was a *modernista,* a vanishing race then. But Barba was famous in Havana for a verse and a reversal. The poet wrote, "I believe in nothing. In nothing!" In real life he was a poor poet and a pederast. Terribly ugly, he was called a "horse without a rider." As he was a night-hawk, he was also called "the Nightmare." He had an equine face, but he wasn't equanimous.

Not only was Barba a very ugly man, but one of his front teeth was missing. This is not such a terrible fate for a face. George Eliot, a lady who looked like a horse, had two front teeth missing. Balzac had only one tooth left in his smile, making him into some sort of unicorn. But those are novelists. Barba was a poet and was very unhappy with his wandering minstrel of a tooth, here today and gone tomorrow. He found a device to cover up the dental absence by making himself a tooth with cotton mostly, sometimes with writing paper, but never with half a cigarette, as a half-wit once suggested.

Let me tell you about a typical soiree with Barba in downtown Havana. They usually began early in the evening at the Louvre Promenade. The Louvre was a café and for Barba a *café con leche,* as with most poets then. *Café con leche* was ambrosia for Barba. He loved to talk. How he loved to talk! He usually began with any vesper (this was his word for the evening), as described by Lezama: "Noche insular, jardines invisibles." But as Barba began to weave it like nightfall, some Sophocles sent a word of doom in a sudden cloud—or rather in a suddenly missing cloud. Barba's tooth had disappeared, seemingly forever, in his garrulous mouth. It used to go like this. There it was, the ersatz tooth, whiter than any other teeth, shining in the Havana night, and then, all of a sudden, the tooth wasn't there any more. Then it visibly came back, as white as Moby Dick, swimming on the other side of midnight or of the mouth. Sometimes the shining, soft tooth came to rest on Barba's livid lower lip, or, in a quantum leap, it flew over the bush of his beard. "Ah, here it is!" Barba would exclaim as of a prodigal son and retrieve the wayward tooth from his bard's beard. The poet took himself for a fascinating raconteur (though his conversation was a raccoon's tour, if we judge by his listener's mien). Fascination came, if at all, from watching that daring false tooth on the flying trapeze of his spittle. Some other time it was more like a castaway sailor in white drifting on the raft of the poet's tongue to negotiate his dire passage between the Charybdis of his teeth and the Scylla of his gums. Barba was the stuff myth and missing teeth are made of.

Now for "Barba in Love," or "Bluebeard Hides a Secret." Barba fell in love as suddenly as the sun sets in the tropics. The *modernista* poet found his last love, literarily, when he "covered the waterfront." The lovers ill met by moonlight by the docks: the two were locked in love near the harbor. He, the lover, was a sailor, and Barba used to sing: "By the sea, by the sea, by the sea by Debussy." He was, as you can hear, happy. But he believed in nothing, not even in fate, and he was ugly,

poor, and thin. Thin because he was tubercular. To his chagrin (that's how he used to call his grin), it was 1930, a year of misfortunes or missed fortunes for Barba. Anyway, fate came to the archpoet when Barba was promenading down the Prado with his sailor, and he was intercepted by Lorca by chance. The Andalusian was the opposite of the Colombian: rich, famous, and charming, and with a set of shining white teeth and a tanned face to match. While Barba was no match, Lorca stole Barba's silent sailor with a smile. Barba tried to be sporting and smiled too. Lorca found himself a sailor, but Barba's tooth was missing in action.

There was one occasion when Lorca blended a Havana institution into his ars poetica. There was in Old Havana an important branch of Western Union, the cable company then busier than a whorehouse on Saturday. The manager was a tall, bulging blond man known, I don't know why, by the name of Mae West. Our Mae West didn't care for tall, dark men, and his messengers were all cute and coy boys. They went everywhere on their bicycles sporting a smile. They used to cruise the city at incredible speed and sometimes seemed to fly. Lorca saw the messengers speeding up and down Havana, all pretty and levitating, and he said, "In Havana the angels ride on a bicycle."

Here comes the end. The culmination of Lorca's visit came when a few Habaneros gave him a farewell dinner in the dining room of the Inglaterra Hotel, at the end of the Louvre Promenade. At the table were Lorca and his discombobulated disciples, the three-penny poets. There also was the literary litter ready to write prose the way Lorca wrote poems: the penny dreadful. Through the open doors (air conditioning, like the best, was yet to come) you could see the innumerable Greek columns of the hotel, now white in the setting sun. In the background there was the square called, for reasons unknown, Parque Central, and in the middle of it the statue of another poet killed in his prime by the bullet that killed Lorca. (The poet of course didn't know this.) The name of the older poet is José Martí. There was a name on both bullets.

Suddenly it started to rain—rain, real rain, unannounced, unexpected, flooding rain. It rained everywhere. It rained behind the evening's colonnade and on the pavement, on the cement and on the asphalt, and even on the cement of the park, and you couldn't see the trees from the doors of the hotel. You couldn't see the trees even if you were in the park. It rained on the statue and on the long white pedestal under the hero. Now his indicting hand and the index finger became livid and then liquid, as the rains came for all. It rained in the park and on the building across called Gómez Square and even further down the street in the small square where the Hemingway beggars drank water from a faucet in the morning and across the square where Hemingway himself drank firewater to spit flames and brimstone in writing. It rained on the Cytherea Hergesheimer had discovered and on the black-and-white urban landscape that Walker Evans had developed and then printed forever. It rained all over Havana.

Meanwhile, in the dining room, the brave eaters devoured their heavy meal. Spain in the tropics, indifferent to a rain that was now liquid curtains on the windows, a breath of nature on the opaque mirrors and waterfalls beyond the doors. Nobody noticed. Only Lorca saw the rain. He stopped eating to look at it. Then, all of a sudden, he jumped from his seat, stepped aside, and went quickly to the enormous doors to see the rain. He hadn't seen such a rain before. The Granada rain transformed the dust into mud like bull's blood, the Madrid rain only watered the public gardens, and the rain in New York was like cold death. Other kinds of rain he had seen before were not rain, if you compared them with this ungodly flood. The hotel instantly became an ark with its eating menagerie, and of course Lorca was now Noah.

Lorca stayed on his watchtower, seeing all the rain falling as naturally as the sun was shining bright only a few minutes before. He forgot all about dinner in watching this spectacle that was part dream and part nightmare. But the other guests noticed his absence and left their meals as leftovers to approach Lorca and see through his eyes whatever he was looking at now. They came in pairs, then more of them came to make the noise Habaneros love best: the din that tried to cancel the roar of the rain. To talk, to talk! Lorca took a finger (it was the index to become a double of the poet in the rain), took it to his lips to silence his hoity-toity hosts. They all stopped talking, but it didn't stop raining. Lorca was hung between a glass and quicksilver.

The noise of the banquet had ended in the thunder of the rain. For the first time many has-been writers and would-be poets were gathered in a solemn ceremony. Federico García Lorca the poet (and *poet* means "maker" in Greek) had made them see rain in Havana as a poetic phenomenon. Nobody has really seen rain before—or after. Lorca was our local rainmaker. It seems as if the rain has not stopped ever since, and we see him through a mirror of water. That's what *pristine* means: "through a glass transparent."

Guillermo Cabrera Infante, Autumn 1987

---

[1] "Brief Encounters in Havana" was delivered by Cabrera Infante to an audience of approximately one hundred at the University of Oklahoma on the evening of 19 March 1987—*Ed.*

[2] Joseph Hergesheimer, *San Cristóbal de la Habana,* New York, Knopf, 1923, pp. 9–10. Subsequent quotes are indicated by page numbers in parentheses—*Ed.*

Vistas of Dawn in the (Tristes) Tropics: History, Fiction, Translation

All of Europe is a museum just as all of Oklahoma is a theatre for Kafka.

▨ **SEVERO SARDUY**

■ HISTORY IS A STORY

Vista del amanecer en el trópico (1974; Eng. *View of Dawn in the Tropics,* 1978) was one of the original titles of the book that became *Tres tristes tigres* (1964; Eng. *Three Trapped Tigers,* 1971), a novel that was going to counterpoint Guillermo Cabrera Infante's *carnevale* to the satyrs and nymphs of Havana nightlife with somber documentary vignettes of history in the making—the revolution against Batista which ended in the victory of Fidel Castro. "Both a chronicle and a Utopian vision of that moment, the original novel was a view of the tropical dawn of Cuba, the dawn of a new historical age," Emir Rodríguez Monegal wrote in a review for *Plural* of the work that finally did become *Vista del amanecer en el trópico* in 1974.[1]

However, in 1965 the self-exiled Infante, convinced that the revolutionary government was turning into a repressive regime, particularly after the censorship of the film *P.M.* and after other restrictive measures, disengaged from his work-in-progress the politically engaged vignettes. The documentary *P.M,* filmed by his brother Sabá Cabrera and Orlando Jiménez, was a vivid testimony in black-and-white to the nightlife in Old Havana, though most of the characters were black or mulatto, dancing to hypnotic cha-cha-chas, rumbas, mambos, and boleros, drinking, and occasionally getting into a brawl.

It was not a vision of the "reformed" Cuba that the regime wished to publicize. Also, it was the first time, GCI noted, that an artistic work was censored in Cuba "not for expressing counterrevolutionary ideas, but because of its form as well as content."[2] What his brother Cabrera was not allowed to show in film, Infante would tell in literature.

Literary or esthetic politics, even more than Cuban politics, motivated the transformation of *Vista* into *TTT,* however. The original project followed the formula of GCI's first work of fiction, his collection of "lyrical" stories and "epic" vignettes titled *Así en la paz como en la guerra* (In Peace As in War; 1958); in a similar fashion fiction and history conjoined to form another total or totalitarian Sartrean fiction, a Utopian project proposing a view of history and fiction as a continuum. The text that finally turned into *TTT,* however, recognized no other counterpoint than its own verbal music, making history and politics into a barely audible basso continuo.

Several years later GCI collected the vignettes— which now began with the earliest chronicles of Cuba and ended in the early 1970s, since he had continued to compose new vignettes—and, by means of the cinematic technique of montage, he created out of them a book. Or rather, in making a readerly discovery, he was finally able to write the book, as he explains in his 1986 interview with Danubio Torres Fierro.

> One day, upon reading the new vignettes, which had been published in places as diverse as Mexico and Czechoslovakia, I realized that they had a common denominator: violence. Cuba's history seemed wrought out of a violence which contradicted its peaceful tropical geography. Using these vignettes and others which I wrote on Cuba's most remote and most recent history, plus actual testimonies (for example, in the last part of the book), another *View of Dawn in the Tropics* arose, this time turning the exemplary title into an ironic one: History now viewed as a simple story, historical life transformed into mere writing into versions of reality—or rather "reality." (86)

Completed during somber years for GCI, *Vista* was also a less joy(ce)ful book than *TTT.* The vignettes are concise Hemingwayesque glimpses of a moment, an incident, a place, a character, or a text, as William Kennedy observed, "in the tradition of the vignettes of *In Our Time.*"[3] Many of them are descriptions of photographs or engravings—literally moments captured in time in which the still, the visual image, becomes dramatized for an instant, petrifying History in a graphic referent. Some are oral testimonies, transcripts of conversations that actually took place. Inscriptions on photographs, fragments of recorded speeches, national hymns, legends, hearsay, official reports, transcripts—these are the ruins, the textual remains of History which constitute history-as-told in *Vista.*

The counterpoint between lyricism (Cuba's nature and geography) and the epic (history) had now become a subtle fugue. But Infante—a fanatic subverter of academic or journalistic clichés, even his own—hated the term *vignettes.* First it seemed because he didn't want to appear to be repeating literary strategies, having used vignettes in his collection of stories. There was another

reason, though, suggested in a letter early on in our correspondence concerning the book (I translate).

> I promised Prometheus [alluding to a Havana theatre group in the 1950s] not to use that word any more with *View of Dawn in the Tropics,* but I don't know what to call these fragments: perhaps *viewgnettes?* And there's a critic in Spain who insists that the book is a novel, with all the generals and the comandantes becoming one captain. What do you think? (4 October 1975)

GCI's main concern here was that *vignettes* spoiled the structural *view* (that is, the reading) of the book as a long poem and not as a series of brief narratives—a serious concern from a pragmatic as well as a more purely literary perspective, if such a distinction is necessary. After the Spanish publisher had mistakenly advertised the work as "una serie de relatos," Cass Canfield Jr. hesitated to publish the book, insisting (correctly) that volumes of stories do not sell well and that *View* should come out when GCI's new novel was ready to roll too. The editor finally agreed to publish it when GCI carefully went over the book with him and showed him its undeniable unity. GCI writes in a letter dated 18 September 1976 that "Cass had the idea . . . they were a series of vignettes about Cuba under Batista and not what the book is: a history which denies history and an epic told in lyrical terms about the history imposed upon the geography of that long unhappy island." These last words *long unhappy island* allude to Hemingway's passing description of Cuba in a kind of elegy to the Gulf Stream which appears in his book *Green Hills of Africa.* This elegy, as I'll discuss further, turned out to be the "subtext" of the last vignette of the book.

▪ FROM VISTA TO VIEW

Though GCI participated less in this translation than in that of either *TTT* or, later, *Infante's Inferno*—wordplay and excessive elaboration would have upset its delicate balance, the grave contrapuntal effect of its lyricism, understatement, and straightforward violence—he still collaborated significantly. He added some new vignettes which—like one about a black general and another about a failed attack on the presidential palace— underscore an ironic, pathetic view of the "best intentions" of revolution.[4] He also maintained a correspondence with me over a period of four years (1974–78), which dealt with all aspects of the translation, from the most practical issues (getting the book published, pondering over its reception) to answering my many translation questions, discussing the concept of the book, and offering numerous corrections and editorial suggestions.

The subtle variations of style and language in *View of Dawn in the Tropics,* and also its demands for documentary authenticity, provided a challenge, whereas its elegant concision made it both pleasurable and more manageable than GCI's more voluminous undertakings. Regarding its deceptive simplicity (in comparison with *TTT*), GCI warned me in a letter of 12 November 1977 (I translate literally):

> *View*, despite its apparent easiness, has a lot of tricks to it, of style but also language. In the first pages I use many archaic documents mixed into the narration; some of the pages which seem as if they were mine—like that extraordinary graffiti we've already discussed—are really historical documents.

Italo Calvino once said that a real collaboration between author and translator begins with the translator's questions, and that "a translator with no doubts cannot be a good translator."[5] The translator Alastair Reid once pointed out to me an experience I immediately identified with, that of looking up words one already knew—that is, translators have doubts even when they have the answers.

Anyway, my first questions to GCI when I'd already begun to translate *Vista* were:

> Dr. Livingston, I presume that on pp. 13–14 of *Vista* the quotations from Columbus are from his first voyage, correcto? On p. 17, do you remember from what section of Padre de las Casas' writings comes the quotation? Since both those works are translated, I thought it worthwhile to quote from the translations, if possible. Also, if possible, could you give me a list of the other works you quote from. Most of them probably aren't translated but, if so, I should check into the translations. (My letter, 28 November 1975)

His response, dated 13 December 1975 was prompt, despite protestation to the contrary. (These letters are irresponsibly bilingual, so I've translated most of the Spanish segments.)

> Dear Jill, forgive my delay in answering your letter in turn, but yours had gotten mislaid (in this universe filled with papers that is my *mundo infame* [infamous world], not to be confused please with *mondo cane* or with *inmundo infante* [filthy Infante, but a pun, hence a better translation would be: Infante's underworld—underwear, get it?] and I couldn't answer yours without having it in view [in sight]: Land! shouted Rodrigo de Triana from the crow's nest—and you're right the quotation is from Columbus's first voyage, but I don't know if it [Columbus's letter] was translated from the Italian or from *hispaniolo antico*. I can't tell you anything about Las Casas—called "Bartolomeo" by C. L. Sulzberger!—I got that quotation (like many of the others [dealing with

the Conquest and colonial Cuba]) from Portuondo's history of Cuba. All the quotations come from there, and those that don't come from that history, I've forgotten whence they come since I wrote those vignettes years ago. (For example, the one where the general's mother refuses to recognize him because he surrendered and only accepts him when she finds out that he tried to commit suicide first, and others like that vignette. I don't think there are references to other universal works other than the obvious, Borges and Hemingway, for example, both of whom have written about history and about Cuba; remember the "odious rumba The Peanut Vendor.") [This last quotation is from Borges's *Universal History of Infamy*, translated into English by Norman Thomas Di Giovanni and Borges as "the deplorable rumba" (*A Universal History*, pp. 19–20).]

At first glance, question and answer seem redundant—that is, that most of the historical quotations came out of Portuondo's book was already known. Still, the author 1) confirms this in detail, a comfort to the ever-doubtful painstaking translator, and 2) he underscores the tentativeness of his originals, or rather his translations' origins, since a) Columbus's letters were translated from the Italian or . . . , and in any case scholars have noted that "Columbus's prose is an imperfect mixture of Italian, Spanish and Portuguese" which, one imagines, the king and queen of Spain—or their secretary—had some difficulty in deciphering.[6] Moreover, to begin with, b) GCI has forgotten—unavoidably or conveniently—the origins of his "quotations"; and finally, c) he alludes to the inevitable mistranslations of History (Sulzberger's version of Las Casas's name, and of course Portuondo's "History of Cuba," an official textbook read by Cuban children in grade school). Infante also mentions in this letter literary quotations: Borges and the pervasive influence of Hemingway, particularly the Hemingway quotation (in the last vignette), which Infante brooded over in a previous letter (27 September 1975).

> Do you think that the vignettes (or whatever they're called) are coming out too Hemingwayan in English? I'm worried about that with some of them, particularly the older ones (like those you're translating now, the one with the two generals), that were written around 1963 or even before. It worries me because of the possible American reader (and especially critic). I know that in others they'll find influences of Borges, though in reality they are homages to the Argentinian—or direct quotations, as you know. But Hemingway is really so dead to me that it would be like performing funeral rites to name him among the influences of the book—although I chose for the end a direct quotation from him, this time con-

sciously, since he is one of the few writers who have written on Cuba, not with the immediacy of the revolution in mind but rather the permanence of the island, which is really the theme of *View,* as you well know.

There is more than perhaps meets the eye in this exchange. The real theme of *View* turns out to be—via Hemingway—a subversion of the original intention of the heavily Hemingwayesque vignettes: in effect, four centuries of violence are framed by first and last vignettes which speak of the island's permanence. The repeated incidents of violence—though the causes, from conquest to revolution, seem so varied in ideology—also speak of another permanence: the age-old adage, still true, "History repeats itself."

There is, however, another "transgression" which comes into view here. In my letter I ask what amounts to a metatranslational question—that is, am I to respect the original of GCI's "translation" (original, that is) and quote faithfully, by quoting faithfully the (inevitably unfaithful) translation of that original "pretext" already written in English? Or am I, like him (the author), to rewrite the "original," quoting "freely," that is, writing? In his "quotations" of Borges and Hemingway, GCI is really paraphrasing (i.e., rewriting) more than quoting. For example, the phrase "Before dying, did the last hostage think he was dreaming" (*VDT,* 76) alludes to "Did he . . . resume his sleep . . . so that the murderers would be a dream . . .?" from two sentences in Borges's story "La espera" ("The Waiting," from *Labyrinths*), which I've condensed here into one for the purpose of comparison.

GCI was doubtlessly directing me toward the writerly course while at the same time denying (unconscious) influence in favor of (conscious) homage to Borges and Hemingway, two literary Vergils he could not ignore, though he had exorcised at least one of them, Hemingway, through the exorcising (and homaging) device of parody in *TTT:* for example, in the figure of Mr. Campbell, the supposed author of a supposed story that is parodied through translation. Mr. Campbell, apparently a hack writer, is a silly avatar of Hemingway or of a Hemingwayesque character, the hero or antihero now a kvetching, prejudiced American tourist.

Still, not completely exorcised, the "anxiety of influence" lingers on, now multiplied in the dimension of translation. In *View* GCI is concerned about the reception of his work in English, the native language of Hemingway. How was GCI to avoid being read as secondary, perpetrating the odious relationship between a mainstream culture and marginal Cuba? He had already been unjustly burned over this issue in John Updike's parochial, prejudiced panning of *TTT* on the grounds that "we" (the English language) did not need a Cuban Joyce.[7]

GCI phrases his concern here, however, not as anxiety but as a parricidal criticism of Hemingway, "because of the bad reputation Hemingway has now" (27 August 1977)—i.e., the fact that Hemingway is passé.

> The particularly vulnerable zones are those written in Brussels. Those written in London are more *mine* [my italics]. What was written in 1963 is too much under the aegis of Borges (aside from the textual quotations), and the form of my vignettes in that period owes a lot to Hemingway.

The distinctions between the "derivative," earlier vignettes and the more "original" later ones (particularly "the originality of paralyzing history in photographs, graphic referents") certainly concern the writer. (Indeed, what GCI defines as his original, final conception of the book, that of "de-signifying history, converting History into stories," could also "derive," in this instance from Borges's "timid games" in *A Universal History of Infamy.*) Perhaps more relevant to the reader, however, is how histories and fictions are transformed into a text whose *originality* lies in its critical dialogue with these urtexts.

I would therefore like to retrace briefly the process of translating the last vignette, GCI's "translation" of Hemingway back into its purloined language, in order to give, if not a view, at least a glimpse of how the translation attempts to continue the dialogue between texts that constitutes the original, at the same time that it marks a critical difference, like all effective translations, parodies, *and* originals.

◼ A SUBTEXT

Let's begin by taking a look at the original's original, not the island of Cuba but Hemingway's now much-prefaced description of the island in the stream. For brevity's sake, I shall transcribe the particular segments of Hemingway's elegy to the Gulf Stream "cited" by Infante, thus unfortunately butchering poor Hemingway, much like the sharks did to the Old Man's big fish. Anyway:

> When, on the sea, you . . . know that this Gulf Stream you are living with . . . has moved, as it moves, since before man, and that it has gone by the shoreline of that long, beautiful, unhappy island since before Columbus sighted it and that . . . those that have always lived in it are permanent and of value because that stream will flow, as it has flowed, after the Indians, after the Spaniards, after the British, after the Americans and after all the Cubans and all the systems of governments, the richness, the poverty, the martyrdom, the sacrifice and the venality and the cruelty are all gone as the high-piled scow of garbage . . . spills off its load into the blue water . . . with no

significance against one single, lasting thing—the stream.[8]

Now here is GCI's "translation":

> Y ahí estará. Como dijo alguien, esa triste, infeliz y larga isla estará ahí después del último indio y después del último español y después del último africano y después del último americano y después del último de los cubanos, sobreviviendo a todos los naufragios y eternamente bañada por la corriente del golfo: bella y verde, imperecedera, eterna. (233)

The "changes" are interesting: 1) Hemingway's "long, beautiful, unhappy" island becomes emphatically more unhappy in GCI's "sad, unhappy and long"; 2) the "after the Indians" series is translated faithfully (GCI's addition of *último* is needed to give the dramatic emphasis that Hemingway's rhetorical repetition makes vivid in English), except GCI omits the British—who perhaps played a more minor role in his view of Cuba's history—and adds the Africans—a principal racial group in Cuba, omitted here by Papa Hemingway, ironically in a book about Africa; 3) GCI condenses all the evils into *naufragios,* literally "shipwrecks," metaphorically to be taken as disasters, all the shipwrecked explorers and refugees signifying, after all, both individual and historical disaster. "Eternally bathed by the Gulf Stream" condenses all that Hemingway is saying about the beauty, power, and permanence of nature, the stream, in opposition to humanity's waste. More significantly, however, the narrator shifts the focus from the stream to the island, which becomes nature, beautiful, green, lasting, eternal, except that *imperecedera* is stronger, more active—more directly associated with the history of violence just told—than the tranquil adjective *lasting.*

GCI is both quoting and paraphrasing Hemingway, thus paying homage but also subtly subverting, switching emphasis, marking a difference by using Hemingway's words to sing not the stream but the island. GCI indicates without saying it that he is not an American adventurer out on his fisherman's yacht, but rather a beached, now-exiled Cuban who has really known this "unhappy" island. Hemingway's nostalgic "long, beautiful, unhappy" becomes more poignant in the words of one who lived it from within.

Here, finally, is the English translation:

> And it will always be there. As someone once said, that long, sad, unfortunate island will be there after the last Indian and after the last African and after the last American and after the last of the Cubans, surviving all disasters, eternally washed over by the Gulf Stream: beautiful and green, undying, eternal. (141)

Here one can observe a process similar to the original "rewriting." *Always,* like *último,* is added—or intuitively retraced back to the original's original—for the necessary rhetorical emphasis on permanence that the strong formal future tense gives in Spanish, just as the first sentence is turned around so that "always be there" is stressed at the strongest point, the end of the sentence. "Long, sad, unhappy" becomes "long, sad, unfortunate," displacing the simple, original *unhappy,* not only because *unhappy* picks up other connotations in its passage through Spanish—*infeliz* by a contiguity of notions means "mis-" or "unfortunate"—but because, unlike "triste, infeliz," there is no progression between the synonymous *sad* and *unhappy* in English, in either meaning or emotional intensity.

Those of us who translate know that *y* doesn't always translate automatically as "and," since *y* can gracefully disappear between two words, whereas *and* can sometimes stick out like a sore thumb. But here *y,* as GCI (5 December 1977) insisted, "should be 'and,' tying up with the unfinished first vignette"—that is, as the "end" of a long or interrupted sentence, giving the book, again, its "undeniable unity."

On the question of *shipwrecks* versus *disasters* GCI expressed the same doubt as myself: "If we put 'disasters' we lose the connection with the waters and if we put 'shipwrecks' it's too dramatic, metaphoric. Toss a coin, girl, toss a coin." I did toss one, a wooden nickle, and came up with *disasters,* but precisely because *naufragios* serves a metonymic function: i.e., it literally denotes "shipwrecks," but it connotes, in common speech, disasters in general, shipwrecks being one of many possible disasters (and a very common one around Cuba, but not the only one, as *VDT* vividly tells). Again, the general term *disasters* made more sense in this final "eternal" summing up, a summing up which subsumes Hemingway's list of disasters. The word marks a three-way dialogue involving the English translation, the original, and the original's Hemingwayan original, just as "after the last" in the American translation marks the subversion of the "subtext" by accepting the "contamination" of the Spanish "translation."

GCI seems to have taken from Hemingway's version both what effective writing in Spanish permitted, and what he interpreted—from his *view*—as the truer version. An act of translation, of criticism, of creation. Hemingway's elegant meditation on nature's truth and human folly is quoted in homage, but the Cuban writer subverts the other's discourse to criticize the "white father's" distanced, estheticized view: the island is finally not a backdrop but very much the foreground. GCI estheticizes too, of course, both in translating and in rewriting Hemingway in his own style. Writing always "falsifies" and/or "magnifies," Borges once whimsically complained.

The American translation of *Vista* incorporates, perhaps without intending to, a double vision: Hemingway's original and GCI's interpretation, both by quoting and by misquoting. The linguistic difference—between the original and its urtext—is of course lost in translation, but the critical difference has made its mark.

Hemingway believes he is telling it like it is in his version. GCI's view—critically subsuming Hemingway's—recognizes that all writing is secondary, which may mean that he is closer to telling it like it is. One way to see this view is to look back in laughter at *TTT*, where Hemingway's influence is exorcised in countless ways. The foreword to *Green Hills* was—it would seem, but GCI's the only one who can tell us, if he remembers—the source of one of the satiric epigraphs in *TTT*. Hemingway, taking himself—and realism—quite seriously, writes with humor:

> Unlike many novels, none of the characters or incidents in this book is imaginary. Any one not finding sufficient love interest is at liberty, while reading it, to insert whatever love interest he or she may have at the time. The writer has attempted to write an absolutely true book to see whether the shape of a country and the pattern of a month's action can, if truly presented, compete with a work of the imagination.

The "action" of which the "work of the imagination" falls short, by the way, includes the glorified slaughter of African animals by the stoic, heroic Great White Hunter. Why GCI would wish to bury the American patriarch under numerous parodies would not be difficult to understand. GCI writes a row of nonsequiturs in his *TTT* epigraph.

> The characters, though based on real persons, appear as fictional beings. The proper names mentioned all through the book must be considered pseudonyms. The facts are, at times, taken from reality, but are finally resolved as imaginary. Any similarity between literature and history is accidental.

GCI is pulling everybody's leg—seriously—including Hemingway's. The first sentence is pleonastic play, perhaps making fun of the movie industry's fear of law-

suits. The second sentence is a half-lie, since some of the names are real (like Rine Leal, René Jordan, Jesse Fernández), but a pithy lie, since names (particularly Infante, which means "speechless") are linguistic conventions: even when "real," do they *really* signify? (But let's leave Derrida in peace.) The third sentence makes quite clear that GCI is questioning Hemingway's privileging of the real over the imaginary, and the fourth mocks not only Hemingway's machismo but also Marxist social realism. GCI takes Hemingway's text (and cinematic and sociological clichés) and—as in dream speeches—repeats the words but gives them a different meaning, revealing language's elusiveness despite all intentions to the contrary.

The epigraph "got lost" in translation; neither GCI nor his editor considered it funny enough to clutter up the front of the book, perhaps. Also perhaps, *View of Dawn in the Tropics* carries over what GCI is saying (despite language's nonsense) in *TTT*, but this time the joke is dead serious.

Both GCI and I were fairly content—and I suppose relieved—with the translation when it finally came out. Among his comments toward the end of the translation process: "What is coming out very well is the tone, between ironic and factual and often deadpan *écriture*—how do you like the polyglotism?"

Suzanne Jill Levine, Autumn 1987

[1] Emir Rodríguez Monegal, review of *Vista del amanecer en el trópico*, in *Plural*, Mexico City, May 1975, p. 66. See also *WLT* 50:1 (Winter 1976), p. 123.

[2] Danubio Torres Fierro, "Guillermo Cabrera Infante," in *Memoria plural: Entrevistas a escritores latinoamericanos*, Buenos Aires, Sudamericana, 1986, p. 87.

[3] William Kennedy, "Island of Luminous Artifact," *Review*, 25–26 (1979), p. 136.

[4] Guillermo Cabrera Infante, *View of Dawn in the Tropics*, New York, Harper & Row, 1984, pp. 42, 86. Subsequent references use the abbreviation *VDT*.

[5] Italo Calvino, "Statement on Translation," *Translation*, special issue on the Italian book in America, Columbia University, 1986, pp. 109–10.

[6] *Noticias secretas y públicas de América*, Emir Rodríguez Monegal, ed., Barcelona, Tusquets, 1984, p. 32.

[7] *New Yorker*, 29 January 1972, p. 91.

[8] Ernest Hemingway, *The Green Hills of Africa*, New York, Scribner's, 1935.

Asia

East Asia

CHINA

Walking Toward the World: A Turning Point in Contemporary Chinese Fiction

The truth is that we share many ideological beliefs and political interests. In contrast to the previous generation, we were all individualists, trying to detach ourselves as writers from the collective "we" and to break taboos. We wanted to write about the sexual and psychological aspects of life and free ourselves from the kind of old-fashioned realism that defined the previous generation.

▓ A. B. YEHOSHUA (ISRAELI NOVELIST)[1]

Chinese fiction has changed more rapidly and profoundly during the twelve years since the reform Plenum of the Eleventh Central Committee (December 1978) than anyone could have predicted. As political restrictions on literature fell by the wayside, writers began once again to express their individual moral and intellectual visions of Chinese culture and society in narratives informed by personal esthetic standards.[2] Beginning in 1984 with the publication of Zhong Ah Cheng's novella "The Chess Master" ("Qi wang"),[3] the last half of the 1980s represented a major turning point in contemporary Chinese fiction. From that time on, contemporary Chinese fiction has been "walking toward the world" (zouxiang shijie), a phrase that may be taken to mean approaching the quality of the finest in world fiction.

According to the highly perceptive critic Li Tuo (editor of Beijing Literature until June 1989), two very different kinds of literature have been and still are competing with each other for domination of the contemporary Chinese literary stage. On the one side there is the conservative, traditionalistic, mostly party- or party-faction-approved triad consisting of literature of the wounds, reform literature, and reportage. In all three of these genres the message, usually one of social amelioration, is more important than any considerations of structural or linguistic artistry. On the other side, and far more interesting both thematically and artistically, is the triad of misty (obscure) poetry, nativist (return to roots) fiction, and experimental (sometimes called avant-garde) fiction. These three genres are concerned first and foremost with the innovative and artistic use of language, and two elements they all share are the development of a modern Chinese language to replace the Maospeak of the last thirty-five years and the deconstruction of the dominant ideology of the Maoist and communist era in China.[4] This is only an introductory essay, and in it I can only discuss very briefly a number of my personal favorites from the large amount of nativist and experimental narratives that have appeared since the second half of 1984. I shall limit my synopses and comments primarily to as yet untranslated works.

A notable breakthrough in mainland Chinese fiction was the novella "The Chess Master" ("Qi wang"), the first published work of a thirty-six-year-old writer named Zhong Ah Cheng. First discussed outside China in the Hong Kong magazine The Nineties, it was instantly acclaimed by scholars, critics, and general readers as a work greatly superior to the vast majority of its contemporary literary productions. Ah Cheng originally planned to write a series of "eight kings," but only managed to produce two other extremely intriguing novellas, "The King of Trees" ("Shu wang," 1985) and "The King of Children" ("Haizi wang," 1985).[5]

In these three novellas Ah Cheng discards Maospeak for the diction of traditional Chinese vernacular fiction to depict the moral tensions inherent in the lives of spiritually impoverished educated youth and materially impoverished rural people—not necessarily all peasants—who inhabit a traditional milieu that has been greatly disrupted by the modern ideology of Maoism. The three stories are set in the Cultural Revolution decade, but their thematic import presents a direct challenge to the dominant discourse of contemporary China. The beauty of Ah Cheng's stories lies in his mastery of language, both scenic description and dialogue, in order to create the living ambience of China's teeming countryside. He is interested in presenting the simple goodness of a number of rural people in contrast both to the callow urban youth who have been thrust into their midst and also to the unbelievably "progressive" caricatures of peasants found in much of Maoist fiction. The common decency of these well-developed characters, combined with the refreshing newness of Ah Cheng's paradoxically more traditional diction, renders his stories immensely appealing.

Thematically these stories also present a frontal attack on impersonal and instrumental Maoist values through a reaffirmation of a whole range of traditional Chinese values. "The Chess Master" emphasizes filial piety, human dignity, loyalty, friendship, and the importance of art and a spiritual life. "The King of Trees" emphasizes human dignity, friendship, and self-sacrifice in the context of humanity's closeness to nature. Finally, "The King of Children" powerfully reaffirms the Confucian value of learning and genuine education for the cultivation of the individual and the production of meaning in life.

Wang Zengqi, the oldest of the writers discussed here, has also adapted many traditional Chinese narrative techniques in the creation of lyric but not idyllic stories embodying a view of traditional Chinese culture as an unbroken circle. In the process he has also offered a gentle critique of some of the more unsavory aspects of traditional society. "Ordination" ("Shou jie," 1980)[6] is a typical example of a Wang Zengqi story. He has said it represents "a dream of forty-three years ago," when he was seventeen. It is a charming story of the coming of age of a young monk named Ming Hai. Having grown up in one place with his childhood sweetheart, he becomes a monk for economic reasons. In the course of the story he goes off to visit a large monastery for his ordination. There he finds that the monastery is a grand and wealthy world unto itself in which the monks eat meat, drink wine, marry, and have children, completely confirming the standard prejudices of the laity. The Chinese Buddhist life is thus shown to be a Confucianized or Sinified one which leaves ample room for ordinary human needs and desires while at the same time continuing to serve important spiritual and ceremonial functions in society: marking the key stages of life and death, and providing entertainment and financial services. In the comic and heartwarming denouement Ming Hai returns home to tell his childhood sweetheart Xiao Yingzi of the wonders he has seen, and she surprises him with a proposal of marriage ("Let me be your old lady"), which, after a moment's hesitation, he gladly accepts. And perhaps they live happily ever after.

Han Shaogong blends the modernistic narrative and structural techniques of "magic realism" with a jaundiced-eye vision of ancient Chu (southwestern) culture in a series of stories focused on rural life in West Hunan and highly critical of traditional Chinese culture. His best-known story, "The Mute" ("Ba ba ba," 1986),[7] based on an inventive fictional reconstruction and blending of Han and Miao customs from West Hunan, is a chronological narrative of a series of events in the life of Bing Zai, the resident idiot of Chicken Head Village. It is primarily an allegory of the circular, repetitive, meaningless history of traditional Chinese culture. Bing Zai, whose only utterances are "Baba" (Daddy) or "F—— your mother," is the epitome of the idiocy of popular traditional beliefs. He becomes the focus of a series of tragicomic incidents of collective ignorance. Chosen by the village elders for human sacrifice to appease the God of Grain and end a famine, Bing Zai is saved by a thunderclap, and his salacious mumblings are subsequently regarded as oracular pronouncements predicting victory in war. The battle between two starving villages ends in disaster for both, the aged and infants are deliberately poisoned, and the strong young men and women of both villages burn their huts down and move away. Only Bing Zai, the symbol of all of this ignorance and misery, is left alive, a sure indication that the whole meaningless tragedy will be repeated over and over again.

Mo Yan has employed modern narrative and structural techniques, heavily influenced by William Faulkner, to create both a naturalistic rural nightmare—the Chinese countryside—and a nostalgic saga of a race of heroes, the "red sorghum clan." In stories like "The Crystal Carrot," ("Touming de hong luobo," 1986) "The Dry River" ("Ku he," 1986), "White Dog and the Swings" ("Baigou qiuqianjia," 1986), and "Happiness" ("Huanle," 1987) he has depicted a rural China which is deliberately opposed to that found in the dominant discourse of Zhao Shuli, Zhou Libo, Li Zhun, Hao Ran, and other post-1949 party-supported writers of rural fiction.[8] In contrast to his Maoist predecessors, Mo Yan's Chinese countryside is a nightmarish world of ignorance, poverty, and cruelty, full of suffering, sadness, and misery temporarily relieved by minute doses of kindness, friendship, and love. Irrational violence generally engulfs his protagonists and leads to tragic misfortune or death. For example, the young stonemason of "The Crystal Carrot" is beaten by the bitter young blacksmith in a fight in which his lover Chrysanthemum has one of her beautiful dark eyes put out by a poorly aimed handful of gravel while the little mute, Black Child, is caught stealing sweet potatoes and sent home naked by the cruel Brigade Leader. The protagonist of "Happiness" can only recall one solitary act of tenderness in his entire life: once an older woman led him to a secluded place in the fields, opened her blouse, and let him gaze at her breasts.

Mo Yan's first novel, *Hong gaoliang jiazu* (The Red Sorghum Clan; 1987),[9] nostalgically explores the character of the Chinese people—"the greatest heroes and the biggest bastards"—of the first four decades of this century. The author is consciously trying to reestablish a link between the bigger-than-life aspect of the Chinese past and the seriously flawed Chinese present. The film version of the first parts of this epic novel has been very successful, but the novel itself, though containing some fascinating material, suffers from a certain lack of unity. Mo Yan's second novel, *Tiantang suantai zhi ge* (Paradise County Garlic Song; 1988),[10] returns to his earlier depictions of rural Shandong and is a much more mature work both in its ideological vision and in its artistic use of language.[11]

The young Tibetan writer Zhaxidawa's short story "Soul Tied to the Knots on a Leather Cord" ("Xizai pishengkou shang de hun," 1985)[12] seems to me to be a surprising example of what Linda Hutcheon in her 1980 book *Narcissistic Narrative* called "Metafiction." As she wrote: "'Metafiction,' as it has now been named, is fiction about fiction—that is, fiction that includes within itself a commentary on its own narrative and/or linguistic identity." She dubbed such fictional narratives "narcissistic" due to their "textual self-awareness," their "self-reflective, self-informing, self-reflexive, autoreferential, [and] auto-representational" nature.[13] Metafiction is also said to be characteristic of "postmodernism" in literature. Hutcheon describes the "metafictional paradox" as follows:

> Its central paradox for readers is that, while being made aware of the linguistic and fictive nature of what is being read, and thereby distanced from any unself-conscious identification on the level of character or plot, readers of metafiction are at the same time made mindful of their active role in reading, in participating in making the text mean. They are distanced, yet involved, co-producers of the novel. (xii)

Zhaxidawa's story seems to me to embody this central paradox and, like other postmodernist metafiction described by Hutcheon, "tends more to play with the pos-

sibilities of meaning (from degree zero to plurisignification) and of form (from minimalist narrative to galloping diegesis) . . . [and] to explore the impossibility of imposing [any] single determinate meaning on a text" (xiii). Given the fact that a "single determinate meaning" was the sine qua non of fiction for the first thirty years of the People's Republic, and that such fiction still makes up the bulk of published work there, such paradoxical, ambiguous, and exploratory fiction may be seen as a new phenomenon on the literary scene in the People's Republic in the 1980s. Readers are referred to the translation for confirmation of my idea that this is a rare early postmodern story in China.

I shall end this essay with a brief consideration of a writer whose works represent some of the finest of recent experimental fiction. Born in 1963 in Suzhou in Jiangsu province, a graduate of Peking Normal University, and now an editor at *Zhongshan* magazine in Nanjing, Su Tong is the author of many short stories and novellas, two collections of which have been published in Taiwan as *Qi qie chengqun* (Wives and Concubines; 1990) and *Shangxin de wudao* (A Sad Dance; 1991).[14] The following statement from the introduction to "Wives and Concubines" both illustrates Su Tong's particular approach to fiction and is characteristic of the contemporary writers of experimental fiction: "My own particular failing is that I am always buried in the minor details of the life of the past but lack any plans for the future. The realm of art is a kind of light; it may be bright or it may be dark; it may exist or it may not. The world that I hope to attain has several elements; I hope for naturalness, simplicity, peacefulness, and breadth; I also hope for abundance, complication, and multiple changes. All these elements have one aspect in common: they must be purely artistic" (10). It is hard to understand just what Su Tong means by *simplicity* and *peacefulness,* but a short discussion of the three novellas included in "Wives and Concubines" should demonstrate the breadth of his vision and the abundance, complication, and great variability of his imagination. The naturalness of his language could only be conveyed in an excellent translation.

"Wives and Concubines" contains a trilogy of novellas which Chinese critics have called a fictional "family history" and in Western terms could be considered a form of "historiographic metafiction."[15] The metafictional dimension is maintained throughout, as the narrator frequently interrupts to tell the readers that he "does not know" what he has imaginatively narrated, or he "knows" something, or he "must" put some character in or take some character out of the "family history." He repeatedly uses "it is said" and also variations of a phrase like "grandfathers told the grandsons."

The first story, "Nineteen Thirty-Four Escape" ("Yi jiu san si nian de taowang"), is told by a first-person narrator who introduces himself paradoxically by saying "I am my father's son; I am not called Su Tong" (16). He also says that he is given to studying his own shadow and that he once tried unsuccessfully to escape from his father's shadow. His father's shadow extends from the family's rural origins to the city in which they now live. After these preliminary introductions, the narrator proceeds to narrate the events of 1934, a "year of calamity," of a cholera epidemic in his "old home," Maple Tree Village. The year was followed in 1935 by a flood; it was also the year his father was born to his grandmother, née Jiang, and stolen away (taken to the city where the family now lives) by "the little woman Huanzi," mistress of the narrator's grandfather Chen Baonian. Perhaps it is only a coincidence that 1934 was also the year of the Chinese Communist Party's Long March. Perhaps not.

At the end of the story the narrator says, "What I have narrated is really only a story of escape" (77). There are many escapes: he, at nineteen, escapes into the city. His grandfather Chen Baonian escapes to the city and grows rich running a bamboo handicraft store, also avoiding the cholera epidemic in the countryside. His father escapes the cholera that killed off his five brothers and sisters. His uncle Dog Pup escapes to the city to be with his father Chen Baonian. His grandmother Jiang escapes her life of poverty by giving herself to a lecherous old landlord, Chen Wenzhi, who had once before kidnapped her and tossed her in the Pool of Corpses to die; thus she escapes death twice.

Through his narration of a cholera epidemic, the hunger and poverty of the rural people, the venality of the men, the concubinage of the women, and the inveterate will to survival of his grandmother (symbol of the Chinese race as a whole), who saved his father and thus their family line from plague and famine and who eventually married a lecherous old landlord, all without the slightest mention of the glorious history of the revolutionary party, Su Tong's fictional history gives a new meaning to "the minor details of the life of the past." This new meaning is either totally unrelated to or in complete opposition to the dominant discourse of the past forty-two years.

Set in Maple Tree Village from 1948 to 1950, the second story of "Wives and Concubines," "Opium Poppy Family" ("Yingshu zhi jia"), presents both characters and incidents that testify to Su Tong's abundance of imagination. The carefully and strikingly delineated characters include Liu Laoxia, landlord and opium grower; his "son" Liu Chencao (really the natural son of their hired hand Chen Mao); his daughter Liu Suzi; his real son, a mentally retarded idiot named Chen

Yanyi; his brother Liu Laoxin; his wife, the Cat-Eyed Woman who was probably murdered by him or his concubine, the ex-prostitute Cui Huahua, mother of Chencao by Chen Mao; Chen Mao, the hired hand who aspires to be a rural revolutionary; the rural bandit Jiang Long, Chencao's former schoolmate Jiang Tianhong; and the revolutionary land-reform leader and communist cadre Lu Fang, also Chencao's former schoolmate.

Told by a third-person omniscient narrator, the story relates the decline of a southern landlord family whose land is totally devoted to the cultivation of opium poppies. Chencao is forced by his crafty, greedy, and totally unscrupulous "father" to leave school and come home to work and inherit the land. He hates the opium business, is so allergic to the smell of opium that it sends him into fits of itching, and longs nostalgically to return to school and a civilized, genteel life. That is not to be, however, and a major element of "Opium Poppy Family" is his progressive decline into decadence as he is forced to adapt to a life he never wanted. In a fit of anger, and in self-defense, he kills his crazy and always hungry half-brother Yanyi. In 1948 he reluctantly receives the keys to the grain storage bins, a symbol of his ancestors' patrimony, because his "father" is aging. He immediately begins to squander the family fortune by giving land away to the tenants. He hates his natural father Chen Mao but does not know why Chen has a strange effect on him. As the revolution approaches, his sister is taken away and raped for three days and three nights by the local bandit Jiang Long.

When the revolution comes, Chencao knows the opium trade is over; at that point he starts to eat opium and to decline into a dreamlike state. During the land-reform campaign Chen Mao, newly made an agricultural cadre, rapes Chencao's sister; she commits suicide after charging Chencao to kill Chen Mao. Chencao finally kills his real father Chen Mao, shooting him once in the genitals and once in the head; he dies from the head wound, but his genitals are not shot off. The land-reform leader Lu Fang then shoots Chencao dead as he lies in an opium stupor in a crock of opium powder. Just before he dies Chencao utters an awful prediction: "I'm going to be born into the world again." The vicious cycle of Chinese history is going to be repeated despite what the official ideology says about the ultimately progressive nature of that history.

The final novella in the trilogy, "A Profusion of Wives and Concubines" ("Qi qie chengqun"), is the story of Lotus, a nineteen-year-old schoolgirl who becomes the fourth wife of Chen Zuoqian, a rich and raunchy fifty-year-old whose family is on the decline, although we are never told how it becomes so rich in the first place. In one year she goes from being Chen's most favored concubine to being rejected and going insane. Her insanity has two causes. The first is a lack of love or, more specifically, sex, something she enjoyed very much until the old man grew impotent. She prudishly rejects his whispered invitations to perform kinky sex. The second is the more immediate cause. Looking out her bedroom window early one morning, she sees the family servants drown Chen's third wife Meishan in a well in the back courtyard for having an affair with a local doctor. The well is specially built for the purpose of disposing of any of the Chen family wives or concubines who commit the unpardonable crime of adultery. The story ends on the day that Chen Zuoqian's new wife (his fifth) arrives at the family compound. Noticing Lotus's strange behavior, she asks the servants about her and is told, "She was originally the fourth wife; something's wrong with her mind." She listens and then is told that Lotus is saying, "I won't jump, I won't jump, she says she won't jump into the well" (230). The circular ending of this story also seems to imply that the terrible family history of Chinese women will also continue into the present era.

The eighteen short stories of "The Sad Dance" continue to probe the sexual and psychological aspects of life in a highly imaginative and often shocking fashion. I will mention only three of them here.

The prepubescent I-narrator of "Breaking Away in a Coaster" ("Cheng hualunche yuan qu") arrives late for the first day of school on September 1st because he has discovered that his little brother has broken his coaster. At Red Flag Middle School an ugly girl classmate seated next to him has her first menstruation in class, and the teacher blames him and makes him leave the classroom. He chases a white rabbit into an old warehouse and blunders into the local party secretary and the music teacher making love on the ground. Then he runs into Shorty Zhang, who takes him to watch—actually to participate in—a fight between two rival gangs. There is no overt mention of the Cultural Revolution; this is just ordinary rural teen violence of the 1970s. The narrator then tries to save the beautiful but insane wife of their next-door neighbor when she runs into the river naked to the waist and tries to commit suicide; she does this so often, usually with her clothes on, that they are all used to it. His father has to save both of them when the woman wraps her arms around him so he cannot swim. At that point he goes to have his coaster repaired by the eighteen-year-old Cat Head, the best coaster maker in town, probably an unemployed youth. He peers through Cat Head's window and catches him masturbating. Some time later Cat Head's mother tells him Cat Head said he has a score to settle with him, but he blurts out naïvely that he did not see anything. Just then news

arrives that Cat Head has been killed by a car when his coaster went out of control. Cat Head is the best coaster driver in town, his death is highly suspect, and there is a hint of suicide due to shame at being caught masturbating. In the last scene the young man has a dream in which his coaster drives far away on a deserted road, which I would interpret as breaking away into the imagined freedom of adulthood.

The I-narrator of "Reminiscence of Mulberry Grove" ("Sangyuan liunian") remembers when he was fifteen he was a go-between for a tough older boy named Xiao Di, who struck up a relationship with a beautiful girl named Cinnabar Jade. Following the older boy's example, he also tried to have a relationship with a girl named Xinxin, his first sexual relationship, but he failed. After Cinnabar Jade became pregnant by Xiao Di, she and another boy named Fuzzy Head were found dead in a lovers' embrace. Cinnabar Jade had tooth marks on her face where Fuzzy Head bit her. How they died is not stated, but there is an indication they were killed by adults or committed suicide. Some time later, when he returns from the Harbin, where his parents are sent to work, the narrator sees the now-pregnant Xinxin, and he remarks to himself that he never could figure out what "that bitch" (gou nüren) was all about.

The I-narrator of "A Strange Visitor" ("Guai ke") tells of a beautiful girl from the local fruit store, whom he and every other young man was naturally in love with. She is raped by the local tough, Third Hegemon, who has recently returned from a labor-reform farm. Soon after that, a one-eyed stranger comes into the fruit stand, sits down, and eats two apples. When the young woman asks him what else he wants, he replies "an eye" (yanjing), but she thinks he means "eyeglasses" (yanjing, different tone). Later that day, when Third Hegemon comes in, the stranger shouts "An eye!" and attacks him, but Third Hegemon beats him off. The woman then believes Third Hegemon must have put the man's eye out, but Third Hegemon swears he's never seen the stranger before. One night a few days later, the stranger comes up the stairs of the fruit shop, attacks the woman with a knife, and puts out her eye. Third Hegemon comes in and strikes the stranger in his one good eye, whereupon the stranger heaves a sigh of relief. In the denouement the woman goes on to work at another fruit stand and has nothing more to do with Third Hegemon. The narrator's final comment is: "I think men and women for the most part share the same common experiences, but men have absolutely no comprehension of how women come to be women" (75).

I cannot offer any ultimate interpretation of these stories at this time, but I hope that this brief survey of the best of contemporary Chinese fiction has both convinced readers that Chinese fiction has certainly taken its place in the march of world fiction and whetted their appetite for more of it in English translation.

Michael S. Duke, Summer 1991

[1] Jay Parini, "The Land of Oz," *New York Times Magazine,* 14 April 1991, p. 46.

[2] This literary resurgence attracted a tremendous amount of Western scholarly interest, resulting in the publication of a number of anthologies in English translation. Among them are Michael S. Duke, ed., *Contemporary Chinese Literature: An Anthology of Post-Mao Fiction and Poetry* (Armonk, N.Y., Sharpe, 1985) and *Worlds of Modern Chinese Fiction: Chinese Short Stories and Novellas from the People's Republic, Taiwan, and Hong Kong* (Armonk, N.Y., Sharpe, 1991). Several conferences have been held on this body of work. One conference volume of critical articles (Jeffrey C. Kinkley, *After Mao,* Cambridge, Ma., Harvard University Press, 1985) and one overall survey of the period from 1978 through the spring of 1984 (Michael S. Duke, *Blooming and Contending,* Bloomington, Indiana University Press, 1985) have been published. Besides my own books, the following English works have been published in the 1980s: Helen Siu and Zelda Stern, eds. & trs., *Mao's Harvest: Voices from China's New Generation* (Oxford University Press, 1983); Mason Wang, ed., *Perspectives in Contemporary Chinese Literature* (Green River Review, 1983); Perry Link, *Stubborn Weeds: Popular and Controversial Chinese Literature After the Cultural Revolution* (Indiana University Press, 1983), *Roses and Thorns: The Second Blooming of the Hundred Flowers in Chinese Fiction, 1979–1980* (University of California Press, 1984), and *People or Monsters? Reportage and Stories of Present-day Chinese Society* (Indiana University Press, 1983); Lee Yee, *The New Realism: Writings from China After the Cultural Revolution* (Hippocrene, 1983); and Jeanne Tai, ed. & tr., *Spring Bamboo: A Collection of Contemporary Chinese Short Stories* (New York, Random House, 1989).

[3] Ah Cheng, "Qi wang" (The Chess Master), *Shanghai Wenxue,* 1984, no. 7.

[4] Li Tuo (as edited by Yu Xiaoxing), "Haiwai Zhongguo zuojia taolunhui jiyao" (Brief Record of Overseas Chinese Writers' Seminar), *Jintian,* 1990, no. 2, pp. 94–103.

[5] Ah Cheng, "Shu wang" (The King of Trees), *Zhongguo Zuojia,* 1985, no. 1; and "Haizi wang" (The King of Children), *Renmin Wenxue,* 1985, no. 2, pp. 4–19. All three novellas and several short stories are in *Qi wang* (The Chess Master), Beijing, 1985. See Bonnie McDougall, *Three Kings,* London, Collins Harvill, 1990.

[6] Wang Zengqi, "Shou jie" (Ordination), in *Wang Zengqi duanpian xiaoshuo xuan,* Beijing, Beijing Chubanshe, 1982, pp. 195–218.

[7] Han Shaogong, *Youhuo* (Temptations), Changsha, Hunan Wenyi Chubanshe, 1986, pp. 155–99.

[8] "Touming de hong luobo" (The Crystal Carrot), "Ku he" (Dry River), and "Baigou qiuqianjia" (White Dog and the Swings) are all reprinted in Mo Yan, *Touming de hong luobo* (The Crystal Carrot), Beijing, Zuojia Chubanshe, 1986, pp. 136–201, 213–29, and 265–90 respectively; "Huanle" (Happiness) is in *Renmin Wenxue,* 1987, nos. 1–2, pp. 6–42.

[9] Mo Yan, *Hong gaoliang jiazu* (The Red Sorghum Clan), Beijing Jiefangjun Chubanshe, 1987. Parts of "Red Sorghum" and "Sor-ghum Wine" formed the background for the 1988 film *Red Sorghum,* for which Mo Yan wrote the screenplay.

[10] Mo Yan, *Tiantang suantai zhi ge* (Paradise County Garlic Song), Beijing, 1988. Howard Goldblatt will be bringing out a translation of *Red Sorghum* in late 1991 and of *Garlic Song* in 1992.

[11] For a full analysis of this novel, see Michael S. Duke, "Paradise County: Mo Yan's *Tiantang suantai zhi ge* (1988) and Its May Fourth Precursors," in Ellen Widmer and David Der-wei Wang, eds., *From May Fourth to June Fourth,* forthcoming from Harvard University Press.

[12] Zhaxidawa, "Xizai pishengkou shang de hun" (Soul Tied to the Knots on a Leather Cord), *Xizang Wenxue* (Tibetan Literature), 1985, no. 1. Reprinted in Ah Cheng et al., eds., *1985 xiaoshuo zai Zhongguo,* Beijing, Zhongguo Wenlian Chuban Gongsi, 1986, pp. 1–24. Translated in Jeanne Tai, ed. & tr., *Spring Bamboo.*

[13] Linda Hutcheon, *Narcissistic Narrative: The Metafictional Paradox,* London, Methuen, 1984 (first published 1980), pp. 1–2.

[14] Su Tong, *Qi qie chengqun* (Wives and Concubines), Taipei, Yuanliu, 1990; *Shangxin de wudao* (A Sad Dance), Taipei, Yuanliu, 1991.

[15] Meng Yue, "Su Tong de 'jiashi' yu 'lishi' xiezuo" (Su Tong's 'Family History' and 'History' Writing), *Jintian,* 1990, no. 2, pp. 84–93. Linda Hutcheon, *A Poetics of Postmodernism,* New York, Routledge, 1988.

Fresh Flowers Abloom Again: Chinese Literature on the Rebound

Slightly more than a year ago I reported on the reemergence in China of the literary periodical *Wenyi Bao* (Literary and Arts Gazette), two years after the fall of the Gang of Four and the termination of the decade-long Cultural Revolution.[1] It was a signal event, one which prompted expressions of relief and optimism by observers throughout the world and by China's literary establishment. Much has happened in Chinese literary circles in the intervening period, most of which serves to bear out this optimism and redirect attention to the literary activities of the world's most populous nation.

Of utmost significance was the convening in Beijing of the Fourth Congress of Chinese Writers and Artists from 30 October to 16 November 1979, nineteen years after the previous one.[2] More than 3,200 writers and artists representing the eleven affiliate organizations of the China Federation of Literary and Art Circles (Chinese Writers Association, Chinese Dramatists Association, et cetera) were in attendance, many of them appearing in public for the first time in over a decade. During my recent trip to China I was told that many tearful reunions occurred as the Congress got underway, with the standard greeting being, "So, you're still alive!" More than a hundred writers and artists did not survive the Cultural Revolution; their names were solemnly intoned by the dramatist Yang Hansheng during a speech that constituted the emotional high point of the gathering.

Following the opening addresses by the Vice-Chairman of the Federation, novelist Mao Dun, and Vice-Premier Deng Xiaoping, the major address was given by Zhou Yang, who was subsequently elected as the new Chairman of the Federation. Over the following two weeks the most important speeches were analyzed and debated during meetings by the affiliate organizations. Further speeches and reports were given,[3] and the Congress was closed following the revision of charters, the election of officers and a final address by the octogenarian playwright Xia Yan.

Among the highlights of Vice-Premier Deng's speech were his implied refutation of Mao Zedong's line that literature and the arts are merely tools of class struggle, his call for a broadening of themes to include views from both positive and negative perspectives, and an admonition to return to literary (as opposed to or in addition to) political criteria. Zhou Yang went into greater detail during a four-hour speech in which he advocated a return to realism and a rejection of revolutionary romanticism (which held sway during the Cultural Revolution); he recommended that Mao's literary policies, first outlined in his famous "Talks at the Yenan Forum on Literature and the Arts" in 1942, be subjected to an intense reevaluation, that writers be given new freedoms and that all forms of dogmatism be abolished. His speech was hotly debated, with the majority of attendees either agreeing with his recommendations or faulting him for not going far enough.[4]

The first major evaluation of the Congress occurred during a playwrights' conference held in Beijing in January-February 1980, at which the newly elevated General Secretary of the Central Committee of the Chinese Communist Party, Hu Yaobang, repeated the official view that Mao's literary policies need to be reevaluated and liberalized. In speaking for the Central Committee, Hu made a number of concrete proposals regarding the selection of themes, the production of more and better literary works, methods of swelling the ranks of writers, and writers' responsibilities. He seemed most intent on reassuring members of the literary community that debate was to be encouraged, that society is better served by honesty and integrity than by rigid dogma, slogans and the mechanical application of current political orthodoxies in literary works. The most enthusiastic receptions followed his repeated guarantees of a more humanitarian position by the Party in regard to writers and artists.

During his report Hu stressed China's backwardness, emphasized the important role of intellectuals in improving upon this situation and made repeated references to the fallibility of Mao. He gave official sanction for writers to continue with exposé literature, as long as its goal continued to be constructive and supportive of modernization; and in this vein he promised a policy of noninterference in literary matters by the government and the Party.

In echoing a slogan that appeared in the mid-1950s, Hu and other literary figures called for a renewal of the "Hundred Flowers Blooming" campaign.[5] In celebration of this trend, the Shanghai Literature and Arts Publishing House brought out a collection of stories from that period; entitled *Chong Fang de Xianhua* (Fresh Flowers Abloom Again), the anthology is comprised exclusively of stories that were critical of government policy and societal trends and were subsequently labeled as "poisonous weeds." Many of the authors of these relabeled "fresh flowers" spent fifteen years or more paying the penalty of overt criticism.

▪ ▪ ▪

As a result of the Congress and the follow-up speech by Hu Yaobang, cautious optimism seems to be called for in the treatment of writers and intellectuals and in the upgrading of literature in China over the coming years. What began in 1976 with the fall of the Gang of Four and led to the gathering in 1979 seems to have produced a spirit of cooperation in the 1980s between two historical antagonists—government and the literary community—and the immediate future holds some promise.

In literary terms, things have improved considerably in recent months. Although it is too early to expect a rash of high-quality writings in either the creative or scholarly vein, progress is being made. The immediate post-Gang-of-Four trend of accusational literary exercises, long on emotion and short on artistic sophistication, known collectively as "Scar Literature" (shanghen wenxue) and constituting a national cleansing of the soul, has now run its course, and the writers have begun to experiment with a multitude of literary forms and devices. The greatest achievements to date have been in the short story, journalistic writings and drama, the latter including movie and television scripts. Few substantial novels have been produced, and those that have appeared to date are mostly of a historical nature, focusing on other than contemporary events.[6]

Literary scholarship and criticism show indications of renewed vigor, although conservatism still holds sway. It is no longer a problem of breadth (which characterized the Cultural Revolution period, when the acceptable objects of study were severely limited), but of approach. It appears that the scholars and critics are allowing the creative writers to test the winds before setting their own course; in the meantime standard Marxist esthetic criteria continue to be applied, with the concomitant neglect of artistry still in evidence. Nonetheless, it is encouraging to note that previously proscribed areas of activity, such as literature from the 1930s and contemporary literature from Taiwan, are now attracting the attention of scholars and critics; and if the results thus far published still prove unsatisfying, it is at least a beginning.

The overall impression I gained from my recent visit and the discussions I had with literary figures of all ages and from diverse spheres of activity was that, although no one feels that past losses can be recouped, renewed dedication to literary ideals and an affirmation of the role of writers are essential to the modernization of China. All are bending their efforts toward producing high-quality, socially significant literature and literary scholarship in the shortest possible period of time. In this they are being aided by the long dormant publishing industry.

The current amount of activity in publishing circles astonishes not only those of us who have long thirsted for more and better creative writings as well as critical and historical works, but writers in China as well, who are being virtually swamped with requests for manuscripts in an already highly competitive industry. For all it is an unprecedented boon. The writers have reacquired vehicles for expression and experimentation and are now assured of increasingly lucrative remuneration for their labors. The standard rate of payment for literary publications currently is Renminbi (RMB) $9 (U.S. $6.30) per thousand words, running to nearly double that figure for the best-known writers, such as the octogenarian novelist Ba Jin (Pa Chin).

Book publishing has, until recently, been somewhat less attractive, but as of 1 July 1980, royalties are being paid in place of standard fees—this in a country where the number of volumes in a single printing often runs into the hundreds of thousands. A popular, energetic writer can now make a living with his pen, earning perhaps as much as RMB $5,000 (U.S. $3,500) annually from magazine publication and book royalties. Another indication of official encouragement of literary activities is the paid vacation (for up to several months or longer) offered established writers as well as those who want to try their hand at writing for the first time. One hopes that these measures will speed up the process of fostering a new generation of young writers to fill the void created by a decade of anti-cultural fanaticism.[7]

Even the most casual observer of the contemporary Chinese literary scene cannot but be overwhelmed by the abundance of literary magazines and journals now being published in China. The Chinese phrase "like the sprouting of bamboo after a spring rain" certainly applies here. The precise number as of this writing is 108, a figure that is increasing monthly (this does not include the general-interest publications, which usually incorporate a section on literature and the arts). But that only tells part of the story, for many of the periodicals tend to increase their frequency once they are fairly well established. Two cases in point: the monthly *Wenyi Bao,* which is now in its third year following a resumption of publication in mid-1978, will soon become a semimonthly journal, partly to lessen the backlog of articles and partly as a means of shortening the time lag between the appearance of creative works and the publication of reviews and critical articles; another major new periodical, *Xin Wenxue Shiliao* (Historical Materials on Modern Literature), began publication as an occasional series but has now become a quarterly and could conceivably be published even more frequently in the future. As a result, the amount of available material is increasing on two separate fronts (three, if one considers the expansion of literary coverage in general-interest publications), and one is hard put to keep abreast of all the developments.

The distribution of literary periodicals, most of which are exportable, is based in part upon geographical considerations: each province and autonomous region publishes a literary monthly under the auspices of the Chinese Writers Association; in addition, a literary journal is published by the representative organization of each provincial capital and several other major cities. To these are added journals issued by universities, scholastic institutions (such as the various bodies that comprise the Chinese Academy of Social Sciences), publishing houses (such as the People's Literature Publishing House in Beijing) and national literary organizations (such as the Writers Association, which, in addition to *Wenyi Bao,* publishes *Xin Guancha* [The New Observer] and will soon begin publication of *Xiaoshuo Xuankan,* a monthly collection of the best fiction that has appeared throughout the country). Finally, there are specialty publications such as *Xiaoshuo Yuebao* (Short Story Monthly), a new magazine that will find itself in competition with *Xiaoshuo Xuankan,* and *Sanwen* (Prose), a monthly journal published in Dalian (Dairen). Although the average printing of literary journals is about 150,000 copies per issue, some run as high as a million.

The subject matter and types of China's literary magazines are equally diverse. Journals such as *Renmin Wenxue* (People's Literature) and *Shikan* (Poetry) are devoted exclusively to creative writing, while others, like *Wenyi Bao* and *Wenxue Pinglun* (Literary Criticism), are almost exclusively critical and theoretical. Certainly the majority of the provincial journals emphasize local creative works, but they will publish other types of articles and essays that deal with some aspect of their provincial literary scene. Specialty publications, generally monthly or quarterly, are designed for studies of classical or foreign literature, while others are devoted to folk literature, juvenile literature, drama and the like.

Perhaps of greatest interest to scholars involved in research on modern Chinese literature are the several journals devoted to historical materials, of which *Xin Wenxue Shiliao* is the most important. Beginning publication for internal consumption only (as is so often the case with such magazines and books, once a copy reaches Hong Kong, it is quickly reproduced and made available internationally) and issued irregularly, it is now a quarterly available for export; the same can probably be expected to occur in the cases of similar regional publications. Included in such periodicals are the reminiscences of literary figures from the 1920s, 1930s and beyond, as well as historical documents and analyses that have surfaced only in the past few years, and extensive bibliographies, all of which are invaluable aids to contemporary research.

Magazines, journals and books from China are inexpensive and, although occasionally somewhat poorly printed and generally slow in getting off the presses, carefully edited and extremely broad in scope. The quantity published is invariably inadequate to the demand, so that book buying is an activity that relies heavily on punctuality and determination. This holds true for reprintings of older works as well as first printings, the latter of which now include science fiction, novels of romance, anthologies of poetry and many other types. In particularly high demand are translations of foreign works, old and new, and works from Taiwan, where the high degree of sophistication will most likely serve as a model for younger potential writers in China.

The importance placed upon the continued, even expanded publication of literary magazines, the state goals of which are to promote the development of socialist thought among their readers and to encourage more people to choose writing as a career, was manifested by the convening of a conference of editorial workers in April-May 1980, at which Zhou Yang gave the major address. Organized by the Chinese Writers Association, the conference constituted a forum for examining the successes and failures of literary periodicals over the past three years and afforded the Central Committee yet another opportunity to express its enthusias-

tic support for publishers, editors and writers in their important work.

Even with the knowledge that shifting political winds tend to dictate the direction of literary endeavors and the degree of freedom allowed writers, artists and intellectuals, it is easy to be heartened by the renewed literary activity in China and optimistic about the prospects for the future, both in terms of artistic excellence and the increasing societal influence of dedicated writers. One cannot be faulted, however, if one finds it difficult to avoid holding one's breath, given the mercurial nature of Chinese politics.

Howard Goldblatt, Winter 1981

1   "Contemporary Chinese Literature and the New *Wenyi Bao*," *World Literature Today*, 53:4 (Autumn 1979), pp. 617–18.

2   The first Congress was held on 2 July 1949, at which time the China Federation of Literary and Art Circles was created and the Chinese Writers Association formed. The second Congress was held in September 1952, the third in July 1960. A large-scale literary forum was called by Jiang Qing (Chiang Ch'ing) in Shanghai in 1966, which ushered in the Cultural Revolution.

3   The majority of speeches and reports, with an introduction and analysis, is now being prepared under my editorship and will be available from M. E. Sharpe, Inc. sometime in 1981.

4   For further details on the Congress, see recent issues of the Beijing Foreign Languages Press monthly publication *Chinese Literature*, particularly nos. 2, 3 and 4 of 1980.

5   Mao Zedong's slogan "Let a hundred flowers bloom and a hundred schools contend" ushered in a brief period of open criticism of the Party. It was quickly and abruptly terminated by an anti-rightist campaign that witnessed the end of many literary careers.

6   A sampling of recent literary works in English translation can be found in issues of *Chinese Literature* and in the following anthologies: Kai-yu Hsu, ed., *Literature of the People's Republic of China*, Bloomington, In., Indiana University Press, 1980; Lu Xinhua, Liu Xinwu, et al., *The Wounded: New Stories of the Cultural Revolution, 77–78*, Geremie Barmé and Bennett Lee, trs., Hong Kong, Joint Publ. Co., 1979; Winston L. Y. Yang and Nathan K. Mao, eds., *Stories of Contemporary China*, New York, Paragon, 1979. Two additional anthologies are in preparation and will be published by Indiana University Press.

7   At present the most active and successful creative writers, many of whom began their writing careers in the mid-1950s, are in their forties and early fifties. The older writers, who suffered most bitterly during the Cultural Revolution, are devoting most of their time and energy to the writing of personal histories.

Chinese Literature and the Nobel Prize

It is not surprising that out of the literature of a people that make up a quarter of mankind, no Nobel Prize writer has yet emerged.* Those critics and scholars of

Bei Dao *(Meulenhoff Publishers)*

modern Chinese literature who could have molded opinion have been generally apologetic that the literature cannot be judged by purely literary standards. Trained or teaching in the West for the most part, they would measure the achievement of Chinese writers against "Western" standards, whatever these might be, at the same time requiring that the literature be distinctively "Chinese," as if it could be anything else. The problem is that modern Chinese literature goes against almost all the tenets of modernism. It is not a literature that celebrates esthetic or technical excellence or the impassioned but detached contemplation of life; nor is it a literature that believes in the realm of the political and economic power play. It "makes nothing happen" (to use the famous statement that Auden makes in his elegy on Yeats), its power residing rather in analogical sublimations, in a kind of colonizing symbolization extended by the creative imagination. On the other hand, it *is* a literature *engagée,* passionately so most of the time, a literature that believes it can make things happen and insists that it cannot be read detached from the political and social turmoil of its time.

Modern Chinese literature began as a part of a general movement for reform toward the end of the last century, when such intellectual leaders as Yan Fu and Liang Qichao saw in literature a powerful weapon for

political agitation and decided to adopt it as a means for "arousing people's hearts." Literature in twentieth-century China has never relinquished this formative role. In it is felt the pulse of a great nation in transition, a transition that has brought with it all the agonies and expectations of continued national rebirth. By using literature as a means of expression, therefore, many writers have exercised great influence not only on Chinese thought but also on events.

Thus Chinese writers are keenly aware of their responsibilities as citizens of an awakening nation. No longer cherishing "dreams of the western chamber" or enjoying themselves in "the breeze in the moonlight," they bring to their writings a social consciousness and spirit of realism unmatched in any other literature. They are not averse to using literature as a powerful means of propaganda, even for the improvement of mankind. The writers are deeply moved by the spectacle of human misery around them, and their writings are restless and agitating, constantly in search not so much of new form as a new form of life.

It is arguable whether literature can be judged in purely literary terms, and the insistence in Alfred Nobel's will that the works to be rewarded should be of benefit to mankind and should display an "ideal tendency" is a recognition of the contextual nature of both literary art and its assessment. If such terms of Nobel's will are interpreted as a search for works that impress not just by artifice but also by a full expression of true feeling, not by the eloquence of rhetoric but by the eloquence derived from the mainsprings of experience, impelled by the pressure of circumstances toward some saving vision, then there is no lack of modern Chinese writers worthy of the Nobel Prize in Literature.

Among twentieth-century Chinese writers, the most outstanding is undeniably Lu Xun (1881–1936). There are other writers of major importance, however, writers of whom it can be said that they have, through their writings, changed the temper of the time, bared to four billion people the truth of their soul and its poetry. In their works is revealed the major trend of a century: a revolutionary cataclysm which has wrecked the foundations of Chinese society and uprooted family and human ties and which, as soon as it has spent its strength, leaves behind a nightmare of violence, horror, and despair, with no dawn glimmering but an obstinate hope, an undying vision.

It has been said that the shortest route to China is Lu Xun. Lu Xun's madman, Ah Q, and Kong Iji[1] have become deathless images in the national imagination of the wretchedness, sickness, and pathos of the Chinese soul, enmeshed in a mind-set of stultifying and corrupting cultural and moral habits that seduce through fear and ignorance. Characters and landscape come alive with passionate lucidity in his writings, which are also impressive in their penetration of the human psyche; but his vision of life, though bitter, is humane. He puts trust in clear perception, understanding, and compassion, though the surrounding reality that he depicts answers none of man's dreams and reflects the chaotic, selfish, dehumanizing social and ethical order that is life's condition. He is the first and probably the greatest Chinese fiction writer in the twentieth century.

Toward the last years of Lu Xun's life and in the years following, many fine writers emerged. Any assessment of twentieth-century Chinese fiction cannot ignore the achievements of Yu Dafu, Zhang Tianyi, Xia Jun, Shen Congwen, Duan-mu Hongliang, Jian Zhongshu, Bing Xin, Ding Ling, Guo Meruo, and Shi Tuo, or such vividly crafted "proletarian" works as *The Sun Shines over the Sangkan River* by Ding Ling, "Hungry Guo Su'e" by Lu Ling, and *Moving Force* by Cao Ming.[2] However, the most prominent among these writers are three diverse talents: Lao She, Mao Dun, and Ba Jin.

Lu Xun died in 1936, and by the rules of the Nobel Prize, he has long been rendered ineligible for the award. By the same token, Lao She, who was driven to suicide during the Cultural Revolution in 1966, and Mao Dun, who died in 1981, are out of the running. Both have created classics whose absence would have left an impoverishing gap in modern Chinese literature. Lao She composed some two dozen works, the first, "The Philosophy of Old Zhang," in 1928 and the last, among them the plays *Dragon-Beard Ditch* and "Teahouse," in the late fifties. Lao She is commonly viewed as a satirist; but his range is much wider, and his vision of man and society has an epical feel about it. His novels, notably *Ma and Son* and *Camel Xiangzi,*[3] are tight architectonic structures that examine, in a language that is now humorous and witty, now satirical and darktinged, but always vigorous and impassioned, and with an unswerving dramatic focus that reveals an astonishing moral and psychological acumen, the question of what makes a man what he is. Through characters that are memorably human, even though they may be studies of meanness and servitude, he depicts the atrophy of good impulses in the pursuit of material well-being, the frustration of environment and personality, the moral and physical exhaustion that attends even individual effort, thus crystallizing a generation's shame, anger, inadequacy, and yearning that still reverberates in the new writings of China today.

In contrast to Lao She, Mao Dun uses an ornate literary vocabulary to create works of great scope and tragic insight, exploring the chasm between personal commitment and reality, the discrepancy between the futility of individual effort and the general prevalence of anarchy, reflected as a caricature of purposeful action. Novels such as "Rainbow," "The Wild Roses," and *Midnight*[4] are works of sustained psychological drama enacted against a turbulent background of historical events. Change—for example, the decline of Confucian and other values—is seen as both the acting out of the corrupt force of an imprisoning past and the manifestation of fundamental human limitations, so that history and human nature collaborate, as it were, in engendering the tragic reality of the present.

Ba Jin made his literary debut in 1929 with "Destruction."[5] A prolific writer whose works are being collected into ten volumes containing his more than twenty novels, numerous short stories, essays, criticism, and travel literature, he received high critical acclaim in the forties but found himself unenviably placed between physical survival and artistic compromise when the Chinese communists took over in 1949. His reputation plunged as his readers felt betrayed when he allowed himself to be used as a propaganda tool, while his communist masters remained suspicious of his bourgeois liberal-humanist values. Nevertheless, Ba Jin remains a distinguished and significant writer. As late as 1979 he brought out a noteworthy collection of essays, *Suixiang lu,* (Random Thoughts), which glimmer with his characteristic moral fervor, passion, subdued indignation, and tender sympathy. Among these is a deeply moving recollection of his wife, a victim of the Cultural Revolution, entitled "Remembering Xiaoshan." He is reportedly completing a sequel to his "Turbulent Stream" trilogy entitled *Qun* (The Masses).

What impresses most about Ba Jin's work is its passionate idealism, yet an idealism grounded in sharply observed social structures and interactions and psychologically penetrating scrutiny of human drives and actions. In thematic range he is perhaps unrivaled; in novels such as "Destruction," the two trilogies "Turbulent Stream" and "Love Trilogy," "Fire," *Cold Nights,* "Ward No. 4," "Leisure," "Snow," and "Flame" he explores the personal conflict of individuals, the dissolution of families, the fates of miners, the horrors of war, the soul-destroying conditions in hospitals, the struggle of the little man. Though focusing on particular events of a particular period, his oeuvre surveys the worlds of the individual, the family, and society, generalizing the national predicament into a universal predicament. Admittedly, there are strong, overt social concerns in his work—the oppression of women, the tyranny of hereditary structures, the injustice and inhumanity of bureaucratic systems, the moral cowardice of intellectuals, the indifference of the social order—but it is the tragic vision of life that his writing conveys rather than the so-cial criticism it is informed by that gives it depth and memorableness. Ba Jin has been criticized for allowing his exuberance, his deeply felt humanism, and his ro-mantic-revolutionary fervor to run away with him, so that his stories are flawed by sensationalism, melodra-ma, and a lack of concern with form and technique. By the same token, however, these very qualities impart to the human fates he summons an irresistible sense of in-evitability. This feeling comes from an expression of a unique sense of history, grasped as an overwhelming, confusing, inexplicable collective experience, an experi-ence of a vividly realized present which bears with it the burden of a past felt as displacement, exile, separation, bitter betrayal, and loss. Each novel is a massive move-ment that gathers up as it goes a dense body of physical and moral details, adding particle to particle and build-ing layer upon layer with irresistible power. Ba Jin's characters often must invent their own illusions to give themselves reality, and his work attacks the convention-al values, empty language, and sterile emotion which constitute the fictions modern man uses to evade his own authenticity while centrally engaged in authenti-cating the individual's bewildering quest for a viable identity.

Modern Chinese drama and poetry have developed more slowly: the first because in its modern-day form it is completely new, with no traditional precedents or models; the second because of the long-persistent prob-lem of molding the new vernacular (baihua) into a musi-cal and expressive medium, a problem exacerbated by a genuine antitraditional fervor, the attempt to wrestle with at times overwhelming Western influences, and the need to be socially engaged. Early dramatists like Guo Meruo, Tian Han, Cao Xuesong, Hong Shen, and Ouyang Yuqian have shown the way, and among them Cao Yu is still acknowledged to be the first and foremost modern Chinese dramatist. Cao Yu's theater had been the awakener and educator of many young men and women of the thirties and forties. Dramas such as *Thun-derstorm, Sunrise,* "Wilderness," *Peking Man,* and "Meta-morphosis"[6] are works of great power and passion, fo-cusing on the decadence and corruption of the traditional Chinese morality and social system and delv-ing into unconscious, primitive emotions, but at the same time evoking characters and situations that often transcend their realistic basis to assume symbolic pro-portions. Powerful and well crafted as his plays are, however, they constitute a drama of pathos rather than of tragedy; they are so often bogged down by the influ-ence of Freudian psychology and O'Neillian symbolism that the unresolved conflict between the writer's social concerns and his artistic integrity results in melodrama,

weak characterization, and an incoherent moral view-point. Up to this day, Chinese dramatists, while groping their way in the new dramatic form, have resorted to foreign models for guidance, with Goethe, Ibsen, O'Neill, Brecht, and Miller serving as catalysts at differ-ent periods. Though there are promising dramatists writing now—Wu Zuguang, Huang Zuling, Bai Fengxi, Gao Xingjan, and Yang Jiang among them—dramatic identity is still fluid, while a complex theater has yet to develop.

In poetry, pioneers such as Zang Kejia, Tian Jian, Guo Meruo, Bian Zhilin, Xu Zhimo, Wen Yiduo, Dai Wangshu, Li Jinfa, and He Qifang have run the whole gamut of romantic, symbolist, metaphysical, bal-ladesque, didactic socialist, and enigmatic personal verse. Ai Qing, in his late seventies now, appears to be the most enduring among them, finishing his first long poem in 1935 while in prison[7] and, after an imposed silence of almost twenty years between 1957 and 1975, still writing today. His "Dayan River," a sustained narra-tive in vivid, racy, vigorous language about the struggles and sufferings of the peasant wet nurse who raised him, is still profoundly moving. At its best, his poetry has the vibrant simplicity one finds in Blake and the elegiac so-nority of Whitman, but he lacks their complexity of vi-sion, which is his great weakness as much as his strength. As exemplified in works such as "Message from Dawn," "Wilderness," "Diamond in the Snow," "The North," "Spring," and "Black Eels," his poetry draws on elements of folk literature: a lively colloquial language, sharp contrasting colors, a narrative form in which verse alternates with prose and the expressive beats of drum ballads, an epical treatment of the life of laboring people, minute observations of common ob-jects and scenes, interweaving of lyricism, sarcasm, cari-cature, and didacticism. Still, there seems to be a delib-erate avoidance of complexity of thought, so that his language is often rhetorically thin and his perspective one-dimensional. In terms of achievement in the con-text of Chinese literature, Ai Qing has perhaps gone as far as one can in exploring the poetic possibilities of the truly ordinary language spoken by men.

The fiction produced in China after the 1949 com-munist liberation has been generally dismissed as lack-ing in literary quality, written to political coercion and formula; but from the literary-historical point of view, the works of writers like Zhao Shuli, Zhou Libo, Hao Ran, Ai Wu, Du Pengcheng, and Hu Wanchun during this period form a significant corpus nonetheless, signif-icant because they mark a logical culmination of the lit-erary trend set by the earlier literature. The efforts of the earlier writers to find a language and form to evoke the new society and thereby reinvigorate the Chinese soul congeal into a literature whose sole aim becomes the celebration of the new society. In other words, earlier experiments to explore the most effective combination of fiction and reality culminate in acts of identification of fiction with reality. If such literature is minor, it is minor perhaps in a way comparable to the formulaic court poetry of the earlier Tang dynasty. Such writings turn against literature's first virtue, which is its ability to create alternative worlds. At the first signs of political liberalization, therefore, reaction sets in, resulting in a stream of interesting works. Critics, concerned more with the charting of political movements than with a genuine assessment of the quality of such works, have labeled them sequentially as "literature of the hundred flowers," "dissent literature," "literature of the wounded," "literature of introspection," and "literature of the second renaissance." Undoubtedly, there are writers worthy of notice who have emerged, and names like Lu Xinhua, Wang Meng, Liu Binyan, Bai Hua, Zhang Jie, Shen Yung, Wu Zuguang, Shen Rong, Jian Zilong, Feng Jicai, Gu Hua, Zhang Xinsin, Zhang Xianliang, Wang Zhaojun, and Li Cunbao have come to international attention. None of them is of undisputed achievement, however. Their writings are marked by seriousness of purpose and commitment, often moving and passionate as they explore the huge backlog of social, political, and interpersonal problems left over since the founding of the communist new society. There is subtle and penetrating character portrayal in Shen Rong, effective pathos in the depiction of situations and individuals in Zhang Ji. The old masters too enjoy a revival during this period, so that Feng Jicai's stories, for example, remind one of Mao Dun in his less-bitter moments, whereas Gu Hua's idyllic work "The Log Cabin Overgrown with Creepers" recalls Shen Congwen.[8] On the whole, however, the works of these writers are of uneven literary quality, focused as they usually are on a cause of human suffering that is fatalistic, lying outside the characters ultimately, in the political and social chaos of the time. Thus, moving as much of the literature is, it lacks tragic scope and a sense of authenticity.

At various times, writers like Wang Meng and Bai Hua have been mentioned as possible candidates for the Nobel Prize. Wang Meng is a writer best known for his experiments in developing refreshing perspectives in narrative art, and stories such as "Eye of the Night" ("Ye de yen"), "Butterfly" ("Hudie"), "Voices of Spring" ("Chun zhi sheng"), and "Dreams of the Sea" ("Hai de meng")[9] show skillful control of composition. He undercuts and juxtaposes chronological events in montagelike fashion, uses narrative ellipses and compression, and employs extensive monologue and plotless narration to explore the inner feelings and thoughts of his

characters or to filter external description and events through their consciousness. Bai Hua's compositions— "Bitter Love" ("Kulian") being a typical example[10]—similarly display sophisticated narrative technique in the use of allusion, flashback, symbolic landscape and situations, and complicated plot structure. Both these writers are intensely concerned with the expression of humanistic values and the struggle for human dignity, but their work is characterized more by sense and sincerity than by vibrancy and memorableness. The characters who inhabit their work are often not fully developed, caught in shrill gestures, or are stock figures lacking independent vitality. Like much of the literature of the seventies and eighties, their writings seem content (to use a phrase from Proust) with "describing things, offering a summary of their lives and surfaces."[11]

For political more than for literary reasons, one suspects, the literature written in China in the late seventies and eighties has received a great deal of attention in the West, and not a small degree of misplaced adulation. Amid this scholarly euphoria it has generally been overlooked that writers working outside China— notably in Taiwan—have been producing similar, if not more interesting work for quite a number of years. In terms of technical sophistication and mastery, depth of feeling, range of intellect, and understanding of their milieu and of the human situation, writers like Chen Ruoxi, Zhang Ailing, Qi Dengsheng, Wang Zhenhe, Huang Chunming, Wang Wenxing, Chen Yingzhen, Chang Xiguo, XiXi, and Li Yongping certainly rival any of the fictionists writing in China today.

A leading talent, not only among writers in Taiwan but also among writers in China, is Bai Xianyong. A political ideology built around the myth of eventual recovery of the mainland and tacitly put to rest only after the death of Chiang Kai-shek in 1975 generated a sense of impermanence and unreality on which writers in Taiwan have built a literature of nostalgia and exile. Bai Xianyong's work must be seen in such a context. What is remarkable is that his stories, depicting as they do the spiritual, moral, and psychological exile of mainlanders who fled to Taiwan when the communists took over China, become profoundly vivid symbolizations of modern man trapped in his memory and dreams, wandering ghosts whose yearning for actualization of their true selves is defeated as much by themselves as by the impersonal force of history. His figures seek desperately to reshape the world they inhabit, and it is the gulf between this factitious world and the one that threatens to pull them into its coercive influence that generates the anxious energy of his work. Through daring juxtaposition of echoes and allusions with a vivid vernacular "gutter" language and dialects, one hears not only the modern but the classical masters, the voice of China's present and past. It is paradoxically this insistence on the historicity of his fiction, which combines an almost documentary precision of detail in characterization and setting with a poetic evocation of the characters as usual types, that makes each of his stories unique, firmly embedded in a specific historical context yet rendering a universal stereotype of endlessly repetitive human behavior and fate. In the history of postwar Chinese literature, his "Taibei Characters"[12] may well be comparable in importance to Joyce's *Dubliners*. This work, together with the collections of short stories "The Exiled Celestial," "The New Yorkers," "Nightmare in the Park," and the novels "In the Realm of Our Kingdom" and "The Illegitimate," make up some of the best fiction produced by any writer since the May Fourth era.

The poetry scene in both China and Taiwan has been in greater ferment since 1949. As the novelty of Western modernism wears off and the indigenous classical tradition is rediscovered, poetry in Taiwan has taken on a new musicality and depth of timbre. Over the last twenty-five years several accomplished voices have emerged: notably Yang Mu, Le Fu, Zheng Chouyu, Ya Xian, Zhou Mandie, Zhang Cuo, Wu Sheng, Luo Qing, Wu Teliang, and Xiang Yang. The unofficial poet laureate among them, in the eyes of many readers outside China, is Yu Guangzhong, a prolific poet who has been actively writing since his first poems came out in the early fifties.[13] Yu is a combination of many paradoxes. He is one of the most traditional of living Chinese poets yet the most experimental, and each of his volumes of poetry shows some new development; he lives on the classics yet is steeped in his own time and is thoroughly familiar with contemporary English and American literature, of which he has produced some able translations; he is deeply patriotic in sentiment yet cosmopolitan in outlook. His poetry is nurtured by a vibrant grafting of classical verse onto a living vernacular, richly musical and complex yet thoroughly accessible. He is interested in what lyric poets of all ages have been interested in—encounters with nature, reflections on the human condition, time and death, and the meaning of existence—but the one great note in his poetry is man's essential solitude. It is the solitude of loneliness, alienation, and exile, but also the solitude of meditation, peace, and purity of heart. Above all, Yu's poetry describes the solitude of essence. Man is alone in his very ability to experience and to know, but through the music he makes in language, he turns that loneliness into a celebration of his uniqueness and the uniqueness of each of his creations: nature, love, companionship, culture, society, country, history. The pathos of time's

changes is always with him, as is the maddening crassness of his destructive nature; but the ability to make music, to utter the possibility of withstanding the pressure of existence, subsumes all.

In China it is only from the early 1970s that we see poetry taking fresh energy. Among the promising personalities that have come to notice—Gu Cheng, Yuan Kejia, Shu Ting, Mang Ke, Li Ying, Ye Wenfu, Yan Li, Zhu Ziqi, Ke Yan, and Yang Lian—Bei Dao is one of the most outstanding and exciting talents. Although Bei Dao has not published very much,[14] his poetry has generated a great deal of discussion and controversy among literary and official circles in China.[15] His work, like that of his modern Chinese predecessors, displays what C. T. Hsia calls "an obsession with China . . . [and the] nightmare images of [the] national situation,"[16] but it projects that "obsession" from an intensely introverted vision and in a medium that is dense, even obscure, in thought yet vibrantly lucid in evocation—modes of composition that depart significantly from the orthodox esthetics of most of his contemporaries. In his successful poems this tension between a transparent outer form, which is often painfully realistic and actual, and a self-centered inverted vision of personal fulfillment traps the reader in a double bind, suggesting that it cannot be resolved in its own terms but only by transcending both toward some new, now shared vision. Bei Dao does not always succeed, however. The tension sometimes breaks down, as in a poem like "Love," so that the experience is trapped within the text or a psychological release is forced through the rhetorical situation, putting the authenticity of the experience in question. One suspects that these scintillatingly dark, somber, lyric elegies mark but an important stage in Bei Dao's promising career; for it is difficult to see how, with an increasingly restricted emotional and stylistic range, he can avoid working himself into a poetic cul-de-sac.

Twentieth-century Chinese literature has suffered from the grave vicissitudes of its social and political circumstances, it is true, but not least, one might perhaps add, also from the benign neglect, misplaced motivation, and eager patronization of its own scholars. We need more critics like Jaroslav Prusek and C. T. Hsia, who can approach their subjects with respect, enthusiasm, a confident sense of literary history, a humanistic catholicity, and a dispassionate, disciplined assessment of the achievements. There is no lack of creative talent, and talent of the first order, in twentieth-century Chinese literature; but we require critics who are willing to approach these writers as writers (even if writers with a mission) and not as ideological polemicists or political dissenters. It does not do to elevate a writer because he dares to speak against the political system, however oppressive, just as it does not do to dismiss one because his writing is narrowly ideological without undertaking an adequate critical analysis and providing explication of the esthetic grounds for doing so. For a proper assessment of contemporary Chinese literature, we need critics who are not ideologically biased one way or the other and who can bring themselves to validate a literature that is highly contextualized, a literature whose structure, against the accepted current post-structuralist critical tenet, is not self-reflexive, an exciting commentary on its own epistemological problematics, but which is in fact highly referential of the extratextual world.

John Kwan-Terry, Summer 1989

This essay, written and typeset prior to the events of 4 June 1989 in Beijing, continues the discussion begun in WLT's Spring 1988 "Nobel Prize Symposium II: Choices and Omissions 1967–1987" (62:2, pp. 197–241). For reference, see also William Riggan, "The Swedish Academy and the Nobel Prize in Literature: History and Procedure," WLT 55:3 (Summer 1981), pp. 399–405.—Ed.

1 *Nahan* (The Outcry), Beijing, 1923, a collection of short stories containing "The Diary of a Madman," "Kong Iji," and "The True Story of Ah Q." Lu Xun's short fictional work includes *Panghuang* (Hesitation), Beijing, 1925; *Yecao* (Wild Grass), Beijing, 1926; *Zhaohua xishi* (Morning Flowers Picked in the Evening), Beijing, 1927; *Gushi xinbian* (Old Legends Retold), Shanghai, 1936. His stories have been widely translated: e.g., *The Complete Stories of Lu Xun*, Yang Xianyi and Gladys Yang, trs., Bloomington, Indiana University Press, 1981; for a review, see WLT 57:1 (Winter 1983), p. 170.

2 Ding Ling, *Taiyang zhaozai Sangganhe shang* (The Sun Shines over the Sangkan River), Shanghai, 1949; translated into English by Yang Xianyi and Gladys Yang, Beijing, 1954. Cao Ming, *Yuandongli* (Moving Force), Beijing, 1948; translated into English by the Peking Cultural Press, 1950. Lu Ling, *Ji'e de Guo Su'e* (Hungry Guo Su'e), Shanghai, 1946.

3 Lao She, *Erh Ma* (The Two Ma's), Shanghai, 1939, translated as *Ma and Son* by Jean M. James, San Francisco, 1980; and *Letuo Xiangzi* (Camel Xiangzi), Shanghai, 1937, translated in *Chinese Literature,* November 1978, pp. 3–58, and December 1978, pp. 13–72. Among Lao She's works are *Lao Zhang di zhexue* (The Philosophy of Old Zhang), Shanghai, 1932; *Zhao Ziyue,* Shanghai, 1933; *Lihun* (Divorce), Shanghai, 1933, translated as *The Quest for Love of Lao Lee* by Helena Kuo, New York, 1948; *Huozang* (Cremation), Shanghai, 1946; *Maocheng ji* (Cat Country), Shanghai, 1946, translated by William Lyell, Columbus, 1970; *Sishi tongtang* (Four Generations under One Roof), Shanghai, 1946, translated as *The Yellow Storm* by Ida Pruitt, New York, 1951; *Niu Dienci zhuan* (Biography of Niu Dienci), Shanghai, 1947, translated as *Heavensent* by Gene Z. Hanrahan, London, 1951; *Longxugou* (Dragon-Beard Ditch), Beijing, 1953, translated by Liao Hung-ying, Beijing, 1955; and *Chaguan* (Teahouse), Beijing, 1958. Translations of Lao She's short stories can be found in *Chinese Wit and Humour,* George Kao, ed., New York, 1946; Yuan Chia-hua and Robert Payne, *Contemporary Chinese Short Stories,* London, 1946; Wang Chi-chen, *Contemporary Chinese Stories,* New York, 1944; Daniel Milton and

W. Clifford, *A Treasury of Modern Asian Stories,* New York, 1961; Gene Z. Hanrahan, *50 Great Oriental Stories,* New York, 1965; W. J. F. Jenner, *Modern Chinese Stories,* Oxford, 1970; Liu Wu-chi, *K'uei Hsing,* Bloomington, 1974; *Renditions,* Autumn 1978. Chapters of an unfinished novel, *Zhen hongqi xia* (Beneath the Red Banner), have been translated in *Chinese Literature,* February-March 1981.

4 Mao Dun, *Hung* (Rainbow), Shanghai, 1929; *Yeqiangwei* (Wild Roses), Shanghai, 1931; *Ziye* (*Midnight*), Shanghai, 1933, translated by Hsu Mengh-hsiung and A. C. Barnes, Beijing, 1953; *Baofengyu* (The Storm), Shanghai, 1925; *Huainanzi,* Shanghai, 1926; *Shi* (The Eclipse)—trilogy consisting of *Huanmie* (Disillusion), *Dongyao* (Vacillation), and *Zhuiqiu* (Pursuit)—Shanghai, 1927–28; *Huisema* (Pale Horse), Shanghai, 1931; *Lu* (Road), Shanghai, 1932; *Chuncan* (Spring Silkworms), Shanghai, 1933. Translations of Mao Dun's stories can be found in Hanrahan, *50 Great Oriental Stories;* Jenner, *Modern Chinese Short Stories;* Wang Chi-chen, *Contemporary Chinese Stories;* Yeh Chun-chan, *Three Seasons & Other Stories,* London, 1946; Ch'u Chai and Winberg Chai, *A Treasury of Chinese Literature,* New York, 1965; Harold Isaacs, *Straw Sandals,* Cambridge, 1974; Sidney Shapiro, *Spring Silkworms & Other Stories,* Beijing, 1956; Edgar Snow, *Living China,* London, 1936.

5 Ba Jin, *Miewang* (Destruction), Beijing, 1929. Among Ba Jin's huge output of novels, short stories, autobiographical writing, travel notes, essays, and translations are the following fictional works: *Aiqing di sanbuqu* (The Love Trilogy), consisting of *Wu* (Fog), *Yu* (Rain), and *Leidien* (Thunderstorm), Shanghai, 1939; *Jiliu* (The Turbulent Stream)—a trilogy consisting of *Jia* (Family; translated by Sidney Shapiro, Beijing, 1958), *Chun* (Spring), and *Qiu* (Autumn)—Shanghai, 1931–40; *Chuntian li di qiutian* (Autumn in Spring), Shanghai, 1932; *Xue* (Snow), Shanghai, 1933; *Ba Jin Duanpian xiaoshuo ji* (Collected Short Stories of Ba Jin), Shanghai, 1940; *Qiyuan* (Garden of Leisure), Shanghai, 1944; *Di si bingshi* (Ward No. 4), Shanghai, 1946; *Huo* (Fire), Chungking, 1946; *Hanye* (Cold Nights), Shanghai, 1947, translated by Nathan K. Mao and Liu Ts'un-yan, Seattle, 1979. Translations of the short stories can be found in Wang Chi-chen, *Contemporary Chinese Stories;* Snow, *Living China;* Richard L. Yen, *Modern Chinese Literature: Bilingual Series,* vol. 3, Shanghai, 1941; Joseph S. M. Lau et al., *Modern Chinese Stories & Novellas, 1918–1948,* New York, 1982; Wen I, *Short Stories by Pa Chin,* Shanghai, 1941; *Chinese Literature,* May 1962, June 1963, July-August 1979. On Ba Jin, see also WLT 55:4, pp. 632–33.

6 Cao Yu, *Leiyou* (Thunderstorm), Shanghai, 1934, translated by Wang Tso-liang and A. C. Barnes, Beijing, 1960; *Richu* (Sunrise), Shanghai, 1936, translated by A. C. Barnes, Beijing, 1960; *Yuanye* (Wilderness), Shanghai, 1937; *Beijingren* (Peking Man), Shanghai, 1940, translated by Leslie N. K. Lo et al., New York, 1986; *Shuibien* (Metamorphosis), Shanghai, 1940. Cao Yu also wrote *Jia* (Family), Shanghai, 1942, and *Qiao* (The Bridge), Shanghai, 1947.

7 Ai Qing, *Dayanhe* (Dayan River), Shanghai, completed in 1935 but not published until 1939. Among his other works are *Xueli zuan* (Diamond in the Snow), Chungking, 1945; *Kuangye* (Wilderness), Shanghai, 1947; *Liming de tongzhi* (Message from Dawn), Shanghai, 1948; *Beifang* (The North), Shanghai, 1949; *Heiman* (Black Eels), Beijing, 1955; *Chuntian* (Spring), Beijing, 1956; *Guailai de ge* (Songs of Return), Shanghai, 1980; *Leye ji* (Falling Leaves), Shanghai, 1982; *Ai Qing suan ji* (Ai Qing's Poems), Beijing, 1984. *Selected Poems of Ai Qing,* Eugene Eoynag, tr., Bloomington, 1982, has a good selection; for a review, see WLT 57:4 (Autumn 1983), p. 685.

8 Some of Feng Jicai's fictional works are *Gaonuren he ta di aizhangfu* (Tall Wife and Short Husband), Shanghai, 1984; *Wu zhong ren* (Man in the Mist), Beijing, 1984; *Feng Jicai zhongduanpian xiaoshuo* (The Short Stories of Feng Jicai), Beijing, 1981. A selection of his stories in English is available in *Chrysanthemums and Other Stories*, Susan W. Chen, tr., San Diego, 1985. Gu Hua's story "The Log Cabin Overgrown with Creepers" appeared originally in *Shiyue,* October 1981, and is available in translation in *Chinese Literature,* December 1982, pp. 5–35.

9 Some of Wang Meng's fiction is collected in *Wang Men xiaoshua baogao wenxue xuan* (An Anthology of Wang Meng's Fiction and Reportage Literature), Beijing, 1981. "Hudie" ("Butterfly") is published in *Shiyue* (October), October 1980, and is translated into English in *Chinese Literature,* January 1981, pp. 3–63. Other translations can be found in *Prize-Winning Stories from China 1978–1979,* Beijing, 1981, and *Butterfly and Other Stories,* Beijing Foreign Languages Press, 1983.

10 Bai Hua, "Kulian" (Bitter Love), *Shiyue* (October), 3 September 1979. Some of Bai Hua's fiction is included in *Bai Hua jinzuo xuan* (Selections from Bai Hua's Recent Works), Bi Hua, ed., Hong Kong, 1981, and *Bai Hua juan* (A Book of Bai Hua), Hong Kong Movement for the Support of Chinese Writers, 1981. A few stories by Bai Hua are translated into English in *Chinese Literature.* See also *Bai Hua's Cinematic Script: Unrequited Love,* T. C. Chang et al., eds. & trs., Taipei, 1981.

11 Marcel Proust, *Remembrance of Things Past,* London, 1941, vol. 12, p. 239.

12 Bai Xianyong's fictional work includes *Zhexian ji* (The Exiled Celestial), Taipei, 1967; *Youyuan jingmeng* (Nightmare in the Park), Taipei, 1969; *Taibeiren* (Taipei Characters), Taipei, 1971; *Niuyue ke* (The New Yorkers), Hong Kong, 1974; *Jimode shiqisui* (Lonely Seventeen), Taipei, 1976; *Yujizhong de fenghuanghua* (Phoenix Blossom in the Rainy Season), Taipei, 1980; *Niezi* (The Illegitimate), Hong Kong, 1981; *Zai womende wangkuoli* (In the Realm of Our Kingdom), Hong Kong, 1981; *Yongyuande Yin Xueyan* (Yin Xueyan Never Dies), Hong Kong, 1981. Translations of Bai's short stories appear in *Twentieth Century Chinese Stories,* C. T. Hsia, ed., New York, 1971; *An Anthology of Contemporary Chinese Literature,* Chi Pang-yuan et al., eds., Taipei, 1975; *Chinese Stories from Taiwan, 1960–1970,* Joseph S. M. Lau, ed., New York, 1976; *Wandering in the Garden: Waking from a Dream,* George Kao et al., trs., Bloomington, 1982; *Literature East & West,* December 1965; *Renditions,* Autumn 1975; *The Chinese P.E.N.,* Spring and Autumn 1976; *Stone Lion Review,* no. 2, 1978; *Tamkang Review,* Spring 1979.

13 Among Yu Guangzhong's works are *Zhangshangyu* (Rain on the Palm), Taipei, 1964; *Qiaoda yue* (Percussive Music), Taipei, 1969; *Lianzhi lianxiang* (Association of the Lotus), Taipei, 1964; *Zai lengzhan de niandai* (In Time of Cold War), Taipei, 1964; *Yu yongheng bahe* (Tug of War with Eternity), Taipei, 1979; *Yu Guangzhong shixian* (Collected Poems of Yu Guangzhong), Taipei, 1981. Translations have appeared in Yu Kuang Chung, *Acres of Barbed Wire,* Taipei, 1971; Yip Wai-lim, *Modern Chinese Poetry,* Iowa City, 1970; Angela C. Y. Jung Palandri, *Modern Verse from Taiwan,* Los Angeles, 1972; Dominic Cheung, *The Isle Full of Noise,* New York, 1987.

14 Only a handful of Bei Dao's poems are published every year since 1978 in national, local, and provincial magazines in China. He has two published volumes of poetry: *Mosheng de haitan* (Unfamiliar Shore), Beijing, n.d.; and *Bei Dao shixuan* (Selected Poems), Beijing, 1986. An excellent translation is

Bonnie S. McDougall, *Notes from the City of the Sun: Poems by Bei Dao,* Cornell University Press, 1983. Other translations can be found in David S. G. Goodman, *Beijing Street Voices,* London, 1981; *Contemporary Chinese Literature: An Anthology,* Michael Duke, ed., New York, 1985; *Renditions,* special issue on "menlong" (misty) poets, nos. 19/20, (Spring 1983), pp. 195–208; *Bulletin of Concerned Asian Scholars,* July-September 1984, pp. 27–30.

15 See "Introduction" to McDougall, *Notes from the City of the Sun.*

16 C. T. Hsia, *History of Modern Chinese Fiction,* New Haven, Ct., 1971, p. 533.

Poetry in Hong Kong: The 1990s

▪ INTRODUCTION

Hong Kong literature has often been considered a marginal phenomenon on the fringe of developments in Motherland China, the British Commonwealth, or even other societies (L. Lee, 80). Hong Kong culture has even been identified as a culture of disappearance, transience being its very essence: "The city is not so much a place as a space of transit" (Abbas, 4). Adjectives like *hybrid, transitional,* or *homeless* have been used to describe its culture (Leung, 1996, 55). Such a label arises partly because Hong Kong is perceived to be a marginal society, at the crossroads of at least two cultures and two histories, with political and social change forever imminent. This perspective is more or less imposed on Hong Kong writers rather than one they enthusiastically adopt for themselves (Leung, 1995, 73).

In view of Hong Kong's history, the sociopolitical framework of analysis (and its related emphasis on cultural concerns of transience, identity, or the lack thereof) is not irrelevant, especially at times of highly salient events such as the 1997 handover. While not invalid, this perspective is not entirely fortunate, because if we subscribe to it too much, we shall fail to see the diversity of themes and the full range of human concerns explored by Hong Kong writers. Now, in the 1990s, the time has certainly come—if it had not come before—for literature in Hong Kong, and hence its poetry, to be considered worthy of investigation in itself rather than as another mode of social history. Historical and political events do have an impact on the concerns of writers, but they are not the only forces molding writers' collective psyche. Hence they cannot be the only themes articulated in view of the much-noted vibrancy in the literary world in the Hong Kong of the 1990s (Parkin, 1995, xix; "Hong Kong Nineties," 7; Cheung, ix).

In this paper I shall try to present a fuller range of themes articulated by poets in Hong Kong and illustrate the diversity of their poetry, a diversity that is essential and to be expected with the maturation of a literary genre. The discussion will focus specifically on the current work of poets of ethnic Chinese origin who write in English or who have had their works translated into English. A brief introduction to the poetry scene in Hong Kong is given as background to the thematic discussion. I shall conclude with a redefinition of what Hong Kong poetry is.

▪ THE POETS, THEIR READERS, AND OTHER SUPPORT

Poetry in Hong Kong could be discussed in four categories: 1) poetry written in Chinese by Chinese poets; 2) poetry written in English by ethnic Chinese poets; 3) poetry written in English by non-Chinese poets residing in Hong Kong; and 4) poetry in translation.

Poetry Written in Chinese. In Hong Kong there are many more poets writing in Chinese than in English. In the recent literary history of Hong Kong, there have been at least three generations of poets writing in Chinese: those who left China to reside in Hong Kong during the 1940s and 1950s; those who were born and grew up in Hong Kong during the postwar baby boom; and the present generation who grew up in the shadow of the 1997 transition. In a recent bibliography introducing 187 Chinese literary works by Hong Kong writers (Youth Literary Book Store, 1995) from the 1940s to the 1990s, the number of poetic works cited has grown steadily. Of the seventy-one works cited to represent the 1990s, fifteen (21.13 percent, or about one-fifth) are either poetry collections or anthologies which include some poetry. The volume of poetic output throughout the entire period also amounts to 19.79 percent (37 out of 187).

Poetry Written in English by Ethnic Chinese. In contrast, where poets writing in English are concerned, if we focus only on ethnic Chinese poets writing in English, then there are comparatively few who are currently visible on the literary scene. Louise Ho, teaching at the Chinese University of Hong Kong (CUHK), is noted for her two recent collections *Local Habitation* (1994) and *New Ends, Old Beginnings* (1997) and for her appearance in several anthologies such as *Hong Kong: Somewhere Between Heaven and Earth* (White, 1996). Another poet, Agnes Lam, who teaches at the University of Hong Kong (HKU), published her first collection, *Woman to Woman and Other Poems,* in 1997, and that same year saw a translation of sixty poems by Joseph Lee, an established Hong Kong artist and a poet writing in Chinese. Apart from these two, there are several others. Juliette Chen, born of Vietnamese and Taiwanese parents, came to Hong Kong when she was two years old and now lives in San Francisco (Parkin, 1995, 63). Yuen Che Hung writes mainly in Chinese but also occasionally in English. Their work in English can be found in the 1995 anthology of Hong Kong poetry edited by Andrew Parkin. There are also some young poets like Karen Cheung among the student population in the universities.

Further back in time was the work of Joyce Hsia (1965, 1973), who also edited an anthology in English together with Lai Tim Cheong in 1977. The ethnic Chinese poets featured in this 1977 volume included Louise Ho, Joyce Hsia, Monica Lai, Gregory Leong, and Herbert Leung. Hsia and Lai also featured several non-Chinese writers in their volume. In another, more recent anthology of Hong Kong poetry written in English, *Vs: 12 Hong Kong Poets* (1993), fewer ethnic Chinese poets were included. Of the twelve poets represented, apparently only three are of Chinese descent: Louise Ho, Yuen Che Hung, and Liam Fitzpatrick, born in Hong Kong of Irish and Chinese parentage.

Poetry Written in English by Non-Chinese Poets Residing in Hong Kong. From time to time, some non-Chinese poets from abroad have spent time in Hong Kong. Edmund Blunden was the legendary example, with a much-cited volume entitled *A Hong Kong House: Poems 1951–1961,* published in 1962. He began teaching at HKU in 1953 and was highly influential in the Hong Kong literary world—and, of course, beyond. The label "Blundenians" was coined for the generations of his students (W. C. Chan et al., 137). Following Blunden's sojourn came Joseph Jay Jones, a Fulbright lecturer in American literature at HKU and CUHK from 1965 to 1966. He published his first poetry collection, *Handful of Hong Kong: A Visitor's Verses,* in 1966.

In current times there is Andrew Parkin, who teaches at CUHK. In 1995 he published *From the Bluest Part of the Harbour: Poems from Hong Kong,* an anthology mentioned earlier which features two ethnic Chinese poets writing in English (Louise Ho and Juliette Chen), nine writing in Chinese but translated into English, and one who did both (Yuen Che-hung). In 1997, Parkin also published his own work in the bilingual volume *Hong Kong Poems in English and Chinese* with Laurence Wong, a poet writing in Chinese and teaching at Lingnan College. Other non-Chinese poets can be found in *Vs: 12 Hong Kong Poets,* also mentioned earlier: they are Brent Ambacher, Simon Beck, Ulrikka Gernes, Jeremy Hardingham, Richard Lawrence, Gerard Tannam, Deirdre Tatlow, and Gordon Osing. Periodically, individual collections such as those by Gladys Palmer (1978) and Raymonde Sacklyn (1993) have appeared as well. Jimmy McGregor's collection of mainly short stories (1995) also included several poems.

Poetry in Translation. Translation tends to go only one way, from Chinese into English, apparently for the benefit of the international community literate in English. Of the Chinese poets who have been translated into English, Leung Ping-kwan, who taught at HKU for many years but now teaches at Lingnan, is internationally well known for both his own work and his critical reviews. His bilingual collection *City at the End of Time* (1992) was translated by Gordon Osing, an American poet. Examples of the translated work of other Chinese poets can be found in Andrew Parkin's 1995 anthology, which includes verse by Yu Kwang-chung, Leung Ping-kwan, Woo Kwok-yin, Yuen Che Hung, Laurence Wong, Wu Xubin, Chung Waiman, Chan Tak-kam, Wong Leung-wo, and Ng Mei-kwan. Other poets writing originally in Chinese but translated into English are featured in "Hong Kong Nineties," a special 1997 issue of *Renditions,* a CUHK journal devoted to the publication of Chinese writing translated into English. The eleven poets represented in this issue are Fan Sin Piu, DEL, Heather Tu, Lau Wai Shing, Chan Chi Tak, Cheung Siu Por, Choi Chi Fung, Qiu Cheng, Cheung Kwok Man, Xiao Xi, and Gu Cao. Seven of these (Fan, Tu, Lau, Chan, Cheung, Xiao, and Gu) are young poets working on *Huxi Shikan,* the Chinese journal of the Fresh Air Poetry Society. (All of this subgroup except Gu Cao are also featured in another 1997 anthology of fifteen young poets brought out in Chinese by Heung Kong Publishing [Wong, Chan, & Lau, 1997].) The large number of poets now accessible in English translation marks quite a change from the situation ten years ago in another special issue of *Renditions,* "Hong Kong" (1988). At that time, alongside several poems selected from the 1930s, only four poets were featured: Shu Xiangcheng, Huang Kuo-Pin (Laurence Wong, mentioned above), Leung Ping-kwan, and Zhong Weimin (Chung Wai-man, mentioned above).

The Readership. Because there are more poets writing in Chinese than in English, there is conceivably more local interest in poetry written in Chinese than in verse written in English. This is to be expected in view of the language competence or preference in the general population. At school, English is increasingly taught as a foreign or auxiliary language even though it is still officially the medium of higher education, at least for several disciplines at most universities. The four categories of poetry mentioned above also attract slightly different groups of readers, with some overlap. Readers of Chinese poetry in Hong Kong are likely to be young students or the artistic, intellectual, or literary community locally. There is also some interest in Hong Kong Chinese writing among the Chinese-speaking population outside Hong Kong. It has been reported that in the last few years Hong Kong literary histories and authors' series have appeared in China with some momentum ("Hong Kong Nineties," 7). The readers of Hong Kong writing in English could be young or older returnees from English-speaking countries, Hong Kong residents who have been educated in English either locally or overseas, the non-Chinese community in Hong Kong, and some overseas Chinese. The readership of non-Chinese visiting poets writing in Hong Kong tends to be similar to that for English literature in general. Chinese writing in Hong Kong can be studied as Chinese literature. English writing in Hong Kong by ethnic Chinese writers, however, is likely to be viewed as postcolonial literature, commonwealth literature, or part of what is termed world literature written in English. For all of them, there is also the wider interest of scholars interested in Hong Kong society or culture or, from an even more generic perspective, the culture of an Asian society. Poets writing in Chinese whose work has been translated into English have contributed in no small measure to this international understanding and dissemination of Hong Kong culture.

Other Support. As for other types of support, among Chinese writers, a possible focal point is a poets' organization such as the Fresh Air Poetry Society. For those poets writing in English, there is no formal association of poets, at least not one that is well known. Sometimes an enthusiastic poet may be able to gather several other poets together periodically for group readings (see e.g. the readings listed in Parkin, 1995, xv-xvi), but these meetings tend to be rather informal. In any case, as people come and go, groups form and disband rather quickly. As far as official organizations are concerned, the Hong Kong Arts Development Council and the Hong Kong Arts Centre have the mission of promoting artistic development and appreciation in Hong Kong, the literary arts included. Unlike the visual arts or drama, poetry is not readily "visible." The idea of a poetry reading or a literary discussion as an artistic activity to be supported by these two organizations was recently promoted in a program titled "Meeting Hong Kong Writers This Life" as part of the festivities during the handover period in the summer of 1997. This program introduced readers to the works of Hong Kong writers in a series of Saturday-evening meetings over a period of three months and featured poets such as Leung Ping-kwan, Agnes Lam, Louise Ho, and Chan Sui Hung.

Another important type of support that is needed for the development of poetry in Hong Kong is assistance in publication. For the Chinese poets, there are several journals, magazines, and newspaper supplements that have come and gone over the last twenty years. Two current periodicals are *Huxi Shikan* and *Shishuang Yuekan.* In addition, *Renditions* (as mentioned above) publishes English translations of Chinese poetry but not vice versa. For poetry written in English, one periodical, *Imprint,* was started in 1980 but ceased publication within the year (Lam, 1988, 75). At present there is no such periodical for Hong Kong poets writing in English, and so they often submit their work to periodicals outside Hong Kong.

Apart from periodicals, support for publishing individual collections or anthologies is also needed. In recent years the Hong Kong Arts Development Council has funded the publication of some poetry collections written in Chinese. Poets writing in Chinese or in English are all eligible to apply, but it appears that poets writing in English have not done so to any appreciable degree. Two 1997 publications, Agnes Lam's *Woman to Woman and Other Poems* and Louise Ho's *New Ends, Old Beginnings,* were issued by a commercial publisher, Asia 2000, interested in promoting English writing in Asia. Parkin's 1995 anthology of largely translated works *From the Bluest Part of the Harbour* was published by Oxford University Press. For the Chinese poets, publishers currently providing support can be found in the Youth Literary Book Store's 1995 bibliography of Hong Kong literature; they include Shishuang Yuekan Publishing, Joint Publishing (HK), Su Ye (or Su Yeh), Oxford University Press, and Cosmos, among others. Counting all the publishers listed in this bibliography for all seventy-one literary works (not just poetry) published in Chinese in the 1990s, there are twenty-one major publishers and several smaller ones. Local publication support for poetry written in Chinese is therefore appreciably greater than is that for poetry written in English. But then there are more poets writing in Chinese than in English. This has been so for some years (M. Chan, 51) and is unlikely to change in the near future, if ever.

▪ DIVERSITY OF THEMES

With that background introduction to the poetry scene, I should now like to discuss the themes explored by Hong Kong poets. I shall focus on the work of ethnic Chinese poets writing in English or those writing originally in Chinese but having their work translated into English. It has been argued that, for the ethnic Chinese poets, whether they write in Chinese or in English, their themes are likely to be similar (M. Chan, 54). I would add that the emphasis on one theme or another may vary with the background or personality of the poet. Poets are also likely to write about different concerns at different times of their lives.

In the discussion below, while it is not possible to be exhaustive in the themes investigated or definitive in the categorization of poems, I hope to illustrate that sociopolitical concerns, though important, are not the only ones explored. Several other themes recur in the poetry published in the 1990s: 1) historical reference and political or cultural identity; 2) lives in exile or dislocation; 3) the charm of the place, and nostalgia for it; 4) affluence and poverty in a cosmopolitan city; 5) love, sex, and marriage; 6) family and people; and 7) the human condition.

Historical Reference and Political or Cultural Identity. I do not deny that there has always been a certain political awareness among Hong Kong poets. In the years leading up to 1997, several poets had dealt in differing degrees with the changeover issue. Louise Ho's poem "Island" (1997, 60) captures the fluidity in identity as this deadline drew near.

We are a floating island
We have no site
Nowhere to land
No domicile

Come July this year
We may begin to hover in situ
May begin to settle
May begin to touch down
We shall be
A city with a country
An international city becoming national

In another poem, "A Good Year" (1997, 66), Ho calls 1997 "a good year" because, while "deadly deadlines kill," "it is here."

Another poet, Agnes Lam, tries to express her complex feelings toward the associated changes in "Shanghai Tang" (1998). The poem begins with an announcement for a new radio station in Putonghua from 31 March 1997 and a new language-education policy. In the face of such changes, she asks:

Why should I feel responsible?
What could be better for Hong Kong?
A child born of political assault,
legitimized by a treaty, returned by another.

If only
I could just buy myself
a cheongsam of white silk
from Shanghai Tang in vogue,
wait for 1st July
to ride the tide,
enjoy the scenery
as we cross the century.

It would have been easy if she could face these changes by simply putting on a cheongsam from the new boutique in Central, after which the poem is named. But for her, and probably for many Hong Kong residents, although there is no fear about the changeover—and indeed, some are looking forward to it—the scenery is not just for enjoyment.

There are other poems portraying the cultural images of Hong Kong in these changing times. Gu Cao's "Images of Hong Kong in the Tourist Association's Publicity Films" (1997) is a complaint against the superficiality of the images "forever under the curse of the junk . . . evolving from Susie Wong into / dressy dames" at Club Volvo (considered the leading nightclub in Hong Kong) and incorporating not just "a cheongsam accompanied by the compulsory lute" but also imported musicals like *Cats* and *The Phantom of the Opera*. To Gu Cao, these images are but "postcards blown all over the place like pieces of confetti," disintegrating and dispersing the inhabitants of the city. Leung Pingkwan's poem "Images of Hong Kong" (1992, 32–35) does not deny the images per se. He just wants to know "How does it add up?" and points to the need for "a new angle" so that we can find our way through "factories of images and songs" even though the search for a complete but nontrivial identity may not be entirely fruitful: "We need a fresh angle, / nothing added, nothing taken away, / always at the edge of things and between places. / Write with a different color for each voice; / OK, but how trivial can you get? / Could a whole history have been concocted like this?"

Lives in Exile or Dislocation. That Hong Kong people live "at the edge of things and between places" culturally, psychologically, and geographically is a common theme with Hong Kong poets. Several have written about their sense of exile as immigrants to other shores. "Migratory" by Louise Ho (1997, 31–33) touches upon the very core of the exile's pain.

The neighbours are kind, the dogs are friendly
The land is veritable Eden, the roads are straight
Tender is the meat, tasty is the fruit
It is the loss, the loss
That grips like a vice
That tightens the spine
And the legs go soft
Space-tost, land-lost
I float, I drift, I hover
Cannot settle
Cannot come to stay

As keenly aware of the exile's loss, if less evidently painful, is Laurence Wong in "Autumn Thoughts" (1997, 50–51), which begins with a description of the Tolo Harbour flowing through other scenic spots in Hong Kong but ends with the realization that the poet has

"forever lost the harbour at Tolo" now that he resides in Toronto.

In contrast to this pain and loss is Agnes Lam's lighter poem, "Petals" (1997, 19–20), which allows for growth "without roots" each time she transplants. She accepts this growth "with but the scent / for a season / even a moment / translucent petals / dancing in a raindrop spectrum," though she is well aware of the tenuousness of this growth, which can be dissipated by a mere afternoon storm even as "pedestrians cross in their umbrellas."

The theme of exile refers back to some Hong Kong poetry of the 1940s and 1950s by poets who had come from China. The difference is that whereas those poets longed for China, these contemporary emigrants long for Hong Kong, which speaks volumes against the thesis that Hong Kong is but a place of transit. If it is, why should so many of its people long for it as home wherever they may be? The theme of exile is part of the theme of Hong Kong as home. To be homesick, one must first know what home is like.

The Charm of the Place, and Nostalgia. Not only is the Hong Kong of today valued as a place to belong to, but its past is sought after as well. Leung Ping-kwan's poem "The Clogs" (1992, 24–25) takes readers on a journey back in time to a way of life on Ladder Street, an old road on Hong Kong Island.

It got to be magic, old clogs in Ladder Street,
my shadow and I scraping along, down, clacking
  back into the years,
noting solely ankle speaking to ankle.
Clothes poles pointed to the years, their days hung
  out to dry.
("Clothes poles! Get your clothes poles here!")
Memory is like scissors. ("Any scissors to grind?
  Knives to sharpen?")
Memory cut lots of things into silhouettes.

But then one cannot "make appointments with bygone voices."

Chan Chi Tak's "Boat and Home" (1997, 182–85) portrays another bygone way of life, this time on a fishing boat, home of a friend who gave the poet a Christmas card which he lost while moving house. With this friend, he had once savored the serenity of a night in the boat's cabin "as the yellow bulb gently swayed" and "the radio played pop tunes": "faulty memory has let slip your name just this remains / on the card no hackneyed Hong Kong junk returning in the sunset / but a home / a boat / braving the elements, making a living." How different is this life "with its dangers, vast waters" and "the stink of fish" from the city landscape in Choi

Chi Fung's "Sleepwalk in the Suburbs" (1997, 202–3), where "fruit trees hang heavy with cans" and "bottles of drinkable water float down the river." Not surprisingly, the poet asks, "will there be mountains of tissues in the city one day?"

So disgusted is one poet with the modern additions to the Hong Kong landscape that he erases them completely in his imagination. In Joseph Lee's poem illustrating his paintings on Lamma Island (1997, 79), he removes the power station with this plea: "Don't ask me where / did those three hideous columns go? / I see only / a clear sky and waters / of midnight blue, / flickers of light where houses are, / half awake, half asleep. / Has not the power plant / stopped its generation?"

Affluence and Poverty in a Cosmopolitan City. In contrast to Joseph Lee, Heather Tu takes us right to the heart of the city in "Lunch at a Five Star Hotel in Central" (1997b, 168–71). Her portrayal is as disturbing as it is attractive. In one breath, she points out how "the decor is very elegant" and "the environs are high-tech," though "we are surrounded / we are surrounded on all sides / by steel and concrete." While buildings confront each other, she tells us, it is still an afternoon to be enjoyed "a couple of times in a year . . . doing nothing thinking of nothing." The poem ends with a question/comment: "Yes, yes, aren't we very glad / That this big city is so accessible / And so very very affluent."

Leung Ping-kwan is less indulgent toward such affluence, though humorously so. In "Lucky Draw" (1992, 80–85) he uses several lists of things both material and immaterial that people count it their luck to accumulate, all in an effort to illustrate the consumerism and vanities of Hong Kong society. Here is a partial list of what a lady desires, somewhat surrealistic for comic effect:

She gets a canned husband,
and a bunch of motorized relatives.
She gets a new set of fingernails,
eyebrows and nose.
She gets the title of vice-chairman
of all associations.
She gets four crocodiles that can sing,
a hippopotamus that sends flowers regularly . . .

The acquisition of things is a competition, and the poet has no wish to participate: "The dice I throw / score the lowest total. / I buy a newspaper / and miss the ferry."

The "I" in Leung Ping-kwan's poem is not the only one "left empty-handed." Louise Ho goes to the very brink of the poverty line in her portrayal of a streetsleeper in "City" (1994, 24). As this man opens his palm to beg, "His digits / Do not rend the air, / They merely touch / As pain does, effortlessly." In another poem, "Meeting" (1997, 70), before a man "With a withered face and yellowed teeth / Thinking or not thinking / Of the next meal or the next shelter," Ho questions the intellectual basis of her own life: "How dare I / Find value to reside / Only in the works of the human intellect."

To these several treatments of the affluent-city theme, Agnes Lam adds her poem "Nerissa's Cage" (1997, 58), portraying a woman who has everything yet wishes to escape the cage of "a life of charm and wonder": "but where is there to go / if the sky itself is closed?"

Love, Sex, and Marriage. As multifaceted as the treatment of the city theme is the realization of the general theme of love, sex, and marriage in Hong Kong poetry. In "Denial of the Flesh" (1997, 166–67) Heather Tu's description of suppressed sexual desire is honest and vivid, alive like a cat teasing and twirling "the white hidden nape behind your neck" and making you "a fish gripped inside the cat's mouth" if you resist. Chung Wai-man's "Porcelain Fragments" (1995, 114–16) speaks of another aspect of love: "If youth also is a fragile porcelain vase / Then I have fed the flower in the vase / With love, watered it with wine, / Believed it was the most beautiful flower in the world." With the fading of the dream, petals scattered, worms bred, and mold grew, and he could only laugh aloud: "Making the vase my cup I drank to the hills outside the window, / Downed the tea whose taste I couldn't place / A tea infused from those petals."

Another version of disillusionment is played out in Juliette Chen's "Dinner with an Eligible Bachelor," though the disappointment here is probably more the father's than the young lady's. To the young lady, the Chinese banquet to which she was brought had but the ghost of an eligible husband, though the father could have wished otherwise. Just as satirical is Louise Ho's treatment of a mutual seduction on campus involving a professor and "a graduate student admirer" through close observation of their body language in "Tilting" (1997, 82).

Probing more deeply into the core of marital tension in spite of love, Agnes Lam tries in the poem "Dandelions" (1997, 68) not to question "quiet coexistence / amidst difference," while Leung Ping-kwan in "Papaya" (1992, 90–93) traces the complex history of a relationship symbolized by the sharing of papayas. A final picture of mature love without such conflict is given in Agnes Lam's poem "For My Husband" (1997, 108), in which a husband expresses love for his wife by making sure that there is always enough boiled water for her to drink.

Family and People. The value of family and people is never felt more deeply than at times of separation and loss. Agnes Lam's poem "The Flowerpot" (1997, 23–26) illustrates a sister's yearning for her brother "married to another country, half a world away." Aside from geographic distance, death is the ultimate divider. Elegies for deceased parents, relatives, and friends are common in traditional Chinese poetry and they are also found in contemporary Hong Kong poetry. In Louise Ho's "Upon Hearing of a Friend's Death" (1997, 72) she mourns: "Gentle born of gentle clans / One more lost of the so few / Of the 'old stock' / I now walk silent among the busy crowds / I cower under their collective might."

Sad as the passing away of a friend may be, that of a parent is often more so. In Agnes Lam's poem in memory of her mother (1997, 89–90) the children try to love their mother beyond death by dressing her in "silk underwear, embroidered shoes." After the elaborate rituals, the poet's loss is felt in her realization that her mother is no longer behind her as she climbs the hill for the burial.

Love and mercy and rest bestow—
up the hill my mother would go.

Brothers and sister following,
I, the youngest, trailing.

How you yelled behind in schooldays past
for them to wait as I was last.

Mother, this hill we now climb—
you are not behind me.

The Human Condition. Just as death is inescapable, so too are certain circumstances in life. A common theme in Hong Kong poetry is the lack of control over the context of one's life. Joseph Lee's poem about his paintings of flower pots (1997, 107) is a direct comment on the boundaries of life.

In the mountain, flowers are too wild.
In a vase, they wait but to wither.
These several styles
of pots and bowls made
to hold your life
yet mark your boundaries.
Who asked God to create man
on a weekend?

Louise Ho's poem "Tree of Life" (1997, 52) presents an even bleaker picture: "All torn and twisted shredded and confused / Meandering tree of life a weak pattern / On a brick wall's worn whitish grey grouting / Mere seepage along the way of least resistance / And towards no end in particular."

A more splendid scene is painted in "Cloud Travel" by Leung Ping-kwan (1992, 120–25), but the human condition remains the same. As he looks at the clouds outside his airplane window, he tells us, "The clouds are amazing, but you can't live there. / No, we've got to come down somewhere, / pass documents, / show one of this world's passports / and stand in line, / present the baggage of your life / carried from country to country."

A variation on this theme of being trapped in life is the search for the meaning of life itself. In Agnes Lam's poem "My Cerebral Child" (1997, 46) a mother, thinking of all the dangers and sorrows awaiting children on this earth, questions whether it is truly loving of her to plan the birth of a child not yet conceived. Life itself may be a burden that is hard to bear, as in this poem by Joseph Lee (1997, 57): "On my shoulders, / a heavy burden. / Not ingots of gold / or sins of mankind. / Nor vanities of a thousand years. / Uncovering, I only see / my life and me."

The seven themes illustrated by the thirty-two poems cited here are of course not the only ones portrayed in Hong Kong poetry. Others include old age, death, religious faith, animals, plants, scenery, environmental pollution, art and music, life and landscape in other countries, poetic imagination, and so forth.

■ A COHERENT STORY OR MANY MESSAGES

Taking all the themes discussed, it is not difficult to string them together into some logical story of Hong Kong. That story could be something like this and could even begin with a political premise: because Hong Kong is always living on the edge of political change, Hong Kong people are unsure of their identity (Theme 1). Always in transit (Theme 2), they try to look for permanence in the physical landscape, at times becoming nostalgic about the disappearance of its charms (Theme 3). This yearning is accentuated by the pace of life in an affluent cosmopolitan city, a pace which tends to leave a void. Those who manage to get to the top find nothing else worth striving for, whereas others have difficulty just surviving (Theme 4). In the face of such emptiness, relationships often take on more meaning than they are capable of achieving (Theme 5). Still, the wish for emotional fulfillment remains; hence, family and friends are highly valued (Theme 6). The story of Hong Kong is the story of the human condition. Life goes on, with all its limitations (Theme 7). Now that was not difficult at all to string together. But is the story entirely logical, and is it necessary to have one?

The many scholars who have discussed literature in Hong Kong have provided a wealth of metaphors. Mimi Chan (1982, 48) points out the truth of the clichéd description of Hong Kong as the "melting pot of east and west." Andrew Parkin (1995, xix) calls the city "a crucible for the modern writer" and likens its poetry to "a truly important piece of the Chinese epic." To Martha Cheung (1998, ix), the diversity in Hong Kong literature is best presented as "a collage," and literary works are likened to "matches struck in the dark" (1998, xii-xiii). Leung Ping-kwan (1998, 13) offers the metaphor of a chorus of many voices. None of these critics is arguing for homogeneity among writers. Their vivid metaphors are merely attempts to find some coherence amid the many and varied expressions, some harmony in the apparent dissonance. Yet why should we expect there to be coherence or harmony? Why should there be one grand Hong Kong story or several smaller ones contributing to it?

I offer instead the metaphor of communication on the Internet, a metaphor which allows for local expression while maintaining regional and global communication. Each poet is at an e-mail address communicating with others. Some do so in Chinese and some in English. Some are based in Hong Kong and some are outside. Some of them talk about politics in their messages. Some talk about the beauty of the view outside their window: if not a junk in the setting sun, then at least the setting sun itself. Others speak of love or death. Each message is a poem, literary merits varying as letters do. As messages, why should all these "communiqués" necessarily form a coherent whole? Should they not be saying different things in different words for different people at different times? This reminds us of the ethnography of communication in the tradition of Hymes (1964). The whole point is that poetry as communication is always a new act, and communication about life is always full of variation.

■ **POETIC COMMUNITIES AND HONG KONG POETRY**

In the midst of the many messages, what then is Hong Kong poetry? The core Hong Kong poetry will be the verse written by poets based in Hong Kong, geographically or psychologically. Poets in this core forge links with poets and readers locally, regionally, or internationally to the extent that they communicate with them personally or through publications. They may do so through translation, if necessary.

Who then are the Hong Kong poets? Citizenship or passports cannot define this. If they do, then several ethnic Chinese poets in Hong Kong will not qualify. Period of residence may be a more useful index. What about ethnicity? Must Hong Kong poets be ethnic Chinese? I would suggest not necessarily, as long as they can identify with Hong Kong and Hong Kong readers find that they can identify with these writers' poetry.

This mutual identification and acceptance is necessary because poetry is a communicative act. We can borrow from sociolinguistics the concepts of speech communities and speech fellowships (Hudson, 25–30) in our attempt to understand poetic communities. A person is a member of a community insofar as he identifies with it and is able to communicate with other members in that community. A poet can belong to more than one community, the Hong Kong poetic community (or a subgroup within it) being but one of them. Different poets and different readers may identify different communities for themselves. Poets then, whether ethnic Chinese or not, do not even have to be talking about local topics all the time for them to be counted within the Hong Kong poetic community.

Some may object to my inclusion of non-ethnic Chinese poets residing in or identifying with Hong Kong into the poetic community of Hong Kong. They are likely to say that these writers do not really know the real Hong Kong because they suffer the disadvantage of looking at Hong Kong outside the local life. Although there have been some extravagant stereotypes of Hong Kong created by writers passing through, these are images of Hong Kong nonetheless and need not be rejected for being unrepresentative. Those who care to speak more representatively for the majority of Hong Kong inhabitants should present their work more often and be given every opportunity to do so. A more proportional picture will then emerge, and exaggerated accounts can be seen for what they are.

■ **CONCLUSION**

I have tried to do several things in this paper. I have introduced both the poets and some of their poetry. In doing so, I have also tried to work toward a redefinition of Hong Kong poetry and Hong Kong poets, a redefinition which I hope can be useful for other, similar communities. Hong Kong in the 1990s is actually more like many other bilingual and bicultural communities than some people would think. Hong Kong poets are no more on the fringe than are poets in other countries. At least they need not be. Hong Kong people are no more at the crossroads of two languages and cultures than are many other communities. As we enter the twenty-first century, monolingual and monocultural communities constitute the exception rather than the norm. Every place has a history. Hong Kong is not unique in that. It is high time that we let go of the tyranny of the sociopolitical approach so as to fully appreciate poetry in Hong Kong for what it is. Hong Kong poetry does reflect sociopolitical concerns. That is entirely natural because poets do not live in a sociopolitical vacuum. But their lives are not premised merely on the sociopolitical context; their poetic communication goes beyond that. Hong Kong poetry is as diverse as the lives of its poets and readers and as cosmopolitan as to be expected of an international city communicating with the rest of the world. To try to interpret its entire culture through the political window of its colonial past or its new city-adjunct-to-China destiny is to deny the vitality of life and culture in a city teeming with individuals living, communicating, loving, and dying in a place they call home. Hong Kong is a place of transit only insofar as man is a pilgrim on earth.*

Agnes Lam, Winter 1999

*This paper was first presented at the Department of English Language and Literature, the National University of Singapore, on 17 April 1998 during the author's visit on a fellowship sponsored by the Association of Southeast Asian Institutions of Higher Learning (ASAIHL), the National University of Singapore, and the University of Hong Kong. The support of the Association and of both universities as well as that of several poets, especially Leung Ping-kwan and Heather Tu, who supplied useful references for poetry written in Chinese, is gratefully acknowledged.

■ WORKS CITED

Abbas, A. (1997). *Hong Kong: Culture and the Politics of Disappearance*. Hong Kong. Hong Kong University Press.

Blunden, E. (1962). *A Hong Kong House: Poems 1951–1961*. London. Collins.

Chan, C. T. (1997). "Chuan he jia" [Boat and Home]. In "Hong Kong Nineties," special issue of *Renditions: A Chinese-English Translation Magazine*, nos. 47/48, pp. 182–85.

Chan, M. (1983). "Creative Writing in English in Hong Kong." In *The Teaching of Literature in ASAIHL Universities: Proceedings of a Seminar of the Association of Southeast Asian Institutes of Higher Learning (ASAIHL) Held at the University of Hong Kong, 13–15 December 1982*. A. Tatlow, ed. Hong Kong. Hong Kong University Press. Pp. 48–58.

Chan, W. C., K. M. Lo, and K. K. Yung, eds. (1961). *Edmund Blunden: Sixty-five*. Hong Kong. Hong Kong Cultural Enterprises, for the English Society, University of Hong Kong.

Chen, J. (1995). "Dinner with an Eligible Bachelor." In *From the Bluest Part of the Harbour: Poems from Hong Kong*. A. Parkin, ed. Hong Kong. Oxford University Press. Pp. 68–69.

Cheung, M., ed. (1998). *Hong Kong Collage: Contemporary Stories and Writing*. Hong Kong. Oxford University Press.

Choi, C. F. (1997). "Mengyou jiaowai" [Sleepwalk in the Suburbs]. In "Hong Kong Nineties," special issue of *Renditions: A Chinese-English Translation Magazine*, 47/48, pp. 202–3.

Chung, W. M. (1995). "Porcelain Fragments." In *From the Bluest Part of the Harbour: Poems from Hong Kong*. Pp. 114–16.

Gu, C. (1997). "Luyou xiehui xuanchuan duanpian zhong de xianggang xingxiang" [Images of Hong Kong in the Tourist Association's Publicity Films]. In "Hong Kong Nineties." Pp. 218–19.

Ho, L. (1994). *Local Habitation*. Hong Kong. Twilight Books, in association with the Department of Comparative Literature, University of Hong Kong.

———. (1997). *New Ends, Old Beginnings*. Hong Kong. Asia 2000.

"Hong Kong." (1988). Special issue of *Renditions: A Chinese-English Translation Magazine*, nos. 29/30.

"Hong Kong Nineties." (1997). Special issue of *Renditions: A Chinese-English Translation Magazine*, nos. 47/48.

Hsia, J. (1965). *Lost Light: Poems in Memory of Her Little Son George*. Hong Kong. Ye Olde Printerie.

———. (1973). *On Wind and Water*. Hong Kong. Privately printed.

———, and T. C. Lai, eds. (1977). *Hong Kong: Images on Shifting Waters*. Hong Kong. Kelly & Walsh.

Hudson, R. A. (1980). *Sociolinguistics*. Cambridge, Eng. Cambridge University Press.

Hymes, D. (1964). "Introduction: Toward Ethnographies of Communication." *American Anthropologist*, 66 (6:2), pp. 12–25.

Jones, J. J. (1966). *Handful of Hong Kong: A Visitor's Verses*. Hong Kong. Department of Extramural Studies, Chinese University of Hong Kong.

Lam, A. (1988). "Language Education and Literary Creativity in English: A Tale of Two Cities." In *Asian-Pacific Papers*. B. McCarthy, ed. Wollongong. Applied Linguistics Association of Australia. Pp. 70–78.

———. (1997). *Woman to Woman and Other Poems*. Hong Kong. Asia 2000.

———. (1998). "Shanghai Tang." *Plus Zero*, 2, p. 53.

Lee, J. (1997). *Joseph Lee: The First Ten Years*. A. Lam, tr. Hong Kong. University Museum and Art Gallery, University of Hong Kong. (Bilingual Chinese/English.)

Lee, L. O.-F. (1995). "Xianggang wenhua de bianyuanxing chu tan" [On the Marginality of Hong Kong Culture]. *Jintian* [Today], 28, pp. 75–80.

Leung, P.-K. (1992). *Xingxiang xianggang* [City at the End of Time]. G. T. Osing, tr. Hong Kong. Twilight Books, in association with the Department of Comparative Literature, University of Hong Kong. (Bilingual Chinese/English.)

———. (1995). "Yinyan" [Introduction]. *Jintian* [Today], 28, pp. 71–74.

———. (1996). *Xianggang wenhua kongjian yu wenxue* [The Cultural Space and Literature of Hong Kong]. Hong Kong. Youth Literary Book Store.

———. (1998). "The Story of Hong Kong." In *Hong Kong Collage: Contemporary Stories and Writing*. M. Cheung, ed. Hong Kong. Oxford University Press.

McGregor, J. (1995). *Life and Death*. Hong Kong. Privately printed.

Palmer, G. (1978). *The Magic Circle of Hong Kong*. Hong Kong. United Publishers.

Parkin, A., ed. (1995). *From the Bluest Part of the Harbour: Poems from Hong Kong*. Hong Kong. Oxford University Press.

———, & L. Wong. (1997). *Hong Kong Poems in English and Chinese*. E. Almberg et al., trs. Vancouver. Ronsdale. (Bilingual Chinese/English.)

Sacklyn, R. M. (1993). *Some Little Thoughts*. Hong Kong. Kaylloyd.

Tu, H. (1997a). "Guanyu jinyu" [Denial of the Flesh]. In "Hong Kong Nineties," pp. 166–67.

———. (1997b). "Zai zhonghuan wuxingji jiudian wucan" [Lunch at a Five Star Hotel in Central]. In "Hong Kong Nineties," pp. 168–69.

Vs: 12 Hong Kong Poets. (1993). Hong Kong. Big Weather.

White, B. S., ed. (1996). *Hong Kong: Somewhere Between Heaven and Earth.* Hong Kong. Oxford University Press.

Wong, C. Y., C. T. Chan, & W. S. Lau, eds. (1997). *Cong bentu chufa: Xianggang qingnian shiwu jia* [From This Earth: 15 Young Hong Kong Poets]. Hong Kong. Heung Kong Publishing.

Youth Literary Book Store. (1995). *Xianggang wenxue shumu* [Hong Kong Literature: A Bibliography]. Hong Kong. Youth Literary Book Store.

Literature in the Service of Politics: The Chinese Literary Scene since 1949

"There is in fact no such thing as art for art's sake, art that stands above classes or art that is detached from or independent of politics. Proletarian literature and art are part of the whole proletarian revolutionary cause; they are, as Lenin said, cogs and wheels in the whole revolutionary machine.... Literature and art are subordinate to politics, but in their turn exert a great influence on politics."[1] Thus Chairman Mao laid down his guidelines on art and literature in his famous "Yenan Talks" in 1942, which were to become one of two philosophical bases of the new literature of the People's Republic of China (founded in 1949). The other base—or the underpinnings of the same base really—was the Soviet theory of socialist realism (defined by Gorky as "the realism of men who transform and rebuild the world") with its emphasis on "positive" heroes and class struggle. The new literature was to be written for the masses and to conform to Marxist-Leninist principles. As interpreted by implementers of Mao's cultural policies, this literature was to reflect the Party's policies working smoothly, to depict "revolutionary realism plus revolutionary romanticism." It was not to portray love between the sexes across class lines, nor what was cynically referred to as "the so-called love of humanity," because such things were considered inappropriate or impossible in a classless society. Above all, the literature was to be optimistic in tone.

Kai-yu Hsu has made a major contribution to the study of contemporary Chinese literature by putting together in a single volume, *Literature of the People's Republic of China,*[2] translations of representative works of about 140 poets and writers, which give an excellent overview of the sort of literature produced in Mainland China during the period 1949–79. Because of the inseparability of literature and politics in the view of the Chinese Communists, the selections naturally reflect the changing aims and emphases in the Chinese political

Scene. Thus the literary fortunes of individual writers are curiously tied to the political fortunes of the writers and their works, a fact which explains the abruptness of entrance and exit of many a writer. To guide the reader through the intertwining labyrinths of literature and politics, the editor and the contributors have thoughtfully provided invaluable commentaries, biographical sketches and an indispensable "Chronology of Major Events." The need for all this becomes clear when one recalls Marx's conception of a dialectical relationship between form and content in art: forms are *historically* determined by the content they embody.

In accordance with the direction of politics in recent Chinese history, Hsu has organized his anthology into these divisions: 1) the period from Yenan to Peking, 1942–55; 2) the Hundred Flowers Movement (an official drive to encourage literary and artistic activity) and the subsequent Anti-Rightist Campaign, 1956–58; 3) the Great Leap Forward (an ambitious drive to increase industrial and agricultural production) and Anti-Revisionism, 1959–61; 4) the Socialist Education Campaign, emphasizing selfless dedication to socialist ideas; 5) the Cultural Revolution of 1964–70 which, ostensibly aimed at correcting all undesirable tendencies in the new society, degenerated into a factional political struggle and the denunciation, even persecution, of "undesirable" writers and intellectuals (i.e., the vast majority); and 6) the Aftermath—the Fall of the Gang of Four (Chiang Ch'ing, wife of Mao, and her close supporters), the rehabilitation of denounced authors and a regeneration of creative writing.

Hsu's periodization seems to me to be more useful (because it is more refined) than that adopted in a recent history published in Mainland China, the *Zhongguo dangdai wenxue shi* (History of Contemporary Chinese Literature),[3] whose highly emotive language and labels of absolute judgment ("correct viewpoint," "wrong," "conspiratory literature," et cetera) say much about the contemporary literary scene in China. It is interesting to see how the editors of *Wenxue shi* view the same decades covered by Hsu's book. The reader is told that during the period 1949–56 Mao's literary guidelines "were correctly carried out on the whole," that 1957–66 saw much development of literature "reflecting the revolutionary struggle and eulogizing the Party and socialism" but that serious mistakes were made (including "blind direction" and "the equating of literature with politics"!), that the Hundred Flowers Movement "was not conscientiously carried out," that during the period 1966–76 Lin Piao and the Gang of Four "assumed Fascist cultural dictatorship of the literary scene," bringing untold suffering to writers and intellectuals as a prelude to their planned usurpation of Party leadership, but that happily during 1976–79 the Gang was defeated and "the Party corrected the direction of the literary movement." The editors warn that "struggle still exists" and that one should be wary of the dangers coming from the extreme Left as well as from the Right.

Consistent with the Marxist emphasis on the interrelationship between history and literature, the settings for the literature of the last thirty years have been mainly those of historical significance: the Communist revolution up to 1949, the Korean War, socialist education, reconstruction, the land reform experience and, more recently, oppression under the Gang of Four. A handful of historical novels and plays, however, are set in the more distant past, notable examples being Yao Hsüeh-yin's multivolume *Li Tzu-ch'eng* and Wu Han's "Hai Jui Dismissed From Office" (1961), a play with satirical political undertones. Criticism of the latter by Yao Wen-yüan, one of the "Gang," indeed ushered in the Cultural Revolution. No longer making the exposure of contemporary social evils their concern as in the thirties (because, some would say, there were none), nor the psychological probing of life, writers of this period turned their energy to portraying the class struggle, the production struggle, or simply singing the praise of the Party and the victory of socialism. A new folk hero, capable of emerging triumphant over all difficulties in the end, has been created. Certain kinds of subject matter hitherto ignored either because they were considered too ordinary or because of a lack of firsthand knowledge (the construction of a factory, frontier exploits, et cetera) became popular with the official elevation of physical labor and the broadening of frontier experience.

As to language, Hsu has pointed out the new use of familiar imagery to relate to material needs. All the same, scholars have noted the persistence of the past in the literature of the present—the narrative style of the traditional storyteller, the presentation of characters in the novel in the manner of Yüan opera, even Wu Han's veiled criticism of the present through the past. Much of the residual past at the narrative-stylistic level is rooted in the folk tradition and thus adds to the proletarian flavor of the new literature. But one can hardly say the same of Mao's use of the classical form in his poems, let alone explain it by the Marxist argument of unity of form and content. A significant development of the period is the emergence of several ethnic minority writers on the national scene (Malchinhu, Rabchai Tsa-zang and others).

The nationwide imposition of a set of prescriptive guidelines designed to harness literature in the service of politics was something unprecedented in the China of 1949. To be sure, the Chinese have within their own Confucian tradition a pragmatic concept of literature:

namely, that literature has its moral and political functions, both for the ruler and his subjects. But Confucian humanism is in many ways the very antithesis of Marxist dialectics, and there never has been a well-organized movement to propagate a literary theory in Chinese history, certainly none supported by punitive campaigns against the nonconformist. Controversy over the "Yenan Talks" has surfaced from time to time. Those who advocated a broader realism (Hu Feng, Shao Ch'üan-lin, et al.) or those who directly or indirectly challenged the Party's concept of "typicality" with their less than positive portraits (Wang Meng, Liu Pin-yan, K'ang Cho) were eventually silenced. By the time the Cultural Revolution reached its climax in the late sixties, nearly all post-1949 writings had been condemned, leaving behind nothing but the most impeccable in doctrine, such as the handful of model revolutionary operas written under Chiang Ch'ing's guidance.

In the last few years, following the downfall of the Gang of Four and the rehabilitation of vilified writers, a spirit of renaissance has infused the whole literary scene (see *WLT* 53:4, pp. 617–18). The fourth National Assembly of Writers and Artists met in October-November 1979, after a lapse of almost twenty years. In his congratulatory message Vice-Premier Teng Hsiao-p'ing stressed the "need for the literary artist to express his individual creative spirit." Numerous short stories and poems appeared in the literary magazines; many of these used oppression under the Gang as theme ("Class Teacher," "The Scar," poems by Liu Sha-he, the novels of Mo Ying-feng) and soon came to be known as "Literature of the Scars." Going one step beyond the mere exposure of "scars," some writers delved into the larger issues of bureaucratism and the darker forces in man and society, the conflict between the individual and his environment: e.g., Chao Tzu-hsiung's "The Future Beckons," touching on the obstacles to modernization; "Between Human Being and Demon," an excellent work of reportage by the controversial Liu Pin-yan; and Chiang Tzu-lung's "Director Ch'iao Assumes Office," rated among the best works of fiction for 1979. Despite their bold treatment of bureaucratism, which drew flak from the hardline critics, these works have earned praise in Chinese literary circles. In the same vein, Yeh Wen-fu's poem "General, you can't behave like this!" (*Shikan*, 8/1979) caused quite a stir. But the greatest controversy was in the area of film literature. Two movie scripts— "In the File of Society," depicting the abuse of a girl by a bureaucrat and his son during the Cultural Revolution, and "Woman Thief," showing how family upheaval in the same period has turned a girl into a thief whose unmatched skills range from knife-throwing to making fun of bureaucrats—have drawn accusations of using naturalistic techniques, "unhealthy description," "ignoring the true expression of typicality," "incorrect viewpoint," even "questioning the validity of socialism," though defenders of the two works have not been few.[4]

On the theoretical level, there is much healthy discussion and debate in the literary magazines on such key issues as the relationship between literature and politics, the need for legal protection in literature, the function of criticism, the lifting of all restrictions on subject matter, the "social effects" of literature, heroic models, typicality and realism. While quite a few writers have argued against simplistically subsuming literature under politics, many affirm that despite the excesses of the Cultural Revolution, literature should not be detached from politics—as long as this politics is "class politics" and not that of "a few ambitious conspirators" (*Wenxue shi,* p. 25). Chou Yang[5] recently summed up the present official position by stressing a determination to carry out Mao's once professed policy of "letting a hundred flowers bloom" (which developed into an antirightist campaign), deemphasizing the subservience of literature to politics (while reiterating the inseparability of the two) and calling upon all writers to "be truthful in their reflection of life," to dare criticize others and to accept criticism, to exercise restraint (bearing in mind the "social effects" of their work), to guard against dangers from both the Left and the Right and to focus their attention on socialist reconstruction and modernization. Regarding the technique of fiction, it is interesting to note that Wang Meng's recent work ("The Eyes of Night," "Voice of Spring") shows characteristics of the "stream of consciousness" technique.

The last thirty years have not produced in China a writer of the stature of Lu Hsün. It is hoped that recent relaxation of control will lead to a true blossoming of a hundred flowers. Owing to restriction of publication date, Kai-yu Hsu's anthology does not reflect the latest literary harvests; but in terms of "typicality" for the period covered, one could hardly ask for more.

K. C. Leung, Winter 1981

---

[1] *Selected Works of Mao Tse-tung,* vol. 3, Peking, Foreign Languages Press, 1967, p. 86.

[2] Kai-yu Hsu, ed. Bloomington, Indiana University Press, 1980, xiv + 976 pages, $37.50

[3] Fu-chou, Fu-chou Jen-min, 1980. Compiled by the faculty of twenty-two universities and colleges. For the quotes following see vol. 1, pp. 2–10.

[4] See e.g. *Wenyi Bao* (Peking), 1980, no. 4, pp. 49–53; 1980, no. 8, pp. 20–23; and 1980, no. 9, pp. 33–41.

[5] Currently President of the All-China Federation of Literary and Art Circles. I refer to his address to the editorial staffs of literary magazines on 5 May 1980, reprinted in *Wenyi Bao,* 1980, no. 7, pp. 2–7.

Gao Xingjian *(Harper Collins)*

Between the Individual and the Collective: Gao Xingjian's Fiction

When the winner of the Nobel Prize in Literature was announced on 12 October 2000, many people in the United States and in the People's Republic of China were wondering just who Gao Xingjian was. It was not a totally invalid question for American observers, since he was virtually unknown here outside of academic circles. What was unusual was the excitement in China over the selection of a Chinese Nobel laureate of whom most had never heard. As a self-exiled writer and naturalized French citizen, Gao Xingjian has witnessed the erasure of his name from the literary scene and the national collective memory in China for reasons that will be briefly explained in the following pages.

This is not to say that Gao's selection went unnoticed in the country of his birth; the Shanghai novelist Wang Anyi, for instance, announced that she was "very happy a Chinese writer won this award, no matter where he lives."[1] And the internationally renowned novelist Mo Yan has spoken of Gao's enormous contributions. But this essay does not concern itself with the

Chinese—either the nation's youth, who were ecstatic over the choice but had no idea who the man was, or representatives of the official establishment, who were furious at what they viewed as an intentional provocation by the Swedish Academy or were utterly dismissive of his talents ("a very very average" writer, some said). Rather, I shall use this opportunity to introduce Gao's fictional works to Western readers.

Gao Xingjian was born in Jiangxi Province in 1940. As a French major in college, he obtained a broad knowledge of Western literary theories, particularly modernist writings, which prompted the publication of *A Preliminary Discussion of the Art of Modern Fiction* in 1981.[2] Published during the thaw immediately following the Cultural Revolution (1966–76), this treatise aroused heated debate among scholars and writers in China and "awakened a self-awareness in literature,"[3] but also sparked attacks of "spiritual pollution" on Gao, who was then put under surveillance.

In July 1983, his short play *Bus Stop* was banned after ten performances, for it was considered by some to be "the most pernicious work since the establishment of the People's Republic."[4] *Bus Stop*, in the vein of Beckett's *Waiting for Godot*, portrays a group of people waiting for a bus to take them to the city, although their bus never comes. During their ten-year wait, the individual riders reveal their dreams and desires; this was later viewed by Gao's detractors as a direct criticism of the Communist Party, which had failed to take the people into the city, the symbol of prosperity. The ten-year waiting period can also be read as a metaphor for the Cultural Revolution, during which Gao himself had burned mounds of his writings for fear of persecution, particularly since his wife at the time had reported to the authorities on the "unsavory" content of his writings.[5]

Political pressure was further compounded by a diagnosis of lung cancer, the cause of his father's death only a few years earlier. Although an X-ray later proved the diagnosis wrong, the impact on Gao was life-changing; meanwhile, the nightmare of persecution remained persistent in the form of a rumor of his imminent consignment to a prison farm in the remote province of Qinghai. Gao quickly decided to leave Beijing and set out on a roaming journey in Southern China. In 1987 he went to Germany on a fellowship and vowed not to return to Communist China until the totalitarian system was overthrown. He would go even further, by denouncing a system that allows for no dissent; in 1989 he publicly condemned the crackdown on the student movement in Tiananmen Square, an act that sealed his fate in China. His works were banned and his name was never mentioned again, except privately among small groups of intellectuals. When the October 2000 an-

nouncement came, the Chinese government dismissed the news as "a Frenchman with a Chinese name winning the Nobel." No wonder people in China did not know who he was, let alone have any familiarity with his works.

Although Gao Xingjian and his works have been politicized by supporters and detractors alike, he insists that he does not subscribe to any particular literary school of thought or align himself with any political faction, including nationalism and patriotism. "I consider literary creation to be a kind of challenge against society waged by an individual's existence," he has written; "even though this challenge may be insignificant, it is at least a gesture."[6]

In August 1989, soon after the Tiananmen massacre, a performing-arts center in Los Angeles contacted Gao with a request to write a play in support of the students' movement. When Gao gave them the play, they told him it wouldn't work for an American audience because it didn't have a hero. They needed a hero in the American fashion, but his play didn't have a single one. So they asked him to revise it; Gao responded that since the Chinese Communist Party could not make him alter his plays, he was not about to do so for the American theater.[7] It is, in part, this challenge against society and an uncompromising attitude toward his beliefs and creative principles that won such high praise from the members of the Swedish Academy.

One of the qualities that place Gao Xingjian squarely in the ranks of the most respected Nobel laureates is the universal appeal of his works, which are distinctively Chinese and yet transcend national boundaries. Unlike so many modern and contemporary Chinese writers, who seem "obsessed with China,"[8] Gao, though drawing his inspiration from Chinese culture, nevertheless ponders more fundamental issues of human existence. Among his favorite themes is the relationship between the individual and the collective entity, which can be a society or a small group of people. In addition to the famous (or "infamous") *Bus Stop*, which incurred official censorship, his other plays, equally well received in Europe, also tackle this issue. *Absconding*,[9] for instance, the play rejected by the Los Angeles Center for the Performing Arts, deals with three characters who hide in a small warehouse on the night of the Tiananmen massacre. Coming from disparate backgrounds, the characters express different views on political movements. One of them, a middle-aged man, even goes so far as to claim that all mass movements are controlled by a political power from behind the scenes and thus become games of political struggle. According to Gao, when the play was performed in Germany, the setting was changed from Tiananmen Square in 1989 to Germany during the Nazi era.[10] To his European adapters, it was obvious that the choice between resistance and collaboration, as well as an individual's role in any kind of movement, is by no means uniquely Chinese, and easily finds historical resonance elsewhere; nevertheless, the Communist Party chose to read his plays as an open attack on its authority.

The conflict between individual and collective rights and responsibilities is prominently featured in Gao's plays predating the Tiananmen massacre as well. In early 1986, he completed a short play titled *The Other Shore,* which was immediately banned in the People's Republic and was performed only in Taiwan and Hong Kong. The notion of the other shore comes from the Buddhist concept that human life (on this shore) is full of suffering, and that one can expect salvation only after reaching the other shore. What complicates this play is the fact that the playwright does not allow the characters to obtain salvation or happiness even after they reach the other shore. Worse yet, they are further mired in manipulation and power struggles. The main character, Man, is sought out to lead the others, but then is persecuted when he refuses to be part of the collective. Representing the ultimate individualist, Man yearns for independence, but fails when the collective demands a total surrender of his individuality. Even his search for love is thwarted. Like Gao the playwright, Man becomes an outcast and leaves the stage in the form of a withered heart.

> MAN: (*Weakly*) Who are you?
>
> SHADOW: Your heart.
>
> (*As the crowd watches the drooping, blind, and deaf heart slouch past them, Shadow quietly drags Man away. The crowd slowly follows behind the heart, which is extremely old and actually invisible. All exit.*)[11]

Readers and viewers of Gao's plays in China (if the librettos were available and the plays could be staged, of course) would undoubtedly recognize them as criticisms of Chinese society, in which the individual is constantly required to participate in collective activities. It is no wonder then that the Communist Party regards Gao's work as pernicious, since such a totalitarian entity can allow no dissenting voice or quest for individuality. What readers need to bear in mind, however, is that this is by no means a uniquely Chinese problem. As shown in Gao's plays, man cannot exist alone, for he needs the Other. The Other is like a fire on a cold night; one builds a fire to keep warm, but gets burned if one gets too close to it. How to achieve a balanced, comfortable distance between Self and Other is, as Gao's works invariably demonstrate, a perennial problem for people all over the world.

This distance is essential in any society, be it Christian, Confucian, or something else, in which the dominating thought seeks to encroach upon marginal ideologies. This, however, does not mean that Gao Xingjian is a propagandist who wages a frontal attack on any dominant ideology. Rather, he approaches this issue by reflecting upon traditional Chinese culture, which, contrary to general perception, is anything but homogeneously Confucian. His long novel *Lingshan* (Eng. *Soul Mountain*) is the perfect example. Instead of questioning the impact of totalitarian Communist rule on the individual, Gao elevates the focus of examination to the level of individual versus collective in the context of dominant Confucian tenets versus marginalized cultures.

In *Soul Mountain* Gao employs two narrators, "I" and "you," clearly the two halves of one self; the absence of "we" makes this abundantly clear.[12] While the "I" explores the connection between man and nature in a wandering journey into the natural preserves of Western and Southern China, the "you" delineates the relationship between man and woman through an encounter with a "she":

> You know that I am just talking to myself to alleviate my loneliness. You know that this loneliness of mine is incurable, that no-one can save me and that I can only talk with myself as the partner of my conversation.
>
> As I listen to myself and you, I let you create a she, because you are like me and also cannot bear the loneliness and have to find a partner for your conversation. . . . Like me, you wander wherever you like. As the distance increases there is a converging of the two until unavoidably you and I merge and are inseparable. At this point there is a need to step back and to create space.[13]

Such an experiment with technique may not please every reader, but it allows Gao to reflect upon the relationship between Self and Other (be it a woman or nature itself), which is reminiscent of the existentialist question expounded in Sartre (incidentally, also a Nobel selectee, but one who refused the prize).

Through the narrator's journey in search of Soul Mountain, a physical locale and a spiritual site as well, the author incorporates local legends and supernatural tales from traditions of the Han Chinese and Chinese minorities on the borders. The critic Henry Zhao has argued that, in Gao's mind, there is an official culture represented by power and symbolized by rationalism, male power, and inculcation. This has been the dominant culture in Chinese society for centuries, one that can only be countered with an opposite culture represented by antirationalism, woman, and nature.[14] Such a view, if indeed it is held by Gao, may strike feminists and postcolonial theorists as chauvinistic and imperialistic, for the gender Other—woman—and the ethnic Other—China's minorities—can be regarded as mere foils for the Han Chinese man in quest of self-discovery. If that were the case, then this work could be considered just another male-centered intellectual exercise. But we cannot deny that in Chinese society, Confucian rationality, represented by Northern orthodoxy and the imperial government, has always been suspicious of the South and of that segment of Chinese culture that is imaginative and has an investment in the supernatural. In this sense, Gao's spiritual journey to return to nature serves the higher purpose of recognizing the legitimate status of minority cultures that are an integral part of Chinese civilization. Moreover, it is an implicit criticism of the dominant ideology—be it Communist or Confucian—and the latter's relentless demand for conformity and submission.

An inherent prerequisite for questioning the orthodox ideology and restoring the legitimacy of minority traditions is skepticism. One must reexamine ideas and beliefs that have been accepted for generations as "truth" and acknowledge that the foremost object of skepticism is history. Toward the end of the novel, the narrator "I" comes to the "historical" site where the legendary Yu, one of the earliest Chinese kings, is rumored to have eliminated the problem of flooding for the Chinese populace:

> In Yu's tomb there are now artefacts for reference but the experts still cannot decipher the tadpole-like script on the stone epitaph opposite the main hall. I look at it from various angles, ruminate for a long time, and suddenly it occurs to me that it can be read in this way: history is a riddle,
>
> it can also be read as: history is lies
> and it can also be read as: history is nonsense
> and yet it can be read as: history is prediction
> and then it can be read as: history is sour fruit
> yet still it can be read as: history clangs like iron
> and it can be read as: history is balls of wheat-flour dumplings
> or it can be read as: history is shrouds for wrapping corpses
> or taking it further it can be read as: history is a drug to induce sweating
> or taking it further it can also be read as: history is ghosts banging on the walls
> and in the same way it can be read as: history is antiques
> and even: history is rational thinking
> or even: history is experience

> and even: history is proof
> and even: history is a dish of scattered pearls
> and even: history is a sequence of cause and effect
> or else: history is analogy
> or: history is a state of mind
> and furthermore: history is history
> and: history is absolutely nothing
> even: history is bad sighs
> Oh history oh history oh history oh history

> Actually history can be read any way and this is a major discovery! (450–51)

Such a skeptical attitude is, of course, not permitted under Communist rule, for the latter promotes a single interpretation of history that serves the Party and rejects dissent. But for Gao, it is precisely this skeptical attitude that preserves the integrity of his work; that is, his skepticism goes beyond a criticism of Communist society or even Confucian culture, as he does not subscribe to any single political belief. He questions the authoritarian view because it is only human to do so, whether one lives in China or elsewhere.

Soul Mountain is considered a highly autobiographical work, as it relates to Gao's search for a utopia after being given a second chance in life, while simultaneously dealing with the increasing pressure of political persecution. His second novel, *Yige ren de Shengjing* (One Man's Bible), is even more autobiographical; and yet, like *Soul Mountain,* it seeks to reach a higher level of truth and a broader humanity. As its title suggests, though it may be but one man's Bible, it is a Bible nonetheless, and deals with one man's life during a turbulent era of Chinese history while he searches for the meaning of existence in the face of human cruelty, trauma, and memory.

Read against *Soul Mountain,* "One Man's Bible" is strikingly different in its realistic portrayal of historical events. The major narratological difference is that the "I," "you," and "she" in *Soul Mountain* are here reduced to "you," "he," and "she." The critic Liu Zaifu argues that, as the novel deals with the Cultural Revolution, the "I" is inevitably strangled by merciless reality.[15] In other words, in the frenzy of the Great Proletarian Cultural Revolution, the individual "I" cannot survive. Unlike the "I" in *Soul Mountain,* who can embark upon self-imposed exile, the "I" in the latter novel must be eliminated. Such a narrative technique clearly sets Gao apart from the authors of the many Cultural Revolution memoirs that have flooded the market (Chinese and Western alike) in recent years. Gao's work is not an attempt to condemn the large-scale persecution so prevalent in modern Chinese history, but a sincere and sometimes brutally honest examination of the human psyche.

The story begins with an encounter between "you" and a Jewish woman in Hong Kong on the eve of the crown colony's turnover to the motherland, and cuts back and forth between the current "you" and the past "he." "You" is Gao's alter ego, one who has been living in the West and appears in Hong Kong for performances of his plays. His meeting the Jewish "she," an old acquaintance from China, calls to mind historical similarities between the Jews' fate in World War II and the fate of the Chinese during the disastrous ten-year Cultural Revolution (often referred to in China as its own "holocaust"). But the two individuals deal with the past very differently; "she" needs to remember and seems to enjoy the masochistic pleasure of shouldering the sufferings and sorrows of all Jews, while "you" wants to forget everything, which inevitably leads to the creation of "he," who travels back to the past. "He" recalls how he was once a fervent participant, until finally realizing that he was nothing but a pawn in a political struggle among higher powers. "He" tries to flee from the cruelties that one person inflicts upon another for no obvious reason other than hysteria motivated by mass madness. While "he" relives the past, "you" is also forced to reflect upon his former self and the process of writing.

> You have to liberate from memory that he, that child, that boy, that man who had yet to reach adulthood, that lucky surviving daydreamer, that insolent fellow, the one who was growing trickier by the day, the past you who had not lost your conscience, cruel and yet not without sympathy. Don't defend him and repent for him. When you observe him and listen to him, you naturally feel an uncontrollable sorrow and regret, but don't let the emotion spread and become sentimental feelings. If you stripped him of his mask to examine him, you'd have to turn him into a fictional construct, someone completely unrelated to you, awaiting your discovery. Only then would this narrative bring you the pleasure of writing, and curiosity and exploration would come naturally.[16]

> You write this book for yourself. This book about exile is your One Man's Bible and you are your own God and disciple as well. You don't sacrifice yourself for others, so don't expect others to sacrifice for you. That is only fair. Everyone wants happiness; how could you have it all? You must know that there has never been much happiness in this world to begin with. (203–4)

Critics of Gao's work have generally focused on his techniques and themes, and not much has been written about women, though they play a significant role in his novels. As mentioned earlier, feminists might find his treatment of women in *Soul Mountain* bordering on male chauvinism. While I agree that Gao gives women

a prominent role in countering the male-centered Chinese culture in *Soul Mountain,* one might nonetheless find the portrayal in "One Man's Bible" less satisfying, even disturbing. Appearing in a series of encounters fraught with sexual overtones, the female characters in this long novel are somewhat flat and lack autonomy.

Gao has indicated in a private conversation with a writer friend, Ma Jian, that "of course this world could not exist without women. Men would find it impossible to survive without them, and so do I. Without women, a literary work would be boring to write, let alone to read."[17] Some might also argue that sexual desire is an integral part of the human psyche, one which should be included in an expose of the darkest aspects of the Cultural Revolution. However, what remains debatable is the significance of juxtaposing the portrayal of relentless persecution of the individual with sexual encounters in which most of the women are passive objects for sexual gratification.

Like *Soul Mountain,* "One Man's Bible" does not have a clear, linear story line, but incorporates a juxtaposition of episodic recollections and meditations on life, love, and suffering. Obviously, Gao Xingjian does not intend for his two novels to be read merely as stories of the Cultural Revolution or as fantastic travelogues. Both are difficult texts because the author constantly forces readers away from the plots and into his reflections on larger issues. In this sense, they have the quality of the "alienation effect" made famous by Brecht, one of Gao's favorite Western playwrights. They also show how Gao combines dramatic techniques with novelistic themes; ultimately, he would like readers to regard him as a disciple of modernism and a practitioner of "art for art's sake," one who views his responsibility as a writer as both passionately personal and nonideological. He himself has written:

> Literature itself generally has no mission, no group, no movement, no ideology; the writer is solitary, unique. The placards of various ideologies have been attached to him by others so that he can be easily identified and put into archives or else put up for sale.[18]

For Gao, of course, those placards have also led to exile and excommunication from his homeland. The ultimate significance of Gao Xingjian's selection as winner of the 2000 Nobel Prize in Literature, one whose nationalistic and political overtones often obscure the act of writing itself, may well rest in at least one apparent victory of the individual over the collective. I suspect that "China's" first Nobel laureate takes considerable pleasure in that possibility.

Sylvia Li-Chun Lin, Winter 2001

[1] See Jonathan Mirsky, "Chinese Writers Rejoice Over Nobel Prize to Gao," *International Herald Tribune,* 20 October 2000, p. 11.

[2] This work has not been translated into English; the title is taken from Mabel Lee's introduction to *Soul Mountain,* Sydney/New York, HarperCollins, 2000, p. vii.

[3] Chen Sihe, "The First Kite of Modernism," *China Times* (Taipei), 30 October 2000.

[4] From *Theater & Society: An Anthology of Contemporary Chinese Drama,* ed. Haiping Yan, New York, Sharpe, 1998, p. xviii. This was uttered by a senior Party member, as quoted in Mabel Lee's introduction, p. viii.

[5] From the Hong Kong newspaper *Ming Pao,* 15 October 2000.

[6] Gao Xingjian, "My View on Creative Writing," *United Daily* (Taipei), 13 October 2000.

[7] "I'm a Chinese After All," interview with Gao Xingjian in *Ming Pao* (Hong Kong), 15 October 2000.

[8] This comment, widely quoted among scholars of Chinese literature, was made by C. T. Hsia, Emeritus Professor of Chinese at Columbia University.

[9] "Absconding" is Mabel Lee's translation of the original title, *Taowang,* also rendered as "Exile" by Gilbert C. F. Fong, in the appendix to *The Other Shore: Plays by Gao Xingjian,* Hong Kong, Chinese University Press, 1999. It is also sometimes referred to as "Fugitives."

[10] "I'm a Chinese After All."

[11] *The Other Shore: Plays by Gao Xingjian,* p. 40.

[12] See Mabel Lee, "Pronouns as Protagonists: Gao Xingjian's *Soul Mountain* as Autobiography," in *Gao Xingjian: Critical Assessments,* ed. Kwok-kan Tam, forthcoming from the Chinese University Press in Hong Kong, 2001, n.p.

[13] *Soul Mountain,* tr. Mabel Lee, pp. 312–13.

[14] Henry Yiheng Zhao, introduction to *Selected Works of Gao Xingjian,* Hong Kong, Mingchuang chubanshe, 1999, p. 4.

[15] Liu Zaifu, "Epilogue," in Gao Xingjian, *Yige ren de Shengjing* (One Man's Bible), Taipei, Lianjing chuban shiye youxian gongsi, 1999, pp. 451–56.

[16] *Yige ren de Shengjing* (One Man's Bible), p. 188. The translation here is mine. A complete translation by Mabel Lee will be published in late 2001.

[17] Ma Jian, "Wuxian de xiaxiang" (Dreams with No Limits), *Ming Pao yuekan* (Hong Kong), 11/2000, p. 48.

[18] Gao Xingjian, "Bali suibi" (Jottings from Paris), in his *Meiyou zhuyi* (Without Isms), Hong Kong, Tiandi tushu youxian gongsi, 1996. Quoted and translated in Mabel Lee, "Gao Xingjian on the Issue of Literary Creation for the Modern Writer," in *Gao Xingjian: Critical Assessments,* n.p.

PRC Politics and Literature in the Nineties

By the end of the 1980s, "liberalization" in Chinese literary circles had reached the point where Chinese writers at international symposia in Shanghai and Beijing were complaining of a wrongful lack of world recognition. They hinted at a foreign conspiracy to deny them that most individual and bourgeois symbol of acclaim, the Nobel Prize. At the turn of the 1990s, following the student demonstrations in Tiananmen Square in May and June 1989, Chinese literature was again under the thumb of the hard Marxist Left. Leading writers were either in exile abroad or in disgrace at home. Officers from top to bottom of literary, media, and cultural organizations were dismissed and replaced. The rank and file of the Chinese literary world, as they had done in earlier movements and purges, penned condemnations of the decade of "bourgeois liberal" writings and denounced their fellows. The issues that emerged during the government cleanup from June 1989 into the new decade included reevaluations of literary theory and the reaffirmation of Maoist views, the vilification of "gadfly" writers like Liu Binyan, the denunciation of targeted works like the controversial TV serial "Yellow River Elegy" and their authors, the reaffirmation of socialist journalism, and intensified campaigns against all suspect publication lumped under the general rubric *pornography.* "Anti-bourgeois liberalization" was the unifying objective.

By mid-1990, a year after the demonstrations, much of the fuss over these issues had given way to a more pressing concern that had emerged. The dismissals and replacements in the senior echelons of the party had upset the balance of power between the more liberal "reform" faction and the hard-line Marxist Left. Since most of the turnovers had occurred in the ideological and cultural fields, literary concerns were the most directly affected. The situation crystallized into a conflict between the newly appointed overseer of propaganda and ideology, Li Ruihuan, representing the "reform" faction, and the newly appointed acting minister of culture, He Jingzhi, supported by the hard-liners. The resolution of this struggle will be the principal factor affecting the nature of Chinese literature in the current decade.

On 31 August 1989 He Jingzhi, deputy director of the Central Committee Propaganda Department, concurrently took over the post of acting minister of culture following the dismissal of the incumbent, the novelist Wang Meng. He Jingzhi had been a close friend of Mao Zedong and is noted as a "Maoist poet." He enjoys the patronage of the emerging hard-line patriarch, Vice President General Wang Zhen, and is supported by the hard-line faction led by Premier Li Peng and propaganda chief Wang Renzhi. As the new acting minister of culture, he immediately set about purging the ministry of its dissident voice and is reported to have "disciplined the 2,800 staffers who supported the student activists."[1]

Li Ruihuan came to archpatriarch Deng Xiaoping's attention as the energetic, economic-reform-minded Mayor of Tianjin and earned political good grace by his crackdown on student dissidents in 1986–87 and again in 1989. He was elevated to the ruling Standing Committee of the Politburo, with the portfolio of ideology and propaganda. However, Li immediately showed different colors by dismissing two of the five members of Wang Renzhi's hard-line Leading Group on Propaganda in an attempt to balance the overly conservative nature of the unit. (The two men were eventually replaced by similarly hard-line ideologues.)

Coming into the new decade, Li increasingly found disfavor with the hard Left. By August 1990, as maneuvering among the factions for influence in the upcoming Seventh Plenary Session of the Thirteenth CPC Central Committee intensified, contradictions between Li Ruihuan and Premier Li Peng were said to be "sharpening," and the premier was reported to have made private contact with the old-timer leadership such as Wang Zhen, Bo Yibo, and Li Xiannian to denounce Li Ruihuan's speeches as "unscientific and irresponsible." Bo Yibo publicly criticized Li Ruihuan for "acting in an uncouth way." Added Bo, "There is no one standing guard by his mouth."[2]

By the second half of 1990 Li seemed to have shot his bolt. His patron Deng Xiaoping was seriously ailing and had virtually disappeared from the political scene. The Marxist economist Chen Yun, now in his nineties, assumed Deng's mantle and observed the formation of a new propaganda leadership group consisting of Party Secretary Jiang Zemin; the Leftist ideologue Deng Liqun, most recently rehabilitated by Chen and other left-wing supporters like President Yang Shangkun; Propaganda Minister Wang Renzhi; and Xu Weicheng, who runs the day-to-day work of the Central Propaganda Department and is the controlling voice of Gao Di's *Renmin Ribao* (People's Daily). The Leftist ideologue Hu Qiaomu was included as advisor to the group.

Li Ruihuan, although holding the ideological portfolio of the Party Standing Committee, was entirely excluded from membership "for not adopting a clear attitude in criticizing bourgeois liberalization, for not working resolutely, and for having catered to the resentment of those who had made serious political mistakes." Furthermore, Li's antipornography drive was criticized as a ploy to sidestep the real campaign against ideological relaxation. Deng Liqun was tipped to replace Li in the Standing Committee ideology post; but even without the active support of Deng Xiaoping, by the end of 1990 Li had survived the onslaught. His antipornography movement revived in provincial and national discussion and was instated as a draft resolution in the Sixteenth Session of the Seventh National People's Congress Standing Committee, presided over by Wan Li. Wan Li and other "reform" faction members continued to oppose He Jingzhi's confirmation as minister of culture.

The arena is the public press. He Jingzhi controls the official organ of the Ministry of Culture, *Zhong-guo Wenhua Bao* or *China Cultural News.* Li Ruihuan has to present his prolific views on literature through the party-controlled *People's Daily,* which, Li claims, tampers with his speeches. Matters came to a head in the 24 June 1990 edition of the *China Cultural News,* wherein an editorial titled "Leaders' Directions on Ideology" failed to include anything Li Ruihuan had said. Since Li was officially in charge of ideology, such deliberate omission by He was regarded as an attack on Li. Li counterattacked by convening various newspaper editors to hear Wang Renzhi announce that a formal investigation into the 24 June edition was being undertaken. Wang charged that by ignoring Li Ruihuan's views, He Jingzhi was guilty of "splitting the party," a most serious accusation that had been leveled at Zhao Ziyang at the time of his confinement under house arrest during the 1989 Tiananmen disturbances. The Cultural Revolution ultra-Leftist and now deputy minister of propaganda Xu Weicheng was appointed to lead the investigation.[3] Li Ruihuan followed up this initiative by installing a "work team" at the *China Cultural News* offices to monitor future publications, but this team was soon withdrawn under orders from the hard-Left patriarch Wang Zhen.

Another massive left-wing campaign against "bourgeois literature" was launched in *Wenyi Bao* (Literary News; 13 October 1990), the organ of the Chinese Writers Association. This attack focused on the controversial 1985 play *WM* (We). However, the production had not attracted the universal audience that had watched the televised "Yellow River Elegy," and the scope of the new discussion was limited to intellectual literary circles. Instead, coming into 1991, both He Jingzhi and Li Ruihuan turned their attention to the National Forum on Opera Performance and pursued their ideological squabbling through that medium.[4]

Since the demonstrations the orthodox line on literature has been reiterated ad nauseam. Essays published in both the popular and the specialized literary press by leading littérateurs and party and government officials resurrect Mao's talks at the Yenan Forum on Literature and Art as the guiding principles. Criticisms of these half-century-old theories had reached unprecedented intensity just prior to the June 1989 demonstrations. Current spokesmen for the old line are diligent in defending Mao's ideas of the 1940s against prede-monstration charges that they "laid lopsided emphasis on the political function of literature and neglected its esthetic nature," that literature was "primarily to serve the peasants,"[5] and that Mao's dictates are "outdated, stagnant theories of mechanical reflection and vulgar social science which summon only the outer laws of lit-erature but fail to address their inner laws." Instead, typifying the rhetoric of the mid-1990s hard line, He Jingzhi decreed that "studying the basic theories of so-cialism and grasping Marxist-Leninist-Mao Zedong Thought is an extensive and strategic task of literary cir-cles."

Currently highlighted is a Maoist literary principle that has perennially caused confusion: i.e., the doctrine "Let a hundred flowers blossom and a hundred schools of thought contend." This aphorism is coupled with other Maoist pronouncements like "Make the past serve the present and foreign things serve China" and "Weed through the old to let the new grow." At face value the ideas seem to imply that writers are free to express their own views and opinions in whatever form they choose. Mao himself, however, tempered such license with the warning that it would nevertheless be "wrong to allow erroneous ideas to spread unchallenged so that they monopolized the field," and he further dictated criteria for distinguishing between "fragrant flowers and poi-sonous weeds."

Spokesmen for the Left in the 1990s are diligent in further defining the parameters of "literary freedom." Relating Mao's "foreign things serving China" to the current campaign against bourgeois liberalization, they warn writers against picking up Western ideas that were "dumped in the garbage bin years ago and prizing them as precious gems." They call for vigilance against works that reveal "erroneous trends," that oppose or vilify the Communist Party, and that deviate from the socialist road. Criticism and diversity in form and content and healthy development from literary predecessors may be permitted. However, says one clever dialectician, the "double hundred" was a policy of "conscious manage-ment" on the part of the CCP and the socialist regime to "promote China's socialist cultural prosperity." Thus the policy is to "implement socialist culture rather than culture of another nature" and to "safeguard and devel-op socialism rather than shake and subvert socialism." A writer may then express himself freely—within the scope of China's constitution and laws.[6] Other articles hold that only Marxism, whose basic tenets reveal the laws of literary development, can effectively guide di-verse thought, creation, and competition along the so-cialist road. Since Marxism is defined by the CCP, litera-

ture itself should therefore be under the guidance of the party. A summary in He Jingzhi's *China Cultural News* (16 July 1990) blames the disorders of the late 1980s precisely on deposed Party Secretary Zhao Ziyang for his policy of "less control over and less interference in literature" and, perhaps attacking Li Ruihuan, states to the contrary that it is necessary to "tighten control over the world of literature and make sure that power re-mains in the hands of those loyal to Marxism."

Literary freedom is linked with literary "value," which in turn is related to the ongoing campaign against pornography. The problem is progressive. Lenin's anal-ysis that bourgeois literary freedom is dependent upon the "wallet" is cited as the reason why recent literature in China, infected with the bourgeois liberalization of personal inclination, has become a "commodity." That is to say, the success and value of a publication has be-come assessed by its box-office receipts. An article of faith of communist government is that socialist ideas cannot generate spontaneously among the masses and working classes, especially in China, whose small pro-ducers strongly incline toward capitalism and feudal-ism. In the lax ideological administration of the Zhao Ziyang era (1987–89), decent books and magazines were denied circulation because they could not make money, while publications that propagated sex and vio-lence were popular. The function of literature, though, is to promote socialist spiritual civilization. Therefore, it is argued, the government will have to invest in the support of socialist literature to squeeze out pornogra-phy, and writers themselves should uphold the Four Cardinal Principles and submit to the party for guid-ance in the "Two Serves." For literature and art to flour-ish, said acting Culture Minister He Jingzhi (28 July 1990), it must adhere to the socialist road.

Leftist literary ideologues are further charged with observing the paradox between this "flourishing" and the "rectification" of literature demanded by the new cultural authorities. The principle also has its locus clas-sicus in Mao's Yenan talks. "Rectification" and "flourish-ing" must be complementary and mutually promoting. They are not sequential but represent unity. "Rectifica-tion" or "shaking up" is defined as helping the broad masses of literary workers to understand correct orien-tation, to distinguish right from wrong, to strengthen their determination and make concerted efforts to de-velop socialist literature in a healthy and persevering way. Literature "flourishes" when the ideological and cultural front is seized with healthy and fine literary works, in which case the thirst of the broad masses for outstanding works is quenched, the influence of bour-geois liberalization in literature is curbed and eliminat-ed, and achievements in "wiping out pornography" are consolidated and enhanced. The practical problem lies with the literati themselves, who are susceptible to various degrees of error. To improve their quality, they must learn Marxist-Leninist-Mao Zedong Thought and conscientiously study Mao's Yenan talks and Deng Xiaoping on literature under the correct leadership of the Central Committee of the party. Whether literature is properly rectified or not, or whether it flourishes, depends upon whether the writers fulfill their task of "serving the people and socialism."

The inclusion of Deng Xiaoping's writings on literature and art at the tail of the Marx-Lenin-Mao *tripitaka* is relatively new. Although based heavily on Maoist theories, Deng's writings place new emphasis on certain principles. For example, in developing arguments about the relationship between literature and the people, that literature serve the people, the aphorisms "People need art, but art needs people more" and "The people are the mother of writers and artists" have become current. Under the criteria for "shaking up," writers must primarily serve their audience by "upgrading the people's thoughts, stimulating their zeal for construction and meeting their varied and ever-increasing cultural needs." If the people are the "mother" of the writers, a telling familial image, the writers are bound to her in loyalty and must treat her well. The lesson is that, for literature to flourish, writers must forgo their individualism, restrain their egos, and "find roots among the masses."

At a forum on socialist arts (3 August 1990) He Jingzhi summed up the duties and expectations of the writer of the 1990s. He announced that writers must have a correct understanding of the history and realities of China's socialist cause and a firm belief that only socialism can save China and that socialism will prevail. This must be both the prime content for the writers' current ideological and political work and also the ideological foundation upon which literary circles will enhance unity, stabilize the situation, arouse enthusiasm, and promote socialist literature. He Jingzhi continued that the Central Committee has called upon ideological and cultural circles to conduct a shake-up on the one hand and a promotion on the other to uphold the socialist road. He added that the study of basic socialist theories must be linked with the struggle against bourgeois liberalization; the self-education of writers must be linked with motivating and unifying the masses; study must be linked with the realities of daily life; and study of socialist theories must be linked with specific measures for upholding the socialist road of literature.

As noted, Li Ruihuan was the visibly successful mayor of the entrepreneurial port city of Tianjin and is a man of sound practical common sense and economic acumen who has been useful in Deng Xiaoping's "reform and opening up to the West." In taking charge of ideology, however, he has exposed a different side of his character, and Li's remarks on literature seem to confirm Deng's puckish whim for promoting loose cannons to senior posts in order to goad the Jumpish hard Left. It is not that Li has refuted the line on literature endorsed by the Left. His pronouncements all condemn pornography, call for vigilance against bourgeois liberalization, acknowledge the validity of the "hundred flowers" thesis, and promote the development of China's national culture. The contention lies in Li's treatment of these themes and the original, unorthodox personal opinions he appends to them.

As a general characteristic, Li Ruihuan exhibits practical rather than theoretical concern. On the elimination of pornography, which he defines as "sex, violence, and superstition," he describes the abuse as "harmful to China's young," who, he notes, constitute half of China's billion-plus population. Li also complains that the importing of pornographic videotapes and other materials damages the reputation of China's "opening up to the West," which is Li's major political and economic interest. On the other hand, Li is the very voice of moderation. He begs the local leadership—which must mobilize the people to the task—to know the limits of the policy. "Overdoing is no good; insufficiency is no good," he reasons. "Better do less than enough for now; there will be time to make it up. If the work is blind and indiscriminate, if decent things are labeled as reactionary or pornographic and are banned or eliminated, if people's decent lives, hobbies, and cultural interests are meddled in, the people will be dissatisfied." The purpose of eliminating pornography, he stresses, is to make literature thrive and invigorate people's lives, not to strike blows at literature.

Li agrees with the orthodox prescription for eliminating pornography and bourgeois liberalization, which is for writers imbued with the spirit of serving the people and socialism to produce such a corpus of outstanding, healthy, socialist-oriented works that those offending publications will simply be squeezed out of the market. Li attenuates the Leftist stress on the political content in these "healthy works," however, by adding that "comrades in literary circles should unite to invigorate literary creation and dominate the cultural sphere with *lively things the people like to watch and hear*" (my italics). Even on the vexed question of reportage Li advises journalists that the "party spirit" demanded of the media by the Marxist Left "should not affect the readability and delightfulness of news reporting." Li suggests that reports be relevant, entertaining, and interesting. They should "promote good relations among the people and the high morale to accomplish the missions of the party," but they must also be "truthful, current, lively, and terse."

Li is in step with the "Double Hundred" principle. He agrees that the "Two Serves" must be adhered to but adds that *exploration in literature must be continued and encouraged* (my italics). Literary works of different styles must be allowed, so long as they do not counter the Four Cardinal Principles and meet the different requirements of the people. Li further adds that particular works or styles *should not be negated on the basis of the opinion of certain leading comrades* (my italics). Works are to be judged by the masses, not by the opinions of the few. Li acknowledges that writers make mistakes but suggests they be allowed to improve gradually in a "democratic and harmonious environment with unity and high morale." Competition and discussion, criticism and countercriticism should proceed "free of personal attacks and label-sticking." Leaders should appreciate that literary activity has its own special laws and characteristics. They should maintain close relations with writers and refrain from dealing with their work in a "crude and oversimplified manner." Cultural forms from overseas such as ballet, symphony, and disco Li observes to be well received, and he considers that they should be permitted to develop smoothly. He likens China to a cultural melting pot or a large socialist garden wherein flowers of all nations may fully blossom. Li sums up the dialectical relationship between the "Two Serves" and the "Double Hundred" by characterizing the former as being orientation and the latter as being the method of performing the former.

Understanding market forces, Li realizes that books of "good educational significance" are unprofitable and agrees with the Left that their publication must be subsidized. Li the economist suggests that to encourage "healthy socialist cultural undertakings," tax relief be afforded for "outstanding spiritual products" and higher taxes be imposed upon best sellers of little academic or cultural value. Outstanding artists should be given preferential treatment in terms of salary and lodgings, and frugality must be observed in cultural undertakings to avoid extravagance and waste.

Li adheres to the Maoist principle that the people are the masters. Since most of the people live in rural areas, orientation to the masses means paying special attention to the peasants. However, in a much less Maoist vein, Li notes that as production develops and standards of material life improve, *people who have become rich* (my italics) will require a richer and more colorful cultural life. During the decade of "opening up," Li complains, culture did not keep pace with economic development. That wasted resources and was detrimen-

tal to the people's interests. He now appeals to writers and artists to observe advances in scientific technology such as the cinema and television and to improve the quality of media presentations.

Overall, Li's plan for ideology and culture is the promotion, under the leadership and close supervision of the party, of a "splendid national culture." Li advocates that all the positive spiritual wealth created by mankind, all the new achievements and developments of human civilization, no matter whether socialist or capitalist, ancient or modern, be incorporated into the Chinese tradition to give it international vision, enrich it, and form a modern culture with Chinese characteristics. To avoid chaotic importing and the resulting bourgeois liberalization, foreign culture must be analyzed, differentiated, selected, and transformed by the Marxist standpoint and methodology. As Li explains it, developing the new from the old is not "going back to the ancients." Feudal thinking is not required, and while the cream is assimilated, the dross must be rejected. "Look to the future rather than cherish the past" is Li's dictum. Suggesting a less happy methodology that is certain to offend almost everyone, Li says that texts from the imperial era be "edited"—bowdlerized—to render them suitable for China's new culture. He does not, however, demand that literature be subservient to temporary, specific, and direct political missions even as it serves socialism; but literature, he says, with a wealth of subject matter on the life and spirit of the socialist era, must portray the universal success of socialism over the last forty years, especially during the recent decade of "opening up."[7]

Thus the two opposing factions of literary ideology led by acting Minister of Culture He Jingzhi and the hard Marxist Left, on the one hand, and the more moderate "reform" member of the Standing Committee of the Politburo with the ideology and propaganda portfolio, Li Ruihuan, on the other express their respective viewpoints. He Jingzhi predictably takes shelter behind the tried and tested orthodoxy of Maoist doctrine, and although he proffers no more than a frozen, dull, backward-looking policy of party and government control over literature, he is nevertheless safe from charges of heresy. Neither should literary circles outside the PRC deceive themselves that Li Ruihuan is any less a Marxist. His views on literary ideology conform with those of the hard Left in every principle. However, Li is also a practical man, committed to economic reform in China. His concern with the development of a national culture is accompanied by original ideas for the practical implementation of such growth. Rather than merely intoning the litany of Maoist doctrine, within the strictures of the Four Cardinal Principles and the "Two Serves," Li bravely, or recklessly, offers hope for freer intellectual and literary discussion, criticism, experimentation, and variety.

John Marney, Summer 1991

[1] *South China Morning Post* (Hong Kong), 7 May 1990, p. 10. For convenient access to these sources, see *Foreign Broadcasts Information Service: China Daily Report* (hereafter abbreviated as *FBIS*).

[2] Chiu Chen, article in *Cheng Ming* (Hong Kong), 1 August 1990, p. 15.

[3] Seth Faison, article in *South China Sunday Morning Post* (Hong Kong), 15 July 1990, p. 13.

[4] *Renmin Ribao*, 6 December 1990; *FBIS*, 4 January 1991, pp. 18–21.

[5] "Nothing in History Should Be Avoided as Taboo," *Wenxue Pinglun*, no. 5 (1989).

[6] Nan Hai, "Comments on Opposing Liberalization and Implementing the 'Double Hundred' Policy," *Renmin Ribao* (People's Daily), 4 December 1989, pp. 1–3.

[7] For Li Ruihuan's views, see the *People's Daily*, 15 May 1990, pp. 2–3, a report of Li's speech delivered on 10 January 1990.

Avant-Garde Poetry in China: The Nanjing Scene 1981–1992

▪ PRELUDE: THE MISTY POETS

Following the climactic events of 1976 that brought a close to the Cultural Revolution, the final years of the 1970s would see the first indications of a new post-Mao literature in mainland China. The new political leadership—whose authority depended on the delegitimization of the Cultural Revolution—found it in their interest to allow, within limits, a more critical literature. For the most part, this new writing was rather unsophisticated, cathartic literature protesting the many injustices of the preceding decade and egregious cases of official corruption. However, at the end of 1978 there appeared in Beijing the first issue of an unofficial literary magazine, *Jintian* (Today), that would prove of seminal importance in the coming decade. Edited by the young poets Bei Dao and Mang Ke, *Jintian* lasted only two years before it was suppressed in the aftermath of the crushing of the Democracy Wall Movement. But already a number of the *Jintian* poets had been appearing in official journals, including the prestigious *Shikan* (Poetry Journal),[1] and the official censure and controversy they aroused only added to their appeal among younger readers and poets. Besides Bei Dao and Mang Ke, the most important of these poets included Gu Cheng, Yang

Liang, Shu Ting, Jiang He, and Duo Duo, who as a group became known as the *menglong shi* or Misty (Obscure) Poets—initially intended as a label of dismissal by their official detractors. It is no overstatement to say that virtually all poetry of significance written in mainland China over the past fifteen years or so has derived from or developed in conscious reaction to Misty Poetry; so, while this paper is primarily concerned with a number of these later poets, a preliminary understanding of Misty Poetry is requisite.[2]

Originally the Misty Poets were brought together less by any specific esthetic program than by their mutual opposition to official verse and the social and political dogma it espoused. What most obviously linked them was simply an insistence on the validity of the individual. Some of their work expressed a defense of the individual against ideological coercion in forms that were little more than a relatively more poetically and allegorically expressed extension of much socialist verse of the preceding decades. More significant, however, was the work that earned them the designation "Misty," poetry which expressed itself in more obliquely symbolist or imagist forms. A typical example is Bei Dao's "Notes from the City of the Sun," a sequence of fourteen very short poems, of which a few follow here:[3]

Love
Tranquillity. The wild geese have flown
over the virgin wasteland
the old tree has toppled with a crash
acrid salty rain drifts through the air

Youth
Red waves
drown a solitary oar

Art
A million scintillating suns
appear in the shattered mirror

Fate
The child strikes the railing at random
at random the railing strikes the night

Living
Net

These titles may initially strike one as a bit portentous, a tendency to which Bei Dao is rather prone, but one ought to keep in mind the context in which the poems were composed; it is part of Bei Dao's strategy to redefine or perhaps undefine these reified terms, which, according to official ideology, ought to have fairly fixed meanings. Such elliptical, imagistic poems are familiar enough to Western readers, but their indeterminate suggestivity, the manner in which they sometimes do and sometimes do not appear to illustrate their titles, posed a challenge to official critics. While detractors accused such work of willful obscurity, it is clear enough that Bei Dao was engaging in the time-honored practice of thinly veiled social criticism. The "red waves" of "Youth," quoted above, uncomfortably suggest both the mindless group-thought of the Cultural Revolution and perhaps of the Red Guards in particular, as well as the bloodied individuals they rolled over. Bei Dao imagines the younger generation he represents as struggling to survive, to hold on to some sense of individual self-worth amid this red tide. "Art" suggests that with the shattering of the utilitarian mimetic mirror of official socialist esthetics, art will be freed to fulfill its manifold subjective possibilities.

The notorious final poem, "Living" (in the original Chinese text, the title has two characters while the poem itself has just one), was dismissed as unworthy of being called a poem at all. But again the implicit social criticism must have been evident enough. The image is exemplary in its openness, suggesting any number of entanglements, relationships, interconnections in which we inevitably find ourselves caught. Or we might read the relationship between title and text as antithetical rather than analogous, so that life in its more authentic sense is that which eludes the net of society that the latter would designate as "living." However, such allegorical translations are less significant in and of themselves than the very indirectness of manner and the purposeful ambiguity that most offended conservative readers—a poetry that defied the ideological instrumentalization that had been dogma since Mao's "Yen'an Talks on Literature and Art" (1942). As is so often the case, what was most politically explosive was precisely that which presented itself as beyond politics.

■ THE THIRD GENERATION POETS IN NANJING (1982–1988)

Although *Jintian* was forced to cease publication in 1980, the nationwide controversy it stirred up only intensified, and it was in this heady atmosphere that the younger poets across mainland China passed the beginning of the 1980s.[4] Inspired by the example of the Misty Poets, whose activities were largely confined to Beijing, the first half of the decade would see the appearance of rival groups in a number of other major cities. Some of the most daring innovations developed in the old capital of Nanjing, and in what follows we will focus principally on two very different tendencies there, as represented by the poetry of Han Dong and Che Qianzi.

In 1981 the nineteen-year-old Han Dong won the most prestigious Chinese literary prize for young writers, the Youth Literary Award, for his sequence "Hold Up the Indomitable Head," but at this point he was still strongly influenced by Misty Poetry. So, it was something of a shock when in the following year he published "Mountain People," which clearly challenged Misty Poetry in its heyday. While Bei Dao's poetry expressed a distrust of society, it nonetheless hoped for society's rational reconstruction, and consequently the poetic subject attempted to shoulder the responsibility of the entire society—a heroicism that tended toward messianism. Bei Dao's work is somber and dignified, with a strong awareness of history and its burdens. His language attempts to build up images and symbols, and, following him, symbolism became the rule among younger Chinese poets.

Han Dong's "Mountain People" deploys a very flat, unadorned language to express the unheroic, even fatalistic consciousness of ordinary people whose concerns are more immediate and limited than the great national and ideological questions that have so preoccupied China's intellectuals and political leaders throughout this century. Rejecting the use of poetic imagery and symbolism, Han Dong undermines the more grandiose pretensions of both official and Misty Poetry. It has been plausibly suggested that Han Dong's position is somewhat analogous to that of William Carlos Williams vis-à-vis Bei Dao as T.S. Eliot. Indeed, in a 1988 essay titled "After Three Worldly Roles" Han Dong castigates Chinese poets in general and Bei Dao in particular for catering to Western expectations. In the early 1980s Western modernisms abruptly poured into China in an unsorted mass and inevitably have had a considerable impact on recent literary, artistic, and intellectual developments. However, it ought to be kept in mind that this influence has been strongly mediated by the haphazard selection and highly uneven quality of translations, and that the critical digestion of Western modernism and postmodernism has lagged far behind the pace of poetic creation. In the case of Han Dong, his colloquialism and concentration on common, often nonurban characters and concerns can be partially understood as a reaction against what he saw as an uncritical enthusiasm for all things Western.

One can better understand the startling impact of Han Dong's work by considering another of his early poems that directly responds to Misty Poetry. A well-known poem by the Misty Poet Yang Lian is entitled "Wild Goose Pagoda," referring to the famous pagoda that still overlooks present-day Xian, the city now most famous for its terra-cotta warriors. The city, formerly called Chang'an, was the capital of the Chinese Empire in its most glorious period, particularly during the Tang dynasty, an era when China produced its greatest poets and was unusually outward-looking (the city was also gateway to the Silk Road). In Yang's poem the ancient pagoda speaks of the glories it has witnessed and laments their loss as China turned inward: "I am held fast in a cage I have myself forged / History of millennia weighs heavy on my shoulders, / Leadweight; my spirit / Shrivels in this venomous solitude." Although alluding to China's long history, such lines also obviously apply rather neatly to the more recent events of the Cultural Revolution and its betrayal of the original hopes of the Chinese Revolution. However, the poem concludes on an optimistic note with hope for a rebirth: "Let me destroy at last this nightmare-cage, / Realign shadow of history, spirit of defiance, / Contiguous, like night and dawn."[5]

Drawing on a classical tradition of poetic lament, Yang's poem is complex in its literary, historical, and mythic allusiveness. The primary point for our purposes is its strong historical and nationalist consciousness, its formal and dignified tone, and its aspiration to be a vehicle for the renewal of Chinese culture. This is Han Dong's response:

About Wild Goose Pagoda
What do we know
About Wild Goose Pagoda
Many come from far away
Just to climb to the top
To be a hero for once
Some will come back a second
Or more times
Those who are frustrated
Those who grow fat
All climb to the top
To be heroes at least once
Then walk down
Go into the broad street
Disappear in an instant
Also a certain type jumps off
Blooming on the steps into a red flower
Becoming a real hero
A present-day hero

What do we know
About Wild Goose Pagoda
We climb to the top
Take a look at the scenery
Then walk down again

Han Dong deflates not only Yang's poem but also a whole classical tradition of poems written on climbing famous heights to meditate on topics of great import. Here the climb, an act of reverence for China's glorious past, is reduced to nothing more than a banal tourist stop, reflecting the ordinary person's lack of historical consciousness or even interest. The only one to climb

for some purpose is the suicide, through whom Han Dong unleashes his most devastating barbs to puncture the rhetorical vacuousness of the nationalist and revolutionary catchwords "red," "blooming flowers," and "heroes." Undoubtedly, behind the Wild Goose Pagoda alluded to by both Yang Lian and Han Dong looms the familiar pagoda at Yen'an, which paradoxically became an icon of the early heroic period of the Communist Revolution. Han Dong's no-nonsense antisentimentalism went well beyond demystifying merely the Misty Poets and offered younger poets a "lost generation" cynicism that has its own sort of exhilaration. Within a few years this sarcasm would be taken to far greater extremes than Han Dong by a number of the younger fiction writers, who in some cases seem intent on nihilistically undermining belief in anything whatsoever.[6]

Similarly, Han Dong's poem "The Ocean Is Before You Now," which purportedly was written in response to Shu Ting's "Morning Songs at the Seaside," ironizes the too predictable and sentimental poetic symbolism of the sea. The heavy use of repetition, so characteristic of Han Dong and many of his followers, tends to undercut any suggestion of lyric flight. But some of Han Dong's most interesting poems, such as "News About a Child" and "A Woman I Don't Know" (see appendix for both), go beyond a demystifying realism to suggest enigmatic parables. In addition to the usual destabilization of perspective, the male speakers of these two poems also appear to be losing their customary patriarchal footing. Merely emphasizing Han Dong's cynicism is to focus too narrowly on one, albeit important, aspect of his work. Even in "About Wild Goose Pagoda," the underlying suggestion is that for the ordinary person there simply is no reason to be much concerned with all the past grandeur associated with the pagoda and the ancient capital. Not only did the common people reap rather limited benefits from these glories, but recent history and the routine demands of everyday survival have effectively erased any meaningful sense of historical consciousness, except to the degree it is evoked for chauvinistic purposes by government propaganda. Many of Han Dong's poems empathize unsentimentally with the ordinary Chinese citizen's ground-level view of life—a view with no grand vistas or extravagant hopes but rather a fatalistic and stoic acceptance of the lot that has been dealt them. It is worth keeping in mind that, for all the dramatic changes that have taken place in recent decades, still today close to 80 percent of the Chinese people live in the countryside—an existence very different from that of urban dwellers and well beyond the ken of even the most sympathetic Western imagination.

Although the designation "Third Generation," used to describe the younger generation of poets following the Misty Poets, would not be introduced into literary circles until 1984 by the Sichuan poet Shang Zhongmin, Han Dong's "Mountain People" (see appendix) can be considered as decisively inaugurating the Third Generation.[7] The "first generation" refers to the largely political poets of the period after 1949, the "second generation" to the Misty Poets themselves. The Third Generation poets are in most cases only a few years younger than the Misty Poets; but given the tumultuous social changes over recent decades, a few years can mean dramatic differences in experience and attitude, and those who came to early maturity after the 1960s tend to take a significantly more cynical perspective than do their slightly older compatriots. While the Third Generation acknowledges the seminal importance of the Misty Poets' break with official poetry and emulate their example of innovation and challenging authority, they are identifiable by their deliberate reaction against the Misty Poetic stance and language, which became sloganized as "anti-sublimity," "anti-expression," and "anti-imagery." Because Han Dong both challenged the newly established idol of the younger poets and opened up a new direction for continuing their revolution, he naturally came to be regarded by many young poets as the leader of the Third Generation. It should be kept in mind, however, that "Third Generation" does not designate a specific group of poets but rather a broad spectrum of different poets nationwide who represent an important shift in orientation or attitude toward poetry.

In 1984, Han Dong and Yu Jian of Kunming (Yunnan Province) joined to found the group "Tamen" (Them), based in Nanjing, and brought out their own underground publication bearing that same name. The designation "Them" was taken from the title of Joyce Carol Oates's 1969 novel to suggest a sense of alienation from mainstream society. Han Dong, Xiao Hai, Xiao Jun, Ding Dang (from Beijing), A' Tong (who later changed his name to Su Tong and became well known as a New Wave fiction writer), Yu Xiao-wei, and Ren Hui formed the backbone of the group. Han Dong's original intention in founding *Tamen* was the same as Bei Dao's in founding *Jintian:* to challenge the official publications. As in the West, it is through these small magazines and presses that the more innovative work is disseminated, and they offer space to young poets relatively free from the distractions and vanities of official success. Throughout mainland China most of the new poetry of importance since 1978 has initially appeared in these unofficial journals.

The group Them can be taken as marking the inception of contemporary modernist poetry in Nanjing, and within a few years of its founding the members' wider impact would become clearly evident. The year 1986 would prove to be a watershed. By then two loyal members of Them, Xiao Hai and Xiao Jun, had established national reputations. *Duihua shijie* (Dialogue Envoy) appeared on the streets of Nanjing, presenting a broad range of underground poets and offering a rival journal to *Tamen.* Although its editor, Zhou Jun, always hoped it would become the focus of a coherent group, it never succeeded in this ambition; despite its initial momentum, many came to feel that the journal was too indiscriminate in its editorial policies, and the more radical poets turned away. Nevertheless, Zhou Jun has been tireless in publishing and promoting Third Generation poets from Nanjing and elsewhere. In the same year, *Shige bao* (Poetry Press) in Hefei (Anhui Province) and *Shenzhen qingnian bao* (Shenzhen Youth Press) sponsored "An Exhibition of Modern Poetry Groups 1986," published in several consecutive issues, the first large-scale revelation of the new underground poetry in official journals. This exhibition not only made Them's poetry known to the public at large, but also stripped Beijing of its status as the sole center of modernist verse. Chengdu, Nanjing, and Shanghai all became rival centers of innovative poetic activity. A couple of years later, much of the work from these exhibitions was collected in *Exploratory Works of the Third Generation Poets,* published in Beijing in 1988, the first official book publication of the Third Generation poets.

■ **LANGUAGE POETRY IN NANJING (1988–92)**

The radical wing of the Third Generation is epitomized by the work of the Suzhou poet Che Qian-zi. Che's "Story of the Crystal Vase," published in 1982, showed inklings of his greater interest in the play of language, which was pushed further in the sequence "My Sculpture," published the following year. Especially the third poem of this sequence, "Three Primary Colors," attracted considerable adverse criticism, because Che seemed wrapped up in the anarchic possibilities of language.

I, on a blank sheet of paper
A blank sheet of paper—there's nothing
With three crayons
Each draws a line
Draw three lines

Without a ruler
The lines are crooked

An adult says (he has grown up):
Red yellow blue
Are three primary colors
Three lines

Stand for three roads

—I don't understand
(What was it he said?)
So sticking to what I like
Draw three round circles

I want to draw the roundest circle

Here Che rejects the automatic metaphorization of poetry and insists on a childlike absorption in the very act of writing, striving for a sort of purity and satisfaction within the medium itself. This does not, however, prevent the poem from suggesting an allegory of the poet's effort to pursue his crooked way in opposition to the straight lines of conventionalized language use and all the social strictures this stands for. Although his concerns are more esthetic, Che's use of unadorned conversational language aligns him with Han Dong against the Misty Poetry.

As an indication of the larger situation within which these younger poets, including the Misty Poets, were working, it is worth taking a brief look at the sort of official reaction this seemingly innocent poem provoked. In *Shikan* (Poetry Journal) the older poet Gong Liu struggled to make sense of the poem.

> "Three Primary Colors" sings of the soul of the younger generation. . . . "Blank paper" is their self-portrayal, and "three lines" represent three different paths in life. "Red" stands for revolution, "yellow" for degeneration, and "blue" for uneventfulness. "Crooked" means things are beyond one's control; "three circles" implies that no matter whether you engage in the revolution, become degenerate, or live a nondescript life, you cannot get out of these pitiful predetermined circles.[8]

However, Gong Liu quickly dismisses this reading, as well as the poem itself, for its hopeless obscurity or, worse, its malignant message. Initially, under such public pressure Che made limited concessions, and his more restrained efforts were much praised by the authorities. Nevertheless, Che could not bridle himself for long, and in the latter half of the 1980s he would rapidly push forward into realms of poetic possibility where even most younger poets have been unable to follow. While his critics complained because they could not readily reduce his poems to stable metaphoric readings, Che would develop a radically metonymic poetry with proliferating perspectives and no obvious coherence.

In association with Che, Lu Hui (later Yi Cun) and Zhou Ya-ping also began more radical experimentation. Initially, they too were more or less followers of the Misty Poets and also, in the case of Zhou, for a while were influenced by Them. But in 1986 appeared Zhou's "New City" and "Youth" (see appendix), expressing an adolescent rebelliousness whose exuberant irreverence and playfulness marked a distinctive new development and hinted at the direction his mature work would take. Around 1987, while both were students at Nanjing University, Che Qian-zi and Zhou Ya-ping joined forces to organize the Formalist Poetry Group, founded to consider the possibilities for a more radically innovative writing. At this time Huang Fan was embarking on related poetic experiments and soon became associated with the Formalist Group. In 1988 Che first proposed his concept of a language-centered poetry he called Original Type, and the following year they formed another group under this designation to put their ideas more rigorously into practice. In early 1991 Che and Zhou brought out the first issue of *Yuanyang* (Original, or Prototype), presenting an initial selection of their own new work. The following year the second issue offered a more substantial presentation, also including poetry by Yi Cun, Huang Fan, Hong Liu, and Xian Meng, along with a group manifesto and critical pieces.[9]

Compared with other Third Generation poets, the Original poets renounce the use of language as a tool and instead concentrate on exploring the literary potential within language itself. In most other Third Generation poetry, language is still transparent, is still the expression of everyday truths or pseudotruths; readability and tangibility are its main concerns, since it begins with a predetermined concept of poetry. However, the Original poets would rather consider "poetry" as a concept waiting to be defined through continual practice. Thus poetry evolves in process, and new practices are constantly being tried out. The Original poets are fascinated with the meanings generated out of the aural and visual relations between Chinese characters and word combinations. This requires a new and more active orientation toward the text on the part of the readers such that their own discoveries become part of the evolving definition of the concept *poetry*. In other Third Generation poetry, idea prevails over form and technique, but in Original poetry this is reversed. Han Dong once made the now-famous remark that "poetry begins and ends in language," but the full implications of this slogan have only been realized in practice by the Original poets.

The Original poets quickly explored a wide range of new possibilities. As usual, this was especially the case with Che Qian-zi, who precociously absorbs and generates a bewildering variety of new and old forms and techniques, ranging from classical-style lyrics to concrete poetry. A couple of stanzas from a long poem entitled "Chair"—Che refers to it as a "five-legged chair"—will give some indication of the radical advance made over work of just a few years earlier.

Countenance in the water, people in the water
Big river flows through flesh, like light penetrating
glass
Carrying silt toward the lower reaches
And boats, loaded with goods
Mathematics, flowers of anti-allegory

Forging gold rings for nipples
Pink human body. Jewelsmith
The village detective raises donkey skins under
lamplight
A paper horse treads the candy-counter, 11:20
Nipple, the eye of the candle sweltering, about to
drop

Water is a recurring image in much of Che's work, which seems appropriate for this verse of swift-flowing transformations. Various images or associations will reappear like elusive threads to bind the myriad possibilities the poem allows. Che once called "Chair" a detective poem, and indeed the "village detective" periodically reappears, as do oblique suggestions of some crime; but whither it all tends is impossible to say. Clearly it is the poet-reader who is the detective pursuing a case without final resolution. Such poetry evokes both the anxiety of instability and the exhilaration of discovery. Perhaps echoing Baudelaire, these "flowers of anti-allegory" refuse to allow themselves to be reductively solved, and the mystery continues. *Anti-allegory* is a key term in the Original poets' manifesto, and their work is clearly an effort to salvage both the language and the reader from the severe deprivations both have suffered under the reign of Mao-speak.

The Originals adamantly resist more or less direct political reflection as a degradation of the poetic. Nevertheless, even if it is frequently indirect, satire is almost irresistible given the situation against which they are reacting, and in general Original poetry is notably humorous. Whereas Che tends toward the mischievously playful, the work of Zhou Ya-ping can be more pointed. In a characteristic piece entitled "University" (see appendix), from *Big Machine* (1990), there are recurring suggestions of phoniness and sterility which presumably might reflect Zhou's feelings about higher education. Yet, while the biting wit is evident enough, neither the target nor the position of the poet is clearly identifiable; indeed, both appear to be in constant motion, with the unnerving result that we cannot be certain whether the poet is aiming his barbs at them, at us, or at himself.

As has been often remarked, traditional Chinese poetry is notable for its paucity of long poems; so, one of the significant developments pursued by a number of Misty and Third Generation poets is the composition of extended poems or sequences, many of which adopt loose narrative or mythic structures. In recent years both Che Qian-zi and Zhou Ya-ping have worked almost exclusively in longer forms or sequences that are startling in their abandonment of predictable structures as well as in their extended musical and visual inventiveness and improvisation. At present, Che seems especially to favor serial poems in which the individual sections often vary markedly in both form and style. By placing such apparently incongruous sections together, Che further stretches the possibilities of connections and conjunctions between the widely dissimilar. Certain sequences, such as the remarkable "Cloth" poems (see appendix), cut across other sequences, with different sections written over many years appearing here and there, grouped with other poems or series.

Although Che is enormously prolific, only a small percentage of his work has seen print, and most of that in unofficial publications with limited circulation. While the general direction Che has taken will undoubtedly strike many readers of contemporary poetry as inevitable, despite the rapid literary transformations taking place in China recently, his work is too far out even for most of his fellow poets. Not surprisingly, Han Dong's work has enjoyed much greater popularity and influence, although few of his epigones can manage his touch, tending to fall into either easy cynicism or sentimentality. Particularly in their handling of language, Han Dong and Che Qian-zi seem to represent two antithetical reactions to the Misty Poets, but there has been an enormous range of other developments by younger poets that fall somewhere in-between. Unfortunately, judging from the translations presently available, the reader can hardly avoid the impression that there has been little going on in China aside from the early work of the Misty Poets, which, despite its seminal importance within the Chinese context, is simply not first-rate poetry. Yet this poetry is constantly recycled in various collections, while the more recent and more mature work of the Misty Poets, much less the great variety of work done by important Third Generation poets, goes largely untranslated and undiscussed. It is to be hoped that along with the current surge in translations of contemporary Chinese fiction, a more representative and interesting offering of contemporary poetry will eventually make itself available.[10]

Jeffrey Twitchell and Huang Fan, Winter 1997

[1] *Shinkan* (Poetry Journal) was the premier poetry magazine in Communist China from 1957 to 1965 and represented the official esthetic inclination of those poets approved by the government, an inclination which manifested itself primarily in ro-

mantic eulogies and revolutionary battle songs in both free verse and ballad form. However, even these works were considered unacceptable by the ultraleftists during the Cultural Revolution, and the journal was suspended in 1965. It was revived in 1976 by the older poets, and because of their own recent experiences they initially took a liberal and benevolent attitude toward the early work of the Misty Poets; however, they soon realized that these younger poets threatened the prestige of their own work, and most turned against them.

2 The most useful selections of translations of early Misty Poetry can be found in *Mists: New Poets from China* (Hong Kong, Renditions, 1983) and *A Splintered Mirror*, tr. Donald Finkel (San Francisco, North Point, 1991). There are also individual volumes of poetry by Bei Dao, Yang Lian, Gu Cheng, and Duo Duo which include more recent work.

3 From Bei Dao, *The August Sleepwalker*, tr. Bonnie S. McDougall, New York, New Directions, 1990. I have modified the translation of the last poem by omitting an indefinite article; the character for "net" (*wang*) can be read as either a verb or a noun.

4 By the late 1980s, most of the major Misty Poets went into self-imposed exile, and after the events of June 1989, *Jintian* (Today) was revived as an exile journal based in Oslo, Norway. See Bei Dao, "The Purposes of the Magazine *Today* (*Jintian*)," *Sulfur*, 34 (1994). A selection of work from the revived *Today* can be found in *Under-Sky Underground*, eds. Henry Y. H. Zhao and John Cayley, London, Wellsweep, 1994.

5 Tr. John Minford with Seán Golden, *Renditions*, 19 & 20 (Spring & Autumn 1983). "Wild Goose Pagoda" is part of a larger poem cycle entitled *Bell on the Frozen Lake*.

6 While throughout the early 1980s the most innovative work was being done by poets, 1985 would see a veritable explosion of startling new fiction, mostly by previously unknown young writers. It has been noted that many of the most experimental and sardonic of these writers come from the Yangtze River valley, and this may reflect Han Dong's early influence; the more notable of these writers include Su Tong from Nanjing (who began as a poet closely associated with Han Dong), Yu Hua from Zhejiang, and Ge Fei from Shanghai. Other leading practitioners of New Wave fiction (*xincao xiaoshuo*) include Ah Cheng, Can Xue, Mo Yan, Han Shaogong, and Liu Heng. Quite a few of the recent films from mainland China that have gained international attention have been based on New Wave works, including Zhang Yimou's *Red Sorghum* (Mo Yan), *Raise the Red Lantern* (Su Tong), and *Ju Dou* (Liu Heng). In the past few years there has been something of a mini-explosion of translations of this fiction as well; good samplings can be found in *The Lost Boat: Avant-garde Fiction from China*, ed. Henry Zhao (London, Wellsweep, 1993), *Running Wild*, eds. David Der-wei Wang and Jeanne Tai (New York, Columbia University Press, 1994), and *Chairman Mao Would Not Be Amused*, ed. Howard Goldblatt (New York, Grove/Atlantic, 1995).

7 A number of different terms are current to designate this younger generation of poets, including "Newborn Generation" and "Post-Misty"; the latter is perhaps the most aptly descriptive, although we will usually prefer "Third Generation" simply because this is the most common usage among the Nanjing poets themselves. Little of this poetry has been translated, but a short selection of a number of major Post-Misty Poets can be found in *Renditions* 37 (1992).

8 Quoted in Michelle Yeh, *Modern Chinese Poetry: Theory and Practice Since 1917*, New Haven (Ct.), Yale University Press, 1991, p. 87.

9 This latter gathering, with an afterword by J. H. Prynne, has been translated as *Original Language-Poetry Group* and published as a special issue of *Parataxis* (Brighton, Eng.), 7 (1995).

10 Thanks must go to Zhen Zhen, Xu Yi, and Ma Ming-qian for their invaluable information and suggestions for this article.

The Literary World of Mo Yan

After more than two decades of vigorous literary development, China has witnessed the emergence of a cadre of talented novelists. Undaunted by a succession of political and economic upheavals, these writers are attracting considerable attention as they fervently weed through the old in order to bring about the new. Mo Yan is a name that stands out amid this wave of creativity. Emerging during the early 1980s with a collection of nativist stories titled *Touming de hongluobo* (The Crystal Carrot), he was labeled as a "root-seeking" (*xungen*) writer. His debut novel, *Honggaoliang jiazu* (1987; Eng. *Red Sorghum*, 1993), a historical romance with bold and unrestrained erotic imagery, propelled Mo Yan's writing into a new creative vista. Yet despite the acclaim by critics and readers, Mo Yan was not content merely to rehash themes or stick with a style with which he had grown familiar. He had another agenda. He followed *Red Sorghum* with an outpouring of short stories and novellas, as well as four powerful novels: *Tiantang suantai zhi ge* (1988; Eng. *The Garlic Ballads*, 1995), *Shisan bu* (Thirteen Steps; 1989), *Jiuguo* (1992; Eng. *The Republic of Wine*, 2000), and *Fengru feitun* (Big Breasts and Full Hips; 1996). Some of these novels are grotesque and bizarre; others are marked by bleak indignation. In the final analysis, Mo Yan's creation is far too complex to be dismissed by such facile labels as "root-seeking" or "avant-garde."

China's preeminent novelist has adopted the nom de plume Mo Yan, meaning "don't speak." Yet from his pen emerges an endless cascade of words. Whatever the subject matter, a torrential flow of rich, unpredictable, often lacerating words remains his trademark. While this claim to silence amid an outpouring of fictional works may signify a contradiction of self-mockery and self-praise, it is precisely why so many literary critics have lent their voices in his support, whether from the perspective of feminism, national discourse, or something else. And yet Mo Yan responds, almost without exception, to this academic and literary clamor with silence. He knows, instinctively, that the written page is where the novelist exists.

Mo Yan's works most compellingly initiate discussions in three areas: 1) the possibility of imagining historical space; 2) the crisscrossing relationship between narration, time, and memory; and 3) the redefining of political and erotic subjectivity. My discussion will focus primarily upon Mo Yan's five full-length novels, in addition to his important novellas, such as the four masterworks in *Hong erdou* (Red Ears; 1998).

■ **FROM PARADISE TO THE OUTHOUSE**

Mo Yan was born to a peasant family in Northeast Gaomi Township in Shandong Province in 1955. Gaomi is situated on the Shandong Jiaodong Peninsula, a place never known to have produced literary talents, an area of barren land and simple people. His formal schooling ended at the fifth grade, when China's disastrous Cultural Revolution broke out in 1966. From the age of eleven to seventeen, he returned to the life of a peasant. Later he was assigned to a temporary position at a factory, eventually leaving the place of his youth to join the army.[1] On the face of it, such a background is not conducive to producing a writer. But after five years of military life, literature became his passion and, ultimately, his career, as a member of the pla Cultural Department. All the while, however, his greatest source of creative inspiration was his hometown, Gaomi, and the people who live there.

When Mo Yan writes of Northeast Gaomi, he is careful to keep in mind that this place is the origin of his creative thought and fertile imagination. Just a few hundred miles from Gaomi is Zichuan, the hometown of Pu Songling,[2] author of the late-seventeenth-century work *Liaozhai zhiyi* (Liaozhai's Records of the Strange). The deeds of heroic brotherhood found in the sixteenth-century novel *Shuihu zhuan* (Eng. *The Water Margin*) also originated in Shandong during the Southern Song Dynasty. With this in mind, when we encounter ancient Chinese war imagery in *Red Sorghum* or monsters and demons in later works, it is easy to spot Mo Yan's literary tip-of-the-hat to his Shandong predecessors. While many modern Chinese nativist writers take their hometown as the chief inspiration for their fiction, there are few who are able to transcend the simple method of imitation and duplication, and consistently provide readers with room to exercise their imagination. With Northeast Gaomi as his focal point, Mo Yan brings together the legendary romances of his red-sorghum forebears, thus providing the most important historical space in contemporary Mainland Chinese fiction.

The "historical space" to which I refer includes, but is not restricted to, the traditional dialectical discourse on space, time, history, and the ontological hometown (*yuanxiang*). "Historical space" refers to how writers like Mo Yan three-dimensionalize a linear historical narra-

tive and imagination, and how they locate concrete people, events, and places into a flowing, kaleidoscopic historical coordinate. Bakhtin reminds us that the meeting point of space and time in a novel is always at the site of the origin of narrative impetus.[3] With Northeast Gaomi, Mo Yan has established a contrast of values, juxtaposing city and country, development and backwardness, civilization and nature. But this sort of thematic analogy has its limitations, and I must stress that Mo Yan's ontological hometown, as found in the pages of his fiction, is a product of narration, the fruits of his historical imagination. Saying that Mo Yan's "root-seeking" works represent the reappearance of various styles and features of a certain geographic environment would not do as much justice to them as saying that they represent the central symbol of another time and space, thus fulfilling the category of dialectical historicism.

And so, in *Red Sorghum,* the wild, open sorghum field is also the stage on which a modern historical revolutionary romance is carried out. We can hear (and seemingly see) the narrator galloping through the "wilderness" of history, memory, and imagination. Mo Yan's scenes—from the erotic glimpse of "My Grand-dad" and "My Grandma" in the sorghum field, the raging conflagration, and the narrator's family's strange and eerie adventures, to the magical method of brewing spirits, the tales of brotherhood and revenge among heroic wanderers, and the blood and tears shed in the struggle against Japan—invariably win the acclaim of readers as vistas of narrative perfection. In Mo Yan's literary world, the past and the future, desire and fantasy are transformed into a flesh-and-blood panorama.

In republican society, where historical (fatalistic) meaning is built on stilts, Mo Yan's method of spatializing and dissecting history goes beyond an affirmation of the importance of life experience. By daring to utilize a durable linguistic symbolism to adorn the native soil of his creation, Mo Yan also provides a historical space with virtually unlimited possibilities for strange and fantastic narrative mutations. Examples in which the coordinates of reality and illusion converge in his fiction include earthshaking madness, a wild spotted dog that searches for human corpses, a locust plague that blots out the sky, and rushing floodwaters.

As a contrast to the splendidly beautiful space of *Red Sorghum,* Mo Yan has created another category of fiction, which insistently returns to the quagmire of realism, expressing a side of nostalgic homesickness that cannot be communicated to those on the outside. These two methods of imagining the ontological hometown reveal the potential for a dialectical discourse. The story "Baigou qiuqianjia" (Eng. "White Dogs and the Swings") is intended as an especially biting satire aimed at literary history. The narrator of the story is an educated young man who has taken time off to return to the country-side. His unchanged hometown is a barren, vulgar place that lacks the power to leave even the slightest favorable impression on him. Only when a chance meeting with a childhood playmate occurs beside the sorghum field are childhood memories of the innocent affection between him and a young girl stirred up. However, the angelic little girl from his youth, blinded after falling off a swing, was forced to marry a mute and bore him three children who similarly cannot speak. In the face of his nostalgic longing for a lost past, the blind woman's response is: "What's there to miss in this run-down place? It's like a goddamned steamer in the sorghum fields, about to suffocate me."[4] No longer are we presented with the rousing romantic spectacle of *Red Sorghum*. Instead, we are left with nothing but a historical degeneration where all one can do is sigh because "things aren't what they used to be."

In recent years Mo Yan has extended his construction of historical space into other areas. In the novel *Thirteen Steps* the protagonist is a madman locked in an iron cage. He relies upon the audience (or listeners) to feed him chalk so that, one after another, he can spit out tales of the miraculous and inconceivable. It is not difficult to imagine where Mo Yan's intentions lie with this work. It is precisely the confines of his protagonist's cage that provide him with a "way out," through his fertile and fantastic imagination. As listeners, "we" are outside the cage, yet are so deeply taken with the caged man's stories that, without realizing it, we become his mouthpieces. This bizarre narrative journey represents the culmination of Mo Yan's meditation on the relative relationship between language and space. One scholar put it well when he said: "Caught up in befuddled logic and a threatening terrain, we are compelled to grope for the sharpest knife or the rarest, strangest piece of chalk, and thus, with a myriad of stories, fight our way out, all the while scribbling an illusion that will help us get back on our feet — an illusionary iron cage."[5] In the end, we are all (historical and linguistic) prisoners in a cage.

The incredible, almost preposterous plot of *Thirteen Steps* leaves readers disturbingly wondering just where it all will end. And it is precisely this tactic that Mo Yan uses to subvert the traditional position to which we are accustomed as readers. In *The Garlic Ballads* (literally "The Garlic Ballads of Paradise") the author adopts a completely different approach. Although on the surface this novel marks a return to traditional realism and the tactics of realism, Mo Yan's satiric intentions hidden within the text are not necessarily weaker than in *Thirteen Steps*. The novel relates the story of officials who

force the people to rise in protest, ultimately leading to a peasant revolt. But setting the story in a certain "Paradise" county of the Republic inevitably leads us to marvel over Mo Yan's irony: in a utopia ruled by workers, peasants, and soldiers, a scandal occurs, and once things get started, they can never be fixed. Without glossing over even the most trifling detail, reality/realism strives to capture and re-create the stitches between social space, form, and consciousness. Mo Yan's narrative exposes the muddleheaded "self-restriction" of official narrative as he presents a biting imitation of the novelist's nonstop attempts to overstep literary boundaries.

Only when Mo Yan's "Paradise" degenerates into a "Republic of Wine" does his literary imagination finally ascend to a higher level. *The Republic of Wine* must be considered the second creative climax for Mo Yan, after *Red Sorghum*. This novel narrates the story of a detective who arrives at the mysterious Republic of Wine to investigate a report of cannibalism. While you will not find the Republic of Wine on any map, visitors who enter will sense a strange, almost *déjà vu* feeling of homely warmth cloaked in the uncanny. This is a place of unbridled consumption, waste, and filth; at the same time, it is the site of carnal indulgence and excessive desire. The Republic rules with a kind of ideological asceticism, yet this "Republic within a Republic" is a world within itself, where nothing is taboo. Within this Republic of Wine the rarest, tastiest delicacy is the flesh of an innocent toddler. With this, Lu Xun's call to "save the children," made in the context of an attack on the cannibalistic nature of Chinese society, is completely reversed. No wonder the descendants of the Red Sorghum family have become the wretchedly base, corrupt entrepreneurs of the Republic of Wine.

Although *The Republic of Wine* is an anti-utopian work, for Mainland Chinese readers whose literary tastes have been suspended for more than forty years, it may also be the utopian release of four decades of pent-up desire. Within this Dionysian space, citizens accustomed to asceticism find themselves suddenly able to swallow, spit, and relieve themselves without hindrance—the engineering of the Republic of Wine's sewage system must have been a major hurdle for the municipal government. Although Mo Yan has exaggerated and fabricated all kinds of marvelous stories and strange tales to leave the reader tongue-tied and dumbstruck, on the most fundamental physiological level he has created a political allegory. Not only is the criminal case never solved, but our drunken cadre investigator ends up falling into a manure pit; from a manure pit to Paradise, on the road to utopia what could be more alluring and enticing than that?[6]

■ FROM OFFICIAL HISTORY TO UNOFFICIAL HISTORY

The second issue raised by Mo Yan's works is that of historical memory and temporal narration. In Chinese Communist artistic and political theory, "history" has always been a major focal point. Under the influence of more than thirty years of Maoist discourse, a codified form of language originating from Mao's revolutionary utterances, "history" has become a self-evident truth. From the revolution to liberation to continual revolution, "a priori history" has interpreted New China's past and foretold her future. Revolutionary historical fiction that began to appear in the 1950s looked back at the Chinese Communist Party's heroic past, carving out the difficult process of founding a republic with the magnanimity of epic narration. Coincidentally, these works served to apotheosize the eternal nature of revolution and prophesy that the glorious days of proletarian dictatorship were just around the corner.

The ability of Mo Yan and writers of his generation to develop a critical voice in the face of this torrent of historical discourse demands our attention. With lofty sentiments, grand aspirations, and a bold sensual vision, the narrator in *Red Sorghum* reflects upon the way in which his Granddad, Grandma, and people of their generation laid the foundation of a family lineage. As the story develops, family history and national history gradually merge, climaxing with "My Granddad and My Grandma's" annihilation of the Japanese in a guerrilla attack. In this respect, Mo Yan appears to be paying tribute to works of revolutionary historical fiction. But on closer examination, we realize that not only does his revolutionary history fail to deliver the promise of ultimate meaning, but it actually reveals a historical degeneration in which each generation fails to live up to the preceding one. As heir to his family line, the narrator of *Red Sorghum* can only imagine the heroic actions of his parents and ancestors, or, with even greater difficulty, record the tribulations and sufferings they endured during the various revolutions and political movements. As stated earlier, Mo Yan has the ability to take us back to the primal scene where history was created; he also has the gift of taking us deep into the consciousness of his characters. At the same time, however, he does not forget to remind us that the ultimate end of narrative is to be found at the fissure between history and revolution, not at their completion.

History can be constantly rewritten, and clues to temporal narration can always be rearranged. *Red Sorghum* navigates through three generations of a family history, solemnly recapitulating a timetable corresponding to the revolution and the founding of the People's Republic. I suspect, however, that what he truly wants to write is just the opposite. After the Cultural Revolution, the destruction of socialist order, and the retreat of the "grand narrative" logic of Maoist discourse, the unbridled, almost deranged legend created by Mo Yan, with his unique literary style, is itself a new kind of historical power. If Maoist historical narrative takes the sublime as its benchmark icon,[7] then what Mo Yan takes as his trademark is a grotesque esthetic and historical view.[8]

The narrative Mo Yan utilizes in his next novel, *The Garlic Ballads,* is completely hybrid and cluttered with different voices, as it moves from folk custom to news coverage, and from stream of consciousness to magic realism. In regard to the work of veteran writers, Mo Yan has brilliantly developed and revived the peasant literature of earlier Communist writers. The satiric element lies in the fact that the target of his peasant uprising is none other than the local government, which legitimates itself with the motto "Serve the People." Moreover, the conclusion of the novel is replete with a heavy dose of official documents to lend weight and justification to governmental suppression and the "injustices" of judicial sentencing (Mo Yan changed the ending after the first edition). Speaking for the "injured and insulted" is one of the major characteristics of Chinese literature from the May Fourth (1919) era through Communist literature under Mao. But Mo Yan's novel inquires into what sort of justice literature can "represent" or "promote." How does it "legally" define the unfair and the unjust? And where is the boundary between poetic justice, legal justice, and historical justice?

Similar questions arise in *Thirteen Steps,* except that they are expressed in a completely different fashion. What the "thirteen steps" refer to is never explicitly defined in the text; however, they can be taken to represent the innumerable variables of life, a defiance of narrative logic, or what one scholar has called a black hole in historical consciousness.[9] The audience in the novel crowds around the caged madman, trying to guess the "meaning" of his frenzied words, so enticed by his ramblings that they cannot tear themselves away: "He pulls you into the story, you collaborate with him to make up the story. You sense you do not have the strength to resist the logic of the story. Your fate is in the hands of the caged man."[10] As we listen to the story and to its constant repetition, we are torn from the caged madman, trapped in a seesaw relationship where each party is confined to its own viewpoints of linguistic meaning, knowledge, and power. It is in this world that language loses the power to express or transmit meaning. And just as these various notions of language and discourse are endlessly enticing, when the moment comes that one is left with no words to utter, "the meaning of history floods one's heart."[11]

With *The Republic of Wine* Mo Yan has carved out yet another literary path. The plot—an investigator's attempt to apprehend a group of cannibalistic villains—faintly reveals a sort of hermeneutic attempt to trace things back to their source and discover their true nature. However, during the course of writing, Mo Yan complicates and clutters his narrative path. In the end, his playful detours through idle talk, bullshit, jokes, and leftover chitchat are more enticing than the main story line. Examples include the strange scene of peasants competing to sell their "meat babies" for the highest price, and the legend of "ape wine," both of which serve to blur the distinction between the true and the false. And it does not stop there. The novel also features a series of letters between Mo Yan (who serves as the narrator) and a third-rate writer in which they discuss the tricks of the trade of literary creation. Good guys and bad guys, good literature and bad literature, the issue of historical justice and historical injustice—all merge in Mo Yan's narrative melting pot. Just as the novel utilizes huge amounts of excretory images, it also becomes more and more unbridled and uncontrollable as the story progresses, finally ending unresolved amid an overwhelming flurry of linguistic mazes and filth. Is Mo Yan's narrative intentionally imitating the process of going from sober to drunk? Or, like the myth of the Greek god Bacchus, is he stirring up the ecstasy of carnal indulgence and chaos, only to be dealt the fate of being dismembered and eaten amid his ecstasy?

In 1993, while writing a number of essays and other types of prose, Mo Yan published a series of short stories titled *Shenliao* (Supernatural Talk). The stories in the volume are terse and forceful; some relate wondrous tales of uncommon men, whereas others relate ghostly tales of the magnificent and incredible. It is as if Mo Yan worked with a literary sketchbook at his fingertips, and although each story is limited in length, they all remain powerful works in their own right. For instance, "Tie hai" (Iron Child), which is set in the iron-smelting movement during the Great Leap Forward (1958), depicts the bizarre tale of two small children who "eat" scraps of copper and iron to survive. In "Ye yu" (Night Fisherman) Mo Yan tells of a fisherman who has a run-in with a voluptuous ghost that has returned from beyond the grave. "Shen piao" (Eng. "Divine Debauchery") relates the story of a country gentleman with an insatiable taste for flesh who hires a score of prostitutes to fulfill his lust for carnal pleasure; his actions are born of desire, but in the end become sanctified in a ritual of exquisite debauchery. Mo Yan himself has admitted that this work has a very heavy *guiqi*, or spectral

mood.[12] Although he grew up on the soil of atheistic Red China, he here pays witness to a world of strange ghouls and supernatural spirits hidden all around him. Wandering through the fissures on the periphery of a grand history, he is left incapable of anything but "supernatural talk."

The spirit of Pu Songling, Mo Yan's fellow townsman of three hundred years ago, refuses to leave: "In a world of peace, man and ghost remain divided. In today's world, man and ghost freely intermingle."[13] The series "Supernatural Talk" appears to have no outward aim, but hidden within the work is Mo Yan's sigh of disillusionment. The short story "Red Ears" takes the ridiculous tale of a prodigal son who loses his family's wealth as its heart, and his huge ears, which function almost as sexual organs, as its soul. At the same time, the story uses the tale of the founding of the Republic as its background. This eccentric and fantastic piece offers a fundamental view into the unique style of "Supernatural Talk."

Big Breasts and Full Hips was Mo Yan's major effort of 1996. The name alone caused a sensation, as did the novel's mammoth size. Nearly 500,000 characters long, it relates the story of a Chinese peasant woman from the North who raises nine children under the most adverse and difficult circumstances. The story, which begins on the eve of the second Sino-Japanese War (1937) and ends in the 1990s, deals with all the stormy changes and hardships that transpired during those years of Communist Chinese history. Using maternal love to extol the heavy gloom of an "obsession with China" has been the specialty of writers ever since May Fourth. In the history of modern Chinese fiction, characters who epitomize the "earthly mother" are so numerous they have become a kind of literary stereotype. Mo Yan, however, has another intention. His mother has in her "all the morally perfect characteristics of the Chinese nation and tradition"; but each of her nine children is a bastard, and after they grow up, they become social failures, never living up to the glorious future for which they seemed destined. This flock of daughters (and one son) follows the Communist Party on its road through the "history of the revolution," capsizing both revolution and history along the way. The spirit of the mother may be grand, but how can her breasts and hips also be grand?

The narrator of *Big Breasts and Full Hips,* Shangguan Jintong, is one of Mo Yan's most unforgettable characters. He is his mother's only son, sired by a Swedish missionary who meets a violent death during the second Sino-Japanese War. Jintong witnesses every tumultuous event in modern Chinese history during his life, yet there is nothing in the world to compare in importance with the breasts of his mother, his sisters, and his wife. Reading through the chapters in which Mo Yan describes 10,000 breasts jiggling in heaven and a breast-fondling banquet on earth is enough to leave readers extolling the praises of the author's literary imagination. While he has always written with a taste for the eerie and magnificent, when looking back at *Red Sorghum* we can see that this debut novel was but the first display of handiwork by a literary master. It is no wonder then that this writer, who grew up on the "milk of the Communist Party," incites never-ending opprobrium from leftist critics.

■ FROM THE SUBJECT TO THE BODY

In the previous two sections I have discussed how Mo Yan has borrowed the coordinated of the ontological hometown to develop a kind of abnormally divergent historical space, and how from the set pattern of realism he has developed a strange and heterogeneous flow of memory and narrative. He not only was present during the "root-seeking" and avant-garde literary movements of the 1980s, but moved freely between them, refusing to be pigeonholed or locked into any one style or movement. To take things a step further, Mo Yan's characters, born of fiction but raised in a world of realism, are extremely difficult to box into any kind of generalization. From the narrative of adolescence in his early work, "The Crystal Carrot," to the later confessions of a breast addict in *Big Breasts and Full Hips,* Mo Yan's characters have continually expressed the ever-changing face of "New China's" citizens. Although virtually every type of character appears in his fiction, we are never presented with the "Red," glorious model citizens that Mao's China would like us to believe are the standard. Mo Yan's characters are merely the possessors of mortal desires and emotions, encapsulating virtually all types of human behavior. To trace this out, we can find examples of his characters' going head to head against one another, passing through metamorphoses, being reincarnated, and even possessing corpses. The actions of these characters not only express the special traits of magic realism and the influence of traditional Chinese legends of the strange, but also display a startling similarity between these two very different literary genres.

We can now begin our discussion of the third main aspect of Mo Yan's fiction: the portrayal of history and subjectivity. Although in the West, academic discussions regarding subjectivity are no longer a hot topic, in post-Maoist China it remains a central issue of debate. Lu Xun's observations of Chinese "national characteristics" have been revisited and brought to the table for discussion along with Liu Zaifu's "theory of characteristic composition," which at one point sparked heated debate.[14] While this debate was raging, Mo Yan was quietly creating his own image for his compatriots; setting small and weak opponents against the big and strong, matching the deformed and disabled against supermen,[15] he went to places no one else could imagine.

In many of Mo Yan's works the "I" characters' looks and appearance are varied and unique, their thinking twisted. One especially noteworthy example is "White Dog and the Swings," where a university student's chance meeting with a childhood playmate leaves him trapped between nostalgic memory and ugly reality. The young man in "Red Locusts" first experiences a sensual encounter, then witnesses a locust attack that blots out the sky. Then there is the little boy in "Ku he" (Eng. "Dry River") who, after being taken advantage of and having no place to vent his anger, goes to the extreme of making a radical accusation against adult society. Then in "Baozha" (Eng. "Explosions") we are presented with a young man trapped in the uncertainty and restlessness of marriage and family, who achieves temporary release by means of explosive bodily movements. Having read all too many Maoist literary works that focus upon the moral superiority of "I" characters, we are taken by the mediocrity of such figures in Mo Yan's fiction, characterized by petty and strange qualities. Thus Mo Yan has redefined the value of being human and recalled his own ability to imagine desire. Nothing takes this further than Shangguan Jintong's first-person narration in *Big Breasts and Full Hips,* where he offers detailed and drawn-out discussions of his Oedipal love for his mother, his breast fetish, and his decadent impotence. There is no shortage of antiheroes in Chinese fiction of the 1990s, but a strange case like Shangguan Jintong, who is not afraid to expose his ugly side, may very well be a first.

Mo Yan intentionally satirizes the turbulent times of "our" generation, for how can our experiences compare with the earthshaking historical storms witnessed by our grandparents' generation? The novella "Fuqin zai minfulian" (Father in the People's Militia) is set in 1948, when Father (like the father in *Red Sorghum*) braves untold dangers in completing his mission to lead a people's militia in transporting army provisions for the People's Liberation Army. Here the formulaic role of the "peasant hero" and knight-errant chivalry are combined with stunning results. The scene where virtually naked people's militiamen transport army supplies across a river in winter is a grand and familiar scene, but more than anything, it is an expression of Mo Yan's power to enchant as a storyteller. At the same time, however, in order to complete their mission, the militiamen endure cold and hunger, even killing starving women who attempt to block their way. The moral predicament in which Mo Yan places his characters cannot but arouse our suspicions. The moment Father delivers the supplies to the destination (he actually takes them past their destination and is nearly dismissed) is when Mo Yan's biting satire makes its appearance. Regardless of how brave and wise Father may have been, when confronted by the military machine of a political party, he must obey orders. To devote one's life to one's country is the supreme goal of "Father's" generation.

Readers familiar with Mo Yan's work may comment that his imagination in portraying female characters is not as strong as with his male characters. The dominance of the male in Mo Yan's fiction surpasses all else; except for mothers and grandmothers (who are also respected in patriarchal society), female characters are generally allowed only minor roles. In some of his fiction, however, we note the author's attempts to strengthen his female characters. The climax of "White Dog and the Swings" takes place when the narrator, fleeing from the countryside, encounters a peasant woman blocking the road. Readers of the story know of the childhood friendship and the adult misfortune between this peasant woman and the narrator. During their final meeting on the country road, the woman has but one request, which is to take her into the sorghum field for an illicit sexual encounter. She and her mute husband already have three mute children, and she wants at least one child who "has a voice." With this female peasant's corporeal request, Mo Yan mocks the habit of idle theorizing on the part of male intellectuals. For the moment that Lu Xun's call to "save the children" is carried out through an illicit desire for sexual pleasure by this peasant woman, the entire narrative of May Fourth humanist realism crumbles.

We have already seen how the citizens in Mo Yan's fictional world are brimming with vitality and determined to take any measures necessary to achieve their goals. For nationalism or brotherhood they willingly endure trials by fire and die without regret; but in the realm of human desire they are equally unstoppable. The reason that *Red Sorghum* stands out is that in tracing his family history, the narrator delves into *how* his granddad raped his grandma; the powerful story then extends from her rape in the sorghum field. But as revolutionary history advances, China's (and men's) desire becomes progressively weaker. In works like *The Garlic Ballads,* repressed desire finds all manner of release and leads to a world of imminent and ever-present danger. By the time we reach *The Republic of Wine,* Mencius' classic lesson that "food and sex are man's nature" is displayed in the most bizarre manner imaginable. The special investigator in the story receives orders to investigate a case, but as he sets out, he falls into a sexual trap,

becoming involved with the wife of his archenemy. As desire takes over, he forgets his mission and ultimately dies in a manure pit; everything rotten and stale ends up where it belongs. Mo Yan often links sexual desire with eating, drinking, urination, and defecation. Specialists in the structure of "deep consciousness" would do well to adopt this phenomenon as instructive in any discussion of the inability of Chinese to leave behind their stage of oral fixation.[16]

But the novel that stands as the true crowning work of Mo Yan's spectacle of desire remains *Big Breasts and Full Hips. If The Republic of Wine* exaggerates the unsavory habit of modern Chinese to stuff themselves full and drink themselves silly, then *Big Breasts and Full Hips* takes things a step further by describing the trembling of another (male) sensory function: the desire and variations of the male sense of touch. Our male protagonist's chief aim in life is to fondle women's breasts; for him, all breasts are created equal. Mo Yan's depiction of a male's obsession with breasts borders on insane organ fetishism. Shangguan Jintong's desire is directed only at breasts—any woman's breasts—and nothing else. In his eyes, females are objectified as a kind of corporeal sexuality. Beneath his breast obsession, however, we know that he is stricken with sexual impotence. Big breasts and full hips represent a sexual totem; how could they not also represent a sexual taboo?

Using history and space, narrative, and the subjective, I have pointed out three of the directions in which Mo Yan's fiction has led us. I have regularly cited the term *history* because I believe that history is the fundamental force moving Mo Yan's fictional world, and is also the object he is trying to replace through his fiction and imagination. Forty years of Chinese historical narrative and practice have left too many scars and examples of brutality. Since the 1980s, the people's ultimate and most sacred point of reliance—communism—has crumbled, decaying before our eyes. Mo Yan has attempted to reconfigure memory and bring the past to life, and in that attempt, his methods have struck a resonant chord with readers and awakened their literary sensibilities. From paradise to the outhouse, from official history to unofficial history, from the subject to the body, Mo Yan spares nothing in his intermingling of narrative styles and forms; this in itself constitutes his most efficient tool in engaging in historical dialogue. If one prepares to undertake a serious study of Mo Yan— this essay included—one cannot underestimate his literary field of vision and potential. Knowing this, we can only sigh and say, "Amid this myriad of endless words and language, how can one say 'Mo Yan' (don't speak)?"

David Der-Wei Wang, Summer 2000, translated by Michael Berry

[1] Mo Yan, *"Shenliao xu"* (Preface to "Supernatural Talk"), Beijing, Beijing shifan daxue chubanshe, 1993, p. 2.

[2] Mo Yan, "Haotan guiguai shenmo" (Love to Talk About Monsters and Demons), in *Cong siling niandai dao jiuling niandai* (From the Forties to the Nineties), ed. Yang Ze, Taipei, Shibao chuban gongsi, 1994, p. 345.

[3] M. M. Bakhtin, *Dialogic Imagination,* trs. Gary Emerson and Michael Holqvist, Austin, University of Texas Press, 1983.

[4] Mo Yan, "White Dog and the Swings," tr. Michael S. Duke, in *Worlds of Modern Chinese Fiction: Short Stories & Novellas from the People's Republic, Taiwan & Hong Kong,* Armonk (N.Y.), Sharpe, 1991, pp. 51–52.

[5] Chen Qingqiao, "Fangxia tudao cheng Fo hou, zai cao xiongqi bian cheng xian: Mo Yan *Shisan bu* de shuohua luoji chutan" (Put Down the Butcher Knife and Become a Buddha; Becoming a Saint After Wielding a Murder Weapon: An Initial Probe into Logical Discourse in Mo Yan's "Thirteen Steps"), *Dangdai,* 52 (August 1990), p. 130.

[6] Wang Dewei (David Der-wei Wang), *"Nihe Miyuan Anxiang, Jiuguo Fucheng Feidu:* Yizhong Wutuobang xiangxiang de bengjie" (Muddy River Labyrinthine Garden Dark Alley, Wine Country Floating City Abandoned Capital: The Collapse of a Kind of Utopian Imagination), *Dialogue jianzhu,* 6 (August 1997), p. 90.

[7] See Ban Wang, *The Sublime Figure of History: Aesthetics and Politics in 20th Century China,* Stanford (Ca.), Stanford University Press, 1997.

[8] Wolfgang Kayser, *The Grotesque in Art and Literature,* Bloomington, Indiana University Press, 1987.

[9] Chen Qingqiao, p. 133.

[10] Mo Yan, *Shisan bu* (Thirteen Steps), Taipei, Hongfan shudian, 1990, p. 203.

[11] Ibid., p. 7.

[12] Mo Yan, "Love to Talk About Monsters and Demons," p. 344.

[13] This quotation is taken from the Song Dynasty work titled "Yang Siwen Yanshan feng guren" (Yang Siwen Meets an Old Friend on Yan Mountain).

[14] See Jing Wang, *High Culture Fever,* Berkeley, University of California Press, 1996, ch. 5.

[15] See my essay "Jiren xing, dangdai Dalu xiaoshuo de zhongsheng 'guai' xiang" (The March of the Disabled Man: The Rebirth of the 'Strange' in Contemporary Mainland Chinese Fiction), in *Zhongsheng xuanhua,* Taipei, Yuanliu chuban gongsi, 1988, pp. 209–20.

[16] Sun Longji, *Zhongguo yishi de shenceng jiegou* (The Deep Structure of Chinese Consciousness), Taipei, Jiegouqun, 1990.

My Three American Books

What follows is the text of a talk given at the Tattered Cover bookstore in Denver, Colorado, on 20 March 2000.

Before I start, I should mention my American translator, Howard Goldblatt. My novels could have been translated by someone else and published in the United States, but the English versions would never have been so beautifully translated, if not for him. Friends of mine who know both Chinese and English have told me that his translations are on a par with my originals. But I prefer to think they've made my novels better. I admit that some people, with dubious motives, have told me he's added things absent in the original, such as descriptions of sex. These people were ignorant of the fact that he and I have an agreement that he'll translate sex scenes in ways that will appeal to American readers, which is why the English and Chinese versions may seem different.

Howard and I began our collaboration in 1988. We've exchanged more than a hundred letters and spoken innumerable times over the telephone. The sole purpose of such frequent contact is to perfect the English translations. Often, we confer over a phrase or an object with which he's unfamiliar. Sometimes, I have to call upon my primitive drawing skills to sketch something for him. From this you can see that he is not only a talented translator, but a serious and conscientious one. It's my good fortune to be able to work with someone like him.

My first novel translated into English was *Red Sorghum.* Before it was rendered into English, it was made into a movie by China's renowned director, Zhang Yimou, and won a major prize at the Berlin Film Festival. The novel became famous because of the movie. In China, when my name is mentioned, people say, "Oh, *Red Sorghum!*" Forgive my immodesty, but, as a matter of fact, *Red Sorghum* evoked strong reactions in China before it was made into a movie. So Zhang Yimou benefited from my novel, then my novel benefited from his movie.

I wrote *Red Sorghum* when I was still at the PLA Art College. It was the early 1980s, the so-called "golden age of contemporary Chinese literature." An enthusiastic readership inspired writers to become passionate about literature. People were no longer content to create or read stories written in traditional styles. Readers demanded that we be more creative, and we dreamed of nothing but becoming more inventive. A critic quipped that Chinese writers were like a flock of sheep being chased by a wolf, a wolf whose name was innovation.

At the time, I had just crawled out of mountain ditches, and didn't even know how to use a telephone, let alone possess any knowledge of literary theories. So the wolf of innovation was not chasing me. I hid out at home, writing whatever I felt like writing. Now that I have some rudimentary knowledge of theory, I realize that slavishly following trends is not true innovation; real creativity is writing honestly about things you're familiar with. If you've had unique experiences, then what you write will be unique. And being unique is new. If you write something different, you will have developed a unique style. It's like singing: training can change your technique, not your voice. No matter how diligently you train a crow, it can never sing like a nightingale.

In other talks I've given, I've brought up my childhood. While city kids were drinking milk and eating bread, pampered by their mothers, my friends and I were fighting to overcome hunger. We had no idea what sorts of delicious foods the world had to offer. We survived on roots and bark, and were lucky to scrape together enough food from the fields to make a humble meal. The trees in our village were gnawed bare by our rapacious teeth. While city kids were singing and dancing at school, I was out herding cows and sheep, and got into the habit of talking to myself. Hunger and loneliness are themes I've repeatedly explored in my novels, and I consider them the source of my riches. Actually, I've been blessed with an even more valuable source of riches: the stories and legends I heard during the long years I spent in the countryside.

In the fall of 1998, when I visited Taiwan, I participated in a roundtable discussion on childhood reading experiences. The other writers on the panel had read many books in their childhood, books I haven't read even now. I said that my experience was different, because while they read with their eyes as children, I read with my ears. Most of the people in my village were illiterate, but such words flew from their mouths that you'd have thought they were educated scholars. They were full of wondrous stories. My grandparents and my father were all great storytellers. But my grandfather's brother—we called him Big Grandpa—was a master storyteller, an old Chinese herbal doctor whose profession brought him into contact with people from all walks of life. He was very knowledgeable and had a rich imagination. On winter evenings, my brothers, sisters, and I would go to his house, where we'd sit around a dusky oil lamp, waiting for him to tell us a story. He had a long, snowy white beard, but not a single hair on top. His bald head and his eyes glinted under the lamplight, as we begged him to tell us a story. "I tell you stories every day," he'd say impatiently. "How many do you think I have? Go on, go home and go to bed." But we'd keep pleading, "Tell us a story, just one." And finally, he'd give in.

I've memorized some three hundred of his stories, and with minor changes, every one of them could become a pretty good novel. I haven't even used fifty of them. I doubt I could ever use up all the stories he told us. And the ones that haven't been written are far more interesting than those that have. It's like a fruit peddler who tries to sell the wormy fruit first. Someday, when the time is ripe, I plan to sell those stories of his.

Most of my Big Grandpa's stories were told in the first person, and they all sounded like personal experience. Back then we believed they were his own stories, and it wasn't till much later that I realized he'd made them up as he went along. His stories sprang from the fact that he was a country doctor who often saw patients in the middle of the night. They always started like this:

"A couple of nights ago, I went over to Old Wang the Fifth's house in East Village to check on his wife. On my way back, as I passed that small stone bridge, I saw a woman in white sitting on the bridge and crying. I said to her, 'Big Sister, it's the middle of the night. Why are you out here all alone, and what are you crying about?' She said, 'Mister, my child is sick, he's dying. Would you go take a look at him?'" My Big Grandpa said, "I know every woman in Gaomi, so this one had to have been a demon." He asked her, "'Where do you live?' The woman pointed under the bridge, 'There.'" My Big Grandpa said, "'You can't fool me. I know you're that white eel demon under the bridge.' Seeing that her ploy had failed, she covered her mouth and smiled. 'You've got it again.' Then, with a jerk of her head, she leaped under the bridge."

Legend had it that a white eel the size of a bucket lived beneath the stone bridge. It had transformed itself into human form to seduce my Big Grandpa. We asked him, "Big Grandpa, why didn't you go with her. Since she was so pretty . . ." He just said, "Dopey kids, if I had, I'd never have come back."

Then he went on to another story. A few nights earlier, he said, a man came to see him, leading a little black donkey with one hand and holding a red lantern in the other. The man said that someone in his family was very sick. Now my Big Grandpa was a very conscientious doctor, so he got dressed and left with the man. The moon was out that night, and that little black donkey shone like fine silk. After the man helped him onto the donkey, he asked, "Sir, are you all set?" My Big Grandpa said he was, so the man slapped the donkey on the rump. Big Grandpa said, "You can't believe how fast that little donkey flew. How fast? All I heard was the wind whipping past my ears, and all I saw were trees on both sides of the road whizzing backward." We were dumbstruck. That donkey must have been like a rocket. He said he knew something wasn't right, and he must have run into demons again.

What kind of demons? He didn't know, so he made up his mind to wait and find out. Before long, the donkey descended from the sky and landed in a magnificent mansion, all lit up by lamps. The man helped my Big Grandpa down as a white-haired old lady came out of the house and led him to the sickroom. It turned out to be a woman about to give birth. Country doctors had to take care of every illness in the world, so delivering a baby was no big deal. He rolled up his sleeves to help the woman deliver her baby. He said this woman was also very pretty, unsurpassingly beautiful—that was his favorite phrase in describing a pretty woman. And not only beautiful, but amazingly fertile. As soon as he grabbed hold of a hairy, furry baby, out came another head. My Big Grandpa thought, "Hey, twins!" But then another furry head poked out, and he thought it must be triplets; then out came another. Just like that, one after another, she delivered eight babies, all furry, with little tails. Cute as can be. It suddenly dawned on him. "Foxes!" he shouted, but the word was barely out of his mouth when ghost-like cries and wolfish howls erupted, as darkness descended around him. Scared witless, he bit his middle finger—a fabled way of exorcising demons—and wound up in a tomb, surrounded by furry little foxes. The adults had fled.

I also heard stories from my grandmother, my father, and other talented storytelling relatives. I've committed many of them to memory. Since they were told by different people, they have distinctively different flavors. If I were to relate all the stories they told, my talk today would be as long as the Great Wall. So now I'll tell you about my novels.

On the surface, *Red Sorghum* seems to be about the war against Japan. But in reality, it's about the folklore and legends told by my kin. Of course, it's also about my longing for the contentment of love and a life of freedom. The only history in my head is the legendary type. Many famous historical figures were actually ordinary people, folks like us. Their heroic accomplishments were nothing but the result of embellishment over a long period of oral transmission. I've read some American reviews of *Red Sorghum*. They struck a resonant chord when they viewed my novel as folklore. This story, which I wrote in the ancient form of storytelling, has been viewed by Chinese critics as a fantastic, new innovation, and I can't help but chuckle to myself. If this is innovation, then being innovative is the easiest thing in the world.

My second novel in English was *The Garlic Ballads,* which I wrote in 1987. In the early summer of that year, a major incident occurred in a Shandong county, a place famous for its garlic. The farmers had a great harvest that year, but were unable to sell their crops, owing to the corruption of officials. Tons of garlic lay rotting in the fields. So the outraged farmers trashed the county government building. There was widespread fall-out,

with lengthy newspaper reports. In the end, the officials were dismissed, but the farmers who led the rebellion were also arrested and jailed. This incident enraged me. I may look like a writer, but deep down I'm still a peasant. So I sat down and wrote the novel; it took me a month. Of course, I moved the setting to the kingdom of my literary production: Northeast Gaomi Township. In reality, this is a book about hunger, and it is a book about rage. I wasn't thinking about innovation when I wrote it, because I felt the need to vent the anger welling up inside me. I wrote it for myself and for all my peasant brethren. But after the book was published, critics continued to insist that I was striving for innovation. They pointed out that the novel was told from three perspectives: first, that of a blind man, a balladeer; second, the objective viewpoint of a writer; and finally, the perspective of the official voice. And they called *that* innovation!

In my hometown, there were indeed balladeers, most of them blind men. They generally performed in groups of three: one to play the Chinese lute, one to beat a drum, and the third to sing. Some were very talented, men who wove current affairs into their songs and improvised as they went along. As a child, I admired them greatly, and considered them to be true artists. When I was writing *The Garlic Ballads,* their hoarse, sad voices echoed in my ears. That, not innovation, was my muse.

My third novel is the recently published *Republic of Wine.* I began writing it in 1989 and finished it in 1992. It was published in 1993, to deafening silence. The clamoring critics had suddenly turned mute. I guess these noisy "experts" were shocked. They had been promoting innovation all along, but when true innovation arrived, they turned a blind eye to it.

There are still many improvements that could be made on both *Red Sorghum* and *The Garlic Ballads,* and if I were to rewrite them, I believe they'd be better. But with *The Republic of Wine,* I couldn't improve it, no matter what I did. I can boast that while many contemporary Chinese writers can produce good books of their own, no one but me could write a novel like *The Republic of Wine.* Deep down I know that even though I may look like a middle-aged man on the outside, my heart is still as young as when I was listening to my Big Grandpa's stories. I realize I'm getting older only when I look in the mirror. When I'm facing a piece of paper, I forget my age, and my heart is filled with the joy of a child. I hate evil with a passion, I ramble, I mutter as if dreaming, I rejoice, I raise hell, I'm getting drunk.

That's about all I have to say about *The Republic of Wine.* Please read this novel, which Howard and I created together. The sex scenes are from the original; he didn't spice it up a bit.

Now, he's translating my next novel, *Big Breasts and Full Hips,* a book as thick as a brick. If you like, you can skip my other novels, but you must read *Big Breasts and Full Hips.* In it I wrote about history, war, politics, hunger, religion, love, and sex. I tell you, if he asks me to cut some of the juicier parts, I won't do it. That's because the sex scenes in *Big Breasts and Full Hips* are among my most gratifying accomplishments. After he finishes the translation, you'll see how well I've done!

I'm pretty drunk now, so I'll stop here.

Mo Yan, Summer 2000, translated by Sylvia Li-chun Lin

JAPAN

The Return of the Gods: Theatre in Japan Today

The sixties in Japan were a period of intense eschatological reflection. Profound questions regarding ultimate ends were being asked in many artistic media. Plays written during this period reflect this trend, which resulted from the profound historical trauma of defeat in World War II, reactivated and exacerbated by the failure of the struggle to prevent renewal of the United States-Japan Mutual Security Treaty in 1960. Disillusioned with both the left-wing political and modern theatre movements, younger theatre people embarked upon a self-conscious attempt to develop an alternative historical mythology that could animate a comprehensive new movement in politics and the arts.

The five plays I have translated and analyzed in *Japanese Drama and Culture in the 1960s: The Return of the Gods* (1988) illustrate this trend.[1] In each play a transhistorical, supernatural character appears, offering salvation to suffering mortals. For example, in Matsuyo Akimoto's *Hitachibō Kaison* (1965; Eng. *Kaison the Priest of Hitachi*) the character is a medieval warrior named Kaison. In Yoshiyuki Fukuda's *Hakamadare wa doko da* (1964; Eng. *Find Hakamadare!*) it is a Robin Hood-like bandit whose exploits span centuries. In Makoto Satoh's *Atashi no Beatles* (1967; Eng. *My Beatles*) hoary archetypes take the form of a certain Liverpudlian quartet. And in Jūrō Kara's *John Silver: Ai no kijiki* (1970; Eng. *John Silver: The Beggar of Love*) it is a peg-legged pirate named Silver. In each play the transhistorical characters offer salvation, the conquest of death, through an assimilation to fabulous time. They are Japanese gods, acknowledged, liberated, and reenfranchised. Their promise of salvation is very real, with roots deep in Japanese culture; but it is a decidedly ambivalent promise, for the price of such salvation is the abandonment of responsibility and creativity in real historical time.

Salvation in each of these plays is indistinguishable from damnation, therefore, and this dilemma is explicitly acknowledged in *Tsubasa o moyasu tenshitachi no butō* (1970; Eng. *The Dance of Angels Who Burn Their Own Wings*), the culminating work of this period. Written as a critique of Peter Weiss's *Marat/Sade* by Makoto Satoh and three other playwrights, the play incessantly repeats the refrain, "We'll be all right if we don't dream." It takes advantage of the manifestation of the Japanese gods and their siren call to salvation in fabulous time to deny their appeal and reaffirm the primacy of historical being.

I refer to this theatrical activity during the 1960s as the "post-*shingeki* movement," because it involved a number of troupes that sought to create an alternative to *shingeki,* the orthodox modern drama of Japan. The post-*shingeki* movement revolutionized Japanese modern drama, and recent developments in the theatre arts have been profoundly influenced by the precedents it set. A few examples of the diverse ways the return of the gods affected Japanese drama in the seventies and eighties will illustrate this influence.

▪ POST-SHINGEKI DRAMATURGY AND LIBERATION THEOLOGY

In 1979 the English-language quarterly *Ampo* (named for the 1960 anti-Security Treaty demonstrations) published a special double issue entitled "Theater as Struggle: Asian People's Drama."[2] With a lead article by Kaitarō Tsuno, a prominent post-*shingeki* critic, the issue contained scripts of four Asian plays, including *The People's Worship,* a play from the Philippines by Reverend J. Elias.[3]

The special issue of *Ampo* grew out of the activities of the Black Tent Theatre 68/71, a representative post-*shingeki* troupe. After spending the years 1972 to 1976 producing Makoto Satoh's trilogy *Kigeki Shōwa no sekai* (Eng. *The World of Shōwa: A Comedy*),[4] the Black Tent Theatre turned its attention to Asian "people's drama," becoming deeply involved with the Philippines Educational Theatre Association (Peta), a group founded in 1967 and based in Manila. The relationship between the Black Tent Theatre and Peta was a fruitful one, and in 1983 the two troupes cooperated to produce a Festival of Asian People's Drama in Tokyo.

Peta was profoundly influenced by the movement within the Roman Catholic Church known as "liberation theology," which proposes that "the religious instinct be defined as a revolutionary urge, a psychosocial impulse, to generate a new humanity";[5] and although it was not originally performed by Peta, *The People's Worship* typifies the movement of which Peta is a part. The play clearly demonstrates how liberation theology reinterprets Christian faith out of the experience of the poor and interrelates spiritual redemption and social revolution.

Tsuno and the Black Tent Theatre were attracted to Asian people's drama as a logical extension of their own theatre activities, which, as I document in *Japanese Drama and Culture in the 1960s,* sought to redefine the concept of political revolution by replacing it in its theological context. That Tsuno and the Black Tent Theatre should have identified with Peta is thus not surprising, for, following their own uniquely Japanese and necessarily tortuous route, Tsuno, Satoh, and the rest of the Black Tent company had combined aspects of Marxism and Judeo-Christian theology in a new dramaturgy that shared much in common with Philippine liberation theology.

▪ TADASHI SUZUKI AND THE SHRINE OF TOGA-MURA

In 1976 Tadashi Suzuki led the Waseda Little Theatre (Waseda shōgekijō) out of Tokyo to take up residence in Toga-mura, an isolated farming village in Toyama prefecture, eight hours by train and bus from Tokyo. Known today as the Suzuki Company of Toga (Scot), the Waseda Little Theatre originated at Waseda University during the 1960 anti-Security Treaty demonstrations.[6] In the 1960s the troupe played a significant part in the post-*shingeki* movement, producing a series of important works, including Minoru Betsuyaku's Zō (1962; Eng. *The Elephant*), an early version of Makoto Satoh's *My Beatles,* and Jūrō Kara's *Shōjo kamen* (Virgin Mask; 1969).[7]

After Betsuyaku left the troupe in August 1969, Suzuki began directing *Gekiteki naru mono o megutte* (Concerning Things Dramatic), a series of three highly original collages composed of great scenes from Western and Japanese drama. After successful performances in Europe in 1972 and 1973, the troupe began producing Greek tragedies—*The Trojan Women* in 1974, *The Bacchae* in 1978, and *Clytemnestra* in 1983—using the unique style of acting the company had begun to develop by adapting Nō and Kabuki techniques to the modern stage.[8]

Shortly after the move to Toga, a rumor began to circulate in Tokyo that Suzuki intended to register the Waseda Little Theatre as a religious organization (shūkyō hōjin), presumably for the preferential tax treatment that would result. I spoke with Suzuki in May 1981 and asked him if there was any truth to the rumor. He replied:

> That was a joke, of course, because no matter how you look at it we're a theatre troupe, not a

religious organization. But what we're doing is close to a religious activity. Every year at the same time in a predetermined space we go through a certain ritual. The form of the place is predetermined, and in that space, the same group performs. It's a prescribed space where the unchanging, the eternal can be introduced, where a changeless something can be performed. That's why we established our theatre in Toga; we wanted to create a fixed, ritual space. That was clear and explicit. As in Nō, although we're different from Nō, the idea was to create our own unique fixed space, our own sacred, purified space, where the continuous memory of the ensemble could work. This is religious. Our idea was to create a religious shrine [*honzan*]. Shingeki isn't doing anything like this. So the idea that we would register ourselves as a religious organization is ridiculous, but I think it would be safe to say that of contemporary theatre groups, as far as the way theatre is produced is concerned, the Waseda Little Theatre is the most "religious" among them.

The eight-hour journey from Tokyo is Toga is nothing less than a pilgrimage to "a religious shrine," where "the unchanging, the eternal" appears. Toga is a sacred space, a *temenos,* to which the gods released by the post-*shingeki* movement can return and where the faithful can go to meet them.

▪ THE BUTOH MOVEMENT AND THE RETURN OF THE GODS

Akaji Maro played the lead role of Miss Safety in Jūrō Kara's production of *John Silver: The Beggar of Love.* In 1972 he left Kara's troupe to found his own dance company, Dai Rakuda Kan (The Great Camel Battleship). Maro had lived for three years (1965–68) with Tatsumi Hijikata. Hijikata (1928–86) was an iconoclastic dancer-choreographer from the Tōhoku region whose debut in May 1959 with an adaptation of the homosexual theme from Yukio Mishima's 1951 novel *Kinjiki* (Eng. *Forbidden Colors*) had caused a scandal. According to Mark Holborn, "The whole dance was performed without music. [Kazuo] Ohno's son, Yoshito, who was still a young boy, enacted sex with a chicken squeezed between his thighs and then succumbed to the advances of Hijikata."[9]

Holborn writes that "Japanese Dadaists, who were pioneering Performance Art in Tokyo in the 1960s, greatly admired Hijikata's theatrical techniques";[10] but Hijikata's dance derived from the same impulses that motivated the post-*shingeki* movement, not some generalized quest for novelty. As he declared in 1985, in what is certainly the definitive expression of his philosophy of dance:

To make gestures of the dead, to die again, to make the dead reenact once more their deaths in their entirety—these are what I want to experience within me. A person who has died once can die over and over again within me. Moreover, I've often said although I'm not acquainted with Death, Death knows me.[11]

Hijikata defined himself shamanistically, as a medium for the appearance of the dead on the stage. Through him, the Japanese gods, the immortal dead, could manifest themselves in the world of the living.

Akaji Maro integrated the perspective of the post-*shingeki* movement into Hijikata's *butoh* dance form. It was Maro and his troupe who first introduced *butoh* to America and with it post-*shingeki* dramaturgy. As Anna Kisselgoff wrote in her review of Dai Rakuda Kan's New York City debut: "Haunted implicitly by the horrors of The Bomb, obsessed with themes of creation and destruction, Butoh pieces bank on the grotesque in their concertedly primeval imagery."[12] The abiding influence of the atomic-bomb experience, the fascination with eschatological issues, the aggressive embrace of anomaly, and the dialectical return to the premodern—the main characteristics of post-*shingeki* dramaturgy are all unmistakable in Kisselgoff's description. One need only look at Ethan Hoffman's recently published photographs of Dai Rakuda Kan and other *butoh* groups to understand that, white-faced, arms extended, faces upturned, eyes vacant, they are ghosts incarnate, that with them the gods have returned to the Japanese stage.[13]

▪ INFLUENCE BEYOND JAPAN

The new mythological formulation that made it possible for the gods to return to the Japanese stage in the 1960s profoundly influenced subsequent developments in the Japanese performing arts. From Asian people's drama to *butoh*, it has been interpreted and articulated in diverse ways and has opened an extraordinary range of possibilities to Japanese theatre.

The influences of the post-*shingeki* movement is already being felt in the United States. Tadashi Suzuki has been working with American actors and is currently touring the United States with a new production of *King Lear; butoh* troupes make frequent appearances in this country; and younger post-*shingeki* troupes continue to debut at world theatre festivals. Today the fundamental and far-reaching shift in the paradigm of modern drama that took place in Japan during the 1960s is making itself felt well beyond Japanese shores.

David G. Goodman, Summer 1988

[1] The present essay is adapted from this volume, published in Armonk, N.Y., by M. E. Sharpe.

[2] "Theater as Struggle: Asian People's Drama," *Ampo* 11:2–3 (1979). *Ampo* is published by the Pacific-Asia Resources Center (Parc) in Tokyo.

[3] The other three plays are *Chinogi* by the Korean dissident poet Kim Chi Ha, *Ugly Jasean* by Areeya Mitrasu of Thailand, and *The House of Man* by Chinen Seishin of Okinawa.

[4] I describe *The World of Shōwa* in "Satoh Makoto and the Post-Shingeki Movement in Japanese Contemporary Theatre," Ph.D. dissertation, Cornell University, 1982, pp. 278–346.

[5] These are the words of the Sri Lankan theologian Aloysius Pieris, quoted in Phillip Berryman, *Liberation Theology*, New York, Pantheon, 1987, p. 167.

[6] Nobuko Albery's *Balloon Top* (New York, Pantheon, 1978) is a roman à clef that presents a firsthand, albeit self-serving, rendition of theatre activities at Waseda at the time of the 1960 demonstrations.

[7] For details regarding Tadashi Suzuki and the Waseda Little Theatre, see my comments in *Theatre Companies of the World*, William C. Young and Colby H. Kullman, eds., Westport, Ct., Greenwood, 1986, pp. 119–22.

[8] See *The Way of Acting: The Theatre Writings of Tadashi Suzuki*, J. Thomas Rimer, tr., New York, Theatre Communications Group, 1986. See also James R. Brandon, "Training at the Waseda Little Theatre: The Suzuki Method," *Drama Review*, 22:4 (December 1978), pp. 29–42; and Tadashi Suzuki, "The Sum of Interior Angles," Frank Hoff and David G. Goodman, trs., *Canadian Theatre Review*, 20 (Fall 1978), pp. 20–27.

[9] Mark Holborn, "Tatsumi Hijikata and the Origins of Butoh," in Ethan Hoffman et al., *Butoh: Dance of the Dark Soul*, New York, Aperture, 1987, p. 11.

[10] Holborn, p. 11.

[11] Hijikata Tatsumi, "Kazedaruma," in *Butoh*, p. 127.

[12] Anna Kisselgoff, "Dance: Dai Rakuda Kan's '5 Rings,'" *New York Times*, 10 April 1987.

[13] Hoffman et al., *Butoh*.

The Nobel Prize in Literature, 1967–1987: A Japanese View

Not until the early part of the period under review of the Nobel Prize in Literature did Japan figure successfully in this particular area of the international sweepstakes. The naming of Yasunari Kawabata (1899–1972) as Nobel laureate in 1968 finally ended a drought that had lasted since the award's inception in 1901. As is generally assumed, authors practicing their craft in languages other than a few prominent Western ones are subject to the vicissitudes of translations into those languages in their competition for the prize. It is in no way inconceivable that, had Sōseki Natsume (1867–1916), a scholar of English literature turned novelist, been available in translation, he might have been tapped for the award. Unanimously recognized by the Japanese as one of their most thoughtful modern authors, he combines artistic sophistication with the sort of "idealistic tendencies" the Nobel Committee would seem to favor. His works probe with astonishing foresight the dilemmas that confront contemporary man, in particular the plight of the intellectual in Meiji Japan (1868–1911) as he enters the hazardous territories of the modern age.

Even before Kawabata was crowned as Japan's first Nobel laureate, apparently two other Japanese writers received serious consideration for the award: Jun'ichirō Tanizaki (1886–1965) and Yukio Mishima (1925–70). The translation of modern Japanese literature into European languages had begun in earnest in the 1950s, and by the early 1960s enough works by these two writers had been rendered into English and French (primarily) to give credence to their worth. In the opinion of many critics and scholars of Japanese literature, both native and foreign, Tanizaki was by far the most deserving of Nobel recognition among Japanese writers of this period.

In a career that spanned a half-century until his death in 1965 at age seventy-nine, Tanizaki produced a succession of memorable works, among them his acknowledged masterpiece, *The Makioka Sisters* (1948), a loving, lyrical evocation of the life of a well-to-do Osaka merchant family in the days prior to the advent of World War II—a work that the military government of the time deemed too frivolous, thus forcing the discontinuation of its serialization in a journal. *The Makioka Sisters,* while sharing many characteristics with his other works, is something of an oddity in Tanizaki's oeuvre, which is often populated—as in *The Key* (1956) and *Diary of a Mad Old Man* (1961–62)—with men obsessed with the sadomasochistic desire to subjugate themselves to beautiful women in the quest for esthetic transcendence. Tanizaki's early works especially reveal shades of Edgar Allan Poe, Oscar Wilde, and Baudelaire, writers with whom he shared an artistic affinity, but from the late 1920s he began to turn more and more in the direction of the native literary tradition for inspiration. In 1933 he published his famous essay, "In Praise of Shadows," which pays homage to the sense of beauty cherished by the ancient Japanese—an esthetic that discovers beauty in that which is understated, indirect, suggestive, shadowy. Thereafter, he combined the craftsmanship he learned from Western literature with a Japanese sensibility to produce a series of brilliant novels that reveal startling psychological perceptions. However, because of his resolutely esthetic focus, meager in what might be called redeeming social values, his Nobel chances were surely greatly reduced, like those of another esthete and consummate artist, Vladimir Nabokov.

National jubilation accompanied the announcement of Kawabata's selection as the 1968 recipient of the Nobel Prize in Literature. At the same time, the Japanese were somewhat perplexed. Why Kawabata, without a doubt the most "Japanese" in his artistry, when there were in their estimation other writers more international in their appeal? Could it have been the "exoticism" the Nobel Committee perhaps perceived in Kawabata's work—not the soundest criterion for a literary award—that was the decisive factor? The Nobel citation naming Kawabata the winner may have fueled such doubts. It reads: "For his narrative mastery which with great sensibility expresses the essence of the Japanese mind."[1] The "Presentation Address" by Anders Österling, Permanent Secretary of the Swedish Academy, dwells on the "Japaneseness" of Kawabata's art, even as it attempts to seek the universal and modern in its particularities; and in the end Kawabata becomes a fashioner of ties between Orient and Occident: "As a writer he imparts a moral-esthetic cultural awareness with unique artistry, thereby in this way contributing to the spiritual bridge-building between East and West."[2]

The supposed "exoticism" notwithstanding, Kawabata must be judged a felicitous choice. Like Tanizaki, though in a different way, Kawabata too began his literary career as an exponent of Western literature, then changed direction toward more native habits. In the 1920s, with Riichi Yokomitsu, a lifelong friend, Kawabata pioneered in introducing to Japan the Western modernist modes and movements (stream of consciousness, automatic writing, dadaism, cubism, expressionism, futurism, and the rest), vestiges of which can be glimpsed in Kawabata's own works, even after his frequently noted turn toward the native tradition in the 1930s. The work that propelled him into the limelight is *The Izu Dancer* (1926), the story of a high-school student who, while on a walking trip to the Izu peninsula, falls captive to the ineffable charms of a little dancer, a member of a party of strolling entertainers. A work that might be described as combining traditional subject matter and modernistic techniques, this early effort already displays a pervasive loneliness rooted in a feeling of homelessness and an unquenchable yearning linked to the Oriental sense of Nothingness or Emptiness that are trademarks of the Kawabata oeuvre.

Edward Seidensticker, the perfect Kawabata translator into English, regards *Snow Country,* published in installments between 1935 and 1937 and brought to its present form in 1947, as perhaps the writer's finest work. The slight story of a Tokyo dilettante named Shimamura and his affair with a hot-spring geisha called Komako on his periodic visits to the "snow country," the novel displays those features for which Kawabata is renowned: a loose, fragmented structure traceable to *renga* or linked verse; sharp, fleeting, and often startlingly modernistic images taken from nature reminiscent of haiku poetry; a dominance of sensual impressions, especially the sense of touch; and a sad, poignant lyricism recalling such Japanese classics as *The Tale of Genji* (from the eleventh century). *Snow Country's* hero, Shimamura, is typically Kawabatan too in his peculiar coldness—a coldness to be associated with detachment from entangling human connections that might impede the attainment of a transcendent realm for which he yearns, obtainable perhaps through art. This detachment, this aloofness, in turn, invests the Kawabata eroticism with a curious quality, intensifying rather than mitigating the sense of isolation and loneliness.

The chef d'oeuvre in the Kawabata canon is *The Sound of the Mountain* (1954). It was, in Kawabata's intermittent manner of composition, preceded by *The Master of Go* and *A Thousand Cranes,* two more masterful works finally brought to a conclusion of sorts in the early 1950s, and followed by such notable novels as *House of the Sleeping Beauties and The Old Capital,* completed in the early 1960s. They all exemplify Kawabata's assertion made in 1947: "Since the defeat, I have but been going back into the sadness that has always been with us in Japan. I have no faith in the appearances and the manners of the postwar world. Perhaps I do not believe in reality. It seems likely that I will move away from the realism that is the basis of the modern novel. Perhaps I have never been there."[3] Certainly the hero of *The Sound of the Mountain,* an old man named Shingo, indulges in flights of esthetic reveries to assuage his keen aversion to reality: his long, boring marriage to a woman he has never truly loved, and disappointment in his two mediocre children, both failures in marriage. He is strongly drawn to his beautiful daughter-in-law, who offers moments of esthetic transcendence and reminds him of another unattainable object of yearning from long ago: his wife's sister, now dead.

That Yukio Mishima coveted international recognition and especially the Nobel Prize is no secret. Apparently under consideration for the award in the same year that Kawabata won, he must surely have received with mixed feelings the news that the prize had gone to the man who, in fact, had served as mentor in his early career. He hastened to send his congratulations from Southeast Asia, where he was on a trip at the time to gather background material for the third volume in his massive tetralogy, *The Sea of Fertility* (1965–71), the work that proved to be the last before his spectacular suicide on 25 November 1970 by the traditional method of disembowelment. Assuming, as some commentators have pointed out, that 1968 was somehow desig-

nated as the year for a Japanese winner, why was Kawabata singled out over Mishima? Was it a case of age before beauty? Were there perhaps elements of "politics" involved? After all, in 1968 Kawabata was serving as president of the Japan PEN Club. Or, more interesting from a literary standpoint, was Kawabata perceived to be more "exotic" than the more "cosmopolitan" Mishima?

Critics regard *Confessions of a Mask,* the great novel that established Mishima as a writer of the first rank in 1949 when he was still only twenty-four years of age, as among the finest to emerge over the course of his very prolific career, spanning roughly a quarter-century. The work is generally assumed to be autobiographical, the account of a young man who becomes gradually aware of his seemingly preternatural proclivities toward homosexuality and his efforts to mask it. This is a far cry, however, from the run-of-the-mill *watakushishōsetsu,* the confessional form that is thought to be a peculiarly Japanese genre in modern Japanese fiction, tending toward a formless expression of the author's feelings and actions, often involving trivial matters. *Confessions of a Mask,* on the contrary, is a tightly controlled work which, especially in the first half, develops along the lines not of a conventional narrative but of a lyrical succession of piquant images associated with homosexual awakening. The novel caused something of a minor sensation on its first appearance, not only because of its subject matter but also because of its unusual treatment.

The Temple of the Golden Pavilion (1956) is by all accounts one of Mishima's supreme accomplishments. The novel fictionalizes an actual 1950 occurrence in which a Zen acolyte, obsessed with the beauty of the temple, set it afire to free himself from its stranglehold. Mishima adroitly weaves into the fabric of this material a number of provocative psychological and philosophical issues—the question, for instance, of what constitutes beauty—that lift the work to a level far beyond what the actual event could have connoted. The narrative method is far more sustained and therefore more Western than Kawabata's haikulike style (for example, the inherently interesting characters are developed polemically in long discourses between the characters), but Mishima too, like Kawabata, has his "exotic" ways (for instance, a Zen *kōan* or riddle serves as a tantalizing motif throughout the novel).

Many other critical and/or popular successes attended Mishima's career, both at home and abroad, not only in the area of fiction writing but in the fields of theater and film as well; one that deserves special mention is *The Sea of Fertility,* the tetralogy that was intended by Mishima himself to cap off his illustrious career. Despite the conspicuous flaws that mar its overall conception and structure, it must all the same be judged a major achievement. It is a work that can be regarded, among the many interpretations attachable to it, as Mishima's view, primarily from an esthetic-cultural (rather than a political) standpoint, of Japan's development in the twentieth century—a development over which he was in no way sanguine. The final volume ends with Honda, the old observer/voyeur who has witnessed the progressive decline of the four incarnations that successively serve as the protagonists for the four books, staring at the Void in the garden of a Buddhist convent.

What to make of that Void or Emptiness is a puzzling question. Marguerite Yourcenar, the eminent late French writer, argues in her recent homage, entitled *Mishima: A Vision of the Void,* that attraction to the Void was ultimately behind Mishima's awesome suicide in 1970, "that void which is also manifest Fullness."[4] Though Yourcenar associates this attraction only with the last years of Mishima's life, the Void in fact recurs in the writer's complete works from the very beginning of his career, a Void or Emptiness become affirmation, something to be striven for. It is the Oriental variety of the Void which, as Kawabata explained in his Nobel Prize acceptance speech, "is not the nothingness or the emptiness of the West. It is rather the reverse, a universe of the spirit in which everything communicates freely with everything, transcending bounds, limitless."[5]

If some flavor of the "exotic" is expected of an Asian writer in his bid for the Nobel Prize, then the chances of Kōbō Abe (b. 1924) may perhaps be slim. There is no question, however, that he has been a towering figure in the world of postwar Japanese belles lettres, as both novelist and playwright in the avant-garde vein. Rather than with his traditionalist countrymen like Kawabata, Abe's affinities lie with contemporary European writers. When he first began producing short stories in the late 1940s and early 1950s, critics pointed to similarities with Kafka because of his thematic concern with metamorphosis; subsequently, and rightly, he has been compared with such authors as Ionesco, Pirandello, and Beckett, who make up the absurdist and existentialist tradition in Western literature.

The work that established Abe's name is *The Woman in the Dunes* (1962), especially after the appearance of its widely applauded film version in 1964 by the director Hiroshi Teshigahara. It tells the story of a Tokyo teacher, an amateur entomologist, who goes in search of a rare insect specimen in the outlying sand dunes, only to be trapped himself at the bottom of a deep pit, where a woman resides as a member of the sand community. His life becomes synonymous with the seemingly absurd task—shared with the woman— of shoveling sand away from the house to resist being buried. When the opportunity to escape finally presents itself, however, the man chooses to remain. The novel raises, in the most palpable terms, such existential issues as the nature of freedom, commitment, and responsibility.

The stunning imagery of sand in *The Woman in the Dunes,* always drifting and never still, which some critics attribute to the Manchurian landscape where Abe spent his youth, becomes transformed in his later works into the ceaselessly shifting cityscape of Tokyo, where his lonely, alienated heroes, bereft of an identity, somehow try to find a foothold in this impersonal, dehumanizing, and stifling labyrinth. In *The Face of Another* (1964) Abe poses the question of what constitutes identity in the story of a man, a scientist, who fashions a mask to hide his badly scarred face, then attempts to seduce his unsuspecting wife with his new "identity." *The Ruined Map* (1967) employs the turnabout or inversion of roles, one of Abe's favorite literary devices, in relating the story of a detective who, hired to hunt down a missing husband in mazelike Tokyo, not only fails to locate the man he seeks, but also becomes the hunted or victim in the process and ends up losing his own identity. *The Box Man* (1973) finds the protagonist taking refuge from his fellow men by holing up in a box that furnishes an anonymity and freedom he could not find in everyday life.

Like Abe, Kenzaburō Ōe (b. 1935) is closer to contemporary Western writers than to his own countrymen in his literary manner and preoccupations. Indeed, he himself acknowledged Jean-Paul Sartre as his spiritual mentor when he embarked on his writing career in the late 1950s. There is in Ōe's works, however, what Japanese critics call *dochakusei,* an indigenous quality that makes his writings unmistakably Japanese, as seen, for example, in the setting and mores of one of his early successes entitled "Plucking Flowers, Killing Kids" (1958): a village in the deep forests where a group of juvenile delinquents, removed there from the city during the heat of World War II, are forced to rely on their own instinctive sense of camaraderie in fending for themselves when the cunning adults abandon them following the outbreak of a plague.

An endlessly inventive writer with a deep-seated antipathy toward authoritarianism, Ōe was frequently at the center of controversy for attacking all manner of sacred cows such as the emperor system and breaking the rules of narrative convention, as in the depiction of sexuality. Then, in 1964, two events of long-lasting significance—the birth of a retarded son and an encounter with the survivors of the Hiroshima holocaust— contributed immeasurably to Ōe's growth as an author. An early work that draws on this material is *A Personal*

Matter (1964), a critical and popular success that permanently fixed Ōe's star in the literary constellation. It relates the story of how Bird, whose chronic desire to escape responsibility is fanned when he discovers that his wife has given birth to a retarded baby, finally learns to tread the path of commitment.

By the time he published *The Silent Cry* (1967), another prizewinning work, Ōe was well on his way to incorporating what he had garnered from his study of Western literary theories, in particular Russian formalism and Mikhail Bakhtin's notion of grotesque realism. A darkly brooding work that pits two brothers against each other in the thick forests of Shikoku (the author's birthplace) as the younger of the two reenacts events in the family's and the village's past, *The Silent Cry* offers Ōe's vision, at once both violent and tender, of Japan's modern history in microcosm. After this novel, Ōe's narrative method becomes progressively more complex to convey a multivoiced discourse in dealing with issues both personal (e.g., his responsibility to his son) and public (e.g., the emperor system, the dangers of power politics in the nuclear age). A collection of short and medium-size fiction entitled *Teach Us to Outgrow Our Madness* (1972) examines from various perspectives the complex relationship between a parent and a child, while engaging such topical questions as the role of the emperor. "And the Flood Reached My Soul" (1973) takes for its background the Japan of the early 1970s, when apocalyptic fear, fueled by predictions of a massive earthquake, the radicalization of the student movement, and the problems created by the nuclear bomb, permeated the society. It asks how the survival of human dignity is possible in the final days of human existence through the portrayal of, again, a father-son pair. The roles of father and son are reversed in "Record of a Pinch-Runner" (1976), reflecting the topsy-turvy milieu of the 1970s as tricksterlike characters struggle with the political issue of nuclear arms. "Contemporized Game" (1979) is a wildly imaginative tour de force which employs folkloric, semiotic, literary, and anthropological theories in presenting Ōe's rendition of Japan's postwar history.

Shūsaku Endō (b. 1923), the current president of the Japan Pen Club, is known as the Japanese Graham Greene because of his Catholic faith. Religious themes without a doubt comprise a major part of his literary works, but Endō is besides a first-rate humorist and playwright. Since his debut as a writer in the mid-1950s, he has built up an impressive body of work that surely puts him in the forefront among Japanese contenders for the Nobel Prize. Much more conventional in his literary manner than either Abe or Ōe, Endō

Shūsaku Endō *(Harper & Row)*

writes novels in which theme, not method, is paramount.

Moral questions, in particular the problem of good and evil, of freedom and responsibility, are frequently at the heart of an Endō work. An early novel called *The Sea and Poison* (1957) confronts the problem of individual responsibility in wartime, as it lashes out at the lack of moral conscience among Japanese doctors who vivisected a captured American pilot for scientific experimentation. The very powerful *Silence* (1966) showcases the grand theme that is sounded in varied forms throughout his oeuvre: the disparity between Eastern and Western spiritual and cultural values that makes the implantation of Western ideas in Japanese soil well-nigh impossible. The backdrop for the story is the persecution of Christians in seventeenth-century Japan, which witnessed the apostasy, under inhuman methods of torture, of Father Ferreira, a celebrated missionary—an apostasy that came about essentially, in the opinion of his persecutor Inoue, because Japan is a "swampland" that will draw in anything (like Christianity) but change it intrinsically in the process. Endō creates, in this and other works, the image of a compassionate Christ, one with whom his countrymen can more readily relate than the stern, demanding father figure that the missionaries had stressed. *Samurai* (1980), while describing the 1614 trade embassy to Mexico and Europe led by a man named Hasekura, in fact deals more profoundly with the arduous path a Japanese must follow in order to encounter Christianity. Endō's latest novel, entitled *Scandal,* centers on a famous Catholic writer rumored to frequent a famous red-light district in contemporary Tokyo. An inquisitive reporter, sensing a scandal, hounds the author, who in turn pursues a shadowy figure that seems to assume his identity.

Two venerable elders of the Japanese literary establishment, Masuji Ibuse (b. 1898) and Yasushi Inoue (b. 1907), are the favorites of the Japanese themselves for receiving the Nobel Prize. Though there is no question that they have enriched modern Japanese literature significantly, both are so intractably Japanese in sensibility and taste, in a way that Kawabata is not, that they resist easy translation into another idiom. The qualities of Ibuse's work—the earthiness, the wry humor, the spareness, and the humanity and compassion—are so tied to aspects of the Japanese language that only in small measure can they be conveyed in translation. Works with a subtle, plebeian flavor, they might be likened to *tōfu* (bean curd), that bland staple of the Japanese diet the people find irresistible. Ibuse's crowning achievement is *Black Rain* (1965), widely regarded as the best literary treatment, free of sentimentality or political stridency, of the atomic bombing of Hiroshima. A quiet, discursive elegy to a people and a landscape, it is in the end, despite the horror and the destruction it depicts, an affirmation of life and a tribute to the human spirit.

Inoue has written numerous short stories and novels with contemporary themes that have received critical approval: for example, *The Counterfeiter* (1951), the story, permeated with human pathos and suffering, of a painter who is reduced to counterfeiting the works of a more gifted and successful acquaintance. Inoue's reputation rests largely, however, on those works based on historical events and personalities that Western readers are likely to find difficult to appreciate, not only because of the subject matter but also because of their intensely Japanese narrative manner, which ignores such Western expectations as carefully fashioned characterization and plot. *The Roof Tile of Tempyō* (1957) tells about the Japanese and Chinese monks in the eighth century who dedicated themselves to the transmission of Buddhist ideals from T'ang China to Japan. *Tun-huang* (1960) is the sorrowful tale of a scholarly young Chinese who buried countless sutras (discovered only in the early part of the twentieth century) in one of the Thousand Buddha Caves at Tun-huang in the eleventh century. As in an Oriental landscape painting, the characters in these works are no more important than the objects, the

landscapes, the events, and the passage of time that envelop them. They are all victims of fate in the sweep of history, mere bubbles on the ocean of time; and it is the awareness of this truth that invests the works with an all-pervasive feeling of sadness.

In the last fifteen to twenty years an extraordinary number of women writers have been active on the Japanese literary scene, often capturing the most prestigious prizes awarded each year—perhaps a not-so-surprising phenomenon in the still male-dominated society of Japan, when the literary vocation is regarded as one of the few outlets where women are allowed to display their prowess. None has to this date compiled a body of work worthy of Nobel recognition, but from their midst may one day emerge a figure who will challenge the preeminence of Lady Murasaki (*The Tale of Genji*) in Japanese belles lettres.

Yoshio Iwamoto, Spring 1988

1 *Nobel Prize Library: Yasunari Kawabata, Rudyard Kipling, Sinclair Lewis,* New York / Del Mar, Ca., Gregory/CRM, 1971, p. 1.

2 Ibid., p. 5.

3 Quoted in Edward G. Seidensticker, "The Life and Works of Yasunari Kawabata," ibid., p. 77.

4 Marguerite Yourcenar, *Mishima: A Vision of the Void,* New York, Farrar, Straus & Giroux, 1986, p. 104. On Mishima, see also *Wlt* 54:3 (Summer 1980), pp. 383–87.

5 Yasunari Kawabata, *Japan the Beautiful and Myself,* Tokyo, Kodansha International, 1969, p. 56. On Kawabata, see *Wlt* 51:2 (Spring 1977), pp. 207–10.

6 On Kenzaburō Ōe, see *Wlt* 58:3 (Summer 1984), pp. 370–73, and 60:1 (Winter 1986), pp. 38–39.

A Voice from Postmodern Japan: Haruki Murakami

Forget everything you know about Japan and enter the postmodern world of Haruki Murakami's *A Wild Sheep Chase,* where people sweat about their careers, drink too much, and drift through broken marriages, all without a kimono in sight.

A postmodern detective novel in which dreams, hallucinations and a wild imagination are more important than actual clues.

As these two quotes—appearing on the back cover and front page of the paperback edition of *A Wild Sheep Chase,*[1] the English translation of Haruki Murakami's novel *Hitsuji o meguru bōken* (1982)—might suggest, the author, perhaps the most popular and widely read, if not the most highly respected, among the current crop of the more "serious" Japanese writers, is frequently identified as a "postmodernist" by both Japanese and Western critics alike. The attribution somehow rings true. Still, what the term *postmodern* signifies exactly, and in what sense (complimentary, derisive, neutral) it is being employed, is not always made clear.

Cutting across a multitude of disciplines, discourse on postmodernism, originated by such European thinkers as Lyotard, Baudrillard, Deleuze, and Guattari, has now been a staple on the Western academic landscape for about the past two decades. Popular usage of the term has not lagged far behind. A recent issue of *Time* (31 August 1992), for instance, reporting on the Woody Allen–Mia Farrow debacle, refers to the prescandal couple as having "produced the portrait of an ideal postmodern family. Unmarried, they lived apart yet loved together." Japanese scholar-critics, taking their cue from Western pronouncements on the subject, have been no less voluble in expatiating on the so-called postmodern condition. An effort in 1987 by a group of Western scholars to draw Japan into a larger orbit of postmodern discourse resulted finally in a volume of essays, edited by Masao Miyoshi and H. D. Harootunian, called *Postmodernism and Japan*.[2] Representing expertise in a variety of fields, the book includes, for example, an insightful piece by the anthropologist Marilyn Ivy, who sees Japanese culture in postmodern terms by virtue of the way knowledge is consumed, like a commodity, via its extensive high-tech information network. The essays as a whole raise a host of provocative issues, among them the role Japan has played in the East-West confrontation that has contributed to the delineation of the premodern-modern-postmodern dialectic.

The question of the literary, artistic, and cultural manifestations of postmodernism has also received considerable attention from many scholars. Among them is Ihab Hassan, whose wide-ranging inquiries into Western postmodernism (as seen, for instance, in his collection of essays entitled *The Postmodern Turn*)[3] include attempts, in somewhat abstract terms, to differentiate between "postmodern" and "modern" literary traits. Hassan, a frequent visitor to Japan, was moved on a recent visit to comment on the postmodern signs suffusing its hybrid East-West culture, specifically identifying, though without any elaboration, Haruki Murakami and Yasuo Tanaka as postmodernist writers.[4]

There is little question that many contemporary Japanese artistic productions exhibit aspects of the numerous characteristics that Hassan identifies as postmodern: for example, "a diffuse self, fugitive forms, a culture open to syntagma and parataxis instead of hier-

Haruki Murakami (*AP/Wide World Photos*)

archic or generative models of organization."[5] Indeed, Tanaka's *Nantonaku kurisutaru* (Somehow Crystal; 1980) is regarded unanimously by Japanese critics as the quintessential postmodern work. Most of the novel shows, in nonlogical fashion, its characters euphorically immersed in the mood, atmosphere, and feelings generated by the brand-name goods of a consumerist society. Their attempt to forge an identity from the acquisition of these brand-name items is complemented by a section of guidebooklike notes, equal in length to the main text, that provides the reader with such information as the special qualitites of the products and where they might be purchased.[6]

An interesting facet of the discussion on postmodernism is the articulation by a number of Japanese scholars, notably Kōjin Karatani,[7] of the presence already in premodern Japanese culture of those elements, such as hostility toward a logocentric system, that Western scholars have called postmodern—a phenomenon that has facilitated the acceptance of postmodernism in Japan, without the resistance to it seen in the modern West. This observation, at the same time, confirms the view that the concept of postmodernism should not be regarded in strictly chronological terms. The assertions of the Japanese scholars accord uncannily in some respects with Roland Barthes's singular "reading" of Japanese culture in *L'empire des signes* (1970; Eng. *The Empire of Signs,* 1982), focusing largely on the traditional aspects (chopsticks, sukiyaki, puppet theater, Zen Buddhism, haiku) still remaining in the contemporary society, where he sees a propensity for decentering and the privileging of the signifier over the signified that tend to produce "silences" and to diffuse "meaning." In literary terms, these characteristics in turn beget such traits as fragmented structures, deemphasis on plot, delight in verbal and rhetorical playfulness, et cetera. Indeed, it might even be argued that the emergence of postmodernist literary modes in the West should help close the gap that Western readers have apparently sensed in approaching Japanese works with their episodic, nonlinear structures—say, those of Yasunari Kawabata—thus rendering them less "exotic."

■ ■ ■

How to situate Haruki Murakami in the scheme of postmodernist literary discourse is somewhat problematic. Whence does his postmodernist penchant derive? It is easy to surmise that, as a Japanese growing up in a postindustrial, late-capitalist society already permeated with so-called postmodern properties from the traditional culture, Murakami (whose parents were teachers of Japanese literature) imbibed osmotically the tendency toward postmodernist modes. Still, it would be remiss to ignore the possible Western sources. Japanese commentaries on Murakami never fail to point out his love affair with Western, especially American, literature and culture.[8] Born in Ashiya, near Kobe, in 1949, the author majored in drama within the Literature Department of Waseda University, where he wrote a thesis entitled "The Ideology of Journeys in American Films" to graduate in 1973. From 1974 to 1982 he managed a jazz bar in Tokyo, during which time he began his writing career, including translation work from American literature. His choices for translation have veered toward authors recognized as somewhat "popular" and/or for their postmodernist leanings: F. Scott Fitzgerald, Raymond Chandler, Raymond Carver, John Irving, Paul Theroux, Tim O'Brien, and Truman Capote. His own work has also been compared with that of Jay McInerney, that chronicler of American yuppie life.

A Wild Sheep Chase, the third of Murakami's novels, displays an abundance of those postmodernist qualities noted above.[9] To begin with, the notion of dispersal and decentering can be sensed in the novel's supreme indifference to the categories of writing into which Japanese works have been habitually and rigidly placed, as though the author were intent on collapsing hitherto sacrosanct boundaries. Is it, for instance, a *tsūzoku-shōsetsu* (popular novel) or *jun-bungaku* (pure literature)?

The story concerns the first-person narrator, "I" (*Boku* in Japanese and so identified in the discussion that follows), the "hero" of the narrative, who is coerced by the secretary of a well-known and powerful (but silent) right-wing figure into abandoning his part-ownership in a small advertising agency in Tokyo to go in search of a sheep with a star-shaped birthmark on its back. The sheep appears in the midst of an idyllic landscape photograph of clouds, mountains, grassy pasture, and sheep that Boku had used in advertising copy for an insurance company. The picture had been taken by an old friend of Boku nicknamed "Rat," who had suddenly disappeared several years earlier and was now apparently roaming aimlessly in Hokkaido. Thus caught in the meshes of an invisible "system," the recently divorced Boku begins a wild sheep chase to Hokkaido, his newly acquired girlfriend, an ear model, in tow. In the pursuit he encounters a motley crew of quirky, oddball characters and learns about the incredible tale of the spirit/soul of the sheep with the star-shaped birth-mark entering the bodies of first the Sheep Professor, then the right-wing leader, and now his lost friend Rat.

The elements of fantasy, mystery, adventure, and detective story, all presented with suspense and humor in a smooth, sophisticated style, nudge the novel in the direction of the "popular." There is enough of the "pure" and "serious" about the work, however, to have held critics back from dismissing it merely as popular stuff—enough, it might be said, of the adversarial role against established norms of all sorts that the distinguished writer Kenzaburō Ōe sees as the defining feature of "pure literature."[10] In other words, it seems to register a concern, albeit in a playfully oblique manner, over the human condition in the contemporary world.

Postmodernist too is *A Wild Sheep Chase's* fragmented, discontinuous structure. It is paratactic, agglutinative, and cavalierly unfaithful to the rules of cause and effect that might be expected in a narrative that carries a detective- or mystery-story line. For instance, part 1, chapter 1 (titled "Prelude: Wednesday Afternoon Picnic" in the translation, "25 November 1970" in the original) bears no organic relationship to the story of the sheep chase, which is loosely launched in chapter 2 that begins part 2 ("July, Eight Years Later" in the translation, "July 1978" in the original). This beginning episode recalls Boku's relationship with a woman who has just died and whose funeral he attends—a relationship that took place in the late 1960s and early 1970s during his university days, when she was still a free-spirited, teenage flower child. At most, what the chapter contributes is a sense of Boku's nature and tastes. He records: "Those were the days of the Doors, the Stones, the Byrds, Deep Purple, and the Moody Blues. The air was alive, even as everything seemed poised on the verge of collapse, waiting for a push" (4). The chapter closes with Boku's indifferent response to the news of Yukio Mishima's suicide on 25 November 1970, an event widely seen by critics as a marker for the end of the politically tumultuous 1960s and the beginning of the politically apathetic, economically prosperous 1970s.

Boku may well be viewed as an exemplar of the diffusion of the ego, the dispersal of the self, the death of the subject, that are an integral part of postmodern discourse. Fredric Jameson, who enunciates such features as the "technological sublime" and "high tech paranoia" as symptoms of the postmodernist mode, puts it in the following way:

> Such terms [the alienation and fragmentation of the self] inevitably recall one of the more fashionable themes in contemporary theory—that of the "death" of the subject itself = the end of the autonomous bourgeois monad or ego or individual—and the accompanying stress, whether as some new moral ideal or as empirical description, on the *decentring* of that formerly centred subject or psyche. (Of the two possible formulations of this notion—the historicist one, that a once-existing centred subject, in the period of classical capitalism and the nuclear family, has today in the world of organizational bureaucracy dissolved; and the more radical post-structuralist position for which such a subject never existed in the first place but constituted something like an ideological mirage—I obviously incline towards the former; the latter must in any case take into account something like a 'reality of the appearance'.)[11]

In Japan the issue has been taken up as a problem of *shutaisei,* a word not readily defined that came into existence in the pre-World War II period to deal with the Western idea of individualism which entered the country in the nineteenth century, when its modernization process began. No doubt in the same lineage with terms like the novelist Sōseki Natsume's *kojinshugi* (individualism) and the critic Hideo Kobayashi's *shakaika-sareta watakushi* (socialized self), *shutaisei* is a compound made up of three characters—*shu* (subject, subjective, sovereign, main), *tai* (body, substance, situation), and *sei* (quality, feature)—which Japanese-English dictionaries define as "subjectivity; subjecthood; independence; identity." Masao Miyoshi in his book *Off Center* notes that "the word means inclusively the agent of action, the subject of speculation or speech act, the identity of existence, and the rule of individualism," while elsewhere glossing the term variously as "confidence," "autonomy," et cetera.[12] He concludes that the establishment of *shutaisei* in Japan is especially

difficult because of, among other reasons, the cultural and social forces of conformism and communalism that envelop the individual. Others have observed that the formation of *shutaisei* is immeasurably hampered in a language where the subject (or, for that matter, the object) need not be explicitly stated so long as it is implied and/or understood.

Does Boku of *A Wild Sheep Chase* possess *shutaisei*? In a recorded conversation (*taiwa*) among three contemporary Japanese critics concerning Murakami where the question is repeatedly raised of whether or not the author and by extension his characters are empowered with *shutaisei,* the answer is ambiguous and inconclusive.[13] Boku, thirty years old, is in many respects an average middle-class citizen who, free from excessive financial worries, enjoys the kind of independence his station bestows. A product of the 1960s, he takes endless pleasure in smoking, drinking, and eating, in bars, coffeehouses, and restaurants. He dresses with casual chic and frequents the movies regularly. His tastes in music and reading materials, though predominantly popular, are disarmingly eclectic—from the Beatles to Mozart, from Sherlock Holmes to Nietzsche—in the postmodern way of leveling elite/popular boundaries. Boku is far from gregarious, yet by no means a true loner; he is by all counts a likable, easygoing fellow, devoid of malice and an overbearing aggressiveness. Indeed, endowed with a sense of humor and self-irony, he is engaging in his displays of sensitivity and tenderness, possesses a wry and ready wit, and evinces a bemused air.

Significantly, however, Boku is a member of the advertising world, that symbol of media-dominated and consumer-oriented contemporary Japanese culture, which is revealed to be under the thumb of the right-wing leader by virtue of his financial holdings; it is this man who indirectly draws Boku into the maelstrom of the sheep chase and robs him of his independence. No wonder, then, that there is no core, only vacuity, to Boku's being. He is literally without a past[14] (or a future, for that matter). Victims of erasure, neither his family nor his divorced wife, for instance, impinges much on his consciousness. Paradoxically, he is often filled with a sense of loss, though the content of that loss is not clearly spelled out. There are, at most, references to the style and climate of the 1960s (as noted earlier), a past that Boku tends to estheticize into an indulgent, wistful nostalgia.

The thinness of Boku's *shutaisei* is exposed by the absence of an interiority and in his relations with other people. If, as Jean-Paul Sartre claims, true identity is forged in the crucible of the dialectic between self and other,[15] Boku fails the test. The "other" is a problematic force for the subjective "I" or self, because it too, unlike inanimate objects, is endowed with a consciousness and subjectivity that often clash with those of the self. Consciously or unconsciously, Boku tries to escape the self-other confrontation by viewing others as objects, no doubt because his own subjective self is wanting in depth.

A case in point is his relationship with his former wife. The divorce effectively takes place early on in the novel, in chapter 2, when Boku returns to their apartment after attending his old girlfriend's funeral to find his wife ready to move out for the final time. The conversation between the two skirts everything that might be thought of as essential for an understanding of their situation. At one point Boku remarks, "I'm not explaining. I'm just making conversation" (16)—summing up the tenor of their relationship. Boku is dejected over and saddened by the failed marriage; but there is no reflection whatsoever on what might have gone wrong, and the matter is soon erased from his consciousness.

The relationship with his new girlfriend is carried out on no firmer ground than that with his former wife. First attracted to her by her beautiful ears glimpsed in a photograph, Boku regards her, perhaps unknowingly, as an object (her ears), thus depriving her of a subjectivity. It is not that Boku is intentionally mean and insensitive, only that he is fundamentally more comfortable with exteriors and averting the deep probe. Indeed, he is fully adept at displaying affection of the surface variety—a candlelight dinner in the romantic setting of a posh French restaurant, for instance. The chitchat they engage in, often bordering on the ridiculous, produces a delightful humor; but in the end it signifies nothing more than the postmodernist "noisy silence." Most telling is his reaction to her sudden disappearance toward the end of the novel. They have finally reached the site in the mountains of Hokkaido where the picture of the grazing sheep had been taken. As Boku naps in the villa, formerly the property of the Sheep Professor and now owned by Rat's family, she mysteriously vanishes. (The reader is informed shortly thereafter that the Sheep Man, who turns out to be the ghost of the now-dead Rat, had urged her to leave.)

> I could not accept the fact of her disappearance. I was barely awake, but even if I were totally lucid, this—and everything that was happening to me—was far beyond my realm of comprehension. There was almost nothing one could do except let things take their course. (244)

Far from chasing after her, Boku proceeds to prepare his dinner—stew, bread, an apple, and wine—which he consumes while listening to a record of the Percy Faith Orchestra playing "Perfidia." The extent of his reflection runs as follows, laying bare his penchant for estheticizing and romanticizing even the very recent past: "I was feeling lonely without her, but the fact that I could feel lonely at all was consolation. Loneliness wasn't such a bad feeling. It was like the stillness of the pin oak after the little birds had flown off" (246).

Boku's attitude toward "others" is perhaps most basically reflected in his aversion to referring to them by their proper names (which are never revealed), as if denying them their independent, subjective identities. (Since Boku ["I"] himself is not assigned a name, the proclivity in turn mirrors that of the author, who in fact has littered his oeuvre with nameless characters.)[16] Thus, Boku's wife is merely "the wife," his girlfriend "the girlfriend with the beautiful ears," and, like the "secretary," the "business partner," and the "hotel clerk," who also inhabit the novel's world, they are reduced to their functional categories. Whatever names do appear are nicknames, such as Rat and Sheep Professor, perhaps suggesting these characters' less-than-human capacities.

The antipathy toward naming is no accident. The topic is taken up within the novel itself and given a comic turn. When Boku is forced to leave Tokyo in search of the special sheep, in a funny scene of reverse bullying, he insists that the right-wing leader's secretary care for his aged cat. Sent to pick up the feline, the secretary's chauffeur asks its name.

> "Nice kitty-kitty," said the chauffeur, hand not outstretched. "What's his name?"
>
> "He doesn't have a name."
>
> "So what do you call the fella?"
>
> "I don't call it," I said. "It's just there."
>
> "But he's not a lump just sitting there. He moves about by his own will, no? Seems mighty strange that something that moves by its own will doesn't have a name." (152)

The conversation continues with an amusing give-and-take on why some things (like ships) are accorded names whereas others are not (like airplanes). The problem goes unresolved, even as the conversants consider the "act of conscious identification with living things" and "non-interchangeability" as possible bases for naming (154).

A symptom of Boku's exteriority is his almost fetishistic attention to trivia, to "things." It is as if a careful tracking of "things" furnishes him with a handle and a grip on a recalcitrant reality. He notes the exact number of steps from the elevator to the door of his apartment, the amount of coffee and cigarettes he consumes, or the time that a particular song was in vogue; he becomes obsessively curious about a whale's penis on display at an aquarium he visits. Even something so intimate as sex turns into a "thing." Concerning his own sexual affairs, about which he is surprisingly reticent, at one point he records perfunctorily, "We returned to the hotel and had intercourse. I like that word intercourse. It poses only a limited range of possibilities" (172). Sex, it would seem, offers him not much more than the sensual gratification he derives from the consumption of "things," like gourmet foods.

Boku's perception of and response to people and things leans heavily on the side of the immediate, the physical, the sensual, mixed with not a little affectation. Riding in the limousine driven by the chauffeur, he comments, "Compared to my fifteen-year-old Volkswagen Beetle I'd bought off a friend, [it] was as quiet as sitting at the bottom of a lake wearing earplugs" (65). He reacts to his girlfriend's ears in the following way:

> She'd show me her ears on occasion; mostly on sexual occasions. Sex with her with her ears exposed was an experience I'd never known. When it was raining, the smell of the rain came through crystal clear. When birds were singing, their song was a thing of sheer clarity. I'm at a loss for words, but that's what it was like. (39)

Anything requiring sustained thought, spiritual input, or a committed stance bores him, perhaps even frightens him. What he finds hard to handle or bothersome, he dismisses with slick, flippant aphorisms, something he remarks Russians are prey to: "Russians have a way with aphorisms. They probably spend all winter thinking them up" (96). Here he is on the matter of sex:

> To sleep with a woman: it can seem of the utmost importance in your mind, or then again it can seem like nothing much at all. Which only goes to say that there's sex as therapy (self-therapy, that is) and there's sex as pastime.
>
> There's sex for self-improvement start to finish and there's sex for killing time straight through; sex that is therapeutic at first only to end up as nothing-better-to-do, and vice versa. Our human sex life—how shall I put it?—differs fundamentally from the sex life of the whale. (25)

It bears reiteration that Boku is by no means a despicable man, out to perpetrate evil. Neither is he coldly indifferent toward those around him—his former wife, his girlfriend, or J the bar owner. He seems genuinely fond of his friend Rat in particular, carrying out with good cheer the curious favors the latter requests. In fact, Rat appears in many ways to be the alter ego of Boku himself—Rat's letters to Boku have the same mannerisms and tone as Boku's speech. Ultimately, however, Boku avoids engagement and commitment, those quali-

ties Sartre deemed so essential in human relations. Short in attention span, he is constitutionally incapable of giving fully of himself to anything. All is surface.

Some Japanese critics have expressed dissatisfaction with Murakami, complaining that his works lack a deep-seated sociopolitico-historical awareness, as if such an awareness were a sine qua non for a fully developed *shutaisei*. There is no denying that Boku, who apparently dodged the turbulent student riots of the 1960s, is mostly uninterested in such matters. However, to assert that Murakami is oblivious to sociopolitical concerns seems extreme. There is enough in *A Wild Sheep Chase* to prove otherwise. What troubles the critics, perhaps, is the teasing, playful, oblique, and incomplete manner—a postmodernist manner—with which they are treated, never allowing them to become central to the narrative. There is, for instance, the matter of the sociopolitico-historical implications of the sheep. A third of the way into the novel, the right-wing leader's secretary furnishes a ponderous summary of the history of sheep in Japan, an animal alien to Japanese soil. The importation of sheep from America began in earnest in the Meiji period (1868–1912), paralleling the country's modernization process. Why, it is logical to ask, is the spirit of the sheep with the star-shaped birthmark made to lodge in the brain of a right-wing nationalist who comes to control politics and the advertising and information industries? And why is it made to find, just before the leader's death, a new host in Rat, who commits suicide in order to kill the sheep? What does the sheep "mean"?

Not a few Japanese critics have taken up the task of sorting out the puzzle of the sheep. To mention but two examples: Kazuo Kuroki, briefly put, interprets the sheep chase as a sentimental journey on Boku's part in search of his lost youth;[17] Mitsuo Sekii sees the sheep as a symbol of Christian, Western society, which Japan tried to emulate in its course of modernization, and its death at the end signifies the demise of modernity.[18] None of the analyses, however, accounts convincingly for, for example, the connection between the sheep and the right-wing leader. Murakami himself has admitted that the sheep as a "key word" was used primarily in the spirit of a game, without any deep significance.[19] There is the temptation to take Murakami at his word, for the "clues" lead nowhere, leaving unanswered what at first looked like a serious historical query about Japanese-Western relations. In the end the novel appears to argue for the postmodern position of decentering and dispersal. The ghost of Rat explains to Boku his reason for murdering the sheep. The sheep, he says, was lusting after "a realm of total conceptual anarchy. A scheme in which all opposites would be resolved into unity. With me and the sheep at the center" (284).

That *A Wild Sheep Chase* found an immense readership in Japan is no surprise. It deftly combines equal measures of hard-boiled realism and beguiling lyricism, of humor and seriousness. It is easy to conjecture that countless readers see mirrored in Boku's breezy, go-with-the-flow attitude their own approach to living in a glossy world dominated by high technology and consumerism. Much more difficult to assess is Murakami's disposition toward Boku and his noncommittal moral posture, or toward the kind of cultural condition that produced him. To be noted, however, is a more openly critical stance discernible in, for example, Murakami's recent collection of short stories called *TV piipuru* (TV People; 1990).

Yoshio Iwamoto, Spring 1993

1 Haruki Murakami, *A Wild Sheep Chase*, Alfred Birnbaum, tr., New York, Penguin/Plume Books, 1990. Page references appearing in the body of this paper will be to this edition. The English translation was first published in 1989 by Kodansha International and was reviewed in *Wlt* 64:4 (Autumn 1990), p. 701.

2 *Postmodernism and Japan*, Masao Miyoshi & H. D. Harootunian, eds., Durham, N.C., Duke University Press, 1989. Reviewed in *Wlt* 64:2 (Spring 1990), p. 364.

3 Ihab Hassan, *The Postmodern Turn*, Columbus, Ohio State University Press, 1987.

4 Ihab Hassan, "The Burden of Mutual Perceptions: Japan and the United States," lecture presented at the International House of Japan on 15 May 1989. The lecture appears in the *International House of Japan Bulletin*, 10:1 (Winter 1990), and is reproduced in *Salmagundi*, 85/86 (Winter-Spring 1990), pp. 71–86.

5 Ihab Hassan, "Parabiography: The Varieties of Critical Experience," in *The Postmodern Turn*, p. 160.

6 There is an interesting analysis of this work by Norma Field in *Postmodernism and Japan*.

7 Karatani Kōjin, *Hihyō to posuto modan* (Criticism and the Postmodern), Tokyo, Fukutake Shoten, 1985, pp. 9–49. (In original-language references the names are given in Japanese sequence, surname first.)

8 Two examples are: Matsuzawa Masahiro, *Haruki, Banana, Gen'ichirō* (the given names of three contemporary Japanese writers), Tokyo, Aoyumisha, 1989; and Sengoku Hideyo, *Airon o kakeru seinen: Murakami Haruki to Amerika* (A Young Man Who Does Ironing: Haruki Murakami and America), Tokyo, Sairyūsha, 1991.

9 Besides *A Wild Sheep Chase*, there is one other Murakami novel in English translation available to American readers: *Hard-Boiled Wonderland and the End of the World* (Alfred Birnbaum, tr., New York, Kodansha International, 1991), a work that was originally published in Japanese under the title *Sekai no owari to hādo-boirudo wandā rando*. Other Murakami novels in English translation, available in Japan, are not sold in the United States.

10 See Kenzaburō Ōe, "Japan's Dual Identity: A Writer's Dilemma," *Wlt* 62:3 (Summer 1988), pp. 359–69. In this article Ōe denies that Murakami's work constitutes "pure literature."

11 Fredric Jameson, "Postmodernism, or The Cultural Logic of Late Capitalism," *New Left Review*, no. 146 (July-August 1984), pp. 53–92.

12 Masao Miyoshi, *Off Center: Power and Culture Relations Between Japan and the United States*, Cambridge, Ma., Harvard University Press, 1991, p. 98.

13 Kasai Kiyoshi, Katō Ten'yō, & Takeda Seishi, *Murakami Haruki o meguru bōken* (Haruki Murakami's Adventures), Tokyo, Kawade Shobō Shinsha, 1991. It is often difficult to fathom the real meaning of the sound-bite-size utterances issuing from the participants in a *taiwa*, where little is discussed in a sustained way.

14 *A Wild Sheep Chase* is regarded as the last volume in a trilogy that began with *Kaze no uta o kike* (Listen to the Wind Song; 1979) and was followed by 1976 *no pinbōru* (Pinball in 1976; 1980); but in these two previous works too not a great deal is revealed about Boku's past.

15 See the section entitled "Being-for-Others" in Jean-Paul Sartre, *Being and Nothingness*, New York, Washington Square Press, 1966.

16 Kōjin Karatani offers a complicated, philosophically oriented explanation for Murakami's avoidance of names and like matters. See the chapter entitled "Murakami Haruki no 'fūkei'" (Haruki Murakami's "Landscape"), in his *Shūen o megutte* (Concerning the End), Tokyo, Fukutake Shoten, 1990.

17 Kuroki Kazuo, *Murakami Haruki: Za rosuto wārudo* (Haruki Murakami: The Lost World), Tokyo, Rokkō Shuppan, 1989, p. 71.

18 Sekii Mitsuo, "'Hitsuji' wa doko e kieta ka" (Where Did the "Sheep" Disappear?), *Kokubungaku Kaishaku to Kyōzai no Kenkyū*, 30:3 (March 1985), p. 124.

19 Quoted in Hisai Tsubaki & Kuwa Masato, *Zō ga heigen ni kaette hi* (The Day the Elephant Returned to the Plains), Tokyo, Shinchōsha, 1991, pp. 183–84.

Mishima's Cosmic Noh Drama: *The Damask Drum*

Yukio Mishima (1925–70), novelist, poet, dramatist, film director, and head of a personal army numbering approximately 100 men, was also the author of successful Noh plays. Rooted in Japanese philosophy, history and culture, characteristics of this form of theatre, Mishima's Noh dramas expanded their focus: they were transposed into modern terms, thereby answering contemporary spiritual needs. Past and present are blended into one symbolic dramatic ritual in *The Damask Drum* (1955): image, line, color and tonality lure and allure the viewer into a complex of mysterious elements.

The product of samurai upbringing, Mishima was educated according to the tenets of his class: the code of strength was uppermost. Courage, will and loyalty to the Emperor had been impressed upon him since his earliest days. Spartan in his ways, honorable in his acts, humble in his attitudes, Mishima was also a specialist in the martial arts of *kendo* (dueling with bamboo staves) and karate. There was, however, another side to this man of iron: that of the poet. Endowed with extraordinary sensitivity, Mishima understood and reacted to the exquisitely delicate aspects of Japanese art. He felt the *livingness* of the Oriental's nuanced universe and entered into complicity with nature in its most elemental ramifications. Mishima set down his thoughts and feelings when a student at Tokyo Imperial University (1944) in a collection of short stories. Kawabata, the future Nobel Prize winner who became Mishima's mentor, encouraged him to pursue a literary course. His advice was accepted by the acolyte. The author of 257 books (fifteen novels, some of which have been translated into English), Mishima emphasized Japan's rich heritage and the poignancy of the confrontation which his culture had to undergo in modern times. At the age of forty-five, Mishima committed *seppuku* (ritual suicide), thus effecting in the real world what had been imagistically and symbolically portrayed in his premonitory work *Runaway Horses*.

The Damask Drum introduces audiences to two different acting areas on stage: the third floors of two office buildings in downtown Tokyo. A law office is visible on one side of the acting area; on the opposite is a couturière's establishment. A street below separates the two: it is marked with the hustle and bustle, neon lights and other brash elements of contemporary life. An old janitor, Iwakichi, is sweeping out the law office. A pretty young clerk, Kayoko, is talking to him. She complains about the difficulties involved in earning a living. During the course of the conversation we learn that Iwakichi has fallen in love with one of the clients of the fashionable dressmaker on the other side of the street whom he had observed only through the window. Kayoko derides the old man for his passion. Suddenly the lights switch off in the law office, only to be turned on in the dressmaking establishment. We now listen to the conversations of a heartless dance master, an unfeeling young man, an arrogant member of the Ministry of Foreign Affairs and the self-satisfied owner of the dressmaking establishment. Irony and satire mark their discourse. We are informed about Iwakichi's love letters, which Kayoko has been delivering daily to the dressmaker's establishment. They mock him, and the dance master creates a plan. He will use one of his props, a drum, to which he will attach a note informing Iwakichi that if he beats the drum his ladylove will hear the sound and be forever his. They throw the drum through the window. Iwakichi receives it, reads the note and is

thrilled at the prospect. What he does not know is that the drum is not made of skin but of damask. No matter how hard he pounds, no sound is emitted. His despair drives him to suicide; and unseen by the audience, he jumps out of the window.

Like many Noh plays, *The Damask Drum* is constructed in two parts, the second of which features Iwakichi's return as a ghost. His ladylove, now present, is no longer the pure idealized image he had believed her to be, but a "whore." Unrequited in her love experiences, she longs for Iwakichi's "real" love as he does for hers. He beats the drum once again, fervently and passionately. Owing to the woman's heartlessness throughout life, however, she is unable to hear the sound. Iwakichi's ghost dies of despair.

In accordance with traditional Noh theatre, *The Damask Drum* is a combination of dance, song and poetic recitation. Although it brings to the stage specific situations and individual beings, an ambiguous condition is experienced. The characters are archetypal in nature; they bathe in a mythical world beyond the space/time continuum. Like weightless entities, they articulate their tensions, and pain grips them in spasmodic sequences. *The Damask Drum* is a play in which the unexpressed is more important than the revealed, silence more predominant than the articulated word, the void prevails over the filled and the amorphous is preferred to the formed.

As traditional Noh drama is religiously oriented, so *The Damask Drum* is imbued with the three most important Japanese philosophical traditions: Taoism, Shintoism and Zen Buddhism. According to the tenets of these sects, the transcendental rather than the individual sphere is experienced—the eternal and not the mortal, the life force (cosmic energy or breath) and not the concrete deity. Noh plays therefore do not bathe in linear time but in cyclical schemes. Although *The Damask Drum* takes place in April, it could be the spring season of any year in any place in the world—that period when the aridity of winter burgeons into hope. Decors are likewise vague; always symbolic, they reflect a mood, a vision, an idealized love, as in *The Damask Drum*: the awakening of powerful emotions which lead directly into pain, controlled yet burning inwardly, altering in accordance with the cosmic life force, so important to the Oriental metaphysician and poet. The visible element on stage reflects not the exterior world, but an inner spiritual and emotional climate. Because of the profoundly spiritual focus, viewers apprehend Noh drama in general and *The Damask Drum* in particular; they penetrate its world intuitively. During the course of its stage life, insights are released, enlightenment is experienced, the mystery of matter becomes discernible—not perhaps in the phenomenological world, but in the deeply spiritual universe of the Japanese soul.[1]

The Damask Drum has maintained the formulae of Noh theatre in its spiritual outlook, its themes, characters, relationship to nature and use of symbol. Like Zen Buddhism and Taoism, *The Damask Drum* is meditative, introspective, slow-paced, subtle and suggestive. The depth and meaning of Iwakichi's love may be apprehended in sudden flashes of illumination; it is not brash or aggressive, but turned inward, felt, sensed. Like conventional Noh drama, *The Damask Drum* has no real plot, and therefore it may take an infinite amount of patience for a Westerner to understand the series of complex images which make up its song-and-dance sequences, tonalities and the inflections included in its choral and orchestral accompaniments. Of import are Iwakichi's sensations; the feelings evoked during the course of the performance; the tensions aroused by the images implicit in his discourse, his gestures and pace (the timing, for example, between the sweeping sequences and the apostrophe to the potted laurel tree in the office which he personifies and cares for with love and affection). All aspects of Iwakichi's stage life, as well as that of the other protagonists, are stylized and predetermined: spatial patterns woven about the stage, poses, interpretations—all add to the fascination of the theatrical experience.

Important in *The Damask Drum,* as it had been in ancient Noh theatre, is the relationship between the stage proceedings and nature. Although the play takes place in two office buildings, there is a symbolic correlation between Iwakichi's feelings and attitudes and nature in general: a correspondence between the cosmic domain and its interaction with regard to the individual in the phenomenological world. These two realms inspire resonance and infinite patterns and distillations of sensations and moods.

The notion of timelessness and eternal becoming implicit in traditional Noh drama is clearly discernible in *The Damask Drum.* Iwakichi lives in a three-dimensional as well as in a four-dimensional sphere. He experiences these worlds interchangeably. In the phenomenological domain, matter and spirit only seem to operate antithetically; in reality, they are manifestations of the Taoist's yin/yang principles, a single universal cosmic force. Since matter and spirit are one in the atemporal sphere, death and life coincide, as do image and reality, fiction and fact. Duality and multiplicity exist only in the existential domain, in Iwakichi's world. The conflicts which arise are stressed by Mishima throughout *The Damask Drum* not only for dramatic purposes, but also for metaphysical reasons: age as opposed to youth, inanimate and animate objects, life and

death, outer and inner domains, solitude and society, business and poetry. These divergent ways are forever intruding one upon the other. "They've switched off the light," Iwakichi says. "Every day at the same time. . . . When this room dies that one comes to life again. And in the morning when this room returns to life, that one dies" (p. 42).[2] The continuity of this duality expresses the eternal play of conflicting forces which must be endured in life.

Iwakichi's "feeling" world stands for ancient ways, spiritual climes as opposed to the harshness of a burgeoning industrial society which is determined to destroy tradition. As the member of the Ministry of Foreign Affairs says when talking about Iwakichi and the world he represents: "It is essential to make him realize that where he lives is a little room nobody will enter" (62). Iwakichi's world is closed, gone, dead to the agents of contemporary culture. Yet the two domains are linked, connected in the form of the clerk Kayoko, who, although a product of twentieth-century ways, still understands traditional views, the nuanced sensitivity of a bygone world. It is she who delivers Iwakichi's love letters to the woman across the way. It is she who can feel the pain involved when one has outlived an age, an approach to life, a society. Two forces which make up the universe according to Taoist doctrine are part of the cosmic flow: it is Kayoko who becomes the catalyst, forcing fusion or dissolution.

That Mishima has situated his drama on the third floor of two office buildings is not surprising. Verticality was always an important factor in Noh drama. The height of the office building corresponds to the mountains which figure so prominently in early Noh theatre. Motionless, still, mountains represent ethereal spheres: heaven, spirit, light circulating about the universe. So the office building in *The Damask Drum* reveals Iwakichi's vision: his love which is too absolute; his desire, overly encompassing; his idealization. The dichotomy between the purity of this image—that is, his ladylove (height)—and the earthiness of the woman of reality (ground) is too great to take on existence in the phenomenological sphere. It can only come to life in the imagination. Iwakichi's earthly fall in suicide at the conclusion of the first part of *The Damask Drum* compels him to take stock of the polarities between fantasy and reality and to rework his vision. Only in death does divergency vanish and oneness prevail.

In the collective and cosmic world of Noh theatre, nature is neither crushed nor violated, nor is it used exclusively for man's benefit, as is so frequently the case in the Western world. In *The Damask Drum* nature is experienced as part of a whole. It is loved and appreciated spiritually, esthetically and physically. When, for ex-

ample, Iwakichi looks at the potted laurel tree in the office, he cares for it, loves it, personifies it, apostrophizes
it. He grasps its spirit, its superworldly aspects; understands its beauty, its mobile attitudes and pulsations.

In accordance with the close correspondence between man and nature characteristic of Noh drama,
Mishima's use of natural forces is implicit in his work.
Wind, for example, to which Iwakichi alludes when he
opens the window, is alive; it enters into the stage ritual
as a turbulent force, a catalyst. Iwakichi describes his
feelings in terms of the wind, thus emphasizing their
transpersonal nature: "I can't stand that dusty wind that
blows at the beginning of spring" (39). He longs for "the
calm of the evening." Spring, although specific, takes on
universality because of the successive seasons implied,
the death/rebirth cycle of which it is a part. It reflects
the rhythms of life; the lives of the societies and civilizations to which the protagonist belongs. Spring is the
symbol of eternal renewal. It mirrors the notion of perpetual becoming: of love forever burgeoning and vanishing.

Iwakichi fears inner chaos, and the wind is an outer
manifestation of this state: a world with which he cannot cope: "the dusty wind" which forces up the dross
and earthiness of life as well as its spiritual counterpart.
He rejects the frightening and sinister character of a
wind which alters nature's seeming stability and longs
for the stillness of the clouds which endow the world
with serenity. As the wind dies down, images of softness
and tenderness appear in Iwakichi's mind's eye, immersing him in the tranquil climate of his own being:
"The wind's died down since evening" (39).

▓ ▓ ▓

Inasmuch as Noh theatre is archetypal and bathes in the
collective domain, specifics such as characters and sets
are to be considered symbolically. Characters in traditional Noh theatre are fixed for the most part. Iwakichi,
the Old Man, corresponds to the *shite,* the main actor.
Although he does not wear a mask (nor does he under
certain circumstances in ancient Noh plays), his face itself remains expressionless: it virtually becomes a mask.
Because of its immobility it stands out in sharp contrast
to his bodily movements, vocal tones and complex of
sculptured spatial forms which he weaves about the
stage as he sweeps the room, tends to the laurel tree and
writes his letters. Iwakichi's expressionless face severs
him from the outside world. He must therefore look inward. In so doing, he injects his part with "emotional
coloring" by means of a variety of poses of the head and
neck and by downward or upward glances and intricate
gestures. The ensemble of accessories used by Iwakichi,
such as his broom, the laurel plant to which he talks,

the letter-writing ceremony and his nuanced vocal
emissions, are integrated into a new unity, thus making
for a total effect. The individual character takes part in
a cosmic drama.[3]

Iwakichi in many respects is reminiscent of a Zen
Buddhist priest who is detached from the material
world, which he considers meaningless. He has swept
it all away, symbolically speaking, and has rid himself
of the dross, the material encumbrances which tie him
to life. His inner riches—his fantasy world, his dream—
the realm of the absolute, are of higher value to him.
Only in the spiritual sphere does he feel the pulsations,
the breath and cosmic rhythms of the universe about
him; only in this domain does he experience the dynamism of life and feelings of belonging. The opposite
world is expressed in the dressmaking establishment
across the way: artifice, materialism, arrogance and cruelty—all forces with which Iwakichi must contend.

Kayoko, the young letter-carrying clerk, may be
considered a kind of contemporary *waki,* a wanderer
throughout the temporal and atemporal realm. She sets
up the dialogue or chemical interchange between the
two views of life. Although specific, the repetition of her
activity takes on cyclical import: that of a perpetual
death/birth ritual. Hope is injected into Iwakichi's life
when she delivers the letters, and despair when no answer is forthcoming. Not only does Kayoko act as a link
between Iwakichi's world and society at large, but she
herself also straddles two civilizations: past and present.
Beset by economic difficulties, she too is a victim of
spiritual crisis: that of the individual who has not yet
discovered her groundbed.

The dancing master, the young man, the government official and the owner of the dressmaking establishment are ironic, satiric and humorous in a rather
grotesque manner. They are modern counterparts of the
kyogen, those ancient clowns who kept audiences
amused by their farces and laughable ways. Anonymous
beings who emerge from nowhere and vanish into darkness, they serve to heighten tension, to explain the stage
happenings in less than poetic language. They infuse
comedy as well as cruelty into Iwakichi's poignant love
situation by relating vignettes and revealing unusual incidents associated with letters delivered by Kayoko.

Although only a stage prop, the damask drum, as
a symbol, is steeped in tradition. It is representational
and yet remains functionless. Comparable to the *koan,*
a device used by Zen Buddhists to banish rational and
syllogistic reasoning (techniques so dear to Western
mentality), it serves as a basis for experience. It allows
Iwakichi to become exposed to the mysteries of existence, to intuit undreamed-of truths, to transcend indi-

vidual understanding. The drum leads to Iwakichi's sudden awakening to the realization of his situation and its impossibility—hence his suicide. When he first takes hold of the drum after it has been tossed out of the office window into his own, he thinks he can win his beloved by pounding on it. He has not yet been initiated into the atemporal sphere of the *koan* and so is incapable of entering into that dimension which would allow him to understand the "foolishness" of his passion.

When Iwakichi strikes the drum—attempting to use it for his own purposes in the existential sphere—he is doomed to failure. As a *koan,* it bathes in its own logic; it participates in cosmic consciousness, which is incompatible with that of worldly spheres. Had Iwakichi been trained by a Zen master, his comprehension of the meaning and focus of this object would have been deeper.[4] As stage property, the drum belongs to the logical and rationally oriented universe, the intellectual sphere and not the archetypal realm. In that it was sent to Iwakichi by those living in the temporal world, the drum represents formalism, convention, geometrical and causal reality. The dimensionless universe sought by Iwakichi and implicit in Zen Buddhism and Taoism implies a world *in potentia*—the notion of perpetual becoming.

The drum which Iwakichi beats, but which remains soundless because of its material, is as alive in his mind as is the potted laurel tree. In keeping with Shinto belief, everthing in nature, whether animate or inanimate, is alive. Shinto deities (*kami*), in the form of spirits of trees, mountains, flowers, ancestors, heroes, the sun or the moon, breathe, act and react in the existential sphere. Man approaches the *kami* without fear and in friendship. A force or *kami* therefore inhabits both the essence of the drum and the laurel tree. Although the drum did not respond to Iwakichi's pleadings, the laurel tree does. It has been transformed in his fantasy world into a princess that takes on life in a garden inhabited by the moon: "She's the princess of the laurel, the tree that grows in the garden of the moon" (40). All the poetry, sensitivity and creative impact of his feelings emerge in this one symbol. Its beauty and gentleness become consoling forces for Iwakichi, who feels his loneliness with such desperation.

The laurel and the moon are recurrent images in Iwakichi's world: they usher in a mood of melancholy. The moon, symbol of transformation, represents biological rhythms and cyclical states. Frequently evoked by Japanese poets, the moon is associated with indirect rather than direct experience and knowledge: passivity, receptivity, and the dream. As it makes its way in the night world of Iwakichi's unconscious, this celestial force conjures up a domain inhabited by spirits, ghosts and images which would allow him to embrace his beloved.

The Japanese have always been "Moon lovers."[5] Iwakichi is no exception. The eerie and mysterious light which emanates from this force suggests a dim, insinuating, shaded domain. It is never brilliant nor filled with glaring lights; rather it is remote, distant, already lived. Objects illuminated by moonlight are not individualized but blend into the environment—hazy, essentially obscure, hiding through the branches of the laurel, stirring the feelings of the onlooker. Its soft light falls lovingly on the complex designs and forms inhabiting the stage. A shadowy world emerges, paving the way for the ghostly encounter in the second part of *The Damask Drum.*

The moon and the laurel are one for Iwakichi. Each injects a sense of belonging or *participation mystique* into the proceedings; each endows the events with painful feeling tones, underscoring the bleakness of Iwakichi's temporal existence and the beauty of his idealization. Yet when Iwakichi's spirit returns, his beloved is no longer that pure being he had created in his mind's eye, but rather a "whore" who longs for the purity of an unborn—unmanifested—love. As he beats the drum once again, hoping this time to breach the gap—to link dichotomies between the invisible and visible spheres—the cold rays of an unfeeling moon envelop the atmosphere, divesting the world of all its warmth and, in so doing, leading to another painful demise.

In contrast to Western theatre, where characters attempt to mark their roles with individuality, the Noh actor focuses his efforts on the creation of emotion—love, anger, revenge, hate—in order to go beyond the individual personality. The facts of the situation to be enacted are stated at the outset of the drama; the atmosphere, mood and poetry conveyed by the role rather than the being itself must be portrayed during the course of the spectacle. For the Westerner, *The Damask Drum* may lack action and conflict. For the Oriental, tension is concentrated and distilled in the images, poetry, gesture and plastic forms which move about the stage. The spatial compositions create the mood, develop and pursue the single emotion which is the sine qua non of Noh theatre.

Just as the Zen painter uses the fewest possible brushstrokes to express the world of multiplicity, so Zen poetry is also known for its sparseness. Mishima maintains this tradition. A word in *The Damask Drum* stands alone, bare, solitary, divested of adjectives and adverbs, and becomes an entity unto itself. As in Bashō's haiku poems, the image delineated becomes "the agent" of cosmic force, bringing illumination to the phenomenological world, making a more profound reality known.

The Damask Drum reflects the Taoist's and the Zen Buddhist's calmness of mind and oneness with nature. It is a manifestation of the Shintoist's animistic beliefs which endow inanimate objects with a *livingness,* thereby enlarging the scope and depth of the dramatic spectacle. Noh theatre, whether ancient or as recreated by Mishima, is unique. It varies from all other forms of performing arts such as song, mime, dance, verse and drama; yet it includes them all. It is the intensity of sustained emotion in *The Damask Drum* which moves audiences and not the realistic portrayals, the sublimated passion with its exquisitely nuanced poetry and its cosmic purpose and design which forces its impress upon the viewer.

Bettina L. Knapp, Summer 1980

¹ Noh theatre began as an earthly replica of a divine adventure: the conflict between the sun goddess Amaterasu and her brother, who terrified her to such an extent by his pranks that she withdrew into a cave in heaven, thus depriving the world of sunlight. The other gods attempted and finally succeeded in enticing her out of her isolation, thus ensuring the return of the sun. Influenced in the course of time by Shinto dances which were performed at various shrines in Japan, by warrior court dances, Buddhist sacred pantomime, song-and-dance routines enacted at religious and festive occasions, humor also became an important factor in Noh theatre or "poetic-dance-monodrama," as it has come to be called. During the spring planting and autumn harvesting of rice, clowning, gymnastic contests and amusing song-and-dance routines were performed to entertain the peasants at work. By the twelfth century the "rustic and the sacred" were unified, and actors began training in structured troupes. By the fourteenth century dialogue was added to both comedy and tragedy routines, creating a veritable theatrical form: gods were transformed into men and women; situations were intense, moods all-pervading.

² Yukio Mishima, *Five Modern No Plays,* Donald Keene, tr. & ed., New York, Vintage, 1973.

³ Daiji Maruoko, Tatsuo Yoshikoshi, *Noh,* Don Kenny, tr., Osaka, Joikusha, n.d., p. 119.

⁴ A typical *koan* is the following: "When both hands are clapped listen to the sound of one hand. If you have heard the sound of one hand, can you make me hear it too?" The acolyte studying Zen is posed this question by his master. D. T. Suzuki, *An Introduction to Zen Buddhism,* New York, Grove, 1964, p. 59.

⁵ Daisetz T. Suzuki, *Zen and the Japanese Culture,* Princeton, N.J., Princeton University Press, 1973, p. 393.

The Seamless Universe of Ōe Kenzaburō

No term or concept appears more frequently in Ōe Kenzaburō's writing than "ambiguity." Ōe made it the

Ōe Kenzaburō (*Robert H. Taylor*)

focus of his 1994 Nobel Lecture, "Japan, the Ambiguous, and Myself," and has acknowledged directly its prominence in his thinking: "I wrote a book entitled 'The Methods of the Novel' (1978) in which I explained that the concept of ambiguity was very important to me" ("Interview" with Yoshida, 372). Closely associated with ambiguity is the idea of simultaneity—of past and present, fact and dream, history and myth—which results in the ambiguity or blurring of distinctions and boundaries that constitutes Ōe's seamless universe. At the same time, however, Ōe counterbalances ambiguity with a vision of human history connected by an underlying structural certitude.

In a discussion of his novel *The Game of Contemporaneity* (orig. *Dojidai Gemu,* 1979), Ōe mentions coming in contact with the Mural Movement during a visit to Mexico:

> Octavio Paz said that Mexico is a place where history is constantly bleeding. And there I found ancient times and the contemporary coexisting. Those colossal murals depict Mexican history from ancient times to the present synchronically. I said to myself, can it be done in literature? If you consider *The Game of Contemporaneity* as a mural, it portrays the history of a village from ancient times to the present. Right beneath the mural is a giant sprawling and looking at the entire history as contemporaneity. Both the writer and the reader can also read the novel in that fashion. (Quoted in Wilson, 125)

As his comment implies, Ōe aimed at a spatial rather than chronological representation of history. The narrator imagines the power of experiencing all of human history simultaneously, thus eliminating the boundaries of past and present and allowing the reorganization of history. As in Faulkner, the same events are related from several different perspectives and in different sequences, resulting in a confusion of fact, memory, fantasy, and chronology. Ōe's intention was, as he says, "to present ambiguity in 'Contemporary Games'—that is to say, one reality conveying many meanings." And he adds, "Since regional folklore and regional myths contain this element of ambiguity, I clearly intended to delve into this matter in the regional myths" ("Interview," 372).

Although an ambitious, clever narrative, much of *The Game of Contemporaneity* is a more contrived, self-conscious elaboration of ideas that Ōe brought together in his earlier, more admired work, *The Silent Cry* (orig. *Man'en gannen no futtoboru,* 1967; Eng. 1974), which is the focus of this essay.[1] Like the later novel, *The Silent Cry* is concerned with history bleeding. The following passage is not from the novel, but it could be:

> He cried the relief he felt at finally seeing the pattern, the way all the stories fit together—the old stories, the war stories, their stories—to become the story that was still being told. He was not crazy; he had never been crazy. He had only seen and heard the world as it always was: no boundaries, only transitions through all distances and time. (Silko, 246)

The passage is from Leslie Marmon Silko's 1977 novel *Ceremony,* and its connection with *The Silent Cry* is strong. Tayo, the central figure of Silko's work, is a mental casualty of World War II, suffering from guilt, loss, and displacement related to the cousin-brother who was killed by the Japanese while Tayo survived. Where modern medicine fails to heal his affliction, the rituals—or ceremony—associated with ancient American Indian myths succeed. Part of Tayo's healing is his realization of the interconnectedness of all human beings and experiences in time and space.

The Silent Cry is a story of two brothers who, like Tayo, are in a sense casualties of the Pacific War and its aftermath and who, also like Tayo, return to their roots for atonement, renewal, a new beginning. Their name, Nedokoro, means "root place." The narrator is twenty-six-year-old Mitsusaburo (Mitsu), a peripheral character who acts as the commentator on his world. He is first encountered sitting in fetal position mired in soil in a pit dug for a septic tank as he contemplates his friend's bizarre suicide and also his wife's alcoholism, which followed the birth of their deformed son. The time is the early 1960s. The younger brother, Takashi, returns from America, where he has been touring in a play, *Ours Was the Shame,* "a penitential piece" meant to atone for the 1960 riots and for mistreatment of the American president when he was in Japan to sign the revised U.S.-Japan Security Treaty. At Takashi's urging, the two head for their native village, Mitsu to find a new beginning, his "thatched hut," and Taka to lead an uprising of young peasant men. He wants to re-create an 1860 episode involving their great-grandfather and especially his younger brother, who led the exploited peasants in their revolt against the wealthy farmers, including the Nedokoro family. Now the enemy is the "emperor," a Korean supermarket czar who is exploiting and impoverishing the peasants. Takashi does not want merely to emulate his great-granduncle, but to "be able to experience as intensely as possible what great-grandfather's younger brother went through spiritually" (183). Because of the story that the great-granduncle had cut a clearing in the forest as a training ground to prepare the men to fight, Takashi decides to organize the young men of the valley for football practice as training for the uprising. As has often been noted, the intention to fuse 1860 and 1960 is clear from the original title of the novel, usually translated as "Football in the Year 1860." Within the novel there is no reference to football in 1860, but the title accurately conveys the novel's tossing the characters back and forth between 1860 and 1960. When Mitsu watches Takashi run naked in a ritual dance in the snow, he thinks:

> The essence of that moment would be drawn out indefinitely; direction in time was swallowed up and lost amid the steadily falling flakes, just as sound was absorbed by the layer of snow. All-pervasive time: Takashi as he ran stark naked was great-grandfather's brother, and my own; every moment of those hundred years was crowded into this one instant in time. (146)

On returning to his native village, Mitsu had experienced a similar sensation of undifferentiated time:

> As I bent down over the spring to drink from it directly, I had a sudden sense of certainty: certainty that everything . . . was just as I'd seen it twenty years before; a certainty, born of longing yet to myself at least, utterly convincing, that the water now welling up so ceaselessly was exactly the same water that had welled up and flowed in those days. (58)

Ōe's treatment of reversible time is informed by the work of Mircea Eliade,[2] who, when distinguishing between sacred and profane time, says:

> One essential difference between these two qualities of time strikes us immediately: *by its very na-*

ture sacred time is reversible in the sense that, properly speaking, it is a primordial mythical time made present. Every religious festival, any liturgical time, represents the reactualization of a sacred event that took place in a mythical past, "in the beginning." Religious participation in a festival implies emerging from ordinary temporal duration and reintegration of the mythical time reactualized by the festival itself. Hence, sacred time is indefinitely recoverable. (68–69)

Echoing Eliade, Ōe uses the ancient Bon [Lantern] Festival, when the spirits of the dead return to earth. In the Nembutsu ritual dance, performed as part of the festival, the dancers are imbued with the spirits of the figures being represented. Each year the "sacred" events of communal myth are reactualized during the dance, and both the spectators and performers are transported to the time of the initial happening. Takashi describes such a happening when as a child he experienced the murder of his brother S during a raid on a Korean settlement:

> As a kid I actually saw, in the Nembutsu dance at the Bon Festival, the 'spirit' of S, in the winter jacket worn by naval air cadets, fighting the men from the Korean settlement at the head of a party of young men, until he was finally beaten to death, stripped of his jacket, and left lying face down in just his white undershirt and shorts. I told you, didn't I, that his arms were raised as if he was dancing, with his legs spread like those of a hurdler in action? (123)

The experience was like that described by Eliade. It was not, Takashi says, "a memory of the real-life raid on the Korean settlement, but an experience in the world of the dance, in which the facts were reworked in visible form through the communal emotions of the people in the valley" (123).

By meticulously reproducing the daily life of 1860, Takashi wants to recover the past even more precisely than in the experience of the Nembutsu dance: "I want to start another rising here, to reproduce the rising of our ancestors a century ago even more realistically than the Nembutsu dance. Mitsu—it's not impossible!" (182). When a young man is expelled from the group and the village after an attempted rape, the 1860 episode is recovered again: "Would you believe it, Mitsu, he was trying to cross the forest in all this snow and get to Kochi! He was identifying with the young fellow in the 1860 rising!" (182).

In *The Silent Cry* the past is not only recoverable, but also continually revised; and each revision makes the past both contemporaneous and ambiguous. Of his aim in literature, Ōe has said: "To create myths, modify myths and deconstruct myths is the most important method of my literature" ("Conversation" with Nathan, 5). One of Mitsu's principal functions is to destroy and reconstruct myths. He is persistent in undermining Takashi's reverence for S and particularly his great-granduncle as heroes. Although acknowledging as dream memories the heroic poses of S, Takashi insists on the truth of the vision of his brother "standing at the head of a group from the valley doing battle with the pick of the men from the Korean village" (75). Mitsu instead portrays S as weak, timid, and a laughingstock: "I found a perverted pleasure in waiting for the fresh flaws that my corrections lured from Takashi's memory and shooting them down as they appeared" (74). Even more important to Takashi is the image of his great-grandfather's younger brother in scenes of heroic resistance as leader of the peasants in the 1860 uprising. Mitsu again imputes Takashi's vision to dream rather than fact and reasons that the ancestor actually fled into the forest and disappeared to escape retribution. Toward the end of the novel, the reader learns that Takashi's dreaming may be closer to the truth than Mitsu's reasoning. S appears more like a hero than a hapless victim, and discovery of a cellar beneath the storehouse reveals evidence that great-grandfather's younger brother did not flee but remained a leader of the resistance. There is no certainty, however; so the past remains suspended in the present, and truth elusive.

This deconstructive handling of history is part of the broader meaning of the novel. Speaking critically of Japan's cultural climate, Ōe says: "Never have we witnessed, in intellectual journalism in our country, the synchronic existence of two opposing new schools of thought—for example, structuralism and deconstructionism—and the resulting combination of antagonism and complementarity, which can lead, in turn, to a mutual deepening of the two schools" ("Japan's Dual Identity," 365). Actually, *The Silent Cry* is itself an example of "the synchronic existence of two opposing new schools of thought." Here, deconstructionism and structuralism exist simultaneously.[3] Even as Ōe is deconstructing village history and myth, he is disclosing their underlying structural connectedness. Whereas Henry Adams searched for a sequence of human history and found it in energy or force, Ōe finds in human history a sequence of violence. In its reactualization of violent events from the village's past, the Nembutsu dance is an acknowledgment and ritual rendering of the legacy of violence. The spirit of destructive malevolence is concretized in the Chosokabe, "a creature of terrifying size that exists everywhere in time and space" and that is an "ever-present reality" in the village (42). Ōe universalizes the sequence of violence by linking the histories of Japan and America. He focuses on three years—1860, 1945, and 1960—which bleed into one another in the course of the novel.

Throughout the 1860s Japan experienced its own civil war in the many, often bloody uprisings of the peasants against economic suppression and exploitation. In choosing the date of 1860 for the fictional uprising in the novel, Ōe intentionally, if obliquely, makes the connection with America on the threshold of its Civil War. There is even the similarity of brother fighting against brother. Although the American Civil War is never mentioned directly, it is recalled in a catalytic incident that is an ironic reminder of the history of blacks in America and the war that should have ended their debasement. Shortly before Takashi returned to Japan from the United States, he encountered Mitsu's friend, who was studying at Columbia, and handed him without comment a pamphlet about the civil-rights movement:

> The frontispiece was a photograph of a black, his body so scorched and swollen that the details were blurred like those of a crudely carved wooden doll, with a number of white men in shoddy clothes standing round him. It was comic and terrible and disgusting, a representation of naked violence so direct that it gripped the beholder like some fearful fantasy. (17)

Recalling the pamphlet later, Takashi remarks: "A terrible picture, the sort of thing that tells you something about the essential nature of violence" (156). The friend believes that the pamphlet was given to him intentionally, and the image of the horribly beaten black man becomes fused with the source of his own condition: "With the inevitability of two drops of water merging into each other, sight linked itself immediately with the ill-defined trouble in his own head" (17). He has suffered from a mental disturbance ever since he was badly beaten in one of the 1960 riots, possibly by Takashi, who fought for a time on both sides. Ironically, the friend had attended the riot not to fight but to rescue his wife. From the beginning of the novel Mitsu has been trying to fathom why his friend had "daubed his head all over with crimson paint, stripped, thrust a cucumber up his anus, and hanged himself" (4). Though horrible, the behavior is understandable if the friend came to recognize, and could not tolerate, the essential human capacity for violence and for victimization of the powerless. His defilement of his body can be seen as an acknowledgment of human degradation, and his suicide an act of atonement—one of several in the novel—for that degradation. After his death, his grandmother connects him with Sarudahiko and, in doing so, affirms

the sequence of human violence by alluding to its presence in the origins of Japan. The reference is to a Japanese creation myth involving Sarudahiko the divine, who met with a representative of gods who were intruding on the earth. In a show of power, the representative of the intruding gods slashed the mouth of one of the inhabitants, a sea slug, "who resisted in silence" and with whom Mitsu identifies his friend (6).

When Takashi gives him the pamphlet, the friend suspects that it is linked also to Takashi's own problems. He is right. Takashi is aware of his own violent nature, admitting, "I've been torn all along between the desire to justify myself as a creature of violence and the urge to punish myself for it" (211). And he links that violent nature to his involvement in the 1960 riots and his fighting on both sides:

> The reason why I deliberately chose to get mixed up in violence during the campaign against revision of the Security Treaty—and the reason why, when I found myself associated with the violence of the weak forced into opposition against unjust violence, I chose to ally myself with unjust violence, whatever its purpose—was that I wanted to go on accepting myself as I am, to justify myself as a man of violence without having to change. (211)

At this point he has not confessed his most compelling reason to punish himself: his culpability in the rape and suicide of his sister. His touring in *Ours Was the Shame* was phony penitence, but the shame he feels and the desire to repent for his treatment of his sister are genuine. Thus, the rape and suicide of his sister are superimposed on the image of the beaten and scorched black man to produce a single image of victimization of the weak and powerless. Takashi finds a means of repentance by leading the uprising against the "Emperor," ironically using violence to atone for violence.

If the 1860 peasant uprising in Japan recalls the American Civil War and the 1960 riots against the U.S.-Japan Security Treaty recall the civil-rights movement in America, the year 1945, especially the atomic bombing of Hiroshima, links the histories of Japan and America even more forcefully and affirms the interconnectedness of history. Mitsu remembers the Nembutsu procession during the war, when "spirits" in army uniforms were introduced:

> They were the ghosts of men drafted from the valley who had been killed in battle. The number of them in uniform increased every year. The "spirit" of a young man who had been working in a Hiroshima factory and was killed by the atomic bomb came down from the forest with his whole body blackened like a lump of used charcoal. (125)

586

Ōe has often discussed and written about the atomic bomb and its implications, and the bombings of Hiroshima and Nagasaki are never far from his consciousness. Here, however, he does not distinguish the bombings significantly and instead includes them as but further instances of the universal, historical pattern of violence and destruction.

In the summer of 1945, after the end of the war, the brother S was killed by the Koreans, and in one version of the incident, related by S's friend, a priest, his death is linked to the 1860 uprising: "There were things in S's behavior that could only suggest he had the 1860 rising in mind when he resolved on his own course of action. I don't think I'm just forcing an analogy in linking 1860 and the summer of 1945" (117). Filling in the blanks of the priest's version, Mitsu concludes that S was bothered that great-grandfather's brother was the only rebel leader not executed, and therefore S, in atonement, decided that he would be the one to die in the raid (117). The year 1945, like 1860 and 1960, commemorates the never-ending sequence of violence that has no boundaries. Another link between Japan and America is the enslaved condition of the Koreans referred to in the novel. The connection with the experience of black Americans is pointed in Mitsu's comment about the Koreans in Japan: "They didn't come here voluntarily in the first place. They were slave labor brought from their own country against their will" (188).

The culminating events of Takashi's failed uprising are in keeping with his violent character. Although Mitsu casts doubt on the accuracy of Takashi's story—another example of the indeterminacy of truth in the novel—Takashi may very well have, as he asserts, raped and brutally murdered a young woman in the village. Believing that he will be arrested and put to death, he commits suicide by shooting himself in the face. Whether he deliberately committed an act that would result in punishment by death as atonement for the violation and death of his sister is one of the uncertainties of the novel, but such behavior would be consistent with his pattern of violence, guilt, and atonement. Once, he said, he had tried to escape the violence which surrounded him. Having been told by Mitsu that he had stood in a dark kitchen calmly chewing candy after learning that S had been killed, Takashi explains his behavior:

> So, though I was only a kid, I found myself surrounded by terrifying violence: after all, corpses and madmen represent violence in its ultimate form. I was driven into a corner from which I couldn't escape no matter how clever I was. By sucking my candy so carefully I was really hoping to make my consciousness burrow down inside

my body, turning its back completely on the violence outside, much as a wound buries itself in swelling flesh. (143)

Tayo, in *Ceremony*, faces a similar challenge against "witchery," his term for the destructive forces which, like the Chosokabe, have existed at all times and in all places. With a weapon in his hand and ready to kill, he decides not to. Choosing not to match violence with violence, he defeats witchery and achieves regeneration through a series of ritual acts that comprise the ceremony of tribal myth. Unlike Tayo, Takashi was not able to turn his back on the violence outside or within himself. In his last conversation with Mitsu, he says that he wants to tell the truth and confesses the relationship with his sister and his responsibility for her suicide. Written on the wall of the room where his body is discovered is his statement in red pencil, "I told the truth." The truth that he told is the only unequivocal truth in the novel, the reality of violence, symbolized by the color red in Takashi's bloodied face and the painted corpse of Mitsu's friend.

The particular form of violence that pervades the novel and creates its atmosphere of despair is the degradation of the flesh. The grotesque suicides of Takashi and Mitsu's friend are the grossest but only two of the many descriptions and incidents, ranging from mild to horrible, in which the body is desecrated. The mildest examples are the comparisons to lower forms: Mitsu describes his wife's hand as "scrawny and stringy as a monkey's" (9); he describes himself as a "vomiting dog" (167) and repeatedly as "just a rat." More serious are the sexual debasement and perversion, deformity, mutilation, and decay that are everywhere in the novel. Takashi has sex with an old, foul-smelling prostitute in a dangerous New York area, deliberately inviting disease and attack. Mitsu's friend descends into orgies of masochistic sex. Takashi seems to revel in describing the decay of S's body as he witnessed or, in his incipient madness, dreamed it: "The ants had completely eaten away the eyes behind the tightly closed lids, leaving red holes the size of walnuts from which a faint, reddish light guided the tiny feet of the ants as they marched to and fro, treading the trifurcated path of ears and nose" (71). Later, with what Mitsu calls "a note of defiant exhibitionism," Takashi describes in detail his murder of the village girl by repeatedly smashing her head with a rock (224). Besides the psychological deformity revealed in the behavior of Takashi and Mitsu's friend, the world's deformity is symbolically represented in the grotesque obesity of the peasant woman Jin, who in her monstrosity and anticipated death is regarded as another scapegoat, atoning for the monstrousness in the world. The implication is that the birth of Mitsu's brain-damaged son is to be expected in such a world.

Ōe has explained the presence of deformity and of sexual depravity in his works more positively than the evidence indicates. One connection he has made alludes to the Russian formalist method of "making strange." Asked about sexual depravity in his novels, Ōe said: "I have simply utilized sexual elements as the most concrete means to defamiliarize the mundane lives of human beings" ("Interview," 373). More often, Ōe identifies his method with the grotesque realism of Rabelais, especially as interpreted by Bakhtin. In his study of Rabelais, Bakhtin says: "Degradation digs a bodily grave for a new birth; it has not only a destructive, negative aspect, but also a regenerating one" (21). Similarly, in his book *The Methods of the Novel,* Ōe says: "Our literature should adopt the image system of grotesque realism as its integral part and, in so doing, should bring about a real regeneration of human life—in this way I intend to formulate the future of Japanese literature" (quoted in "Interview," 373). Ōe may intend to "bring about a real regeneration of human life," but there is a contradiction between what he says and what his works reveal: "Ōe certainly presents pictures grim enough to alarm readers, but instead of suggesting the advent of new hope, he perpetuates an ominous possibility that the outcome of rebirth and regeneration will be worse yet, for example, as in the form of insanity or physical deformity" (Yoshida, 95).

Tayo in Silko's novel recognizes that there are no boundaries, only transitions. *The Silent Cry* goes further to show that in the transitions there is also diminution. As John Barth says in his novel *Giles Goat-Boy,* "Everything only gets worse, gets worse" (xxi). In his understanding of the cyclical process of repetition with diminution, the narrator of this novel, written about the same time as *The Silent Cry* and employing a similar method of grotesque realism, would fit easily into Ōe's world: "There is an entropy to time, a tax on change: four nickels for two dimes, but always less silver" (763). As in Barth's novel, everything in *The Silent Cry* gets worse, becomes trivialized or monstrous. What was once a thriving Korean settlement is now a chicken farm; the storehouse, from which the great-grandfather had defended his family in the 1860 uprising, will now be reconstituted as a restaurant; the "emperor," the moral force to whom the people must now pay homage, is a greedy supermarket czar. Like the 1860 uprising, the 1960 version is a failure; but this time the shame of the peasants' capitulation is "but a squalid, impotent variety" (252). Mitsu in his inert nastiness and Takashi in his tawdry violence are themselves squalid and impotent varieties of their great-grandfather and his younger brother. In a comparison of the two uprisings that recalls Eliade's idea of sacred time, Ōe states that in reenacting the past there is inevitably diminution:

> You mentioned how the sacred is violated in order to keep it sacred. As a historical event, this peasant revolt was also sacralized. But as soon as this resistance is recuperated in a contemporary scenario, as it does in my novel as a grass-roots attack on a supermarket, or rather shopping center, the sacred gets trampled upon, becomes despised, denounced. It is this process that constitutes the theme of my work. ("Conversation" with Pease & Wilson, 23)

After the violence, degradation, and diminution, Ōe's attempts to end his works on a regenerative note lack conviction. In an earlier novel, *A Personal Matter,* Bird emerges from an episode of degraded sex on the threshold of a new beginning. Similarly, *The Silent Cry* is given a happy ending of sorts. Mitsu and his wife, Natsumi, who has been in an alcoholic stupor for much of the novel and who is carrying Takashi's child, will try to salvage their marriage, first at long distance as Mitsu leaves for Africa to build his thatched hut, to begin a new life. Takashi has been incorporated into village myth, another spirit to be invoked at the next Bon festival. The fate of the characters, however, is less important than their function to convey Ōe's multiple perspectives on time and human history. They show the absence of boundaries between past and present, between truth and falsehood, between fact and dream. Further, they show that the structural link in human history is violence, that the present profanes the past, and that there is an entropy to time. These perspectives undermine Mitsu's hope for a new beginning and make the optimistic conclusion ironic.

Ōe's thought has continuity. In his Nobel Lecture, most of which is a collection of ideas that he has expressed over the years, he comments that the title *The Flaming Green Tree,* the last installment in a recent trilogy of novels, was taken from a stanza in Yeats's poem "Vacillation" (27). In that stanza can be found ancient myth, ambiguity, and the merging of past and present, linking the poem to Ōe's earlier fiction as well as to his recent work. Written more than a quarter of a century ago, *The Silent Cry* is indisputably one of Ōe's finest novels and an enduring statement of his art and thought.

Celeste Loughman, Summer 1999

■ **WORKS CITED**

Bakhtin, Mikhail. *Rabelais and His World.* Helene Iswolsky, tr. Bloomington. Indiana University Press. 1984.

Barth, John. *Giles Goat-Boy.* New York. Fawcett. 1968.

Eliade, Mircea. *The Sacred and the Profane: The Nature of Religion.* Willard R. Trask, tr. New York. Harper. 1961.

Mackintosh, Paul St. John, and Maki Sugiyama. "Introduction" to Ōe Kenzaburō's *Nip the Buds, Shoot the Kids.* London. Marion Boyars. 1995. Pp. 5–18.

Ōe, Kenzaburō, *The Silent Cry.* John Bester, tr. New York. Kodansha International. 1981.

———. "An Interview with Kenzaburō Ōe." With Sanroku Yoshida. *World Literature Today* 62:3 (Summer 1988), pp. 369–74.

———. "Japan's Dual Identity: A Writer's Dilemma." *World Literature Today* 62:3 (Summer 1988), pp. 359–369.

———. "A Conversation with Ōe Kenzaburō." With Donald Pease and Rob Wilson. *Boundary 2,* 2:2 (1993), pp. 1–23.

———. "A Conversation with Kenzaburō Ōe." With John Nathan. *Japan Society Newsletter,* July-August 1995, pp. 4–7.

———. "Japan, the Ambiguous and Myself." *Poets and Writers Magazine,* July-August 1995, pp. 25–33.

Pollack, David. *Reading Against Culture.* Ithaca, N.Y. Cornell University Press. 1992.

Silko, Leslie Marmon. *Ceremony.* New York. Penguin. 1977.

Wilson, Michiko N. *The Marginal World of Ōe Kenzaburō.* Armonk, N.Y. Sharpe. 1986.

Yoshida, Sanroku. "Kenzaburō Ōe: A New World of Imagination." *Comparative Literature Studies,* 22 (1985), pp. 80–96.

[1] For further discussion of *The Game of Contemporaneity* (which has not been translated into English), see Michiko N. Wilson, *The Marginal World of Ōe Kenzaburō,* pp. 105–27, and Sanroku Yoshida, "Kenzaburō Ōe: A New World of the Imagination."

[2] Eliade's impact on *The Silent Cry* has been noted by Paul St. John Mackintosh and Maki Sugiyama in their introduction to *Nip the Buds, Shoot the Kids:* "The book was being serialized when Ōe discovered the religious thought of the Romanian scholar-poet Mircea Eliade, with its emphasis on the annihilation/purification of history through ritual repetition, prompting him to withdraw the draft and reshape it into a work which became a watershed in his career as well as probably the greatest postwar Japanese novel" (13).

[3] In David Pollack's view, *The Silent Cry* "can be read quite literally as just such an attempt to confront structuralism with deconstructionism." Pollack, however, sees Ōe as abandoning the attempt by the end of the novel: "After initially distinguishing between two contrasting sorts of time, Ōe seems content in the end to allow the problematic nature of history, memory, and narrative to be entirely subordinated to the invocation of myth-ritual grounded in an autochthonous and unassailable sense of closed community" (206).

Japan's Dual Identity: A Writer's Dilemma

Is Japanese literature decaying? I, as one Japanese writer, stand before you harboring not unfounded suspicions that Japanese literature is indeed decaying. A confession such as this from a writer from the Third World should undoubtedly disappoint an audience that is expecting a genuine "challenge" from our discussion titled "The Challenge of Third World Culture."* There are reasons, however, why I have willingly accepted to act the part of the disappointing clown. There is an element in the Japanese nation and among Japanese that makes us unwilling to accept the fact that we are members of the Third World and reluctant to play our role accordingly. Japan appeared on the international scene clearly as a Third World nation from about the time of the Meiji Restoration (1868). In her process of modernization ever since, she has been a nation blatantly hostile to her fellow Third World nations in Asia, as evidenced by her annexation of Korea and by her war of aggression against China. Her hostility toward her neighbors continues even today.

The destruction we wrought upon China during the invasion is so great that what has been destroyed can never be restored or compensated for. However, even now, more than forty years after the end of the war, I do not think that we Japanese have done enough to compensate for what we *can* compensate for—either economically or culturally. The annexation of Korea in 1910 is no bygone matter when we consider the discriminatory status that some 600,000 Korean residents in Japan are now suffering. Furthermore, when we see our government supporting a South Korean government which oppresses aspirers to democracy in that nation, we see clearly that Japan is indeed one of the powers that oppresses the Third World. Such must also be the national image of Japan not only to seekers of democracy in South Korea but to democratic forces throughout Asia as well.

I must listen with undivided attention to the criticisms of my colleagues, and especially to our participant from the Philippines, Kidlat Tahimik. Japan and the Japanese betray democratic aspirants in Third World countries. We are often aggressors toward nations of the Third World, of which we ourselves are in fact a member. The burden of that image weighs heavily on my back as I stand before you now.

What, then, is the image of Japan and the Japanese in the eyes of the industrialized nations? If I, during my stay here in the United States, am welcomed by neutral smiles, that is because I am a Japanese whose job is to produce Japanese novels and not automobiles, TV sets, or audio equipment—which are highly competitive in the international market. I am free from the hearty welcomes of the happy users of Japanese products. At the same time, I am free from the overt antagonisms of workers engaging in the manufacture of products that must compete with Japanese ones. Nevertheless, when I compare this visit with my first one to this country twenty years ago, I, by the mere fact of my being Japanese, cannot help but feel a strong sense of crisis. Although I have always sensed that crisis in Japan, coming here has made me feel the crisis more acutely.

The crisis that I feel is the crisis of living in a country which, though an economic giant with its huge trade surplus, is dependent on imports for most of its food and resources. It is a nation where the livelihood of its people will be devastated if the balance of imports and exports is disrupted. I feel the crisis of living in a country which, in its process of rising to the status of a technically advanced nation, has spread pollution everywhere and is unable to find a solution to it. I feel the danger of living in a country which, though having experienced the Hiroshima and Nagasaki bombings, is now run by a government that can only support the United States' SDI program, thereby helping spread the nuclear-deterrence myth in the Far East.

Because of her wealth, Japan is now a member of the advanced nations, but, to be sure, she is not an independent nation which implements plans of her own to establish world peace. I feel the crisis of being a citizen of a nation of self-satisfied people—as evidenced in the recent national election (1986) by the landslide victory of the party led by Prime Minister Nakasone, President Reagan's good friend and colleague. As one Japanese intellectual, I have come to sense the crisis stronger than ever through my visit here. I shrink back in fear when I think that the people on those four islands in the Far East are heading for destruction without knowing it, but in a few weeks I will have to go back to those islands and become lost in the crowd there.

Such is the frame of reference with which I, as a Japanese writer taking part in this discussion titled "The Challenge of Third World Culture," will be talking to you. I therefore must admit that my talk may be confusing, because I speak from a standpoint of twofold or perhaps threefold ambiguities. Nonetheless, I wish for myself that I will be able to overcome those ambiguities. I also hope to envisage for myself an idea of Japanese culture that could perhaps play a unique role among the cultures of the Third World. In order to accomplish these wishes, I will present to you the ambiguities as ambiguities and would like to ask my fellow panelists to guide me out of them.

As I mentioned to you in the beginning, I suspect that Japanese literature is decaying. That is to say, I suspect with good reason that the Japanese are losing their power to create an active model for the contemporary age and for the future. I suspect that modern Japanese culture is losing its vital force and that we are seeing, as its outcrop, the waning of Japanese literature. In re-

cent years it is said that the one realm of intellectual activity which has seen the sharpest decline is literature. To the younger generation who respond so sensitively to new cultural developments, literature no longer seems to be within their focus of attention. This, I believe, is already an established theory in cultural journalism. I fear that this is an ominous phenomenon foreboding the total destruction of Japanese culture, let alone cultural journalism.

It is not unusual for Kurt Vonnegut to draw figures of Japanese in his tender, pathos-filled, but inferno-like paintings of the future world. One such piece is a painting of a city destroyed by a neutron bomb: a city in which human life has been terminated but where the machinery of the highly mechanized Matsushita and Honda factories are still in motion. The roof of one of the buildings is painted with a sharp semblance of Mount Fuji, and the apparently Midwestern U.S. city is the Japanese archipelago in metaphor. I cannot deny the possibility wherein Japanese culture, after losing its strength to create a human model to direct its culture toward a new future, shatters and crumbles, only to leave behind in motion such products as automobiles, TV sets, and microcomputers—and the younger generation taking no notice of the oddity of the situation. I would like to examine the present situation of Japanese literature by delving into the foreboding elements of these phenomena.

A characteristic lexical item employed among the writers of Japanese literature is the term *junbungaku*, which in English would translate as "sincere or polite literature" or in French as "belles lettres." It was only after the Meiji Restoration that modern literature, with strong European influences, was established in our country. The precursory treatise that provided the rationale for literature in Japan was Shōyō Tsubouchi's *Shōsetsu shinzui* (The Essence of the Novel), published in 1885—i.e., seventeen years after the Meiji Restoration. By then, Tōkoku Kitamura, the pioneer in modern Japanese romanticism, who was keenly aware of the goings-on of the society of that period, had already started to use the term *junbungaku*. He wrote, "[That man], with his iron hammer named 'Historical Treatise,' preaches that 'junbungaku' needs to be crushed and thus endeavors to assail its realm." From what I have quoted, we are able to know that the term *junbungaku*, as employed by Tōkoku Kitamura, was used as an antithesis to the sciences of philosophy and history with which the Japanese of the early and mid-Meiji era strived to establish the spirit of modernization by borrowing European ideas. Therefore, the term *junbungaku*, when used nowadays, does not denote what it once did. It is used today to refer to, as it were, literature that has passively secluded itself from the literature of the mass media; that is, it is used to denote literature that is not "popular" or "mundane."

My talk on what is "sincere" literature and what is not may ring strange in the ears of a non-Japanese audience, but I, as a Japanese writer, would like to elaborate on it for the purpose of confirming my identity. Although the term *junbungaku* is now used to differentiate the writer's passive withdrawal from mass-media literature, to Tōkoku, the young poet of romanticism and the rationalist of literature who, during the Meiji period, took the matter of the quest for his identity so seriously, even to the point of suicide, *junbungaku* constituted the antithesis to philosophy and history and was an active intellectual genre that he hoped would help create a spirit of modernization among the Japanese. I feel that it is now necessary for us to reevaluate the term *junbungaku* in light of its two definitions.

The role of literature—insofar as man is obviously a historical being—is to create a model of a contemporary age which envelops past and future and a human model that lives in that age. In Japan, where the history of modern and contemporary literature spans a period of over a hundred years, there have been a few men of letters who, as individuals, have created works which surpassed their times. However, it is only for a short period in the history of modern Japanese literature, a period which we refer to as the postwar era, that a group of writers, as a definite literary current, have clearly provided a contemporary age and a human model which inhabited that age. It was a new literary phenomenon that started immediately after the defeat in the Pacific War, in which Japan, in 1945, experienced the bombings at Hiroshima and Nagasaki. This postwar literature was a vital force especially during the first ten years after the war. Although it is hard to say exactly when it ended, I believe it continued to thrive while postwar writers vigorously continued to produce their works, even amid various other literary currents.

Were we to look at specific examples, such as Shōhei Ōoka's novelistic account "The Battle of Leyte" (1969) and Taijun Takeda's "Mount Fuji Sanitarium," the year 1970 seems to serve as a fair guideline. That was also the year Yukio Mishima committed suicide after calling for a coup d'état by members of the Self-Defense Forces—the de facto armed forces of Japan. A comprehensive analysis of the postwar writers brings to light a contemporary age and a human model they created, and it is to that age and model that Mishima tried to produce a counterpart. Mishima too, however, from a broader perspective can be counted as one of the postwar literati.

With this chronology, we find that postwar literature was, in the history of modern and contemporary Japanese literature, the literature that strived to provide a total, comprehensive contemporary age and a human model that lived it. It was literature that endeavored to grapple squarely with the needs of intellectuals, and in fact "postwar literature" did win firm support from intellectuals in various fields. *Junbungaku,* which Tōkoku had proclaimed in defiance of philosophy and history in order to assert his raison d'être, was still in its embryo stage in the middle of the Meiji era. Tōkoku, calling out desperately for the protection of *junbungaku,* built a fence around a lot next to the edifices erected by the philosophy-and-history architects who had imported know-how and material from Europe, so that he and his compatriots would at least later have something on which to build their house. It can rightly be said that Tōkoku's toil and labor bore fruit in the form of postwar literature.

How was it possible for postwar literature to accomplish this? The feat can be attributed to historical reasons. The postwar literati started to publish their works within two or three years after Japan's defeat. Yutaka Haniya's "Ghosts," Hiroshi Noma's "Dark Pictures," Yukio Mishima's "Cigarette," Taijun Takeda's *Saishi kajin,* and Haruo Umezaki's *Sakurajima* are works which appeared only a year after the war. (For Mishima, however, *Confessions of a Mask,* published in 1949, is more characteristic of postwar literature than "The Cigarette.") The year 1947 saw the publication of Rinzō Shiina's "Midnight Feast." A year after that came Toshio Shimao's "Island's End," Shōhei Ōoka's "Prisoner of War," and Kōbō Abe's "Road Sign at the End of the Street"—and here already we have the whole array of the postwar literati. These are writers who had to endure silence while fascism prevailed prior to and during the war years. Their pent-up frustrations became the spring-board for forming their identity as intellectuals. On Japan's day of defeat their ages ranged from twenty to thirty-six; Mishima was the youngest and Shōhei Ōoka the oldest.

During the years of intellectual suppression—that is, during the immediate prewar period and the war itself—Haniya experienced Marxism through the peasant movement, Noma through the liberation movement of the *buraku,* a socially disadvantaged class of people. Takeda and Shiina suffered oppression for having participated in leftist activities while a student and laborer respectively. Ōoka had been taken prisoner by the U.S. forces. Noma, Takeda, and Umezaki had been drafted. When report of defeat reached Shimao, he was a Kamikaze pilot awaiting orders for a suicide attack. Neither Abe nor Mishima—the youngest of the writers—was free from the turmoil of the colonies or from the effects of student mobilization.

Over and beyond their experiences of harsh reality, these writers were either researchers in some special field of interest or, at the least, very careful readers. Haniya and Shiina studied Dostoevsky. Takeda read Lu Xun, Noma immersed himself in French symbolism, and Ōoka read Stendhal. In fact, all the postwar writers were young intellectuals who had endeavored to establish their identity by absorbing the literary impact from Europe. Unable to give vent to self-expression during the war years, these intellectuals honed their intellectualism and lived reality with a spirit of defiance against the battlefields and the fascist government that ruled them. Postwar literature was, in other words, a literary activity which these intellectuals had started simultaneously, once given the freedom to express themselves.

The defeat in the Pacific War, which brought about a decisive period of transition among the postwar writers, was, needless to say, the most important of events that ever took place in Japan's history of modernization since the Meiji Restoration. For Japan, which had pursued modernization all the while and had dared to compete with the imperialist nations of the West, the defeat was nothing less than the revelation of a multifarious impasse for an imperialistically underdeveloped nation. The surrender also led to an examination of askew elements in Japanese culture and tradition of premodernization days. Moreover, the defeat spurred a reform which supplied momentum to Third World-oriented liberation opportunities both within and outside the nation.

Were we to search for a metaphor for this situation in literature, I would suggest Dickens's novels, which are studded with "units" that convey diverse meanings. As we read on, the "units" progress along the path Dickens plots for each of them. When the novel is completed, he affixes to each of the units a retrospective light by means of which each comes to bear full meaning. The individual units are alive already and have significant import in themselves within the story as it progresses, yet the light which emanates from the denouement reveals to us not a contradiction but a new import; and because of the fact that the final light imparts a new significance to the individual units in addition to the one they bore amid the progress of the story, the units take on twofold meanings, thus giving the story itself a new significance.

The diverse units which modernization bore ever since the Meiji Restoration came to reveal twofold meanings upon surrender, that light which shone retrospectively from the finale. That is to say, the Japanese, through defeat in the Pacific War, saw for the first time the entire picture of the modernization of a nation called Japan. At that time it was postwar literature which depicted most sensitively and most sincerely that very picture of Japan and the Japanese.

At the international level Japanese modernization took the form of annexation of Korea, invasion of China, and wars of aggression in other regions of Asia. However, the intellectuals who had had to participate in these incidents and who witnessed the utter downfall of such imperialistic expansion, wrote of what they saw in various ways. Taijun Takeda and Yoshie Hotta wrote about what they saw in China. Hiroshi Noma and Shōhei Ōoka wrote of what they witnessed in the Philippines. The literary activities among Korean nationals in Japan correspond to those by Japanese writers who wrote from the standpoint of Japan as an aggressor nation. Korean writers in Japan wrote in Japanese and delved into the matter of Japan's colonial rule over the Korean peninsula, a matter which has ramifications and legacies even today. Okinawa, under the Ryukyu Empire, long maintained its own political system and a culture with strong cosmological features. After being taken over by Japan, however, Okinawa was victimized in the process of Japan's modernization to an extent incomparable to that of any other prefecture. The fact that Okinawa became the sole battlefield on Japanese soil speaks for itself. The Pacific War culminated in the battles at Okinawa and left the islands in a state of total devastation. Even after the signing of the peace treaty, Okinawa remained under the dominion of the U.S. forces for years to come, but all the while she strived and managed to accomplish her own reconstruction. Because of this experience, Okinawa has a self-expression of her own.

The self-expression of the people of Okinawa is a product of their realistic ideas, efforts, and cultural tradition. We can find, in their expression, direct and important clues by which Japanese can search for a lifestyle which does not pose a threat to any of the nations in Asia. The writers who start by asking how to revive from the experiences of the Hiroshima and Nagasaki bombings bear in mind the movement which seeks the enactment of the A-Bomb Victims' Relief Law. The movement is also one which is making a continuous effort for the eradication of all nuclear weapons. Those writers gaze squarely at the destructive impasse to which Japan's modernization from the Meiji Restoration brought us. It is here that we can discover for ourselves a principle as to how Japan and the Japanese should live in Asia in this new nuclear age. An examination of whether or not this principle has become a general one among the Japanese in the past forty years should be the basis for criticism of Japan and the Japanese today.

If we were to add to the list of postwar writers the name of Tamiki Hara, who wrote of his experiences as an A-bomb victim in Hiroshima and who chose to commit suicide as soon as a new conflict—the Korean War—broke out, it will become all the more clear that the major preoccupation of postwar writers was to examine, with the force of their imagination, what, in pursuit of modernization, Japan and the Japanese had done to Asia and to the vulnerable elements within the nation, how the impasse foreboded defeat, and what means of resuscitation were possible for the nation after it died a national death.

We should also examine how the postwar writers dealt with the problem of the emperor system, for this was the cultural and political axle upon which Japan's modernization revolved. One of the conditions necessary for the nation's modernization was national unity. Thus, the emperor was made the absolute figurehead, and modernization was pursued under the pretext of his inviolable authority. What this actually meant was the deification of the emperor. At the beginning of the new year following the defeat, the emperor issued a proclamation that he was no deity, a proclamation to which MacArthur expressed satisfaction. The fact that soon afterward another "emperor," a certain "Emperor Kumazawa," appeared, claiming to be the descendant of an emperor in the Middle Ages, is an indication of one of the diversities and the astounding amount of total energy which the deified emperor had been suppressing.

The Great Japanese Imperial Army which invaded all regions of Asia was nothing but the emperor's armed forces. In Okinawa, the only Japanese soil on which any battle was fought, many citizens died. Analysts claim that the tragedy the Okinawans had had to suffer was exacerbated by their sense of loyalty to the emperor, a loyalty stronger than that embraced by Japanese on the mainland, for they took greater pride in the fact that they, after the Meiji Restoration, were admitted as children of the emperor for the first time in their history.

The aims of the postwar writers were to "relativize" the value of the emperor, who had had absolute power, and to liberate the Japanese from the curse of the emperor system which haunted their minds, even at the subconscious level. Were we to view the emperor system as positioned at the peak of the structural hierarchy, Hiroshi Noma depicted the lowest, the social outcasts for whom he had been working since before the war. Noma continued to write even after it was common knowledge within journalistic circles that the period of

postwar literature was over. "Ring of Youth," a novel on which he spent many years, was completed a year after Mishima's suicide. The work depicts a scene in which the outcasts demonstrate a show of force in a mass movement and emerge victorious. The victory is a short-lived one, but the mere fact that Noma depicted a victory by those who had been most oppressed is in itself very meaningful.

Mishima's call for a coup d'état in the compounds of the Self-Defense Forces in Ichigaya and his subsequent suicide constituted essentially a theatrical performance. In his later years Mishima's political, ethical, and esthetic principles centered on his deep lamentation for the emperor, who had proclaimed he was not a deity but a human being. Mishima's suicide is an incident which can never be effaced from our memory, for he supposedly had prepared a baleful ghost to appear time and time again whenever Japan encountered a political crisis. This is one of the reasons why I have set 1970 as the year in which the curtain fell for postwar literature—literature which, through Japan's defeat in 1945, was begun as a means of giving vent to cultural energies that had been suppressed since the prewar days. What I mean now by the portents of the decay of Japanese literature is nothing other than the loss of the unique status which postwar literature had established in the realm of Japanese culture. In other words, the literary force which postwar literature had once possessed to enlighten Japan and the Japanese to reality and culture is now being lost.

What, then, is the situation of *junbungaku* in the latter half of the 1980s? Young intellectuals who respond quickly to intellectual fads say that *junbungaku* is already dead, or that it is about to breathe its last. They believe that although there still may be some literary activity shoved away in some bleak corner of journalism where the survivors are barely making a living, the latter will sooner or later fade away as a natural course of events. This group of young intellectuals is composed of critics, playwrights, screenwriters, and introducers of new and diverse literary theories from America and Europe. It even includes writers whose works are not considered to be in the realm of *junbungaku* as well as journalists in various fields and a group who nowadays in our country enjoy the greatest popularity among the younger generation: the copywriters of commercial messages. One might also add almost all the "cultural heroes" of today's grotesquely bloated consumer society in Japan. Lack of activity in the realm of *junbungaku* can be substantiated objectively when we compare the volume of its publication with that of other literature such as popular historical novels, science fiction, mysteries, and various nonfiction categories. Although, obviously, the prewar period and the war years provide no basis for comparison, never have there been so many publications in Japan as in the past forty years. The number of *junbungaku* publications, however, is inversely proportional to the increase in the amount of the other publications. Moreover, there is not one work of *junbungaku* to be found in the 1985 list of the ten best-selling Japanese books in either fiction or non-fiction.

Amidst such a trend, Haruki Murakami, a writer born after the war, is said to be attracting new readers to *junbungaku*. It is clear, however, that Murakami's target lies outside the sphere of *junbungaku,* and that is exactly where he is trying to establish his place. It is generally believed that there is nothing that directly links Murakami with postwar literature of the 1946–70 period. (As a hasty aside here, I believe that any future resuscitation of *junbungaku* will be possible only if ways are found to fill in the wide gap that exists between Murakami and pre-1970 postwar literature.)

Another indicator of the long downward path that *junbungaku* is taking can be seen by the long business slump for literary monthlies peculiar to Japan, those magazines which had helped nurture and develop short stories unique to Japanese literature. I am sure that those literary magazines are periodicals of least concern to the young intellectuals who now are the vanguard of Japan's consumer society. However, looking back on the first ten years after the war, such magazines, together with numerous general-interest publications, played an important role in maintaining high cultural standards. Almost all the representative literary works—e.g., the ones I have mentioned above—were, as was common practice in the publishing system of our nation, first published in literary magazines. It can be said that the slumping literary magazines are eliciting derisive criticism among the young intellectuals who have no direct means of recalling the glory and grandeur of those magazines, except as myth.

Mention must be made of the season of rationality which started to flourish from the latter half of he 1970s and lasted through the first half of the 1980s, a period which coincides with the decline of *junbungaku*. So strong was its force that it overwhemled intellectual journalism. Rationality was the fad among new cultural theories, all of which were imported from Europe and the United States. Here we must not forget that the intellectuals who established postwar literature were those who had been educated before or during the war years and had acquired a certain cultural sophistication. Almost all of them had been greatly influenced by cultural theories of Western Europe or of Russia, whose thoughts reached Japan via Western Europe. The eyes and ears of Japanese intellectuals after the Meiji Restora-

tion had always been directed toward the West. Rare specimens among the postwar writers were Rinzō Shiina and Taijun Takeda. Instead of pursuing higher education, Shiina spent his youth as a laborer. What prepared him for literature was his involvement in the Marxist socialist movement, but what converted him from Marxism was his encounter with Dostoevsky. Takeda studied Chinese classical literature while Japanese imperialism was quickly preparing to invade China. Takeda was greatly influenced by Lu Xun, but for him too Dostoevsky was a thinker without whom he would not have been able to establish his identity.

It is from these writers, and from others who had been influenced by Western literature and thought, that postwar literature was born. Their methodology for delving deep into Japanese traditional thought and culture was also, first of all, Western. The same fact is evident when we examine the manner in which Masao Maruyama established his school of Japanese political thought. Maruyama was a salient contemporary of the postwar writers. By studying those writers, Maruyama in turn opened new horizons for them. The predilection for Western culture which prevailed among the intellectuals who were the vanguard of Japanese modernization carried over to the generation that came after them and continued to characterize their culture.

The Mexican thinker Octavio Paz marks 1968 as an extremely significant year and calls our attention to the series of protest movements and riots that occurred in Prague, Chicago, Paris, Tokyo, Belgrade, Rome, Mexico City, and Santiago. Student riots raged everywhere like a medieval plague, affecting the populace regardless of religious denomination or social class, only on a broader scale. Because the riots were spontaneous, they were all the more universal, and Paz analyzed their significance in light of the situation in which all technological societies, East or West, found themselves. In Japan it was the time when the United Red Army, formed three years after the Tokyo riots, trod the path toward annihilation. The bodies of numerous Red Army members executed in cold blood by their colleagues were dug up after the Asama Mountain Villa Incident of 1972, a year which happens to coincide with the approximate time when postwar literature came to a close. As if in reaction to the political years, the new generation's cultural trend of the 1970s and 1980s swung toward antipolitics. What Paz had pointed out about identical subcultural trends having global horizontal ties had become apparent also in Tokyo.

It must be borne in mind that it was these events which prepared the way for the advent of the season of rationality, a trend for new cultural ideas imported from the United States and from Europe. Speaking for myself,

I, as one writer, evaluate very highly the diversified cultural thoughts springing forth from structuralism, for they provide a strong and vital incentive in the field of literature. Later I shall elaborate on one example of the effectiveness of its introduction. So strong has been its influence that I am even tempted to offer a comparison of the diverse influences of the structuralism-based cultural ideas of the seventies and eighties with the strong galvanizing influence Marxism had exercised on the Japanese mentality when it flourished for a short time before the war.

So great was the influx of new cultural theories following the advent of structuralism that it appeared they were going to permeate the whole of the nation's intellectual climate. An excellent summary of the new cultural theories of the West, "Structure and Power" by a young scholar named Akira Asada, was read everywhere on university campuses. The book sold equally well outside academe and became the most widely read work by any of the postwar writers. "Structure and Power" was by no means easy reading; however, no work of *junbungaku* published during that period was able to generate as much intellectual interest among the younger generation. There followed a time in which many new French cultural ideas—some of which came via the U.S.—were introduced and translated, including poststructuralism and postmodernism and particularly the work of Barthes, Foucault, Derrida, Lacan, Kristeva, and the Yale School of deconstructionists. As far as translations are concerned, aside from those works of mere journalistic faddishness, works of sincere toil and labor started to appear in the latter half of the 1980s. Despite this fact, however, by then intellectual enthusiasm among the younger generation for these new cultural thoughts had come to an end, as it had within the realm of intellectual journalism which had staged, directed, and reflected that enthusiasm. I was by that time no longer a young writer and had never been part of that boom; but as I stand amid the wrack and ruin of the voluminous introductory works and translations and look back upon that age, I notice several interesting characteristics.

First, the young Japanese intellectuals, true to our national character, analyzed and systematized diachronically the various structuralism-based theories and also the criticisms thereof in order to "accept" and—to use an antonym not quite appropriate for this word—"discharge" those theories. For acceptance of Foucault, Barthes had to be discharged. Only after Lacan was dismissed could Derrida be accepted—but only to await the next new thinker. The shuttling of new cultural theories was, up to a point, an easy task for the introducers and translators who advocated their influx.

Cultural heroes came and went. However, the curtain dropped on new cultural trends in our country as soon as these advocates found there was no one thinker or cultural theory for them to shuttle on the American and European conveyor belt.

At the height of the ongoing process of accepting and discharging new cultural theories, very often such phrases as "the performance of ideas" or "the frolicking with texts" came to be used. Without having to refer to any authority on words, I believe that those expressions were indeed very appropriate ones for those who could involve themselves only passively in coping with the kaleidoscope of ideas, for they were, by using those expressions, providing a definition of their identities. Also, amid this cultural trend, a very Japanese connotation was added to the usage of the prefix *post-*. By speaking of "poststructuralism" or "postmodernism," or even of cultural thoughts that were yet to come and for which they were unable to envisage any positive ideas (although obviously we could never expect them to do so, since all they did was passively accept and then discharge), the young Japanese intellectuals conjectured optimistically that, insofar as some cultural theory was in existence, a new one would follow if they simply added the prefix *post-* to the existing one. I am sure that there were not a few young intellectuals who were stricken by a series of self-destructive impulses when they learned that the concept of "post-such-and-such" was in fact insubstantial and when, in turn, they learned that the "such-and-such" thoughts in themselves meant very little, if anything at all.

Second, despite this remarkable trend for absorbing new cultural theories, almost no effort was made to interpret them meticulously in view of specific situations in which Japan found itself. Why then did the new cultural theories from Europe and the United States become so popular among the young intellectuals and in the realm of intellectual journalism? This is indeed the strange part of the story. However, I believe the phenomenon can be attributed mostly to the special characteristic which our nation's intellectual journalism had nurtured ever since the Meiji Restoration. To put it very bluntly, there was an inclination for people to think that an intellectual effort had been accomplished merely by transplanting or translating the new American and European cultural thoughts into Japanese; and both the translators and those who read the translations were inclined to think in the same manner. Such a tendency exists even today.

Since the most important skills required in the task of introducing new cultural ideas were the abilities to read the foreign language in which those thoughts were presented and to translate the works into Japanese, the spokesmen for those ideas were often specialists in literature or languages. Even when cultural theories were replaced in rapid succession, the replacement did not apply to the spokesmen, because they were not necessarily advocates—or critics, for that matter—of what they spoke for. This fact brought about the lukewarm situation whereby a handful of literature and language specialists became the importers of new cultural theories. Obviously, the responsibility does not rest solely with these specialists. If the readers had read their introductions and translations in a way that would have enabled them to apply the new cultural theories in interpreting Japan's reality, their understanding of these theories would have been raised to a higher level. Such an understanding would have fostered the ability even to offer feedback to the sources of those ideas. It would then not have been possible for each new cultural theory itself and for those who had had a hand in introducing it in Japan to remain free from criticism. However, such was not the case. As soon as an introduction or translation was made, the one-way flow from Europe and America to Japan was completed. That is to say, its "acceptance" and "discharge" was over. That is how the continual expectation of new trends in theory became a convention.

This tendency has produced another characteristic phenomenon in today's Japanese cultural climate: namely, the absence of any and all effort to accept a variety of cultural thoughts synchronically. Never have we witnessed, in intellectual journalism in our country, the synchronic existence of two opposing new schools of thought—for example, structuralism and deconstructionism—and the resulting combination of antagonism and complementarity, which can lead, in turn, to a mutual deepening of the two schools. That is why—with the exception of the architect Shin Isozaki, who in his works substantiated his criticism of postmodernism—the cultural anthropologist Masao Yamaguchi, the forerunner among introducers of new cultural theories, stands out as unique and is now being subjected to a reappraisal. Going against the general trend, Yamaguchi, in his work "Periphery and Center," employed a structuralistic methodology and provided substantiation for his unique cultural interpretation of Japan's reality. In his discussion of postwar literature and its importance, his theory, together with its diverse implications, was extremely effective in clarifying the significance of the emperor system. Yamaguchi had been originally a specialist in monarchism, with field-study experience in Nigeria.

Criticism arose claiming that, in any examination of Japanese reality, placing importance on peripheral cultures and energizing them will not lead to the reversal of the relationship between those peripheral cultures and the central one. In other words, Yamaguchi's ideas were attacked as being nonrevolutionary. Critics of his theory asserted that stimulating the periphery would function effectively only in establishing a more solid central authority and that therefore the ideas in Yamaguchi's "Periphery and Center" were reactionary. A political short circuit was the pith and the marrow of their critiques. Their charges overlooked the fact that Yamaguchi's structuralism was one scrupulously calculated—that is to say, that he had something prepared for later which a methodology based on deconstructionism would reveal. Because Yamaguchi's ideas in "Periphery and Center" were based on structuralist methodology but from the outset coexisted synchronically with criticism based on deconstructive methodology, these ideas were made even more profound, thus allowing them to bear more realistic validity. In fact, Yamaguchi proved, by citing from Japanese mythology and from literature of the Middle Ages various examples of ways in which, despite the dichotomy between those who were driven away from society into the periphery and the chosen ones in the center (i.e., the imperial family), that the two often "blended together like fresh ink spots on blotting paper."

Although Yamaguchi's political thought overlaps with that of Yukio Mishima, the two point at diametrically opposite poles. To be sure, Mishima, who lamented the fact that the emperor made his "Human Proclamation" after the defeat and who called for the Self-Defense Forces to rise up in a coup d'état as the emperor's forces, sought to absolutize the emperor system in the context of a cultural principle and in it to seek a paradigm of political unity among the Japanese. In short, if Yamaguchi's ideas as expounded in "Periphery and Center" were to activate the peripheral aspects of Japanese culture and that, in turn, were to result in the strengthening of the center—namely, the emperor system—the resulting system would be totally different from the one Mishima advocated. What is more, Yamaguchi's emperor system would never be the kind which might serve as a guiding principle for the Self-Defense Forces to carry out a coup d'état. When we reread Yamaguchi's cultural theory in light of contemporary reality, we find that there is no room in his thought that would allow for a political short circuit or a political reaction. With its truly free laws of behavior, Yamaguchi's ideas on culture, as evidenced also in his unique "trickster" theory, left no room whatsoever for short-circuited criticism stemming from uncompromising political ideologies. However, Yamaguchi's precursory work leading to the rise in new cultural theories was not followed up well by the introducers of these theories—in other words, the cultural heroes of the late seventies and early eighties. It is precisely here that we can find the means to illuminate the full scope of the question I have raised.

I began my presentation by stating that Japanese literature is decaying and referred specifically to postwar literature, which represents the highest level of literary achievement since the Meiji Restoration and the onset of Japan's modernization. I also noted the evident decline of Japanese literature at that highest level—termed *junbungaku* in Japanese—and how various cultural theories and critical isms, which replaced *junbungaku* in capturing the minds of young intellectuals, came to be accepted and discharged in a manner quite peculiar to our nation. I believe what these phenomena pointed to as a natural course of events was the following situation. Young intellectuals during the late seventies and early eighties felt the decline of Japanese literature most keenly and fell head over heels for new cultural theories from Europe and America. In fact, so great was the number of introductory books and translations that these seemed to outnumber each year's new literary works. However, enthusiasm for new cultural theories was short-lived, coming and going after only a short craze.

In the context of the cultural climate of Japan, the new cultural theories, as one organic part of literature's decline, fell prey to the general flow toward decay faster than that of literature. I believe that the two phenomena—literature and its readers on the one hand, and, on the other, new cultural theories and the young intellectuals who accepted them—should be viewed not as dichotomous adversaries but as one entity "blended together like fresh ink spots on blotting paper."

In a broader perspective, one can say that the young intellectuals were not truly intellectuals as such, but merely young Japanese living a subcultural fad in an urbanized, average consumer culture. Moreover, if one were to extrapolate from the analyses of sociologists which point to the fact that the prevalent middle-class consciousness, though filled with disparities when seen in light of the actual lives of the Japanese on the whole, is shared far and wide in Japan, one could say that such a phenomenon attests to the fact that, in comparison to the days of the student riots, young Japanese have indeed become conservative. Political scientists have attested to the fact that the conservative trend among the younger generation in the large urban areas has played an important role in the recent landslide victory of the ruling conservative party. What this means is that signs of a conservative trend have begun to emerge quite noticeably in the big cities, where the bulk of the younger generation dwells; and such signs will soon start to appear in small cities as well, since the younger generation

is conjoined by an urbanized culture that spans the nation.

Now, the problem, in the context of our discussion, is that this younger generation, so closely conjoined subculturally on a nationwide level, is abandoning literature. Moreover, this is the same younger generation which promptly interred, as things of the past, the trend toward new cultural theories which in many respects overlapped with the subcultural fad they embraced. Akira Asada's treatise "Structure and Power" at one time became a fad on university campuses and occasionally was referred to as the "Asada phenomenon." I cannot simply dismiss this as a mere fad, because it is possible for such a trend among the younger generation to merge with the new cultural theories and then bear positive fruit. When we look back on the various cultural phenomena, that is what actually occurred in many countries after World War II. However, as mentioned earlier, that is not how things turned out in Japan.

The postwar writers and those who created cultural theory for their contemporaries were people who had gone through the hardships of war. Their being one with the younger generation enabled their works to effect a positive influence upon the younger generation, who sought a means of resuscitation at a difficult time in a society that had recently suffered defeat. It is thus that they were able to educate the youth of a generation which followed their own. Speaking for myself, as far as literature is concerned, it is the postwar writers who laid the foundations for my own writing. As far as politics goes, the conservative party has been monopolizing the political scene for a long time. However, I believe that the generation which overlapped with the readers of postwar literature demonstrated its strength by casting enough votes for opposition-party members so that the latter won enough seats to keep the ruling party in check. The people's movement in 1960 to protest the ratification of the new Japan-U.S. Security Treaty was a movement which had actively incorporated the opinions of the postwar writers and those of the cultural theorists. It was a movement which was equally as powerful as, and more animated than, the opposition progressive parties and the labor unions. A comparison of the political and cultural situation of those years—i.e., twenty years ago—with that of today sheds light on what it is exactly that has been lost and how we lost it. The light shines upon the road along which twenty years have taken us and also upon a very symbolic phenomenon: literature treading its path to wrack and ruin.

So, what is to be done? I, as a writer, think of what the critical path has been and what it should be for Japan and the Japanese from the standpoint of literature. I believe that by reflecting on the cultural climate of Japan in the latter half of the seventies and the first half of the eighties, we can see therein glimpses of what course of action we should take. What occurred during that period was the recurrence of short cycles of introductions of new cultural theories from America and Europe. It seemed that the acceptance and discharge of those theories was gradually accelerated, but in the end all enthusiasm for cultural theories died out. Although the diachronic, one-dimensional acceptance and discharge of new cultural theories continued, no effort had been made to interpret those theories in light of Japan's reality and culture. This sort of situation can never occur in societies that produce cultural theories; it can only occur in a country where the vast ocean separates it from the country that produces those theories, where the introduction of theories follows the overcoming of linguistic barriers, where there exists a fad-sensitive intellectual journalism that transmits those ideas, and where there are receivers of what such journalism transmits. In other words, with only a few exceptions, the Japanese were not able to establish a cultural theory of their own—something which could have been realized if they had examined the theories they imported in light of Japan's reality and culture. If that had been done, the resulting feedback from such an examination would have enabled the Japanese to establish a new cultural theory of their own. Though Japan experienced a period of great enthusiasm for new cultural theories, the theories essentially had nothing to do with Japan's reality and culture, and we have today as a result a situation in which those theories have become as remote an existence as they had been from the very outset.

In light of this situation, we see clearly what is lacking in terms of cultural work that is being done by Japanese today. Japan's modernization beginning with the Meiji Restoration had run into a fatal impasse—namely, the Pacific War—and culminated in defeat. Upon very sincere reflection, the Japanese searched for various principles to guide them in making a fresh, new start, and the aim of the postwar writers was to provide literary conviction and expression of such principles. However, the intellectuals of the new generation, those of the seventies and eighties, have not followed up on these principles, nor have they taken a critical stance toward them. They had no intention of developing such principles in the first place. There is indeed a wide gap between the postwar intellectuals and those of the younger generation, as is clear when we look at how the younger intellectuals of the seventies and eighties, by not probing into the various accomplishments of the postwar writers or what they tried to achieve, severed any continuity with the postwar intellectuals.

Many of the postwar writers even went through the bitter experience of fighting in the war as soldiers, and following defeat, they delved into the matter of Japan's new direction, a direction contrary to that which Japan had taken in her process of modernization. In other words, they envisaged a way for Japan to live as one nation in Asia, as one of the Third World nations in Asia. The path Japan had taken prior to the defeat was one in which she had set up the central nations of the world—namely, the U.S. and the European countries—as paradigms to follow. The postwar writers, however, envisaged a path quite the contrary and aimed at establishing an awareness of a principle in which Japan's place in the world would be not in the center but on the periphery. What the Japanese had abandoned in pursuing a center-oriented modernization, the postwar writers endeavored to revive by also learning domestically from Okinawa, which had a cultural tradition of its own, and internationally from Korea, which was instilling a typically Asian prosperity and diversity.

I would add that, as a writer who has engaged in literary activities with the awareness that I carry on the heritage of the postwar writers, I have while writing always borne in mind the island of Okinawa, a peripheral region of Japan, and South Korea, a peripheral nation of the world—and in the latter case especially the works of the modern Korean poet Kim Chi Ha. Also, I have employed in my writing the image system of grotesque realism as my weapon. I would note as well that by considering the cultural characteristics of the peripheral regions of Japan and those of Asia, I have trod a path leading to the "relativization" of an emperor-centered culture. In that regard, I have chosen a course exactly the opposite of that taken by Mishima, who strived to absolutize the emperor system. My novel "Contemporary Games," which I completed at the end of the seventies, is a work in which I aimed at creating a model regarding reality and culture for the kind of Japan I envisage.

I believe that the problem Japanese literature faces today lies in the fact that the attitude toward reality and culture which the postwar writers had nurtured and which was followed up by the writers who came after them was severed completely by the young intellectuals of the seventies and eighties. It was amid such discontinuity in attitude toward reality and culture that the fad for new cultural ideas flourished.

Japan as a Third World nation has an ambiguous place in the world and an ambiguous role to play. The young Japanese intellectuals had a still more ambiguous place in Japan and an equally ambiguous role to play. An examination of these ambiguities in light of the new cultural theories and the providing of an interpretation for them would have been a difficult task but one well worth undertaking, for I believe it would have resulted in the development of a cultural theory unique to Japan; if not, at least it would have taken us beyond the realm of the almost automatic process of "accepting" and "discharging" imported theories.

Among intellectuals of the present new generation, there are some who are taking an increased interest in the singularity of the Okinawan culture, and their interests correspond with the self-expression of the new generation on Okinawa. Many young Japanese who participated in the protest movement for the release of the poet Kim Chi Ha still empathize with the grass-roots movements for the democratization of South Korea. There is also a movement to keep a close watch on Japan's economic aggression against the Philippines and other Asian nations. The youths involved in that movement are now seeking an alliance on a grass-roots level with the younger generation of other nations. A joining of hands with such youths by the young intellectuals who had played a part in introducing new cultural theories can be readily realized, if the latter make an effort to determine how the theories ought to be interpreted in light of Japan's reality and culture, and also if they seek to learn how to plan for the reconstruction of that very reality and culture. Such a merger could bring about direct, concrete results in energizing Japanese literature of the new generation.

The topic of our discussion, "The Challenge of Third World Culture," raises the very relevant question of whether Japanese culture can find a clue for saving itself from the downward path to decline that is so ominously portended by the decline in literature. I can think of no people or nation as much in need of a clue for self-recovery as the Japanese, neither among First or Third World nations; no other people but the Japanese, whose culture evidences a strange blending of First and Third World cultures; no other people but the Japanese, who live that reality.

I would like to close by offering as a hint to the Japanese intellectuals of the new generation a positive directive for embarking upon their self-examination vis-à-vis our topic of our discussion. One reason why I decided to participate in this symposium is the fact that I myself want to learn, for what I have talked to you about is a bigger question for me than for the young intellectuals. There is in Japan a poet and writer of children's stories, Kenji Miyazawa, who had been assigned a peripheral place in contemporary literature and modern history but whose importance is being recognized slowly but steadily. Miyazawa was born in Tōhoku, a peripheral district of Japan. Being an agronomist, he worked for the Tōhoku farmers, who tilled the soil

under adverse conditions. He was a believer in the Saddharma Pundarika Sutra. Under the influence of contemporary Western poetry he established a world of his own expression and imagination. He wrote prolifically while continuing to work as an agronomist, a profession he pursued until his death in 1933 at the age of thirty-seven. His audience was not limited to readers of literature as such, and posthumously he has won—and is winning—an even wider spectrum of readers. Very recently, his epic children's story "The Night of the Galaxy Railway" was made into an excellent animated movie, increasing his popularity even more. The question of what is genuine people's literature has been a topic of debate throughout modern and contemporary Japanese literature, but now people have started to realize that it is Miyazawa who deserves to the fullest degree the title "Writer of People's Literature." Sixty years ago, at the dawn of the Shōwa era (1926–), Miyazawa wrote a treatise titled "Outline of the Essentials of Peasant Art," which epitomizes his ideas both as an agronomist and as a writer. I shall close by quoting its opening paragraph:

We are all farmers—we are so busy and our work is tough.

We want to find a way to live a more lively and cheerful life.

There were not a few among our very ancient forefathers who did live that way.

I wish to hold discussion where there is communion among the facts of modern science, the experiments of the seekers of truth, and our intuition.

One person's happiness cannot be realized unless all the world is happy.

The awareness of the ego starts with the individual and gradually evolves to that of the group, the society, and then the universe. Isn't this the path the saints of yore trod and taught us?

The new age is headed in a direction in which the world shall be one and will become a living entity.

To live strong and true is to become aware of the galaxy within ourselves and to live according to its dictates.

Let us search for true happiness of the world—the search for the path is in itself the path.

Kenzaburō Ōe, Summer 1988

*Ed. Note: Kenzaburō Ōe's paper was delivered at Duke University in Durham, N.C., on 25 September 1986 as one of the featured addresses at the conference "The Challenge of Third World Culture," sponsored by Duke's Center for International Studies. It appears here with the expressed permission of the author. On Ōe, see also *Wlt* 58:3 (Summer 1984), pp. 370–73, and 60:1 (Winter 1986), pp. 38–39.

Contemporary Japanese Poetry

About three years ago the Japan Foundation organized an exhibition of photographs. More than two hundred representative works were selected from photographs of nature and society which had been taken in our country over the course of almost fifteen years. Based on the theme "Japan, Its Life and Ways: 1971–1984," this exhibition traveled to various parts of the world. The selection of works was done in two stages. Representatives of the Japan Professional Photographers Society, after much debate, chose three hundred prints from a group of more than six thousand amateur and professional works which had appeared in newspapers, magazines, and other publications. In order to reduce the number to almost two hundred, a group of people without expertise in photography joined the jury of photography specialists for the final round of competition. I was a member of this final group.

Among the three hundred prints there was a considerable variety of subject matter. Needless to say, there were beautiful photos of nature illustrative of seasonal change, as well as views of life in fishing villages, in farm hamlets, and in the large cities. Both children and oldsters appeared in the photographs; people were working in some cases, enjoying themselves at a picnic or some similar function in others. Current fashion was on display, and ritualistic occasions—the coming-of-age ceremony, weddings, funerals, ancestral services—were also included. Indeed, the prints gave a composite picture of modern Japanese society.

As I examined the photographs, I became aware of something peculiar. Hardly a single one was focused on the image of Japanese society most representative of the seventies and thereafter. Our "high-tech" culture, with its computers and information-processing capabilities, was totally absent. Why was this? I asked the photographers on the jury if they had, in the course of culling these three hundred photos from the six thousand, deliberately excluded those which showed the most advanced sector of our country. Not at all, they replied. In fact, they had located such prints but found them uninteresting as photographs. Most had been taken for promotional purposes by various companies and did not fit into the exhibit. Furthermore, the photographers added, in the most advanced sectors of the economy the principal work was now being performed by robots rather than by people. Even if you took a photo, it looked like something out of a catalogue. Finally, the things a photographer would be most eager to show were precisely those a company was most secretive

about: Photographing them was forbidden, and this was entirely understandable. That was why, the professional photographers concluded, I did not see any such examples in the exhibit.

Adept at managing vast quantities of information and systematized to a high degree, our high-tech "electronic society" is based on delicate machines which do not lend themselves to interesting photography. Needless to say, the machines themselves are operated by specialized engineers of high intelligence. One might take appealing photos of these engineers enjoying their leisure away from the job.

The group which thoroughly understands the complex structure of these delicate machines constitutes a small elite, the great majority being mere workers who are totally ignorant of such things. These workers only operate some appendage of the electronic device. One imagines the everyday lives of this group, lives rendered quite pleasant by those trivial comforts which all of us are gradually acquiring in exchange for handing over our independence and personal dignity to a bureaucratized and standardized society more and more controlled by computers. I might add that, as a consequence of this development, our inner anxieties, instead of getting resolved, become steadily more acute.

Is it not our teams of robots, with their transcendent and highly precise intelligence, which now have the authority once held by humans to make decisions on important questions? Furthermore, the amplification of these robots sometimes gives them access to destructive power beyond the imagination, as can typically be seen in accidents involving nuclear power plants. Against such eventualities the individual person is virtually helpless. Human intelligence can make these delicate machines; but once the machine gets beyond the control of that intelligence and careens toward violence and destruction, the ability to foresee the final issue of the process and to prevent it is almost nil. In using these teams of robots whose destructive power can grow out of control, mankind has achieved a level of prosperity unprecedented in history. Like children frolicking innocently upon the roof of a powder magazine which might explode at any time—that, one might say, describes the people in the so-called advanced countries.

Assuredly this describes the situation in Japan since the seventies. The younger generation in particular has suppressed the anxiety that ought to accompany this condition, opting instead for a hedonistic attitude of living cheerfully in the present. The rise of the new religions and the flourishing of astrology and other forms of divination probably have some necessary connection to the situation.

To my surprise, photos of large political demonstrations were absent from the aforementioned exhibit. The student riots which had kept Japanese society in turmoil until the end of the sixties quickly subsided in the seventies. In their place an indifference, if not animosity, toward declarations of political intent spread among the young people. The hedonistic attitude mentioned above accompanied this development.

The location of commercial and amusement districts in Tokyo popular among the younger generation has shifted. In place of the Ginza, the fashionable quarter of yesteryear, and Shinjuku, the place where the commoners gathered of old, such centers as Shibuya, Roppongi, Aoyama, Kichijoji, and Harajuku have suddenly taken over. Young people throng into these places and remake them in accord with their own tastes. Such districts play a leading role in fashion, in the computer games which the most advanced technology brings into being, and in sports too. The consumer culture which targets the young grows fat as it serves up change with dizzying speed. One fact concerning the rapidly expanding Japanese economy seems undeniable: it has produced a large class of younger people who are hedonistic and affirm the present while avoiding any soical and political responsibilities.

▨ ▨ ▨

Reflecting on the present situation, one cannot avoid the sense of a profound problem for Japan in what has already been said. I can cite here a characteristic phenomenon. Formerly the younger poets—the more enthusiastic ones at least—recognized themselves as an "avant-garde" and prided themselves on composing work that was experimental both in form and in content. It was only natural that few readers understood their poems. For these poets, however, the notion that poetry in particular ought to be in the forefront of literature and the arts was utterly natural.

Since to be of the avant-garde meant necessarily to go beyond the existing framework of poetry and to seek new methods in unknown territory, poets formerly sought ties with other artists, in fields such as music, the plastic arts, film, drama, and radio. The collaboration thus achieved resulted in the creation of works across the old boundaries. For certain individuals like myself at least, born around 1930 and first active in the fifties, one can definitely state that such collaboration was a clear raison d'être for the poet. My friend Shuntarō Tanikawa and I worked out a proposal for collaboration among poets alone. We would sit down at the same table with other poets, even foreign ones, and together compose dozens of pieces in a kind of chain. This practice of "linked poetry" constitutes a protest against existing ways of writing, reading, and criticizing poems. In carrying on this activity, we unquestionably seek something new in an uncharted land, something we Japanese poets have been looking for since the fifties.

Needless to say, we do not accept inferior and unsightly work under the guise of experimentation. We can only shake our heads at this common practice of the avant-garde. To what extent can we change the existing framework of composing? And can we produce superior and persuasive works by these means? Such are the questions that concern us. Poetry must be new in some sense to be worthy of its name.

From this perspective, the year 1970 seems a kind of symbolic watershed. The term *avant-garde* virtually disappeared from discussions of contemporary Japanese poetry, and young poets quit seeking the cooperation of artists from other fields. Those who still aimed toward original work along collaborative lines generally came onstage in the fifties and sixties. I am talking, in this regard, of my own generation and of poets just a decade younger. This is probably closely related to the fact that, among poets presently in their twenties and thirties, criticism which sums up the poetry of the period with compelling persuasion has ceased to exist. During the seventies the poets themselves were acutely aware of how futile their own words were within the great wave that was rapidly transforming Japan into an electronics and information society, and so they restricted their attention to what might be discovered in their immediate surroundings. The poets might write of their private joys and sorrows with sincerity or irony; but the systematized society, with its vast power and its robots, semed something merely to be endured.

This focus of interest is reflected in the photographs from the exhibit which I introduced at the beginning of my essay, most of them either recording the quiet and pleasant lives of people seeking domestic happiness or else showing the scenic beauty of the four seasons. Perhaps the average citizen of contemporary Japan merely clings all the more to his middle-class pleasures for hearing at his back the roar of a revolutionary storm which begins to rage in each country as our century comes to an end. A proverb rooted in Buddhist thought speaks of "the candle in the wind." Our young poets should not be insensitive to the fate of our world, so like this very candle. Indeed, when they express in their subtle way the small joys and pains which they discover within middle-class life, the acute reader can sense in the background a nihilism that wears the mask of cheerfulness. One might even call this feature the key to gauging the honesty and talent of the particular poet.

Just now, then, the term *avant-garde* has become nothing other than an anachronism.

There is another phenomenon closely connected to this state of affairs. For approximately the last ten years there has been a marked revival—some might call it a "boom"—in the traditional forms of verse, the haiku and the tanka. For close to twenty years following Japan's defeat in World War II, our traditional values underwent a rapid decline and lost their credibility. However, along with the miraculous revival of the Japanese economy, the opportunity arose to reassess these same values. With this trend there came a general interest in the traditional forms of poetry. This interest reflected a straightforward desire by people to understand the roots of their country's culture.

An interesting phenomenon occurred after the initial phase of this reevaluation of tradition had passed: for the first time women came forward in large numbers to write in classical verse forms. Because of our economic development and prosperity, many household tasks could now be performed by machines. With more time to spend as they saw fit, women looked to creative activity—in literature or the arts—as a means of self-expression that had been suppressed hitherto. They became very active poets.

In cities throughout Japan and in farm and fishing villages too, schools run by businesses or by local governments, as well as cultural centers similar to colleges, have sprung up in great numbers. What we call the "cultural center" is the best-known example of this development. Such centers offer numerous courses of instruction, sustained to a large extent by the number of women who enroll in them. The courses cover such areas as religion, history, language, literature, art, dance, gymnastics, cosmetics, cooking, gardening, flower arrangement, and the tea ceremony. Included too are courses in the writing of modern verse, tanka, haiku, fiction, and essays. For these latter courses professional critics often serve as instructors, and so do poets who write in various forms. Among the women who take these courses, talented writers and haiku poets emerge in significant numbers.

The classes in tanka and haiku composition are quite popular. The need to write in a brief, set form disciplines the student in the use of language and leads to considerable satisfaction and pleasure. However, it must be said that there is a marked difference in the level of language discipline, depending on the quality of the instruction. It is not only that the teacher who is a haiku or tanka poet can give finer instruction and revise the work of the students. It is the students themselves who positively expect and even demand this of

such a teacher. From the distant days of the Heian period (794 to 1185), the orthodox method of teaching the composition of traditional forms of Japanese poetry has been along these same lines. The clearest proof of this lies in the nature of the best critical writings in these areas. These are not expositions about substance or principles, but manuals of composition and guidebooks which illustrate how to write and appreciate poetry with reference to specific examples. The tanka writings of Shunzei Fujiwara and Teika Fujiwara, the haikai writings of Matsuo Bashō, and the writings on Nō by Zeami—these last composed under the influence of tanka—are all examples of this.

In other words the most widely read and influential works in the area of poetics and art are not those of pure theory; rather, they are precisely the records and accounts of how the best poets instructed their pupils day by day. Women, it might be generally said, readily accept this type of training; and now, in both the tanka and the haiku, the emergence of women poets is very striking.

Speaking of tanka, mention must be made of a volume of poems published early last summer called *Sarada kinenbi* (Salad Days Remembered). Composed by a woman in her midtwenties named Machi Tawara, the book sold two million copies by the end of the year and continues to sell well this year. Such a record is unprecedented in the publishing world generally. Tawara is a recent college graduate and now teaches high school. Closely observing the traditional verse form, her tanka sing lightly of love, of travel, of music, of books—while regularly using the conversational tone of young men and women. These works are modern popular songs in a classical verse form, and they are highly successful.

This poet has caught the public's eye as a cheerful, outgoing, sociable artist, thus reversing the prevailing image of the artist as dark and introverted. Moreover, as her poems are not flippant in the least, mature men who are not in the habit of reading tanka end up greatly admiring them. Perhaps these men believe Tawara's poems provide insight into the opinions and lives of the so-called "new talents," a group such men normally regard as a strange new species. In short, this young woman poet has been accepted by all levels of Japanese society and has become a star of the mass media overnight. People are well disposed toward her because she is young and charming.

A hundred years ago, when Akiko Yosano's tanka appeared on the scene, many older people were scandalized by this woman's contempt for their moral sentiment and sexual respectability. As the author of a volume that has sold over two million copies, Machi

Tawara is much talked about. There is a certain panache to her reception, but not even a hint of scandal. The Platonic notion of the poet as more or less a danger to society would appear to be outmoded in Japan, where mass culture has, in some sense, developed further than in any other country.

Still, even the popularity of Machi Tawara has already begun to abate; but the stage for women of superior poetic talent will be enlarged hereafter. However, we must be aware of the fact that the subject which women poets have commanded until now has, for the most part, been daily life in the home. One might say that this coincides with the point I made in my earlier comment on the photography exhibit.

Tanka and haiku are written and read by many people because their set forms are very approachable. In contrast, modern free verse will always be distant and forbidding. It can never be said that this kind of poetry, lacking a set form and so various in both its themes and techniques of expression, is really accessible. However, inasmuch as poetry is never something merely approachable and easily understood, this alienation of modern verse and reader could be a passing phenomenon.

As for myself, I began writing linked verse together with fellow poets around 1970. (Even some novelists joined in.) During the eighties we carried on the joint creation of linked verse with poets from such Western countries as America, the Netherlands, West Germany, and France. The poets who worked with me included Thomas Fitzsimmons of the United States; J. Bernlef, Willem Van Toorn, and Robert Anker of the Netherlands; Adrian Henri of Great Britain; Antonio Cisneros of Peru; Oskar Pastior, Guntram Vesper, and Karin Kivus of West Germany; H. C. Artmann of Austria; Jean-Pierre Faye and Alain Jouffroy of France; and Hiroshi Kawasaki and Shuntarō Tanikawa of Japan. In a house by a small lake in Michigan, in a garden on the outskirts of Rotterdam, in the Petite Salle of the Centre Pompidou in Paris, beside the Wannsee in West Berlin, or in the Literaturhaus in the center of the same city, we poets sat around a table and jointly composed linked verse.

A gathering of foreign poets essentially unknown to each other until our sessions together, we soon became close friends as we sat for several hours or a few days around a table and composed poetry as a group. We learned that, at some subterranean level, a burst of laughter or silent pause had meaning. On this breeding ground, where language bubbled up from within the participating poets, we shared in a rare experience: confronting one another as collaborative authors of verses that came from each of us.

One thing stood out as most important. We might have had differing notions of reality and diverging techniques of expression; but we could observe these differences in the very process of their formation and respond to them time after time. Ascertaining how heterogeneous we were, we paid due respect to our differences; and there is probably no path to mutual understanding other than transcending our heterogeneity and carrying on the dialogue. At present the world is full of misunderstanding. The struggles are becoming more fierce among the different peoples, religions, cultures, and societies in different stages of development. So long as there is no method for readily resolving these divisions, we must at least cultivate mutual respect by acknowledging our heterogeneity and striving to reach a point where we love one another. This we might call a duty for all people alive today.

From this perspective, the experiment described above does not, in my opinion, amount merely to making linked poetry. This is a challenge: we head toward a realm rich in productive incitements.

Makoto Ōoka, Summer 1988, translated by James O'Brien

An Interview with Kenzaburō Ōe

The following interview took place on 7 June 1986 at Kenzaburō Ōe's residence in Tokyo. The text was translated into English from the Japanese and edited by the interviewer with the permission of Mr. Ōe. The research and the trip to Japan for this interview were supported by a 1986 summer research grant from the Faculty Research Committee of Miami University and by a 1986 travel grant from the Northeast Asia Council of the Association for Asian Studies.

SY: I met with Yōtarō Konaka yesterday. He said that recently Japanese society has created a peculiar mood in which it is rather difficult to discuss matters anti-nuclear, and that one may be considered childish or immature if one is antinuclear. The major theme of your "Flood unto My Soul" (1973), "The Pinchrunner" (1976), and other works is the deracination of mankind by nuclear holocaust. As the author of these novels, do you agree with such an assessment of the social climate?

KO: I published a book called *Hiroshima Notes* (1965; Eng. 1981) twenty-three years ago. So it has been about a quarter of a century since I started to think about "Hiroshima." During that

Kenzaburō Ōe (*Robert H. Taylor*)

time, I have participated in the activities of a group called the Japan Confederation of A-Bomb and H-Bomb Sufferers Organizations; I have written and spoken in public in support of such movements as "Abolishment of Nuclear Weapons" and "Relief for Victims"; I have organized committees and councils for these movements as well; yet I do not think things are particularly difficult today. Twenty-four or twenty-five years ago, they were difficult—oh, well, not really difficult, but I was not supported by the majority of Japanese intellectuals. Many victims talked at those meetings, and they wrote about their ordeals. Nevertheless, Japanese scholars, whether they were scholars of English literature, sociologists, physicists, or well-known writers, seldom paid serious attention to such things—except for a handful of fine scholars such as Kazuo Watanabe, Masao Maruyama, and Professor Shūichi Katō. The situation now is about the same.

Four or five years ago, when American medium-range nuclear missiles put Europe in a very precarious position, an antinuclear movement spread from Europe to the United States. When there are such fervid antinuclear movements in Europe and the United States,

Japanese intellectuals tend to follow their lead. Therefore, we had a large-scale anti-nuclear movement in Japan at that time. Now very little is going on. I have not been influenced by these ups and downs of the movements. I do what I have to do in writing my novels and critical essays.

If Japanese critics say it is childish and naïve to oppose nuclear weapons, let me tell you the following: the American political scientist George Kennan, whose judgment I trust, argues in his book *The Nuclear Delusion* that political figures and nuclear-weapons experts always ridicule antinuclear movements as manifestations of naïveté or childishness. However, it is the naïveté of the expert, in both diplomacy and nuclear weapons, that makes the existence of the world precarious. This is what George Kennan says, and I think this is also true in Japan. So there is no need to keep silent when you are called "childish." To be frank, I have to admit that there is perhaps something indeed quite childish about Japanese antinuclear movements. Nonetheless, one must try to embody one's ideals in one's works. If you don't do this, and you are called "childish," it is in part your own fault.

SY: In your works, Mr. Ōe, there are many themes that had not been treated in Japanese literature before. When you started writing fiction, some readers were shocked because of your unique style, new themes, and new attitudes. I have been reading your works from the earliest ones to the most recent, and I know that your style is gradually changing. For example, in one of your earliest short stories, "Pigeon" (1958), there is this sentence: "A sudden anger ravaged my chest." This is obviously written in the syntax of European languages. Did you create this new style because the traditional Japanese styles could not handle the kind of themes that you wished to treat in your fiction?

KO: First of all, the theme of nuclear deracination is not exactly new. Landing on the moon in a rocket is new. Of course, Edmond Rostand had his character talk about "The Journey to the Moon," and Wells wrote about the moon; but when man actually landed on the moon, that was completely new, and if you use that incident in literature, then you have an entirely new theme. The theme of nuclear deracination, however, is only partly new. The invention of nuclear fission made possible the atomic bomb, which killed many people, and nuclear weapons tend to intensify international tension. True, that is a new turn of events. But at the same time, as far as the notion of human annihilation is concerned, the theme is not new—it is partly in harmony with literary tradition (if I may use the word *tradition* as you used it). What I mean is that the notion of apocalypse in Christian tradition, for instance, or the Indian tradition of eschatology, or our tradition of Buddhist eschatology has been there for a long time. Therefore, I treat in my works the theme of the nuclear apocalypse as something partially rooted in a sort of global human tradition. It's not only me. The American author Bernard Malamud once wrote a novel, *God's Grace* (1982), in which he examines the problems of nuclear apocalypse in the context of the Judeo-Christian tradition.

In the period before I started writing, it was not in the tradition of Japanese literature to write novels in a way similar to that in which a philosopher or historian thinks. After the end of the war in 1945, for about ten years, postwar writers, under the influence of Dostoevsky, Hegel, Heidegger, or Sartre, wrote as the historian writes or the philosopher thinks or the social scientist analyzes. This was a new trend. I was influenced by these writers. I needed to think—think about Japanese society, the world, or about the human being—and when I started to write, I wrote in order to give novelistic expression to my thoughts. I was also reading French philosophers such as Sartre and Camus, so my writing was affected by them too, I suppose. I had an antipathy toward such people as Yasunari Kawabata or Jun'ichirō Tanizaki. I felt antagonistic toward established Japanese authors in general. First of all, they do not think logically. Their thoughts almost always become vague halfway. Furthermore, their thoughts are extremely simplistic. That's the way I thought about them when I was young; I do not necessarily think in the same way now.

I've been reading Kathleen Raine, a British literary critic and poet, who says the following about William Blake: "Blake's thoughts are full of ambiguities, but they are not vague." I thought Tanizaki, Kawabata, and other established writers were not ambiguous but vague. . . . Well, that's what I thought when I was young, anyway. As a rebellion, I tried to write as accurately as possible—for example, without using ellipsis. I tried not to omit any pronouns. As you know,

the Japanese language is very effective when ellipsis is applied, but I was determined not to use it. Then my style became similar to that of a translation. By the way, most translations actually do not have any style. For example, Northrop Frye has been translated into Japanese, but the style is neither Frye's nor the translator's. You have to polish it up until it turns into a new style. I thought that kind of product—that is, something still in the process of translation—was interesting. A draft in which the two languages fight each other is provocative and full of resonance. So, my intention was to destroy the Japanese language by using a kind of syntax that cannot fit into Japanese. I was ambitious. I was writing novels with an extremely destructive intention.

SY: In order to eliminate vagueness . . . .

KO: Yes, in order to eliminate vagueness, I even defined certain words each time I used them in my works. But that was only in the early works. For the past ten years or so, I have been trying to create a new, exemplary Japanese style based on those earlier destructive activities of mine.

SY: Especially in the more recent works, your style is in perfect accord with the rhythms of Japanese speech, isn't it?

KO: That's because I used to compose Japanese *waka* poems.

SY: Oh! That explains it. . . .

KO: My brother is a *waka* poet. And I myself am more versed in classical Japanese literature than critics in general suspect. I am pretty good at haiku or *waka*. I composed quite a few *waka* between the ages of fifteen or sixteen and twenty, or thereabout. Still, I respect contemporary poets more than anybody else. I read a lot of modern Japanese poems. American poets like Auden and other foreign poets such as T.S. Eliot, Yeats, and Blake are very important to me. As you see, I am an avid reader of poetry, and I *am* interested in the rhythm of the Japanese language. I wrote "Contemporary Games" (1979) when I was forty-two or so. It is a kind of conclusion to all of my experimental novels. After that novel, for the past ten years, I've been trying to create yet another new style, a more comfortable one for Japanese; I don't mean to go back to the traditional style but to grope for a more acceptable one.

SY: The role of Shōyō Tsubouchi (1859–1935), for example, was important in that he created a new style for new thoughts. . . .

KO: Yes, but the ambitions of men of letters in regard to their style are always ambiguous. Take Shōyō's style, for instance. The capacity of Shōyō's style for conveying meaning or expressing thought was not as great as that of Enchō Sanyūtei (1839–1900), a popular storyteller and entertainer who was Shōyō's contemporary. Therefore, when Shimei Futabatei (1864–1909), Shōyō's disciple, tried to develop a new style for his *Drifting Clouds* (1889), he studied Enchō's style instead of his teacher's. A writer's thoughts about his style, as is obvious from Shōyō's case, are legitimate only half the time. No matter what the result may be, however, writers have to strive for new thoughts and new styles, especially at the start of a new age. Like Shōyō and Futabatei at the turning point of Japanese history after the Meiji Restoration (1868), I also tried to create a new style under the impact of Japan's surrender in the second world war.

SY: Your use of Gothic or black letters first appeared, I believe, in "Our Age" (1959). Later, in *The Day He Himself Shall Wipe My Tears Away* (1969; Eng. 1977), "The Flood unto My Soul," "The Pinchrunner," and "Contemporary Games," you use that technique profusely. In recent stories, however, you put in Gothics only the dialogue of a character called Eeyore. What is your purpose in doing so? When I first encountered this, I wondered if there were any pictorial meaning on that particular page with the black letters.

KO: Well, any writer in any period or country is interested in typography. For example, Laurence Sterne, who wrote *A Sentimental Journey,* used dashes extensively in his novels. In Japan too, in the Meiji period when typography was introduced, writers tried out various interesting techniques. For example, the critic Chogyū Takayama (1871–1902) put little circles, double circles, dots, and lines around his sentences in order to make these sentences stand out. The Russian critic Mikhail Bakhtin puts uneven spaces between letters by way of emphasis. This is a kind of defamiliarization in typography. I am very much interested in this sort of contrivance. It is possible to use various kinds of type at one time in order to make the pages more expressive. The Japanese language has three scripts: *katakana, hiragana* [two kinds of syllabaries], and *kanji* [Chinese characters], which we usually combine.

SY: In "The Pinchrunner" some parts are all in katakana.

KO: Yes, . . . and there is this interesting thing called *rubi* [the pronunciation key in one of the syllabaries of hard-to-read characters, usually given in small print beside the characters]. For example, if you write the kanji for "defamiliarization" and follow it with either the Russian or French equivalent in Japanese syllabic form as a *rubi,* then you can show in one space both the Japanese word and the foreign term from which the Japanese has originated. You can do the same thing using parentheses. You know, we have so many imported words in Japanese, and it is sometimes important to indicate the source. Thanks to the nature of the writing system, Japanese typography is very diversified. I consciously take advantage of this factor.

SY: Are there any other writers who are doing this kind of thing in Japan?

SY: In *Inter Ice Age 4* (1959; Eng. 1970) Kōbō Abe (b. 1924) filled several pages using only katakana. The translator of this work solved the problem by using capitals. If those works of yours are to be translated, some similar kind of device also has to be developed. How about Gothics or italics?

KO: Yes, I like italics. Those boldface types in my works can be considered as italics in English.

SY: "The Pinchrunner" is unique in that the style is interesting and different from that of other works. You must have invented this particular style to express the atmosphere of farce or slapstick. The major plot device in this work is the identity switch between father and son. How did you come up with such an interesting idea? Is there any particular work that you took as an example?

KO: There is no particular source. I live with my handicapped son. Sometimes our roles somehow get reversed in our conversations—jokingly, of course. The identity switch such as the one between sexes is in the tradition of European grotesque realism as a form of theater, like harlequinades. One example would be *Ferdydurke* by the Polish writer Witold Gombrowicz, in which an adult turns into a child. This is a novel that resembles mine, but it was not a source; I got the idea from my own life with my son. But, of course, I like this kind of novel.

I am also very much interested in slapstick. I like American slapstick movies. Among modern writers, Nathanael West, who wrote *The Day of the Locust,* is my favorite. Another example is *A Cool Million.* This is like an erotic gossip novel but is a slapstick. My interest in these works made me write "The Pinchrunner."

The most important focal point in "The Pinchrunner," however, is its narration by a half-crazed, eccentric man. The problem of narration is certainly very important in the modern novel.

SY: You mean "The plural viewpoint," in which one narrator narrates and another person writes it down?

KO: Yes, that's right. That was a major experiment for me.

SY: You use that technique in various pieces. The most complicated one is . . . .

KO: *The Day He Himself Shall Wipe My Tears Away.*

SY: And "The Trial of Plucking Buds and Shooting Lambs" (1980). This one is very interesting and has an extremely intricate narrative structure.

KO: Critics completely ignored it.

SY: They did? Completely?

KO: Yes, absolutely.

SY: Hmm. I wrote about it for an American journal.

KO: Then that must be the only critical commentary on it in the entire world. *(Laughter)*

SY: Anyway, the purpose of the plural viewpoint is to present reality with all its ambiguities and ambivalences.

KO: Yes, you're right.

SY: In "Contemporary Games" a variety of viewpoints allow the author to present many different images of one reality, which overlap each other. The same episodes told many times by different characters, slightly different each time, create an image that is blurred, just like a picture out of focus. I think this blurred image is intentional and perhaps important. Could you elaborate on this point?

KO: I wrote a book entitled "The Methods of the Novel" (1978) in which I explained that the concept of ambiguity was very important for me. In the same sense of the word as in Kathleen Raine's comment about Blake, I wanted to present ambiguity in "Contemporary Games"— that is to say, one reality conveying many meanings. Since regional folklore or regional myths contain this element of ambiguity, I clearly intended to delve into this matter in the regional myths. Now it's been ten years since I finished that book. I recently finished another

novel on the same subject. The title is simply *M/T,* whose initials stand for "matriarch" and "trickster." This is another "Contemporary Games" told in a straightforward narrative by a reminiscing hero.

These days literary critics talk abut "intertexts," which means the study of the relationship between two or more texts. I intend this recent novel of mine, *M/T,* to be read with such an intertextual connection between it and "Contemporary Games." If you read both of them, you will understand both very well, even if you don't make out each by itself.

SY: Then, the relationship is similar to that between "Plucking Buds and Shooting Lambs" (1958) and "The Trial of Plucking Buds and Shooting Lambs," isn't it?

KO: Yes, except here it is the other way round.

SY: Before "Hiroshima Notes" and *A Personal Matter* (1964; Eng. 1968), I find in many of your works a motif of escape that reminds me of the biblical episode of Noah's ark. Did you have this in mind as the model when you were writing, for example, "A Cry" (1963) or "The Flood unto My Soul"?

KO: No, I didn't. Even though I read the Bible a lot, I have not thought of Noah's ark very much. I read the Bible through William Blake or Dante, and I don't think either of them has much interest in the Noah story.

SY: But "The Flood unto My Soul" has something to do with Jonah, doesn't it?

KO: Yes, I think Jonah is an interesting person. He is angry and prejudiced against God.

SY: Because he is trapped. His situation is a metaphorical presentation of man's entrapment; man's struggle to get out of his confinement points to the leitmotiv of escape in your works.

KO: I have been enchanted by existential philosophies, and naturally I am a very existential author. My main interest has been in examining man's existential situations. Recently, however, I have been more interested in preexistential philosophies—that is to say, my subject matter is not so directly related to existential philosophies any longer. More concrete elements in life, such as how to live with a handicapped child or how to think about the nuclear age, are more important to me now. These days I choose motifs from actual life. I started out very existential, and I still am fundamentally, but to a lesser degree.

SY: The image of Africa is recurrent in your works. To be exact, the heroes in *A Personal Matter,* "Adventures in Everyday Life" (1964), and *The Silent Cry* (1967; Eng. 1974) all try to go to Africa.

KO: And in "Our Age" (1959) too.

SY: In all these novels the image of Africa is ambiguous: sometimes it represents freedom, at other times danger or even death. Mr. Ōe, have you been to Africa?

KO: Strangely enough, I haven't. Africa is a very romantic subject. Also, since I like Conrad, it is a Conradian image for me. A lot of difficulties, full of sufferings, and yet romantic—that is Africa for me. Another thing is that when I was a student, I was (and still am) very much interested in the independence movements of the Third World. Africa has been, for me, a fantasized romantic haven from the real world rather than a place with ontological significance. To me Africa is what India or other Asian countries are to Western authors.

SY: You have seriously treated the theme of sexuality in various novels. In one essay you divided all of humanity into two groups: sexual beings and political beings. Sexual beings live in the shadow of the past and are therefore romantic, whereas political beings are always alert to the changes of the world and look forward to the future. There seem to be two major assumptions about sex: first, humans are incessantly vulnerable to the entrapment of sex; second, the sexual depravity that you often treat is a means of defamiliarization.

KO: Yes, I think you are right. I have used sexuality in my novels as a means of defamiliarization and have attempted to attach various meanings to it. I am different from D. H. Lawrence in that Lawrence at one time treated sex as the central theme of his novels; I have simply utilized sexual elements as the most concrete means to defamiliarize the mundane lives of human beings. I did this especially when I was in my twenties and thirties.

SY: Speaking of defamiliarization, many characters in "The Flood unto My Soul," for example, are maimed: their hands are cut off, say. Some of them are very strangely shaped.

KO: Yes, . . . deformed.

SY: They are like those human figures in Picasso's cubist paintings or like the grotesque people in Hieronymus Bosch's pictures. The prime example in "The Flood" is the Shrinking Man, quite an astonishing invention.

KO: They may resemble Picasso or Bosch, but my interest was in dealing with the possibilities of living together with such strange objects as amputated parts of the human body or deformed persons. I am still writing about this, hoping to discover that it is comfortable to live with those bizarre creatures. At the beginning, I did not intentionally draw difficult and ugly elements into my world, but as I was groping for methods of defamiliarization, they were there. So, yes, you are right. They are a means to defamiliarize the familiar. The Shrinking Man, the example you mentioned, the model for him was Yukio Mishima. I based the character on Mishima. Every time I saw him, I thought of him as a shrinking man.

SY: Could you elaborate on that?

KO: If you realize that the Shrinking Man is a caricature of Mishima, then you will find some new ways to interpret that novel. For example, in things like homosexuality and the desire to punish himself. . . .

SY: I see: you painted Yukio Mishima by using the technique of grotesque realism. In your essay titled "Why Do Human Beings Produce Literature?" (1975) you argue that, if anybody disrupts the fundamental harmony between human beings and their society, the world and the cosmos, literature, based on a humanistic viewpoint, will continue to protest against such violence. When you say "the fundamental harmony," I don't think you mean simply being friendly to each other.

KO: In simple terms, literature should deal with the theme of the ostracized in family and in society. I have extended the theme of ostracism to include the cosmos. The question is how we can change the situation so that nobody is ostracized. That is to say, literature should create a model of the human being and his environment wherein nobody is discriminated against. This is the basis of my literature. The human being conceived by William Blake is not ostracized. The reason I read Blake and Dante is that I wish to see an image of the human being accepted in society and to enlarge my vision further so that I will be able to conceive the model human environment in a cosmic context. At this point the image of nuclear disaster comes in as an extremely disturbing element.

SY: In the essay entitled "The Image System of Grotesque Realism" in your book "The Methods of the Novel" you emphasize the importance of grotesque realism. You say, "Our literature should adopt the image system of grotesque realism as its integral part and, in so doing, should bring about a real regeneration of human life—in this way I intend to formulate the future of Japanese literature."

KO: Yes, that is my fundamental philosophy.

SY: Yes, but in the cosmic context Japan is, of course, a part of the world. As a Japanese author, Mr. Ōe, do you ever write your novels for the sake of world readers?

KO: When one of my pieces was translated into German, the German translator interviewed me. His last question was, "Is the German translation important to you?" I infuriated him by saying "No." I am not very enthusiastic either when a foreign publisher invites me to give a lecture on the occasion of a new publication of my translated work. The reason is that I am not optimistic that my books will find readers in foreign countries. Of course, I grew up under the influence of foreign literature. I have a profound sense of respect for the literatures of Germany, France, America, England, and Latin America as well. I am convinced, however, that literature should be written for people who live in the same country and in the same age as the author. Therefore, I never intentionally write for foreign readers. I strongly feel that I am writing for intellectuals living in this small country with me. If foreign readers happen to find the Japanese model of the human being and society presented in my works interesting, then I would simply be very happy.

With Yukio Mishima, it is a different story, I think. Even though he was very popular and was actually the king of the Japanese literati, Mishima could not trust Japanese criticism and turned to foreign readers. His death was a performance for the foreign audience, a very spectacular performance. The relationship between Mishima and the emperor system was rather dubious; the Japanese knew that. But from foreigners' point of view—say, an American reader's point of view—the Japanese emperor system is something inexplicable. Therefore, that final act by Mishima, tied in with the emperor system, appeared to be a kind of mystical thing. In actuality, he did it in order to entertain foreign readers.

I am always thinking of contemporary Japanese readers. That's why I sometimes get involved in antinuclear movements. If writers of the world became interested in the human models presented in my fiction, I would be very flattered. When I write, however, I only think of the Japanese audience. I am a local writer from the world's point of view. I read worldwide, though. I read Japanese novels, of course; but during the daytime, for about three hours every day, I read whatever I choose to study at the time: for example, Malcolm Lowry, Dante, Yeats, or Bakhtin. When I go to bed, since I quit drinking some time ago, I read Dickens by way of a nightcap. Reading foreign authors is the source of my nourishment. Nevertheless, insofar as I am writing in Japanese, I think I am writing for Japanese readers.

Sanroku Yoshida, Summer 1988

KOREA

From Korean History to Korean Poetry: Ko Un and Ku Sang

The starting point for this paper is two poems, one by Ku Sang and one by Ko Un. Each is a poem to which its author attaches particular importance and which he often reads or quotes. Together they may serve as an example of the ways in which modern Korean poems articulate responses to Korean history. The difference between the two poems and the two poets may be perceived as representing two aspects of the modern Korean poetic response to historical and social realities.

There are a number of features which render the discussion of this matter difficult. Because the Korean language is inaccessible to almost all non-Korean readers, the original poems must remain unquoted and unfelt. (Space permitting, however, photocopies and transliterations of the original Korean texts will accompany my translations of the two poems.) The names and works of the poets, like the outlines of Korean history, are for most non-Korean readers unknown. Korean culture and the evolutions of Korean poetry are similarly remote. No names, categories, or dates offer a familiar reference point. The poems stand alone and may mystify or disappoint. How are they to be read?

The initial response to Ku Sang's work may be that it is not very "poetic." That is certainly the general Korean critics' evaluation of his writing, in a country where poetry is frequently expected to be almost incoherently emotional. Ku Sang's poem number 16 from "Christopher's River" is not intensely witty or lyrical. It comprises a series of tersely epigrammatic phrases, some of which seem farfetched when applied to a river. The implications of will and choice, the abstract and philosophical terminology, the static series of comparisons, all lead the reader away from any naturalistic view of a real river. Yet the river is not simply made a prescriptive model for human behavior. Rather, it is found to embody a vast range of ultimate ideals. Some are familiar Christian ones, such as humility, or giving "and not asking for any reward" (Saint Ignatius); some are completely universal, whereas a few are recognizably Taoist or Buddhist in their stress on flow, impassivity, freedom, and emptiness.

The river is perceived as a symbol, but it is also seen as an enlightened sage itself, transcending history by its particular manner of being in history. None of the individual images of the poem is particularly new or striking; the work depends for its impact on its variations and the cumulative effect, within a very calm emotional scale, of a list of fundamental spiritual attitudes.

In contrast, the poem "Arrows" by Ko Un obviously burns with an intense passion. The rhetoric is exhortatory, militant. The central image is a violent one. Yet there are unexpected turns; the arrows are called on not only to strike their target but to "rot with the pain of striking home" and finally to bleed in union with their victims. This poem is clearly heroic in its call to give up accumulated wealth and ease and even to sacrifice life itself, yet it ends by turning away from the assumed audience to greet those already dead and transfers to them the quality of arrow-ness, hailing them as weapons in a national struggle.

It might be felt that neither of these poems would get very high grades for "well-wrought-urn-ness," that standard New Critical approaches would fail to uncover much to say about them. The rest, as with Hamlet, is silent context. Ku Sang's poem is a textual one first of all. It does not stand alone but instead forms part of a cycle of sixty poems published under the title "Christopher's River." The individual poems are given not titles but numbers, indicating that they are to be seen as elements forming a larger whole. As the poet says in the work's prologue, "I have chosen the river / as a place for conversions of heart."

The prologue addresses Saint Christopher, who unexpectedly found himself carrying the Christ child over the river: "as at the weary end of a certain day you / met long-awaited Love's Incarnation, / so my poetry too may see the light of salvation: / in that hope and belief / I fol-

low you out to the river." The extraordinary comes in the ordinary; the moment of epiphany is embedded in the context of the normal humdrum. Therefore, Ku Sang seems to say, the poet should avoid all attempts at provoked intensity and simulated emotion. His cycle is presented as the record of thoughts rising spontaneously in the course of brief daily visits to the side of a river often more remarkable for its pollutedness than for its natural beauty.

These thoughts, however, are those of an observer preoccupied with ultimate questions, not of an idle onlooker or an ardent romantic eager to find flattering reflections of his own image. The empty mirror held up so that "all things" can "view themselves" is the medieval speculum in which the beholder's true image is revealed and wisdom is gained by the breaking of illusions. Above all, what is hoped for the poetry is not fame or improvement but instead "salvation" by grace. The humility of the poetic form identifies itself as the image of a spiritual stance on the part of the poet. Our poem transfers that stance to the river, which "at all times and in all places / chooses the lowest place."

The humility theme is equally implied in the poem's most challenging stanza: "The river, / unresisting, accepts / every violence, every humiliation, / and never denies itself." This sudden mention of "violence" and "humiliation" functions to dramatize and in a sense to historicize the text. We notice that this is the first stanza of the poem's second half, perhaps a turning point. The challenge alluded to, though not elaborated, is the Gandhian one of nonviolent responses to violence: how is it possible to accept violence without resistance, and without becoming violent, yet without submitting to the will of the violent? How is it possible to remain true to oneself in such situations, neither denying nor betraying one's essential nature or vision?

That challenge is repeated in other terms a moment later: "The river / is its own master, / free despite all bonds." This paradox deepens the invitation to read the poem within history. The constraints that seem to limit or abolish freedom may not after all do so; there is a freedom, as Richard Lovelace said long ago, within the prison cell: "Stone walls do not a prison make, / Nor iron bars a cage."

Looking at the river, Ku Sang evokes the final level of resistance to constraint: freedom within bonds, where the spirit remains unbowed, its own master, refusing to surrender or compromise with the demands of violence, corruption, injustice. It is when one attains that level of authenticity, the poem suggests, that one may see the vision of the next stanza: "Eternity within impermanence," the claim that there is a beyond, an essential meaning to the historical process.

Some Koreans have been shocked by the contrast between this high metaphysical seriousness and the use of the English word *pantomime* in the final stanza. Ku Sang has never seen *Puss in Boots* or *Jack and the Beanstalk,* and the word is surely used here in the sense of "mimed drama" or dumbshow. He brings the poem to a proper close by locating the interpretation of meaning firmly in the onlooker, not in the wordless river. The river, we might say, does not mean; it is. As in the Renaissance emblem tradition, the visual element is a more powerful conveyor of deep meaning than are mere words, so long as the beholding eyes are trained in active, contemplative looking.

This is where Ku Sang positions himself, in the contemplative mode but not on the sidelines of history. His whole life has been marked by the practice of an approach very neatly summed up in this model of the river. He was born in 1919 into a Catholic family, and his brother was a priest in the northern part of the country until 1950, when he is assumed to have been martyred at the start of the Korean War. Ku Sang studied for a while at the Catholic Minor Seminary that formed the local secondary school, but eventually ran away from there. In Japan he studied the philosophy of religions, celebrated "daily funerals of God," and discovered the pantheism of Rilke. He began to write poems evoking the presence he felt within nature. Returning to northern Korea, which had been placed under Russian control after the Japanese withdrawal in 1945, Ku Sang soon had to flee southward to escape arrest for refusing to write in terms pleasing to the supporters of Kim Il-Sung. In the south, he wrote newspaper editorials, and once found himself in prison for denouncing corruption too freely. Untreated tuberculosis cost him the better part of one lung.

Like the river, though, Ku Sang has mostly preferred the quiet flow. His main focus has been to find a center and a focus around which to construct a meaning in the midst of a history, both personal and national, marked by so much chaos and pain. He became reconciled to the Catholic faith through the reading of French philosophers and writers such as Gabriel Marcel, Teilhard de Chardin, and Jean Guiton. To their vision of cosmic order and ultimate hope he added elements of the Eastern religious tradition, Taoist and Buddhist. Above all, in the best Confucian way, he has striven to become a sage. The Eastern sage is often very like a child, and Ku Sang writes his poems like a child, simply, without guile or ambition.

Generally speaking, Ku Sang is neither a raving symbolist nor a rhetorical anarchist, as some Korean poets tend to be. His grammatical structures are usually complete, and his diction is either philosophically abstract or very simply concrete. It might be said that, for him, thought is emotion and coherence is meaning. In this he bridges in a fascinating way the Western and Eastern poetic traditions. It is his deepest conviction that we cannot live or write poetry without having a clear metaphysical vision informing our understanding of events and ourselves.

The authenticity of Ku Sang's life and writing means that today, when he is approaching eighty, he is generally recognized as someone who has always known how to live within a history of corruption without compromising his authenticity. He is widely venerated as a witness to the truth in an age of lies and pretense. His poetry and his person go together. He laughs a lot; and when he collapsed and missed an appointment recently, he kept asking those left waiting to "forgive" him!

In the case of Ko Un, the life and the poetry are very different, although the context is equally modern Korea. "Arrows" was published in a volume containing poems of the usual kind, each one separate and named. The themes of this poem mean that it is going to be necessary to move closer to the details of Korean history in order to locate it than was the case with Ku Sang's poem. Where Ku Sang's text is potentially (although not, of course, actually) general and timeless, the urgency of Ko Un's tone suggests an immediate context of conflict and crisis. Where Ku Sang speaks in solitude, recording thoughts for his own benefit, Ko Un's poem assumes a plural audience, a crowd, and the speaker takes the initiative in exhorting the audience to an action in which he will join as one among many.

That action remains potential, evoked and realized, then fractured, within the poem's text. Whether the poem is read aloud to a crowd or perused while sitting in an armchair, it must evoke at least in part a tension of nonfulfillment. The end turns away from the implied visible audience to salute the dead who have gone before. Anticipating what follows in this paper, we might say that the tone suggests a poem designed to be read to a crowd of demonstrators about to confront battalions of riot police or soldiers armed with tear gas, batons, or, worse, with an oppressive dictator and his corrupt lackeys invisible behind them.

The exalted heroic tone and the themes of resistance and sacrifice are not in fact very characteristic of most of Ko Un's poetry, but they are very characteristic of his popular image. It may be difficult for readers in most of Western Europe or North America, at least, to make anything much of such a text, with the possible exception of those who wish to fight against some fantasy of Evil Empire or Big Government, which is not the

Korean context. What makes this poem challenging is not its poetic process, which is quite transparent, but its reading of history and the way it is rooted in a specific moment of Korean history, challenging readers to decide how they are reading and responding to that history.

"Warriors! Spirits of the fallen!"—in Britain this line must surely be evocative of Poppy Day and war memorials. The enemy of England has for centuries been thought of as the enemy without, the perfidious foreigner. Not in Korea, or at least not in this poem and in those to whom it is addressed. When it was written in the mid-1970s, the struggle was against the dictatorial ex-general Park Chung-Hee, who in 1972 declared himself supreme ruler, abolished all forms of democratic expression, and employed every available means to prevent opposition to his own plans for the country. His plan was essentially to raise South Korea from rural poverty to industrial prosperity within a few years. To do this, low wages, long working hours, and social stability despite harsh living conditions were essential. The youth of the rural villages were recruited to the industrial centers in order to ensure the former, while a machinery of covert surveillance and brutal repression was instituted to maintain the latter.

Many people in Europe and America still recall vivid television images of "Korea's violently demonstrating students," a phrase often pronounced in tones of shocked horror, as if the students clearly had no business being out demonstrating and upsetting people's supper. Ko Un's poem suggests another way of reading modern Korean history, one that expresses shock and horror at the warm welcome given to such grotesque figures as former presidents Chon Doo-Hwan and Roh Tae-Woo in the White House and Buckingham Palace.

The fundamental question is one of legitimacy. In classical Chinese thought, the ruler of a country was considered to possess the "mandate of heaven," which he might lose through behavior contrary to the ways of heaven or Right Principles. In modern Korean history the legitimacy of the regimes installed in Seoul and in Pyongyang has been radically denied by the respective opposing side. More to the point, since the inception of the Republic of Korea in the southern part of the peninsula in 1948, the legitimacy of the regime in power has been a frequent bone of contention.

While regimes have mostly argued that "might is right" and "possession is nine-tenths of the law," these constitutional views have regularly confronted a more democratic definition of the state, seen as a concern of the entire populace. In particular, a long tradition of authoritarian rule rooted in neo-Confucianism has encouraged presidents and would-be presidents to claim more or less unlimited powers and rights, rights often directly opposed to justice and asserted with violence.

Korea's human arrows have a noble and terrible history. It is an ambiguous one, troubled and disputed, a history that produces radically different readings of and responses to the poem and the poet, even within Korea. The most widely recognized flight of arrows in modern Korean history came on 19 April 1960. On that day the college and high-school students of Seoul came out of their schools and went peacefully marching through the city to denounce the corrupt and unpopular president Syngman Rhee's decision to claim a third, unconstitutional term in power. Those unarmed children and youths were mowed down by the regime's guns; hundreds died, and Syngman Rhee was forced to resign.

Since then there have been countless more flights of arrows, and much innocent blood has flowed. On the whole, regimes have not toppled so quickly, but they *have* lost their moral legitimacy. The most wounding incident of all came after Ko Un's poem was written, in May 1980 in the city of Kwangju. Sometimes there have been individual arrows that have had an immense impact, young people whose lives have been taken from them during protests or during torture sessions in police stations. Their names are inscribed in popular memory: Park Chong-chol, Lee Han-yol, and dozens of others. Many are buried in the cemetery at Mangwol-dong, just outside Kwangju, with the victims of that city's massacre.

Behind them, and accompanying them, stand the bleeding arrows of another terrible era of Korean history. In 1909, after ten years of preparation, Japan annexed Korea as a Japanese province and began trying to uproot and destroy the Korean people's national and cultural identity. On 1 March 1919 a movement was launched to demand the independence of Korea, and until 15 August 1945 countless Koreans suffered, were imprisoned, and died for the cause of national liberation. Back further still in the past stand the nameless legions of the Korean poor who from time to time in previous centuries formed a "righteous army" in suicidal protest at the administration's corruption and inhumanity. The last such uprisings occurred in the southwest just a hundred years ago and during the early part of this century on the island of Cheju-do.

The struggle in which Ko Un's arrows fly and bleed is not some kind of simple "protest movement" in the Western sense. It presents itself as a valiant self-sacrifice for the ultimate salvation of the nation. The relationship between arrows and target is complex, because both are part of the same people and both sides claim to be acting for the nation's good. The Korean people's sense of sacred destiny is the legitimizing context; the death of these young people is a martyrdom in the strongest sense. There have even been cases, too painful to discuss, where young people have felt called upon to provoke their own deaths in the struggle.

At this point the discussion can continue in two quite different directions. It is possible to go on and relate the poems as they have so far been read to the poets' lives and to the general Korean life experience. It would be equally possible to "reverse the vapors," as the French would say, to backpedal and become revisionist, for that is part of Korean poetry's complexity. In this paper I have so far been echoing the form of narration of recent history that is conventional among fairly liberal people sympathetic to the students' struggle. Yet if we are going to speak of history, we will have to be rather more historical and shun too simple an idealism. Inevitably, the democracy struggles of the 1970s and 1980s have been open to multiple manipulations. At times the dictatorial regimes have used them to alarm the populace, so that public opinion would move away from opposition. On the other hand, among the activists there were often hidden agendas of a leftist kind, which in Korea leads one to the hidden but never-forgotten face of history, the presence not far north of Seoul of another Korea claiming to be a pure communist regime representing the nation's true future.

There is a large body of conservative opinion in the South which has always automatically condemned the student demonstrations and branded the radical writers, churchmen, and thinkers who supported them as providing irresponsible encouragement, if not direct support, to the North in its intention to take control of the South. This conservative reading of history and literature casts a dark cloud over Ko Un in particular. Therefore, to read Ko Un's poem as I have so far done is in itself a political option, an interpretation of great potential ambiguity, because recent Korean history remains a totally unstable and volatile text. Someone who holds more strongly to conservative ideas might wish to read the poem in a very different, hostile way.

Ko Un claims the right to write this poem because he himself had for a number of years been one of the arrows. Born in 1933, he was a child prodigy who had mastered the traditional Chinese classics by the time he was eight. The horrors of the Korean War, when he was in his late teens, almost drove him to suicide, but instead he renounced the world and became a Buddhist monk. Roaming the country with his master, begging for food, he saw the misery and pain of the war-ravaged land. After ten years he rebelled against the formalism

of the religious traditions, left the order, and immersed himself in life, until its intensity turned against him and suicide again seemed an option. Recovering, he suddenly found himself a leading spokesman for those writers and artists who refused to accept Park Chung-Hee's assumption of absolute power in 1972. Since then he has spoken at every major demonstration and has been arrested many times. For years his passport was confiscated, and he could not travel abroad. He has always been solidly present on one side of the playing field while along the sidelines there have stood the many writers, critics, and intellectuals who did not want to get involved, their heads turned skyward or buried in the sand, if they were not actively licking the generals' boots. Ko Un is a controversial figure.

Returning to a simpler, more romantic mode, we may conclude by saying that the poetry of Korea is immensely varied; there are over two thousand published poets alive in Korea today. Ku Sang and Ko Un should not be seen in isolation. They are very different from each other in the political options they have taken; although they were frequent drinking companions in the 1960s, their responses to the events of the 1970s subsequently placed them in different camps. In the changed situation of recent years they have again drawn closer. Their poetry is different, as they themselves are different: the one intellectual, the other passionate. What they have in common is an awareness of their country's long history of pain.

That is the background without which no reading of Korean poetry is possible. The simple people inhabiting the villages of Korea have never been masters of their destiny. Centuries of arbitrary rule, administrative incompetence, epidemics, invasions from Japan and Mongolia, Chinese and Russian interference, typhoons, bitter winters, poverty, and ignorance have written their own poetic history in the popular Korean soul, a history of tears and unfulfilled yearning that finds expression in the faces and voices of those who survive. *Han* is the Korean word for this burden of inherited grief, and it has its own powerful esthetic in song, dance, gesture, and silence.

It might be thought that such a destiny left its people little cause to rejoice. Yet rejoice they did and do. Rejoicing and suffering are the two poetic poles of the Korean life experience. This may seem obviously true of humanity in general; what is particular about the Korean instance is that the two have been obliged to keep such close company that they are virtually inseparable. The deep energy of the Korean psyche or *Hung* is manifested in the traditional culture by vibrant farmers' music, popular songs, and dances, and in modern life by a frantic rhythm of life, hours spent in discos or karaoke bars, and a lot of collective junketing. Celebration is essentially collective; rice wine, music, and dance are normally necessary components. Through celebration, the ghosts of sorrow are exorcised and the human is united with the heavenly.

The experience of pain by the individual becomes *Han* when it is taken up and understood in the context of the collective national experience of relentless oppression and suffering through the centuries, generation after generation. There are traces of something similar happening in the Scottish ballads before they were collected and turned into printed English literature. The pain, whether it be the sudden loss of a husband or of children, some humiliating social disgrace, or the traditional cruelty of the mother-in-law, is not simply a matter of individual destiny; it raises the suffering individual to the fellowship of all who have shared the experience in the past. The sufferer is frequently female; the arbitrary cruelty of fate cannot be avoided or overcome by quick action but must be endured to the bitter end.

Out of that history, and that manner of experiencing history, it is hardly surprising that poetry is born. That the poetry shuns elaborate esthetic form is hardly surprising as well. The beauty already exists in the people's heart; it does not need to be poeticized to become poetry. Korean history is its own poetry, an ongoing song of grief and endurance.

Brother Anthony of Taizé, Summer 1997

TAIWAN

The Continuity of Modern Chinese Poetry in Taiwan

When we try to delineate the development of a literary genre, we are often faced with choosing a strategy to illustrate the various phases within the definition of that genre. However, there are underlying factors that can influence the formation of a phase, elements which can range from the dominance of a literary movement to the creative ebb and flow of a particular writer. Editors of many poetry anthologies in Taiwan constantly find themselves at the crossroads of having to decide whether to regard an ongoing stage as a special segment of time or to link it to the history of modern Chinese poetry. There is a preference for the former, and the concept of the decade has been introduced as a yardstick to measure a specific period of time. In less than twenty years three anthologies were published under the titles *Poetry of the Sixties, Poetry of the Seventies,* and *Poetry of the Eighties.* However, there are strong indications that

these were more than just temporal demarcations and were in fact recognitions of literary phenomena within the designated time periods. As the editors of *Poetry of the Sixties* admitted in their foreword, the so-called sixties did not explicitly indicate chronicle time but rather a new, modern implication which transcended tradition.[1] Nevertheless, the anthology's editors revealed their "decade mentality" by selecting only works written in Taiwan from 1949 to 1959.

Six years later, *Poetry of the Seventies* was published to include works written between 1962 and 1967. The editors continued to express their awareness of the decadal concept and proclaimed in the anthology's postscript that their basic editorial policy was similiar to that expressed in the foreword to *Poetry of the Sixties:* that is, that a decade does not really imply chronicle time but emphasizes a new, creative, modern definition of poetry. Thus a decadal anthology is not just an edition of poems mechanically issued every ten years, but one whose appearance is caused by the emergence of more progressive and mature works between the previous anthology and the present one.[2]

Whatever verse of "a new, creative, modern" type may mean, as far as the poems selected in *Poetry of the Sixties* are concerned, they are the creative products of various stages of symbolism and modernism. Six years later the editors of *Poetry of the Seventies* indicated that the poets had progressed from adolescence to youth, from experimentation to creativity, and from childhood to maturity. The self-confident tone of the above metaphor led the editors to proclaim further that, in being thus placed among the world poets, these authors were no less significant. Theoretically, the editors of both anthologies strongly advocated the transmogrification of the term *decade* from a meaningless chronological concept to a symbol of literary periodization, and they all admitted that the use of *sixties* or *seventies* in the titles of the volumes was only a practical means and certainly not an indication of their intended ends.

Nine years having elapsed after the publication of *Poetry of the Seventies,* the editors of the succeeding anthology, *Poetry of the Eighties,* felt even more uneasy about using the decade to represent poetic periodization. With a longer list of poets included in their anthology, the editors attempted to utilize a "pastoral mode" to characterize the poetic style of this particular period. In order to retain some of the significance of *decade* in their title, one of the editors, Chang Han-liang, defended the practice in the volume's preface.

> Of course, the periodization in *Poetry of the Sixties* does not imply any chronicle meaning but to present an avant-garde creative attitude, but the succeeding *Poetry of the Seventies* and the present

anthology inevitably bear a significance of the changing and developing of a literary history. The mutation of poetry in these ten years can be traced rather obviously.[3]

Clearly, the editors of this compilation have adopted both a historical outlook and the decadal increment in order to trace the development of poetry from 1966 to 1975. However, they provide us with no explanation as to why they have chosen to start with 1966 and to overlap the last two years covered by *Poetry of the Seventies,* 1966 and 1967. One suspects that the publication date of *Poetry of the Eighties* was 1976 and that editing began in 1975. Pushing back ten years in order to present a full decade would have forced them to begin with 1966; therefore we can see that this year bears no literary significance. It is just a historical convenience, one which allows the editors to use the decade as their structuring temporal unit.

Such a rigid chronological treatment of poetic development did not prove satisfactory in representing the multifarious poetic contents and styles within a ten-year period. Eventually the publication of the "annual anthologies" in the 1980s was undertaken to do away with the incongruity between the "decade anthologies" and ongoing poetic trends. Since the annual anthology is a yearly publication, its chronicle function is well defined, and the editor does not have to bear the literary burden of periodization, in particular the concept of the decade. Beginning in 1983, the Elite Press of Taipei started publishing annual anthologies which used the years from the Chinese Republican-era calendar for their annual titles.[4] As Chang Mo, one of the five rotating editors, recalled in drafting the editorial plan for the first annual anthology, *Poetry 1982,* many details were executed with fixed formats, and individual editors were assigned the task of selecting poems from various sources. Each year the editor in charge collects all the poems published in the literary supplements of daily newspapers, monthly or quarterly literary journals, and poetry magazines. He then solicits other editors for missing poems and further recommendations. As part of this selection process there is both a preliminary screening and a final one: "The preliminary screening goes to the editor in charge, who will seek works from a large variety of sources. Avoiding partisan views as much as possible, he will choose artistic effects as means for his selections."[5] All the editors then assemble to decide upon the final list.

Moving along the same lines as the Elite Press is the Avant-Garde Press, whose annual anthologies are published simultaneously with Elite's but which uses the Gregorian calendar for its standard yearly titles. According to Li Huai-hsien, the editor in charge of *Taiwanese*

Poetry 1982, 1982 was a significant year for Taiwanese poetry. Not only have the works of many senior Taiwanese poets who once flourished during the time of the Japanese occupation reappeared in various journals and anthologies, but many literary journals and poetry magazines with local colors have either published special issues or made efforts to reevaluate the poetry of earlier days. Many poetry journals have resumed publication, and new journals are being formed by younger poets. The tenacious support from the literary supplements of Taiwanese daily newspapers is astounding. In a year's time there were more than four thousand poems published in various newspapers and journals. This is indeed a scene of poetic prosperity. Li unveils his critical criteria for selecting poems as follows:

> *Taiwanese Poetry 1982* may be local-oriented, realistic, social, and even artistic. These are the presuppositions to decide further directives for a critical selection. But we do not deliberately restrict ourselves to a particular viewpoint. Whatever is expressed clearly and precisely as the intentional meaning of a poem will be considered; whether it is published in newspapers, poetry journals, or magazines makes no difference. We don't care too much about authorship either, and we tend to neglect the element of the poet's fame, which we simply don't trust; neither would we care about his background or poetic affiliation.[6]

As regards these two types of anthologies, the decadal and the annual, we may say that the former has long-term assessment in mind, whereas the latter aims at short-range evaluation. Western modernism has been a dominant influence, and poets have congregated in Taiwan for at least twenty years since 1949. Perhaps this is the main reason why early collections like *Poetry of the Sixties* and *Poetry of the Seventies* were able to evaluate a rather unified modernist poetic activity by using the ten-year increment. However, with the emergence of the young poets and their nonconformist practices in the 1970s, the subsequent establishment of a more realistic, native-oriented voice in modern poetry has come to replace the modernists' empty soliloquy. Critics have refused to give credibility to "star poets" whose self-indulgent "obscure poetry" was once fashionable. The whole poetic scene has changed so drastically that the decadal anthology, which used to be highly influential and persuasive, has begun to lose its authority. Unlike in the past, a poet does not now survive on his fame, or on that of the poetry society to which he belongs. With the publication of the yearly collection, his work is judged or selected according to how he performs annually. On the one hand the yearly anthology poses a direct challenge to the dwindling creativity of many senior poets; on the other it serves to replace the editorially ambiguous ten-year compendium, which focuses mainly on the modernist trend. Indeed, many times the emphasis is on the selection of poets rather than on their poetry. In addition, the yearly anthology reaffirms the vital role of poetry in Taiwan along with the nation's flourishing fiction and prose. Modern poetry is accepted as "legitimate" by the general audience—and especially by college students—despite the fact that verse still sells far less than prose or fiction. However, the reclamation of poetry's popularity is not accidental. It represents the vanishing of a nihilistic modernism on the one hand and the steady growth of a more critically oriented poetic audience on the other. The annual anthology functions not only to delineate poetic development from a different perspective, but actually preserves in its selections many poems that are forgotten in daily newspapers or monthly journals. Where these poems would normally last no more than a day or a month, the annually published compendium lengthens their lives in the manner of a historical chronicle.

Still, the yearly anthology has its limitations. First, as we asked of the decadal collection, "Why a decade?," now we may ask, "Why one year?" What is the rationale for beginning with January 1st and ending with December 31st? From where do we derive such a temporal conception of poetry? Is it simply because there *is* a year that there is a yearly anthology? We have noticed that annual publication functions to limit the anthology's coverage to a span of a single year's poetic activity, its changes and representative works. It is perhaps therefore more likely that a young poet will be included, one whose work is more fragmentary and experimental. However, this is not necessarily the case with an established poet, whose career is often built on a much more elaborated scheme, one which may take more than a year to reveal or to establish. Therefore, what is to be considered his "yearly representation" bears little significance to the overall dimensions of his work. He is, in fact, actually misrepresented, since the annual anthology usually selects only one poem per writer. (Sometimes—although it is a rare occasion—the editors select up to three from each poet.) This is perhaps the reason why, after a couple of years, the Elite Press changed its editorial policy to include only young poets, thereby avoiding this misrepresentation of established poets.

In 1989 the Hung-fan Bookstore and Nine Songs Press each published a poetry anthology, using the artistic achievement of the poets as their criterion for selection. Hung-fan's was edited by Yang Mu and Cheng Shu-shen; Nine Songs' was produced under the chief editorship of Yu Kwang-chung as part of *A Comprehensive Anthology of Contemporary Chinese Literature in Taiwan, 1970–1989*. Two volumes of poetry in this edition

were edited by Chang Mo. The publication of the modern literary compendium, of course, can be traced back to Shanghai, to Chao Chia-pi's 1935 edition of the *Comprehensive Anthology of New Literature in China.* Two sets of modern literary compendia were published in Taiwan before the Nine Songs edition. One was the Giant Press edition of *A Comprehensive Anthology of Modern Chinese Literature* (1972); the other was *A Comprehensive Anthology of New Literature in Contemporary China* (1980), published by T'ien-shih Press. So far, the poetry volumes of the Nine Songs edition constitute the most up-to-date representation of modern Chinese poets in Taiwan. They also represent a linkage to the Giant edition published nearly twenty years ago, a connection illustrated by Yu Kwang-chung's statistical count in his general preface: "There were seventy poets included in the Giant edition, from which Nine Songs selected twenty-eight. The survival rate is forty percent. These twenty-eight poets persevere and make up twenty-eight percent of a total of ninety-nine poets."[7] In addition to Yu's observation, Chang Mo also wrote the preface to the anthology's volumes of poetry, clearly delineating the historical development of modern verse in Taiwan starting in the 1970s. Thus it is obvious that the mission of the Nine Songs edition is a historical one and that it is designed to continue the tradition of the previous anthology.

The historicity of modern poetry has been presented by using various editorial schemata—the decadal, the annual, and the comprehensive—and through the development of literary trends and the sorting of poets. There have also been intermittent publications of independent anthologies such as the three-volume *Display of Contemporary Chinese Poetry* (Teh-hua Press, 1981). This edition focused on the poetry from 1970–79 and was jointly edited by Hsiao Hsiao, Hsiang Yang, and Ch'en Ning-kuei. Chang Mo's editions of modern male and female poets, published by the Elite Press in 1981 and 1982 respectively, demonstrate his tenacious efforts to represent different phases of modern verse by variously grouping poets, be it by gender or by poetic affinity. Ya Hsien, in editing the poetry volume of *A Comprehensive Anthology of New Literature in Contemporary China,* arranged the order of the poets according to the number of strokes in their Chinese surnames. Names with fewer strokes come before those requiring more strokes. Chang Mo reverses the order in his edition of the male poets, putting the names with the most strokes before those with fewer strokes. No matter which way it goes, there is little rationale in using the number of strokes in a poet's surname as the criterion for the arrangement of an anthology. It is more appropriate to have these poets ordered according to their dates of birth. An organizational plan such as this at least imparts a sense of chronology and historical development to an edition. Such a disposition is not without flaws, however. For example, Yang Mu was born much later than many senior poets in Taiwan, but he holds a more senior status among his contemporaries. Also, many distinguished poets like Chu Hsiang and Yang Huan were born early and died young, and many anthologies give the false impression that they were merely young poets.

Nearly all the abovementioned compilations focus mainly on the poetry of Taiwan, with the exception of Ya Hsien's T'ien-shih edition, in which he includes the writing of Chinese poets from Singapore, Malaysia, the Philippines, Vietnam, Hong Kong, and the United States. He explains in his introduction that the blood tie between these areas and Taiwan is strong, and he "anticipates that wider attention and concern will be placed upon the literary activity and work of these poets from overseas, so that someday a more comprehensive anthology of Chinese writers will be edited. We can then have peace of mind, telling ourselves that we have expanded the breadth and the depth of Chinese literature."[8] By tracing the origins of modern Chinese poetry in Taiwan, Ya Hsien extols senior mainland poets such as Chi Hsien, Ch'in Tzu-hao, and Chung Ting-wen, who came to settle in Taiwan in the early 1950s. They started a new trend in modern poetry in Taiwan that was different from the mainland tradition. As we recall the resettlement of the Republican government on the island of Taiwan in 1949, and the fact that literary censorship was imposed upon all Leftist writings, we can see why the Chinese poets in Taiwan were forced to seek a new poetics. This is perhaps the reason for the exclusion of mainland Chinese poets from Ya Hsien's anthology. However, after confirming this independent, constructive poetic buildup in those early years, we cannot but wonder at the inevitable influence of mainland Chinese poetry on Taiwanese poets. This is the case regardless of whether we perceive this manifestation to have been implicit or explicit. Senior poets can still remember how those "rare editions" of "hand-copied" banned books were circulated privately among themselves in the early years. Starting in the 1980s, more cultural exchanges took place between the governments of Taiwan and mainland China. Although books published on the mainland and printed with simplified Chinese characters are not allowed to be sold in Taiwan, the works of mainland poets like Ho Ch'i-fang, Feng Chih, Pien Chih-lin, and Hsin Ti, who were once censored and forgotten, are now widely read in reprints and are well remembered.

It is understandable that due to diverse political ideologies, the Republican government in Taiwan cannot afford to risk identifying its modernity with part of the historical consciousness of mainland Chinese literature. There are exceptions, though. In celebration of the sixtieth anniversary of the Republic of China in 1973, the Cheng-chung Bookstore, a cultural enterprise run by the central Kuomintang Party, published an anthology entitled *Poetry of Sixty Years,* with an editorial staff of fourteen writers. The collection started off with Hu Shih heading the list and, together with a few other mainland poets, included poets from Taiwan as a sign of its continuity with the Chinese poetic tradition of the previous six decades. Many important mainland poets were left out, however, and this is understood to be due to the official image of the Cheng-chung Bookstore and the socialist status of these poets. Nevertheless, the anthology represents a quantum leap in the further realization of a poetic reality. Seven years later Lin Ming-teh and his associates edited the *Anthology of New Chinese Poetry* (Ch'ang-an Press, 1980), in which they attempted to broaden their scope by adding more mainland poets. This edition is a collection of poetic groups: Hu Shih and Shen I-mo are called "Poets of the Early Phase"; Hsu Chih-mo, Li Chin-fa, and others are poets of the "Crescent and Symbolist Schools"; and Kao Lan, Feng Ch'eng-chih, and others are "Poets of the War of Resistance." Regarding poets from Taiwan, Chi Hsien, Cheng Ch'ou-yu, and the rest are "Modernists," whereas Ya Hsien, Lo Fu, and others are the "Epoch Poets." Ch'in Tzu-hao and Yu Kwang-chung are the "Blue Stars," and Pai Ch'iu, Lin Huan-chang, and others are poets from the "Bamboo Hats" and the "Dragons." Finally, Lo Ch'ing, Wu Sheng, and others are called "Poets of a New Generation."

Due to limitations of space, the *New Chinese Poetry* volume could not afford to include more poets and their works. However, on the one hand it is gratifying to see an anthology such as this exhibiting the proper attitude toward historical consciousness and thereby acknowledging its mainland maternity. On the other hand it is regrettable that due to unnecessary political restrictions, the anthology still fell victim to political taboos. In order to disguise the Leftist identities of certain poets, the editors deliberately changed their real names or in other instances replaced their pseudonyms with real names. This resulted in a horrendous confusion of identities: Ping Hsin was changed to Hsieh Ying-wan (a distortion of her real name, which is Hsieh Wan-ying); Wen I-to became Wen Chia-hua, which is his real name; Tsang K'e-chia was changed to K'e Chia, Mu Mu-t'ien to Mu T'ien (with another homonym, Mu), Pien Chih-lin to Chi Ling, Li Kuang-t'ien to Kuang T'ien, Ho Ch'i-fang to Ch'i Fang, Ai Ch'ing to Hai Teng. Finally, Feng Chih was changed to Feng Ch'eng-chih, which is his real name. A reader well trained in modern Chinese poetry may find little or no difficulty in determining who is who, but a layman may well find himself walking a labyrinth of historical shadows.

Mention was made earlier that in 1989 the Hungfan Bookstore published *Modern Chinese Poetry,* covering a period of seventy years, from 1917 to 1987. The two editors, Yang and Cheng, attempted to present a more complete picture by including poets from the mainland, Taiwan, and Hong Kong. In doing so, they not only emphasized the fact that modern Taiwanese poetry is indeed part of the mainland tradition, but also indicated that the poets from Hong Kong are used to redefine overseas Chinese poetry within the context of modern Chinese poetry in Taiwan. When Ya Hsien first included overseas poets from Southeast Asia and the United States in his anthology, he was primarily concerned with poetry written in the Chinese language. According to him, overseas poems composed in Chinese deserve a place in the mainstream of Chinese poetry. However, we soon discover that within the past forty years the expressions as well as the national sentiments in many overseas poems are quite different from those found in the verse of either the mainland or Taiwan. As we retrospectively review the development of modern Chinese poetry in the second half of the twentieth century, we see that modern poetry in Taiwan undoubtedly played a leading role. Nevertheless, it should neither fill the role of prodigal son and deny its maternal tradition nor claim independence for the unique features that it has manifested over the past forty years. Obviously, in considering the status of overseas poets, Yang and Cheng claim Taiwan as their home base. Hong Kong poets such as Tai T'ien, Hsi Hsi, Ku Ts'ang-wu, and Liang Ping-chun are included, not because they are identified with British colonialism, but primarily because of their Chinese attachments. Although the anthology has not included poets like K'un Nan or Ma Lang, who, with their modernist tendencies—some dating from the early 1950s—had interacted with the modernists in Taiwan, the collection's inclusion of other young poets certainly widens the spectrum of poetry from Taiwan by including a variety of coherent voices.

As a result of the closer relationship between Taiwan and mainland China in the 1980s, *Modern Chinese Poetry* had the opportunity to present mainland poets exclusively and to use their authentic names. There was no need to disguise the pseudonym with a "false pseudonym," and for the first time Chinese socialist poets could appear before the Taiwanese audience without blemish or political distortion. At the same time, young mainland poets like Bei Dao, Chiang Ho, To To, Shu T'ing, Yang Lien, and Ku Ch'eng were intermingled with Taiwanese poets of the same age group: Su Shaolien, Tu Yeh, Ch'en Yi-chih, Yang Tse, Hsiang Yang, Lo Chih-ch'eng, Hsia Yu, Liu K'e-hsiang, Ch'en K'e-hua, and Lin Yao-teh.

Coupling half a century of closed-door policies with the West and unceasing class struggles and social restlessness (from the rectification movement of the Land Reform in 1952 to the end of the Great Cultural Revolution in 1977), it is not surprising that poetry writing in mainland China has been largely static and governed by political slogans. The emergence of the Misty Poets in the post-Mao period shed some light on the gloomy scene, but their poems are too dim to illuminate the way. After the Tiananmen Square incident of 4 June 1989 many young poets chose exile overseas. Bei Dao is now in Denmark, and Ku Ch'eng is in New Zealand. Taiwan, on the other hand, has enjoyed at least thirty years of political stability and industrial growth, producing an intricate, Western-oriented culture which is different from China's Marxist society. The most obvious token of literary westernization in Taiwan has been the influx of modernist poetics.

The coming of modernism to Taiwan—as well as its reception and repulsion—makes an interesting tale. As noted above, after the nationalist government moved to Taiwan and severed its literary connections with the socialist mainland, the literary vacuum created on the island prompted a quick acceptance of modernism, along with the French symbolist practices of Chi Hsien and Ch'in Tzu-hao. These are the extrinsic factors. Intrinsically, the major reason for the acceptance of modernism lay in the search for a greater creative space. The introduction of Western modernism to Taiwan is the second transplant of westernization after that of 1919, with the former aimed at breaking away from the classical tradition and the liberation of the vernacular Chinese language. Forty years later the use of the vernacular language has proven quite a remarkable success in fiction and prose, but not in poetry of a high linguistic density. The highly condensed language in Western "pure poetry" provided a perfect remedy for the Chinese to ingest. Like Debussy's revolt against the classical eloquence of musical speech through the introduction of spaces or poetic pauses, modernism enhanced the Chinese poetic diction by creating poetic spaces from linguistic density.

Still, we know that modernism is fundamentally a postwar product of the West. It came to Taiwan as a result of a political schism and filled the resultant literary vacuum. In fact, the early social conditions in Taiwan from 1950 to 1960 made the acceptance of the disillusioned modernists problematic; indeed, most Chinese did not even have enough leisure time to harbor illusions. Those were days of hardship and struggle in a preindustrial society that was recovering from Japan's oppressive colonial rule and the remnants of the Pacific War. On the artistic level, where poets were eager to enhance their expression with highly condensed language, the impact of modernism was enormous; however, great disparity existed between the lives of the masses and the artistry of these modernists. While most people were struggling to settle down in Taiwan, many poets were sadly immersed in the "fin de siècle." As a result, although the modernists achieved a high degree of skill in diction and in the dexterous use of images and metaphors, they also became victims of hollow, individual feelings. When Taiwan achieved economic affluence in the 1970s, the rise of "native literature" or the realism of local color as a countervailing movement posed a strong threat to modernist poetics. However, the native literature movement did not last long enough to replace modernism, whose survival into the 1990s has allowed for the arrival of postmodernism to be proclaimed in Taiwan.

If we were to see modernism as a foreign product under the misplacement of time and place (a common modernist paradox), then no matter how vigorously Hassan, Jameson, and the rest promoted the postmodernist phenomenon in Taiwan, it became just another effect of a foreign cause. At least Marxist dialectics cannot convincingly create a discourse to explain the interweaving phenomenon of modernism-realism in the modern poetry of Taiwan, not to mention the fact that Confucian ethics still play a determining role in the cultural matrix. In addition, the once-dominant desire for a native literature as a base for modern Chinese literature and the closer ties between the two political entities of Taiwan and the People's Republic of China have left us in the precarious position of tracing the development of modern Chinese literature through the application of Western literary theory.

In May of 1990 the "Book Reviews" ("K'ai-chuan") section of the *China Times Daily* published a special issue in memory of the Dragon Boat Festival and the classical poet Ch'u Yuan. The editor suggested strategies for reading and understanding five categories of modern poetry: the erotic, the obscure, the unexpected, the eccentric, and the unsensational. Five young writers were asked to explain each of these five categories.[9] Many explanations were made using a heavily postmodernist emphasis. It may be true that these strategies help readers understand more about modern Chinese poetry with a postmodernist orientation, but whether postmodernist poetry exists as a genre of modern Chinese

poetry is still in doubt. So far we have not seen a strong tendency in the young poets to follow any elements of the five categories suggested by the "K'ai-chuan" editor. The crisis of modern poetry's poor readership and marketability is more a sociocultural phenomenon than a literary one. We may have to evaluate and reassess the changing values of an industrial society as the underlying factor rather than attempt to alleviate our "inferiority complex" by playing catch-up with Western avant-garde theory. There is no more literary vacuum, no political interference on the island of Taiwan now. Postmodernism should not be allowed to land there in the guise of a literary savior, although it is undoubtedly true that such external stimuli can prevent the running poetic water from becoming a stagnant pool. The age in which Western thought led the change in modern Chinese poetry is past. Today the critic's mission is not to use obscure theories to explain obscure poems; rather, it is to make his audience aware that obscurity is but one of many poetic tools—though by no means the only one. The main objective of editors and critics—as careful literary arbiters—should be to stabilize and formulate the mainstream of the national poetic tradition. To achieve these ends, there is no need for them to lose either themselves or their audience in the twisting and turning streams of foreign literary-critical methodologies.

Dominic Cheung, Summer 1991

[1] See "Foreword," in *Poetry of the Sixties,* Chang Mo and Ya Hsien, eds., Kaohsiung, Ta Yeh Bookstore, 1961, p. 6.

[2] See "Postscript," in *Poetry of the Seventies,* Chang Mo, Ya Hsien, and Lo Fu, eds., Kaohsiung, Ta Yeh Bookstore, 1967, p. 349.

[3] See "Preface," in *Poetry of the Eighties,* Chi Hsien et al., eds., Taipei, Lien-mei, 1976, p. 1.

[4] For example, the anthology *Poetry 1982* would be more accurately referred to as *Poetry 71,* since the Gregorian year 1982 equates to the Chinese Republican year 71. The easiest way to convert the Gregorian to the Chinese dates is to drop the first two digits, the 19, and to subtract eleven from the remaining two digits. Therefore, if we drop the 19 from 1982, we have just 82. Subtracting eleven from this leaves us with the Chinese Republican year 71. Hence, *Poetry 1982* becomes *Poetry 71.*

[5] See "Introduction," in *Poetry 1983,* Chang Mo, ed., Taipei, Elite, 1983, p. 4.

[6] Li Huan-hsien, "Foreword," in *Taiwanese Poetry 1982,* Taipei, Avant Garde, 1983, p. 6.

[7] See "General Preface," in *A Comprehensive Anthology of Contemporary Chinese Literature in Taiwan, 1970–1989,* Yu Kwang-chung, ed., Taipei, Nine Songs, 1989, p. 3.

[8] *A Comprehensive Anthology of New Literature in Contemporary China,* Ya Hsien, ed., Taipei, T'ien Shih, 1980, p. 27.

[9] See "K'ai-chuan," no. 27, in *China Times Daily,* 25 May 1990, which contains "The Erotic: The Tone of Blackness of Modern Poetry" by Chang Kuo-chih, "The Obscure: The Meanings in

Wordplays" by Ch'en Shu-hsin, "The Unexpected: Reading Poetry as an Exorcist Experience" by Chuang Yu-an, "The Eccentric: The Noneccentricity of Eccentricity" by Hsu Wang-yun,
and, last but not least, "The Unsensational: The Calmness of
a Computer" by Meng Fan. There is also an interview by Wang
Jui-hsiang entitled "Who Killed Modern Poetry?"

From Utopian to Dystopian World: Two Faces of Feminism in Contemporary Taiwanese Women's Fiction

■ INTRODUCTION

With the impact of feminism and the rise of the
women's movement in Taiwan since the 1970s, fiction
written by and about women has grown rapidly, especially in the 1980s. As Taiwan has moved toward modernization and democracy, its reception of feminism has
met with great resistance. Although the first and second
waves of the women's movement laid the groundwork
for diverse women's organizations to sprout in the late
1980s, most of these activities were carried out in a way
that would not appear directly threatening to traditional
Chinese values and mores.[1] As a result, though the
number of women writers increased and sensitive
"taboo" issues related to gender and sex were explored
in their works, few of them challenged directly the underlying patriarchal assumptions and ideologies.

Chinese women writers and their writing have long
been marginalized and classified under the diminutive
term *Gueixiu pai* (feminine group), a category in which
conventional themes of love, marriage, and romantic relationships are dealt with in a predictable, stylized form
and from a sentimental perspective. With the emergence of feminist consciousness, however, some women
writers began expressing their personal experiences and
political concerns openly in their works in a more experimental way. Representative among these writers are
Li Ang, Lu Xiulian (Lu Hsiu-lien), Li Yuanzhen (Lee
Yuan-chen), and Zhen Xinyi. Amid tremendous social
pressure and disapproval, they expose sexual inequality
long embedded in the patriarchal culture by exploring
new themes, images of women, and literary forms.

Lu Xiulian's *Zhe sange nuren* (These Three Women;
1985) and Li Ang's *Shafu* (1983; Eng. *The Butcher's
Wife*) are historic landmarks of fiction by two important
women writers from Taiwan that express female consciousness. On the surface, in terms of characters, subjects, and literary forms, these two novellas are written
from seemingly contrasting points of view. "These
Three Women" focuses on modern Taiwanese intellec-

tual women's search for a new identity, *The Butcher's
Wife* on the sexual exploitation of a peasant woman.
However, each work was created in a self-
acknowledged attempt by the author to be "feminist"[2]—that is, to expose directly and critique the patriarchal oppression and injustice which have victimized
women, on the one hand, and to provide their own visions of gender, sex, and womanhood on the other. Although the receptions accorded the two works in Taiwan represent opposite ends of the spectrum, they
realize, I propose, such an attempt from *different* perspectives: "These Three Women" through reconstructing a new womanhood in a more optimistic, utopian
light; *The Butcher's Wife* through deconstructing the traditional patriarchy from a more pessimistic, dystopian
angle.

The impact of these two works, I believe, is equally
significant, for each not only calls for the end of total
patriarchal domination but also marks the beginning of
a more hopeful era for women in their homeland. In addition to giving strong warnings against gender inequity
and sexual violence toward women, both works impart
empowering messages of the urgent need for consciousness-raising and sociopolitical change. Above all, the
importance of reclaiming the female values of connectedness and mutual understanding is emphasized, explicitly or implicitly.

As a general approach in analyzing these two
works, I have adopted the idea of "gyno criticism" and
apply it here across cultural boundaries.[3] I will focus
mainly on the writings of Lu Xiulian and Li Ang. By discussing these two women authors' distinctive ideas on
feminism and womanhood, on the representations and
new images of women, on the issues of sexuality and
domestic violence, on their relationship to other
women, and on the reception of their own works, I
hope that I may better acquaint readers in the West with
these two women writers, their personal and political
experiences, and their unique literary voices from the
Eastern tradition.

■ LU XIULIAN'S UTOPIAN VISION

A Pioneering Woman and New Feminism. Lu Xiulian (b.1944), commonly known as the "mother" of
the women's movement in Taiwan, is an important activist and writer whose so-called new-feminist ideology
has exerted great influence and caused considerable turmoil on the social, political, and literary scene of her
time. As the leader of the first-wave women's movement
in Taiwan (the "pioneering period," 1972–82), she
challenged patriarchal hegemony and paved the way for
feminism in Taiwan. With a B.A. in political science
from the National Taiwan University and Master's de-

grees in law from the University of Illinois and Harvard University, Lu is vocal and prolific. In addition to writing articles and essays and delivering speeches on equal rights and women's problems, she has also set up hotlines for abused and underprivileged women and organized a publishing house, Tuohuang Zhe (Pioneers), focusing primarily on the discussion of women's issues.

Lu's nonfiction work *Xin nuxing zhui* (New Feminism; 1974, 1986) provides the defining characteristics of her "new feminism" and "new woman," even including a song at the end to rally all women around a new way of life.[4] The book includes a survey of the status of women in America, Japan, Korea, and China, as well as critiques of traditional ideas imposed on women. The characteristics of her new feminism are: first, it emphasizes women as human beings and the importance of their independence and equality; second, it stresses cooperation between the sexes and the birth of "new men" as essential to the emergence of "new women"; and third, it encourages women to develop their intelligence fully and to realize their talents (156–57). In addition to her semiautobiographical works,[5] Lu later created one of her first fictional experiments—"These Three Women"—while in prison due to her political involvement. As an important literary narrative from prison, this fictional trilogy provides surprisingly positive models of intellectual new women and presents an optimistic vision of the feminist ideologies embedded in the author's previous works.

Although some feminists today consider Lu's ideas too "middle-class" and not "radical" enough,[6] her efforts as a pioneer who consciously rejects the total reception of Western feminism, I contend, should not be underestimated.[7] Her special contribution lies in her vision of combining Western and traditional ideas of womanhood and in her charisma, which attracts numerous intellectual volunteers to carry on women's tasks. Among these "recruits" is Li Yuanzhen, who later became the founder of the Awakening Foundation[8] and the leader of the second wave of the women's movement (the "awakening period," 1982 to the present) after Lu.

Recently elected as one of the few female legislative members of Parliament after twenty years as a political outsider, Lu has once again returned to the political arena to continue her work on behalf of democracy and liberation for women.[9] Aside from disagreements over her specific brand of feminism or her particular political strategies, what is worth mentioning is her power in voicing her visions along with her stamina in fighting for them, even under the most difficult situations. As one of the models of a modern new woman herself, Lu has demonstrated the courage and strength to be a female pioneer in her homeland, despite persecution and controversy.

■ **BONDS OF NEW WOMANHOOD**

Written on the toilet seat and the floor of a prison cell, "These Three Women" was intended, according to the novella's preface, to convey and illustrate Lu Xiulian's ideas on "new feminism."[10] In fact, the story is at times filled with didactic passages on women's issues to the extent that Lu herself admits that the book can be read as "nonfiction." Regardless of its genre, the work is important in terms of women's literature in Taiwan in that the author openly proclaims it to be "feminist" by intention, a gesture that still requires much courage in Taiwan.

"These Three Women" is a trilogy on the life of an independent modern new woman, Gao Xiuru, and the inspiration she provides for her two close female friends, Xu Yuzhi and Wang Yun, both in their early forties. The story begins with each of them questioning the prescribed roles for women and the pressure of social expectations and ends with all three women finding their own respective solutions and new way of life. Revealed in the process is the author's optimistic attempt to provide a new map for Chinese womanhood through her intricate weaving of a spiritual female community transcending the boundaries of time and space.[11] The story interconnects the lives and struggles of these middle-aged women, graduated from the same college in search of autonomy and new identity. The setting includes Taipei and San Francisco and spans from the 1960s to the 1970s. The numerous obstacles they each encounter relate in one way or another to sex, money, and race: traditional stereotyped roles in marriage and parenting, prejudices against the single life and widowhood, and cultural conflicts and a sense of displacement in the West, among others. Emotionally relating to and supporting one another, however, these women living on the "margins" of the male-centered Chinese and American context manage to re-create their otherwise restricted existence and cease to be passive, "muted" individuals.[12]

In addition to constructing alternative ways of living for modern women, Lu Xiulian's novella provides a direct critique of traditional values and the injustices they impose on women. For example, according to Xu Yuzhi's mother, Chinese girls are like "vegetable seeds" whose fate, once they have been spread on the ground, is totally out of their own control (24). Other traditional concepts are also questioned during Xiuru's soliloquy, including the "three obediences and four virtues," imposed female chastity, practices such as concubinage, and preference for sons over daughters. Furthermore, modern women's issues such as abortion, teenage pregnancy, sexual abuse, extramarital affairs, and property and inheritance rights, among others, are explored throughout the book, especially through the voices of Gao Xiuru and Wang Yun.

The female characters of "These Three Women" represent different types of new women in the modern world portrayed in a positive light. With different family backgrounds, personalities, and ways of life, each of them eventually fulfills, in one way or another, the author's ideas of new womanhood. For financial and emotional autonomy, they step out of the familiar and secure domain of the kitchen and venture into the male-dominated world of the workplace while at the same time maintaining so-called feminine values and emotional rapport. Combining indigenous and Western ideas, Lu's presentation of their new ways of life emphasizes above all the importance of social service and a sense of community based on the female principles of nonaggression, interconnectedness, and mutual support. These are, I believe, the important characteristics of Lu's writing that have been overlooked by critics in general.

All three women eventually embrace the (Western) idea of autonomy; they manage either to acquire the capability of working independently outside their family or to pursue careers of their own choice. At the same time, they consciously choose to preserve some of the qualities considered typically "feminine" in traditional Chinese culture such as the joy of cooking, raising children, knitting, and taking physical care of oneself. Above all, they learn to reach out to one another and to other sisters and children of the world.

Female Discourse and Style. In an attempt to reconstruct new womanhood and women's spiritual community in her fiction, instead of following the traditional linear narrative form (with a beginning, middle, and end) and male discourse (with its logical, masculine tone), Lu Xiulian invents a nonlinear, open narrative form and adopts female discourse to express her literary vision. The literary form of "These Three Women" is a novella in three parts, a trilogy with the subtitles "You peng zi yuanfang lai" (A Friend from Afar), "Jinsi hesi" (Tonight, Which Night), and "Hui shou" (Looking Back). Each story is narrated from the perspective of one of the three female protagonists as she reflects and muses on bits and pieces of her life and the lives of her women friends in memories and projections. As the heroine of each story speaks in dramatic monologue in the text, the lives of these three women—their dreams, aspirations, and struggles, their past, present, and future—gradually (and almost synchronically) unfold before the reader in a nonlinear, spiral form.

The structure of these three episodes can be seen as a triangle, with each story independent of yet interconnected with the others, just like the lives of the three heroines, separate yet interrelated and ultimately commingled. A spiritual community of women across geographic boundaries gradually evolves as these women learn from one another to reconstruct creatively and to reconnect their individual lives with significant others (women, children, and men) around them. What is worth noting is that each heroine is given her own unique voice and viewpoint. Through the use of first-person internal monologues delivered during the performance of traditional women's everyday activities and chores such as preparing meals, reading letters, bathing, and dressing, the reader is made privy to the meandering flow of their consciousness and thus shares in their most private lives and inner secrets.

The general tone of the three women's language is familiar and conversational, an everyday feminine style: chitchatting, intimate, repetitive, soul-exchanging. It is all soothing, relaxing, almost mesmerizing; the reader is treated as an imaginary confidante with all the secrets and stories poured out from the bosom of these heroines. This also makes their didactic remarks and lessons at times more acceptable for the reader.

The Communal Vision. With "These Three Women," Lu Xiulian has constructed a fictional community of positive new women with a nearutopian vision. In her imaginary Eden her heroines reclaim their female consciousness and find their own identity by venturing into new territory. Although the work is not "great" in terms of literary technique—it was the author's first attempt at writing fiction—it is historically and politically significant in that it not only creates intellectual, independent women characters as counterparts to the traditional ideal, submissive female figures hitherto predominant in Chinese literature, but also provides direct critiques of patriarchal values and inspiring blueprints for a new feminist world.

Lu's vision may seem overoptimistic. For example, she does not directly cut through the biased system of marriage; her model of the "new woman" at times comes dangerously close to an oversimplified "superwoman" syndrome—the double workload, the expectations and pressure from both the family and the job—and her idea of "new men" is never fully developed in her fiction. Nevertheless, her ideas on sexual equality, community support, and cooperation between women and men are timely starting points that suggest various possibilities for women following in her footsteps. Dedicated to her mother and her fellow sisters, "These Three Women" reveals the significance of emotional/spiritual bonding among women and the power and strength of femininity as culturally defined in the East.

■ LI ANG'S DYSTOPIAN WORLD

Another Taiwanese woman writer whose work is intentionally "feminist" is Li Ang. Although she shares a pioneering feminist awareness with Lu Xiulian, Li Ang creates a fictional world which is a near antithesis of that found in "These Three Women." Her dark dystopia in *The Butcher's Wife* carries a powerful message by portraying a male-centered world in which violence and domination rule while female values of connection and understanding are virtually absent.

Gender, Sex, and Violence. Like Lu Xiulian, Li Ang was influenced by Western feminist thinking and the women's movement in Taiwan. As a talented writer, she started out at age seventeen dealing with sensitive topics related to young women from her hometown of Lugang and was especially notable for her depiction of their emotional and sexual world. During the 1970s she apparently came in contact with works by and about Simone de Beauvoir, Virginia Woolf, and Germaine Greer, among other feminist writers, and was fascinated by them.[13] Li followed her sister's footsteps and received her Master's degree in theater from the University of Oregon in the 1980s. It was after her return from the United States that she wrote and published most of her "feminist" works, including fiction such as *The Butcher's Wife* and *Anyeh* (Dark Night; 1985)[14] and nonfiction such as *Nuxing de ijien* (Woman's Opinions; 1984) and *Waiyu* (Extramarital Affairs; 1984). For the latter two works, she wrote newspaper columns expressing her views on modern women's dilemmas within a so-called Taiwanese context and conducted surveys and research on the issue of extramarital affairs (a new form of polygamy and concubinage) to uncover its causes and the effects it has on both women and men. Although she did not participate directly in the women's movement per se, her spiritual involvement is evident from the review she wrote of Lu's work and from her contributions to feminist journals such as *Nuxing Ren* (Woman-Mankind), for which she serves as the managing editor.[15]

As a young female writer entering the male domain of commentary on issues related to gender, sexuality, and power, Li was met with public disapproval.[16] Despite obstacles, however, in the early 1980s she completed *The Butcher's Wife* (the Chinese title literally means "killing one's own husband"), one of the most disturbingly powerful works in the history of Taiwanese literature, exposing patriarchal oppression and exploitation through the subtle manipulation of food, money, and sex.

The Butcher's Wife is a story of the trials and tribulations of Linshi, a young peasant woman from the fishing village of Lugang in southeastern Taiwan at the turn of the century. By presenting the mysterious case of such a peasant woman's "murder" of her husband first through news reports, then through the story proper, the author leads readers through Linshi's life from different perspectives in order to let them form their own conclusions with regard to the cause, effect, and significance of such a tragic event. The unequal relationships between men and women in a marriage system, the biased social customs and religious superstitions, and the powerful control exerted by "gossips," "rumors," and the media in a patriarchal society are all portrayed, questioned, and challenged in the course of uncovering the mystery of the protagonist's intention to kill her husband.[17]

Although the novel won Li Ang a literary award and widespread recognition, it was actually misunderstood and was received rather negatively by the reading public and critics due largely to their perception of the explicit sexual descriptions in the novel as "perverse" and of the climactic act of husband-murdering as "immoral" regardless of the reasons.[18] One of Taiwan's most controversial writers, Li was not only rejected by the conservative "dominant" group for being "outrageous" and promoting disharmony in the family and society, but was also regarded by some local feminists as being too elitist and not sufficiently "radical."[19] Above all, both groups criticized the tragic ending of *The Butcher's Wife* and its pessimistic, gloomy outlook for Chinese women. Suffering from the pressure of severe criticism in the author's homeland, the book was, ironically, much better received in the West by some sympathetic critics,[20] resulting in its translation into several foreign languages, including English, German, French, and Japanese.[21]

Despite her work's being marginalized by critics in her own country, Li nevertheless has continued to pursue such taboo issues as sex, violence, and domination even though the general public still remains silent on such common practices as the keeping of mistresses and concubines, trade in aboriginal adolescent prostitutes, and marital abuse and rape.[22] It is out of her sympathy for and sense of justice toward sexually oppressed women (both poor and rich, rural and urban), I believe, that she launched her attack on the patriarchal evils of her own society by exposing its horrifying "realities" from a woman's viewpoint.

Perhaps the deepest misunderstanding of *The Butcher's Wife* has been the notion of critics that the novel is too pessimistic and therefore lacking in empathy and human bonding. In my view, this reveals a double misapprehension of Li Ang's work. First, the author *does* give important glimpses of such a connection several times in the novel: in the female protagonist Linshi's caring for a small brood of ducklings, in her initial responsiveness to her neighbor Auntie Ahwang's signs of concern, and even in the butcher's gentle, open relationship with his prostitute-friend Jinhua (Golden Flower). Thus Li shows the possibility of empathy and connection even within the dark social nightmare she is presenting. Second, and perhaps more important, she heightens the reader's awareness of the problem she is portraying precisely by leaving these possibilities for compassion and bonding unfulfilled. For example, her ducklings are ruthlessly slaughtered by her husband; her neighbor's concern turns out to be insincere, as she gossips about Linshi's shameless screaming at night without concern for the victim's predicament; and of course the tenderness shown by the butcher toward the prostitute vanishes when he returns home to beat and rape his wife.

The yearning for tender love and understanding and the creation of potential motherly and sisterly figures as sources of redemption in the novel is, I believe, related to the author's personal experiences. As the youngest of three daughters, Li Ang was influenced greatly and encouraged by her mother to think and live independently.[23] Her two literary sisters—Shi Shuqing, a professional writer now residing in Hong Kong, and Shi Shunu, a scholar and literary critic now living with the author near Taipei—also gave her the inspiration and support that she needed to be a writer herself.

Though pessimistic on the surface, *The Butcher's Wife* is a political work which protests sexual violence by depicting it in its fullest reality. Through the novel's metaphorical murder of the patriarchy, the status of women in Taiwan is moved a step forward symbolically. Above all, Li's novella is a subversive work of art that deconstructs the destructive forces of aggression and domination and thereby opens up various possibilities for the feminine principles of communication and compassion.

Femme Fatale or Victim? *The Butcher's Wife* is a powerful piece of feminist fiction that aims to destabilize the subtle patriarchal control and shock readers into consciousness. In contrast to Lu Xiulian's utopian world, it is a dark, dystopian work that serves to deconstruct the phallocentric world of sexual oppression and repression. Ideologically, it provides a critique of several dehumanizing practices involving sex and money, including arranged marriages, the control of food, and sexual assault, both verbal and physical.

In *The Butcher's Wife* the author attempts to subvert a dystopian patriarchal hell through the depiction of the female peasant protagonist Linshi's resistance to and rebellion against its total control. In the news reports at the beginning of the novel before the story proper actually begins, Linshi is condemned by an anonymous newspaper reporter in a "logical," "rational" tone of voice as a "fatal" and "immoral" woman who kills her husband for the sake of another man. According to the news report, "Chen Linshi's confession defies *reason and logic,* for, since ancient times, a murder of this sort has always been the result of an adulterous affair. We urge the *authorities* to launch a thorough investigation to determine the identity and precise role of the secret lover in this case. . . . The killing of a man by his wife is a moral issue that affects all of society. . . . [The] *authorities* must treat this case with the utmost severity" ("News Report #1," emphasis added). The image of Linshi here as a "debauched" woman to be severely punished as a moral lesson for all other women, however, is gradually demystified in the text through the narrator's skillful unfolding of Linshi's life story and the use of recurring symbols and dreams.

Instead of being an evil woman, the female protagonist turns out to be a silent victim in a male-dominated rural village. Readers are told that as a poor orphan, Linshi, together with her widowed mother, was driven out of her own house by relatives claiming that women have no inheritance or property rights. Later we see her as she witnesses at a young age the virtual raping of her mother by a soldier in exchange for food. After her mother is forced to "disappear" from the village, the unprotected, uneducated Linshi is taken in by her uncle and later married off to a butcher in exchange for a monthly supply of pork. In addition to being used as a commodity for trade, she is treated like a sex object, abused, beaten, and harassed by her brutal husband, bringing her ultimately to the brink of insanity. Far from being a bad woman as the news report portrays, Linshi is a victim of patriarchal domination and exploitation.

On a symbolic level, the image of Linshi as a powerless victim is often associated in the main text with that of a dehumanized puppet or a helpless animal. Deprived of proper food and nutrition, she is described as plain and flat in appearance, as if carved out of a piece of wood; she is skinny, with "a long face, long hands, long legs" (81), yellowish dry skin, and a stiff body. Her blank gaze and mechanical motions bespeak her pathetic death-in-life state of being. Deprived of all warmth, joy, and pleasurable human sexuality, she is reduced to the status of a sex object or a frightened animal.

The dystopian world of *The Butcher's Wife* is that of the butcher's slaughterhouse, with Linshi likened to the "bound pig" waiting to be sacrificed and Chen Jiangshui, her husband, associated with a butcher knife, an image of the penis as the essence of phallocentric control. The butcher's brutal slaughtering of pigs thereby symbolizes the aggressive sexual possession and violent victimization of female bodies.

The ultimate control of such an enclosed patriarchal hell is challenged, however, by Linshi's "defiant" act of murder. In a dreamlike, nightmarish atmosphere, we see the starving, harassed, abused wife get up in the middle of the night half-crazed, grab her husband's knife as it shines under the eerie moonlight, and coolly kill the sleeping butcher as if dissecting a pig. The act of taking over and using her husband's knife, a symbol of phallic power, subverts the existing relationship of male and female, of dominant and dominated. The power of a repressed woman's "wild" psyche that has been buried deep inside her unconscious is finally released and reclaimed, albeit in a maddened, surrealistic state.

In contrast to Lu Xiulian's hopeful vision of female community, Li Ang's dystopian vision seems devoid of human contact, true communication, and sisterhood. Although the women in "These Three Women" support one another emotionally, those in *The Butcher's Wife* isolate and persecute one another. Linshi's act of killing is a metaphorical rebellion against the horrible control of the human psyche, the control of body and mind. That is why in her "mad" murderous state Linshi even envisions the villagers' invisible verbal control as "countless bright red tongues noisily jabber[ing] on and on." Eventually she cannot but raise "the knife and hack and hack until the tongues [go] away" (138).

Male Discourse and Subversion. In contrast to Lu Xiulian's use of female discourse in her fiction, Li Ang assimilates mainstream male discourse in *The Butcher's Wife* to depict patriarchal "reality." The main text of the novel presents an enclosed, exclusive, suffocating, male-centered dystopia. Those who follow the patriarchal rules are endowed with the power of "truth" and control. For example, early in the story the elders of the Chen clan, in the name of traditional virtue, condemn Linshi's mother for being "unfaithful," "shameless," and expel her from her society simply because the starving widow exchanged sexual favors for a bowl of rice. The gossiping villagers, who blindly accept and spread rumors about Linshi and her mother for being "tainted" or "possessed" by evil spirits, also reinforce the subtle control of that society. Even the butcher Chen, himself an outcast due to his lowly profession, is given the power of control over his wife by virtue of his being a breadwinning husband. He never looks at Linshi directly, never calls her by her name, and often yells at her or scolds her with dehumanizing and degrading epithets such as "bitch" or simply "woman." In contrast, Linshi and her mother, who do not appear to follow the rigid rules of society voluntarily, are chastised and stripped of any power. They belong to the "muted group," excluded from the dominant one in terms of gender and class.

The formal structure of the text is like that of a frame story, with news reports at the beginning and end serving as secondary texts that introduce and conclude the main text. The news report that openly condemns Linshi and warns all Chinese women against "foreign" and "new" ways of life serves as the first layer of subtle social control. The male discourse of the text which intricately frames the female protagonist is, however, challenged and destabilized through the author's use of irony, through sarcasm in the news reports, and through the dreamlike, Gothic atmosphere of the murder scene itself. The two news reports remarking on female virtues undermine the general social attitude toward Linshi in particular and women in general. The "muted" discourse that emerges at times in Linshi's nocturnal dreams is mostly related to her repressed sexuality. The murder she commits in a state of "madness" can be seen as a symbolic reclaiming of the female psychic power, released only in the realm of the "wild" subconsciousness. The killing of her husband is thus a symbolic gesture subverting patriarchal control.

Beyond the Killing. Linshi's triumph is only transitory. She is eventually sentenced to death for transgressing the patriarchal structure. Meeting violence with violence obviously does not get to the root of the problem in reality, and the function of her action, I believe, lies in its symbolic gesture of resisting complete patriarchal colonization of and control over her body. The moral of the story, I suggest, does not lie in the combative act of murder itself, as some critics maintain, but rather in the gradual revealing of the naked "truth" through the stripping away of the many-layered "lies" that enfold the event. Far from encouraging readers to emulate the heroine's drastic act of revenge, the author opens our eyes by presenting the poignant struggle of a sexually abused woman on the verge. Li Ang's hope lies ultimately in her readers' understanding of the ugly "reality" and their awakening to the urgent need for changing such a dehumanizing, sexist society.

Whether victim or villain, Linshi is seen by some critics as not being a heroine with a feminist consciousness and therefore not a true "victor." Li Ang, however, has argued that it is unrealistic for a peasant woman such as Linshi to be aware of her predicament to such a degree as to rebel.[24] Moreover, several signs of resistance on the heroine's part throughout the novel are neglected by critics. Also, in the news report contained in the epilogue, presumably published after the sentencing of Linshi, readers are told that in reality the woman from Shanghai on whom the entire story is based eventually escaped her death sentence due to the end of the war between China and Japan. Such an arrangement in the frame text, I suggest, is significant in that it indicates a disruption of the patriarchal order's total domination and enclosure and reveals signs of hope for the "resisting" heroine both in fiction and in reality.

■ CONCLUSION

"These Three Women" and *The Butcher's Wife* are two historically important novels, for their appearance signifies the end of patriarchal domination and the beginning of a new era for women of both the middle and the lower class. The shared impact of the two authors Lu Xiulian and Li Ang in helping reshape the values in traditionally patriarchal societies and the possibilities for women in those societies comes from two strikingly different works of fiction. Lu reconstructs womanhood in a contemporary urban world of intellectual women in search of self-actualization. Their idealized progress toward independence and interdependence is conveyed in a trilogy of female narratives. Li Ang, in contrast, deconstructs the Chinese patriarchy through a dark dystopian world. The use of a male-dominated, authoritarian narrative encloses the poor peasant woman in early twentieth-century rural Taiwan without the possibility of self-realization or even of any meaningful degree of autonomy. With her literary subtleties, Li Ang is able to show the implausibility of the dominant group's view of the "evil," "murderous" heroine and to expose the destructiveness of the dominant value system.

In introducing feminist ideas into the Taiwanese context, both authors seem to point in their works to the often marginalized female values of connectedness, understanding, and compassion as constituting an exit: Lu by directly demonstrating the significance of these values through the "communal world" and bonds of her "new women," Li by indirectly presenting the complete lack of and therefore the urgent need for these values through the "phallic hell" of the butcher shop and the murder committed by her "madwoman" on the verge. The juxtaposition of these two works reveals the range and depth of problems confronting women in traditional Chinese societies and the possibilities for fiction as a means by which women can deconstruct and reconstruct the worlds they inhabit.

Ying-Ying Chien, Winter 1994

1   For a detailed discussion of the women's movement in Taiwan, see Ku Yen-lin, "The Feminist Movement in Taiwan, 1972–87," *Bulletin of Concerned Asian Scholars,* 20:1 (January-March 1989), pp. 12–22; and "The Changing Status of Women in Taiwan: A Conscious and Collective Struggle Toward Equality," *Women's Studies International Forum,* 11:3 (1988), pp. 179–86.

2   See Lu Xiulian, "Tiequang xia yiao bigan" [Writing Under the Iron Window], the preface to her *Zhe sange nuren* [These Three Women], Taipei, Zili Evening News, 1986, pp. 2–6; and Li Ang, *Shafu,* Taipei, Lianjin, 1986, pp. 8–9. All translations from Lu's book are my own; citations from Li's novel are based on Howard Goldblatt and Ellen Yeung's translation, *The Butcher's Wife: A Novel by Li Ang,* Berkeley, Ca., North Point, 1986.

3   For a detailed discussion of "gyno critique" or "gyno criticism," see Elaine Showalter, *New Feminist Criticism: Essays on Women, Literature, and Theory,* New York, Pantheon, 1985, pp. 247–50; and Sara Mills et al., *Feminist Readings / Feminists Reading,* Charlottesville, University Press of Virginia, 1989, pp. 83–121.

4   See the revised edition of Lu Xiulian's *Xin nuxing zhui* [New Feminism], Taipei, Dunli, 1986, p. 280. Misperceived by the alarmed government for the author's seemingly militant stance, the book was banned shortly after its first publication in 1974.

5   Among Lu Xiulian's semiautobiographical works are *Shuishu tuohuang de jiaobu* (Counting the Footsteps of Pioneering) and *Xinnuxing hequ hechong* (New Women: Where Are You Going?).

6   Some feminists complain that Lu Xiulian avoids the issue of homosexuality and overemphasizes the "traditional" feminine qualities.

7   According to Lu Xiulian herself, she deliberately includes some of the "feminine qualities" in her new feminist ideologies to counterbalance the so-called "Western feminism."

8   Li Yuanzhen is a professor of Chinese literature at Tamkang University. She organized the "Awakening Foundation," an active and leading local feminist organization in Taiwan. For a detailed discussion, see Ku Yen-lin, 1989, pp. 17–20.

9   See *Ms.,* 3:5 (March/April 1993), p. 10; 17 of Taiwan's 161 members of Parliament are female.

10   Lu Xiulian, *Zhe sange nuren,* p. 8.

11   For a discussion of women's community in literature, see Nina Auerbach, *Communities of Women: An Idea in Fiction,* Cambridge, Ma., Harvard University Press, 1978, esp. pp. 1–32.

12   See Showalter's idea of the "dominant group" versus the "muted group," in *Feminist Readings,* pp. 92–94.

13   Most of these works are translated by Yang Meihui and O Yangzi. See Ying-Ying Chien, "Women, Feminism, and Creativity: An Interview with Li Ang," *Chung-Wai Literary Monthly,* 17:10 (March 1989), p. 185.

14   See Michelle Yeh, "Shapes of Darkness: Symbols in Li Ang's *Dark Night,*" in *Chinese Women Writers: Critical Appraisals,* Michael S. Duke, ed., New York, Sharpe, 1989, pp. 78–95.

15   For Li's review of Lu, see *Zhe sange nuren,* pp. 227–30. *Nuxing ren* [Woman-Mankind] is a feminist journal that includes essays from North America, Taiwan, Hong Kong, and China. It is published in Taipei by Chen Youshi, who currently teaches at the University of Alberta in Canada.

16   See Howard Goldblatt, "Sex and Society: The Fiction of Li Ang," in his *World Apart: Recent Chinese Writing and Its Audience,* New York, Sharpe, 1990, pp. 150–65.

17   The story told in *The Butcher's Wife* reminds us of the "mad housewife" plays in early twentieth-century American literature, such as *Trifles* by Susan Glaspell, in which a stifling marriage and isolated village life lead to the heroine's murder of her husband. I surmise that this play might have been a possible source or inspiration for Li Ang.

[18] See *Fongqi yunyong de nuxing zhui piping* [New Waves of Feminist Criticism], Taipei, Gufong, 1988, pp. 254–90, 344–61.

[19] In the preface to "Women's Opinions" (Shibao, 1987, pp. 2–4) Li Ang explained why she was viewed by a few intellectual friends as "conservative" and "encouraging a bourgeois women's movement."

[20] See, for example, Howard Goldblatt, Carolyn See, and Richard Burgin, among others. Scholars participating in the 1986 "Commonwealth Modern Chinese Literature" conference held in Germany were considered especially "open-minded" by the author with regard to the reception of *The Butcher's Wife*.

[21] See the preface to Li Ang's new novel *Mi-yuan* [Lost in the Garden] (Taipei, Li Ang Series, 1991, pp. 1–2), in which the author explains how, with understanding and support from critics and readers in the West, she overcame inner and outer pressures and picked up her pen to complete the new book.

[22] At a national conference, for example, a female scholar's paper on "domestic violence" was once regarded as "not a professional topic" and unsuitable for inclusion in a formal scholarly meeting.

[23] Chien, p. 194.

[24] Ibid., pp. 184–85.

Central Asia

AZERBAIJAN

Theme and Character in the Azerbaijani Novel, 1930–1957

The modern Azerbaijani novel[1] was largely the product of far-reaching changes in social and economic life following the Bolshevik Revolution of 1917 and the formation of the Azerbaijan Soviet Socialist Republic in April 1920. The new regime was determined to create a "new life" for the inhabitants of the country through rapid industrialization and collectivization of agriculture and through the elimination of all vestiges of "obsolete" customs and mentalities. It reserved an important role for literature in achieving these aims, and during the 1920s party activists were busy mobilizing poets and prose writers for the tasks at hand. But at first in Baku, the political capital and intellectual center of the new republic, as elsewhere in the Soviet Union during this period, literary organization proceeded haphazardly, and writers indulged in a relative creative freedom, showing little inclination toward regimentation. Finally, in 1928 the party succeeded in establishing a single writers' organization—the Azerbaijan Association of Proletarian Writers (Azapp), a branch of the famous Russian association, Rapp. Azapp had as its mission the channeling of creative energies into officially approved projects, but it soon proved unequal to the task of bringing "order" into

the literary ranks. It was replaced in October 1932 by the Union of Soviet Writers of Azerbaijan, the body that henceforth was to oversee all literary activity in the republic. As with the establishment of Azapp, action on the Union in Baku followed the lead of Moscow.

Azapp and, with greater consistency and rigidity, the Union of Writers were responsible for imposing a set of social and esthetic values on Azerbaijani writers which came to be known as socialist realism. Adherence to its principles, which was mandatory, determined an author's choice of subject matter and handling of character. He was expected to depict broad social phenomena and individual personalities from the Marxist-Leninist standpoint. That meant he could not remain neutral toward his subject, but through his art had to show how social change occurred and why it must inevitably lead to a communistic "better world"; in identifying the chief actors in the drama, he was obliged to single out the "progressive forces" for praise while reviling their opponents. Finally, he had also to remember that his art was not only a reflection of reality, but served too as a powerful instrument for changing that reality. He therefore had to be involved in the fundamental issues of his time and had to construct plots and create characters that would explain to his readers what was taking place and inspire them to contribute unstintingly to the strengthening of Soviet power and the fulfillment of economic plans.

Three principles were of paramount importance in determining the content of a literary work. A poem or a novel had, first of all, to reflect *khelgilik* (Russian: *narodnost'*), or closeness to the life of the working masses, and *ideialylyg* (Russian: *idejnost'*), that is, the correct interpretation of current party policies. But by far the most important ideological and esthetic principle (they were never separate) which socialist realism imposed upon the writer was *partiialylyg* (Russian: *partijnost'*), which may be translated as party spirit or the acceptance of party directives in creative work. *Partiialylyg* supplied the proper viewpoint from which the author could observe and judge people and events. Adherence to it was thus essential for a correct understanding of all social phenomena. Together these principles impressed upon the writer that literature could never be divorced from society. Not surprisingly, the idea of art for art's sake was completely foreign to party ideologists and literary directors. They regarded the writer not as a creator of his own ideas or a judge of what was right and wrong, but as a purveyor of the ideas of others—i.e., of the party, which had taken upon itself the burden of revealing truth.

During the quarter-century with which we are concerned there were fluctuations in the degree to which the tenets of socialist realism were applied. During World War II, for example, a notable relaxation of ideological controls occurred in Azerbaijan as elsewhere in the Soviet Union. Then for almost a decade after the war Azerbaijani literature was dominated by the crude dogmatism of Zhdanovism. In a series of articles and speeches Andrei Zhdanov, the chief cultural theoretician of the Soviet Communist Party, elaborated an extreme version of socialist realism that stressed ideological conformity and the didactic functions of literature. He instructed writers to serve the people and the state, to show the superiority of the Soviet system over capitalist society and to shun "decadent" Western literary forms and subject matter.

Beginning in the 1920s, party ideologists promoted the novel as especially suited to achieving their ends because, unlike poetry and the short story, it provided a broad canvas upon which the epic events of revolution and social change could be fully and realistically depicted. Yet, despite this encouragement, no Azerbaijani novel appeared during the first decade of the Soviet regime. The reasons for this absence are complex. First of all, large-scale works of prose fiction had been relatively rare occurrences in Azerbaijani literature. Although cultivated prose in the Azerbaijani language can be traced back to the Middle Ages, poetry was the preferred means of expression in Azerbaijani literary circles, as it was generally in the Muslim world. By the middle of the nineteenth century a realist current began to make significant headway against mystical and romantic traditionalism, an innovation that owed much to increasing Russian intellectual and literary influences following the czarist annexation of Azerbaijan in 1828. Among the most important products of the new realism was the novel. The first Azerbaijani novel was *Aldanmysh kevakib* (Deceitful Stars; 1857) by Mirza Fatali Akhundov (1812–78), the outstanding Azerbaijani man of letters of the nineteenth century.[2] It was followed by such notable works as *Danabash kendinin ehvalatlary* (Events in the Village of Danabash; 1894) by Djalil Mamedkulizade (1866–1932), the great satirist, and *Bahadyr ve Sona* (Bahadyr and Sona; 1896) by Nariman Narimanov (1870–1925), one of the creators of the modern Azerbaijani drama. Nonetheless, poetry continued to be the dominant form of literary expression, and in prose the tale and sketch prevailed.

The absence of the novel in the 1920s may also be explained in part by the fact that all the serious prose of the decade was still being written by authors whose art had matured before the revolution and whose themes and modes of expression belonged to the earlier period. Time was needed to allow a new generation of writers to emerge who could assimilate the momentous

social changes that were taking place and could draw creative inspiration from them. In particular, they had to be convinced that existing genres—the short story and the sketch—were too narrow to encompass mass movements or to allow history its full sweep.

The maturing of the first generation of Soviet Azerbaijani novelists was undoubtedly accelerated by the achievements of Soviet Russian literature in the 1920s, which Azapp actively promoted. The themes and ideological direction of the Soviet Russian novel appeared far more relevant to young Azerbaijani writers than did their own prerevolutionary literature. The publication and subsequent translation into Azerbaijani of *Chapaev* (1923; translated 1929) by Dmitri Furmanov, *Cement* (1924; translated 1930) by Fyodor Gladkov and *The Rout* (1927; translated 1927 and 1929) by Alexander Fadeyev provided models and incentives for the reworking of their themes in accordance with local circumstances.

■ ■ ■

By the end of the 1920s, as a result of a complex process that included social mobilization, the Russian example and individual maturation, a group of Azerbaijani novelists emerged who had assimilated the new creative methods of socialist realism and who drew their themes from contemporary Soviet reality. In the limited space available I have selected for discussion six novelists whose works are representative of our period. The creators of the Soviet Azerbaijani novel were writers who had begun their careers after 1920: Süleiman Rahimov (b. 1900), Alekperzade Abülhasan (b. 1906), Mir Djalal (b. 1908), and Mehdi Hüsein (1909–65). I have also included Mamed Said Ordubady (1872–1950), who had experimented with the novel before 1917, and Mirza Ibrahimov (b. 1911), a short-story writer and dramatist who turned to the novel after World War II.

The themes they chose and the plots they constructed revealed the full extent of their debt to socialist realism. They were totally absorbed in contemporary social problems and adhered wholeheartedly to the interpretation of events provided by the party. Yet their concern with the revolutionary movement and with the collectivization of agriculture and industrialization was not at all extraordinary, because these were matters of overwhelming public concern. In one way or another the entire population had been drawn into the process of building socialism. Novels on these subjects were genuinely popular, for they provided the ordinary reader with a combination of adventure and moral uplift not unlike that found in the American Western novel. The sacrifices of dedicated workers and peasants to create new industries and make barren land bountiful, and the struggles of unselfish revolutionaries against enormous odds to defeat an enemy who stood in the way of a better life for all, could not but have inspired readers to emulate the heroes.

As for style and composition, these novelists remained faithful to traditional realist methods. Their treatment of plot and character was straightforward. They relied heavily upon historical and sociological details and their own observations, and they avoided experimentation with new prose forms. In the delineation of character they left no doubt as to who the heroes and the enemies were, since their main function was to personify good and evil as determined by prevailing ideological requirements. The heroes were usually identified as the "new men" because they represented the forces of constructive change and looked forward rather than backward. They were the individuals who before 1920 fought to overthrow the existing political system and establish a Bolshevik regime in Azerbaijan and who, afterward, led the drive to build a socialist order. In the front ranks were of course the revolutionaries, who were almost always drawn from the urban proletariat and the poorer peasantry. After the revolution the new men were usually the heads of local party organizations and the chairmen of collective farms. In their wake came workers and peasants who had distinguished themselves in defending the revolution and increasing production. Next came the young specialists, usually engineers, who were committed to finding ways of exceeding production goals, and finally there were selected intellectuals who, because they had absorbed the teachings of progressive Azerbaijani and Russian thinkers, could grasp the historical inevitability of socialism.

Whatever his particular function might be, the ideal hero invariably possessed certain essential qualities. Most important of all, he was the personification of *partiialylyg*. He had always to work within the guidelines set by the party; nonconformity or individual initiative that disregarded instructions from above, however well intentioned, was roundly condemned. Next, he had to display complete devotion to the revolution and the socialist transformation of society. For him the revolution was life itself. He was also expected to embody the principle of *khelgilik;* in other words, he had to grow with the masses and to sympathize with their needs and aspirations, while at the same time keeping in mind that his primary duty was to lead. Finally, he had to exercise self-discipline at all times; he could not allow his personal feelings to interfere with the carrying out of the vital tasks entrusted to him by the party.

Evildoers of every kind also abounded. They embodied all the negative aspects of the prerevolutionary social and economic order and served to put in still higher relief the virtues of the heroes. As a group they belonged to the past. In the rural areas they were the landlords, the kulaks and the Muslim clergy—all bearers of a "retrograde mentality" who opposed not only collectivization but every "progressive" change. In the cities the old order was represented by the propertied classes in general and the bourgeoisie in particular. Especially odious characterizations were reserved for persons who were associated with Western capitalism, who espoused Western intellectual and cultural values or who were Azerbaijani nationalists and pan-Turkists. All were held up as prime examples of moral and civic decay.

The treatment of major characters generally left much to be desired. Since they were conceived primarily as composite figures embodying a particular idea or representing an entire social class, their individual personalities tended to be submerged in the broad sweep of mass movements, which in turn were designed to illustrate appropriate interpretations of the nature of historical change. Hence both heroes and villains often seem stilted and artificial, as though drawn according to a preconceived formula. Moreover, their personalities undergo little significant development. The revolutionaries, for example, seem to have been born as such, and therefore, having already reached the highest level the human personality can hope to attain, they can progress no further. When change does occur, it is usually from a lower to a higher state of class (or revolutionary) consciousness, a process brought on by participation in some beneficial collective undertaking. Not surprisingly, then, characterizations were either all positive or all negative, depending upon social class and the degree of receptivity to revolutionary change. There was hardly any middle ground. The one-sidedness with which the hero, for example, was portrayed was also owing in large measure to the failure of the author to explore his inner self or to allow him to express spontaneous emotion. That omission was perhaps not surprising, since the concentration on large-scale movements tended to dwarf individual human feelings. But the essentially didactic function of the hero was also responsible. To plumb the psyche would be to reveal doubts and hesitations, weaknesses hardly befitting the builders of the new socialist order.

One of the staples of the Azerbaijani novel in its first quarter-century was the revolutionary movement before 1917 and the struggle to establish a Soviet regime between 1918 and 1920. An early, classic treatment of the theme was Süleiman Rahimov's *Shamo* (1931), which contains the main elements of the new socialist-realist novel. The author focuses on the role of the peasantry in the revolutionary struggles and its relationship with the urban proletariat. He shows how the peasantry was roused from extraordinary submissiveness toward its traditional masters and from an almost complete absence of social consciousness by the ideas of the Russian Revolution. The Bolsheviks, who were the chief propagators of these ideas, were responsible for the rapid growth of peasant class consciousness, because they alone were able to give form to the aspirations of the oppressed for genuine freedom.

Reinforcing the major theme at the personal level is the story of Shamo, a young shepherd who has come to Baku in search of work. He represents the generation of new men in process of formation. As with the masses, ideas decisively influence his development. Through Mirza Polad, a teacher who had been educated in the spirit of progressive Azerbaijani and Russian social thought (Akhundov, Mamedkulizade, Chernyshevky, Gorky) and who during the revolution of 1917 had joined the Bolsheviks, Shamo becomes acquainted with revolutionary thought, especially the works of Lenin. He joins the Bolshevik Party in Baku, where he develops a close friendship with the worker Eibat, a relationship which symbolizes the indestructible union of the proletariat and the poor peasantry. Now a mature, class-conscious worker, Shamo returns to his village to spread the ideas of communism. Through his tireless labors and their own participation in the revolution the peasants cease to be timid, defenseless beings, and following the lead of the proletariat, represented by Shamo, they finally take their destiny into their own hands.

Mir Djalal's *Dirilen adam* (The Man Who Was Born Again; 1935) is composed of similar ingredients. The time is the Civil War in 1918 and 1919, and the setting is Gandja and the surrounding villages. The contending forces are divided into two camps: the one is composed of Bolsheviks and their sympathizers, who are fighting for the rights of the working masses; the other is supported by landlords and capitalists, who, to save themselves, are ready to sell out the country to foreign imperialists (Turks, British, Germans). The author is especially hard on Azerbaijani nationalists, the so-called Musavatists, who had briefly gained the upper hand; he portrays them as brutish and anarchic and concerned only with self-enrichment. At the center of the action is Kadir, a poor peasant, who is "reborn" as his experiences of civil war accumulate. At first he enrolls in the nationalist army, but he is quickly disillusioned by the corruption of its leaders. His protests land him in prison. There he comes under the influence of Bolsheviks, who remold him into a revolutionary who enthusiastically joins the party.

The above formula for the "revolutionary novel" remained essentially unchanged throughout our period. The post-World War II classic of the genre is *Seher* (Morning; 1949–52) by Mehdi Hüsein. Set in the period between the two Russian revolutions of 1905 and 1917, the first part of the novel describes the life of the working classes of Baku, while in the second the scene shifts to the countryside. The link between them is Bairam, a poor peasant who is drawn to Baku by the promise of work. He quickly falls under the influence of Bolshevik workers, whose ideas about the coming proletarian revolution he accepts enthusiastically. Meshadi Azizbekov, their leader, is mainly responsible for Bairam's conversion. Every inch a Leninist, he is portrayed as the ideal Bolshevik revolutionary, whose humanity and wisdom and sense of civic responsibility prove irresistible to the masses. He is perhaps the true hero of the novel, since it is he who performs the central act—the transformation of a naïve, poorly educated farm boy into a self-conscious worker and proletarian revolutionary. Thus fortified, Bairam returns to his village, where, applying the lessons learned from his master, he stirs a downtrodden peasantry to class-conscious struggle for liberation.

Closely connected to the revolutionary theme was the metamorphosis of the traditional village through the collectivization of agriculture. This was the subject of the first Soviet Azerbaijani novel, Alekperzade Abülhasan's *Iokhushlar* (Ascent; 1930). The plot is simple: two groups—one that stands for a new village based on the needs of the peasant masses, and one which clings to the remnants of old structures—fight over collectivization. Here the new men must even overcome the indifference of the peasants themselves, because the latter have not yet adjusted to the "new tempo" of life and hence cannot appreciate the benefits of the kolkhoz. In the end the forces of progress, led by the chairman of the collective farm, the wise and forceful Aiaz, and the poor peasant Muzdur, prevail.

A major figure in Soviet Azerbaijani fiction—the "new woman"—makes her appearance in *Iokhushlar*. Following Abülhasan's lead, every novelist will henceforth chart the progress of her liberation from the traditions and taboos that had relegated her to perpetual inferiority. In *Iokhushlar* Gumru serves as the prototype of the emancipated woman. Her journey to a consciousness of her worth as a human being is similar to that of Shamo and Bairam. Like them, she finds self-fulfillment through participation in the struggle to create a new economic and social order. Breaking with the past, she joins the kolkhoz, attends a school for party activists in Baku and, as chairman of the village council, leads the drive for collectivization. Her social activism and intellectual achievements differentiate her from all previous Azerbaijani literary heroines.

Another representative novel of collectivization is Suleiman Rahimov's *Sachly* (1941), a broad panorama of the Azerbaijani village in the early 1930s. The plot is a familiar one and requires no elaboration. Of particular interest are the two protagonists, whose conflict reveals the central idea of the novel. Tahir Damirov, the regional party secretary, is a model hero. He is endowed with an enthusiasm and self-abnegation that have become proverbial in the village; he faithfully carries out party directives to strengthen local organizations, to get rid of remaining class enemies and to raise the younger generation in the spirit of communism. In all his acts he is guided by faith in the people and by a vision of the marvelous future promised by communism. By contrast, Gasham Sübhanverdizade, a district bureaucrat and a careerist in the pay of a foreign intelligence service, personifies the emptiness of the old moral system. Devoid of any feelings of responsibility toward the people and sensing the hopelessness of his position, he uses every means available to impede the triumph of socialism.

In all these novels the fate of individuals, heroes or villains, is subordinate to social and political ends. Their thoughts and actions are predictable, for, as in a morality play, good must triumph and evil perish. The heroes are invariably clear-eyed and optimistic; sorrow and discouragement are passing phenomena at best and are never allowed to determine behavior. Azizbekov, Damirov and even Shamo and Bairam are politicized beings who have adopted the party program as the basis of a new code of ethics. Although these men are by no means unattractive, their strict adherence to the code inevitably makes them less than flesh and blood.

After World War II novels continued to reflect the immediate goals of public policy. Special attention was accorded Soviet patriotism, economic recovery and the Cold War. Strangely, for almost a decade after 1945 only one Azerbaijani novel dealing with the Great Fatherland War (as the conflict was called in the Soviet Union) was published: Abülhasan's *Dostlug galasy* (The Bastion of Friendship; 1947–52). The work centers on the defense of Sevastopol by contingents from many Soviet nationalities. Its hero is Kaian Hajijiev, a young Azerbaijani soldier who fights selflessly beside his Russian "brothers." The author draws upon his own experiences in the campaign as an infantry lieutenant, and the finest pages of the novel are the realistic descriptions of battle and the sensitive probings of individual psychologies. Yet the reader is never allowed to forget the all-pervasive theme: the eternal friendship of the nationalities of the Soviet Union.

Representative of the postwar "production novels" is Mehdi Hüsein's *Absheron* (1947–48), which chronicles the rural classes' adjustment to life and work in Baku. The hero is once again a young, inexperienced peasant who has come to work in the oil fields and who is gradually transformed into a skilled, class-conscious worker by older, communist workers who had participated in the 1917 revolution. They are clearly the heroes of the piece, for they have placed the achievement of economic goals above personal ambitions.

The atmosphere of the Cold War suffuses Mirza Ibrahimov's *Gelejek gün* (The Day Will Dawn; 1948). Although the scene is the Azerbaijani-inhabited areas of northern Iran on the eve of World War II, the author clearly has in mind the contest between the Soviet Union and the West for control of Iran after 1945. The story pits the usual starkly differentiated classes against one another, but the enemies—the ruling elements of Iran—besides their corruption and brutality, are also beholden to "predatory Anglo-American imperialists." It is soon apparent that the only way out of misery and oppression for the common people of northern Iran (or, as it is called, southern Azerbaijan) is a democratic revolution and national self-determination for the Azerbaijanis. We find the experienced revolutionary Kurd Ahmed and his protégé—a young Azerbaijani student, Fridun, whom he has convinced of the injustice of the prevailing social system—at the head of workers, peasants and right-thinking intellectuals. Everyone without exception looks to the Soviet Union as the promised land of political and economic progress.

Ibrahimov must have felt especially constrained in writing *Gelejek gün,* because he was dealing with a most sensitive matter: nationalism. Like all Azerbaijani novelists, he had to find a way of integrating the specific customs and aspirations of his people into his work without violating the precepts of Soviet patriotism. In a sense, the party lightened the task by offering guidance within the framework of socialist realism under the banner, "National in form, socialist in content." Here national form was an aspect of *khelgilik,* for it meant continuous contact with the working masses, who were judged to be the true bearers of ethnicity; socialist content was assured by the operation of *ideialylyg,* which enforced a common set of ideological and esthetic values on all Soviet writers regardless of nationality. Andrei Zhdanov, as usual, minced no words. He warned minority writers to avoid glorifying the national past for its own sake and to treat it only within the context of the building of socialism.

The Azerbaijani novelists took these admonitions to heart. They stressed the camaraderie of the various nationalities of the Soviet Untion, as Abülhasan had done in *Dostlug galasy* or Hüsein in *Seher,* where Azerbaijani, Russian and Georgian revolutionaries worked and suffered together to overthrow czarism. Occasionally Azerbaijani nationalism could be an acceptable subject, if it manifested itself outside the borders of Russia or the Soviet Union, as in Ibrahimov's *Gelejek gün* or Mamed Said Ordubady's *Dumanly Tebriz* (Misty Tabriz; 1939–40), which detailed the revolutionary movement in northern Iran before 1917. But any suggestion that the Azerbaijanis might find happiness outside the Soviet Union was taboo. Even praise of those Azerbaijanis who had opposed Russian domination of their country under the czars was a serious violation of Soviet patriotism. Consequently, novelists gave "bourgeois nationalists" no quarter. In *Döiüshen sheher* (The Fighting City; 1933), a novel of the Civil War, Ordubady excoriated the Musavatists as traitors to Western imperialism, and in *Dünia gopur* (A World Collapses; 1933), which deals with the establishment of Soviet power in the countryside after April 1920, Abülhasan even denies their national feeling, portraying them as "cosmopolitans" completely divorced from the language and culture of their own people.

The controversy over nationalism raises the question of what was specifically Azerbaijani in the Azerbaijani novel. Obviously the setting, and the village in particular, was autochthonous and allowed authors to describe at length the mental climate and customs of the Azerbaijani people. The traditional way of life as it had existed before collectivization, although portrayed as backward and oppressive, often comes through in all its color and diversity, thereby enhancing the authenticity of the narrative. The novelists themselves seem more at home in the village than in Baku. Some of the finest work of Süleiman Rahimov and Mehdi Hüsein, for example, consists of descriptions of the rural landscape and portraits of its native inhabitants. In *Shamo* and *Seher* many of the secondary characters especially have preserved their earthiness in contrast to the new men, whose mental outlook and mannerisms betray the homogenizing effects of ideology.

The death of Stalin in 1953 and the relaxation of party controls over literature that followed marked the beginning of a new period in the development of the Azerbaijani novel. Subject matter became more varied and homey than before. Although the great issues of socialist construction could hardly be forgotten, novelists began to pay increasing attention to family life and to the problems of everyday existence. Heroes and even villains became more human, as authors probed deeply into the individual psyche to account for their behavior. Among the first novels to incorporate these innovations was Mirza Ibrahimov's *Böiük daiag* (The Great Bulwark;

1957). At first glance the plot seems to follow the usual formula for kolkhoz novels, where courageous progressives battle against evil to preserve the gains of collectivization and where individual character is transformed through unselfish labor in the public good. But rather than mass movements and symbolic figures, the author focuses his attention on the intimate life of a single family. He makes his hero a creature of flesh and blood. Instead of the ascetic, faultless Tahir Damirovs and Meshadi Azizbekovs, he gives us Rustam-kishi, the head of a collective farm. To be sure, Ruskam-kishi is devoted to the revolution, wise and resourceful; but unlike the heroes of the thirties and forties, he is also arrogant and tradition-bound, and he balks at directives from the party.

These innovations, however, by no means heralded a retreat from the fundamental principles of socialist realism. The publication of a treatise on Leninist esthetics three years after the appearance of *Böiü daiag*[3] suggests how difficult the creative vocation would continue to be. The author attacked "reactionary bourgeois esthetics," notably existentialism, neo-Thomism and Freudianism, and denounced experimentation with form and content in Western literature as "anti-realist" and "dehumanizing." Calling the creative freedom of the artist a "chimera," she reasserted the rights and privileges of *partiialylyg* in literature.

Keith Hitchins, Winter 1983

---

[1] Besides the novels themselves, I have used a number of critical studies and monographs, including: Azerbaijan SSR Elmler Akademiiasy, *Azerbaijan Sovet edebiiiaty tarikhi,* 2 vols., Baku, 1967; Gulu Khalilov, *Azerbaijan romanynyn inkishaf tarikhinden,* Baku, 1973; Iahia Seiidov, *Süleiman Rahimovun romanlary,* Baku, 1975; Valentin Boguslavskij, *Dejanie i ličnost',* Moscow, 1976; Xejrulla Aliev, *Sovremennyj azerbajdžanskij roman,* Baku, 1978; and Iahia Seiidov, *Mehdi Hüsein,* Baku, 1979. I have also profited from numerous studies in *Azerbaijan* (1923-), the monthly literary review in Azerbaijani of the Union of Writers of Azerbaijan, and in *Literaturnyj Azerbajdžan* (1943-), the Union monthly in Russian.

[2] The appearance of the first novel is still a matter of some dispute among Azerbaijani critics.

[3] Šukjufa Mirzoeva, *Kritika sovremennoj reakcionnoj buržuaznoj èstetiki,* Baku, 1960.

Past, Present, Future, and Postcolonial Discourse in Modern Azerbaijani Literature

To gain an understanding of the modern literature of Azerbaijan, one must bear in mind two important factors that have influenced the country's artistic and cultural life: the colonial condition of Azerbaijan under the Soviet empire, and the control of the means of communication through censorship. Although restrictions on speech and thought have been the common experience throughout this empire's history, the peripheral nationalities have been restricted even further as regards the expression of their indigenous national identity.

In their experience of colonialism and their resistance to it, Azerbaijanis have much in common with other colonized peoples who have been dominated by European empires. Under the guise of narratives of equality, the Soviet regime continued the colonial relationships that had existed within the czarist empire. If the Russians were masters during the czarist period, in the new regime of federal states the Russians were, in George Orwell's words, "more equal than the others." In the name of "civilization" and "modernization," Soviet Russia secured its political, economic, and cultural dominance over the "backward" peripheries, including Azerbaijan. After recovering (with military might) territories lost to the czarist empire, the new Soviet regime offered enticements, such as formal self-governments, for the new republics; however, the policies that were carried out with such narratives, using such slogans as "equality among nations" and "friendship of peoples," were in fact unchanged. Russia assumed its dominance over these other nationalities, who were compelled to give up their independence once the Soviet empire consolidated its power.[1]

The narratives of the Soviet empire, however, did not go completely unchallenged. Despite the restraints of censorship and the control of communication, some Azerbaijani writers found ways of presenting a critical view of social conditions, challenging the Soviet narratives in their works as well as engaging in postcolonial discourse. The work of these writers shares much with that of other writers who have experienced colonial domination and whose works reflect expressions of cultural resistance.

Criticism of social conditions in Azerbaijan under Soviet rule has been reflected in a variety of artistic and literary genres. Azerbaijani prose writers during the Soviet period practiced such criticism through the use of symbols, metaphors, parables, and allegories. These devices were most useful in circumventing the prohibitions of censorship. Works such as Anar's *Dantenin Jubilasi* (Dante's Jubilee; 1968), Akram Eilisli's *Gilanar Agajina Dediklarim* (My Words to the Sour Cherry Tree; 1981) and *Adamlar Va Agajlar* (People and Trees; 1987), and Isi Malikzada's *Goyu* (The Well; 1976), along with the writings of Elchin, Movlud Suleymanov, Sabir Ahmadli, Isa Husseynov, Alaviyeh Babayeva, Is-

mail Shikhli, and the poet Bakhtiyar Vahabzada are examples of such challenges. The postcolonial discourse in literary texts, however, is seen most readily and most strongly in historical fiction. It is in Azerbaijani works of this genre produced during the Soviet era until just before the breakup of the USSR and the independence of Azerbaijan that a channel was opened through which the postcolonial nation has been imagined by contemporary Azerbaijani writers and readers.

Through the use of historical narratives, Azerbaijani writers have attempted to reconstitute the cultural and national identity damaged by the colonial experience. Writing the history of peripheral nationalities in a way that would suit the demands of Moscow was a key to the Soviet empire's maintenance of power. Although Russian expansion during the czarist era was first condemned, as the Soviet regime consolidated its power, particularly under Stalin, this expansion was presented as beneficial for the peripheral nationalities, who were made to believe in Russia's "enlightening missions." And although the tight grip on the writing of history was relaxed somewhat after Stalin's death, this view continued in the Soviet Union until the mid-1980s under Gorbachev, whose general programs of *perestroika* (restructuring) and *glasnost'* (openness) resulted in the relaxation of censorship. It was then that the opportunity arose for a rewriting of the history of the outlying nations of the USSR. Before this time, conventional historical texts had been produced under Moscow's considerable restraints. Forbidden postcolonial discourses and historical narratives from the point of view of indigenous Azerbaijanis were expressed through historical fiction. In Pratha Chatterjee's words, "Anticolonial nationalism creates its own domain of sovereignty within colonial society well before it begins its political battle with the imperial power."[2]

Through the historical novel, Azerbaijani writers attempted to retrieve and make accessible the historical knowledge that had been censored and distorted due to the politics of the times. In order to circumvent the prohibitions imposed by Soviet censorship, authors focused mostly on foreign powers' past invasions and occupation of Azerbaijan and on the heroic resistance of the Azerbaijanis against those powers, which allegorically represented the Soviets and their colonial domination over Azerbaijan. Thus the historical novel above all provided an outlet for the construction of a national identity and became a source for the imagined postcolonial national community. Wrapping nationalist themes around a temporal narrative—what Benedict Anderson calls "calendrical time"—these texts have helped shape the imagination of historical time and nationalist history with the ultimate goal of independence.

The novels are engaged on three temporal levels: set in the past, the narratives engage in the present through the device of historical allegory while becoming an outlet for imagining the future.

Historical novels have been used to convey nationalist sentiment in Azerbaijan in different eras, but it is important to bear in mind that the word *nation* has carried a variety of meanings. Whereas during the time of consolidation of the Soviet empire and the years of World War II (two periods during which nationalist themes were common), *nation* predominantly meant the Soviet Union, it is during the decades after Stalin, especially during the 1970s and 1980s, that *nation* in the historical novel indicated an independent Azerbaijan—the decades, in fact, that set the stage for the Soviet Union's breakup. Interest in the writing of historical novels focused on the nationalist theme increased after the relaxation of censorship and the policies of *perestroika* of the mideighties and continued until Azerbaijan's official attainment of independence in 1991 with the collapse of the Soviet empire. Temporalities—past, present, and future—and the way they relate in texts vary depending on the political atmosphere and the prohibitions imposed by censorship at the time. All these texts, however, have been influential in the construction of the Azerbaijani national identity.

The 1970s and 1980s marked a period of awakening of the Azerbaijani national consciousness. The policies of the Soviet empire underwent considerable changes during this time, and more power was accorded to the local leaders in the outlying republics. During this period "the local party bosses were allowed free rein on their own turf. Russian 'colonial' apparatchiks were less watchdogs than co-operative partners."[3] This held true, of course, only so long as Moscow was not challenged and its authority was left intact. The situation, however, provided an opening for the resurgence of national and native assertions in the various republics on the periphery, albeit coded and discreet. One of the forums for this resurgence was the official publication of the Azerbaijan Writers Union, *Azarbaycan*. The Union published many "standard items on the importance of Russian influence on Azerbaijan's culture. But the journal also published some subtle, ambiguous pieces whose implications for national identity and consciousness were powerful and, to the Azerbaijani accustomed to code words, unmistakable."[4]

It was in this atmosphere that themes from national history became a preoccupation of Azerbaijani writers and national heroes of the precolonial past became central characters of literary texts. Among such works were *Mahshar* (Doomsday; 1979) by Isa Husseynov, *Heykalsiz Abida* (The Idol Without a Statue; 1982) by Nabi

Khazri, *Alamda Sasim Var Manim* (I Have a Voice in This World) and *Vatana Gayit* (Come Back to the Homeland; 1977) and *Yad Et Mani* (Remember Me; 1980) and *Baki 1501* (Baku 1501; 1981) by Aziza Jafarzada, *Gizilbashlar* (The Gizilbashes; 1983) by Alisa Nijat, and *Khudafarin Corpusi* (The Khudafarin Bridge; 1983) by Farman Karimzada. The last three novels revolve around the life of Shah Ismail Khatayi, a sixteenth-century king who founded the Safavid dynasty and established a centralized Azerbaijani state with Azeri as its official language. While these novels were important in the revival of national history, they were often allegories for contemporary situations as well, since, despite all the changes that had taken place, the means of communication were still heavily controlled and censored. In his article "Azerbaijan Romani: Dunan, Bu Gun" (The Azerbaijani Novel: Yesterday, Today) the Azerbaijani literary critic Vagif Yusufli writes:

> During the last part of the 1970s and early part of the 1980s, interest in historical themes began. Novels were written about Shah Ismail Khatai, Mirza Shafi Vazeh, and other heroes from our past. Our people's history was reflected in literary works. Of course, this interest in historical subjects was not accidental. It had a sociopolitical reason. Going back to popular folklore, mythology, and roots was a tendency among many Soviet nationalities. The fount of folklore never stopped flowing during those years. The quest for history reflected in the novel was the same. The use of historical themes created numerous possibilities for writers.[5]

Aziza Jafarzada's *Vatana Gayit* provides a good example of this type of novel. Set in the eighteenth century, the account revolves around the life of the Azerbaijani poet Nishat Shirvani. The most important themes of the novel, however, relate not so much to Shirvani's life story as to the constant threats to and occupation of Azerbaijan by the Persians and Ottomans. Later on, Russia joined in the attempt at occupying and controlling the region. It is in just this setting that the most important theme of the novel is revealed: the Azerbaijanis' heroic resistance against the invading imperial powers and their efforts to preserve their national culture and history so that it might be passed intact to the next generation. Jafarzada further attempts to recapture the indigenous life lost to her colonized generation by depicting scenes of the traditional bazaar and various forgotten ceremonies and rituals.

In the prologue to *Vatana Gayit* Azerbaijan has been invaded by the Ottomans, who are leading Azerbaijani men and women away as slaves in a caravan that remains in motion throughout the first chapter. The caravan is a central symbol signifying Azerbaijan's continued predicament as an occupied and exploited people subjugated by imperial powers throughout history. Among those in the caravan is a female poet who writes about these events in *bayaties* or couplets, an important element in Azerbaijani folklore. Her couplets are passed from generation to generation and record the history of invasion and resistance. In the same way as the poet in her story, Jafarzada gives us a narrative of contemporary Azerbaijan, using the past as a means of conveying some sense of the present situation in Azerbaijan under Soviet rule: "In all my novels and stories I have brought up the important issues of today in the disguise of the old times because of the imposition of censorship. In all my creative work I have sought refuge in history."[6]

Jafarzadeh was not completely successful in *Vatana Gayit:* one entire chapter was censored because it contained themes considered dangerous to the existing colonial status quo. This chapter recounts the singlehanded resistance of an Azerbaijani woman against one of the Russian imperial army leaders who wanted to set up his military command post in front of her house. The woman lured the army chief into her home and finally saw to it that he was killed. For the Soviet authorities, writing of the invasion of Azerbaijan by the Ottomans and Persians was not a threat; however, once the invading power was the Russian empire, the chapter had to be banned not only because of the allusion to the Russian conquest of Azerbaijan but also due to the fact that the account contradicted the colonial narrative of the "preenlightened, backward, and passive" Azerbaijani woman: "This woman was not what [the army chief] had imagined the 'Muslim Woman' to be; she was a well-educated woman, aware of world affairs."[7]

Historical novels became very popular once again following enactment of the 1985 policy relaxing censorship; however, in contrast to the period in which Jafarzada wrote *Vatana Gayit,* the connections now made between past and present were much clearer. Contemporary problems were discussed openly as a direct result of colonial history, and the repressions of the Stalinist era were emphasized. It was under Stalin that the truly international nature of the Soviet Union faded and national policies secured the dominance of Russia over the outlying republics, including Azerbaijan. This was the era when purges suppressed any voice of national aspiration, giving local power to Moscow's puppets through such policies as adopting the Cyrillic alphabet in non-Slavic as well as Slavic regions, establishing the primacy of the Russian language in education, and limiting sovereignty in the non-Russian republics, whose histories were interpreted and rewritten as narratives favoring the interests of Moscow.

Literary works produced after the mid-1980s reexamined the history of Azerbaijan and explored the roots of contemporary social problems. Among these works were *Gatl Gunu* (The Day of Murder; 1987) by Yusuf Samadoglu, *Abaddiyat* (Eternity; 1988) by Isa Husseynov, *Yasak Edilmish Oyun* (The Forbidden Game; 1988) by Sabir Ahmadly, *Gara Orpak* (The Black Headscarf) by Manzar Nigarly, and *Olum Hokmu* (The Death Sentence; 1989) by Elchin. In contrast to the pre-1985 narratives' use of the remote past, writers after the mid-1980s tended to incorporate more recent history into their narratives. Although criticism of the present and references to repressive periods in history were now allowed, writers were still inhibited somewhat in presenting a truly postcolonial discourse. The new openness engendered questions about the power relationship between each republic and the center. Criticism was allowed, but the empire remained. In an article about the literary texts published after the relaxation of censorship, one Azerbaijani literary critic wrote:

> The hidden issues were so many that their disclosure within a short period created chaos, which is very natural. One of the functions of literature is to draw on social circumstances as a source of narrative . . . and to analyze the facts about our past and present. That is why today we seem to be asking the general question: where have we come from and where are we going? What is shared in the literary texts under study is an attempt to find an answer for this very question in one way or another. What is the recent past, the present, and the future of this belligerent nation that occupies such a small space on the global map, Azerbaijan?[8]

Elchin's *Olum Hokmu* is a perfect example of the novels written during this period, involving itself with a quest for the past, its relation to the present, and the hope it engenders for the future. Elchin focuses here on two time periods: the era of repression and terror under Stalin, and the years of bureaucratic stagnation and corruption under Brezhnev. The background and family history of the many characters that populate this novel serve as a major theme in Elchin's multiepisodic saga, establishing cause-and-effect connections between past and present. Although these connections are freely discussed and the criticism of corruption is openly and continually voiced, postcolonial discourse is expressed only indirectly.

Throughout its history, both under the Soviet regime and in its aftermath, Azerbaijani society, as portrayed here, is divided and polarized between two groups: the collaborators (brokers of the ideology of the Moscow regime) and the ordinary people (mostly affected, repressed, and controlled by that ideology). The dividing line between the groups is demarcated by opposing political and economic positions as well as by national, religious, cultural, and linguistic identities. Connections to Moscow are expressed through the local collaborators, whose loyalties are with the center of power: they speak the language of power (Russian) and identify mainly with its culture. In contrast are the common citizens who have resisted the colonial power by preserving the marks of their national identity, their religion, their language, and their culture. The opposing groups are brought together through a central plot involving an old cemetery, "Tulki Galdi Gabistani" (The Fox-Ridden Graveyard), a metaphorical designation for a colonized Azerbaijan removed from its traditions. The cemetery director, Abdul Ordokhanovich Ghafarzada, uses the site to make money. It houses a semifactory during the day, producing goods to be sold on the black market. By night it becomes a profitable tavern and gambling house. Bribes, which travel up the ladder of connections to reach the center of power, are obtained for the empty gravesites, providing Ghafarzada with additional income.

> From that money, he will take a little for himself and will give the rest to his superior. What will his superior do then? He will also take a little of the money for himself and give the rest to the minister. What will the minister do? He will take his own portion and give the rest to his own superiors. They will take their own portions, and where do you think the rest will go? To Moscow.[9]

Elchin carefully weaves into his postcolonial narrative an episode involving the death of an old woman and a neighbor's attempts to have her buried in the cemetery, an ancestral burial site. This endeavor ends in failure, since the graveyard, having been invaded by the "foxes," is no longer accessible to the community's common citizens. A young student, Murad Ildrimly, dreams that the neighbors have gathered in front of the director's office.

> The office was crowded with people, most of whom Murad Ildrimly could not recognize because they did not have any faces. Ghafarzada, however, could be seen clearly. In his mind, Murad Ildrimly could hear whispers saying, "Tulki burdadir" [The fox is here]. Ghafarzada was standing in his office behind his desk singing the Soviet national anthem, his color dark yellow like that of a fox. The room was decorated with red banners bearing slogans like "Long live the friendship of the Soviet people" and "Long live the Soviet Communist Party." Portraits of Brezhnev and all the other members of the Politburo were hung on the wall above Ghafarzada's head. The color of the faces in the portraits was also dark yellow, like that of a fox.[10]

The episode ends with the old woman being buried not in the graveyard of her ancestors but in a newly created one, suggesting that Azerbaijan is not accessible for Azerbaijanis who resisted colonial domination. At the conclusion of the novel, Elchin expresses hope for the future, when the imposed power will be eliminated and the people will have access to what was once theirs. In the final scene, one of the outraged neighbors, a victim of the past who spent years in prison during Stalinist times, strangles the graveyard director.

"Calendrical time," the passage of time involving past, present and future, is used in both *Vatana Gayit* and *Olum Hokmu*. However, neither of these works directly expressed criticism of the colonial domination of Azerbaijan. It is only during the independence movement and the final years of the breakup of the Soviet empire that historical novels have involved postcolonial narrative with direct references to the invasions of Azerbaijan by the Soviet army. Also during this time, the theme of independence is no longer discussed as a wish for the future but rather as a reality in the making.

Soon after the reforms of the Gorbachev era, and starkly contrasting with the "friendship of nationalities" myth, a conflict arose between Azerbaijan and the Armenian Republic over the disputed mountainous region of Karabakh. Moscow's stance in this dispute brought thousands of protesting Azerbaijanis to Lenin Square (now Freedom Square), an initiative taken by various grass-roots groups. Although the reason for the formation of these groups was the Karabakh conflict, other issues—such as the damages caused by cultural and linguistic russification, the economic advantages and natural wealth (oil) taken from Azerbaijan to benefit Moscow, and environmental disasters caused by colonial policies—lent force to the angry Azerbaijani protesters. From these grass-roots initiatives, different political parties sprang up, the most popular of which has been the People's Front of Azerbaijan. The Karabakh conflict, then, was in fact "a catalyst for the rise of the national movement"[11] that finally led, in January 1990, to a direct confrontation between the Azerbaijanis and the military might of the Soviet empire, a confrontation resulting in the massacre of hundreds of Azerbaijanis.

The events of these most recent years provide the major theme of many of the literary works of this period, among them Ali Amirli's *Meydan* (The Square; 1992), Sabir Ahmadli's *Danizdan Galan Sas* (The Voice from the Sea; 1990), Mammad Oruj's *Izrailla Gorush* (Meeting with Azrael; 1992), Agshin Babayev's *Dunyanin Akhiri* (The End of the World; 1992), and Isi Malikzada's *Girmizi Sheytan* (The Red Satan; 1991). In Isi Malikzada's short novel *Girmizi Sheytan* parallel narratives represent two time periods and the two major

Soviet invasions: the events of 1920, when the Bolshevik army took over the short-lived independent Republic of Azerbaijan (established in 1918); and those of the independence movement of the late 1980s and the 1990 Soviet attack.

To make direct connections between the two events and emphasize the continuity of colonial invasion and domination, the author makes the characters involved in the independence movement of the 1990s the grandchildren of the characters from the 1920s, representing both groups as victims of colonial oppression. One striking difference, however, lies in the portrayal of the characters present during the 1920s invasion, whom the writer depicts as having collaborated with the Soviets against their own people. Their grandsons, on the other hand, are at the forefront of the nationalist movement: "I want to die on the battlefield, pay my dues to my country, and wash away my grandfather's sins,"[12] says one character. Another, the protagonist Samandar, is the one who actually makes the connection with the past, sharing an image—the Soviet soldier who kills him as a red Satan—with his grandfather. In this novel the connection with the past is the reality of the present. Malikzada also provides a glimpse of the future. When Samandar is ready to leave his house and join the protesters (on the night he will be killed), his young son gives him his toy gun for protection.

If in *Vatana Gayit* and *Olum Hokmu* the nationalist postcolonial theme is arranged in a temporal narrative giving the sense of time and its passage and shaping the thinking about national history with the imagination of a future independent nation as its goal, *Girmizi Sheytan* blends past and future in the present moment when the goal is being fulfilled. The nationalist zeal and passion of the 1990s has given way to the realities of individuals struggling in a post-Soviet, postcolonial Azerbaijani society with all its economic, social, and political instabilities.

The hardship of life in an unstable environment with an uncertain future is the dominant theme in contemporary Azerbaijani literature, as reflected in the works of Sara Nazirova, Mehriban Vazir, Rafig Tagi, Manzar Nigarly, Afagh Massud, Sabir Azeri, and many others.[13] The short stories collected in Anar's *Otel Otagi* (Hotel Room; 1995) provide excellent examples of this trend, as in "Vahima" (Fright), which depicts the life of a nouveau-riche character who loses his sanity out of fear of losing his accumulated wealth, or in "Otel Otagi," which describes the exodus of many Azerbaijanis to other countries, or in "Red Limousine," which tells the story of an individual who is caught in the uncertainties and unfamiliarities of the present: "He raised his head and looked at the clouds. The clouds were fa-miliar. A familiar rain was pouring from the familiar clouds. It looked like the rain was pouring not from the clouds but from the past, a past that had been lost forever."

Shouleh Vatanabadi, Summer 1996, translated by Peter Rollberg

1 Michael Rywkin, *Moscow's Lost Empire,* New York, Sharpe, 1994, p. 4.

2 Partha Chatterjee, *The Nation and Its Fragments,* Princeton (N.J.), Princeton University Press, 1993, p. 6.

3 Rywkin, p. 181.

4 Audrey L. Altstadt, *The Azerbaijani Turks,* Stanford (Ca.), Hoover Institution Press, 1992, p. 188.

5 Vagif Yusufli, "Azerbaijan Romani: Dunan, Bu Gun," *Azarbaican Adabi-Badii Jurnal,* 1987, no. 12, p. 177.

6 Tahira Mammadova, "Sozum Hala Chokhdur," *Azarbaycan,* 1992, nos. 3–4, p. 180.

7 Aziza Jafarzada, unpublished manuscript provided by the author, p. 4.

8 Nizamaddin Mustafa, "Dord Roman Bir Problem," *Azarbaycan,* 1989, no. 6, p. 170.

9 Elchin, *Olum Hokmu,* Baku, Yaziji, 1989, p. 32.

10 Ibid., pp. 315–16.

11 Tadeusz Swietochowski, *Russia and Azerbaijan,* New York, Columbia University Press, 1995, p. 218.

12 Isi Malikzada, "Girmizi Sheytan," *Azarbaycan,* 1992, nos. 9–10, p. 49.

13 Because of financial problems and a shortage of paper, many of these writers have difficulty publishing their works.

IRAN

Poetry against Piety: The Literary Response to the Iranian Revolution

The revolutionary movement of 1978–79 in Iran occurred at a time when the break between the creative minds and the ruling body of the country was very nearly complete. A generation of Iranian writers had witnessed the gradual stifling of all hopes for the establishment of a free, democratic state, the growth of an increasingly elaborate system of censorship and surveillance, and the rise of an arrogantly pretentious yet culturally insensitive elite whose traditional respect for literature and the arts had been replaced by a rampant desire to ape Western customs and cultures. It had further been subjected to a classic policy of pushing the writer into conformity with the state through increased pressures and redoubled restrictions on intellectual and artistic expression.

Although no Iranian writer remained unaffected by policies and practices of the monarchical state regarding the intellectual community in general and the writer in particular, consequences varied in each case, ranging from total withdrawal by the writer from the public domain to a head-on clash with the state, ending in exile, imprisonment, or execution. The literature of the period reveals a double-pronged response adopted by a majority of writers and poets. First, in an attempt to conceal from the censor what he feels he must reveal to his readers, the writer seems to have taken refuge in ever-deeper layers of symbolic expression. I have referred to this phenomenon, in one particularly illustrative instance, as the "grand internalization" of literature during the last two decades of Pahlavi rule.[1] Second, the writer and the poet gradually came to mingle in their works the role of the chronicler of reality with that of the visionary idealizer capable of transforming any movement on the social front into a personal romance of the future. Revolution was no longer a sudden radical change, but a new push toward an ideal future, often just around the corner of Iranian history. On a plane almost independent of objective reality, the writer gave expression to his heartfelt desires and dreams, as if by expressing them he could assume the power to make them come true.

The advent of the revolutionary movement—a process in which Iranian writers themselves played no small part[2]—externalized the antagonistic feelings of the writer toward the state and objectified the former's romance of the revolution. Many Iranian writers saw in an imminent revolution a unifying cause, a historic opportunity, and an idea into which they could channel their creative energies. The revolutionary situation seemed naturally to open before them new vistas of possibility whose exact definitions eluded comprehension. If revolution as a cognitive concept appeared too complex a notion to grasp, however, the wonder that came to pass day after eventful day in the streets of Tehran and other Iranian cities throughout 1978 was a definitely palpable spectacle to delight in, a new subject to write about. Moreover, the Iranian revolution imposed itself with unusual immediacy, force, and speed, demanding to be recorded as the realization of a long-awaited intellectual fantasy. In other words, the event of the revolution—as distinct from revolution as an idea—constituted a radically new phenomenon, before which the writer stood in awe. The key word in all this is *new*, with all its connotations of strangeness and novelty, for it was these very attributes, so dear to the literary imagination, which at this juncture concealed many anomalies inherent in the literary response to the various stages of the Iranian revolution.

A quick glance at the literary works written between October 1977, when the Writers Association of Iran held ten evenings of readings at the Goethe Institute in Tehran, and the collapse of the Iranian monarchy in February 1979 reveals that literature has become more kinetic, more image-centered and event-oriented, and of course more buoyant. In fact, the most notable outward sign of the poetry of the Iranian revolution remains its tendency to paint the scene, to gloat in the sight, to celebrate the concrete event of the revolution. That the revolution itself should emerge as the dominant theme of a multitude of poems and stories of the period is perhaps to be expected in a country where for almost a generation the writer could not address social issues directly. However, stylistically too, these writings give the distinct impression that the writer is witnessing something momentous, extraordinary, and dazzling. Such powerful images as red carnations implanted in the barrel of a wavering soldier's gun as a metaphor for the wound his bullet may plant in a demonstrator's body begin to appear side by side with the more familiar image of red tulips symbolizing the reincarnation of political martyrs. All sorts of sounds, from the loud screeching of gunfire to the still-louder chorus of people chanting revolutionary slogans, break the long lull of the poetic line. Scents of rose water and incense—ceremonially sprinkled or burned by women as they send their men off to great undertakings or welcome them back—blend with the stench of blood in the gutter. A wealth of new figures of speech are summoned to capture and record the moment when one more man falls in another encounter between state troopers and demonstrating revolutionaries.

It has my brother's smell
                this corpse
it has the smell of my brothers.
From side streets still come
cries of wounds, blood and bullets,
the smell of my brothers.
My blessed people
plant tulips
         in this bloodied soil.[3]

That burgeoning sense of oneness, whose purpose remains unspecified, is celebrated in numerous poems commemorating the demonstrations and strikes that quickly brought the revolution to its successful culmination. The poet who for years had lamented his isolation, his inability to reach out in the gloom of the ruling repression, could now welcome the dark as a cover for a long-delayed togetherness.

How glorious is our night
when bullets
tattoo it,

and cries of "God is great"
bring together
our hearts
our anxious hearts
from the two corners of the night.

. . . .

How glorious is our night
when darkness
unites the town.[4]

The familiar picture of the autumnal garden, where the slow dying of flowers had for years symbolized the withering of the poet's spirit of freedom in the chill of oppression, is now reversed to contain promises of vernal blossoming and growth. In the emblematic garden of Iranian society on the eve of the revolution, tulips grow, jasmines bloom, and "every night a rose yields / on its deathbed / the pollen of the new will to the garden."[5] Touched by the magic wand of the revolution, in short, the symbolism of alienation is transformed almost overnight into the imagery of integration.

Of course, certain traditional images of modern Persian poetry, forged and shaped in the years of repression, continue. There are countless red banners, spun of the flame of popular wrath, raised against the backdrop of the fading night to herald the approaching dawn. There are still red stars, red gallows, red hands, red throats, and an ever-present red horizon in the landscape of this literature. The loud clanking of the chains of slavery becomes even louder, the noisy onrush of the masses running toward the palace of the paper man gathers new strength, and a mere raising of clenched fists or chanting of a slogan causes many flaccid walls to crumble or rotten doors to give way. These images, so expressive of the social situation only a decade earlier, now appear mechanical in flow and metallic in flavor, devoid, to a large extent, of engaging intellectual reflections on the meaning and significance of the imminent revolution in comparison with the emerging poetry of possibility. In a collection of poems fittingly titled *Nabz-i Vatanam ra Migiram* (I Take the Pulse of My Country), M. A. Sepanlu echoes this new motif when he summons a miraculously new power of transformation.

Blessed is the tree
which in the solitude of this landscape
points to the root of the possible
and in its extremities
promises to bestow upon us
a recognizable identity.[6]

That uncharted world of the possible, that undefined yet recognizable sense of identity, most clearly typifies the mental attitude behind much of the litera-

ture of the period. Intellectual ambiguities and uncertainties are neither resolved in the mind of the poet nor overcome in his poetry. Rather, they are either buried out of sight behind the delight of the moment or clad in vague generalities. Even those poets and writers who perceived something deeply threatening in the gradual ascendancy of religious elements in the course of the revolution seem to have felt compelled by the force of events to murmur their reservations privately even as they marveled publicly at the spectacle that was unfolding before their eyes. In a fine long poem titled "Mardum Hamārih Haq Dārand" (People Are Forever Right) Isma'il Kho'i, a prominent poet now in his forties, commemorated the homecoming of the frail old clergyman who had by now become the voice of a revolutionary movement. Witnessing the scene where crowds, estimated in the millions, fill all public thoroughfares, side streets, alleyways, and rooftops and even climb tree branches to welcome their new idol, the poet ponders the power of their unity and their unquestionable allegiance to the revolution in a series of dialogues between his public and private selves. In the end, the poet's public voice concludes that "doubts and suspicions are useless," that people are always right "because they are many" and because they forever seek the 'shall be.'" Still, the poet's inner voice, in an obvious mood of lonely meditation, observes: "I / do not believe / that any force / can build tomorrow / out of the stuff of yesterdays."[7]

That poem provides a particularly vivid illustration of the intellectual response to the onset of the revolution. Caught between uncertainties about the revolution's course and cast of characters, on the one hand, and a deeply detested status quo on the other, many members of the Iranian intelligentsia decided to throw their lot in with the revolution. The shape of the revolution could neither affirm their sense of historical direction nor synthesize the dichotomy between their ideals and the reality of their social situation. Nevertheless, in breaking through the social stagnation and political bankruptcy that characterized the existing order, it promised to create a dynamic atmosphere in which such goals as movement toward social justice, greater individual and civil rights and liberties, and, most of all, a meaningful balance of modernity and identity could be achieved, much as the alliance of the secular intellectual and progressive clergy had brought about in the Constitutional Revolution. For the present, the Iranian writer felt compelled to respond with a momentary nod of approval. Thus it was, in spite of all obvious contradictions and complications, that many writers were co-opted into the revolutionary process. At any rate, the revolution had magically turned into a mirror in which everyone looked for the image of his own ideals.

With the revolution as an accomplished fact, and as the earliest indications of the Islamic state's cultural bearings surfaced through the awesome pageantry of revolutionary events, diverse misgivings began to find expression in literary works. Within the first few months after the February 1979 insurgency that toppled the Iranian monarchy, those writers who had counted on the revolutionary process to cleanse itself of whatever impurities may have gotten mixed up with it, began to realize to their dismay that what was most repulsive to them seemed to constitute the most essential elements in the world view of the religious revolutionists now in constant ascendancy in the hierarchy of power. In the summer of 1979, in the midst of such blatant aberrations as summary executions of political enemies, public flogging and stoning in strict accordance with the Islamic practice of medieval times, and organized attacks on unsympathetic intellectual activities, Ahmad Shamlu wrote his now-famous poem entitled "Dar Īn Bunbast" (In This Blind Alley). Aside from its thematic significance, the poem reflects the poet's determination to confront a naked situation in as straightforward a manner as possible.

They smell your mouth
lest you may have said: I love you,
they smell your heart.
       Strange time, my dear.
And they flog love
by the road-block.
       Hide love in the larder.
In this crooked blind alley, at the turn of the chill
they feed the fire
with logs of song and poetry.
Hazard not a thought.
       Strange times, my dear.
He who knocks at the door in the noon of night
has come to kill the light.
       Hide light in the larder.

There! butchers
stationed in streets
with bloody chopping-woods and cleavers.
       Strange times, my dear.
And they chop smiles off lips
       songs off the mouth.
       Hide joy in the larder.

Canaries barbecued
on a fire of lilies and jasmines.
       Strange times, my dear.
Satan, drunk with victory
squats at the feast of our undoing
       Hide God in the larder.[8]

The poem begins by presenting a series of images depicting facets of daily life, interrupted by an almost involuntary refrain testifying to the ineffable nature of the situation: "strange time, my dear." At the same time, scenes of naked violence, unbridled repression, and the most flagrant invasion of private corners of human existence are interspersed with statements concerning the poet's sense of an impending danger threatening basic and native social values. The two threads—one lyrical, the other elegiac—culminate in the feast of Satan, celebrating the demise of intellectual dreams. Interestingly, the defense mechanism on which the poem stands is structured on a dialectical movement toward the source of all unity, as envisioned in Persian mysticism. The poet bids his beloved—and his audience—to hide away first love, then light, then joy, and finally God himself. Thus, in a sort of poetic peripeteia, the agnostic poet points to a native principle of transcendence and mystical alliance with God in the face of evil upon the earth.

It would of course be erroneous to imply that the nascent theocracy succeeded quickly and quietly in stifling artistic expression. Indeed, the period between February 1979 and June 1981, when the Islamic Republic can be said to have finally succeeded in consolidating its sway over the country, must be considered a period of feverish productivity in contemporary Persian literature. A good many of the works written in the 1970s saw the light of public attention during this period. Dramatic works such as Moshen Yallfāni's Davandih-yi Tanhā (The Lone Runner), Sa'id Soltanpour's Abbas Āqā, Kārgar-i IranNational (Abbas Āqā, the Iran-National Worker), and Bahrām Bayzā'ī's Marg-i Yarzdgird (The Death of Yazdgird), as well as such works of prose fiction as Ahmad Mahmūd's Dastan-i Yik Shahr (A Tale of One City), Reza Barāheni's Chah bih Chah (From Well to Well), Nassīm Khāksār's Gamhā-yi Paymūdan (Steps to Tread), and Ali Ashraf Darvishiyan's Sillūl-i 18 (Cell 18) are among the most notable literary products conceived or written before the collapse of the monarchical regime and published after the revolution. In them the reader confronts a fresh look at the past, a new interpretation of life under the rule of monarchy, and the impact of that rule on the fabric of Iranian society. In these and other creations of the period, the reader occasionally comes face to face with a genuine intellectual desire to comprehend the unfolding reality in terms of social experiences of the past. What was the historical stage through which Iranian society was passing? What kind of phenomenon was the Iranian revolution? What was the cultural identity of the religious revolutionists? Answers to these and related questions in fact form the central preoccupation of writers in postrevolutionary Iran.

The most convenient answer suggesting itself to the mind of the writer seems to stem from the all-too-obvious emphasis the revolutionary leaders laid on religion as the new basis for national life. Furthermore, the religious revolutionists had come to public viewing with a new old language that had long disappeared from public parlance. All this, coupled with the populist, anti-intellectual rhetoric of revolutionary authorities and the missionary zeal with which they advocated a manner of governance thought long dead, reinforced a sense of alienness, a basic incongruity between the new rulers and what was perceived as the quintessence of Iranian culture. As a result, the perception of the revolution as a second Arab invasion of Iran begins to permeate many literary works of the period. In an angry outburst of emotion against the cultural attitudes of the new state, Isma'il Kho'i refers to "these uncultured conquerors" as "crossbred descendants from the seed of Changiz and the house of Abu-Jahl,"[9] thus coupling two despised alien figures: the Mongol invader of Iran, whose name is virtually synonymous in the Iranian consciousness with unbridled brutality; and an uncle to the prophet Muhammad whose name actually means "the father of ignorance."

More immediate than the new rulers' identity was the question of their attitude toward the existing culture. Here a combination of religious zeal and cultural callousness is perceived as the motive inspiring the new rulers in sullying the revolution on the cultural front. Hushang Golshiri's short story "Fathnāmah-yi Mughān" (The Magi's Victory Chronicle), by far the best work of short fiction from the period, typifies this attitude by following the fortunes of a group of men in a provincial town from the noontime joy of popular revolt against the monarchy to the midnight of total submission to the Draconian savagery of the religious revolutionists. As the story opens, the townspeople have already broken windowpanes at movie houses and banks in protest against what such institutions stand for. "When we shattered those windows," one observes, "we did not think that it was movies we were breaking down. We were attacking the banality they symbolized, and the perpetrators of that kind of banality."[10] What remains to be destroyed, then, is the imposing statue of the horseman at the Shah Square. In a masterly tour de force, the author introduces Barāt, a tavern owner, as the man who finally decides to pull down the shah's statue with the help of the townsfolk. A cultivated, popular, and honest man who loves poetry and loathes all kinds of hypocrisy, Barāt has been a political prisoner and possesses an inner capacity for leadership. In a well-structured sequence of focused actions and pointed dialogues, the story depicts Barāt's worsening situation after the revolution, as religious elements turn against him because of his unholy occupation.

Eventually, Barāt is arrested and flogged in public because of his continued defiance of the ban on the sale and consumption of alcohol. His cache of wines and spirits is discovered and entrusted to a local bulldozer driver for destruction. The man buries the precious find in an open field, word goes from mouth to mouth, and at night townsmen congregate at the site. There, having partaken in the sacred ritual of unearthing these symbolic remains of their worldly culture, they begin, their fingers cut, their hands scarred, and their bodies bruised, to nourish themselves with this "water of life," so dearly celebrated in Persian literature and lore. For a brief moment, in the dim light of lanterns and candles, the assembly achieves the status of a grand symbol reminiscent of so many life-and-death struggles against bigotry and despotism in Iranian history. Soon, however, the revolutionary guards, clad in the emblematic *keffiyeh* and *akal*, arrive on the scene, guided by a flickering light and the distant din of human voices singing sad, sinuous songs. The drinkers, violators of a most severe religious injunction, are subjected to the inevitable verdict. "They ought to be flogged," the commanding officer orders, "every one of them! Start, even if it takes until doomsday."

The ending of the story depicts an archetypal mélange of the literal and figurative layers of the story's meaning in a memorable image-ensemble.

> They stretched one from our midst on the ground, two guards holding his feet, two others his hands. They covered his head with a black cloth, gathered its hems into a knot, stuck the lump in his mouth, and started to flog him. No noise could be heard, from anybody. Then they too squatted all around us, encircling the fringes of the light from our lanterns, their heads covered in keffiyehs. We could see their eyes only. And we, all of us, lay down outstretched, humble and earthy, our backs turned on ancient stars—still ancient stars—waiting for these men, clad in keffiyehs and akals, to get to us. Our feet outstretched, we were awaiting our turn to receive our Islamic punishment. And while waiting, we pressed the mouth of the bottle into our mouths, sucking in the very last drops of that bitter-tasting mother-of-evil. And then, drunk, we rested our faces on the soil, the cold, damp, frost-covered soil, and waited. (6)

That Golshiri's story reads like a prose rendition of the motifs, topoi, and themes of Shamlu's poem testifies to the remarkable consistency of the writer's perception of and response to the course of the Iranian revolution in this period. Golshiri's men in Arabian headbands recall Shamlu's sniffing dogs and bloodthirsty butchers of official orthodoxy, as well as many other personages portrayed in the fiction and poetry of Iran in the early years of the Islamic Republic. Indeed, Persian literature of the period is replete with impressions of invasion by an alien force, a sense of being exiled at home, of feeling foreign in the ancestral land. Filled with an alienation much deeper than he had ever experienced under the monarchy, the Iranian writer gives to his readers an increasingly distinct feeling that the matter of his work is being served in a posture of wide-eyed bewilderment. At times it is as if the writer feels that in order to convey an impression of the unbelievable reality around him, he has to plunge into hitherto unexplored domains.

In several separately published episodes which promised to constitute portions of a larger work, the playwright and fiction writer Gholam-Hossein Sa'edi oversteps limits of time and place to present a narrative of pure action. Just at a time when torture was being reinstated as an instrument of state policy in dealing with political dissidents, he portrayed naked violence as an internal constant in Iranian history. The narrative, an account of the emissaries of the great Khedive of Egypt on their way to the court of the glorious Emir of the Tartars, culminates in the scene where the convoy witnesses an orgy of actual skinning of strange beasts in the valley of the "emerald cup."

> Brandishing his sharp, shiny budkin, the dark muscular man ran forward, jumped up in the air, and, while turning around full circle, his tongue hanging out like a bloody cut of meat, sliced the skin around the beast's neck with expert craftsmanship. So exquisitely was this done, with such ordered grace, that it looked as if in the blink of an eye the animal had been adorned with a wreath of white flowers interspersed with red bulbs.[11]

Toward the end of this episode, the travelers ask the kindly, hospitable, bearded skinners whether they know the glorious Emir and his court. "Of course we do," replies the master skinner. "We have learned the art of skinning animals alive from him and from his courtiers—especially from the glorious Emir himself" (59). The embassy continues on its way.

Such was the writer's growing realization of the heritage of violence in the "emerald cup," which vaguely recalls the Iranian plateau. Indeed, cruelties of such magnitude, conducted with such natural ease—and born of the idea of liberating revolution—form the thematic nexus of much of the imaginative literature of the time. The fact that violence can be legitimized as a natural psychic state indistinguishable from the daily activities of life gives rise to the possibility—and the writer's fear—of the continuation of age-old historical mechanisms in new forms. That possibility and that fear finally

materialized in the summer of 1981, when the Islamic Republic—now in the midst of a foreign war—finally made public its undeclared war on intellectual dissidents at home. Shortly after President Banisadr's ouster, the Revolutionary Guards raided and ransacked the office of the Writers Association of Iran. The most active members of the association were arrested shortly afterward; others were soon purged from the bureaucracy, the universities, and the mass media. Sa'id Soltanpur, a poet and playwright and a member of the association's executive board, was executed on 29 June. Many member writers thought it advisable to go into hiding, some never to resurface until they had crossed the country's borders into safety, a majority to end up in Paris, where they now reside. In the battle against the Islamic theocracy, Iranian writers had not only lost their dream of a better future; they had in fact lost their very voice.

Thus begins a period of clandestine life at home or forced exile for Persian literature. Literary writings in exile in the course of the past few years and the unpublished literature created in Iran occupy, in my judgment, a significant place in the annals of twentieth-century Persian literature. Within the former category such collections of poetry as Nader Naderpur's *Subh-i Durūghīn* (False Dawn; Paris, 1982), Isma'il Kho'i's *Kābūs-i Khūn Sirishtah-yi Bīdārān* (Blood-Molded Nightmare of the Wakeful; London, 1984), and Nemat Mirzazadeh's *Beh Havā-yi Mīhan* (Longing for the Fatherland; Paris, 1983), as well as many works published in *Alefbā,* a periodical edited by Sa'edi and published in Paris, are only the most outstanding among scores of volumes of poetry, drama, and prose fiction published outside Iran in recent years. I have also been fortunate in being the recipient of a good deal of the writings that have no possibility of publication under the present conditions. Meanwhile, having silenced the intellectual community in Iran, the Islamic Republic is beginning to allow the publication of some literary works with no direct bearing on its policies and practices. Simin Behbahani's *Dasht-i Arzhan* (Millet Field; Tehran, 1983), another volume of ghazals with veiled but felicitous observations on life in the Islamic state, and Isma'il Fasih's *Sorayya in Coma* (Tehran, 1983; Eng. 1985), the narrative of a journey from the war-stricken southwestern province of Khuzestan to Paris and the Iranian exile community, are among the most notable works in this cateogry. Finally, Reza Baraheni's *Āvāz-i Kushtigān* (Song of the Slain; Tehran, 1984), by far the best work by the author to date, is a gripping account of cultural decadence and brutal repression, chronologically set in the last years of monarchical rule, but with palpable undertones of relevance to the Islamic Republic's attitude toward the intellectual opposition. The common denominator in all these works is the writer's full realization of the relevance of past experiences to present circumstances and the courageous portrayal of the essential continuity of mechanisms of repression and despotic rule.

■ ■ ■

Based on all this, what general observations can be made about the nature and significance of the literary response to the Iranian revolution? Obviously, literature does not admit of the kind of sudden radical change that effects itself on the social scene. The formal and structural conventions of contemporary Persian literature, moreover, having historically evolved from a need to tackle social issues, have demonstrated great resilience, vitality, and flexibility in treating the theme of the revolution. On the other hand, the idea and experience of the Iranian revolution can in turn be said to have changed the contemporary literature of Iran, now broadening its scope and deepening its concerns, now modifying or negating the very bases on which it stands. Doubtless, the revolution has affected the creative minds behind that literary tradition. Aside from a gradual thaw in the symbolic landscape of literature, a perceptible loosening of the diction, and a remarkable sharpening of the formal rhetorical posture, we occasionally come across bold new attempts at direct, naked expression of a naked, unambiguous situation. The widening field of experience has, in turn, resulted in an obvious expansion of the range of moods and messages communicated through literature. The Persian literature of the 1980s embodies greater fears and hopes, greater hopes and anticipations, and a more self-assured sense of the dialectics of reality and the creative imagination than ever before recorded. Once again, the desire for social change is being incorporated into the creative process, this time accompanied by a fresh realization that that desire must be united with the pounding beat of the national will to forge a new reality.

Finally, even though he is still basically a visionary idealizer, the Iranian writer no longer seems to view such complex phenomena as revolution with uncritical acceptance. An exile at home or an outcast abroad, he now seems more conscious than ever before of the need to anchor his dreams in the roots of his history and the depths of his culture. The distance between Paris and Tehran in 1985 is much greater in miles than in mood. Whether roaming the banks of the Seine or brooding over the silence that reigns in his realm, the Iranian writer of this decade appears more than ever determined to set out on a long new journey in search of a novel sense of himself and the world around him. In

this lies an impression of painful growth, as palpable as pain and as gratifying as growth itself.

Ahmad Karimi-Hakkak, Spring 1986

[1] See Ahmad Karimi-Hakkak, "A Well amid the Waste: An Introduction to the Poetry of Ahmad Shamlu," *Wlt* 51:2 (Spring 1977) pp. 201–206.

[2] For a detailed account of the role of Iranian writers in the course of the Iranian revolution, see my essay "Protest and Perish: A History of the Writers Association of Iran," *Iranian Studies*, 18:1–4.

[3] Mīrzā Āqā Askarī, "Tashyi'i Jināzah-yi Shahīd" (A Martyr's Funeral Procession), *The Journal of the Writers Association of Iran,* 1 (Spring 1979), p. 199. All translations are mine.

[4] Siyāvush Kasrā'ī, "Az Qurug ta Khurūskhān" (From Dusk to the Cock-Crow), ibid., p. 139.

[5] Mahmud Azad, "Farāz-ha-i az Shi'ri Buland-i 'Iman Hamīshih Rāzi-st'" (Fragments from the Long Poem "Faith Is Always a Mystery"), ibid., p. 141.

[6] M. A. Sepanlu, "Fardā, bih Mīhanam" (Tomorrow, to Iran), in *Nabz-i Vatanam ra Mīgīram* (I Take the Pulse of My Country), Tehran, Zaman, 1978, p. 78.

[7] Isma'il Kho'i, "Mardum Hamārih Haq Darand" (People Are Forever Right), *Andishah-yi Āzād*, 4 (15 April 1980), p. 33.

[8] Ahmad Shamlu, "Dar īn Bunbast" (In This Blind Alley), in *Little Homesick Songs,* Tehran, Mazyar, 1980, pp. 30–32.

[9] Isma'il Kho'i, "Āmīzigān-i Tukhmih-yi Changīz o Dudmān-i Abujahl" (Crossbred Descendants from the Seed of Changiz and the House of Abu-Jahl), *Andishah-yi Āzād,* 4 (15 April 1980), p. 33.

[10] Hushang Gulshiri, "Fathnameh-ye Moghan," *Kasgah-e gesseh,*1 (undated), pp. 1–6. Only one issue of this journal was published. The story is dated November-December 1980.

[11] Gholam-Hossein Sā'edi, "Dar Sarāchah-yi Dabbāghān" (The Magi's Victory Chronicle), *Būstān*, 2nd series, 1 (June-July 1981), pp. 52–59. Sa'edi died in Paris on 23 November 1985.

The Quince-Orange Tree, or Iranian Writers in Exile

Exile is not a particularly recent phenomenon in Persian literary history. Long before the 1979 revolution many Iranian writers had been forced into or had chosen exile—Mirza Malkum Khan, Adbul-Rahim Talibuff, and Mohammad Ali Jamalzadeh, to name a few—but the emergence of a body of literature which is at once the product and the *expression* of Iranian exile is unique to the past decade. I will leave to experts the analysis of the historical, political, and sociological factors which have precipitated this literary occurrence and instead focus on the effects of exile on contemporary Iranian literature. Moreover, I will limit my discussion to the linguistic manifestations of Iranian exile.

As Iranian literature in exile is no longer being written exclusively in Persian, the very classification of works by Iranian writers has become problematic. Some critics argue that works written in a Western language cannot be placed within the mainstream of Persian literature. They are better classified as immigrant literature in the national and linguistic tradition from which they emerge. My contention is that the texts written in a language other than Persian form one of the three categories of Iranian exile literature and play a significant role in the evolution of that literature.

Most Iranian writers, regardless of the language in which they write, agree that exile leads to cultural and linguistic deracination. In his most recent novel, *The Pilgrim's Rules of Etiquette,* Taghi Modarressi has given full expression to this sentiment. The following passage is from the opening chapter of the novel, in which the protagonist, Hadi Besharat, explains to an American colleague his misgivings about remaining in the West:

> "To be sure there are common features between the Easterner and the Westerner, and in certain respects each can benefit the other. But in the end their encounters remain barren. It's like the quince-orange tree, which is a graft between a quince and an orange, or the mule, which is the result of horse-and-donkey copulation. Of course each has some use. But they themselves are barren and fruitless."[1]

This type of cultural graft may appear barren in the logic of the novel itself, but if we go beyond the character of the protagonist, we realize that these words issue from the pen of a writer who has defied this dictum by establishing himself in two linguistic and cultural realms. Beginning with *The Book of Absent People,* published in 1986, Modarressi has been translating his own works into English. Both *The Book of Absent People* and *The Pilgrim's Rules of Etiquette* have appeared almost simultaneously in Persian and English. What I mean by "almost" is that the Iranian censorship laws have in both cases delayed the publication of the Persian texts in Iran until after the English edition's release by Doubleday.

Modarressi belongs to that group of Iranian exiles who have begun to explore the creative possibilities of expatriation. I place him in the third category of my typology and shall return to him in the final section of my presentation.

The first group is composed of those writers who, although living in exile, continue to write primarily in Persian and for an Iranian audience. Ths most well-known representative of this group is Bozorg Alavi, who since 1953 has lived in what used to be East Germany. In a speech delivered in November of 1989 at the Middle Eastern Studies Association conference in Toronto, Alavi lamented his exile and spoke of isolation from his community of readers: "A writer must have readers. If there is ever a defeat for a writer, it is being deprived of readers. In exile, I did not have readers. Everything I wrote, before seeing the light of day, would be forgotten and exiled."[2] In a different speech delivered in October 1989 at American University, Alavi extended his own experience of exile to that of other Iranian writers living in Europe and North America.

> As I have gathered, there are currently a few hundred Iranian poets and writers in North America and Europe. They write poems and short stories, some of them excellent. I would not dare claim that the work of a given writer living in Iran, which I have also enjoyed, is better than that produced in exile. But I am certain that if some of these exiles lived in Iran, they would have markedly better productions.[3]

Normative as this statement may sound, it reflects the sentiment of not only the majority of Iranian writers but also of many of their expatriate readers. It is important to emphasize that, in his judgments, Alavi is not motivated merely by nationalist fervor. In this same speech he pointed out that it is imperative for Iranian writers to familiarize themselves with international literary trends and to broaden their horizons beyond the limits of their own national literature. He also argues that, in a literary context, being "plagued by the West"[4] is not derogatory.[5]

Alavi's's apprehension does not stem from any lack of confidence in the ingenuity and talent of the Iranian writer. Instead, he believes that cultural and linguistic isolation erodes those ties which make it possible for an Iranian writer to forge his or her own unique identity. Alavi's own fate as a writer is a case in point. After only one attempt at writing a short story in German, Alavi returned to writing in Persian. His most recent novel, *Ants,* awaits the approval of Iranian censors.

Expatriate Iranian readers by and large echo Alavi's sentiments. At the panel of Iranian writers in Toronto in November 1989 a few exiled writers read from their works in English. Some in the audience vehemently protested the very use of English. A similar disappointment, albeit more subtle, is reflected in an article on the same event published in the magazine *Iranian Woman.* The author of this article wonders aloud what makes someone who writes in English an Iranian writer.[6]

The response offered by those belonging to the second group of exile writers is: the content and the spirit of their works. Donné Raffat, whose first novel *The Caspian Circle* was published in English in 1978 and who was not present at the above-mentioned meeting, offers this insight into and justification of his unique Iranian heritage:

[This story] could have only happened in Iran, on Iranian soil, with Iranian people, and with a novice Iranian writer, his language notwithstanding, doing the writing. If I had known enough Farsi, I would likely have written in Farsi; if I had been raised in France or Germany, I would have done the same in French or German. But as it was, I was brought up in America and schooled in England, and thus I wrote in English.

Yet at the moment of the writing, I was Iranian to my core and marrow; for what I had, in lieu of the language, was the vision: more than that, the experience of the vision. From nowhere else could that vision have come: this was the country's gift to me. Not the language—which I was fated to lose—but the vision.[7]

For Raffat and Iranian writers like him, language is not the sole link to a cultural and literary heritage. Raffat suggests that the loss of Persian need not be regarded as detrimental to the creative identity of the Iranian writer. Unlike Alavi, Raffat places emphasis on the creative act rather than on those who receive it. In both cases there nevertheless remains a gulf between the writer and his homeland. It is the different strategies which Alavi and Raffat take in bridging that gulf which place them in two distinct categories of exile: the one continues to write in Persian but laments his lack of psychological contact; the other has opted for English but claims a transcendental psychological bridge back to Iran.

The affinity between the two is better brought out by Manoucher Parvin, who formulates the problem thus: "I am an exile. I have been exiled from Iran. I have been exiled from my son who speaks English to me. I am even exiled from myself, but I am alive and I write."[8] Here the act of writing itself is posited as a means of transcending exile. What is implicit in Parvin's confession is that if exile implies a severing of linguistic ties, then its recognition may well be uttered in a second language. The question Raffat and Parvin seem to be asking themselves is whether, as Iranian writers, they should cling to a fading past or begin a fusion of past and present. To borrow and adapt a phrase from Nabokov's *Pale Fire,* for them "exile [has not] become a bad habit."[9]

Other Iranian writers such as Nahid Rachlin and F. M. Esfandiary have moved further away from this dilemma by declaring national specificities irrelevant. Rachlin, who launched her literary career in English, dismisses the question that a writer's cultural ties are determined in purely linguistic terms. Both of her novels, *Foreigner* and *Married to a Stranger,* although written in English, are set in Iran. Rachlin may not insist on being labeled an Iranian writer, yet she too is preoccupied with memories of an Iranian past. In *Foreigner,* on

the occasion of the protagonist's visit to a shrine, we read:

Echoes, faraway, vibrated in my head, my whole body. Surges of memory, of going from chamber to chamber in mosques and shrines, clinging to my mother, flowed over the surface of my mind. Suddenly, in spite of myself, I stopped, leaned my head against a wall and kissed it, tears filling my eyes and rolling down my cheeks.[10]

Esfandiary has problematized the same issue in his own name. Admitting to being a writer first and an Iranian second, he has changed his name to FM-2030, like a radio station. In other words, for him the Persian name is interchangeable with any other North American cultural symbol. The title of his latest book, *Are You Transhuman?,* is an unequivocal response to the question of identity.

The writers who have chosen a second language as their medium of expression seem to accept the disruption of exile, recognize their discarded identity, and embark upon creating a new one. However, the new persona they create for themselves is determined by remnants of the old. They become pioneers of the type described by Salman Rushdie:

Our identity is at once plural and partial. Sometimes we feel that we straddle two cultures; at other times, that we fall between two stools. But however ambiguous and shifting this ground may be, it is not an infertile territory for a writer to occupy. If literature is in part the business of finding new angles at which to enter reality, then once again our distance, our long geographical perspective, may provide us with such angles.[11]

For an example of this type of new vision in Persian literature, I would cite the Iranian singer and artist Shusha Guppy's autobiography *The Blindfold Horse: Memories of a Persian Childhood.* In the following passage Guppy weaves together wanderlust and exile and demonstrates the artist's ability to forge a new existence out of a historical necessity:

Of all the hawkers, the most popular was the *Shahre-Farang* (a City in Europe) man. He pushed his big black box on a wheelbarrow shouting: "Come and see the *Shahre-Farang!* Travel with me to the land of the *Farangi* and see its marvels!" . . .

Children rushed from all directions and offered the *Shahre-Farang* man their coins. . . .

The first four tiny spectators would crouch and glue their eyes to the little windows that opened on to the magical world within, their hands cupped around the rims better to shut out light and reality. Presently the man would set his machine in motion turning a handle at the back, and a marvelous tapestry would unfold. . . .

It was all over in a second! But the seed of curiosity and desire had to be planted: I longed to see those beautiful and exotic places, meet the strange people who lived beyond the Seven Mountains and the Seven Seas. It was the first stirring of an urge to move, search, perhaps in the end find a place where the soul would feel at home. Of such yearnings, exiles are made. *Le bonheur est ailleurs*—happiness is elsewhere. . . . The *Shahre-Farang* ignited a flame which nothing but time and experience could contain.[12]

By tracing her expatriation to childhood memories of the *Shahre-Farang,* Guppy accords herself a new vision of exile, one which reaches beyond the present and places her experience—and, by extension, that of other Iranians—in a universal poetic context. Her expatriation, which began with glances into an enticing and imaginary unknown, bears within it the seeds of a new creativity. As pointed out throughout her autobiography, Guppy's artistic career was not launched until after her departure from Iran; that is to say, her art became a vehicle for repatriation: "I recorded that lullaby on my first LP in London, which was a collection of Persian folk-songs and mystic chants. It became the signature tune of the Children's Hour on Persian Television."[13] What emerges from Guppy's reflections on her art is an ever-shifting set of juxtapositions: past and present, self and other, insider and outsider. It is precisely the tension inherent in such polarities which provides Guppy with a creative impulse.

With this type of juxtaposition, to say nothing of the dualism so deeply embedded in the Iranian spirit, we have entered the third category of Persian exile discourse. The writer who best represents this group is Taghi Modarressi. As I have implied in reference to Shusha Guppy's text, the boundary between the second and the third category cannot always be rigidly marked and maintained. It may be easier to grasp the differences between these two classifications in linguistic terms. Whereas the writers in the second category write in a second language and maintain ties, tenuous though they may be, with Iranian culture, the writers in this third category move with some ease from Persian to their adopted language. Their works are informed by a double perspective and reflect this duality on many levels.

This tendency is made clear in Modarressi's essay "Writing with an Accent." Describing his arrival in the United States and his first few months in Kansas, Modarressi hints at the first manifestations of his desire for

exact translations, for a perfect delineation of the self and the other.

If I wanted to say something, I compared Persian and English words, as dictionaries do. Persian and English words arranged themselves in two parallel lines like dancers in a nineteenth-century ballroom, bowing to each other and trying to find a mate. I had not yet mastered a linguistic consciousness that I could consider my own. I knew that if I were to comprehend the new culture, it was not enough to rely on memorized phrases.[14]

The new phase of recognition was, for Modarressi, accompanied with the discovery of what he calls his "internal voice." He regards this as an "artifact," a construct which allowed him to bring together the past and the present. Far from suggesting that this process leads to a perfect synthesis, Modarressi argues that his new voice liberates him from choosing between the self and the other, the foreigner and the native, the Iranian and the immigrant.

On the plane returning from Iran to the US, a strange idea kept occurring to me. I thought that most immigrants, regardless of the familial, social, or political circumstances causing their exile, have been cultural refugees all their lives. They leave because they feel like outsiders. Perhaps it is their personal language that can build a bridge between what is familiar and what is strange. They may then find it possible to generate new and revealing paradoxes. Here we have our juxtapositions and our transformation—the graceful and the awkward, the beautiful and the ugly, sitting side by side in a perpetual metamorphosis of one into the other. It is like the Hunchback of Notre Dame trying to be Prince Charming for strangers.[15]

This vision has allowed Modarressi to write works for an Iranian and American audience at once. There is no doubt that *The Pilgrim's Rules of Etiquette* or *The Book of Absent People* will be read and discussed very differently in Iran and North America. However, what is certain is that Modarressi has transcended the earlier self-imposed exile which prevented him from writing. Better to be read by two very different audiences than not be read at all.

Modarressi now uses these juxtapositions to his advantage. His new role reveals itself on both the thematic and the linguistic levels of his novels. In *The Pilgrim's Rules of Etiquette* the protagonist Hadi Besharat, a scholar of ancient Iranian history and culture, flees the horrors of the Iran-Iraq war by immersing himself in the study of third-century Manichaean texts in Parthian, Sogdian, and Middle Persian. Modern Persian, the language of his immediate reality, becomes displaced by dead languages in which Besharat finds echoes of the present. In the English version of the book Besharat speaks and writes yet another language, a blending of modern Persian and American English. Modarressi's insistence upon direct renderings of Persian idioms into English is a signal to his readers that the untranslated and the untranslatable form the essence of his work. In the following passage, for example, the flavor of the original is preserved:

> [The general] lamented that foreigners couldn't read Farsi and discover what sort of treasures are buried in this ancient land. He complained, "Agha, why is it that the instant our young people's feet reach the shores of America and Europe they roll up two pieces of toilet paper, tuck them under their arms like diplomas, and descend on the homeland? No sooner have they returned, the sweat of travel not dry on their bodies, than they go to the podium and, without a smidgen of knowledge of the cultural treasures of this land, let words bigger than themselves come out of their mouths and affect everyone." (12)

Most reviewers of the English translation of *The Pilgrim's Rules of Etiquette* have remarked on the double nature of the author's language. In her review, for instance, Anita Desai points out: "The quick, light, glancing manner in which [Modarressi] achieves this 'double-writing' or arabesque surely has to do with the fitting of his Iranian self into his American setting, of the remembered Persian tongue into the practiced English one. This produces a language—and a way of thinking—that is not Western, nor quite Eastern, but a shimmering amalgam of the two."[16] This particular expression of exile indicates that contemporary Iranian literature can withstand exile. More important, Modarressi's example indicates that exile may, in fact, lead to the type of expansion and internationalization advocated by Alavi. Far from being isolated and condemned to oblivion, exiled Iranian writers are becoming part of a new international literary phenomenon: i.e., a class of writers who are not limited by their nationality and do not write for a single national audience. For them the loss of a homeland and a nationality is a difficult yet exuberant step toward self-definition. The transformation such writers undergo is aptly outlined in Salman Rushdie's essay "Imaginary Homelands."

> It may be argued that the past is a country from which we have all emigrated, that its loss is part of our common humanity. Which seems to me self-evidently true; but I suggest that the writer who is out-of-country and even out-of-language may experience this loss in an intensified form. It is made more concrete for him by the physical fact of discontinuity, of his present being in a dif-

ferent place from his past, of his being "elsewhere." This may enable him to speak properly and concretely on a subject of universal significance and appeal.[17]

This vision has already enabled exiled Iranian writers to reclaim their loss and to reimpose themselves upon their homeland. Even in its most passionate form of longing for return and frustration with the loss of a heritage, Persian literature of exile has created a new esthetic norm within the Persian literary system. That the literature produced outside Iran is being imported into Iran is indicative of its acceptance within the mainstream of Persian literature and its significance for the Iranian audience.

It may now be possible to respond to the question which has plagued critics and readers alike. Is literature written in a second language Persian literature? If the answer is a categorical no, then there is little room for creativity. On the other hand, if the answer is yes, Iranians may be able to plant their quince-orange trees anywhere and watch them blossom.

Nasrin Rahimieh, Winter 1992

[1] Taghi Modarressi, *The Pilgrim's Rules of Etiquette,* New York, Doubleday, 1989, p. 8.

[2] Ali Sajjadi, "A Conference Report: 'Iranian Writers Writing in a Second Language' in Toronto, Canada," *Par,* 4:12 (January 1990), p. 16. The English translation of the quotation derived from the above Persian text is my own.

[3] Mohammad Sharif Kashani, "A Report of the Session to Honor Bozorg Alavi," *Par,* 4:11 (December 1989), p. 44. The English translation is my own.

[4] This phrase is derived from *Plagued by the West* (Paul Sprachman, tr., Delmar, N.Y., Caravan Books, 1982), a treatise by the Iranian writer Jalal Al-e Ahmad in which he argued against the indiscriminate adoption of Western standards and norms in Iran.

[5] Kashani, p. 44.

[6] Nima Naguibi, "Writing in a Second Language: The Panel of Iranian Writers in Toronto" (in Persian), *Iranian Woman,* 4:4 (Jaunuary 1990), p. 8.

[7] Donné Raffat, "Writing in English: What Oft Was Thought but Ne'er So Well Expressed in Persian, Or When a *Nom de Plume* Is Not a Pseudonym," talk delivered at the Middle Eastern Studies Association conference, Toronto, 1989, p. 13.

[8] Naguibi, p. 8.

[9] Vladimir Nabokov, *Pale Fire,* New York, Wideview/Perigree, 1962, p. 292.

[10] Nahid Rachlin, *Foreigner,* New York, Norton, 1978, p. 124.

[11] Salman Rushdie, "Imaginary Homelands," in *Imaginary Homelands: Essays and Criticism 1981–1991,* London, Granta Books, 1991, p. 15.

[12] Shusha Guppy, *The Blindfold Horse: Memories of a Persian Childhood,* Boston, Beacon, 1988, pp. 94–95.

[13] Ibid., p. 126.

[14] Taghi Modarressi, "Writing with an Accent," talk delivered at the Middle Eastern Studies Association conference, Toronto, 1989, p. 3.

[15] Ibid., p. 6.

[16] Anita Desai, "Head to Come," *New Republic,* 4 December 1989, p. 45.

[17] Rushdie, p. 12.

Literary Developments in Iran in the 1960s and the 1970s Prior to the 1978 Revolution

In the fall of 1977, ten nights of public readings and speeches by prominent Iranian writers and poets and literary critics were sponsored by the Iran-German Cultural Society in Tehran.[1] This festival of words took place in an atmosphere of freedom and a lack of formalized restraint uncharacteristic of the previous two decades. For the audience, dominated by young students, the occasion provided an opportunity to hear at first hand writers and poets whose works censorship had relegated to virtual anonymity.

Censorship was a handmaiden of the Pahlavi government's program for the revitalization of Iran. In the government's rush to push Iran into a new era of prosperity, and in the face of what the government perceived to be widespread "obstinacy," dissenting opinions were not tolerated. For a short period of time the grip of censorship was loosened, however, due in part to a crisis in the government brought about by economic troubles and social unrest, and also to the issue of human rights spreading throughout the world. Iranian writers and journalists, among other concerned groups (such as lawyers and judges), wrote open letters to the government which were circulated underground.[2] Such letters urged an end to the government's arbitrary actions, censorship, and cultural stagnation.

By August of 1978 "the public was no longer silent on issues of major concern, such as the need for social and political reform."[3] Books which had never been published appeared in print. The Iranian writer Bozorg Alavi gauged the political situation in Iran from his home in East Germany by whether or not he received any books from Iran. In the period from 1975 to August 1977, all his requests for books were unanswered or refused. However, copies of his novels, unavailable in Iran in 1970, appeared in print in Tehran in 1978, and by the spring of 1979, many of his books, some 100,000 copies, were finally in print after twenty-five years of censorship. By July of 1979, the celebration of words, in the form of news, editorials, novels, stories, poems, and opposition publications, was sadly coming to an end. After the first presidential election in December 1979, a new machinery of censorship was once again in place. Many Iranian writers were forced to flee Iran.

Although Iranian governments have curtailed free artistic expression throughout the twentieth century, new features of artistic repression became evident in the 1960s and 1970s. After the fall of the Mosadegh government in 1953 and the subsequent strengthening of the shah's political power, not only was opposition suppressed, but it was done so with increasing efficiency and ruthlessness. In 1957 and 1958 laws were passed which gave the political police (SAVAK) the power to deal with all forms of opposition to the government. In the 1960s even these laws (which were in themselves violations of the 1906 Iranian Constitution and the Universal Declaration of Human Rights) were ignored. There were arrests, detentions, torture, and executions. Writers and poets did not escape government control or reprisals.

Increasingly effective government control of culture had an insidious effect on Iranian artistic life, for at the same time that the government acted to suppress critical comment on its activities, it patronized an officially sanctioned culture which propped up the government's image of itself or depicted values to which the government felt Iran and Iranians should aspire. Very often the source of these values was the West, because the government itself sought inspiration and models for progress outside Iran. This situation left out in the cold those serious writers who saw it as their duty to depict Iranian life in all its poverty, unhappiness, and ignorance.

"Censorship crushes the true artists and scatters the seeds of the 'pseudo-artists,'" the writer Gholam-Hossein Sa'edi (1935–85) told his audience on the fourth night of the "Ten Nights." Sa'edi divided the artistic community of past years into two groups: true artists and fake artists. The latter group looked for their inspiration outside Iran. As such, they were only capable of producing "fake art," because their art had a base neither in Iran nor in the West. Art which sprang from a non-Iranian milieu was necessarily superficial and imitative. The pseudoartists were uninterested in the culture of Iran and the culture of the Iranian people and their problems and concerns. Sa'edi ascribed the astounding growth of "fake art" entirely to the social environment and to the patronage of "so-called art" by "leaders" and "people in charge." The audience for Iranian art, he continued, cannot be made up of a select few (who are in any case uninterested in the indigenous culture). The Iranian people are capable of judging a true work of art, and it is in the heart of the people that a true work of art must find a place. Unfortunately, as Sa'edi pointed out, it was the fake artist who received wide exposure in the government-controlled media.

The writer Behazin (b. 1915), speaking in 1968 and 1969 to the Association of Iranian Writers (formed by Iranian writers in 1968 to give a legal character to writers' fight with the censor and to provide moral support for writers who were in trouble), voiced some of the concerns expressed by Sa'edi in 1977: "Art which is acceptable to the censor grazes with ease in the government's exclusive pastures and is never subjected to critical appraisal."[4] Government art thus becomes decadent and lifeless, Behazin pointed out, while "oppositional art" does not gain exposure. He went on to say that, in this situation, the intellectual growth of the nation's young was stunted. Writers were at present "worn out, excluded from what is going on, and out of touch with reality and with information."

Writers such as Simin Daneshvar (b. 1923) and Behazin, considered "progressive" figures in the Iranian cultural milieu of the 1960s and 1970s, and writers who belonged to the AIW were officially discredited in news releases. Perhaps even more effective in relegating these authors to the status of nonentities was the fact that their work was ignored by the media (unlike the government-patronized artists, who were unhampered in presenting their work to the public). "For every Behazin and Daneshvar and Golshiri, there are scores of hacks and would-be short-story writers and so-called translators[5] who supply the material for cheap books and newspapers," Sa'edi told his audience.

Freedom of expression became, for serious/progressive writers, the freedom to express their country's true culture and true aspirations. Freedom of expression meant the freedom to depict society as it was rather than as it should be. Writing about certain aspects of Iranian life thus became a political act in itself and brought the writer into conflict with the censor.[6] In Bozorg Alavi's view, writing and imprisonment were sacrifices made for political ends.

No matter if the actual machinery of censorship was careless and disorganized. The illegality, ruthlessness, and arbitrariness of its practice made censorship a formidable enemy for creative writers and introduced an element of fear into the cultural life of the 1960s and 1970s. The publishers feared for their livelihood, the writers for their lives.

Sa'edi's "Ārāmesh dar huzūr-e dīgarān" (Eng. "Composure in the Presence of Others")[7] is a novella about middle-class Iranians living in the Iran of the late 1950s (although the situation of the characters would apply to the Iran of the 1960s and even 1970s). The subject of Sa'edi's scrutiny, the middle class, is a departure from the author's more usual look at villagers and the urban poor. The story was adapted for the screen by Sa'edi and Naser Taqva'i in 1972 but was banned for a period of time.

The story opens with a sudden summer storm, the sky filled with ragged, menacing clouds. A retired colonel makes a hasty decision to sell his small chicken business and move from the town where he lives with his young second wife to the town where his two young daughters by his first marriage reside. The latter town is large enough to have a hospital, where the young girls work, but open socializing between males and females is not sanctioned. The young daughters, who obviously do not usually wear traditional clothing, put on chadors to wander about certain sections of town.

All the characters in the story could conceivably be the patients of their creator, a psychiatrist as well as a creative writer. The colonel (he is not given a name) is a retired army officer, alienated from a world which no longer values him (ten to twenty years ago, as the colonel tells us, army officers were in the driver's seat and were treated with reverential respect). He flits in and out of the day-to-day existence of his daughters but does not play a meaningful part in their lives. Moreover, he is separated from the younger generation by a change in social behavior: his daughters socialize with the young men they meet at work (albeit in a surreptitious manner), whereas the colonel's second marriage (after the death of his first wife) was arranged by the principal of the school where his wife worked. Unappreciated by either society or family, the colonel finds death looming large. He is unable to sleep without having confused dreams in which weird phantoms pursue him. He is irritable; he stares off into the darkness and writes letters to no one in particular, tears streaming down his face. Growing increasingly demented, he is finally taken to a mental hospital. Only in madness does the world finally become less menacing to him. Upon entering the mental hospital, the colonel shouts to the crows lined up in the hospital's garden, "Hello friends, at last I'm saved."

The young people too are alienated from their world. The doctor (again, no name is given to the character) is "the hope of the nation's future," but he is a cynical, opportunistic, uncaring young man, interested in women and uninterested in his patients. None of the younger generation is able to find any meaning in life. One of the daughters complains that she feels useless and ineffective; she is not like the old or the new. Another character, known only as "the man with blue eyes," says that all the high hopes of the past, "all the things that keep a person going," have come to nothing: "What can we do with this icy, cold, dead existence?" The young men seek escape in alcohol, drugs, and suicide and the women in shopping and primping. Only the colonel's wife is a study in "complete composure." She is the colonel's good helpmate, forever subdued, docile, meek, drawn along in spite of herself, in her husband's rash decisions. Her one dread is to be left homeless, without shelter. She pushes away problems and denies her feelings. She is viewed by her young stepdaughters as a "sad case," a bird whose wings have been clipped by her husband's jealousy. She has no appetite, is listless, depressed, and anxious, but only she is perfectly serene amid the confusion of the others. She is the only kind character in the story. In the final scene, in the colonel's messy, forsaken hospital room, she offers him water from her hands.

The characters are like animals caught in an unforgiving trap, thrashing about to no avail. They seek escape, but their lives remain essentially unchanged, a feature of the majority of stories of this period. The characters, however varied their milieu, move about like so many pieces of a kaleidoscope, shifting position slightly but never leaving the circumference of the kaleidoscope.

The world as pictured by Sa'edi is one in which clocks are forever marking the passage of time, a world with no clear lines, where shadows and shapes merge together. It is a world where clouds obscure the sky, where sounds of music are muffled and muted. It is an unfriendly world where neighbors peek out at the trials and tribulations of others from behind the curtains of their own homes. Doors in the houses are closed, and windows look out into darkness, the "disquieting darkness of the night." It is a world where the clanging of the itinerant blacksmith's chains give comfort to the women but "aggravate the colonel's terror and excesses." Images of suffocation, death, and burial abound. Strange noises and phantoms invade the lives of the characters, symbols of their fears and anxieties.

If, on first reading, the characters are faceless and seemingly harmless, gradually the reader is drawn in by Sa'edi to feel the sadness of the world that the characters inhabit. The only "happy" character is the servant Ameneh, who quietly goes about her chores and waits patiently for her orders. Sa'edi is a social critic, but primarily the poet of people's suppressed feelings of emptiness, fear, and yearning. Thus his characters become powerful images of suppression, in spite of their lack of "name or place," and his writing a powerful indictment of a "system" that produces psychological and emotional distress.

The serious writers of the 1960s and 1970s were forced to deal with a lack of public support, both material and spiritual. Writers earned a living from jobs other than writing. "We are not professional writers," Simin Daneshvar told a recent interviewer. "We all had jobs, and we did not earn a living by writing; it was not possible to do so. We have never been able to get organized. We are continually in a state of turmoil and excitement, and we are unable to write."[8] As a young woman, Daneshvar wrote articles for Radio Tehran and for newspapers. She did translation work (which she later regretted, because it took her away from writing) and taught at the University of Tehran until she retired in 1977.[9] Behazin went to France to attend university on a government scholarship and became thoroughly acquainted with French language and literature. With this knowledge, he was able to abstain from, in his words, the "disgrace of selling oneself" and to support his family by translating. Sa'edi, trained as a psychiatrist, ran a clinic in the slums of South Tehran.

Readership for works by the serious writers, though still small, was growing and primarily young.[10] Even the reading public was affected by censorship. A reader might buy a book that was available in the bookstores and take it home, only to find that he had fallen into a trap set by the authorities. The reader was then arrested and sent to prison, where he might languish for months. By all estimates, censorship and the lack of intellectual stimulation should not have provided an atmosphere conducive to creative writing and the development of Persian prose, which was in any case a relatively recent phenomenon, dating back only to the 1920s. Still, Persian prose (which is "essentially poetic," in Alavi's view) had come into its own by the 1960s and 1970s and was (again in Alavi's view) "on a par with poetry as a means of expression—maybe in some ways even more vigorous."

Iranian writers showed amazing fortitude, resilience, and, above all, ingenuity in dealing with their handicaps. As Daneshvar has pointed out, art does not necessarily flourish only in times of artistic freedom; sometimes one sees water lilies blossoming in slimy pools. When an artist puts her mind to it, she can create interesting symbols to escape from the "invisible net." In the final event, serious writers thought for themselves. They made use of allegory and symbolism and allusion, even vague writing that could be taken in a hundred different ways, to say what they wanted to say. And although these methods had their dangers (i.e., thoughts were often not taken to their logical conclusion) and caused writers to run the risk of losing their audience, most still said what they felt they had to say.

Their readers, after all, had had a long apprenticeship in deciphering evasive and symbolic language.

Those writers who continued writing in the Iranian milieu of the 1960s and 1970s were imbued with a deep sense of their artistic mission. Bozorg Alavi's "strong sense of mission" to enlighten the Iranian people helped him continue writing in spite of censorship. "I know I cannot write about flowers and nightingales," he has said, in part as a reaction to the content of much of traditional writing, and in part as a response to his immediate milieu. The poet Ahmad Shamlu (b. 1925) echoes these sentiments.[11] The modern poet, unlike the poet of olden times, shares the life of his fellow citizens ("poets are trees in humanity's forest / not hothouse flowers in some patron's protected garden"). As such, the modern poet can (and must) speak for humanity ("poetry today is mankind's weapon"). Sa'edi closed his speech to his young audience with the words "three hundred red roses but one real flower / if we feared for our lives, we would not be dancing in the lovers' assembly."

Daneshvar makes use of surreal settings when the occasion calls for it, but she prefers real settings. True artists have a mission to make a statement about their world, she says. Artists must look at their world, describe it, respond to it, and explain it. Her particular mission is to defend society's "afflicted" (which she interprets in a different sense than Sa'edi). She connects her characters to actual circumstances and often shows them dealing with historical situations. At times she places her characters in political situations so that they have a right to make choices.

In her story "Mudel" (The Model),[12] for example, she describes a small corner of Iranian life: namely, a recently opened coeducational high school for training painters and sculptors. The story takes place in the 1960s. The model of the story's title is a young French teacher, Farideh, who risks her job to stand up to an authoritarian principal. The principal is obsessively worried about the likelihood of a scandal, any hint of which would close the school. Farideh befriends two star-crossed lovers: a young girl "accused" of receiving anonymous love letters, and a young boy who is afraid to own up to his "crime." The innocent love of these two young people is portrayed against the background of the principal's callousness and suspicion and the girl's mother's worry over the family's loss of reputation. In this tightly knit society, an individual's actions necessarily have an impact on others.

The culprit of the story is made evident by the author. The culprit is not "love," as the principal and the young girl's conservative and religious mother would have us believe, but rather a fearful society, which regards natural human occurrences such as adolescent love with hostility. The story is not one-sided, however, for Daneshvar demonstrates her humanism and understanding of human foibles in conveying a man's fear of losing his job and a widow's fear of jeopardizing her good name.

The other "model" in the story is a young night watchman for the Department of Education, who moonlights by taking work as a model during the day, leaving him time for only a quick nap between jobs. Yet another "afflicted" character is the school janitor, who monotonously expresses his fears for the coming winter and his family's lack of warm clothes. He complains to no one in particular about his wife's illness; only Farideh hears what he is saying.

Although Farideh is willing to sacrifice her job for her pupils, and although she is a model human being, kind and devoted to her charges, she cannot change the system. She can only make life a little more pleasant for those who are victimized by that system. Farideh is not the stereotype of the weak, helpless female found in much of Persian writing by male authors (the socially concerned writers). She is strong-minded and independent. In fact, she is a model for Iranian women (although Daneshvar does not take her out of one situation and put her into a totally different one). Farideh is capable of moral and humanistic behavior, but not of changing her world, personally or politically. Daneshvar too is something of a model for Iranian female writers. She wrote the first novel by a female (when she was twenty-eight) and advocated the description of the female mentality by women. The focus of her scrutiny was not only the world of intellectuals like herself, but the world of lower-class women as well.

The language and thinking of the story are simple, as is appropriate for the ordinary person whom Daneshvar was attempting to reach in her writing. She felt it was an author's duty to write in a simple style due to the low rate of literacy in Iran. In order to accomplish this, she tried hard to forget what she was taught during six years of study at Tehran University's Faculty of Literature and to find her own language for each story to match the social setting and class of her characters. The lack of freedom that she experienced in writing was not due particularly to censorship or political repression. She speaks of a "conservative and hypocritical" society which inhibited frankness and sincerity in writing (particularly a female's writing). Her perception of life's "bitter truths" and "bad times" embraces all aspects of life, from poverty and personal problems to Iran's place in the world and its unique history.

Sa'edi and Daneshvar, both well known in the decade prior to the Iranian revolution, had very different experiences of state control. Although Daneshvar was kept back from attaining her rightful rank in the university and her works were occasionally revised because of interference from the censor, she was never imprisoned. Alavi speaks of becoming politicized in prison, where truth is revealed as it cannot be in the world outside. From his exile in Paris, Sa'edi urged the act of writing as a highly effective political weapon against the government of the Islamic Republic.

The writer Behazin suffered imprisonment also,[13] and like Sa'edi, he viewed literature as an instrument of change. Sadly, his creative works were relatively unknown in Iran before the period when censorship eased. He was recognized primarily in his capacity of translator (most likely because of his membership in the Tudeh Party), and his work could best be described as community-oriented. For Behazin, the writer's mission is to describe his world in all its variety, whether his topics are acceptable or unacceptable to the censor. As the best-educated, most aware, and even most courageous element in society, writers must show people the flaws in the system and point them in a new direction. The variety of Behazin's writing attests to his courage in carrying through with his mission, in spite of the loneliness and isolation that this action entailed.

The story "Az dehāneh-ye chāh" (Through an Opening in the Well),[14] written in the first person and based on incidents in Behazin's personal life (as is much of his writing), acquires social significance through the author's treatment of the material. The storyteller informs the reader that all his life he has been trying to escape from dark and enclosed spaces. In order to accomplish this task, he is continually imagining and striving for an ideal to ease the pain of earthly existence. He must, simply by virtue of being human, experience the world's loneliness, separation, death, and terror, but he can aspire to something else. Although the work is somewhat unspecific and elliptic, the author seems to be parrying ignorance with a gradually awakening enlightenment, possibly a social conscience, which has its beginnings in Europe. The seven short episodes in the story take the reader back and forth between France and Iran, which seems extremely poverty-stricken and sad to the author upon his return from Europe. Only the dark Iranian sky, filled with a myriad of shining stars, gives him comfort.

In the final episode, a family friend, a noble sayyid brimming with life and vitality as he entertains the author and his father in his country garden, becomes lost. He is finally dragged from the bottom of an irrigation channel, half alive. The sayyid is placed in a dark room with drawn curtains, and a thin piece of black cloth is put over his eyes. Each time the door opens to let a bit of light into the room, he lets out a weak cry of pain and tries to cover his eyes with his bony hands. There is not much hope of his survival, but the doctor tries hard and prays to God for help. The author feels sadness and embarrassment when he witnesses the sayyid's fear of light. He feels suffocating hatred and terror upon seeing the noble figure embracing darkness. The author runs out into the light and immediately feels rejuvenated. The sayyid is buried three days later, satisfying his "desire for the dark."

■ ■ ■

The stories touched upon in this article, as well as scores of other works of the prerevolutionary period, are emphatically Persian in locale and spirit, but the content is very often inspired by the political and social milieu of that period. The works of writers such as Behazin, Daneshvar, and Sa'edi, meant as teaching vehicles, treat problems and situations that were specific to a certain period in Iranian history. The government of the Islamic Republic wants officially to negate that period. Prerevolutionary poetry is deemed by the new government to be Western-inspired, and many poets who wrote in the decade or so before the revolution are living in exile. Similarly, Sa'edi, Shamlu, and all the women writers were decreed by the Islamic Republic's Ministry of Guidance (the agency which granted the seal of approval for publication) to have been corrupted by Western influence. In spite of Alavi's desire to write for "the people," the reality of his situation was such that writers of the 1930s wrote for themselves and for each other. Thirty to forty years later, artists still complained of isolation from the reader, who was a necessary component of the perfect circle formed by the writer, his or her writing, and the audience. However, the profusion of interesting and varied writing attests to the richness of Persian creativity and of the Persian milieu, and also to ingenuity in the face of restraining influences.

Rivanne Sandler, Spring 1986

[1] These readings and speeches were published in the anthology *Dah Shab* (Ten Nights), Tehran, Amir Kabir, 1978.

[2] Writers sent two letters to the prime minister in June 1977. Writers, lawyers, and intellectuals banded together for a second time in 1980 to denounce censorship and the abuse of human rights, but to no avail.

[3] Donné Raffat, *The Prison Papers of Bozorg Alavi: A Literary Odyssey,* Syracuse, N.Y., Syracuse University Press, 1985, p. 204. For a review, see this issue, p. 357.

[4] Behazin, *Goftār dar Āzādī* (Talks on Freedom), Tehran, Agah, 1977; 4th printing, 1979.

[5] The government supported translations of works whose contents tallied with its priorities.

[6] Behazin was a member of the Tudeh (Communist) Party, which was ineffective in Iranian political life after 1959. Sa'edi's political affiliations are unclear, but he was imprisoned on many occasions from the 1950s to just before the revolution. Daneshvar was deliberately nonpolitical.

[7] Gholam-Hossein Sa'edi, "Ārāmesh dar huzūr-e dīgarān," in Vāhemeh-hā-ye bī nām o neshān, Tehran, 1967. Translated as "Calm in the Presence of Others," in Sa'edi's Dandil: Stories from Iranian Life, New York, Random House, 1981. For a review, see WLT 56:4 (Autumn 1982), p. 745.

[8] "Pā-ye Suhbat-e Sīmīn Dāneshvar" (An Interview with Simin Daneshvar), Alefbā (Paris), no. 4, 1983.

[9] Daneshvar was living in Paris at the time of the interview with Alefbā.

[10] In Alavi's time, 200–300 copies of a novel would be sold, "and then who would read it with any critical interest," he asks, "aside from a few literary people?"

[11] On Shamlu, see Ahmad Karimi-Hakkak, "A Well amid the Waste: An Introduction to the Poetry of Ahmad Shamlu," WLT 51:2 (Spring 1977), pp. 201–206.

[12] Sīmīn Dāneshvar, "Mudul" (The Model), in Shahrī chūn behesht, Tehran, Mauj, 1975; first printing, 1966.

[13] Behazin has also been detained by the government of the Islamic Republic.

[14] Behazin, "Az dehāneh-ye chāh" (Through an Opening in the Well), in Shahr-e Khodā, Tehran, Agah, 1978; first printing, 1970.

The Woman Who Sings No, No, No: Love, Freedom, and Rebellion in the Poetry of Forugh Farrokhzad

Persian women are perceived as veiled, repressed prisoners of a culture that traditionally inhibits the movement and growth of females. Certainly no brave, audacious Scheherazade comes to most Westerners' minds as they try to identify any outstanding Persian female poets or artists. Nevertheless, Forugh Farrokhzad's work distinguishes her as a daring, innovative writer who challenges the traditions of her Middle Eastern world, producing a poetry that addresses poignantly and forcefully the sensuality and grace of love, the sweetness of personal and social freedom, and the imperatives of rebellion and renewal. In one of her later poems she unburdens herself with words whose simplicity and obstinance mask an eloquence and passionate directive that characterize the unconventional, lyric style of her mature work.

—I must say something
I must say something
in the shivering moment at daybreak

when space blends with something strange
like the portents of puberty
I want
to surrender to some revolt
I want
to pour down out of that vast cloud
I want
to say no no no.
(FF, 53)

The titles of Farrokhzad's books published during her short lifetime (1935–67) reveal her interests: *The Captive, The Wall, Rebellion,* and *Another Birth.* As Farzaneh Milani points out, the first three collections, printed between 1955 and 1957, indicate the "general mood" of Farrokhzad's attraction to the themes of "women's independence and intellectual growth," but the poems in these early volumes are "fraught with conflicts: between sensuality and the safety of puritanical morality, between freedom and its accompanying anxieties and uncertainties. There is resentment of men's absolute right to give free rein to their sexual whims, and [the poet's] demand that pleasure be woman's right as well" (FM, 372–73). The early poems, therefore, explore repeatedly the nature of love—not just idealized love but sexual intimacy and romantic enjoyment. Farrokhzad ponders the nature of sex and gender, constructing an art that confronts the traditions of her background, and by the time she publishes *Another Birth* in 1963, she offers an image of a new, liberated, thoughtful Iranian woman: sensual, caring, complex, confident, and free. The intensity of expression in her poetry becomes the fierce cry of a woman seeking identity in the repressive world of twentieth-century Iran, a world heir to centuries of closed opportunities for women in all endeavors but particularly in art. Her work is strongly autobiographical, "honest, unposturing, and reflective of her innermost thoughts and feelings ... open, frank, and intimate," qualities that "might not have a place" in the "authoritarian, patriarchal Iranian environment" (MH90, 42–43, 34–35). "Everyone's afraid / Everyone's afraid," she writes (FF, 71), but poetry is the great liberator: "I don't search for anything in my poems; rather / in my own poems I discover myself" (MH77, 291).

When *The Captive* first appeared, Farrokhzad was twenty; the volume "exploded like a bombshell in Persian society and created intense controversy," according to Shireen Mahdavi, because "for centuries the subject matter of Persian poetry had been love, the suffering of the lover, the fickleness of the beloved, and the joys of reunion, but the poets had been men." No female poet had ever bared her soul "in frank and uninhibited confessions of romantic and physical love. In a culture where female sexuality was feared, [Farrokhzad's] poems brought the subject to the forefront." Mahdavi adds that this "bold expression of passion and emotion by a woman was absolutely revolutionary" (SM, 393–94), and Michael C. Hillmann declares that in 1955 Farrokhzad "published the first volume of verse in the history of Persian literature exhibiting a poetic speaker recognizable throughout as a female" (MH90, 41). In "The Hidden Dream," for example, Farrokhzad ignores literary and cultural traditions as she addresses a lover in the explicitly sensual yet casual, familiar tones of woman: "O, hey, man who has burned / My lips with the sparkling flames of kisses, / Have you seen anything in the depth of / My two silent eyes of the secret of this madness?" Social convention may force a woman to hide her passion, but external strictures of decorum can never extinguish the reality of desire: "Do you have any idea that, in my heart, I / Hid a dream of your love? / Do you have any idea that of this hidden love / I had a raging fire on my soul?"

The strain of hidden love may drive a woman mad, but the exuberant and bold "I" of the poem, the yearning female self, denies restraint and yields to the urges of immediate love, which in *The Captive,* as Hillmann observes, "makes the heart ache and . . . satisf[ies] all needs" (MH77, 295).

They have said that that woman is a mad woman
Who gives kisses freely from her lips;
Yes, but kisses from your lips
Bestow life on my dead lips.

May the thought of reputation never be in my head.
This is I who seeks you for satisfaction in this way.

I crave a solitude and your embrace;
I crave a solitude and the lips of the cup.

The insistent "I," reminiscent of Walt Whitman's pressing and audacious "Me myself" in *Leaves of Grass* (1.65), celebrates ultimately the endless fount of sexual desire and vitality that runs as a strong current through the poem and through the volume in general: "O, hey, man who has burned my lips / With the flames of kisses, / This is a book without conclusion, / And you have read only a brief page from it" (MH77, 295).

In another poem Farrokhzad conveys through the central image of a caged bird the desperate longing of a woman caught in a struggle against "suffocating cultural confinement" (SM, 394): "From behind the cold, darkened bars / I look, desiring and perplexed, toward you, / Dreaming of a hand that comes toward me, / And suddenly I can fly toward you." The speaker yearns for escape from the imprisonment of her cage. She is vexed, however, for she knows that the bars are cold and very

real; only in a dream or in the creative act of imaginative will does she move toward freedom and fulfillment—"toward you"—and toward self and wholesome identity: "toward me." Farrokhzad is no romantic, however; her posture often is one of craving without, necessarily, satisfaction or completion.

I ponder a moment of his neglect
When I may fly from this silent place
And laugh in my captor's face,
And beside you start my life again.

I ponder, but I know
I will never escape this cage,
For even if the jailer let me go,
I have no strength to fly.

Finally, in the personal darkness of her distinct, woman's dilemma, Farrokhzad finds illumination in the inviolable, irreducible power of her own private desire and imagination: "Oh sky, if I could one day / Leave this silent place, / What would I say to the crying child / Who passes me? I am the captive bird. // I am the candle that burns itself, / I make luminous what I destroy" (tr. John Zubizarreta with Moeineh Seyedin).

Farrokhzad defines her early poetry as the expression of her "outer world," which, Amin Banani explains, is how the poet describes the awakening in her of a "defiant consciousness of a woman's predicament" (FF, 5). Her disregard for the conventions and mores of male-dominated Persian society expresses her considerable scorn for expected patterns of outer behavior and traditional morality, both of which, of course, are dictated by men. Woman's predicament is that she is captive in the alien world of men, who prescribe her outer and inner agendas, her social and spiritual boundaries. Farrokhzad's defiance of these limitations is obvious in a poem such as "The Sin."

I sinned, a sin full of pleasure,
In an embrace which was warm and fiery;
I sinned surrounded by arms
Which were hot and avenging and iron . . .

In that dark and silent seclusion,
I sat dishevelled at his side;
His lips poured passion on my lips,
And I escaped from the sorrow of my crazed heart
. . .

I sinned, a sin full of pleasure,
Next to a shaking, stupefied form;
O God, who knows what I did
In that dark and quiet seclusion.
(MH77, 297)

The speaker has shared a carnal experience that would be labeled a sin by the keepers of the traditional moral code; yet the act is more than physical contact, for it engenders new life and the mystery of genuine human intimacy. The lover's eyes are "needful" and "secret-full," and the speaker's "heart impatiently shook . . . In response to the requests." The lover is "shaking, stupefied," transformed by the gesture of love, which is approved apparently even by God, who witnesses the moment and seems to condone the "positive and vital . . . natural urgency and pleasure of it all" (MH77, 297). The "dramatic and challenging individuality" of Farrokhzad's feminism in such poems shows why "Farrokhzad the poet has more often been called Farrokhzad the individualist, Farrokhzad the kept woman, Farrokhzad the whore" and why one commentary of her work includes "a photograph of Brigitte Bardot, with a caption quoting her view about appearing nude on the screen" (MH90, 51–52).

Still, the poet calls her experience a sin, revealing the painful dilemma of being caught between the heavy burdens of her millennia-old Persian past and the compelling call of new, predominantly Western ideas. As Mahdavi notes, Farrokhzad "grew up during a period when Iran was ambitious for modernization. . . . However, despite the fact that her poems are a revolt against conventional Persian relationships she is haunted by the indoctrination of her early upbringing" (SM, 395). In the poem "The Sin," for example—a work that flaunts its avant-garde feminism in brash, confident tones—the poet "does not call the act of making love by any name other than sin," and, according to Mahdavi, in Farrokhzad's personal life the same "conflict and spiritual dilemma recurs in her decision to divorce, losing her son" (SM, 395). When she was twenty-two, Farrokhzad's marriage, arranged six years earlier, ended in divorce, and Muslim law consequently forbade her officially from ever again seeing her only son; Mahdavi claims, "This separation left a permanent mark on her life," for essentially the young Farrokhzad was "faced with the choice of either becoming a free woman and pursuing her poetic career or remaining enslaved with her child. Having made the choice, she is doomed to feel 'the old grave of this endless grief'" (SM, 393, 395).

The awful dilemmas experienced by Farrokhzad in her personal life and revealed through her art express her strong desire not to be captive to the old ways and her inability often not to remain caught within the walls of established definitions of her gender and her art form. The first three volumes, for instance, though radical in tone and bold in feminist subject matter, remain rather conventional in form, adhering to the literary tradition of rhymed quatrains in Persian verse. Mahdavi says, "The poems follow the classical Persian format of rhyming couplets in quatrain stanzas" (SM, 396), and

Hillmann figures that "of eighty-six poems in her first three collections, seventy-five are series of quatrains" (MH77, 302). Farrokhzad herself seems discontent with the absence of formal ingenuity in her early work, for she repeatedly comments about her naïveté as crafter, as if she knows that her verse is unequal to the revolutionary content of the poems. In a 1964 interview, less than three years before her untimely death, she quips, "I have just begun the business of poetry in a serious way" (FF, 3). About her first three volumes, she says: "In those days poetry had not yet settled in me. It was cohabiting with me, like a husband, a lover, like all the people who stay with you for a while. But later poetry took roots in me" (FF, 4–5).

Farrokhzad's restlessness in her early work and her impatience with the "sheer weight of a 1000-year-old poetic tradition . . . [which] had reduced art into artifice and debased poetry into versification" (FF, 8) are evident in a few early poems in *The Wall*. "The World of Shadows," for instance, is unique among the youthful pieces in that its form consists of stanzas and lines of unequal length and no perceptible rhyme scheme.

At night on the damp road
  how often have I said to myself
    does life within our shadows assume colors, or
    are we ourselves the shadows of our shadows?

O you thousands of wandering spirits,
    sliding about me on the waves of darkness,
  where is my shadow?
  "The light of terror gleams in the crystal of my
silent cry."
  where is my shadow?
  where is my shadow?

I don't want
  for a moment to separate my shadow from
myself
I don't want
  her to slip far from me on the paths, or
    fall heavy and weary under the feet of
      passers-by. . . .
O . . . O sun
  why do you keep my shadow at a distance
from me? . . .
What does the sun say?
What does the sun say?
  Weary
  Bewildered
  Astonished
  I race down the road of endless questions.
(MH77, 298–99)

Clearly, the poet is ready for personal growth and for development of her craft. The impulsiveness and bravado of *The Captive* are missing here; instead, the persona is brooding, reflective, anxious, searching. Her shadow, her second self, her double eludes her; the world is "cold and alien"; the moonlight is "fading" and "ominous . . . cold and heavy"; and the tone is distinctly restive (MH77, 298–99).

In the poems of *Rebellion,* however, Farrokhzad moves further along by addressing more frequently the larger themes of fuller "human identity" and completion of the whole self, a shift that "forcefully draws attention to stages in Furugh's developing and expanding awareness and convictions" (MH77, 299). Hillmann cites Girdhari Tikku's examination of Farrokhzad's poems as "the only comprehensive study in English" of the poet's work, and it is Tikku who traces carefully the poet's growth through her first three volumes and who says that *Rebellion* "represents . . . a sort of natural development out of the poet's earlier poetic issues" (see MH77, 299). Moving from an acknowledged captivity to a self-conscious awareness of the nature of the particular barriers around her and then to a rebellious, complex struggle with wide-ranging issues of human value and human identity, Farrokhzad must have sensed in 1957 that she was on the verge of great personal and artistic change.

Consequently, Farrokhzad's personal, social, and artistic rebirth is the focus of *Another Birth,* the collection published in 1964. In this volume, according to Farzaneh Milani, the poet "emerges as a different character, one privileged with emotional and intellectual complexities, actively involved in a redefinition of her life." Milani adds that the "vacuum created by the dissolution of inadequate social values is filled with her own new substitutes," and we notice that poetry—because of its self-consciousness, its self-creating potential, and its imperatives for order—becomes Farrokhzad's keenest substitute (FM, 374). In fact, in an interview just a few months before her death Farrokhzad answers the question "Why do you write poetry?" this way:

> Because I need to. For me poetry is a need higher than the order of eating and sleeping, something akin to breathing. . . . Poetry for me consists of words living inside me—and the writing out of these words on paper in a living form. . . . Suddenly you see that just as you are turning inward, the words, like ants coming out of their hole on a sunny day, come out one after another and line up with a logical order. This order of words, if at that same instant they could express your mental intent, will undoubtedly become a poem. This is how I write poems now. For some time now I don't go searching for words. Rather, I wait for words to find their own place, to come into exis-

tence. Then I invite them to an order, to a kind of harmony. (FF, 7–8)

In *Another Birth* the poet comes as close as she ever came to complete harmony with her inner compulsions toward personal, social, and artistic freedom. We sense her development in these lines from the title poem:

> My whole being is a dark chant
> that will carry you perpetuating you
> to the dawn of eternal growths and blossomings
> in this chant I sighed you, oh
> in this chant
> I grafted you to the tree, to the water, to the fire.
> (SM, 397)

As Mahdavi points out, "The love described is neither guilt-ridden nor oppressed, but liberated" (SM, 397). The contrast with the earlier piece "The Sin" is telling, for in "Another Birth" there is no conflict or dilemma, no hint of self-deprecation or veiled agony over the nature of sexual love. In "The Garden's Victory" two lovers are "joined together symbolically by water, mirror, and light, traditional components of a Persian marriage ceremony" (SM, 397).

> Everybody knows
> Everybody knows
> you and I saw the garden
> through that dour, cold embrasure
> and picked the apple
> from that happy branch out of bounds
> Everyone's afraid
> Everyone's afraid, but you and I
> who were joined to the lamp, the water, the mirror
> and were not afraid.
> (FF, 71)

This Adam and Eve are fulfilled, not punished. Milani argues that the archetypal lovers "see the apple and, to pick it up, they enter the garden. . . . The forbidden fruit admits them to the garden rather than expels them. Subtly, the poet turns the familiar myth around. It is not the woman who tempts the man. Instead, they pick the apple together and deliberately. Neither is responsible for the other; there is no devil" (FM, 378). The rest of the poem is full of positive images of burgeoning life: "gamboling wild hares," "pearlfilled oysters," "phoenixes," "open windows," "fresh air," "a world pregnant with new seedlings," "lovelocked hands," "moving air" (FF, 72). Because of the reversal of the traditional Edenic story, the poem, then, is better titled by Hassan Javadi and Susan Sallee; their translation, "The Conquest of the Garden," conveys more directly Farrokhzad's intent to suggest the triumph of human love over Eden's ordinary doom and guilt.

Even the earlier shame and anguish over a lost son and lost potential are resolved to a degree in *Another Birth*. In "A Red Rose" Farrokhzad sings a fitting counterpart to her startling and defiant "no no no."

Red rose
Red rose
Red rose

He took me to the red rose garden
and in darkness set a red rose in my fearful hair
and then
made love to me on the petal of a red rose

O you fearstruck doves
O you fruitless virgin trees, O blind windows
Under my heart now, and in the corner of my womb
the red rose grows
Red rose
red
as a bloodstain

Ah, I'm pregnant, pregnant.
(FF, 73)

We remember, however, that despite the private and artistic resolutions evident in her more mature poems of rebirth, Farrokhzad's themes are still rooted in her strongly rebellious nature. "Rebellion," Milani reminds us, "is the very stuff of Forugh's life and the galvanizing principle behind her art" (FM, 369). The directives of "—I must say something / I must say something . . . I want / to say no no no," after all, come from the same imagination as "A Red Rose." Farrokhzad never denies the compulsions of her gender's cry for freedom, despite the greater number of poems in *Another Birth* that offer moments of reconciliation with the outer world of society, culture, religion—man's world. On the one hand we read these lines from the last stanza of "Another Birth":

I know a sad little nymph
who lives in the sea
and plays the wooden flute of her heart
tenderly, tenderly
Sad little nymph
dying at night of a kiss
and by a kiss reborn each day.
(FF, 92)

On the other we read the scathing, bitter tones of "Mechanical Doll," a poem that resembles "Barbie Doll," the American writer Marge Piercy's satire on the same subject.

Even more, oh yes
you can be even more silent than this
You can stare at cigarette smoke
hours at a time

staring the frozen stare of the dead . . .
You can stand stock still at the curtain
but blindly, but unhearing

You can cry with a voice
utterly false, utterly strange
"I love you"
In some man's overwhelming embrace
you're a beautiful healthy woman
a leather tablecloth for body
with a pair of big, tough tits
You can foul love's chastity
in the bed of a drunk, a maniac, a bum . . .

You can be like mechanical dolls
gazing at your world with glassy eyes
Your strawstuffed form
can sleep through the years in its velvet case
dressed up with sequined voile
To the pressure of any passing hand
you can squeak inanely
"Oh, how happy I am!"
(FF, 44–45)

The dry humor of the last line is as devastating an indictment of woman's passivity as the wry sarcasm of Piercy's closing stanza: "In the casket displayed on satin she lay / with the undertaker's cosmetics painted on, / a turned-up putty nose, / dressed in a pink and white nightie. / Doesn't she look pretty? everyone said. / Consummation at last. / To every woman a happy ending" (11.19–25).

Farrokhzad's later poems, then, are complex and dichotomous, reflecting the poet's shift from private warfare upon her predominantly masculine Persian world to consideration of greater issues of general human isolation, universal order, and spiritual rebirth from a more truly feminist perspective, in that she arrives at a more inclusive rather than exclusive understanding of the human condition. Still, she continues with "audacity to trespass boundaries and to follow her inner promptings" as she explores the nature of love and intimacy between men and women, staying true to her unconventional style and openness in discussing sexual relationships (FM, 368). In "Mates," for example, she ascribes new meaning to the so-called afterglow of sex.

Night approaching
and darkness after night
and after dark
eyes
hands
and breathing breathing breathing
and water sounding
dripping drop drop drop from the spigot

Then two dots of red
two cigarettes
the clock's ticktock
and two hearts
and two solitudes.
(FF, 70)

The tension and contest of sex, the emptiness of mere physical contact, the incommunicativeness in darkness are reminiscent of many of the poems in the earlier volumes, but we notice that the perspective is widened: "*two* hearts / and *two* solitudes" (italics mine). Both man and woman are dehumanized and isolated by the limited carnality of sex, which results only in disembodied presences—eyes, hands—in an equally fragmented world: dripping spigots, smoldering cigarettes. The sexual disingenuousness and spiritual aridity portrayed in "Mates" remind us of parts of T. S. Eliot's *Waste Land,* a relationship perhaps not so arbitrary, for one of the strongest influences on Farrokhzad's poetry was the work of Nimā Yushij, a "solitary voice . . . raised in the 1920's" (FF, 8). Nimā's *Afsāna* (Myth) was published in 1922, the same year as Eliot's great mythic poem of personal and cultural collapse, and it "heralded a new beginning in the history of Persian poetry . . . [and] led . . . to the birth of modernistic poetry" (FM, 375). These are intriguing intertextual connections, for we also hear in Eliot's poem the drip drop of water used as a similar sign of the dry human condition in the modern world devoid of private, historical, and mythical foundation: "If there were the sound of water only / Not the cicada / And dry grass singing / But sound of water over a rock / Where the hermit-thrush sings in the pine trees / Drip drop drip drop drop drop drop / But there is no water" (11.353–59). Evidently, Farrokhzad was a poet very much alive to the themes and formal innovations of the modern art that had taken shape in her lifetime in Iran and that had swept world literature in the earlier decades of modernism.

In February 1967 Farrokhzad was killed tragically in an automobile accident, just a few weeks after her thirty-second birthday, when she swerved her Jeep to avoid a school bus. Amin Banani recounts that in "the afternoon of her burial in a small cemetery in the foothills of the Alborz mountains, a heavy snow was falling—an eerie enactment of a recurrent theme in her poems" (FF, 3). Banani refers us to one of Farrokhzad's poems, which Milani also identifies as the poet's affirmation of her art, as "a promise of blossoming and growth, eternity itself" (FM, 367).

Perhaps those two young hands were true, those two
    young hands
buried below the never ending snow
And next year, when Spring

sleeps with the sky beyond the window
and shoots thrust from her body
the green shoots of empty branches
will blossom O my dearest one, my dearest only one.
(FF, 3)

After Farrokhzad's death, Muhammad Riza Shafi'i Kadkani wrote a powerful tribute: Forugh's "special genius and distinctive poetic personality . . . will assuredly give [her] permanent recognition as the most important woman poet in the thousand-year history of Persian literature, and as one of two poets of prominence in the present century" (quoted in MH77, 314).

Clearly, Forugh Farrokhzad's poetry invites further critical attention, and there are more translations and more accurate, complete bibliographies to be done in English. Her four published volumes, the posthumous collection *Let Us Believe in the Oncoming Season of Cold,* and her ventures into theater and film (she collaborated with Ebrahim Golestan on the internationally acclaimed 1963 documentary *The House Is Black,* made two short films for UNESCO, and produced or assisted in the making of several other documentary films from 1959 to 1964; see FF, 5–6, and MH77, 312) remain yet to be studied fully in the context of modern Persian artistic accomplishments. She offers her readers not only an impressive and sensitive treatment of the bold themes of modern feminist concerns but also—in a daring, singular, and compelling poetic voice—a generous and perceptive study of the greater, wider mysteries of human love, of the human ache for freedom, and of the transfiguring vitality of spiritual renewal.

John Zubizarreta, Summer 1992

■ **SELECTED BIBLIOGRAPHY IN ENGLISH**

Davaran, Ardavan Hamid. "Modern English and Persian Poetry: A Comparative Study." Dissertation, University of California at Berkeley. 1973.

Farrokhzad, Forugh. *Another Birth.* Hassan Javadi, Susan Sallee, trs. Emeryville, Ca. Albany. 1981.

———. *Bride of Acacias: Selected Poems of Forugh Farrokhzad.* Jascha Frederick Kessler with Amin Banani, tr. Amin Banani, intro. Ehsan Yarshater, foreword. Farzaneh Milani, afterword. Delmar, N.Y. Caravan. 1982. (References use the abbreviation FF.)

Hillmann, Michael C., ed. "Major Voices in Contemporary Persian Literature." *Literature East and West,* 20 (1976).

———. *Twentieth Century Persian Literature in Translation: A Bibliography.* Washington, D.C. Imperial Embassy of Iran. Cultural Department, publication no. 3. 1976.

———. "Furugh Farrukhzad: Modern Iranian Poet." In *Middle Eastern Muslim Women Speak.* Elizabeth Warnock Fernea, Basima Qattan Bezirgan, eds. Austin. University of Texas Press. 1977. Pp. 291–317. (References use the abbreviation MH77.)

———. *A Lonely Woman: Forugh Farrukhzad and Her Poetry.* Washington, D.C. Mage / Three Continents. 1987.

———, ed. "Forugh Farrokhzad a Quarter-Century Later." *Literature East and West,* 24 (1988).

———. "An Autobiographical Voice: Forugh Farrokhzad." In *Women's Autobiographies in Contemporary Iran.* Cambridge, Ma. Harvard University Press. 1990. Pp. 33–53. (References use the abbreviation MH90.)

———. *Iranian Culture: A Persianist View.* Lanham, Md. University Press of America. 1990.

Mahdavi, Shireen. "Captivity, Rebellion, and Rebirth." *Parnassus: Poetry in Review,* 12–13 (1985), pp. 393–400. (References use the abbreviation SM.)

Milani, Farzaneh. "Formation, Confrontation, and Emancipation." In Forugh Farrokhzad, *A Rebirth.* David Martin, tr. Lexington, Ky. Mazda. 1985. Pp. 123–33.

———. "Forugh Farrokhzad." In *Persian Literature,* Ehsan Yarshater, ed. Albany, N.Y. Bibliotheca Persica. 1988. Pp. 367–80. (References use the abbreviation FM.)

KAZAKSTAN

A Dilettante's Marginal Notes on National Literature

We are living under the sign of Change. It is a time of hope and of alarm. Life is becoming palpably more crowded and complicated, the order of things is changing sharply, the space of culture is being transformed. The reality we call national literature is living out a crisis of muteness, for it has lost its landmarks and cannot work out its position. And the entity we call the Text is absent altogether—or it is present only in a fragmented way. Of late there has been an attempt to approach, aspire to, comprehend the secret of modernity; but either the fatigue from the hopeless verbal constructions that have gone before is so great, or the need for the everlasting Word is so small—either way, local literature is in an unmistakable stupor.

It's a disease, of course, a grave and chronic one, and the organism's resistance to it weakens with the years. To resist requires constant effort. Until now we have only dimly guessed that it was a disease. Now we know for sure. And we are afraid to consider the consequences, for what might be the consequences of nonlife? To realize the present trouble and still try to find a way out of the almost hopeless situation, we must explain the reasons—that is, the history of the disease. The danger that threatens us is so great that, in the face of it, we must look honestly and soberly at our own condition and admit that our fall from the realm of the Spirit, from the realm of the Word, has, alas, effectively taken place. Without an analysis of what has happened, it is impossible to hope for the revival we so desire. Let us turn to the "facts of the time."

From time immemorial on the steppe, the Word has been all. The Kazakh nomad, with an equal mastery of the spear and the Word, knew that where language is powerless, all the rest is useless. With the Word, they routed enemies and won the hearts of beauties; with the Word, they reconciled and healed. Composers of verses and songs had a special status: to lift a hand against a poet was considered sacrilege. On his death, a father would leave his son a horse, the boundless expanse of the steppes, and—the Word. And the words in which son and father took leave of each other were handed down, discussed, compared, evaluated, remembered.

Oral literature had its own rich traditions. Today not one scholarly study is dedicated to them. The heroic epics *Alpamys, Koblandy,* and *Er-Targyn,* the lyric poems "Kyz-Zhibek," "Kozy-Korpesh," and "Bayan-Slu" exist in numerous variants. Ceremonial-ritual songs, legends, tales—there is no end to them. The poetic, figurative speech of our forefathers was their natural speech. People came from all around to gather at *aitysy,* competitions of improvisational poets. (My ninety-year-old grandfather Bilyal used to tell how, in his youth, he traveled fifty kilometers on foot to listen to such an *aitys:* the verbal duel went eight hours straight before it was broken off late in the evening by general agreement; but in the morning it was resumed, and only toward noon did it end with the victory of one of the *akyns* or bards, whose prize was a bay racehorse. Against this background, the mentions in songs and verses of heated verbal duels lasting three days and three nights turn out to be less metaphor than statement of fact.)

The air itself was poetry. For a horseman, unfettered by belongings, the world was unified, continually created before one's very eyes, like a manifestation of the infinite divine essence. The nomad, sensing the absolute harmony of existence, connected the past, present, and future effortlessly in every instant (more than likely, the "compression," the mixing and drawing together of events separated by centuries, in ancient texts is not a flaw but rather a consequence of a cosmic way of thinking that we have now lost); life was organized by uninterrupted movement, and if other peoples were faced with disaster, the fact was here received with tranquillity and resignation, as inevitable. Life was part of a voyage, a journey with an unknown end on which one must set out in an unwaveringly positive frame of mind, with full readiness to receive any outcome whatsoever. (It is not for nothing that the expression for "died" in the Kazakh language—*kaitys boldy*—literally translates as "returned"; after all, the Return to the Maker was the finding of everlasting life.) Love without fear, self-realization without calculating self-interest, gave rise to beauty and freedom. This is the stuff poetry is made of. And this was the truth of life—intoxicating, joyous, full of magic, of immortal wisdom. For the nomads, the situation of Fate presupposed not submissive waiting and not melancholy impending doom, but a wonderful possibility of power over one's own destiny within the framework of the inevitable.

The epic power of the legends, tales, poems, and songs of that time strikes the imagination; the energy of the lines captivates and, possessed of magical effect, makes visible the image of the ancient steppe, like an image of a lost paradise. Beyond all doubt, the epoch in which these things arose was a period of galvanic shock to the ethnic space of the steppe, an epic time with an epic hero, solid, fearless, not stopping for any obstacle, pursuing an ideal interest and always achieving victory. The words have no authors, they are anonymous. More precisely, their creator is the people itself. The fifteenth and sixteenth centuries, the epoch of the formation of Kazakh ethnic identity, left us an extremely rich and diverse artistic heritage. It was then that the genre of historical legend came into being, and from that time *shezhire* began to be formed: genealogies that even to the present day have a place in the traditional Kazakh family. There arose the concept of *menginik el,* the eternal country of the Kazakhs. (*El* is a word that means simultaneously "people" and "land.") The beginning was brilliant. Harmony was almost the organizing principle of life. The only reality left over from that time is the literature, which creates that world anew out of nonexistence.

Different times make for a different literature. The Great Disaster—*ak taban shubyryndy*—the Mongol-Dzungar invasion of 1723, sweeping the Kazakhs far outside the bounds of their ethnic territory, gave rise to a different hero, one who charted his place in history through pain and suffering: the man of history changed the epic hero of literature. The poetry of that time is an experience of disaster, a demonstration of despair and hope. The conquered, exiled, and ruined people was now uniting not in the usual manner of life, not through racial or tribal ties, not through the old traditions, not through material or rational means, but only through the Word. (Isn't it surprising? A people scattered throughout the world, among numerous races and tribes, so different one from another both in externals and in mentality—this difference exists even today—had practically no dialects; language was the only refuge and salvation.)

A fundamental turn took place: from contemplation to deed, from appeasement to struggle, and its defining inception was not esthetic but ethical and moral nature; honor and valor increased hope. The former syncretic unity with nature, the harmony regarded as a given, gave way to a sense of the ruin and catastrophe

the world contained, and, as a consequence, the artist's need to fix his presence in this world led to self-assertion. The keen sense of intense consciousness, as of a correlation, a connection with another reality, put forth the problem of a new embodiment, for the old world as a state of being was lost forever. The elevated mood, the mastery of the essence of all things—this was a happy moment, a flash of Light; but the once-revealed harmony strayed from its path in the soul for good, and the Word became a reminiscence of it, keeping everyday life from disintegrating. A new genre was born: *tolghau,* the "reflection" or "essay." The Word became personified, poetry found a concrete author, and behind the verse there was now a face. Of course, as the soil on which the artist came of ideological and spiritual age, there remained a collective way of thinking, a national folk body of work, but now the artist was guided by Providence; he was becoming a Prophet, a Hero, a Leader. He was taking on himself the labor and the responsibility of testifying before History. His word was becoming the fact of his people's existence.

Let us be frank: over the centuries that followed (right up to the twentieth), in the framework of the Russian empire, the Word remained the Kazakhs' only deed; and if it is true that the word *Kazakh* translates from the Arabic as "free, valiant," then it is not surprising that at the head of the anti-Russian uprisings and mutinies there stood, for the most part, the people of the Word—that is, poets. Appealing directly to Aruakh, the Spirit of the forefathers, they aspired to transcendence for their own opinions and judgments; they became *batyry,* heroes. Thanks to them, life became a matter of semantics; they created with the Word a space for history, through their eyes the people came to know itself, and in this way there sprang up other perspectives for society as a whole. The poet himself became an event, a cultural phenomenon.

On the boundary between the nineteenth and twentieth centuries, the key figure was that of Abai Kunanbaev, whose work became the crystallization of the soul of the Kazakh steppe. It was in his work, the work of the founder of Kazakh literature, that a propitious opening of national borders took place; proclaiming a Trinity of existence—love, reason, and free will—he developed a conception of a modern man who needed God and an idea of a God who needed man as a manifestation of Himself. Abai represents the renaissance of Kazakh culture. One fact of his presence in literature justifies our existence: his very appearance, a flashing awareness of generations' unconsciousness of our history.

The bourgeois-democratic February Revolution of 1917 evoked—and we will accept this without skepticism—an "explosive" wave of spiritual renewal: the surge in national self-awareness was unusually powerful and clear. The first Kazakh political party, "Alash," was headed by a sort of spiritual aristocracy which included Alikhan Bukeikhanov, Mustafa Chokai, Mukhamedzhan Tynyshpaev, Magzhan Zhumabaev, and Mirzhakyp Dulatov. Their names became a symbol of honor and courage. All of them were born intellectuals, and their main business was the Word. From their oeuvres, mythlike, there arose—I dare to assert—a different country. They tried, however strange it may sound, to build a new Kazakhstan out of their own selves, out of their own work, out of literary history. They tried, by their own impetus, to bring the steppe out of its torpor, the helpless deadlock of expectation. Of course, this attempt (leaving personal sympathies aside, one should say "utopian attempt") was instantly quashed by the Soviet regime; it was practically nipped in the bud. The new regime mercilessly wiped out everything original, suppressing the individual, obliterating the genuine; and it feared the living Word like fire, for the Word was Truth.

Real words were being uttered but, for the most part, to all intents and purposes, were not being heard—and therefore not assimilated. The steppe dozed again. In place of the former Kazakh national literature, an official Kazakh-Soviet literature developed: a new "socialist" content flowed into the traditional forms. The initial disharmony and disjunction failed to disturb anyone, and remarkable imitators soon appeared, offering their services to "neoliterature." The Soviet years were an epoch of stagnation; the most talented transmitters of language, tradition, culture—the flower of the nation—were persecuted and annihilated, and when it became clear that their Word had already taken root among the people, even the people themselves were half wiped out, methodically and in succession, in the course of the collectivization of the 1930s. (Of almost 6 million Kazakhs, 2.7 million perished in those years.) The total aggression resulted in wholesale reversal and regression.

At the close of the nineteenth and the beginning of the twentieth century, however, a new movement of the Word began in the field of Kazakh culture. Blood finally began to circulate through the whole organism again: the flexible, malleable, and open nomadic consciousness, having let Russian imperial reality "pass through it," was finding its former clarity of thinking, its ability to manifest its own history, and the few texts by poets and writers from those years that have come down to us—and are only now becoming a fact of social consciousness—show what promising possibilities native literature held. Alas, that which is not realized and as-similated in time generally fails to take root at all. (With this in mind, it is understandable why some Kazakh writers were absorbed in historical chronicles for many long years: the present reality was so destructive that it was necessary, obeying the instinct of self-preservation, to fix the past for presentation to future generations. This is one point of view; from another, this same self-preserving impulse created the illusion of regaining a former world, in a different dimension—a saving, but ultimately false, position.)

Amazed in our hearts at ourselves, demonstrating surprising adaptability, we accustomed ourselves to a new life. But to express it artistically?! That surely called for genius. It is impossible to describe in familiar words a life that has been turned inside out; after all, this through-the-looking-glass movement was very much a Soviet sociohistorical phenomenon. You don't express an upside-down world with the usual ideas (but a different form of expression was developing into caricature, cartoon, and protest). The paradox lay in the fact that the whole situation was culturally indescribable. The literature of that period (with print runs in the hundreds of thousands!) is striking precisely for its . . . lifelessness. (Schematism, the substitution of ideology for psychology, solemn proclamation, the automation of thought, the loss of the essence of the word—we have here all the signs of the violent demise of language.) All of that "Soviet Kazakhstan" literature, if we are to look at it with detachment, recalls a sick man's feverish dream. We drifted out of the dream, but the sickness still remained, and it was the sickness of consciousness. I have the conviction—strange, perhaps, but immutable—that between the Word (that is, language, thought) and actual reality there exists a direct physical connection. Not only do life and events create language, but the reverse is true as well. Placebo words engendered phantom people. The signs of things changed their very essence. The crisis of the Word brought on a crisis of identity: there appeared un-people, a zombie-like consciousness—no fantasy this, but only a sad statement of what had come about. The horror of it lies in the fact that it is irreversible.

A sadly logical fact: with the advent of the country's sovereignty—amid a number of publications and re-publications from the last century and the beginning of the twentieth—there came to light, in truth, not one single work by a contemporary writer that sparked a reaction from the reading public. (As for the "inner recesses," as for what was written—as in Russia—privately, "under the table," we had nothing of the sort. What kind of commentary is that?) There are only unwarranted expectations, the illusion that our Word is about to be reborn. In order for that to take place today, however, the Word needs support, and we must not look for this core outside but create it anew. It has to be created, as things stand, not from the best, but from what is at hand; and what there is, in the overall sense, is leftover, secondhand, derivative—that is, a barren breed. The result of such work is not hard to predict.

The present situation with the Word is a situation of good motives. But intentions and deeds, as we know, are two entirely different things. It is strange to think, but it seems that we have lost forever our taste for normal life (in point of fact, we don't understand what that is), for true values, for genuine things; we move by guesswork, totally worn out from our former senselessness, having lost our very creative capacity. We cannot grasp what has happened. In trying now to fix our own landmarks in the history of our literature, we see terrible gaps, yawning holes—voids that nothing fills (or that are filled with yesterday's husks, with a substitute for thoughts and feelings). We are out of step with our own structure. We ourselves have become barbarized. We are trying to restore our memory; grain by grain we are gathering the authentic Word (and we are not always sure we will recognize it). Alas, it seems to us that we are not actually ourselves—a guess, but not without foundation. Repeatedly we have tried to remain in the bosom of the Word. Time has tested us. We passed through the first checkpoint at the dawn of the birth of the nation, having been subjected to the Dzungar invasion, having preserved the homeland of the Word. The second attempt at separating us from language—in the framework of the Russian empire—did not take hold either: a handful of people, at the cost of their lives and despite their own neglect, managed to hold on to the native Word. The next ordeal—total annihilation under the Soviet system—resulted in tragedy.

Between the literature of the Past (even the quite recent past) and the present Word there is a gulf, for that literature was the product of another consciousness, to all intents and purposes—at last we're coming to it!—the product of another world, another existence. We ought to admit it: we were like hamsters on the treadmill of someone else's history, and now that, by the will of fate, we have jumped off that treadmill with a desocialized, radically simplified consciousness, we vaguely understand: now we are something other than we were. We have Another History. And this history demands its own language. Like Münchhausen dragged out of the swamp by his hair, we must pull ourselves out of the darkness, take the trouble to know ourselves, whatever inner convulsions and pain it requires—to "turn our eyes into our soul" and try to comprehend the fact of existence, our own and others'. Disregarding accustomed beliefs, abstracting ourselves from former

outlooks and assumptions of the transcendent, we must make ourselves aware of the contemporary condition of the Word: Sickness—that is, impotence and despair, emanating from the crisis in the state of existence, the crisis in the foundations of the absolute.

Kazakh film and painting, in this regard, resolved upon a deadly risk: Operation "Self." Young directors and artists of the 1980s and 1990s reported their own personal experience as evidence of the path to truth in the context of general human culture. In this way there arose "a new Kazakh wave" in the cinema and there appeared an avant-garde group in art which overstepped the barrier of the national spirit and won the recognition of a worldwide public. Native literature, meanwhile, writhes dumbly: the need for new forms is acknowledged, but the essence of the modern Word has still not been brought to light. Thus (once again, the dependence of reality on the Word!) the reality of our life has still not been revealed to us, for until now it has not been named or grasped. Everything that happens demands to be articulated, fixed in the realm of language; but we, childish and fainthearted, are afraid to look at ourselves and see what in fact we are.

Very likely, this is also the drama of freedom. We have to pull through, to return from the realm of specters, back to reality again. How are we to do this in a situation of disintegration, eating away at our eschatology? (We are broken down, leveled. We are in a state of entropy.) Only by overcoming ourselves, whatever the strain on the soul. It is clear that we today exist as an opportunity, a blueprint; but to make it a reality would be conceivable only at the pinnacle of selfhood, and the question now—since it calls not for spurious but rather for continuous efforts—is: do we have strength enough?

In the first place, we must prove to ourselves that we ourselves actually exist. Only then is further movement possible—of the Word, of language, of conscious existence. That is, of real life.

Asiya Baigozhina, Summer 1996

KYRGYZSTAN

Post-Socialist Kyrgyz Literature: Crisis or Renaissance?

The cultural sphere always reacts sensitively to shifts between sociopolitical formations. After all, the disappearance of an old society and the emergence of a new order constitute a painful process in any nation, for such a formational shift is frequently accompanied by revolutionary unrest, cruelty, and oppression. The communist empire, which not so long ago seemed to be a powerful monolith occupying one-sixth of the earth, was forced to leave the arena of history, having been defeated in the merciless competition between social systems and by ideological pressure from outside. The socioeconomic ties among he former Soviet republics were severed, and a "parade of sovereignty" began.

The destruction of traditional cultural and economic relations and the immense difficulties that came with the emergence of a new society have resulted in symptoms of crisis. Some of these symptoms can be observed in the intellectual sphere, particularly in literature. Deprived of constant material support and ideological guidance from the state, Kyrgyz national literature is experiencing a very problematic period of development. The quality and diversity of books has declined sharply, and professional literati have been forced to find occupations in other fields. In the past, the state took care of the publication and distribution of books, regardless of their quality.

Kyrgyz literature, as an organic part of Soviet literature, grew under the powerful influence of Russian and other developed literatures. At the same time, Kyrgyz literature maintained its national originality and distinctiveness, which might be characterized succinctly by the formula "Unity in diversity." In its essence, however, it was a literature of socialist realism. The artistic method of socialist realism—announced by Maksim Gorky and accepted at the First Congress of Soviet writers in 1934—presumes a description of reality in its revolutionary transformation and must be rendered in the spirit of populism (*narodnost'*) and party-mindedness (*partūnost'*). In other words, this method was based on a class-oriented approach which in itself is part of communist ideology and thus possessed authority over the new literature.

The growth and development of Kyrgyz literature was closely linked to the method of socialist realism, but interpreted in a simplified manner, so that this method limited the full blooming of artistic imagination and thinking. This schematic and dogmatic approach, characteristic of socialist-realist literature, produced a large number of colorless works which have become mere footnotes in literary history. In these works, reality is shown in a one-sided manner and from a rigid point of view. For example, the so-called "theory of conflict-lessness," which dominated literature for a long time, was based on the claim that conflict could exist only between the good and the better and that life should be presented as a festivity of labor, involving all people.

Later, such a simplified approach to artistic imagination was replaced by a more analytic attitude toward poetics and the description of characters, one in which the individual and his psyche, his emotions and doubts, became the main object of literary analysis. Over a certain period of time, this shift improved the quality of literature and raised the esthetic criteria to a higher level. Of course, this process did not evolve without inner contradictions, tensions, and conflicts, but it also brought about achievements. Thus, alongside official and pompous works, there developed another literature which determined the overall quality of Kyrgyz literature.

Liberation from ideological dogma and socialist homogeneity opened the path to the long-awaited artistic freedom, which under the Bolshevik regime had been interpreted as service to the people and to the party. Finally, after the disappearance of socialism as a system, several new states are now striving to create genuinely democratic societies under the rule of law, in which the individual human being and his interests, dreams, and thoughts are considered a main priority. Undoubtedly, in these new circumstances literature must also renew itself, yet the question is: how? Unfortunately, seventy years of Bolshevik rule, the worshiping of communist ideas and ideals, did not pass without consequences. And the current ideological vacuum will have an impact on people's thinking and actions for a long time to come.

The crisis which permeates the socioeconomic sphere of society influences the literary sphere as well. State funding has ceased to exist, and the various artists' and writers' unions which both united creative individuals in the past and loyally served the state have lost status and influence. Currently the Kyrgyz Writers Union is split in two. It has lost its former fame and authority and is more occupied with the division of property than with questions of literary creativity. However, even in the past the union was rarely involved with the actual creative process; after all, this institution had more important business.

Recently a number of literary journals and newspapers have proved unable to cope with the free-market competition and have closed down. The market dictates its own conditions, causing immense financial problems for a number of literary periodicals. Book publishers are in no better shape, since the works of Kyrgyz authors are not popular with the general public. Although the circulation of books is very small, unsold copies remain on the shelves of bookstores for a long time. For this reason, publishing houses mostly print books by those authors who themselves come up with the money for the production costs. One might say that Kyrgyz literature under current conditions resembles a wanderer at a crossroads who is afraid to move forward, since he does not want to make another mistake.

Among the literary genres, the one that reacts most sensitively and quickly to new realities is journalistic essayism (*publitsistika*). In many periodicals this genre is experiencing a genuine boom, and the critical statements of well-known essayists evoke a lively response from the reading public. This notwithstanding, the definitive genre by which to judge the quality of present-day literature is the novel. Compared to other epic genres, the art of the novel entered Kyrgyz literature at a late stage. For a long time, the dominant view was that a novel must be a lengthy narrative with huge crowds of characters and manifold events. This simplified concept of the novelistic genre contributed to the appearance of voluminous, short-lived novels in our literature. At the same time, a number of important novels that promoted the advancement of Kyrgyz literature appeared in print, among them *The Long Path* by Elebayev, *In the Mountains* by Sydykbekov, *The Battle* by Abdukaimov, *The Broken Sword* by Kysymbekov, *Days of Trouble* by Danikeyev, and *A Day Lasts Longer Than a Hundred Years* by Aitmatov.

If the concept holds true that the level of a national literature is determined to a great extent by the art of the novel, then the logical question arises about the Kyrgyz novel's current state. The answer is that due to the general economic crisis and the sharp decline in book production, the state of the novel is uncertain. Nevertheless, several novels have been published in the last few years, including Chingiz Aitmatov's *Place of the Skull* and *The Mark of Cassandra,* which were received with much acclaim throughout the world. This success does not come as a surprise, since in every new work Aitmatov reveals previously unseen sides of his talent. His most recent novels touch upon the deepest questions of modernity and force the reader to relate seemingly eternal problems to the involved network of our time.

As many critics have stated, *The Mark of Cassandra* is doubtless a novel of warning. The inner world of humankind, facing cosmic challenges, is undergoing encounters with its own self. Humans are reminded of their status as carriers of intelligence and tolerance and of their responsibility for everything in their environment. As the circumstances for human life become harsher, the cosmic challenge to grasp the meaning of global catastrophes and apocalyptic clashes becomes more urgent. Where does the threat to humankind come from? Obviously from man's inner self, since he incorporates good and evil and has the ability to destroy himself completely. Global wars, ecological catastrophes, genocides, conflicts between ethnic groups and tribes, and other symptoms of self-destruction are all the work

of humans themselves. In this respect the encoded signals of embryonic Cassandras who pass unnoticed in the stressful life of ordinary humans acquire symbolic meaning and global relevance. Aitmatov's novel certainly inspires deep thoughts about the future of our world.

Along with Aitmatov's novels, the works of several other leading Kyrgyz authors evoke a lively response from readers. One such work is the novel *Tengri Manas* by the late A. Dzhakybekov, in which the central character embodies the ideal figure from the Kyrgyz national epos and appears in reality almost like an ordinary human being. The novel strictly follows its own esthetic framework and thus makes the introduction of the hero of an epos artistically legitimate.

Another noteworthy novel is K. Dzhusubaliev's *Cold Walls,* which was written in 1969 during a period that is now called "the time of stagnation." Although the novel—an original and esthetically unique work—does not contain any episode or allusion directly criticizing the socialist system, it could only be published after socialism was abolished and Kyrgyzstan acquired its independence. The novel's esthetic quality derives from a narrative technique similar to the "stream of consciousness" and resembles the works of Joyce, Camus, Kafka, and others. The central character of *Cold Walls* is an isolated man who lives in the reclusive world of his own thoughts, fantasies, and memories. The "cold walls" of the title symbolize human alienation and the individual's withdrawal into his interior after having been excluded from the world of the majority.

K. Osmonaliev's novel *The Enmity of Nomads* was published with newly implemented changes and additions. It tells the story of conflicts between Kyrgyz tribes in the nineteenth century, before Kyrgyzstan became part of Russia. A similar topic is the focus of S. Dzhusuiev's novel in verse *Kurmandzhan Datkha.* Its central character is a historical figure, a woman who succeeded in keeping peace and unity between the southern Kyrgyz people in the first millennium of our era.

The Queen of Snakes by E. Omurakunov and *A World of Lies* by S. Sarygylov are examples of crime and adventure fiction. Apart from novels, an impressive number of novellas and short stories in this genre by D. Malyanov, M. Makenbayev, K. Berdikeyev, B. Arakeyev, and others have been published. The novellas of the young prose writer Melis Makenbayev deserve special mention for their insightful social and psychological analyses of life in prison zones. In the past, this topic was taboo and was only treated by dissidents such as Alexander Solzhenitsyn in *The Gulag Archipelago.* Makenbayev shows the life of people who are not given any understanding or compassion by their fellow human beings—the underdogs of society—and he does not smooth the painful aspects of the reality they experience.

The publication of poetry has decreased due to limited demand from the public and the problems in finding benefactors for this type of literature. Those Kyrgyz poets who in their verses praised the Communist Party and Lenin, the friendship of peoples, and the triumph of communism immediately adjusted their writings to the changing circumstances. Consequently, new words emerged in their poetic terminology in order to describe the transformed society adequately. Voluminous collections are now devoted to the theme of love, including Egembergy Ermatov's *Love,* N. Alymbekov's *Love Will Not Be Sung,* and Suyunbay Eraliev's *Letter to the Beloved.* In Ermatov's book of poems, love is presented as the sphere of authentic human feelings, one in which mutuality is required. The poet emphasizes the most subtle emotions, which are often invisible from outside. Ermatov never declares the intensity of feelings in a loud, overly explicit, or exaggerated fashion.

On the opposite side of the poetic spectrum, A. Omurkanov's poetic collection *Traces on the Sun* is characterized by an almost journalistic directness in which the poet reflects on the period of transition to a new society and comes to the conclusion that present problems are the result of all the accumulated shortcomings of decades under communist rule.

The above list is far from complete, but it certainly shows that Kyrgyz literature is not dead. Rather, the painful process of societal renewal is directly reflected in Kyrgyz letters. Unlike in the past, party permission is no longer needed to publish a book. Instead, the free market dictates conditions, conditions that are harsh and merciless. The increase in book prices has dramatically reduced the number of potential readers. This reduction makes the publication of books in the Kyrgyz language unprofitable for publishing companies, and this factor in turn brings the vicious circle to a close: good authors usually lack generous sponsors; thus, only those authors who maintain stable connections with the financial world can publish their books. The commercialization of book publishing has moved forward, a factor which also contributes to the nature and quality of literature. As a result, the shelves in bookstores are filled with low-quality works of dubious reputation, written in a primitive style.

Kyrgyz literature is preserving its identity, but it is under great pressure during this difficult period of our development. The Kyrgyz literature of socialist realism is gradually being replaced by a literature of realism, but how long this process will take is difficult to say.

Bektash Shamshiev, Summer 1996

TAJIKISTAN

Tajik Literature: Seventy Years Is Longer Than the Millennium

The Tajik language and its literature are a tangle of paradoxes. Tajikistan covers much of the region where the earliest Iranian civilizations of the Silk Road flourished, even before that of the Medes and Persians on the plateau to the southwest; relics of much earlier Iranian languages are still spoken in the mountains. The written language and spoken lingua franca, however, has long been a variety of Persian, which spread to these parts from the Iranian plateau with the expansion of Islam in the eighth century. At the Samanid court of Bukhara this evolved into the vehicle of a great literature, replacing Arabic in the East as the voice of humanistic scholarship, mysticism, and poetry, of Avicenna and al-Ghazali, Omar Khayyam and Hafiz. Rudaki, the father of Persian verse, was born in Tajikistan late in the ninth century. Nobody else of truly international note has surfaced since.

From the eleventh to the sixteenth century, successive waves of invaders (the Mongols, Tamerlane, the Uzbeks) from Inner Asia massacred, ruled, settled, and intermarried in this zone of passage. Much of the Iranian population was driven into the mountains or marooned in the ancient oasis cities of the Oxus basin, Bukhara and Samarkand. The rank and file of the invaders eventually settled down to farm and trade among the Iranians. By the middle of the nineteenth century, when the Russian empire rolled into Central Asia, this ethnolinguistic cauldron had simmered down into a peasantry of turcophone Uzbeks and persophone Tajiks, a small urban commercial and intellectual class (chiefly Tajiks), and a ruling Uzbek elite that struck even the czar's generals as one of the more bloodthirsty and reactionary regimes of the age.

Illiteracy and bilingualism were widespread; Uzbek Turkish was gaining ground as the vernacular. Persian was still the principal written language of government, and classical Persian poetry was cultivated among the less devout and more iranized of the Uzbek khans. The spoken Persian of the north, including the dialect of the Jews of Bukhara, was heavily influenced by Turkic vocabulary and structures. Some literate Bukharans, with the ambivalent support of the Russians against fierce opposition from the Muslim clerics, introduced a modern curriculum and methods of education for both Uzbek and Tajik children, modeled on the so-called Jadid schools devised by Tatar intellectuals of Kazan. By the eve of the Bolshevik Revolution, the khanate of Bukhara was already undermined by indigenous teachers and poets such as Sadriddin Aini (1878–1954), who were writing a more vernacular style of Persian with a reformist content.

After the Bolshevik dust settled, Uzbeks and Tajiks were packaged in 1929 into separate republics. There were several problems with this neat arrangement, apart from the sizable minorities of each ethnos that were left in the other's SSR. "Tajikistan" was allotted the Pamir Mountains and their western foothills, with its capital at Dushanbe, a Russian colonial city; Bukhara and Samarkand, the traditional centers of the Tajiks' literature and culture, were now located in "Uzbekistan." Nevertheless, Aini and other reformers-turned-revolutionaries (including the Uzbek, Fitrat) turned with enthusiasm and considerable debate to devising a new Persian literary language, "Tajik," in a new Latin alphabet. A concerted educational campaign dramatically increased literacy throughout Central Asia. Then, a mere decade later, in 1939, Moscow decreed a change from the Latin to the Cyrillic alphabet, in order to facilitate education in Russian and consolidate the revised version of the Soviet Union. This time there was no debate. Persian materials in Arabic script were no longer allowed into Tajikistan.

The new literary models were to be Gorky and socialist realism. Aini led the obligatory parade of rags-to-revolution autobiographies. Some of his contemporaries and fellow reformers, such as Sadri Ziyo, did not change step adroitly enough and perished in the purges of the 1930s. Pairav Sulaimoni (1899–1933), whose poetry at first followed both the form and the content of classical lyrical and mystical verse, was fiercely criticized and in 1930 abruptly switched to a martial brand of socialist realism. His daughter Gulchehra became an established writer who translated Russian verse and whose own poetry was widely translated in the Soviet Union.

The second generation of Tajik writers may be represented by Sotym Ulughzoda and Mirzo Tursunzoda. Both were born in 1911; Ulughzoda learned classical Persian poetry at school, while Tursunzoda, the son of poor peasants, was brought up in an orphanage. Each joined the Communist Party in 1941 and dedicated his talents to its service. Ulughzoda produced exemplary plays, screenplays, translations, novellas, and short stories (e.g., "The Morning of Our Life," which paints a glowing picture of the future of a prosperous socialist Tajikistan). He fell from favor after his son "defected" to London, and lives now in a small apartment in Moscow. Stalin Prize winner Tursunzoda (d. 1977) was a peripatetic propagandist, reading from his collection of poems ("International Friendship" and "Ballad of

India") to Third World audiences. His poetry was also issued in an Arabic-script edition, for export only. In their footsteps, an impressive quota of Tajik novelists, essayists, historians, and poets from all classes and regions converged within the unerring guidelines of the writers' unions in Moscow and Dushanbe to define the republic's literary personality.

As compensation for political subordination, the Tajiks even in prerevolutionary times had developed a cultural superiority complex. Was not Persian, their own language, the literary vehicle of Iran and (in its heyday) India too? Aini confirmed the trend with his "Sample of Tajik Literature" (1926, in Arabic script), which laid claim to most of the classical Persian canon, making no distinction between writers of Central Asia and of Iran. Under Soviet rule, the Tajiks were at the same time indulged in this anachronistic posturing and (except for university students in the "philological stream") deprived of the materials and training to study their classical and international heritage. Iran and the rest of the world ignored them; Tajikistan was integrated into the Soviet system but remained the poorest republic in the Union.

The dialect base for the Tajik literary language had been conceived as essentially that of Bukhara and the north, which had some literary precedents. Inevitably, with Bukhara and Samarkand gerrymandered from the map, younger writers from the south and center of Tajikistan have since contributed their own idioms and genres. Folk genres—riddles, tales, ballads—were collected and imitated, and alien European genres—drama and opera—were imported and emulated as vehicles of both new fiction and traditional tales infused with a communist message. Despite the uniformity of approved themes, prose style has not yet settled into a standard mold. Poetry was (and is) the heart of Persian literature, for Tajiks no less than for Iranians or Afghans; its diction and lexicon have remained closer to an international Persian literary norm. However, since the new writing system did not distinguish the traditional long and short vowels (an opposition which forms the basis of Persian prosody), neither the odes of Hafiz nor the verses of new poets, whether lyrical or socialist, could be fully appreciated or taught by someone who had no grounding in the Arabic script. It was not until the era of *glasnost'* in the late 1980s that this small item of dirty linen was publicly aired by Tajik critics.

The most dangerous challenge to Tajik literature and culture came, however, from the fraternal Russian presence itself. Stalin had imposed the yoke, but even Khrushchev exhorted all to grin and bear it: "The sooner everyone learns Russian, the sooner we'll build socialism." Accordingly, the business of government and industry was carried on increasingly in Russian, the upwardly mobile younger generation went to Russian rather than Tajik schools, and the intelligentsia read Tolstoy or Solzhenitsyn in preference to Sa'di or Bedil. Tajik literature began to take on the aspect of an approved folkloric relic, like one of those Central Asian folk orchestras modeled on the balalaika band. At a Writers Union meeting in Moscow in 1988, Chingiz Aitmatov, the world-famous Kyrgyz writer, and Muhammadjon Shukurov, a leading Tajik scholar (son of the ill-fated Sadri Ziyo), declared the national languages of Central Asia to be in danger of extinction and called for a campaign of conservation and revitalization.

The response to this, and to the sudden opportunities for genuine criticism of the system permitted by Gorbachev's *glasnost'*, was an enthusiastic, grassroots language movement which in 1989 forced through the lethargic Soviet of Deputies a language-status law, the first in the Central Asian republics. This declared Tajik Persian to be the state language and promulgated measures to increase its use in public life; among these was an undertaking to revert to the use of the Perso-Arabic alphabet at some future date. (The Latin alphabet, now viewed by pan-Iranists as part of the pan-Turkic plot to absorb the Tajiks, was not considered.) A flood of independent newspapers and magazines, some already printing articles, poems, and teach-yourself columns in Arabic script, carried the public into an unexpected, and largely unwished-for, independence in 1991. Scholars, journalists, and poet-politicians (notably Loyiq Sherali, Bozor Sobir, and Gulrukhsor) disowned the fabrications of Soviet literature and vowed to draft a new Tajik identity as full members of the Persian-speaking world. Renewed contact with Iran and with the Iranian diaspora in North America, and the importation of books of classical and modern Persian literature, gave promise of a literary renaissance.

Came the civil war of 1992 and polarization between the neocommunists, who have regained power, and the Islamists, who continue an implacable opposition from across the Afghan border, with the pan-Iranists uncomfortably in between. With political and economic life in a downward spiral, language policy has taken a back seat. "Persian" has been dropped from the new constitution, and "Tajik" has resumed its place as the national language, still in Cyrillic (though orthographically reformed); in practice, Russian prevails again, despite the out-migration of tens of thousands of Russian and other European ex-Soviet citizens. The independent press has been closed down, and paper is in short supply. Yet Tajik literature, oddly enough, is far from dead. Poetry is increasingly published in Perso-Arabic script; the tenor of cultural debate has become

less truculent and irredentist than during the 1988–92 redrafting of Tajik language and history, with more moderate voices seeking an accommodation between the polarities. The leitmotiv remains the continuing quest for a true Tajik identity.

The prescribed themes of communism no longer provide an automatic framework for literature, but the Islamic revolutionary alternatives offered by Iran are hardly more attractive. The Tajiks are not Shi'is, though their history too—and daily life in Dushanbe—has its share of martyrs; today's citizens want a future of their own, without having to toe the line of either of their Big Brothers. Writers, while still exercising political self-censorship, need no longer submit to collective self-criticism before they publish. Prose fiction may now thumb its nose at the sacred cows of the establishment, as, for example, Ūrun Kūhzod's "Mother" subverts the idealistic, Stakhanovite views of selfless socialist labor, rural modernization, and women's liberation. It may (as in the stories by Sattor Tursun and Bahmanyor) explore the realms of the spiritual and the supernatural, which were automatically excluded from Soviet discourse as remnants of religion.

Poetry is a different matter. As the senior partner, more overtly humiliated in service to an impersonal propaganda machine (cf. Gulrukhsor's "Epitaph"), it must more consciously reinvent itself. In his essay, Askar Hakim contemplates the responsibilities and the craft of a new breed, the independent Tajik poet. This individual may never be as famous as Rudaki, but he is determined at least to be his own master.

John R. Perry, Summer 1996

TURKMENISTAN

Toward a New Maturity

The connection between literature and the fate of the nation on whose language it is based is indisputable. The truth of this fact is revealed most clearly during moments of sudden turns and cataclysms which result in fundamental changes to the established social order and spiritual life of a nation, as the latter is forced to confront once again a most complicated and fateful task: which new path in the sociopolitical system should it choose, and how should it make certain of moving in that direction in a dependable fashion? One such cataclysm in the twentieth century, without any doubt, was the dissolution of the USSR, at one and the same time disinheriting and dispersing populations which until that moment had made up the multinational, unified, and mighty Soviet Union. Many of the peoples affected were totally unprepared for such a violent shock. Furthermore, the conformist style of life under the Soviet system did not encourage habits of independent thinking, neither as individual human beings nor as a nation. Salvation lay in the unity of the nation, in the cohesion of all its social layers. But each country from the former "brotherhood of nations" sought this salvation in its own way.

The Turkmens are a nation with very ancient roots. Their ethnogenetic ties reach down to peoples and tribes preceding our era: to the Dakhs, the Massagetae, the Alans, the Huns, and others. They were famous in the Middle Ages when they took an immediate part in the formation of the great Seljuk Empire at the beginning of the current millennium. Many tribal groups became detached from the core of their fraternal tribes and penetrated into Asia Minor, where the Kharagoyunlies and the Akhoyunlies in the fifteenth and sixteenth centuries created their large independent feudal states. Many of those who had cut themselves off settled in Egypt, in Syria, in Iraq, in the Caucasus, in Turkey, and in Iran. Those, however, who valued the hot but native and familiar sands—the hills where their umbilical cord was buried, as the natives would say—remained in the original home territory, the huge region from the Khazar lands (Caspia) up to the Amu-Daryia. Immeasurable amounts of blood and other sacrifices were the price to be paid for this tribal scattering, for the absence of an independent nation-formation. Through these severe, ages-long trials the nomad warrior's sense of freedom was hardened like steel, and he refused to yield his free spaces to foreign hordes, however great their power might be. That is why he was able to proclaim with pride, "I prefer the scalding hot winds of my land to the cool spaces of palace gardens." Testimony to this pride and determination is found in the words of the heroes of our finest literary works, our ancient epic creations, the *destans*. These speak of the love of freedom of the Turkmens, for whom a life apart from any cabalistic dependence on palaces and shakhinshahs was a measure of national honor and dignity.

Then came October 1991. What the Turkmens had been nurturing in their soul for ages now became reality. The constitutional promulgation of national independence for Turkmenistan roared like spring thunder through all four corners of the sunny country. This was a triumph of the brightest hopes and of the dreams of generations past and present. There was universal joy, genuine and unaffected. There was an untrammeled feeling of broad expanse and of rebirth and prosperity. The idea and the practical aspects of independence seized everyone. To speak metaphorically, in the hearts of people as on the strings of the dutar, melody-mukans rang, different in sound yet all proclaiming independence, optimistic hopes, and fiery faith. A national leader emerged from the ranks of the people who astutely and sensibly directed the universal patriotic enthusiasm in the necessary direction. And literature, the artistic word, like all other forms of art, could not but join in this triumph of national harmony.

The themes and ideas of independence served to increase the new unity and stability, expressed in poems of joy, ringing poetic appeals, and publicistic passions. Like an image, a symbol of national unity, people took to the outstanding personality of the first president of independent Turkmenistan, Sapamurat Niyazov, a personality that instilled respect and love in the Turkmen people. In this multivoiced manifestation, which had taken shape in a sort of elemental way, everyone participated, even those whose professional habits were quite unrelated to it. The pathos of recognizing one's civic duty and dignity was heard unanimously.

There was nothing surprising in all this. To tell the whole world as soon as possible about that innermost secret—namely, the marvelous opportunity for the whole nation henceforth to breathe the fresh "sweet" air of national freedom—was a heartfelt need for everyone. The spiritual revelations about independence, about the homeland, and about the national leader merged into a rapturous paean to the greatest event in the nation's history. Like children who, upon seeing a rainbow in the sky, rush to embrace and caress it, so the adults too rushed to express in song their universal joy, stirring feelings of satisfaction and delight. Others, for some reason, were inclined to see in this some sort of subjection to political opportunities aimed at pleasing those in power. But can literature avoid politicization when a nation's entire life is politicized? Furthermore, it is well known that vociferous propaganda, sloganeering, and the self-righteousness of passions compose the "genetic" quality of any revolution, especially in its early stages. To the extent of the maturing of cognitive reason, a revolution begins gradually to comprehend and grasp more fundamentally and deeply the significance of its ideals. Our "Turkmen revolution" too is apparently no exception in this regard.

True, the old nation had created a literature of ancient traditions. Monumental epics such as the *Gorkut ata* and the *Gyorogly* were born as the embodiments of the permanent values of our national spirit, works containing the wisdom of the collective mind, the common accumulated comprehension of the world, the unique signs of artistic convention and imagination. Models of the lyrical-epic genre—the *destans*—came to us as the literary fruits of artistic endeavor. Here the erotic-romantic story is enhanced through genuine poetic mastery and the ideals of elevated human relationships are proclaimed in song: the triumph of the purity of love, of truth and justice. Such works as *Shasenem and Harib, Zokhre and Takhir, Layla and Majnun, Sayat and Khemra,* and many others played and continue to this day to play an enormous role in the improvement of the artistic consciousness of the Turkmens. Our classical literature was shaped in the best traditions of the poetry of the East. The names of such Eastern giants as Firdawsi, Jami, Rumi, Nesimi, Nizami, and Omar Khayyam speak for themselves. Our famous poet-classics Andalib, Azadi, and Magtymguly, who lived in the seventeenth and eighteenth centuries, learned from them the great craft of versification and a philosophical-mystical comprehension of the world.

An enumeration of the poets of the past who have enriched Turkmen classical literature with their contributions would make a long list. I shall speak here of only one great poet-thinker whose work has raised the level of Turkmen poetic thought to its highest summit: Magtymguly-Pyragy, who left for his successors a veritable treasure trove of poetry, thought, and philosophy. We commonly assume that 1733 was the year of this poet's birth: "I am a Circassian by birth, my home country is the Atrek, and my name is Magtymguly." His father, whom he revered with profound filial piety, was Dovletmammed-Azadi, a highly educated man for his time, a poet and philosopher and author of the treatise "Vagzy-Azat," extremely rich in its moral-philosophical content. Dovletmammed's son set himself apart from other contemporary poets by the incomparable patriotic greatness of his thoughts and sufferings, conception and promulgation of human love, goodness and purity. Once, having ascended to the very highest ridge of his native mountains, he proclaimed with his mighty voice: "All you Turkmens, unite! You Teke, Yomudy, Yazyrs, Alils, all you tribal brothers related by blood, unite!" And against the background of his consistent, profound humanism, this appeal gains a clearly broad philosophical significance when it is seen as a call to unite all humanity.

Magtymguly is convincing in his agonizing search for answers to the question as to how to make human beings better and morally more perfect in their deeds and actions, as to how to do this so that each person should constantly carry in his thoughts a desire to give peace and tranquillity to all as children of the human family. How to let reason, that rarest of nature's gifts, serve not the decline but the ascent of man—these ideal beliefs would unfortunately collapse, but the poet-thinker would remain faithful to his humanism: "Whoever does not value humankind, while himself a human

being, / Such a creature is worse than a cow that mindlessly stuffs its stomach."

The poet relentlessly speaks of the goal of spiritual perfection. Here the main intent had to be the preservation of a firm link with the people. Outside this link with one's people, with the nation, there would be no life at all, no human values. With the people comes that power which "warms like the sun." Rulers who have grown distant from their people also lose their thrones. Therefore, in thy striving to improve, thou art summoned to serve thy people: "Think of me as a coward if I am afraid of the raging stream, / Think of my love as worthless if it is unable to light the world with its flame." Magtymguly is an eternally fertile ground that nourishes a Turkmen's reason and conscience. I shall claim that it was precisely on this ground that in the eighteenth and nineteenth centuries a whole constellation of classical writers was born: Kemine, Mollanepes, Zelili, Seidi, Shabende, Sheydai, Myatadzhi, and others.

These then were the basic foundations of Turkmen literature before the events of the year 1917: a classical literature, a national epos, and a rich folklore tradition. Proletarian literature scorned this heritage and refused to acknowledge the "feudal admixture." A philosophical depiction of contemporary life from a primitively prejudicial position was characteristic of the early experiments by proletarian writers. Socialist realism followed as a program for creative activity, obligatory for all literatures of the national republics. This meant that a writer had to depict the phenomena of reality not as they actually were but in their "revolutionary development." Thus, ideological tendentiousness and the dependence of the creative process on party directives became entrenched—a sort of historical epos which lasted almost half a century.

One must admit that, along this path, Turkmen literature passed through a period of realism. Certain genres of realist prose appeared which previously—i.e., before the Revolution—had not existed. Our links with Russian and other literatures which possessed a great realist tradition exerted a beneficial influence. Furthermore, socialist realism did not mean simply the rote learning of ready-made creative principles. Rather, it was a complicated process whereby writers were urged toward the development of their own vision of the world, toward the spiritual perfection of their own artistic intellect and talent. As a result, huge prose works appeared, novel trilogies and tetralogies which bore witness to the vast intellectual horizons of their authors, their high levels of artistic thought, the elevation of the culture of realism. Here mention should be made of Berdy Kerbabayev, Khydyr Deryaev, Beki Stytakov, Ata Koushutov, Klych Kuliev, and others whose names are linked to the appearance of multilevel canvases representing Turkmen reality both past and present in bright and sharp outline. Kerbabayev's *Reshaiushchii shag* (The Decisive Step) is a novel which has received widespread recognition and has been published in many countries of the world in various languages. Here a realistic maturity is combined with a genuine palette of vital, attractive characters, psychologically convincing and embellished with nationalist attributes. This, to be sure, is not by accident. Kerbabayev, taught by the experience of a multifaceted life and gifted with a supreme talent deemed worthy of the highest honors of his time, was one of the originators of Turkmen literature during the Soviet period. Always ahead of the literary process and his coevals, he boldly demonstrated through his own creative work how to free oneself from the fetters of socialist realism in spite of the ideological prescriptions established for the novel in the forties. Kerbabayev's name could adorn the literature of any country, even the most developed artistically.

In the following decades such slogans as "The artist and power" and "The artist and his people" were adhered to by each writer in his own way according to the extent of his creative intellect and his drive toward self-affirmation by looking through the prism of existence to view and display his own position in life. Nevertheless, the Damocles' sword of control and censorship still hung over the writer's head, demanding the faithful execution of directives sent down from above.

Let it be understood: I am not about to describe the history of our literature, but I *am* talking about certain moments in the course of its development which have determined its present image. Seen in this light, it was the decades from the 1950s to the 1970s which brought a trend toward innovation, specifically in the intensification of personal stimuli in poetry and the appearance of creative individuals. The latter were concerned above all with the quality of the poetic thought expressed and with its spiritual weight. They revealed the inner world of people, their erotic passions and heroic deeds. Conflicts were presented in convincing contexts and in the clashes between characters. A certain distancing from the use of conventionalized devices in the imagery of traditional Eastern poetry became noticeable. Briefly put, the recognition took hold that poetry is the single most sensitive instrument leading to the comprehension of the mystery of the inner life of a human being, of the inaccessible nuances of his feelings and passions. Similar visions were attained in their works in varying degrees of spiritual depth by the poets R. Seyidov, A. Kekidov, Ch. Ashirov, K. Seyitlev, A. Atadzhanov, K. Kurbannepesov, M. Seidov, B. Khudaynazarov, Y. Durdyev, A. Khaidov, N. Bayramov, and others.

These were followed by a pleiad of talented young artists who thought in contemporary ways. They arrived on the scene with an undisguised desire to speak their own word, to introduce a living current of innovative tendencies into the literary process. With their university educations, seduced by the achievements of international poetry, they absorbed the traditions of the national past with the goal of rethinking these traditions in a creative way, of transforming the established canonical forms and the means of creating images. They were drawn to the emotional brilliance of language, to the capaciousness and multiple semantic layers of poetic thinking. Several of these poets have meanwhile passed on, including G. Ezizov, Kh. Kuliev, and I. Nuryev, but others continue to thrive and work, among them A. Atabayev, S. Orayev, B. Dzhutdiev, N. Redzhepov, A. Bugaev, and others. Their poetry promoted a broadening of horizons as regards themes and ideas, the enrichment of verse with a national-poetic spirit, and innovations in form, poetic meter, and rhythm.

Playwriting has also enjoyed distinct success. Its experience during the past two decades has been crowned by works of truly great artistic merit, which have exerted a genuine influence on the professional level of the national theater. And incidentally, legitimate Turkmen theater is at present one of the better-known regional theaters abroad.

To repeat, I have sketched here only a very general picture of the present state of Turkmen literature. It boasts very real accomplishments and possesses considerable potential. Its development and orientation are conditioned, as I have said, by the fundamental change in the historical context which our people are undergoing at the present time. The difficulties of this period of transition from socialism to a market-oriented system are in fact reflected in the general atmosphere of our spiritual culture, in literary developments in particular. Furthermore, the independence of the country as a nation-state opens up totally new and favorable conditions for a complete assimilation—without any ideological obstacles or interdictions—of the history and present life of the nation, including aspects of religion and religious customs. There are no longer any taboo subjects, personages, or events, no ideological or other limitations to restrict the creative freedom of the writer.

The euphoria and the strong emotions occasioned by the achievement of independence is slowly fading, and the creators of artistic literature face new tasks. Coming to terms with these tasks is much more complicated and more difficult than was the case under socialism. It means being able to look at life in all its fullness and variety, without facile solutions and falsifications—that is, in a bright, emotionally exciting, and absorbing way. We are talking then about fundamental changes which must occur in the artistic consciousness of the writer, in his view of his mission under conditions of great popular agitation on the path to the discovery of genuine freedom and independence.

The period after the collapse of totalitarian power has confronted the postsocialist writer with a phenomenal moment of truth, about which Chingiz Aitmatov wrote in this same journal in 1993 (see *WLT* 67:1, pp. 11–17). Turkmen literature, like the other literatures that survived the totalitarian era, has turned its face toward truth, the truth of history and of the nation, which has chosen its own form of development and progress. As a writer, I am convinced that only the effort toward the artistic assimilation of the social experience and national character of the people, the condition of its spirit and soul, will permit our literature to make its contribution in a confident and productive way to contemporary world literature.

Khudayberdy Durdyev, Summer 1996, translated by
Joachim T. Baer

UZBEKISTAN

Uzbek Literature

Today more than a hundred countries have recognized the Republic of Uzbekistan, which has the longest history of any of the newly independent states of the former Soviet Union. It is a country with more than 120 ethnic groups.

It is well known that czarist Russia, starting in the 1850s, occupied the territory of Turkistan; as a result of the agreement between the Russians and the Chinese and a policy of colonization and occupation, West Turkistan became subject to Russia and East Turkistan became subject to China. The changes instituted by the Bolsheviks in 1917 did not bring freedom to the people of Turkistan; on the contrary, they successfully maintained the former colonial oppression with false laws, continuing the policies of russifying and secularizing the Turkistan peoples and draining their material resources and spiritual wealth. West Turkistan was completely dissolved in 1924, and in its place puppet republics such as the Uzbek Soviet Socialist Republic, Kazakhstan, Kyrgyzstan, Turkmenistan and Tajikistan were formed. The designations "Turkistan" and "Turk" were banned from use. As a result, the history and concept of the Turkish people were crushed in the cogs of the Soviet ideological machine.

Historians of Greek antiquity beginning with Herodotus disdained the term "ancient Turk," referring to Turks instead as "Scythian," "Sak" or "Soghdian," and "Massagetae." For a thousand years following the Arab invasion, Arabic and Persian had ruled. In the states formed from the old Turkistan, the Turkish peoples—Turkmen, Kazakhs, Uzbeks, Kyrgyz, Karakalpaks, and Uighurs, descendants of the ancient Turks who for 10,000 years had lived as the Turks of Turkistan—were revived and designated by the Russians as "young nations." Actually, the Russians were the young nation; Russian literature and history began a mere three hundred years ago with Karamzin and Kantemir. Turkistan is acknowledged the world over as the cradle of civilization and humanity.

Despite the policy of colonization continued in the Uzbek SSR and other republics, national consciousness and national movements did not die out completely. Historians and writers continued to let the people know that the Uzbek civilization was an ancient one and taught people about great historical figures and their writings and deeds. World-renowned scholars such as Beruni, Ibn Sina, Farabi, and Ulughbek as well as great wordsmiths such as Nawaii and Babur were written about. Five-volume collections of Beruni's and Ibn Sina's works and a ten-volume edition of Nawaii's works were published in Russian and Uzbek. By 1990 a forty-volume set of fairy tales and epic songs from Uzbek folk literature was published, and currently a 100-volume edition of Uzbek folktales is being compiled. This in itself attests to the great cultural heritage of the Uzbek civilization.

Encyclopedias written in almost all languages hold to the one-sided idea that Uzbeks are descended from Uzbek Khan, the khan of the Golden Horde from 1313–42, and from the Shaybanids, who arrived in West Turkistan in the fifteenth century. (Shaybani Khan brought down the Timurid dynasty and established Uzbek rule in its place.) True, tribal Turks called Uzbeks did arrive with the Shaybanids, but they dwelled in the territory of Turkistan during the Timurid era, in that of the Khorazmshahs before that, during the Karakhanids and during the reigns of all the Turk khans, because they, after all, were the original Turkish people of Turkistan, right? Why is this not openly acknowledged? Because if the aggressors who have conquered this part of the world let these facts be known, then the mask of colonization would be torn. If this truth were made known to the modern ancestors of the ancient inhabitants of Turkistan and they fully comprehended their interests and rights, the claim could be put forward that "as there is one India, one China, one Iran, and one Russia in the world, in the land between these countries there should be one country of Turkistan, known to the world for the past ten thousand years." Fine, we will address this in a future history. For now let us continue with the main topic.

When our president, Islam Karimov, announced the independence of the Republic of Uzbekistan in parliamentary session in 1991, no one made a sound. Only after he said, "Well, is there no applause?" did our People's Deputies shout and clap. This in itself shows how deeply colonization had etched its stamp into the minds of the people. Today the people of Uzbekistan march bravely toward independence. But the path of freedom and independence is difficult; one cannot make a man who has been a slave for forty years into a free man in five years; this is too difficult. The reference in the Koran to "their hearts having been sealed" means that some people's hearts will never open up to the proper path; and when this is taken into account, as a people which has been freed from colonization travels down the path followed by the rest of the world, the well-meaning countries of the world supporting our young independent country with sincere and practical aid are doing something beneficial for the history of all mankind. The Uzbekistan of today is composed of the descendants of the old Uzbeks and ancient Turks, and their forefathers brought benefits to the world for thousands and thousands of years. One can learn this starting with the books of Herodotus, whose remains repose in the territory of modern Turkey, and from the epic tales of the ancient Sumerians. (The Sumerians headed west from the Sumer and Yulduz valleys near the Tien Shan mountains of Turkistan and founded a world civilization.)

In short, in all encyclopedias, including the Oxford University edition, we read: "Uzbeks, Uzbekistan—one of the republics of the Soviet Union, not just one of the Turkish peoples of Central Asia, but the Uzbeks are the Turks of ancient Turkistan, in other words an ancient civilized people born of the fusion of the Turks of the Timurid era with the Shaybanid 'Uzbeks'." As for Shaybani Khan, he was a Turk and wrote so in his works. Uzbekistan is a part of Turkistan; in other words, Uzbekistan is Turkistan—that is, Turan. Our history and ethnic and spiritual existence are tied to Turkistan and to Turan. Today, when Uzbekistan stands as an independent republic, not to accept what is our due is to signal that the oppression of colonization continues to exert an effect.

The history of Uzbekistan is not just the period 1924–91; the history of Uzbekistan is the history of Turkistan. Stone Age relics from a million years ago have been found in the Selunghur caves of the Ferghana Valley, one of Turkistan's ancient cradles of civilization. The 150,000-year-old Teshiktash man (Surkhandarya) is famous the world over. Five years ago the Japanese

found the oldest statue of Buddha in Surkhan and declared that Uzbekistan is one of the cradles of Buddhist civilization. The *Avesta* was written in our land. The tales, stories, and poems from the seventh to the third century B.C. of Shiraq, Tomaris, Alp Er Tonga, Zarina and Strangio, Odatida and Zariadr are not just history but are also examples of the first written literature; they are considered the modern Uzbeks' national treasures. This is why this truth was stated openly in all the textbooks and books on literary history written during the Soviet era.

There is a theory that written Uzbek literature began with the Yassavids (eleventh century). In my opinion, Uzbek literature, or Turkish literature of Turkistan (including Kazakh, Kyrgyz, Uighur, Karakalpak, and Turkmen), started as written literature in the seventh century before Christ. What is the basis for this claim? Here it is: "Alp Er Tonga oldimi? / Issiz achun qaldimi? / Oksiz ochin aldimi? / Endi yurak yirtilur." The poem from which these lines are taken was written in the year 626 B.C. and is dedicated to the death of Alp Er Tonga, referred to as "Scythian" by European historians and as "Soghdian" by Persian historians, but actually the leader of the ancient Turkish people. (In 626 B.C. Alp Er Tonga Khan was tricked into coming as a guest to the Shah of Iran Kaykhusrav and was poisoned and killed.) Although 2,620 years have passed, this poem is still comprehensible to a modern Uzbek. In N. Rahimov's "Uzbekified" translation in the 1993 book *Turk Khaqanligi* (Turk Khanate), only three words were changed: "Alp Er Tonga oldimi? / Yâmân dunyâ qâldimi? / Zamâna ochin âldimi? / Endi yurak yirtilur."

True, in the Sumerian epic tale written four thousand years ago, in the Alp Er Tonga epic, in the writings on the petroglyphs found in the ancient territory of Turkistan, Tonyaquq (712 A.D.), Kultegin (731 A.D.), and Bilge Khaqan (735 A.D.), there are many words still used by today's Uzbeks. These relics give us a basis for saying that Uzbek poetry began being produced in written form in the seventh century before Christ. In the *Shahname* as well, written by Firdawsi in Persian one thousand years ago, Alp Er Tonga is called "Afrasiyab"; Alp Er Tonga says, "Two-thirds of the world is in my hands, both Iran and Turan are my palaces." In other words, the ancient Turks, the forefathers of today's Uzbeks, ruled over two-thirds of the known world seven centuries before Christ, and such a historical and literary relic was left behind as proof.

In the histories of 2,500 years ago, both the struggle of the ancient Turks of Turan against the Persians of Iran and the heroic deeds of Tomaris and Shiraq against invaders have been preserved in reports and epic tales. These too can be considered the modern Uzbeks' historical and literary national treasures. Or let us take the history of the Kanglis. Before Christ, in the territory of Turan, the Kangli state (which lasted from the third century B.C. to the fifth century A.D.) included the territory of modern Uzbekistan. Judging from archeological excavations, from history books such as those of Greek and Aryan historians, and from other works, this state's great civilization had a huge effect on all of Turan, and naturally it left a great mark on human history. The Kanglis were the first people in the world to build horse-drawn carts (*kang* means "wagon").[1] As the great twentieth-century Azerbaijani poet Khalil Riza Uluturk said, "The father of the rocket and the first pioneers of space were the Kanglis, since it was they who discovered how to use the horse-drawn cart as a battle weapon." Even today in the Tashkent province some Kangli villages remain inhabited by Kanglis. Their appearance, language, and mannerisms are like those of the ancient Turks: they are straightforward, do not bargain, are frank and stern.

I am using these examples in order to connect history with the present. In the realm of Khorazm, located in the territory of ancient Turan, numerous great states were formed. Khorazm had its own system of writing. It is said that the Khorazm Turks controlled nearly all the lands of Turan in the sixth and seventh centuries B.C. There were many books and manuscripts written in the Khorazmian alphabet; the writings in this script were kept in people's homes and, in the third century B.C., in Khorazmian libraries. The ancient Eastern books and religious texts in Khorazmian script were burned and lost after the Arab invasion. Thus, in the territory of Khorazm, which is considered just one province of Uzbekistan, the fact that there were libraries 2,300 years before the present, and glorious religious books like the *Avesta* and other philosophical and literary works, shows that the forefathers of the modern Uzbeks were among the world's oldest civilized people.

An important event in the history of Uzbekistan (ancient Turan and Turkistan) was its conquest by Alexander the Great and his subsequent death there. The building of an empire by the Greeks, its fall, and the subsequent establishment of the Salavki state (third century B.C.), the Greco-Bactrian state (250–140 B.C.), the Evtidem empire (250–155 B.C.), and the Tokharian state (second to first century B.C.) complete the history of the states connected to Uzbekistan two thousand years ago. It would be possible to discuss them, but one would have little time left to discuss the following two thousand years.

The powerful state which held sway in the first to the fourth century A.D. was that of the Kushans. A great civilization was also formed during the time the Afri-

gians ruled (fourth to eighth century A.D.). Those referred to as the "Ephthalites," who actually made up the state peopled by ancient Turks called the White Huns, left important traces in world history in the fifth century. This was an age when the Huns established their own empires in the East, the West, and in Europe. Then came the Turk khanates. In Turan, the Turks' weakening, disintegration, and invasion by the Arabs took place in the seventh century. As a result, in 704, the Turks became subject to the Arabs. As Beruni wrote, and as is stated in the history of Narshakhi, the temples of the ancient Turks were destroyed and mosques were built in their places; books composed in the old Turkish language, all written materials, statues, and images were lost; religious books inscribed on animal skins were also burned. Thus, objects of the ancient Turk civilization were incinerated, buried, and lost. Over the next thousand years the history and culture of the indigenous people, the Turks, was taken away from them and history began to be written to serve not them but the Arabs and the Persians.

The Persians, who were slaves to the Arabs and served as interpreters (they had, since ancient times, been our forefathers' opponents in war), also played an important role in the Arab rule and promoted the slogan "The language of science is Arabic, the language of literature is Persian." Because of this, Turk scholars wrote their works in Arabic. Abu Mansur as-Saalibin's book *Yati matut dahr,* containing examples of the work of more than a thousand of Turkistan's scholars, writers, and poets of the tenth century, is a testament to this. Or recall that the works of Beruni and Ibn Sina, Farabi, and the father of algebra, Al-Khorazmi, were all written in Arabic. The writing of literature in Persian—Nizami, for example, with his Turkish blood, and the composing of Khusraw Dehlavi's first "Khamsa" in Persian—alienated the Turanian and Turkistanian Turks from their own national consciousness, and as a result they were not able to participate actively in the workings of state in their own lands. No matter how amazing it is that Dehlavi's poem reached a million lines, Turks read these only in Persian, and the majority of the people could not read them at all. In my opinion, the fact that Persian served as the official language in the states formed in Turkistan, and even in the khanates which were toppled at the beginning of this century, can be traced to this early history.

The first writer and thinker to comprehend this situation was Ahmad Yassavi: in his Hikmat book (the *Devan-i Hikmat*) he wrote the essential meaning of the Koran, the Hadith, and Persian histories in Turkish poetry that the ordinary Turk could understand. Yassavi (1091–1129) lived nine hundred years ago, and the book he left us, the *Devan-i Hikmat,* constitutes one of the oldest written works which is still read and memorized by our people to this day. Yassavi did not write in Arabic or in Persian but instead composed his beautiful poems in his mother tongue, Turkish, an act which must be considered symbolic of his love for his people and his nationalist feelings. The Turks, who had their own religious book in the *Avesta* even before the Arabs and before Christ and who conceived of the world as composed of a hundred layers of sky and with a single creator and master of all existence in the hundredth layer, Tangri (they called him Oghan), in other words who had a fear and love of God in their hearts, became ignorant and less civilized and backward as a people due to the successive invasions and wars and the loss of their language with the strengthening of the status of Arabic and Persian. Yassavi put a stop to this process with his book. Poetry in Turkistan was revived once again through his work, and national consciousness began to flow in people's veins. During this same era, the books of Yassavi's predecessors from a century earlier, Yughnaki and Yusuf Khas Hajib, written in Old Turkish, played a significant role in the formation of a national literature in Turkistan.

In Turkistan in those times the Ghaznavids, Karakhanids and Khwarazmshahs (tenth to eleventh century) ruled with might and power; they left behind a great civilization, including the magnificent scientific institution, the Ma'mun Academy, created during this period. As a result of the Turkistan renaissance which was taking shape at this time, the European Renaissance of the fifteenth century was born.

The subsequent era in the history of Turkistan and Turan, even the history of the world, is associated with the empire of Genghis Khan and the states formed by his sons. It is fashionable in historical literature to refer to Genghis Khan as a Mongol and to portray his campaigns of uniting the lands of Turan as only an invasion. But Genghis Khan, like the Turk emperors Oghuz Khan and Attila before him, united the lands of ancient Turan, where the kindred tribes of the Mongols and Turks were brought under one rule, and built capitals in Karakurum and Otukent. This was a tradition inherited from Oghuz Khan. Was Genghis Khan really a foreigner? Were the Mongols really enemies to the Uzbeks? Before answering this question, recall that in Babur's famous *Baburname,* the Shaybanids and the Uzbeks were portrayed as enemies. What Babur wrote was right: the Uzbeks who arrived with Shaybani Khan were an army which came this way from the Golden Horde. The Turkish homeland in which Babur lived was a land of the Turks that belonged to the West Turkistan Timurid state; what brought an end to the Timurid dynasty was

the Uzbek state. But the Uzbeks were a "tribe" who are traced back to Uzbek Khan. In other words, Uzbek is not the name of a nation but instead designates those who were the troops of Uzbek Khan. Uzbek Khan was a descendant of Batu Khan, who was the son of Genghis Khan. So who is enemy to whom?

Today, in my mind, these histories need to be stated and written openly. Only in this way can we put a stop to thoughts which serve the ideology of those who divided and conquered Turkistan and which were deliberately distorted and confused so as to work against us. That is, there will be no more chauvinistic words which bewilder our people such as those of seven or eight years ago: "Neither Timur nor Samarkand and Bukhara have any relationship to modern-day Uzbeks." Or if we hear that "Nawaii was not Uzbek, he was Uighur," we need not be at a loss. If we look at history, and at the age when Nawaii lived, this great poet, who was connected to the Timurid dynasty, referred to himself as a Turk, not as an Uighur or Uzbek; on the contrary, the Uzbeks deposed the Timurids, to whom he was connected; however, today it is clear that the Turks to which Nawaii and the Timurids belonged were forefathers to both the Uzbek Genghisid descendants belonging to Shaybani and the Shaybanids and to the nation referred to as the modern Uzbeks. Disputes have broken out in the West over these very questions. Considering how certain works which were written expressly to leave our national existence in the shadows are referred to in those disputes, the need for clarification is evident.

Indeed, in the literature of the era following Yassavi there appeared dozens of great poets such as Lutfi, Sakkaki, Ataii, Yaqini, and Gadaii. The five hundred years from the tenth to the fifteenth century boasted such authors and works as Mahmud Kashghari's *Devan-i Lughat at-Turk,* Yusuf Khas Hajib's great philosophical and historical text *Qutadghu Bilig,* Ahmad Yugnaki's *Hibat ul-Haqa'iq,* Ahmad Yassavi's *Devan-i Hikmat,* and Sulayman Baqirghani's *Baqirghan Kitabi.* Khwarazmian Rabghuzi's *Qissa-i Rabghuzi,* the first Uzbek prose work, along with the poems and epic tales of Qutb, Sayfi Sarayi, and Dukbek, were great steps forward in Uzbek literature up to Nawaii. When regarded from a linguistic standpoint, the literature of these five hundred years shows little difference between the language used by poets beginning with Yassavi and the modern Uzbek language. All their works can be understood even today without translation or explanations. But the prose works and historical epics (Hajib and Yugnaki, Rabghuzi) retain strong elements of old Turkish, and for this reason as well, considering the Arabic and Persian vocabulary which subsequently entered the language of the Turks of Turkistan, some distance is felt between these works and today's readers. Therefore some of these are published today in a form modified to correspond to the modern language.

Nawaii in his own time perceived this change and composed his *Muhakamat ul-Lughatayn* in response to those who claimed that Persian was superior and that one could not create literature in Turkish. In this work he shows how rich Turkish is and gives proof not only that it is superior as a language of poetry, but also that it is the oldest and richest such language. The writings which were included in the fifteen-volume edition of Nawaii published during the Soviet era (1960–70) and then later in the twenty-volume "Complete Collected Works" (begun in 1987) are considered literary gems showing the embodiment, development, and crowning achievement of the Turkish literary tradition up to his time. His ghazals written in prose used and improved upon all the widespread forms of poetic verse practiced up to that time in Arabic and Persian literature, and stand apart in their conveyance of Islamic and global ideas and in their wealth of meaning. Nawaii was the first to create a *khamsa* or five-volume collection of poetry in Turkish. Each of these volumes—*Hayrat ul-Abrar, Farhad wa Shirin, Layli wa Majnun, Sab'a-i Sayyar,* and *Sadd-i Iskandari*—is a philosophical-historical-metaphorical novel written in verse.

It must be said that any European or American who has not been schooled in the East and knows nothing of Islamic civilization, science, history, and arts, no matter how "great" a scholar he may be, will naturally understand nothing of Nawaii's poetry and works. The task is similar to someone ignorant of Japan's literature, history, and national experience trying to comprehend Japanese poetry. In short, in order to understand the meaning of the poetry of Turkistan which began with Yassavi and continued to the nineteenth century, especially prose poetry and Sufi verse, it is imperative that one be knowledgable of the Koran, the Hadith, and Islamic and Turkish civilization. This requirement is no different than the prerequisite that a person have eyes, intelligence, and developed thought processes in order to read a book. In a word, if we wish to explain the scale for measuring a work, we can say this: in their poems the classic poets of Turkistan basically speak of the beauty of the beloved. They understood the "beloved" (*yār*) as this world and other worlds known and unknown to us, human beings, animals and all animate and inanimate beings, and the creator of all: God. They understood this world, human life, beauty, and all conditions as miracles created by God. They summoned others to love God, no matter what befalls them, to be patient and love God more, to love everything that God

has created, every human being, every living creature, every day and every night. They conveyed this meaning using various traditional methods and metaphors. People were reared with this very meaning and outlook, and these brought about moral unity and a unity of outlook in society—in other words, ideological unity, and states became strong and developed. Because it is one God that created all Creation, he is the owner of all things, and the feeling of all humans as one family and one society took shape from this.

The writers listed above were studied well in the past; in Soviet times too their books were printed in many editions (with the exception of Yassavi, Rabghuzi, and Bakirghani, who were not published in their entirety because they were deemed "harmful" and "religious"). Today they are being studied more thoroughly, with the new outlook born of independence. Research is currently being carried out on their works.

Nawaii lived in Herat in the fifteenth century, and he is buried there; the works he wrote have been read for some five hundred years throughout Turkistan, even by the Uighurs of East Turkistan, which was later overrun by the Chinese, in Afghanistan, the land in which Nawaii lived and wrote, south of the dismembered Turkistan, in Azerbaijan, and in Turkey. His works were copied by hand and later distributed widely as lithographs. Nawaii became the common poet of the turcophone peoples living in the lands which stretch like a belt from the Great Wall of China to the territory of modern-day Turkey. For example, the thousand-year-old *Twelve Maqam* have been performed using only the lyrics of Nawaii, in itself a unique musical theater in the world and something truly ethnic in character. Nawaii's works are also the subject of intense study in Afghanistan and have been published dozens of times in Turkey over the past fifteen years. However famous Shakespeare is in Europe, Nawaii is loved to an equal degree among the turcophone peoples.

From the sixteenth to the nineteenth century, when Turkistan was divided, wrapped in its own shell, and separated from the rest of the world, a decline set in. The literature created during this period conformed to the times, but several truly national and great writers were also produced, among them Mashrab, Abulghazi Bahadir Khan, Pashshakhoja, Munis, and Agahi. Traditions developed in history, literature, and in the arts, and hundreds of historical and literary works were created. It would not be incorrect to say, however, that literary development was able neither to rise to nor even approach that of Nawaii's time.

At the time of the invasion of West Turkistan by the Russians in the 1850s, the Khokand Khanate, the Khiva

Khanate, and the Emirate of Bukhara ruled the lands that make up most of present-day Uzbekistan. From a historical as well as literary perspective, the legacy of these khanates and the emirate belongs mostly to the inhabitants of Uzbekistan, and perhaps for this reason it was primarily scholars in Uzbekistan who revived and published the literary heritage of West Turkistan during the Soviet era. It is also the Uzbeks who have published (without translation) and read the works of Ahmad Yassavi from nine hundred years ago, which are considered today to be the legacy of the entire Turkish world. All our kinsmen, Kazakhs as well as Turks in Turkey, publish his works only after adapting them to their own modern languages. What does this show us? To my mind, it shows modern Uzbek to be the closest language to Old Turkish.

But I digress. European thought, culture, and technical development arrived concurrently with the encroachment of Russia into West Turkistan, and of course not without oppression and pillage. One cannot ignore that a positive European influence also took place, however. It is for this reason that the famous nineteenth-century poet Zakirjan Furkat, in his newspaper articles and in his poems, called on Turkistanians to learn the Russians' advanced way of thinking, culture, language, and technology. What lay behind Furkat's slogan "Learn from the Russians"? Furkat's day coincided with a time when Russian colonization had become firmly situated in Turkistan, and with the increased oppression it was not possible to say anything openly against them. For this reason, the poet, who was thinking of his people's freedom and benefit, entreated them to learn from the Russians, saying that first they should learn the colonizers' language, that if they learned Russian they would come to know the Russians better and to discern their strengths and weaknesses, and thereby learn how to free themselves from the Russian yoke. For this reason it is possible to consider Furkat to be the father of Jadidist thought in Turkistan.

One could also name Muqimi, Zavqi, and Awaz Otar among the poets who, like Furkat, lived in the last century and were studied widely during the Soviet period. While these were called "democrats," there were other great poets who were branded as "court poets," though this was a biased and incorrect characterization. It will always be proper to judge each author according to the times he lived in. The poets, writers, and historians of the past are all ours, the democratic ones, sycophants, religious, and agnostic ones—all of them belong to us equally.

The strengthening of the policy of colonization at the beginning of the twentieth century in Turkistan naturally gave rise to opposition forces. According to what historians have written, during the czarist era there were some forty-five hundred uprisings against oppression. How many more such revolts occurred only in people's minds? Doubtless, these millions of revolts and waves of emotion in people's hearts have been reflected in popular songs and poetry. The writers known in history as Jadidists—Mahmudkhoja Behbudi, Munawwar Qari, Hamza, Sadriddin Ayni, Batu, Elbek, Abdulla Qadiri, Cholpan, and Fitrat—played a significant role in the development of national thought and literature. But with the exception of Hamza and Ayni, who went over to the Soviet side, all were purged or killed. Like Turkey's Ziya Gökalp and the Caucasus's Ismailbek Gasprali, who initiated the intellectual and spiritual awakening in the Turkish world at the beginning of the twentieth century, Turkistan had the great Jadidist (*jadid* = "new") educator and writer Mahmud Behbudi (1875–1918). In addition to his mother tongue, Turkish,[2] Behbudi knew Arabic and Persian. He also understood life in Russia and her colonies very well. He founded schools, a library, and in 1913 produced the newspaper *Samarkand* and the periodical *Kozgu* in Persian and Turkish[3] (in Persian, this was called *Ayna*). He was the first to write a play in Uzbek: his *Padarkush* (Patricide) was performed on many stages in Turkistan. In this play the idea is put forth that a child who has no education my kill his father as a result of his ignorance. In other words, the message is conveyed that an uneducated people could bring about their own demise and the fall of their homeland. With the advent of *perestroika*, the play was published for the first time in the journal *Sharq Yulduzi* in the 1990s. History, geography, and other textbooks written by Behbudi were also important contributions in their day.

Another author who, like Behbudi, carried on the ideas of the awakening and liberation of Turkistan was Abdulla Awlani (1878–1934), known as an educator, poet, and playwright. Among the several science textbooks and poetry collections he published was the popular *Turki Gulistan* (Turkic Flower Garden or Paradise; 1913), wherein he wrote of what was necessary to cultivate national spirit. This work was reissued in condensed form in the 1970s, then again later in its entirety. Awlani founded the periodicals *Asiya* and *Shuhrat* in Tashkent. His plays such as *Advokatlik Asanmi* (Is It Easy to Be a Lawyer?), *Ikki Muhabbat* (Two Loves), *Toy* (Wedding or Ceremony), *S'ezd* (Legislative Session), and *Oliklar* (Dead Bodies) contributed greatly to the development of Uzbek national playwriting and literature.

A literary personality who fought with his pen for Turkistan's independence and who was finally killed by the Soviets was Abdurauf Fitrat (1886–1938). Fluent in Turkish, Arabic, Persian, and Russian, this very talented writer taught at Petersburg University and ultimately earned a professorship there. He had studied in Turkey, in Istanbul, and it was there that his early books appeared. In my opinion, Fitrat stands first in his portrayal of national thought and attitudes in literature and in his open expression of national interests. In *Yurt Qayghisi* (The Homeland's Distress) he says, "I was born for you, I live for you, oh holy cradle of the Turks!" He summoned people to the cause of Islam and Turkness in his numerous articles in *Hurriyat* and *Ulugh Turkistan*. Plays such as *Chin Sevish* (True Love), *Hind Istilalchilari* (Hindu Invaders), *Oghuzkhan* (Oghuz Khan), and *Temur Saghanasi* (The Tomb of Timur) are priceless for Uzbek literature in their nationalist ideology and literary value.

Another author who performed a great service for Uzbek national life and literature and who was ultimately killed by the Soviets was Abdulla Qadiri (1894–1938). He began his creative works with the play *Bakhtsiz Kuyaw* (The Hapless Son-in-Law; 1913), in which he was influenced by Behbudi. Afterward he wrote stories. *Otgan Kunlar* (Bygone Days), considered the first Uzbek novel, first appeared in serial form in a newspaper starting in 1922. This novel was widely read and loved in his own time as well as later. His second novel, *Mehrabdan Chayan* (The Scorpion from the Pulpit),[4] was issued in 1928. In these novels certain historical events which took place in the Khokand Khanate, in Tashkent, Marghilan, Khokand, and in Turkistan in general, as well as Turkistanians' traditional and everyday life, are depicted beautifully and with great care. After the author was purged, his books were not printed for another twenty years. Later they were reissued in multiple editions, and several of his novels were turned into beautiful Uzbek films.

A great poet who took twentieth-century Uzbek poetry to its heights and who was shot in 1938 by the Soviets was Abdulhamid Sulayman Cholpan (1897–1938). His first poems appeared in such newspapers as *Sadayi Farghana* and *Sadayi Turkistan*. By the 1920s and 1930s, collections of his verse such as *Bulaqlar* (Springs), *Uyghanish* (Awakening), *Tang Sirlari* (Secrets of the Dawn), *Saz* (Lute), and *for* (Skylark) had appeared. Cholpan also published a number of plays, including *Chorining Isyani* (The Revolt of the Slave Woman) and *Ortaq Qarshibaev* (Comrade Qarshibaev), as well as a good many articles of literary criticism and the novel *Kecha wa Kunduz* (Night and Day). After Cholpan was executed, he was essentially blacklisted and his works were not published. It was only in the early 1990s that his poems and his novel were reissued.

Uzbek nationalists such as Behbudi and Fitrat in their initial creative works, Sadriddin Ayni (1878–

1954), and Hamza (1889–1929), under pressure from the Soviet government, went over to "the Soviet side," and for this reason their works were published in ten-volume sets in Uzbek, Russian, and Tajik and were carried around like flags. Nothing was said, however, about their initial nationalistic work and their ideas concerning the liberation of Turkistan. Perhaps this complicated issue will eventually be investigated during the era of independence.

During the Soviet Uzbekistan era thousands of writers, poets, and playwrights grew and matured. Today as well in Uzbekistan, more than a thousand authors continue to create literary works. Among the hundreds of writers who became famous in the years 1930–90 one might cite Hamza, Kamil Yashin, Hamid Alimjan, Uyghun, Aybek, Maqsud Shaykhzada, Mirtemir, Mirkaram Asim, Mirmukhsin, Turab Tola, Habibi, Sabir Abdulla, Asqad Mukhtar, Shukrulla, Adil Yaqubov, Pirimqul Qadirov, Erkin Wahidov, Shukur Khalmirzaev, Abdulla Aripov, Rauf Parfi, Jamal Kamal, Aman Matjan, and Muhammad Ali. Their poems and novels have been translated into many of the world's languages, and among the recurring themes in their works are the history of Turkistan and particularly such figures as Shiraq, Tomaris, Alexander the Great, Genghis Khan, Timur, Babur, Nawaii, Beruni, and Muqana. Although these works were written in the Soviet era, they contributed greatly in their unique literary quality, their exposition of various stages of history, and their cultivation of the moral and spiritual issues of the Uzbek nation. Any listing of the finest individual works from this period would have to include the national poet Aybek's novel *Nawaii*, Maqsud Shaykhzada's tragic play *Mirza Ulughbek*, all of Mirkarim Asim's historical tales, Uighun and Izzat Sultan's play *Alisher Nawaii*, Adil Yaqubov's and Pirimqul Qadirov's historical novels, Mirmukhsin's novel *Me'mar* (The Architect), Shukur Khalmirzaev's hundreds of stories, and Erkin Wahidov's and Abdulla Aripov's poems.

Just as the division of Turkistan during the 1920s and the wooing of nationalist writers to the Soviet cause was a complicated affair, I am of the opinion that it is equally difficult to get the public as well as writers who were brought up in the Soviet system to think, write, and live in the new nationalistic mode. But as the idea of independence becomes more familiar and more widespread, there is no doubt that the Uzbek state will become stronger and our people more united.

Tahir Qahhar, Summer 1996, translated by William Dirks

---

[1] The modern Uzbek word for "wagon" is *arawa*, which is of Arabic origin.—*Translator.*

[2] That is, Uzbek.—*Translator.*

[3] See note 2.

[4] *Mehrab* actually refers to the niche in a mosque pointing toward Mecca which is in front of the imam as he leads the prayer.—*Translator.*

South Asia

INDIA

Revisioning History: Shashi Tharoor's *Great Indian Novel*

In a recent article titled "Figures, Configurations, Transfigurations" Edward Said suggests that contemporary postcolonial literatures express "ideas, values, emotions formerly suppressed, ignored or denigrated by, and of course in, the well-known metropolitan centers" (1). He goes on to claim that these literatures have "played a crucial role in the re-establishment of national cultural heritage, in the re-installment of native idioms, in the re-managing and re-figuring of local histories, geographies, communities." Although Said overestimates the emancipatory potential of postcolonial literatures and conveniently generalizes a diverse body of work, there is clearly an attempt by writers from former colonies to rearticulate their colonial and postcolonial experience and write themselves back into history. Indeed, such acts of recovery are essential, since one of the most damaging legacies of colonialism is its textual appropriation of communities' pasts, where the native becomes the passive subject of history. Frantz Fanon elaborates on this point in *The Wretched of the Earth*: "Colonialism is not satisfied merely with holding a people in its grip and emptying the native's head of all form and content. By a kind of perverted logic, it turns the past of the oppressed people, and distorts, disfigures and destroys it" (161). While both Said and Fanon denounce the cultural imperialism of the former colonizers, their pronouncements are relevant beyond the period of "colonialism."

Political independence for the former colonies has not translated into economic or cultural freedom. Contemporary efforts to articulate an "authentic" postcolonial voice are often mapped within the terms of past power relations. It is quite apparent, for instance, that the unequal relationship between the metropolitan centers (London, New York, and Paris) and their former colonies still exists. A glance at the abundant Euro-American critical discourse on postcolonial writing, for example, generally shows some recurring patterns. On the one hand, there is the complete absence of the post-

colonial subject in the postmodern narrative. Gayatri Spivak, analyzing Gilles Deleuze's comments on a universalized workers' struggle, points out that such statements constitute a "disavowal"; they disregard "the international division of labor, a gesture that often marks poststructuralist political theory" (272). The postcolonial subject is also absent in the work of such critics as Jean-François Lyotard, who have been quick to point out the theoretical contradictions of the Western master narrative. However, unlike other theorists from the West and from the former colonies, Lyotard does not acknowledge the specific reasons for its diminished influence. He does not attempt to theorize the postwar anti-imperial stance of the former colonies and its effect on that narrative. The Western narrative, according to Lyotard, has been replaced only by "petits récits" or smaller local narratives.

The other, more insidious trend in contemporary theories of postcolonial literature is the assumption by Western critics that postcolonial cultural production operates fundamentally and inevitably as a form of resistance to Western cultural hegemony. Such a critical stance allows Western critics, however unwittingly, the privilege of universalizing postcolonial cultural production and excluding those that do not conform to their definitions. This act of cultural appropriation, which has been encouraged by institutional and pedagogic practices, results in the recolonization of postcolonial literatures and thereby negates their rich cultural and political diversity.

These scholarly views are undoubtedly damaging, but they are further reinforced by Western capital's control over marketing techniques which preclude the "normal" circulation of any text written originally in or translated into a European language. The postcolonial writer is therefore faced with the metropolitan center's attempts to control her discourse and regulate her production. The writer has to break out of a limiting universe with its own discursive rules in order to produce any oppositional discourse. Indeed, as Michel Foucault has shown, these discursive rules are characterized by the fixing of terms for the elaboration of concepts and theories. Only certain "speaking subjects . . . may enter into discourse on a specific subject. . . . More exactly, not all areas of discourse are open and penetrable; some are forbidden territory while others are . . . open to all" (225).

In this essay I would like to examine the efforts of a contemporary Indian writer, Shashi Tharoor, to break out of Western discursive constrictions in order to recover and rearticulate events on the subcontinent in this century. My comments on Tharoor's work are largely restricted to the condition of the middle-class Indian writer who has a specific tradition to draw upon and are not designed to be pronouncements on the efforts made by writers from the Caribbean or the African continent. It is important to recognize that literary texts emerge from a complex set of historical circumstances and "competing ideological and cultural clusters" (Ahmed, 23). Any claims about postcolonial texts must be negotiated through an intricate mapping of specific social and cultural conditions that accompany the production of a particular text. An analysis of the historical legacy of colonialism, however, does display a certain degree of uniformity in the postcolonial condition. A common history of economic and cultural bondage results in similar political and cultural expressions. Thus Tharoor's project may well be close to other rewritings in the postcolonial tradition and may subsequently contribute to a broader understanding of writers for whom "the re-reading and rewriting of the European historical and fictional record [remains] a vital and inescapable task, [a task which is] at the heart of the post-colonial enterprise" (Ashcroft, 196).

This essay, however, will not deal only with salvaging Tharoor as a representative postcolonial writer. In the first section I will demonstrate that postcolonial writers, such as Tharoor, are themselves the victims of divided allegiances and ambivalent loyalties: their class position among largely illiterate populations, the material and discursive attractions of metropolitan centers, and the lure of recognition and publication offers from London and New York, among other factors, contribute to their unavoidable involvement in Western cultural systems. Said, Fanon, and Ashcroft, in their urgency to celebrate the recovery of the "national" or "native" voice, avoid highlighting the inevitable contradictions that must accompany any process of cultural recovery. An attempt to recover a "national" past is necessarily exclusive and can only succeed by eliminating other oppositional voices. I examine Tharoor's own, perhaps somewhat deficient, acknowledgment of the historical inconsistencies of his project. Ultimately, it is my contention that any effort to establish, define, or locate a historical past is never only a project for "re-managing and re-figuring . . . local histories, geographies, and communities," but also a creative cultural act fraught with its own contradictions (Said, "Figurations," 1).

▨ WRITING BACK TO THE EMPIRE: A DIALOGUE WITH THE PAST

In *The Political Unconscious* Fredric Jameson suggests an interpretive move which would effectively (re)cover the political subtext of a work and would perhaps subvert the dominant narrative:

[One must rewrite] the literary text in such a way that the latter may itself be seen as the rewriting or restructuration of a prior historical or ideological sub-text, it being always understood that that "subtext" is not immediately present as such, not some common-sense external reality, nor even the conventional narratives of history manuals, but rather must itself always be (re)structured after the fact. (81)

While Jameson's comments are related to the analysis of literary texts, they also include the actual process of rewriting any prior historical or ideological text. In this context, Tharoor's work is an attempt to recover a subtext by breaking away from the dominant European narrative. Tharoor's "restructuration" of the events preceding Indian Independence and after defies the "conventional narratives of history manuals." His appropriation of the great Indian epic, the *Mahabharata,* in order to rewrite Indian history and to restore groups to their historical being is what Homi Bhabha would perhaps call "sly civility," where the "native refuses to satisfy the colonizer's narrative demand" (78).

According to Bhabha, the writer, in this instance, occupies a position which is neither openly rebellious nor apparently compliant. A portion of this "sly civility" is Tharoor's use of an alien language to give shape to past events. The language question is complicated, since theoretically Tharoor has three choices: he can write in Sanskrit, the original language of the epic; alternatively, he can write in Hindi or any other regional language; finally, he can write in English, a language of preference for writers from his class.[1] Tharoor, unlike the ancient scribes, has too many options. His ultimate linguistic choice is not merely dictated by his familiarity with English, but also situates his audience, which is composed primarily of westernized Indians and the international bourgeoisie. His decision, then, is drastically different from a writer like Ngũgĩ wa Thiong'o, who feels that "the real language that one is looking for is the language of struggle, the language of the transformation of our various societies. And eventually this language can only be found in the actions and feeling and thoughts and experiences of the working people" (150). However, Ngũgĩ's idealistic statement belies the fact that his choice to write in Kikuyu excludes a large number of Kenyan "working people" who speak either Luo or Maasai.

Neither Tharoor nor Ngũgĩ, despite their ideological differences, can claim to have found the "correct" formula for liberating the so-called working people. Obviously, Tharoor's literary objectives are far less clear. Perhaps he realizes the impossibility of making a sharp and violent break with the dominant culture of the metropolitan center. Any such attempt would have to erase two hundred years of history and also deny that both the colonizer and the colonized have been permanently changed through their encounter. The alternative, however, is not simply to accept the master's language but to decolonize it, as the British dub poet Linton Kwesi Johnson has so effectively done.[2] Tharoor's recourse is to "begin by co-opting the entire properties of that [alien] language as correspondences to properties in [his] matrix of thought and expression" (Soyinka, quoted in Gates, 40). His counterhegemonic strategy, then, is to adapt a compelling and popular Indian epic so that he may "negate the prior European negation of [his] culture and adopt and creative(ly) modif(y) . . . western languages and artistic forms in conjunction with indigenous languages and forms" (JanMohamed, 103). According to Mikhail Bakhtin, such a move at the linguistic level is particularly relevant and applicable to the genre of the novel.

> Language upon entering the novel establishes its own special order within it, and becomes a unique artistic system, which orchestrates the intentional theme of the author. [The author] can make use of language without wholly giving himself up to it, he may treat it as semi alien or completely alien to himself while compelling language ultimately to serve all his own intentions. (299)

The prose writer, in Bakhtin's words, distances himself from the language of his work and speaks "through" language. Such a writer draws from other languages, creating a heteroglot novelistic language. Of course, according to Bakhtin, the choice here is not so much between available distinct languages, but between the specific sociolects within a "given" language.

However, despite Tharoor's creative use of the master's language, he does not and cannot reverse the course of history. He cannot create a new master narrative, a legitimizing monolithic discourse. His history has to differ from those "official, orthodox, authoritatively national and institutional versions [which] tend principally to designate provisional and highly contestable attempts to freeze these versions of history into identities for use" (Said, "Figurations," 12). Tharoor's narrator, Ved Vyas, who is also the narrator of the *Mahabharata,* aptly sums up his views on such nationalist versions of history: "Some of our more Manichean historians tend to depict the British villains as supremely accomplished—the omniscient, omnipresent, omnipotent manipulators of the destiny of India. Stuff and nonsense, of course" (116). Tharoor/Vyas's rejection of Manichean dualities also suggests that the *Mahabharata* cannot be used as a vehicle to look back nostalgically

at a "pure" precolonial past. This would be an ahistorical move, since it would deny the last few centuries of historical involvement. The *Mahabharata* itself must pass through the filter of colonial experience. The text, as Ved Vyas tells Ganapati, like India, like history, is constantly changing.

> History, Ganapati—indeed the world, the universe, all human life, and so, too, every institution under which we live—is in a constant state of evolution. The world and everything in it is being created and re-created even as I speak . . . going through the unending process of birth and rebirth which has made us all. India has been born and reborn scores of times, and it will be reborn again. India is forever; and India is forever being made. (245)

Tharoor's (dis)claimer of nationalist histories does not, however, imply that his version is a disinterested one. The India to which Tharoor refers is seen through his eyes—narrow eyes that largely ignore the plight of the vast underclass for whom independence merely suggested a ceremonial shift in power. In a sense, Tharoor's project of writing back to the center sadly enacts the erasure of the subaltern or the underclass. Jenny Sharpe, in a perceptive analysis of figures of colonial resistance, points out the inherent contradictions of a middle-class "liberating" discourse such as Tharoor's: "To think of the relation between the discourse centering on the production of the colonial subject and what it occludes as an eclipse is to see that the subaltern classes are not situated outside the civilizing project but are caught in the path of its trajectory. . . . For the colonized subject who can answer the colonizers back is the product of the same vast ideological machinery that silences the subaltern" (143). Tharoor's effort to answer the colonizer is dependent upon the material and discursive tools that are provided by the colonizer. The same ideological apparatus that provides him with a voice is inevitably caught up in silencing those who are less fortunate than Tharoor.

Clearly, Tharoor's work is not "resistance literature" in the way Barbara Harlow describes it. *The Great Indian Novel* does not call "attention to itself as a political and politicized activity . . . [nor is it] *immediately* and *directly* involved in a struggle against ascendant or dominant forms of ideological and cultural production" (Harlow, 29). The choice of a single narrator who recounts the deeds of great men denies that the "struggling oppressed class itself is the depository of historical knowledge" (Benjamin, 260). Tharoor's epic historical perspective is necessarily exclusive and detracts from the liberatory potential of what is otherwise a notable act of cultural recovery. His narrative is not the testimony of a whole people. The historical version he offers concerns great men and is fashioned by a grand moral and ethical design: "In my epic I shall tell of past, present and future, of existence and passing, of efflorescence and decay, of death and rebirth; of what is and of what was, of what should have been" (18). Such declarations are made in order to capture the mood of the epic, not to pose as counterhegemonic challenges.

But perhaps it is Tharoor's historical selection which makes any attempt to recover the struggles of the subaltern finally irrelevant. The banality of everyday life does not interest Tharoor or his narrator. Their India is the India of great men, of Gandhis and Nehrus. Tharoor, in his emphasis on Gandhi and Nehru, ignores one fact: "That such and such a man and precisely that man arises at a particular time in a particular country is, of course, pure chance" (Marx, 767–68). The all-pervasive figure of Gandhi/Gangaji, the so-called enigmatic individual genius, is a diversion from the collective social forces that shape any age. His omnipresence is also juxtaposed, somewhat contradictorily, against mass spontaneous revolution. In this instance Tharoor presents a falsified notion of a spontaneous movement detached from a conscious leadership. Such beliefs only perpetuate historical myths and give the "masses a 'theoretical' consciousness of being creators of historical and institutional values, of being founders of a state" (Gramsci, 198).

Tharoor's revisionist history, a history from a privileged vantage point, thus ultimately remains "traditional," for he fails to recover the history of the silenced voices, the voices which made the national struggle possible. "Traditional" historiography has been dominated by this elitism, "colonialist elitism and bourgeois-nationalist elitism. . . . Both these varieties of elitism share the prejudice that the making of the Indian nation and the development of the consciousness—nationalism—which informed this process were exclusively or predominantly elite achievements" (Guha, "On Some Aspects," 1). Such historical versions further the "great men" myth of history and erase the politics of the people. Indeed, as Partha Chatterjee has pointed out, the "unique achievement of Gandhism [was] the political appropriation of the subaltern classes by a bourgeoisie aspiring for hegemony in a new nation state" (176). The struggle for national independence, as in so many other dependent nations, saw the national bourgeoisie begin to organize itself to slip into the ranks soon to be vacated by the British. The national bourgeoisie with its incomplete version of a war of independence assured a qualified independence: a transference of power without a transference of autonomy. India remained dependent upon the West while the native ruling class used the existing state apparatus to maintain their dominance. Meanwhile, the Indian peasants and the urban workers remained disempowered by the machinations of the national bourgeoisie. These subaltern groups were "always subject to the activity of the ruling groups, even when they rebel[led]. . . . Only 'permanent' victory breaks their subordination, and that not immediately" (Gramsci, 55).

As in the *Mahabharata,* where we learn nothing about the slaughtered soldiers on the battlefield of Kurukshetra, so in Tharoor's India we learn very little about the underprivileged foot soldier. Tharoor the novelist/historian cannot "rescue from out the colonial history the suppressed native voice, attempting also to derive new historiographical insights not only for comprehending the past but also for discussing . . . the weaknesses in native societies" (Said, "Third World," 39). He can only make a feeble attempt at recognizing the unreliability of his historical knowledge: "There is no story and too many stories; there are no heroes and too many heroes. What is left out matters almost as much as what is said" (Tharoor, 411). But it is not enough to legitimize exclusion by claiming that the "political and governmental process in our country has always been distant from the vast mass of the people [and that] this has been sanctified by tradition and reinforced by colonialism" (370). These words diffuse the nature of the problem within a vortex of "traditions" and sustain oppression.

Ultimately, Tharoor is bound by his ideological position in modern India. As a westernized, middle-class Hindu, he is unable to get beyond the habitual preoccupations of his class. His nostalgia for the past, a past when India was the "land of Rama, . . . the land where truth and honour and valour and dharma were worshipped as the cardinal principles of existence" (411), is juxtaposed against his distaste for postindependence failures. Tharoor's longing for a return to past glories, however, is based on a created, static notion of "tradition."

In the following section I would like to demonstrate that Tharoor's romantic, monolithic "land of Rama" is a contradiction to his otherwise skeptical approach to the past and his acknowledgments about the impossibility of recovering that past. I also intend to point out that in his skepticism, Tharoor does depart from "traditional" historiography. He generally has an "ironic" (Hayden White's term) distance from the past and displays elements of both "documentary objectivism" and "relativist subjectivism" (Dominique LaCapra's terms).

■ THAROOR'S MAHA/GREAT BHARATA/INDIA

In a recent interview Tharoor quite clearly states his reasons for using the *Mahabharata* to fore/background events in modern India:

> [The *Mahabharata*] struck me as a work of such contemporary resonance, it helped crystallize my own inchoate ideas about issues. I wanted a vehicle to transmit some of my political and historical interests in the evolution of modern India. I saw the recasting of the *Mahabharata* as a perfect vehicle for the two Indias. ("Interview," 18)

Tharoor's choice is a significant one, because the *Mahabharata* has been and remains embedded in the Hindu national consciousness as *the* great epic. Even in the West, viewers have been exposed to its depth and scope through versions such as Peter Brook's theatrical production and his six-hour film. However, a text as complex and as "foreign" as the *Mahabharata* can only be given limited exposure in the West; Brook's film, for example, was shown in the United States only in so-called art houses and on viewer-supported television. It is exactly the reverse in India. The world of the *Mahabharata* is "the national heroic past: it is the world of 'beginnings' and 'peak times' in the national history, a world of fathers and of founders of families, a world of 'firsts' and 'bests'" (Bakhtin, 13). Bakhtin's characterization of the epic is undoubtedly true of the *Mahabharata,* but his somewhat imperious dismissal of the epic form is in complete contradiction to the fluidity of the great Indian epic. According to Bakhtin, the epic is marked by its "closedness" and "conclusiveness": "Because it is walled off from all subsequent times, the epic past is absolute and complete. It is as closed as a circle; inside it everything is finished, already over. There is no place in the epic world for any openendedness, indecision, indeterminacy. . . . It suffices unto itself, neither supposing any continuation nor requiring it" (16). Bakhtin's generalizations about the epic form, of course, should be understood within the context of his discussion of the novel. He valorizes the latter form, since he claims that it is "determined by experience, knowledge, and practice (the future)" (15). The novel also, because of its polyglossia, is open and continuous; the epic, on the other hand, has "absolute conclusiveness and closedness" (16).

The *Mahabharata,* however, has not existed merely as a "closed" text. It has undergone numerous forms of revisions; its "meanings" have been constantly reinterpreted and revised. Its primary battle, the battle of Kurukshetra, is marked by its inconclusiveness. Throughout generations the epic has been translated and transformed in different versions. Part of the "inconclusiveness" of the *Mahabharata* is thus celebrated through its numerous translations and transcreations in various regional languages. One of the more recent "transformations" of the epic has been a highly successful presentation for a mass television audience. The obscurities of the epic have been rewritten within the framework of a popular narrative mode, and the result has enthralled television audiences in India. Anil Chopra's *Mahabharata,* made for Doordarshan India, uses narrative styles from popular cinema to convert a complicated tale into a spicy treat for viewers. However, it is not the mere trappings of a Bombay melodrama which captivate the viewer: the characters in the *Mahabharata* exist as symbols of virtue; the concept of "dharma" informs the text and is an important part of Hindu religious/philosophical doctrine; filmmakers and playwrights often use characters and events from the epic (Shyam Benegal's *Kalyug* is a good example of this tradition); and perhaps more important for Tharoor, "There's hardly a political controversy where there isn't somebody making some allusion to characters of the *Mahabharata* and describing a politician as Karna, or as Duryodhana" ("Interview," 25).

Tharoor's fascinating combination of history, mythology, and politics thus remains close to an indigenous living tradition; but perhaps it is Tharoor's anecdotal recounting of events in all their farcical and tragic tones that separates the novel from other historical accounts. His narrative methodology is that of the carnivalesque historians, and he uses Bakhtinian festive laughter to disrupt and displace colonial hierarchies; neither the English nor the Indians are spared as objects of ridicule. Like the traditional Indian clown-narrator (the "Viduksha"), Tharoor can take all kinds of narrative liberties as long as he adheres to the core of his tale.

But perhaps the most significant manner in which Tharoor parts company with traditional histories of India is his recognition of the difficulty of translating past events into an "objective" narrative. Vyas/Tharoor confesses that perhaps the "true" history of India can never be suitably recovered; all one has are biases and distortions.

> Every tale I have told you, every perception I have conveyed, there are a hundred equally valid alternatives I have omitted and of which you are unaware. . . . This is my story of the India I know, with its biases, selections, omissions, distortions, all mine. . . . Every Indian must for ever carry with him, in his own head and heart, his own history of India. (373)

Here Tharoor almost completely echoes the words of Hayden White:

> There is no such thing as a single correct view of any object under study but . . . many correct

views, each requiring its own style of representation. . . . The historian operating under such a conception could thus be one who, like the modern artist and scientist, seeks to exploit a certain perspective on the world that does not pretend to exhaust description or analysis. (*Tropics of Discourse*, 46–47)

Any attempt to describe historical events always includes ordering and arranging certain narrative strategies, which then aid in fulfilling the historian's intentions. White suggests an apparent alternative to this manipulative strategy and argues that an "ironic" view of history enables historians to take a skeptical view of the past, since they have distance. Such "irony presupposes the occupation of a 'realistic' perspective on reality [i.e., the historian's], from which a non-figurative representation of the past might be provided" (*Metahistory*, 38). Ironic distance provides perspective and avoids romanticizing. It is quite clear, however, that "irony" also gives the historian a certain sense of superiority over his so-called naïve counterparts. And in Tharoor's case, as we have seen, "irony" does not preclude romantic essentializing. The "ironic" narrative strategy can even consolidate such essentializing by ignoring contesting "historical" voices which accompany any form of "presupposition."

In many ways, Tharoor the novelist/historian is performing what is primarily a creative act. He reinterprets and re-presents "popular" stories about the past and, like a historian, gives shape to the unknown. Hayden White makes a similar point in his essay "The Historical Text as Literary Artifact."

History—the real world as it evolves in time—is made sense of in the same way that the poet or novelist tries to make sense of it, i.e., by endowing what originally appears to be problematical and mysterious with the aspect of a recognizable, because it is a familiar, form. It does not matter whether the world is conceived to be real or only imagined; the manner of making sense of it remains the same. (*Tropics of Discourse*, 98)

This process of making familiar is a creative way of reinterpreting selected moments of the past and ordering history.[3] Tharoor's narrator, Ved Vyas, is also conscious about such artificial methods of recounting history—a history which is always imposed and ordered: "We tend, Ganapati, to look back on history as if it were a stage play, with scene building upon scene, our hero moving from one action to the next in his remorseless stride to the climax. Yet life is never like that . . . and so the recounting of history is only the order we artificially impose upon life to permit its lessons to be more clearly understood" (101).

The tendency to "order" events or produce meanings is what LaCapra has referred to as "relativistic subjectivism." According to LaCapra, the relativist historian "places himself or herself in the position of 'transcendental signifier' that 'produces' or 'makes' the meanings of the past" (138). The objectivist, on the other hand, "places the past in the 'logocentric' position of . . . 'transcendental signified.' It is simply there in its sheer reality, and the task of the historian is to use sources as documents to reconstruct past reality as objectively as he or she can" (137). Clearly, both positions are equally prone to a "misreading" of past events. Any effort to recover the past is mediated by the ideological position of the historian. Tharoor himself alternates between the subjectivist and the objectivist roles. He attempts to order the random events in history by contextualizing them through the language of an epic tradition, but ultimately even he recognizes the impossibility of organizing the past. He then claims to report only "facts." His narrator takes care to emphasize, "Facts, that is all I intend to record, facts and names. This is history" (86), but then concedes that these supposed facts are equally unreliable.

As Tharoor and Vyas order history, so too do they fashion the characters and events from the *Mahabharata*. It is not important for Tharoor to have an "authentic" rendering of the epic. Tharoor's characters do not so much reflect or imitate the "real" figures; they act as symbolic personalities and present the reader with associative images, which then must be decoded through apparently shared cultural experiences. It therefore becomes unnecessary to question Tharoor's choice of characters or to decide whether Subhas Chandra Bose's role in the Indian national movement is as important as Pandu's role in the epic, or if the absence of Abhimanyu (Arjuna's son) is significant. As Vyas puts it, the point of the story is in the telling: "I did not begin the story in order to end it; the essence of the tale is in the telling. . . . There is no end to the story of life. There are merely pauses" (162–63).

Clearly, for Tharoor, "faithfulness to [the] idea" is far more important than "faithfulness to the novelistic depiction of characters" ("Interview," 19), and a significant part of Tharoor's "faithfulness to the idea" is to show the idealism and the hope of the years preceding independence. Bhisma/Ganga Dutta/Gandhi dominates the narrative, but his deeds, in postcolonial India, have been reduced to the realm of textual experience.

It is in the history books now, and today's equivalent of the snot-nosed brats of Motihari have to study it for their examinations on the nationalist movement. But what can the dull black-on-white of their textbooks tell them of the heady excitement of those days? (50)

Tharoor, as a student in postcolonial India, has also been presented with textual versions of the independence struggle and its moments of heady idealism. For many writers of his generation, therefore, the failure of independence becomes the greatest tragedy of modern India. India, like the majority of colonized nations, overestimated the emancipatory potential of independence. The misplaced priorities of its leaders created a state which "was well on the way to becoming the seventh largest industrial power in the world, whatever that may mean, while 80% of her people continued to lack electricity and clean drinking water" (Tharoor, 293). The "blind" Dhritarashtra/Nehru led the country toward a form of "progress" but was incapable of providing housing, food, or employment for the vast majority of his people.

The greatest postindependence betrayal, however, comes when Dhritarashtra/Nehru's daughter, Indira Gandhi / Priya Duryadhoni, declares a state of emergency. The subsequent struggle for democracy then becomes, for Tharoor, the battle of Kurukshetra or the great Bharata war. Tharoor's choice for the modern analogy to the ancient war is a revealing one. The 1977 parliamentary elections which saw the defeat of the authoritarian Indira Gandhi were undoubtedly a triumphant moment for Indian democracy, but as Tharoor knows, the electoral victory achieved very little. Within three years the opposition to Gandhi had collapsed and she was returned to her previous position. Certainly, in terms of human suffering, the partition of the subcontinent remains the most tragic event in modern Indian history, and the scars of that separation still remain on both sides of the divide. Thus, Tharoor's choice for the great contemporary battle is problematic; however, Tharoor/Vyas does concede that the 1977 election following the emergency is not meant to be the single most important event in recent times.

> Life is Kurukshetra. History is Kurukshetra. The struggle between Dharma and adharma is a struggle our nation, and each one in it, engages in on every single day of our existence. That struggle, that battle, took place before this election; it will continue after it. (391)

Indeed, as anyone who is familiar with the current political violence in India knows, "battles" have become part of our daily existence. The various religio-ethnic schisms have made the turmoils of the emergency recede in the national imagination. Tharoor, however, is surprisingly cavalier about these struggles. Perhaps a failure to revive a "politics of the people" makes Tharoor blind to other political factors in his homogenized Maha/Great Bharata/India. On 4 April 1990 some 300,000 Hindus affiliated to the Vishwa Hindu Par-

ishad, a militant Hindu organization, gathered on the lawns of the Delhi Boat Club to pledge their electoral support to the Bharatiya Janata Party.[4] Such a spectacle can only be terrifying to the Muslims and other minorities in India. And the recent gains of that same party in the parliamentary elections of 1991 aggravated the already existing tensions between the majority Hindus and other minority communities.[5] Thus, to say "I have been on the whole a good hindu in my story" (412) or to regret "how far we have travelled from the glory and splendour of our adventurous mythological heroes" (411) has a somewhat frightening resonance in contemporary Indian politics. Also, given the various regional crises in India, with secessionist movements breaking out in Assam, Jammu and Kashmir, and Punjab, it is simply naïve to claim that "the regionalists and autonomists and separatists and secessionists . . . are of no consequence in the story of India" (412).[6] Can the lessons of the *Mahabharata* give shape to the chaos that is modern India? Is it enough to slip into a mindless idealism where the only goal is a hopelessly intangible one? "Let each man live by his own code of conduct, so long as he has one. Derive your standards from the world around you and not from a heritage whose relevance must be constantly tested" (418).

Notwithstanding these serious inconsistencies, *The Great Indian Novel* is still a notable example of a postcolonial writer's attempting to break free of the restraints of a metropolitan culture. Through his innovative use of the English language and in his effort to recover an indigenous epic "tradition," Tharoor effectively recovers a version of India for a portion of its people. His revisioned History provides a "site of intersection" (Said, "Narrative," 83) where the postcolonial writer can refigure dominant European narratives. It must be remembered that traditional European historiography, both before and after independence, consisted of "colonialist knowledge . . . its function was to erect that past as a pedestal on which the triumphs and glories of the colonizers and their instrument, the colonial state, could be displayed to best advantage" (Guha, "Dominance," 211).

In the light of these years of imposed colonialist "knowledge," Tharoor's work, despite all its contradictions and failures, creates a postcolonial space which celebrates the possibilities of revisioning colonialist knowledge. The battle between the center's imposition of discursive restrictions on the postcolonial writer and the writer's creative efforts to break free from this imposition will continue. And writers such as Shashi Tharoor will be caught between the contradictions of their class position and their efforts to "redraw" frontiers and rewrite histories. They are trapped in an inevitable predicament: even as they attempt to challenge the hegemonic entailments of metropolitan culture, they simultaneously renew their cultural contract with the metropolis. However, despite their inevitable complicity in past and contemporary systems of colonialist knowledge, writers like Tharoor succeed insofar as they provide a corrective for the epistemic violence of the European colonizers. Perhaps Chinua Achebe's thoughts on the "novelist as teacher" sum up what Tharoor at best can hope to achieve from his work: "I would be quite satisfied if my novels (especially the ones set in the past) did no more than teach my readers that their past—with all its imperfections—was not one long night of savagery from which the first Europeans acting on God's behalf delivered them" (45).

Kanishka Chowdhury, Winter 1995

■ WORKS CITED

Achebe, Chinua. *Morning Yet on Creation Day.* New York. Anchor. 1975.

Ahmed, Aijaz. "Jameson's Rhetoric of Otherness and the "National Allegory." *Social Text,* 17 (Fall 1987), pp. 3–25.

Ashcroft, Bill, et al. *The Empire Writes Back: Theory and Practice in Post-Colonial Literature.* London. Routledge. 1989.

Bakhtin, Mikhail. *The Dialogic Imagination.* Caryl Emerson and Michael Holquist, trs. Austin. University of Texas Press. 1981.

Benjamin, Walter. "Theses on the Philosophy of History." In his *Illuminations.* Harry Zohn, tr. New York. Schocken. 1969. Pp. 253–64.

Bennett, Tony. *Outside Literature.* New York. Routledge. 1990.

Bhabha, Homi. "Sly Civility." *October,* 34 (1985), pp. 71–80.

Chatterjee, Partha. "Gandhi and the Critique of Civil Society." In *Subaltern Studies III: Writings on South Asian History and Society.* Ranajit Guha, ed. New Delhi. Oxford University Press. 1984. Pp. 153–95.

Fanon, Frantz. *The Wretched of the Earth.* Constance Farrington, tr. New York. Grove. 1968.

Foucault, Michel. *The Archaeology of Knowledge.* A. M. Sheridan Smith, tr. New York. Pantheon. 1972.

Gates, Henry Louis Jr. "Authority, (White) Power and the (Black) Critic: It's All Greek To Me." *Cultural Critique,* 7 (Fall 1987), pp. 19–46.

Gramsci, Antonio. *Selections from the Prison Notebooks of Antonio Gramsci.* Quintin Hoare and Geoffrey Nowell Smith, eds. & trs. New York. International Publishers. 1971.

Guha, Ranajit. "On Some Aspects of the Historiography of Colonial India." In *Subaltern Studies: Writings on South Asian History and Culture I.* Ranajit Guha, ed. New Delhi. Oxford University Press. 1982. Pp. 1–7.

———. "Dominance Without Hegemony and Its Historiography." In *Subaltern Studies: Writings on South Asian History and Culture VI.* Ranajit Guha, ed. New Delhi Oxford University Press. 1989. Pp. 210–35.

Jameson, Fredric. *The Political Unconscious: Narrative as a Socially Symbolic Act.* Ithaca, N.Y. Cornell University Press. 1981.

JanMohamed, Abdul. *Manichean Aesthetics: The Politics of Literature in Colonial Africa.* Amherst. University of Massachusetts Press. 1983.

LaCapra, Dominique. *History and Criticism.* Ithaca, N.Y. Cornell University Press. 1985.

Lyotard, Jean-François. *The Postmodern Condition: A Report on Knowledge.* Geoff Bennington and Brian Massumi, trs. Minneapolis. University of Minnesota Press. 1984.

Marx, Karl, and Friedrich Engels. *The Marx-Engels Reader.* Robert C. Tucker, ed. New York. Norton. 1978.

Ngũgĩ wa Thiong'o. "The Language of Struggle." *Transition,* 54 (1991), pp. 142–54.

Said, Edward. "Figurations, Configurations, Transfigurations." *Race and Class,* 32:1 (1990), pp. 1–16.

———. "Narrative, Geography and Interpretation." *New Left Review,* 180 (March/April 1990), pp. 81–97.

———. "Third World Intellectuals and Metropolitan Culture." *Raritan,* 9:3 (1990), pp. 27–50.

Sharpe, Jenny. "Figures of Colonial Resistance." *Modern Fiction Studies,* 35:1 (Spring 1989), pp. 137–55.

Spivak, Gayatri. "Can the Subaltern Speak?" In *Marxism and the Interpretation of Culture.* Cary Nelson and Larry Grossberg, eds. Urbana. University of Illinois Press. 1988. Pp. 271–313.

Tharoor, Shashi. *The Great Indian Novel.* New Delhi. Penguin Books India. 1989.

———. Interview. *India Currents,* 4:8 (1990), pp. 18+.

———. "The Revenge of History." *New York Times,* 11 December 1992, p. A21.

White, Hayden. *Metahistory: The Historical Imagination in Nineteenth Century Europe.* Baltimore. Johns Hopkins University Press. 1973.

———. *Tropics of Discourse: Essays in Cultural Criticism.* Baltimore. Johns Hopkins University Press. 1978.

[1] Sanskrit, of course, is not a realistic choice for Tharoor. For writers such as he, who have been educated in westernized institutions, Sanskrit remains largely an alien language. As far as Tharoor is concerned, the English language remains the most practical, though necessarily limiting, option.

[2] Linton Kwesi Johnson's distinctive style is best seen in his many albums and in such poetry collections as *Inglan Is a Bitch.*

[3] Tony Bennett makes a similar point in *Outside Literature:* "The past, in so far as the historian is concerned with it, is never the past as such—not everything that may be said of it—but only the past as a product of the specific protocols of investigation which characterize the discipline of history in its concern to establish, classify and order the relations between events pertinent to the inquiry in hand" (56).

[4] The Bharatiya Janata Party (BJP) has attained national recognition since the 1991 elections. Smaller militant Hindu organizations such as the Vishwa Hindu Parishad, the Jana Sangh, and the Shiv Sena have aligned themselves to the BJP in order to attain some degree of political clout. The BJP now walks the fine line between being a mainstream party and appeasing these smaller militant groups.

[5] Since I wrote this essay, events in India have taken a turn for the worse. The destruction of the Ayodha mosque by Hindu militants and the consequent riots across the country have forever shattered the confidence of millions of India's citizens, both Hindu and Muslim.

[6] Tharoor's response to the 1992 riots is characteristic of his faith in a democratic, secular India: "The raging battle is for India's

soul. For my sons, the only possible idea of India is the one their parents grew up with, that of a nation greater than a sum of its parts. That is the only India that will allow them to continue to call themselves Indians" (A21).

Indian Writing Today: A View from 1994

1. Twenty years ago, in his introduction to the Penguin anthology *New Writing in India* (1974), Adil Jussawalla identified two common qualities in the literatures of the various Indian languages. One was the predominance of "metaphors of dismemberment and dislocation," for which he located the source in the Indian experience of the Partition of the subcontinent at the end of British rule in 1947.

> Partition caused a major crack in the Indian personality, and the subsequent linguistic divisions of India, communal riots, territorial losses, unstable borders and big-power rivalries on the subcontinent have, if anything, widened the crack and caused several more to appear. To the extent that an Indian takes his country's lack of integration personally, any disintegration of it, whether threatened or actual, will be regarded as a separation of different parts of a single body.

The other quality was the presence of "a strong smell of death about contemporary Indian writing." In this instance Jussawalla perceived a parallel between "the obsession with death" and "the treatment of political, social and personal paralysis."

> In other words, this writing reflects the Indian petty bourgeoisie's present inability to find a dynamic role for itself in a society which is slowly transforming itself from the semi-feudal to the capitalist. Wedged between the class that employs it and the broad masses of peasants and the growing urban proletariat, it can only torment itself with its own contradictions or turn on itself in a fury of self-destruction. This is the writing of a bourgeoisie at a dead end.

In the two decades since Jussawalla wrote these words, the contemporary Indian writer's obsessions with death, dismemberment, and dislocation have become more intense and have acquired other meanings. In Mahasveta Devi's "Draupadi," for instance, a short story first published in Bengali in 1978, the heroine, Dopdi, is a twenty-seven-year-old woman of the Santal tribe in eastern India. Like her husband, she becomes a tribal revolutionary who is wanted by the Indian government's special armed forces for insurrectionary activity. She is tracked down and arrested, questioned about her collaborators, and then raped successively by half

a dozen or more of her male captors. In the process, "her breasts are bitten raw, the nipples torn," and she is reduced to "a compelled spread-eagled still body," her thighs and "pubic hair matted with dry blood," her "ravaged lips" bleeding. Not quite dead, but no longer humanly alive, Dopdi passes beyond allegorical personifications of the Partition. Her mutilation and apportionment evoke not only the kind of Balkanization practiced by departing colonial powers—in this case, the segregation of the so-called tribal ("non-Aryan") and mainstream ("Aryan") populations in India—but also the violence enacted by men on women, postcolonial nation-states on their own citizens, armed forces on civilians, canonical on noncanonical cultures, classical norms on folk practices, and those in power on those who offer resistance.

2. The continuities and differences between the metaphors Jussawalla detected in the writing of the 1960s and early 1970s and the complex representations we find in the Indian literatures of the past two decades signify a many-layered shift in literary quality. One crucial feature of the shift is that various forms of nonrealistic or antirealistic writing have now (re)surfaced in the different Indian languages. This has happened partly in reaction to the dominance, over the last one hundred years or so, of the realistic mode in fiction, drama, and nonfictional prose. The dominance of realism was a consequence of the British colonization of the subcontinent, which brought with it a cultural imperialism centered on "the great tradition" of the nineteenth-century English novel and, by parallel, the French and the Russian novel. The Indian reaction against realism after about 1960 was therefore anticolonial and, at the same time, nationalistic. It led to two kinds of searches: one for an uncontaminated precolonial Indian or non-European "high" literary past, and the other for a common Indian "folk" culture. Both searches led to a return to Indian and non-European models of nonrealistic representation, ranging from the modes of fantasy in Sanskrit epic and episodic narrative and Arabic frame stories, to the mode of the marvelous in Indian folktales and mythology.

In Indian-language drama after 1960, for example, the alternative to the realistic theater of Chekhov, Ibsen, and Shaw was the antirealism of Indian myth and Indian folk theater. In an interview with Aparna Dharwadker recorded in Chicago in July 1993 the Kannada playwright Girish Karnad explained the antirealist element in his own work in terms that are symptomatic of the contemporary Indian literary situation as a whole.

> In the 1960s, theatre people in India talked endlessly about "going back to the roots." There was an entire conference organized by the Sangeet

Natak Akademi [the national academy of music, drama, and the performing arts] in New Delhi, in the late '60s, where this point was passionately debated, but without reference to a single play, because at that time no contemporary playwright had used folk forms. It was all a theoretical discussion about what could or should be or should not be done, whether one could be "modern" and still use traditional forms and whether traditional techniques would not mean a return to unscientific medievalism. When *Hayavadana* was published, two modern Kannada writers, Gopalakrishna Adiga and P. Lankesh, savaged it as "retrograde," because scientifically it is not possible to graft a head back onto a body!. . .

Actually, I didn't start off by saying: "Let me use folk techniques. How shall I go about it?" I remember I was telling B. V. Karanth [subsequently the director of the National School of Drama] the story of *Hayavadana,* and saying it would make a marvellous film, when he said: "It will make even better theatre. We are always talking about how to use masks. Why don't you write a play for masks?" I knew he was right. So I began with the simple question: How to justify the use of masks? By using a nonrealistic, possibly traditional form in which the use of masks won't look absurd. But traditional performances begin with the worship of Ganesh, a god with a human body and an elephant's head. And suddenly, the theme of a human body bearing a head unrelated to it started developing as the basis of the form of the play. So there were the men who got their heads mixed up; there was the god; what about animals? That's how the framing story of *Hayavadana* emerged—the man with the horse's head. It was literally worked out like that! What I am particularly happy about is the fact that *Hayavadana* does not merely apply folk techniques to an otherwise realistic story. The play goes right through from the divine to the animal. So does *Naga-Mandala.* There's no way of telling these tales realistically.

Since the late 1970s, other strategies of antirealistic representation, such as allegory and magic realism, also have surfaced in Indian writing, partly because they have become predominant after World War II in other parts of the world, from Latin America and the Caribbean to Europe.

The (re)emergence of antirealism in recent Indian writing has been accompanied by a persistence of social realism and psychological realism from the middle of this century. These two kinds of realism appear in the writing of the 1970s and 1980s as modes separable from each other, and also as modes that combine to revitalize literature, particularly in prose genres, as a form of effective social critique. In fact, Mahasveta Devi's meticulously researched, remarkably detailed stories in Bengali about life in urban and rural India (mainly in and around West Bengal) raise social realism to a new level of criticism. As she says in one of her prefaces, "Life is not mathematics and the human being is not made for the sake of politics. I want a change in the present social system and do not believe in mere party politics." Similarly, the exceptional experiments of Indian and Pakistani short-story writers in Urdu—from Balraj Manra, Surendar Parkash, and Naiyer Masud to Abdullah Hussein, Khalida Asghar, Enver Sajjad, and Zamiruddin Ahmad—have given psychological realism a cutting edge it did not have earlier. The same is true of fiction in other languages, from Bengali, Gujarati, and Marathi to Tamil and Malayalam, in which writers combine the devices of social and psychological realism to produce unprecedented representations of contemporary Indian reality.

3. In "Some Contexts of Modern Indian Poetry," an essay published in *Chicago Review* in 1992, I suggested that three contexts are particularly important for an understanding of twentieth-century verse in the Indian languages: the history of various local, regional, and national literary movements; the web of Indian and foreign influences which provides the intertextual basis for poetic writing; and the social backgrounds of the poets and their audiences, including their involvements in some recent social movements on the subcontinent. K. Satchidanandan, a major Malayalam poet and scholar of the twentieth century and currently the editor of *Indian Literature,* the official journal of the Sahitya Akademi, India's national academy of letters, extended and modified my account in several ways in "Turning Iron into Gold: Poetry's Alternative Nationhoods," his introduction to the special issue of the journal on younger Indian poets, published at the end of 1993. Satchidanandan argued that Indian poetry today is "more polyphonic than ever before, perhaps because of a break-down of unifying concerns, and homogenizing ideologies" (such as the quest for national independence in the first half of this century). This "destruction of a central voice . . . has made poetry more various, more democratic, capable of reflecting . . . plurality," and the resulting heterogeneity signifies "a collapse of neat categories like the Romantic and the Progressive, the Modern and the post-Modern." From Satchidanandan's perspective, the modern poet is "always a dissenter" in society, whether that society is shaped by late capitalism and consumerism, as in the United States, or by a totalitarian political system, as in the former Soviet Union. Using very different means, both kinds of societies systematically erase the dissenting poet's individuality because it threatens

the system in place. According to Satchidanandan, as poets in post-Independence India have tried to counter the commodification or the censorship of the individual, they have succeeded in creating at least four kinds of "poetic nations." One is the nation of the "modernist poetry" of the 1950s and 1960s, which "tried to resist the commodification of the individual by a dynamic assertion of individual identity"; a second is that of the women's movement, which has been striving "consciously or unconsciously . . . to subvert our phallocentric order"; a third is the nation or "imagined poetic community" of "insurrectional poetry" produced by the Dalit movement in Maharashtra and Gujarat and the Bandaya movement in Karnataka; and a fourth is the still-emergent one of *uttar adhunik kavita,* postmodern poetry, in languages like Bengali, Kannada, Oriya, and Malayalam, which "seeks an indigenous alternative to what its practitioners call the 'Eurocentric modernism' of the fifties and sixties" and which "may be called postmodern in a specifically Indian sense."

Building on Satchidanandan's insights, and broadening the references of my earlier essay beyond poetry to include fiction and drama, I would now emphasize that, in the postcolonial decades, Indian writing has remained a predominantly middle-class institution. Within it we can distinguish broadly, on one side, between the literature produced by dominant groups, such as urban, educated, professional, and/or upper-caste men, and that produced by subaltern groups, such as middle-class women, or recently literate, lower-caste men and women outside or on the fringes of the middle class. On the other side, we can differentiate prosubaltern writing from writing that remains disengaged from subalterneity and therefore seems to be antisubaltern, elitist, or "comfortably middle class." These four categories—though suspect, like all other categories—intersect with one another in interesting ways in the contemporary literatures in the Indian languages. For instance, a large prosubaltern (and antielitist) literature has emerged from the post-Independence left-wing movement in India, which has been peopled mainly by men and women writers from dominant groups, who are driven by the guilt of belonging to a protected and privileged urban middle class in a country where a very high proportion of the population still lives in dehumanizing poverty. This literature includes the writing about "tribals"—the oldest indigenous inhabitants of the subcontinent, who still lead extremely "primitive" lives, even though they number more than seventy million—by writers like Mahasveta Devi in Bengali and Sitakant Mahapatra in Oriya (the latter the winner of India's highest literary honor, the Jnanapith Award, in early 1994). It also includes the work of a large number of

activist-writers who, though belonging to the urban middle class, have devoted their careers in various ways to the poor and the oppressed in the Indian countryside. In 1963 the Hindi novelist Krishna Baldev Vaid, a prosubaltern middle-class writer, suggested that the goals of Indian fiction ought to be: "portrayal of poverty, hunger and disease; portrayal of widespread social evils and tension; examinations of the survival of the past; exploration of the hybrid culture of the educated middle class; analysis of the innumerable dislocations and conflicts in a tradition-ridden society under the impact of an incipient, half-hearted industrialization." Surprisingly—or perhaps not so—Vaid's prescription from three decades ago describes quite precisely what a great deal of prosubaltern Indian writing, as practiced by writers who themselves are not subaltern, has actually accomplished between the 1960s and the present.

Of the movements involving writers who actually belong to subordinated, disenfranchised, or oppressed groups in contemporary Indian society, two are especially significant, as both Satchidanandan and I have already observed. One is the women's movement in the literatures of the Indian languages, which has brought together women writers with a range of feminist and other women-centered perspectives. (Some male writers, like Raghuvir Sahay in Hindi and A. K. Ramanujan in English, stand on the edges of this body of writing, since they have written works from women-centered perspectives or have worked extensively—as editors, translators, and commentators—with texts produced by women.) In many instances, women's writing since about 1970 focuses mainly on the unequal distribution of power across gender differences within middle-class Hindu, Muslim, and Sikh societies (e.g., the poems of Amrita Pritam in Punjabi, Gagan Gill in Hindi, and Rajani Parulekar in Marathi). In other instances, however, this literature also deals with more complicated situations in which gender inequities combine with asymmetries between upper and lower classes, higher and lower castes, urban and rural environments, older and younger generations, and so on (e.g., the short stories of Amrita Pritam in Punjabi).

The other movement involving subaltern writers is that linking various communities of present and former untouchables in Hindu caste society, most notably the Dalits who write in languages like Marathi, Gujarati, and Kannada. In this case, subaltern writers and groups produce a prosubaltern literature that is sometimes, or often, virulently anti-middle-class and, since high literature is largely a middle-class institution, even antiliterary. At the hierarchical bottom of this pyramid is Dalit women's writing, in which women violently subordinated by men in the lowest stratum of Indian society attempt to overturn gender domination as well as caste and class domination (e.g., the Marathi poetry of Jyoti Lanjewar and Hira Bansode). In practically all the cases of prosubaltern writing—whether by subalterns themselves or by their supporters and sympathizers in the dominant groups—we see the articulation of an intricate vision of social justice, not unlike the ones found in the corresponding revolutionary and subaltern movements in, say, Latin American, Caribbean, and African literatures of the postwar period.

4. Since the 1930s, Indian-language writers and critics have quite bitterly and consistently attacked Indian English writers on several grounds. One basis for the criticism is that, in the colonial period as well as in postcolonial times, Indians who choose to write in English consciously collaborate with the colonizer. Besides being the cultural "toadies" of their Western masters, Indian English writers—so the argument goes—also embody the alienation from their origins and cultural traditions that results from colonial, and now postcolonial, westernization. Since such writers write in a language that is not their own, they can only imitate or mimic those whose native tongue it is. Moreover, since English is foreign to Indian soil, it cannot naturally and effectively represent the real life of the subcontinent. Indian English writers have had to defend themselves against such an argument repeatedly during the past fifty or sixty years, which is precisely the period over which their writing has shaped itself into a recognizable literature in its own right.

Ironically, between about 1975 and 1985, it was Indian English writing, rather than writing in the Indian languages, which broke through Western skepticism about its literary viability and its originality and achieved international recognition. The extraordinary quality of new works in English by Anita Desai, Nissim Ezekiel, Arun Kolatkar, Jayanta Mahapatra, Bharati Mukherjee, R. K. Narayan, A. K. Ramanujan, and Salman Rushdie, among others—together with G. V. Desani and Raja Rao earlier, and Amitav Ghosh and Vikram Seth a little later—placed Indian English literature on par with the best new writing in the British Commonwealth and Anglo-Irish and American traditions. This was the kind of cultural breakthrough that writers in Bengali, Hindi, Kannada, Marathi, Tamil, and Urdu, for example, could not have achieved on their own, even if they had been lucky enough to find first-rate English, French, or German translators.

The explosion of high-quality new writing in English by Indians, in poetry in the 1970s and in prose fiction in the 1980s, has altered the relations between Indian English and the indigenous Indian languages quite irreversibly. The achievements of the Indian English poets and novelists have eroded the long-standing complaint that, since Indians are foreigners to the English language, they cannot produce great or original works in it. These achievements have also dismantled the unsympathetic view that Indian English literature is essentially a *comprador* literature that merely reproduces the prototypes of Anglo-American literature without subverting the old or new colonial authority of the latter. Most interestingly, the recent accomplishments of Indian English writing have undermined the prejudice that it cannot adequately or authentically represent India, Indian life, or Indian reality and cannot invent ways of representing Indian experience accurately and imaginatively. Perhaps the sharpest irony is that, following its recent successes in the international literary marketplace, Indian English literature now provides some of the unacknowledged models for writing in the Indian languages. Since about 1980, for example, the modes of allegory, fantasy, and magic realism have become commonplace in the various Indian languages to a significant extent because of their success in Indian English fiction. This relationship between English and the Indian languages is a reversal of their relationship, say, thirty years ago, because throughout the nationalist phase the indigenous Indian languages claimed the first right to authentic representations of India.

The exclusive access to the indigenous, the traditional, and the authentic that Indian-language writers appropriated for themselves until very recently has a significant history. Starting in the 1840s and 1850s or soon after, writers in languages such as Bengali, Braj Bhasha, Gujarati, Malayalam, Tamil, and Urdu seized upon authenticity as their defining characteristic chiefly in reaction to European colonization and Orientalism. As an oppositional and subaltern discourse within the order of the raj, nineteenth- and early-twentieth-century writing in the Indian languages created a literary space that neither colonial administrators nor Orientalist scholars could censor, regulate, or appropriate effectively. That is, the rapidly developing modern Indian literary languages remained outside the cultural reach of most Western specialists, even as they do now (which is why, in the last fifty years, European and Anglo-American scholars have remained so deeply alienated from contemporary Indian-language writing). Between about 1850 and 1950, as a representational space that stood within an imperial regime but did not fall into the hands of the colonizer, Indian-language writing became one of the principal sites of anticolonial nationalism. As a collective nationalistic enterprise that lasted more than a century, the literatures in the Indian languages thus were able to legitimize themselves easily by claiming to possess the native, authentic, and traditional sources of Indian identity and culture.

In the past ten or twenty years that claim to authenticity has been undermined, not only by the accomplishments of Indian English literature, but also by the inescapable modernity and cosmopolitanism of Indian-language writing itself, and by the emergent diaspora of the Indian languages among immigrant communities around the world. In the outpouring of discourse in print and other media in the 1980s and 1990s, Punjabi poets have now appeared in California and British Columbia, Urdu short-story writers in Toronto and London, Marathi and Gujarati novelists in Washington, D.C., and Chicago, and Bengali poets in Heidelberg, Paris, and Boston. At the end of the twentieth century, after being confined for several hundred years to fairly fixed regions on the subcontinent, the literatures of the Indian languages seem to be dispersed all over the globe.

5. Almost exactly twenty-five years ago, *Books Abroad*—the former avatar of *World Literature Today*—published a special issue titled "The Letters of India in Transition," in honor of the centenary of Mahatma Gandhi's birth. If what I have outlined above is placed beside the introduction to that issue by Nissim Ezekiel, who was then the leading Indian English poet and critic of his generation, we begin to get a glimmer of how much has happened in India since 1969. Ezekiel wrote his piece without being aware of either the women's movement or the Dalit movement, both of which had already appeared in their early forms on the subcontinent. He also wrote without reference to the gap between "comfortably middle-class" writing and "guilt-ridden" left-wing writing in English and the Indian languages, which has become so evident subsequently. From his position at the end of the 1960s, Ezekiel could view his fellow writers in a skeptical-humanist framework, built out of elements in the liberal rather than the Marxist tradition.

Nevertheless, Ezekiel noted several features of post-Independence Indian writing that are visible down to the present day. It is still true that few Indian writers are of world stature; that the complexities of the Indian literary situation defy generalization, and are not only literary but also linguistic, social, and cultural; that literature, especially in the indigenous languages, is still a social force on the subcontinent, even though the writing in each language tends to be isolated from writing in the others; and that Indian English writers fare far better than their counterparts in the Indian languages. Some of Ezekiel's other observations from 1969, however, need to be modified substantially. We need to recognize now that the relationships between English and the Indian languages are multilinear and reversible rather than binary and fixed; that the apparent parochialism

of the Indian reading public in each language really masks a potentially dangerous regional and cultural chauvinism, capable of fueling a violent separatism; that the opposition between Indianness and westernization is now an entangled rather than a straightforward one; and that, despite everything, Indian-language literatures can make a greater impact in translation than they could twenty-five years ago. Most important, perhaps, contrary to Ezekiel's benign hope, the best Indian writing—whether in English or in an Indian language—can no longer avoid the extremes of Indianness and westernization, or traditionality and cosmopolitanism.

The breakdown in the 1980s and 1990s of Nehru's post-Independence secular socialism and the concomitant rise of regional separatism, religious fundamentalism, and communal violence have made it impossible for writers to find a simple humanistic middle ground. Unless one retreats into middle-class comfort and obliviousness, or into pure estheticism, one cannot escape facing up to the extremes in the local, regional, and national situations on the subcontinent. Unfortunately, those extremes now are extreme enough to encroach on the space of literature and to force some forms of contemporary Indian writing to aspire to the condition of silence.

Vinay Dharwadker, Spring 1994

Trends in Modern Indian Fiction

Literary trends do not emerge full-blown, like Minerva from Jupiter's head, nor do they vanish suddenly and completely, leaving not a trace behind. Rather, while some old trends continue unabated, others, out of sheer exhaustion, or else in response to the changing social or literary situation, lose their energy, sometimes dying a natural death, but more often continuing in a muted form, leading a subterranean existence, or else appearing under new guises, or disguises. New trends, earlier anticipated, gradually gather strength, become vigorous, occupy the center of the stage for a while, until they too are pushed into the background. In literature it is thus a matter more of links and continuities with the past than of making a clean break with it.

It is only in this limited sense, without dogmatism—and, one might add, with considerable trepidation—that one can venture to speak of trends in modern Indian fiction (since Indian fiction in effect means the fiction of twenty-two languages recognized by the Sahitya Akademi and a great deal more). It is by no means as if in modern Indian fiction earlier concerns and preoccupations have been abruptly and completely replaced by new ones. In fact, many old trends continue to lead a vigorous life: exploration of the experience of love in all its richness, complexity, and variety; delicate play of individual sensibility; preoccupation with the self and with one's moods and emotions (often in philosophical and existential frames); and, above all, a brooding concern with historical, legendary, and mythical themes—these have remained strong and effective as in the past. Still, even as these trends have continued, others, making a tentative appearance at first, have acquired a new energy, a new shape and form, sometimes a new context, and have become dominant, more articulate, asserting themselves more strenuously.

1. A major development in modern Indian fiction has been the growth of a feminist or woman-centered approach, an approach which seeks to project and interpret experience from the viewpoint of a feminine consciousness and sensibility. Feminism assumes that women experience the world differently from men and write out of their different perspective. As Patricia Meyer Spacks remarks, "There seems to be something that we might call a woman's point of view, . . . an outlook sufficiently distinct to be recognizable through the centuries" (4–5).

It must not be imagined that feminism suddenly burst upon the Indian literary scene in recent years. Rather, it has grown slowly and steadily, some of its features having been anticipated by earlier writers such as Bankimchandra Chatterji and Rabindranath Tagore in Bengali and Jainendra Kumar in Hindi. Saratchandra Chatterji, who created perhaps the most memorable portraits of women in Indian literature, was something of a feminist by conviction, as were some of his heroines, such as Kamal and Kiranmoyee. In Urdu, Ismat Chugtai had scandalized many by her outspoken themes, while as early as the 1930s the now almost completely forgotten Rashid Jahan, in her stories in *Angare* (Embers) and *Aurat* (The Woman), had dealt with the problems of women, especially Muslim women, with daring un-conventionality. In Marathi, Vasumati Dharker published a number of stories from the 1930s to the 1950s in which, says Rani Dharker, "the strong women characters she portrays and the ideas about women . . . are far ahead of her time" (79).

Thus what may be called the faint foreshadowings and premonitions of feminism become visible in Indian fiction as early as in the 1920s and 1930s. It is, however, only in the post-Independence period, and especially since the 1960s, that Indian novelists have begun to question seriously and systematically, and at times to reject outright, traditional interpretations of women's role and status in society. Ideals of womanhood firmly entrenched—often imposed by men and unconsciously internalized by women—are now losing their sanctity and are being critically assessed.

Oppression and exploitation of women in what is now often called a patriarchal society has been an ever-present theme in Indian fiction. The theme is a recurrent one in Premchand and Saratchandra Chatterji, although in Saratchandra it is often suffused in a romantic glow which blunts its sharp edge. Whereas earlier writers had often glorified women's suffering, however, Indian novelists in the last two or three decades have on the whole presented it unpalliatively, with much greater realism, and without minimizing its impact by giving it the halo of noble self-sacrifice. Recent Indian novelists tend to present oppression of women with greater self-consciousness, a deeper sense of involvement, and not infrequently a sense of outrage. The theme takes on sharpness and urgency, and is developed with great diversity of situations and characters, in Nayantara Sahgal's novels *The Day in Shadow* and *Rich Like Us*. In the Dalit or "oppressed" writer Baburao Bagul's nightmarish Marathi novel *Sood* (Revenge) Janaki, the daughter of a devadasi, finally seeks to destroy her femaleness as the only way to escape being degraded by men, and therefore offers her female body to the River Ganga. Mrinal Pande's story "Girls" (in Hindi) brings out the discrimination women themselves practice in the upbringing of girls and boys. The unnamed eight-year-old narrator is told by a female relative: "You are born a girl and you will have to bend for the rest of your life, so you might as well learn" (59). The narrator is finally driven to expostulate: "When you people don't love girls, why do you pretend to worship them?" (63). In Shashi Deshpande's justly celebrated English novel *That Long Silence,* the matric-failed Dilip is given a favored position over his much more talented sister Kusum. Manorama Mathai's story "The Marriage of Aley" in her collection of short prose in English *Lilies That Fester,* shows the unenviable fate of even well-educated Christian women of Kerala, and the writer Kamala Das recalls how even in her matriarchal society a man could force his niece to divorce her husband, whom she loved, and marry another man (155).

The celebrated Oriya writer Binapani Mohanty, whose avowed aim is to uphold "femininity" and "woman-consciousness" and who excels in presenting the plight of village women, and the leading Gujarati novelist Kundanika Kapadia, who has taken a sustained interest in the Women's Liberation movement, graphically and at times polemically depict the fate of women wronged by men. More restrained is the Assamese writer Sneha Devi, whose collection of stories *Sneha Devir Ekunki Galpa* is remarkable for its presentation of images of women's life with insight and sensitivity. As Bhaben Barua remarks, at the heart of each of her stories "there is the voice of a woman. The significance of her contribution to Assamese fiction partly lies in the expression of this sensibility. . . . Various aspects of feminine sensibility have . . . been presented in her stories with remarkable authenticity" (15–16).

To be sure, portrayal of women's suffering has been an eternal theme in Indian literature, going as far back as the *Mahabharata* and the *Ramayana*. What is innovative and unprecedented is the perspective and point of view from which it is now presented. No longer extolled as noble sacrifice or enveloped in an aura of misty romanticism, women's suffering is now portrayed, especially by women writers, with bleak realism for what it often is: an outcome of male egotism, selfishness, and heartlessness.

Increasingly in recent Indian fiction women refuse to put up passively with oppression and injustice, choosing rather to resist them with courage and determination, often coming out victorious in the end. Although some writers may persist in showing women in traditional roles in society, many present women in active and assertive roles. Recent Tamil fiction, for example, deals pervasively with the theme of emancipation of women, the tone ranging all the way from muted to strident, from placid to doctrinaire. Jayanti Naik's stories in *Garjan* (in Konkani) present village women fighting against male authoritarianism with firmness and success. In the title story of Gangadhar Gadgil's collection *The Woman and Other Stories* the main character is a strong-willed woman committed to asserting and defending her integrity as an individual. In Sindhi, Soni Mulchandani portrays women who fight against injustice with persistent courage in her aptly titled collection *Shakti* (Strength). Rita Shahani's novel *Chanda Khan Sija Taeen* (From the Moon to the Sun) shows the protagonist gradually shedding her dependence on external props and becoming self-reliant, thus ceasing to be the moon which reflects the light of the sun in order herself to become the sun. Qurratul-Ain Haider's Urdu novel *Chandni Begum* presents a new and emerging face of the Muslim woman after long years of repression.

A major strength of Shashi Deshpande's *That Long Silence* is its sensitive and realistic presentation of the married life of the narrator Jaya and her husband Mohan. The searching critical examination to which the institution of marriage has been subjected in recent Indian fiction may to some extent well be an offshoot of the growth of a feminist outlook. Marital relationships, and the oppression that often exists in them, have been a subject of great concern for recent Indian novelists, both men and women, although it is women writers

who have felt most strongly and passionately about them, for understandable reasons. Writers such as Shivani, Amrita Pritam, Binapani Mohanty, and Sneha Devi effectively show the frequently oppressive nature, from a woman's point of view, of such relationships, and the legitimization of women's exploitation which they too often involve. In a well-known poem, "Pati" (Husband), the Punjabi woman poet Manjit Tiwana wryly remarks: "The husband is a hungry wolf who saves you from other wolves, but devours you in the end" (cited by Ashok Kumar). Dina Mehta's finely chiseled stories of married life are peopled by women who boldly question male values and often totally reject male hegemony. In her delicately ironic story "Absolution" the narrator, a conventional middle-class housewife tellingly named Sita, responds to her husband Ram's persistent infidelity by what may be called retaliatory infidelity. Her husband, who had flowers left for his wife in the lacquered bowl on the breakfast table after his acts of infidelity, is totally discomfited when he finds, in an ironic reversal of situation, a glorious bouquet of red carnations left for him by—who else but his wife!

Feminism as manifested in modern Indian fiction suffers from certain limitations. Too often it has led to the portrayal of passive, unrelieved suffering of women, their stark misery. Many women writers have been afflicted with excessive self-pity and have failed to extricate themselves from the vale of tears. For example, in Shashi Deshpande's novel *That Long Silence* the spectacle of women suffering without resistance or struggle becomes unbearably oppressive. The fact is that passive suffering, no matter how true to life, does not go a very long way as a theme in narrative or dramatic literature.

Moreover, feminism in modern Indian fiction has often been too descriptive and not sufficiently critical. While it has effectively played with the surface, it has not sufficiently provided insight into the deep social and psychological factors which produce the environment in which exploitation of women becomes possible. Sometimes man is blamed too easily as the ubiquitous villain to whom can be traced back all the suffering and oppression of women, and women's role in the oppression of women is not brought out, except through the cruel-mother-in-law syndrome. Arguably, in India at least, women themselves have been great oppressors of women. To attribute this entirely to the patriarchal system is, I think, overly deterministic and undercuts the individual's autonomy and freedom of action.

Such lack of criticism can easily lead to exaggeration and sentimentality. But, as Krishna Kripalani remarks, "Wails of anguish or thunder of curses or growls of anger do not by themselves turn into great literature"

(109). They can in fact lead to reductive, unidimensional approaches toward reality. In India, however, militant, programmatic feminism of the kind common in the West, when it has appeared at all, has tended to be confined to academics and socialites, its literary manifestations having been minimal. Not having achieved the occasional militancy of the West, literary feminism in India has also largely escaped the excesses of the Western model: a simplistic and doctrinaire view of reality and an aggressive and passionate conviction in the infallibility of one's own point of view, as well as an outright rejection of all that militates against it.

For all its limitations, feminism remains one of the most significant developments in modern Indian fiction. It has brought about an insistent, searching revaluation of the role and status of women in society and thus may justly be considered an exciting and innovative approach which has vitalized and enriched Indian fiction of recent years in many, many ways.

2. Pressing socioeconomic problems of the day have always been a rich source of material in literature. In India some of the great writers have compassionately dealt with the paramount socioeconomic problem of modern India: the plight of working-class people, the lower castes, the oppressed and the disadvantaged. In Hindi, Premchand had dwelled at length on the vices of the zamindari system and the wretched condition of farmers and landless laborers in the villages. In Malayalam, T. S. Pillai had dealt with social injustice and economic disparities in such novels as *Scavenger's Son* ("Forty is the biggest age we can expect to reach," Palani says of scavengers [13], and Chudalamuttu's tireless efforts to save his son from becoming a scavenger like himself fail) and *Chemmeen* (Shrimp), a study of the eternally hungry and poverty-stricken fishermen of coastal Kerala. Shivaram Karanth had dealt with similar problems in his Kannada novels *The Whispering Earth* and *Choma's Drum,* while in Oriya, Gopinath Mohanty had portrayed the misery of the tribals, most saliently in his classic novel *Paraja* and in *Amrutar Santan* (Children of Immortality). Krishan Chander in Urdu and Mulk Raj Anand in English had analyzed poverty and exploitation from a leftist ideological slant. Anand's *Untouchable* and *Coolie* study characters hopelessly mired in poverty due to a flawed social system, whereas his novella *The Road* continues the crusade against social injustice through the protagonist Bhikhu, an untouchable who embodies the most positive values of the story. In fact, as early as 1936 the manifesto of the first All-India Progressive Writers Conference had unequivocally affirmed: "The new literature of India must deal with the basic problems of our existence today—the problems of hunger and poverty, social backwardness and

political subjection" (cited by Jain, 106), thus conceiving of literature as an effective instrument of social change and in the vanguard of the fight against injustice and oppression.

Modern Indian writers have continued to show deep involvement with socioeconomic problems and issues. To be sure, there are writers who have chosen to stand aloof from social and economic turmoil in order to cultivate a personal sensibility and to explore the individual psyche (Ajneya and Mohan Rakesh in Hindi) or to make excursions into the mythic and the historic (Kalki and Na. Parathasarathy in Tamil). Nevertheless, social issues, concerns, and problems remain the major preoccupation of a whole host of modern Indian writers of fiction in many languages. India's freedom, far from improving the lot of the poor, unleashed greed, selfishness, and hypocrisy to an unprecedented degree, breeding disenchantment with the social system as well as a sense of expectations unfulfilled and legitimate aspirations thwarted. In fact, in the very first decade after Independence, Gopinath Mohanty's novels of city life, *Harijan* and *Danapani* (Bread and Water), the latter of which tells of a man's rise through sordid and unscrupulous means, had given a foretaste of what was to come. In the course of time the gentle irony with which social vices were targeted gave way to a harsher, more severe tone, gradually hardening into hopeless indignation, savage satire, and bitter cynicism.

Novels and stories showing the suffering and humiliation of the downtrodden and the disinherited have in recent years become too prolific to permit exhaustive discussion. In Hindi, Sanjiv's novel *Dhar* (The Sharp Edge) deals with the life of coal miners in Bihar, among the most oppressed of working people: as the woman character Maina remarks, theirs is the life of a dog—from this heap to that heap of dirt. Yogesh Gupta's collection of stories *Mere Antariksh* (My Horizons) brings out the agony of the working class in the face of unemployment and rising prices.

Social and consciousness-raising themes have also dominated modern Bengali fiction, especially the work of such writers as Mahasveta Devi and Samaresh Basu. Lakshminandan Bora's Assamese novel *Patal Bhairavi* presents rampant corruption and degeneration of values in modern Assam. In Oriya, Surendra Mohanty's novel *Phatamati* shows how the rot has spread to engulf village life also. The retired schoolteacher Hrushikesa goes back to his village in search of a peaceful environment, only to find that the villages have now become like city suburbs. The novel reminds me of Shrilal Shukla's celebrated study of village politics, *Raag Darbari* (in Hindi), set in Shivpalganj in the Awadhi-speaking region of Uttar Pradesh. In a somewhat similar vein, but focused on the communal divide, Tejasvi's novel *Chidambara Rahasya* (in Kannada) shows the disintegration of a whole way of life in the village of Kesaruru. In the frenetic struggle for power, the Harijans are reduced to being mere pawns.

Depiction of social reality is the major preoccupation of Punjabi writers of the 1970s and 1980s. This is also true of Telugu writers, says the critic Indrakanti Srikantasharma: "The Telugu short story today has gained a new tempo and brevity. It sounds, of course, bitter and cynical, as the writers do not see anything but bitterness and frustration in the society around them" (cited by Srinivasacharyulu, 40). In Tamil, however, one often finds a more hopeful note. In Su. Samuddiram's novella "Oru Nal Poduma" Annam, the young widow of a construction worker, decides to carry on the fight with the help of the labor union and face an uncertain future rather than be trapped into an immediate profitable settlement. In another novella, "Veril Pazhutha Pala" (The Jackfruit That Ripens Off the Root), Samuddiram shows the successful struggle of a low-caste office head against his corrupt uppercaste staff.

Social oppression and social change are also major themes in other Indian languages. In Nepali, Lil Bahadur Chettri's novel *Brahmaputraka Chheuchhau* deals with the plight of Nepali settlers in Assam. The main character Gumansimha reminds one of Hardy's Jude in that a malignant fate seems to dog his every step and frustrate all his efforts to improve his lot. The four stories in Om Goswami's *Pagdandi Par Suraj* (in Dogri) show lower- and middle-class society in the process of change. Two of the stories vividly portray the life and customs of low-caste *mhashas* ("Nhere Modai Di Lo") and *chamars* (cobblers; "Pagdandi Par Suraj").

Thus it will be seen that urgent social issues and problems of the day continue to be a major source of literary inspiration for writers of fiction in various Indian languages. In fact, it may well be asserted that the current state of society is perhaps the most persistent theme in modern Indian fiction.

3. A salient problem of modern Indian life has been the process of urbanization, the migration of large populations from the relative stability of rural society to the turmoil and insecurity of urban life. The price of urbanization—the pain and travail it brings in the wake of what too often turns out to be the mirage of a better life, the gradual loss of innocence and dignity, the slow but certain erosion of old values and decencies one had clung to in the midst of poverty and deprivation in the village, the inevitable sinking into the mire of urban crime and squalor—these are subjects which have en-

gaged the attention of modern Indian writers of fiction in many languages. Concurrently, the loneliness, the loss of communication, the feeling of alienation which pervasively afflicts modern city dwellers has also interested these writers as a subject for literary exploration.

Kamala Markandaya's novels *Nectar in a Sieve* and *A Handful of Rice* poignantly study the suffering of village people migrating to cities. *Nectar in a Sieve* shows the evils of industrialization through the declining fortunes of Nathan, the farmer, and his wife Rukmani. Nathan's land is swallowed by the newly established tannery, forcing him to seek employment in the city, where he and his family fall easy victims to ruthless men who exploit them. In *A Handful of Rice* the exodus of villagers to the city becomes the primary theme, and industrialization is the culprit which ruins Indian artisans and peasants. Ravi, who leaves his village to go to Madras in search of employment, comes symbolically to represent the unemployed village youth drawn to the city by the lure of the good life, only to become embroiled in its vices, ending up totally disillusioned. R. R. Borade's Marathi novel *Charapani* shows the drastic changes in the character and mode of village life due to rapid urbanization and industrialization. Jayawant Dalvi's celebrated Marathi novella *Chakra* graphically portrays life in urban slums to which migrants are often condemned.

Rajendra Yadav's Hindi novel *Ukhare Huye Log* (The Uprooted) is a study of the nightmarish quality of city life. The prevailing mood is one of unalloyed cynicism, with no hope of redemption held out. The same is true of Samaresh Basu's Bengali novellas *Manus Ratan* and *Patak*. In *Manus Ratan* some rickshaw-pullers pick up an unclaimed corpse near the station and beg money from passers-by, ostensibly to cremate it, their real intention being to use the money to enjoy themselves. A sense of hopelessness and futility pervades, however, and at the cremation ground they all burst into tears, involuntarily. In *Patak* the narrator is a twenty-three-year-old collegian who has murdered his mother for no clear reason one can see and now wanders the streets of Calcutta. The story is told through a series of flashbacks, with the focus on prevailing moral and sexual permissiveness, particularly among college students, both male and female. A revolting spectacle is what one sees: aimlessness, decadence, loss of conviction, a total collapse of values.

More recently, in some of his stories in *Prabhasak Katha* (in Maithili), Prabhas Kumar Choudhary shows how the pressures of life in the city play havoc with human relationships. In the fine story "Sambandheen" the burden of living brings about estrangement between husband and wife. Sirshendu Mudhopadhyay's Bengali novel *Manab Jamin* deals with the tragedy of the Indian middle class in an urban milieu. Debes Ray's novel *Tista Parer Vrittanta* (also in Bengali) vividly and poetically portrays the price of development, the process of uprooting and unsettling that it involves, and the disruption of man's harmonious relationship with nature that it causes. The scale is truly epic, although the tone is unmistakably nostalgic and elegiac.

4. India's independence had raised people's expectations sky-high, some legitimate, others—since political freedom cannot by itself be a panacea for all social and economic ills—perhaps exaggerated and unrealistic. In India, as in many African countries with a colonial past, the new native rulers turned out to be no less rapacious than the colonial masters they had supplanted, a typical *Animal Farm* situation. The disenchantment to which this gave rise found in Africa its classic expression in the works of such writers as Chinua Achebe and Wole Soyinka of Nigeria and Ngũgĩ wa Thiongo of Kenya. In India the sense of hopes belied and aspirations not fulfilled began to appear as a literary theme soon after 1947. T. S. Pillai's Malayalam novel *Rungs of the Ladder* brings out in detail the machinations of politicians and bureaucracy through the case study of a middle-class Nair who rose to the position of Chief Secretary of Travancore. Political satire gradually became an increasingly familiar theme in Indian fiction even as the tone hardened into cynical despair. Deshbandhu in Rajendra Yadav's *Ukhare Huye Log* comprehensively epitomizes the corrupt and manipulative politician.

Increasingly, political issues have become a rich and fertile source for literary exploration. Nayantara Sahgal's interest in politics is deep and abiding: each of her novels, she says, "more or less reflects the political era we are passing through." She adds: "Fiction is my abiding love. But I need to express myself on vital political issues. Political and social forces shape our lives. How can we be unaware of them? I believe there is what the American writer E. L. Doctorow has called 'a poetics of engagement' where commitment and aesthetics meet and give each other beauty and power" ("A Truly Wonderful Moment"). Her novel *Rich Like Us* deals with the time of the Emergency—which she aptly calls "a collective will to cowardice"—when opportunists prospered while the honest and upright suffered. Shashi Tharoor's justly acclaimed work *The Great Indian Novel* burlesques the *Mahabharata* to comment upon current events. The Congress split, for example, represents the fratricidal war between Kauravs and Pandavs. Arun Joshi's novel *The City and the River* is a political allegory about the rise and fall of governments and the abuse of power. O. V. Vijayan's Malayalam novel *The Saga of Dharmapuri* also deals with the perversion of the political process during the Emergency.

An exceptionally forceful indictment of political corruption and manipulation is Satakadi Hota's Oriya novel *Rajdhanira Ranga* (The Capital in Its True Colors), in which the writer effectively brings out the complete degeneration of values behind the glittering façade of the capital. Om Goswami's collection of Dogri stories *Sunne di Chiree* (The Golden Bird) also targets the current political situation, with the title story being an all-embracing castigation of complete loss of decency in every sphere of life in modern India. The story "Magarmuchh" satirizes the way the rich manipulate government officials and labor leaders to oppress the poor. "Nark Joon" and "Mhatamdari" expose dishonest recruitment procedures. E. Sonamani's Manipuri stories in *If the Front Door Is Closed, Enter Through the Back Door* revealingly anatomize dishonest ministers and legislators. Sonamani's portrait of Minister Ibochaoba in the title story is an exceptionally fine representation of the corrupt politician. Rafiq Zakaria's novel *The Price of Power* is a somewhat transparent political allegory, its characters and events thinly disguised versions of real people and real situations. Much more effective and sophisticated as political satire is Ranga Rao's *Fowl-Filcher*, in which the protagonist, unjustly nicknamed "Fowl-Filcher" for a crime he did not commit, graduates after a highly checkered career to become a politician's trusted assistant, ironically getting killed in the riots he himself had engineered.

Many modern Indian novels deal with specific political issues. O. V. Vijayan's *Gurusagaram* (in Malayalam) is set against the backdrop of the Bangladesh war and the growth of the Naxalite movement. Novels dealing with issues such as the antireservation agitations, terrorism, and various reformist movements are many. However, the very topicality which adds to the relevance of such works also often makes them ephemeral, unless they are anchored by a more enduring component, as is the case with *Gurusagaram*, for example, in which the strong element of spirituality has a broadening and universalizing effect.

5. The intricate web of family relationships, especially in a joint or extended family, has perpetually interested Indian writers. Exploration of these relationships as literary themes continues in modern Indian fiction with undiminished vigor, although the nature of the issues dealt with may have changed in response to the current social situation.

Harmony within the family has been an ideal traditionally cherished by Indian writers. In the early decades of the century Premchand and Saratchandra had come down heavily on those who sowed seeds of dissension in the family for selfish ends. The discomfiture and ultimate rout of such people is gleefully presented in many of Saratchandra's stories. Later, Rajendra Yadav's Hindi novel *Sara Akash* became the definitive study of the pains and pleasures of living in a joint Indian family. *Sara Akash* is a triumph of modern Indian fiction in its graphic and sensitive portrayal of the close, convoluted, sometimes stifling nature of family relationships in a joint middle-class Indian family, the petty envies and intrigues, the perpetual bickerings, and also the warmth, the affection, the magnanimous self-sacrifice.

Although interest in problems of the joint family system has remained unabated in recent Indian fictional works, the treatment has become much more serious, even somber. Whereas the earlier writers had often dealt with family discord in a more or less light vein, bringing out its comedy, writers in recent years have tended to treat it with solemnity, showing a brooding concern with its darker aspects. In Punjabi, Ram Sarup Ankhi and Inder Singh Khamosh have dealt with dissensions in family relationships and brought out how greed and selfishness of individuals leads to disintegration of the family. Stories of the domineering mother-in-law and the bullied daughter-in-law have been extremely common in Indian fiction, Prabhas Kumar Choudhary's "Sheetyuddha" (Cold War) in Maithili being a fine recent example. But now the reverse side of the relationship, with sons and daughters-in-law showing, in their headlong pursuit of the pleasures of life, callous disregard of the welfare of the parents, is also being explored. The breakup of the joint family under the impact of modernization and economic pressure has bred a new and major social problem: the insecurity and widespread neglect of the elderly. Stories dealing with the plight of old people left destitute and emotionally insecure crowd the pages of fictional works in many Indian languages. The generation gap and the problems of old age have been vividly presented, for example, in Homen Borgohain's Assamese novel *Asta Rag.* The author himself says: "In the past, old age was not like this. People were afraid of death, but not of growing old. But now there is a change and man is afraid of growing old, not of death" (cited by Sarma, 26).

6. The East-West encounter has ever been a theme rich in possibilities for literary exploration. The great literary potential of the theme has been recognized and exploited not only by Indian but also by British and American writers. Rudyard Kipling's extensive but condescending and simplistic treatment of the theme offended many. Later, E. M. Forster, M. M. Kaye, and other English writers explored the theme with greater understanding and sensitivity.

Among Indian writers, Rabindranath Tagore's *Gora* is a pioneering study of Indo-British encounter in the context of Bengal. More recently, Kamala Markandaya has dealt with the unresolved conflicts of Indo-British relations in many of her novels. In *Some Inner Fury* the love between Mira and Richard fails because they belong to the different nations of the ruled and the ruler. In *Possession* Lady Caroline's pursuit of Valmiki, an illiterate peasant boy with a passion for painting, ends in failure. *The Nowhere Man* shows the ambiguous situation of Indians settled in England, who have lost their roots in native India but have not been assimilated or accepted in British society and are often objects of suspicion and ridicule.

The earlier writers usually dealt with the theme of the East-West encounter with high seriousness, dwelling mainly on the stresses and strains in personal relationships (as between Aziz and Fielding in Forster's *Passage to India*), the basic incompatibility, the problems which they saw not only as unsolved but also as insoluble. Thus it is the dark side of the Indo-British encounter which has usually occupied writers both Indian and British. For example, the Jnanapith Award-winning Telugu writer Visvanatha Satyanarayana seems to take a totally negative view and to stress the irreconcilable incompatibility between the East and the West in his allegorical story "Maklidurgamio Kukka," in which the mating of a bitch of British breed with an Indian country dog ends in disaster (cited by Srinivasacharyulu, 37).

Much lighter in intent and approach is R. K. Narayan's story "A Horse and Two Goats," which brings out mutual incomprehension through interaction between the down-and-out goatherd Muni and a visiting American tourist. In *The Vendor of Sweets* the Americanized Indian Mali and the American girl Grace are similarly treated with mild irony. In the recent novel *The Shadow Lines,* however, Amitav Ghosh takes a positive view of the possibility of interpersonal relationships between East and West. The novel, which explores relationships among three generations of the Datta-Chowdharys of Bengal and the Prices of London, concludes that national borders are mere illusions—"shadow lines"—beyond which exist enormous possibilities for fruitful intercultural communication.

The playful element of the East-West encounter, more perceptible in recent Indian fiction than ever before, is beautifully—and hilariously—brought out by Anurag Mathur in *The Inscrutable Americans.* The story line of this immensely delightful book is woven around twenty-year-old Gopal's one-year sojourn at the small American university campus in Eversville to study chemical engineering. Incredibly naïve and callow in many ways, Gopal, from Jajau in Madhya Pradesh, is, however, as he himself tells his long-suffering American friend Randy, "more clever than I look." The comedy arises out of Gopal's getting into all kinds of bizarre situations due to his doggedly literal-minded application of his own expectations and cultural conventions to his American experience. The result is often misunderstanding and mutual incomprehension, but not unbridgeably, as shown by the warm relationship which grows between Gopal and Randy.

To cite but one example of the hilarious situations which develop when Gopal comes face to face with Americans who are all, in his judgment, "too advanced," here is his encounter with U.S. Customs in New York as he writes about it to his younger brother back home:

> "At Customs, brother, I am getting big shock. One fat man is grunting at me and looking cleverly from small eyes. 'First visit?' he is asking. 'Yes,' I am agreeing. 'Move on,' he is saying making chalk marks on bags. As I am picking up bags he is looking directly at me and saying 'Watch your ass.'

> "Now, brother, this is wonderful. How he is knowing we are purchasing donkey? I think they are knowing everything about everybody who is coming to America. They are not allowing anybody without knowing his family and financial status and other things. And we are only buying donkey two days before my departure. I think they are keeping all information in computers. Really these Americans are too advanced." (11–12)

7. Modern Indian fiction, though rich and complex, suffers from a certain lack of variety, which, to begin with, can be seen in its thematic range. Prolific in exploring such themes as political and socioeconomic issues, personal relationships, and various aspects of individual sensibility, it yet more or less neglects many areas of human experience. Ecology and environment-related themes, travel and adventure, science fiction and other forms of fantasy, utopias and dystopias (technological and otherwise)—these are rarely dealt with in modern Indian fiction, although they have provided excellent literary material in many Western literatures.

The lack of variety can also be seen in the tone, the approach, the interpretation. On the whole, modern Indian fiction tends to be solemn and staid, and, barring exceptions such as Anurag Mathur, rather deficient in humor. Modern Indian writers of fiction tend to be too serious, and to cultivate a largely negative and pessimistic, if not downright denunciatory, outlook. The current situation is held to be hopeless, and there is hardly any indication of how things can be improved. Whatever hope is held out is often of a facile, irrational kind, not implicit in the logic of events, sometimes amounting to no more than wishful thinking or taking the form of a Dickensian (and Premchandian) inexplicable change of heart.

There is, moreover, a certain lack of depth in the way modern Indian writers of fiction analyze social and political maladies in the country. The blame is too easily laid on "others"—on politicians, industrialists, businessmen, and bureaucrats—and not on the collaborative, all-but-universal apathy of the so-called silent majority which enables political knavery to succeed and often worthless elements to rise to the top. There is not much insightful analysis of the process or of the factors and circumstances which produce such self-seeking and predatory attitudes in society and make the corrupt what they are.

The writers also lack self-criticism, since they seldom show concern with their own—the artists' and the intellectuals'—responsibility in social life. The way many modern Indian writers have, in practical life, isolated themselves from social problems, weaving whenever they can a web of comfort and security around them, amounts to a kind of willful secession from the society which sustains them. But modern Indian writers show little awareness of and introspection about this aspect of the situation.

For all that, there is no denying the richness, the plenitude, of modern Indian fiction, its frequently high quality in content and form, its sensitive and imaginative projection of both the universal and the narrowly contemporary and topical elements in the Indian experience, its graphic presentation of social and economic realities. Modern Indian fiction is full of vigor, vitality, and boundless creative energy, which makes the modern period an exciting, exhilarating epoch in Indian literary history.

R. K. Gupta, Spring 1994

■ **WORKS CITED**

Anand, Mulk Raj. *Coolie*. Bombay. Kutub-Popular. 1933.

———. *Untouchable*. Bombay. Kutub-Popular. 1935.

———. *The Road*. Bombay. Kutub-Popular. 1961.

Bagul, Baburao. *Sood*. Bombay. Abhinav Prakashan. 1970.

Barua, Bhaben. "Sensitive and Reflective." *Indian Literature,* 34:6 (November-December 1991), pp. 15–19.

Basu, Samaresh. *"Patak" aur Do Laghu Upanyas* ("Patak" and Two Novelettes). Prayodhkumar Majumdar, tr. (into Hindi). Delhi. Akshar Prakashan. N.d.

Bora, Lakshminandan. *Patal Bhairavi*. Guwahati. Sahitya Prakash. 1986.

Borade, R. R. *Charapani*. Pune. Mehta. 1990.

Chettri, Lil Bahadur. *Brahmaputraka Chheuchhau*. Darjeeling. Shyam Prakashan. 1986.

Choudhary, Prabhas Kumar. *Prabhasak Katha*. Darbhanga. Jayotsana Choudhary. 1989.

Dalvi, Jayawant. *Chakra*. Gauri Deshpande, tr. Bombay. Sangam Books. 1974 (first published in Marathi, 1964).

Das, Kamala. "My Instinct, My Guru." *Indian Literature*, 33:5 (September-October 1990), pp. 155–62.

Deshpande, Shashi. *That Long Silence*. New Delhi. Penguin India. 1988.

Devi, Sneha. *Sneha Devir Ekunki Galpa*. Guwahati. Bani Prakash. 1988.

Dharker, Rani. "Getting Out of the Groove." *Indian Literature*, 35:1 (January-February 1992), pp. 79–85.

Gadgil, Gangadhar. *The Woman and Other Stories*. New Delhi. Sterling. 1990.

Ghosh, Amitav. *The Shadow Lines*. Delhi. Ravi Dayal. 1988.

Goswami, Om. *Sunne di Chiree*. Jammu. Jot. 1983.

———. *Pagdandi Par Surai*. Jammu. Jot. 1989.

Gupta, Yogesh. *Mere Artariksh*. Delhi. Sachin Prakashan. 1988.

Haider, Qurratul-Ain. *Chandni Begum*. New Delhi. Educational Publishers. 1990.

Hota, Satakadi. *Rajdhanira Ranga*. Cuttack. Nalanda. 1988.

Jahan, Rashid. *Angare*. Lucknow. Sajjad Zahir. 1931.

———. *Aurat*. Lahore. Hashmi Book Depot. 1937.

Jain, S. P. "'Angare': A Reappraisal." *Indian Literature*, 30:4 (July-August 1987), pp. 101–7.

Joshi, Arun. *The City and the River*. New Delhi. Vision Books. 1990.

Karanth, K. Shivaram. *Choma's Drum*. U. R. Kelkur, tr. Delhi. Hind. 1978 (first published in Kannada, 1933).

———. *The Whispering Earth*. A. N. Murthy Rao, tr. Delhi. Vikas. 1975 (first published in Kannada, 1942).

Kripalani, Krishna. *Modern Indian Literature: A Panoramic Glimpse*. N.p. Nirmala Sadanand. 1968.

Kumar, Ashok. "Passionate Poetess from Punjab." *The Hindustan Times*, 22 June 1992, p. 10.

Markandaya, Kamala. *Nectar in a Sieve*. London. Putnam. 1954.

———. *Some Inner Fury*. London. Putnam. 1955.

———. *Possession*. London. Putnam. 1963.

———. *A Handful of Rice*. New Delhi. Orient. 1966.

———. *The Nowhere Man*. London. Allen Lane. 1973 (first published, 1972).

Mathai, Manorama. *Lilies That Fester*. Calcutta. Writers Workshop. 1988.

Mathur, Anurag. *The Inscrutable Americans*. Calcutta. Rupa. 1991.

Mehta, Dina. "Absolution." In *Contemporary Indian Short Stories in English*. Shiv K. Kumar, ed. New Delhi. Sahitya Akademi. 1990. Pp. 123–31.

Mohanty, Gopinath. *Harijan*. Cuttack. Students' Store. 1948.

———. *Amrutar Santan*. Cuttack. Bharati Vihar. 1949.

———. *Danapani*. Cuttack. Rashtrabhasha Pustak Bhandar. 1955.

———. *Paraja*. Bikram K. Das, tr. New Delhi. Oxford University Press. 1987 (first published in Oriya, 1945).

Mohanty, Surendra. *Phatamati*. Cuttack. Friends. 1988.

Mukhopadhyay, Sirshendu. *Manab Jamin*. Calcutta. Ananda. 1988.

Mulchandani, Soni. *Shakti*. Bombay. Privately printed. 1989.

Narayan, R. K. *The Vendor of Sweets*. Mysore. Indian Thought. 1967.

———. *A Horse and Two Goats*. Mysore. Indian Thought. 1970.

Pande, Mrinal. "Girls." In *The Inner Courtyard: Stories by Indian Women*. Lakshmi Holmstrom, ed. Calcutta. Rupa. 1991. Pp. 56–64.

Pillai, T. Sivasankara. *Chemmeen*. New Delhi. Jaico. 1988 (first published in Malayalam, 1956).

———. *Rungs of the Ladder*. C. Paul Verghese, tr. New Delhi. Arnold-Heinemann. 1976 (first published in Malayalam, 1964).

———. *Scavenger's Son*. R. E. Asher, tr. New Delhi. Orient. N.d. (first published in Malayalam, 1948).

Rao, Ranga. *Fowl-Filcher*. New Delhi. Penguin India. 1987.

Ray, Debes. *Tista Parer Vrittanta*. Calcutta. Deys. 1988.

Sahgal, Nayantara. *The Day in Shadow*. New Delhi. Vikas. 1971.

———. *Rich Like Us*. London. Heinemann. 1986.

———. "'A Truly Wonderful Moment'" (interview with Nergis Dalal). *The Hindustan Times Sunday Magazine,* 11 January 1987, p. 7.

Samuddiram, Su. *Veril Pazhutha Pala*. Madras. Manivasakar Padhipaghim. 1989.

Sanjiv. *Dhar*. New Delhi. Radhakrishna Prakashan. 1989.

Sarma, Arabinda Nath. "Neither Rosy, Nor Bleak." *Indian Literature*, 30:6 (November-December 1987), pp. 25–32.

Shahani, Rita. *Chanda Khan Sija Taeen*. Pune. Privately printed. 1989.

Shukla, Shrilal. *Raag Darbari*. Gillian Wright, tr. New Delhi. Penguin India. 1991 (first published in Hindi, 1968).

Sonamani, E. *If the Front Door Is Closed, Enter Through the Back Door* (in Manipuri, title translated from Manipuri). Imphal. Manipuri Sahitya Parishad. 1985.

Spacks, Patricia Meyer. *The Female Imagination*. New York. Knopf. 1975.

Srinivasacharyulu, B. V. "The Short Story in Telugu Literature." *Indian Literature*, 26:1 (January-February 1983), pp. 34–42.

Tagore, Rabindranath. *Gora*. New Delhi. Macmillan. 1980 (first published, 1910).

Tejasvi, K. P. Purnachandra. *Chidambara Rahasya*. Bangalore. Patrika Prakashan. 1985.

Tharoor, Shashi. *The Great Indian Novel*. New Delhi. Penguin India. 1989.

Vijayan, O. V. *Gurusagaram*. Kottayam. D.C. Books. 1987.

———. *The Saga of Dharmapuri*. New Delhi. Penguin India. 1988 (first published in Malayalam as *Dharmapuranam*, 1985).

Yadav, Rajendra. *Sara Akash*. Delhi. Hind. 1971.

———. *Ukhare Huye Log*. Delhi. Akshar Prakashan. 1975 (first published, 1956).

Zakaria, Rafiq. *The Price of Power*. Bombay. India Book Rest. 1987.

Raja Rao's Inimitable Style and Art of Fiction

A visit to South India and Mysore in 1978 confirmed for me the importance and significance of Raja Rao's novels. He is quintessentially, I think, an Indian novelist, perhaps the most remarkable and disturbing of his generation. In this article I shall speak only of *The Serpent and the Rope.* I had read the novel before visiting India. I glimpsed a world of conservatism there that was unlike Western conservatism—much as one resembled the other—in that the vested interests of South India lay, it seemed to me, less in class and property and much more in an ingrained twilight or ritualization of hierarchical shadow rooted in legacies of nonevolutionary stasis and conformity to fate.

The appeal of such a sanction administered—if I may so put it—by a sovereign nondual tradition or Ego was everywhere in South India, I felt, and it aroused in me profound uneasiness and misgiving, so much so that a question mark seemed to tremble on the lips of the grave and beautiful sculptures one contemplated in the temples. To what degree did the enormity of stasis possess a subversive or hidden otherness that lay in a state of eclipse within the unconscious of art, the unconscious of history, despite art's passivity, history's conformity to nondual Ego?

Such subversive or hidden otherness—if indeed it existed at all within the tremor of palatial sculptures inside ancient temples—was marginal, I knew, but by no means irrelevant, I felt, to the continuing life of the creative imagination through and beyond the closures of the past. Indeed, such marginality could subtly dislodge, one felt, the prepossessions of a bureaucratic orphanage of spirit enshrined everywhere: so enshrined, how could it do otherwise but belittle the womb of origins and diminish the mystery of cross-cultural marriage between the past and the present, the past and the future?

My sensation was that such marginality was akin to an agent of illumination within a blocked evolutionary process in the ritual demeanor of the sculptures around me. Did there lie in that blockage and faint tremor or smile of tradition the forfeit of diversity and duality now aligned to mental incest within the sovereign Ego?

Take Rama, the protagonist of *The Serpent and the Rope.* On reflection it seemed to me that the ruined or ruinous smile of tradition within palace or temple in involuntary intercourse with incestuous spirit had left its seal upon him not so much in guilt as in a creative amnesia, a paradox of memory. He was the veiled child of

Raja Rao *(Gil Jain)*

South India. He was an orphan of a bureaucratic, veiled eternity. His grief or remorse was inevitably tinged therefore with hubris—with a kind of fabricated, proud sorrow for the womb of origins, the feminine body, whether mother or wife—even as such prideful fabrication subtly undercut itself into genuine passion as the novel progressed within the pathos of an odyssey in which pain and sorrow, however rarefied, possessed their subtle menace, their subtle proportions of the abyss.

> I was born an orphan, and have remained one. I have wandered the world and have sobbed in hotel rooms and in trains, have looked at the cold mountains and sobbed, for I had no mother. One day, and that was when I was twenty-two, I sat in a hotel—it was in the Pyrenees—and I sobbed, for I knew I would never see my mother again.[1]

Rama's hubris is, I find, a matter of tone, the music of karma. That hubris lies in the claims that he makes for himself at various stages of his odyssey (in which India appears to sound or resonate within him): claims that attest a veil he may only lift to fantasize others and other places, an absolute veil that is himself, a veil nevertheless that, despite its woven intention, becomes the shadow of pathos and forbidden duality. It is as a dark Narcissus therefore that he sees his mother in himself in fantasizing sorrow or passion for one who exists to confirm her nonexistence in him.

Rama's celebration of the veil within which he cradles the passing of his mother is almost akin to Western sublimation in a Freudian sense. Forbidden desires, it is hoped, will remain forever repressed and the harmony of sublimation achieved within a potentially doomed but one-sidedly triumphant civilization. Such a reading of Rama's relationship to tradition, however, would be false. It is not repression and sublimation in a Freudian context that he symbolizes. His malaise is, one would imagine, far older than Freud's (venerable and ritual-oriented as the latter may be), so old it is steeped in a play with appearances, a play with the shadow of karma, his own shadow. The play with that shadow, with repressed instinct, with the suffering world, voids repression, voids suffering. They do not exist save as bubbles in the tapestry of incestuous tradition that runs into a shroud within the birth of memory. To conceive of birth is to conceive of death, karma declares, except in the degree that birth and death are illusions within an orphanage of metaphysical security. We see the shroud in all its peculiar Indian/Brahmin/European tapestry repudiating feminine beauty as a paradisiacal illusion.

> Beatrice, O Beatrice is beautiful in Paradise. But what an impossible tyrant she becomes. It is she who wants to show the Truth to Dante. . . . She who should see light through him, now wants to show the light to him. It is the inversion of Truth. Where the world cannot annihilate itself . . . it has to make the world feminine. Just as progeny is through woman, child after child, generation after generation, you may have as many paradises as you care to have. Buddhism went to Tibet, and gave itself many paradises. Tantra entered Hinduism, and worshipping the women, made the world real. Man became thus the everlasting, the superman, the slave of himself, and all such supermen must end in stink. . . . Ravana was defeated by his ten heads. *The miracle must for ever end in emptiness.* (377–78; italics mine)

We see the shroud as a way of interpreting "superman" experience into a peculiar distinction between what Rama *is* from the day he was born into self-deceptive paradise, into paradox, into "born orphan," and what Rama *carries* as the necessary fabrication of tradition. On one side of the fabric (the fabricated genesis of the "real" world, "generation after generation") lies therefore the harlequin irony of an unconscious/subsconscious dualism within the womb of origins. On the other side lies "the miracle that must for ever end in emptiness." The two sides appear to resemble each other, but they are not the same. Still, since they are

both native to Rama's "truth," or to the "inversion of Truth," dualism feeds on a capacity for pregnant or subversive moment, even as "emptiness" unhinges that capacity into subtle menace, subtle abyss.

"Emptiness" is the poverty of true change in an unhinged world, poverty masquerading nevertheless as princely male fantasy, princely male legend, princely male enchantment, and music within a disequilibrium of appearances.

> They say my mother was very beautiful and very holy. Grandfather Kittanna said, "Her voice, son, was like a *vina* playing to itself, after evensong is over, when one has left the instrument beside a pillar in the temple. Her voice too was like those musical pillars at the Rameshwaram temple—it resonated from the depths, from some unknown space, and one felt God shone the brighter with this worship. She reminded me of concubine Chandramma. . . . That was long before your time," Grandfather concluded, "it was in Mysore, and I have not been there these fifty years."

> Grandfather Kittanna was a noble type, a heroic figure among us. It must be from him I have this natural love of the impossible—I can think that a building may just decide to fly, or that Stalin may become a saint, or that Mahatma Gandhi is walking with us now. I sometimes feel I can make the railway line stand up, or the elephant bear its young one in twenty-four days; I can see an aeroplane float over a mountain and sit carefully on a peak. (4)

Grandfather Kittanna's tale is filtered through a language of echoing tradition "playing to itself" within a paradox, within a mirror of the disequilibrium of appearances. "It was in Mysore, and I have not been there these fifty years" endorses an insecure testament "long before [Rama's] time" within a tapestry of "buildings that may decide to fly" or "railways that stand up" or "aeroplanes floating over a mountain . . . sitting on a peak."

The "beautiful and holy mother" dissolves—one is tempted to imagine—to reappear as "concubine Chandramma" within the great man's adventures as perceived by Rama within his bright/dark Narcissus mirror.

> Grandfather Kittanna was heroic in another manner. He could manage a horse, the fiercest, with a simplicity that made it go where it did not wish to go. I was brought up with the story how Grandfather Kittanna actually pushed his horse into the Chandrapur forest one evening—the horse, Sundar, biting his lips off his face; the tiger that met him in the middle of the jungle; the leap Sundar gave, high above my Lord Sher, and the

custard-apples that splashed on his back, so high he soared—and before my grandfather knew where he was, with sash and blue-Maratha saddle, there he stood, Sundar, in the middle of the courtyard. . . . When Atchakka asked, "Sundar is all full of scratches . . . ?" then Grandfather spoke of the tiger, and the leap. For him, if the horse had soared into the sky and landed in holy Brindavan he would not have been much surprised. Grandfather Kittanna was like that. He rode Sundar for another three years, and then the horse died—of some form of dysentery, for, you know, horses die too—and we buried him on the top of the Kittur Hill, with fife and filigree. We still make an annual pilgrimage to his tomb. (4–5)

The element of play within one / within all, "generation after generation," the element of heroic mock epic, enhances Rama's withdrawal into the gloom of echoing reflection, gloomy but ancestral, beloved palaces that compete with Sundar's tomb as the goal of pilgrimages. Mock-heroic exploits become the ridiculous substance of change that is no change at all within a hierarchical establishment. All becomes communal dust, the dust of communal fear, and Rama suffers the contamination of communal disaster despite himself. He confesses wryly even as he revisits the legendary heights of Grandfather Kittanna's greatness embodying the state: "But I, I've the fright of gun and sword. . . . I do not really have the fear of fear. I only have fear" (5).

Such fear—let us note immediately—is a curious fear woven of communal dust, communal mock epic, fear that becomes a proud pageant, proud fear that sustains the practice of nonviolence as if "Mahatma Gandhi is walking with us now," communal lighthouse in communal dust. Such ironies permit Rama to build a self-deprecating family tree upon Grandfather's exploits, a family tree of implicit nonviolence embracing Mahatma Gandhi. That family tree is the abode of orphans of family, orphans of eternity, "orphan to orphan," embracing the robe of compliant relations and antecedents whose fate it is to inspect the cosmos as play with the shadow of the unhinged self.

It would be easy to identify all this with European theater of the absurd, but such identification misses the Indianness of Raja Rao's art, the elusive fixture of the Ego whose play with dust, in Brahmin and Brahman logic, is intended to veil inviolable inner Truth rather than—as with the theater of the absurd—a cult of despair. In a keynote address given at the South Asian Language Association Conference at the University of Texas in Austin in the spring of 1984, Raja Rao makes his objectives clear: "The poet is the sage, I am. The 'I' of the I. He is. Is is. And so it. Call it, Brahman, if you like . . . the Brahman . . . from whom the creation of the world (*seems to*) proceed" (italics mine).[2] This is a fascinating confession, and I would hazard a guess that the casual parenthesis "seems to" provides a lead into a genuine coincidence that is much more telling than a comparison with Freud's repression/sublimation syndrome or with twentieth-century theater of the absurd, Ionesco and Beckett.

The coincidence between Raja Rao's India and Western Europe is reflected in the Gnostic movement. Among the many historical curiosities to which Rama is drawn as he journeys in Europe is the Cathar heresy. The Cathars were an ascetic sect of Gnostic heretics existing in Europe between the tenth and fourteenth centuries. They suffered a cruel extermination at the hands of the orthodox Catholic Church. The crux of the Cathar heresy in Roman eyes was their rejection of nature. Not to put too fine a point on it, they saw nature as an evil creation founded by a Demiurge rather than by true Spirit. Thus they entertained the notion of abstention from childbearing. Though this may have implied an equality of divorce from nature by both men and women committed to ascetic vocation, it drew, in practical terms, a shadow of dread across the womb and the female body.

The Brahman—if I may quote from Raja Rao's address—is one "from whom the creation of the world (seems to) proceed." It is legitimate therefore to ask: is the Brahman Truth or Lie? If Truth in the Cathar sense, then the fantastication of appearances proceeding from him is a Lie. "Seems to" is the thorn in Rama's side.

The absolute rejection of fertile nature by the Cathars is tempered in Rama's philosophy, one would think, by his genuine immersion in misgiving. Nature is not a vessel of evil in *The Serpent and the Rope,* but it becomes, if I read the novel aright, part and parcel of the shroud that Rama carries within the birth of memory. The shroud possesses an involuntary power to secrete a cradle within it and brings therefore a harlequin dimension into Rama's marriage to the Frenchwoman Madeleine and to her pregnancy by him. True pregnancy? Ephemeral pregnancy? The shroud endorses the predicament of the Brahman. Is the Brahman Truth or Lie? Does the Brahman impregnate the world *or merely seem to do so?*

Such questions make it necessary for me to return to a point I made earlier in this article and which—may I also say now?—is implicit in my approaches to *The Serpent and the Rope* in a cross-cultural study I wrote some years ago. I referred to Rama there as an "unconscious harlequin."[3] The shroud of the harlequin in the context of what I said then and am saying now is so fissured by intuitive and contradictory psyche that it runs against the absolute ideology or strict intention that the author of the novel entertains.

Let me restate what I have just said a little differently. The fissure of which I am speaking helps to illumine, I find, a consolidation or blockage between the drama of tradition and the web of nature—nature's diverse roots yet nature's economy or density or paradoxical unity. It helps to illumine, however marginally, a nature that trembles on the brink of revisionary narrative possibilities within and through itself as genuine mystery, genuine creation. I need to stress all this, though it is inconsistent with an absolute logic that *The Serpent and the Rope* seeks to affirm, for it is in the light of such nebulous fissures, such elusive inconsistencies, that one rereads the novel and discovers a haunting, revisionary edge secreted in the narrative and particularly within the anguish Rama displays when he rejects Madeleine even as he tries to comfort her and is filled with the knowledge that she is, *or seems to be,* pregnant by him. He shelters himself from such knowledge within the persona of sterile parenthesis, and fatherhood becomes a lie. In equating himself with a lie, he relinquishes, I would suggest, an acute possibility to transform the entire narrative of his life. I say "narrative" to imply a sensation that Rama rebels against his author's or creator's will and that such rebellion, however marginal it appears, is a premise of revolutionary possibility within the "narrative life" of the character Rama. Rama may be on the point at times of overturning his author's will. He does not ultimately do so, but the paradox enriches the life of the narrative.

> "What a very beautiful night, Rama," she said, and led me to the window, and took me in her arms. I could feel the full joy of her presence in myself, and I suspected that there was another, an additional presence, that would grow, as this night, in the texture of being: *a third presence,* more real than our own, more lasting, and from that on to another, created through other presences, and thus more lasting again—like those olives which had been planted and made real to us by some Roman citizen of another age whose presence, unknown to himself, may have been felt that night—an embryo that had no eyes and no feet yet, but had lit the congress of circumstance *in which two beings had known a truth,* which had a beginning, a middle and an end, yet had been consecrated for an instant at the edge of the "I." Discovery is a whisper to oneself, and *the night of love is an embalmment,* a holiness that we place outside of time, in the knowledge that *creation is truth.*
>
> When I woke to myself, I heard Madeleine crying, as though the womb bore a light that was too difficult to carry. I slipped her back to bed, and

lay by her hour after hour, touching her forehead and wiping her perspiration, as though her pain was the first, the only one of mankind. There is no pain more acute than a pain unnameable, and all the shine of the world is only a prophecy, *a shout that death is,* that one loses another, that a tight breast has a pain no husband can take away, were he even within you. *Who is within after all? No one. It is one's own pain that sobs to oneself. To be woman is to suffer, to bear the yoke* of man. The rains will break before the door of the barn is reached. *Night alone exists and the exhaustion of an empty day.*

> Madeleine's body had reached out to its full womanhood, *and I was the lie.* (130–31; italics mine)

This eloquent and beautiful passage comes close, I think, to identifying the tapestry of the shroud in the birth of memory by which—if I read the novel aright—one may perceive the emblematic scope of *The Serpent and the Rope.* If "the night of love is an embalmment," then creation's truth becomes questionable.

Each reader must decide for himself or herself on implications that cross-cut, undermine, even as they appear to fertilize each other. The passage tends, I feel, to show in the midst of its ambiguities how close Rama may have moved to an erasure of the parenthesis "seems to" in the annunciation of "creation." Had that erasure occurred, would it not have borne on the "ultimate word" or narrative of his life to embody "he is" in equality with "she is"? At the summit of such rich mutuality or duality, however, Rama dispossesses himself of the "embryo" of community: "Who is within after all? No one. . . . *I was the lie.*"

Nevertheless, he does so with pain and regret, for "Madeleine's body had reached out to its full womanhood." That sudden declaration, "I was the lie," is crucial and decisive. It endows the Brahman's fantastications of the impregnation of the world with tragic playfulness that seems so real, so steeped in the magic of the senses, that it turns tragedy around into a romance within the depleted sovereign Ego. Rama is left to savor Madeleine's "full womanhood," beside which the climax of illusion he has experienced exacts a penalty upon fertile nature: "To be woman is to suffer, to bear the yoke of man."

How can hollow romance prevail as the climax of suffering? It does so when the lie is a play and the play in essence (whatever dramatic penalties it exacts) is an embroidery of appearances to lighten the brute burden of tragedy. It is as if thereby they subsist (play and tragedy, romance and the "shout that death is") upon the cancellation one of and by the other into absolute—however depleted—identity, absolute fate.

We have arrived, I think, at the crossroads of Raja Rao's major Indian novel. What karmic price does civilization pay to the enigmatic Brahman of whom Raja Rao speaks in the address from which I have quoted? Fertility exacts its price. Technology exacts its price. But if "creation is truth," then that price undermines the ground of fate, overturns the Brahman, to enhance— rather than diminish—the responsibilities that men and women bear toward one another and toward the animal species on planet Earth. If, on the other hand, nature's fertility, nature's labor, is wrought from the climax of illusion, then the Brahman is restored. The fate of suffering generations becomes a matter of coping with fear, with emptiness, and with perverse romance.

It is here—where fear, emptiness, and perverse romance cross—that *The Serpent and the Rope* establishes its symbolic negatives within tapestries of mood, temper, and parenthesis. Fear, as we have already seen, takes paradoxical root in mock epic and grandfather legend to build the pageantry of nonviolence as a temporary expedient against evil. The lie or perverse romance becomes the playful colonization of Madeleine's Europe by Rama's India in that Cathar or Gnostic heresy ceases to be a heresy and becomes the embalmment of love.

Emptiness is the ultimate seal on paradise. A lust for paradise as Rama interprets his desires is followed by a withdrawal from Madeleine's full womanhood. But therein lies a catch. The greed for continuing paradise continues, and Rama hits out by indicting Dante's Beatrice as the tyrant of heaven. Unwittingly it seems "the yoke of man" upon "suffering woman" is overturned. The inferno appears and man becomes "the slave of himself"—a creature of mental incest—and "the inventor of gas chambers and concentration camps" (377– 78).

The "I" of the I builds a hierarchy of symbolic negatives to restrain the scope of terror. He builds that hierarchy on a play of constitutional weaknesses: namely, mock epic, mock colonization, and perverse romance. However, in equating perverse romance with lust or greed for paradise, he suffers himself, it seems, the torments of the damned. How real or unreal those torments are in the body politic of societies such as India— plagued by poverty and the injustices of caste—is a vital question one would imagine for the sage who broods on the nonevolutionary premises of the Brahman.

Wilson Harris, Autumn 1988

[1] Raja Rao, *The Serpent and the Rope*, New York, Overlook, 1986 (© 1960), p. 4. Subsequent parenthetic page references are to this edition.

[2] Raja Rao, "The Ultimate Word," *Temenos* (London), no. 9 (1988).

[3] Wilson Harris, *The Womb of Space: The Cross-Cultural Imagination,* Westport, Ct., Greenwood, 1983, p. 79.

Shakuntala's Daughters: Women in Contemporary Indian Drama

When at the end of act 1 in Kalidasa's play, Shakuntala explains to her friends that her dress is caught on an amaranth twig, she not only allows herself the pleasure of one last lingering glance at King Dushyanta but exhibits a natural coyness that is immediately attractive to the king and to us as readers. The king has already noticed the "budding charms" that caused the guileless Shakuntala to complain petulantly that her dark dress was fastened so tightly that it hurt. Having complete faith in her small world, where innocence is protected and truth and happiness certain to be recognized and eventually rewarded, Shakuntala emerges as a delightful ingenue who enjoys toying with her own emotions, which, translated into acts and feelings, are reflected in Kalidasa's nature imagery.

"A girl is held in trust, another's treasure," explains Shakuntala's adoptive father, the hermit priest Kanva (act 4), but when that treasure goes unrecognized and is rejected and scorned by a bewitched King Dushyanta, Shakuntala shows that she is not at a loss in a masculine world of treachery. "Wretch," she screams angrily at the king when he condemns "the female's untaught cunning" and accuses her of being "selfish, sweet, false" as one who entices fools. "You," she tells him; "you judge all this by your own false heart." Still, there is another side to Shakuntala. "You self-willed girl," shouts one of Kanva's pupils who had brought Shakuntala to the king; "do you dare show independence." Thereupon Shakuntala, a woman of her time, shrinks back in fear (act 5). She has friends in high places, however, and can escape her agony until she and the king are united through the gods' will and the appearance of their son. Like many a woman of modern times, her man "had done her wrong," yet there is some truth to Shakuntala's later admission that "it was some old sin of mine that broke my happiness" (act 7). Charmingly competent to deal with the world she understands and perhaps strong enough to deal with the larger world, she eventually and happily accepts her place beside the king.

Shakuntala's story, like the stories in all Sanskrit plays, has a happy ending—happy, that is, in traditional terms of a woman's place in society and a woman's happiness. Shakuntala's daughters, women in today's Indian drama, have not always had that luxury of happiness, whether or not they have accepted a proscribed role in society, whether or not the dramatist set his scene in modern times or in the legendary past.

In a play entitled *Hayavadana* (1970) Girish Karnad—Rhodes Scholar, actor, director, film writer, producer, and playwright—once again tells the story of the transposed heads that is found in several literatures, east and west. It is the story of two friends, Devadatta the delicate intellectual and Kapita the muscular man of power. The heroine of the play, Padmini, a delightful and clever girl, is discovered by Devadatta, who swears that to have her he would sacrifice his head to Lord Rudra, the Prince of Demons and God of the Dead. Charming, witty, with a fine sense of humor, Padmini is described by Devadatta as "Yakshini, Shakuntala, Urvashi and Madhumati—all rolled into one" (act 1). When the lovers are united and Padmini is heavy with child, Devadatta feels that her condition with their first child warrants canceling a planned trip with Kapita. "What do you mean first?" Padmini retorts: "How many babies can one have in six months?" Devadatta persists: "I don't like the idea of your going so far in a cart in this present condition; that's all." Padmini responds with the lightheartedness her character projects. "Ordinarily," she says, "I would have replied that I have a womb of steel, but I won't—under the present condition" (act 1). Then they both laugh. Later, when Padmini must deal with Kapita's head on Devadatta's body as well as the serious question as to whose wife she is, her lightheartedness disappears. Pointing an accusing finger, Kapita says: "I know what you want, Padmini. Devadatta's clever head on Kapita's strong body." "Shut up, you brute!" Padmini screams back at him (act 1). An appropriate resolution is obviously difficult, and finally, when Kapita and Devadatta die, Padmini is burned on the funeral pyre by her own decision. Spirited and charming, modern in many ways, Padmini chooses nonetheless to follow the Indian tradition.

Mohan Rakesh was a strong force in modern Indian literature and drama before his untimely death in 1972 at the age of forty-seven. Although he wrote only three plays, his contribution to the theater has been highly praised by many Indian critics and playwrights, in particular Rajinder Paul, playwright and editor of *Enact* magazine, a major source of information on modern Indian drama. One of Rakesh's plays, *One Day in Ashadha,* describes the love of Kalidasa the poet and Mallika, the simple village girl who loves him and, dreaming of his rise to greatness, persuades him to seek his fortunes in the capital. There time passes, and Kalidasa marries a princess who, sensing the influence Mallika had over

Kalidasa, comes to visit the village in an attempt to understand the atmosphere that has been so important to Kalidasa's poetry. Later Kalidasa returns to the village, trying to find "where he belongs," still filled with the self-love that made it impossible for him to comprehend Mallika's all-encompassing devotion. Now, however, things have changed: Mallika's mother is dead, she is very poor, she is married and has a child. Life has been hard for her, and she complains. For both of them, the illusions of their youth are gone. Recognizing that time never waits, Kalidasa steals away, leaving his past and the love he never understood. Indian critics have judged this portrayal of a painful relationship between a man and a woman to be the first realistic play written in Hindi.

Social problems in India have occupied the thoughts of Badal Sircar, whose one-act play *Marital* (1969) presents some of the frustrations of married life and a reaction by a wife who is not encumbered either by Shakuntala's innocence or by her inhibitions. As the husband searches the classified ads for an apartment they can afford, the wife deals with the children. "Mummy, Mummy," one of them calls, "Dada is beating me." Mother has a ready answer: "Why do you let him beat you, you fool. Can't you run away?" Finally, the toilet column exhausted, the husband reads another kind of popular ad in Indian newspapers: "Wanted, slim, fair-complexioned, educated girl bride." With cynical expediency, both husband and wife attach some importance to the career girl bride. As the husband leaves for the bazaar and the child cries out again, the wife takes her own advice and provides the curtain line: "Mummy is dead. Career girl mummy will come. Complain to her." Surely this is an escape that would never have occurred to Shakuntala, whose theatrical retreat from unpleasantness with the aid of a heavenly nymph appears to be unavailable to a modern wife. If there is a comparable touch of the romantic dream in Sircar's climax, the reality of sober thought is more chilling for the modern woman.

In fact, sober thought and social realism go hand in hand in contemporary Indian drama, where the activities of woman are sometimes the primary issue. Such a play is *A Touch of Brightness* (1965) by Partap Sharma. Because the action of the seven scenes is set in "one of the most infamous localities of Bombay City," the well-known brothel cages, the Indian government prevented the play from being staged at the first Commonwealth Arts Festival in London in 1965 and banned performances in India the following year. *A Touch of Brightness* was finally seen in London in 1967, a stimulating example of the playwright's powerful art. Throughout the play it is clear that "there is no idea more frightening than reality" (scene 3), a concept particularly relevant to those Indian women whose lives are described by the opening lines of the play: "This is a road / With nowhere to go."

The play dramatizes the passage from innocence to manhood of a street urchin, Pidku, the adopted son of a pavement dweller in Bombay. The stimulating force in his growth is a young girl, Prema, whose very name means "love." Some say she is touched in the head. If so, says Pidku, it is "a touch of brightness" (scene 1). To Benarsi Baba, the pavement dweller, Prema is a distraction in his efforts to make Pidku a champion chess player, and he arranges her sale to a madam of one of the prostitution cages. There Prema becomes Ruhkmani, the beloved of Lord Krishna. In her new surroundings the strangeness of her character that people had recognized surfaces in her visions, her fear of a great calamity, her expressed wish to be "the perfect balance." The other girls in the brothel cannot understand this visionary's Whitman-esque attitude, this strange young person who claims to be both man and woman. "I am all," she preaches with Christ-like compassion; "Come with your suffering. Accept" (scene 4). Certain that she is feeling the ebb and flow of the universe, Ruhkmani passionately pursues her cause, assuming the godhead itself and preaching an acceptance of god which Pidku cannot understand, as he vainly tries to rescue her from her destiny. From his association with Ruhkmani—his sorrow for her poverty and the way she must live, his youthful love and their bond as sworn brother and sister—Pidku learns a new road to travel which does not include Benarsi Baba and the life so vividly illustrated by the night life of the street dwellers and the prostitution cages of Bombay. A woman, not a man, has been his teacher, "a touch of brightness" in an otherwise desolate and depraved world.

Traditional society in India defined the roles that women would play. The extremely complex caste system dominated life, and as critics have suggested, there could be no Cinderella role in traditional Hindu literature. Whether or not the Cinderella motif represents a romantic ideal or male sexism, in India one does not move from one social level to another. That does not mean, of course, that in contemporary society such moves have not been contemplated or achieved, but there has usually been a price to pay. These varied roles that women assume in modern society are well illustrated in the plays of Asif Currimbhoy, a "karma yogi" whose more than thirty plays show the tremendous energy that underlies his frequently agonizing compassion for mankind, male and female, for the people of India.

For Western audiences and students of modern Indian drama, Currimbhoy is a playwright of social purpose and, as Faubion Bowers once wrote, "the authentic voice of India." Because man reveals himself through social and political institutions, Currimbhoy searches the social-political world for his themes. Generally, he writes about man, but the strength and force of women in his plays are inescapable. In fact, his women characters, major or minor, are frequently more memorable than his male characters. Razia, for example, is a dominating force in *The Hungry Ones,* (1965), that relentless and frustrating search by two Americans for an understanding of and admission to the mysteries of India. A woman controls the plot of *The Doldrummers* (1960), wherein trendy questioners search for meaning in Indian daily life. Women also determine the life that Currimbhoy ridicules in a comedy entitled *'Darjeeling Tea?'* (1971).

In Currimbhoy's best plays his women characters are central to the provocative and sensitive issues that stimulate his creativity. Senhora Miranda is such a character in *Goa* (1970), his play about the Indian takeover of the Portuguese colony. She embodies the personal struggle as well as the spiritual force with which Currimbhoy frequently endows his women characters. Driven by her personal needs yet sensitive to the larger political issues involved, Miranda is a carefully realized woman of India as well as a symbolic force in the coup.

Currimbhoy wrote *An Experiment with Truth* in 1969 to dramatize Gandhi's struggle. He also emphasized the unrecognized importance of Kasturba, Gandhi's wife. When Gandhi talks about his vows, even his vow of celibacy which "transcends all restraints," she reminds him softly: "I took the vows, too, or have you forgotten, Bapu?" With a certain serenity, buttressed by great forbearance and inner strength, she tells him forthrightly: "What you sow, I reap, and it isn't always glorious" (1.2). Sometimes more aware of the real world than her husband, Kasturba complains that Gandhi's actions have made them poorer, that the experiments he considers restraints she considers indulgence. She worries about their children, who were not educated as she would have wished, whereas he was more absorbed with his "many children." "It was difficult," she says from her deathbed, "for me to become . . . everyone's mother" (3.1). Still, she always saw Gandhi, not as the failure he sometimes imagined, but as a great man with whom she was "mortally bound" throughout the life he was driven to live.

Currimbhoy's *Inquilab* (1970) is a highly political play dramatizing the Naxalite revolt in Calcutta, which involved many students and took place mainly on the university campus. Emphasizing the man's world of

India, the argument of the play contrasts Professor Datta, the traditionalist who believes in authority, with his son Amar, a callow rebel against that authority, caught up by the terrible conditions of India's poor and manipulated by power-hungry revolutionaries. Amar's bitter challenge to his father reflects the youthful dream: "You," he shouts, "were the Gods that failed" (1.1). Professor Datta's wife plays a minor role in the basic conflict between landholders and landless laborers, but her superstitious, passionate, and demanding nature reflects her generation. In a manner characteristic of many successful nineteenth-century Western melodramas, *Inquilab* pits honor against love: Amar's passionate belief in justice for all versus his love for Suprea, the daughter of a friend of the Datta family who is also an authoritarian landowner. As an innocent and romantic zealot, Amar places his cause before his love: "I must realize myself first, you understand." "Yes, yes, Amar," Suprea answers; "I understand" (1.1). However, neither understands the horrors of the riot in which Amar is involved or the suffering it brings, although Amar finally recognizes and confesses to Suprea that "there's something merciless about a cause" (3.1). The intensifying struggle, though, involves only the masculine world of India. The women are not allowed to participate in the action, but only to suffer the consequences of man's acts.

If Currimbhoy concentrates upon the man's world in *Inquilab,* he shows another approach to Indian life in *This Alien . . . Native Land* (1975). Here women control the action of the play, and men are merely toys—helpless, used, defeated, impotent. An overly refined Jewish family in India fights vainly for its identity as the struggle rages between the possessive and manipulating mother Rachel and Tara, the Indian girl who has married Jacob, favored son of Rachel and Joseph. As a counterpoint to Tara's destructive force, there is a sister in the family, Sarah, a strong, vulgar, and intimidating girl whose rebellion against her orthodox family has propelled her to a married man, a Muslim in fact, to whom she degrades herself in sensual pleasure, only to be rejected. Tara, clever and arrogant, crude, determined, and scornful of others, asserts her control over all but Rachel—even David, whose jealousy of his brother Jacob and cynical approach to life make him a betrayer. To Joseph, old and lost in dreams, Tara becomes the naked Salomé who taunts his impotence. Her extreme sensuality and insidious power also traduce the frustrations of Sarah, as the playwright creates the image of a possessive and unsatisfied India from within the disturbing specter of the Indian woman, Tara. Surely evident in this highly theatrical work is the revelation of the modern woman as a commanding social and spiritual force in India.

Shakuntala, charming and beautiful, enjoyed an innocent faith in her world. Happiness and security, however, were not problematic in her life. If treated badly, she could simply show a temper, but she also knew her traditional place and accepted her lot, as provided either by men or by the gods. Most modern dramatists in India have abandoned a romantic philosophy and offer mainly the social realism of the propaganda stage, where issues and problems can be easily presented. Seen in terms of these prevailing social issues, some Indian women, as portrayed by modern dramatists, accept their traditional place in Indian culture; others reject traditions and demand to be individuals in a complex society. Neither singled out for heroic treatment, as was the modern woman in Maoist China, nor forgotten among the confusing voices of modern India, Indian women are carefully presented onstage as victims and perpetrators, traditionalists and rebels, part and parcel of a developing world where social realism in the theater has become the dramatic style.

Walter J. Meserve, Summer 1989

■ WORKS CITED

Currimbhoy, Asif. *Complete Works.* Calcutta. Writers Workshop. 1973. (Includes '*Darjeeling Tea?',* The Doldrummers, An Experiment with Truth, Goa, The Hungry Ones,* and *Inquilab.*)

———. *This Alien . . . Native Land.* Calcutta. Writers Workshop. 1977.

Kalidasa. *Shakuntala.* Available in numerous editions, including *Three Sanskrit Plays,* Michael Coulson, ed. & tr., New York, Penguin, 1981, and *Theater of Memory: The Plays of Kālidāsa,* Barbara Stoler Miller, ed. and tr., New York, Columbia University Press, 1984.

Karnad, Girish. *Hayavadana.* Translated by the author from the Kannada. Delhi. Oxford University Press. 1975.

Rakesh, Mohan. *One Day in Ashadha.* Enact (Delhi), 1971.

Sharma, Partap. *A Touch of Brightness.* New York. Grove. 1968.

Sircar, Bidal. *Marital.* Enact (Delhi), 1970.

Tamil Literature

Of the many spoken and written languages on the Indian subcontinent, the constitution recognizes fifteen. They are Assamese, Bengali, Gujarati, Hindi, Kannada, Kashmiri, Malayalam, Marathi, Oriya, Punjabi, Sanskrit, Sindhi, Tamil, Telugu, and Urdu. Hindi has been given the status of India's official language, along with English. These fifteen languages belong to the two main language families: Indo-Aryan and Dravidian. Contemporary Indian literature includes, therefore, literature in any one of the fifteen languages, not excluding English. My understanding of literatures in other Indian languages, except Tamil, Sanskrit, and Hindi, has been only through English.

Tamil is the oldest of the four major Dravidian languages and is spoken by 56 million people (1991 census), mainly in Tamil Nadu in southeastern India. It is also spoken outside India in Sri Lanka, Malaysia, Burma, South Africa, the Fiji Islands, and the Caribbean Islands. The language was regulated around 250 B.C.

The earliest Tamil literature goes back to a period between 150 B.C. and 250 A.D. and is found in numerous anthologies that were later gathered together in two great collections, *The Eight Anthologies* and *The Ten Long Poems.* These, together with *The Tale of the Anklet* (fifth century A.D.), *The Descent of Rama* (twelfth century A.D.), and the medieval devotional hymns of the Saiva and Vaishnava poets, are the outstanding productions of the Tamil genius. The Tamils, in two thousand years, have not surpassed this achievement.

What, then, is the state of contemporary Tamil literature? The poet Ka. Naa. Subramanyam (1912–89) sums it up in the poem "Three Strains." His opinion is wholly unorthodox and is not accepted by most Tamils. The Tamils live in a euphoric past, and this euphoria expresses itself in an excessive glorification of the Tamil language to the exclusion of almost everything else. The situation is rather dispiriting. Let us look at the poem.

Arab
mongol
tartar
three strains
go to make
this jade
dragging the jutka
grazing the tarmac
of Madras streets.

Three sangams
and twice three
go to make this
Tamil language
I handle
and speak
and manhandle
and teach
derived
from of old.

The strains are weak,
wearing out;
arab or mongol
or tartar elements
are rarely
to be recognized
in this
tottering
but willing
jade.

The "jade" is "tottering / but willing," and it would appear that there is little that is significant in contemporary Tamil writing.

1: Fiction. Popularity, rather than literary quality, is what characterizes Tamil literature today. Periodicals such as *Ananta Vikatan, Kalki,* and *Kumutam* encourage and patronize pulp fiction. In the 1930s R. Krishnamurti (pseud. "Kalki," 1899–1954) specialized in historical romances. They are insignificant as literature but nevertheless fed the pride of the Tamils in their awesome exultation over their past glories.

Two writers in particular reacted strongly to Kalki's romances, and so pioneered the new Tamil writing: C. Vriddhachalam ("Pudumaippittan," 1906–48) and S. Mani ("Mowni," b. 1907). Through the periodical *Manikkoti* (The Jeweled Banner) they and others such as N. Pichamurti (1900–78) and K. P. Rajagopalan (1902–44) made the short story the dominant form of Tamil writing. Both Pudumaippittan and Mowni explored the psychological overtones of character and situation. Their stories are entirely intellectual in content, and the average Tamil reader, fed on Kalki's romances, found both Pudumaippittan and Mowni hard to stomach. In the words of Subramanyam, Mowni "put the Tamil language to uses to which it had never been exposed and, in the process, became difficult, though not obscure."

Subramanyam himself is one of the pioneers of modern prose fiction in Tamil. In his novels from *Hunger* onward to *Demon Breed* he reexamines the Tamil tradition, and it is this inquiry that has given his novels their unique importance. They are anything but popular. He does not sing the praises of the Tamils, or of their two-thousand-year-old heritage. Tamils find the questions he asks about them embarrassing and uncomfortable. In earlier Tamil novels the approach was passive, and this prevented any reexamination of tradition and its relevance to contemporary life. Therefore, self-questioning or the quest for identity or God were problems too remote for Tamil fiction to bother itself about. In Subramanyam's novels there is, on the other hand, a conscious reacceptance of tradition. A sense of bewilderment, even anguish, before the forces of life and therefore the need for roots, as situations inherent in the human condition, are explored in his novels. *Demon Breed,* for instance, is an inquiry into the forces behind life, and how tradition, rightly understood and activated, helps human beings organize these forces and fulfill themselves as individuals. The novel may be regarded as a fable of our times. It offers insights into the relationship of men and women to themselves, society, and God. No other novel in recent Tamil literature has attempted this task so honestly and imaginatively.

Subramanyam's earlier novels, such as *False Gods, One Day,* and *When the Favored Fall into Ruin,* are skillful modulations on the theme of *Demon Breed,* that of reexamining the basic aspects of the Tamil tradition. In his novels, prose fiction in Tamil reached its apotheosis. Other novelists whose work I consider significant are L. S. Ramamirtham (b. 1916), T. Janakiraman (b. 1921), Rajam Krishnan (b. 1925), Sundara Ramaswamy (b. 1931), J. Thyagarajan ("Ashokamitran," b. 1931), Chudamani Raghavan (b. 1931), D. Jayakanthan (b. 1934), Neela Padmanabhan (b. 1938), and C. S. Lakshmi ("Ambai," b. 1944).

More than any other Tamil writer, L. S. Ramamirtham has taken it upon himself to "purify the dialect of the tribe," to rescue the language from the accretions that surround it, so that words obey his call. His poetics is founded upon the belief that there should be no distance separating the word from the object it represents. "When I say 'fire,'" he writes, "it should burn my mouth." This explains why he is obsessed with the mystique of the word, its texture and nuances. Writing for him is an act of meditation. In *Son* he exploits Tamil folklore and evokes without any sentimentality the life of a woman on whose family a curse has been placed. His language is rich in poetry, unlike the insipid brew of the popular magazines. From the earliest times there have been two varieties of Tamil in use: a formal or literary variety used in writing, and an informal variety with many spoken dialects. The situation is not unlike that of Greek with its standard, *katharévusa,* and its vernacular, *dhimotiki.* The gap between the two varieties of Tamil is enormous. The language used in writing is still literary. The spoken language has not been fully exploited, except perhaps by Ramamirtham. In the process his Tamil has achieved the rarified state of poetry. This has, however, made him difficult to read. The Tamil middle-class Brahmin household, with its intricate network of family relationships, is the focus of Ramamirtham's work. In *The Ocean of Milk* he evokes for us three generations of his family. Especially striking are the cameos that he offers of his grandfather and of the family deity. His fiction thus centers on the family saga.

T. Janakiraman's novels *The Thorn of Passion* and *Mother Came* represent the realistic and humanistic trends in contemporary Tamil writing. *Mother Came* is a satire on traditional, sentimental attitudes toward the mother. The novel is psychologically interesting in its observations on urban life in Tamil Nadu today. Many of Rajam Krishnan's novels are social documents that chronicle the lives of isolated communities, such as those of the coastal fisheries of Tamil Nadu that are vividly evoked in *On the Seashore.* Others, such as *The Battlefield,* revolve around the politics of the family, and es-

pecially of a woman's role in it. Sundara Ramaswamy's *Story of a Tamarind Tree* is about the disappearance of an idyllic, pastoral society and its replacement by an artificial world. In *Dissolving Shadows* Ashokamitran explores levels of urban society as they interact with one another. He particularly exposes the unreality of the Tamil film world. His vision is unsentimental and austere.

In Chudamani Raghavan's fiction women are free spirits. They refuse to buckle under the pressures of society in their need to fulfill themselves as individuals. Marriage does not put them under a spell. They turn their backs on husband and family to become persons in their own right. Raghavan's novels from *The End of the Ordeal* to *Mother* speak eloquently about women's empowerment and their right to be themselves. They illustrate the truth of Adrienne Rich's statement in "Conditions for Work": "Feminism means finally that we renounce our obedience to the fathers and recognize the world they have described is not the whole world." Essentially a short-story writer, D. Jayakanthan, in his novels *Some Men at Certain Times* and *A Man, a Home, and a World,* interprets life in the context of social change.

Neela Padmanabhan's novel *The Generations* chronicles three generations of a family of merchants who have fallen on evil days. Within a few months of her marriage, Nagammai is sent back to her father's house by her impotent husband on the suspicion that she is barren. Everyone is reconciled to her fate except her brother Diraviam, who fights back against the forces of orthodoxy in order to rehabilitate his sister. He fails in the end, and his failure enlarges the novel's tragic dimensions even more than Nagammai's fate. There is something elemental about the novel, and it is a landmark in Tamil fiction.

Ambai writes in the tradition of Krishnan and Raghavan on familial themes. Her work explores the tensions women experience in a patriarchal society where fathers and husbands do everything in their power to oppress women, as in the stories collected in *Wings Must Break.* In *The Face Behind the Mask* Ambai undertakes one of the first extended discussions of women in Tamil literature. The study is a milestone in Indian feminist criticism.

Prose fiction in Tamil has come into its own only in the last fifty years. The time is not yet ripe to critically evaluate its contribution to Tamil literature. The death of Pudumaippittan in 1948 at the age of forty-two deprived Tamil literature of the one writer who could have given it a sense of direction.

2: Poetry. Although prose fiction in Tamil is little over a hundred years old, Tamil poetry goes back to the second century B.C. The poems from *The Eight Antholo-gies* are of such breathtaking sophistication that one would be hard put to find parallels in contemporary Tamil poetry. They remain unsurpassed to this day.

The ghost of C. Subramania Bharati (1882–1921) hovers over every contemporary Tamil poet. Though a traditional poet, Bharati broke away from the received forms and, singlehandedly, invented the idiom and metric of twentieth-century Tamil verse. He defamiliar-ized the current language of poetry, which was elitist and static, by exploiting the spoken language as the ve-hicle for lyric expression. By his innovations, Bharati was able to overcome the diglossia that traditionally characterized the Tamil language. For the first time, po-etry was no longer the exclusive preserve of the elite. It flourished on the tongues of the illiterate and unedu-cated. It was set to music and sung or chanted in films and at political rallies. The poem "Autobiography" epit-omizes the widespread disaffection brought about by education in a foreign language like English, as in these lines, for example: "No climbing back from this bottom-less pit / This hell of foreign learning— / Into which my father pushed me / For my own good, simple-minded that he was."

The innovations begun by Bharati, notably in his *Prose Poems,* were carried forward by Pichamurti, Raja-gopalan, Pudumaippittan, and Subramanyam, who ex-perimented in nontraditional forms. However, it was Subramanyam who, as writer, editor, and apologist, es-poused new verse and helped establish its poetics.

> It was in 1959 that I made a critical statement on what I called new poetry in the magazine *Saraswathi* in which I pleaded for an intellectual content in poetry apart from the emotional, a harking back to the oldest strata of Tamil poetry, the sangam poems, which are in recognizable conversational phrases, and for the hard image shorn of adjectives of any kind. It was easy for the Tamil poet to indulge in mysticism and I called for avoiding it.

By focusing attention on the classical Tamil poems, Subramanyam urged his contemporaries to return to the wellspring of their own poetic tradition and cre-atively exploit it. He thus helped establish a poetics as well as provide a sense of direction to new verse in Tamil. It was therefore the poets themselves rather than the professional scholars who took the lead in exploring the secrets of their craft and formulating a poetics. In a rather outspoken poem, "Situation," Subramanyam describes the limbo inhabited by the Tamil poet:

Introduced to
the Upanishads
by T. S. Eliot;

and to Tagore
by the earlier
Pound;

and to the Indian
tradition by
Max Müller
(late of the Bhavan);

and to the Indian
dance by
Bowers;

and to Indian
art by
what's-his-name;

and to the Tamil
classics by
Daniélou
(Was he Pope?);

flesh nor fish
blood nor stone
totempole;

vociferous in
thoughts not
his own;

eloquent in
words not
his own
(The age demanded. . .)

In fact, this is true of all Indian writers. They owe their discovery of India and of themselves as Indians to Euro-pean scholars.

In his search for new thresholds, Pichamurti appro-priated for Tamil the free verse of Walt Whitman (1819–92). "*Leaves of Grass,* by the American poet Walt Whitman, was in fact," he wrote, "the germ from which my own efforts in free verse blossomed. Reading it I dis-covered the wellspring of poetry. Afterwards I read Bharati's *Prose Poems.* They strengthened my resolve." It was Pichamurti, and not Bharati, who won attention for free verse in Tamil. The form freed him from the re-straints of an obsolete prosody. He began to explore un-conventional subjects. "Naranan the Shopkeeper," "The Wild Duck," and "The Guide" are in the nature of forays into unknown territories. At the same time, he invests ordinary and familiar things with the breath of poetry, as in these lines from "Seeing": "In the oppressive sun / big with child, a sweeper / finds no end of pleasure / in a sprig of tobacco." "The Wild Duck," for one in-stance, breathes with Whitman's voice and presence. The irreverent tone is there, as are the open, expansive rhythms. Consider these lines, which halt in their flight the Siberian wild ducks as they heave into view at Ve-dantangal, the bird sanctuary near Madras:

They follow their own nature to reproduce their
  kind.
They abide by no law.
They have no tall stories of the past,
No tradition or pride.
Untaught, and by instinct alone,
They fly three thousand miles to nest here.
And now, the flapping of their wings.

Free verse in English was itself an offshoot of the French
vers libre, which was the most enduring feature of the
revolution in poetic form initiated by the symbolist
movement in the late nineteenth century. In "Reflections on *Vers Libre*" T. S. Eliot wrote: "But the most interesting verse which has yet been written in our language has been done either by taking a very simple
form, like the iambic pentameter, and constantly with-
drawing from it, or taking no form at all, and constantly
approximating to a very simple one. It is contrast between fixity and flux, this unperceived evasion of monotony, which is the very life of verse." The rationale
for free verse was sought in the development of an appropriate modern poetic idiom."

   In the absence of an official, public status as a poet,
the Tamil poet's universe of discourse came to be centered in his own inner world, in the complexities of his
own experiences—sexual, emotional, and psychological. Experience itself is depersonalized as it shapes into
a poem. Every once in a while the poet steps out amd
bares his chest to the world in a gesture of defiance,
only to retreat awkwardly. One such occasional poem
is Subramanyam's "The Latecomer."

I had, in fact, set out for the play.
But it was all over
When I got there.
The house was empty
And littered with chairs.
Even as I stood wondering
Where to sit,
The day was upon me.

The truism that, unprepared as we are, life passes most
of us by and then it is too late to do anything is embedded in the text. The image of the theater is the only hint
offered to the reader in his attempt to make explicit the
theme of the poem. The analogy between theater and
life is not suggested. The reader is expected to supply
the equation and thus complete the poem. The interpretation is the result of a mediation between the explicit
and implicit features of the poem, whose philosophic
thrust thus remains unobtrusive—in fact, unsaid. The
thematic indeterminacy is further reinforced by the indeterminacy of the prosodic form, free verse. A traditional meter would have imposed a more formal pattern.

Little magazines in Tamil have helped not only to
foster new verse but also to keep it alive. It was in the
pages of *Eluttu* (Letters), edited by C. S. Chellappa (b.
1912), that the new voices were first heard and talked
about. Founded in 1959 as a critical review, its 119 issues comprise a history of the new verse movement in
Tamil. Chellappa's Eluttu Press published *New Voices* in
1962, an influential anthology that contained the work
of twenty-four poets. What is refreshingly new about
these poems is not only their informal tone, or their employment of colloquial language and unconventional
images, but their impressive use of irony. Often the
poems are brief aphoristic or epigrammatic statements.
Thus, a whole new dimension was added to Tamil poetry. Besides Subramanyam, the poets who best represent
the new poetic are T. K. Doraiswamy ("Nakulan," b.
1922), Shanmuga Subbiah (b. 1924), T. S. Venugopalan (b. 1929), S. Vaidheeswaran (b. 1935), S. Palanisa-
my ("Si. Manee," b. 1936), R. Ranganathan
("Gnanakoothan," b. 1938), and T. K. Somasundaram
("Kalapriya," b. 1950). The important critical study *The
Origin and Development of New Verse* by R. S. Krish-
naswami ("Vallikkannan," b. 1920) offered the first serious consideration of the new poetry, and thus helped
legitimize the movement.

   Nakulan's poems walk a tightrope between verse
and prose, creating an edginess of tone that is unusual
in Tamil poetry. He exploits the power and resilience
of the spoken language, uninflated by metaphor. This
gives his poems their characteristic starkness. A poem
by Nakulan is an invitation to observe the general drift
of a thought as it discovers the extraordinary in the
midst of the ordinary. In "Step Aside," for instance, the
speaker wrestles with the unreality of his multiple identities. It is vintage Pessoa.

In this great house
I have no room of my own.
No known face in this big town.
And when the known face
Shows its true colors,
It turns out to be
The face of a stranger.
When will I stop being
What I appear to be?
The thought crossed my mind.
A voice said: "Step aside."

Again, Nakulan is perhaps the only Tamil poet I know
who is comfortable with exploring intimate relationships between men and women, as in the exquisite
"Sushila" poems. The absence of love poetry is intriguing, especially since the genre dominates classical Tamil
literature. Here is a well-known poem by Pālaipātiya

Perunkatunkō (second century A.D.) that poignantly evokes the situation of a woman abandoned by her lover: "He avoids our street though he lives / in the same town. Should he visit us, / he won't take me, lovingly, in his arms. / Unseeing, he walks past me as if I were / the burning ground of strangers. Once, / I was unashamed when passion had robbed me / of my senses. But now, like an arrow / sent flying from a bow, it has landed far off." Nakulan does not hesitate to tap into this rich vein. His tone, however, is low-keyed and ruminative, as in the poem "It Is Me."

Out of habit I was sitting up
In the room with myself:
I heard someone
Knock on the door.
"Who is it?" I asked.
"It is me, Sushila.
Open the door."
Who can foretell which door
Will fly open, and when?

What distinguishes Shanmuga Subbiah as a poet is his unobtrusive voice, heard almost as an afterthought. His poetry represents a breakthrough for Tamil verse. In "To Those Who Inquired After My Welfare" the reader overhears the speaker in the poem talking to his interlocutors.

Yes, I've been through it all!
Thank Heaven!
I have also two kids.
Who should take credit for them, I wonder?
Both are sons.
Moreover, I'm rheumatic
And she, consumptive.
It's a pity
The older of the two is ill
Most of the time.
As for the younger one,
There's been nothing to complain of,
At least so far.
Of tomorrow, who can say?
Above all,
I'm a clerk.
Will this do?
Or, is there anything else
You wish to know?

It is a familiar situation, the urban hell that we all inhabit, where the boredom and horror of a middle-class existence are sharply etched. His cup is full, but he refuses to complain. The culture itself has become desacralized. The poem chokes on the burden of the unsaid. It is irony that redeems it from turning melodramatic. The use of casual, everyday discourse produces a surface calm that is totally at odds with the intention of the text. The meaning is thereby foregrounded.

Subbiah's language has the force and simplicity characteristic of oral societies where the power of the spoken word is feared and respected. Again, the poem "Dog Show" is remarkable for its understatement and economy. Something as uneventful as a dog show provokes the poet to an ironic social comment. The pariah dogs, after all, represent for him the inescapable Indian reality. On the other hand, the pedigreed dogs, though equally real, are an aberration, because Indians are not particularly known for their kindness to animals. Dog shows were part of the social entertainment of upper-class Indians under the raj. Like the SPCA, they ironically survive even today. Still, the poet does not scorn them. His irony is gentle and inoffensive throughout: "I too saw / The dog show. / It was amusing. / But coming out, / I walked into a rabble / Of pariah dogs."

"After Reading the Daily" gives the politician a rap on the knuckles for his indifference and lack of feeling. Subbiah is keenly alive to the tensions to which modernization has given rise in a traditional society such as India. He takes the West to task for this in "To the Westerners" by exposing the contradictions inherent in its way of life. At the same time, he also sees unerringly the contradictions in the Indian way of life. But the poem stops there. No attempt is made to examine the contradictions and relate them to a broad pattern of human behavior. The poem raises expectations that remain unfulfilled. This failure to sustain an argument at length perhaps explains that thinness of much of contemporary Tamil poetry about which Subramanyam had complained. More than any other poet, however, Subbiah briefly and poignantly encapsulates in his poems the daily embarrassment of living in urban India, and of being at odds with the orthodox Tamil establishment.

T. S. Venugopalan's collection *A Paddy Field in Summer* is unusual in style and content. Tamil poetry traditionally has been dominated by the pundits with their strict enforcement of stylistic and prosodic conventions. Seen in this context, Venugopalan's verse represents a breakthrough for Tamil. His tone is neutral throughout. He is content to state rather than explain: hence the total absence of metaphors in his poems. Partly on account of this, they lack any complex structure. They possess, on the other hand, the hard, grainy quality of proverbs. They are epigrammatic, often with an ironic twist at the end, throwing light on an obscure corner of experience. Take the poem "Family Pride." It opens with a proverb, and like all proverbs, it epitomizes a story. In addition, the story has an unexpected ending. The movement of the poem is thus linear throughout, except toward the end, where it curves abruptly, almost turning a somersault. Through a sort of double-edged irony, the poem deflates, on the one hand, the pride of the Tamils in their possibly non-Aryan ancestry (as represented by the mango-stone) and comments, on the other hand, on their unfortunate position today, as represented by the worm. The poem can therefore be read as a historical exercise that is symbolically realized—an exercise that ranges, however superficially, over the entire gamut of Tamil experience. And to have said all this in just twelve words (in Tamil) is no small achievement.

The curried mango-stone
Boasted of its pedigree.
I sowed
And waited.

The huge tree and its fruits
Dissolved into a shadow.
What wriggled out
Was a worm.

The edifice of S. Vaidheeswaran's poems is built almost entirely on images. The effect is invariably visual rather than aural. "Shedding" is an example, inspired by the repulsive posters that foul the streets of Madras.

The city walls lie
Inert as snakes.

The poster skins
Often expand and turn brittle.
The walls, still and erect,
Citified snakes that they are,
Peel off their skins hastily
At dead of night,
And stir themselves about, glittering,
In their fresh coat of scales.

Si. Manee's long poem "Hell" is a showpiece of the new verse movement in Tamil. The poem examines the state of Tamil culture today as represented by the urban hell that is Madras, in which relationships between men and women are unreal. Torn between the past and the present, the Tamils inhabit a wasteland. Manee speaks of the despair precisely and without emotion.

Tamil Nadu is not in the east,
Neither is it wholly in the west.
She put the vessel on the stove
To cook rice, but went no further.
The result: starvation and ruin.
She does not turn back,
Nor does she move forward.
The present is a toss-up.
A tradition hard as nails, and
Beliefs under lock and key—
Both refuse to give a hand
To untie the knot.

What's to be done?

Unlike the other poets, Gnanakoothan has not opted out of traditional metrics. Except occasionally, his verse moves heavily with the burden of the past. He is by far the most literary of the seven poets discussed here, and the only one seriously preoccupied with the state of the language. His two-line poem "Tamil" is almost the manifesto of new poetry in Tamil: "It's true Tamil is the breath of my life, / But I won't brag about it to others." He uses colloquial Tamil, even slang, forcefully and with ease. His irony is often directed at himself. He says with disarming candor, "Nothing remarkable happened in my life. This is the problem both for me and my poetry." The poem may be viewed as an ironic response to Bharati's eulogy on Tamil, as in the following lines: "Be sure to make the thunder / Of Tamil resound in every street."

Kalapriya's poems are brief dispatches about life in rural Tamil Nadu. They bring to life the immemorial rhythms of village India in all their beauty and simplicity, as in the poem "The Path."

A train speeds past a hut.
A bull crouches inside a shed:
The hair on its thighs stands up.
Utterly naked, a little girl
Blows her new whistle
And waves to the train.

On the threshing floor,
Stretched in cradles,
The young ones lie scared
Of the dust: their eyes
And mouths shut tight.
Butterflies are all they dream about.

By the edge of the paddy field,
A rattlesnake is beside itself with pain:
Unable to move, a mute frog
In its belly.
A schoolboy casts about for a rock:
His bag and packed lunch
Do penance by the side of the path.

A prominent feature of new verse in Tamil is that most of the poets favor a short poem (six or eight lines) as opposed to a long one. This is perhaps a conscious effort to appropriate the formal excellence of classical Tamil verse. However, no one will dispute its relevance to contemporary Tamil life. Herein lies its potential for further growth.

I began translating the Tamil poets included here in the winter of 1978 while a guest of the University of Iowa's International Writing Program in Iowa City as one more step in the dialogue between myself and my

Tamil past. I used to pelt the frozen Iowa River with verses from Andal and Ilango. Of Tamil, I had written in *Rough Passage:* "To live in Tamil Nadu is to be conscious / every day of impotence. / There is the language, for instance: // the bull, Nammalvar took by the horns, / is today an unrecognizable carcass, / quick with the fleas of Kodambakkam." It was that bull I was keen on taking by the horns. I set aside the contemporary poets for a time and turned my attention to *The Tale of the Anklet.* I envied Ilango his great epic, and the only way I could possess the poem, make it my own, was to rewrite it in English. My assimilation of Ilango is a form of translation—rewriting a poem in English that I could not myself write in Tamil. Again, it was at the hospitable campus of the University of Texas at Austin, during the four years that I was there from 1982 to 1986, that I began and completed the translation of the 5,730-line epic. By making Ilango speak in the accents of English, I hope I have breathed life into the poem and awakened it from its enforced sleep in Tamil. The translation was published in 1993 by Columbia University Press in its series "Translations from the Asian Classics." *The Tale of the Anklet* is India's finest epic in a language other than Sanskrit. It is to the Tamils what the *Iliad* is to the Greeks: the story of their civilization. It is precisely this burden of the past that the Tamil poet has to wrestle with, unlike poets in other modern Indian languages, and one which sets him apart. The situation is unique to Tamil literature. The Greek example once again comes to mind, as the work of poets such as Dínos Christianópoulos (b. 1931) demonstrates. They are not rendered speechless by Homer's patrimony. Neither should the Tamil poets be by Ilango's.

Poets from Bharati onward attempted to breathe life into Tamil. Poetry for them was a "struggle for breath." Their voices faltered and stumbled as they tried to free themselves from the past. Not even Bharati was up to the task. The fruits had already been picked. There was nothing left in the barrel to scrape. Yet Bharati, in his *Prose Poems,* indicated the directions that poets after him were to follow.

No contemporary Tamil poet is totally free of tradition, however emphatically he might swear to the contrary, for the poetic tradition asserts itself most vigorously through language. The Tamil poet finds himself at the center of a linguistic triangle which imposes on him varying degrees of allegiance to classical Tamil, Sanskrit, and English. The situation is true for other contemporary Indian literatures as well. As a result of the encounter with the West, we can speak of a dissociation of sensibility in India in the nineteenth century. The origin of modernity in India can be traced to that historic event. This led to the desacralization of the In-

dian languages and to the eventual secularization of the literatures in them.

R. Parthasarathy, Spring 1994

Contemporary Indian Poetry in English

Regular readers of *World Literature Today* will have noticed the infrequency with which Indian books from one of the twenty or so major regional languages are reviewed; only occasionally do reviews appear of work translated from those major, though multiply fragmented, Indian cultural resources. Instead, India is represented here, as elsewhere abroad, almost solely by Indian English writing. Unlike Caribbean or African literatures, however, those flourishing in India are not consistently written in some postcolonial language, some form or other of Arabic, English, French, Spanish, or Portuguese. Given that publications in Indian English account for less than half the total print production and that Hindi dominates the centrally controlled radio and television, criticism from abroad, as indeed in India, deals at best sketchily with the full range of contemporary Indian literary and oral culture. Accurate, if not full, representation would require a minimal sampling of fiction, poetry, and belles lettres in Hindi, Bengali, Marathi, Gujarati, Tamil, Kannada, Telugu, Malayalam, and Urdu. Fullness would require sampling also Punjabi, Oriya, Assamese, Sanskrit, and several other Hindi-related tongues like Bhojpuri or Maithili, together with some indication of work done in the major tribal languages, especially from the Northeast, for at least thirty-three indigenous languages are each used by over a million of the now nearly one billion Indians. Though probably sixty percent of Indians are unable to read any of the dozen or so different alphabets, ignorance of poetry is mitigated by frequent oral recitations, not merely at regional-language educational and religious festivals but at ordinary political and social events as well. The bimonthly journal of the national literary academy, *Indian Literature,* still attempts annually a critical survey in Indian English of the year's work in the twenty or so major languages; a double issue in 1980, entitled "Indian Poetry Today," included English-translated poems from nineteen regional languages plus an "Indo-English" selection. *WLT* surely cannot aspire to such full reviewing, but at least in treating Indian English, it can indicate for interested but uninformed readers the peculiar circumstances for that narrowly selective part of Indian literary production.

Though the percentages are several times higher in the largest cosmopolitan centers—Bombay, Delhi, Calcutta, Madras, Ahmedabad, Bangalore, Hyderabad—perhaps only three or four percent of Indians (close to twenty-five million persons concentrated in the larger urban centers) speak English with some fluency. Over ninety-five percent of that group use it as a second language, preponderantly for practical professional purposes: in science, the law, engineering and higher technology, international or interstate commerce, academe. Since eight percent of Indian youth now seek higher education, where English is commonly the medium of instruction, that academic use looms especially large in the culture, and more and more children of the upper classes (say, the fifteen percent of households which pay income tax) go at an early age to English-medium schools. Thus, when Indian English is used for literary purposes, particularly for poetry, the writer is generally not writing in a language spoken in the kitchen, nursery, or bedroom, certainly not at the temple or on the street or in the fields. Thus, unlike a poet in English-dominant cultures, an Indian English poet is stretching his or her linguistic resources (and those of his indigenous readers) far beyond what is enlisted in their common everday life; in America the reading of Shakespeare by nonspecialists makes comparable demands.

It was, therefore, crucial historically that almost all the postcolonial Indian English poets who first achieved some recognition in India live in the two or three major metropolitan centers. There, amid a cosmopolitan mélange of people and tongues, a large coterie—usually academic or otherwise professional, many in advertising, publicity, or mass-media work—speaks Indian English regularly outside the home and is available to support poetry writing and societies. Through extensive stays in Britain or, especially in the two more recent decades, in America (the U.S. or Canada), a large proportion of the best-known poets have undergone supplemental saturation experiences with English where it is the surrounding culture's common language. It is also a significant fact that, unlike most published poets in America, the professional work of Indian English poets does not involve teaching contemporary poetry and poetry writing, and if they are teachers in college or university English departments, as several are, the prescribed syllabus of British and American poetry is slight; Indian English poetry only very recently was admitted as good enough and, indeed, uniquely useful for advanced linguistic and cultural study. Even for a postgraduate (M.A.) degree in English literature—still considered almost a requisite preparation for passing exams for prestigious Indian administrative positions—students read in poetry only the major anthology pieces by the top twenty or so British and American poets. For example, *Advanced College Poems* (Oxford University Press, 1989), designed for those studying English as a language through the B.A. or B.Comm. courses, includes sixteen poems; an even more traditional list of twenty poems, from Shakespeare's "All the World's a Stage" and Gray's "Elegy. . ." to Frost's "The Road Not Taken" and Dylan Thomas's "Do Not Go Gentle into That Good Night," was published by Orient Longman the year before, also "specially prepared for undergraduate general English courses . . . with detailed explanatory notes and an exhaustive vocabulary geared to the students' linguistic ability." One result of the marginality of Indian English poetry in its own culture (and much more so abroad) is that realistically or practically there is little opportunity or motivation to be very productive. Only a few poets write or publish regularly, and only quite recently have three or four new, well-edited, and selective poetry journals and chapbook series appeared to supplement the seventeen-year-old New Poetry in India series sponsored by Oxford University Press. Several other, usually irregularly issued indigenous poetry journals and publishers' (or independent poets') series are now mostly defunct, suffering from general failures of distribution and the failure of occasional readers or libraries to subscribe or purchase.

A more qualitative consequence of this situation is the critical cliché that Indian English verses quite often "smell of the lamp." That is to say, an academic and exaggeratedly intraliterary, often imitative or derivative, quality constitutes a distinct hazard avoided by only the most accomplished Indian English poets. Narrowly trained in English poetry, both writers and readers enjoy, accept, and expect that Indian English poetry sound recognizably like the little that they have already experienced. Furthermore, critics and even the poets themselves have repeatedly complained that Indian English poetry is thematically isolated, alienated from the cultural mainstream, written from an "ivory tower" that is politically and socially irresponsive, if not irresponsible. Again, part of the reason is a tradition-bound expectation that poetry be removed from daily life and reach for sublime feelings and truths. In addition, everyday critics and reviewers still assume, correctly for the many lesser practitioners, that fundamental linguistic difficulties—lexical, syntactic, rhythmic, even grammatical—need to be overcome by all those trying to write authentically Indian poetry in English. Especially "nativist" critics, those dedicated to regional-language literary cultures, still characterize the clearly Indian form of English as "the enemy's tongue," as if it were unchanged from the language inherited from and impregnated with British colonial oppression or, in more recent nativist analyses, with American or Eurocentric neo-imperialist values. Thus, Indian English is supposedly incapable of authentically representing Indian experience, except perhaps that of a tiny, alienated Anglophilic minority. Meanwhile, most present-day regional-language poetry tends to be conservative, employing traditional patterns and themes and formulaic diction with hardly perceivable contemporary touches, or else it strains toward a violent modernism, for few have achieved postmodern colloquial easiness with free verse.

A nonspecialist foreign critic possessed of a little basic information and writing about Indian English poetry, say, for the *TLS* or, if it were ever to occur, the *New York Times Book Review* or the *New York Review of Books,* all too easily begins with elementary questions of the Indian English poet's linguistic competence. Most Indian critics support this perspective of supposed outside experts in English and, like them, go on to focus almost exclusively on issues of authenticity and thematics, ultimately seeking an undefinable "Indianness" of content and attitude. Critical reviews rarely examine a poet's personal techniques, such as skill in bending the ordinarily quite bureaucratized Indian English language. Indeed, individual styles, including distinctive influences from each poet's surrounding cultural environment of regional-language literature or from classical Indian traditions, are scarcely discernible except among a very few poets. Again, a vexed relationship between tradition and individual talent, including considerable confusion introduced by academic reverence for T. S. Eliot's theory, impinges on Indian English critics and poets alike, resulting in their valorizing tradition, myth, and legend, while minimizing individuality, creativity, and a personal rather than a group consciousness.

In consequence, considerable importance and often intense controversy have over the years surrounded the selection of the top-ranking Indian English poets for national anthologies, usually edited by one of the poets themselves and destined for academic use or at least read largely from an academic perspective. An amusing, if media-hyped report by Sunaina Lowe of supposedly vindictive poet-editors' anthology choices and their targets' ripostes appeared with cartoon caricatures of the pugilistic combatants in the August 1982 *Imprint.* Four recent anthologies, however—by Vilas Sarang for Orient Longman (1989), by K. Ayyappa Paniker for the Sahitya Akademi (1991), by Arvind Mehrotra for Oxford University Press (1992), and by Makarand Paranjape for Macmillan (1993)—have generally avoided similar slanderings by following, on the whole, now well-established lines with only one or two eccentric omissions and unconventional new choices. Examining anthologies by provincially based poets which heavily emphasize obscure minor poets of a par-

ticular region[1] reveals that, indeed, the second rank of performance is distinctly inferior, with much of the work being nearly worthless. Thus, exactly as provincial poets have long complained, the poetry publishing scene in India has been not only highly centralized in Bombay, with New Delhi and Calcutta recently gaining stronger importance, but it is also very narrowly limited, sharply hierarchical, prone to self-publication, and liable to exceedingly poor national distribution and biased selectivity. Still, that the Indian English literary scene is supportive of only a dozen or so mostly cosmopolitan, well-anthologized poets seems more critically justifiable than if, for instance, such an evaluative situation eliminated all but a few of the hundreds of highly skilled, sometimes well-individuated, contemporary American academic poets.

Given this cultural, literary, and linguistic context as well as widely deplored critical failures of responsibility, sensitivity, and judgment, what criteria would be appropriate and just for judging contemporary Indian English poetry? Should the criteria exhibit the perspective of the operative indigenous cultural context? That is, should criticism be concerned with the geographically if not socially varied, preeminently *multiculturally mixed* Indian English interpretive community in which this poetry must ordinarily succeed or fail? Without a doubt, the better Indian English poets have attempted to break out of the parochial, elitist, and academic boxes created by their hypereducated high-class audiences and by their own ordinarily also narrow experience. Rather than pursue the conventional kinds of esthetically and emotionally esoteric poetry long revered in Indian traditions, they have espoused, for the most part, a modern poetics, but not necessarily one committed to other Western values, like individualism or progressivism. Perhaps the most influential of all these poets, Nissim Ezekiel, has fairly directly addressed imminent civic and moral and personal concerns, on the somewhat abstract model of British "Movement" poets of the 1950s, only occasionally with an identifiably Indian or postcolonial perspective.[2] Perhaps the most unreservedly British-seeming of these poets, however, is Dom Moraes, until middle age a U.K. resident and youthful prizewinner, but after returning to Bombay and later to a looser form of poetry, he essayed, besides his usual Eurocentric mythologies, those of Sri Lanka and other poems with distinct national, regional, or Bombay concerns.[3] A number of self-exiled or expatriate Indian English poets have lived mainly in the United States: e.g., off and on, Shiv K. Kumar;[4] or the late A. K. Ramanujan[5] for thirty years; or, more recently, R. Parthasarathy, the first widely successful anthologist;[6] and, fairly briefly, Dilip Chitre and Arvind Krishna Mehrotra (who have also, as translators, mined medieval Marathi and ancient Prakrit poets respectively);[7] as well as two somewhat younger émigrés, Meena Alexander and Aga Shahid Ali.[8] Each of the latter two, as well as several other émigrés with lesser talents, like Darius Cooper, Uma Parameswaran, or the older G. S. Sharat Chandra, has explored his or her particular Indian cultural and family background and alienated psyche using traditionally concrete modernist techniques and a distinctly "international" (i.e., American) perspective.

Still, there are many Indian English poets who, usually without being intimately confessional, seem committed to drawing their poetry from distinctly non-alienated Indian sources. They have often forged their verse from Indian history, legend, and myth; besides the two translators just mentioned, several others stand out as most successful. Though a heritage Parsi, a role he explores in only two or three poems, Keki Daruwalla has drawn heavily on the harsh geography and the often violent Muslim and Mughal past and rituals of North India, where he was long stationed in the Indian police forces.[9] Less brilliantly, but with sharp details and convincing emotion, Man Mohan Singh has mined his Punjabi childhood village experiences to good poetic effect.[10] From his Cuttack home Jayanta Mahapatra draws on not only his Orissan landscape, culture, and family background but also ancient Indian myths and legends, for example, confabulating his second long poem, *Relationship,*[11] with the nearby thirteenth-century Sun Temple at Konarka. In 1981 the Sahitya Akademi for the first time awarded its annual prize in Indian English literature to a poet, convinced at last by this poem of Mahapatra's that authentically Indian work could be done in that once-alien medium. Gieve Patel, another avowed heritage Parsi, is also recognizably Indian English, at least in his many specific poems that use the autobiographical perspective of a physician working in the Bombay slums.[12] Both Kamala Das and Imtiaz Dharker, as well as still younger feminist poets like Charmayne D'Souza and some other women noted below, clearly reveal their particular indigenous circumstances in dealing with the peculiar oppressions of women in India, whether among Hindus, Muslims, Catholics, or supposed secular sophisticates.[13] Totally satisfactory results are predictably rare when poets try to comment directly on current Indian events: the assassination of Mrs. Gandhi, the Bhopal chemical-cloud tragedy, even the endemic horrors of destitution, as Jayanta Mahapatra, generally a highly personal meditative poet, has attempted in *Dispossessed Nests: The 1984 Poems;* he was more successful, as also less journalistic, in his lengthy *Temple,* drawing on an impoverished octogenarian woman's suicide, and in many poems from

his latest collection, *The Whiteness of Bone.*[14] Only Arun Kolatkar, a bilingual poet in Marathi, has written a long poem (really a sequence of short lyrics) that could conceivably be called popular within the limited potential readership; first published almost twenty years ago and at least twice reprinted, it traces a modernized youth's ironic pilgrimage to a famous Hindu temple at Jejuri in the mountains near Bombay.[15]

Seeking current relevance and modernistic liveliness, Kolatkar famously attempted to put Bombay criminal argot into a few of his Indian English poems (possibly translated from his Marathi poems), and others less talented than Salman Rushdie—e.g., Makarand Paranjape—or more obscurely difficult—e.g., the earlier Adil Jussawalla[16]—have experimented in poetry with urban or collegiate slang. Nevertheless, the kind of *colloquial ease* which marks later twentieth-century American poetry should perhaps not be demanded in order to admire what is most distinctive of contemporary Indian English poetry. For one thing, the general Indian esthetic continues to expect poetry to use a special high register of language and feeling, subject and expression, even when it is "modernistic"—that is, very internal and symbolic-imagistic—so that it often comes across initially, especially to outsiders, as "romantic" or even sentimental, rather exaggerated in technique and tone, as is readily apparent in Mahapatra's early work. Notwithstanding this caution, most of the Indian English poetry one sees nowadays has a natural-seeming, everyday poise, from Vikram Seth's joking-poking rhymes[17] and the prosaic-ironic self-and-society castigations of other young or youngish poets like Menka Shivdasani,[18] Tara Patel,[19] or Saleem Peeradina,[20] to the perhaps more complex work of the older generation of poets like Eunice de Souza[21] and the others mentioned above.

Similarly, the common Western critics' demand that each poet demonstrate an *individual* voice may also need to be modified for the Indian writer and reader, in part because, again, their society generally does not value or even define individuality in the West European way. It is difficult to overemphasize the pressure of tradition in Indian culture, so much so that a poet is frequently enjoyed more for imitating a recognizable style or conventional thought than for the wit, imagination, and/or originality of the writing. However, just because "anxiety of influence" has rarely troubled these writers in a Western way, critics should not therefore helplessly approve the crudely derivative pastiches regularly heard in second-rate Indian English poetry, echoing T. S. Eliot, Yeats, Stevens, Frost, or any other supposedly authoritative poet from Shakespeare and Milton to Alien Ginsberg, or even, quite recently, their own countrymen, Jayanta Mahapatra and Nissim Ezekiel!

Rather than a personal voice, in reading an Indian English poem one may dimly sense and want to understand better a whole literary world lying behind it, or at least it may seem that some special poetic style or other is being used, but not necessarily one recognized outside India. Yet the requisite knowledge—for example, of how India's many, relatively conservative regional-language literary traditions may now be operating in contemporary poetry—cannot readily be assumed among either poets or critics, whether using Indian English or not. The consequence is, as so astute a foreign observer as Syd. C. Harrex has noted, that readers—I would emphasize whether Indian or foreign—may "detect a special Indian nuance when it isn't there or miss one when it is."[22] For example, though the figure appears repeatedly in two long poems by Jayanta Mahapatra, I have found no Indian critic able to identify "the golden deer," which, among other, more narrowly localized possibilities, may draw on Buddhist doctrine (the fire sermon was delivered in a deer park) or, with quite different and ambiguous meanings, on the Hindu epic, the *Ramayana,* where Sita is seduced from her charmed protective circle by golden deer.

Most foreign critics and many foreign-trained Indian ones tend to ignore these issues concerning the cultural context of contemporary Indian English poetry and to impose or assume Western literary values irrelevant to the authorship or the predominant readership of this body of work. Using an internationally based medium that is more flexible, one that has a developed modern tradition and is more widely read (in India as well as abroad) than poetry in their mother tongue, Indian English poets have composed a diverse body of work, but is the effectiveness of any piece to be determined only by so-called international terms? Harrex's caution cannot be ignored, as, for example, when one reads the Browningesque dramatic poems of Keki Daruwalla and wonders whether his many hawk poems and motifs should be related to Hopkins's "Windhover," Ted Hughes's "Hawks Roosting," or (and?) the Mughal and later maharajas' traditional sport of falconry. Furthermore, the overwhelming majority of Indian English poetry readers reside, after all, in India, not abroad; even though scattered throughout the many multicultural states, they do not represent demographically the nation as a whole, and certainly do not constitute a single idealized interpretive community with a unified esthetic perspective. The highly specialized Indian audience for Indian English poetry, for the most part, is academically but narrowly trained in the language and related literatures and comes from a politically dominating cultural elite that is also undeniably isolated socially, complacently overprivileged, and willing to exploit

its neocolonialist power for consumerist values not sharable with eighty percent of the people, the poverty-impacted agricultural majority living in small villages.

Individual members of that audience may have adopted or are sympathetic with an ethos that transcends their class psychology, bias, and interests, but few can be expected to live as self-sacrificing social reformers. India, as a so-called "developing nation," is nevertheless straining intermittently and erratically toward economic and democratic institutions that give voice and power to all sections of society; the most visible struggles are those to accommodate oppressed minorities—women, Muslims, Sikhs, tribals, and outcastes—within an overwhelmingly caste-Hindu, male-dominated culture. By developing its capacities for cultural criticism, Indian literature, even poetry, which fortunately is still commonly revered in the general culture, must serve a primarily social, even political function. It is and must be more than an entertaining diversion or interesting social and personal revelations, must go beyond conserving cultural values, building a national consciousness or offering visionary alternatives, for a crucially important function is to provide concrete cultural critiques for a society undergoing rapid changes that threaten both its diversity and its unity.

Still, an esthetic emphasizing social responsibility runs exactly counter to the long-standing, widely revered Indian literary and critical tradition, which emphasizes, in conventional Hindu religious terms, the transcendental quality of poetry, its capacity to express or induce the nine classically defined esthetic emotions and, at its best, to achieve a supreme mystical state of bliss, overarching and generally ignoring everyday concerns. Thus, despite general parallels, the estheticism of most twentieth-century Western critical perspectives—current theory and varieties of deconstruction, structuralism, mythicism, and New Criticism, but not the Marxian, the feminist, the ethnocentrist, and the neohistoricist—accords only very slightly with the mainstream classical Indian critical tradition and not at all with the contemporary cultural and social situation. A recent revivalist bent among Indian critics, allied, however reluctantly, with the current Hindu nationalist fanaticism, has also sought principled sustenance in regional literary traditions. Yet current research reveals that critical theories have for centuries been largely absent from regional literatures, even classical Sanskritic roots being forgotten or ignored there.[23] "Nativism," the accepted term for a regionally based cultural bias that might in theory seem critically promising, thus has in fact little to build upon beyond recent, admittedly splintered and diminished literary practice in the regional languages, or else rather irrelevant ancient Sanskritic or Western modernist/postmodern criticism.

In this critically disintegrated and democratically threatened cultural context, what is required, it seems, is a flexible and inclusive perspective, particularly with regard to potentially powerful, nationally privileged Indian English literary products. Even though contemporary poetry may appear a minor cultural genre in the West, where television and other print media eclipse its ancient oral influence, in India, still a largely nonliterate, perhaps soon a postliterate, civilization, poetry still has an authoritative place as an instrument of cultural expression. Even though that status does not regularly accrue to Indian English poetry by virtue of its demographically limited readership and the preponderantly elitist, alienated attitudes of its practitioners, still something of the traditional reverential attitude remains for these recent linguistic products composed in the single tongue learned and practiced throughout the socially dominating classes of the nation. It behooves those concerned about this nation, struggling toward democratic liberalism and soon to be the most populous country on earth, to attend to the poetry of its ruling elite insofar as it reveals a variety of perspectives on the current and future course of Indian society.

■ ■ ■

Having already listed a wide selection of the presently most valued Indian English poets, this survey can best demonstrate their interest and worth by focusing finally on three or four preeminent practitioners. Judging only from the attention they have received in their own country and abroad, one would immediately cite Nissim Ezekiel and Jayanta Mahapatra, adding possibly Professor P. Lal, an effective publicist, publisher, and translator (he would say "transcreator") of epic classics. However, to most contemporary tastes, Lal is a rather sentimental poet whose imagery and themes are exceedingly conservative, expressing, it may be said in his defense, the highly emotional esthetic of most Indian readers.[24] A heroic speech the poet himself selected from his 1975 long poem, *The Man of Dharma & the Rasa of Silence,* should suffice as illustration of a mode of Indian English writing widely practiced but not highly valued by the major Indian anthologists or journal editors.

"Born of the sun, my radiant child,
Wrapped in yoga in the sun-tinted
Shades of the cowdust hour near Kuruksetra,
Armour-skinned son, dearest fruit of the
Pleasures of virginal concupiscence,
I am your mother, look at me.
Fruit of the spear of the sun,

Do not forsake me now, my eldest son."
(From "Karna and Kunti," *Collected Poems,* 161)

In the place of Professor Lal, one could set a more interesting, tough-minded poet of Indian life like Keki Daruwalla, mentioned before, or a more sophisticated, somewhat alienated one like A. K. Ramanujan. The latter spent most of his adult life as a professor of South Asian languages and civilizations at the University of Chicago and was discovered and given a "genius grant" by the MacArthur Foundation in 1983; so his work has, no doubt, benefited greatly from the affluent resources of our English-dominant culture. Like many Indian expatriates, throughout his career he periodically returned to his home base in the Mysore area, and in 1976 he was awarded the Padma Shri by the government of India for his dedicated and delicate translations and folklore studies. Though his family language (and alphabet) was Tamil—and he has translated both ancient and medieval sacred (Vaisnavite) and erotic classics from that left-branching, agglutinative, punctuationless language—the regional language of his home in Mysore (Karnataka State) is Kannada. And though Kannada is also a pre-Sanskritic Dravidian tongue with its own alphabet, he has also translated poetry from this language copiously, most notably the tenth-to-twelfth-century Kannada free-verse *vacanas* to the god Siva.[25] Two examples, predictably, do not suggest the wide range of feelings and situations that these fine translations recapture, the first playing with Vaisnavite metaphysics, the second with erotic strangenesses, in order to revel in worldly plenitude.

It's true
even I am you
even the unbearable hell
    of this world
    is you:
    this being so
        what's the difference?
One may go to paradise
    and reach perfect joy
or go the other way
    and fall into hell
yet I being I
    even when I remember
    I am you
I still fear hell:
lord in perpetual paradise
let me be at your feet.
("Waxing and Waning," 3)[26]

Good woman,
your waist is higher

than your head, your face a stork,
plucked and skinned, with a dagger for a beak,
                    listen to me.
If I take you in the front, your hump
juts into my chest; if from the back
it'll tickle me in odd places.
                              So I'll not
even try it. But come close anyway and let's touch
side to side.

    Chi, you're wicked. Get lost! You half-man!
As creepers hang on only to the crook of a tree
there are men who would love to hold this hunch
of a body close, though nothing fits. Yet, you lecher,
you ask for us sideways. What's so wrong
with us, you ball, you bush of a man?
Is a gentle hunchback type far worse than a cake
of black beans?
(From "The Hunchback and the Dwarf: A Dialogue," st. 5–6)[27]

Ramanujan's own poems deal with negatings, often
of previous selves: e.g., "Highway Stripper," "Moulting,"
or "Chicago Zen," which ends, "and watch / for the last
/ step that's never there." Those lines and their lineation
suggest Ramanujan's urbane wit that marks these and
other poems from *Second Sight* (1986), while earlier
poems from *The Striders* and *Relations* achieve their
more intense effects with precise imagery, compound
verbal ambiguities, and especially with richly nostalgic
memories of family life and lore in India, which by no
means should be interpreted as uncritical of Hindu traditions and attitudes.

And who can say I do not bear,
as I do his name, the spirit

of Great Grandfather, that still man,
untimely witness, timeless eye,

perpetual outsider,
watching as only husbands will

a suspense of nets vibrate
under wife and enemy

with every move of hand or thigh:
watching, watching, like some

spider-lover a pair
of his Borneo specimens mate

in murder, make love with hate,
or simply stalk a local fly.
(End of "The Hindoo: He Doesn't Hurt a Fly or a Spider
Either")[28]

Tearing away from these addictive poems, we can
recognize the greater historical importance of a more
overtly moralistic poet, Nissim Ezekiel, a Bene Israel
Jew educated with Muslims, Parsis, Christians, and Hin-

dus in Bombay English-medium schools and now unable adequately to translate, much less compose, poems
in the Marathi language that they all spoke and speak
at home. After polishing his poetic craft in England for
several years, Ezekiel returned to Bombay in the early
1950s, where he wrote:

The Indian landscape sears my eyes.
I have become part of it
To be observed by foreigners.
They say that I am singular.
Their letters overstate the case.

I have made my commitments now.
This is one: to stay where I am,
As others choose to give themselves
In some remote and backward place.
My backward place is where I am.
(Conclusion of "Background Casually")

Though stressing for semantic differentiation—the basis
for English metricality—is quite alien to Indian languages, including, often confusingly, much Indian English, Ezekiel's incisive lines and thinking for two decades were generally, indeed rather abstractly, expressed
within exceedingly strict metrical limits. This practice,
however, offered a model of restraint and craftsmanship, an even-tempered poise of moral seriousness and
good-humored sanity, for at least a generation of younger Bombay writers, who might otherwise have fallen
into the exaggerations of attitude, feeling, and technique which commonly mar inept Indian English poetry. In a continuing line of love poems Ezekiel rarely, as
Vilas Sarang has remarked, achieves insightful details,
intense emotion, or unclichéd thought, but many
scenes of love and lust can be devastatingly effective if
placed among his several kinds of social satire: "She
gave me / six good reasons / for saying No, / and then
/ for no reason at all / dropped all her reasons / with her
clothes" ("Passion Poems, IV: On Giving Reasons"). Evidently Ezekiel looks to sexual encounters to measure
the limits of the liberal rationalism he reveres, just as
he has written a number of hymns and prayers, again
by no means always mocking.

I don't mind singing, though,
thanksgiving and all that.
It saves time to worship
One [rather] than many.

To tempt God and seek to
prove him is sheer folly.
If that's what our fathers
did, I'm sorry for them.
I suspect they merely voiced
a doubt or two, which our

Psalmist exaggerates, as usual.
(Second half of "Latter Day Psalms, VII")

From poetry of statement like Ezekiel's—reprised most closely by Manohar Shetty[29]—we can shift radically to the darkly evocative meditative poetry of Jayanta Mahapatra. Coming to write Indian English poems only at age forty, Mahapatra has moved from the purposely obscure romantic mode of *Swayamvara* and *Close the Sky, Ten by Ten* (both 1970) through a long phase where ambiguously complex syntax, surreally linked imagery, and a fairly simple diction wove interior landscapes of weary confusion and unfocused yearning, sometimes associated with an idealized feminine presence (or, more probably, absence) that approaches ghostly or ghastly spirituality. Along the way, though a heritage Christian, he has caught burning moments and provocative images of the Hindu manners, thought, and ritual that flourish and decay around him. An oft-quoted example is unaccountably entitled "Taste for Tomorrow":

At Puri, the crows.
The one wide street
lolls out like a giant tongue.

Five faceless lepers move aside
as a priest passes by.

And at the street's end
the crowds thronging the temple door:

a huge holy flower
swaying in the wind of great reasons.

Less visualizable scenes of thoughtful combat among evanescent feelings dominate his later work, with confusing evocations as in "Dust," which concludes:

This dust is the good eye which teaches its visions:
the time when there's nobody home when you
    return,
and museums are unable to see further than
    tomorrow,
when the poor will float at the edges of the spirited
    sea—
as awakening outside my own life
I watch the dust go down on its knees to clean my
    wasted house,
to let me see where the light had wandered,
among ashes, desk tops and sad trouser pockets,
in the shadows on my son's lips and brow, inside the
    nets
which had never made a catch, and back to darkness
where the dust does not show those things
that fumble still among our forgotten desires.

Despite characteristic questionings, "Harvest" seems less uncertain of itself, beginning: "What does my world

say? / I follow the substance of my shadow / in the procession of light on the leaves; / and I watch myself, standing in shadow, / afraid to step out of it. / But then the sun comes down on me. // And I sit all alone, waiting / for my joys to come back. / Ah, the monarchy of the morning lily, / its eye narrow with love!" In especially the later poems from *A Whiteness of Bone* (1992) a more direct, confident, and economical voice rises from the usually oppressive, perhaps neurotically self-effacing, self-pitying, self-destructive situations, winning through lately to a new clarity and consequent strength without compromising the bleak vision. Various levels of social relevance are distinguishable as the poems work to become less obsessively self-absorbed, as assuredly in "Shadows," which needs to be seen whole.

Ash-white mists of mornings
will soon turn dark against the heat.
Peace. The earth-odour is a burden
which one cannot lay down
because there is no one to pick it up again.
This longing for darkness,
resenting its need that holds,
like a frightened hare
seeking the refuge of the woods.
Yet the beating of the heart
makes one impatient, one becomes
a little child who is hurt not only by a word,
but even by a short pause of indecision.
Shadows will soon reach over
and stroke the skin under the eyes.
And opportunities are hampered by the hour,
by fate. Warm dust rises. Even in sleep
to recognize defeat, to let the arms
do their useless tasks they have been doing,
to refuse to lie to one's heart and call it peace.
(From *A Whiteness of Bone*, 14)

In that last line Mahapatra encapsulates perhaps the core motivation for his often rambling, complaining meditations. For comparison, Ezekiel decides, "All I want now / is the recognition of dilemma / and the quickest means of resolving it / within my limits" ("Transparently," *CP*, 150). Mahapatra too goes on experiencing pain, failure, futility, but resists resolution, asks rhetorically, "Which is the wisdom I could use?" ("A Death," *Whiteness*, 18), and draws out his poems, moods, moments, not seeking meaning or reason or light.

Just another morning,
and my neighbor's wave of greeting
is a gift, entering
my body without reason or belief.

. . . .

Love: let me not try to defend myself.
If this love of mine is light, a grace,
let it be unimportant and uninteresting
to inspire me through the long way
into nowhere, to tell them I am *here*.
(Ending of "Light," *Whiteness*, 20)

Like Ramanujan, Meena Alexander (b. 1951 in Al-
lahabad) has spent most of her adult life outside her native India, which she has visited annually since adolescence. For the past dozen years she has lived in New
York City, where she is now a professor of English literature (with a Ph.D. at twenty-one from Nottingham) in
the City University graduate-studies program, occasionally teaching creative-writing classes. Unlike Mahapatra,
therefore, she has enjoyed the many advantages of intensive and extensive experiences with English as the
primary language around her and of advanced studies
in the Amero-British poetic tradition, at least from
Wordsworth to the present. However, among fellow Indian English poets, it is Mahapatra whom she recognizes as a major influence in her work, and she has written sensitively about his poetry, including poems to him
and his wife. Unlike Ezekiel or Dom Moraes or Ramanujan and so many others wrestling with and absorbing the influences of Eliot, Yeats, Pound, Auden,
Empson, and unlike Daruwalla, who, raised as the son
of an English teacher, now contentedly harkens to still
earlier British voices (and perhaps to Theodore
Roethke), Mahapatra, taking cues, no doubt, wherever
he could find them in his native Oriyan tradition, now,
late in his career, seems to have incorporated into his
intensely romantic outlook the cooler fruits of contemporary Amero-British poetic style from Wallace Stevens
(with perhaps something of Yeats) forward. Of a distinctly younger, postmodern generation, Meena Alexander has almost from the start been able to explore the
fertile possibilities for her poetry that are indicated not
only by writers of international repute but also by her
most successful Indian English precursors as well as by
sophisticated contemporary criticism of postcolonialist
writing, some of which she has written herself. Besides
Mahapatra, Ezekiel early encouraged her, P. Lal first
published her, and, no doubt, as a fellow expatriate in
American academe, A. K. Ramanujan offered her a pattern, though he exploits his Hindu family heritage while
she almost ignores her Syrian Christian roots. Familial
and village mythologies similar to Ramanujan's underlie
Alexander's two major poetic achievements: *The Storm*
and *Night-Scene, the Garden,* poems evoking respectively
the legend-laden life at her paternal and her maternal
grandparents' ancestral homes in south-central Kerala.

It is almost as if in a meditation

in a time of war
we turned to pluck
the strings of dusty lutes,
the fallen harp surrendered its grace
to our impenitent fingers,
and the ancestral houses of our dead
and these ceremonial motions of the damned
healed us of ourselves,
all exile ended, the faces
in lamplight rejoicing.
(End of IV, "Returning Home," section 21, from *Storm*)

Beginning inevitably with modernistically obscure
romantic self-imaginings, Alexander's manner has remained evocative, elusive, evolving, but a central principle in her work is the gift of place. As one of the most
literally unhoused of postcolonial writers—or, one
might say, multiply displaced and replaced—Alexander
reveals throughout her mature work a repeated fixation
on not only her two ancestral homes in Kerala but all
manner of other spaces wherein human relationships
can occur. Still, the gift of potential life within those
spaces—wombs for human interaction, substantial bodies for inwardness, for imaginative consciousness—is
never accepted without hesitation, reservation, for there
seems always a holding back in consequence of feeling,
and sometimes being, exiled from the source of light,
from unqualified love, from limitless life. Some impetus
for her at times breathless, breakneck, frustrating pursuit of perception or insight, even of sheer phenomenological sensation, perhaps derives from Alexander's
heady academic and writing career. It was begun in
French among Arabic speakers, stalked into a nervous
breakdown in a British university, brought to fruition
at age twenty-six or so when, back for a few years teaching in India, she was interviewed as a promising poet
in Mahapatra's literary journal, soon married an American Indologist and returned with him to Minneapolis,
quickly settling in New York City. All along, while creating a bicultural family, she has thrown herself headlong into imaginative creative activity, amassing an impressively varied bibliography, including most recently
a richly complex female immigrant artist's autobiography, *Fault Lines,* for the Feminist Press. In that book one
recognizes how the revelation of intimate personal relationships is resisted not only because potentially distorting and oppressive of an intensely driven self, but
also because they presumably could not express the
hidden spirit seeking its own secret, if much broken,
way.

The first of Alexander's poems ever chosen (by K.
Ayyappa Paniker) for an Indian English anthology, "Sidi
Syed's Architecture," appeared in *House of a Thousand
Doors* (1988) and later in an Indian journal. The six-

teenth-century architect brought to India to build palaces, mosques, and tombs for the great Mughal/Afghani
emperors, Sidi Syed, is projected by Alexander as, like
herself, "a man unhoused / yet architect of himself, / his
genius still smouldering." Of the fifty-two lines, the
opening and close will suggest Alexander's imaginative
power, freedom, and circumstantiality. The poem begins with dissembling simplicity:

I sometimes wonder what he was like
Sidi Syed, a small man
come all the way from Abyssinia,
his skin the colour of earth
before the waters broke loose
from the Sabarmati river.
It was Ahmed's city then, in the year 1500.
Loitering by the river
he watched infants with blackened eyes
swinging in their cradles,
mothers with chapped hands laundering.
He saw skins of cattle and deer
laid out to dry on the sharp rocks;
heard voices in them calling him,
crying out
as if home were nothing
but this terrible hunger
loosed between twin earths,
one underfoot by the river bed,
the other borne in the heart's hole.

> [After becoming a successful architect—one
> guesses also the source for the architectural style
> that culminates in the Taj Mahal—Sidi Syed
> builds his own tomb.]

Was it for him
this starry palm
with vine on vine still tumbling,
a tumult of delight
struck from a stonecutter's hands?
Fit elaboration of a man unhoused
yet architect of himself,
his genius still smouldering?
The mosque was hollow though
like a sungod's tomb;
it tracked his hunger
the madness of stretched skin
still so close
on those noisy river beds.

More than two earths offer their spaces to Meena Alexander's poetic architecture; so, as each opening constitutes a new consciousnesses of being, we can anticipate
from her word-shaping imagination further starry "elab-
orations of a man unhoused."

The following poem is also by Meeng Alexander:

Sweet Alyssum

I.

'I am grateful' she said to me
'for the room a bomb makes when it falls'— she
    said this
sitting straight under a tree
what tree, I have forgotten now.

She said she was your sister.

I listened to her, burying my head in my hands.
She did likewise.

The olive root from your childhood
its colour spent in dreams,
an arrowhead from a bronzed
hillside in Jerusalem
terrible city of the deity
where children pound fists against
rocks coloured like cheap plastic balls,

crimson, phosphorus, ivory
the ballast of desire you discovered so early,
casting its gravity against
the skeletal forms of love we bear within.

'Wen Beitak?' they asked 'Nad Evida?'
'Where is your home?'
        the child battling the fourgated wind
hair blown back, crying into his own eyes
in the schoolyard rough with golden mustard bloom
at the edge of no man's land.

■ ■ ■

In your dream you came to Ellis Island,
to a humpbacked apple tree
        right where the boats stop,
it stoops over, casting its fruit into black water.
The dream doubled up like a pregnancy
you saw yourself a child again,
at the gates of great Jerusalem.

'He has no home now,
you know that, don't you?'
She said turning towards me,
the woman who claims to be your sister
'As for me, I am grateful
for what I have.'

As she moved, digging her heels into rock
I saw the left side of her face
where skin had fused into bone

so deep the burning went

'Maria Nefeli who loves the cloud gatherer'
I whispered
        'or Draupadi born of fire
                surely you are she
or Demeter even, poised at the bramble pit

where love drove her
or Sita clinging to stone

'Look here is flowering mustard he brought me
from Bethlehem
from the old schoolyard filled
with children, before
        it fell.
           Sweet alyssum too.
Take it, please.'

▪ ▪ ▪

Doubtless there will be still other poetries coming more directly from India as well. These too will continue reflecting the eclectic mélange in every Indian English poet of his or her multiple cultural traditions, not merely the Greater and Lesser Hindu ones, so ancient and manifold, nor the other indigenous religious and cultural strains—Muslim, Sikh, Syrian Christian, Buddhist, Parsi with Mughal-Persian, Bene Israeli—but each of these religious heritages variously modified according to whatever the regional-language oral and literary traditions may do with them, together with the many powerful and varied, mostly secular, Western influences, which in turn are secularizing all those older indigenous forces working in their unique and often mysterious ways. Adhering to and adumbrating, re-creating and re-interpreting one another, these rich admixtures of thought and feeling, imaginative perception and mythic vision, will produce in the years ahead a confusing cacophony of voices with the many other Indian literatures in the other indigenous languages. Sorting out and selecting from these will remain a daunting task for concerned readers, especially without the critical construction of an appropriately discontinuous, dissonant critical understanding and multivalent appreciation of contemporary Indian poetries.

John Oliver Perry, Spring 1994

[1] One of the better recent anthologies by a provincially based poet is *Voices: Indian Poetry in English,* collected largely from Orissan sources by a competent poet who has appeared in no other anthology, Niranjan Mohanty. Teaching English at Berhampur University in Orissa, Mohanty had earlier edited an overtly regional anthology, *The Golden Voices: Poets from Orissa Writing in English* (1986), and for almost two decades a biennial journal, *Poetry,* which is also quite uneven in its selections but measurably better than both *Poetry Time* and *Poesie,* issued irregularly from the same university. Another center for Indian English poets, though much of their stale, imitative, trivial production hardly qualifies as verse, has arisen at a provincial university in Amravati; there Professor O. P. Bhatnagar, another poet-editor-academic not highly respected outside his area, has emphasized culturally appropriate, nonelitist standards of clarity, humility, rationality, secularity, and sociopolitical relevance, apparently with little success, as his several mainly

Hindi-belt anthologies, like *Rising Columns: Some Indian Poets in English* (1981), unfortunately indicate. One of the most egregious types of Indian English anthology issues from various world societies of poets, publishing otherwise unprintable writers from the U.S., the U.K., et cetera, to substantiate the pretentious claims of Indian versifiers; examples are *East-West Winds (An International Anthology of Selected Poetry in English),* edited by G. R. Krishna (Mangalore, 1982), and several by Krishna Srinivas, editor of *Poet,* a so-called "international" journal from Madras.

[2] Nissim Ezekiel, *Collected Poems 1952–1988,* New Delhi, Oxford University Press, 1989. Reviewed in *WLT* 64:2, p. 361.

[3] Dom Moraes, *Serendip,* New Delhi, Viking, 1990 (reviewed in *WLT* 65:4, p. 769); see also *Collected Poems 1957–1987,* New Delhi, Penguin, 1987.

[4] Shiv K. Kumar, *Subterfuges,* New Delhi, Oxford University Press, 1976; and *Trapfalls in the Sky,* Madras, Macmillan, 1986. See also the Kumar issue of the *Journal of South Asian Literature,* 25:2 (Summer-Fall 1990).

[5] A. K. Ramanujan, *Selected Poems,* New Delhi, Oxford University Press, 1976; and *Second Sight,* New Delhi, Oxford University Press, 1986 (reviewed in *WLT* 61:2, p. 349).

[6] R. Parthasarathy, *Rough Passage,* New Delhi, Oxford University Press, 1977; also *Ten Twentieth Century Indian Poets,* R. Parthasarathy, ed., New Delhi, Oxford University Press, 1975/76.

[7] Dilip Chitre, *Traveling in a Cage,* Bombay, Clearing House, 1976; and *Says Tuka: Selected Poetry of Tukaram,* New Delhi, Penguin, 1991. Arvind Krishna Mehrotra, *Middle Earth,* New Delhi, Oxford University Press, 1984 (includes selections from two earlier volumes); and *The Absent Traveler: Prakrit Love Poetry from the Gathasaptasati of Satavahana Hala,* New Delhi, Ravi Dayal, 1991. Since A. K. Ramanujan is among the best three or four Indian English poets, his celebrated translations from both Kannada and Tamil classics only diversify his reputation; less intensively, Jayanta Mahapatra has also translated considerable amounts of Oriya poetry, mainly contemporary, and has also lately ventured "into a strongly Oriya literary territory" with poems in his mother tongue.

[8] Meena Alexander, *House of a Thousand Doors,* Washington, D.C., Three Continents, 1988 (reviewed in *WLT* 63:1, p. 163); *The Storm,* New York, Red Dust, 1989; and *Night-Scene, the Garden,* New York, Red Dust, 1992 (reviewed in *WLT* 67:2, p. 444). Agha Shahid Ali, *The Half-Inch Himalayas,* Middletown, Ct., Wesleyan University Press, 1987; and *A Nostalgist's Map of America,* New York, Norton, 1991.

[9] See especially Keki N. Daruwalla, *Crossing of Rivers, and The Keeper of the Dead* (reissued together), New Delhi, Oxford University Press, 1991; in the former book North Indian Hindu experience and narrative predominate.

[10] Man Mohan Singh, *Village Poems,* New Delhi, Arnold-Heinemann, 1982.

[11] Jayanta Mahapatra, *Relationship,* Greenfield Center, N.Y., Greenfield Review, 1980; and Cuttack, Chandrabhaga, 1982. See also other works cited below.

[12] Gieve Patel, *How Do You Withstand, Body?,* Bombay, Clearing House, 1976; and *Mirrored, Mirroring,* New Delhi, Oxford University Press, 1991.

[13] Kamala Das, *Collected Poems,* vol. 1, Trivandrum, privately printed, 1984; Imtiaz Dharker, *Purdah,* New Delhi, Oxford University Press, 1988; and Charmayne D'Souza, *A Spelling Guide to Woman,* Hyderabad, Disha/Orient Longman, 1990.

[14] Jayanta Mahapatra, *Selected Poems,* New Delhi, Oxford University Press, 1987 (drawing from six of nine previous volumes; reviewed in *WLT* 62:2, p. 333); *Dispossessed Nests: The 1984 Poems,* Jaipur, Nirala, 1986 (reviewed in *WLT* 61:3, p. 491); *Temple,* Adelaide, Dangeroo, 1989 (reviewed in *WLT* 64:2, p. 362); and *A Whiteness of Bone,* New Delhi, Viking, 1992 (reviewed in *WLT* 67:2, p. 445).

[15] Arun Kolatkar, *Jejuri,* Bombay, Clearing House, 1976 (reviewed in *WLT* 61:4, p. 680).

[16] Adil Jussawalla, *Missing Person,* Bombay, Clearing House, 1976; Makarand Paranjape, *The Serene Flame* and *Playing the Dark God,* Calcutta, Rupa, 1991 and 1992 (reviewed respectively in *WLT* 65:4, p. 769, and 66:3, p. 588).

[17] Vikram Seth, *The Humble Administrator's Garden,* New Delhi, Oxford University Press, 1987 (London, Carcanet, 1985); and *The Golden Gate,* New Delhi, Oxford University Press, 1986 (New York, Random House, 1986), among others.

[18] Menka Shivdasani, *Nirvana at Ten Rupees,* Bombay, Praxis, 1990 (reviewed in *WLT* 66:3, p. 581).

[19] Tara Patel, *Single Woman,* Calcutta, Rupa, 1991 (reviewed in *WLT* 66:2, p. 404).

[20] Saleem Peeradina, *Group Portrait,* New Delhi, Oxford University Press, 1992 (reviewed in *WLT* 67:2, p. 448); and *First Offence,* Bombay, Newground, 1980.

[21] Eunice de Souza, *Fix,* Bombay, Newground, 1979; and *Woman in Dutch Painting,* Bombay, Praxis, 1988.

[22] Syd. C. Harrex, "Small-Scale Reflections on Indian English-Language Poetry," *Journal of Indian Writing in English* (Gulbarga), 8:1–2 (1980), pp. 137–38 (verb forms adjusted).

[23] See G. N. Devy, *After Amnesia: Tradition and Change in Indian Literary Tradition,* Bombay, Orient Longman, 1992.

[24] P. Lal, *The Collected Poems,* Calcutta, Writers Workshop, 1977; and editor of the influential and fulsome *Modern Indian Poetry in English: An Anthology and a Credo,* Calcutta, Writers Workshop, 1969 and (rev. exp. ed.) 1971.

[25] A. K. Ramanujan, *Speaking of Siva* (Kannada *vacanas*), Baltimore, Penguin, 1973; *Hymns for the Drowning: [Tamil] Poems for Visnu by Nammalvar,* Princeton, N.J., Princeton University Press, 1981; and *Poems of Love and War: From the Eight Anthologies and the Ten Long Poems of Classical Tamil,* New York, Columbia University Press, 1985.

[26] A. K. Ramanujan, tr. & ed., *Hymns for the Drowning,* p. 39; (8.1.9 of Nammalvar's *Tiruvaymoli*).

[27] A. K. Ramanujan, tr. & ed., *Poems of Love and War,* p. 209.

[28] Ramanujan, *Selected Poems,* p. 24.

[29] Manohar Shetty, *A Guarded Space,* Bombay, Newground, 1981; and *Borrowed Time,* Bombay, Praxis, 1988.

New Indian Poetry: The 1990s Perspective

Introduction. The 1980s were certainly the decade for the Modern Indian Novel in English, but the 1990s seem to be, from all worthwhile published evidence, the decade for Modern Indian Poetry in English. Without doubt, Vikram Seth's novel in verse *The Golden Gate* (1986) marked the watershed for the modern movement in Indian poetry. Not only does the book figure on the center-stage of the New Formalist movement in America, but its prodigious global success (followed by an even more overwhelmingly successful novel, *A Suitable Boy* [1993]), has put new Indian poetry on the international map.

The contemporary English-language Indian poetry scene has never been so prolific in its energy and innovation, just as much as it has been in its output (at least as far as the number of excellent volumes that have been published by mainstream publishers are concerned). Added to this, a sizable number of good poetry collections have emerged from reputed small presses. This is true not only for India but also for the broad Indian diaspora: in the USA and Canada, the UK, the Caribbean, Southeast Asia, the South Pacific, and East and South Africa. Corroborating all that, the success of and interest in Indian writing (though so far primarily in fiction), both nationally and internationally, coupled with an ever-increasing audience of book buyers and a newfound special interest of the mainstream media, have contributed to this rather welcome situation. It is especially heartening for the health of poetry, as it has finally spilled out from the garret and graduated to a more widespread and growing audience of readers.

India is the third-largest English-language publishing market in the world after America and the United Kingdom. Therefore it is not unusual that a national interest in indigenous contemporary English writing has been firmly established and is steadily making its presence felt internationally. An important development as regards publishing Indian poetry globally is the establishment of a new publishing house in London, Aark Arts. With publishing associates in Washington, Canberra, Durban, Bombay, and New Delhi, Aark Arts plans to bring out, in its initial stages, half a dozen titles of new Indian poetry over the next two years.

The New Generation. When in 1992 I was commissioned by Peter Forbes, the editor of London's *Poetry Review,* to do an exhaustive piece on the "New Generation" for their special India issue (Spring 1993, 83:1), I scoured and waded through over two hundred volumes of new poetry (as well as journals). In the end I shortlisted about forty collections (by nearly thirty poets), predominantly from India, and a selection by writers from the broad Indian diasporas who had produced good, substantial poetry. In an attempt to present the true pulse of new Indian poetry, I was to a certain extent fairly generous in including a reasonable cross section from an infinitely diverse group, primarily because it was really the first time (certainly in Britain) that a premier poetry journal was devoting an entire issue to Indian poetry.

Looking back with considered retrospection, taking into account the interim two-and-a-half-years, and having rummaged diligently through innumerably more volumes by newer or younger Indian poets who have published since then, I would make certain additions and deletions to that original list. There are poets I would drop (on the basis of their inferior newer work or their absolute dormancy or repetitiveness) and poets I would add who have emerged since or for some technical reason or other were not included in the earlier piece. But as far as some of the larger issues are concerned (as well as specific comments on previously published volumes), I have drawn here upon the observations from my earlier *Poetry Review* essay, especially on aspects which have remained unchanged since then. The poets featured in this essay/review include: Meena Alexander, Bibhu Padhi, Vikram Seth, Rukmini Bhaya Nair, Prabhanjan Mishra, Manohar Shetty, Imtiaz Dharker, Sujata Bhatt, Jeet Thayil, Vijay Nambisan, Ian Iqbal Rashid, Tabish Khair, and Ranjit Hoskote.

Poetry Publishing in India. The Indian mainstream commercial publishers, spurred primarily by the international success of Indian novelists such as Amitav Ghosh, Salman Rushdie, Upamanyu Chatterjee, Shashi Tharoor, Bharati Mukherjee, Firdaus Kanga, and others, enthusiastically entered the arena of creative-writing publishing in a big way—first fiction, and then, in the last few years, poetry. In poetry, Rupa & Co. / Indus HarperCollins certainly led the field in capitalizing on the new literary scene. In 1991, their first year, when they launched the New Poetry series, they published six titles, followed by another half a dozen in 1992 and a similar number the year after. Their emphasis (for the most part) has been on truly young talents rather than middle-aged writers touted as young. Viking Penguin have been slow and tentative in terms of what one expects of a major publisher. They primarily stuck to the established safe bets like Moraes and Seth, except for one two-poet volume (another one forthcoming) and a first book. Orient Longman, under their Disha Books imprint (marketed in the UK as Sangam Books), have yielded three new collections and an anthology. The Oxford University Press (India) list remains conservative, incorporating a couple of older poets a year, though they recently added one new poet to their list. And as mentioned earlier, London's Aark Arts, with their Indian bases in New Delhi and Bombay, will add to the overall contribution significantly.

Among the small presses, Praxis, Konarak, and Seagull need worthy mention. The Writers Workshop in Calcutta continues to spew out sari-wrapped hand-bound volumes with more efficiency than a motorized modern press. One wishes that they concentrated on quality rather than quantity. Of course, there is no denying that P. Lal's press is of historical importance, because he published many of the older and middle-generation poets at a time when no one else was publishing poetry, especially in the 1970s.

Contemporary Poetic Climate, Language, and Style. The most striking features of the new generation of poets are their range of concerns and themes and their use of language. They use English as an Indian as well as a global language, without the "peculiar hang-ups" exhibited by many in the earlier generations, whose work went "under many ludicrous names—Indo-English, India-English, Indo-Anglian, and even Anglo-Indian and Indo-Anglican" (A. K. Mehrotra). Thankfully, the last traces of archaic forms of British English have finally vanished. The new generation of poets are unafraid, motivated, clearsighted, and they use English with a sense of ease. Their language, style, rhythms, and forms are inventive, original, and contemporary.

Even the poetic climate among the younger poets seems to be changing. No longer are the dividing lines between different camps or centers (Delhi, Bombay, Calcutta, Orissa) starkly demarcated or distinct; no longer are the antagonisms or group loyalties so severe. A fairly professional and keen "friends in war" attitude seems to prevail among the younger poets from different cities (or, for that matter, other parts of the world). In my personal experience, the poets of my own generation seem very open, supportive, and interested in one another's work, at the same time possessing an acute sense of vibrant criticism. Even some of the older-generation poets are now rather forthcoming and encouraging and treat the young poets as colleagues in the same trade. This is a marked difference from the earlier attitudes of some of the older writers, who possessed a condescending attitude toward younger practitioners. Many of them then were busy praising and publishing one another—i.e., writers of their own generation—with the result that from the mid-1970s to about the late 1980s, hardly any new work by young poets was allowed to flower. Some who did publish consistently were publishing abroad. For an average young Indian poet, however, the task was an arduous one: first, the general lack of support; then the exorbitant process of sending poems to journals abroad, as there were very few journals or poetry publishing outlets in India and fewer still that were not controlled by the older mafia. Even the anthologies edited by different poets that appeared in the last couple of decades contained the same retinue of poets (more or less), with few if any young poets represented.

Poetry Criticism and Teaching. Contemporary poetry criticism, by and large, has been a weak spot in Indian literature. The material on this subject that has come out, published mainly by poet/editors, has been either self-congratulatory or absolutely servile vis-à-vis the compilers' peers within the mafia. Poetry reviewing is in great danger, for a goodly number of the poetry reviewers operate within the ever-increasing context of "pop journalism." Many of them are general journalists reviewing a film one day, a fashion show the next, a volume of poems the third. Most seem to lack the knowledge of craft and nuances that goes to form a basic poem. Of course, I can think of exceptions, though only very few, like Arvind Krishna Mehrotra, Adil Jussawalla, Sandeep Bhatnagar, and others, who do perform the task with precision and rhythm. At the end, it seems, a poet is usually the best reviewer of poetry, as long as he maintains the poem as the primary text and keeps his personal jealousies and dislikes aside.

The teaching of contemporary poetry is another weakness, both in schools and in the universities. Whereas the teaching of "classic poets" belonging to the "Eng Lit Canon" like Milton, Shakespeare, Spenser, Donne, and Wordsworth is of high caliber (in a strictly academic sense), the actual aspect of craft and prosody is almost always left out. In terms of modern poetry, my experience as an undergraduate at the University of Delhi left me utterly frustrated. T. S. Eliot was as modern as the syllabus got, as if to say that nothing worthwhile had been written in the post-Eliot era.

New Global Interest. It is time to redraw the literary map of India and Indian poetry. Certainly of late there has been an ever-increasing interest in the poetry from the subcontinent. New anthologies have appeared: Kaiser Haq's in America, Vilas Sarang's and Mehrotra's in India; I myself am working on one that will appear in England and elsewhere. More and more special issues (or sections) of magazines and journals are being or have been devoted to Indian poetry: *Wasafiri* and *Poetry Review* in England; *Kunapipi* in Denmark; *Kyk-over-al* in Guyana; *Toronto South Asian Review* and the *Malahat Review* in Canada; *Nimrod, Chicago Review, World Literature Today, International Quarterly,* and *New Letters* in the USA. In addition, I am currently on commission to guest-edit a portfolio of contemporary Indian poetry for the *Paris Review* (New York) and the Spring 1995 issue of *Wasafiri* (London) on "India and Indian Diaspora Writing," just to name a few.

With all this historical background in perspective, let us sample thirteen Indian English-language new-generation poets who have published in recent years.

Meena Alexander (b. 1951). Meena Alexander brings to her work a varied range of landscapes—India, Sudan, England, America—as well as a strong sense of being a woman and the issues of being a minority/black poet in a primarily white American community. Her first book, *Stone Roots,* appeared many years back, in 1980. She has since published a book of criticism, a novel, and a memoir. Her newer poetry is available in the form of two pamphlets, *The Storm* (1989) and, most recently, *Night Scene, the Garden* (1992). These work as companion long poems—the first relating to the tearing down of her father's house (to be replaced by a new one) and the second about her mother's home. These two houses are located in the landscape of her childhood, in Kerala, only twelve miles from each other. "After the First House," the opening poem in *The Storm,* begins with a mix of drama and sadness.

Father's father tore it down
heaped rosewood in pits
as if it were a burial

bore bits of teak
and polished bronze
icons and ancient granary;

the rice grains clung
to each other
soldered in sorrow,

syllables
on grandmother's tongue
as she knelt.

Alexander's poems tend to have a languorous feel about them. She uses the sequence form to build scene after scene, weaving characters with feelings that gradually heighten the further you travel with her. Myth, language, warfare—all collide. "And in the empty hold of air / whispers of children born into this garden" closes *Night Scene.*

Bibhu Padhi (b. 1951). Bibhu Padhi is a poet who uses language with strength and originality. His first book, *Going to the Temple* (1988), reveals his poetic talent amply. In "Indian Evening" he shows how well one can handle local color with subtlety without getting messy or prosaic or deliberately Indian: "Its quiet puts us in touch / with creatures of dust and heat. // The crows fly about the pale sky / with a homely noise, // while the gods float by effortlessly / with the first evening chants. // There is peace here, regardless / of every single, separate pain." His second book, *Lines from a Legend* (1992), and his third, *A Wound Elsewhere* (1992), appearing almost back to back, confirmed his strengths further. Padhi's concerns range from the local Cuttack winter to America, from the peculiarities of a power cut in the summer to a dead sparrow. Some of his best poems are those where he uses sparse couplets, such as "Trees," "Pigeons," "I Hear a Small Voice Speaking," "Footprints," and "The Farther Shore."

One disturbing habit of Padhi's is that of repeating individual poems from previous books in his new ones without actually acknowledging that fact. If they were acknowledged, that would be fine, because then the reader would not feel cheated. Padhi's next book, *Painting the House,* is forthcoming, and one looks forward to more pleasure from his quill. His individual signature, his deft handling of language, and his quiet sensibility place him most certainly among the superior poets in the 1950s group.

Vikram Seth (b. 1952). Vikram Seth is one of the very few contemporary authors who, with every new book, tries something different: travelogue (*From Heaven Lake*), novel in verse (*The Golden Gate*), pure poetry (*Mappings, The Humble Administrator's Garden, All You Who Sleep Tonight*), children's verse (*Beastly Tales*), drama, and, most recently, poetry translation (*Three Chinese Poets*) and a novel in prose (*A Suitable Boy*). His choice of genres, as is evident, spans the whole literary spectrum, and each one with his unique signature and a definite formal necessity. *The Golden Gate* was set in tetrameter sonnet stanzas à la *Eugene Onegin,* the play in alexandrine couplets; and, what is not entirely unbelievable, Seth is contemplating writing his dissertation in economic demography in sestinas.

Since all of Seth's other books have been reviewed widely, I shall discuss the latest in his poetic oeuvre, *Three Chinese Poets* (1992). This volume contains new translations of poets from the period between 701 and 770 in China—Wang Wei, Li Bai, and Du Fu—three Tang Dynasty poets who lived in the period of "great cultural glory interrupted by a disastrous civil war" during the eighth century A.D. This triumvirate of lyric poets, even though they share the same period in history, are very different in their sensibility.

Wang Wei is a poet of introspection and seeks seclusion in the quietude of nature: "Empty hills, no man in sight—/ Just echoes of the voice of men. / In the deep wood reflected light / Shines on the blue-green moss again" ("Deer Park"). The poems of Li Bai (or Li Po in older transliterations), on the other hand, are full of energy and show. His canvas is wide-ranging and grand. His indulgence in epicurean delights invites the vastness of the galaxy; the waterfall at Lu Shan in the poem of that name plunges three thousand feet "As if the sky had dropped the Milky Way." Elsewhere, the poet drinks with the moon as his companion: "A pot of wine among the flowers. / I drink alone, no friend with me.

/ I raise my cup to invite the moon. / He and my shadow and I make three" ("Drinking Alone with the Moon"). Du Fu (or Tu Fu) writes poems that are reflective and sometimes sad, commenting on the Confucian times with "wry self-deprecation." In the changing political climate of the time, he reminisces, "I've heard it said Changan is like a chessboard, where / Failure and grief is all these hundred years have brought. . . . My ancient land and times of peace come to my thoughts" ("An Autumn Meditation"). Seth's translations are fresh, precise, and moving, adding to the worthy list of works by other important translators like Gill Holland, David Hawkes, and Pauline Yu, and of course Jeanne Larsen's *Brocade River Poems* of the Tang Dynasty.

Rukmini Bhaya Nair (b. 1952). Rukmini Bhaya Nair's debut collection *The Hyoid Bone* (1993) brings to light another poet of talent, another poet in whose work the woman's point of view is discussed with authority. Nair also brings to her poetry a background in linguistics, fusing lexical rules and variations in unusual ways. In the poem "Genderole" all this is displayed with great skill: "Considerthefe-malebodyyourmost / Basictextanddontforgetitsslokas // Whatpalmleafmscandoforusitdoes / Therealgapsremainforwomentoclose." There is no flinching as far as her questioning stance is concerned as she challenges: "Sankarayouoldmisogynisttellme / Whatssocontemptibleaboutfleeting / Splendour? / . . . Itmaybebeneathyoutopriseapartthisgimmick / Butrememberthethingawomanchangesbestishersex." Nair's endings are always unpredictable and sometimes quite witty. Another interesting aspect of the poem just quoted is its form, the way the "couplets" are used in the Sanskritic tradition of *slokas,* with the *poornaviram* or "full-stop" marking the end of the two-line stanzas.

In "Moondrop, Javadweep" we see the effectiveness with which Nair paints the fury of an equatorial rainstorm: "Drenching rain, and the blindness / That goes with it, pushed us down. / We went so quickly on our knees, / The long soak of road squelching. // Closest thing to stoning it was—/ Small, stinging pebbles of rain // And then—fist-sized rock-hammers / Loosed wrath of some invisible mob." In spite of her skill with words and patterns, however, she can go overboard with her cleverness. Parenthetic puns like "Wor(l)d," (W)omen," "Convers(at)ion," and "Ma(i)nstream," or forced linguistic and visual gymnastics on the page in "Language Lessons* Related Reading" and "Malviya Nagar—Sissinghurst" actually detract rather than add to her poetry. Used in moderation, such wordplay would be fine, but too much of it comes across as gimmickry. Nair could easily do with less of that, as there is much going for her poems otherwise.

In *The Hyoid Bone* Nair uses mythology, everyday life, travel experiences and her imagination with power. Her poems "God From Bankura," "Maya-Mriga—California," "Flame," "Perchance to Dream," and "Quartet" are among my favorites. She is a poet whose work is exciting, and one looks forward to the new poems in her next collection, currently in progress and to be titled *Gargi's Silence*.

Prabhanjan Mishra (b. 1952). Prabhanjan Mishra's first book, *Vigil* (1993), contains poems that arise predominantly from an Oriyan sensibility, an interest in local folklore and myth, and the poet's experiences as a twentieth-century suburban Bombay dweller. In the rural landscape of Orissa, where "The smell of ripe paddy / churns hungry stomachs," we see the peasant's "sad buttocks / and shrunken breasts / peer through the tattered cloth." In this poem, "Peasants of Orissa," the stark reality is brought into sharp focus in a sad vein: "Only day-dreams sustain their smiles."

The postcolonial response to a colonial past is ironically and effectively explored in a poem such as "The Foreign Tourist": "For you to come and plunder, / rape and massacre / and return centuries later / to applaud the splendid ruins." Quite in contrast, the plight of metropolitan suburbia is explored vividly with an underlying ironic ring: "It is not Bombay / unless one looks / at the postal addresses, / the varicose city growing elsewhere / like a pestilence. // In the east the salt pan bask. / The creek, languid in the north, is a well-fed boa; having swallowed the city's garbage / at the mouth of the belching drains. // At the nearby station / tired trains stop for a drink or smoke. / One hears them grunt and gasp, / the announcer urging them to take to the tracks" ("Suburb").

When Mishra chooses to be lyrical, however, he can be a pure delight. Consider the opening stanza of "Weeds of Hope": "The night is an impenetrable mask, / the sharp shapes of feminine footfalls / cut slices of nostalgia. / Across a quiet pool of waiting / the numb senses crawl / on the bellies of turtles." The jacket blurb of *Vigil* highlights the author's "one-page poems," where he "puts across one basic emotion or feeling in each poem." I tend to think that Mishra is much more complex than that. In fact, in his six-part long poem "Moon Is a Neon Lamp" (not in this book), his real strengths with narrative are displayed, including a rich use of imagery, lyricism, tension, and specificity.

Manohar Shetty (b. 1953). Manohar Shetty's poems in his three books *A Guarded Space* (1981), *Borrowed Time* (1988), and *Domestic Creatures* (1994) use with unusual effect the spatial element that pervades everyday life. Whether in a cramped train—"the lines /

Rustle unchecked through his hands" ("Epitaph")—or looking inward—"I weave myself / a cocoon breathe / the air in the inky / gloom" ("Cocoon")—or opening a lid—a cockroach "tumbles out / Like a family secret; / Scuttles back into darkness" ("Domestic Creatures")—Shetty has full control of the movements of his characters in the areas he has outlined. In the poem "Floorshow, Bombay," executed in tight tercets, the performer feels a sense of a trap's having been laid by the leering eyes of the audience.

Her unpeeled costume is heaped
Like fishscales, and she
No longer glistens, a mermaid.

Smoke-screened sighs escape
From the redly-lit audience when she bends
Crabwise instead, unwinds a ream

Of ribbon from the cleft
Of her sex, the tantalising yards
Cheered like a victory parade.

Away from the vicarious climax
Her suppleness swaddles her waist,
Her facial a pink mash.

The sense of claustrophobia the dancer feels is finely juxtaposed as an antithesis both to the visual energy of her pirouettes and to the movement created by the lines' internal rhymes, as "Her unpeeled costume is heaped . . . ." This poem, like many others in Shetty's books, uses metaphors rather refreshingly.

Even though in his forty years he has only produced three volumes, what he has written is to be savored. The new collection, *Domestic Creatures* (1994), actually contains poems from his first two books that have been thoroughly revised, along with a few new poems.

Imtiaz Dharker (b. 1954). In *Purdah* (1989) Imtiaz Dharker "brings to her poetry a very specific and tightly-wrought Muslim sensibility, one that is further enhanced in strength by her individual point of view, indeed any woman's point of view." Consider the opening lines of "Purdah II": "The call breaks its back / across the tenements. 'Allah-u-Akbar' . . . / Your mind throws black shadows / on marble cooled by centuries of dead. / A familiar script racks the walls. / The pages of the Koran / turn, smooth as old bones / in your prodigal hands." Further on, she says, "They have all been sold and bought, / the girls I knew / unwilling virgins who had been taught, / especially in this strangers' land, to bind / their brightness tightly round, / whatever they might wear, / in the purdah of the mind. // They veiled their eyes / with heavy lids. / They hid their breasts, / but not the fullness of their lips." The quiet juxtposition of passion and protest eventually strikes a social note of tension, one that is couched in the reserve energies of an uncoiled spring. Added to this sensibility is an innate feel for the visual media, especially the fine arts. Many of Dharker's poems—"Living Spaces," "Outline," "No-man's Land," "Image"—contain an inner force that is carefully etched, a sharp-line quality of sketches derivative from her own work as an artist.

Dharker's poetry arises out of both the peculiarity and the particularity of living in a coupled exile— residing both inside and outside a culture, within both the Islamic and the Hindu tradition, and eventually resting as much in the traditional as in the modern. The short poem "Exile" exemplifies much of this: "A parrot knifes / through the sky's bright skin, / a sting of green. / It takes so little / to make the mind bleed / into another country, // a past that you agreed / to leave behind." Dharker's second collection of poems, *Postcards from God,* is due this year.

Sujata Bhatt (b. 1956). Sujata Bhatt is by far one of the best of the 1950s poets. She uses free verse with delicacy, poise, and effect. Her lines are tight, her metaphors unusual, and her range of themes wide. In her first book, *Brunizem* (1988), the continents where she has lived—Asia, Europe, and North America—are used as her poetic landscapes. In "Udaylee" she explores with haunting sentiment the state of menstruating women, who are deemed untouchable during that period according to the beliefs and practices in the Gujarati community of her childhood: "Only paper and wood are safe / from a menstruating woman's touch. / So they built this room / for us, next to the cowshed." Further, she describes, "This aching is my blood flowing against, / rushing something— / knotted clumps of blood, / so I remember fistfuls of torn seaweed / rising with the foam, rising."

Bhatt's mother tongue, Gujarati, figures prominently in her poems in both of her books. In her second collection, *Monkey Shadows* (1991), the protagonist in the poem "Devibhen Pathak" says at different points in the poem, "(Chaal, chaal! Sapat Payhri lay!) Let's go! Put on your slippers," then later, "(aray bhen, tamnay khabar nathi . . . ?) Oh bhen, don't you know . . . ?" Bhatt goes one step further by using the actual Devnagari Gujarati script on the page. Though it may appeal visually to some readers, I tend to think it distracts and can even appear gimmicky if used too often. Bhatt is an accomplished poet, however, using her multicultural background to its fullest effect: her growing up in America, her Indian family background, her German marriage. Her next collection, *A Stinking Rose,* is expected to appear in England later this year.

Jeet Thayil (b. 1959). Jeet Thayil occupies half the space in the two-poet volume *Gemini* (1992), the first attempt by Viking Penguin India to publish young poetry. His work is mostly urban, where unusual angles of sex prevail, and he likes using rhymes. Take the poem "Oneroid," for instance:

This woman, her milk is black
she feeds me lying back.
Strange countries stop her in-betweens
lazy with crime, softnesses, sin.

Her phallus is a Chinese pipe,
I suck upon it hollow-cheeked,
eunuched in the lamplit dark
as she sputters and spits and shrieks.

She fills me up with moving space.
I lie still and I'm gone
on nodding, neon, perfect dreams.
I pine for places never seen.

In "India Mother" we see delightful irreverence couched in innocence, as "Her hands round out your anus, a hand / wets you there and powders you, hands / busy themselves with your sex." This volume only serves as an introduction, and one looks forward to Thayil's forthcoming first full-length collection, *Apocalypse.*

Vijay Nambisan (b. 1963). Vijay Nambisan occupies the second half of *Gemini* (1992), sharing the volume with Thayil. His poems can appear soft-hearted at first glance, but he has a keen sense of sarcasm, wit, and humor, qualities that are lacking in most of the younger poets: "When my grandfather grew to be an old man, / he was a little mad: / his hair turned black again / and his voice held its own, and his eyes / asked incessantly for answer, an answer" ("Poetic Licence"). His grandfather, family, friends, and his own people appear frequently in his poems, as do the smells of alcohol, the despair of loneliness, rejection and loss. Nambisan's strength lies in his predominantly unsentimental tackling of such themes. The first stanza of "Holy, Holy" illustrates this: "The rain threatens this ordinary day / With magic. Things that grow manifest, / Plainly, the unnatural: more sure / And permanent is the unwalked way, / Lifeless air, stone unencumbered / With feelings; not obsessed, therefore pure." This volume only provides a glimpse of what is to follow. If the signs Nambisan shows are anything to go by, then I am excited about what his future poems might hold.

Ian Iqbal Rashid (b. 1964). Ian Iqbal Rashid's first collection, *Black Market White Boyfriends and Other Acts of Elision* (1991), essentially wrestles with a variety of struggles: the struggle of growing up in different cultures, the struggle of language and identity, and the struggle of the homosexual world. The book opens with startling candor with "An/other Country," wherein the poet and his white lover are watching "The Jewel in the Crown" on television. The narrative onscreen is cleverly interwoven with the suggested narrative of his own life: "Now I watch you watch Sergeant Merrick watch poor Hari Kumar. / And follow as the white man's desire is twisted, / manipulated into a beating." Further, the poet is willing to be the submissive black man mirroring what happens onscreen: "My beauty is branded into the colour of my skin, / my strands of hair thick as snakes, / damp with the lushness of all the tropics, / My humble penis cheated by the imperial wealth of yours. / Hari's corporal punishment, mine corporeal: / Yet this is also part of my desire."

The element of sexuality is seeping in abundance, oozing out of most of the poems. In "Civilities" we see the poet's own experience of racism and gay rape: "policeman on me says paki / bare hand on billy stick, / gloved hand pulling at my cock." In "A Redefinition" the poet lies on the "vast rumpled ocean" which is his lover's bed, "completely naked but for [his] skin / which is also a sheath. . . . It gleams nut-brown or bronze or cocoa / or such other magazine words." In "Bewitched, Bothered and Bewildered" he says, "I will allow you again, come in, come / inside, further and further / until you are in," but all this is often couched with a muted air of serious questioning, issues that are often difficult to confront directly. Sometimes, however, Rashid's syntax appears awkward, line breaks seem random, and words tend to ramble. Whether it is his enthusiasm about the content of his poems rather than their form will be apparent in his future books.

Rashid's strengths lie in the cinematic quality of his verse as well as in his use of dialogue in poetry. His newer poems, as evidenced in journals, show considerable maturity and growth. A chapbook, *Song of Sabu,* and his second collection, *The Heat Yesterday,* will be published later this year.

Tabish Khair (b. 1966). Tabish Khair brings a reporter's eye to his poems. In his first book, *My World* (1991), "My India Diary" presents us with a series of snapshots of scenes he has observed and recorded in plain, simple, fragment phrases.

> II. the stifling heat
>   of too many men of too little space
>
>   hunched houses on both sides brawling boys
>   the anger of being bricked in
>
> IV. puja procession
>   clay god carried to the ghats
>   dancing in the streets
>   happiness like a summer cloud

today
man will triumph over gods.

Many of these vignettes (I suppose one could call them phrase-poems) draw upon minute and ordinary details in everyday life and are used as comments on larger issues in society. Sometimes Khair achieves this with a haunting effect, as in "Second-hand Books," where "There is something sad about second-hand books: / Their creased covers have seen a little too much, / Their yellow pages promise yet another story. // If you shake them lightly or shuffle the pages, / Something is sure to fall out—a piece of paper, / A letter, a receipt, an unused ticket; // Something that seems to hint at a world you cannot enter." There is always a peculiar kind of poignancy in his poems—sometimes wise, sometimes naïve, sometimes fatalistic, but always moving.

In Khair's second book, *A Reporter's Diary* (1993), he takes some of the minute observations further. Many of his poems are personal ("To Gyanendra," "For Smriti"), others contain experience of his travels ("An Peels Onions in Europe," "At Theresienstadt"), and there are those that explore aspects of fear while experimenting with the sonnet form. His language has developed more, and we see him tackling certain harder issues such as death ("Nanijan's Cupboard," "When Someone Dies," "Death in a Muddy Pond," "Shraddhanjali") and the futility of language itself ("Preface").

Ranjit Hoskote (b. 1969). As far as first books go, I would certainly rate Ranjit Hoskote's *Zones of Assault* (1991) among the most promising ones. He uses poetic diction with effective accuracy, images with clarity, and metaphors with originality. In his elegy "Two Women in Midsummer" he portrays grief juxtaposed with a scene of calm: "Two women in midsummer / Sharing their loss / In traditional white. // Walls, their bricks baked brown, / Relieved now and then / By pictures fading into cool green remembrances." The city of Bombay is presented with postindustrial venom and futility in many of his poems. In "Reclamation" we read: "The land is a wolf's grey paw reaching out to grab / Bay and breakwater. It grips hurt headlands / above seabite and claws out / The grasping promontories of reclamation." Further in the same poem we see "drills drone and shop-basements begin / To be ploughed. / The crane vanguards the offensive, advancing / Boom by beam from the bare angle of the road. / Its herald the jet blast of asphalt and fuel / Chokes sea-tush, grass, breath."

Hoskote's themes range widely, from political violence to Renaissance art, to figures such as Safdar Hashmi and Hannibal, and portrays landscapes as different as Kashmir and Hardwar. Sometimes Hoskote can become extremely convoluted and trip over his own syntax and cleverness, but that seems somewhat acceptable, considering there are many good poems here.

Conclusion. In addition to the poets mentioned above, there are others who have been published in magazines and anthologies but have not yet brought out their first collections: C. P. Surendran, Maya Chowdhry, Taj Masud, Sanjeev Richhariya, Rajneesh Dham—promising names who will vie for space in the future. Then there are others who have published volumes to their credit—Melanie Silgardo, Debjani Chatterjee, Suma Josson, Menka Shivdasani—and who could have just as easily been featured in this piece. If the poets discussed in this essay represent the vibrant generation of new Indian poets, then the future of modern English-language poetry in India is certainly in mature hands, a force to reckon with in the wider arena of contemporary world poetry.

Sudeep Sen, Spring 1994

PAKISTAN

Poetry, Pakistani Idiom in English, and the Groupies

My fascination with myths is akin more to Edith Hamilton's than to Bulfinch's; and like Gilbert Murray and Humphrey Kitto, I enjoy exploring the artistic and ideational continuum between the myth and its sociopsychological antecedents. I am also painfully aware of what I lack: Lawrence Durrell's devotion to reliving the myth beyond its natural time. Here I shall be partly exploring and partly commenting on the art-myths and the presupposed as well as resultant sociolinguistic configurations as given in my title.

No doubt, Pakistanis have produced a considerable quantity of poetry in English which is of a high standard. It can be said safely that in general the South Asian epic tradition and other metaphysical poetics joined to the facile romanticism learned in English by nineteenth-century South Asian English writers combined to make them excessively imitative of both the main traditions without the individual excellences of either, and made them at best the experimental go-betweens or "pioneers," as we are prone to call them. Much of that kind of writing lacked the precision, the conciseness, and the enhanced subjectivity of the ghazal. The present-day work of Pakistani poets, as of the writers in other genres in English, finds its beginnings in the 1930s in the modern and witty, if austere, compositions of Shahid Suhrawardy. His *Essays in Verse,*[1] drawing on the fine precision of Muslim art and often an English neoclassical taste, represents a high-water

mark of South Asian poetry in the first half of the twentieth century. Like many writers in English as well as in other languages of the subcontinent, Suhrawardy moved to Pakistan after its founding and eventually settled in Karachi as a Pakistani writer of poetry, art criticism, and general prose. He has had his keen followers, even if such an acknowledgment is made through critical evasions supplanted by poetic echoes.[2] Indeed, poetry since 1947 has achieved its distinctive voice: modern, at times modernist, but contemporary, relevant, and genuinely of the place, a voice that carries both the responsibility and the authority of an ancient civilization recomposed part by part in its newer settings.

If some of the best English poetry today is being written in Pakistan, it is not by virtue of adherence to any particular brand of poetry or any given method which is recognizably outstanding; rather, it is due to the fact of the diversity, the richness, and the spare fullness of its practice here and there that we come to appreciate its quality, its range, and its depth as a genre. However, it was not always seen like this. The need of a Pakistani idiom in the English poetry written in Pakistan was a substantial topic of literary discussion in the 1960s in such cities as Lahore, Karachi, Dhaka, Chittagong, Rajshahi, and Peshawar.[3] The focus narrowed relatively in the 1970s, and proponents such as Ahmed Ali, Shahid Hosain, Syed Ali Ashraf, Syed Sajjad Husain, Taufiq Rafat, and others saw historical forces transform the cultural continuum that was to be built in Pakistani English. The post–1971 situation in Pakistan (without the former East Pakistan) changed the priorities of literary discussion in Pakistani literary societies, but such discussion was always ancillary to actual literary practice anyway; for a Pakistani English idiom, however limited its registers and social range, did exist in these parts of South Asia even before it was proffered somewhat "officially" and earnestly in the 1960s. What remains to be answered critically is: to what extent did the interested poets achieve their objective? Also, what techniques did they employ to "get there"? Indeed, it is my observation that there has been more sloganizing in this regard than actual probing. When I queried a recent writer on the subject as to what constitutes a "Pakistani idiom in English" besides the local-colorist techniques and atonal translation from other Pakistani languages, the answer came in the form of silence, which convinced me that I had asked a silly question.[4] Another relevant inquiry would be to see if "Pakistani idiom in English" was not equally well or better achieved in work originating from quarters where it has been least talked about.

It may be noted that the best English verse by Pakistani poets in Pakistan and abroad was being written in the 1970s, when already the "talk" about "Pakistani idiom" was dying down. Poets whose work has been established in both literature and in the criticism about it are mainly those anthologized in my book *Pakistani Literature: The Contemporary English Writers*.[5] I would particularly cite Taufiq Rafat's and Daud Kamal's work of the period 1970–85, Shahid Hosain's work of the 1960s and the 1970s, Ahmed Ali's and G. Allana's poetry of several decades which will require elaborate periodization, and Zulfikar Ghose's work published during 1964–84. Kaleem Omar was the most prolific though variable of poets during the 1970s. Then and during the early 1980s he produced work of considerable quality and gusto. Maki Kureishi, also a fine poet, wrote during the 1970s and the early 1980s. Her work, like that of Kaleem Omar, has been anthologized, though neither has yet published a book. Taufiq Rafat has published a collection of his own, and Daud Kamal published two before his death in 1987,[6] whereas both Ahmed Ali and G. Allana have several volumes each to their names.[7] Unlike Ahmed Ali, or G. Allana until he died, however, both Kureishi and Omar, as well as Rafat, have been given more and more to poetic silence or to the salon-side seductions of *vers de société* since the early 1980s. Nevertheless, it is these poets, basically, who laid the groundwork for building the monument of Pakistani English poetry, a monument whose excellence and accelerated merit may possibly be seen elsewhere, in another decade. My own poetry[8] was not written alongside theirs, but I would be a churlish Switzer not to acknowledge many years of friendship and literary conversation with several of them. Similarly, Zulfikar Ghose's work has been written abroad, although he has been in touch with his country.[9] Mention should be made also of the work developing in the literary societies in Lahore, Karachi, Peshawar, and Rawalpindi-Islamabad and of such poets as M. Athar Tahir, Adrian Hussain, Salman Tarik Kureishi, Nadir Husain, Waqas Ahmad Khwaja, Jocelyn Ortt-Saeed, Raja Changez Sultan, Alys Faiz, Hina Faisal Imam, and Mansoor Sheikh. Despite all manner of intellectual manifestos, poetic credos, and similar social cliff-hangers, Pakistani English poetry remains a mélange of Pakistani—or generally Asian—and Western poetic forms and language resources.

I mention this because recognizing this particular aspect of our total cultural situation has a bearing on many other important activities related to both poetry and life. In an expurgated section of my letter to the editor of the *Pakistan Times,* which I cited earlier, I had queried their contributor on "Pakistani idiom in English" if the displacement (or replacement) of the River Ravi in a poem with, say, the Euphrates would make the perpetrator fall outside Pakistani idiom and beyond the pale. As there was no answer, I could then only guess. Proof has not been long in coming, however, since a number of writers are now clearly on record concerning Zulfikar Ghose, whose physical distance from the land of his birth as well as his subject matter—rather, the "setting" of his work, it seems—has provided the grounds for declarations depriving this finest of Pakistani writers of the natural citizenship of Pakistani letters.[10] In other words, the proponents of the idea of a Pakistani idiom are not only interested in certain literary techniques but also try to assume an active role in the politics of culture, which is equally rife in other Pakistani languages; for to decide who is a Pakistani writer—irrespective of the exigencies of actual residence—and who is not or may not be, I must admit, is a sobering undertaking for anyone and quite an awesome decision for poets to make for others. These declarations also reveal, under their own stark light, the fact that the critical culture, at least in certain quarters, is still more tribal and ethnographic than national-cosmopolitan—and not quite sufficiently well equipped to deal with the more sensitive issues of expatriation and exile.[11] The matter should thus make one raise questions not only about a Pakistani idiom in English but also about "Pakistaniness": what constitutes this, that, and the other? And who may best exemplify these?

Although most—or all—discussion of a Pakistani idiom in English has been confined to the genre of poetry, it may be borne in mind that the limitations of the discussion so far are not actually the limitations of the subject. We must consider also its uses in prose, fictional and otherwise. A certain local color of northwestern India, with the relevant vocabulary/diction and tone, was already present even before any of the writers first mentioned began to draw the lines or erect barricades. Kipling, as a writer of both prose and poetry, may justifiably be seen as the first genuine practitioner of a Pakistani idiom in English. Ahmed Ali's *Twilight in Delhi* (1940) followed and perfected that kind of language practice, injecting our Urdu-related idiom into English fiction as well as certain indigenous rhythms of speech and sentiment in the main narrative. Much of Ali's poetry also readily exhibits these features, though we cannot ignore the Far Eastern and Western influences on his work. He is probably the only writer in Pakistan who has thus successfully incorporated the Pakistani idiom into his English, whereby it represents the entire sensibility rather than being relegated solely to selective situations. Shahid Suhrawardy's romantic credentials and wit are as much indebted to the Urdu-Persian-Bengali background of his Pakistani existence as to his English education and long residence abroad. So there is the admixture of his romantic and neoclassical idioms in this Pakistani poetry, though the character of his idiom is more conceptual, cerebral, textural, and poetic than, say, a visually referential proof of locality. Bapsi Sidhwa (in *The Crow Eaters* [1978] and *The Ice-Candy Man* [1988]) relies a good deal on the special effects created by language mixing—between English and her Punjabi-Gujarati-Urdu resources—and strops her comic tongue on this new banana-splitting idiom, which, embedded in its particular setting, is recognized as Pakistani. Shuaib bin Hasan's prose in his essays and travelogue *A Passage to England* has the syntax and textures of educated Pakistani speech. Zulfikar Ghose may not use the Pakistani-language idiom; but he certainly has drawn on much Pakistani material, and his Punjabi-Urdu (and largely Mughal-British) heritage is quite evident in both his poetry and his fiction.

The dialogue between the characters in certain works of fiction by Ghose (e.g., *The Murder of Aziz Khan,* 1967) has the resonance of actual speech, some of it Pakistani in the relevant settings, even though this cannot be a rule for a writer working in a broader culture or setting. What are we really to think of Joyce, Auden, Mann, Pound, and Brodsky? Which spoken idiom did Nabokov or Conrad draw upon? Where should Beckett locate his characters' speeches, and in what language idiom should the connecting narration be? Evidently a new solution must arise from the context of the work and the literary choices available. Ghose's work demonstrates these issues. Nevertheless, some of the major currents in his oeuvre—the place of emotion in human life, the relationship of the mind to the matter, of the reality to the art of dealing with it, of the appearance to the reality, of the mind to the heart, of the language to the subject—are essentially part of a greater Muslim and South Asian tradition in our letters, and the sooner his work is recognized for what it is, the better. In fact, Shahid Suhrawardy, Ahmed Ali, and Zulfikar Ghose, in their particular strengths and literary rights, remain eminently Pakistani as writers in the English language, for they share many of their concerns, themes, and struggles as well as a stylistic awareness among themselves and with several other Pakistani writers who have had to deliberate about both language and form and what they will do within the genre and the world.

Further, besides the localistic claims made for the Pakistani idiom in English, it has been said often enough that this idiom has been an effective means of replacing "borrowed poeticisms." That is perhaps an unhappy choice of phrase, but replacing a borrowed poeticism with another poeticism, though certainly an indication of change, would not go beyond exchanging

one mannerism for another if the program to create a "local mould" goes through in its merciless entirety and thus begins to obviate the experience it set out to capture. The new modish embellishments would certainly recall the earlier, perhaps contrary, mannerisms of the colonial period, because, despite definite departures, the language, though spoken widely, does not have sufficient social depth. Therefore the desire to indigenize, it appeared, could be turned into native constraint and, in certain cases, as discussed earlier, something just a hop away from the correct-culture syndrome.

What is obvious, nevertheless, is that the major practitioners of the 1960s felt that it was obligatory to have a program—even one to disavow any specific objectives—for the practice of poetry. A certain reservation was that unknown objects were foreign quantities: their gods were Greek, their myths were unrelated, and their authority was untenable. The Pakistani idiom in English was offered as an apology both to "native" and "nonnative" speakers of English: for the former, it was *distinctive;* for the latter, it represented *their own* selection of language and culture. By the mid–1970s, however, the energy generated by the idea was exhausted, as the set pieces made from it were also a doctored wood with plastic roots, and the results were not highly appreciated by readers and critics. The broader cultural idiom, range of allusion, and formal restructuring, as seen in the poetry of the 1950s, had found a connection across this decade and a half. Furthermore, around then, liberal thinking and a national-cosmopolitan outlook began to transform Pakistani poetry, an outlook which led to the less apologetic and more confident and accomplished work of the late 1970s and the 1980s.

Now, when all the original proponents and friends of the idea, including Taufiq Rafat, are noticeably quiet about it,[12] it will not be improper to wonder why there is so much talk by others being heard about it. For one thing, it is an indication that the event is nearly over as a program and all but consigned to the interests of history, the stuff of scholarship and journalism. For another, it is not yet a fully dead horse being flogged for mere poetic amusement: there are moves afoot to form new groups, circles, and societies, some of which are well-intentioned literary exaggerations of a social kind, whereas others are pure hot water spiked with the lime of heart trouble or politics. These moves recall similar earlier exercises, mainly of the 1960s, a decade of groupies of various kinds and of circle buffs. These circles always had the tendency to bend all straight lines and parallel routes (the modern highway structure) to suit their circling and enclosing movement (the old local-alley traffic). The Writers Guild flourished during this time, along with many other writers' groups. So did the

Pakistani-idiom groupies. In the wake of the 1950s language riots in East Pakistan, English was then increasingly seen as a bridge spanning the two distant, disparate parts of the country, and the perception grew stronger with the institution of the One (administrative) Unit (of West Pakistan). With the secession of East Pakistan and the redistributed power structure among the federated units of the renamed Pakistan, Urdu became the undisputed challenger to the confederal hegemony of official English, while the languages of the provinces began also to demand and assert an existence for themselves.

Thus English remains the seesaw partner of the area gang, and its present vicissitude makes it again a language to reckon with in our national structures. Hence the new groupies, of whom I spoke just a while ago. English is there, but does the Pakistani idiom in English, as we understand it from the 1960s, have a chance of literary revival in 1990? I think not. Taufiq Rafat has been quiet about it—and many observers have testified to that—because the sixties have long been over, and also because the work does not bear out the worth of the proclamations. The work confirms only the older, more solid, and more self-evident truths: that all genuine writing addresses itself to its natural and social environment, and that each writer will evolve his own idiom in the (English) language of common use to communicate his particular perception, personality, perhaps also meaning, and their adumbrations, elisions, mutations, indulgent equivocations, contractions, expansions, absence(s), or hesitations. As the language of common use in this country increasingly becomes Pakistani in its natural linguistic progression,[13] the Pakistani idiom in English will cease to be an embellishment or, alternatively, an indulgence and a constraint.

Finally, a word about the mythical Poets' Group at Lahore.[14] The only correct statement about it can be that it never existed.[15] Some of us poets, who were like-minded in certain ways, met together occasionally to share our poems and chat about them; and many of us in our daily lives saw one another socially or professionally too. There certainly was the pleasure of the company and conversation, but there never was a program, a manifesto, a forum, a magazine or journal, or even a regular schedule, curriculum, or agenda to qualify us as a "group." In time—by the early 1970s—each fabled beast, which appeared in the Yeatsian illusion as slouching toward Bethlehem, was actually seen buying an airline ticket and taking off for either New York or London. These random, though the more enjoyable for being unplanned, meetings came to an end when our respective lives—or the further tasks and volitions that awaited them—took us elsewhere, out of Lahore. The

friendships, nevertheless, have continued in the seasonal round and are a fine reward by themselves for not grouping up and then giving up within the time frame Lahore afforded us then. Poetry has flourished, both in and outside Lahore, and beyond the 1960s and 1970s. This is due most of all—or perhaps only—to the individuals who have written and still continue to do so. Should we be surprised? After all, even the poets who declaimed about their Pakistani idiom and formed groups grew up in time and began to write freely again.[16]

Alamgir Hashmi, Spring 1990

1 Shahid Suhrawardy, *Essays in Verse,* Cambridge, Eng., Cambridge University Press, 1937.

2 See the comments on Shahid Suhrawardy and Taufiq Rafat in my "Counterpoint in the Arts: The Example of *Dover Beach,"* *Explorations,* 12:1–2 (1988–89), pp. 65–75. The article dates from 1978 and has been reprinted from an earlier issue of *Explorations.*

3 For an indication of the cultural and linguistic discussion in the literary societies of the period, see the early bibliography issues (with country reports) of the *Journal of Commonwealth Literature* (U.K.); *Pakistan Quarterly* (Karachi), 17:2 (1970); and *Venture* (Karachi), 6:1 (1970). There is little impression of it in my own critical writings of the early 1970s, evidently because my poetic practice was stronger than my critical confessions or claims, and I was content with the situation. I can cite, for example, my article "The Basic Issue: Some Theoretical Bases of English Writing in Pakistan," which was written in 1970 but, following emendations, was published later in *The Ravi* as "The Basic Issue," 64:3 (May 1973), pp. 20–25. However, as late as January 1989, Ahmed Ali, a major practitioner of the Pakistani idiom in English, during the first International Conference on English in South Asia, denied ever writing—or wishing to write—Pakistani English. He described himself as a Pakistani writer who wrote in English (not Pakistani English, the idiom notwithstanding).

4 "Pakistani English Poetry and Taufiq Rafat," M. Athat Tahir, *Pakistan Times Magazine Section,* 1 May 1986, p. 3. A cramped and reworded version of my comment and query was published in "Letters to the Editor," *Pakistan Times,* 8 May 1986, p. 4. The original text of my letter is in the Pakistani Literature Archive. It may be added that most writers on the subject exhibit a highly visible vagueness about the concept and role of an "idiom" in poetic language, particularly as it may constitute a Pakistani English. W. A. Khwaja's longish introduction to his anthology *Mornings in the Wilderness: Readings in Pakistani Literature* (Lahore, Sang-e-Meel, 1988) likewise repeats, reviews, and augments the uncritical nebula surrounding linguistic and poetic activity today.

5 Alamgir Hashmi, *Pakistani Literature: The Contemporary English Writers,* New York, 1978; 2d ed., Islamabad, Gulmohar, 1987. Reviewed in *WLT* 61:3 (Summer 1987), p. 494.

6 Taufiq Rafat, *Arrival of the Monsoon,* Lahore, Vanguard, 1985. Daud Kamal, *Recognitions,* Budleigh Salterton, 1979; and *A Remote Beginning,* Budleigh Salterton, 1985.

7 Beginning with *The Purple Gold Mountain* (London, Keepsake, 1960), Ahmed Ali's latest poetry publication is *Selected Poems,* Gulbarga, India, JIWE, 1988. For a handy collection by G. Al-

lana, see *The Hills of Heaven: Selected Poems,* Karachi, Royal Book Company, 1980.

[8] Apart from my critical works, my seven poetry collections to date are: *The Oath and Amen,* Philadelphia, 1976; *America Is a Punjabi Word,* Zürich, 1979; *An Old Chair,* Bristol, 1979; *My Second in Kentucky,* Lahore, 1981; *This Time in Lahore,* London, 1983; *Neither This Time / Nor That Place,* London, 1984; *Inland and Other Poems,* Islamabad, 1988. For reviews of the last three, see *WLT* 59:4 (Autumn 1985), p. 661, and 62:4 (Autumn 1988), p. 731.

[9] Zulfikar Ghose's fourth poetry publication, *A Memory of Asia: New and Selected Poems* (Austin, Tx., 1984), will be superseded soon by a new *Selected Poems,* to be published in 1990 by Oxford University Press in Karachi. For a review of *Memory of Asia,* see *WLT* 59:2 (Spring 1985), p. 317.

[10] See Waqas Ahmad Khwaja's introduction to *Mornings in the Wilderness.* Athar Tahir once again expressed himself so on the matter in his paper on Taufiq Rafat, delivered at the National Seminar on Pakistani Literature in English, University of the Punjab, Lahore, 5–6 November 1989. Taufiq Rafat has expressed—and possibly initiated—the same opinion concerning Ghose on a number of both recorded and informal occasions. The politicking and manipulation to nudge out Ghose have gone to incredible lengths, so much so that recent book-jacket blurbs for Rafat's works, as well as a number of speakers in the Lahore seminar mentioned earlier, began thus: "When Taufiq Rafat started writing in 1947. . ." A number of earlier informal as well as written statements gave the age of fourteen to be his starting point, which would make the year 1941, as Rafat was born in 1927. It appears that the said quarters are doing what they can to make him out as one of the one thousand "midnight's children" *switched* during the poetically productive night of 14 August 1947.

[11] Some outstanding examples of critical incapacity are to be seen concerning the work of Faiz Ahmed Faiz, Ibne Insha, and Noon Meem Rashed, not to mention the problems caused by Rashed's views about the final disposal of the body and burial, which were also related to his exile. I may add to this list my own work during the years of exile.

[12] During a radio conversation between Kaleem Omar and myself ("Pakistan Calling," Radio Pakistan, Islamabad, Spring 1989) Omar stated that a Pakistani idiom in English was an idea of that period (the 1960s) and had excited interest, but that one could not subscribe to any such restricting language theorem.

[13] Cf. Alamgir Hashmi, "Prolegomena to the Study of Pakistani English and Pakistani Literature in English," unpublished conference paper, First International Conference on English in South Asia, University Grants Commission, Islamabad, 1989.

[14] I gave a detailed account of the writers/poets and their interests and association at Lahore during the late 1960s and the early 1970s while replying to some interview questions sent to me in the U.S. in the mid–1970s by Rukhsana Ismail (University of Karachi) for her book concerning Pakistani poetry in English.

[15] Later writers have tried to perpetuate the myth of the Lahore Poets' Group. See Tariq Rahman, "Pakistani English Poetry: A Survey," *Journal of Indian Writing in English,* 16:2 (1988), pp. 27–44; and Waqas Ahmad Khwaja, "Introduction," *Mornings in the Wilderness.* Both Rahman and Khwaja speak of the Lahore Group as a historical formation completed by its presupposed hierarchy, tradition, styles, and manners and foreclosed by a logical beginning and an inevitable end.

[16] This article is based on a lecture on the critical and historical approaches to the historiography of Pakistani poetry in English, delivered at the National Seminar on Pakistani Literature in English, University of the Punjab, Senate Hall, 5–6 November 1989.

"A Stylized Motif of Eagle Wings Woven": The Selected Poems of Zulfikar Ghose

Born in Sialkot in 1935, Zulfikar Ghose moved with his family to Bombay in 1942 and to England following the Partition. His first book of poems appeared in London in 1964, and he became well known as a poet from Pakistan. In quick succession came short stories, novels, and an autobiography, as well as journalism and other writings. By the time he left England for the United States in 1969, he was already a writer to reckon with in several genres.

Although during the last twenty-five years his fiction list has come to dominate the publishers' charts and the reviewers' prime slots, he remains a writer who has practiced poetry consistently since the late 1950s, when his early poems began to be published in British magazines. Ever since, his poems have appeared regularly in magazines, anthologies, textbooks, broadcasts, and individual collections. Over the years Pakistani magazines and anthologies have also carried some of his work, though hardly any of his books has been issued in Pakistan as yet. The *Selected Poems** therefore fills a crying gap.

The fifty-three poems chosen by Ghose for this volume have been drawn from his three poetry collections and a previous "New and Selected Poems" published in the United States. He has added substantially to the number chosen for the latter stateside volume, and not only with new, uncollected poems. Some items in the earlier collections which he excluded from *A Memory of Asia: New and Selected Poems* (declaring that "the ones not included in this volume do not now strike me as worthy of anyone's attention") have happily made their way back here and will survive. On the other hand, the twenty new poems carried in *A Memory of Asia* are reduced here to eleven, whereas the twelve uncollected and included here for the first time are a treat over previous decisions of immediate excision and removal whose only remedy for the faithful reader was either the original editions or the now equally hard-to-obtain *Penguin Modern Poets 25.*

Still, excision, removal, and survival are not just the practical aspects of compiling Ghose's book(s); these are forces which have informed both his life and his creative work. As a child he suddenly found himself chucked out of his original habitat; as a youth he had to leave the landscape to which he was accustomed and cope with a new environment with which he could never be at one without the doubtful aid of "external" interferences and attachments; as a man he had to consider his roots, rely on memory, and invent a language that would make sense of the contemporary world for him who has all but lost his "home." Partition and exile, and the attendant socioreligious traumas, have not been written about enough in our literature, particularly in verse of any significance, and there is yet to develop a sense of the transition of the 1940s, with its confused options and a "lost generation" on both sides of the Indo-Pakistani border and beyond. Although of that enduring generation—like Khwaja Ahmad Abbas, Quratul-Ain Haider, Saadat Hasan Manto, Abdullah Hussain, and Aziz Ahmad—Ghose, in the literary sense, has hardly been lost, has always described himself as Pakistani, and remains a poet of national, international, and universal dimensions.

In the early poems the personal and the historical coincide in a verse which abounds in animals juxtaposed to mechanical imagery and an inhospitable landscape characterized as India, where the old order has given way to one that looks new but is actually quite ancient: "in a bazar donkeys speak into carrots / like crooners miming into microphones" ("Across India: February 1952"). "Asoka's wheel" and the "vote," in "A Short History of India," mix and unmix Western and Eastern symbols into further definitions of order. Some recent comment concerning *A Memory of Asia* has made much of Ghose's attachment to India,[1] without realizing of course that the India of the poems is ostensibly not the state but rather the place designated so poetically, almost like the heath in *King Lear*. Likewise, in the same poem the eagles may be real but are quite beyond that: "Above us the sun is still, / the eagles are motifs of the air."

And not just motifs. With the poetic progress, from the car journey in the earlier poem to "Flying over India," the sight improves with the intelligence at work: "The point of the eagle's introspection / or its lonely watch-tower withdrawal / is also my point of view." Both the motif and the point of view, as universal as they obviously are, closely belong to the Pakistani poetic tradition. What could be more Iqbal-like than the lines just quoted? Or consider these lines from the same poem, concluded with an ironic comment made the sharper for its perfect rhyme:

Give me the purer air. The flat earth is awful.
Give me height, height, with its cold perspective
of forms of the earth. Senseless now to dive

like eagles to the earth's sparrows. The jungle's beasts are unseen from here. From these heights, one can almost believe in human rights.

Besides broad observation, many of the poems are autobiographical, indeed historical in a material and artistic sense. Their symbolic strategies lend a universal credence to their experience. An early poem, "The Body's Independence," illustrates this in its self-evident three-part structure, which is common to a number of other early poems as well. The biology lesson in the first part of that poem is autobiographical and tends to become symbolic in that the teacher's "voice, a lesson in prosody, / told us of the secrets of the heart. / . . .We furtively laughed at the shape of man, / but his eyes saw farther than the chart." In the second part the speaker's personal illness is gradually healed "with the oil of life to anoint my head." As Ghose has stated, he fell seriously ill at the time of Independence.[2] The country then was in no better condition, and symbolic means are employed to indicate that. The means of personal recovery from illness are also symbolic, equated to the Mughal prince Humayun's recovery through parental sacrifice and consecration: "My body took shape like the chart, I found / the outline of my bones fill with flesh and blood." In the third part of the poem coalesce all three elements of the self in a reversal of fair possibility, and the earlier narrative is flinched: "India was at civil war, / the crow excreted where he pleased. And I, / reborn from my fairy tale, saw bones charred / in mounds on pavements. It was no country / for princes, and the eagle soared."

"The Body's Independence," a complete reflection on art's healing power and the modes of civil existence, is concerned with the close relation of the human body to the body politic and is an excellent exemplification and enhancement of a principle first enunciated by Rousseau: "The body politic, like the human body, begins to die from its birth, and bears in itself the causes of its destruction."[3] The poem ends with a precise twopronged comment: "The blood of India ran out with my youth." Other Pakistani poems have addressed themselves to the theme of Independence from a similar analytic standpoint,[4] though they have not spawned a culture of resistance or revolution like the Urdu poetry of the 1940s and its later development.[5] The symbols achieved have also the power to contain other forms of social action.

As I said earlier, the symbolic is rooted in the autobiographical and historical hold on reality; and on the other side of the opaque glass of exile is printed its universal, international, and national character in an essential symmetry of liminal relations. Poems like "The Attack on Sialkot" and "The Mystique of Roots" still address these concerns, but "The Alien" and "This Landscape, These People" paradoxically locate the speaker in England. Nearly all the poems in Ghose's second collection, *Jets from Orange*, tend to be more open-ended, or pointed outward from the specific contexts of imagery, and they define their subjects in frames of cultural breadth which are new, whether the subject is a picnic in Jammu ("The Picnic in Jammu"), the compunctions at the composition of art on account of the decomposition of the human body ("Decomposition"), or the culture lost between Bombay and London whose music is "hybrid jazz of no tradition" ("The Lost Culture"). The eagle or the hawk of the earlier poems has been replaced by the jet plane, while the new dog-weary existence, "as if suspended mobility," is conveyed in intricately rhyming regular lines in "Kew Bridge" and "history's fashionable misconceptions" and other romancing find a temporary correction in lines like "we make spring-mattressed love with its / Kleenex anti-climax, hearing the planes descend" ("Don't Forget the Pill, Dear"). The earlier pun has an abortive purpose, but the clenched consonantal landing, with its iambic movement, sounds convincing enough.

Like the poem mentioned last, the poems in Ghose's third volume, *The Violent West,* evince an interest more in certain philosophical propositions than in the images which seem to suggest them. The excellent measure and rhyme of "Of Self-Hatred" can well examine "a stylized motif of eagle wings woven / in subtly differentiated colours on dacron that feels / like silk." And in the last stanza, "One by one, / consider the hypotheses that come / from the undergrowth or from the cold ocean." The search for home, as such, should prove to be even more difficult, since the propositions lead to still other images—of enticements that lead away—in these poems written since Ghose's taking up residence in the U.S. "Old Ragged Claws," for example, ends with the telling line, "I have come so far West, the East is near." "On Owning Property in the U.S.A." underlines the contradictions of pursuing dreams, whereas "It's Your Land, Boss" brings home the irrelevance and unfruitful nature of one's relations to land. "An Imperial Education" considers the "subtle corruption" of the situation of the excolonies man in the West and the compulsions to engage in the dual conspiracy of silence and speech, none of which will lead one home.

Following a recent visit to Pakistan, Ghose published an article titled "Going Home," in which he said:

It was my first visit to Pakistan in twenty-eight years but when I climbed up the stupa at Dharmarajika in Taxila on a beautifully clear May morning and looked at the land stretching to the mountains on the horizon I had the sensation that my absence from that soil had been of a far longer duration and, at the same time, now that I had my feet planted in it, I had existed continuously on that earth for two thousand years. . . . There are moments in our lives when we can hear the soul whisper its contentment that the long torment of being has been stilled at last. The air in Taxila filled my brain with that serenity. I felt I was at home.[6]

An earlier statement about being at home in Texas[7] is here superseded by a feeling that approximates belonging to the place, not just to the landscape. That may be qualified, arguably, by the memory of how the Ghose text ekes out its own satisfactions from the very contradictions set up by it—and by the memory of the last two lines of "The Pursuit of Frost": "a lost-and-found / civilization (a home, wanderer!), an ancient fraud." Still, the discovery of a perfect symbol in Peshawar which seems to capture all that it is about can evoke a sense of belonging.

At the Peshawar Museum I was struck by the power of the incomplete statue of the fasting Buddha to fix the itinerant self in a timeless and bodiless space. . . . That which is not there startles the mind with the certainty of its being; . . . the broken incomplete Buddha is the mirror the soul looks at when the body has been compelled to recognize its inconsequentiality; . . . he is the man in exile whose body must forever be incomplete because a part of it resides in the place of his origin. . . . He is and is not, simultaneously a pure idea of the ambiguity of life which is now solidly real and now an empty dream.[8]

The poems from *A Memory of Asia* evidence a discursive shift; memory is made up of language and perception, and the finely modulated verse paragraph of the title poem is a suitable vehicle for their permutations. "Notes Towards a Nature Poem," "E.g.," and "I.e." describe a sort of theory of poetry, in this case nature poetry; and poems like "Among Other Things," "A Young Girl Diving," and "A Dragonfly in the Sun" carry out the principles in precisely apprehended images. In "I.e." is advanced the notion of the name and a particular, detailed registering of the object of beauty instead of the cultivating of an idealism of the nothing—viz., Saint-John Perse's reflection on Braque's birds. The birds in the Ghose poem suggest their shapes from their names. If Perse tried to unfold a total view of man in union with the universe and tortured by history, Ghose names the subject without the epic resources and relies on it as man's only relation to his reality; but in the meantime several texts (Braque, Perse, Ghose) have overlapped and converged in a "radiance" ("E.g.") of "the abstract group" ("I.e."). "Trees" and "Sounds" are further explorations and fine poems in this vein. "The Oceans" is a reflection on the oceans' beauty, power, and mystery, as well as their role in our world, but the poem is a trifle overexplained.

"Flying over the Extinct Volcanoes" has transparent images, though these are not without the symbolic resonances (religion, stock market, weather chart) which must deny narrative comfort. The last poems, hitherto uncollected, generally carry forward this style. The mood is somber when not bitter. The concerns with the deceptive nature of reality ("The Sun and the Lizard"), revisionist history ("The Monument to Sibelius in Rio de Janeiro"), futility ("The Counter Riddle"), and false assumptions ("Destiny"), and with an unnatural and barren existence ("Surprising Flowers," "Lady Macbeth's Farewell to Scotland") continue, though not without some vague vibrations from "perfumed landscapes."

Clearly, Ghose is a poet with a moral passion, writing from a split-screen vision of himself in a consensus society. Several continents and cultures have shaped his outlook and the subjects of his verse, and there is a remarkable unity of idea and tone across his later writings in several forms. Whereas his fiction now exhibits a familiarity with Latin American literature, his poetry has remained largely untouched by the "Southern" experience, which has imparted certain changes in the work of some of his North American contemporaries—say, the later Mark Strand. Still, Ghose may not have been inclined to having two strings to his bow, which already had South Asia in place, even if South Asian English poetry itself has largely been quite parochial.[9]

In Ghose's poetry the Western formal influences have thus remained paramount. His association with the British poets known as the Group[10] may not have been a decisive factor, as he has disavowed any such implication himself, naming his reading of Robert Lowell's *Life Studies* (1959) as a turning point in his career.[11] Lowell's "influence," in the early poems particularly, is highly visible, in that, like Lowell, Ghose effectively evokes large landscapes of memory embedded with personal, family, communal, and national histories. Further, the turn of phrase and the ease with the subjective image are owed more to Lowell and the American "confessional" poets than to contemporary British practice. These thematic choices and structural strategies, of memory and making, were to continue until almost the 1980s, when Ghose took to the indeterminate text and open structures as practiced by American poets like Wallace Stevens and John Ashbery. His reading of Wittgenstein, Proust, and Beckett has fostered not so much the *form* as the attitude,[12] and Ghose has made the language itself the source of substance and beauty, the

writer's ideal home. It can be argued with point, nevertheless, that Ghose's ear was affected by the (British) Group's loud reading habits and that he hardly could outgrow the staple pentameter (even when it fluctuates), the structured stanza, the seductions of rhyme, and the overall measured if not austere movement of rather academic verse. Add to this the stress on experience (and experience as reading, as Ghose indicated to Bruce Meyer)[13] as well as Ghose's rational intelligence, sharp irony, learning, and craftsmanship, and you might think you have been reading (or listening to) a Movement poet.[14] Not so: there is greater variety and expanse in his work; his images are fresh, his voice is unique, and he has made the intercontinental terrain his province. Land (as a place to belong to, not to buy or sell), self, beliefs, and relationships are the leitmotivs— in his poetry as well as his fiction—crowned by a graceful introspective language, which is Zulfikar Ghose's counter against the chaos of our civilization.

Alamgir Hashmi, Winter 1992

*Zulfikar Ghose. Selected Poems. Karachi. Oxford University Press. 1991.

[1] K. S. Narayana Rao, review of Ghose's *Memory of Asia,* in *WLT* 59:2 (Spring 1985), p. 317.

[2] Bruce Meyer, "An Interview with Zulfikar Ghose," in Zulfikar Ghose, *Selected Poems,* Karachi, Oxford University Press, 1991.

[3] Jean-Jacques Rousseau, *Du contrat social* (1762), Good translations can be seen in *Social Contract,* Maurice Cranston, tr., Harmondsworth, Penguin, 1969; and *Social Contract and Discourses,* 2d rev. ed., J. H. Brumfit and J. C. Hall, eds., G. D. H. Cole, tr., London, 1973.

[4] See "Freedom's Dawn (August 1947)," in *Poems by Faiz,* V. G. Kiernan, tr., London, 1971; and Alamgir Hashmi, "Pakistan Movement," in *Pakistan Times,* Pakistan Resolution Golden Jubilee Celebrations Supplement, 23 March 1990.

[5] See "Introduction," in *The Penguin Book of Modern Urdu Poetry,* Mahmood Jamal, ed. & tr., Harmondsworth, Penguin, 1986.

[6] Zulfikar Ghose, "Going Home," *Weekend Post* (Lahore), 10 August 1990, p. 3.

[7] Meyer, op. cit.

[8] Ghose, "Going Home," p. 3.

[9] See the discussion of poetry in Alamgir Hashmi, *Commonwealth Literature,* Lahore, 1983; Alamgir Hashmi, "Poetry, Pakistani Idiom in English, and the Groupies," *WLT* 64:2 (Spring 1990), pp. 268–71; and also Alamgir Hashmi, "Poetry in Contemporary India" (review article), *Journal of South Asian Literature,* 19:1 (1984), pp. 219–22.

[10] See *A Group Anthology,* Philip Hobsbaum and Edward Lucie-Smith, eds., London, 1963.

[11] Meyer, op. cit.

[12] In his discussion of Ghose's fiction, Bruce King correctly states that "the similarities of Ghalib and Iqbal to Ghose's view of the

relationship of language to reality. . .possibly are explained by cultural heritage." Bruce King, "From *Twilight* to *Midnight:* Muslim Novels of India and Pakistan," in *The Worlds of Muslim Imagination,* Alamgir Hashmi, ed., Islamabad, 1986, pp. 243–59.

[13] Meyer, op. cit.

[14] See *New Lines,* Robert Conquest, ed., London, 1956; see also Blake Morrison, *The Movement,* London, 1980.

SRI LANKA

Sri Lanka's "Ethnic" Conflict in Its Literature in English

The situation is a nightmare. . . . There is my Western side that wants a solution and there is my Eastern side that doesn't expect a solution.[1]

▨ MICHAEL ONDAATJE

The Western world is aware of what is termed the ethnic conflict in Sri Lanka, but I am not sure to what extent the facts are known, because the media emphasis is naturally on the sensational. Sri Lanka is a multiracial and multireligious nation. According to the most recent census, which was carried out in 1981, the population of Sri Lanka is over fifteen million, comprising 73.98 percent Sinhalese, 12.6 percent Tamils, 7.12 percent Moors, 5.56 percent Indian Tamils, 0.29 percent Malays, 0.26 percent Burghers (descendants of the Portuguese and Dutch), and 0.20 percent others. Of the Tamils, less than a half live in the North of Sri Lanka; the majority live among the Sinhalese. The Tamil minority enjoys a much better position in Sri Lanka than most minorities in other countries, and also, partly because of favored treatment ensuing from the classic colonial policy of "divide and rule" during a century and a half of British occupation, they became, in the words of Sri Lanka's leading historian, K. M. de Silva, "a minority with a majority complex."

After Independence (1948) the Sinhalese majority began to feel keenly that the balance should be righted, whereas the Tamil minority wanted their privileged position to continue. This led to occasional outbreaks of communal violence. The Tamils were aggrieved when Sinhalese was made the official language of Sri Lanka in 1956, though in practice they enjoyed the same language rights as the Sinhalese; the legal fiction was politically useful to the Sri Lanka Freedom Party to win the votes of the Sinhalese and score a landslide victory over the dominant United National Party in the general election of that year, but it had an unfortunate estranging effect on the Tamils. This was exploited by the Tamil United Liberation Front in the 1970s in opting for a separate state for the Tamils, *Eelam* as it was called in Tamil; in the general election of 1977 the Tamils in the North and the East voted overwhelmingly for this party. The Eelam goal was a major threat to the sovereignty and territorial integrity of the country; this added to the resentment already felt by the Sinhalese, because the Tamils still held more than two or three times their ethnic proportion in the most important positions in public and private employment and because the charges of discrimination against the Tamils in education, employment opportunities, and development assistance to the North were unfounded. Although the Tamil United Liberation Front may have intended to use the demand for Eelam only as a bargaining device to secure a greater devolution of power, a chasm developed between the leaders of this party, who belonged to the older generation, and the Tamil youths, who adopted the Eelam cry with complete seriousness.[2] This led to the radicalization of Tamil politics, terrorism being employed as a legitimate means, Indian involvement, and international ramifications. The result is the present so-called ethnic crisis.

If one looks around the world—Cyprus, Canada, Belgium, Spain, Malaysia, Nigeria, India, Sri Lanka—it soon becomes clear that so-called ethnic tension and conflict is a common feature of our times and is often deeply built into the structure of these societies; people in Britain need look no further than Ulster in Ireland to see the phenomenon manifesting itself daily. Its real source and condition lies in the patterns of incorporation of diverse cultures, races, and classes in the hierarchies of power, opportunity, resources, and access to these.[3] It is this core of structural tension that is crucial, and, strictly speaking, it is not ethnic as such; ethnicity provides only symbols for conflict.

Much of the world is unaware that there exists a sharp division of Sri Lanka into two sections not on grounds of religion or race or even of Sinhalese-speakers and Tamil-speakers. There are both Sinhalese and Tamils who are Christians. We have both Sinhalese and Tamils who embrace Islam, sometimes through conviction and sometimes frivolously in order to avail themselves of the convenience of a multiplicity of wives. Some Sinhalese, particularly those of Negombo on the West coast, speak Tamil as fluently as many Tamils speak Sinhala. There are no absolute differences of attitude and perception between these people such as often exist between the bilingual (i.e., Sinhala or Tamil and English) and monolingual of both communities.

We must remain aware of this divide when considering a cross section of the writing prompted by the "ethnic" conflict. The writers in English are obviously on the sidelines, sensitive souls responding to a situation engendered by politicians, who are not likely to consider their viewpoints, and by militants and soldiers who do not read the language in which they write and in any case would not be influenced by either the pity or the propaganda of a comfortable and cushioned class who share neither their privations nor their perceptions. These writers seem to write for one another, for the local critics, for a few readers of their own class, and for a corresponding class in the developed world rather than for those actively engaged or involved in the struggle. Barriers of class prevent communication more effectively between Sinhalese and Sinhalese and between Tamil and Tamil than between Sinhalese and Tamils of corresponding classes.

Though tension in Sri Lanka erupted into outbreaks of communal violence sporadically after 1958, the only notable effort in earlier years to put it into writing was James Goonewardene's "Sow a Storm," an extract from an unpublished novel. Goonewardene portrays the Sinhalese and Tamils in terms of shallow stereotypes current in the popular imagination. The Sinhalese trader is fat, greasy, and feckless. The Tamil clerk scorns delights and lives laborious days, piling up coin against coin; he is a pillar of Jaffna's "postal-order economy."[4] Here we see the tendency of writers to avoid portraying any direct confrontation between characters belonging to the two communities, a forbearance prompted both by tact and by ignorance of the fundamental views and attitudes of those directly involved: the nationalist or Marxist rebels and the security forces ordered out to face them.

In the late 1970s and early 1980s increasing terrorism in the North resulted in the regular deaths of policemen and soldiers who were attempting to contain it. When thirteen Sinhalese soldiers were killed in a single attack by Tamil terrorists in July 1983, however, there was a backlash in the South, the worst instance of communal violence to date. The government felt that much of the violence was engineered by an extremist political party. Richard de Zoysa's poem "Apocalypse Now," written two years earlier, was deep and prophetic.

Divide and rule. And pendulous to the North
Hangs *Jambudipa,* stained with her own blood
Bleeding heart red as ripe pomegranate
And bitter as the damson. All the fruits of hate
Quivering she holds. Waiting to drop
Into our gaping mouths.
(*Jambudipa* means "India" in Sinhala)

In "Shere Khan Age" Devika Brendon is shattered by the sheer carnage of July 1983.

Where there were memories

now ruins—a charred body,
and scavengers come to kill
each other for the pieces of
a dying nation.
Bloodstained, O island of gentle
welcomes and temple flowers,
your red sands are now more
red. Tear-shaped, you are
now also fear-swept.

The allusion to Kipling, introduced in the title and continued later, and to Wilfred Owen's war poem "Greater Love" here add intensity to the communication of the poet's horror as her own earlier, and customary, views of Sri Lanka are torn to shreds. This response of a young Sri Lankan girl, now settled in Australia, is sensitive though without historical perspective and balance. Yasmine Gooneratne, also in Australia now, reveals these latter qualities too, as she responds quickly to the same situation in "Big Match." The image of a cricket match is ironic and, though not functioning throughout the poem or centrally as an organizing, controlling presence, helps the poet avoid vagueness in expressing her horror and pathos. She is impartial and sees both races as to be blamed: "and Big Match fever, flaring high and fast, / has both sides in its grip and promises / dizzier scores than any at the Oval."

The creative writers in English found July 1983 and the later escalation of strife to the proportions of a civil war in the North and East of the country a traumatic new experience (like their earlier experience of the 1971 insurgency) which they were impelled to express and interpret, even if they were unable to come to terms with it. Jean Arasanayagam, the most prolific writer on this subject, said: "July '83 was my regeneration."[5] Her experience of the communal disturbances that month and, for a short while, as a refugee in a camp is the subject of her collection of poems *Apocalypse '83* (1984), and under the pressure of this experience she departs from the ornate, lush manner of her earlier verse. In "Nallur 1982" she writes:

It's there
    beneath the fallen fronds dry crackling
    pile of broken twigs, abandoned wells of brackish
    water lonely dunes
        It's there
the shadows of long bodies shrunk in death
the leeching sun has drunk their blood and
bloated swells among the piling clouds
        It's there
            death,
                smell in the air
Its odour rank with sun and thickening blood
mingling with fragrance from the frothy toddy

pots swinging like lolling heads from
blackened gibbets.

Arasanayagam's new style is an improvement on the
earlier and includes occasional striking phrases, but unfortunately its basis is a kind of rhetoric that is constantly high-pitched and given to repetition and wordiness.
The poet's dwelling on the same feelings reduces the
value of those feelings, however worthy in themselves.
It is true that Wilfred Owen said, "Above all I am not
concerned with Poetry. / My subject is War, and the pity
of War. / The Poetry is in the pity,"[6] but Owen's good
poetry, as in "Anthem for Doomed Youth," works as poetry and is beautifully disciplined, unlike Arasanayagam's verse. It has been argued that T. S. Eliot's *Waste
Land* deals with the modern world, which is disorderly,
and that therefore the poem's disorderliness is justified.
This seems to me a fallacious argument, however; even
chaos has to be presented in organized poetic form. By
the same token, one should not argue that Arasanayagam's lack of control and form is justified by the chaotic
nature of the situation which is her subject.

Arasanayagam is a member of the Burgher community (that is, of mixed Dutch and native descent), the
smallest and most Westernized community in Sri
Lanka, very different from the mass of the people. Thus,
it is wholly natural for her, in *A Colonial Inheritance*
(1985), to feel herself an alien in our society and to be
preoccupied with exploring her identity and heritage,
adopting an anticolonial stance. She married a Tamil,
and the other major interest in this volume of poetry of
hers lies in her presentation of the problems caused by
the hatred directed at her by her husband's family because she belonged to a different community. Still, she
identifies herself with her husband's community to the
point of being partisan on their behalf in her presentation of the "ethnic" conflict. In "Remembering Nallur—
1984" the imagery suggested by the fact that Nallur is
the site of the most celebrated temple of the Hindu god
of war, Skanda or Murugan, exalts the conflict to the
level of a religious sacrifice: "now they come bearing
weapons / the spears of Murugan turned / to guns and
grenades in celebration / of the great festival of Death."
The poet, in her fervor, romanticizes and simplifies the
complicated conflict.

In her two most recent poems, published in 1987,
Arasanayagam reveals a new maturity. In "A Question
of Identity" she faces squarely the fact of her Catholic
Burgherness, and "A Country at War" is almost as good,
much more restrained than her earlier efforts in this
field and more complex: "This time the explosions did
not go off / for the nonce things still stand intact / but
it's only a matter of time, the foundation's / wired perhaps tomorrow the edifice comes down." Arasanayagam
suggests the tottering of the whole state.

The writing which rises from this situation of "ethnic" conflict is very different from the writing that
stemmed from the Spanish Civil War. It is not only that
many of the writers who belonged to the International
Brigade possessed genuine gifts; they were committed
to the ideals and shared the experiences of those at the
battlefront, whereas in the present case, prompted as it
is by gushes of emotion and frequently physically remote from its actual background where the terrorists
ambush or lay land mines for soldiers and massacre civilians, much of the writing gains its impetus from
newspaper reports, hearsay, and memories of the 1983
backlash. This writing is consequently very openly and
simply an attempt to express and generate pity and horror. Unfortunately, much of it lacks the selectivity that
sharpens the impact of prose or poetry, so that we become aware of the writer's strenuous efforts to move our
feelings: for example, Kamala Wijeratne says in "Farewell," "I hung down my head / in misery and shame /
the weight of history sagged down my shoulders / its
pages heavy with the grim saga of our war-torn races,"
or writes in "A Soldier's Wife Weeps," "They gave you
a hero's burial / with all military honours / the band
played / and your body passed from hand to hand." In
"The Dance" Premini Amerasinghe ponders the fact that
religion has proved impotent in the conflict, even a
source of evil; Hinduism and Buddhism seem rallying
points for opposing forces instead of serving as agents
of reconciliation.

The lotus withers
in a lake of blood
A Bo-tree weeps
impotently

Christ writhes in agony
once more
and Krishna bows his head
in shame.

There is a little writing based on some firsthand experience of the conflict, hardly any better artistically but
opening up more aspects of it and more points of view.
In "Dirge for Corporal Premaratne" Suresh Canagarajah
shows himself to be an angry young Tamil and writes
straightforward propaganda. In "A Room in Frankfurt"
V. I. S. Jeyapalan laments exile, the squalid lodgings as
well as the grief and weariness: "Wandering mongrel /
dog-tired, prone in bed / scavenging for a living / His
days crawl." In "To a Student" Kamala Wijeratne dramatizes a moment of professional interaction distorted by
an awareness of communal disharmony, danger, and violence in simple idealistic terms.

But why can't your irises lock with mine?
Our ears stop all unkind sound?
Let us shake off these brand names
And search for a herb that heals,
And make a cooling poultice to cure mass lunacy.
Leave behind those Ilions and Carthages to antique
    dealers,
Let us plan fresh methodology to stop other
    Hiroshimas.

The "ethnic" conflict has been dealt with mainly in more or less short poems, but Gamini Akmeemana published a fragment of a novel in volume 4 of the *New Lankan Review* (1986) relevant to this theme and of interest. Nihal, an archeologist, trusts Anandan, a Tamil apothecary married to a Sinhalese, whereas Mr. Fernando, a schoolteacher, thinks, "Nowadays you can't trust those Tamil fellows." Still, Nihal says of Fernando, "He's a good sort really." That the author makes Nihal, an unprejudiced speaker, pass this judgment suggests that despite Mr. Fernando's openly stated, almost obsessive distrust of Tamils, Mr. Fernando himself was not likely to be actively hostile or destructive, but the conflict has generated distrust.

Maureen Seneviratne, in her story "Mirage," presents a glimpse of a high-living Sinhalese gunrunner whose imports do not, of course, reach the government forces, and an officer's awaking to this kind of treachery and totally unscrupulous greed (the "lamppost" killings[7] of Tamils adjudged traitors by the terrorists provide proof of corresponding features in the North). Seneviratne's sustained juxtaposition of two situations, the gunrunner in the plush hotel with the officer, on the one hand, and the officer in the jungle in an operation against the terrorists on the other, makes the moral significance very clear; but the lameness of her prose robs the novel of the force that could have been imparted by this clever tactic, and the situations themselves are not really re-created but only thinly described.

T. Arasanayagam has written the only play so far published which takes the "ethnic" conflict as its setting and subject, *The Intruder*. The work is a concoction of pale imitations of other plays: the dialogue of Ernest MacIntyre's absurdist dramas *The Loneliness of the Short-Distance Traveller* and *A Somewhat Mad and Grotesque Comedy,* the gunman of Pinter's Gus in *The Dumb Waiter,* the old woman of Maurya in Synge's *Riders to the Sea,* and Cathleen ni Houlihan in Yeats's play of that name, the crazed girl who, with white flowers in her hair, sings of Shakespeare's Ophelia. The play makes suggestions as it proceeds, but these remain vague and are never organized into a meaningful whole. The only notable point, it seems to me, is the placing of the Boy, an em-

bodiment of violence and death: his stupidity is a criticism of what he stands for.

The writers in English stress the pathetic aspect of the "ethnic" conflict, whereas the teledrama and film in Sinhala emphasize positive aspects such as good personal relations among individual Sinhalese and Tamils, which makes for ethnic harmony. Kamala Wijeratne's poem in English, "Foster Brothers," is exceptional in being the latter vein. We are never permitted by the writers in English, whether they be Sinhalese, Tamil, or Burgher, to see a presentation of the actual conflict in all its complexity, with its tangled web of wrongs—economic, political, and physical—perpetrated not by one side or the other but both. It is as though prudence, moral cowardice, or sheer superficiality has prevented writers of all communities from analyzing or even facing the complexity of the situation.

A possible and hopeful exception is Chandani Lokuge, who shows in her short story "A Pair of Birds" a readiness to confront the complexities that engender conflict—but she is an exception. The artistic weakness of the poetry is, I think, partly because our recent poets do not draw upon the Western traditions available to them, as Yasmine Gooneratne and Patrick Fernando did. Conflict and crises in history do not necessarily produce good or plentiful literature: World War II was the biggest conflict in modern history, but it begat little literature in English and nothing of outstanding quality. On the other hand, conflict and crises are not always portrayed well in art out of the immediacy of the experience: it was only many years after the Vietnam War had ended that remarkable films about it began to appear in the United States. This may or may not apply to Sri Lankan literature in English about our "ethnic" conflict. To date, generally speaking, Wilfred Owen's words hold true: "The Poetry is in the pity."

D. C. R. A. Goonetilleke, Summer 1992

[1] Michael Ondaatje, "Canadian Pacific," *The Guardian* (U.K.), 9 December 1988, p. 32.

[2] Mr. V. Prabakaran, the leader of the Liberation Tigers of Tamil Eelam, has said time and again, "We will not stop short of Eelam." See Rohan Gunaratna, *War & Peace in Sri Lanka,* Kandy, Sri Lanka, Institute of Fundamental Studies, 1987, p. 6.

[3] Dr. Hema Goonatilake's recent study of two multiethnic slums in Colombo provides relevant evidence; it suggests that ethnic antagonism is minimal among the lower strata of society and appears increasingly as one moves up the socioeconomic ladder and that it is born mainly out of socioeconomic competition, not the other way round. See T. Sabaratnam, "No Communalism in City's Multiethnic Slums," *Daily News* (Colombo), 11 December 1987, p. 1.

[4] Jaffna is the northern region of Sri Lanka, which has a predominantly Tamil population. Those Tamils who worked in Colom-

bo and whose families were in Jaffna used to support their families by sending remittances in the form of postal orders.

[5] Quoted by D. C. R. A. Goonetilleke, "Sri Lanka" (1984), *Journal of Commonwealth Literature*, 20:2 (1985), p. 124.

[6] C. Day Lewis, "Preface," in Wilfred Owen, *Collected Poems*, London, Chatto & Windus, 1968, p. 31.

[7] The victim is killed and tied to a lamppost, or tied to a lamppost and killed, in a method of execution that is also meant to deter others.

Poverty, Pride, and Memory: On the Writings of Basil Fernando

On the west coast of Sri Lanka, just north of the capital Colombo, there is a small village where the majority of the inhabitants are poor people belonging to the fisher and the washer castes. The name of the village, Palliyawatte, indicates that it is Christian, for in Sinhala *palliya* means "church" and *watta* means "property." It became Christian—Catholic—after the Portuguese conquest of the coastal provinces of Sri Lanka in the early sixteenth century.

Even today the west coast as a whole makes up a Catholic core area in otherwise Buddhist Sri Lanka, Catholicism having struck deeper roots than might be explained by the violence of the conquerors. It even stood the test when Catholics themselves were persecuted, after the Portuguese (following one hundred years of rule) were chased out by the Reform Dutch. When *their* time had come to its end, and when after another 150 years the more tolerant English took over, the Catholic Church again emerged as the strongest of the Sri Lankan Christian churches, while the Reformed Church collapsed like a house of cards.

But back to Palliyawatte. In this village, fifty-one years ago, the writer Basil Fernando was born. In those days the village certainly lived up to its name: the village church was a natural center, the priest the foremost authority, the bishops more well known than politicians. People went to church regularly, and on Good Friday the women dressed in black. Especially in the drama of Passion Week, the villagers lived through their own exposed position and agony, their poverty and the threat of illness and death.

The church statues of Jesus Christ on the cross were especially easy for the fishermen and washers to identify with: a suffering and lonesome human being, clothed in a simple loincloth like themselves, but also a Christ who, according to Fernando, radiated helplessness—and submissiveness. Submissiveness was exactly what the church, the offspring of foreign conquerors, preached. Neither did it ever seriously try to resist the caste system; it even stirred up bad blood when a new priest, a Frenchman, allowed low-caste boys to participate in the altar service.

The priest never let the villagers get to know him intimately, and he considered himself their benefactor, not their liberator. "He helped the poor, / But disliked / A tailor's son becoming a doctor," to quote from *Evelyn My First Friend and Other Poems* (1985, 28). When Basil Fernando was a child, however, poverty in Palliyawatte was not as deep as it is today. Perhaps this helped make it easier for the church to play the role of benefactor. People could dress better and had more to eat than either before or after; there was even meat every day of the week, except Fridays, when Catholics traditionally do not eat meat.

Poverty, humiliation, and the agony of self-contempt, however, were always present, as were the screams of those who where beaten up in the police station. They too have remained present in the writings of Basil Fernando. Even his first published short story, from 1968 and in Sinhala, deals with the sense of relief felt by a low-caste boy: the monsoon rain forces him to stay at home, and he does not have to go outside into a world where his value is always questioned. In another short story, from the 1990 collection *Six Short Stories of Sri Lanka,* the writer lets a disillusioned revolutionary, a former priest, observe: "Poverty is no abstraction. It is something which eats into you, into your nerves, eyes, ears, anything that may be called the soul and body" (150).

Moreover, times grew worse. With the fifties came rising prices and massive protests, a Buddhist renaissance with nationalist overtones, ever more severe antagonism between the Sinhalese and the Tamil minority. The Catholic Church too was gradually given new signals. The Second Vatican Council (1962–65) emphasized the responsibility of all Christians "toward the poor and all the suffering" and opened the Catholic Church to non-Catholics as well as non-Christians. It also demanded an end to poverty and oppression. The Archbishop of Colombo could, for the very first time, put on a red cardinal's hat, but a theology with a stress on the liberation of the poor and oppressed was not welcomed by the leaders of the church. That at least is how Basil Fernando understood it. "Bishops of Asia, we appeal to you. . . . Dispossess yourselves of your wealth and possessions," was the demand formulated in the late sixties at a bishops' meeting in the Philippines—attended by Basil Fernando—but it was not received with sympathy.

Basil Fernando lived his life, figuratively speaking, close to the church, in that he went to schools controlled by it. Eventually he felt he had lost his Christian faith: "I saw too much blood and hypocrisy" (*Death and Rebirth,* 10). But it has come back, stronger than ever, although not accompanied by any confidence in the established church. Several poems from the collections of the eighties allude to the suffering and death of Christ, and they all deal with a Christ who belongs to the poor and afflicted. In one of them, the poet dreams of a mob that persists in roaring, "We have no king but Caesar," and votes to condemn Jesus to death (*Sharing Betel,* 35). In another poem a soldier hears his prisoner whisper, "I thirst," and has a sensation of the crucified behind him; however, he silences the prisoner as well as his own inner voice by shooting the man—and by crossing himself afterward (32). A third poem deals with Pontius Pilate, the shrewd lawyer who shifts his own responsibility onto the masses (33).

In a fourth poem we meet Peter, the apostle, warming himself by the fire in the courtyard of the high priest. Three times he denies all knowledge of Jesus; here, though, this does not happen "out of shame" but "out of necessity" (*Evelyn,* 17). Facing manipulated opinion, a poor man must protect himself with lies and accept being slandered by later popes and theologians. Above all, he must bide his time, "with patience of a fisherman / taught by the sea" (ibid.).

The Christian element is strongest in the later collection *Death and Rebirth* (1993), which opens with a sequence of poems in the form of a prayer to God. These are poems dealing with evil and violence, with bureaucrats and poverty, but also expressing the certainty that God is greater than his churches and has not only patience but also love and a sense of humor.

Basil Fernando was born in a time when the older generation was still in possession of the heritage of traditional poetry, a common phenomenon in the homes of poor Sinhalese people. Modern poetry flourished as well: "the Colombo poets" with their rhymed patriotic poems were read (and sung) by many, free verse was gaining ground, and all newspapers carried a poetry column. Basil Fernando was not the only child who dreamed of becoming a poet; so did most of his schoolmates.

Basil Fernando, a boy from the washers' caste, also had the opportunity to continue his studies. It was his mother's wish: she herself had wanted to become a teacher but had instead been forced (according to custom) to marry the husband of her deceased sister and submit to a life of poverty. She defied prejudice, worked her will, and inspired other villagers to do the same. In

a long poem from the collection *Sharing Betel,* Basil Fernando pays homage to his mother for all she meant to him: "And I who carried / The cloth bundles with you / Am carrying your spirit within me / Your pride / And the determination / Never to bow down" (16–17). In fact, English schools offered low-caste children new opportunities. Here Basil Fernando was to conquer a new language, a language that was to help him break with poetic forms and their power over thought and to express experiences that traditional Sinhalese self-understanding could not contain.

In 1972, the year after the suppression of the armed insurrection of Sinhalese leftist youth, Basil Fernando passed his examination at the faculty of law. In the seventies he was a university teacher in English and intensely engaged in the work of revolutionary socialist groups. He had begun to write, and in 1973 his first book appeared: *A New Era to Emerge,* a collection of poetry. Three years later followed a collection in Sinhala, *Koluwa Maleya* (The Young Man Died). In 1982 he became a lawyer, in a situation where law and order were increasingly threatened by collapse. In 1984 he began to work with violations of human rights and also published two more volumes of poetry and a collection of short stories. The persecution of Tamils became more and more violent, and the Tamil Tiger guerrillas emerged. The police and the military grew increasingly powerful. People began to disappear and were later found murdered, among them priests with undesirable opinions. One lawyer was arrested by the police and died in hospital from his wounds and from maltreatment. The lawyers' association took the unique decision not to represent the police in any legal instance.

In 1989, within a short period of time, four of Basil Fernando's colleagues were murdered and he himself was warned by a police officer who was kindly disposed toward him that his safety could no longer be guaranteed. That same year, in connection with a legal conference abroad, Basil Fernando left Sri Lanka. In one of his prayer poems in *Death and Rebirth* he thanks God "For helping me to see danger / To flee in time / And for the strangers I met on the way / Who turned out to be / Such good friends / Theirs and your company" (6). Since then he has represented (among others) Vietnamese refugees in Hong Kong and has monitored elections in Cambodia. He is a member of the editorial board of an Asian journal of creative writing, *Asia: Culture Links* (Hong Kong), and he has also continued to publish: in addition to poems and short stories, he has produced two books on refugee issues and human rights and one on Sri Lanka. In the latter he emphasizes the fatal legacy of colonial times, which has contributed to the development of a police and military state within the state, to the persecution of trade unions and minorities, and to continual violations of human rights.

Even in his first collection of poems there are scenes from Basil Fernando's adolescence, and such scenes have become a permanent feature of his work. In fact, Palliyawatte, the village of his childhood, emerges as the life-giving center of his writings: "I am left / To tell the stories" (*Evelyn,* 15). His recollections have grown to almost symbolic dimensions. The fortunes of Palliyawatte's people and the questions of poverty, pride, and faith are still waiting for an answer.

Basil Fernando's style is unobtrusive and restrained. His strong feelings are disciplined by a terse, austere, and sometimes ironic matter-of-factness. His abruptness may sometimes seem excessive, making his poems look more like drafts than finished products, but his sense of rhythm seldom fails. His verse is almost always free, with but a few sudden, singing rhymes inserted here and there. He comes straight to the point, his choice of words is simple, and strikingly often he uses a direct form of address to the person about whom he is writing.

A lot of what he writes revolves around *friendship,* one of the finest words he seems to know (along with others like *sharing*). The titles of both of his collections of poems from the eighties are significant: *Evelyn My First Friend* and *Sharing Betel.* The long memorial poem dedicated to his mother (mentioned and quoted above) speaks of the relationship between mother and child as a form of friendship (*Sharing,* 8). His parents' involuntary marriage meant "a permanent state of suffering and shock" (10), but nevertheless, "what friends, you two later became" (9). A city may be a friend, as may the shade under the trees; Catholic priests develop strong ties of friendship, and the writer wishes to think of God not as his Lord but as his friend. Perhaps we find the most moving expression of friendship in the title poem of *Evelyn My First Friend,* a memorial poem to the poet's little sister, who died at the age of six from wrongly treated pneumonia.

They brought you back,
Dressed like a little angel.

I did understand
The meaning.
That day is more
Vivid to me
Than any other,
Before or after.

You were my first friend
And the best.
Even decades after
You are so much about the place.
That'll be so

Till into silence
I too would go. (7)

The struggle to ease the sense of loneliness and anonymity, to overcome the distance in time and space, is constant. The process of memory itself is a decisive sign of life, a sign of solidarity with the world to which the writer once naturally belonged. Fragments of memory and of faces in his dreams stand out as revelations, and, as if it were an invocation, he continually repeats his refusal to forget them. Even a poem seemingly registering everyday impressions, including sounds from neighboring apartments, seems in a concentrated way to deal with that which is too easily lost. In several of Basil Fernando's best texts it is as if human destiny itself had received an aura of anonymity—an ambiguous anonymity, in certain respects universal but also the result of poverty and of enforced modesty. One of the nameless dead by the roadside, perhaps fallen in the insurrection of 1971, arouses feelings of guilt. The unknown young man of whom the poet catches a glimpse during the curfew also affects him: "Stop, and tell me at least tomorrow" (*Evelyn,* 22). His agony and despair are also great in a poem dedicated to the memory of his murdered neighbor, a poem wherein the dead man visits the poet and laughs at him: "Every night, I feel / I should pass away too / And be reborn, again and again / Till I prove capable / Of winning your friendship / Once more" (quoted in *The Village at the Mouth of the River,* part 5, March 1993).

Compared with the former longing for friendship and solidarity, there is now a "savage indifference" (*Evelyn,* 31) leaving its mark on life in Sri Lanka today. "I'm deeply interested in the destructive role the Sri Lankan middle class has played and still is playing against the best interests of the mass of people here," Basil Fernando stated in a recent interview. Calculation and greed stand out as virtues acquired by long practice in his society, together with envy and submission. Violence is smoldering, and from time to time it breaches the surface and bursts into flame.

Basil Fernando's first collection of short fiction, *Four Short Stories of Sri Lanka* (1986), deals with the gangster system in politics, with graft and corruption. Politicians and police officers, ultimately responsible for much of the murdering and plundering that goes on, are constantly trying to shunt their own guilt onto ordinary people. In one of his most powerful protest poems, written after the massacre of Tamils in July 1983, the writer refuses to take this guilt upon himself. In the prizewinning poem "Just Society" from *Evelyn My First Friend* he speaks in the name of all Sinhalese people:

You burned the buildings
And put me in prison

You threw their infants into fire
And called me inhuman
You murdered in open daylight
And blamed me for wanting blood
You turned my neighbour into a refugee
And said I am responsible
You looted his hard-earned property
And called me a thief
You imprisoned him and killed him
And named me a brute.
You befriended thugs and I the victims
But you made me the accused. (10)

In other poems, sometimes in a deceptively good-humored tone of voice, he gives us almost unbearable pictures of the ravages of the murderous mob in Colombo. However, Basil Fernando also seems to feel a need to give oppression new proportions, to bring it down to earth, so to speak. In a kind of playful fable, the career politician is reduced to a conceited little ant, the government to a pig ready for slaughter and hanging on a spit or to a fish on the hook. There is a clear connection between animal and imagination; in one poem the writer depicts himself as breaking out of his isolation and being transformed into a bird.

In the abovementioned "Just Society" Basil Fernando also writes, "Wounds of defeat / Will live with me long / And the memory / Of this insult" (*Evelyn,* 11). In another poem he compares his countrymen to cattle with the brand of submission burned in them early, by the European conquerors, or possibly even earlier. Already in his first collection of poetry he speaks of "ages of suffering" connecting the lives of the anonymous poor with the past. Individual memory is fused into a collective one. To remember is to expose oneself to something difficult and painful, but memories also pave the way to pride and resistance. A fight against a ruthless local landowner, one short story tells us, lived on in legend. In an interview the author quotes a priest who once found that the memory of the rebellion of 1818 still survives in the minds of people in a distant part of Sri Lanka!

In his latest and best collection of short fiction, *Six Short Stories of Sri Lanka,* the long-term perspective stands out clearly. In some of his stories Basil Fernando depicts proud men of his native village causing bitter envy; it required persecution and violence to break them. His prose has now changed. In spite of the spare and foreshadowing style and in spite of the anonymous contours of the human lot, these recent short stories are more full-length portraits than were the tales of his earlier, more satiric collection. The climax comes in a noteworthy, concentrated story about an old man who seems to have a great deal in common with the author's own father. Throughout his life, this man has lived in the very same village. Every day, after work, he walks down to the canal for a short rest. Half of his eighty-year life he has lived under British rule, the other half under independence. He never speaks about colonial times. He has buried them somewhere along with his deepest pain and sense of humiliation, far down in the lower recesses of his mind and the collective subconscious. He is like a tortoise, pulling his head into his shell; he sees nothing but cannot help registering impressions.

It is in this unconscious way, over unimaginable distances of time, that the experiences and outlook of generations are passed on. The independence of 1948 brought no significant change; the police and the military continued to protect the powerful and the rich. In the short story, dead bodies suddenly appear floating along the canal, in increasing numbers—bodies of murdered people no one dares to bury, victims of unknown massacres in unknown places. Eventually the old man is no longer capable of walking down to the canal. He starts to have nightmares. He sees himself and his son lying dead in the water on either side of the big church statue of Christ, like the two thieves depicted in the Gospels. All the people he has ever known and loved appear in his dreams, also dead in the water. He is frightened and retreats into himself. In a final dream, he reaches the very core of memory, a core of shock and shame; men of a foreign race with swords and guns are running amok in his village.

This short story may be compared with another text dealing expressly with Basil Fernando's own father. In a poem from *Sharing Betel* the long-term perspective of the father stands out as a foothold the son feels he is lacking.

You, Father, are eternity
And I am impermanence
You are quietness, the strength
Of silence. I am only noise
The weakness of urgency.
You tend the garden, look after
Little ones, reflecting backward
To eight decades or so.
I, just stare blank into nothingness. (37)

In many texts it is precisely the absence of a foothold—a state of emptiness, apathy, and discouragement—that stands out as the great threat, as the death of spirit. In a poem from *Death and Rebirth* the writer asks God if it is He who has left people in a void or if the people have left Him. It is probably no coincidence that, in the poem above, we see the image of the father, bearing the weight of eight decades, joining with the image of God.*

Anders Sjöbohm, Winter 1999

*This essay is based on information supplied by the writer himself and on the rich material LeRoy Robinson has published in various university magazines in Nagasaki, Japan. These include primarily the journal *Keiei to Keizai,* an interview in three parts (1985–88), and a biography in six parts, *The Village at the Mouth of the River* (1992–93). Robinson has also edited and, in the same magazine, published the two collections of short stories by Basil Fernando. My essay is dedicated to LeRoy Robinson, as an expression of appreciation and gratitude for all his unselfish work and for his friendship over the years.

▪ WORKS CITED

Fernando, Basil. *A New Era to Emerge.* Nugegoda. 1973.

———. *Koluwa Maleya.* 1976.

———. *Evelyn My First Friend and Other Poems.* Wattala. 1985.

———. "Four Short Stories of Sri Lanka." LeRoy Robinson, ed. *Keiei to Keizai* (Nagasaki University), 65:4 (March 1986).

———. *Sharing Betel.* Colombo. 1987.

———. "Six Short Stories of Sri Lanka." LeRoy Robinson, ed. *Keiei to Keizai,* 70:3 (December 1990).

———. *Sri Lanka—Modernization Vs. Militarization: Ethnic Conflict and Labour.* Hong Kong. Asia Monitor Resource Center. 1991.

———. *Asian Refugees: A Search for Solutions.* Hong Kong. International Affairs / Christian Conference of Asia. 1991.

———. *The Inability to Prosecute: Courts and Human Rights in Cambodia and Sri Lanka.* Hong Kong. Future Asia Link. 1993.

———. *Death and Rebirth.* Hong Kong. 1993.

———. *The Cynics and the Owls.* Hong Kong. 1994.

Robinson, LeRoy. "An Interview with Basil Fernando on Aspects of Culture in Sri Lanka." 3 parts: *Tonan Ajia Kenkyu Nenpo* (Nagasaki University), 27 (20 December 1985), pp. 127–41; *Keiei to Keizai* (Nagasaki University), 66:1 (June 1986), pp. 123–42; *Keiei to Keizai,* 68:2 (September 1988), pp. 141–62.

———. "The Village at the Mouth of the River: A Biography of Basil Fernando." Published in six installments in *Keiei to Keizai* and *Tonan Ajia Kenkyu Nenpo* from March 1992 to September 1993.

Southeast Asia

MALAYSIA

A Survey of Malaysian Poetry in English

Every fortnight, for two and a half years from 1991 to 1993, I wrote a poetry column in the *New Straits Times,* the main national daily newspaper in Malaysia. I had the intention of introducing poets and poetry to Malaysians and took as my brief the discussion of particular poems by poets I found interesting. During those two and a half years I naturally discussed some Malaysian poets who wrote in English. When Professor Edwin Thumboo requested a survey article of Malaysian poetry in English for *World Literature Today,* I decided that I should draw on the pieces that went into my column for what must really be a personal perspective on this corpus of poetry. I have tried to pick out the concerns of the individual poets, which have also been the more general concerns of the group as a whole.

Shirley Lim is arguably the most famous writer of Malaysian origin. Having twice won the American Book Award (in 1990 for *The Forbidden Stitch: An Asian American Women's Anthology* and again in 1996 for her memoir, *Among the White Moonfaces*), she is obviously one of the most prominent Asian American writers today. Way back in 1980 she won the Commonwealth Literature Prize for the best first book with *Crossing the Peninsula.* Lim had written it as a Malaysian. Ironically, in the year the prize was announced, she became an American citizen: "On Saint Valentine's day, 1980, four months pregnant, I stood in a hall in White Plains and swore allegiance to the flag and to the republic for which it stands" (*Moonfaces,* 295).

Notwithstanding the leaving (I discussed this in a public lecture in September 1994 at the Singapore Festival of Books, a lecture titled "The Poetry of Departures: Ee Tiang Hong and Shirley Lim"), Shirley Lim has returned repeatedly to Malaysia and Asia. Her most recent book, *What the Fortune Teller Didn't Say,* was published in 1998 and was launched in the United States and also in Malaysia at the Triennial of the Association for Commonwealth Literature and Language Studies (ACLALS) held in Kuala Lumpur in December of that same year.

And yet, being at home in America does not preclud the resurgence of longing for the original home. One simply doesn't give one's history away by adopting another passport. One striking poem from the 1980 prizewinning volume best speaks of this nostalgia for home:

Thoughts from Abroad
Late through October the leaves change colour.
The season has been around so long most
Do not see it go to winter.
From our window-height we watch the year close
In the trees. About us, the rural land
Reflects the sunlight. Far away,
Unglimpsed, the Atlantic makes a band
Of mirrors for Massachusetts. Today,
The scene is exulting: to air and light
Houses, trees and highways seem sensible
Moment to moment; till we can quite
Imagine this world invisible
As instinct on the flood for home
From which all exiled landscapes come.

Shirley Lim's sonnet is clearly set in New England. With its rhymes that do not all rhyme perfectly, we are reminded of Robert Lowell, the New England and Massachusetts connection. This lovely and somewhat loose sonnet recalls the fourteen-line unrhymed sonnets of Lowell. One might say that the spelling of "colour" in the British form already proclaims the origins of the sonneteer as elsewhere. By itself it may not be worth noticing, and indeed it may be attributed to the different orthographic conventions of publishing in the British Commonwealth and the United States. However, since other features of the sonnet drive home the same point, one can say that Lim declares her origin to have been in Malaysia. She is a Commonwealth poet, who speaks and writes a variety of English which harks back to metropolitan English.

"Most / Do not see it go to winter," but not the poet, to whom the vibrant colours of autumn are still not dulled by familiarity. Rhyming "colour" with "winter" underlines by its contrast the privation that is winter with its absence of rich colours. It also prepares us for the hankering after the landscapes of which the poet has been deprived in being abroad. Lim's sonnet turns a little earlier than the conventional sonnet usually does—i.e., at the last word of the eighth line rather than at the beginning of the sestet. "Today" is rhymed with "away," and again we catch the suggestion of the poet's being abroad, away. The landscape of New England is described in rich detail, yet all these details fade in the face of the longing for home, for the absent, exiled landscapes. "Home" and "come" form an eye-rhyme pair. This failure to rhyme in the clinching couplet at the end of Lim's sonnet points to a thematic dislocation and proclaims a displaced persona haunted by "exiled landscapes." The imperfect rhymes bespeak displacement, a "home" elsewhere. It is when, in Massachusetts, "to air and light / Houses, trees and highways seem sensible / Moment to moment" that the poet longs most strongly for the exiled landscape, so that even the animated, exulting New England landscape before her fades and becomes invisible, as those which have been exiled come flooding back.

Ee Tiang Hong also left Malaysia, but for Australia rather than the United States. His leaving was not so strongly tinged with nostalgia. Some of his poems speak somewhat bitterly of discrimination and disillusionment. In "Patriotism" (from *Myths for a Wilderness*, Kuala Lumpur, 1976) he asks plaintively: "Surely by the time one reaches / The seventh generation, / The seventh heaven, / One is no longer subject / To all these?" (52). "All these" included many things, but certainly the bewilderment and anger of being treated unequally in the land of his ancestors: "With all these, goodness, /

How shall I breathe with dignity / What air of freedom there is / Here in my motherland?"

Ee's departure was thus more decisive than Shirley Lim's. Part of this must be due to the fact that he saw less than Lim did which he might work lovingly into poetry. Malacca, the hometown of both Ee and Lim, was more sensuously and intimately imprinted in Lim and also more forcefully described by her. She speaks of her childhood that "imprinted on me the sense of Malacca as my home, a sense I have never been able to recover anywhere else in the world" (*Moonfaces,* 41). I wonder whether this lighter engagement with his homeland puts Ee in a better position to see the comic possibilities of the English spoken here in Malaysia. At any rate, it is Ee who exploits the language for comic purposes in "Song of a Young Malayan":

Not say I don't appreciate poetry
But you speak of poetry which have no rhyme,
Not like the ones I sometimes quote:
"What is our life so full of care
We got no time to stand and stare?"
But I still must admit
I don't like poetry
Very much. I like music.

Not jazz American stuff,
Classical music worse still, too long and dull.
I like music to be sentimental,
Like at night while dim light in my room
I turn on the radio.
O Russ Hamilton is my favourite,
His words so full of meaning:
"I'll go out in the night
But you a dream."

But I never like painting in school
I hated Art like anything.
And Modern Art
I cannot understand. Like Picasso —
Why he always show
A man with funny shape
Head and body all mixed up?
I think
It's all nonsensical.

The well of Malaysian English is perhaps too shallow to yield clear poetic water fit for drinking in large draughts. When we grapple with our profoundest problems, we probably do so in Malay or in our respective vernacular languages, unless English happens to be our most proficient language. But it is very unlikely that we do our deepest thinking in Malaysian English such as we find in Ee Tiang Hong's poem.

Salleh Ben Joned, who was taught by Ee in school, salutes his teacher in the poem "Malchin Monologue," which begins with a striking similarity to "Song of a Young Malayan":

not say I don't speak english well
but you speak of english that got no
kick lah!
Not like the real malaysians talk;
No guli-in-the-mouth
Tongue-twisting tricks
Like that funny fellow on the telly
That kereta lembu appleby
Talks to his minister
Always with a slow trick up his tongue

Salleh Joned uses Malaysian English mockingly. The point is obviously to send up the Malaysian accent in this half-serious defence of it. He uses the Malaysian knack for unusual stress placement to make multilingual jokes: "we stress the du in education / 'cause we just like to do what we like / with words and their meanings / we tekan the ni in fornication / for the same reason — understand tak? / In purchase we always stress the chase / In bargain the gain of course." The "fornication" line is an inside joke for Malaysians in that it assumes the reader's awareness of a little Malay and a little Hokkien. One imagines a properly clued-in coterie at a pub roaring over the wisecrack. The poem concludes: "How dare you say we misplace our stresses! / We always have them about us / Everytime we talk english."

After decades of political independence, teacher and pupil can still be seen to be doing the same thing with Malaysian English. It seems not to be a variety of the English language which has been properly naturalised and elaborated as a literary language. The limitations of this variety are all the clearer when set against the success of the two poems we have looked at. These serve only to underline the failure of Malaysian English to acquire the status of a literary language.

Muhammad Haji Salleh's poetry in English (and he is a poet in two languages, with Malay as a second and now dominant poetic medium) is an interesting case for this discussion of the particular contribution of Malaysian poets to a literary language. Having studied English literature at the Universities of Singapore and Malaya, he is interesting to look at from the point of view of his diction. His poem "death like conception (for father)" speaks of the passing of his father. Death in the poem is seen to be in the hands of God, like the beginning of life, coming unbidden and ultimately beyond the reach of human intervention.

death like conception
arrives with the whims of fate
or the gentleness
of the moment.

now death stood in your soul
the tenant body has surrendered
its blood and life-redness
to its last owner,
stock-taker.

but death should not come
to the pulsating cells,
not after convalescence,
the rest of renewal.
but it came
and it took you along.
home is where

you return at last,
at the end of the truncated
winding road.
in life you knew your way,
death should be a journey
along the hopes and beliefs
that have overshot
into the undergrowth,
shadow-bound and earth-bound.

now, through these eyes
of sight and blindness,
I pray, as I have never
called to god before
for a father's soul,
god-given and god-taken.

Obviously, any poet who sits down to write a poem chooses from a hoard of available words. Equally important with the choice of suitable words is the task of deflecting words which come crowding in too easily, to ensure that the clichés and the threadbare words do not get into the poem to mar it. The strategy of deflecting words is very clear in this poem. "Undertaker," a word which is natural in the context of the poem's subject, is never allowed in. The hackneyed phrase "Rest in peace" is also not admitted. Instead, we have "stock-taker," "took," "god-taken," and "the rest of renewal." Deflecting a word can, in the context of this poem, amount to rejecting an emotion or wishing for a certain outcome, in this case the hope of delaying the death of the father: "but death should not come / to the pulsating cells, / not after convalescence, / the rest of renewal."

The poet pays tribute to the faith of his father, as the poem is finally a falling back on the ancestral faith. There is a sense in which the poet has never yet called on God ("I pray, as I have never called to God before"). The word as can be read as "since." But equally strong is the sense of as understood to mean "in the way"— "since I have never prayed before" as well as "in a manner I have never used in prayer before." The faith of the poet is not an easy faith. He prays with his eyes of sight and of sight obscured by tears—or, figuratively, of rational belief coupled with blind faith. The poet prays through his eyes also perhaps because he is unused to praying in the usual way. The alternative meaning is equally viable: i.e., that he prays through his eyes because in the profound grief of losing one's father, that is how one naturally prays on top of praying with the prescribed sacred prayers.

The spatial image of death as a journey is anticipated by the use of "arrives" (line 2) and "return" (line 17). Set in this context, there is instability in the word *bound* which, even without the poet's collusion, at once suggests stability in the sense of "tied down" and instability in the sense of "headed for." This latter sense is more strongly suggested by the imagery of the journey in the second stanza, which also suggests another word, "heaven-bound," a word which is strongly implied and which receives strong encouragement from the image of the way and the journey and a suggestion that is completely justified by the last line, "god-given and god-taken." There is a resolution in "god-taken," the unusual compound word that ends the poem: the poet's father is not carried away by the undertaker, but rather he is taken back into the presence of God. He is not conveyed underground but taken up to God; he returns to God. The father comes from God and returns to God; his soul is "god-given and god-taken." The chimed ending "god-given and god-taken" provides suitable closure. It completes a scheme of very spare rhyming which starts with last owner/stock-taker in the first stanza and shadow-bound/earth-bound in the second, in an essentially free-verse form. The affirmative statement of the ending is a resolution that both possesses some charm and carries conviction.

Wong Phui Nam is the most serious Malaysian poet still writing in English. The register of his English is highbrow and proper. But the seriousness I want to focus on signifies worthiness of serious critical consideration as well as seriousness in the sense of being grave, commonly manifested in solemnity or a lack of humor. Poems of death crowd Wong's published collections of poetry. Indeed, *how the hills are distant* (1968), the first of his two books, opens with such a poem: "When I am dead / and the old man, the river, / after a night of rain among the hills / should come upon me, / I shall only stir / like stones that drag the muddy bed. . ."

Poems published in the "Poet's Place" section of the *New Straits Times* by Wong Phui Nam have restated different aspects of the theme of death. "Terminal Ward" (from *Waking to the Prospect of a Dangerous Passage*), published on 11 March 1992, is a striking instance. It is all the more pointed for appearing on the same page as an obituary for the late lamented Keris Mas, a Malay writer of national fame. "For Another Birthday (for Joseph)" (Literary Page, 4 September 1991) is a graphic forward look to death and the attendant decomposition, which will make even the least squeamish stomach turn away from the birthday cake.

One complex poem titled "For THH" is about a birth that feels like death ("being dropped with split caul / into the wide maw of the cold and watery world"). It has an epigraph ("We Poets in our youth begin in gladness") which seems to be challenged by the opening poem in *how the hills are distant* and a large number of others in the volume, including a tender elegiac piece for the aged amah dying surrounded by old newspapers, biscuit tins, and faded photographs. The closing poem is another example in this vein. It speaks of the death of the heart in the dusun: "When you walk in the dusun, / the flying foxes gone, / mangosteens tightened up in knots / on shrivelled boughs, be glad / the heart too can turn up root / and die."

Though not a juvenile work at all, *how the hills are distant* is the product of Wong Phui Nam's youth, and the gladness of the epigraph of "For THH" is not much in evidence. The gladness that exists is the gladness that the death of the heart is possible. This strain in Wong's poetry is a form of resolute meditation on death. A poet like Omar Khayyam can also think about mortality, but in a different way. In Omar Khayyam one sees that there can be humour in such contemplation, if the focus on death is not too resolute, if thinking on death drives one back to life. Witness this quotation, from Edward Fitzgerald's translation:

For in the Market-place, one Dusk of Day,
I watch'd the Potter thumping his wet Clay:
   And with its all-obliterated Tongue
It murmur'd: "Gently, Brother, gently, pray!

Ah, fill the Cup — what boots it to repeat
How Time is slipping underneath our Feet:
   Unborn Tomorrow, and dead Yesterday,
Why fret about Them if Today be sweet!

Life after death is spent not in hell but in the potter's shop, and the punishment in death consists not in the torments of hellfire but in the thumping of the potter, whom the lump of clay addresses in terms of matey fellowship! So Omar Khayyam imagines before he turns his back on the potter's shop to run into the tavern for a drop of cheer. I believe Wong in his poems about death to be, among other things, instructing himself and his readers in facing the inevitable "dangerous passage" and practising mortification in the religious sense.

Ooi Boo Eng is the best of the occasional poets from Malaysia—i.e., those poets who, over the years, have published poems but have not brought out a *collection* of verse. There are a number of them. Kee Thuan Chye, though primarily a playwright, is another such poet worthy of mention. When Ooi left for Australia in 1983, Malaysia lost a poet of talent and an academic of distinction. Ooi was a trained teacher before he joined the University of Malaya in the sixties. He had been taught by Anthony Burgess at the teacher training college and earned himself a berth in one of Burgess's novels as a communist by the name of—what else?—Ooi Boo Eng. The real Ooi was not and is not a communist. After acquiring degrees in English literature at the Universities of Durham and Newcastle in England, he was happy to come back to the Malay College for a spell to teach the sons of the nobility as well as the brighter sons of Malay commoners, boys such as Anwar Ibrahim.

In the early seventies Ooi taught me English literature. I found his lectures on Metaphysical poetry particularly interesting. The Metaphysical poets are of course a group of writers habitually making unobvious connections and often given to elliptical reasoning. Himself a subtle thinker and writer, Ooi was able to illuminate the subtleties of Metaphysical poetry for his undergraduate audiences. Not for him, in writing as in teaching, the plodding of the pedestrian pedant. His syntactically difficult prose and lecturing style equally suited that subtle race of seventeenth-century writers. That style is clearly found in his poems.

They had form.
They had a manner, the manner.
Bred to it, granted,
caught, maybe, from that air
from which, as Nashe says,
    himself catching it,
brightness falls.
But carried to the manner born —
    a simple magnificence
    that made history
        and eternity
    with a gesture.

When Sidney and soldier met
At Zutphen, for example —
    Sidney bleeding, soldier too,
        'ghastly casting his eyes at the bottle'.
It isn't what he did —

Ooi is not so well known as he deserves to be, because he has never published collections of his verse. What we have are distinguished poems in academic journals here in Malaysia and abroad. These are difficult for readers to locate, and his actual readers are usually scholars who come upon his poems en passant in their professional reading.

Several poets I do not have the space to deal with here are Cecil Rajendra, a practising lawyer with a few volumes to his name (*Bones and Feathers,* Kuala Lumpur, 1978), and Hilary Tham, who now lives in the United States. There are some younger poets now writing in Malaysia who have published their work since I gave up my column in August 1993. Among those who have issued volumes of poetry are Charlene Rajendran (*Mangosteen Crumble,* Kuala Lumpur, 1999), Bernice Chauly (*going there and coming back,* Kuala Lumpur, 1997), and Rahel Joseph (*beginnings,* Kuala Lumpur, 1997). The scene is not overcrowded by any stretch of the imagination. Then as now, there is practically no sponsorship from either the public or the private sector. The audience for poetry in multilingual Malaysia is small in any case, and it is even smaller for poetry written in English.

This year literature has been made an integral part of the study of the English language, so that theoretically all Malaysian school students will have read some literary texts by the time they leave school. Since Malaysia has universal education up to the lower secondary level, one hopes that a new generation of readers, but particularly of readers of poetry, will be emerging in the near future.

C. S. Lim, Spring 2000

Traversing Boundaries: Journeys into Malaysian Fiction in English

Much of Malaysian literature has dealt with the problem of psychic displacement of migrant communities settling in a new land. Certainly, Malaysian literature written in English has identified very closely with this concern over the decades of postindependence Malaysia. The complexity involved is intensified by the fact that English is an acquired second language, rather than the first language, of the writers themselves. Choosing a colonial and non-native tongue to write about questions pertaining to identity and struggles of integration within a multicultural and pluralistic social context is, to say the least, fraught with difficulty that writers in a monocultural setting would be quite unfamiliar with. As with most marginalised communities, Malaysian writers in English are faced with the onerous task of creating a place for themselves in a setting which may not always regard them as possessing a crucial voice in the evolution of a people or a country. English, once the predominant language of administration, now no longer harbours hegemonic designs on the majority who speak the local and national language, Malay, with greater ease than ever they did English.

So far, Malaysia resembles any postcolonial, postindependence country, with its attendant problems of the loss and recovery of native cultures and language. With the inflow and settling of migrant groups from neighbouring countries as part of the colonial answer to the need for cheap labour in the nineteenth century, Malaysian society is now no different from many of its Asian neighbours in its spread of multicultural groups and its varieties of Asian languages existing alongside the dominant indigenous tongue and culture. The development and evolution of Malaysia have taken turns which have fostered, at least in cross-cultural communication, a greater willingness on the part of the nonindigenous (non-Malay) migrant communities to use Malay as their lingua franca. The displacement of English from the administrative and educational centers of Malaysian life itself has had implications on the receptivity of the average Malaysian to Malaysian literature written in English. The move downward from common administrative language to a language used by an urban minority has meant that users and writers of English have become increasingly marginalised; simultaneously, English has contributed to an increasingly fragmented context in which it stands alongside other local (and limited) vernaculars such as Tamil or Chinese. Most speakers of English are educated and middle-class urban dwellers. Many, though not all, of them are non-Malays who may have little access to their own native tongues, or most probably prefer instead the internationality of English as a means of effective communication, though they are familiar enough with Malay as the medium of communication locally.

Shirley Lim, a Malaysian-born writer and academic now resident in the United States, sums up very well the complex situation of language choice among the Chinese Malaysians; for example, "If Bahasa [Malaysia] is seen as an instrument for empowering one racial group and consequently for disempowering the Chinese Malaysians, the language itself may rouse strong feelings of disaffiliation, to be used only when necessary. The same Chinese Malaysians may turn to the language of descent to express their resistance to a national formation that appears to erase their identity. . . . Or . . . rejecting both Malay and Chinese cultural nationalisms based on paradigms of racial descent, assent to an international language . . . English" (1994a, 46–47). Such complications dog the immigrant communities, whether Chinese or Indian in descent, in their relations with the dominant language of discourse, the national language, known as Bahasa Malaysia (Malay) or Bahasa, for short.

Those who resort to English are of course regarded sometimes unfavourably as Malaysians heavily influenced (and still colonised) by the fashions of the West and who have no real sense of rootedness in the land. The situation is compounded by the fact that such Malaysians, many of them nonindigenous, have never resolved the problem their migrant fathers / mothers encountered earlier in the century: estrangement and alienation from the adopted new land. In fact, English serves quite well as the language to carry the ideas and metaphors of alienation occurring within migrant communities. Its alienness lends to its use a peculiar suitability, a deliberate dissonance and distancing between text and reader that only emphasises the extent of alienation experienced. For the Malaysian writer in English, this is amplified in the content of the writing itself, which is usually to do with the migrant consciousness struggling for integration and authenticity. Writing from the fringes of a predominantly urban and therefore cha(lle)nging landscape, the Malaysian writer in English exemplifies the dispossessed engaged in confronting the fragmented historical and cultural sense in a postindependence, postcolonial state.

In speaking of several Malaysian novels, Shirley Lim writes incisively and insightfully of the place of English in the Malaysian setting:

> English is an ethnic-neutral instrument whose international character counters a national-language / cultural dominance to express fragmentations resulting from exclusions and suppressions. In a monolingual, monocultural situation, minorities delegitimatized national-language processes [sic] use the former colonial language's "otherness" to give themselves a voice and identity. In oppressive national cultures, writers may turn to the strongly metropole function of English to criticize their societies' provincialism and chauvinism. . . . For Malaysian minority ethnic writers whose participation in the national literary scene has been severely marginalized, English serves as a counter-identification with a more accepting international culture. (1994b, 136–37)

Though there is a growing use of English among the Malay urban and elite class, most of the current Malaysian writers in English write from non-Malay, immigrant perspectives. The scene has not evolved all that much from the tightly culture-bound considerations of the different ethnic communities of preindependence Malaya to postindependence Malaysia. Writers of note continue to grapple with the notion of a national identity and a national culture, no matter how subtly or otherwise this is worked through. The traceable novelistic attempts emerge from ethnic categories, first and fore-

K. S. Maniam *(Robert H. Taylor)*

most; fidelity to these "ethnic surface[s] and social interactions" (Lim, 1994b, 138) provides the Malaysian writer with a well-worn familiarity that frames the deep, ongoing sense of dispossession well. For the purposes of this essay, the Malaysian fiction writers considered will include the major voices writing in English, such as Lee Kok Liang, Lloyd Fernando, and K. S. Maniam. It must be noted that Malaysian literature in Malay (the national literature), despite its prolific and rich nature, will have to be excluded.

Movements in Malaysian fiction have been occasioned by the immigrant's need to make sense of his new land. In a writer like K. S. Maniam, the almost inchoate need and desire for rootedness is most thoroughly expressed in his autobiographical novel *The Return* (1981). As a bildungsroman, it retells the story of the young narrator's life as he struggles to escape the oppressiveness of his small-town South Indian culture into greater freedom as a young schoolteacher working in a bigger city. Identity conflicts between first-generation and second-generation immigrants are described in terms of the narrator Ravi's escape from the paternalistic and chauvinistic stranglehold of the *Ayah*[1] figure of the novel. His education is felt to be the most crucial aspect of his young life, because it represents the fulfilling of his individuality and his overcoming the repressive social system of his inherited culture which has kept his family poor: "This is a community of Indian immigrants dependent on a system of colonial patronage and cowed by the circumstances of the rubber plantation economy

from which they draw their livelihood. It is a community turned in on itself, angry, shrewish, violent, engaged in unremitting conflict, and dominated by the seemingly arbitrary viciousness of the menfolk" (C. W. Watson, introduction to *The Return,* xi). Ravi's gradual empowerment is (ironically) effected through his mastery of the English language, the language of the colonialist. In fact, he is ridiculed by his community for trying to be a white. Finally, Ravi's conflict is between his Asian past and quasi-Western present self, a self that is "phantasmagoric, absorbed in fantasies insidiously propagated by an aggressively colonizing culture" (Lim, 1994b, 140). The vision of the land which his grandmother Periathai had, and the obsessive madness of his father-to-be, likewise anchored in the land, form part of the uneasiness of Ravi's life. He desires this rootedness, while seeing little beyond his own sense of dislocation as a second-generation South Indian immigrant and Western-trained English-language schoolteacher.

We see the same agonised negotiation of the individual through the labyrinthine passages of initiation in Maniam's other works, such as the title story in the collection *Haunting the Tiger,* "The Pelanduk" in *Plot, The Aborting, Parablames and Other Stories,* and particularly in his 1993 novel *In a Far Country.* Evaluating ethnic traditions in a multicultural and pluralistic postmodern context, and attempting to redefine and even transcend these social and psychological geographies, remain, for Maniam and other writers like him, crucial challenges. Reading isolated writers in Malaysian literature gives the impression that Malaysia is in the main monocultural, either comprising Indian or Chinese or Malay peoples. Cursory references to other cultures and races in literary texts further such an impression, which is erroneous but perhaps unavoidable in writings which begin from very clear and concrete cultural settings. In much of the depiction of cultures not the writer's own, it is all too clear how superficial and stereotyped the descriptions can be. Maniam, for instance, works remarkably well in his astute renditions of the Tamil Indian scene, but is less confident and less successful otherwise. Directing the tide of thinking therefore toward a culture that is vital and hybrid seems to be the desired requisite in novelistic concerns in Malaysian fiction. This Maniam does attempt, especially in the later work *In a Far Country.*

Lloyd Fernando in *Scorpion Orchid* (1976) and *Green Is the Colour* (1993) tries this, but the focus in *Scorpion Orchid,* for instance, on ethnically representative figures during the political troubles of the 1950s in Singapore (when it was still part of Malaysia), tends toward mere stereotype. *Green Is the Colour* explores the trauma of the 13 May 1969 racial riots, with the central concerns again being located in characters from the Chinese, Malay, Indian, and Eurasian communities in Malaysia. These contiguous communities are forced together into an uneasy alliance after the riots. This is reflected in the four friends, as Fernando takes pains to emphasise. But the artificiality of their togetherness is not always intentional. The friends remain surface figures, stereotypes: "The author has to deal with a range of characters of different races without privileging anyone. . . . He does not stay long enough with any one character for us to know that character well. Although his characters are memorable collectively, no one individual arrests our attention" (Wong Soak Koon, 1994, 188). In spite of the government push toward *Muhibah*,[2] and certainly in spite of authorial intent, these friends remain bound within their ethnic and cultural contexts. The effort toward a dynamic and organic national community is stillborn.

There is a lack of penetration into the core of the Malaysian struggle suggested by such potentially stereotyped novels. While Fernando looks toward introspection to understand the troubles which afflicted Malaysia in the 1950s and 1960s, there is little deliberation beyond the obvious race and culture observations. Integration stemming from the deeply conscious need for a kind of identity loss as necessary in the process of transcending race / culture bounds occurs in Maniam's novel *The Return,* where we see an initial engagement of this sort in Kannan, Ravi's deranged father. At the work's conclusion, Ravi pens a poem to his late father and intimates that his "words will not serve" (173). His mastery of the coloniser's tongue has gained great freedom for him, but does not settle the deep and underlying malaise of his dispossession. Ravi is both marginalised and deracinated, fundamentally withdrawn from the heart of his history / past. Kannan, on the other hand, with the unself-consciousness of the madman (or the schizophrenic here), finally "degenerates" linguistically into a kind of glossolalia: "He began to chant in a garbled language. It embarrassed me to hear him recite a rhythm mounted on Tamil, Malay and even Chinese words. It was a secret language, like the one we invented among ourselves when we were adolescents . . . with additional consonants or dropped vowels" (170–71).

Kannan's withdrawal from the realities of the social world reflects the inchoate need to enter into himself, to meditate, for "he was a man possessed by a special, esoteric dream" (171). His chants and rituals, for instance, support such a reading of the events of his life leading to his suicide. In fact, Kannan's deranged tongue may not be so insane as Ravi thinks; fruit of his maddened contemplations, it may even be legitimately

seen as a "garbled attempt to grapple with a multi-racial environment" (Wong Soak Koon, 1995, 94), distant and apart from his son's mastery of the English language. The crux of Kannan's somewhat quixotic quest (which finally drives him mad) is the inexpressible need for landedness and rootedness: "He had lost touch with reality completely. Now he not only increased his visits to the river, but he also brought pebbles, clay and lallang[3] to the house. These he laid out on a banana leaf before Nataraja. 'Breathe your spirit into them!' he chanted. 'Make them the clay and grass of my body!'" (168). He fights against government officials who tell him he is a squatter and will be evicted soon, just as his mother Periathai had done earlier. The pathos of the repetitive cycles which oppress mother and son only stresses the ongoing dispossession of all the characters and underlines ironically Ravi's supposed triumph over his repressive society as simply an evasion of the challenge facing migrant communities. Kannan dies at last in the house he builds with his own hands, burned by the flames he himself ignites, literally consumed by the land he so longed to possess.

The human enterprise is viewed with deep irony and fatalism; it appears that integratedness is too remote an illusion to entertain. Lee Kok Liang's work, with its Buddhist undertones, describes the desire for coherence within a backdrop that continually renders all action impotent. His narration is often detached: the sufferings of human life are inevitable, part of the tedious cycle of *samsara*[4] and *karma*[5] from which humanity struggles to emerge through death. *Death Is a Ceremony* was Lee's last published work before he died in 1992. The title sounds portentous in retrospect; certainly, in this collection of short stories, death reaches inexorably into the lives of men and women, unapologetic about its interference. Such a framework or backdrop of impersonal universal powers and forces at work resonates in the context of Malaysian fiction as continual reverberations of those political and social dynamics which drive individuals to madness and dissolution. In the wheels of a greater determining force, Lee's characters emerge as strange players executing their roles in a painful scene, uncomprehending of purpose and futile in their bid for transcendence.

Lee describes a fear-ridden cast attempting to take the narrative eye away from their necessary end (death and dissolution). However, his characters are not without will. *Flowers in the Sky* (1981) and *The Mutes in the Sun* (1981), Lee's other books, resist helpless defeat in their stories about "alarming, powerful profiles of individuals brutalised, ostracised, alienated by authority figures or fellow victims" (Harrex, 144). These "paradigms of social evils" are nevertheless "mitigated by gestures of compassion or love" (144). This is also a point Fernando picks up, incidentally, in *Green Is the Colour,* suggesting therefore that human gestures forging interracial communications express the "glimpses of hope" in the collective struggle toward integration and identity (Wong Soak Koon, 1994, 185).

Lee's use of the mute in the title story (actually a novella) of *The Mutes in the Sun* and "Dumb Dumb by a Bee Stung" (from *Death Is a Ceremony*) is an interesting rendition of the dumbfounded individual in a situation of psychic displacement within a pluralistic context. The mute is the silenced Other, marginalised by nature and society, yet ironically, he "articulates" the inadequacies of the dominant ideology / culture by his gaze in "Dumb Dumb by a Bee Stung," for instance. The mute hunchback intrudes disturbingly into the funeral of Mr. Tze Tai Yuen. The deformed child's presence provides a curious dissonance amid the gathering of the cultural elite awaiting Mr. Tze's euphemistic departure to the "yellow springs." It is his incongruously steady gaze that proves unsettling and unnerving.

> The little hunchback was really annoying him, staring at him; his right cheek twitched. There was something in that fellow's eyes that disturbed him — a stare as questioning as a cat's but glazed over by a film of resignation, defeat or acceptance. Hin Too glanced around and it seemed to him that the whole atmosphere of the place had been compressed into the stare of the boy. He shook off the feeling. It was hot and he was getting tired. (153)

In retaliation for his intrusion, the boy is thrown out of the hall, to be tormented by the street youths and stung by a hive of bees. As a description of marginalised man, the hunchback who intrudes into such frames of ritual and ceremony becomes, through a reversal, a frightening figure which relays to the characters at large their own illusory sense of dominance. He reminds them of bad karma and the ephemeral nature of human striving for power. Mr. Tze's death, which has been ceremonialised and is the "euphemistically applied 'journey' he is about to take" (M.Y. Wong, 28), cracks the moment the characters face the uncompromising reality of the hunchback's undermining gaze.

Lee appears to confine himself to depicting the human condition in such terms. But, as Syd Harrex points out, "Politics permeate most spheres of human activity and relationships in Lee's fictional world" (144). Ever mindful of the local sensitivities, Lee conveys his sense of the conflicts of the Malaysian individual subtly and indirectly; certainly, this gentle refusal to confront another directly is typical of the fastidious refinement of his Straits Chinese background and culture. His technique of "applied introspection" which "reveals the inward brooding of a world and its inhabitants" (Harrex, 145) does seem, in fact, to be the general direction to which other writers like Maniam and Fernando are also pointing. But there is no prescription about Lee's fiction. He offers not so much a method as a meditative consideration of life through his characters' internal conflicts.

Taking up this idea of introspection and consciousness as a means toward transformation and transcendence of race/culture bounds, Maniam in *In a Far Country* moves away from the simpler structure and concerns of *The Return* and experiments with an inward retrieval of the dispossessed individual's past before any transcendence or transformation can occur. The protagonist, Rajan, tells his wife Vasanthi, "We must go back again and again" (186). The liveliness of the past is sustained through such connectedness with it. In the linearity of human continuity and evolution, the past remains open and accessible, revitalising through its influence on the shaping mind and spirituality of the individual who seeks. Rajan's exploration of his past requires a drastic minimalising and a deliberate shrinking of his immediate world. In what appears to be some imminent breakdown, he shuts himself up in a room in his house to initiate this inner journey: "It was on such a bright morning, some time back, that I left my office premises, abruptly, and shut myself up in this room in my house. My wife and children didn't know what to make of my behaviour the first few days, then fell into a routine that emerged from the crisis" (1). The difficulty of the enterprise is underscored by Maniam's prose, "dense, obscure" (Wong Soak Koon, 1995, 95); the departure from realism and the dependence on mind and dreamscapes is destabilising, fostering the continued heightening of an expanding consciousness and understanding of the present in the revelatory use of visions from the past. Rajan's breakdown is transfiguring; it transforms him as he "enters those mindscapes . . . dormant in the mind . . . to re-experience with fresh empathy and understanding past relationships" (Ibid., 95).

Rajan's delving into his past involves his recall of his father and his friend Lee Shin, Zulkifli, Wali Farouk, vagrant philosopher Sivasurian, and Vasanthi. His father represents the obvious, Rajan's cultural heritage; Lee Shin and Zulkifli represent the Chinese and Malay consciousness respectively. Zulkifli and Sivasurian also act as Rajan's spiritual guides as he undertakes the journey inward, and it is important to see Zulkifli, the indigenous Malay guide, as the one who assists in Rajan's discovery of the land (symbolised by the spirit of the tiger) through the lens of an essentially migrant consciousness. But Rajan now moves beyond even what Zulkifli shows him in the inward and symbolic journey which he takes back to the land of the tiger (this time alone). In depicting these interracial communications, however, Maniam avoids "nationalist realism" (Paul Sharrad, introduction to *In a Far Country,* xv) and stereotyping: his novel, while about "trying to become a Malaysian" (ix), shifts its attention from externally imposed views of national identity. Identity for Rajan / Maniam begins at the point of spiritual blackness encroaching upon the country of the soul. In the far country of his mind and past, Rajan is engulfed by the darkening realisation of his dispossession. Only as he comes to new understanding of the characters he recollects, and replaces their actions and lives in the refreshing context as individuals rather than racial representatives or stereotypes, does Rajan fully appreciate how he has himself shifted from the stifling insularity of cultural boundedness to an expanding and encompassing sympathy and knowledge of others.

Rajan's purgatorial breakdown voices the deathliness Lee Kok Liang's characters fear. Its necessity is evident in Rajan's final recovery of the self, and of the tempered hopefulness at the novel's conclusion. The theme is not new: by choosing loss and death, Rajan emerges a phoenixlike figure, imbued with a depth of empathy for the struggles of his friends and an undeniable connection with the land. This is crucial to the novel. Rajan's earlier foray into the interior of the jungle, or the land of the tiger, had been effected with Zulkifli as his guide; but now, his inward and symbolic rejourneying to the same place is to understand what he could not years ago, and, finally, to transcend it: "Without anyone to guide or impose on me, I am travelling with an agility of my own. There is no more an eye, neither Zulkifli's nor the tiger's, watching. I've suddenly become the eye itself. A lidless eye so that nothing can be distorted" (138).

Rajan's consciousness becomes concentrated in the eye, all-seeing and all-understanding. It is through this spiritual awakening that he reaches even beyond the tiger's boundaries, the symbol of "some central ordering principle" (Wong Soak Koon, 1995, 104) or authority: "I am relieved I don't hold on to any authority, in whatever sense, and merely allow the stream of experience to reveal all the various shades of experience and meaning. . . . My only wish now is that I never try ever again to impose my will or beliefs on others. And in return, I hope others will do the same" (144). Fernando's acts of compassion and Lee's saddened gaze of the Other resonate in Rajan's words. Maniam's renewed protagonist is practical: emerging out of the crisis, he redefines his relationship with his wife, coming to see how she, and the women before her, have suffered from the oppressiveness of male discourse within dominant social / cultural structures. In *In a Far Country* there are these little acts of kindness, and the Other no longer seems quite so threatening in the light of his or her humanity. Legitimizing the Other is not an act which frees Vasanthi, or the countless suppressed Indian women Rajan can think of, so much as it certainly frees him from the rigidities of his cultural biases.

> Then, as I watched her, she began to sob and then to cry. It wasn't a woman who was crying. Her body didn't just shake; it was convulsed with tremors from a deeper source. Was it because I was so near her that I saw and felt a straining? Was it because I was near the nearness that I couldn't help myself from releasing her from the straining?
>
> Something helped me to begin the unworking. Unworking the sari folds tucked so tightly, neatly, into her flesh. Undoing the cross-stitches of her and my sari-bordered life. It comes to me now, even as I write, this strange, unlooked for energy that dares to undo the network of inhibitions, prohibitions, history and predilections that we have cast about us: a nakedness that reaches beyond the flesh. (196)

Using the woman to describe the Other provides focus for Maniam to deal with the wider social scenario. He does not go beyond this point in his conclusion, but the implications are more than evident.

Malaysian fiction in English has always contained a core sense of the anguish of the dispossessed. Indeed, the novels examined are "identity-haunted books spiraling from their fringe locations" (Lim, 1994b, 154). Constructing fictions to voice that alienation remarks on these movements toward a healing resolution. Maniam's point, especially in *In a Far Country,* is to take the attention away from (and even reject) externally imposed views of group or collective identity, and rightly suggests that culture, being dynamic and organic, arises first from the growth of the assenting individual consciousness. For migrant consciousness to be absorbed into the land (the far country, surely), the Malaysian writer in English must grapple hard with the willingness to lose cultural boundedness in the deeper desire and struggle for an assimilating and encompassing consciousness. Wrestling the sinewy antagonist, fragmentation, does call up great unease, deep anguish, but out of the unyielding blackness emerges "an endless landscape the ridges of which lead you into fresher and fresher valleys of discovery" (*In a Far Country,* 196).

Wong Ming Yook, Spring 2000

■ **WORKS CITED**

Fernando, Lloyd. *Scorpion Orchid.* 1976. Singapore. Times Books International. 1992.

———. *Green Is the Colour.* Singapore. Landmark Books. 1993.

Harrex, Syd. "Obituary: Lee Kok Liang (1927–1992)." *Centre for Research in the New Literatures in English Reviews Journal,* no. 1 (1993, special New Zealand issue), pp. 143–45.

Lee, Kok Liang. *Flowers in the Sky.* 1981. Singapore. Federal Publications. 1991.

———. *The Mutes in the Sun and Other Stories.* 1981. Singapore. Federal Publications. 1991.

———. *Death Is a Ceremony and Other Short Stories.* Singapore. Federal Publications. 1992.

Lim, Shirley Geok-lin. "Language, Gender, Race and Nation: A Postcolonial Meditation." In *Writing Southeast / Asia in English.* London. Skoob Books. 1994a.

———. "Centers and the Fringe: Novels in English from Malaysia and Singapore." In *Writing Southeast / Asia in English.* London. Skoob Books. 1994b.

Maniam, K. S. *The Return.* 1981. London. Skoob Books. 1993, 1996.

———. *In a Far Country.* London. Skoob Books. 1993, 1994.

———. *Haunting the Tiger.* London. Skoob Books. 1996.

Sharrad, Paul. Introduction to *In a Far Country* by K. S. Maniam. 1993. London. Skoob Books. 1994.

Watson, C. W. Introduction to *The Return* by K. S. Maniam. In *S.E. Asia Writes Back! Skoob Pacifica Anthology No. 1.* C. Y. Loh, and I. K. Ong, eds. London. Skoob Books. 1993.

Wong, M. Y. "Behind the Ritual." *Centre for Research in the New Literatures in English Reviews Journal,* no. 2 (1993), pp. 27–29.

Wong Soak Koon. Review of *Green Is the Colour* by Lloyd Fernando. In *The Pen Is Mightier Than the Sword: Skoob Pacifica Anthology No. 2.* C. Y. Loh, I. K. Ong, eds. London. Skoob Books. 1994.

———. "Journeying into K. S. Maniam's *In a Far Country.*" In *Challenges of Reading the New and Old.* Lim Chee Seng, ed. Kuala Lumpur. University of Malaya. 1995.

[1] Honorific for a man of high social standing.

[2] Malay for harmony and unity.

[3] Tall, wild grass.

[4] *Samsara* refers to the Buddhist / Hindu concept of a continuous cycle of life, death, and rebirth of the individual soul.

[5] *Karma* refers to the Buddhist / Hindu doctrine of reincarnation and rebirth.

PHILIPPINES

One Hundred Years of Filipino Poetry: An Overview

By way of showing the main outlines of the course of Filipino poetry in English from 1905 to the present, we

Nick Joaquin *(Philippine Graphics)*

might say that during the first forty years or so, the creative struggle was with both the new language, English, and the poet's subject: i.e., the native or Filipino matter, both sense and sensibility, that is to be expressed in and through that language. Then, from the 1950s to the 1970s, the artistic concern focused on the formal perfection of the poem as "verbal icon." For it was in the fifties that the American New Criticism began to hold critical sway; indeed, to the present, its influence is still conspicuous in writers' workshops, critical reviews, and judgments in literary contests. By the seventies, however, it had become inevitable that, with facility in the language and mastery of poetic form, new ways would be found for forging—in a double sense, to fashion and to feign—the work called poem.

There are thus, in this quick overview, roughly three overlapping phases or, more precisely, dominant strains: an inveterate romantic spirit from our first published literary attempts in the *Filipino Students' Magazine* (Berkeley [Ca.], April 1905) to José Garcia Villa's *Have Come, Am Here* (New York, Viking, 1942); an enduring formalist or New Critical concern from the 1950s to the 1970s; and finally, an open, liberative, or poststructuralist space from the 1970s to the present. These are of course only convenient labels as starting points toward a possible description, for we do not mean to suggest, for example, that during the romantic phase there was no concern for excellence of "poetic form" (as even the New Critics understood that term to mean an organization of the poetic elements, such as rhythm and imagery, in relation to the poem's total effect), nor that, until the "open clearing," as it were, in the 1970s, the poets had little social commitment (for indeed, our first poem in English, "The Flood" by Ponciano Reyes [1905], speaks of the plight of our working people in a natural disaster).

We should therefore insist on the overlap of those phases and the imbrication of those strains, because a century is too short for a literature and it is impossible to set definite time-boundaries to the poetic course. A poet like Bienvenido N. Santos (1911–96) continued to write through all those so-called phases, from the 1930s through *The Wounded Stag* (1956) to *Distances: In Time* (1983). A number of poems by Nick Joaquin (b. 1917) in *Prose and Poems* (1952) were written as early as the midthirties but were already quite different from the usual romantic verses of the time; and with most of his *Collected Verse* (1987), Joaquin is definitely in our "open clearing." What I would particularly stress is that the poetic course was a long and creative struggle with both the poet's medium (an adopted language) and the poet's subject—a struggle that repeats itself with every individual poet, although unfortunately not too many persevere in that "starving career" in our culture. By the poet's subject I do not mean any specific topic or theme, but the poet's insight into his own humanity and the culture which nurtures and sustains it; I mean the poet's own deepest thought and feeling, which always long for a language by which their meaningfulness is achieved. What "Filipino matter," what humanity as Filipino— what as individuals and as a people we have become through our colonial experience with Spain and America and our own democratic experiment—is simply inexpressible, but that precisely is the occupation of poetry, what Wallace Stevens calls "musing the obscure."

For the poet, the language comes alive, be it English or Tagalog, not from the words that are already there and their meanings in daily usage, but from their tillage, the particular uses to which they are put, by which our sense of our own reality in our historical circumstances is achieved. Both language and history are the crucial factors ("makers") from which our writers forge that "Filipino matter"—our mythology or imagination of ourselves.

■ THE ROMANTIC SPIRIT: FROM FERNANDO MARAMÁG TO JOSÉ GARCIA VILLA

Indisputably, the twentieth century is English in our history, as well over two centuries before then was Spanish. Our literary works, our textbooks, our mass media—if nothing else—show that, to all intents and purposes, for good or ill, English was in fact, and still is, a national language with us. If language fixes the forms of the world we inhabit and forges there our sense of our own native reality, then it can be said that through Spanish and English, as we had adopted them to our image and purposes, we have in fact shaped our Filipino consciousness with much the same force (if not more potent) as through our own native tongues. Indeed, our own various languages had also in their own way indigenized the alien grammars so that, over time, the native Indio freed himself through a kind of spiritual homesteading in the imperial backcountry.

In our early verses, such as those in our first anthology, Rodolfo Dato's *Filipino Poetry* (1924), both language and subject were borrowed, almost as though we had no thought or feeling of our own, so that skylark and nightingale in English Romantic poetry were simply converted into our *kuliawan* (oriole) and *maya* (rice bird). But it would be quite misleading to speak of a "literary apprenticeship," because we already had accomplished writers in Spanish, Tagalog, and our other native languages. The apprenticeship was linguistic and cultural, but not in the literary or poetic art. Precisely, the inevitable tension which obtained between the creative struggle with the new language and the poet's individual response to his new situation cleared that poetic terrain where the Filipino poet subdued the tutelary spirits of English Romanticism to his own perception of his circumstances and history.

And thus, before World War II bloodied our shores in 1941, Filipino romantic poetry had come into full flower in the poems of Doveglion (José Garcia Villa), Luis G. Dato (1906–83), Angela C. Manalang-Gloria (1907–95), and Trinidad L. Tarrosa-Subido (1912–94), even as our poets in Spanish before the Americans came had already transformed both the sensibility and idiom of the Spanish romantic spirit into our own native clearing. It was of course José Garcia Villa whose poetry, strongly influenced by E. E. Cummings, made a clearing within English which the poets showed how, through craft and cunning, a language might be reinvented. In *Many Voices* (1939) and *Poems by Doveglion* (1941), having rejected the Romantic and Victorian molds in poetry as early as "Man-Songs" (1929) and "Poem for an Unhumble One" (1933), he achieved a breakthrough by way of an individual poetic idiom to his own distinctive subject—a kind of dialectic between the I-Genius God, and Death—in *Have Come, Am Here* (1942) and in volume 2 (1949). It can fairly be said that, before Villa, our poets wrote in English, but after Villa, our poets wrought from English. He was also the first to break the taboo on explicit sex, passion, and homosexuality in our fiction and poetry (e.g., his story "Wings and Blue Flame," 1938), even as the dominant male ideology in romantic poetry, where woman's idealization serves to keep her subject, was subverted in the pseudonymous Nacing's "Crisalidas" (1914), Manalang's "Revolt from Hymen" (1940), and Tarrosa-Subido's "Love Is My Need" (1945).

Most certainly, the Filipino romantic poets did not limit themselves to romantic love, sunsets, and roses as S. P. Lopez and Arturo Rotor charged in 1939 in our first national literary controversy. Their engagement with their own cultural and social milieu, already signaled by Reyes's poem "The Flood" in 1905, appears in our early patriotic verses (e.g, Justo Juliano's "Sursum Corda" [1907], Maramág's "Moonlight on Manila Bay" [1912], Juan Pastrana's "America, Hear" [1922]) and reaches clear and powerful expression in such poems as "Man of Earth" (1932) and "Land of Our Desire" (1934) by Amador Daguio (1912–66), "Memorial to America" (1940) by Conrado B. Rigor (1914–60), and "If You Want to Know What We Are" (1940) by Carlos Bulosan (1911–56). Among other notable poets during this romantic phase are M. de Gracia Concepcion (1895–1954), Procopio L. Solidum (1901–40), Cornelio F. Faigao (1908–59), Virgilio F. Floresca (1908–44), A. E. Litiatco (1908–43), Conrado V. Pedroche (1909–80), Maximo Ramos (1910–88), Celestino M. Vega (1910-?), S. P. Lopez (1910–90), Conrado S. Ramirez (1910-?), Guillermo Castillo (1911–45), Guillermo V. Sison (1911–79), Fidel D. de Castro (1911-?), Aurelio S. Alvero (1913–58), N.V.M. Gonzalez (1915–99), and Francisco Arcellana (b. 1916).

With *Like the Molave* by Rafael Zulueta y da Costa (1915–90), which could very well mark the end of the romantic phase in our poetry, it had become important for the poet to reshape the romantic idiom and imagery in order that he might find his own voice and address more directly his own time and circumstances. Villa found his own voice, but in 1929 he had exiled himself to America. Then the war came and the romantic efflorescence of the 1930s wilted. wrote his last poem, "The Anchored Angel," in 1953, continued to be a strong influence in the craft of poetry well into the seventies, as one might see in the poems of Jolico Cuadra (b. 1937) and Luis H. Francia (b. 1945). More important, we find in Bienvenido Santos's collection *The Wounded Stag* (1956) and Edith Tiempo's *Tracks of Babylon* (1966) that the romantic idiom had only been transformed into a new mode of expression by which the poet gave form and substance to his own insights.

▪ THE FORMALIST STRAIN: FROM EDITH L. TIEMPO TO CIRILO F. BAUTISTA

By the 1950s we have a modern poetry in full swing. Leonard Casper's *Six Filipino Poets* (1954), coming two years after Nick Joaquin's *Prose and Poems* (1952), signaled the advent of the American New Criticism. This critical mode, with its stress on organic unity, emotional restraint, and metaphor, irony, and ambiguity, shaped the poetic sensibility from the 1950s well into the 1980s and 1990s, especially through the Silliman University Writing Program (1962 to the present) and the University of the Philippines National Summer Writers Workshop (1964 to the present).

Of Casper's six poets, three—Ricaredo Demetillo (1920–98), Dominador I. Ilio (b. 1913), and Edith L. Tiempo (b. 1919)—were graduates of the University of Iowa Writing Program, after which "Mom" Edith, with her husband Edilberto K. Tiempo, patterned the Silliman Writers Workshop. Apart from Brooks, Purser, and Warren's *Approach to Literature* (1936), which was used from the 1950s to the early 1980s as the standard textbook in the collegiate introductory course to literature, also noteworthy are the formalist critiques of Philippine literature in English by Leonard Casper in *The Wayward Horizon* (1951) and *The Wounded Diamond* (1964).

Nevertheless, despite the potent and on the whole salubrious effect of New Criticism, I would insist that the poetic transformation of both language and sensibility since the 1950s owes more to the poet's creative toil with language in response to his circumstances than to the New Critical ideology, as may well be observed in the poetry of Oscar de Zuñiga (1912–79), Manuel A. Viray (1917–97), Carlos A. Angeles (b. 1921), Virginia R. Moreno (b. 1925), Alejandrino G. Hufana (b. 1926), Leonidas V. Benesa (1928–84), Hilario S. Francia Jr. (b. 1929), Tita Lacambra Ayala (b. 1931), Bienvenido Lumbera (b. 1932), Emmanuel Torres (b. 1932), Ophelia Alcantara Dimalanta (b. 1933), Ernesto D. Manalo (1936–62), Rolando S. Tinio (1937–97), Alfredo O. Cuenca Jr. (b. 1937), Jose M. Lansang Jr. (b. 1939), Federico Licsi Espino (b. 1939), Artemio Tadena (1939–77), and Cirilo F. Bautista (b. 1941).

If we compare our poets of the 1950s and 1960s with the earlier romantics, we would immediately notice a greater number who have their own individual mode of expression and their own distinctive subject. The generation of Maramág especially, but also Villa's in the thirties and forties, would seem to write alike because they were drawing from a common hoard of romantic themes and employing a widely accepted kind of poetic diction and imagery. The way through the changing poetic terrain since the 1950s is poet to poet, because each one who perseveres in the craft constantly achieves through metamorphosis of his idiom and subject a full individual voice. Each one's poetic career— e.g., Edith Tiempo, our finest New Critical poet, from *Tracks of Babylon* (1966) to *The Charmer's Box* (1993) and *Extensions, Beyond* (1995); or Cirilo F. Bautista, the most outstanding of his generation, from *The Cave* (1968) and *The Archipelago* (1970) to *Charts* (1973) and *Telex Moon* (1981) to *Boneyard Breaking* (1992) and *Sunlight on Broken Stones* (1999)—shows that the poet constantly makes new discoveries in his own field of vision and transforms his mode of expression conformably to them. Thus, whatever be the poetic influences in his work or the regnant critical theory of his time, the work of imagination is achieved chiefly by the poet's own solitary labor, the long and stubborn creative struggle to forge from one's chosen medium a language in which to discover and express one's subject.

A number of poets also seemed to show how, since the New Criticism put a premium on the poet's rhetorical legerity, language could be so polished or reworked as to disfigure it—but also how, at the same time, a poetic breakup of linguistic usage, or even a breakdown of sense, might perhaps presage a new poetic transformation. Ricaredo Demetillo's *No Certain Weather* (1956) has all the rhetorical vigor and poetic fire that the New Criticism demanded, yet the poet is not trapped in the poem's rhetoric, for, in such poems as "Poet in a Time of Darkness" (1952) and "Rebellious Sonnets" (1954), he excoriates the moral hypocrisy and sensuality of the bourgeois and inveighs against greed and corruption in high places. But after that first collection, he seems to have exhausted his moral and religious lode with *La Via: A Spiritual Journey* (1958); his too close following of Villa on "the Gospel Truth: God's male sensuality!" may have vitiated his poetry. In his later verses, from *Masks and Signature* (1968) to *Lazarus, Troubadour* (1974), he seems to be in search of a simpler mode of expression, less thick with rhetoric, such as we find in "Lines to a Novitiate" (1972) and "I Don't Invite the Tigers, Augustine" (1974).

Like Demetillo, both Dominador Ilio and Manuel Viray have a remarkable first collection of verse, Ilio's *The Diplomat and Other Poems* (1955) and Viray's *After This Exile* (1965), but their later verses endure a kind of poetic breakdown, as though the language hewn by New Critical dicta can no longer sustain the poet's vision. Looking for a new language then becomes the primary occupation. Ilio finds a fresher, more natural expression in such poems as "Prokosch in Tehran, 1978" (1979) and "Hakim Popolzai on the Road to the Hindu Kush" (1980). In Viray's later verses, from *When Blood*

with *Light Collides* (1975) to *The Automatic Glass Door* (1991), a kind of disintegration of language and sensibility sets in, as though the poet's quest has entered a labyrinth without clew. The poet's large abstractions seem to whir through the text like bees desperate for blossoms. Alejandrino Hufana's poetry, too—from *13 Kalisud* (1955) and *Sickle Season* (1959), to *Poro Point* (1961) and *The Wife of Lot* (1971), to *Obligations: Cheers of Conscience* (1975), *Shining On* (1985), and *Ennuegs* (forthcoming)—is exemplary as regards that poetic breakup of sense and imagery which teeters perilously on the edge of gibberish; yet it may be the language of oracle.

■ THE OPEN CLEARING: FROM THE 1970S TO THE PRESENT

Our poetry since the 1970s flourishes in that open, liberative, poststructuralist clearing where seemingly there does not exist any formal constraint in the writing of poetry. It was as though the poet needed to free himself from New Criticism, not indeed from the discipline of craftsmanship which it stresses, but rather from its obsession both with the ideology of the poem as autonomous and with the rhetoric of figures (tension, irony, paradox, ambiguity). Moreover, as an effect of the political activism in the midsixties and the Martial Law regime, it had again become an urgent issue with the poet that his poems connect with the social reality even while he recognized the requirement of formal excellence. We might see this move in the poems of Gelacio Guillermo (b. 1939) and Alfredo Navarro Salanga (1948–88), which of course only stresses the fact that since 1905, despite the trance of the English poetic and critical sensibility, our poets stood upon their own native ground.

Our writers began to be aware in the 1980s of new critical theories which seem to affect their poetry: the structuralists who fostered an extreme type of formalism and, almost in the same breath, the poststructuralists who ravish still the voids in language. Yet our poets are not academics, even if a number find their home in universities. It would be closer to the truth to say that, as poets tilling the soil of language, they make their own discoveries about poetry in their own way which the academic critic later finds conformable with some artistic criterion or other theoretical aspect of literary creation.

Our poetry from the 1980s to the present is marked by a more heightened consciousness of language in the way it creates its own reality, together with a deep sense of the poem as artifice or a kind of double forgery: a forgery from language which itself is already a fiction of reality, and a forgery in one's own consciousness from the reality outside language. As the poet Alfred A. Yuson (b. 1945) puts it, our poetry today is marked by "the consistent projection of a personal voice whose treatment of experience and insight is couched in either hard-edged or tender understatement. . . . The quiet image, the ironic engagement, the subtle verbal gesture have come to the forefront as favored contemporary devices for lyric or cerebral identification." Among the notable poets from the 1970s to the present are Luis Cabalquin-to (b. 1935), Alfred A. Yuson, Jaime An Lim (b. 1946), Edgardo B. Maranan (b. 1946), Simeon Dumdum Jr. (b. 1948), Ricardo M. de Ungria (b. 1951), Marne Kilates (b. 1952), Ramon C. Sunico (b. 1955), Eric T. Gamalin-da (b. 1956), J. Eugene Gloria (b. 1957), Juaniyo Arcel-lana (b. 1959), Fidelito C. Cortes (b. 1959), Danton Re-moto (b. 1963), DM Reyes (b. 1968), Jim Pacual Agustin (b. 1969), J. Neil C. Garcia (b. 1969), Ruel S. De Vera (b. 1973), Ramil Digal Gulle (b. 1973), and John Labella (b. 1975).

One other remarkable thing about our poetry today is the number of women poets who re-create their sensi-bility, carving from language a reality that is truer to their "inner promptings," as Edith Tiempo says. Among the most notable are Myra Peña-Reyes (b. 1938), Merlie M. Alunan (b. 1943), Marra Pl. Lanot (b. 1944), Elsa Martinez Coscolluela (b. 1945), Rowena Tiempo Tor-revillas (b. 1951), Marjorie M. Evasco (b. 1953), Isabela Banzon (b. 1954), Bing Caballero (b. 1954), Lilia N. Lopez-Chua (b. 1956), Grace R. Monte de Ramos (b. 1956), Merlinda C. Bobis (b. 1959), Ma. Fatima V. Lim-Wilson (b. 1961), Ma. Luisa B. Aguilar-Cariño (now Luisa Igloria; b. 1961), Lina Sagaral Reyes (b. 1961), Isabelita Orlina Reyes (b. 1962), Nerisa del Carmen Guevara (b. 1973), and Conchitina R. Cruz (b. 1976).

By way of conclusion, it bears stressing that, to create our own literature (poetry), English had to be naturalized, so to speak, and become Filipino—become nothing short of a national language. We had to find ourselves again and found a country that had been lost. We had, as it were, to colonize English in and by our own turn of phrase; that is, we ourselves had to inhabit the new language so that our own way of looking, our own thinking and feeling in our own historical circum-stances, could become the nerves and sinews of that language. From the beginning to the present, that is in fact the poet's job.

Gémino H. Abad, Spring 2000

■ **WORKS CITED**

Gémino H. Abad, Edna Z. Manlapaz, eds. *Man of Earth: An Anthol-ogy of Filipino Poetry and Verse from English, 1905 to the mid–'50s.* Quezon City, Phil. Ateneo de Manila University Press. 1989.

Gémino H. Abad, ed. *A Native Clearing: Filipino Poetry and Verse from English since the '50s to the Present / From Edith L. Tiempo to Cirilo F. Bautista.* Quezon City, Phil. University of the Philip-pines Press. 1993.

———, ed. *A Habit of Shores: Filipino Poetry and Verse from En-glish, '60s to the '90s / The Sequel to A Native Clearing.* Quezon City, Phil. University of the Philippines Press. 1999.

Postcolonial Visions and Immigrant Longings: Ninotchka Rosca's Versions of the Philippines

Ninotchka Rosca, one of the major players in the saga of Filipina American writers, may have been the model for Elleke Boehmer's description of the 1990s generic postcolonial writer: "more likely to be a cultural travel-ler, or an extra-territorial, than a national. Ex-colonial by birth, 'Third World' in cultural interest, cosmopoli-tan in almost every other way, he or she works within the precincts of the Western metropolis while at the same time retaining thematic and/or political connec-tions with a national background" (233). Her novels *State of War* (1988) and *Twice Blessed* (1992) re-create the multifariousness of Philippine culture as they look back at the country's history and more recent political life, highlighting personal contingencies and cultural choices. As the term *postcolonial* "does not imply an au-tomatic, nor a seamless and unchanging process of re-sistance, but a series of linkages and articulations" (Ash-croft et al., 3), this writer's primary focus—the two colonial experiences undergone by the Filipinos, the political upheavals that took place during the Marcos dictatorship, and the country's history of migration to the West—converts the telling of Philippine history and culture into a resource for fictionally constructing a dis-course of nationalism. Rosca speaks with the voice of the economically and politically displaced immigrant of the twentieth century, transported into alien contexts from where she defines and constructs alternative iden-tities and communities. In this manner, by presenting literary versions of a homeland and its history, Rosca ul-timately composes a portrait of the creation of the Filipina.

This writing simultaneously provides an epiphany for Filipino American writers in general. E. San Juan Jr. has pointed to the problem and the need of reinventing the Filipino in the United States, articulating the long-suffered silence and invisibility of creative artists: the master narrative of the migrant worker's odyssey used by Carlos Bulosan and the interior monologues of Bien-venido Santos's expatriates marooned in the megalopo-lis can no longer serve as generic models (123). San

Juan believes that a beginning must be made from the experience of Filipino Americans born in the sixties and seventies and from the realities of the immigrants of the eighties. In this regard, Oscar Campomanes argues for a literature of exile and emergence rather than a literature of immigration and settlement whereby life in the United States serves as the space for displacement, suspension, and perspective. Exile becomes a necessary, if inescapable, state for Filipinos in the United States—at once susceptible to the vagaries of the (neo)colonial U.S.-Philippine relationship and redeemable only by its radical restructuring (Campomanes, 1992, 51). Nonetheless, San Juan claims,

> . . . this cannot be done without evoking the primal scene coeval with the present: the neocolonial situation of the Philippines and its antecedent stages, the conflicted terrain of ideological struggle which abolishes the distinction/distance between Filipinos in the Philippines and Filipinos in the U.S. Continuities no less than ruptures have to be articulated for an oppositional practice to emerge. The terrain is less geographical than cultural—culture defined as the complex network of social practices signifying our dominant or subordinate position in a given social formation. (123)

The complex network of social and cultural practices in the Philippines is generally characterized by its palimpsestic nature, the process of history and the creation of culture having been inscribed and reinscribed by successive generations and manifold colonizations. The country has been described by historian Horacio de la Costa as "an Asian nation of Malay stock, socially structured on a basically Indonesian pattern, containing a large infusion of Chinese blood and attitudes, but with a cultural heritage in part Spanish, in part Anglo-Saxon" (103). Christianity is the dominant religion, a legacy from three-plus centuries of Spanish colonial administration (1565–1898) and nearly five decades of American administration (1898–1946); the Philippines is the only Catholic nation in Asia. Until the ratification of the Constitution in 1986, there were three official languages: Filipino, English, and Spanish. Today, the first two are the official languages of education, justice, the press, and the street, with interventions from the languages of the diverse provinces.

The cultural consequences of these influences have been described in various ways. Shirley Geok-lin Lim, in her study on Philippine and Singaporean literature in English, *Nationalism and Literature,* shows how both writers and critics in postcolonial, newly independent societies like the Philippines have become increasingly conscious of the possibility of a disjuncture: a gap lying between critical expectations and operational defini-

tions carried over from older colonizing and still culturally dominant and powerful societies and the literature produced in recently independent countries which are still in the process of evolving national and cultural identities (1993b, 2). The Filipino writer N. V. M. González has classified the Philippines as a victim of the "cross-roads syndrome," a collision of Asian and Western cultures leading to a sense of discontinuous history and cultural hybridization (35). As a consequence, Rosca, like other postcolonial/immigrant writers and critics, works within a "cultural simultaneity" or a heterogeneous overlapping of cultures with their attendant myths, religious and ethical philosophies, esthetic ideologies, political systems, and economic modes, "a restless product of a long history of miscegenation, assimilation and syncretization as well as conflict, contradiction and cultural violence" (Sangari, 217).

One of the most striking characteristics of this literature is the manner in which the writers use and manifest various modes of ambivalence. The diasporic formation of most Filipino American writers has made them privilege, in their creative endeavors, implicit "figurations of exilic displacements, nostalgia for the old country, leavetaking, dispossession and imagined 'homecomings'" (Campomanes, 1997, 85). These themes are converted into an unprecedented source of "creative and oppositional energy, as generative questions of language and form/genre, and as obsessive thematic modes such as exilic displacements, local subjectivities, Philippine-oriented nationalist imaginings, and U.S.-based postcoloniality or Filipino *American* reckonings with colonialism's legacies" (Campomanes, 1997, 76). Literary repossession of the homeland and its history may be a manner of subverting the conditions of inherited culture, a symbolic attempt to reverse the workings of time and migration.

On different levels, Rosca's novels project a desire to come to terms with a past that is both personal and collective: the fiction will explore the Filipino character and history of their community as reflections on both personal odysseys of displacement and a search for self. The between-world situation leads the writer to engage in an intense reworking of questions such as oppositionality, marginality, boundaries, displacement, and authenticity, a process that requires constant variation and review. Donald Goellnicht points out that "rather than thinking in binary terms of inside/outside, we should perhaps think of hybrid positions as a web of multiply intersecting and shifting strands in which the precise location of the subject is extremely difficult to map. . . . Subject positions are not the result of essential determinants but are culturally produced (in relation to other positions) and socially learned, a complex and continuous process" (340). From her position as a Filipina writer in English, therefore, Rosca may be revising—through the intermingling of creative imagination and the facts of history within what has been a largely orientalist framework of literary and cultural studies—the boundaries of that subjectivity, recognizing its contingencies and therefore sustaining its validity and authenticity. The definition of *nation,* using the Philippines' volatile cultural pluralism as starting point, therefore becomes one of the major preoccupations in the creative development of her work. Taken on and debated as an intrinsic part of her imaginative vision, the issue of the nation becomes a topic worthy of full fictional realization. Timothy Brennan suggests that nations are "imaginary constructs that depend for their existence on an apparatus of cultural fictions in which imaginative literature plays a decisive role" (157). Because of the multiplicity of cultures that make up the Philippines, the process of national self-making in story and symbol is vital. The nation must be constructed again and again in the collective imagination, the elusive identity constructed anew. Fictional narrative, with its potential to penetrate into existing situations and compose alternative realities, provides a rich medium for the purpose.

Central to the reimagining of the country's identity is an emphasis on geographic position. As Linda Warley has written, a preoccupation for setting has particular valency for postcolonial subjects, since their home locations have been historically constructed as peripheral: the writer's charge is "imaginative possession of place, an act of self-articulation at once necessitated by and working in opposition to the invasion of both territory and mind enacted by Europe upon colonial space" (25). A major feature of all postcolonial literatures is the concern with either developing or recovering an appropriate identifying relationship between self and place, because it is precisely within the parameters of place and its separateness that the process of subjectivity can be conducted. "Place" is characterized first by a sense of displacement in those who have moved to the colonies, or the more widespread sense of displacement from the imported language, of a gap between the experienced environment and the descriptions the language provides, and second by a sense of the immense investment of culture in the construction of place (Ashcroft et al., 391). Thus, the narratives to be analyzed inhabit a social and conceptual space in which the problems of meaning and form acquire both personal and political significance. The defining characteristic of the novels, nonetheless, is not strictly a matter of place, but rather a matter of consciousness; social and cultural determinants of a specifically Filipino kind inform the novels,

giving them vast importance in terms of ideological and linguistic difference. Rosca's fiction, which focuses on the evolution of a particular place, acknowledges that the "culture" of a nation is shaped by the complex processes of memory and language as well as by obvious and identifiable historical events. The country itself, subject to historical change and psychological disturbance—portrayed as social structure and configuration of consciousness and memory—becomes the recurring motif and unifying principle of her novels, profoundly affecting those who live there, those who leave, and those who wish to return.

The formation of the Filipinos' elusive, problematic, palimpsestic identity as a people and as a nation lies at the thematic center of the novels. Ultimately, one may argue, they are also discourses on Rosca's position as a woman and an artist, caught in a world of binary oppositions: Filipino/American, Filipino/Spanish, home/exile, past/present, personal/political, real/fantasy. In an essay entitled "Myth, Identity and the Colonial Experience," Rosca explores the creation of the Filipino self in literature, claiming that the collective nature of the fictional self in much Filipino fiction results not only from the historical evolution of writing in the country but also from the country itself. Like most writers of the Third World, Filipino writers have a well-developed sense of the national self, of national life, and of the contradictions that make it problematical even to have a "self" in this context at all. The attempt to resolve, for instance, the conflict between the orientation of the bedrock culture and the fragmenting effect of colonialism is a dominant theme in Philippine writing and, in particular, in the writing by Filipinos outside the Philippines (1990, 240). Rosca explains that what one finds in Filipino fiction is

> . . .a self that shares in all of the contradictoriness of the national self. It is difficult for a Filipino writer to conceive of judging events solely from a personal, individual point of view. . . . What he or she attempts to do, consistently throughout the years, is to locate himself or herself within the collective self and to look at the world with the eyes of his or her people and his or her history. . . . By representing this self in fiction, the writer assumes part of the responsibility for defining it even as he or she reflects it—as he or she defines it, so it becomes more his or her definition. . . . We do not have objective manifestations of the self that have been evolving since prehistory. . . . Our materials are perishable: language and memory—uncertain, imperfect. But they fit well the volatile nature of this, our self, for they can change as fast as we can, as we flicker through myths and identities, unravel the impact of colonialism on our selves, and go through our

metamorphosis. Memory, most of all, anchors us, for, though it is fragile, it is also the longest umbilical cord. (1990, 242)

In this regard, irony as the predominant tone in the narratives becomes one mode of self-defining discourse. Much of Philippine life and culture is itself intrinsically doubled and therefore at least structurally ripe for irony. The country's history, which offers many binary oppositions—native/colonizer, East/West, indigenous superstitions/Roman Catholicism—was made more complex when the arrival of the Americans added a third pole to the conflict. Furthermore, the Philippines is a country of expatriation, a condition brought on by successive histories of colonization and which has become both a form and an inseparable part of Filipino identity (Lim, 68). Doubleness—of identity, of culture, of loyalties, often of language—is the basis of the experience of immigration. The very doubleness inherent in irony—the need to keep literal and ironic meanings afloat together—disrupts any notions of meaning as single, stable, or complete. Linda Hutcheon suggests that irony is one way of coming to terms with that duplicity, for it is the trope that incarnates doubleness, and it does so in ways that are particularly useful to the "other": irony allows the other to address the dominant culture from within that culture's own set of values and modes of understanding, without being co-opted by it and without sacrificing the right to dissent, contradict, and resist, opening up new space, literally between opposing meanings, where new things can happen (49). The experimentation with the doubled structure of irony as a strategy of authorship manifests how Rosca, as well as other Asian American writers, have "moved beyond the conventional dichotomous, binary construction of white and Asian-national to a positioning of ethnic identity as interrogative, shifting, unstable, and heuristic" (Lim, 1993a, 160). Rosca's novels demonstrate how the process of establishing identity from within, independently of imposed definitions, has reached a turning point clearly resonant with the phenomenological reality of the Filipina American.

The irony in Ninotchka Rosca's novels is evident, in the first place, in the fact that *State of War* and *Twice Blessed* are romans à clef. Through the use of metaphors and allusive names, the writer demands a second-level reading of the works as both historical and political statements and cultural critique. As Rosca states, "The problem was how to tell a story that was not anybody's story and yet was everybody's story" (Mestrovic, 90). As communal biographies (a distinctive postcolonial genre), the novels prepare homogenous cultural ground out of which national symbols could be extracted. In this manner, the cultural life of a particular group can

be made to represent a broader history (Boehmer, 191–92). *State of War* and *Twice Blessed* revision centuries of Philippine cultural and imaginative history through the metaphor of familial relations. The author merges the facts of history with violent and surreal events in the present to emphasize the effects of foreign colonization on the Filipino psyche. In her first novel she implies that Filipinos have been locked in a continual state of war against military, economic, and cultural invasions ever since Magellan intervened in Lapulapu's tribal affairs and lost his life at Mactan. Using as a frame the Festival (Ati-Atihan) celebrated annually on the Visayan island of K-, her time scheme moves from the late stages of the dictatorship of the Commander (a clear allusion to Marcos), to a review of centuries of colonial influence on Philippine bloodlines—apparent in such families as the Banyagas, Villaverdes, and Batoyans—with a final return to the Festival as it deteriorates into a wild, frustrated assassination attempt. Leonard Casper believes that the intent of this strategy is to provide an indirect but nevertheless dramatic appeal for a truly independent nationalism (203).

The relationships of the major characters in the novel are emblematic of the complexities of the Philippine conflict. *State of War* focuses on three protagonists: Adrian Banyaga, the wealthy heir; Anna, the vengeful widow of a revolutionary, and Eliza, the frivolous and independent mistress of a millionaire. Their genealogies provide the most complex maze in the novel, an analogy for the direction the novel will take in charting entangled identities. Old Andy, grandfather of Adrian Banyaga, is the grandson of a Capuchin monk who is also the father of Carlos Lucas de Villaverde, husband of Mayang Batoyan. She later has an illegitimate child, Luis Carlos, with the German chemist Hans Zangroniz. Luis Carlos is to be the father of Anna Villaverde, who marries Manolo Monreal, whose father Jake betrays Luis Carlos during the Japanese occupation and is eventually killed by Luis Carlos. Hans Zangroniz, meanwhile, has changed his name to Chris Hansen, gone to the southern part of the archipelago, and become the grandfather of Eliza Hansen. No one seems to realize that this complicated web of relationships exists, and that the three main characters are actually related. In the present, Adrian and Anna are lovers while Eliza and Anna are friends who appear to share a sort of sentimental sisterhood but never quite the recognition of their being cousins. The genealogies and symbolic stories of these main characters intertwine in a series of historical wars and developments symbolized by a twenty-four-hour period of festivity and political conspiracies. The interrelated merrymaking and political conflict is emphasized by narrative pattern and design, as exemplified by the three-"book" structure of the novel. The first and last books, "Acts" and "Revelations," follow the movements of the three central characters during the Festival. The middle section, "Numbers," traces the genealogy of these characters and thus the history of Spanish occupation to the present day. Oscar Campomanes has pointed out that the novel is an obvious footnote to the triangulated characteristic of Linda Ty-Casper, another Filipina American writer, whose preface to her novel *Awaiting Trespass* points to "a small book of hours about those waiting for their lives to begin . . . a book of numbers about those who stand up to be counted . . . a book of revelations about what tyranny forces people to become; and what, by resisting, they can insist on being" (quoted in Campomanes, 1992, 71).

History provides the structure to both of Rosca's narratives. In *State of War* emphasis is constantly laid on the idea of the Philippines as a land of beginnings, and of the importance of the knowledge of a historical past in order to progress in time. The diverse biological and cultural influences that formed the Filipino are of concern to the writer: "But where Eliza was of that rare fortuitous sienna skin, accidentally bred by a mingling of Caucasian and Malay blood, Anna was fair, of a gold tint that testified to an indefinable mixing of Chinese, Malay and other strange bloods. A true child of the Philippine archipelago" (*SW,* 12). Anna Villaverde's first solemn declaration as a child, "Everything in this country happens in the morning. . . . Because it is a country of beginnings" (*SW,* 328), is an echo of the Chinese guerrilla's declaration to Mayang that "this country—it has no continuity. It is only a country of beginnings. No one remembers" (*SW,* 292). The need to preserve and know history obsesses the characters, just as its opposite, not to know the past, proves to be a condemnation. After the war against the Japanese, Luis Carlos and the soldiers who surrendered to the Americans realized that "in the newness to come, it was important . . . that a little of history remain" (*SW,* 307). The manipulation of history poses another danger. Anna, named thus in her father's hope that she would be "the start of better things" (*SW,* 326), laments: "'They monkeyed around with the language, Eliza, while we were growing up. Monkeyed around with names. Of people, of places. With dates. And now, I can't remember. No one remembers. And even this'—she waved a hand toward the Festival—'even this will be forgotten. They will hide it under another name. No one will remember'" (*SW,* 149). Rosca seems to suggest that, as Ashcroft, Griffiths, and Tiffin have noted, "what it means to have a history is the same as what it means to have a legitimate existence: history and legitimation go hand in hand; history legitimates 'us' and not others" (355).

The author implies, in *State of War,* that because most of the persons involved are not aware of their history or their bloodlines, they are condemned to repeat the errors of the past. Illegitimacy breeds illegitimacy; Manolo Monreal will betray the guerrillas, as his father Jake did before him, and die for this at the hands of his wife, daughter of the man who had killed his father in revenge. Rosca introduces a cyclical and deterministic view of history through metaphors of time looping in and out and by lyrical descriptions of characters hurled into a sort of time warp of the past, their "young minds already twisted by the histories to be learned" (*SW,* 338). The characters, their ancestors and descendants are destined to meet again and again in a series of extraordinary coincidences; Anna Villaverde laughs at this "fractured history," marked by "war treading on the heels of a just-concluded war in a country of beginnings" (*SW,* 339). In a surreal scene toward the end of the novel, she mentally revisions the events from the time Magellan's boats sailed to Mactan, where he met his death, to the time Dewey steamed into Manila Bay and sank the Spanish fleet: "So it began, the country's confusion over language and memory, so that in this Festival of commemoration, there remained no more than this mangled song" (*SW,* 338).

The novel ends tragically, with shattered dreams and death. Eliza is murdered, her body washed ashore four days after the Festival; Adrian is crippled, his mind fixed "forever in a maze of words, a verbal account of four hundred years, tortured and tormenting" (*SW,* 376). Only Anna survives and goes to teach children in a small village in the mountains. Pregnant with Adrian's child, she awaits the birth of her son, "who would be nurtured as much by her milk as by the archipelago's legends . . . and he would be the first of the Capuchin monk's descendants to be born innocent, without fate. . . . Her son would be a great storyteller, in the tradition of children of priestesses. He would remember, his name being a history unto itself, for he would be known as Ismael Villaverde Banyaga" (*SW,* 382). The vital importance of the oral narrative as a medium for the transmission of the past comes through at this point. The storyteller, who describes and preserves networks of racial and ancestral affiliation, protects communal memory as part of the process of identity-building. Only when one has a history, and can recount it, Rosca suggests in the novel, can one, and one's country, be made whole.

Twice Blessed, though more limited in scope, also offers a general revision of recent Philippine history. Using as its frame the preparations for the presidential inauguration of Hector Basbas, Rosca retells the creation and propagation of the Marcos dynasty. Hector and his twin Katerina, the twice-blessed, power-hungry, and despotic, are the protagonists of this dismal recollection of the years of the dictatorship, characterized by violence, perverse relationships, corruption, and tragedy. The writer makes few attempts to disguise her characters and the more scandalous events and details of the Marcos dictatorship: the possession of thousands of pairs of shoes, the diamond rosaries, the tragic deaths of workmen. This travesty of the events and characters nonetheless also points to the consequences of a colonial past and its overwhelming effect on the present in the form of strict social codes and uneven distribution of wealth.

The narrative centers on the perverse relationship between the twins and those who surround them. Rosca alludes to a mystical and degenerate relationship between the twins as the dramatic center of the novel. As orphaned children, they were united in their revulsion at their poverty and in their desire for revenge upon relatives who had humiliated them. Now that they are adults, all others are merely peripheral, threads in the weaving of the fabric of the self-reinforcing illusions of the two who find fulfillment only in each other, their rise in the world, and the unnatural propagation of their bloodline. The repeated image of deformed and monstrous children, results of inbreeding, prevail in the novel, sometimes as morbid signs of luck and fortune. An obsession for power and control, and an awareness and appropriation of the intricacies of the culture that has resulted from the repeated experiences of colonization, characterize the protagonists. Spanish-descended aristocratic families with fortunes from sugar and tobacco who have gone to absurd extremes to preserve their Caucasian genes are the center of society and must be courted in order to find acceptance. American dollars are equally essential in the greedy rise to power. Rosca takes advantage of the indigenous Filipino and adopted Spanish names to delineate and define relationships: Teresa Tikloptuhod ("bended knee") is Katerina's "childhood friend and official confidante" (*TB,* 10); Armand Gloriosa, Katerina's husband, son of one of the wealthiest and most influential families, is merely a tool used by the twins; the names of their offspring are parodies of the Marcos children's names.

Rosca satirizes, in *Twice Blessed,* the cultural idiosyncrasies resulting from the effects of colonial interventions, the understanding that there are "two countries in this country" (*TB,* 163). She highlights the often contradictory elements of the culture: the supremacy of family matriarchs; the elegance of the "crisp accents of a city-trained mixed-blood society matron" (*TB,* 19); the inauguration in a "palace, which isn't a palace but a humbler summer retreat, two hundred years old, of

Spanish governor-generals" (*TB,* 9); the inauguration area which was formerly "an execution ground during the reign of the now long departed Spanish governor-generals and villains, bandits and heroes alike had been strangled, shot, knifed and garroted there" (*TB,* 258–59). The upper classes who strive to "bring civilization to Manila" by planning to stage the latest Broadway show (*TB,* 110) are caricatured by the author to force reflection on the multifarious nature of the Filipino. The different characters are acutely aware of the workings of history on the present, and use them to their advantage: social codes elaborately worked out serve as political tools for progress or subtle hints at a downfall.

The country itself becomes a protagonist in the narrative, a force to be reckoned with. The twins' real tragedy, in their fight for power, lies in their being blind to and failing to understand the real adversary. Once again, the past weighs on the present, as the main characters analyze the question of destiny for themselves and for the Filipino people. Katerina, obsessed with beginnings in her desire to forget her shameful past, shows a marked "preference for blank walls and what she called *tabula rasa*" (33): her world is the immediate future, that of power and glory. Hector's downfall arises from the fact that he "was actually a simple man, an ordinary man, one who could love very deeply, without compromise; indeed, that was the stuff of his personal tragedy, because he lived in a country of compromise" (137). He had misjudged the hidden strength of the country he dreamed of dominating. Although "he was a true child of the archipelago and knew that survival had to be paid for . . . and that every opportunity should be used for one's benefit" (*TB,* 207, 215), he miscalculated the country's obsession with its own destiny. Believing, as did Armand, that the Filipinos were "a people without destiny" (*TB,* 114), he chose to ignore the outgoing president's extraordinary premonition: "In the last two years, I caught a glimmer of something so surprising, so entrancing, I forgot to prepare for my retirement. . . . I saw a nation struggling to be born" (*TB,* 256–57). Rosca's theme is ultimately the dramatic birth of a nation, and the role and destiny of the players who assisted in that birth.

An overwhelming sense of tension pervades the novel: people hide behind masks, dangerous facts are buried in rhetoric, no one trusts anybody, treachery is constantly expected. Even with one's closest allies, secrets are folded "into secrets like elaborate origami constructs, until they themselves lost the ability to tell truth from falsehood" (*TB,* 171). One of the major deceptions is the creation and re-creation of identities. The twins renew themselves repeatedly, according to need: they have to be what is demanded of them at each moment of the struggle for power. When they discuss a scheme to attract attention away from the president, Hector suggests various possibilities that he says must be lived, as he says:

> "Only for a while, only for a while. Then maybe we can drop all this pretense and be what we really are."
>
> Which was—what? Teresa found she could not complete the thought.
>
> "What happens," Katerina blurted out, "if we become what we pretend to be?"
>
> Hector was genuinely surprised. He studied his sister and then shrugged. "So much the better," he said after a while. "It won't be such a strain anymore." (*TB*, 77)

But tragedy looms in the future for those who believe they can arrest the turning wheel of history. Once again, Rosca predicts grief for those who have not learned the lessons of the past and how to read the signs of the times. Premonitions of tragic deaths, of disease, of sin, and of exile threaten the staged felicity of the main characters. Teresa Tikloptuhod, for instance, "who asked for nothing more of fate than her fate realized, acquired a sense of time so acute that she began to be able to unravel the future from the skeins of the present. Much good it did her, since no one listened, anyway" (*TB*, 81). In a manner reminiscent of Anna's surreal vision at the end of *State of War*, Teresa perceives her future, and that of those who surround her, in a seemingly impassive manner: her father's murder, Epee's twin children, San Custodio's end, her own destiny. Looking at her house, she discerns that she "would miss it years from now when she was pinned down, immobilized, disgraced, and exiled in a foreign country" (*TB*, 88). And from her lips comes the ultimate foreshadowing of the Marcos family's downfall and the future of the Philippines: "Every widow who's run in her husband's place has won" (*TB*, 171).

The author's own situation as a writer exiled during the Marcos dictatorship adds a personal dimension to an understanding of *Twice Blessed* and its theme. Rosca's political denunciation of the Marcos regime in her second novel shrouds a deeper reflection on the situation, past and future, of the Philippines and its people. The voice of the exile is heard clearly, looking back on "a beautiful country; you find out only when you've been away" (*TB*, 112), as she re-creates the fear and tension that characterized the dictatorship years. Her description of the drama of the insurgent is vivid: "That was how it was in this country . . . everyone lived in terror, not daring to stop, not daring to look back if only to check whether the adversary was far or near of indeed

if there even was one, not daring to take stock lest the little havens of safety they'd patched together over their heads came crashing down" (*TB*, 29). The shelter Rosca has chosen for herself is her fiction, her version of her country viewed and reimagined with the perspective offered by time and distance, her valedictory for a homeland she was forced to leave behind.

These narratives, as Rosca has shown, have the capacity to establish new metaphors of nationhood: "not only to rewrite history, but to create and frame defining symbols for the purpose of imagining the nation" (Boehmer, 198). She uses the analysis of the cyclical histories and destinies of the characters—the reminder of the dangers of forgetting, the invention of identities, and the revelation of the overwhelming intricacies of the political system—to develop metaphors of reconstruction. The Chilean writer Isabel Allende, whose themes mirror Rosca's, has explained that "in a novel we can give an illusory order to chaos. We can find the key to the labyrinth of history. We can make excursions into the past, to try to understand the present and dream the future. In a novel we can use everything: testimony, chronicle, essay, fantasy, legend, poetry and other devices that might help us to decode the mysteries of our world and discover our true identity" (45). Ninotchka Rosca's novels, a Filipina American's views of her complex country, are powerful discourses of the discovery and construction of personal and national identity through an incisive analysis of the postcolonial/immigrant condition. Themes such as the creation of identity, the loss of memory, and the limitations of not knowing history emphasize the effects of colonial interventions and the diasporic destiny of the country. The narration of the postcolonial immigrant's elusive story arises from the interaction of historical facts and memory, the compulsion to read beyond superficial accounts in order to offer new interpretations and, ultimately, create alternative versions of history.*

Rocío G. Davis, Winter 1999

*The author would like to thank the Spanish Ministry of Science and Education for funding that helped in the research for this article, part of a project entitled "Historical and Fictional Worlds: The New Relation Between History and Literature in the Last Quarter of the 20th Century" (PB 94–0578), directed by Dr. Ignacio Olábarri.

■ **WORKS CITED**

Allende, Isabel. "Writing as an Act of Hope." In *Paths of Resistance: The Art and Craft of the Political Novel*. William Zinsser, ed. Boston. Houghton Mifflin. 1989. Pp. 41–63.

Ashcroft, Bill, Gareth Griffiths, and Helen Tiffin, eds. *The Post-Colonial Studies Reader*. London. Routledge. 1995.

Boehmer, Elleke. *Colonial and Postcolonial Literature*. Oxford, Eng. Oxford University Press. 1995.

Brennan, Timothy. "The National Longing for Form." In *Nation and Narration*. Homi K. Bhabha, ed. London. Routledge. 1990.

Campomanes, Oscar V. "Filipinos in the United States and Their Literature of Exile." In *Reading the Literatures of Asian America*. Shirley Geok-lin Lim and Amy Ling, eds. Philadelphia. Temple University Press. 1992. Pp. 49–78.

———. "Filipino American Literature: Looking Homeward." In *An Interethnic Companion to Asian American Literature*. King-Kok Cheung, ed. New York. Cambridge University Press. 1997. Pp. 73–124.

Casper, Leonard. "Minoring in History: Rosca as Ninotchka." *Amerasia*, 16:2 (1990), pp. 201–10.

De la Costa, Horacio. *Literature and Society: A Symposium*. Carlos P. Romulo, ed. Manila. Florentino. 1964.

Goellnicht, Donald C. "Blurring Boundaries: Asian American Literature as Theory." In *An Interethnic Companion to Asian American Literature*. King-Kok Cheung, ed. New York. Cambridge University Press. 1997. Pp. 338–65.

Gonzalez, N. V. M. "Imagination and Literature of Emerging Nations." *Solidarity*, 9:5 (May-June 1975), pp. 34–38.

Hutcheon, Linda. *Splitting Images: Contemporary Canadian Ironies*. Toronto. Oxford University Press. 1991.

Lim, Shirley Geok-lin. "Assaying the Gold; or, Contesting the Ground of Asian American." *New Literary History*, 24 (1993a), pp. 147–69.

———. *Nationalism and Literature: English-Language Writing from the Philippines and Singapore*. Quezon City, Phil. New Day. 1993b.

Mestrovic, Marta. "Ninotchka Rosca." *Publishers Weekly*, 6 May 1988, pp. 90–91.

Rosca, Ninotchka. *State of War*. New York. Norton. 1988.

———. "Myth, Identity and the Colonial Experience." *World Englishes*, 9:2 (1990), pp. 237–43.

———. *Twice Blessed*. New York. Norton. 1992.

San Juan, E. Jr. "Mapping the Boundaries: The Filipino Writer in the U.S.A." *Journal of Ethnic Studies*, 19:1 (Spring 1991), pp. 117–31.

Sangari, Kumkum. "The Politics of the Possible." In *The Nature and Context of Minority Discourse*. David Lloyd and Abdul JanMohammed, eds. Oxford, Eng. Oxford University Press. 1990.

Philippine Literature in English: Tradition and Change

With the influx of American influence into Philippine soil, primarily on account of the Spanish American War and the ceding of the Philippines to America in 1898, writers began to use English as their medium of expression, since it became the medium of instruction in all schools and was the preferred tongue among the intellectual elite, who were challenged into adopting a foreign tongue with a measure of adeptness. Understandably, Philippine literature, from the opening of the twentieth century until the outbreak of the Pacific War in 1941, was patterned after Anglo-American models, romantic readings of nineteenth-century vintage saturating the literary scene. English became the primary tool for communication, not only in education but also in literature.

The almost four centuries of foreign domination had made Filipinos proficient in several tongues. By learning English and Spanish, educated Filipinos came in contact with the humanistic and scientific works of the most advanced countries of the world. On the other hand, some scholars claim that the development of this Western cultural orientation resulted in the submergence of those Asian values which are the bases of a national culture in evolution. With American textbooks, instructors, and writers as models, Filipinos started to learn not only a new language but also a new way of life alien to their tradition. Thus began their Western education, or miseducation, the onset of colonial orientation or disorientation depending on how one looks at it.

Even before World War II, nationalism had seeped into the country's literature because of political movements which demanded that writers begin weaning themselves from American influence and shaping their own national identity or psyche, that they become more aware of social realities beyond subjects of a romantic flavor, such as moonlight and roses, the birds, the bees, the flowers, and the trees, that they stop flaunting their bleeding hearts—products of a febrile imagination, so antiromanticists claimed. This was triggered by the establishment of a commonwealth kind of government in 1935, the first step toward a semblance of self-rule, with the promise of independence in 1946.

Generally, part of the literary ferment that appeared before World War II as it affected Philippine shores was fostered by the dynamic tension in the history of literary evolution and the brush with Western culture and politics. The granting of political independence did not in fact end American domination. On the contrary, many features of colonialism remain even today: greater confusion in the language situation, for example, as the better writers down to the present day continue to write in English. For many years after Philippine "independence," the educational system was still American-oriented. But somehow, the more important writers of this period tried to prove that even while they wrote in English, they remained essentially Filipino at heart.

Still, the critic Petronilo Daroy observed another aspect of Philippine literature being written after the war: "Indeed, the national sensibility after World

II is characterized by indignant perceptions which often manifest themselves in stories which base their claim to realism on the mere fact of their brutal treatment of evil." At any rate, this attention to the unsmiling aspects of Philippine life liberated our literature from maudlin emotionalizing and excessive sentimentalism.

After the war, in 1945, writers in the Philippines began to be discernibly more westernized, in the name of cultural advancement. American professors and authors visited the country and conducted seminars, and Filipino writers started their exodus to the United States to drink in the wisdom of the American literary masters. They became seriously modernized in the process. And after decades of a so-called cultural time-lag, they had now started to keep pace with trends abroad and, from the 1950s onward, were already truly westernized, in the sense of being predominantly formalistic and craft-conscious. This was largely courtesy of the New Criticism, a tendency which has continued to the present day in the form of an emphasis on craft, on certain set standards and formulas for both poetry and prose, although other approaches and ideologies have begun to seep in and to rock the boat of modernism, this so-called call to form.

Because of the sociopolitical upheavals during the 1970s, the infamous dictatorial regime of Ferdinand Marcos, and the upsurge of unrest and activism even in universities, resulting in the so-called parliament of the streets, writers began to deviate from artistic preoccupations and wrote protest or committed literature. This frenzied, restive, agitated atmosphere led to the famous EDSA revolution in 1986, a four-day phenomenon aptly called People Power, a bloodless revolution fought with songs, prayers, and flowers, climaxing in the Cory Aquino miracle. The rest, as the cliché goes, is history.

More than a decade has passed since then. Writers have now gone back to honing their craft in the service of excellence, aware that before being political, they must first write well. The great divide lies in the schism between writers writing in English, on the one hand, and those whose brand of nationalism demanded that they write in their own tongue, Filipino, on the other.

Today, it seems, it is not so much the writer's personal sense of artistic commitment that is questioned as his choice of literary medium. The big issue for so-called nationalists who doubt the validity and viability of English as a medium in the wake of a significant surge of good writers working in Filipino: will the Filipino writer writing in English continue to survive, and for how many more decades? The fact remains that several good writers are still working in English, the language in which they are more comfortable and one that

has become part of their cultural history, which cannot just be rejected and ignored as if it never happened.

In the meantime, a number of the better writers, unfazed by this controversy over language, have gone past formalism without rejecting it altogether, into more generalized commitments to both truth and beauty, the two great imperatives of significant literature in whatever period, climate, or persuasion. While some continue to write under the colonial heritage of Spanish and American domination, a heritage they cannot disown or ignore without unwriting or reinventing Philippine history, several robust and dynamic groups of university-based young writers, proudly armed with contemporary literary theories, have now discerned a need to break free from so-called colonial straitjackets.

Philippine contemporary literature is moving on, aware of its inherited culture at the same time and holding on to what is ethnically or locally its own. While it considers the legitimacy of indigenous traditions, undeniably significant in the shaping of national identity, it does not ignore opportunities for cross-cultural encounters which could broaden exposure to literary materials, leading to values, meanings, sentiments previously muffled by extreme traditionalism.

At this point, certain grim realities are inevitably reflected in Filipino authors' writings, even as the country continues to be mired in mass poverty, graft, and criminality, encouraging the growth of an esthetics of despair but never hopelessness. Still, the more recognizable voice is one of affirmation in spite of this sense of alienation which plagues Third World countries like the Philippines. Add to this an essentially romantic temperament that has allowed the use of a rich imagination to produce that compelling power of summoning the better sensibilities toward more than mere broodings or exaggeratedly bleak literary scenarios, into rendering more dramatic moments in history on the vaster canvas of the universal human condition.

■ PHILIPPINE POETRY IN ENGLISH

Early Philippine poetry in English was used as vehicle for self-expression, often very personal, romantic outbursts, and later on, before the outbreak of the Pacific War, became an expression of a dawning nationalistic fervor based on a growing social commitment which reminded the poet to get out of his ivory tower, open his eyes to social realities, and begin to write as a Filipino writing for the Filipino reader and not for a Western audience. Recognized poets then were Angela Manalang Gloria, known for her exquisite verses on love and other very female experiences; R. Zulueta da Costa, who at that point in time had already begun to temper his romanticism with poetry which celebrated national destiny, eloquently affirming the need for Filipinism. Already way ahead of his time, José Garcia Villa started to write a new kind of poetry, but it was not until after the war that he was recognized and hailed in his own country, and this only after his recognition by peers and masters abroad. An exponent of art for art's sake, he produced works which dazzled with their intensity, their lyricism, their unorthodox mysticism, their sheer magic in the luminosity of language, and their virtuosity and originality of style.

Modernism in poetry started during the 1950s and continued onward. The fifties saw the strong influence of modernism on most Philippine poets, especially those who had gone abroad to study under the masters. The influences of several modernist movements inevitably seeped into Philippine poetry: namely, the metaphysical school, which resulted in the combined poetic workings of the intellect and the emotion; imagism, which emphasized the visual image, the tight line, the wringing of rhetoric's neck, so to speak; impressionism, which capitalized on suggestiveness, musicality, subjective description, symbolism; and the New Criticism, which upheld a strong preoccupation with form and craftsmanship.

Carlos Angeles and Emmanuel Torres wrote with such technical precision, particularly in the handling of poetic imagery, that they were usually called poets' poets. Edith Tiempo was able to combine the cerebral and emotional qualities of poetry, vision, and controlled passion in perfect poetic tension. Cirilo Bautista's achievement is phenomenal, evincing a mastery of the epic line like nobody else, combining the epical and the historical, the impressionistic and the surrealistic, the lyrical and the narrative.

Ricardo de Ungria, on the other hand, has mastered the tight form, with short, striking lines that pack in a wealth of intensity, passion, energy, and dynamism, using language to the nth degree, so to speak. Alfred Yuson's poetic ingenuity lies in the turning of wittily, scintillatingly, strangely singing phrases, reveling in language's vaunted new autonomy. Gémino Abad masters the cerebral tone, the clean, clear, chiseled line, the startling imagery, and the right degree of evocativeness, exploiting the poem's being-ness, affirming the integrity of language, and shunning the "wilder shoots." To date, he has brought out three very significant anthologies, which together trace the evolution and development of poetry in English, the most comprehensive and scholarly compilation of such verse yet assembled.

Marjorie Evasco, Rowena Torrevillas, Merle Wenceslao, and Maria Luisa Carino, a new breed of fe-

N. V. M. Gonzalez (*Robert H. Taylor*)

male poets, continue the romantic tradition, effectively infused with an awareness of contemporary imagery and rhythm and strengthened by a sense of regionalism and even feminism, while at the same time attuned to the quality, depth, and breadth of poetry's more vital concerns. The younger poets who have become the voice of today's brand of poetic sensibility are not much different from their predecessors, many of whom were their mentors and even their inspiration. They are just as careful with form, having attended workshops and seminars with these mentors as lecturers, are just as Western in their influences, and are equally as conscious of their sociohistorical roots and milieu, having come a long way from the unrestrained, unbridled expression of personal emotions and naïve outpourings of the past era.

■ PHILIPPINE FICTION

Prior to the 1920s, Philippine short stories are better classified as tales rather than stories, mostly ghost tales or folktales explaining natural phenomena with a theme in which a moral was brought home to the reader. Plot structure was worked along the easy, chronological, "and then" method, to use E. M. Forster's terminology. The short-story writers of that era drew mostly on Western culture and Western models. By the 1930s the market for Philippine short stories in English was no longer confined solely to the home front but had started to break into print abroad as well. Among the prominent writers were Paz Marquez Benitez, Paz Latorena, Arturo B. Rotor, Amador Daguio, Loreto Paras Sulit, Carlos Bulosan, and Manuel Arguilla. Bienvenido Santos and N.V.M. Gonzalez, although writing at that time, were not to gain wider recognition and a larger audience until after World War II. The years immediately before the war were characterized by a desire to create a "national literature," not merely by writing about simple rustic life, Philippine flora and fauna, and Philippine national heroes, but by attempting to define the national psyche or identity, however evasive that might be. By the end of the 1930s the Philippine short story had already improved in quality, offering plausible characterization, a stricter control of language, and interesting situations and themes. The "modern" short story (in the sense of "contemporary" or "twentieth-century") was not to be written until after the war.

Manuel Arguilla, who died before the war, wrote the most significant prewar collection, *How My Brother Leon Brought Home a Wife and Other Stories,* exemplifying a dynamic tension between social commitment and artistic excellence—the objective of good literature both before the war and for all time. The social note was pursued in Carlos Bulosan's *America Is in the Heart,* in the choice of subject matter and characters like the peasants and the laborers, and in the portrayal of the effects of politics on the private lives of people, the interrelation between economic conditions and political power.

N.V.M. Gonzales began writing in the 1930s, but his first short-story collection was not published until 1947, when *Seven Hills Away* appeared. Other distinguished collections followed, all products of serious artistic effort and of an artistic creed which upheld the belief that art must involve working with material (a serious craft) and must be a thing of beauty (artistic). The social note in Gonzalez's fiction never called attention to itself and never took precedence over the artistic objective, and Gonzalez was long considered the supreme craftsman, training many of his students at the University of the Philippines and the University of Santo Tomas always to labor with loving attention over every line and detail.

Likewise, Francisco Arcellana started his literary career before the war, but his influence and reputation as one of the Philippines' finest writers did not spread until after the war. His artistic ingenuity is most apparent in *Divide by Two,* with its strong emotional impact, its subtle manipulation of symbols, and the powerful rhythm of its language. Bienvenido Santos was another prewar youth and postwar writer whose first book of short stories, *You Lovely People,* about Filipino exiles in

America during the war, was not published until well after the war's end, in 1955. Like Gonzalez and Arcellana, he wrote mostly about loneliness, alienation, and homesickness, all postwar maladies. And of course there was Nick Joaquin, who stood above his contemporaries both as craftsman and as cultural historian. His mastery of the language is manifested in his flexible style, one that could be lush and exuberant one moment, slangy or colloquial and very contemporary the next, depending on his subject, his vision matched only by a creative power that was quite unsurpassed in its sense of history, tradition, and art.

Gregorio Brillantes, in his volume of short fiction titled *Distance to Andromeda* and in other short stories, wrote particularly about the generation under thirty, adolescent and postadolescent youths who suffered alienation from family, from society, and from themselves. Brillantes writes with a sure hand, frequently offering rich insights about the Catholic faith as it illumines the lives of countless Filipino families.

These were the big names in the field of the short story, the artists who never used their art as a tool for social and political propaganda. More than mere preoccupation with form, their writings showed that they had significant truths to express and personal visions to share. More names shone on the horizon: Kerima Tuvera, Gilda Cordero Fernando, Aida Rivera Ford, Juan Gatbonton, and Andres Cristobal Cruz, to name but a few.

The 1960s were, summarily, a period when writers seriously grappled with problems of art. The early 1970s saw a proliferation of politically motivated or committed writing and protest literature. Short-story writers became more conscious of the political milieu and of social issues in the wake of the increased activism all over the world and right in their country, especially during the troubled days of a dictatorial government. Some of the more recent fiction writers include Paulino Lim, Alfred Yuson, Jose Dalisay, Mario Eric Gamalinda, and Cristina P. Hidalgo.

In the meantime, what about the novelists? The war provided postwar novelists with a subject. Stevan Javellana's *Without Seeing the Dawn* focuses on an antiheroic protagonist hardened and embittered by the war, but ultimately vindicating himself and becoming almost heroic in the process. Edilberto Tiempo, the fiction writer and critic, wrote with an awareness of social history but remained strictly formalistic in his firm grasp of craft and his handling of history. Bienvenido Santos worked with a sense of pathos, irony, and realism, and took up the theme of personal and sociocultural alienation, especially among Filipinos stranded in America during the war, suffering from intense homesickness but somehow managing to endure with strength and fortitude and "loveliness" of spirit.

Francisco Sionil José's monumental Rosales saga, which is made up of five novels, has, more than any other series of works, touched on this Filipino search for roots, as well as on class struggle, social corruption, and the fight for social justice in postcolonial times. No other writer has been more widely translated in his own country and in other countries. N.V.M. Gonzalez's novels also reflect discipline, control, and irony, best reflected in his portrayal of the harsh world of the fisherfolk and peasants who endured and prevailed with dignity and grace in the face of pressure and want. His novels are manifestations of reality turned art.

Recent novelists have ventured into the murky terra incognita of postmodernism, rejecting the traditional concepts of fiction, portraying a world devoid of value and meaning, interweaving literature with journalism, history, biography, and even criticism. The objective is merely "pleasure of the text" through verbal or psychological constructs, a totality of vision. Examples of such avant-garde Filipino fictionists are Mario Eric Gamalinda, Jessica Hagedorn, and Alfred Yuson, to name but three of the more prominent figures.

Meanwhile, the influence of literature in the country is imperiled by the impact of modern technology on life and culture, and the Filipino writer feels it his responsibility to put literature back on track and in the center of life, aware of the perpetual need to upgrade and transform it into a meaningful social yet artistically forward-moving activity, opening up to a large interdependent world, listening to the polyphony of voices which could add to their own largeness of spirit and understanding, aware that they cannot continue to write in isolation, that each of the writings of all writers of the world is but a mere episode within that one general experience of the universal person forever in the process of unfolding and evolving.

Ophelia A. Dimalanta, Spring 2000

The Philippine Novel in English into the Twenty-first Century

In 1965, the critic Leonidas Benesa complained that when he was asked to prepare a paper on the Filipino novel in English from 1941 to 1962, he had to spend the greater part of the five weeks given him on "a frantic expedition that looked more archaeological than historico-literary" (Benesa, 53–54). In the end, he had

come up with only eleven novels published during those twenty-one years—half a novel per year. Today, if someone were to construct a list of the novels in English published during the last two decades, he would come up with at least sixty titles—roughly three novels per year. Contrary to the gloomy predictions of the militant student-led movements of the late sixties, Philippine fiction in English has not merely survived; it appears to have thrived.

Philippine fiction written in English belongs to a long and rich narrative tradition of literary works in several languages. The novel in the Philippines was modeled after Western prototypes, but its roots lie deep in native soil. There is a tradition of local narratives—oral epics, ballads, tales, and other folk materials—to which were later added other narrative types introduced by the Spaniards, including metrical romances (*corridos*), saints' lives, fables, parables, and folk epics (*pasyons*). The novel in the Philippines developed by combining elements from these different traditions, producing such noted works as *Florante at Laura* by Francisco Baltazar or Balagtas (1788–1862) and ultimately leading to José Rizal (1861–96), whose novels *Noli Me Tangere* (1887) and *El Filibusterismo* (1891) were the first works of realistic fiction produced by a Filipino. They are the work of a man steeped in both his native traditional literature and the major European literatures.

By the 1920s English was firmly established as a medium of both education and literary expression. Nonetheless, the early novels in English are not appreciably different from their predecessors in Spanish and Tagalog. For instance, the first Philippine novel in English, *A Child of Sorrow* (1921) by Zoilo Galang (1895–1959), is a simplistic and melodramatic story of thwarted love—in essence, a Tagalog novel written in English. On the other hand, *The Filipino Rebel* (1927) by Maximo Kalaw (1891–1955) is a historical novel about the American conquest of the islands and the establishment of the new colonial regime, very much in the tradition of Rizal, though far less successful. With N.V.M. Gonzalez's *Winds of April* (1940) "the Filipino novel takes on a definite qualitative change, manifesting the stylistic and thematic traits that have been taken to be distinctive of the English branch of Philippine fiction" (Mojares, 345).

In the 1950s and early 1960s, the intellectual milieu of the urban, university-educated English writer in the Philippines became even more sophisticated and cosmopolitan. Foremost among the postwar novelists are Bienvenido Santos (1911–96), N.V.M. Gonzalez (1915–99), and Nick Joaquin (b. 1917). These three offer an interesting study in the different directions which the Philippine novel in English has taken: Joa-

Bienvenido Santos (*Wig Tysmans*)

quin's language borrows the cadences and the exuberance of Spanish; Gonzalez's deliberately attempts to capture the syntax and rhythms of the local languages; Santos's comes closest to American English.

Joaquin's novel *The Woman Who Had Two Navels* (1961) is an impressive achievement, both for its dazzling use of English and for its mastery of narrative technique in rendering the search for a national identity. *Cave and Shadows* (1983) is structured like a mystery thriller, yet it explores the same theme, drawing on a rich store of myth and legend but locating the action in the thick of contemporary events and using a middle-class intellectual as protagonist. Joaquin's style has been described as "tropical baroque," a reference as much to his choice of unusual protagonists in rather melodramatic situations as to his prose.

Gonzalez's novel *The Bamboo Dancers* (1959) draws on the author's urban experiences, and on his expatriate years. His earlier *Season of Grace* (1956), on the other hand, drew on his earlier life in the province of Romblon and Mindoro, bending English to the shape and sense of the language of the Visayan peasant with admirable simplicity and economy.

Santos's earlier novels—*Villa Magdalena* (1965), about a decaying family and class differences; *The Volcano* (1965), about Philippine-American relations; and *The Praying Man* (1982), about corruption in high places—are set in the Philippines, but his two later nov-

els *The Man Who (Thought He) Looked Like Robert Taylor* (1983) and *What For You Left Your Heart in San Francisco* (1987) are deeply moving portraits of "wounded men," Filipinos in America. It is in these two novels that his distinctive use of the English language is most obvious: his choice of idioms, the clipped, brisk pace, the consistent understatement.

Perhaps the most important woman novelist of the postwar period is Kerima Polotan. *The Hand of the Enemy* (1962), the story of a woman's search for love, but a search solidly grounded in contemporary social and political realities (including a *sakdalista* movement in Pangasinan), has been lavishly praised for its impeccable handling of English, an elegance perhaps matched only by Gregorio Brillantes and Gilda Cordero Fernando, younger fiction writers who have not produced full-length novels.

Edith Tiempo, named National Artist only last year, is best studied through her poetry. Still, her novels—*A Blade of Fern* (1979), *His Native Coast* (1979), *The Alien Corn* (1991), and *One, Tilting Leaves* (1995)—are interesting in that they focus on a different Philippines—the provincial towns and cities, the world of loggers, miners, small-town academics—and in that they are told in a rather quaint, almost mannerist English, the effect perhaps of the relative isolation of Silliman University, where she is based.

▪ THE CONTEMPORARY NOVEL IN ENGLISH

Most contemporary Philippine novels are historical novels. In these, history does not merely provide the setting, but enters into the motivation of the characters, propels the plot. The characters are political beings; their conflicts are engendered by political events. I would even claim that the real protagonist here is the nation itself, and the real conflict its desperate struggle for survival. This, it seems to me, is the most important change in the last two decades.

This tradition of writing has always existed in the Filipino novel in all languages. But, while it may not have been the dominant trend in the Filipino novel in English in the past, of late it clearly has been so. Contemporary novelists have all gone beyond the recording of their protagonists' personal conflicts to focus on the larger problems plaguing the nation. The protagonists of many of these novels are in many ways reincarnations of Rizal's Crisostomo Ibarra, perhaps an indication of both the enduring power of Rizal on the imagination of Filipino middle-class writers and the inescapable aftermath of the historical situation that gave rise to his novels. Here then, over and over again, is the middle-class intellectual, unable to escape his or her roots, determined to save his or her country, thwarted both by the sinister power of the enemy (in some cases still the colonial master of old, in others his surrogate) and by the tragic flaw in his or her own character, which often is indecision.

In their attempt to (re)write the story, contemporary Filipino novelists have appropriated a number of different strategies, ranging from those of conventional realistic fiction (as in Jose Y. Dalisay's *Killing Time in a Warm Place,* Renato Madrid's *Devil Wings,* Carlos Cortes's *Longitude,* and the novels of Edilberto Tiempo, F. Sionil José, and Antonio Enriquez), to those associated with marvelous realism and postmodernism (as in Eric Gamalinda's *Confessions of a Volcano* and *Empire of Memory* and Alfred Yuson's *Great Philippine Jungle Energy Café*). They explore Philippine mythical material, an important part of the work of retrieval, of reconstruction, of the retelling of the story (as in Erwin Castillo's *Firewalkers* and Cecilia Manguera Brainard's *Song of Yvonne*). They employ such postmodern techniques as the collage, a variety of language registers, discontinuity of narration, et cetera, to depict the fragmentations and carnivalesque quality of modern Philippine life (as in Gina Apostol's *Bibliolepsy* and Alfred Yuson's *Voyeurs and Savages*). And, though some of the novels end on an ambiguous note, with the protagonist still trapped in indecision, most—including the one comic novel in the group, *The Great Philippine Jungle Energy Café*—finish on a note of affirmation.

A few novels actually conclude with a statement of what the author perceives as the role the writer must play within the postcolonial context. And what is that role? The writer must protest; he must resist his own alienation, his own marginalisation, for s/he is the conscience of his race. And the writer must remember, for s/he is its memory. Thus, these novels are steps toward retrieving the nation's fragmented past and making it whole, rewriting the story written by the conquerors so that we, the conquered, and our descendants might know it and be healed. Through imaginative reconstruction, our novelists have undertaken the reexamination and reinterpretation of our long, complex colonial history, as well as our more recent history under the Marcos dictatorship. In this they are simply being absolutely true to tradition.

▪ THE FUTURE

It should be mentioned that many of the contemporary Philippine writers in English are expatriates, like Villa, Bulosan, and Santos, and like Rizal and his comrades before them. Some of this new generation of expatriate writers have partly penetrated the mainstream in the USA, among them Jessica Hagedorn and Bino Realuyo.

Jessica Hagedorn (*Karen Dacker*)

Unlike the Bulosan generation, however, they are not writing American immigrant novels. Many are writing historical Philippine novels, something which Oscar V. Campomanes sees as a strategy for making themselves "visible," a means of coping with their exile that is different from that taken by the first generation of expatriate writers (Campomanes, 163–65).

I see this as a significant trend—namely, the increasing importance of the diaspora—in Philippine literature. The attention given to ethnic American studies and minority discourse in universities in the U.S. has opened a window for Asian-American writers. On the one hand, it has created an audience for ethnic American literature, including Asian American literature; on the other hand, it has stimulated U.S.-born Filipino-American writers to return to the Philippines in search of their roots. Among the Fil-Am fiction writers now published in the U.S. are: Ninotchka Rosca with *State of War* (1998) and *Twice Blessed* (1999), Jessica Hagedorn with *Dogeaters* (1990), Cecilia Manguera Brainard with *When the Rainbow Goddess Wept* (1995), Arlene Chai with *The Last Time I Saw Mother* (1995) and *Eating Fire and Drinking Water* (1997), Michele Skinner with *Mango Seasons* (1996), Rinehart Zamora Linmark with *Rolling the R's* (1995), Peter Bacho with *Cebu* (1991), Bino Realuyo with *Umbrella Country* (1999), and the short-story writers Marianne Villanueva, Evalina Galang, and Eric Gamalinda.

In Philippine classrooms, students will sometimes raise the issue of why these writers are being taught in Philippine literature courses, when in fact they are now Americans. My response has always been that I do not see the difference between them and Jose Garcia Villa, Carlos Bulosan, and Bienvenido Santos. There was never any objection raised to teaching those authors as Filipino writers. The diaspora is an aspect of the Philippine reality which cannot be ignored. A more important question might be: will we cease to regard these newer authors as "Filipino" when they switch to America as subject and theme, as indeed Jessica Hagedorn has done in *The Gangster of Love* (1996)?

Another trend in the new millennium will be the growing importance of the Internet. Access to cyberspace has already made possible the forging of stronger ties between Filipino and Filipino-American writers. Naturally, this is both a plus and a minus. On the one hand, we can today, more than ever, speak of belonging to a community of writers. Writers based both in the Philippines and in the U.S. and other countries are in direct personal contact through e-mail and contribute to Internet magazines such as *Likhaan on Line,* hosted by the University of the Philippines Creative Writing Center, and *Legmanila,* hosted by a group of young UP professors, as well as to other electronic 'zines hosted by Filipinos living in different countries. On the other hand, these close connections could have the result of alienating Philippine writing in English even farther from Philippine writing in Filipino and the other Philippine languages; for of course, it is the writer in English who is likely to be most drawn to the Internet, since the overwhelming majority of the material there is in English.

The fact that the Net is interactive adds yet another dimension, and now we are able to download novels from the Internet. All this, and other as yet unforeseeable developments, will inevitably affect the type of novels being written. Already computer games, e-mail, and the concept of virtual reality have entered into fiction, affecting not just subject matter but narrative strategy as well. Yuson's *Voyeurs and Savages,* for example, combines actual e-mail messages from people like Eric Gamalinda, Rowena Torrevillas, Evalina Galang, and Eileen Tabios with newspaper clippings and other texts along with a straightforward—albeit fragmented—narrative. Fragmentation and collage are also characteristics of *Bibliolepsy* and *Rolling the R's.* In the future, we will perhaps see serial novels on the Internet, or novels on CD, which will be regularly revised and updated, or interactive novels, or a new type of

graphic novel produced completely by the writers themselves working with computer graphics and scanners.

According to Jose Y. Dalisay Jr., we have now achieved "a degree of performance and sophistication that we can rightly be proud of, wherever our aesthetic, philosophical or ideological preferences may incline" (Dalisay, 145). Though he was speaking of the Philippine short story, I think his assertions may be made of the novel in English as well. Describing the younger generation of Philippine fiction writers, he says they are "generally well-schooled, well-read, and well-travelled, which lends their work a certain consciousness of form, a deliberation of design" (Dalisay, 150).

> Their chosen issues tend to be those of gender and sexuality, the environment, cultural identity, and individual freedom. They have material aplenty, but seemingly no single, defining experience, in the way the War or the First Quarter Storm was for their predecessors. . . . Their response to aggravation is rarely anger, but irony and wit, perhaps withdrawal. . . . They possess a deftness of language that comes not only from reading, but also from speaking and listening to the language all the time; it is an English inflected with the resonances and accents of pop culture, the internet, the stock market, and yet also of that home in the province that no one ever quite leaves behind. (Dalisay, 151)

Realism remains the dominant style, but many writers are experimenting with marvelous realism, science fiction, the comic book, horror, parody, and other forms of metafiction. One result is a blurring of the boundaries between fiction and nonfiction, between fiction and drama. The writers no longer seem to feel bound to defend their choice of English. After all, many of them are bilingual. "Indeed, we are witnessing the continuing de-Americanisation of English, its appropriation by Filipino writers for Filipino subjects and purposes" (Dalisay, 151). It is not unlikely that in the future some novels will be written not in just one language but in two or three, a reflection of the way most Filipinos experience the world. Quite possibly, the language of narration might be a form of "standard English" (I enclose the term in quotation marks to underline the fact that it is problematic), but the dialogue, and even the characters' thoughts, may well be rendered in a mixture of Taglish, Engalog, Cebuano, Iluko, *swardspeak, colegialaspeak, El-Shadai-speak,* et cetera, as demanded by the character.

■ CONCLUSION

Is it true that Philippine literature in general is enjoying a kind of "golden age"? Well, that may be too grandiose a claim. But if one is to judge by the publishing scene, which has never been so vigorous, or by the appearance of bookstores which not only carry Philippine literary titles but often carry *only* Philippine literary titles, or by the number of literary contests or, particularly, the proliferation of creative-writing workshops and courses both inside and outside academe, and lately even of creative-writing centers, the answer would have to be that it is not doing badly at all.

And what of its audience? Is there a larger audience now for Philippine literature? Paradoxically, the answer to this question would have to be "Just a little, not much." This is to be regretted, of course, but it has its advantages. Since very few writers in English are dependent on their writing for a living, they are, in a rather paradoxical way, free—free to write in any way they please, free to be as outrageous, as innovative, as daring as they choose to be. This ensures that, although the audience for their works may not be growing as fast as one would wish it, the literature itself is in constant flux. It is growing, changing, transforming. We can only hope that, in one of its transformations, it will find, finally, that it is speaking to and for not just a faithful band of literati but a mass audience as well.

Cristina Pantoja Hidalgo, Spring 2000

■ WORKS CITED

Benesa, Leonidas V. "The Filipino Novel from 1941–1962." In *Literature at the Crossroads*. Manila. Florentino. 1965.

Campomanes, Oscar. "Filipinos in the United States and Their Literature of Exile." In *Discrepant Histories*. Vincent Rafael, ed. Pasig, Phil. Anvil. 1995.

Dalisay, Jose Y. Jr. "The Filipino Short Story in English: An Update for the '90s." In *Likhaan Anthology of Philippine Literature in English*. Gémino H. Abad, gen. ed. Quezon City, Phil. University of the Philippines Press. 1999.

Ileto, Reynaldo C. *Pasyon and Revolution: Popular Movements in the Philippines, 1840–1910*. Quezon City, Phil. Ateneo de Manila University Press. 1979.

Lumbera, Bienvenido, and Cynthia N. Lubera. *Philippine Literature: A History and Anthology*. Manila. National Book Stores. 1982.

Mojares, Resil. *Origins and Rise of the Filipino Novel*. Quezon City, Phil. University of the Philippines Press. 1983.

Reyes, Soledad. *The Romance Mode in Philippine Popular Literature*. Manila. De La Salle University Press. 1994.

SINGAPORE

Dissenting Voices: Political Engagements in the Singaporean Novel in English

■ HISTORIES

Few countries can be said to have their literary development forcibly redirected in its course by politics, as Singaporean literature was by the separation of Singapore from Malaysia on 9 August 1965. Until the peninsula of Malaya attained independence from the British on 31 August 1957, Singapore and Malaya had been governed as one political entity. In 1959, Singapore had become an internally self-governing colony, the British taking responsibility for defence. In 1963, Singapore, together with Sabah and Sarawak, became member states of the newly formed Federation of Malaysia.

With the island's departure from Malaysia in August 1965 to become a republic, the literature of Singapore assumed its own path, after several decades of literary commonality with its peninsular neighbour. The shared beginnings of this literature in English can be traced to the University of Malaya in Singapore, where small groups of undergraduates had come together to discuss writing and to write creatively.[1] It was primarily poetry that was discussed, written, and published, either in anthologies or subsequently in individual collections.[2] When fiction first came to be published, it was similarly as anthologies of short stories.[3]

It is not difficult to explain the preeminence of poetry over short fiction from the sixties and even into the eighties. Aspiring writers could have found it less inhibiting and formidable a task to produce thirty or more poems for a collection, where a novel would have required a social setting and a cast of characters whose lives had to be followed over several hundred pages. Drama was then dominated by productions of Western plays by theatre groups on campus, and from the British Armed Forces stationed in Singapore. Where the poet was free to explore the landscapes of his mind, as Edwin Thumboo indicates, the inadequate variety of social types in a nascent society disadvantages both the fictionist and dramatist: "The fiction cannot go beyond the parameters set by the material. And the material will grow only as a society expands, as life expands" (Thumboo, v). The creation of short fiction which marks the beginnings of Singaporean fiction in English may also be viewed as a product of the insecurity or absence of a fictive tradition which makes the rendering of "episodic" narratives the preferred form. Writers like Catherine Lim, Goh Sin Tub, and Lim Thean Soo probably felt comfortable with the manageable demands of short stories, which could also provide the training ground for the novels they would subsequently write.[4]

▪ "EVERY GOVERNMENT REWRITES THE PAST TO SUIT THE NEEDS OF THE PRESENT"

Where the short fiction of the early years of independence was not particularly concened with politics, Singapore's more recent fiction demonstrates the reality that "the individual in Singapore is not extricable from the social or political" (Haskell, 147). In short stories like Simon Tay's "Stand Alone" and "Exiles" (1991) and in novels like Suchen Christine Lim's *Fistful of Colours* (1993), Gopal Baratham's *A Candle or the Sun* (1991), and Philip Jeyaretnam's *Abraham's Promise* (1994),[5] the narrative engagement with history and politics is indicative of the realism underlying much of the fiction of Singapore.

The smallest country and the only island nation in Southeast Asia, the main island of Singapore is 584.8 square kilometres in area.[6] Singapore's urban character, good roads, and public transport define a microcosm that is highly efficient, highly organized, and easily controlled. The PAP (People's Action Party) has been the ruling party since 1959. Given that Singapore is virtually a one-party state, with opposition parties having always had and continuing to have little (and thus ineffectual) representation in Parliament, the voice of government is loud and clear, the hand of government strong and perceived to be authoritarian and omnipresent. Politics has a palpable presence in this city-state.

Compactness enhances the sense of political presence, as well as vulnerability: Singapore's forcible birth as a republic has made it continually conscious of the necessity and politics of survival, that initial period of insecurity being recalled and addressed in Tay's short story, aptly titled "Stand Alone." As Colonel Singh tells Charlie, the narrator, "The sudden separation of Singapore from Malaysia in 1965 forced Singapore to stand alone, before it was ready." Then, as the story also recounts, Singapore's defence preparedness was aided by Israeli expertise. Goh Keng Swee, then Deputy Prime Minister and Minister of Defence, recalls that although several friendly Asian and African countries were asked, it was the government of Israel which "responded willingly and sent a small but talented team of advisers to help us build up the army" (Goh, 56).

"Stand Alone" is set against a geopolitical backdrop of Singapore's vulnerability: the withdrawal of British forces from the region in the late 1960s, the "Confronta-

tion" against Malaya and Singapore launched by Indonesian President Sukarno on 20 January 1963 (in the hope of incorporating the two countries into a Greater Indonesia), the communist threat from Vietnam, and those guerrillas who still lingered in the Malayan jungle despite the declaration of the end of the (Communist) Emergency in 1960. Charlie comes to learn, through his father's military background,

> . . . a fear of much bigger threats: of the Vietnamese, of Communists still in the Peninsula jungle, of neighbouring nations that we had recently been part [of] or confronted by. . . . Maybe "fear" is not the right word. It was an emotion — call it what you will — that made us take courage, determined to be prepared for an onslaught and to survive any odds. A fear that made us bold. (*SA*, 217)

Despite these sentiments, which could be taken to justify the necessity of compulsory National Service[7] for men, the recollection of his army days in the eighties furnishes Charlie with a critique of the unquestioned power and hierarchy in the military. Charlie's discontent with the unyielding, unexplained codes of conduct in the army implies a sense of unease and helplessness before the faceless power of official and established machinery, or forces perceived as beyond an individual's control.

So too in *Fistful of Colours, A Candle or the Sun,* and *Abraham's Promise,* the relative powerlessness of the individual against the impersonal, crushing forces of power (as manifested in party politics or the larger overriding forces of history) emerges through narratives of the state and, correspondingly, narrative exposures of the drastic consequences which follow when the state (or party) is challenged or interrogated. The espousal of a different or dissenting view often results in disproportionately retributive treatment meted out by an authoritarian, even vindictive state. Often, then, the individual is intimidated into conformity or silence, whatever his convictions may really be.

Both the multiple narratives and the narratives within narratives provide structural means for embedding the linked (and then "delinked") history and politics of Singapore and Malaya/Malaysia in *Fistful of Colours.* From the contemporaneous to the past, Lim delineates the entanglements of ordinary lives with the historical and political life of their countries. The four friends who are the main characters in the novel are all in their thirties or, as in the case of Mark the expatriate teacher, already forty. Both Su Wen, a painter and art teacher, and Nica, a sculptor of Indian and Chinese ancestry, were originally from Malaysia. The fourth member, Jan, Su Wen's colleague in junior college, is engaged to Zul, a Malay journalist. Through this deliberately multiracial fraternity (the Malaysian-born) Lim explores the problems which underlie identity formation and national identity, her many shifts in locale and recollection between Malaysia and Singapore affording the linkages between the two countries—now separate and sovereign but still tied to each other by a shared past too recent to be forgotten by those who had lived it.

The discourse of resistance to an official view of what it means to be a Singaporean Chinese (or Chinese Singaporean) is best summed up by Mark:

> "Every government rewrites the past to suit the needs of the present."
>
> "Yes, I know. We remember some and forget some. What we don't want, we forget, cut it out."
>
> "I doubt it's as clear-cut as that," he smiled. (FC, 221)

This may be read as the questioning of an imposed, therefore contrived and constructed sense of cultural (or even national) identity by a government which, for reasons of expedience, chooses to equate "Chinese" with "Mandarin-speaker," for the presumed purpose of a unified ethnic identity. Besides the resulting marginalisation of non-Mandarin, dialect-speaking Chinese (as lesser Chinese), the implied linguistic link to the mother country may be alienating for some as well. As Jan tells her fiancé Zul, she, unlike her father, has never felt she was from China, because she "grew up here." Indeed, recalling a university lecturer, she links the settlement of Singapore by immigrant Chinese to the rejection of "certain things in the home country."

Then too, in her resistance to a reductive national definition and national ideology which privilege their own exclusive elitism over a more accurate truth, Su Wen sees the (Chinese) immigrant virtues of "survival, hard work, thrift and the accumulation of wealth and property" as having been marginalised in favour of the promotion of the Confucian high ideals of a Mandarin class.

> "I am as Chinese as my Cantonese-speaking grandparents have brought me up to be. And they were illiterate non-Mandarin speakers. And it wouldn't have occurred to anybody at that time in the fifties to label them as less Chinese or what! But nowadays to be Chinese, you must know Mandarin and read these characters. How can I? I can't read these. And my grandparents couldn't." (FC, 218)

Like many English-educated Chinese, Su Wen is not literate in Chinese. She describes her generation as "a lost generation," in reference to the political changes which accompanied Singapore's separation from Malaysia, resulting in the consequent artificial division of people related by ties of kinship and race into two politically separate peoples. Before coming to Singapore, she had studied the national language, Malay, but had moved from Malaysia to Singapore at twelve. The precipitate birth of Singapore as a republic brought in its wake political definitions and redefinitions which imposed discontinuities on ordinary lives and compelled revisions of identity, of which the imposition of Mandarin as a "mother tongue" for all Chinese, regardless of their home dialect, is but one striking example.

■ "A MATTER OF SECURITY"

As Baratham and Jeyaretnam show, political compliance is expected by the state. Anything that is perceived to threaten the status quo is to be demolished. This overreaction to difference and dissent (no matter how apparently mild) characterises the portrayal of the government or the ruling party in A Candle or the Sun and Abraham's Promise.

Hernando Perera, the protagonist of A Candle or the Sun, is an aspiring writer and manager of the furniture department at Benson's, a department store. Already married to Sylvie, he has an affair with Su-May and comes to know a religious group, Children of the Book, to which Su-May belongs. The politically proactive group prints and distributes a clandestine streetpaper which, while being critical of the government and its highhandedness, urges Singaporeans to regain their "essential freedoms." Whereas in another country such a streetpaper would not be much noticed, "this was Singapore, where the most trivial publication required a special permit from the Ministry of Culture and where contravention of this regulation was dealt with swiftly and severely" (CS, 55).

The streetpaper takes the government to task for subjecting its citizens to social engineering—"Your masters kennel you in neat boxes, doctor your females, control litter size according to pedigree and tell you what names you can give your pups" (a reference to the government policy of encouraging less well educated women to sterilize themselves after one or two children)[8]—and depriving them of the most precious gift, "the right to talk and mingle freely with your fellow men; your right to control your destiny." The streetpaper convinces Perera that "Singaporeans were denied essential freedoms," and he begins "vicariously to share their deprivation."

At work, the reorganization of Benson's may cost Perera his job. In a satiric swipe at "Asian values"[9] about which much has been earnestly made by the Singapore government over the past decade, Baratham has Chuang, Perera's boss, pronounce:

> "We must fling out false Western values leading to moral decay, unemployment and social welfare. No more imitating falsity. Right here in furniture department," he waved his arms expansively, "we install traditional Asian values. Soon we sell antique Chinese furniture —" (CS, 45)

Perera subsequently accepts a job from his friend Samson Alagaratnam, writing progovernment articles in the Ministry of Culture, and is enlisted to help Sam unearth the culprits behind the streetpaper, Sam himself having been assigned the responsibility of designing "counter-measures." One possible strategy of intimidation, as pointed out by Anuita, Sam's girlfriend, is to flood the market with their own newspaper written to "create a bit of violence here, a bit of racial trouble there." Even more horrifying is her bland suggestion that they could pin the blame on scapegoats, "people we've wanted to get for a long time, . . . innocent of producing streetpapers, but maybe guilty of other things." When Hernie comes to know that the leader, Peter Yu, and Su-May plan to leave Singapore to work in a hospital in Tanzania, he feels betrayed by Su-May and contacts Samson to tell him of the people behind the streetpaper, including Peter's intention of "encouraging displays of defiance during Culture Week."

Perera's exposure leads to Samson's plan to arrest the Children of the Book on New Year's Eve for "our A-One, top-secret, fully-modern, electronic, staffed-by-specialists detention centre" (151). As the enormity of his betrayal of the Children of the Book dawns on him, Perera argues—in vain—that the most one could do with the misguided Children of the Book "would be to fine them or impose some minor deterrent sentence." But he is told by Anuita that the men at the top would demand more.

In assisting Su-May and Peter's escape to freedom via Malaysia and Thailand, Perera is caught, taken in for interrogation, and detained without trial. The repeated beatings he receives at the hands of his guardians (sardonically described by Baratham as "young gymnasts, . . . [who] do whatever they have to do to me with consummate grace and in tune to harmonies I cannot hear") have rendered him toothless. The conclusion of Candle plays the improbability of Hernie's release from torture and detention against the probability of Peter and Su-May's freedom, with Hernie's vision of the couple working in a hospital located on the slopes of Mount Kilimanjaro, where "grassland gives way to rain forest, the air becomes cool, and here a well-worn trail leads to a line of hospital buildings."

Baratham makes the perceived sensitivity of the Singapore government to national security an object of satiric attention. As Anuita tells Perera, not only is culture a matter of security, but "Did they never tell you that on this island paradise of ours trade is a matter of security, education is a matter of security, health is a matter of security, how you wash your underwear is a matter of security?" (CS, 104). As Ban Kah Choon argues, Candle is not "just an attack on a particular government but an exposé of the way systems work to instill a general sense of fear." Peter Yu's attempt to subvert the status quo of compliance and conformity does not have so much to do with whether he is right in doing so as the degree of reaction his action provokes: "The fact of the matter is that organs of political control, sensing danger to their controlled orderliness, react with all the power at their disposal" (Ban, 95).

The conclusion of Candle recalls "Exiles," the concluding story in Stand Alone. Like Hernie Perera's conjuring of Kilimanjaro, Steven, one of the two narrators in Tay's story, invents Patagonia, a similarly far country of the imagination to which he can escape from his present misery of solitary confinement in prison, a state to which he seems to have been consigned for several years. For Steven, speaking (or thinking) in prison, and in apparent reference to the garden image that is associated with his Garden City (an image actively promoted by the Singapore government at home and its tourism board abroad),

> I don't have anything to do with this garden. . . . In the middle of this land which is my concern and care, this garden is an island I leave to the care of another, and is a place I take without having sown, admire without having tilled and pruned. All that is asked is that I admire and enjoy, and that I love this woman who is my wife. The garden is the heart of my land. (SA, 248)

Lyrical, allusive, and subtly critical of compliance, Tay implies that the garden (or gardener or government) would brook no assistance or interference in cultivation, though one is welcome to partake of the garden's yield. Where Steven escapes to a remote part of South America, and Hernie envisions Kilimanjaro in Tanzania for Peter and Su-May, Mothi, the other narrator of "Exiles" and Steven's friend, is contemplating emigration. Like numerous Singaporeans squeezed together on an island whose size gives many things a claustrophobic as well as exaggerated importance, Mothi recalls an earlier time when he and Steven wanted to go on holiday together to get away from it all by trekking "to the end of the world, Patagonia," especially when their articles had changed nothing.

Commenting on the nature of political power in Singapore, Nirmala PuruShotam writes:

> In Singapore, power is located centrally in a paternalistic state. Any difference from state-designed conceptions of the normal and the moral must negotiate with a feared power. . . . To negotiate with authority is to reformulate one's position so that it is closer to what is or seen to be the official view of morality and normalcy. (PuruShotam, 43)

PuruShotam sees the accommodation which underlies negotiation as creating self-censorship, which is compounded by the presence of the Internal Security Act (which permits arrest and detention without trial) and the Public Entertainment Licensing Unit (under which all scripts for public performance are required to secure prior official approval): "If we are serious about being a nation then, we must be serious about allowing the nation to be."

■ "I WANTED ONLY TO BE A SINGAPOREAN"

As Baratham notes, "There are more things in this world than the carrot and the stick, and the PAP have worked on the assumption that is all there is to human behaviour" (Baratham, *Fay*, 145). Nevertheless, the ubiquitous message that filters "top down" is to quell the conscience rather than risk the fallout. Abraham Isaac, the elderly protagonist of *Abraham's Promise*, believes in standing up for his conscience, and he suffers grievously for it. In Jeyaretnam's retrospective narrative, the former teacher of Latin reminisces about a life that has been more failure than success and feels partly responsible for the suicide of his sister, Mercy, and the failure of his marriage to Rani.

On the social and political level, though Isaac, teacher of Latin, may be regarded as a classicist by training, a man familiar with the ideals and assumptions which underpin democratic political systems in Britain and Western Europe, he is not unaware of the sins of colonialism. When the party of which Isaac is a member (teachers in government schools were not allowed to join political parties, but Isaac, as a teacher in a mission school, could do so) sweeps into power, he rejoices that while "the city had always been prosperous, genuine political self-direction could alleviate problems, such as housing and sanitation, that had been glossed over by our imperial masters" (*AP*, 115).

However, when the new leadership begins asserting its control to the extent of plotting the removal of the head of the Civil Service Union, who had objected to the changes it wanted, Isaac confides his disquiet to his former colleague, Krishna. Now a politician in the ruling party, Krishna argues for the precedence power must have over truth and conscience, the practical necessity of fear: "Only if we're feared can we do what has to be done." Despite Krishna's advice to observe silence, Isaac writes a "blistering defence" of the Civil Service Union leader which appears in the Teachers' Union newsletter. In the furore that ensues, Isaac's refusal to retract his views or apologise to the Ministry of Education leads to his suspension and subsequent dismissal. Despite the common knowledge that the charges of abandoning his class and threatening the principal are false, no one in the school—teacher or student—is willing to bear witness for him. As his colleague, Chong confesses, he has to toe the line because he has a wife and children to support.

The naïveté of Isaac's childlike faith in politics, religion, and his fellow men, that otherworldliness that gives priority to principle over expediency and makes Isaac a victim of his own idealism, recalls the remark made by his wife: "You are soft, a dreamer. I don't know if politics will be good for you." A second opportunity at compromise chances his way when Krishna is arrested in a security swoop by his party for suspected communist sympathies, and Isaac is approached by men from Internal Security who wish to work out a deal: in exchange for an affidavit pointing out that Krishna, even during his schoolteaching days, had been a communist sympathiser, Isaac will be able to teach again.

> "Look upon him as a sacrifice, a ram that must die — figuratively speaking, of course — for the good of the nation. We must show Malaya, and the British, that we can keep law and order, keep Communism in check. Krishnasamy is proof of our ability to do so." (*AP*, 163)

The affidavit would have been used as an instrument of intimidation, to make Krishna, his former colleague and his ex-wife's lover, realise the helplessness of things in the hope of extracting a confession. Isaac refuses to write; Krishna refuses to confess and is detained without trial. By the time he is released, Rani is already (prematurely) dead, and Victor, Isaac's son by her, has already come to live with his father.

Rajeev Patke observes of Isaac that "duty to God is introjected into duty towards one's nation. When that fails, the drive turns first to the duty to educate the young, then to duty towards the son" (Patke, 132). It should be noted, however, that once Isaac is suspended and dismissed from teaching, there is little opportunity for him to nurture the young other than as a private tutor to a small number of individuals. There is an elegiac quality about *Abraham's Promise*, particularly as the "old and grey and melancholy." Abraham Isaac recalls a life marked more by disappointment than by achievement. Even though his son is a successful lawyer, he is disappointed to discover—though he learns to accept—his homosexuality. In his very name, the man bears both the love and sacrifice of his biblical namesakes. Relating the story of Abraham and Isaac to his tutee, he asks if the latter has appreciated the young Isaac's point of view: the boy must have realised what his father planned and could not have realised that God had spoken to his father. Isaac was ready to die "because he loved his father. . . . Love, boy, it leads you to sacrifice."

Arguably, it was love for the principle of truth and the truth of principle, a love linked to his love for his country, that led Isaac to sacrifice his career (his lifeblood); it is love for his son that makes him sacrifice the prospect of having his son marry and raise a family, for the fact—which he comes to accept—of its impossibility. The sacrifice may be seen as given by Abraham into two generations: his own, and his son Victor's.

▪ IN DENIAL, BUT AFFIRMING

Underlying the authorial critique present in these texts is a concern that the state or the government provide its citizens with a threshold for difference and dissent, a concern too with the need to be sensitive to the spirit rather than retributive with the letter of the law. Criticism of the government (or the ruling party) should not be equated with disloyalty toward one's country; as PuruShotam remarks, "A commitment to the nation is larger than a commitment to the government."

While Lim's *Fistful of Colours* is more concerned with one's sense of identity and selfhood and the disruptions it suffers as a result of political change, and "Stand Alone" captures conflicts between individual freedom and national service, "Exiles," *A Candle or the Sun,* and *Abraham's Promise* point to a repressive political system intolerant of difference and dissent, obsessed as it is with what it reads, rightly or wrongly, as threats to its security. None of these narratives offers an amicable resolution to the tensions which characterise not only Singapore but also modern states and their governance: between the need for freedom and the need for order, between openness and intimidation, between idealism and pragmatism, even as these authors demonstrate that history and politics are integral to Singaporean narrative and text.

For Tay, Lim, Baratham, and Jeyaretnam too, it is the ordinary Singaporean who needs to be empowered and entrusted with accountability by a more mature and sensitive political leadership, and in a climate where transparency is reciprocal—not seen only as issuing from the rulers but also as invited from the ruled. Underlying the prescription, of course, is a belief in the virtues of freedom of speech. As Singaporeans become increasingly well educated (with English as the medium of instruction), and as the electorate matures in sophistication and expectation, Singaporeans will likely want to be seen and treated as capable of responsible and creative dissent. The more educated and informed you are, the more likely are you to speak up.

Victor Savage has pointed out the use of geographic smallness as legitimising the continuation of one-party domination and the endorsement of the People's Action Party (PAP)[10] rule. Savage characterises the irony of Singapore's survival dilemma thus:

> In order to maintain its national viability, Singaporeans must effectively be "biosphere people" — a people regional and cosmopolitan in outlook. The key to this biosphere viability is adaptation. This has been translated over the years in many ways by the leadership as "entrepreneurship," maintaining an open and flexible economy, seizing on opportunities and maintaining competitiveness, and being global in the economic sector. (Savage, 212)

Though the vulnerability of Singapore by virtue of its size, its lack of a hinterland, and the circumstances of its birth is embedded in the mindset of the governing elite, the four fictionists examined here would affirm, by its very absence, the need for a more open political culture founded on trust in the citizen, and an acceptance of criticism in the spirit in which it is given.

One can hardly be global—i.e., open and flexible economically, and entrepreneurial in outlook—without also opening up cultural and intellectual areas of discourse. The borders of the world are increasingly porous; global competitiveness is likely to include worldwide competitiveness of ideas, life-styles, and the practice of human rights. Though the liberalisation of policy and attitude is likely to be "evolutionary rather than revolutionary" (Tan, 136), it does not appear to be a process that can be suppressed in the long run.[11]

> There is an endless sky, there is a goodness that defies pragmatism, there is a gentleness that is unconnected with retribution. These things have been denied in Singapore. They are real and important if we want to make our society workable. (Baratham, *Fay,* 146)

Baratham's remarks, romantic and unreal for a society so struck by the pragmatic and utilitarian, nevertheless express a sufficient(ly Singaporean) seriousness of ideal and intent to make them worthy of bearing in mind and pursuing for a future that must now be foreseen.

Leong Liew Geok, Spring 2000

■ WORKS CITED

Ban Kah Choon. *Of Memory and Desire: The Stories of Gopal Baratham*. Singapore. Times Books International. 2000.

Baratham, Gopal. *A Candle or the Sun*. London. Serpent's Tail. 1991. [CS]

———. *The Caning of Michael Fay*. Singapore. KRP Publication. 1994. [Fay]

Brewster, Anne. *Towards a Semiotic of Post-Colonial Discourse: University Writing in Singapore and Malaysia, 1949–1965*. Singapore. Heinemann Asia (for Centre for Advanced Studies, National University of Singapore). 1989.

Chua Mui Hoong. "Speakers' Corner details in a few months." *The Straits Times,* 20 March 2000, p. 3.

Ee Tiang Hong. *Responsibility and Commitment: The Poetry of Edwin Thumboo*. Leong Liew Geok, ed. Singapore. Singapore University Press (for Centre for Advanced Studies, National University of Singapore). 1997.

Goh Keng Swee. "National Service and Defence Policy." In *Towards Tomorrow: Essays on Development and Social Transformation in Singapore*. Singapore. The Singapore National Trades Union Congress. 1973. Pp. 55–61.

Haskell, Dennis. "Memory and Romanticism in Philip Jeyaretnam's *Abraham's Promise.*" In *Interlogue: Studies in Singapore Literature*. Volume 1: *Fiction*. Kirpal Singh, ed. Singapore. Ethos Books. 1998. Pp. 145–56.

Jeyaretnam, Philip. *Abraham's Promise*. Singapore. Times Books International. 1995. [AP]

Lee Kuan Yew. *The Singapore Story: Memoirs of Lee Kuan Yew*. Singapore. Times Editions. 1998.

Lim, Suchen Christine. *Fistful of Colours*. Singapore. EPB Books. 1993. [FC]

Ng, Irene. "Govt. looks to non-grads to boost births." *The Straits Times,* 16 March 2000, p. 1.

Patke, Rajeev S. "*Abraham's Promise:* Violence, Critique, and the Birth of a Nation." In *Interlogue: Studies in Singapore Literature*. Volume 1: *Fiction*. Pp. 117–43.

Patten, Chris. *East and West: The Last Governor of Hong Kong on Power, Freedom and the Future*. London. Macmillan. 1998.

PuruShotam, Nirmala. "Speaking Out of the Ordinary." *The Sunday Times,* 20 February 2000, p. 43.

Savage, Victor. "Human-Environment Relations: Singapore's Environmental Ideology." In *Imagining Singapore*. Pp. 187–217.

Singapore: Facts and Pictures. Ng Poey Siong and Ng Siew Hong, eds. Singapore. Ministry of Information & the Arts. 1997.

Singh, Bilveer. "A Small State's Quest for Security: Operationalizing Deterrence in Singapore's Strategic Thinking." In *Imagining Singapore*.

Tan, Kevin Y. L. "Fifty Years of the UDHR: A Singaporean Reflects." In *Human Rights Perspectives*. Tan Ngoh Tiong and Kripa Sridharan, eds. Singapore. United Nations Association of Singapore & Pagesetters Services. 1999. Pp. 108–40.

Tay, Simon. "Asia's Contribution to Human Rights." In *Human Rights Perspectives*. Pp. 103–17.

———. "Exiles." In his *Stand Alone*. Singapore. Landmark. 1990. Pp. 209–45.

———. "Stand Alone." In his *Stand Alone*. Pp. 247–68.

Thumboo, Edwin, et al. *The Fiction of Singapore*. Singapore. UniPress at the Centre for the Arts, National University of Singapore. 1993. [1990]

1 See Anne Brewster, *Towards a Semiotic of Post-Colonial Discourse: University Writing in Singapore and Malaysia, 1949–1965,* Singapore, Heinemann Asia (for Centre for Advanced Studies, National University of Singapore), 1989; and Ee Tiang Hong, *Responsibility and Commitment: The Poetry of Edwin Thumboo,* ed. Leong Liew Geok, Singapore, Singapore University Press (for Centre for Advanced Studies, National University of Singapore), 1997, pp. 9–13, for the beginnings of Malayan/Malaysian and Singaporean literature in English.

2 The first collection of poetry, Wang Gungwu's *Pulse,* was published in 1950. In 1956 Edwin Thumboo's *Rib of Earth* was published, and *I of the Many Faces* by Ee Tiang Hong appeared in 1960. There were other individual collections, e.g., by Lim Thean Soo, who published his *Selected Verses* in 1951 and *Poems, 1951–1953* in 1953.

3 *Compact: A Selection of University of Malaya Short Stories: 1953–1959* was edited by Herman Hochstadt for the University's Raffles Society. Lloyd Fernando edited *Twenty-Two Malaysian Stories* (1968), and Geraldine Heng compiled *The Sun in Her Eyes: Stories by Singapore Women* (1976). Chandran Nair edited *Singapore Writing* (1977), an anthology of poetry and prose, and Robert Yeo the two-volume *Singapore Short Stories* (1978). The first Singaporean novel in English was *If We Dream Too Long,* published in 1972 by its author, Goh Poh Seng.

4 *Little Ironies: Stories of Singapore* (1978) was Catherine Lim's first collection of short stories. This was followed by a second, *Or Else, the Lightning God & Other Stories,* in 1980, and subsequent collections. Lim's first novel, *The Serpent's Tooth,* was published many years later, in 1992. Of the considerable fiction that Lim Thean Soo produced, only two are novels: *Destination Singapore* (1976) and *The Towkay of Produce Street* (1991). Similarly, *The Nan-Mei-Su Girls of Emerald Hill* (1989) remains Goh Sin Tub's only novel among a good number of collections of short fiction.

5 Where appropriate, the following abbreviations will be used in the text: *SA* for *Stand Alone,* FC for *Fistful of Colours,* CS for *A Candle or the Sun,* and AP for *Abraham's Promise.*

6 *Singapore: Facts and Pictures,* 1997, eds. Ng Poey Siong and Ng Siew Hong, Singapore, Ministry of Information & the Arts. 1997, p. 1.

7 Singapore began its defence build-up in 1967, by relying on a National Service Scheme which was founded on national conscription, a Ministry of Defence having been established in 1966. See Bilveer Singh, "A Small State's Quest for Security: Operationalizing Deterrence in Singapore's Strategic Thinking," In *Imagining Singapore,* eds. Ban Kah Choon, Anne Pakir, and Tong Chee Kiong, Singapore, Times Academic Press, 1992, p. 115.

8 In August 1983, Lee Kuan Yew, then Prime Minister, drew attention to the growing number of single graduate women and the long-term effects their unmarried state would have on the future of Singapore. A range of incentives was quickly introduced by the government to encourage better-educated women to marry or to have more children. These included priority in school admission for their children and enhanced child relief. The former proved very unpopular because of its elitism, and was phased out. Over the years too, child relief has been extended to cover women with three "O" Level passes in the General Certificate of Education, where originally they benefited women with five. The latest development in demographic engineering, the need to target a broader base of women, made front-page news. See Irene Ng, "Govt looks to non-grads to boost births," *The Straits Times,* 16 March 2000, p. 1.

9 See Chris Patten, "Asian Values," In *East and West: The Last Governor of Hong Kong on Power, Freedom and the Future,* London, Macmillan, 1998, pp. 146–72, which begins with his account of his exchange with Lee Kuan Yew over the matter. See also Simon Tay, "Asia's Contribution to Human Rights," In *Human Rights Perspectives,* eds. Tan Ngoh Tiong and Kripa Sridharan, Singapore, UN Association of Singapore & Pagesetters Services, 1999, pp. 109 ff.

10 Savage quotes Brigadier-General Lee Hsien Loong (the son of Lee Kuan Yew), currently Minister of Trade and Industry and First Deputy Prime Minister, as saying, "Singapore is too small for a system of two balanced political parties either to develop or to work well" and "'small and vulnerable' Singapore could only prosper with a 'strong government,' preferably a one-party dominant government and certainly the continuities of PAP rule" (*The Straits Times,* 4 July 1986, p. 20). See Victor Savage, "Human-Environment Relations: Singapore's Environmental Ideology," in *Imagining Singapore,* pp. 199, 203.

11 The most recent development in liberalisation: a Speaker's Corner, modeled on Hyde Park corner in London, is to be set up shortly for Singaporeans to speak out on anything except religion and race. Speakers however, would need to apply for a permit from the Public Entertainment Licensing Unit (PELU), though approval would be given within an hour or so. Reported in *The Straits Times,* 20 March 2000, p. 3.

Poetry in English from Singapore

The history of the English and their language in Singapore goes back to the early nineteenth century, when the commercial interests of the East India Trading Company in the Malaya peninsula transformed the island first into trading outpost, then into settlement and colony. The history of poetry in English from Singapore, however, has a more recent provenance. The period from the 1830s to the 1940s provides little evidence for the use of English for purposes other than the pragmatic needs of everyday discourse, business, and trade. The first attempts at poetry in English were fostered by the opportunities represented by a university education in the late 1940s, and the university, along with the mentoring power of older poets and the canon they have fostered, has continued to play a decisive role in the development of talent in a country whose history has been synonymous with its growth as a small, rapidly modernizing metropolis, in which the community of readers and poets has always been fairly close, the collective commitment to material and technological betterment firm, and the paternal presence of the state ubiquitous.

The first book of poems in English to be published from the region was Wang Gungwu's *Pulse* (1950), followed by collections from Lim Thean Soo (1951, 1953) and Edwin Thumboo (1956). The first anthologies of poetry in English, *Litmus One* (1958) and *30 Poems* (1958), followed soon after. Since then the corpus of Singapore poetry has grown to over a hundred volumes from more than fifty poets.[1] The continued vitality of English as a creative language in a postnationalist era is indebted to the retention of English by the state, a significantly pragmatic choice for an island with four languages, a population of just over three million, and surrounded by countries which have reverted to their regional languages. During the 1950s and 1960s, despite the show of individual talent, the Singaporean interest in writing in English remained intermittent and isolated, finally coming into its own during the 1970s, when a number of poets emerged and matured and the interest in writing found a wider base, allied to relative ease in finding regional publishers willing to invest in poetry. During the last two decades this interest has grown exponentially, and the end of the century has seen lively poetic activity, especially from young writers, supported by sympathetic media and an audience within Singapore that continues to increase, in spite of the fact that writing from Singapore has yet to receive the international recognition it deserves.

The early poetry was preoccupied with learning how to incorporate indigenous elements of culture and language into an adopted idiom, persuading its pre-established conventions of form and style to make room for localized self-expression. At its most literal, this involved the forcing of English to accommodate expressions in Malay and Chinese into the poetic context. The result—*Engmalchin*—was largely unsatisfactory, as in the following example from Wang Gungwu (who was to give up writing in English):

Thoughts of Camford fading,
Contentment creeping in;
Allah had been kind;
Orang puteh has been kind.
Only yesterday his brother said,
'Can get *lagi satu* wife *lah!*'[2]

The problem of how a local idiom might grow in relation to the language of the former colonizer has continued to remain a challenge for writers in Singapore, as elsewhere. The state retention of an idealized norm based on British English has had the effect of forcing all local variants into the category of *Singlish,* thus politicising any choice of idiom by a writer between the standard and the local. In contrast to the failure of *Engmalchin,* a poem like "Singapore" by Goh Sin Tub (b. 1927) four collections spread over as many decades: *Rib of Earth* (1956), separated by a long gap from *Gods Can Die* (1977), followed by *Ulysses by the Merlion* (1979), and then, with another gap, by *A Third Map: New and Selected Poems* (1993). The series of anthologies he has edited—*The Flowering Tree* (1970), *Seven Poets* (1973), *The Second Tongue* (1976), *Anthology of ASEAN Literatures* (1985), and *Journeys* (1995)—has also made him the most influential factor in the formation of the Singapore canon. Thumboo's early poems are few and far between, making up in quality for what they lack in quantity. When he essays traditional forms, the stanzaic self-possession aspires to a Yeatsian assurance and poise.

Days squeeze my thoughts
And time transfigured lies
Orion dropped your captive hand
The merbak lonely cries[4]

Images are used sparingly, but can be striking, as in "Lallang trimmed with fire" (95) or "Navel wet before the world was old" (96), or as in "Dregs":

Day loses its transparency,
The winds fold up and die;
Clouds grow distant in slow streaks
And shadows wither by. (109)

This fluency with traditional metre never deserts Thumboo's poetry, but is often held in abeyance by a preference for free verse, which enables an exorcism of literary ghosts through the flexibility of the irregular line and the sparing use of rhyme.

Thumboo's variations on the lyric mode are held together by an integrative vision focused on two themes: the interpenetration of the personal by the historical imagination, and the role of friendship in the private and the public realms. Myth, symbol, allusion, fable, and anecdote all are harmonized by the overarching consistency of these twin concerns. History, for Thumboo, bridges the gap between the personal and the communal, just as friendship is the communion of the personal with that which it shares outside the self. History as a textual narrative and a sequential ordering of events in memory is harmonized into a knowledge lived in the body of one's thoughts and feelings. It exacts its measure of awareness as a form of remembering (of the self in relation to other selves), and is inversely allied to the forgetting we know as indifference to or abandonment of the Other. Likewise, friendship is not treated merely as shared experiences, attitudes, and memories, but as the sublation of differences (of the kind that must be an immanent and imminent part of any alliance or friendship) in responsibility and care, as these are allied, inversely, to guilt (as in betrayal) or fear (not of death, but of being dead to one another).[5]

Edwin Thumboo *(Gil Jain)*

can be taken as representative of the more moderate spirit that prevailed among poets of his generation.[3] It begins with an image which has an aura of the familiar: "Day here hurls its light." The poet moves quickly from this evocative image to a more prosaic poetry of statement, which addresses his relation to the changes being undergone by his country in an earnest and self-preoccupied tone. The parental community is addressed from a position that bespeaks an isolation whose romanticism has been dispelled by the sombre fear of social marginalisation. The poem enacts the process of developing an attitude to the nation while nursing palpable designs on the reader. The homeland is treated as a landscape and a seascape transformed from "fresh salt" and "simple hills" into "a commercial waterway / greased with waste." The poem illustrates how Singapore poets are prone to address the nation in hortatory tones mingled with the anxiety that they speak helplessly in the wake of the national pursuit of a chimerical progress.

The poet who has mediated most successfully and the longest between the private and the public voices in Singapore poetry is Edwin Thumboo (b. 1933), with

Thus, "The Immigrant" acknowledges the migrant's choice as a form of gain-in-loss: "Days and Indian days stretch / Beyond the grasping of his hands" (115). "9th of August – II" recognizes the loss-in-gain of Singapore's enforced independence from Malaysia: "For us what then? / Make strangers out of friends / To face each other till the bitter end" (125). In the wake of the separation of Singapore from Malaysia (in the early 1960s), "Ibrahim Bin Ahmad" offers recognition of what is owed in knowledge and fellowship between communities:

. . .That Hang Jebat
Broke the selfishness of victory
To put such pride in giving
Was counted among us
These three hundred years or so.
We stood for much. (126)

In Nairobi, "A Brother" recognizes that "The African can be my brother / When he is most himself" (127). In "A Letter" friendship is retrievable even though friends forget to write, just as return to abandoned homelands is still possible in one of the other poems addressed to the same friend, "After the Leaving" (188). A poem like "Conversation with my friend Kwang Min at Loong Kwang of Outram Park" (161) dramatizes historical time through personalized locales, and the metonymic fragments of art that can shore up the self against time and its attritions. Later poems like "Grand Uncles: Kang to Sinnathamby at Monk's Hill Terrace" ironise self-reflexivity more thoroughly by refracting it through ventriloquised selves: "To Orchard Mall . . . perturbed by the new, / Missing the old . . . with reservations" (180).

Thumboo has come to represent the formative phase in Singapore's history, as the poet laureate of Singapore's growth into nationhood. His poems give poetic expression to the drive toward a progressive harmonization of the four ethnic components of Singapore (Chinese, Malay, Indian, and Eurasian) into a single collectivity. At a specific time in the historical development of his country, he understood the task of poetry in terms of explaining the formation of the nation to its people. Poets not inclined to take this path have felt that it entailed a preference for the public over the personal and the hortatory over the lyrical. The poem by Thumboo that gets the most attention, in this respect, is "Ulysses by the Merlion." It sets up an interaction between Western and local myth as a way of representing Singapore's aspiration for unity in diversity, and for the histories of migration and the struggle for economic prosperity to be sublated in an achieved identity. The poem has attracted considerable attention among subsequent poets, who have all felt obliged to write their own Merlion (or anti-Merlion) poems, illustrating their anxiety of influence, as well as the continuing local fascination with the dialectic between a public and a private role for poets, which Thumboo (as Yeats before him, in the Irish context) has wanted to sustain as a fruitful rather than a tense relation between the personal and the public.

Poets of the next generation, however, have generally taken up positions antithetical to what they perceive as the drives channeling the resources of their society. Here, for instance, is Robert Yeo (b. 1940):

Father prosperity dispenses
Priorities to his children.
Most things pragmatic prosper
But art (lower-case) has to defer.[6]

Such an antithesis forces poetry into a corner, "as if being lonely / Is the alternative to living / In Singapore" (132). But the poet is honest enough to admit that

Yes, it feels good to be
Able to come back to
A still rather chaste
Absolutely safe
Absurdly clean
Incredibly green
Familiar and cosy
Home. (134)

Such honesty is scrupulous and characteristic of Yeo, who is well known locally as a playwright as well as a novelist. But such honesty also dissipates the sharpness of critique.

Yeo's friend and slightly younger contemporary, Kirpal Singh (b. 1949), the author of three volumes of poetry, has been sharper and less ameliorative in his resistance. In a poem like "Making Omelettes" he plays up to the role of temperamental (and, in his case, also ethnic) insider-as-outsider, making a meal of a typecasting he cannot resist, thus giving new teeth to an old saw. The humour disguises no part of what is being treated allegorically as a fable of power and powerlessness in a multiracial society that has worked hard at making the ethnic pieces of the jigsaw hold together without cutting one another too obviously.

. . . and I begin now to think about the eggs we crack and how sometimes the shell is so hard the egg refuses to crack as if to say, not me, no me — get him, get her but not me and so the story goes on about the eggs which are small and big, brown and white, chickens and ducks and eggs which invite cracking and make you feel very hungry . . .[7]

The temptations to which poets often succumb in Singapore are the romantic notion that one can achieve selfhood by separating oneself from the commonality, and its corollary belief that a self alienated from the drives of its society can subsist by making a value of that alienation. The most original and interesting such poet is Arthur Yap (b. 1943), whose poetic career stretches over more than a quarter-century, from *only lines* (1971), through the collective *five takes* (1974), *commonplace* (1977), and *Down the Line* (1980), to *Man Snake Apple & Other Poems* (1986).

On the surface, Yap's poems can appear odd, weird, eccentric, or willfully obscure and oblique: they drop the upper case and, with it, many of the forms of syntax and cohesion by which the conventions of interpersonal communication are normally sustained. This e.e. cummings aspect of deliberately dressing as a private (a rebel in an army full of beribboned officers) makes the point that nonconformity is as much a matter of principle as of temperament. Beyond affect, what it accomplishes is a mimesis or correspondence between a fractured syntax and a newly and gingerly put-together sense of the world, as if the shattered bits of what might once have been whole had been pieced together with care, wonder, pain, and amazement, into configurations which add up to meaning in a new way that revises our notions of how meaning is constituted in poems out of words arranged as lines. Here is a part of "things":

chair
wall
window
desk
bed. . .

in being hung up like a portrait, truly dead.
medium shot: window. Open it.
let the sun in, let suicide out.
before hitting the ground, frame it in slow motion.
Reverse repeat, pan it back to window, its source. . .[8]

But many Yap poems are not dependent on such a redrawing of the wheel. Their novelty resides not in telescopic syntax but in how metaphors merge in synesthesia. Here, for instance, is a traditional poetic motif transfigured by "dawn":

dawn in the quiet key of light
utters a whole paragraph of hues
in the early mutter of an aviary. . . .

The lively key to morning
is mysteriously sharp, already laden
with the still, angular mirrors of noon. (63)

Yap's poems are alert to the nuances of the spoken idiom, making him particularly skillful in his delineation of the objects of implicit social satire. "2 mothers

Kirpal Singh (*Peter Nazareth*)

in a h d b playground" has justifiably become a classic, immediately accessible, enormously funny, and devastating in its implicit critique. Yap has a keen and neutral ear for mimicry, and can ventriloquise intonation as fluently as he can disguise his own in studied ambiguity. The poem "an afternoon nap" castigates the mother castigating her child:

the ambitious mother across the road
is at it again. Proclaiming her goodness
she beats the boy. Shouting out his wrongs, with raps
she begins with his mediocre report-book grades. . . .
Swift are all her contorted movements,
Apt for every need; no soft gradient
Of a consonant-vowel figure, she lumbers
& shrieks, a hit for every 2 notes missed. (60)

The resistance offered by Yap is directed not at national entities like State and Nation, but at the ordinary people whose lives conform to denials of faith in and responsiveness to what their conformity blinds them to. The poetry is full of perceptiveness rather than anger or reproach, and leavened by a sharp verbal wit and wryly sardonic irony, alert to the treacherous aspects of the promise held forth by language that it can be adequate to every quirk of feeling, thought, and idea, and not simply leave us stranded with the feeling that "the word swallows up the world" (129). Yap also offers the honesty of a deep ambivalence about much that is reflected troublingly in the mirror of his sensibility, aware of the distortions to be found there, unwilling to resolve them into more clarity than honesty would live with.

Yap, Yeo, and Singh could be said to belong to the second generation of poets from Singapore, along with Chandran Nair (b. 1944) and a handful of others like

Geraldine Heng, who was the first woman from Singapore to publish a volume of poetry in English (*white-dreams,* 1976). Wong May (b. 1943) grew up in Singapore, and published *A Bad Girl's Book of Animals* earlier than Heng's volume, in 1969, but she is originally from New York. Nair and Heng practically abandoned poetry after the 1970s; but all of these poets began writing in the late 1960s, and all of them reinforced the dissident tradition of voicing anxieties about the poetic self in relation to the community and the cost of some of its aspirations. Lee Tzu Pheng (b. 1946) belongs to the same generation, but began publishing poems a decade later, rapidly achieving widespread recognition through four slim volumes: *Prospect of a Drowning* (1980), *Against the Next Wave* (1988), *The Brink of an Amen* (1991), and *Lambada by Galilee & Other Surprises* (1997). Lee writes in a poetic idiom based loosely on the British poetic tradition, in the sense that her diction and syntax are chaste, and her progress through a poem is always decorous and well managed, enriching the reader's awareness without ruffling the poem's deportment, as in, say, Elizabeth Barrett Browning or Christina Rossetti or Elizabeth Jennings.

The entire tradition of poetry in Singapore works within the conventions of the lyric poem, and Lee is its neatest exponent. Her poems yield richly to the literate reader accustomed to close reading, sympathetic to resonant images, sensitive emotions, and feelings delineated with clarity and precision, through a structured argument that pleases by not being obvious. In her early poems the poetic voice was always close to the poet's self, although in her most recent volume she has diversified the monologic effect of personal statement with the oblique ironies of dramatized voices.

Two poems stand out from the even tenor of subdued personal feelings that characterize Lee's first volume: "Bukit Timah, Singapore" and "My Country and My People." Both offer memorable utterances on the public theme so dear to poets in Singapore: the changes that have rapidly transformed a sleepy kampong village culture into "the megapolitan appetite."[9] Both start a poet's quarrel with the country, commemorate a past that has vanished ineluctably, and gaze apprehensively on the future already unfolding steadily across the body politic. Both acknowledge a need to resist, but also a need to acknowledge the logic of what cannot simply be resisted. Scrupulous, descriptive, and fair-minded, they resist resistance even as they access critique, without straining the resources of either.

Lee's second volume shows an expansion of scope. Her interest in children's literature and in the power of myth and fairy tale to animate human suffering, and the knowledge acquired through pain, finds expression in

poems like "Grimm Story" and "Thorn-Rose: The Bad Fairy's Version." Here is the beginning of the latter poem:

Deep within the womb of sleep
Her innocence and beauty she surrenders
To no one; life breathes unhurried
In a peaceful deathlessness;
And who is free
As she is in seclusion
Where none can fall or weep
Because of her, whose enchantment keeps her
Inviolate, in that safehold of thorns
Her fate conjures?[10]

Lee's Christianity comes to the fore in her third volume, *The Brink of an Amen:* the reader encounters it as a process personal to the poet, shared without presumption. The language acquires a confidently quiet force considerably more effective than the somewhat subdued manner of the first two volumes. Here, for instance, is "Babel":

Even as we taste
the powerful lure of words
our speech fails on our tongues
to dialects of blood.

Where have we the skill
to tell the human lot,
when all our words divide
and cannot make us whole?[11]

The range of topics and techniques is considerably enlarged, giving us one of the most richly satisfying of volumes in English from Singapore. Irony makes a humorous and perceptive entry. The elegiac poems balance feeling with repose. The play on words is precise and resonant in an economical way, as in "Inventory":

headstern
heartstrong
fine-eyed
footlong
softmouthed
selfweaned
wakesome
wisemined
youngblood
youthsbane
lastfound
lifesgain (60)

Lee's most recent volume consolidates the achievement of her third book, with sharper ironies and a keener sense of the feminine. Here is the ending of "Graffiti in the Ladies":

You wonder if it's shock or shame

that you feel. Or maybe both.

It's easy to say
someone hysterical did this.

Does violence have a gender?
Has woman been clapped so much in her place
she has no room to face her demons
but the public lavatory?
Surely this vandalizing speaks much more
than the writing on the wall?[12]

Yeo, Singh, Nair, and Lee represent the second generation of poets writing in English from Singapore.
Writers like Leong Liew Geok (b. 1947) and Hoh Poh
Fun (b. 1946) have made their appearance on the stage
of Singapore poetry in English at a later date. Leong is
the author of two volumes, *Love Is Not Enough* (1991)
and *Women Without Men* (1999). Despite the titles,
Leong does not write on lesbian or feminist themes, but
works out a position from which men can be perceived
in a more down-to-earth way and women can develop
independent selves without becoming typecast in sexist
roles. Hoh's *Katong and Other Poems* (1994) is the work
of a person with a subdued yet refined sensibility,
which is at its most pleasing when it deals with nature.

A third, younger generation, most of them born
after 1960, is currently very active in Singapore, comprising Angeline Yap, Simon Tay, Desmond Sim, Koh
Buck Song, Felix Cheong, Paul Tan, Gwee Li Sui, Aaron
Lee Soon Yong, Yong Shu Hoong, and several others.
Other poets of interest, who do not quite fit in within
the otherwise plausible three-generation narrative, include Elangovan—primarily a writer in Tamil, though
also the author of *Transcreations* (1988), a bilingual collection of poems in Tamil and English—and Robert
Vaughan Jenkins (born in Singapore, and a Singapore
citizen since 1992), the author of *From the Belly of the
Carp: Singapore River Voices* (1996), which breaks free
of the otherwise dominant local preference for the lyric
form to give voice to a series of dramatized monologues
which offer a discursive survey of local character types
and several partly overlapping personalized histories
centred on the Singapore River.

From the diverse group who began writing in the
already affluent, technocratic, and efficient society of
1980s Singapore, Boey Kim Cheng (b. 1965) is perhaps
the most interesting. The author of three volumes, he
currently lives away from Singapore, in Australia. Boey's
poetry is characterized by three features: intensity, restlessness, and a prodigal gift for metaphor. The intensity
with which he takes himself and his themes has something almost Rilkean in its self-absorbed introversion,
its lack of irony, and its portentous striving for a larger
significance to the life of things and persons, which

would be religious were it less turbulent. Here is the
brief "Sunset" from his first volume:

The house of man
sits on a quiet hill
and meditates,
absorbing the last words:
the hard membrane
of its windows
suddenly moistening.[13]

The poetry is sophisticated, capable of absorbing a
broad cultural awareness into its fabric. The relation of
the poet to his country has an abrasive element that can
be sampled from "The Planners":

The country wears perfect rows
of shining teeth.
Anaesthesia, amnesia, hypnosis.
They have the means.
They have it all so it will not hurt,
so history is new again.
The piling will not stop.
The drilling goes right through
The fossils of last century.[14]

Beyond the animus against Singapore, there is the temperament of a wanderer: "I am swayed by an inner
music / of irresolution. There will be a lot of pondering
/ up and down the length of this street, and other
streets, / beyond this American dream, before the rolling stops / and I come home, wherever, whatever, that
is."[15] Boey is a gift that has yet to accommodate itself
properly with the world.

Of the younger poets with one or more volumes to
their credit, the most interesting are Alvin Pang (b.
1972) and Alfian Sa'at (b. 1977), whose second volume
is to appear in late 2000. Pang's *Testing the Silence*
(1997) is characterized by a sensitive restraint of feeling
combined with tact and delicacy of expression. He handles the short irregular line in free verse with skill, and
makes a virtue of understatement.

Light
like an Impressionst's brush
dapples
the glistening
fish-skin
of water
one   bright   scale
at a time.[16]

The poetry stands close to silence, aware of the burden
of words, as in "Sound and Fury": "We reach out / into
the superfluity of words / Silence. And bring back / ourselves and our burdens emptied / of real value. Emptied" (27).

In contrast, Sa'at is more vigorous and energetic. His ear for language as sound is acute in respect of social nuance as well as poetic rhythm. He harnesses syntactic repetition as a principle of organization very effectively in a number of poems that use the technique of listing a catalogue to build up the momentum of poems into powerful litanies of expressiveness. His "Singapore You Are Not My Country" takes the tradition of the poet's engagement with his country to a new level of rhetorical excitement:

Singapore I am on trial.
These are the whites of my eyes and the reds of my
  wrists.
These are the deranged stars of my schizophrenia.
This is the milk latex gummy moon of my sedated
  smile.
I have lost a country to images, it is as simple as
  that.
Singapore you have a name on a map but no maps
  to your name.
This will not do. . .[17]

This is the final entry in one of the most exciting volumes of poetry to come out of Singapore. It bespeaks the health of what, in a Yeatsian frame of mind, one may speak of as a necessary lover's quarrel with the world, or, in a Marvellian frame of mind, as a dialogue between Created State and Resolved Soul.

Rajeev S. Patke, Spring 2000

[1] *Celebrations: Singapore Creative Writing in English,* ed. Gene Tan, Singapore, National Library, 1994, pp. 44–67. Lists 84 volumes of poetry in English from 48 poets, and 34 anthologies and collections.

[2] Quoted in Anne Brewster, *Towards a Semiotic of Post-Colonial Discourse: University Writing in Singapore and Malaysia 1949–1965,* Singapore, Heinemann Asia / Centre for Advanced Studies, 1989, p. 4.

[3] Goh Sin Tub, "Singapore," in *Seven Poets: Singapore and Malaysia,* ed. Edwin Thumboo, Singapore, Singapore University Press, 1973, pp. 97–99.

[4] Edwin Thumboo, "Louise," in Ee Tiang Hong, *Responsibility and Commitment: The Poetry of Edwin Thumboo,* ed. Leong Liew Geok, Singapore, Centre for Advanced Studies / Singapore University Press, 1997, p. 107.

[5] An entire thematics of care is alluded to in Martin Heidegger, "Care is being-toward-death," *Being and Time,* tr. Joan Stambaugh, Albany, State University of New York Press, 1996, p. 303.

[6] Robert Yeo, *Leaving Home, Mother: Selected Poems,* Singapore, Angsana Books, 1999, p. 131.

[7] Kirpal Singh, *Catwalking and the Games We Play,* Singapore, Ethos Books, 1998, p. 31.

[8] Arthur Yap, *the space of city trees: selected poems,* London, Skoob Books, 2000, p. 67.

[9] Lee Tzu Pheng, "Bukit Timah, Singapore," in *Prospect of a Drowning,* Singapore, Heinemann, 1980, p. 50.

[10] Lee Tzu Pheng, *Against the Next Wave,* Singapore, Times Books, 1988, p. 47.

[11] Lee Tzu Pheng, *The Brink of an Amen,* Singapore, Times Books, 1991, p. 29.

[12] Lee Tzu Pheng, *Lambada by Galilee & Other Surprises,* Singapore, Times Books, 1997, p. 35.

[13] Boey Kim Chang, *Somewhere-Bound,* Singapore, Times Books, 1989, p. 40.

[14] Boey Kim Chang, *Another Place,* Singapore, Times Books, 1993, p. 63.

[15] Boey Kim Chang, *Days of No Name,* Singapore, EPB, 1996, p. 51.

[16] Alvin Pang, *Testing the Silence,* Singapore, Ethos Books, 1997, p. 53.

[17] Alfian Sa'at, *One Fierce Hour,* Singapore, Landmark Books, 1998, p. 41.

Australia and New Zealand
GENERAL

Patrick White: Prophet in the Wilderness

How will Patrick White be remembered by his readers and by academe? As the prophet in the wilderness, the failed Christian, the neoromantic, the vehement satirist, the homosexual recluse, the accursed artist, by his readers? Or as staunch republican and socialist, supporter of Aboriginal rights, environmentalist, antinuclear campaigner, rich patron of the arts, of Australian writers and the deprived, by those who did not read him? In the minds of some Australians he was a deservedly despised eccentric, a cantankerous old gossip, paranoid, vindictive, uncompromising, a cussed quarreler (there certainly was something of the constipated Mother Superior about him). Or will White be remembered as the untypical Australian, the giant of Aust. Lit., unsurpassed in his country in talent, scope, and vision?

If most people agree that White is the greatest Australian writer of this century, there seems to be difficulty in defining the exact nature of his "greatness." One could suggest quite simply that White had more to say, and said it better, than any other novelist, poet, or playwright of his generation. This, of course, is true. The immense outpouring of prose—twelve novels, three collections of short stories, eight plays, and a short autobiography—were published over a period of fifty years. The White canon impresses first of all by its weight, grandeur, variety, and scale. Here is a Proust, or a Henry James, who suffered a lifelong battle with language, producing and creating until the end. There was a compulsion, a necessity, to continue writing,

Patrick White *(Don Edwards; courtesy: Australian Information Service)*

which White fought against, but succumbed to unwillingly. He often spoke of the writer's gift as a scourge rather than a blessing, an onerous, pain-filled, daily wrestling match. White's fight with himself, and with words, is more interesting and of another dimension than that of his Australian contemporaries. The intensity of his soul-searching, the nature of his contradictions and ambiguities, the catharsis he made public, and the manner in which his "confession" is conveyed are all of major interest for the light they shed on what it is to be human. Now that the first biography has been written, now that White's work is complete, now that the author's ashes have been scattered in the park opposite his house, there remains the task of valuing the achievement, of investigating the art and the artist.

Although White started to capture the critics' attention in the late sixties, it was not till the seventies and eighties that an explosion in the White industry took place. The first guides, such as that by Geoffrey Dutton, (one of the first Australians to notice White's talent), are schematic and elementary. The first European study, by the Swede Ingmar Björkstén, later translated into German and Norwegian, is a clear and intuitive guide, which brought White to the attention of European read-

ers and showed how the author interpreted the theme of suffering. The New Zealander Peter Beatson was the first critic to suggest that White's greatness relied on the religious and theological concerns of the oeuvre, a critical approach later developed by the Australian academic Veronica Brady. Other critics chose to concentrate on the theme of failure, the Nietzschean influence, or to apply a Jungian grid to the text. Modern literary theory has not yet been brought to bear on the oeuvre. Since White does not easily lend himself to a poststructuralist analysis, he has been saved from the feminists, the Lacanians, and the deconstructionists.

One of the most enlightening approaches to reveal the major qualities of the oeuvre would seem to be the metaphysical, religious enquiry begun by Beatson. I would like to look at some of the essential aspects of White's poetic imagination following this direction: the use of mythopoesis, the two-dimensional vision of reality, the author's exactitude in observing human beings and the natural world, the celebration of the flamboyant and the grotesque. These qualities allow us to gauge the full import of what White has bequeathed to future generations.

Part of White's greatness lies in his ability to invent and give expression to mythopoesis. He is one of the outstanding mythmakers of the twentieth century. White's sources are classical and biblical myth, Plato and the Kabbala, Eastern religions and Jung, as well as Aboriginal mythology. Examples are the quest myth, based on Homeric odyssey and the idea of geographic and psychological exploration, which he used in *The Aunt's Story, Voss, The Tree of Man, A Fringe of Leaves,* and *The Twyborn Affair,* the genesis myth in *The Tree of Man;* the crucifixion in *Riders in the Chariot;* the mandalic quaternary and Ezekiel's Four Living Creatures in *The Solid Mandala* and *Riders in the Chariot;* and the Lear myth in *The Eye of the Storm.* What is significant about European myth in White's work is the author's ability to use different elements of the post-Platonic, Judeo-Christian tradition especially, in an Australian context, and give it meaning. As well as imparting a recognisable mythic structure to most novels, White's main characters gain a mythic dimension which gives them weight and a certain heroism. Theodora Goodman in *The Aunt's Story* is partly modeled on Ulysses, Stan and Amy Parker in *The Tree of Man* on Adam and Eve; Voss is both Christ-like and a Nietzschean superman, Himmelfarb imitates Christ and is "crucified" on a jacaranda in *Riders in the Chariot,* and Elizabeth Hunter in *The Eye of the Storm* is a feminine, Australian version of King Lear rediviva.

Plato's cave myth is effective in *The Eye of the Storm,* where the bunker on the island, the bedroom of Mrs.

Hunter, indeed Australia itself, is seen in terms of Plato's cave, in which a puppet show of reality contents the ignorant inhabitants. Eden as an earthly paradise is used in numerous novels. The incongruity of *terra australis* as a garden of Eden, with eucalyptus and Moreton Bay figs, works to insist on the unspoiled nature of Australia and the relatively late arrival of the white man as a threatening presence in 1788. The myth of the outsider, the scapegoat, or the freak is central to White's imaginary universe. He used it in many forms: the artist, the Jew, the homosexual, the madman, the Aborigine, the divine fool, and the deformed person. That White felt himself to be a misfit is evident from his autobiography, as well as from his constant need to rework the idea of exclusion, the community versus the individual, and the xenophobic, often cruel treatment of the person who is different.

Two examples of the successful way in which White adapts myth to an Australian context are the seven black swans in *The Eye of the Storm* and the Southern Cross in *Voss*. In the first novel White uses the symbol of the swan when describing Mrs. Hunter during the eye of the storm, but he manages ingeniously to bring out the negative, darker side of the symbolic meaning usually contained in the swan image by having seven *black* Australian swans fed bread by the protagonist in a eucharistic manner. The starry cross that Voss observes in the sky at the end of the novel is a constellation prominent in the southern hemisphere, but it is also an adumbration of Christ's cross and is an effective image of Voss's figurative cross.

White raises the question of specifically Australian myths in his two historical novels, *Voss* and *A Fringe of Leaves*. Both are attempts to analyse the present by delving into the history of the nineteenth century. *Voss* uses allegory in the tradition of Bunyan. The eponymous hero is a sort of Everyman; he represents white European man who sets out to conquer space—the continent of Australia, as the British had done after 1788. Future, for this Nietzschean megalomaniac, is will: to subjugate, to colonise, to vanquish. *Voss* is a difficult, penetrating investigation of the explorer quest myth. The power of the novel comes partly from an elaborate metaphysical interpretation of this myth. The huge continent of Australia becomes a metaphor of the self; Voss's physical movement toward the interior, his journey inland, is a means of suggesting a concomitant discovery of man's humanity and divine resemblance. The huddlers on the southeast coast (proportionately now about 80 percent of the population) represent those who are content to remain "on the surface," who balk at the hardship of discovering their true selves.

Another essential element of White's oeuvre is the double vision of man and reality evident in almost all of the corpus. As a first epigraph to *The Solid Mandala* White chose a translation from the French surrealist poet Paul Eluard: "There is another world, but it is in this one." This epigraph could preface all of White's work. White's imitation of "this world," what he calls the "actual sphere" at the end of *The Solid Mandala,* reveals both delight and disgust. White's attitude toward the physical, phenomenological world of sense and feeling—the world of "tables and chairs," to take up a typical metaphor of the author—is ambivalent. There is a Dionysian celebration, an ecstatic rendering of the natural world, whether it be the Australian outback, the countryside, a suburban garden, or a garden in the South of France. The author takes pleasure in natural description and imitates the Romantic idea of showing man as an integral part of nature. We think of Theodora Goodman and the volcanic hills of Meroë in *The Aunt's Story*, the Australian bush in *The Tree of Man*, the desert interior of Australia in *Voss*, Miss Hare and Himmelfarb under the flowering plum tree in blossom in *Riders in the Chariot*, Sister de Santis and her morning rite with the birds in Mrs Hunter's garden in *The Eye of the Storm*, Ellen Roxburgh's trek through the bush in *A Fringe of Leaves*, and Eddie Twyborn's healing epiphany in the countryside of New South Wales in *The Twyborn Affair*.

At the same time, White insists on man's physical, fleshy, humanity. It is simplistic and inexact to say that White suffered from a Gnostic disgust of the flesh and all his attempts at describing the body are to show man's bestiality. It is true that there is a fascination for the physically ugly (Voss, Himmelfarb, Rhoda Courtney, Theodora Goodman are all called ugly), for hunchbacks and harelips, for farting dogs and putrefying flesh, but this sordid aspect must be seen in the context of an attempt to give as complete a picture as possible of man's *human* nature. This is not to deny a Swiftian strain, to be seen in the piles of excrement found by Hurtle and Hero on the altar on the island of Perialos in *The Vivisector,* or the shitting moon observed by Cutbush in the same novel. White, like Dorothy de Lascabanes in *The Eye of the Storm*, enjoys lifting the lid of the rubbish bin to show us putrefaction, decay, and disintegrating flesh, what Hero calls "Dreck." In *The Vivisector* Hero exclaims, "Well I will learn to live with such Dreck as I am: to find a reason and purpose in this Dreck."[1] In the same way, behind the exhibition of the seamy lies a reason and purpose for White. The body, the physical, the actual sphere, the taking on of flesh is an essential part of White's double vision of man—a vision based on the idea of incarnation.

In the chapter devoted to Patrick White in her book *A Crucible of Prophets* Veronica Brady speaks of Australian twentieth-century literature centred upon a one-dimensional sense of the world. This leads other authors to be locked into a vacuous and trite social realism, characteristic of contemporary Australian literature. "Kitchen-sink" dramas are revealed, often in a jejune literalism, with the hope of portraying life as it is, or was: drugs, sex, and war predominate, together with expletives, showing what White once called the "sewage and plastic of the late Twentieth Century."[2] In contrast to this one-dimensional sense of reality, White's vision of what it means to be human, together with that of some Australian poets, is profoundly metaphysical. He gives us the "kitchen-sink" side of life. We only have to read part 4 of *The Solid Mandala*, "Mrs. Poulter and the Zeitgeist," to see how White, even better than the "social realists," managed to capture the zeitgeist of the sixties and seventies. But beyond this the author sees another dimension of human life, the metaphysical or religious side, which places his work alongside that of major novelists of the nineteenth-century tradition.

The second dimension of White's work discussed by Veronica Brady, and previously by Peter Beatson, is the religious, metaphysical aspect of life. This is Eluard's "other world . . . in this one." White's condemnation of his native country when he returned to live there in 1948 has now become well known. After nearly twenty years of exile in his youth, the author returned after World War II and found that "in all directions stretched the Great Australian Emptiness, in which the mind is the least of possessions . . . and the march of material ugliness does not raise a quiver from the average nerves."[3] White was shocked in the fifties by an exaltation of the "average" and the mediocre, by a materialistic and possession-obsessed culture celebrating muscles and sport, and by an anti-intellectual, bookless, mindless drudgery based on the banal. White's novels from *The Tree of Man* onward are an attempt to fill up the spiritual void he detected in Australian life, and in the Australian novel, which he termed "the dreary, dun-coloured offspring of journalistic realism."[4] Unfortunately, this journalistic ugliness, the "bags and iron of Australian life," as White also called it, is still prevalent in contemporary Australian literature, marked as it is by artistic and intellectual impoverishment.

Before writing *The Tree of Man,* White underwent a religious conversion in the early 1950s. He had thrown away religion, especially institutionalised Anglicanism, in his teens. After falling on his back in the mud and rain on his way to feed the dogs one day, White cursed a God in whom he started to believe. The farce

of his "fall," and its subsequent humbling, led White to have inklings of the divine Presence *in* this world. Henceforth he sought an elusive, difficult God. White's novels, plays, and stories of the next forty years are the testimony of a private-made-public search for the sacred and the transcendental, for the imprint of God's intervention in human affairs: "I wanted to discover the extraordinary behind the ordinary, the mystery and the poetry which alone could make bearable the lives of an ordinary man and woman, and incidentally, my own life since my return."[5] The use of the terms *extraordinary* and *mystery* helps situate White's work as the product of an artistic and intellectual but also religious quest. White is one of the major religious writers of this century. In 1969 he said during an interview: "Religion. Yes, that's behind all my books. What I am interested in is the relationship between the blundering human being and God."[6] There are parallels between White's work and that of the Catholic writer Flannery O'Connor. White, however, denied being a Christian. Perhaps it is safer to compare him with the visionary artist William Blake: both lie outside orthodox Christianity, but their work reveals a constant use of traditional Christian myth, symbol, and terminology. White freely uses terms such as *soul, fall, sin, suffering, grace,* and *cross.* The Christian theme of fault, expiation, and redemption is common to most of his novels. It is easy to see White's characters fighting with the problems of evil and suffering, to detect a preoccupation with the idea of caritas—Christian love—and to follow the search of each protagonist for God.

Various problematics of a metaphysical nature lie at the centre of White's oeuvre: sin, evil, and cruelty; the incarnation of the soul into the body; the mystery of suffering; the tragicomedy of sex; the model of the Christ-like suffering servant, the *zaddikhim* of Judaism or the "Burnt Ones" of White's private mythology; man's postlapsarian, divided nature and his attempt to reach physical, spiritual, or mystic union; the humble everyday saint; the manifestation of God in the world, the theophany; man's two-dimensional reality, the world he knows and feels and the world some intuit (the sacred or the transcendent). Unlike most Australian novelists of this century, White chose a spiritual quest as being the most important thing that moves man. He left aside problems of power and politics, the drug subculture of the sixties and its related sexual liberation, which still haunts some minor Australian novelists; he usually disregarded money (except in *The Eye of the Storm,* where it motivates the new Goneril and Regan, the two grown-up children of Mrs. Hunter), and romantic love is marked by its near absence. In giving such a predominant place to metaphysical considerations, White, avoiding the "philosophical novel" reminiscent of Dostoevsky, manages to give his fictional creations a depth and dignity lacking in so much contemporary fiction. The latter tends to be like the Australia that White described in 1958: empty, thin, spiritually void, ephemeral, and weightless—in other words, to quote Qohelet the Ecclesiast, vain.

Part of White's power as a novelist lies in the exactitude or precision with which he observed human beings, and in his descriptions of the natural environment. For someone known to be a recluse, who spent eighteen years on a farm on the outskirts of Sydney and the rest of his life in inner-city Sydney (after 1948 he only traveled to Europe occasionally), the extent of White's imaginary world is astonishing. His rendering of Judaism and the Jew surviving the Holocaust in *Riders in the Chariot* has intrigued Jewish readers for its accuracy and sincerity. It comes as a surprise to learn, after reading *Voss,* that White never traveled to the centre of Australia but relied instead on his experiences in the Egyptian desert and on his reading and imagination to give a convincing account of the Australian desert. Backgrounds for his works extend from suburban Sydney, the Australian countryside, Greece, the United States, the South of France, and Nazi Germany to London of the 1930s. The author had personal knowledge of all these places, and he used the South of France and London several times in different novels. Greece had a particular fascination for White, due in part to his Greek-speaking companion of fifty years, Manoly Lascaris. The Parthenon, White once wrote, was the symbol of everything he, as a solitary artist, aspired to. In *Flaws in the Glass* he wrote: "I have come closest to what one always hopes for in Ayia Sophia, Constantinople, alone in the Parthenon . . . in a garden full of birds, in my silent room."[7] The principal background for his fiction, however, is still Australia. No other contemporary novelist has been able to give such an exact, poetic, truthful, and extensive rendering of antipodean *natura naturans* as White, and no other novelist observes Australians so closely.

Some of the different "types" that White depicted with astounding verisimilitude are the suburban, countrified Australian housewife with her down-to-earth qualities and occasional lapses of grammar; the urban socialite, rich, extravagant, and sometimes intellectually ignorant (the portrait seems to be based on White's mother, Ruth White); the selfless do-gooder; the divine fool; the artist as freak and prophet; the honest-to-God one-track Australian male; the rejected, suffering scapegoat; and the physically deformed, lonely outcast. These recurring types show the wide range of human experience which intrigued the author. In some cases White was projecting aspects of his own personality.

Lacking flamboyance, cursed with reserve, I chose fiction . . . as the means of introducing to a disbelieving audience the cast of contradictory characters of which I am composed . . . I see myself not so much a homosexual as a mind possessed by the spirit of man or woman according to actual situations or the characters I become in my writing.[8]

White was particularly successful in creating feminine characters. Some of the outstanding portraits are Elizabeth Hunter, Dorothy de Lascabanes, Joanie Golson, Mrs Courtney, and all the housewives, who, in the author's words, were inspired from the feminine side of his own nature. A believer in man's psychic androgyny, White considered the balance between the masculine and the feminine sides of the individual to be of vital importance.

White's evocation of place is exceptional. From the mythic, remembered, rural Australia of *Happy Valley*, written in exile in London of the 1930s, to the middle section of *The Twyborn Affair,* written in Sydney some forty years later, White returned in every novel to the country landscape of Australia, which was a major source of inspiration, fascination, and love. It was landscape which brought White back to his homeland in 1948, and which he celebrated immediately in writing *The Tree of Man* and *Voss.* The general historical movement in Australia from small country towns toward a growing, alien suburbia and urban life distressed White. He traces this demographic and social phenomenon in the epic *The Tree of Man,* in *The Solid Mandala,* and in *Riders in the Chariot.* Seeing the modern Australian city as a bastion of false values, a latter-day Babylon where Mammon was worshiped, White, like some Latin and later Romantic poets, associated the countryside with childhood innocence and natural beauty. There is an elegiac, lyric strain throughout the oeuvre, more present in some contemporary Australian poetry than in the novelistic tradition, a yearning for a "communion of soul and scene," as White termed it in *The Tree of Man.* Far from the bucolic tranquillity of European pastoralism, here White presents a harsh, disaster-bringing, treacherous, and menacing landscape, to be seen in Voss's fatal expedition into the desert and Ellen Roxburgh's trials with the indigenous people in *A Fringe of Leaves.* When White is not dealing with the great outback of Australia, he describes country scenes nearer the cities as a sort of *locus amoenus,* places of "Romantic" retreat, where nature gives solace and temporary respite from the passions and conflicts of the city.

White possessed an encyclopedic knowledge of Australian flora and fauna. A taxonomy of flowers, shrubs, plants, and trees weaves its way into the work, providing passages of natural description such as the following, taken from *Riders in the Chariot,* which are remarkable for their figurative use of language and poetic beauty:

> Only precariously alive, the trees were the greener for their sickliness, moodily defiant of the strong light, with little, wizened oranges radiating a feverish gold. All was most extraordinarily exposed to mind and view from beneath the plum, and could have appeared to challenge hope, if it had not been for the evidence of continuity: a bird cupped in the grey goblet of her nest, a litter of young rabbits moving by clockwork into grass, the eyelids of a lizard denying petrifaction by the sun. It was perfectly still, except that the branches of the plum tree hummed with life, increasing, and increasing, deafening, swallowing them up.[9]

The particularity of White's vision has much to do with a veering toward the exuberant, the flamboyant, and even the grotesque. This is true as much for the characters and situations he imagines as it is for his prose style, often thought to be difficult and idiosyncratic. We see a similar grotesqueness of situation in the work of Flannery O'Connor, or in the paintings of Francis Bacon. The decrepit, aging, and physically repugnant Elizabeth Hunter in *The Eye of the Storm* is vividly described by elaborate patterns of animal imagery and unusual metaphors. Her death on a commode is apt, horrifying, and cruel in its truth to life—the mother of Patrick White died in the same way. Rhoda Courtney, the hunchback of *The Vivisector,* is another grotesque product of White's imagination. Through inventive metaphors, the author brings to life this birth-marked Cranach figure, vivisecting her ugliness and deformity. Unusual, evocative, even horrible situations abound: Himmelfarb's "crucifixion" in *Riders in the Chariot;* the strangled, drowned dog in *The Eye of the Storm* or the vivisected dog in *The Vivisector,* the brutal killing of a cockatoo in the short story "The Cockatoos"; Doll Quigley's murder of her brother in *The Tree of Man.* Excess, blasphemy, perversion, and evil make their appearance in often startling and original form.

Patrick White's legacy to future generations of Australian writers is immense. As White plunged his intellectual, religious, and artistic roots in a distinctly European tradition, future Australian writers have the choice of following such a post-Platonic, postromantic tradition, or finding their inspiration in less Eurocentric modes of thought. The seriousness and consummate skill of White's art provide an unavoidable model and a storehouse of language for any later writer living in the society White knew and imitated in his fiction. Modern secularism, the championing of the mediocre in Austra-

lia, the small canvases which content most contemporary novelists of this country, the obsession with the irrelevant paraphernalia of living—all vindicate White's achievement yet foreshadow the difficulty of finding another Australian artist to match the master.

David Coad, Summer 1993

[1] Patrick White, *The Vivisector,* Harmondsworth, Eng., Penguin, 1977, p. 392.

[2] Patrick White, *Flaws in the Glass,* Harmondsworth, Eng., Penguin, 1985, p. 116.

[3] *Patrick White Speaks,* Christine Flynn & Paul Brennan, eds., Sydney, Primavera, 1989, p. 15.

[4] Ibid., p. 16.

[5] Ibid., p. 15.

[6] Ibid., p. 19.

[7] White, *Flaws in the Glass,* p. 74.

[8] Ibid., pp. 20, 80–81.

[9] Patrick White, *Riders in the Chariot,* Harmondsworth, Eng., Penguin, 1984, p. 91.

Open, Mixed, and Moving: Recent Australian Poetry

1. What happens when we join two plain words and come up with "Australian poetry"? It seems that we have grafted something very new onto something very old. We think of a country that celebrated its bicentennial as recently as 1988, and of writers who work in, around, or partly against a long history of European poetics. Yet in saying "Australian poetry" we also bring into sight another kind of art: the traditional songs of the land's Aboriginal peoples. We bring them into sight, though not into sharp focus. We may begin to see that *Australian* reaches as far back as *poetry,* if not farther; but only when we realise that both words distort as they reveal, can we truly approach the songs themselves. The word *Australian* derives from a seventeenth-century coinage, *Terra Australis,* that identifies an unknown space—Australasia, Polynesia, and "Magellanica"—as viewed from a European perspective. It is from that same viewpoint that Captain James Cook observed the land in 1788 and, declaring it *terra nullius,* could possess it for the Crown. So to call traditional Aboriginal chants "Australian" is to conceive them in the very terms that have brutalised and often endangered those traditions. In a similar way, to construe them as "poetry" is implicitly to measure them against esthetic norms that remain wholly exterior to them.[1]

One could organise a reading of Australian poetry around *Australis* and *nullius.* How the land is differently experienced and mapped by Europeans and Aboriginals is a familiar theme, as is the settlers' apprehension of a spiritual emptiness at the heart of the land. In order to develop such a reading, thematic criticism has tended to reduce the uncertainties in the expression "Australian poetry" as quickly as possible. Criticism of Australian literature has been inclined to be empirical rather than dialectical, a bias that applies to conservatives, liberals, and radicals alike. (If there are conservatives and liberals who do not question received notions of *Australian,* there are Marxists who cheerfully dissolve *poetry* into social categories.) Still, we might learn more about the country's writing by dwelling in those uncertainties for a little longer than usual. For example, to take a current doxa, we might wonder if a firm insistence on the complete alterity of Aboriginal ceremonial songs could have the effect of removing them from white people's attention altogether, with who knows what political consequences. Perhaps the analysis of "Australian poetry" can be taken further, without denying the importance of its first, corrective phase. Perhaps the expression can be widened and deepened so that, in time, it can include what it now seems to exclude.

This expansion of meaning can happen only if the word *Australian* is used affirmatively in many contexts: cultural, political, religious, and social. The price of such an expansion is clear: the nation's presumed self-identity would be set at risk. The challenge, though, is to imagine that rise as positive; and that means, among other things, recognising a range of idioms as Australian. For if our image repertoire is allowed to be regulated solely by a narrative of British discovery and colonial exploration, *Australian* will become an impoverished word, unequal to the diversity of the country it names. The same sort of point might be made about *poetry,* except that this word has already taken its chances in a wide range of circumstances and is still taking them: think of "computer poetry," "language poetry," "performance poetry," and "street poetry." Not all these subgenres will survive, but in granting any one of them a chance (which includes the chance of criticism), one is also underwriting the survival of poetry at large. The word *Australian* is much younger than *poetry,* but even so it has more immediate and overt ideological forces pulling it this way and that. It needs to be kept in play for as long a time as possible, given generous chances, so that it will not readily lend itself to dark aspects of nationalism or be pressed into the service of racism.

We do not usually talk of "Australian languages," not because there is just the one but because English is linguistically and culturally predominant. The land has 150 or so Aboriginal tongues (it once had many more) and over a hundred others drawn from Asia and Eu-

rope. Thinking about these figures complicates the expression "Australian poetry." To judge from local anthologies, it has come to mean a canon of verse written in English by Anglophones living in or born in Australia. That canon has never been inert, yet over the last twenty years it has been vigorously stretched or tightened under the hands of various poetry schools and pressure groups. One outcome is that some ancient Aboriginal chants, such as the Wonguri-Mandjigai "Moon-Bone Song," appear more often in anthologies. Nevertheless, the category "Australian poetry" is undoubtedly larger than that specified by the normative and revisionary canons. We know that verse is composed here in German, Greek, and Italian; but we have no coordinated knowledge of talented poets who may be writing in Arabic, Chinese, Hungarian, Polish, Spanish, Vietnamese, or any other of the community languages.

Even if we were to restrict ourselves to verse written in English, Australian poetry would not be all of a piece. How could it seem so? Taken by themselves, historical markers are unreliable: 1788 may signal the start of British colonialisation, yet it can hardly mark the origin of the country's poetry. On the one hand there are writers whose ethnic background sets them at variance with the myth of national origin. The verse of Antigone Kefala and Dimitris Tsaloumas, for example, moves to the rhythms of quite other historical and mythological times. On the other hand, there are poets from British stock whose central influences are Asian, American, or European. Robert Gray's imaginative world, for instance, has been formed by his reading of Francis Ponge, Charles Reznikoff, and Japanese Zen poets. In much the same way, geographic markers can generate tricky marginal cases that turn out to be important. Peter Porter is thought by some to be our finest living poet. He was born in Brisbane and returns there from time to time; but for the last forty years he has lived in London and made a solid reputation there. Where does the Australia in "Australian poetry" begin and end? Who may draw its border lines?

We might get farther more quickly by agreeing that "Australian poetry" designates an economy of concepts: cultural, geographic, and historical, but also political and social. That economy can be described though not rigorously defined. It is very doubtful whether some poetic gestures can rightly be ventured as more authentically Australian than others. This is so even when—or, better, especially when—the question of esthetic value is raised, for there are different sorts of good poetry written in the country. This is not an idea that pleases everyone. Some people believe there are determining traits in "Australian," depending on, though more elusive than, geographic and historical criteria. "*Australian* poetry," people say, with a clear stress and a knowing look, even when there is no danger of confusing it with American or English poetry. The adjective can be pronounced as though it indicated an essence or quality, one that can be suggested far more easily than cashed out. When one asks what *Australian* means in this context, the answer can be simple or complex, depending on how many elements are involved. Here are four common ones: thematic (discovery, farming, mateship, the outback), topic (Bondi Beach, Gallipoli, New England, Sydney Harbour), linguistic (the poem uses or mentions colloquial speech and/or "characteristic" figures such as irony and litotes), or literary historical (the writer in question can be cued into a feasible national sequence—for instance, one that begins with Lawson and Patterson).

Attempts to restrict the meaning of *Australian* usually specify one or more of these elements as determining traits, thereby reducing an internal difference at work in the adjective. When that happens, we can begin to see the effects of an ideology at work. Sometimes it can be heavily marked, as when the adjective in "Australian poetry" bespeaks an ethereal content, a spirit of the land or of the people, that is absorbed by a writer and then uniquely expressed by him or her. When Les Murray's publishers describe his *Collected Poems* (1991) in terms of "profound perceptions of natural and spiritual truth," they are responding—consciously or unconsciously—to the intense political work those poems do. "I am not European. Nor is my English," he says, a tad anxiously; and elsewhere, "It will be centuries / before many men are are truly at home in this country." Murray's poetic depends on his readers' believing that he is one of those people and that he is one with the land.

"I am looking at the place where the names well out of field stone," Murray writes. While decoding the proper names of the land and its people, though, he quietly encodes a certain culture as natural. "The vernacular republic," as he calls it, is the community of authentic Australians. These are not necessarily country folk, although he often takes them as a reference point. You join the vernacular republic by recognising your spirit land all about you. On the surface of the poems this spirit is given in rare moments of ethnic convergence and moral openness, when people drop their differences and talk together on a human level. Meanwhile, beneath the surface, the poems work hard to define *human* by way of closure, self-identity, and patriarchy. No surprise, then, to find modernity cast as the enemy throughout, or even that it converges with a Pauline notion of "the world" as fallen and stubbornly turned toward death. It is from here that we get Murray

the sermoniser and polemicist, the man who talks chillingly of how society cannot survive without male blood sacrifices. Although he laments that Australia has "vanished into ideology," he has transformed himself into the most ideological of our poets, and to the detriment of his verse. Over the last decade his work has turned increasingly *entêté,* animated more by linguistic dexterity than by feeling, and given to indulge hobbyhorse theories of poetry. While he has occasionally regained form, sometimes with considerable verve, his later work often seems more like material for poetry rather than finished poems.

Murray marks an extreme of those writers who seek entry to "Australian poetry" through the adjective as well as the noun. By and large, most local writers prefer to write poetry and let "Australian" take care of itself. If one could arrange for a fish-lens photograph of Australian poetry to be taken today, it would include a great deal more than I can show here. There would be all the verse written in the community languages I have mentioned; there would be translations by local poets of Apollinaire, Bobrowski, Mandelstam, and Ungaretti, among others; and of course there would be Australian poets living thousands of miles from Australia. One would see marks of old hostilities between rival groups formed in the 1960s (national versus international, Sydney versus Melbourne, advocates of closed form versus proponents of vatic freedom). Looking closely, you could pick out A. D. Hope publishing his latest collection, *Orpheus,* at the ripe age of eighty-four; and everywhere, younger poets trying their first powers in magazines and pamphlets. You would see *Scripsi,* the country's premier literary journal, and *bystander,* the latest little magazine; and you would see anthologies and counteranthologies. Poetry readings in building sites, pubs, and universities would be registered in the photograph, as would the "writers' train" that takes groups of authors for brief visits to the outback, and there would also be the blurry trails of visiting poets, including Miroslav Holub from Czechoslovakia and John Ashbery from the U.S.

I will be using a far more narrow lens than the fisheye as I look at several volumes of selected and collected poems that have lately appeared. This means bypassing Aboriginal and ethnic writing (little of which is gathered into selected or collected editions) and some fine individual books—Alex Skovron's *Sleeve Notes,* for one—but perhaps one can see more by concentrating on a few large features of the landscape. Publishers of Australian verse cannot profit from large print runs, with the consequence that two or three years after publication successful books can prove hard to find. Over the past few years, however, the two main publishers of poetry—

Angus & Robertson and the University of Queensland Press—have issued a number of engaging collectanea. Some of these, like David Campbell's *Collected Poems,* Shaw Neilson's *Selected Poems,* and Francis Webb's *Cap and Bells,* preserve the work of writers who died over a decade ago; others, like selecteds by Robert Adamson and Robert Gray, show us the work of writers in full flight. These volumes are vivid contributions to Australian letters. Still, in order to give more of the tenor of what is happening today, I will focus on books fresh from the warehouse.

2. It is a journalistic commonplace that the late 1960s were a time of loosening up and experiment in Australian poetry. Literary modernism did not take firm root here in the 1920s and 1930s, and when it tried again in the 1940s, it was pounced upon by James Mc-Auley and others, who perpetrated the "Ern Malley" hoax (an oeuvre of modernist verse that was instantly acclaimed until it was revealed to be the afternoon's work of two antimodernist writers). With all the force of something long repressed, the modern impulse eventually returned. As Laurie Duggan writes in a song, "(Do) the Modernism," new things were happening in America and Europe, but not here: "Well, b-back in Australia they c-couldn't cope / they do the James Mc-Auley, do the A. D. Hope / they never busted a pentameter or stayed up late / until the g-g-generation of s-s-sixty-eight."[2] A steady series of "modernisms" attracted attention, most deriving from the United States. Enthusiasms for the Black Mountain School and the New York School, set against the sombre backdrop of the Vietnam War, temporarily inspired a number of poets, most of them ephemeral. Traces of this period remain in the best of "the generation of sixty-eight"—John Forbes, John Scott, and Alan Wearne—and, sometimes more interestingly, in the work of poets who had amply established themselves by the early seventies. John Blight, Vincent Buckley, David Campbell, and Chris Wallace-Crabbe all opened themselves to new energies and new disciplines in their collections of the 1970s without forgetting who they were and what they had already learned.

Other writers remained more or less untouched by the bright fashions: whatever changes were to appear in their later writing were already marked as possibilities in earlier publications. Slighted in the sixties and seventies, their work now seems more likely to last than what was then applauded for its Australian content or American style. Of no one is this more true than Gwen Harwood (b. 1920), whose *Collected Poems* (1991) places her in the first rank of Australian poets. Harwood was never ignored; she was sometimes lauded (and achieved notoriety in 1961 for publishing an acrostic sonnet in

the *Bulletin* which, when grasped, read "Fuck all editors"). For all that, until the late seventies and early eighties her value was given only notional assent by all but a few devoted admirers. There are several reasons for this. She has been a relatively isolated female writer, spending almost all her adult life in Tasmania, a long way from the centres of literary fashion. Far from promoting herself, she has occasionally published under pseudonyms (Francis Geyer, Walter Lehmann, T. F. Kline, and Miriam Stone), has worked in formal modes when they were least in vogue, and has bidden her time: her first book, *Poems,* appeared in 1963 when she was forty-three, and it has taken a quarter of a century for three more slim volumes to join it.

Thinking of Harwood's geographic isolation tells us very little about the poetry itself. It may have been a condition for her writing as she does, but beyond that there is nothing much to say. Still, the words *independence* and *solitude* keep coming to mind as one reads poem after poem. "I want to report how *I* found the world"—so Wittgenstein confided to his notebook in 1916, and so Harwood, for whom Wittgenstein is a touchstone, might say too. Certainly she would agree with another of his notebook remarks: "The philosophical I is not the human being, not the human body or the human soul with the psychological properties, but the metaphysical subject, the boundary (not a part) of the world. The human body, however, my body in particular, is a part of the world among others, among beasts, plants, stones etc., etc."[3] Much of Harwood's writing explores that space between the metaphysical subject and the body, the self abiding in the solitary state of the *cogito* and the self's liturgy, its unique movement toward the Other. And Harwood indicates how concertinaed, stretched, and striated that space can be. The *Collected Poems* begins with "Alter Ego," in which the speaker announces a quest to find the one "whom I greet / yet cannot name, or see," a journey that must be "on paths of love and pain." The Other she seeks is herself, and while her quest goes by way of love of friends and family, it always returns her to herself, to a deeper sense of self. That cycle of return can be felt throughout "Bone Scan," the final section of *Collected Poems,* and is artfully pointed in the book's concluding lyric, "Carapace," where the speaker asks us to hold a protective shell in the hollow of a palm: "I hold," she says, "in my unhoused continuing self / the memory that is wisdom's price / for what survives."

That "continuing self" is partly revealed in the solitude of meditation and music, to be sure, but also in the body's rounds of pleasure and pain, and its steadily accumulating credits and debits to time. The other person finally remains unknown and unknowable: "bone to my bone I grasp the world. / But what you are I do not know," concludes "Carnal Knowledge I." And in "Dialogue" a stillborn child asks its mother, "Where is my grave?" and is told "in my head." No mourning is ever fully successful, despite the poem's disclaimer ("Do you mourn for me every day? / Not at all it is more that thirty years"), and when her child stops questioning, the mother looks about her only to find "wings of cloud / burning and under my feet / stones marked with demons' teeth." Perhaps the intensity of Harwood's personal lyrics, her apprehension of being "unhoused," begins to explain why she has had recourse to that literary carapace, the pseudonym. To this, though, I should add that she often presents herself under the guise of imagined characters, Professor Eisenhart and Professor Kröte, two tragicomic intellectuals by means of whom she offers keen satire of suburban life and materialistic values. Like Descartes, the author of the *cogito*, Harwood can say *Lavartus prodeo*, I go forward masked.

At first it is tempting to say that Rosemary Dobson (b. 1920) also advances in disguise, for she too speaks through other characters. Yet the description does not quite fit. Descartes observed in the *Préambules* that "when I go into this theatre of a world, where hitherto I have been a spectator, I go forward masked." The distinction is apt. In Dobson's poetic world the figure of the spectator is more important than that of the masked actor. "There is a being alone in a crowd, a chosen withdrawal / A singling apart of the mind," we hear in one poem, and indeed the theme of the spectator surfaces in a fair number of her lyrics. Sometimes the observer gazes at a work by Calvi, Crivelli, Vereist, or Vermeer and ponders the relations between representation and presence. Once, in "The Bystander," a stock character speaks from several paintings: "I am the one who looks the other way." It is a rare echo of Auden, and equally rare are confidences that, as she gets older she finds herself not giving a damn, "looking slantwise / at everyone's morning."

Dobson's characteristic stance links observation to compassion. One of her quests is, as she says, "To keep their memory from the rage of time," and the very title of the moving final section of her *Collected Poems* (1991), "Untold Lives," speaks eloquently of those gathered in that anonymous word *their*. A biographical poet, then, though not one given simply to autobiography. Only very seldom is the surface of the poems taken up with self-description or overt self-reflection. This is a poetry of truth rather than correctness, as Heidegger might say, a poetry that derives its peculiar charge and charm by letting a truth proper to a life unfold in its own time and in its own way (which might on occasion involve withdrawal). A lyric like "Being Called For" speaks from a layer of the self beneath that of personality.

Come in at the low-silled window,
Enter by the door through the vine-leaves
Growing over the lintel. I have hung bells at the
Window to be stirred by the breath of your
Coming, which may be at any season.
In winter the snow throws
Light on the ceiling. If you come in winter
There will be a blue shadow before you
Cast on the threshold.
In summer an eddying of white dust
And a brightness falling between the leaves.
When you come I am ready: only, uncertain—
Shall we be leaving at once on another journey?
I would like first to write it all down and leave the
   pages
On the table weighted with a stone,
Nevertheless I have put in a basket
The coins for the ferry.

The lyric seals traces of Emily Dickinson and Georg Trakl, among others, into a unique idiom. Here "among others" is not a formula but a positive sign of the calm assurance with which Dobson has negotiated powerful influences.

The final image in "Being Called For," reserving coins for Charon, reminds us of a classicism that runs through Dobson's writing. It can be sensed directly in lyrics like "Knossos" and "Poems from Pausanias," and indirectly in the questioning of art's relations to the real world (which includes a worrying away at Platonic distinctions). But her classicism is not all of a piece; it is diverted by reading and translating Osip Mandelstam— himself a lover of Greek austerity—and by adapting the quite different classicism of Chinese poetry. Drawing threads from these two traditions, and knotting them together in her own way, enables Dobson to speak with an achieved dignity that takes the side of the ordinary. Her voice is at once formal and informal, scrupulous and casual. Nowhere is this seen to more advantage than in "Folding the Sheets," where two people are pictured "Advancing towards each other / From Burma, from Lapland" as well as from India and China.

We meet as though in the formal steps of a dance
To fold the sheets together, put them to air
In wind, in sun over bushes, or by the fire.
We stretch and pull from one side and then the
   other—
Your turn. Now mine.
We fold them and put them away until they are
   needed.
A wish for all people when they lie down to sleep—

Smooth linen, cool cotton, the fragrance and stir of
  herbs
And the faint but perceptible scent of sweet clear
  water.

Dobson's idiom ties together various influences, mainly
Western but also, and more recently, Eastern. For those
who know what to listen for, it is an unmistakably Australian voice. All the same, when one tries to unravel the
knot to find out where its Australianness lies, nothing
can be found. It is the same in trying to isolate Americanness or Englishness.

"I, who always find / In anticlimax pleasure"—the
lines are spoken by one of Dobson's characters, though
they can orient us in the world of Elizabeth Riddell's *Selected Poems,* (1992). In one of her most memorable
poems, "The Letter," Riddell (b. 1910) takes her tendency to subtraction as a starting point. The verse letter
consists of two texts: one, plain and rather reserved,
that forms the actual content of the letter; and another,
unwritten and more passionate, that moves in counterpoint to the first, unsettling its discretions and silences.
I interrupt the poem about halfway through.

It has been a long time since I wrote. I have no
  news.
*I put my head between my hands and hope
my heart will choke me. I put out my hand
to touch you and touch air. I turn to sleep
and find a nightmare, hollowness and fear.*

And by the way, I have had no letter now
For eight weeks, it must be
*a long eight weeks
because you have nothing to say, nothing at all,
not even to record your emptiness
or guess what's to become of you, without love.*

As the letter ends, so, on one level, convention and
emotion come closer while remaining just as distant on
another level: "I will end this letter now. I am yours
with love / *Always with love, with love.*"

Riddell's *Selected Poems* falls into two halves, "First
Life" and "Second Life," the division marking well over
a decade of poetic silence. Without the blank pages in
the middle of the book it would be hard to tell that so
many years had passed. The writing insists on a clear,
steady surface; indeed, it verges on denying that language has a density of its own, a solidity that forces the
world to be refracted through it or (if one were to believe the worst) to be dismissed from it. The dangers of
such a plain style are everywhere present, for the poems
run the risk of being inconspicuous or deprecated as
journalism. (In fact, Riddell *has* been overlooked and
has been a journalist for many years.) All styles have

their attendant dangers, however, and this is one poet
who forces her readers to distinguish between complexity and richness, to learn how to find the latter in clarity
and, in the end, to value it the more highly.

For all their continuities with the past, Riddell's
later poems show a fresh engagement with the physical
world. "In Dar-es-Salaam the morning lay on us like wet
silk," begins one section of "Occassions of Birds," which
ends by evoking pink pigeons of Mauritius with their
"tiny heads and supplicating voices, / poor flakes of
pink driven out when the forest was felled." Riddell
treats verbal precision almost as a categorical imperative, much like Robert Gray; yet where Gray travels to
Japan, translates haiku, and brilliantly evokes life in an
increasingly industrialised and Americanised Tokyo,
Riddell resolutely stays at home. "We Might Go to
Japan" is the title of a recent poem. Its drama involves
two people over lunch, looking at fish (are they real or
not?) and slowly talking each other out of the trip.
There is no point flying to Japan; it is too late, since "we
will miss the Emperor's dying / amid blossom frozen on
black branches." No interest in registering local colour
here: everything that "Japan" might mean is consumed
in a stark image of a passing culture. The difference between real and painted fish is hardly worth remarking,
since the Japanese have so successfully blurred the distinction between nature and culture.

Where a queering of the nature/culture dichotomy
marks a limit for Riddell's poetics, it forms the condition of possibility for John Forbes (b. 1950) to write at
all. Perhaps the most striking thing about his *New and
Selected Poems* (1992) is its uniform manner; the kind
of poetry that attracted him in his twenties remains his
sole model in his forties. Not unfamiliar, this model in-
terlaces two fascinations: the writing of Frank O'Hara,
and modern critical theory. They are not of equal importance in this case. A close knowledge of O'Hara informs everything Forbes writes, while he collects glittering pieces of critical theory like a magpie. Although he
admires O'Hara, Forbes is not influenced by him evenly
at every point. One way of viewing the New Yorker is
to see him drawn partly by Walt Whitman and partly
by Pierre Reverdy, his work pulling now toward a celebration of the self and now toward a programme of fragmentation and reconstruction. They are not incompatible impulses, though they set up strange patterns of
mutual interference which can be moving (in "To the
Harbormaster," say) or tedious (in "Second Avenue").
There is no Whitmanesque elation in Forbes; his poetics
turns tightly around cubism. Tightly, because it overrides the surrealist interest in the unconscious and focuses intently on the cubist demand to reconstitute perception, and because Forbes is a perfectionist,

preferring to manicure lyric form rather than to venture forth on a long haul.

Contemporary critique of representation, whether by Baudrillard or Rorty, aids and abets Forbes's poetics. An early lyric like "TV" elaborates itself by calculatingly overrunning the divisions between presence and representation: "dont bother telling me about the programmes / describe what your set is like," we are instructed, only to find that the speaker is already doing precisely that, picturing the "curved screen its strip of white stillness like / beach sand at pools where the animals come." Any firm contract between writer and reader is broken before it can be signed, and we are left ungrounded, in a world where image and reality have been disconnected from each other.

Australia is part of that world, of course, which means it is put into question. Hence "On the Beach: A Bicentennial Poem," Forbes's ironic contribution to the stage-managed festivities of 1988. "Your vocation calls / & you answer it," the poem begins, but Forbes understands his vocation (as poet and as Australian) in anything but a received high style. His proclaimed task is "to fake a flashy ode," although he knows full well that the lines between original and forgery are never clearcut and that his poetics derives much of its appeal from being flashy. "On the Beach" cleverly shows that "Australia" is always and already a cultural construction, put together from what happens to be on hand. Part of the ode deforms one of our literary culture's prime icons, Les Murray's poem "An Absolutely Ordinary Rainbow," about a man who suddenly begins weeping, for no apparent reason, in Martin Place, Sydney. Murray's poem offers itself as a study of Grace. Forbes responds by decelebrating its central event.

> astonished
> trade union delegates
> watch a man behead a chicken
> in Martin Place—isn't there
> a poem about this
> & the shimmering ideal
> of just walking down the street?
> not being religious
> we bet on how many circles
> the headless chook will complete
> & won't this do for a formal
> model of Australia, not
> too far-fetched, not too cute?

"Not being religious," Forbes writes, glancing at the end of Murray's poem, when the weeping man wipes his eyes and hurries away down Pitt Street, evading believers. Animal sacrifices are performed in some sacred ceremonies, and trade unions have roots in Christianity.

Forbes amusingly testifies to the locals' lack of belief in transcendence but perhaps plays on the etymology of *religious* (from the Latin *religare*: to tie back, tr. to form into a community). It is the heartless bet that gathers the observers into a larrikin group: a model of secular, materialistic Australia.

It is this nihilist view of antipodean life, in which no value can escape devaluation and no poppy can grow too tall, that once led Australian writers to seek cultural asylum in Europe. There are different ways of being an expatriate writer, and David Malouf (b. 1934) has not taken the path of either Peter Porter or Randolph Stow, both of whom make their homes in England. For well over a decade now Malouf has divided his time between Tuscany and Sydney, and whether he has two homes or no home is a question that surfaces in his writing. "We are all of us exiles of one place / or another, even those / who never leave home," he writes, thinking of Dante in Ravenna and doubtless also of himself. The linked values of home and exile regularly traverse his work, along with other oppositions, for Malouf is finely alert to the ways in which a world, his own, answers to a grid of meshing polarities: the present and the past, high and popular culture, young Australia and old Europe, the great and the tiny. The pressure of these competing forces can be felt in the opening lines of "Among the Ruins," from *Poems 1959–89* (1992). "A late arrival on the scene, I stood in '59 / in the shadow of Titus' arch, watching pigeons / in their brief season fluff / and preen among the columns, inheriting / old nesting-places high in a dung-patched cornice. There were ruins / everywhere that year, though the war was fourteen years behind us and the Fall / of Rome further back still. I had missed the best of / it. . ." To feel oneself a latecomer, cast in the shadows, without an inheritance, yet longing for a true home: the experience is common in Malouf's generation of writers, and it informs a dimension of his verse. The celebrations of Queensland exotica ("The Pacific / breaks at our table"), of consummation ("I taste moonlight / transformed into flesh"), and of the sheer wonder of the "is-ness of things" create another dimension that permeates the first.

All those elements come together in "Early Discoveries," a double portrait of the poet as a child and of his Lebanese grandfather. "I watch him practise his odd rites, hatchet in hand / as he martyrs chickens in the woodblock's dark," he writes, in an image that John Forbes would be quick to ironise. "This is his garden," the adult speaker declares, "a valley in Lebanon; you can smell the cedars on his breath / and the blood of massacres, the crescent flashing from ravines / to slice through half a family. He rolls furred sage between /

thumb and stained forefinger, sniffs the snowy hills: bees shifting / gold as they forage sunlight among stones, churchbells wading / in through pools of silence. He has never quite migrated." And so both "his" and "garden" are divided and recombined as we begin to understand the grandfather's circumstances. This image of Malouf's forebear living partly in Lebanon and partly in Queensland can stand for many others of its kind in Australian poetry. A sense of dislocation presses on the collective imagination: Antigone Kefala, Peter Skrzynecki, and Ania Walwicz have each brooded on experiences of European migration. It has two phases, often separated by a generation: a passage from the old world to the new, and a quest for one's roots on the far side of the globe.

John Blight (b. 1913), on the other hand, quests inward, tracking down his roots in the imagination. Although his *Selected Poems 1939–1990* (1992) gives us an opportunity to see where that journey begins, in books that have long been out of print, he comes into his own as a poet a little later with his two rich volumes of beachcombing sonnets. The sea here does not simply provide an occasion for describing a beached whale, a jellyfish, or an island. Rather, it functions as the condition of possibility for poetic experience. Having no meaning in itself, but rich in human projections, the sea offers itself to a ceaseless meditation. "The wave is something, yet—nothing," begins one sonnet, in a philosophical key; another starts, "These are the first shapes: stonefish and starfish." The most anthologised of these lyrics, "Death of a Whale," is also the most programmatic, with its neat moral, "Sorry we are, too, when a child dies; / But at the immolation of a race who cries?" By contrast, "A Dog to Tie Up" remains open to the chances thrown its way. "If the sea must beat my door, hungry animal," it is because "it has no words to frame its speech; / but speaks cunningly nevertheless." All of Blight's beachcombing sonnets are a response to that dialectic: the sea, as Other, cannot speak (and so must be given voice) yet speaks in its own way (which must be respected).

"I am at no loss its meanings to guess," Blight goes on. (Confidence is one of his traits as a writer, even when the poems themselves seem hesitant.) And his understanding of the sea gives him a greater possession than property; it gives him "a guest." The sonnet then moves into its brilliant sestet: "And who has a guest at his door has / all wisdom for his learning; has / the sea, as he says, 'sighing or storming'; has / another's problems to exclude his own; has / the ocean at his door to deal with; has / a dog to tie up each tide—his dinghy; has. . ." This is not only a technical tour de force but

also a prime example of how a brief lyric can circumnavigate a complex theme. To detail all the modalities of possession implied by those six *has*'s would take some time.

Blight's later poems, from *Hart* (1975) to *Holiday Sea Sonnets* (1985) and beyond, attest an effulgence of poetic energy. Searching for a parallel, I can think only of A. R. Ammons's work over the same period. For both writers, individual poems shine more brightly when read in the context of their whole endeavour. By the 1970s we find that Blight has entered so profoundly into his imagination that he can only think poetically. This does not mean that everything he writes succeeds, but rather that his successes tend to be more inward and more artless. One sign of great craft is simplicity; another is idiom. Blight has both. Thus in "The Geese" he muses over the birds' directions that he sees "as a maze and can never / follow in my groping hour by / hour of daylight," and so comes to this illumination: "Black out the sun / for ever, if I were gifted / with familiarities as / theirs with orbs and galaxies . . . / as though each sipped of stars all night. // Chained with them I may get drunk a / little—but have their pinions / to ferry me beyond all comment."

3. As a coda, I take a sentence from A. D. Hope, still the country's finest living poet. In 1963, writing a short survey of recent Australian literature, he observed that, for contemporary writers, "The country is something they start from and not something they feel they have to aim towards."[4] Neither a goal nor an origin, "Australia" is an economy of experiences, ideas, and promises; and, among others, it falls to Australian writers and critics to keep it open, mixed, and moving.

Kevin Hart, Summer 1993

[1] T. G. H. Strehlow, in *Songs of Central Australia* (Sydney, Angus & Robertson, 1971), argues that the Arunda songs are akin in complexity to biblical and Nordic poetry. However, see Stephen Muecke et al., *Reading the Country* (Fremantle, W.A., Fremantle Arts Centre Press, 1984), for a different understanding of Aboriginal songs and the dreaming in general.

[2] Laurie Duggan, *The Great Divide: Poems 1973–83,* Sydney, Hale & Iremonger, 1985, p. 50.

[3] Ludwig Wittgenstein, *Notebooks 1914–1916,* 2d ed., G. H. von Wright and G. E. M. Anscombe, eds., G. E. M. Anscombe, tr., Oxford, Blackwell, 1979, p. 82e.

[4] A. D. Hope, *Australian Literature, 1950–1962,* Melbourne, Melbourne University Press, 1963, p. 4.

Who Is the Colonist? Writing in New Zealand and the South Pacific

As the last part of the world to be overwhelmed by "the expansion of the West," the various islands of the Pacific present different examples of the effects of colonialism. I shall focus here on those islands where the British were the imperial power. Further differences could be found among the various islands taken over by the French, in particular a contrast in the way the latter were seen as part of France rather than as "alien" colonies. Even in New Zealand, where one might expect a classic example of colonial domination over an indigenous civilization, it proves to be at least a partial exception. The many island groups became commercially dependent but were never fully subordinate to the imperial culture, at least in part because their smallness and limited resources never attracted a sizable white settlement. Instead, government officials, missionaries, and a few traders offered a more or less transient white presence without dramatically changing the indigenous way of life—except in the matter of religion. Tonga, for example, is probably the only Methodist kingdom in the world, not in the sense of an established church but because the royal family converted and so did most of the population. To underline the diversity, Fiji represents a classical case of imperial change. In much the same way as in Trinidad, natives of India were brought in to work on the sugar plantations, with the result that they now outnumber the native Fijians, a fact which has underlain the recent political turmoil in that country.

To some extent this difference from other colonial experiences reflects both the timing of the colonial takeover and the facts of geography. Although in the early part of the nineteenth century the Pacific was mostly the haunt of whalers and sealers, the middle of the century was a prime time for missionary endeavor, and the various missionary groups had great influence on the British Parliament. The history of the British Pacific represents a continuing battle between the Colonial Office, the various missions, and economic interests. To this was added an American presence, notably in Samoa, Fiji, and New Zealand, where an American, John B. Williams of Salem, observed the signing of the Treaty of Waitangi in 1840. He was later appointed as a consul and has left behind a record of his experience.

Recent revisitation of the contact experience (e.g., Obeyesekere) has suggested that change was not a one-way affair. The local indigenes adopted with great alacrity the ideals of free trade and economic competition. As Bernard Smith (1992) has suggested, Captain Cook may have opened the Pacific to free trade rather than to Enlightenment civilization. As an example, the Maori, in New Zealand, quickly became agrarian entrepreneurs, supplying much of the food for the local white settlers and the convict colonies in Australia. The subsequent collapse in a general economic downturn almost destroyed this enterprise and added to Maori suspicion of the Pakeha (whites), even if the later land wars had not entirely changed the relationship, but it is an early and startling example of cultural adaptation. A more sinister adaptation was the Maori's ready turning to trade in guns, clearly more efficient tools for warfare.

The same adaptation took place in religious affairs. Most Polynesians quickly adopted the ideas and trappings of the missionaries (even to wearing Mother Hubbards). How deep this was remains open to question, but it is clear that indigenous religious traditions declined rapidly. Many of the myths and traditions were recorded by government officials and missionaries and were certainly transformed in the process (Binney, Brown, Luomala, Orbell, Simms). There are widespread local cults and sects, the most bizarre perhaps being the various cargo cults of the Solomons and other island groups; but in New Zealand many Maori versions of Christianity emerged, including the Ringatu faith, which was largely Old Testament-based and became a major factor in the later campaigns of the Land Wars under the leadership of Te Kooti Rikirangi. Even today, the Ratana movement (a Maori sect comparable to European charismatic sects) exerts significant political influence (Turner and the *Australian Religion Index*).

Historically speaking, Polynesians have always been adaptable, reflecting perhaps the nature of oral as opposed to written traditions. As Witi Ihimaera expressed it in a letter to this author, the Maori after the wars retreated for a while to reassess how they should incorporate the best in the new (British) tradition into their own. A parallel change took place in the Pacific Islands, as the islanders paused to see how best they could continue their traditional ways but with less settler pressure. In Samoa, however, there was considerable opposition to proposed colonial changes in traditional local government, and even ongoing guerrilla warfare (the first use of the term *Mau Mau*, though it is actually cognate to the Maori *Hau Hau*), which forms the background to several of Albert Wendt's novels, where he excoriates the Samoans for their sloth and the British for their duplicity. In Fiji the presence of a sizable Indian population has caused a great deal of friction, since they were seen as taking control of trade (see Subramani). These disparate examples suggest that there is no single resolution.

New Zealand, which provides the clearest example of parallel and interacting developments, allows the reader to see: early colonial views of the cultures as separate; the evolving view of what constitutes a New Zealander, and consequently what it means to be a New Zealand writer; and the hard-won decision to express New-Zealandism via several cultural paths (Pearson, Ihimaera, Walker). This process is complicated by the need of most Pakeha writers to distance themselves from Britain. Although most early writing is distinctly derivative, later writers began seeking ways to address their placement at the end of the world, and since the 1930s a continuing sequence of writers has sought to remake the colonial myths (Curnow in poetry and Sargeson in prose provide outstanding examples). In very recent times, even these founding myths have come under fire. Maurice Shadbolt in *Strangers and Journeys* sought with mixed success to revisit the myth of the laconic settler, and further undermined it in *The Lovelock Version* (Martin, 1992). Moreover, both ethnic groups have had to come to grips with how they should write about their shared history. This is nowhere more evident than in the works of historians and novelists about the Land Wars (formerly, in the colonial tradition, "the Maori Wars"). James Belich and M. P. K. Sorrenson, as historians, have reconstructed the earlier, accepted history to incorporate a more balanced view of the Maori side, whereas Ihimaera and Shadbolt have undertaken literary reconstructions.

Although New Zealand's population is preponderantly of British stock, there are other ethnic groups—for example, Scandinavians—and the Maori population approaches in visibility that of African Americans in the United States. Whereas the other European traditions have not yet emerged to the extent so clear in Australia (Gunew's bibliography of other writings is extensive), some at least have produced important writing: for example, Yvonne Dufresne, who is of Danish descent. All minorities—and in this sense even the Pakeha majority is a minority in terms of worldwide English—have had to learn how to write within a major tradition without simply becoming provincial.

Early on, the Maori took advantage of the new written language to conduct their own propaganda campaigns via newspapers, but after their defeat they retreated into the backblocks, where they began to regroup. The oral traditions dwindled because there were few qualified to carry on the task; however, a renaissance at the turn of the century saw new leaders emerge who were determined to incorporate the Maori in the new Dominion on equal terms, if possible. The result was the emergence of Maoritanga, a neologism intended to convey the sense of Maoridom (see *Tihe Mauri Ora,* 1978). Incidentally, the very term *Maori* is of postcolonial construction, since the Maori were in fact prenational and tribal rather than national. *Maori* simply means "the people." Of great significance is the adoption of Maori as an official language, a first among ex-colonial countries. No matter how superficial, it allows, among other things, for the Maori to use their own language in judicial proceedings.

There has been recent Pakeha acknowledgment of former oppression, notably in the setting up in 1975 of a Waitangi Tribunal to determine how to restore proper land rights. There is a significant difference from the Native American rights movement in that the treaty is unique in having been signed as between equals and having recognized basic Maori rights, albeit with great problems because of the differences between the two texts (English and Maori). The Maori version was a missionary product and may have been faulty (see Hackshaw and Kingsbury). The textual reexamination of the treaty has become a symbol of the reexamination of relations between the two cultures (Sorrenson, Kawharu), engendering a significant (in both senses) literature.

The wars have long been a topic for writers (Martin, 1993), but the most important works have been the novels by Ihimaera and Shadbolt. In *The Matriarch* Ihimaera began a trilogy meant to explore the postcolonial development of the Maori, in its way a companion journey to that of his other novels and short stories, which had looked at the current Maori way of life and its contrast between town and country, tradition and adaptation (Martin, 1983). The novel is set at the time of Te Kooti's campaign for justice and land rights, even though the war itself only provides the groundwork for a much more extensive review of Maoritanga (Wertheim). It is a retelling of the accepted history from a Maori view-point, and also follows Maori models of discourse, particularly the protocols which govern speech at a public meeting; in one magnificent scene the matriarch faces down other craven Maori participants in a meeting with the (Pakeha) prime minister. The book also makes use of the Maori concept that all times are always present (Durix [1983] explores this in relation to the earlier novel, *Tangi*). In the mode of fact-fiction it also incorporates quotations from speeches by Maori members of Parliament and (unacknowledged) from historians. These have been challenged because they "distort" the original meaning, but the challenge fails to understand the differences between the oral tradition on which the novel is based and the superficial requirements of academic discourse.

Shadbolt, on the other hand, although he appears to revisit the Pakeha tradition (along the lines of Belich as a historian), takes a very different approach to some of the actual incidents. A comparison of the two novelists' accounts of the "Massacre at Matawhero" is instructive. The picture given in *Season of the Few* is of the Maori corrupted, but in a later novel about another, earlier campaign (*Monday's Warriors*), Shadbolt is much more sympathetic toward the Maori and ridicules the pretensions of the colonial forces. Together these two novelists show how New Zealand authors from both cultures are recasting the accepted history of their country. These major works are accompanied by many others, which range from a painstaking and far from pretty reconstruction of the Maori on the eve of European discovery, *Behind the Tattooed Face* by Heretaunga Pat Baker, to modern thrillers such as *Broken October* by Craig Harrison.

Although most major Maori writers of recent years have chosen to write in English, this decision has not been a rejection of their heritage but rather a way of extending that heritage to the Pakeha population (Ihimaera, 1966), which also needs to find a home in a new place. Ihimaera's early novels and short stories deal with the problems of adapting to a different way of regarding work and time and adapting the extended family to the single-family European approach. Similarly, Hone Tuwhare subtly changes European poetic forms to enable him to express Maori attitudes toward experience. Keri Hulme shares with Janet Frame a feminine view of life, which has been characterized by Lawrence Jones as the use of mirrors, suggesting both reflection and distortion, in contrast to the Pakeha male's use of "barbed wire," a symbol of a very different approach to land ownership and individualism (Jones, 1992). There have been some differences of critical opinion over Hulme's approach. Even as Ihimaera has been accused of antifeminism, Hulme has been accused of being anti-Maori, a writer using Pakeha forms to discuss Maori concerns (Stead and Fee). These critical reactions indicate how intermingled the various approaches have become.

In both traditions there has been a male-female contest. For many years New Zealand literature was dominated by a male coterie of academic writer/critics, and the contribution of women writers was downplayed as "female" writing. Despite the fact that much writing of New Zealand content was by women—e.g., Nelle Scanlan's Pencarrow series—and that some women writers such as Robin Hyde explored a totally different aspect of life from that written about by males, this contribution was largely overlooked (Stevens). Heather Roberts (1989) has sought to redress this balance by recovering much of the hidden history. While it has been impossible to ignore Janet Frame, earlier writers have not been given due recognition for their attempts to uncover for the general reader the role of women in a colonial society. Only now are Robin Hyde's works being accorded serious critical treatment. Katherine Mansfield represents a special case, as the only New Zealand writer who has been taken into the international canon. Even here, Witi Ihimaera's *Dear Miss Mansfield,* intended as a Maori retelling of many of her stories, particularly those surrounding the mystery of Maata, was seen as a less than desirable contribution to the centennial adulation, perhaps because it transgressed both racial and sexual divides.

These changing views of what constitutes New Zealand literature also imply a new view of what it means to be a contributor to a new literary tradition. There remains a need to reexamine the ways in which the various strands of New Zealand writing reinforce one another. Further critical attention should be given to the ways in which the races have been depicted in the literature. Here it is significant that the *New Zealand National Bibliography* omitted most writing in Maori. That omission has been remedied, and the new *Dictionary of New Zealand Biography* (in progress) will also appear in a Maori version. Moreover, the major *Oxford History of New Zealand Literature* carries the subtitle "In English"!

Pacific writing also reflects the coalescing of traditions. Additionally, it also illustrates the effects of geography, since the Pacific nations are, in effect, microstates separated by vast distances. Several collections of stories and poems are available which suggest that yet another kind of English literature is emerging. To date this has received only limited critical attention. Several essays in Chris Tiffin's *South Pacific Images* look at multiple views of Fijian society, and Subramani has explored the subculture of the imported Indian majority; but so far there has been no true critical overview. Even Norman Simms's *Silence and Invisibility* is now quite old, in terms of a very recent literature. Simms does point out quite properly that these literatures do not follow blindly either genre or mode of expression and show clearly the effects of orality.

Albert Wendt has been the most prominent of South Pacific writers. His several essays and collections of poems explore the world of the South Pacific islander. I have suggested elsewhere (1984) that there are parallels between Wendt and V. S. Naipaul. A Samoan of mixed German-Samoan heritage and educated in New Zealand, Wendt has given form to the ambivalent relationships not only within the islands but also with other powers, such as New Zealand and Australia. Since his move back to Fiji from New Zealand, his writing has grown in power and originality. These and other writings are in clear contrast to the langourous tales by Stevenson and Loti, the schoolboy stories of R. M. Ballantyne, and even James Michener's *South Pacific*. It is no longer possible to conceive of any basic book on the South Pacific as being confined to works by European authors, though A. Grove Day's *Pacific Islands Literature* will remain a useful compilation about the European Pacific.

In global power terms the island nations of the South Pacific have been overlooked, even while the new importance of the Pacific has been emphasized. They represent the first group of states that has sought a truly nuclear-free zone, which of course has brought them into conflict not only with France but also with the U.S. Few indeed have looked at the extensive literature surrounding the Greenpeace incident (when French saboteurs sank an ecological organization's vessel headed for the French nuclear-testing grounds), but they indicate just how little progress has been made in answering the very real concerns of the world's ministates. In this setting New Zealand has taken on the role of Pacific leader, even to the extent of endangering its relationship with the U.S., and there have been some signs of an emerging anti-Americanism. Access to the very limited South Pacific literature has been restricted by a European-centered view of literature, yet it shows one more example of the ways in which cultural traditions have adapted to the world surrounding them (Simms, 1986). The clash between cultures is not limited to the African or Asian continents, but extends to the ocean world of the Pacific and may suggest alternative ways of examining cultural adaptation.

Murray S. Martin, Summer 1994

▪ WORKS CITED

Australasian Religion Index. Vol. 1: 1989-. Wagga Wagga, NSW. Center for Information Studies, Charles Sturt University. Includes religious publications on racial/cultural issues.

Belich, James. *The New Zealand Wars and the Victorian Interpretation of Racial Conflict.* Auckland, N.Z. Auckland University Press. 1986.

A Bibliography of Australian Multicultural Writers. Sneja Gunew et al., eds. Geelong, Vic. Center for Studies in Literary Education, Deakin University. 1992.

Binney, Judith. "Maori Oral Narrative, Pakeha Written Texts: Two Forms of Telling History." *New Zealand Journal of History,* 20:1 (1987), pp. 16–28.

Brown, Ruth. "Maori Spirituality as a Pakeha Construct." *Meanjin,* 48:2 (1989), pp. 252–58.

Day, A. Grove. *Pacific Islands Literature: One Hundred Basic Books.* Honolulu. University Press of Hawaii. 1971.

Durix, Jean-Pierre. "Time in Witi Ihimaera's *Tangi.*" *Journal of New Zealand Literature,* 1 (1983), pp. 101–14.

Fee, Margery, "Why C. K. Stead Didn't Like Keri Hulme's *the bone people:* Who Can Write as Other." *Australian and New Zealand Studies in Canada,* 1 (Spring 1989), pp. 11–32.

Hackshaw, Frederika. "Nineteenth Century Notions of Aboriginal Title and Their Influence on the Interpretation of the Treaty of Waitangi." In *Waitangi: Maori and Pakeha Perspectives of the Treaty of Waitangi.* I. H. Kawharu, ed. Auckland, N.Z. Oxford University Press. 1989. Pp. 92–120.

Henderson, J. McLeod. *Ratana: The Origins and the Story of the Movement.* Wellington, N.Z. Polynesian Society. 1963.

Ihimaera, Witi. "Te Taha Maori (The Maori Side Belongs to Us All)." *New Zealand Bookworld,* 1966, pp. 3–6.

Jones, Lawrence. "Versions of the Dream: Literature and the Search for Identity." In *Cultural Identity in New Zealand.* David Novitz, Bill Willmott, eds. Wellington, N.Z. GP Books. 1984. Pp. 187–211.

———. *Barbed Wire and Mirrors.* 2d rev. ed. Dunedin, N.Z. Otago University Press. 1992.

Kingsbury, Benedict, "The Treaty of Waitangi: Some International Law Aspects." In *Waitangi: Maori and Pakeha Perspectives of the Treaty of Waitangi.* Pp. 121–57.

Luomala, Katherine. *Voices in the Wind: Polynesian Myths and Chants.* Rev. ed. Honolulu. Bishop Museum. 1986.

Martin, Murray S. "The Blending of Traditions: Witi Ihimaera's Contribution to New Zealand Literature." *International Fiction Review,* 1983, pp. 53–55.

———. "Rage, Order, and Disorder in the Islands: The Novels of Albert Wendt and V. S. Naipaul." *Perspectives on Contemporary Literature,* 10 (1984), pp. 33–39.

———. "*A Fair Enough Try: Strangers and Journeys.*" *Australian and New Zealand Studies in Canada,* 5 (Spring 1992), pp. 72–80.

———. "Cultural Reconsiderations in New Zealand Literature: The New Zealand Wars." Paper presented at the American Comparative Literature Association Conference, 1993.

Obeysekere, Gananath. *The Apotheosis of Captain Cook: European Mythmaking in the Pacific.* Princeton, N.J. Princeton University Press. 1992.

Orbell, Margaret. *Maori Poetry: An Introductory Anthology.* Auckland, N.Z. Heinemann. 1978.

———. "The Religious Significance of Maori Migration Traditions." *Journal of the Polynesian Society,* 84:3 (1990), pp. 1460–64.

Pearson, Bill. "Attitudes to the Maori in Some Pakeha Fiction." In his *Fretful Sleepers and Other Essays.* Auckland, N.Z. Heinemann. 1974. Pp. 46–71.

Roberts, Heather. *Where Did She Come From? New Zealand Women Novelists 1882–1987.* Wellington, N.Z. Allen & Unwin. 1989.

Simms, David R. *The Great New Zealand Myth: A Study of the Discovery and Origin Traditions of the Maori.* Wellington, N.Z. Reed. 1976.

Simms, Norman. *Silence and Invisibility: A Study of the Literatures of the Pacific, Australia, and New Zealand.* Washington, D.C. Three Continents. 1986.

Smith, Bernard. *Imagining the Pacific. In the Wake of Captain Cook.* New Haven, Ct. Yale University Press. 1992.

Sorrenson, M. P. K. "Toward a Radical Reinterpretation of New Zealand History: The Role of the Waitangi Tribunal." *New Zealand Journal of History,* 21:2 (1987). Reprinted in *Waitangi: Maori and Pakeha Perspectives of the Treaty of Waitangi.* Pp. 155–79.

South Pacific Images. Chris Tiffin, ed. St. Lucia, Qld. South Pacific Association for Commonwealth Literature and Language Studies. 1978. See especially the two essays on Fiji.

Stead, C. K. "Keri Hulme's 'the bone people' and the Pegasus Award for Maori Literature." *Ariel,* 16 (1985), pp. 101–8.

Stevens, Joan. *The New Zealand Novel 1860–1965.* 2d rev. ed. Wellington, N.Z. Reed. 1968.

Tihe Mauri Ora: Aspects of Maoritanga. Michael King, ed. Auckland, N.Z. Methuen. 1978.

Turner, Harold W. *Bibliography of New Religious Movements in Primal Societies.* Vol. 3: *Oceania.* Boston. G. K. Hall. 1990. Provides a remarkable overview of an extensive literature.

Walker, Dennis. "The Ethos of Place: Criticism, the Canon and the Literary Conversation of New Zealand." *Landfall,* 46:1 (March 1992), pp. 65–73.

Wertheim, Albert. *"The Matriarch"* (review). *CRNLE Journal,* 1 (1989), pp. 53–55.

Williams, John Brown. *The New Zealand Journal 1842–1844.* Salem, Ma. Peabody Museum of Salem / Brown University Press. 1956.

■ **LITERARY REFERENCES**

Baker, Heretaunga Pat. *Behind the Tattooed Face.* Whatmongo Bay, N.Z. Cape Catley. 1978.

Frame, Janet. *Intensive Care.* Wellington, N.Z. Reed. 1970. This is but one of many novels.

Harrison, Craig. *Broken October: New Zealand 1985.* Wellington, N.Z. Reed. 1976.

Hulme, Keri. *the bone people.* Wellington, N.Z. Spiral/Hodder & Stoughton. 1984.

Ihimaera, Witi. *Tangi.* London. Heinemann. 1973.

————. *Dear Miss Mansfield: A Tribute to Kathleen Mansfield Beauchamp.* London. Viking Penguin. 1989.

————. *The Matriarch.* London. Heinemann. 1989.

Into the World of Light: An Anthology of Maori Writing. Witi Ihimaera, D. S. Long, eds. Auckland, N.Z. Heinemann. 1982.

Seaweeds and Constructions. No. 7: *A Pacific Islands Collection.* Honolulu. 1983. Contains, as well as poems and stories, an essay by Albert Wendt titled "Towards a New Oceania" and an extensive bibliography.

Shadbolt, Maurice. *Strangers and Journeys.* New York. St. Martin's. 1956.

————. *Season of the Jew.* London. Hodder & Stoughton. 1986.

————. *Monday's Warriors.* London. Hodder & Stoughton. 1990.

Subramani. *The Fantasy Eaters: Stories from Fiji.* Washington, D.C. Three Continents. 1988.

Wendt, Albert. *Sons for the Return Home.* Auckland, N.Z. Longman Paul. 1973.

————. *Flying Fox in a Freedom Tree.* Auckland, N.Z. Longman Paul. 1974.

————. *Pouliuli.* Auckland, N.Z. Longman Paul. 1977.

————. *Leaves of the Banyan Tree.* Auckland, N.Z. Longman Paul. 1979.

Australian Literature since Patrick White

Back in the 1970s, James McAuley—poet, critic, and editor of the journal *Quadrant*—projected a scheme which he called Poets Anonymous. He had observed many troubled souls scattered around Australia who earnestly wanted to be poets, but he judged that most wrote poorly: sincerity is after all a hallmark of bad verse. McAuley believed that such an organisation as Poets Anonymous might help cure them of the desire to write. Sufferers would meet regularly to discuss their affliction. Moreover, the government would intervene constructively by paying them money *not* to write. This droll notion still has resonance in the 1990s, in the Australian literary scene after the death of Patrick White. McAuley's caustic, unfashionable perception of how little good Australian writing there was at the time deserves honest scrutiny again. So does his skepticism concerning the most appropriate kinds of subsidy which should be given to the arts.

Although his achievement is sometimes begrudged by local literary critics, White is one of the greatest and most uncomfortable artistic talents Australia has to show. He died in 1990, but his last significant novel, the marvelous romance *The Twyborn Affair,* had been published in 1979. In the 1980s his autobiography *Flaws in the Glass* (1981), which aroused antagonisms as it sought to settle scores, was the only substantial work that he produced. Years before his death, then, White had left other Australian novelists to their own courses and devices. All were sensible of his influence. Few resented it. He was a great enabler: principally because of White's efforts, all forms of Australian literature gained a surprising degree of popular and institutional recognition abroad. Foe of academics White assuredly was, yet he had done more than any other Australian writer to ensure that his national literature would not only be central to syllabuses at home but also become a subject of study in more than forty overseas countries. It is not altogether coincidence that fiction, which form he favoured, despite a long, inventive, and productive career as a playwright and an apprenticeship as a poet, is in an apparently more robust condition in contemporary Australia than is drama or verse.

All these literary kinds—or, more exactly, their practitioners—have for two decades benefited from financial assistance through the Literature Board of the Australia Council. This has been disbursed as writers' fellowships and as grants-in-aid to publishers. On 6 January 1993 the Literature Board was subjected to a vigorous attack in the Melbourne *Age* newspaper by Les

Murray, Australia's most accomplished and internationally its best-regarded poet. After acknowledging that without money from the Board "I could not have had the career in poetry I have had," Murray called nevertheless for its abolition. His central objection to the performance of the Board was that it had ill-treated a number of authors, awarding "niggardly and very sporadic support on unadmitted but obviously political grounds." Murray discerned a conspiracy: the penalising of writers for being his friends, for their supposed alignment with him "in a literary faction which in fact doesn't exist." On the other hand, he argued, the work of many of the beneficiaries of the largesse of the Literature Board exhibited "a scandalous lack of literary achievement."

Aggrieved and angry supporters of the Board retorted. The poet and novelist Rodney Hall, chairman of the Australia Council, attacked Murray's "wild and unconscionable statements." Others questioned the financial viability of Murray's alternative scheme of support for writers. Blood had been drawn. Murray's case did not lack advocates. In a column in the *Australian* newspaper of 25 February, "Scroungers Who Claim to Be Artists," Padraic P. McGuinness opened by declaring, "What a shabby lot our writers, artists, actors, book sellers and book publishers are!" His main target of attack was adjacent: "a whole new class of professional arts administrators of no talent whatsoever who can now make a living out of being hangers-on of the publicly-funded arts." He found this "milieu" to be "increasingly hermetic, uninterested in coming to terms with its 'public,' but rather self-sustaining and self-justifying on the government teat."

Stepping back from the personal acrimonies involved in this dispute, one can discern large and vexed issues concerning the present state of literature in Australia. The ills which Murray and McGuinness alleged are not special to Australia, but may be aggravated by the intestine nature of its cultural life. Consider a crucial aspect of cultural production: although there are numerous and fugitive publishers of poetry in Australia, Angus & Robertson (a famous, old, and honoured name, but not part of the HarperCollins group) has been by far the largest publisher of contemporary verse. For years Murray was the chief adviser for this programme, in which position his patronage and power became in their turn a cause of hostility from some other poets. In 1991, having found his recommendations persistently refused, Murray severed his connections with the firm. A number of poets on the old Angus & Robertson list subsequently moved elsewhere.

It remains the case, as it has long been, that thanks to Angus & Robertson, tyro poets found their way into

Thomas Keneally (*Gil Jain*)

print while established authors were kept there. Nevertheless, a recent sample of first volumes of verse under the Angus & Robertson imprint suggests a disturbing lack of discrimination about what is published. As one instance, two of the volumes of verse from this firm which appeared early in 1993 were Lynn Hard's *Dancing on the Drainboard,* which with technical accomplishment negotiated an austere tonal range from the sardonic to the mordant, and S. K. Kelen's jumbled, occasionally ranting, and intermittently competent *Dingo Sky.* Such a disparity of performance is not untypical of verse published anywhere. What it indicates, however, is not so much the variegated landscape of Australian poetry, but a lack of courage to make judgments of its quality, whether these should have come initially from publishers or later from reviewers and academics with a professional stake in the heart of Australian literature.

Unpalatable as the suggestion may be in several quarters, it is perhaps too easy to be published in Australia, whether poetry or fiction is in question. Murray trenchantly made a similar point in his *Age* article, where he regretted a situation "in which publishers to ten multinationals indifferently bring out good and bad Australian literary books and scarcely bother to market them because the Literature Board pays for them anyway." Only the University of Queensland Press, among large-scale publishers of works of Australian literature and criticism, is not owned overseas. The multinational publishers, in Murray's view, maintain token Australian lists in order to be able to dump other stock in the local market.

This is not altogether a fair account of the activities of Penguin Australia, which for many years has been the leading publisher of new Australian fiction, besides being a keen promoter of what it has acclaimed as fresh writing talent. Vital as its enterprise has been, Penguin is also open to Murray's blanket charge of publishing "indifferently" good and bad books. This is not only a matter of individual taste and judgment. In the present climate, perhaps more readily since White's death, and under factional pressures from within university departments of literature, questions of quality, issues of evaluation have been rendered hard to pose and confront. Some particular instances may point to the extent of the problem.

White's durability made critics to a degree neglectful of or at times too sanguine about the sustained and successful careers of novelists who were his juniors: Morris West, Thea Astley, Jessica Anderson, Thomas Keneally, and David Malouf among them. In the restless, envious, modish cultural climate of Australia, long-haul and financially well-remunerated careers have tended to be over-looked or disparaged. The fault, snobbishly discerned, of some of these authors has indeed often been to write copiously, to exploit the genres of popular fiction, to sell well, in paperback and at airports. Jon Cleary, Colleen McCullough, and Peter Corris, besides Keneally and West, have suffered most in this way, so that their versatility and iconoclasm have been neglected, let alone the salutary example of craft and dedication which they have set.

Instead, busloads of Australian writers have been puffed briefly, then soon forgotten, and for reasons at times extrinsic to their literary merit. Penguin published Mark Henshaw's first novel, *Out of the Line of Fire,* jubilantly in 1988, the nation's bicentennial year. Intelligent, intricate, and erotic, capable of being put (in several estimates) in Calvino's company, the book became a token of Australian cultural maturity, of its emancipation from parochial concerns at long last, and at age two hundred. Sadly, there is no news of Henshaw in the 1990s. Wherever he has gone (perhaps along the old expatriate's route to Europe, or the more recently trodden wisdom trails of Asia), Henshaw's first novel has had no successor. That may be, not least, because

of the burden of expectation which was placed upon him.

Out of the Line of Fire sold well in Australia. Abroad, it seemed less exotic and received less warm regard. Encouraged by this measure of success, however, Penguin puffed even harder (as the next Henshaw) Julian Davies, author of the feeble and pretentious *Revival House* (1991). Literary judgment was being asked to surrender not only to a promotion campaign but also to the presumption that Australia ought to be able to produce experimental, self-referential, postmodern fiction. It is in a similar cause that some academics have sought to advance the reputation of the increasingly opaque fiction of Gerald Murnane, whose most recent novel was *Velvet Waters* (1990). Inspecting such business, it is difficult not to feel that some modern Australian novels are being written to order for institutionally occupied or hampered literary theorists, who can then impose these "texts" on their hapless students.

In consequence of these processes, talented writers of fiction, capable of resistance to literary fashion, regularly receive less than their critical due in Australia. By Murray's reckoning, they are the ones who are also more likely to be given less public money to continue with their labours. Perhaps every culture belatedly celebrates its unaccommodating talents. Those who deserve recognition among Australian novelists include Marion Campbell and Kate Grenville (both for several years silent), Brian Castro (whose *Double-Wolf* of 1991 deservedly won him a couple of literary-prize cheques), and Alan Gould. The latter had to cope at first with that evasive label "poet novelist." Regarded less slickly, his novel *To the Burning City* (1991) is a serious engagement with the interrelation of provenance and conscience in Australia.

In so abstract a statement, that might be admitted as a master theme of modern Australian writing. It has not always led to such accomplished fiction as Gould's, Astley's, or Hall's, to name three pertinent figures. Too many poems, slabs of too many novels are obliged exercises in spurious guilt, most frequently concerned with the mistreatment of the Aboriginal peoples by the ancestors of some Australians. The question which Northrop Frye contended was the dominant one in a postcolonial culture, not "Who am I?" but "Where is here?," has been glibly answered too often in Australia. A burden of blame has been shouldered so avidly as to point to a death wish near the heart of Australian literature and in the talkative reaches of the public life of the nation. As an unfortunate corollary, Aboriginal authors such as Oodgeroo Noonucal (formerly Kath Walker) and Mudrooroo Narogin (once Colin Johnson) have suffered from the suspension of critical judgment of their work. In effect, they have been put on cultural reservations, where they are privileged but not free.

In 1993 Morris West declared closed his career as a novelist. He introduced *The Lovers* by asserting that "this is the last novel which I shall write." In both positive and negative respects, West's has been an exemplary Australian literary life. Benefiting from no government sponsorship but from good fortune (a pope's timely death), West became a best-selling author with such books as *The Shoes of the Fisherman* (1963). His reward at home was an envy-inspired critical disdain. One searches without profit for his name in the *Oxford History of Australian Literature* (1981) and finds an offhand mention—coupling West with another internationally successful author, Thomas Keneally—in the *Penguin New Literary History of Australia* (1988). Disciplined exercises of craft, if in the forms of popular fiction, have not recommended West to the academic community. Yet his grasp of geopolitics, his subtle analysis of the nature of diplomacy, let alone the exclamations of generous anxiety concerning the fate of Australia in his novels, deserve more than benign neglect.

Not that West, or Keneally, has suffered from want of appreciative readers. Keneally's rapacious imagination, the historical span of his fiction from the Hundred Years' War to World War II, and his mannerist style and intuitive grasp of the procedures and terrors and melodrama make him—with appropriate hyperbole—Australia's Balzac. Accordingly, he has been stigmatised as unruly and too prolific. *A Woman of the Inner Sea* (1992) was a daring success, being at once a dissection of political evil, fond vitalisation of Australian myth, and terrible encounter with domestic pain. Turning aside from picaresque adventures in Australia's past (*Illywhacker,* 1985; *Oscar and Lucinda,* 1988), Peter Carey—with Keneally, Australia's only winner of the Booker Prize for fiction—also addressed suburban horrors with his latest novel, *The Tax Inspector* (1991).

By comparison with Keneally's prodigal output and the massive span of two of Carey's novels, David Malouf's production has been taut and measured. Known first as a poet, he has turned increasingly to fiction. In *The Great World* (1990) he reinvigorated the saga form (as White had done in the 1950s with *Voss* and *The Tree of Man*). Doing so, he reckoned with elemental features of Australian society and culture which have been incompletely or reluctantly expressed, among them the mental and physical warring between men and women across a chasm of differing aspirations and perceptions; the contradictory yearnings for roots and rootlessness, for provenance and anonymity; the desire to be part of history yet free of its burdens.

The notion that they are prisoners of history, inordinately bearing the burden of memories of the past, has hampered weaker Australian novelists but liberated stronger ones. Carey, Keneally, Malouf, as well as Anderson, Hall, Robert Drewe (with his version of the Ned Kelly story, *Our Sunshine* [1991]), and Jean Bedford, have emphatically and often turned to Australia's past for their materials and have explored the confines of the abstract prison house of history. Sometimes they have written veritable captivity narratives. Malouf's most recent novel, *Remembering Babylon* (1993), and Hall's latest, *The Second Bridegroom* (1991), venture into the origins of Australia by means of tales of the convict system and of first encounters between Europeans and Aborigines. Malouf's *Great World* encompassed both the literal imprisonment of two Australian soldiers, Digger and Vic, after the fall of Singapore to the Japanese, and the sequestration of Australia from international affairs and from the possibilities of epic at which the title of the novel gestures. Malouf examines a resonant matter in the national history: the ambiguous returns for Australia at those times when it has sought to enter the wider world by going to war. That for many men this enabled escape from the prison of domesticity and marriage is another of the novel's disquieting suggestions.

It would be gratifying warmly to second the applause which Elizabeth Jolley's fiction regularly receives. Her novel *Cabin Fever* (1990) dourly extended the strain of autobiographical fiction which she had begun with *My Father's Moon* (1989). Droll, grim, an astute analyst of loneliness, Jolley survived the twoscore rejections of her first novel to become the most uncritically praised of contemporary Australian authors. A consistent producer of fiction, she has not risked slipping from fickle and amnesiac public consciousness in the manner of such accomplished writers as C. J. Koch (whose last novel, *The Doubleman,* appeared in 1984) or Helen Garner (who broke a long silence with *Cosmo Cosmolino* in 1992). Writing in a season when women authors tend to receive a relatively privileged hearing which few of them seek, Jolley may now loom as the biggest name among Australian novelists since Patrick White, but she may prove to be one of the soonest forgotten.

In the field of drama, where White, Malouf, and Keneally among novelists have all strayed, the 1990s present a barren prospect. Only David Williamson has prospered since the renaissance of Australian drama, which had its beginnings in Melbourne in the 1960s, based on the Australian Performing Group and the La Mama companies. Disgruntled with the response to his experimental theatre, Jack Hibberd abandoned playwriting for fiction in the 1980s. Undeterred by critics of the slickness of his plays, Williamson (Australia's Alan Ayckbourn) continues to produce a successful work each year, most recently *Top Silk* (1990), *Siren* (1991), and *Money and Friends* (1992). He has by now created the fullest account of middle-class mores (those of his audience) and the largest body of cheerless comedy which Australian drama has to show.

Of younger dramatists who exhibit signs of stamina, Stephen Sewell had two plays performed in 1991, *Sisters* and *King Golgrutha,* while Michael Gow's *Furious* was staged in the same year. It is hard not to feel that the brio of the 1960s and 1970s has been lost. The Australian Performing Group has long been disbanded. Dramatists' energies are increasingly channeled into television (Gow wrote the script for "Edens Lost" in 1989) and film (where Williamson has numerous credits). The 1960s now take their place as another of Australian drama's false dawns, while the audiences won then to radical and aggressive theatre have withered away.

The landscape of Australian poetry seems to be dotted with argumentative figures at various stages of their progress through middle age. Their public profiles may unfortunately be determined more by the rancorous disputes in which they are engaged about funding bias (as Mark O'Connor was before Murray) than by their poetry. Besides Murray, whose most recent volumes are *Dog Fox Field* (1990) and *Translations from the Natural World* (1992), the subtle, witty, and intellectually strenuous verse of Gwen Harwood commands the local scene. Her *Collected Poems* appeared in 1991. Another writer of stature (and one more adversary of Murray), Robert Gray, had his revised and expanded *Selected Poems* published in 1990. In recent years, bitter feuding within poetry's small world has been carried on by means of anthology (among others), notably in the *Penguin Book of Modern Australian Poetry* (1991), edited by John Tranter and Philip Mead.

Standing sardonically apart from such squabbling is one of White's many ex-friends, and the only modern Australian writer to bear comparison with him as a savagely comic anatomist of his contemporary society. That is Barry Humphries, whose *Neglected Poems and Other Creatures* (1991) gathered his satiric sour apples from the last three decades. In the following year Humphries ventured into autobiography, a genre that has attracted and distracted some of Australia's finest writers during the last quarter-century. His *More Please* chronicled those early years in Melbourne which since have ripely furnished his satire. The upsurge of autobiographical writing dates from the 1960s, when Australian authors began to feel that the fabric of their history and society was sufficiently rich to form a background for the work

of romantic introspection. White's *Flaws in the Glass* belongs to this movement, as do the much-celebrated *A Fortunate Life* (1981), by the World War I veteran and working-class autodidact Bert Facey, and *My Place* (1987), another work concerned with the painful search for origins, written by the part-Aboriginal Sally Morgan. Facey found his book turned into a television miniseries. Morgan's was soon fodder for school and university syllabuses. Amnesia may afflict Australian culture, but opportunism is its complement.

The literary weather of the 1990s is acrid and unsettled. Writers who have mastered their craft find themselves jostled aside by one-book wonders, who, promoted too hard too early, are then abandoned. Those of the few who have enjoyed commercial success—a handful of novelists, Williamson among playwrights—find that their other, ambiguous rewards include critical suspicion and envy. Reputations, however honorably won, are begrudged and undermined. A terrible want of generosity obtains. In such circumstances it is all the more necessary to salute the durable achievements of those writers who have welcomed the liberties which White's success afforded them, then made their solitary ways.

Peter Pierce, Summer 1993

Dreaming Wholeness: David Malouf's New Stories

In 1998, David Malouf delivered the Boyer Lectures, an annual radio series sponsored by the Australian Broadcasting Corporation; his presentations were later published as *The Spirit of Play: The Making of Australian Consciousness.* "Play," that fine postmodern term, broadens wonderfully in the postcolonial atmosphere of Australia, denoting most usefully, along with drama and other circumstances of production, the deliberate slackness that is built into a ship's rigging to let masts and spars flex without damage, where taut trim in a storm would shatter them. This play, in turn, feeds into the subtitle's similar implication of continuing process, in which "making" suggests an ongoing construction and the avoidance of a definite article suggests that multiplicity and variation have replaced the uniformity in what older fashions of national characterization would have styled "*the* Australian consciousness." This maneuvering is highly representative of Malouf's style as a writer of fiction, especially in the new story collection, *Dream Stuff* (2000). But it goes more deeply than that.

The "spirit of play," of course, echoes the most common description of Aboriginal consciousness as "the spirit of place," a conjunction that Malouf wants his auditors to take seriously. To substitute "play" for "place" is to do exactly that: to play with words, to suggest intersecting modes of consciousness and methods of learning, to exchange the suppositions of permanence and objectivity implied by fixed location for admissions of contingency and self-consciousness. It is also to claim that the phrase, and the indigenous consciousness it describes, may be translated meaningfully by later participants. Even so, the notion of play, however vital and energizing to contemporary societies, has here built into it a disturbing reminder of colonial appropriation, as indeed the exploration of historical influences upon a present consciousness has been an ongoing concern in Malouf's work.

Aboriginal culture, as Malouf has referred to it recently, is most notable for types of dynamism and regeneration that challenge monopolistic European cultural definition, while suggesting, on the other hand, that the dominant culture may forget how important its own forms of rapid adaptation can be.

> This capacity to re-imagine things, to take in and adapt, might be something we should learn from, something that comes closer than a nostalgia for lost purity to the way the world actually is, and also to the way it works. It might remind us of something we need to keep in mind: which is the extent to which Aboriginal notions of inclusiveness, of re-imagining the world to take in all that is now in it, has-worked to include *us*. (*Spirit*, 59)

This clever *re*-appropriation of indigenous culture, which replaces descriptions of "timeless" tribal identity, ultimately licenses the "play" by means of the "spirit" that precedes and surrounds it. Such a process may initiate deep changes within human character, which may, for all their contingency and even violence, include redemptive possibilities for happiness and health.

Dynamism, and the continuing sense of individuality in progress, are central to the models of consciousness in Malouf's fiction. These processes of play are clear, for example, in Malouf's praise of Australian poets of his generation: they

> . . . created a body of poetry in which all the common phenomena of our Australian world — flowers and trees and birds, and helmet shells and ghost-crabs and bluebottles — had been translated out of their first nature into the secondary and symbolic one of consciousness in that great process of culture, and also of acculturation, that creates a continuity at last between the life without and the life within. It is one of the ways — a necessary one — by which we come at last into full possession of a place. Not legally,

David Malouf (*Robert H. Taylor*)

and not just physically, but as Aboriginal people, for example, have always possessed the world we live in here: in the imagination. (*Spirit*, 39)

Meaning is not inherent, then, but emerges through translation within the structured yet emphatically accommodative symbolism of an individual consciousness; Aboriginal process becomes a great "example" for postcolonial Australia "as it painstakingly redefines itself, reclaiming its history and implanting a homegrown culture" (Conrad, 25). But possible frameworks of translation must be limitless, as the mind moves "towards what is, in effect, a convergence of indigenous and non-indigenous understanding, a collective spiritual consciousness that will be the true form of reconciliation here" (*Spirit*, 39–40).

Reconciliation, however, cannot come easily, for uplifting translation and convergence imply their opposite, resistant or restrictive mediation by means of rationalization and solipsism. Throughout *Dream Stuff*, individuals struggle within their perceptions of the world: they work to acknowledge, first, that conscious construction of identity is very difficult; second, that self-knowledge often results in a reflexive distrust that threatens esteem and accommodation; and third, that the recognitions achieved through translation and convergence are severely limited by failures of enactment, and above all by mortality.

Dream Stuff is another playful title, an intersection of Western high culture and Aboriginal influence. Its glancing reference to *The Tempest* ("We are such stuff as dreams are made on," 4.1.156–57) embeds the postcolonial inheritance of high-cultural irony; the suggestion of the Aboriginal Dreaming or Dreamtime, the ongoing spiritual regeneration that manifests itself in seemingly continuous physical reality, characterizes an Australian present informed by converging influences and intersecting mythologies. In between, the pettiness of "stuff" is both a playful deflation and a warning that serious human possibilities can be reduced by frustration and deflection: when circumstances offer enough routine, enough well-being, enough self-esteem, the easiest way to cope with the enormous burden of the convergent present is to ignore it.

The most extreme form of bland ignorance, along with its most shocking reversal, is in "Lone Pine," the story of an elderly couple murdered at an outback campsite. The brutality of the killing, however, is not as shocking as the irreversibility it represents, the realization that Harry and May Picton have done so little with their time before—or, allegorically, during—"the first real trip they had ever taken, the trip of their lives" (102).

> Back in Hawthorn they had a paper run. Seven days a week and twice on weekdays, Harry tossed the news over people's fences on to the clipped front lawns: gun battles in distant suburbs, raids on marijuana plantations, bank holdups, traffic accidents, baby bashings, the love lives of the stars. (102)

The Pictons have managed to evade translation, disseminating information from which they do not benefit. The world of clipped front lawns (introduced species) and routinized experiences (artificial upkeep) can be safely maintained as the sum of existence, and this containment of events and circumstances imposes its small scale upon all information. Harry's paper route becomes the equal of the continent:

> He had reckoned it up once. In twenty-seven years bar a few months he had made his round on ten thousand seven hundred occasions in twelve thousand man-hours, and done a distance of a hundred thousand miles. That is, ten times around Australia. Those were the figures. (103)

If every mile equals every other mile, all days are the same, all experience contained within an understood range, there is no need for self-examination and no such

thing as wider inquiry. Where differentiation begins to occur, it can be reduced to nullity. May relates to Harry a constant run of gossip, to which "he did not listen," a list of "victims of life's grim injustice, or of man's unpredictable cruelty" in which individual tragedies can be deadened by the sheer length of their reiteration; but she too limits the challenge of experience by joining a fundamentalist church which reduces all events to sin or blessing.

With no interest in imaginative translation of raw event into meaning, Harry and May caravan through the interior in a bubble of sameness.

> Driving up here was dreamlike. As the miles of empty country fell away with nothing to catch the eye, no other vehicle or sign of habitation, your head lightened and cleared itself — of thoughts, of images, of every wish or need. Clouds filled the windscreen. You floated.
>
> The clouds up here were unreal. (101–2)

Actually, Malouf is tricky here, inserting just enough of the language of incipient transcendence, enough of Harry's mind clearing itself beyond ego and material, to imply the possibility of a leap where none actually occurs; the exalted vocabulary simply collapses, reduced to postcard size in a world where the unfamiliar is pushed away into emptiness and unreality. Where Malouf traces imaginative growth to the landscape of his childhood—"I think it's wonderful to have grown up beside something called Deception Bay"(Koval)—the Pictons reduce the outback to the banality of home. They play at being "explorers, each day pushing on into unknown country" (104), and then crush that awesome possibility into cuteness, naming their campsites "according to whatever little event or accident occurred that made it memorable—Out-of-Nescaf Creek, Lost Tin-opener, One Blanket Plains." Their vision is impoverished by familiarization, because for Malouf "Australian social forms seem to have little depth or substance when set against the compelling continuities of the natural world" (Indyk, 87). While it is certainly not their fault that a young man shoots them in a place they were going to call Lone Pine "unless something unexpected occurred," there may be complicity in such severe reduction of the world to crises of instant coffee and canned food, and perhaps in the willingness to give the name Lone Pine to yet another spot on earth. The slightness of their domestic realm makes the violence of their murders all the more shocking (Kellaway), but the point is how little they have made of their time, how small has been the compass of their world—and worse, of their curiosity about it.

In *Dream Stuff,* the brutality of such stories as "Lone Pine" and "Night Training," along with the sudden violence in "Dream Stuff" and the slower psychological erosion in "Sally's Story," suggests a metaphysical reciprocity at work: not that characters deserve what erupts upon them, but that, electively or not, they subscribe to a world view in which violence is one of the elementary structures of experience. Such a regime prefers narratives based upon conflict, not mutuality or reciprocity. Problems are arranged in patterns resolved through competitions which result in victors and vanquished; these reinforce themselves by overwhelming other possibilities so thoroughly that eventually individuals assume there is no other narration in which to participate, and assume their places, without actual combat, in hierarchies that are then said to be natural or instinctual. The irreversibility of such a structure, the characterization of past and present as competitions so violent that it is impossible to envision a future in other terms, describes a constant jettisoning of elements perceived to be "defeated"—objects, concepts, and narrations that have become outworn, inefficient, or irrelevant. Yet the after-images of these discards retain a certain power in their absence, as unanswered questions, unattempted recourses, or, as Malouf says, "unfinished business" (Koval; also Skea). Because the historical dimension of conflict is unidirectional, there can be no return to gather discards, even though they may later seem desirable; the resulting sense of irrecoverability generates increasing senses of alienation and frustration, which search in the present for something or someone to blame and thus produce yet more desperately perceived conflict. Reconciliation therefore requires a different model, not simply of operations and analogical perceptions, but a new basic structure that permits recovery through visions of reversibility and inclusion.

One of the characters in "Great Day," the last and most expansive story of *Dream Stuff,* advances such a new vision of continuity and encompassment toward its ultimate. Clem Tyler describes a reverse extension of current radio astronomy, a receiver deep in space gathering sounds from Earth that, given the distance they travel, are historical by now—a factor that places Australia in a particular position of coming-into-being:

> "What it picks up, it's made that way, is heartbeats, just that. Every heartbeat on the planet, it doesn't miss a single one, not one is missed. . . .
>
> "Once upon a time, all this bit of the planet, all this — land mass, this continent — was silent, there was no sound at all, you wouldn't have known it was here. Silence. Then suddenly a blip, a few little signs of life. . . . Then a rush, till there are millions. . . . Only it takes such a long time for the sound to travel across all that space that the receiver doesn't even know as yet that we've arrived — us whites, I mean. But that doesn't matter . . . because we *are* here, aren't we?. . . If we imagined ourselves out there and concentrated hard enough, really concentrated, we could hear it too, all of it, the whole sound coming towards us, all of it. It's possible. Anything is possible. Nothing is lost. Nothing ever gets *lost*." (179–81)

The leap of imagination to extend the viewpoint seems both ordinary, a common extrapolation of time and space beyond direct observation, and marvelous, a view of human existence from a baseline so long that perspective becomes panoptic and synchronous.

In fact, Clem's metaphor of encompassed space and time establishes the first principle necessary for building a definitional structure to liberate consciousness from the failures of self-defensiveness. Essentially nonverifiable through logical distinctions of factuality and denotation, the first-principle unity here described as "nothing is lost" is nonetheless measurable in terms of responses that approach nearer to or recede farther from its implications of inclusiveness. Such a model copes with play more successfully than orders based upon categorical limitation and hierarchy. It accommodates contemporary spatializations of fractal patterning and sensitive dependence, and temporal factors of layering and synchronicity. Validly translating scientific terms to discursive ones (Oliver, 126), it signals the collapse of rhetorical figures of analogy and simile, as the neutrality that permits the mind to look in one direction and then to look comparatively in another disappears into simultaneous affective unity; individual differentiation is retained, perhaps even accentuated—the receiver hears every heartbeat—by the breakdown of systems that previously licensed divisive generalizations based upon origin, affiliation, or activity.

With "nothing is lost" as the first principle, the territory of consciousness in *Dream Stuff* is established by Henry James's discussion of writing from experience, which Malouf cites in an interview with Ramona Koval.

> The power to guess the unseen from the seen, to trace the implication of things, to judge the whole piece by the pattern, the condition of knowing life in general so completely that you are well on your way to knowing any particular corner of it — this cluster of gifts may almost be said to constitute experience, and they occur in country and in town, and in the most differing stages of education. If experience consists of impressions, it may be said that impressions *are* experience, just as (have we not seen it?) they are the very air we breathe. Therefore, if I should certainly say to a novice, "Write from experience and experience only," I should feel this was rath-

er a tantalizing monition if I were not careful immediately to add, "Try to be one of those on whom nothing is lost!" (James, 427)

Just try—the effort needed to apprehend unity involves extreme effort: guessing and tracing patterns, separating and then synthesizing a vastness of sources including the unexpected, scrutinizing and validating the flow of impressions as they coalesce into what can be articulated as experience, followed by pushing that articulation toward the verifiability which an audience can acknowledge as meaning. Play, indeed.

Clem Tyler's image of the cosmic heartbeat receiver follows a car accident—perhaps echoing the one that nearly killed Robert Hughes—in which the space and time of the continent are summed up in a terrible instant. Late at night, three years before, a Aboriginal child playing "chicken" had leaped in front of Clem's car.

> Clem swung the wheel, narrowly avoiding the boy, and the whole continent — the whole three million square miles of rock, tree-trunks, sand, fences, cities — came bursting through the windscreen into his skull. The remaining hours of the night had lasted for fourteen months. It had taken another year to locate the bit of him that retained the habit of speech. (142)

Nearly every other character in *Dream Stuff*, except those we have seen retreating into limitation and defensiveness, pays a more or less heavy price for acquiring a sense of inclusiveness and proof from loss.

The first story in the volume, "At Schindler's," first raises issues of continuity through their opposite, the differences between the young protagonist's routine life and the "broken" or varied rhythm of a resort holiday during World War II: "Jack loved these broken continuities. They were reassuring. You let things drop out of sight, then you picked them up again further on. Nothing was lost. Even a single day could have that pattern" (9). Reassurance amid brokenness is an important term of experience, offering Jack a vision of potential wholeness to begin accommodating his father's death, his mother's affair with an American soldier (importantly, Lorenzo notes, an aircraft navigator), and his own developing consciousness of psychological and physical boundedness. The other component of Jack's recognition is just as important, however: the sense that the pattern could be discerned in a single day, and expand from there to a larger ordering of time and space that proposes ultimately to encompass all experience—and thus to provide a metaphysical structure that moves beyond the defensive world-models of categorical limitation and unabating competition.

In a pivotal incident, Jack inadvertently sees his mother and the American making love. Often said to be traumatizing for a child, the scene instead turns to reconciliation as Jack donates to the adults his own thrill in sheer physicality:

> What Jack was reminded of was moments when, in a kind of freedom that only his body had access to, he ceased for a time to be a boy and became a porpoise, rolling over and under the skin of sunlight all down the length of the Bay. Under the waves, then over. Entering, emerging. From air to water, then back again. (20)

In this moment of animal self-location, Jack understands the lovers not as elders or authorities, but in their full animation; through this Jamesian "trying," the information is moved to a new level, as Jack's mind earns the wisdom that only his body has known until then.

In a flash of lightning, Jack believes he sees his absent father watching the lovemaking as well.

> Jack strained to make him out there, to hold on to the sight of him. And realized, with a little shock, what the apparition really was. Not a ghost, but himself, fantastically elongated in the glass of the old-fashioned wardrobe. (21)

Having worked to synthesize the present, the physical and emotional being of others along with himself, Jack's vision expands to receive the past, as acceptance of his father's continuing influence, and to project a future, in the figure of himself at adult size. "His father would not be coming back" (22), and he must acknowledge in his mother the kinds of emotions and appetites that he knows he will later claim for himself as an adult. Jack earns his vision when he accepts that reconciliation involves effort and even pain: for other characters, the lesson is more direct.

In the title story, Colin, an author, returns to Brisbane for a reading nearly thirty years after he left as a teenager.

> He had long understood that one of his selves, the earliest and most vulnerable, had never left this place, and that his original and clearest view of things could be recovered only through what had first come to him in the glow of its ordinary light and weather. (36)

Evocation, however, has become suspiciously easy; the layers of identity, in Colin's initial version, are too heavily controlled by a present persona which is "always 'distinguished'" (61). Distracted by self-defensiveness, he is vulnerable to the real, dangerous slippage that occurs in events "he would have rejected outright if they had presented themselves to him as the components of a plot. They were too extravagant for the web of quiet incident and subtle shifts of power that were the usual stuff of his fiction" (49). Colin's "usual stuff" has distracted him from the "dream stuff"—the world revealed in the true range of "its constituent elements, its details" (Indyk, 92)—so that he is unprepared for the shock that follows. A deranged man attacks him, convinced that Colin is his wife's lover, and then draws a knife and begins to slash himself. Colin grapples with the man, is slightly injured before the police arrive, and spends the night in jail before the incident can be clarified.

The gap between events and Colin's ability to explain himself is the territory of Jamesian experience, presumably the area that Colin never considered in his fiction: it certainly matches both the flaws in his analysis of childhood in Brisbane and the faults in the assumptions he brings to his return there. Released, finished with his public appearance, Colin falls asleep in his hotel room and dreams "in a stretch of time where before and after had no meaning" (62). He returns to his earliest memory, a scene in which he cradles the family dog as it dies in the space under a Brisbane house built on piles, much like the ones Malouf describes in *12 Edmondstone Street*. In his dream, Colin holds the dog, and its heart makes "a regular, reassuring thump against his ribs" (63)—not the dog's own ribs but Colin's. He returns in that timeless dreaming to the earliest sympathy he has known, a space where physicality and affect are inseparable; dreaming now in the clarity following reduction and fear, Colin can begin the difficult work of recovering a unity that could have been his all along.

The recognition earned by the protagonist in "Sally's Story" is equally dependent upon acknowledging pain. In the belief that it will help her train as an actress, Sally Prentiss becomes a "widow," a prostitute specializing in long-term relationships; for "a week or ten days as required" (74), she lives with American soldiers on leave in Australia during the Vietnam War. "She did not think it would be damaging" (75), but the men are all alike in hoping or demanding that sharing an apartment with "a wife out of the porno magazines" (75) would offer an illusion of normalcy solid enough to protect them from their recent experience. Based upon denial, such images of completion are unstable, obviously, but Sally is surprised that she is victimized almost as effectively as her combat-scarred clients. Her defenses are surprisingly thin.

> "Oh Delilah," she said to herself in a voice of commiseration, "not another one!" She had a whole cast of voices that she used for bucking herself up or giving herself a good talking-to, or for commenting, in a half-mocking way, on the irony of things and the rebounds and reversals that made up her world. (75)

As in "Lone Pine," Malouf's narration here emphasizes the character's own limited vocabulary—her silly evasions of self-examination—and then leads into a recognition which remains true to that language. Indeed, the play of inclusiveness must permit such a character to "try" for the Jamesian center from her own point of view, using the tools realistically available to her, and here it does: "She began to feel haunted. By so much that remained unfinished, unresolved in her relations with this or that one of them" (80). The first authentic move Sally makes to close the gap of unfinished business is to visit the country town from which she escaped.

At a wedding, Sally's mother points out Brad Jenkins, a man whose wife has left him with two children, and begins to generalize about "these happy-go-lucky fellers" (84) before abruptly stopping. Sally, "with her new understanding of these things," realizes that her mother is actually describing her own life, her own husband who abandoned the family when the children were small. Thus, Sally's prostitution here is the key to re-envisioning her mother with the same kind of humane allowance that Jack finds in "At Schindler's." Of course, Sally and Brad come together, but the approach to intimacy here includes a four-year-old and a baby, which means that definitions of love and characterizations of lovers must broaden considerably. In the middle of their first night together, Brad gets up to comfort the little girl and brings her back to bed with him.

> So there was that, too.
>
> She began to laugh.
>
> "What is it?" he asked; "what's so funny? She won't be in the way. You go on back t' sleep. I'm used to it." And reaching across the baby, he had another hand for her, his fingers gently stroking her cheek. (91–92)

Here, Malouf shows the assembly of a new order, where the ability to comfort is genuine and boundless, where nothing need be lost and physicality leads to understanding that accommodation can be made for all, small and large, at the same time.

Colin's imagination expands through contact with hard, mad pain; Sally's experience as a prostitute translates into humane acknowledgment. Acknowledgments of dislocation and instability seem ironically basic in attempts to envision the center where nothing is lost (Butler, 192); however, the basis of these movements—that is, the position from which one is alienated or dislocated—must be nonrestrictive. Any set of circumstances should be capable of producing the necessary movement, and any voice should theoretically provide the vocabulary for expressing the changes of scale and awareness that accompany it: given enough time, even Harry Picton's postcard language might have expanded beyond its self-described limits. Malouf tests this implication of the basic Jamesian principle by setting several stories in *Dream Stuff* within first-person narrations of very limited, highly structured points of view.

Amy, the narrator of "Closer," is a nine-year-old girl in an extended Pentecostal family. The language she knows is heavy with biblical phrasing, and the structures it articulates are based upon the unquestioned authority of the adults around her and the enclosed space of their farm. Within these, she attempts to understand the exclusion of her Uncle Charles, who at Christmas and Easter drives from Sydney in his silver BMW and stands outside the fence while the family eats the holiday dinner. Amy does not understand his license plate, GAY 437, or his apparent exile, but she senses, within the structures she knows, that the adults' conflict is elemental and their emotions are genuine.

> Because Uncle Charles lives in Sodom we do not let him visit. If we did, we might be touched. He is one of the fools in Israel — that is what Grandpa Morpeth calls him. He has practiced abominations. Three years ago he confessed this to my Grandpa and Grandma and my Uncle James and Matt, expecting them to welcome his frankness. Since then he is banished, he is as water spilled upon the ground that cannot be gathered up again. (26)

The conflict occurs within conflations of time and space—biblical and current, Sodom and Sydney—that are initially devastating; in fact, however, they can become useful terms of the first-principle unity, if they can be translated away from projections of ongoing universalized conflict and toward apprehensions of equalized inclusiveness. Both ethical and narrative issues, therefore, depend upon Amy's vocabulary containing enough play to articulate the necessary alienation from the closure of her current circumstances.

Although the terse phrasing of Amy's language tends to reduce subtle and complex indicators, it is certainly capable of expressing paradox through accumulation and proximity.

> When we sit down to our meal, with his chair an empty space, the food we eat has no savour. I watch Grandpa Morpeth cut pieces of meat with his big hands and push them between his teeth, and chew and swallow, and what he is eating, I know, is ashes. His heart is closed on its grief. And that is what love is. That is what death is. (30)

Amy's training has emphasized that God's love is stronger than death, and now it is exactly the absolut-

ism of her vocabulary that prompts her to question whether the family seems intent upon rejection. Her interrogation cannot develop under routine circumstances, where adult rule would stifle it, so her search proceeds in dream. When her uncle fails to appear as usual—the suggestion is AIDS—Amy dreams of him in a new, translated mode: he emerges from the BMW naked, and "you could see his bare feet in the grass, large and bony, and he glowed, he was smooth all over, like an angel" (31). He walks right through the fence that had excluded him in the waking world, which seems proper to Amy since "the lumpy coarse-stemmed grass was the same on both sides, so why not?" Again, conflation is turned into play, a structure that permits speculation: if nature is the same on one side of the fence as the other, then the fence is contingent and artificial, a human construction unacknowledged by the grass (or by the little flowers that sprout around Uncle Charles's feet in the dream), and the family's other attributions of what is natural and unnatural, as they relate to him, must be questionable likewise. Returned to a waking world—but one no longer so distinct from dream—Amy can use this flexibility to measure her insight precisely in terms of the distance between the outmoded exclusivity and the newly developed inclusion, and thus to direct her vision through increasingly accurate self-awareness. All of this is possible within the vocabulary to which she already has access—in, ironically, a voice "whose value lies precisely in the demonstration of its own limits" (Indyk, 107).

As "Closer" describes transcendental continuity in spatial terms, similar narrations examine the temporal persistence of events as affective values. Since the past is received as narrative, historical definition is based upon ongoing interpretation and self-conscious hermeneutic inquiry, mythologizing in a present which currently asks the past to admit multiple sources and a layering of voices. "Blacksoil Country" is narrated by Jordan McGivern, a twelve-year-old boy—actually, his 150-year-old ghost—whose family are pioneers in Queensland. The exposition follows the pattern of nineteenth-century bush tales: Jordan's father is a bitter, broken man, undone as much by angry pride as by hardship and bad luck; his mother is long-suffering and silent, and the boy combines their gifts by following his father's general lead even while seeing his shortcoming and self-defeat. The suggestion of colonial allegory, in the family's work on behalf of a landowner who remains in Sydney, "too comfortable out at Double Bay" (117), likewise recalls Australian figurations of long standing. But the story forks, and the narrator's simultaneous maintenance of the several versions demonstrates the potential values of play in historical interpretation.

Jordan is killed by Aboriginals. First, his father shoots an Aboriginal who approaches while carrying a dead sheep: he assumes the sheep is stolen and construes the approach, as all acts by Aboriginals, as hostile. "He did not know that black was a messenger. Who had the right to pass through all territories without harm" (126–27), to bring him a neighboring settler's gift. One fork of the story, then, follows the persistence of ideas that led to the event, ideas which do not include admission of a mistake: "How could he know that? And even if he had, he mightn't have cared anyway that it was a consideration in their world. It wasn't one in ours" (127). This maintenance of racially bounded stances requires the simplistic, entrenched division of space into "ours" and "theirs," along with the peremptory overriding of "theirs." From here, the outcome seems causal: Jordan is killed in reprisal, and in return the Aboriginals are killed or driven off. The public version of the story, duly reported "in the newspapers at Maitland and Moreton Bay and beyond" (130), is characterized by "fear and justified rage and the unbridled savagery of slaughter"—the usual stuff. The settlers conform to it despite their low opinion of the father: racist distinction offers images of solidarity and success in a harsh land, at least temporarily, "for a season" (130). Again, the undercutting of high claims through limitation and irony constitutes a familiar part of the "laconically, humorously tragic" tradition in Australian literature (Conrad, 34).

Less commonly, the narrator shows his father's personal transformation. Grief, expressed in public, gives the father clarity, focus, and stature beyond any he could have earned on his own.

> He is a new man. He has discovered one of the ways at last to win other men to him and he blazes with the power it brings him. He is monstrous. And because he believes so completely in what he must do, is so filled with the righteous ferocity of it, others too are convinced. (129)

Malouf's exposition of these two directions, both leading to violence and monstrosity, suggests that, however contested, the divisive structures of self-evaluation and actualization incorporated into early phases of Australian culture remain sufficiently strong to need undercutting yet again. A century and a half later, nothing is lost: not brutalization, not racism, not the killing of twelve-year-olds. And nothing is lost: possibilities for understanding, for interacting, for amalgamating Australian consciousness that acknowledges the experience of all.

Jordan's version of the story overarches the others, narrating them with faithfulness to traditions of historical reporting and bush writing, but reducing their values. The public story and the father's psychological act-

ing-out are denied their former exclusive claim to telling the story of Australia. The national dreaming now looks toward its "democratic purpose" (Butler, 195) by broadening into complex and layered subjects that also include Jordan's mother, Aboriginals of several different orders, and a ghostly guide who ensures that possibilities remain open: "I can show you this country. I been in it long enough" (116). He has earned his vision of transcendent unity by becoming literally one with the land, part of what is now always meant by "Australia": "And me all that while lying quiet in the heart of the country, slowly sinking into the ancientness of it, making it mine, grain by grain blending my white grains with its many black ones" (130). Jordan's voice acknowledges the pain of history and nation-building, and then translates it to the redemptive dislocation that carries him away from limitation and defensiveness, toward an inclusivity that enables the present to "reread the past for the sake of a different future" (Oliver, 113).

Children such as Jack, Amy, and Jordan have always been important in Malouf's writing (Koval); they are at once the most vulnerable components of present society, and the most resilient agents of the future. Despite impediments of historical boundedness and social limitation, their voices and their participation indicate an expanding present moment, a space with enough play to allow alternative—yes, hopeful—visions of a future. These, in turn, loop back to the present to generate further expansiveness and—even—comfort: in "Sally's Story," Brad Jenkins snuggles his baby on one arm and pats Sally with his other hand, in a playful, physical, kind gesture of unanticipated wholeness. Time and again, in *Dream Stuff* and in his writing "all that while," David Malouf offers narrations of broad human possibility that draw readers into wise and complex visions of human dreaming.

John Scheckter, Autumn 2000

■ **WORKS CITED**

Butler, Judith. *Bodies That Matter: On the Discursive Limits of "Sex."* New York. Routledge. 1993.

Conrad, Peter. "New New World." *Granta*, 70 (Summer ["Winter in Australia"] 2000), pp. 11–37.

Indyk, Ivor. *David Malouf.* Melbourne. Oxford University Press. 1993.

James, Henry. "The Art of Fiction" (1884). In *The Critical Tradition: Classic Texts and Contemporary Trends.* David H. Richter, ed. New York. St. Martin's. 1989. Pp. 422–33.

Kellaway, Kate. "Landscape Artist." *The Observer,* 9 April 2000. 1 September 2000 at http://booksunlimited.co.uk/Print/0,3858,3983859,00.html.

Koval, Ramona. "Books and Writing with Ramona Koval: David Malouf — *Dream Stuff.*" *ABC Online.* Transcript of radio program, 14 April 2000. 1 September 2000 at http://www.abc.net.au/rn/arts/bwriting/stories/s117284.html.

Lorenzo, Olga. "The Rhythm of Life." *The Age*, 20 May 2000. 1 September 2000 at http://theage.com.au/books/20000320/A19212–2000Mar19.html.

Malouf, David. *A Spirit of Play: The Making of Australian Consciousness*. 1998 Boyer Lectures. Sydney. ABC Books, for the Australian Broadcasting Corporation. 1998.

———. *Dream Stuff: Stories*. New York. Pantheon. 2000.

Oliver, Kelly. *Subjectivity without Subjects: From Abject Fathers to Desiring Mothers*. Lanham, Maryland. Rowman & Little-field. 1998.

Skea, Ann. Review of *Dream Stuff. Eclectica*, 4:2 (April-May 2000). 1 September 2000 at http://www.eclectica.org/v4n2/skea_malouf.html.

Maori Literature in English: An Introduction

One of the most exciting aspects of New Zealand writing during the 1970s has been the emergence of a Maori literature in English. For too long relegated by critics to the realm of the tourist curiosity and the anthropological specimen, the Maori tradition has persisted in the period since European contact as a dynamic part of Maori culture. The oral tradition—formal speeches, songs, chants and a variety of long and short narrative forms—continues essentially in the Maori language and has undergone many changes under the influence of European music, religion and material culture. A written literature began in the Maori language early in the nineteenth century but until recently was limited to non-narrative writings such as political speeches, religious tracts and genealogical lists. Informally, unpublished diaries and other memoranda were written but by and large remained the private heirlooms of families and tribal groups. In the last decade more and more Maori writing has turned to genres familiar to the European canon of literature: lyrical verse, short stories and longer prose works, both in fiction and nonfiction areas. Unfortunately, much of this has not yet been published or given the general distribution such writing deserves. The current trend to teach Maori in the secondary schools of New Zealand and to develop university courses in Maori to the graduate level will assure a widening of the readership for such modern Maori poetry and prose writing.

Outside New Zealand, for the foreseeable future, however, Maori writing will be of interest primarily in English. To anthropologists and folklorists, the main consideration will be in the English translations and versions of traditional Maori oral culture. While this material will also be interesting to those concerned with the development of Third World literatures, especially as contextual reading, the real focus will be on the Maori authors using English as their main vehicle. Few though they are yet, these writers have the skill and insight of good writers, and interest in their work need not be confined to that of an intellectual travelogue.

Before I give brief sketches of the work of three leading prose writers and a small group of the poets, it may be useful to list some of the more accessible and reliable texts on Maoritanga (i.e., the full spirituality of Maori culture). Two standard books by Sir Peter Buck (Te Rangi Hiroa) remain useful in providing a background to Maori writers: *Vikings of the Sunrise* (1938) and *The Coming of the Maori* (1949); these works, while challenged in some detail by recent studies, nevertheless offer a broad overview of Polynesian culture in the Pacific and the place of the Maoris within that larger grouping. The best of the new synthesizing texts must be the second edition of Joan Metge's *The Maoris of New Zealand: Ratahi* (1976), a book which, though by a Pakeha (a European New Zealander), captures the spirit and essence of Maoritanga. In terms of more day-to-day aspects of Maori life, a small pamphlet published by Harry Dansey—a Maori of great intellectual stature, a dramatist, journalist and public spokesman for the Maori cause—introduces his people to the European with sympathy for both sides: *Maori Custom Today* (1971).

Two further aspects of Maoritanga which are often seen but misunderstood by the European and which form a strong element in the frame of identity implicitly referred to in the Maori writers in English are the carved meetinghouse and the formal ceremonials of Maori occasions. W. J. Phillipps's *Maori Carving Illustrated* (1955) offers a readable and reliable introduction to the subject and many well-chosen photographs to demonstrate the elements discussed in the text. The formal ceremonials of Maori life, whether in funeral, wedding, greeting or dedication, are cogently set out by Anne Salmond in a book called *Hui: A Study of Maori Ceremonial Gatherings* (1976).

A. W. Reed's 1963 *Treasury of Maori Folklore* is full of interesting material but is set out from the European point of view and hence lacks the Maori sense of organization. To take a somewhat different instance, the home marae (meetinghouse) of the Maori Queen, Turangawaewae, at Ngaruawahia, has a "museum"; but unlike a Pakeha museum, where exhibits are set out and labeled so as to show types of objects and are arranged by categories of use, structure or period, the Maori "museum" shows objects in terms of their owners and the tribal connections they manifest. Their value is to living members of families involved in historical circumstances surrounding the making or donating of the tikis,

feather cloaks and other objects. Thus, despite its somewhat archaic Victorian flavor in the translations, the
three volumes of *Nga Moteatea,* begun by Sir Apirana
Ngata and revised and completed by Pei Te Huirini
Jones (1959), offer a goodly selection of Maori poetry
in the traditional vein; each poem—they are chants, laments, satirical jibes, challenges and so on—is identified as to the maker of the song, his tribal connections
and the occasion for the performance. John Caselberg's
Maori is my Name (1976) offers a fine selection of translations from nineteenth-century Maori prose works.

In the light of the continuing Maori tradition, it is
surprising that Allen Curnow's *Penguin Book of New Zealand Verse* has only a few lines of Maori myth in translation to stand as an introduction to the history of New
Zealand poetry, and Vincent O'Sullivan's *Oxford Anthology of Twentieth Century New Zealand Verse* has only one
Maori writer represented, Hone Tuwhare. Prose writers
have fared a little better, but still by and large it is only
rarely that any other than the three main prose writers
to be looked at now find space in the "establishment"
journals of New Zealand literature or the standard texts
of short story collections. Two journals, however,
should be noted as correcting the above situation. *Koru,*
edited by the Maori poet Haare Williams, is an annual
which publishes stories, poems and essays by Maori
writers, whether in English or in Maori. Closely associated with the new Maori Writers and Artists Society,
Koru is a major force in this renaissance of Maori culture
we are describing. The other journal taking part in this
development, though its aims are much wider, is *Pacific
Quarterly* (formerly *The New Quarterly Cave*), which is
based on principles of multiculturalism and multilingualism.

The three prose writers most deserving of attention
today are Patricia Grace, Witi Ihimaera, and Heretaunga
Pat Baker. The first and last of this group have so far
published only one book each, while Ihimaera is the
most prolific with three books to his credit and more
on the way. Each writer offers a unique approach to the
problem of establishing a Maori tradition in English-
language prose, each depending upon an approach to
bilingualism, the structure of narrative events and the
relevance of Maori history and legend. What is most
amazing is that until these three writers appeared, the
New Zealand Maori's literary image was entirely shaped
by European authors; sympathetic as they may have
been (and yet so often the concerns with the love or
rape of young nubile Maori *wahines* in potboilers and
the comic "nigger" touch appearing in the background
of sentimental tales were not in the least sympathetic),
the Maori was not given "a fair go." His customs were

traduced, and his oral traditions reduced to children's
tales. But that is another story.

Patricia Grace's one book of short stories, *Waiariki,*[1]
shows a self-conscious sensibility in the process of discovering a proper medium for self-expression. The
twelve tales in the collection tend to become concerned
with the very language of their own making, and that
language becomes the theme and central image of the
book itself. The opening story is even called "A Way of
Talking" and concerns the contrast, first, between a
young Maori girl who has stayed at home and still
speaks in the dialect of the region, and her older sister,
who has gone to the big city and learned to speak in the
manner of the Pakeha; second, there is a contrast between the language of those who are not aware of what
they are saying and those who, like the older sister (and,
after an initial misunderstanding, the younger sister as
well), speak with a control over their tone and vocabulary, so as to be in control of the situation. Behind these
contrasts lies another: the way of talking of the title,
which refers to a picturesque phrase used by both girls'
grandmother, a phrase which draws from the understated richness of the oral Maori tradition. It is a deep
and rich tradition, and its strength quietly underlies the
more noisy and superficial concerns of the two main
characters and their dealings with a rather silly Pakeha
woman down the road.

This and the last story we can call the "English
tales." They are told all in English, with the rhythms of
English prose, and clearly use the techniques of the
standard European short story. The final story, "Parade," takes a young, educated Maori girl back from the
city to her small town, where she is asked to take part
in a local fair. The Maoris dress in their traditional costumes and, while on a float in the parade, dance and
sing action songs. The city girl realizes quickly that the
townsfolk are exploiting the Maoris, and she tries to object to the fact that her people are being stared at like
circus freaks. But her old uncle Hohepa says: "It is your
job, this. To show others who we are." Not until the ride
home, exhausted, as she and the others sing the traditional Maori songs, however, does she understand what
Hohepa and her Granny Rita mean. If the Pakeha are
exploiting the Maori in this parade, the Maori are
proudly asserting their Maoritanga: while others may
stare in ignorance, the performers themselves are fully
aware of their place in the land and in history, and their
public performance, singing and dancing, being together, is a manifestation of the enduring quality of their
way of life.

The other stories in *Waiariki* fall into two other categories, and in these Patricia Grace puts the burden of
her craft. She has shown in the opening and closing

tales, which frame the collection, her ability to handle the European-type story very well indeed. In the stories between she experiments with language. One type, which I call the "Maori tale," is written in a form of English which follows Maori syntax and vocabulary; it has an appearance of being a literal translation. The other type, in which there is a high frequency of Maori words and phrases, I call the "macaronic tale"; this has three registers of language—the normal English of the narrator, the dialect rhythms and syntax of the characters, and the use of Maori itself.

The Maori tales are of limited esthetic value and show only why this mode should not be followed. They prove, if it needed to be proved, that one language is not a grid of words interchangeable with the words of another language; grammatical structures and thought patterns are distinct. Hence, for the Maori, living in two linguistic and cultural realms of experience, two separate ways of feeling and measuring reality must be accommodated. A short paragraph from "At the River" will demonstrate the nature of these tales:

> To the tent to rest after they had gone to the river, and while asleep the dream came. A dream of death. He came to me in the dream, not sadly but smiling, with hand on heart, and said, "I go but do not weep. No weeping, it is my time."

> If there is any other value in these Maori tales it is in the patterning of events, which come through with that sense of time more fluid than the modern European's sense of distinctness and relativity; the past and the present flow into one another. Yet finally, this deliberately non-English prose is an annoyance.

The macaronic tales have another approach. By trying to capture the reality of Maori speakers in their ambiguity and dual registers, Patricia Grace tends toward an illusion of that reality which goes beyond the bounds of propriety. For while it is certainly permissible to ask a reader not merely to keep checking a glossary of Maori words or footnotes of explanation or even to build up a memory of Maori phrases and terms once explained and later used without English paraphrase in the text, I think the overloading of the text in one language with passages in another language also becomes more an irritation than an asset to the stories.

The literary artist, if he or she chooses one language rather than another, must retain a coherence and a control that includes respect for the inner dynamic of that language itself. Giving an illusion of Maori phrases and whole speeches is part of the craft of the writer. If, in reality, the Maori of today thinks and speaks in a mixture of languages, does the writer have the right to produce that reality without artistic modification? The argument is a tricky one, but I feel that an illusion based on the retention of a few key Maori words for feelings and things not normally part of Pakeha experience would work as well as a Zolaesque fictional representation of life in progress.

Certainly the stories told in this macaronic way depend on a few Maori words at best, with their real strengths lying rather in the nonverbal qualities of Maori friendship and the valuing of things in common. "The Dream," for instance, is an extended anecdote about a fellow who has a dream about an eel and then tries, first on his own and then with the advice of his mates, to make that dream applicable to a bet on the horses. While the joke in the tale turns on some Maori puns, the real essence of the story lies in Raniera's relations with his friends. The wordplay could be told and the familiar discourse amongst the characters could be reproduced without any heavy reliance on macaronics.

We can see this in the writings of Witi Ihimaera. His suggestion of Maori dialect rhythms and his use of key words in Maori are not intrusive, and he does not even feel called upon to offer the reader a glossary, in the manner of Patricia Grace. The literary problem he seems to have set himself, rather, is at another level, and that is the fusing of the Maori sense of time and place and the communal sense of identity which the Maori feels with European techniques of narrative presentation, such as flashback and overlap. The result is, I feel, that technique begins to override content and the insights of the author are lost in excessive verbiage and sentimentality.

While this may seem paradoxical, the exaggerated concern with technique results in the failure of the writer to follow through the inner dynamic of his situations and characterizations, so that they remain on the level of superficial or incomplete implication, analogy or emotional consequence. *Pounamu, Pounamu*[2] is a collection of short stories covering much the same ground as Patricia Grace's *Waiariki* but concentrating more on character and theme than on language. Ihimaera has a clear grasp of the basic techniques of the plotting, pacing and focal points of the genre; but he does not go any farther than Grace in sounding the basic Maori themes—*aroha, whanau* and identity, that is, of social love, of emotional ties between family and tribe both living and dead, and of the modern Maori caught between loyalty to Maoritanga and the necessity of accommodating to a Pakeha-dominated society.

Even more than Grace, though, Ihimaera sees that the literary problem can be solved by focusing attention not on language but on objects and customs. Unfortunately, he tends to deal with these only in vague emotive terms. For example, in a story of *Pounamu, Pounamu* the protagonist-narrator speaks of the loss of a family heirloom, the greenstone of the title:

> It was a big piece of greenstone, not the valuable dark green kind, but a smoky green like opal. But I used to like to hold it to the sun and look into it, and feel the soft luminous glow flooding around me. And I used to whisper to myself, "Pounamu . . . pounamu . . . pounamu . . . ," and almost hear the emerald water rushing over the clay from where the greenstone had come.

The effect is sentimental. It deals with sentiments, in a good sense, but also manipulates technique only to rouse sentiments without exploring other significances, and this is sentimentality in the bad sense.

The two novels that grew out of the short story collection, *Tangi* and *Whanau*,[3] make only minimal advances in terms of theme, character and situation and actually are novels only insofar as they integrate fragments, sketches and episodic tales. *Tangi* is most ambitious, attempting as it does to depict a Maori funeral in terms of a modern European novel, and gains what coherence it has from the character of the narrator and the focusing of attention on the *hui*, the funeral of the main figure's father. *Whanau* takes a less avant-garde approach and seeks to integrate the realistic portrayal of village life into a novel of social issues. This latter novel, however, misses its opportunity for unique Maori expression and for greater artistic unity by only skirting the central image, the local meetinghouse, and by forcing a most contrived and melodramatic conclusion onto the diverse events in order to bring them together.

Tangi is a moving tale nonetheless, recounting the maturation of Tama, a young man in his twenties who has left the small village near Gisborne to live and work among the Pakehas in Wellington; when he is called home to his father's funeral, the flood of emotion that engulfs him must be given a shape and a direction. It is guilt and fear mixed with love for his father and family: guilt at leaving home, at not helping out with the family farm and at not participating in the communal life of the *whanau;* and fear of facing the uncertainties of the future without the wise counsel of his father. What Tama comes to know through the experience is that the wisdom of his father lies in the shared Maori identity of the whole *whanau* and that he can undertake full responsibilties as a means of gaining the identity and security he longs for.

Unfortunately, the flashback and overlap techniques used by Witi Ihimaera are excessive and detract from the strength of the novel, particularly in deflecting attention from the ceremonies and myths associated with the funeral. Three main time schemes overlap: Tama returning to the village from Wellington; the events of the tangi itself; and Tama in the train on the way back to the city. Flashback memories of his father and mother are interspersed with these overlapped plot lines, each told in a repetitive and almost incantatory rhythm. Such is, for instance, the refrain-like recollection of the proverb taught to Tama by his father: "To manawa, a ratou manawa. / Your heart is also their heart." Instead of deepening the awareness in both Tama and the reader, the techniques merely label the experience: we do not see the changes coming about in Tama, nor do we understand how they interconnect with the complications of life both in the village and in the city.

Whanau is even more disappointing, though it has many interesting moments—moments which, were they worked out as short stories on their own, would have great esthetic value. The small village is at once boring and tedious to the people who live in it and the spiritual basis of their lives, a spirituality signaled by the meetinghouse called Rongopai. Built in the last century in expectation of a revival of Maori strength and identity through integration of Christian values and European techniques called for by Te Kooti, the house is decorated with a mixture of traditional carvings and brightly painted European-influenced realistic scenes and characters; but the meetinghouse has fallen into decay, unused since Te Kooti failed to appear. There are hints throughout *Whanau* that the author wants to relate the diverse people and situations to this meetinghouse, but it is only in a sentimental way that he does this at the very end of the book. A child runs off in the middle of the night with his ailing grandfather in order to prevent the old man from being sent to a hospital; the petty squabbles and drunken selfishness of various individuals are forgotten in the communal effort to find the child and old man on a dark and stormy night. Of course, the old man leads the boy to Rongopai, dreaming he is returning to the good old days. He and the child are found, and the *whanau* decides to keep the elder at home; even the daughter married to a Pakeha overcomes her European desire to see the sick man in a hospital; and for a moment, as of old, the *whanau* is united by *aroha*.

Sensationalism in the form of sex and violence is to be found aplenty in *Behind the Tattooed Face*,[4] Heretaunga Pat Baker's novel of Maoris on the eve of "the fatal impact," the arrival of the Europeans. But the novel works with a coherence and a distinctly Maori sense of thematic unity in a way that both of Ihimaera's more self-consciously literary novels fail to do. In imagining a totally Maori society, Baker largely frees himself from the problem of depicting the Maori in the midst of a Pakeha world. Though using English as his main medium, he is not concerned with language: except for a few phrases and the citation of some chants, the assumption is that he is translating into normal English an experience that took place wholly in Maori. As a historical novel this one is no less accurate than any European version in the nineteenth century; present mentality is projected back on the past, and by and large the concerns of the modern Maori are worked out in a setting well stocked with nostalgia. But precisely because of this anachronism, we gain from Baker's novel a better and clearer picture of Maori sensibility today.

The story itself is a complicated account of intertribal warfare in the Bay of Plenty area during the eighteenth century. Baker's forte seems to be, on the one hand, describing the building of *pas* (fortified villages), the performance of all sorts of traditional ceremonies in what he imagines their pristine form to have been, and the sensationalism of sacrifice, battle, rape and feats of endurance and courage. On the other hand, he seeks to tell a well-made, fast-moving story, and this he does with alternating moods—intimate moments of delicacy, public declamations, quiet or rollicking comedy. His characters are diverse, and there is no sense of dealing with noble savages or indeed with savages of any kind; his old-time Maoris are normal people, even the *tohunga* (a priest or craftsman), homosexual though he be. The characters are no more developed than in a good popular novel, but this seems to be appropriate for a people in a tribal society where identity is less subjectively involved than communally determined. In other words, Baker has turned Maori legend into a well-constructed, unpretentious popular book. Where Grace and Ihimaera have undertaken more complicated literary tasks, Baker has succeeded in creating a Maori novel in English. It is not at a very high level, but it is competent. Grace and Ihimaera have shown skill and insight but have not yet worked out the mode for a "serious" Maori literature; still their works are no less interesting for the failures or at least the relative failures so far. And certainly in comparison with Pakeha New Zealand prose writers, they can be valued with no condescension.

The area of Maori poetry in English can only be touched very briefly here. Most of the writers, when identified as Maori, tend to write much closer to their native traditions than do the prose writers, perhaps because the introspective and confessional nature of most New Zealand poetry in English enforces this expectation of ethnicity; or, perhaps even more, because the poetic tradition in Maori—in action songs, chants, laments and satirical verse—is still very much a functioning aspect of living Maori culture.

It would be possible to classify the poems, rather than the poets, into those completely in English, those in a macaronic style (that is, mixing Maori and English, though with the latter dominant) and the bilingual versions (two poems in close relationship, one in English and one in Maori, neither really a translation of the other). A good example of the first kind of poem is "Koha"[5] by Haare Williams. The title is glossed by the author thus: "The principle of giving and reciprocity is universal—what do we understand about giving— when Earth or Trees give, they give their very best . . . do we?" Here is the text in full:

Our
Nanny Wai
sang
to orchard trees
calling each
by name;

we didn't really know
why . . .

"Trees give their best—
for them
to hold back is to
die . . .

you give little
when you give
things—
give of yourselves,
like trees . . .
that's giving!
Learn from them!

With Earth
for mother—and
Sky
for father
they hold back
Nothing!"

The year
Nanny Mai went
the trees grew old
and died . . .
we didn't really know
why.

The language here is simple, the short lines forcing attention on the key thoughts, which drive deeply into the nature of Maori attitudes toward the land, people and *aroha*.

A poem moving into the category of macaronics is "Waiata of My Tipuna" by Rowley Habib (Nga Pitiroirangi),[6] a recent winner of a grant from the Maori Purposes Fund Committee as the best Maori writer of the year. To understand the poem one must know some Maori words: *waiata* (songs, poems), *tipuna* (ancestors) and *mauri* (life principle).

Waiata of my tipuna
(now made alien sound)
waft to me yet
from ancient rivers
from beginnings
deep in my country's soil.

Mauri of my tipuna
(now made dissipated force)
reach me yet
through the aged tree
through roots / which / reach down
deep in my country's soil.

With a more abstract language than Williams, Habib gives strength to the lines by the use of the actual words for the Maori feelings he is expressing.

In the third category, the bilingual versions, I would like to cite from two authors. The first is a section of a poem sequence by Van Phillipps called "Three River Poems / Nga Waio o Wanganui."[7]

Kia mimiti ra ano nga waio Whanganui.
E pahemo ai taku aroha ki te po.

Kia mutu ra ano to waiata a te tui,
Ka pahemo haere aku maharatanga.

Kia timata mai te po mutunga kore,
A reira ra ano taku ngakau ke i tenei pakohu.

Koia nei. Naku e nei kapu.

When the waters dry from Whanganui,
Then will my love die.

When the *tui* ceases to sing,
Then will my memories fade.

When the last night begins,
Then will my heart turn from this valley.

These are my words.

The straightforward incremental repetition of the poem has a classical simplicity to it, which gains from its relationship to the Maori text and the rich associations of the places and things referred to.

The other bilingual poem I would like to offer here as evidence for the beauty and excitement in the present development of a Maori literature in English is by the late Arapeta Awatere. (A hero of World War II, Awatere died in March 1976, much mourned by the people of New Zealand.) It is a poem called "He Raiona / Lion"[8] and dedicated to Peter A. Williams, barrister and solicitor "whom I observed on many occasions in action at the bar."

He rooia kei te kooti
mataara matapopore matahi
tohunga waananga
maarama ki te koorero
pokarare taana taki koorero

He raiona toona rite
mataara matapopore
kararehe paptu muurere
rere ana te ihi
rere ana te wehi

Me he uira toona nakawhiti
oona wheeue oona rei
kua ngangau kua mate te hoariri
kua miti i oona taotuu . . .
kua haere!

Counsel at the bar
vigilant poised meticulous
devastating debator
exquisite in expression
precise in presentation

Lion in the jungle
vigilant poised majestic
cunning prowling predator
serene in meditation
fierce in concentration

Lightningspeed in action
brain and brawn flexed
locked in mortal combat
licks his wounds . . . is gone!

The turning of traditional Maori epithets to a modern situation is an important part of the development of a unique variant in English.

While the best-known Maori poet today in New Zealand and perhaps overseas is Hone Tuwhare, his verse remains very much a part of the English tradition proper and is not directed toward a specific Maori variant. This comment is not meant to detract from his merits; but it is from the poets cited above and from men and women such as the names that follow that a new Maori literature in English will emerge: Georgina Kamiria Kirby, Raina Tibble, Apirana Taylor, Dinah Rawiri-Steele, Ruth Hera Lee, Robin Kora, Katerina Mataira. There are many others, and it is significant that of these quite a few are now choosing to write only in Maori. While this approach has its own special virtues, I think it would not be amiss to see, paradoxically, in this phenomenon a sign that Maori poetry in English will remain close to its dynamic Maori sources.

Norman Simms, Spring 1978

[1] Auckland, Longman Paul (Pacific Paperbacks), 1975.
[2] Auckland, Heinemann, 1972.

3 *Tangi,* Auckland, Heinemann, 1973; *Whanau,* Auckland, Heinemann, 1974.

4 Whatamongo Bay, Queen Charlotte Sound, Cape Catley, 1975.

5 *New Quarterly Cave* 2:4 (1977), p. 371.

6 *New Quarterly Cave* 1:3 (1976), pp. 60–61.

7 *New Quarterly Cave* 1:4 (1976), p. 91.

8 *New Quarterly Cave* 1:2 (1976), p. 57.

Latin America

Contesting the Boundaries of Exile: Latino/a Literature

As if there were not already enough confusion and slippage in the term Latino/a (referring most commonly to people from Spanish-colonized countries now living within the United States, but sometimes applied more loosely to the peoples of those Spanish-speaking countries themselves), the categorization "Latino/a literature of exile" has been making increasing appearances in college course titles. Do such titles imply (as they would seem to) that the literature being studied is a subset of Latino/a literature of the USA? Existing scholarship on the subject would seem to indicate otherwise, generally positing two presumably distinct categories: Latino/a "exile" literature and Latino/a "ethnic" (U.S.) literature. The ambiguity of the term Latino/a persists here, since this delineation actually suggests that literature by exiles from Spanish-speaking countries is not U.S. Latino/a at all. Thus articles meant to draw the parameters of the body of U.S. Latino/a literature (such as those by Juan Bruce-Novoa or Eliana Rivero, both significantly called "Hispanic Literature in the United States") exclude exile literature entirely (and explicitly) from consideration.[1]

Significantly, critical discussions of "exile" Latino/a writing have focused predominantly on authors of Cuban origin, as Cubans have represented by far the largest group of Latino/a exiles immigrating to the United States.[2] "Ethnic" Latino/a literature, generally understood more broadly as writing produced by Americans of Mexican, Cuban, Puerto Rican, Dominican, and Central/South American descent, is treated by critics as a separate and quite distinct category—a distinction that, in practice, tends to *exclude* much Cuban writing in the USA from the label "U.S. Latino/a writing." This essay proposes to challenge the construction of mutual exclusivity between exile and ethnic writing, and to reexam-ine the relationship between a fairly narrowly defined body of work (exile writing, primarily Cuban although hypothetically including other exile groups such as Dominican) and the more heterogeneous (although, as I have already indicated, presumably nonoverlapping) production of writing labeled ethnic U.S. Latino/a literature, by looking at the work of a few writers who blur the boundaries of these distinctions.

According to the dominant critical perspective, what defines "Latino/a literature of exile," as opposed to U.S. Latino/a *ethnic* literature, is that it is characterized by "nostalgia," a "looking back" to the country and culture of origin that have been "lost" by the political circumstances forcing emigration to the United States. Critics define Latino/a literature of exile as written by those who arrived in the U.S. as adults and as focused on the country and culture of origin, while suggesting that writers who were born in the U.S or who arrived as children produce *ethnic* (not exile) writing, which is bicultural and focused on experiences of cultural transition and "hybridity." Reviewing some of the scholarship specifically on Cuban literature of exile, Karen Christian presents an accurate summary of critical efforts to draw distinctions between ethnic and exile writing:

> Gustavo Pérez-Firmat describes exile sensibility as being retrospective, with a powerful fixation on the culture of origin. . . . Eliana Rivero similarly asserts that exile writers, who were often writers before being immigrants, tend to re-create social, political, and personal "landscapes" of their native land in their nostalgia-tinged works. . . . Both critics view U.S. Cuban *ethnic* writing, on the other hand, as more likely to engage questions of biculturalism and cultural transformation. (56)

Although Juan Armando Epple, another critic mentioned by Christian, includes both kinds of writing in his discussion of "Hispanic Exile in the United States," he still claims that, in contrast to writing that can be considered "Cuban *American*," "literature of exile" *strict-*

ly speaking (*sensu stricto*) is "thematically and aesthetically tied to the respective national traditions" (336). Isabel Alvarez Borland conjoins both labels into a single one in the title of her book, *Cuban-American Literature of Exile,* which addresses authors typically considered "exiles," such as Reinaldo Arenas, as well as those typically considered "ethnic," such as Achy Obejas and Cristina García. But within the covers of the book, Alvarez Borland is still centrally concerned with "the differences between an ethnic and an exilic perspective" (2), and she preserves throughout her discussion the separate labels "Cuban exile and Cuban-American writing" (4). Her attempt to delineate these separate categories, predictably, falls back on the definitions drawn by other critics: in exile writing, "the presence of the adopted country is not central to these writers' narratives since most of them write from the sometimes bitter and nostalgic perspective of exile" (7), while "*Cuban-American ethnic writers* . . . who came from Cuba as infants or who were born in the United States to parents of the first exile generation . . . set about the task of constructing a U.S. identity" (8–9; emphasis Borland's).[3]

These categorizations are presented with a vocabulary of trends and tendencies; thus this body of critics seems to be suggesting that people who are exiled as adults will *tend* to write one way, while their children who grow up primarily in the U.S. will *tend* to write another way. But to then distinguish the two *kinds* of writing by name (exile writing versus ethnic writing) is to begin to construct a more essentialist definition of the terms: e.g., exile writing is nostalgic and backward-looking, whereas ethnic writing is focused on U.S. experiences of biculturalism and hybridity.[4] I suggest that a reformulation of the terms of discussion allows us to consider both the heterogeneity and the constructedness of what we think of as the "Latino community"; thus we ought (for reasons I will elaborate upon below) to be able to talk about a subset of U.S. Latino/a ethnic literature that is *also* "of exile"—that is, *about* exile and springing *from* it. And while my main concern in this paper will be the writing of second-generation U.S. Latina/os (those whom the critics I have mentioned above call "ethnic" writers), these writers themselves suggest the ways in which their predecessors (the "exiles") have also been profoundly influenced by a U.S. context, thus blurring the boundaries between the exile and the ethnic in the other direction as well. The writing of authors such as the Cuban Americans Achy Obejas, Cristina García, and Roberto Fernández, as well as of the Dominican American Julia Alvarez (whose attention to the "exile" experience of Dominican immigrants serves as a corrective for a critical discussion that has, up to now, ignored this particular group of "exiles"), provides a

fruitful counterpoint to the discussions of exiles and ethnics found in recent literary criticism. I propose to problematize the exile/ethnic dichotomy by setting the critical discussions against some of the "ethnic" texts to which they refer.

A revealing starting point in an interrogation of the assumptions behind the exile/ethnic opposition is provided by Eliana Rivero's article "Hispanic Literature in the United States: Self-Image and Conflict," which is particularly overt in moving beyond a general description of the shifting concerns in texts of exiles versus children of exiles, to a much more prescriptive definition of terms based on ideological perspective. As Rivero puts it, "If we define ethnic minority art and literature in the United States as a form of cultural resistance and/or protest" (187)—and she does define them this way—"then the works by Cuban immigrants *can never be considered*" as ethnic minority U.S. literature (187; emphasis mine).[5] Cuban exiles, Rivero explains, having left Castro's communist regime, "oppose the socialist revolutionary process taking place in their homeland" (183) and embrace the "selfish, materialistic middle class values" (187) of the U.S. dominant culture. On the other hand, texts by writers of Cuban heritage which can be read as "cultural resistance or protest" apparently qualify as Cuban *American* literature, rather than as "exile" literature. But Rivero's definition begs the question: just what is literature that qualifies as "ethnic" protesting *against?* While at times Rivero is quite specific that it occupies an oppositional stance vis-à-vis the "dominant white Anglo culture" (179) of the U.S., at other times she posits a vaguer, more general protest against "the establishment" (183). But here lies a problem, since even conservative Cuban exile literature could conceivably be read as protest against the current "establishment" in Cuba. "Social protest," in Rivero's terminology, then, must mean "protest" against *conservative* ideologies, cultures, and establishments. But this is to define a body of literature by a particular, preferred ideological leaning. (It doesn't count as "ethnic" unless it's *Left.*)

It would seem that Rivero is engaged in a project of what Werner Sollors calls the invention of ethnicity. Drawing on Benedict Anderson's writings on the formation of nations and nationalism, Sollors calls attention to the premise that ethnicities, like nations, are "imagined communities" rather than peoples connected by any essential, natural, or unchanging relations. What connects these communities is a set of "collective fictions" that, far from being themselves stable, are "intensely debated" and "continually reinvented" (xi). Ethnicity, in other words, is not born but made; and furthermore, it is not made once and for all, but is always being remade. The "markers" of ethnicity—of what makes someone "authentically" a member of a given ethnic group—are not set in stone, but can change to suit current needs and pressures. (One of the functions of "collective fictions," however, is to make such markers seem obvious and "given," so that we assume, for example, that Spanish-speaking residents of the United States are "of course" Latino/a and share a common culture. Here Spanish becomes one of the "obvious" markers of ethnicity.) And the phrase "collective fictions" draws our attention to the fact that ethnicity (like "nation" in Homi Bhabha's postulation of "nation as narration")[6] is *narrated:* "Texts are not mere reflections of existing differences but also, among many other things, productive forces in nation-building [and ethnicity-building] enterprises" (Sollors, xv). That is to say, the writings from a given ethnic group do not simply "reflect" that group's ethnicity in some unproblematic way; rather, they actively "produce" it, by engaging in the making of a collective fiction of what that ethnic group "is."

These insights are especially powerful in understanding the formulation of "Latino/a" ethnicity. As several critics have observed, there are no necessary, essential qualities that link people of Chicano/a, Puerto Rican, Cuban, Dominican, or other Central or South American descent into a single, and singular, ethnicity labeled "Latino" or "Hispanic."[7] U.S. Hispanics, Geoffrey Fox writes, include "some 25 million people who don't know or care much about one [an]other, don't think or talk alike, and have not until recently thought of themselves as having any common interests" (22). While such a statement may seem extreme, it is in many ways accurate; the interests and sensibilities of the different groups labeled by the term *Hispanic* certainly do not always coincide, and might even be opposed.[8] Indeed, some critics and authors reject such a label outright, preferring to be understood by their specific heritage.[9] Nevertheless, there are clearly certain advantages to linking these groups together under a single label;[10] thus Latino/as have at times participated in the construction of a single "ethnicity" which binds peoples of Spanish-speaking descent in the U.S.—a construction which, in order to be persuasive, often seeks to "ignore the deep differences concealed within the census's metanational category 'Hispanics'" in order to convert the "statistical fiction" into a "social reality" (Fox, 22–23).

Fox suggests that there are different versions of the "constructed" category of "Hispanics" as a singular people. One version—Fox associates it with the "Right"— has, as its goal, to gain access to power within existing social and political structures; but another more "Left" (Fox's word) version is built around "solidarity for the other 'little guys'" and is directly antagonistic to the white "power structure" (Fox, 11–12). It is this version of constructed Latino/a ethnicity which, I suggest, is furthered by Rivero's quite specific distinctions between Cuban exiles and Cuban American ethnics. Rivero's article is itself one of the texts which narrates ethnicity, linking Cuban *American* writing to the "Third World stance of many Chicano and Nuyorican writers" (183) in defining a Latino/a ethnicity which will always, by its very "nature," advance a progressive ideology (Rivero declares, for example, that "Chicano literature . . . is *by essence and definition* a literature . . . of social protest" [178–79; emphasis mine]), while leaving out the troubling literature by Cuban exiles that might seem to contest such an understanding of Latino/a literature. As Rivero puts it: "The closer [Cuban-American writers] get to an appreciation of minority life in American society, and the more they empathize with Chicanos and Neoricans, the more alienated they become with respect to their original 'exile culture'" (187). Empathy with other U.S. Latino groups makes a writer of Cuban origin a Latino/a writer, rather than a writer "of exile"; the labels are mutually exclusive. We need never again question or challenge the politics of U.S. Latino/a ethnic texts, since if they are conservative, they are by definition not U.S. Latino/a literature but rather literature of exile. (Thus there is no reason to study them in a class on U.S. Latino/a literature or U.S. ethnic literature, not to mention a class in U.S. literature more generally.)

But it is not only Cuban exiles that are excluded by virtue of such a definition. Where would Rivero put Richard Rodriguez, born and raised in the U.S. and one of the most recognized of Mexican American writers, whose work has been criticized for its conservative and assimilationist attitudes? Do those attitudes disqualify him as a Latino writer? (He is certainly not an "exile" writer.) While the goal of creating solidarity around issues of marginalization and (dis)empowerment is of central concern for many in the (imagined) Latino/a community, it seems to me that to use literary classifications in this way is to "essentialize" ethnic writing ("by *essence* . . . a literature of social protest") in a way that does not allow for alternative and less popular or less attractive expressions of ethnic experience, such as the desire to assimilate.

The Dominican-American writer Julia Alvarez's second novel, *In the Time of the Butterflies,* poses another challenge to these critically constructed categorizations. Although Alvarez came to the U.S. as a young child and is therefore presumably an "ethnic" writer, *In the Time of the Butterflies* does not explicitly "engage questions of biculturalism and cultural transformation" that are said to be the characteristics of U.S. ethnic Latino/a literature. Rather, the text, set entirely in the Dominican Republic, attempts to imaginatively recreate the stories of three sisters, the Mirabals, who have become historical figures because of their efforts in the resistance to the dictator Rafael Trujillo. Alvarez's subject matter would seem, according to the critics who distinguish between "exile" and "U.S. ethnic" literature, to place her quite firmly in the "exile" camp; the novel is "about" the political situation in the country of origin that propelled Alvarez's own exile. But these critics don't *expect* Alvarez to be writing an exile novel; as someone who came to the U.S. as a *child,* not an already developed writer, she "should" be writing U.S. ethnic literature. Roberto González Echevarría, a prominent scholar of Latin American literature, begins his *New York Times* review of *In the Time of the Butterflies* by echoing the assumptions of other critics on the appropriate and even definitional concerns for ethnic U.S. literature: "The central concern of Hispanic writers in this country [is] the pains and pleasures of growing up in a culture and a language outside the mainstream."

Based upon this apparently descriptive, but actually (as we shall see) quite prescriptive, characterization, González Echevarría privileges Cristina García's *Dreaming in Cuban* and Julia Alvarez's first novel, *How the García Girls Lost Their Accents.* Conversely, González Echevarría criticizes *In the Time of the Butterflies* on the grounds that in this novel Alvarez writes "as if she needed to have her American self learn what it was really like in her native land, the Dominican Republic." He notes the metafictional figure in *Butterflies* who is "a thinly disguised version of Ms. Alvarez, an Americanized Dominican woman who wants to write something about the Mirabals and is looking for information. . . . *In the Time of the Butterflies* reads like the project the Americanized Dominican woman at the beginning of the novel . . . would have come up with after pondering the fate of the Mirabal sisters from her perspective as a teacher on a United States college campus today." Although González Echevarría seems to think this a scathing criticism, it is clear that this is *precisely* the project of *In the Time of the Butterflies;* the function of the "Americanized Dominican woman" in the novel is to remind readers of how Alvarez's perspective on her country of origin is highly conditioned by her having been "Americanized." We can see the difficulties critics have in responding to a work by an "ethnic" writer that does not fit the definitional parameters of ethnic writing (it is not centrally concerned with biculturalism), and then in dealing with the elements of biculturalism that resurface, after all, in what looks like an "exile" text.[11]

As I have already discussed, one assumption of critics who treat "exile" and "ethnic" as distinct and non-

overlapping categories is that literature of exile strictly speaking does not significantly "engage questions of biculturalism and cultural transformation"—that is, that it is somehow "monocultural" and not significantly "transformed" by virtue of being produced in the U.S. In fact, the *only* influence the move to the U.S. has had, in the logic of this critique, is that the country of origin is no longer immediately accessible and must be looked back to in longing—hence the "nostalgia." What is interesting about this construction of "nostalgia" is that it seems to contain within it two paradoxical assumptions: first, that the culture is "lost" to the person who must therefore feel nostalgia for it (it is no longer practically accessible); and second, that it is not lost at all, that it is in fact still basically the *only* culture shaping the person's perspective. In turn, this second assumption implies an *essential* relationship to the country and culture of origin. Thus Latino/a literature of exile is assumed to have an authoritative, authentic relationship to a Latin American country and culture; it is "thematically and aesthetically tied to the respective national traditions" (Epple, 336).

Yet it is surely the case that exile writing produced in the U.S. bears the stamp of its new context; no work can be divorced from the historical and social conditions under which it is written. Exile constructions of their own ethnicity *within a U.S. context* may, for example, be affected by the need to assert, in a foreign land, a certain authority of speech, as Salvador Jiménez Fajardo observes. Such an authority might be granted by the "testimonial sense, [in which] exilic speech bears the stamp of personal witnessing that brings a 'true' picture of past events" (184–85; quoted in Epple, 335). Writing which suggests an untroubled, essential, and even representative relationship to a home country might then be construed as an effort to "authorize" one's voice within the new U.S. setting. U.S. popular culture perpetuates an understanding of "Hispanics" generally as essentially linked to their culture of origin, as Christian suggests in noting that book jackets and reviews of U.S. Latino/a writers will repeatedly compare them to prominent Latin American writers such as Borges or García Márquez (121–22). Thus asserting the "authority" to speak for a culture of origin left behind is one permissible way to claim authority within a new U.S. cultural context.

Conversely, it is also surely the case that much writing termed "ethnic" is shaped by the experience of exile. Writers such as Alvarez, Obejas, García, and Fernández—to name just a few—are all products of exile who are now considered "ethnic" authors, having immigrated to the U.S. as children. Literature by these authors is often *strongly* backward looking, even though it is *also* about "biculturalism and cultural transformation"—that is, it willfully and self-consciously occupies the expected position of "nostalgia" in order to *say something* about the way that nostalgia has been constructed in previous texts, both literary and critical. To exclude the work of certain authors from the category of "literature of exile" when their writing has in fact been shaped by the experience of exile is thus to attempt to impose boundaries which will make literature of exile look amazingly homogeneous and without internal critique (much the same as saying that all "ethnic" literature is literature of "social protest" without conservative elements). A careful examination of the narratives of writers who were exiled as children and have grown up in the U.S. suggests that "nostalgia" marks their texts just as surely as it does those of adult exiles; but such an examination also encourages a reconsideration of nostalgia, which is often represented in this literature as itself a "constructed" version of ethnicity which has everything to do with being located in U.S. culture.

Roberto Fernández's novel *Raining Backwards* is one effort by a Cuban exile/ethnic to problematize the cultural authority of the "exile" position. The first vignette in the novel is called "Retrieving Varadero," referring to the famous Cuban "Varadero Beach." In this hilarious vignette, which I quote at length to convey a sense of its sexually suggestive momentum, an exiled Cuban woman uses her idealized nostalgic stories of her Cuban past to elicit increasingly intimate favors from a much younger Cuban exile hungry for stories of the homeland he does not remember.

> Eloy had been serving Mirta faithfully for the last two months in exchange for tidbits of the past. He was thirsty for learning about the golden-roofed cities of that enchanted island. . . . Very slowly, Mirta came to realize that her words had a narcotic effect upon the youth, and shrewdly opted to trace her remembrances of memories for practical favors that could ease the burden of living. . . .
>
> "Why don't you bathe me before you go?" . . .
>
> "Okay, Miss Mirta, but tell me more. Tell me more" . . .
>
> "It was on Varadero Beach that I met my only fiancé. It was a week after the 1943 storm . . . and the breezes were warm . . . a little bit more to the right, lather me right down there . . . but the breezes were never hot and you didn't need suntan lotion and the white seals would play happily with the swimmers . . . and when it rained, it rained molasses and rice so you just needed to open your mouth and eat and if you wanted more to eat you just simply said: 'Sea creatures, I'm hungry,' and the fish and the mollusks would

> jump from the water to your pan and the sand had the texture of baby powder and the breezes were warm but . . ."
>
> "Miss Mirta, you already told me about the breezes and the sand." . . .
>
> For the first time, Mirta realized that the well of remembrances that she had been exploiting was about to run dry. . . .
>
> "Tell me more! If you don't continue, I won't either."
>
> Mirta, alarmed by his attitude, tried to lure him again with her all but exhausted memories.
>
> "The white seals then came accompanied by yodelers. . . ." [Another extended series of nostalgic "memories" follows.]
>
> "What's the matter, Miss Mirta? You're sweating! Are you okay? Do you want me to call my aunt?"
>
> "It's nothing. It's just that I get excited when I remember so many beautiful memories. But please, please don't stop lathering me, but now a little bit toward the left . . . please."
>
> "But Miss Mirta. I'm too tired and my aunt . . ."
>
> "I'll tell you more, my love. I'll tell you so much. . . ." (41–45)

Fernández is obviously having fun here, first of all by parodying Cuban exile nostalgia as an always-already idealized *construction* of the past that is driven by *desire,* so that we can read Mirta's sexual desire, which produces romanticized narratives of the homeland, as a metaphor for desire for the lost homeland itself. Further, the production of memories is actually driven by their exchange value: Mirta can exchange her memories for other benefits, and she wields a certain power, as long as she is producing narratives of her homeland, that she loses if she withholds those narratives. Nostalgia, Fernández's text suggests, can in no way result in an "authoritative" representation of the culture of origin, since its precondition is the U.S. context that drives desire and rewards the production of "testimony" about the homeland. Contrary to the assumption of an essential cultural identity preserved and transmitted through memories, Fernández suggests that memories of the country of origin are themselves a U.S. cultural product, and therefore always already hybrid.

Other Latino/a writers confirm such a view of memory. In a recent interview, for example, Julia Alvarez tells of her sisters' memories of their last day in the Dominican Republic:

> One sister had written that we had pushed the car down the drive so that the secret police wouldn't hear the car. And my older sister said,

"That's silly, that never happened! That was in *The Sound of Music!*" We had seen that movie soon after coming to this country and were deeply moved by it. So that one sister had adapted her memory to the scenes in that movie. (Caminero-Santangelo, 18)

The sister's memory marks the simultaneous condition of exile and ethnicity; while focusing on the land of origin and the situation of exile, it is filtered through her current U.S. context. (Dominican exile resulting from Trujillo's dictatorship is imagined through an American movie's representation of Austrian exile resulting from Hitler's invasion.) Achy Obejas's novel *Memory Mambo* also addresses the theme of the unreliability of memory and the ways in which present context shapes remembering in particular ways. Obejas's narrator, Juani, starts out: "I've always thought of memory as a distinct, individual thing. I've read with curiosity about the large parts of our brains where memory resides" (9). These opening lines invoke the idea of memory as a physical repository for "facts" (a notion that would lend "authority" to memory) in order to spend the rest of the novel undermining this understanding of memory. The opening continues:

> My family and I came from Cuba to the U.S. by boat when I was six years old, in 1978. These are the facts: It was a twenty-eight-foot boat; there were fourteen of us; the trip lasted two days; we were picked up by the Coast Guard just a few miles from Key West.
>
> . . . The whole time this was happening, I didn't know what was going on. . . . So, if these are the facts, why do I remember so much more? Why do I remember foggy meetings around the kitchen table[?]. . . . Why do I remember driving around senselessly for days, in and out of the beaches outside *La Habana* . . .? My father planned our escape this way, but I never went along on these excursions. So why is it I can see my father's body, gleaming like larvae, vanishing into the water just off the shore? . . . How can I remember my father shaking the water off like a dog, . . . the hurried, nervous way he unearthed the street clothes he'd buried in newspapers in the sand? If these aren't my memories, then whose are they? Certainly not my father's—he always casts himself as the stoic hero in his stories, unshakable and inscrutable. He would have said his body shone like a blade; he would have quoted compatriots and collaborators applauding his brilliance. If these were my father's stories, they would be wholly congratulatory and totally void of meaningful detail. (11)

Juani criticizes her father's stories of the past for idealizing him—that is, for being constructed in such a way

as to grant him a certain authority. But it is entirely possible that her own memories, which position her as a "witness" to the subversive, conspiratorial meetings and excursions in preparation for escape, similarly work to grant her a certain cultural authority or prestige within the U.S., where her "authority" as a foreigner and as a lesbian will be limited at best. Memories are no guarantor of cultural authenticity; rather, they are just one more story we tell about ourselves as a way of *constructing* the meanings of our ethnicity and, in certain cases, of granting ourselves a certain cultural authority.

Latino/a writers problematize the "exile" versus "ethnic" dichotomy, and its attendant notions of static identity and rigid critical boundaries, in other (perhaps more overt) ways as well. In Cristina García's *Dreaming in Cuban,* for instance, the character who would logically be characterized as an "exile"—Lourdes Puente, who leaves Cuba with her husband and small daughter after the revolution—is in fact an instant, and willing, "ethnic," who adapts to her new country without the slightest trace of nostalgia: "Lourdes considers herself lucky. Immigration has redefined her, and she is grateful. Unlike her husband, she welcomes her adopted language, its possibilities for reinvention. . . . She wants no part of Cuba, no part of its wretched carnival floats creaking with lies, no part of Cuba at all, which Lourdes claims never possessed her" (73). As an exile, Lourdes is immediately "redefined" by her new surroundings; she holds no dreams of return. Though it may certainly be true that, as Kathleen Brogan suggests, "memories of Cuba . . . , despite her disavowals, still possess" Lourdes (98–99), this reading only underscores the argument that exile and ethnic are permeable and overlapping categories. Though Lourdes, as an adult "exile," "reinvents" herself in her new country (thus challenging critical understandings of exile), she also continues to bear the traces of her country of origin; she becomes, in other words, an ethnic hybrid.

The metaphor of "invention" is also deployed in Alvarez's representation of an adult exile in *How the García Girls Lost Their Accents.* Once again, invention stands for the possibilities of cultural adaptation and hybridity, as embraced by the *mother,* an adult exile from the Dominican Republic. In the chapter "Daughter of Invention," Laura García, who spends her time "inventing gadgets to make life easier for the American Moms" (138), speaks in a language that cross-pollinates English with Spanish: "'With patience and calm, even a burro can climb a palm.' This last was one of her many Dominican sayings she had imported into her scrambled English" (138). Further, though she, along with her husband Carlos, supposedly resists her daughters' increasing Americanization, unlike Carlos (and against his wishes), she speaks in English to them: "And her English was a mishmash of mixed-up idioms and sayings that showed she was 'green behind the ears,' as she called it" (135). Laura's "mixed-up" metaphors, splicing together distinct idiomatic expressions in the creation of a new linguistic "invention," are highly suggestive of exactly the sort of hybridity that is a signpost of ethnic "hyphenated" or "in-between" identity. This linguistic hybridity speaks to her desire to reinvent herself (like Lourdes Puente) in her new country. In contrast to Carlos, who still wonders "whether or not he might move his family back" now that the conditions of their exile (the dictatorship of Trujillo) are no longer present, Laura "had gotten used to the life here. She did not want to go back to the old country where . . . she was only a wife and mother. . . . Better an independent nobody than a high-class house-slave" (143–44). Though Laura's role as the protective mother seems to cast her as an "exile" who resists a sinister Americanizing influence on her daughters, she embraces this influence for herself, suggesting both the ways in which exile and ethnic categorizations can overlap, and the ways in which other aspects of identity, such as gender, can intersect with and complicate these categorizations.

In contrast, in terms of the supposed characteristics of "exile" sensibility, the most strikingly exilic characters in both *Dreaming in Cuban* and *García Girls* are in fact the young protagonists who came to the U.S. as small children—who, in other words, should be the novels' "ethnic" characters. (And indeed, they are this as well.) It is Lourdes's daughter Pilar in *Dreaming in Cuban* whose memories are laden with inescapable nostalgia: "I'd run through great heaps of leaves just to hear them rustle like the palm trees during hurricanes in Cuba. But then I'd feel sad looking up at the bare branches and thinking about Abuela Celia. I wonder how my life would have been if I'd stayed with her" (32). Indeed, the desire to "go back" for Pilar is so strong that, early in the novel's narrative, she snaps, "That's it. My mind's made up. I'm going back to Cuba. I'm fed up with everything around here" (25). And the central character of Alvarez's *García Girls* is similarly driven back to her country of origin by a painful and lingering sense of what she has "lost," so that this novel opens with her return to the Dominican Republic, possibly to stay: "Let this turn out to be my home, Yolanda wishes. . . . This is what she has been missing all these years without really knowing that she has been missing it. Standing here in the quiet, she believes she has never felt at home in the States, never" (11–12). Like Pilar, Yolanda "believes," in stereotypically exilic fashion, that she can only be "at home" in the land of origin. (Notice, however, that this notion of home is conveyed in highly

tentative terms: Yolanda "wishes" and "believes," rather than knowing, recognizing, or realizing.) The desire to return is much stronger, and more feverishly felt, for this second generation of American immigrants than for the first, in both novels. As both Alvarez and García make palpably clear, their own literature is centrally about the experience of exile, which affects the second generation in ways as powerful and profound as it does the first generation. To categorize this literature as "ethnic" *rather than* "exile" is to preempt serious consideration of the contribution it makes to a larger body of exile literature, or to the critical conversation about exile.[12]

Of course, the larger narrative structures of both *García Girls* and *Dreaming in Cuban* undermine the young protagonists' naïve views that somehow they are culturally tied solely or even primarily to their countries of origin. The logic of both narratives leads these characters to understand the ways in which they have already been inescapably influenced by their second land, so that homecomings of the sort they imagine will never be possible for them. Thus, when Pilar finally returns to Cuba, years later—in a section titled "The Languages Lost"—she recognizes, "Sooner or later I'd have to return to New York. I know now it's where I belong — not *instead* of here, but *more* than here" (236).[13] And Yolanda, no matter how *she* perceives herself, is perceived as distinctly American by her extended family in the Dominican Republic, who greet her with a chorus of "Here she comes, Miss America!" (4); thus she herself is rendered into a striking symbol of U.S. nationalism that contrasts dramatically with the cake, in the shape of the Dominican Republic, that is brought out to celebrate her return, with a candle "for each year you've been away" (6). The repeated emphasis in both novels' homecomings is on the realization that the country of origin is no longer "home" for the young exiled protagonists.

But in the context of both characters' extreme nostalgia for their homelands and poignant emphasis on "loss," such reminders of their Americanization do far more than confirm their "ethnic" status. It is vital to keep in mind that these young protagonists are themselves the most obvious exile figures of the novels; thus the undermining of their idealized assumptions that "home" is still the homeland in some unproblematic way is in fact a larger commentary about the repressions necessary in any formulation of exile nostalgia, and a broader critique of the assumption that *any* exile can remain monocultural, uninfluenced by the land of transplantation. (Recall that each character's mother is in fact *more* dramatically influenced by the new culture than is her daughter, at least in the early period of the move to the U.S.) As Salman Rushdie has written, exiles "are haunted by some sense of loss, some urge to reclaim, to look back. . . . But if we do look back, we must also do so in the knowledge — which gives rise to profound uncertainties — that . . . we will not be capable of reclaiming precisely the thing that was lost; that we will, in short, create fictions . . . imaginary homelands" (10). Rushdie's comments remind us, once again, of Roberto Fernández's *Raining Backwards,* in which the paradigmatic exile, Mirta, represents her homeland through highly imaginative fictions constructed by desire. But even further, Rushdie's representation of exile (like Alvarez's and García's) undermines the assumption of exilic monoculturalness implicit in the critical distinctions between exile and ethnic, and suggests that to be an exile is *always already* to be an ethnic, one whose profound encounter with another culture will make it forever impossible to "return home" — to resume the old existence and former ways of seeing — even if a geographic return becomes possible.

What my analysis of texts by "ethnic" U.S. Latino/as has demonstrated, I hope, is that these texts vigorously resist the rigid and dichotomous characterization of exile versus ethnic that has come to be reified in critical studies, such that it often goes unquestioned even for literary critics whose studies actually suggest a more complex relationship between the two categories. This is not to suggest, however, that the texts I have examined reject the affiliation with disempowered minorities and concern with the "Third World" that form the basis of Eliana Rivero's construction of U.S. Latino/a ethnicity (and of U.S. ethnicity in general). Rather, it is to suggest that the texts propose a larger vision of constructed U.S. Latino/a ethnicity, one which, while it often works to connect itself to other ethnic minorities in the U.S., also potentially includes the first generation of U.S. exiles. Thus, in these texts, diverging views on the nature of exile or the relationship to the country of origin are portrayed as debates *within* the Latino/a community, rather than as arguments the community has with something outside of itself. That is, the vision of Latino/a ethnicity offered by such texts is far more diverse and heterogeneous than critics like Rivero or González Echevarría would have it.

The labor required to construct and maintain such a community is thus acknowledged as more difficult and necessarily more self-conscious than an essentialist definition recognizes; connections among Latino/a groups within the U.S., as well between U.S. Latino/as and disempowered "Third World" populations in countries of origin, are represented as strategic and coalitional rather than essential and defining. As Félix Padilla has explained, "Latino ethnic conscious behavior is *situa-*

tionally specific, crystallized under certain circumstances of inequality experience shared by more than one Spanish-speaking group at a point in time" (13). To ignore the strategic nature of Latino ethnic consciousness — to assume that Latino ethnicity, by definition (even if that definition excludes "exiles"), automatically signifies empathy for the often differently disempowered positions of every Latino/a group — is in fact to ignore the work that must be done in bridging such differences to construct a strategic Latino/a community. As Suzanne Oboler cautions: "The present dynamics within the Latino groups sometimes seem to suggest that the continued lack of recognition of the implications of differences within the group may ultimately hinder efforts to unite in the various and ongoing struggles for social justice" (xviii). Critics such as Rivero, who hope to solve the problem of differences by simply removing a predominantly conservative exile population from consideration, implicitly assume that the remaining constituents of the group are tied together by fundamental similarities. But only by starting from the understanding that U.S. Latino/as are always already riven by at times overwhelming differences can the real work of forging community out of those differences begin.[14]

Marta Caminero-Santángelo, Summer 2000

■ WORKS CITED

Alvarez, Julia. *How the García Girls Lost Their Accents.* New York. Plume/Penguin. 1991.

———. *In the Time of the Butterflies.* 1994. New York. Plume/Penguin. 1995.

Alvarez Borland, Isabel. *Cuban-American Literature of Exile: From Person to Persona.* Charlottesville. University Press of Virginia. 1998.

Anderson, Benedict. *Imagined Communities: Reflections on the Origin and Spread of Nationalism.* Revised edition. New York. Verso. 1991.

Anzaldúa, Gloria. *Borderlands/La Frontera: The New Mestiza.* San Francisco. Spinsters/Aunt Lute. 1987.

Bhabha, Homi K. *The Location of Culture.* London. Routledge. 1994.

Brogan, Kathleen. *Cultural Haunting: Ghosts and Ethnicity in Recent American Literature.* Charlottesville. University Press of Virginia. 1998.

Bruce-Novoa, Juan. "Hispanic Literature in the United States." In *American Writing Today.* Richard Kostelanetz, ed. Troy, N.Y. Whitston. 1991.

Caminero-Santangelo, Marta. "Seeing Difference: Murdering Mothers in Morrison, García, and Viramontes." In *The Madwoman Can't Speak: Or Why Insanity Is Not Subversive.* Ithaca, N.Y. Cornell University Press. 1998.

———. "Speaking for Others: Problems of Representation in the Novels of Julia Alvarez." *Antipodas,* 10 (1998), pp. 53–66.

———. "'The Territory of the Storyteller': An Interview with Julia Alvarez." *Antipodas,* 10 (1998), pp. 15–24.

Christian, Karen. *Show & Tell: Identity as Performance in U.S. Latina/o Fiction*. Albuquerque. University of New Mexico Press. 1997.

Epple, Juan Armando. "Hispanic Exile in the United States." In *Handbook of Hispanic Cultures in the United States: Literature and Art*. Francisco Lomelí, ed. Houston. Arte Público. 1993. Pp. 333–59.

Fernández, Roberto G. *Raining Backwards*. Houston. Arte Público. 1988.

Fox, Geoffrey. *Hispanic Nation: Culture, Politics, and the Constructing of Identity*. Secaucus, N.J. Carol Group. 1996.

García, Cristina. *Dreaming in Cuban*. New York. Ballantine. 1992.

Giménez, Martha E. "'Latino/Hispanic'—Who Needs a Name? The Case Against a Standardized Terminology." *International Journal of Health Services*, 19:3 (1989), pp. 557–71.

González Echevarría, Roberto. "Sisters in Death" (review of Julia Alvarez's *In the Time of the Butterflies*). *New York Times Book Review*, 18 December 1994, p. 28.

Jiménez Fajardo, Salvador. Review of Michael Ugarte's *Shifting Ground: Spanish Civil War Exile Literature*. *Siglo XX/20th Century*, 8:1–2 (1990–91), pp. 183–91.

Novas, Himilce. *Everything You Need to Know About Latino History*. New York. Plume/Penguin. 1994.

Obejas, Achy. *Memory Mambo*. Pittsburgh. Cleis. 1996.

Oboler, Suzanne. *Ethnic Labels, Latino Lives: Identity and the Politics of (Re)Presentation in the United States*. Minneapolis. University of Minnesota Press. 1995.

Padilla, Félix. *Latino Ethnic Consciousness: The Case of Mexican Americans and Puerto Ricans in Chicago*. Notre Dame, Indiana. University of Notre Dame Press. 1985.

Rivero, Eliana. "Hispanic Literature in the United States: Self-Image and Conflict." *Revista Chicano-Riqueña*, 13:3–4 (Fall-Winter 1985), pp. 173–91.

Rushdie, Salman. "Imaginary Homelands." In his *Imaginary Homelands: Essays and Criticism 1981–1991*. New York. Viking Penguin. 1991.

Santiago, Fabiola. "A People Ask: Who Are We?" *Miami Herald*, 6 October 1996, pp. A1, A2.

Sollors, Werner. "Introduction: The Invention of Ethnicity." In *The Invention of Ethnicity*. Werner Sollors, ed. New York. Oxford University Press. 1989. Pp. ix-xx.

Stavans, Ilán. *The Hispanic Condition: Reflections on Culture and Identity in America*. New York. HarperCollins. 1995.

[1] The term *Hispanic* does not in any way correct the ambiguity of the term *Latino,* with which it is synonymous and like which it is generally understood to refer to ethnics in the U.S. but sometimes to "Hispanic" (that is, Latin American) countries and peoples.

[2] Although people of other Spanish-speaking countries have also come to the United States as exiles, they are currently virtually invisible in the discussion of "exile" Latino/a literature. This may be attributed in part to their relatively small representation in the body of published literature by "Latino/as" living in the States. The Chilean-born writer Isabel Allende, who since 1988 has resided and written in the USA, represents one notable exception. The Dominican-born writer Julia Alvarez, who came to the U.S. in exile with her family when she was a child, is generally considered an "ethnic" rather than an "exile" writer, as we shall see. Another writer of Dominican background, Junot Diaz, is a relative newcomer to the scene of Latino/a publishing in the U.S.

[3] Alvarez Borland also identifies, and discusses at some length, a group she refers to (following Pérez-Firmat) as the "'one-and-a-half' generation": "writers who left Cuba during their early adolescence and thus had Cuban childhoods and U.S. adulthoods" (7). For Alvarez Borland, this group serves a transitional role between exiles and ethnics.

[4] Alvarez Borland sticks most closely to a descriptive, rather than a prescriptive, discussion of common characteristics within each body of writing, and to a distinction based upon age of immigration rather than upon the characteristics of the writing itself. Perhaps as a result, her analysis of individual texts does not support a rigid "ethnic" versus "exile" dichotomy.

[5] Juan Bruce-Novoa apparently concurs with this assessment: "We can eliminate immediately from our discussion the Cuban literary production in the United States. Their main literary activity comes from writers who consider themselves exiles more than U.S. citizens or permanent residents" (469). In this critical proclamation, even more extreme than Rivero's in its gestures of inclusion and exclusion, both first-and second-generation Cuban exile writers are dismissed from the body of U.S. Latino/a literature on the basis of an assumed presumption about the self-perception of a majority of them.

[6] Karen Christian, in her own explication of the construction of Latino/a ethnicity, applies Homi Bhabha's concept of "nation as narration" to the category of ethnicity, much as Sollors applies Anderson's theory of "imagined communities." See Bhabha, p. 142; cited in Christian, pp. 14–15.

[7] See for example Alvarez Borland, p. 149; Oboler, pp. xi-xii, 1–2; Giménez, pp. 557–71.

[8] Fox explains, for example, that, "until the end of the 1960s," U.S. newspapers for Spanish-speaking audiences catered to specific Latino ethnic groups that "had little contact with one another, separated by geography, dialect, and radically different social and political concerns. The Cubans seemed to care about nothing but overthrowing the revolution in Cuba, the Puerto Ricans debated their island's political status (as commonwealth, republic, or state) . . . , while the Mexicans were concerned about immigration law, anti-Mexican discrimination, and other local problems" (41–42). Fox makes a compelling argument that one of the pivotal factors in the construction of a sense of Latino peoplehood was the growth of media (such as television) that attempted to appeal to *all* Hispanic groups at once in an effort to increase audiences.

[9] Like Fox, Pérez-Firmat argues that the term *Latino* does not refer to an actual ethnicity; but for Pérez-Firmat, this means that such umbrella terms should therefore be rejected in favor of more specific ethnic categories: "Latino is a statistical fiction, a figment of the imagination of ethnic ideologues, ad executives and salsa singers. I am not a Latino. I am Cuban. . . . To me, Latino is an empty concept. Latino doesn't have a culture, a language, a place of origin" (quoted in Santiago and cited in Alvarez Borland, p. 150). The prominent Chicana writer Gloria Anzaldúa seems to suggest that umbrella terms such as *Latino* or *Hispanic* undermine a specific politicized Chicano/a community: "We call ourselves Hispanic or Spanish-American or Latin American or Latin when linking ourselves to other Spanish-speaking peoples of the Western hemisphere and when cop-

ping out" (62). Other writers/critics who present skeptical views of the value of an overarching term include (but are certainly not limited to) Alvarez Borland, Oboler, and Giménez. A quite different debate, of course, concerns the preference for *Latino* over *Hispanic;* the latter is an argument about which umbrella term is preferable, rather than about whether to use one at all. For an explanation of the debate between terms, see Fox, pp. 12–15; Stavans, pp. 24–27; and Oboler, pp. 3–4. A basic discussion useful in the teaching of undergraduate courses is also found in Novas, pp. 2–4.

[10] As Fox observes of the evolution of the umbrella term, "It was in the interests of Hispanics to be counted—the more there were, the more attention they would get. . . . Mexican Americans, Puerto Ricans, Cubans, and others . . . were eager to be grouped together to get the largest possible numbers for purposes of congressional redistricting and for the allotment of federal funds" (30, 32).

[11] A version of my discussion of González Echevarría's review of Alvarez's *In the Time of the Butterflies* appeared, in a different context, in my article "Speaking for Others: Problems of Representation in the Novels of Julia Alvarez," *Antipodas,* 10 (1998), pp. 53–66.

[12] Alvarez Borland rectifies this damaging exclusion by treating works by García, Fernández, Obejas, and others as part of a larger tradition of Cuban exile writing beginning with a first generation of exile writers such as Reinaldo Arenas and Guillermo Cabrera Infante. As Alvarez Borland rightly states, "Cuban-American literary expression is firmly grounded in the experience of exile" (149). In light of this view, her preservation of the terms *exile* and *Cuban American ethnic* as fairly mutually exclusive seems puzzling.

[13] See Caminero-Santangelo, "Seeing Difference," for a more extended discussion of the ways in which the narrative of *Dreaming in Cuban* ultimately undermines Pilar's assumption of intimate and even immediate connections between herself and Cuba.

[14] Special thanks to the University of Kansas Faculty General Research Fund for supporting this project; and to Roy Boland, the editor of *Antipodas: Journal of Hispanic and Galician Studies of Australia and New Zealand,* for graciously granting permission to reproduce here, in revised form, a brief portion of the discussion from my article "Speaking for Others: Problems of Representation in the Novels of Julia Alvarez."

The Nobel Prize and Writers in the Hispanic World: A Continuing Story

The relationship between the Nobel Prize in Literature and the writers of the Hispanic world has not been, on the whole, a happy one. Many writers, critics, and readers in Spanish-speaking countries have decried the fact that several giants of Hispanic letters—the names of Benito Pérez Galdós, Rubén Darío, Miguel de Unamuno, Antonio Machado, Federico García Lorca, Julio Cortázar, and Jorge Luis Borges come to mind—went to their graves without having received the Nobel, and

they resent the fact that the first prize awarded to a Spanish writer was squandered on a mediocre playwright, José Echegaray (honored in 1904), whose melodramatic and bombastic plays are unreadable and unperformable today. (More than one graduate student has complained bitterly about the inclusion of plays by Echegaray in the Ph.D. reading lists, where he had been placed due to his international reputation based upon his receipt of the Nobel.)

On the other hand, similar mistakes in the choice of writers have been made by the Swedish Academy in the case of other literatures and, I hasten to add, since literary criticism is not an exact science, will continue to be made in the foreseeable future. Reading old lists of awards is a most melancholy and depressing pastime, since most of the writers celebrated by their contemporaries have long become passé and been totally forgotten. The Spanish Academy and the various committees and institutions that award prizes in the Hispanic world have also committed their share of mistakes. *Errare humanum est.*

What makes the Nobel Prize in Literature so remarkable is that by conferring instant international fame to the writer to whom it is awarded, it creates high expectations on the part of every potential reader. The writer is no longer compared to his peers, to the members of his literary generation or group, and is placed instead inside a magic circle, a sacred space which he inhabits in the company of the happy few, the handful of writers selected over the years as representing the highest embodiment of modern literary art. By separating the writer from the social and cultural environment that nurtured him, the Nobel Prize has created an artificial climate, much like a lush tropical garden kept alive by glass and steam.

The Hispanic world is not a well-organized entity. Separate trends are easy to observe: on the one hand, the peninsular culture of Spain, with its medieval roots and its great flowering in the Golden Age and beyond; then, across the ocean, dozens of Spanish-speaking countries whose presence in contemporary culture has become more prominent during recent decades. A friendly rivalry has developed between these two great branches of Hispanic culture, a vying for international attention, and of course the competition for the gold of the Nobel Prize is as keen as any Olympic Games sports rivalry. The Swedish Academy is, after all, a European institution and was perhaps slow in turning its attention to the growing achievements of Spanish American culture. When it finally awarded a prize to a Hispanic writer from across the Atlantic, the year was 1945 and the recipient was Gabriela Mistral, a woman of exquisite personality and undeniable poetic talent but whose verse was too reminiscent of the Rubén Darío *modernista* trend, as interpreted by Amado Nervo, to be a real leader. The prize should have gone instead to a real pioneer, to a Vicente Huidobro or a César Vallejo. The Swedish Academy was twenty-five years behind the times.

Another prize was squandered in 1922. The laurel went that year to the Spanish playwright Jacinto Benavente, whose vast production is now mostly obsolete and was already out of phase with modern times when the medallion was conferred. Technically effective, often witty, Benavente reminds us of an early George Bernard Shaw, or of Pinero, or perhaps James Barrie, and even occasionally Oscar Wilde. Fin-de-siècle mannerisms and conventions are very much part of his background. Perhaps two of his plays are still worth reading: *Los intereses creados* (1907; Eng. *The Bonds of Interest,* 1916) and *La Malquerida* (1913; Eng. *The Passion Flower,* 1917). Once more the Academy chose a writer whose work pointed toward the past, not the future.

To make matters worse, there is one important aspect of Hispanic letters that the Swedish Academy has ignored throughout the history of the prize: Catalan literature. No Catalan writer has ever received a Nobel Prize, in spite of a remarkable renaissance that has produced first-rank poets such as Joan Maragall, Josep Carner, Carles Riba, Salvador Espriu, Agustí Bartra, and J. V. Foix, and novelists such as Mercè Rodoreda and Llorenç Villalonga.

▪ ▪ ▪

All these remarks are a necessary preface to an account of the most recent prizes awarded to Hispanic writers: when the situation is as bad as it was in 1945, when all the mistakes appeared to have been made, one could perhaps hope for some improvement, and indeed the future did become brighter. I am tempted to state that in essence the Swedish Academy may have started from the wrong premise: it may have planned and intended for the Nobel Prize to educate the world about the basic values of literature and yet ended being educated itself by the arduous task it had undertaken. Its judgment has improved steadily.

In 1956 the prize went to the Spanish poet Juan Ramón Jiménez, and most responsible readers and critics in the Hispanic world stood up and cheered: for the first time, after so many years, the Academy had found a worthy Hispanic recipient for its prize. It had taken fifty-five years, since the first prize was awarded in 1901. Jiménez was a master, his prose poem *Platero y yo* (1917, Eng. *Platero and I,* 1946) a landmark, and his

later poems would transcend his symbolist origins into pantheistic experimental "pure" poetry. Nobody had praised the Academicians for speed; they proved to be slow but steady. After this success the rest of the way seems to have been relatively easy.

Still, many questions, doubts, and reservations are possible. The next prize conferred upon a Spanish-speaking writer went in 1967 to the Guatemalan novelist Miguel Ángel Asturias, the author of *El señor presidente* (1946; Eng. *Señor Presidente),* *Hombres de maíz* (1949; Eng. *Men of Corn),* and *Leyendas de Guatemala* (Legends from Guatemala; 1930). I do not claim that Asturias was a bad choice, but other names possibly carried more literary prestige and were unjustly overlooked by the Swedish Academy. Borges, for instance, had become internationally famous. Cortázar had already published many of his best short stories, and his novel *Rayuela* (Eng. *Hopscotch)* had appeared in 1963. Other good writers available were, for instance, the Mexican poet Octavio Paz and, in Spanish peninsular letters, the poets Jorge Guillén, Rafael Alberti, and Vicente Aleixandre (who was eventually to receive the prize). Pablo Neruda, the Chilean poet, was also a strong presence; he would have to wait a few more years.[1] Asturias had undeniable literary quality, however, and his masterpiece was both stylistically experimental (influenced by surrealism in some of its more memorable pages) and socially committed, a bitter satire and denunciation of dictatorship in Latin America. His retelling of Guatemalan legends was poetic and graceful.

A general feeling of enthusiasm greeted the next Nobel Prize given to a Hispanic writer: the recipient was Neruda, in 1971. It was obvious that the aim of the Swedish Academy was becoming more accurate. The feeling of pleasure and gratitude in the Spanish-speaking world was not shared by everybody: Neruda was perhaps too controversial, a real card-carrying member of the Chilean Communist Party and an outspoken champion of all the leftist causes in Latin America and elsewhere—and also, let us face it, a diehard Stalinist. Still, his poetic genius and his warm personality could not be ignored. This was a prize awarded to a great poet, to the author of *Veinte poemas de amor y una canción desesperada* (Twenty Love Poems and a Song of Despair; 1924), of *Canto general* (1950), of the *Odas elementales* (Elemental Odes; 1954). Briefly, his creative power and his influence upon other Latin American poets were at their peak. The Nobel Prize was applauded even by many readers and critics who were opposed to Neruda's political ideology. The choice had been right, and totally beyond politics. It was also a risky one: a few years before, in 1964, another leftist writer, Jean-

Paul Sartre, had been awarded the Nobel and had declined it. Would Neruda do the same? He did not, to the great relief of the Swedish Academy.

One must therefore applaud each right choice—without, however, abandoning a rigorous critical viewpoint. For each right choice it is possible to point out a wrong one. Let us never forget that the people who awarded the laurels to Neruda (and to Juan Ramón Jiménez, and later to Vicente Aleixandre and to Gabriel García Márquez, all outstanding writers, all worthy of the honor) belonged to the same institution that said no to Benito Pérez Galdós, the great Spanish novelist who was briefly considered in the same year in which the prize went jointly to Echegaray and Frédéric Mistral (1904), the same Academy that overlooked Marcel Proust and Franz Kafka but honored many writers whose names and works have been forgotten: for example, Karl Gjellerup and Henrik Pontoppidan (1917), Carl Spitteler (1919), Wladistaw Stanistaw Reymont (1924), Grazia Deledda (1926), and Erik Axel Karlfeldt (1931).

Vicente Aleixandre of Spain was the next Hispanic writer to receive the Nobel Prize, gaining the honor in 1977. Born in 1898, Aleixandre belongs to the brilliant Generation of '27, which included such great poets as Lorca, Guillén, Salinas, Alberti, and Cernuda. The prize was a fitting reward for a long and fruitful life wholly committed to poetry. Inspired by the German romantic poets and by surrealism, Aleixandre had developed a unique and powerful version of Spanish surrealism, a style especially adept at creating vast frescoes and cosmic visions. There is no doubt that Aleixandre is a major poet, and it is therefore difficult to quarrel with the choice. On the other hand, several other major poets belonging to the same generation also deserved recognition: Jorge Guillén, perhaps the most exquisite and serene of contemporary poets writing in Spanish; Rafael Alberti, who was Lorca's close friend and is a great poet himself; and the distinguished scholar-poet Dámaso Alonso.[2] Several Spanish critics have stated that it would have been far better to have Aleixandre and Guillén share the prize. In an essay I wrote for *WLT* soon after the Nobel was awarded to Aleixandre, I said much the same thing.

> Why Aleixandre? More explicitly, why should the Nobel Prize for Literature be awarded to Vicente Aleixandre in 1977? Barbara Walters, speaking through a nationwide television program, declared that the poet was virtually unknown outside his native Spain (which only proves the lack of intellectual preparedness of our television announcers). And yet, if Lorca had been alive today, there is no question that the

prize would have been his. The prize belongs not to a man, in this case, but to a whole generation, the generation of Lorca, Jorge Guillén, Rafael Alberti—perhaps the brightest and most original poetic generation in twentieth-century Western Europe. Not a restricted, disciplined group, as the French surrealists became, but rather a band of friends open to all influences.[3]

It was, in any case, the right time to award a prize to a Spanish poet: much was happening in Spain beneath the still hard-and-cold political surface, much that had to be encouraged, as I pointed out in the same essay.

> In his recent work Aleixandre, once more, renews himself without changing his poetic personality. His last two books, *Poemas de la consumación* and *Diálogos del conocimiento,* with their short sentences, their paradoxes, their moments (flashes) of illumination, remind me of Heraclitus, of the Oriental mystics, of Schopenhauer. Wisdom, resignation, a sad acceptance, a stubborn resistance. From surrealism to wisdom: this is the trajectory—a long and fruitful journey—of our poet. As Robert Bly has written: "For the Nobel Prize to come to Aleixandre now is fitting, not only because of the energy and intensity of his own poetry, but because it comes at this moment in Spanish history. Spain is waking up after years of sleep, and Aleixandre's poetry and stubborn presence have a strong part in that awakening." (207)

We are now coming to the end of our story: the last Nobel Prize to be conferred upon a Hispanic writer went to the Colombian novelist Gabriel García Márquez, the celebrated author of *Cien años de soledad* (1967; Eng. *One Hundred Years of Solitude,* 1970), born in 1928 and without any doubt the most famous novelist in the Hispanic world as well as one of the most prominent authors in international literary circles. The prize was awarded to him in 1982. Many other awards had come his way previously, including Colombia's Esso Literary Prize (1961) and most especially the Neustadt International Prize for Literature (1972), one of the most prestigious honors that can be obtained in our century and, as has been pointed out repeatedly, a prize that has become a "waiting room" or "antechamber" of the Nobel, since many of its candidates and recipients later have become winners of the Swedish prize.

It would be futile to cast any shadow of a doubt or criticism upon the presentation of the Nobel to such a distinguished author. García Márquez's novels have been received with rare unanimous enthusiasm by critics and the general reading public alike. They have been translated into many languages and have become part of our cultural horizon. García Márquez is, as a novelist, a paragon, a rara avis: both robust and sophisticated, he sometimes appears to be folksy and naïve but at second glance turns out to be subtle and complex. In other words, he can please all audiences. He has lived in many countries in addition to his native Colombia, especially Mexico and France, and is an outstanding member of that circle of Latin American writers responsible for the so-called Boom (Carlos Fuentes, Mario Vargas Llosa, Julio Cortázar, José Donoso, et cetera), a literary group that has revolutionized Hispanic fiction and established new benchmarks for contemporary prose. If this set has a leader, García Márquez would seem to be it. For the first time in many years fiction written in Spanish has commanded international attention and been translated time and time again. Viewed in terms of the sociology of culture, this is a phenomenon that has few precedents in our century. Academic critics of the highest sophistication attest to the quality and subtlety of the works produced by this group. Could there be any doubt that the Nobel awarded to García Márquez was an excellent choice and that with it the Swedish Academy was redeeming itself from past mistakes?

Alas, there can indeed be serious doubts that the choice made in 1982 was the right one. I am not simply trying to play the role of devil's advocate, although it is a necessary and useful one which someone has to play. I would appeal instead to the reader's common sense. Let us think of the Nobel Prize in Literature as a powerful lighthouse projecting its beam into a vast dark night. Its light is intermittent: it comes to us only once a year. Moreover, it moves and rotates, projecting its beam in what the French would call a *tour d'horizon*: after it has lit a certain cultural (and geographic) area, it will proceed onward until a few years later (five? ten? fifteen? more?) it will shine again with benevolence upon the same geographic-cultural area. It would be inconceivable—and it has never happened—that a Nobel Prize in Literature would be awarded in two successive years to two writers belonging to the same cultural and linguistic area (let us say, for instance, two French writers). Therefore an award to a relatively young author (García Márquez was fifty-four when chosen) almost unavoidably dooms much-older Hispanic writers to die unrewarded. Let us for a moment identify ourselves with such older Spanish-language writers as the great Argentine prose writer and poet Jorge Luis Borges (1899–1986), or the outstanding Spanish critic and poet Dámaso Alonso (b. 1898), or the Mexican poet and essayist Octavio Paz (b. 1914), or the Argentine fiction writer Julio Cortázar (1914–1984). No matter how much they applauded the choice of García Márquez in 1982, each one of them in his innermost thoughts must have

cursed it, since it practically eliminated any possibility of their ever receiving the prize themselves. (And in fact Borges died in 1986, having waited years in vain for a Nobel Prize he amply deserved, and Cortázar preceded him in death in 1984, also deprived of the award.) It would have been much better to have chosen Borges in 1982 and at that moment to have placed García Márquez on a "waiting list" that would have brought him the laurels at a later date, possibly eight to ten years afterward, especially if we consider that he is in some ways Borges's pupil and follower and that some of the most subtle and philosophical structures and devices in his masterpiece owe much to Borges's own conception of time and space. Without Borges's bold yet exquisite imagination we would not have the opening and closing chapters of *One Hundred Years of Solitude*. From the viewpoint of literary history it is Borges who turns out to be the seminal artist, the major thinker and theoretician, without whom neither García Márquez nor Cortázar (nor many other Boom writers) makes much sense. It would have helped immensely if the *real* leader of the new generation of Latin American fiction writers had been rewarded in 1982. It was obvious then that Borges would not be with us many more years. It was therefore a mistake, a miscalculation, not to give him the prize in 1982, when the attention of the Swedish Academy had become focused on Hispanic writers and a choice had to be made among them.

It would be unwarranted to end this essay on a negative note. The Swedish Academy's choice in 1982 was justified on many grounds, and certainly the recipient of the prize has continued to publish interesting and valuable novels, though none of the caliber of his earlier masterpiece. No critic (or group of critics) is infallible. Good will and hard work cannot be denied the Swedish Academy. It has learned much from previous mistakes. Its motto from now on should be that of one of our TV networks: "The best is yet to come."

Manuel Durán, Spring 1988

[1] On the writers listed here, see the following articles and special issues: on Borges, *BA* 45:3 (Summer 1971), pp. 383–470; *WLT* 58:1 (Winter 1984), pp. 57–58, and 62:1 (Winter 1988), pp. 5–10; on Cortázar, *BA* 50:3 (Summer 1976), pp. 503–608; on Paz, *BA* 46:4 (Autumn 1972), pp. 543–614, *WLT* 55:4 (Autumn 1981), pp. 628–29, and 56:4 (Autumn 1982), pp. 589–643; on Guillén, *BA* 42:1 (Winter 1968), pp. 7-60, *WLT* 56:4 (Autumn 1982), pp. 589–90, and 58:2 (Spring 1984), pp. 228–29; on Aleixandre, *WLT* 52:2 (Spring 1978), pp. 203–8; on Neruda, *BA* 46:1 (Winter 1972), pp. 49–55.

[2] On Dámaso Alonso, see *BA* 48:2 (Spring 1974), pp. 231–320.

[3] Manuel Durán, "Vicente Aleixandre, Last of the Romantics: The 1977 Nobel Prize for Literature," *WLT* 52:2 (Spring 1978), p. 203. Subsequent citations will be parenthetic by page number.

Mario Vargas Llosa *(Gil Jain)*

Social Commitment and the Latin American Writer

The Peruvian novelist José María Arguedas killed himself on the second day of December 1969 in a classroom of La Molina Agricultural University in Lima. He was a very discreet man, and so as not to disturb his colleagues and the students with his suicide, he waited until everybody had left the place. Near his body was found a letter with very detailed instructions about his burial—where he should be mourned, who should pronounce the eulogies in the cemetery—and he asked too that an Indian musician friend of his play the *huaynos* and *mulizas* he was fond of. His will was respected, and Arguedas, who had been, when he was alive, a very modest and shy man, had a very spectacular burial.

But some days later other letters written by him appeared, little by little. They too were different aspects of his last will, and they were addressed to very different people: his publisher, friends, journalists, academics, politicians. The main subject of these letters was his death, of course, or better, the reasons for which he decided to kill himself. These reasons changed from letter to letter. In one of them he said that he had decided to commit suicide because he felt that he was finished as a

writer, that he no longer had the impulse and the will to create. In another he gave moral, social and political reasons: he could no longer stand the misery and neglect of the Peruvian peasants, those people of the Indian communities among whom he had been raised; he lived oppressed and anguished by the crises of the cultural and educational life in the country; the low level and abject nature of the press and the caricature of liberty in Peru were too much for him, et cetera.

In these dramatic letters we follow, naturally, the personal crises that Arguedas had been going through, and they are the desperate call of a suffering man who, at the edge of the abyss, asks mankind for help and compassion. But they are not only that: a clinical testimony. At the same time, they are graphic evidence of the situation of the writer in Latin America, of the difficulties and pressures of all sorts that have surrounded and oriented and many times destroyed the literary vocation in our countries.

In the USA, in Western Europe, to be a writer means, generally, first (and usually only) to assume a personal responsibility. That is, the responsibility to achieve in the most rigorous and authentic way a work which, for its artistic values and originality, enriches the language and culture of one's country. In Peru, in Bolivia, in Nicaragua et cetera, on the contrary, to be a writer means, at the same time, to assume a social responsibility: at the same time that you develop a personal literary work, you should serve, through your writing but also through your actions, as an active participant in the solution of the economic, political and cultural problems of your society. There is no way to escape this obligation. If you tried to do so, if you were to isolate yourself and concentrate exclusively on your own work, you would be severely censured and considered, in the best of cases, irresponsible and selfish, or at worst, even by omission, an accomplice to all the evils— illiteracy, misery, exploitation, injustice, prejudice—of your country and against which you have refused to fight. In the letters which he wrote once he had prepared the gun with which he was to kill himself, Arguedas was trying, in the last moments of his life, to fulfill this moral imposition that impels all Latin American writers to social and political commitment.

Why is it like this? Why cannot writers in Latin America, like their American and European colleagues, be artists, and only artists? Why must they also be reformers, politicians, revolutionaries, moralists? The answer lies in the social conditions of Latin America, the problems which face our countries. All countries have problems, of course, but in many parts of Latin America, both in the past and in the present, the problems which constitute the closest daily reality for people are not freely discussed and analyzed in public, but are usually denied and silenced. There are no means through which those problems can be presented and denounced, because the social and political establishment exercises a strict censorship of the media and over all the communications systems. For example, if today you hear Chilean broadcasts or see Argentine television, you won't hear a word about the political prisoners, about the exiles, about the torture, about the violations of human rights in those two countries that have outraged the conscience of the world. You will, however, be carefully informed, of course, about the iniquities of the communist countries. If you read the daily newspapers of my country, for instance—which have been confiscated by the government, which now controls them—you will not find a word about the continuous arrests of labor leaders or about the murderous inflation that affects everyone. You will read only about what a happy and prosperous country Peru is and how much we Peruvians love our military rulers.

What happens with the press, TV and radio happens too, most of the time, with the universities. The government persistently interferes with them; teachers and students considered subversive or hostile to the official system are expelled and the whole curriculum reorganized according to political considerations. As an indication of what extremes of absurdity this "cultural policy" can reach, you must remember, for instance, that in Argentina, in Chile and in Uruguay the Departments of Sociology have been closed indefinitely, because the social sciences are considered subversive. Well, if academic institutions submit to this manipulation and censorship, it is improbable that contemporary political, social and economic problems of the country can be described and discussed freely. Academic knowledge in many Latin American countries is, like the press and the media, a victim of the deliberate turning away from what is actually happening in society. This vacuum has been filled by literature.

This is not a recent phenomenon. Even during the Colonial Period, though more especially since Independence (in which intellectuals and writers played an important role), all over Latin America novels, poems and plays were—as Stendhal once said he wanted the novel to be—the mirrors in which Latin Americans could truly see their faces and examine their sufferings. What was, for political reasons, repressed or distorted in the press and in the schools and universities, all the evils that were buried by the military and economic elite which ruled the countries, the evils which were never mentioned in the speeches of the politicians nor taught in the lecture halls nor criticized in the congresses nor

discussed in magazines found a vehicle of expression in literature.

So, something curious and paradoxical occurred. The realm of imagination became in Latin America the kingdom of objective reality; fiction became a substitute for social science; our best teachers about reality were the dreamers, the literary artists. And this is true not only for our great essayists—such as Sarmiento, Martí, Gonzáles Prada, Rodó, Vasconcelos, José Carlos Mariátegui—whose books are indispensable for a thorough comprehension of the historical and social reality of their respective countries, but it is also valid for the writers who only practiced the creative literary genres: fiction, poetry and drama. We can say without exaggeration that the most representative and genuine description of the real problems of Latin America during the nineteenth century is to be found in literature, and that it was in the verses of the poets or the plots of the novelists that, for the first time, the social evils of Latin America were denounced.

We have a very illustrative case with what is called *indigenismo,* the literary current which, from the middle of the nineteenth century until the first decades of our century focused on the Indian peasant of the Andes and his problems as its main subject. The indigenist writers were the first people in Latin America to describe the terrible conditions in which the Indians were still living three centuries after the Spanish conquest, the impunity with which they were abused and exploited by the landed proprietors—the *latifundistas,* the *gamonales*—men who sometimes owned land areas as big as a European country, where they were absolute kings who treated their Indians worse and sold them cheaper than their cattle. The first indigenist writer was a woman, an energetic and enthusiastic reader of the French novelist Emile Zola and the positivist philosophers: Clorinda Matto de Turner (1854–1909). Her novel *Aves sin nido* opened a road of social commitment to the problems and aspects of Indian life that Latin American writers would follow, examining in detail and from all angles, denouncing injustices and praising and rediscovering the values and traditions of an Indian culture which until then, at once incredibly and ominously, had been systematically ignored by the official culture. There is no way to research and analyze the rural history of the continent and to understand the tragic destiny of the inhabitants of the Andes since the region ceased to be a colony without going through their books. These constitute the best—and sometimes the only—testimony to this aspect of our reality.

Am I saying, then, that because of the authors' moral and social commitment this literature is good literature? That because of their generous and courageous goals of breaking the silence about the real problems of society and of contributing to the solution of these problems, this literature was an artistic accomplishment? Not at all. What actually happened in many cases was the contrary. The pessimistic dictum of André Gide, who once said that with good sentiments one has bad literature, can be, alas, true. Indigenist literature is very important from a historical and social point of view, but only in exceptional cases is it of literary importance. These novels or poems written, in general, very quickly, impelled by the present situation, with militant passion, obsessed with the idea of denouncing a social evil, of correcting a wrong, lack most of what is essential in a work of art: richness of expression, technical originality. Because of their didactic intentions they become simplistic and superficial; because of their political partisanship they are sometimes demagogic and melodramatic; and because of their nationalist or regionalist scope they can be very provincial and quaint. We can say that many of these writers, in order to serve better moral and social needs, sacrificed their vocation on the altar of politics. Instead of artists, they chose to be moralists, reformers, politicians, revolutionaries.

You can judge from your own particular system of values whether this sacrifice is right or wrong, whether the immolation of art for social and political aims is worthwhile or not. I am not dealing at the moment with this problem. What I am trying to show is how the particular circumstances of Latin American life have traditionally oriented literature in this direction and how this has created for writers a very special situation. In one sense people—the real or potential readers of the writer—are accustomed to considering literature as something intimately associated with living and social problems, the activity through which all that is repressed or disfigured in society will be named, described and condemned. They expect novels, poems and plays to counterbalance the policy of disguising and deforming reality which is current in the official culture and to keep alive the hope and spirit of change and revolt among the victims of that policy. In another sense this confers on the writer, as a citizen, a kind of moral and spiritual leadership, and he must try, during his life as a writer, to act according to this image of the role he is expected to play. Of course he can reject it and refuse this task that society wants to impose on him; and declaring that he does not want to be either a politician or a moralist or a sociologist, but only an artist, he can seclude himself in his personal dreams. However, this will be considered (and in a way, it is) a political, a moral and a social choice. He will be considered by his real and potential readers as a deserter and a traitor, and his poems, novels and plays will be endangered. To be an artist,

only an artist, can become, in our countries, a kind of moral crime, a political sin. All our literature is marked by this fact, and if this is not taken into consideration, one cannot fully understand all the differences that exist between it and other literatures of the world.

No writer in Latin America is unaware of the pressure that is put on him, pushing him to a social commitment. Some accept this because the external impulse coincides with their innermost feelings and personal convictions. These cases are, surely, the happy ones. The concidence between the individual choice of the writer and the idea that society has of his vocation permits the novelist, poet or playwright to create freely, without any pangs of conscience, knowing that he is supported and approved by his contemporaries. It is interesting to note that many Latin American men and women whose writing started out as totally uncommitted, indifferent or even hostile to social problems and politics, later—sometimes gradually, sometimes abruptly—oriented their writings in this direction. The reason for this change could be, of course, that they adopted new attitudes, acknowledging the terrible social problems of our countries, an intellectual discovery of the evils of society and the moral decision to fight them. But we cannot dismiss the possibility that in this change (conscious or unconscious) the psychological and practical trouble it means for a writer to resist the social pressure for political commitment also played a role, as did the psychological and practical advantages which led him to act and to write as society expects him to.

All this has given Latin American literature peculiar features. Social and political problems constitute a central subject for it, and they are present everywhere, even in works where, because of the theme and form, one would never expect to find them. Take the case, for example, of the "literature of fantasy" as opposed to "realist literature." This kind of literature, whose raw material is subjective fantasy, does not reflect, usually, the mechanisms of economic injustice in society nor the problems faced by urban and rural workers which make up the objective facts of reality; instead—as in Edgar Allan Poe or Villiers de L'Isle-Adam—this literature builds a new reality, essentially different from "objective reality," out of the most intimate obsessions of writers. But in Latin America (mostly in modern times, but also in the past) fantastic literature also has its roots in objective reality and is a vehicle for exposing social and political evils. So, fantastic literature becomes, in this way, symbolical literature in which, disguised with the prestigious clothes of dreams and unreal beings and facts, we recognize the characters and problems of contemporary life.

We have many examples among contemporary Latin American writers of this "realistic" utilization of unreality. The Venezuelan Salvador Garmendia has described, in short stories and novels of nightmarish obsessions and impossible deeds, the cruelty and violence of the streets of Caracas and the frustrations and sordid myths of the lower middle classes of that city. In the only novel of the Mexican Juan Rulfo, *Pedro Páramo* (1955)—all of whose characters, the reader discovers in the middle of the book, are dead people—fantasy and magic are not procedures to escape social reality; on the contrary, they are simple alternative means to represent the poverty and sadness of life for the peasants of a small Jalisco village.

Another interesting case is Julio Cortázar. In his first novels and short stories we enter a *fantastic* world, which is very mischievous because it is ontologically different from the world that we know by reason and experience yet has, at first approach, all the appearances—features—of real life. Anyway, in this world social problems and political statements do not exist; they are aspects of human experience that are omitted. But in his more recent books—and principally in the latest novel, *Libro de Manuel* (1973)—politics and social problems occupy a place as important as that of pure fantasy. The "fantastic" element is merged, in this novel, with statements and motifs which deal with underground militancy, terrorism, revolution and dictatorship.

What happens with prose also happens with poetry, and as among novelists, one finds this necessity for social commitment in all kinds of poets, even in those whom, because of the nature of their themes, one would expect not to be excessively concerned with militancy. This is what occurred, for instance, with religious poetry, which is, in general, very politicized in Latin America. And it is symptomatic that, since the death of Pablo Neruda, the most widely-known poet—because of his political radicalism, his revolutionary lyricism, his colorful and schematic ideology—is a Nicaraguan priest, a former member of the American Trappist monastery of Gethsemane: Ernesto Cardenal.

It is worth noting too that the political commitment of writers and literature in Latin America is a result not only of the social abuse and economic exploitation of large sectors of the population by small minorities and brutal military dictatorships. There are also cultural reasons for this commitment, exigencies that the writer himself sees grow and take root in his conscience during and because of his artistic development. To be a writer, to discover this vocation and to choose to practice it pushes one inevitably, in our countries, to discover all the handicaps and miseries of underdevelopment.

Inequities, injustice, exploitation, discrimination, abuse are not only the burden of peasants, workers, employees, minorities. They are also social obstacles for the development of a cultural life. How can literature exist in a society where the rates of illiteracy reach fifty or sixty percent of the population? How can literature exist in countries where there are no publishing houses, where there are no literary publications, where if you want to publish a book you must finance it yourself? How can a cultural and literary life develop in a society where the material conditions of life—lack of education, subsistence wages et cetera—establish a kind of cultural apartheid, that is, prevent the majority of the inhabitants from buying and reading books? And if, besides all that, the political authorities have established a rigid censorship in the press, in the media and in the universities, that is, in those places through which literature would normally find encouragement and an audience, how could the Latin American writer remain indifferent to social and political problems? In the practice itself of his art—in the obstacles that he finds for this practice—the Latin American writer finds reasons to become politically conscious and to submit to the pressures of social commitment.

We can say that there are some positive aspects in this kind of situation for literature. Because of that commitment, literature is forced to keep in touch with living reality, with the experiences of people, and it is prevented from becoming—as unfortunately has happened in some developed societies—an esoteric and ritualistic experimentation in new forms of expression almost entirely dissociated from real experience. And because of social commitment, writers are obliged to be socially responsible for what they write and for what they do, because social pressure provides a firm barrier against the temptation of using words and imagination in order to play the game of moral irresponsibility, the game of the enfant terrible who (only at the level of words, of course) cheats, lies, exaggerates and proposes the worst options.

But this situation has many dangers, too. The function and the practice of literature can be entirely distorted if the creative writings are seen only (or even mainly) as the materialization of social and political aims. What is to be, then, the borderline, the frontier between history, sociology and literature? Are we going to say that literature is only a degraded form (since its data are always dubious because of the place that fantasy occupies in it) of the social sciences? In fact, this is what literature becomes if its most praised value is considered to be the testimony it offers of objective reality, if it is judged principally as a true record of what happens in society.

On the other hand, this opens the door of literature to all kinds of opportunistic attitudes and intellectual blackmail. How can I condemn as an artistic failure a novel that explicitly protests against the oppressors of the masses without being considered an accomplice of the oppressor? How can I say that this poem which fulminates in assonant verses against the great corporations is a calamity without being considered an obsequious servant of imperialism? And we know how this kind of simplistic approach to literature can be utilized by dishonest intellectuals and imposed easily on uneducated audiences.

The exigency of social commitment can signify also the destruction of artistic vocations in that, because of the particular sensibility, experiences and temperament of a writer, he is unable to accomplish in his writings and actions what society expects of him. The realm of sensibility, of human experience and of imagination is wider than the realm of politics and social problems. A writer like Borges has built a great literary work of art in which this kind of problem is entirely ignored: metaphysics, philosophy, fantasy and literature are more important for him. (But he has been unable to keep himself from answering the social call for commitment, and one is tempted to see in his incredible statements on right-wing conservatism—statements that scare even the conservatives—just a strategy of political sacrilege in order not to be disturbed once and for all in his writings.) And many writers are not really prepared to deal with political and social problems. These are the unhappy cases. If they prefer their intimate call and produce uncommitted work, they will have to face all kinds of misunderstanding and rejection. Incomprehension and hostility will be their constant reward. If they submit to social pressure and try to write about social and political themes, it is quite probable that they will fail as writers, that they will frustrate themselves as artists for not having acted as their feelings prompted them to do.

I think that José María Arguedas experienced this terrible dilemma and that all his life and work bears the trace of it. He was born in the Andes, was raised among the Indian peasants (in spite of being the son of a lawyer) and, until his adolescence, was—in the language he spoke and in his vision of the world—an Indian. Later he was recaptured by his family and became a middle-class Spanish-speaking Peruvian white. He lived torn always between these two different cultures and societies. And literature meant for him, in his first short stories and novels (*Agua* [1935], *Yawar Fiesta* [1949], *Los ríos profundos* [1958]), a melancholic escape to the days and places of his childhood, the world of the little Indian villages—San Juan de Lucanas, Puquio—or towns of the Andes such as Abancay, whose landscapes

and customs he described in a tender and poetic prose. But later he felt obliged to renounce this kind of lyric image to fill the social responsibilities that everybody expected of him. And he wrote a very ambitious book, *Todas las sangres* (1964), in which he tried, escaping from himself, to describe the social and political problems of his country. The novel is a total failure: the vision is simplistic and even a caricature. We find none of the great literary virtues that made of his previous books genuine works of art. The book is the classic failure of an artistic talent due to the self-imposition of social commitment. The other books of Arguedas oscillate between those two sides of his personality, and it is probable that all this played a part in his suicide.

When he pressed the trigger of the gun, at the University of La Molina, on the second day of December in 1969, José María Arguedas was too, in a way, showing how difficult and daring it can be to be a writer in Latin America.

Mario Vargas Llosa, Winter 1978

ARGENTINA

Borges, Postcolonial Precursor

1. Postmodernism holds center stage as the major critical practice of the moment. And Borges is there, of course.[1] Critics working in Latin American literature, however, have noted the discomforts of fitting Borges, along with other Latin American authors, into the postmodern mold; as one critic asked graphically, if with some gender bias: "Is the corset too tight for the fat lady?"[2] One place where the corset pinches is in its elision of the Latin American condition of the texts. Typically, these are subsumed into Euro-U.S. concerns. The traits that mark their "postmodernism" are employed to illustrate trends in "late capitalist, bourgeois, informational, postindustrial society" and are said to respond to Western needs: for example, the "totalizing forces" of mass culture."[3] What is forgotten is the peripheric, ex-centric position. The "postmodern" characteristics of Latin American and Borgesian literature enthusiastically embraced by U.S. and European critics—self-reflexivity, indeterminacy, carnivalization, decanonization, intertextuality, pastiche, hybridity, the problematizing of time and space and of historical and fictional narration—are primarily a correlative of a colonized history and an uncohered identity, of incomplete modernity and uneven cultural development, rather than postindustrialization and mass culture. Their uncritical incorporation into a metropolitan repertoire indicates

that the centering impulse of a "decentered" postmodernism is far from gone.[4]

It is at this point that postcolonialism becomes an effective heuristic tool. Like all concepts, it is a tool, and one must take care lest it too become a corset squeezing the fat lady. There are many colonialisms, diverse postcolonial situations, significant overlaps between postcolonialism and other theoretical modes, disparate and antagonistic strands of postcolonial criticism, interrogations about *post*colonialism's continuing enmeshment in the colonial gaze.[5] Nevertheless, *grosso modo,* postcolonial theory has done much in its shift of focus from the "center" to the "margins," with the core of interest on conditions and developments at the "margins"; it has made valuable contributions to a comparative approach that contests the usual North-South perspective of literary studies and connects cultures and literatures that have infrequently, if ever, spoken to each other; and it has provided important insights for "identifying and articulating the symptomatic and distinctive features" of postcolonial texts, *from* the condition of postcoloniality.[6]

This work is exceedingly relevant to Latin American writers, first and foremost Borges. Traits of Borges that have been understood (or misunderstood) within the two regnant contexts of study, Eurocentric or national-Latin American, acquire new sharpness when read from the perspective of postcolonialism. A postcolonial perspective brings into focus Borges's strengths and Borges's lacks. It allows for a renewed appreciation of Borges's role as a forerunner to what is significant in present literary-critical practice, particularly the writing of such "Third World" authors as Salman Rushdie, Tahar Ben Jelloun, Anton Shammas, and Sergio Chejfec, who see in the Argentine master a postcolonial precursor.

2. Postcolonial critics underscore the theoretical hegemony of Europe, a hegemony that has utilized the texts of the "margins" to construct itself—Latin American literature and postmodernism is a case in point—yet has frequently ignored the theoretical explorations of the "margins." These explorations, in the literary texts themselves and in essays and works of criticism, more than once prefigure issues that have since become crucial to the "center," as in the case of postmodernism; and this prefiguring results precisely from the "marginal" status, with its intense sensitivity to problems of textuality and reality, to troubling epistemological questions.

Borges illustrates the elision, despite the fact that he has attained canonical rank in Euro-U.S. critical-literary discourse. Certain Borges writings are cited to buttress, say, Genette or Bloom or Foucault, whereas

Jorge Luis Borges *(Robert H. Taylor)*

others are little mentioned. "Kafka and His Precursors" and "Pierre Menard, Author of the *Quixote*" fall into the first category; "The Argentine Writer and Tradition" into the second. Then too, what we might call the postcolonial implications of even the cited works are ignored; this is true of Borges's essays and his fictions.

Let us look at "El escritor argentino y la tradición." Originally delivered as a lecture in the fifties, the essay contains many of the questions that are important to postcolonial criticism and that intersect with the preoccupations of the "center." The issue of tradition itself, with the related issue of the canon, is one. Borges's purpose in the essay is to define Argentina's literary tradition in order to guide contemporary Argentine writers in their task. The title of the piece recalls Eliot's "Tradition and the Individual Talent," an essay that Borges refers to in "Kafka and His Precursors" to develop the now well-known idea that "every writer *creates* his own precursors."[7] But to continue with tradition. Nowhere in his discussion does Eliot interrogate what tradition is for the English writer. He declares: the "historical sense compels a man to write . . . with a feeling that the whole of the literature of Europe from Homer and within it the literature of his own country has a simultaneous existence and composes a simultaneous order."[8] Although Borges attempts to project an analogous sense of security and order, opening his essay by calling the problem of defining Argentine literary tradition a "pseudoproblem" and concluding with what has been read as a submission to Europe, the fact is that there is a great deal more probing of the meaning of tradition, as well as heterogeneity in describing it and subversiveness in treating it.

Borges reflects upon a number of possible traditions: the tradition of gauchesque poetry, the tradition of Spanish literature, and the Western tradition as a whole. The gauchesque receives particular attention, in large measure because it has been considered Argentina's "authentic," "native" literary tradition, and its masterwork, José Hernández's *Martín Fierro,* Argentina's canonical book. Borges's pointed analysis dwells on the primary claim to authenticity of the gauchesque, its language, supposedly derived from the spontaneous oral poetry of the gauchos. His examination in effect dismantles this claim; he indicates that the gauchesque poets, city men, cultivated a "deliberately popular language never essayed by the popular poets themselves." In the constructed idiom there was a purposeful "seeking out of native words, a profusion of local color," whereas the gaucho singers tried to express themselves in nondialectal forms and to address great abstract themes. Borges's conclusion is that gauchesque poetry, which had produced admirable books, not least Hernández's "lasting work," was nevertheless a "literary genre as artificial as any other" (178–80).

The discussion is enormously suggestive. What is the relationship between orature and literature in conforming a literary tradition? Questions about the continuities and discontinuities between oral and written forms are at the heart of literary-critical discourse in Africa, for example, with the unexamined championing of the oral tradition as *the* model for contemporary African writing an area of debate. There is likewise the matter of an essentialized nativism as the basis of contemporary cultural tradition, what the Nigerian critic Chidi Amuta terms "raffia, calabash, and masquerade culture."[9] The seeking out of a profusion of local color, including fixed "native" linguistic codes, is seen by Amuta and other critics as a retrograde maneuver that perpetuates the "exotic" view of the non-European and ignores the essence of postcolonial cultures and their languages as dynamic, dialectical, hybridized formations.

If a limited, conversational nativism could not form the basis for Argentine literary tradition (in the essay Borges recalls that early in his career he had been a "raffia and calabash" man), neither could the literature of the former "mother country." Borges states categorically: "Argentine history can be unmistakeably defined as a desire to become separated from Spain" (182). Instead of positing a smooth interface between Spanish literature and Argentine literature as one grandly unbroken

master narrative (a position more than once perpetuated in the teaching of Latin American literature), Borges posits rupture. For an Argentine to write like a Spaniard is testimony to "Argentine versatility" in assuming a persona rather than indication of a natural state (183). Of course, Borges returned again and again to the masterwork of Spanish literature, the *Quixote,* as he dialogued with Spanish writers—Quevedo, Gracián—and as he rewrote the *Martín Fierro* in his fictions; but his selective manipulation of elements of these traditions can best be explicated in the framework of the third tradition he examines, Western culture.

In their studies the Australian critics Bill Ashcroft, Gareth Griffiths, and Helen Tiffin, who are among the most prolific researchers in postcolonial theory, underscore that it "is inadequate to read" postcolonial texts "either as a reconstruction of pure traditional values or as simply foreign and intrusive."[10] These texts are constituted in the shuttle space between the two illusory absolutes, "within and between two worlds." Postcolonial texts can further be conceived as an alternate reading practice whose aim is the revisionist appropriation and abrogation of the Western canon (196, 193). These thoughts are helpful in approaching Borges's approach to the Western tradition, because his posture has been construed as nothing if not "foreign and intrusive." Borges writes: "I believe our tradition is all of Western culture," but the statement does not lead to a reiteration of the authority of the "center" to "write" Borges. Instead, Borges turns the Western tradition against itself by appropriating the right to write back to the "center." "We have a right to this tradition," he asserts, *"greater than that* which the inhabitants of one or another Western nation might have" (184; emphasis added). The assertion is the takeoff point for a model of difference and a strategy of subversion.

Dialoguing with another essay, Thorstein Veblen's 1919 article "The Intellectual Pre-eminence of Jews in Modern Europe," Borges applies to the Argentine and Latin American circumstance the American thinker's notion of Jewish difference as the breeding ground for innovation. Long before Derrida's *différance,* Borges anchors his attitude toward Western discourse in "not feel[ing] tied to it by any special devotion," in "feel[ing] different," like the Jews or the Irish. Difference makes for deferral. To quote Borges again: "I believe that we . . . can handle all European themes, handle them without superstition, with an irreverence which can have, and already does have, fortunate consequences" (184).

There is in these statements of "The Argentine Writer and Tradition" all the creative *chutzpah* and, yes, the ambiguity—if not anxiety—of the postcolonial situation. On the one hand, the speaking back, the challenge to the metropolis, and the installation of irreverent difference as the modus operandi of fortunate literary labor; on the other the pervasive concern, common to postcolonial societies, with myths of identity and authenticity, with establishing a linguistic practice, with place and displacement, with canonicity and "uncanonicity." Borges's lifelong Hebraism, exemplified in the essay, correlates with this double movement. It was not merely the Jewish condition, traversed as it was with many similar complexities, that attracted Borges. It was also the Jewish textual tradition, some of whose views were displaced by the dominant Greek-Western logos as inauthentic—in Borges's words, "alien" to the Western mind.[11] (What the dominant logos judged "authentic" in Jewish textuality was authenticated by its appropriation, not by its Jewish roots.)

One such view was the conception of writing as inevitably *inter*textual, constituted in the bold interaction—not decorous separation—of Torah and scholia, of canon and commentary, through an ongoing process of interpretive reconstitution. Another was the idea, carried to an extreme by the mysticism of the Kabbalah, that audacious revisionism masked as faithful reproduction formed the proper stance toward tradition. Borges's exploration and radicalization of these beliefs—vindicated decades later by "Hebraist" iconoclasts at Yale and elsewhere as a way of dislodging a still-classicist criticism—was clearly an attempt to find precedents, from the edge of the world, for alternative literary models: models of strategic "marginality" with the interplay of the standard and the subversive that became Borges's stance.

It is not incidental that Bloom connects Jewish hermeticism to Borges via a secularized, parodic version of the principle of "reading old texts afresh,"[12] for in his nonsuperstitious handling of Western themes the "parodic miniaturization of a vast work of art" constituted one of Borges's favorite revisionary operations.[13] We are now so familiar with these Borgesian manipulations that we scarcely stop to consider their implications, particularly in a postcolonial context.

The biblical urtext, whose questioning "to absurdity" by the Kabbalists Borges so admired, is not the least of the vast parodied works;[14] in Borges, Cain becomes Abel, Judas becomes Jesus, the Crucifixion of Jesus becomes the crucifixion of a medical student, Golgotha becomes an obscure Argentine ranch. The event occurs after the student "brings light" to the "heathen," in a tale audaciously entitled "The Gospel According to Mark." One cannot help but think here of works like Yambo Ouologuem's *Devoir de violence,* Chinua Achebe's *Things Fall Apart,* Ngũgĩ wa Thiongo's *Petals of Blood,* Timothy Findley's *Not Wanted on the Voyage,* and Gabriel García

Márquez's *Cien años de soledad*—all postcolonial novels in which scripture is parodically repositioned, its orthodox presuppositions (often in the setting of the missionizing endeavor in the imperialized area) disrupted. In "The Gospel According to Mark" Borges gives narrative substance to the linguistic-interpretive relativization that necessarily occurs in new and hybridized settings: the student Baltasar Espinosa, whose name already bespeaks Judaic heresy and whose background and religious beliefs are already impure, cannot exert interpretive control either over the text—not accidentally an English Bible—or over events, and it is ultimately the even more mestizo Guthries/Gutres who have the last word at tale's end.

Other master myths and works, and systems of knowledge, are subjected to parallel carnivalistic-reductive techniques, frequently in an Argentine milieu: the ineffable godhead is viewed, flat on the back, in a Buenos Aires cellar; the sublime Dante Alighieri is the flatulent Carlos Argentino Danieri; Erik Lönnrot meets death in a spectral *porteño* Southside after a rigorous Spinozan quest; Qaphqa is a latrine in Babylon, synonym of Babel, synonym of Buenos Aires, as in the line from Borges where he sings to his "babelic" home city, "texted" out of cultural and linguistic fragments from the four corners of the earth.[15] Indeed, in many of Borges's texts it is not merely the inversion of a specific writer or system that "writes back" to the "center." There is the freewheeling pastiche of authors, epochs, languages, philosophies that is equally undermining, since the very juxtaposition short-circuits metropolitan notions of linearity, epistemological security, temporal-spatial coherence, historical and fictional progression, and mimetic accuracy.

A pastiche of associations suggests itself at this point: Foucault's heterotopic reading of the signs in teacups of Western history and thought "out of a passage in Borges" from "The Analytical Language of John Wilkins" that contains the kind of juxtaposition just noted; a Chinese taxonomy of beasts, many fabulous (more shortly about postcolonialism and imaginary beings); or Homi Bhabha's positing of the lack of mimetic correspondence as a postcolonial strategy for shattering the mirror of Western representation, which brings to mind Borges's early championing of irrealism, a frequent recourse, he points out, of non-Western writing; or even Ngũgĩ's comment about space, time, and progress in the "Third World," in Kenya, and in Argentina: "Skyscrapers versus mud walls and grass thatch . . . international casinos versus cattle-paths and gossip before sunset. Our erstwhile masters had left us a very unevenly cultivated land: the centre was swollen with fruit and water sucked from the rest, while the outer parts were progressively weaker and scragglier as one moved away from the centre."[16] In Borges one finds the "unevenness," the clashing orders, the disjunctive language of narration that results in large measure from the disorder left behind by colonialization; but it is a disorder that calls to answer established rhetorics so as to fashion novel discourses out of the challenge.

It is not for nothing that in "Kafka and His Precursors," where heterogeneous pieces nudge each other, Borges fabricates a more provocative, postcolonial version of Eliot's majestic proposition that every writer's work *modifies* our conception of the past and future. According to Borges, every writer goes further: he *creates* his own forerunners.[17] And appropriately so, for at the "periphery," where things have as yet to cohere, one must create a genealogy, an identity, and a place. Still, Borges experienced the uncoherence of the edge at a time when the Western "center" itself could not hold, as a young man beholding the spectacle of the Western order disintegrating in the trenches of the Great War, and as a writer at the height of his powers observing, from far-off Buenos Aires, the even greater falling apart of things during World War II. The postcolonial world emerged out of these conflicts; Borges, with his outsider's antennae, foresaw and registered many of the seismic shifts in the realms of thought and literature.

At the same time, however, he registered the contradictions of an intellectual caught in the divide, one whose background and formation continued to enmesh him, at many moments, in the colonial gaze. The repeated dislocations at the Casa Rosada and at the Plaza de Mayo, messy and equivocal as some might have been, were in large measure the correlatives of what Borges was chronicling in his texts; but more often than not he did not see this. At the divide, Borges was crucial in shattering time-honored, dominant codes of recognition, clearing the ground; it remained for his postcolonial ephebes to carry on the work and build in the clearing through the very process that Borges had advocated: by realizing, transforming, and transgressing the precursor.

3. For postcolonial writers Borges is a reference point beyond his general preeminence in a European-North American repertoire of culture—although there is undoubtedly that aspect as well. In a number of important recent "Third World" novels, from the most diverse regions, Argentina is part of a geography of the imagination, a territory away from the "center" that conjures up a cluster of postcolonial topoi: colonization, linguistic displacement, exile, cross-culturality. It appears in the Hebrew-language *Arabeskot* (Eng. *Arabesques*), by the Palestinian Anton Shammas, in Rushdie's *Satanic Verses,* in the Moroccan Tahar Ben Jelloun's

Enfant de sable (Eng. *The Sand Child*), and in Sergio Chejfec's, *Lenta biografía* (Slow Biography). Chejfec is an Argentine living in Venezuela, but in his book Argentina is a zone not much different from that found in the other works listed here.

Borges himself is also a presence in all these novels. He is a character, unnamed but mistakable, in Ben Jelloun, where he travels from Buenos Aires to Marrakesh to weave the final threads in the fabric of tales that is the text, including the tale of the enigmatic and androgynous Moroccan hero, who travels to visit him in Buenos Aires. He is quoted by Shammas, who closes the novel—made up of twin parts, twin narrators, and twin heroes—"with a paraphrase of Borges: 'Which of the two of us has written this book I not know.'"[18] He is acknowledged as a source in Rushdie, who thanks him for the description of the imaginary manticore, the man-tiger whom Rushdie places in a British detention center-sanatorium for all manner of monstrous "Third World" mutants.[19] And he is cited as a major inspirer of Chejfec, according to a "Retroductory Note" placed at the slow biography's end. The note says that the ambiguating narrations of Borges, and of Juan Carlos Onetti, both literary masters from the River Plate, enact the area's temporal-spatial disjunction and lack of a firm past: are we exiled Europeans, are we descendants of gauchos? These narrations likewise suggest the impossibility of ironclad mimetic reconstructions of history, and of grand canonical narratives. *Lenta biografía,* ends the "retroduction," is inserted in the space between paragraphs from Onetti and paragraphs from Borges.[20]

To trace the visible Borges in these novels is not an exercise in the inventorying of evident markings, but an opening to the other, subterranean Borges, whose identity, to paraphrase Rushdie, is clear in the successor texts, even when he remains anonymous (549); for as the exoteric clues indicate, Borges is there in the text milieu in which the novels operate: in the sense of feeling different, in the clash of discourses, in the deferral of canons, in the undoing of hallowed representations. Each one of these books is centered in difference and hybridity. To quote Rushdie again: "An idea of the self as being (ideally) homogeneous, nonhybrid, 'pure',—an utterly fantastic notion!" (427). Like *The Satanic Verses,* the novels by Shammas, Ben Jelloun, and Chejfec tell the story of "mestizo" heroes, whose indeterminate, usually doubled identity is the indeterminate identity of the postcolonial. Gibreel Farishta and Saladin Chamcha, floating in the "most insecure and illusory of zones, illusory, discontinuous, metamorphic," changing countries, changing names, shifting languages, shifting accents, half-Indian, half-British, devilish, angelic.[21] "For are they not conjoined opposites, these two?" writes

Rushdie. "One seeking to be transformed into the foreignness he admires, the other preferring, contemptuously, to transform" (426). Both are what the author calls "chimeran grafts," the type of fantastic beasts that Chamcha, transformed into a devilish man-goat, meets in the sanatorium (406).

In *The Sand Child* the chimeran graft is Ahmed-Zahra, created Borgesianly by his father. Writes Ben Jelloun, echoing "The Circular Ruins": "His idea was a simple one, but difficult to realize, to maintain in all its strength: the child to be born was to be male, even if it was a girl!"[22] The female-male, a piteous Minotaur, a circus freak, is Morocco, her birth announcement annoying to the French, his tribulations reflecting the violences of "Third World" life: abiding feudalism, particularly toward women; the murders, abuse of confidence, unstable identity, theft of inheritance (141).

Shammas's hybrid is Anton Shammas–Mich(a)el Abyad, an Israeli Arab, a Lebanese Palestinian; but he is also Anton Shammas–Yehoshua Bar-On, a Jewish Israeli writer, and Anton Shammas-"Paco," a "pure" Palestinian (168). In this novel the real "Anton Shammas" does not stand up—or perhaps he is standing up throughout—because, as the Borgesian ending of the book indicates, there is no homogeneity or oneness. The same is true of the nameless Argentine-Jewish protagonist of *Lenta biografía,* possibly the mirror image of "Anton Shammas," shuttling between his Jewish condition and his Argentine condition, struggling to conjecture an identity through his immigrant father's Yiddish stories of the Holocaust, which the son hears in Buenos Aires at the edge of the father's table—the image of the periphery is recurring—and renders in a Spanish full of verbal and iconic gaps.

Such linguistic equivocalness is reflected in all the other novels, where a variety of Englishes, "tainted" with Indian and other idioms, jostle the Queen's; where Arabic jostles French; Arabic, Hebrew; Hebrew and Yiddish, Spanish; and, maybe, through Borges, Spanish jostles everything. Borges's line about the language of the book in the Library of Babel is pertinent: "He showed his find to a wandering decoder who told him the lines were written in Portuguese; others said they were Yiddish. Within a century, the language was established: a Samoyedic Lithuanian dialect of Guaraní, with classical Arabian inflections."[23]

Clearly the poetics of the pastiche is at work in these books of Borges's continuers. Borges himself is part of a collage of cultures (Western and Eastern), of times (linear, circular, arabesque), of stories (oral, written, European, Middle Eastern), of locales (skyscrapers versus mud or stone walls), of citations (Proust, Joyce, Willa Cather, Onetti, Hudson, García Márquez, Amos Oz, Rabbi Nahman of Bratslav [in Shammas], the Bible, the Koran). As in the master, the shock of discourses insinuates a postcolonial heterotopia, but one that takes Borges's undermining strategies even further, because it is more heterotopic, embracing more multifarious and more far-flung cultural ingredients. The "empire" that "writes back" to the "center" has been enlarged, as has the notion of what is the "center," which may now be not only the culture of Europe or North America, but dominant cultures within the "margin" itself. Concomitantly, there are enlarged possibilities for irreverence with fortunate consequences.

This is evident if we consider the employment of Borges's preferred maneuver, the parodic deflation of canons. The Bible continues to be questioned, in Shammas, for instance, where linguistic-interpretive relativization occurs on the very ground meant to eliminate it: Israel. Shammas, as he puts it, uses Hebrew, the language of the Bible, the language of Grace, to build his Tower of Babel, of confusion (92). Scriptural verses in Hebrew frequently employed to buttress the Jewish claim to the land are cited against themselves to relativize that claim as they are spoken, with evident irony, by an Arab, who at the same time questions the Arab-Christian piety of village life and further muddies the ground by portraying persecution by Muslims devoted to the Koran.

Indeed, when Rushdie, in *The Satanic Verses,* uses a preferred Borgesian symbol to speak of "that labyrinth of profanity," he is talking about an "anti-mosque" and an anti-Koran (383). His "satanic verses" are not only the Prophet's, wherein, manipulated by Shaitan, Mohammad allegedly entertained the heterodox possibility of other gods but Allah; they are also Rushdie's hardly superstitious handling of the holy writ, wherein the scribe, named Salman, changes the verses dictated by the Prophet. "I rewrote the Book," he audaciously says (368). Ben Jelloun is similarly not above tampering with the Koranic-Islamic tradition. His man-who-is-really-a-woman enters the hallowed, male precinct of the mosque to hear the "collective reading of the Koran." She comments: "I got great pleasure out of undermining all that fervor, mistreating the sacred text" (25).

To mistreat the sacred text, to rewrite the book—the Borgesian modus operandi is additionally hybridized, additionally indigenized, turned against other canons that can oppress and imperialize. But, following the Borgesian example, these very canons, seen uncanonically, can also be liberating vis-à-vis the West. Borges's vindication of textual modes alien to the Western mind served to release the subversive potential of these modes for writers brought up in Islamic traditions, for instance, yet writing in Western languages. Borges provided a model of literary postcoloniality: a writer writing in a Western language, both within and without the West, who used the potential of non-Western elements, or elements at the edge of the West's table—Judaic notions about literature as a series of Midrashic versions, Eastern traditions of irrealism, books such as the Koran and the *Thousand and One Nights*—to undermine and enrich Western literature. In Shammas, Rushdie, Ben Jelloun, and Chejfec, versions give way to versions, dreams to dreams, tales to tales, because, thanks to authors like Borges, these previously strange esthetic-textual strategies have become the means to take apart and to rebuild. Even as the ephebes use Borges to enlarge creative opportunities, however, the very enlargement, which evidences his prophetic role, points to areas of limitation.

Faced with the genuine articles, authors who know the Koran at first hand, in Arabic; writers for whom Judaism is existential, not only bookish; intellectuals brought up in the cultures of India, North Africa, or the Middle East—faced with these, the bounds of Borges's vindications become more obvious. He advocates the Orient at a distance, filtered through the European translations of Lane and Burton, Waley and Kuhn, with inevitable elements of Orientalism. (Borges, however, is always aware of the dangers of translation; see "The Translators of the 1001 Nights" and "The Enigma of Edward FitzGerald.") Analogously, his Judaism, as he often admitted, is secondhand, marked by "an invincible ignorance" of Hebrew, Aramaic, and Yiddish, unmarked by the physical pain of "three thousand years of oppression and pogroms."[24]

The same is true of his handling of sociopolitical issues. Rushdie takes the manticore from Borges; but whereas Borges discusses the beast's Plinian and Flaubertian sources, Rushdie anchors him squarely in a postcolonial address, a diminished yet still imperial Britain, an independent yet still colonized "Third World." "Borges and I" is the inspiration for the closing of Shammas's novel; but whereas Borges deals with the hesitation between the literary persona and the flesh-and-blood individual, Shammas delves into the tortuous and violent web of Middle Eastern identity, with the conflict of individuals a metonymy for the conflict of communities. Ben Jelloun uses "The Circular Ruins" to explore how a man dreams a man and imposed him on reality; but in Ben Jelloun the simulacrum is a man imposed on the reality of a *woman*, a Moroccan woman, and on an Islamic "Third World" reality of incomplete independence, especially for women.

The successors, as noted earlier, realize and transgress Borges. They create him as their postcolonial precursor by contextualizing and modifying. In their hands the Borgesian conception of the past as an open, dynamic system is applied to Borges himself. Borges is hybridized and indigenized, but as a kindred spirit: a fiction maker who decades ago helped forge the idiom in which these disciples now do their own, pointed, writing back to the "center."

Edna Aizenberg, Winter 1992

[1] For discussions of postmodernism in which Borges is central, consult Douwe Fokkema, *Literary History, Modernism and Postmodernism*, Amsterdam, 1984; Brian McHale, *Postmodernist Fiction*, New York, Methuen, 1987; and John Barth, *The Friday Book: Essays and Other Nonfiction*, New York, Putnam, 1984.

[2] Fernando Calderón, ed., "Identidad latinoamericana, premodernidad, modernidad y postmodernidad, o . . . Le queda chico el corsé a la gorda?," *David y Goliat*, 17:52 (1987).

[3] Linda Hutcheon, *A Poetics of Postmodernism: History, Theory, Fiction,*, London, Routledge, 1988, pp. 7, 6.

[4] Critics who point this out include Jean Franco ("The Nation as Imagined Community," in *The New Historicism*, H. Aram Veeser, ed., London, Routledge, 1989), Stephen Slemon ("Modernism's Last Post," *Ariel*, 20:4 [1989], pp. 3–17), and Hutcheon ("'Circling the Downspout of Empire': Post-Colonialism and Postmodernism," *Ariel*, 20:4 [1989], pp. 149–75).

[5] Hutcheon, "Circling," p. 161.

[6] Bill Ashcroft, Gareth Griffiths, Helen Tiffin, *The Empire Writes Back: Theory and Practice in Post-Colonial Literatures*, London, Routledge, 1989, p. 115.

[7] Jorge Luis Borges, *Labyrinths: Selected Stories and Other Writings*, Donald A. Yates and James E. Irby, eds., New York, New Directions, 1962, p. 201.

[8] Ibid., p. 49.

[9] Chidi Amuta, *The Theory of African Literature: Implications for Practical Criticism*, London, Zed, 1989, p. 2.

[10] Ashcroft et al., p. 110.

[11] Edna Aizenberg, "Borges and the Hebraism of Contemporary Literary Theory," in *Borges and His Successors*, Edna Aizenberg, ed., Columbia, University of Missouri Press, 1990, p. 250.

[12] Ibid., pp. 255, 257.

[13] Emir Rodríguez Monegal, *Jorge Luis Borges: A Literary Biography*, New York, Dutton, 1978, p. 416.

[14] *Borges, a Reader: A Selection from the Writings of Jorge Luis Borges*, Emir Rodríguez Monegal and Alastair Reid, eds., New York, Dutton, 1981, p. 24.

[15] Jorge Luis Borges, "El tamaño de mi esperanza," cited in Edna Aizenberg, *The Aleph Weaver: Biblical, Kabbalistic and Judaic Elements in Borges*, Potomac, Md., Scripta Humanistica, 1984, p. 26.

[16] Ngũgĩ wa Thiongo, *Petals of Blood*, New York, Dutton, 1977, p. 49.

[17] Emir Rodríguez Monegal, *Borges: Hacia una lectura poética*, Madrid, Guadarrama, 1976, p. 64.

[18] Anton Shammas, *Arabesques*, Vivian Eden, tr., New York, Harper & Row, 1988, p. 259.

19 Salman Rushdie, *The Satanic Verses,* New York, Viking Penguin, 1988.

20 Sergio Chejfec, *Lenta biografía,* Buenos Aires, Puntosur, 1990, p. 170.

21 Rushdie, *The Satanic Verses,* p. 5.

22 Tahar Ben Jelloun, *The Sand Child,* Alan Sheridan, tr., San Diego, Harcourt Brace Jovanovich, 1987, p. 12.

23 Borges, *Labyrinths,* p. 54.

24 Jorge Luis Borges, "Preface," *The Book of Imaginary Beings,* Norman Thomas di Giovanni with the author, tr., New York, Dutton, 1969, p. 11.

A Last Interview with Manuel Puig

The last time I talked to Manuel Puig, he was calling from the airport, as he usually did when just passing through New York; this time he especially wanted to know about our friend Gregory Kolovakos. That was April 1989, and Gregory was dying of AIDS, as we all knew. Already grieving the recent death of another friend, Enrique Pezzoni, the brilliant editor and publisher in Buenos Aires, we commiserated; and he came as close to raging as I ever heard: "Will this plague ever end?" In less than six months Manuel himself was dead, not an AIDS victim but a postoperative casualty in a relatively backwater hospital, like one of his characters. There had been no difficulty in removing the source of Manuel's gall, if indeed he ever really had any; but his heart relinquished him.

Gregory had also linked us ten years before, when he suggested to the relatively new gay magazine *Christopher Street* that I might be the person to interview Manuel. *Kiss of the Spider Woman* was big at the time, and I knew the book well. Earlier, Seaver Books had been interested in Puig but unable to see the worth of his latest novel, and so I suggested my editing the early chapters over a weekend in order to demonstrate that the translation, not the novel, was the problem. Jeanette Seaver liked the result, considered it, but finally begged off; so the translator revised his work, more or less in line with my initial editing, and the novel predictably came out from Dutton. In those days Gregory and I worked together at the Literature Department of what was then the Center for Inter-American Relations, and his recommendation to *Christopher Street* only extended our daily endeavor in one more useful, friendly way.

For me this interview turned out like the others I had done with Manuel—hilarious hard work—but with differences: his earnestness replaced the cautious defensiveness I knew so well; his effort exceeded the usual

Manuel Puig *(Jerry Bauer)*

pickiness, and he revised laboriously, when we talked (having me turn off the machine while we worked something out, rehearsed a line); later he rewrote, cut, and expanded everything; and still later he had us recite it to make sure his script "worked." On one hand, certain points truly mattered to him: he wanted to clarify the political importance of the notorious footnotes in *Kiss of the Spider Woman,* for instance. On the other, he cared about getting the star attributions right.

The latter worry I first encountered on a flight back from the University of Wisconsin in Madison, where Manuel and I had participated in one of the many conferences organized there by Zunilda Gertel. I was apologizing to him for having perhaps spoken too long during my section of the program (I had seen his lips twitch, pulled on individual strings, and his mouth jerk as I did the critic's job of comparisons, literary history, and the like). He wasn't interested. "Who was I *like?*" he asked. Guessing, I mumbled some old actress's name. "*How?*" I tried again. Better: "Well, but don't you think I had just a little Claudette Colbert?" Telling him I hadn't thought about it, but, yes, when he answered the question from that dark-haired fellow about halfway back, he had tilted his head—to the side, chin slightly up, eyes big, bright—and telling him that suited. "And you? *How* were you?" Turned out *how* I was was a mix too, and none too flattering, in my eyes, at the time at least. Of course this was all twinkling, yet as we refined more and more *how* we were like this one or that, I saw the serious critical purpose: he was judging, denotatively as well as connotatively, according to a scale as delicate and intricately calibrated as that used to appreciate the Japanese tea ceremony or the tango. Years later, in the interview, his seeming jokes on star readings engaged his full intelligence and sensibility no less, just as in *Under a Mantle of Stars* the Daughter's line to the effect that it does not matter who you are but *how* you are represents Puig's profound superficiality to a *T*. (By the way, we read every line of that translation aloud too, switching parts, changing inflections, discussing, and there's only one phrase I left in that I think he was wrong about.)

After all our rush and work, the interview appeared without our seeing galleys, without the section on the footnotes—and without our ever being paid. Manuel gnashed, Gregory sulked a little, and I finally deposited the papers, along with lots more, at the University of Texas's Humanities Research Center in Austin, which has generously assisted me in preparing this definitive version. The record straight, my promise kept, I dedicate it to Manuel and Gregory, whose stubborn frailty gave us so much.

■ ■ ■

A homosexual affair in an Argentine prison makes quite a jump from your previous fiction.

I wouldn't call it a "homosexual affair." In that cell there are only two men, but that's just on the surface. There are really two men, and two women. I agree with Theodore Roszack when he says that the woman most desperately in need of liberation is the woman every man has locked up in the dungeons of his own psyche.

Where did you get the idea for having the gay prisoner tell the plots of films to the political prisoner?

That was the very first idea I had for the novel: that these two guys would meet through a mediator—films; that otherwise they couldn't talk to each other. One is heterosexual, the other isn't; they're both defensive. The gay one doesn't have much education, but a *great* fantasy.

He's been educated at the movies.

Yes, so he tells the other one films at night, to help him fall asleep. They can't face certain subjects directly. Slowly, and unconsciously, they reveal themselves.

But that's true in almost all your fiction, isn't it? The meeting of people in popular art forms, like films, tangos, radio programs. Right from the little boy in Betrayed by Rita Hayworth *who goes to the movies every day with his mother and writes about them at school.*

Yes, the beginning of *Kiss of the Spider Woman* is all there in the boy's composition class from *Rita Hayworth*. In a repressive society some people only dare discuss matters metaphorically.

But now we can see how you've developed the theme from a little boy in school to adults in jail, from provincial life out on the pampas to urban life in Buenos Aires.

Sure, because I moved to the city. My childhood was in this small town in the pampas, and my later experiences are all city experiences. I started going to a boarding school in the capital at thirteen, and then my family moved to Buenos Aires when I was seventeen. So, I can't say much more about small towns, because I've got this impression that in the first two novels I've said everything about them that I've got to say.

You started your career wanting to write movie scripts, and, in a sense, Kiss of the Spider Woman *returns to that wish since it's almost entirely in dialogue.*

That was not intentional at all. My two previous novels had used a lot of technical narrative devices—stream of consciousness, letters, diaries, classical third person—and I thought this new novel would need all those again. Anyhow, I thought that the first chapter could be handled more easily in pure dialogue. And once I got started, I just couldn't stop! I saw that the dialogue was the real vehicle for the narration, that dialogue where what isn't said is very important, where what's skipped expresses maybe more than the rest.

That's another constant in your books, isn't it? Like the one-sided conversation in Rita Hayworth *or the passages in* The Buenos Aires Affair *describing what the characters don't* see, *don't* consider.

Here it's especially important, since we have two characters, and they meet only in words: they almost cannot look at each other, let alone touch each other, because they are men and that's forbidden. The communication is only verbal in the prison; but what characters do without paying attention always interests me: what's not in the focus of your attention but is there anyhow.

While you were writing the novel, did you ever think of turning it into a play?

Technically, that would be very difficult. The development of the plot is too long and fragmented to be fit into a play. I've been approached to make a theatrical adaptation, but it's hard for me to forget the novelistic structure the plot was born with. I'd need to think of a totally new structure, a theatrical one.

So you started with a movie set in New York, the 1943 Cat People.

But it wasn't *Cat People* in the first draft. It was more of a *Dracula* thing in the first chapter. The structure of the novel was all set. I was here in New York around the end of '73, when I'd left Argentina, and I was gathering all the materials for the novel . . . I'd done a certain amount of research.

What kind?

First of all, I'd met with prisoners in Argentina.

Political prisoners?

Yes, it was very easy in June of '73, because when the Peronists came into power again, the president was Campora, and he freed all political prisoners. I asked a lawyer friend who defended political prisoners to help me meet some of them, and that was very useful. Two months later the political equilibrium tilted to the right, and I decided to leave the country.

Did you interview gays too, like the prisoner Molina?

No. I knew that type very well, and I wanted to work with an unsophisticated type, a reactionary, in a certain way. The type of homosexual who rejects all experimentation, all new trends. They've accepted the models of behavior from the '40s—you know: the subdued woman and the dashing male—and they have, of course, identified with the subdued though heroic woman, and they don't want to change that fantasy—or they can't. Although they're film-crazy, these types would even reject all the new kinds of movie heroines and heroes. They're still attached to the prototypes of *One-Way Passage* and *Now Voyager*. I think that's one of the main topics of the novel: can people change their eroticism after a certain age? I believe it's almost impossible. Those sexual fantasies have crystallized during adolescence and imprison you forever. I'm saying all this with a Claude Rains cocked eyebrow.

All right, the cocked eyebrow, but if there's a kind of parody of the homosexual . . .

No, not parody. *Parody* is a word I don't trust too much, because it carries some degree of scorn. I don't let myself go in the direction of scorn very often. The character is parodic in itself. If he's mimicking a woman of the '40s, a film character of the '40s, he's already parodic. It's not me who's doing the parody. Greer Garson wouldn't have liked me to do that.

What about the revolutionary, Valentin?

Oh, no, there's no space for parody in his case. I've tried to give realistic portraits. Sure, both, in their own ways, are excessive; but the excess is not in my treatment of their nature.

The revolutionary learns a lot from the homosexual. What about the homosexual from the revolutionary?

That I leave up to the reader. But personally, I think that Molina just *uses* the melodramatic possibilities offered to him by the revolutionary, the possibilities of becoming an underground heroine.

But the homosexual comes to be protective of the revolutionary. For example, he doesn't give the authorities all the information he could.

Yes, but *not* for ideological reasons, for sentimental ones.

And in a way that prepares for his death, which is melodramatic, staged.

Yes, a movie death. And the character chose, I didn't.

What made you give up on Dracula *and choose Jacques Tourneur's* Cat People?

I was doing research—here in New York at the Public Library—for the Nazi language I needed for chapters 3 and 4 of *Spider Woman*, the characteristics of the language of Nazi propaganda. Around then I saw *Cat People* on TV. I had seen it many times, and it was a favorite; but somehow I hadn't thought of it, and now I just couldn't resist. I said to myself: this *has* to be in the book, because the character would have chosen it. The choice was an imposition by the character. He would have told that story.

Did you have the other movies in mind already?

Yes. The Nazi film was almost ready, but I have to explain that it's an invented movie. It happened like this: I couldn't find just one, a single Nazi film that would serve my purposes, so I invented one that has pieces from many—mainly from *Die große Liebe* (The Great Love) with Zarah Leander, from 1942, you know. And the Mexican film I hadn't got ready yet. For that I went to Mexico a few months later and saw a lot of Mexican cabaret films, a genre in itself, which is unfortunately almost unknown in the States.

So quite a bit of research went into Spider Woman?

Yes, but for each of my books I have to do that.

Which inevitably leads us to those footnotes in Spider Woman.

I had to read a lot. I realized the reader wouldn't be able to judge the action without the appropriate information on the origins or causes of homosexuality. At the beginning I thought all this information should come through the mouths of the characters; these quoted texts should be present there in the cell somehow. Since one of the characters is learned, an avid reader, I thought of having those books in the cell; but it wasn't possible, simply because that kind of information had been violently denied to people. It's only recently that we're starting to see books that present an organized explanation of the origins of homosexuality. In Freud, in Jung, in all the main psychoanalytic texts the information is fragmented; and, of course, it's destined to an elite audience, to a very few specialists. General information is very recent. In this respect I very much like Dennis Altman's *Homosexual: Oppression and Liberation*. It's easy to read and covers a lot. For instance, it makes very clear, accessible comment on hard-to-read books like Marcuse's.

Do you expect readers of Spider Woman *to take the views in the footnotes seriously?*

Of course, of course. This information's been denied *violently* to people, as I was telling you. Only now, in the States, in the last ten years, are these subjects starting to be discussed openly with a certain orderliness. It's very recent, and it's restricted to this part of the world. And you must remember that my novel was destined, first of all, to a Spanish-speaking reader. So I said to myself: well, the information's been violently denied, so I'll violently incorporate it into the narration; it will be there as an explanation, a footnote, having nothing to do with the text—the literary text, I mean.

It's the only point in the novel where the narrator intrudes on the text.

Yes, it's my voice, but not my judgment. I simply repeat, in a condensed form, the judgments of specialists.

How did you decide when to add a footnote?

I thought that there were moments when the lack of information in the characters reinforced the dramatic potential, the conflict.

A little like a chorus in classical drama, giving background for the protagonists, heightening the conflict. But, you know, the information's been violently denied here in the States as well. A number of people I've talked to have asked, "Are those footnotes real?" They suspect that the notes are fiction too.

I didn't anticipate that. All the notes are quotations—except for one.

Are you willing to say which one?

Well, I . . . you see . . . I . . . I advanced an idea of my own; but I wanted to present it under a very respected name, not a fiction writer's name, and well . . . it's there . . .

And we have to find it for ourselves. Another detective mystery, like your other works. But are the notes authentic quotations?

For the English, I gave the translator the texts, but I don't know what he did. But, no, they're not direct quotes, anyhow. They're paraphrases.

How have the footnotes—the whole homosexual topic, for that matter—been received in Latin America and Spain?

Some of the critics have assumed, very pedantically, that the notes are common knowledge and that,

really, they were not necessary. Can you believe that? "We *all* know those things," they say. In the Spain of 1976! In the Mexico of 1977! And that's totally untrue! In those countries people have very little information about the origins of homosexuality. Or none at all.

Do you have a theory?

No, not really. I've chosen, in the book, to present those that seem to me to be the most interesting.

Are the attitudes toward homosexuality in Latin America very different from those here?

Well, to begin with, the rejection is universal. Universal. But here in this country there's been an advance, a very great advance, in the way homosexuals want to work up a new self-respect. The liberation movements, et cetera. The way they create their own places. All that has, for me, one very positive aspect: the self-respect. But, at the same time, I see a great danger in the American attitude, and that's in the way homosexuals tend to think of themselves as *totally* different from heterosexuals and segregate themselves drastically. Which means denying the true origin of it all. For me, the only natural sexuality is bisexuality; that is, *total* sexuality. It's all a matter of *sexuality,* not homosexuality, not heterosexuality. With a person of your own gender, with a person of the opposite gender, with an animal, with a plant, with anything. Just as long as it's not offensive to the other party. I see both homosexuality and heterosexuality as specializations, as limiting matters. I see exclusive homosexuality and exclusive heterosexuality as cultural results, not as a natural outcome. If people were really free, I think they wouldn't choose within the limits of one sex. At the same time, I believe in the couple, whether heterosexual or homosexual. I think that with one person you develop things in time, sex also becomes much, much richer, more refined. I don't mean monogamy necessarily, but . . .

But going back to the rejection business, I believe gays shouldn't imitate the mistakes of heterosexual people, who are so frightened by their latent homosexuality and have to think of themselves as totally different from gays. Segregation is wrong. Ghettos are wrong. Of course, I realize that a minority has to get together in order to demand respect with a certain strength; but anyhow, the basic issue—no matter how ideal and remote it may sound—of a sexual community, neither hetero nor homo, should not be forgotten.

The problem's reflected in the book, where there can't be any free choice, and the cell is a microcosm of society—a cell.

The characters have no choice at all.

Which means that the novel, like your others, is critical of society.

Yes. You see, I wanted to reproduce in the cell what the situation is outside: that we're restricted by cultural conditioning, restricted to a very limited choice.

Do you think some readers will misread and think you're representing homosexuals as silly queens?

No, no, I hope not. There's enough discussion inside the book to show that all homosexuals are not like that. Molina's just the last of the romantics, the last of the romantic women. That interests me. In the '70s the only women who can still cling to the old cliché are the people who adopted those models of behavior and have no way to experiment with them. Molina wants to get married to a straight man and become a subdued wife. Since' the experience is impossible, he will never be able to kill the illusion. In present society, or at least until very recently, you didn't have much choice: you either followed your mother or you followed your father. And they were very typed. A woman's behavior in the '40s was determined by the mystique of the era, and a man's too: it was either Myrna Loy or Clark Gable. If those parents had been free people, their children would be free too. There wouldn't be such delimitation. After all, why should the field of the mother be so separated from the field of the father? Two absolutely separated planets? You know, the orbit of sensitivity was the mother's, and the orbit of action was the father's.

Doesn't this show up in the way Molina is formed almost exclusively by films and the revolutionary by books? With the difference that the reader never learns precisely which books the revolutionary reads.

Of course. And the reader isn't told those titles because he already has information on all that. We know what a young man on the Left is like, what his world is, what he reads.

But while the revolutionary's formation, his reading, is respected in silence, there's a criticism, implicit at least, in the camp sensibility of the queen.

I don't agree. I don't deal much with the revolutionary's formation, but I do with his resulting reflexes. And if there's some conscious criticism on my part, it's of the "extremist" or "segregationist" attitude of both the revolutionary and the homosexual. What's more, I don't know how it sounds in the book, but my intention was to be more severe with the educated character, since he'd had more access to information. For the other character, the only available models of behavior were film romances. Films were his spiritual food.

Now they're becoming that food for educated people as well.

Yes, but with a different perspective. Back then it was an attitude of total belief. Films were taken as the real world, especially for people living in underdeveloped countries. These phony fantasies coming from the developed countries were looked at as the reality, as what the world should be like.

So the queen has her eye out for the foreign, the exotic, while the revolutionary is looking to his own country.

Since the rejection is total in Latin American countries, the homosexual has no other way out except for escape, so there's great difficulty in developing liberation movements. Don't forget that most of these countries are under military rule.

Last summer Dennis Dollens and I were watching the Gay Pride march with Luisa Mercedes Levinson, and she said she wished she could show that parade to the generals running her country. You can't have that sort of event in Argentina, can you?

Look, it's not possible to have a gathering of over twenty people! The perennial state of siege thing. What's more, in my country there's active persecution now. There can be no homosexuals, for instance, on TV; they can't be interviewed, they can't act. I don't mean open homosexuals only; I mean the closet cases as well. Censorship knows about them.

It's official?

No, no. *Nothing's* official.

And your books are banned there.

Yes, with the exception of the first two, *Betrayed by Rita Hayworth* and *Heartbreak Tango*.

Not banned throughout Latin America though.

Now get ready for something special: I'm not distributed in Cuba either. So Argentina on the Right and Cuba on the Left: they both have something to object to in my books. In Cuba none of my books could appear. Extraofficially I was told my work was too concerned with eroticism. Even worse, *Kiss of the Spider Woman* is concerned with homoeroticism, and that Castro certainly doesn't like. The harassment of homosexuals in Cuba is well known, and, I hate to say that, because there are aspects of the Cuban revolution I respect and admire.

Still, there is, after all, one positive aspect to sexual life in Latin American countries. And it's true of Latin countries in general. Well . . . let's go by stages: the fact that mothers are really subdued by their husbands in those countries gives rise to a decidedly "feminine" type of homosexual son, one who will in general try to be his mother, be compelled to repeat the subdued-female role. So, the straight macho tends to see the majority of this kind of homosexual as women. The Latin macho, to top it all, has no doubt about his "manhood," so he goes ahead and has sex with a gay man—exclusively an active role, of course, at the beginning—without feeling "contaminated" at all. All this has one horrible side: the fact that what makes it possible is that the roles are so stiff—or, better, say rigid. But anyhow, there is a form of bisexuality achieved on the part of the macho. It's a sick formula, but the contact is established. In many cases what starts as a shady affair ends up as a friendship: the straight eventually marries, and the gay designs the bride's gown while waiting to be godmother to the children. In the States I guess a straight man would feel he's a closet case forever if he once had a locker-room escapade with a buddy. One more example: in machismo countries a straight woman would more easily accept a lesbian's proposal too, because a woman there is so stripped of any sexual threat that it arouses no great fears.

I've met many Latin American homosexuals who are married, have children, live an ostensibly heterosexual life, but maintain a homosexual life on the side.

Among the higher classes. It used to be almost standard but never spoken about. The homosexual side would be thought of in the following way: "He's a nice person, but once he killed somebody; still, he's basically nice." It would be a stigma of which nobody speaks. But I think that's true among the higher classes in all countries.

But when Valentín has sex with Molina, it doesn't reflect what we've just been talking about.

No. Valentín does it *rationally*. This guy's really a very honest person, someone who hates oppression, and he ends up in that cell with a screaming queen. But, unknowingly, he reproduces a system of exploitation in the cell. When he realizes he's exploiting the weaker person in that tiny world, he becomes truly guilty, and he tries to remedy the situation. The rational excuse for him to act sexually—of course, he acts sexually because he *needs* to: the queen's not attractive, maybe she's a middle-aged person; but you know, a body's a body on a desert island—the excuse he gives himself is more Christian charity than justice, but . . .

What about the emphasis on pain in their intercourse? I recall Molina's expressing pain and Valentín's saying that if it didn't hurt, he'd let the queen do it to him.

There's this cliché among women, women of the '40s or '50s, who'd always say, it *hurts!* It was part of the act. A frail romantic woman had to be equipped with a very narrow vagina. But in the novel it's part of the female act the gay character's putting on.

Both are caught in their ignorance and conditioning: a victim of mass fantasy and someone deluded into thinking he understands the structure when he doesn't even grasp the power of his cellmate. But the story's not a parable.

If you tell a real story, the criticism is implied. If you choose a good situation, a representative story, then the situation, the situation itself, is critical. But not all "real" stories have meaning—or even interest.

So your virtual absence as narrator in no way implies that you're absent so far as social criticism goes.

Well, I'm present from the moment I choose to tell this story and not some other, and I've chosen this one because I think it has meaning. I try to give the reader all the possible data. I don't want my judgment to be oppressive. The reader should have space in which to make up his own mind. And there I'm in the hands of the fates.

How did you reach your decision, from your first novel on, to stay outside the narrative as much as possible?

I think that's because I'm *veddy moderne*. No, really, it's because I'm convinced that Freud killed the novel of the nineteenth century. Before Freud you thought a person's psychology was entirely contained in his conscious, with a little margin for those obscure things that were hardly talked about: the instincts! So the authors who thought they knew a character's conscious—what was *there* to be shown—felt really in command of the situation. Those authors acted outrageously but innocently; they were innocent, and that bathed them in grace. But they were shrewd: they dealt mainly with heroes, not with the enslaved little man. Then Freud comes along and reveals the whole back room! To which we have no direct access. Which means that you can never, never say, "I'm sure about this character. I'm sure of why he behaves like this." You can present fragments of behavior but never the totality. You can never say, as Tolstoy did, "Anna was jealous" or "Anna hated" or "Anna loved," because now we know that those feelings are so much more complex than they were supposed to be. Among the twentieth-century writers, I admire Kafka especially. What is he interested in? Cobwebs, the world of the unconscious, the system that somehow manipulates us, the bars we're not aware of but which are there and don't let us act freely. What the reader is mainly searching for now is not heroes but the man in the crowd and why he can't act otherwise. But it's extremely difficult to capture that invisible net of repression. Anyhow, that's what interests me: to try to capture the unconscious of the characters. And the more common the characters are, the more archetypal they are, the more they interest me. Because they're in the same cell with millions. Heroes don't interest me. Not really. I know I can't approach the unconscious contents directly; they won't reveal themselves. One has to beat around the bush.

But sometimes you do go after unknowable material, as at the end of Spider Woman, *where we read the unconscious fantasy of Valentín.*

I thought it would be interesting to have access to his mind at a moment when he's free; and, with a very controlled person like him, that can only happen under sedation.

That's the only time he has any happiness, where the last words of the novel read, ". . . this dream is short but this dream is happy."

Yes, that's right, but there's also the film he completes in his nightmare in chapter 7.

So, as a narrator, you must not be omniscient.

Sure, how can I be omniscient, how can I be a masterful third person, an authoritarian third person, if I'm not certain of so much?

To be omniscient is to reproduce the repression?

Exactly.

And the dramatic method of plays and films is less repressive?

Well, let's see . . . I wouldn't go *that* far. But what can I say? Since films have to be accepted by such vast audiences, they are devised, not unconsciously but in a very special way; so they become part of the imprisoning bars and are consequently limiting fantasies, and, in a way, they can be restrictive.

Whom do you design your fiction for?

It's always to please one person in particular. To convince one person of something. It has always been like that. I don't know, for me writing is always an act of seduction. At a certain point there's an important person in my life—doesn't need to be a sexual challenge—someone I respect who doesn't respect me. We disagree about something. And I write to show that person I'm not as dumb as I sound. By the time I finish the novel or the novel comes out, that person isn't important any more. By writing, I've exorcised some kind of devil that was there. At least, it's been like that with my five novels.

Going back to Kafka, is he important to you in your own writing?

You see, I was exposed to literature *after* I was exposed to films. The films were really the big, big artistic influence in my life. But I have to say there are two modern literary wizards for me: Kafka, as I said, and Faulkner, who can fascinate me *almost* as much as von Sternberg or Hitchcock. Kafka resorted to fantasies for his comment on the manipulation of the unconscious, but Faulkner dared go into reality; and somehow, his descriptions of environment give us an access to that unknown swamp of the unconscious. I would have liked to say that with a Michael Chekhov accent: he played the kind analyst in *Spellbound* beautifully.

What about nonliterary writers?

I find the new French school of psychoanalysis very interesting. Very hard to follow, but interesting. Lacan and his disciples.

What interests you, the notion of "mirroring"?

Yes. It's hard enough to try to understand it, let alone say anything about it, but I have the impression that there's definitely something there. But films are the real influence—von Sternberg and the whole MGM look, if I can define it that way. No especially great directors at MGM, but a certain visual style, contributed by producers like Thalberg and Mayer and second-rate directors like Fleming, Leonard, Mervyn Leroy. And the faces of their women.

So, for you, it's the stars, the fantasy, that matters rather than the qualities that cinéastes discover in films?

Yes. For me it is the fantasy that stars embody. The constellation of vices and virtues. As a child I was afraid of Harlow, but I adored the subdued-though-heroic woman, who in the '30s was Norma Shearer and in the '40s became Greer Garson. I protected the waif Louise Rainer. As for Garbo and Lamarr, they were too strong and too beautiful; they didn't need me. Unless they died in the end, like Garbo in *Camille* or Lamarr in *Lady of the Tropics.* Then they suffered glamorously. They died, and I died with them, only to go to heaven along with them. Very, very dangerous clichés. Because the enjoyment of suffering was there; there was a streak of masochism.

But very different from the fantasies of masochism you see today.

Oh, I hate that! I'm glad we came to that. I think it's awful, and it has a simple explanation: since in the States nobody punishes homosexuals any more, they have to punish themselves. I find it extremely silly. And it's just a fad—the exploitation of the sicker side of the homosexual condition. I hope this phase will be over soon.

If your character were growing up today, who'd be his model?

What wouldn't I give to know! But for that you must be twelve! I ought to have a son in Argentina now in order to know how Laura Antonelli impresses him.

All your fiction presents this generational conflict, doesn't it?

Well, yes. In the new book the heroine is over thirty and belongs to that group who can't identify with the older models but can't identify with the models who arose after the sexual revolution either.

How was Spider Woman *received in Spain?*

With respect, or should I say "respectful distance"? Part of my interest in giving all the information on homosexuality came from thinking about the young reader in Spain, who has suffered the most violent denial of information of any reader in Western Europe in our time. They had censorship for almost forty years! And I thought: what about people with sexual problems? The young people, the teenagers who really haven't even had access to Freud! Not to mention Marcuse. So, what about giving them some information about sexuality? Because I really have something against specialization. When I say that somebody's "homosexual," I think I'm not saying the total truth. It should be said: *homosexual / latent heterosexual.* Recently a newspaperman who'd read *Spider Woman* asked me if I'm a writer for homosexuals. It made me so mad, this need for ghettos, as if a novel about a homosexual wouldn't be interesting to a heterosexual! As if the novel wouldn't speak to that imprisoned woman in the man's body we talked about before. (And let's not forget about the man bottled up in every woman!) In a free society, though, where women and men would stop acting within the limitations of roles, their children would be free too. But certainly not people of our generation. Maybe the adolescents of '79—in America—yes, but not in other countries. Seeing the relaxation of roles, they may be able to enjoy the body of any human being. These days, for people raised in the '40s, there's not much room for bisexuality, not because it's unnatural but because of cultural castration.

So the book is really subversive in relation to the system of sexual repression.

I hope so.

And that fits in with what we once discussed: the sexual repression of older people, of unattractive people.

That's the subject of my new novel! The one that's coming out in Spain in March, *Pubis angelical.* It's all another form of discrimination. The state should take care of that. The sexual satisfaction of the old, the ugly, and the deformed.

Socialized sex, like socialized medicine?

Yes, yes. Certainly. . . . I'm saying it with a straight face.

May I quote that: "a straight face"?

Yes! And, if possible, add a Ronald Colman idealistic stare into the void, as in the last close-up in *Tale of Two Cities.*

Ronald Christ, Autumn 1991

Manuel among the Stars (Exit Laughing)

. . . and luckily after the airplane crashed Ginger Rogers and Fred Astaire dance transparent in the memory, since nobody can keep them apart any more.

▓ *BETRAYED BY RITA HAYWORTH* ("TOTO, 1939")

Manuel Puig dancing among the stars in a billowy heaven—that's how I'd like to remember him, doing his fey imitation of Fred Astaire, or of Rita Hayworth's steamy, classy striptease from *Gilda.* Twenty years ago I translated these words uttered by Toto, Manuel's six-year-old alter ego, but I was also translated by them, by Manuel's playful, poignant reconstructions of silver-screen fantasies and the emotions they evoked in their zealous spectators.

Manuel's death came as a shock. Suddenly I would no longer have the chance to hear his voice, to see his smile; he was an original, and now the original has vanished. Manuel once prophesied, all too accurately, that I would be surrounded by ghosts because I had established close ties with an older generation of writers at a young age.

It was with the Uruguayan literary critic Emir Rodríguez Monegal that I first met Manuel Puig on a wintry New York night in 1969, at a now-extinct dragon-bedecked Chinese restaurant in Greenwich Village. Over the years restaurant dates with Manuel would be rare occasions, not because we didn't get together often in the early seventies but because Manuel, who in struggling youthful years in Europe had worked as a restaurant dishwasher, was convinced that eateries were unhygienic gyp joints. Manuel was on the parsimonious side, justified no doubt by his modest means until success came his way with *Kiss of the Spider Woman.* Emir had told me that Manuel was handsome, so I already recognized him when an Italian-looking version of Tyrone Power with thinning hair entered the restaurant with a sprightly step.

Manuel's first impression upon meeting me was basically his first impression of Emir and me; he commented with mischievous precision that we were "una pareja llamativa," a striking couple. *Llamativa* was one of those fulminating euphemisms he borrowed from his mother's lexicon, giving the spoken cliché a new life in mimicry. Indeed, when I met Elena, his mother, I was hearing the speech of characters in *Rita Hayworth.* Manuel explained my giggle of recognition to his bemused mom: "You sound just like my novel!"

More than restaurants, whenever Manuel showed up in New York, we would go to movies together, and when he was living in his little studio on Carmine Street, visitors would often be invited, even obliged, to join him in front of the TV, his time machine back to the glorious thirties and forties.

Manuel's own personal brand of film criticism was as unconventional as his novel personality and his personable novels. In 1970 we went to a special showing of Ben Hecht's fierce satire on journalism, *Nothing Sacred* (1937), starring Carole Lombard and Fredric March. Manuel sat silent staring as the audience repeatedly cracked up at the rapid-fire, cynical dialogue. Suddenly—during a nightclub scene in which an inebriated Lombard stood up tottering and the audience sat silently waiting for the next witty line—his face lit up as he exclaimed, a solo voice pitched in the dark and vast hall, "Ay qué traje divino!" (Oh, what a beautiful dress!). *Divino* is another of those marvelous Argentine clichés, and as far as he was concerned, the luminous gown clinging to the immortal Carole's svelte curves was the only worthwhile moment in the whole flick.

Manuel, who often had a need to instigate fights with close and dear friends, didn't speak to Emir for three years because of a dispute over Susan Hayward. Emir had made the mistake of calling her acting corny, which Manuel thought heartless, considering her hard life and, at the time, her recent death. Manuel and I were estranged over another detail: he didn't like the concept of sharing royalties with the translator. But affinities and mutual respect finally won over these trivial spats. In one of the many editions of his books he gave me, the first Seix Barral edition of *Rita Hayworth* (1972), he inscribed, parodying the Peronist motto, "Emir cumple, Jill dignifica, eternos en el alma de su Manuel," substituting Emir for Perón, myself for the immortal Evita, and himself for the Argentine people in a phrase roughly signifying "Perón achieves, Evita dignifies, eternal in the heart of their people." Nothing was sacred to Manuel except the silver screen, and to be his friend meant sharing his (com)passionate (ir)reverence for movies.

Guillermo Cabrera Infante prefaced an eloquent homage to Manuel, published in the *Guardian* (London) and in *El País* (Madrid), by saying that he would have much preferred not to write anything, to have Manuel still among us. I feel the same as I look back at our friendship and particularly our partnership in translation. I translated his first three novels into *Betrayed by Rita Harworth, Heartbreak Tango,* and *The Buenos Aires Affair.* Years and books were to pass before I translated Manuel again. Not only Manuel's parsimony over royalty-sharing, but my academic career intervened at the moment Manuel asked me to translate *Kiss.* After a hiatus of over ten years we were reunited to work on what is now his last novel, *Cae la noche tropical,* just pub-

lished by Simon & Schuster as *Tropical Night Falling.* The book is portentously concerned with mortality and the hope for transcendence. On a first reading I found it gloomy, but the deeper connection that translation requires brought home to me its redemptive, even at times exhilarating impact.

But back to the beginning: *La traición de Rita Hayworth.* Manuel would sometimes call the book "Cansino," alluding to Ms. Hayworth's real surname (he would often call people as well as books by another name, maybe their real but hidden name, invariably a feminine one). Because of the homosexual sensibility implied in the title—or in spite of its refreshing originality—the book had great difficulties finding its publisher in Spanish. The cinematographer Néstor Almendros and such lucid literati as Juan Goytisolo, Emir Rodríguez Monegal, and Guillermo Cabrera Infante urged Carlos Barral—the most innovative literary editor in Spain at that time—to publish the book. He was unwilling to take the risk, however, and only after the success of *Boquitas pintadas* (Eng. *Heartbreak Tango*), published by Sudamericana in Argentina in 1968, did Seix Barral begin publishing Manuel's works.

Betrayed by Rita Hayworth clearly reflected a homosexual sensibility: what male or even female writer in the Hispanic world dared then to write about the mediating presence of Hollywood's myths, such an ideologically suspect subject? Though nobody said so in public, the book affronted moral as well as literary conventions. Manuel had discovered new territory and would be followed by more mainstream writers such as the Peruvian Mario Vargas Llosa and the Parisian-Argentine Julio Cortázar, who could now write about supposedly debased subject matter as soap operas (Vargas Llosa's *Aunt Julia and the Scriptwriter*), movie stars (Cortázar's *We Love Glenda So Much*—Glenda Jackson, that is), and homosexuality (Vargas Llosa's *Real Life of Alejandro Mayta*).

La traición de Rita Hayworth was finally published in 1967 in Argentina by Jorge Álvarez, a small press. When the moment came to find a translator for *Rita* in English, E. P. Dutton was willing to try, if their then star translator, Norman Thomas di Giovanni—who had so effectively promoted Borges—would give the book a whirl. Di Gi refused. Unable to extort 50 percent royalties from Manuel, he thought it wouldn't be mercantile enough for his efforts—and he was also daunted by the book's uncompromising Argentine speech. So, for an unknown writer, an unknown translator was chosen, but Manuel and I would have to present samples before the book was accepted.

When I read the first chapters of *Rita Hayworth,* I too was daunted: one-sided dialogues and thick Argentine monologues made it impossible to know who the characters were. Manuel Puig subverted here the communicative function of spoken language by transforming it, with all its grammatical violations, into writing. His hyperrealist technique of recording spoken language was a mimetic tour de force, but only an Argentine could understand what he wrote, I thought.

La traición de Rita Hayworth had begun as a screenplay, but its author soon realized that the autobiographical material "was too complicated to be analyzed in film." As he explained in an interview: "I needed more space and freedom. I wasn't sure about any of those characters. The kick was to find the truth about these [people] who had been with me during my childhood: my cousin, my mother, my father, my closest friends."[1] Monologues, conversations, letters, and diaries would serve here to retrace his past, the relationships, the Hollywood musicals and melodramas at the root of his identity and sexuality, from Toto's monologues culminating in his "rewriting" of "The Movie I Liked Best," to the borrowed language of everyday life, as in a telephone conversation between the traveling saleswoman Choli and Mita, Toto's mother. Choli speaks to Mita about "interesting women" who are "hiding a past," leading exciting and adventurous lives, in an effort to represent or fantasize about her own life, as if she were an avatar of Joan Crawford or of her idol Mecha Ortiz, Argentina's answer to Joan Crawford or Norma Shearer. Interesting was another loaded euphemism for Manuel's aunt and mother figures, meaning attractive or, in plainer language, sexy.

It wasn't until reading Puig's second novel, the more accessible Boquitas pintadas (1968), laughing and emoting with a cast of soap-opera characters whose pleasures and pains transcended the language barrier, that I could gain entrance to his fictive town of Colonel Vallejos and attempt to translate the words uttered in his unique voice(s). I was fascinated by the possibility of creating a bridge through a shared (though radically different) "American" experience. Buenos Aires evolved, like New York, as a haven for exiles, or for the grandchildren of exiles; both are cities where immigrants and natives, peoples of different colors and classes mingled and invented a common living language and culture. These cities assimilated the cultural products of Europe and North America. This bridge between North and South, which made it initially possible for a North American translator to cross over—with the negative cargo of economic and cultural imperialism but also with the positive charge of a shared energy and sensibility—created an ambivalence that Puig was to articulate definitively in Kiss of the Spider Woman. Like the young Toto (Manuel was actually called "Coco" as a kid) in a

small pampas town, I too (brought up in a neighborhood in north Manhattan) was nourished on the words and images of the American movies of the thirties and forties. My childhood as the youngest in a family of much-older siblings put me in touch with this recent past, its values, emotions, and motion pictures.

My first translations were close collaborations, or "closelaborations," a neologism coined by Guillermo Cabrera Infante. Working with him, and later with Manuel Puig, I observed that the problem of one word versus another was not unique to translation. The original writer constantly chooses words and phrases, compelled by intuitions and reasons that often have more to do with language's limitations than with his own intentions.

The dialogued chapters (1, 2, 4) in Rita Hayworth presented what initially seemed like insurmountable difficulties. In the very first chapter ("Mita's Parents' Place, La Plata, 1933") and chapter 2 ("At Berto's, Vallejos, 1933") conversations are transcribed without any descriptive or narrative context, and the names of the speakers are omitted. The reader gradually figures out who's who from the casual hints dropped by the speakers, speaking from within their world and not to the author or reader, who both play the role of eavesdropper. And we "hear"—in chapter 4—only Choli's side of the conversation, from which we are forced to infer Mita's possible responses. This dialogue device—uncompromising to the reader—has always been problematic for Puig's English-language publishers. I spent a good deal of time trying to persuade the editor at Simon & Schuster to retain its use in Tropical Night Falling, rather than explain it, by inserting the characters' names at the beginning of each utterance.

Manuel provided me with missing identities of characters and parts of dialogue in Rita Hayworth, without which I couldn't have understood completely the implications of remarks that were confusing precisely because they were so real. In "natural" conversation people convey meaning more through intonations and facial expressions than through actual words, and the characters at Mita's parents' house and at Berto's represent either uneducated people or Italian immigrants whose brand of Spanish is often awkward if not ungrammatical. The translation had both to communicate and to obscure meaning by imitating conversational language in its rawest form, had to border on the ungrammatical yet use a speech that sounded "natural," idiomatic.

As we worked through the translations, pop references and Spanglish irreverently pervaded our epistolary conversations, letters that Manuel signed as a series of female correspondents, notably "Greta," the Garbo he imitated so well in voice and gesture, particularly her famous lines in *Grand Hotel*. "Miss Gustafson," or simply "Gustafson," referring to Garbo's real last name, was a common signature during the period we were working on "Cansino." (All those who have seen and especially heard Manuel intone "I want to be alone" agree that they experience the original Greta as a mere effigy of her translation, Manuel.)

In this period Manuel and I were calling each other S.W. for Suffering Woman, but "she" also called me (I had gone to Europe for two weeks) V.W. for Vacationing Woman. Other monikers for me ranged from simple-peasant-girl names like Teresita to those of "interesting" dark-haired foreign actresses like Silvana Mangano and Harriet Andersson.

Apart from the guidance I received in these letters—guidance that went beyond explaining the meaning of words into the realm of literary mentorship—Manuel's humor, encouragement, and flattery gave me tremendous moral support as I took on what was, for a beginner, an extraordinary challenge. There almost seemed to be a continuity between his correspondence and the novel, since in these letters his anxieties about love life, economic survival, and literary success rang as clear—and often in the same tone—as in the documents scribbled by his characters.

Having broken my leg skiing in February 1970, I joked about having my own "original B'way cast" in a letter to Manuel in which I asked his advice about what sections of *Rita Hayworth* to present to the publisher as samples. His reply, cited below, refers to Marian Skedgell, the editor at Dutton in Latin American fiction, as "la Unfaithfull," alluding to Mick Jagger's then-girlfriend Marianne Faithfull. Marian was an extremely nice person and a very conscientious editor but was a bit overwhelmed by Manuel's innovative quirks; his names always implied some form of criticism, either praise or mockery, and those which follow are no exception.[2]

Rome, April 6 1970

Jill!

Poor darling with your original B'way cast, how terrible!!!! I hope it will be OK soon. I'm consoled by the idea that the *ski bum* who ran into you could have hurt your head, and then you would have suffered amnesia and forgotten me forever. . . . If you want to present samples to *la . . . Unfaithfull* I'll suggest some pieces a) Chapter II, almost all of it, they're only eight pages, not difficult and rather seductive, b) Chapter V, from the beginning until for example line 16 of page 83, c) Chapter 8 from the beginning to line 4 of page

150, d) Chapter 15 from the beginning to line 7 of page 294—

That's 8 pages + 10½ + 4 + 4⅓, a lot of work if then nothing will happen. . . . But anyhow please try, more pages, less pages, but try, I have the feeling it will be tough at the beginning but then a more bearable job. The first monologue you'll do will kill you, but then it will all go well. Of Chapter I and IV I'll give you all the clues so you have no problems (who's speaking at which point—Chapter I—and what does Mita say—Chapter IV). . . . It will be great if you send me the chapters before showing them to the Horror, that's Marian Skeleton, for some possible super polish that we may do together. Again thank you for trying and best wishes!!

Cariñísimos,

Greta

Manuel had a way of being so precise, so demanding, yet so modest and self-effacing, that the initiate (like myself), and even his more seasoned friends and collaborators, would often find it hard to refuse his wishes. As a beginning translator, I was certainly motivated, if not to dignify, at least to achieve. Manuel was also an acute critic not only of others but of himself, and like a good critic he did indeed choose a wise array of excerpts for the sample, to display the book's diversity as well as some of its finest, or funniest, moments.

The following excerpted letter is typical of those I received during the course of translating *Rita Hayworth*. Of all the writers I collaborated with, his responses were the quickest, his handwritten revisions the neatest.

Buenos Aires, August 26 1970

Divina: I've just reread Ch. 5 and I'm *enchanted*. I think that wonders can occur if the translation continues to go so well. . . . I answer your questions:

p. 125: "Quien se los toca" *means he's so high, unattainable, that we common people have no chance to object to anything he does.*

p. 131: "cartonazo" *was a word (slang) used in the 40s meaning big fool, idiot, dope.*

p.150: "Alma en la sombra" [Soul in the Shadows] *is "Rage in Heaven" Bergman-Robert Montgomery.*

[Movie-title reference: The Spanish titles were almost always different from the English titles, usually more melodramatic, more corny.]

p. 151: "Hasta que la muerte nos separe" [Till Death Do Us Part] *is "The Great Man's Lady"* [movie reference].

P. 168: "chacar" *is slang for "to steal."*

p. 171: "pulastro" *is a very terrible word to name a pansy, "faggot" or something like that.*

p. 218: pastel caucaso: *A russian or jewish cold dish that can be sold at any delicatessen (cooked with eggs and spinach).*

[With this description I was able to find out from my sister Alice that the dish was *schave*.]

p. 220: "clavando" = *slang for fucking.*

***

Love,

Miss Gustafson

When the project was finally completed, toward the end of 1970, I received the following:

Buenos Aires, December 20

Dear Suzanne:

How incredible it seems to have finished "Cansino." Are you content? What always happens to me after a big effort is a depressed stage, I'm sad and exhausted. I had a lot of work all together with "Aquella bocca di pinta mi ingannava!," possible title of "Boquitas" Feltrinellified [reference to the Italian translation of *Heartbreak Tango*, whose final title was a tango in Italian, "una frase, unrigo appena"], with the Brazilian publication of "Boquinhas pintadas," with the Sudamericana edition of "Cansino," etc. I'll send you after the holidays a copy of "Consino," and also "Boquinhas" Sudamericana, it came out okay [hard to please perfectionist Manuel]. *And what is Suzanne, that talented woman, doing? Is she already preparing her vehicle co-starring prim Miss Kerr?*

In Manuel's Metro-Goldwyn-Mayer galaxy-of-stars chart he assigned to each of the Latin American writers of the pre-Boom, Boom, and post-Boom a female star according to his appraisal of their key characteristics. Deborah Kerr was the code name for José Donoso, with the caption "Why is she always refused an Oscar? But she still waits." These codifications were quite biting, to say the least—again the intuitions of an acute critic. Donoso is a fine writer who has never received top billing, even though he has written books as ambitious, powerful, and complex as any by Gabriel García Márquez or Carlos Fuentes.

Manuel would relentlessly track the publishing process, which produced in him emotions ranging from elation to high anxiety, often juxtaposed in his letters to updates on the ups and downs of his love life, as in the following:

B.A. January 27, 1971

Sweetest ever:

How fortunate that la Schedule is reading [the manuscript of *Rita Hayworth* in English] with interest, what suspense. I also have the suspense of

"Boquinhas pintadas," it came out in early December and the atrocious publisher has still not sent me a single review, and I know from others that piles of them have come out. *Suffer, woman, suffer!* . . . I'm working a little better the last few days on the novel, it's not called "Yeta" any more [*yeta* means "bad luck"], we'll see what name we'll give it. [It was to become *The Buenos Aires Affair*.] I think by the end of the year it will be finished, I'm already fed up with the theme. . . . Well, enough career talk, I'll tell you about a tremendous sentimental run-in: a Brazilian journalist came to visit in B.A. and I fell madly in love, he *just had fun, me indian girl lost heart to white hunter, he back home me cry, tears good for book, plenty pathos, he 25, me 38, but career must go on.* Well, dear, I wish you a nice winter with many fireside scenes. Love forever

Ayesha

[He is referring to the immortal Amazon/queen in *She*, H. Rider Haggard's famous adventure story.]

Manuel was always worried about the visual presentation of his books, a well-grounded concern, since editors tended to pinch the budget on "prestige" (versus profitable) items such as Latin American fiction. For his Spanish editions he furnished the cover art by such famous illustrators as Maxfield Parrish, Erté, Tamara de Lempicka, and Leyendecker. "Fabulous" below doesn't quite capture the supercorny Argentine adjective *regio* (literally, maybe, "regal") in the original letter.

Buenos Aires, May 23 1971

Dear Jill:

I found your lovely letter days after landing in the land of Evita Duarte. . . . Monday I sent you the new "Rita," but it's a scandal that in N. York they can't find something FABULOUS for the cover. One idea: the forties still have not been exploited, only the brilliant Yves de San Lorenzo [read Yves St. Laurent] has taken them up again, wouldn't a cover with 40s fashions be marvelous? [Here he doodled some female figures in forties getups.]

Well, I beg you to tell the superFaithfull to think of the 40s if she hasn't already gotten something 30s. The cover of the new "Rita" is a copy of a famous French design. . . . Something ingenious from the 40s were Vargas's drawings, *always girls*, drawn very very well as if they were photographs. They usually came in calendars. . . .

Kisses,

Gustafson

In this last excerpt—another love-life update from the *Rita Hayworth* correspondence—the Garbo *Grand Hotel* motif resurfaces.

Buenos Aires, July 7

Dear Jill: My hand is trembling, I'm waiting for the Baron's call, nothing less. I'm madly in love, he seems to be changing now, great news my dear Silvana, Baron von Geigern didn't die after the poker, my Flix is still breathing. . . .

▪ ▪ ▪

Heartbreak Tango. Manuel always had deeply mixed feelings about Argentina, the land where he had experienced repression and homophobia since childhood, and the jokes he makes in his letters—"the land of Evita Duarte," and below referring to Buenos Aires with the popular cliché "Queen of the Plata"—are, like all jokes, serious. This letter, written toward the end of translating *Heartbreak Tango,* begins with obsessive concern about the inefficient mail. He then responds to my suggestion that our names appear in collaboration, since major changes, notably the epigraphs to each episode but also song lyrics and Gypsy card reading, were the product of Manuel's participation. This excerpt reveals clearly that Manuel cared about the reader's response and knew that readers preferred not to be reminded that they were reading a translation. His nickname for me here combines "Jill" with "large female scoundrel."

Reina del Plata, 26 August 72

Jillastruna:

I don't think it would be appropriate to put "in collaboration with the authoress" what for? wouldn't it give the impression that too many things had been changed?

For the sake of preserving the book's humor, Manuel encouraged and suggested many changes, including the names of characters—for example, of the maid, La Raba. *Rabadilla* (Raba for short), "tail of a chicken," alludes at once to the maid's prominent rear, which signals her "biological" destiny and ultimately her social role: her anatomy is her downfall, perpetrated by the seducer Pancho. "Goose Ass" and "Bunny Tail" came futilely to mind, but suddenly a brainstorm: I remembered "Fanny," the name of a large, warmhearted woman who had been like a grandmother to me. Manuel thought the correspondence between Fanny and Rabadilla was "perfect," acceptable women's names in two different languages that could serve the same "end."

Manuel also liked "Dr. Nasti" for Dr. Aschero, though he later changed "Nasti" to "Nastini." "Aschero" functions as a proper name of Italian origin— identifying his immigrant origins, suggesting nouveau vulgarity as opposed to native-born gentility—and associates him with *asco,* disgust. He is a vile villain who

takes advantage of his position of power to seduce young women in his employ. With the help of the telephone directory, I found an Italianate name that would suggest a similar meaning. "Nasti," though not as visceral as "Aschero" (*asco* is synonymous with "nausea"), nevertheless describes this scoundrel. But Manuel thought "Nasti" was too obvious and decided to tone it down to "Nastini," a ridiculous Italianate name producing a comic *effect* for the American reader, just as "Aschero" makes the Spanish reader chuckle.

In this same letter Manuel also mentions the principal problem, the need to find the book's title in order to decide on the epigraphs to the subdivisions and episodes. As he says (and I translate): "I don't know what to say to you about the divisions Part I and Part II; I think that it's useless to rack our brains before deciding on the title, which they will be derived from."

In the original *Boquitas* quotations of familiar tango lyrics appear as epigraphs to each episode, a phrase or a few words that immediately touch the Argentine reader by invoking a well-known melody, and hence a mood or theme. The original quotations prefigure the characters, plot, and/or narrative form of each chapter. The Spanish-speaking and particularly the Argentine reader, whose feelings have been awakened by a musical memory, immediately captures the intonation of these words, what is implied between the said and the unsaid. Their exaggerated "bad taste" and the popular singer Carlos Gardel's sarcastic interpretations add a self-reflexive dimension, a distancing effect heightened by the novel's historicity. Their function as both nostalgic and ironic counterpoint is "heard" by the Argentine reader, but for the American reader, for example, a literal translation of poetic clichés like "She was my whole life" would ring hollow. It could be a line from a popular song, but the specific tone, the contact between speaker and listener, is lost.

The tango "means" something else anyway outside the "River Plate" (as the British nicknamed the Argentina-Uruguay region). For Europeans and North Americans, Latin American dance music has always had a stylized *Latin* connotation, whereas in Argentina the tango is as homespun as blues and jazz are in the United States. It would have been absurd, however, to substitute Billie Holiday's singing for Libertad Lamarque's, or Cole Porter's lyrics for Alfred Le Pera's. The cultural source would have been completely erased by such a drastic transposition. And American popular music, according to Puig's portrayal of Argentina in the thirties and forties, did not invade the popular media and consciousness as significantly as the Hollywood cinema and consumer-oriented advertising. The solution we finally came up with—thanks to Manuel's vast knowledge of

United States mass culture—was to translate some tango lyrics that were *essential* to the plot but to replace at least half of the epigraphs with either taglines from Hollywood films or Argentine radio commercials, originally borrowed from Madison Avenue inventions—that is, artifacts relevant to the original context but which rang a funny, familiar, exaggerated bell for American readers, as he comments in an interview we did together.

> Because we couldn't use one-line epigraphs, as in the original, we found ourselves with too many complete songs, most of them unknown. They are sometimes picturesque, but without music they are not much as poetry. We thought of using other materials, such as taglines from American films. These are often quite funny and many of them ring a bell for Americans who went to movies in the 30s and 40s.[3]

These substitutions added a new dimension of interpretation, bringing out certain implied elements in the text. By highlighting commercial advertising, as in the epigraph to episode 2, we underlined Puig's observations on mass culture as well as the intent, throughout his writing, to show how popular media have dissipated traditional distinctions between consumerism and art. What follow are some alternative epigraphs, before we decided on the final ones:

Episode 10 (in which Fanny and Nené discover nasty truths about each other's life; in which Mabel's desperate affair with Pancho begins): "I wish I could say I was sorry" (tagline for *The Letter,* starring Bette Davis and Gale Sondergaard). The final choice was "A woman's lips set the frozen north aflame" (tagline for *Northern Pursuit,* starring Errol Flynn and Julie Bishop).

Episode 12 (in which police report Fanny's killing of Pancho; in which Juan Carlos's sister Celina performs what is for her the humiliating task of visiting the widow to beg her not to reveal to anyone in town that she's going off to be with Juan Carlos in the mountains near the sanatorium): "I wish I could say I was sorry" was finally used here, appropriate because of Fanny's crime of passion and also because of the hatred between the two women, Celina and the widow. Earlier solutions suggested by Manuel were: 1) "Sometimes there's a terrible penalty for telling the truth" (tagline for *The Great Lie,* starring Bette Davis and Mary Astor), which also would have been appropriate, since Mabel coerces Fanny to tell a lie in order to conceal Mabel's relationship with Pancho; 2) "Her eyes of blue did open wide, / my timeless sorrow she understood, / and with a snarl of woman piqued / said life plays tricks and left for good" (from Le Pera's tango "She Returned One Night"). All the women—Mabel, Fanny, especially Celina and

the widow—are piqued or snarling in this chapter, but this latter choice was finally used for episode 13, where blue-eyed Nené and foxy Mabel reveal and discover mutual fears, defects, and secrets and come to the sad conclusion that life indeed plays tricks. Other tagline treasures which Manuel suggested but finally discarded were: "The men in her life sometimes lived to regret it" (tagline for *Temptation,* starring Merle Oberon); "Maybe I'm just a dame and didn't know it!" (*Thelma Jordan,* starring Barbara Stanwyck); and "The nearer they get to their treasure, the farther they get from the law" (*The Treasure of the Sierra Madre,* starring Humphrey Bogart).

Manuel's "found objects"—taken from popular mass culture—cover a broad range of possible quotations, some of which appear in his originals. Many other tangos could have been incorporated into the original *Boquitas.* The fact that one tango can replace another, that a tagline can even substitute for a tango, reminds us not so much of translation's inadequacy as of the provisional, makeshift nature of the original. As Borges tentatively concluded in his essay on the versions of Homer, "The concept of a definitive text pertains either to fatigue or to religion." What matters here is not the monolithic value of a quoted text but rather the relationship between texts, and between the novel and its reader.

Here is a fragment from one of Manuel's last letters on *Heartbreak Tango:*

Buenos Aires, June 21 1973

Lady sings the tangos:

How are you? . . . Well, let's hope that our "Tango" is going well, the galleys had some tremendous errors, cursed touches from the copy desk, I pointed it all out to Jack [Macrae]. But you know how those things are, "che sará, sará" . . . Doris Day once sang wisely. . . .

■ ■ ■

The Buenos Aires Affair. The title *The Buenos Aires Affair* obviously did not present any problems in English translation. Indeed, Manuel claimed to me that one of the reasons he chose this "Hitchcockian" title was to avoid the complications of *Boquitas.* Even though this was, if anything, a secondary motive, these words "The Buenos Aires Affair" are only one more sign of the interdependence of translation and original throughout Manuel's work.

Changes wrought in the making of *Heartbreak Tango* provoked choices made in *The Buenos Aires Affair* (1973), both original and translation, as well as in the edition of *Boquitas pintadas* published in Spain and in

El beso de la mujer araña (1976; Eng. *Kiss of the Spider Woman,* 1979). *The Buenos Aires Affair,* subtitled "A Detective Novel," followed *Boquitas* as a formal parody of yet another popular genre, structured by a suspenseful plot centered on an (apparent) crime. Just as Manuel chose the serial romance to explore and explode provincial middleclass values in *Boquitas,* so did he choose the detective story as a frame to analyze the repressive psychosexual causes and consequences of fascism in Argentina. He wanted to confront the political violence that marked the Buenos Aires of the seventies, an atmosphere that he embodies in his two principal characters: Leo, an art critic, and Gladys, an artist. This detective novel, a mock case study of an archetypal sadomasochistic relationship, confirms with parodic precision the nexus Freud first perceived between psychoanalysis and detective work.

Each chapter is headed by a filmic quotation, snippets of dramatic dialogue from mostly American films, highlighting Manuel's favorite iconic stars of the era such as Rita Hayworth and Joan Crawford. Quotations from movie ads, a strategy begun in the translation of *Boquitas,* inspired the epigraphs in *The Buenos Aires Affair.* These dialogues exhibit glamorized models of conduct that, again, contradict or parallel ironically the events in each chapter. The female star's dilemma—or destiny—in each quote relates to some aspect of the psychodrama in the novel. Precisely because the women Manuel depicts have "bought" the messages communicated by the movies, their lives are mediated by these images. Making women the dominant, pivotal figures in his books "was a revolutionary proposition," Manuel once said: "In a pampas town, to see everything revolving around a feminine figure was quite subversive."[4]

In the "translating" of these quotations of dialogues back into their original language, many changes occurred which reveal how interconnected all Manuel's works were, by a vast network of pop or mass-media materials, and how translating and the original writing were part of one continuous creative process. For example, chapter 5 of the original *Buenos Aires Affair* begins with a quotation from *Dinner at Eight* starring Jean Harlow, the glamorous or reckless "dumb blonde" par excellence headed for a tragic destiny. Suspense and the novel's sinister atmosphere intensify in this episode, in which an anonymous caller (Leo's older-woman confidante, a sort of surrogate mother) dares to inform the police of the possibility that Leo may commit a psychopathic crime but fearfully refuses to reveal either Leo's name or her own.

The original quotation features a comical argument between Jean Harlow and her potbellied husband (Wallace Beery), a fraudulent businessman, in which he gloats over his sinister power while she persists in asserting her own, perhaps recklessly. The epigraph insinuates a tension between vulnerability and power that develops in the chapter. Manuel suggested that we quote from another Jean Harlow classic, *Red Dust.* We had already used the tagline from that film in episode 3 of *Heartbreak Tango* to epitomize the clichéd relationship in which the woman is swept off her feet by a macho stud. In the movie Clark Gable (despite real-life insecurities) played, as always, a tough guy whom women couldn't resist. The comic dialogue quoted in *The Buenos Aires Affair* emphasizes not the thrill, however, as in *Heartbreak's* third episode, but rather the danger the reckless Harlow risks in the middle of the jungle, surrounded by savage beasts.

> Jean Harlow, a platinum blonde in a Chinese prostitute's kimono, at night walks out onto the veranda of white hunter Clark Gable's house, and upon seeing a ferocious tiger, says: "Who are you looking for, alley cat?" The plantation's drunkard thinks the sound of the beast had frightened and awakened her, to which she responds "I'm not used to sleeping nights anyhow." (65)

Danger is undercut by her risqué joke, but the ironic play between danger and frivolity serves to highlight the tension created by the banal phone conversation between Leo's confidante and the police officer, and by the danger lurking, that of classic stud Leo turned psychopathic killer. *Red Dust* provided complementary materials that served to emphasize both the alienating gaps between men and women in *Heartbreak Tango* and the potentially destructive consequences of that alienation in *The Buenos Aires Affair.*

I could present infinite examples of the continuity between Manuel's translations and originals but will limit myself to one: the *Cat People* motif. We adopted the tagline from the movie *Cat People* as the epigraph to episode 15 in *Heartbreak Tango,* which later blossomed, under Manuel's green thumb, into the first movie narrated by Molina in chapter 1 of *Kiss of the Spider Woman:* "She was one of the dreaded Cat People / —doomed to slink and prowl by night . . . / fearing always that a lover's kiss might / change her into a snarling, crawling killer!" In *Heartbreak Tango* this quotation exaggerates the cattiness and frustration of Juan Carlos's sister Celina, who, thinking Nené is responsible for Juan Carlos's death, takes petty revenge in this episode. The *Cat People* theme deepens in *Kiss of the Spider Woman* into a metaphorical representation of sexual repression and its flip side, violence. Like Toto's "revisions" of movie plots, the device that turned into Molina's narratives in *Kiss,* Manuel's novels interpret themselves as well as a broad range of cultural artifacts.

■ ■ ■

Coda. Manuel's last letter to me was typical, celebrating the end of one project, thinking about the next. He was trying (without success) to get me involved in a screenplay project on the life of Vivaldi, but I was certainly looking forward to further collaborations.

Cuernavaca, Thursday 19 April 90

Jillastra amorosa:

The translation's divine; I'm delighted! Only needs a few minimum touches that I'm proposing, along with some minimal additions so that it will be better understood in Gringoland. . . . But your talent shines! Please finish "Vivaldi," don't be lazy,

Kisses, Manuel

Like Greta Garbo, Manuel stepped out of the limelight at the height of his career. Unlike some fellow Latin American novelists, whose continuing works seem to grow weaker or resemble pastiches of early successes, Manuel produced seven novels that were true originals, each one an exploration of yet another uncharted territory. We can replay on our mental VCR's Manuel's life as a version of *The Story of Vernon and Irene Castle,* the 1939 film whose exalted ending Toto so poignantly describes. Poor boy struggles for success in the arts, makes good, dies tragically while still youthful, handsome, and triumphant. He even went out with a posthumous tagline, an obituary reported in the *New York Times* which, like Juan Carlos's obituary in the opening chapter of *Heartbreak Tango,* could have been fabricated by him, fusing fact and fiction: "Manuel Puig is survived by his two sons." Javier Labrada and Agustín García Gil, the two "sons," are in reality two Mexican friends whom Manuel nicknamed affectionately, after Rita Hayworth's daughters, Rebecca and Yasmín. Manuel had the last laugh, getting in one more satiric wink and wave of his baton as the curtain fell. But we still miss him, much too much.[5]

Suzanne Jill Levine, Autumn 1991

[1] Manuel Puig, interview in *City,* 5, pp. 69–70.

[2] Manuel's English will be cited in italics; my translation of the Spanish in the letters—I'll try to leave in Argentine flavor—will remain in roman type. My asides will be contained in brackets.

[3] Manuel Puig and Suzanne Jill Levine, "Author and Translator: A Discussion of *Heartbreak Tango,*" in *Translation,* New York, Columbia University Press, 1974, p. 37.

[4] From the *City* interview, p. 72.

[5] I would like to thank Douglas Woodyard for his editorial suggestions. Some of the material in this piece will appear in my book *The Subversive Scribe: Translating Latin American Fiction,* to be published by Graywolf Press in late 1991. This piece also contains excerpts from my essay "From Little Painted Lips to *Heartbreak Tango,*" in *The Art of Translation: Voices from the Field,* Rosanna Warren, ed., Boston, Northeastern University Press, 1989.

Dangerous Messianisms: The World According to Valenzuela

In the beginning was the Word, and the Word was with God; and the Word was God.

■ —THE GOSPEL ACCORDING TO SAINT JOHN

As reflected in her work, Luisa Valenzuela's main preoccupation throughout the years has been the repressive character of our primarily masculinist Western culture. Thus the fate of women—perhaps the archetypal repressed—as well as that of all marginalized peoples, is at the center of the fictional realms she creates. So is the fate of peoples victimized by the cruel repression of dictatorial regimes.

Keenly aware that it is through language—that is, through the institutionalization of a privileged discourse—that repression is effected, Valenzuela has obsessively defied the established order with her own fictional practice, a practice that chiefly aims at releasing the meaning-producing potentiality of language. Since early on in her career, the author has exhibited a deep understanding of the dual nature of the linguistic medium: it possesses the power to construct and make absolute a given truth as well as the power to deconstruct and make that same truth relative. Valenzuela has likewise noted that, whatever their nature, the canonized truths invariably establish themselves as privileged centers around which experience is organized. More important, they also become objects of veneration and of cults, instituting rituals and demanding sacrifices.

In this reductive world, where people end up worshiping ideas that they themselves produce, any truth may become an object of veneration. For Valenzuela, in fact, anybody or anything may be sacralized. In "A Story About Greenery,"[1] a text written early in her career satirizing this proclivity to worship, a green thistle is revered. Having sprung up quite unexpectedly in a city which, under the rule of a repressive mayor, had "eradicated green [the color green] by decree,"[2] the thistle is gradually sacralized as it develops into an emblem of defiance and ultimately into a symbol of liberation. In this story Valenzuela also alludes to the fact that invariably the initial impetus of a liberating movement is perverted at some point, when its adherents become fanatics and must themselves repress others in order to impose their own truth: at the close of the story the worshipers of the thistle plan to force the city-dwellers to privilege the color green. What is crucial here, however, is that in most cases the venerated object (person or truth) takes on quasi-divine qualities, and that observance of the cult created around it supposedly leads to redemption, while nonobservance leads to eternal damnation. This recalls the figure of the messiah, important here because, embodying the mythical figure of the Father, the messiah speaks the truth, demands sacrifices, condemns or redeems. The question of the messiah leads us to the three short stories which are the main focus of this essay.

Included in *Simetrías*[3] (Symmetries), one of Valenzuela's recently published works, the three stories are grouped together under the general rubric of "Mesianismos" (Messianisms) and are entitled "Transparencia" (Transparency), "El enviado" (The Messenger), and "La risa del amo" (The Master's Laugh). Pointing to the figure of Christ, the archetypal messiah, and addressing the problem of damnation and redemption, these texts are unmistakably satiric. It must be noted, however, that Valenzuela's satire is not so much directed against traditional Christianity with its myths and rituals; rather, it is aimed at the seemingly unavoidable proclivity of the Western mind to organize experience (at whatever level) around a messiahlike figure and in terms of a virtually incontestable discourse. It is a primarily univocal and essentially patriarchal discourse that establishes the rules of the game and anticipates transgressions as well as retributions. It could hardly be otherwise, since the messiah has traditionally been interpreted as God the Father incarnate.

To be sure, Valenzuela detects a religious substratum in *all* the dominant discourses in the Western world. Not only a religious leader but also an astute politician or even a member of the armed forces (especially a member of the armed forces) may play a messianic role. Dominated by the mighty presence of the Father and erected in His name (Jacques Lacan's *nom du père*),[4] our patriarchal culture endlessly revives the symbols and reenacts the rituals associated with the Christian or, rather, the Judeo-Christian tradition. For the author, this is particularly true in the case of authoritarian regimes such as the military dictatorships she has so passionately denounced in her work. Thus, for example, confession and penance as well as self-flagellation in the Church have their counterparts in the confession and punishment in the torture chamber; a religious procession (of the soldiers of God) finds an echo in military parades or in marches honoring a leader or a cause; the worship of the deity in the Church is replicated by the "worship" of the tyrant, who, more often than not, as-

Luisa Valenzuela (*Gil Jain*)

sumes the role of savior. In the world according to Valenzuela, the traditional Church has consistently shown the way.

For the author, to conduct human affairs in the way we deal with the gods is highly problematic, for it imprisons human beings in a closed system of neverending rituals and empty discourses which are altogether disempowering. Quite often these rituals and discourses justify murder and countless other atrocities and damn humans to the eternal hell they have traditionally sought to elude. In Valenzuela's world, hell exists primarily in the human mind, that is, in a subjectivity constituted by a common language which is laden with the truths of the Father and accordingly robbed of its life, deadened, rendered transparent. Thus "Transparency," the first of the three stories examined here, addresses the problem of a language (any language) which has become transparent—that is, dispossessed of its intrinsic ambiguity and meaning-producing power and forced to speak only the consecrated truths. The story focuses on the making of a despot who, in the guise of the messiah, attempts to impose his truth upon the world.

Narrated in the first person, "Transparency" describes the process whereby a leader, who is presented as the president of a club or association, gradually becomes possessed by an uncontrollable thirst for power, which he satisfies by making his control as president absolute and, in turn, by assuming a messianic role. (Here Valenzuela hints at the process whereby a person, alienated by blind ambition, transforms into a Christ-like figure in his own eyes.) Intent on spreading his word throughout the universe and on silencing all other voices with his own, he appropriates language to render it transparent and ensure univocality in his kingdom: "Delicate thing, language: we must tune up our instrument to perfection in order to eradicate doubts and invalidate ambiguities or uncertainties [of meaning]" (89). Implicitly declaring the act of doubting a blasphemy and banishing ambivalent and/or poetic language from his realm, he proclaims the need for a unifying language that will bring together all peoples under the unifying presence of an absolute leader: himself.

This absolute leader echoes the demonic witchdoctor in *Cola de lagartija* (Eng. *The Lizard's Tail*),[5] a novel in which Valenzuela forcefully denounces the crimes perpetrated by the military during the recent dictatorship in Argentina. Characteristically, the witchdoctor is possessed by what the author has described as the "messianic madness" of tyrants of all times, which she sees as inextricably linked to the lust for power.[6] (Let us recall that the army officers who successively assumed power in Argentina saw themselves as saviors called upon to redeem the country from the subversive forces, real or imaginary, that threatened the established order. The "dirty war" that passionately occupied them was made to appear as a sacred one.) Like the protagonist of "Transparency," the witchdoctor in the novel aspires to rule over a univocal realm where the act of doubting has been eradicated "by decree."[7] Moreover, his thirst for power and absolute control is reflected in his plan to absorb the entire world in his own being. The fact that his plans of absolute supremacy go awry is significant: in the world according to Valenzuela, even the most repressive regime is condemned to undermine itself at a given moment. This is also illustrated in "Transparency." Let us now return to the story.

In a realm like the one conceived in "Transparency," where there is no room for ambiguities or uncertainties of meaning, for symbols or metaphors, poetic language is anathema. It epitomizes the possibility of subversion. Ironically, however, even the poetic language that has enshrined the truth of the archetypal Christ is here in jeopardy. "From now on, we shall call bread, bread, and wine, wine, as it should have always been," affirms the president turned messiah, who then adds, "The bread shall not be my Body, neither the wine my Blood" (91–92). Anticipating the final results of his repressive discourse, the narrating Christ states that in the end "there will not even be a reason for people to

call me God" (92). He also predicts that as a consequence, the day will come when he will be able to retire to the country, "although to retire will no longer be the word [and] neither will country be the word" (92). The play on the term *word* suggests that in the long run all words, including "the Word that was in the beginning," will fade into silence, will invalidate themselves.

To sum up, if the transparency of language proclaimed by the fictionalized messiah in this story implies the abolition or silencing of all other voices, it ultimately suggests the abolition or silencing of his own. Said differently, carrying repression to its final consequences, the authoritative (authoritarian) discourse of the messiah turns against itself; it becomes self-parodic and in the end self-invalidating. Transparency of language is indeed tantamount to its death.

This leads us to the second story, "The Messenger," in which transparency of language is likewise the goal and in which tradition once again leads the way. If "Transparency" focuses on the creation of a self-proclaimed messiah, "The Messenger" centers on the making of one by a third party, the mythmaker. In addition, the story also calls attention to the fact that although the mythmaking process faithfully reiterates the same internalized mental and linguistic structures that have sustained the patriarchal order throughout the centuries, the mythmaker may freely draw upon the internalized structures to suit his own ends. Let us focus on the story.

As the omniscient narrator in "The Messenger" is silenced and the narrative is taken over by one of the characters, language is forced to shed its ambivalence and its poetic, meaning-producing possibilities and to become transparent. In fact, it could hardly be otherwise, since the appropriating narrative voice here attempts to articulate a univocal and incontestable discourse, one that establishes and consecrates a messianic, almost divine being. It is worth noting that in "The Messenger," as in the story previously examined, transparency of language also has unfavorable consequences. For example, one of the recurring motifs here is the metaphor that alludes to the Christian rite of communion. As language becomes transparent as a result of the impact of the appropriating narrative voice, the metaphor is robbed of its poetic implications and taken literally: the metaphor, in fact, becomes reality, and the rite of communion turns into an invitation to murder and cannibalism. Let me clarify this by focusing on the text itself.

"The Messenger" vaguely evokes the true story of a number of young Latin American athletes whose airplane crashed in the snow-covered Andes Mountains a decade or so ago. The fact that some of the men survived the crash and escaped death by consuming the flesh of their dead companions captivated people's imagination. Many saw the traditional rite of communion in this essentially cannibalistic act. In Valenzuela's narrative the survivors return home to a tumultuous welcome, only to be struck shortly thereafter by a mysterious illness that threatens progressively to kill them all. Apparently only one will be spared, Pedro, whose father lucidly confronts his son's illness and saves him by reenacting the cannibalistic act in the mountains. A nurse "in the service of his country" (94) in his youth—that is, in the service of the army—the father understands the nature of Pedro's illness and feeds him a small portion of his own flesh. In due course the entire family is forced to join the father in the secret mission of feeding Pedro with their own flesh. In the end, however, a human sacrifice (ostensibly, the first in a never-ending series) is required to satisfy Pedro's now insatiable need for human flesh. Equating his son's experience to that of a *tigre cebado* (a tiger that feeds only on human flesh), Pedro's father obscurely understands that the events in the Andes have modified Pedro's organism "in such a way as to require unimaginable tributes" (94), the tribute of a human life, among others. The mythmaker here has deified his son, and, as tradition dictates, the deity often requires sacrifices.

Interestingly, the person sacrificed is a young man whose fair hair and limpid eyes clearly evoke the beauty of the traditional Christ. Just as Pedro, for having survived the crash, is seen as the chosen one by his progenitor—that is, as the messiah appointed by God "to redeem us all" (96)—so is the young stranger viewed as a sacrificial victim sent from heaven to keep the new deity alive. In the father's eyes, not only has the Lord saved Pedro's life, but He has likewise decreed that he (Pedro) would survive by consuming human flesh. Stripping the traditional rite of communion of its symbolic implications, he concludes that "the Lord has shown him [Pedro] the way of his flesh, which is the flesh of us all" (95), including that of the young stranger who has served the divine will "with his body" (97).

Playing havoc with the traditional myth, Pedro's father has turned his son, now a bona fide cannibal, into a Christ-like figure. He has also transformed the sacrificed stranger into a Christ. If tradition has shown him the way, Pedro's father has succeeded in arbitrarily adapting tradition to his own purposes. To be sure, the confusion between the redeemer and the redeemed that results from the protagonist's mythmaking process invalidates the Christ myth as we know it. Likewise, his interpretation of Christ as "showing the way of his flesh, which is the flesh of all" in a discourse that aims at being transparent justifies cannibalistic acts. In this story Valenzuela persuasively argues against the blindness with which we confront both our myths and the myth-making process. Since the mechanics of this process are internalized—that is, embedded in the psyche and deposited in language—the process is experienced unconsciously as an integral aspect of the "natural" order. This is the reason why the proclivity to worship appears to be inescapable in our world.

On the other hand, what must not be overlooked here is that in his youth, the mythmaker had served his country and had been associated with the army, a place where men serve with their bodies and with the bodies of others the will of their superiors, worthy representatives of the powerful Father. Clearly, Valenzuela indicts the army here, which she links to brutal dictatorial regimes. Rather than embodying the ideals of valor, justice, and freedom, the army represents the desire for power and domination of those who assume on earth the role of the gods in heaven. In the name of the Father, even cannibalistic acts such as torture, destruction, and violation are amply justified by the military "messiahs." The *tigre cebado* functions as a metaphor for the army and its insatiable need for human flesh.

Ironically, however, the discourse produced by Pedro's father is ultimately undermined by his own doubting, a transgressive act he appropriately sees as blasphemous. On one occasion he unexpectedly reveals that at times he considers Pedro's sacred mission as merely an "addiction" (96) to human flesh. Even more important, at the close of the story he voices his concern about the legitimacy of the myth he has erected around Pedro, whose early mystical propensities now appear on the wane. Furthermore, in order to justify his cannibalism, Pedro appears now to be trying to convince his father he is indeed consuming the body of Christ—engaged in the sacred act of communion. His horrified progenitor begins to suspect that by murdering the young stranger to feed his son, he has once again sacrificed the original Christ, and that through this sacrifice, Pedro has been but an "intermediary" (98), an accomplice, in fact. If in this story Valenzuela clearly exposes the sham of the mythmaking process, in the third narrative examined here, "The Master's Laugh," she challenges the central myth of our culture: that of God the Father.

"The Master's Laugh" satirizes the fabrication of a deity, the indoctrination of his followers, and the rekindling of the hope of salvation. It likewise focuses on the inevitable immolation of those opposed to an emerging creed. Twelve men (who may or may not have been prelates or high dignitaries of the Catholic Church) meet in a palacelike mansion built somewhere on the slopes of the Andes Mountains, presumably in Argentina. It is midwinter, and the warmth of the fires burning all over the mansion, the luxurious furniture, and the excellent wines contrast with the desolate, snow-covered landscape outside. At some point near midnight, the men, having forced the women they have brought with them to retreat to an inner chamber, gather in a large hall ostensibly to bond. A séance improvised sometime after midnight turns serious (deadly serious) when the medium (who had been faking his role) senses that a foreign presence has perhaps possessed him and has begun to speak through him. A bright yellow light which explodes at that moment and almost blinds them appears to confirm the ghostly presence.

Faithful to tradition, the men interpret the voice, which promises them everlasting life if they subscribe to a new creed, as that of the Divinity. Quite arbitrarily, the creed rejects fire as a purifying and hence sacralizing agent and instead adopts coldness (the cold of winter, of ice, of snow) as "the vital principle" (103) and hence as an object of adoration. All the fires in the house are then obediently extinguished by the twelve men turned apostles, and all the windows are opened to let in the cold. Not surprisingly, the butler, who sensibly opposes this madness, is sacrificed to the new god. The women, who neither accept nor reject the new cult (in fact, they know nothing about it), are also sacrificed merely on account of their being women; as tradition would have it, they are seen as witches, the embodiment of evil. In the end, however, rather than achieving salvation, the twelve men apparently achieve eternal damnation, as the earth opens up and the flames of hell engulf them. As they sink into darkness, they hear the deafening laughter of their newly consecrated god and once again are blinded by the yellow brilliance they have previously perceived and interpreted as an attribute of the deity.

In this story Valenzuela exposes the myth of God the Father by creating an arbitrary and cruel divinity who misleads (blinds) humans with his promise of redemption and eternal life. Even more important, the author appears to denounce here the uncritical passivity with which the men accept the new god and his injunctions and commit murder in his name. In doing so, they reenact a ritual that is central to Western culture: as the men themselves admit, tradition, represented here by the Inquisition, "has already showed them the way" (105). In the final analysis, however, Valenzuela problematizes the existence of God the Father in this story by implying that the men have objectified and projected onto the improbable divinity the power that is rightfully theirs to shape their destiny in accordance with a design of their own. In other words, Valenzuela brings home the point that the deities people worship (like the ideas

or theories they idolize) are their own creations. At the same time, she also suggests that men create their gods in their own image. Worthy representatives of the Father, the twelve men in the story may be dignitaries of the Church, but they may also be high-ranking officers in the army. Whatever the case, the story points to segments of society, the army and the Church, that have traditionally wielded extraordinary power in Latin America: the power to differentiate themselves from others and to subjugate and even destroy them in the name of the Father and in accordance to his Law.

In "The Master's Laugh" Valenzuela further elaborates on this issue by arguing that the gods created by men—that is, the ideas or objects they worship—acquire a life of their own and in the end exercise power over their creators, metaphorically cannibalizing them. Even more important, she also suggests that since these idols are the product of man's imagination, their metaphoric cannibalism proves to be in reality self-cannibalism on man's part. In this regard let us recall the self-annihilating discourse of the leader-turned-messiah in "Transparency," the first story examined here. As language is rendered transparent by the discourse of the master in this story—that is, as it is dispossessed of its ambiguities, poetic qualities and meaning-producing potentiality—so too are the users of this language, *including the messiah himself,* disempowered. Interpreted in terms of a metaphorical self-cannibalism, disempowerment is the only possible damnation in the world according to Valenzuela. It follows that empowerment and salvation are contingent upon the restoration to language of its meaning-producing and meaning-dissolving essence: only by wielding a discourse that defies the transparency of the official word may people reclaim their own power and rebel against the established order. This defiance is illustrated in "The Master's Laugh."

Told by an impersonal narrative voice, "The Master's Laugh" reveals a text laden with ambiguities. Parodying Christ's apostles, the twelve men gathered in the mansion may be Church dignitaries or high-ranking army officers; the medium conducting the séance may be a genuine psychic or a clever impostor; the residence where the twelve men gather may be a stately mansion or some luxurious army barracks. Unlike the narrative voice in "Transparency," which preaches univocality, and unlike the voice of Pedro's father in "The Messenger," which attempts to produce an incontestable discourse, the impersonal narrator in "The Master's Laugh" articulates a bivocal and even multivocal text. Fraught with uncertainties, the story affords several interpretations, a practice condemned as heretical in "Transparency." Even in the narrative by Pedro's father in "The

Messenger," which aims at univocality, there is room for ambiguity of meaning. As stated earlier, at least twice the narrator of this story expresses doubts about his own supposedly incontestable truths. Of crucial importance here is the fact that the narrator *doubts* his own truth, for, in the world according to Valenzuela, doubting is the first step toward empowerment and redemption. The need to doubt—that is, to problematize persistently the sacred truths of our culture—has been a constant "message" in the author's imaginary realms.

It is true that Valenzuela has consistently exhibited a dynamic conception of truth, a conception that accords both with her vision of the world as dynamic and ever-changing and with her view of language as dynamic and ever-productive. In the *ideal* world envisioned by the author, commonly held truths are continually made relative and the proclivity to worship forever curbed. In this ideal world, where language is infused with life and its transparency forever averted, there is no room for privileged discourses or messianisms, for cannibalisms or self-cannibalisms. Instead, there is room for empowerment and for deliverance from the incontestable truths and the tyrannical deities we ourselves create in the name of the Father. If tradition has shown the way, it has also provided humans with the means to counteract tradition: the use of language itself, and the potential to doubt, question, and expose falsity and myth.

Z. Nelly Martínez, Autumn 1995

[1] Included in Luisa Valenzuela, *Open Door,* trs. Hortense Carpentier et al., San Francisco, North Point, 1988.

[2] Ibid., p. 127.

[3] Luisa Valenzuela, *Simetrías,* Buenos Aires, Sudamericana, 1993. Translations from this book are my own. Page references will be given parenthetically in the text.

[4] The embodiment of transcendent authority, the Father is interpreted here as the author of the Law (that constitutes and institutes human society) and hence as linked to the order of language and thereby to the order of the symbolic. See Jacques Lacan, *Ecrits: A Selection,* tr. Alan Sheridan, New York, Norton, 1977. Among others, chapter 6, "On a Question Preliminary to Any Possible Treatment of Psychosis," is of interest here. For further inquiry into the figure of the Father, the following two works are essential reading: Gerda Lerner, *The Creation of Patriarchy,* New York, Oxford University Press, 1986; and Mary Daly, *Beyond God the Father: Toward a Philosophy of Women's Liberation,* Boston, Beacon, 1973.

[5] Luisa Valenzuela, *Cola de lagartija,* Buenos Aires, Bruguera, 1983. As is now amply recognized, the Argentine army, which stayed in power from 1976 to 1983, committed acts of unspeakable cruelty against the citizens of that country. Valenzuela attempts to capture the horror in *Cola de lagartija.* The novel is also available in English: *The Lizard's Tail,* tr. Gregory Rabassa, New York, Farrar Straus Giroux, 1983.

[6] In an interview, Valenzuela stated the following: "Another theme that's very important to me is messianic madness and

lust for power, the insanity of Nero and Caligula, of the blacks of Ethiopia. We see that insanity so often in the people of Africa, but it is also present, more veiled and less primitive, though at the same level of intensity, in our own military." Magdalena Garcia Pinto, *Women Writers of Latin America: Intimate Histories,* trs. Trudy Balch and Magdalena Garcia Pinto, Austin, University of Texas Press, 1991, p. 220. Valenzuela called my attention to the fact that the phrase "of the blacks of Ethiopia" in this quotation should read "of the negus of Ethiopia".

[7] Valenzuela, *Cola de lagartija,* p. 56.

BRAZIL

Biblical Correspondences and Eschatological Questioning in the Metafiction of Murilo Rubião

The idea of an all-powerful divine being is present everywhere, if not consciously recognized, then unconsciously accepted.[1]

▨ C. G. JUNG

To Frazer, magic is compulsion; religion is propitiation; a combination of the two exists side by side since neither method proves fully successful alone.[2]

▨ MELVILLE JEAN HERSKOVITS

Contemporary Brazilian fiction is beginning to receive the kind of critical attention that has previously been reserved for the "boom" years of Brazil's Spanish-speaking neighbors. Translations of important works are now internationally well received. Though not yet generating the kind of cult following enjoyed by a García Márquez or a Vargas Llosa, Brazilian fiction is being intensely reviewed by professional scholars. Most recent Brazilian fiction is strongly couched in sociopolitical meaning. Writers such as Márcio Souza, Ivan Ângelo, João Ubaldo Ribeiro, Roberto Drummond, Ignácio de Loyola Brandão, Luiz Vilela, and others have created a literature of international interest by seizing the meaning of a sociopolitical present and recasting it in transnationalized literary techniques.

However, one very singular writer, Murilo Rubião, has maintained a consistent tradition of undefinable personalism in his short fiction since the 1940s. His is a unique esthetic focus, related to the "metafictions" of Barth, Kafka, and Borges, but still richly framed in the writer's personal vision and concerns. It is generally the case that most discussions of Rubião's works underscore the surrealistic or magically realistic qualities of his writings. His fantastic visions and magical worlds are usually alluded to and described, but very rarely is there an attempt to analyze the underlying oneiric logic and thematic unity in his fiction.

A detailed exploration of two of Rubião's famous stories—two pieces that lend their names to collections—may offer an insight into the fictional world view of one of Brazil's most original writers. The evolutionary philosophical focus that these two stories portray is an interesting one and worthy of further study. Bobby J. Chamberlain relates that Rubião was born in Silvestre Ferraz, Minas Gerais, in 1916 and worked as a journalist, government bureaucrat, and commercial attaché.[3] *O ex-mágico* (The Ex-Magician from the Minhota Tavern) was published in 1947; *O pirotécnico Zacarias* (Zacarias, the Pyrotechnist) came out in 1974. Although there exist parallels in style and structure, Rubião's thematic and eschatological focus during the passing decades has altered dramatically.

Raymond S. Sayers considers Rubião "one of the two or three outstanding writers of fantastic fiction, a genre that occupies a strong place in modern Brazilian writing."[4] Sayers observes that Rubião's characters are depersonalized and that there exists no real tension or empathy between reader and text. The reader "is forced to remain an outsider—that is precisely the effect which the author desires and which contributes to his originality."[5] Utilizing Sayers's reading of Rubião's fiction as a point of departure, the present study calls attention to the seminal importance of these short narratives in the development of contemporary Brazil's postmodern anti-realistic fiction. While underscoring the historical importance of this fiction, the study will also analyze Rubião's use of biblical correspondences and inversions to tender an evolving vision of eternal eschatological questions.

■ I

The idea of creating or recasting a parallel religious text, one that complements and may run contrary to traditional theological thinking, is not new. In sixteenth-century Portugal and Spain there existed an abundance of ascetic and mystical writings: "Jewish religious thought has had two major . . . aspects. One has been that of down-to-earth rationalism represented by the *Talmud* and its vast commentary literature. The other has been that of mysticism embodied in the literature of the *Cabala*. While the Talmudists sought to apprehend God, wisdom, and righteousness by means of logic, the cabalists sought the same objectives by means of the 'hidden wisdom' and esoteric practices. . . . Denied the natural means for coping with reality they grasped at the magical."[6]

Rubião's fictive imagination constructs an ingenious parallel text that is, in essence, a parodistic inversion of important biblical motifs and themes. The biblical layer is especially strong in "The Ex-Magician from the Minhota Tavern." No element of Rubião's fiction is extraneous. He is a conscious and deliberate artist. Elizabeth Lowe states that "Murilo Rubião claims to have rewritten 'O Convidado' for twenty-six years."[7] The author himself affirms, "I never worried about giving an end to my stories. Using ambiguity as a fictional means, I try to fragment my stories to the utmost to give the reader the certainty that they will go on indefinitely" (*CBL*, 196). Thus one must assume that the biblical correspondences are consciously planned and that the creation of a magical reality is not merely an end in itself. Lowe's reading of these works stresses the theme of "the sentence to infinite repetition, or the condemnation to eternal life" (*CBL*, 149). Jorge Schwartz also highlights the "theme of the infinite, rendered by repetitive and circular action, [which] reduces the alleged future to an eternal present. This, in turn, becomes the 'mask' of the Apocalypse" (*CBL*, 154).[8] The masterful aspect of Rubião's minimalist and carefully constructed fiction is that it is accomplishing exactly what the author has stated that he intended to accomplish: "using ambiguity as a fictional means," that is, to generate active reader participation and critical interpretation.

Theodore Ziolkowski, in discussing novelists like Günter Grass, Gore Vidal, and John Barth in his book *Fictional Transfigurations of Jesus,* states: "It is hardly surprising to find a strong strain of parody in . . . their . . . fictional transfiguration. . . . These sophisticated talents of the twentieth century with their jaded sensibilities, who know everything and have lost all naïveté, must agree with this modern Faustian view that all the devices of art 'are suitable today only for parody.'"[9] In the way that John Barth's *Giles Goat-Boy* "exploits the Bible for the sheer aesthetic fun of structural parody" (*FTJ*, 257), Rubião's fiction is a parodic analogue of biblical occurrences. However, Rubião's use of fantasy and magicality has a deeper, more theological focus: a concern with the problematics of eschatology. Rubião's stories explore universal theological questions. Ziolkowski refers to "the vast neo-baroque splendor of Barth's zany cosmos" (*FTJ*, 257); Rubião's esthetic vision is anything but zany, for it is steeped in melancholy and anguish. He has created two companion pieces of short fiction wherein death has no finality and the central question—even though presented in an antirealistic and avant-garde manner—is the eternal relationship between the divine and the human.

▪ II

Rubião's fiction blurs the distinction between illusion and reality, magic and religion, the human and the divine. The God figure's realization of his eternal nature and the subsequent burden that this discovery causes form the axis upon which both pieces turn. The ex-magician comes into existence abruptly, and his miraculous genesis is depicted in flat, colloquial, and prosaic terms: "I found myself one day, with light gray hair, in the mirror of the Minhota Tavern, a discovery which in no way frightened me, any more than it astonished me to take the owner of the restaurant out of my pocket."[10] The magician's story continues in a narratively detached fashion. It consciously accommodates and exploits the creation myth. The story's tone inverts biblical hyperbole and grandiloquence, for this modern-day deity's manner is anything but godlike. Rubião's story tenders important metaphysical questions from the perspective of the God figure's inability to explain his capacity to create: "He, rather perplexed, asked me how could I have done such a thing. What could I answer, given my situation, a person who lacked the least explanation for his presence in the world?" (*EM*, 109). This same ironically colloquial tone and an extreme openness of meaning is now found in much of the antirealistic fiction of Ignácio de Loyola Brandão, Moacyr Scliar, and Luiz Vilela: "I said to him that I was tired, that I was born tired and weary" (109).

Rubião's stories are tightly constructed analogues and purposefully vague allegories. A historical and sociopolitical dimension is added, as the magician is employed to entertain the customers at the very tavern where he was created: "So I began, from that time on, to entertain the clientele of the establishment with my magical activity" (*EM*, 109). In an overt accommodation of Jesus's first manifestation of his divine power at the wedding feast at Cana, Rubião burlesques the fact that in contemporary society the profit motive outweighs religious revelation.

> The man himself, however, failed to appreciate my habit of offering onlookers a variety of free lunches, which I would mysteriously draw forth from the inside of my own jacket. Judging it to be not the best of transactions merely to increase the number of customers—without a corresponding growth in profits. . . . (*EM*, 109–10)

The story continues to explore and exploit the brooding God figure's conception of himself. Although he possesses the ability to perform supernatural feats, he is not at peace, for he is envious of others: "Why be moved, though, if those innocent faces, destined to endure the suffering inflicted upon any man's coming of age, aroused no pity in me, much less any anger, over their

having everything I longed for but did not myself possess: birth, and a past" (*EM*, 110).

The contemporary irony of Rubião's inverted mythic perspective is that the God figure is not presented as all-knowing and all-powerful but is instead as racked with self-doubts as his human counterparts. His powers become a burden: "As I grew more popular, my life became intolerable" (*EM*, 110). He longs to put an end to all the attention that he continually receives. In an act of self-mutilation he decides to try to remove the source of his anguish: "On one of these occasions, completely furious, and resolved never again to practice magic, I cut off my hands. To no purpose. As soon as I moved, they reappeared, fresh and perfect, on the ends of the stump of each arm!" (*EM*, 111). Having failed, he merely wishes to die: "I had to resolve my despair somehow. After weighing the matter carefully, I concluded that only death would put a proper end to my misfortune." Rubião then incorporates the motif of Daniel in the lions' den: "Steadfast in my decision, I took a dozen lions out of my pockets and, crossing my arms, waited for the moment when I would be devoured." Here even the lions are filled with a parallel sense of anguished ennui: "'This world is tremendously tedious,' they declared" (*EM*, 112). Upon learning this, the magician turns violent and slays them in a grotesque manner: "I failed to restrain my outright rage. I killed them all, and began to devour them myself. I had hopes of dying the victim of a fatal indigestion." The magician comes to realize that he is immortal; he can find no way to kill himself. Theological inversions and ironies are sharply drawn.

> I pulled the trigger, expecting a loud report and the pain of the bullet tearing through my head.
>
> There was no shot, and no death: the handgun turned into a pencil.
>
> I rolled to the floor, sobbing. I who could create other beings had no means to liberate myself from existence. (*EM*, 112)

The story's most profanely ironic twist occurs as the magician-God figure finally does discover a means of dying, a quotidian form of death, so to speak: "From a sad man I heard that to be a civil servant was to commit suicide little by little. I was in no condition to determine which form of suicide was best suited to me: slow or quick. As a result, I took a job in the Department of State" (*EM*, 112). As in much Brazilian fiction, sociopolitical reality is viewed here with a fine sense of absurdist black humor: "1931 began cheerlessly, with threats of mass dismissals in our department and a refusal by the typist to consider my proposal. Faced with the possibility of being discharged, I tried somehow to look after my own interests" (*EM*, 113). Work, love, and friends are only "momentary distractions." The magician is still racked with anguish: "I struggle with uncertainties." However, he now wishes to remain at his trivial job and reverts to magic, attempting to deceive his supervisor; yet, when he most needs his magic, when it is intrinsically important to him, it fails: "I was forced to admit defeat. I had trusted too much in my powers to make magic, which had been nullified by bureaucracy" (*EM*, 113). He now can only feign his "miraculous gift of wizardry." At the story's end he is left alone contemplating his existence: "Of course, the illusion gives me no comfort. It only serves to intensify my regret not to have created a total magical world" (*EM*, 114).

The central symbols in Rubião's fiction are color, light, and brilliance. Fireworks, seminally important as an emblem of divine presence and knowledge, also constitute a motif that is underscored in both pieces of short fiction. In a poignant soliloquy the magician laments his inability to cover the earth with magically polychromatic displays that emanate from his own being. He yearns for the love and attention of all men. In essence, he seeks the transcendence of divine affirmation.

> At certain moments I imagine how marvelous it would be to extract red, blue, white, and green handkerchiefs from my body, fill the night with fireworks, turn my face to the sky and let a rainbow pour forth from my lips, a rainbow that could cover the earth from one extremity to the other. Then the applause from the old men with their white hair, and from gentle children. (*EM*, 114)

The tale ends on this note of pathos, with the God figure dreaming of radiant transcendental displays of color. Rubião's story evolves as an inverted spiritual quest, a theological enigma in which both God and man suffer and dream of revelation within the "Kenoma," the nonplace of emptiness.

■ **III**

It is possible to view Murilo Rubião's fictional world as an esthetic continuance of the absurdist and antilogical elements that were contained in the novels of Mário de Andrade and Oswaldo de Andrade. His fantasist's imagination has also inspired and influenced younger writers, laying the groundwork for the popularity of the Brazilian absurdist antinovel. In essence, his fictional poetics have expanded existing Brazilian literary traditions while remaining firmly rooted in the collective spirit of the absurd that has constituted such a strong world view from colonial times to the present. His narrative obsession with metaphysical issues, the offhand, colloquial, and ironic presentation of his stories, and his characters' comic-strip thinness and quasi-allegorical nature are all antecedents of such present-day novels as Ignácio de Loyola Brandão's *Zero*. Rubião's serious metaphysical musings are presented in an absurdist narrative form. Inverted biblical motifs evolve as contemporary "cabalistic" enigmas filled with magic, mystically ambiguous meaning, and evanescent flashes of pure metaphysical illuminations.

In his essay "The Christian Novel Now" Peter S. Prescott observes, "One need not profess the faith to recognize the mythic structure that Christian themes can lend a narrative, or the fine opportunities for moral perplexity that they afford."[11] Within the fictive world that Rubião creates are the stirrings of the "metafictional vogue" that was to occur some twenty years after the publication of "O ex-mágico." It was Robert Scholes and William Gass who defined the term *metafiction*. Gass, the American philosopher, critic, and novelist, points out metafiction's affinity to antiliterature.

> The use of philosophical ideas in the construction of fictional works—in a very self-conscious and critical way, I mean—has been hastened by the growing conviction that not only do these ideas often represent conceptual systems of considerable complexity, they have the further advantage of being almost wholly irrelevant as accounts of the real world. They are, that is, to a great degree *fictional* already, and ripe for fun and games. . . .

> Indeed, many of the so-called antinovels are really metafictions.[12]

The more recent of the two narratives, "Zacarias, the Pyrotechnist," begins, as do all of Rubião's stories, with a biblical epigraph, in this case from the Book of Job (11:17): "And thine age shall be clearer than the noonday; thou shalt shine forth, thou shalt be as the morning star"[13] (*EM*, 87). Job, a contemporary emblem of suffering and anguish, gives voice to his strong faith in God and the future. His vision of divine revelation is expressed by the symbol of intense light. In *The Art of Biblical Narrative* (1981) the critic Robert Alter, while discussing the historical interweaving of biblical events and characters, states, "The only evident exceptions to the rule are [Jonah and] Job, which in its very stylization seems manifestly a philosophic fable (hence the rabbinic dictum, 'There was no such creature as Job; he is a parable')."[14] Rubião's approach to his fiction is very much in the fabulist's tradition. He creates characters and situations that fall outside the realm of objective reality. His is a distorted, fantastical vision which his readers explore with the dedication of the ancient cabalists.

With the centrality of the symbology of light established, the story of Zacarias begins. The tension in the work is created from the opening query: "Rare is the occasion when, in conversations among friends of mine or people of my acquaintance, this question doesn't arise: was the pyrotechnist Zacarias actually dead?" (*EM,* 87). Zacarias recounts the events of his physical death. However, in death life continues. A physical paradox is tendered, and an enigmatic fictional game is set in motion: "The individual whom they persist in calling Zacarias is nothing but a tormented soul wrapped in some pitiable human garb"; "To live, to get muscles good and tired, walking along streets filled with people, empty of men" (*EM,* 87, 89). As in the work of Clarice Lispector, every element in Rubião's polished fictions is conceived with endless care. His selection of the name "Zacarias" evokes the figure of the biblical priest of the same name (Luke 1:5–67, 3:2), who was struck dumb by the angel Gabriel for his skepticism. He recovers his speech as his son John the Baptist is born; at that moment he praises God in an effusive blessing often referred to as the Benedictus. Another overt use of symbolism is the choice of the name "Acaba-Mundo Road" (End-of-the-World Road). The apocalyptic connotation here is also employed to convey biblical resonance instantly.

After Zacarias's (non)death, life's sensual pressures continue: female companionship, alcohol, and particularly the presence of color. Zacarias calls his love of light and color a "polychromatic delirium," stating, "I never want to live without color" (*EM,* 89). As the months pass, he grows to accept his state. With physical death comes an awakening and a deepening of experiences. He now endures a heightened sense of anguish and compassion for all men. His anxiety also includes concern for his present state of being.

> Only one thought really troubles me: what events will fate hold in store for a dead man, if the living breathe such agonizing lives? And my anxiety increases on sensing, in all its fullness, how my capacity to love, to discern things, is far superior to that of the many who pass me by so fearfully. (*EM,* 92–93)

In what can only be described as a very uncustomary vision for a contemporary writer, Rubião's narrative concludes, not on an anguished note, but with the hopeful vision that was reflected in the opening quote from the Book of Job. The ending is affirmative and joyous, one that is somewhat unexpected in a splenetic age of predominantly alienated writings.

> Still, a clear day might dawn tomorrow, the sun brilliant as never before. And at such an hour men may come to realize that, even on the mar-

gin of life, I am still alive, because my existence has been transmuted into colors, and whiteness is already drawing close to the earth, to the exclusive delight of my eyes. (*EM,* 93)

Rubião brings together these two pieces of short fiction under the unifying images of light and color. The ex-magician, who two decades earlier lamented his inability to cover the earth with a rainbow of color, is fictionally reincarnated in the character of Zacarias, who "can not live without color." Zacarias, at work's end, attains an anthropomorphic diffusion of his being into cosmic and Divine Light.

Though much contemporary literary criticism utilizes the term *apocalyptic* in the sense of a highly negative warning, the term in its original Greek meaning of "disclosure" or "revelation" in a positive sense is applicable to Rubião's metafiction. "Zacarias, the Pyrotechnist" prefigures the power and sensuous splendor of the Book of Revelation. Like Saint John before the blinding light of the New City descending to earth, Zacarias senses an existence in which his being will be "transmuted into colors." The intense rapture, delight, and hope of the Book of Revelation mirror the narrative's final paragraph: "I am still alive . . . the sun brilliant as never before . . . a clear day might dawn tomorrow . . . whiteness is already drawing close to the earth" (*EM,* 93). Rubião is consciously constructing a correspondence with one of the world's most beautiful and influential pieces of literature in order to convey his contemporary gospel of hope.

Murilo Rubião's prose evolves as an existential rethinking of man's place in the universe. He attempts to engender a new fiction, one which continually seeks to define the unique nature of contemporary man's existence. He has moved beyond the now clichéridden concept of the encounter with nothingness to a metaphysical stance that stresses a strong element of faith. However, it is difficult to equate the metaphysical impulses in Rubião's writings to any traditional concept of religion. His metafictions ask readers to coparticipate actively in the creative process. Through his conscious and lyric accommodation of biblical correspondences, he imparts to his narrative resonances of the universal literary experience, what Coleridge calls "the film of familiarity." In "Zacarias, the Pyrotechnist" he employs these correspondences to convey, in magically poetic terms, a hopeful vision of contemporary man's eschatological situation.

Robert E. DiAntonio, Winter 1988

---

[1] Carl Gustav Jung, *Psychological Reflections,* Jolande Jacobi, ed., New York, Harper, 1961, p. 301.

[2] Melville Jean Herskovitz, "Magic," in *The Standard Dictionary of Folklore, Mythology and Legend,* Maria Leach, ed., New York, Funk & Wagnalls, 1975, p. 660.

[3] Bobby J. Chamberlain, "Murilo Rubião," in *A Dictionary of Contemporary Brazilian Authors,* David William Foster and Roberto Reis, eds., Tempe, Arizona State University Center for Latin American Studies, 1982, p. 131.

[4] Raymond S. Sayers, review of *The Ex-Magician and Other Stories, WLT* 54:2 (Spring 1980), p. 264.

[5] Ibid.

[6] Nathan Ausubel, *Pictorial History of the Jewish People,* New York, Crown, 1984, p. 39.

[7] Elizabeth Lowe, *The City in Brazilian Literature,* Rutherford, N.J., Fairleigh Dickinson University Press, 1982, p. 196. Subsequent references use the abbreviation *CBL.* For a review, see *WLT* 57:1 (Winter 1983), p. 82.

[8] Lowe is paraphrasing Jorge Schwartz's "Obra Muriliana do fantástico como máscara," *Minas Gerais Suplemento Literário,* 15 March 1975, p. 14.

[9] Theodore Ziolkowski, *Fictional Transfigurations of Jesus,* Princeton, N.J., Princeton University Press, 1972, p. 231. Subsequent references use the abbreviation *FTJ.*

[10] Murilo Rubião, *The Ex-Magician and Other Stories,* Thomas Colchie, tr., New York, Avon, 1979, p. 109. All subsequent references are to this edition and use the abbreviation *EM.* For a review of Harper & Row's 1979 hardcover edition, see *WLT* 54:2 (Spring 1980), p. 264.

[11] Peter S. Prescott, *Never in Doubt,* New York, Arbor House, 1986, p. 83.

[12] William H. Gass, "Philosophy and Form of Fiction," in his *Fiction and the Figures of Life,* New York, Knopf, 1970, p. 25.

[13] The biblical quotation actually ends with ". . . as the morning" and not "the morning *star*" included in the epigraph in the English version of the story—Ed.

[14] Robert Alter, *The Art of Biblical Narrative,* New York, Basic Books, 1980, p. 33.

Women Writers in Brazil Today

Despite the presence of a military dictatorship in Brazil from 1964 to 1979, women experienced an increasingly favorable position in Brazilian society and in literary art. Some male authors reacted to the violence of the military regime with strong criticism of its bureaucratic and repressive nature. Rubem Fonseca's *Feliz ano novo* and Ignacio Loyola Brandão's *Zero* were among the works suppressed during the 1970s. The most successful books published after the political *abertura* (opening) in 1979 that dealt with the guerrilla movements during the dictatorship were social documents: Fernando Gabeira's *O que é isso, companheiro?* and Alfredo Syrkis's *Os carbonários.* The best of the lot was the novel *Em câmera lenta* by Renato Tapajoz. Women's literary reaction to the regime was not so explicit, although many participated in the guerrilla groups.

Repression has always played an important part in Brazilian society. Only after 1920 did women reach a certain independence beyond housework and tertiary activities through a release of sorts from their roles in a patriarchal society and through a better level of education. Even now, the great majority of women writers belong to the upper and middle clases. In 1950 one university graduate in ten was a woman—10 percent in relation to men. In 1964 the figure was one in three; by 1974 more women than men finished university, but mostly in the humanities.[1] Historically, this pattern of repression may be traced to the nation's Jesuit background, from colonial times through the middle of the eighteenth century. Also, the agricultural and rural face of the country restrained women from exerting a freer role in society until its change through urbanization and industrialization in the 1950s. Women, either confined within themselves or actually locked inside the space of their homes, became prisoners of their own bodies, dwellings, or within the walls of their gardens. As Chombart de Lauwe writes, "The house corresponds to a certain image of the family and the distant relatives in a society. . . . Space expresses not only social structures, but also the tensions, the conflicts, the domination between classes, ethnic groups, age groups, and sex categories."[2] *Les coins de la maison,* the intimate spaces in the house pointed out by Gaston Bachelard, serve as a hiding place to which women retreat in memory and psychological time. "Time in memory" is the negation of the outside world, according to Irma Garcia. Inner space is related to the perception of the family and its inescapability, the only universe women know from childhood,[3] and Luce Irigaray asserts that "there is a long love story between a woman and her objects."[4]

Current French theory stresses the distinctions between feminine voice and female voice. Hélène Cixous, in "Castration or Decapitation?," draws parallels between the anatomy of the female body and the types of responses that women make to the external world.[5] This is a very reductive statement, for women would be determined a priori by their sex in their interrelations in life. In Viviane Forrestier's words, "There can be a feminine writing produced by women, but neither masculine nor feminine exists. The text must contain this differentiation in itself."[6] As Mary Jacobus puts it, the discussion of a feminine voice would occupy itself with the essential definition of feminine writing. However, it seems more important to define what effect a female voice can have as a new reality and a counterideological force in society and in literature.[7]

The only possibility for women to express themselves in a new, inventive way is to exert a counterideological perspective on society. As Lukács states,[8] there is always a relationship between class and ideology; it is also true that most Brazilian women writers belong to the upper and middle classes. Nonetheless, through a transformation of society in fiction, and a statement of new points of view, it is possible to escape into, or at least indicate, new directions for society and literature. Therefore, humor can be considered one of the most effective counterideological techniques in writing since symbolism, and even more so since surrealism. It functions as a way of reversing the givens, the conscious rules and social meanings, coming from inner sources of the mind and independent of external repressive forces in society.

As in many stories by Kafka, humor introduces a new reality, as it subdivides meaning into conscious (allowed, accepted, logical, given) and unconscious (unexpected, surprising, extra-ordinary, absurd, analogical) and displaces the signifier (the unconscious, for psychoanalysis) onto the signified (social, denotative meaning). The method employed here departs from quotations of the works and not from a reliance on any a priori theory. "Quoting authors is much less reductive than paraphrasing or interpreting them," states Wolfgang Iser.[9]

An examination of the last fifteen years in Brazilian literature, the period of particular interest here, reveals five main tendencies: existential, discourse experimentation, political allegory, the humorous diary or correspondence, and eroticism. The writers of the first group were highly influenced by the existential prose of Clarice Lispector, one of the leading Brazilian authors of post–1922 modernism. The narrator's voice accompanies an autobiographical reflection of the individual protagonists—women who recount their feelings through continuous descriptive monologues, as if seeing themselves in a mirror. One could agree here with Lacan that identity only merges upon recognition of the self through reflection in a mirror, the figure of the Other.[10] This plaintive, descriptive voice basically speaks of the decay of the body, loneliness, wrinkles, and perplexity in the face of existential questions. These characters have failed in their relationships and have lost hope for the future, almost without reference to any activity besides family or home life. In typical monologues, the author-character in Rachel Jardim's *Inventário das cinzas* contemplates failure, with no shift in tone between the three parts of the novel.

> To me, to break up my marriage meant to thrust myself headlong into emptiness.
>
> I looked for a job. Up to then I had never considered the possibility of supporting myself.
>
> I decided to lose weight in order to establish my appearance as an old woman. . . . I eat sparingly,

I cultivate the pleasure of delineating the meager version of the bony figure that starts to walk toward its own ashes.[11]

A sameness of tone and perspective permeates both the female and male voices in Patrícia Bins's novel *Antes que o amor acabe,* narrated by a frustrated bourgeois woman who thinks she is wasting away in a childless love.[12]

The ultimate loss, death, pervades many of these writers' novels and short stories. Characters brood, suggesting a feeling that Freud calls "mourning and melancholy," which occurs due to deprivation of a loved one through death or abandonment. *O quarto fechado* by Lya Luft treats death in all its appearances: destruction of the self and of art, disease, madness, the suicide of one of her twin children; in fact, the story takes place during the boy's funeral.[13] In *Inventário das cinzas,* quoted above, Rachel Jardim shares this sense of death.

> No one answers for me. What a strange sensation. Yesterday, at bedtime, I locked up the house and thought: it is as if I were locking my own tomb. And the idea did not disturb me. (120)
>
> Teeth. Small tombs, sepulchers painted white on the outside, rotten on the inside. They offer little resistance to old age. In them decomposition sets in. (132)
>
> I cannot imagine myself old in a coffin. I would like to die with my present face. I think it is very fitting; it is, as one says of carmelized sugar, at the exact point, ready to die. (209)

Death likewise obsesses Agda, the title character of a short story by Hilda Hilst. Her decrepit, repulsive body so impresses and depresses her that she chooses to drown herself in a well: "The greatest pleasure is to drown my yellow and aged flesh in this slime and never more have anybody TOUCH ME, NEVER MORE NEVER MORE."[14]

Fragmentation is another aspect of these writers' discourse. In Adélia Prado's poems and novels, again, the first-person-singular narrator centers autobiographically on the author's life. This voice differs somewhat from that of other female authors because Adélia Prado lives in a small town in the backlands of Minas Gerais, far from urban centers such as Rio and São Paulo. Her more naïve and more spontaneous narrative depicts the simple habits and humble people of her surroundings. Fragmentation—a sense of inferiority that may characterize a feminine voice—is her narrative technique in *Cacos para um vitral.*

> In Glória's notebook: a novel is made up of leftovers. Poetry is a nucleus. However, it is necessary to be patient with the remnants, with the fragments. Skilled people make baskets, orna-

ments, stained glass out of them, which then form new nuclei. Is this a vain thought? Of course. I want to be an extraordinary poet and to be able to write a very funny play so that everyone can laugh until they become brothers.[15]

Fragmentation takes place in female discourse, even before outward objective observation occurs, because of broken social roles. This augments Walter Benjamin's argument that fragmentation, as exemplified in the modern work of art, is an effect of capitalist society.[16]

Family life becomes a trap in Lya Luft's *Reunião de família,*[17] where a woman faces "the ruins and the fragmentation of the feminine world."[18] This accounts for Norma Pereira Rego's failed description of Rio in the sixties and seventies in *Ipanema dom divino.*[19] Surprisingly enough, Francisca Souza da Silva more vividly conveys a sense of the city and the life therein; from a directly opposite class standpoint, her book *Ai de vós!* is a realistic, day-to-day experience of a poor domestic living in the slums.[20]

Mere language experimentation, as practiced by the writers of this second group, is not enough to effect an inversion of the roles assigned women by society. Shifts in time, development of imagination, and inventiveness in plot do not break established standards. These writers try to differentiate themselves from the literary tradition by experimenting with new techniques of narration and dramatization, often based on Spanish America's so-called magic realism. Male authors develop fantastic literature and magic realism most successfully, as evidenced, for example, in works by J. J. Veiga, Dalton Trevisan, and Vitor Giudice. Among women, Nélida Pinon has employed imaginary plots in her novels and stories; an abstract, detached narrator often serves a critical function in the text, using a rational language aloof from the literary language. Regina Célia Colônia experiments with the vocabulary and visual resources of concrete poetry. In her book of poems *Sumaimana* she plays with the semantics of the Quechua language of the Andean Indians. In *Canção para o totem,* a collection of short stories, her words are more permeated with visual connotation than with meaning corresponding to the dictionary.[21]

Lygia Fagundes Telles is an experienced writer whose first published work was *Praia viva* in 1944. Her psychological stories, often based on family life, use suspense and shifts in time, and her narration, often in the third person, almost always includes a critical outward perspective on the characters, as in her book of short stories *Antes do baile verde* (1970). In her novels *Verão no aquário* and *As meninas* she became more experimental in language. Her most recent books of short stories,

Seminário dos ratos (1977) and *Mistérios* (1981), have dealt with magic realism, the latter being her best.[22]

A third tendency could be labeled "political allegory." In spite of the promising potential of this genre, women have not, up to now, developed it in any outstanding fashion. One is tempted to note, as Hélène Cixous does, that a fearful atmosphere of suspense is peculiar to women, for "old stories consist of the repressed of culture" (HC, 52). In these short stories women can project their own fear, a result of their repressed superego, provoked by society and the family, and this projection functions as an outlet for their anxiety. Brazil's last years of dictatorship could very well serve as a pattern and inaugurate a new mode of storytelling: "The economy of the return of the libido" might "bring about a true revolution in a savage tongue" (HC, 49), which unfortunately has not yet taken place. *Memórias do medo* by Edla van Steen[23] alludes metaphorically to the military regime when, at the beginning of the novel, one of the characters disappears at the hands of the police. Another novel written as a political allegory, but in such a dreamlike atmosphere that it falls short of any political representation, is *Sortilegiu* by Myriam Campello.[24] The book which best succeeds as an allegorical reference to the military dictatorship, however, is *O pardal é um pássaro azul* by Heloneida Studart, who is today a federal deputy from Rio, elected in 1983.[25] The plot centers on a love affair between a guerrilla fighter and a girl who hides him. A simple, straightforward narrative conveys the work's antigovernment political message.

We now come to the fourth group of writers, who have developed a new voice among Brazilian women today, employing humor as an unrepressed language, often in diary or letter form applied to prose or free verse. Playing with puns and situations, in her recent book of poems *Finesse e finura* Ledusha inverts social norms, syntax, and grammar and ridicules the roles women have had to exert in modern urban society.

lace
In general
I'm at ease in leisure
I read Proust
I adolesce eternally
I comb the clouds

en retard
Winds of January
penetrate the apartment
stir discreet veils
that love has woven
only now did I learn
Lucio loved me
there in Barcelona

démodé
Ulysses didn't blow
according to form[26]

For this new type of woman, staying at home is not a sinking experience of identity loss, but rather an opportunity for reading and recalling travels, in summertime. Dispensing with capital letters, Ledusha divests literature of its aura, making women confront reality, a most frightening experience for those who cannot progress beyond their individual selves to reach culture as a whole.

lady
what frightens me
is love without fear (26)

the bride of prometheus
stealing fire from men
to give to the gods
in the plural
i burn (27)

Humor effects a total reversal of the social values traditionally attributed to women. The poet's voice here shuns quiet, familylike, or exclusive love relationships; in "bold-faced," playing with the meaning of the word *fire,* she aligns herself with Prometheus in the circular structure of the poem: "my darling, Anthony, / I couldn't go / I had a flat / I couldn't change" (45). The title of this poem is employed like a newspaper headline, a technique often used by the modernist poet Oswald de Andrade in his books *Pau-Brasil* (1925) and *Primeiro caderno do aluno de poesia Oswald de Andrade* (1927). The title "deslavada" (bold-faced) refers metonymically to the expression "mentira deslavada" or "bold-faced lie" and provides the poem with a second reading, as Oswald de Andrade practiced in his poetry.

insolent mosquitoes
paint tragedy humorously
so long awaited
ledusha a false madwoman
finds herself in love
(L, 72)

new-mayakovsky
I prefer toddy to tedium. (88)

easy-going
a feminist on Saturday Sunday Monday Tuesday
  Wednesday Thursday and on Friday
a wolf-woman. (87)

These poems from *Risco no disco* employ humor and sometimes an ironic, external voice, as also seen in Márcia Denser's erotic stories. It is one of the best tools to break the rigidity of modern urban society and its fixed roles. Denser attempts to create an unrepressed female narrator in *O animal dos motéis* and *Exercícios para o pecado.*[27] However, her descriptions of sex and eroticism follow a male pattern and a masculine point of view, as in the ironic, cynical voice encountered in Henry Miller, Rubem Fonseca, and Raduan Nassar and in some of Hemingway and the beat generation. It would seem that women have to adopt a masculine voice to survive a male-dominated society.

Side by side with humor, the diary or letter form serves an innovative purpose in the shift of tone in female literature. Ana Cristina Cesar (1952–83) can be considered to have taken part in the liberating "mimeogaph generation" movement of the 1970s. In *A teus pés, Cenas de abril, Correspondência completa,* and *Luvas de pelica*[28] she shows a fondness for intimate diaries and love letters in free verse or poetic prose. She wrote as if a hidden onlooker were observing her from within the walls of her own room. Her poetry, which was extremely autobiographical, employed what Georges Bataille called *l'expérience intérieure,*[29] a term he preferred to *mysticism.* By this he meant inner sensation and knowledge of the self, when the human being, and especially the artist, overcomes the feeling of silence and of solitude. Bataille stated that the consciousness of solitude and death is the only path to communciate art. Art then becomes the victory of Eros (life, love) against Thanatos (death, repression). In "Carnival: Independent Youth" the ego identifies itself with the liberating experience of carnival in the modern, though often solitary, city.

For the first time I broke the golden rule and got
  spaced out
upward without measuring the consequences. Why
do we refuse to be a prophetess, and what dialect is
  that
to the small evening gathering? I got spaced out:
it's now, my heart, in the chariot of fire in the
air, no grace crossing the state of
São Paulo, at daybreak, furiously, and all for you: it's
now, in this dead end.
(ACC, 15)

Cesar's poems in *Cenas de abril* are filled with recollections and references to travels, as in a diary. Her two other books are also written in diary form. The taste for travel is an outlet for women's fear of losing their identity when they are locked up (IG, 329). To cope with this longing for an escape, diaries and letters are a perfect form, for they have no boundaries, no limitations, no sense of space. As Anaïs Nin once wrote, "Sadness led me to construct a cavern to protect myself: my diary."[30] The main characteristic of such writing is that "one can cut off a letter or a diary at any point, at any length. The diary accompanies the rhythm of life" (IG, 164).

Breaking up the famous metaphorical lines on death and navigation by the French symbolists, the poems below convey the same imaginary sensation of failure in adventure and in action felt by those nineteenth-century poets toward woman in modern times.

Recovery from Adolescence
it's always easier
to anchor a ship in space
(ACC, 57)

A-B-C of Healing
Women and children are the first to stop dreaming of
  sinking ships.
(ACC, 17)

Questioning oneself as a writer through a blank space of inquiry opened between writer and reader—the basis for modern *écriture,* in Paul Ricoeur's hermeneutics—may be another form of asking what it means to be a woman. This blank space can be inserted in the text by humor or by a questioning position on the part of the narrator-author, as Edla van Steen does at the end of each chapter of *Memórias do medo,* quoted above.

One of the most promising trends in Brazilian women's literature is erotic writing, the realm of the fifth and last group to be examined here. These writers began to appear under the impact of literary contests promoted by the erotic magazine *Status* and under the influence of Rubem Fonseca's erotic style. The only prior known instance of Brazilian women writing artistically in the erotic "genre" were the love letters by Sister Mariana de Alcoforado from her convent to a French lover. First published in France in 1669, the letters went through many editions but were later judged inauthentic and to have been written by a man. Among the erotic poets, Bruna Lombardi is the most daring, sometimes so overcome by her intentions and meanings that she forgets to polish the form and employ more sophisticated solutions in her rhyming.[31] Olga Savary is one of the most mature and recognized poets producing erotic poems; she frequently employs the image of wild beasts to represent women's feelings.[32]

Poetry, in its lyrical qualities, helps to convey better the meanings of eroticism through its metaphors. Prose has the disadvantage of using a more metonymic vocabulary, if we still accept today Jakobson's terminology. Two anthologies, both compiled by Márcia Denser, may serve as examples. In the first, *Muito prazer,* the task of coming to grips with paper and having to describe eroticism in metonymic, denotative, and rather explicit language to achieve a plot led many of the authors to shun the subject and use their space only to tell the sources of their repression. As in "Tanganica" by Judith Grossmann and "A chave na fechadura" by Cecília Prada,[33]

most of these stories could equally well have been included in nonerotic anthologies. Although there is more about how Brazilian women feel repressed by their families, their husbands, and society, there is little or no eroticism in the writing. The second anthology, *O prazer é todo meu,* is more successful in its aim. Authors like Sônia Coutinho and Myriam Campello manage to combine the erotic with a refined and sophisticated narrative technique.[34]

Erotic writing is one of the tools for acting out the "hysterical side of women," as Hélène Cixous states. If Lacan is correct when he asserts that women are outside the symbolic order, then, she contends, the agenda is speak, speak, and speak (HC, 47). Edla van Steen also builds up an intense atmosphere between a couple struggling not to see one another any more in her story "*Carol* cabeça *lina* coração" (PA, 171–73n). It is in her latest book of short stories, *Antes do amanhecer,* that she is able to combine an atmosphere of suspense with one of eroticism in a highly imaginative plot. Outstanding stories are "O Sr. e a Sra. Martins," "Aluga-se apartamento," and "Intimidade."

The author who most develops the quest for a free female voice is Sônia Coutinho. *Os venenos de Lucrécia*[35] shows the inordinately intricate and intimate problems of a solitary woman in a large city like Rio. Her feelings and expectations in relation to work, personal fulfillment, and desire to overcome the external limitations of her sex are conveyed in a sensual tone and rich dialogues. Although not focusing on eroticism, Coutinho's last book, *O jogo de Ifá,*[36] shows the search for identity in the androgynous characters Renato and Renata, brother and sister, whose destinies run parallel in the plot. The initial reference to Virginia Woolf's *Orlando* is explained at the end of the book when the two protagonists perceive their selves as both masculine and feminine, female and male. The elliptical structure of cross and double references matches Cortázar's plot construction in *Hopscotch.*

From what has been examined, it could be concluded that an innovative voice among women writers in Brazil exists in those who employ humor or the day-to-day recounting of feelings and experiences through the use of a narrator who is both intimate and critical. This has been the tool best suited to develop a counterideological movement within the literary tradition. Besides providing an original feminine discourse, these authors were also able to reach what Wolfgang Iser considers to be the true aim of literary discourse as an esthetic object: the achievement of representation.[37]

The problem of representation of one's self through its projection into another self, according to Luce Irigaray in *Speculum de l'autre femme,* must be linked in a totality of identity in women's discourse. This identity can only be achieved when women first define their own roles in literature and in society, especially in one that is still so repressed and male-dominated as Brazil's. In a society ruled seriously by men, women have yet to become sufficiently liberated to play and to laugh. Up till now, women have been treated as sex objects— witness the continued popularity of *Gabriela,* a case compounded with the myth of the mulatta, someone between races, whose role in society is in flux.

Humor could be the outlet, the breaking out from all structures. Women should start to laugh at themselves, as Cixous says,[38] instead of going on mourning for all eternity. Like the Mario de Andrade character who left his conscience (meaning traditional roles) far away on the island of Marapatá, in the Amazon delta, women should be the Macunaímas of Brazilian society. Women should laugh in earnest and find more pleasure than did Ci, one of Macunaíma's first lovers, who soon was to pay for her pleasure by becoming a heavenly constellation. Before discussing a possible development of a feminine or a masculine voice, or perhaps an androgynous voice, women should begin by discussing rules, syntax, and social norms and by deciding what they hope to achieve through writing, and then ask whether they can finally overcome class limitations and exert a truly counterideological role in what they do and write.

Luiza Lobo, Winter 1987

[1] Maria Inácia d'Avila Neto, *O autoritarismo e a mulher, o jogo de dominação macho e fêmea no Brasil,* Rio de Janeiro, Achiamê, 1978, p. 14.

[2] Chombert de Lauwe, "Ethnologie de l'espace humain," in *De l'espace écologique à l'espace corporel,* Paris, PUF, 1975, as quoted by Maria Inácia d'Avila Neto, pp. 238, 240. All translations are my own unless otherwise indicated. My thanks to Charles Martin, Cliff Landers, Debora Truban, and Claire Johnson for their help in revising this article in English.

[3] Irma Garcia, *Promenade femmilière: Recherches sur l'écriture féminine,* Paris, Des Femmes, 1981, 2 vols. All quotations refer to vol. 1. Subsequent references use the abbreviation IG.

[4] Luce Irigaray, "Face-à-Femmes," in *Alternatives,* p. 94. as quoted in Garcia, pp. 367–68.

[5] Hélène Cixous, "Castration or Decapitation?," Annette Kuhn, tr., *Signs,* 7:1 (Autumn 1981), p. 47. Subsequent references use the abbreviation HC.

[6] Viviane Forrestier, "Féminin pluriel," *Tel Quel,* 74, p. 12.

[7] Mary Jacobus, "Is There a Woman in This Text?," *New Literary History,* 14:1 (Autumn 1982), pp. 117–41.

[8] Georg Lukács, *Histoire et conscience de classe,* Paris, Minuit, 1960.

[9] Wolfgang Iser, "Narrative Strategies as a Means of Communication," in *Interpretation of Narrative,* Mario J. Valdés and Owen

[10] J. Miller, eds., Toronto, University of Toronto Press, 1981, p. 101.

[10] Jacque Lacan, "Le stade du miroir," in his *Ecrits,* Paris, Gallimard, 1966.

[11] Rachel Jardim, *Inventário das cinzas,* Rio de Janeiro, Salamandra, 1984, pp. 57, 58, 117. Subsequent references use the abbreviation RJ.

[12] Patrícia Bins, *Antes que o amor acabe,* Rio de Janeiro, Nova Fronteira, 1984. For the husband's viewpoint, see p. 39.

[13] Lya Luft, *O quarto fechado,* Rio de Janeiro, Nova Fronteira. 1984.

[14] Hilda Hilst, "Agda," in *O papel do amor,* Edla van Steen, ed., São Paulo, Indústria de Papel Simão, 1978/79, p. 163. Subsequent citations from this anthology use the abbreviation *PA.*

[15] Adélia Prado, *Cacos para um vitral,* Rio de Janeiro, Nova Fronteira, 1980, p. 79.

[16] Walter Benjamin, "The Work of Art in the Age of Its Mechanical Reproduction," in his *Illuminations,* Harry Zohn, tr., New York, Schocken, 1969.

[17] Lya Luft, *Reunião de família,* Rio de Janeiro, Nova Fronteira, 1982.

[18] Donaldo Schüler, review of *Reunião de família,* in *Colóquio-Letras* (Lisbon), 72 (March 1983), p. 105.

[19] Norma Pereira Rego, *Ipanema dom divino,* Rio de Janeiro, Nova Fronteira, 1984.

[20] Francisca Souza da Silva, *Ai de vós!,* Rio de Janeiro, Civilização Brasileira, 1983.

[21] Regina Célia Colônia, *Sumaimana,* 2d ed., Rio de Janeiro, Alves/Pró-Memória/INL, 1984. In other stories of *Canção para o totem* (Rio de Janeiro, Civilização Brasileira, 1975) the atmosphere is more one of language experimentation than of eroticism.

[22] Lygia Fagundes Telles, *Mistérios,* Rio de Janeiro, Nova Fronteira, 1981, and *Seminário dos ratos,* Rio de Janeiro, Olympio, 1977. For a review of the latter, see *WLT* 52:2 (Spring 1978), p. 276.

[23] Edla van Steen, *Memórias do medo,* São Paulo, Melhoramentos, 1974. Subsequent references use the abbreviation EVS.

[24] Myriam Campello, *Sortilegiu,* Rio de Janeiro, Civilização Brasileira/MEC/INL, 1981.

[25] Heloneida Studart, *O pardal é um pássaro azul,* Rio de Janeiro, Civilização Brasileira, 1981. See also *O estandarte da agonia,* Rio de Janeiro, Nova Fronteira, 1981.

[26] Ledusha, *Finesse e fissura* (including *Risco no disco* and *Nocaute*), São Paulo, Brasiliense, 1984, pp. 18, 21, 63. Her poetry relates to the so-called mimeograph generation. Subsequent references use the abbreviation L.

[27] Márcia Denser, *O animal dos motéis,* Rio de Janeiro, Civilização Brasileira / Massao Ohno, 1981, and *Exercícios para o pecado: Duas novelas,* Rio de Janeiro, Philobiblion, 1984.

[28] Ana Cristina Cesar, *A teus pés* (including the other three books), 2d ed., São Paulo, Brasiliense, 1983. Subsequent references use the abbreviation ACC.

[29] Georges Bataille, *L'expérience intérieure,* in his Œuvres complètes, vol. 5, Paris, Gallimard, 1973.

[30] Anaïs Nin, *Journal,* vol. 1, p. 319, as quoted in Garcia, p. 310.

[31] Bruna Lombardi, *O perigo do dragão,* 3d ed., Rio de Janeiro, Record, 1984.

[32] Olga Savary, *Magma,* São Paulo, Massao Ohno / Kempft, 1982, pp. 28, 29.

[33] *Muito prazer: Contos eróticos femininos,* Márcia Denser, ed., Rio de Janeiro, Record, 1982. See also Marina Colasanti, "Menina de vermelho, a caminho para a Lua," pp. 49–58.

[34] *O prazer é todo meu: Contos eróticos femininos,* Márcia Denser, ed., Rio de Janeiro, Record, 1984.

[35] Sônia Coutinho, *Os venenos de Lucrécia,* São Paulo, Atica, 1978.

[36] Sônia Coutinho, *O jogo de Ifá,* São Paulo, Atica, 1980.

[37] Wolfgang Iser, "The Interplay between Creation and Interpretation," *New Literary History,* 15:2 (Winter 1984), p. 387.

[38] Hélène Cixous, *LA,* Paris, Gallimard, 1976. See also "The Laugh of the Medusa," Keith and Paula Cohen, trs., *Signs,* 1 (Summer 1976), p. 887.

Carlos Drummond de Andrade and the Heritage of *Modernismo*

To a large extent, the work of Carlos Drummond de Andrade is *the* poetic legacy of *modernismo*.* Born in 1902, he published his first volume of verse, *Alguma poesia* (Some Poetry), in 1930; others, like Manuel Bandeira (1886–1968) and Mário de Andrade (1893–1945), came from that no-man's-land sometimes called *pré-modernismo,* which means that they had to make the revolution and to fight at the barricades. Not so with Carlos Drummond de Andrade; for him *modernismo* was a war already won, and the only task left was to occupy and explore the conquered territories—which he did, masterfully.

Of course, he is much more than a faithful follower and an adherent; it would be more correct to see him as one of the Apostles who went about spreading the Message. All these theological metaphors are authorized by Mário de Andrade, who christened Manuel Bandeira as "*modernismo*'s Saint John the Baptist"; if that is true, Drummond has been its Beloved Son in whom the gods of literature are well pleased. In fact, being anti-Brazilian, or at least a-Brazilian, in some aspects (his introversion and reserve, his horror of rhetoric and bombast), he is on the other hand eminently Brazilian, with an acute eye for the ridicule, steely irony, skepticism tempered by tenderness and vice-versa and, above all, his flawless congeniality to the complex and contradictory state of mind and soul that is "to be Brazilian."

Although he wrote in one of his *arts poétiques,* "Do not make lines out of events," it is impossible to dissociate his poetry from the "events" of literary and social history since 1922. Not that he took facts as themes, but in the sense that facts created an atmosphere, intellectual and emotional, which reflected and certainly conditioned the "atmosphere" of his poetry. His career, like Roman highways, is marked with successive milestones that signal not only the journey and the distance but also, in this case, the landscape. Each one of his main volumes corresponds to a particular moment in the history and evolution of literary principles and moral concepts. In 1930 *Alguma poesia* was the book of victorious *modernismo* and the no less victorious inauguration of the Second Republic. Times were ripe for simplicity and directness of expression, for snapshots of the "real Brazil," for tireless exercises in self-criticism, for repudiation of the past and for the poetry of the common man (both as author and reader).

Everything was clear and familiar, or was it? Under the species of the poem "In the Middle of the Road" the closet's skeleton was found in one room of the colonial house, spotlighted by the brilliant tropical sun and incredibly fascinating. Unexpectedly, it caught the imagination of the readers, rejected the everyday poetry of the volume and gave it its "real" meaning.

In the middle of the road there was a stone
there was a stone in the middle of the road
there was a stone
in the middle of the road there was a stone.

Never should I forget this event
in the life of my fatigued retinas.
Never should I forget that in the middle of the road
there was a stone
there was a stone
there was a stone in the middle of the road
in the middle of the road there was a stone.
(Elizabeth Bishop, tr.)

What in the world could that possibly mean? Written about 1925—that is, at the very beginning of Drummond's career—the poem anticipated and announced (which, of course, no one could have known at the time) the hermeticism of Brazilian poetry in the 1930s and 40s and beyond, represented in his own work by *Claro enigma* (Clear Enigma; 1951). Meanwhile, all the philistines had their day: roaring laughter was heard all over the country, and everyone proposed a mock explanation, going from pure and simple mental derangement to the very well-known writer's urge to baffle the bourgeois. Later on, with good humor and superlative cunning, the author himself would write the history of the whole episode in *Uma pedra no meio do caminho: Biografia de um poema* (A Stone in the Middle of the Road: Biography of a Poem; Rio de Janeiro; 1967).

The Second Republic, in literature as well as in politics, was rapidly disintegrating, however, as *Sentimento do mundo* (Sense of the World; 1940), with the first intrusion of "events," showed with insistent urgency. The war was *there,* and "the war was in us" (to recall the title of Marques Rebelo's novel); Drummond was no longer the parochial dweller of the small *Brejo das almas* (Morass of Souls; 1934), in the State of Minas Gerais, but a citizen of the world. Long before Marshall McLuhan, poets were aware of the global village; polarized to the right and the left, Brazilian intellectuals fought with words the same war others were fighting with swords; Drummond entered the second phase of his career as a poet, going through a process of ever-increasing sympathy with socialist ideas without ever accepting full regimentation in any extremist party.

One may even consider the whole episode a misunderstanding in semantics: since the political situation of the time was viewed and felt as "fascist," to oppose it was inevitably to seem "leftist"; later on, when the unfathomable political interests made strange bedfellows of democracy and communism, it was only normal, if somewhat naïve, to celebrate Russian resistance against Nazism. In all that, we must keep in mind the peculiarity of the Brazilian situation: Drummond was, ideologically, sincerely and openly opposed to the regime, while at the same time being one of its high officials (Director of the Cabinet in the Ministry of Education); and when the Communist Party stormed an election for the board of the recently formed Writers Guild (Associação Brasileira de Escritores), likewise seen as a center of political opposition, Drummond and many others resigned immediately.

This resignation, along with general trends in poetry (the replacement of Modernist generations by the so-called Generation of '45), signaled Drummond's gradual but steadfast withdrawal from "events" and correspondent immersion in personal, emotionally autobiographical and hermetic poetry. The consequence was a period of "pure poetry," if we can call it that, represented by *Claro enigma.* It must be noted, however, that, having developed his poetry in progressively transcending stages, Drummond never disavowed any of his successive selves, integrating each instead into the next. This is well documented by the *opera omnia* that symbolically close each period. In 1942 *Poesias* marked the end of the properly Modernist poetry of *Alguma poesia* and *Brejo das almas* (including *Sentimento do mundo,* which, as noted, responded to a new line of inspiration); in 1948 *Poesia até agora* (Poetry until Now) did the same for all the preceding books, including *A rosa do povo* (The People's Rose), whose nature and character of political "engagement" corresponded symmetrically to *Sentimento do mundo.*

What comes next is *Claro enigma,* i.e. the surpassing of both Modernist poetry (nationalist, picturesque,

colloquial) and ideological verse (ephemeral, journalistic, partisan) in favor of broader concepts: man and his fate, literature as a reality in its own right. But the dialectics of Drummond's spirit demanded that he "reintegrate" this world of abstractions and pure intellectual hedonism into his national roots and his own personal origins—and the next *opera omnia* was called *Fazendeiro do ar & poesia até agora* (Farmer of the Clouds and Poetry until Now; 1953). Why "farmer of the clouds"? One might think that that title, in light of the foregoing poetic corpus, suggests a new state of mind, something like Drummond's *petit testament,* a sardonic admission of failure in the struggle for the goods of this world. In fact, it points to the permanent obsession of his poetry: namely, a mythical past forever lost in the fog of memory, the dearly departed in their dusty frock coats, family albums where Time has left the yellowed footprints of its passage, Minas Gerais and its old ghosts floating in almost inaudible murmurs of incomprehensible voices. As early as *Sentimento do mundo* (1940), in the extraordinary poem "Confidência do itabirano," Drummond had intoned, like a phrase in a symphony, the theme of the "farmer of clouds": "I owned gold, and cattle, and plantations. Now I am a bureaucrat." The full emotional impact of those lines can only be felt and appreciated within the context of a semantic antagonism extremely acute in the conscience of Brazilians, the antagonism that opposes the nobility of the gentleman farmer to the petty nature of bureaucratic work.

Thus there is a strong central current that unifies and nourishes the whole of Drummond's work, beyond and above all the changes of inspiration and esthetic concepts it went through along the years. The sardonic fairy leaning over his cradle cast an evil spell on him but also traced the outline of his career: "Go, Carlos, and be awkward in life." The poet himself does not see his own successive avatars as so many variations in poetic personality, but rather likes to have them organized in clusters of large thematic lines. Editing his own anthology in 1962, he intended it to be a "faithful mirror," reflecting "certain characteristics, preoccupations and tendencies" that "condition or define" his work as a whole. Chronological order seemed to him less significative than the nine psychological "sections": 1) the individual, 2) the land, 3) family, 4) friends, 5) the impact of society, 6) carnal knowledge, 7) poetry proper, 8) playful exercises and 9) the existential vision or an attempt at one.

If we accept that view—and, provided the other is not excluded, there is no reason why we shouldn't— Drummond's poetics developed like a complex living organism, continually incorporating without really rejecting its successive ages and stages. It is not unreasonable to think that Drummond considered his poetic work substantially complete in 1953, for thereafter not only were his subsequent books, in a sense, minor ones and mostly in prose, but the *opera omnia* of the later years bore the "neutral" titles *Poemas* (1959) and *Reunião* (1967; 7th ed., 1976)—to which we may add, for the record, *Obra completa* (1964) and *Poesia completa e prosa* (1973).

Drummond's celebrated irony is in fact a defense against emotion, particularly against sentimental pathos. Brazilian readers were never fooled by that, and what touches them deeply is the submerged strain of melancholy, even despair and anguish, that pervades the whole work. But irony takes care of all that. Life is what it is— no use for grand gestures or solemn proclamations on the mountain. All of Drummond's work could be interpreted in that perspective, if we take as a springboard the two final strophes of "Poem of Seven Faces." Here is one of them, including a second-degree irony, since it is also a mock reference to Tomás Antô-nio Gonzaga (1744–1810), one of the greatest lyric poets in the Portuguese language.

Mundo mundo vasto mundo
se eu me chamasse Raimundo
seria uma rima, não seria uma solução.

This of course loses its pun in translation.

World, world, vast world,
if my name was Twirled
it'd be a rhyme, it wouldn't be a solution.
(John Nist, tr.)

The unfortunate Gonzaga wrote to his beloved Marília, "Eu tenho o coração maior que o mundo" (My heart is larger than the world), to which Drummond pinned the ridicule of a "Raimundo" that, besides being a perfect rhyme, is also a proper name generally associated with black slaves in old colonial Brazil. He goes even further: *his* heart is, in fact, at least as large as Gonzaga's: "World, world, vast world, / even vaster is my heart." But at this point he perceives the danger of over-sentimentality lurking behind every word; the situation is getting out of hand, the ambiance is pushing him to tears, like a good old romantic poet; so the best course is to find another explanation for this moment of weakness.

I shouldn't tell you
but this moon
but this cognac
shake a person up like hell.

Drummond's critical status is privileged too; not only is he one of the rare poets about whom all judg-

ments that count are favorable, but he has also attained an uncommon audience in the public at large—due in part, it must be said, to his regular column in one of Rio de Janeiro's leading newspapers. Aside from innumerable articles and essays in books, magazines, literary histories and the like, his work has been the subject of very sophisticated analyses by a number of specialists: Oton Moacir Garcia (*Palavra puxa palavra,* 1955), Hélcio Martins (*A rima na poesia de Carlos Drummond de Andrade,* 1968), Emanuel de Morais (*Drummond rima itabira mundo,* 1972), Afonso Romano de Santana (*Drummond, o "Gaúche" no tempo,* 1972), Joaquim-Francisco Coelho (*Terra e família na poesia de Carlos Drummond de Andrade,* 1973) and Gilberto Mendonça Teles (*Drummond: A estilística de repetição,* 2nd ed., 1976), to name only a few. Today Drummond is unquestionably the dean of Brazilian poetry. The singularity of his situation can be well evaluated by the fact that it could not be challenged, even remotely, by any of the younger poets or by the clutches of the more or less indistinguishable ones regimented under the banner of such collective enterprises such as concretism, praxism and the like.

Wilson Martins, Winter 1979

*On Brazilian *modernismo* see Wilson Martins, *The Modernist Idea,* Jack E. Tomlins, tr., New York, New York University Press, 1970. Selections of Drummond's poetry in English are easily accessible in Carlos Drummond de Andrade, *In the Middle of the Road: Selected Poems,* John Nist, ed. & tr., Tucson, University of Arizona Press, 1965; Elizabeth Bishop, Emanuel Brasil, eds., *An Anthology of Twentieth-Century Brazilian Poetry,* Middletown, Cn., Wesleyan University Press, 1972; and José Neistein, ed., *Poesia brasileira moderna: A Bilingual Anthology,* Manoel Cardozo, tr., Washington, D.C., Brazilian-American Cultural Institute, 1972. Moreover, Drummond has twice been nominated for *WLT*'s biennial $10,000 Neustadt International Prize for Literature: in 1972 by Jorge de Sena (see accompanying essay), and in 1978 by Brazilian critic Antônio Cândido.

Feijoada, Coke and the Urbanoid: Brazilian Poetry since 1945

An intellectual hardened in the fray of the heroic "Modern Art Week," São Paulo's revolutionary "Semana de Arte Moderna" of 1922, proudly confided what he considered to be one of the major achievements of the Modernism movement. Thanks to his generation, the humble Brazilian national staple of rice and black beans, transformed into a succulent dish of great subtlety called *feijoada completa,* now had become sociably acceptable fare at restaurants as well as at family gatherings of the bourgeoisie.[1] Not too long ago, he felt, lobster with "mayonnaise," roast beef garnished with potatoes "sautées" and "petits pois," cheese "soufflé," "charlotte russe" and "chartreuse" had been "de rigueur." Like the culinary plane, Brazilian poetry since the end of World War II has distinguished itself by the refinement, evaluation, analysis and assimilation of the legacy of *modernismo* on the one hand, and by the rupture with the old order on the other. The acceptance of the major tenets of the Modernist credo, a peculiar mixture of populism, erudition and revolutionary vanguard esthetic in search of the African, European and American components of Brazilian culture in order to create an authentic national artistic expression, has occurred in virtually all places and on all levels: in the *ginásios,* university lecture halls, newspapers, magazines and reviews as well as on radio and television. However, the first major break with the past since 1922 began in the early fifties when a number of heterogeneous, often contradictory, experimentalist schools bearing different labels (e.g., concretism, neo-concretism, praxis-poems, semiotic poetry, process-poems, tropicalism, et cetera) sought new idioms, systems and signs as well as new media of communication.[2]

The gradual assimilation of the Modernist theories acted as a leaven and fostered greater refinement and introspection resulting in a more accurate assessment of Latin American reality as well as a more precise definition of Brazil's identity, culture and past. In addition, it contributed considerably to the acceptance of new schools of thought, such as the New Criticism of the early fifties and the structuralism of the late fifties. Thus *Tristes tropiques* (1955) was translated into Portuguese and became part of the university curriculum long before the English edition of 1961. Perhaps a more pertinent example would be the retrospective reassessment of Mário de Andrade (1893–1944), the guiding influence of the Modernist generation. In the literary supplement to the *Jornal do Brasil* of Sunday, 3 March 1957, devoted exclusively to his work, Andrade was praised as "the most complete intellectual organizer and the most efficient leader of our literary history." The same Rio de Janeiro newspaper later featured other similar articles such as "Oswald de Andrade and Anthropophagy" (20 October 1957) and "Letter of Mário de Andrade to Manuel Bandeira" (21 November 1958). By 1976 Eduardo Escorel's *Lição de amor* (A Lesson in Love), a film based on one of Mário's short stories, and another based on his major novel *Macunaíma* (1969; directed by Joaquim Pedro de Andrade) had become very popular. Meanwhile the legend of anthropophagy lived on in Nelson Pereira dos Santos's hilarious gourmandist-gluteous production "Como era gostoso o meu frances" (1971), whose suggestive meaning can only be approximated by the title "How Tasty Was My Frenchman."

More formal scholarship of *modernismo* began, in part, with Manuel Bandeira's (1886–1966) *Apresentação da poesia brasileira* (An Introduction to Brazilian Poetry). Mário da Silva Brito's impeccably researched first volume on the history of Modernism "Antecedentes da Semana de Arte Moderna" (Forerunners of the Modern Art Week) and the extremely useful anthology *Panorama da poesia brasileira, VI: O modernismo* (1959) followed later on. The sixties brought the reprinting of the first polemic phase of Oswald de Andrade's (1890–1954) work *Memórias sentimentais de João Miramar* (Sentimental Memoirs of João Miramar; 1964), the *Poesias reunidas de Oswald de Andrade* (Collected Poems of Oswald de Andrade; 1966) and *O rei da vela* (The King of the Candle; 1967). Facsimiles of two crucial Modernist reviews, *Klaxon* (1922–23) and the *Revista de Antropofagia* (Anthropophagous Review; 1928–29), published in São Paulo in two *dentições* or "teethings," came out in 1972 and 1976 respectively, sponsored by José Mindlin. In 1972 Murilo Mendes published *Poliedro,* and the intellectual *Revista de Cultura Vozes* dedicated its January-February issue to "50 anos de modernismo brasileiro" (50 Years of Brazilian Modernism), with an interview and commentary by Alceu Amoroso Lima, one of the most respected critics of the movement, who stated that, "finished or in the process of renewal, the Modernist cycle represents the richest legacy of all our cultural evolution." That same year the 28 February issue of the popular newsmagazine *Veja* brought in-depth coverage of "A Semana aos 50 anos" (The Week 50 Years Old), concluding that, "like its hero Macunaíma, it assumes a different appearance according to who looks at it." In 1973 Marta Rosetti Batista, Tele Porto, A. Lopez and Yone Soarez de Lima unearthed some fundamental documentation in *Brasil: 1° tempo modernista—1917/29* (Brazil: The First Modernist Period—1917/29); and in 1976 an avant-garde literary magazine paid the ultimate compliment to one of the key figures of the movement by calling itself *JOSÉ* (1976–78).

Although the title of the review literally means "Joseph," the most common given name in Portuguese, and could loosely be translated as "Joe" or "Everyman," it is also a tribute to one of the more famous existential poems of the same title by Carlos Drummond de Andrade (b. 1902) in *Fazendeiro do ar & poesia até agora* (Farmer of the Clouds & Poetry until Now; 1953). With contributions by its founder and editor Gastão de Holanda as well as by Luis Costa Lima, Haroldo de Campos, Mário Pontes, Jorge Wanderley, Ferreira Gullar, Geraldo Carneiro, Sabastião Uchoa Leite, Silviano Santiago, Benedito Nunes, Alceu Amoroso Lima, Antonio Houaiss, Otto Maria Carpeaux, Carlos Drummond de Andrade, Emir Rodríguez Monegal and many other distinguished writers and critics, it published some of the finest traditional, established and innovative poetry, criticism, essays and short fiction of the seventies. Dedicated to excellence within severe existing financial limitations, it even had a conscience and never closed its eyes to government censorship or to fearful social realities such as the shantytown on the hill of Cantagalo, fifteen blocks from the editorial offices in Ipanema.

15. Free flight
The seagulls coming from São Conrado
divert their course to Cantagalo
drawn by a special smell.
Over there, dead buildings, devoid of stone ornament
where mud, shit and garbage slide,
the continuum of time, the space, the flux
of accepting the world in the image of the water
  hole,
where the rare light confuses flight
with the shadow of the Mardi Gras dancer.[3]

Of course, a large amount of the systematic evaluation, analysis and assimilation of *modernismo* in *JOSÉ* and elsewhere was made possible by the fact that a number of its most formidable figures such as Bandeira, Drummond, Jorge de Lima (1893–1953), the individualistic Cecilia Meireles (1901–64) and Murilo Mendes (1902–75) remained active or had works published between 1945 and 1978. To this group of the most eminent we could add two singular members. After an early start as a poet, Vinícius de Moraes (b. 1913), a latecomer to Modernism, was to achieve enviable popularity as a composer of bossa nova and samba lyrics and to lead the sort of life that many of his contemporaries fantasized about but did not actually dare to live. Pedro Nava (b. 1903), a medical doctor by profession, was always respected in literary circles as a member of "O Grupo Mineiro, *A Revista*" (The Minas Gerais Group from *The Review*; 1925) and as an occasional poet; his sinister "O defunto" (The Deceased; 1946) is a good example. When he devoted a great amount of time to writing in his seventies and published the monumental trilogy *Báu de ossos* (Trunk of Bones; 1972), *Balão cativo* (Captive Balloon; 1973) and *Chão de ferro* (Iron Ground; 1976) the *poeta bisexto* or "leap-year poet," as Bandeira aptly called him, was to become the unrivaled memorialist of his generation. Paradoxically, by incorporating the legacy of *modernismo* into the mainstream of Brazilian life and thereby giving its theories wider diffusion and popular acceptance, these authors continued to grow in individual reputation, but their movement was finished as a collective enterprise.

The so-called Generation of 1945 was to pave the way to the future and to distinguish itself from the hard-core Modernists by slight changes in form, tone and occasionally theme more than by actual changes of direction. The essayist Eliane Zagury was known for her remark that "São Paulo's Modern Art Week had a granddaughter who went astray and a legitimate grandson—concretism." The year 1945 might then seem arbitrary, since the shrewd Bandeira had noted that most of the "forty-fivers," João Cabral de Melo Neto (b. 1920), Mauro Mota (b. 1912), Paulo Mendes Campos (b. 1922), Ledo Ivo (b. 1924) and Geir Campos (b. 1924)—the group later to cluster around *Orfeu* (Orpheus; 1947)—had already published before or after that date.[4] Melo Neto launched his literary career with the poems of *Pedra do sono* (Sleepstone; 1942), actually written between 1939 and 1941. João Guimarães Rosa (1908–69; see accompanying article by Gregory Rabassa) premiered with the short stories of *Sagarana* (Saga-Like Tales; 1946). These were the two major figures of prose and poetry whose influence was to dominate Brazilian letters in the fifties. If the "Generation of 1945" still seems a convenient label for us today, this might be due to its symbolic character—the fact that the death of Mário de Andrade, the principal propagandist and undisputed leader of *modernismo,* virtually coincides with the end of World War II and the first fall of the strongman Getúlio Vargas. Then again, 1945 marks the appearance of some fundamental works by prominent authors: *Poesias reunidas* (Collected Poems) by Oswald de Andrade, Drummond's *A rosa do povo* (The People's Rose), Emílio Moura's *Cancioneiro* (Book of Ballads), *Mar absoluto* (The Absolute Sea) by Cecilia Meireles and Murilo Mendes's *Mundo enigma* (The World an Enigma). All of the works are significant, and in the best we can already detect the end of an era, or rather the echoes of notes more clearly sounded by the inheritors of *modernismo*—the "forty-fivers," with their shift in emphasis toward more rigorous form, greater introspection and a corresponding preoccupation with psychic experiences as well as a stress on community and collective values that are at the origin of poetry.[5] The title of Drummond's book "The People's Rose" illustrates this, and in one of his major poems, "Procura da poesia" (In Search of Poetry), first published in Rio's *Correio de Manhã* on 16 January 1944 as a "Metapoema" or poetic manifesto, he speaks of form, but above all of the very essence of words: "Don't make verses about events . . . / Enter silently into the realm of words. There you'll find the poems waiting to be written."[6] Sound advice indeed, and not too far removed from the credo of the neo-concretists, who expressed the significance which a word's semantic field generates in the following terms: "The motor of the poem is the word itself, its energy is diffused in all directions and founds verbal time."[7]

Although various critics have brought to light examples of the "poetry of figures" in antiquity and ingenious games of wit seem to have flourished during the Baroque period, Brazilian concretists are fond of tracing their lineage to more immediate sources.[8] Moacy Cirne, one of the best-informed observers of contemporary poetry in Brazil, has noted how the initial wave of concretism began in the years 1953–54 and took three fundamental directions: the *Noigandres* group of São Paulo, composed of Augusto de Campos (b. 1931), his brother Haroldo de Campos (b. 1929) and Décio Pignatari (b. 1927); Rio and the rest of the country contributed Wlademir Dias-Pino and Ferreira Gullar (b. 1930).[9] Some of the main reviews of concretist expression were *Noigandres, Invenção, Ponto, Etapa, Projeto* and *Vírgula.* However, from the January 1957 issue until 1961 the literary supplement to the *Jornal do Brasil,* under the editorial guidance of Reynaldo Jardim, was to be the principal organ for the diffusion of the theories and polemics of the São Paulo and Rio factions. The paper then proceeded to publish a series of articles on the tenets of concretism and to explore the origins of twentieth-century poetry. A few of the more important topics discussed were Huidobro's *Altazor,* Pound's *Cantos* and the imagists, futurism and the *Parole in libertà* of Marinetti, the syntactic-semantic experimentation in Joyce's *Finnegan's Wake,* Mallarmé's "Un coup de dès jamais n'abolira le hasard," cubism and the *Calligrammes* of Apollinaire. The poet Ferreira Gullar, in charge of the section on fine arts with which the literary movement was closely associated, grew into the most articulate advocate of the experimental vanguard. Indeed, along with Waldemar Cordeiro's "O objeto" (The Object), Pignatari's "Forma, função e projeto geral" (Form, Function and the General Project), A. de Campos, Pignatari and H. de Campos's "Plano piloto para a poesia concreta" (Pilot Plan for Concrete Poetry) and Gullar's "Manifesto neoconcreto" (Neo-Concrete Manifesto), "Teoria do não-objeto" (Theory of the Non-Object), "Arte concreto" and "Da arte concreta a arte neo-concreta" (From Concrete to Neo-Concrete Art) stand today as some of the basic manifestos crucial to the understanding of the period. Manuel Bandeira, Theon Spanudis and José Lino Grünewald also collaborated in the pages of the *Jornal do Brasil,* as did Oliveira Bastos and Wlademir Dias-Pino, along with many others.

The length of this article precludes examining numerous significant poets of the different experimentalist schools mentioned—concretism, neo-concretism, praxis-poems, semiotic poetry, process-poems and tropicalism. Moreover, scholars are just beginning to map out the main literary coordinates of the fifties and sixties. With this in mind, it seems appropriate to focus on a few representative figures and some of the controversial works still unfamiliar to American readers.[10] One which seems to have circulated widely is a short poem by Décio Pignatari from *Noigandres 4,* a nonsense term borrowed from Ezra Pound. (In Canto 20 Professor Levy of Freiburg fields a question about the meaning of *noigandres,* a key word in the work of the Provençal poet Arnaut Daniel: "'Yes, Doctor, what do they mean by *noigandres?*' / And he said: 'Noigandres! Noigandres! . . . Now what the DEFFIL can that mean!'") Although a disarmingly simple derivative of the well-known advertisement "Drink Coca Cola," Pignatari's six-letter anagram neatly defies translation into English. If we consider that it was first published in 1958 in Brazil, at that time a not overly industrialized country of the Third World, it bears an almost premonitory, multi-referential message, much like Augusto de Campos's more direct and visually richer creation "Luxo-Lixo" (Luxury-Garbage; 1965), a frontal attack on the waste generated by the programmed obsolescence of a consumer society.

beba coca cola
beba   cola
beba coca
babe cola caco
caco
cola
　　c l o a c a[11]

In Pignatari's poem *beba* (drink) is transposed by metathesis to *babe,* "drool" or "slobber" in Portuguese, and by the omission of the second word of the slogan into "drool cola." In the third line the elimination of the last part gives "drink coca," bringing to mind the tropical coca shrub, the source of the white, toxic, alkaloid powder popularly known as "snow" or cocaine. The fourth line is a perverse variant of the initial slogan, now altered by the double metathesis of *babe* and *caco* as well as by the change of the word order into "drool cola bit." However, *caco,* which in Brazilian Portuguese also signifies "piece" or "fragment," as in "caco de vidro" (a piece of broken glass), is intentionally only a phoneme removed from *caca* and *cocô,* both baby talk for excrement. The sequence of the last two words of the fourth line, *cola* and *caco,* is changed and repeated in the fifth and sixth, in order to prepare for the final transposition of sounds culminating in the punch line *c l o a c a* or "sewer." By now the initial message has been irremediably deformed and its deformation visually stressed even further by expansion or distribution of the six letters of *cloaca* into a space which would normally accommodate nine of the same size and typeface. However, there still exists a certain logical, implicit relation to the original meaning, which now could be reformulated as "Coca Cola = sewage."

Given the social, chronological and literary context of Pignatari's work, the concrete poem panning the standard advertisement of a synthetic beverage is more than a clever manipulation of sounds, meanings and word arrangements. It is a powerful indictment of a society ruled by imported Madison Avenue publicity techniques. Since Coca Cola, Inc., along with the United Fruit Co. and Ford Motors, too often has become associated with North American economic penetration and hegemony—as in Pablo Neruda's devastating "La United Fruit Co." of *Canto general* or Billy Wilder's satiric film *One, Two, Three*—Pignatari's poem has another dimension. Because one of the characteristics of concrete poetry is that its visual and oral structures reflect content and form, on the symbolic plane it also protests the "Coca-Colazation" of Latin American culture by foreign products. The allusion to the United States is portrayed graphically by the visual disposition of the thirteen alternating black and white linear spaces, which bring to mind the alternating red and white stripes representing the thirteen original colonies in the American flag. If we disregard for a moment the word *cloaca*, which achieves its own independence at the end of the poem, we will also find the reference in the twelve four-letter words, which total forty-eight letters, the number of states in the Union. (Alaska and Hawaii were admitted as the forty-ninth and fiftieth states in 1959, one year after the poem had been published.)

Although this might seem farfetched, it becomes less so if we take into account the fact that the nationalist anti-capitalist and anti-commercial theme also appears in Pignatari's other visual poetry. (One of the principal pieces of *Invenção* 5 [1967] consists of a huge one-dollar bill, enlarged on a scale of 5:1, where the head of Washington has been replaced by the head of a bleeding Christ crowned with thorns.[12] The label under the picture, however, still reads "Washington." On the back of this item, which actually folds out of the text of the book, we read "Cr$isto é a solução," or "Chr$ist is the solution," a dig at United States as well as Brazilian currency, considering that the initials "Cr" also stand for the abbreviation of "Cruzeiro," thus giving another possible reading of "Cr[uzeiro], $ [dollar], this is the solution.") Finally, the last word *cloaca* is inextricably linked in the poem with a semantic field of synthetic/ toxic substances and excrement and carries an implicit statement about a run-rampant, industrialized technology applied to human nutrition. Thus it very possibly is an early protest against the ersatz or junk-foodstuffs of a mechanized world which progressively prods human beings away from the cycles of nature by robbing them of their taste and pumping them full of noxious surrogates. The brave new world is one of "enriched" food, "fortified" with sodium acid pyrophosphate, L-cysteine, thiamine mononitrate, calcium propionate, hydroxypropyl methylcellulose, monoglycerides, locust bean, xantham, guar and karaya gums, polisorbate 80, carcinogenic red dyes and similar delights. In sum, Pignatari's poem is a cry against the computerized, ciphered, labeled, punched and spindled existence in which we are forced to ingest standardized, homogenized fare, man-made materials and non-dairy creamers.

Ferreira Gullar is the pseudonym of José Ribamar Ferreira, born and raised in São Luis do Maranhão, an old colonial city founded by the French in 1612. In the winter of 1975, during his political exile in Buenos Aires, the author paid the bittersweet tribute of a native son to his hometown by writing a haunting remembrance of things past. The result of this catharsis was the long, 103-page *Poema sujo* (Dirty Poem), an oneiric vision of the landscape of childhood and adolescence in provincial northeastern Brazil. When the book first appeared in Rio de Janeiro the following year, with a first printing of 4,000 copies, the volumes were sold out and the editor of Civilização Brasileira had to print another 5,000 copies. Considering the limited market for poetry in Latin America, this was a remarkable feat, particularly when we realize that another two editions soon followed the first. After his return from exile in 1976 Gullar wrote "Lessons from Architecture," dedicated to Oscar Niemeyer, the architect of Brasilia (1960), the Museum of Caracas (1965), the Mosque of Algiers, (1968) and a man respected for his social conscience.

On the planet's shoulder
(in Caracas)
Oscar placed
for ever
a bird　　　a flower

(he doesn't build our houses
out of stone:
but of wing)

In the heart of long-suffering Algeria
one afternoon he landed
a star ship
　　　　beautiful
as life is yet bound to be

(with his future design
Oscar teaches us
that dreaming is popular)

He teaches us to dream
even if we have to struggle
with harsh matter:
the iron the cement the hunger
of human architecture

He teaches us to live
within that which he transfigures:
in the sugar of stone
in the dream of the egg
in the clay of dawn
in the feather of snow
in the pure whiteness of the new

Oscar teaches us
that beauty is light.[13]

Even though much of Gullar's career developed in Rio, he has somehow remained true to Maranhão, where he wrote his first successful piece, *Luta corporal* (Hand-to-Hand Combat), without any contact with the literary establishment of Rio de Janeiro. Possibly the most famous and revolutionary poem of the book is "Roçeiral," a kind of pre-concrete "Jabberwocky," finished on 5 April 1953. After discarding five versions, Gullar settled on the final form, conceived as in a trance or as if under the influence of marijuana. This is why the poet considers the work the *carro chefe,* the first float of a carnival parade, the point of departure from the "Generation of 1945" for the constructivist venture.

The concrete poetry and related movements which appeared in São Paulo, Rio de Janeiro and the North had symbiotic relationships with painting (Picasso, Malevitch, Braque, Mondrian, Klee, Volpi, Torres Garcia), plastic arts (Palatnik), sculpture (Max Bill, Giacometti, Moore, Calder), ballet (Pape, Jardim) and music (Webern, Stockhausen, Boulez, Cage, Berio Nono) as well as an intimate connection with cinema (Eisenstein, Resnais, Godard, Antonioni), advertising, architecture and industrial design (Le Corbusier, Gropius, Bauhaus, Hochschule für Gestaltung). The neo-concretists (Amilcar de Castro, Claudio Mello e Souza, Ferreira Gullar, Franz Weissman, Lygia Clark, Lygia Pape, Reynaldo Jardim, Theon Spanudis) eventually rebelled against the more rationalist, objectivist and ideologically dogmatic postulates of the São Paulo school (A. de Campos, H. de Campos, Pignatari, Waldemar Cordeiro, Wollner, Maluf, Nogeira Lima, Geraldo de Barros).

In their attempt to achieve a fourth-dimensional psycho-psychic unity of space, time, color, sound and motion, the neo-concretists tried to break out of the limiting confines of the page and to consider for the first time alternatives such as utilizing not only the area of a page for the composition of poetry, but also its reverse side. An act such as turning a page would enable a reader to participate in the creation of a poem and eventually would lead to the invention of the *livro poema* or book poem, the *poema espacial (não objeto)* or spatial (non-object) poem, the *livro universo (ou livro sem fim)* or universe book (or book-without-end), and even to the *poe-sia buraco* or poetry of the hole.[14] Although here we can only glimpse the complexities of the experimentation, the spatial poems provide interconnected, mobile, square and triangular plaques which can be raised and lowered to reveal or hide a word written on the next one. Gullar describes one of the best examples of the "poetry of the hole" as "built in the backyard of Hélio Oiticica's house in the Gavea section of Rio de Janeiro: a room below ground level which could be reached by a flight of stairs. In the center of the softly lit room stood a bright red cube, half a meter wide, which, when lifted, revealed a smaller green cube, under which finally appeared a solid, compact white cube, quite a bit smaller than the last. On the bottom of this cube, on the side facing the ground, was the word *rejuvenesca,* 'grow younger.'"[15] Gullar's most bizarre project, which literally never got off the ground, was the "ultimate" poetry exhibition. After careful planning and with invitations sent out to all participants, the actual showing would last precisely one hour, since a time clock would detonate a bomb, causing an explosion. Needless to say, friends dissuaded him from pursuing this idea any further. If it had occurred, it would have been a happening before happenings became popular. Gullar now feels that constructivism was a worthwhile enterprise in its time, a phase through which he had to pass in order to grow in other directions such as social poetry, praxis-poems, tropicalism and so forth, and that somehow it still is a part of what he does today. However, poetry ultimately needs to communicate, and in his opinion many of the concretist experiments too often amounted to formalism raised to the third power. Concretism exhausted itself when it did not have any further message: it became an exquisite spectacle for the initiate and an erudite game for an overly reduced minority.

Although its founders remain active critics who continue exploring the visual dimensions of poetry and although texts of yesteryear are assiduously published and attractively packaged in poetic objects such as the *Caixa preta* (Black Box), concretism, as well as most of the schools associated with it, is dead and enshrined as a movement.[16] Its canonization took place in the retrospective exhibition "Projeto construtivo brasileiro na arte (1950–1962)" (Brazilian Constructivist Project in Art [1950–1962]), a collective enterprise sponsored in 1977 by the Museu de Arte Moderna in Rio de Janeiro and the Pinacoteca do Estado (State Gallery) of São Paulo, with a remarkable catalogue meticulously edited by Aracy Amaral. Perhaps the contributions of constructivism to literature are best summarized in "A escola de Ulm" (The School of Ulm) by Cabral de Melo Neto, who did not take part in the movement but who like Bandeira and Murilo Mendes was ultimately sympathetic to some of its goals. The poet from Pernambuco, a great admirer of the lucidity and clarity of the best work of Le Corbusier and Niemeyer, speaks here about the "Hochschule für Gestaltung":

Against the sticky humors
of a bloated, carnal, fat art,
of stale air, bad breath,
dirty stains which go together,

Ulm flings open a thousand windows
to a luminous, fresh wind:
a clean wind, light
as a September sun

washed by a rain that has left
its crystal on burnished metal,
its metal with the light-giving,
cutting edge of a cricket's chirp.[17]

After the demise of constructivism and related movements as a coherent force, the future belongs to the girls and boys of Brazil, those bratty newcomers surfacing everywhere, ready to spit on their elders or to defile the latter's graves in order to assure themselves a place in the tropic sun. The enfants terribles of Rio de Janeiro write poems with such endearing titles as "Me segura q'eu vou dar um troço" (Hold Me, I'm Gonna Have a Fit), "Revolução" (Revolution), "Make love, not beds ou é isso mesmo" (. . . or Yeah That's It), "Já já" (Right now), "The Plot Thickens," "Kitsch-as-Kitsch-Can," "Lúcifer," "1974 (desentranhado do poema 1914 de Carlos Drummond de Andrade)" (1974 [Disemboweled from the Poem 1914 of Carlos Drummond de Andrade]), "Fug 42," "Your/Yher," "Ficar maluco de beijo" (Go Nuts Kissing), "Mandala (o querer da arte questionado)" (Mandala [The Wish of Art Put to the Test]), "Ensolarado de metralhadoras" (Sundrenched by Machine-Gun Fire), "Light-Cock-Song," "Crash cardíaco," (Cardiac Crash), "Vida bandida" (Rip-Off Life), "O miolo do sonho e o dente de alho" (The Stuff Dreams Are Made of and the Garlic Clove), "A pombinha e o urbanoide" (The Lil' Pigeon and the Urbanoid) and "Polis I, II, III."[18] Their authors often carry such anonymous nicknames as Chacal, Charles, Cesar, Adauto and Waly Sailormoon, possibly one of the more cryptic, considering it might be an English parody of Wadi Salomão, Brazil's proverbial pawnshop Jew. Too often the poems show the alienation, anonymity and contained rage of frustrated individuals unable to control their own destiny in the midst of a megalopolis.

my poetry sings nothing
—how could it?—
it screams out all our suppression
like a maniac in a straitjacket.[19]

Although it is too early to generalize on the limited information available, there are evident common characteristics of Rio's younger poets of the seventies. Among the first would undoubtedly be a desire to accept "Kulchur" or perhaps to reexamine "high culture" and restructure it by incorporating elements of "pop" or "counter culture," previously considered nonliterary. The anti-intellectual aversion to *Kultur* with a kapital *K* also embraces high-sounding postulates of academic culture vultures and, at times, applies equally to the elitist experimentation of different vanguard schools. The second involves the anti-literary bias of the young Turks or their ambivalent attitude with regard to classic or established literature. Although we may find echoes of Lorca, Hölderlin, Castro Alves, Camões, Drummond, Machado, Mário de Andrade, Rilke, Murilo Mendes, Kant and Baudelaire, allusions range in tone from the mildly ironic to the mordant or subversive. Camões's sonnet to the Portuguese language "A língua portuguesa" becomes "Oflor dolacio in kult y bela" (roughly, "Oflower oflatium rud e en' beautiful"), Poe returns as "Edgar Allan PUM," and the impact of "BUMBA-meu-BRECHT" could conceivably be rendered as "FLICK-Brecht's-BIC." A third common denominator might well be linguistic hybridism, a sort of *Promenadenmischung* or heterogeneity of tone and styles reflecting, in turn, contradictory views of reality. Thus a great mixture of levels of discourse is apparent in the texts, where the concrete alternates with the abstract, the transcendent with the ordinary, the tragic with the comic. Not surprisingly, the third category we have mentioned is directly related to the fourth, which is the progressive incorporation of colloquial, journalistic and advertising language into poetic diction.

In sum, a conscious leveling process, determined to break down linguistic and class barriers between formal written and casual oral usage, seems to be at work. In addition, the emphasis in the poems of the new generation is on specific, everyday images, giving a direct apprehension of the urban environment and immediate sense gratification, a "Paradise Now" whose possible precedents lie in the works of Ginsberg, Ferlinghetti, Patrice Lumumba and Abbie Hoffman. Finally, since heterogeneous groups are notoriously more unstable and violent than homogeneous ones, another common denominator is bawdiness, the casual use of profanity and a deliberate, aggressive use of obscenity, as in the arch "Conto de fadas" (Fairy Tale): "O ratão transformara-se num príncipe encantado de pau dura / A bocetinha falante de Cinderela babava pelos bigodes."[20]

As with the constructivist experiments, the difficulty of evaluating and judging the new work often lies in finding an adequate critical terminology, what Sebastião

Uchoa Leite has called the "esthetic of the garbage can." Since raw emotion, ideology or pornography is no substitute for talent, and since the road to poetic oblivion may be paved with the best of intentions, ultimately only strength and quality count. As we know from Baudelaire, Borchert or Jerome Liebling's macabre still-lives "Examination at the Womb Door" (*Aperture,* no. 79, 1977), they may appear anywhere and everywhere, whatever the subject matter, as in this orgiastic brothel scene of "Lira dos 20 anos" (Lyre of the 20-Year-Old) by an uninhibited, *machão* Geraldo Carneiro:

ó minha amada dança como as putas
a luz dos lupanares langue louca
no lodaçal dos luares
                              &
eu, lírico Orfeu com minha espada
tangendo tua túrbida trevosa
                    ardente
eu, bardo eloquente: eu, o espadarte.[21]

(o my beloved dance like the whores
wane weirdly in the brothels' glow
under the mire of moonlights
                              &
I, lyrical Orpheus, woo thee with my sword,
strumming your fiery dark
                    folds
I, the eloquent bard: I the swordsman.)

Luiz Carlos Verzoni Nejar (b. 1939), a lawyer who has become State Attorney in his native city of Porto Alegre, provides a diametrically opposed sensibility to the anguished, anarchic, U.S.-geared cultural awareness of the enfants terribles of Rio de Janeiro. Raised in the state of Rio Grande do Sul, where he attended the Colégio N. Senhora do Rosário and studied law at the Catholic University of Porto Alegre, he possesses, not surprisingly, both *gaúcho* heritage and forensic background as essential parts of his poetic diction. The roots of this profoundly regional and universal voice are evident from the titles of his books—*O campeador e o vento* (The Plainsman and the Wind; 1966), *Canga* (Yoke; 1971), *Casa dos arreios* (Harness Shed; 1973) —and even from the cover of *Árvore do mundo* (Tree of the World; 1977), where a huge tree anchored in the earth evokes the stylized silhouette of the umbu (*Spondias tuberosa*), with a tenuous outline of the southern half of the Western Hemisphere as part of the leaf pattern. "Corda e faca" (Rope and Knife), one of the poems from this last volume, ends with the following verse: "Faca e corda. Corda de dor que se corta / como a vida vai cortando / o pouco que a vida solta"[22] (Knife and rope. Rope of pain we cut / as life cuts / the little life lets loose). In the rural economic context of southern Brazil

and the River Plate countries the rope and knife of the poem's title immediately bring to mind the everyday instruments of farm laborers working with livestock or grazing animals. The regional term *guitarra* for guitar, instead of the usual Brazilian Portuguese equivalent *violão* or "viola" as well as the earlier *moenda* (here probably a wheat or corn mill as contrasted with a northern sugar-cane mill) or *tempo ponteado,* time plucked on the guitar, while not intrinsically local, also reveal southern cultural overtones. But it is characteristic of Nejar's lyrical style that concrete, traditional terms such as *corda, faca, diarista* (a day laborer) and *pampa,* existentially linked with the culture of his native habitat, immediately gain additional, abstract, universal meaning.

Canga, a tribute to a workingman named Jesualdo Monte, ultimately acquires the dimension of man's fate, as becomes evident from a quotation of Saint-John Perse which precedes it. And in *Casa dos arreios,* a title which initially suggests a concept or metaphor derived from horse or cattle raising, assumes a new perspective with the texts of the book as well as with the epigraph from *Don Quijote* which introduces them: "Mis arreos son las armas, mi descanso el pelear." As Nelly Novaes Coelho so well observes in the preface to the volume, "man is seen as a knight errant (= the noblest category of hero). His tools in trade of acting on the world, metaphorically *arreos* [raiments], actually become 'weapons' (= instruments of the realization of the warrior). His moments of quiet introspection, here expressed by rest or *descanso,* are seen as an act amounting to conflict (*pelear*) or struggle."[23]

Nejar's law background often surfaces in the shifting interplay between precise philological and technical terminology equivocally contrasted with itself or analogous concepts. "Inquirição" (Inquest), "Arras" (Pledge, or Dowry), "Ajuizamento" (Judgment), "Uti possidetis" and "Jurisdição" (Jurisdiction), all poems exploring dimensions of self, carnal knowledge and conjugal love, are a good indication; and the multiple meanings of the term *execução* or "execution" from "O sopro da execução" (The Breath of Execution) are an even better example. Of all the poets of his generation, Carlos Nejar is the only one who has begun to achieve some degree of national and international recognition for his linguistic verve, the consistently high level of work, as well as the wide range of themes he employs: time, love and the sea, solitude, death, South America, the cycle of seasons. Two volumes of his poetry have recently come out in Lisbon; two German Latin Americanists, Günter Lorenz and Curt Meyer-Clason, have edited his poems; and this very Lusophone issue of *World Literature Today* includes "Deus era a selva" (God Was the Jungle) and "As coisas viam" (Things Used to See).[24] In addition,

Nejar has helped to break down the built-in resistance to anything coming from the Spanish-speaking world by translating a neighbor from next door, Jorge Luis Borges's *Ficciones* (1970) and *Elogio de la sombra* (1971). This is not surprising, since *riograndenses* have traditionally been among the most politically aware and internationally minded; and it is fitting and by no means coincidental that Nejar be, with Ferreira Gullar, one of the few Brazilian poets who has a conscience of Latin American solidarity, as may be seen from "Dentro da noite veloz" (In the Rapid Night) and *Somos poucos* (We Are Few). Fortunately poets are not a scarce commodity; that is why I would like to dedicate these pages to the many new voices I was unable to include but would welcome hearing from and writing about on future occasions.

Klaus Müller-Bergh, Winter 1979

[1] For the origins of the *feijoada* see Pedro Nava, *Bâu de ossos: Memórias 1*, Rio de Janeiro, Olympic, 1974, p. 71, and *Chão de ferro: Memórias 3*, Rio de Janeiro, Olympio, 1976, pp. 18–21. Purists willing to sample it should consult the legendary Dona Benta's *Comer bem: 1001 receitas de bans pratos*, 50th ed., São Paulo, Nacional, 1965, pp. 142–43. Trendier types might prefer to inquire at the omniscient C.I.A., the Culinary Institute of America.

[2] The principal manifestos of these schools can be found in Gilberto Mendonça Teles's *Vanguarda europeia e modernismo brasileiro: Apresentação dos principals poemas, manifestos, prefácios e conferências vanguardistas de 1857 até hoje*, 3rd rev. & enl. ed., Petrópolis, Vozes, 1976.

[3] Gastão de Holanda, "Trobar Clus de Cantagalo: 28 momentos de favela," *JOSÉ* (Rio de Janeiro), May-June 1977. This and all other translations are my own.

[4] Giovanni Pontiero, "Manuel Bandeira in the Role of Literary Critic," *Annali dell'Instituto Universitario Orientate*, Romance Section XX, Naples, Gennaio, 1978, p. 218.

[5] WLT readers interested in exploring this period further might consult Giovanni Pontiero's article (note 4) as well as his forthcoming book on the Brazilian poet. On Carlos Drummond de Andrade, consult Wilson Martins's "Carlos Drummond de Andrade and the Legacy of *Modernismo*" in this issue. On João Cabral de Melo Neto, see the poet's own *Museu de tudo: Poesia 1966–1974*, Rio de Janeiro, Olympio, 1975, and his *Poesias completas*, 2nd ed., Rio de Janeiro, Olympio, 1975, as well as Benedito Nunes's *João Cabral de Melo Neto*, Petrópolis, Vozes, 1971; French critic André Camlong of the Université de Toulouse is currently also involved in substantial research on the poet, and Elizabeth Bishop's *The Complete Poems*, New York, Farrar, Straus & Giroux, 1969, contains translations from his work. On Cecilia Meireles, see Henry Keith and Raymond Sayers, *Cecilia Meireles: Poemas em tradução*, Washington, D.C., Brazilian-American Cultural Institute, 1976, as well as Eliane Zagury, *Cecilia Meireles*, Petrópolis, Vozes, 1973. The Italian critic Luciana S. Picchio is currently editing the complete works of Murilo Mendes.

[6] Carlos Drummond de Andrade, *Fazendeiro do ar & poesia até agora*, Rio de Janeiro, Olympio, 1954, pp. 212–13.

[7] Ferreira Gullar, "Da arte concreta a arte neo-concreta," in *Projeto construtivo brasileiro na arte 1950–1962*, Aracy A. Amaral, ed., Rio de Janeiro/São Paulo, Museu de Arte Moderna/Pinacoteca do Estado, 1977, p. 113.

[8] Armando Zarate, "Devenir y síntoma de la poesía concreta," *Revista Iberoamericana*, 98–99 (January-June 1977; special "Letras brasileiras" issue), pp. 117–47. Also, Wilson Martins, "Tendencias da literatura brasileira contemporánea," ibid., pp. 17–26.

[9] Moacy Cirne, *Vanguarda: Um projeto semiológico*, Petrópolis, Vozes, 1975, pp. 30, 28.

[10] In addition to the valuable book by Gilberto Mendonça Teles and the outstanding collection by Aracy A. Amaral, Mário Chamie's "Instauração praxis: Vanguarda nova," in *Tempo Brasileiro*, 26–27 (January-March 1971; issue on "Vanguarda e modernidade"), pp. 60–69 is very useful. The best document of a dialogue with more responsible members of the younger generation is "Vanguarda em questão," *Tempo Brasileiro*, ibid., pp. 40–59, as well as "Debate: Poesia hoje," *JOSÉ*, 2 (August 1976), pp. 3–9, and R. Schwartz, *Les temps modernes*, 1970.

[11] Décio Pignatan, *Poesia pois é poesia 1950–1975*, São Paulo, Duas Cidades, 1977, p. 113.

[12] Ibid., p. 153.

[13] Ferreira Gullar, unpublished poem, printed with theoermission of the author.

[14] Ferreira Gullar, "A poesia neo-concreta," in *Projeto construtivo brasileiro na arte 1950–1962*, pp. 339–40.

[15] Ibid., p. 339.

[16] Augusio de Campos, Julio Plaza, *Caixa preta: Textos objetos + disco poemas de Augusta de Campos*, Caetano Veloso, reader, São Paulo, Invenção, 1975; Haroldo de Campos, *Xadres de estrelas: Percurso textual 1949–1974*, São Paulo, Perspectiva, 1976; Décio Pignatari, *Poesia pois é poesia 1950–1975*; and *Teoria da poesia concreta: Textos crítical e manifestos 1950–1960*, São Paulo, Duas Cidades, 1975. For the relationship of constructivism and the fine arts, particularly the work of Tarsila do Amaral, Milton Dacosta, Alfredo Volpi, Arnaldo Ferrari, Rubem Valentim, Valdeir Maciel and Jandyra Waters, see the pamphlet edited by Theon Spanudis, São Paulo, 1977.

[17] João Cabral de Melo Nelo, *Museu de tudo*, p. 71; also *Projeto construtivo brasileiro na arte*, pp. 176–81.

[18] Heloise Buarque de Hollands, *26 poetas hoje*, Rio de Janeiro, Labor do Brasil, 1976.

[19] Ibid., p. 199.

[20] Ibid., p. 73.

[21] Geraldo Carneiro, "Lira dos 20 anos," *JOSÉ*, 10 (July 1978), p. 33.

[22] Luis Carlos Verzoni Nejar, "Corda e faca," in his *Árvore do mundo*, Rio de Janeiro, Nova Aguilar, 1971, p. 60.

[23] Nelly Novaes Coelho, "*Casa dos arreios*: Uma poética antropológica," in Carlos Nejar's *Casa dos arreios*, Porto Alegre, Globo, 1973, p. 44.

[24] *Dois poetas novos do Brasil: Carlos Nejar e Armindo Trevisan*, Lisbon, Moraes, 1972; Carlos Nejar, *O poço do calabouço*, Lisbon, Moraes, 1974; Günter W. Lorenz, *Die zeitgenössische Literatur in Lateinamerika*, Tübingen, Erdman, 1971; Curt Meyer-Clason, *Brasilianische Poesie des 20. Jahrhunderls*, Munich, DTV, 1975.

João Cabral de Melo Neto: "Literalist of the Imagination"

Ma nature a horreur du vague.

▓ **PAUL VALÉRY**

The award of the latest edition of the Neustadt Prize to the Brazilian poet João Cabral de Melo Neto confirms what poetry lovers in that country and foreign specialists in Latin American literature have known for a long time: namely, that the author of works such as *O Cão sem Plumas, Morte e Vida Severina, Uma Faca só Lâmina, A Educação pela Pedra,* and *Auto do Frade*—to name but a few of his nineteen individual titles in verse—is one of the major poets of this second half-century. I myself concluded the second of two articles on João Cabral, published in the Portuguese journal *Colóquio/ Letras* in 1976, with the certainty that he was *the* major Latin American poet since World War II.

When those articles were written, *A Educação pela Pedra* (Education by Stone), published in 1966, was still Cabral's most recent volume of verse, and it was not yet clear what direction his poetry might take during the next ten years or so. The publication of his *Poesias Completas,* dated 1968, added no further material, and the poet, who on an earlier occasion had been close to giving up writing poetry (Freixeiro, 188), had confessed himself sucked dry by what was then his thirteenth individual title. And indeed, after his earlier struggle to eliminate the fortuitous, the sentimental, and the influence of lyric fantasy from his verse, João Cabral had reached such a peak of discipline, both in self-control and in the control of his creative "machine," and so great a power of formal compression, that one might be forgiven for wondering what he could add to his achievement. In the event, by the time my articles appeared, a further volume of verse, with the engaging title *Museu de Tudo* (Museum of Everything; 1975), bringing together compositions written in the intervening years (1966–74), offered some sort of answer to one's query. Any doubts that João Cabral might have abandoned—or been abandoned by—poetry have been further set to rest by the regular appearance of subsequent titles throughout the 1980s. But before asking if the last quarter-century's production has seen changes in the poet's attitudes, toward poetry and toward the world about him, and in his technical discipline, some considerations on the first twenty-five years are in order.

Cabral has recounted[1] how, in his late teens, he was introduced to the poetry of Apollinaire and the French

João Cabral de Melo Neto (*Robert H. Taylor*)

surrealists, so that when he began to write poetry himself, theirs were the footsteps he attempted to follow. On an earlier occasion, however, he had declared that the starting point for the poems of his first book, *Pedra do Sono* (Stone of Sleep; 1942), published when he was twenty-two years old, was the influence of Murilo Mendes, often regarded as close to the surrealists in the oneiric nature of his visual landscape and the fortuitous manner in which persons and objects appear and interact. Certainly the poems of *Pedra do Sono* invoke a world more akin to the substance of dreams than to the ordered expectations of everyday reality, a world in which women swim back and forth in invisible rivers and flowers grow out of photographs or are the heads of saints. Still, as the poet recognized, although the imagery of these poems might be termed surrealist, the type of poem associated with that movement, with its recourse to automatic writing and lack of formal discipline, was quite alien to Cabral's temperament. He added the book was a hybrid, remarking on the discernment of the critic Antônio Cândido, whose contemporary review had classed it rather as cubist: in fact, though one of the poems is entitled "A André Masson" and is thereby dedicated to the French surrealist painter, another rather more pointedly addresses a "Homenagem a Picasso."

Cabral referred to *Pedra do Sono* as a "false book" (Freixeiro, 1971), rejecting a number of the poems for his *Poesias Completas,* and critics tended to accept the poet's statement at face value. A subsequent consensus, however, may be summed up in the closing sentence of a useful reappraisal of the collection's status: "*Pedra do Sono* is not prehistory: it is the first stage of [an] unending process" (Gledson, 1978). Or rather part of the first stage, for we find ourselves in somewhat similar territory in parts, at least, of *Os Três Mal-Amados* (The Three Ill-Loved Ones; 1943) and *O Engenheiro* (The Engineer; 1942–45), which do nevertheless mark the beginnings of a critical attitude toward the matter and nature of poetry. In the first the "interwoven monologues" (Reckert, 1986) of the three speakers, or the monologue-plus-*diálogo implícito* equation preferred by another scholar (Secchin, 34), present different attitudes toward poetry. One of these, devoured by passion, constitutes a political dead end; the other two offer a dialectic between imagination, over which the poet has little control, and discipline, in which poetry becomes a pre-established system, a "lucidity alone capable of allowing us a complete new way of seeing a flower, of reading a line of poetry" (Cabral, 372).[2]

The poems of *O Engenheiro,* as the dates show, were to some extent contemporaneous with those of *Os Três Mal-Amados* and share similar concerns. As Stephen Reckert comments (171), "*O Engenheiro* does not immediately cast off the lexical and imagistic legacy of its predecessors, with their *nuvens, sonhos, fantasmas,* and general vague air of menace." The title poem, however, though it uses the word *dream* as noun and verb, in its first verse surrounds it with light, sun, open air, and what the poet calls "bright things" (*coisas claras*); and by the second verse the engineer—Cabral's metaphor for the poet—is thinking, thinking about "a world not masked by any veil" (Cabral, 344), where everything is in its appointed place and the building (i.e., the poem) grows organically, of itself ("out of nothing but its own strength"), as if it were part of the natural scene. If this means what it seems to,[3] "A Lição de Poesia" presents a less optimist view, urging the need for vigilance, which was to be so important for Cabral's future creative work, and introducing for the first time the idea of extreme concision ("twenty words, always the same"), while emphasizing the constructive process in the metaphor of the "useful machine" (*máquina útil*).

Still, the dialectic between inspiration, with its unpredictability, and purposeful control was far from decided. The opposing forces were lined up once more in the seminally important *Psicologia da Composição* (Psychology of Composition), which, together with "Fábula de Anfion" and "Antiode," first appeared in a version

hand-printed by the poet himself. The order of the title page is not obeyed by the texts, which open with the "Fábula de Anfion" in a version clearly intended to counteract the *poésie pure* connotations of Valéry's "Amphion." A glance at the three poems immediately reveals an important innovation, in that each of them is organized in sections, but following a different pattern in each case: "Fábula" is in three parts, indicated by Arabic numerals, with further subdivisions shown by asterisks; "Psicologia da Composição" is arranged in eight numbered parts, this time using Roman numerals; the five sections of "Antiode" are marked A to E. The title poem of *O Engenheiro* already refers to "the design, the project, the number," and this virtual obsession with order was to mark all Cabral's subsequent poetry in one way or another. In the interview referred to earlier (see endnote 1) the poet explained that being a constructivist, he follows in his poems a rigid, mathematically preordained scheme, which starts as an empty framework, to be filled slowly and methodically. The three long poems which make up *Psicologia da Composição* constitute, in essence, an attack on lyric excess, on romantic inspiration, and on poetic diction, in the name of constraint, understatement, and rigor.

By this time João Cabral had entered his country's diplomatic service and soon left Brazil on his first posting, as vice-consul in Barcelona (1947–50). There began a relationship with Spain and Spanish culture the influence of which cannot be excluded from any reading of his poetry. At the same time, his absence from the Brazilian literary scene preserved him from involvement in the literary "politics" enjoyed by various of his contemporaries, the young lions who had begun to call themselves the "Generation of '45" and to engage in skirmishes with the established poets (Drummond de Andrade, Manuel Bandeira, Augusto Frederico Schmidt, et alii), from whose influence they dearly wished to free themselves. Cabral did in fact intervene, publishing a series of articles under the title "A Geração de '45" in the Rio daily *Diário Carioca* in late 1952, upon his return to Brazil. With a degree of objectivity, he criticized both sides, his main argument being that the young poets had not found an established poetic vision, a definition of poetry valid for their time, but rather a number of individual poets, each with his personal manner, which the younger writers had tended to follow in an initial phase. It was his judgment that this stage had been passed and that the "Generation of '45" poets had extended the repertoires of their immediate predecessors while largely reconciling the differences between them in a way Cabral felt could produce what he called a "modern Brazilian expression."

Part of what Cabral wrote in these articles can be found, more fully developed but shorn of specific allusions to the Brazilian literary scene, in a lecture he delivered to the São Paulo Poetry Club (Clube de Poesia) in November of the same year. The lecture was entitled "Poesia e Composição: A Inspiração e Trabalho de Arte" and clearly reflected the problems which had afflicted his own poetry. He also introduced a further problem, remarking on the absence of communication in contemporary poetry, whether this was created under the aegis of inspiration or was the result of disciplined artisanship. He spoke of the hermeticism of contemporary verse, and it must be admitted that most of his own poetry up to that time is not of easy access, certainly not to the general reading public.

This is true even of *O Cão sem Plumas* (1949–50), a tightly woven narrative poem almost as long as the three poems of *Psicologia da Composição,* in which Cabral turns to the physical and social reality of his native state, Pernambuco, and its capital city, Recife. The "featherless dog" of the title is in fact a metaphor for the Capibaribe River, whose course becomes the poem's discourse, transferring its nakedness to the poverty-stricken inhabitants of the *mangues* or mud flats on the city's outskirts.

Like the river
those men
are like featherless dogs
(a featherless dog
is more
than a plundered dog;
is more
than a murdered dog . . . .) (309)

The poem's final section concentrates its discourse around the words *live* (verb and adjective) and *dense*—the Portuguese word is *espesso,* meaning "thick," as in thick soup or when we say that blood runs thicker than water, so that *espesso* is used here for the solid density of real things: a man's blood is "much thicker . . . than a man's dream," and an apple is "much thicker / if a man eats it / than if a man sees it" (317). In the final instance the notion of *thickness,* having hammered the claims of reality, sordid social reality, to poetic treatment of a wholly unsentimental nature, is installed, it seems, as a precept for the poet himself to follow: "the day that is gained / each day / (like a bird / second by second / achieving its flight)" (318).

The period of some five or six years beginning with the composition of *O Cão sem Plumas* was a particularly productive one for João Cabral, as well as being important for his reputation. His feeling that contemporary poetry had given priority to expression over communi-

cation, in the process abandoning such publicly more accessible forms as the fable and narrative poetry, led him to compose two works intended for general consumption: another narrative poem, *O Rio* (The River; 1954), more descriptive in nature, and the reverse drama *Morte e Vida Severina* (1955; Eng. "Death and Life of a Severino"), cast in a popular dramatic mold. In the already-quoted interview he admitted wryly that his plan to produce "poetry for the people" did not work out quite as he had intended, since he wrote both works with the idea that they would be read aloud in Recife's São José market. Ironically, *Morte e Vida Severina* has found its way to a wider public than any other of Cabral's works and provides an interesting example of the way different sociopolitical contexts can impose new readings on texts. Written during an open phase of Brazil's recent political history, it was later performed by the São Paulo University drama group, with music by Chico Buarque de Holanda, at the University Theater Festival in Nancy (France), where it was awarded first prize. This was in 1966, two years after the military coup in Brazil introduced an oppressive political regime, severely restricting the democratic rights achieved after the fall of Getúlio Vargas. In such a climate the play's central character, Severino, a symbol of the poor peasant fleeing the drought of his native *sertão* (badlands), could acquire the much wider connotation of a whole oppressed populace, and its final message of optimism could be seen to offer more hope than in the original circumstances. The play was also performed in the poor districts of São Paulo as well as in towns in the interior.

At the same time as he was engaged in the play's composition, Cabral continued to write verse intended for the individual reader, poems, as he himself put it, "to be read in silence . . . requiring more than one reading." Such are the poems of the short collection *Paisagens com Figuras* (Landscapes with Figures; 1956), eighteen texts on topics evenly divided between the poet's native Northeast and that Spain which was to occupy an increasingly large place in his poetry, cast for the most part in the traditional Portuguese quatrain form (heptasyllables rhyming a b c b). To class these as descriptive vignettes would do the poems little justice, for what Cabral does is rather to define, metaphorically, the real places or people he takes as his starting point, seeking a lesson in the appropriateness of the chosen analogy. In the long poem *Uma Faca só Lâmina* (1956; Eng. *A Knife All Blade*), which he wrote almost simultaneously, he was to conclude that reality is too violent to be grasped by any image. Here, however, he had started not from real referents but from the semantic features of linguistic signs, three in number—bullet, clock, and knife—in accordance with the poem's subtitle, "The Usefulness of Fixed Ideas."

The two books thus seem to complement each other, as if the discourse of *Uma Faca só Lâmina* had germinated from the argumentative "Diálogo" of *Paisagens com Figuras,* in which two speakers, A and B, seek to define the nature of the Andalusian *cante hondo* (deep song). The method is oddly reminiscent of the *desafios* and *repentes* still popular in Brazil's Northeast and which have much to do with the choice of words and images, suggested by one participant and put in doubt or corrected by the other, continuing back and forth until one of the participants fails to respond—all intoned in a droning chant which Cabral's quatrain seems to simulate. So here speaker A, who suggests the first comparison, also completes the dispute, picking up the knife image proposed by B and limiting it first to the blade, then to "the purpose which completes a knife," which is, however, to be found "on the reverse side of nothing."

Uma Faca só Lâmina is clearly a work of great importance in Cabral's poetic production. He had already rejected the "poetic word" and experienced the need to strip words of all prior associations. He had, as we saw earlier, begun to do things by numbers, creating a rigid framework, mathematically designed, within which to compose his text. Theme as such is of less importance, perhaps because "the medium is the message," which is to say that the process of composition is, in a sense, its own theme, for Cabral's poetry henceforth is essentially metapoetic and metalinguistic. Recent studies have stressed the concrete nature of his poetic language (Peixoto) or his constant struggle to excise what Antônio Carlos Secchin calls the "*overflow* of the signified." The poet himself, to quote once more from the 1968 interview, considered that, for him, creation was not "the spilling of an excess of being, but a lack of being," which seems similar to his image of "the reverse side of nothing."

In a poem entitled "Autocrítica," from the later volume *Escola das Facas* (School of Knives; 1980), Cabral considered that two things alone had forced him into poetry, and both were Pernambuco; but one was the real Pernambuco, his home state, whereas the other was Andalusia. The former vaccinated him against "rich speech"; the other made him a "mad challenge," which was to show the *sertão* and Seville in verse. After *Uma Faca só Lâmina* João Cabral's poetry does indeed center almost obsessively on topics related to Pernambuco and Seville. Over the next ten years he composed the texts which make up the four titles published between 1960 and 1966: *Quaderna, Dois Parlamentos, Serial,* and *A Educação pela Pedra.* The first three appeared together

in 1961 under the title *Terceira Feira* (Third Fair), the fourth in 1966; in 1968 came the first edition of his complete poems, and in 1969 he was elected to Brazil's Academy of Letters.

The title *Quaderna,* referring to the four-spot on a die or, alternatively, to each of the quarters on a coat of arms, seems to be justified by the constant use of the quatrain form and the organization of the texts in multiples of four, not forgetting their total, which numbers twenty. Cabral, by his own account, was always fond of the number four, which seemed to him "the rational number par excellence"; and *Serial,* with its sixteen poems, is even more rigorously based on it, whereas the forty-eight poems of *A Educação pela Pedra* (Education by Stone) all have sixteen or twenty-four lines, always divided into two parts, suited to the argumentative binarism which is a mark of his poetry. The division into parts or sections, already observed in the longer poems, is carried over into *Quaderna* and *Serial,* each of which contains a number of poem sequences in which Cabral explores different aspects of a topic, testing the semantic capacity of the linguistic sign to equate to the features he discerns in the object[4] in question (the flamenco dancer, the *cante hondo,* the city of Recife, a goat, et cetera) or to define the creative processes of writers and artists with whom he identifies (Graciliano Ramos, Marianne Moore, Francis Ponge, Joan Miró, Mondrian). Now in his forties, João Cabral had reached great maturity as a poet, and these volumes are so full of magnificent poetry that one hesitates to single out individual poems; the choice is almost inevitably one of personal favorites.

Among the best known of the poem sequences in *Quaderna* are the "Estudos para uma Bailadora Andaluza" (Studies for an Andalusian Dancer), forty-eight quatrains divided into six equal sections which test six images for their appropriateness as analogies for the dancer, who is compared in turn to fire, a mare, a telegraph operator, a tree, a statue, and the spike of a maize plant. At the same time, the *bailadora* and her dance must be understood as offering analogies with the poet and his text, or the creative process, at least as Cabral would have them. So the image of the mare immediately includes that of the rider and the impossibility of distinguishing between the two or separating them, which invites comparison either with the poet engaged in creating or with the content and form of the text. The telegraphist analogy, suggested by the foot tapping, deals more overtly with messages and the emitter-receiver relationship, while the final comparison introduces what was to be a productive image for Cabral, with decided erotic overtones, as he sees the unfolding of the dance as the "undressing" of the maturing maize spike. The importance of the image is emphasized by the repetition, in the poem's closing verse, of the word *espiga* and the participial adjective *espigada:* analogous to the image which the dancer's final movements will engrave on the mind's eye, we may infer, should be the reader's sense of revelation as the poem's final lines release its total communicative thrust.

João Cabral started out with a stone, though it was merely part of the name of a backwater town somewhere in Pernambuco (Pedra do Sono), and the "Pequena Ode Mineral" of *O Engenheiro* already warned him to "Seek the order / you see in a stone"; but we have to wait until *A Educação pela Pedra* for the stone to, as it were, bear fruit. Over the years the poet has shown a marked tendency to favor things that are dry and spare, sun and fire, naked or clear-cut shapes, metal objects, sharp instruments, which somehow equate to his rational manner and his need to rationalize his poetic process. The stone which was destined to appear in the title of the collection published in 1966 is such a thing. A thing: simultaneously object and instrument, challenge and example, metaphor and metonym. Although the poet was from the humid, fertile coastal area of Pernambuco, born and educated in Recife, accustomed to life on the family sugar estates, he identified strongly with the dry, barren *sertão,* more akin to the "lack of being" he saw in himself. He similarly identified, poetically, with the way of speech of the inhabitants of the *sertão,* which he called their "idioma pedra," as if there were a language called "Stonish," since he refers to the "native speaker of this tongue" in the poem "O Sertanejo Falando" (The Way a *Sertanejo* Speaks). In "stone language" the words are so hard, "stony almonds," that they form ulcers in the mouth, so that the speaker, "that stony tree," must articulate them slowly and with the utmost care, which explains why he is anything but loquacious. The analogy is clear but is given a more obviously social dimension in the title poem, "A Educação pela Pedra," for if the first part of the text extols the virtues of the stone—its "unemphatic, impersonal voice," its "cold resistance . . . to being shaped," its "concrete flesh"—the shorter second part transports us to the *sertão,* where the stone has nothing to teach, because the inhabitants are born with it in their very souls.

The writing of poetry has clearly been a serious business for João Cabral de Melo Neto, but this does not mean that his verse is ponderous or plodding. In fact, one of the words I would use when speaking or writing about it is *wit,* not with that term's more recent connotations of facetiousness, but in its older sense as we relate it, for instance, to the intellectual ingenuity of so-called metaphysical poetry. For all the discipline and rigor and the extremely rational cast of his verse, there is nothing

classical in Cabral's choice of metaphor and comparison, as the example of the Andalusian dancer will have shown. In a Penguin anthology of Latin American writing published all of twenty-five years back (Cohen, ed., 1967), the notes on João Cabral advised the English reader that he would "see some resemblances to the wittily fantastic poetry of Marianne Moore." Cabral may have come into contact with Moore's poetry during his spell of diplomatic duty in Great Britain, between 1950 and 1952, since her *Collected Poems* appeared in 1951 under the Faber imprint. However, the first reference to her in Cabral's verse occurs in *Serial,* a collection of poems written between 1959 and 1961, and more specifically in the poem sequence "O Sim Contra o Sim" (Yes Against Yes), four texts of eight verses each, invoking alternately two poets, then two painters, and the same again, so that in all the poet focuses on creative processes in eight artists (Moore, Ponge, Miró, Mondrian, Cesário Verde, Augusto dos Anjos, Gris, Dubuffet). The poem's title indicates Cabral's approval of his "models," despite the differences among them, but it is hardly necessary; for although there is no direct linguistic (i.e., grammatical) evidence of the poet's presence, the impersonal affirmations betray his systematic preferences in the choice of words like *scalpel, clean, economical, learn anew, discipline, clear water, firmness, geometry, simple, cohesive, magnifying glass, microscope, stethoscope, auscultation.*

The scalpel is obviously another form of the knife, or rather the naked blade, which Cabral used to such effect in *Uma Faca só Lâmina,* the "angry blade" as he called it then; but in the case of Marianne Moore the blade becomes the writing implement, substituting for the pencil, and the poet a surgeon. Although the Brazilian poet clearly admires Moore, one infers that her skill is wholly dependent on the choice of instrument, viewed not so much as an object but rather as a metaphor for a process. Cabral's admiration was by no means a momentary homage, but we must wait until *A Escola das Facas* (1975–80) for the next direct reference. Not only is the poem "A Imaginação do Pouco" (Imagination on a Small Scale) prefaced by an epigraph from one of Moore's poems ("imaginary gardens with real toads in them"), but she herself is mentioned by name, giving Cabral the opportunity to stress his own limited capacity in relation to things of the imagination. *Agrestes* (1981–85) opens with a Moore epigraph ("Where there is personal liking we go. / Where the ground is sour") and contains no fewer than three poems which take Moore and her poetry as their subject. "Ouvindo Marianne Moore em Disco" (On Hearing a Recording of Marianne Moore) praises Moore's undeclamatory reading of her own poetry as being very much in tune with the poetry itself; "Homenagem Renovada a Marianne Moore" (Renewed Homage to Marianne Moore) is more metapoetic in pointing up the formal, constructive nature of poetry as practiced by Moore and Cabral. There is also a hint here of poetry as an aid to self-construction, "a crutch for a gammy leg," but the personal identification is to be found in the aptly entitled "Dúvidas Apócrifas de Marianne Moore" (Apocryphal Doubts of Marianne Moore). Spoken in the first person, as though by Moore herself, the voice can be identified with Cabral, who uses this device to express his awareness that "talking about things" in poetry can be just another way of talking about oneself.

The choice of what Cabral elsewhere calls "a luva sósia" (a glove's double) tells us more about ourselves, but any choice—as when one compiles an anthology—is meaningful; and although the Brazilian poet has generally preferred to write about those in whom he detects similarities, his more recent volumes have been less rigorous in this respect. After *A Educação pela Pedra* there is a noticeable lessening of the tension which reached its high-water mark in the metaphorical dialectic of that work. Marta Peixoto sees a different sort of dialectic in the long-awaited *Museu de Tudo* (1966–75), between "discouraging effort and spiritual renewal." It seems to me that the poet himself puts his finger on the problem in the opening text, where he more or less explains the title. As he tells us, a museum can be a "garbage can or an archive," and his book "is the warehouse of what's inside," lacking a presiding design. Cabral ranges wide in subject matter in this collection of what often seem little more than comments but which on closer perusal bear the epigrammatic stamp that is a frequent mark of his art. People, places, books, works of art, and even soccer all find their way into this collection of eighty texts—perhaps not all that surprising in a poet who had elevated chewing gum and aspirin to poetic respectability in his previous book. Pride of place, however, goes to artists: no fewer than thirty-five texts bring the manner of other poets or, quite as often, painters, sculptors, and architects under the microscope.

A Escola das Facas (1975–80) covers a much shorter period, and although it contains little more than half the total of poems found in *Museu de Tudo,* the texts occupy approximately the same amount of printed space. There are few of the eight-liners so frequent in the previous collection, but poems arranged in sequences are again in evidence, such as the ten-part "Descrição de Pernambuco como um Trampolim" (Description of Pernambuco as a Trampoline), the eight-part "Prosas da Maré na Jaqueira" (Chatting with the Tide at Jaqueira), or the six-part "Tio e Sobrinho" (Uncle and Nephew). The nephew in this last sequence

is certainly the poet himself, for the first time explicitly and systematically present in his own verse. Often, it is true, this is done through the oblique third person; but significantly, the opening poem, "Menino de Engenho" (Plantation Boy), makes no bones about using the first person and, at the same time, with its intertextual nod to Lins do Rego's famous novel, points to the other systematic bases of *A Escola das Facas,* which might almost have been entitled "Memories of Pernambuco." Moreover, the book's title includes allusions to the titles of two earlier collections, *Uma Faca só Lâmina* and *A Educação pela Pedra,* as if to remind us that a possible *recherche du temps perdu* will not mean giving in to mere sentiment. Still, the poet himself suggests that this retrospective view is less critical ("De Volta ao Cabo de Santo Agostinho" [Going Back to Cape Santo Agostinho]), because he now appears to doubt the usefulness of his earlier critical vision, of the debates and the protests for which it was in some way responsible.

João Cabral prefaced *A Escola das Facas* with a poem addressed to his publisher in which he hinted that this might be his last book. In the event, it was, to date, the last but four, and the next showed that the vein of poetry was far from exhausted. Furthermore, the doubts implied at the end of the previous collection are well and truly silenced, as the poet comes back in the full force of a dramatic poem, a "poem for voices" as he calls it, but certainly intended as a public poem, establishing an irresistible link with *Morte e Vida Severina* almost thirty years on. *Auto do Frade* (The Friar's Way; 1984)—the word *auto* doubling for "play" and "auto da fé"—narrates, dramatically, the martyrdom of Frei Caneca, the liberal Carmelite friar condemned to death for sedition due to his activities in the Pernambucan revolution of 1824. This is a text one imagines Cabral would have wanted to publish during the dark days of military oppression in Brazil, for despite its historical context one cannot misinterpret the allusion to an authoritarian power which transforms the armed forces into an instrument of oppression against the country they were intended to defend. Caneca is shown as a luminous figure, in stark contrast with the darkness of his prison, an obvious reference to the obscurantism of his surroundings. He has to suffer ecclesiastical degradation before he can be led to the scaffold, to be executed as a common criminal, but the authorities are unable to make anyone perform the execution and are obliged to recognize Caneca as a military opponent, worthy of a military death by firing squad. *Auto do Frade* is an exhilarating performance, a text of enormous dignity in which we recognize the qualities of luminosity, precision, and compression which we have come to associate with João Cabral de Melo Neto's poetry.

In the same period as one assumes he was working on *Auto do Frade* the poet continued to write the shorter poems which he published in 1985 as *Agrestes,* a title with two meanings: the adjective means "wild" or merely "rustic," whereas the noun refers to the area of rocky land with low vegetation situated between the fertile *mata* and the arid *sertão* in northeastern Brazil. Not that the poetry describes this landscape, suggesting that the word, used in the plural, is essentially metonymous, reminding us of Cabral's penchant for the dry, the stony, and the unemphatic. There is, admittedly, a section of the book entitled "Do Outro Lado da Rua," made up of poems associated with the poet's years in West Africa, which include desert conditions; but when the epigraph from Marianne Moore, mentioned earlier, talks of "Where the ground is sour," such is a chosen territory, for it corresponds to a "personal liking." However, one cannot expect all the poems in a total of some ninety texts to be directly related to an introductory epigraph, the more so since the book's final section consists of poems on death.

Poems on Spain, more specifically on Andalusia and Seville, began to appear in Cabral's works as far back as 1956, and any consideration of his verse needs to take this into account. The poet was fascinated by bullfighters, by Andalusian Gypsies, particularly the flamenco dancers, and by the city of Seville itself. The bullfighters, Manolete in particular, impressed him with their technique, in which he sought those qualities he admired in poets and painters. Manolete is remembered in a text in *Agrestes,* "Lembrando Manolete" (Recalling Manolete), in which Cabral stresses bullfighting as running the most terrible risks "with the coolness of one whose life is not on a knife's edge." In other words, the bullfighter (i.e., the poet) constantly exposes himself to danger while being in control of the situation—not the sort of social control referred to in "Conversa de Sevilhana," whose talkative female speaker sends all policemen, doorkeeper, and petty bureaucrats to hell. Flamenco dancing is also a form of risk: in "Uma Bailadora Sevilhana" the speaker criticizes another dancer because she "dances without taking chances, without danger" and defines the style of dancing as "always a doing, never a done." Exactly as poetry should be, for, as Cabral puts it in a closing poem, "Postigo" (Back Gate), "writing is always from scratch / and the old hoe is no use this time." The flamenco singer similarly exposes himself in the *cante hondo,* for his voice, as it were, carries him to the top of a mast and the slightest miscue will bring him crashing down. Poems like these should, of course, be read intertextually with those of earlier books, particularly, in the present cases, the justly famous "Estudos para uma Bailadora Andaluza" and "A Palo Seco," both from *Quaderna.*

Cabral was also fascinated by the women of Seville, whose mixture of provocative elegance and imaginative verve he used as a figure of comparison for others, as in the hyperbolic opening of "Portrait of a Lady" (*Agrestes*)—"I've never seen even an Andalusian woman / use her legs as you do"—or the riposte to a would-be compliment: says he, "Sleeping with you would be great," to which she replies, "Is that all you would do? / Sleep? Do I perhaps have a face like a sleeping pill?" He was also attracted by the Andalusian habit of the *infundio,* the white lie or tall story, exemplified in the poem "As Infundiosas" in his next collection of verse, *Crime na Calle Relator* (Crime on Relator Street; 1987). Interestingly, he vouches for the truth of what he recounts when he parenthetically states that the three speakers were known to him personally, being friends of his: thus, imagination can run wild without the poet's running the risk of being accused of wild fantasy. The poems of this collection are mainly narrative, stories with a point to them, though the point may be left to the reader, as in the slightly macabre "Funeral na Inglaterra," where a lady diplomat apologizes to her hosts for having stepped unintentionally on what she took to be a flowerbed covered over with fertilizer, only to be told that the "fertilizer" was the ashes of the deceased, who had wished to be among friends. Cabral can be humorous, as this book reveals, but never hilarious!

By this time (1987) the poet had been widowed and had remarried, wedding another poet, Marly de Oliveira, for whom he wrote the poem "A Sevilhana que Não se Sabia" (The Seville Woman Unknown to Herself)—which appears in his last two books of verse—and whose qualities as muse are attested by her undoubted presence in other poems in his most recent book. Retired from the diplomatic service after a final stint in Portugal, Cabral has settled with his wife in Rio de Janeiro. After *Crime na Calle Relator,* with its mixture of poems once more devoted to Pernambuco and Andalusia, in 1989 he gave us *Sevilha Andando,* with its fifty-two poems all about aspects of Seville or anything that reminds him of Seville, as in "Na Cidade do Porto," with its chance view of "uma mulher de andar sevilha" (a woman with a Seville walk), with her determined elegant step, head held high like the maize spike at its spikiest—an allusion which takes us back again to the metaphor used in the "Estudos para uma Bailadora Andaluza." Here we find Cabral being, as it were, forced by the very circumstances of his discovery into a most unexpected oxymoron: the simile of the "chama negra" (black flame) for the woman's hair, which fuses with the "sol negro" (black sun) in which he discovers a "farol às avessas" (inside-out lighthouse) to light his way with each new waking day.

Seville, then, has become a composite metaphor for many qualities which the poet admires, and which he otherwise found in isolated objects, places, or people. On the evidence of this most recent volume, it is more than that, particularly in the first of the two unequal parts into which the poet divides the collection, "Sevilha Andando"; for if the book as a whole is dedicated simply "Para Marly," it is this first part that is most marked by her presence, the poet's "novo álcool," the woman whose presence "like Sevilha / is within-without, is nightday." However, the book's longer second part, "Andando Sevilha" (Around Seville), is no less alive, for there is no hint of its being in the past, no suggestion of nostalgic recollection. Instead, these latest poems by João Cabral are almost all in the present tense, as if the poet were present at the instant of penning the diverse moments of his travelogue.

One is tempted to ask what Brazilian readers who have never visited Seville might make of these poems about places unknown to them and whether they would gain by prior knowledge. The poet's answer might be that the places only begin to exist in his verse, since description is not his purpose, and despite the "literariness of his imagination," the vision is a very personal one. Certainly, it is not the chance construction effected more than forty years before, in the "Fábula de Anfíon," when Anfíon's flute raised the walls of Thebes, because João Cabral never forgot that lesson. It would require, however, a much more detailed and specialized study of his poetry to illustrate his unremitting labor to build those walls with his own hands, brick by brick, and to discover where, if at all, his vigilance may have flagged. When Vinicius de Moraes classed him as a diamond, João Cabral preferred to define himself, or his poetry, in terms of an industrial diamond, lacking the rarity value of the precious stone but having qualities similar to a cactus ("Resposta a Vinicius de Moraes," *Museu de Tudo*). The poet has undoubtedly mellowed since then; the diamond may have lost its abrasiveness but not its cutting edge.

John M. Parker, Autumn 1992

■ WORKS CITED

Cabral de Melo Neto, João. *Poesias Completas.* Rio de Janeiro. José Olympio. 1986.

Cohen, J. M., ed. *Latin American Writing Today.* Harmondsworth, Eng. Penguin. 1967.

Freixeiro, F. *Da Razão à Emoção II.* Rio de Janeiro. Tempo Brasileiro. 1971.

Gledson, J. "Sleep, Poetry, and João Cabral's 'False Book': A Revaluation of *Pedra do Sono.*" *Bulletin of Hispanic Studies,* 55, pp. 43–57.

Parker, John M. "João Cabral: 'Um Sistema para Abordar a Realidade.'" *Colóquio/Letras,* 32, pp. 31–39, 33, 40–50.

Peixoto, Marta. *Poesia com Coisas.* São Paulo. Perspectiva. 1983.

Reckert, Stephen. "João Cabral: From *Pedra to Pedra.*" *Portuguese Studies,* 2, pp. 166–84.

Secchin, Antônio Carlos. *João Cabral: A Poesia do Menos.* São Paulo. Brasília. 1985.

[1] The interview was recorded in 1968 and was published in the *Diário de Pernambuco* on 21 October 1979.

[2] All the translations in this article are my own unless otherwise indicated.

[3] Stephen Reckert judges "the tools and materials" for the building of prior concern to the poet, but the last verse does emphasize natural forces.

[4] As Reckert (183) rightly observes, "An object, for Cabral, may equally well be a city or region, or the society that inhabits them, or an individual member of that society: a plantation worker, a writer, a dancer."

Who's Afraid of (Luso-) Brazilian Literature?

It has become a commonplace for Brazilians to say that if Machado de Assis (1839–1908) had written in another language like English or French, he would be acclaimed worldwide and recognized as a major nineteenth-century author of Western literature. More or less the same, one assumes, could be said by the Portuguese about the great fictionist Eça de Queirós (1845–1900), who also wrote in the second half of the last century.

Although the Portuguese language is spoken by over 220 million people on four continents,[1] it does not have the same impact and political relevance that other languages do; and since Portuguese-language literature, whether in the original or in translation, is less well known, it stands apart not only for general readers, scholars, and students, but also for an international recognition like the Nobel Prize. Even in nonliterary considerations, which seem also to be important with an award like the Nobel, this is an unfair situation. It is amazing how people in the United States are unaware that Portuguese and not Spanish is spoken in Brazil, that the capital is not Buenos Aires but Brasília, and that Brazil is the fifth-largest country in the world and the eighth economic power in the West; or that Rio is not in the jungle, with snakes crawling down the streets; or, for those who have heard something about the country, that Brazil means more than carnival, samba, and beautiful mulatta women, or soccer, torture (in the recent past), or foreign debt (today).

Brazil has around 140 million inhabitants, covers eight and a half million square kilometers, and stretches

4,300 kilometers from the northern Amazon basin to the Uruguayan border in the south, a distance equivalent to that from London to Tehran. To fill the Brazilian portion of the Amazon basin would require five states the size of Texas. This huge giant, larger than the forty-eight continental states of the U.S., is awakening: its gross national product is around $280 billion and ranks first among developing countries. Brazil produces more than India, just over half the output of Britain, and fifty billion dollars more than Spain, its nearest rival. A large part of this goes to service the foreign debt, however—a hundred billion dollars in 1984, "so enormous that the nation's trade surplus could barely pay the interest."[2]

On the political level, Brazil is undergoing a difficult economic crisis, with an incredible inflation rate and the failure of the Cruzado plan. One might say that the country is learning (again or for the first time?) to live democratically, after twenty-nine years of dictatorship (the Estado Novo from 1937 to 1945 and the military government from 1964 to 1985). Pluralization, the creation of a society where all segments would be represented, is in progress, but this will of course take a while, since politicians still seem to pursue basically their own interests and those of the dominant groups. In any case, even if one realizes that there are problems like hunger, health, and education in Brazil, what deserves recognition is how Brazilian culture as a whole is extremely alive, yielding significant contributions in music, cinema, sports, technology (yes, Brazil manufactures computers and sophisticated airplanes), and literature.

A brief panorama of Brazilian literature is in order. First of all, there are some writers who play an important role within the literature to which they belong (having, say, an intrinsic and historical significance), and there are others who would be great in any literature, such as the aforementioned Machado and Eça. One of the major trends in Brazilian literature has been the search for cultural identity, for an affirmation that would differentiate it and free it from European influence. Authors like Machado assimilated influences in a parodic fusion, transforming them and, as a result, generating another literary and cultural discourse in which influence is mixed with autochthonous elements. Therefore, one cannot speak of cultural dependence, at least not in the same terms that this might be appropriate, say, for the romantics.

Brazilian modernism (which is more or less the equivalent to vanguardism in Spanish American literatures and the modernism of European literatures) was more successful in the 1920s both in borrowing a language from Europe (the several isms of the avant-garde) and in trying to capture the peculiarities of Brazilian re-

ality, culture, and society. It is important to stress that with modernism Brazilian literature became "itself," so to speak, in the sense that the influences were not taken as copies but were appropriated parodically, assimilated, and transformed. On the other hand, Brazilian literature had by then its own tradition, and it would be correct to say that modernism was romanticism double-checked, once the modernist writers had undertaken the romantics' project and pushed it further.

If we keep in mind this summary, Graciliano Ramos (1892–1953) stands out as the first Brazilian writer forgotten in this century by the awarders of the Nobel Prize. Apart from his dry style and the almost classical concision of his writing (which seems to be very appropriate for the reality it describes), Ramos's work is important because it encompasses the contradictions of Brazilian modernization: characters like Paulo Honório, from *São Bernardo* (1934), stand midway between traditional values and capitalist ones. Besides any localized social commitment in his fiction, Ramos is universal when he lashes out against social injustice and the exploitation of the poor by the powerful.

If we focus our attention only on the last twenty years, two Brazilian poets and three novelists have deserved at least nomination for the Nobel Prize in Literature: Carlos Drummond de Andrade, João Cabral de Melo Neto, João Guimarães Rosa, Clarice Lispector, and Autran Dourado. Andrade (1902–87) is important for the same reason as Ramos: he too represents Brazil's transition from a rural society to an urban and industrialized one. However, his fine poetry also explores the anguish of contemporary individuals in a contemporary world, menaced by the bomb, anonymous in the midst of monstrous cities, suffering from failures in communication, love, and human solidarity. If we examine his poetry as a whole, we read the story of the prodigal son who leaves his provincial hometown, repudiates his family and the father figure, and comes to live in a metropolitan context, where he encounters all the problems and anxieties of modern man. Gradually, and more intensively after *Boitempo* (Ox-Time; 1968), Andrade's poems return to his father and to his childhood in Itabira (in the interior of the state of Minas Gerais), to the family and the values of the clan, recovering in the process his past in the space of a literary representation. Andrade's writings range over many themes and subjects, from love to ecology, with a poetic diction that can easily be considered that of one of the greatest Portuguese-language poets of all time. Andrade's poetry is notably sparse and stands out in a culture not characterized by sobriety.[3]

In the verse of João Cabral de Melo Neto (b. 1920) we discover the northeast and its problems, but social denunciations are expressed here in a very sophisticated and refined esthetic way. João Cabral profits from the *cordel,* the popular marketplace verses, and from medieval Spanish poetry as well as from constructivists like Miró, Mondrian, Le Corbusier, Valéry, or Jorge Guillén. Cabral's poems not only speak about the presence of death in the poor Brazilian northeast, but also about poetry/art in metalinguistic texts, and about eroticism in poems like "Estudos para uma bailadora andaluza" (Studies for an Andalusian Dancer).

Situated at one extreme of Brazilian poetry, an extreme whose major characteristic is the progressive erosion of emotive lyricism, Cabral's poetry is antilyrical. Determinedly lucid, a geometrician and engineer of verses, Cabral has turned more and more to the landscape of the northeast, with a spare diction and a constant process of rethinking the metaphors out of which his poems are made. What is most remarkable and unique in Cabral's literature, however, is the fact that he identifies the northeastern Brazilian landscape with Spain, its dryness with Castile, its sunniness with Andalusia. More recently, these comparisons also include Africa. Cabral is a diplomat and has lived many years in Spain and Senegal; these contacts and the commitment of his poetry to contemporary art in general make him a very important figure.[4]

Perhaps João Guimarães Rosa (1908–67) is the Brazilian writer of this century most known abroad. His fiction is a true synthesis of Brazilian literature, and it reveals a convergence of various currents: regionalism/ universalism, esthetic consciousness/social preoccupation, and baroque/modernism, to mention only a few of the main elements brought together in the vast mural which the creator of *Sagarana* (1946) left as a legacy. Moreover, Rosa evokes the entire European tradition, which he amalgamates in a magical alchemy with the Brazilian literary tradition. In *Grande sertão: Veredas* (1956; Eng. *The Devil to Pay in the Backlands,* 1963) we find echoes of both themedieval gesta and the language of the Western novel, of traditional myths and popular stories, and all the principal outlines of our literary heritage distilled in the saga of Riobaldo Tatarana. This structure of refracted forms is used by Rosa to draw together possibilities already present in the modernist project, of which his writing is such an admirable summa.

We can discover two planes in Rosa's literary production: one of life on a small scale, made up of common happenings, a contingent space in which life seems to be a tangle of random pieces; and another of life on a large scale, occupied by the large issues that hound Rosa's characters, questions that have no answers, although they signal to a certain extent a Utopian dimension of life. Most often Rosa's characters move from the first to the second plane, and madness, love, poetry, and infancy function as the transition from the privation of contingency to the plenitude of the transcendent; yet it is a transcendent located within the immanent. Rosa's emphasis is on the process and on the attempt to reground man in the world, on the root meaning of religiosity, and on the reintegration of men with the totality.

All of Rosa's rivers have three banks. His careful working of language provokes a "stylistic shock" in the novice reader. By exploring the potentialities of the linguistic system, by incorporating words from other languages into Portuguese, by revitalizing terms and expressions that have fallen into disuse, by taking up the language of the backlands of Minas Gerais, by creating neologisms, forging syntax, and experimenting with new resonances of alliteration, Rosa elaborates his own unmistakable diction. He turns Portuguese inside out, confers on it a new expressivenness, and liberates language (in his own words) "from the mountains of ashes under which it lay."

Nevertheless, the care taken in linguistic matters reaches beyond the esthetic and the ludic in that, for Rosa, language possesses a metaphysical dimension. Words have their own "third bank." Rosa sees language as a weapon in the defense of human dignity. Through the renovation of language, the world is renovated. The sense of life may be recovered via a reconstruction of language whereby the latter has restored to it its naming and creative power, the original act of *poiesis* by which being is founded through the word. Concomitantly, Rosa rejects Cartesian rationality in favor of a greater role for intuition, revelation, inspiration, enchantment, and magic. As a consequence, there is a rejection of certain weaknesses of Western thought and its habit of binary oppositions: reason versus emotion, good versus evil, and so on. Rosa shows how "everything is and nothing is," how each thing carries within itself its own opposite, and how the "third bank" is a privileged space, a Utopian territory in which contradictions are abolished. Neither this bank nor that, nor both at the same time, the "third bank" is the place where the individual wanders, where he explores the different-same waters of the river of life, free from the confines of temporality.

In *Grande sertão: Veredas* Diadorim represents this privileged space, the (metaphorical) outback, denied to the human Riobaldo, who heavily treads the "human" outback in order to find transcendence in immanence. In accord with these metaphysical outlines, which assume universal dimensions, Rosa's work is a multifaceted panorama of the modus vivendi of the rural inhabitant and of the "condition of the bandit," a complex and vast mural of the outback with its customs, its language, its particular economy, and its flora and fauna. In an effort at representing the transition in Brazilian society from the rural to the urban, the mural painted by Rosa pinpoints in all its mythic dimensions the archaic culture of the outback subdued by urban civilization. Social denunciation thus appears mediated also by language. By setting aside a fossilized language and rejuvenating the poetic word's power of revelation, Rosa's fiction constitutes a protest against society that has institutionalized degraded speech.

Rosa left a body of writing that not only synthesizes Brazilian literature; it also places it in the context of Western culture. That literature is endowed with a metaphysical shape, but it is a metaphysics against metaphysics; in this way Rosa speaks with a voice identical to that of the most innovative philosophical contributions of our time and in tune with writings that reject the whole cultural heritage of the West, whose gaps are only too visible.

Rosa's work could be called baroque in the sense that it is a universe "full" of ingredients and allusions. Clarice Lispector (1926–1977) shares with Rosa more or less the same concerns, but with some notable differences. Her fiction is urban, strongly influenced by philosophy (especially existentialism), and the search by characters like GH in *A paixão segundo GH* (1964; Eng. *The Passion According to GH*) evokes a phenomenological operation, in the sense that it is based on a kind of peeling away, in a "somnambulic language" that attempts to express the inexpressible. The discussion of the very nature of language and meaning (and interpretation and history) is crucial in this novel in particular and in Lispector's fiction in general. Standing on a "third leg," GH always shields herself from the jeopardizing chaos of the world. Savoring the cockroach, her communion with nature, she demonstrates her nonhumanness and seeks contact with "nonbeing" in order to prepare herself to know what it is to "be" human. Again, as in Rosa's literature, the binary oppositions are neutralized: coming into nature, after the deconstruction of culture and the meanings imposed on words, GH finds in fact "the human beyond the human," God in mankind. In other words, her passage is a sort of returning, but in such a way that this new space is the human condition re-created and in plenitude. Language plays a very important role in this process, and the writing of the novel is continually aware of it. Lispector's diction does not produce a "stylistic shock" like Rosa's. What is apparent, however, is an intense working of language in order to verbalize the unnamable. The recent translation of Lispector into French and the forthcoming publication of the English version of *GH* will undoubtedly

inscribe her as one of the most important writers of this century.

The other Brazilian writer deserving of the Nobel Prize is Autran Dourado (b. 1926). Mainly a novelist but also the author of short stories and nonfiction books wherein he demonstrates his solid knowledge of theory, philosophy, and literature and "explains" his own works' architecture and symbology, Dourado is considered the best living prose writer in Brazilian letters today. His fiction is set in general in his home state of Minas Gerais, with its baroque heritage, the ghosts of its past, and the shadows of its myths. Historically speaking, it focuses mainly on the aforementioned transition of Brazilian society and on the decadence of the landlords. Despite the presence of some nostalgic echoes, this is done in a critical way, since the mythical implications are seen as an obstacle for dealing more critically with reality. Dourado is extremely adept in stream-of-consciousness techniques, and he builds his novels with what may be called a passionate lucidity. *Opera dos mortos* (1967; Eng. *Voices of the Dead*) is one of Brazilian literature's masterpieces, a work which could become a very good movie in the hands of a filmmaker such as Visconti or Bertolucci.

Some will have noticed my omission of the famous Jorge Amado (b. 1912) from this list of past and present Brazilian writers worthy of Nobel consideration. It is not necessary to subscribe to the opinion that Amado is simply a popular novelist, undeserving of any attention within the framework of "serious literature," whatever such a phrase may mean. Amado must be taken into account as practically the only Brazilian writer who lives from his literature, with a legion of readers. His best works are those wherein he explores cultural contradictions, a concept so important for understanding Brazilian society: *Gabriela, cravo e canela* (1958; Eng. *Gabriela, Clove and Cinnamon*), *Os velhos marinheiros* (1960; Eng. *Home Is the Sailor* and *The Two Deaths of Quincas Wateryell*), *Dona Flor e seus dois maridos* (1966; Eng. *Dona Flor and Her Two Husbands*) are his best books by far. What is most bothersome in Amado's writing is that he offers an emphatically exotic view of Brazil: sensual women, Afro-Brazilian religious rituals, spicy foods, and so on. An accurate examination of his fiction would reveal that he has a Manichean understanding of mankind: the poor and black are good; the white, rich, and bourgeois are bad. There is a radical populist empathy toward the lower classes and a male-luxurious comprehension of women, who seem to appear in his novels only to make love (if they are black or mestiza) or to serve as a pain in the neck (if they are white and/or middle-class). One has a real problem with Brazilianists who see Brazilian culture only through the exotic lens of Jorge Amado, although he does deserve respect as a writer.[5]

Turning briefly to the literature of Portugal, Fernando Pessoa (1888–1935) undoubtedly stands out as a poet who deserved the Nobel. Being at least four poets in one, Pessoa is a contemporary also in the sense that his poetry is, by definition, a displacement of the subject and truth.[6] Pessoa lived at the beginning of this century, however. In recent Portuguese literature the reader's attention is called to authors such as Carlos de Oliveira (1921–81), Sophia de Mello Breyner Andresen (b. 1919), Miguel Torga (b. 1907), José Saramago (b. 1922),[7] and Augustina Bessa-Luís (b. 1922) as possible candidates for the Nobel Prize. Vitorino Nemésio (1901–78) and Jorge de Sena (1919–78)[8] introduced new dictions in Portuguese poetry, in the sense that they fought against the strong flood of post-Pessoa versification.[9]

Whoever may be nominated, the fact remains that in the past twenty years the Luso-Brazilian literatures have gone unrecognized by the Swedish Academy.[10] The writers who received the Nobel during this period, for instance, were not well known in Brazil (with the exception of García Márquez), and they were translated more or less immediately after their respective awards on the basis of the Nobel Prize's prestige, as in the case of Elias Canetti. In conclusion there is no reason at all to be afraid of the Luso-Brazilian literatures.

Roberto Reis, Spring 1988

[1] See *WLT*'s special issue, "The Three Worlds of Lusophone Literature," 53:1 (Winter 1979), pp. 5–69.

[2] Priit J. Vesilind, "Brazil: Moment of Promise and Pain," *National Geographic,* 171:3 (1987), p. 368. Other recent articles in English about Brazil: Robert Harvey, "Brazil," *The Economist,* April 1987; Richard Martin, "Brazil: Where Tomorrow Never Comes," *Insight,* August 1987.

[3] On Carlos Drummond de Andrade, see *WLT* 51:4 (Autumn 1977), pp. 571–72, and 53:1 (Winter 1979), pp. 16–18.

[4] On João Cabral de Melo Neto, see *WLT* 62:1 (Winter 1988), pp. 73–74.

[5] On Jorge Amado, see *WLT* 58:1 (Winter 1984), pp. 49–50.

[6] On Fernando Pessoa and his legacy, see *WLT* 53:1 (Winter 1979), pp. 5–9.

[7] On José Saramago, see *WLT* 61:1 (Winter 1987), pp. 27–31.

[8] On Jorge de Sena, see *WLT* 53:1 (Winter 1979), pp. 9–15.

[9] I am thankful to Miguel Tamen for the suggestion of these two names.

[10] Apologies are in order for not including the Luso-African literatures here as well. On these literatures, see *WLT* 53:1 (Winter 1979), pp. 40–56.

Gabriel García Márquez: Labyrinths of Love and History

After his first surprise best seller, *Cien años de soledad* (Eng. *One Hundred Years of Solitude*), burst on the literary scene in 1967 and transformed a group of writers (Carlos Fuentes, Mario Vargas Llosa, José Donoso, and others) into a phenomenon known as "elboom," bringing him and them worldwide fame, every work by Gabriel García Márquez has been published to great fanfare and has been widely reviewed. The books under joint discussion here, *El amor en los tiempos del cólera* (Eng. *Love in the Time of Cholera*) and *El general en su laberinto* (Eng. *The General in His Labyrinth*),[1] have been met mostly by laudatory reviews in all three Americas. Differences in the reception are generally of tone and enthusiasm. In North America the reviews, though almost all positive, usually have been elegantly detached and even scholarly.[2] In Latin America both the praise and the criticism have been more passionate. "A chain of repugnant and sick sexual passions," fulminates Francisco Lemos Arboleda in *El País,* a Colombian newspaper, in late December 1985, on greeting *El amor en los tiempos del cólera*. In his opinion, the novel is "pornographic" and not worthy of being compared with "the immortal *María,*" a nineteenth-century Colombian novel. Though *María* mostly mimics breathy and exclamatory French romances, in the eyes of many Colombian critics and ordinary readers *María's* author, Jorge Isaacs, is untouchable. Every Colombian, however, seems willing to take on García Márquez. When the subject is a continental hero like Simón Bolívar, the contentious voices, pro and con, are multiplied by many from the rest of Latin America. *El general en su laberinto* occasioned fierce national and even continental debates after it was published on García Márquez's sixty-first birthday (28 March 1989).

At first glance, *Love in the Time of Cholera* and *The General in His Labyrinth* could not be more different from each other. The first chronicles the undying love of an octogenarian, Florentino Ariza, who, having loved Fermina Daza in her youth, secretly worships her for more than half a century and then courts her a second time after her husband dies, triumphantly consummating his passion on a river-boat during a trip on the Magdalena River. The novel celebrates, therefore, the vitality possible in old age, love over despair, health over sickness, life over death. The second novel deals with a much younger but much sicker man, Simón Bolívar, who, one day in May 1830, having renounced the presidency of Colombia, embarks on his final journey down the Magdalena. In *The General in His Labyrinth* despair, sickness, and death inevitably win out over love, health, and life. The first novel deals with ordinary people, the second with a continental hero. The first comes out of the writer's imagination, its sources being his life and memory as well as his observations of older people in love, including—García Márquez has said—his own parents. The second, though born, of course, of García Márquez's imagination, comes also from the library. A thoroughly researched book, its sources are documents, letters, histories, and biographies. Indeed, somewhat like a graduate student before his dissertation committee, the author proudly parades his research efforts in a three-page afterword entitled "My Thanks." Here we find out, among other things, how García Márquez learned to take notes, how his friends in many countries helped him with his research, and how he double-checked his facts and eliminated anachronisms, all in the interest of accurately depicting Bolívar's "tyrannically documented life" (272).

Historical accuracy is not an idea one usually associates with fiction, much less with an author like García Márquez. Let us not be misled, however, by the scholarship of his afterword to consider *The General in His Labyrinth* uniquely "realistic" among García Márquez's works. He has always been—as he has repeatedly insisted—a realist. That is, he portrays life as he has observed it and as he believes it to be. Moreover, in seeking the enduring patterns behind the detail, he agrees with the Aristotelian conception of poetic truth. For Aristotle, poetry, since it deals with universals, possesses the deepest kind of truth. Such a spirit of poetic truthfulness has certainly moved García Márquez in *The General in His Labyrinth* as well as in such major works as *One Hundred Years of Solitude* and *El otoño del patriarca* (1975; Eng. *The Autumn of the Patriarch*), works which presented recognizably "true" though undocumented pictures of Latin American life and of the Latin American dictator type.

This poetic realism is also, in a somewhat different style, the mode of *Love in the Time of Cholera*. The book reads like a nineteenth-century novel in the grand narrative tradition. That anachronistic approach allies García Márquez with masters like Defoe, Fielding, Balzac, Tolstoy, Conrad, and even the early Thomas Mann. Such narrative traditionalism upset some Latin American reviewers, who somehow expected García Márquez to write something stylistically daring and innovative. Critical expectations are fickle. Earlier, when *The Autumn of the Patriarch* was published, critics were disturbed because it was too innovative, too different from

One Hundred Years of Solitude, a work that some expected him to rewrite forever.[3] *Love in the Time of Cholera* may differ stylistically from much of the previous fiction by García Márquez; but it focuses on one of his most enduring themes, love, and the story that it tells is bold, touching, and finally exuberant.

García Márquez was inspired to write *Love in the Time of Cholera,* he tells Marlise Simons in an interview published in the *New York Times Book Review* (7 April 1985), by something he once saw: an elderly couple, very much in love, happily dancing on the deck of a ship, oblivious to their surroundings. This image took root in his mind, much like other images which inspired previous novels: a man on a porch in the Colombian city of Barranquilla, waiting for something (*El coronel no tiene quien le escriba* [Eng. *No One Writes to the Colonel*]); a small boy being taken by an old man to see a block of ice, exhibited as if it were part of a circus sideshow (*Cien años de soledad*); an incredibly old man alone in a presidential palace, which is full of cows (*El otoño del patriarca*). From that image of the dancing couple García Márquez created a story about passion eventually reciprocated, a reflection on old age much in the spirit of Simone de Beauvoir's 1970 work *La vieillesse* and in the manner of Tolstoy's reflections on death and dying in *The Death of Ivan Ilyich,* and a meditation on the art of love.

Let me list the ways—some of them, at least—in which García Márquez portrays love in this novel: love between old people, love between adolescents, love between an old man and a young virgin, love with prostitutes, love as infidelity, epistolary love, platonic love, interracial love, masochistic love—in fact, almost every kind of love except (so complains Enrique Fernández in his December 1986 review in the *Village Voice*) homosexual love. In this Colombian *Kama Sutra* García Márquez even mentions some unusual sexual positions, though he does not describe them: that of the angel on the rack, or that of the chicken on the grill. In some senses also he has produced a taxonomy of love through brief descriptive phrases: love is, for example, a cataclysm, a martyrdom, an instance of madness, a pain in the heart, a rebirth, a fever, a disease, an attack of cholera (these last three showing, in part, how "love as illness" is one of the controlling metaphors of the book). These and other details point to a fundamental quality of this novel. Unlike Jorge Isaacs, García Márquez does not envelop love in a haze of sentimentality. We come away from *Love in the Time of Cholera* convinced that, indeed, this is what love must be like—or can be like—at age eighty or at fifty, at forty or at twenty, convinced that García Márquez has sounded the depths of the human heart.

For all its surprising freshness in the García Márquez canon, *Love in the Time of Cholera* nevertheless shares thematic preoccupations with previous works, especially the theme of old age. But there are significant differences. The secret of a good old age, believes Colonel Aureliano Buendía in *Cien años de soledad,* is an honorable pact with solitude.[4] In *Love in the Time of Cholera* the secret seems to be the ability to love. In earlier works old age itself is a time of wisdom, as in the case of Ursula Buendía, or a time of terrible power, as in that of the deathless dictator of *El otoño del patriarca,* or a time of decrepitude, as it is in the story of the old man with enormous wings. Before *Love in the Time of Cholera* García Márquez had not depicted old age very positively. Its zesty portrayal in this novel leads Roberto González Echevarría to conclude that it is "not only a great book, but one of the few optimistic ones to have come along in many years."[5]

That optimism, that zest about sexuality and love in old age, has bothered some critics uncomfortable with the idea of physical passion between people whose skin is no longer tight, whose hair (what there is of it) no longer shines, whose bones may now creak with arthritic pain, and whose eyes can no longer see clearly. That, however, is precisely what García Márquez describes in the last fifth of his novel, and the pages devoted especially to the consummation of the passion between Florentino and Fermina are poignant, magisterial, and unforgettable. Moreover, behind the description of that and other loves in the novel lies a deeper love, a love of life itself. It is an attitude which, simply, says "yes" to life and to all that it may bring.

The "yes" becomes a "no" in *The General in His Labyrinth.* "Let us go," the general tells his trusted servant José Palacios on the very first page of the novel, "as fast as we can. No one loves us here" (in the Spanish, "aquí no nos quiere nadie")—words which the Liberator had apparently actually spoken many times in his life and which have also been attributed to his final delirium.[6] Bolívar may indeed have died from tuberculosis, as is generally thought (the exact cause of death has never been established conclusively enough for some people), but for García Márquez, Bolívar really dies from a lack of love. Despised by many of his countrymen, abandoned by all but a few aides and associates, left—during the final seven months of his life—without even the companionship of his longtime mistress Manuela Sáenz, Bolívar had no choice but to die of a broken heart. Historically and medically, there may be another explanation. In the world of philosophic universals and poetic truths, however, love, or its lack, can kill.

The General in His Labyrinth seems to me to be a labyrinthine summation in historical fiction of certain of García Márquez's long-standing obsessions and ever-present topics: love, death, solitude, power, fate. Love is but one of the themes that link this novel with previous books. In interviews the author calls attention to some of those links. It is as if, increasingly conscious of the geographic and historical unity of all his previous work, he wishes to make sure that readers understand how intimately, despite appearances to the contrary, *The General in His Labyrinth* is related to all the other fiction. "At bottom," García Márquez tells María Elvira Samper in an important interview published in the Colombian weekly *Semana* (20 March 1989), "I have written only one book, the same one that circles round and round, and continues on." In that same interview he seeks to ground *The General in His Labyrinth* in the world of his previous fiction.

> *El general* is more important than the rest of my work put together. It demonstrates that my work as a whole is founded on a geographic and historical reality. That reality is not that of magical realism and all those other things which people talk about. When you read [this novel], you realize that everything else in some way has a documentary, geographic, and historical basis that is borne out by *El general.* It is like *El coronel no tiene quien le escriba* all over again, but historically grounded this time.[7]

Such an avowal of the novel's ties to the past goes hand in hand with numerous details which proclaim its kinship with prior fiction. Like the Patriarch, Bolívar was a dictator (indeed that was one of his official titles for a while) with the power to give absolute commands which were actually carried out. That power was first consolidated—and believed in by others—in 1814, when Bolívar ordered the mass execution of all the captured royalists in the Guayra; and yet, throughout his career, while reveling in such power and not hesitating to use it, Bolívar stated his distaste for it. Such an ambivalent attitude made him into that most contradictory of leaders: the unwilling despot. In this he resembles Colonel Aureliano Buendía, reluctant hero of Colombia's civil wars and never more ferocious a warrior than in his battles to secure peace. Like Colonel Aureliano Buendía, Bolívar escapes numerous assassination attempts, seems to lead a charmed life, and is destined to die of natural causes. Like Colonel Aureliano Buendía, Bolívar believes the wars he has waged to have been "fruitless" ("guerras inútiles" in the Spanish; 13) and the "disillusionments of power" ("los desengaños del poder"; 13) to have been many and overwhelming.

Some phrases either call attention to previous works, both fictional and not, or sound as if they have been lifted from them. Such intertextuality is evident when Bolívar, on coming into a room, is "surprised by the scent of the guavas lying in a gourd on the window-sill" ("sorprendido por el olor de las guayabas expuestas en una totuma sobre el alféizar de la ventana"; 113). (*El olor de la guayaba* is the title of a book of reminiscences and conversations between García Márquez and Plinio Apuleyo Mendoza, published in Barcelona by the Editorial Bruguera in 1982.) The following sentence from *The General in His Labyrinth* could well have been written for *One Hundred Years of Solitude:* "Fourteen years of wars had taught him [Bolívar] that there was no greater victory than being alive" (27). *The General in His Labyrinth* even ends with a sentence whose final rhythmic phrases recall *One Hundred Years of Solitude.*

> Then he [Bolívar] crossed his arms over his chest and began to listen to the radiant voices of the slaves singing the six o'clock *Salve* in the mills, and through the window he saw the diamond of Venus in the sky that was dying forever, the eternal snows, the new vine whose yellow bellflowers he would not see bloom on the following Saturday in the house closed in mourning, the final brilliance of [the] life that would never, through all eternity, be repeated again. (267)[8]

Such a resemblance is intentional, of course, and it seems to me to be a canny message to his readers: "Look," García Márquez seems to be saying, "the story of Bolívar is of a piece with that of the Buendías, and both are the story of Latin America itself."

The message goes deeper than this, however. Here, as so often in his work, García Márquez's sensibility is close to that of the ancient Greeks. For him, Bolívar's is a fated life. That sense of fatality is portrayed through the constant use of sentences which foreshadow an end known to us all (e.g., "The last visitor he received the night before was Manuela Sáenz, the bold Quiteña who loved him but was not going to follow him to his death"; 6), through phrases like "it was the end" (37) and "they never saw each other again" (41), and through such foreshadowing techniques as the repeated appearance of a clock that is stopped at seven minutes past one, the exact time of Bolívar's death. García Márquez also frames the entire novel with an epigraph which might have been written by Homer, Aeschylus, or Sophocles: "Parece," Bolívar writes to Francisco de Paula Santander, "que el demonio dirige las cosas de mi vida." Edith Grossman's translation, "It seems that the devil controls the business of my life," narrows the interpretive range of Bolívar's comment. Bolívar did not write "el diablo" but rather the more suggestive "el demonio." *Demonio* comes from the Greek *daímon,* a term with several related meanings. According to Liddell and Scott's *Greek-English Lexicon,* "divine power" is one of them (*theós* is

the term usually used to personify a god). More often, *daímon* simply means "fate" or "destiny," as in "óti daímones thélosin" (what [the] gods ordain). In believing himself to be controlled by the forces of fate, and in submitting to the will of the *daímon,* the Liberator resembles many of García Márquez's heroes, from the Buendías in *One Hundred Years of Solitude* to Santiago Nasar in *Crónica de una muerte anunciada,* (1981; Eng. *Chronicle of a Death Foretold*).[9] It is worth recalling at this point that García Márquez prefaced his very first novel, *La hojarasca* (Eng. *Leaf Storm*), first published in 1955, with a long quotation from Sophocles' *Antigone.*

The theme of fate is also linked to that of love, and both are related in turn to the image of the labyrinth. For this "novelist of love," as Eugene Bell-Villada has described him,[10] or this "nymphomaniac of the heart," as García Márquez identified himself in an interview for *Playboy* magazine (February 1983, p. 178), the lack of love pushes Bolívar to his death. García Márquez uses love also as a barometer of Bolívar's heart and health. Bolívar had the reputation of being a womanizer, and books have been written on the subject (e.g., Cornelio Hispano's *Historia secreta de Bolívar*); but during his final months of life he was really too ill to add to that reputation. The novelist of love, instead of recounting Bolívar's sexual exploits during those months and thereby straining the credulity of his readers, portrays love mostly through Bolívar's memory. Women, most of them beautiful and almost all of them invented by García Márquez (e.g., the charming Miranda Lindsay) but some not (Manuela Sáenz and Anita Lenoit), weave through Bolívar's life like talismanic presences, now protecting him from harm (especially assassination attempts), now comforting him in his solitude. Every few pages García Márquez inserts another woman. Their very presence, since most of them are said to belong to Bolívar's glorious past, allows a labyrinthine exploration of his life before his final journey, and the ebbing of his passion in bed (or in the hammock), as in the episode of the young girl who leaves him in the morning as virginal as she was the night before (181–83), mirrors the ebbing of his life. Inexorably, just as the Magdalena River winds its way to the sea, Bolívar is drawn through the darkening maze of life, until at the end, just before his final moments, he curses his inability to find a way out of "the labyrinth" (267)—the first and only time the word is used in the book. There is no Ariadne's thread for him as there was for Theseus, no thread of love—or of hope—to lead him back to life.

This wise book, superbly translated by Edith Grossman, deserves to be read and reread, taught again and again, and written about—as it will be—for many, many years. By choosing to portray Bolívar's life the way he does, García Máquez summarizes so much: the life of a great man, an era, a culture. However, García Márquez has also portrayed himself in portraying Bolívar, and has admitted as much. "I identify myself in many ways with Bolívar," he tells María Elvira Samper in *Semana.* For example, he says that he has "loaned" Bolívar his own "choleric personality, and he [Bolívar] controls his anger as well as I control mine. The truth is that a novelist builds a character with pieces of himself." Those pieces are both biographical and philosophical in this case. Biographically, both Bolívar and García Márquez are men of the Caribbean; both live much of their lives in high-altitude urban areas; both feel nostalgia for their native haunts; both are uncomfortable among "cachacos," a pejorative term for *Bogotanos* used by those from the coastal regions of Colombia. Philosophically, García Máquez is like Bolívar also, he says, in that neither of them "pays much attention to death, because that distracts one from the most important thing: what one does in life" (32–33).[11] What García Márquez has done in life is magnificent indeed.

Written in the author's maturity, *Love in the Time of Cholera* has the freshness of someone looking at old places with new understanding. Here García Márquez seems to be rediscovering joyfulness, reveling in the knowledge that old age can have some of the wonderment and passion of youth. In all this, *Love in the Time of Cholera* is very much like *One Hundred Years of Solitude,* despite the apocalyptic ending of that book. By contrast, *The General in His Labyrinth* is written in an elegiac mode, and critics have commented on its lack of humor. It is a valediction, not forbidding mourning. If *Love in the Time of Cholera* is high comedy, then *The General in His Labyrinth* is tragedy. If *Love in the Time of Cholera* is like *One Hundred Years of Solitude,* then *The General in His Labyrinth* is like *The Autumn of the Patriarch,* dark in its mood, somber in its message. Taken together, these two most recent novels demonstrate once again the astonishing range of García Márquez's work and the empathetic flexibility of his mind and heart.

Michael Palencia-Roth, Winter 1991

[1] Gabriel García Márquez, *El amor en los tiempos del cólera,* Bogotá, La Oveja Negra, 1985; translated by Edith Grossman as *Love in the Time of Cholera,* New York, Knopf, 1990; and *El general en su laberinto,* Bogotá, La Oveja Negra, 1989; translated by Grossman as *The General in His Labyrinth,* New York, Knopf, 1990. Parenthetic page numbers refer to the Spanish-language editions.

[2] For *Love in the Time of Cholera,* see, for example, Jean Franco in *The Nation,* 23 April 1988; Walter Clemons in *Newsweek,* 25 April 1988; Michael Wood in the *New York Review of Books,* 28 April 1988; David Castronovo in *America,* 3 September 1988; and Roberto González Echevarría in the *Yale Review,* Spring 1989. For *The General in His Labyrinth,* see Joseph Coates in "Tribune Books" of the *Chicago Tribune,* 9 September 1990; Margaret Atwood in the *New York Times Book Review,* 16 September 1990; R. Z. Sheppard in *Time,* 17 September 1990; Tim Padgett in *Newsweek,* 8 October 1990; and Robert Adams in the *New York Review of Books,* 11 October 1990. The exception to the elegant detachment in the reviews is the lively, loosely written, and finally negative review by John Leonard in *The Nation,* 3 December 1990.

[3] It is possibly that difference that led some Latin American critics to denounce *El otoño del patriarca* on its publication. One critic lamented García Márquez's forgetfulness about the virtues of punctuation ("las virtudes del punto"—Rubén Gamboa, in *Handbook of Latin American Studies,* 1976, p. 425), apparently himself overlooking such masters of scarce punctuation as Proust and Joyce. Another, Jaime Mejía Duque, delivered himself of a long diatribe entitled *El otoño del patriarca o la crisis de la desmesura* (Bogotá, La Oveja Negra, 1975). The length of the criticism about García Márquez's excessive length was itself excessive.

[4] Gabriel García Márquez, *Cien años de soledad,* Buenos Aires, Sudamericana, 1967, p. 174. Unless otherwise noted, the translations in this review are my own.

[5] González Echevarría, p. 478.

[6] See Jean Descola, *Los libertadores,* Barcelona, Juventud, 1960, p. 306.

[7] From an interview with García Márquez conducted by María Elvira Samper, *Semana* (Colombia), 20 March 1989, p. 28. The original text reads: "*El general* tiene una importancia más grande que todo el resto de mi obra. Demuestra que toda mi obra corresponde a una realidad geográfica e histórica. No es el realismo mágico y todas esas cosas que se dicen. Cuando lees el Bolívar te das cuenta de que todo lo demás tiene, de alguna manera, una base documental, una base histórica, una base geográfica que se comprueba con *El general.* Es como otra vez *El coronel no tiene quien le escriba,* pero fundamentado históricamente. En el fondo yo no he escrito sino un solo libro, que es el mismo que da vueltas y vueltas, y sigue."

[8] "Entonces cruzó los brazos contra el pecho y empezó a oír las voces radiantes de los esclavos cantando la salve de las seis en los trapiches, y vio por la ventana el diamante de Venus en el cielo que se iba para siempre, las nieves eternas, la enredadera nuev? cuyas campánulas amarillas no vería florecer el sábado siguiente en la casa cerrada por el duelo, los últimos fulgores de la vida que nunca más, por los siglos de los siglos, volvería a repetirse."

[9] For an analysis of the relationship between *Crónica de una muerte anunciada* and Greek tragedy, see my article, "*Crónica de una muerte anunciada:* El Anti-Edipo de García Márquez," *Revista de Estudios Colombianos,* 6 (1989), pp. 9–15.

[10] Eugene Bell-Villada, *García Márquez: The Man and His Work,* Chapel Hill, University of North Carolina Press, 1990, pp. 176 ff.

[11] "Me siento identificado en muchas cosas con Bolívar. Por ejemplo, en esa cosa de no pararle muchas bolas a la muerte, porque lo distrae a uno de lo fundamental, que es lo que está haciendo uno en la vida. . . . [García Márquez le prestó al personaje Bolívar] lo colérico, que lo controlaba tan bien como lo controlo yo. La verdad es que un novelista hace un personaje con retazos de sí mismo."

García Márquez's New Book: Literature or Journalism?

When Gabriel García Márquez announced that he was abandoning literature for journalism until the Pinochet dictatorship disappeared from Chile, people expected him to keep his word, and many were surprised when he published *Crónica de una muerte anunciada* (Chronicle of a Death Foretold). He was not really breaking his pledge, however, as can be seen from what he said in an interview with Rosa E. Peláez and Cino Colina published in *Granma* (Havana) and reprinted in *Excelsior* of Mexico City (31 December 1977). In the interview he is asked what aspect of journalism he likes best, and his answer is reporting. He is subsequently asked about the *crónica* genre and answers that it is all a matter of definition, that he can see little difference between reporting and the writing of chronicles. He goes on to say that one of his ultimate aims is to combine journalism and fiction in such a way that when the news item becomes boring he will embellish it and improve upon it with inventions of his own. So when he wrote this latest book of his, a short, tight novella, by his lights he was not returning to fiction but carrying on journalism as usual, even though his uncramped definitions could well apply to everything that he had written previously and supposedly had put in abeyance.

The chronicle has long been the primitive method of recording events and people and passing them on into history. Most of what we know about medieval Europe has come from chronicles, and in Africa history has been kept through the oral chronicles of the griots. In Latin America, Brazil in particular, the "chronicle" is a recognized and broadly practiced form, offspring of the more ancient variety, that lies somewhere between journalism and "literature." In the United States certain newspaper columns of a more subjective and personal nature correspond to the Latin American chronicle, which almost inevitably makes its first appearance in the press before going into book form. Therefore García Márquez is correct when he says that it is all a matter of definition in the question of whether or not he has abandoned literature and whether or not he has returned.

This new book shows many aspects of life and literature and how one is essentially the same as the other: life imitates art.[1] It starts off in good journalistic style with the "when" and the "what."

> On the day they were going to kill him, Santiago Nasar got up at 5:30 in the morning to wait for the boat the bishop was coming on. He'd dreamt he was going through a grove of timber trees where a gentle drizzle was falling, and for an instant he was happy in his dream, but when he awoke he felt completely spattered with bird shit. "He was always dreaming about trees," his mother told me 27 years later, recalling the details of that unpleasant Monday. "The week before he'd dreamt that he was alone in a tinfoil airplane and flying through the almond trees without bumping into anything," she told me. Plácida Linero had a well-earned reputation as an accurate interpreter of other people's dreams, provided they were told her before eating, but she hadn't noticed any ominous augury in those two dreams of her son's, or in the other dreams of trees he'd told her about on the mornings preceding his death.[2]

This use of the temporal to begin the narration reminds one immediately of *One Hundred Years of Solitude,* which begins in a similar if not identical vein and sets the stage for the necessary retrospect: "Many years later, as he faced the firing squad, Colonel Aureliano Buendía was to remember that distant afternoon when his father took him to discover ice."[3] The difference is that *One Hundred Years of Solitude* begins in medias res, in good epic fashion, while this "chronicle" opens almost at the end of the action, not quite so far as the end of life as in *The Autumn of the Patriarch,* but close to it. This might well show the influence of journalism in the direction that García Márquez's style has been taking through these last three longer works. The first is more legendary and historical as it develops toward its inevitable and fated climax, while the last two depend on journalistic investigation for their development.

Julio Cortázar has spoken about that nightmare for authors (and typesetters) in Spanish: *casualidad/ causalidad* (chance/causality). There is no need to worry about such a slip in the interpretation of this story, as the two elements coincide quite neatly. It is known from the beginning of the tale that the Vicario twins are planning to kill Santiago Nasar for having deflowered their sister Angela, thus ruining her marriage to the strange but wealthy newcomer Bayardo San Román. Many people in the town are aware of the Vicarios' intentions, but through a concatenation of quite normal, even banal, bits of happenstance, nothing is ultimately done to stop them. Indeed, one gathers that even they have little heart for the dirty job that honor is forcing them to do and are only waiting for the authorities or someone to prevent them from bringing it off, since they are prevented by the code from backing down themselves. The title is quite fitting, therefore, in that the death in question has been announced and is foretold. García Márquez has managed to keep the shock and horror of surprise, however, by seeing to it also that the one person who is blithely unaware of what has been ordained, almost until the moment of the act itself, is Santiago Nasar. In the end chance has become the cause of the inexorable deed: *casualidad/causalidad*.

The format used for the narration of the tale is quite journalistic. The narrator, García Márquez himself, perhaps genuine, perhaps embellished, as he mentioned in the interview cited above, is investigating the murder some twenty years later in order to ascertain how such a thing could have happened, how in the end no one was in a position to stop what nobody, including the perpetrators, wanted to happen. The matter of imperfect memory (there are great discrepancies as to the weather) helps lend uncertainty to a tale or event that had become certain because of uncertainty itself. The narrator also relies upon his own memory; he was home from school at the time of the killing and was a friend and contemporary of Santiago Nasar, having caroused with him the night before the murder. In addition, he interviews the participants and several observers, tracking some of them down to more remote places. The narration is a kind of complicated act of turning something inside-out and right-side-out again in that it resembles the application of fictive techniques to the narration of true events in the manner of Norman Mailer and Truman Capote, but here fiction is treated like fact treated like fiction. This swallowing of his own tale by the snake gives a very strong feeling of authenticity to the story.

One would have to investigate further, and perhaps it would be impossible to ascertain how much of the tale is based on fact. García Márquez has always maintained that most of his stories, especially the ones that seem most fantastic, are all based on fact and human experience; hence the validity of Alejo Carpentier's description of this whole body of Latin American literature as *lo real maravilloso* (the marvelously real). A great deal of the background obviously comes from the author's youth, for he includes his family in it. The town is not identified as Macondo, but the doctor is Dionisio Iguarán, the family name of Úrsula in *One Hundred Years of Solitude*. The bridegroom's father is tied in directly to events in the earlier novel.

But the main attraction was the father: General Petronio San Román, hero of the civil wars of the past century, and one of the major glories of the Conservative regime for having put Colonel Aureliano Buendía to flight in the disaster of Tucurinca. My mother was the only one who wouldn't go to greet him when she found out who he was. "It seems all right to me that they should get married," she told me. "But that's one thing and it's something altogether different to shake hands with the man who gave the orders for Gerineldo Márquez to be shot in the back."[4]

The Caribbean geography of marshes, seascapes and ships is very much that mystical yet real world that García Márquez evokes in his other works.

Instead of giving us a linear narration of the episodes leading up to the final tragedy, García Márquez divides the novella into chapters, each of which follows the trajectory from a slightly different angle and involves a different combination of characters. The fictive structure is therefore a web of crisscrossed story lines, and in the center (or on the bias) is the hole of solitude and impotence where the killing takes place, uncrossed by any of the lines that would have plugged it and prevented the tragedy. This reminds one of the suicide attempt by Colonel Aureliano Buendía in *One Hundred Years of Solitude* when, in emulation of the poet José Asunción Silva, he asks his doctor friend to make a dot on his shirt where his heart is. We later find that the wily physician, on to the colonel's intentions, has designated the one spot in the area of the heart where a bullet can pass without being fatal. As in so many other aspects of this book when compared to the others, and as García Márquez does so many times with a technique that links all of his tales but at the same time differentiates among them, we have mirror images, reverse and obverse.

There is a richness of characters, as one would expect from this author. While he borrows some from his other books, as is his wont, he invents new ones that have great possibilities for expansion into tales of their own, the same as innocent Eréndira and her heartless grandmother, conceived in *One Hundred Years of Solitude* and developed at length in their own novella. As it is, García Márquez is adept at weaving different and seemingly unconnected stories together in order to make the webbing of his complete tale, and any of the tangents that he uses to devise the whole chronicle could be followed off into a separate narrative. There are also intriguing characters on the fringes that we hope to see more of. The wedding and the murder coincide with the bishop's passage up the river (there are always rivers in García Márquez). This episcopal worthy was passing through early in the morning on the day after the abortive wedding and on the day of the killing. The atmosphere, rather than being tetric in advance of the slaughter (the brothers were butchers and killed him with their pig-sticking knives), is ludicrous; for it seems that the bishop's favorite dish is cockscomb soup, and the townspeople have gathered together hundreds of caged roosters as an offering to his grace. At dawn a cacophony ensues as the captive creatures begin to crow and are answered by all the cocks in town. As it so happened, and as predicted by Santiago Nasar's mother, the bishop did not even deign to stop, and his paddlewheeler passed by as he stood on the bridge and dispensed mechanical blessings to the sound of the congregated roosters. This was the comic atmosphere that would surround the death foretold.

What unites so much of García Márquez's writing is the sense of inexorability, of fatefulness. Things often come to an end that has been there all the while, in spite of what might have been done to avoid it, and often mysteriously and inexplicably, as with the death of José Arcadio, the son, in *One Hundred Years of Solitude*. Here the hand of doom is unavoidable, but the path is tortuous, as it would logically appear that there were ever so many chances to halt the assassination. There is a touch of mystery too, however, in the fact that the narrator-investigator was never able to find out if Angela Vicario and Santiago Nasar had been lovers. All evidence and logic said that the dashing young rancher, already betrothed to the daughter of one of his Arab father's compatriots, could not possibly have been interested in a brown bird like Angela Vicario. She had her own mystery, however, because in the end, years later, she and Bayardo San Román come back together again as strangely as they had been joined the first time. He appears one day at her new home in "exile" beyond Riohacha with a suitcase full of the letters she had been writing him—all unopened.

From the beginning we know that Santiago Nasar will be and has been killed, depending on the time of the narrative thread that we happen to be following, but García Márquez does manage, in spite of the repeated foretelling of the event by the murderers and others, to maintain the suspense at a high level by never describing the actual murder until the very end. Until then we have been following the chronicler as he puts the bits and pieces together ex post facto, but he has constructed things in such a way that we are still hoping for a reprieve even though we know better. It is a feeling that makes us understand why *King Lear* was altered in the nineteenth century in order to spare those sentimental audiences the ultimate agony of Cordelia's execution. García Márquez has put the tale together in the down-to-earth manner of Euripides, but in the final pathos he comes close to the effects of Aeschylus.

The little slips of fate that seem so unimportant until they end in tragedy are the blocks that he builds with. Coincidence or lack of it is not so patently contrived as in Mario Vargas Llosa's novel *The Green House,* where we have the same characters wearing different masks on different stages. Instead, the epiphanies mount up and reveal the characters and the circumstances (never completely; there is always something

unknown) by a succession of banal delights and contretemps. In his latest and as yet unpublished piece, a short story entitled "El rastro de tu sangre en la nieve" (The Trail of Your Blood on the Snow), García Márquez tells of the trip by car of a newly wedded tropical couple from Madrid to Paris and the strange death of the bride at the end as she bleeds to death in a Paris hospital as the result of having been pricked by a thorn in the bouquet of roses presented her on their arrival in Madrid from Cartagena de Indias. In this chronicle of a death unforetold the girl dies as her unfortunate bridegroom, confused and astray in Paris, is completely out of touch with the impossible situation. It is another string of confusions similar to that in this novella, even though the locale is much more Cortazarian and the characters seem almost out of Luis Rafael Sánchez. The first sentence, though, is vintage García Márquez: "At dusk, when they reached the frontier, Nena Daconte realized that the finger where she wore her wedding ring was still bleeding."

"Chronicle of a Death Foretold" might well be the book that García Márquez was projecting in his Havana interview when he said that he wanted to write the false memoirs of his own life. He is not the protagonist of the story, but he is not only the author; he is the narrator. He even tells how he first proposed marriage to his wife and mentions her by name. In this way he is following the tradition of Cervantes, who mingled the real and the fictional to the degree that all levels came together in a time that only Proust could understand, and he is also very close to what Borges is up to in his story "The Other Borges." When Gabriel García Márquez said that he was abandoning literature for journalism, he probably did not realize the ambiguity of his statement, and since then, as he has done in his reportage, he has come to the conclusion that in technique at least—and possibly in many other ways as well—they are the same.

Gregory Rabassa, Winter 1982

[1] A scam recently brought off by persons involved in the conduct of the Pennsylvania state lottery is almost identical with that manipulated by the aged dictator in *The Autumn of the Patriarch*.

[2] Although the novella has appeared in Spanish, the publication of the English translation has been delayed. Thus I am quoting from the manuscript of the version that I finished last year.

[3] Gergory Rabassa, tr., New York, Harper & Row, 1970, p. 1.

[4] Manuscript, pp. 24–25.

Fabián Dobles: Memories of a Costa Rican Novelist

To those readers and critics unfamiliar with the life of the Costa Rican writer Fabián Dobles, his last novel, *Los años, pequeños días* (1988),[1] translated into English by Joan Henry as *Years Like Brief Days* (1996), is a fictional account of a seventy-year-old man in the process of re-membering his youth, of retelling those formative experiences that made him a man, and of re-creating those crucial moments that forged his political ideology and world view. Nevertheless, for anyone familiar with the Dobles clan, the people and places in the narrative are real and the novel seems less a fiction than an autobiography. The use of the term *autobiography,* however, does not intend to lessen the literary value of the work, but rather to open the critical space for understanding it. For, indeed, the case has been made that "all writing that aspires to be literature is autobiography and nothing else . . . for behind every work of literature there is an 'I' informing the whole and making its presence felt at every critical point, and without this 'I,' stated or implied, the work would collapse into mere insignificance."[2]

In his remembering and recounting of the past, the first-person narrator of Dobles's tale takes the position of analytic observer, watching himself as a youth, as "other," acting simultaneously as both subject and object of his narrative. The subject/object complication becomes more vexed as the narrator watches the old man, who in turn watches the youth. As Dobles explores this maze of relationships among multiple presents and multiple pasts, he exposes the various psychological exigencies of remembering: the need to reconcile one's present with the recollection of the past; the need to speak the past, to tell what has been buried in memory; the need to negotiate the past, to corroborate memory, to review, to remember, to reremember; the need to complete or fulfill the past, to finish what was left undone or unsaid and to respond to it on an emotional and psychological level. Overall, his narrator underlines the need to view one's multiple selves over the diachrony of time. The memories of the main character—a fictional persona for Dobles himself—are clearly drawn from Dobles's life and experience, although he contemplates them from the point of view of the "other." While the characters are unnamed, their discernible historical referents indicate the ambiguity of delineating between novel and autobiography, between history and fiction, and between objective fact and subjective memory. The present, Dobles suggests, is not mediated by any objective sense of the past or by static, univocal memories of it, but rather by the complex and continual psychological process of recalling.

Dobles's story begins with an old man's compulsion to revisit a landmark of his youth, an actual place in Costa Rica: the Customs House built by Don Braulio Carrillo, one of the Republic's former presidents. As the narrator describes in the novel, the site still exists near a one-hundred-year-old stone bridge and arch. The river the old man remembers, however, has been drained: "He knew that, but it didn't matter to him" (14). His memory of it, "unassailable by time," coexists in the present alongside the actual "river bed, now almost without water, small and dirty" (14). His obsessed visit to the site acts as a catalyst for inducing memories so that present and past exist simultaneously in the same space: "There he was with the enjoyment of youth caressing the stones as if they were flesh and not granite. The river was really filling up with torrents and foam as it did in the thirties" (14). This dual vision of present and past, this unavoidable interplay of memory and actuality, constitutes the fundamental complexity of the "self" which paradoxically exists from present moment to present moment while also maintaining a life over the continuity of chronological time: "But this lad is alive as I am alive, and I don't know if I or he or we both are the ones who get up now, go out to the entrance hall and walk to the street" (37).

It is never enough, Dobles's narrator suggests, to remember silently and alone. The mental image, in order to reveal itself fully to the subject, must be spoken, must be consciously remembered and told. The isolated incident in the past must be linked by the subject/narrator to the overall life/story, so that the lived experience, incompletely understood at the moment it occurs, takes a formative place in the growth and development of the self over time. In order to speak the past and attempt to fix the fluidity of memory, Dobles's narrator writes a fictional letter to his mother, now long dead, in which he reveals to her what he never could tell her while she was alive. The cumulative effect of the multitude of stories and memories included in this epistle helps to explain and justify the narrator's present state of mind. He (as subject of the action) essentially writes the letter to himself (as object). Not only we the readers, then, but he himself can trace the beginnings of his loss of faith in the Catholic Church, his questioning of authority, both parental and religious, and his disillusionment with what he sees as a hypocritical society. The tone of the letter, despite his mother's obvious ignorance regarding the major events that affected him as a youth, is neither resentful nor bitter. Instead, he reveals a sympathetic understanding of her and writes in a gentle, evocative tone—"Do you remember that, Mama?" (44)—as Dobles reveals "the secret story of every more or less normal lad" (45), as he recounts the multiple tales of youthful lusts and disillusionments, of the hypocrisy of the priest who attempts to seduce him, of his anxiety when he believed his father was dying of cancer, and as he learns the lessons of adulthood: "From now on you're going to feel initiated" (100).

Speaking the past, however, assumes a clearly understood past that can be spoken, a univocal consistency of memory, an objectified representation of what once was. The issue, of course, is much more complicated, as the old narrator comes to realize when he shows his elder brother the letter he has written to his mother. The letter becomes the point of departure for the two old men to reminisce, but as they do so they are forced to see the past from the perspective of each other's unique memories. The brothers disagree, and each is surprised at how the other remembers their collective past: "Do you understand me, brother? No, of course not" (69). Thus, the negotiation of the past begins: "But why, why didn't you consult me?" Each brother defends his memories in order to maintain the integrity of his own "self": "But I sang, brother, I sang. . . . I used to dream, too. Do you think I didn't?" (74). From this conversation in the present, we understand the fluidity of the past and the instability of memory. The retelling of history, rather than an objective recounting, becomes a negotiated re-creation: "Do you remember? . . . Have you forgotten? . . . Look, I'd completely forgotten that, how awful of me" (79).

As the two old men corroborate and revise each other's memories of their youth, as they review their stories and reremember their individual lives which occupied the same historical space, each adds details from his memory to complement and complete the recollections of the other. As they do so, both experience a concomitant affective response in the present to the experiences they have evoked from the past. They discuss, they laugh, they sing old songs, and they come to know each other more intimately than they have ever been able to do before. In the process they also come to know themselves at a deeper and more sympathetic level. Later, as the old man goes through a similar process of remembering with his wife "because you are a part of the story too," he allows himself the affective outlet he denied himself in front of his brother when he "overcame [his] desire to sob, though [he] had a lump in [his] throat." Instead, "the man who is relating this to his wife sitting beside him cannot now refrain from sobs when she is moved to tenderness and cherishes his memories" (97). This psychological completion of the past in the present as one shares one's past with another

and asks for forgiveness—"For goodness' sake forgive me, old boy, even though it's a long time ago. / —No, no. You must forgive me" (102)—allows the self to regenerate, to move forward as it sheds resentment, bitterness, and pride. Speaking the past acts as a catharsis for the soul, which must live in the present even while it comes to terms with the memories of itself. In the words of Atahualpa Yupanqui, whose song is simultaneously played and remembered in Dobles's text, "He who wants to live a happy life must not remain silent" (102).

Many of the old narrator's memories center on the autocratic figure of his father, a countryside medical doctor trained in New York. He recalls his father's quick and violent temper, his severity, his rigorous Catholic devotion, and his unquestioned position as the patriarchal authority of a large (ten children) family. It is this rigid and volatile man who ignites his son's passions and spurs his class consciousness, producing a political and social awareness which ultimately results in his conversion to a Marxist political ideology, despite the fact that such a position was clearly contrary to his father's fervent Catholic beliefs. The narrator vividly remembers his father's fury at being unable to save the children in his community who died, not from disease but from hunger. Initially, the father feeds the narrator's early misanthropy: "I felt deeply bitter and this made me lose faith in other people. Who was telling the truth? who was lying? who was sincere? who was a hypocrite? when the one you trusted was being deceitful and lying to you and the insincere one was telling you the truth" (106). Through the process of remembering, crosschecking those memories against the memories of others, and emotionally responding to the spoken image, the narrator eventually comes to terms with the distant father he never really understood: "It was really he who, thanks to his bad-tempered constraints, prepared me for life" (106).

This review and subsequent reevaluation of the significance of the past deconstructs any sense of objective history.[3] Memory is clouded in confusion and ambiguity, in inaccuracies and forgetfulness. Moreover, the significance of the past must necessarily unfold in the present. As the present changes, so does its concomitant relationship to the past, making reevaluation a continual and renewable enterprise. Likewise, the sense of a univocal, fixed, and coherent self which moves through time disappears as the narrator discovers "that one is not only one, but multitudes in time and space" (106). The old man's task in the narrative, as in life itself, is to "rearm [his] being, to try to love and understand, and so [he says] I began to look for the other side, invisible and unknown, of my close family tribe, and to listen for sonorities hidden from the world and history, as my Papa did when he placed the hollow of one hand on the skin of a patient's body and tapped with the other on the back of the hollow to feel reactions from inside" (107).

One of the characteristics of autobiography is that it is by nature open-ended. The story not only does not finish, since the "I" (both subject and object, both teller and told) is still alive at the end of his tale, but the narrative must also perforce delineate a context for the "I" which acquires a life of its own and continues even after an author's death. The "I" of this narrative has a place, Heredia—"This is certainly my valley, the place I can never forget" (105)—and a family, the Dobles clan, which in the course of the novel stretches backward for two generations to Dobles's maternal grandparents, forward to his nieces and nephews, and laterally to his wife, who understands that "it was a long time since [her husband] had been the young man of the thirties and who now went on repeating episodes that he had talked about so many times and that reminded her of parts of her own life and her family" (112). The wife and nieces and nephews, in turn, have places and families of their own, some of them important players in Dobles's narrative, and some who spill over outside the confines of the text itself.

The suspicion, voiced by James Olney, a well-known literary critic of autobiography, that "the student and reader of autobiographies . . . is a vicarious or a closet autobiographer"[4] is particularly relevant in this case. It is not unimportant or insignificant that the "I" of this analytic study, the supposed "literary critic" here, is also a niece by marriage of the "I" in Los años, pequeños días. As a daughter-in-law of the "sister who sang like a lark" (67), I too have a relationship to the story. As an American, a "gringa," I too have a historical responsibility for the deplorable conditions and racist practices in the hospitals of New York at the turn of the century described in the novel by Dobles's father, the doctor who trained in the United States. The doctor's memories, which then become part of his son's memories, reflect a time from my national history and converge with a piece of my collective past. Some of the stories that Dobles's narrator tells I have heard from my mother-in-law, from her perspective, or from my husband's aunt (the sister who almost drowned Fabián as a little boy while pretending he was a doll and giving him a bath [66], from her perspective, or from other family members. As all of our stories in their various versions intersect at various points on the continuum of history, Dobles's narrative comes full circle. His novel, initially written perhaps like the narrator's letter to his mother, as an attempt at personal clarification—"all this is and

was no more, and I've changed" (13)—transcends the limitations of the author's unknowable purposes and extends to the reader, in this case to me, who cannot read divorced from my own present, my own context, and my own memories, both personal and collective. In this way, I become an integral part of the story itself, of the continuous narrative which overflows the boundaries of the pages of Los años, pequeños días and awaits the next story to be artificially and momentarily fixed, remembered, and objectified in the pages of literary history.

Ann González, Summer 1999

■ **BIOGRAPHICAL NOTE ON FABIÁN DOBLES AND THE DOBLES FAMILY.** Fabián Dobles was born on 17 January 1918 in San Antonio de Belén, a small country town in Costa Rica, to Dr. Miguel Dobles Sáenz, who was indeed, as the novel indicates, trained at Johns Hopkins at the turn of the century. His maternal grandmother Micaela Solera, known to her grandchildren and great-grandchildren as Mamita Quela, and his maternal grandfather Santiago Rodríguez, called Papá Santiago, had seven children besides Fabián's mother, Carmen Rodríguez Solera, three of whom were the unmarried aunts in the novel: Lucila, Marta, and Otilia. Another daughter, Margarita, married José Manuel Peralta, the rich uncle who appears in the novel. Fabián had six sisters, all of whom appear briefly in the novel: Carmen is the eldest, and Rosario is the married sister who saves him as he tries to escape his angry brother; Alicia is the daughter with the voice of a lark who almost dies in a typhoid epidemic that Fabián recounts; Susana is another of Fabián's older sisters, along with Margarita, the sister who almost drowns him by accident. Marielos is the baby sister he mentions who is sent away with him to a neighboring house during the typhoid epidemic. His elder brother Miguel, who has such a pivotal role in the novel, managed Papá Santiago's farm and business and had a passion for horses, which Fabián faithfully portrays. His two younger brothers Alejo and Alvaro are not even born for most of the novel's childhood memories. Fabián's wife, who also plays a prominent role in the novel, is Cecilia Trejos.

Fabián Dobles published his first novel, *Ese que llaman pueblo,* in 1942. Most of his fiction falls under the category of social realism, a popular form of Spanish American narrative in the 1940s and 1950s which focuses on the life and problems of the agrarian "campesinos" and lower classes, works filled with antiheroes and human tragedy. Particularly striking about Dobles's style is his effort to imitate and phonetically reproduce the speech patterns of his countrymen. He claimed in interviews not to write for the "ancho mundo / wide world" but rather to communicate with "su gente / his people" in the Costa Rican vernacular. Nevertheless, the fact that he provides a glossary of Costa Rican expressions at the end of each of his novels (except for the last one) would indicate that he, at least, intended for non-Costa Ricans to have access to his work. Indeed, his works have been translated into a variety of languages, among them Russian, German, Portuguese, and English. The translation into Italian of his collection of short stories *Historias de Tata Mundo* (1955) was funded by UNESCO.

Dobles is considered one of Costa Rica's finest writers. Among his many national and international awards is the Magón National Prize for Culture (1993). In addition, he was honored in his lifetime with the publication of his complete works in a five-volume set, a joint project of the Editorial de la Universidad de Costa Rica and the Editorial de la Universidad Nacional in 1993. He died in San José in March 1995, survived by his wife, five daughters, and numerous grandchildren.

[1] Fabián Dobles, *Los años, pequeños días,* Costa Rica, Farben Grupo Editorial Norma, 1993; translated by Joan Henry as *Years Like Brief Days,* London, Peter Owen, 1996. All citations are from the translation and are indicated in the text in parentheses.

[2] *Autobiography: Essays Theoretical and Critical,* ed. James Olney, Princeton (N.J.), Princeton University Press, 1980, pp. 4 and 21.

[3] This is not a new argument either in the field of history or in literary criticism. See, for example, Hayden White's essay "The Historical Text as Literary Artifact," in *The Tropics of Discourse: Essays in Cultural Criticism,* Baltimore, Johns Hopkins University Press, 1978. I have reversed White's thesis here to argue that Dobles's novel—a "literary artifact"—also works as a historical (autobiographical) text.

[4] Olney, p. 26.

MEXICO

Octavio Paz: Nobel Laureate in Literature, 1990

A welcome surprise, a pleasant surprise: this is how most readers and critics have received the news of the awarding of the 1990 Nobel Prize in Literature to Octavio Paz. The element of surprise was due mostly to the fact that no one, or almost no one, thought that a Nobel could be accorded to a Hispanic writer so soon after the 1989 selection of the Spanish novelist Camilo José Cela.[1] After all, this is not the way—or so we surmised—the Swedish Academy thinks and acts: after an

award to a representative of a certain cultural or linguistic area, attention is displaced to another area.[2] We expected the prize to go to a writer from Asia, Africa, Eastern Europe, anywhere else in the world. Moreover, Paz had been bypassed so often, he was such an obvious candidate yet had been ignored for such a long time, that we were beginning to imagine a dark plot, a mysterious conspiracy that had managed to sabotage his candidacy in the past and would continue to do so in the future.

Paz himself had no inkling that the prize would go to him until the very last minute. I remember clearly having dinner with him, together with a group of professors and graduate students at Silliman College (one of the colleges that are part of Yale University) the night before the award was announced. Someone—tactlessly, I thought—mentioned the Nobel Prize and asked him what were his chances of winning it. He answered briefly that he did not think he would ever get it, adding that he never thought about the prize any more, then changing the conversation to another subject. I must conclude that either he is an excellent actor, which I doubt, or else he was as much in the dark about the impending announcement as was everybody else in that room.

The obvious fact is that for many years Paz's poetic voice has been a major contribution to world literature, his many-faceted talent a force to be reckoned with on several continents. He comes closer than anyone else I can think of to being the ideal candidate for a distinction such as the Nobel Prize, and the list of the literary awards and honors he has received is a long one: among many others the Jerusalem Prize, the Cervantes Prize, and the Neustadt Prize—this last one considered by many the antechamber of the Nobel Prize, since so many of its recipients, candidates, and jurors have gone on to receive the Swedish Academy's accolade.[3]

Perhaps the first question that we must ask, therefore, is not why Paz has been awarded the prize, but why it has taken so long. This question is essentially fruitless, however, as it can only be answered by an insider, by a member of the Swedish Academy, and these gentlemen seldom talk about their deliberations and the motives that lead them to their choices. Let us ask ourselves instead what is the place in world literature of Paz as a writer, what impact he has had so far, and what we can expect of him in the future.

The core of Paz's output, his compelling vocation, has always been, from the very beginning, poetry. If we want to start with the barest of definitions, one limited to a minimum of words, we have to state that Paz is a Mexican poet. After that we should add: Paz is a great Mexican poet whose poetry transcends the barriers of nationalism and can be effective even outside his language area, since it deals with feelings, intuitions, ideas, and sensations that can be called truly universal. Born in a Mexico that had become, after the turmoil of the 1910 revolution, inward-looking and often suspicious of foreign ideas, Paz has managed to open the windows of Mexican culture to all influences: he is at home in the Orient, in Western Europe, in the United States, not to mention countries such as Spain and Argentina, which are essentially part of his cultural and linguistic area. He is the very opposite of the chauvinistic Mexican intellectual caricatured by Carlos Fuentes who recommended to his friends only Mexican authors, avoiding all foreign influences, for "those who read Proust, proustitute themselves."

Some of the most important titles in Paz's vast production are deeply rooted in the Mexican experience, the Mexican psyche, and Mexican history. A book such as *The Labyrinth of Solitude,* for instance, could not have been written by anyone outside the mainstream of Mexican culture. In it Paz defines values, outlines a collective experience, explores the conscious and unconscious mind of his country. A book as easy to read as it is difficult to classify, *Labyrinth* approaches the Mexican present through insights into the past, carried out with the skills of an anthropologist, a historian, a poet, a visionary: Paz speaks to us with many voices, for he realizes that a difficult subject has to be tackled from many sides. The circular patterns of ancient Mexican culture are present in Paz's long poem *Sun Stone;* the baroque tensions and beauty of colonial Mexico are an integral part of his book on Sor Juana Inés de la Cruz, *The Traps of Faith.* Contemporary Mexico is the subject of innumerable poems by Paz, yet often the conclusions of his books, whether long poems or volumes of essays, allow him to express something that connects Mexican experience and culture to a more general pattern. His exploration of Mexican existential values is illuminating in and by itself and also as a path toward a wider understanding, a more general approach. No real understanding can be achieved when we start with generalities, Paz seems to be saying, and at the same time the concrete experience is properly lived and examined, it can become the transcendent path toward a universal horizon.

Paz is therefore, as I have stated more than once, a poet-philosopher, a philosophical poet.[4] As Anna Balakian points out, he "belongs to the new breed of humans, more numerous each day, who are freeing themselves of ethnic myopia and walking the earth as inhabitants of the planet, regardless of national origin or political preferences."[5]

This polarity, provincial-universal, could be illustrated by a tree, with deep roots in the Mexican soil and branches, flowers, fruits, and leaves spreading out in all directions. Without in any way diminishing Paz's merit, we may point out that there is always an element of luck to every success story. Part of Paz's new poetic vision can be attributed to the fact that he was born at the right time: 1914, a fateful year that saw the beginning of World War I and the dramatic highlight of the Mexican Revolution, with the ragged armies of Villa, Zapata, and Obregón marching toward Mexico City. It was a very good year for the literary and artistic avant-garde: the guns of August in Europe, like Villa's and Zapata's cavalry charges in Mexico, were about to shake to its foundations the establishment that had dominated Western culture during most of the nineteenth century and the first years of the twentieth. The Mexican Revolution plays the same role as World War I in the cultural field: in both cases it cannot be said the upheaval creates a new system of values, and it is possible to find important forerunners of the new avant-garde styles before the beginning of the bloody years; yet the changes in dynasties and political regimes, the rise of minorities to power, and, above all, the failure of the system of values prevalent before 1914 make it possible for the avant-garde to spread inexorably and displace the old styles, the entrenched sensitivities that had been prevalent in many instances since the early nineteenth century. Paz was born in the year when true modernity in literature and the arts began for most of the Western world.

A sense of openness to the world, of old structures crumbling away and affording a glimpse of a wider horizon, is part of Paz's childhood remembrance. Paz has said about himself:

> As a boy I lived in a place called Mixcoac, near the capital. We lived in a large house with a garden. Our family had been impoverished by the revolution and the civil war. Our house, full of antique furniture, books, and other objects, was gradually crumbling to bits. As rooms collapsed we moved the furniture into another. I remember that for a long time I lived in a spacious room with part of one of the walls missing. Some magnificent screens protected me inadequately from wind and rain. A creeper invaded my room. . . . A premonition of that surrealist exhibition where there was a bed lying in a swamp.[6]

If there is a message I see in most of Paz's writings, it is that man is both a wide-eyed receiver of messages reaching him from all directions and a giver of messages and a ruler through his language and his mind. If the German philosopher Ernst Cassirer defined man as the animal who can create language and myths, we can also state that it is language, myths, and poetry that have created man. Man is a speaking, mythmaking, poetry-writing animal. A vast shuttle is at work, back and forth, between our mind, the inner recesses of our minds, and the world around us, including the remote galaxies far beyond our telescopes. Paz knows by instinct what the German philosophers of the romantic era, Fichte, Schelling, Hegel, found out through a lifetime of reasoning, and what in our century Martin Buber has restated: there is no "I" without a "Thou," no individuality without an otherness; we are all a plurality without giving up our individual selves. (*Plural* is the title Paz decreed for the magazine he founded in Mexico after his return from India.) As Paz put it in his acceptance speech at the Neustadt Prize presentation ceremony in 1982:

> In esthetic terms, Plurality is a richness of voices, accents, manners, ideas and visions; in moral terms, Plurality signifies tolerance of diversity, renunciation of dogmatism and recognition of the unique and singular value of each work and every personality. Plurality is Universality, and Universality is the acknowledging of the admirable diversity of man and his works. . . . To acknowledge the variety of visions and sensibilities is to preserve the richness of life and thus to ensure its continuity.[7]

Plurality means also tolerance, acceptance of other viewpoints, freedom to make statements that others may accept or reject. Only in a society committed to freedom and democracy can plurality flourish, and with it our best chance to reach fuller integration with the vast world around us, to influence it and be influenced by it. Language is at the center of a vast movement, language that expresses our mind and expands it, language as a tool that allows us to delve into ourselves and into the world around us, language as a mirror that shows us our own face, language as a shuttle that goes back and forth, weaving reality, weaving the whole world around us, as a vast cocoon, as a cradle that may bring forth other worlds. Being and Becoming are the two sides of the coin, both real, each influencing the other. The shuttle again goes back and forth in Paz's most ambitious philosophical poem, *Blanco*.

The spirit
Is an invention of the body
The body
An invention of the world
The world

An invention of the spirit

Lines pregnant with meaning, part of a long poem that has few parallels in contemporary literature. The shuttle in its huge unstoppable movement, back and forth, creating worlds and erasing them, mixing and blurring what we thought permanent, has become a symbol of our history and our destiny. Hope and fear are intermingled. We are part of history, part of being, also part of the destruction and death of history and of becoming. Everything depends on another aspect of being coming to the rescue, inventing our reality, so that we in turn can invent a reality that will sustain our creator and, by doing so, save ourselves from utter collapse; yet our anguish is not warranted, since as part of the shuttle we are also part of the circle of being and creation—and destruction—part of the never-ending process and, as such, truly immortal.

The preceding paragraph is not necessarily the only reading of Paz's lines; his poem can well be interpreted in other different ways. What I mean by my reading is simply that Paz is a true philosophical poet, that his visions are deep and sustaining, that his gift is a special one, a gift few other poets possess. How many philosophical poets can we find in the traditional Western canon? Dante certainly, also Lucretius, Shakespeare, Quevedo, Calderón, Milton, Donne, T. S. Eliot, and a few others. Not many. Coleridge, Keats, Novalis among them. The hallmark of the philosophical poet is always that he is not alone, even when he thinks he is. He is constantly urged by an inner demon to go forth and explore, to find his place, his role, in the cosmos—not only for himself but for all of us.

Of course Paz is not only a philosophical poet. His voice can be intimate, occasionally ironic. His love poems are erotic and refined. Moreover, the importance of Paz as a literary theoretician and critic has grown constantly during the last decades, and some of his titles (*The Bow and the Lyre* comes to mind) have become indispensable. His public persona is also much in evidence of late, with frequent appearances on Mexican television, his founding and organizing of magazines (*Plural, Vuelta*), and his contribution to newspapers with articles and notes dealing with current events. If we are to compare Paz's total impact with that of other famous poets, we might say that he is as much a philosophical poet as T. S. Eliot was, but he is more intimate, more erotic, warmer than Eliot.[8] We might add that he has become as much of a public poet and writer as Victor Hugo was in the nineteenth century, although Paz's style is less grandiloquent than Hugo's; Paz never overacts.

In any case, Paz's place in the literary canon of our century is secure: I would like to point out in conclusion that occasionally the Nobel Prize calls attention to an unknown writer and may be helpful, for a while, to the writer's influence, whereas at other times, when judiciously given to a deserving writer, it helps restore credibility in the value and importance of the prize itself. The Nobel Prize awarded to Paz belongs to the latter category: since it was so obviously deserved by the recipient, it has helped renew our confidence in the award-giving process, and therefore we should congratulate not only Paz but most especially the members of the jury who made such a wise choice.

Manuel Durán, Winter 1991

[1] On Cela's Nobel, see *WLT* 64:1 (Winter 1990), pp. 5–8.

[2] See William Riggan, "The Swedish Academy and the Nobel Prize in Literature: History and Procedure," *WLT* 55:3 (Summer 1981), pp. 399–405.

[3] In addition to Paz, Czesław Miłosz (Neustadt 1978, Nobel 1980) and Gabriel García Márquez (1972, 1982) have gone on to receive the Nobel after winning the Neustadt Prize. Seven other Neustadt candidates and three jurors also received the Nobel subsequent to their involvement with the Neustadt, and a fourth juror later received the Nobel Peace Prize.

[4] See specifically my article "Octavio Paz: The Poet as Philosopher," *WLT* 56:4 (Autumn 1982), pp. 591–94.

[5] Anna Balakian, "Focus on Octavio Paz and Severo Sarduy," *Review* 72, Fall 1972.

[6] Rita Guibert, "Paz on Himself and His Writing: Selections from an Interview," in *The Perpetual Present: The Poetry and Prose of Octavio Paz*, Ivar Ivask, ed., Norman, University of Oklahoma Press, 1973, p. 25. The book edited by Ivask is still one of the best introductions in English to Paz's works and personality.

[7] Octavio Paz, "Laureate's Words of Acceptance," *WLT* 56:4 (Autumn 1982), p. 596.

[8] For a perceptive account of the relationship between Paz and Eliot, on the one hand, and between Paz and surrealism on the other, see Manuel Ulacia, "Octavio Paz o el árbol milenario," *¡Siempre!,* 7 November 1990, pp. 42–45.

The Return of the Past: Chiasmus in the Texts of Carlos Fuentes

Throughout his career, the texts of Carlos Fuentes have revealed a relentlessly dialectical mode of thought coupled with a strong sense of the return of the past. I would like to investigate here a persistent rhetorical figure in Fuentes's prose that, besides being fascinating in its own right, constitutes a linguistic analogue for both these characteristics of Fuentes's work. This is the device of chiasmus, most simply defined as an A B B A structure of words or ideas in a sentence, a reversal in the order of two otherwise parallel phrases, images or concepts.[1] It is an ancient design; Fuentes's use of it constitutes an example of the presence of the past its structure represents. Pierre Fontanier discusses it very briefly in *Les figures du discours* (The Figures of Discourse), classifying it as a "réversion" (a reversal) and giving several well-known examples: "One must not live [A] to eat [B], but rather eat [B] to live [A]." This is the most basic form, but the number of reversed elements can increase: "It is not places [A] which honor [B] men [C] but rather men [C] who honor [B] places [A]." Fontanier explains that "reversals cause all the words, or at least the most essential ones, in a proposition to turn back on themselves with a different and often a contrary meaning."[2]

Though it does appear in his fiction, this chiastic structure occurs most frequently in Fuentes's essays, and so I will begin with those. There it is most easily recognized in sentences, but as we shall see, it also operates as a recurrent conceptual pattern in the fiction.[3] A few examples from the essays: Young people in Mexico, Fuentes maintains, "ven [A] lo que no quieren [B]; quieren [B] lo que no ven [A]."[4] With regard to Mexico's history, Fuentes says that "no podemos [A] regresar [B] a Quetzalcóatl [C]; Quetzalcóatl [C] tampoco regresará [B] a nosotros [A]. Como Godot, Quetzalcóatl [A] se fue [B] para siempre y sólo regresó [B] disfrazado de conquistador español o de príncipe austriaco [A]" (*TM,* 33). The first triple chiasmus, we-return-Quetzalcóatl/Quetzalcóatl-return-we, is quite clear; the second less so. One needs to generalize the terms to god-travel/travel-god. A particularly striking instance of the pattern is the following pair of chiasmi:

> México [A] impuso a Cortés [B] la máscara de Quetzalcóatl. Cortés [B] la rechazó e impuso a México [A] la máscara de Cristo. Desde entonces es imposible saber a quién se adora en los altares barrocos de Puebla, de Tlaxcala y de Oaxaca. Pero la confusión ha sido superada por la sangre: los indios, acostumbrados a que los hombres [A] muriesen en honor [B] de los dioses [C], se sintieron maravillados y vencidos por un dios [C] que había muerto en honor [B] de los hombres [A]. (*TM,* 22–23)

A humorous example comes from Fuentes's essay on Faulkner. Fuentes maintains that a recurrent theme in the literature of the American South

> ha sido la oposición entre la "inocencia" norteamericana [A] y la "corrupción" europea [B]. (Había que llegar al gabinete de los horrores del Doctor Nabokov para asistir a la inversión de los términos: Humbert Humbert, el europeo [B] inocente, es la víctima de Lolita, la corrupta ninfeta norteamericana [A] cuyo libido se alimenta de popcorn y Coca-Cola.)[5]

Celestina's palindrome at the end of chapter 1 of *Terra Nostra* fits conceptually into this group because of its acrostic design, cutting out a circular pattern within the line of the prose. It reverses the words as if in a mirror: "Este es mi cuento. Deseo que oigas mi cuento. Oigas. Oigas. Sagio. Sagio. Otneuc im sagio euq oesed. Otneuc im se etse."[6] The reversed pattern stands as a linguistic emblem, a sign over the door of the narrative, warning readers who enter there to abandon all hope of traditional linear time.

These conceptual reversals tend to make Fuentes's expository prose opaque; they disrupt the linear arguments that generally characterize political writing. The chiastic design of the text forces the reader to double back on what has been read and consider alternatives. The process suggests a discourse that takes more than one line of thought into account, one that plays with words. This circular design in the line of prose draws attention to language; in some sense it turns us from referent to sign or from story to discourse and back out again before we know it.[7]

Interestingly enough, Hugh Kenner discovers a similar tendency toward chiasmus in Joyce's work and associates it with what he calls (after Douglas Hofstadter's *Gödel, Escher, Bach*) "strange loops."[8] These "loops" are instances when we go from language to thing to language or vice versa; they constitute a character's coming into consciousness of language and out of it again. Kenner takes an example from the beginning of *A Portrait of the Artist as a Young Man,* a chiastic poem which Stephen makes out of something that has been said to him.

Pull out his eyes,
Apologise,
Apologise,
Pull out his eyes.

Apologise,
Pull out his eyes,
Pull out his eyes,
Apologise.

Kenner maintains that Stephen's presence tends to produce chiasmus, presumably because of his growing sensitivity to words as words, a sensitivity revealed also by its presence in Fuentes's essays.

On the most general level, Fuentes's repeated use of this rhetorical pattern, particularly in the essays, indicates a hortatory stance. It forms part of Fuentes the demagogue, the journalist, willing always to coin a catchy phrase.[9] Paradoxically, even though—as I've suggested—the design incorporates reversals of thought, its very symmetry also gives a sense of inevitability to a pronouncement and in many cases combines playfulness with authority.[10]

Fuentes even sees the development of his fiction in chiastic terms, albeit in retrospect: he has said that *"Cruz* es una historia de la muerte de la vida. *Aura* es una historia de la vida de la muerte."[11] Within the fiction, a pervasive structure of reversal related to the

chiastic reversals is the movement from an anchor place or time (A), excursions into various pasts (B) (B), and a return back out to end in the initial space (A). In *La muerte de Artemio Cruz* the "yo" of the dying present begins and ends the story, enclosing the "tú" and the "él" of the past, both more desirable alternatives to itself. In *Cambio de piel* the dusty streets of Cholula enclose the European and American pasts of the three principal figures. Similarly, in *Una familia lejana,* autumnal Paris begins and ends the story of excursions into the pasts of the same two continents.

Zona sagrada contains a continual series of chiastic progressions for Guillermo: the self (A) encounters Claudia (B), is transformed in some way into her (B) and then is returned to a diminished self (A). The chiastic design seems especially appropriate here because the novel centers on two figures and their permutations. The pattern of Guillermo's seemingly inescapable transformations in and out of himself toward his mother is disrupted at the end of the novel by a final, definitive metamorphosis. All of this takes place in a sacred space that allows such transformational reversals, the holy place of reversible time, which exists only as long as the fiction. At one point Guillermo's musings on the palindrome of Rome takes on a chiastic form: "Amor-Roma. ¿Te das cuenta? Roma-Amor. / Y tu nombre regresa a mí."[12] He applies the design to himself and Claudia, signaling his entrapment in an incestuous love.

The structure of the monumental *Terra Nostra* can also be seen as a kind of chiasmus: we begin in Paris in 1999 (A), go on to "The Old World" (B) and then to "The New World," which in some ways is a mirror image of the Old (B), and finally return to the initial scene (A). Within the novel there are many chiastic movements. Of the old La Señora, who finally has her dead husband all to herself, we might say that her love (A) is dead (B) but out of this death (B) love (A) is recreated. Similarly, El Señor is alive (A), yet thinks mainly of death (B), but when he is dying (B), the organic life (A) of his material body takes over (in the form of pus and crawling worms) so that he ends up where he started in spite of himself. The opposite of El Señor's exclusive control and power, articulated also in a chiasmus—this one presumably designed by more benevolent, cosmic forces—is the expression of the earth's power over man rather than the reverse, which is what El Señor attempts to achieve: the ancient in the palm basket explains to the pilgrim that his companion Pedro "quiso adueñarse [A] de la tierra [B]. Pero la tierra [B] es una divinidad y no puede ser poseída [A] por nadie. Es ella que nos posee" (*TN,* 394). Just preceding this, the problematic idea of "discovery" in the New World is expressed in repeated chiasmi—the structure of paradox. When the pilgrim and Pedro encounter natives on the beach, "Nos [A] miraron [B]. Los [B] miramos [A]." And again, in the next paragraph, "Nos miraron. Los miramos. Lo primero que cambiamos fueron miradas. Y de ese trueque nació mi veloz, silente pregunta: "¿Nos [A] descubren ellos [B] . . . o les [B] descubrimos nosotros [A]?" (*TN*, 384). This is followed by looser chiastic structures, as if to signal the perennially puzzling nature of life in both New World and Old. The pilgrim explains that "habiendo aprendido a querer al viejo Pedro, rogaba ahora que no me [A] heredase su destino [B], sino que su muerte [B] me [A] liberase para hallar el mío, así fuese peor que el suyo. Común [A] fue nuestra suerte [B] desde que nos embarcamos juntos. Ahora nuestros destinos [B] se separaban [A] para siempre" (*TN*, 386).

Philippe Ariès traces the development of the cult of tombs as places to be visited where the lives of "loved ones" are preserved beyond death.[13] He claims that the cult of the dead increases as the number of the faithful declines, and he elaborates the thought in a suitably chiastic pattern: "When God [A] is dead [B], the cult of the dead [B] may become the only authentic religion [A]." In the most general sense, Fuentes's novels, with their increasingly intertextual mode, operate in the literary realm like Ariès's Parisian cemeteries. Ariès, by quoting a popular version of Comtian philosophy which argued that since "the tomb develops the sense of continuity within the family and the cemetery the sense of continuity within the city and the human race," points out that the cemetery must be "in the city itself, so as to facilitate the worship of the dead, which is an element of civic life of the utmost importance." The isolated and final, nonprogressive nature of El Señor's Escorial provides the most obvious negative analogue for this attitude. It is a foil, as has often been pointed out, for the text that contains it—a communal literary afterlife where past texts are revived and transformed. In Ariès's chiastic contention that in "secular France in the 19th and early 20th century, the intensity of memory and its constant preservation had created for the dead [A], in the minds of the living [B], a second existence [B], which was less active than, but just as real as, the first [A]," one cannot help thinking of Proustian memory and its continuation in Fuentes's recent novel, *Una familia lejana,* and of Fuentes's notions of parallel lives and second realities.

Una familia lejana establishes what we might regard as an essentially chiastic relationship between Latin America and France. Writers like José María Heredia, Jules Supervielle and others were born in Latin America (A) of French (B) parents, wrote and gained fame in France (B) but are included here primarily because of their Latin American origins (A). More specifically, within the novel, at the beginning, the French setting is infiltrated by the New World; Count Branly has just visited Mexico, and Fuentes—a Mexican—sits talking to him in his club overlooking the Place de la Concorde. Throughout the novel we see instances of the New World infiltrated by French culture: the French cultural center in Mexico City, the Frenchwoman Lucie's marriage to Hugo Heredia. At the end of the novel, in unseasonably warm weather when Fuentes enters the pool area of Branly's club, the French atmosphere seems to have been taken over by a tropical American rain forest.

> . . . crecen las plantas entretejidas, revueltas, los árboles de tronco oloroso cubiertos de hiedras y lianas que suben por las pilastras de mosaico verde hacia la gran bóveda de fierro y cristal ciego, tapado por la espesa trabazón de los follajes. Las flores huelen fuertes, envenenadas, hambrientas. Árboles de pólvora: los había olvidado y ahora su olor me recuerda las cortezas que sirvieron para fabricar las municiones de Indias.[14]

Again, French atmosphere infiltrated by the New World.

As the story draws to a close, a cluster of chiastic designs reinforces the configuration of two entities crossing over, which stands behind the idea of parallel lives that Fuentes develops as he confronts Lucie Heredia—or her ghost—setting up her candelabra in the dying Branly's house.

> ¿tenemos todos un fantasma que nos acompaña a lo largo de nuestra vida sin que jamás lo veamos? ¿es nuestra muerte [A] la condición para que nuestro fantasma [B] encarne? ¿quién [B], entonces, va a acompañarnos en nuestra muerte [A]? ¿el fantasma de nuestra vida, el único que nos recuerda verdaderamente? (*FL*, 208)

Fuentes keeps on thinking about Branly and Lucie Heredia.

> Si en algún lado estaba la realidad de la mujer [A] eternamente inconclusa que caminó sin gravedad por todos los senderos mágicos del Parc Monceau era en el rostro de cera, en las manos pálidas, en la mirada inteligente del hombre [B] que debió ignorar la muerte de la mujer para recibir su presencia espectral. Branly [B]: sólo en él resucitaban todos los tiempos de la mujer [A] de Hugo Heredia que fue la novia de los parques infantiles de mi amigo. (*FL*, 208)

He decides that "no es una hipótesis; Lucie [A] va a vivir [B] apenas muera [B] mi amigo Branly [A]" (*FL*, 209). While person A lives, person B is a ghostly presence; then person B installs herself and comes alive as A dies. Fuentes leaves Branly (A) dying in one room, passes into "the neighboring room" ("la chambre voisine" of Supervielle), sees increasingly clearly the ghostly figure of Madame Heredia (B) with her candelabra coming more and more alive (B), then thinks about Branly (A) and wishes to return to his room. On his way to Branly's club he asks himself, "¿Fui yo [A] el amigo que le faltó, por haberme quedado a vivir en la Argentina, a Hugo Heredia [B]? ¿Fue él [B] el amigo que yo [A] no tuve en la numerosa soledad porteña de mi juventud?" (FL, 212). Earlier, Branly explains how he has intervened in Hugo Heredia's temporal games to achieve a compensatory chiastic design: "Hugo Heredia [A] quiso condenar [B] a su hijo al pasado. Yo me he encargado, al contarle a usted la historia que debió permanecer oculta, de condenar [B] a Hugo Heredia [A]" (FL, 194). And finally, Fuentes's own ghost whispers to him in typically chiastic fashion, "Heredia [A]. Tú [B] eres [B] Heredia [A]" (FL, 214).

When questioned about this chiastic pattern in his work, Fuentes himself pointed out that it resembles a mirror—a self-reflexive space, we might add.[15] This is a fascinating idea, when we contemplate it in the context of Fuentes's use of mirrors in his fiction. His mirrors are generally not like masks, though characters like Artemio Cruz or Claudia (in Zona sagrada) or Elizabeth (in Cambio de piel) may wish they were. A mirror is often terrifying because it returns a character to himself, to a presence that he may have wished to forget or to go beyond. Artemio Cruz's reflections at the beginning and the end of his book remind him that he is old, not immortal; they show a single, aged, physical self, not the numerous possible selves of the imagination. Like the circular chiastic pauses in the prose of the essays, mirrors in La muerte de Artemio Cruz provide moments of reflection in a life of action. In Terra Nostra the ancient New World sage in the palm basket dies of terror when he views himself in a mirror. The chiastic nature of these returns to the self via mirrors is perhaps clearest near the end of Zona sagrada: Guillermo (A) dresses up in Claudia's (B) clothes, sees his reflection as Claudia (B) in her mirror but then finally stumbles and falls, tearing the clothes, rediscovering himself (A). During this scene, Guillermo thinks that "ella [A] me [B] permite verme [B] como ella [A]" (ZS, 186).

Most significantly, perhaps, these linguistic mirrors of chiasmus are miniature examples of making the past present. This space that Fuentes cuts out of linear prose works against the linear time of progress he claims has been superimposed on indigenous time in Mexico.[16] In doubling back on itself to end where it began, this progress suggests a continuous series of cyclical transformations. The chiastic reversals quoted above describing the repeated patterns of conquest and sacrifice in Mexi-

co, like the persistence of myth in Fuentes's works as a whole, reveal yet again his concern with a return of the past. They are one of the tricks of history: their sense of inevitable progression and return reminds you that what you thought you controlled controls you. Your plans for the future turn out to duplicate the past. Ancient sacrifice persists through history and resurfaces as modern repression. In this example from Fuentes's essay "De Quetzalcóatl a Pepsicóatl," Spain is the victim of the chiastic progression: "La suprema paradoja de la colonización española es que fuimos colonizados [A] por un país [B] que pronto se convirtió en país [B] colonizado [A] por las potencias mercantiles del norte de Europa" (TM, 30).

For the most part, the chiastic design is a frightening one and suggests an ominous return of the past or of the self. In this sense the chiasmus represents a "mythic" pattern in the most general way; it returns us momentarily to a kind of textual illo tempore, abolishing linear progression. This is the aspect of the design that structures Aura. That story seems to represent an exception to the many frightening returns of the past—depending, of course, on whose point of view we adopt. Consuelo achieves her desired return of the past; she progresses, in chiastic terms, from Consuelo to Aura and then from Aura to Consuelo. For Felipe, on the other hand, until the very end, when he too seems to be transformed, the experience is disturbing, so that the frightening aspects of the pattern are by no means entirely submerged.

If we wish to consider Aura as a chiastic design, there is also the problem of where to start the series: with Consuelo young? Consuelo old? And whom to include in it: Consuelo alone or Consuelo and the General—and Felipe as well? and Aura? Since the terms of the progression change, it is difficult to constitute a single pattern. Even so, several rough formulations of events incorporate our uncanny sense of a return to the past that conforms to the chiastic design. The youth (A) of Felipe and Aura confronts the age (B) of Consuelo; Aura ages (B), and then all participate in the project of mutual rejuvenation (A). With regard to Felipe and Aura, Felipe (A) imagines he will save Aura (B), when it is Aura (B) who saves him (A); and Felipe (A) intends to take Aura (B) out of Consuelo's house, when in fact Aura (B) draws Felipe (A) inside. Perhaps the most essential design is the following one, which encompasses the broadest time scheme: Consuelo and the General as young lovers (A); Consuelo alone when the General has died (B); Consuelo alone, but having conjured Aura (B); and finally, Consuelo and Felipe-as-the-General rejuvenated (A). Here we have a double chiasmus: young-old/old-young and together-apart/apart-together.

Within the narrative discourse, several smaller chiastic progressions reinforce these larger conceptual reversals. In the description of Aura's eyes—which present us with a landscape of youth—we move from Felipe to the green eyes, mentioned twice, then back to Felipe, who has now decided to remain in the house on Donceles Street: "Tú los ves y te repites que no es cierto, que son unos hermosos ojos verdes idénticos a todos los hermosos ojos verdes que has conocido o podrás conocer. Sin embargo, no te engañas: esos ojos fluyen, se transforman, como si te ofrecieran un paisaje que sólo tú puedes adivinar y desear."[17] At the center of the novel, a group of chiastic designs describes the interactions of Felipe and the two women.

> Miras rápidamente de la tía [A] a la sobrina [B] y de la sobrina [B] a la tía [A], pero la señora Consuelo [A], en ese instante, detiene todo movimiento y, al mismo tiempo, Aura [B] deja el cuchillo sobre el plato y permanece inmóvil [B] y tú recuerdas que, una fracción de segundo antes, la señora Consuelo [A] hizo lo mismo. (A, 35)

And again:

> Te preguntas si la señora [A] no poseerá una fuerza secreta sobre la muchacha [B], si la muchacha [B], tu hermosa Aura vestida de verde, no estará encerrada contra su voluntad en esta casa vieja [A], sombría. . . . Recuerdas a Aura [A] minutos antes, inanimada, embrutecida por el terror: incapaz de hablar enfrente de la tirana [B], moviendo los labios en silencio, como si en silencio te implorara su libertad, prisionera al grado de imitar todos los movimientos de la señora Consuelo, como si sólo lo que hiciera la vieja [B] le fuese permitido a la joven [A]. (A, 36)

These are of course premonitions of the final conflation, representing the return of the past and also magically tightening the circle around all three figures, suggesting Felipe's hidden emotional involvement in the plan. The fictional magic of love in Aura, the desired return of the past, contrasts with the implacable reality of history, the unexpected—and often undesired—return of the past.

As one contemplates the chiastic designs within Fuentes's texts, two problems arise, both of them concerning the tendency of the chiasmi to mediate between two opposing concepts. The first problem is whether chiasmus is an open or a closed form. The passage from A to B represents an opening up to possible change, but then the remaining elements return it to the original point. The question centers on whether the original point is desirable and also on whether it is transformed. In a sense, still thinking of Aura, Felipe-as-the-General is rather like the little doll whose potent sawdust trick-

les out to achieve a transforming effect yet which retains its ritual shape—both an open and a closed form.[18]

The other problem concerns volition. What force achieves the turnaround, the mysterious shift in direction that seems to occur between the two B's in the chiasmus?[19] As we have seen, often the human figures appear to be caught in the design, a design conjured by forces beyond their control. Magic enters Fuentes's work in two distinct yet related capacities: to underline extreme psychological power and to suggest the presence of ancient cosmic forces. (Compare the final magical transformations in Aura and Zona sagrada with the events in La región más transparente and Cambio de piel.) Both kinds of forces reach beyond ordinary human capacities and are frequently combined—hence the compelling power of magical realism's most compelling images. In the chiasmic design we sense both these compulsions, forces both within and beyond normal human powers. Again, the formality of the pattern—a recognizably human, an ancient rhetorical construct—contrasts with its frequent implications of the triumph of an implacable time over human will.

Out of this latter notion comes the desire to rewrite history, to restructure it rhetorically, a desire which stands behind Fuentes's essayistic chiasmi as well. Those designs then represent a delicate combination of human volition and historical coercion. This insertion of poetic form in historical discourse, as well as the notion of return of the past, necessitates a brief consideration of Fuentes's relationship to Vico.

The connection between the chiastic tendency in Fuentes's work and the theories of Vico is problematical. Two issues are at stake. First, the famous ricorsi—or the returns of the past—take a more consistently utopian form in Vico than in Fuentes. Vico does in many cases posit a return to the forms of the past.[20] But as A. Robert Caponigri maintains, he also proposes a complex incorporation of past into present. Caponigri's description of Vico's vision might well apply to Fuentes's ideas for reform: "The effort which can send a nation back upon its origins to grasp anew, in idea, the principles of its own spontaneous life and power is the greatest spiritual effort a nation can make. It is criticism in its purest, that is, its most concrete and historical form." In sum, for Caponigri, the ricorso, like a chiasmus, is "an advance which is yet a return upon itself."[21] In Fuentes's fictions—and his essays—this would be the ideal, usually unrealized in Mexico: to build on the past rather than being engulfed by it. The A B B A structure, while it can imply Vico's pattern, seems to me to project a harsher, a more fatalistic design. In the second place, as Hayden White has pointed out, perhaps Vico's most original contribution is to correlate modes of linguistic competence with stages of history, a project which motivates Fuentes's equations of hierarchical forms of government and of writing in his essays and in *Terra Nostra*.[22]

With regard to the chiastic return of the past, as is often the case, Fuentes's ideas parallel closely those of Octavio Paz. In an essay defining "El tiempo de Octavio Paz," Fuentes postulates a poetic present, a moment which recalls a past and envisions a future that repeats the past. It is as if that poetic present were at the center of a chiastic design (between the two B's). He has encountered a peasant who calls his town by one name in times of peace and by another in times of war. According to Fuentes, the man knew that there was "otro tiempo" and that "podía aspirarse, simultáneamente, a un tiempo lejano, el del origen, el del ser primero; y también a un tiempo futuro que, de manera cierta, sería el cumplimiento de aquél. Encuentro y transfiguración de la edad rememorada y de la edad deseada" (*CDP,* 152). Fuentes goes on to distinguish Paz's sense of the temporal play of civilizations from the linear systems of Toynbee or Spengler, claiming that Paz's formulations resemble the circle, spiral and permanent present of Lévi-Strauss's mythologies.

It seems to me that in this essay, as occasionally elsewhere in his work, Fuentes's attraction to the chiastic design of his discourse almost overshadows its subject. (This is one reason why I believe the design itself is important conceptually in his texts, beyond the particular ideas it may express at a given moment.) After his observations on Toynbee and Spengler versus Paz and Lévi-Strauss, Fuentes adds: "las civilizaciones como obra del lenguaje; el lenguaje como obra de las civilizaciones." Chiasmus certainly, but puzzling. One finds it difficult to extract more than a general sense of the interplay between language and action. Similarly, after agreeing with Paz that we are contemporaries of all men, he says that "para decirnos [A], debemos decir al mundo [B]; y el mundo [B], para decirse, debe decirnos [A]" (*CDP,* 157). In a final—and confusing—flourish, it becomes apparent that the chiastic design does indeed reflect Fuentes's and Paz's ideas about cyclical time. In Paz's writings, Fuentes says,

> el mundo [A] de la palabra [B] de Blake engendra la palabra [B] del mundo [A] de Mallarmé. Los signos están en rotación. La historia de los hombres es una sola. La sostiene, padece y goza, una pareja primigenia y última, la persona amada y natural que es principio y solución del mundo. (*CDP,* 157)

The rotation of signs in the chiastic structures of reversal posits their dependence on position, affirms a linguistic relativism, implicitly questioning any simple kind of semiotic system, any automatic correlation of sign and referent. Appropriately enough, in his essay on "Los signos en rotación" Paz himself describes literary ideals in chiastic form.

> Una poesía sin sociedad sería un poema sin autor, sin lector, y, en rigor, sin palabras. . . . Los dos términos buscan una conversión mutua: poetizar [A] la vida social [B], socializar [B] la palabra poética [A]. Transformación de la sociedad [A] en comunidad creadora, en poema vivo [B]; y del poema [B] en vida social [A], en imagen encarnada.[23]

A mutual conversion, an interpenetration of two entities that modify without abolishing each other. In similar fashion, Paz's description of André Breton, one of his own masters in poetic form, typically yokes poetry and passion in chiastic form to suggest the magical power of language: "Para [Breton] los poderes de la palabra [A] no eran distintos a los de la pasión [B] y ésta [B], en su forma más alta y tensa, no era sino lenguaje [A] en estado de pureza salvaje: poesía. Breton: el lenguaje de la pasión—la pasión del lenguaje."[24]

I have suggested that in the domain of story, chiasmus can be seen to represent the implacable return of the past, of cyclical time, but that it can also suggest—in the domain of discourse—a desire for control over this mythical time, a harnessing of its strength. In this context it is interesting to consider Paz's discussion of "Revuelta, revolución, rebelión" in his *Corriente alterna*. Paz explains that all the meanings of the Spanish word *revuelta* "están regidos por la idea de regreso asociada a la de desorden y desarreglo" (*CA,* 147). As we have seen, the formality of a chiastic design might attempt to channel this chaotic kind of recurrence, to achieve a more orderly, more benevolent *ricorso,* the imposition of linguistic order on historical chaos. Paz believes that the popular term *revuelta* was replaced by *revolución,* which had philosophical prestige: "En revolución las ideas de regreso y movimiento se funden en la de orden; en revuelta esas mismas ideas denotan desorden" (*CA,* 148). According to him, both the reformist and the revolutionary "son intelectuales, los dos creen en el progreso, los dos rechazan el mito: su creencia en la razón es inquebrantable" (*CA,* 151). But for Paz, the word *revolución* has changed in modern times. Originally, *revolution* was a word that implied

> la idea del tiempo cíclico y, en consecuencia, la de regularidad y repetición de los cambios. Pero la acepción moderna no designa la vuelta eterna. . . . El tiempo cíclico se rompe y un nuevo tiempo comienza, rectilíneo. . . . La segunda acepción postula la primacía del futuro: el campo de gravitación de la palabra de desplaza del ayer conocido al mañana por conocer. . . . El tiempo

cristiano era finito: comenzaba en la Caída y terminaba en la Eternidad, al otro día del Juicio Final. El tiempo moderno, revolucionario o reformista, rectilíneo o en espiral, es infinito. (CA, 152)

Paz claims that now the rebel, like the poet, absorbs the old meanings of both *revuelta* and *revolución;* he incarnates spontaneous protest against power and the notion of cyclical time. His action "no se inscribe en el tiempo rectilíneo de la historia, dominio del revolucionario y del reformista, sino en el tiempo circular del mito: Jupiter será destronado, volverá Quetzalcóatl, Luzbel regresará al cielo" (CA, 152). In this scheme the closure of the chiastic pattern would seem to belong to the earlier kind of *revolución,* the one that affirms cyclical time, mythic time. Thus again here, as it can be seen to represent both an orderly project and an inevitable process, chiastic designs underline the double imperative behind Fuentes's texts: the vision of social reform and the vision of implacable forces, where the time of history is temporarily usurped by the time of myth, the time of poetry.[25]

As suggested earlier, the tradition of chiasmus reaches far back in time, and in Mexico, for example, Sor Juana provides Fuentes with a distinguished precursor in its use. There seems to be a change since the seventeenth century, though. In the religious and courtly poetry of Sor Juana, chiasmus reflects the paradoxes of religious or amorous ecstasy from inside; the mind is churned about from within. In Fuentes's prose we sense a more cerebral anguish at the imposition of a pattern from the outside. The mind is rolled around by history and responds by duplicating the pattern. The disquieting reversal of chiasmus may achieve its ultimate—though indirect—effect on the reader by suggesting the Borgesian inversion of reader and read as we experience it in such texts as "Las ruinas circulares" or "Magias parciales del *Quijote.*"

¿Por qué nos inquieta que el mapa esté incluido en el mapa y las mil y una noches en el libro de *Las Mil y Una Noches?* ¿Por qué nos inquieta que Don Quixote sea lector del *Quijote,* y Hamlet, espectador de *Hamlet?* Creo haber dado con la causa: tales inversiones sugieren que si los caracteres de una ficción [A] pueden ser lectores [B] o espectadores, nosotros, sus lectores [B] o espectadores, podemos ser ficticios [A]."[26]

Paz maintains that the idea of modernity itself is an exclusively Western idea, based on the medieval Christian concept of irreversible linear time. This he of course contrasts with the cyclical time of the Greeks, the Chinese and the Aztecs.[27] In this context, Fuentes's chiastic designs may represent an attempt to get beyond the modernity that contains him. Chiasmus is a rhetorical structure that yearns for the cyclical time of myth to conquer the linear time of history. Ancient and postmodern conquer modernity. Furthermore, as already suggested, the mixture of this ancient design with contemporary slang achieves yet another kind of return of the past in the linguistic texture of the present, perhaps even conflating the sacred and the profane.[28] Fuentes once claimed that chiasmi were a frequent ingredient in Mexican political rhetoric.[29] I have not been able to verify that, but in any case, his use of the form constitutes a fruitful contamination of private by public discourse.

Finally, the chiastic temporal pattern corresponds also to the political desires of both Paz and Fuentes—and Zapata—for an eventual fulfillment of the utopian dreams of community with which the New World began.[30] This would provide an agrarian happy ending for the chiastic progression of Mexican history, which has gone from pre-Conquest communal lands (A) to the large haciendas of the colony (B), essentially repeated in the same structures of ownership after independence (B), to the desired result of the revolution (A)—accomplished or subverted and thus not yet arrived, depending on who is speaking to whom. More fancifully, perhaps the structure of chiasmus works something like the windows of dream through which Fuentes claims Milan Kundera asks the reader to enter his houses of fiction.[31] We feel as if we might be situated inside one of their panes of glass, looking in and out at once, backward and forward, toward the worlds of the first and the second realities that Fuentes portrays in his fiction.

Wendy B. Faris, Autumn 1983

[1] According to the *Princeton Encyclopedia of Poetics, chiasmus* is technically a figure where each of two subordinate clauses in a sentence could modify each of two main clauses, so that the elements might be switched around. *Antimetabole* is defined as a similar figure where two words of an early part of a sentence are repeated in reverse order later on. Richard Lanham, in his *Handlist of Rhetorical Terms,* gives *antimetabole* as a synonym for *chiasmus* and gives a pattern of A B B A in verse as an example. The essential feature I am concerned with is not the original interchangeability of the parts of a sentence but rather the repetition in reverse order, so that comes last. In his recent introduction to a volume of essays entitled *Chiasmus in Antiquity* (Hildesheim, Gerstenberg, 1981, p. 9), John W. Welch defines *chiasmus* as "inverted parallelism."

[2] Pierre Fontanier, *Les figures du discours,* Gérard Genette, intro., Paris, Flammarion, 1968, pp. 381–82. Translations from this work are my own.

[3] Needless to say, as Welch recognizes in discussing ancient texts, the detection and analysis of these larger and modified chiastic forms is more complex and controversial than in the case of smaller and more easily classified forms.

[4] Carlos Fuentes, *Tiempo mexicano,* Mexico City, Mortiz, 1971, p. 149; subsequent references use the abbreviation *TM.*

5 Carlos Fuentes, *Casa con dos puertas*, Mexico City, Mortiz, 1970, p. 64; subsequent references use the abbreviation *CDP*.

6 Carlos Fuentes, *Terra Nostra*, Mexico City, Mortiz, 1975, p. 35; subsequent references use the abbreviation *TN*. José Miguel Oviedo considers the sentence central. For him it suggests the mobility of events, their rapid transformations into others often opposite to themselves; see "Sinfonía del nuevo mundo," *Hispamérica* 6:16 (1977), p. 27.

7 The focalization of the process is necessarily difficult to separate out, since it generally operates more in an interlinguistic rather than in an intersubjective context. It is a speech habit of the text itself rather than of one character within it.

8 Hugh Kenner made these points in an address to the New Mexico James Joyce Symposium in Albuquerque, June 1981.

9 In his discussion of chiasmus in antiquity, Welch points out that the "inherent mnemonic capacities" of the design served the needs of an oral tradition; it was suited to use in ritual settings, perhaps even facilitating alternate recitation in Jewish worship p. 12.

10 William Wimsatt recognizes this tendency with regard to chiastic rhymes: in a chiastic design, "the meaning is locked in a pattern of inevitability"; see *The Verbal Icon: Studies in the Meaning of Poetry*, Lexington, University of Kentucky Press, 1954, p. 162.

11 Fuentes in James R. Fortson, *Perspectivas mexicanas desde París: Un diálogo con Carlos Fuentes*, Mexico City, Corporación Editorial, 1973, supplement to *El*, p. 14.

12 Carlos Fuentes, *Zona sagrada*, Mexico City, Siglo XXI, 1979, p. 65; subsequent references use the abbreviation *ZS*.

13 Philippe Ariès, *The Hour of Our Death*, Helen Weaver, tr., New York, Knopf, 1981, pp. 541–43.

14 Carlos Fuentes, *Una familia lejana*, Mexico City, Era, 1980, p. 213; subsequent references use the abbreviation *FL*.

15 Fuentes made this point in an interview with me in September 1980.

16 See Fuentes's discussion in "De Quetzalcóatl a Pepsicóatl," in *Tiempo mexicano*, pp. 17–42.

17 Carlos Fuentes, *Aura*, Mexico City, Era, 1962, p. 20; subsequent references use the abbreviation *A*.

18 Fuentes expressed this tension between origin or progression in fiction as he discussed the puzzling image of the twin fetuses at the end of *Una familia lejana*: "Once Victor and André have been reunited they go back to the origin;. . . the origin is sperm. But death is the price of recovering this image of unity. The origin is death. . . . There is a tension there, between the perfection of death at the origin, the unity, and the narration, which wants to go forward and tell its story" (from the interview with me in September 1980).

19 In his discussion of chiasmus in the New Testament, Nils W. Lund notes that "at the centre of a chiasmus there is often a change in the trend of thought, and an antithetic idea is introduced. After this, the original trend is resumed and continued until the system is concluded." He designates this feature "the law of the shift at the centre" and believes that in such structures "the centre was regarded as a turning point"; see *Chiasmus in the New Testament*, Chapel Hill, University of North Carolina Press, 1942, p. 41.

20 "In countless passages scattered throughout this work and dealing with countless matters we have observed the marvelous correspondence between the first and the returned barbarian times. From these passages we can easily understand the recourse of human institutions which the nations take when they arise again"; *The New Science of Giambattista Vico,* rev. tr. of 3rd ed., Thomas G. Bergin and Max H. Fisch, eds. & trs., Ithaca, N.Y., Cornell University Press, 1968, p. 397.

21 A. Robert Caponigri, *Time and Idea: The Theory of History in Giambattista Vico*, London, Routledge & Kegan Paul, 1953, pp. 133–36. I am indebted to Lois Parkinson Zamora of the University of Houston for pointing out to me the application of Caponigri's ideas on Vico to Fuentes's texts.

22 See Hayden White, "The Tropics of History: The Deep Structure of the *New Science*," in his *Tropics of Discourse: Essays in Cultural Criticism*, Baltimore, Johns Hopkins University Press, 1978, pp. 197–217.

23 Octavio Paz, *El arco y la lira*, Mexico City, Fondo de Cultura Económica, 1956, p. 254.

24 Octavio Paz, *Corriente alterna*, Mexico City, Siglo XXI, 1967, p. 53; subsequent references use the abbreviation *CA*.

25 For a good discussion by Fuentes of his position "equidistant between Mallarmé and Joseph Stalin," see "An Interview with Carlos Fuentes" by Herman P. Doezma, *Modern Fiction Studies,* 18:4 (Winter 1972–73), pp. 491–503.

26 Jorge Luis Borges, *Otras inquisiciones*, Buenos Aires, Emecé, 1960, pp. 68–69.

27 Octavio Paz, "La revuelta del futuro," *Los hijos del limo*, Barcelona, Seix Barral, 1974, p. 44.

28 That chiasmus has long been a sacred form is well established by Lund. Many of the chiasmi he studies have numerous terms (i.e., A B C D E F F E D C B A). Indeed, he sees this as a distinguishing feature of the scriptures. He posits the origin of chiasmus as a Hebrew influence on the Greek text of the New Testament. Welch has subsequently shown that the complexity of chiasmus diminishes in later Latin and Greek writers, "setting the style for most Western writing ever since"; see *Chiasmus in Antiquity,* p. 250.

29 Fuentes made this suggestion in conversation with me in August 1982.

30 According to Fuentes, America was discovered and invented as a utopia; that was immediately denied by the concrete necessities of history, and the land was forced to enter the epic mode under whose sign it has lived during most of its existence. The only way out of this worn-out epic mode is a mythic possibility of reactivating the past and reducing it to human proportions; see Fuentes in Emir Rodríguez Monegal, *El arte de narrar: Diálogos*, Caracas, Monte Ávila, 1969, p. 133.

31 See Carlos Fuentes, "El otro K," *Vuelta,* 28 (March 1979), p. 24.

On Reading and Writing Myself: How I Wrote *Aura*

To my immortal friend, Lillian Hellman

One, yes, One Girl, twenty years of age, in the summer of '61, over twenty-two years ago, crossed the threshold between the small drawing room of an apartment on the Boulevard Raspail and entered the bedroom where I was waiting for her.

Carlos Fuentes *(Gil Jain)*

There was a rumor of discontent and a smell of explosives in the French capital. These were the years when De Gaulle was finding a way out from Algeria and the OAS, the Secret Army Organization, was indiscriminately blowing up Jean-Paul Sartre and his concierge: the bombs of the generals were egalitarian.

But Paris is a double city; whatever happens there possesses a mirage which seems to reproduce the space of actuality. We soon learn that this is a form of deceit. The abundant mirrors of Parisian interiors do more than simply reproduce a certain space. Gabriel García Márquez says that with their army of mirrors the Parisians create the illusion that their narrow apartments are double their real size. The true mystery—Gabriel and I know this—is that what we see reflected in those mirrors is always *another* time, time past, time yet to be. And that, sometimes, if you are lucky, a person who is *another* person also floats across these quicksilver lakes.

I believe that the mirrors of Paris contain something more than their own illusion. They are, at the same time, the reflection of something less tangible: the light of the city, a light I have attempted to describe many times, in political chronicles of the events of May 1968 and of May 1981 and in novels such as *Distant Re-*

lations, where I say that the light of Paris is identical to "the expectation that every afternoon . . . for one miraculous moment, the phenomena of the day—rain or fog, scorching heat or snow—[will] disperse and reveal, as in a Corot landscape, the luminous essence of the Île de France."

A second space: A second person—the other person—in the mirror is not born *in* the mirror: she comes from the light. The girl who wandered in from her living room into her bedroom that hot afternoon in early September more than twenty years ago was another *because* six years had gone by since I first met her, in the budding grove of her puberty, in Mexico.

But she was also another because the light that afternoon, as if it had been expecting her, defeated a stubborn reef of clouds. That light—I remember it—first stepped through timidly, as if stealing by the menace of a summer's storm; then it transformed itself into a luminous pearl encased in a shell of clouds; finally it spilled over for a few seconds with a plenitude that was also an agony.

In this almost instantaneous succession, the girl I remembered when she was fourteen years old and who was now twenty suffered the same changes as the light coming through the windowpanes: that threshold between the parlor and the bedroom became the lintel between all the ages of this girl: the light that had been struggling against the clouds also fought against her flesh, took it, sketched it, granted her a shadow of years, sculpted a death in her eyes, tore the smile from her lips, waned through her hair with the floating melancholy of madness.

She was another, she had been another, not she who was going to be but she who, always, was being.

The light possessed the girl, the light made love to the girl before I could, and I was only, that afternoon, "a strange guest in the kingdom of love" ("en el reino del amor huésped extraño"), and knew that the eyes of love can also see us with—once more I quote Quevedo—"a beautiful Death."

The next morning I started writing *Aura* in a café near my hotel on the rue de Berri. I remember the day: Khrushchev had just read his twenty-year plan in Moscow, where he promised communism and the withering away of the state by the '80s—here we are now—burying the West in the process, and his words were reproduced in all their gray minuteness in the *International Herald Tribune* which was being hawked by ghostly girls, young lovers jailed in brief prisons of passion, the authors of *Aura*: the dead girls.

Two, yes, Two Years Before I was having a few drinks with Luis Buñuel in his house on the Street of

Providence, and we talked about Quevedo, a poet the Spanish film director knows better than most academic specialists on baroque poetry of the seventeenth century.

You have already noticed, of course, that the true author of *Aura* (including the dead girls I have just mentioned) is named Francisco de Quevedo y Villegas, born on 17 September 1580 in Madrid and supposedly deceased on 8 September 1645 in Villanueva de los Infantes; the satirical and scatological brother of Swift, but also the unrivaled poet of our death and love, our Shakespeare, our John Donne, the furious enemy of Góngora, the political agent for the Duke of Osuna, the unfortunate, jailed partisan of fallen power, the obscene, the sublime Quevedo dead in his stoical tower, dreaming, laughing, searching, finding some of the truly immortal lines in the Spanish language:

Oh condición mortal Oh dura suerte
Que no puedo querer vivir mañana
Sin la pensión de procurar mi muerte.

(Oh mortal state Oh man's unyielding fate
To live tomorrow I can have no hope
Without the cost of buying my own death.

Or maybe these lines, defining love:

Es yelo abrasador, es fuego helado,
es herida que duele y no se siente,
es un soñado bien, un mal presente,
es un breve descanso muy cansado.

(It is a freezing fire, a burning ice,
it is a wound that hurts yet is not felt,
a happiness desired, a present evil,
a short but oh so tiring rest.)

Yes, the true author of *Aura* is Quevedo, and I am pleased to represent him here today.

This is the great advantage of time: the so-called "author" ceases to be such; he becomes an invisible agent for him who signed the book, published it and collected (and goes on collecting) the royalties. But the book was written—it always was, it always is—by others. Quevedo and a girl who was almost dust in love, *polvo enamorado.* Buñuel and an afternoon in Mexico City, so different from an afternoon in Paris but so different also, in 1959, from the afternoons in Mexico City today.

You could see the two volcanoes, Popocatépetl the smoking mountain and Iztaccíhuatl the sleeping lady as you drove down Insurgentes Avenue, and the big department store had not yet been erected on the corner of Buñuel's house. Buñuel himself, behind a minimonastery of very high brick walls crowned by crushed glass,

had returned to the Mexican cinema with *Nazarín* and was now playing around in his head with an old idea: a filmic transposition of Gericault's painting *Le radeau de la Méduse,* which hangs at the Louvre and describes the drama of the survivors of a naval disaster in the eighteenth century.

The survivors of the good ship *Medusa* at first tried to behave like civilized human beings as they floated around in their raft. But then, as the days went by, followed by weeks, finally by what seemed like an eternity, their imprisonment on the sea cracked the varnish of good manners and they became salt first, then waves, finally sharks: in the end they survived only because they devoured each other. They needed one another to exterminate one another.

Of course, the cinematic translation of the terrible gaze of the Medusa is called *The Exterminating Angel,* one of Buñuel's most beautiful films, in which a group of society people who have never truly needed anything find themselves mysteriously incapable of leaving an elegant salon. The threshold of the salon becomes an abyss and necessity becomes extermination: the shipwrecks of Providence Street only need each other to devour each other.

The theme of necessity is profound and persistent in Buñuel, and his films repeatedly reveal the way in which a man and a woman, a child and a madman, a saint and a sinner, a criminal and a dreamer, a solitude and a desire need one another.

Buñuel was inventing his film *The Exterminating Angel* and crossing back and forth, as he did so, over the threshold between the lobby and the bar of his house, looking for all the world like a pensioned picador from old Cagancho's cuadrilla. Buñuel's comings and goings were, somehow, a form of immobility.

A todas partes que me vuelvo veo
Las amenazas de la llama ardiente
Y en cualquier lugar tengo presente
Tormento esquivo y burlador deseo.

(Everywhere I turn I see
The menace of the burning flame
And everywhere I am aware
Of aloof torment and mocking desire.)

Since we had been talking about Quevedo and a portrait of the young Buñuel by Dalí in the '20s was staring at us, Éluard's poetic formula imposed itself on my spirit that faraway Mexican afternoon of transparent air and smell of burnt tortilla and newly sliced chiles and fugitive flowers: "Poetry shall be reciprocal"; and if Buñuel was thinking of Géricault and Quevedo and the film, I was thinking that the raft of the *Medusa* already contained two eyes of stone that would trap the characters of *The Exterminating Angel* not only in the fiction of a shadow projected on the screen, but within the physical and mechanical reality of the camera that would, from then on, be the true prison of the shipwrecks of Providence: a camera (why not?) on top of Lautréamont's poetical meeting of an umbrella and a sewing machine on a dissecting table.

Buñuel stopped midway between lobby and bar and asked aloud: "And if on crossing a doorsill we could instantly recover our youth; if we could be old on *one* side of the door and young as soon as we crossed to the *other* side, what then . . . ?"

Three, yes Three Days After that afternoon on the Boulevard Raspail I went to see a picture that all my friends, but especially Julio Cortázar, were raving about: *Ugetsu Monogatari: The Tales of the Pale Moon After the Rain,* by the Japanese filmmaker Kenji Mizoguchi. I was carrying around with me the first feverish pages of *Aura,* written in that café near the Champs Élysées as I let my breakfast of coffee and croissants grow cold and forgot the headlines of the morning *Figaro.* "You read the advertisement: this kind of offer is not made every day. You read it and then reread it. It seems addressed to you and to nobody else."

Because "You are Another," such was the subjacent vision of my meetings with Buñuel in Mexico, with the girl imprisoned by the light in Paris, with Quevedo in the freezing fire, the burning ice, the wound that hurts yet is not felt, the happiness desired, the present evil which proclaims itself as Love but was first of all Desire. Curiously, Mizoguchi's film was being shown in the Ursulines Cinema, the same place where, more than thirty years before, Buñuel's *Andalusian Dog* had been first screened to a vastly scandalized audience. You remember that Red Cross nurses had to be posted in the aisles to help the ladies who fainted when Buñuel, on the screen, slashes the eye of a girl with a razor as a cloud bisects the moon.

The evanescent images of Mizoguchi told the beautiful love story adapted by the Japanese director from the tale "The House Among the Reeds," from the collection of the *Ugetsu Monogatari,* written in the eighteenth century by Ueda Akinari, born in 1734 in the red-light district at Sonezaki, the son of a courtesan and an unknown father. His mother abandoned him when he was four years old; he was adopted and raised by a family of paper and oil merchants, the Ueda, with infinite love and care, but also with a profound sense of nostalgia and doom: the happy merchants were unclassed by commerce from their former military tradition; Akinari contracted the pox and was saved perhaps by his adop-

tive mother's contracting of the disease: she died, he was left crippled in both hands until the God of Foxes, Inari, permitted him to hold a brush and become a calligraphist and, thus, a writer.

But first he inherited a prosperous business; it was destroyed by fire. Then he became a doctor: a little girl whom he was treating died, yet her father continued to have faith in him. So he gave up medicine. He could only be a lame writer, somehow a character in his own stories, persecuted by bad luck, poverty, illness, blindness. Abandoned as a child, Akinari spent his late years dependent on the charity of others, living in temples or the houses of friends. He was an erudite. He did not commit suicide, yet died in 1809.

So with his sick hand miraculously aided by the God of Foxes, Ueda Akinari could take a brush and thus write a series of tales that are unique because they are multiple.

"Originality" is the sickness of a modernity that wishes to see itself as something new, always new, in order continually to witness its own birth. In so doing, modernity is that fashionable illusion which only speaks to death.

This is the subject of one of the great dialogues by the magnificent Italian poet and essayist of the nineteenth century, Giacomo Leopardi. Read Leopardi: he is in the wind. I was reading him with joy in the winter of '81, then met Susan Sontag in New York the following spring. She had been surprised by a December dawn in Rome reading Leopardi: like Akinari, infirm; unlike him, a disillusioned romanticist turned pessimistic materialist and maybe, because he knew that in mankind, "outside of vanity, all is pain," he could write some of the most burning lyrical marvels in the Italian language and tell us that life can be unhappy when "hope has disappeared but desire remains intact." For the same reason, he could write the biting dialogue of Fashion and Death:

Fashion: Lady Death! Lady Death!

Death: I hope that your hour comes, so that you shall have no further need to call me.

Fashion: My Lady Death!

Death: Go to the Devil! I'll come looking for you when you least desire me.

Fashion: But I am your sister, Fashion. Have you forgotten that we are both the daughters of decadence?

Ancient peoples know that there are no words that do not descend from other words and that imagination only resembles power because neither can reign over *Nada,* Nothing, *Niente.* To imagine Nothing, or to believe that you rule over Nothing, is but a form—perhaps the surest one—of becoming mad. No one knew this better than Joseph Conrad in the heart of darkness or William Styron in the bed of shadows: the wages of sin are not death, but isolation.

Akinari's novella is set in 1454 and tells the story of Katsushiro, a young man humiliated by his poverty and his incapacity for work in the fields who abandons his home in order to make his fortune as a merchant in the city. He leaves his house by the reeds in the care of his young and beautiful wife Miyagi, promising he will return as the leaves of autumn fall.

Months go by; the husband does not return; the woman resigns herself to "the law of this world: no one should have faith in tomorrow." The civil wars of the fifteenth century under the Ashikaga shoguns make the reencounter of husband and wife impossible. People worry only about saving their skins, the old hide in the mountains, the young are forcibly drafted by the competing armies; all burn and loot; confusion takes hold of the world and the human heart also becomes ferocious. "Everything" says the author, reminding us that he is speaking from memory, "everything was in ruins during that miserable century."

Katsushiro becomes prosperous and manages to travel to Kyoto. Once settled there, seven years after he has bade farewell to Miyagi, he tries to return home but finds that the barriers of political conflict have not fallen, nor have the menaces of assault by bandits disappeared. He is fearful of returning to find his home in ruins, as in the myths of the past. A fever takes hold of him. The seven years have gone by as in a dream. The man imagines that the woman, like himself, is a prisoner of time and that, like himself, she has not been able to stretch out her hand and touch the fingers of the loved one.

The proofs of precarious humanity surround Katsushiro; bodies pile up in the streets; he walks among them. Neither he nor the dead are immortal. The first form of death is an answer to time: its name is forgetting, and maybe Katsushiro's wife (he imagines this) has already died; she is but a denizen of the subterranean regions.

So it is death that, finally, leads Katsushiro back to his village: if his wife has died, he will build a small altar for her during the night, taking advantage of the moon of the rainy season.

He returns to his ruined village. The pine that used to identify his house has been struck by lightning. But the house is still there. Katsushiro sees the light from a lamp. Is a stranger now living in his house? Katsushiro crosses the threshold, enters and hears a very ancient voice say, "Who goes there?" He answers, "It is I, I have come back."

Miyagi recognizes her husband's voice. She comes near to him, dressed in black and covered with grime, her eyes sunken, her knotted hair falling down her back. She is not the woman she had been. But when she sees her husband, without adding a word, she bursts out crying.

The man and the woman go to bed together and he tells her the reason why he has been so late in returning and of his resignation; she answers that the world had become full of horror, but that she had waited in vain: "If I had perished from love," she concludes, "hoping to see you again, I would have died of a lovesickness ignored by you."

They sleep embraced, deeply sleeping. As day breaks, a vague impression of coldness penetrates the unconsciousness of Katsushiro's dream. A rumor of something floating by awakens him. A cold liquid falls, drop after drop, on his face. His wife is no longer lying next to him. She has become invisible. He will never see her again.

Katsushiro discovers an old servant hidden in a hut in the middle of a field of camphor. The servant tells the hero the truth: Miyagi died many years ago. She was the only woman who never quit the village, in spite of the terrible dangers of war, because she kept alive the promise: we shall see each other once again this autumn. Not only the bandits invaded this place. Ghosts also took up their lodgings here. One day Miyagi joined them.

Mizoguchi's images told a story similar yet different from Akinari's tale. Less innocent, the contemporary filmmaker's story transformed Miyagi into a sort of tainted Penelope, a former courtesan who must prove her fidelity to her husband with greater conviction than a virgin.

When the village is invaded by the troops of Governor Uesugui sent from Kamakura to fight a ghostly and evasive shogun in the mountains, Miyagi, to save herself from the violence of the soldiers, commits suicide. The soldiers bury her in her garden, and when her husband finally returns, he must appeal to an old witch in order to recover the spectral vision and the spectral contact with his dead wife.

Four, no, Four Years After seeing the film by Mizoguchi and writing *Aura*, I found in an old bookshop in the Trastevere in Rome, where I had been led by the Spanish poets Rafael Alberti and María Teresa León, an Italian version of the Japanese tales of the *Togi Boko*, written by Hiosuishi Shoun and published in 1666. My surprise was quite great when I found there, written two hundred years before Akinari's tale and three hundred before Mizoguchi's film, the story called "The Courtesan Miyagino," where this same narrative is told, but this time around with an ending that provides direct access to necrophilia.

The returning hero, a Ulysses with no heroism greater than a recovered capacity for forgetting, does not avail himself of a witch to recover his embodied desire, the courtesan Miyagino who swore to be faithful to him. This time he opens the tomb and finds his wife, dead for many years, as beautiful as the day he last saw her. Miyagino's ghost comes back to tell her bereaved husband this tale.

My curiosity was spurred by this story within the story of *Aura,* so I went back to Buñuel, who was now preparing the script for his film *The Milky Way,* reading through the 180 volumes of the Abbé Migne's treatise on patristics and medieval heresies at the National Library in Paris, and asked him to procure me right of entry into that bibliographical sanctuary, more difficult to penetrate, let me add, than the chastity of a fifteenth-century Japanese virgin or the cadaver of a courtesan of the same era and nationality.

Anglo-Saxon libraries, I note in passing, are open to all, and nothing is easier than finding a book on the shelves at Oxford or Harvard, at Princeton or Dartmouth, take it home, caress it, read it, take notes from it and return it. Nothing more difficult, on the contrary, than approaching a Latin library. The presumed reader is also a presumed kleptomaniac, a convicted firebug and a certified vandal: he who pursues a book in Paris, Rome, Madrid or Mexico City soon finds out that books are not to be read but to be locked up, become rare and perhaps serve as a feast for rats.

No wonder that Buñuel, in *The Exterminating Angel,* has an adulterous wife ask her lover, a dashing colonel, to meet her secretly in her library. What if the husband arrives? asks the cautious lover. And she answers: We'll tell him I was showing you my incunabula.

No wonder that Juan Goytisolo, when he invades a Spanish library in his *Count Julian,* fruitfully employs his time by squashing fat green flies between the pages of Lope de Vega and Azorín.

But let me return to that bibliographical Leavenworth which is the Bibliothèque Nationale in Paris: Buñuel somehow smuggled me in and permitted me to grope in the dark, with fear of imminent discovery, for the ancestry of the Japanese tales of the *Togi Boko,* which in their turn were the forebears of Akinari's tales of the moon after the rain, which then inspired the film by Mizoguchi that I saw in Paris in the early days of September 1961, as I searched for the form and intention of *Aura.*

Is there a fatherless book, an orphan volume in this world? A book that is not the descendant of other books? A single leaf of a book that is not an offshoot of the great genealogical tree of mankind's literary imagination? Is there creation without tradition? But again, can tradition survive without renewal, a new creation, a new greening of the perennial tale?

I then discovered that the final source of this story was the Chinese tale called "The Biography of Ai'King," part of the collection called the *Tsien teng sin hoa.*

Yet, could there conceivably be a "final source" for the story that I saw in a Parisian movie house, thinking I had found in Mizoguchi's dead bride the sister of my Aura, whose mother, I deceived myself, was an image of youth defeated by a very ancient light in an apartment on the Boulevard Raspail and whose father, deceitful as well, was an act of imagination and desire on crossing the threshold between the lobby and the bar of a house in Mexico City's Colonia del Valle?

Could I, could anyone, go beyond the "Biography of Ai'King" to the multiple sources, the myriad, bubbling springs in which this final tale lost itself: the traditions of the oldest Chinese literature, that tide of narrative centuries that hardly begins to murmur the vastness of its constant themes: the supernatural virgin, the fatal woman, the spectral bride, the couple reunited?

I then knew that my answer would have to be negative but that, simultaneously, what had happened did but confirm my original intention: Aura came into this world to increase the secular descent of witches.

Five, At Least Five, Were The Witches who consciously mothered Aura during those days of my initial draft in a café near the rue de Berri through which passed, more or less hurried and/or worried by the urgent, immediate events of this world, K. S. Karol the skeptical reporter, Jean Daniel the questioning journalist, and Françoise Giroud, the vibrant First Lady of the French press, all of them heading toward the pressroom of *L'Express,* the then great weekly that they made against bombs and censorship and with the close cooperation—it is hallucinatory to imagine it today—of Sartre and Camus, Mendès-France and Mauriac.

These five bearers of consolation and desire, I believe today, were the greedy Miss Bordereau of Henry James's *Aspern Papers,* who in her turn descends from the cruelly mad Miss Havisham of Charles Dickens's *Great Expectations,* who is herself the English daughter of the ancient countess of Pushkin's *Queen of Spades,* she who jealously keeps the secret of winning at cards.

The similar structure of all three stories only proves that they all belong to the same mythical family. You invariably have three figures: the old woman, the young woman and the young man. In Pushkin, the old woman is the Countess Anna Fedorovna, the young woman her ward Lisaveta Ivanovna, the young man Hermann, an officer of the engineering corps. In Dickens, the old woman is Miss Havisham, the girl Stella, the hero Pip. In Henry James, the old woman is Miss Juliana Bordereau, the younger woman her niece Miss Tina, the intruding young man, the nameless narrator H.J.— "Henry James" in Michael Redgrave's staging of the story.

In all three works the intruding young man wishes to know the old lady's secret: the secret of fortune in Pushkin, the secret of love in Dickens, the secret of poetry in James. The young girl is the deceiver—innocent or not—who must wrest the secret from the old woman before she takes it to the grave.

La señora Consuelo, Aura and Felipe Montero joined this illustrious company, but with a twist: Aura and Consuelo are *one,* and it is *they* who tear the secret of desire from Felipe's breast. The male is now the deceived. This is in itself a twist on machismo.

And do not all three ladies descend from Michelet's medieval sorceress who reserves for herself, be it at the price of death by fire, the secrets of a knowledge forbidden by modern reason, the damned papers, the letters stained by the sperm of candles long since gone dead, the cards wasted by the fingers of avarice and fear, but also the secrets of an antiquity projecting itself with greater strength than the future?

For is there a secret more secret, a scandal more ancient, than that of the sinless woman, the woman who does not incite toward sin—Eve—and does not open the box of disgrace—Pandora? The woman who is not what the Father of the Church, Tertulian, would have her be, "A temple built on top of a sewer," not the woman who must save herself by banging a door like Nora in Ibsen's *Doll's House,* but the woman who, before all of them, is the owner of her time because she is the owner of her will and of her body; because she does not admit any division between time, body and will and this mortally wounds the man who would like to divide his mind from his flesh in order to resemble, through his mind, his God, and through his flesh, his Devil?

In John Milton's *Paradise Lost* Adam rebukes the Creator, challenges him, asks him:

Did I request thee, Maker, from my Clay
To mould me Man, did I sollicitte thee
From darkness to promote me, or here place
In this delicious Garden?

Adam asks his God, and even worse,

. . . to reduce me to my dust,
Desirous to resigne, and render back
All I receav'd, unable to performe
The terms too hard, by which I was to hold
The good I sought not.

This man divided between his divine thought and his carnal pain is the author of his own unbearable conflict when he demands, not death, but at least, because she is worse than death, life without Eve—that is, life without Evil, life among men only, a wise creation peopled by exclusively masculine spirits, without this fair defect of nature: woman.

But this life among masculine angels shall be a life alienated, mind and flesh separated. Seen as Eve or Pandora, woman answers from the other shore of this division, saying that she is one, body inseparable from soul, with no complaints against Creation, conceived without sin because the apple of Paradise does not kill: it nurtures and it saves us from the schizoid Eden subverted by the difference between what is to be found in my divine head and what is to be found between my human legs.

The secret woman of James, Dickens, Pushkin and Michelet who finds her young granddaughter in Aura has, I said, a fifth forebear. Her name is Circe. She is the Goddess of Metamorphosis and for her there are no extremes, no divorces between flesh and mind, because everything is transforming itself constantly, everything is becoming other without losing its anteriority and announcing a promise that does not sacrifice anything of what we are because we have been and we shall be: "Ayer se fue, mañana no ha llegado, / Hoy se está yendo sin parar un punto; / Soy un fue, y un seré, y un es cansado" (Yesterday is gone, tomorrow has not come, / Today is endlessly fleeing; / I am an I was, an I shall be, an I am tired).

Imitating old Quevedo, I asked the *Aura* papers, feverishly written as the summer of '61 came to an end, "Listen life, will no one answer?" And the answer came in the night which accompanied the words written in the midst of the bustle of commerce and journalism and catering on a grand Parisian avenue: Felipe Montero, the false protagonist of *Aura,* answered me, addressing me familiarly:

You read the advertisement. Only your name is missing. You think you are Felipe Montero. You lie to yourself. You are You: You are Another. You are the Reader. You are what you Read. You shall be Aura. You were Consuelo.

"I'm Felipe Montero. I read your advertisement."

"Yes, I know. . . . Good. Please let me see your pro-file, . . . No, I can't see it well enough. Turn toward the light. That's right. . . ."

You shall move aside so that the light from the can-dles and the reflections from the silver and crystal re-veal the silk coif that must cover a head of very white hair and frame a face so old it must be almost childlike. . . .

"I told you she'd come back."

"Who?"

"Aura. My companion. My niece."

"Good afternoon."

The girl will nod and at the same instant the old lady will imitate her gesture.

"This is Señor Montero. He's going to live with us."

Six, Only Six Days before her death, I met La Traviata. My wife Sylvia and I had been invited in Sep-tember of 1976 to have dinner at the house of our old and dear friends Gabriella and Teddy van Zuylen, who have four daughters with the green eyes of Aura who spy on the guests near four paintings by Roberto Matta, Wifredo Lam, Alberto Gironella and Pierre Alechinsky, without anyone being able to tell whether the girls are coming in or out of the paintings.

"I have a surprise for you," said our hostess, and she sat me next to Maria Callas.

This woman made me shake violently, for no rea-son I could immediately discern. While we dined, I tried to speak to her at the same time that I spoke to myself. From the balcony of the Theatre of Fine Arts in Mexico City I had heard her sing *La Traviata* in 1951, when she was called Maria Mennighini Callas and ap-peared as a robust young woman with the freshest, most glorious voice that I had ever heard: Callas sang an aria the same way that Manolete fought a bull: incompara-bly. She was already a young myth.

I told her so that night in Paris. She interrupted me with a velocity at once velvet-smooth and razor-sharp in its intention: "What do you think of the myth now that you've met her?" she asked me.

"I think she has lost some weight," I dared to an-swer.

She laughed with a tone different from that of her speaking voice. I imagined that for Maria Callas crying and singing were acts nearer to song than to speech, be-cause I must admit that her everyday voice was that of a girl from the less fashionable neighborhoods of New York City. Maria Callas had the speaking voice of a girl selling Maria Callas records at Sam Goody's on Sixth Avenue.

This was not the voice of Medea, the voice of Norma, the voice of the Lady of the Camelias. Yes, she

had slimmed down, we all knew it, without losing her glorious and warm voice, the voice of the supreme diva. No: no one was a more beautiful woman, a better ac-tress or a greater singer on an opera stage in the twenti-eth century.

Callas's seduction, let me add, was not only in the memory of her stage glory: this woman I now saw, thinned down not by her will but by her sickness and her time, nearer every minute to her bone, every second more transparent and tenuously allied to life, possessed a hypnotic secret that revealed itself as *attention*. I really think I have never met a woman who lent more atten-tion to the man she was listening to than Maria Callas.

Her attention was a manner of dialogue. Through her eyes (two black lighthouses in a storm of white pet-als and wet olives) passed images in surprising muta-tion: her thoughts changed, the thoughts became im-ages, yes, but only because she was transforming ceaselessly, as if her eyes were the balcony of an unfin-ished and endless opera that, in everyday life, pro-longed in silence the suffused rumor, barely the echo, of the nights which had belonged to Lucia de Lamerm-oor and Violetta Valéry.

In that instant I discovered the true origin of *Aura*: its anecdotal origin, if you will, but also its origin in de-sire, since desire is the port of embarkation as well as the final destiny of this novella. I had heard Maria Callas sing *La Traviata* in Mexico City when she and I were more or less the same age, twenty years old perhaps, and now we were meeting almost thirty years later and I was looking at a woman I had known before, but she saw in me a man she had just met that evening. She could not compare me to myself. I could: myself and her.

And in this comparison I discovered yet another voice, not the slightly vulgar voice of the highly intelli-gent woman seated at my right; not the voice of the singer who gave back to belcanto a life torn from the dead embrace of the museum; no, but the voice of old age and madness which, I then remembered (and con-firmed it in the Angel record I went out hurriedly to buy the next morning), is the unbelievable, unfathomable, profoundly disturbing voice of Maria Callas in the death scene of *La Traviata*.

Whereas the sopranos who sing Verdi's opera usu-ally search for a supreme pathos achieved thanks to ago-nizing tremors and attempt to approach death with sobs, screams and shudders, Maria Callas does some-thing unusual: she transforms her voice into that of *an old woman* and gives that ancient voice the inflection of madness.

I remember it so well that I can almost imitate the final lines: "E strano! / Cessarono / Gli spasmi del dolore."

But if this be the voice of a hypochondriac old lady complaining of the inconveniences of advanced age, immediately Callas injects a mood of madness into the words of resurgent hope in the midst of a hopeless malady: "In mi rinasce—m'agita / Insolito vigore / Ah! Ma io rittorno a viver'." Only then does death, and nothing but death, defeat old age and madness with the exclamation of youth: "Oh gioia!"

Maria Callas invited Sylvia and me to see her again a few weeks later. But before that, one afternoon, La Traviata died forever. But before, also, she had given me my secret: Aura was born in that instant when Maria Callas identified, in the voice of one woman, youth as well as old age, life along with death, inseparable, convoking one another, the four, finally, youth, old age, life, death, women's names: *"La* juventud," *"la* vejez," *"la* vida," *"la* muerte."

Seven, yes, Seven Days were needed for divine creation: on the eighth day the human creature was born and her name was desire. After the death of Maria Callas, I reread *The Lady of the Camelias* by Alexander Dumas *fils*. The novel is far superior to Verdi's opera or to the numerous stage and film adaptations because it contains an element of delirious necrophilia absent from all the descendants.

The novel begins with the return to Paris of Armand Duval—A.D., certainly the double of Alexander Dumas—who then finds out that Marguerite Gautier had died. Marguerite Gautier, his lover lost through the suspicious will of Duval *père*, who says he is defending the family integrity by demanding that Marguerite abandon Armand, but who is probably envious of his son and would like Marguerite all for himself. Anyway, Duval *fils* desperately hurries to the woman's tomb in Père Lachaise. The scene that follows is surely the most delirious in matters of narrative necrophilia.

Armand obtains permission to exhume the body of Marguerite. The graveyard keeper tells Armand that it will not be difficult to find Marguerite's tomb. As soon as the relatives of the persons buried in the neighboring graves found out who she was, they protested and said there should be special real estate set apart for women such as she: a whorehouse for the dead. Besides, every day someone sends her a bouquet of camelias. He is unknown. Armand is jealous of his dead lover: he does not know who sends her the flowers. Ah, if only sin saved us from boredom, in life or in death! This is the first thing that Marguerite told Armand when she met him: "The companion of sick souls is called boredom." Armand is going to save Marguerite from the infinite boredom of being dead.

The gravediggers start working. A pickax strikes the crucifix on the coffin. The bier is slowly pulled out; the loose earth falls away. The boards groan frightfully. The gravediggers open the coffin with difficulty. The earth's humidity has made the hinges rusty.

At long last, they manage to raise the lid. They all cover their noses. All, save Armand, fall back.

A white shroud covers the body, revealing some sinuosities. One extreme of the shroud is eaten up and the dead woman's foot sticks out through a hole. Armand orders that the shroud be ripped apart. One of the gravediggers brusquely uncovers Marguerite's face.

The eyes are no more than two holes. The lips have vanished. The teeth remain white, bare, clenched. The long black tresses, dry, smeared onto the temples, cover up part of the green cavities on the cheeks.

Armand kneels down, takes the bony hand of Marguerite, and kisses it.

Only then does the novel begin: a novel that, inaugurated by death, can only culminate in death. The novel is the act of Armand Duval's desire to find the object of desire: Marguerite's body. But since no desire is innocent—because we not only desire, we also desire to change what we desire once we obtain it—Armand Duval obtains the cadaver of Marguerite Gautier in order to transform it into literature, into *book,* into that second-person singular, the You that structures desire in *Aura.*

You: that word which is mine as it moves, ghostlike, in all the dimensions of space and time, even beyond death.

> *"You shall plunge your face, your open eyes, into Consuelo's silver-white hair, and she'll embrace you again when the clouds cover the moon, when you're both hidden again, when the memory of youth, of youth reembodied, rules the darkness and disappears for some time.*
>
> *"She'll come back, Felipe. We'll bring her back together. Let me recover my strength and I'll bring her back."*

Felipe Montero, of course, is not You. You are *You.* Felipe Montero is only the author of *Terra Nostra.*

I published *Aura* in Spanish in 1962. The girl I had met as a child in Mexico and seen re-created by the light of Paris in 1961 when she was twenty, died by her own hand, two years ago, in Mexico, at age forty.

Carlos Fuentes, Autumn 1983

PERU

"O Tempora, O Mores": Time, Tense and Tension in Mario Vargas Llosa

Time present and time past
Are both perhaps present in time future,
And time future contained in time past.
If all time is eternally present
All time is unredeemable.

—T. S. Eliot, "Burnt Norton," I

It is meet that Mario Vargas Llosa should have recently considered the novelistic art of Flaubert,[1] for the French master, powerful tradition that he has become for the whole narrative craft, would appear to hold the Peruvian novelist in a degree of thralldom. Like his fellows in Spanish America, Vargas Llosa attempts the break-through into a new expression that aims to portray or perhaps even to create what he calls "total reality" by means of the "total novel." This outlook on the creative process of fiction is contained in his earlier study of the techniques of Gabriel García Márquez.[2] One wonders whether the very ungraspable nature of García Márquez's art might not have led Vargas Llosa to the consideration of the more reductive qualities of the French novelist. In his own novels Vargas Llosa seems to be struggling toward something new, something more apt as an expression of contemporary Spanish American reality. But the experimentation often seems to be only that, an attempt at the "new," which of course does reflect the Latin American zeitgeist exceedingly well. The problem with his methods is that he is working with elements tried and true handed down by the nineteenth century as daring innovations which, however, have become our regnant canon. We no longer riot over Brahms.

Robert Brustein, in a recent piece, has touched upon this question as it concerns the theatre.[3] The gist of what he says can be extended to take in any number of art forms, particularly the novel, which is so close to drama. What Brustein posits is a clash between Newtonian and Einsteinian outlooks as concerns human behavior. If only indirectly, the new vision of the universe (or pluriverse) is open-ended at both ends, Janus inside-out. Our symbols have changed and by them our other means of expression. Previously we went around in circles, trying to isolate our moment as an arc of that ring. The mystery often lay in our inability to determine the direction of flow of that circular route. In spite of this, however, we were comfortable with our agoraphobic state, pondering such things as the myth of eternal return, *plus ça change* . . . , et cetera. Brustein has seen

in what he calls Newtonian theatre a structure based on cause and effect, on the inexorability of laws. Einsteinian theatre is, on the contrary, unsure, insecure, a theatre more interested in effects than in causes. This has been the route, too, of a great deal that has been done in the novel, from Gide's gratuitous act to Cortázar's pataphysical adventures, particularly in *Hopscotch,*[4] which act as a kind of salubrious intubation for the congested Spanish American novel.

It is now writ that space is curved and that space and time are one and the same. The trouble is that all of this is visually (even "humanly") inconceivable, as Earl Russell once warned a friend, and can only be conveyed by rather recondite ciphers. In artistic expression this needs must have recourse to a new set of symbols or a readjustment of the old, much as one must adjust an alphabet to the requirements of a new tongue, as St. Cyril did. The circle, then, can no longer obtain because of its limitations, its finitude. A much better structure or anti-structure is the spiral, infinite at both "ends," which is the literal base upon which the Brazilian Osman Lins has laid out his novel *Avalovara.*[5] Our moment is a segment of a spiral, not the arc of the circle (the covenant?); our cosmography is more Miltonic than Dantean.[6]

Mario Vargas Llosa has sought out the simultaneity suggested by the space-time continuum in his novel *Conversation in The Cathedral.*[7] This long book encompasses any number of moments, which the author has daubed for identity through the use of three verbal tenses or times. After a rather banal prologue in present time which fittingly sets the tone for the whole novel, action ultimately moves to the brothel-bar named La Catedral because of the proximity of the episcopal see, although the symbolic possibilities are obvious and legion. It is precisely this beginning which imparts the genius loci of Lima, which cannot help but be affected by the dank and dismal gray cloud cover that so often cloaks the city and which drove the writer Sebastián Salazar Bondy to denunciation, despair, drink and destruction. Vargas Llosa sees to it that this atmosphere of gray mediocrity is maintained throughout the book. There is no excitement here; everything is inept, both morally and mentally, from violence and murder on down.

This is the present tense, the time of the beginning and the time of the conversation between Zavalita and Ambrosio as they drink beer and dredge up the past in La Catedral. In most languages including Spanish the present tense suggests immediacy, thus livening up the narration. This is not so in the case of *Conversation in The Cathedral;* here it serves as little more than an indicator of who is speaking right now, and indeed, in the nonvocal parts of the beginning and end of the novel, its effect is to dampen the action, make it more drab. It is possible that Vargas Llosa has meant to use the tense here as a sort of descriptive device, to show the banality of the present of which he writes; and in a larger sense, as the conversational present is here responsible for all that is retold and recalled from the past, this banality is properly imposed on preterit events as they pass through the alembic of the here and now. Recollection is expressed in the past tense, with the aorist and imperfect aspects serving their normal grammatical functions. Once within past time, further recollection or delving is then put into the pluperfect tense. After the reader has come to the meeting between Zavalita and Ambrosio early in the book, he must be aware of the careful use of tense employed by the author and he must be continuously on the qui vive lest he be plunged like some Wellsian adventurer into a different time warp.

It is difficult to say whether or not Vargas Llosa has been successful in his use of this technique. Perhaps it is too much of a contrivance which only serves to oppilate the narrative flow. It is also possible, however, that this is precisely what the author seeks: a sense of sameness that obtains between time present and time past, both recent and remote. Eliot's time future is not evident grammatically, but as the novel ends, it would appear that Ambrosio (and Zavalita by implication) has come to the taffrail and all that is left to do is take another turn about the deck:

> And when the rabies scare was over, would your work at the pound be through, Ambrosio? Yes, son. What would he do? What he'd been doing before the supervisor had Pancras bring him in and told him, O.K., give us a hand for a few days even if you haven't got any papers. He would work here and there, maybe after a while there'd be another outbreak of rabies and they'd call him in again, and after that here and there, and then, well, after that he would have died, wasn't that so, son? (601)

It is the circle again, chaos within order, the atmosphere of Latin America's jerry-built military regimes and their wakes.

The abeyance of an expectant tautness in the novel is never resolved. Recognitions are diluted by their placement within the parallel flows of time, and although there are some near misses, there are no really blatant Dickensian epiphanies. Only at the start, with the encounter between Zavalita and Ambrosio, the former family chauffeur, do we have the recognition scene from which the whole narrative emerges. Again one wonders whether or not this plain lack of adventure

might not be a deliberate attempt by the author to stress the drabness of it all. If that is so, then Vargas Llosa has succeeded only too well. The novel is much too long, and at times the reader must indeed have a certain *Einfühlung* with those Peruvians who were suffered to endure General Odría's dictatorship longer than they should have. The failure of what at first blush purports to be an adventurous and inventive style might also be a reflection of the absurdity of expecting permanence from such political structures, so flimsy in spite of their concomitant brutality, as was the case with the Reich that was built to last a thousand years and missed its mark by 987. We must always look to the other side of this stylistic aspect of the "absurd," however, and wonder if what we can call Cortazarian intent will serve a writer who is really more at home with Flaubert. It is back to the circle versus the spiral once more. Vargas Llosa's novel is nice and round; it slices well.

As with basic matter itself, human life and its portrayal in artistic form still have too many missing features; even the constants are incomplete The verities of the nineteenth-century novel, Newtonian as they are, no longer obtain; types and samples are still flat and only give us a partial view of the human figure. If time is the fourth dimension (and this is improbable), then it must be seen in its latest contexts in relation to space and not as it had been seen before. The time in this novel is not relative, or at least it is not shown to be so in a cogent way. There is no blending of Proustian time with Joycean space as is done so skillfully in José Lezama Lima's novel *Paradiso*.[8] There is too much certitude in the use of time here; we receive the technique ex cathedra, even through the nominal coincidence of a local shebeen. The novelist who works with time should be aware that of the two long-sought quarks in particle physics, we have finally been given proof of the existence of the one called "beauty." The one called "truth" remains elusive. A reliance upon accepted temporal divisions will render Veeck's Law[9] operative, but it will also limit its effect to an acceptance of the customs and manners of the industrial society upon which it is based.

Vargas Llosa was more successful with the impact of parallel structure and connective characters in his earlier novel *The Green House*.[10] In it we have a displacement in space that serves thereby as a mutual displacement in time, and the woof and the warp of the two "elements" are thus quite congenial. Character is preserved as people change roles and even names with a dislocation in space. Bonifacia passes from jungle to mission to marriage to brothel, a series of way stations which underlines the fact that her destiny would have been patterned in a similar way regardless of specifics. Cause and effect are seen inexorably at work here; the creatures are Darwin's, their variations in nomenclature are only superficially relevant to their being. In *The Green House* Vargas Llosa is more successful when he leaves things unknown, incomplete. This may be closer to "total reality" than attempts at rounding out characters in order to render the reader omniscient. The god-like reader has to be the most superficial, for he will have to ignore what he cannot know. His omniscience is really partiscience, calibrated to his limited ken. This is the reader who must contribute, the one for whom Cortázar's guru-like Morelli wishes to write in the "expendable chapters" of *Hopscotch.*

In *The Green House* Vargas Llosa does address himself to this reader in one aspect of the novel, and that is why it is a more "advanced" work than *Conversation in The Cathedral.* The title of the novel itself is the connective theme that links the primitive world of the jungle to the primal lusts of "civilization" which are enclosed by the green walls of the whorehouse. There has to be some connection here with W. H. Hudson's outwardly more idyllic *Green Mansions,* and the figure of Rima is as hermetic in many ways as that of the pathetic blind Antonia, whom Anselmo the harp player has kept hidden in the Green House in a kind of perverted purdah. The reader is given his opportunity here, then, to create feelings, to impute them or to ignore them. Even before reaching "total reality" (which can only be a vision or a dream), we must first come to that ambiguous or ambivalent reality sought by Machado de Assis and presented to us through his untrustworthy characters.[11]

It is precisely this mystery, this world which is not explained or cannot be, that is missing in *Conversation in The Cathedral.* There the pieces do fall neatly together at the end, or even sooner if the reader's powers of ratiocination are sufficiently acute. The only question remaining is the "why," the cause again, and this is not the *Urfrage* of reality, which in its human aspects becomes tabescent in the light of explanation. If the ending of *Conversation in The Cathedral* is pessimistic in that it predicts more of the same with the grave as goal, *The Green House* ends on a note which, while similarly unprogressive, at least is an acceptance of mystery, if we will, as theology tells science to leave it to its own devices:

> "I'll stop by and pick you up," Dr. Zevallos says. "We'll go to the wake together. Try to get at least eight hours of sleep."
>
> "I know, I know," Father García says with a grunt. "Don't be giving me advice all the time." (405)

This aspect could have been what attracted Vargas Llosa to a considered and detailed study of the work of García Márquez, and of all of the Peruvian's works, *The Green House* comes closest to the outlook too vaguely called "magic realism" and epitomized by *One Hundred Years of Solitude.*[12] *The Green House* is open-ended; Don Anselmo's gramarye remains unexplained, even though the narrative flow has left it accepted in one way or another. In like manner *One Hundred Years of Solitude,* in spite of the inexorable tone of its close,

> . . . and that everything written on them was unrepeatable since time immemorial and forever more, because races condemned to one hundred years of solitude did not have a second opportunity on earth. (422)

is also unfinished in the larger sense: the time entailed is but a segment of the never-ending (-beginning) spiral, one hundred years' worth.

Those who have read Cortázar's *Hopscotch* are tempted (if they have learned their lesson well) to take the chunks of narration which are the bricks of *The Green House* and rearrange them, as Cortázar invites the reader to do with his novel. It can be done with some success, for Vargas Llosa has already made a start in that direction. It can be done because in this novel, unlike the case of his later one, he has not reduced time to a device of measurement or location, a practical tool, but has conjoined it with space, so that the characters carry their space with them too (green jungle/Green House), inseparable from their time, which bears more resemblance here to Proust's Time. More real too is the world we do not see, the one we accept by fiat from custom. We take it for granted that "normal" things are happening out of sight and behind closed doors. Part of the shock in this novel is that what has been going on behind closed doors in the Green House is not normal, is almost eerie, a moment of *esperpento* worthy of Valle-Inclán or Luis Buñuel. Yet from the union of Don Anselmo and Antonia we have Chunga, one of the most "realistic" and *ordinary* characters in the whole novel. The quotidian, then, is born of unlikely elements that remain partially mysterious to us. Its time is not turned dead center on the tailstock.

Vargas Llosa's most recent novel at this writing, *Pantaleón y las visitadoras,*[13] misses an opportunity to make better use of the cinematographic technique essayed. In this comic rather than humorous book, the author tells the story almost completely by means of dialogue, using the identifying phrases as a kind of stage direction to describe the character's action or attitude. The result is more a dialogued novel like the *Celestina* or Galdós's *Realidad* than it is a movie put onto the printed page. This is strange in that of late Vargas Llosa has become interested in film and has even acted and directed. Outside of dialogue there is little evidence of cinematographic effects. The kaleidoscopic succession that was used by Dos Passos and Joyce and later cultivated in Latin America by Cortázar and Cabrera Infante is not often present in the works of Mario Vargas Llosa, least of all in *Pantaleón,* seemingly written with the screen in mind. There seems to be a very promising step in this direction with *The Green House,* but with *Conversation in The Cathedral* it is as if the author had not realized how close he was to handling the modern view of time, so close to the helter-skelter pace of our customs, and he returned to earlier temporality, taking rhythm for tempo and following its regularity. It is as if there is a drive for neatness, for aliquot parts, not the aliquants that keep Cortázar's work swirling. The characters in *The Green House* left remainders, those in *Conversation in The Cathedral* do not and therefore disappear in our imagination. This is in large measure because time is a function in the first novel, while in the second it is a tool, such a treacherous one that we should be careful as to whom we let pick it up.

Gregory Rabassa, Winter 1978

1 *La orgía perpetua: Flaubert y* Madame Bovary, Barcelona, Seix Barral, 1975.

2 *García Márquez: Historia de un deicidio,* Barcelona, Barral, 1971).

3 "Drama in the Age of Einstein," *New York Times,* 7 August 1977, Section 2, pp. 1,22.

4 *Rayuela,* Buenos Aires, Sudamericana, 1963; *Hopscotch,* Gregory Rabassa, tr., New York, Pantheon, 1966.

5 *Avalovara,* São Paulo, Melhoramentos, 1973; English translation by Gregory Rabassa in progress for Knopf.

6 We must remember that the souls whom Dante encounters in Hell can remember the past and foresee the future but cannot know the present for having had it too much with them. Milton's time is more truly eternal.

7 *Conversación en La Catedral,* 2 vols., Barcelona, Seix Barral, 1969; *Conversation in The Cathedral,* Gregory Rabassa, tr., New York, Harper & Row, 1975.

8 *Paradiso,* Mexico City, Era, 1968; *Paradiso,* Gregory Rabassa, tr., New York, Farrar, Straus & Giroux, 1974.

9 "Always live east of where you work" (so that the sun will not be in your eyes while driving). Promulgated by Bill Veeck, owner of the Chicago White Sox.

10 *La Casa Verde,* Barcelona, Seix Barral, 1965; *The Green House,* Gregory Rabassa, tr., New York, Harper & Row, 1968.

11 The entire story of *Dom Casmurro* is given us through the eyes of the protagonist, whose neuroses render him completely unreliable. We should also note that all of the fantastic episodes in the *Odyssey* are narrated by Odysseus himself, a notorious prevaricator.

12 *Cien años de soledad,* Buenos Aires, Sudamericana, 1967; *One Hundred Years of Solitude,* Gregory Rabassa, tr., New York, Harper & Row, 1970.

13 *Pantaleón y las visitadoras,* Barcelona, Seix Barral, 1973. Harper & Row will soon publish an English translation by Ronald

Christ and Gregory Kolovakos. The title was still undecided when last I heard. I still stand by my own suggestion, "Pantaleón and the Visitationists," which was turned down by all hands. (Ed. Note: During production of this issue we learned that the English translation will be entitled *Captain Pantoja and the Special Service.*)

URUGUAY

Juan Carlos Onetti (1909–1994): An Existential Allegory of Contemporary Man

Now that Juan Carlos Onetti has left us—when we had already come to believe that he was immortal—we ask ourselves, from where within a country in which narrative is traditionally polarized between rural realism and modest urban incursions did this writer emerge? What was his literary heritage? And, most important, how could he establish, based on a "territory of the imaginary," Santa María, a fictional tradition in which a good many Uruguayan and many other Latin American writers can recognize themselves, an exclusive world that today is the inheritance of universal literature?

If going from the regional to the universal is the privilege of good literature, then in Onetti's case everything began in 1939, in the unkempt room of a tenement house, where a man smokes and paces incessantly through a hot and humid summer night, after a day of celebration. Bored with lying in bed and with smelling alternately one armpit then the other while grimacing in disgust, the man takes stock of his life on the eve of his fortieth birthday: he has no work or friends, he has just divorced, and his neighbors seem "more repugnant than ever"; it's been more than twenty years since he lost his ideals, and, according to news he has heard on the radio, "it appears that war is imminent."

Any human being confronted with a similiar life circumstance could not avoid the most somber of reflections. Nevertheless, Eladio Linacero, the protagonist of *El pozo* (1939; Eng. *The Pit,* 1991), Juan Carlos Onetti's first novel, succeeds in evading his sad reality. For him, it is enough to begin writing a dream ("the dream of the log cabin"), although to do so he feels obliged to recognize that, in his words, "I am a solitary man who smokes anywhere in the city," a confession with which he ends his monologue. In the space of fifty-six pages, narrated in the first person throughout that insomniac night, he not only frees himself from the most menacing ghosts of solitude but also establishes another reality, thanks to his simple formula of acceptance: "I am a man who turns toward the shadow on the wall at night in order to think of foolish and fantastic things."

This salvation through writing portends a destiny that Onetti would fulfill with exemplary precision. Twelve years later, in 1951, another man also paces while suffering insomnia in a small apartment in the San Telmo district of Buenos Aires, "a small and timid man" who has said "no to alcohol, no to tobacco" and that there is "nothing like women." José María Brausen, the protagonist of La vida breve (1951; Eng. A Brief Life, 1976), appears to be the direct descendant of Linacero. Like the latter, Brausen maintains a mediocre existence and, after five years of marriage, comes to discover the end of his relationship, ruined by indifference. The pretext of this sudden revelation has been the mastectomy which his wife Gertrudis has just undergone, but the reality of his solitude appears much more profound than the scar that cruelly marks her amputation. Without feeling compassion or affection and while listening to her moan as she dreams, Brausen accepts his failure with "the expected resignation that comes with being forty."

Nevertheless, within the four walls of his apartment and through successive nights during which, plagued by insomnia, he paces between the kitchen, the bedroom, and the bathroom, Brausen is capable also of freeing himself from his present circumstance. "Any sudden and simple thing was going to happen, and I could save myself by writing," he says the night he decides "to do something." He sits at a table where, by his own account, "I had under my hands the paper necessary to save myself, a blotter, and a fountain pen." Unlike Linacero, for whom it sufficed "to tell a dream" with the "event" that preceded it, Brausen simultaneously undertakes a twofold escape. On the one hand, he doubles as Arce, a makeshift macró (pimp) who bursts into the apartment of his neighbor, a prostitute whose noises he has heard through the thin partition walls that separate their bedrooms, as if their two beds were end to end. At the same time, he assumes the identity of a character he has created (Díaz Grey) in a city (Santa María) imagined with such perfection that at the end of the novel he is able to flee to it without forcing the ambiguous reality of the fiction he invented. Beginning with La vida breve, this mythical city with recognizable archetypes of the River Plate region—synthesized by Onetti as a true paradigm—becomes the setting for the rest of his work. Brausen, its "founder," will have a monument erected in his honor in the principal plaza in La novia robada (The Stolen Bride; 1968), and in Cuando ya no importe (When It No Longer Matters; 1993) his name will be invoked during religious processions.

Through the evasion of the sad personal circumstances of Eladio Linacero and José María Brausen, Onetti establishes a formal, tense universe, a world enclosed existentially on itself, rigorous in style and without concessions yet saved by the act of writing placed at the disposal of its antiheroes. Disoriented beings (when not frustrated), uprooted noncomformists, outsiders, and marginal figures face the difficulty of communicating with others and feel that authenticity is repressed by society. They take refuge with their anguish in the space of a small room and carry out a solitary, intense "descent into themselves," having been preceded by the first outsider in modern literature, the protagonist of Dostoevsky's Notes from Underground.

Born 1 July 1909 in Montevideo, Uruguay, Onetti is a member of a kind of lost generation of the River Plate that reached maturity in the 1940s and could be characterized as somewhat nihilistic. To the extent that he was able to create characters who were authentic spiritual pariahs, morally banished and politically disenchanted, his total rejection of the ruling values is among the most radical. His anti-heroes go much further in their forsaking all belief. Abandoned beings, "amoral, indifferent" men "without faith or interest in their destiny," as he would define them in his foreword to Tierra de nadie (No Man's Land; 1941), they are depicted, Onetti admits, "with an equal spirit of indifference," although in reality he has always been empathetic to their sadness through an expressive pity and has discovered with them that the freedom such characters as Linacero or Brausen attained only served to make their isolation more obvious.

In Onetti, solitude is the result not of a deliberate calling for independence but rather of a kind of paralyzing lucidity. All impulse to "action" is denied by a thoroughgoing introspective analysis. In this position there is an inevitable failure, a negation of all that could become delightful, vitalistic enthusiasm, a call to analyze and reflect instead of openly enjoying life. Protagonists who are confined to their rooms like Linacero and Brausen, uncommitted observers of other people's business like Díaz Grey or Jorge Malabia, impresarios destined for defeat like Larsen, eternal planners of projects that are never carried out like Aranzuru—all seem to have come to the conclusion that, as H. G. Wells said, "there is no escape or getting around it or getting through it."

In Onetti's work there is no place for a man of universal values, even if these values appear to be threatened, problematic, or alternative. His disillusionment is total and absolute; there is no possible faith, no imaginable response to crisis, no question worth posing. His dispossession brings him close to the essential dead-end truths of Samuel Beckett's characters. Linacero is, in effect, not unlike Molloy.

Onetti's characters, moreover, live "marginalized" on the muddy banks of the River Plate, "expelled" from Europe, and "fallen" into "an uncharted land, void of spirit." H. A. Murena defines the situation of the River Plate in *El pecado original de América* (America's Original Sin): "America is made up of exiles, is the land of exile, and all who are exiled know profoundly that in order to live, one must be done with the past, must erase memories of this world to which one's return is forbidden, for to do otherwise is to remain suspended from memories, unable to live." Therefore, Onetti ironically asks himself, "Why here? Preceding us there is nothing. One gaucho, two gauchos, thirty-three gauchos," making a clear, irreverent allusion to the Uruguayan national myth, historically founded on the landing of the "thirty-three gauchos from the east bank of the River Plate."

Onetti not only affirms the lack of a perceptible historical past, but he also disavows the expression of traditional culture. In a weekly newspaper column, symptomatically called "La Piedra en el Charco" (The Rock in the Puddle), he severely criticizes his era for lacking originality, for the sterility into which regionalism, *costumbrismo,* and social realism have fallen. Devoid of all rhetorical weight, history is transformed into a tabula rasa, where everything remains to be written, but where, in reality, nothing is worth writing.

Onetti's antiheroes proclaim that "nothing can be done," or, what seems more serious still, that "nothing is worth doing." Far from anguish, nausea, and even *détresse,* one can speak only of fatalism and resignation. Onetti himself declared as an elemental philosophical principle that "the whole art of living lies in the simple ease of accommodating ourselves within the hallow of events that we have not provoked by our own will; not forcing anything; simply being each minute."

In conclusion, it is not worth struggling for some other future, since "An enlightened man should do nothing. Look at construction workers, at any number of things. It breaks your heart. All life wallowing in misery. Look at politics, literature, or what have you. All is false, and the autochthonous is the falsest of all. If there's nothing to do here, don't do anything. If gringos like to work, let them break their backs. I don't have any faith; we don't have faith. Some day we'll have a mystique, for sure; but in the meantime, we're happy."

The formulation of a philosophy of existence in Onetti can, consequently, seem weak. One must wade through sundry isolated paragraphs of his works in order to construct a scheme that surprises by its simplicity and its coherence. For the moment, one discov-

ers that, like a good inhabitant of the River Plate region, Onetti understands that synonymous with virility is a certain contentiousness, a certain obligatory terseness of emotional expression and its mysterious reasons—a constant that appears in the works of authors as diverse as Macedonio Fernández, Jorge Luis Borges, and Julio Cortázar, as well as in many tango lyrics.

In essence, more than a form of deracination, Onetti translates the profound frustration of the inhabitants of the River Plate region, maladjusted as a result of expectations and legitimate aspirations and the sad proof of their surrounding reality, a reality which he judges with a severe, hypercritical focus. His is a criticism that opens its doors to the skepticism of "withdrawn men who shun the masses with taciturnity," about whom Juan Carlos Ghiano has written. In this self-reflection one recognizes not only a single esthetic stance but also a generalized attitude, even at the popular level, where one vacillates between denunciation and acceptance, the confirmation that "things are as they are and there is no recourse but to accept them as such."

One reality Onetti himself had to face came in 1973, when, during the coup d'état of 27 June, he was forced to leave Uruguay and take refuge in Spain, where he resided until his death. In Madrid, far from the Buenos Aires where he had worked as a correspondent for the Reuters news agency, or from his native Montevideo, where he had written for the weekly *Marcha* and the daily *Acción* and where he was director of the municipal library, he received the 1978 Cervantes Prize and, thanks to numerous translations, international recognition.

The fame that was to arrive late did not change Onetti's view of life at all, that vision that Díaz Grey outlined in *El astillero* (1961; Eng. *The Shipyard,* 1968): life "is nothing more than this: what we see and what we know." There is no transcendence or philosophical meaning worth insisting upon. The important thing is that "nothing makes sense." The meaning of this view of existence is quite simple: men are beings who, refusing to accept clarity, complicate everything with "words and anxieties." Resignation, not at all anguished, must lead to admitting death itself as part of a routine.

Onetti's fatalism seems to lead to a certain passivity. Here we are far from all demonic existential anguish; we are close to a kind of beatific, transcendent understanding of all human and earthly anxieties, an attitude that could be religious had it been nurtured by faith. This insistence on the precariousness of existence, which provides the basis for the title of one novel, *La vida breve,* and is implied by the title of another, *Los adioses* (The Good-byes; 1954), makes one recall the lyrics of a song which points toward maturity: "Las marionetas, dan, dan / dan tres vueltas y se van" (The marionettes turn, turn, / turn three times and are gone).

From the impersonal rooms or boarding houses the evasion projected by solitary men has led to boredom or sadness, the expression of a resigned fatalism, far from all anguish and despair. At the end of the dream there is nothing left but to "watch oneself parsimoniously, calmly, growing old without drawing conclusions," or perhaps to "bore oneself smiling," as Díaz Grey suggests with a certain sadness—a sadness which can also be a "state of love" that assures a balance between hopelessness and rebelliousness and foretells a possible individual salvation.

And for what purpose is one saved? The answer rests in literature alone, that form of writing which frees Linacero and Brausen and which Onetti makes his own with a rigorous vocation, for what matters is to write, but not in any old way. In Onetti, beneath the guise of anti-intellectualism, one discovers a compendium of many of the techniques of the best contemporary narrative: the ambiguity of Herman Melville, the multiple points of view of Henry James, the interior monologue of James Joyce, the collective characters of Sherwood Anderson (Does *Winesburg, Ohio* influence Santa María?), the rounded perfection of a story by Stephen Crane, the atmosphere of William Faulkner. The lack of faith in any philosophical, religious, or political dogma does not keep Onetti from believing in the essential condition of the writer. As Lucien Goldmann would say of Jean Genet, one could also say of Onetti:

"Only art and appearance can constitute the esthetic compensation of a deceptive and insufficient reality." The exaltation of the powers of imagination through literature would, therefore, constitute more than escape; it would constitute authentic liberation. One could add, from a gnostic point of view, that if to tell a story is to understand, then to understand is to create—an understanding and a creation that, in Onetti's literary praxis, has been translated into a brief yet intense saga. If his work appears to be an enterprise of evasion, made acute with mechanisms that go along with the able management of the best techniques and procedures of writing, it does not constitute an easy escapism, for to escape from one specific reality does not imply abandoning man's essential reality, to let fall into "moral indifference" his existential problematic, which is valid in all time and space.

Herein lies the true meaning of Onetti's work: to arrive at the crux of the individual's intimate solitude, at the metaphysical sadness of the human condition, through the progressive awareness of the uselessness of most human action and through the stripping away of all the trappings that surround us and create for us false dependencies on our surrounding reality; and, in arriving at this crux, to grasp the essence of the human condition in order to distill in an original and solitary way a true existential allegory of contemporary man, not just of the River Plate region or of Latin America but of universal man.

Fernando Ainsa, Summer 1994, translated by David Draper Clark